Spain

Damien Simonis

Sarah Andrews, Stuart Butler, Anthony Ham, John Noble

Josephine Quintero, Miles Roddis, Arpi Armenakian Shively

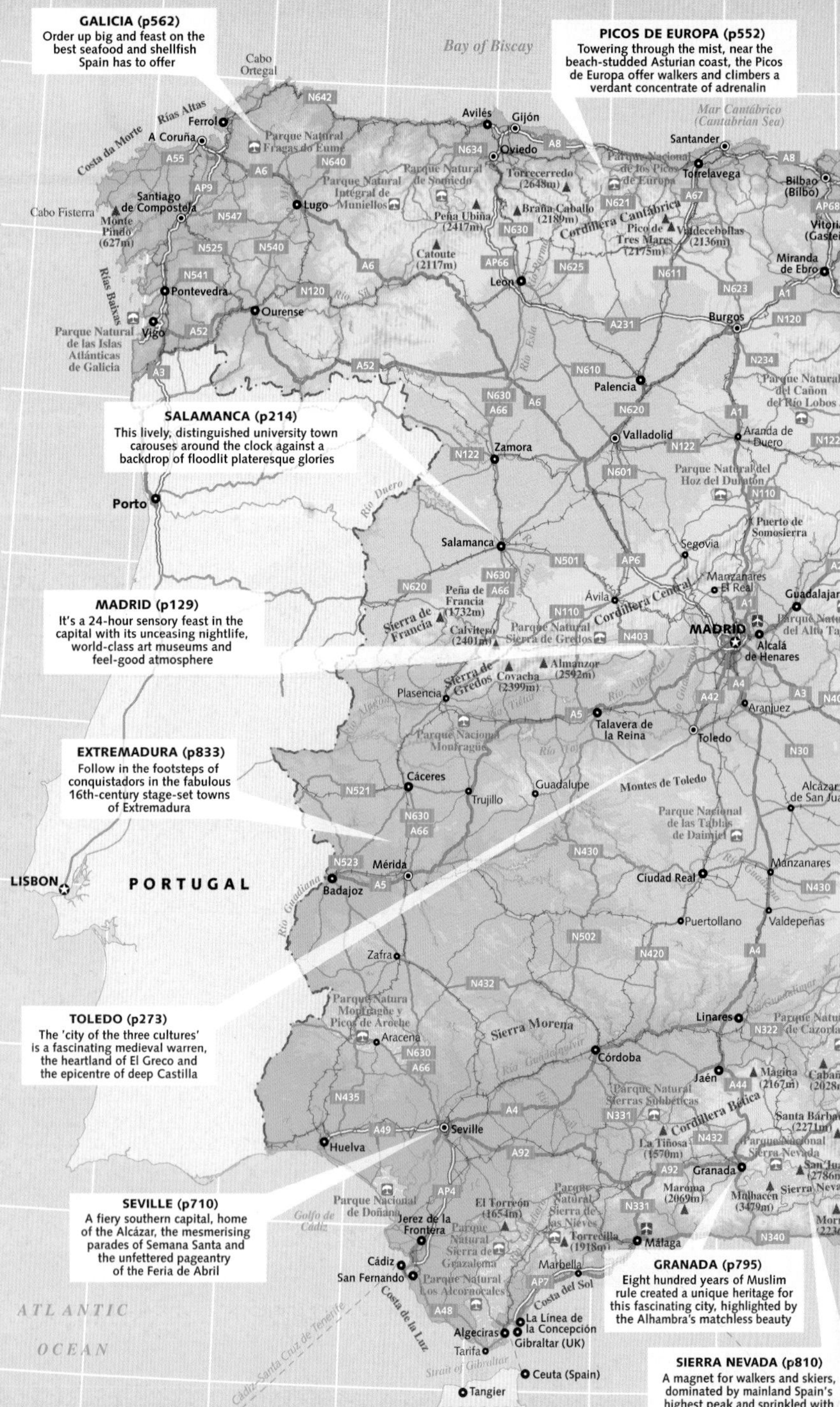
GALICIA (p562)
Order up big and feast on the best seafood and shellfish Spain has to offer
PICOS DE EUROPA (p552)
Towering through the mist, near the beach-studded Asturian coast, the Picos de Europa offer walkers and climbers a verdant concentrate of adrenalin
SALAMANCA (p214)
This lively, distinguished university town carouses around the clock against a backdrop of floodlit plateresque glories
MADRID (p129)
It's a 24-hour sensory feast in the capital with its unceasing nightlife, world-class art museums and feel-good atmosphere
EXTREMADURA (p833)
Follow in the footsteps of conquistadors in the fabulous 16th-century stage-set towns of Extremadura
TOLEDO (p273)
The 'city of the three cultures' is a fascinating medieval warren, the heartland of El Greco and the epicentre of deep Castilla
SEVILLE (p710)
A fiery southern capital, home of the Alcázar, the mesmerising parades of Semana Santa and the unfettered pageantry of the Feria de Abril
GRANADA (p795)
Eight hundred years of Muslim rule created a unique heritage for this fascinating city, highlighted by the Alhambra's matchless beauty
SIERRA NEVADA (p810)
A magnet for walkers and skiers, dominated by mainland Spain's highest peak and sprinkled with the Alpujarras hamlets
Bay of Biscay
Mar Cantábrico (Cantabrian Sea)
ATLANTIC OCEAN
PORTUGAL
MOROCCO
LISBON
Porto
MADRID
Cabo Ortegal
Rías Altas
Costa da Morte
Cabo Fisterra
Rías Baixas
Ferrol
A Coruña
Santiago de Compostela
Lugo
Pontevedra
Vigo
Ourense
Avilés
Gijón
Oviedo
Santander
Torrelavega
Bilbao (Bilbo)
Vitoria (Gasteiz)
Miranda de Ebro
Burgos
León
Palencia
Valladolid
Zamora
Salamanca
Aranda de Duero
Segovia
Ávila
Manzanares El Real
Guadalajara
Alcalá de Henares
Aranjuez
Toledo
Talavera de la Reina
Plasencia
Cáceres
Trujillo
Guadalupe
Mérida
Badajoz
Ciudad Real
Puertollano
Manzanares
Valdepeñas
Alcázar de San Juan
Zafra
Aracena
Linares
Córdoba
Jaén
Seville
Huelva
Granada
Málaga
Jerez de la Frontera
Cádiz
San Fernando
Marbella
La Línea de la Concepción
Algeciras
Gibraltar (UK)
Tarifa
Ceuta (Spain)
Tangier
Parque Natural Fragas do Eume
Parque Natural de las Islas Atlánticas de Galicia
Parque Natural de Somiedo
Parque Natural Integral de Muniellos
Parque Nacional de los Picos de Europa
Parque Natural del Cañon del Río Lobos
Parque Natural del Hoz del Duratón
Parque Natural Sierra de Gredos
Parque Natural del Alto Tajo
Parque Nacional Monfragüe
Parque Nacional de las Tablas de Daimiel
Parque Natural Sierras Subbéticas
Parque Natural de Cazorla
Parque Nacional Sierra Nevada
Parque Nacional de Doñana
Parque Natural Sierra de Grazalema
Parque Natural Los Alcornocales
Parque Natural Sierra de las Nieves
Monte Pindo (627m)
Torrecerredo (2648m)
Peña Ubiña (2417m)
Braña Caballo (2189m)
Catoute (2117m)
Pico de Tres Mares (2175m)
Valdecebollas (2136m)
Cordillera Cantábrica
Cordillera Central
Sierra de Francia
Peña de Francia (1732m)
Calvitero (2401m)
Sierra de Gredos
Covacha (2399m)
Almanzor (2592m)
Puerto de Somosierra
Montes de Toledo
Sierra Morena
Cordillera Bética
Mágina (2167m)
Cabañas (2028m)
Santa Bárbara (2271m)
La Tiñosa (1570m)
Maroma (2069m)
Mulhacén (3479m)
San Juan (2786m)
Sierra Nevada
Morrón (2236m)
El Torreón (1654m)
Torrecilla (1918m)
Golfo de Cádiz
Costa de la Luz
Costa del Sol
Strait of Gibraltar
Cádiz–Santa Cruz de Tenerife
Río Sil
Río Esla
Río Duero
Río Tajo
Río Guadiana
Río Guadalquivir

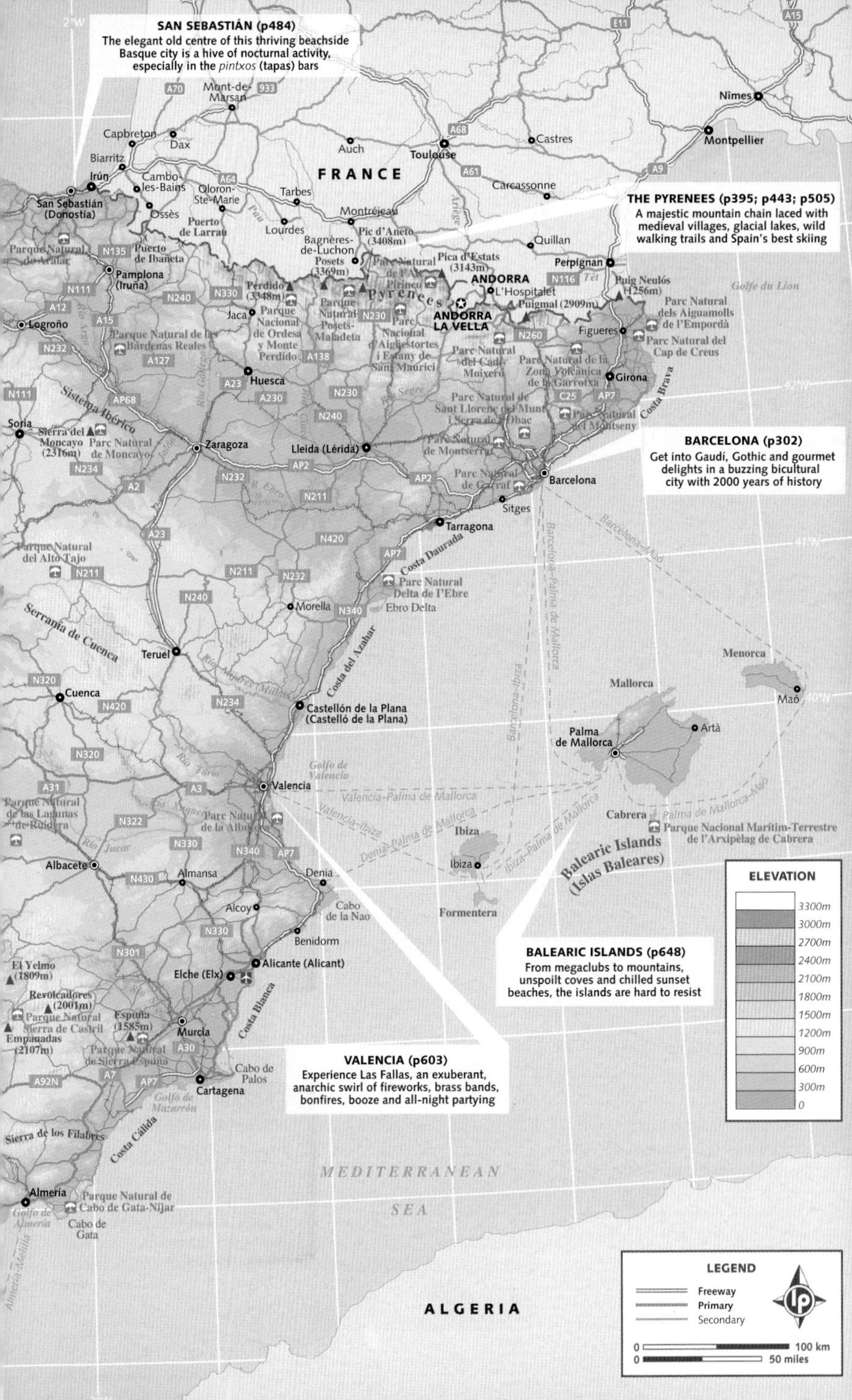

SAN SEBASTIÁN (p484)
The elegant old centre of this thriving beachside Basque city is a hive of nocturnal activity, especially in the *pintxos* (tapas) bars
THE PYRENEES (p395; p443; p505)
A majestic mountain chain laced with medieval villages, glacial lakes, wild walking trails and Spain's best skiing
BARCELONA (p302)
Get into Gaudí, Gothic and gourmet delights in a buzzing bicultural city with 2000 years of history
BALEARIC ISLANDS (p648)
From megaclubs to mountains, unspoilt coves and chilled sunset beaches, the islands are hard to resist
VALENCIA (p603)
Experience Las Fallas, an exuberant, anarchic swirl of fireworks, brass bands, bonfires, booze and all-night partying
FRANCE
ANDORRA
ANDORRA LA VELLA
ALGERIA
MEDITERRANEAN SEA
Golfe du Lion
Balearic Islands (Islas Baleares)
Mont-de-Marsan
Capbreton
Dax
Biarritz
Irún
San Sebastián (Donostia)
Cambo-les-Bains
Ossès
Oloron-Ste-Marie
Auch
Toulouse
Castres
Nîmes
Montpellier
Carcassonne
Tarbes
Lourdes
Montréjeau
Bagnères-de-Luchon
Pic d'Aneto (3408m)
Posets (3369m)
Pica d'Estats (3143m)
Quillan
Perpignan
L'Hospitalet
Puigmal (2909m)
Puig Neulós (1256m)
Figueres
Girona
Pamplona (Iruña)
Logroño
Jaca
Huesca
Zaragoza
Soria
Lleida (Lérida)
Barcelona
Sitges
Tarragona
Morella
Ebro Delta
Teruel
Cuenca
Castellón de la Plana (Castelló de la Plana)
Valencia
Albacete
Almansa
Alcoy
Denia
Cabo de la Nao
Benidorm
Alicante (Alicant)
Elche (Elx)
Murcia
Cartagena
Cabo de Palos
Almería
Cabo de Gata
Mallorca
Palma de Mallorca
Artà
Menorca
Maó
Cabrera
Ibiza
Formentera
Costa Brava
Costa Daurada
Costa del Azahar
Costa Blanca
Costa Cálida
Sistema Ibérico
Serranía de Cuenca
Sierra de los Filabres
Golfo de Valencia
Golfo de Mazarrón
Golfo de Almería
Parque Nacional Marítim-Terrestre de l'Arxipèlag de Cabrera
Parc Natural dels Aiguamolls de l'Empordà
Parc Natural del Cap de Creus
Parc Natural Delta de l'Ebre
Parque Natural de Cabo de Gata-Níjar
Parque Natural del Alto Tajo
Parque Natural de Moncayo
Parque Natural de las Bardenas Reales
Parque Nacional de Ordesa y Monte Perdido
Parc Nacional d'Aigüestortes i Estany de Sant Maurici
Barcelona–Palma de Mallorca
Barcelona–Maó
Barcelona–Ibiza
Valencia–Palma de Mallorca
Valencia–Ibiza
Denia–Palma de Mallorca
Ibiza–Palma de Mallorca
Palma de Mallorca–Maó
Almería–Melilla
ELEVATION
3300m
3000m
2700m
2400m
2100m
1800m
1500m
1200m
900m
600m
300m
0
LEGEND
Freeway
Primary
Secondary
0 100 km
0 50 miles

On the Road

DAMIEN SIMONIS Coordinating Author
All work and no play makes Damien a dull boy, and in Formentera how could I not take time to slither into the turquoise waters of one of my favourite beaches, Es Arenals (p680)? My thoughts were fixed on an impending paella, in a shady spot a 2km scooter ride away.

JOSEPHINE QUINTERO Here I am pretending to be just as wacky as Don Quijote! Tilting at windmills is essential to the La Mancha (p272) experience. They're just one of the delights of this great region. I wish I could stuff one in the boot of the car and plonk it in my garden – it sure beats a garden gnome!

SARAH ANDREWS I'd spent the morning touring the village of Ribadavia and the Ribeiro wine country (p600). As I was pregnant, I couldn't indulge in much wine tasting, but I did find the wonderful winery-restaurant-hotel Casal de Armán, where I had a memorable meal and then explored the gardens and vineyards.

ANTHONY HAM After long months of research, I'd saved the jewel of Islamic architecture, La Aljafería (p436), for last. I was enjoying a quiet moment with my daughter, Carlota, who was born a *madrileña* just prior to research for the book. My wish is that she'll come to know Spain's wonderful richness as encapsulated by places like this.

STUART BUTLER What a glorious summer day in the Pyrenees (p505), you might think. Wrong. Despite confident statements to my wife about how weather forecasts are always incorrect and it would in fact be sunny all day, within 15 minutes we were utterly lost in a dense fog and soaked to the skin in a storm.

MILES RODDIS I'm no frequenter of cat houses. But this one's special. It appeared one morning, set into a graffiti-covered wall in Valencia (p604). Someone had forged a hole and built a facade no more than knee high for the neighbourhood's feral cats to slink through. It expresses how with small, imaginative gestures individuals can make their mark on their environment.

ARPI ARMENAKIAN SHIVELY
Shhh! Don't tell anyone I'm having such a good time among the agonised-looking antiquities at El Garlochi (p727), Andalucía's most over-the-top bar, decorated with religious relics. What you can't see is the incense and the choir of angels – cheers!

For full author biographies see p911.

EXPERIENCE SPAIN

From mountains to sea, Spain is a smorgasbord. Hedonists are in for a treat whether taking in the *pintxos* (Basque tapas) routes of San Sebastián, boutique-hopping in Barcelona or burning the midnight oil in Madrid. Some of the country's Mediterranean beaches are well known, but the wild beauty of the north coast is for most a joy yet to be unveiled. Of equally savage beauty are the mountain ranges, offering hiking challenges such as the Parque Nacional de Ordesa y Monte Perdido in the Pyrenees. Roman walls, ancient mosques, Gaudí kookiness and contemporary genius dot the nation from north to south.

Architectural Wonders

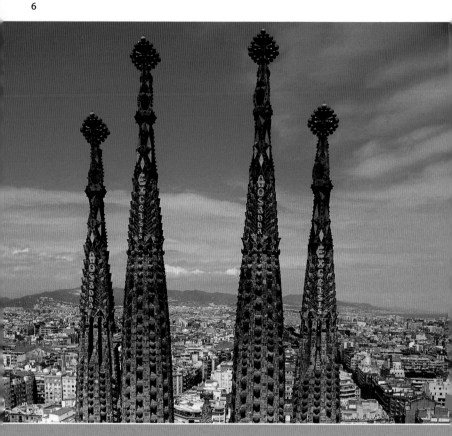

Celtiberian tribes, Roman legions, Muslim princes, Christian kings and modern designers have all left indelible marks across Spain. Gothic, Gaudí and Gehry unite in a sublime and eclectic architectural cocktail that's unique. You could immerse yourself for years and still not see all its riches.

❶ La Sagrada Família (Barcelona)

One of Spain's top sights, the Modernista brainchild of Antoni Gaudí remains a work in progress more than 80 years after its creator's death. Inspired by nature and Gothic style, Barcelona's quirky temple (p330) soars skyward with fanciful majesty.

❷ Alhambra (Granada)

Even Emperor Carlos V realised that the palace complex of the Alhambra (p797) left behind in Granada after 800 years of Muslim rule was an extraordinary treasure. It is perhaps the most refined and exquisite example of Islamic art in the world.

❸ Ciudad de las Artes y las Ciencias (Valencia)

One of the nation's star architects, Santiago Calatrava, created this City of Arts and Sciences in Valencia (p607). A daring and visually stunning piece of contemporary architecture, the complex includes a state-of-the-art theatre, grand aquarium, planetarium and science museum.

❹ Museo Guggenheim (Bilbao)

Not to be outdone by Valencia, Bilbao enlisted Frank Gehry to create the mind-blowing Museo Guggenheim (p473) on a bend in the river in the heart of the city. For many visitors, the dreamlike shimmering silhouette outshines the fine art collections it houses.

❺ El Acueducto (Segovia)

The Romans built things to last. Without a drop of mortar, they assembled this gigantic but elegant aqueduct of granite blocks to supply Roman Segovia (p227) with water. This engineering feat has stood the test of time – almost 2000 years!

❻ Catedral de Santiago de Compostela

Bearing an unusually rich Romanesque facade, the splendid cathedral (p565) is the objective of pilgrims traversing the Camino de Santiago across northern Spain.

❼ Plaza Mayor & Catedral Nueva (Salamanca)

The elegant central square of Salamanca, Plaza Mayor (p215), is possibly the most comely in all Spain. Nearby, the Catedral Nueva is an extraordinary melding of Gothic and Renaissance art.

❽ Mezquita (Córdoba)

One of the world's most outstanding mosques under Muslim control, Córdoba's Mezquita (p788) was later rendered unique when its Christian conquerors created a church within the ranks of its horseshoe arches.

❾ Roman Walls (Lugo)

The Romans made it to the four corners of Iberia. The largely intact walls that millennia later still surround the ancient city of Lugo (p601), in Galicia, are proof of their power.

Senses in the City

Spaniards live their cities to the max. Few other peoples spend as much of their leisure in the streets, hopping from bar to bar or from store to store. Across the board, Spain's cities display extraordinary variety, from the cosmopolitan style of Barcelona to the fire and Arab airs of southern Granada.

1 Madrid Nightlife

Where else has traffic jams in the wee hours? Madrid's not the only European city with nightlife but few can match its intensity and street vibe. Stumble around Huertas, Malasaña, Chueca and La Latina for wall-to-wall bars to suit all tastes (p184).

2 Shopping in Barcelona

Shop till you drop along Barcelona's boulevards (Passeig de Gràcia, Rambla de Catalunya and Avinguda Diagonal) as well as in countless independent stores and bijou boutiques in the Barri Gòtic, around Passeig del Born and Gràcia (p358).

3 Easter in Seville

Return to Spain's medieval Christian roots and join Seville's masses for the dramatic Easter celebration of Semana Santa. Religious fraternities parade elaborate *pasos* (sculptural representations) of Christ and the Virgin Mary around the city to the emotive acclamation of the populace (p723).

4 Tea & Tapas in Granada

East still meets West in the last of Spain's Muslim cities to fall to the Christian reconquest. In the teahouses of the Albayzín quarter (p804) you could almost be in Morocco. Elsewhere, the tapas bars around Plaza Nueva fill to bursting point with good-natured, loud-talking locals (p807).

5 Pintxos in San Sebastián

Chefs here have turned bar snacks into an art form. *Pintxos* are piles of flavour often mounted on a slice of baguette, and form the backbone of any central San Sebastián (p490) bar crawl – a uniquely tasty and sociable night out.

6 Hanging Out in Cádiz

Possibly Europe's oldest city, Cádiz (p738) has a laid-back, almost rakish live-for-the-present vibe that makes its somewhat decayed 18th-century centre instantly likeable. Locals party the sweltering summer nights away in the old town squares and waterfront bars.

7 Three Cultures in Toledo

Symbolic home to Spain's Catholic Church and the army, the medieval core of Toledo (p273) is an extraordinary piece of world heritage. Known as the city of the three cultures (where Muslims, Jews and Christians once rubbed shoulders), it remains a fascinating labyrinth today.

Into the Blue

There's something in the clichés. Indeed, the Spanish coast is an infinite source of marvel and surprise. From the impossibly clear turquoise waters of the Balearic Islands beaches to the vertigo-inducing heights of Cabo Ortegal, plunging into the Atlantic in the northwest, the sea exerts a magnetic attraction.

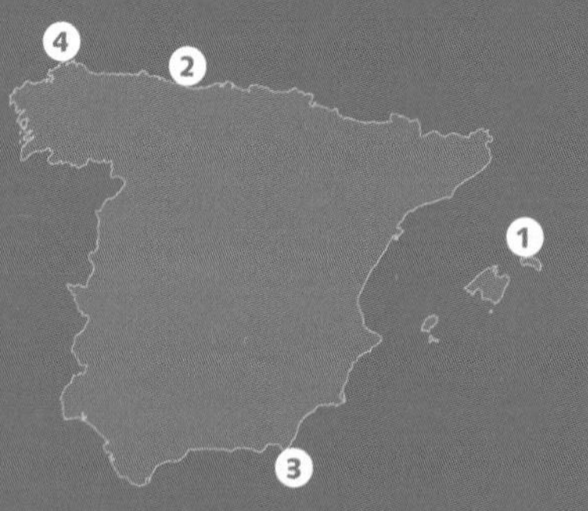

Author Tip

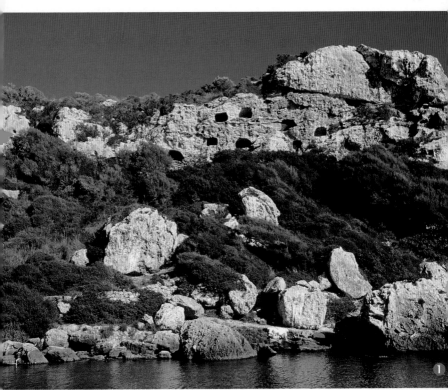

The rain may fall mainly on the plain, but the sun takes a direct hit on its worshippers. Sunscreen, hat, sunglasses and water are all musts at the beach. Watch for red or yellow flags, which warn against taking a dip.

❶ Beaches of Menorca

Menorca is a Unesco Biosphere Reserve with beaches that defy description. Some assert that reaching them by sea is the height of pleasure, but happening upon them from the interior brings equal joy. Among the best are Cala Macarelleta and Cala en Turqueta (p694).

❷ Asturias

According to one count, the emerald green northern Spanish region of Asturias boasts 211 beaches! While the coolness of the Atlantic is a drawback, the beauty of many of these frequently wild and unspoiled stretches, such as those around Llanes (p547), is utterly breathtaking.

❸ Cabo de Gata

Cabo de Gata (p828), a wild stretch of protected coastline east of Almería, is legendary among Spaniards. For most of the year the beaches, strung between imposing cliffs, are nearly deserted. They offer some decent diving, too.

❹ Cabo Ortegal

The wild Atlantic bluffs of this magnificent cape in Galicia (p579) remind us of how small we are. While powerful winds whip around you, great Atlantic rollers seem little more than sea spray as they crash against the walls of Cabo Ortegal far below.

3

Natural Highs

Hikers and climbers have myriad options at altitude. The Pyrenees offer countless possibilities; the Sierra Nevada has skiing around mainland Spain's highest peak; and lesser-known ranges, such as the emerald green Picos de Europa and central Sierra de Gredos, abound with rugged hiking trails.

❶ Parque Nacional Sierra Nevada

Dominated by the Mulhacén (3479m), mainland Spain's highest peak, this national park (p810) makes a stunning backdrop to the warm city of Granada. Skiing in winter and hiking in summer can be mixed with exploration of the fascinating villages of Las Alpujarras.

❷ Parque Nacional de Ordesa y Monte Perdido

One of the high points (pun intended) of the Pyrenees, this national park (p451) is a hikers' dream. Centred on Monte Perdido (3348m), it offers plenty of opportunities for tough excursions along great rock walls and glacial cirques, accompanied by the occasional chamois.

❸ Picos de Europa

Jutting out in compact form just back from the rugged and ever-changing coastline of Cantabria and Asturias, the Picos (p552) comprise three dramatic limestone massifs, unique in Spain but geologically similar to the Alps and jammed with inspiring trails.

❹ Sierra de Gredos

Walkers, mountain bikers and climbers have a whole enchanted world of lakes and granite mountains to explore in this extensive mountain chain west of Madrid (p213). Various villages and the occasional castle dot this at times tough and forbidding range.

Contents

Regional Map Contents

Asturias p534
Cantabria p520
Galicia p563
Basque Country, Navarra & La Rioja p470
Castilla y León p207
Catalonia p371
Aragón p432
Barcelona pp306–7
Madrid p132
Castilla-La Mancha p273
Valencia p605
Extremadura p834
Balearic Islands p649
Murcia p696
Andalucía pp708–9

Destination Spain

Spain may be a modern European country, but it's never lost its whiff of the exotic. The stereotypes by which it's known – *bailaors* (flamenco dancers) stamping and swirling in flounces of colour; *toreros* (bullfighters) flaunting their courage in the bullrings; and beach-lovers soaking up pitchers of sangria over steaming paella – just happen to be true. But Spain is also so much more.

For a start, few countries can match the diversity of the Spanish landscape. If mountains give you frisson, Spain has them in abundance. In the north, the Pyrenees and the Picos de Europa are as beautiful as any mountain range on the continent, while the snowcapped Sierra Nevada rises up from the sun-baked plains of Andalucía like an unlikely apparition of the Alps. Stunning coastlines, the horizonless gravitas of the *meseta* (high tableland of central Spain) and the captivating semideserts of the south combine to create an extraordinary picture.

FAST FACTS

Population: 45 million

Area: 504,782 sq km

GDP: €1348 billion (world's eighth-largest economy)

GDP per head: €19,226

GDP growth: 1.8%

Inflation: 4.6%

Unemployment rate: 9.63%

Average life expectancy: 79.92 years

Highest point in peninsular Spain: Mulhacén (3479m)

Biggest paella: made in Valencia in 1992 in a pan 20m in diameter; it was eaten by 100,000 people

Everywhere you go, villages of rare and timeless beauty perch on hilltops and huddle in valleys. Vestiges of Old Spain cling to traditions that the rest of Europe lost long ago and to the stone-and-timber architecture that never goes out of style. Spend as long as you can in places such as these. Better still, use them as bases for hiking, skiing and all manner of stirring outdoor pursuits.

A world away, Spain's dynamic cities are temples to all that's modern and cool. Madrid, Barcelona, Valencia and Seville have become bywords for that peculiarly Spanish talent for living the good life, and for doing so at full volume and all night. Most cities also promise a daytime feast of exceptional sites, from world-class art galleries to graceful Islamic-era monuments, from *barrios* (districts) overflowing with medieval charm to zany Gaudí flights of fancy.

Speaking of feasts, food and wine are what Spaniards really get excited about. Variety is the touchstone of Spanish cooking and every region, nay, every Spanish village seems to have its own speciality. Often the recipes have been intact for centuries; sometimes they've just emerged from the laboratory. You may experience the best meal ever over tapas in an earthy bar where everyone seems to be shouting, or in the refined surrounds of a Michelin-starred restaurant. Either way, the breadth of culinary experience that awaits you is astonishing.

Fascination also resides in the fact that Spain is a work in progress, a country wrestling with its place in the modern world. Spain's rapid rise to become one of Europe's most progressive countries – remember it's only been a democracy for 30 years – finds daily expression as Spaniards confront a host of modern problems.

Ask any Spaniard what they're most concerned about and they're likely to reply: 'the economy, of course'. Spaniards are struggling: how to buy a house, how to pay the mortgage, how to survive on some of Europe's lowest salaries while prices reach parity with the rest of the continent are national obsessions. In this economy, where stellar recent growth has been fuelled by booming construction, the Europewide economic downturn is rocking Spain to its foundations. Immigration, too, is increasingly at the forefront of Spaniards' minds.

And then there are those issues with a more local focus. Since Spain's Socialist government returned to power with a narrow victory in national polls in March 2008, Spaniards have been watching and hoping that the next four years won't be as bitter as those that preceded them. Although the government and opposition have promised to end the politics of confrontation, the divisive issues that plagued the last legislature remain open wounds and no one's holding their breath.

The raft of social reforms pursued with such zeal by the Socialist government, and opposed with equal fervour by the opposition, are, it seems, here to stay. But with the government promising to make abortion laws 'more flexible', remove Christian symbols from government ceremonies and open debate on laws allowing a limited form of euthanasia, it's hard to see how the two sides can be reconciled. The election of the Archbishop of Madrid, arch-conservative Antonio María Rouco Varela, to lead the powerful Spanish Bishops' Conference in 2008 suggests that the road ahead will be anything but boring.

Euskadi Ta Askatasuna (ETA; Basque Homeland and Freedom) may be on the decline but, after a nine-month 'permanent' ceasefire, it showed it was still around with the bombing at Madrid's Barajas airport on 30 December 2006. Two people died – the first deaths attributed to ETA in almost four years – and the killing of a former Basque councillor followed during the 2008 election campaign. 'No more negotiations' was the message from both the ruling Socialists and the opposition Partido Popular (People's Party). But negotiate they must on at least one front: the Basque regional government has promised a referendum on plans for far-reaching autonomy.

'Spain's dynamic cities are temples to all that's modern and cool.'

But for all the issues that confront and divide, Spaniards seem intent on staring down the doomsayers and living life in a way that seems to say 'Crisis? What crisis?' The shops are full, Spaniards are travelling more than ever and it's often said that the current young generation is the first in a very long while to be truly proud of its country. Spain is all the rage around the world, from its cuisine and celebrity chefs to its architecture and design. The national football team finally shook off the mantle of perennial underachiever by winning the 2008 European Championships, its first major trophy since 1964, and Rafael Nadal's epic Wimbledon victory was the first by a Spaniard since 1966. In the aftermath of sporting success, the feel-good factor was palpable in just about every corner of the land and, despite the undoubted problems the country faces, there's a newfound confidence, an overwhelming sense that Spain's time is now.

Getting Started

Getting the most out of a visit to Spain is partly a matter of timing. If you hope to enjoy the outdoors (walking, skiing, diving and so on), you need to plan around the weather but avoid the crowded seasonal peaks. You may want to be around to witness some of the country's extraordinary festivals. Some visitors aim for a taste of luxury and gourmet indulgence; in this case it is worth planning which castles to stay in and which avant-garde restaurants to book. Whether it's a lazy beach holiday or a strenuous cycle tour you're craving, whatever your budget, anything is possible.

WHEN TO GO

See Climate Charts (p868) for more information.

Depending on what you're after, Spain is a year-round destination. The ideal months to visit are May, June and September (plus April and October in the south). At these times you can rely on good to excellent weather pretty much throughout the country, yet avoid the main crush of Spanish and foreign tourists and the sometimes extreme heat. During July and August, temperatures can climb to 45°C in inland Andalucía; at this time Madrid is unbearable and almost deserted.

Winter (from December to February) along the south and southeast Mediterranean coasts is mild. In the height of summer (from June to August), retreat to the northwest, to beaches or high mountains, anywhere to escape excessive heat. You can be sitting outside enjoying a beer in a T-shirt in Granada in February, or rugged up against the cold while trekking the Picos de Europa in July.

Swimming in the Mediterranean is pleasant from about mid-May to early October, although the Costa Brava can be a touch chillier. The ski season in the Pyrenees generally runs from mid-December to early April, depending on snowfalls, which in recent years have been patchy.

See the Events Calendar (p24) to plan around the countless fiestas that dot the Spanish calendar.

COSTS & MONEY

Spain is, as locals will quickly tell you, not as cheap as it once was. What you spend on accommodation (probably your single greatest expense) will depend on various factors, such as location (Madrid is pricier than Murcia), season (August along the coast is packed and expensive), the degree of comfort you require and a little dumb luck. At the budget end you'll pay €12 to €27 for a bed in a youth hostel (depending on the hostel, season and your age).

The cheapest bearable *pensión* (small private hotel) or *hostal* (budget hotel) is unlikely to cost less than €20 (single) or €35 (double) a night; reckon on more in the cities and resorts. Depending on where you are, you can stumble across good single or double rooms with attached bathroom from as little as €30 or €45 (€60 or €80 in the more popular locations).

Eating out is still more variable. A *menú del día* (daily set menu) can cost as little as €8 to €12. Bank on spending at least €20 on a full dinner (including house wine).

Most sights are fairly cheap. Keep an eye out for free days (especially Sundays and set days for EU citizens).

Public transport is reasonably priced, although high-speed trains can be expensive. See the Transport chapter (p883) for more details.

A backpacker sticking to youth hostels, lunchtime snacks and travelling slowly could scrape by on €40 to €50 a day. A more comfortable midrange

HOW MUCH?

El País newspaper €1.10

Admission to dance clubs €10-20

Cocktail €6-10

Seat at a Real Madrid or FC Barcelona match €15-170

City metro ride up to €1.30

DON'T LEAVE HOME WITHOUT...

- Valid travel insurance (p874)
- Your ID card and passport or visa if required (p880)
- Driving licence and car documents if driving, along with appropriate car insurance (p892)
- A concealed money belt or shoulder wallet to help save you from being a petty-theft victim (p871)

budget, including a sandwich for lunch, a modest evening meal, a couple of sights and travel will be anything from €100 to €150 a day. From there, the sky's the limit. It is possible to spend hundreds on five-star lodgings and even in the occasional gourmet paradise.

TRAVELLING RESPONSIBLY

Spain's history, location, lack of mineral wealth and dependence on tourism for a sizeable chunk of its national income (more than 10% of GDP) combine to make environmental issues a key to its future.

The presence of millions of tourists in Spain every year is both a boon and a burden on resources. Take care not to waste water; tread carefully in parks, on the coast and other sensitive areas; avoid littering everywhere; and keep an eye open for local products rather than succumbing to mass imports (from food to fashion). Staying in rural accommodation can provide a source of income to otherwise slowly dying country communities. Travelling in the interior away from the standard locations can be rewarding and it helps spread the tourist burden more evenly around the country!

'Whether it's a lazy beach holiday or a strenuous cycle tour you're craving, anything is possible.'

Bear in mind that much of the overly dense, barely controlled construction of holiday housing on the coast is not for Spaniards. Much of the damage is already done, but anyone considering buying coastal apartments might want to consider the implications. The same is true of the nation's golf-course frenzy. Golf tourism is on the rise but is hardly compatible with the semidesert nature of parts of southern Spain, where scarce water would be better directed at irrigation.

Keep in mind that water is at a premium in much of the country. Drought threatened water restrictions along much of the Mediterranean coast in 2008 until, much to everyone's relief, abundant unseasonal downpours in May filled the dams. Despite this, of course, prudent consumption remains the order of the day. Reining in those long showers is good for everyone! For more on environmental issues, see p106.

A motorised vehicle is advantageous for getting to some parts of the country but by making judicious choices you can give your drivers, the vehicles and the atmosphere a rest. Public transport, including the country's growing high-speed rail network, makes it easy to get around between major destinations. In cities, park your car and use public transport instead.

You are what you eat! Seeking out better restaurants that use fresh local products or shopping at produce markets is a way of contributing to both your well-being and the local economy.

Giving your custom to local businesses, especially those with ecofriendly credentials, in and around parks and protected areas helps sustain rural economies without recourse to potentially noxious alternatives.

In parks and other protected areas, stick to established routes, obtain permits for restricted areas and don't damage vegetation or scare wildlife. Take extreme care to avoid starting fires, which every summer ravage large

TOP PICKS

Portugal • Madrid SPAIN

SPANISH CINEMA

A handful of silver-screen classics slipped through the general drivel produced during the long Franco era, but since the dictator's demise in 1975 Spaniards have been cheekily adventurous with celluloid. Check out p67 for more on this topic.

- *Todo Sobre Mi Madre* (Pedro Almodóvar; 1999)
- *Amantes* (Vicente Aranda; 1991)
- *¡Bienvenido, Mr Marshall!* (Luis García Berlanga; 1952)
- *Flamenco* (Carlos Saura; 1995)
- *Volver* (Pedro Almodóvar; 2006)
- *Lucía y el Sexo* (Julio Medem; 2001)
- *Un Chien Andalou* (Luis Buñuel; 1929)
- *Jamón, Jamón* (José Juan Bigas Luna; 1992)
- *Mar Adentro* (Alejandro Amenábar; 2004)

THE GREAT OUTDOORS

Spain's scenery is as varied as its history, food and weather, and is often the backdrop for exciting activity. To get your adventurous side into action, see what's on offer in Spain Outdoors (p110). Our pick for top spots include the following:

- Baqueira-Beret (p413) – top-class skiing in the Pyrenees.
- Illes Medes (p385) – pretty diving near the islands off the Costa Brava.
- Tarifa (p758) – powerful windsurfing near the Straits of Gibraltar.
- Vall de la Noguera Pallaresa (p406) – the country's best white-water rafting.
- Aneto (p450) – hiking around the highest peaks of the Spanish Pyrenees.
- Cabo de Gata (p828) – a wild coastal stretch perfect for swimming and diving.
- Parque Nacional Monfragüe (p843) – the place to look out for the *águila imperial* (imperial eagle) and other rare large birds.
- Menorca (p683) – the entire island is a tranquil Unesco Biosphere Reserve.
- Parque Nacional Sierra Nevada (p810) – an area offering skiing, walking and horse riding, not to mention mainland Spain's highest mountain, Mulhacén.
- Camino de Santiago (p118) – the famous spiritual walking trail from the French border to Santiago de Compostela.

areas of Spain. Consider walking as an alternative to disruptive activities such as quad biking.

Just as walkers should tread softly and leave no refuse behind them, so divers should be careful not to disturb the seabed, coral and marine life. Boaters should not drop anchor in areas where Poseidon grass grows on the seabed, as they will tear up this sea flora when weighing anchor. Look for a sandy bottom.

Littering remains a problem and a big issue on crowded beaches. It is incredible but true that awareness campaigns are still needed to remind people not to leave cigarette butts, cans and other refuse on the beach. The lesson, it appears, is yet to be learned by all. Bin your rubbish!

Look out for discount cards that support environmental and sustainability projects, for instance the Targeta Verda in the Balearic Islands (see the boxed text, p673).

TRAVEL LITERATURE

Much ink has been spilled on the subject of Spain by its observers, both foreign and local. For books on Spanish history, art and architecture, see the recommendations in the History, Culture and Architecture chapters.

Ghosts of Spain, by Giles Tremlett, looks at contemporary Spain, a country in overdrive to catch up with the rest of the West but with its heart still planted in its tumultuous past.

Between Hopes and Memories: A Spanish Journey, by Michael Jacobs, is an amusing and personal reflection on contemporary Spain. Jacobs sets out from Madrid and criss-crosses the country, dipping into its historical, literary and cultural dimensions.

Tuning Up at Dawn, by Robert Graves' son Tomás, looks at Mallorca (and Spain) since the civil war, with an emphasis on the music world in which he was caught up.

Spanish Steps sees author Tim Moore and his donkey, Shinto, undertaking the walk from France to Santiago de Compostela, offering no shortage of laughs along the way. A more serious and superbly written account of the Camino can be found in Cees Nooteboom's *Roads to Santiago*.

Written in 1845, Richard Ford's classic *A Handbook for Travellers* not only tells us how things once were in places we see now, but also has us chortling as its irascible English author is by turns witty, informative and downright rude.

There is no shortage of expats churning out émigré memoirs in Spain. One of the more amusing is *Mañana, Mañana, Viva Mallorca*, by Peter Kerr, one of four books he wrote during his family's three-year stint running an orange orchard on the island.

'Much ink has been spilled on the subject of Spain by its observers, both foreign and local.'

INTERNET RESOURCES

EuroResidentes (www.euroresidentes.com) A multilingual portal aimed at foreign residents in Spain, detailing everything from mortgage advice to Spanish travel blogs.

Fiestas.net (www.fiestas.net) Good site on fiestas worth checking out.

LonelyPlanet.com (www.lonelyplanet.com) Can get you started with info on Spain, links and a forum of travellers trading information on the Thorn Tree.

Renfe (Red Nacional de los Ferrocarriles Españoles; www.renfe.es) Timetables and tickets for Spain's national rail network.

Spanish Fiestas (www.spanish-fiestas.com) Has little on fiestas but does have everything from events listings to links for active holidays.

Turespaña (www.spain.info) This is the Spanish tourist office's site, which offers lots of general information and useful links.

Vayafiestas.com (www.vayafiestas.com) Spanish-only site with month-by-month info on fiestas around the country.

Events Calendar

From San Sebastián to Seville, Spaniards share a zest for the fest. The country's calendar creaks beneath the weight of an unending parade of feast days and celebrations that, whether of religious or pagan origin, share the common aim of providing an excuse for much drinking, eating and merrymaking.

JANUARY

FESTIVIDAD DE SAN SEBASTIÁN 20 Jan

During this festival (p488) everyone in San Sebastián dresses up and goes somewhat berserk.

FEBRUARY

ARCO mid-Feb

Madrid hosts Arco (Feria Internacional de Arte Contemporánea; www.arco.ifema.es in Spanish), one of Europe's biggest contemporary art fairs (p173), at the tail end of winter.

FEBRUARY–MARCH

CARNAVAL

This event involves several days of fancy-dress parades and festivities. It is at its wildest in Cádiz (p741) and Sitges (p365), but is also good in Ciudad Rodrigo (p223). It usually ends just before Lent, on the Tuesday 47 days before Easter Sunday. An especially odd celebration takes place in Solsona, Catalonia (p415). Townsfolk celebrate Carnaval by hoisting a donkey (nowadays made of plastic) up the central clock tower and dropping it onto the crowded square below! Another little-publicised version is the Batalla de Caramels (Battle of the Sweets), the high point of very rowdy Carnaval celebrations in Vilanova i la Geltrú (p420) in which locals hurl countless sweeties at one another.

MARCH

LAS FALLAS 12-19 Mar

This festival consists of several days of all-night dancing and drinking, first-class fireworks and processions. Its principal stage is Valencia city (p611), but it is also celebrated in Gandia (p629) and elsewhere in the Valencia region. The festivities culminate in the ritual burning of (sometimes enormous) effigies in the streets. See www.fallas.es (in Spanish) for more.

MARCH–APRIL

SEMANA SANTA (HOLY WEEK)

The week leading up to Easter Sunday (which changes each year) entails parades of *pasos* (holy figures) and huge crowds. It is most extravagantly celebrated in Seville (p723), but it is also big in Málaga (p772), Córdoba (p791), Toledo (p280), Ávila (p211), Cuenca (p295), Lorca (p704) and Zamora (p240).

DANSA DE LA MORT

In the fairly nondescript Catalan village of Verges (p384), the Dansa de la Mort (Dance of Death) on Holy Thursday is a chilling experience. This nocturnal dance is the centrepiece of Easter celebrations and is much bigger in numbers than the town that hosts it!

LOS EMPALAOS

The village of Villanueva de la Vera, in northeast Extremadura, plays out one of the most extraordinary acts of Easter abnegation you are ever likely to witness. Taking place on Holy Thursday, the devotion and self-inflicted suffering of the barefoot penitents who walk the Way of the Cross leaves most onlookers breathless (see p836 for details).

APRIL

MOROS Y CRISTIANOS 22-24 Apr

Colourful parades and mock battles between Christian and Muslim 'armies' in Alcoy (p644), near Alicante, make this one of the most spectacular of several similar events staged in Valencia and Alicante provinces (see www.portalfester.com in Catalan).

FERIA DE ABRIL late Apr

This is a week-long party (p723) held in Seville, kicking off after the religious fervour of Semana Santa. *Sevillanos* ride around on horseback and in elaborate horse-drawn carriages by day and, dressed up in their best traditional finery, dance late into the night. For more details, see http://feriadesevilla.andalunet.com (in Spanish). The city also stages its biggest bullfight series this week.

ROMERÍA DE LA VIRGEN DE LA CABEZA last Sun in Apr

Hundreds of thousands of people make a mass pilgrimage to the Santuario de la Virgen de la Cabeza (www.santuariovirgencabeza.org in Spanish) near Andújar, in Jaén province (p816). As a small statue of the Virgin Mother is paraded about, people pass clothes and even small children over the crowd to have a priest touch them to the statue's mantle.

FERIA DEL QUESO last weekend in Apr

The streets of Trujillo, in Extremadura, are filled with an overwhelming aroma as multitudes of cheeses from all over Spain are displayed at this gourmet fest (p851). The fair is sometimes held at the beginning of May. See www.feriadelqueso.com for details.

MAY

FERIA DEL CABALLO early May

A colourful equestrian fair in Andalucía's horse capital, Jerez de la Frontera (p749), the Feria del Caballo features parades, bullfights and plenty of music and dance.

WOMAD early May

For three days Cáceres is taken by musical storm for the World of Music, Arts and Dance festival (p845). You could hardly hope for a greater concentration of performers from all over the planet, nor for a more beautiful setting than the medieval squares of this city.

CONCURSO DE PATIOS CORDOBESES early to mid-May

Scores of beautiful private courtyards are opened to the public for two weeks in Córdoba (p790). For more information, check out www.patiosdecordoba.net (in Spanish).

ES FIRÓ around 11 May

Sóller, in northern Mallorca, is invaded by Muslim pirates in early May. This gives rise to a 'battle' between townsfolk and invaders known as Es Firó (p662). It recreates an infamous assault on the town that was repulsed on 11 May 1561, in which Ses Valentes Dones (Valient Women) played a key part in victory.

FIESTA DE SAN ISIDRO 15 May

Madrid's major fiesta (p173) features bullfights, parades, concerts and more. Some of the events, such as the bullfighting season, last for a month. Indeed, this is the major bull fiesta – *toreros* (bullfighters) the world over dream of being able to fight here at the Las Ventas ring.

MAY–JUNE

ROMERÍA DEL ROCÍO 7th weekend after Easter

Focused on Pentecost weekend, the seventh after Easter, this is a festive pilgrimage made by up to one million people to the shrine of the Virgin at the Andalucian village of El Rocío (p734); see www.portalrociero.com (in Spanish).

CORPUS CRISTI 9th week after Easter

On the Thursday in the ninth week after Easter, religious processions and celebrations take place in Toledo (p280) and other cities. Those in Toledo (www.corpuschristitoledo.es) are most impressive.

JUNE

HOGUERAS DE SAN JUAN 23 Jun

Midsummer bonfires and fireworks feature on the eve of the Fiesta de San Juan (24 June; Dia de Sant Joan), notably along the Mediterranean coast – especially southeast and south – but also as far north as Barcelona (p344). It's celebrated with particular gusto in Ciutadella, Menorca (p691), where you can see splendid horsemanship in multitudinous parades. See www.santjoanweb.com.

ROCK IN RIO late Jun

Launched in 2008 over two weekends in Arganda del Rey (30km from Madrid), this enormous rock festival attracted 200,000 spectators to see national and international acts. A repeat is planned for 2010.

SÓNAR

Performers and spectators come from all over the world for Sónar (www.sonar.es), Barcelona's two-day celebration of electronic music (see p344). Dates vary each year.

JULY

FIESTA DE SAN FERMÍN (SANFERMINES) 6-14 Jul

For many, the highlight of this week-long non-stop festival and party in Pamplona (p502) is the

FINDING YOUR FIESTA

As well as the fiestas listed here (and others in the course of the guide), there are numerous sources listing the events, both traditional and modern, that go on throughout the year in Spain. You could start with the national tourist office website (www.spain.info): click on What to Do? and then Events and Fiestas. Some upcoming events are listed immediately and you can search by type of event, region, town, dates and so on. Regional and local tourist offices also tend to have copious information on the events in their regions – check the relevant websites to get started. Another more 'homemade' website is www.portalfiestas.com (in Spanish). Again, you can search by place and date. Punters provide many of the listings. If you can deal with the Spanish, you may well uncover some weird and wonderful events in the remotest towns and villages. Spainforyou.es (www.spainforyou.es in Spanish) is a similar tool. Less exhaustive but a good starting point is Spanish Fiestas (www.spanish-fiestas.com). A good book resource is the illustrated *Popular Fiestas, Spain Day by Day* by María Ángeles Sánchez. It covers, to a greater or lesser extent, thousands of Spanish fiestas.

encierro (running of the bulls), an activity also pursued in dozens of other cities and towns through the summer.

FESTIVAL DE ORTIGUEIRA 2nd weekend in Jul

Groups from as far off as Nova Scotia come to celebrate their Celtic roots with the *gallegos* in this bagpipe- and fiddler-filled music fest in Galicia's Ortigueira (p579). See www.festivaldeortigueira.com for info.

DÍA DE LA VIRGEN DEL CARMEN 16 Jul

Around this date in most coastal towns the image of the patron of fisherfolk is carried into the sea or paraded on a flotilla of small boats.

DÍA DE SANTIAGO 25 Jul

The Feast of St James marks the national saint's day and is spectacularly celebrated in Galicia at Santiago de Compostela (p569), the site of St James' tomb.

FESTIVAL INTERNACIONAL DE JAZZ E BLUES DE PONTEVEDRA late Jul

Top jazz and blues musicians converge on the pretty Galician town of Pontevedra for four days of good listening (p586) near the end of July. The international get-together is preceded by several days of local acts.

FESTIVAL INTERNACIONAL DE BENICÀSSIM late Jul

Spain is awash with outdoor concert festivals attracting big-name acts from around the country and abroad. This one, in the Valencian town of Benicàssim (p623), remains one of the original and best.

JULY–AUGUST

FESTIVAL DE TEATRO CLÁSICO

The Roman theatre and amphitheatre in Mérida, Extremadura (p856), become the stage for the classics of ancient Greece and Rome, and the occasional newbie such as Will Shakespeare. What better setting for the works of Sophocles and Euripides? Performances are held most nights during July and August.

AUGUST

FESTES DE LA PATRONA 1-2 Aug

In northwest Mallorca, Pollença is the scene of fierce mock combat between invading Muslim pirates and townsfolk armed mostly with poles (p663). The afternoon of processions and combat in the streets of the town is preceded by a night of revelry in which music and drink fire up souls until dawn.

SEMANA GRANDE OR ASTE NAGUSIA 1st Sat after 15 Aug

Bilbao is touched by a little summer madness for about 10 days with processions, cultural events, music and much partying, especially in the streets of the old town (see p475). Similar events take place in various towns along the Bay of Biscay coast. Gijón (p543) is particularly frenetic.

LA TOMATINA 2nd-last or last Wed in Aug

This massive tomato-throwing festival in Buñol, Valencia (p619) must be one of the messiest get-togethers in the country. Thousands of people launch about 100 tonnes of tomatoes at one another in just an hour or so!

CERTAMEN DEL QUESO 2nd-last or last Sun in Aug
In Arenas de Cabrales (p557) at the foot of the Picos de Europa, cheese-lovers are treated to cheese tasting, making, judging and more.

SEXENNI 2nd half Aug
In the high-country inland town of Morella, the good folk come together every six years (next in 2012) for nine days of exuberant baroque festivities in honour of the Virgin (p627). The town is decorated in preparation for the grand processions of a *paso* of the Virgin Mary from a chapel 24km away, to give thanks for her saving Morella from the plague in 1672.

SEPTEMBER

FIESTA DE LA VIRGEN DE GUADALUPE 6-8 Sep
The pretty town of Guadalupe in Extremadura celebrates its very own Virgin Mary (p853). A statue is paraded about on the evening of the 6th and then again in the monastery on the 8th, which also happens to be Extremadura's regional feast day.

FERIA DE PEDRO ROMERO 1st half Sep
The honouring of Pedro Romero, one of the legends of bullfighting, is a good excuse for the people of Ronda to host weeks of partying (p782). Highlights include a flamenco festival and a program of bullfighting, all liberally washed down with plenty of all-night eating and drinking.

FIESTA DE SAN MATEO 21 Sep
For one week, Logroño celebrates the feast day of St Matthew and the year's grape harvest (p512). There are grape-crushing ceremonies and endless opportunities to sample the fruit of the vine in liquid form.

FESTES DE LA MERCÈ around 24 Sep
Barcelona's gigantic party (p344) marks the end of summer with four days of parades, concerts, theatre, fire running and more.

OCTOBER

DÍA DE NUESTRA SEÑORA DEL PILAR 12 Oct
In Zaragoza the faithful mix with the hedonists to celebrate this festival dedicated to Our Lady of the Pillar (p437). The pillar in question, upon which the Virgin Mary is said to have appeared, is in the cathedral, but much of the fun happens in the bars nearby.

FIESTA DE SANTA TERESA 15 Oct
The patron saint of Ávila (p211) is honoured with 10 days of processions, concerts and fireworks around her feast day.

Itineraries

CLASSIC ROUTES

HEADING SOUTH

One Month/Barcelona to Algeciras

The sun glitters on the Mediterranean as your flight glides in to **Barcelona** (p302), Spain's second-biggest city. Explore the architecture and sample the food, then embark on a coast crawl with stops in **Tarragona** (p421) for the Roman ruins, **Peñíscola** (p624) for the beach, and **Valencia** (p604) for another dose of nightlife and the 21st-century wonders of the Ciudad de las Artes y las Ciencias. From here, flee deep into Castilla-La Mancha and halt at craggy **Cuenca** (p292). Push on to the capital, mighty **Madrid** (p129), for the hedonism and museums before continuing to **Toledo** (p273), a medieval jewel. The road sweeps through La Mancha's plains and olive groves to **Ciudad Real** (p285). Make a left for the striking village of **Almagro** (p287), in Almodóvar territory, then take the A4 for **Jaén** (p816) and its gorgeous cathedral. Nearby are the Islamic glories of **Granada** (p795) and **Córdoba** (p787). The colourful capital of the south, **Seville** (p710), also beckons. Hear the call of Africa? Drop down to **Cádiz** (p738) and proceed east to **Algeciras** (p761) for the boat to Morocco and a whole new adventure.

This 1767km route slices right across Spain, from the sparkling northern seaside metropolis of Barcelona, via the pulsating capital of Madrid to the fiery south of Andalucía. En route, make coastal stops in Tarragona and Valencia, and the Castilian strongholds of Cuenca, Toledo and Almagro.

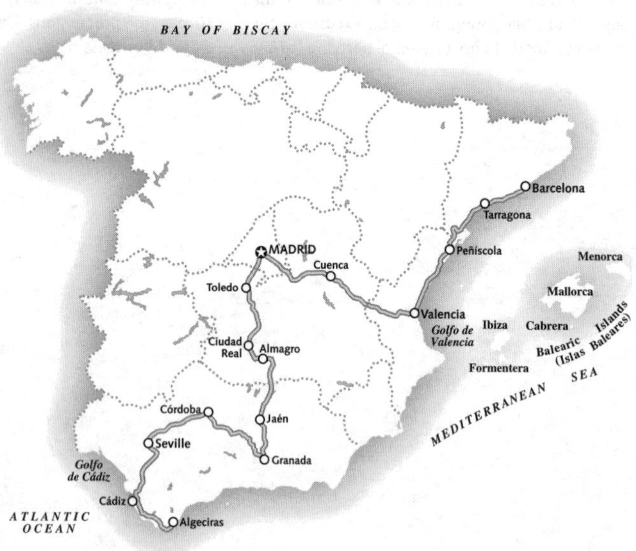

ANDALUCIAN ADVENTURE

Three Weeks / Málaga to Tarifa

Capture the colour, excitement and variety of Spain's vibrant southernmost region by combining visits to its three great World Heritage cities – **Seville** (p710), **Córdoba** (p787) and **Granada** (p795) – with an exploration of some of its most beautiful countryside and a refreshing beach spell to finish your trip. If flying in or out of **Málaga** (p768), don't miss its excellent **Museo Picasso** (p768).

Andalucía was the heartland of medieval Islamic Spain and each of the main World Heritage cities is home to one of Spain's three great Islamic monuments: Granada's **Alhambra** (p797), Córdoba's **Mezquita** (p788) and Seville's **Alcázar** (p718). Modern Andalucian culture and entertainment, too, are at their most effervescent in the university cities of Seville and Granada, both centres of the flamenco scene and bursting with bars serving some of the most delectable tapas in the region. These cities also boast an array of other treasures, from Granada's historic **Capilla Real** (p802) and old Muslim quarter, the **Albayzín** (p802), to Seville's massive **cathedral** (p717) and baroque churches. For a change of key, venture out from Granada to the otherworldly valleys of **Las Alpujarras** (p812), which also provide easy access to mainland Spain's highest mountains, the **Sierra Nevada** (p810), great for walking in summer and skiing in winter.

Having done your cultural bit, turn south from Seville for **Jerez de la Frontera** (p746), the sherry, equestrian and flamenco hub of Cádiz province, and the historic, vivacious port city of **Cádiz** (p738), before winding down on the sandy Atlantic beaches of the Costa de la Luz between Cádiz and Spain's internationally hip southernmost town, **Tarifa** (p757).

The route from Málaga to Tarifa is 840km. Add another 170km if you must return to Málaga at the end. Three weeks allows enough time to savour the places you visit; with four weeks you can linger as you like and make your own discoveries.

GREEN SPAIN **One Month / San Sebastián to Santiago de Compostela**

Spain's well-drenched northern coast forms a green band from the Basque Country to Galicia, backed by the Cordillera Cantábrica. Either **San Sebastián** (p484), with its crescent bay and tapas bars, or **Bilbao** (p469), with its Guggenheim museum, will make a fine introduction. Heading westwards, hug the coast of Cantabria and Asturias, making forays to inland valleys and mountains. Following Cantabria's eastern coast, drop by the old centre of **Castro Urdiales** (p528), surf at **Oriñón** (p528) and cruise the bars of **Santander** (p521). Explore the cobblestone medieval marvel of **Santillana del Mar** (p529), admire the Modernista architecture in **Comillas** (p532) and catch some waves at sprawling **Playa de Merón** (p533). The eastern Asturias coast is best travelled by train, stopping off at **Llanes** (p547) and **Ribadesella** (p546). **Arriondas** (p555), the next stop, is one gateway to the majestic **Picos de Europa** (p552). Straddling Cantabria and Asturias, these peaks offer fabulous hiking. Next head for **Oviedo** (p535), Asturias' capital, for its pre-Romanesque architecture, and **Gijón** (p541), a substantial port where cider flows copiously. West of Gijón, secluded beaches await between the picturesque fishing harbours of **Cudillero** (p548) and **Luarca** (p549). One approach to Galicia is to follow its *rías* (estuaries), a route that covers dynamic cities such as **A Coruña** (p572) and **Vigo** (p590), as well as low-key resorts, islands and protected areas. Between the Rías Altas (north) and Rías Baixas (west) are the untamed beaches of the **Costa da Morte** (p581). **Santiago de Compostela** (p564) makes a suitable end point for a Green Spain trek. Those with more time could make the final approach on foot along the **Camino de Santiago** (p118) pilgrim route. Alternatively, discover the area with the Transcantábrico scenic train (see the boxed text, p895).

The sea sets the agenda for the Iberian Peninsula's emerald fringe. This sweep of coastline crosses some 600km, dotted with hundreds of beaches. Cosmopolitan Bilbao and tall peaks present bracing alternatives. All roads lead to Santiago de Compostela in Galicia, Spain's culturally distinct northwest extremity.

ROADS LESS TRAVELLED

EXTREME WEST

One Week / Salamanca to Seville

For many travellers, the plateresque joys of the university town of **Salamanca** (p214), in western Castilla y León, are well known, but relatively few venture south into what was long one of the poorest regions of Spain. A back highway leads into the hill territory of the Peña de Francia, whose main village is pretty **La Alberca** (p225). You would never guess that until recent decades misery ruled in this quiet rural retreat. The road continues to climb and then suddenly drops through woods into Extremadura, passing into the once equally poor Las Hurdes region to reach **Plasencia** (p841) to the southeast. Jammed with noble buildings, churches and convents, it was for centuries the region's principal city, and makes a good base for excursions up the northeast valleys and to **Monasterio de Yuste** (p835). From Plasencia, a circuit takes you first to the charming hill town of **Guadalupe** (p852), lorded over by the monastery complex dedicated to Our Lady of Guadalupe. Country roads then lead westwards to the medieval town of **Trujillo** (p849), a warren of cobbled lanes, churches and the newer Renaissance-era additions that were the fruit of American gold. A short drive further west lies the ochre-coloured medieval jewel of **Cáceres** (p844), a town with a lively student nightlife scene, too. To the south stand some of Spain's most impressive Roman ruins in **Mérida** (p854). Further south again across the dry plains lies the white town of **Zafra** (p861). Rather than continue straight into Andalucía, make a westwards detour to the hilly town of **Jerez de los Caballeros** (p862) before finally heading south for magical **Seville** (p710).

This 810km route opens up the treasures of Extremadura, wedged between the Castilian university town of Salamanca and the south's sultry mistress, Seville. Along the way, discover the Roman wonders of Mérida, fine medieval cities, and the enchanting towns of La Alberca, Guadalupe and Zafra.

LA MANCHA TO EL MAESTRAZGO

One to Two Weeks / Toledo to Peñíscola

Start this adventure in nonconformist fashion with a couple of nights in **Toledo** (p273), rather than the typical day trip from Madrid. Wander further from convention by taking the road south to **Orgaz** (p283) and then a detour southeast to **Consuegra** (p289), one of many villages associated with Don Quijote. From there you plunge south past olive groves to **Ciudad Real** (p285) and east to **Almagro** (p287), an enchanting stop for a night or two. While here, make the excursion for the hilltop castle ruins outside **Calzada de Calatrava** (p288). From Almagro, the trail takes you east towards **Ruidera** (p288) and its lagoon park. From Ruidera, swing back northwest to Quijote territory, checking out **Campo de Criptana** (p289), **El Toboso** (p290) and **Mota del Cuervo** (p290). The road continues east to **Belmonte** (p290) and its castle. For a castle you can sleep in, press on to **Alarcón** (p297). Make the loop southeast to reach **Alcalá del Júcar** (p291), on the stunning Río Júcar, which you can then follow west before heading back north for **Cuenca** (p292) and its hanging houses. A pretty riverside route takes you north along the CM2105 road into the hilly territory of the Serranía de Cuenca and the **Ciudad Encantada** (p297) and then east across the Montes Universales to the ochre town of Muslim origin, **Albarracín** (p465). Next stop is **Teruel** (p461), remarkable for its old town's architecture. To the east lies a route past hamlets of the high country of El Maestrazgo, including **La Iglesuela del Cid**, **Cantavieja** and **Mirambel** (see p466). Crossing into Valencia (but still in El Maestrazgo), our route takes you to the breathtaking **Balma monastery** (p629), on to the pretty, castle-dominated town of **Morella** (p627) and finally to the coast at **Peñíscola** (p624).

Think you've been there and done that in Iberia? This 1185km meander across the back-blocks of central Spain will delight with Quijotic villages, castles, broad plains and the remote high country of El Maestrazgo – all far from tourist trails – before emerging at pretty, coastal Peñíscola.

TAILORED TRIPS

PASSING THROUGH PARADORES

Spain's chain of *paradores* (luxurious, state-owned hotels) offers the chance to reside in grand mansions, former convents and formidable castles. Just south of Madrid in Chinchón, the **Parador Nacional** (p203) is set in a 17th-century former monastery. To the south, among the best in Andalucía are the **Parador de Granada** (p806) within the Alhambra complex, the castle location of the **Parador de Jaén** (p818) on Santa Catalina Hill and the 16th-century Renaissance mansion of **Parador Condestable Dávalos** (p821) in Úbeda. A cluster of fine *paradores* is scattered west of Madrid. In Extremadura, the most tempting include 15th-century **Parador de Guadalupe** (p854) in Guadalupe; the 16th-century **Parador de Trujillo** (p851) in a former convent; and the **Parador de Cáceres** (p847), a 14th-century town house. To the north, León's **Hostal de San Marcos** (p249) is one of the finest *paradores* in the land, housed in the Monasterio de San Marcos. Equally fine is the luxury 15th-century **Parador Hostal dos Reis Católicos** (p570), a former pilgrims' hospice in Santiago de Compostela, northwest Galicia. East in Olite, Navarra, the **Principe de Viana** (p509) is another gem, occupying a wing of a 15th-century palace. In Catalonia, the hilltop castle–monastery complex of the **Parador Ducs de Cardona** (p415), in Cardona, stands out.

KIDS' SPAIN

Spain's generous diet of beaches, fiestas, castles and double-decker city tours keep under-14s content much of the time. Unique local attractions provide the icing on the cake. Barcelona has a great aquarium and other amusements at **Port Vell** (p328), along with the CosmoCaixa interactive science museum (p334). Around Catalonia, kids will enjoy the *cremallera* (rack and pinion) train ride to **Montserrat** (p367) and its weird rock pillars, and Spain's biggest amusement/adventure park, **Port Aventura** (p426).

Down the Mediterranean coast, activate those little brain cells at Valencia's marvellously entertaining *and* educational **Ciudad de las Artes y las Ciencias** (p607), which includes Europe's largest aquarium. Gijón, in Asturias, is home to another fine **Acuario** (p543), among whose stars are the sharks and a lively pair of otters.

Estepona's wildlife park **Selwo Aventura** (p779) stands out among the Costa del Sol's many kid-friendly attractions. In **Gibraltar** (p763) youngsters love the cable car, the apes, the dolphin-spotting trips and the tunnels in the upper rock. Next stop: **Jerez de la Frontera** (p746) for its zoo and the prancing horses of the Real Escuela Andaluza del Arte Ecuestre. **Isla Mágica** (p721), in Seville, thrills the white-knuckle brigade.

Up in Madrid, check out **Faunia** (p164) and the **Parque del Buen Retiro** (p156), with its boat rides and street performers. Many kids will go loco for the locos at the **Museo del Ferrocarril** (p164).

GOTHIC SPAIN

Wherever you find yourself in Spain, the majesty of Gothic construction can be admired. Start your tour in **Barcelona** (p302), which boasts one of the most extensive Gothic city cores in Europe. Its splendours include the Església de Santa Maria del Mar, the Reials Drassanes medieval shipyards and Saló del Tinell. From the Catalan capital you can make a grand sweep west to admire some of the country's landmark Gothic monuments. **Burgos** (p255) is home to a soaring Gothic cathedral much influenced by the French style and, further west still, **León** (p246) hosts another grand Gothic cathedral. Near Madrid, **Segovia** (p226) and **Ávila** (p207) also make the grade with their fine Gothic cathedrals; Ávila's was the earliest raised in the country. There's more Gothic to be found in lesser-known centres, such as pretty **Sigüenza** (p299). In Andalucía there are delights in store, such as the grand cathedral in **Seville** (p710) and Capilla Real in **Granada** (p795). They weren't just building cathedrals in those days. The Castilian countryside in particular is littered with castles of all shapes and sizes. Some, like the all-brick construction in **Coca** (p233), are all the more extraordinary for their mix of Gothic and Mudéjar styles. That mix continues in many monuments in medieval **Toledo** (p273), south of Madrid, where stands yet another Gothic pearl, in the form of the cathedral. Finally, the Balearic Islands also sport a Gothic cathedral in **Palma de Mallorca** (p653).

WATER WORLDS

One of only two European countries to possess both Atlantic and Mediterranean coast (the other, of course, being France), Spain's extraordinarily varied coastline offers the visitor a little bit of everything. Swimming is clearly an option all over the place, but some of the most beautiful beaches and water are to be discovered in the **Balearic Islands** (p648), especially on **Menorca** (p683) and **Formentera** (p678). You'll find one of the best ways to get around the Balearic Islands is by sailing. It is possible to hire charter yachts (with or without skipper) from places such as **Barcelona**, where you can take sailing and windsurfing classes (p340) before you set off. Divers will be eager to explore the depths around the **Illes Medes** (p385), an incredible protected archipelago of islets off Catalonia's Costa Brava. Another popular beach spot that is certain to attract divers is the start of **Cabo de Gata** (p828). Windsurfers, on the other hand, consider **Tarifa** (p757) to be their mecca. Surfers without sails make for the north coast, especially spots such as **Zarautz** (p484) and **Mundaka** (p482), which is known for its mythical left wave. Wild and woolly spots abound along the Atlantic coast. Among the most intriguing water-borne excursions in Galicia is a trip to the **Illas Cíes** (p593). There's more to enjoy than just sea water, however; those who like white-water adrenalin should make for **Ribadesella** (p546) or **Llavorsí** (p406) and climb aboard for a bumpy ride.

History

The massive wave of immigration that Spain has experienced in the last decade – the number of foreign-born residents has surged from less than 1 million to almost 5 million – has amazed many Spaniards and become a hot political issue. But a look at the country's history shows that immigration is nothing new here. Even before the recent influx of Africans, Latin Americans and northern and eastern Europeans, any Spaniard who could trace their family tree back far enough would unearth a tangle of roots that could include Stone Age hunters from Africa; ancient Greeks and Romans; Visigoths and other Germanic tribes; Berber tribespeople from Morocco; Phoenicians, Jews and Arabs from the Middle East; and *gitanos* (Roma people) of uncertain origins.

Spain has dealt its share of emigration too. The ancestors of a good half of the people living in the Americas today were Spaniards and as recently as the mid-20th century Spaniards were flocking in their hundreds of thousands to northern Europe and the Americas in search of a better life.

The key to this great ebb and flow of peoples is Spain's pivotal location just a stone's throw from Africa and as close to America as anywhere in Europe. Sitting at the meeting point of two continents and of two great bodies of water – the Mediterranean and the Atlantic – it has been soaking up influences from a vast array of peoples and cultures for thousands of years. Even its occasional periods of relative isolation were shaped by its relations with external powers and cultures.

For a colourful survey of the whole saga of Spanish history, read *The Story of Spain* by Mark Williams.

The impact of this great cultural melange is still present throughout the country – not only in the physical heritage of monuments, architecture, archaeological sites and landscape, but in language, food, music, dance, work and the big regional differences that still enthral travellers today.

THE FIRST IMMIGRANTS

Spain's history of outside contact goes back a long way indeed. In 2008 archaeologists discovered an assortment of bones and stone tools unearthed at Sima del Elefante (Elephant Chasm) in the Sierra de Atapuerca, near the northern city of Burgos. Dating revealed that a fossilised human jawbone and eight teeth were between 1.1 and 1.2 million years old – the oldest human remains ever found in Western Europe. Scientists reckon these bones come from an early type of human that later evolved into the species Homo antecessor, which might in turn have given rise to the later Neanderthals or Homo sapiens. The Atapuerca finds don't mean that the first non-African people were Spaniards – older human remains have been found in Georgia, from where scientists speculate that humans may have moved west into Western

TIMELINE

Before 1 million BC

Early humans reach Spain, possibly from Eastern Europe, and leave their fossilised remains in the Sierra de Atapuerca hills near the northern city of Burgos.

c 22,000 BC

Neanderthal humans die out on the Iberian Peninsula – possibly due to climatic changes during the last Ice Age, possibly because they were displaced by Homo sapiens arriving from Africa.

c 3000–1900 BC

Spaniards begin to work metal: people at Los Millares near Almería smelt and shape local copper deposits. Then people at El Argar, also in Almería, learn to alloy copper with tin, initiating the Bronze Age.

Europe. But they do prove the enormous length of human occupation on the Iberian Peninsula.

Caves and archaeological sites all round Spain have revealed plenty more about Spain's later prehistoric inhabitants. Even in those far-off days Spain's contacts with other regions, especially Africa and the eastern Mediterranean, catalysed many important steps on the long road to civilisation here. The Cueva de Nerja (p786) was one of many haunts of the first anatomically modern humans in Iberia, the Cro-Magnons, who probably arrived from Africa around 35,000 years ago and hunted mammoth, bison and reindeer. After the end of the last Ice Age in about 8000 BC further new peoples arrived, again probably from North Africa, and their rock-shelter paintings of hunting and dancing survive in eastern Spain.

The most famous and impressive cave art however – sophisticated images of bison, stags, boars and horses – is at Altamira (p532) near Santander, and dates from around 12,000 BC. Altamira was part of the Magdalenian hunting culture of southern France and northern Spain, an Old Stone Age culture that lasted from around 20,000 to 8000 BC.

The Neolithic (New Stone Age) reached Spain from Mesopotamia and Egypt around 6000 BC, bringing revolutionary innovations such as the plough, crops, livestock, pottery, textiles and permanent villages, especially in the east of the country. Contacts with northern Europe are also evident with the appearance of megalithic tombs (dolmens), constructed of large rocks, in several places around the perimeter of the peninsula between 3000 and 2000 BC – the same era as the megalithic age in France, Britain and Ireland. The best dolmens in Spain are at Antequera (p784) in Andalucía. At the same time the southeastern province of Almería saw the beginnings of metal technology in Spain.

The beautiful Iberian statue Dama de Elche (Lady of Elche), near Alicante), dates from around the 5th century BC and can be seen in Madrid's Museo Arqueológico Nacional.

TRADERS & INVADERS

Spain's rich natural resources and settled societies eventually attracted early seafaring traders from more-sophisticated societies around the Mediterranean. This series of newcomers arrived between 1000 and 500 BC, bringing further technological advances and introducing many elements that still characterise Spain today.

Traders were then replaced by invaders as emerging imperialist states sought not only to tap the wealth of places like Spain but also to exert military control – again leaving their own indelible marks on Spanish life and identity.

Phoenicians, Greeks, Celts

By about 1000 BC a flourishing culture rich in animals, agriculture and metals had arisen in western Andalucía. Phoenicians, a Semitic people from present-day Lebanon, first came to exchange perfumes, ivory, jewellery, oil,

c 800–500 BC

The fabled Tartessos culture, influenced by Phoenician and Greek traders, flourishes in western Andalucía. Carthage then replaces the Phoenicians and Greeks as the major trading power in the western Mediterranean.

218 BC

Roman legions arrive in Spain during the Second Punic War against Carthage, initiating the 600-year Roman occupation of the Iberian Peninsula. It takes Rome two centuries to subdue the last local resistance.

1st to 3rd centuries AD

The Pax Romana (Roman Peace), a period of stability and prosperity. The Iberian Peninsula is divided into three provinces: Baetica (capital: Córdoba); Lusitania (capital: Mérida) and Tarraconensis (capital: Tarragona).

wine and textiles for Spanish silver and bronze, but soon established coastal trading colonies at Cádiz (which they called Gadir), Huelva (Onuba), Málaga (Malaca) and Almuñécar (Ex or Sex). Around 700 BC the colonists introduced iron-making technology into the lower Guadalquivir valley and Spain entered the Iron Age. The Phoenician-influenced culture that developed was very likely the fabled Tartessos, mythologised by later Greek, Roman and biblical writers as a place of unimaginable wealth. No one knows whether Tartessos was a city, a state or just an area. Some argue it was a trading settlement near modern Huelva; others believe it may lie beneath the marshes near the mouth of Río Guadalquivir.

Cádiz is the oldest continually inhabited city in the whole of the Iberian Peninsula, dating back to at least the 9th century BC.

In the 7th century BC Greek traders reached Spain too, establishing settlements mainly up the Mediterranean coast – the biggest was Emporion (Empúries; p386) in Catalonia.

As well as iron, the Phoenicians and Greeks brought with them several things now considered quintessentially Spanish – the olive tree, the grapevine and the donkey – along with other useful skills and items like writing, coins, the potter's wheel and poultry.

Around the same time as the Phoenicians brought iron technology to the south, the Celts (originally from Central Europe) brought it – and beer-making – to the north when they crossed the Pyrenees. In contrast to the dark-featured Iberians (the general name given to most inhabitants of the peninsula at this time), the Celts were fair. Celts and Iberians who merged on the *meseta* (plateau; the high tableland of central Spain) are known as Celtiberians. Celts and Celtiberians typically lived in sizable hill-fort towns called *castros*.

The Carthaginians

From about the 6th century BC the Phoenicians and Greeks were pushed out of the western Mediterranean by Carthage, a former Phoenician colony in modern Tunisia that established a flourishing settlement in Ibiza.

Carthage naturally didn't see eye to eye with the next rising Mediterranean power, Rome, and after being defeated in the First Punic War (264–241 BC, fought for control of Sicily), the Carthaginians invaded the Iberian Peninsula in 237 BC. The Second Punic War (218–201 BC) saw the Carthaginian general Hannibal march his elephants over the Alps towards Rome, but also brought Roman legions to Spain. Hannibal was finally routed in North Africa in 202 BC.

The Romans

The Romans held sway in Iberia for 600 years, but it took them 200 years to subdue the fiercest of local tribes. By AD 50, however, most of Hispania (as the Romans called the peninsula) had adopted the Roman way of life. The major exceptions were the Basques who, though defeated, were never Romanised like the rest.

53

Future Roman Emperor Trajan is born in Itálica, near modern Seville, to a wealthy senator and general. His imperial rule will begin in 98 and see the Roman Empire reach its greatest extent.

4th to 7th centuries AD

Germanic tribes enter the Iberian Peninsula, ending the Pax Romana, but one of them, the Visigoths, establishes control and brings 200 years of relative stability in which Hispano-Roman culture survives.

711

Muslims invade Iberia from North Africa, overrunning it within a few years. They become the dominant force on the peninsula for nearly four centuries, a potent one for four centuries after that.

Rome's legacy was huge, giving the country a road system, aqueducts, temples, theatres, amphitheatres and bathhouses, along with the religion that still predominates today, Christianity. The basis of most of the languages still spoken here – Castilian, Catalan, Galician and Portuguese – are all versions of the vernacular Latin spoken by Roman legionaries and colonists, filtered through 2000 years of linguistic mutation. It was also the Romans who first began to cut (for timber, fuel and weapons) the extensive forests that in their time covered half the *meseta*. The Roman era also saw the arrival of Jews in Spain who were to play a big part in Spanish life for over 1000 years. In return, Hispania gave Rome gold, silver, grain, wine, soldiers, emperors (Trajan, Hadrian, Theodosius) and the literature of Seneca, Martial, Quintilian and Lucan. Another notable export was *garum*, a spicy sauce derived from fish and used as a seasoning. The finest of Spain's Roman ruins are at Empúries (p386), Itálica (p730), Mérida (p854), Tarragona (p421) and Segovia (p226).

Segovia's stunning aqueduct still provides the city with water, just as it has done since being built around the beginning of the 2nd century AD.

The Pax Romana in Spain started to crack when two Germanic tribes, the Franks and the Alemanni, swept across the Pyrenees in the late 3rd century AD, causing devastation. When the Huns hit Eastern Europe from Asia a century later, further Germanic peoples moved westwards. Among these were the Suevi and Vandals, who overran the Iberian Peninsula around 410.

The Visigoths

The Visigoths, another Germanic people, sacked Rome itself in 410. Within a few years, however, they had become Roman allies, being granted lands in southern Gaul (France) and fighting on the emperor's behalf against the barbarian invaders in Hispania. When the Visigoths were pushed out of Gaul in the 6th century by yet another Germanic people, the Franks, they settled in the Iberian Peninsula, making Toledo their capital.

The rule of the roughly 200,000 long-haired Visigoths, who had a penchant for gaudy jewellery, over the millions of more-sophisticated Hispano-Romans was at first precarious and undermined by strife among their own nobility. The Hispano-Roman nobles still ran the fiscal system and their bishops were the senior figures in urban centres. The ties between the Visigoth monarchy and the Hispano-Romans were, however, strengthened in 587 when King Reccared converted to Roman Christianity from the Visigoths' Arian version (which denied that Christ was identical to God). Culturally, the Visigoths tended to ape Roman ways and their lasting impact on Spanish culture was limited to certain names like Roderigo and Leovigildo, and a few churches in the north. One, at Baños de Cerrato (p245) near Palencia, dates from 661 and is probably the oldest surviving church in the country.

718

Pelayo, a Visigothic Christian nobleman, establishes the Kingdom of Asturias in the north of the country. With victory over a Muslim force at the Battle of Covadonga around 722 the Reconquista (Reconquest) of Spain begins.

756

Córdoba begins to dominate Al-Andalus (the Islamic areas of the peninsula) as Abd ar-Rahman arrives here after the collapse of the Omayyad Empire in Syria and defeats the local Muslim rulers.

801

Barcelona is taken by Frankish troops and becomes a buffer between the Christians to the north and the Muslims to the south.

MUSLIM SPAIN

Following the death of the prophet Mohammed in 632, Arabs had spread through the Middle East and North Africa, carrying Islam with them. With the disintegration of the Visigothic kingdom through famine, disease and strife among the aristocracy, the country was ripe for invasion. If you believe the myth, the Muslims were ushered into Spain by the sexual adventures of the last Visigoth king, Roderic, who reputedly seduced Florinda, the daughter of Julian, the Visigothic governor of Ceuta in North Africa. Julian sought revenge by approaching the Muslims with a plan to invade Spain and in 711 Tariq ibn Ziyad, the Muslim governor of Tangier, landed at Gibraltar with around 10,000 men, mostly Berbers (indigenous North Africans). Roderic's army was decimated, probably near Río Guadalete or Río Barbate in Cádiz province, Andalucía, and he is thought to have drowned while fleeing the scene. Visigothic survivors fled north and within a few years the Muslims (often referred to as Moors) had conquered the whole Iberian Peninsula, except small areas in the Asturian mountains in the north. Their advance into Europe was only checked by the Franks at the Battle of Poitiers in 732.

Richard Fletcher's *Moorish Spain* is an excellent short history of Al-Andalus (the Muslim-ruled areas of the peninsula).

The name given to Muslim territory on the peninsula was Al-Andalus. Its frontiers shifted constantly as the Christians strove to regain territory in the stuttering 800-year Reconquista (Reconquest). Up to the mid-11th century the frontier lay across the north of the peninsula, roughly from southern Catalonia to northern Portugal, with a protrusion up to the central Pyrenees. Political power and cultural developments centred initially on Córdoba (756–1031), then Seville (c 1040–1248) and lastly Granada (1248–1492). These cities boasted beautiful palaces, mosques and gardens, universities, public baths and bustling *zocos* (markets). Al-Andalus' rulers allowed freedom of worship to Jews and Christians (known as *mozárabes* or Mozarabs) under their rule. Jews mostly flourished, but Christians had to pay a special tax, so most either converted to Islam (to be known as *muladíes* or *muwallads*) or left for the Christian north. The Muslim settlers themselves were not a homogeneous group. Beneath the Arab ruling class was a larger group of Berbers, and tension between these two groups broke out in numerous Berber rebellions.

The Muslim Legacy

Muslim rule not only set Spain's destiny quite apart from that of the rest of Europe but left an indelible imprint on the country. Al-Andalus developed the most cultured society of medieval Europe and great architectural monuments such as the Alhambra in Granada and the Mezquita (mosque) in Córdoba are the stars of the Muslim legacy. The characteristic tangled, narrow street plans of many a Spanish town and village, especially in the south, owe themselves to the Muslims, and they also developed the Hispano-Roman agricultural base by improving irrigation and introducing new fruits and crops, many of which are still widely grown today. The Spanish language contains many

854

The Muslims establish a chain of forts along the frontier with the Christian areas of the north of the country. One of these strongholds is Magerit, which will go on to become Madrid.

10th century

The Cordoban Caliphate reaches its zenith and the city is home to nearly half a million people, becoming famous across Europe for its art, architecture and library of around 400,000 books.

1085

The northern Christian kingdom of Castilla captures the major Muslim city of Toledo (and Magerit/Madrid) after infighting among the Muslim *taifas* (small kingdomss) has left them vulnerable to attack.

common words of Arabic origin including the names of some of those new crops – *naranja* (orange), *azúcar* (sugar) and *arroz* (rice). Muslim and local blood quickly merged after the conquest, adding a new ingredient to the Spanish genetic mix. It was also through Al-Andalus that much of the learning of ancient Greece – picked up by the Arabs in the eastern Mediterranean – was transmitted to Christian Europe.

The Cordoban Emirate & Caliphate

Initially Al-Andalus was part of the Caliphate of Damascus, which ruled the Muslim world. In 750 the Omayyad caliphal dynasty in Damascus was overthrown by a rival clan, the Abbasids, who shifted the caliphate to Baghdad. However, one aristocratic Omayyad survivor managed to make his way to Spain and establish himself in Córdoba in 756 as the independent emir of Al-Andalus, Abd ar-Rahman I. He began constructing Córdoba's Mezquita, one of the world's greatest Muslim buildings. Most of Al-Andalus was more or less unified under Cordoban rule for long periods. In 929 the ruler Abd ar-Rahman III gave himself the title caliph, launching the Caliphate of Córdoba (929–1031), during which Al-Andalus reached its peak of power and lustre. Córdoba in this period was the biggest and most dazzling city in Western Europe. Astronomy, medicine, mathematics and botany flourished and one of the great Muslim libraries was established in the city.

Córdoba's renowned 10th-century caliph Abd ar-Rahman III had red hair and blue eyes; one of his grandmothers was a Basque princess.

Later in the 10th century the fearsome Cordoban general Al-Mansour (or Almanzor) terrorised the Christian north with 50-odd forays in 20 years. He destroyed the cathedral at Santiago de Compostela in northwestern Spain in 997 and forced Christian slaves to carry its doors and bells to Córdoba, where they were incorporated into the great mosque. But after Al-Mansour's death the caliphate collapsed in a devastating civil war, finally breaking up in 1031 into dozens of *taifas* (small kingdoms). The most powerful of these included Seville, Granada, Toledo and Zaragoza.

The Almoravids & Almohads

Political unity was restored to Al-Andalus by the invasion of a strict Muslim sect of Saharan nomads, the Almoravids, in 1091. The Almoravids had conquered North Africa and were initially invited to the Iberian Peninsula to support the Seville *taifa* against the growing Christian threat from the north. Sixty years later a second Berber sect, the Almohads, invaded the peninsula after overthrowing the Almoravids in Morocco. Both sects roundly defeated the Christian armies they encountered.

Almohad rule saw a cultural revival in Seville and the great Cordoban philosopher Averroës (1126–98) exerted a major influence on medieval Christian thought with his commentaries on Aristotle, trying to reconcile science with religion.

1091

The Almoravids, an increasingly powerful Muslim dynasty from North Africa, invade the peninsula, destroying the *taifas*, unifying Muslim Spain and bringing a temporary halt to Christian expansion.

1147

The Almoravids are defeated by the Almohads who gain control over Al-Andalus. Their rule is short-lived however – with victory at the battle of Las Navas de Tolosa in 1212 the momentum swings decisively in favour of the Christians.

1218

The University of Salamanca is founded by Alfonso IX, King of León, making it the oldest – and still the most prestigious – university in the country.

The Last Redoubt: Granada

Almohad power eventually disintegrated because of internal disputes and Christian advances. Seville fell to the Christians in 1248, reducing Muslim territory on the Iberian Peninsula to the Emirate of Granada, which occupied about half of modern Andalucía. Ruled from the lavish Alhambra palace by the Nasrid dynasty, Granada saw Muslim Spain's final cultural flowering, especially in the 14th century under Yusuf I and Mohammed V, both of whom contributed to the splendours of the Alhambra (p797).

Following his 1959 success in *Ben-Hur*, Charlton Heston turned to the Spanish Reconquista for his follow-up Hollywood epic, *El Cid* (1961).

THE RECONQUISTA

The Christian Reconquest of the Iberian Peninsula began in about 722 at Covadonga, Asturias, and ended with the fall of Granada in 1492. It was a stuttering affair, conducted by Christian kingdoms that were as often at war with each other as with the Muslims. But the Muslims were gradually pushed south as the northern kingdoms of Asturias, León, Navarra, Castilla and Aragón developed. Spain owes many of its hundreds of picturesquely impressive castles to this era.

An essential ingredient in the Reconquista was the cult of Santiago (St James), one of the 12 apostles. In 813, the saint's supposed tomb was discovered in Galicia. The city of Santiago de Compostela (p564) grew here, to become the third-most popular medieval Christian pilgrimage goal after Rome and Jerusalem. Christian generals experienced visions of Santiago before forays against the Muslims, and Santiago became the inspiration and special protector of soldiers in the Reconquista, earning the sobriquet Matamoros (Moor-slayer). Today he is the patron saint of Spain.

The pre-Romanesque churches of the northern region of Asturias are unique, pre-dating the rest of Europe in the introduction of this architectural style by over two centuries.

Castilla Rises

Covadonga, in Asturias, is where Visigothic nobles took refuge after the Muslim conquest. Christian versions of the battle there tell of a small band of fighters defeating an enormous force of Muslims; Muslim accounts make it a rather less important skirmish. Whatever the facts, by 757 Christians occupied nearly a quarter of the Iberian Peninsula.

The Asturian kingdom eventually moved its capital to León, which spearheaded the Reconquista until the Christians were set on the defensive by Al-Mansour in the 10th century. Castilla, initially a small principality within the kingdom of León, developed into the dominant Reconquista force as hardy adventurers set up towns in the no-man's-land of the Duero basin, spurred on by land grants and other *fueros* (rights and privileges). It was the capture of Toledo in 1085, by Alfonso VI of Castilla, that led the Seville Muslims to call in the Almoravids.

Alfonso I of Aragón, on the southern flank of the Pyrenees, led the counterattack against the Almoravids, taking Zaragoza in 1118. After his death Aragón was united through royal marriage with Catalonia, creating

1236

Córdoba falls to Fernando III of Castilla, with Seville following 12 years later, leaving the Nasrid Emirate of Granada as the last surviving Muslim state on the peninsula.

1258

The King of France formally relinquishes control over Catalonia, leading to a Catalan golden age as the region becomes the dominant power in the western Mediterranean.

1366–69

Civil war erupts in Castilla as Pedro (nicknamed 'the Just' by his supporters but 'the Cruel' by his enemies) fights his half-brother Enrique for the throne. Enrique eventually kills Pedro and becomes king.

a formidable new Christian power block known as the Kingdom of Aragón.

In 1212 the combined Christian armies routed a large Almohad force at Las Navas de Tolosa in Andalucía. This was the beginning of the end for Al-Andalus: León took the key towns of Extremadura in 1229 and 1230; Aragón took Valencia in the 1230s; Castilla's Fernando III El Santo (Ferdinand the Saint) took Córdoba in 1236 and Seville in 1248; and Portugal expelled the Muslims in 1249. The sole surviving Muslim state on the peninsula was now the Emirate of Granada.

Spanish History Index (vlib.iue.it/hist-spain/index.html) provides countless internet leads for those who want to dig deeper.

The Lull

Fernando III's son, Alfonso X El Sabio (the Learned; r 1252–84), proclaimed Castilian the official language of his realm and gathered around him scholars of all religions, particularly Jews who knew Arabic and Latin. Alfonso was, however, plagued by uprisings and plots, even from within his own family. Indeed, the Castilian nobility repeatedly challenged the crown until the 15th century. In a climate of xenophobia spawned by the struggle against the Muslims, intolerance also developed towards the Jews and Genoese, who came to dominate Castilian commerce and finance while the Castilian nobility were preoccupied with low-effort, high-profit wool production. In the 1390s anti-Jewish feeling culminated in pogroms around the peninsula.

Castilla and Aragón laboured under ineffectual monarchs from the late 14th century until the time of Isabel and Fernando (Isabella and Ferdinand), whose marriage in 1469 merged the two kingdoms. Isabel succeeded to the Castilian throne in 1474 and Fernando to that of Aragón in 1479, and together they would become an unbeatable team.

Granada Falls

In 1476 Emir Abu al-Hasan of Granada refused to pay any more tribute to Castilla, spurring Isabel and Fernando to launch the Reconquista's final crusade, against Granada, with an army largely funded by Jewish loans and the Catholic Church. The Christians took full advantage of a civil war within the Granada emirate, and on 2 January 1492 Isabel and Fernando entered the city of Granada at the beginning of what turned out to be the most momentous year in Spanish history.

The surrender terms were fairly generous to Boabdil, the last emir, who got the Alpujarras valleys south of Granada and 30,000 gold coins. The remaining Muslims were promised respect for their religion, culture and property, but this didn't last long.

UNITED SPAIN & THE AMERICAN EMPIRE

Christopher Columbus' voyage to the Americas, in the very same year as Granada fell, presented an entire new continent in which the militaristic and

1469

Isabel, the 18-year-old heir to Castilla, marries Fernando, heir to Aragón and one year younger than his bride, uniting Spain's two most powerful Christian states.

1478

Isabel and Fernando, the Reyes Católicos (Catholic Monarchs), stir up religious bigotry and establish the Spanish Inquisition that will see thousands killed between now and 1834 when it's finally abolished.

1492 (January)

After a long siege, Isabel and Fernando capture Granada and the Reconquista is complete. Boabdil, the last Muslim ruler, is scorned by his mother for weeping 'like a woman for what you could not defend like a man'.

crusading elements of Spanish society could continue their efforts. It also opened up vast new sources of wealth for the Spanish crown (which spent it on costly European wars), the nobility and the Church (which built opulent palaces, cathedrals and monasteries) and foreign merchants (who siphoned off a large profit from Spanish trade). The great majority of the population, however, reaped little benefit, and many in this new Christian society found they were not welcome at all.

Goodbye Jews & Muslims

The Christian zeal of the Catholic Monarchs led to the foundation of the Spanish Inquisition as a way to root out those who didn't practise Christianity as the Church desired. It focused first on *conversos* (Jews converted to Christianity), accusing many of continuing to practise Judaism in secret, and then, in April 1492, under the influence of Grand Inquisitor Tomás de Torquemada, Isabel and Fernando ordered the expulsion of all Jews who refused Christian baptism. Up to 100,000 converted, but some 200,000 – the first Sephardic Jews – left Spain for other Mediterranean destinations. The bankrupt monarchy seized all unsold Jewish property. A talented and valuable middle class was gone.

The Iberian Peninsula's best-known Neanderthal relic is 'Gibraltar woman', a skull found in 1848.

Cardinal Cisneros, Isabel's confessor and overseer of the Inquisition, tried to eradicate Muslim culture too. In the former Granada emirate he carried out forced mass baptisms, burnt Islamic books and banned the Arabic language. After a revolt in Andalucía in 1500, Muslims were ordered to convert to Christianity or leave. Most (around 300,000) underwent baptism and stayed, becoming known as *moriscos* (converted Muslims), but their conversion was barely skin-deep and they never assimilated. The *moriscos* were finally expelled between 1609 and 1614.

Hello America

In April 1492 the Catholic Monarchs granted the Genoese sailor Christopher Columbus (Cristóbal Colón to Spaniards) funds for his long-desired voyage across the Atlantic in search of a new trade route to the Orient.

Columbus set off from the Andalucian port of Palos de la Frontera (p733) on 3 August 1492, with three small ships and 120 men. After a near mutiny as the crew despaired of sighting land, they finally arrived on the island of Guanahaní, in the Bahamas, and went on to find Cuba and Hispaniola. Columbus returned to a hero's reception from the Catholic Monarchs in Barcelona, eight months after his departure. Three more voyages saw him founding the city of Santo Domingo on Hispaniola, finding Jamaica, Trinidad and other Caribbean islands, and reaching the mouth of the Orinoco and the coast of Central America, but he died impoverished in Valladolid in 1506, still believing he had reached Asia.

Brilliant but ruthless conquistadors followed Columbus' trail, seizing vast tracts of the American mainland for Spain. Between 1519 and 1521

1492 (April)

Isabel and Fernando expel around 200,000 Jews who have refused Christian baptism. They will go on to establish Sephardic Jewish communities around the Mediterranean while Spain's economy suffers through the loss of their business knowledge.

1492 (October)

Christopher Columbus, funded by Isabel and Fernando, lands in the Bahamas, opening up the Americas to Spanish colonisation. The shift in maritime trade from the Mediterranean to the Atlantic has a devastating impact on ports like Barcelona.

1494

The Treaty of Tordesillas divides recently discovered lands outside Europe between Spain and Portugal, giving the Spanish control of vast territories in the Americas.

Hernán Cortés conquered the fearsome Aztec empire with a small band of adventurers. Between 1531 and 1533 Francisco Pizarro did the same to the Inca empire, and by 1600 Spain controlled Florida, all the biggest Caribbean islands, nearly all of present-day Mexico and Central America, and a large strip of South America. The new colonies sent huge cargoes of silver, gold and other riches back to Spain, where the crown was entitled to one-fifth of the bullion (the *quinto real,* or royal fifth). Seville enjoyed a monopoly on this trade and grew into one of Europe's richest cities.

Entangled in Europe

Fernando and Isabel embroiled Spain in European affairs by marrying their four children into the royal families of Portugal, Burgundy and England. When Isabel died in 1504 the Castilian throne passed to her daughter Juana, whose husband, Felipe El Hermoso (Philip the Handsome), was heir to the Low Countries and the lands of the powerful Habsburg family in Central Europe. However, Juana, dubbed Juana la Loca (the Mad), proved unfit to rule and, when Felipe died soon after Isabel, Fernando took over as regent of Castilla until his death in 1516. It was his annexation of Navarra in 1512 that brought all of Spain under one rule for the first time since Visigothic days.

The minor country town of Madrid was selected in 1561 by Felipe II as the new capital from which he would mould his kingdom.

Fernando was succeeded by his grandson Carlos I (Charles I), son of Juana la Loca and Felipe El Hermoso, who arrived in Spain from Flanders in 1517, aged 17, to take up his Spanish inheritance. In 1519 Carlos also succeeded to the Habsburg lands in Austria and was elected Holy Roman Emperor (as Charles V), meaning he now ruled all of Spain, the Low Countries, Austria, several Italian states, parts of France and Germany, and the expanding Spanish colonies in the Americas.

Carlos spent only 16 years of his 40-year reign in Spain and at first the Spanish did not care for a king who spoke no Castilian, nor for his appropriations of their wealth. Castilian cities revolted in 1520–21 (the Guerra de las Comunidades, or War of the Communities), but were crushed. Eventually the Spanish came round to him, at least for his strong stance against the threat of Protestantism and his learning of Castilian.

European conflicts soaked up the bulk of the monarchy's new American wealth and a war-weary Carlos abdicated shortly before his death in 1556, dividing his many territories between his son Felipe II (Philip II; r 1556–98) and his brother Fernando. Felipe got the lion's share, including Spain, the Low Countries and the American possessions, and presided over the zenith of Spanish power, though his reign is a study in contradictions. He enlarged the American empire and claimed Portugal on its king's death in 1580, but lost Holland after a long drawn-out rebellion. His navy defeated the Ottoman Turks at Lepanto in 1571, but the Spanish Armada of 1588 was routed by England. He was a fanatical Catholic, who spurred the Inquisition to new persecutions, yet readily allied Spain with Protestant England against Catholic

1517–56

Reign of Carlos I, Spain's first Habsburg monarch, during which the country will be part of a huge empire spanning large parts of Europe and South and Central America.

1556–98

Reign of Felipe II, the zenith of Spanish power. The American territories expand into the modern United States and the resulting enormous amounts of money are ploughed into grandiose architectural projects.

1561

The king chooses the relative backwater of Madrid as the capital of his empire. The nobility rush to build suitable residences in the city but the overwhelming impression of the new capital is one of squalor.

France. He received greater flows of silver than ever from the Americas, but went bankrupt.

THE LONG DECLINE

Spain's impotent response to its American windfall came steadily home to roost over the following centuries. Though the arts enjoyed a golden age, a series of mostly weak, backward-looking monarchs and a wealthy, highly conservative Church and idle nobility allowed the economy to stagnate, leading to food shortages. Spain lost most of its European possessions and its sea power was terminated during the Napoleonic Wars, during which it suffered the humiliation of several years' occupation by French forces.

Felipe IV and his family (sans mistresses) have been preserved for posterity in Velázquez's world-famous family portrait, *Las Meninas,* which can be seen in Madrid's Museo del Prado (p153).

Hapless Habsburgs

Seventeenth-century Spain was like a gigantic artisans' workshop, in which architecture, sculpture, painting and metalwork consumed around 5% of the nation's income. The age was immortalised on canvas by artists such as Velázquez, El Greco, Zurbarán and Murillo, and in words by Miguel de Cervantes, the mystics Santa Teresa of Ávila and San Juan de la Cruz (St John of the Cross) and the prolific playwright Lope de Vega. But the last three Habsburg kings who presided over all this were notoriously ineffectual. Felipe III (Philip III; r 1598–1621) left government to the self-seeking Duke of Lerma. Felipe IV (Philip IV; r 1621–65) concentrated on his mistresses and handed over affairs of state to Count-Duke Olivares, who tried bravely but retired a broken man in 1643. Spain lost Portugal and faced revolts in Sicily, Naples and Catalonia. Silver shipments from the Americas shrank disastrously. And Carlos II (Charles II; r 1665–1700) failed to produce children, a situation that led to the War of the Spanish Succession.

Bumbling Bourbons

Carlos II bequeathed his throne to his young relative Felipe V (Philip V; r 1700–46), who also happened to be second in line to the French throne. Meanwhile the Austrian emperor Leopold wanted to see his own son Charles (a nephew of Carlos II) on the Spanish throne. The resulting War of the Spanish Succession (1702–13) was a contest for the balance of power in Europe. Spain lost its last possessions in the Low Countries to Austria, and Gibraltar and Menorca to Britain, while Felipe V renounced his right to the French throne but held on to Spain. He was the first of the Bourbon dynasty, still in place today.

Santa Teresa of Ávila was brought to the silver screen by the rising star of Spanish cinema, Paz Vega, in the 2006 release *Teresa, Vida y Muerte* (Teresa, Life and Death), directed by Ray Loriga.

Under Felipe's successor, Fernando VI (Ferdinand VI; r 1746–59), the economy took an upturn thanks to a revitalised Catalonia and the Basque shipbuilding industry. But agricultural Castilla and Andalucía were left behind due to a lack of land reforms. The enlightened despot Carlos III (Charles III; r 1759–88) expelled the backward-looking Jesuits, transformed

1580

Spain rules over Portugal after the death of the Portuguese king leads to internal disputes over the succession. John, Duke of Braganza, will eventually restore Portuguese independence as John IV in 1640.

1588

Felipe II's 'invincible Armada' sails to England as part of a Spanish invasion force. English attacks and bad weather destroy up to half the fleet, while the rest limps home in defeat.

Early 1600s

Spain enjoys a cultural golden age with the literature of Cervantes and the paintings of Velázquez, Murillo and El Greco reaching new heights of artistic excellence just as the empire is declining.

the capital Madrid, established a new road system out to the provinces and tried to improve agriculture, but food shortages still fuelled unrest among the masses.

The Peninsular War

Carlos IV (Charles IV; r 1788–1808) was dominated by his Italian wife, Maria Luisa of Parma, who saw to it that her favourite, the handsome royal guard Manuel Godoy, became chief minister. When Louis XVI of France, a cousin of Carlos IV, was guillotined in 1793, Spain declared war on France only for Godoy to make peace two years later, promising military support against Britain. In 1805 a combined Spanish–French navy was beaten by the British fleet, under Admiral Nelson, off the Cabo de Trafalgar (south of Cádiz), putting an end to Spanish sea power.

In 1807 Napoleon and Godoy agreed to divide Britain's ally Portugal between them. French forces poured into Spain, supposedly on the way to Portugal, but by 1808 this had become a French occupation of Spain and Carlos was forced to abdicate in favour of Napoleon's brother Joseph Bonaparte (José I). In Madrid crowds revolted and across the country Spaniards took up arms guerrilla-style, reinforced by British and Portuguese forces led by the Duke of Wellington. The French, hopelessly stretched by Napoleon's Russian campaign, were eventually driven out after their defeat at Vitoria in 1813.

José Bonaparte might not have been a popular king but he left behind some great urban architecture in Madrid, including the Plaza de Oriente and Puerta de Toledo.

THINGS START TO FALL APART

An increasingly backward and insular Spain knew little about the great economic and political motors of 19th-century Europe – industrialisation, democratisation, national unification and colonial expansion. In fact Spain moved in pretty much the opposite direction. It lost the last of its overseas possessions and suffered a series of debilitating internal conflicts, and though its liberal factions took feeble steps in the direction of democracy, the mass of the populace sank into depths of poverty and exploitation that spawned deepening social unrest.

Fernando Marches Backwards

During the Peninsular War a national Cortes (parliament) meeting at Cádiz in 1812 had drawn up a new liberal constitution for Spain, which incorporated many of the principles of the American and French prototypes. This set off a contest that lasted most of the 19th century between conservatives (the Church, the nobility and others who preferred the earlier status quo) and liberals (who wanted vaguely democratic reforms).

Fernando VII (Ferdinand VII; r 1814–33) revoked the Cádiz constitution, persecuted liberals and cheerily re-established the Inquisition. Meanwhile the American colonies took advantage of Spain's problems to strike out on

1609–14

The *moriscos* (converted Muslims) are finally expelled from Spain in a final purge of non-Christians that undermines an already faltering economy.

1676

The devastation caused by the third Great Plague to hit Spain in a century is compounded by poor harvests. In all, more than 1.25 million Spanish die through plague and starvation during the 17th century.

1700

Felipe V, first of the Bourbon dynasty, takes the throne after the Habsburg line dies out with Carlos II. The fact that Felipe is second in line to the French throne causes concern across Europe.

their own. By 1824 Spain's only remaining overseas possessions were Cuba, Guam, the Philippines and Puerto Rico.

My Throne – No, Mine

Fernando's dithering over his successor resulted in the First Carlist War (1833–39), between supporters of his brother Carlos and those loyal to his infant daughter Isabel. Carlos was supported by the Church, other conservatives and regional rebels, together known as the Carlists, while the Isabel faction had the support of liberals and the army.

During the war violent anticlericalism emerged. Religious orders were closed and, in the Disentailment of 1836, church property and lands were seized and auctioned off by the government. As usual, only the wealthy benefited, and it was the army that emerged victorious from the fighting.

In 1843 Isabel, now all of 13, declared herself Queen Isabel II (Isabella II; r 1843–68). One achievement of sorts during her inept reign was the creation of a rural police force, the Guardia Civil (Civil Guard), which mainly protected the wealthy in the bandit-ridden countryside. Business, banking, mining and railways brought some economic progress, and there were some reforms in education, but relatively few benefited. Eventually radical liberals, and discontented soldiers led by General Juan Prim, overthrew Isabel in the Septembrina Revolution of 1868.

But Spain still wanted a monarch and in 1870 a liberal-minded Italian prince, Amadeo of Savoy, accepted the job. Needless to say, the Spanish aristocracy opposed him, which led to another Carlist War (1872–76), fought between not just two but three mutually opposing factions: Amadeo loyalists, conservatives wanting Isabel II's son Alfonso on the throne, and other conservatives who backed Carlos' grandson Carlos.

During the First Republic some Spanish cities declared themselves independent states, and some, such as Seville and nearby Utrera, even declared war on each other.

The First Republic

Amadeo abandoned Spain in February 1873 and the liberal-dominated Cortes proclaimed the country a federal republic. Within less than two years, though, it had lost control of the regions and the army put Alfonso on the throne as Alfonso XII (r 1874–85), in a coalition with the Church and landowners.

THE GREAT DIVIDE

By the late 19th century industry had finally arrived in Barcelona, Madrid and some Basque cities, attracting large-scale migration from the countryside and bringing both prosperity and squalid slums to the cities. In rural areas, the old problems of underproduction, oligarchic land ownership and mass poverty persisted. Many Spaniards emigrated to Latin America, while those who stayed were only too ready to seize on revolutionary ideas arriving from elsewhere in Europe. Society and politics became increasingly polarised and

1702–13

The War of the Spanish Succession begins with Britain supporting Charles of Austria as a counter claimant to Felipe V. The Treaty of Utrecht in 1713 leaves Felipe as king but Spain loses Gibraltar and the Low Countries.

1761

Spain becomes involved in the Seven Years War (1756–63), fighting alongside the French against Britain and her allies. The latters' eventual victory sees Spain hand over Florida to the British.

1793

Spain declares war on France after Louis XVI is beheaded, but within a couple of years the country is supporting the French in their struggles against the British.

though the mild dictatorship of Primo de Rivera in the 1920s put a temporary lid on unrest, it only served to delay the slide into full-scale civil war.

Revolutionaries & Separatists

The anarchist ideas of the Russian Mikhail Bakunin had reached Spain in the 1860s and rapidly gained support. Bakunin looked forward to a free society in which people would voluntarily cooperate with each other – a state of affairs that was to be achieved through strikes, sabotage and revolts. Anarchism appealed to both rural peasants and city workers and in the 1890s and the 1900s anarchists bombed Barcelona's Liceu opera house, assassinated two prime ministers and killed 24 people with a bomb at King Alfonso XIII's wedding in 1906. In 1910, the anarchist unions were organised into the powerful Confederación Nacional del Trabajo (CNT; National Labour Confederation).

Spain lost the last of its once vast overseas possessions – Cuba, Puerto Rico, the Philippines and Guam – in the humiliating Spanish-American War of 1898.

Socialism grew more slowly than anarchism because of its less dramatic strategy of steady change through parliamentary processes. The Unión General de Trabajadores (UGT; General Union of Workers), established in 1888, was moderate and disciplined. Its appeal was greatest in Madrid and Bilbao, where people were fearful of Catalan separatism.

Parallel with the rise of the left was the growth of Basque and Catalan separatism. In Catalonia, this was led by big business interests. In the Basque country, nationalism emerged in the 1890s in response to a flood of Castilian workers into Basque industries: some Basques considered these migrants a threat to their identity.

In 1909 a contingent of Spanish troops was wiped out by Berbers in Spanish Morocco, leading the government to call up Catalan reservists to go and fight. This sparked off the so-called Semana Trágica (Tragic Week) in Barcelona, which began with a general strike and turned into a frenzy of violence. The government responded by executing many workers.

Spain stayed neutral during WWI and enjoyed an economic boom, but anarchist and socialist numbers grew, inspired by the Russian Revolution, and political violence and mayhem continued, especially in lawless Barcelona.

First Dictatorship

Alfonso XIII (r 1902–30) had a habit of meddling in politics (there were 33 different governments during his reign), and when, in 1921, 10,000 Spanish soldiers were killed by a small force of Berbers at Anual in Morocco, the finger of blame pointed directly at the king. However, just as a report on the event was to be submitted to parliament in 1923, General Miguel Primo de Rivera, an eccentric Andalucian aristocrat, led an army rising in support of Alfonso and established his own mild, six-year dictatorship.

Primo was a centralist who censored the press and upset intellectuals but gained the cooperation of the socialist UGT. He founded industries, improved

1805

In October a combined Spanish-French fleet is defeated by British ships under Nelson at the Battle of Trafalgar. Spanish sea power is effectively destroyed and discontent grows against the king's pro-French policies.

1808–13

Carlos IV abdicates and French occupation begins, with Napoleon's brother, Joseph, on the throne. The ensuing Peninsular War (Spanish War of Independence) sees British forces under the Duke of Wellington helping the Spanish defeat the French.

1809–24

Most of Spain's American colonies win independence as Madrid's priorities turn towards ousting the French. By 1824 only Cuba, Puerto Rico, Guam and the Philippines will still be under Spanish rule.

roads, made the trains run on time and built dams and powerplants, but eventually, with an economic downturn following the Wall St crash and discontent in the army, Alfonso XIII took the chance to dismiss him.

Second Republic

Unfortunately, Alfonso had brought the monarchy into too much disrepute to last long himself. When a new republican movement scored sweeping victories in local elections in 1931, the king left for exile in Italy. The tumultuous Second Republic that followed – called La Niña Bonita (Pretty Child) by its supporters – split Spanish society down the middle and ended in civil war.

National elections in 1931 brought in a government composed of socialists, republicans and so-called radicals (who were actually centrists). A new constitution in December that year gave women the vote, granted autonomy-minded Catalonia its own parliament, legalised divorce, stripped Catholicism of its status as official religion, stopped the government paying priests' salaries, and banned priests from teaching. It also promised land redistribution, which pleased the Andalucian landless, but failed to deliver much.

The left-wing government then lost the election of 1933. Anarchist disruption, an economic slump, the alienation of big business, the votes of women and disunity on the left all contributed to the defeat, and a new Catholic party, the Confederación Española de Derechas Autónomas (CEDA; Spanish Confederation of Autonomous Rights), won the most seats. Another new force on the right was the fascist Falange, led by José Antonio Primo de Rivera, son of the 1920s dictator.

The Oscar-winning film *Belle Epoque*, telling the story of a Spanish army deserter finding love in 1930s rural Spain, was actually filmed in Portugal.

By 1934 violence was spiralling out of control. The socialist UGT called for a general strike, Catalonia declared itself independent (within a putative federal Spanish republic) and workers' committees took over the northern mining region of Asturias after attacking police and army posts. A violent campaign against the Asturian workers by the Spanish Foreign Legion (set up to fight Moroccan tribes in the 1920s), led by generals Francisco Franco and José Millán Astray, firmly split the country into left and right.

In the February 1936 elections the right-wing National Front was narrowly defeated by the Popular Front, a left-wing coalition with communists at the fore. Violence continued from both sides. Extremist groups grew and peasants were on the verge of revolution, but when the revolt actually came, on 17 July 1936, it was from the other end of the political spectrum. On that day the Spanish army garrison in Melilla, North Africa, rose up against the left-wing government, followed the next day by garrisons on the mainland. The leaders of the plot were five generals, among them Francisco Franco, who on 19 July flew from the Canary Islands to Morocco to take charge of his legionnaires. The civil war had begun.

1814

Fernando VII becomes king and revokes the Cádiz Constitution – an attempt by Spanish liberals to introduce constitutional reforms – just weeks after agreeing to uphold its principles.

1833–39

The First Carlist War is triggered by disputes over the succession between the daughter of Fernando VII, Isabel, and his brother, Carlos. Isabel will eventually become queen.

1860s

Anarchist ideas reach Spain and soon gain a wide following. In 1868 Isabel II is overthrown and goes into exile in Paris.

THE SPANISH CIVIL WAR

Some pundits postulate that the civil war might not have happened without the Great Slump: Primo de Rivera might have stayed in power and somehow succeeded in holding Spain together. Others see the civil war as a long-term consequence of Spain's failure to modernise and distribute at least some wealth beyond the ruling class. Most agree that given the extreme polarisation of society and politics by the beginning of the 20th century, Spain could not work out its internal contradictions without a conflagration of some kind.

Ernest Hemingway's tersely magnificent novel *For Whom the Bell Tolls* is full of the emotions unleashed in the Spanish Civil War.

Wherever the blame lies, the civil war split communities, families and friends, killed an estimated 350,000 Spaniards (some writers put the number as high as 500,000), and caused untold damage and misery. Both sides committed atrocious massacres and reprisals, and employed death squads to eliminate opponents. The rebels, who called themselves Nationalists because they believed they were fighting for Spain, shot or hanged tens of thousands of supporters of the republic. Republicans did likewise to Franco sympathisers, including some 7000 priests, monks and nuns. Political affiliation often provided a convenient cover for settling old scores.

At the start of the war many of the military and Guardia Civil went over to the Nationalists, whose campaign quickly took on overtones of a crusade against the enemies of God. In Republican areas, anarchists, communists or socialists ended up running many towns and cities: social revolution followed.

British director Ken Loach's *Tierra y Libertad* (Land and Freedom), made in 1995, is one of the most convincing treatments of the civil war on film.

Nationalist Advance

The basic battle lines were drawn within a week of the rebellion in Morocco. Most cities with military garrisons fell immediately into Nationalist hands – this meant almost everywhere north of Madrid except Catalonia and the north coast, as well as parts of Andalucía. Franco's force of legionnaires and Moroccan mercenaries was airlifted from Morocco to Seville by German warplanes in August. Essential to the success of the revolt, they moved northwards through Extremadura towards Madrid, wiping out fierce resistance in some cities. At Salamanca in October, Franco pulled all the Nationalists into line behind him.

Madrid, reinforced by the first battalions of the International Brigades (armed foreign idealists and adventurers organised by the communists), repulsed Franco's first assault in November and endured, under communist inspiration, over two years' siege.

Foreign Intervention

The International Brigades never numbered more than 20,000 and couldn't turn the tide against the better armed and organised Nationalist forces.

Nazi Germany and Fascist Italy supported the Nationalists with planes, weapons and men (75,000 from Italy, 17,000 from Germany), turning the

1872–74

Another Carlist War begins and the First Republic, a federal union of 17 states, collapses. The monarchy is ultimately restored in the shape of Isabel II's son, who becomes Alfonso XII in 1874.

1898

Spain loses Cuba, Puerto Rico, Guam and the Philippines, its last remaining colonies, after being defeated by the United States, which declared war in support of Cuban independence.

1909

The Semana Trágica (Tragic Week) in Barcelona begins after the army calls up Catalan reservists to fight in Morocco. A general strike turns into a violent riot and dozens of civilians are killed.

war into a testing ground for WWII. The Republicans had some Soviet planes, tanks, artillery and advisers, but the rest of the international community refused to become involved (although some 25,000 French fought on the Republican side).

Homage to Catalonia recounts George Orwell's personal involvement in the civil war, moving from euphoria to despair.

Republican Quarrels

With Madrid besieged, the Republican government moved to Valencia in late 1936 to continue trying to preside over the fractious diversity of political persuasions on its side, which encompassed anarchists, communists, moderate democrats and regional separatists.

In April 1937 German planes bombed the Basque town of Guernica (called Gernika in Basque), causing terrible casualties; this became the subject of Picasso's famous pacifist painting. All the north coast fell to the Nationalists that year, giving them control of Basque industry. Republican counterattacks near Madrid and in Aragón failed.

Meanwhile divisions among the Republicans erupted into fierce street fighting in Barcelona in May 1937, with the Soviet-influenced communists completely crushing the anarchists and Trotskyites who had run the city for almost a year. The Republican government then moved to Barcelona in autumn 1937.

Hugh Thomas' *The Spanish Civil War* is the classic account of the war in any language: long and dense, yet readable and humane. Helen Graham's *The Spanish Civil War: A Very Short Introduction* does its different job well, too.

Nationalist Victory

In early 1938 Franco repulsed a Republican offensive at Teruel in Aragón, then swept eastwards with 100,000 troops, 1000 planes and 150 tanks, isolating Barcelona from Valencia. In July the Republicans launched a last offensive as the Nationalists moved through the Ebro valley. This bloody encounter, won by the Nationalists, resulted in 20,000 dead.

The USSR withdrew from the war in September 1938 and in January 1939 the Nationalists took Barcelona unopposed. The Republican government and hundreds of thousands of supporters fled to France.

The Republicans still held Valencia and Madrid, and had 500,000 people under arms, but in the end the Republican army simply evaporated. The Nationalists entered Madrid on 28 March 1939 and Franco declared the war over on 1 April.

FRANCO'S SPAIN

The 36-year Franco dictatorship began in merciless fashion. Instead of postwar reconciliation, more blood-letting ensued. An estimated 100,000 people were killed or died in prison after the war. The hundreds of thousands imprisoned included many intellectuals and teachers; others fled abroad, depriving Spain of a generation of scientists, artists, writers, educators and more. Eventually even Franco's supporters wearied of his absolute, intolerant rule, and by the time he died in 1975 Spain was more than ready for a transition to democracy.

1914–18

Spain remains neutral during World War I and experiences a financial boom as the shift from an agricultural to an industrial economy increases to meet wartime needs.

1923–30

After parliamentary criticism of the king and military, General Miguel Primo de Rivera launches a coup and establishes himself as dictator. Early successes are followed by a lack of support and he retires and dies in 1930.

1931–36

The Second Republic is declared when Alfonso XIII is deposed and goes into exile. Regions are granted autonomy under the new constitution, but society is polarised and political violence spirals.

Until then Franco kept hold of power by never allowing any single powerful group – the Church, the Movimiento Nacional (the only legal political party), the army, monarchists or bankers – to dominate. The Cortes was merely a rubber stamp for such decrees as he chose to submit to it. Regional autonomy aspirations were simply not tolerated.

The army provided many government ministers and enjoyed a most generous budget. Catholic supremacy was fully restored, with secondary schools entrusted to the Jesuits, divorce made illegal and church weddings compulsory. Despite endemic corruption among the country's administrators, Franco won some working-class support offering job security and paid holidays, though workers had no right to strike.

David Trueba's 2003 movie *Soldados de Salamina* (Soldiers of Salamis) and Javier Cercas' identically named 2001 novel tell how a Republican soldier helps a Falangist leader escape execution in the last days of the civil war. Both were big successes.

WWII & the Years of Hunger

A few months after the civil war ended, WWII began. Franco promised Hitler an alliance but never committed himself to a date. In 1944 Spanish leftists launched a failed attack on Franco's Spain from France; small leftist guerrilla units continued a hopeless struggle in the north, Extremadura and Andalucía until the 1950s – a little-known story that is only now starting to be properly told.

After WWII Spain was excluded from the UN and NATO, and suffered a UN-sponsored trade boycott that helped turn the late 1940s into Spain's *años de hambre* (years of hunger). With the onset of the Cold War, however, the US wanted bases in Spain and Franco agreed to the establishment of four, in return for large sums of aid. In 1955 Spain was admitted to the UN.

Economic Miracle

In 1959 a new breed of technocrats in government, linked to the Catholic group Opus Dei, engineered a Stabilisation Plan, with devaluation of the peseta and other deflationary measures, which brought an economic upswing. Spanish industry boomed and thousands of young Spaniards went abroad to study. Modern machinery, technology and marketing were introduced; transport was modernised; new dams provided irrigation and hydropower.

Franco styled himself Generalísimo (Supreme General) and, later, *caudillo,* which is roughly equivalent to the German *Führer.*

The recovery was funded in part by US aid, and remittances from more than a million Spaniards working abroad, but above all by tourism, which was developed initially along Andalucía's Costa del Sol and Catalonia's Costa Brava. By 1965, the number of tourists arriving in Spain was 14 million a year.

A huge population shift from impoverished rural regions to the cities and tourist resorts took place. Many Andalucians went to Barcelona. In the cities, elegant suburbs developed, as did shantytowns and, later, high-rise housing for the workers.

The Final Decade

The year 1964 saw Franco celebrating 25 years of peace, order and material progress. However, the jails were still full of political prisoners and large gar-

1936–39

The Spanish Civil War starts when Nationalist rebels led by General Francisco Franco rise up against the elected government. The fighting and atrocities on both sides leave about 350,000 Spaniards dead.

1939

Franco enters Madrid in March and his dictatorship begins. Keeping Spain out of WWII, he manages to avoid an Allied invasion and stay in power, though guerrilla attacks on his regime continue into the 1950s.

1959

ETA is founded with the aim of gaining Basque independence. The terrorist group will go on to murder more than 800 people (according to estimates by the Spanish government), including Franco's prime minister in 1973.

risons were still maintained outside every major city. Over the next decade, labour unrest grew and discontent began to rumble in the universities and even in the army and Church.

Regional problems resurfaced too. The Basque-nationalist terrorist group Euskadi Ta Askatasuna (ETA; Basque Homeland and Freedom) gave cause for the declaration of six states of emergency between 1962 and 1975; heavy-handed police tactics won ETA support from some Basque moderates.

Franco chose as his successor Prince Juan Carlos, the Spanish-educated grandson of Alfonso XIII. In 1969 Juan Carlos swore loyalty to Franco and the Movimiento Nacional. Cautious reforms by Franco's last prime minister, Carlos Arias Navarro, provoked violent opposition from right-wing extremists. Spain seemed to be sinking into chaos when Franco died on 20 November 1975.

Paul Preston's *Franco* is the big biography of one of history's little dictators – and it has very little to say in the man's favour. Preston has also written *Juan Carlos: Steering Spain from Dictatorship to Democracy*, about the present king.

DEMOCRATIC SPAIN

Juan Carlos I, aged 37, took the throne two days after Franco died. The new king's links with the dictator inspired little confidence in a Spain now clamouring for democracy, but Juan Carlos had kept his cards close to his chest and can take most of the credit for the successful transition to democracy that followed. He sacked Navarro in July 1976, replacing him with Adolfo Suárez, a 43-year-old former Franco apparatchik with film-star looks. To general surprise, Suárez got the Francoist-filled Cortes to approve a new, two-chamber parliamentary system, and in early 1977 political parties, trade unions and strikes were all legalised and the Movimiento Nacional was abolished.

Since then Spain has cast barely a backward glance. Spaniards seemed to agree on a kind of instinctive pact to bury old differences and get on with building a better future together. Everyone had had enough of conflict and division, and to this day most Spaniards are still reluctant to rake over past grievances.

The country now has a democratic, semifederal constitution and a multiparty political spectrum; it's an important member of the European Union (EU); and Spaniards are richer, better educated and more liberated than ever before. Of course not everything in the orchard is orange blossom. Terrorism, on an ongoing basis by ETA and on one occasion by Islamic militants, has cost many hundreds of lives; hundreds more people have died trying to reach Spain as immigrants in dangerous sea crossings; economic progress has been stained by corruption; and right now democratic Spain is enduring probably its worst economic downturn yet. But compared with the drama of the switch from dictatorship to democracy, public affairs since the 1970s have been less spectacular – a few orderly changes of elected government, plenty of exaggerated mud-slinging between the parties, some economic ups and downs (but mostly ups), the odd scandal, an ongoing tussle between Madrid and some regions over autonomy. In short, just the kind of non-news that makes for steady improvement in ordinary people's lives.

1960s

Tourism takes off with millions of northern Europeans flocking to the Mediterranean coasts. The economy, in tatters since the Civil War, finally begins to recover.

1973

Franco's prime minister, Carrero Blanco, is blown up in his car in Madrid by a remote controlled bomb planted by ETA. The assassination further destabilises an already weakened regime.

1975

Franco dies and is succeeded by King Juan Carlos I. The monarch had been schooled by Franco to continue his policies but soon demonstrates his desire for change.

A New Constitution & Social Liberation

Adolfo Suárez's centrist party, the UCD (Democratic Centre Union), won nearly half the seats in the new Cortes in 1977. The left-of-centre Partido Socialista Obrero Español (PSOE; Spanish Socialist Worker Party), led by a charismatic young lawyer from Seville, Felipe González, came second. One of the new government's first acts was to grant a general amnesty for acts committed in the civil war and under the Franco dictatorship. There were no truth commissions or trials for the perpetrators of atrocities.

25 Años sin Franco (25 Years Without Franco; http://www.elmundo.es/nacional/XXV_aniversario) is a special 2000 supplement of *El Mundo* newspaper published online – in Spanish, but the photos and graphics tell their own story.

In 1978 the Cortes passed a new constitution making Spain a parliamentary monarchy with no official religion. In response to the fever for local autonomy after the stiflingly centralist Franco era, the constitution also provided for a large measure of devolution to Spain's regions. By 1983 the country was divided into 17 'autonomous communities' with their own regional governments controlling a range of policy areas.

Personal and social life enjoyed a rapid liberation after Franco. Contraceptives, homosexuality and divorce were legalised, and the Madrid party and arts scene known as the *movida* formed the epicentre of a newly unleashed hedonism that still looms large in Spanish life.

Felipe in Charge

In 1982 Spain made a final break from the past by voting the PSOE into power with a big majority. Felipe González was to be prime minister for 14 years. The PSOE's young and educated leadership came from the generation that had opened the cracks in the Franco regime in the late 1960s and early 1970s. It persuaded the unions to accept wage restraint and job losses in order to streamline industry. Unemployment rose from 16% to 22% by 1986. But that same year Spain joined the European Community (now the EU), bringing on a five-year economic boom. The middle class grew ever bigger, the PSOE established a national health system and improved public education, and Spain's women streamed into higher education and jobs.

The Spanish government can be found on the web at www.la-moncloa.es, while Juan Carlos I has his site at www.casareal.es.

Around halfway through the boom, the good life began to turn a little sour. People observed that many of the glamorous new rich were making their money by property or share speculation or plain corruption (something that hasn't changed much since). By 1992, when Spain celebrated its arrival in the modern world by staging the Barcelona Olympics and the Expo 92 world fair in Seville, the economy was in a slump and the PSOE was mired in scandals. Most damaging was the affair of the Grupos Antiterroristas de Liberación (GAL), death squads that had murdered 28 suspected ETA terrorists (several of whom were innocent) in France in the mid-80s. A stream of GAL allegations contributed to the PSOE's election defeat in 1996. In 1998 a dozen senior police and PSOE men were jailed in the affair.

1976

The king appoints Adolfo Suárez as prime minister who engineers a return to democracy. Left-wing parties are legalised, despite military opposition, and the country holds free elections in 1977.

1978

The new Spanish constitution is approved in a referendum on 6 December and establishes Spain as a parliamentary democracy with Juan Carlos as head of state. The day becomes a national holiday.

1981

On 23 February a group of soldiers attempts a military coup by occupying the parliament building. The king appears on national television to denounce their actions and the coup collapses.

José María in Charge

The 1996 general election was won by the centre-right Partido Popular (PP; People's Party), led by José María Aznar, a former tax inspector from Castilla y León. The party had been founded by a former Franco minister, Manuel Fraga, something its opponents never let it forget. Aznar promised to make politics dull, and he did, but he presided over eight years of solid economic progress, winning the 2000 election as well, with an absolute parliamentary majority.

The PP cut public investment, sold off state enterprises and liberalised sectors such as telecommunications. During the Aznar years Spain's economy grew by an average of 3.4% a year, far outstripping the EU average, and unemployment fell from 23% in 1996 to 8% in 2006 (still the highest in Western Europe, though many officially jobless people were actually working in a big black economy).

Spain uses more cement than any other country in Europe.

Aznar took a hard line against ETA, refusing to talk with it unless it renounced violence. He also lined up firmly behind US and British international policy after the 11 September 2001 attacks on the USA. However, his strong support for the US-led invasion of Iraq in 2003 was unpopular at home, as was his decision to send Spanish troops to the conflict.

The major social change of the Aznar years was a tripling of the number of foreigners, especially from South America, Morocco, sub-Saharan Africa and Eastern Europe, in the population: see p60 for more on this profoundly important development.

As the 2004 general election approached, Aznar decided to retire from politics, handing the PP reins to Mariano Rajoy. The opposition PSOE had an amiable, sincere, new leader; a young lawyer from Valladolid named José Luis Rodríguez Zapatero, who had successfully managed to distance himself from his party's less than pristine past. But Rajoy still seemed certain to lead the PP to a third victory. All expectations were confounded, however, by the most violent, tragic and dramatic turn of events in Spain's three decades of democracy.

The Madrid Bombings

Early on Thursday 11 March 2004, three days before the general election, bombs exploded on four crowded commuter trains in and near Madrid, killing 191 people and injuring 1800. A quarter of Spain's population, 11 million people, poured onto the streets in demonstrations of peace and solidarity the following day. Accompanying the national shock and grief was the question, 'Who did it?' The PP government pointed its finger at ETA, which had recently been foiled in two attempts to carry out devastating bombings. The evidence, however, pointed at least equally strongly to Islamic extremists, and investigating police were certain by the following day that ETA was not the culprit. The government continued to maintain that

1982–96

Spain is governed by the centre-left Partido Socialista Obrero Español (PSOE) led by Felipe González. The country experiences an economic boom but the government will become increasingly associated with scandals and corruption.

1986

Spain joins the European Community (now the EU). Along with its membership of NATO since 1982, this is a turning point in the country's reacceptance around the world since the Franco years.

1992

Barcelona holds the Olympic Games, putting Spain firmly in the international spotlight and highlighting the country's progress since 1975. In the same year, Madrid is European Capital of Culture and Seville hosts a Universal Expo.

ETA was the prime suspect until Saturday 13 March, when police in Madrid arrested three Moroccans and two Indians.

The following day the PSOE, which had lagged a distant second in the opinion polls before 11 March, won the election. This shock result was attributed to the PP's unpopular policy on Iraq, which most Spaniards believed was the reason terrorists had attacked Madrid, and to the PP's perceived attempts to mislead the public by blaming the bombings on ETA.

By March 2005, 75 people, mostly Moroccan, had been arrested for suspected involvement in the bombings. Seven others, suspected ringleaders, had blown themselves up when cornered by police in Madrid three weeks after the bombings. Many of the 75 arrested were released, but in 2007 21 of them were found guilty in a Madrid court on charges including murder, forgery and conspiracy to commit a terrorist attack. Two of the Moroccans and a Spaniard who supplied the explosives received jail sentences of thousands of years for murder. Investigators concluded that the attackers had been a local group of North Africans settled in Spain, inspired by, but without direct links to, Al-Qaeda.

Ghosts of Spain (2006) by Giles Tremlett of the *Guardian* gets right under the skin of contemporary Spain, and its roots in the recent past. If you read only one book on Spain, make it this one.

The New PSOE

Within two weeks of taking office in April 2004, the Zapatero government honoured its campaign pledge to pull Spanish troops out of Iraq. Zapatero then forged on with a series of social reforms that predictably angered the Spanish right but largely pleased his party's supporters, including the many young voters who chose the PSOE in the wake of the Madrid bombings.

The new government legalised gay marriages, made divorce easier, took religion out of the compulsory school curriculum, gave dissatisfied Catalonia an expanded autonomy charter, and declared an amnesty for illegal immigrants that allowed 500,000 non-EU citizens to obtain legal residence and work permits in Spain. In 2007 parliament also passed the 'Historical Memory Law' designed to officially honour the Republican victims of the civil war and the Franco dictatorship. The law ordered the removal of any remaining Francoist symbols from public buildings, opened archives and provided for the exhumation of those buried in anonymous graves after Francoist atrocities. (Surely not by coincidence, a few weeks later the Vatican beatified 498 Spaniards, mainly priests, monks and nuns, who had fallen victim to leftists during and after the civil war.)

A majority of the new Zapatero cabinet announced after the 2008 election were women, including the defence minister Carme Chacón, who took office when she was seven months pregnant.

Zapatero also tried to start peace negotiations with ETA – something the PP had refused to do. ETA, which wants an independent state covering the Spanish and French Basque Country and Navarra, declared a 'permanent ceasefire' in March 2006, but resumed violence with a bomb that killed two people at Madrid airport nine months later. Zapatero then called off any moves towards dialogue. While the Spanish government estimates that ETA has killed more than 800 people in its five decades of existence, it is

1996–2004

Disaffection with PSOE sleaze gives the centre-right Partido Popular (PP), led by José María Aznar, a general election victory. His government presides over eight years of economic progress but support for the Iraq War is deeply divisive.

2004 (11 March)

Four commuter trains in Madrid are bombed during the morning rush hour by Islamic terrorists. One hundred and ninety-one people are killed and 1800 are wounded.

2004 (14 March)

PSOE, led by José Luis Rodríguez Zapatero, wins a surprise election victory after Aznar's government wrongly accuses ETA of the bombings. Many blame his government's support of the US invasion of Iraq for the attacks.

currently much weakened by a series of arrests of its top leaders and police seizures of its arms.

Come the next elections in March 2008, the only significant cloud over prospects of a repeat Zapatero victory was cast by the economy. Fortunately for the PSOE, the worst economic news did not emerge till after the election, which it won with an increased majority over the PP. But the international financial crisis of 2007–08 had ominously coincided with a slump in Spain's construction and property industry, on which the country's amazing 10-year boom had been based. Zapatero's second term of office looked likely to be a lot harder going than the first.

2004–06

Zapatero introduces a range of liberal measures including same-sex marriages and greater autonomy for the regions. Most popular is the withdrawal of Spanish troops from Iraq.

2006

ETA declares a permanent ceasefire in March and talks take place with the government. These are immediately stopped in December after a bomb at Madrid's airport causes a building to collapse and kills two people.

2008

Zapatero wins the general election with an increased majority. His victory comes just as problems with the Spanish economy are becoming more of a concern.

The Culture

THE NATIONAL PSYCHE

More than five centuries of national unity have done little to erode the regional ticks that distinguish one group of Spaniards from another. Even so, it's possible to make the occasional national generalisation. A visitor to Franco's Spain in the 1960s might have found Spaniards uniformly dour and frumpy, but that's no longer the case.

A long parade of fiestas and fun during the year, provide Spaniards with plenty of excuses for merrymaking. Not that they need an excuse. Urban Spain in particular attaches great importance to what the Irish would call *craic*. From the international rave clubs of Ibiza to the rivers of revellers in the narrow Siete Calles of Bilbao, a live-for-the-moment attitude prevails. Perhaps it's a precariousness about daily life down the centuries in this long-troubled country that has engendered the need for momentary escape.

A trip around the country reveals a broad spectrum of regional traits. While the people of deep Spain, in the two Castillas, tend to be taciturn and dry, their neighbours to the south in Andalucía are the height of instant affability. Your average Andalucian loves a chat over a sherry in an extroverted and often fickle fashion. In the northeast, the Catalans are famed for their unerring sense of business and a rather Protestant style of work ethic. Further west, the proud Basques can at first seem unapproachable, but quickly prove effusively hospitable once the ice is broken.

For centuries a magnet for Spaniards from all corners of the country, Madrid comes closest to providing a picture of the amalgam. Its people have that air of those who live in a capital city, burning candles at both ends by working and partying hard, and keeping a curious eye open for newcomers.

Sebastian Balfour's *The Politics of Contemporary Spain* gives a highly informed rundown of the issues that move Spain, ranging from tensions between the central government and the regions to corruption and ETA terrorism.

LIFESTYLE

When Spain passed its new constitution in 1978, 40% of Spanish homes had neither bath nor shower and a quarter of the population above 16 was illiterate. Now, most families have all the standard white goods, a car and take annual holidays at home and abroad – indeed, since the early 1990s especially, the Spanish mania for foreign travel has exploded. It's true, however, that household debt has never been so high.

The rapid rise in living standards has been accompanied by deep social change. Although the official birth rate rose to 1.37 children per woman in 2006, the highest since 1991, Spanish women are nevertheless having fewer children than they were a couple of generations ago. Divorce is on the rise, as is the number of single-parent families.

The Partido Socialista Obrero Español (PSOE; Spanish Socialist Worker Party) government shook the conservative elements of society to the core when it legalised same-sex marriage in 2005. A little over a year later, two male soldiers in the Spanish army married in Seville. By mid-2007, same-sex marriages represented 2% of the total.

Children still tend to stay in the parental home longer than their counterparts in northern Europe. The reasons given range from unemployment (almost 20% of university graduates take four years or more to find work) to low salaries combined with the high cost of rent.

The average annual salary for employees is around €17,000, although many people tend to get by on around €1000 a month. Thus the term *mileurista,* describing those who just manage to scrape by, has entered common usage. The official minimum wage is €600 a month. In real terms (after inflation), the average buying power of Spanish wage-earners dropped 4% from 1995 to 2005. Spain is the only OECD country in which this occurred. As the economy slowed in 2008, more and more people began to feel the pinch.

ECONOMY

After more than a decade of boom times, Spain was given an ice-cold shower in 2008. The word 'crisis' has filled the pages of the Spanish finance press since José Luis Rodríguez Zapatero's Socialist Party government was re-elected in March 2008. His laconic finance minister, Pedro Solbes, prefers to talk of a 'slowdown'.

From strong growth of up to 4% in 2007, the outlook was looking as bleak as just 1% growth in 2008. Solbes was hanging on tight to International Monetary Fund projections of Spanish growth bouncing back to 3% by 2010. At the same time, inflation shot up to 5.1% (well above the EU average of 3.6%). The collapse of the construction industry (which at the height of the good times accounted for 16% of the economy), has already led to massive lay-offs. Unemployment, at 9.6% in mid-2008 (after highs of more than 20% in the early 1990s), could, according to some analysts, shoot back up to 14% by 2009.

Is there any bright news? The tourism industry (accounting for 11% of the economy) brought in a record 59.2 million visitors (27.5% of them from the UK) to the country in 2007. The outlook for 2008 was also good (15.2 million tourists arrived in the first quarter).

POPULATION

Spain is one of the least densely populated of Western European countries, with about 91 of its 46.1 million people per square km.

Spaniards were long considered to be among the shortest and slimmest people in Europe but a 2008 study showed that the average height of the male Spaniard had grown 14cm since the beginning of the 20th century. The youngest generations of Spaniards are, on average, about the same height as most other Europeans.

According to a study by the Organisation for Economic Cooperation and Development (OECD), Spain is the second-noisiest country in the world after Japan.

A Eurostat report in 2006 indicates that Spain is expected to be the EU country with the highest percentage of population over 65 by 2050.

In recent years, immigration has bolstered the population. By the end of 2006 it was estimated that immigrants accounted for more than 5.2 million people, more than 11% of the population.

Spaniards like to live together in cities, towns or *pueblos* (villages), a habit that probably goes back to past needs for defence. Only in the Basque Country (and to some extent Galicia) do you see countryside dotted with single farmsteads and small fields. Cities such as Madrid and Barcelona have among the highest population concentration in the world, while the countryside is bereft of people.

Regional differences persist today. The peoples with the strongest identities – the Catalans, Basques and, to a lesser extent, the Galicians – are on the fringes of the Spanish heartland of Castilla and have their own languages and minority independence movements.

Some consider Spain's Roma people to be its only true long-standing ethnic minority. They are thought to have originated in India and reached Spain in the 15th century. As elsewhere, they have suffered discrimination. There are about 600,000 to 700,000 Roma in Spain, more than half of them in Andalucía.

GITANOS – A PEOPLE & THEIR LANGUAGE

José Santos Silva, 53, is president of the Federació d'Associacions Gitanes de Catalunya, which groups some 60 Roma associations in Catalonia, representing about 100,000 *gitanos*, or Roma people.

People don't generally associate gitanos with Catalonia but more with Andalucía? The earliest written evidence of *gitano* presence in Spain is a Catalan document of 1425.

Is the word gitano (gypsy) pejorative? It's not the word but how it's used. It depends on the tone. We ourselves use it.

How did you get involved in groups defending gitanos? I started off in workers' rights and trade unions when working for a multinational around the transition (the period leading to democracy after General Franco's death in 1975). Later, with democracy, it became possible to talk about defending *gitanos*. In Franco's time, *gitanos* were forbidden to stay in the same town for more than 24 or 48 hours and had no access to permanent jobs. All of that is finished now, but since democracy arrived, advances have been timid. In housing, for instance, there is a tendency to group *gitanos* together in certain *barrios* (districts), such as La Mina in Barcelona. As a result, schools have a high percentage of *gitano* children, *payos* (non-*gitanos*) take their children away and the schools become isolated. There should be a nationwide plan for the integration of *gitanos*. We are some one million in Spain.

Are things better now than they were? Sure, Spain in general is better off and things have improved. Racism remains a problem but *gitanos* and *payos* rub along. Now there are mixed marriages. Curiously, regardless of whether the husband or wife is *payo,* the couple are welcomed with greater solidarity by the *gitano* community.

Roma people are migrating to Spain from Eastern Europe. Does the gitano community help them? We'd like to but don't really have the means.

What are the biggest challenges for the gitano community? Education and training. Some things are being done and the Catalan government is pioneering… In April a program was put in place to train teachers of the Romanó language (the universal language of the Roma people).

Did the Spanish gitanos lose their language? Until the 18th century, *gitanos* continued to speak Romanó but then it was banned. A few words have remained in what we call Kaló. But many have been changed and influenced by Spanish. With this training program, things will change, I think, in five or so years. Imagine! *Gitanos* communicating in Romanó with other Roma in Europe and the US!

MULTICULTURALISM

Long an exporter of its people (the 'Moroccans of the 1950s' in the words of writer Rosa Montero, one of the country's best-known journalists and novelists), Spain has been confronted since the mid-1990s by a new reality: multiculturalism.

The massive influx of immigrants has changed the once seemingly homogeneous make-up of the country. The national population has grown from around 40 million to more than 46 million since 2000, almost entirely due to immigrants. Of them, 1.7 million come from other EU countries. The Balearic Islands have the greatest percentage of foreign residents – almost 20% (mostly Britons and Germans). Speculation on the presence of illegal immigrants in Spain ranges from 200,000 to one million – it is virtually impossible to know.

Some 1.5 million Muslims (around 650,000 from Morocco) live in this once ultra-Catholic country. More than one million nationals from Spain's former South American colonies have come to claim their birthright in the *madre patria* (mother country).

While some cases of racial tension have made the headlines, so far the Spanish experiment in receiving immigrants has been largely trouble free. The streets of Spain's cities have taken on new hues. Madrid in the 1980s had a largely uniform feel but today it hums to the sounds of many languages, whose speakers have brought new tastes to the dining table. Kebab stands and Peruvian restaurants abound. You'll find, for example, Argentines staffing call centres, Filipinos waiting in restaurants or Eastern Europeans working in bars. Hordes of retired and wealthy EU citizens are catered for by co-nationals on the holiday coasts.

The image of illegal immigrants crossing the Straits of Gibraltar, and the more dangerous Atlantic route (to the Canary Islands) from Mauritania and even Senegal, in barely seaworthy boats has been a daily reminder of a litany of suffering. The alarmed cries over this 'deluge', however, ring hollow. Far more illegal migrants arrive by more mundane means: over the French border and by air.

Border controls are generally cursory and many South Americans do not need a visa to travel to Spain. Pretending to be a tourist is all a prospective *clandestino* (illegal immigrant) needs to do to get past passport control. Many businesses have connived in this, as illegal labour comes cheap.

The slowdown in the economy, however, has had an immediate impact and is likely to put a brake on immigration. According to one 2007 study, the immigrant population was responsible for half of the country's robust economic growth in the years 2001–05; immigrants now make up 40% of those to have joined the ranks of the unemployed since 2007. Indeed, in June 2008, the government announced a program to encourage unemployed migrants to return to their home countries. The government expected, perhaps optimistically, that up to one million people might opt for this carrot, but at the time of writing few had taken up the offer.

SPORT

In June 2008 Madrid was confirmed as an official candidate to host the 2016 Olympic Games. The city was one of the finalists in the fight for the 2012 event.

Football

Fútbol seems to be many a Spaniard's prime preoccupation. Hundreds of thousands of fans attend the games in the *primera división* (first division) of the *liga* (league) every weekend from September to May, with millions more following the games on TV.

Mites de Barça is a trilingual coffee-table book covering one of Spain's most glorious football sides, FC Barcelona.

Spain went into delirium when it won the European Cup against Germany in 2008, the first time it had managed this since beating Russia in 1964.

Almost any *primera división* match is worth attending, if only to experience the Spanish crowd. Those matches involving eternal rivals Real Madrid and FC Barcelona stir even greater passions. These two clubs have large followings and something approaching a monopoly on the silverware: between them they have carried off the league title 48 times (Real Madrid has won 31 times). In 2008 Real Madrid took the title with relative ease. Barcelona, on the other hand, had an awful year, collapsing in the latter half of the season.

Real Madrid has its home in the **Estadio Santiago Bernabéu** (☎ 913 98 43 00, 902 32 43 24; www.realmadrid.com; Avenida de Concha Espina 1), near metro Santiago Bernabéu. FC Barcelona's home is at **Camp Nou** (☎ tickets national 902 18 99 00, international +34 93 496 36 00; www.fcbarcelona.com; Avinguda Aristides Maillol s/n), near Metro Collblanc.

Other leading clubs include Valencia, Athletic Bilbao, Deportivo La Coruña, Real Betis (of Seville), Málaga and Real Sociedad of San Sebastián.

Bullfighting

Bullfighting occurs in Portugal, southern France and parts of Latin America, but Spain is its true home. The most important fight season takes place in

Madrid for a month from mid-May as part of the city's celebrations of its patron saint, San Isidro.

To aficionados the fight is an art form and to its protagonists a way of life. To its detractors it is little more than ghoulish torture and slaughter. If we call it here a spectator sport, it is more for lack of another obvious 'category'.

For the latest information on the next bullfight near you, biographies of *toreros* (bullfighters) and more, check out www.portaltaurino.com (in Spanish).

La lidia, as bullfighting is known, took off in the mid-18th century. King Carlos III stopped it temporarily late in the century, but his successors dropped the ban. By the mid-19th century, breeders were creating the first reliable breeds of *toro bravo* (fighting bull), and a bullfighting school had been launched in Seville.

The bullfighting season begins in the first week of February with the fiestas of Valdemorillo and Ajalvir, near Madrid, to mark the feast day of San Blas. All over the country, but especially in the two Castillas and Andalucía, *corridas* (bullfights) and *encierros* (running of the bulls through town), as in Pamplona, are part of town festivals. As a rule, *corridas* take place on weekends from about 6pm. On the card are six bulls, and hence six fights, faced by three *cuadrillas* (teams) of *toreros* (bullfighters).

The matador is the star of the team. Above all it is his fancy footwork, skill and bravery before the bull that has the crowd in raptures, or in rage, depending on his (or very occasionally her) performance.

The Asociación para la Defensa de los Derechos del Animal (ADDA) – www.addaong.org (in Spanish) – is a Spanish animal-rights and anti-bullfighting organisation.

A complex series of events takes place in each clash, which can last from about 20 to 30 minutes. *Peones* dart about with grand capes in front of the bull; horseback *picadores* drive lances into the bull's withers and *banderilleros* charge headlong at the bull in an attempt to stab its neck. Finally, the matador kills the bull, unless the bull has managed to put him out of action, as sometimes happens.

The most extraordinary matador of the moment is Madrid's José Tomás who, at the fiestas of San Isidro in Madrid on 5 June 2008 (after five years in retirement), cut four bulls' ears (the cutting off of an ear, or in rare cases both ears, of the dead bull is a mark of admiration) for his performance – something that hadn't been seen for decades. *El País* declared on page one: 'He's a Legend.' Says the austere Tomás: 'Living without bullfighting isn't living.' Two weeks later, in another epic afternoon, bulls gored him severely in the thighs three times.

Other great fighters include El Cordobés, El Juli, Manuel Jesú (El Cid) and Miguel Ángel Perera. That day in Madrid, Tomás fought bulls of the equally legendary breeder, Victoriano del Río, one of several who has opted to try cloning top-class fighting bulls, although many observers are sceptical about the potential results.

La lidia is about many things – death, bravery, performance. No doubt the fight is bloody and cruel, but aficionados say the bull is better off dying at the hands of a matador than in the *matadero* (abattoir). To witness it is not necessarily to approve of it, but might give an insight into the tradition and thinking behind *la lidia*.

Basketball

Baloncesto (basketball) is an increasingly popular sport, and Spain's first ever world championship victory (over Greece) in September 2006 in Japan doubtless won it more aficionados. The national side qualified for the Beijing Olympics in 2008, with star Barcelona player, Pau Gasol (also a hit in the US NBA competition with the Los Angeles Lakers) leading the way. They had a magnificent result, going down 118–107 to the unstoppable USA team in the final and taking a silver medal. From late September to late June, 18 clubs contest the Liga Asociación de Clubes de Baloncesto (ACB) national league. Leading teams include Barcelona and Real Madrid

GREAT ANGLO-AMERICAN BULLFIGHTERS

Ernest Hemingway loved watching the bullfight, but some of his countrymen preferred action to observation. Sidney Franklin was the first English-speaking *torero* (bullfighter) to take the alternative, in 1945 in Madrid's Las Ventas, one of the largest rings in the bullfighting world. He was followed by Californian John Fulton (a painter and poet) in 1967. Best of all was Arizona-born Robert Ryan. Now retired, he is man of many facets – writer, poet, painter, sculptor and photographer. Englishman Henry Higgins, known in Spain as Enrique Cañadas, something of an adventurer and pilot, was also keen to take the ring, while his countryman, Mancunian Frank Evans (known as 'El Inglés'), only retired in 2005.

(attached to the football clubs), Tau Vitoria, Unicaja of Málaga, Pamesa of Valencia, Caja San Fernando of Seville and Estudiantes of Madrid. For details on upcoming matches around the country, check out the Spanish-language league website www.acb.com.

Motor Racing

Every year around April or May the dashing Formula One knights in shining motorised armour come to Montmeló, about a 30-minute drive north of Barcelona, to burn rubber. For more information, see p358. In August 2008, a new circuit entered action in Valencia.

Spain's champion driver, Asturias-born Fernando Alonso, was twice world champion with the Renault team in 2005 and 2006. After a disastrous year with McLaren in 2007 (in which he was pipped for the championship by Kimi Raikkonen), he returned to Renault in 2008, only to find that the quality of the vehicles was not up to par.

Spain is motorcycle mad, especially with world-class rider Dani Pedrosa to inspire the public. It stages a Grand Prix tournament in the world 500cc championship (as well as in the 250cc and 125cc categories) in May each year at the Jerez de la Frontera track **Circuito Permanente de Velocidad** (☎ 956 15 11 00; www.circuitodejerez.com; Carretera de Arcos, Km10) in Andalucía. A second Grand Prix round is usually held at the Montmeló circuit a month later.

Other antibullfighting organisations are the World Society for the Protection of Animals (WSPA; www.wspa.org.uk) and People for the Ethical Treatment of Animals (PETA; www.peta.org).

Cycling

Spain's version of the Tour de France cycling race is the three-week **Vuelta a España** (www.lavuelta.com), which is usually held in September. The course changes each year. Following in the footsteps of the former champion cyclist Miguel Indurain (who won the Tour de France five times in a row and is considered one of the greatest cyclists of all time), Alberto Contador won the Tour de France in 2007 and became the second Spaniard (after Indurain) to take the Giro d'Italia in 2008.

Tennis

Spanish tennis is attracting a growing following of fans, most of whom concentrate their attention on the young left-handed champion, Rafael Nadal, the wonder boy from Manacor (Mallorca) and champion of the clay court (he has taken the French Open, on clay, four times in a row). He replaced Swiss champion Roger Federer as world No 1 seed after beating Federer in a cliffhanger at Wimbledon in 2008 and, en passant, taking gold in the men's singles at the Beijing Olympics. Other Spanish players worth following include Carlos Moyá, Juan Carlos Ferrero and David Ferrer. Spanish women players have stood out less in recent years, with the exception of doubles pair Vivi Ruano and Anabel Medina, who won the women's doubles at the French Open in 2008. Spain's strength in men's tennis also won it the Davis Cup in 2000 and 2004.

Golf

Spaniards are also increasingly taken with golf. José Marí Olazábal and Sergio García are the stars of the moment (and a killer combination for Europe in the Ryder Cup), although no one can forget the triumphs of Severiano (Seve for short) Ballesteros, who dominated the Spanish, and indeed much of continental Europe's, golf scene in the 1990s. Spain is peppered with more than 350 golf courses, which attract a lot of tourists in addition to local players.

MEDIA

The word 'internet' was finally accepted as a Spanish word by the Real Academia Española in late 2003.

Media observers in Spain lament the poor quality of much TV news reporting and its frequent partiality. The state-run channels, notably TVE1, tend to toe the line of whichever party is in power.

In print, things are healthier, although the main newspapers each have their political leaning. If *El País* (www.elpais.com), the country's most prestigious newspaper, is centre-left and closely associated with the PSOE, *ABC* (www.abc.es) is conservative right wing. In the years of political tension from 2004 to 2008 between the ruling PSOE and right-wing opposition PP (Partido Popular; People's Party), the even more right-wing *El Mundo* (www.elmundo.es) teamed up with COPE (a radio station run by the Spanish Episcopal Conference) in a campaign to discredit not only the PSOE but also moderate members of the PP. It remains to be seen whether, after the 2008 elections (won by the PSOE), these two will soften their approach.

Some regional titles have their own axes to grind. A good example is a Catalan-language daily published in Barcelona, *Avui* (www.avui.com), which pushes an openly Catalan-nationalist line.

RELIGION

Second to Rome, Spain has long been thought of as the world's greatest bastion of Catholicism. The Church in Spain, however, still a powerful institution in spite of the constitutional separation of Church and State since 1978, is anxious. On paper, 80% of the population claims to be Catholic, but only 20% regularly attend Mass. In a recent poll of EU countries, Spaniards were asked if religion was important in their lives. Only 34% replied 'yes', and only four of the EU's 27 member states came in with lower results.

The arrival to power of José Luis Rodríguez Zapatero and his PSOE government in 2004 was unwelcome news for the men in purple. The legalisation of gay marriages, the easing of divorce laws and the decision to drop the previous government's secondary-school reforms (which included compulsory religious education) all met with vigorous criticism from the country's bishops, led by the ultraconservative Cardinal Antonio María Rouco.

Indeed the church, whose headquarters is in the small conservative town of Toledo, the 'Rome of Spain', is tetchy. In a 2006 paper, the Episcopal Conference declared that 'the Church considers masturbation, fornication, pornographic activities and homosexual practices to be serious sins against chastity'. The condom, of course, is considered 'immoral'. In the 2008 election campaign, the Spanish church hierarchy openly attacked the PSOE government and recommended a vote for the Partido Popular. Zapatero's normally restrained foreign minister, Miguel Ángel Moratinos, described the cardinals as 'fundamentalists' and the government warned that in the coming years there would be changes (without specifying them) in the model of state financing for the Catholic church. State funding (including for private Catholic schools, salaries for religion teachers, direct subsidies and more) amounts to more than five billion euros a year. Other forecasted changes could include an easing of restrictions on abortion (a touchy subject) and advances in the law (passed in 1980) on religious freedom.

Spain's most significant (and growing) religious communities after Catholics are Protestants (around 1.4 million) and Muslims (around 1.5 million). Plenty of other religions, from Judaism through Buddhism to the Mormons are also present. Religious freedom is guaranteed under the constitution but leaders of the minority faiths frequently claim that they are victims of discrimination, especially in terms of state funding and religion lessons in school.

WOMEN IN SPAIN

Since the demise of Franco in 1975, Spanish society has evolved in leaps and bounds, and women have quickly conquered terrain in what was (and in many respects remains) a profoundly male-dominated society. In the Franco years, the woman's place was in the home. Nowadays, 54% of university students are women.

In the workplace, women continue to fight against the odds. On average, women are paid 15% to 48% less than men. Some 80% of those in part-time work are women. Few women make it to the top levels of business (about 20% of directors are women).

In 2007 the PSOE government approved a law aimed at promoting equality of the sexes. It provides for a minimum of 40% of women candidates at all elections. The law, which met with some employer and PP opposition, would also oblige larger companies to favour the employment and promotion of women.

Putting his money where his mouth his, Zapatero, upon re-election in 2008, appointed more women ministers (eight) than men (seven) – a first in Spain. Another first was the appointment of Carme Chacón as the first ever female defence minister in the country's history.

A more controversial law passed in 2004 was aimed at tackling domestic violence and built in an element of positive discrimination by applying tougher penalties to male aggressors than their (infinitely fewer) female counterparts. Years later, the Spanish constitutional court still has not decided whether or not the law is anticonstitutional.

ARTS

Literature

It is difficult to talk of a 'Spanish' literature much earlier than the 13th century, if one means literature in Castilian. Before this, troubadours working in Vulgar Latin, Arabic and other tongues were doing the rounds of southern Europe, and the great writers and thinkers in a Spain largely dominated by Muslims produced their treatises more often than not in Arabic or Hebrew.

Of all the works produced in Spanish in the Middle Ages, the *Poema de Mio Cid,* which has survived in a version penned in 1307 (although first written in 1140), is surely the best known. This epic tale of El Cid Campeador, or Rodrigo Díaz, whose exploits culminated in mastery over Valencia, doesn't let the facts get in way of a good story of derring-do.

Perhaps the greatest of all the Spanish poets was Luis de Góngora (1561–1627). He manipulated words with a majesty that has largely defied attempts at critical 'explanation'; his verses are above all intended as a source of sensuous pleasure. This was during the greatest period of Spanish letters, known as El Siglo de Oro (Golden Century), which stretched roughly from the middle of the 16th century to the middle of the 17th century.

For a gripping account from the losing side of Nelson's famous victory over the Franco-Spanish fleet, it is hard to beat the prose of Benito Pérez Galdós in *Trafalgar*.

The advent of *comedia* (comedy) in the early 17th century in Madrid produced some of the country's greatest playwrights. Lope de Vega (1562–1635) was perhaps the most prolific: more than 300 of the 800 plays and poems attributed to him survive. He explored the falseness of court life and roamed political subjects with his historical plays. Less playful is the work of Tirso de Molina (1581–1648), in whose *El Burlador de Sevilla* (Trickster of Seville) we meet the immortal character of Don Juan, a likeable seducer who meets an unhappy end.

For Ernest Hemingway's exhaustive study of a subject he loved dearly, the bullfight, reach for *Death in the Afternoon*.

With a life that was something of a jumbled obstacle course of trials, tribulations and peregrinations, Miguel de Cervantes Saavedra (1547–1616) had little success with his forays into theatre and verse. Today, however, he is commonly thought of as the father of the novel. *El Ingenioso Hidalgo Don Quijote de la Mancha* started life as a short story, designed to make a quick *peseta*, but Cervantes found he had turned it into an epic tale by the time it appeared in 1605. The ruined *ancien régime* knight and his equally impoverished companion, Sancho Panza, embark on a journey through the foibles of his era – the timelessness and universality of which marked the work for greatness.

It was some centuries before Cervantes had a worthy successor. Benito Pérez Galdós (1843–1920) is Spain's Balzac. His novels and short stories range from social critique to the simple depiction of society through the lives of his many players. His more mature works, such as *Fortunata y Jacinta*, display a bent towards naturalism.

Miguel de Unamuno (1864–1936) was one of the leading figures of the Generation of '98, a group of writers and artists working around and after 1898 (a bad year for Spain with the loss of its last colonies and an economic crisis at home). Unamuno's work is difficult, but among his most enjoyable prose is the *Tres Novelas Ejemplares*, which is imbued, like most of his novels and theatre, with a disquieting existentialism.

A little later came the brief flourishing of Andalucía's Federico García Lorca (1898–1936), whose verse and theatre leaned towards surrealism, leavened by a unique musicality and visual sensibility. His many offerings include the powerful play *Bodas de Sangre* (Blood Wedding). His career was cut short at the hands of Nationalist executioners in the early stages of the civil war.

Arturo Pérez-Reverte has built up a following for his series of rollicking tales from 17th-century Spain that feature Capitán Alatriste.

One of the few writers of quality who managed to work through the years of the Franco dictatorship was the Nobel Prize–winning Galician novelist Camilo José Cela (1916–2002). His most important novel, *La Familia de Pascual Duarte*, appeared in 1942 and marked a rebirth of the Spanish realist novel. It is said to be the most widely read and translated Spanish novel after *Don Quijote*.

CONTEMPORARY WRITING

The death of Franco in 1975 signalled the end of the constraints placed on Spanish writers. Many of those who became able to work in complete freedom had already been active in exile during the Franco years. Juan Goytisolo (b 1931) started off in the neorealist camp but his more mature works, such as *Señas de Identidad* (Signs of Identity), are decidedly more experimental (some might say impenetrable).

Murcia's Arturo Pérez-Reverte (b 1951), long-time war correspondent and general man's man, has become one of the most internationally read Spanish novelists. His latest novel, *Un Día de Colera* (A Day of Rage; 2007), is a vivid account of Madrid's uprising against Napoleon's occupying troops in May 1808.

Another writer with a broad following at home and abroad is Javier Marías (b 1951). He has kept the country in thrall these past years with his 1500-page trilogy *Tu Rostro Mañana* (Your Face Tomorrow), greeted by some critics (but by no means all) as the best Spanish novel in decades. It recounts the story of Jaime Deza, a Spanish academic who worked for MI6 in Oxford and returns to Spain after divorcing.

Madrid's Almudena Grandes (b 1960) is another regular contributor to *El País* and one of the country's best-known female authors. In *El Corazón Helado* (Frozen Heart), she delves into the dark past of a prominent businessman in the days of Franco and the Spanish Blue Division, sent to fight with the Nazis in Russia.

Manuel Vázquez Montalbán (1939–2003), one of Barcelona's most prolific writers, is best known for his Pepe Carvalho detective novel series and a range of other thrillers.

La Ciudad de los Prodigios (City of Marvels) by Eduardo Mendoza (b 1943) is an absorbing and at times bizarre novel set in Barcelona in the period between the Universal Exhibition of 1888 and the World Exhibition in 1929. His latest novel, *El Asombroso Viaje de Pomponio Flato* (Amazing Journey of Pomponius Flatus; 2008), is a mix of historical novel set in Roman times, detective story and biting satire of modern popular literature.

Pérez-Reverte's swashbuckling Capitán Alatriste was the subject of a blockbuster film, *Alatriste*, in 2006 – at €24 million, the most expensive movie ever made in Spain.

After the runaway success of *La Sombra del Viento* (Shadow of the Wind), Barcelona-born, US-based Carlos Ruiz Zafón (b 1964) cranked up the publicity machine to promote his second best-seller, *El Juego del Ángel* (The Angel's Game), in 2008. The first is an engaging, multilayered mystery story set in 20th-century history Barcelona. The latter is a fantasy novel centred on the Cemetery of Forgotten Books that appeared in his first novel.

Julia Navarro (b 1953) has had huge success with her three historico-religious novels: *La Hermandad de la Sábana Santa* (Brotherhood of the Holy Shroud); *La Biblia de Barro* (Bible of Clay) and her latest, *La Sangre de los Inocentes* (Blood of the Innocent). Indeed, the historical novel is all the rage, with hitherto unknown writers pouring out mystery and intrigue. They include: Ildefonso Falcones (b 1945) and his *La Catedral del Mar* (Cathedral of the Sea); Javier Serra (b 1971), who hit the bestseller lists with *La Cena Secreta* (Secret Supper); and Matilde Asensi (b 1962), who has seven novels under her belt.

Cinema & Television

Mention cinema and Spain in the same breath nowadays and just about everyone will say: Pedro Almodóvar (b 1949). The Castilian director with the wild shock of hair, and whose personal, camp cinema was born in the heady days of the Madrid *movida* (the late-night bar and club scene) in the years after Franco's death, is inimitable.

Spanish cinema has evolved in leaps and bounds, but Spanish films still only attract around 15% of audience share in Spain (60% goes to US films). State aid is limited and the average Spanish flick is made on a budget of approximately €3 million, peanuts compared with the average Hollywood production.

The Good, the Bad and the Ugly, a great spaghetti western by Italian director Sergio Leone, was largely shot in the Tabernas desert in southeastern Andalucía.

Almodóvar's *Volver* (Return; 2006), is a trip back in time and space for the director, who explores aspects of life in his homeland of southern Castilla-La Mancha. In a typically unhinged tale partly set (as usual) in Madrid, Almodóvar lines up a series of his favourite actresses (including Carmen Maura and Penélope Cruz) to rattle the skeletons in a village family's closet. At the time of writing he was working on his next production, *Los Abrazos Rotos* (Broken Embraces).

In terms of strangeness, a link could perhaps be made between Almodóvar and one of the earliest great names in Spanish film, Luis Buñuel (1900–83). This icon started off with the disturbing surrealist short *Un Chien Andalou*

(An Andalucian Dog; 1929), made with Salvador Dalí ('nuff said). Much of his later film-making was done in exile in Mexico.

One classic to slip through the net of Franco's censorship was *¡Bienvenido, Mr Marshall!* (1952), by Luis García Berlanga (b 1921), a satire of the folkloric genre beloved of the regime, and at the same time a critique of the deal done with the USA to provide Marshall Plan aid to Spain in return for military bases. About the only tangible result for the villagers in the film is a rain of dust as Marshall's VIP cavalcade charges through.

The WWII blockbuster movies *The Battle of the Bulge* and *Patton* were both shot on location in Spain in the 1960s using Spanish army material, including 75 tanks and 500 infantrymen.

Carlos Saura (b 1932) has been incredibly prolific, with more than 35 films to his name, ranging from the dance spectacular *Flamenco* (1995) to the civil war tragicomedy *¡Ay, Carmela!* (1990).

In 2000 Almodóvar became one of the few Spaniards to take an Oscar, in this case for possibly his best movie, *Todo Sobre Mi Madre* (All About My Mother; 1999). José Juan Bigas Luna (b 1946) is another quirky director who has had foreign audiences a-giggle with his hilarious *Jamón, Jamón* (Ham, Ham; 1992), a story of crossed love and murder starring two (at the time) unknowns, Javier Bardem and Penélope Cruz. Both are now regulars in Hollywood, and Bardem won the Oscar for Best Supporting Actor in the Coen brothers' disturbing *No Country for Old Men* in 2008.

Bardem has had plenty of success. In the landmark *Mar Adentro* (Out to Sea; 2004), by Alejandro Amenábar (b 1972), he played the lead role in a touching true story of a man's 30-year struggle to win the right to end his own paralysed life.

Vicente Aranda (b 1926) found acclaim with *Amantes* (Lovers; 1991), set in 1950s Madrid and based on the real story of a doomed love triangle. In 2007 he produced *Canciones de Amor en Lolita's Club* (Love Songs at Lolita's Club), a story of love in a mafia-run brothel based on a tale by the Barcelona writer Juan Marsé.

Julio Medem (b 1958) takes us on complex interior journeys into the lives of his characters, mirrored by real journeys. Perfect examples of this are his slow-moving, poetic films *Los Amantes del Círculo Polar* (Lovers of the Arctic Circle; 1998), *Lucía y el Sexo* (Sex and Lucia; 2001) and *Caótica Ana* (Chaotic Ana; 2007).

Films on the Franco years pop up regularly. One of the better ones is Emilio Martínez Lázaro's *Las 13 Rosas* (13 Roses; 2007), on the beginning of the dictatorship in Madrid after the civil war.

Indy Rock (www.indyrock.es in Spanish) is a good source for upcoming gigs and festivals, and Clubbing Spain (www.clubbingspain.com in Spanish) has the deal on house and techno events.

For decades, a key figure in the Spanish film business was Rafael Azcona (1926–2008), the country's most prolific screenwriter, responsible for numerous scripts in landmark films.

Spanish TV is dominated by chat shows that often border on gossipy shouting matches, but several series have carved out a big chunk of audience share during the past few years. *Cuéntame Cómo Pasó* (Tell Me How It Happened) is set in a *barrio* (district) of Madrid and recounts tales of the city from 1940 to the 1980s. Starring Imanol Arias, it is one of the most watched shows on the *caja tonta* (silly box).

Also popular is *El Comisário,* a cop show starring Tito Valverde as *comisário* (police chief) Gerardo Castilla, who's in charge of a young police team investigating anything from baby kidnappings to street crime.

The late-night American-style chat show *Buenafuente* (hosted by Andreu Buenafuente) is a mix of interviews with personalities and slightly silly humour.

Music

Spain pulsates with music – and not just flamenco. The country's intense musicality will be one of your abiding memories. The rock, pop and electronic scene, while not always wildly original or hugely successful beyond Spanish shores, is busy and energetic – a good deal more so than in many other European countries – and has a big following.

Meanwhile flamenco (see p73), the music most readily associated with Spain, is enjoying a golden age.

POPULAR MUSIC

Each summer throws up a danceable, catchy hit that takes the country by storm. Perhaps the most ridiculous of all time was *Baila el Chiki Chiki*, a silly reggaeton spoof performed by Chikilicuatre (David Fernández Ortiz). A part-time actor posing as an Argentine inventor (with huge toupee and thick-rimmed glasses), he appeared on the late-night *Buenafuente* show and achieved such notoriety that he was selected as Spain's entry to the 2008 Eurovision song contest. Unsurprisingly, Chiki's humour didn't translate too well.

The undoubted King Midas of Spanish pop, writer of countless hit ballads for himself and others, is Madrid-born Alejandro Sanz (b 1968). The wistful quality of his earlier songs has given way to an edgier more urban sound.

Evergreen singer-songwriters include the iconoclastic Joaquín Sabina, a prolific producer of rock-folk with a consistent protest theme for more than two decades, and Joan Manuel Serrat, one of Barcelona's favourite sons, who has a croonier feel. The two are immensely popular in Spain and Latin America and actually toured together in 2007.

Nacha Pop, whose lead performers are Nacho García Vega and Antonio Vega, were the pop hit of the 1980s Madrid *movida* and recently hit the comeback trail, with concert tours in 2007 and 2008, much to the pleasure of nostalgic fans.

> Many home-grown bands in Catalonia sing in Catalan rather than Spanish, and since 1998 the annual Senglar Rock festival has celebrated Catalan rock.

A popular young band serving up more mainstream pop-rock is the Madrid foursome El Canto del Loco, which provides great, high-energy live performances. The group's album *Zapatillas* (Trainers) was the big success of 2005–06.

Bilbao-born Fito Cabrales is possibly the biggest rock solo phenomenon of the moment. Appearing as Fito & Fitipaldis, he offers a clean, soft rock with personal lyrics.

A hit in Spanish dance clubs, Melendi is an Asturian whose music has connotations of Barcelona rumba (an offshoot of flamenco that is again flowering after virtually dying out in the 1980s). His best album is *Mientras No Cueste Trabajo*.

Jarabe de Palo, a group led by Pau Donés, got its lucky break with the hit song *La Flaca* in 1996 on their first, self-titled album. With ironic lyrics and a relaxed melodic sound, Jarabe de Palo's pop-rock is instantly likeable. Their disk album is *Adelantando*.

The hard postindustrial rock known as *bakalao* in the 1980s and *mákina* in the 1990s seems to be making another comeback, led by the likes of Chimo Bayo, the DJ who gave us the *exta-sí, exta-no* tune that was an essential part of 1990s raves across Europe.

FOLK

Although you're likely to find the odd group playing traditional folk music in several regions, Spain's real folk hotbed is Galicia. The region's rich heritage is closely related to that of its Celtic cousins in Brittany and Ireland and has nothing in common with other Spanish music such as flamenco. Emblematic of the music is the *gaita*, Galicia's version of the bagpipes. Top bagpipers are popular heroes in Galicia, and some of the younger generation have broadened the music's appeal by blending it with other genres.

One highly versatile performer – not just of the *gaita* but also of other wind instruments – is Carlos Núñez. He presents a slick show involving violins, percussion, guitar and lute, and often invites a wide range of guest artists, as on his successful and award-winning 2004 album *Carlos Núñez y Amigos*. Other exciting Galician pipers are Susana Seivane, Mercedes Peón (who mixes the pipes with vocals and many other instruments in a spectrum of ethnic styles) and Xosé Manuel Budiño.

Lluís Llach (b 1948), Catalonia's Bob Dylan, led the way as a protest singer in the Franco years.

Galicia's most successful Celtic group is the highly polished Milladoiro. Other groups to seek out are Berrogüetto, Luar Na Lubre and Fía Na Roca. Uxía is a gutsy female solo vocalist.

Neighbouring Asturias also has distant Celtic roots. You'll come across the *gaita* here, too, especially at country fiestas in the west where you might see locals dancing *baile vaqueiro,* brisk traditional folk dances.

CLASSICAL

All Spanish cities have active classical-music scenes but little of the music you'll hear will have been written by Spanish composers.

Outsiders have made at least as much serious music as Spaniards themselves from the country's vibrant rhythms. Who hasn't heard of *Carmen,* an opera whose leading lady epitomises all the fire and flashing beauty conjured up by the typical image of Andalucian women? Its composer, Frenchman Georges Bizet (1838–75), had been mesmerised by the melodies of southern Spain in much the same way as Claude Debussy (1862–1918), whose penchant for the peninsula found expression in *Iberia*. Another Frenchman, Maurice Ravel (1875–1937), whipped up his *Bolero* almost as an aside in 1927. Russians, too, have been swept away by the Hispanic. Mikhail Glinka (1804–57) arrived in Granada in 1845, fell under the spell of *gitano* song and guitar, and returned home to inspire a new movement in Russian folk music.

Spain itself was more or less bereft of composers until the likes of Cádiz-born Manuel de Falla (1876–1946) and Enrique Granados (1867–1916) in the early 20th century. Granados and Isaac Albéniz (1860–1909) became great pianists and interpreters of their own compositions. The blind Joaquín Rodrigo (1901–99) was one of Spain's leading 20th-century composers. His celebrated *Concierto de Aranjuez* for guitar yielded what for some is the greatest jazz rendering of any classical-music work – Miles Davis' 1959 version on his *Sketches of Spain* album.

Velázquez so much wanted to be made a Knight of Santiago that in *Las Meninas* he cheekily portrayed himself with the cross of Santiago on his vest, long before his wish was finally fulfilled.

Andrés Segovia (1893–1987), from Linares in Andalucía, was steeped in flamenco. He probably did more than any other musician to establish the guitar as a serious classical instrument, taking this formerly humble instrument to dizzying heights of virtuosity.

In opera, Spain has given the world both Plácido Domingo (b 1934) and José Carreras (b 1946). They have long been among the world's top male opera singers. Catalonia's unstoppable Montserrat Caballé (b 1933) is one of the world's outstanding sopranos.

Painting & Scuplture

Humans have been creating images in Spain for at least as long as 14,500 years, as the cave paintings in Altamira (p532) attest. Later, the Celtiberian tribes were producing some fine ceramics and statuary, perhaps influenced by the presence of Greeks, Carthaginians and ultimately Romans.

Mostly anonymous, the painters and decorators of Romanesque churches across the north of the country left behind extraordinary testaments to the religious faith of the early Middle Ages. Some remain in situ but the single best concentration of 12th-century Romanesque frescoes, possibly in all Europe, can be seen in Barcelona's Museu Nacional d'Art de Catalunya (p337).

Artists began to drop their modesty in the 14th century, and names such as Ferrer Bassá (c 1290–1348); Bernat Martorell (c 1400–52), a master of chiaroscuro; Jaume Huguet (1415–92); and Bartolomé Bermejo (c 1405–95) are thus known to us, and their works identifiable. At this time Gothic painting, more lifelike and complex than the seemingly naive, didactic Romanesque, took hold.

One of the most remarkable artists at work in the latter half of the 16th century was an 'adopted' Spaniard. Domenikos Theotokopoulos (1541–1614), known as El Greco (the Greek), was schooled in his native Crete and Italy, but spent his productive working life in Toledo (see the boxed text, p278). His slender, exalted figures can be seen in various locations in that city, as well as in Madrid's Museo del Prado (p153).

THE GOLDEN CENTURY

As the 16th century gave way to the 17th century, a remarkably fecund era opened. A plethora of masters, in the service of both the Church and the State, seemed to appear out of nowhere.

In Italy, José (Jusepe) de Ribera (1591–1652) came under the influence of Caravaggio. Many of his works found their way back to Spain and are now scattered about numerous art galleries, including a solid selection in the Museo del Prado.

The star of the period was the genius court painter from Seville, Diego Rodríguez de Silva Velázquez (1599–1660), who stands in a class of his own. With him any trace of the idealised stiffness that characterised a by-now spiritless mannerism fell by the wayside. Realism became the key, and the majesty of his royal subjects springs from his capacity to capture the essence of the person, king or *infanta* (princess), and the detail of their finery. His masterpieces include *Las Meninas* (Maids of Honour) and *La Rendición de Breda* (Surrender of Breda), both in the Museo del Prado.

A less-exalted contemporary, and close friend of Velázquez, Francisco de Zurbarán (1598–1664) moved to Seville as an official painter. Born in Extremadura, though probably of Basque origin, he is best remembered for the startling clarity and light in his portraits of monks. He travelled a great deal and a series of eight portraits can still be seen hanging where Zurbarán left them, in Guadalupe's Hieronymite Real Monasterio de Santa María de Guadalupe (p853). Zurbarán fell on hard times in the 1640s and was compelled by the plague to flee Seville. He died in poverty in Madrid.

Reach into the tortured mind of one of Spain's greatest artists with the help of Robert Hughes' riveting work on *Goya*.

Zurbarán has come to be seen as one of the masters of the Spanish canvas, but in his lifetime it was a younger and less-inspired colleague who won all the prizes. Bartolomé Esteban Murillo (1618–82) took the safe road and turned out stock religious pieces and images of beggar boys and the like, with technical polish but little verve. Again, you can see many of his works in the Museo del Prado.

GOYA & THE 19TH CENTURY

Francisco José de Goya y Lucientes (1746–1828), a provincial hick from Fuendetodos in Aragón, went to Madrid to work as a cartoonist in the Real Fábrica de Tapices (p157). Here began the long and varied career of Spain's only truly great artist of the 18th (and for that matter the 19th) century. By 1799 he was Carlos IV's court painter.

Several distinct series and individual paintings mark the progress of his life and work. At the end of the 18th century he painted such enigmatic masterpieces as *La Maja Vestida* and *La Maja Desnuda,* identical portraits of un unknown woman but for the lack of clothes in the latter. At about the same time he did *Los Caprichos*, a series of 80 etchings lambasting the follies of court life and ignorant clergy.

The arrival of the French and the war in 1808 profoundly affected his work. He makes unforgiving portrayals of the brutality of war in *El Dos de Mayo* (Second of May) and, more dramatically, *El Tres de Mayo* (Third of May). The latter depicts the execution of Madrid rebels by French troops and both hang in the Museo del Prado.

An obvious precursor to many subsequent strands of modern art, Goya was an island of grandeur in a sea of artistic mediocrity in Spain. He marked a transition from art being made in the service of the State or Church to art as a pure expression of its creator's feeling and whim.

Long after Goya's death, the Valencian Joaquín Sorolla (1863–1923) set off on his own path, ignoring the fashionable French Impressionists and preferring the blinding light of the Valencian coast to the muted tones favoured in Paris. He is known for his cheerful, large-format images of beach life and much of his work can be admired in Madrid's Museo Sorolla (p160).

THE SHOCK OF THE NEW

Like a thunderclap came the genius of the mischievous *malagueño* (person from Málaga), Pablo Ruiz Picasso (1881–1973). A child when he moved with his family to Barcelona, Picasso was formed in an atmosphere laden with the avant-garde freedom of Modernisme (see p89).

Anthony Hopkins starred as the genius artist from Málaga in *Surviving Picasso* (1996), concentrating on one of Picasso's numerous affairs. Hopkins is brilliant, the film less so.

Picasso must have been one of the most restless artists of all time. His work underwent repeated revolutions as he passed from one creative phase to another. From his gloomy Blue Period, through the brighter Pink Period and on to cubism – in which he was accompanied by Madrid's Juan Gris (1887–1927) – Picasso was nothing if not a surprise package.

By the mid-1920s he was dabbling with surrealism. His best-known work is *Guernica*, a complex canvas portraying the horror of war and inspired by the German aerial bombing of the Basque town Guernica (Gernika) in 1937. Picasso consistently cranked out paintings, sculptures, ceramics and etchings until the day he died. A good selection of his early work can be viewed in Barcelona's Museu Picasso (p326). Other of his works are scattered about different galleries, notably Madrid's Centro de Arte Reina Sofía (p152).

Separated from Picasso by barely a generation, two other artists reinforced the Catalan contingent in the vanguard of 20th-century art: Dalí and Miró. Although he started off dabbling in cubism, Salvador Dalí (1904–89) became more readily identified with the surrealists. This complex character's 'hand-painted dream photographs', as he called them, are virtuoso executions brimming with fine detail and nightmare images dragged up from a feverish and Freud-fed imagination. Preoccupied with Picasso's fame, Dalí built himself a reputation as an outrageous showman and shameless self-promoter. The single best display of his work can be seen at the Teatre-Museu Dalí (p391) in Figueres.

Slower to find his feet, Barcelona-born Joan Miró (1893–1983) developed a joyous and almost childlike style that earned him the epithet 'the most surrealist of us all' from the French writer André Breton. His later period is his best known, characterised by the simple use of bright colours and forms in combinations of symbols that represented women, birds (the link between earth and the heavens), stars (the unattainable heavenly world, source of imagination) and a sort of net, which entraps all these levels of the cosmos. Galleries of his work adorn Barcelona (p338) and Palma de Mallorca (p656).

FROM FRANCO TO THE CONTEMPORARY SCENE

The two main artistic movements of the 1950s, El Paso and the Catalan Dau el Set, launched names such Antonio Saura (1930–98), Manuel Millares (1926–72) and Barcelona's tireless Antoni Tàpies (b 1923). The art of Madrid's Eduardo Arroyo (b 1937) is steeped in the radical spirit that kept him in exile from Spain for 15 years from 1962. His paintings, brimming with ironic socio-political comment, tend, in part, to pop art.

The death of Franco acted as a catalyst for the Spanish art movement. New talent sprang up, and galleries enthusiastically took on anything revolutionary, contrary or cheeky. The 1970s and 1980s were a time of almost childish self-indulgence. Things have since calmed down but there is still much activity.

www.arteespana.com is an interesting website (in Spanish) that covers broad swathes of Spanish art history (and where you can buy art books or even models of monuments).

The Basques Eduardo Chillida (1924–2002) and Jorge Oteiza (1908–2003) were two of Spain's leading modern sculptors, active throughout their lives almost to the end of their days.

Joan Hernández Pijuan (1931–2005) was one of the most important abstract painters to come out of Barcelona in the latter decades of the 20th century. His work is often referred to as informalist and it concentrates on natural shapes and figures, often with neutral colours on different surfaces.

Seville's Luis Gordillo (b 1934) started his artistic career with surrealism, from where he branched out into pop art and photography. His later work in particular features the serialisation of different versions of the same image. Antonio López (b 1936) is considered the father of the so-called Madrid hyperrealism. One of his grandest works is the incredibly detailed *Madrid desde Torres Blancas* (Madrid from Torres Blancas), which he painted from 1976 to 1982.

Mallorcan Miquel Barceló (b 1957) is one of the country's big success stories. His work is heavily expressionist, although it touches on classic themes, from self-portraiture to architectural images. His most public creation is the fantasy world remake of a chapel in Palma de Mallorca's cathedral (p653).

Barcelona's Susana Solano (b 1946) is a painter and above all sculptor, considered to be one of the most important at work in Spain today, while Jaume Plensa (b 1955) is possibly Spain's best contemporary sculptor. His work ranges from sketches through sculpture and to video and other installations that have been shown around the world.

Flamenco World (www.flamenco-world.com), Flama (www.guiaflama.com in Spanish), Centro Andaluz de Flamenco (www.centroandaluzdeflamenco.es in Spanish), esflamenco.com (www.esflamenco.com) and Deflamenco.com (www.deflamenco.com) are all great resources on flamenco, and include calendars of upcoming events.

Seville's Curro González (b 1960) creates big canvases full of hallucinatory figures, allegory and allusions to contemporary society. Distortion, surrealism and a good dose of irony are among his arms.

The figure of the woman lies at the heart of much of the recent work by Madrid's José Manuel Merello (b 1960), paintings full of broad sweeps of primal colour and blurred detail.

Flamenco

The passionate and uniquely Spanish constellation of singing, dancing and instrumental arts known as flamenco first took recognisable form in the late 18th and early 19th centuries among Roma people in the lower Guadalquivir valley of Andalucía (still flamenco's heartland). The first flamenco was *cante jondo* (deep song), an anguished instrument of expression for a group on the margins of society. *Jondura* (depth) is still the essence of pure flamenco. It's not something that's universally appreciated: to the unsympathetic ear, flamenco song can sound like someone suffering from excruciating toothache. But love it or hate it, a flamenco performer who successfully communicates their passion will have you on the edge of your seat. The gift of sparking this kind of response is known as *duende* (spirit).

GREAT FLAMENCO & FUSION ALBUMS

- *Paco de Lucía Antología* – Paco de Lucía (1995)
- *Una Leyenda Flamenca* – El Camarón de la Isla (1993)
- *Cañailla* – Niña Pastori (2000)
- *Del Amanecer* – José Mercé (1999)
- *Niña de Fuego* – Concha Buika (2008)
- *Noche de Flamenco y Blues* – Raimundo Amador, BB King et al (1998)
- *Blues de la Frontera* – Pata Negra (1986)
- *Cositas Buenas* – Paco de Lucía (2004)
- *Lágrimas Negras* – Bebo Valdés and Diego El Cigala (2003)
- *Sueña La Alhambra* – Enrique Morente (2005)

A flamenco singer is known as a *cantaor* (male) or *cantaora* (female); a dancer is a *bailaor/a*. Most of the songs and dances are performed to a blood-rush of guitar from the *tocaor/a* (male or female flamenco guitarist). Percussion is provided by tapping feet, clapping hands and sometimes castanets. Flamenco *coplas* (songs) come in many different types, from the anguished *soleá* or the intensely despairing *siguiriya* to the livelier *alegría* or the upbeat *bulería*.

FLAMENCO TODAY

Rarely can flamenco have been as popular as it is today, and never so innovative. While long-established singers such as Enrique Morente, Carmen Linares, Chano Lobato and José Menese remain at the top of the profession, new generations continue to broaden flamenco's audience.

Universally acclaimed is José Mercé, from Jerez. Estrella Morente from Granada (Enrique's daughter), Miguel Poveda (from Barcelona) and La Tana from Seville are young singers steadily carving out niches in the first rank of performers.

Dance, always the readiest of flamenco arts to cross boundaries, has reached its most adventurous horizons in the person of Joaquin Cortés, born in Córdoba in 1969. Cortés fuses flamenco with contemporary dance, ballet and jazz in spectacular shows with music at rock-concert amplification. The most exciting younger dance talent is Farruquito (Juan Manuel Fernández Montoya), born into a legendary flamenco family in Seville in 1983 (he made his Broadway debut at the age of five). Other top stars to look out for – you may find them dancing solo or with their own companies – include Sara Baras, Antonio Canales, Manuela Carrasco, Cristina Hoyos and Eva La Hierbabuena.

Among guitarists, listen out for Manolo Sanlúcar from Cádiz; Tomatito from Almería; and Vicente Amigo from Córdoba and Moraíto Chico from Jerez, who both accompany today's top singers.

FLAMENCO FUSION

Given a cue, perhaps, by Paco de Lucía (see opposite), musicians began mixing flamenco with jazz, rock, blues, rap and other genres in the 1970s and they're still doing it today. This 'flamenco fusion' presents perhaps the easiest way into flamenco for newcomers and can be great music in its own right.

The seminal recording was a 1977 flamenco-folk-rock album *Veneno* (Poison) by the group of the same name, centred on Kiko Veneno and

Raimundo Amador, both from Seville. Kiko remains an icon of flamenco fusion, mixing rock, blues, African and flamenco rhythms with witty lyrics focusing on snatches of everyday life. Amador later formed the group Pata Negra, which produced four fine flamenco-jazz-blues albums, before going solo.

The group Ketama, originally from Granada, has successfully mixed flamenco with African, Cuban, Brazilian and other rhythms for two decades. Cádiz's Niña Pastori (b 1978) arrived in the late 1990s with an edgy, urgent voice singing jazz- and Latin-influenced flamenco.

Eleven-strong Barcelona-based band Ojos de Brujo mixes flamenco with reggae, Asian and even club dance rhythms. *Techarí* (2006) is a great album. They're great live performers and have gained wide popularity outside as well as inside Spain.

Málaga's Chambao successfully combines flamenco with electronic beats on its albums such as *Flamenco Chill* (2002) and *Pokito a Poko* (Little by Little; 2005).

Mala Rodríguez (b 1978), born in Jerez de la Frontera, no doubt upsets some of the purists with her wild combination of flamenco and rap. Her latest album, *Malamarismo* (2007), is a classic of her unique genre.

Concha Buika, a Mallorcan of Equatorial Guinean origin, not only possesses a beautiful, sensual voice but also writes many of her own songs. Her albums *Buika* (2005) and *Mi Niña Lola* (2006) are a captivating melange of African rhythms, soul, jazz, hip hop, flamenco and more!

In his first book, *Duende,* Jason Webster immersed his body and soul for two years in Spain's passionate and dangerous flamenco world in search of the true flamenco spirit.

FLAMENCO LEGENDS

The great singers of the 19th and early 20th centuries were Silverio Franconetti and La Niña de los Peines, from Seville, and Antonio Chacón and Manuel Torre, from Jerez de la Frontera. Torre's singing, legend has it, could drive people to rip their shirts open and upturn tables.

La Macarrona and Pastora Imperio, the first great *bailaoras,* took flamenco to Paris and South America. Their successors, La Argentina and La Argentinita, formed dance troupes and turned flamenco dance into a theatrical show.

The dynamic dancing and wild lifestyle of Carmen Amaya (1913–63), from Barcelona, made her the *gitana* dance legend of all time. Her long-time partner Sabicas was the father of the modern solo flamenco guitar, inventing a host of now-indispensable techniques.

After a trough in the mid-20th century, when it seemed that the *tablaos* (touristy shows emphasising the sexy and the jolly) were in danger of taking over, *flamenco puro* got a new lease of life in the 1970s through singers such as Terremoto, La Paquera, Enrique Morente and, above all, El Camarón de la Isla (whose real name was José Monge Cruz) from San Fernando near Cádiz. El Camarón's incredible vocal and emotional range and his wayward lifestyle made him a legend well before his tragically early death in 1992. As his great guitar accompanist Paco de Lucía observed, 'Camarón's cracked voice could evoke, on its own, the desperation of a people'.

Some say that Madrid-born Diego El Cigala (1968) is El Camarón's successor. This powerful singer had a rare hit with his *Lágrimas Negras* (Black Tears) album, done with Cuban piano legend Bebo Valdés, in 2003, and followed up with another album that mixes flamenco with Cuban influences, *Dos Lágrimas* (Two Tears) in 2008.

Paco de Lucía, born in Algeciras in 1947, is the flamenco artist known most widely outside Spain, and with good reason. So gifted that by the time he was 14 his teachers had nothing left to teach him, de Lucía has transformed the flamenco guitar into an instrument of solo expression with new techniques, scales, melodies and harmonies that have gone far beyond traditional limits.

SEEING FLAMENCO

Under the artistic direction of Nacho Duato since 1990, the Compañía Nacional de Danza has performed to critical acclaim around the world and won many awards.

Flamenco is easiest to catch in Andalucía, Madrid and Barcelona. In many towns in the south, summer *ferias* (fairs) and fiestas include flamenco performances, and some places stage special night-long flamenco festivals. Bigger events include the two-week Festival de Jerez in Jerez de la Frontera (www.festivaldejerez.es in Spanish) in late February/early March every year; the Festival Internacional del Cante de las Minas (www.fundacioncantedelasminas.com in Spanish), in La Unión, Murcia, over several days mid-August; and the month-long Bienal de Flamenco (p724) held in Seville. Otherwise, look out for big-name performances in theatres, check seasons of concerts, and you can visit regular flamenco nights at bars and clubs in some cities – often just for the price of your drinks. Flamenco fans also band together in clubs called *peñas,* which stage live performance nights; most will admit interested visitors and the atmosphere here will be authentic and at times very intimate.

Theatre & Dance

Thanks mainly to a big development program by the PSOE governments of the 1980s and 1990s, most Spanish cities boast at least one theatre worthy of the name, and drama is now a vibrant field. Larger cities such as Madrid, Barcelona and Seville have plenty of smaller locales staging avant-garde and experimental productions as well as larger venues for straighter productions. Unadulterated drama, though, is unlikely to appeal if your understanding of Spanish – or, in Barcelona, Catalan – is less than fluent.

Federico García Lorca's dramatic play, *Bodas de Sangre* (Blood Wedding), was brought to the screen in a modern flamenco remake by Carlos Saura with dancers of the calibre of the late Antonio Gades in 1981.

Dance thrives and not just in the context of flamenco. Barcelona is Spain's capital of modern dance, with several shows to choose from almost any week. Madrid is closing the gap and its Compañía Nacional de Danza, under the direction of Nacho Duato (b 1957), is one of Europe's most exciting contemporary ensembles and has performed to great acclaim around the world. The Ballet Nacional de España, founded in 1978, mixes classical ballet with Spanish dance. Spain's most gifted classical dancer for aeons, *madrileña* Tamara Rojo (b 1974), is the prima ballerina for London's Royal Ballet since 2000, garnering ever more superlative reviews as the years pass.

Here and there you'll find the occasional regional folk dance, such as Catalonia's *sardana* round-dance; *baile vaqueiro* (various styles, some very lively, for couples, accompanied by *gaita,* percussion and song) in western Asturias; or the Málaga area's *verdiales,* flag dances done to exhilarating fiddle and percussion music.

Local Flavours

A cool glass of Spanish white is the perfect accompaniment to architectural magnificence

Spanish food and wine are topics about which Spaniards could wax lyrical for hours – usually while enjoying said food and wine. We're inclined to agree with them and hence couldn't confine ourselves to covering the Spanish staples alone (see p92). This section goes a little deeper, exploring the extraordinary regional varieties of Spanish cuisine, peeling back the layers of the distinct culinary cultures that make travelling in the country such a memorable feast.

BASQUE COUNTRY & CATALONIA

The Basque Country and Catalonia are Spain's undoubted culinary superstars. Partly this is because of the area's gastronomic innovation; its avant-garde chefs – Ferran Adrià, Sergi Arola, Mari Arzak, Oriol Balaguer and Pedro Subijana, to name just a few – are famous throughout the world for their food laboratories, their commitment to food as art and their crazy riffs on the themes of traditional local cooking. But the Basque Country and Catalonia are also a gastronomes' paradise because food here runs deep into every aspect of culture. If Spaniards elsewhere in the country love their food, the Basques and Catalans are obsessed with it. They talk about it endlessly. They plan their day around it. And then they spend the rest of their time dreaming about it. One taste and you're likely to be doing the same.

The confluence of sea and mountain has bequeathed to the Basque Country an extraordinary culinary richness, a cuisine as much defined by the fruits of the Bay of Biscay as by the fruits of the land. You're as likely to find great *anchoas* (anchovies), *gambas* (prawns) and *bacalao* (cod) as you are heaving steaks and *jamón* (ham), and often in surprising combinations. The food is exceptional wherever you go in the region, but San Sebastián is the Basque Country's, and perhaps even Spain's, true culinary capital. It's here that you understand how deeply ingrained food is in Basque culture, home as the city is to everything from secret gastronomic societies and exclusive sit-down restaurants with the full complement of Michelin stars to the more accessible *pintxos* (Basque tapas) bars of the Parte Vieja. If we could choose one place to sample the creativity, variety and sheer excitement of Basque cuisine, it would be here. It's from the kitchens of San Sebastián that *nueva cocina vasca* (Basque nouvelle cuisine) has emerged, announcing Spain's arrival as a culinary superpower. The results are, quite simply, extraordinary.

top five BASQUE EATING EXPERIENCES

Pintxos (Basque tapas; p490) in the bars of San Sebastián's Parte Vieja, washed down with *txacoli* (a sharp, local white wine).

Bacalao al pil-pil (salt cod and garlic in an olive-oil emulsion) at Kasazuri and Restarante Alberto (p491) in San Sebastián.

Chipirones en su tinta (baby squid served in its own ink) at Rio-Oja (p477) in Bilbao.

Chuleton de buey (enormous steaks) at various *sidrerías* (cider bars) in the mountains around San Sebastián.

Nueva cocina vasca (Basque nouvelle cuisine) at Arzak (p491), one of Spain's best restaurants.

Considered by many to be the Basque Country's equal when it comes to food excellence, Catalonia blends traditional Catalan flavours and extraordinary geographical diversity with an openness to influences from the rest of Europe, a trait that Barcelona has turned into a way of life. All manner of seafood, paella, rice and pasta dishes are regulars on Catalonian menus and, this being Catalonia, always with a creative local twist. Sauces are more prevalent here than elsewhere in Spain, and the further you head inland, the more likely you are to see the mainstays of Pyrenean cooking with *jabalí* (wild boar), *conejo* (rabbit), *caracoles* (snails, especially in Lleida) and delicious hotpots such as *suquet* (fish and potato stew). If you prefer to self-cater, with the finest produce in the land, look no further than Barcelona's Mercat de la Boqueria (p352). Here you'll find *botifarra* (the local version of cured pork sausage) and *garrotxa*, a formidable Catalan cheese that almost lives up to its name. Desserts are also a feature, notably *crema catalana* (the Catalan version of crème brûlée).

top five SPOTS FOR CATALAN SPECIALITIES

Casa Leopoldo (p350), Barcelona – Catalan seafood.

Xiringuito d'Escribà (p350), Barcelona – rice and *fideuá* (noodles with fish and shellfish).

Restaurant Elche (p352), Barcelona – paella, *fideuá*, *suquet* (fish and potato stew), *sarsuela* (seafood stew).

Hotel Durán (p393), Figueres – *suquet*, and rabbit with snails.

Restaurant El Roser II (p387), L'Escala – *suquet*.

INLAND SPAIN

Central Spain's high *meseta* (plateau) has a food culture all its own. The best *jamón ibérico* (cured ham made from the hindquarters of wild pigs that have fed exclusively on acorns) comes from Extremadura and Salamanca, while *cordero asado lechal* (roast spring lamb) and *cochinillo asado* (roast suckling pig) are winter mainstays right through the heart of Spain to such an extent that Spaniards will travel for hours on a winter weekend in search of the perfect *cochinillo* or *cordero*.

Beyond these iconic dishes, each region has its own speciality.

In Aragón it's all about meat, where a love for *ternasco* (suckling lamb, usually served as a steak or ribs with potatoes) is elevated almost to the status of a local religion. Teruel's *jamón* is considered to be among Spain's finest, and the Pyrenean fare in the north closely

Excitement abounds for roasted meats of all varieties in Castilla y León and throughout inland Spain
IONAS KALTENBACH

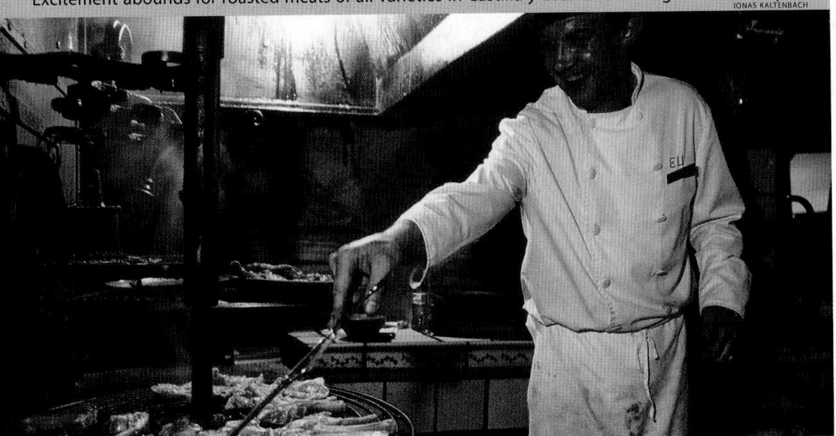

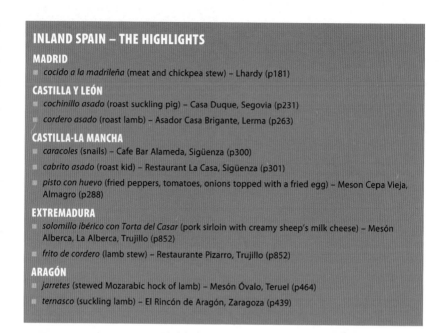

INLAND SPAIN – THE HIGHLIGHTS

MADRID

- *cocido a la madrileña* (meat and chickpea stew) – Lhardy (p181)

CASTILLA Y LEÓN

- *cochinillo asado* (roast suckling pig) – Casa Duque, Segovia (p231)
- *cordero asado* (roast lamb) – Asador Casa Brigante, Lerma (p263)

CASTILLA-LA MANCHA

- *caracoles* (snails) – Cafe Bar Alameda, Sigüenza (p300)
- *cabrito asado* (roast kid) – Restaurant La Casa, Sigüenza (p301)
- *pisto con huevo* (fried peppers, tomatoes, onions topped with a fried egg) – Meson Cepa Vieja, Almagro (p288)

EXTREMADURA

- *solomillo ibérico con Torta del Casar* (pork sirloin with creamy sheep's milk cheese) – Mesón Alberca, La Alberca, Trujillo (p852)
- *frito de cordero* (lamb stew) – Restaurante Pizarro, Trujillo (p852)

ARAGÓN

- *jarretes* (stewed Mozarabic hock of lamb) – Mesón Óvalo, Teruel (p464)
- *ternasco* (suckling lamb) – El Rincón de Aragón, Zaragoza (p439)

resembles that of neighbouring Catalonia. For more on mouthwatering Aragonese cuisine, see the boxed text, p439.

In Extremadura, you should always order *solomillo ibérico con Torta del Casar* (pork sirloin with creamy Torta del Casar cheese made from sheep's milk) if it's on the menu, while *frito de cordero* (lamb stew), *migas* (breadcrumbs, often cooked with cured meats and served with grapes) and even frog legs are other delicacies to watch for.

Castilla-La Mancha is famous for its *queso manchego* (a hard cheese made from sheep's milk), as well as snails and quirky dishes such as bread embedded with sardines that you'll find in Alcalá de Júcar. Castilla y León is even more devoted to the cult of meat with *carnes asadas* (roasted meats) and *embutidos* (cured meats) weighing down every bar and restaurant across the region.

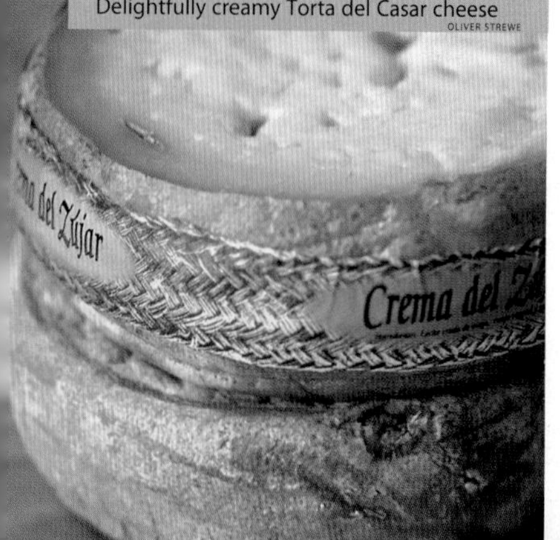

Delightfully creamy Torta del Casar cheese
OLIVER STREWE

In Madrid the local *cocido a la madrileña* (meat and chickpea stew) inspires considerable passion; it's echoed in Astorga in northern Castilla y León, where the elements (soup, meats etc) are eaten in reverse order and known as *cocido maragato*. *Madrilieños* are also passionate about fish and seafood; it's often said Madrid is the best 'port' in Spain because the seafood arrives fresh daily from both the Atlantic and the Mediterranean.

GALICIA & THE NORTHWEST

Perhaps more than any other Spaniards, *gallegos* (Galicians) are defined by their relationship with the sea. A large proportion of them make their livelihoods from fishing, and their cuisine, their fiestas and, some would say, their whole reason for living revolves around fish and seafood. Yes, they're proud of their *empanadas* (savoury pies) and *pimientos de padron* (grilled and often spicy green capsicum). But these are merely diversions from the main event, which is *pulpo gallego* (spicy boiled octopus), a dish whose constituent elements (octopus, oil, paprika and garlic) are so simple yet whose execution is devilishly difficult. The trick is in the boiling; dipping the octopus into the water, then drawing it out and dipping again cooks it at just the right rate. Other Galician mainstays include a litany of bewildering sea creatures such as *navajas* (razor clams), *coquinas* (large clams), *percebes* (goose barnacles), *mejillones* (mussels), *berberechos* (cockles), *almejas* (baby clams) and *vieiras* (a form of scallop). We hope you like shellfish…

Pucker up for some *pulpo* (octopus) in Galicia
OLIVER STREWE

Not to be outdone, neighbouring Asturias and Cantabria also give to Spain a handful of seafood delicacies, the best known of which are *anchoas*. If you're anywhere in Spain and you spy *anchoas de santoña* on the menu, don't hesitate for a second. Better still, go straight to the source and visit Santoña (p527) where the little fellas come ashore.

ATLANTIC CHEESES

The moist, cool climate of northwestern Spain produces rich grasses that make for fat, contented cows and flavour-filled milk. Some of the more widely available varieties of cheese:

- **San Simón** – a slightly smoked Galician mountain cheese that's dense, yellow and has a creamy texture.
- **Cabrales** – a creamy, powerful blue cheese from Asturias cured in the cool, deep caves of the Picos de Europa. To learn about how it's made, visit the Cueva El Cares (p535).
- **Afuega'l Pitu** – an Asturian valley cheese that's drier and nuttier than most Atlantic cheeses and sometimes made with paprika.
- **Tetilla** – literally 'nipple', this Galician cheese is so-named for its remarkable resemblance to a perfectly shaped breast; it's mild, sweet and creamy.
- **Ahumado de Aliva** – a Cantabrian cheese smoked over juniper wood and with a mild, smoky taste.

In the high mountains of the Cordillera Cantábrica in the coastal hinterland, the cuisine is as driven by mountain pasture as it is by the daily comings and goings of fishing fleets. Cheeses are particularly sought-after, with special fame reserved for the untreated cows' milk cheese, *queso de Cabrales*. River fish (trout, eels and salmon in particular) are also popular. But if *asturianos* (Asturians) get excited about one food above all others, then it would have to be *fabada asturiana* (a stew made with pork, blood sausage and white beans). This is winter food, the sort of meal that will have you rising from the table on suddenly heavy legs and longing for a siesta. The saving grace is that the fresh taste of *sidra* (cider) straight from the barrel will not, unless you overindulge, cast such a long shadow over the rest of your afternoon.

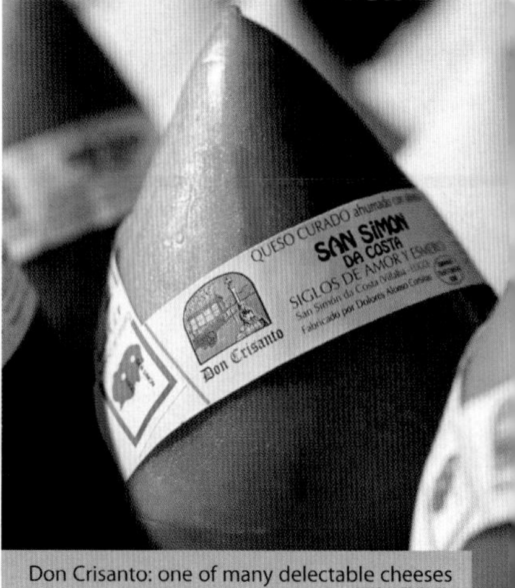

Don Crisanto: one of many delectable cheeses
JONAS KALTENBACH

VALENCIA, MURCIA & THE BALEARIC ISLANDS

There's so much more to the cuisine of this region than oranges and paella, but these two signature products capture the essence of the Mediterranean table. There's no dish better suited to a summer's afternoon spent with friends overlooking the sea than paella, a dish filled with flavour and, very often, full of seafood. You can get a paella just about anywhere in Spain, but to get one cooked as it should be cooked, look no further than the restaurants lined up along Valencia's Paseo Marítimo Neptuno or La Pepica (p616). For the noodle variety of *fideuá* (noodles with fish and shellfish), the alternative that many travellers prefer with a dollop of *alioli* (garlic mayonnaise), your first stop should be Restaurante Emilio (p630) in Gandia.

The cooking style of the Balearic Islands owes much to its watery locale and to its cultural similarities with Catalonia and Valencia. As such, paella, rice dishes and lashings of seafood are recurring themes, with a few local variations, notably the preponderance of eel, sometimes in the most unlikely places (the Mallorcan *espinagada*, eel and spinach pie, for instance). One particularly tasty local dish in Ibiza is *arròs caldós* (saffron rice cooked in the broth of local fish, herbs and potatoes).

PAELLA

Easily Spain's best-known culinary export, paella well deserves its fame. The base of a good paella always includes short-grain rice, garlic, parsley, olive oil and saffron. The best rice is the *bomba* variety, which opens out accordion fashion when cooked, allowing for maximum absorption while remaining firm. Paella should be cooked in a large shallow pan to enable maximum contact with the bottom of the pan where most of the flavour resides. And for the final touch of authenticity, the grains on the bottom (and only on the bottom) of the paella should have a crunchy, savoury crust known as the *socarrat*. Beyond that, the main paella staples are *paella valenciana* (from Valencia, where paella has its roots and remains true to its origins), which is cooked with chicken and beans, and the more widespread *paella de mariscos* (seafood paella), which should be bursting with shellfish.

Authentic paella is served with a crunchy crust
GREG ELMS

Murcia's claim to culinary fame brings us back to the oranges. The coastal littoral of this region is known simply as 'La Huerta' ('the garden'). This is one of Spain's most prolific areas for growing fruit and vegetables and has been since Moorish times. Citrus fruits do indeed account for much of the region's output, but you'll also come across rice, tomatoes, peppers and olives. Great plates of grilled vegetables are, not surprisingly, a common order, but *arroz caldoso* (rice cooked in fish stock), *arroz con conejo* (rice with rabbit) and *zarangollo* (omelette of courgettes, onion and potatoes cooked in olive oil) are tasty variations on the theme.

ANDALUCÍA

It's difficult to reduce a region as large and diverse as Andalucía to a few words, but there are a few overarching culinary themes. Seafood is an obvious and consistent presence the length and breadth of the coast. While many of the national and well-known Mediterranean varieties of seafood are found here, the long reach of local fishing fleets into deep Atlantic waters adds depth to your eating experience. The result is all the usual suspects, alongside *pez espada* (swordfish), *cazón* (dogfish or shark that feeds on shellfish to produce a strong, almost sweet flavour), *salmonetes* (red mullet) and *tortilla de camarones* (shrimp fritters).

Another governing principle is that the temperature rarely drops below tolerable and in summer the region bakes with a ferocity unmatched elsewhere on the peninsula. As such, a primary preoccupation of its inhabitants is keeping cool, and there's no better way to do so than with a *gazpacho andaluz* (Andalucian gazpacho), a cold soup with many manifestations. The base is almost always tomato, vinegar and olive oil, but also often incorporates green peppers and soaked bread, and you'll find cooks who won't use anything but sherry vinegar. Our opinion? They're all good. Other similar cold soups typical of the region include *ajo blanco* (white gazpacho, cooked using almonds and no tomato), and *salmorejo cordobés* (a cold tomato-based soup from Córdoba where soaked bread is essential). And one final thing: yes, it's supposed to be cold. *Please* don't make the mistake of one traveller in Seville who returned his gazpacho and asked for it to be heated.

GAZPACHO ANDALUZ

Ingredients

- 1kg ripe tomatoes, peeled, seeded and chopped
- 1 green pepper
- 2 cloves of garlic
- 6 tablespoons of olive oil
- 1 tablespoons of vinegar
- 1 tablespoon of salt
- 3 tablespoons of iced water

Blend all the ingredients with one tablespoon of the iced water in a mortar with pestle, or in a food processor. Refrigerate for two hours. Stir in enough of the water to maintain a soupy consistency.

Andalucía is also Spain's spiritual home of bullfighting. In season (roughly May to September), bars and restaurants will proudly announce '*hay rabo de toro*', which roughly translates as, 'yes, we have bull's tail for those of you who not only like to see the bull chased around the ring but also like to pursue it to its ultimate conclusion'. If you don't think about where it came from, it's really rather tasty.

SPANISH WINE

All of Spain's autonomous communities, with the small exceptions of Asturias and Cantabria, are home to recognised wine-growing areas. With so many areas to choose from, and with most Spanish wines labelled primarily according to region or classificatory status rather than grape variety, a little background knowledge can go a long way.

Spanish wine is subject to a complicated system of wine classification with a range of designations marked on the bottle. These range from the straightforward *vino de mesa* (table wine) to *vino de la tierra,* which is a wine from an officially recognised wine-making area. If an area meets certain strict standards for a given period and covering all aspects of planting, cultivating and ageing, it receives Denominación de Origen (DO; Denomination of Origin) status. There are currently 65 DO-recognised wine-producing areas in Spain. An outstanding wine region gets the Denominación de Origen Calificada (DOC), a controversial classification that some in the industry argue should apply only to specific wines, rather than every wine from within a particular region. At present, the only DOC wines come from La Rioja (p515) in northern Spain and the small Priorat area (see the boxed text, p416) in Catalonia.

Other important indications of quality depend on the length of time a wine has been aged, especially if in oak barrels. The best wines are often, therefore, marked with the designation '*crianza*' (aged for one year in oak barrels), '*reserva*' (two years ageing, at least one of which is in oak barrels) and '*gran reserva*' (two years in oak and three in the bottle).

An outstanding wine relies on careful harvesting in Ourense, Galicia

OLIVER STRE

Architecture

As you look up at the arches of the great Roman aqueduct in Segovia, you can almost see centurions marching beneath it. The mesmerising beauty of the Alhambra soothes with the gentle bubbling of its cool fountains, inducing a dream sense of a long-past Arab world. On a grey winter's day, along the echoing corridors of the Monasterio de Santo Domingo de Silos' Romanesque cloisters, the Middle Ages seem to return with all their mystical fervour. Towering, at times half-ruined, castles dot the countryside from Catalonia to Castilla. To gaze up, eyes turned to God, at the great Gothic cathedrals of Burgos, Palma de Mallorca and Toledo, you can feel the awe they must have inspired when first raised. And who cannot be carried away by the whimsy of Gaudí's Modernista fantasy in Barcelona's La Sagrada Família and Casa Batlló?

Spain's architecture presents one of the broadest and richest testimonies in Europe to thousands of years of building ingenuity. Starting with the simple stone housing of the Celtiberian tribes, primarily scattered across northern Spain, we pass to a handful of reminders of the presence of Greek trading populations at key coastal points. The Carthaginians left nothing behind them but the Romans certainly did, including bridges, aqueducts, city walls and theatres. Ruins of several towns and settlements have also survived.

Unique within Europe is Spain's rich Islamic cultural heritage. The Muslim–Christian division of the peninsula gave rise to other unique styles, from the pre-Romanesque of a long isolated Asturias to spin-off styles with Islamic influences, such as Mozarabic and Mudéjar.

The great movements in medieval construction, Romanesque and then Gothic, are amply represented across the country. While not as rich as in countries such as Italy, Spain also shows off plenty of Renaissance-era and baroque jewels. Closer to modern times, Modernisme, the Spanish (largely Catalan) version of art nouveau, threw up the eccentric genius of Gaudí.

Today, both local and foreign architects are peppering the nation with daring new icons.

Ciudades Patrimonio de la Humanidad España is a beautiful volume (in Spanish) covering those cities that are or contain World Heritage sites.

ANCIENT SPAIN

The tribes that first inhabited the Iberian Peninsula, collectively known as Celtiberians, left behind a wealth of evidence of their existence. The most common living arrangement, called the *castro*, was a hamlet surrounded by stone walls and made up of circular stone houses. Several have been partly preserved in locations mostly across northern Spain. Among the better known are those at A Guarda (La Guardia; p595) on Galicia's southern coast, and near Coaña (p549) in Asturias.

The Greeks and Carthaginians rarely made it far into the Spanish interior. Greek remains at Empúries (p386) in Catalonia are the most impressive reminder of their Iberian presence.

The Romans left more clues. Among the more spectacular sites are the aqueduct in Segovia (p226), the bridge at Alcántara (p848) and the stout walls of Lugo (p600).

Vestiges of some Roman towns can also be seen. Among the more important are the ancient town of Augusta Emerita in Mérida (p854); ancient Tarraco, now known as Tarragona (p421); the amphitheatre and other ruins at Itálica (p730) near Seville; and Sagunto (p620) in Valencia. Modest remains have been imaginatively converted into underground museums

Museu d'Història de la Ciutat in Barcelona (p323) and Museo del Foro de Caesaraugusta in Zaragoza (p436).

EARLY CHRISTIANITY

An exhaustive website covering monasteries old and new in Spain, www.catolicos.com/monasteriosespana.htm (in Spanish), has links that will lead you to many sites of great architectural interest around the country.

Filling the vacuum left by the departing Romans, the Visigoths employed a more humble but remarkably attractive style, which survives in a handful of small churches. The 7th-century Ermita de Santa María de Lara, at Quintanilla de las Viñas (p260) in Burgos province, is one of the best. Fragments of this unique style can be seen in several cities across Spain, including Toledo.

Reputedly the oldest church in Spain is the 7th-century Basílica de San Juan in Baños de Cerrato (p245), while the crypt of the cathedral in nearby Palencia (p243) has Visigothic origins. The horseshoe arch, later perfected by the Arabs, is characteristic of the Visigoth aesthetic.

When Spain was swamped by the Muslim invasion of AD 711, only the unruly northern strip of the country in what is today Asturias (and probably parts of Cantabria and the Basque Country) held out. During the 9th century a unique building style emerged in this green corner of Spain cut off from the rest of Christian Europe. Of the 30-odd examples of pre-Romanesque architecture scattered about the Asturian countryside, the Palacio de Santa María del Naranco and Iglesia de San Miguel de Lillo, in Oviedo, are the finest (see the boxed text, p539). These buildings offer a foretaste of the Romanesque style.

THE MARK OF ISLAM

The Alhambra comes alive in the entertaining and learned study *Alhambra*, by Michael Jacobs; it's beautifully illustrated with photographs of one of Andalucía's most emblematic buildings.

Córdoba was the centre of Islamic political power and culture for its first 300 years in Spain, but Muslims remained for almost another 800 years in their longest-lasting enclave, Granada.

The Syrian Omayyad dynasty that set up shop in Spain brought with it architects imbued with ideas and experience won in Damascus. This was soon put to use in the construction of the Mezquita (p788) in Córdoba, the style of which was echoed across Islamic Spain. Horseshoe-shaped and lobed arches, the use of exquisite tiles in decoration (mostly calligraphy and floral motifs), complex stucco, peaceful inner courtyards and stalactite ceiling adornments are all features reminiscent of Damascus.

Remnants of this Islamic legacy abound across Spain, although many grand examples have been lost. The most striking piece of Islamic architecture in northern Spain is the palace of the Aljafería (p436) in Zaragoza.

In the 12th century the armies of Morocco's Almohad dynasty stormed across the divided lands of Islamic Spain. To this we owe some of the marvels of Seville, in particular the square-based minaret known as the Giralda (p717), even more beautiful than the minaret of the Koutoubia mosque in Marrakesh.

The Alhambra, one of the world's most remarkable Islamic monuments, was used as a barracks by Napoleon's troops during the Peninsular War.

Islamic art reached new heights of elegance with the construction of the Alhambra (p797) in Granada. Built from the 13th to the 15th centuries, it is symptomatic of the direction taken by Islamic art at the time. Eschewing innovation, the Alhambra expresses a desire to refine already well-tried forms (geometric patterns, use of calligraphy in decoration, stalactite decor). It is one of the Islamic world's most beautiful creations.

MOZARABIC & MUDÉJAR

Already in the 10th century, Mozarabs – Christians practising in Muslim territory – began to adopt elements of classic Islamic construction and export them to Christian-held territory. Although Mozarabic artisans contributed to many buildings, there are few 'purely' Mozarabic structures. Among the outstanding examples are the Iglesia de San Miguel de Escalada (p251), east of León; the Ermita de San Baudelio (p266), beyond Berlanga de Duero in Soria province; and the Iglesia de Santa María de Lebeña (p560) on the east side of the Picos de Europa mountains.

More important was the influence of the Mudéjars, Muslims who remained behind in the lands of the Reconquista. Their skills were found to be priceless (but cheap) and their influence is evident throughout Spain.

One unmistakable Mudéjar feature is the preponderance of brick: castles, churches and mansions all over the country were built of this material. Another telltale feature is in the ceilings. Extravagantly decorated timber creations, often ornately carved, are a mark of the Mudéjar hand. Several different types get constant mention. The term *armadura* refers to any of these wooden ceilings, especially when they have the appearance of being an inverted boat. *Artesonado* ceilings are characterised by interlaced beams leaving regular spaces (triangular, square or polygonal) for the insertion of decorative *artesas*. The term *techumbre* (which can simply mean 'roof') applies more specifically to the most common of *armaduras,* where the skeleton of the ceiling (when looked at from the end) looks like a series of As.

FROM ROMANESQUE TO GOTHIC

As the Muslim tide was turned back and the Reconquista gathered momentum, the first great medieval European movement in design began to take hold in Spain, spreading from Italy and France. From about the 11th century churches, monasteries, bridges, pilgrims' hospices and other buildings in the Romanesque style mushroomed in the north.

A replica of Seville's Giralda minaret once stood in Madison Square, New York, along with another in Kansas City. Neither exists any more.

The first wave came in Catalonia, where Lombard artisans influenced by Byzantine building techniques soon covered the countryside with simple churches – the church of Sant Climent de Taüll (p409) and others scattered around nearby are emblematic.

Romanesque is identified by a few basic characteristics. The exteriors of most edifices bear little decoration and tend to be simple, angular structures. In the case of churches in particular, the concession to curves comes with the semicylindrical apse – or, in many cases, triple apse. The single most striking decorative element is the semicircular arch or arches that grace doorways, windows, cloisters and naves. The humble church of the **Monasterio de Sigena** (☎ 974 57 81 58; www.villanuevadesigena.com in Spanish; Villanueva de Sigena; closed for restoration), 93km east of Zaragoza, has a doorway boasting 14 such arches, one encased in the other.

The Camino de Santiago (Way of St James) is studded with Romanesque beauties. These include (travelling from east to west) the Monasterio de Santo Domingo de Silos (p262), the smaller cloister (Las Claustrillas) in the Monasterio de las Huelgas (p257) in Burgos and the restored Iglesia de San Martín (p245) in Frómista.

During the 12th century, modifications in the Romanesque recipe became apparent. The pointed arch and ribbed vault of various kinds are clear precursors of the Gothic revolution to come.

The Monasterio de la Oliva (p510) in Navarra was among the first to incorporate such features, and other buildings followed. Cathedrals in Ávila (p208), Sigüenza (p299), Tarragona (p423) and Tudela (p510) all display at least some transitional elements.

A peculiar side development affected southwest Castilla. The cathedrals in Salamanca (p217 and p217), Zamora (p240) and Toro (p239) all boast Byzantine lines, particularly in the cupola.

Everyone in northern Europe marvelled at the towering new cathedrals built from the 12th century, made possible by the use of flying buttresses and other technical innovations. The idea caught on later in Spain, but three of the most important Gothic cathedrals in the country, in Burgos (p256), León (p248) and Toledo (p277), were built in the 13th century.

The first two owe much to French models, but the Spaniards soon introduced other elements. The huge decorative altarpieces towering over the high altar were one such innovation. And, although not an exclusively Spanish touch, the placing of the choir stalls in the centre of the nave became the rule rather than the exception in Spanish Gothic style.

The main structural novelty in Spanish Gothic was star-vaulting, a method of weight distribution in the roof in which ribbed vaults project outwards from a series of centre points.

Spanish Splendour: Palaces, Castles & Country Homes (Roberto Schezen, photographer) is a sumptuous photographic presentation of some of the most spectacular noble buildings in Spain.

In Catalonia another variant of the style, Catalan Gothic, was largely bereft of the pinnacles and other decorative touches more common in French and northern European styles. Catalan architects favoured breadth over height and stretched the limits of the possible by creating incredibly broad, unsupported vaults. Their use of supports like flying buttresses was minimal.

Monuments often belong to several styles. Many great buildings begun at the height of Romanesque glory were not completed until long after Gothic had gained the upper hand. And although, for instance, the cathedral in Burgos was one of the first to go up, its spires were a result of German-inspired late-Gothic imagination. In many cases, these Gothic or Romanesque-Gothic buildings later received a plateresque or baroque overlay.

Mudéjar influences still made themselves felt, particularly in the use of brick rather than stone. Toledo and the region of Aragón, particularly in Zaragoza, Teruel, Tarazona and Calatayud, boast many gloriously original and unique buildings of a Gothic–Mudéjar combination.

The so-called Isabelline style was a late ingredient. Taking some cues from the more curvaceous traits of Islamic design, it was in some ways an indirect precursor to plateresque. Its ultimate expression would be Toledo's San Juan de los Reyes (p278), originally destined to be the final resting place of the Reyes Católicos (Catholic Monarchs). Designed by French-born Juan Güas (1453–96), it is a medley of earlier Gothic and Mudéjar elements, with a final decorative Isabelline flourish.

The 16th century saw a revival of pure Gothic, perhaps best exemplified in the new cathedral in Salamanca (p217), although the Segovia cathedral (p227) was about the last, and possibly most pure, Gothic house of worship raised in Spain.

It wasn't only religious buildings that flourished. Most of the innumerable castles scattered across the country went up in Gothic times. Many never saw action and were not intended to – an extraordinary example of Mudéjar castle-building from this era is the sumptuous castle at Coca (p233). In Barcelona some marvellous civil Gothic architecture can be admired, including the Saló del Tinell (p323) in the one-time royal palace in the Barri Gòtic and the Reials Drassanes, the once-mighty shipyards now home to the Museu Marítim (p321).

Ildefonso Falcones' 2006 novel, *La Catedral del Mar* (Cathedral of the Sea), tells the story of the building of this singular Catalan Gothic 'peoples' church' in Barcelona.

THE RENAISSANCE

The Renaissance in Spain can be roughly divided into three distinct styles. First was the Italian-influenced special flavour of plateresque. To visit Salamanca is to receive a concentrated dose of the most splendid work in the genre. The university facade (p217), especially, is a virtuoso piece, featuring busts, medallions and a complex floral design. Not far behind in intensity comes the facade of the Convento de San Esteban (p218). Little of the work can be convincingly traced to any one hand, and it appears that the principal exponent of plateresque, Alonso de Covarrubias (1488–1570), was

THE CHURRIGUERA CLAN

José Simón de Churriguera (d 1679) was a well-considered sculptor from Barcelona who worked in Madrid. He was something of a specialist in *retablos* (huge, carved wooden altar backdrops), a speciality he handed down to his three sons, José Benito (1665–1735), Joaquín (1674–1724), and Alberto (1676–1750).

Of the three sons, José Benito had perhaps the most illustrious career, being appointed court architect by Carlos II in 1690, a job he held down until 1702. As a sculptor, he carried out various extraordinary *retablos*. Their memorable works feature twisting gilded columns, burdened with all manner of angels and saints. He was dubbed 'the Michelangelo of Spain' in his obituary. José Benito was also busy as an architect. He built what is now the stately late-baroque Real Academias de Bellas Artes de San Fernando in Madrid (p150). Meanwhile, Alberto (who completed the Academia after his brother's death) and Joaquín both worked on Salamanca's late-Gothic Catedral Nueva (p217). It was a real family business, as one of their nephews also contributed. Alberto also designed that city's grand golden-hued Plaza Mayor (p217), a jewel of restrained baroque.

busier in his home city of Toledo (with the Alcázar, p276, and the Capilla de Reyes Nuevos in the cathedral, p277).

Next came the more purist Renaissance style that prevailed in Andalucía and had its maximum expression in the Palacio de Carlos V (p800) in Granada's Alhambra. Diego de Siloé (1495–1563) and his followers are regarded as masters of the style. Siloé made his mark with Granada's cathedral (p802); others followed him with such masterpieces as the Jaén cathedral (p816).

Juan de Herrera (1530–97) is the last and perhaps greatest figure of the Spanish Renaissance, but his work bears almost no resemblance to anything else of the period. His austere masterpiece is the palace–monastery complex of San Lorenzo de El Escorial (p199).

BAROQUE BAUBLES

The heady frills and spills of baroque can be seen all over Spain, but usually in the form of additions rather than complete buildings. Cádiz's cathedral (p740) is an exception (although some neoclassical work was added). Three loose phases can be identified, starting with a sober baroque still heavily influenced by Herrera, followed by a period of greater architectural exuberance and finally running into a mixture of baroque with the beginnings of neoclassicism.

The leading exponents of this often overblown style were the Churriguera brothers. Alberto Churriguera designed Salamanca's Plaza Mayor and had a hand in the city's cathedral (see the boxed text, above).

Baroque reached new heights of opulence with the Sagrario in Granada's Monasterio de La Cartuja (p803) and the Transparente in Toledo's cathedral (p277). Seville is jammed with gems. But baroque appears elsewhere, too: the facade superimposed over the Romanesque original in the cathedral of Santiago de Compostela (p565) and the cathedral in Murcia (p697) are notable.

For a good introduction to the Modernista genius Antoni Gaudí, have a look at www.gaudiallgaudi.com. It has links to photographic sections on a range of his works, as well as that of other Modernista architects, designers and artists.

MODERNISME MADNESS

Catalonia, at the end of the 19th century, was the powerhouse of the country. And over its capital was unleashed one of the most imaginative periods in Spanish architecture by a group of architects who came to be known as the Modernistas. Leading the way was Antoni Gaudí (1852–1926), who sprinkled Barcelona with jewels of his singular imagination. They range from his immense, and still unfinished, La Sagrada Família (p330) to the simply weird Casa Batlló (p331) and only slightly more sober La Pedrera (p332).

Hot on Gaudí's heels were two other Catalan architects, Lluís Domènech i Montaner (1850–1923) and Josep Puig i Cadafalch (1867–1957). Domènech i Montaner's works include the Palau de la Música Catalana (p325), while Puig i Cadafalch built town houses such as Casa Amatller (p332).

Elsewhere in Spain, Modernisme (the local version of art nouveau) made little impact, although Gaudí and Domènech designed a handful of playful buildings in northern Spain.

CONTEMPORARY CREATIONS

If Barcelona is the seat of Modernisme, Madrid is the capital of Spanish art deco. In the 1920s the newly created Gran Vía provided a perfect opportunity for architectural creation. A number of art deco caprices raised in that era still line the boulevard today; one of the more overwhelming is the Palacio de Comunicaciones (p156) on Plaza de la Cibeles.

Gaudí: The Man & His Work, by Joan Masso Bergos, is a beautifully illustrated study of the man and his architecture, based on the writings of one of his confidants.

Ambitious building and urban redevelopment programs continue to change the main cityscapes. In Barcelona, for instance, the 1992 Olympics provided an enormous impulse for new construction and urban renewal. The Macba art museum (p324), opened in 1995, shines white and bold, bright in the once slummy El Raval district. More recently, Jean Nouvel added the spangly gherkin-shaped Torre Agbar (p333), just off Plaça de les Glòries Catalanes, in 2005; the controversial and costly blue triangular Edifici Fòrum (p330) was deposited on the waterfront in 2004 by Swiss architects Herzog & de Meuron; and Enric Miralles (1955–2000) made a colourful splash in 2005 with the Mercat de Santa Caterina (p326). His posthumous Gas Natural building (2006), a poetic skyscraper in glass, is a major addition to the waterfront. His architect widow, Italian Benedetta Tagliabue, saw Miralles' projects through to completion.

Further south, Valencia chimed in with its futuristic Ciudad de las Artes y las Ciencias (City of Arts and Sciences; p607) complex, by Santiago Calatrava (b 1951). Frank Gehry (b 1929) is responsible for the single most eye-catching modern addition to the Spanish cityscape (so far) with his Museo Guggenheim (p473) in Bilbao, where Calatrava has also been busy designing the city's airport. Not to be left out, Sir Norman Foster (b 1935) designed the city's new metro system.

In a similar vein, Lord Richard Rogers (b 1933) provided the dreamy, wavy new Terminal 4 at Madrid's Barajas airport.

The 2008 Expo in Zaragoza converted the city into a hive of architectural activity. Of the many (in some cases loopy) buildings created for the event, Zaha Hadid's whalelike bridge-cum-pavilion is impossible to miss, as is the soaring, glittering Torre del Agua, by Enrique de Teresa (b 1951) and Julio Martínez Calzón (b 1938). With glass surfaces and sober, triangular lines, the

NIEMEYER'S GIFT

Brazil's extraordinary architect Oscar Niemeyer (b 1907), who gave birth to his home country's capital, Brasilia, might manage to upstage Gehry's Bilbao Guggenheim museum with his plans for the Centro Niemeyer (p548), on which work began in 2008, in the Asturian coastal industrial city of Avilés. A recipient of a Príncipe de Asturias prize for his work, Niemeyer reciprocated by donating the design to the northern region. Looking like something that could have been dreamed up as a moon base in a Hollywood space epic, a pair of elegant white flying-saucerish mounds will house cultural and congress centres, and possibly a museum. It's being built on former industrial land on the east side of the estuary. It will be Niemeyer's only work in Spain.

Palacio de Congresos, by the *madrileño* pair Fuensanta Nieto (b 1957) and Enrique Sobejano (b 1957), is another key structure designed to last.

INTO THE FUTURE

In Madrid, the Cuatro Torres business area (CTBA) near the Paseo de la Castellana to the north of the city is nearing completion. Featuring four towers soaring up to 250m, the zone is due for completion in 2009. Sir Norman Foster and Argentina's US-based César Pelli (who designed Malaysia's Petronas Twin Towers in the 1990s) are leading the way with, respectively, the Torre Caja Madrid and Torre Cristal, both 250m high and Spain's highest buildings. Already complete is the Torre Espacio (223m) by Pei Cobb Freed & Partners. Only the fourth tower, the Torre Sacyr Vallehermoso, was designed by Spanish architects (Carlos Rubio Carvajal and Enrique Álvarez-Sala Walter).

In January 2008 two base jumpers managed to get onto the site of Madrid's still incomplete 250m Torre Cristal and launched themselves off the top with parachutes.

Barcelona also continues to power ahead with projects. Zaha Hadid (b 1950) has designed a novel building that will look like many rectangular dinner plates stacked in precarious fashion and serve as the campus of the Universitat del Llevant in the city's Fòrum area. Nearby, the national telecommunications company, Telefónica, will get a daring new sliver of a skyscraper as headquarters for its Catalonia operations, designed by Enric Massip-Bosch. Elsewhere in the nascent hi-tech zone of 22@, a giant cube of a building, with partly inflatable facade to reduce energy consumption, will be part of the Parc Barcelona Mèdia multimedia complex and is due to open in late 2009.

Frank Gehry has plans for five twisting steel-and-glass towers that will feature a large degree of solar energy self-sufficiency for the new railway station and transport interchange planned for Barcelona's until-now neglected La Sagrera district. Lord Richard Rogers is transforming the former Les Arenes bullring on Plaça d'Espanya into a singular, circular leisure complex, with shops, cinemas, jogging track and more.

Not to be left out, Sir Norman Foster won the design competition in 2007 for FC Barcelona's planned new-look Camp Nou stadium. The overhaul will create a kind of glow-in-the-dark sponge-cake affair and is planned for completion in 2012, although problems within the club may delay the project.

Come 2009, the new Fira 2 trade fair on the road to Barcelona's airport will be marked by two landmark twisting towers (one a hotel, the other offices) designed by Japanese architect and Gaudí fan, Toyo Ito (b 1941). The jellyfishlike entrance to the new fairgrounds is already eye-catching.

Barcelona architect Ricard Bofill (b 1939) is creating an 88m spinnaker-shaped hotel (Hotel W, owned by the Starwood chain) right on the Mediterranean shoreline at the southern end of the Barceloneta beaches. It is due to open in 2009. Bofill, who has handled much of the restructuring of the city's airport over the years, also designed the new south terminal.

Over in Logroño, in La Rioja, Fuensanta Nieto and Enrique Sobejano will create their Centro Temático del Vino, a meandering, angular building due to be completed in 2010.

Food & Drink

Spanish cuisine is, quite simply, wonderful. Paella, sangria, the wines of La Rioja and tapas are all the rage in restaurants around the world, and Spanish chefs such as Ferran Adrià are undisputed global superstars. These icons of the Spanish kitchen are merely the tip of an extremely large iceberg; few countries can match Spain's gastronomic variety, innovation and sheer culinary excellence.

Spaniards spend more on food per capita than anyone else in Europe.

Spaniards love to travel in their own country and, given the riches on offer, they especially love to do so in pursuit of the perfect meal. Tell a Spaniard that you're on your way to a particular place and they're sure to start salivating at the mere thought of the local speciality and a favourite restaurant at which to enjoy it. That's because eating is more than a functional pastime to be squeezed between other more important tasks; it's a great and fundamental pleasure, a social event to be enjoyed with friends, always taken seriously enough to have adequate hours allocated for the purpose and savoured like all good things in life.

Having joined Spaniards for years around the table, we've come to understand what eating Spanish-style is all about. If we could distil the essence of how to make food a highlight of your trip into a few simple rules, it would be this: *always* ask for the local speciality; *never* be shy about looking around to see what others have ordered before choosing; *always* ask the waiter for his or her recommendations; and, wherever possible, make your meal a centrepiece of your day.

Rich in anecdotes and insight, *A Late Dinner – Discovering the Food of Spain*, by Paul Richardson (2007), is arguably the best and most readable book in English about Spanish food.

¡Buen provecho! (Enjoy your meal!)

For more information on Spain's regional cuisines and some of its better-known wine-producing regions, turn to p77.

THE LAWS OF SPANISH COOKING

The laws of traditional Spanish cooking are deceptively simple: take the freshest ingredients and interfere with them as little as possible. While the rest of the world was developing sophisticated sauces, Spanish chefs were experimenting with subtlety, creating a combination of tastes in which the flavour of the food itself was paramount. Nowhere is this more evident than in the humble art of tapas – bite-sized morsels whose premise is so simple as to have all the hallmarks of genius – where carefully selected meats, seafood or vegetables are given centre stage and allowed to speak for themselves. Such are the foundations on which Spanish cooking is built.

Climate and history have also played important roles in the development of the Spanish diet, which is typically Mediterranean with its liberal

THE ORIGIN OF TAPAS

Medieval Spain was a land of isolated settlements and people on the move – traders, pilgrims, emigrants and journeymen – who had to cross the lonely high plateau of Spain en route to elsewhere. All along the route, travellers holed up in inns where the keepers, concerned about drunken men on horseback setting out from their village, developed a tradition of putting a 'lid' *(tapa)* of food atop a glass of wine or beer. The purpose was partly to keep the bugs out, but primarily to encourage people not to drink on an empty stomach.

In this sense, little has changed. The tapa continues to serve the dual purposes of providing enjoyment while acting as a lid to enable you to reach new levels of stamina during long Spanish nights.

ORIOL BALAGUER, PASTRY CHEF & CHOCOLATE REVOLUTIONARY

Your father was also a pastry chef? I was born wrapped in the smell of chocolate. I became impregnated by it.
You worked with master chef Ferran Adrià. What did you learn? A way of cooking and thinking that I had never seen before and to always believe that you can go one step further.
In 2001 you won the prize for the Best Dessert in the World. What was it? I amalgamated seven different textures of chocolate. It's a dessert for lovers and for those obsessed with chocolate.
What's your philosophy of desserts? A dessert must create happiness, excitement.
What role does tradition have in your cooking? I have a series of recipes based around memories of my childhood that I have updated for the 21st century. But I am much more motivated if I start with something unknown.
Why is Spanish food all the rage? We are a country with great designers, sculptors, creators, painters and architects and this creative atmosphere has spilled over into the world of gastronomy.
If your work were to have a parallel in music, what would it be? There are moments when it could be jazz, others classical music and, occasionally, Bruce Springsteen.

use of olive oil, garlic, wine (three culinary legacies the Spaniards owe to the Romans), onions, tomatoes and peppers. The country's long Muslim occupation is reflected in the use of spices such as saffron and cumin and in honeyed desserts. Spain was also once the centre of an empire, and from its South American colonies came potatoes and tomatoes (not to mention coffee and chocolate).

As Spain grew in wealth, meat (especially roasts) became an integral ingredient of the Spanish table, particularly inland where game became common. Roast lamb or suckling pig still dominate the cuisine of Castilla, especially in winter when hearty meals serve to fortify Spaniards against the bitter cold. The obsession with *jamón* (ham), not to mention chorizo, *lomo* (loin, usually pork) and *salchichón* (salami-like sausage), came from the south (as did olives). Many of the coastal specialities in such high demand today – from the astonishingly varied Atlantic offerings of Galicia in the northwest or the Basque Country in the north to the seafood-rich paellas and other rice dishes of the Mediterranean – were considered staple meals perfectly suited to the local climate long before they acquired world-superstar status.

Spain is the world's largest producer of olive oil and much of the Italian olive oil sold around the world is made from Spanish olives.

If simplicity is the cornerstone of Spanish cooking, it's the innovation and nouvelle cuisine emerging from Spanish kitchens that has truly taken the world by storm. Chefs such as Ferran Adrià, Mari Arzak and Oriol Balaguer (see the boxed text, above) have developed their own culinary laboratories, experimenting with all that's new while never straying far from the principles that underpin traditional Spanish cuisine.

This blend of strong tradition and cutting-edge cuisine is illustrated by a simple fact: Spain is home to both the world's oldest restaurant, Restaurante Sobrino de Botín (p179) in Madrid, and El Bulli (see the boxed text, p388) in Catalonia, a temple of gastronomic experimentation that's consistently voted the world's best restaurant by *Restaurant* magazine.

In January the country's most prestigious chefs showcase the latest innovations in Spain's world-famous cuisine at the Madrid Fusion (www.madridfusion.net) gastronomy summit.

STAPLES & SPECIALITIES

Desayuno (breakfast) is generally a no-nonsense affair taken at a bar on the way to work. A *café con leche* (half coffee and half warm milk) with a *bollo* (pastry) is the typical breakfast. Croissants or a cream-filled pastry are also common. Some people prefer a savoury start – try a *sandwich mixto,* a toasted ham and cheese sandwich; a Spanish *tostada* is simply buttered toast. Others, especially those heading home at dawn after a night out, go for an all-Spanish favourite, *churros y chocolate,* a deep-fried stick of plain pastry immersed in thick hot chocolate.

The typical *carta* (menu) begins with starters such as *ensaladas* (salads), *sopas* (soups) and *entremeses* (hors d'oeuvres). The latter can range from a mound of potato salad with olives, asparagus, anchovies and a selection of cold meats – a meal in itself – to simpler cold meats, slices of cheese and olives.

Another essential presence on the Spanish table is cured ham from the high plateau, known as *jamón serrano.* Every *tasca* (tapas bar) has it. *Jamón ibérico de bellota* is the best ham in Spain; it's made from the hindquarters of wild pigs that have fed exclusively on acorns. The *jamón* from Extremadura or Salamanca is considered to be the finest, although the Teruel region of Aragón makes a convincing claim for membership to such an elite group. Highly seasoned chorizo (pork sausage) is also made from acorn-fed pigs. Spanish cured meats are a bit like Italian prosciutto, but are deep red rather than blushing pink, offer more to the teeth, have a richer aroma and last longer in the mouth.

The recipe for cured meats such as *jamón* (ham) is attributed to a noble Roman, Cato the Elder, who changed the course of Spanish culinary history with his tome *De Re Rustica.*

The basic ingredients of later courses can be summarised under the general headings of *pollo* (chicken), *carne* (meat), *mariscos* (seafood), *pescado* (fish) and *arroz* (rice). Meat may be subdivided into *cerdo* (pork), *ternera* (beef) and *cordero* (lamb). If you want a *guarnición* (side order), such as *verduras* (vegetables), you may have to order separately.

When it comes to fish, the Spanish mainstays are *bonito* (tuna), *sardinas* (sardines), *anchoas* (anchovies), *merluza* (hake), *dorada* (bream) and *lenguado* (sole). Shellfish is another favourite. But the fish with which Spaniards have the closest relationship, historically (indeed almost spiritually), is *bacalao* (dried and salted cod). For many centuries roving Spanish fishermen have harvested the codfish from the grand banks of Newfoundland and Norway, salting it and bringing it home looking more like a rock than food. After soaking it several times in water it's rehydrated and relieved of its salt content, which enriches the flavour and improves the texture. Originally it was considered food for the poor and some called it 'vigil day beef' for its use during fasts. The best place to enjoy it is in the Basque Country, where it's revered. Try sweet red peppers stuffed with *bacalao* and we're sure you'll be inclined to agree.

JAMÓN – A PRIMER

Jamón (ham) is Spain's culinary constant and one of the few things that unites the country. If there is a national dish, this is it. Nearly every bar and restaurant in Spain has at least one *jamón* on the go at any one time, strapped into a cradlelike frame called a *jamónera.* More often, a bar will have several hams, the skin and hooves still attached, hanging from the walls or ceiling.

Spanish *jamón* is, unlike Italian prosciutto, a bold, deep red and well marbled with buttery fat. At its best, it smells like meat, the forest and the field. Like wines and olive oil, Spanish *jamón* is subject to a strict series of classifications. *Jamón serrano* refers to *jamón* made from white-coated pigs introduced to Spain in the 1950s. Once salted and semidried by the cold, dry winds of the Spanish sierra, most now go through a similar process of curing and drying in a climate-controlled shed for around a year. *Jamón serrano* accounts for approximately 90% of cured ham in Spain.

Jamón ibérico – more expensive and generally regarded as the elite of Spanish hams – comes from a black-coated pig indigenous to the Iberian Peninsula and a descendant of the wild boar. Gastronomically, its star appeal is its ability to infiltrate fat into the muscle tissue, thus producing an especially well-marbled meat. If the pig gains at least 50% of its body weight during the acorn-eating season, it can be classified as *jamón ibérico de bellota,* the most sought-after designation for *jamón.*

Inland, you're far more likely to encounter *legumbres* (legumes) such as *garbanzos* (chickpeas), *judías* (beans) and *lentejas* (lentils). Of the hearty stews, the king is *fabada* (pork and bean stew) from Asturias, although *cocido,* a hotpot or stew with a noodle broth, carrots, cabbage, chickpeas, chicken, *morcilla* (blood sausage) beef and lard is a special favourite in Madrid and León. Other popular staples in Spain's interior include *cordero asado* (roast lamb), *cochinillo asado* (roast suckling pig) and *patatas con huevos fritos* (baked potatoes with eggs).

The Food of Spain & Portugal – A Regional Celebration, by Elisabeth Luard (2005), demystifies the food and wine of the various Spanish regions with recipes and the context from which they arise.

If you opt for tapas, your choice is endless because anything can be a tapa: a handful of olives, a slice of ham and cheese on bread, a bit of *tortilla de patatas* (potato and onion omelette). Other common orders include: *boquerones en vinagre* (fresh anchovies marinated in white vinegar, which are delicious and tangy); *boquerones fritos* (fried fresh anchovies); *albóndigas* (good old meat balls); *pimientos de Padrón* (little green peppers from Galicia – some are hot and some not); *gambas* (prawns, either done *al ajillo,* with garlic, or *a la plancha,* grilled); *chipirones* (baby squid, served in various ways); *calamares a la Romana* (deep-fried calamari rings)…the list goes on.

And last, but by no means least, there's paella. For everything you need to know about what makes a good paella, see the boxed text, p82. But in the meantime we'll let you into a secret: a *really* good paella can be surprisingly hard to come by in Spanish restaurants. Why? For a start, saffron is extremely expensive, prompting many restaurants to cut corners by using yellow dye number 2. Secondly, many restaurant owners play on the fact that every second foreign visitor to Spain will order a paella while in the country, but few will have any idea about what a good paella should taste like. Spaniards are much more discerning when it comes to their national dish, so check out the clientele before sitting down and ordering – if there are plenty of locals in residence, you can order with more confidence. The places where we recommend the paella throughout this book are also among the better places to try.

DRINKS

Wine

Spaniards invariably accompany their meal with a Spanish wine. Extremely loyal to the local drop, they often wonder, with considerable justification, what need they have for foreign wines when their own vineyards produce it prodigiously and to such high quality.

Wines from Spain (www.winesfromspain.com) is the best website covering Spanish wine, with detailed but accessible sections on history, grape varieties and all the Spanish wine-producing regions.

Probably the most common premium red table wine you'll encounter will be from La Rioja, in the north. The principal grape of Rioja is the Tempranillo, widely believed to be a mutant form of the Pinot Noir. Its wine is smooth and fruity, seldom as dry as its supposed French counterpart. Look for the 'DO Rioja' classification on the label and you'll find a good wine. Not far behind are the wine-producing regions of Ribera del Duero (Castilla y León), Navarra and Aragón (see the boxed text, p448), and the Valdepeñas area (see the boxed text, p289) of southern Castilla-La Mancha, which has less variety but is generally well priced and remains popular.

For white wines, the Ribeiro wines of Galicia are well regarded. Also from the area is one of Spain's most charming whites – Albariño. This crisp, dry and refreshing drop is a rare wine as it's designated by grape rather than region. The Penedès area in Catalonia produces whites and sparkling wine such as *cava,* the traditional champagnelike toasting drink of choice for Spaniards at Christmas.

Sherry, the unique wine of Andalucía (especially around Jerez), is Spain's national dram and is found in every bar, *tasca* and restaurant in the land. Dry sherry, called *fino,* begins as a fairly ordinary white wine of the Palomino

SPAIN'S BEST WINE MUSEUMS

Although tourist offices in Spain's major wine regions can help point you in the direction of local bodegas (wineries) and many also organise winery tours, the following museums are where you really should start your journey in getting to know the local drop. Most are interactive, allowing you to familiarise yourself with the various grape aromas; many host tastings; and all put the wineries you're about to visit into their proper historical context.

- Museo del Vino, Haro (p516) – La Rioja
- Dinastía Vivanco, Briones (Museo de la Cultura del Vino; p517) – La Rioja
- Museo Provincial del Vino, Peñafiel (p265) – Ribera del Duero
- Museo del Vino, Olite (p509) – Navarra
- Espacio de Vino, Barbastro (p447) – Somontano, Aragón
- Museo del Vino, Cariñena (p441) – Cariñena, Aragón's largest wine-growing area

grape, but it's 'fortified' with grape brandy. This stops fermentation and gives the wine taste and smell constituents that enable it to age into something sublime. It's taken as an *aperitivo* (apéritif) or as a table wine with seafood. Amontillado and Oloroso are sweeter sherries, good for after dinner. Manzanilla is grown only in Sanlúcar de Barrameda (p745) near the coast in southwestern Andalucía and develops a slightly salty taste that's very appetising. When ordering it be sure to say *'vino de Manzanilla'*, since *manzanilla* alone means chamomile tea.

Spain has the largest area (1.2 million ha) of wine cultivation in the world and accounts for over 30% of land under vine in the EU, followed by France and Italy (around 25% each).

Then there is that famous Spanish wine drink, sangria. Don't expect too much from it and remember that it was developed as a way to make use of bad wine. It's usually a red wine mixed with citrus juice and zest, a bit of cinnamon, sometimes some rum and always diabetes-inducing amounts of sugar.

For more information on Spanish wines, see p84.

Other Drinks

Spaniards' love of *cerveza* (beer) makes perfect sense given that the weather is often fiercely hot and the food salty. In bars and *tascas* almost all the beer is on tap, so sidle up to the bar and order *una caña* for a small beer, or *una jarra* for a greater thirst. Common brands are Cruzcampo, Mahou and San Miguel; the latter is the strongest, at 5.4%.

Similar to beer, *sidra* (cider) is the speciality of Asturias, although Galicia and the Basque Country also claim it as their own; you can enjoy it fresh in a *sidrería* (cider house), often poured straight from the barrel.

More than half of Spain's wine production comes from Castilla-La Mancha, with Catalonia, Extremadura and Valencia making up the top four. Better-known wine-producing regions such as La Rioja and Castilla y León trail in fifth and sixth place respectively.

Aguardiente is the term for strong spirits, the most famous being Ponche Caballero, while a *copa* generally refers to spirits. If you've ordered a whisky with coke *(whisky con coca cola)*, or just about any other *copa*, you'll be expected to watch while the bartender pours your spirit of choice…and continues pouring until you tell them to stop. You pay no extra regardless of the amount!

Horchata is a sweet, milky drink made from pressed *chufas* (tiger nuts) and sugar. Tea and coffee are unremarkable in Spain, but the hot chocolate is thick, rich and delicious.

CELEBRATIONS

In addition to the feasts of the calendar, Spaniards will find plenty of other reasons to have a fiesta, most of which revolve around the important rites of passage in Spanish life – birthdays, anniversaries, first communions, graduations and weddings. Spanish fiestas will almost always be accompanied by groaning tables of food and by music, whether a live group or a more impromptu performance.

The most important week of the year culminates in Easter, and there are special dishes associated with Semana Santa (Holy Week). In some communities there are Good Friday processions in which heavy floats are borne by penitents. In order to keep up their strength, they may breakfast on *bacalao a la vizcaína* (dried and salted cod with chillies and capsicum).

The New Spain – Vegetarian & Vegan Restaurants, by Jean Claude Juston, should be a bible for vegetarian and vegan visitors. It's available from L'Atelier (www.ivu.org/atelier).

As this is the biggest and most important holiday on the Spanish calendar, it's an important time for families and friends to come together to eat. Dishes that are often served during this period include *monas de pascua* (chocolate figurines), *torta pascualina* (spinach and egg pie) and *torrija* (French toast). A popular Easter dish in Mallorca is *flan de pascuas* (Easter cheese flan), and *cordero pascual* (spring lamb) is common fare everywhere.

At Christmas, *turrón* is a countrywide favourite. It's a uniquely Spanish kind of nougat, whose recipe goes back to the 14th century and incorporates honey, almonds and sugar.

VEGETARIANS & VEGANS

Such is their love for meat, fish and seafood, many Spaniards, especially the older generation, don't really understand vegetarianism. As a result, dedicated vegetarian restaurants are still pretty thin on the ground outside the major cities.

The discovery of *cava* (sparkling wine) is credited, at least in France, to Dom Pérignon – upon tasting it for the first time he called out to his brethren, 'Come quickly! I am drinking stars!'

That said, while vegetarians – especially vegans – can have a hard time, and while some cooked vegetable dishes can contain ham, the eating habits of Spaniards are changing; an ever-growing selection of vegetarian restaurants is springing up around the country. Barcelona and Madrid in particular have plenty of vegetarian restaurants to choose from. Restaurants offering a good vege selection are easy to find throughout this book – they're marked with a Ⓥ symbol.

Otherwise, salads are a Spanish staple and, in many restaurants, are a meal in themselves. You'll also come across the odd vegetarian paella, as well as dishes such as *verduras a la plancha* (grilled vegetables); *garbanzos con espinacas* (chickpeas and spinach); and numerous potato dishes, such as *patatas bravas* (potato chunks bathed in a slightly spicy tomato sauce) and *tortilla de patatas*. The prevalence of legumes ensures that *lentejas* and *judías* are also easy to track down, while *pan* (bread), *quesos* (cheeses), *alcachofas*

A BAR OR RESTAURANT BY ANY OTHER NAME

Plenty of places that serve food and drink go by the name of *bar* or *restaurante,* but there are variations on the theme.

- *asador* – a restaurant specialising in roasted meats.
- *bar de copas* – gets going around midnight and primarily hard drinks are served.
- *cervecería* – the focus is on *cerveza* (beer) and there's plenty of the foamy stuff on tap.
- *horno de asador* – a restaurant with a wood-burning roasting oven.
- *marisquería* – a bar or restaurant specialising in seafood.
- *tasca* – a tapas bar.
- *terraza* – an open-air bar, for warm-weather tippling only.
- *taberna* – usually a rustic place serving tapas and *raciones* (large tapas): expect to see barrels used as tables and tile decor.
- *vinoteca* – slightly more upmarket wine bars where you can order by the glass.

(artichokes) and *aceitunas* (olives) are always easy to find. *Tascas* usually offer more vegetarian choices than do sit-down restaurants.

If vegetarians feel like a rarity among Spaniards, vegans will feel as if they've come from another planet. To make sure that you're not misunderstood, ask if dishes contain *huevos* (eggs) or *productos lácteos* (dairy).

EATING WITH KIDS

Food and children are two of the great loves for Spaniards, which means that children are always welcome, whether in a sit-down restaurant or in a chaotically busy bar. If highchairs aren't available, staff will improvise and you shouldn't be made to feel uncomfortable as your children run amok. As for the food, children's menus may be rare, but Spanish fare is rarely spicy and kids tend to like it. Toddlers are usually fed straight from their parents' plate. When kids get hungry between meals it's easy to zip into the nearest *tasca* and get them a snack and there are also sweet shops every few blocks. The only restriction you might find on where you can take the kids is if the bar or restaurant permits smoking. In theory, children are not permitted in places that allow smoking. In practice, this being Spain, most places simply look the other way and can live with the kids' presence if you can live with the smoke. See p868 for further information on travelling with children.

Despite Spain's reputation as a country of wine-lovers, beer sales surpassed wine sales in Spain in the early 1990s.

HABITS & CUSTOMS

Spanish waiters – love them or hate them, they're unlikely to leave you indifferent. In smarter establishments, waiters are often young, attentive and switched on to the needs of patrons. In more traditional places, waiting is a career, often a poorly paid one, which is the preserve of old men (sometimes one old man, sometimes one grumpy old man) in white jackets and bow ties and for whom service with a smile is not part of the job description. In such places, they shuffle amid the tables, the weight of the world upon their shoulders, struggling with what seems a Sisyphean task. Getting their attention can be a challenge. On the other hand, they know their food and, if you speak Spanish, can help tailor your order in the best possible way.

For an authoritative and comprehensive periodical on Spanish gastronomy, check www.spaingourmetour.com, which overflows with recipes and ideas for culinary explorations of Spain.

Somewhere in between are Spanish bartenders, who can be as informal as they are informed and who love to shout their orders to the kitchen and generally create a breezy atmosphere.

In simpler restaurants you may keep the same knife and fork throughout the meal. As each course is finished you set the cutlery aside and your plates will be whisked away.

Most visitors complain not about the quality of Spanish food but its timing. *Comida/Almuerzo* (lunch) is the main, leisurely meal of the day and rarely begins before 2pm (kitchens usually stay open until 4pm). For *cena* (dinner), few Spaniards would dream of turning up before 9.30pm. In the

TRAVELLERS' FRIEND – MENÚ DEL DÍA

One great way to cap prices at lunchtime Monday to Friday is to order the *menú del día*, a full set-menu (usually with several options), water, bread and wine. These meals are priced from around €8.50, although €10 and up is increasingly the norm. You'll be given a menu with five or six starters, the same number of mains and a handful of desserts – choose one from each category and don't even think of mixing and matching.

The philosophy behind the *menú del día* is that during the working week few Spaniards have time to go home for lunch. Taking a packed lunch is just not the done thing, so most people end up eating in restaurants, and all-inclusive three-course meals are as close as they can come to eating home-style food without breaking the bank.

THE ART OF ORDERING TAPAS

Too many travellers miss out on the joys of tapas ('high cuisine in miniature' as some restaurants like to call it) because, unless you speak Spanish, the art of ordering can seem one of the dark arts of Spanish etiquette. Fear not – it's not as difficult as it first appears.

In the Basque Country, Zaragoza and many bars in Madrid, Barcelona and elsewhere, it couldn't be easier. With so many tapas varieties lined up along the bar, you either take a small plate and help yourself or point to the morsel you want. If you do this, it's customary to keep track of what you eat (by holding on to the toothpicks for example) and then tell the bar staff how many you've had when it's time to pay. Otherwise, many places have a list of tapas, either on a menu or posted up behind the bar. If you can't choose, ask for '*la especialidad de la casa*' (the house speciality) and it's hard to go wrong. Another way of eating tapas is to order *raciones* (rations; large tapas serving) or *media raciones* (half-rations; smaller tapas serving). These plates and half-plates of a particular dish are a good way to go if you particularly like something and want more than a mere tapa. Remember, however, that after a couple of *raciones* you'll almost certainly be full; the *media ración* is a good choice if you want to experience a broader range of tastes. Tapas are always taken with a drink, and almost always while standing at the bar. In some bars you'll also get a small (free) tapa when you buy a drink.

For more on regional tapas, see the boxed texts, p182 and p490.

meantime, many bars serve tapas and *raciones* (large tapas) throughout the day. *Bocadillos* (filled rolls) are another option. If you can't face a full menu, a simpler option is the *plato combinado*, basically a meat-and-three-veg dish.

When it comes to tipping, most Spaniards leave small change or around €1 per person.

One final thing: don't jump out of your seats if people passing your table address you with a hearty '*¡buen provecho!*' They're just saying '*bon appétit*' or 'Enjoy your meal!'.

COOKING COURSES

There are numerous terrific cooking courses throughout Spain:

Alambique (Map pp142–3; ☎ 91 547 42 20; www.alambique.com; Plaza de la Encarnación 2, Madrid) Cooking classes start at around €50, with English-speaking courses from €70.

Catacurian (☎ USA 1 800 945 8606, Spain 93 511 07 38; www.catacurian.com; Carrer del Progres 2, El Masroig, Tarragona, Catalonia) Head down to the rural wine region of Priorat for three- to 10-day wine and cooking classes. Catalan chef Alicia Juanpere and her American partner Jonathan Perret lead tours and teach the classes (in English). Three-day courses start at €1250.

Cook and Taste (Map pp316–17; ☎ 93 302 13 20; www.cookandtaste.net; La Rambla 58, Barcelona) Learn to whip a paella or stir a gazpacho; a half-day workshop starts at €60.

Cooking Club (Map p133; ☎ 91 323 29 58; www.club-cooking.com in Spanish; Calle de Veza 33, Madrid) The regular, respected program of classes here encompasses a range of cooking styles.

Dom's Gastronom Cookery School (☎ 93 674 51 60; www.domsgastronom.com; Passeig del Roser 43, Valldoreix) Cordon-bleu chef Dominique Heathcoate runs the full gamut of Catalan, Spanish and French cuisine. Eight hours of classes over four days costs €100; groups are catered for.

L'Atelier (☎ 958 85 75 01; www.ivu.org/atelier; Calle Alberca 21, Mecina Fondales, Granada) Award-winning vegetarian chef Jean-Claude Juston (formerly of Neal's Yard Bakery and other celebrated veggie eateries in London) runs vegetarian cookery courses at his welcoming little guesthouse in the magical Alpujarras valleys of Andalucía. One day costs €50.

To the Heart of Spain, by Ann and Larry Walker (1997), is a cookbook, wine book and travelogue of their food-inspired travels through Spain.

The New Spanish Table, by Anya Von Bremzen (2006), has 275 recipes dedicated to the fusion of tradition and nouvelle cuisine that is taking the world by storm.

EAT YOUR WORDS

Want to know *pil pil* from *pimiento*? *Salsa* from *sandía*? Get behind the cuisine scene by getting to know the language. For pronunciation guidelines, see p900, and for a complete rundown on useful phrases check out Lonely Planet's *Spanish Phrasebook*.

Useful Phrases

Table for ..., please.
Una mesa para ..., por favor. — *oo*·na *me*·sa *pa*·ra ..., por fa·*vor*

Can I see the menu, please?
¿Puedo ver el menú, por favor? — *pwe*·do ver el me·*noo*, por fa·*vor*

Can I see the wine list, please?
La lista de vinos, por favor — la *lee*·sta de *vee*·nos por fa·*vor*

Can you recommend a good local wine?
¿Me recomienda un buen vino del país? — me re·ko·*myen*·da oon bwen *vee*·no del pa·*ees*

Can I have (a beer), please?
¿(Una cerveza), por favor? — (*oo*·na ther·*ve*·tha), por fa·*vor*

Good health/Cheers!
¡Salud! — sa·*loo*

Do you have children's meals?
¿Tienen comidas para niños? — *tye*·nen ko·*mee*·das pa·ra *nee*·nyos

The bill, please.
La cuenta, por favor. — la *kwen*·ta, por fa·*vor*

I'm vegetarian.
Soy vegetariano/a. (m/f) — soy ve·khe·ta·*rya*·no/a (m/f)

Food Glossary

a la parrilla	a la pa·*ree*·lya	grilled
aceitunas	a·thay·*too*·nas	olives
adobo	a·*do*·bo	marinade
aguacate	a·gwa·*ka*·te	avocado
ajo	*a*·kho	garlic
albóndigas	al·*bon*·dee·ga	meatballs
arroz	a·*roth*	rice
asado	a·*sa*·do	roasted
bacalao	ba·ka·*low*	dried and salted cod
berenjena	be·ren·*khe*·na	aubergine, eggplant
bistec	bis-*tek*	steak
bocadillo	bo·ka·*dee*·lyo	bread roll with filling (usually without butter)
boquerones	bo·ke·*ro*·nes	fresh anchovies, served either *fritos* (fried) or *en vinagre* (marinated in white vinegar)
butifarra	boo·tee·*fa*·ra	sausage
cabrito	ka·*bree*·to	kid, baby goat
calamares	ka·la·*ma*·res	squid rings
caldo	*kal*·do	broth, stock
callos	*ka*·lyos	tripe
camarón	ka·ma·*ron*	small prawn, shrimp
caracol	ka·ra·*kol*	snail
cebolla	the·*bo*·lya	onion
cerdo	*ther*·do	pork
chorizo	cho·*ree*·tho	cooked spicy red sausage
chuleta	choo·*le*·ta	chop, cutlet
churro	*choo*·ro	long, deep-fried doughnut
cochinillo	ko·chee·*nee*·lyo	suckling pig
codorniz	ko·dor·*neeth*	quail
coliflor	ko·lee·*flor*	cauliflower
conejo	ko·*ne*·kho	rabbit
confitura	kon·fee·*too*·ra	jam
cordero	kor·*de*·ro	lamb
empanadillas	em·pa·na·*dee*·lyas	small pie, either savoury or sweet
ensalada	en·sa·*la*·da	salad

escabeche	es·ka·*be*·che	pickle, marinade
estofado	es·to·*fa*·do	stew
frito	*free*·to	fried
galleta	ga·*lye*·ta	biscuit
granada	gra·*na*·da	pomegranate
helado	e·*la*·do	ice cream
langosta	lan·*gos*·ta	lobster
langostino	lan·gos·*tee*·no	king prawn
leche	*le*·che	milk
lechuga	le·*choo*·ga	lettuce
lomo	*lo*·mo	loin (pork unless specified otherwise)
maíz	ma·*eeth*	corn
mantequilla	man·te·*kee*·lya	butter
manzana	man·*tha*·na	apple
mejillones	me·khee·*lyo*·nes	mussels
menú del día	me·*noo* del *dee*·a	daily set menu
merluza	mer·*loo*·tha	hake
miel	myel	honey
morcilla	mor·*thee*·lya	black pudding
naranja	na·*ran*·kha	orange
ostra	*os*·tra	oyster
paella	pa·e·lya	rice dish that has many regional variations
pan	pan	bread
pastel	pas·*tel*	cake
pato	*pa*·to	duck
pescaíto frito	pes·ka·*ee*·to *free*·to	fried fish
pil pil	peel peel	garlic sauce spiked with chilli
pimentón	pee·men·*ton*	paprika
pimiento	pee·*myen*·to	pepper, capsicum
plátano	*pla*·ta·no	banana
platija	pla·*tee*·kha	flounder, plaice
plato combinado	*pla*·to kom·bee·*na*·do	combination plate
queso	*ke*·so	cheese
raciones	ra·*thyo*·nes	large tapas serving
relleno	re·*lye*·no	stuffing
riñón	ree·*nyon*	kidney
salsa	*sal*·sa	sauce
sandía	san·*dee*·a	watermelon
sesos	*se*·sos	brains
seta	*se*·ta	wild mushroom
solomillo	so·lo·*mee*·lyo	sirloin (usually of pork)
sopa	*so*·pa	soup
tarta	*tar*·ta	cake
ternasco	ter·*nas*·ko	lamb ribs
ternera	ter·*ne*·ra	veal
tortilla de patatas	tor·*tee*·lya de pa·*ta*·tas	potato and onion omelette
tostas	*tos*·tas	toasted bread, often with a savoury topping
trucha	*troo*·cha	trout

Environment

THE LAND

The Iberian Peninsula (Spain and Portugal), having previously floated around off the western end of Europe for millions of years, joined hands with the rest of the continent about 70 million years ago. Its collision at that time with the European and African landmasses caused the peninsula's main mountain chains to rise up, most obviously the Pyrenees. The resulting rugged topography not only separated Spain's destiny from the rest of Europe's for long periods, but also encouraged the rise of separate small states in the medieval period.

The Meseta

Located at the heart of Spain and occupying 40% of the country, the *meseta* is a sparsely populated (apart from a few cities, such as Madrid) tableland that is much given to grain growing. Contrary to what Professor Henry Higgins taught Eliza Dolittle, the *meseta* is not where most of Spain's rain falls. In fact it has a continental climate: scorching in summer, cold in winter, and dry year-round. Nor is it really a plain: much of the *meseta* consists of rolling hills and it is split in two by the Cordillera Central mountain chain. Three of Spain's five major rivers – the Duero, the Tajo and the Guadiana – flow west across the *meseta* into Portugal and, ultimately, into the Atlantic Ocean. Like other Spanish rivers, these three are dammed here and there to provide much of the country's water and electricity.

The Mountains

The *meseta* is bounded by mountain chains on all sides except the west (where it slopes gradually down across Portugal).

Across the north is the damp Cordillera Cantábrica, which rises above 2500m in the spectacular Picos de Europa. The Sistema Ibérico runs down from La Rioja in the central north to southern Aragón, peaking at 2316m in the Sierra del Moncayo. The southern boundary of the *meseta* is the low, wooded Sierra Morena, rolling across northern Andalucía.

But you will find it's at or near Spain's extremities that the country's highest mountains rise up. The Pyrenees stretch for 400km along the French border, rising to numerous 3000m-plus peaks in Catalonia and Aragón, the highest of these being Pico de Aneto (3408m). Across Andalucía stretches the Cordillera Bética, a rumpled mass of ranges that includes Mulhacén (3479m) – mainland Spain's highest peak – in the Sierra Nevada, southeast of Granada.

The highest peak in the whole of Spain isn't on the mainland at all, but is actually Teide (3718m), 1400km southwest of the mainland on the Canary island of Tenerife.

The Lowlands

Around and between all the mountains are five main lower-lying areas.

The basin of the Río Ebro, Spain's most voluminous river, stretches from the central north to the Mediterranean coast, yielding a variety of crops, although parts of central Aragón are near-desert.

The lower Ebro flows through fertile Catalonia, composed mainly of ranges of low hills (but rising up to the mighty Pyrenees in the north). Further south, the coastal areas of Valencia and Murcia are dry plains that have been transformed by irrigation into green market gardens and orchards.

The basin of Spain's fifth major river, the Guadalquivir, stretches across central Andalucía. The summer here sees high temperatures, with a daily average high of 36°C in Seville in July and August.

In northwest Spain is the region of Galicia, which is hilly, rainy and green, with mixed farming.

The Coasts

Spain's coast is as varied as its interior. The Mediterranean coast alternates between rocky coves and inlets, and flatter, straighter stretches with some long beaches and heavy tourism development, as on the Costa del Sol.

Sea temperatures along the Mediterranean coast average 19°C or 20°C in June or October, and a reasonably comfortable 22°C to 25°C between July and September – slightly more in the Balearic Islands and around Alicante.

The Atlantic coast has cooler seas and whiter, sandier beaches. The Costa de la Luz, from the Strait of Gibraltar to the Portuguese border, is blessed with long sandy beaches. In the northwest, Galicia is deeply indented by long estuaries called *rías*, with plenty of sandy beaches. Along the Bay of Biscay, the Cordillera Cantábrica comes almost down to the coast, and the beaches are mostly coves and small bays, though still sandy.

WILDLIFE

Spain's animal life is among Europe's most varied, and for the dedicated naturalist a wildlife-spotting trip to Spain can be as rewarding as one to the plains of Africa – but you have to be patient and you have to know where to look. Sadly, many species are now in perilously small numbers. Spain's plant life is astonishing in its variety, as the spectacular wildflower displays on roadsides and in pastures in spring and early summer testify.

If you can find a copy, *Spain (Wildlife Travelling Companion)*, by John Measures, is an excellent guide to the wildlife and wild places of the country.

Animals

There are about 130 *osos pardos* (brown bears) in the Cordillera Cantábrica, and about 20 in the Pyrenees (in France and Andorra as well as Spain). Hunting or killing Spain's bears has been banned since 1973, and expensive conservation programs have started to pay off in the last few years, at least in the western Cordillera Cantábrica, where the population is considered viable for future survival. It still faces some threats, however, including the decline of natural food sources and unregulated tourism (see the boxed text, p551). Bears are slowly being introduced from Slovenia to boost the Pyrenean population; so far this is looking to be successful.

The *lobo* (wolf) is also on the increase. From a population of about 500 in 1970, Spain now has between 2000 and 2500. Their heartland is the mountains of Galicia and northwestern Castilla y León (Zamora is the province with the most wolves). Though heavily protected, wolves are still considered an enemy by many country people.

Wild Spain, by Frederic V Grunfeld (1999), is a useful practical guide to Spain's wilderness and wildlife areas, with illustrations of both animals and plants. It's getting a little dated but still does the job.

The outlook is even brighter for the *cabra montés* (ibex), a stocky mountain goat species whose males have distinctive long horns. Almost hunted to extinction by 1900, the ibex was protected by royal decree a few years later (though is still subject to controlled hunting today). There may now be 30,000 in the country, chiefly in the Sierra de Gredos and the mountains of Andalucía.

More common beasts – all widely distributed – include the *jabalí* (wild boar); the *ciervo, corzo* and *gamo* (red, roe and fallow deer); the *gineta* (genet), a catlike creature with a white-and-black coat; and the *ardilla* (red squirrel). The chamois *(rebeco, sarrio, isard* or *gamuza),* a small antelope, lives mainly above the tree line in the Pyrenees and Cordillera Cantábrica. Southwestern Spain is home to the Egyptian *meloncillo* (mongoose). Gibraltar's 'apes' – actually Barbary macaques – are the only wild monkeys in Europe.

Twenty-seven marine mammal species live off Spain's shores. Dolphin- and whale-spotting boat trips are a popular attraction at Gibraltar (p763) and nearby Tarifa (p757).

Of all the protected areas in Spain, probably the most rewarding one for wildlife viewing is the Parque Nacional de Doñana in Andalucía (p733).

Try birdwatching field guides such as *Collins Field Guide: Birds of Britain & Europe,* by Roger Tory Peterson, Guy Mountfort and PAD Hollom, or the slimmer *Collins Bird Guide: The Most Complete Guide to the Birds of Britain & Europe,* by Lars Svensson et al.

Birds

With 390 resident species and subspecies, Spain has easily the biggest and most varied bird population in Europe. Around 25 species of birds of prey, including the *águila real* (golden eagle), *buitre leonado* (griffon vulture) and *alimoche* (Egyptian vulture), breed here. Monfragüe in Extremadura (p843) is the single most spectacular place to observe birds of prey. You'll often see them circling or hovering in mountain areas or on the *meseta*. Almost as good are the Pyrenees, where hundreds of lofty eagles, vultures and other birds cruise on the thermals.

Another spectacular bird that you're certain to see if you're in western Andalucía, Extremadura or either of the Castillas in spring or summer is the white stork. Actually black and white, this creature makes its large and ungainly nests on electricity pylons, trees and towers – in fact, any vertical

LAST OF THE LYNX

The Iberian lynx (also known as the pardel lynx), Europe's only big-cat species, is without doubt the most majestic large creature in Spain. This beautiful cat once inhabited large areas of the peninsula, but in a tale we all know only too well, humans have done their utmost to wipe the cat out. Today only three populations remain: one in the Parque Nacional de Doñana (p733), another in the Sierra Morena, and a small group of 15 or so discovered in Castilla-La Mancha as recently as 2007. Numbers are so critically low that there is now a very real possibility that the Iberian lynx will become the first big cat to become extinct since the sabre-tooth tiger.

In 2000 it was estimated that 400 lynx remained throughout Spain and Portugal, but by 2005 that number had dropped to a mere 100 individuals. This dramatic reduction began with a crash in the rabbit population, the cats' main prey, thanks to disease. The situation was further worsened by habitat destruction through a change in farming techniques and road and housing developments. In fact, between 1960 and 1990 the lynx suffered an 80% reduction in its range.

However, there is a glimmer of hope. The Sierra Morena population currently seems to be stable (though not much higher than Doñana's), and populations have begun to be vaccinated against Feline Leukaemia Virus. Projects are also under way to increase the rabbit population. Most encouragingly, the first captive breeding projects have started to bear fruit, with 14 baby lynx born in the last few years. Further captive breeding centres are being constructed or have recently opened in different parts of Spain and Portugal, and the first cubs born from these are expected to be released into the wild in 2009–10.

For more on the fate of the lynx, see the excellent website, www.soslynx.org.

protuberance it can find, even right in the middle of towns – and your attention will be drawn by the loud clacking of chicks' beaks from these lofty perches. Thousands of *cigüeña blanca* (white storks) migrate north from Africa across the Strait of Gibraltar in January and February – as do much smaller numbers of Europe's only other stork, the *cigüeña negra* (black stork), which is down to about 200 pairs in Spain.

Spain's extensive wetlands make it a haven for water birds. The most important of the wetlands is the Parque Nacional de Doñana (p733) and surrounding areas in the Guadalquivir delta in Andalucía. Hundreds of thousands of birds winter here, and many more call in during the spring and autumn migrations. Other important coastal wetlands include La Albufera (p619) and the Ebro delta (p428). Inland, thousands of *patos* (ducks) and *grullas* (cranes) winter at Laguna de Gallocanta in Aragón (p461), Spain's biggest natural lake. Laguna de Fuente de Piedra (p785), near Antequera in Andalucía, is one of Europe's two main breeding sites for the *flamenco* (greater flamingo), with as many as 20,000 pairs rearing chicks in spring and summer (the other main breeding ground is France's Camargue).

Practical birdwatching guides include John R Butler's *Birdwatching on Spain's Southern Coast*, Ernest Garcia and Andrew Paterson's *Where to Watch Birds in Southern & Western Spain*, and Ernest Garcia and Michael Rebane's *Where to Watch Birds in Northern & Eastern Spain*.

Plants

Mainland Spain and the Balearic Islands contain around 8000 of Europe's 9000 plant species, and 2000 of them are unique to the Iberian Peninsula (and North Africa). This abundance is largely due to the fact that the last ice age did not cover the entire peninsula, enabling plants killed off further north to survive in Spain.

Mountain areas claim much of the variety. The Pyrenees have about 150 unique species and the much smaller Sierra Nevada in Andalucía about 60. When the snow melts, zones above the tree line bloom with small rock-clinging plants. The alpine meadows of the Picos de Europa are home to 40 orchid species.

A variety of pines flourishes on Spain's hills and mountains. The lovely umbrella pine, with its large spreading top and edible kernel, grows near coasts.

BACK FROM THE BRINK?

The *quebrantahuesos* (lammergeier or bearded vulture), with its majestic 2m-plus wingspan, is still a threatened species but is recovering slowly in the Pyrenees, where about 80 pairs now breed (the largest population in Europe). It has also been sighted in the Picos de Europa mountains after a 50-year absence, and an attempt is being made to reintroduce it to Andalucía's Parque Natural de Cazorla. The name *quebrantahuesos,* meaning 'bone breaker', describes the bird's habit of dropping animal bones on to rocks from great heights, so that they smash open, allowing the bird to get at the marrow.

Another emblematic and extremely rare bird is the *águila imperial ibérica* (Spanish imperial eagle). Long thought to be a subspecies of the imperial eagle, it's now widely regarded as a separate species and is unique to Spain. With the help of an active government protection plan, its numbers have increased from about 50 pairs in the 1960s to some 220 pairs today, in such places as Monfragüe and Andalucía's Sierra Morena.

Spain's several hundred pairs of *buitre negro* (black vulture), Europe's biggest bird of prey, probably make up the world's largest population. Its strongholds include Monfragüe and the Sierra Pelada in western Andalucía.

The rare but beautiful Spanish fir is confined to the Sierra de Grazalema and a few other small areas in western Andalucía.

The natural vegetation of many lower slopes in the east and south is Mediterranean woodland, with trees such as the wild olive, carob, holm oak and cork oak that are adapted to a warm, fairly dry climate.

The best guide to Spain's flowers and shrubs is *Flowers of South-West Europe*, by Oleg Polunin and BE Smythies. In the south, Betty Molesworth Allen's *Wildflowers of Southern Spain* is very helpful.

NATIONAL & NATURAL PARKS

Much of Spain's most spectacular and ecologically important country – about 40,000 sq km or 8% of the entire country, if you include national hunting reserves – is under some kind of official protection. Nearly all of these areas are at least partly open to visitors, but degrees of conservation and access vary. For example, *parques naturales* (natural parks), the most widespread category of protected area, may include villages with hotels and camping grounds, or may limit access to a few walking trails with the nearest accommodation 10km away. Fortunately, the most interesting parks and reserves usually have helpful visitors centres where you can obtain decent maps and information on local accommodation, walking routes and activities.

The *parques nacionales* (national parks) are areas of exceptional importance for their fauna, flora, geomorphology or landscape, and are the country's most strictly controlled protected areas. They are declared by the national parliament but managed by Spain's regional governments. Spain has 14 national parks – nine on the mainland, four on the Canary Islands and one on the Balearic Islands. The hundreds of other protected areas, declared and administered by Spain's 17 regional governments, fall into at least 16 classifications and range in size from 100-sq-metre rocks off the Balearics to Andalucía's 2140-sq-km Parque Natural de Cazorla.

The English-language Iberianature (www.iberianature.com) is a terrific source of up-to-date information on Spanish fauna and flora.

ENVIRONMENTAL ISSUES

Human hands have been wreaking radical change in Spain's environment for more than two millennia. It was the Romans who began to cut the country's woodlands, which until then covered half the *meseta*. Deforestation since then, along with overtilling and overgrazing (especially by huge sheep herds), has brought substantial topsoil erosion; most of the fertile Doñana wetlands and the 300-sq-km delta of Río Ebro have been formed by eroded deposits. Urban and industrial growth, intensive tourism development along the

SPAIN'S HIGHLIGHT PARKS

Park	Features	Activities to visit	Best time	Page
Parc Nacional d'Aigüestortes i Estany de Sant Maurici	beautiful Pyrenees lake region	walking, wildlife-spotting	Jun-Sep	p407
Parque Nacional de Doñana	bird and mammal haven in Guadalquivir delta	4WD tours, walking, wildlife-watching, horse riding	year-round	p733
Parque Nacional de Ordesa y Monte Perdido	spectacular section of the Pyrenees, with chamois, raptors and varied vegetation	walking, rock climbing	mid-Jun–Jul, mid-Aug–Sep	p451
Parque Nacional de los Picos de Europa	beautiful mountain refuge for chamois, and a few wolves and bears	walking, rock climbing, caving	May-Jul, Sep	p552
Parques Nacional and Natural Sierra Nevada	mainland Spain's highest mountain range, with many ibex, 60 endemic plants and the beautiful Alpujarras valleys on its southern slopes	walking, rock climbing, mountain biking, skiing, horse riding	depends on activity	p810
Parque Natural de Cazorla	abundant wildlife, 2300 plant species and beautiful mountain scenery	walking, driving, wildlife-watching, mountain biking, 4WD tours	Apr-Oct	p823
Áreas Naturales Serra de Tramuntana	spectacular mountain range on Mallorca	walks, birdwatching	late Feb-early Oct	p659
Parque Nacional Monfragüe	spectacular birds of prey	birdwatching	Mar-Oct	p843
Parque Natural Sierra de Grazalema	lovely, green, mountainous area with rich bird life	walking, caving, canyoning, birdwatching, paragliding, rock climbing	Sep-Jun	p752
Parc Natural del Cadí-Moixeró	steep pre-Pyrenees range	rock climbing, walking	Jun-Sep	p403
Parc Natural de la Zona Volcànica de la Garrotxa	beautiful wooded region with 30 volcanic cones	walking	Apr-Oct	p396
Parque Natural Sierra de Gredos	beautiful mountain region; home to Spain's biggest ibex population	walking, rock climbing, mountain biking	Mar-May, Sep-Nov	p213
Parque Natural de Somiedo	dramatic section of Cordillera Cantábrica	walking	Jul-Sep	p551
Parque Natural de Cabo de Gata-Níjar	sandy beaches, volcanic cliffs, flamingo colony and semidesert vegetation	swimming, birdwatching, walking, horse riding, diving, snorkelling	year-round	p828

coasts, and the construction of hundreds of dams for hydroelectricity and irrigation have caused further change. And over the centuries many animal species have been drastically depleted by hunting and habitat loss.

The good news is that wind and solar energy are taking off. The latter attracts government subsidies and by 2010 will cover 1% of Spain's energy needs. Investors are buying up unused farmland to create solar energy parks. Wind energy attracts less state help but, in key areas such as Galicia (by one account, the region occupies the sixth place in the world in terms of wind-energy production), Asturias, north Catalonia and the area around Tarifa in Andalucía, windmills abound.

For tips on reducing your environmental impact while in Spain, see Travelling Responsibly, p21.

Conservation

Environmental awareness took a huge leap forward in the post-Franco 1980s. The Partido Socialista Obrero Español (PSOE) government spurred a range of actions by regional governments, which now have responsibility for most environmental matters. In 1981 Spain had just 35 environmentally protected areas, covering 2200 sq km. Now there are more than 400, covering some 40,000 sq km. But different regions give varied priority to conservation: Andalucía has more than 80 protected areas, while neighbouring Extremadura has just three. Nor are protected areas always well protected, often because their ecosystems extend beyond their own boundaries. And environmentalists and dedicated officials still have to struggle against illicit building, quarrying and hunting in some protected areas.

For official information on national parks, visit the website of Spain's environment ministry (www.marm.es; click on 'Red de Parques Nacionales'). It's in Spanish, French and English, and full of pretty graphs and pictures.

According to the 2007 International Union for Conservation of Nature (IUCN) *Red List of Threatened Species,* of Spain's animal species 35 vertebrates (including 15 birds and 20 mammals) and 135 invertebrates are considered in danger of extinction. In the plant realm, of the 8000 species on the mainland and Balearic Islands, 49 are in danger of extinction. Plants are threatened by such factors as ploughing and grazing, as well as by tourism and collection.

Water

Potentially Spain's worst environmental problem is drought. It struck in the 1950s, 1960s and 1990s, and threatens again in the late 2000s. This is despite a gigantic investment in reservoirs (which number around 1300, covering a higher proportion of Spain than of any other country in the world) and projects such as the Tajo-Segura water-diversion system, which can transfer 600 million cubic metres of water annually from the Tajo basin in central Spain to the heavily irrigated Valencia and Murcia regions on the Mediterranean coast. Although Spain's many dams and reservoirs provide irrigation and hydroelectricity (reducing the need for nuclear or dirtier forms of power) and conserve water, they inevitably destroy habitats.

Intensive agriculture and the spread of towns and cities (including tourist resorts) have lowered water tables in some areas. Growing vegetables under huge areas of plastic in the southeast, especially Almería province, with intense fertiliser and pesticide use, and water pumped up from deep underground, is drying up some of the underground aquifers it depends upon.

Sunseed Desert Technology, based in Almería, works to find sustainable solutions to living in a dry, semidesert environment. It accepts volunteers in a number of fields. See the website www.sunseed.org.uk for more.

After agriculture it's the tourist industry that consumes the most water and, ironically, it's the south (the region that can least afford to waste water) that seems to be the most blasé about water use. Golf courses are a particular problem in this area, with the average 18-hole course consuming as much water as a town of 20,000 people. Despite this, golf courses continue to breed along the southern coasts.

The situation was eased slightly in the spring and early summer of 2008, which was the wettest in Spain since 1971 and temporarily eased the strain on reservoirs.

Other Problems

Coastal development, often slackly controlled, has degraded many of the country's coastal environments and added to the pollution of the seas, although sewage-treatment facilities are being steadily improved. The coastal building boom has accelerated in the past decade, fuelled by second-home buyers from Spain and abroad. In the southern region of Andalucía 59% of the coastline is already urbanised. The voracious construction and property industry plans ever more developments: *El País* newspaper reported in late

2005 that plans had been approved for at least 1.65 million more homes along the Mediterranean coast between Andalucía and the Valencia area in the east, with some towns and villages planning to multiply their populations by 10. Most of these projects are now nearing completion but, with the property market crash and the poorly performing economy, it is likely that many will remain empty for some time.

In 2008 Spain was awarded 527 blue flags for beach cleanliness – 49 less than in 2007, but still the most in the world. For more information, see www.blueflag.org.

Spain's beaches still get creditable numbers of 'blue flags', which indicate that they meet certain minimal standards of hygiene, facilities and environmental management.

Valencia, Granada and Madrid have the dubious distinction of being the three cities with the dirtiest air in Spain, chiefly because of vehicle emissions, according to the environmental group Ecologistas en Acción.

Spain Outdoors

Few countries in Europe can match Spain's diversity of landscapes. Its never-ending coastline takes in everything from the snakelike *rías* (inlets or estuaries) of rugged Galicia to the olive-backed shores of the Mediterranean, while jagged mountain ranges such as Andalucía's mighty Sierra Nevada and the Pyrenean peaks in the north reach for the skies. This landscape makes for a wonderful adventure playground; there's something for everyone no matter what age or fitness level. You could enjoy these from afar with a glass of Rioja wine in hand, but diving in (sometimes literally) adds a whole new dimension to your Spanish adventures. As well as burning off all those excess tapas, the numerous activities and sports on offer provide the best opportunities for making local friends.

So what can you do to get the sweat glands working? Spain is famous for superb walking and mountain-biking trails. More unlikely, high-adrenalin pursuits include downhill skiing and hang-gliding. If you prefer your fun to be wet, Spain is also one of the best places in Europe to engage in all manner of water sports including superb surfing and windsurfing, canoeing, diving and sailing.

Depending on your level of experience, you have the option of striking out on your own or joining an organised tour; the latter has the advantage of hooking you up with like-minded people. As a rule, the operators along the Mediterranean coast are more plentiful and have more experience in dealing with English-speaking clients than those in the north, although high standards of professionalism are pretty uniform wherever you go.

WALKING

Spain is one of the premier walking destinations in Europe and a snapshot of the possibilities shows why: conquering Spain's highest mainland peak, Mulhacén (3479m; p810) above Granada; following in the footsteps of Carlos V in Extremadura (p837); walking along Galicia's Costa da Morte (Death Coast; p581); or sauntering through alpine meadows in the Pyrenees (p395).

GRs, PRs & Other Paths

Spain's long-distance walking trails (GRs) follow old Roman, royal and pilgrimage roads, cart trails and shepherds' migratory paths.

Spain's extensive networks of short and long-distance trails are called *senderos de pequeño recorrido* (PRs) and *senderos de gran recorrido* (GRs), respectively. PRs are marked with yellow-and-white slashes, while GRs are signposted in red and white. While these are a great concept, maintenance of the trails is sporadic. Local or regional groups also create and maintain their own trails using their own trail marking. Tourist offices may have pamphlets describing nearby walks, and trailheads sometimes have informative panels. There are also many excellent walking guides to specific regions, though most of these are in Spanish only and, as they tend to make comments like 'Turn left at the farm with the red rooster in the yard' (amazingly the rooster is normally where it's supposed to be!), it would prove very hard to follow these sort of instructions without speaking excellent Spanish.

When to Go

Spain encompasses a number of different climate zones, ensuring that, unlike in much of Europe, it's possible to hike here year-round. In Andalucía conditions are at their best from March to June and in September and October; they're downright unbearable in midsummer, but in winter most trails remain open, except in the high mountains. If you prefer to walk in summer, do what Spaniards have traditionally done and escape to the north. The Basque Country, Asturias, Cantabria and Galicia are best from June to September. The Pyrenees are accessible from mid-June, while July and August are the ideal months for the high Sierra Nevada. August is the busiest month on the trails, so if you plan to head to popular national parks and stay in *refugios* (mountain refuges), book ahead.

Prime Spots

For good reason, the Pyrenees, separating Spain from France, are most famous for walking. The range is utterly beautiful: prim and chocolate-box pretty on the lower slopes, wild and bleak at higher elevations, and relatively unspoilt in comparison with some European mountain ranges. The Pyrenees contain two outstanding national parks, Aigüestortes i Estany de Sant Maurici (p407) and Ordesa y Monte Perdido (p451). The spectacular GR11 (Senda Pirenáica) traverses the range, connecting the Atlantic (at Hondarribia in the Basque Country) with the Mediterranean (at Cap de Creus in Catalonia). Walking the whole 45-day route to appreciate its beauty is unnecessary, as there are day hikes in the national parks that coincide with the GR11.

Breathtaking and accessible limestone ranges with distinctive craggy peaks (usually hot climbing destinations, too) include Spain's first national park, the Picos de Europa (p552), which straddles the Cantabria, Asturias and León provinces and is fast gaining a reputation as *the* place to walk in Spain. Less well known, but just as rewarding, are Valencia's Els Ports area (p629), and the Sierra de Cazorla (p823) and Sierra de Grazalema (p752) in Andalucía.

To walk in mountain villages, the classic spot is Las Alpujarras (p812), near the Parque Nacional Sierra Nevada in Andalucía. Galicia has some interesting possibilities, including the Camino Real (PR-G4; p598) in the monastery-laden natural paradise of A Ribeira Sacra. The Pyrenean foothills in Navarra offer superb village-to-village hiking, in particular around the oh-so-pretty Valle del Baztán (p506).

With an average altitude of 660m, Spain is the second-highest country in Europe, after Switzerland.

Great coastal walking abounds, even in heavily visited areas such as the south coast (try Cabo de Gata; p828) and Mallorca (p651). The latter's most commonly hiked routes are in the north and west of the island; for more info, see www.mallorcanwalkingtours.puertopollensa.com. The easy walking on Galicia's Illas Cíes (p593), part of Spain's newest national park, makes it ideal for families. The Galician coastline is crammed full of possibilities, including the GR-50 (p579), a well-known trail that begins in Betanzos and bounces up and down valleys and through forests before finishing in La Serra da Capelada, and shorter, kid-friendly hikes around the Cabo Ortegal (p579). Another good trail heads out to Spain's 'Land's End', Cabo Fisterra (p582). The Basque coast also has plenty of possibilities, especially along the quieter central section (p483).

Spain's most famous long walk is the pilgrim's route of Camino de Santiago (p118), but the Don Quijote trail (see the boxed text, p290), which for some almost counts as a pilgrimage, offers a less trodden path in Castilla.

For more information on parks and protected areas, see p106.

Information

Region-specific walking (and climbing) guides are published by **Cicerone Press** (www.cicerone.co.uk) for Mallorca, the Cordillera Cantábrica, the Vía de la Plata pilgrim's route from Sevilla to Santiago, the Costa Blanca, the Sierra Nevada and the GR11 route across the Spanish Pyrenees. In Barcelona, **Quera** (Map pp316-17; ☎ 93 318 07 43; Carrer de Petritxol 2) is a map and guidebook specialist. Madrid's **La Tienda Verde** (Map p133; ☎ 91 535 38 10, 91 533 07 91; www.tiendaverde.es;

Calle de Maudes 23 & 38) and **Librería Desnivel** (Map pp142-3; ☎ 902 24 88 48; www.libreriadesnivel.com in Spanish; Plaza de Matute 6) both sell maps (the best Spanish ones are Prames and Adrados) and guides. In Spanish, the website www.andarines.com gives route descriptions and useful links for books, sports shops and Spanish mountaineering associations.

CYCLING

Spain has a rich variety of cycling possibilities, from gentle family rides to challenging two-week expeditions. If you avoid the cities (where cycling can be somewhat nerve-wracking), Spain is also a cycle-friendly country, with drivers accustomed to sharing the roads with platoons of Lycra-clad cyclists. The excellent network of secondary roads, usually with a comfortable shoulder, is ideal for road touring.

An excellent English-language website, with articles on wildlife, outdoor sports and conservation, is www.wild-spain.com.

When to Go

In terms of when to go, the same information holds true for cycling as it does for walking (see p110).

What to Take

Bike hire along the popular Mediterranean coastal areas, on the islands and in major cities is relatively easy, but is hit-and-miss just about anywhere else. Bring your own helmet (helmets are required by law but enforcement is inconsistent) and bicycle if you're planning to do serious touring. Bicycle shops are common everywhere, making it unnecessary to load yourself down with supplies.

Prime Spots

Every Spanish region has both off-road (called BTT in Spanish, from *bici todo terreno* or mountain bike) and touring trails and routes. Mountain bikers can head to just about any sierra (mountain range) and use the extensive *pistas forestales* (forestry tracks). A challenging off-road excursion takes you along the Altiplano across the Sierra Nevada (p810). Classic long-haul touring routes include the Camino de Santiago (p118), the Ruta de la Plata (see the boxed text, p838) and the 600km Camino del Cid, which follows in the footsteps of Spain's epic hero from Burgos to Valencia. Guides in Spanish exist for all of these, available at bookshops and online.

Information

An indispensable website for readers of Spanish is www.amigosdelciclismo.com, which gives useful information on restrictions, updates on laws, circulation norms, contact information for the hundreds of cycling clubs all over the country and lists of guidebooks, as well as a lifetime's worth of route descriptions organised region by region. There are more than 200 cycling guidebooks published (the vast majority in Spanish). *España en Bici,*

SLEEPING BENEATH THE STARS

Camping outside designated camping grounds is generally not permitted in Spain, but despite this many people park their vans up for the night along remote beaches or in rural areas and have a peaceful night's kip. If you try this, keep your chosen campsite clean and don't be noisy or drunken, and you'll be more likely to get away with it for a night. If you get caught you'll be moved on by the police, and if you've made a mess or are disorderly the consequences could be more severe. In the mountains, wild camping by trekkers is much more accepted. The website www.campingsonline.com can help you locate campsites anywhere in the country.

AIRLINE BAGGAGE CHARGES

Visitors flying into Spain can expect a hefty surcharge for carrying anything that can even vaguely be labelled 'sports equipment'. You should always check the rules before purchasing your ticket. Be aware that it's normally cheaper to pay the baggage charges online when purchasing the ticket rather than leaving it until you get to the airport. Most of the budget airlines charge somewhere in the region of €30 to €50 per piece of sporting equipment, per flight, but rules vary widely for the big airlines. Iberia and Air France, for example, charge so much to carry surfboards, windsurfers, bikes, diving equipment and even bodyboards that it's often cheaper to buy a new board in Spain and give it away at the end of the trip! Other airlines, such as British Airways, have banned surfing and windsurfing equipment from their flights altogether. If you're carrying golf clubs then you'll be pleased to know that many scheduled airlines charge significantly less – despite a set of golf clubs being heavier, larger and more delicate than a bodyboard!

by Paco Tortosa and María del Mar Fornés, is a good overview guide, but it's quite hard to find. *Cycle Touring in Spain: Eight Detailed Routes*, by Harry Dowdell, is a helpful planning tool, as well as being practical once you're in Spain. Another good resource is *The Trailrider Guide – Spain: Single Track Mountain Biking in Spain*, by Nathan James and Linsey Stroud.

For information on bicycle purchase and transport in Spain, see p891. **Bike Spain** (Map pp142-3; www.bikespain.info) in Madrid is one of the better cycling tour operators. The **Real Federación Española de Ciclismo** (☎ 91 540 08 41; www.rfec.com) provides contact information for bicycle clubs.

SKIING & SNOWBOARDING

For winter powder, Spain's skiers (and the royal family) head to the Pyrenees of Aragón and Catalonia. Outside of the peak periods (the beginning of December, 20 December to 6 January, Carnaval and Semana Santa), Spain's top resorts are relatively quiet, cheap and warm in comparison with their counterparts in the Alps. Resorts now also cater to snowboarders, with shops, schools and the installation of on-slope half-pipes. The season runs from December to April, though January and February are generally the best, most reliable times for snow. However, the Pyrenees winter seasons of 2006–07 and 2007–08 were dreadful, with the former in particular having almost no snow and many of the lower resorts barely able to open.

The website www.spainforvisitors.com is a good all-purpose site that provides links to a host of activities in Spain, including ballooning, skiing, walking, sailing and windsurfing.

Prime Spots

In Aragón, two popular resorts are Formigal (p458) and Candanchú (p457); just above the town of Jaca, Candanchú has some 42km of runs with 51 pistes (as well as 35km of cross-country track). In Catalonia, Spain's first resort, La Molina (p402), is still going strong and is ideal for families and beginners. Considered by many to have the Pyrenees' best snow (especially in January), the 72-piste resort of Baqueira-Beret (p413) boasts 30 modern lifts and 104km of downhill runs for all levels (and 7km of cross-country track). The aprés-ski scene also gets high ratings. Further west, the resorts of Navarra offer low-key but reliable midwinter skiing conditions. The best-known area is around Isaba (p508).

Spain's other major resort is Europe's southernmost: the Sierra Nevada (p810), outside Granada. With completely overhauled facilities for the 1996 World Cup ski championships, the 80km of runs are at their prime in March. Despite their World Cup status, the slopes are particularly suited for families and novice-to-intermediate skiers.

Of the minor ski stations with poorer snow and a shorter season, Navacerrada (p205) is just 60km from Madrid and has 16 runs that cater to beginners and intermediates. It can be overwhelmed by crowds on winter weekends. In La Rioja, Valdezcaray, in the Sierra de la Demanda just 45 minutes from Santo Domingo de la Calzada, has 14 runs reaching a maximum altitude of 1530m. Manzaneda, 90km northeast of Ourense in Galicia, boasts a 230m elevation drop, extensive snow-making machines and 15 runs along treeless trails from 1500m to 1800m.

Information

If you don't want to bring your own gear, Spanish resorts have equipment hire, as well as ski schools. Lift tickets cost between €30 and €40 for adults, and €24 and €26 for children; equipment hire costs around €18 to €20 a day. If you're planning ahead, Spanish travel agencies frequently advertise affordable single- or multiday packages with lodging included. An excellent source of information on snowboarding and skiing in Spain (and the rest of Europe) is www.skisnowboardeurope.com.

For a list of hyperbaric chambers and diving-accident facilities in Spain, check www.scuba-doc.com/divsp.htm.

WATER SPORTS

Scuba Diving & Snorkelling

There's more to Spain than what you see on the surface – literally! Delve under the ocean waves anywhere along the country's 4000km of shoreline and a whole new Spain opens up, crowded with marine life and including features such as wrecks, sheer walls and long cavern swim-throughs. The numerous Mediterranean dive centres cater heavily to an English-speaking market and offer single- and multiday trips, equipment rental and certification courses. Their Atlantic counterparts (in San Sebastián, Santander and A Coruña) deal mostly in Spanish, but if that's not an obstacle for you, then the colder waters of the Atlantic will offer a completely different, and very rewarding, underwater experience.

A good starting point is the reefs along the Costa Brava, especially around the Illes Medes marine reserve (p385) off L'Estartit (near Girona). On the Costa del Sol (p775), operators launch to such places as La Herradura Wall, the *Motril* wreck and the Cavern of Cerro Gordo. Spain's Balearic Islands are also popular dive destinations with excellent services.

Paco Nadal's *Buceo en España* provides information province by province, with descriptions of ocean floors, dive centres and equipment rental.

There are a number of excellent surf guidebooks to Spain. Check out Stuart Butler's English-language *Big Blue Surf Guide: Spain*, José Pellón's Spanish-language *Guía del Surf en España* and Low Pressure's superb *Stormrider Guide: Europe – the continent.*

Surfing

The opportunity to get into the waves is a major attraction for beginners and experts alike along many Spanish coastal regions. The north coast of Spain has, debatably, the best surf in mainland Europe, while the Canaries, Spain's Atlantic islands, have probably the best island-based surf.

The main surfing region is the north coast, where numerous high-class spots can be found, but Atlantic Andalucía and even the Mediterranean get decent winter swells. Despite the flow of vans loaded down with surfboards along the north coast in the summer, it's actually autumn through to spring that's the prime time for decent swell, with October probably the best month overall. The variety of waves along the north coast is impressive: there are numerous open, swell-exposed beach breaks for the summer months, and some seriously heavy reefs and points that only really come to life during the colder, stormier months. In general, many of these spots are fairly quiet in comparison with neighbouring France.

In summer a shortie wetsuit (or, in the Basque Country, just board shorts) is sufficient along all coasts except Galicia (which picks up the icy Canaries current – you will need a light full suit here). In winter you will need a thicker 4mm wetsuit and boots for everywhere but the Costa de la Luz and the southern Mediterranean, where a 3mm full suit will suffice.

Though most spots are hassle-free, the locals do demand respect at many of the better spots – learners, inexperienced surfers or just plain rude surfers will not be tolerated at places like Mundaka in the Basque Country (p482), Rodiles in Asturias (p546) and Liencres in Cantabria. During the hectic summer months local surfers at any beach can get a bit testy over the incredible number of surf schools filling the line-up with learners. If you're joining a surf-school course, ask the instructor to explain the rules and to keep you away from the more experienced surfers. Surf shops abound in the popular surfing areas and usually offer board and wetsuit hire.

The Billabong Pro Mundaka brings the world's best surfers to northern Spain for a crucial stop on the World Championship Tour over the first 10 days of October. If you can't be there in person catch it live on www.aspworldtour.com.

The most famous wave in Spain is the legendary river-mouth left at Mundaka (p482), and on a good day there is no doubting that it is one of the best waves in the world. However, it's not very consistent, and when it's on it's always very busy and ugly. In 2005 upriver dredging and a conservation project resulted in the famous sandbar being washed away for a while. A World Championship Tour event had to be cancelled, and surfers and local businesses were up in arms about the dredging, but fortunately the wave has returned and the conservation project has not suffered.

Heading east, good waves can be found throughout the Basque Country, and even in downtown San Sebastián at the city beach, Playa de Gros (Playa de la Zurriola; p488) Neighbouring Cantabria and Asturias also have a superb range of well-charted surf beaches and a number of mystery spots… we'll leave you to discover them. If you're looking for solitude, along Galicia's Costa da Morte (p581) some isolated beaches remain empty even in summer. This is also the most consistent place in Spain for waves. On the Mediterranean, southwest Spain gets powerful, winter beach breaks, and weekdays off Conil de la Frontera (just northwest of Cabo de Trafalgar; p755) can be sublimely lonely.

You'll find decent surfing info at www.3sesenta.tv (in Spanish) and www.gruposr.com (in Spanish; click on Surfer Rule).

Windsurfing & Kitesurfing

Spain is blessed with excellent windsurfing and kitesurfing (kiteboarding) conditions along much of its Mediterranean coast. Up on the rougher north coast conditions are normally not so good, though Galicia has superb conditions for wave sailing, with frequent, strong, cross-shore winds and good surf.

An excellent glossy guidebook to wind- and kitesurfing spots across Spain and the rest of Europe is Stoked Publications' *The Kite and Windsurfing Guide: Europe*.

The best sailing conditions are to be found around Tarifa (p757), which has such strong and consistent winds (caused by funnelling through the Straits of Gibraltar) that it's said that the town's formerly very high suicide rate was due to the wind turning people mad. Whether or not this is true, one thing is without doubt: Tarifa's 10km of white, sandy beaches and perfect year-round conditions have made this small town the windsurf capital of Europe. The town is crammed with windsurf and kite shops, windsurfing schools and a huge contingent of passing surfers. However, the same wind that attracts so many devotees also makes it a less than ideal place to learn the art.

If you can't make it as far south as Tarifa, then the less-well-known Empuriabrava in Catalonia also has great conditions, especially from March to July, while the family resort of Oliva near Valencia is also worth considering. If you're looking for waves, try Spain's northwest coast, where the northeast trade winds keep the wind constant all year. The Spanish-language website www.windsurfesp.com gives very thorough descriptions of spots, conditions and schools all over Spain.

SPAIN FOR SKATERS

If you're a keen skater, you'll be pleased to know that several larger Spanish cities, as well as many of the surf-obsessed coastal towns, are generally fairly skater-friendly (at least as skater-friendly as any town council is!), so it might be worth bringing your skateboard or rollerblades along. Bilbao (p469), Madrid and Pamplona (p499) are all kitted out with good skate parks and some decent street-skating opportunities, but it's Barcelona, with a couple of excellent skate parks (try the Forum area, p330) and a progressive local crew, that really leads the way in the Spanish scene. Local skaters everywhere will often be happy to adopt you and show you where to go.

Kayaking, Canoeing & Rafting

With 1800 rivers and streams, opportunities abound in Spain to take off downstream in search of white-water fun. As most rivers are dammed for electric power at some point along their flow, there are many reservoirs with excellent low-level kayaking and canoeing, where you can also hire equipment. The downside is that following a river's course to the sea means you'll end up carrying your boat.

In general, May and June are best for kayaking, rafting, canoeing and hydrospeeding (water tobogganing). Top white-water rivers include Catalonia's turbulent Noguera Pallaresa (p406), Aragón's Gállego, Cantabria's Carasa and Galicia's Miño. For fun and competition, the crazy 22km, en-masse Descenso Internacional del Sella canoe race (p555) is a blast, running from Arriondas in Asturias to coastal Ribadesella. It's held on the first weekend in August. Kayaking in the Parque Natural Fragas do Eume (p577) is a great opportunity for families to get paddling together on a beautiful reservoir in the middle of a dense Atlantic forest.

Bring your running things – the Spanish love jogging and people will happily tell you good running routes. Footballers will also find impromptu games taking place everywhere, and players will often be happy for you to join in.

Patrick Santal's *White Water Pyrenees* thoroughly covers 85 rivers in France and Spain for kayakers, canoers and rafters.

For more tranquil sea kayaking around cliffs, the Costa Brava's shore by Cala Montgó, Tamariu (p379) and Cadaqués (p388) is tops. Guided excursions, classes and equipment hire from beaches are easy to locate.

Sailing

Spain has some 250 harbours for sport sailing and stages many regattas. There are also many companies that specialise in chartering sailing boats both with and without a skipper and crew. The **Real Federación Española de Vela** (☎ 91 519 50 08; www.rfev.es in Spanish) maintains a calendar of windsurfing and sailing regattas, as well as regulations governing sailing in Spanish waters.

Canyoning & Puenting

If walking, sliding, diving, jumping and swimming down canyons is your thing, Spain's top *barranquismo* (canyoning) centres are found in Aragón's Sierra de Guara (p446), which, with its 200-odd canyons, is famous for its deep throats, powerful torrents and narrow gorges. It's generally regarded as one of the best places in Europe for the sport. The Río Verde north of Almuñécar (p815) in southern Spain is also a decent area to explore. May to September are generally the best months.

Another popular activity run by adventure outfits all over Spain is swing jumping or *puenting* (which is the Spanglish way of saying 'jumping from a very high and very scary bridge'). Unlike bungee jumping, where there's rebound, the idea is to jump out far, snug in two harnesses and two cords, and free fall (reaching up to 170km/h) into a pendulum-like swing action. Well, it certainly sounds more exciting than a day spent mowing the lawn!

HANG-GLIDING & PARAGLIDING

If you want to take to the skies either *ala delta* (hang-gliding) or *parapente* (paragliding), there are a number of specialised clubs and adventure-tour companies. The **Real Federación Aeronáutica España** (www.rfae.org in Spanish) gives information on recognised schools and lists clubs and events. The best places for paragliding in Spain are Castejón de Sos (p449) in Aragón, Zahara de la Sierra (p754) and Grazalema (p753) in Andalucía, Almuñécar (p815), and a number of places along the Mediterranean coast. For hang-gliding try Montsec in Catalonia (p420) as well as the places listed here for paragliding.

For the lowdown on skydiving courses, drop zones (Seville is one of the most popular spots) and equipment hire, look no further than www.skydiveworldwide.com/europe/spain.php.

Camino de Santiago

Nancy Frey

Traversing northern Spain to the tomb of James the Greater in Santiago de Compostela, the Camino de Santiago (Way of St James) pilgrimage is considered to be Europe's premier cultural itinerary. In the latter quarter of the 20th century, the Camino experienced a remarkable renaissance as people took to recreating the medieval journey, following the old trails marked by the traditional pilgrimage symbols of scallop, shell and staff on foot and by bicycle (and, more rarely, on horseback). The key to the Camino's immense appeal is its accessibility. A 13th-century poem from a remote Pyrenean monastery says it all: 'The door is open to all, to sick and healthy, not only to Catholics but also to pagans, Jews, heretics and vagabonds.' Not much has changed. Modern pilgrims are not primarily religiously motivated but come from every possible background, age and nationality. The Camino continues to attract all sorts – culture hounds, soul searchers, those longing for a great physical challenge, food and wine enthusiasts, as well as lovers of natural landscapes and back roads. Whether you walk for just one day or for 50 – the Camino is ready to give, if you're ready to receive.

The word *'compostela'* comes from either 'campus stellae' meaning starry field or 'compostium' meaning burial ground.

HISTORY

Before people could fly or drive to Santiago, millions of pilgrims from across Europe simply walked out their doors and headed for Santiago de Compostela along a vast network of trade routes, royal roads and trails that eventually came together in Spain. Goethe's comment that 'Europe was born on the pilgrim road to Santiago' thus makes sense. But what originally set Europe's feet moving? Tradition tells us that in AD 813 Pelayo, a religious hermit living in the boondocks of northwestern Iberia, followed a shining star and angelic voices to a Roman mausoleum hidden under briars.

Scallop shells are worn by Santiago pilgrims as the symbol of their journey to Compostela; in the iconography you will recognise St James by the scallop shells on his hat and tunic.

Inside were the remains of the apostle James the Greater (in Spanish, Santiago). Once confirmed by the local bishop Teodomiro and Asturian king Alfonso the Chaste, the earth-shaking discovery spread like wildfire and put the incipient Compostela indelibly on European maps. Today it's hard to imagine the impact of this news, but in that age pilgrimage to holy sites with relics was tantamount to obtaining a ticket to eternal salvation through the system of penance and indulgences. Relics were sacred commodities: the more important the relic, the more important the shrine that held them. Santiago's relics were gold: nearly intact and belonging to one of Jesus' favourite apostles, making them Europe's finest. When word got out, the devoted began the arduous journey to Spain, especially when the Crusades made it too dangerous to reach Jerusalem.

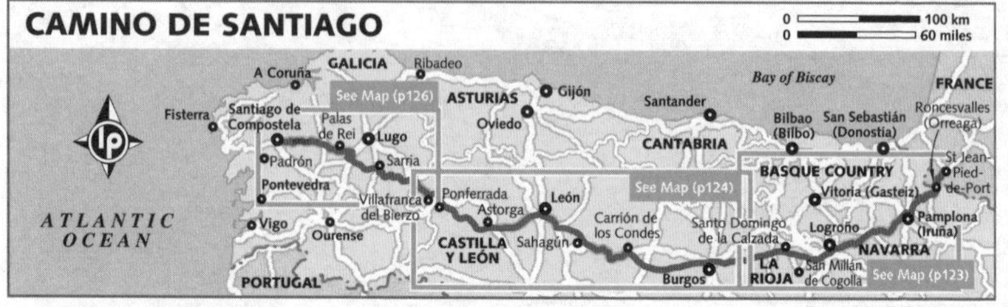

SCALLOP SHELL

Many theories abound as to why the scallop shell is associated with St James. Some say the scallop, already linked with a local pagan Venus cult, was recycled when Christianity made headway in the area. Picture Botticelli's Venus rising out of her shell in *The Birth of Venus*. Similarly, the symbol of rebirth is apt for St James as his pilgrimage ideally offers regeneration of the soul. But the best story goes like this: as the stone boat carrying Santiago's body reached the Galician coast there was a pagan wedding taking place on shore. The groom, mounted on a horse, was racing along the beach. Catching sight of a floating stone boat was so unsettling that he and the horse fell into the crashing waves and began to drown. Santiago, in his first act of postmartyrdom mercy, righted the groom and his horse, and when they emerged out of the waves they were covered in scallop shells.

How Santiago's remains reached present-day Compostela must rank among medieval Europe's greatest legends. Originally a fisherman, James took up Jesus' call and became one of his first apostles. Apocryphal tradition instructs us that James then preached in Iberia before returning to Jerusalem where he met his violent end. The Bible explains that James has the dubious honour of being the first apostle martyred (decapitated) by Herod Agrippa, in AD 44. Debate, however, surrounds the remainder of the story. Apparently, James' followers secreted his body to Jaffa and set sail in a stone boat on a miraculous sea voyage through the Strait of Gibraltar back to Galicia at Padrón. Queen Lupa, the local pagan ruler, set wild bulls onto the disciples when they requested permission to bury their Christian martyr. Not about to be daunted, the disciples prayed to Santiago, who calmed the bulls' ire, allowing them to be peacefully yoked. Santiago was then buried and forgotten until Pelayo followed the star seven centuries later.

While the spiritual rewards of pilgrimage were infinite, the hazards were too. In the 10th century there was no actual 'road' to Compostela; the Camino needed to be built and settled to provide pilgrims with safe trails, bridges, shelter, towns, churches and first aid. To encourage able-bodied souls to the area, monarchs offered enormous privileges to settlers, who soon populated town after town. Northern Spain was additionally plagued by Christian versus Muslim skirmishes, which made the going hazardous. Monarchs and ecclesiasts were no fools and they quickly put the apostle's image to work – he was reborn as the legendary Santiago Matamoros (Moor-slayer), heading up the Christian troops mounted on a white charger at key Reconquista (Reconquest) battles.

Benedictine monks from Cluny in France also recognised the advantage of close ties to the Camino. They founded many monasteries and attendant churches along the trail, which populated the way with Romanesque art forms and helped to spread the order's power. In the 12th century a French cleric compiled the *Liber Sancti Jacobi* (aka the Book of St James). A masterwork on the Santiago pilgrimage, it includes a remarkable guidebook that divides the route from the Pyrenees into 13 stages. This was instrumental in spreading Santiago's fame.

A further boon for Compostela was the Pope's 1189 granting of Holy Year status to the shrine, further increasing its prestige as a pilgrimage destination. Consequently, as a major focus of European traffic, northern Spain was blessed with an abundance of first-rate architecture from Romanesque to baroque styles.

After its 11th-to-13th-century heyday (which rivalled even Rome and Jerusalem), the Camino suffered through the Protestant Reformation,

Years in which 25 July falls on a Sunday are considered 'Holy Years' (Año Santo/Jacobeo). In these years pilgrims can earn plenary indulgences (erasing all one's sins), partly explaining the Camino's popularity. The next occurrences are 2010 and 2021.

nearly dying out until its late-20th-century revival. The route's current success has pumped new life into some lost little corners of northern Spain.

INFORMATION

Although in Spain there are many *caminos* (paths) to Santiago, by far the most popular is, and was, the Camino Francés, which originated in France, crossed the Pyrenees at Roncesvalles and then headed west for 750km across mountains, wheat and wine fields, and forests of the regions of Navarra, La Rioja, Castilla y León and Galicia.

Travelling the Camino by car brings greater flexibility to explore many additional sites as well as to enjoy day walks. Tourist offices along the Camino are all stocked with brochures highlighting local information.

Waymarked with cheerful yellow arrows on everything from telephone poles to rocks and trees, the 'trail' is a mishmash of rural lanes, paved secondary roads and footpaths all strung together. Scallop shells, stuck in cement markers or stylised on blue-and-yellow metal signs, also show the way.

There is no official starting point. Nowadays many people walk or cycle varying lengths based on different criteria: time, interest or challenge. Starting at Roncesvalles, the Camino takes roughly two weeks cycling or five weeks walking.

A very popular alternative is to walk only the last 100km (the minimum distance allowed) from Sarria in Galicia in order to earn a Compostela certificate of completion given out by the Catedral de Santiago de Compostela. Modern pilgrims carry a Credencial del Peregrino (Pilgrim's Credential), which they can get stamped daily in churches and bars, and at *albergues* and *refugios* (refuges).

For more information about the Credencial and the Compostela certificate, visit the cathedral's **Oficina de Acogida de Peregrinos** (Pilgrim's Office; ☎ 981 56 88 46; Rúa do Vilar 1; www.archicompostela.org/Peregrinos/default.htm; 🕑 9am-9pm), in person or via the web.

Websites

Many websites cover planning, history, maps, newsgroups and information on all the alternative *caminos*. Some great sites:

www.caminolinks.co.uk A complete, annotated guide to many *camino* websites.
www.csj.org.uk Confraternity of St James online bookshop offering historical and practical information, and detailed guides to the alternative *caminos*.
www.mundicamino.com Excellent, thorough descriptions and maps of all of the *caminos*.
www.santiago-today.com A huge selection of news groups from where you can get all of your questions answered plus planning information.

PILGRIM HOSTELS

Following the same spirit of charity as the medieval monasteries that gave hospitality to pilgrims, the *refugio* (refuge) system developed during the Camino's renaissance in the early 1990s. After making the pilgrimage herself, Lourdes Lluch, a Catalan woman, decided that the Camino needed more facilities for pilgrims. During the summer of 1990, she rented a run-down house in Hornillos del Camino – one of the bleakest parts of the Camino – set up a makeshift shelter, and pulled pilgrims in off the street, offering them food, drink and a clean place to rest their weary bodies. The idea took off and there are now some 300 *refugios* along the Camino, owned by parishes, Friends of the Camino associations, private individuals, town halls and regional governments. While in the early days these places were run on donations and provided little more than hot water and a bed, today's pilgrims are charged €5 to €10 and expect showers, kitchens and washing machines. Some things haven't changed though – the *refugios* still operate on a first come, first served basis and are intended for those doing the Camino solely on their own steam.

CAMINO BOOKS

Camino books abound! The best of each category is suggested below.

- Background history: William Melczer's essential history and translation of the 12th-century *Pilgrim's Guide to Santiago de Compostela.*
- Culture: David Gitlitz and Linda Davidson's *The Pilgrimage Road to Santiago*: *The Complete Cultural Handbook* is well worth its weight.
- Analysis: Anthropologist Nancy Frey explores the pilgrimage's modern resurgence in *Pilgrim Stories: On and Off the Road to Santiago.*
- Guidebook: Millán Bravo Lozano's *A Practical Guide for Pilgrims* provides great maps and route descriptions.
- Religious/Spiritual Account: Joyce Rupp gives a compelling account of the inner journey in *Walk in a Relaxed Manner.*
- Esoteric: Paulo Coelho's mystical journey described in *The Pilgrimage* is an international bestseller.

Tours

If you want a guided trip, there are numerous outfits that organise walking and cycling tours of varying duration. **On Foot in Spain** (www.onfootinspain.com) offers guided cultural walking tours along the Camino Francés and Camino Portugués. Flexible, self-guided options where you walk on your own but are provided with maps, route notes, reserved accommodation and luggage transfers are offered by **World Walks** (www.worldwalks.com). **Bike Spain** (www.bikespain.info) specialises in guided and self-guided cycling tours from León, and **Great Explorations** (www.great-explorations.com) runs cycling options from Pamplona.

Friends of the Camino associations worldwide also provide invaluable information, especially the **Confraternity of St James** (☎ 020 7928 9988; www.csj.org.uk; 27 Blackfriars Rd, London, SE1 8NY, UK).

The yellow arrow waymarkers were invented back in the 1980s by O Cebreiro's energetic priest Elías Valiña Sampedro. He and his nephews went out with cans of yellow paint (leftovers from highway road repairs) and marked the historical ways.

PLANNING

This chapter is a mere sampling of what the Camino has to offer and can't possibly go into the kind of detail needed to tackle the full distance. For comprehensive information, see the boxed text, above, on Camino books, or the websites listed in the Information section, opposite.

When to Go

People walk and cycle the Camino year-round. In May and June the wildflowers are glorious and the endless fields of cereals turn from green to toasty gold, making the landscapes a huge draw. July and August bring crowds of summer holidaymakers and scorching heat, especially through Castilla y León. September is less crowded and the weather is generally pleasant. From November to May there are fewer people on the road as the season can bring snow, rain and bitter winds. Santiago's feast day, 25 July, is a popular time to converge on the city.

Take a virtual tour of one of the Camino's many magnificent cathedrals. The website http://santiago-today.com offers a downloadable audioguide of the Santiago cathedral.

Getting There & Around

The Camino Francés has no fixed starting point, which means you can pick up the trail anywhere you choose. See city sections in the Basque Country, Navarra & La Rioja, Castilla y León and Galicia chapters for transport details. Covering the entire route by public transport is difficult, unless you are simply travelling from one major town to the next and skipping the smaller villages.

TOP DAY WALKS ALONG THE CAMINO FRANCÉS

- Forests and family-friendly: Puerto de Ibañeta to Espinal (below)
- For solitude: Rabé de las Calzadas to Hontanas (p124)
- Views and inspiration: Rabanal del Camino to Molinaseca (p125)
- For a challenge: Herrerías to O Cebreiro (p126)
- Landscape and villages: Sarria to Portomarín (p127)

CAMINO FRANCÉS

Outlined below are the major stages and highlights of the main route, the Camino Francés. Each stage can take as long as you like but we've suggested the best day walk for each section, which you'll see outlined in the sidebars as you read. Specific information on the major towns in each of these regions is found in the corresponding chapters.

Roncesvalles to Pamplona

Just north of Roncesvalles at Puerto de Ibañeta, the Camino Francés dramatically enters Spain at the same Pyrenean pass that was immortalised in the 12th-century French epic poem *Song of Roland* and that Napoleon used to launch his 1802 occupation of Spain. Dominated by its great, imposing abbey, and embraced by soaring beech forest and green pastures dotted with sheep, Roncesvalles admirably sets the tone for this extraordinary route. Inside the heavily restored 13th-century Gothic church, you'll find the first statue of Santiago dressed as a pilgrim (with scallop shells and staff), and a finely sculpted 14th-century silver-encased Virgin and child.

DAY WALK

Summary Enchanting beech forest, village and farmland walk steeped in medieval history. Good for families.

Start Puerto de Ibañeta

Finish Espinal

Distance 8.4km

Duration 2.5 hours

Difficulty Easy

The Camino trail traverses dense mixed forests, rural farmland and picturesque villages (especially Burguete and Espinal). Three-storey whitewashed houses with huge ashlar stone corners, brightly coloured shutters and steep peaked roofs (for the winter snows) line the undulating road.

Pamplona became an official stop along the Camino in the 11th-century, cementing its prosperity. Just inside the cathedral's bland neoclassical facade are the pure, soaring lines of the 14th-century Gothic interior. The 15th-century alabaster tombs of Pamplona's 1423 uniter, the Navarran king Carlos III El Noble and his wife, Doña Leonor, are particularly fine.

Pamplona to Logroño

Heading west out of Pamplona via Zariquiegui, the Sierra del Perdón, with its long line of electricity-producing windmills, looms ahead. The sierra's pass reveals a bird's-eye-view of the long valley leading to Puente la Reina, where the Camino Aragonés, coming from the east, joins up with the Camino Francés. Nestled below in the patchwork quilt of wheat, white asparagus, grapes and olive trees, Eunate is a stunning 12th-century, octagonal chapel silently reigning over a desolate wheat field. Of probable Templar origin, the chapel once served as a pilgrim's graveyard.

DAY WALK

Summary Hilly walk with diverse agricultural crops, gorgeous spring flowers and quiet villages. Detour to the Romanesque Eunate chapel. Bring a walking stick.

Start Zariquiegui

Finish Puente la Reina

Distance 15km

Duration Five hours

Difficulty Medium to Hard

The multistorey houses along Puente la Reina's main street have enormous wooden doors and finely carved eaves, lining the way to the town's striking 11th-century bridge. The diamond-shaped piers and hollows in the bridge's arches help reduce water resistance when the Río Arga rises during floods.

You'll find unusual Mudéjar-influenced Romanesque doorways, all with lobed arches, complicated knots and fascinating sculpture, in Puente la Reina's Iglesia de Santiago, in picturesque hilltop Cirauqui's Iglesia de San Román, and in Estella's Iglesia de San Pedro de la Rúa. In spring and early summer enormous roses, geraniums and grapevines blanket the houses in these villages.

Estella contains exceptional monumental Romanesque architecture: the outstanding portal of the Iglesia de San Miguel; the cloister of the Iglesia de San Pedro de la Rúa; and the Palacio de los Reyes de Navarra. On the Palacio, look for the vices of arrogance (a donkey playing a harp while a dog listens), lust (snakes sucking on the breasts of a woman) and avarice (naked people with money bags around their necks) high up on the street-corner capital.

Outside Estella, at the Bodega de Irache, the winery owners tempt virtuous pilgrims with a free wine and water fountain. Both are also sold cheap in an adjacent vending machine! Evergreen oaks and wine groves fill undulating landscapes until a long, barren stretch leads through the sleepy towns of Los Arcos, Sansol and Torres del Río. In hillside Torres you'll find another remarkably intact eight-sided Romanesque chapel, the Iglesia del Santo Sepulcro. To see inside, which is complete with a rare 13th-century Christ figure (crucified with four nails), it's necessary to locate the local key lady. There's a sign on the door indicating the woman's address, the hours of opening and requested donation.

Logroño to Burgos

The Camino heads through rolling, expansive stretches of Riojan wine and wheat fields, avoiding looming mountains to the south and north. At first urban and open, the constantly changing trail becomes rugged and wooded, eventually transforming into high, open tableland. Much of the area's surprisingly red earth holds the secret to some of Spain's finest red wines. In September the vineyards paralleling the Camino burst with huge bunches of rich red Garnacha and Tempranillo grapes.

The great Río Ebro marks the entrance (once a major obstacle for pilgrims) to Logroño and explains its wealth and size. The dour Gothic Iglesia de Santiago houses a large Renaissance altarpiece depicting unusual scenes from the saint's life, including run-ins with the wicked necromancer Hermogenes. The facade's odd 17th-century Santiago Matamoros image appears to be a musketeer cutting Mt Rushmore–style heads. Michelangelo's crucifixion painting behind the main altar in the Catedral de Santa María de La Redonda is a must-see.

DAY WALK

Summary Challenging ascent, wooded trails and quiet hills lead to the remote Romanesque monastery. Take plenty of water and a walking stick.

Start Villafranca Montes de Oca

Finish Monasterio de San Juan de Ortega

Distance 12.5km

Duration Four hours

Difficulty Medium to hard

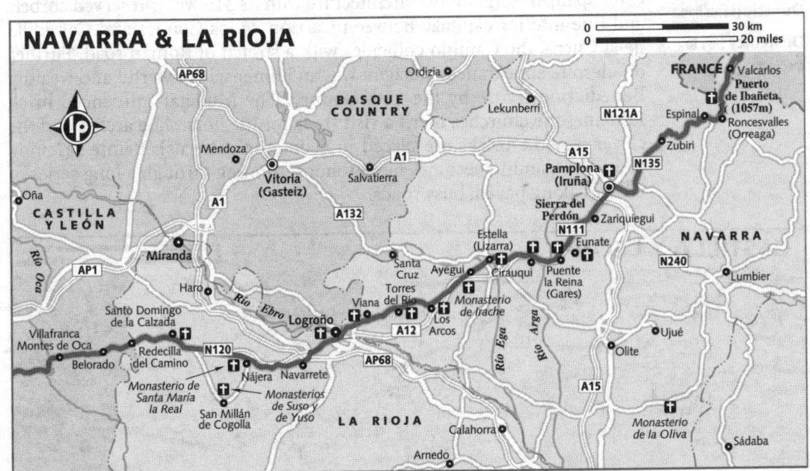

Nájera literally grew out of the town's red cliff wall when 11th-century king Ramiro discovered a miraculous statue of the Virgin in one of the cliff's caves. He built the Monasterio de Santa María la Real around it and Nájera became Navarra's splendiferous capital. Look for the fine, flamboyant Gothic tombs of Navarra's early nobility.

Ultreya, a popular Camino word of cheer, comes from the chorus of the oldest known Santiago pilgrim song 'Dum Pater Familias'. Discovered as sheet music stuffed into the Liber Sancti Jacobi, the word translates as 'onward ho' or 'go forward with courage'.

Santo Domingo de la Calzada is one of the road's most captivating places. It is named for its energetic 11th-century founder, Santo Domingo, who cleared forest, built roadways, a bridge, a pilgrim's hospice, and a church, and who performed many wondrous miracles depicted masterfully in Hispano-Flemish paintings in the cathedral.

After entering Castilla y León province, the Camino climbs through the open scrub (spring brings abundant purple heather) and dense woods (first Pyrenean oak and then plantation pine) of the Montes de Oca, once a thieves' haven, to the isolated Romanesque church and monastery at San Juan de Ortega. At every vernal and autumnal equinox a shaft of light hits a Romanesque capital depicting the Annunciation, drawing thousands of visitors.

Burgos overwhelms with its art and architectural riches. Not to be missed is the 13th-century Gothic cathedral, with its three eight-pointed-star vaults magnificently illuminating the main aisle and two chapels.

Burgos to León

There's a dramatic visual shift after Burgos. For the next 200km across Burgos, Palencia and (most of) León provinces, seas of wheat and other cereals dominate the horizon in this area known as the *meseta* (the high tableland of central Spain). The *meseta* is not flat. Villages are set low in long valleys (intermittently bisected by small, poplar-lined rivers), which rise up to the high, barren plains. There are large limestone rocks everywhere (pilgrims frequently pile up these white stones alongside the trails in eerie, large cairns). People usually either love or hate this section of open, exposed territory where trees and lonely adobe villages are few and far between. Flocks of sheep led by solitary shepherds are a common sight in the stretch between Rabé de las Calzadas and Sahagún.

DAY WALK

Summary Best in spring, this rolling *meseta* (tableland) walk brings solitude amid the wheat, allowing you to appreciate the region's lonely landscapes and villages.

Start Rabé de las Calzadas

Finish Hontanas

Distance 18.8km

Duration Five hours

Difficulty Easy to medium

Rising majestically from the valley floor, the crumbling ruins of Castrojeriz' castle dominate the town where four large churches attest to more prosperous times. In Frómista, the Iglesia de San Martín is one of the jewels of early Spanish Romanesque architecture with its 315 well-preserved corbels and fine interior capitals. Between Carrión de los Condes and Calzadilla de la Cueza, the Camino coincides with a stretch of Roman road. Further on, despite appearances Sahagún was an immensely powerful and wealthy Benedictine centre by the 12th century. The Mudéjar-influenced brick Romanesque churches merit a visit (look for the horseshoe arches and the clever way the bricks are placed in geometric patterns). Before reaching León, the Camino becomes monotonous, running through a long series of villages along paved, busy roads.

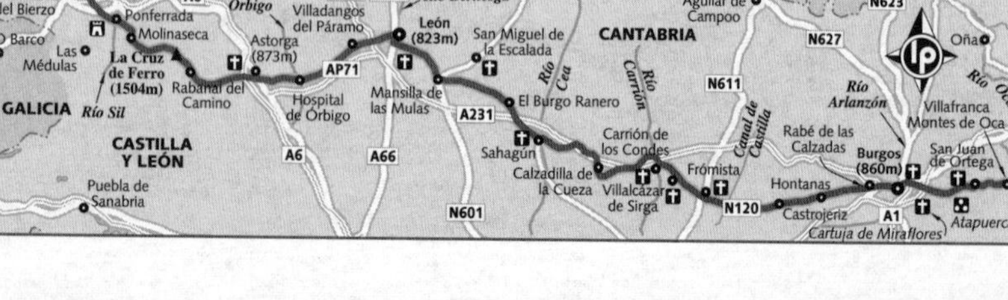

CASTILLA Y LEÓN

THE PILGRIM HELPER

John, a 68-year-old retired Englishman, has spent seven years travelling along the Camino Francés in his campervan, helping hundreds of pilgrims on their way to Compostela. But how did a former theatre and TV stage manager get into this?

Tell me about your own pilgrimage... I first went to the Camino as a pilgrim in the spring of 2001. I wanted to walk and reflect in quiet peaceful surroundings because I was grieving for the death of a loved one. Long before I reached Santiago, I had learned to accept and reconcile myself to the fate of the one whose life was cut short. Then I started noticing and thinking about the problems that many of the other pilgrims were suffering as they walked. I wanted to help them if I could.

How did this lead to the campervan? There are some bleak, barren stretches of the Camino Francés… So I began to think 'Why don't I try to help?' I had plenty of free time on my hands. I speak five European languages. I know something about how to give first aid. So I decided that a rescue vehicle was needed, and I went and bought a campervan! Now I spend a good part of each summer, parked for up to eight hours each day, in the middle of a lonely stretch. I offer first aid… But on very hot days what most of the pilgrims ask for is only cool drinking water…up to 500 pilgrims pass by between early morning and midafternoon.

Why do you do this? I have a lot of fun, and I get a lot of satisfaction doing this voluntary unpaid work. I have made a lot of friends and I intend to continue for many years to come.

Why do you think many people walk to Santiago today? My impression is that a very large proportion have suddenly been confronted with a grave problem with home, work, family, career, their physical health or love life… and they are so overwhelmed by their everyday preoccupations that they don't know what to do about it. Walking the Camino is a unique kind of therapy. I call it 'Self-administered Ambulatory Psychotherapy'. Troubled minds heal themselves – by walking the Camino de Santiago.

Considered to be the Sistine Chapel of Romanesque painting, the royal pantheon in León's Iglesia de San Isidoro contains magnificently preserved 11th-century frescoes depicting the most important scenes from Christ's life. Also sublime, the city's Gothic cathedral boasts nearly 1800 sq metres of stained-glass windows dating from the 13th to the 19th centuries, making them the best collection in Europe after Chartres in France.

León to Villafranca del Bierzo

Hospital de Órbigo has an impressive medieval bridge and is famed for its association with the outlandish chivalry of a 15th-century knight, Don Suero de Quiñones. In one of Europe's last grand tournaments, for a month he jousted with all comers, breaking 300 lances in order to free himself from his self-imposed 'prison' (an iron collar he wore around his neck, symbolic of the unrequited love that bound him). After Hospital de Órbigo, the Camino runs headlong into the western end of the Cordillera Cantábrica. Gateway to the mountain villages (which are collectively known as the Maragatería), Astorga has good Roman ruins, and an excellent Camino museum inside Gaudí's fantastical neo-Gothic Palacio Episcopal.

From Astorga the Camino progressively ascends through open scrub hills (covered with aromatic lavender and thyme in spring) and small villages nearly abandoned before the pilgrimage's revitalisation in the early 1990s. At this point you're once more amid wood and stone houses, these ones sporting vibrant blue, green and red shutters. A favourite stopover, Rabanal del Camino even has a tiny Benedictine monastery founded in 2001. The Camino's high point (in more ways than one) is La Cruz de Ferro (1504m); this tiny iron cross is lodged in a long wooden pole set into an ancient pile of rocks. Pilgrims leave stones – sometimes brought from home and

DAY WALK

Summary Reach La Cruz de Ferro, enjoy the high ridge's impressive views and descend to picturesque, riverside Molinaseca. Bring a walking stick for the long, tough descent.

Start Rabanal del Camino

Finish Molinaseca

Distance 24.5km

Duration Seven hours

Difficulty Hard

Peregrino means 'pilgrim' in Spanish and is often one of the first words learned on the Camino.

sometimes gathered a few yards away – on this pile, and also leave behind personal items of every sort: photos, bandanas, braids of hair, cigarette lighters, messages etc.

Coasting along the high hills, the trail offers spectacular views of the expansive, fertile El Bierzo valley, surrounded entirely by mountains, before making a long, steep descent to Molinaseca. The Camino cuts straight across the industrialised valley, through the large city of Ponferrada, most famous for its impressive castle, and a series of unmemorable towns to its western limit at Villafranca del Bierzo.

At Villafranca's Romanesque Iglesia de Santiago, pilgrims too ill to go further could once upon a time receive pardon at the Puerta del Perdón (the church's north door), just as if they had reached Santiago.

Villafranca del Bierzo to Sarria

Flanked by steep wooded hills, the long Valcarce river valley leads to Herrerías, from where the Camino abruptly rises to the O Cebreiro pass and village. Nine *pallozas* (circular, thatched-roof dwellings used since pre-Roman times) and adjacent stone houses (nearly every second one is a bar or hostel) make up this singular village. Famous not only for attracting terrible weather, for the foundation of a monastery here in 836, and as the legendary locale of the Holy Grail, O Cebreiro is also the confirmed centre of a 14th-century miracle in which the host and wine literally turned into the flesh and blood of Christ.

In Galicia everything changes: the area is permanently green and hilly; villages and hamlets abound; the grand monuments disappear and are replaced by small country churches, beautiful *cruceiros* (stone crosses), and *hórreos* (traditional stone grain stores); the houses are all stone and their roofs are all slate; and the rural people speak Galego. Throughout Lugo province emerald pastures, rushing clear streams and old-growth oak and chestnut stands embrace the trail. If you take a sneaky peek through barn doors you'll see cobwebbed remnants of Galicia's rural heritage and its late move towards mechanisation, such as wooden ploughs and carts. Don't be surprised to see wizened elderly folk (the women dressed in black) carrying huge scythes to the field or trundling high wheelbarrow-loads of hay, greens or potatoes.

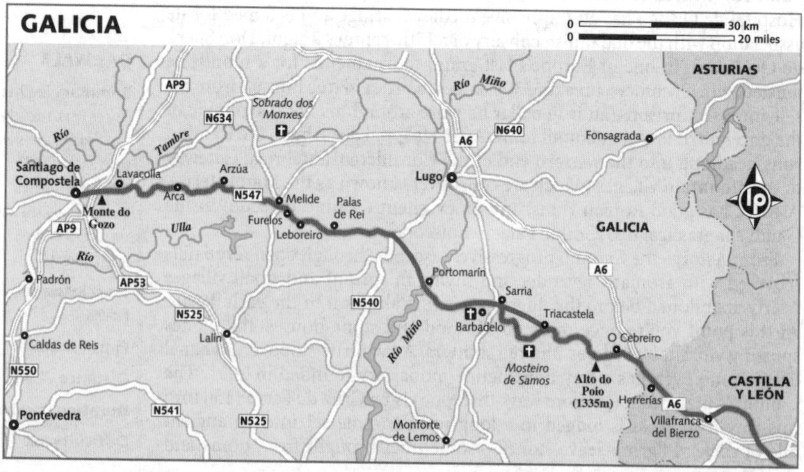

DAY WALK

Summary Exhilarating ascent, offering great views, through chestnut and oak woods, villages and then open hills to O Cebreiro. Beware: weather can vary from bottom to top.

Start Herrerías

Finish O Cebreiro

Distance 8.4km

Duration 3.5 hours

Difficulty Medium

TO THE END OF THE WORLD

Some medieval pilgrims continued trekking from Santiago to the end of the known world, Fisterra (Finisterre in Spanish; p582). They still do today, but most take the bus. Off the end of Fisterra's lighthouse, pilgrims burn stinking bits of clothing while watching the sun set over the endless blue abyss. Santiago's city tourism office runs day tours to Fisterra, which can be booked online (www.santiagoreservas.com).

In Triacastela the Camino diverges, with both paths reuniting in Sarria. Going via Samos you'll see the grand Benedictine Mosteiro de Samos, founded in the 6th century. It has two lovely cloisters (one with odd, busty mermaids and the other filled with roses); an imposing 18th-century church; and four walls of murals detailing St Benedict's life painted after a horrendous 1950 accident in which the monastery's still exploded, burning everything (including most of the library) except for the church and sacristy.

Sarria to Melide

People who want to undertake the last 100km usually start in Sarria, which is built on a hill topped by a crumbling castle. The Camino winds through village after hamlet after village (such as Barbadelo, with its well-preserved Romanesque church); through forest and field, divided by every imaginable type of stone fence; and then steeply descends to Portomarín, set on a hill above the Río Miño. Flooded in the 1960s to make way for a hydroelectric plant further downriver, Portomarín was re-established uphill and its key buildings, such as the fortresslike Romanesque Iglesia de San Juan, were moved stone by stone to the new town. Little attracts one's attention en route to or in Palas de Rei. But from Palas to Melide there are lovely rural lanes, and the villages of Leboreiro and Furelos are particularly well preserved.

In Melide, you'll find Galicia's oldest *cruceiro* along the main drag, excellent *pulpo* (octopus) prepared in huge copper vats, and a good ethnographic museum in the small historical quarter. The museum covers the area's pre-Roman and Roman history as well as local trades practised for centuries but lost in the last 50 years.

DAY WALK

Summary Hilly with beautiful rural lanes lined with ivy- and fern-covered stone walls, granite villages; intimate view of Galicia's rural life and verdant countryside.

Start Sarria

Finish Portomarín

Distance 23km

Duration 6.5 hours

Difficulty Medium

Melide to Santiago de Compostela

Santiago's historical quarter starts at the Rúa de San Pedro and leads to the Porta do Camiño gateway. Millions have tread the pedestrian street's enormous granite slabs, hemmed in by impressive stone houses and churches, that soon reach the Catedral de Santiago de Compostela's northern facade. A few more steps down the tunnel staircase under the Archbishop's Palace (street musicians' favourite venue) and you reach the magnificent cathedral square, the Praza do Obradoiro. Pilgrims' most important rituals revolve around the 12th-century Pórtico de la Gloria at the cathedral's western end and the area behind the main altar, where pilgrims climb stairs to hug a Romanesque Santiago statue and then descend to the crypt to pay respect to the relics. A fitting end to the pilgrimage is witnessing the cathedral's big finale staged before Mass ends: the swinging of the mighty Botafumeiro incense burner (see the boxed text, p565).

DAY WALK

Summary The final steps to the cathedral through the historical quarter inevitably produce goosebumps.

Start Rúa de San Pedro

Finish Catedral de Santiago de Compostela, Praza do Obradoiro

Distance 500m

Duration 15 minutes

Difficulty Easy

OTHER CAMINOS DE SANTIAGO

Many alternative *caminos* lead pilgrims to Santiago. They too have yellow arrows (more sporadic), *refugios* (fewer) and important pilgrimage monuments, but lack the marvellous infrastructure and crowds of the Camino Francés.

A short detour north from Melide, the Cistercian monastery of Sobrado dos Monxes features an ornate Galician baroque facade. Though it fell into disrepair in the 19th century, the monastery has been restored and offers hospitality to pilgrims travelling the Camino Primitivo.

Historically, pilgrims coming via Toulouse in southern France crossed the Pyrenees at the Somport Pass (1632m) and took the Camino Aragonés through Jaca and Sangüesa to join the main route at Puente la Reina.

Crossing into Spain at Irún or sailing down to ports such as Santander, San Vicente de la Barquera and Avilés, pilgrims connected up with the Caminos del Norte, following the Basque, Cantabrian and Asturian coasts, and turned inland at any number of spots to join up with the Camino Francés. The oldest known pilgrimage route to Santiago, the Camino Primitivo, connected the Asturian city of Oviedo with Compostela.

The Ruta de la Plata brought pilgrims north from southern Spain via Seville, Zafra, Mérida, Cáceres, Salamanca and Zamora along old Roman trade roads. This *camino* either heads north to Astorga or enters Galicia via Puebla de Sanabria.

The Camino Portugués had inland and coastal versions and reached Galicia at Verín or Tui. British pilgrims popularised the Camino Inglés by sailing to the Galician ports of A Coruña and Ferrol then proceeding south on foot to Santiago de Compostela.

Madrid

No city on earth is more alive than Madrid, a beguiling place whose sheer energy carries a simple message: this city knows how to live. Madrid is cross between Penélope Cruz (beautiful and quintessentially Spanish), Madonna (sassy and getting better with age) and an ex-convent schoolgirl who grew up, got sophisticated but never forgot how to have a good time.

It's true Madrid doesn't have the immediate cachet of Paris, the monumental history of Rome or the reputation for cool of that other city up the road. But it's a city that becomes truly great once you're under its skin and get to know its *barrios* (districts). There you'll discover a diverse city whose contradictory impulses are legion, the perfect expression of Europe's most passionate country writ large.

This city has transformed itself into Spain's premier style centre and its calling cards are many: astonishing art galleries; relentless nightlife; an exceptional live music scene; a feast of fine restaurants and tapas bars; and a population that's mastered the art of the good life. It's not that other cities don't have these things. It's just that Madrid has all of them in bucket-loads.

HIGHLIGHTS

- Watch the masterpieces of Velázquez and Goya leap off the canvas at the world-famous **Museo del Prado** (p153)
- Search for treasure in the Sunday **El Rastro flea market** (p151) then join the crowds in the **Parque del Buen Retiro** (p156)
- Soak up the buzz with a *caña* (small beer) or glass of Spanish wine on **Plaza de Santa Ana** (p152)
- Go on a **tapas crawl** (p182) in the medieval *barrio* of La Latina
- Immerse yourself in Madrid's extraordinary **live music scene** (p191)
- Make a sporting pilgrimage to see the stars of Real Madrid play at **El Estadio Santiago Bernabéu** (p193)
- Enjoy some of the friendliest bars in Spain in **Huertas** (p185) or **Malasaña** (p187)
- Soak up the glamour and spend your hard-earned euros in the exclusive *barrio* of **Salamanca** (p158)
- Feast on roast suckling pig at **Café de la Iberia** (p203) in Chinchón

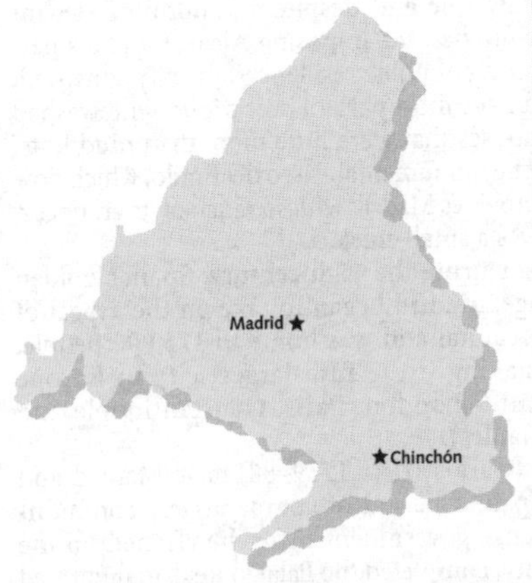

AREA: 505 SQ KM (MADRID)	AVE SUMMER TEMP: HIGH 32°C, LOW 16°C (MADRID)	POP: 3.1 MILLION (MADRID)

HISTORY

When Iberia's Christians began the Reconquista (Reconquest) – the centuries-long campaign by Christian forces to reclaim the peninsula – the Muslims of Al-Andalus constructed a chain of fortified positions through the heart of Iberia. One of these was built by Muhammad I, emir of Córdoba, in 854, on the site of what would become Madrid. The name they gave to the new settlement was Mayrit (or Magerit), which comes from the Arabic word *majira*, meaning water channel.

A Worthy Capital?

Madrid's strategic location in the centre of the peninsula saw the city change hands repeatedly, but it was not until 1309 that the travelling Cortes (royal court and parliament) sat in Madrid for the first time. Despite the growing royal attention, medieval Madrid remained dirt-poor and small-scale: 'in Madrid there is nothing except what you bring with you,' observed one 15th-century writer. It simply bore no comparison with other major Spanish, let alone European, cities.

By the time Felipe II ascended the Spanish throne in 1556, Madrid was surrounded by walls that boasted 130 towers and six stone gates, but these fortifications were largely built of mud and designed more to impress than provide any meaningful defence of the city. Madrid was nonetheless chosen by Felipe II as the capital of Spain in 1561.

Madrid took centuries to grow into its new role and despite a handful of elegant churches, the imposing Alcázar and a smattering of noble residences, the city consisted, for the most part, of precarious whitewashed houses that were little more than mud huts. The monumental Paseo del Prado, which now provides Madrid with so much of its grandeur, was a small creek.

During the 17th century, Spain's golden age, Madrid began to take on the aspect of a capital and was home to 175,000 people, making it the fifth-largest city in Europe (after London, Paris, Constantinople and Naples).

Carlos III (r 1759–88) gave Madrid and Spain a period of comparatively commonsense government. After he cleaned up the city, completed the Palacio Real, inaugurated the Real Jardín Botánico and carried out numerous other public works, he became known as the best 'mayor' Madrid had ever had.

Madrileños (Madrid residents) didn't take kindly to Napoleon's invasion and subsequent occupation of Spain in 1805 and, on 2 May 1808, they attacked French troops around the Palacio Real and what is now Plaza del Dos de Mayo. The ill-fated rebellion was quickly put down by Murat, Napoleon's brother-in-law and the most powerful of his military leaders.

Wars, Franco & Terrorism

Turmoil continued to stalk the Spanish capital. The upheaval of the 19th-century Carlist Wars was followed by a two-and-a-half-year siege of Madrid by Franco's Nationalist forces from 1936 to 1939, during which the city was shelled regularly from Casa de Campo and Gran Vía became known as 'Howitzer Alley'.

After Franco's death in 1975 and the country's subsequent transition to democracy, Madrid became an icon for the new Spain as the city's young people – under the mayoral rule of Enrique Tierno Galván, a popular socialist professor – unleashed a flood of pent-up energy. This took its most colourful form in the years of *la movida* (see the boxed text, opposite), the endless party that swept up the city in a frenzy of creativity and open-minded freedom that has in some ways yet to abate.

On 11 March 2004, just three days before the country was due to vote in national elections, Madrid was rocked by 10 bombs on four rush-hour commuter trains heading into the capital's Atocha station. When the dust cleared, 191 people had died and 1755 were wounded, many seriously. Madrid was in shock and, for 24 hours at least, this most clamorous of cities fell silent. Then, 36 hours after the attacks, more than three million *madrileños* streamed onto the streets to protest against the bombings, making it the largest demonstration in the city's history. Although deeply traumatised, Madrid's mass act of defiance and pride began the process of healing. Visit Madrid today and you'll find a city that has resolutely returned to normal.

On 20 August 2008, however, the city was again shaken by tragedy, after a Spanair flight from Madrid to the Canary Islands crashed upon take-off. The crash killed 153 people and plunged the city into mourning.

ORIENTATION

In Spain, all roads lead to Madrid's Plaza de la Puerta del Sol, kilometre zero, the physical and emotional heart of the city. Radiating out from this busy plaza are roads – Calle Mayor, Calle del Arenal, Calle de Preciados, Calle de la Montera, Carrera de San Jerónimo and Calle de Alcalá – that stretch deep into the city, as well as a host of metro lines and bus routes.

South of the Puerta del Sol is the oldest part of the city, with Plaza Mayor and Los Austrias to the southwest and the busy streets of the Huertas *barrio* to the southeast. Also to the south lie La Latina and Lavapiés.

North of Plaza de la Puerta del Sol is a modern shopping district and, beyond that, the east–west thoroughfare Gran Vía and the gay *barrio* Chueca, gritty Malasaña, then Chamberí and Argüelles. East of the Puerta del Sol, across the Paseo del Prado and Paseo de los Recoletos, lie El Retiro park and Salamanca.

INFORMATION

Bookshops

The Museo del Prado, Centro de Arte Reina Sofía and Museo Thyssen-Bornemisza have excellent bookshops for art lovers.

Altaïr (Map pp134-5; ☎ 91 543 53 00; www.altair.es in Spanish; Calle de Gaztambide 31; ⏲ 10am-2pm & 4.30-8.30pm Mon-Fri, 10.30am-2.30pm Sat; Ⓜ Argüelles) Cosy travel bookshop, with a range of maps, guides and travel literature.

Casa del Libro (Map pp142-3; ☎ 91 524 19 00; www.casadellibro.com in Spanish; Gran Vía 29; ⏲ 9.30am-9.30pm Mon-Sat, 11am-9pm Sun; Ⓜ Gran Vía) Spain's answer to Borders has a large foreign-language (including English) literature section on the ground floor at the back.

Cuesta de Moyano bookstalls (Map p145; Cuesta de Claudio Moyano; ⏲ 9am-dusk Mon-Sat, 9am-2pm Sun; Ⓜ Atocha) A row of 30-odd bookstalls bursting with secondhand books.

De Viaje (Map p140; ☎ 91 577 98 99; www.deviaje.com in Spanish; Calle de Serrano 41; ⏲ 10am-8.30pm Mon-Fri, 10.30am-2.30pm & 5-8pm Sat; Ⓜ Serrano) Madrid's largest travel bookshop, with travel agency, travel gear section and exhibitions.

J&J Books & Coffee (Map pp138-9; Calle del Espíritu Santo 47; ⏲ 10pm-10pm Mon-Thu, 10am-midnight Fri & Sat, 2-10pm Sun; Ⓜ Noviciado) They claim to have 150,000 (mostly English-language) books.

Pasajes Librería Internacional (Map pp138-9; ☎ 91 310 12 45; www.pasajeslibros.com; Calle de Génova 3; ⏲ 10am-8pm Mon-Fri, 10am-2pm Sat; Ⓜ Alonso Martínez) One of the best English-language bookshops in Madrid.

Petra's International Bookshop (Map pp142-3; ☎ 91 541 72 91; Calle de Campomanes 13; ⏲ 11am-9pm Mon-Sat; Ⓜ Santo Domingo) A lively expat community is drawn to this excellent (mostly secondhand) English-language bookshop.

LA MOVIDA MADRILEÑA

Anyone who went wild when they first moved out of their parents' house can identify with *la movida madrileña* (literally 'the Madrid scene'). After the long, dark years of dictatorship and conservative Catholicism, Spaniards, especially *madrileños,* emerged onto the streets in the late 1970s with all the zeal of ex-convent schoolgirls. Nothing was taboo as *madrileños* discovered the '60s, '70s and early '80s all at once. Drinking, drugs and sex suddenly were OK. All-night partying was the norm, cannabis was virtually legalised and the city howled.

La movida was presided over by Enrique Tierno Galván, an ageing former university professor who had been a leading opposition figure under Franco and was affectionately known throughout Spain as 'the old teacher'. A socialist, he became mayor of Madrid in 1979 and, for many, launched *la movida* by telling a public gathering '*a colocarse y ponerse al loro*', which loosely translates as 'get stoned and do what's cool'. Not surprisingly, he was Madrid's most popular mayor ever. When he died in 1986, a million *madrileños* turned out for his funeral.

But *la movida* was not just about rediscovering the Spanish art of *salir de copas* (going out to drink). It was also accompanied by an explosion of creativity among the country's musicians, designers and film-makers.

The most famous of these was film director Pedro Almodóvar. Still one of Europe's most creative directors, his riotously colourful films captured the spirit of *la movida,* featuring larger-than-life characters who pushed the limits of sex and drugs. When he wasn't making films, Almodóvar immersed himself in the spirit of *la movida,* doing drag acts in smoky bars. Among the other names from *la movida* that still resonate, the designer Agatha Ruiz de la Prada (p195) stands out. Start playing anything by Alaska, Los Rebeldes, Radio Futura or Nacha Pop and watch *madrileños'* eyes glaze over with nostalgia.

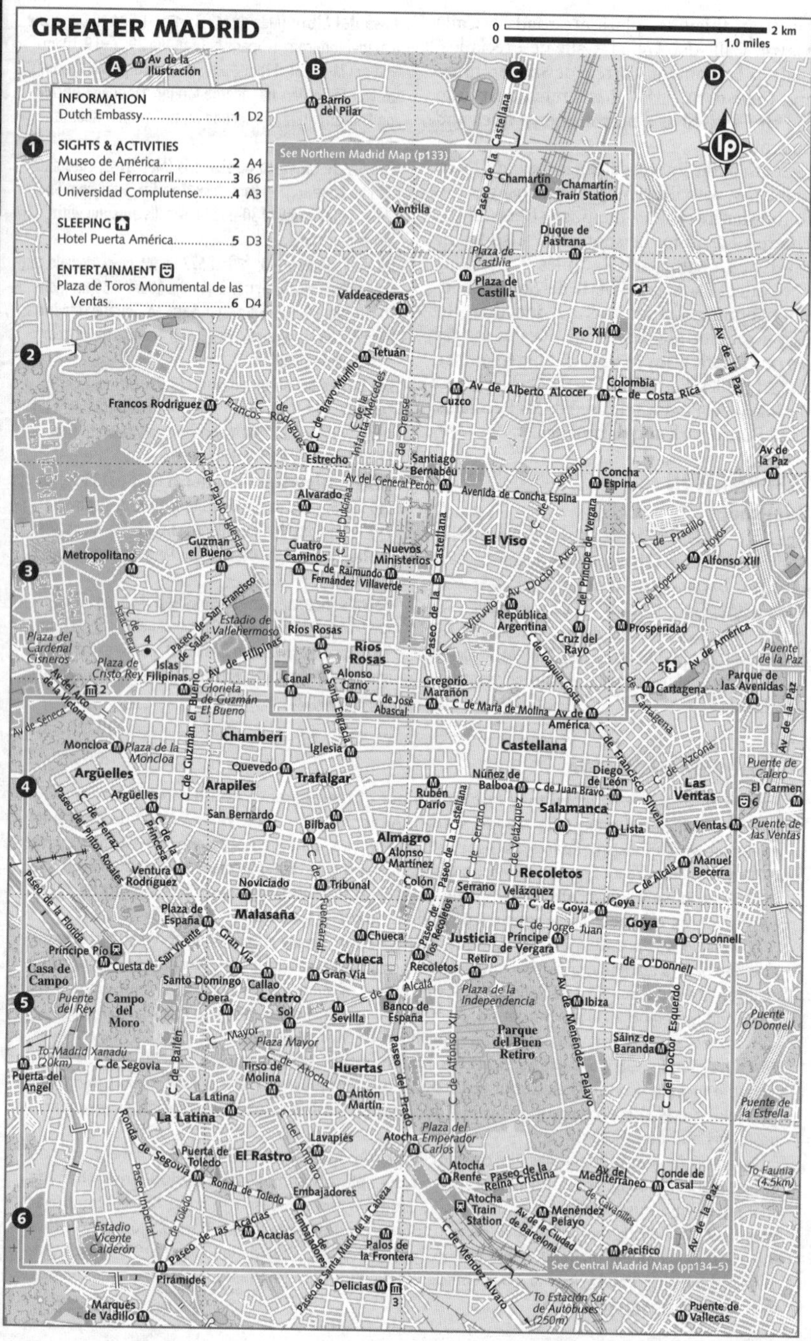
GREATER MADRID
0 2 km
0 1.0 miles
INFORMATION
Dutch Embassy 1 D2
SIGHTS & ACTIVITIES
Museo de América 2 A4
Museo del Ferrocarril 3 B6
Universidad Complutense 4 A3
SLEEPING
Hotel Puerta América 5 D3
ENTERTAINMENT
Plaza de Toros Monumental de las Ventas 6 D4
See Northern Madrid Map (p133)
See Central Madrid Map (pp134–5)
Av de la Ilustración
Barrio del Pilar
Paseo de la Castellana
Chamartín
Chamartín Train Station
Ventilla
Duque de Pastrana
Plaza de Castilla
Valdeacederas
Pío XII
Tetuán
Av de Alberto Alcocer
Cuzco
Colombia
C de Costa Rica
Av de la Paz
Francos Rodríguez
C de Francos Rodríguez
C de Bravo Murillo
C de la Infanta Mercedes
C de Orense
Estrecho
Santiago Bernabéu
Av del General Perón
Concha Espina
Avenida de Concha Espina
C de Serrano
Alvarado
C del Dulcinea
Av de Pablo Iglesias
Guzman el Bueno
Metropolitano
Cuatro Caminos
Nuevos Ministerios
El Viso
C de Pradillo
Alfonso XIII
C de López de Hoyos
C de Raimundo Fernández Villaverde
Av Doctor Arce
C del Príncipe de Vergara
República Argentina
Av de Vitruvio
Paseo de San Francisco de Sales
Estadio de Vallehermoso
C de Isaac Peral
Plaza del Cardenal Cisneros
Plaza de Cristo Rey
Islas Filipinas
Av de Filipinas
Ríos Rosas
C de Santa Engracia
Cruz del Rayo
Prosperidad
Av de América
Puente de la Paz
Av del Arco de la Victoria
Glorieta de Guzmán El Bueno
Canal
Alonso Cano
C de José Abascal
Gregorio Marañón
C de María de Molina
C de Joaquín Costa
Av de América
Cartagena
C de Cartagena
Parque de las Avenidas
Av de Séneca
Moncloa
Plaza de la Moncloa
Chamberí
Iglesia
Castellana
C de Francisco Silvela
C de Azcona
Puente de Calero
Argüelles
Quevedo
Trafalgar
Arapiles
Núñez de Balboa
C de Juan Bravo
Diego de León
Las Ventas
El Carmen
Paseo del Pintor Rosales
C de Ferraz
C de la Princesa
C de Guzmán el Bueno
San Bernardo
Rubén Darío
Salamanca
Lista
Ventas
Puente de las Ventas
Bilbao
Almagro
Alonso Martínez
C de Serrano
C de Velázquez
C de Alcalá
Manuel Becerra
Ventura Rodríguez
Noviciado
Tribunal
Colón
Recoletos
Serrano
Velázquez
C de Goya
Goya
Paseo de la Florida
Plaza de España
Malasaña
C de Fuencarral
C de Jorge Juan
Príncipe Pío
Chueca
Paseo de los Recoletos
Justicia
Príncipe de Vergara
O'Donnell
Casa de Campo
Cuesta de San Vicente
Gran Vía
Retiro
C de O'Donnell
Santo Domingo
Callao
Puente del Rey
Campo del Moro
Ópera
Centro
Sol
Sevilla
C de Alcalá
Banco de España
Plaza de la Independencia
Av de Menéndez Pelayo
Ibiza
Puente O'Donnell
C Mayor
Plaza Mayor
Parque del Buen Retiro
Sáinz de Baranda
C de Segovia
To Madrid Xanadú (20km)
Puerta del Ángel
C de Bailén
Tirso de Molina
C de Atocha
Huertas
Antón Martín
Paseo del Prado
C de Alfonso XII
C del Doctor Esquerdo
La Latina
Puente de la Estrella
Ronda de Segovia
C del Amparo
Lavapiés
Atocha
Plaza del Emperador Carlos V
Puerta de Toledo
El Rastro
Atocha Renfe
Paseo de la Reina Cristina
Av del Mediterráneo
Conde de Casal
To Faunia (4.5km)
Paseo Imperial
Ronda de Toledo
Embajadores
Atocha Train Station
C de Cavanilles
Menéndez Pelayo
Av de la Ciudad de Barcelona
C de Toledo
Paseo de las Acacias
Acacias
Paseo de Santa María de la Cabeza
Paseo de Embajadores
Palos de la Frontera
C de Méndez Álvaro
Pacífico
Estadio Vicente Calderón
Pirámides
Delicias
Marqués de Vadillo
To Estación Sur de Autobuses (250m)
Puente de Vallecas

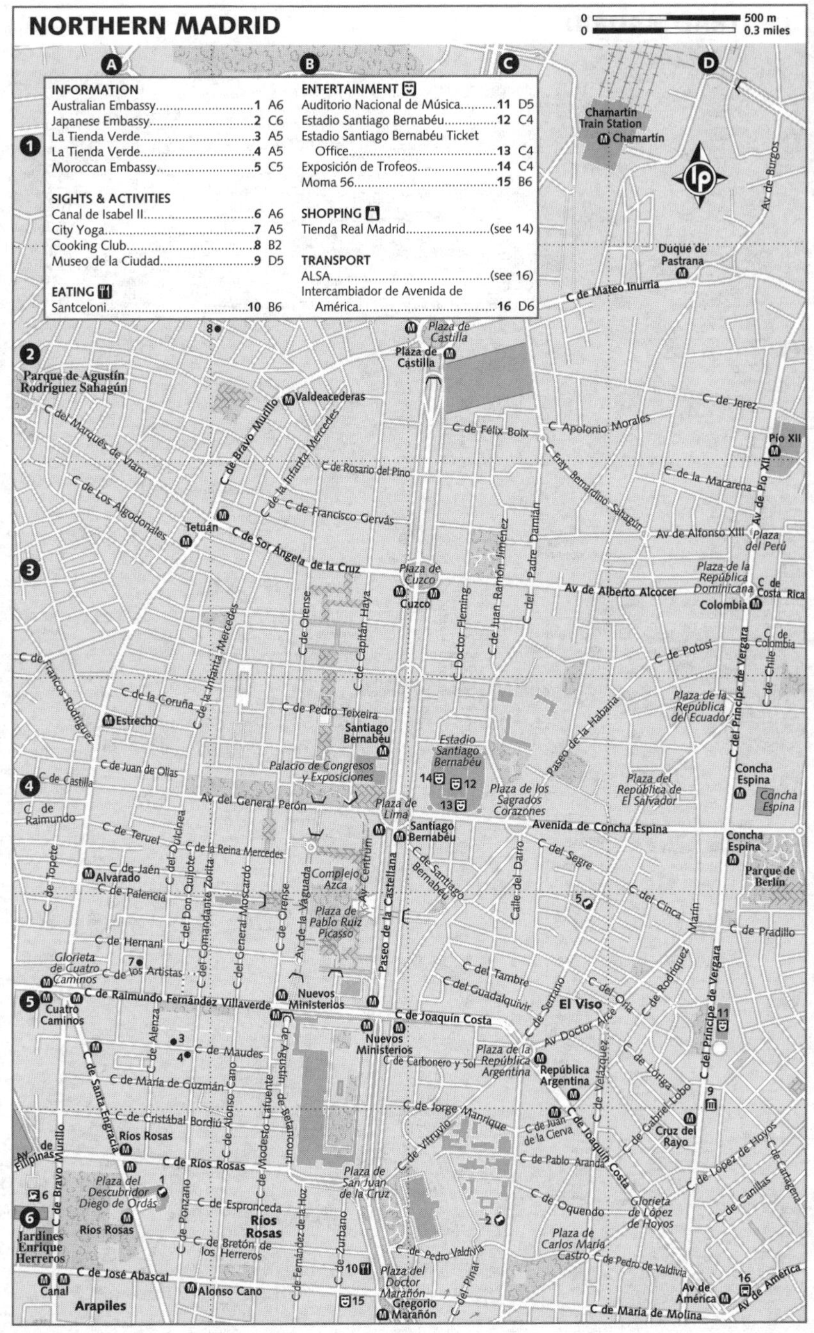
NORTHERN MADRID
0 500 m
0 0.3 miles
INFORMATION
Australian Embassy 1 A6
Japanese Embassy 2 C6
La Tienda Verde 3 A5
La Tienda Verde 4 A5
Moroccan Embassy 5 C5
SIGHTS & ACTIVITIES
Canal de Isabel II 6 A6
City Yoga 7 A5
Cooking Club 8 B2
Museo de la Ciudad 9 D5
EATING
Santceloni 10 B6
ENTERTAINMENT
Auditorio Nacional de Música 11 D5
Estadio Santiago Bernabéu 12 C4
Estadio Santiago Bernabéu Ticket Office 13 C4
Exposición de Trofeos 14 C4
Moma 56 15 B6
SHOPPING
Tienda Real Madrid (see 14)
TRANSPORT
ALSA (see 16)
Intercambiador de Avenida de América 16 D6
Chamartín Train Station
Chamartín
Av de Burgos
Duque de Pastrana
C de Mateo Inurria
Plaza de Castilla
Plaza de Castilla
Parque de Agustín Rodríguez Sahagún
Valdeacederas
C de Bravo Murillo
C de la Infanta Mercedes
C del Marqués de Viana
C de Rosario del Pino
C de Los Algodonales
C de Francisco Gervás
Tetuán
C de Sor Ángela de la Cruz
C de Jerez
C de Félix Boix
C Apolonio Morales
C Fray Bernardino Sahagún
C de la Macarena
Pío XII
Av de Pío XII
Av de Alfonso XIII
Plaza del Perú
C de Juan Ramón Jiménez
C del Padre Damián
Plaza de Cuzco
Cuzco
Av de Alberto Alcocer
Plaza de la República Dominicana
C de Costa Rica
Colombia
C de Orense
C de Capitán Haya
C Doctor Fleming
C de Colombia
C de Potosí
C de Francos Rodríguez
C de la Coruña
C de Pedro Teixeira
Estrecho
Santiago Bernabéu
Paseo de la Habana
Plaza de la República del Ecuador
C del Príncipe de Vergara
C de Chile
C de Juan de Olías
Palacio de Congresos y Exposiciones
Estadio Santiago Bernabéu
Plaza de los Sagrados Corazones
Plaza del República de El Salvador
Concha Espina
Concha Espina
C de Castilla
Av del General Perón
Plaza de Lima
C de Raimundo
C de Teruel
C de la Reina Mercedes
Santiago Bernabéu
Avenida de Concha Espina
C de Santiago Bernabéu
C del Segre
Parque de Berlín
C de Jaén
Alvarado
C de Palencia
C de Topete
C del Dulcinea
C del Don Quijote
C del Comandante Zorita
C del General Moscardó
Complejo Azca
Av de la Vaguada
Av Centrum
Plaza de Pablo Ruiz Picasso
Paseo de la Castellana
Calle del Darro
C del Cinca
Marín
C de Pradillo
C de Hernani
Glorieta de Cuatro Caminos
C de los Artistas
C del Tambre
C del Guadalquivir
C de Serrano
El Viso
C del Oria
C de Rodríguez
C de Raimundo Fernández Villaverde
Nuevos Ministerios
Cuatro Caminos
C de Joaquín Costa
Nuevos Ministerios
Av Doctor Arce
C de Alenza
C de Maudes
C de Agustín de Betancourt
C de Carbonero y Sol
Plaza de la República Argentina
República Argentina
C de Velázquez
C de Lóriga
C de Santa Engracia
C de María de Guzmán
C de Cristóbal Bordiú
C de Alonso Cano
C de Modesto Lafuente
C de Jorge Manrique
C de Vitruvio
C de Juan de la Cierva
C de Joaquín Costa
C de Gabriel Lobo
Cruz del Rayo
Ríos Rosas
Av de Filipinas
C de Bravo Murillo
C de Ríos Rosas
C de Pablo Aranda
C de López de Hoyos
C de Cartagena
Plaza del Descubridor Diego de Ordás
C de Espronceda
Plaza de San Juan de la Cruz
C de Oquendo
C de Canillas
Glorieta de López de Hoyos
Jardines Enrique Herreros
Ríos Rosas
C de Ponzano
Ríos Rosas
C de Bretón de los Herreros
C de Fernández de la Hoz
C de Zurbano
C de Pedro Valdivia
Plaza de Carlos María Castro
C de Pedro de Valdivia
C de José Abascal
Canal
Alonso Cano
Plaza del Doctor Marañón
C del Pinar
Av de América
Av de América
Arapiles
Gregorio Marañón
C de María de Molina

CENTRAL MADRID

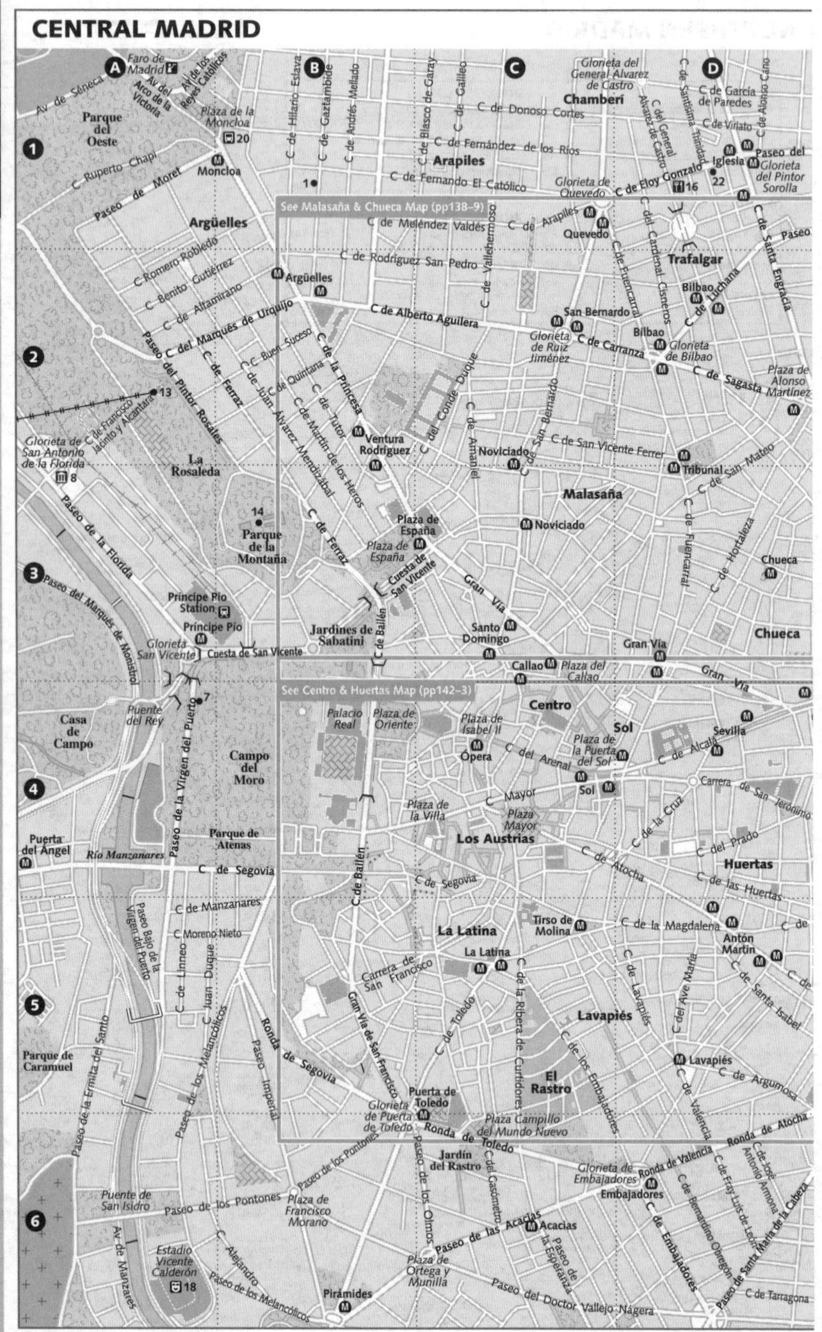

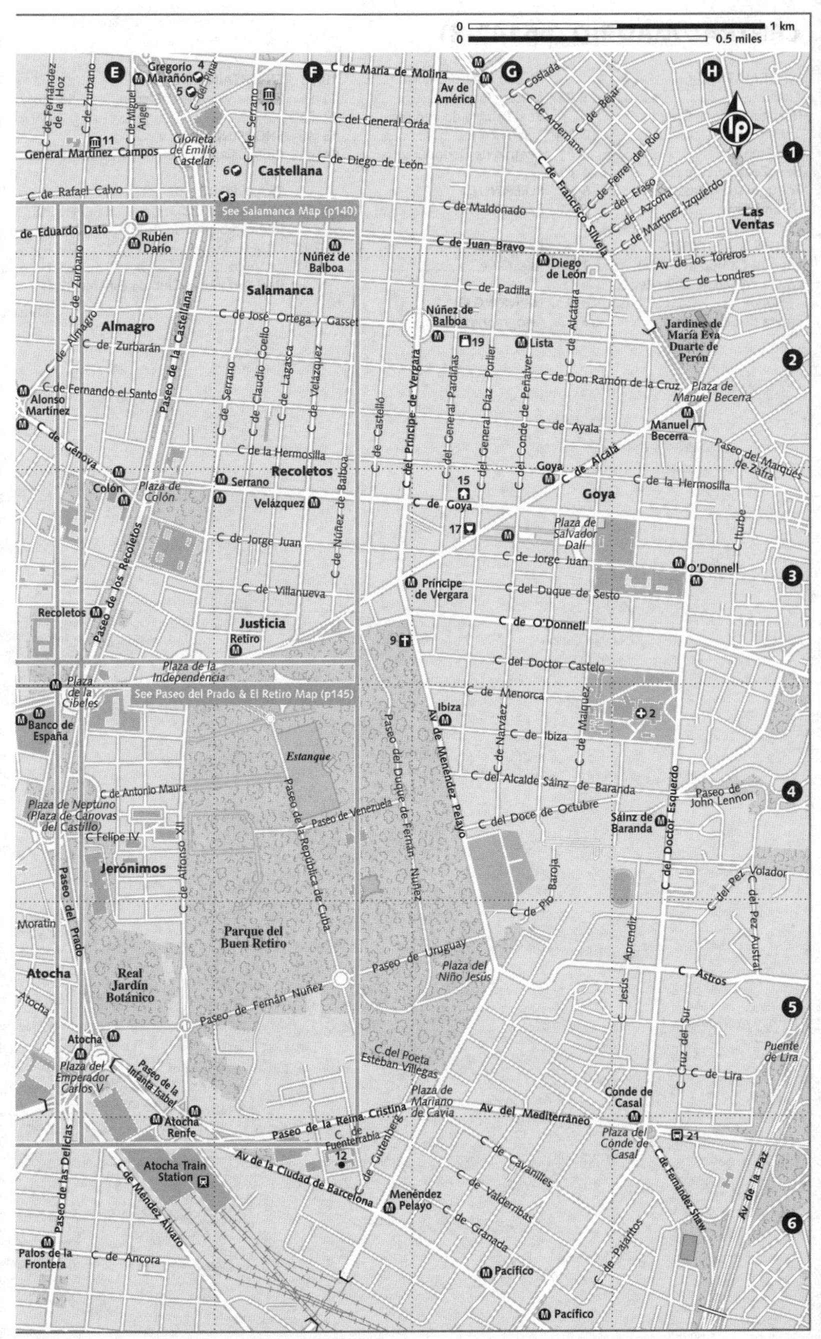
0 1 km
0 0.5 miles
E
F
G
H
1
2
3
4
5
6
Gregorio Marañón
C de Fernández de la Hoz
C de Zurbano
C de Miguel Ángel
C del Pinar
C de Serrano
C de María de Molina
Av de América
C Coslada
C de Béjar
C de Ardemans
C del General Oráa
General Martínez Campos
Glorieta de Emilio Castelar
C de Diego de León
Castellana
C de Francisco Silvela
C de Ferrer del Río
C del Eraso
C de Azcona
C de Martínez Izquierdo
C de Rafael Calvo
See Salamanca Map (p140)
C de Maldonado
Las Ventas
de Eduardo Dato
Rubén Darío
Núñez de Balboa
C de Juan Bravo
Diego de León
Av de los Toreros
C de Londres
C de Zurbano
Salamanca
C de Padilla
C de Almagro
Almagro
C de José Ortega y Gasset
Núñez de Balboa
Jardines de María Eva Duarte de Perón
C de Zurbarán
19
Lista
C de Alcántara
Paseo de la Castellana
C de Serrano
C de Claudio Coello
C de Lagasca
C de Velázquez
C de Castelló
C del Príncipe de Vergara
C del General Pardiñas
C del General Díaz Porlier
C del Conde de Peñalver
C de Don Ramón de la Cruz
Plaza de Manuel Becerra
Alonso Martínez
C de Fernando el Santo
C de Ayala
Manuel Becerra
C de Génova
C de la Hermosilla
Recoletos
Goya
C de Alcalá
Paseo del Marqués de Zafra
Colón
Plaza de Colón
Serrano
15
C de la Hermosilla
Velázquez
C de Goya
Goya
C de Núñez de Balboa
17
Plaza de Salvador Dalí
C de Jorge Juan
C de Jorge Juan
C Iturbe
Paseo de los Recoletos
O'Donnell
C de Villanueva
Príncipe de Vergara
C del Duque de Sesto
Recoletos
Justicia
C de O'Donnell
Retiro
9
C del Doctor Castelo
Plaza de la Independencia
Plaza de la Cibeles
See Paseo del Prado & El Retiro Map (p145)
C de Menorca
C de Máiquez
2
Banco de España
Ibiza
C de Narváez
C de Ibiza
Estanque
Paseo del Duque de Fernán Núñez
Av de Menéndez Pelayo
C de Antonio Maura
C del Alcalde Sáinz de Baranda
Paseo de John Lennon
Plaza de Neptuno (Plaza de Cánovas del Castillo)
Paseo de Venezuela
C del Doce de Octubre
Sáinz de Baranda
C Felipe IV
C de Alfonso XII
Paseo de la República de Cuba
C del Doctor Esquerdo
C del Pez Volador
Jerónimos
C del Pez Austral
Paseo del Prado
C de Pío Baroja
C Aprendiz
Moratín
Parque del Buen Retiro
Paseo de Uruguay
C Astros
Atocha
Real Jardín Botánico
Plaza del Niño Jesús
C Jesús
Atocha
Paseo de Fernán Núñez
Atocha
C del Poeta Esteban Villegas
Puente de Lira
Plaza del Emperador Carlos V
Paseo de la Infanta Isabel
C Cruz del Sur
C de Lira
Plaza de Mariano de Cavia
Conde de Casal
Atocha Renfe
Paseo de la Reina Cristina
Av del Mediterráneo
C de Fuenterrabía
Plaza del Conde de Casal
21
12
Paseo de las Delicias
Atocha Train Station
C de Gutenberg
C de Cavanilles
C de Fernández Shaw
Av de la Paz
C de Méndez Álvaro
Av de la Ciudad de Barcelona
Menéndez Pelayo
C de Valderribas
C de Granada
C de Pajaritos
Palos de la Frontera
C de Ancora
Pacífico
Pacífico

CENTRAL MADRID (pp142–3)

INFORMATION
Altaïr......1 B1
Hospital General Gregorio Marañón......2 H4
Irish Embassy......3 F1
New Zealand Embassy......4 E1
Portuguese Embassy......5 E1
US Embassy......6 F1

SIGHTS & ACTIVITIES
Entry to Campo del Moro......7 A4
Ermita de San Antonio de la Florida......8 A3
Ermita de San Isidro......9 F3
Museo Lázaro Galdiano......10 F1
Museo Sorolla......11 E1
Real Fábrica de Tapices......12 F6
Teleférico......13 A2
Templo de Debod......14 B3

SLEEPING
Bauzá......15 G3

EATING
Sagaretxe......16 D1

DRINKING
Geographic Club......17 G3

ENTERTAINMENT
Estadio Vicente Calderón......18 A6

SHOPPING
Oriol Balaguer......19 G2

TRANSPORT
Herranz......(see 20)
Intercambiador de Autobuses de Moncloa......20 B1
La Veloz......21 H6
Real Automóvil Club de España......22 D1

MALASAÑA & CHUECA (pp138–9)

INFORMATION

A Different Life **1** G5
Berkana **2** G5
Café Comercial .... (see 39)
Drop & Drag **3** G5
J&J Books & Coffee **4** D4
Pasajes Librería Internacional **5** H3
Servicio de Atención al Turista Extranjero **6** C6

SIGHTS & ACTIVITIES

Antiguo Cuartel del Conde Duque **7** C3
Casa de las Siete Chimeneas **8** G6
Museo Municipal **9** F4
Museo Municipal de Arte Contemporáneo de Madrid .... (see 7)
Palacio de Buenavista **10** H6
Parque Secreto **11** D2
Sociedad General de Autores y Editores **12** G4
Spa Relajarse **13** H4
Telefónica Building **14** F6

SLEEPING

Albergue Juvenil **15** F3
Hostal América **16** F6
Hostal Don Juan **17** F6
Hostal La Zona **18** E6
Hotel Abalú **19** D5
Hotel Óscar **20** G6

EATING

4 de Tapas **21** G6
A Dos Velas **22** E4
Bazaar **23** G6
Bocaito **24** G6
El Lateral **25** F5
Fresc Co **26** G3
La Isla del Tesoro **27** E3
La Musa **28** E3
La Taberna de San Bernardo **29** D3
Laydown Rest Club **30** C5
Nina **31** E3
Restaurante Momo **32** G6
Restaurantes La Giralda **33** F2
Ribeira Do Miño **34** F4

DRINKING

Antik Café **35** F6
Areia **36** G4
Café Acuarela **37** G5
Café Belén **38** G4
Café Comercial **39** F3
Café Pepe Botella **40** E4
El Jardín Secreto **41** B4
La Vía Láctea **42** E3
Mamá Inés **43** F6
Ojalá Awareness Club **44** E4
Stop Madrid **45** F6

ENTERTAINMENT

Café La Palma **46** D3
Cinesa Proyecciones **47** E1
Clamores **48** F2
Cool **49** C6
El Berlín Jazz Club .... (see 57)
El Junco Jazz Club **50** G4
Honky Tonk **51** G2
Kabokla **52** D4
La Enana Marrón **53** G4
La Fulanita de Tal **54** H5
Las Tablas **55** B5
Morocco **56** D5
Oba Oba **57** D6
Ohm **58** D6
Penta Bar **59** F4
Princesa **60** B4
Renoir **61** B4
Siroco **62** D3
Stromboli Café **63** G4
Sunrise **64** G6
Supersonic **65** B1
Tupperware **66** F4
Why Not? **67** G6

SHOPPING

Antigua Casa Talavera **68** C6
Mercado de Fuencarral **69** F5
Patrimonio Comunal Olivarero **70** G4
Poncelet **71** H4
Reserva y Cata **72** H5

TRANSPORT

Avis **73** C5
Europcar **74** C4
Hertz **75** B4
National/Atesa **76** C5
Pepecar **77** B5

MALASAÑA & CHUECA

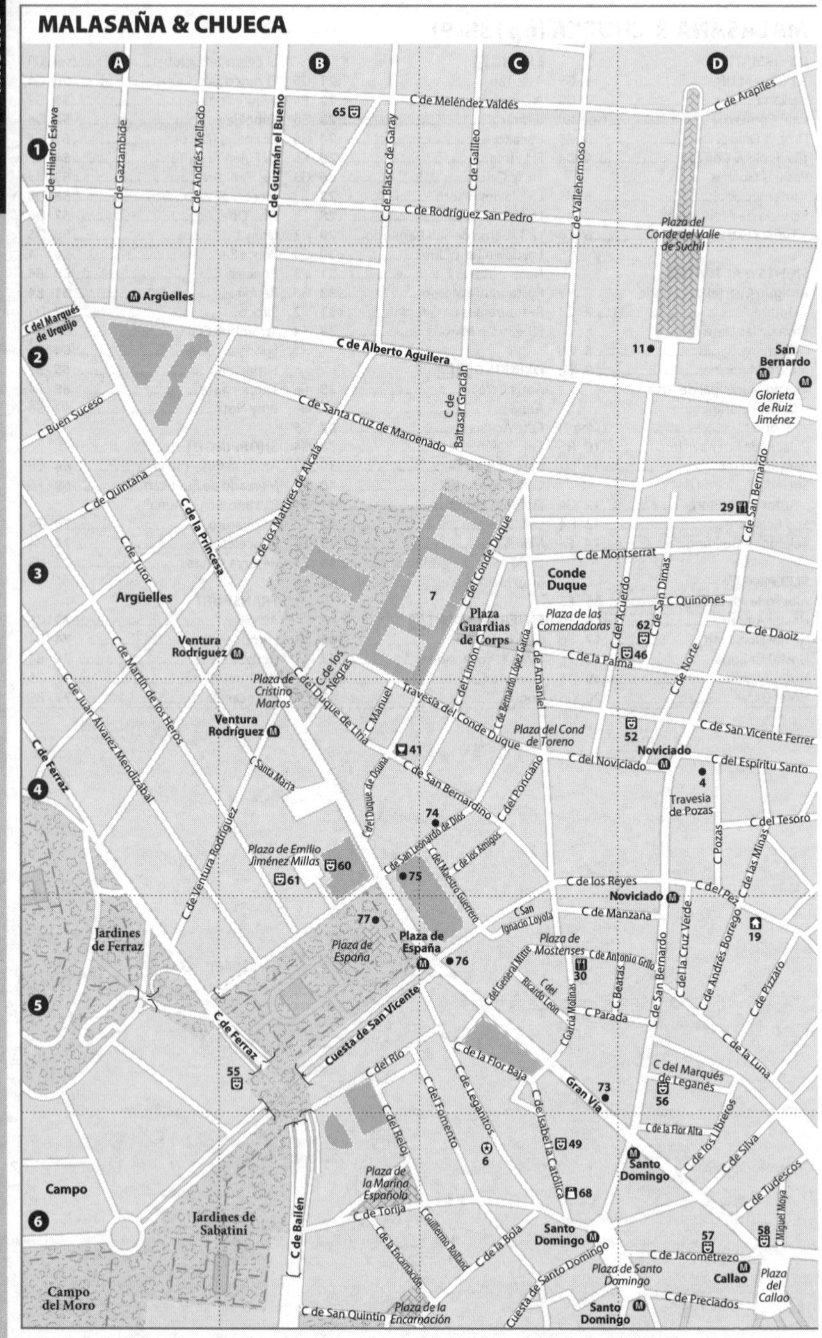

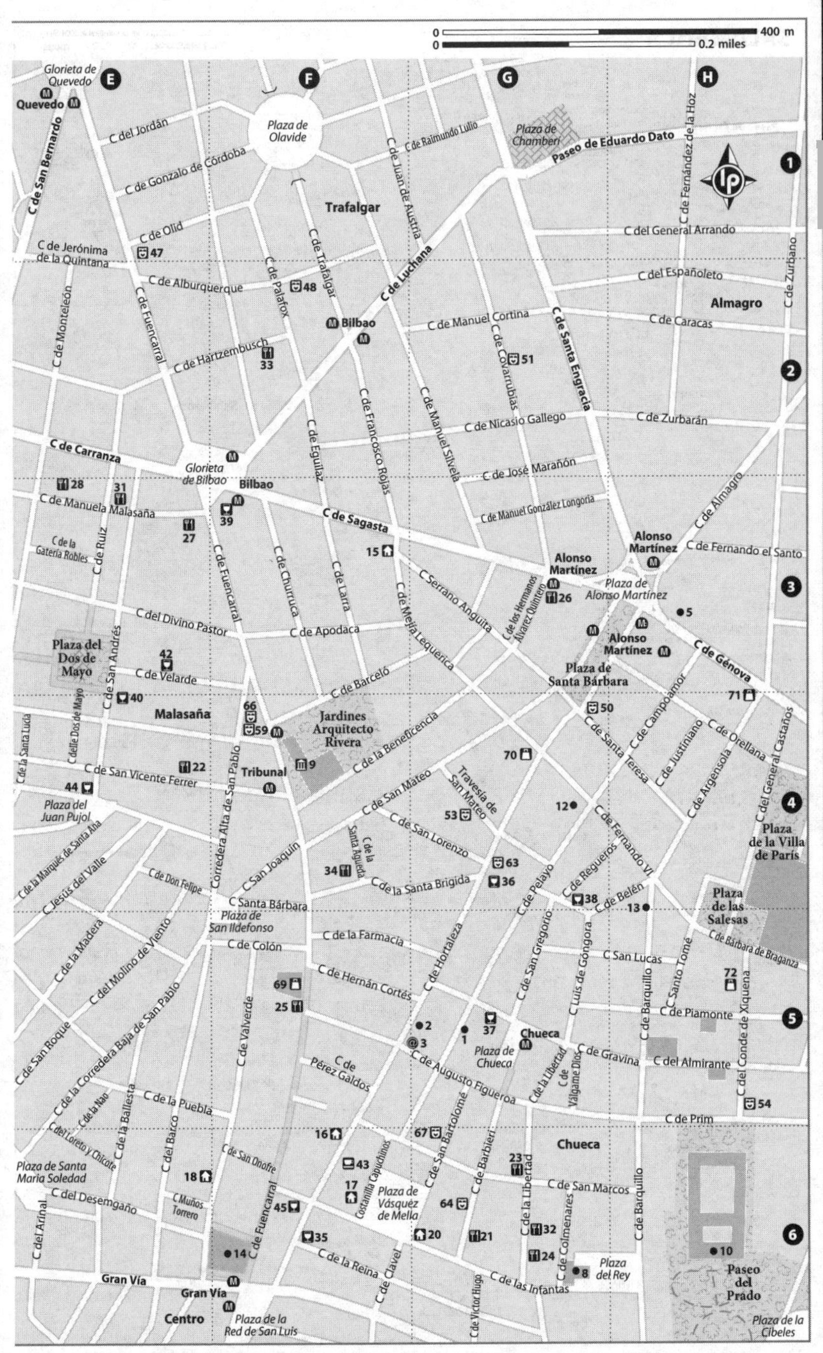

Plaza de Olavide
Trafalgar
Plaza de Chamberí
Paseo de Eduardo Dato
Almagro
Glorieta de Bilbao
Bilbao
C de Sagasta
Alonso Martínez
Plaza de Alonso Martínez
C de Génova
Plaza de Santa Bárbara
Plaza del Dos de Mayo
Malasaña
Jardines Arquitecto Rivera
Tribunal
Plaza de la Villa de París
Plaza de las Salesas
Plaza de San Ildefonso
Chueca
Plaza de Chueca
Plaza de Vásquez de Mella
Plaza del Rey
Paseo del Prado
Gran Vía
Centro
Plaza de la Red de San Luis
Plaza de la Cibeles

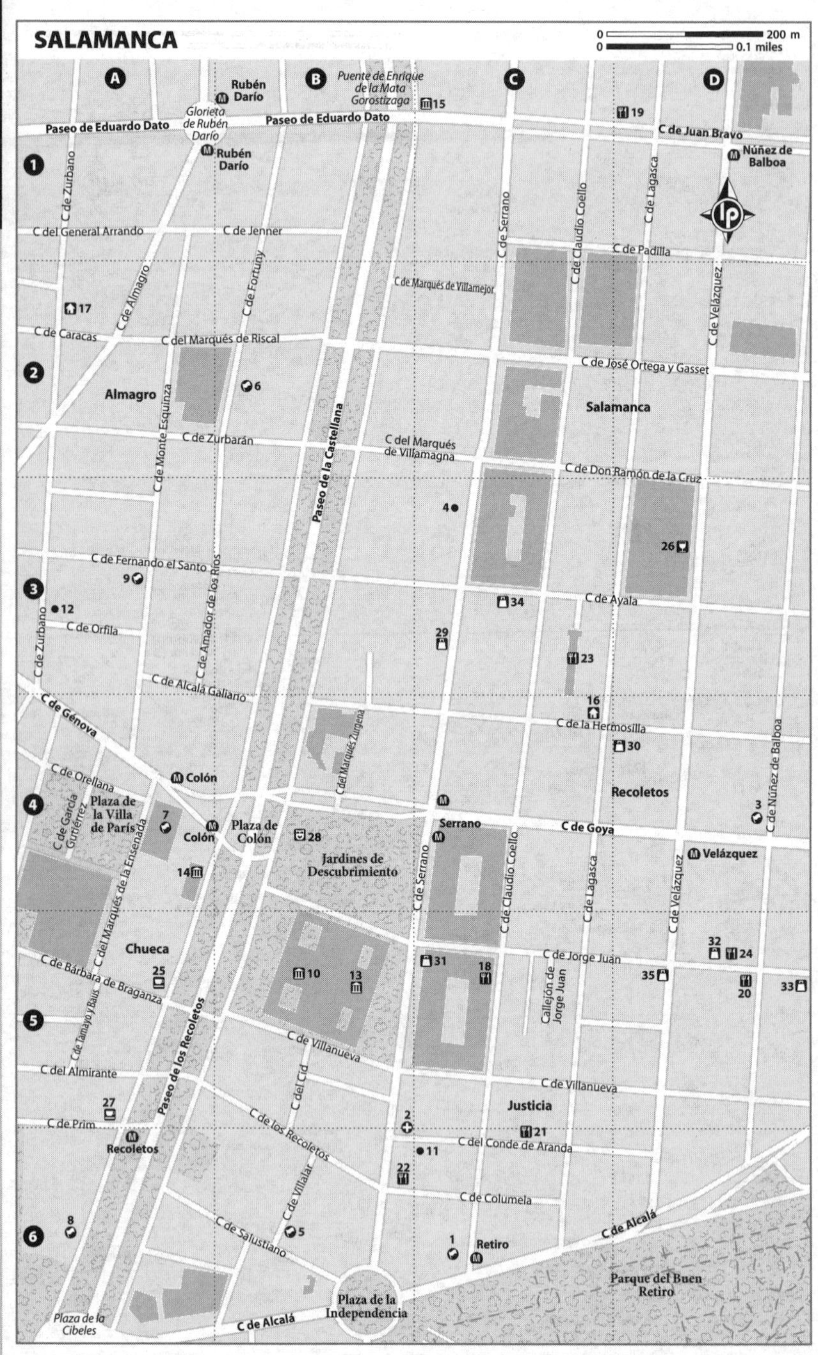
SALAMANCA
0 200 m
0 0.1 miles
A
B
C
D
1
2
3
4
5
6
Rubén Darío
Puente de Enrique de la Mata Gorostizaga
15
19
Glorieta de Rubén Darío
Paseo de Eduardo Dato
C de Juan Bravo
Núñez de Balboa
Rubén Darío
C de Zurbano
C de Lagasca
C de Claudio Coello
C de Serrano
C del General Arrando
C de Jenner
C de Padilla
C de Almagro
C de Fortuny
C de Marqués de Villamejor
C de Velázquez
17
C de Caracas
C del Marqués de Riscal
C de José Ortega y Gasset
Almagro
6
Salamanca
C de Monte Esquinza
Paseo de la Castellana
C de Zurbarán
C del Marqués de Villamagna
C de Don Ramón de la Cruz
4
26
C de Fernando el Santo
9
C de Amador de los Ríos
34
C de Ayala
12
C de Orfila
29
23
C de Alcalá Galiano
16
C de Génova
C de la Hermosilla
30
C del Marqués Zurgena
C de Orellana
Colón
Recoletos
C de Núñez de Balboa
Plaza de la Villa de París
7
Colón
Plaza de Colón
28
Serrano
C de Goya
3
C de García Gutiérrez
Velázquez
14
Jardines de Descubrimiento
C del Marqués de la Ensenada
Chueca
C de Jorge Juan
32
24
C de Bárbara de Braganza
25
10
13
31
18
35
20
33
Callejón de Jorge Juan
C de Tamayo y Baus
Paseo de los Recoletos
C de Villanueva
C del Almirante
C del Cid
C de Villanueva
Justicia
27
C de Prim
C de los Recoletos
2
21
Recoletos
C del Conde de Aranda
11
22
C de Villalar
C de Columela
C de Salustiano
5
8
1
Retiro
C de Alcalá
Parque del Buen Retiro
Plaza de la Independencia
Plaza de la Cibeles
C de Alcalá

SALAMANCA (p140)

INFORMATION
Andorran Embassy........ **1** C6
Anglo-American Medical Unit........ **2** B5
Canadian Embassy........ **3** D4
De Viaje........ **4** C3
French Embassy........ **5** B6
German Embassy........ **6** B2
UK Consulate........ **7** A4
UK Consulate-General........ **8** A6
UK Embassy........ **9** A3

SIGHTS & ACTIVITIES
Biblioteca Nacional........ **10** B5
Chi Spa........ **11** C6
International House........ **12** A3
Museo Arqueológico Nacional........ **13** B5
Museo de Cera........ **14** A4
Museo de la Escultura Abstracta........ **15** C1
Museo del Libro........ (see 10)

SLEEPING
Hesperia Hermosilla........ **16** C4
Hotel AC Santo Mauro........ **17** A2

EATING
Biotza........ **18** C5
Fast Good........ **19** D1
La Colonial de Goya........ **20** D5
La Galette........ **21** C6
Mallorca........ **22** B6
Mercado de la Paz........ **23** C3
Sula Madrid........ **24** D5

DRINKING
Café-Restaurante El Espejo........ **25** A5
El Lateral........ **26** D3
Gran Café de Gijón........ **27** A5

ENTERTAINMENT
Centro Cultural de la Villa........ **28** B4

SHOPPING
Agatha Ruiz de la Prada........ **29** C3
Amaya Arzuaga........ **30** D4
Camper........ **31** C5
Davidelfín........ **32** D5
Gallery........ **33** D5
Mantequería Bravo........ **34** C3
Sara Navarro........ **35** D5

CENTRO & HUERTAS

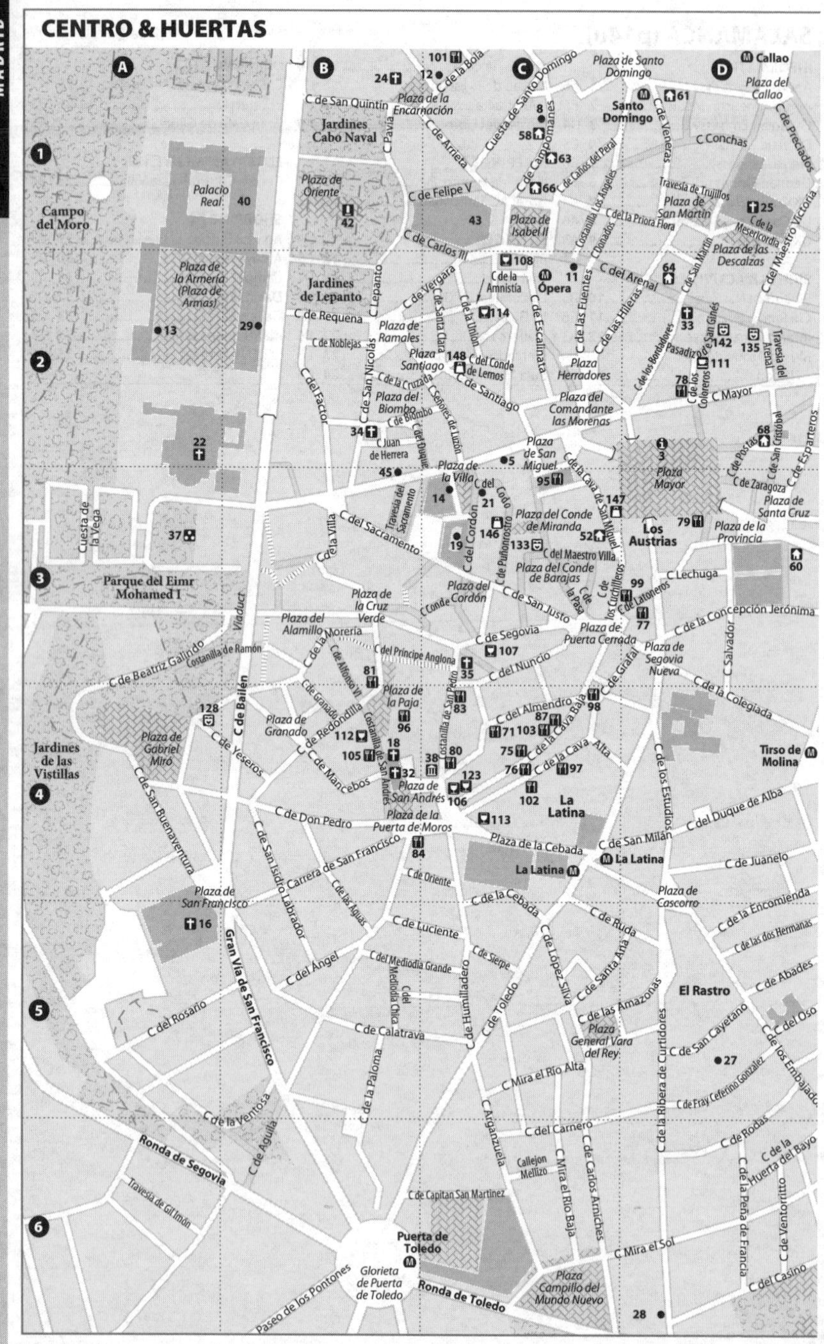

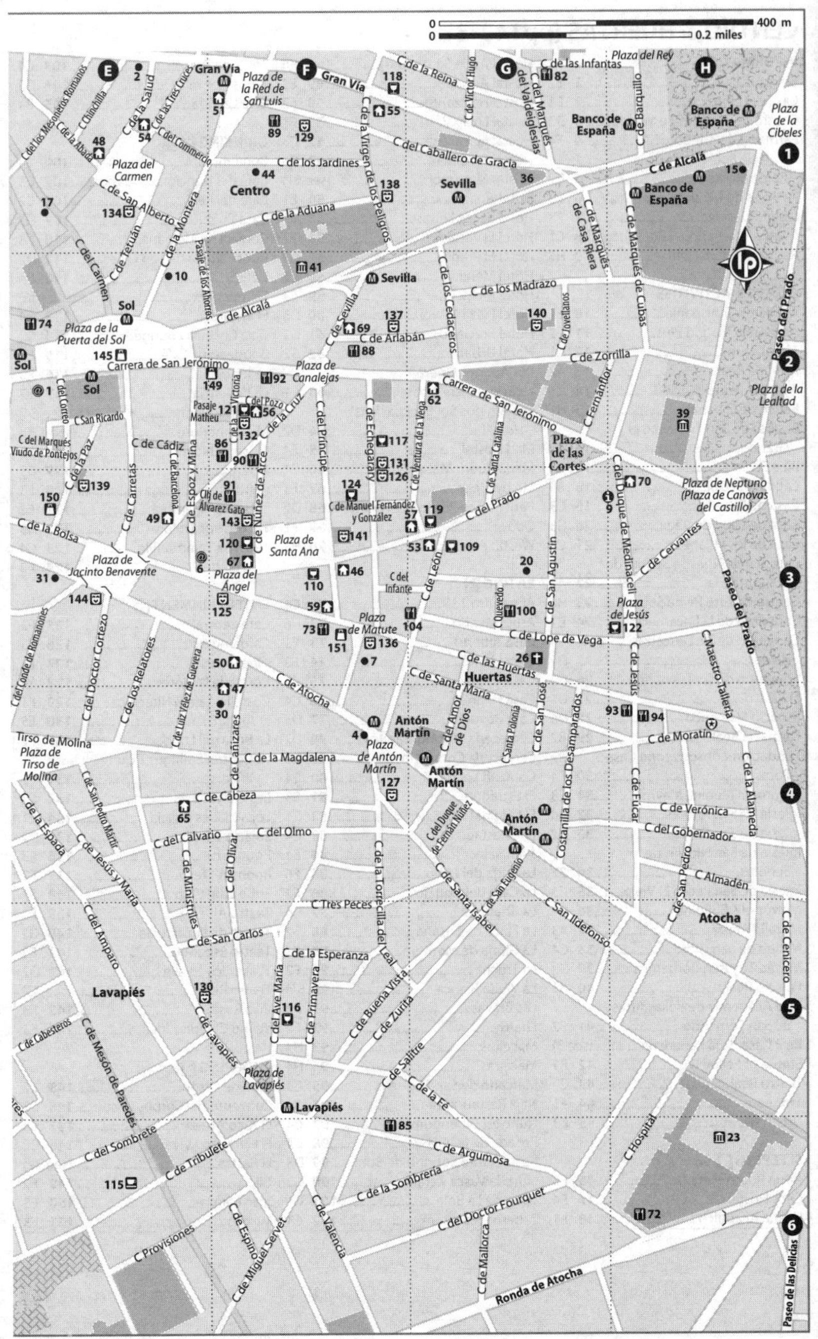

Gran Vía
Plaza de la Red de San Luis
C de la Reina
C de las Infantas
Plaza del Rey
Banco de España
Plaza de la Cibeles
C de Alcalá
C del Caballero de Gracia
C de los Jardines
Centro
Sevilla
Plaza del Carmen
C de la Aduana
C de los Madrazo
Sol
Plaza de la Puerta del Sol
C de Arlabán
Carrera de San Jerónimo
Plaza de Canalejas
C de Zorrilla
Paseo del Prado
Plaza de la Lealtad
Plaza de las Cortes
C de Cádiz
C del Prado
Plaza de Neptuno (Plaza de Canovas del Castillo)
C de Cervantes
Plaza de Santa Ana
C de la Bolsa
Plaza de Jacinto Benavente
Plaza del Ángel
Plaza de Matute
Plaza de Jesús
C de Lope de Vega
C de las Huertas
Huertas
C de Santa María
C de Atocha
Antón Martín
Plaza de Antón Martín
C de Moratín
Tirso de Molina
Plaza de Tirso de Molina
C de la Magdalena
C de Cabeza
C del Olmo
C de Verónica
C del Gobernador
C Almadén
C Tres Peces
C de San Carlos
C de la Esperanza
Atocha
Lavapiés
Plaza de Lavapiés
C de Argumosa
C del Doctor Fourquet
Ronda de Atocha
Paseo de las Delicias
400 m
0.2 miles

CENTRO & HUERTAS (pp142–3)

INFORMATION

Bbigg **1** E2
Casa del Libro **2** E1
Centro de Turismo de Madrid **3** D2
Farmacia del Globo **4** F4
Farmacia Real Botica de la Reina Madre **5** C2
La Bolsa de Minutos **6** E3
Libería Desnivel **7** F3
Petra's International Bookshop **8** C1
Regional Tourist Office **9** H3

SIGHTS & ACTIVITIES

Academia Inhispania **10** E2
Academia Madrid Plus **11** C2
Alambique **12** C1
Armería Real **13** A2
Ayuntamiento **14** C3
Banco de España **15** H1
Basílica de San Francisco el Grande **16** A5
Bike Spain **17** E1
Capilla del Obispo **18** B4
Casa de Cisneros **19** C3
Casa de Lope de Vega **20** G3
Casa de los Lujanes **21** C3
Catedral de Nuestra Señora de la Almudena **22** A2
Centro de Arte Reina Sofía **23** H6
Convento de la Encarnación **24** B1
Convento de las Descalzas Reales **25** D1
Convento de las Trinitarias **26** G3
El Rastro **27** D5
Espacio Flamenco **28** D6
Farmacia Real **29** B2
Fundación Conservatorio Casa Patas **30** F4
Hammam Medina Mayrit **31** E3
Iglesia de San Andrés **32** B4
Iglesia de San Ginés **33** D2
Iglesia de San Nicolás de los Servitas **34** B2
Iglesia de San Pedro El Viejo **35** C3
Metrópolis Building **36** G1
Muralla Árabe **37** A3
Museo de San Isidro **38** C4
Museo Thyssen-Bornemisza **39** H2
Palacio Real **40** B1
Real Academia de Bellas Artes de San Fernando **41** F2
Real Casa de la Panadería (see 3)
Statue of Felipe IV **42** B1
Teatro Real **43** C1
Trixi.com **44** F1
Urban Movil **45** B3

SLEEPING

Alicia Room Mate **46** F3
Cat's Hostel **47** F4
Hostal Acapulco **48** E1
Hostal Adria Santa Ana (see 49)
Hostal Adriano **49** E3
Hostal Horizonte **50** F3
Hostal Luis XV **51** F1
Hostal Macarena **52** C3
Hostal Sardinero **53** G3
Hostel Metropol (see 51)
Hotel Anaco **54** E1
Hotel de las Letras **55** F1
Hotel El Pasaje **56** F2
Hotel El Prado **57** G3
Hotel Meninas **58** C1
Hotel Miau **59** F3
Hotel Plaza Mayor **60** D3
Hotel Preciados **61** D1
Hotel Urban **62** G2
Los Amigos Ópera Backpackers' Hostel **63** C1
Los Amigos Sol Backpackers' Hostel **64** D2
Mad Hostel **65** E4
Mario Room Mate **66** C1
Me by Melía **67** F3
Petit Palace Posada del Peine **68** D2
Quo **69** F2
Westin Palace **70** H3

EATING

Almendro 13 **71** C4
Arola Madrid **72** H6
Casa Alberto **73** F3
Casa Labra **74** E2
Casa Lucas **75** C4
Casa Lucio **76** C4
Casa Revuelta **77** D3
Cervecería 100 Montaditos **78** D2
Cervecería Compano **79** D3
Corazon Loco **80** C4
El Estragón **81** B3
El Original **82** G1
Ene Restaurante **83** C4
Juanalaloca **84** B4
La Buga del Lobo **85** F6
La Casa del Abuelo **86** F2
La Chata **87** C4
La Finca de Susana **88** F2
La Gloria de Montera **89** F1
La Trucha **90** F2
La Viuda Blanca (see 64)
Las Bravas **91** F3
Lhardy **92** F2
Maceiras **93** H4
Maceiras **94** H4
Mercado de San Miguel **95** C3
Naïa Restaurante **96** B4
Nunc est Bibendum **97** C4
Posada de la Villa **98** C4
Restaurante Sobrino de Botín **99** D3
Sidrería Vasca Zeraín **100** G3
Taberna La Bola **101** C1
Taberna Matritum **102** C4
Taberna Txacoli **103** C4
Vinos Gonzalez **104** G3
Viva La Vida **105** B4

DRINKING

Bonanno **106** C4
Café del Nuncio **107** C3
Café del Real **108** C2
Casa Pueblo **109** G3
Cervecería Alemana **110** F3
Chocolatería de San Ginés **111** D2
Delic **112** B4
El Imperfecto (see 136)
El Viajero **113** C4
Gaia Cocktail Lounge **114** C2
Gaudeamus Café **115** E6
La Inquilina **116** F5
La Venencia **117** F2
La Viuda Negra (see 64)
Midnight Rose (see 120)
Museo Chicote **118** F1
Ølsen **119** G3
Penthouse **120** F3
Taberna Alhambra **121** F2
Taberna de Dolores **122** H3
Taberna Tempranillo **123** C4
Viva Madrid **124** F3

ENTERTAINMENT

Café Central **125** F3
Cardamomo **126** F3
Cine Doré **127** F4
Corral de la Morería **128** A4
Costello Café & Niteclub **129** F1
El Juglar **130** E5
La Boca del Lobo **131** F2
La Central Bullfight Ticket Office **132** F2
Las Carboneras **133** C3
Localidades Galicia **134** E1
Palacio Gaviria **135** D2
Populart **136** F3
Room at Stella **137** F2
Suite Café Club **138** F1
Teatro Albéniz **139** E3
Teatro de la Zarzuela **140** G2
Teatro Español **141** F3
Teatro Joy Eslava **142** D2
Teatro Real (see 43)
Villa Rosa **143** F3
Yelmo Cineplex Ideal **144** E3

SHOPPING

Casa de Diego **145** E2
Convento del Corpus Cristi **146** C3
El Arco Artesanía **147** C3
El Flamenco Vive **148** C2
El Rastro (see 27)
Gil **149** F2
José Ramírez **150** E3
México **151** F3

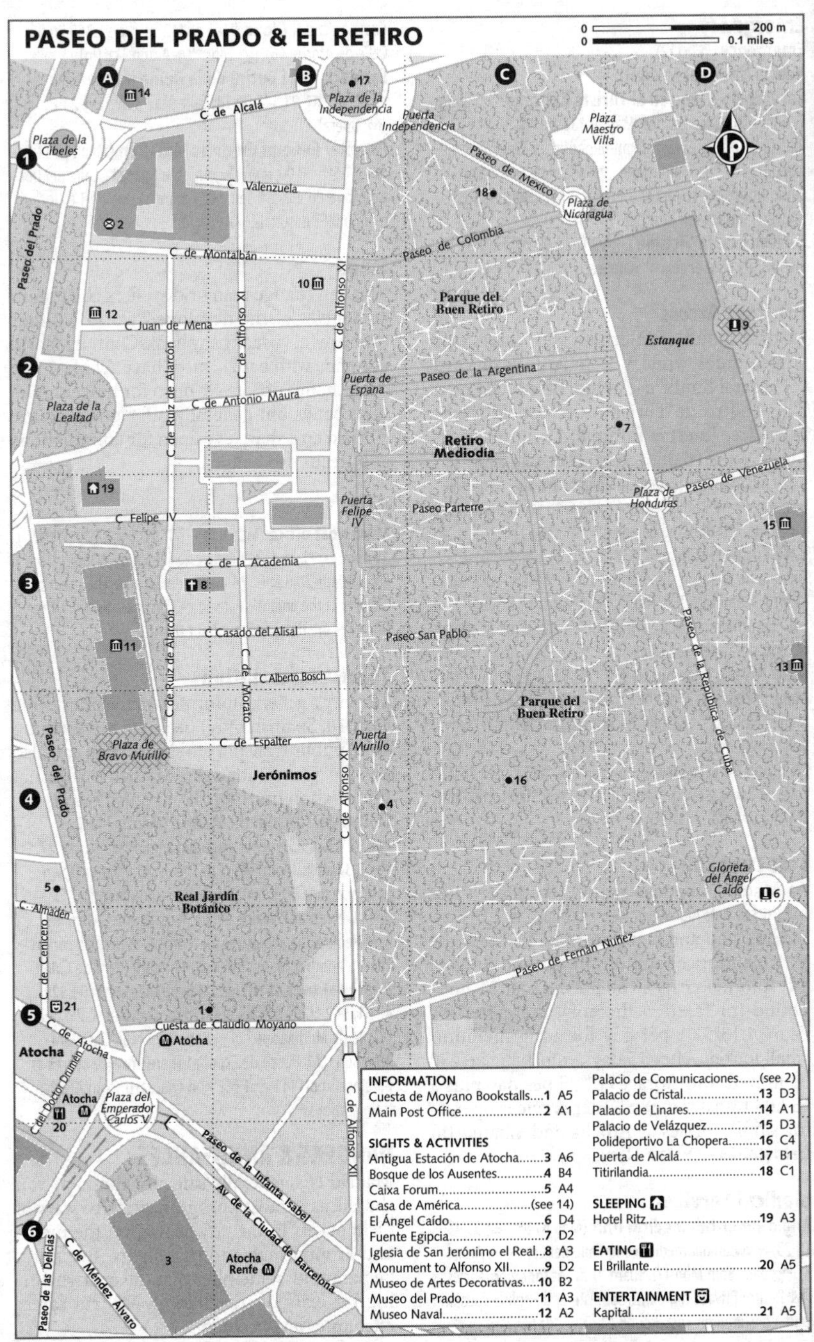
PASEO DEL PRADO & EL RETIRO
0 200 m
0 0.1 miles
A
B
C
D
1
2
3
4
5
6
Plaza de la Cibeles
C de Alcalá
Plaza de la Independencia
Puerta Independencia
Paseo de México
Plaza Maestro Villa
Plaza de Nicaragua
C Valenzuela
Paseo del Prado
C de Montalbán
Paseo de Colombia
Parque del Buen Retiro
Estanque
C Juan de Mena
C de Alfonso XI
Puerta de Espana
Paseo de la Argentina
Plaza de la Lealtad
C de Antonio Maura
C de Ruiz de Alarcón
Retiro Mediodía
Plaza de Honduras
Paseo de Venezuela
Puerta Felipe IV
Paseo Parterre
C Felipe IV
C de la Academia
C Casado del Alisal
Paseo San Pablo
C de Morato
C Alberto Bosch
Paseo de la República de Cuba
Puerta Murillo
C de Espalter
Plaza de Bravo Murillo
Jerónimos
Glorieta del Ángel Caído
Real Jardín Botánico
C Almadén
C de Cenicero
Paseo de Fernán Nuñez
Cuesta de Claudio Moyano
Atocha
C de Atocha
C del Doctor Drumen
Plaza del Emperador Carlos V
Paseo de la Infanta Isabel
Av de la Ciudad de Barcelona
Paseo de las Delicias
C de Méndez Álvaro
Atocha Renfe

INFORMATION
Cuesta de Moyano Bookstalls....1 A5
Main Post Office....2 A1

SIGHTS & ACTIVITIES
Antigua Estación de Atocha....3 A6
Bosque de los Ausentes....4 B4
Caixa Forum....5 A4
Casa de América....(see 14)
El Ángel Caído....6 D4
Fuente Egipcia....7 D2
Iglesia de San Jerónimo el Real...8 A3
Monument to Alfonso XII....9 D2
Museo de Artes Decorativas....10 B2
Museo del Prado....11 A3
Museo Naval....12 A2
Palacio de Comunicaciones....(see 2)
Palacio de Cristal....13 D3
Palacio de Linares....14 A1
Palacio de Velázquez....15 D3
Polideportivo La Chopera....16 C4
Puerta de Alcalá....17 B1
Titirilandia....18 C1

SLEEPING
Hotel Ritz....19 A3

EATING
El Brillante....20 A5

ENTERTAINMENT
Kapital....21 A5

Emergency

Emergency (☎ 112)
Policía Nacional (☎ 091)
Servicio de Atención al Turista Extranjero (Foreign Tourist Assistance Service; Map pp138-9; ☎ 91 548 85 37, 91 548 80 08; satemadrid@munimadrid.es; Calle de Leganitos 19; 9am-10pm; M Plaza de España or Santo Domingo) To report thefts or other crime-related matters, this is your best bet.
Teléfono de la Víctima (☎ 902 18 09 95) Hotline for victims of racial or sexual violence.

Internet Access

Madrid is full of internet cafes. Some offer student rates, while most have deals on cards for several hours' use at much-reduced rates. The Centro de Turismo de Madrid (right) offers free internet for up to 15 minutes.
Bbigg (Map pp142-3; ☎ 91 531 23 64; Calle Mayor 1; 1/5hr €2.50/3; 9.30am-midnight; M Sol) A massive internet centre in the heart of town with separate sections for Skype, internet and games.
Café Comercial (Map pp138-9; ☎ 91 521 56 55; Glorieta de Bilbao 7; per 50min €1; 7.30am-midnight Mon, 7.30am-1am Tue-Thu, 7.30am-2am Fri, 8.30am-2am Sat, 9am-midnight Sun; M Bilbao) Surf the net in one of Madrid's grandest old cafes.
Drop & Drag (Map pp138-9; ☎ 91 532 93 72; Calle de Augusto Figueroa 7; per hr €2; noon-1am Mon-Fri, 3pm-midnight Sat & Sun; M Tribunal or Chueca) Handy if you're in Chueca.
La Bolsa de Minutos (Map pp142-3; ☎ 91 532 26 22; Calle de Espoz y Mina 17; per hr €2; 9.30am-midnight; M Sol or Antón Martín)

Left Luggage

At Madrid's Barajas airport, there are three **consignas** (left-luggage offices; 24hr): in T1 (near the bus stop and taxi stand), in T2 (near the metro entrance) and on the ground floor of T4. A locker costs €3.60 for the first 24-hour period (or fraction thereof); thereafter it's €4.64/4.13/3.61 per day for a big/medium/small locker. After 15 days your luggage will be moved into storage (€1.85 per day plus a €37.08 transfer fee). Similar services operate for similar prices at Atocha and Chamartín **train stations** (7am-11pm).

Medical Services

Anglo-American Medical Unit (Map p140; ☎ 91 435 18 23; www.unidadmedica.com; Calle del Conde de Aranda 1; 9am-8pm Mon-Fri, 10am-1pm Sat for emergencies; M Retiro) Private clinic with Spanish- and English-speaking staff. Consultations cost around €120.
Farmacia del Globo (Map pp142-3; ☎ 91 369 20 00; Calle de Atocha 46; 24hr; M Antón Martín)
Farmacia Real Botica de la Reina Madre (Map pp142-3; ☎ 91 548 00 14; Calle Mayor 59; 24hr; M Ópera)
Hospital General Gregorio Marañón (Map pp134-5; ☎ 91 586 80 00; www.hggm.es in Spanish; Calle del Doctor Esquerdo 46; M Sáinz de Baranda) One of the city's main public hospitals.

Money

You can change cash or travellers cheques in currencies of the developed world without problems at virtually any bank. Central Madrid abounds with banks; most have ATMs.

Exchange offices are open for longer hours than banks but generally offer poorer rates. Also, keep a sharp eye open for commissions at bureaus de change.

Post

Main post office (Map p145; ☎ 91 396 27 33; www.correos.es; Plaza de la Cibeles; 8.30am-9.30pm Mon-Fri, 8.30am-2pm Sat; M Banco de España) The main post office is in the gigantic Palacio de Comunicaciones. Other branches are dotted throughout the city.

Tourist Information

The city's general-information telephone line (☎ 010, Spanish only) deals with everything from public transport to shows. You can also try the Comunidad de Madrid's regional information line (☎ 012, Spanish only).
Centro de Turismo de Madrid (Map pp142-3; ☎ 91 429 49 51; www.esmadrid.com; Plaza Mayor 27; 9.30am-8.30pm; M Sol) The *ayuntamiento* (town hall) also runs bright-orange information points at Plaza de la Cibeles, at Plaza de Callao, outside the Centro de Arte Reina Sofía and at the T4 terminal at Barajas airport. There's another tourist office underneath Plaza de Colón.
Regional tourist office (Map pp142-3; ☎ 91 429 49 51, 902 10 00 07; www.turismomadrid.es; Calle del Duque de Medinaceli 2; 8am-8pm Mon-Sat, 9am-2pm Sun; M Banco de España) There are also offices at Barajas airport (T1 and T4), and Chamartín and Atocha train stations.

DANGERS & ANNOYANCES

Madrid is a generally safe city although you should, as in most European cities, be wary of pickpockets in the city centre, on the metro and around major tourist sights. But don't be paranoid: remember that the overwhelming majority of travellers to Madrid rarely encounter any problems.

MADRID CARD

If you intend to do some intensive sightseeing and travelling on public transport, it might be worth looking at the **Madrid Card** (☎ 91 360 47 72; www.madridcard.com). It includes free entry to more than 40 museums in and around Madrid (including the Museo del Prado, Museo Thyssen-Bornemisza, Centro de Arte Reina Sofía, Estadio Santiago Bernabéu and Palacio Real) and free Descubre Madrid walking tours, as well as discounts on public transport, on the Madrid Visión tourist bus and in certain shops and restaurants. The ticket is available for one/two/three days (€42/55/68). There's also a cheaper version (€28/32/36), which just covers cultural sights. The Madrid Card can be bought online, over the phone, or in person at the tourist offices on Plaza Mayor and in Calle del Duque de Medinaceli, and in some tobacconists and hotels – a list of major sales outlets can be found on the website.

You need to be especially careful in the most heavily touristed parts of town, notably the Plaza Mayor and surrounding streets, the Puerta del Sol, El Rastro and the Museo del Prado. Tricks abound and they usually involve a team of two or more (sometimes one of them is an attractive woman to distract male victims). While one diverts your attention, the other empties your pockets.

More unsettling than dangerous, the central Calle de la Montera has long been the haunt of prostitutes, pimps and a fair share of shady characters, although the street has recently been pedestrianised, and furnished with CCTV cameras and a police station. The same applies to the Casa de Campo, although it, too, has been cleaned up a little.

The *barrio* of Lavapiés is a gritty, multicultural melting pot. We love it, but it's not without its problems, with drug-related crime an occasional but persistent problem. It's probably best avoided if you're on your own at night.

SIGHTS

Madrid has three of the finest art galleries in the world – if ever there existed a golden mile of fine art, it would have to be the combined charms of the Museo del Prado, the Centro de Arte Reina Sofía and the Museo Thyssen-Bornemisza. Beyond the museums' walls, the combination of stunning architecture and feel-good living has never been easier to access than in the beautiful plazas, where *terrazas* (cafes with outdoor tables) provide a front-row seat for Madrid's fine cityscape and endlessly energetic streetlife. Throw in some outstanding city parks (the Parque del Buen Retiro, in particular) and areas like Chueca, Malasaña and Salamanca, which each have their own identity, and you'll quickly end up wondering why you decided to spend so little time here.

Los Austrias, Sol & Centro

These barrios are where the story of Madrid began. As the seat of royal power, this is where the splendour of Imperial Spain was at its most ostentatious and where Spain's overarching Catholicism was at its most devout – think expansive palaces, elaborate private mansions, ancient churches and imposing convents amid the raucous clamour of modern Madrid.

This is Madrid at its most riotous and diverse: the tangle of streets tumbling down the hillside of Madrid de Los Austrias (named for the Habsburg dynasty, which ruled Spain from 1517 to 1700); the busy shopping streets around Plaza de la Puerta del Sol (more commonly known as Puerta del Sol, the Gate of the Sun); the monumental Gran Vía, marking the northern border of central Madrid. If other *barrios* have their own distinctive character traits, then Los Austrias, Sol and Centro are the sum total of all Madrid's personalities. It's also where the *madrileño* world most often intersects with that of tourists and expats drawn to that feel-good Madrid vibe.

PLAZA MAYOR

The stunningly beautiful **Plaza Mayor** (Map pp142-3; Ⓜ Sol) is a highlight of any visit to Madrid. The grandeur of its buildings is one thing, but this is a living, breathing entity, from the outdoor tables of the *terrazas* to the students strewn across the cobblestones on a sunny day.

Designed in 1619 by Juan Gómez de Mora, the plaza's first public ceremony was the beatification of San Isidro Labrador, Madrid's patron saint. Thereafter, bullfights watched by 50,000 spectators were a recurring spectacle

MADRID IN TWO DAYS

You've a hectic day ahead of you so plan it around the best places (and plazas) to relax en route. Begin in **Plaza Mayor** (p147), with its architectural beauty, fine *terrazas* (terraces) and endlessly fascinating passing parade. Wander down Calle Mayor, passing the delightful **Plaza de la Villa** (opposite), and head for the **Palacio Real** (below). By then you'll be ready for a coffee or something stronger, and there's no finer place to rest than in **Plaza de Oriente** (below). Double back up towards the **Puerta del Sol** (p150), and then on to **Plaza de Santa Ana** (p152), the ideal place for a long, liquid lunch. Time for some high culture, so stroll down the hill to the incomparable **Museo del Prado** (p153), the home of a grand collection of predominantly Spanish old masters and one of the best art galleries in Europe. In anticipation of a long night ahead, catch your breath in the **Parque del Buen Retiro** (p156) before heading into **Chueca** or **Malasaña** for great restaurants (p181), followed by some terrific live music (p191).

On day two, cram in everything you didn't have time for on day one. Choose between the **Centro de Arte Reina Sofía** (p152) and the **Museo Thyssen-Bornemisza** (p155), then jump on the metro for a quick ride across town to the astonishing Goya frescoes in the **Ermita de San Antonio de la Florida** (p159). Finish off with tapas in **La Latina** (p182) and end up with drinks at **Museo Chicote** (p187).

until 1878, while the autos-da-fé (the ritual condemnation of heretics) of the Spanish Inquisition also took place here. Fire largely destroyed the square in 1790, but it was rebuilt and became an important market and hub of city life. Today, among the uniformly ochre apartments with wrought-iron balconies, you can still see the exquisite frescoes of the 17th-century **Real Casa de la Panadería** (Royal Bakery).

PALACIO REAL

Spain's lavish **Palacio Real** (Royal Palace; Map pp142-3; ☎ 91 542 69 47; www.patrimonionacional.es; Calle de Bailén s/n; adult/child, student & EU senior €10/3.50, adult without guide €8, EU citizens free Wed; 🕑 9am-6pm Mon-Sat, 9am-3pm Sun & holidays Apr-Sep, 9.30am-5pm Mon-Sat, 9am-2pm Sun & holidays Oct-Mar; Ⓜ Ópera) is a jewel box of a palace, although it's used only occasionally for royal ceremonies; the royal family moved to the modest Palacio de la Zarzuela years ago.

When the Alcázar burned down on Christmas Day 1734, Felipe V, the first of the Bourbon kings, decided to build a palace that would dwarf all its European counterparts. Felipe died before the palace was finished, which is perhaps why the Italianate baroque colossus has a mere 2800 rooms, just one-quarter of the original plan.

The official tour leads through 50 of the palace rooms, which hold a good selection of Goyas, 215 absurdly ornate clocks and five Stradivarius violins still used for concerts and balls. The **main stairway** is a grand statement of imperial power, leading first to the Halberdiers' rooms and eventually to the sumptuous **Salón del Trono** (Throne Room), with its crimson-velvet wall coverings and Tiepolo ceiling. Shortly after, you reach the **Salón de Gasparini**, with its exquisite stucco ceiling and walls resplendent with embroidered silks.

Outside the main palace, visit the **Farmacia Real** (Royal Pharmacy) at the southern end of the patio known as the **Plaza de la Armería** (or Plaza de Armas). Westwards across the plaza is the **Armería Real** (Royal Armoury), a shiny collection of weapons and armour, mostly dating from the 16th and 17th centuries. The Armería is included in the Palacio Real ticket or you can visit it on its own (adult/child, student and EU senior €3.40/1.70).

PLAZA DE ORIENTE

A royal palace that once had aspirations to be the Spanish Versailles. Sophisticated cafes watched over by apartments that cost the equivalent of a royal salary. The **Teatro Real**, Madrid's opera house and one of Spain's temples to high culture. Some of the finest sunset views in Madrid. Welcome to **Plaza de Oriente** (Map pp142-3; Ⓜ Ópera), a gloriously alive monument to imperial Madrid.

At the centre of the plaza, which the palace overlooks, is an equestrian **statue of Felipe IV**, designed by Velázquez. This is the perfect spot to take it all in, with marvellous views wherever you look. If you're wondering how a heavy bronze statue of a rider and his horse rearing up can actually maintain that stance, the answer is simple: the hind legs are solid while the front ones are hollow. That idea was Galileo Galilei's.

Nearby are some 20 marble statues of mostly ancient monarchs. Local legend has it that these ageing royals get down off their pedestals at night to stretch their legs.

The adjacent **Jardines Cabo Naval**, a great place to watch the sun set, adds to the sense of a sophisticated oasis of green in the heart of Madrid.

CAMPO DEL MORO & JARDINES DE SABATINI

In proper palace style, lush gardens surround the Palacio Real. To the north are the formal French-style **Jardines de Sabatini** (Map pp142-3; 9am-9pm May-Sep, 9am-8pm Oct-Apr; M Ópera or Plaza de España). Directly behind the palace are the fountains of the **Campo del Moro** (Map pp134-5; 10am-8pm Mon-Sat, 9am-8pm Sun & holidays Apr-Sep, 10am-6pm Mon-Sat, 9am-6pm Sun & holidays Oct-Mar; M Príncipe Pío), so named because this is where the Muslim army camped before a 12th-century attack on the Alcázar. Now shady paths, a thatch-roofed pagoda and palace views are the main attractions.

CATEDRAL DE NUESTRA SEÑORA DE LA ALMUDENA

Paris has Notre Dame and Rome has St Peter's Basilica. In fact, almost every European city of stature has its signature cathedral, one that is a stand-out monument to the city's glorious Christian past. Not Madrid. It's **Catedral de Nuestra Señora de la Almudena** (Map pp142-3; ☎ 91 542 22 00; Calle de Bailén; 9am-9pm; M Ópera), south of the Palacio Real, is cavernous and laden with more adornment than charm, its colourful, modern ceilings doing little to make up for the lack of old-world gravitas that so distinguishes the world's great cathedrals.

Carlos I first proposed building a cathedral here back in 1518, but construction didn't get underway until the 1880s. Other priorities got in the way and it wasn't finished until 1992. Not surprisingly, the pristine, bright-white neo-Gothic interior holds no pride of place in the affections of *madrileños*.

MURALLA ÁRABE

Behind the cathedral apse, down Cuesta de la Vega, is a short stretch of the so-called **Muralla Árabe** (Arab Wall; Map pp142-3; M Ópera), the fortifications built by Madrid's early medieval Islamic rulers. Some of it dates as far back as the 9th century, when the initial Islamic fort was raised. Other sections date from the 12th and 13th centuries, by which time the city was in Christian hands.

PLAZA DE LA VILLA

There are grander squares elsewhere, but the intimate **Plaza de la Villa** (Map pp142-3; M Ópera) is one of Madrid's prettiest. Enclosed on three sides by wonderfully preserved examples of 17th-century *barroco madrileño* (Madrid-style baroque architecture: a pleasing amalgam of brick, exposed stone and wrought iron), it has been the permanent seat of the city government since the Middle Ages.

On the western side of the square is the 17th-century **ayuntamiento** (town hall), in Habsburg-style baroque with Herrerian slate-tile spires. On the opposite side of the square is the Gothic **Casa de los Lujanes**, whose brickwork tower is said to have been 'home' to the imprisoned French monarch François I after his capture in the Battle of Pavia (1525). The plateresque **Casa de Cisneros**, built in 1537 with later Renaissance alterations, also catches the eye.

CONVENTO DE LAS DESCALZAS REALES

The grim, prisonlike walls of the **Convento de las Descalzas Reales** (Convent of the Barefoot Royals; Map pp142-3; ☎ 91 542 69 47; www.patrimonionacional.es; Plaza de las Descalzas 3; adult/child €5/2.50, EU citizens free Wed, incl Convento de la Encarnación €6/3.40; 10.30am-12.45pm & 4-5.45pm Tue-Thu & Sat, 10.30am-12.45pm Fri, 11am-1.45pm Sun; M Ópera or Sol) offer no hint that behind the plateresque facade lies a sumptuous stronghold of the faith.

Founded in 1559 by Juana of Austria, the widowed daughter of the Spanish king Carlos I, the convent quickly became one of Spain's richest religious houses thanks to gifts from Juana's noble friends. On the obligatory guided tour you'll see a gaudily frescoed Renaissance stairway, a number of extraordinary tapestries based on works by Rubens, and a wonderful painting entitled *The Voyage of the 11,000 Virgins*. Some 33 nuns still live here and there are 33 chapels dotted around the convent.

CONVENTO DE LA ENCARNACIÓN

Founded by Empress Margarita of Austria, the **Convento de la Encarnación** (Convent of the Incarnation; Map pp142-3; ☎ 91 542 69 47; Plaza de la Encarnación;

adult/child €3.60/2, EU citizens free Wed, incl Convento de las Descalzas Reales €6/3.40; ⌚ 10.30am-12.45pm & 4-5.45pm Tue-Thu & Sat, 10.30am-12.45pm Fri, 11am-1.45pm Sun; Ⓜ Ópera) occupies a 17th-century mansion built in *barroco madrileño*. It's still inhabited by nuns of the Augustine order (Agustinas Recoletas). Inside there is a unique collection of 17th- and 18th-century sculptures and paintings, as well as a handful of silver and gold reliquaries. The most famous contains the blood of San Pantaleón, which purportedly liquefies every year on 27 July, drawing throngs of the curious and the faithful.

IGLESIA DE SAN NICOLÁS DE LOS SERVITAS

Considered Madrid's oldest surviving church, **Iglesia de San Nicolás de los Servitas** (Map pp142-3; ☎ 91 548 83 14; Plaza de San Nicolás 6; ⌚ 8am-1.30pm & 5.30-8.30pm Mon, 8-9.30am & 6.30-8.30pm Tue-Sat, 9.30am-2pm & 6.30-9pm Sun & holidays; Ⓜ Ópera) may have been built on the site of Muslim Magerit's second mosque and offers a rare glimpse of medieval Madrid. Apart from the restored 12th-century Mudéjar bell tower, most of the present church dates back to the 15th century.

IGLESIA DE SAN GINÉS

Due north of Plaza Mayor, **Iglesia de San Ginés** (Map pp142-3; Calle del Arenal 13; Ⓜ Sol or Ópera) is one of Madrid's oldest churches: it has been here in one form or another since at least the 14th century. What you see today was built in 1645 but largely reconstructed after a fire in 1824. The church houses some fine paintings, including El Greco's *Expulsion of the Moneychangers from the Temple* (1614), which is beautifully displayed: the glass is just 6mm from the canvas to avoid reflections. Sadly, the church opens to the public only once a week (at the time of writing, Saturday).

PLAZA DE LA PUERTA DEL SOL

The official centre point of Spain is a gracious hemisphere of elegant facades that's often very crowded. It is, above all, a crossroads. People here are forever heading somewhere else, on foot, by metro (three lines cross here) or by bus (many lines terminate and start here). In Madrid's earliest days, the **Puerta del Sol** (Gate of the Sun; Map pp142–3) was the eastern gate of the city.

Plaza de la Puerta del Sol comes into its own on New Year's Eve, when all Madrid packs into the square, waiting for the clock that gives Spain its official time to strike midnight, as the rest of the country watches on TV. Look out for the statue of a bear nuzzling a *madroño* (strawberry tree); this is the symbol of the city.

REAL ACADEMIA DE BELLAS ARTES DE SAN FERNANDO

In any other city, the **Real Academia de Bellas Artes de San Fernando** (Map pp142-3; ☎ 91 524 08 64; http://rabasf.insde.es in Spanish; Calle de Alcalá 13; adult/senior & under 18yr/student €3/free/1.50; ⌚ 9am-7pm Tue-Fri, 9am-2.30pm & 4-7pm Sat, 9am-2.30pm Sun & Mon Sep-Jun, varied hr Jul & Aug; Ⓜ Sevilla) would be a standout attraction, but in Madrid it too often gets forgotten in the rush to the Prado, Thyssen or Reina Sofía. An academic centre for up-and-coming artists since Fernando VI founded it in the 18th century (both Picasso and Dalí studied here), it houses works by some of the best-loved old masters. Highlights include works by Zurbarán, El Greco, Rubens, Tintoretto, Goya, Sorolla and Juan Gris, not to mention a couple of minor portraits by Velázquez and a few drawings by Picasso.

GRAN VÍA

It's difficult to imagine Madrid without Gran Vía, the grand boulevard that climbs through the city centre from Plaza de España down to Calle de Alcalá, but it has only existed since 1911, when it was bulldozed through what was then a lively labyrinth of old streets. On a rise about one-third of the way along stands the 1920s-era **Telefónica building** (Edificio Telefónica; Map pp138–9), which was for years the tallest building in the city. During the civil war, the boulevard became known as 'Howitzer Alley' as shells rained down from Franco's forces in the Casa de Campo. At the southern end of Gran Vía, the stunning French-designed **Metrópolis building** (Edificio Metrópolis; Map pp142–3; 1905), has a winged statue of victory sitting atop its dome.

La Latina & Lavapiés

La Latina combines some of the best things about Madrid: arguably the Spanish capital's best selection of tapas bars and a medieval streetscape studded with elegant churches. The *barrio*'s heartland is centred on the area between (and very much including) Calle de la Cava Baja and the beautiful Plaza de la Paja.

Lavapiés, on the other hand, is a world away from the sophistication of modern Madrid.

This is one of the city's oldest and most traditional *barrios*. It's at once deeply traditional and home to more immigrants than any other central Madrid *barrio*. It's quirky, alternative and a melting pot all in one, both a long-standing community and one constantly in the making. It's not without its problems and the *barrio* has a reputation both for antiglamour cool and as a no-go zone.

EL RASTRO

A Sunday morning at **El Rastro** (Map pp142-3; 8am-3pm Sun; M La Latina), Europe's largest flea market, is a Madrid institution. El Rastro (the Stain) owes its name to the blood that once trickled down these streets from the slaughterhouses, which sat up the hill. It's been an open-air market for half a millennium.

The madness begins at Plaza de Cascorro, near La Latina metro stop, and you could easily spend an entire morning inching your way down Calle de la Ribera de Curtidores and the maze of streets branching off it. Cheap clothes, luggage, antiques, old photos of Madrid, old flamenco records, faux designer purses, grungy T-shirts, household goods and electronics are the main fare, but for every 10 pieces of junk, there's a real gem waiting to be found. For many *madrileños,* the best of El Rastro comes after the stalls have shut down and everyone crowds into nearby bars for an *aperitivo* (aperitif) of vermouth and tapas, turning the *barrio* into the site of a spontaneous Sunday fiesta.

A word of warning: pickpockets love El Rastro as much as everyone else.

VIADUCTO & JARDINES DE LAS VISTILLAS

For a great view out to the west, take a stroll down Calle de Segovia, where a **viaducto** (viaduct) provides a good vantage point. The outdoor tables in the adjacent **Jardines de las Vistillas** (Map pp142–3) are another good spot, with views out towards Sierra de Guadarrama. During the civil war, Las Vistillas was heavily bombarded by Nationalist troops from the Casa de Campo, and they in turn were shelled from a Republican bunker here.

LA MORERÍA

The area stretching southeast from the viaducto to the Iglesia de San Andrés was the heart of the *morería* (Moorish quarter). Strain the imagination a little and the maze of winding and hilly lanes even now retains a whiff of the North African medina. This is where the Muslim population of Magerit was concentrated in the wake of the 11th-century Christian takeover of the town.

BASÍLICA DE SAN FRANCISCO EL GRANDE

One of the largest churches in the city, the **Basílica de San Francisco el Grande** (Map pp142-3; ☎ 91 365 38 00; Plaza de San Francisco 1; admission €3; 8-11am Mon, 8am-1pm & 4-6.30pm Tue-Fri, 4-8.45pm Sat; M La Latina or Puerta de Toledo) dominates the skyline at the southern reaches of La Latina, its pretty dome lording it over the rooftops. The baroque basilica has some outstanding features, including frescoed cupolas and chapel ceilings by Francisco Bayeu. Goya's *The Prediction of San Bernardino of Siena for the King of Aragón* is here, too. According to legend, the basilica sits atop the site where St Francis of Assisi built a chapel in 1217.

IGLESIA DE SAN ANDRÉS & AROUND

The stately **Iglesia de San Andrés** (Map pp142-3; Plaza de San Andrés 1; 8am-1pm & 6-8pm; M La Latina) crowns the plaza of the same name, providing a lovely backdrop for the impromptu parties that fill this square on Sunday afternoons as the El Rastro crowd drifts in. Gutted during Spain's civil war, it was restored to its former glory and is at its best when illuminated at night.

Around the back, overlooking the delightful Plaza de la Paja, is the **Capilla del Obispo**, considered the best Renaissance church in Madrid, though it's not strictly of the period. Look out for the mostly Gothic vaulting in the ceilings, the plateresque tombs and the fine Renaissance reredos. It was long the resting place of San Isidro Labrador until his remains were moved to the Basílica de San Isidro. Restoration of the chapel was nearing completion at the time of writing.

The nearby **Museo de San Isidro** (Map pp142-3; ☎ 91 366 74 15; www.munimadrid.es/museosanisidro in Spanish; Plaza de San Andrés 2; admission free; 9.30am-8pm Tue-Fri, 10am-2pm Sat & Sun; M La Latina) occupies the spot where San Isidro Labrador (the patron saint of Madrid) is said to have ended his days around 1172. Displays range from archaeological finds from the Roman period to maps, scale models, paintings and photos of Madrid down through the ages. A particular highlight is the large model based on Pedro Teixera's famous 1656 map of Madrid.

MOST BEAUTIFUL PLAZAS

- **Plaza Mayor** (p147) – the elegant focal point of central Madrid.
- **Plaza de Oriente** (p148) – the glorious centrepiece of imperial Madrid.
- **Plaza de Santa Ana** (below) – the heartbeat and cultural hub of Huertas.
- **Plaza de la Villa** (p149) – a cosy square surrounded by stunning local architecture.
- **Plaza de la Paja** (p151) – the villagelike intimacy of Old Madrid.
- **Plaza de la Puerta del Sol** (p150) – the clamorous crossroads of the city centre.
- **Plaza de la Cibeles** (p156) – a monument to Madrid's cults of excess and extravagance.

IGLESIA DE SAN PEDRO EL VIEJO

With its clearly Mudéjar bell tower, **Iglesia de San Pedro El Viejo** (Map pp142-3; ☎ 91 365 12 84; Costanilla de San Pedro; Ⓜ La Latina) is one of the few remaining windows onto the world of medieval Madrid. The church was built atop the site of the old Mezquita de la Morería (Mosque of the Muslim Quarter), in the days when Madrid was still influenced by its Muslim occupation.

Huertas & Atocha

If Huertas is known for anything, it's for nightlife that never seems to abate once the sun goes down. Such fame is well deserved, but there's so much more to Huertas than immediately meets the eye. Enjoy the height of sophisticated European cafe culture in the superb Plaza de Santa Ana, then go down the hill through the Barrio de las Letras to the Centro de Arte Reina Sofía, one of the finest contemporary art galleries in Europe. Across the Plaza de Emperador Carlos V from the gallery, the Antigua Estación de Atocha marks the beginning of the Atocha district and is as much a landmark for architects as for train travellers.

PLAZA DE SANTA ANA

A delightful confluence of elegant architecture and irresistible energy, **Plaza de Santa Ana** (Map pp142-3; Ⓜ Sol, Sevilla or Antón Martín) is a gem. What it lacks in a distinguished history (it was laid out in 1810 during the reign of Joseph Bonaparte, giving breathing space to what had hitherto been one of Madrid's most claustrophobic *barrios*), it more than compensates for as a focal point of the *barrio*'s intellectual life, overlooked by the Teatro Español and surrounded by a host of live music venues.

BARRIO DE LAS LETRAS

The area around Plaza de Santa Ana is often referred to as the Barrio de las Letras (District of Letters), because of the writers who lived here during Spain's golden age of the 16th and 17th centuries. Miguel de Cervantes was originally buried in the baroque **Convento de las Trinitarias** (Map pp142-3; Calle de Lope de Vega 16; Ⓜ Antón Martín) and a commemorative Mass is held for him every year on the anniversary of his death, 23 April. The convent is closed to the public. Cervantes' house, at Calle de Cervantes 2, is long gone, but just down the street is the **Casa de Lope de Vega** (Map pp142-3; ☎ 91 429 92 16; Calle de Cervantes 11; adult/concession €2/1, Sat free; ⌚ 9.30am-2pm Tue-Fri, 10am-2pm Sat; Ⓜ Antón Martín), the former home of Lope de Vega (1562–1635), Spain's premier playwright. It's now a museum containing memorabilia from Lope de Vega's life and work.

ANTIGUA ESTACIÓN DE ATOCHA

The **Antigua Estación de Atocha** (Old Atocha Train Station; Map p145; Plaza del Emperador Carlos V; Ⓜ Atocha or Atocha Renfe) is a towering iron-and-glass relic from the 19th century. Lovingly preserved and artfully converted in 1992 into a surprising tropical garden with more than 500 plant species, it now feels more like a lush greenhouse than a transport hub, although the cavernous ceiling resonates with the grand old European train stations of another age.

CENTRO DE ARTE REINA SOFÍA

Adapted from the shell of an 18th-century hospital, the **Centro de Arte Reina Sofía** (Map pp142-3; ☎ 91 774 10 00; www.museoreinasofia.es; Calle de Santa Isabel 52; adult/child & senior/student €6/free/4, 2.30-9pm Sat & Sun free, audioguide €3; ⌚ 10am-9pm Mon & Wed-Sat, 10am-2.30pm Sun; Ⓜ Atocha) houses the best in modern (predominantly) Spanish art, principally spanning the 20th century up to the 1980s.

The main gallery's permanent display ranges over the 2nd (Rooms 1 to 12) and 4th (Rooms 13 to 39) floors. Note that the room numbers have recently been changed to accommodate temporary exhibitions and may change again, so pick up a floor plan from the information desk just inside the museum's entrance.

The big attraction for most visitors is Picasso's *Guernica* in Room 6 on the 2nd floor, which alone is worth the entrance price. Alongside this masterwork is a plethora of the artist's preparatory sketches.

Primary among the other stars in residence is the work of Joan Miró (1893–1983), which adorns Room 12, a long gallery adjacent to the Picasso collection. Amid his often delightfully bright primary-colour efforts are some of his equally odd sculptures. You'll also want to rush to Room 10 to view the 20 or so canvases by Salvador Dalí (1904–89), especially the surrealist extravaganza *El Gran Masturbador* (1929). Amid this collection is a strange bust of a certain *Joelle* done by Dalí and his pal Man Ray (1890–1976). Other surrealists, including Max Ernst (1891–1976), appear in Room 11.

For lesser-known 20th-century Spanish artists, Room 12 concentrates on the *madrileño* José Gutiérrez Solana (1886–1945), while Room 3 hosts works by the better-known Juan Gris; these spill over into Room 4. Among the bronzes of Pablo Gargallo (1881–1934) in Room 5 is a head of Picasso. Also on the 2nd floor, in Room 1, you'll find the excellent works of Basque artist Ignazio Zuloaga (1870–1945).

The collection on the 4th floor ranges from the 1940s to the 1980s. Rooms 20 to 23 in particular offer a representative look at abstract painting in Spain, including Eusebio Sempere (1923–85) and members of the Equipo 57 group (founded in 1957 by a group of Spanish artists in exile in Paris), such as Pablo Palazuelo. Rooms 24 to 35 lead you through Spanish art of the 1960s and 1970s. Some external reference points, such as works by Francis Bacon (1909–92) and Henry Moore (1831–95), both in Room 24, are thrown in to broaden the context.

Closer to the present day, Room 38 is given over to work by Eduardo Arroyo, while beautiful works of the Basque sculptor Eduardo Chillida (1924–2002) fill Rooms 42 and 43.

The state-of-the-art Reina Sofía is itself a work of art, especially the stunning extension that spreads along the western tip of Plaza del Emperador Carlos V and hosts temporary exhibitions, auditoriums, the bookshop, a cafe and the museum's library.

Paseo del Prado & El Retiro

If you've just come down the hill from Huertas, you'll feel like you've left behind a madhouse for an oasis of greenery, fresh air and high culture. The Museo del Prado and the Museo Thyssen-Bornemisza are among the richest galleries of fine art in the world, and plenty of other museums lurk in the quietly elegant streets just behind the Prado. Rising up the hill to the east are the stately gardens of the supremely enjoyable Parque del Buen Retiro.

MUSEO DEL PRADO

One of the world's top museums, the **Museo del Prado** (Map p145; ☎ 91 330 28 00; http://museoprado.mcu.es; Paseo del Prado; adult/under 18yr & over 65yr/student €6/free/4, Sun free, audioguide €3.50; 🕑 9am-8pm Tue-Sun; Ⓜ Banco de España) has a peerless collection of Spanish and European art. Spend as long as you can here or, better still, plan to make a couple of visits because it can be a little overwhelming if you try to take it all in at once.

The more than 7000 paintings held in the Museo del Prado's collection (just over half are currently on display) are like a window on the historical vagaries of the Spanish soul: grand and imperious in the royal paintings of Velázquez; darkly tumultuous in the Pinturas Negras (Black Paintings) of Goya; and outward-looking in the collection of sophisticated works of art from all across Europe.

The building in which the Prado is housed is itself a masterpiece. Completed in 1785, the neoclassical Palacio de Villanueva served, somewhat ignominiously, as a cavalry barracks for Napoleon's troops during their occupation of Madrid between 1808 and 1813. In 1814 King Fernando VII decided to use the palace as a museum. Five years later the Museo del Prado opened with 311 Spanish paintings on display, and it's never looked back. In late 2007 the long-awaited extension of the Prado opened to critical acclaim.

Entrance to the Prado is via the western Puerta de Velázquez (in the old part of the Prado) or the eastern Puerta de los Jerónimos (the extension), but first, tickets must be purchased from the ticket office at the northern end of the building, opposite the Hotel Ritz.

Entering via the Puerta de Velázquez, turn right into Room 75, home to works by Tintoretto and Titian. Your primary aim should be Rooms 66 and 67, where the darkest and most disturbing works of Francisco

José de Goya y Lucientes reside. Las Pinturas Negras are so called because of the dark browns and black that dominate, and for the distorted animalesque appearance of their characters. *Saturno Devorando a Su Hijo* (Saturn Devouring His Son) captures the essence of Goya's genius, and *La Romería de San Isidro* (Pilgrimage of San Isidro) and *El Akelarre (El gran cabrón)* – which translates as Witches' Sabbath (The Great He-Goat) – are profoundly unsettling.

It's time for a dramatic change of pace. There is no more weird-and-wonderful painting in the Prado than *The Garden of Earthly Delights* by Hieronymus Bosch (c 1450–1516) in Room 56A. While it's undoubtedly the star attraction of this fantastical painter's collection, all his work rewards inspection.

Before heading upstairs, don't miss the paintings by German artist Albrecht Dürer (1471–1528) in Room 55B, or Italy's Rafael (1483–1520) in Room 49.

The first floor is where the Prado really struts its stuff. In Room 39 are two of the museum's greatest masterpieces, Goya's *El Dos de Mayo* and *El Tres de Mayo*. Among Madrid's most emblematic paintings, they bring to life the 1808 anti-French revolt and subsequent execution of insurgents. In the same room are two more of Goya's best-known and most intriguing oils, *La Maja Vestida* and *La Maja Desnuda*. These portraits of an unknown woman, commonly believed to be the Duquesa de Alba (who may have been Goya's lover), are identical save for the lack of clothing in the latter. You can enjoy the rest of Goya's works in Rooms 32, 29 and 16B.

From Room 16B, it's a short stroll to Room 12, where you'll encounter the extraordinarily life-filled paintings of one of the greatest figures of Spanish art. Of the many paintings by Diego Rodriguez de Silva y Velázquez that so distinguish the Prado, *Las Meninas* is what most people come to see. Completed in 1656, it's more properly known as *La Família de Felipe IV* (The Family of Felipe IV). Velázquez' mastery of light and colour is never more apparent than here. It depicts the infant Margarita in the centre and, on the left, Velázquez himself. An interesting detail of the painting, aside from the extraordinary cheek of painting himself in royal company, is the presence of the cross of the Order of Santiago on the artist's vest. Velázquez was apparently obsessed with being given a noble title. He got it shortly before his death, but in this oil painting, he has awarded himself the order years before it would in fact be his!

There are more fine works by Velázquez in Rooms 14, 15, 16 and 18. Watch out in particular for his stunning paintings of various members of royalty – Felipe II, Felipe IV, Margarita de Austria (a younger version of whom features in *Las Meninas*), El Príncipe Baltasar Carlos and Isabel de Francia – on horseback: they seem to spring off the canvas.

If Spanish painters have piqued your curiosity, the stark figures of Francisco de Zurbarán dominate Rooms 18 and 18A, while Bartolomé Esteban Murillo (Room 28) and José de Ribera (Rooms 25 and 26) should also be on your itinerary. The vivid, almost surreal works by the 16th-century master El Greco, whose figures are characteristically slender and tortured, can be seen in Rooms 9A to 10A.

An alternative is the Prado's outstanding collection of Flemish art. The fulsome figures and bulbous cherubs of Peter Paul Rubens (1577–1640) provide a playful antidote to the darkness of many of the other Flemish artists and can be enjoyed in Rooms 8 to 11. His signature *Las Tres Gracias* (The Three Graces) is in Room 9, while the stand-out *Adoración de los Reyes Magos* (Adoration of the Magi) is in Room 9B. Other fine works in the vicinity include those by Anton van Dyck (Rooms 9B, 10A and 10B). On no account should you miss Rembrandt in Room 7.

From the 1st floor of the Edificio Villanueva, passageways lead to the Edificio Jerónimos (Jerónimos Building), the Prado's modern extension. The main hall (where you enter if coming through the Puerta de los Jerónimos) contains information counters, the Prado's excellent new bookshop and its cafe. Rooms A and B (and Room C on the 1st floor) host temporary exhibitions, often including many Prado masterpieces that were held in storage for decades for lack of wall space. If you continue up to the 2nd floor you'll reach the cloisters, the undoubted architectural highlight of the extension. Built in 1672 of local granite, they were until recently attached to the adjacent Iglesia de San Jerónimo el Real (p157) but were stripped to the ground and rebuilt to stunning effect.

MUSEO THYSSEN-BORNEMISZA

The favourite art gallery of many visitors to Madrid, the **Museo Thyssen-Bornemisza** (Map pp142-3; ☎ 91 369 01 51; www.museothyssen.org; Paseo del Prado 8; adult/concession €6/4; 10am-7pm Tue-Sun; Ⓜ Banco de España) has something for everyone, with a breathtaking breadth of artistic styles, from the masters of medieval art to the zany world of contemporary painting. All the big names are represented here, sometimes with just a single painting, but the Thyssens' gift to Madrid and the art-loving public is to have them all under one roof. Its easy-to-follow floor plan also makes it one of the most easily navigable galleries in the capital.

The collection is the legacy of Baron Thyssen-Bornemisza, a German-Hungarian magnate. Spain acquired the prestigious collection when the baron married Carmen Tita Cervera, a former Miss España and ex-wife of Lex Barker (of *Tarzan* fame). The deal was sealed when the Spanish government offered to overhaul the neoclassical Palacio de Villahermosa specifically to house the collection. Almost 800 works have hung here since October 1992. Although the baron died in 2002, his glamorous wife has shown that she has learned much from the collecting nous of her late husband. In early 2000 the museum acquired two adjoining buildings to house approximately half of Carmen Thyssen-Bornemisza's collection.

The 2nd floor is home to medieval art, predominantly Italian, German and Flemish religious paintings and triptychs, mostly from the 13th and 14th centuries. There are some real gems hidden here. Unless you've a specialist's eye, pause in Room 5, where you'll find one work by Italy's Piero della Francesca (1410–92) and the instantly recognisable *Henry VIII* by Holbein the Younger (1497–1543). Continue to Room 10 for the evocative, Brueghel-like *Massacre of the Innocents* (1586) by Lucas van Valckenberch. Room 11 is dedicated to El Greco (with three pieces) and his Venetian contemporaries Tintoretto and Titian, while Caravaggio and the Spaniard José de Ribera dominate Room 12. A single painting each by Murillo and Zurbarán add further Spanish flavour in the two rooms that follow, while the exceptionally rendered views of Venice by Canaletto (1697–1768) should on no account be missed.

But best of all on this floor is the extension (Rooms A to H) built to house the burgeoning collection, with more Canalettos hanging alongside Monet, Sisley, Renoir, Pissarro, Degas, Constable and Van Gogh.

Before heading downstairs, a detour to Rooms 19 to 21 will satisfy those devoted to 17th-century Dutch and Flemish masters, including Anton van Dyck, Jan Brueghel the Elder and Rembrandt.

If all that sounds impressive, the 1st floor is where the Thyssen really shines. English visitors may want to pause in Room 28, where there's a Gainsborough, but if you've been skimming the surface of this at-times overwhelming collection, Room 32 is the place to linger over every painting. The astonishing texture of Van Gogh's *Les Vessenots* is a masterpiece, but the same could be said for *Woman in Riding Habit* by Manet, *The Thaw at Véthueil* by Monet and Pissarro's quintessentially Parisian *Rue Saint-Honoré in the Afternoon*.

Rooms 33 to 35 play host to Modigliani, Picasso, Cezanne, Matisse and Egon Schiele, while the baronness' eye for quality is nowhere more evident than in the extension (Rooms I to P). Juan Gris, Matisse, Picasso, Kandinsky, Georges Braque, Toulouse-Lautrec, Degas, Sorolla, Sisley and Edward Hopper are all present, but our favourites include the rich colours of Gauguin's *Mata Mua,* Monet's dreamlike *Charing Cross Bridge* and the rare appearance of Edvard Munch with *Geese in an Orchard*. Quite simply, it's an outrageously rich collection.

BEST MUSEUMS FOR SPANISH ARTISTS

- **Museo del Prado** (p153) – Goya, Velázquez, Zurbarán and all the biggies
- **Centro de Arte Reina Sofía** (p152) – Picasso, Dalí, Miró...
- **Ermita de San Antonio de la Florida** (p159) – Goya
- **Real Academia de Bellas Artes de San Fernando** (p150) – Goya, Velázquez, Picasso, Juan Gris
- **Museo Sorolla** (p160) – Joaquín Sorolla
- **Museo Municipal de Arte Contemporáneo de Madrid** (p159) – contemporary artists

On the ground floor, the foray into the 20th century that began in the 1st-floor extension continues with a fine spread of paintings from cubism through to pop art. In Room 41 you'll see a nice mix of the big three of cubism: Picasso, Georges Braque and Madrid's own Juan Gris. Picasso pops up again in Room 45, another one of the gallery's stand-out rooms. Its treasures include works by Marc Chagall, Kandinsky, Paul Klee and Joan Miró.

Room 46 is similarly rich, with the splattered craziness of Jackson Pollock's *Brown and Silver I* and the deceptively simple but strangely pleasing *Green on Maroon* by Mark Rothko taking centre stage. In Rooms 47 and 48, the Thyssen builds to a stirring climax, with Salvador Dalí, Francis Bacon, Roy Lichtenstein, Edward Hopper and Lucian Freud (Sigmund's Berlin-born grandson) all represented.

PARQUE DEL BUEN RETIRO

A Sunday walk in **El Retiro** (Map p145; 6am-midnight May-Sep, 6am-11pm Oct-Apr; M Retiro, Príncipe de Vergara, Ibiza or Atocha) is as much a Madrid tradition as tapas and terrace cafes. Littered with marble monuments, landscaped lawns, the occasional elegant building and abundant greenery, it's quiet and contemplative during the week, but comes alive on weekends.

Laid out in the 17th century by Felipe IV, the park was once the preserve of kings, queens and their intimates, but *madrileños* from all walks of life have long since made it their own. Apart from strolling, people come here to read the Sunday papers in the shade, take a boat ride (€4 for 45 minutes) or enjoy a cool drink at the numerous outdoor *terrazas*. Puppet shows for the kids are another summertime feature (look for **Titirilandia**, or Puppet Land).

The *estanque* (lake) is watched over by the massive ornamental structure of the **Monument to Alfonso XII** on the eastern side, complete with marble lions. If you want to catch the essence of Madrid, come here as sunset approaches on a summer Sunday afternoon – as the crowd grows, bongos ring out across the park and people start to dance.

Legend has it that an enormous fortune buried by Felipe IV in the mid-18th century rests beneath the **Fuente Egipcia** (Egyptian Fountain) on the western side of the lake. Other highlights include the 1887 **Palacio de Cristal** (91 574 66 14; 11am-8pm Mon-Sat, 11am-6pm Sun & holidays May-Sep, 10am-6pm Mon-Sat, 10am-4pm Sun & holidays Oct-Apr), a charming metal-and-glass structure south of the lake, which hosts temporary exhibitions; the 1883 **Palacio de Velázquez**, which was closed for renovations at the time of research; and, at the southern end of the park, a statue of **El Ángel Caído** (the Fallen Angel, aka Lucifer), one of the world's few statues to the devil.

In the southwestern corner of the park is the moving **Bosque de los Ausentes** (Forest of the Absent), also known as the Bosque del Recuerdo (Memorial Forest), an understated memorial to the 191 victims of the 11 March 2004 train bombings. For each victim stands an olive or cypress tree.

In the northeastern corner of the park are the pleasing ruins of the 13th-century **Ermita de San Isidro** (Map pp134–5), a small country chapel that's noteworthy as one of the few, albeit modest, extant examples of Romanesque architecture in Madrid. When it was built, Madrid was a little village more than 2km away.

REAL JARDÍN BOTÁNICO

With its manicured flowerbeds and neat paths, the **Real Jardín Botánico** (Royal Botanical Garden; Map p145; 91 420 30 17; Plaza de Bravo Murillo 2; adult/child/concession €2/free/1; 10am-9pm May-Aug, 10am-8pm Apr & Sep, 10am-7pm Oct & Mar, 10am-6pm Nov-Feb; M Atocha) is more intimate than El Retiro. First created in 1755 on the banks of Río Manzanares, the garden was moved here in 1781 by Carlos III. These days you can see thousands of plant species.

CAIXA FORUM

The extraordinary **Caixa Forum** (Map p145; 91 330 73 00; www.fundacio.lacaixa.es in Spanish; Paseo del Prado 36; admission free; 10am-10pm; M Atocha), which opened in early 2008 at the southern end of the Paseo del Prado, is one of the most exciting architectural innovations to emerge in Madrid in recent years. Seeming to hover above the ground, this brick edifice is topped by an intriguing summit of rusted iron. On an adjacent wall is the *jardín colgante* (hanging garden), a lush vertical wall of greenery almost four storeys high. Inside are four floors of exhibition and performance space awash in stainless steel and with soaring ceilings.

PLAZA DE LA CIBELES

Of all the grand roundabouts that punctuate the elegant boulevard of Paseo del Prado,

Plaza de la Cibeles (Map p145; Ⓜ Banco de España) most evokes the splendour of Imperial Madrid.

The jewel in the crown is the astonishing **Palacio de Comunicaciones**. Completed in 1917 by Antonio Palacios, Madrid's most prolific architect of the belle époque, it combines elements of the North American monumental style of the period with Gothic and Renaissance touches. Newcomers find it hard to accept that this is merely the central post office, although the city council is gradually taking it over as the *ayuntamiento*. Other landmark buildings around the plaza's perimeter include the **Palacio de Linares**, **Casa de América**, **Palacio de Buenavista** (Map pp138–9), **Casa de las Siete Chimeneas** (Map pp138–9) and the national **Banco de España** (Map pp142–3; 1891). The views east towards the Puerta de Alcalá or west towards the Metrópolis building are some of Madrid's finest.

The spectacular fountain of the goddess Cybele at the centre of the plaza is also one of Madrid's most beautiful. Ever since it was erected in 1780 by Ventura Rodríguez, it has been a Madrid favourite. Carlos III tried to move it to the gardens of the Granja de San Ildefonso, near Segovia, but the *madrileños* kicked up such a fuss that he abandoned the idea. The Cibeles fountain has also long been the venue for joyous and often destructive celebrations by players and supporters of Real Madrid whenever the side wins anything of note.

MUSEO NAVAL

Boat lovers will get a thrill from the **Museo Naval** (Map p145; ☎ 91 379 52 99; www.museonavalmadrid.com in Spanish; Paseo del Prado 5; admission free; 🕑 10am-2pm Tue-Sun; Ⓜ Banco de España), but it's also of interest to those who've always wondered what the Spanish Armada really looked like. Apart from its extraordinary model ships, the museum's highlights are the antique maps, especially Juan de la Cosa's parchment map of the known world, put together in 1500 – it's supposedly the first map to show the Americas.

MUSEO DE ARTES DECORATIVAS

Give your inner antique dealer a thrill at the **Museo de Artes Decorativas** (Museum of Decorative Arts; Map p145; ☎ 91 532 64 99; http://mnartesdecorativas.mcu.es; Calle de Montalbán 12; adult/child €2.40/1.20, Sun free; 🕑 9.30am-3pm Tue-Sat, 10am-3pm Sun; Ⓜ Retiro). A fascinating window onto the life of the upper classes from the 15th to the 19th centuries, the museum is awash with sumptuous period furniture, ceramics, carpets, tapestries and the like. Spread over five floors, it could keep you occupied for hours but probably only deserves one.

IGLESIA DE SAN JERÓNIMO EL REAL

Tucked away behind the Museo del Prado, the lavish **Iglesia de San Jerónimo el Real** (Map p145; ☎ 91 420 35 78; Calle de Ruiz de Alarcón 19; 🕑 10am-1pm & 5-8pm Mon-Sat; Ⓜ Atocha or Banco de España) was largely destroyed during the Peninsular War. The interior was reconstructed during the 19th-century, however, and is just exquisite. The chapel was traditionally favoured by the Spanish royal family and it was here, amid the mock-Isabelline splendour, that King Juan Carlos I was crowned in 1975 upon the death of Franco. Being a chapel of royal choice did little to protect it from the Museo del Prado's inexorable expansion – what remained of its cloisters next door was demolished (despite vociferous local protests) and then rebuilt as part of the Museo del Prado extension.

PUERTA DE ALCALÁ

The first triumphal **gate** (Map p145; Plaza de la Independencia; Ⓜ Retiro) to bear this name was built in 1599, but Carlos III was singularly unimpressed and had it demolished in 1764 and replaced by another, the one you see today. Twice a year, in autumn and spring, cars abandon the roundabout and are replaced by flocks of sheep being transferred in an age-old ritual from their summer to winter pastures (and vice versa).

REAL FÁBRICA DE TAPICES

Fancy a wall tapestry or a rug based on some of Goya's sketches? The **Real Fábrica de Tapices** (Royal Tapestry Factory; Map pp134-5; ☎ 91 434 05 51; www.realfabricadetapices.com in Spanish; Calle de Fuenterrabía 2; admission €2.50; 🕑 10am-2pm Mon-Fri Sep-Jul; Ⓜ Menéndez Pelayo) can whip one up for you in just a few months for a mere €10,000 or so. Founded in 1720 to provide the royal family and other bigwigs with tapestries befitting their grandeur, it counts the Hotel Ritz and the current royal family as regular clients. Many works are based on cartoons by Goya, who was a long-time employee here, creating 63 different drawings to use as models for elaborate tapestries.

Salamanca

The *barrio* of Salamanca is Madrid's most exclusive quarter, defined by grand and restrained elegance. This is a place to put on your finest clothes and be seen (especially along Calle de Serrano or Calle de José Ortega y Gasset), to stroll into shops with an affected air and resist asking the prices, or to promenade between the fine museums and parks that make you wonder whether you've arrived at the height of civilisation.

MUSEO ARQUEOLÓGICO NACIONAL

The rather forbidding entrance to the **Museo Arqueológico Nacional** (National Archaeology Museum; Map p140; ☎ 91 577 79 12; http://man.mcu.es in Spanish; Calle de Serrano 13; admission €3, free Sun & after 2.30pm Sat; ⌚ 9.30am-8pm Tue-Sat, 9.30am-3pm Sun & holidays; Ⓜ Serrano) little resembles what lies within. Presented with typically Spanish flair (the lighting is perfect and the large collection of artefacts is never cluttered), this delightful collection spans everything from prehistory to the Iberian tribes, Imperial Rome, Visigothic Spain and the Muslim conquest, and includes specimens of Romanesque, Gothic and Mudéjar handiwork.

The museum's ground floor is the most interesting. Highlights include the stunning mosaics taken from Roman villas across Spain (those in Rooms 22 and 24 particularly catch the eye); the magnificent, gilded, Mudéjar domed ceiling in Room 35; and the more sombre Christian Romanesque and Gothic paraphernalia of Room 33. Elsewhere, sculpted figures, such as the *Dama de Ibiza* and *Dama de Elche*, reveal a flourishing artistic tradition among the Iberian tribes – no doubt influenced by contact with Greek and Phoenician civilisations. Outside, stairs lead down to a partial copy of the prehistoric cave paintings of Altamira in Cantabria (see p532).

The basement contains displays on prehistoric man and spans the Neolithic period to the Iron Age – it's probably more of interest to dedicated archaeology buffs. Modest collections from ancient Egypt, Etruscan civilisation in Italy, classical Greece and southern Italy under Imperial Rome take their place alongside finds from the ancient civilisations of the Balearic and Canary Islands.

The 1st floor contains all sorts of items pertaining to Spanish royalty and court life from the 16th through to the 19th centuries.

The museum was undergoing major renovations at the time of writing so the location of some of the exhibits may have changed by the time you read this. Admission is free until the renovations are complete.

BIBLIOTECA NACIONAL & MUSEO DEL LIBRO

One of the most outstanding of the many grand edifices erected in the 19th century on the avenues of Madrid, the 1892 **Biblioteca Nacional** (National Library; Map p140; ☎ 91 580 77 59; Paseo de los Recoletos 20; admission free; ⌚ 10am-9pm Tue-Sat, 10am-2pm Sun; Ⓜ Colón) dominates the southern end of Plaza de Colón. The reading rooms are more for serious students, but the recently overhauled Museo del Libro is a must for bibliophiles. Downstairs and entered via a separate entrance, it has interactive displays, illuminated manuscripts and priceless original works, such as a 1626 map of Spain and Picasso's *Mademoiselle Léonie en un sillón*.

MUSEO LÁZARO GALDIANO

In an imposing early-20th-century Italianate stone mansion, the **Museo Lázaro Galdiano** (Map pp134-5; ☎ 91 561 60 84; www.flg.es in Spanish; Calle de Serrano 122; adult/student €4/3, Sun free; ⌚ 10am-4.30pm Wed-Mon; Ⓜ Gregorio Marañón) has some 13,000 works of art and objets d'art. Apart from works by van Eyck, Bosch, Zurbarán, Ribera, Goya, Claudio Coello, El Greco, Gainsborough and Constable, this is a rather oddball assembly of all sorts of collectables. In Room 14 some of Goya's more famous works are hung together to make a collage, including *La Maja* and the frescoes of the Ermita de San Antonio de la Florida.

MUSEO DE LA ESCULTURA ABSTRACTA

This fascinating open-air collection of 17 **abstract sculptures** (Map p140; Ⓜ Rubén Darío) includes works by the renowned Basque artist Eduardo Chillida and the Catalan master Joan Miró, as well as Eusebio Sempere and Alberto Sánchez, one of Spain's foremost sculptors of the 20th century. The sculptures are beneath the overpass where Paseo de Eduardo Dato crosses Paseo de la Castellana.

Malasaña & Chueca

The inner-city *barrios* of Malasaña and Chueca are where Madrid gets up close and personal. Yes, there are rewarding museums and examples of landmark architecture sprinkled throughout. But these *barrios* are more about doing than seeing; more about experiencing life as it's lived by *madrileños* than ticking off a list of wonderful, if more static, attractions. These attractions may have made the city famous, but they only tell half the story. These are neighbourhoods with attitude and personality, where Madrid's famed nightlife, shopping and eating take you under the skin of the city. Each of these *barrios* has its own personality: Malasaña is streetwise and down to earth, while Chueca, as Madrid's centre of gay culture, is more stylish and flamboyant.

MUSEO MUNICIPAL

The fine **Museo Municipal** (Map pp138-9; ☎ 91 588 86 72; www.munimadrid.es/museomunicipal in Spanish; Calle de Fuencarral 78; admission free; ⏰ 9.30am-8pm Tue-Fri, 10am-2pm Sat & Sun Sep-Jun, 9.30am-2.30pm Tue-Fri, 10am-2pm Sat & Sun Jul & Aug; Ⓜ Tribunal) has an elaborate and restored baroque entrance, raised in 1721 by Pedro de Ribera. The interior is dominated by paintings and other memorabilia charting the historical evolution of Madrid, of which the highlight is Goya's *Allegory of the City of Madrid*. Also worth lingering over is the expansive model of 1830s Madrid on the ground floor. Sadly, the museum was due to close for extensive renovations in October 2008 and may not reopen until 2010.

SOCIEDAD GENERAL DE AUTORES Y EDITORES

The swirling, melting wedding cake of a building that is the **Sociedad General de Autores y Editores** (General Society of Authors & Editors; Map pp138-9; Calle de Fernando VI 4; Ⓜ Alonso Martínez) is as close as Madrid comes to the work of Antoni Gaudí. It's a joyously self-indulgent ode to Modernismo and one of a kind in Madrid. It's far more impressive from the street, which is just as well because it's only open on the first Monday of October (International Architecture Day) and during the Noche en Blanco festivities.

ANTIGUO CUARTEL DEL CONDE DUQUE

Dominating the western edge of the Malasaña district, this formidable former **barracks** (Map pp138-9; ☎ 91 588 57 71; Calle del Conde Duque 9; Ⓜ Plaza de España, Ventura Rodríguez or San Bernardo) houses government archives, libraries and the Hemeroteca Municipal (the biggest collection of newspapers and magazines in Spain) behind its 228m facade. Also contained within its walls is the **Museo Municipal de Arte Contemporáneo de Madrid** (☎ 91 588 29 28; www.munimadrid.es/museoartecontemporaneo in Spanish; admission free; ⏰ 10am-2pm & 5.30-9pm Tue-Sat, 10.30am-2.30pm Sun), with contemporary Spanish and international paintings, sculpture, photography and graphic art. Now and then in summer the one-time barracks also does a night gig as a music venue.

Chamberí & Argüelles

You don't come to Chamberí or Argüelles for the sights, although there are some fine museums, as well as outstanding places to eat, drink and watch live music. Chamberí and, to a lesser extent, Argüelles may be fairly well off today, but they lack the snootiness of Salamanca. As such, it's here perhaps more than anywhere else in Madrid that you get a sense of the city as the *madrileños* experience it, away from the tourist crowds.

ERMITA DE SAN ANTONIO DE LA FLORIDA

The frescoed ceilings of the **Ermita de San Antonio de la Florida** (Map pp134-5; ☎ 91 542 07 22; Glorieta de San Antonio de la Florida 5; ⏰ 9.30am-8pm Tue-Fri, 10am-2pm Sat & Sun Sep-Jun, varied hr Jul & Aug; Ⓜ Príncipe Pío) are one of Madrid's most surprising secrets. Recently restored and also known as the Panteón de Goya, the southern of the two small chapels is one of the few places to see Goya's work in its original setting, as painted by the master in 1798 on the request of Carlos IV.

The frescoes on the dome depict the miracle of St Anthony, who is calling on a young man to rise from the grave and absolve his father, unjustly accused of his murder. Around them swarms a typical Madrid crowd. Usually in this kind of scene the angels and cherubs appear in the cupola, above all the terrestrial activity, but Goya, never one to let himself be confined within the mores of the day, places the human above the divine.

The painter is buried in front of the altar. His remains were transferred in 1919 from Bordeaux (France), where he died in self-imposed exile in 1828.

TEMPLO DE DEBOD

Remarkably, this authentic 4th-century-BC Egyptian temple sits in the heart of Madrid, in the Parque de la Montaña. The **Templo de Debod** (Map pp134-5; ☎ 91 366 74 15; www.munimadrid.es/templodebod in Spanish; Paseo del Pintor Rosales; admission free; ⏰ 10am-2pm & 6-8pm Tue-Fri, 10am-2pm Sat & Sun Apr-Sep, 9.45am-1.45pm & 4.15-6.15pm Tue-Fri, 10am-2pm Sat & Sun

Oct-Mar; Ⓜ Ventura Rodríguez) was saved from the rising waters of Lake Nasser, formed by the Aswan High Dam, and sent block by block to Spain in 1968. The views from the surrounding gardens towards the Palacio Real are quite special.

MUSEO DE AMÉRICA

Travel to, and trade with, the newly discovered Americas was a central part of Spain's culture and economy from 1492 until the early 20th century. The **Museo de América** (Map p132; ☎ 91 549 26 41; http://museodeamerica.mcu.es in Spanish; Avenida de los Reyes Católicos 6; adult/child/student €3/free/1.50, Sun free; 🕑 9.30am-3pm Tue-Sat, 10am-3pm Sun; Ⓜ Moncloa) has a representative display of ceramics, statuary, jewellery and instruments of hunting, fishing and war, along with some of the paraphernalia brought back by the colonisers. The Colombian gold collection, dating back to the 2nd century AD, and a couple of shrunken heads are particularly eye-catching.

MUSEO SOROLLA

The Valencian artist Joaquín Sorolla immortalised the clear Mediterranean light of the Valencian coast. His Madrid mansion, now a **museum** (Map pp134-5; ☎ 91 310 15 84; http://museosorolla.mcu.es in Spanish; Paseo del General Martínez Campos 37; adult/child/student €2.40/free/1.20; 🕑 9.30am-3pm Tue-Sat, 10am-3pm Sun; Ⓜ Iglesia or Gregorio Marañón), is home to the largest collection of his works.

On the ground floor you enter a cool *patio cordobés,* an Andalucian courtyard off which is a room containing collections of Sorolla's drawings. The 1st floor was mostly decorated by the artist himself and Sorolla used the three separate rooms as studios. In the second one is a collection of his Valencian beach scenes. Upstairs, works spanning Sorolla's career are organised across four adjoining rooms.

Northern Madrid

The **Museo de la Ciudad** (Map p133; ☎ 91 588 65 99; www.esmadrid.com; Calle del Príncipe de Vergara 140; admission free; 🕑 10am-2pm & 4-7pm Tue-Fri, 10am-2pm Sat & Sun; Ⓜ Cruz del Rayo) has outstanding scale models of various Madrid landmarks, among them Plaza de Toros. Others cover whole *barrios* or features such as Plaza de la Villa and Paseo de la Castellana. The theme running through the museum is 'Discover your city'; it's a topic well worth exploring as the exhibits take you from Madrid's beginnings up to the Enlightenment, through the 19th century and to the present.

Beyond the Centre

Casa de Campo (Ⓜ Batán), a 1700-hectare, somewhat unkempt semi-wilderness, stretches west of Río Manzanares. There are prettier and more central parks in Madrid, but such is its scope that nearly half a million *madrileños* visit every weekend, when cyclists, walkers and picnickers overwhelm the byways and trails that criss-cross the park.

Inside the Casa de Campo is the **Zoo Aquarium de Madrid** (☎ 91 512 37 70; www.zoomadrid.com; adult/3-7yr & senior €16.90/13.70), home to around 3000 animals, and the **Parque de Atracciones** (☎ 91 463 29 00; www.parquedeatracciones.es in Spanish; admission €9.30, incl unlimited rides adult/under 7yr €27.50/18), a decent amusement park sure to keep the kids entertained. Opening hours vary at both places.

A fun way to get to the Casa de Campo is the **teleférico** (cable car; Map pp134-5; ☎ 91 541 74 50; www.teleferico.com in Spanish; adult one-way/return €3.50/5, 3-7yr one-way/return €3.40/4). It starts at Paseo del Pintor Rosales, on the corner of Calle del Marqués de Urquijo, and ends at a high point in the middle of the park. Hours of operation vary.

ACTIVITIES

Cycling

Madrid is not Europe's most bicycle-friendly city, but a ride in the Casa de Campo or El Retiro is a fantastic way to spend an afternoon. The following places rent bikes:

Bike Spain (Map pp142-3; ☎ 91 559 06 53; www.bikespain.info; Plaza de la Villa 1 (Calle del Codo); half-/full day/weekend €10/15/25; 🕑 10am-2pm & 4-7pm Mon-Fri, 10am-2pm Sat & Sun; Ⓜ Ópera) Also organises cycling tours.

Trixi.com (Map pp142-3; ☎ 91 523 15 47; www.trixi.com; Calle de los Jardines 12; 4/8/24hr €8/12/15, helmet €2.50; 🕑 10am-2pm & 4-8pm Mon-Fri, 10am-8pm Sat & Sun Mar-Oct, 10am-3pm daily Nov, Dec & Feb; Ⓜ Gran Vía)

Urban Movil (Map pp142-3; ☎ 91 542 77 71; Calle Mayor 78; 1hr/half-day/full day €4.50/14/19; Ⓜ Ópera)

Swimming

If you're clamouring for respite during the dry heat of Madrid's endless summer, head to the huge outdoor pool at **Canal de Isabel II** (Map p133; ☎ 91 554 51 53; Avenida de Filipinas 54; admission €4; 🕑 11am-8pm Jun-early Sep; Ⓜ Ríos Rosas or Canal) in northern Madrid. You could also try the large outdoor pools at **Casa de Campo** (☎ 91 463 00 50; Avenida Ángel; admission €4.50; 🕑 11.30am-9pm May-Sep, 9am-noon, 3-7pm & 9-10pm Oct-Apr; Ⓜ Batán), where the indoor and outdoor swimming pools are some of Madrid's best.

Tennis

Polideportivo La Chopera (Map p145; ☎ 91 420 11 54; Parque del Buen Retiro; court rental from €5; 9am-8pm Mon-Fri; M Atocha) is the most atmospheric place to play tennis, surrounded by trees and open spaces in the southwestern corner of El Retiro.

Skiing

Madrid Xanadú (☎ 902 36 13 09; www.madridsnowzone.com in Spanish; Calle Puerto de Navacerrada, Arroyomolinos; 10am-10pm Sun-Thu, 10am-midnight Fri & Sat) is the largest covered ski centre in Europe. Open year-round, it's kept at a decidedly cool -2°C. Within the same complex is a mammoth mall, cinemas, a kart track and an amusement park. Madrid Xanadú is approximately 23km west of Madrid, just off the A5. To get here, take bus 529, 531 or 536 from the Estación Sur de Autobuses.

Fitness Clubs

You'll find there are public gyms and indoor pools (normally for lap swimming only) scattered throughout Madrid. They generally charge a modest €3.50 to €7 for one-day admission and they can get pretty crowded on weekends and after work hours. Privately owned health centres are more expensive (€10 to €15), but will usually have less-crowded workout rooms.

Polideportivo La Chopera (Map p145; ☎ 91 420 11 54; Parque del Buen Retiro; workout €5; 9am-8pm Mon-Fri; M Atocha), in the southwestern corner of El Retiro, is one of Madrid's most complete and more central sports centres, boasting a fine new workout centre.

Spas & Yoga

Madrid's best day spas and yoga centres include the following:

Chi Spa (Map p140; ☎ 91 578 13 40; www.thechispa.com; Calle del Conde de Aranda 6; 10am-9pm Mon-Fri, 10am-6pm Sat; M Retiro)

City Yoga (Map p133; ☎ 91 553 47 51; www.city-yoga.com in Spanish; Calle de los Artistas 43; 10am-10pm Mon-Fri, 10am-2pm Sat; M Cuatro Caminos or Nuevos Ministerios) There's a €30 joining fee.

Hammam Medina Mayrit (Map pp142-3; ☎ 902 33 33 34; www.medinamayrit.com; Calle de Atocha 14; 10am-midnight; M Sol) A traditional Arab bath; bookings required.

Spa Relajarse (Map pp138-9; ☎ 91 308 61 48; www.sparelajarse.com in Spanish; Calle de Barquillo 43; 11am-11pm Mon-Sat, 1-9pm Sun; M Chueca)

WALKING TOURS

Walk 1: Historic Madrid

Start in the pulsating, geographic centre of Spain, **Plaza de la Puerta del Sol** (**1**; p150), then head northwest along Calle de Preciados. The second street on the left will bring you out onto Plaza de las Descalzas, home to the **Convento de las Descalzas Reales** (**2**; p149). Moving south, you come to the **Iglesia de San Ginés** (**3**; p150), the site of one of Madrid's oldest places of Christian worship. Behind it is the wonderful **Chocolatería de San Ginés** (**4**; p184), a place of worship for lovers of *chocolate con churros* (deep-fried doughnut strips dipped in hot chocolate).

Continue up to and across Calle Mayor until you reach **Plaza Mayor** (**5**; p147), then turn west and head down the hill to the historic Plaza de la Villa, home of Madrid's 17th-century **ayuntamiento** (**6**; p149). On the same square stand the 16th-century **Casa de Cisneros** (**7**; p149) and the Gothic **Casa de los Lujanes** (**8**; **p149**), one of the city's oldest surviving buildings.

Take the street down the left side of the Casa de Cisneros, cross Calle del Sacramento at the end, go down the stairs and follow the cobbled Calle del Cordón out onto Calle de Segovia. Almost directly in front of you is the Mudéjar tower of the 15th-century **Iglesia de San Pedro El Viejo** (**9**; p152), whereupon the narrow, almost medieval streets of Old Madrid close in and twist down the hill. Proceeding up Costanilla de San Pedro, you reach the **Museo de San Isidro** (**10**; p151). Next door is the **Iglesia de San Andrés** (**11**; p151), where the city's patron saint, San Isidro Labrador, was once interred.

From here, twist down through lanes that time forgot to Calle de Bailén and the wonderful, if expensive, *terrazas* on the edge of the **Jardines de las Vistillas** (**12**; p151), where you can contemplate the sweeping views out towards Sierra de Guadarrama.

After a soothing *cerveza* (beer), follow the viaduct north to the **Catedral de Nuestra Señora de la Almudena** (**13**; p149), the **Palacio Real** (**14**; p148) and the supremely elegant **Plaza de Oriente** (**15**; p148). The eastern side of the square is closed off by the **Teatro Real** (**16**; p192).

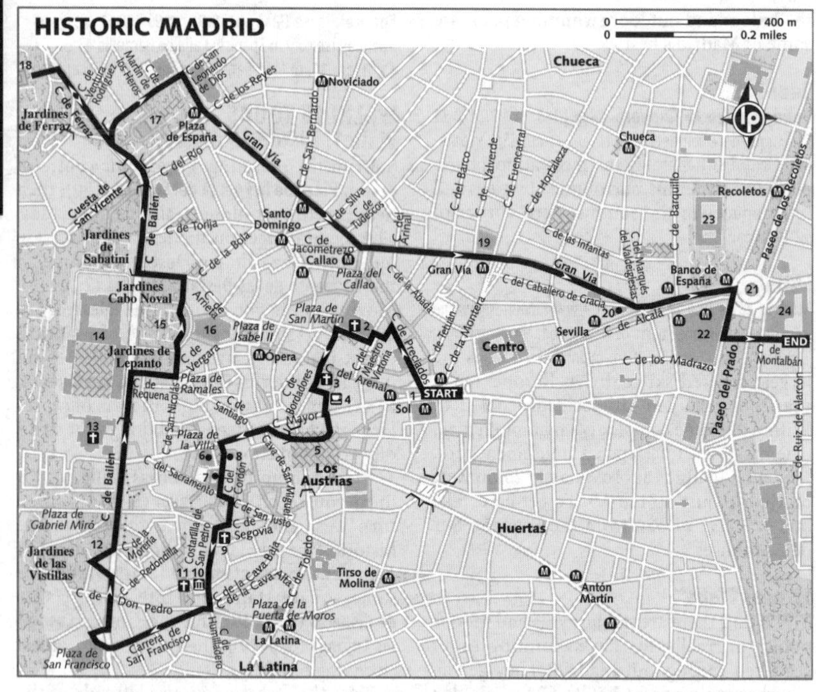

WALK FACTS

Start Plaza de la Puerta del Sol
Finish Palacio de Comunicaciones (Plaza de la Cibeles)
Distance Approximately 5km
Duration Three hours to full day

Return to the western side of the square and follow the walkway extension of Calle de Bailén, which leads into **Plaza de España (17)**, surrounded by monumental towers and featuring a statue of Don Quijote. Calle de Ferraz leads northwest to the ancient Egyptian **Templo de Debod** (**18**; p159), from where there are more fine views.

Return to Plaza de España, the eastern flank of which marks the start of **Gran Vía** (p150), a Haussmannesque boulevard that was slammed through the tumbledown slums to the north of Sol in the 1910s and 1920s. Today it's a busy thoroughfare, chock-full of traffic and humming with passers-by darting in and out of side streets, shops and eateries. About two-thirds of the way along is the mighty **Telefónica building** (**19**; p150), still easily visible from its hilltop perch. Head down past the elegant facades to the superb dome of the **Metrópolis building** (**20**; p150), where Gran Vía meets Calle de Alcalá. Down the hill you go to **Plaza de la Cibeles** (**21**; p156), Madrid's favourite roundabout. As you approach, look out for the late-19th-century **Banco de España (22)** on your right and the **Palacio de Buenavista (23)** on your left. Impossible to miss is the ornate **Palacio de Comunicaciones** (**24**; p157), facing you in all its glory from across the plaza.

Walk 2: Artistic Madrid

Before setting out, pause in the splendid old **Café Comercial** (**1**; p187) on Glorieta de Bilbao, a favourite haunt of writers, artists and intellectuals for more than a century. From here, walk northeast along Calle de Luchana, northwest up Calle de Santa Engracia and then down the hill of Paseo del General Martínez Campos to the **Museo Sorolla** (**2**; p160), home to the works of Joaquín Sorolla, one of the major Spanish painters of the early 20th century.

Continue down to Paseo de la Castellana and the **Museo de la Escultura Abstracta** (**3**;

p158), an outdoor exhibition of fine modern sculptures by some of the big names in Spanish contemporary art. As you continue southwest along this grand boulevard – shun the outer footpaths and wander under the shade of the trees that run almost through the centre – pause at either the **Café-Restaurante El Espejo** (**4**; p187) or **Gran Café de Gijón** (**5**; p187), both of which are steeped in history, atmosphere and the ghosts of writers and artists past.

At **Plaza de la Cibeles** (**6**; p156), turn right up the hill to the **Real Academia de Bellas Artes de San Fernando** (**7**; p150), which in any other city would be considered reason enough to visit on its own. Cross the elegant Plaza de Canalejas and keep going along Calle del Príncipe to **Plaza de Santa Ana** (**8**; p152), where a statue of the poet Federico García Lorca looks towards the **Teatro Español** (**9**; p191). From the plaza, take Calle del Prado, turn right on Calle de León, then left down Calle de Cervantes. At No 11 is the **Casa de Lope de Vega** (**10**; **p152**), the playwright's house. You're now in the heart of the Barrio de las Letras, where many famous Spanish writers spent their days. Just around the corner (Calle de Quevedo, then Calle de Lope de Vega) is the 17th-century **Convento de las Trinitarias** (**11**; p152), where Miguel de Cervantes was laid to rest and, depending who you believe, still lies today.

Return to Calle de Cervantes and turn left at the grand **Plaza de Neptuno (12)** roundabout – watched over by the two grand old dames of the Madrid hotel scene, the **Westin Palace** (**13**; p177) and the **Hotel Ritz** (**14**; p177) – for the extraordinary **Museo Thyssen-Bornemisza** (**15**; **p155**). Diagonally across the square is the gracious, low-slung Palacio Villanueva, better known to art lovers as the peerless **Museo del Prado** (**16**; p153), where you could spend hours or days. Behind the Prado are the verdant **Real Jardín Botánico** (**17**; p156) and the long-standing **Cuesta de Moyano bookstalls** (**18**; p131), both of which are pleasant detours as you continue south en route to Madrid's other extraordinary gallery, the **Centro de Arte Reina Sofía** (**19**; p152).

WALK FACTS

Start Café Comerciál
Finish Centro de Arte Reina Sofía
Distance Approximately 5km
Duration Three hours to full day

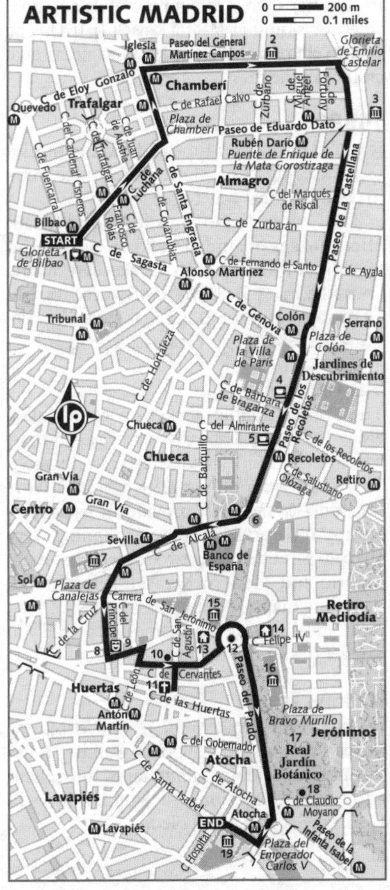

COURSES

Language

Madrid is jammed packed with Spanish language schools of all possible categories. Non-EU citizens who are wanting to study at a university or language school in Spain should, in theory, have a study visa. Some language schools worth investigating include the following.

Academia Inhispania (Map pp142-3; ☎ 91 521 22 31; www.inhispania.com; Calle de la Montera 10-12; Ⓜ Sol)

Academia Madrid Plus (Map pp142-3; ☎ 91 548 11 16; www.madridplus.es; 6th fl, Calle del Arenal 21; Ⓜ Ópera)

International House (Map p140; ☎ 91 319 72 24; www.ihmadrid.es; Calle de Zurbano 8; Ⓜ Alonso Martínez)

Universidad Complutense (Map p132; ☎ 91 394 53 36; www.ucm.es/info/cextran/Index.htm; Secretaria de los Cursos para Extranjeros, Facultadole Filologia [Edificio A] Universidad Complutense, Cuidad Universitaria; Ⓜ Cuidad Universitaria)

Flamenco

There are plenty of places where you can learn to dance *sevillanas* or strum the guitar like the greats.

Espacio Flamenco (Map pp142-3; ☎ 91 298 19 55; http://espacio.deflamenco.com; Calle de la Ribera de Curtidores 26; 🕑 11am-2pm & 5.30-8.30pm Mon-Fri, 11am-2.30pm Sat & Sun; Ⓜ Puerta de Toledo)

Fundación Conservatorio Casa Patas (Map pp142-3; ☎ 91 429 84 71; www.conservatorioflamenco.com in Spanish; Calle de Cañizares 10; Ⓜ Antón Martín or Tirso de Molina)

Cooking

Alambique (Map pp142-3; ☎ 91 547 42 20; www.alambique.com; Plaza de la Encarnación 2; Ⓜ Ópera or Santo Domingo) Cooking classes start from around €50, with English-language courses from €70.

Cooking Club (Map p133; ☎ 91 323 29 58; www.club-cooking.com in Spanish; Calle de Veza 33; Ⓜ Valdeacederas) Regular classes encompassing a range of cooking styles.

MADRID FOR CHILDREN

Madrid has plenty to keep the little ones entertained. A good place to start is **Casa de Campo** (p160), where there are swimming pools, the Zoo Aquarium de Madrid and the Parque de Atracciones, which has a 'Zona Infantil' with sedate rides for the really young. To get to Casa de Campo, take the *teleférico*, one of the world's most horizontal cable cars, which putters for 2.5km out from the slopes of La Rosaleda.

Another possibility is **Faunia** (☎ 91 301 62 35; www.faunia.es in Spanish; Avenida de las Comunidades 28; adult/under 12yr €23/17; Ⓜ Valdebernardo), a modern animal theme park with an 'Amazon jungle' and 'Polar Ecosystem'. Opening hours vary.

At the mammoth indoor playground **Parque Secreto** (Map pp138-9; ☎ 91 593 14 80; www.parquesecreto.com in Spanish; Plaza del Conde del Valle de Suchil 3; admission per 30min from €2.50; 🕑 5-9pm Mon -Fri, 11.30am-2pm & 4.30-9pm Sat & Sun; Ⓜ San Bernardo), you'll find 800 sq metres of indoor playgrounds (labyrinths, floating castles, pits filled with plastic balls, toboggans etc) for kids aged up to 11.

All aboard! The **Museo del Ferrocarril** (Railway Museum; Map p132; ☎ 902 22 88 22; www.museodelferrocarril.org; Paseo de las Delicias 61; adult/child €4/2.50; 🕑 10am-3pm Tue-Sun Sep-Jul; Ⓜ Delicias) is home to old railway cars, train engines and more. It's definitely guaranteed to fascinate budding engineers. The **Museo Naval** (p157) will appeal to those fascinated by ships.

The **Museo de Cera** (Wax Museum; Map p140; ☎ 91 319 26 49; www.museoceramadrid.com; Paseo de los Recoletos 41; adult/under 10yr €15/9; 🕑 10am-2.30pm & 4.30-8.30pm Mon-Fri, 10am-8.30pm Sat & Sun; Ⓜ Colón) is Madrid's modest answer to Madame Tussaud's, with more than 450 wax characters.

Other possibilities include seeing Real Madrid play at the **Estadio Santiago Bernabéu** (p193), wandering through the soothing greenery of the **Parque del Buen Retiro** (p156), where in summer there are puppet shows and boat rides, or skiing at **Madrid Xanadú** (p161). The **Centro Cultural de la Villa** (p191) has occasional children's theatre.

TOURS

If you're pushed for time and want to fit a lot of sightseeing into a short visit, guided tours may be the ideal way to see the city.

The Centro de Turismo de Madrid (p146) offers dozens of guided walking, cycling and bus itineraries through its **Descubre Madrid** (Discover Madrid; ☎ 91 588 29 06; www.esmadrid.com; walking tours adult/concession €3.30/2.70, bus tours €6.45/5.05, bicycle tours €3.30/2.70 plus €6 bike rental) program.

Bus Tours

The orange double-decker buses of **Madrid Vision** (☎ 91 779 18 88; www.madridvision.es; 1-/2-day ticket adult €16/20.50, 7-16yr & over 65yr €8.50/11, under 7yr free; 🕑 9.30am-midnight 21 Jun-20 Sep, 10am-5pm 21 Dec-20 Mar, 10am-6.30pm rest of year) provide the usual hop-on-hop-off overview of the city, running every 10 to 20 minutes along two routes, Historical Madrid and Modern Madrid. Information, including maps, is available at tourist offices, most travel agencies and some hotels, and you can get tickets on the bus.

Walking Tours

Letango Tours (☎ 91 369 47 52; www.letango.com; weekdays/weekends €98/138) offers walking tours through Madrid, including tapas tours, with additional excursions to San Lorenzo El Escorial, Segovia and Toledo.

(Continued on page 173)

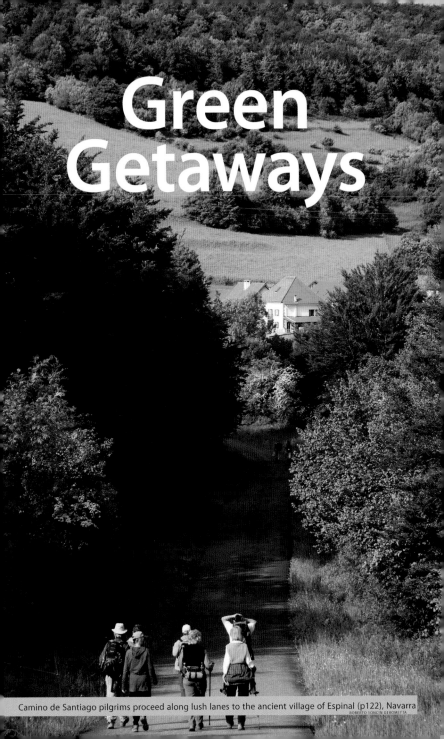

Green Getaways

Camino de Santiago pilgrims proceed along lush lanes to the ancient village of Espinal (p122), Navarra
ROBERTO SONCIN GEROMETTA

Imagine spending a week walking the wilderness and returning each night to a log fire in a remote ecolodge. Or a journey spent entirely in quiet little villages, slowing down to the rhythms of rural life and as far away from the crowded *costas* (coasts) as you could get. Or coming to understand the real Spain as you chug through the countryside on a slow train filled with gossiping locals.

Sustainable travel has come a long way since the days of hair-shirts and hippie communes. Spain is an easy country to explore in a manner that minimises your impact upon the environment without compromising comfort. That doesn't mean the country's overflowing with ecofriendly resorts and enlightened environmental policies. It's not – in fact, Spain is a little slow coming to the party in that regard. What it does mean, however, is that its outstanding public transport, its vast wilderness areas and its ample opportunities to lose yourself in local villages make sustainable travel a viable option.

Taking time to traverse the rural side of Spain above Pampaneira (p813) in Andalucía

KEVIN FOY / AL

A VILLAGE ITINERARY – THE SPANISH HEARTLAND

Although by no means exhaustive, the following route would require months of slow travel to take in all of these villages. Visiting even a handful locales, however, will initiate you into the joys of village life, Spanish-style. You can easily mix and match from this itinerary to suit your time and inclination.

Starting in the foothills of the Pyrenees, **Aínsa** (p450) is the medieval village par excellence of northern Aragón, complete with stone walls and stone everything else. Further west, the hill town of **Sos del Rey Católico** (p460) is a splendid place in which to lose yourself. It's also one that you'll hesitate to tell others about lest the secret get out. Heading south, skirting clamorous Zaragoza, onto the windswept plains that lead down to Teruel, **Daroca** (p461) is surrounded by concentric circles of medieval walls and has that changeless quality that always makes us want to stay longer than we planned. Further south again, an epic history weighs lightly upon gorgeous **Albarracín** (p465), but it did leave behind a castle, fortress walls that snake across the surrounding hills and views that even Tuscany would struggle to match.

Not far west, but across the frontier into Castilla-La Mancha, **Pastrana** (p298) is your honey-coloured introduction to the charming villages of Castilla, while further north, evocative little **Atienza** (p301) has just a few hundred inhabitants and more than enough Romanesque churches for a village of ten times its size. Quiet little back roads lead into the easternmost reaches of Castilla y León and **Medinaceli** (p271), close to the Madrid–Barcelona highway yet a world away, high on its hilltop perch and awash with light-stone architecture. Travelling west takes you to **Calatañazor** (p270), population at last count just 63; it has surprisingly significant history, and its streetscapes are everything you dreamed of in a Spanish *pueblo* (village). Veer northwest and you'll hear the call of **Covarrubias** (p261), which you'll enter through an arch in the old village walls, and then try to find excuses (of which there are many) to postpone your departure. **Puebla de Sanabria** (p242) is a fair geographical hike away to the west but, if you've the time, you won't regret the detour. Otherwise, you have stop at **Candelario** (p226), high in the hills of the Sierra de Béjar in Castilla y León's far southwest, before exploring the forgotten villages of the **Sierra de Francia** (p225). Wondering which village we had in mind when discussing the village mayor and the gossiping old folk at the beginning of the Village Life section (overleaf)? It could have been any of the villages we've travelled through on this itinerary, but it was actually **Villanueva del Condé** (p225) in the Sierra de Francia.

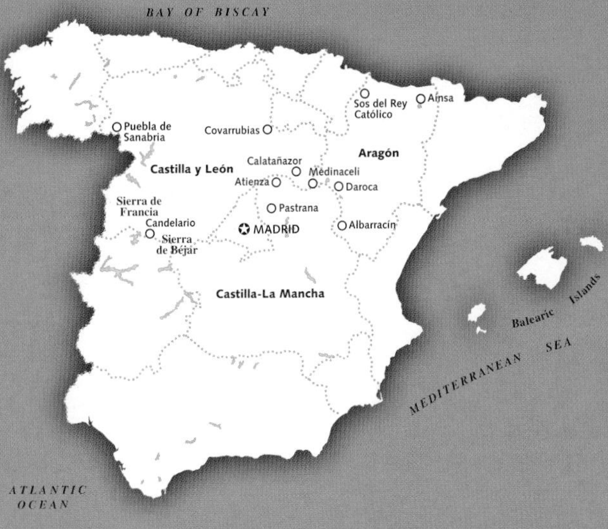

Historical fortress walls, Albarracín, Aragon (p465)
BRUCE ESBIN

VILLAGE LIFE

Spain's cities may have been rushing headlong into the 21st century long before it arrived, but visit village Spain and you'll wonder if time has stood still. These time capsules of an older way of living are the perfect getaways, not least because every euro you spend in a village supports the local economy and slows the inexorable migration of Spaniards towards the cities. The process of urbanisation has placed countless (some estimates suggest as many as 2000) villages under threat. For more information on the decline of village life, see the boxed text, p245.

But don't escape to this wonderful world for noble reasons alone. Do it because villages are gentle antidotes to the crazy pace of modern life and are of rare beauty. They're the sort of place where the mayor rides through town astride a horse and announces the latest news in the cobblestone Plaza Mayor or Plaza de España. Just down the lane, the elderly of the village gather on doorsteps to gossip and simply to pass the time. And then, as night falls, a brief hubbub may arise from the local bar, but soon everyone heads home and silence envelopes the quiet, narrow streets. This is how Spain used to be. This is how Spain still is, if you know where to look.

Many of the more beautiful villages have been discovered by Spanish tourists, it's true, but most tourists start to move on as the sun nears the horizon, which is when you'll really appreciate your surroundings if you stick around. Just about every Spanish village worth its salt boasts a smattering of *casas rurales,* literally 'rural homes', in which owners have opened up a couple of rooms for travellers looking for lodgings. Some of these *casas rurales* are simple; some are *extremely* comfortable with period touches and an attention to traditional detail emanating from every wooden beam. But forget reception desks, forget minibars and forget the sort of impersonal service that so many hotels seem to specialise in. Here you'll often find the family living just up the hall, many of whom just love to sit down over breakfast and tell you all about life in the village. It's as if they've all the time in the world.

Markets are a great way to partake in a slice of village life in Basque Country (p468)

KEITH LEWIS / ALAMY

SLOW TRAVEL

Slow travel is about far more than just how you get from A to B. It's about staying for as long as possible in each place, slowing down to the pace of village or rural life, making friends and leaving with more than a fleeting understanding of the places you've visited. The philosophy of slow travel may make for environmentally sustainable trips, but it's above all a reimagining of your journey, a recognition that the depth to which you explore and engage with the places you visit is ultimately more important than how many places you can cover in a short period of time. Fast travel ticks the boxes. Slow travel produces memories that last a lifetime.

Those committed to slow travel are helped by the fact that an extraordinary network of trains fans out across Spain from Madrid, reaching every conceivable corner of the country. While admittedly some of these are high-speed AVE services that race across the countryside, the majority are regional trains that take the slowest route possible. Either way, if we could offer one piece of advice to lessen your environmental footprint and travel in comfort at the

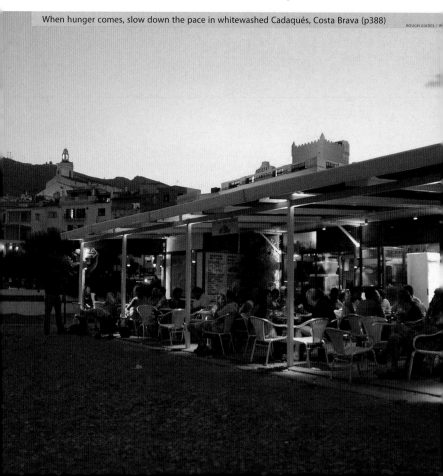

When hunger comes, slow down the pace in whitewashed Cadaqués, Costa Brava (p388)

ROUGH GUIDES /

TRAVEL SLOW & MAKE A DIFFERENCE

- **Camino de Santiago** (p118) Follow the endless trails of the faithful, whether as a pilgrim or as someone eager to get under the skin of northern Spain.
- **Lodge** (www.holisticdecisions.com) Located in the Sierra Nevada National Park, this ecofriendly place is all about immersing yourself in nature, but in a comfortable house that encourages you to stay for up to one week. The attention to sustainable principles extends to using sustainable resources for the wood-burning stoves to the opportunity you're given to view Spain's wildlife in the surrounding hills.
- **Sunseed Desert Technology** (www.sunseed.org.uk) An alarming UN report suggests that 90% of Spanish regions bordering the Mediterranean could soon become desert. Sunseed is doing something about it. The group set up shop in a previously abandoned village in Almería in 1986, planting crops using dry-land regeneration techniques and basing its small community on practices of sustainable living, including solar power and recycling. They accept part-time and full-time volunteers for periods of two to seven weeks.
- **Adventure Travel Abroad** (www.adventuretravelabroad.com) This US group organises ecovolunteering programs on Ibiza where a group of local environmentalists, mindful of the impact of tourism on the island's ecology, have set up a centre to provide education, conduct research and actively protect local ecosystems. Programs for volunteers last from one to 12 weeks.
- **Aparthotel & Restaurante Venus Albir** (www.raycons.com) Given the overdevelopment rampant along Spain's Mediterranean Coast, a visit to the Costa Blanca normally involves a guilty look back at your carbon footprint. Not any more – at least not at the Venus Albir. One of very few places in Spain to receive European certification as a 'Bio Hotel', this place is ecofriendly to its foundations (built using natural local materials). Solar panels, rainwater tanks and organic food in the restaurant are also part of the deal. Stay a week, stay as long as you want, but do so with a clear conscience. See p634 for more.
- **L'Atelier** (www.ivu.org/atelier) This exclusively vegetarian guesthouse in the village of Mecina, near Granada, prepares all its meals using organic local produce and donates a share of its profits to street children in Colombia. See p814 for details.
- **Tren de la Fresa** (Strawberry Train) You could take the fast route to Aranjuez from Madrid if you're eager to escape city life from April to June, but the strawberry train is slower and so much more fun. Attendants in period dress hand out strawberries. See the boxed text, p202.

same time, it would be this: wherever possible, take the train. It's true that there are many villages that lie beyond the end of the line. If that's where you're headed, consider hopping on a local bus or, better still, setting off on your bicycle or having a go at walking.

Within towns themselves, and some larger cities such as Valladolid (see the boxed text, p235) and Zaragoza (see the boxed text, p431), schemes of low-cost or even free bicycle rental are available. Madrid may not seem like the most bike-friendly capital, but its tourist office organises bicycle tours (p164) of the city. For more information on cycling in Spain, turn to p112 and p891.

In addition to spending longer in each place and taking the slow road to get there and around, another worthwhile option is spending time in a place where you can make a positive contribution that extends beyond supporting the local economy. The most obvious way to do this is to volunteer at a place making serious efforts to reverse the environmental mistakes of the past and live in a way that's committed to zero environmental impact. There aren't many of them, but those that are around deserve to be supported. Check out the boxed text, above.

Take a slow chug north to Sóller from Palma de Mallorca (p653)

(Continued from page 164)

The **Wellington Society** (☎ 609 143203; www.wellsoc.org; tours €50-85) operates a handful of quirky historical tours laced with anecdotes and led by the inimitable Stephen Drake-Jones. Possibilities include Bullfights, Hemingway's Madrid and Curiosities & Anecdotes of Old Madrid.

The privately run **Adventurous Appetites** (☎ 639 331073; www.adventurousappetites.com; 4hr tours €50; 8pm-midnight Mon-Sat) organises English-language tapas tours through central Madrid from the bear statue in Puerta del Sol. Prices include the first drink but exclude food.

Cycling Tours

Londoner Mike Chandler organises **Madrid Bike Tours** (☎ 680 581782; www.madridbiketours.com; 4hr tours incl picnic lunch €65), offering a range of guided four-hour tours.

Bike Spain (Map pp142-3; ☎ 91 559 06 53; www.bikespain.info; Plaza de la Villa 1 (Calle del Codo); tours €30; 10am-2pm & 4-7pm Mon-Fri, 10am-2pm Sat & Sun; M Ópera) is another possibility for English-language guided city tours.

Urban Movil (Map pp142-3; ☎ 91 542 77 71; www.urbanmovil.com; Calle Mayor 78; 1/2hr tours €35/60; 10am-8pm; M Ópera) runs Segway tours around Madrid.

FESTIVALS & EVENTS

Madrid loves to party, and seemingly any excuse is good for a fiesta. For details about national festivals see p24, but here in the city be sure to look out for the following events. There's more information online at www.esmadrid.com.

February

Arco (Feria Internacional de Arte Contemporánea; www.arco.ifema.es) One of Europe's biggest celebrations of contemporary art, Arco draws galleries and exhibitors from all over the world to the Parque Ferial Juan Carlos I exhibition centre near Barajas airport. It's held mid-February.

Festival Flamenco A combination of big names and rising talent comes together for five days of fine flamenco music in one of the city's theatres.

March–April

Jazz es Primavera (www.sanjuanevangelista.org) Three weeks of jazz in the leading jazz venues across the city.

May

Suma Flamenca (www.sumaflamenca.com in Spanish) Another soul-filled flamenco festival that draws some of the biggest names in the genre.

Dos de Mayo On 2 May 1808, Napoleon's troops put down an uprising in Madrid, and commemoration of the day has become an opportunity for much festivity, often called the Fiesta de la Comunidad de Madrid. The day is celebrated with particular energy in the bars of Malasaña.

Fiesta de San Isidro Around 15 May, Madrid's patron saint is honoured with a week of nonstop processions, parties and bullfights. Free concerts are held throughout the city, and this week marks the start of the city's bullfighting season.

June

Día del Orgullo de Gays, Lesbianas y Transexuales The colourful Gay Pride Parade sets out from the Puerta de Alcalá in the early evening, and winds its way around the city in an explosion of music and energy, ending up at the Puerta del Sol.

July–August

Veranos de la Villa Madrid's town hall stages a series of cultural events, shows and exhibitions, known as Summers in the City.

August–September

Summer Festivals Small-time but fun, the neighbourhood summer festivals, such as San Cayetano in Lavapiés, and San Lorenzo and La Paloma in La Latina, are great for cheap entertainment from mid-August to September.

La Noche en Blanco On September's White Night, first held in 2006, Madrid stays open all night with a citywide extravaganza of concerts and general revelry in 120 venues.

October–November

Fiesta de Otoño Music, dance and theatre take over Madrid from mid-October to mid-November, during the fantastically cultural weeks of the Autumn Festival.

Emociona Jazz Madrid loves its jazz too much to be confined to just one festival. In November groups from far and wide converge on the capital for concerts across town.

SLEEPING

Madrid once trailed far behind Barcelona when it came to cool accommodation, but not any more. Having undergone something of a hotel revolution, the city now has high-quality accommodation across all price ranges and caters to every taste.

Each *barrio* has its own distinctive identity and where you decide to stay will play an important role in your experience of Madrid, although all are just a few metro stops from each other. Los Austrias, Sol & Centro put you in the heart of the busy downtown area, while La Latina (the best *barrio* for tapas), Lavapiés, Huertas (good for nightlife) and Atocha are good for those who love Madrid nights and

TOP SLEEPS

From buzzing backpackers' to swish temples of style, Madrid has something for everyone. These are our favourites across a range of budgets:

- **Albergue Juvenil** (p177) – everything's supernew at this terrific youth hostel
- **Cat's Hostel** (opposite) – backpackers' hostel with a stunning courtyard and filled with life
- **Hotel Meninas** (opposite) – designer rooms on one of our favourite streets
- **Hotel Óscar** (p178) – outrageously stylish rooms in a wonderful location
- **Quo** (p176) – one of the city's longest-standing boutique hotels
- **Hotel Abalú** (p178) – high-quality boutique hotel tucked away in Malasaña
- **Hotel Puerta América** (p178) – Madrid's style temple, with rooms by world-famous architects
- **Hotel Urban** (p177) – oh-so-sleek, with antiques strewn throughout a supermodern tower of glass

don't want to stagger too far to get back to their hotel in the wee small hours. Staying along the Paseo del Prado is ideal for those here to spend most of their time in galleries, while Salamanca is quiet, upmarket and perfect for serial shoppers. You don't have to be gay to stay in Chueca, but you'll love it if you are, while Malasaña is another inner-city *barrio* with great restaurants and bars. Chamberí removes you from the tourist scrum and lets you experience Madrid as the locals do.

Accommodation prices in Madrid vary with the not-always-discernible seasons. In general, most midrange and some top-end places have separate price structures for high season *(temporada alta)*, midseason *(temporada media)* and low season *(temporada baja)*, but there's little agreement among hoteliers about when the seasons actually begin and end.

Los Austrias, Sol & Centro

With a wealth of historical sites, this area is probably where you'll spend the most time, making it a good place to be based. There's accommodation across a range of budgets, and traditional taverns, restaurants and shops within a stone's throw.

BUDGET

Los Amigos Sol Backpackers' Hostel (Map pp142-3; ☎ 91 559 24 72; www.losamigoshostel.com; 4th fl, Calle de Arenal 26; dm €16-19; Ⓜ Ópera or Sol; 💻) A couple of blocks away from Los Amigos Backpackers' Hostel, this place offers a similar deal.

Los Amigos Ópera Backpackers' Hostel (Map pp142-3; ☎ 91 547 17 07; www.losamigoshostel.com; 4th fl, Calle de Campomanes 6; dm €17-19; Ⓜ Ópera; 💻) If you arrive in Madrid keen for company, this could be the place for you – lots of students stay here, the staff are savvy (and speak English) and there are bright dorm-style rooms that sleep four to 12 people (with free lockers).

Hostel Metropol (Map pp142-3; ☎ 93 231 20 45; www.metropolhostel.com; 1st fl, Calle de la Montera 47; dm/s/d €17/45/60; Ⓜ Gran Vía; 💻) This place attracts a host of young travellers, not because of its rooms (which are simple and don't have a whole lot of character), but because it offers a special something that few hostels have: attitude.

Hostal Luis XV (Map pp142-3; ☎ 91 522 13 50; www.hrluisxv.net in Spanish; 8th fl, Calle de la Montera 47; s/d/tr €45/59/75; Ⓜ Gran Vía) Everything here – the views, the spacious rooms and the attention to detail – makes this family-run place feel pricier than it is. Exterior rooms have balconies from where the views are superb (especially from the triple room 820); you'll find it hard to tear yourself away.

Hostal Acapulco (Map pp142-3; ☎ 91 531 19 45; www.hostalacapulco.com; 4th fl, Calle de la Salud 13; s/d/tr €52/62/79; Ⓜ Gran Vía; ❄ 💻) This immaculate little *hostal* (budget hotel) is a cut above many in Madrid, with marble floors, recently renovated bathrooms, double-glazed windows and comfortable beds. Street-facing rooms have balconies overlooking sunny Plaza del Carmen and are flooded with natural light.

Hostal Macarena (Map pp142-3; ☎ 91 365 92 21; www.silserranos.com in Spanish; 1st fl, Cava de San Miguel 8; s/d €60/74; Ⓜ Sol; 💻) On one of the old cobblestone streets that runs past Plaza Mayor, this *hostal* is at once homely and loaded with impeccable, old-style charm. The rooms are nicely spacious and decorated in warm colours, with the occasional antique writing desk.

MIDRANGE & TOP END

Hotel Plaza Mayor (Map pp142-3; ☎ 91 360 06 06; www.h-plazamayor.com; Calle de Atocha 2; s/d from €65/85; M Sol or Tirso de Molina; ❄) Sitting just across from Plaza Mayor, here you'll find stylish decor, charming original elements from the 150-year-old building and extremely helpful staff. The rooms are attractive, some with a light colour scheme and wrought-iron furniture. The attic rooms boast minimalist dark-wood floors and beams, and designer lamps, and have lovely little terraces with wonderful rooftop views of central Madrid.

Hotel Anaco (Map pp142-3; ☎ 91 522 46 04; www.anacohotel.com; Calle de las Tres Cruces 3; s/d from €80/95; M Gran Vía; ❄) We like a place that spends its renovation dollars on the rooms rather than the lobby. The latter is of a tired 1970s vintage, but the rooms are decorated in neutral tones, with touches of red and modern fixtures like stainless-steel basins.

Mario Room Mate (Map pp142-3; ☎ 91 548 85 48; www.room-matehoteles.com; Calle de Campomanes 4; s €90-120, d €100-140; M Ópera; ❄ 💻) Entering this swanky boutique hotel is like crossing the threshold of Madrid's latest nightclub – staff dressed all in black, black walls and swirls of red lighting in the lobby. Rooms are spacious, with high ceilings and simple furniture, light tones contrasting smoothly with muted colours and dark surfaces.

Petit Palace Posada del Peine (Map pp142-3; ☎ 91 523 81 51; www.hthotels.com; Calle de Postas 17; d €115-150; M Sol; ❄) This outstanding hotel combines a splendid historic building (dating to 1610), a brilliant location (just 50m from the Plaza Mayor) and modern hi-tech rooms. The bathrooms sparkle with stunning fittings and many historical architectural features remain in situ in the public areas. It's just a pity some of the rooms aren't larger.

Hotel Preciados (Map pp142-3; ☎ 91 454 44 00; www.preciadoshotel.com in Spanish; Calle de Preciados 37; s/d from €122/125; M Santo Domingo or Callao) This hotel has a classier feel than many of the other business options around town and it gets rave reviews for its service. Soft lighting, light shades and plentiful glass personalise the rooms and provide an intimate feel.

Hotel Meninas (Map pp142-3; ☎ 91 541 28 05; www.hotelmeninas.com; Calle de Campomanes 7; s/d from €109/129; M Ópera; 💻) Opened in 2005, this is the sort of place where an interior designer licked his or her lips and created a masterwork of minimalist luxury. The colour scheme is blacks, whites and greys, with dark-wood floors and splashes of fuchsia and lime-green. Flat-screen TVs are in every room, along with the latest bathroom fittings and internet access points (there's even a laptop in some rooms), all rounding out the effect of clean lines and the latest innovations.

Hotel de Las Letras (Map pp142-3; ☎ 91 523 79 80; www.hoteldelasletras.com; Gran Vía 11; d from €165; M Gran Vía) If you want to cause a stir with a new hotel in Madrid at the moment, make sure it has a rooftop bar overlooking the city. They're all the rage, but Hotel de las Letras started the craze. The bar's wonderful, but the whole hotel is excellent, with individually styled rooms, each with literary quotes from famous writers on the walls.

La Latina & Lavapiés

Places to stay are pretty thin on the ground in these two *barrios*. What's here is just back from the clamorous streets of downtown but close enough to get around the centre on foot. It's a good choice for budget travellers.

our pick **Cat's Hostel** (Map pp142-3; ☎ 91 369 28 07; www.catshostel.com; Calle de Cañizares 6; dm €19, d from €24; M Antón Martín; ❄ 💻) Now here's something special. The internal courtyard is Madrid's finest – lavish Andalucian tilework, a fountain, a spectacular glass ceiling and stunning Islamic decoration, surrounded on four sides by an open balcony. There's also a softly lit and supercool basement bar, where occasional live flamenco cohabits with free internet connections.

Mad Hostel (Map pp142-3; ☎ 91 506 48 40; www.madhostel.com; Calle de Cabeza 24; dm €20; M Antón Martín; ❄ 💻) From the same people who brought you Cat's Hostel, Mad Hostel is similarly filled with a buzzing vibe. The 1st-floor courtyard – with retractable roof – is a wonderful place to chill, while the four- to eight-bed rooms are smallish but new and clean. There's a small rooftop gym equipped with state-of-the-art equipment.

Hostal Horizonte (Map pp142-3; ☎ 91 369 09 96; www.hostalhorizonte.com; 2nd fl, Calle de Atocha 28; without/with bathroom s €29/40, d €44/55; M Antón Martín) Billing itself as a *hostal* run by travellers for travellers, Hostal Horizonte is a well-run place. The rooms have far more character than your average *hostal*, with high ceilings, deliberately old-world furnishings and modern bathrooms.

Huertas & Atocha

If you're opening a swish new designer hotel in Madrid, Huertas seems to be the place to do it. Some of the most exciting new upmarket hotels are to be found here, in a *barrio* that seems hell-bent on reinventing itself as the Spanish capital's home of accommodation chic. Huertas nights will, however, quickly bring you back down to earth, filled as they are with the roar of Madrid at play. Going to sleep in Huertas can seem like something of a lost cause on weekends.

BUDGET

Hostal Adriano (Map pp142-3; ☎ 91 521 13 39; www.hostaladriano.com; 4th fl, Calle de la Cruz 26; s/d/tr €49/63/83; Ⓜ Sol) They don't come any better than this bright and cheerful *hostal* wedged in the streets that mark the boundary between Sol and Huertas. Most rooms are well sized and each has its own colour scheme.

Hostal Sardinero (Map pp142-3; ☎ 91 429 57 56; fax 91 429 41 12; Calle del Prado 16; s/d from €47/67; Ⓜ Sol or Antón Martín;) More than the cheerful rooms (which have high ceilings, air-conditioning, a safe, hairdryers and renovated bathrooms), it's the friendly old couple who run Hostal Sardinero that gives it its charm. They love it if you take the time to sit down for a chat.

Hostal Adria Santa Ana (Map pp142-3; ☎ 91 521 13 39; www.hostaladriasantaana.com; 4th fl, Calle de la Cruz 26; d/tr €70/90; Ⓜ Sol) The owners of Hostal Adriano also run this one. It's on the same floor, but a step up in price, style and luxury. Put the two *hostales* together and they're a great combination.

MIDRANGE & TOP END

Hotel El Pasaje (Map pp142-3; ☎ 91 521 29 95; www.elpasajehs.com; Calle del Pozo 4; d incl breakfast €90-110; Ⓜ Sol) If you were to choose your ideal location in Huertas, Hotel El Pasaje would be hard to beat. Set on a quiet lane largely devoid of bars, yet just around the corner from the Plaza de la Puerta del Sol, it combines a central location with a quiet night's sleep, at least by the standards of Huertas. The feel is intimate and modern (except for the tired-looking bedspreads – what were they thinking?), with good bathrooms, minibars and enough space to leave your suitcase without tripping over it.

Quo (Map pp142-3; ☎ 91 532 90 49; www.hotelesquo.com; Calle de Sevilla 4; s €90-160, d €90-195; Ⓜ Sevilla;) Quo is one of Madrid's homes of chic, with black-clad staff, minimalist designer furniture, tall ceilings and huge windows that let light flood in. The colour scheme is black and red, with light surfaces providing perfect contrast and a resolutely contemporary look. We're also big fans of the bathrooms, with glass doors, glass benches and stainless-steel basins. All rooms have flat-screen TVs, black-and-white photos of Madrid, dark-wood floors and comfy armchairs; rooms on the 7th floor have Jacuzzis and private terraces with terrific views over the rooftops.

Alicia Room Mate (Map pp142-3; ☎ 91 389 60 95; www.room-matehoteles.com; Calle del Prado 2; d €90-200; Ⓜ Sol or Antón Martín;) One of the landmark properties of the designer Room Mate chain of hotels, Hotel Alicia overlooks Plaza de Santa Ana with beautiful, spacious rooms. The style (the work of Pascua Ortega) is a touch more muted than in other Room Mate hotels, but the supermodern look remains intact, the downstairs bar is oh-so-cool, and the service young and switched on.

Hotel Miau (Map pp142-3; ☎ 91 369 71 20; www.hotelmiau.com; Calle del Príncipe 26; s/d incl breakfast €85/95; Ⓜ Sol or Antón Martín;) If you want to be close to the nightlife of Huertas or you can't tear yourself away from the beautiful Plaza de Santa Ana, then this is your place. Light tones, splashes of colour and elegant modern art adorn the rooms, which are large and well equipped. Bring ear plugs if sleep is something you value.

Hotel El Prado (Map pp142-3; ☎ 91 369 02 34; www.pradohotel.com; Calle del Prado 11; s €80-120, d €125-195; Ⓜ Antón Martín or Sol;) This hotel is one of Madrid's most welcoming and offers style and service beyond its three stars. There's a wine theme running throughout the spacious rooms, which have parquetry floors, white-and-cream tones, and places to sit and write. The double-glazed windows are also a bonus, especially if you're here on a weekend.

Me by Melía (Map pp142-3; ☎ 91 701 60 00; www.mebymelia.com; Plaza de Santa Ana 14; d from €200; Ⓜ Sol or Antón Martín) Once the landmark Gran Victoria Hotel, the Madrid home of many a famous bullfighter, this audacious new hotel is fast becoming a landmark of a different kind. Overlooking the western end of Plaza de Santa Ana, this luxury hotel is decked out in minimalist white with curves and comfort in all the right places. This is one place where it's definitely worth paying extra (€50) for a room with a view. Its two bars are among the most sophisticated in town.

our pick **Hotel Urban** (Map pp142-3; ☎ 91 787 77 70; www.derbyhotels.com; Carrera de San Jerónimo 34; d €200-350; Ⓜ Sevilla;) The towering glass edifice of Hotel Urban is the epitome of art-inspired, superstylish designer cool. With its clean lines, modern art and antiques from around the world, it's a wonderful antidote to the more classic charm of Madrid's five-star hotels of longer standing. Dark-wood floors and dark walls are offset by plenty of light, while the bathrooms have wonderful designer fittings – the wash basins are sublime. The rooftop swimming pool is Madrid's best and the gorgeous terrace is heaven on a candlelit summer's evening.

Paseo del Prado & El Retiro

The artistic splendour of the art galleries along the magnificent Paseo del Prado is a fine reason for choosing to stay here. This former *barrio* of choice for Madrid's royalty now hosts two of the city's most luxurious hotels.

Westin Palace (Map pp142-3; ☎ 91 360 80 00; www.westinpalacemadrid.com; Plaza de las Cortes 7; d €369-470; Ⓜ Banco de España or Antón Martín;) An old Madrid classic, this former palace of the Duque de Lerma opened as a hotel in 1911 and was Spain's second luxury hotel. Ever since it has looked out across Plaza de Neptuno at its rival, the Ritz, like a lover unjustly scorned. Its name may not have the world-famous cachet of the Ritz, but it's not called the Palace for nothing and is extravagant in all the right places.

Hotel Ritz (Map p145; ☎ 91 701 67 67; www.ritzmadrid.com; Plaza de la Lealtad 5; d €562-675; Ⓜ Banco de España;) The grand old lady of Madrid, the Hotel Ritz is the height of exclusivity. One of the most lavish buildings in Madrid, its classic style and impeccable service are second to none. Not surprisingly, it's the hotel of choice for presidents, kings and celebrities. The public areas are palatial and awash with antiques, while the rooms are extravagantly large, opulent and supremely comfortable.

Salamanca

Salamanca is Madrid's most exclusive address, home to suitably grand sights and the best shopping that the city has to offer. It's generally a quieter choice than anywhere else in the capital and good restaurants abound.

Hesperia Hermosilla (Map p140; ☎ 91 246 88 00; www.hesperia.com; Calle de la Hermosilla 23; s/d from €125/135; Ⓜ Serrano;) If you're here on a mission to shop in Salamanca, or you value quiet, exclusive streets away from the noise of central Madrid, this modern and subtly stylish hotel is a terrific choice. The furnishings are vaguely minimalist, especially in the public areas, and LCD flat-screen TVs and other creature comforts are rare luxuries in this price range.

Bauzá (Map pp134-5; ☎ 91 435 75 45; www.hotelbauza.com; Calle de Goya 79; s/d/ste from €150/200/340; Ⓜ Goya;) Minimalist and modern, the new Bauzá would be right at home in New York's Soho. The generous rooms boast dark-wood floors, soothing greys and blues, and occasional flashes of originality like Indian textile prints. Computers, plants, sound systems and designer lamps add to the appeal without crowding the rooms.

Malasaña & Chueca

Staying in Malasaña or Chueca keeps you within walking distance (or a short metro ride) of most of Madrid's major sights, but immerses you in the sometimes gritty, usually cool personalities of these two inner-city *barrios*. There's not a lot to see here – a few museums is about it – but both *barrios* are wonderful places to eat out or drink the night away.

our pick **Albergue Juvenil** (Map pp138-9; ☎ 91 593 96 88; www.ajmadrid.es; Calle de Mejía Lequerica 21; dm €18-24; Ⓜ Bilbao or Alonso Martínez) If you're looking for dormitory-style accommodation, you'd need a good reason to stay anywhere other than here while you're in Madrid. Opened in 2007, the Albergue's rooms are spotless, no dorm houses more than six beds (and each has its own bathroom), and facilities include a pool table, a gymnasium, wheelchair access, free internet, laundry and a TV/DVD room with a choice of movies. All the facilities are supermodern and breakfast is included in the price.

Hostal Don Juan (Map pp138-9; ☎ 91 522 31 01; 2nd fl, Plaza de Vázquez de Mella 1; s/d/tr €38/53/71; Ⓜ Gran Vía) Just because you're paying cheap rates for your room doesn't mean you can't be treated like a king. This elegant two-storey *hostal* is filled with art (each room has original works) and antique furniture that could grace a royal palace. Rooms are simple but luminous and large, and most have a balcony facing out onto the street.

Hostal América (Map pp138-9; ☎ 91 522 64 48; www.hostalamerica.net; 5th fl, Calle de Hortaleza 19; s/d €40/55; Ⓜ Gran Vía) This place is run by a lovely mother-son-dog team who preside over superclean, spacious and IKEA-dominated rooms. As most rooms face onto the usual interior 'patio' of the building, you should get a good night's sleep in this busy area. For the rest of the time, there's an expansive terrace with tables, chairs and a coffee machine.

Hostal La Zona (Map pp138-9; ☎ 91 521 99 04; www.hostallazona.com; 1st fl, Calle de Valverde 7; s/d/tr €50/60/85; Ⓜ Gran Vía;) Catering primarily to a gay clientele, the stylish Hostal La Zona has exposed brickwork, wooden pillars and a subtle colour scheme. We like a place where a sleep-in is encouraged – breakfast is from 9am to noon, which is exactly the understanding Madrid's nightlife merits. Other highlights include free internet, helpful staff and air-conditioning/heating in every room.

our pick **Hotel Óscar** (Map pp138-9; ☎ 91 701 11 73; www.room-matehoteles.com; Plaza de Vázquez de Mella 12; d €90-200, ste €150-280; Ⓜ Gran Vía) Simply outstanding. Hotel Óscar's designer rooms ooze style and sophistication. Some have floor-to-ceiling murals, the lighting is always funky and the colour scheme is awash with pinks, lime-greens, oranges or a more minimalist black-and-white.

our pick **Hotel Abalú** (Map pp138-9; ☎ 91 531 47 44; www.hotelabalu.com; Calle del Pez 19; s/d from €74/105, ste €140-200; Ⓜ Noviciado) At last, Malasaña has its own boutique hotel, an oasis of style amid the *barrio*'s time-worn feel. Each room has its own design drawn from the imagination of Luis Delgado, from retro chintz to Zen, baroque to pure white, and most aesthetics in between. Some of the suites have Jacuzzis and large-screen home cinemas. You're close to Gran Vía, but away from the tourist scrum.

Chamberí & Argüelles

Chamberí has bars, shops, cinemas and restaurants in just the right measure, and you'll quickly feel less like a tourist and more like a local by staying here. There aren't many places to stay, but those that are here are excellent, and you're only a short metro ride from the main sites of interest.

Hotel AC Santo Mauro (Map p140; ☎ 91 319 69 00; www.ac-hoteles.com; Calle de Zurbano 36; d €279-355; Ⓜ Alonso Martínez) Everything about this recently renovated place oozes exclusivity and class, from the address – one of the elite patches of Madrid real estate – to the mansion that is the finest in a *barrio* of many. This is a place of discreet elegance and warm service, and rooms are suitably lavish; the Arabian-styled indoor pool isn't bad either. David Beckham may be derided for many things, but the fact that he chose to make this his home for six months certainly suggests a high degree of taste.

Beyond the Centre

our pick **Hotel Puerta América** (Map p132; ☎ 91 744 54 00; www.hoteles-silken.com/hpam; Avenida de América 41; d from €239; Ⓜ Cartagena; Ⓟ) When the owners of this hotel looked at its location halfway between the city and the airport, they knew they had to do something special. Their idea? Take some of world architecture's most innovative names and give them a floor each to design. The result? An extravagant pastiche of styles, from curvy minimalism and zany montages of 1980s chic to bright-red bathrooms that feel like a movie star's dressing room. Even the bar ('a temple to the liturgy of pleasure'), restaurant, facade, gardens, public lighting and parking garage each had their own architect (including Jean Nouvel, Ron Arad, David Chipperfield, Sir Norman Foster and Zaha Hadid).

EATING

After holding fast to its rather unexciting local cuisine for centuries (aided, it must be said, by loyal locals who never saw the need for anything else), Madrid has finally become one of Europe's culinary capitals.

There's everything to be found here, not least the rich variety of regional Spanish specialities from across the country. And there's not a *barrio* where you can't find a great meal. Restaurants in Malasaña, Chueca and Huertas range from glorious old *tabernas* (taverns) to boutique eateries across all price ranges. For more classically classy surrounds, Salamanca and Northern Madrid are generally pricey but of the highest standard, and ideal for a special occasion or for spotting royalty and celebrities. In the central *barrios* of Los Austrias, Sol and Centro there's a little bit of everything. Splendid tapas bars abound everywhere, but La Latina is the undoubted queen.

Los Austrias, Sol & Centro

Downtown Madrid has a little bit of everything: from the world's oldest restaurant to downtempo fusion eateries, from regional tapas to Asian flavours, from old Spanish bars where the ambience owes everything to impromptu theatre to brightly painted vegetarian restaurants.

Cervecería 100 Montaditos (Map pp142-3; ☎ 902 19 74 94; www.cerveceria100montaditos.com; Calle Mayor 22; small bocadillos €1.20; Ⓜ Sol) This terrific chain of bars serves up no fewer than 100 different varieties of mini *bocadillos* (filled rolls) that span the full range of Spanish staples in more combinations than you could imagine. You fill out your order and take it up to the counter, and your name is called in no time.

Cervecería Compano (Map pp142-3; Calle de Botaneros; bocadillos €2.30; Ⓜ Sol) Spanish bars don't come any more basic than this, but it is the purveyor of an enduring and wildly popular Madrid tradition – the *bocadillo de calamares* (a large roll stuffed with deep-fried calamari) – at any hour of the day.

La Gloria de Montera (Map pp142-3; ☎ 91 523 44 07; Calle del Caballero de Gracia 10; meals €20-25; Ⓜ Gran Vía) La Gloria de Montera combines classy decor with eminently reasonable prices. The food's not especially creative, but the tastes are fresh, the surroundings are sophisticated and you'll get a good initiation into Spanish cooking without paying over the odds. They don't take reservations, so turn up early or be prepared to wait.

La Viuda Blanca (Map pp142-3; ☎ 91 548 75 29; www.laviudablanca.com; Calle de Campomanes 6; meals €35; ⏲ lunch & dinner Tue-Sat, lunch Mon; Ⓜ Ópera) Calle de Campomanes is fast becoming one of central Madrid's coolest streets and La Viuda Blanca is an essential part of its charm. The dining room is flooded with sunshine through the glass roof by day, the crowd is young and trendy, and the cooking of *madrileño* chef César Augusto is filled with flavour.

Taberna La Bola (Map pp142-3; ☎ 91 547 69 30; www.labola.es; Calle de la Bola 5; meals €35; ⏲ closed Aug; Ⓜ Santo Domingo) In any poll of food-loving locals, Taberna La Bola (going strong since 1880) always features near the top for most traditional Madrid cuisine. We're inclined to agree, and if you're going to try *cocido a la madrileña* (Madrid-style meat and chickpea stew; €20), this is a good place to do so.

Restaurante Sobrino de Botín (Map pp142-3; ☎ 91 366 42 17; www.botin.es; Calle de los Cuchilleros 17; meals €35-45; Ⓜ La Latina or Sol) It's not every day that you can eat in the oldest restaurant in the world (1725), which also appears in many novels about Madrid, most notably Hemingway's *The Sun Also Rises*. The secret of its staying power is fine *cochinillo* (suckling pig; €21) and *cordero asado* (roast lamb; €21) cooked in wood-fired ovens. Eating in the vaulted cellar is a treat.

WHAT'S COOKING IN MADRID?

- *Cocido a la madrileña* (Madrid-style meat and chickpea stew) – Taberna La Bola (left) or Lhardy (p181)
- *Callos a la madrileña* (tripe casserole with chorizo and chillies) – Casa Revuelta (see the boxed text, p182)
- *Sopa de ajo* or *sopa castellana* (garlic broth with floating egg and bread) – Posada de la Villa (p180)
- *Chocolate con churros* (deep-fried doughnut strips dipped in hot chocolate) – El Brillante (p180) or Chocolatería de San Ginés (p184)
- *Bocadillo de calamares* (a roll stuffed with calamari) – Cervecería Compano (left)

La Latina & Lavapiés

Although it faces stiff competition elsewhere, La Latina is simply the best *barrio* in Madrid for tapas – if you're only planning one tapas crawl while in Madrid, do it here. La Latina also ranks up there with Malasaña and Chueca for stylish dining and innovative cooking; you could just about take your pick of any of the restaurants around Calle de la Cava Baja and not leave disappointed.

Lavapiés is more eclectic and multicultural. Generally speaking, the further down the hill you go, the better it gets, especially along Calle de Argumosa.

Viva La Vida (Map pp142-3; ☎ 91 366 33 49; www.vivalavida.vg; Costanilla de San Andrés 16; veg buffet €1.80 per 100g; ⏲ 11am-midnight; Ⓜ La Latina; Ⓥ) This organic food shop has as its centrepiece an enticing vegetarian buffet with hot and cold food that's always filled with flavour. On the cusp of Plaza de la Paja, and with a laid-back vibe, it's a great place at any time of the day, especially outside normal Spanish eating hours when your stomach's rumbling.

El Estragón (Map pp142-3; ☎ 91 365 89 82; Plaza de la Paja 10; meals €20-25; Ⓜ La Latina; Ⓥ) A delightful spot for crêpes and other vegetarian specialities, El Estragón is undoubtedly one of Madrid's best vegetarian restaurants, although attentive vegans won't appreciate the use of butter.

La Buga del Lobo (Map pp142-3; ☎ 91 467 61 51; www.labocadellobo.com in Spanish; Calle de Argumosa 11; meals €25-30; 11am-2am Wed-Mon; Ⓜ Lavapiés) La Buga del Lobo has been one the 'in' places in gritty Lavapiés for years now and it's still hard to get a table. The atmosphere is bohemian and inclusive, with funky, swirling murals, contemporary art exhibitions and jazz or lounge music. The food's good and traditional, featuring meat and fish dishes for mains and *croquetas* (croquettes) cheeses or salads for starters.

Naïa Restaurante (Map pp142-3; ☎ 91 366 27 83; www.naiarestaurante.com in Spanish; Plaza de la Paja 3; meals €25-30; lunch & dinner Mon-Sat; Ⓜ La Latina) On the lovely Plaza de la Paja, Naïa has real buzz about it, with a cooking laboratory overseen by Carlos López Reyes, delightful modern Spanish food and a chill-out lounge downstairs. The emphasis throughout is on natural ingredients, healthy cooking and exciting tastes.

Nunc est Bibendum (Map pp142-3; ☎ 91 366 52 10; Calle de la Cava Alta 13; meals €30-35; lunch & dinner Mon-Sat, lunch Sun; Ⓜ La Latina) Nunc est Bibendum combines a classy, clean-lined look with a varied menu that defies categorisation – sometimes it's a Basque base, other flavours come from the south or from France – but is always good. The wine list is thoughtfully chosen, with some lesser-known Spanish wines.

Ene Restaurante (Map pp142-3; ☎ 91 366 25 91; www.enerestaurante.com; Calle del Nuncio 19; meals €30-35; Ⓜ La Latina) Just across from Iglesia de San Pedro El Viejo, one of Madrid's oldest churches, Ene is anything but old-world. The design is cutting-edge and awash with reds and purples, while the young waiters circulate to the tune of lounge music. The food is Spanish-Asian fusion and there are also plenty of *pintxos* (Basque tapas) to choose from. The chill-out beds downstairs are great for an after-dinner cocktail or even a meal, although they're always reserved well in advance.

Posada de la Villa (Map pp142-3; ☎ 91 366 18 60; Calle de la Cava Baja 9; meals €35-40; lunch & dinner Mon-Sat, lunch Sun, closed Aug; Ⓜ La Latina) This wonderfully restored 17th-century *posada* (inn) is something of a local landmark. The atmosphere is formal, the decoration sombre and traditional (heavy timber and brickwork), and the cuisine decidedly local – *cocido* (meat and chickpea stew), *callos* (tripe) and *sopa de ajo* (garlic soup).

Casa Lucio (Map pp142-3; ☎ 91 365 32 52; www.casalucio.es in Spanish; Calle de la Cava Baja 35; meals €35-45; lunch & dinner Sun-Fri, dinner Sat closed Aug; Ⓜ La Latina) Lucio has been wowing *madrileños* with his light touch, quality ingredients and home-style local cooking for ages – think seafood, roasted meats and eggs (a Lucio speciality) in abundance. Casa Lucio draws an august, always well-dressed crowd that has included the king of Spain, former US president Bill Clinton and Penélope Cruz.

Huertas & Atocha

The noise surrounding Huertas nightlife can obscure the fact that the *barrio* is a terrific place to eat out. Like the *barrio* itself, its culinary appeal lies in a hotchpotch of styles rather than any overarching personality. It's a state of affairs perhaps best summed up by the presence of restaurant Arola Madrid, one of the home kitchens of master chef Sergi Arola, and down-and-dirty tapas bars selling *oreja* (pig's ear). In between, there's Basque, Galician, Andalucian, Scandinavian and Italian to choose from.

El Brillante (Map p145; ☎ 91 528 69 66; Calle del Doctor Drumén 7; bocadillos €4-6, raciones €6-10; 6.30am-12.30am; Ⓜ Atocha) Just by the Centro de Arte Reina Sofía, this breezy and no-frills bar-eatery is a Madrid institution for *bocadillos* (the *bocadillo de calamares* is an old favourite) and other snacks. It's also famous for *chocolate con churros* or *porras* (deep-fried doughnut strips).

La Finca de Susana (Map pp142-3; ☎ 91 369 35 57; Calle de Arlabán 4; meals €20-25; Ⓜ Sevilla) Just because you're paying relatively low prices for your meal doesn't mean you have to dine in *cutre* (rough-and-ready) surrounds. The softly lit dining area here is bathed in greenery, and the sometimes innovative, sometimes traditional food draws a hip young crowd.

Maceiras (Map pp142-3; ☎ 91 429 15 84; Calle de las Huertas 66; meals €20-25; lunch & dinner Tue-Sun, dinner Mon; Ⓜ Antón Martín) Galician tapas (think octopus, green peppers etc) never tasted so good as in this agreeably rustic bar down the bottom of the Huertas hill, especially when washed down with a crisp white Ribeiro. The simple wooden tables, loyal customers and handy location make for a fine atmosphere. There's another branch around the corner at Calle de Jesús 7, which keeps the same hours.

Casa Alberto (Map pp142-3; ☎ 91 429 93 56; www.casaalberto.es in Spanish; Calle de las Huertas 18; meals €20-25; ⌚ noon-1.30am Tue-Sat, noon-4pm Sun; Ⓜ Antón Martín) One of the most atmospheric old *tabernas* of Madrid, Casa Alberto has been around since 1827. The secret to its staying power is vermouth on tap, excellent tapas and fine sit-down meals; *rabo de toro* (bull's tail) is a good order.

Vinos Gonzalez (Map pp142-3; ☎ 91 429 56 18; Calle de León 12; meals €20-25; ⌚ 9am-midnight Tue-Thu, 9am-1am Fri & Sat; Ⓜ Antón Martín) Ever dreamed of a deli where you could choose a tasty morsel and sit down and eat it right there? Well, here you can. On offer are a tempting array of cheeses, cured meats and other typically Spanish delicacies.

Sidrería Vasca Zeraín (Map pp142-3; ☎ 91 429 79 09; Calle Quevedo 3; meals €30-40; ⌚ lunch & dinner Mon-Sat; Ⓜ Antón Martín) In the heart of the Barrio de las Letras, this sophisticated Basque restaurant is one of the best places in the area to sample the region's cuisine. The staples include cider, *bacalao* and wonderful steaks, while there are also a few splashes of creativity thrown in (the secret's in the sauce).

Arola Madrid (Map pp142-3; ☎ 91 467 02 02; www.arola-madrid.com in Spanish; Calle de Argumosa 43; meals €50; ⌚ 10am-9pm Mon & Wed-Sat, 10am-5pm Sun; Ⓜ Atocha) What do you get if you cross one of Spain's most celebrated young chefs and a designer, blood-red space in one of Europe's most innovative galleries? A terrific place to eat, drink or simply hang out and feel stylish in one of the great art cities of the world. Housed in the Centro de Arte Reina Sofía, Arola Madrid offers nouvelle cuisine with an emphasis on presentation and variations on a traditional Spanish base.

Lhardy (Map pp142-3; ☎ 91 522 22 07; www.lhardy.com; Carrera de San Jerónimo 8; meals €50-60; ⌚ lunch & dinner Mon-Sat, lunch Sun; Ⓜ Sol or Sevilla) This Madrid landmark (since 1839) is an elegant treasure-trove of takeaway gourmet tapas. Upstairs is the upscale preserve of house specialities such as *callos*, *cocido*, pheasant in grape juice and lemon soufflé. It's expensive, but the quality and service are unimpeachable and the great-and-good of Madrid have all eaten here at some stage.

Salamanca

Eating out in Salamanca is traditionally as exclusive as the shops that fill the *barrio*, featuring the sorts of places where the keys to Jags and BMWs are left for valet parking, only the impeccably dressed are allowed through the doors, and prices and quality are high. But Salamanca is also home to some of Madrid's best-kept eating secrets, from *pintxos* to fusion restaurants to intimate dens of creative home cooking.

Fast Good (Map p140; Calle de Juan Bravo 3; meals €10-15; ⌚ noon-5pm & 8pm-midnight Mon-Fri, 12.30-5.30pm & 8pm-midnight Sat & Sun; Ⓜ Núñez de Balboa) Fast Good is a simple concept (food that's fast but healthy) from masterchef Ferran Adrià. It's a terrific place for a freshly prepared hamburger using Spanish ground beef with an olive tapenade, sandwiches with Spanish ham, paninis, roast chicken or French fries cooked in fresh olive oil. We also love the curvy white and lime-green decor.

La Galette (Map p140; ☎ 91 576 06 41; Calle del Conde de Aranda 11; meals €30-35; ⌚ lunch & dinner Mon-Sat, lunch Sun; Ⓜ Retiro; Ⓥ) This lovely little restaurant combines an intimate dining area with checked tablecloths and cooking that the owner describes as 'baroque vegetarian'. The food is a revelation, blending creativity with a strong base of traditional home cooking. The *croquetas de manzana* (apple croquettes) are a house speciality, but everything on the extensive menu is good. The only problem is that the tables are too close together.

Sula Madrid (Map p140; ☎ 91 781 61 97; www.sula.es; Calle de Jorge Juan 33; meals €70-80; ⌚ lunch & dinner Mon-Sat; Ⓜ Velázquez) If you want to catch Salamanca's happening vibe, head for Sula, a gourmet food store, superstylish tapas bar and clean-lined restaurant where gastronomic wunderkind Quique Dacosta (voted Spain's best chef in 2005) serves up a range of Mediterranean dishes that you won't find anywhere else. Design touches added by Amaya Arzuaga help to make this one of Madrid's coolest black-clad spaces.

Malasaña & Chueca

Cool *barrios*. Cool places to eat. Chueca and Malasaña may be radically different, one newly modern, the other rooted firmly in the past, but their restaurants are remarkably similar. Blending old *tabernas* with laid-back temples to nouvelle Spanish cuisine, the eating scene here revolves around an agreeable buzz, innovative cooking and casual but stylish surrounds. Some streets stand out, especially Calle de Manuela Malasaña in Malasaña and Calle de la Libertad in Chueca.

A TAPAS TOUR OF MADRID

Madrid's home of tapas is La Latina, especially along Calle de la Cava Baja and the surrounding streets. **Almendro 13** (Map pp142-3; ☎ 91 365 42 52; Calle de Almendro 13; meals €15-25; Ⓜ La Latina) is regularly voted among the top tapas bars in Madrid for traditional Spanish tapas, with an emphasis on quality rather than frilly elaborations. A few doors up, **Corazon Loco** (Map pp142-3; ☎ 91 366 57 83; Calle del Almendro 22; meals €15-25; ⏲ lunch & dinner Tue-Sun; Ⓜ La Latina) is similarly popular, with canapés a speciality and well-priced wines. Down on Calle de la Cava Baja, **Taberna Txacoli** (Map pp142-3; ☎ 91 366 48 77; Calle de la Cava Baja 26; meals €15-20; ⏲ lunch & dinner Tue & Thu-Sat, lunch Sun, dinner Wed; Ⓜ La Latina) does Basque 'high cuisine in miniature', although these are some of the biggest *pintxos* (Basque tapas) you'll find. On the same street, **Casa Lucas** (Map pp142-3; ☎ 91 365 08 04; Calle de la Cava Baja 30; meals €20-25; ⏲ lunch & dinner Thu-Tue, dinner Wed; Ⓜ La Latina) and **La Chata** (Map pp142-3; ☎ 91 366 14 58; Calle de la Cava Baja 24; meals €25-30; ⏲ lunch & dinner Thu-Mon, dinner Wed; Ⓜ La Latina) are also hugely popular. Not far away, **Juanalaloca** (Map pp142-3; ☎ 91 364 05 25; Plaza de la Puerta de Moros 4; meals €30-35; ⏲ lunch & dinner Tue-Sun, dinner Mon; Ⓜ La Latina) does a magnificent *tortilla de patatas* (potato and onion omelette), and **Taberna Matritum** (Map pp142-3; ☎ 91 365 82 37; Calle de la Cava Alta 17; meals €20-30; ⏲ lunch Mon-Fri, lunch & dinner Sat & Sun; Ⓜ La Latina) serves great *tostas* (toasts) and other tapas.

Most famous for *bacalao* (cod) is **Casa Labra** (Map pp142-3; ☎ 91 531 00 81; Calle de Tetuán 11; meals €15-20; ⏲ 11am-3.30pm & 6-11pm; Ⓜ Sol), which has been around since 1860 and was a favourite of the poet Federico García Lorca. However, many *madrileños* wouldn't eat *bacalao* anywhere except **Casa Revuelta** (Map pp142-3; ☎ 91 366 33 32; Calle de Latoneros 3; meals €10-15; ⏲ lunch & dinner Tue-Sat, lunch Sun; Ⓜ La Latina or Sol), clinched by the fact that the owner painstakingly extracts every fish bone in the morning.

BUDGET

Fresc Co (Map pp138-9; ☎ 91 521 60 52; Calle de Sagasta 30; meals €9-10; ⏲ 12.30pm-1am; Ⓜ Alonso Martínez) If you just can't face deciphering another Spanish menu or are in dire need of a do-it-yourself salad, Fresc Co is a fresh, well-priced, all-you-can eat antidote. An extensive buffet of salads, soups, pasta and pizza is on offer, and the price includes a drink. Queues often form out the door at lunchtime.

La Taberna de San Bernardo (Map pp138-9; ☎ 91 445 41 70; Calle de San Bernardo 85; meals €15-20; ⏲ 2.30-4.30pm & 8.30pm-2.30am; Ⓜ San Bernardo) The *raciones* (large tapas servings; around €6 to €8) here include plenty of Spanish favourites with a few surprising twists thrown in – the *berenjenas con mile de caña* (deep-fried aubergine with honey) is brilliant.

MIDRANGE

Restaurante Momo (Map pp138-9; ☎ 91 532 73 48; Calle de la Libertad 8; meals €20; ⏲ Mon-Sat; Ⓜ Chueca) Momo is a Chueca beacon of reasonably priced home cooking for a casual crowd. It has an artsy vibe and is ideal for those who want a hearty meal without too much elaboration. The three-course dinner *menú* (set menu; €12.80) is one of Madrid's best bargains, and the famous chocolate *moco* (chocolate 'snot', but really homemade chocolate pudding) is the tastiest of dessert dishes despite the worrying name.

A Dos Velas (Map pp138-9; ☎ 91 446 18 63; www.adosvelas.net in Spanish; Calle de San Vicente Ferrer 16; meals €20-25; ⏲ lunch & dinner Mon-Sat; Ⓜ Tribunal) The food here is always creative, with Mediterranean cooking fused with occasional Indian or even Argentinian flavours. There's a lovely dining area with soft lighting and exposed brick, and service is attentive without being intrusive. The lime-marinated swordfish with avocado salad is among our many favourites.

Ribeira Do Miño (Map pp138-9; ☎ 91 521 98 54; Calle de la Santa Brigida 1; meals €20-25; ⏲ lunch & dinner Tue-Sat; Ⓜ Tribunal) This riotously popular seafood bar and restaurant is where *madrileños* with a love for seafood indulge their fantasies. The *mariscada de la casa* (€30 for two) is a platter of seafood so large that even the hungriest of visitors will leave satisfied. Leave your name with the waiter and be prepared to wait for up to an hour for a table.

our pick **La Musa** (Map pp138-9; ☎ 91 448 75 58; www.lamusa.com.es; Calle de Manuela Malasaña 18; meals €25-30; Ⓜ San Bernardo) A local favourite of Malasaña's hip, young crowd, La Musa has designer decor, lounge music and food that will live long in the memory. The fried green tomatoes with strawberry jam and great meat dishes

In Huertas, **La Casa del Abuelo** (Map pp142-3; ☎ 91 521 23 19; Calle de la Victoria 12; meals €15-25; 🕑 11.30am-3.30pm & 6.30-11.30pm; Ⓜ Sol) is famous for *gambas a la plancha* (grilled prawns) or *gambas al ajillo* (prawns sizzling in garlic on little ceramic plates) and a *chato* (small glass) of the heavy, sweet El Abuelo red wine. For *patatas bravas* (fried potatoes lathered in a spicy tomato sauce), **Las Bravas** (Map pp142-3; ☎ 91 532 26 20; Callejón de Álvarez Gato 3; meals €15; 🕑 10am-11.30pm; Ⓜ Sol) is the place, while **La Trucha** (Map pp142-3; ☎ 91 532 08 82; Calle de Núñez de Arce 6; 🕑 lunch & dinner Tue-Sat; Ⓜ Sol) has a counter overloaded with enticing Andalucian tapas.

In Chueca, don't miss **Bocaito** (Map pp138-9; ☎ 91 532 12 19; Calle de la Libertad 4-6; 🕑 lunch & dinner Mon-Fri, dinner Sat; Ⓜ Chueca), another purveyor of Andalucian *jamón* (ham) and seafood and a favourite haunt of film-maker Pedro Almodóvar. Nearby, **4 de Tapas** (Map pp138-9; ☎ 91 532 94 64; Calle de Barbieri 4; meals €20; 🕑 9am-5pm & 8pm-2.30am Mon-Sat; Ⓜ Chueca or Gran Vía) has a lounge-bar atmosphere and terrific *tostas* and *cazuelas* (food cooked in a small ceramic pot). Where Chueca meets Malasaña, **El Lateral** (Map pp138-9; ☎ 91 531 68 77; www.cadenalateral.es; Calle de Fuencarral 43; meals €15-25; 🕑 1pm-1am; Ⓜ Tribunal) is sophisticated and has a wide range of choices.

Away to the east in Salamanca, **Biotza** (Map p140; ☎ 91 781 03 13; Calle de Claudio Coello 27; 🕑 9am-midnight Mon-Thu, 9am-2am Fri & Sat; Ⓜ Serrano) offers creative Basque *pintxos* in stylish surrounds, while **La Colonial de Goya** (Map p140; ☎ 91 575 63 06; Calle de Jorge Juan 34; meals €20; 🕑 8am-midnight Mon-Fri, 8am-1am Sat; Ⓜ Velázquez) serves up 68 different varieties of *pintxos*. Similarly good, in Chamberí, is **Sagaretxe** (Map pp134-5; ☎ 91 446 25 88; Calle de Eloy Gonzalo 26; meals €15-20; 🕑 noon-5pm & 7pm-midnight Sun-Wed, noon-5pm & 7pm-12.30am Thu, noon-5pm & 7pm-1am Fri & Sat; Ⓜ Iglesia), where the *surtido de pintxos* (your own selection of tapas) costs €15/24 for eight/12.

are fun and filled with flavour. They don't take reservations so sidle up to the bar, put your name on the waiting list and soak up the ambient buzz of Malasaña at its best.

Bazaar (Map pp138-9; ☎ 91 523 39 05; www.restaurantbazaar.com; Calle de la Libertad 21; meals €25-30; Ⓜ Chueca) Bazaar's popularity among the well-heeled and often-famous shows no sign of abating. Its pristine white interior design with theatre lighting may draw a crowd that looks like it stepped out of the pages of *Hola!* magazine, but the food is extremely well priced and innovative. They don't take reservations so get here early or be prepared to wait, regardless of whether you're famous or not.

El Original (Map pp142-3; ☎ 91 522 90 69; www.eloriginal.es in Spanish; Calle de las Infantas 44; meals €25-30; 🕑 lunch & dinner Mon-Sat; Ⓜ Chueca or Banco de España) With the best products and signature dishes from each of the regions of Spain, you might expect El Original to be a bastion of traditionalism. Indeed, they describe their food as classic Spanish cooking. But the classic theme ends when you step into the restaurant and find trees growing in the sleek dining room.

our pick La Isla del Tesoro (Map pp138-9; ☎ 91 593 14 40; Calle de Manuela Malasaña 3; meals €30; Ⓜ Bilbao; Ⓥ) La Isla del Tesoro is loaded with quirky charm – the dining area is like someone's fantasy of a secret garden come to life. The cooking here is assured and wide-ranging in its influences; the jungle burger is typical in a menu that's full of surprises. The weekday, lunchtime *menú del día* (daily set menu) is more varied than most in Madrid, with Indonesian, Lebanese, Moroccan, French and Mexican, among others, all getting a run.

our pick Nina (Map pp138-9; ☎ 91 591 00 46; Calle de Manuela Malasaña 10; meals €30-35; Ⓜ Bilbao) This is one of our favourite restaurants in Madrid, with fantastic food, great service and a stylish dining area. The cooking is similarly cool; the *foie fresco a la plancha* (grilled foie gras) is rich and divine. Popular with a sophisticated local crowd, Nina can be a hard place to get a table and booking on weekends is essential. English-language menus are available.

Laydown Rest Club (Map pp138-9; ☎ 91 548 79 37; www.laydown.es in Spanish; Plaza de Mostenses 9; meals €30-35; 🕑 2-4pm & 9.30pm-2.30am Tue-Fri, 9.30pm-2.30am Sat & Sun, 2-4pm Mon; Ⓜ Plaza de España) The name says it all. Part of the ongoing craze in concept dining, Laydown Rest Club is whiter than white and completely devoid of tables – you eat Roman-style while reclining on beds, where you're served by toga-clad waiters with huge feather fans. The menu changes daily, but never strays too far from a Mediterranean theme.

Chamberí & Argüelles

At first glance, Chamberí and Argüelles seem more like residential areas than great places to go out. With so many young and upwardly mobile *madrileños* clamouring to live here, however, there are some fine choices if you know where to look. There's rarely another tourist in sight and you'll feel much more a part of the *barrio* than in the town centre.

Restaurantes La Giralda (Map pp138-9; ☎ 91 445 17 43; www.restauranteslagiralda.com in Spanish; Calle de Hartzembusch 12 & 15; meals €20-25; 🕑 lunch & dinner Mon-Sat, lunch Sun; Ⓜ Bilbao) The two Restaurantes La Giralda face each other across the road, and feel like you've landed in Sevilla or Cádiz. Great for just about every kind of fried or fresh Mediterranean seafood you can imagine (and many you can't). The quality is high so it's hugely popular, but the downstairs dining area is surprisingly large.

Northern Madrid

The business and well-to-do clientele who eat in the restaurants of northern Madrid know their food and are happy to pay for it. It can be a fair metro or taxi ride north of the centre, but well worth it for a touch of class.

our pick **Santceloni** (Map p133; ☎ 91 210 88 40; www.restaurantesantceloni.com; Paseo de la Castellana 57; meals from €100, menús €125-155; Ⓜ Gregorio Marañón) The Michelin-starred Santceloni is one of Madrid's best restaurants, with luxury decor that's the work of star interior designer Pascual Ortega, and nouvelle cuisine from the kitchen of master Catalan chef Santi Santamaría. Each dish is an exquisite work of art – try the lobster with vegetables and an oil-mint emulsion. But we'd recommend one of the set menus to really sample the breadth of tastes on offer.

Self-Catering

Some of the better fresh-food markets in town include **Mercado de San Miguel** (Map pp142-3; Plaza de San Miguel; 🕑 9am-2.30pm & 5.15-8.15pm Mon-Fri, 9am-2.30pm Sat; Ⓜ Sol) and **Mercado de la Paz** (Map p140; 🕑 9am-8pm Mon-Sat; Ⓜ Serrano).

For fine takeaway food, head to **Mallorca** (Map p140; ☎ 91 577 18 59; Calle de Serrano 6; 🕑 9.30am-9pm; Ⓜ Retiro), a Madrid institution. Everything here, from gourmet mains to snacks and desserts, is delicious. There are branches throughout the city.

Other specialist gourmet food stores include Mantequería Bravo (p195) and Poncelet (p195).

DRINKING

You've seen the great paintings, you've eaten an outstanding meal and, if you have any sense, you'll have taken a siesta. Now it's time for your initiation into Europe's most dynamic nightlife. To get an idea of how much *madrileños* like to go out and have a good time, consider one simple statistic: Madrid has more bars than any city in the world – six, in fact, for every 100 inhabitants.

If you're after the more traditional, with tiled walls and flamenco tunes, head to the *barrio* of Huertas. For gay-friendly drinking holes, Chueca is the place. Malasaña caters to a grungy, funky crowd, while La Latina has friendly bars that guarantee atmosphere most nights of the week. In summer, head to the outdoor cafes in the city's squares.

Los Austrias, Sol & Centro

Old taverns and the odd hidden gem rub shoulders in Madrid's centre. As a general rule, the further you stray from Plaza Mayor, the more prices drop and the fewer tourists you'll see.

Chocolatería de San Ginés (Map pp142-3; ☎ 91 365 65 46; Pasadizo de San Ginés 5; 🕑 9am-7am Wed-Sun, 6pm-7am Mon & Tue; Ⓜ Sol) Perhaps the best-known of Madrid's *chocolate con churros* vendors, this Madrid institution is at its most popular from 3am to 6am as clubbers make a last stop for sustenance on their way home. Only in Madrid.

Café del Real (Map pp142-3; ☎ 91 547 21 24; Plaza de Isabel II 2; 🕑 9am-1am Sun-Thu, 10am-2am Fri & Sat; Ⓜ Ópera) One of the nicest cafes in central Madrid, this place serves a rich variety of creative coffees and a few cocktails to a soundtrack of chill-out music. The best seats are upstairs, where the low ceilings, wooden beams and leather chairs make a great place to pass an afternoon.

La Viuda Negra (Map pp142-3; ☎ 91 548 75 29; Calle de Campomanes 6; 🕑 5-9pm Sun & Mon, 9pm-2am Tue & Wed, 9pm-3am Thu-Sat; Ⓜ Ópera) This all-dressed-in-orange, loungelike cocktail bar ('The Black Widow') is minimalist enough for Manhattan and genuinely cool enough to satisfy the sophisticated crowd of the new Madrid. If you're the sort that likes to settle in for the night, you can first eat at the sister restaurant, La Viuda Blanca (p179), next door, then ease over to the bar for funky house music until late. Sunday afternoons are jazzy and very mellow.

Gaia Cocktail Lounge (Map pp142-3; ☎ 610 737 639; www.gaiacocktail.com in Spanish; Calle de la Amnistía 5; ⏰ 10pm-3am Tue-Thu, 8.30pm-3.30am Fri & Sat; Ⓜ Ópera) Heartbreakingly sleek and oh-so-cool, Gaia is one of the best bars in the centre, serving up delicious cocktails to a DJ soundtrack of jazz, funk, lounge and occasional house music.

La Latina & Lavapiés

Two different *barrios*, two very different vibes. Most nights (and Sunday afternoons), crowds of happy *madrileños* hop from bar to bar across La Latina. This is a *barrio* beloved by discerning 20- and 30-something urban sophisticates who ensure there's little room to move in the good places and the bad ones don't survive long. The crowd is a little more diverse on Sundays as hordes fan out from El Rastro. Most of the action takes place along Calle de la Cava Baja, the western end of Calle de Almendro and Plaza de la Paja. Working-class, multicultural Lavapiés is a completely different kettle of fish – quirky bars brimful of personality that draw an alternative, often bohemian crowd. Not everyone loves Lavapiés, but we do.

Bonanno (Map pp142-3; ☎ 91 366 68 86; Plaza del Humilladero 4; ⏰ noon-2am Sun-Thu, noon-2.30am Fri & Sat; Ⓜ La Latina) If much of Madrid's nightlife starts too late for your liking, Bonanno could be for you. It made its name as a cocktail bar, but many people come here for the great wines and it's usually full with young professional *madrileños* from early evening onwards. Be prepared to snuggle up close to those around you if you want a spot at the bar.

Café del Nuncio (Map pp142-3; ☎ 91 366 08 53; Calle de Segovia 9; ⏰ 12.30pm-2.30am Sun-Thu, 12.30pm-3.30am Fri & Sat; Ⓜ La Latina) Café del Nuncio straggles down a stairway passage to Calle de Segovia. You can drink on one of several cosy levels inside or, better still in summer, enjoy the outdoor seating. On summer weekends, this place hums with the sort of clamour that newcomers to Madrid find utterly irresistible.

Delic (Map pp142-3; ☎ 91 364 54 50; Costanilla de San Andrés 14; ⏰ 11am-2am Tue-Sun, 8pm-2am Mon; Ⓜ La Latina) We could go on for hours about this long-standing cafe-bar, but we'll reduce it to its most basic elements: nursing an exceptionally good mojito or three on a warm summer's evening at an outdoor table on one of Madrid's prettiest plazas is one of life's great pleasures. Bliss.

Gaudeamus Café (Map pp142-3; ☎ 91 528 25 94; www.gaudeamuscafe.com in Spanish; 4th fl, Calle de Tribulete 14; ⏰ 3.30pm-midnight Mon-Fri, 8pm-midnight Sat; Ⓜ Lavapiés) Decoration that's light and airy, with pop-art posters of Audrey Hepburn and James Bond. A large terrace with views over the Lavapiés rooftops. A stunning backdrop of a ruined church atop which the cafe sits. With so much else going for it, it almost seems incidental that this cafe serves great teas, coffees and snacks.

El Viajero (Map pp142-3; ☎ 91 366 90 64; Plaza de la Cebada 11; ⏰ 2pm-2am Tue-Thu & Sun, 2pm-3am Fri & Sat; Ⓜ La Latina) This landmark of La Latina nights may have lost a little of its glamour, but it's nonetheless an essential place for a drink in the *barrio*. Its undoubted highlight is the open-air, rooftop *terraza* that boasts fine views down onto the thronging streets, although when the weather's warm, it's nigh-on impossible to get a table.

La Inquilina (Map pp142-3; ☎ 627 511 804; Calle del Ave María 39; ⏰ 7pm-2am Tue-Thu, 1-4pm & 8pm-3am Fri-Sun; Ⓜ Lavapiés) This could just be our favourite bar in Lavapiés. It's partly about the cool-and-casual vibe, partly because it's a bar run by women and partly because of its community spirit with deep roots in the Lavapiés soil. Contemporary artworks by budding local artists adorn the walls and you can either gather around the bar or take a table out the back.

Taberna Tempranillo (Map pp142-3; ☎ 91 364 15 32; Calle de la Cava Baja 38; ⏰ 1-4pm & 8pm-midnight; Ⓜ La Latina) You could come here for the tapas, but we are recommending Taberna Tempranillo primarily for its wines, of which there is a selection that puts most other Spanish bars to shame. It's not a late-night place, but it's always packed with an early-evening crowd.

Huertas & Atocha

Huertas comes into its own after dark and stays that way until close to sunrise. Bars are everywhere, from Sol down to the Paseo del Prado hinterland, but it's in Plaza de Santa Ana and along Calle de las Huertas that most of the action is concentrated.

Cervecería Alemana (Map pp142-3; ☎ 91 429 70 33; Plaza de Santa Ana 6; ⏰ 10.30am-12.30am Sun-Thu, 10.30am-2am Fri & Sat, closed Aug; Ⓜ Antón Martín or Sol) If you've only got time to stop at one bar on Plaza de Santa Ana, let it be this classic *cervecería,* renowned for its cold, frothy beers.

It's fine inside, but snaffle a table outside in the square on a summer's evening and you won't be giving it up without a fight. This was one of Hemingway's haunts, and neither the wood-lined bar nor the bow-tied waiters have changed since his day.

Casa Pueblo (Map pp142-3; ☎ 91 420 20 38; Calle de León 3; ⏲ 8.30pm-2.30am Tue-Sun; Ⓜ Antón Martín) Jazz may be all the rage in Madrid, but Casa Pueblo was onto it long before the fad started and will remain so long after it passes. As such, it has a whiff of authenticity about it. Tango is also a staple of the bar and there are occasional live acts.

El Imperfecto (Map pp142-3; Plaza de Matute 2; ⏲ 3pm-2am Sun-Thu, 3pm-3am Fri & Sat; Ⓜ Antón Martín) Its name notwithstanding, the 'Imperfect One' is our ideal Huertas bar, with live jazz on Tuesdays (and sometimes other nights) and a drinks menu as long as a saxophone, ranging from cocktails (€6.50) and spirits to milkshakes, teas and creative coffees.

La Venencia (Map pp142-3; ☎ 91 429 73 13; Calle de Echegaray 7; ⏲ 1-3.30pm & 7.30pm-1.30am Sun-Thu, 1-3.30pm & 7.30pm-2.30am Fri & Sat; Ⓜ Sol) This is how sherry bars should be – old-world, drinks poured straight from the dusty wooden barrels and none of the frenetic activity for which Huertas is famous. La Venencia is a *barrio* classic, with fine sherry from Sanlúcar and Manzanilla from Jeréz. There's no music, no flashy decorations; it's all about you, your *fino* (sherry) and your friends.

Ølsen (Map pp142-3; ☎ 91 429 36 59; Calle del Prado 15; ⏲ 1-4pm & 8pm-2am Tue-Sun; Ⓜ Antón Martín) This classy and clean-lined bar is a temple to Nordic minimalism and comes into its own after the Scandinavian restaurant out the back closes. We think the more than 80 varieties of vodka are enough to satisfy most tastes. You'll hate vodka the next day, but Madrid is all about living for the night.

Taberna Alhambra (Map pp142-3; ☎ 91 521 07 08; Calle de la Victoria 9; ⏲ 10am-2am; Ⓜ Sol) There can be a certain sameness about the bars between Sol and Huertas, which is why this fine old *taberna* stands out. The striking facade and exquisite tilework of the interior are quite beautiful; however, this place is anything but stuffy and the vibe is cool, casual and busy. Late at night there are some fine flamenco tunes.

Taberna de Dolores (Map pp142-3; ☎ 91 429 22 43; Plaza de Jesús 4; ⏲ 11am-1am Sun-Thu, 11am-2am Fri & Sat; Ⓜ Antón Martín) This Madrid institution is known for its blue-and-white tiled exterior, and for an older, 30-something crowd that often includes the odd *famoso* (celebrity) or two. You get good house wine, great anchovies and some of Madrid's best beer for prices that haven't been seen elsewhere in the city since the euro sent prices soaring.

Penthouse (Map pp142-3; ☎ 91 701 60 20; 7th fl, Plaza de Santa Ana 14; ⏲ 9pm-4am Wed-Sat, 5pm-midnight Sun; Ⓜ Antón Martín or Sol) High above the clamour of Huertas, this exclusive cocktail bar has a delightful terrace overlooking Plaza de Santa Ana and the rooftops of downtown Madrid. It's a place for sophisticates, with chill-out areas strewn with cushions, funky DJs and a dress policy designed to sort out the classy from the wannabes. If you suffer from vertigo, consider the equally sybaritic Midnight Rose on the ground floor.

Viva Madrid (Map pp142-3; ☎ 91 429 36 40; www.barvivamadrid.com; Calle de Manuel Fernández y González 7; ⏲ 1pm-2am Sun-Thu, 1pm-3am Fri & Sat; Ⓜ Antón Martín or Sol) A beautifully tiled bar, some of the best mojitos in town, a friendly atmosphere, a mixed crowd and scattered tables – what more could a *madrileño* want? Not much apparently, as it's famous on the Huertas late-night scene.

Salamanca

Salamanca is the land of the beautiful people and it's all about gloss and glamour: heels for her and hair gel for him. As you glide through the *pijos* (beautiful people), keep your eyes peeled for Real Madrid players, celebrities and designer clothes. If nothing else, you'll see how the other half lives.

Geographic Club (Map pp134-5; ☎ 91 578 08 62; Calle de Alcalá 141; ⏲ 1pm-1.30am Sun-Thu, 1pm-3.30am Fri & Sat; Ⓜ Goya) With its elaborate stained-glass windows, wooden African masks and photos from around the world, the Geographic Club feels like an Irish bar by day (it's the wood panelling that does it), but it gets noisy after midnight with a more mixed crowd than most of Salamanca can muster.

El Lateral (Map p140; ☎ 91 435 06 04; Calle de Velázquez 57; ⏲ 1pm-1am; Ⓜ Velázquez or Núñez de Balboa) It doesn't get much more *pijo* than this chic wine bar, where wearing hair gel seems to be a prerequisite for entry. Don't bother coming here after work's out unless you're in an Armani suit; at other times, the excellent wines and other drinks loosen up the crowd (if not the ties) more than you'd think.

Café-Restaurante El Espejo (Map p140; ☎ 91 308 23 47; Paseo de los Recoletos 31; 🕑 10.30am-1am Sun-Thu, 10.30am-2am Fri & Sat; Ⓜ Colón) Once a haunt of writers and intellectuals, this Modernista gem could well overwhelm you with its mirrors, chandeliers and bow-tied service of another era; it's quiet and refined, although the outdoor tables are hugely popular in summer.

Gran Café de Gijón (Map p140; ☎ 91 521 54 25; Paseo de los Recoletos 21; 🕑 8am-2am; Ⓜ Chueca or Banco de España) This graceful old café has been serving coffee and meals since 1888 and has long been a favourite with Madrid's literati. You'll find yourself among intellectuals, conservative Franco diehards and young *madrileños* looking for a quiet drink. Come for the history, but prepare to pay above the odds for the experience.

Malasaña & Chueca

Drinking in Malasaña and Chueca is like a journey through Madrid's multifaceted past. Around the Glorieta de Bilbao and along the Paseo de los Recoletos you encounter stately old literary cafes that revel in their grandeur and late-19th-century ambience. Throughout Malasaña, *rockers* (rockers) nostalgic for the hedonistic Madrid of the 1970s and 1980s will find ample bars to indulge their memories. At the same time, across the *barrios* but especially in gay Chueca and away to the west in Conde Duque, modern Madrid is very much on show, with chill-out spaces and swanky, sophisticated bars.

Café Pepe Botella (Map pp138-9; ☎ 91 522 43 09; Calle de San Andrés 12; 🕑 10am-2am Sun-Thu, 10am-3am Fri & Sat; Ⓜ Bilbao or Tribunal) As good in the wee small hours as it is in the afternoon, this is a classy bar with green velvet benches, marble-topped tables, old photos and mirrors covering the walls. The faded elegance gives the place charm that's made it one of the most popular and enduring drinking holes in the *barrio*.

Areia (Map pp138-9; ☎ 91 310 03 07; www.areiachillout.com in Spanish; Calle de Hortaleza 92; 🕑 12.30pm-3am Mon-Thu, 12.30pm-3.30am Fri-Sun; Ⓜ Chueca or Alonso Martínez) The ultimate lounge bar by day (cushions, chill-out music and dark, secluded corners where you can hear yourself talk, or even snog quietly), this place is equally enjoyable by night. That's when groovy DJs take over (from 11pm Sunday to Wednesday, and from 9pm the rest of the week) with deep and chill house, nu jazz, bossa and electronica. It's cool, funky and low-key all at once, although the cocktails can be pricey.

La Vía Láctea (Map pp138-9; ☎ 91 446 75 81; Calle de Velarde 18; 🕑 7.30pm-3am; Ⓜ Bilbao or Tribunal) A living, breathing and somewhat grungy relic of *la movida*, La Vía Láctea remains a Malasaña favourite for a mixed, informal crowd who seem to live for the 1980s – eyeshadow for boys and girls is a recurring theme. There are plenty of drinks to choose from and by early on Sunday morning anything goes. Expect long queues to get in on weekends.

Café Belén (Map pp138-9; ☎ 91 308 24 47; Calle de Belén 5; 🕑 3.30pm-3am; Ⓜ Chueca) Café Belén is cool in all the right places – lounge and chill-out music, dim lighting, a great range of drinks (the mojitos are as good as you'll find in Madrid and that's saying something) and a low-key crowd that's the height of casual sophistication.

Stop Madrid (Map pp138-9; ☎ 91 521 88 87; Calle de Hortaleza 11; 🕑 12.30-4pm & 6.30pm-2am; Ⓜ Gran Vía) The name may be incongruous, but this terrific old *taberna* is friendly and invariably packed with people. It wins the vote of at least one Lonely Planet author for the best sangria in Madrid.

El Jardín Secreto (Map pp138-9; ☎ 91 541 80 23; Calle de Conde Duque 2; 🕑 5.30pm-12.30am Mon-Thu & Sun, 6.30pm-2.30am Fri & Sat; Ⓜ Plaza de España) 'The Secret Garden' is all about intimacy and romance in a *barrio* that's one of Madrid's best-kept secrets. Lit by Spanish designer candles, draped in organza from India and serving up chocolates from the Caribbean, it's at its best on a summer's evening, but the atmosphere never misses a beat. It attracts a loyal and young professional crowd.

Café Comercial (Map pp138-9; ☎ 91 521 56 55; Glorieta de Bilbao 7; 🕑 7.30am-midnight Mon, 7.30am-1am Tue-Thu, 7.30am-2am Fri, 8.30am-2am Sat, 9am-midnight Sun; Ⓜ Bilbao) This glorious old Madrid cafe proudly fights a rearguard action against progress with heavy leather seats, abundant marble and old-style waiters. As close as Madrid came to the intellectual cafes of Paris' Left Bank, Café Comercial now has a clientele that has broadened to include just about anyone. See the boxed text, p188.

Museo Chicote (Map pp142-3; ☎ 91 532 67 37; www.museo-chicote.com; Gran Vía 12; 🕑 8am-4am Mon-Sat; Ⓜ Gran Vía) The founder of this Madrid landmark is said to have invented more than a hundred cocktails, which the likes of Hemingway, Sophia Loren and Frank Sinatra all enjoyed at one time or another. It's still

FERNANDO, WAITER AT CAFÉ COMERCIAL

This cafe's been around for a while? It was first opened in 1860 by a priest and it's been in my family for four generations.

How long have you been a waiter here? I grew up in here, but 20 years as a waiter and behind the bar.

Has the cafe changed over the years? Not a bit. The last renovations were in 1958.

No changes at all? Ten or 12 years ago we put an internet cafe upstairs. Downstairs is now nonsmoking. And, as of three years ago, we finally have female waiters!

Has the clientele changed? We've always had customers from children to old people, which is very typical of Madrid. Many famous people as well.

And what do they order? People are now more health-conscious than before – decaffeinated coffee, water. Even though later they go out and smoke.

You must have seen some changes. Look at this cafe and you see Madrid.

frequented by film stars and socialites, and it's at its best after midnight when a lounge atmosphere takes over, couples cuddle on the curved benches and some of the city's best DJs do their stuff.

Ojalá Awareness Club (Map pp138-9; ☎ 91 523 27 47; Calle de San Andrés 1; 🕒 8.30am-1am Sun-Wed, 8.30am-2am Thu-Sat; Ⓜ Tribunal) Ojalá is funky. We love it first and foremost for a drink (especially a daiquiri) at any time of the day. Its lime-green colour scheme, zany lighting and a hip, cafe-style ambience all make it an extremely cool place to hang out, but the sandy floor and cushions downstairs take chilled to a whole new level.

ENTERTAINMENT

For the lowdown on upcoming concerts and showings at Madrid's theatres, cinemas and football stadiums, check out the following:

EsMadrid Magazine (www.esmadrid.com) Monthly tourist office listings for concerts and other performances; available at tourist offices, some hotels and online.

Guía del Ocio (www.guiadelocio.com in Spanish) A Spanish-only weekly magazine available for €1 at news kiosks.

In Madrid (www.in-madrid.com) The monthly English-language expat publication is given out free at some hotels, original-version cinemas, Irish pubs and English bookshops, and has lots of information about what to see and do in town.

La Netro (http://madrid.lanetro.com) Comprehensive online guide to everything that's happening in Madrid.

Metropoli (www.elmundo.es/metropoli in Spanish) *El Mundo*'s Friday supplement magazine has information on the week's offerings.

On Madrid (www.elpais.com in Spanish) *El País* also has a Friday supplement with listings for the week.

Salir Urban (www.salirsalir.com) The magazine (€2.50) is mostly for bars, restaurants and live music, but the online version has a section on theatres.

What's on When (www.whatsonwhen.com) The Madrid page covers the highlights of sports and cultural activities, with some information on getting tickets.

Clubs

No *barrio* in Madrid is without a decent club or disco, but the most popular dance spots are in the centre. For intimate dancing or quirky decor, head to Chueca or Malasaña. Don't expect the dance clubs or *discotecas* to really get going until after 1am, and some won't even bat an eyelid until 3am, when the bars elsewhere have closed.

Club prices vary widely, depending on the time of night you enter, the way you're dressed and the number of people inside. The standard entry fee is €10, which usually includes the first drink, although megaclubs and swankier places charge a few euros more. Even those that let you in free will play catch-up with hefty prices for drinks, so don't plan your night around looking for the cheapest ticket.

LOS AUSTRIAS, SOL & CENTRO

Cool (Map pp138-9; ☎ 902 499 994; Calle de Isabel la Católica 6; 🕒 11pm-6am Thu-Sat; Ⓜ Santo Domingo) Cool by name, cool by nature: think gorgeous people, gorgeous clothes and a strict entry policy. One of the hottest clubs in the city, it features curvy white lines, discreet lounge chairs in dark corners and a pulsating dance floor. Things don't really get going until 3am and the music's a mix of electronica and house, with themed gay and rock nights.

Costello Café & Niteclub (Map pp142-3; www.costelloclub.com; Calle del Caballero de Gracia 10; 🕒 6pm-3am; Ⓜ Gran Vía) Costello Café and Niteclub has an innovative mix of pop, rock and fusion in smooth-as-silk, Warholesque surrounds.

It may close earlier than we'd like, but we still think this is one of the coolest places in town.

Oba Oba (Map pp138-9; Calle de Jacometrezo 4; 🕑 11pm-5.30am Sun-Thu, 11pm-6am Fri & Sat; Ⓜ Callao) This nightclub is Brazilian down to its G-strings, with live music some nights and dancing til dawn every night of the week. You'll find plenty of Brazilians in residence, which is the best recommendation we can give for the music and the authenticity of its caipirinhas.

Palacio Gaviria (Map pp142-3; ☎ 91 526 60 69; Calle del Arenal 9; 🕑 11pm-4am Sun-Wed, 10pm-6am Thu, 11pm-7am Fri & Sat; Ⓜ Sol) An elegant palace converted into one of the most popular dance clubs in Madrid, this is the kind of place where the crowd can be pretty young and boisterous and the queues long. Thursday is international student and house music night – international relations have never been so much fun.

Teatro Joy Eslava (Map pp142-3; ☎ 91 366 54 39; www.joy-eslava.com in Spanish; Calle del Arenal 11; 🕑 11.30pm-6am; Ⓜ Sol) The only things guaranteed at this grand old Madrid dance club (housed in a 19th-century theatre) are a crowd and the fact that it will be open. (The club claims to have opened every single day for the past 27 years.) The music and the crowd are a mixed bag, but queues are long and invariably include locals and tourists, and even the occasional *famoso*.

LA LATINA & LAVAPIÉS

El Juglar (Map pp142-3; ☎ 91 528 43 81; www.salajuglar.com; Calle de Lavapiés 37; 🕑 9pm-3am Sun-Wed, 9pm-3.30am Thu-Sat; Ⓜ Lavapiés) One of the hottest spots in Lavapiés, this great venue caters for a largely bohemian crowd with a rock-dominated program, leavened with flamenco on Sunday and occasional rumba, jazz and soul beats. Concerts begin around 9.30pm and then it's DJ-spun Latin tunes after midnight.

HUERTAS & ATOCHA

Kapital (Map p145; ☎ 91 420 29 06; www.grupo-kapital.com in Spanish; Calle de Atocha 125; 🕑 6-10pm & midnight-6am Thu-Sun; Ⓜ Atocha) One of the most famous megaclubs in Madrid, this massive seven-storey nightclub has something for everyone: from cocktail bars and dance music to karaoke, salsa, hip hop and more chilled spaces for R&B and soul. The crowd is sexy, well heeled and up for a good time. On Sunday, 'Sundance' (otherwise known as 'Kapital Love') is definitely for those who have no intention of appearing at work on Monday, while other nights belong more to the Real Madrid set.

Room at Stella (Map pp142-3; ☎ 91 531 63 78; www.theroomclub.com; Calle de Arlabán 7; 🕑 1-6am Thu-Sat; Ⓜ Sevilla) If you arrive here after 3am, there simply won't be room and those inside have no intention of leaving until dawn. The DJs here are some of Madrid's best and the great visuals will leave you cross-eyed, if you weren't already from the house, electronica, new wave or funk in this vibrant, heady place.

Villa Rosa (Map pp142-3; ☎ 91 521 36 89; Plaza de Santa Ana 15; 🕑 11pm-6am Mon-Sat; Ⓜ Sol) The extraordinary tiled facade of this long-standing nightclub is a tourist attraction in itself; the club even appeared in the Pedro Almodóvar film *Tacones Lejanos* (High Heels; 1991). The music is what they call *comercial*, which basically means the latest dance hits with nothing too challenging. As such, it's more about Madrid's energy than its latest trends.

MALASAÑA & CHUECA

There's more information about Chueca's nightclubs in the boxed text, p190.

Morocco (Map pp138-9; ☎ 91 531 51 67; Calle del Marqués de Leganés 7; 🕑 midnight-3am Thu, midnight-5.30am Fri & Sat; Ⓜ Santo Domingo) Owned by the zany Alaska, the stand-out musical personality of *la movida*, Morocco has decor that's so kitsch it's cool, and a mix of musical styles that never strays too far from 1980s Spanish and international tunes. The bouncers can be a bit shirty, but then it's not the most amiable profession in the world, now is it?

Penta Bar (Map pp138-9; ☎ 91 447 84 60; www.elpenta.com in Spanish; Calle de la Palma 4; 🕑 9pm-3am; Ⓜ Tribunal) A night out here and you could be forgiven for believing that *la movida* never died down. It's an informal place where you can groove to the '80s music you love to hate. Don't even think of turning up before midnight.

Siroco (Map pp138-9; ☎ 91 593 30 70; www.siroco.es in Spanish; Calle de San Dimas 3; 🕑 10pm-6am Thu-Sat; Ⓜ Noviciado) One of the most eclectic nightclubs in Madrid, Siroco does everything from reggae to acid jazz, from 1970s to funk, house and hip hop. As such it gets a diverse crowd and queues can be long. The one unifying theme is the commitment to Spanish music (sometimes live); it's a good place to hear local music before it becomes too mainstream.

GAY & LESBIAN MADRID

Madrid has always been one of Europe's most gay-friendly cities. The city's gay community is credited with reinvigorating the once down-at-heel inner-city *barrio* of Chueca, where Madrid didn't just come out of the closet, but ripped the doors off in the process. But there's nothing ghetto-like about Chueca. Its extravagantly gay and lesbian personality is anything but exclusive and the crowd is almost always mixed gay/straight. As gay and lesbian residents like to say, Chueca isn't gay-friendly, it's hetero-friendly.

It's a great time to be gay in Madrid. Under laws passed by the Spanish Congress in June 2005, same-sex marriages now enjoy the same legal protection as those between heterosexual partners. At the time there was a conservative backlash, but opinion polls showed that the reforms were supported by more than two-thirds of Spaniards. The best time of all to be in town if you're gay or lesbian is around the last Saturday in June, for Madrid's gay and lesbian pride march (p173).

Chueca has an abundance of gay-friendly bars, restaurants and shops. **A Different Life** (Map pp138-9; ☎ 91 532 96 52; www.lifegay.com in Spanish; Calle de Pelayo 30; 🕑 10.30am-9.30pm Mon-Thu, 10.30am-10pm Fri & Sat, 12.30-9.30pm Sun; Ⓜ Chueca) is a bookshop geared towards gays and lesbians, while **Berkana** (Map pp138-9; ☎ 91 522 55 99; www.libreriaberkana.com in Spanish; Calle de Hortaleza 64; 🕑 10.30am-9pm Mon-Fri, 11.30am-9pm Sat, noon-2pm & 5-9pm Sun; Ⓜ Chueca) operates like an unofficial information centre for gay Madrid; here you'll find the bi-weekly *Shanguide*, jammed with listings and contact ads, and the *Mapa Gaya de Madrid,* as well as books, magazines and videos.

Another good place to get the low-down on gay Madrid is the laid-back **Mamá Inés** (Map pp138-9; ☎ 91 523 23 33; www.mamaines.com in Spanish; Calle de Hortaleza 22; 🕑 10am-2pm Sun-Thu, 10am-3.30am Fri & Sat; Ⓜ Gran Vía or Chueca), a cafe where you'll hear the gossip on where that night's hot spot will be. **Café Acuarela** (Map pp138-9; ☎ 91 522 21 43; Calle de Gravina 10; 🕑 2pm-3am; Ⓜ Chueca), just up the hill from Plaza de Chueca, is a dimly lit centrepiece of gay Madrid – a huge statue of a nude male angel guards the doorway. Also good for a low-key night out is the sophisticated **Antik Café** (Map pp138-9; ☎ 620 427 168; Calle de Hortaleza 4 & 6; 🕑 5pm-2am Sun-Thu, 5pm-3am Fri & Sat; Ⓜ Gran Vía), where the dark interior is all about intimacy and discretion.

For something a little more upbeat, the cosy **Why Not?** (Map pp138-9; Calle de San Bartolomé 7; 🕑 10.30pm-6am; Ⓜ Chueca) is the sort of place where nothing's left to the imagination (the gay and straight crowd who come here are pretty amorous) and it's full nearly every night of the week. Pop and top-40s music are the standards here.

Two of the more outrageous gay nightspots in Madrid are **Sunrise** (Map pp138-9; www.sunrisechueca.com in Spanish; Calle de Barbieri 7; 🕑 midnight-6am Thu-Sat; Ⓜ Chueca) and **La Fulanita de Tal** (Map pp138-9; ☎ 91 360 47 02; www.fulanitadetal.com in Spanish; Calle del Conde de Xiquena 2; 🕑 10pm-3am Sun-Wed, 10pm-4am Thu-Sat; Ⓜ Chueca).

Other clubs popular with a predominantly gay crowd include **Ohm** (Sala Bash; Map pp138-9; Plaza del Callao 4; 🕑 midnight-6am Fri & Sat; Ⓜ Callao), **Cool** (p188) and **Suite Café Club** (Map pp142-3; www.suitecafeclub in Spanish; Calle de la Virgen de los Peligros 4; 🕑 9pm-3am Tue-Sat; Ⓜ Sevilla).

For a place to rest your head, look no further than the excellent **Hostal La Zona** (p178), which has a mainly gay clientele.

Stromboli Café (Map pp138-9; ☎ 91 319 46 28; Calle de Hortaleza 96; 🕑 4pm-3am Thu & Fri, 4pm-3.30am Sat; Ⓜ Chueca or Tribunal) One of Chueca's best smaller clubs, Stromboli somehow manages to stay hip and happening with lounge, nu jazz and deep house beats from some of the best local DJs, who love the cosy lounge feel almost as much as the punters do.

Tupperware (Map pp138-9; ☎ 91 446 42 04; Corredera Alta de San Pablo 26; 🕑 8pm-3.30am Sun-Wed, 9pm-3.30am Thu-Sat; Ⓜ Tribunal) A Malasaña stalwart, Tupperware draws a 30-something crowd, spins indie rock with a bit of soul and classics from the '60s and '70s, and generally revels in its kitsch (eyeballs stuck to the ceiling, and plastic TVs with action-figure dioramas lined up behind the bar).

CHAMBERÍ & ARGÜELLES

Moma 56 (Map p133; ☎ 91 395 20 59; Calle de José Abascal 56; 🕑 midnight-6am Wed-Sat; Ⓜ Gregorio Marañón) Two words: beautiful people. Get your Prada gear on and that studied look of sophistication, and join the small-time celebrities and owners of the flashy sports cars parked out front. The decor (red padded walls, red lighting) is as sleek as the too-cool crowd, who shake off their pretensions once the live percussion fuses into DJ house. There's nowhere quite like it in Madrid.

Supersonic (Map pp138-9; Calle de Meléndez Valdés 25; 9.30pm-3.30am Thu-Sat; M Argüelles) Madrid has nightclubs in the most unlikely places… On a quiet residential Argüelles street, this great little *discoteca* is one of the best places for indie music, from 1970s glam rock to everything that we loved to hate about '80s and '90s British pop (The Smiths, Oasis etc).

Cinemas

Cine Doré (Map pp142-3; ☎ 91 369 11 25; Calle de Santa Isabel 3; Tue-Sun; M Antón Martín) The National Film Library offers fantastic classic and vanguard films for just €2.

Cinesa Proyecciones (Map pp138-9; ☎ 902 33 32 31; Calle de Fuencarral 136; M Bilbao or Quevedo) Wonderful art-deco exterior; modern cinema within.

La Enana Marrón (Map pp138-9; ☎ 91 308 14 97; www.laenanamarron.org; Travesía de San Mateo 8; M Alonso Martínez) There's no beating this great arty, alternative theatre, showing documentaries, animated films, international flicks and oldies.

Princesa (Map pp138-9; ☎ 91 541 41 00; Calle de la Princesa 3; M Plaza de España) Screens all kinds of original-version films, from Hollywood blockbusters to arty flicks.

Renoir (Map pp138-9; ☎ 91 541 41 00; Calle de Martín de los Heros 12; M Plaza de España) Plenty of latest-release films, as well as some interesting documentaries and Asian flicks.

Yelmo Cineplex Ideal (Map pp142-3; ☎ 902 22 09 22; Calle del Doctor Cortezo 6; M Sol or Tirso de Molina) Close to Plaza Mayor; offers a wide selection of films.

Theatre & Dance

Madrid's theatre scene is a year-round affair, but it really gets going in autumn. Most shows are in Spanish, but those who don't speak the language may still enjoy musicals or *zarzuela*, Spain's own singing and dancing version of musical theatre. Tickets for all shows start at around €10 and run up to around €50.

Compañía Nacional de Danza (☎ 91 354 50 53; http://cndanza.mcu.es) Under director Nacho Duato, this dynamic company performs worldwide and has won accolades for its innovation, marvellous technicality and style. The company, made up mostly of international dancers, performs original, contemporary pieces and is considered a leading player on the international dance scene. When in town, which is not often, they perform at various venues, including the Teatro de la Zarzuela.

Ballet Nacional de España (☎ 91 517 46 86; http://balletnacional.mcu.es) A classical company that's known for its unique mix of ballet and traditional Spanish styles, such as flamenco and *zarzuela*.

Teatro Albéniz (Map pp142-3; ☎ 91 531 83 11; Calle de la Paz 11; M Sol) Staging both commercial and vanguard drama, as well as big-name musical concerts, this is one of Madrid's better-known theatres.

Centro Cultural de la Villa (Teatro Fernán Gómez; Map p140; ☎ 91 480 03 00; www.esmadrid.com; Plaza de Colón; M Colón) Located under the waterfall at Plaza de Colón, this cultural centre stages everything from classical music concerts to comic theatre, opera and quality flamenco performances.

Teatro de la Zarzuela (Map pp142-3; ☎ 91 524 54 00; http://teatrodelazarzuela.mcu.es; Calle de Jovellanos 4; M Banco de España) This theatre, built in 1856, is the premier place to see *zarzuela*. It also hosts a smattering of classical music and opera, as well as the cutting-edge Compañía Nacional de Danza.

Teatro Español (Map pp142-3; ☎ 91 360 14 80; Calle del Príncipe 25; M Sevilla, Sol or Antón Martín) This theatre has been here since the 16th century and is still one of the best places to catch mainstream Spanish drama, from the works of Lope de Vega to more recent playwrights.

Live Music

FLAMENCO

Seeing flamenco in Madrid is, with some exceptions, expensive – at the *tablaos* (small-stage theatres that usually double as restaurants), expect to pay €30 to €35 just to see the show. The admission price usually includes your first drink, but you pay extra for meals (up to €50 per person) that, put simply, are rarely worth the money. For that reason, we suggest you eat elsewhere and simply pay for the show (after having bought tickets in advance), albeit on the understanding that you won't have a front-row seat. The other important thing to remember is that most of these shows are geared towards tourists. That's not to say that the quality isn't top-notch – often it's magnificent, spine-tingling stuff. It's just that they sometimes lack the genuine, raw emotion of real flamenco, and the atmosphere is not as spontaneous as being surrounded by a knowledgeable crowd who can lift a performer to new heights.

Cardamomo (Map pp142-3; ☎ 91 369 07 57; www.cardamomo.es in Spanish; Calle de Echegaray 15; admission €10; 9pm-3.30am, shows 10.30pm Tue & Wed; M Sevilla) If you believe that flamenco is best enjoyed in a dark, smoky bar where the crowd is predominantly local and where you can clap, shout *'Olé!'* and even sing along (the crowd is so thick no one will mind), Cardamomo is brilliant.

Corral de la Morería (Map pp142-3; ☎ 91 365 84 46; www.corraldelamoreria.com; Calle de la Morería 17; admission €32-35; 8.30pm-2.30am, shows 10pm; M La Latina) This is one of the most prestigious places in Madrid, with 50 years as a leading flamenco stage and top performers most nights. The stage area has a rustic feel, and tables are pushed up close.

Las Carboneras (Map pp142-3; ☎ 91 542 86 77; www.tablaolascarboneras.com in Spanish; Plaza del Conde de Miranda 1; admission from €33; shows 9pm & 11.30pm Mon-Thu, 8.30pm & 11pm Fri & Sat; M Sol or La Latina) Like most of the *tablaos* around town, this place sees far more tourists than locals, but the quality is top-notch. It's not the place for gritty, soul-moving spontaneity, but it's still an excellent introduction and one of the few places that flamenco aficionados seem to have no complaints about.

Las Tablas (Map pp138-9; ☎ 91 542 05 20; www.lastablasmadrid.com in Spanish; Plaza de España 9; admission €10-30; shows 10.30pm; M Plaza de España) Las Tablas has quickly earned a reputation for quality flamenco. Most nights you'll see a classic flamenco show, with plenty of throaty singing and soul-baring dancing.

CLASSICAL MUSIC & OPERA

Auditorio Nacional de Música (Map p133; ☎ 91 337 01 40; www.auditorionacional.mcu.es; Calle del Príncipe de Vergara 146; M Cruz del Rayo) Resounding to the sounds of classical music, this modern venue offers a varied calendar of performances, often by Madrid's Orquesta Sinfonía (www.osm.es) and led by conductors from all over the world.

Teatro Real (Map pp142-3; ☎ 902 24 48 48; www.teatro-real.com in Spanish; Plaza de Oriente; M Ópera) The Teatro Real is as technologically advanced as any venue in Europe, and is the city's grandest stage for elaborate operas and ballets. You'll pay as little as €15 for a spot so far away you'll need a telescope, although the sound quality is consistent throughout. For the best seats, don't expect change from €100.

JAZZ

Madrid was one of Europe's jazz capitals in the 1920s. It's taken a while, but it's once again among Europe's elite for live jazz. You'll pay about €10 to get into most places, but special concerts can run up to €20 or more.

Café Central (Map pp142-3; ☎ 91 369 41 43; www.cafecentralmadrid.com in Spanish; Plaza del Angel 10; admission €9-15; 1pm-2.30am Sun-Thu, 1pm-4am Fri & Sat; M Antón Martín or Sol) This art-deco bar has consistently been voted one of the best jazz venues in the world by leading jazz magazines, and with more than 8000 gigs under its belt, it rarely misses a beat. Big international names like Chano Domínguez, Tal Farlow and Wynton Marsalis have all played here, and there's everything from Latin jazz and fusion to tango and classic jazz. Shows start at 10pm and tickets go on sale an hour before the set starts.

Populart (Map pp142-3; ☎ 91 429 84 07; www.populart.es in Spanish; Calle de las Huertas 22; admission free; 6pm-2.30am Mon-Thu, 6pm-3.30am Fri & Sat; M Antón Martín or Sol) One of Madrid's classic jazz clubs, this place offers a low-key atmosphere and top-quality music – mostly jazz, but with occasional blues, swing and even flamenco thrown into the mix. Think Compay Segundo, Sonny Fortune and the Canal Street Jazz Band and you'll get an idea of the quality on offer here. Shows start at 11pm, but if you want a seat get here early.

El Berlín Jazz Club (Map pp138-9; ☎ 91 521 57 52; www.cafeberlin.es in Spanish; Calle de Jacometrezo 4; admission €6-12; 7pm-2.30am Tue-Sun; M Callao or Santo Domingo) El Berlín is a Madrid jazz stalwart and the kind of place that some serious jazz fans rave about as the most authentic in town. The atmosphere is vaguely cabaret and the headline acts a who's who of world jazz.

El Junco Jazz Club (Map pp138-9; ☎ 91 319 20 81; Plaza de Santa Bárbara 10; admission free; 11pm-6am; M Alonso Martínez) El Junco appeals as much to jazz aficionados as to clubbers. Its secret is high-quality live jazz gigs from Spain and around the world at 11.30pm every night, followed by DJs spinning funk, soul, nu jazz and innovative groove beats.

OTHER LIVE MUSIC

Café La Palma (Map pp138-9; ☎ 91 522 50 31; www.cafelapalma.com in Spanish; Calle de la Palma 62; admission free-€6; 4pm-2am Sun-Thu, 4pm-3.30am Fri & Sat;

(M Noviciado) It's amazing how much variety Café La Palma has packed into its labyrinth of rooms. Live shows featuring hot local bands are held at the back, while DJs mix up the front. You might find live music other nights, but there are always two shows at 10pm and midnight from Thursday to Saturday. Every night is a little different.

Clamores (Map pp138-9; ☎ 91 445 79 38; www.clamores.es in Spanish; Calle de Alburquerque 14; admission €5-20; ⌚ 6pm-3am Sun-Thu, 6pm-4am Fri & Sat; M Bilbao) This one-time classic jazz cafe has morphed into one of the most diverse live music stages in Madrid. Jazz is still a staple, but world music, flamenco, soul fusion, singer-songwriter, pop and rock all make regular appearances. Live shows can begin as early as 9pm.

Honky Tonk (Map pp138-9; ☎ 91 445 61 91; www.clubhonky.com in Spanish; Calle de Covarrubias 24; admission free; ⌚ 9pm-5am; M Alonso Martínez) Despite the name, this is a great place to see local rock 'n' roll, though many acts have a little country or blues thrown into the mix too. It's a fun vibe in a smallish club that's been around since the heady 1980s. Arrive early as it fills up fast.

Kabokla (Map pp138-9; ☎ 91 532 59 66; www.kabokla.es in Spanish; Calle de San Vicente Ferrer 55; admission free; ⌚ 9pm-3am Tue-Thu, 9pm-5am Fri & Sat, 2.30pm-midnight Sun; M Noviciado) Run by Brazilians and dedicated to all things Brazilian, Kabokla is terrific. Live Brazilian groups (from percussion to samba and cover bands playing Chico Buarque) play most nights from around 10pm. When there's no live music, the DJ gets the crowd dancing. They also serve Madrid's smoothest caipirinhas.

La Boca del Lobo (Map pp142-3; ☎ 91 429 70 13; Calle de Echegaray 11; admission free-€10; ⌚ 9.30pm-3am Tue-Thu & Sun, 9.30pm-3.30am Fri & Sat; M Sevilla) Known for offering mostly rock and alternative concerts, La Boca del Lobo (The Wolf's Mouth) is as dark as its name suggests. It has broadened its horizons, adding country and jazz to the line-up, with weekly roots and groove jam sessions on Wednesdays. Concerts start at 10.30pm most nights and DJs take over once the live acts leave the stage.

Sport

BULLFIGHTING

From the Fiesta de San Isidro in mid-May until the end of October, Spain's top bullfighters come to swing their capes at **Plaza de Toros Monumental de las Ventas** (Map p132; ☎ 91 356 22 00; www.las-ventas.com in Spanish; Calle de Alcalá 237; M Ventas), one of the largest rings in the bullfighting world. Las Ventas has a grand Mudéjar exterior and a suitably Colosseum-like arena surrounding the broad, sandy ring. During the six weeks of the fiesta's main bullfighting season that begins with the Fiestas de San Isidro in May, there are *corridas* (bullfights) almost every day.

Tickets for *corridas* are divided into *sol* (sun) and *sombra* (shade) seating. The cheapest tickets (around €5) are for standing-room *sol*, though on a broiling-hot summer day it's infinitely more enjoyable to pay the extra €4 for *sombra* tickets. The very best seats – in the front row in the shade – are the preserve of celebrities and cost more than €100.

Ticket sales begin a few days before the fight, at the Las Ventas **ticket office** (⌚ 10am-2pm & 5-8pm). A few ticket agencies sell before then, tacking on an extra 20% for their trouble; one of the best is **Localidades Galicia** (Map pp142-3; ☎ 91 531 27 32, 91 531 91 31; www.eol.es/lgalicia; Plaza del Carmen 1; ⌚ 9.30am-1pm & 4.30-7pm Tue-Sat; M Sol). You can also buy tickets at the authorised **La Central Bullfight Ticket Office** (Map pp142-3; Calle de la Victoria; M Sol). For most bullfights, you'll have no problem getting a ticket at the door, but during the Fiesta de San Isidro or when a popular *torero* comes to town, book ahead. For information on who'll be in the ring, check out the colourful posters tacked up around town or the daily newspapers.

For further discussion of Spain's most controversial pastime, see p61.

FOOTBALL

The Estadio Santiago Bernabéu, home of Real Madrid, is a temple to football and one of the world's great sporting arenas; watching a game here is akin to a pilgrimage for sports fans. When the players strut their stuff with 80,000 passionate *madrileños* in attendance, you'll get chills down your spine. If you're fortunate enough to be in town when Real Madrid wins a major trophy, head to Plaza de la Cibeles (p156) and wait for the all-night party to begin.

Named after the club's long-time president, the **stadium** (Map p133; ☎ 91 398 43 00; www.realmadrid.com; Avenida de Concha Espina 1; tour adult/under 14yr €10/8; ⌚ 10am-7pm Mon-Sat, 10.30am-6.30pm Sun; M Santiago Bernabéu) is a mecca for *madridistas* (Real Madrid football fans) worldwide. For a self-guided tour of the stadium, buy your ticket at ticket window 10 (next to gate 7). The tour takes you through the extraordinary **Exposición de Trofeos** (Trophy Exhibit), the presidential box, the press room, dressing rooms and the players' tunnel, and even onto the pitch itself. There are no tours on match days.

Tickets for matches start at around €15 and run up to the rafters for major matches. Unless you book through a ticket agency, turn up at the ticket office at Gate 42 on Avenida de Concha Espina early in the week before a scheduled game. The all-important telephone number for booking tickets (which you later pick up at Gate 42) is ☎ 902 32 43 24, which only works if you're calling from within Spain. If you're booking from abroad, try **Localidades Galicia** (Map pp142-3; ☎ 91 531 27 32, 91 531 91 31; www.eol.es/lgalicia; Plaza del Carmen 1; 9.30am-1pm & 4.30-7pm Tue-Sat; Ⓜ Sol). Numerous websites also sell tickets to Real Madrid games, including www.madrid-tickets.net, www.madrid-tickets.com and www.ticket-finders.com.

The city's other big club, Atlético de Madrid, may have long existed in the shadow of its more illustrious city rival, but it has been one of the most successful teams in Spanish football history in its own right. The first-division team's home, **Estadio Vicente Calderón** (Map pp134-5; ☎ 91 366 47 07; www.at-madrid.com; Paseo de la Virgin del Puerto; Ⓜ Pirámides), isn't as large as Real Madrid's (Vicente Calderón seats a mere 60,000), but what it lacks in size it makes up for in raw energy. To see an Atlético de Madrid game, try calling the stadium, but you're more than likely to get a ticket if you turn up at the ground a few days before.

SHOPPING

Eager to change your look to blend in with the casual-but-sophisticated Spanish crowd? Tired of bull postcards and tacky flamenco posters? Convinced that your discerning friends back home have taste that extends beyond a polka-dot flamenco dress? In Madrid, you'll find it all, including English-language bookshops, stores selling Spanish food delicacies and cutting-edge homewares. This is a fantastic city in which to shop and *madrileños* are some of the finest exponents of the art.

The key to shopping Madrid-style is knowing where to look. Salamanca is the home of upmarket fashions, with chic boutiques lining up to showcase the best that Spanish and international designers have to offer. Some of it spills over into Chueca, but Malasaña is Salamanca's true alter ego, home to fashion that's as funky as it is offbeat – ideal for that studied underground look that will fit right in with Madrid's hedonistic after-dark crowd. Central Madrid – whether it's Sol, Huertas or La Latina – offers plenty of individual surprises, although there's little uniformity in what you'll find. That sense is multiplied a hundred-fold in El Rastro (p151), where *madrileños* converge in epic numbers on Sundays to pick through the junk in search of treasure.

The peak shopping season is during *las rebajas*, the annual winter and summer sales when prices are slashed on just about everything. The winter sales begin around January 7, just after Three Kings' Day, and last well into February. Summer sales begin in early July and last into August.

All shops may (and most usually do) open on the first Sunday of every month and throughout December.

Books

For a list of bookshops in Madrid, see p131.

Fashion & Shoes

Mercado de Fuencarral (Map pp138-9; ☎ 91 521 41 52; Calle de Fuencarral 45; 11am-9pm Mon-Sat; Ⓜ Tribunal) Madrid's home of alternative club-cool revels in reverse snobbery. It's funky, grungy and filled with more torn T-shirts, black leather and silver studs than you'll ever need. Sadly, it looks likely to be shut down and moved to Valencia in 2009. Check the web for more details.

Camper (Map p140; ☎ 91 578 25 60; www.camper.es; Calle de Serrano 24; 10am-8.30pm Mon-Sat; Ⓜ Serrano) Spanish fashion is not all haute couture, and this world-famous cool and quirky shoe brand from Mallorca has shops all over Madrid. The designs are bowling-shoe chic, with colourful, fun styles that are all about comfort. There are other outlets throughout the city.

Sara Navarro (Map p140; ☎ 91 576 23 24; www.saranavarro.com; Calle de Jorge Juan 22; 10.30am-8.30pm Mon-Sat; Ⓜ Velázquez) Spanish women love their shoes and, perhaps above all, they love Sara Navarro. This designer seems to understand that you'll buy expensive shoes like these only rarely, so why not make each into a perfect work of art. The shop is a temple to good taste, with fine bags, belts and other accessories as well.

Amaya Arzuaga (Map p140; ☎ 91 426 28 15; Calle de Lagasca 50; 10.30am-8.30pm Mon-Wed, 10.30am-9pm Thu-Sat; Ⓜ Velázquez) Amaya Arzuaga, one of Spain's top fashion designers, has sexy, bold options. She loves mixing black with bright colours (one season it's 1980s fuchsia and turquoise, the next it's orange or red) and has earned a reputation as one of the most creative designers in Spain today.

Agatha Ruiz de la Prada (Map p140; ☎ 91 319 05 01; Calle de Serrano 27; 10am-8.30pm Mon-Sat; M Serrano) This boutique has to be seen to be believed, with pinks, yellows and oranges everywhere you turn. It's fun and exuberant, but it's not just for kids: it's also serious and highly original fashion. Agatha Ruiz de la Prada is one of the enduring icons of Madrid's 1980s outpouring of creativity known as *la movida madrileña* (see the boxed text, p131).

Davidelfín (Map p140; ☎ 91 700 04 53; www.davidelfin.com; Calle de Jorge Juan 31; 10.30am-2.30pm & 4.30-8.30pm Mon-Sat; M Velázquez) This young Spanish designer combines catwalk fashions with a rebellious spirit. The look is young, sometimes edgy and an enthusiastic nod to the avant garde.

Gallery (Map p140; ☎ 91 576 79 31; www.gallerymadrid.com; Calle de Jorge Juan 38; 10.30am-8.30pm Mon-Sat; M Príncipe de Vergara or Velázquez) This stunning showpiece of men's fashions and accessories (shoes, bags, belts and the like) is the new Madrid in a nutshell – stylish, brand-conscious and all about having the right look. With an interior designed by Tomas Alia, it's one of the city's coolest shops for men.

Tienda Real Madrid (Map p133; ☎ 91 458 74 22; Estadio de Santiago Bernabéu, Avenida de Concha Espina 1; 10am-9pm Mon-Thu, 10am-8pm Fri & Sat, 11am-8pm Sun; M Santiago Bernabéu) The club shop of Real Madrid sells replica shirts, posters, caps and just about everything under the sun to which they could attach a club logo. From the shop window, you can see down onto the stadium itself.

Food & Drink

Convento del Corpus Cristi (Map pp142-3; Plaza del Conde de Miranda 3; 9.30am-1pm & 4-6.30pm; M Ópera) The cloistered nuns at this convent also happen to be fine pastry chefs. You make your request through a door, then through a grille on Calle del Codo and the products are delivered through a little revolving door that allows the nuns to remain unseen by the outside world.

Patrimonio Comunal Olivarero (Map pp138-9; ☎ 91 308 05 05; Calle de Mejía Lequerica 1; 10am-2pm & 5-8pm Mon-Fri, 10am-1.30pm Sat; M Alonso Martínez) To catch the real essence of Spain's olive oil varieties, Patrimonio Comunal Olivarero is perfect. With examples of the extra virgin variety (and nothing else) from all over Spain, you could spend ages agonising over the choices. The staff know their oil and are happy to help out.

Mantequería Bravo (Map p140; ☎ 91 576 76 41; Calle de Ayala 24; 9.30am-2.30pm & 5.30-8.30pm Mon-Fri, 9.30am-2.30pm Sat; M Serrano) Behind the attractive old facade lies a connoisseur's paradise, filled with local cheeses, sausages, wines and coffees. The products here are great for a gift, but everything's so good that you won't want to share. Mantequería Bravo won the 2007 prize for Madrid's best gourmet food shop or delicatessen – it's as simple as that.

Oriol Balaguer (Map pp134-5; ☎ 91 401 64 63; www.oriolbalaguer.com; Calle de José Ortega y Gasset 44; 10am-2.30pm & 5-8.30pm Mon-Sat; M Lista) Catalan pastry chef Oriol Balaguer has a formidable CV – he worked with Ferran Adrià and won the prize for the World's Best Dessert in 2001. His much-awaited chocolate boutique opened in Madrid in March 2008 and is a combination of small art gallery and fashion boutique, except that it's dedicated to exquisite chocolate collections and cakes. You'll never be able to buy ordinary chocolate again after a visit here.

Reserva y Cata (Map pp138-9; ☎ 91 319 04 01; www.reservaycata.com in Spanish; Calle del Conde de Xiquena 13; 11am-2.30pm & 5-9pm Mon-Fri, 11am-2.30pm Sat; M Colón or Chueca) This old-style wine shop stocks an excellent range of local wines, and the knowledgeable staff can help you pick out a great one for your next dinner party or a gift for a friend back home. They specialise in quality Spanish wines that you just don't find in El Corte Inglés and there's often a bottle open so that you can try before you buy.

Poncelet (Map pp138-9; ☎ 91 308 02 21; www.poncelet.es in Spanish; Calle de Argensola 27; 10.30am-8.30pm Mon-Sat; M Alonso Martínez) For Spanish and other European cheeses, this place should be your first stop.

Handicrafts

Antigua Casa Talavera (Map pp138-9; ☎ 91 547 34 17; Calle de Isabel la Católica 2; 10am-1.30pm & 5-8pm Mon-Fri, 10am-1.30pm Sat; M Santo Domingo) The extraordinary tiled facade of this wonderful old shop conceals an Aladdin's Cave of ceramics from all over Spain. This is not the mass-produced stuff aimed at the tourist market, but comes from the small family potters of Andalucía and Toledo, and ranges from the decorative (tiles) to the useful (plates, jugs and other kitchen items).

El Arco Artesanía (Map pp142-3; ☎ 91 365 26 80; www.elarcoartesania.com; Plaza Mayor 9; 11am-9pm; Ⓜ Sol or La Latina) This superstylish shop in the southwestern corner of Plaza Mayor sells an outstanding array of homemade designer souvenirs, from stone and glasswork to jewellery and home fittings. The papier-mâché figures are gorgeous, but there's so much here to turn your head.

José Ramírez (Map pp142-3; ☎ 91 531 42 29; www.guitarrasramirez.com; Calle de la Paz 8; 10am-2pm & 4.30-8pm; Ⓜ Sol) José Ramírez is one of Spain's best guitar makers and his guitars have been strummed by a host of flamenco greats and international musicians (even the Beatles). In the back of this small shop is a little museum with guitars dating back to 1830.

El Flamenco Vive (Map pp142-3; ☎ 91 547 39 17; www.elflamencovive.es; Calle del Conde de Lemos 7; 10am-2pm & 5-9pm Mon-Sat; Ⓜ Ópera) This temple to flamenco has it all, from guitars, songbooks and well-priced CDs, to polka-dotted dancing costumes, shoes, colourful plastic jewellery and literature about flamenco. It's the sort of place that will appeal as much to curious first-timers as to serious students of the art.

Gil (Map pp142-3; ☎ 91 521 25 49; Carrera de San Jerónimo 2; 9.30am-1.30pm & 4.30-8pm Mon-Fri, 9.30am-1.30pm Sat; Ⓜ Sol) You don't see them much these days, but the exquisite fringed and embroidered *mantones* and *mantoncillos* (traditional Spanish shawls worn by women on grand occasions) and delicate *mantillas* (Spanish veils) are stunning and uniquely Spanish gifts. Inside this dark shop, dating back to 1880, the sales clerks still wait behind a long counter to attend to you; the service hasn't changed in years and that's no bad thing. They also sell *abanicos* (Spanish fans).

Casa de Diego (Map pp142-3; ☎ 91 522 66 43; www.casadediego.com; Plaza de la Puerta del Sol 12; 9.30am-8pm Mon-Sat; Ⓜ Sol) This classic shop has been around since 1858, selling and repairing Spanish fans, shawls, umbrellas and canes. Service is old-style and the staff occasionally grumpy, but the fans are works of antique art.

México (Map pp142-3; ☎ 91 429 94 76; Calle de las Huertas 20; 9am-2pm & 5-8pm Mon-Fri, 9am-2pm Sat; Ⓜ Antón Martín) A treasure chest of old maps, this is a great place to find a unique souvenir of Spain. Some 160 folders hold maps of Madrid, Spain and the rest of the world. These are all originals or antique copies, not modern reprints, so prices range from a few hundred euros to thousands.

GETTING THERE & AWAY

Air

Madrid's **Barajas airport** (Aeropuerto de Barajas; Map p200; ☎ 902 40 47 04; www.aena.es) lies 15km northeast of the city. It's Europe's fourth-busiest hub (more than 52 million passengers pass through here annually), trailing only London Heathrow, Paris Charles de Gaulle and Frankfurt.

The airport's architecturally stunning Terminal 4 (T4) deals mainly with flights of Iberia and its partners (eg British Airways, American Airlines and Aer Lingus), while other intercontinental or non-Schengen European flights leave from T1. Spanair and Air Europa operate from both T1 and T2, depending on the destination. Air Berlin, Alitalia, Austrian Airlines, SAS and TAP Air Portugal also operate from T2. At the time of writing, only the tiny Lagun Air was operating out of T3. Iberia's Puente Aereo (air shuttle) between Madrid and Barcelona, which operates like a bus service with no advance booking necessary, operates from T4, while Spanair's equivalent service leaves from T3. For a full list of which airlines operate from which terminals, visit www.esmadrid.com – click on 'Services' then 'Transport'.

Although all airlines conduct check-in *(facturación)* in the airport's departure areas, some also allow check-in at the Nuevos Ministerios metro stop and transport interchange in Madrid itself – ask your airline.

Increasingly, airlines have abandoned their shop-front offices in Madrid so, in most cases, you'll have to go online, call the following numbers or contact a travel agent. Major airlines operating at Barajas include the following:

Aer Lingus (☎ 902 50 27 37; www.aerlingus.com)
Air Berlin (☎ 902 32 07 37; www.airberlin.com)
Air Europa (☎ 902 40 15 01; www.aireuropa.com)
Air France (☎ 902 20 70 90; www.airfrance.com)
Alitalia (☎ 902 10 03 23; www.alitalia.it)
American Airlines (☎ 902 11 55 70; www.aa.com)
British Airways (☎ 902 11 13 33; www.britishairways.com)
British Midlands (☎ 902 10 07 37; www.bmibaby.com)
Continental Airlines (☎ 900 96 12 66; www.continental.com)
easyJet (☎ 807 26 00 26; www.easyjet.com)

German Wings (☎ 91 625 97 04; www.germanwings.com)
Iberia (☎ 902 40 05 00; www.iberia.es)
KLM (☎ 902 22 27 47; www.klm.com)
Lufthansa (☎ 902 88 38 82; www.lufthansa.com)
MyAir.com (www.myair.com)
Royal Air Maroc (☎ 902 21 00 10; www.royalairmaroc.com)
Ryanair (☎ 807 22 00 32; www.ryanair.com)
Spanair (☎ 902 13 14 15; www.spanair.com)
TAP Air Portugal (☎ 901 11 67 18; www.flytap.com)
Transavia (☎ 902 01 01 05; www.transavia.com)
Turkish Airlines (☎ 902 11 12 35; www.turkishairlines.com)
Vueling (☎ 902 33 39 33; www.vueling.com)

Bus

Estación Sur de Autobuses (☎ 91 468 42 00; www.estaciondeautobuses.com in Spanish; Calle de Méndez Álvaro 83; Ⓜ Méndez Álvaro), just south of the M30 ring road, is the city's principal bus station. It serves most destinations to the south and many in other parts of the country. Most bus companies have a ticket office here, even if their buses depart from elsewhere.

Major bus companies include **ALSA** (☎ 902 42 22 42; www.alsa.es) and **Avanza** (☎ 902 02 00 52; www.avanzabus.com); some of the former's buses heading north leave from the Intercambiador de Avenida de América (Map p133).

Car & Motorcycle

If you arrive by car, be prepared to face gridlock traffic. The city is surrounded by three ring roads, the M30, M40 and M50 (still not 100% completed). You'll probably be herded onto one of these, which in turn give access to the city centre.

CAR HIRE

The big-name car-rental agencies have offices all over Madrid. Avis, Budget, Hertz and Europcar have booths at the airport and some have branches at Atocha and Chamartín train stations. See the Transport chapter (p893) for more information.

Recommended companies:
Avis (Map pp138-9; ☎ 902 180 854; www.avis.es; Gran Vía 60; Ⓜ Santo Domingo or Plaza de España)
Europcar (Map pp138-9; ☎ 902 105 055; www.europcar.es; Calle de San Leonardo de Dios 8; Ⓜ Plaza de España)
Hertz (Map pp138-9; ☎ 902 402 405; www.hertz.es; Edificio de España, Plaza de España 18; Ⓜ Plaza de España)
National/Atesa (Map pp138-9; ☎ 902 100 101; www.atesa.es; Gran Vía 80, 1st fl; Ⓜ Plaza de España)
Pepecar (Map pp138-9; ☎ 807 414 243; www.pepecar.com; underground parking area, Plaza de España; Ⓜ Plaza de España)

Train

Madrid is served by two main train stations. The bigger of the two is **Atocha train station** (Antigua Estación de Atocha; Map pp134-5; Ⓜ Atocha Renfe), at the southern end of the city centre. **Chamartín train station** (Map p133; Ⓜ Chamartín) lies in the north of the city. The bulk of trains for Spanish destinations depart from Atocha, especially those going south. International services arrive at and leave from Chamartín, as do several services for northern destinations. Be sure to find out which station your train leaves from. For bookings, contact **Renfe** (☎ 902 24 02 02; www.renfe.es) at either train station.

High-speed Tren de Alta Velocidad Española (AVE) services connect Madrid to Seville (via Córdoba), Valladolid (via Segovia), Toledo, Málaga and Barcelona (via Zaragoza).

GETTING AROUND

Madrid is well served by an excellent and rapidly expanding underground rail system (metro) and an extensive bus service. In addition, you can get from the north to the south of the city quickly by using *cercanías* (local trains) between Chamartín and Atocha train stations. Taxis are also a reasonably priced option.

To/From the Airport

The easiest way into town from the airport is line 8 of the metro (entrances in T2 and T4) to the Nuevos Ministerios transport interchange, which connects with lines 10 and 6. It operates from 6.05am to 2am. A single ticket costs €1 (10-ride Metrobús ticket €7); there's a €1 supplement if you're travelling from T4. The journey to Nuevos Ministerios takes around 20 minutes from T2; around 30 minutes from T4.

Alternatively, from T1, T2 and T3 take bus 200 to the transport interchange *(intercambiador)* on Avenida de América (Map p133). From T4, take bus 201; going to T4, take bus 204. The same ticket prices apply as for the metro. The first departures both to and from the airport are at 5.20am. The last scheduled service from the airport is 11.30pm; buses leave every 12 to 15 minutes. There's also a free bus service connecting all four terminals.

A taxi to the centre will cost you around €25 (up to €35 from T4), depending on traffic and where you're going; in addition to what the meter says, you pay a €5.25 supplement. There are cab ranks outside all four terminals.

Bus

Buses operated by **Empresa Municipal de Transportes de Madrid** (EMT; ☎ 902 50 78 50; www.emtmadrid.es) travel along most city routes regularly between about 6.30am and 11.30pm. Twenty-six night-bus *búhos* (owls) routes operate from midnight to 6am, with all routes originating in Plaza de la Cibeles.

Car & Motorcycle

At first, driving in Madrid can be a little hair-raising. The grand roundabouts of the major thoroughfares sometimes require nerves of steel as people turn left from the right-hand lanes or right from the centre. The morning and evening rush hours frequently involve snarling traffic jams, which are even possible in the wee hours of the morning, especially towards the end of the week when the whole city seems to be either behind the wheel or in a bar. The streets are dead between about 2pm and 4pm, when people are either eating or snoozing.

PARKING

Most of Madrid is divided up into clearly marked blue or green street-parking zones. In both areas, parking meters apply from 9am to 8pm Monday to Friday and from 9am to 3pm on Saturday; the Saturday hours also apply daily in August. In the green areas, you can park for a maximum of one hour (or keep putting money in the metre every hour) for €1.80. In the blue zones, you can park for two hours for €2.55. There are also private parking stations all over central Madrid.

Should your car disappear, call the **Grúa Municipal** (city towing service; ☎ 91 787 72 92). Getting it back costs €138.70 plus whatever fine you've been given.

Cercanías

The short-range *cercanías* regional trains operated by **Renfe** (www.renfe.es/cercanias in Spanish), the national railway company, go as far afield as El Escorial, Alcalá de Henares, Aranjuez and other points in the Comunidad de Madrid. Tickets range between €1.15 and €3.80 depending on how far you're travelling. In Madrid itself, they're handy for making a quick, north–south hop between Chamartín and Atocha mainline train stations (with stops at Nuevos Ministerios and in front of the Biblioteca Nacional on Paseo de los Recoletos only). Another line links Chamartín, Atocha and Príncipe Pío stations.

Metro

Madrid's modern **metro** (☎ 902 44 44 03; www.metromadrid.es) is a fast, efficient and safe way to navigate the city, and generally easier than getting to grips with bus routes. The metro covers 284km (with 282 stations), making it Europe's second-largest metro system, after London.

There are 11 colour-coded lines in central Madrid, in addition to the modern southern suburban MetroSur system, as well as lines heading east to the major population centres of Pozuelo and Boadilla del Monte. The metro operates from 6.05am to 2am. A single ticket costs €1; a 10-ride Metrobús ticket is €7.

The back of this book contains a colour map of the main central Madrid metro system and the MetroSur (although the latter's unlikely to be of interest to visitors).

Taxi

Madrid's taxis are inexpensive by European standards. Flag fall is €1.95 from 6am to 10pm daily, €2.15 from 10pm to 6am Sunday to Friday and €2.95 from 10pm Saturday to 6am Sunday. Several supplementary charges, usually posted inside the taxi, apply; these include €5.25 to/from the airport, €2.75 from cab ranks at train and bus stations, €2.75 to/from the Parque Ferial Juan Carlos I and €6.50 on New Year's Eve and Christmas Eve from 10pm to 6am. There's no charge for luggage.

Among the 24-hour taxi services are **Radio-Taxi** (☎ 91 405 55 00), **Tele-Taxi** (☎ 91 371 21 31) and **Radio-Teléfono Taxi** (☎ 91 547 82 00; www.radiotelefono-taxi.com in Spanish); the last runs taxis for people with a disability.

AROUND MADRID

The Comunidad de Madrid may be small but there are plenty of rewarding excursions that allow you to escape the clamour of city life without straying too far. Imposing San Lorenzo de El Escorial and graceful Aranjuez guard the western and southern gateways to Madrid. Also to the south, the beguiling village of Chinchón is a must-see, while Alcalá de Henares is a stunning university town east of the capital. To the north, picturesque villages (and skiing opportunities) abound in Sierra de Guadarrama and Sierra del Pobre.

SAN LORENZO DE EL ESCORIAL

pop 16,600 / elev 1032m

The imposing palace and monastery complex of San Lorenzo de El Escorial is an impressive place, rising up from the foothills of the mountains that shelter Madrid from the north and west. The one-time royal getaway is now a prim little town overflowing with quaint shops, restaurants and hotels catering primarily to throngs of weekending *madrileños*. The fresh, cool air here has been drawing city dwellers since the complex was first ordered to be built by Felipe II in the 16th century.

History

Kings and princes have a habit of promising extravagant offerings to God, the angels, saints and anyone else who'll listen, in return for help in defeating their foes. Felipe II was no exception before the Battle of St Quentin against the French on St Lawrence's Day, 10 August 1557.

Felipe's victory was decisive, and in thanks he ordered the construction of the complex in the saint's name above the hamlet of El Escorial. Several villages were razed to make way for the huge monastery, royal palace and mausoleum for Felipe's parents, Carlos I and Isabel. It all flourished under the watchful eye of the architect Juan de Herrera, a towering figure of the Spanish Renaissance.

The palace-monastery became an important intellectual centre, with a burgeoning library and art collection, and even a laboratory where scientists could dabble in alchemy. Felipe II died here on 13 September 1598.

In 1854 the monks belonging to the Hieronymite order, who had occupied the monastery from the beginning, were obliged to leave during one of the 19th-century waves of confiscation of religious property by the Spanish state, only to be replaced 30 years later by Augustinians.

Orientation & Information

You can't miss the monastic complex that marks the town's southern border. Running parallel to the monastery's main wall is Calle de la Floridablanca, close to which you'll find the **tourist office** (☎ 91 890 53 13; www.sanlorenzoturismo.org; Calle de Grimaldi 2; 🕑 10am-6pm Mon-Fri, 10am-7pm Sat & Sun) as well as some shops and restaurants.

Sights

The main entrance to the **Real Monasterio de San Lorenzo** (☎ 91 890 78 18; www.patrimonionacional.es; admission €8, EU citizens free Wed; 🕑 10am-6pm Apr-Sep, 10am-5pm Oct-Mar, closed Mon) is on its western facade. Above the gateway a statue of St Lawrence stands guard, holding a symbolic gridiron, the instrument of his martyrdom (he was roasted alive on one). From here you'll first enter the **Patio de los Reyes**, which houses the statues of the six kings of Judah.

Directly ahead lies the sombre **basilica**. As you enter, look up to the unusual flat vaulting below the choir stalls. Once inside the church proper, turn left to view Benvenuto Cellini's white Carrara marble statue of Christ crucified (1576).

Next you'll be led through several rooms containing tapestries and an El Greco, and then downstairs to the northeastern corner of the complex, where you'll find the **Museo de Arquitectura** and the **Museo de Pintura**. The former tells the story (in Spanish) of how the complex was built, while the latter contains a range of Italian, Spanish and Flemish art from the 16th and 17th centuries.

At this point you are obliged to head upstairs into a gallery around the eastern extension of the complex known as the **Palacio de Felipe II** or **Palacio de los Austrias**. You'll then descend to the 17th-century **Panteón de los Reyes** (Crypt of Kings), where almost all Spain's monarchs since Carlos I lie interred with their spouses. Backtracking a little, you'll find yourself in the **Panteón de los Infantes** (Crypt of the Princes).

Stairs lead up from the **Patio de los Evangelistas** to the **Salas Capitulares** (chapter houses) in the southeastern corner of the monastery. These bright, airy rooms, the ceilings of which are richly frescoed, contain a minor treasure chest of works by El Greco, Titian, Tintoretto, José de Ribera and Hieronymus Bosch (El Bosco to Spaniards).

You can wander around the **Huerta de los Frailes**, the orderly gardens just south of the monastery. In the **Jardín del Príncipe**, which leads down to the town of El Escorial (and

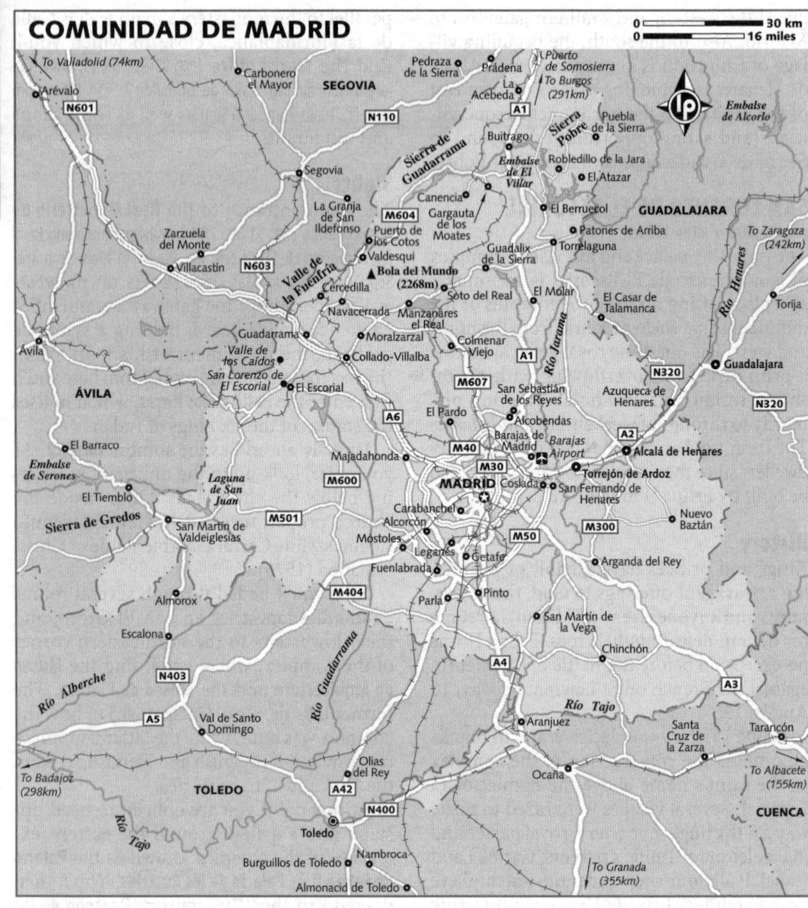

the train station), is the **Casita del Príncipe**, a little neoclassical caprice built under Carlos III for his heir. The **Casita de Arriba** (Casa del Infante; ☎ 91 890 59 03; admission €3.40; ⏰ 10am-1pm & 4-6.30pm Tue-Sun Jul-Sep, 10am-1pm & 4-6.30pm Sat & Sun Oct-Jun), another 18th-century neoclassical gem, is along the road to Ávila.

Sleeping & Eating

Hotel Parrilla Príncipe (☎ 91 890 16 11; www.parrillaprincipe.com; Calle de la Floridablanca 6; s/d from €50/60) Rooms here are nicely turned out with a vaguely old-world style and some have views of the monastery. The hotel's restaurant – where great grilled meats abound – is one of the best in town. It's open Wednesday to Monday and meals cost around €30.

La Cueva (☎ 91 890 15 16; www.mesonlacueva.com; Calle de San Antón 4; meals €35-40; ⏰ lunch & dinner Tue-Sun) Just a block back from the monastery complex, La Cueva has been around since 1768 and it shows in the heavy wooden beams and hearty, traditional Castilian cooking. Roasted meats and steaks are the mainstays, with a few fish dishes.

Getting There & Away

Every 15 minutes (every 30 minutes on weekends) **Herranz** (Map pp134-5; ☎ 91 896 90 28) sends buses 661 and 664 to El Escorial (€3.15, one hour) from platform 30 at the Intercambiador de Autobuses de Moncloa.

San Lorenzo de El Escorial is 59km northwest of Madrid and it takes 40 minutes to drive there. Take the A6 highway to the M600, then follow the signs to El Escorial.

A few dozen **Renfe** (☎ 902 24 02 02; www.renfe.es) C8 *cercanías* make the trip daily from Madrid's Atocha or Chamartín train station to El Escorial (€2.45, one hour).

SOUTH OF MADRID

Warner Brothers Movie World

Disney World it ain't, but this **movie theme park** (☎ 902 02 41 00; www.parquewarner.com in Spanish; San Martín de la Vega; adult/child & senior €35/26.50; ⏰ from 10am, closing hr vary), 25km southeast of central Madrid, has much to catch the attention. Kids will love the chance to hang out with Tom and Jerry, while the young-at-heart film buffs among you will be similarly taken with the Wild West or remakes of the studio sets for such Beverly Hills greats as *Police Academy*. Entrance to the park is via Hollywood Blvd, not unlike LA's Sunset Blvd, whereafter you can choose between Cartoon World, the Old West, Hollywood Blvd, Super Heroes (featuring Superman, Batman and the finks of Gotham City) and finally Warner Brothers Movie World Studios. It's all about the stars of the silver screen coming to life as life-sized cartoon characters roam the grounds, and rides and high-speed roller coasters (up to 90km/h!) distract you if attention starts to wane. There are also restaurants and shops. Opening times are complex and change – always check before heading out here.

To get here by car, take the A4 (the Carretera de Andalucía) south out of Madrid and turn off at Km22 for San Martín de la Vega, about 15km east of the exit. Follow the signs to the car park, where parking is available for €5.

You can also catch one of the C3 *cercanías* that leave Atocha train station regularly, headed towards Pinto. In Pinto change trains and get on the C3A line that goes to Parque de Ocio.

Aranjuez

pop 49,500 / elev 489m

Aranjuez was founded as a royal pleasure retreat, away from the riff-raff of Madrid, and it remains a place to escape the rigours of city life. The palace is opulent, but the fresh air and ample gardens are what really stand out.

ORIENTATION & INFORMATION

Getting around here is easy. When you come into town, you cross Río Tajo and immediately enter a large traffic circle. The palace and its gardens are to your right, while the rest of town spreads out to your left and in front of you. The bus station is right off the central throughway on Calle Infantas. The **tourist office** (☎ 91 891 04 27; www.aranjuez.es in Spanish; Plaza de San Antonio 9; ⏰ 10am-6.30pm Nov-Apr, 10am-8.30pm May-Oct) is in the heart of town, a few hundred metres southwest of the Palacio Real.

SIGHTS

The **Palacio Real** (☎ 91 891 07 40; www.patrimonionacional.es; adult/child, senior & student €5/2.50, EU citizens free Wed; ⏰ 10am-5.15pm Tue-Sun Oct-Mar, 10am-6.15pm Tue-Sun Apr-Sep) started as one of Felipe II's modest summer palaces, but took on a life of its own as a succession of royals, inspired by the palace at Versailles in France, lavished money upon it in the 18th century. With more than 300 rooms, this sprawling box of a palace is filled with a cornucopia of ornamentation. Of all the rulers who spent time here, Carlos III and Isabel II left the greatest mark.

Taking the obligatory guided tour (in Spanish) gives an insight into the palace's history and the art that fills it. The **Sala de Porcelana** (Porcelain Room) is extravagant, its walls covered in handcrafted porcelain figures, echoing a similar chamber in Madrid's Palacio Real (p148). The **Sala Fumadora** (Smoking Room) is almost as extraordinary: it's a florid imitation of an Alhambra interior, with Arabic inscriptions in stucco and an intricate stalactite ceiling carved in wood.

Afterwards, stroll in the lush **gardens** (admission free; ⏰ 8am-6.30pm Tue-Sun Oct-Mar, 8am-8.30pm Tue-Sun Apr-Sep). They're a mix of local and exotic species that have rubbed along nicely since Spanish botanists and explorers started bringing back seeds from all over the world in the 19th century (an audio guide is available). Within their shady perimeter, which stretches a few kilometres from the palace base, you'll find a man-made attraction: the **Casa de Marinos**, which contains the **Museo de Falúas** (☎ 91 891 03 05; admission €2; ⏰ 10am-5.15pm Oct-Mar, 10am-6.15pm Apr-Sep), a museum of royal pleasure boats from days gone by. Reservations are required to visit the museum.

Further away, towards Chinchón, is the **Casa del Labrador** (☎ 91 891 03 05; admission €5), a tasteless royal jewellery box crammed to the rafters with gold, silver, silk and some second-rate art. It sits in the Jardín del Príncipe, an extension of the massive Palacio Real gardens,

THE STRAWBERRY TRAIN

You could take a normal train from Madrid to Aranjuez, but for romance it's hard to beat the **Tren de la Fresa** (Strawberry Train; ☎ 902 24 02 02, 902 22 88 22; adult/child return €24/16; ⏲ late March or early April to mid-or late-June). Begun in 1985 to commemorate the Madrid–Aranjuez route – Madrid's first and Spain's third rail line, inaugurated in the 1850s – the Strawberry Train is a throwback to the time when Spanish royalty would escape the summer heat and head for the royal palace at Aranjuez.

The journey begins at 10.05am, when an antique Mikado 141F-2413 steam engine pulls out from Madrid's Atocha station, pulling behind it four passenger carriages that date from the early 20th century and have old-style front and back balconies. During the 50-minute journey, rail staff in period dress provide samples of local strawberries – one of the original train's purposes was to allow royalty to sample the summer strawberry crop from the Aranjuez orchards. Upon arrival in Aranjuez, your train ticket entitles you to a guided tour of the Palacio Real, Museo de Falúas and other Aranjuez sights, not to mention more strawberry sampling. The return train leaves Aranjuez for Atocha at 6pm.

Tickets can be purchased at any Renfe office or at any travel agency that sells train tickets.

and was closed for restoration at the time of writing.

Several walks begin on the historic paths that run through the Jardín del Príncipe or other palace gardens before branching off into forests or fields. One of the most popular leads past the Mar de Ontígola, a swampy area with unusual vegetation, and along the banks of Río Tajo.

Offering a fun tour around town and a very practical way to get to the Jardín del Príncipe, the **Chiquitren** (☎ 902 08 80 89; www.arantour.com; adult/child €5/3; ⏲ 11am-5.30pm Tue-Sun Oct-Feb, 10am-8pm Tue-Sun Mar-Sep) is a tourist train that loops around Aranjuez. It leaves from near the Palacio Real entrance, and makes stops at the Casa del Labrador and the Casa de Marinos.

The **museum** (☎ 91 892 16 43; admission €1.20; ⏲ 11am-5.30pm Tue-Sun Oct-Mar, 11am-7.30pm Tue-Sun Apr-Sep) housed in Plaza de Toros has displays on the history of bullfighting, the natural attractions of Aranjuez and the entertainments to which the royal court once treated itself.

SLEEPING & EATING

Hostal Castilla (☎ 91 891 26 27; www.hostalesaranjuez.com; Carretera Andalucía 98; s/d €42/55) A short walk from the palace and the town centre, this friendly, charming *hostal* offers impeccable little rooms with attached bathrooms.

NH Príncipe de la Paz hotel (☎ 91 809 92 22; www.nh-hoteles.com; Calle de San Antonio 22; d from €95) Sleek, modern design and attentive service make this the best hotel in town.

El Rana Verde (☎ 91 891 13 25; www.aranjuez.com/ranaverde; Plaza Santiago Rusiñol; meals €25-35) The 'Green Frog' is a classic riverside restaurant that specialises in frogs' legs, but it offers all sorts of local dishes, including, of course, strawberries for dessert.

Casa José (☎ 91 891 14 88; www.casajose.es; Calle de Abastos 32; meals €35-40; ⏲ lunch & dinner Tue-Sat, lunch Sun) The quietly elegant Casa José is the proud owner of a Michelin star and is packed on weekends with *madrileños* drawn by the beautifully prepared meats and local dishes.

GETTING THERE & AWAY

The **AISA** (☎ 902 19 87 88; www.aisa-grupo.com in Spanish) company's bus 423 runs to Aranjuez from Madrid's Estación Sur every 15 minutes (€3.20, 45 minutes).

If you're driving from Madrid, take the A4 south to the M305, which leads to the city centre. Aranjuez is about 50kmfrom Madrid.

C3 *cercanías* leave every 15 or 20 minutes from Atocha train station (€2.45, 45 minutes). On weekends in spring the Strawberry Train is another, albeit slower, option (see the boxed text, above).

Chinchón

pop 5080

Chinchón is just 45km from Madrid but worlds apart. Although it has grown beyond its village confines, visiting its antique heart is like stepping back into another era and into a charming, ramshackle world. Chinchón's main attractions are its plaza and the smorgasbord of traditional *mesón*-style (tavern-style) restaurants scattered around town. The **tourist office** (☎ 91 893 53 23; www.ciudad-chinchon.com; Plaza Mayor 6; 🕑 10am-6pm Mon-Fri, 11am-3pm & 4-6pm Sat & Sun, longer hr in summer) is small but the staff are extremely helpful.

SIGHTS

The heart of town is its unique, almost circular **Plaza Mayor**, which is lined with sagging, tiered balconies – it wins our vote as one of the most evocative *plazas mayores* in Spain. In summer the plaza is converted into a bullring, and it's also the stage for a popular passion play shown at Easter.

Chinchón's historical monuments won't detain you long, but you should take a quick look at the 16th-century **Iglesia de la Asunción**, which rises above Plaza Mayor, and the late-16th-century Renaissance **Castillo de los Condes**, out of town to the south. The castle was abandoned in the 1700s and was last used as a liquor factory. Both are usually closed to the public, but the local tourist office has recently begun a program allowing sporadic visits. Ask at the tourist office for details.

To get an idea of the traditional lifestyle in the area, head to the **Museo Etnológico La Posada** (☎ 91 894 02 07; Calle Morata 5; adult/child €3/2; 🕑 11am-2pm & 4-8pm Mon, Tue, Thu & Fri, 11am-8pm Sat & Sun), a well-run museum exhibiting old farm equipment, household items and traditional garb.

FESTIVALS & EVENTS

The **Fiesta Mayor** is held from 12 to 18 August, when the town's main plaza is turned into a bullring that dominates the centre, and morning bullfights are held daily. If you're drawn to the spectacle, watch from the surrounding balconies over breakfast and coffee.

SLEEPING

Hostal Chinchón (☎ 91 893 53 98; www.hostalchinchon.com in Spanish; Calle Grande 16; s/d/tr €35/45/60; 🏊) The public areas here are nicer than the smallish rooms, which are clean but worn around the edges. The highlight is the surprise rooftop pool overlooking Plaza Mayor.

Parador Nacional (☎ 91 894 08 36; www.parador.es; Avenida Generalísimo 1; d from €148) The former Convento de Agustinos (Augustine Convent), Parador Nacional is one of the town's most important historical buildings and can't be beaten for luxury. It's worth stopping by for a meal or coffee (and a peek around) even if you don't stay here.

EATING

Chinchón is loaded with traditional-style restaurants dishing up *cordero asado* (roast lamb). But if you're after something a little lighter, there is nothing better than savouring a few tapas and drinks on sunny Plaza Mayor.

Mesón Cuevas del Vino (☎ 91 894 02 06; www.cuevasdelvino.com; Calle Benito Hortelano 13; meals €30-35; 🕑 lunch & dinner Wed-Mon) From the huge goatskins filled with wine and the barrels covered in famous signatures, to the atmospheric caves underground, this is sure to be a memorable eating experience with delicious home-style cooking.

Café de la Iberia (☎ 91 894 08 47; www.cafedelaiberia.com; Plaza Mayor 17; meals €35-40; 🕑 lunch & dinner Tue-Sun) This is definitely our favourite of the *mesones* on the Plaza Mayor perimeter. It offers wonderful food, attentive staff and an atmospheric dining area – eat in the light-filled internal courtyard or on the balcony. The speciality is succulent *cochinillo asado* (roast suckling pig).

GETTING THERE & AWAY

La Veloz (Map pp134-5; ☎ 91 409 76 02) has half-hourly services (bus 337) to Chinchón (€3.20, 50 minutes). The buses leave from Avenida del Mediterráneo, 100m east of Plaza del Conde de Casal.

Sitting 45km southeast of Madrid, Chinchón is easy to reach by car. Take the A4 and exit onto the M404, which makes its way to Chinchón.

ALCALÁ DE HENARES

pop 198,800

So close to Madrid and just off an unappealing highway, Alcalá de Henares is full of surprises. It's like a smaller Salamanca, with historical sandstone buildings seemingly at every turn. Throw in some sunny squares and the legendary university, and it's a terrific place to escape the capital. The **tourist office** (☎ 91 881 06 34; www.turismoalcala.com in Spanish; 🕑 10am-2pm & 5-7.30pm Jun–mid-Sep, 10am-2pm & 4-6.30pm Sep -May) is on Plaza de los Santos Niños.

Sights

The city entered an era of prosperity when Cardinal Cisneros founded a **university** (☎ 91 883 43 84; 🕑 9am-9pm) here in 1486. Now centred on a much-restored Renaissance building, the university was one of the country's principal seats of learning for a long period. You can wander around various faculty buildings, dating mostly from the 17th century, but more interesting is the guided tour (free; six per day Monday to Friday, 11 per day Saturday and Sunday), which gives a peek into the Mudéjar **chapel** and the magnificent **Paraninfo** auditorium, where the king and queen of Spain give out the prestigious Premio Cervantes literary award every year.

The town is also dear to Spaniards as the birthplace of the country's literary figurehead, Miguel de Cervantes Saavedra. The site believed to be Cervantes' birthplace now houses the **Museo Casa Natal de Miguel de Cervantes** (☎ 91 889 96 54; www.museo-casa-natal-cervantes.org; Calle Mayor 48; admission free; ⏰ 10am-6pm Tue-Sun Jun-Sep), which lies along the beautiful, colonnaded **Calle Mayor**. It's filled with period furniture and bits and pieces relating to his life.

Sleeping & Eating

Husa El Bedel (☎ 91 889 37 00; www.husa.es; Plaza San Diego 6; d from €60) A sophisticated hotel that offers spacious accommodation and a perfect location.

El Ruedo (☎ 91 880 69 19; Calle de los Libreros 38; meals €20-25; ⏰ 9am-11pm Thu-Tue) With a quiet patio for outdoor eating, this is a great place to get informal fare such as salads and mixed plates.

Hostería del Estudiante (☎ 91 888 03 30; Calle de los Colegios 3; menú €30-35) Run by the national *parador* hotels, this elegant restaurant is considered the best in town. With its wooden beams, open fireplace and adjacent courtyard, it's an atmospheric place to eat. It's very near the main university building and a nearby building is being converted into a *parador* hotel.

Getting There & Away

Alcalá de Henares is just 35km east of Madrid, heading towards Zaragoza along the A2.

Several buses leave Madrid regularly (every five to 15 minutes) from the Intercambiador de Avenida de América (Map p133) and Estación Sur (€1.55, one hour).

A constant stream of C1, C2 and C7 Renfe *cercanías* make the trip from Atocha station to Alcalá de Henares (€1.15, 50 minutes) daily.

SIERRA DE GUADARRAMA

To the north of Madrid lies the Sierra de Guadarrama, a popular winter ski destination and the home of several charming towns, such as Manzanares El Real and Cercedilla, which make great bases for exploring the mountains.

Manzanares el Real

pop 6620 / elev 908m

This is a sweet little mountain town, but what makes it stand out from others like it is the 15th-century storybook **Castillo de los Mendoza** (☎ 91 853 00 08; admission incl guided tour €2; ⏰ 10am-5pm Tue-Sun Oct-Mar, 10am-2pm & 3-6pm Tue-Sun Apr-Sep). The perfectly preserved castle looks like something out of a Disney cartoon with its evenly spaced turrets and strong round towers. There are great views of the sierra from the summit.

Near town, several trails lead into the Parque de la Pedriza, one of which brings you to freshwater pools. Rock climbers have a wealth of options, with 1500 climbing routes in the park. For advice check out the **Centro de Educación Ambiental de Manzanares el Real** (Environmental Education Centre of Manzanares el Real; ☎ 91 853 99 78; Camino de la Pedriza; ⏰ 9am-6pm).

Bus 724 runs regularly to Manzanares from Plaza de Castilla (Map p133) in Madrid (€2.75, 40 minutes).

Cercedilla

pop 6780 / elev 1188m

This mountain town and its surroundings are popular with walkers and mountain bikers. Several trails are marked out through the hills, the main one known as the **Cuerda Larga** or **Cuerda Castellana**. This is a forest track that takes in 55 peaks between the Puerto de Somosierra in the north and Puerto de la Cruz Verde in the southwest. It would take days to complete, but there are several options for shorter walks, including day excursions up the Valle de la Fuenfría and a climb up Monte de Siete Picos.

Mountain bikers can take their bikes up on the local train to Puerto de los Cotos (a lovely ride in itself), scoot across to the Bola del Mundo (in good winters the top end of Guadarrama's best ski piste) and pedal downhill to Cercedilla.

You can get information at the **Centro de Información Valle de la Fuenfría** (☎ 91 852 22 13; Carretera de las Dehesas, Km2; ⏰ 10am-6pm), a couple of kilometres from Cercedilla train station. Accommodation is scarce in this area.

From Madrid's Chamartín train station, the C2 *cercanías* line goes to Cercedilla (€1.30, 80 minutes, 15 daily), or you can take bus 684 from platform 15 of Madrid's Intercambiador de Autobuses de Moncloa (€3, one hour).

Nearby in Guardarrama, **Sala de Guadarrama** (☎ 91 854 21 21; Carretera de los Molinos, Km2, Guadarrama; meals €35-40; closed 20 Sep-20 Oct) is a solid bet for a bite. It's known for its pricey but delicious and (given the location) surprising seafood dishes. It's a popular place, so you'll need to reserve far in advance if you plan to come on a weekend.

Ski Resorts

If you're here in winter, you may want to head up to the modest ski resorts in the Guadarrama. Snowless years are common and the available pistes are not extensive, but it's popular on weekends, when the area is best avoided.

The main centre is **Navacerrada** (☎ 902 88 23 28; www.puertonavacerrada.com in Spanish; lift tickets €20-30), with 13km of mostly easy runs. The **Valdesqui Ski Resort** (☎ 91 570 12 24; Puerto de los Cotos; lift tickets €25-40) is another option.

From Madrid's Chamartín train station, you can get to Puerto de Navacerrada on the C8B *cercanías* line (€1.85, two hours with train change in Cercedilla, four daily). Bus 691 from platform 14 of Madrid's Intercambiador de Autobuses de Moncloa (Map pp134–5) also runs here regularly (€2.75, one hour).

Tucked into a picturesque valley, the large **Hotel La Barranca** (☎ 91 856 00 00; www.hotellabarranca.com; Valle del Pinar de la Barranca, Navacerrada; s/d incl breakfast from €65/84;) offers all the comforts, including pool and tennis courts. Its restaurant also comes recommended for excellent Castilian fare.

NORTH OF MADRID

Palacio Real de El Pardo

Built in the 15th century and remodelled in the 17th, this opulent **palace** (☎ 91 376 04 52; www.patrimonionacional.es; Calle de Manuel Alonso; admission €5; 10.30am-4.45pm Mon-Sat, 10am-1.30pm Sun Oct-Mar, 10.30am-5.45pm Mon-Sat, 9.30am-1.30pm Sun Apr-Sep) was Franco's favourite residence. It's surrounded by lush gardens (they close one hour later than the palace) and on Sunday fills with *madrileño* families looking for a bit of fresh air and a hearty lunch. Of the art on display inside, the tapestries stand out, particularly those based on cartoons by Goya.

If you're driving from Madrid take the M40 to the C601, which leads to El Pardo. The 13km trip takes just 15 minutes. You can also take bus 601 (€1.25, 25 minutes), which leaves every five to 10 minutes from the Intercambiador de Autobuses de Moncloa (Map pp134–5).

Buitrago & Sierra Pobre

Buitrago is the entryway into the Sierra Pobre (Poor Mountains), a quiet stretch of mountains east of the busier Sierra de Guadarrama. Popular with hikers and others looking for nature without quite so many creature comforts, the sleepy Sierra Pobre has yet to develop the tourism industry of its neighbours. And that's just why we like it.

In Buitrago you can stroll along part of the old **city walls**. You can also take a peek into the 15th-century Mudéjar and Romanesque **Iglesia de Santa María del Castillo**, and the small **Picasso Museum** (☎ 91 868 00 56; Plaza Picasso; admission free; 11am-1.30pm & 4-6pm Wed-Mon), which contains a few works that the artist gave to his barber, Eugenio Arias. For more information, visit the **Buitrago tourist office** (☎ 91 868 16 15; 9am-3pm Jul-Sep).

Tiny hamlets are scattered throughout the rest of the sierra. Some, like **Puebla de la Sierra** and **El Atazar**, make for pretty walks from Buitrago and serve as starting points for winding hill trails.

Housed in a tastefully converted barn, **Posada de los Vientos** (☎ 91 869 91 95; Calle Encerradero 2, La Acebeda; r from €65; Sat, Sun & holidays winter only) is a charming, small, family inn where the rooms have exposed stonework and wooden beams. The owners are a friendly lot.

The best restaurant in the area is in nearby Villavieja del Lozoya. **El Arco** (☎ 91 868 09 11; Calle Arco 6; meals €25-35; hlunch Fri-Sun mid-Sep–mid-Jun) is known for its fresh, creative cuisine based on local ingredients and traditional Spanish dishes. Villavieja del Lozoya is 5km northwest of Buitrago.

The **Continental Auto Company** (☎ 91 745 63 00) has a dozen daily buses connecting Madrid's Plaza de Castilla (Map p133) with Buitrago (€4.55, 1½ hours).

Castilla y León

While package tourists head for the beaches, discerning travellers looking for a window onto the Spanish soul make for Castilla y León. This is Spain without the stereotypes. Some of the country's most beautiful cities are here, rising up from the lonely plains of the central plateau with dazzling architecture that provides a backdrop to night-time carousing of the highest order. Salamanca is a glorious temple to plateresque and Renaissance sandstone, but its vibrant student population ensures that it doesn't live in the past. Segovia is similarly alive, its buzzing streets watched over by an astonishing Roman aqueduct and a fairy-tale castle that seems to belong (and once did) in Disneyland. Elsewhere, the cathedrals of León and Burgos are among Europe's most impressive, while the multi-turreted walls of Ávila are everything you dreamed they would be.

But the story of Castilla y León is just as accurately told through quiet back roads, isolated villages and captivating castles that appear in the most unlikely places. The tourist hordes have yet to discover these riches. From the scenic Sierra de Francia in the southwest to Covarrubias, Calatañazor and Medinaceli in the east, this is the hidden Spain that most foreign travellers never imagined still existed.

Spaniards travel from all over the country to sample a feast perfectly suited to the extremes of climate atop central Spain's *meseta* (tableland): *cordero asado* (roast lamb), *cochinillo asado* (roast suckling pig) and some of the country's most prestigious cured meats. Try for yourself!

HIGHLIGHTS

- Spend as long as you can amid the architectural elegance and irresistible energy of **Salamanca** (p214)
- Immerse yourself in Disneyland legends and marvel at the ingenuity of the ancients in **Segovia** (p226)
- Savour the sepulchral light in León's **catedral** (p248), a kaleidoscopic vision of glass and stone
- Lose yourself in the land time forgot amid the stone-and-timber villages of the **Sierra de Francia** (p224)
- Dine on *cordero asado* (roast lamb) like a Castilian in the pretty hilltop towns of **Lerma** (p263) or **Sepúlveda** (p264)
- Escape city life in the charming village of **Covarrubias** (p261)

- AREA: 94,224 SQ KM
- AVE SUMMER TEMP: HIGH 31°C, LOW 14°C
- POP: 2.5 MILLION

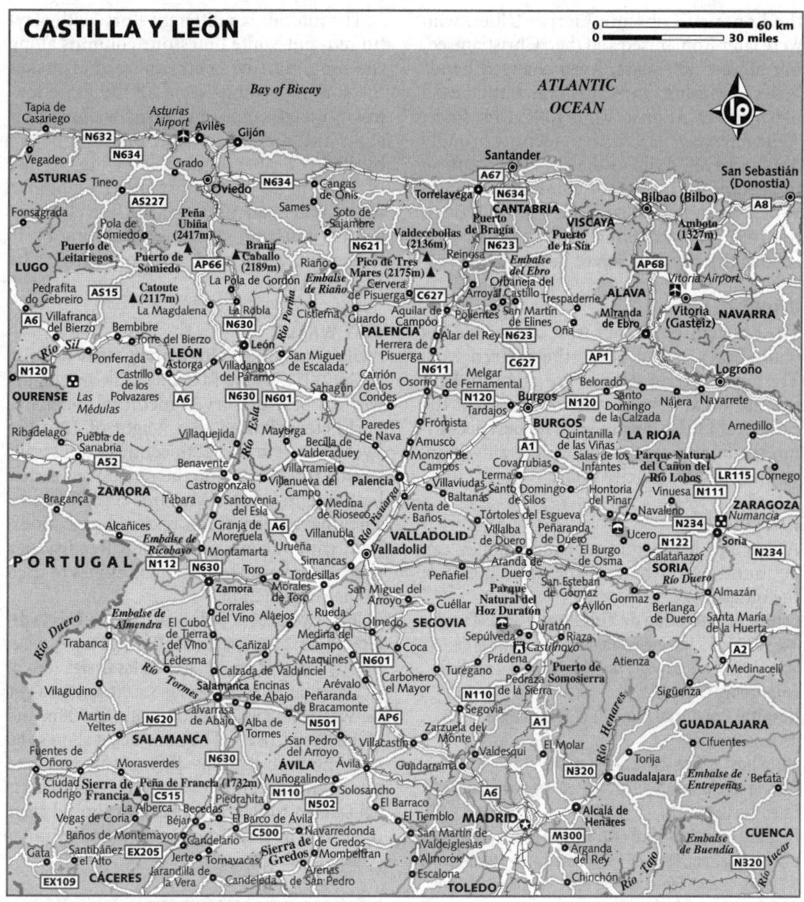

THE SOUTHWEST

You could easily spend a week or more in southwestern Castilla y León, one of the region's most engaging corners. Salamanca and Ávila are two of the most appealing towns in central Spain, but the beautiful Sierra de Gredos and the time-worn villages of the Sierra de Francia and Sierra de Béjar promise fascinating breaks from city life.

ÁVILA

pop 53,800 / elev 1130m

Ávila's old city, surrounded by imposing city walls comprising eight monumental gates, 88 watchtowers and more than 2500 turrets, is one of the best-preserved medieval bastions in all Spain. In winter, when an icy wind whistles in off the plains, the old city huddles behind the high stone walls as if seeking protection from the harsh Castilian climate. At night, when the walls are illuminated to magical effect, you'll wonder if you've stumbled into a fairy tale.

Within the walls, Ávila can appear caught in a time warp. It's a deeply religious city that for centuries has drawn pilgrims to the cult of Santa Teresa de Ávila, with many churches, convents and high-walled palaces. As such, Ávila is the essence of Castilla, the epitome of Old Spain.

History

According to myth, one of Hercules' sons founded Ávila. The more prosaic truth gives the honour to obscure Iberian tribes, who were later Romanised and then Christianised. For almost 300 years, Ávila changed hands between Muslims and Christians, until the fall of Toledo to Alfonso VI in 1085. Ever since, Ávila has worn its Christian identity proudly on its sleeve. 'Ávila of the Knights' went on to become an important commercial centre with a well-established noble class, although the 1492 edict expelling all Jews from Spain robbed the city of much of its lifeblood.

Orientation

The old centre fans out west of the *catedral* (cathedral), which abuts the eastern wall. The bus and train stations are a five- and 10-minute walk, respectively, northeast of the cathedral in the new town. The best accommodation and eating options are all within, or just outside, the city walls.

Information

ATMs and banks that exchange money can be found everywhere in the eastern end of the old town.

Centro de Recepción de Visitantes (tourist office; ☎ 902 10 21 21; www.avilaturismo.com; Avenida de Madrid 39; 🕒 10am-6pm Nov-Mar, 9am-8pm Apr-Oct)
Emergency (☎ 112)
Hospital Provincial (☎ 920 35 72 00; Calle de Jesús del Gran Poder 42)
Main post office (Plaza de la Catedral 2)
Policía Nacional (☎ 920 25 10 00, emergencies 091; Paseo San Roque 34)
Regional tourist office (☎ 920 21 13 87; www.turismocastillayleon.com; Plaza de Pedro Dávila 4; 🕒 9am-2pm & 5-8pm daily mid-Sep–Jun, 9am-8pm Sun-Thu, 9am-9pm Fri & Sat Jul–mid-Sep)

Sights

CATEDRAL

Ávila's 12th-century **catedral** (☎ 920 21 16 41; Plaza de la Catedral; admission €4; 🕒 10am-7pm Mon-Fri, 10am-8pm Sat, noon-6pm Sun Jun-Sep, shorter hours rest of year) is not just a house of worship, but also an ingenious fortress: its stout granite apse forms the central bulwark in the heavily fortified eastern wall of the town. Although the main facade hints at the cathedral's 12th-century, Romanesque origins, the church was finished 400 years later in a predominantly Gothic style, making it the first Gothic church in Spain. The sombre grey facade betrays some unhappy 18th-century meddling in the main portal.

The interior is a different story, with playful red-and-white limestone columns along the long, narrow central nave that makes the soaring ceilings seem all the more majestic. Renaissance-era carved walnut choir stalls and a dazzling altar painting begun by Pedro de Berruguete, showing the life of Jesus in 24 scenes, are other highlights of the inner sanctum. Off the fine cloisters, a small museum contains a painting by El Greco and a splendid silver monstrance by Juan de Arfe.

CITY WALLS

Ávila's splendid **12th-century walls** (murallas; ☎ 920 21 13 87; adult/child €4/2.50) rank among the world's best-preserved medieval defensive perimeters. Raised to a height of 12m between the 11th and 12th centuries, the walls stretch for 2.5km atop the remains of earlier battlements of the Muslims and Romans. They have been much restored and modified, with various Gothic and Renaissance touches and even some Roman stones re-used in the construction.

The two access points are at the **Puerta del Alcázar** (🕒 11am-6pm Tue-Sun Oct-Apr, 11am-8pm Tue-Sun May-Sep) and the **Puerta de los Leales** (Casa de las Carnicerias; 🕒 10am-6pm Tue-Sun Oct-Apr, 10am-8pm Tue-Sun May-Sep), which allow walks of 300m and 800m, respectively. The same ticket allows you to climb both sections. By the time you read this, a third section of the wall, from **Puerta del Carmen** to **Puerta del Puente**, should have opened. The last tickets are sold 45 minutes before closing time.

BASÍLICA DE SAN VICENTE

So much of Ávila's religious architecture is brooding and sombre, but the graceful **Basílica de San Vicente** (☎ 920 25 52 30; Plaza de San Vicente; admission €1.80; 🕒 10am-1.30pm & 4-6pm) is a masterpiece of the subdued elegance of Romanesque style. A series of largely Gothic modifications in sober granite contrast with the warm sandstone of the Romanesque original. Work started in the 11th century, supposedly on the site where three martyrs – San Vicente and his sisters – were slaughtered by the Romans in the early 4th century. Their canopied cenotaph is an outstanding piece of Romanesque with nods to the Gothic; don't forget to pop down into the crypt. The **Jardín de San Vicente** across the road was once a Roman cemetery.

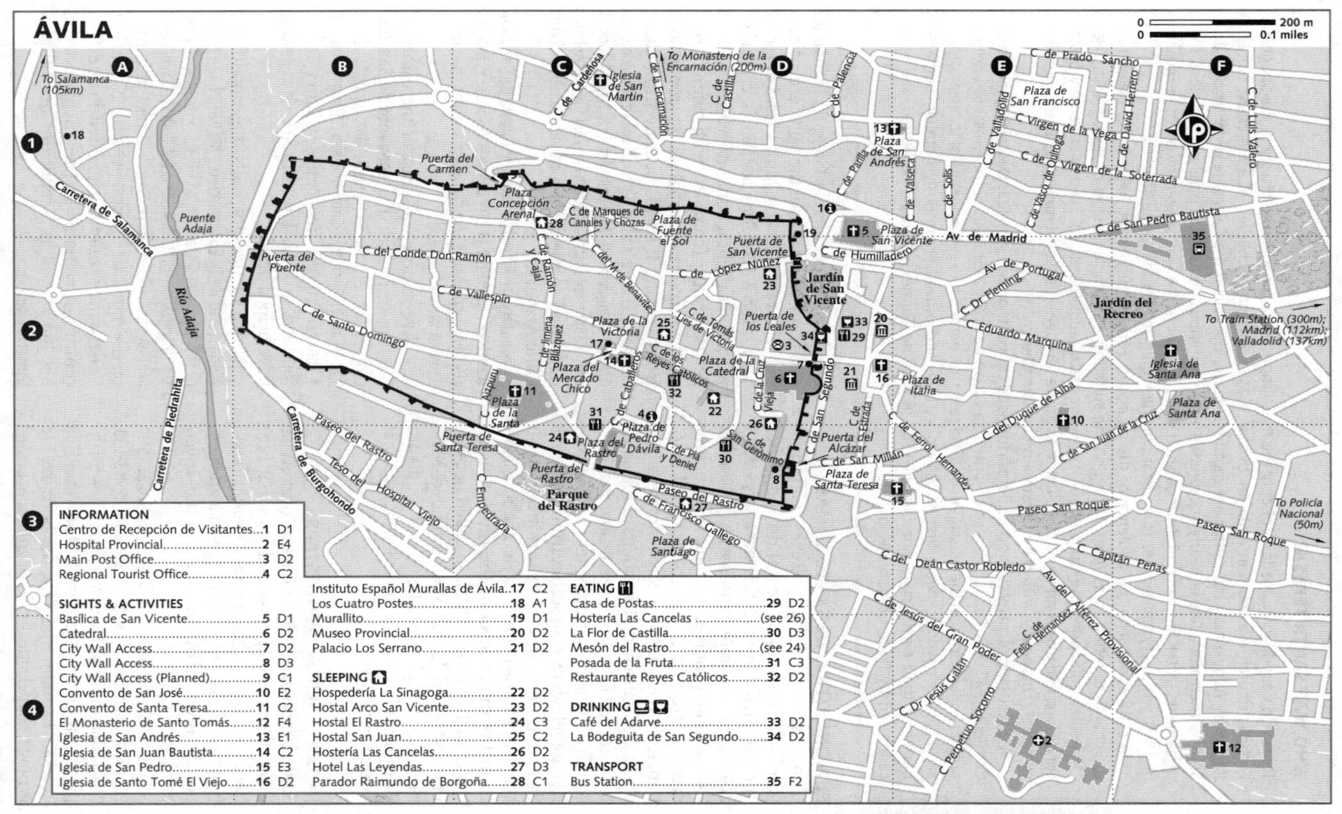
ÁVILA
CASTILLA Y LEÓN
INFORMATION
Centro de Recepción de Visitantes 1 D1
Hospital Provincial 2 E4
Main Post Office 3 D2
Regional Tourist Office 4 C2
SIGHTS & ACTIVITIES
Basílica de San Vicente 5 D1
Catedral 6 D2
City Wall Access 7 D2
City Wall Access 8 D3
City Wall Access (Planned) 9 C1
Convento de San José 10 E2
Convento de Santa Teresa 11 C2
El Monasterio de Santo Tomás 12 F4
Iglesia de San Andrés 13 E1
Iglesia de San Juan Bautista 14 C2
Iglesia de San Pedro 15 E3
Iglesia de Santo Tomé El Viejo 16 D2
Instituto Español Murallas de Ávila 17 C2
Los Cuatro Postes 18 A1
Murallito 19 D1
Museo Provincial 20 D2
Palacio Los Serrano 21 D2
SLEEPING
Hospedería La Sinagoga 22 D2
Hostal Arco San Vicente 23 D2
Hostal El Rastro 24 C3
Hostal San Juan 25 C2
Hostería Las Cancelas 26 D2
Hotel Las Leyendas 27 D3
Parador Raimundo de Borgoña 28 C1
EATING
Casa de Postas 29 D2
Hostería Las Cancelas (see 26)
La Flor de Castilla 30 D3
Mesón del Rastro (see 24)
Posada de la Fruta 31 C3
Restaurante Reyes Católicos 32 D2
DRINKING
Café del Adarve 33 D2
La Bodeguita de San Segundo 34 D2
TRANSPORT
Bus Station 35 F2

WHO WAS SANTA TERESA?

Teresa de Cepeda y Ahumada, probably the most important woman in the history of the Spanish Catholic Church, was born in Ávila on 28 March 1515, one of 10 children of a merchant family. Raised by Augustinian nuns after her mother's death, she joined the Carmelite order at age 20. Shortly thereafter, Teresa nearly succumbed to a mysterious illness that paralysed her legs for three years. After her early, undistinguished years as a nun, she was shaken by a vision of hell in 1560, which crystallised her true vocation: she would reform the Carmelites.

In stark contrast to the opulence of the church in 16th-century Spain, her reforms called for the church to return to its roots, taking on the suffering and simple lifestyle of Jesus Christ. The Carmelites demanded the strictest of piety, went *descalzadas* (barefoot), lived in extremely basic conditions and even employed flagellation to atone for their sins. Not surprisingly, all this proved extremely unpopular with the mainstream Catholic Church.

With the help of many supporters, Teresa founded convents of the Carmelitas Descalzas (Shoeless Carmelites) all over Spain. She also co-opted San Juan de la Cruz (St John of the Cross) to undertake a similar reform in the masculine order, a task that earned him several stints of incarceration. Santa Teresa's writings were first published in 1588 and proved enormously popular, perhaps partly for their earthy style. She died in 1582 in Alba de Tormes, where she is buried. She was canonised by Pope Gregory XV in 1622.

EL MONASTERIO DE SANTO TOMÁS

Commissioned by the Reyes Católicos (Catholic Monarchs), Fernando and Isabel, and completed in 1492, this **monastery** (☎ 920 22 04 00; Plaza de Granada 1; admission €3; 10am-1pm & 4-8pm) is an exquisite example of Isabelline architecture and is rich in historical resonance. Three interconnected cloisters lead up to the church that contains the alabaster tomb of Don Juan, the monarchs' only son. It's backed by an altarpiece by Pedro de Berruguete depicting scenes from the life of St Thomas Aquinas. The magnificent choir stalls, in Flemish Gothic style, are accessible from the upper level of the third cloister, the Claustro de los Reyes, so called because Fernando and Isabel often attended Mass here. It's thought that the Grand Inquisitor Torquemada (see the boxed text, p237) is buried in the sacristy.

IN SANTA TERESA'S FOOTSTEPS

Santa Teresa casts a long shadow over Ávila. From the convent, plaza and gate that bear her name, to the sweet *yemas de Santa Teresa* (yummy cookies made with egg yolk and supposedly invented by the saint), her trail covers every inch of the city.

The **Convento de Santa Teresa** (☎ 920 21 10 30; Plaza de la Santa; admission free; 8.45am-1.30pm & 3.30-9pm Tue-Sun), built in 1636 over the saint's birthplace, is the epicentre of the cult surrounding Teresa. The room where she was born in 1515 is now a chapel smothered in gold; it is lorded over by a baroque altar by Gregorio Fernández and features a statue of the saint. An adjoining **relics room** (10am-2pm & 4-7pm daily Apr-Oct, 10am-1.30pm & 3.30-5.30pm Nov-Mar) is crammed with Teresa relics, some of which, such as her ring finger (complete with ring), border on the macabre (but that didn't stop Franco from keeping it by his bedside throughout his rule). There's also a small **museum** (admission €2; 10am-2pm & 4-7pm daily Apr-Oct, 10am-1.30pm & 3.30-5.30pm Nov-Mar, 10am-2pm & 4-7pm Tue-Sun Apr-Oct) dedicated to the saint and accessible from Calle Aizpuru.

Nearby, the 16th-century **Iglesia de San Juan Bautista** (☎ 920 21 11 27; Plaza de la Victoria; before & after mass) contains the baptismal font in which Teresa was baptised.

A five-minute walk east of the cathedral lies the unremarkable **Convento de San José** (☎ 920 22 21 27; Calle del Duque de Alba; admission €1.20; 10am-1.30pm & 3-6pm Nov-Mar, 10am-1.30pm & 4-7pm Apr-Oct), the first convent Santa Teresa founded, in 1562. The saint herself is said to have helped build it.

North of the city walls, the unadorned **Monasterio de la Encarnación** (☎ 920 21 12 12; Calle de la Encarnación s/n; admission €1.70; 9.30am-1.30pm & 3.30-6pm Mon-Fri, 10am-1.30pm & 4-6pm Sat & Sun, longer hours in summer) is where Santa Teresa fully took on the monastic life and lived for 27 years. A Renaissance complex modified in the 18th century, it contains further mementoes of her life as well as a replica of her suitably Spartan cell.

CHURCHES & MANSIONS

The Romanesque **Iglesia de Santo Tomé El Viejo** (Plaza de Italia; admission €1.20; 10am-2pm & 4-7pm Tue-Sat, 10am-2pm Sun) dates from the 13th century, and it was from this pulpit that Santa Teresa was castigated most vehemently for her reforms. It has been impressively restored to house mostly Roman foundation stones and a splendid floor mosaic. It's an annexe of the **Museo Provincial** (920 21 10 03; admission €1.20, free Sat & Sun; 10am-2pm & 4-7pm Tue-Sat, 10am-2pm Sun Oct-Jun, 10am-2pm & 5-8pm Tue-Sat, 10am-2pm Sun Jul-Sep), housed in the adjacent granite 16th-century Mansión de los Deanes. Both can be entered on the same ticket.

The **Iglesia de San Pedro** (920 22 93 28; Plaza de Santa Teresa; 10.30am-noon & 7-8pm) was built a little later and its light, sandstone exterior is a pleasant complement to the granite austerity that reigns inside the city walls. North of the old city, the 12th-century **Iglesia de San Andrés** (Plaza de San Andrés; 10am-2pm & 4-6pm Mon-Sat May-Oct) is Ávila's oldest church and a pure example of the Romanesque.

Palacio Los Serrano (920 21 22 23; Plaza de Italia; admission free; 7.30-9.30pm Mon-Fri, noon-2pm & 7.30-9.30pm Sat & Sun) is used for contemporary art exhibitions.

MURALLITO

The cutesy little train-on-wheels *(tren turístico)* works especially well in Ávila, making a circuit of the city walls with a few other sights thrown in. The **Murallito** (630 945021; www.murallitoavila.com in Spanish; adult/child €4/3) runs daylight hours (30 minutes duration) for most of the year, with a night tour (50 minutes) at 10pm on Fridays and Saturdays in July and August.

LOS CUATRO POSTES

Northwest of the city, on the road to Salamanca, this spot affords fine views of Ávila's walls. It also marks the place where Santa Teresa and her brother were caught by their uncle as they tried to run away from home (they were hoping to achieve martyrdom at the hands of the Muslims). The best views are at night.

Courses

The **Instituto Español Murallas de Ávila** (920 22 27 73; www.iema.com; Calle de Martín Carramolino 6; 9am-2pm & 4-8pm Mon-Fri) offers Spanish-language courses.

Festivals & Events

Ávila's principal festival, **Fiesta de Santa Teresa**, honours the city's patron saint with processions, concerts and fireworks in the second week of October.

Ávila is one of the best places in Castilla y León to watch the solemn processions of **Semana Santa** (Easter Holy Week). It all begins on Holy Thursday and the most noteworthy event is the early-morning (around 5am) Good Friday procession, which circles the city wall.

Sleeping

Staying overnight in Ávila, as opposed to taking a day trip from Madrid, immerses you in the medieval tranquillity that is the city's hallmark.

Hostal San Juan (920 25 14 75; www.hostalsanjuan.es; Calle de los Comuneros de Castilla 3; s €24-30, d €38-48) With warm tones throughout, Hostal San Juan is pleasant, friendly and close to everything in Ávila. The rooms don't have a lot of character, but they're terrific value.

Hostal El Rastro (920 21 12 18, 920 35 22 25; www.elrastroavila.com in Spanish; Plaza del Rastro 4; s/d from €33/50) Eight quaint rooms overlook a quiet square, providing a great location and a certain old-world charm in the upper budget range.

Hostal Arco San Vicente (920 22 24 98; www.arcosanvicente.com; Calle de López Núñez 6; s €45-50, d €60-70) Another terrific option, this engaging *hostal* (budget hotel) has lovely, brightly painted rooms and friendly owners. The rooms at the back are quieter and have a private terrace. The location, just inside Puerta de San Vicente, is also a winner.

our pick **Hotel Las Leyendas** (920 35 20 42; www.lasleyendas.es; Calle de Francisco Gallego 3; s €55-67, d €67-85;) Occupying the house of 16th-century Ávila nobility just outside the city walls, this beautiful, intimate hotel overflows with period touches (original wooden beams, exposed brick and stonework) wedded to modern amenities. Some rooms have marvellous views out across the plains, while others look onto an internal garden. Highly recommended.

Hospedería La Sinagoga (920 35 23 21; lasinagoga@vodafone.es; Calle de los Reyes Católicos 22; s/d/tr from €53/74/106) This delightful little hotel hidden down a quiet lane incorporates details from Ávila's main 15th-century synagogue, with bright, spacious rooms. Rates for doubles can drop as low as €42 on winter weekdays.

Hostería Las Cancelas (☎ 920 21 22 49; www.lascancelas.com; Calle de la Cruz Vieja 6; s/d/tr from €53/76/107; ⏲ Feb-Dec) Tucked away behind the cathedral, close to Puerta del Alcázar, this place has large rooms (some are huge) with traditional furniture. Touches like ladders to reach the higher windows are typical of the thoughtfulness with which this place is run.

Parador Raimundo de Borgoña (☎ 920 21 13 40; avila@parador.es; Marques de Canales y Chozas 2; d/ste from €127/285;) Occupying a 16th-century palace hard up against the wall in the north of the old town, Parador Raimundo de Borgoña has all of the essential elements of the *parador* chain: elegant public areas, helpful staff and stylish bedrooms.

Eating

Ávila is famous for its *chuleton de Ávila* (T-bone steak) and *judías del barco de Ávila* (white beans, often with chorizo, in a thick sauce).

La Flor de Castilla (☎ 920 25 28 66; Calle de San Gerónimo; ⏲ 10am-2pm & 5-8pm Mon-Sat) This is a fine place to buy a *yema de Santa Teresa,* a sticky, ultrasweet cookie made of egg yolk and sugar, and said to have been invented by the saint.

Posada de la Fruta (☎ 920 22 09 84; www.posadadelafruta.com in Spanish; Plaza de Pedro Dávila 8; meals €10-18) This restaurant has a split personality. Simple, informal meals can be had at the cafe-bar in a light-filled, covered courtyard, while the traditional *comedor* (dining room) serves *menús* (set menus) and à la carte dishes.

Casa de Postas (☎ 920 35 21 53; www.casadepostas.com in Spanish; Calle de San Segundo 40; menú del día €12, meals €30-35; ⏲ lunch & dinner Wed-Mon) Just outside Puerta de los Leales, Casa de Postas has a busy tavern for tapas downstairs and a more formal restaurant upstairs.

our pick **Restaurante Reyes Católicos** (☎ 920 25 56 27; www.restaurante-reyescatolicos.com in Spanish; Calle de los Reyes Católicos 6; menú del día from €17, meals €25-35) Most *asadores* (restaurants specialising in roasted meats) in Ávila are old-school, with dark, wood-panelled dining areas. This slick, modern restaurant is a refreshing change. The cuisine is a mix of traditional and fusion dishes, with a range of set menus (€17 to €48).

Mesón del Rastro (☎ 920 21 12 19; Plaza del Rastro 1; menú del día €20; ⏲ lunch & dinner Thu-Sat, lunch only Sun-Wed) The dining room at Mesón del Rastro, with its dark-wood beams, announces immediately that this is a bastion of Castilian cooking. Expect hearty, delicious mainstays such as *chuleton de Ávila* (€13), *judías del barco de Ávila* (€7) and *cordero asado* (roast lamb; €15).

Hostería Las Cancelas (☎ 920 21 22 49; www.lascancelas.com; Calle de la Cruz Vieja 6; meals €30-40; ⏲ lunch & dinner Feb-Dec) Occupying a delightful interior patio dating back to the 15th century, this place is a mainstay of Ávila cuisine. If you're going to indulge in hearty local food, this is a good place to do so.

Drinking

Ávila nights aren't particularly lively, but there are a few spots worth seeking out.

La Bodeguita de San Segundo (☎ 920 22 59 17; www.vinoavila.com in Spanish; Calle de San Segundo 19; ⏲ 11am-midnight Thu-Tue) This gem of a wine and tapas bar is standing-room only most nights and more tranquil in the quieter afternoon hours. The setting, in the 16th-century Casa de la Misericordia, is superb and the wines are outstanding.

Café del Adarve (Calle de San Segundo 40; ⏲ 5pm-late) About as lively as Ávila gets, Café del Adarve has quirky decor, weekend DJs and occasional live music during winter.

Getting There & Away

BUS

From Ávila's **bus station** (☎ 920 22 01 54; Avenida de Madrid 2), services run by **Larrea/La Sepulvedana** (☎ 902 22 22 82; www.lasepulvedana.es in Spanish) go to Madrid's Estación Sur (€7.09, one hour 20 minutes); there are up to nine daily Monday to Friday, and around five daily on weekends. **Avanza** (☎ 902 02 09 99; www.avanzabus.com) has buses to Segovia (€4.30, 55 minutes, five daily Monday to Friday, one or two on weekends) and Salamanca (€5.58, 1½ hours, four daily Monday to Friday, one to three on weekends). Buses also leave for the Sierra de Gredos, including Navarredonda de Gredos (€4.15, 1¼ hours, two to three daily) and Arenas de San Pedro (€5.30, 1¼ hours, twice daily Monday to Saturday).

CAR & MOTORCYCLE

From Madrid, take the A6 motorway northwest, then the N110 west. Driving time is around one hour; the toll costs €6.85. From Ávila, the N501 heads north to Salamanca, the N110 east to Segovia and the N403 north to Valladolid. For the Sierra de Gredos, take the N502.

TOP VILLAGES OF OLD CASTILLA

- **San Martín del Castañar** (p225) – Sierra de Francia's prettiest village
- **Candelario** (p226) – stone-and-wood village huddling beneath the Sierra de Béjar
- **Pedraza de la Sierra** (p232) – lovely walled hamlet watched over by a castle
- **Puebla de Sanabria** (p242) – a return to the past with medieval streetscapes
- **Castrillo de los Polvazares** (p254) – vivid colours emblematic of northwestern Castilla y León
- **Covarrubias** (p261) – arguably Castilla y León's most postcard-perfect village
- **Santo Domingo de Silos** (p261) – quiet streets, a stunning cloister and Gregorian chants in the Burgos hinterland
- **Peñaranda de Duero** (p264) – a palace, churches and a ruined castle on the banks of the Río Duero
- **Calatañazor** (p270) – movie-set, cobbled charm just off the highway but a world away
- **Medinaceli** (p271) – splendid old-world feel high above eastern Castilla y León

There's free street parking just outside the northern wall.

TRAIN

From the **train station** (☎ 902 24 02 02; Paseo de la Estación), more than 30 trains run daily to Madrid (from €6.50, 1¼ to two hours) and a handful to Salamanca (€8.40, one to 1½ hours).

Getting Around

Local bus 1 runs past the train station to Plaza de la Catedral.

SIERRA DE GREDOS

West of Madrid and south of Ávila, the plains of Castilla yield to the precipitous Sierra de Gredos, a secret world of lakes and granite mountains rising up to the Pico de Almanzor (2592m). While the occasional castle or sanctuary may catch the eye, the overriding appeal is the scenery. The sierra is also popular with walkers, mountain bikers and rock climbers, and is at its best for these activities in spring (March to May) and autumn (September to November). Summer (June to August) can be stifling, while in winter (December to February) the trails are covered in snow. The region overflows with Spanish tourists on weekends but sees very few foreign tourists, which is, of course, part of its charm.

Public transport to and throughout the sierra is intermittent at best (and almost nonexistent on weekends), so renting a car is essential to getting the best from the region. Of the three main routes through the sierra, the N502 travels north–south, paralleling an old Roman road (still visible in parts) through a steep valley. Cutting across the northern foothills, the C500 affords scenic views of the mountains, while the C501 follows the southern flank and passes through some outstanding scenery en route to Extremadura's La Vera.

Arenas de San Pedro & Around

A convenient gateway to the southern Sierra de Gredos, **Arenas de San Pedro** (population 6778, elevation 620m) does have its pretty corners, but it's more the sort of place you'd use as a base than visit for its own sake.

The **tourist office** (☎ 920 37 23 68; Plaza de San Pedro; 🕓 10am-1pm & 4-8pm) in Arenas has walking suggestions, as does Ávila's regional tourist office (p208).

In the town centre, sights worth a quick look include the stout 15th-century **Castillo de la Triste Condesa**, the sober 14th-century Gothic **parish church** and the **Roman bridge**. A 10-minute walk north of here is the neoclassical **Palacio del Infante Don Luis de Borbón**, a gilded cage for Carlos III's imprisoned brother.

Not far from Arenas de San Pedro, **Guisando**, **El Hornillo** and **El Arenal**, a trio of villages at a distance of 5km, 6km and 9km from Arenas, respectively, have access to walking trails. All three are served by a bus (weekdays only).

One popular walking trail leads from El Arenal to Puerto de la Cabrilla. Gaining some

1000m over a distance of 4.5km, it's a strenuous five- to seven-hour workout.

SLEEPING & EATING

Hostal El Castillo (☎ 920 37 00 91; Carretera de Candeleda 2, Arenas de San Pedro; s/d €23/35) On the main road through Arenas, Hostal El Castillo has pleasant, clean rooms with heating and TV.

Hostal El Fogon de Gredos (☎ 920 37 40 18; Calle Linarejo 6, Guisando; s/d €45/60) This is the most attractive option in Guisando, offering pretty rooms with minibar, heating and satellite TV. It's even better known as a restaurant (meals €20) for hearty, meat-dominated local cuisine.

Hostería Los Galayos (☎ 920 37 13 79; www.losgalayos.com; Plaza de Condestable Dávalos 2, Arenas de San Pedro; s/d from €48/64) At this comfortable three-star place in the heart of Arenas de San Pedro, the tired decor distracts only momentarily from the fact that rooms are good and spacious, and the location is a winner.

CASTILLA Y LEÓN

GETTING THERE & AWAY

At least two buses run daily from Arenas de San Pedro to Madrid (€10.60, 2½ hours), except on Sunday. Two daily buses do the trip to Ávila (€5.30, 1¼ hours) from Monday to Saturday.

Northern Flank of the Sierra de Gredos

To escape the weekend and summer crowds, the Sierra de Gredos' less-frequented northern flank has some spectacular views, fine walks and excellent hotels. Public transport is even less frequent here than further south.

Running west off the N502, near Puerta de Pico, the scenic C500 leads past Navarredonda de Gredos and on to Hoyos del Espino, from where the small AV931 leads into the sierra, ending after 12km at La Plataforma. This is the jumping-off point for one of the most picturesque walks, leading to the **Laguna Grande**, a glassy mountain lake in the shadow of the Pico de Almanzor. The easy-to-moderate walk along a well-marked 8km trail takes about 2½ hours each way. Next to the lake is a *refugio* (mountain shelter), which is often full, and good camping. From here it's possible to climb to the top of the **Pico de Almanzor** (2592m; difficult) in about two hours or continue for two hours west to the **Circo de Cinco Lagunas** (easy to moderate). From there you could either backtrack or descend via the Garganta del Pinar towards the town of Navalperral de Tormes, a rigorous undertaking that can take five hours. For maps and further information on these routes, visit the tourist office in Arenas de San Pedro (p213) or Ávila (p208).

SLEEPING & EATING

Navarredonda de Gredos has the best choice of accommodation, although Hoyos del Espino is another reasonable base.

Albergue Juvenil (☎ 920 34 80 05; albngredos@dvnet.es; Navarredonda de Gredos; dm under/over 26yr €10/15; 15 Mar-15 Dec;) This place offers spotless rooms, its own Olympic-sized swimming pool and breathtaking mountain views for those who are counting their euros.

Hostal Refugio de Gredos (☎ 920 34 80 47; www.refugiodegredos.com in Spanish; Navarredonda de Gredos; s/d €45/60) Housed in a lovely old building with sturdy stone walls, this well-run place has good rooms with hints of character and an excellent restaurant.

La Casa de Arriba (☎ 920 34 80 24; www.casadearriba.com; Calle de la Cruz 19, Navarredonda de Gredos; s/d €67/79) Brimful with rustic charm, La Casa de Arriba is a touch of class with wooden beams, wood floors, antique furnishings and thick stone walls. The restaurant is one of the best in the area.

El Milano Real (☎ 920 34 91 08; www.elmilanoreal.com; Calle de Toledo s/n, Hoyos del Espino; d from €102) This is a gorgeous place to stay, with stylish, spacious rooms hiding behind the old-world facade. Each room is different, but the attic rooms have a stylish Japanese feel. Wonderful views, a delightfully peaceful setting and a fine restaurant (meals around €35) are other highlights.

SALAMANCA

pop 156,000

Whether floodlit by night or bathed in midday sun, there's something magical about Salamanca. This is a city of rare architectural splendour, awash with sandstone overlaid with Latin inscriptions in ochre, and with an extraordinary virtuosity of plateresque and Renaissance styles. The monumental highlights are many, with the exceptional Plaza Mayor (illuminated to stunning effect at night) an unforgettable highlight. But this is also Castilla's liveliest city, home to a massive Spanish and international student population who throng the streets at night and provide the city with so much life. In short, this is one place you'll never want to leave.

History

In 220 BC Celtiberian Salamanca was besieged by Hannibal. Later, under Roman rule, it was an important staging post on the Via Lata (Ruta de la Plata, or Silver Route) from the mines in Asturias to Andalucía. After the Muslim invasion of Spain, it changed hands repeatedly. The greatest turning point in the city's history was the founding of the university in 1218. It became the equal of Oxford and Bologna, and by the end of the 15th century was the focal point of some of the richest artistic activity in the country. The city followed the rest of Castilla into decline in the 17th century, although by the time Spanish literary hero Miguel de Unamuno became rector at the university in 1900, Salamanca had essentially recovered. Throughout the 20th century, especially during the Civil War and the almost four decades of Franco's rule that followed, Salamanca's university became both the centre for both liberal resistance to fascism and the object of Franco's efforts to impose a compliant academic philosophy in Spain's most prestigious university. To a small degree, that liberal-conservative tension still survives and defines the character of the town.

Orientation

The old centre, north of Río Tormes and with Plaza Mayor at its heart, is compact and easily walked. The train and bus stations are equidistant from the centre of town, the former northeast and the latter northwest. Buses connect both to the town centre. Most accommodation and eating options, and major monuments, are close to Plaza Mayor.

Information

EMERGENCY

Emergency (☎ 112)
Policía Nacional (☎ 091; Ronda de Sancti-Spíritus 8)

INTERNET ACCESS

Ciberplace (Plaza Mayor 10; per hr €1; 🕑 11am-midnight Mon-Fri, noon-midnight Sat & Sun)
Laundry (Pasaje Azafranal 18; per hr €2; 🕑 10am-2pm & 4-8pm Mon-Fri, 10.30am-2pm Sat)

LAUNDRY

Laundry (Pasaje Azafranal 18; per wash €3.15; 🕑 10am-2pm & 4-8pm Mon-Fri, 10.30am-2pm Sat) Coin-operated with free soap powder.

> **BEST CITY FOR...**
>
> - **Medieval walls** – Ávila (p207)
> - **Cathedrals** – León (p246), Burgos (p255), Palencia (p242) and Salamanca (opposite)
> - **Stunning architecture** – Salamanca (opposite), Zamora (p240) and Segovia (p226)
> - **Restaurants and nightlife** – Salamanca (opposite), León (p246), Segovia (p226) and Valladolid (p233)
> - **Pretty plazas** – Salamanca (opposite) and Valladolid (p233)
> - **Provincial atmosphere** – Soria (p267)

MEDICAL SERVICES

Hospital Clínico Universitario (☎ 923 29 11 00; Paseo de San Vicente 58)
Hospital Santísima Trinidad (☎ 923 26 93 00; Paseo de las Carmelitas 74-94)

MONEY

There is no shortage of banks around the centre, particularly along Rúa Mayor.

POST

Main post office (Calle Gran Vía 25-29)

TOURIST INFORMATION

Both of Salamanca's tourist offices organise guided tours of the city. These depart at 11am daily (at 11am and 4.30pm on Fridays and Saturdays) and cost from €6 to €7. Summer tours include English- and/or French-speaking guides.
Municipal tourist office (☎ 923 21 83 42; www.salamanca.es; Plaza Mayor 14; 🕑 9am-2pm & 4.30-8pm Mon-Fri, 10am-8pm Sat, 10am-2pm Sun)
Regional tourist office (☎ 923 26 85 71; Casa de las Conchas, Rúa Mayor s/n; 🕑 9am-2pm & 5-8pm daily mid-Sep–Jun, 9am-8pm Sun-Thu, 9am-9pm Fri & Sat Jul–mid-Sep)

Sights

Salamanca is an easy city to explore on foot (see p218), but a good way to get an overview is to climb aboard the **tren turístico** (tourist train; ☎ 638 004967; Plaza Anaya; adult/child €3.75/1.75; 🕑 10am-2pm & 4-8pm). Trips last for 20 minutes, and the service runs for longer hours in summer.

SALAMANCA

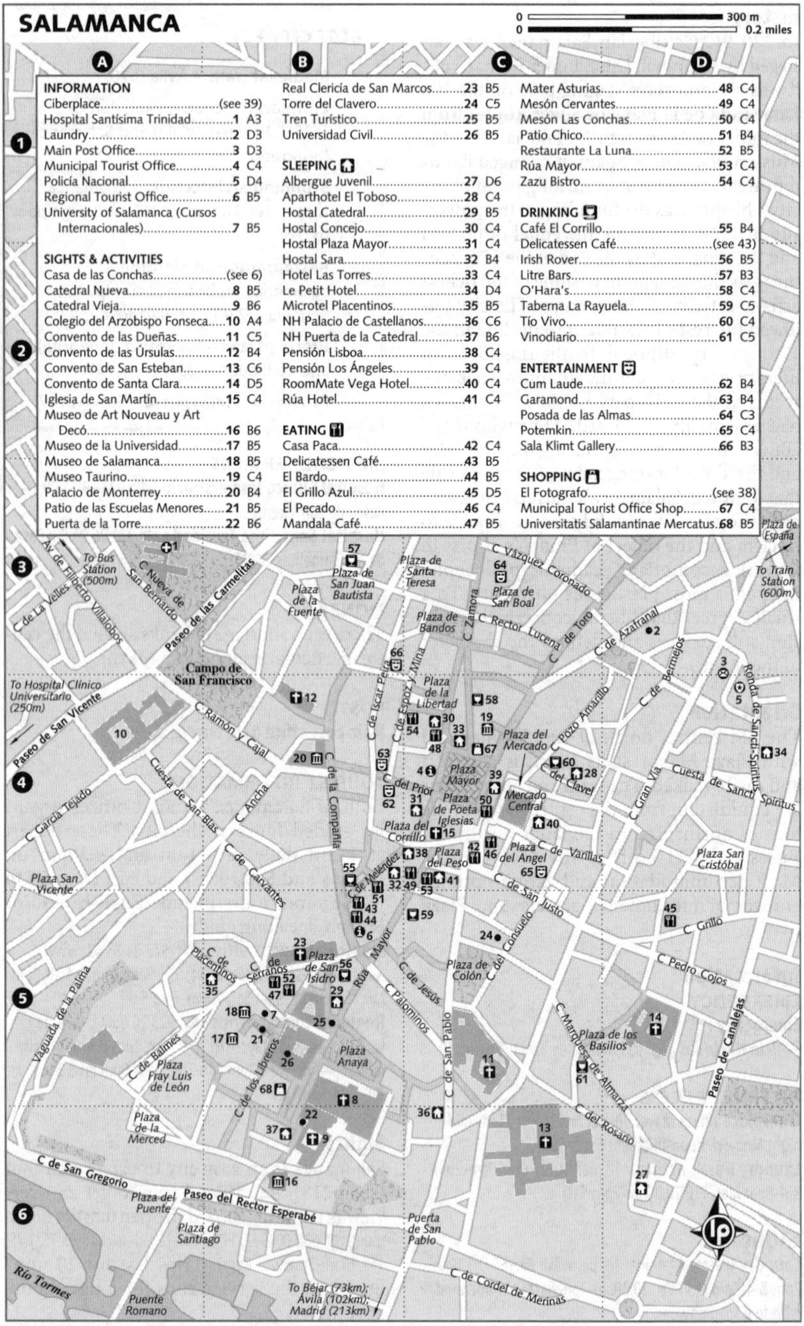

0 — 300 m
0 — 0.2 miles

INFORMATION
Ciberplace.....(see 39)
Hospital Santísima Trinidad.....1 A3
Laundry.....2 D3
Main Post Office.....3 D3
Municipal Tourist Office.....4 C4
Policía Nacional.....5 D4
Regional Tourist Office.....6 B5
University of Salamanca (Cursos Internacionales).....7 B5

SIGHTS & ACTIVITIES
Casa de las Conchas.....(see 6)
Catedral Nueva.....8 B5
Catedral Vieja.....9 B6
Colegio del Arzobispo Fonseca.....10 A4
Convento de las Dueñas.....11 C5
Convento de las Úrsulas.....12 B4
Convento de San Esteban.....13 C6
Convento de Santa Clara.....14 D5
Iglesia de San Martín.....15 C4
Museo de Art Nouveau y Art Decó.....16 B6
Museo de la Universidad.....17 B5
Museo de Salamanca.....18 B5
Museo Taurino.....19 C4
Palacio de Monterrey.....20 B4
Patio de las Escuelas Menores.....21 B5
Puerta de la Torre.....22 B6
Real Clericía de San Marcos.....23 B5
Torre del Clavero.....24 C5
Tren Turístico.....25 B5
Universidad Civil.....26 B5

SLEEPING
Albergue Juvenil.....27 D6
Aparthotel El Toboso.....28 C4
Hostal Catedral.....29 B5
Hostal Concejo.....30 C4
Hostal Plaza Mayor.....31 C4
Hostal Sara.....32 B4
Hotel Las Torres.....33 C4
Le Petit Hotel.....34 D4
Microtel Placentinos.....35 B5
NH Palacio de Castellanos.....36 C6
NH Puerta de la Catedral.....37 B6
Pensión Lisboa.....38 C4
Pensión Los Ángeles.....39 C4
RoomMate Vega Hotel.....40 C4
Rúa Hotel.....41 C4

EATING
Casa Paca.....42 C4
Delicatessen Café.....43 B5
El Bardo.....44 B5
El Grillo Azul.....45 D5
El Pecado.....46 C4
Mandala Café.....47 B5
Mater Asturias.....48 C4
Mesón Cervantes.....49 C4
Mesón Las Conchas.....50 C4
Patio Chico.....51 B4
Restaurante La Luna.....52 B5
Rúa Mayor.....53 C4
Zazu Bistro.....54 C4

DRINKING
Café El Corrillo.....55 B4
Delicatessen Café.....(see 43)
Irish Rover.....56 B5
Litre Bars.....57 B3
O'Hara's.....58 C4
Taberna La Rayuela.....59 C5
Tío Vivo.....60 C4
Vinodiario.....61 C5

ENTERTAINMENT
Cum Laude.....62 B4
Garamond.....63 B4
Posada de las Almas.....64 C3
Potemkin.....65 C4
Sala Klimt Gallery.....66 B3

SHOPPING
El Fotografo.....(see 38)
Municipal Tourist Office Shop.....67 C4
Universitatis Salamantinae Mercatus.....68 B5

PLAZA MAYOR

Built between 1729 and 1755, Salamanca's exceptional grand square is widely considered Spain's most beautiful central plaza, particularly at night when it's illuminated (until midnight) to magical effect. Designed by Alberto Churriguera, it's a remarkably harmonious and controlled baroque display. The medallions placed around the plaza bear the busts of famous figures (including Franco in the northeastern corner). Bullfights were held here well into the 19th century; the last ceremonial *corrida* (bullfight) took place here in 1992. The plaza's outdoor tables are a place to linger, watch the passing parade and marvel at the beguiling beauty of the architecture. Chances are you'll find yourself drawn here again and again.

Just off the square, the pretty 12th-century Romanesque **Iglesia de San Martín** (Plaza del Corrillo; 11am-2pm & 4-7pm Tue-Sun) is wedged among a huddle of houses.

CATEDRAL NUEVA

The tower of the late-Gothic **Catedral Nueva** (923 21 74 76; Plaza Anaya; 9am-8pm) lords over the centre of Salamanca, its compelling *churrigueresco* dome visible from almost every angle. It is, however, the magnificent Renaissance doorways, particularly the Puerta del Nacimiento on the western face, that stand out as one of several miracles worked in the city's sandstone facades. The Puerta de Ramos, facing Plaza Anaya, contains an encore to the 'frog spotting' challenge on the university facade (see the boxed text, p218): look for the little astronaut and ice-cream cone chiselled into the portal by stonemasons during recent restorations.

Inside, the most notable features include the elaborate choir stalls, main chapel and retrochoir, all courtesy of the prolific José Churriguera. The ceilings are also exceptional.

For fine views over Salamanca, head to the **Puerta de la Torre** (Ieronimus; Plaza de Juan XXIII; admission €3.25; 10am-7.15pm), at the southwestern corner of the cathedral's facade. From here, stairs lead up through the tower, past labyrinthine but well-presented exhibitions of cathedral memorabilia, then along the interior balconies of the sanctuaries of the Catedral Nueva and Catedral Vieja and out onto the exterior balconies. There's another entrance inside the Catedral Vieja.

CATEDRAL VIEJA

The Catedral Nueva's largely Romanesque predecessor, the **Catedral Vieja** (adult/student €4.25/2; 10am-7.30pm) is adorned with an exquisite 15th-century altarpiece, with 53 panels depicting scenes from the lives of Christ and Mary, topped by a representation of the Final Judgment – it's one of the most beautiful Renaissance altarpieces beyond Italy's shores. The cathedral was begun in 1120 and remains something of a hybrid: there are Gothic elements, while the unusual ribbed cupola, the Torre del Gallo, reflects a Byzantine influence. The cloister was largely ruined in the 1755 earthquake, but the Capilla de Anaya houses an extravagant alabaster sepulchre and one of Europe's oldest organs, a Mudéjar work of art dating from the 16th century. The entrance is inside the Catedral Nueva.

UNIVERSIDAD CIVIL

The visual feast of the entrance facade to Salamanca's **university** (923 29 44 00; Calle de los Libreros; adult/student €4/2, free Mon morning; 9.30am-1pm & 4-7pm Mon-Fri, 9.30am-1pm & 4-6.30pm Sat, 10am-1pm Sun) is a tapestry in sandstone, bursting with images of mythical heroes, religious scenes and coats of arms. It's dominated in the centre by busts of Fernando and Isabel. It's the elusive frog that draws the crowds (see the boxed text, p218), but don't let that distract you from the overall magnificence.

Founded initially as the Estudio Generál in 1218, the university came into being in 1254 and reached the peak of its renown in the 15th and 16th centuries. Behind the facade, the highlight of an otherwise modest collection of rooms lies upstairs: the extraordinary **university library**, one of the oldest university libraries in Europe. With some 2800 manuscripts gathering dust, it's a real cemetery of forgotten books. Note the fine late-Gothic features and beautiful *techumbre* (carved wooden ceiling).

Among the small lecture rooms arranged around the courtyard downstairs, the **Aula de Fray Luis de León** was named after the celebrated 16th-century theologian and writer whose statue adorns the Patio de las Escuelas Menores outside. It conserves the original benches and lectern from Fray Luis' day. Arrested by the Inquisition for having translated the *Song of Solomon* into Spanish, the sardonic theologian returned to his class after five years in jail and resumed lecturing with the words, 'As I was saying yesterday…'.

The **Escalera de la Universidad** (University Staircase) that connects the two floors has symbols carved into the balustrade; to decode them was seen as symbolic of the quest for knowledge.

CONVENTO DE SAN ESTEBAN

Rising above the southeastern corner of the old city, the Convento de San Esteban's **church** (☎ 923 21 50 00; adult/concession €3/2; 🕑 10am-2pm & 4-8pm) has an extraordinary altarlike facade with the stoning of San Esteban (St Stephen) as its central motif. Inside is a well-presented museum dedicated to the Dominicans and their missionary work in the Americas. The splendid Gothic-Renaissance cloister has strategically placed mirrors that enable you to fully appreciate the fine ceiling. Climb to the 1st floor, from where you can access the church's choir stalls. In the church's main sanctuary, the centrepiece is a *retablo* (altarpiece), an ornate masterpiece by José Churriguera.

Walking Tour

Start your exploration of Salamanca in the incomparable **Plaza Mayor** (**1**; p217). Heading west off the southwestern corner of the plaza, take Calle del Prior, which leads to the **Palacio de Monterrey** (**2**), a 16th-century holiday home of the Duques de Alba and a seminal piece of Spanish Renaissance architecture. It's not open to the public but the facade is superb. A short detour north yields the **Convento de las Úrsulas** (**3**; ☎ 923 21 98 77; Calle de Úrsulas 2; admission €2; 🕑 11am-1pm & 4.30-6pm, closed last Sun of month), a late-Gothic nunnery founded by Archbishop Alonso de Fonseca in 1512 and now home to his magnificent marble tomb, sculpted by Diego de Siloé. Across the Campo de San Francisco, the 16th-century **Colegio del Arzobispo Fonseca** (**4**; ☎ 923 29 45 70; Paseo de San Vicente; admission free; 🕑 10am-2pm & 4-7pm) is a sober plateresque structure notable for its fine entrance, pleasing courtyard and antique clock collection.

Climb the Cuesta de San Blas and then wind your way southeast to the **Real Clericía de San Marcos** (**5**; Universidad Pontificia; ☎ 923 27 71 00; Calle de la Compañia; admission €2.50; 🕑 10.30am-12.45pm & 5-6.45pm Tue-Fri, 10am-1.15pm & 5-7.15pm Sat, 10am-1.15pm Sun), a colossal baroque church where obligatory guided tours run every 45 minutes. Directly opposite is the **Casa de las Conchas** (**6**; ☎ 923 26 93 17; Calle de la Compañia 2; admission free; 🕑 9am-9pm Mon-Fri, 9am-2pm & 4-7pm Sat & Sun), one of the city's most endearing buildings, named after the scallop shells clinging to its facade. Its original owner, Dr Rodrigo Maldonado de Talavera, was a doctor at the court of Isabel and a member of the Order of Santiago, whose symbol is the shell. It now houses the public library, entered via a charming bi-level courtyard.

From Plaza de San Isidro, head southwest along Calle de los Libreros to the **Universidad Civil** (**7**; p217), which faces onto the **Patio de las Escuelas Menores** (**8**), a small square where you'll find the **Museo de Salamanca** (**9**; ☎ 923 21 22 35; Patio de las Escuelas Menores 2; admission €1.20, free Sat & Sun; 🕑 10am-2pm & 4-7pm Tue-Sat, 10am-2pm Sun). Housed in the former residence of Queen Isabel's doctor, it's more interesting for the picture of tranquil Salamanca residential life in its attractive patios than for the paintings and sculptures within. Almost next door, off a small cloister, the main attractions of the **Museo de la Universidad** (**10**; Patio de las Escuelas Menores; incl Universidad Civil €4; 🕑 9.30am-1pm & 4-7pm Mon-Fri, 9.30am-1pm & 4-6.30pm Sat, 10am-1pm Sun) are the ceiling fresco of the zodiac and two *techumbres*, one clearly Mudéjar and the other with Italian Renaissance influences.

After visiting the **Catedral Nueva** (**11**; p217) and the **Catedral Vieja** (**12**; p217), and climb-

FROG SPOTTING

A compulsory task facing all visitors to Salamanca is to search out the frog sculpted into the facade of the Universidad Civil. Once pointed out, it's easily enough seen, but the uninitiated can spend considerable time searching.

Why bother? Well, they say that those who detect it without help can be assured of good luck and even marriage within a year. Some hopeful students see a guaranteed examinations victory in it. If you believe all this, stop reading now. If you do want help, look at the busts of Fernando and Isabel. From there, turn your gaze to the largest column on the extreme right of the facade. Slightly above the level of the busts is a series of skulls, atop the leftmost of which sits our little amphibious friend (or what's left of his eroded self).

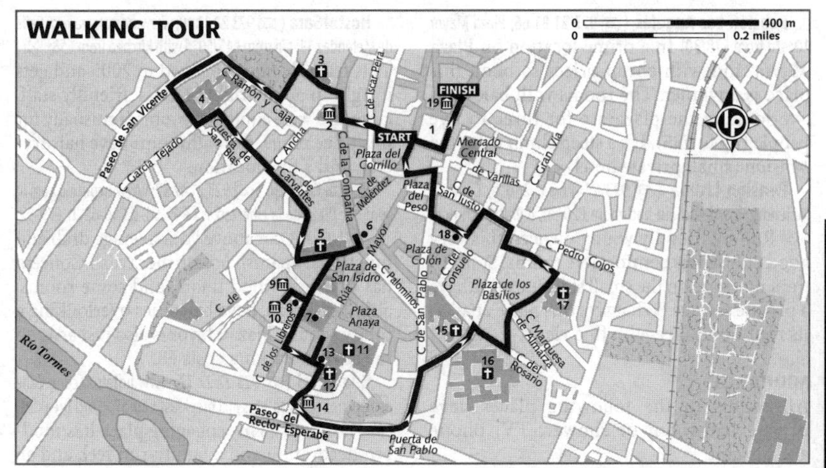

WALK FACTS

Start Plaza Mayor
Finish Museo Taurino
Distance 3.5km
Duration Three hours

ing up through the **Puerta de la Torre** (**13**; p217), head southwest down the hill to the **Museo de Art Nouveau y Art Decó** (**14**; Casa Lis; ☎ 923 12 14 25; Calle de El Expolio 14; adult/concession €3/2, free Thu morning; 11am-2pm & 5-9pm Tue-Fri, 11am-9pm Sat & Sun), a gallery devoted to both styles in a Modernista (Catalan art nouveau) house.

Walking east along Paseo del Rector Esperabé, then north along Calle de San Pablo, brings you to the Dominican **Convento de las Dueñas** (**15**; ☎ 923 21 54 42; Calle Gran Vía; admission €1.50; 10.30am-12.45pm & 4.30-6.45pm Mon-Fri, 10.30am-12.45pm Sat), home to the city's most beautiful cloister, with some decidedly ghoulish carvings on the capitals. Directly opposite is the sublime **Convento de San Esteban** (**16**; opposite), while quiet streets lead away to the northeast to the **Convento de Santa Clara** (**17**; ☎ 923 26 96 23; adult/child €2/1; 9.35am-2pm & 4.20-7pm Mon-Fri, 9.30am-3pm Sat & Sun). This much-modified convent started life as a Romanesque structure, and you can climb up some stairs to inspect at close quarters the 14th- and 15th-century *artesonado* (wooden Mudéjar ceiling).

As you make your way northwest to the old town, pause at the **Torre del Clavero** (**18**; Calle del Consuelo), a 15th-century octagonal fortress with an unusual square base and smaller cylindrical towers. Continue up Calle de San Pablo, skirt Plaza Mayor and then seek out the **Museo Taurino** (**19**; ☎ 923 21 94 25; Calle de Doctor Piñuela 2; adult/child/senior €3/free/2; 11.30am-1.30pm & 6-8pm Tue-Sat, 11.30am-1.30pm Sun), packed with bullfighting memorabilia.

Courses

Salamanca is one of the most popular places in Spain to study Spanish, and the **University of Salamanca** (Cursos Internacionales, Universidad Civil; ☎ 923 29 44 18; www.usal.es; internat@cursos.usal.es; Patio de las Escuelas Menores) is the most respected language school. Courses range from a six-hour course spread over two weeks (€335) to a 10-week course of five hours a week (€1530). It can also arrange accommodation with local families.

The municipal tourist office (p215) has a list of accredited private colleges.

Sleeping

Salamanca has outstanding accommodation, especially in the midrange and top-end categories. Prices in just about all places increase on weekends.

BUDGET

Albergue Juvenil (☎ 923 26 91 41; www.alberguesalamanca.com; Calle de Escoto 13-15; dm €13, s/d €25/36) Salamanca's youth hostel is ideal for those looking for travel buddies as it's a popular, well-run place with large, clean dorms. It's a 10-minute walk down the hill from the old town and breakfast costs €2.

Pensión Los Ángeles (☎ 923 21 81 66; Plaza Mayor 10; s/d from €18/30) In a prime location on Plaza Mayor and with cheap prices to boot, this place is a winner. The rooms with balconies overlooking the plaza are for three to five people (up to €95). It's a steep climb up to the *pensión* (small private hotel).

Pensión Lisboa (☎ 923 21 43 33; 2nd fl, Calle de Meléndez 1; s/d without bathroom €20/30, d with bathroom €35) Run by friendly young owners, this very good choice has comfortable rooms. Some of the singles are on the small side but some have a private terrace. What sets this place apart is its rooftop terrace with fine views.

MIDRANGE

All rooms in the following places have private bathroom or shower, TV, phone and air-con.

Aparthotel El Toboso (☎ 923 27 14 62; www.hoteltoboso.com; Calle del Clavel 7; s/d from €30/45, 3-/4-/5-person self-contained apt €76/84/93; ❄) Even if the rooms are ageing at this friendly place, they're super value, especially the enormous apartments, which come with kitchens and renovated bathrooms. It's ideal for families or if you're planning to stay in Salamanca for more than a night.

our pick **Hostal Catedral** (☎ 923 27 06 14; Rúa Mayor 46; s/d €30/48; ❄) Just across from the cathedrals, this lovely *hostal* has a few extremely pretty, clean-as-a-whistle, bright bedrooms with showers. All look out onto the street or cathedral, which is a real bonus, as is the motherly owner, who treats her visitors as honoured guests.

Le Petit Hotel (☎ 923 60 07 73; www.lepetithotel.net in Spanish; Ronda de Sancti-Spíritus 39; s/d/tr €36/49/59; ❄) Overlooking a peaceful square in a quiet part of town, this splendid place has individually designed rooms that are worth far more than what the owners ask for them, especially the renovated ones on the 4th and 5th floors. Some of the rooms are smallish and the floral wallpaper in some may not be to everyone's taste, but the welcome is warm and the quality high.

Hostal Plaza Mayor (☎ 923 26 20 20; www.hostalplazamayor.es in Spanish; Plaza del Corrillo 20; s €30-36, d €50-60; ❄) A few steps from Plaza Mayor, this *hostal* has a fabulous location and is one of the best in this price range. The stylish, clean rooms come with satellite TV and some have a touch of character. If you're a light sleeper, ask for a room at the back.

Hostal Sara (☎ 923 28 11 40; www.hostalsara.org; Calle de Meléndez 11; s/d from €45/50, d with kitchen from €58; ❄) This friendly *hostal* opened in 2005 and gets it right in all the right places – friendly staff, large and well-equipped rooms (unusually for this price range, the bathrooms have hairdryers), and a fine location.

Hostal Concejo (☎ 923 21 47 37; www.hconcejo.com in Spanish; Plaza de la Libertad 1; s €45-54, d €56-69, tr €79-92; P ❄ 💻) A cut above your average drab and functional Spanish *hostal*, the stylish Concejo has polished wood floors, and some rooms, although small, have balconies overlooking a pretty square. Plaza Mayor is also just around the corner. Parking costs €8.

Rúa Hotel (☎ 923 27 22 72; www.hotelrua.com; Calle de Sánchez Barbero 11; s incl breakfast €50-57, d incl breakfast €67-115; ❄ 💻) This engaging place has modern decoration and a family-run feel, and all rooms are apartments/suites (with kitchen) of around 30 sq metres. All are filled with light, but the best rooms are those facing north, with terrific views. The breakfast room in the basement includes a 13th-century stone arch.

our pick **Microtel Placentinos** (☎ 923 28 15 31; www.microtelplacentinos.com; Calle de Placentinos 9; s €54-80, d €67-92; ❄) One of Salamanca's most charming boutique hotels, Microtel Placentinos is tucked away on a quiet street and has rooms with exposed stone walls and wooden beams. The service is faultless, and the overall atmosphere one of intimacy and discretion. Some rooms have a Jacuzzi.

TOP END

Room Mate Vega Hotel (☎ 923 27 22 50; www.room-matehotels.com; Plaza del Mercado 16; d from €80; ❄ 💻) The Room Mate chain of hotels has taken Spain by storm, with the hallmarks being originality, a personal touch and a highly refined sense of style. The Salamanca outpost, which opened in early 2008, is all of these things, although the aesthetic is more subdued than elsewhere.

Hotel Las Torres (☎ 923 21 21 00; www.hthotels.com; Calle de Concejo 4-6; d from €85; ❄ 💻) Part of the quality High-Tech chain, this stylish hotel has lovely dark-wood floors, designer lamps and bathrooms, and a generally classy feel. The rooms overlooking Plaza Mayor (Salamanca's best view) start at €120, depending on the season. Some rooms on the interior (facing the internal patio or lightwell) are a little small.

Housed in an old palace just down from the cathedrals, **NH Palacio de Castellanos** (☎ 923 26 18

18; www.nh-hotels.com; Calle de San Pablo 58-64; s from €99, d €106-210;) is all lofty patios and antique staircases. The character doesn't spill over much into the rooms, but they're supremely comfortable. If it's full (and it often is), try the equally good **NH Puerta de la Catedral** (923 28 08 29; www.nh-hotels.com; Plaza de Juan XXIII 5; d €95-210;), next to the Catedral Vieja.

Eating

El Grillo Azul (923 21 92 33; Calle Grillo 1; menú de día €9, meals €15-20; lunch & dinner Tue-Sat, lunch only Sun; V) Vegetarian visitors to Salamanca have a treat that's rare in Castilian towns – a real-life vegetarian restaurant. It's a quiet place with creative salads, organic rice and pasta.

Restaurante La Luna (923 21 28 87; Calle de los Libreros 4; lunch & dinner menús €11; lunch & dinner Tue-Sun, lunch only Mon) We like this place almost as much as we like Mandala (below). Downstairs is crowded and intimate; upstairs is bright and modern. The food is a good mix of hearty meat staples and fresh lighter meals.

our pick **Mandala Café** (923 12 33 42; Calle de Serranos 9-11; meals €15-20; V) Cool, casual and deservedly popular, Mandala specialises in a wide range of *platos combinados* (combination plates; €4.20 to €9). There are also salads and plenty of vegetarian choices. The feel is contemporary but laid-back and the food excellent.

Mesón Las Conchas (923 21 21 67; Rúa Mayor 16; meals €20-30) The atmospheric Mesón Las Conchas has a choice of outdoor tables (in summer), an atmospheric bar and an upstairs, wood-beamed dining area. The bar in particular caters less to a tourist crowd than to locals who know their *embutidos* (cured meats). For sit-down meals, there's a good mix of roasts, *platos combinados* and *raciones* (large tapas servings). The wine servings are generous.

Mater Asturias (923 21 83 86; Calle de Concejo 3; menú asturiano €22, meals €25-30) 'Mother Asturias' is a slick bar-restaurant all decked out in lime-green, with chain mail hanging above the bar. They've won prizes here for their *sidra* (cider) and even let you pour it yourself. The tastes are fresh and straight from Spain's northern coast, with a few staples from the Asturias mountain hinterland. We especially enjoyed the *surtido de brochetas* (selection of brochettes; €20).

our pick **Mesón Cervantes** (923 21 72 13; Plaza Mayor 15; meals €25-30; 10am-midnight) This is another great place where you can eat at the outdoor tables on the plaza, but the dark wooden beams and atmospheric buzz of the Spanish crowd on the 1st floor should be experienced at least once. The food's a mix of *platos combinados* (€9 to €14), salads (€5.50 to €11.50) and *raciones* (€7 to €18); vegetarians won't have much choice among the last.

Casa Paca (923 21 89 93; Plaza del Peso 10; meals €35-40) Established in 1928 and still going strong, Casa Paca is rumoured to be where the king dines when in town. Both the restaurant and its most famous patron are known for their love of hearty dishes like *cochinillo asado* (roast suckling pig; €18).

El Pecado (923 26 65 58; Plaza de Poeta Iglesias 12; meals €40, menú de degustación €45) One of the trendy places to regularly attract Spanish celebrities (eg Pedro Almodóvar and Ferran Adrià) in recent times, El Pecado ('The Sin') has an intimate dining room and quirky, creative menu. The hallmarks are fresh tastes, intriguing combinations and a menu that changes regularly.

Other choices around the city centre:

Delicatessen Café (923 28 03 09; Calle de Meléndez 25; menú del día €15, meals €20-25; 9am-late) A cool place to be seen, whether for breakfast, an afternoon snack or dinner.

El Bardo (923 21 90 89; Calle de la Compañía 8; menú del día €15, meals €25-35) High-calibre tapas restaurant.

Patio Chico (923 26 86 16; Calle de Meléndez 13; menú del día €15, meals €20-25) Hugely popular for tapas.

Rúa Mayor (923 26 06 10; Rúa Mayor 9; dinner & lunch menús €15) Wildly popular cafe-bar-restaurant.

Zazu Bistro (923 26 16 90; www.restaurantezazu.com in Spanish; Plaza de la Libertad 8; menú del día €22, meals €30-35) *Hôtel Costes* on the stereo and Mediterranean fusion cooking (with Thai, North African and South American flavours thrown in).

Drinking

Salamanca, with its myriad bars and large student population, is the perfect after-dark playground. Nightlife here starts very late, with many bars not filling until after midnight. Clearly many of Salamanca's students have better things to do than hit the books.

Taberna La Rayuela (Rúa Mayor 19; 6pm-1am Sun-Thu, 6pm-2am Fri & Sat) This low-lit upstairs bar buzzes with a 20-something crowd and is an intimate place. It's probably our favourite spot in town for first drinks.

Vinodiario (Plaza de los Basilios 1; 10am-1am) Away from the crowds of the old-city centre, this delightfully chilled wine bar is staffed by knowledgeable bar staff and loved by locals, who fill the outdoor tables when the weather's warm. The tapas are good and it's another favourite for early-evening drinks.

Café El Corrillo (☎ 923 27 19 17; www.cafecorrillo.com in Spanish; Calle de Meléndez 18; ⏲ 8.30am-late) Café El Corrillo is great for a beer and tapas at any time, and live music on Friday nights from 11.30pm. The *terraza* (terrace) out the back is the place to be on a warm summer's evening.

Tío Vivo (Calle del Clavel 3; ⏲ 4pm-late) Here you can sip drinks by flickering candlelight. It's in the must-visit category, not least to peek at the whimsical decor of carousel horses and oddball antiquities.

Delicatessen Café (Calle de Meléndez 25; ⏲ 9am-late) This supercool cafe is all curves, soft lighting and minimalist fusion decor. It's more *pijo* (beautiful people) than student hang-out.

Salamanca has two lively Irish pubs, **O'Hara's** (Calle Zamora 14) and the **Irish Rover** (Calle Rúa Antigua). At the latter Monday is international night, but, then again, so are most nights…

The so-called 'litre bars' on Plaza de San Juan Bautista are fun night-time hang-outs with a young crowd. Here you can guzzle a 1L *cerveza* (beer) for €3 or a *cubalibre* (rum and coke with lemon juice) for €6.

Entertainment

Many of Salamanca's cafe-bars morph into dance clubs after midnight; there's usually no cover charge.

Posada de las Almas (Plaza de San Boal; ⏲ 6pm-late) Decked out in a curious design mix of looming papier-mâché figures, dollhouses and velvet curtains, this place attracts a mixed crowd – gay and straight, Spanish and foreign.

Potemkin (Calle del Consuelo; ⏲ 11pm-late) Salamanca's grungy alternative to the sophisticates elsewhere can be found at Potemkin, where you'll catch live rock music most nights. The neighbouring bars are similar, so dress down.

Most of the best *discotecas* (clubs) are on Calle del Prior or around the corner on Calle de la Compañia. Places where you can wave your hands in the air like you just don't care include the following:

Cum Laude (Calle del Prior 7; ⏲ 10pm-late Tue-Sun) Sprawling mock-palace interior and a crowd that knows all the words. Look elsewhere on the nights when they ask €30 admission…

Garamond (Calle del Prior 24; ⏲ 9pm-late) Rather baronial decor and a great selection of music.

Sala Klimt Gallery (Calle de Iscar Peira 30; ⏲ midnight-6am Fri & Sat) House, electro or techno creates one helluva good time.

Shopping

Salamanca overflows with souvenir shops, running the whole gamut from the tasteful to the tacky.

Universitatis Salamantinae Mercatus (☎ 923 29 46 92; Calle de Cardenal Plá y Deniel s/n; ⏲ 10am-2pm & 4.30-8pm Mon-Sat, 10.15am-2pm Sun) The official shop of the University of Salamanca has a stunning range of stationery items, leather-bound books and other carefully selected reminders of your Salamanca visit.

El Fotografo (☎ 923 26 64 92; Calle de Meléndez 5; ⏲ 10.30am-1.30pm & 5-8.30pm Mon-Fri, 11am-2pm & 6-8.30pm Sat) This small photography shop sells beautiful B&W photos of Salamanca, coffee-table books and photographic equipment.

Municipal Tourist Office Shop (Plaza Mayor 27; ⏲ 10am-2pm & 5-8pm Mon-Sat, 10am-2pm Sun) In addition to the small range of souvenirs sold in the municipal tourist office, there's another shop, under the arches on the north side of Plaza Mayor. It has more to choose from and it's all good.

Getting There & Away

BUS

The **bus station** (☎ 923 23 67 17; Avenida de Filiberto Villalobos 71-85) is northwest of the town centre. **Auto Res** (☎ 902 02 00 52; www.auto-res.net) has hourly departures to Madrid (regular/express €11.82/17.40, three/2½ hours), with other buses going to Valladolid (€7.40, 1½ hours), Ávila (€5.58, 1½ hours) and Segovia (€9.88, 2¾ hours).

El Pilar (☎ 923 22 26 08) has up to 13 daily services (fewer on weekends) to Ciudad Rodrigo (€5.65, 1½ hours), while **Cosme Autocares** (☎ 923 12 08 00) has at least one daily bus, except on Sunday, to La Alberca (€4.75, around 1½ hours), with stops in villages of the Sierra de Francia such as Mogarraz and San Martín del Castañar.

Almost hourly buses operate to/from Zamora (€4.25, one hour), with less-frequent departures to Candelario (€5.60, 1¾ hours).

CAR & MOTORCYCLE

The N501 leads southeast to Madrid via Ávila; the N630 heads north to Zamora. For Portugal, take the N620 west via Ciudad Rodrigo. For the Sierra de Francia, take the C512.

There are few underground parking stations (€9 to €13 for 12 hours) in the old part of town – your best bet is along or just off Calle Gran Vía.

TRAIN

Up to eight trains depart daily for Madrid's Chamartín station (€16.50, 2½ hours) via Ávila (€8.40, one hour). There are also frequent services to Valladolid (from €7.50, 1½ hours).

Getting Around

Bus 4 runs past the bus station and around the old town perimeter to Calle Gran Vía. From the train station, the best bet is bus 1, which heads into the centre along Calle de Azafranal. Going the other way, it can be picked up at the Mercado Central.

AROUND SALAMANCA

The town of **Alba de Tormes** makes for quite an interesting and very easily accomplished half-day excursion from Salamanca. People come here from far and wide to pay homage to Santa Teresa, who is buried in the **Convento de las Carmelitas** she founded in 1570. There's also the stout and highly visible **Torreón**, the only surviving section of the former castle of the Duques de Alba. There are regular buses (every two hours on weekends) from Salamanca's bus station to Alba de Tormes.

CIUDAD RODRIGO

pop 14,000

Close to the Portuguese border and away from well-travelled tourist routes, somnambulant Ciudad Rodrigo is one of the prettier towns in western Castilla y León. It's an easy day trip from Salamanca, 80km away, but sleeping within the sanctuary of its walls enables you to better appreciate its medieval charm – and you'll have the sloping Plaza Mayor all to yourself after the tourist crowds return home.

Information

Post office (Calle de Dámaso Ledesma 12)

Tourist office (☎ 923 49 84 00; www.ciudadrodrigo.net; Plaza Mayor 27; 10am-1.30pm & 4-7pm Tue-Sun, longer hours Jul & Aug)

Sights

The **catedral** (Plaza de San Salvador; admission €2, free Wed afternoon; 10am-1pm & 4-9pm), begun in 1165, towers over the old walled town. Of particular interest are the Puerta de las Cadenas, with Gothic reliefs of Old Testament figures; the elegant Pórtico del Perdón; and, inside, the exquisite carved-oak choir stalls.

Even if you've nothing to post, the **correos** (post office; Calle de Dámaso Ledesma 12) is worth passing by to admire the *artesonado*, while the 1st-floor gallery of the **ayuntamiento** (town hall) is a prime vantage point overlooking Plaza Mayor. The fusion of 12th-century Romanesque-Mudéjar elements with later Gothic modifications makes the **Iglesia de San Isidoro** worth seeking out. The 16th-century **Palacio de los Castro** (Plaza del Conde 3; admission free; 9am-7pm Mon-Sat) boasts one of the town's most engaging plateresque facades; only the patio is open to visitors.

You can also climb the **city walls** and follow their length of about 2.2km around the town for good views over the surrounding plains.

Festivals & Events

Carnaval in February is celebrated with great enthusiasm in Ciudad Rodrigo. In addition to the outlandish fancy dress, you can witness (or join in) a colourful *encierro* (running of the bulls) and *capeas* (amateur bullfights).

Sleeping

Pensión París (☎ 923 48 23 49; Calle del Toro 10; s with washbasin €16-20, d with washbasin €28-40) There's nothing inspirational about these simple rooms with shared bathroom, although they're well kept and tidy (if a little overpriced in summer). The location is ideal, down a quiet street within sight of Plaza Mayor.

Hostal Puerta del Sol (☎ 923 46 06 71; fax 923 46 08 02; Rúa del Sol 33; s/d from €38/43) One of the better *hostales* within the city walls, the Puerta del Sol has comfortable rooms with satellite TV.

our pick **Hospedería Audiencia Real** (☎ 923 49 84 98; www.audienciareal.com in Spanish; Plaza Mayor 17; d €40-80;) Right on Plaza Mayor and with lovely rooms with wrought-iron furniture and exposed brickwork, this fine *hospedería* (inn) could just be our favourite spot in town. The more expensive rooms come with balconies overlooking the plaza.

Parador Enrique II (☎ 923 46 01 50; www.parador.es; Plaza del Castillo 1; d from €155;) Ciudad Rodrigo's premier address is a plushly renovated castle built into the town's western wall. The views are good, the rooms brimful of character and the restaurant easily the best in town.

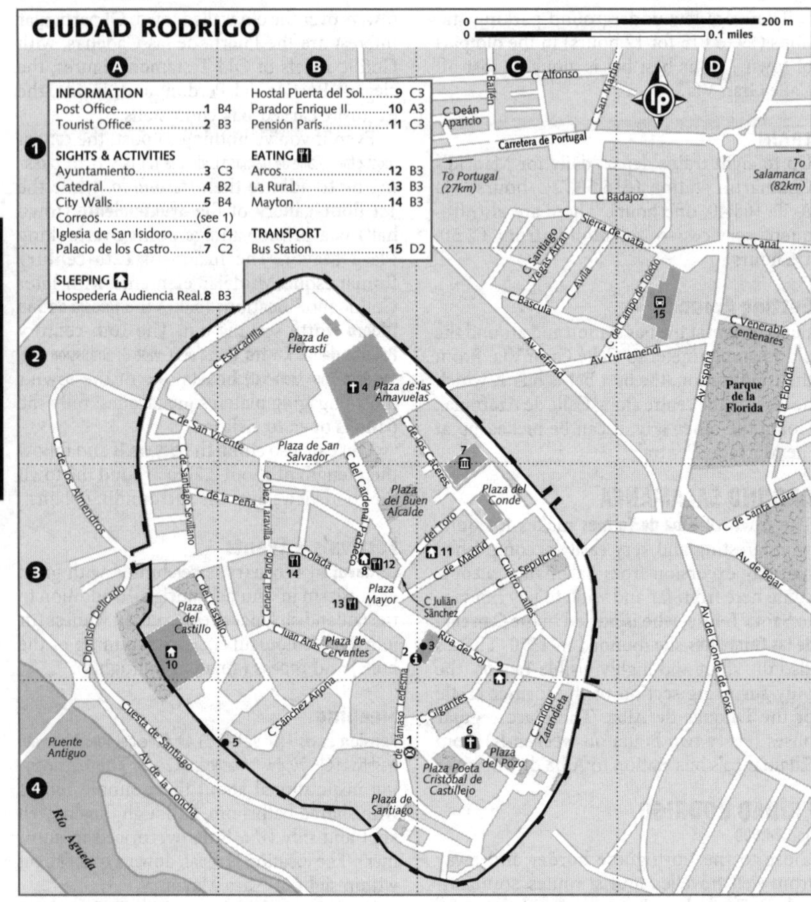

Eating

Arcos (Plaza Mayor; 🕑 9am-late) A good spot for breakfast and snacks or just a coffee, this is a fine front-row seat for watching the town's goings-on.

La Rural (Plaza Mayor; tapas from €0.75, raciones €3.50-5; 🕑 8am-midnight Mon-Sat) Across the square from Arcos, La Rural is always busy and deservedly so for its cheap tapas.

Mayton (☎ 923 46 07 20; Calle Colada 9; menú del día €10, meals €25) Set in an old stone mansion – but without the prohibitive price tag you would expect to find – Mayton promises quality home-style cooking. The region's outstanding *embutidos* feature alongside *cordero,* and there is an overflowing, atmospheric wine cellar.

Getting There & Away

El Pilar (☎ 923 22 26 08) has up to 13 daily services (fewer on weekends) to Salamanca (€5.65, 1½ hours). For the Sierra de Francia, you'll need to go via Salamanca.

SIERRA DE FRANCIA

Hidden away in a remote corner of southwestern Castilla y León, this mountainous region with wooded hillsides and pretty stone-and-timber villages is among Castilla y León's best-kept secrets. Quiet mountain roads connect villages that you could easily spend days exploring and where the pace of life remains untouched by the modern world. Best of all, its architecture is yet to succumb to the ill-conceived developments that have come to blight other once-idyllic corners of Spain.

This was once one of Spain's most god-forsaken regions. Malaria-ridden until the early 20th century, the region hadn't improved much in 1932 when Luís Buñuel came to film *Las Hurdes – Terre Sans Pain* (Land Without Bread). When King Alfonso XIII visited in June 1922, the only milk available for his coffee was human! Touched by this abject misery, or perhaps hoping for something a little more palatable on his next visit, he was supposedly responsible for the introduction of the area's first cows.

La Alberca

pop 1160 / elev 1048m

La Alberca is one of the largest and most beautifully preserved of the Sierra de Francia's villages, a historic and harmonious huddle of narrow alleys flanked by gloriously ramshackle houses built of stone, wood beams and plaster. Numerous stores sell local products such as *jamón* (ham) and *turrón* (nougat), galleries of local artists abound, and cosy bars and restaurants cluster on the pretty-as-a-postcard Plaza Mayor and along Calle de Tablado. Spanish tourists threaten to overwhelm the town on summer weekends, so plan to come during the week and make an overnight stop to see La Alberca at its best.

Housed in one of La Alberca's most evocative half-timbered buildings, **Hostal La Alberca** (☎ 923 41 51 16; www.hostallaalberca.com; Plaza del Padre Arsenio; s/d €25/35) is a charming place with comfortable, renovated rooms.

La Alberca's classiest hotel, **Hotel Doña Teresa** (☎ 923 41 53 08; www.hoteldeteresa.com in Spanish; Carretera Mogarraz; s/d from €60/80) is a perfect fit for the village's old-world charm and is just a short stroll from Plaza Mayor. The large rooms combine character (wooden beams and exposed stonework) with all the necessary mod cons (minibars and newly renovated bathrooms). Check out the offers on the website for the best deals. It also has a good restaurant.

Buses travel between La Alberca and Salamanca (€4.75, around 30 minutes) twice daily on weekdays and once a day on weekends.

Around La Alberca

Having your own car enables you to immerse yourself in quiet villages such as **Mogarraz**, east of La Alberca, which has some of the most evocative old houses in the region and is famous for its *embutidos*. **Miranda del Castañar**, further east again, is similarly intriguing, strung out along a narrow ridge, but **San Martín del Castañar** is the most enchanting, with half-timbered stone houses, flowers cascading from balconies, a bubbling stream and a small village bullring at the top of the town.

Hotels are rare in these parts, but *casas rurales* (village or farmstead accommodation) abound, with a handful in each village. Alternatively, **Hostal Las Madras** (☎ 923 43 71 15; www.lasmadras.com; Calle de Barrionuevo 27; d €45), in the quiet, pretty little village of **Villanueva del Condé**, is a wonderful choice. The rooms are warm and filled with wood and tiles, the owners are friendly and there are views from the balconies over the village square or to the surrounding hills. The restaurant is also top quality. You can even see the village mayor riding through town on a horse and announcing the latest news to the men passing the day by the fountain.

For further information and maps of this area, visit the tourist offices in Salamanca (p215) or Ciudad Rodrigo (p223).

Valle de las Batuecas

The drive south into Extremadura through this dreamy valley is spectacular. Just beyond La Alberca, a sweeping panorama of cascading lower mountain ranges opens up before you. The road corkscrews down into the valley before passing through beautiful terrain that has been praised by poets and the playwright Miguel de Unamuno, and which is especially nice in spring when purple heather blankets the hillsides and wildflowers are in bloom.

Peña de Francia

Head north from La Alberca along the C512 and you'll soon strike the turn-off to the highest peak in the area, Peña de Francia (1732m), topped by a monastery and reached by a road that turns perilous after rain. Views extend east to the Sierra de Gredos, south into Extremadura and west towards Portugal.

SIERRA DE BÉJAR

Between the Sierra de Francia and the Sierra de Gredos, the Sierra de Béjar is home to more pretty villages, rolling mountain scenery and a character all its own.

The centre of the region is **Béjar**, whose partly walled old quarters line up at the western end of a high ridge. Among the worthwhile sights is the eye-catching 16th-century **Palacio Ducal**, just west of Plaza Mayor. A charming place to stay in Béjar is the **Antigua Posada** (☎ 923 41 03 33; Calle Victor Gorzo 1; d €49), close to the centre of town and in a lovely old building, while **Hospedaría Real de Béjar** (☎ 923 40 84 94; www.hospederiarealdebejar.com; Plaza de la Piedad 34; s/d from €69/80) is a step up in both price and quality, with stylish rooms and supermodern amenities.

Just east of the mountains, the C500 leads to **El Barco de Ávila**, which has a pretty setting on Río Tormes and is lorded over by a proud if ruinous castle.

The most scenic village in the region is tiny **Candelario** (population 1020), a 5km detour from Béjar. Rubbing against a steep mountain face, this charming enclave is a popular summer resort and a great base for outdoor activities. Like the villages of the Sierra de Francia, the village is dominated by mountain architecture of stone-and-wood houses clustered closely together to protect against the harsh winter climate.

Hotel Cinco Castaños (☎ 923 41 32 04; www.candelariohotel.com; Carretera de la Sierra s/n; s €39-54, d €54-60) has two stars and is our pick of the places to stay in Candelario. It's set amid the hills within walking distance of the village, and has simple but pleasant rooms, great views and a fine restaurant. **Mesón La Romana** (☎ 923 41 32 72; Calle de Núñez Losada; menú del día €11, meals €15-20) does reasonably priced meats cooked on an open wood-fire grill.

Béjar and Candelario are served by sporadic bus services from Salamanca and various other destinations, including Madrid and Plasencia.

THE CENTRAL PLATEAU

There's something soul-stirring about the high *meseta* (plateau) with its seemingly endless horizon. But from the plains spring the delightful towns of the Castilla y León heartland – magical Segovia, energetic Valladolid, the Romanesque glories of Zamora and the exceptional cathedral of Palencia.

SEGOVIA

pop 56,100 / elev 1002m

Unesco World Heritage–listed Segovia has always had a whiff of legend about it, not least in the myths that Segovia was founded by Hercules or by the son of Noah. It may also have something to do with the fact that nowhere else in Spain has such a stunning monument to Roman grandeur (the soaring aqueduct) survived in the heart of a vibrant modern city. Or maybe it's because art really has imitated life Segovia-style – Walt Disney is said to have modelled Sleeping Beauty's castle in California's Disneyland on Segovia's Alcázar. Whatever it is, the effect is stunning: a city of warm terracotta and sandstone hues set amid the rolling hills of Castilla and against the backdrop of the Sierra de Guadarrama.

History

Founded by Celtiberian tribes, Segovia was occupied by the Romans in 80 BC and rose to become an important town of Roman Hispania. As Christian Spain recovered from the initial shock of the Muslim attack, Segovia became something of a frontline city until the invaders were definitively evicted in 1085. Later a favourite residence of Castilla's roaming royalty, the city backed Isabel and saw her proclaimed queen in the Iglesia de San Miguel in 1474. After backing the wrong side in the Guerra de las Comunidades (War of the Communities) in 1520, Segovia slid into obscurity until the 1960s, when tourism helped regenerate the town. This rebirth gained added momentum in 1985 when the old town and aqueduct were added to Unesco's World Heritage list, bringing Segovia to the attention of the world and sparking a tourist boom that has not yet abated.

Orientation

The old town of Segovia rises in the east and ends in the fanciful towers of the Alcázar (Islamic-era fortress) to the west. If you arrive by train, bus 2 will take you to Plaza Mayor, site of the cathedral and tourist office, and close to plenty of hotels, restaurants and bars. From the bus station, it's about a 15-minute walk north. Calle de Juan Bravo, the road connecting Plaza Mayor and the aqueduct, is a pedestrian thoroughfare that locals know simply as Calle Real.

Information

Banks abound along Calle de Juan Bravo, near Plaza Mayor, and on Avenida de Fernández Ladreda.

Centro de Recepción de Visitantes (tourist office; ☎ 921 46 67 20; www.turismodesegovia.com; Plaza del Azoguejo 1; 🕓 10am-7pm Sun-Fri, 10am-8pm Sat)

Emergency (☎ 112)
Hospital General (☎ 921 41 91 00) About 2.5km southwest of the aqueduct on the road to Ávila.
InternetCaf (☎ 921 42 51 58; Calle de Teodosio El Grande 10; per hr €2; 9am-11pm) Internet access.
Main post office (Plaza del Doctor Laguna 5)
Policía Nacional (☎ 091; cnr Paseo de Ezequiel González & Carretera de Ávila)
Regional tourist office (☎ 921 46 03 34, 902 20 30 30; www.segoviaturismo.es; Plaza Mayor 10; 9am-2pm & 5-8pm daily mid-Sep–Jun, 9am-8pm Sun-Thu, 9am-9pm Fri & Sat Jul–mid-Sep)

Sights

EL ACUEDUCTO & AROUND

Segovia's most recognisable symbol is El Acueducto (Roman aqueduct), an 894m-long engineering wonder that looks like an enormous comb plunged into Segovia. First raised here by the Romans in the 1st century AD, the aqueduct was built with not a drop of mortar to hold the more than 20,000 uneven granite blocks together. It's made up of 163 arches and, at its highest point in Plaza del Azoguejo, rises 28m high. It was most probably built around AD 50 as part of a complex system of aqueducts and underground canals that brought water from the mountains more than 15km away. By some accounts, it once reached as far as the Alcázar. The aqueduct's pristine condition is attributable to a major restoration project in the 1990s. Sadly, the aqueduct and other monuments are only illuminated at night on weekends and during Easter.

Before delving into the old town, there are a few churches worth your time. **Iglesia de San Millán**, off Avenida de Fernández Ladreda, is a time-worn example of the Romanesque style typical of Segovia, with porticoes and a Mudéjar bell tower. A couple of other late-Romanesque churches around here are the **Iglesia de San Justo** (Plaza de San Justo; admission by donation; 11am-2pm & 4-6pm Mon-Sat) and the **Iglesia de San Clemente** (Plaza de San Clemente).

TO THE CATEDRAL

From Plaza del Azoguejo, beside the aqueduct, Calle Real winds up into the heart of Segovia. About a quarter of the way up to Plaza Mayor is the **Casa de los Picos** (☎ 921 46 26 74; admission free; noon-2pm & 6-8pm Mon-Fri Sep-Feb, noon-2pm & 7-9pm Mon-Fri Mar-Aug), a Renaissance mansion with a diamond-shaped facade that's home to a school of applied arts and hosts free exhibitions.

A little further on you reach **Plaza de San Martín**, one of the most captivating little squares in Segovia. The square is presided over by a statue of Juan Bravo and the 14th-century **Torreón de Lozoya** (☎ 921 46 24 61; admission free; 5-9pm Tue-Fri, noon-2pm & 5-9pm Sat & Sun), a tower that was once an armoury and now houses exhibitions. The pièce de résistance, however, is the Romanesque **Iglesia de San Martín**, with the *segoviano* touch of a Mudéjar tower and arched gallery. The interior boasts a Flemish Gothic chapel.

In a perfect marriage of space and function, the **Museo de Arte Contemporáneo Esteban Vicente** (☎ 921 46 20 10; www.museoestebanvicente.es; Plazuela de las Bellas Artes s/n; adult/concession €2.40/1.20, free Thu; 11am-2pm & 4-7pm Mon & Wed, 11am-2pm & 4-8pm Thu & Fri, 11am-8pm Sat, 11am-3pm Sun) occupies a 15th-century palace of Enrique IV, complete with Renaissance chapel and Mudéjar ceiling. Some 148 abstract paintings and sculptures by Segovia-born artist Esteban Vicente (1903–2000), a fine painter of the abstract expressionist school, form the core of the exhibit.

The shady **Plaza Mayor** is the hub of old Segovia, lined by an eclectic assortment of buildings, arcades and cafes with an open pavilion in its centre. The **Iglesia de San Miguel**, where Isabel was proclaimed Queen of Castilla, recedes humbly into the background before the splendour of the cathedral across the square.

CATEDRAL

Started in 1525 after its Romanesque predecessor had burned to the ground in the War of the Communities, the **catedral** (☎ 921 46 22 05; Plaza Mayor; adult/concession €3/2, free Sunday 9.30am-1.15pm; 9.30am-5.30pm Oct-Mar, 9.30am-6.30pm Apr-Sep) is a final, powerful expression of Gothic architecture in Spain that took almost 200 years to complete. The austere three-naved interior is anchored by an imposing choir stall and enlivened by 20-odd chapels. One of these, the Capilla del Cristo del Consuelo, houses a magnificent Romanesque doorway preserved from the original church. The Capilla de la Piedad contains an important altarpiece by Juan de Juni, while the Capilla del Cristo Yacente and Capilla del Santísimo Sacramento are also especially beautiful. The Gothic cloister is lovely, while the attached

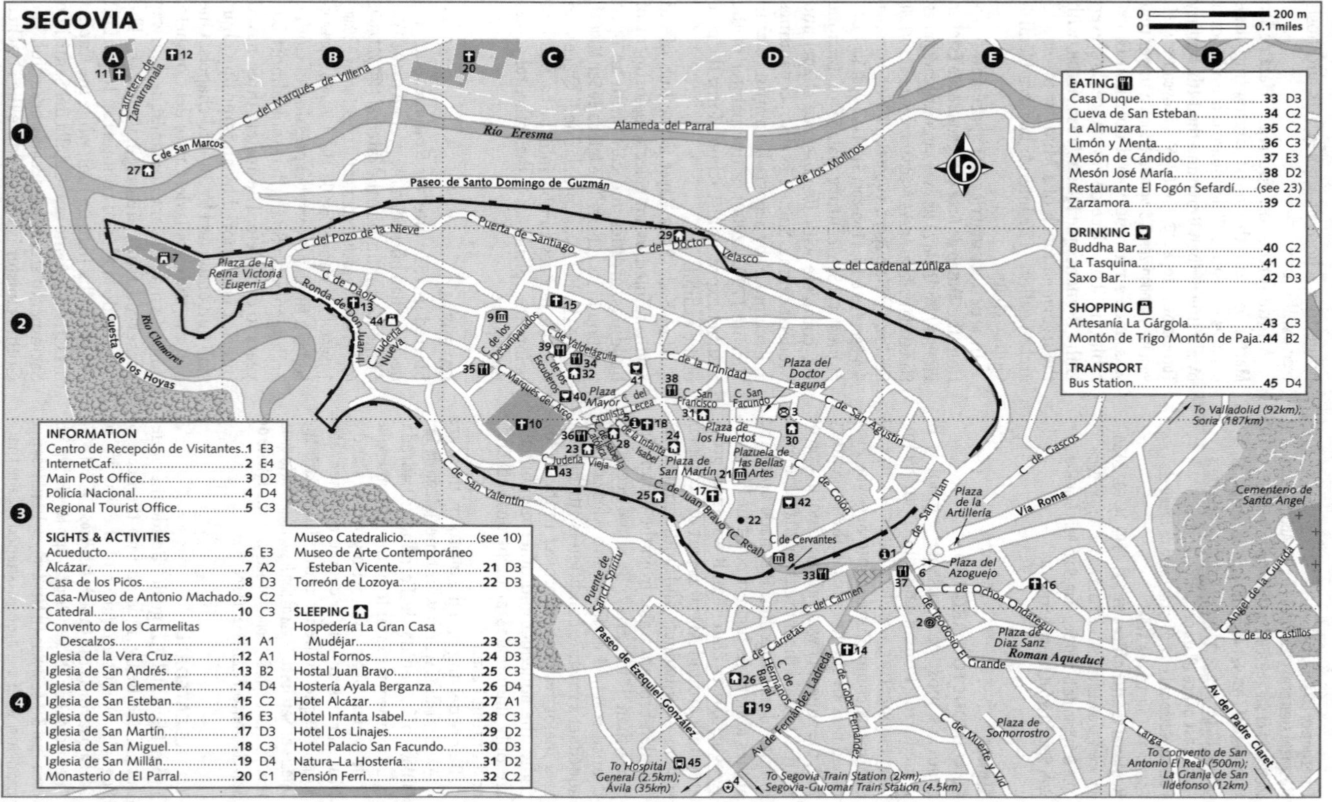
SEGOVIA
0 200 m
0 0.1 miles
INFORMATION
Centro de Recepción de Visitantes..1 E3
InternetCaf..................2 E4
Main Post Office..................3 D2
Policía Nacional..................4 D4
Regional Tourist Office..................5 C3
SIGHTS & ACTIVITIES
Acueducto..................6 E3
Alcázar..................7 A2
Casa de los Picos..................8 D3
Casa-Museo de Antonio Machado..9 C2
Catedral..................10 C3
Convento de los Carmelitas Descalzos..................11 A1
Iglesia de la Vera Cruz..................12 A1
Iglesia de San Andrés..................13 B2
Iglesia de San Clemente..................14 D4
Iglesia de San Esteban..................15 C2
Iglesia de San Justo..................16 E3
Iglesia de San Martín..................17 D3
Iglesia de San Miguel..................18 C3
Iglesia de San Millán..................19 D4
Monasterio de El Parral..................20 C1
Museo Catedralicio..................(see 10)
Museo de Arte Contemporáneo Esteban Vicente..................21 D3
Torreón de Lozoya..................22 D3
SLEEPING
Hospedería La Gran Casa Mudéjar..................23 C3
Hostal Fornos..................24 D3
Hostal Juan Bravo..................25 C3
Hostería Ayala Berganza..................26 D4
Hotel Alcázar..................27 A1
Hotel Infanta Isabel..................28 C3
Hotel Los Linajes..................29 D2
Hotel Palacio San Facundo..................30 D3
Natura–La Hostería..................31 D2
Pensión Ferri..................32 C2
EATING
Casa Duque..................33 D3
Cueva de San Esteban..................34 C2
La Almuzara..................35 C2
Limón y Menta..................36 C3
Mesón de Cándido..................37 E3
Mesón José María..................38 D2
Restaurante El Fogón Sefardí......(see 23)
Zarzamora..................39 C2
DRINKING
Buddha Bar..................40 C2
La Tasquina..................41 C2
Saxo Bar..................42 D3
SHOPPING
Artesanía La Gárgola..................43 C3
Montón de Trigo Montón de Paja..44 B2
TRANSPORT
Bus Station..................45 D4
Río Eresma
Río Clamores
Alameda del Parral
Paseo de Santo Domingo de Guzmán
C del Marqués de Villena
C de San Marcos
Carretera de Zamarramala
C de los Molinos
C del Cardenal Zúñiga
C del Pozo de la Nieve
C Puerta de Santiago
C del Doctor Velasco
Plaza de la Reina Victoria Eugenia
Ronda de Don Juan II
C de Daoiz
C Judería Nueva
Cuesta de los Hoyas
C de los Desamparados
C de Valdeláguila
C de los Escuderos
C Marqués del Arco
Plaza Mayor
C del Cronista Lecea
C de la Trinidad
C San Francisco
C San Facundo
Plaza del Doctor Laguna
C de San Agustín
Plaza de los Huertos
Plazuela de las Bellas Artes
Plaza de San Martín
C de la Infanta Isabel
C de Isabel la Católica
C Judería Vieja
C de San Valentín
C de Juan Bravo (C Real)
C de Colón
C de Cervantes
C de San Juan
Plaza de la Artillería
Vía Roma
C de Gascos
Plaza del Azoguejo
C de Ochoa Ondategui
C de Teodosio El Grande
Plaza de Díaz Sanz
Roman Aqueduct
C del Carmen
C de Carretas
C de Hermanos Barral
Av de Fernández Ladreda
C de Gober Fernández
C de Muerte y Vid
Plaza de Somorrostro
C Larga
Av del Padre Claret
C Ángel de la Guarda
C de los Castillos
Cementerio de Santo Ángel
Puente de Sancti Spíritu
Paseo de Ezequiel González
To Valladolid (92km); Soria (187km)
To Convento de San Antonio El Real (500m); La Granja de San Ildefonso (12km)
To Segovia Train Station (2km); Segovia-Guiomar Train Station (4.5km)
To Hospital General (2.5km); Ávila (35km)

Museo Catedralicio will appeal to devotees of religious art.

TO THE ALCÁZAR
The direct route to the Alcázar from Plaza Mayor is via Calle Marqués del Arco. About halfway along you pass yet another Romanesque church, the **Iglesia de San Andrés**. Away to the right is the **Casa-Museo de Antonio Machado** (☎ 921 46 03 77; Calle de los Desamparados 5; admission €1.50, free Wed; 🕑 11am-2pm & 4.30-7.30pm Wed-Sun). Machado, one of Spain's pre-eminent 20th-century poets, lived here from 1919 to 1932 and his former home contains his furnishings and personal effects. A few paces further down the road rises the lovely six-level sandstone tower of the 13th-century Romanesque **Iglesia de San Esteban**, which has a baroque interior.

ALCÁZAR
Rapunzel towers, turrets topped with slate witches' hats and a *deep* moat at its base make the **Alcázar** (☎ 921 46 07 59; www.alcazardesegovia.com; Plaza de la Reina Victoria Eugenia; adult/concession €4/3, tower €2, EU citizens free 3rd Tue of month; 🕑 10am-6pm Oct-Mar, 10am-7pm Apr-Sep) a prototype fairy-tale castle, so much so that its design inspired Walt Disney's vision of Sleeping Beauty's castle. Fortified since Roman days, the site takes its name from the Arabic *al-qasr* (fortress). It was rebuilt and expanded in the 13th and 14th centuries, but the whole lot burned down in 1862. What you see today is an evocative, over-the-top reconstruction of the original.

Highlights include the **Sala de las Piñas**, the ceiling of which drips with a crop of 392 pineapple-shaped 'stalactites', and the **Sala de Reyes**, featuring a three-dimensional frieze of 52 sculptures of kings who fought during the Reconquista. The views from the summit of the **Torre de Juan II** are truly exceptional, and put the old town's hilltop location into full context.

CHURCHES & CONVENTS
Another smorgasbord of religious buildings stretches across the luxuriant valley of Río Eresma to the north of the city.

The most interesting of Segovia's churches, and one of the best-preserved of its kind in Europe, is the 12-sided **Iglesia de la Vera Cruz** (☎ 921 43 14 75; admission €1.75; 🕑 10.30am-1.30pm & 4-7pm Tue-Sun Apr-Aug, 10.30am-1.30pm & 4-6pm Tue-Sun Sep-Mar, closed Nov). Built in the 13th century by the Knights Templar and based on the Church of the Holy Sepulchre in Jerusalem, it long housed what is said to be a piece of the Vera Cruz (True Cross), now in the nearby village church of Zamarramala (on view only at Easter). The curious two-storey chamber in the circular nave is where the knights stood vigil over the holy relic. For fantastic views of the town and the Sierra de Guadarrama, walk uphill behind the church for approximately 1km.

Just west of Vera Cruz is the **Convento de los Carmelitas Descalzos** (☎ 921 43 13 49; admission by donation; 🕑 10am-1.30pm & 4-7pm Tue-Sun, 4-7pm Mon, closed 1hr earlier in winter), where San Juan de la Cruz is buried. The area immediately south of the convent affords fine views up to the Alcázar. A little further east is the **Monasterio de El Parral** (☎ 921 43 12 98; admission by donation; 🕑 10am-12.30pm & 4.15-6.30pm Mon-Sat, 10-11.30am & 4.15-6.30pm Sun). Ring the bell to see part of the cloister and church; the latter is a proud, flamboyant Gothic structure. The monks chant a Gregorian Mass at noon on Sundays, and at 1pm daily in summer.

About 1.3km southeast of the aqueduct, the **Convento de San Antonio El Real** (☎ 921 42 02 28; off Avenida de Padre Claret; adult/child €3/free, admission free 9.30am-1.15pm Sun; 🕑 10am-2pm & 4-7pm Tue-Sat, 9.30am-2pm Sun) was once the summer residence of Enrique IV. Its Gothic–Mudéjar church has a splendid ceiling.

THE DEVIL'S WORK
Although no one really doubts that the Romans built the aqueduct, a local legend asserts that two millennia ago a young girl, tired of carrying water from the well, voiced a willingness to sell her soul to the devil if an easier solution could be found. No sooner said than done. The devil worked through the night, while the girl recanted and prayed to God for forgiveness. Hearing her prayers, God sent the sun into the sky earlier than usual, catching the devil unawares with only a single stone lacking to complete the structure. The girl's soul was saved, but it seems like she got her wish anyway. Perhaps God didn't have the heart to tear down the aqueduct.

Festivals & Events
Segovianos let their hair down for the **Fiestas de San Juan y San Pedro**, celebrated from 24 to

29 June with parades, concerts and bullfights. On San Juan's day, a pilgrimage takes place to a hermitage outside town, where, says a tourist office handout, 'according to tradition and owing to the profound state of merriment caused by the abundant consumption of spirits, the sun is supposed to rise going around in circles'. We make no comment.

The **Fiesta San Frutos**, on 25 October, celebrates the town's patron saint, who is said to be the healer of hernias and bodily fractures. The event is marked in the cathedral with choral singing.

Sleeping

Segovia's accommodation just gets better all the time, whatever your price range, whatever your taste, but especially in the midrange category.

BUDGET

Pensión Ferri (☎ 921 46 09 57; Calle de los Escuderos 10; s/d without bathroom €18/28) Occupying an old house in a superb location, this is a good budget choice. The rooms are simple but quaint and incorporate some of the building's original wood and brickwork.

our pick **Hostal Juan Bravo** (☎ 921 46 34 13; Calle de Juan Bravo 12; d with washbasin/bathroom €35/43) Another excellent choice with sparkling rooms, Hostal Juan Bravo has rooms at the back with stunning views of the Sierra de Guadarrama. The friendly owners round out a great package.

Hostal Fornos (☎ 921 46 01 98; www.hostalfornos.com in Spanish; Calle de la Infanta Isabel 13; s €34-41, d €48-55) This tidy little *hostal* is a cut above most places in this price category. It has a cheerful air thanks to rooms that have that fresh white-linen-and-wicker-chair look. Some are larger than others, but the value is unimpeachable.

MIDRANGE & TOP END

Natura – La Hostería (☎ 921 46 67 10; www.naturadesegovia.com in Spanish; Calle de Colón 5-7; d from €60; ❄) An eclectic choice a few streets back from Plaza Mayor, it has contemporary art on the public walls (think Dalí) and brightly painted rooms with old wooden furnishings. It won't be to everyone's taste, but it does have personality.

our pick **Hospedería La Gran Casa Mudéjar** (☎ 921 46 62 50; www.lacasamudejar.com; Calle de Isabel La Católica 8; d €60-160; ❄ 💻) Spread over two buildings, this place has been magnificently renovated, blending genuine, 15th-century Mudéjar ceilings in some rooms with modern amenities. In the newer wing, where the building dates from the 19th century, the rooms on the top floors have fine mountain views out over the rooftops of Segovia's old Jewish quarter.

Hotel Infanta Isabel (☎ 921 46 13 00; www.hotelinfantaisabel.com; Plaza Mayor 12; s €64-128, d €83-128; ❄) Right on Plaza Mayor, this charming hotel is a fine choice. The colonnaded building provides some hint to the hotel's interior, where most rooms have period furnishings and plenty of character. Rooms are large and those with balconies overlooking Plaza Mayor are best, if a little noisy on weekends.

Hotel Los Linajes (☎ 921 46 04 75; www.hotelloslinajes.com; Calle del Doctor Valesco 9; s €66-78, d €89-106; ❄) For some of the best views in Segovia, Hotel Los Linajes is exceptionally good. The rooms are large and filled with character, and all look out onto the hills; many also have cathedral and/or Alcázar views.

Hotel Palacio San Facundo (☎ 921 46 30 61; www.hotelpalaciosanfacundo.com; Plaza San Facundo 4; s/d from €82/102; ❄ 💻) Segovia's hotels are proving adept at fusing stylishly appointed modern rooms onto centuries-old architecture, and this place is one of the best. A gorgeous courtyard, warm colour schemes, friendly service and a central location add up to a great package.

Hostería Ayala Berganza (☎ 921 46 04 48; www.partner-hotels.com; Calle de Carretas 5; d €115-150; ❄ 💻) This boutique hotel has elegant, individually designed rooms (all have tiled floors, beautiful bathrooms and rustic accents) within a restored 15th-century palace. It's not far from the aqueduct, but it's quiet and oozes style. Watch for internet offers, as doubles can fall as low as €60.

Hotel Alcázar (☎ 921 43 85 68; www.alcazar-hotel.com; Calle de San Marcos 5; d €125-165; ❄) Sitting by the riverbank in the valley beneath the Alcázar, this charming, tranquil little hotel has lavish rooms beautifully styled to suit those who love old-world luxury. Breakfast (€10) on the back terrace is a lovely way to pass the morning, and there's an intimacy and graciousness about the whole experience.

Eating

Segovianos love their pigs to the point of obsession. Just about every restaurant proudly boasts its *horno de asar* (roasts) and they say that 'pork has 40 flavours – all of them good'. The main speciality is *cochinillo asado* (roast suckling pig), but *judiones de la granja* (lima beans with pork chunks) also looms large on menus. The local dessert is a rich, sweet concoction drenched in *ponche*, a popular Spanish spirit, and hence known as *ponche segoviano*.

Limón y Menta (☎ 921 44 21 41; Calle de Isabel La Católica 2; 🕑 8am-11pm) This is the place to head for a mouthwatering array of biscuits and pastries, including some of the best *ponche segoviano* around.

Zarzamora (☎ 921 46 12 47; Calle de Valdeláguila s/n; meals €10-15; 🕑 6pm-midnight Tue-Sun) Down the hill from Plaza Mayor, Zarzamora is a gem offering healthy pasta and meat dishes, fruit tarts and other home cooking. It's like eating in your own cosy kitchen.

La Almuzara (☎ 921 46 06 22; Calle Marqués del Arco 3; meals €15; 🕑 lunch & dinner Tue-Sat, dinner only Sun; V) If you're a vegetarian, you don't need to feel like an outcast in this resolutely carnivorous city. La Almuzara features lots of vegetarian dishes, pastas and salads, and the ambience is warm and artsy.

Casa Duque (☎ 921 46 24 87; www.restauranteduque.es; Calle de Cervantes 12; menús del día €21-40) They've been serving *cochinillo asado* (€19) here since the 1890s and long ago mastered the art. For the uninitiated, try the *menú segoviano* (€31), which includes *cochinillo*, or the *menú gastronómico* (€40), which gives a taste of many local specialities. Downstairs is the informal *cueva* (cave), where you can get tapas and yummy *cazuelas* (stews).

Mesón José María (☎ 921 46 11 11; www.rtejosemaria.com in Spanish; Calle del Cronista Lecea 11; meals €30-40) Close to Plaza Mayor, this respected *mesón* (tavern) offers great tapas in the bar and five dining rooms serving exquisite *cochinillo* (€21) and other local specialities.

our pick **Restaurante El Fogón Sefardí** (☎ 921 46 62 50; www.lacasamudejar.com; Calle de Isabel La Católica 8; meals €30-40) This is one of the most original places in town, serving Sephardic cuisine in a restaurant with an intimate patio or a splendid dining hall with original, 15th-century Mudéjar flourishes. There are also cheaper Sephardic tapas in the bar downstairs, as well as *cochinillo* in the main restaurant.

Mesón de Cándido (☎ 921 42 59 11; www.mesondecandido.es; Plaza del Azoguejo 5; meals €30-40) Set in a delightful 18th-century building in the shadow of the aqueduct, Mesón de Cándido is another place famous throughout Spain for its suckling pig and roast lamb.

Cueva de San Esteban (☎ 921 46 09 82; www.lacuevadesanesteban.com in Spanish; Calle de Valdeláguila 15; meals €35; 🕑 11am-midnight) One of the only restaurants in Segovia not devoted to suckling pig, this popular spot focuses on seasonal dishes, with a few Galician treats and an excellent wine list.

WHAT'S COOKING IN CASTILLA Y LEÓN?

Castilla y León's cuisine owes everything to climate. There's no better way to fortify yourself against the bitterly cold winters of the high plateau than with *cordero asado* (roast lamb), a signature dish from Sepúlveda to Burgos and every town in between. *Cochinillo asado* (roast suckling pig) is a speciality of Segovia. Other regional specialities include *morcilla de Burgos* (blood sausage mixed with rice, from Burgos), *chuleton de Ávila* (T-bone steak, from Ávila) and *embutidos* (cured meats such as *jamón* and chorizo). The *jamón* from Guijelo, south of Salamanca, is recognised throughout Spain as belonging to the elite.

Drinking & Entertainment

In fine weather, Plaza Mayor is the obvious place for hanging out and people-watching. Calle de la Infanta Isabel is one of those Spanish streets that you'll definitely hear before you see it; locals call it 'Calle de los Bares' (Street of the Bars). Another good street for bars and nightclubs in the same area is Calle de los Escuderos.

La Tasquina (☎ 921 46 19 54; Calle de Valdeláguila 3; 🕑 9pm-late) This wine bar draws crowds large enough to spill out onto the pavement nursing their good wines, *cavas* (sparkling wines) and cheeses.

Saxo Bar (Calle de Seminario 2; 🕑 9pm-3am Wed-Sat) Down the hill a little, this place sometimes has live music, usually jazz.

On Calle de los Escuderos at No 3 you'll find **Buddha Bar** (🕑 9pm-late), with lounge music that can turn more towards house as the night wears on.

Shopping

Artesanía La Gárgola (☎ 670 747080; www.gargolart.com in Spanish; Calle Judería Vieja 4; 🕑 11am-2pm & 5-8pm) There are many shops worth browsing in Segovia, but make sure you check out these unusual, high-quality handmade crafts and souvenirs in ceramic, wood and textile.

Montón de Trigo Montón de Paja (☎ 921 46 07 69; www.montondetrigomontondepaja.com; Plaza de la Merced 1; 🕑 11am-2.30pm & 3.30-7.30pm) With handcrafted handbags, block prints of Segovia and a host of other artsy, locally made items, this shop is ideal for creative gifts.

Getting There & Away

BUS

The bus station is just off Paseo de Ezequiel González, near Avenida de Fernández Ladreda. **La Sepulvedana** (☎ 921 42 77 07; Paseo de Ezequiel González), which is based at the bus station, has half-hourly buses to Segovia from Madrid's Paseo de la Florida bus stop (€5.87, 1½ hours). **Avanza** (☎ 902 02 00 52; www.avanzabus.com) has buses to Ávila (€4.30, 1¼ hours, five daily) and Salamanca (€9.88, 2¾ hours, two daily). **Linecar** (☎ 921 42 77 06; www.linecar.es) has buses that run almost hourly to Valladolid (€7.25, 2¾ hours), with just six departures on Sunday.

CAR & MOTORCYCLE

Of the two main roads down to the AP6, which links Madrid and Galicia, the N603 is the prettier. The alternative N110 cuts southwest across to Ávila and northeast to the main Madrid–Burgos highway. There's only street parking in the old town.

TRAIN

There are two options by train, both operated by **Renfe** (☎ 902 24 02 02; www.renfe.es). Up to nine normal trains run daily from Madrid to Segovia (€5.90 one way, two hours), leaving you at the main train station 2.5km from the aqueduct. The faster option is the high-speed AVE (€9 one-way, 35 minutes), which deposits you at the new Segovia-Guiomar station, 5km from the aqueduct.

Getting Around

Bus 9 (€0.80, half-hourly 10am to 1pm and 4.30pm to 7pm) does a circuit through the old town from just outside the aqueduct, while bus 11 (€0.80, every 15 minutes 6.45am to 9.45pm) connects Segovia-Guiomar station with just outside the aqueduct.

AROUND SEGOVIA

La Granja de San Ildefonso

It's not hard to see why the Bourbon King Felipe V chose this site to recreate in miniature his version of Versailles, the palace of his French grandfather Louis XIV. In 1720 French architects and gardeners, together with some Italian help, began laying out the elaborate and decidedly baroque **gardens** (🕑 10am-6.30pm Oct & Mar, 10am-7pm Apr, 10am-8pm May–mid-Jun & Sep, 10am-9pm mid-Jun–Aug, 10am-6pm Nov-Feb) in the western foothills of the Sierra de Guadarrama, 12km east of Segovia. La Granja's centrepiece is 28 extravagant fountains that depict ancient myths such as those featuring Apollo and Diana. Due to the ageing pipes, they're rarely running, except briefly during Easter.

The 300-room **Palacio Real** (☎ 921 47 18 95; www.patrimonionacional.es), once a favoured summer residence for Spanish royalty and restored after a fire in 1918, is impressive but perhaps the lesser of La Granja's jewels. The palace, including the **Museo de Tapices** (Tapestry Museum), was closed for major restoration works at the time of research.

Up to a dozen daily buses to La Granja depart regularly from Segovia's main bus station (€1.15, 20 minutes).

Pedraza de la Sierra

pop 490

The captivating walled village of Pedraza de la Sierra, about 37km northeast of Segovia, is eerily quiet during the week; its considerable number of restaurants and bars spring to life with the swarms of weekend visitors. At the far end of town stands the lonely **Castillo de Pedraza** (admission €5; 🕑 11am-2pm & 5-8pm Wed-Sun Mar-Aug, 11am-2pm & 4-6pm Wed-Sun Sep-Feb), unusual for its intact outer wall. For a wonderful rural shopping experience, visit **De Natura** (☎ 921 50 98 52; www.casayjardin.es/denatura.htm in Spanish; Calle Calzada 8), a three-storey barn-house filled with quality Castilian bric-a-brac, including furnishings and traditional clay and porcelain crockery.

On the first and second Saturdays of July, Pedraza hosts the atmospheric **Conciertos de las Velas**, when the electricity is shut down and live music is performed in a village lit only by candles.

The excellent **Hospedería de Santo Domingo** (☎ 921 50 99 71; www.hospederiadesantodomingo.com; Calle Matadero 3; s/d from €95/114) has terrific rooms with balconies, most of which overlook a small garden. The terracotta-tiled floors are a nice touch.

Bus services to Pedraza are sporadic at best.

Turégano

pop 1160

Turégano, about 30km north of Segovia, is dominated by a unique 15th-century **castle-church** complex built by the then Archbishop of Segovia, Juan Arias Dávila, who decided to make a personal fortress of the town. At once cutesy and formidable, the castle walls, with their sturdy ramparts and rounded turrets, are built around the facade of the Iglesia de San Miguel; ruined sections of the wall fan out across the surrounding countryside.

Coca

pop 2100

A typically dusty, inward-looking Castilian village, 50km northwest of Segovia, Coca is presided over by a stunning all-brick **castle** (guided tours €2.50; tours 10.30am-1pm & 4.30-7pm Mon-Fri, 11am-1pm & 4-7pm Sat & Sun), a virtuoso piece of Gothic–Mudéjar architecture. Built in 1453 by the powerful Fonseca family, it's surrounded by a deep moat. Entry is by guided tour only during the times listed above – tours start when there is enough people in a group – and it closes one hour earlier in the evening in winter. Up to five buses run daily between Coca and Segovia (€3.15, one hour).

VALLADOLID

pop 316,600

Connected by air to London, Brussels and Milan, and by fast train to Madrid, Valladolid is a city on the upswing and a convenient gateway to northern Spain. An attractive place with a very Spanish character, the city's appeal is in its sprinkling of monuments, the fine Plaza Mayor and its excellent museums. By night, Valladolid comes alive as its large student population overflows from the city's boisterous bars.

Information

You'll find banks with ATMs along Calle de Santiago.

Hospital de Valladolid Felipe II (☎ 983 35 80 00; Calle de Felipe II 9)

Main post office (Plaza de la Rinconada)

Policía Nacional (☎ 091, 983 26 37 04; Calle de Felipe II 11)

Tourist office (☎ 983 21 93 10; www.asomateavalladolid.org; Acera de Recoletos; 9am-2pm & 5-8pm daily mid-Sep–Jun, 9am-8pm Sun-Thu, 9am-9pm Fri & Sat Jul–mid-Sep)

Sights

MUSEO NACIONAL DE ESCULTURA

This **museum** (☎ 983 25 03 75; http://museoescultura.mcu.es; Calle de San Gregorio 2; adult/child/concession €2.40/free/1.20, free Sat afternoon & Sun; 10am-2pm & 4-9pm Tue-Sat, 10am-2pm Sun mid-Mar–Sep, shorter hours rest of year), Spain's premier showcase of polychrome wood sculpture, is housed in the former Colegio de San Gregorio (1496), a flamboyant example of the Isabelline Gothic style where exhibition rooms line a splendid two-storey galleried courtyard.

Works by Alonso de Berruguete, Juan de Juní and Gregorio Fernández are the star attractions, especially some enormously expressive fragments from Berruguete's high altar for Valladolid's Iglesia de San Benito. Downstairs is a small wing dedicated to

IT COULD HAVE BEEN SO DIFFERENT

Wondering why some of the great names of Spanish history – El Cid, Cervantes, Christopher Columbus and the merciless Inquisitor General Fray Tomás de Torquemada – were all connected with Valladolid? It's because the city was considered Spain's capital-in-waiting. In short, Valladolid could have been Madrid.

Fernando of Aragón and Isabel of Castilla discreetly married here in 1469. As Spain's greatest-ever ruling duo, they carried Valladolid to the height of its splendour. Its university was one of the most dynamic on the peninsula and Carlos I made Valladolid the seat of imperial government. Felipe II was born here in 1527 but, 34 years later, chose to make Madrid the capital, even though Madrid was considerably smaller. Valladolid, which had become too powerful for its own good, was aghast. In 1601 Felipe III moved the royal court back to Valladolid, but the move was so unpopular that the court returned to Madrid, there to remain in perpetuity.

With Spain's return to democracy after 1975, the *vallasoletanos* (people from Valladolid) had to be content with their city becoming the administrative capital of the Autonomía de Castilla y León.

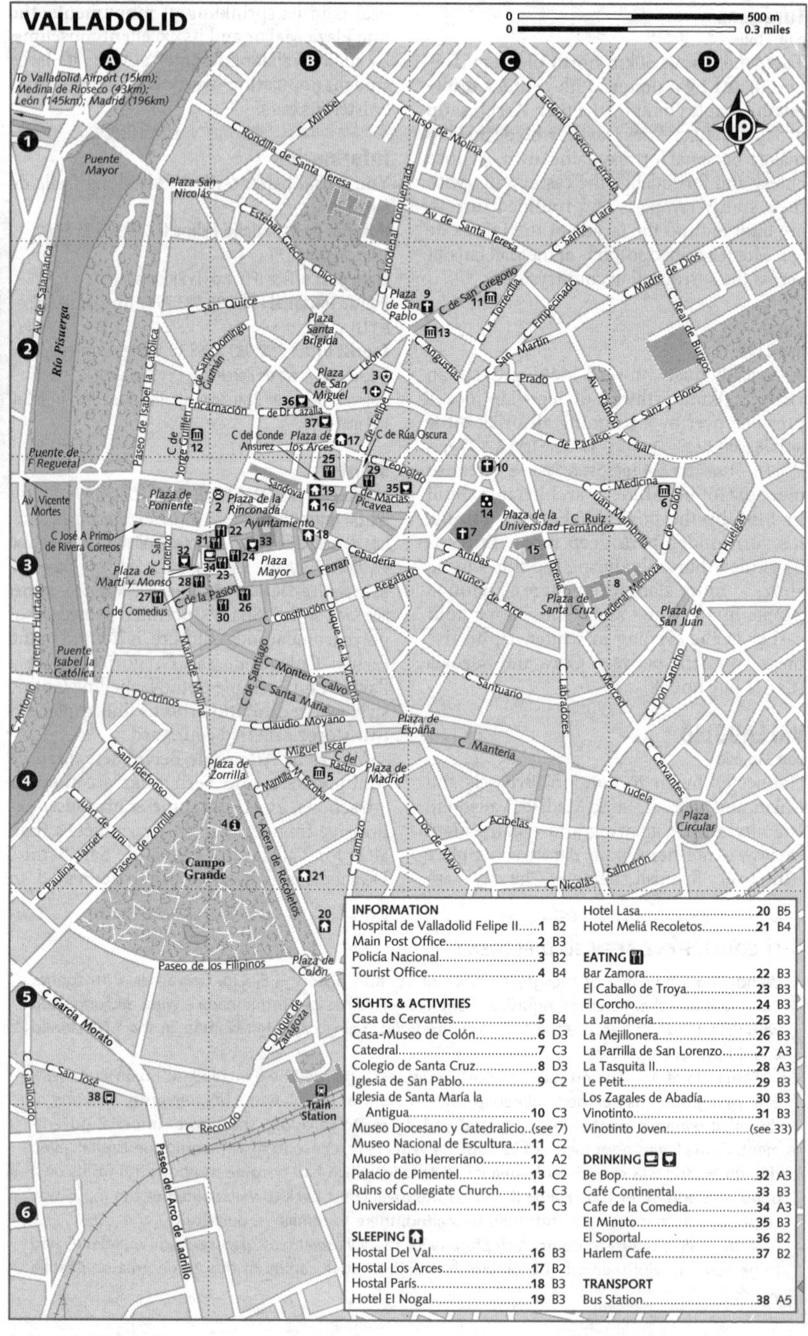
VALLADOLID
0 500 m
0 0.3 miles
A
B
C
D
1
2
3
4
5
6
To Valladolid Airport (15km); Medina de Rioseco (43km); León (145km); Madrid (196km)
Puente Mayor
Río Pisuerga
Plaza San Nicolás
C Rondilla de Santa Teresa
C Mirabel
C Tirso de Molina
C Cardenal Ciseros Cerrada
Av de Santa Teresa
C Santa Clara
C Esteban Grecia Chico
C Carodenal Torquemada
Av de Salamanca
C San Quirce
Plaza de San Pablo
C de San Gregorio
C La Torrecilla
C Empecinado
C Madre de Dios
C Real de Burgos
Plaza Santa Brígida
C Angustias
C San Martín
C Prado
Av Ramón y Cajal
C Sanz y Flores
C de Paraíso
C de Santo Domingo Guzmán
Plaza de San Miguel
C León
C Encarnación
C de Dr Cazalla
C del Conde Ansurez
Plaza de los Arces
C de Felipe II
C de Rúa Oscura
C Leopoldo
C de Jorge Guillén
Paseo de Isabel la Católica
Puente de F Regueral
Av Vicente Mortes
C José A Primo de Rivera Correos
Plaza de Poniente
Plaza de la Rinconada
C Sandoval
C de Macías Picavea
Ayuntamiento
C Medicina
C Juan Mambrilla
C de Colón
C Huelgas
Plaza de la Universidad
C Ruiz Fernández
C San Lorenzo
Plaza de Martí y Monsó
Plaza Mayor
C Cebadería
C Ferrari
C Arribas
C Núñez de Arce
C Librería
Plaza de Santa Cruz
C Cardenal Mendoza
Plaza de San Juan
C de la Pasión
C de Comedius
C Regalado
C Constitución
C Duque de la Victoria
C Lorenzo Hurtado
Puente Isabel la Católica
C Mantadé Molina
C de Santiago
C Montero Calvo
C Santa María
C Santuario
C Labradores
C Merced
C Don Sancho
C Antonio
C Doctrinos
C Claudio Moyano
Plaza de España
C Mantería
C San Ildefonso
C Miguel Iscar
C del Rastro
Plaza de Zorrilla
C Mantilla
C M Escobar
Plaza de Madrid
C Tudela
C Cervantes
Plaza Circular
C Juan de Juni
C Paulina Harriet
Paseo de Zorrilla
C Acera de Recoletos
C Gamazo
C Dos de Mayo
C Acibelas
Campo Grande
C Nicolás Salmerón
Paseo de los Filipinos
Plaza de Colón
C García Morato
C Duque de Zaragoza
C Gabilondo
C San José
Train Station
C Recondo
Paseo del Arco de Ladrillo
INFORMATION
Hospital de Valladolid Felipe II......1 B2
Main Post Office......2 B3
Policía Nacional......3 B2
Tourist Office......4 B4
SIGHTS & ACTIVITIES
Casa de Cervantes......5 B4
Casa-Museo de Colón......6 D3
Catedral......7 C3
Colegio de Santa Cruz......8 D3
Iglesia de San Pablo......9 C2
Iglesia de Santa María la Antigua......10 C3
Museo Diocesano y Catedralicio..(see 7)
Museo Nacional de Escultura......11 C2
Museo Patio Herreriano......12 A2
Palacio de Pimentel......13 C2
Ruins of Collegiate Church......14 C3
Universidad......15 C3
SLEEPING
Hostal Del Val......16 B3
Hostal Los Arces......17 B2
Hostal París......18 B3
Hotel El Nogal......19 B3
Hotel Lasa......20 B5
Hotel Meliá Recoletos......21 B4
EATING
Bar Zamora......22 B3
El Caballo de Troya......23 B3
El Corcho......24 B3
La Jamónería......25 B3
La Mejillonera......26 B3
La Parrilla de San Lorenzo......27 A3
La Tasquita II......28 A3
Le Petit......29 B3
Los Zagales de Abadía......30 B3
Vinotinto......31 B3
Vinotinto Joven......(see 33)
DRINKING
Be Bop......32 A3
Café Continental......33 B3
Cafe de la Comedia......34 A3
El Minuto......35 B3
El Soportal......36 B2
Harlem Cafe......37 B2
TRANSPORT
Bus Station......38 A5

Fernández, whose melodramatic intensity is especially well reflected in his painfully lifelike sculpture of a dead Christ.

PLAZA DE SAN PABLO

Virtually next to the Museo Nacional de Escultura, this open square is dominated by the exquisite **Iglesia de San Pablo**. The church's main facade is an extravagant masterpiece of Isabelline Gothic, with every square inch finely worked, carved and twisted to produce a unique fabric in stone. With major restoration work under way when we visited, we hope you won't have to take our word for it. Also fronting the square is the **Palacio de Pimentel**, where, on 12 July 1527, Felipe II was born. A tiled mural in the palace's entrance hall depicts scenes from the life of the king. The palace hosts occasional exhibitions.

MUSEO PATIO HERRERIANO

Dedicated to post-WWI Spanish art, this **museum** (☎ 983 36 29 08; www.museopatioherreriano.org in Spanish; Calle de Jorge Guillén 6; adult/concession €3/2, admission €1 Wed; ⌚ 11am-8pm Tue-Fri, 10am-8pm Sat, 10am-3pm Sun) contains works by Salvador Dalí, Joan Miró, Basque sculptor Eduardo Chillida, Jorge Oteiza, Antoni Tápies and Esteban Vicente, arrayed around the cloisters of a former monastery.

CATEDRAL & AROUND

Valladolid's 16th-century cathedral is not Castilla's finest, but it does have a fine altarpiece by Juní and a processional monstrance by Juan de Arfe in the attached **Museo Diocesano y Catedralicio** (☎ 983 30 43 62; Calle de Arribas 1; admission €2.50; ⌚ 10am-1.30pm & 4.30-7pm Tue-Fri, 10am-2pm Sat & Sun). Arguably more interesting are the 13th-century **ruins** of the old Collegiate Church (atop which the cathedral was built) on the cathedral's northeastern perimeter.

Immediately north of the cathedral is the beautiful **Iglesia de Santa María la Antigua**, a 14th-century Gothic church with an elegant Romanesque tower. The baroque facade to the east of the cathedral belongs to the main building of the **universidad** and was the work of Narciso Tomé.

East of the cathedral and the church is the early-Renaissance **Colegio de Santa Cruz** (1487). The main portal is early plateresque; wander inside to see the three-tiered and colonnaded patio and, in the chapel, Fernández' super-realistic *Cristo de la Luz* sculpture.

> **VALLADOLID BY BIKE**
>
> Hats off to Valladolid's tourist authorities, who've initiated the **Valladolid en bici** (Valladolid by bike; www.ava.es) program whereby you can borrow a bicycle from 10 places around town (the tourist office and Plaza Mayor are the most convenient) and leave it at any of the 10 when you're done. And it's free. All you have to do is fill out a form with your passport or ID card details and you're ready to explore one of Spain's most bike-friendly cities. The tourist office also has a bike map of the city, highlighting cycling lanes and routes.

CASAS DE CERVANTES & COLÓN

Cervantes was briefly imprisoned in Valladolid, and his **house** (☎ 983 30 88 10; Calle del Rastro; adult/under 18yr & senior €2.40/free, admission free Sun; ⌚ 9.30am-3pm Tue-Sat, 10am-3pm Sun) is happily preserved behind a quiet little garden.

The **Casa-Museo de Colón** (☎ 983 29 13 53; Calle de Colón; admission €2, Wed €1; ⌚ 10am-2pm & 5-8.30pm Tue-Sun) is our favourite museum in Valladolid. Reopened after a major overhaul in 2006, the museum is spread over four floors with interactive exhibits and wonderful old maps taking you on a journey through Christopher Columbus' (Cristóbal Colón in Spanish) journeys to the Americas. The top floor describes Valladolid in the days of the great explorer (who died here in 1506). The explanations are in Spanish only.

Sleeping

Valladolid's hotels see more businesspeople than tourists during the week, so prices at many hotels drop considerably from Friday to Sunday.

Hostal Los Arces (☎ 983 35 38 53; www.hostaldelval-losarces.com in Spanish; Calle de San Antonio de Padua 2; s/d with washbasin €18/33, with bathroom €33/42) This place is outstanding value, with pleasant, renovated rooms with TV, most of which overlook a reasonably quiet street. The owner is friendly in an understated, Castilian kind of way.

Hostal Del Val (☎ 983 37 57 52; www.hostaldelval-losarces.com in Spanish; Plaza del Val 6; s/d with washbasin €18/33, with bathroom €33/42) Run by the same owner as Los Arces. Decent rooms overlooking a quiet square.

Hotel Lasa (☎ 983 39 02 55; www.hotellasa.com; Acera de Recoletos 21; s €42-50, d €54-86; P ❄ 💻)

Handy for the train station and geared towards business travellers, Hotel Lasa's warmly decorated rooms have a nice blend of antique furnishings, shiny parquet floors and modern bathrooms, with a sharp attention to detail. Parking costs €13.

Hostal París (☎ 983 37 06 25; www.hostalparis.com in Spanish; Calle de la Especería 2; s/d from €51/69; P) One of the closest places to Plaza Mayor, Hostal París has comfortable rooms with all the trimmings (including satellite TV) and good service, although travellers with babies won't appreciate paying €13 for a cot. Some rooms are quite simple, but most look onto the street. There's parking from 8pm to 10am for €11.

Hotel El Nogal (☎ 983 34 03 33; www.hotelelnogal.com in Spanish; Calle del Conde Ansúrez 10-12; s/d from €50/72; P) Hotel El Nogal has a mixture of old and new, with most of the rooms sporting polished floorboards, ample space (even the singles) and modern bathrooms, some with hydro-massage showers. All face out onto either a plaza or a quietish street, and the older rooms are gradually disappearing. Parking costs €11.

Hotel Meliá Recoletos (☎ 983 21 62 00; www.solmelia.com; Acera de Recoletos 13; s/d from €70/90; P) This excellent four-star hotel has a touch of class that elevates it above other hotels in this category. Part of a chain but with a boutique-hotel intimacy, it offers large luxurious rooms and impeccable service. With a predominantly business clientele, the hotel lowers its rates considerably from Friday to Sunday. Parking costs €14.

Eating

TAPAS

Valladolid is a great town to get into the tapas habit and you need look no further than the bars west of Plaza Mayor. **Bar Zamora** (Calle de Correos 5; lunch & dinner Thu-Tue) has won prizes for its tapas with flavours from western Castilla, while **El Corcho** (Calle de Correos 2), a few doors up, wins the prize of public opinion from many locals.

It's said that Spaniards consume 30 million kilograms of mussels every year and it's our guess that a fair proportion of these are downed in **La Mejillonera** (Calle de la Pasión 13). A good place to try for its range of *tostas* (toasts) is the popular **La Tasquita II** (Calle Caridad 2).

If you're willing to stray a little further, the tiny **Le Petit** (Calle de Rúa Oscura 4) has more than 50 varieties of canapés and a great deal offering a glass of wine and a canapé for €2. Around the corner, **La Jamónería** (Calle del Conde Ansúrez 11) is popular for cured meats.

RESTAURANTS

All of the following places are also good for tapas.

OUR PICK El Caballo de Troya (☎ 983 33 93 55; www.elcaballodetroya.com; Calle de Correos 1; menús €13-22, meals €25-45; lunch & dinner Mon-Sat) The 'Trojan Horse' is a Valladolid treat, ranged around a stunning interior courtyard with a *taberna* (tavern) downstairs for brilliant *raciones* – we recommend the *bandeja surtidas* (tasting platters) for a rich and varied combination of tastes. The restaurant is as sophisticated in flavours as the dining room is classy in design.

La Parrilla de San Lorenzo (☎ 983 33 50 88; Calle de Pedro Niño; meals €25-30; bar 10.30am-late, restaurant lunch & dinner) Both a rustic stand-up bar and a much-lauded restaurant with vaulted ceilings, La Parilla de San Lorenzo has upmarket Castilian cuisine (hearty stews, legumes and steaks play a leading role) with a relaxed ambience. The menu looks like a medieval religious document!

Los Zagales de Abadía (☎ 983 38 08 92; Calle de la Pasión 13; meals €25-30; lunch & dinner Tue-Sun) The bar here is awash with hanging local produce and it's not averse to the occasional pig's head mounted on the wall – all are also represented in the tapas varieties along the bar, along with salmon and *bacalao* (cod). But Los Zagales is best known for its restaurant, where the servings are generous and the food excellent.

Vinotinto (☎ 983 34 22 91; www.vinotinto.es in Spanish; Calle de Campanas 4; meals €25-30) This is where wine bar meets steakhouse, sizzling nightly with local gossip, spare ribs and other grilled meats. We especially enjoyed the local *jamón ibérico*, which was sliced so finely as to melt in the mouth (as it should be but rarely is). Vinotinto Joven, opposite, has a more intimate, younger feel.

Drinking

Central Valladolid brims with welcoming bars and cafes, and you'll quickly find a personal favourite.

El Minuto (Calle de Macias Picavea 15; 9am-late) Near the cathedral, this smooth cafe-bar is popular with students and is flanked by several other prospects for late-night drinking.

THE DARK PRINCE OF THE INQUISITION

There were few more notorious personalities of the Spanish Inquisition than the zealot Fray Tomás de Torquemada (1420–98). Immortalised by Dostoevsky as the articulate Grand Inquisitor who puts Jesus himself on trial in *The Brothers Karamazov,* and satirised by Monty Python in the *Flying Circus,* Torquemada was born in Valladolid to well-placed Jewish *conversos* (converts to Christianity).

A Dominican, Fray Tomás was appointed Queen Isabel's personal confessor in 1479. Four years later, Pope Sixtus IV appointed this rising star to head the Castilian Inquisition.

Deeply affected by the Spanish cult of *sangre limpia* (pure blood), the racist doctrine that drove the 800-year struggle to rid Spain of non-Christian peoples, Torquemada gleefully rooted out *conversos* and other heretics, including his favourite targets, the *marranos* (Jews who pretended to convert but continued to practise Judaism in private).

The 'lucky' sinners had their property confiscated, which served as a convenient fund-raiser for the war of Reconquista against the Muslims. They were paraded through town wearing the *sambenito,* a yellow shirt emblazoned with crosses that was short enough to expose their genitals, then marched to the doors of the local church and flogged.

If you were unlucky, you underwent unimaginable tortures before going through an auto-da-fé, a public burning at the stake. Those who recanted and kissed the cross were garrotted before the fire was set, while those who recanted only were burnt quickly with dry wood. If you stayed firm and didn't recant, the wood used for the fire was green and slow-burning.

In the 15 years Torquemada was Inquisitor General of the Castilian Inquisition, he ran some 100,000 trials and sent about 2000 people to burn at the stake. Many of the trials were conducted in Valladolid's Plaza Mayor; the executions in Plaza de Zorrilla. On 31 March 1492, Fernando and Isabel, on Torquemada's insistence, issued their Edict of Expulsion, forcing all Jews to leave Spain within two months on pain of death.

The following year, Torquemada retired to the monastery of Santo Tomás in Ávila, from where he continued to administer the affairs of the Inquisition. In his final years he became obsessed with the fear that he might be poisoned, and refused to eat anything without having (what he believed to be) a unicorn's horn nearby as an antidote. Unlike many of his victims, he died in his sleep in 1498.

The nearby Calle de Librería is an epicentre of early-evening student drinking.

Café Continental (Plaza Mayor 23; ⌚ 8am-3am) This hip spot is our pick of the bars and *terrazas* (terraces) that surround the delightful Plaza Mayor. It features live music upstairs some nights.

Plaza de San Miguel draws bar-hoppers like moths to a flame. The options around here can be pretty generic, but the sophisticated **El Soportal** (Plaza de San Miguel; ⌚ 4pm-1am Sun-Thu, 4pm-3am Fri & Sat) and **Harlem Cafe** (Calle de San Antonio de Padua; ⌚ 4pm-1am Sun-Thu, 4pm-3am Fri & Sat), around the corner and with music from America's Deep South, are a real cut above the rest.

Plaza de Martí y Monsó also has a sprinkling of bars. **Cafe de la Comedia** (Plaza de Martí y Monsó; ⌚ 10am-1am) is noisy with people and a convivial atmosphere, while **Be Bop** (Plaza de Martí y Monsó; ⌚ 4pm-late) is all pink stilettos and a supercool crowd.

Getting There & Away

AIR

Ryanair (www.ryanair.com) has flights to Valladolid from London (Stansted), Brussels (Charleroi) and Milan (Orio al Serio). **Iberia** (www.iberia.es) operates up to five daily flights to Barcelona, with connections to other cities in Spain.

BUS

With such good train connections, it's hard to see why you'd need the bus. For the record, buses travel to Madrid almost hourly between 6.30am and 9.30pm (€12.10, 2¼ hours), while others go hourly to Palencia (€3.10, 45 minutes).

CAR & MOTORCYCLE

The N620 motorway passes Valladolid en route from Burgos to Tordesillas, where it connects with the A6 between Madrid and A Coruña in Galicia. The N601 heads northwest to León and south to hit the A6 west of Segovia.

TRAIN

Five daily high-speed AVE train services connect Valladolid with Madrid (€31.20, one hour), but there are slower services (2½ hours) for as little as €14.60. Other regular trains run to León (from €9.60, about two hours), Burgos (from €8.20, about 1½ hours), Palencia (from €3.15, 45 minutes), Salamanca (from €7.50, 1½ hours) and Bilbao (from €22.80, about 3½ hours).

Getting Around

Valladolid's airport is 15km northwest of the city centre. **Linecar** (☎ 983 23 00 33) has up to five daily bus services from Valladolid to the airport (€3.50) and three services going the other way. A taxi between the airport and the city centre costs around €20, a little more on Sunday and holidays.

Local buses 2 and 10 pass the train and bus stations on their way to Plaza de España.

AROUND VALLADOLID

Medina de Rioseco

pop 5010

Medina de Rioseco, a once-wealthy trading centre, is a shadow of its former medieval self, but retains a handful of worthwhile sights. The **tourist office** (☎ 983 72 03 19; www.medinaderioseco.com in Spanish; Calle La Dársena del Canal de Castilla s/n; 10am-2pm & 5-8pm Tue-Sat, 10am-2pm Sun), close to Plaza Mayor, can point you in the right direction.

The **Iglesia de Santa María de Mediavilla** (☎ 983 70 03 27; 11am-2pm & 4-7pm Tue-Sun Oct-Apr, 11am-2pm & 5-8pm daily May-Sep) is a grandiose Isabelline Gothic work with three star-vaulted naves and the famous **Capilla de los Benavente**. Anchored by an eye-popping altarpiece by Juan de Juní, it's sometimes referred to as 'the Sistine Chapel of Castilla'. Down the hill, the portals of the light-flooded **Iglesia de Santiago** (admission €1.80; 11am-2pm & 4-7pm Tue-Sun Oct-Apr, 11am-2pm & 5-8pm daily May-Sep) blend Gothic, neoclassical and plateresque architectural styles.

Medina de Rioseco is famous for its Easter processions, but if you can't be here during Holy Week, the **Museo de Semana Santa** (☎ 983 70 03 27; www.museos-medinaderioseco.com; Calle de Lázaro Alonso s/n; adult/under 14yr €3/free, admission free first Thu of month; 11am-2pm & 4-7pm Tue-Sun Sep-May, 11am-2pm & 5-8pm daily Jun-Aug) provides an insight into the ceremonial passion of Easter here. Like its sister museum in Zamora (p240), it's dedicated to *pasos* (figures carried in Semana Santa processions) and an extensive range of other Easter memorabilia.

Hostal Duque de Osuna (☎ 983 70 01 79; Avenida de Castilviejo 16; s/d from €20/35), not far from the bus station, is excellent value, especially as the rooms come with private bathroom. The rooms aren't anything special but they're clean. Prices can double during high season and Semana Santa.

Hostal La Muralla (☎ 983 70 05 77; Plaza de Santo Domingo 4; d €28-32) offers huge, bright rooms with small bathroom, TV, balcony and fan.

Two places for a great feed are **Restaurante La Rúa** (☎ 983 70 07 83; Calle de San Juan 25; menú €9) and **Restaurante Pasos** (☎ 983 72 00 21; Calle de Lázaro Alonso 44; menú €13). The latter has a classier feel, with Castilian fare that's easily Medina de Rioseco's best.

Each day up to eight buses run to León (€5.90, 1¼ hours) and up to 10 go to Valladolid (€3.25, 30 minutes).

Tordesillas

pop 8710

Commanding a rise on the northern flank of Río Duero, this charming little town has a historical significance that belies its size. Originally a Roman town, it later played a major role in world history when, in 1494, Isabel and Fernando, the Catholic Monarchs, sat down with Portugal here to hammer out a treaty determining who got what in Latin America. Portugal got Brazil and much of the rest went to Spain.

The **tourist office** (☎ 983 77 10 67; www.tordesillas.net; 10am-1.30pm & 4-6.30pm Tue-Sat, 10am-2pm Sun Oct-Apr, 10am-1.30pm & 5-7.30pm Tue-Sat, 10am-2pm Sun May-Sep) is in Casas del Tratado, near the Iglesia de San Antolín.

SIGHTS

The history of Tordesillas has been dominated by the Mudéjar-style **Real Convento de Santa Clara** (☎ 983 77 00 71; adult/concession €3.60/2, EU citizens free Wed; 10am-1.15pm & 3.45-5.45pm Tue-Sat, 10.30am-1.15pm Sun, shorter hours Oct-Mar), still home to a few Franciscan nuns living in near-total isolation from the outside world. First begun in 1340 as a palace for Alfonso XI, it was here, in 1494, that the Treaty of Tordesillas was signed. A guided tour (included in the entry fee) of the convent takes in some remarkable rooms, including a wonderful Mudéjar patio left over from the palace, and the church – the stunning *techumbre* is a masterpiece. The

Mudéjar door, Gothic arches and Arabic inscriptions are superb, as are the **Arab baths** (☎ 983 77 00 71; admission €2.25, incl convent €4.60; 🕒 by appointment).

The **Museo del Tratado del Tordesillas** (☎ 983 77 10 67; Calle de Casas del Tratado; admission free; 🕒 10am-1.30pm & 4-6.30pm Tue-Sat, 10am-2pm Sun Oct-Apr, 10am-1.30pm & 5-7.30pm Tue-Sat, 10am-2pm Sun May-Sep) is dedicated to the 1494 Treaty of Tordesillas and the informative displays look at the world as it was before and after the treaty. There's a reproduction of the treaty itself and a map that suggests Spain did very well out of the negotiations.

The **Museo de San Antolín** (Calle de Tratado de Tordesillas s/n; admission €1.80; 🕒 10.30am-1.30pm & 4.30-6.30pm Tue-Sun, 10.30am-1.30pm Sun), in a deconsecrated Gothic church, houses a collection of religious art.

The heart of town is formed by the pretty, porticoed **Plaza Mayor**, its mustard-yellow paintwork offset by dark-brown woodwork and black grilles.

SLEEPING & EATING

Hostal San Antolín (☎ 983 79 67 71; sanantolin@telefonica.net; Calle San Antolín 8; s/d €27/45) This is the best place to stay in the old town, although the overall aesthetic and rooms are modern. The attached restaurant, the Mesón San Antolín, is one of the most popular eateries in town, with good *raciones* downstairs and a fancy restaurant upstairs. It's just off Plaza Mayor.

Parador de Tordesillas (☎ 983 77 00 51; www.parador.es; Carretera de Salamanca 5; d €160) Tordesillas' most sophisticated hotel is the ochre-toned *parador*, just outside town, where some rooms have four-poster beds (it's that sort of place) and many look out onto the tranquil gardens. This is one of the flagship *paradores* and is worth every euro. The set menu in the restaurant costs €30.

A few pleasant cafes and restaurants surround the perimeter of Plaza Mayor, including **Don Pancho** (☎ 983 77 01 74; Plaza Mayor 9; menú €9, meals €20-25), which is known for its homely atmosphere and home cooking, including meats roasted in a wood-fire oven. For tapas, try **Viky** (☎ 983 77 10 61; Plaza Mayor 14; menú €8.20, meals €25; 🕒 lunch & dinner Tue-Sun).

GETTING THERE & AWAY

The **bus station** (☎ 983 77 00 72; Avenida de Valladolid) is near Calle de Santa María. Regular buses depart for Madrid (€10.50, 2¼ hours), Salamanca (€5.25, 1¼ hours), Valladolid (€2.25, 30 minutes) and Zamora (€4.95, one hour).

Toro

pop 9740

Toro is your archetypal Castilian town in more than just name. Modern Toro, which lies north of Río Duero, is one of those Castilian towns whose past overshadows its present – it was here that Fernando and Isabel cemented their primacy in Christian Spain at the Battle of Toro in 1476. Since then, the town has settled rather comfortably into provinciality at the heart of a much-loved wine region, but it does have a few architectural gems to detain you for half a day if you're in the area.

The **tourist office** (☎ 980 69 47 47; Plaza Mayor 6; 🕒 10am-2pm & 4-7pm Tue-Sat, 10am-2pm Sun Oct-Jun, 10am-2pm & 4-8pm Tue-Sun Jul-Sep) organises two-hour **guided walking tours** (☎ 686 639551; €5) of the town's sights. Pick up a program here or from the regional tourist office in Zamora (p240).

SIGHTS

Romanesque churches appear on seemingly every street corner in Toro. The **Colegiata Santa María La Mayor** (🕒 10.30am-2pm & 5-7.30pm Tue-Sun Feb-Sep, 10am-2pm & 4.30-6.30pm Tue-Sat Oct-Jan) rises above the town and boasts the magnificent Romanesque–Gothic Pórtico de la Majestad. Treasures inside include the famous 15th-century painting called *Virgen de la Mosca* (Virgin of the Fly); see if you can spot the fly on the virgin's robe.

From behind the church you have a superb view south across the fields to the Romanesque bridge over Río Duero. The nearby **Alcázar**, dating from the 10th century, conserves its walls and seven towers.

Southwest of town, the **Monasterio Sancti Spiritus** (☎ 980 10 81 07; 🕒 tours 10.30am-12.30pm & 4.30-6.30pm Tue-Sun) features a fine Renaissance cloister and the striking alabaster tomb of Beatriz de Portugal, wife of Juan I. Guided tours run variously during the hours indicated.

SLEEPING & EATING

Hostal Doña Elvira (☎ 980 69 00 62; Calle Antonio Miguelez 47; s/d with washbasin €12/18, d with bathroom €28) One of the cheapest *hostales* in Toro, Hostal Doña Elvira has a few floors of simple, clean rooms, all with TV.

Hotel Juan II (☎ 980 69 03 00; http://hoteljuanii.com; Paseo del Espolón 1; s/d from €51/69; ❄) With fine balcony views from some rooms, parquetry floors and plenty of space, Hotel Juan II is probably Toro's best; the same can be said for the attached restaurant. It's in the heart of town and has a lovely rooftop terrace.

Plaza Mayor and nearby streets bustle with plenty of places to eat.

GETTING THERE & AWAY

Regular buses operate to Valladolid (€3.60, one hour) and Zamora (€2.45, 25 minutes), and there are two direct services to Salamanca (€5.40, 1½ hours) on weekdays.

ZAMORA

pop 66,200

As in so many Spanish towns, your first introduction to provincial Zamora is likely to be nondescript apartment blocks, but don't be put off: the *casco historico* (old town) is awash with beautiful medieval monuments that have earned Zamora the popular sobriquet 'Romanesque Museum'. It's a subdued encore to the monumental splendour of Salamanca and one of the best places to be during Semana Santa.

Information

Emergency (☎ 112)
Hospital Virgen de la Concha (☎ 980 54 82 00; Avenida Requejo s/n) Two and a half kilometres east of the old town.
Municipal tourist office (☎ 980 53 36 94; Plaza de Arias Gonzalo; 🕑 10am-2pm & 4-7pm Oct-Mar, 10am-2pm & 5-8pm Apr-Sep)
Policía Nacional (☎ 091, 980 53 04 62; Calle San Atilano 3)
Post office (Calle de Santa Clara 15)
Regional tourist office (☎ 980 53 18 45; oficinadeturismodezamora@jcyl.es; Avenida Príncipe de Asturias 1; 🕑 9am-2pm & 5-8pm daily mid-Sep–Jun, 9am-8pm Sun-Thu, 9am-9pm Fri & Sat Jul–mid-Sep) Organises guided tours (free to €5); check with the office for timing.

Sights

CATEDRAL & AROUND

Crowning medieval Zamora's southwestern extremity, the largely Romanesque **catedral** (☎ 980 53 06 44; adult/concession €3/1.50; 🕑 10am-1pm & 5-8pm Tue-Sun Mar-Sep, 10am-2pm & 4.30-6.30pm daily Oct-Feb) features a square tower, an unusual Byzantine-style dome surrounded by turrets, and the ornate Puerta del Obispo. To enter the cathedral, you pass through the **Museo Catedralicio** (🕑 same hours), where the star attraction (on the 2nd floor) is the collection of Flemish tapestries. The oldest tapestry depicts the Trojan War and dates from the 15th century.

Inside the 12th-century cathedral itself, the early-Renaissance choir stalls are a masterpiece: carvings depict clerics, animals and a naughty encounter between a monk and a nun. The other major highlights are the **Capilla de San Ildefonso**, with its lovely Gothic frescoes, and some fine Flemish tapestries in the adjoining antechamber.

For a look at what's left of the city wall and its **castillo** (castle), head to the little park just west of the cathedral. The castle was cordoned off for repairs at the time of writing.

CHURCHES

Zamora's **churches** (🕑 10am-1pm & 5-8pm Tue-Sun Mar-Sep, 10am-2pm & 4.30-6.30pm daily Oct-Dec) are of Romanesque origin, but all have been subjected to other influences. Among those churches retaining some of their Romanesque charm are the **Iglesia de San Pedro y San Ildefonso** (with Gothic touches), **Iglesia de la Magdalena** (the southern doorway is considered the city's finest, with its preponderance of floral motifs) and **Iglesia de San Juan de Puerta Nueva** on Plaza Mayor. **Iglesia de Santa María La Nueva** (Calle de San Martín Carniceros) is actually a medieval replica of a 7th-century church destroyed by fire in 1158.

If you're here in January or February, apart from being *extremely* cold, you'll find most of Zamora's churches closed while church authorities sort out the year's opening hours. Check with either of the tourist offices.

MUSEO DE SEMANA SANTA

This **museum** (☎ 980 53 22 95; Plaza de Santa María La Nueva; adult/concession €3/1.50; 🕑 10am-2pm & 5-9pm Mon-Sat, 10am-2pm Sun) will initiate you into the weird-and-wonderful rites of Easter, Spanish-style. It showcases the carved and painted *pasos* that are paraded around town during the colourful processions. The hooded models are eerily lifelike.

Festivals & Events

If you're in Spain during **Semana Santa**, make your way here to Zamora, a town made famous for its elaborate celebrations; it's one of the most evocative places in the country to view the hooded processions. Watching the penitents weave their way through the historic streets, sometimes in near-total silence, is an

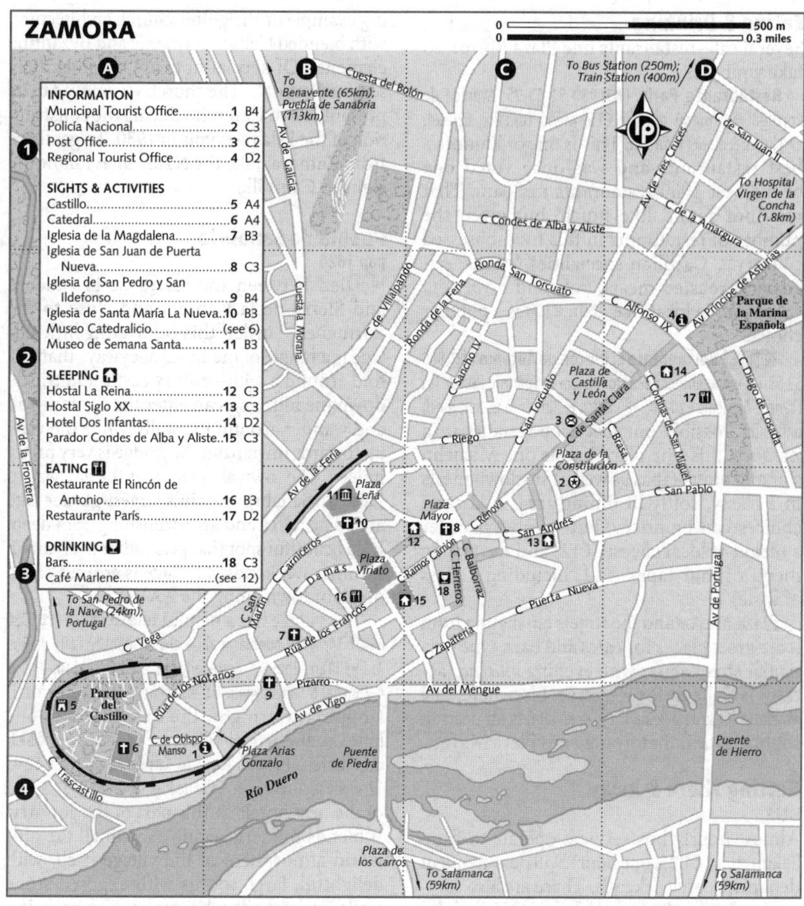

experience you'll never forget. During the rest of the year, the Museo de Semana Santa will provide initiation (opposite).

Sleeping

Zamora has a decent spread of accommodation. Prices can almost double during Semana Santa.

Hostal La Reina (☎ 980 53 39 39; Calle de la Reina 1; s/d without bathroom €20/27, with bathroom €25/35; Ⓟ) Watched over by delightful older owners, Hostal La Reina offers large rooms, the best of which have balconies overlooking Plaza Mayor. Prices drop by as much as €5 in winter. Parking costs €8.

Hostal Siglo XX (☎ 980 53 29 08; Plaza del Seminario 3; s/d with washbasin €22/35) Located in a secluded nook, Hostal Siglo XX has five bright, simple rooms. It's close to the main sights on a quiet street.

Hotel Dos Infantas (☎ 980 50 98 98; www.hoteldosinfantas.com in Spanish; Calle Cortinas de San Miguel 3; s €40-60, d €50-160; ❄) They won't win any style awards here, but the rooms are large and comfortable and you're not too far from the old town.

Parador Condes de Alba y Aliste (☎ 980 51 44 97; www.parador.es; Plaza Viriato 5; s/d from €113/143; ❄ 💻) Set in a sumptuous 15th-century palace (previous 'guests' included Isabel and Fernando), this is modern luxury with myriad period touches (mostly in the public areas). There's a swimming pool out the back and, unlike many *paradores,* it's right in the heart of town.

Eating & Drinking

Several cafe-restaurants line Plaza Mayor, so take your pick.

Restaurante París (☎ 980 51 43 25; Avenida de Portugal 14; menú del día €15, menú turístico €20-24; ⌚ lunch & dinner Mon-Sat) This is one of Zamora's best restaurants and was once voted one of the best 1000 restaurants in Spain. That may not sound like much, but given the number of restaurants in this food-obsessed country… Castilian specialities (steaks, salads and roasted meats) rule and *arroz a la zamorana* (a local rice dish; €10) is a popular choice.

our pick **Restaurante El Rincón de Antonio** (☎ 980 53 53 70; www.elrincondeantonio.com in Spanish; Rúa de los Francos 6; meals €20-50; ⌚ lunch & dinner Mon-Sat, lunch only Sun) Possibly our favourite restaurant in Zamora, this fine place boasts one Michelin star and offers tapas as well as sit-down meals in a classy, softly lit dining area. À la carte choices can be pricey, but we always order a *ración* of local cheese (€12) and the tasting menu of four tapas (€11, including a glass of wine).

Plaza Mayor and the streets emanating from it are great places for cafes and bars. One particular street abuzz with evening *marcha* (action) is Calle de los Herreros. Elsewhere, **Café Marlene** (Calle de la Reina 1; ⌚ 4pm-1am) is an oasis of sophistication that fronts onto Plaza Mayor.

Getting There & Away

BUS

Almost hourly bus services operate to/from Salamanca (€4.25, one hour), with less-frequent departures on weekends. There are also services to León (€7.15, 1½ hours), Valladolid (€6.40, 1½ hours), Burgos (€14.04, 4½ hours), Bilbao (€23.55, six hours, one daily) and Madrid (via Toro and Tordesillas; normal/express €13.76/20.50, 3¼/2¾ hours).

TRAIN

Trains head to Valladolid (€7.70, 1½ hours, one daily), Madrid (€25.90, 3¾ hours, three daily), Ávila (€19, two hours, two daily) and Ourense (€23.90, two hours, three daily).

AROUND ZAMORA

San Pedro de la Nave

This lonely 7th-century **church** (☎ 980 56 91 62; ⌚ 10am-1pm & 5-8pm Tue-Sun Mar-Sep, 10am-2pm & 4.30-6.30pm Fri & Sat, 10am-2pm Sun Oct-Dec), about 24km northwest of Zamora, is a rare and outstanding example of Visigothic church architecture, with blended Celtic, Germanic and Byzantine elements. Of special note are the intricately sculpted capitals. The church was moved to its present site in Campillo during the construction of the Esla reservoir in 1930. To get there from Zamora, take the N122, then follow the signs to Campillo.

Puebla de Sanabria

pop 1620

Nestled between the Sierra de la Culebra and Sierra de la Cabrera and close to the Portuguese border, this captivating little village is a tangle of medieval alleyways that unfold around a 15th-century castle and trickle down the hill. You can enter the castle at will and wander around the walls, while the view up towards town from the bridge is very pretty indeed. The town also serves as the gateway to Lago de Sanabria, Spain's largest glacier lake at 368 hectares and an astonishing 55m deep. It's a beautiful spot that gets rather overrun on summer weekends. The lake is around 15km north of town along the ZA104.

The village has a helpful **tourist office** (☎ 980 62 07 34; www.pueblasanabria.org in Spanish; Calle de Rúa 3; ⌚ 11am-2pm & 5-8pm daily Apr–mid-Oct, 11am-2pm & 4-7pm Sat & Sun only mid-Oct–Mar) and it's well worth stopping overnight: the quiet cobblestone lanes make it feel like you've stepped back centuries. **Posada Real la Cartería** (☎ 980 62 03 12; www.lacarteria.com; Calle de Rúa 16; d €70-115) is one of the best hotels in this part of the country. It blends modern comforts with all the old-world atmosphere of the village itself, with delightful, large rooms with exposed stone walls and wooden beams, not to mention a gym, a good restaurant and professional service.

There are sporadic bus services to Puebla de Sanabria from Zamora (from €6.75, 1¼ hours). If travelling by car, leave Zamora on the N630, then pick up the N631 at the Embalse de Ricobayo, which eventually merges with the N525.

PALENCIA

pop 82,300

Quiet Palencia boasts an immense Gothic cathedral, the sober exterior of which belies the extraordinary riches that await within; it's widely known as 'La Bella Desconocida' (Unknown Beauty). Otherwise, you'll find some pretty squares, a colonnaded main street

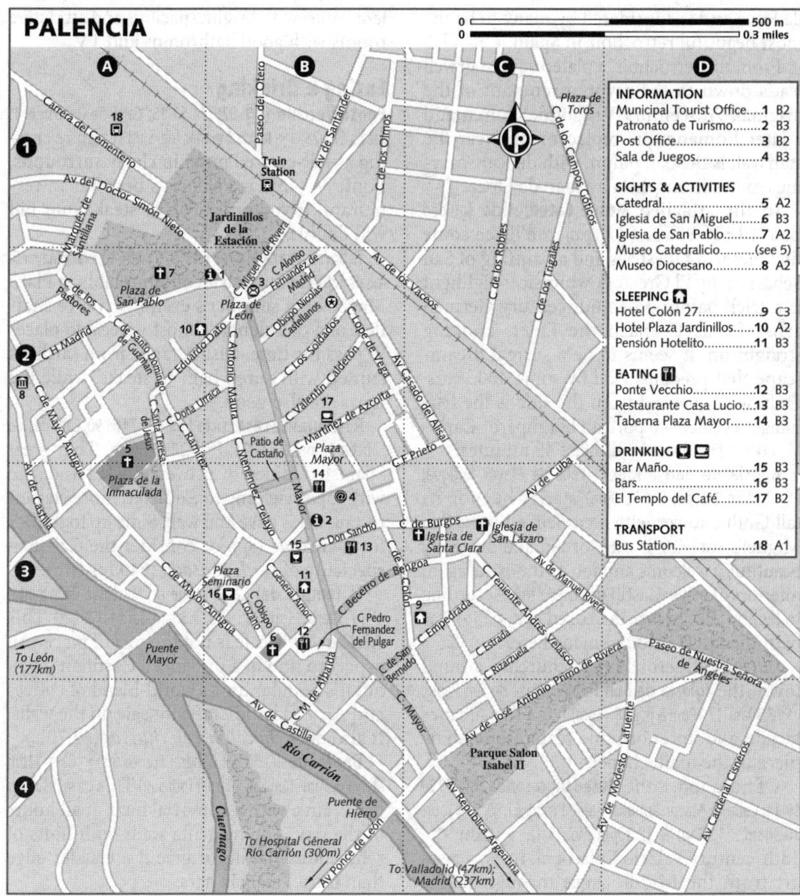

(Calle Mayor) and a slew of other churches. King Alfonso VIII founded Spain's first university here in 1208.

Information

Emergency (☎ 112)
Hospital Géneral Río Carrión (☎ 979 16 70 00; Avenida Donantes de Sangre s/n)
Municipal tourist office (☎ 979 74 99 74; www.palencia-turismo.com; Plaza de San Pablo; 🕑 10.30am-2pm & 5-8.30pm Jul-Sep, shorter hours rest of year)
Patronato de Turismo (☎ 979 70 65 23; Calle Mayor 31; 🕑 9am-2pm & 5-8pm Mon-Sat, 9am-2pm Sun) Information about Palencia province.
Post office (Plaza de León 4)
Sala de Juegos (Plaza Mayor; per hr €1; 🕑 10am-10pm Mon-Fri, 10am-2.30pm & 5-9pm Sat & Sun) Internet access.

Sights

The Puerta del Obispo (Bishop's Door) is the highlight of the facade of the imposing **catedral** (☎ 979 70 13 47; admission €1.50; 🕑 8.45am-1.30pm & 4-6.30pm Mon-Sat, 11.15am-1pm Sun Oct–mid-May, 10am-1.30pm & 4.30-7.30pm Mon-Fri, 10am-5.30pm Sat, 11.15am-1pm & 4.30-8pm Sun mid-May–Sep), which, at 130m long, 56m wide and 30m high, is one of the largest of the Castilian cathedrals.

The interior contains a treasure trove of art. One of the most stunning chapels is the Capilla El Sagrario: its ceiling-high altarpiece tells the story of Christ in dozens of exquisitely carved and painted panels. The stone screen behind the choir stalls, or *trascoro*, is a masterpiece of bas-relief attributed to Gil de Siloé and is considered by many to be the most beautiful retrochoir in Spain.

From the retrochoir, a plateresque stairwell leads down to the crypt, a remnant of the original, 7th-century Visigothic church and a later Romanesque replacement. Near the stairwell is the oak pulpit, with delicate carvings of the Evangelists by Juan de Ortiz.

In the attached **Museo Catedralicio** (guided tours €1.80; 9am-2pm & 4-8pm) you'll see some fine Flemish tapestries and a painting of San Sebastián by El Greco. A whimsical highlight is a trick painting by 16th-century German artist Lucas Cranach the Elder. Looking straight on, it seems to be a surreal dreamscape that predates Dalí by some 400 years. Only when viewed from the side is the true image revealed – a portrait of Emperor Carlos V. Tours run hourly and last 45 minutes.

Iglesia de San Miguel (Calle de Mayor Antigua; 9.30am-1.30pm & 6-7.30pm) stands out for its tall Gothic tower with a castlelike turret. San Miguel's interior is unadorned and austerely beautiful, a welcome antidote to the extravagant interiors of other Castilian churches. According to legend, El Cid (see the boxed text, p258) was betrothed to his Doña Jimena here.

Of the numerous other churches around town, the **Iglesia de San Pablo** (Plaza de San Pablo; 7.30am-12.30pm & 6.30-8.15pm) has a Renaissance facade and an enormous plateresque altarpiece in the main chapel.

Of note, too, is the **Museo Diocesano** (979 70 69 13; Calle de Mayor Antigua; guided tours €1.80; tours 10.30am, 11.30am & 12.30pm Mon-Sat), within the 18th-century Palacio Episcopal. It showcases art from the Middle Ages through to the Renaissance. Pride of place goes to works by Pedro de Berruguete and an altarpiece starring the Virgin (attributed to Diego de Siloé).

Sleeping

Pensión Hotelito (979 74 69 13; hotelito03@yahoo.es; Calle del General Amor 5; s/d without bathroom €19/30, d with bathroom €35) The best of Palencia's budget digs, this *pensión* is tidy, friendly and quiet, despite being quite central.

Hotel Plaza Jardinillos (979 75 00 22; Calle de Eduardo Dato 2; s/d €29/34) You don't find value for money like this very often. Some of the rooms come with splashes of colour, most are spacious (including the singles) and the overall sense is of a midrange hotel at budget prices.

Hotel Colón 27 (979 74 07 00; www.hotelcolon27.com; Calle de Colón 27; s/d €33/45) This place is excellent value, with bright, spacious and attractive rooms with good bathrooms and TV.

Eating & Drinking

Ponte Vecchio (979 74 52 15; Calle de Doctrinus 1; meals €15-25; lunch & dinner Tue-Sun) If you're craving a well-cooked pasta in classy surrounds, Ponte Vecchio is Palencia's best Italian restaurant. If you order fish or steak, your bill will double.

Taberna Plaza Mayor (979 74 04 10; Plaza Mayor 8; meals €20) If you grab an outdoor table in Plaza Mayor on a summer's evening, you've snaffled one of Palencia's most agreeable places to pass the time. Dishes range from sardines stuffed with cured ham to steaks, while the tapas are also good.

Restaurante Casa Lucio (979 74 81 90; Calle de Don Sancho 2; meals €20-25; 1.30-11.30pm) That great Spanish tradition of an overcrowded bar laden with tapas yielding to a quieter, more elegant restaurant is alive and well. Sidle up to the bar for a creative tapa or consider the Castilian speciality of *cordero asado* (€40 for two).

El Templo del Café (Calle de Martínez de Azcoita; 7.30am-11pm Sun-Thu, 7.30am-1am Fri & Sat) This African-style cafe is not the sort of place you expect to find in a provincial Castilian town, but it's popular for its world-blend of coffees and African handicrafts for sale on the walls. It also does *chocolate con churros* (€2.70).

Bar Maño (Calle del General Franco 5; 8am-11pm Mon-Fri, 9am-3am Sat, 10am-11pm Sun) This casual, hip bar is alive with a convivial buzz at all hours of the day. The magenta walls with hints of semi-industrial decor give it a classier edge than most Palencia bars.

Drinking is taken seriously by the late-night crowd who frequent the handful of bars that encircle the tiny Plaza Seminario. Drinks are cheap and the decor is the sort that you drink to forget.

Getting There & Away

BUS

From the **bus station** (979 74 32 22; Carerra del Cementerio) there are regular services to Valladolid (€3.10, 45 minutes), Madrid (€15.26, 3¼ hours), Aguilar de Campóo (€4.80, 1½ hours), Frómista (€2.45, 30 minutes) and Paredes de Nava (€1.45, 25 minutes).

TRAIN

Trains are usually a good bet, with regular departures from Palencia's busy little **train**

A SLOW DEATH

Many tranquil villages of Castilla y León have a dark secret: they could soon be extinct. Spain's economic boom in the late 1990s and beyond drove a massive shift from rural villages into urban centres. In the last 50 years, Spain's largest autonomous region has lost a million inhabitants. Its population of just over 2.5 million people is now the same as it was in 1901.

Award-winning documentary film-maker Mercedes Alvarez is one of just 43 inhabitants in the village of Aldealsenor and, in an interview with *El País* newspaper in 2005, warned of 'the dying without sound of a culture with over a thousand years of history'. At the same time, the renowned Spanish writer Julio Llamazares, a Castilla y León native, blamed 'the uncontrolled development of the 1960s and 1970s, which generated a total disdain for everything rural'.

The regional Castilla y León government has set up a commission to study the problem and attempts are being made to lure more immigrants to smaller communities – just 2.5% of Castilla y Leon's population are immigrants, compared with a national average of around 10%.

station (☎ 979 74 30 19) throughout the day to Madrid (€18.35, 3¼ hours), Burgos (from €4.40, one hour), León (from €7.15, 1¾ hours) and Valladolid (€3.15, 45 minutes).

AROUND PALENCIA

Baños de Cerrato

Close to the singularly unattractive rail junction of Venta de Baños lies Spain's oldest church, the 7th-century **Basílica de San Juan** (admission €1, free Wed; ⏲ 10.30am-1.30pm & 4-6pm Tue-Sun Oct-Jun, 10am-1.30pm & 5-8pm Tue-Sat Jul-Sep) in Baños de Cerrato. Built by the Visigoths in 661 and modified many times since, its stone-and-terracotta facade exudes a pleasing, austere simplicity and features a 14th-century alabaster statue of St John the Baptist. To get there, take a train from Palencia to Venta de Baños, then walk the final 2km.

Paredes de Nava

pop 2150

The eminent 16th-century sculptor Alonso de Berruguete was born in Paredes in 1488. Sadly, most of the town's churches are in great disrepair, save for the eclectic 13th-century **Iglesia de Santa Eulalia** (☎ 979 83 04 40; Plaza de España; admission €2; ⏲ 10.30am-1.30pm & 4-7pm Mar-Sep, by appointment rest of year), with its pretty steeple with arched windows. Its museum contains several pieces by Berruguete.

Several trains travel daily to Palencia (€2.20, 15 minutes), and a couple of buses (€1.45) also ply the route.

Frómista

pop 840

The main (and some would say only) reason for stopping here is the exceptional Romanesque **Iglesia de San Martín** (☎ 979 81 01 28; admission €1; ⏲ 10am-1.30pm & 4.30-8pm May-Sep, 10am-2pm & 4-6pm Oct-Apr). Dating to 1066 and restored in the early 20th century, the squat facade of this harmoniously proportioned church is adorned with a veritable menagerie of human and zoomorphic figures, while the capitals inside are also richly decorated.

If you get stuck here overnight, **Pensión Marisa** (☎ 979 81 00 23; Plaza Obispo Almaraz 2; s/d/tr without bathroom €17/28/37) has spotless, bright rooms and great home cooking, while **Hotel San Martín** (☎ /fax 979 81 00 00; Plaza San Martín 7; s/d €30/45) promises a little more comfort.

There are two buses daily from Palencia (€2.45, 30 minutes).

MONTAÑA PALENTINA

These hills in the far north of Castilla y León offer a beautiful preview of the Cordillera Cantábrica, which divides Castilla from Spain's northern Atlantic regions.

Aguilar de Campóo

pop 7270

Aguilar de Campóo wouldn't win a beauty contest, but it does boast a medieval **castle** and serves as a good base for exploring the region: there are no fewer than 55 Romanesque churches in the cool, hilly countryside.

The **tourist office** (☎ 979 12 36 41; Plaza de España 30; ⏲ 10am-1.45pm & 4-5.45pm Tue-Sat, 10am-1.45pm Sun) is on the elongated Plaza de España, which is capped at its eastern end by the **Colegiata de San Miguel**, a 14th-century Gothic church with a fine Romanesque entrance.

Downhill from the castle is the graceful Romanesque **Ermita de Santa Cecilia**. Just outside town, on the highway to Cervera de

Pisuerga, is the restored **Monasterio de Santa María la Real** (☎ 979 12 30 53; Carretera de Cervera; admission €5; 🕒 10.30am-2pm & 4.30-8pm daily 26 Jun–mid-Sep, 4-7pm Tue-Fri, 10.30am-2pm & 4.30-7.30pm Sat & Sun rest of year), of Romanesque origin. Its 13th-century Gothic cloister with delicate capitals is glorious.

There's plenty of accommodation around town and the square is swarming with cafes, bars and a couple of restaurants. The sprawling, central **Hotel Restaurante Valentín** (☎ 979 12 21 25; www.hotelvalentin.com; Avenida Ronda 23; s €36-45, d €52-59) is easily the best choice, with large rooms.

Regular trains link Aguilar de Campóo with Palencia (€5.70, 1¼ hours), but the station is 4km from town. Buses bound for Burgos, Palencia and Santander depart at least once daily.

Romanesque Circuit

The area around Aguilar is studded with little villages and churches. At **Olleros de Pisuerga** there's a little church carved into rock, while further south, on a quiet back road, the Benedictine **Monasterio de Santa María de Mave** (admission free; 🕒 10am-2pm & 4-7pm Tue-Sun) has an interesting 13th-century Romanesque church. The **Monasterio de San Andrés de Arroyo** (guided tours €2.50; 🕒 10am-12.30pm & 3-6pm) is an outstanding Romanesque gem, especially its cloister, which dates from the 13th century. Admission is by guided tour, run hourly.

The C627 highway heading to **Cervera de Pisuerga** is lined with still more little churches dating from as far back as the 12th century. Cervera de Pisuerga itself is dominated by an imposing late-Gothic church, the **Iglesia de Santa María del Castillo**.

The N621 north from Cervera is a lovely road into Cantabria and to the southern face of the Picos de Europa.

THE NORTHWEST

The city of León stands like a sentinel at the rim of the great Castilian heartland and its breathtaking cathedral provides a major focal point for pilgrims along the Camino de Santiago, before the trail climbs west into the sierras that separate Castilla from Galicia. León's hinterland is full of gems such as Astorga and the otherworldly minescapes of Las Médulas.

LEÓN

pop 135,100 / elev 527m

León is one of our favourite cities in the region, combining stunning historical architecture with an irresistible energy. Its standout attraction is the cathedral, one of the most beautiful in all of Spain. By day you'll encounter a city with its roots firmly planted in the soil of northern Castilla, with its grand monuments, loyal Catholic heritage and role as an important staging post along the Camino de Santiago. By night León is taken over by its large student population, who provide it with a deep-into-the-night soundtrack of revelry that floods the narrow streets and plazas of the picturesque old quarter, the Barrio Húmedo. It's a wonderful mix.

History

A Roman legion set up camp here in AD 70 as a base for controlling the goldmines of Las Médulas (p254). In the 10th century the Asturian king Ordoño II moved his capital here from Oviedo and, although it was later sacked by the Muslim armies of Al-Mansour, León was maintained by Alfonso V as the capital of his growing kingdom. As the centre of power shifted south, León went into decline; in 1780 John Adams wrote that 'Nothing looked either rich or cheerful but the churches and churchmen'. Mining brought the city back to life in the 1800s. Throughout the 20th century, León's fame revolved around its role as a major staging post along the Camino de Santiago. The city came within the newly autonomous region of Castilla y León in 1983, which some locals saw as an indignity after its proudly independent history. To see how León has grown, look for the historical relief map in Plaza de San Marcelo showing the city in the 1st, 10th and 20th centuries.

Orientation

The train and bus stations lie on the western bank of Río Bernesga, while the heart of the city is on the eastern side. From the river to the cathedral it's about 1km. The old town, the Barrio Húmedo, lies immediately south of the cathedral.

Information

Banks with ATMs and exchange services are concentrated along Avenida de Ordoño II.

Emergency (☎ 112)

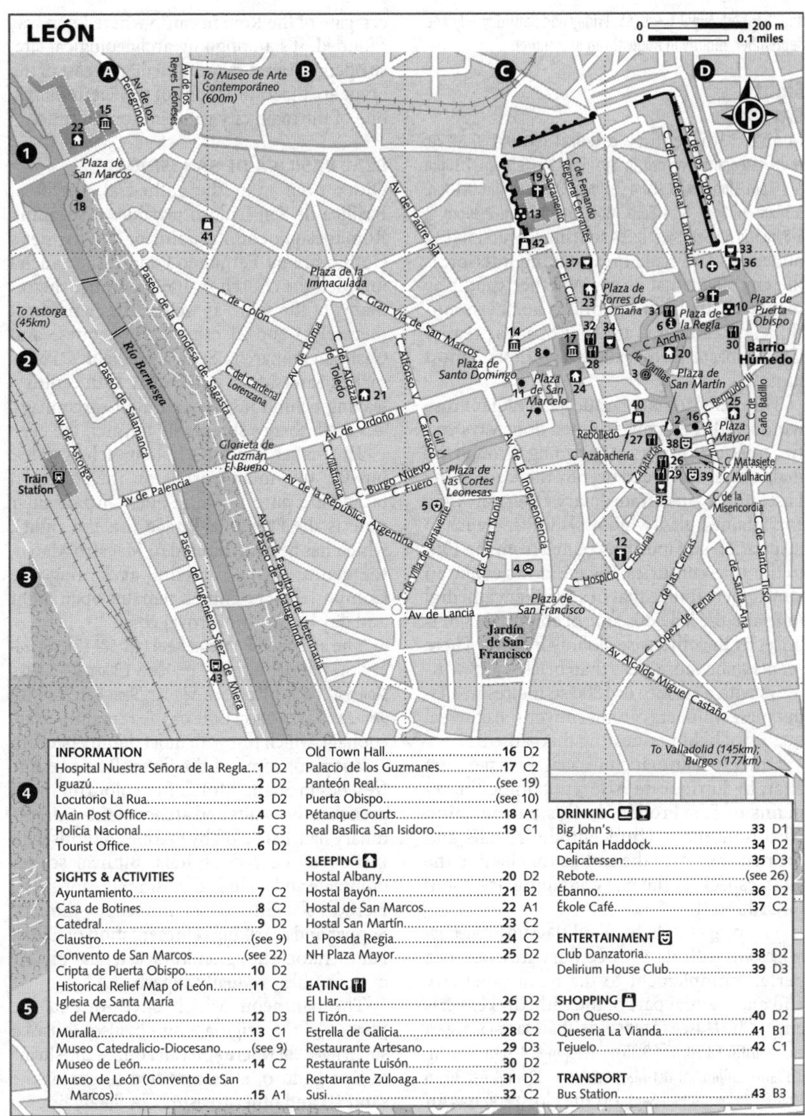

Hospital Nuestra Señora de la Regla (☎ 987 23 69 00; Calle del Cardenal Landázuri 2)

Iguazú (☎ 987 20 80 66; Calle de Plegarias 7; 🕑 10am-2pm & 5-8.30pm Mon-Fri, 10.30am-2.30pm Sat) A fine little travel bookshop.

Locutorio La Rua (☎ 987 21 99 94; Calle de Varillas 3; per 1/5hr €2/5; 🕑 9.30am-9.30pm Mon-Fri, 10.30am-2.30pm & 5.30-9.30pm Sat) Internet access.

Main post office (Avenida de la Independencia)

Policía Nacional (☎ 091, 987 20 73 12; Calle de Villa de Benavente 6)

Tourist office (☎ 987 23 70 82; Plaza de la Regla; 🕑 9am-2pm & 5-8pm Mon-Fri, 10am-2pm & 5-8pm Sat & Sun Oct-May, 9am-8pm daily Jul-Sep) The tourist office organises guided city tours (€8; twice daily July to September, and twice each Saturday and Sunday March to June and October). Night tours (€5; Friday and Saturday July and September, nightly in August) run in summer.

Sights

CATEDRAL

León's 13th-century **catedral** (☎ 987 87 57 70; www.catedraldeleon.org in Spanish; 8.30am-1.30pm & 4-7pm Mon-Sat, 8.30am-2.30pm & 5-7pm Sun Oct-Jun, 8.30am-1.30pm & 4-8pm Mon-Sat, 8.30am-2.30pm & 5-8pm Sun Jul-Sep), with its soaring towers, flying buttresses and truly breathtaking interior, is the city's spiritual heart. Whether spotlit by night or bathed in the glorious northern sunshine, the cathedral, arguably Spain's premier Gothic masterpiece, exudes a glorious, almost luminous quality.

The extraordinary facade has a radiant rose window, three richly sculpted doorways and two muscular towers. After going through the main entrance, lorded over by the scene of the Last Supper, an extraordinary gallery of *vidrieras* (stained-glass windows) awaits. French in inspiration and mostly executed from the 13th to the 16th centuries, the windows evoke an atmosphere unlike that of any other cathedral in Spain; the kaleidoscope of coloured light is offset by the otherwise gloomy interior. There seems to be more glass than brick – 128 windows with a surface of 1800 sq metres in all – but mere numbers cannot convey the ethereal quality of light permeating this cathedral.

Other treasures include a silver urn on the altar, by Enrique de Arfe, containing the remains of San Froilán, León's patron saint. Also note the magnificent choir stalls and the rich chapels in the ambulatory behind the altar, especially the one containing the tomb of Ordoño II.

The peaceful, light-filled **claustro** (cloister; admission €1), with its 15th-century frescoes, is a perfect complement to the main sanctuary and an essential part of the cathedral experience. The **Museo Catedralicio-Diocesano** (admission incl claustro €3.50; 9.30am-1.30pm & 4-7pm Mon-Fri, 9.30am-1.30pm Sat Oct-May, 9.30am-1.30pm & 4-7.30pm Mon-Fri, to 7pm Sat Jul-Sep), off the cloisters, has an impressive collection encompassing works by Juní and Gaspar Becerra alongside a precious assemblage of early-Romanesque carved statues of the Virgin Mary.

CRIPTA DE PUERTA OBISPO

Beneath the footpath below the southern wall of the cathedral is the **Cripta de Puerta Obispo** (admission free), the foundations from the northern gate of the Roman camp where León was founded. It's an ongoing archaeological site, so opening times vary. Immediately east of the crypt are the foundations of the **Puerta Obispo**, one of the main city gates in Roman times.

REAL BASÍLICA DE SAN ISIDORO

Older even than the cathedral, the Real Basílica de San Isidoro provides a stunning Romanesque counterpoint to the former's Gothic strains. Fernando I and Doña Sancha founded the church in 1063 to house the remains of the saint, as well as the remains of themselves and 21 other early Léonese and Castilian monarchs. Sadly, Napoleon's troops sacked San Isidoro in the early 19th century, leaving behind just a handful of sarcophagi, although there's still plenty to catch the eye.

The main basilica is a hotchpotch of styles, but the two main portals on the southern facade are pure Romanesque. Of particular note is the **Puerta del Perdón** (on the right), which has been attributed to Maestro Mateo, the genius of the cathedral at Santiago de Compostela. The church remains open night and day by historical royal edict.

The attached **Panteón Real** (☎ 987 87 61 61; admission €4, free Thu afternoon; 10am-1.30pm & 4-6.30pm Mon-Sat, 10am-1.30pm Sun Sep-Jun, 9am-8pm Mon-Sat, 9am-2pm Sun Jul & Aug) houses the remaining sarcophagi, which rest with quiet dignity beneath a canopy of some of the finest Romanesque frescoes in Spain. Motif after colourful motif drenches the vaults and arches of this extraordinary hall, held aloft by marble columns with intricately carved capitals. Biblical scenes dominate and include the Annunciation, King Herod's slaughter of the innocents, the Last Supper and a striking representation of Christ Pantocrator. The agricultural calendar on one of the arches is equally superb.

The pantheon, which once formed the portico of the original church, also houses a small **museum** where you can admire the shrine of San Isidoro, a mummified finger of the saint (!) and other treasures. A **library** houses a priceless collection of manuscripts.

Abutting the southwestern corner of the basilica is a fragment of the former **muralla** (old city wall), a polyglot of Roman origins and medieval adjustments.

HOSTAL DE SAN MARCOS

More than 100m long and blessed with a glorious facade, the Convento de San Marcos (lying within the Hostal de San Marcos) looks more like a palace than the pilgrim's hospital it was from 1173. The plateresque exterior, sectioned off by slender columns and decorated with delicate medallions and friezes, dates to 1513, by which time the edifice had become a monastery of the Knights of Santiago.

Much of the former convent is now a supremely elegant *parador* (p250). Although you need to stay here to appreciate its full splendour, the former chapter house, with its splendid *artesonado,* and the exquisite cloister are both open to the public. The cloister is technically part of the **Museo de León** (☎ 987 24 50 61; adult/student €0.60/free, free Thu; 🕑 10am-2pm & 4-7pm Tue-Sat, 10am-2pm Sun Oct-Jun, 10am-2pm & 5-8pm Tue-Sat, 10am-2pm Sun Jul-Sep), accessible through the church at the eastern end of the convent and serving as an interpretation centre.

If you're here on a weekend, head to the riverbank, next to the Puerta de San Marcos, where you may find old men with balls of steel playing *pétanque*.

MUSEO DE ARTE CONTEMPORÁNEO

León's showpiece **Museo de Arte Contemporáneo** (Musac; ☎ 987 09 00 00; www.musac.org.es; Avenida de los Reyes Leóneses 24; admission free; 🕑 11am-8pm Tue-Thu, 11am-9pm Fri, 10am-9pm Sat & Sun) belongs to the new wave of innovative Spanish architecture. A pleasing square-and-rhombus edifice of colourful glass and steel, the museum won the Spanish architecture prize in 2003. It has been acclaimed for the 37 shades of coloured glass that adorn the facade; they were gleaned from the pixelisation of a fragment of one of the stained-glass windows in León's cathedral. Although the museum has a growing permanent collection, it mostly houses temporary displays of cutting-edge Spanish and international photography, video installations and other similar forms. For many, the building may appeal more than the works it contains. Musac also hosts musical performances and is fast becoming one of northern Spain's most dynamic cultural spaces.

MUSEO DE LEÓN

After years of looking for a suitable home, the **Museo de León** (☎ 987 23 64 05; Plaza de Santo Domingo 8; admission €1.20, free Sat & Sun; 🕑 10am-2pm & 4-7pm Tue-Sat, 10am-2pm Sun Oct-Jun, 10am-2pm & 5-8pm Tue-Sat, 10am-2pm Sun Jul-Sep) has finally found a space worthy of the city's history. Spread over four floors, the exhibits begin with stunning stone artefacts in the basement, and thereafter journey through the Middle Ages up to the 19th century. It's wonderfully presented and the informative descriptions are in Spanish and English. The much-touted 3rd-floor views of León aren't up to the hype.

BARRIO HÚMEDO

On the fringes of León's old town (also known as the Barrio Gótico), Plaza de San Marcelo is home to the **ayuntamiento**, which occupies a charmingly compact Renaissance-era palace. The Renaissance theme continues in the form of the splendid **Palacio de los Guzmanes** (1560), where the facade and patio stand out. Next door is Antoni Gaudí's contribution to León's skyline, the castlelike, neo-Gothic **Casa de Botines** (1893). The zany architect of Barcelona fame seems to have been subdued by sober León.

Down the hill, the delightful **Plaza de Santa María del Camino** (also known as Plaza del Grano) feels like a cobblestone Castilian village square and is overlooked by the Romanesque **Iglesia de Santa María del Mercado**.

At the northeastern end of the old town is the beautiful and time-worn 17th-century **Plaza Mayor**. Sealed off on three sides by porticoes, this sleepy plaza is home to a bustling fruit-and-vegetable market on Wednesday and Saturday. On the west side of the square is the superb late-17th-century baroque **old town hall**.

Festivals & Events

León is famous for its solemn **Semana Santa** processions of hooded devotees, while the city really lets its hair down from 21 to 30 June for the **Fiestas de San Juan y San Pedro**.

Sleeping

Hostal Bayón (☎ 987 23 14 46; Calle del Alcázar de Toledo 6; s/d with washbasin €15/28, with shower €25/35) At this long-standing León favourite, the laid-back owner presides over cheerful, brightly painted rooms with pine floors. You're surrounded by modern León, but just a five-minute walk from the old town.

Hostal San Martín (☎ 987 87 51 87; www.sanmartinhostales.com in Spanish; 2nd fl, Plaza de Torres de Omaña 1; s without bathroom €20, s/d/tr with bathroom €28/40/52) In a splendid, recently overhauled 18th-century building, this engaging little place is an outstanding choice with light, airy and modern rooms (most with balcony). The owners are friendly, the location central but quiet and the rooms immaculate.

Hostal Albany (☎ 987 26 46 00; www.albanyleon.com; Calle de la Paloma 13; s/d €35/50; 💻) The sort of place you'd expect to find in Barcelona or Madrid, Hostal Albany is a high-class *hostal* with a designer touch. Clean lines, plasma TVs, great bathrooms and cheerful colour schemes abound. Some rooms have partial cathedral views.

NH Plaza Mayor (☎ 987 34 43 57; www.nh-hoteles.es; Plaza Mayor 15; d from €87; ❄ 💻) Part of the stylish NH chain, which has a knack for finding a great location in need of tender loving care, the NH Plaza Mayor has the perfect combination of comfort, muted colour schemes, great service and an intimate ambience. Nineteen rooms overlook the plaza.

our pick La Posada Regia (☎ 987 21 31 73; www.regialeon.com in Spanish; Calle de Regidores 9-11; s €55-65, d €90-120) You won't find many places better than this in northern Spain. The secret is a 14th-century building, magnificently restored (wooden beams, exposed brick and understated antique furniture), with individually styled rooms, character that overflows into the public areas and supremely comfortable beds and bathrooms.

Hostal de San Marcos (☎ 987 23 73 00; www.parador.es; Plaza de San Marcos 7; d from €198; ❄ 💻) León's sumptuous *parador* is one of the finest hotels in Spain. With palatial rooms fit for royalty and filled with old-world charm, this is one of the *parador* chain's flagship properties. See also p248.

Eating

Restaurante Luisón (☎ 987 25 40 29; Plaza Puerta Obispo 16; menú del día €8, meals €15-20) This place could only exist in Spain – basic surrounds, offhand waiters and terrific, hearty food that keeps the locals fortified during cold winters. You'll need to book ahead, especially at lunchtime, when *leonéses* can't get enough of the local *botillo berciano*, a succulent pork dish, or *cocido leónes* (León-style chickpea stew).

Estrella de Galicia (☎ 987 24 08 32; Calle Ancha 20; menú del día €11, meals €20-25; 🕒 lunch & dinner Tue-Sun) All that's good about northwestern Spanish cuisine can be found here, with Galician seafood, Cantabrian fish and cured meats from the northern interior. The *pulpo* (octopus) is a great order but Estrella also does salads, mini-rolls and a host of *raciones*.

Susi (☎ 987 27 39 96; Calle de López Castrillón 1; menú del día €12, meals €25-30; 🕒 lunch & dinner Mon-Sat, lunch only Sun) Intimate dining and creative cooking make for a fine experience at this stylish temple to good taste. The service is attentive, the wine list is long, and the menu has some dishes that will live in the memory – the *solomillo relleno con foie y datiles* (sirloin filled with foie gras and dates) stands out.

our pick El Tizón (☎ 987 25 60 49; Plaza de San Martín 1; menú del día €13, meals €25-30; 🕒 lunch & dinner Mon-Wed, Fri & Sat, lunch only Sun) The tapas are good here, but the small sit-down restaurant, with an abundant set lunch, is even better. House specialities include the local *embutidos* and there's an extensive wine list. No wonder it's always full.

Restaurante Zuloaga (☎ 987 23 78 14; Sierra Pambley 3; menú del día €14, meals €25-30; 🕒 lunch & dinner Tue-Sun) This fabulous place in the vaults of an early-20th-century palace has a well-stocked cellar and classy menu. The walls feature original mosaics by the artist Ignacio Zuloaga.

Restaurante Artesano (☎ 987 21 53 22; www.palaciojabalquinto.com in Spanish; Calle de Juan de Arfe 2; menú del día €18, meals €35) One of the classier places to eat in León, Restaurante Artesano combines creative food, modern art and the renovated 17th-century Palacio Jabal Quinto. It's the ideal spot for a special occasion, and the choices are many and varied, from *embutidos* to *brocheta de pato* (duck brochettes).

El Llar (☎ 987 25 42 87; Plaza de San Martín 9; meals €25-30) This old León *taberna* is a great place to *tapear* (eat tapas) or dine upstairs in the sit-down restaurant. Either way, you'll come across an abundance of local wines, cheeses and other specialities of the region. For a typical León taste, order the *tabla de embutidos* (plate of cured meats).

Drinking & Entertainment

The Barrio Húmedo's night-time epicentre is Plaza de San Martín – prise open the door of any bar here or in the surrounding streets (especially Calle de Juan de Arfe and Calle de la Misericordia), inch your way to the bar and you're unlikely to want to leave until closing time. The crowds will tell you where the buzz is, but a good night could begin at **Rebote** (Plaza de San Martín 9; 🕒 8pm-1am), then move on to funky **Delicatessen** (Calle de Juan de Arfe 10; 🕒 10pm-3am Wed-Sat) before ending up at the **Delirium House Club** (Calle de la Misericordia

9; 🕑 11pm-5am Thu-Sat) or **Club Danzatoria** (Calle de Ramirez III 9; 🕑 11pm-3am Wed-Sat).

Tucked away behind the cathedral to the east, **Big John's** (Avenida de los Cubos 4; 🕑 7pm-2am) is a jazz hang-out with occasional live jazz at 10.30pm, while **Ébanno** (Avenida de los Cubos 2; 🕑 4pm-late) is classy and as good for laptop-toting wi-fi hunters as for late-night sophisticates.

Elsewhere, **Ékole Café** (☎ 987 22 57 02; Plaza de Torres de Omaña s/n; 🕑 4.30pm-1.30am Sun-Thu, 4.30pm-3.30am Fri & Sat) is one of our favourite León drinking holes, with cocktails (€5), ice creams, hot drinks and a lovely interior patio.

A great place for a drink, day or night, is **Capitán Haddock** (Calle Ancha 8; 🕑 noon-late), with red velvet curtains, candlelight, mirrors and an ambience somewhere between boudoir and retro.

Shopping

Don Queso (Calle Azabachería 20; 🕑 10am-2pm & 5.30-8pm Mon-Fri, 9.30am-2.30pm Sat) Cheese-lovers will want to make a stop here; you'll find every imaginable variety.

Queseria La Vianda (☎ 987 24 03 70; Calle Gran Vía de San Marcos 45; 🕑 10am-3pm & 6-9pm Mon-Fri, 10am-3pm Sat) This small shop overflows with *productos artesanales* (homemade products), from chestnuts in cinnamon to trout cake to *nicanores* (a local sweet pastry).

Tejuelo (☎ 987 23 88 22; Calle de Ruiz de Salazar 18; 🕑 10.30am-2pm Mon-Fri, 11am-2pm Sat) Handmade paper products, fountain pens, leather-bound books and a small but rich range of classically upmarket stationery make this place stand out.

Getting There & Away

BUS

From the **bus station** (Paseo del Ingeniero Sáez de Miera), **ALSA** (☎ 902 42 22 42; www.alsa.es) has numerous daily buses to Madrid (€20.74, 3½ hours), Burgos (€13.31, 3¾ hours), Astorga (€3.15, 45 minutes), Ponferrada (€7.65, two hours), Oviedo (€8.04, 1½ hours) and Valladolid (€8.47, two hours).

CAR & MOTORCYCLE

The N630 heads north to Oviedo, though the AP66 *autopista* (tollway) that runs parallel to the west is faster (the two roads merge at Campomanes). The N630 also continues south to Salamanca. The N120 goes west to Galicia via Astorga, where it merges with the A6.

Parking stations (€9 to €13 for 12 hours) abound in the streets surrounding Plaza de Santo Domingo.

TRAIN

Regular daily trains travel to Valladolid (from €9.60, two hours), Burgos (from €17.90, two hours), Oviedo (from €7.15, two hours), Madrid (from €22.40, 4¼ hours) and Barcelona (from €43.20, 10 hours).

EAST OF LEÓN

Iglesia de San Miguel de Escalada

Rising from Castilla's northern plains, this beautifully simple treasure was built in the 9th century by refugee monks from Córdoba on the remains of a Visigothic church dedicated to the Archangel Michael. Although little trace of the latter remains, the **church** (🕑 10.15am-2pm & 4.30-8pm Tue-Sun May-Oct, 10.40am-2pm & 4-5.50pm Tue-Sat, 10am-2pm Sun Nov-Apr) is notable for its Islamic-inspired horseshoe arches, rarely seen so far north in Spain. The graceful exterior porch with its portico is balanced by the impressive marble columns within. The entrance dates from the 11th century.

To get here, take the N601 southeast of León. After about 14km, take the small LE213 to the east; the church is 16km after the turn-off.

Sahagún

pop 2850 / elev 807m

An unremarkable place today, Sahagún was once home to one of Spain's more powerful abbeys. Today the abbey is a crumbling ruin, evocative in an abandoned kind of way. Its more important remnants are kept in the small **Museo Benedictinas** (☎ 987 78 00 78; admission by donation; 🕑 10am-noon & 4-6pm Tue-Sat, 10am-noon Sun).

Next to the former abbey is the early-12th-century **Iglesia de San Tirso** (🕑 10.15am-2pm & 4.30-8pm Wed-Sat, 10.15am-2pm Sun Apr-Sep, 10.40am-2pm & 3-5.30pm Wed-Sat, 10.40am-2pm Sun Oct-Mar), an important stop on the Camino de Santiago, known for its pure Romanesque design and Mudéjar bell tower laced with rounded arches. The **Iglesia San Lorenzo**, just north of Plaza Mayor, has a similar bell tower.

For more information visit the local **tourist office** (☎ 987 78 21 17; www.sahagun.org; Calle del Arco 87; 🕑 10am-2pm & 4.30-7pm Oct-Jun, 10am-10pm Jul-Sep).

Low on charm but high on comfort, the modern **Hotel Puerta de Sahagún** (☎ 987 78 18 80; www.hotelpuertadesahagun.com; Calle de Burgos; s €40-45, d €70-75) seems a bit out of place in provincial Sahagún, but it's spick, span and a haven from dusty Camino trails.

Trains run regularly throughout the day from León (€4.10, 40 minutes) and Palencia (€4.10, 35 minutes).

WEST OF LEÓN

Astorga

pop 12,200 / elev 870m

Perched on a hilltop on the frontier between the bleak plains of northern Castilla and the mountains that rise up to the west towards Galicia, Astorga is a fascinating little town with a wealth of attractions far out of proportion to its size. In addition to its fine cathedral, the city boasts a Gaudí-designed palace, a smattering of Roman ruins and a personality dominated by the Camino de Santiago.

HISTORY

The Romans built the first settlement, Astúrica Augusta, here at the head of the Ruta del Oro. During the Middle Ages Astorga was well established as a waystation along one of Europe's most important pilgrimage routes. By the 15th century its growing significance inspired the construction of the cathedral and the rebuilding of its 3rd-century walls.

Astorga is the capital of a district known as the Maragatería. Some historians claim the *maragatos*, who, with their mule trains, dedicated themselves almost exclusively to the carrying trade, were descendants of the first Berbers to enter Spain in the Muslim armies of the 8th century.

INFORMATION

The **tourist office** (☎ 987 61 82 22; turismo@ayuntamientodeastorga.com; ⌚ 10am-2pm & 4-8pm daily May-Oct, 10.30am-1.30pm & 4-6.30pm Mon-Sat Nov-Apr) is in the northwestern corner of the old town.

SIGHTS

Catedral

The most striking element of Astorga's **catedral** (☎ 987 61 58 20; ⌚ 9.30am-noon & 5-6.30pm Oct-Mar, 9am-noon & 5-6.30pm Apr-Sep) is its plateresque southern facade, made from caramel-coloured sandstone and dripping in sculptural detail. Work began in 1471 and proceeded in stop-start fashion over three centuries, resulting in a mix of styles. The mainly Gothic interior has soaring ceilings, with the 16th-century altarpiece by Gaspar Becerra monopolising your gaze among the many gilt-edged flourishes. The attached **Museo Catedralicio** (admission €2.50, incl Museo de los Caminos €4; ⌚ 10am-2pm & 4-8pm Apr-Sep, 11am-2pm & 3.30-6.30pm Oct-Mar) features the usual religious art, documents and artefacts.

Palacio Episcopal

The Catalan architect Antoni Gaudí may have spurned Madrid, but he left his mark on Astorga in the fairy-tale turrets, frilly facade and surprising details of the Palacio Episcopal. Built for the local bishop from the end of the 19th century, it now houses the **Museo de los Caminos** (☎ 987 61 82 22; admission €2.50, incl Museo Catedralicio €4; ⌚ 10am-2pm & 4-8pm Tue-Sat, 10am-2pm Sun Apr-Sep, 11am-2pm & 4-6pm Tue-Sat, 11am-2pm Sun Oct-Mar). It's an eclectic collection with Roman artefacts and coins in the basement; contemporary paintings on the top floor; and medieval sculpture, Gothic tombs and silver crosses dominating the ground and 1st floors. The highlight (apart from the playful Gaudíesque interior) is the chapel, with its stunning murals, tilework and stained glass.

Museo del Chocolate

Proof that Astorga does not exist solely for the virtuous souls of the Camino comes in the form of this small and quirky private **museum** (☎ 987 61 62 20; Calle de José María Goy 5; admission €1, incl Museo Romano €3; ⌚ 10.30am-2pm & 4-6pm Tue-Sat, 11am-2pm Sun). Chocolate ruled Astorga's local economy in the 18th and 19th centuries, as evidenced by this eclectic collection of old machinery, colourful advertising and fascinating lithographs. It offers a refreshing, indulgent (some would say sinful) break from Castilla's religious-art circuit. Best of all, you get a free chocolate sample at the end.

Ruta Romana

Housed in the Roman *ergástula* (slave prison), the **Museo Romano** (☎ 987 61 69 37; Plaza de San Bartolomé 2; admission €2.50, incl Museo del Chocolate €3; ⌚ 10am-1.30pm & 4.30-7pm Tue-Sat, 10.30am-1.30pm Sun Jul-Sep, 10.30am-1.30pm & 4-6pm Tue-Sat, 10.30am-1.30pm Sun Oct-Jun) has a modest selection of artefacts and an enjoyable big-screen slide show on Roman Astorga.

Ask at the tourist office about the Ruta Romana Spanish-language guided tours (€3.10, noon Tuesday to Sunday from Easter to October), which seek out the other Roman ruins dotted around town. Among these are the **town walls**, **thermal baths**, **sewers** and **Las**

Domus del Mosaico; the last is a Roman floor plan with a few mosaics just 100m southeast of the museum. The tours last for 1½ hours.

FESTIVALS & EVENTS

During the last week of August, Astorga awakes from its customary slumber to celebrate the **Festividad de Santa Marta** with fireworks and bullfights.

SLEEPING

Pensión La Peseta (☎ 987 61 72 75; www.restaurantelapeseta.com; Plaza de San Bartolomé 3; d €50-55) Although it's a touch overpriced (the rooms are fine if a little uninspiring), the owners are superfriendly and keen to make your stay comfortable. They readily admit that the attached restaurant (p254) is their passion, so you should spend more time there than in your room.

Hotel Gaudí (☎ 987 61 56 54; www.hotelgaudiastorga.com; Calle de Eduardo de Castro 6; s/d from €48/65; ❄) There aren't many places in the world where you can see a Gaudí flight of fancy from your bed, so ask for a street-facing room. The large carpeted rooms are otherwise reasonable, although the decor could do with a fresh look.

Hotel Astur Plaza (☎ 987 61 89 00; www.asturplaza.com; Plaza de España 2; s/d/ste from €65/90/100; ❄ 💻) This modern hotel is comfortable and while you may lament the lack of character in the rooms, if you have one facing the pretty Plaza de España, you'll leave more than happy. It's worth asking for special offers as prices can drop when things are quiet.

EATING

The local speciality is *cocido maragato*, a stew of chickpeas, various meats, potatoes and cabbage. Unlike elsewhere, Astorgan tradition dictates that you first eat the meat, then the vegetables before finishing up with the broth. Portions are huge, so one order usually feeds two.

Cervecería La Esquina (☎ 987 61 57 97; Plaza de España 5; meals €10-20) For tapas, this is probably the best place, with local *leónes* specialities and a wonderful house dish called *patatas esquinadas* (lightly seasoned potato slices). You'll also get service with a smile, not to mention 18 varieties of beer to choose from.

La Peseta (☎ 987 61 72 75; www.restaurantelapeseta.com; Plaza de San Bartolomé 3; meals €20) Famous for its *cocido* (€17.50), the excellent La Peseta also has other local specialities, including *morcilla* (blood sausage) and *alúbias* (small white beans). Service is friendly and obliging and, unusually, the cut-price *menús* also run at night. La Peseta offers cheaper *menús* for pilgrims.

Restaurante Las Termas (☎ 987 60 22 12; Calle de Santiago Postas 1; meals from €20) Renowned for the quality of its *cocido* (€18), Las Termas also does a great *ensalada maragata* (salad of chickpeas and cod).

Restaurante Serrano (☎ 987 61 78 66; Calle de la Portería 2; meals €30; lunch & dinner Tue-Sun) The upmarket Restaurante Serrano is a little different to the other darkish, wood-panelled restaurants around town. Decor is bright and the menu creative.

Pastry shops all over town churn out the local *mantecadas,* a cakelike sweet peculiar to Astorga. Places to try include **Confitería Alonso** (Plaza de España) and **La Mallorquina** (cnr Calles de Los Sitios & de Santiago Postas), both of which keep erratic hours. A small/large box costs €3/6.

GETTING THERE & AWAY

Regular bus services connect Astorga with León (€3.15, 45 minutes, up to 16 daily) and Ponferrada (€4.65, 1¼ hours, up to 10 daily). There are also departures for Oviedo (€10.50, 2½ hours, two daily) and Madrid (€21, 4½ hours, five daily). The train station is inconveniently a couple of kilometres north of town.

Around Astorga

Castrillo de los Polvazares, 6km west of Astorga, is a 17th-century hamlet built from vivid ferrous stone, its blazing orange colour made all the more striking by the brilliant green paint job on the doors and window frames. **Hostería Cuca La Vaina** (☎ 987 69 10 34; www.cucalavaina.com; Calle de Jardín; d from €55) is a well-run place with warm service and rooms filled with character. The restaurant serves up the local speciality *cocido maragato*. Semiregular buses (€1, 15 minutes) run from Astorga's bus station.

Ponferrada

pop 66,900 / elev 508m

Ponferrada, 60km west of Astorga, is not the region's most enticing town, but its castle and remnants of the old town centre (around the stone clock tower) make it a worthwhile stop en route to or from Galicia. The **tourist office** (☎ 987 42 42 36; Calle de Gil y Carrasco 4; 10am-2pm & 4.30-6.30pm Mon-Fri, 10.30am-1.30pm & 4.30-6.30pm Sat, 10.30am-1.30pm Sun) lies in the shadow of the castle walls.

SIGHTS

Built by the Knights Templar in the 13th century, the walls of the fortress-monastery **Castillo Templario** (adult/concession €3/1.50; 11am-2pm & 5-9pm Tue-Sat, 11am-2pm Sun May-Aug, 11am-2pm & 4-7pm Tue-Sat, 11am-2pm Sun Sep-Apr) rise high over Río Sil, and the square, crenellated towers ooze romance and history. The castle has a lonely and impregnable air, and is a striking landmark in Ponferrada's otherwise bleak urban landscape.

Among Ponferrada's churches, the Gothic–Renaissance **Basílica de Nuestra Señora de la Encina** (☎ 987 41 19 78; 9am-2pm & 4.30-8.30pm), up the hill past the tourist office, is the most impressive, especially its 17th-century painted wood altarpiece from the school of Gregorio Fernández.

SLEEPING & EATING

Hostal Santa Cruz (☎ 987 42 83 51; hsantacruz@wanadoo.es; Calle Marcelo Macias 4; s/d with washbasin €25/30, with bathroom from €30/40) A largish place with reasonable rates, Hostal Santa Cruz is a good budget choice. The rooms all come with TV and the friendly service comes free.

Hotel AC Ponferrada (☎ 987 40 99 73; www.ac-hoteles.com; Avenida de Astorga 2; s/d from €106/111;) Part of the quality AC Hotels chain, this modern four-star place won't win any prizes for personality, but the service is attentive and the rooms supremely comfortable.

For meals, both **Mesón Mosteiro** (☎ 987 42 68 05; Calle del Reloj 10; meals from €8) and **Mesón El Quijote** (☎ 987 42 88 90; Calle de Gregoria Campillo 3; menú €8), in the new town, offer cheap set meals.

GETTING THERE & AWAY

The bus station is at the northern end of town (take local bus 3 to/from the centre). Regular buses connect Ponferrada with León (€7.65, two hours), via Astorga (€4.65, 1¼ hours, up to 10 daily), Madrid (€24.50, five hours, seven daily) and most Galician cities, including Lugo.

Las Médulas

The ancient Roman goldmines at Las Médulas, about 20km southwest of Ponferrada, once served as the main source of gold for the entire Roman Empire – the final tally came to a remarkable 3 million kilograms. An army of slaves honeycombed the area with canals and tunnels (some over 40km long!) through which they pumped water to break up the rock and free it from the precious metal. The result is a singularly unnatural natural phenomenon and one of the more bizarre landscapes you'll see in Spain. It's breathtaking at sunset.

To get to the heart of the former quarries, drive beyond Las Médulas village (4km south of Carucedo and the N536 highway). Several trails weave among chestnut patches and bizarre formations left behind by the miners.

THE EAST

Eastern Castilla y León is where you can leave behind tourist Spain and immerse yourself in a world of charming villages, isolated monasteries and castles, quiet roads and scenic landscapes. Beautiful Burgos and provincial Soria serve as bookends to the region if you're in need of urban life.

BURGOS

pop 174,100 / elev 861m

The extraordinary Gothic cathedral of Burgos is one of Spain's glittering jewels of religious architecture. It looms large over the city, and not just its skyline. On the surface, conservative Burgos seems to embody all the stereotypes of a north-central Spanish town, with sombre grey-stone architecture, the fortifying cuisine of the high *meseta* (plateau) and a climate of extremes. But this is a city that rewards deeper exploration: below the surface lies vibrant nightlife, good restaurants and, when the sun's shining, pretty streetscapes that extend far beyond the landmark cathedral. There's even a whiff of legend about the place: beneath the majestic spires of the cathedral lies Burgos' favourite and most roguish son, El Cid.

History

Burgos began life in 884 as a strategic fortress on the frontline between the Muslims and the rival kingdom of Navarra. It was surrounded by several *burgos* (villages), which eventually melded together to form the basis of a new city. Centuries later, Burgos thrived as a staging post for pilgrims on the Camino de Santiago and as a trading centre between the interior and the northern ports. During the Spanish Civil War, General Franco used Burgos as the base for his government-in-waiting.

Orientation

Old Burgos, dominated by the cathedral, is wedged between Río Arlanzón and the hill to the northwest on which stands the town's old castle. Most of the hotels and restaurants lie north and east of the cathedral. South of the river, in the newer part of town, are the bus and train stations.

Information

There are banks all over central Burgos.

Caja España (Calle de la Paloma 4) One of the most central places to change money.

Ciber-Café Cabaret (Calle de la Puebla 21; per hr from €2.50; noon-1am Sun-Thu, 7pm-4am Fri & Sat) Internet access.

Emergency (☎ 112)

Hospital General Yagüe (☎ 947 28 18 00; Avenida del Cid Campeador 96)

Main post office (Plaza del Conde de Castro)

Municipal tourist office (☎ 947 28 88 74; www.aytoburgos.es in Spanish; Plaza del Rey Fernando 2; 10am-2pm & 4.30-7.30pm Mon-Fri, 10am-1.30pm & 4-7.30pm Sat & Sun mid-Sep–Jun, 10am-8pm daily Jul–mid-Sep)

Policía Nacional (☎ 091, 947 22 04 66; Avenida de Castilla y León 3)

Regional tourist office (☎ 947 20 31 25; www.turismocastillayleon.com; Plaza de Alonso Martínez 7; 9am-2pm & 5-8pm daily mid-Sep–Jun, 9am-8pm Sun-Thu, 9am-9pm Fri & Sat Jul–mid-Sep)

Sights

OLD QUARTER

Burgos' old quarter, on the north bank of Río Arlanzón, is stately rather than grand, austerely elegant in the manner of so many cathedral towns of old Castilla. Coming from the south, it can be accessed via two main bridges. One of these is the **Puente de San Pablo**, beyond which looms a romanticised **statue of El Cid** with his swirling cloak and sword held aloft. About 300m to the west, the **Puente de Santa María** leads to the splendid **Arco de Santa María** (☎ 947 28 88 68; admission free; 11am-1.50pm & 5-9pm Tue-Sat, 11am-1.50pm Sun), once the main gate to the old city and part of the 14th-century walls. It now hosts temporary exhibitions. Running along the riverbank between the two bridges is the **Paseo del Espolón**, a lovely

CASTILLA Y LEÓN

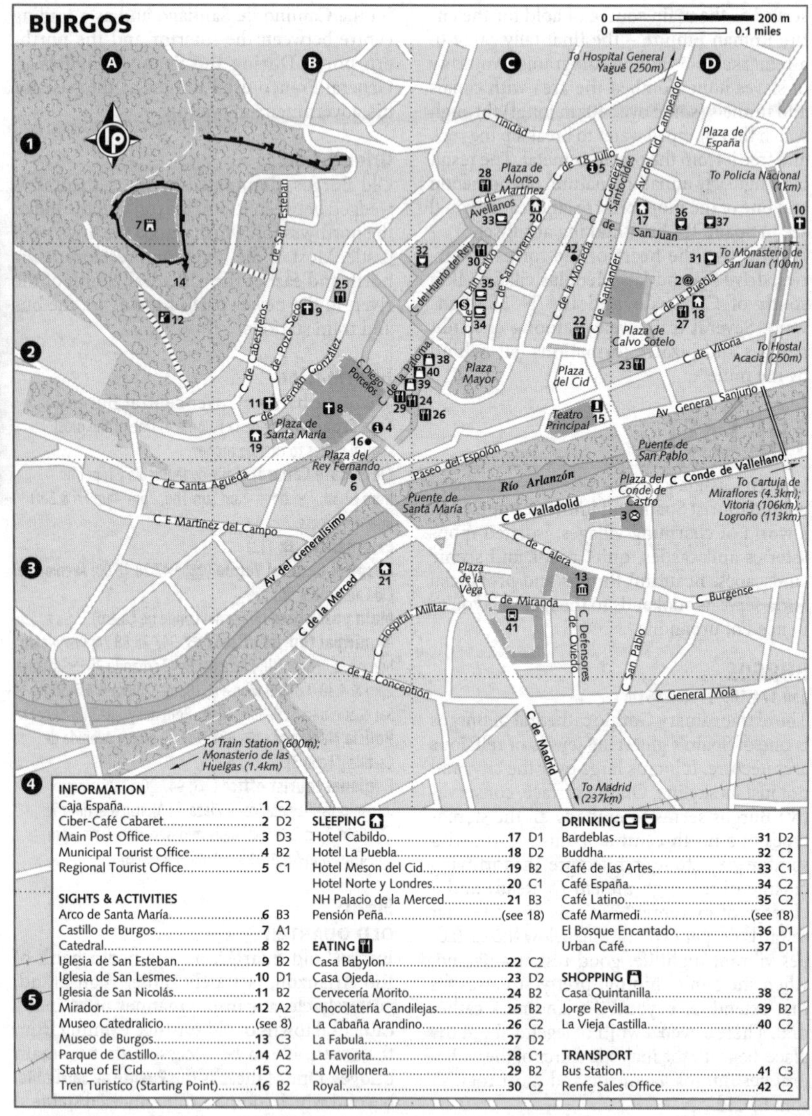

tree-lined pedestrian area. Just back from the *paseo* (promenade) is the oddly shaped **Plaza Mayor**, with some lovely facades.

CATEDRAL

The Unesco World Heritage–listed **catedral** (☎ 947 20 47 12; Plaza del Rey Fernando; adult/child/pilgrim & student/senior €4/1/2.50/3; 🕑 9.30am-7.30pm 19 Mar-Oct, 10am-7pm Nov-18 Mar) is a masterpiece that's probably worth the trip to Burgos on its own. It had humble origins as a modest Romanesque church, but work began on a grander scale in 1221. Remarkably, within 40 years most of the French Gothic structure that you see today had been completed. The twin towers, which went up later in the 15th century, each represent 84m of richly decorated Gothic fantasy and they're surrounded by a sea of similarly intricate spires. Probably the most impressive of the portals is the **Puerta del Sarmental**, the main entrance for visitors, although the honour could also go to the **Puerta de la Coronería**, on the northwestern side, which shows Christ surrounded by the Evangelists.

It's possible to enter the cathedral from Plaza de Santa María for free, but doing so leaves the most worthwhile sections off-limits. Nonetheless, you'll still have access to the **Capilla del Santísimo Cristo**, which harbours a much-revered 13th-century crucifix (known as the *Cristo de Burgos*) made from buffalo hide, and the **Capilla de Santa Tecla**, with its extraordinary ceiling.

Inside the main sanctuary, a host of other chapels showcase the diversity of the interior, from the light and airy **Capilla de la Presentación** to the **Capilla de la Concepción** with its impossibly gilded, 15th-century altar. The main altar is a typically overwhelming piece of gold-encrusted extravagance, while directly beneath the star-vaulted central dome lies the **tomb of El Cid**. Another highlight is the **Escalera Dorada** (Gilded Stairway; 1520) on the cathedral's northwestern flank, the handiwork of Diego de Siloé.

The **Capilla del Condestable**, on the eastern end of the ambulatory behind the main altar, is a remarkable late-15th-century production. Bridging Gothic and plateresque styles, its highlights include three altars watched over by unusual star-shaped vaulting in the dome. The sculptures facing the entrance to the chapel are astonishing 15th- and 16th-century masterpieces of stone carving, portraying the passion, death, resurrection and ascension of Christ.

Also worth a look is the peaceful **cloister**, with its sculpted medieval tombs. Off the cloister is the **Capilla de Corpus Cristi**, where, high on the northwestern wall, hangs the coffin of El Cid. The adjoining **Museo Catedralicio** has a wealth of oils, tapestries and ornate chalices, while the **lower cloister**, downstairs, covers the history of the cathedral's development, with a scale model to help you take it all in.

CHURCHES

Between the cathedral and the climb up to the castle, the **Iglesia de San Esteban** is a muscular 14th-century Gothic structure with an unusual porch, while the neighbouring **Iglesia de San Nicolás** (☎ 947 20 70 95) boasts an enormous stone-carved altar by Francisco de Colonia, with scenes from the life of St Nicolas. It was closed for major restoration when we visited.

Across town, the delightfully unadorned **Iglesia de San Lesmes** (Plaza de San Juan; 🕑 before & after Mass) dates to the 15th century and is notable for its three naves and rustic charm. Adjacent is the **Monasterio de San Juan** (Museo Marceliano Santamaría; ☎ 947 20 56 87; Plaza de San Juan; admission free; 🕑 11am-1.50pm & 5-9pm Tue-Sat, 11am-1.50pm Sun), with an evocative shell that has been converted into a museum for local artists.

MONASTERIO DE LAS HUELGAS

A 30-minute walk west of the city centre on the southern bank of Río Arlanzón, this **monastery** (☎ 947 20 16 30; guided tours adult/student €5/4, free Wed; 🕑 10am-1pm & 3.45-5.30pm Tue-Sat, 10.30am-2pm Sun) was once among the most prominent monasteries in Spain. Founded in 1187 by Eleanor of Aquitaine, daughter of Henry II of England and wife of Alfonso VIII of Castilla, it's still home to 35 Cistercian nuns.

If you've come this far, join a guided tour (otherwise only a small section of the church is accessible), which takes you through the three main naves of the church. This veritable royal pantheon contains the tombs of numerous kings and queens, including those of Eleanor and Alfonso. Also here is a spectacular gilded

BURGOS CARD & TREN TURÍSTICO

The **Burgos Card** (☎ 902 08 89 08; www.burgoscard.com; 1/2 days €13/17) covers entrance for all the sights mentioned in this section, and offers discounts at a range of shops, hotels and other businesses around town.

Also covered by the Burgos Card is the cutesy **tren turístico** (tourist train; adult/child €4/2), which leaves from outside the tourist office and runs past all the major sights in town. The only stop it makes on the 45-minute journey is at the mirador next to the *castillo* (castle), so it's a good way to get an overview of the town rather than get from place to place. It runs Friday evenings, Saturday and Sunday, with more-frequent departures in summer. Buy your ticket at the tourist office.

EL CID: THE HEROIC MERCENARY

Few names resonate through Spanish history quite like El Cid, the 11th-century soldier of fortune and adventurer whose story tells in microcosm of the tumultuous years when Spain was divided into Muslim and Christian zones. That El Cid became a romantic, idealised figure of history, known for his unswerving loyalty and superhuman strength, owes much to the 1961 film starring Charlton Heston and Sophia Loren. Reality, though, presents a different picture.

El Cid (from the Arabic *sidi* for 'chief' or 'lord') was born Rodrígo Diaz in Vivar, a hamlet about 10km north of Burgos, in 1043. After the death of Ferdinand I, he dabbled in the murky world of royal succession, which led to his banishment from Castilla in 1076. With few scruples as to whom he served, El Cid offered his services to a host of rulers, both Christian and Muslim. With each battle, he became ever more powerful and wealthy.

It's not known whether he suddenly developed a loyalty to the Christian kings or smelled the wind and saw that Spain's future would be Christian. Either way, when he heard that the Muslim armies had taken Valencia and expelled all the Christians, El Cid marched on the city, recaptured it and became its ruler in 1094 after a devastating siege. At the height of his powers and reputation, the man also known as El Campeador (Champion) retired to spend the remainder of his days in Valencia, where he died in 1099. His remains were returned to Burgos, where he lies buried along with his wife, Jimena, in the cathedral.

Renaissance altar topped by a larger-than-life Jesus being taken off the cross. The highlight, though, is the **Museo de Ricas Telas**, reached via a lovely Romanesque cloister known as Las Claustrillas. It contains bejewelled robes and royal garments.

CARTUJA DE MIRAFLORES

The **church** (🕑 10.15am-3pm & 4-6pm Mon-Fri, 11am-3pm & 4-6pm Sat & Sun) of this strict Carthusian monastery, in peaceful woodlands 4km east of the city centre, contains a trio of 15th-century masterworks by Gil de Siloé. The most dazzling of these is the ornate, star-shaped alabaster tomb of Juan II and Isabel of Portugal, the parents of Isabel la Católica. Gil de Siloé also carved the tomb of her brother, the Infante Alfonso, and helped with the giant *retablo* that forms a worthy backdrop to the royal mausoleum. The walk to the monastery along Río Arlanzón takes about one hour.

MUSEO DE BURGOS

This **museum** (☎ 947 26 58 75; Calle de Calera 25; adult/student & under 18yr €1.20/free, Sat & Sun free; 🕑 10am-2pm & 4-7pm Tue-Sat, 10am-2pm Sun Oct-Jun, 10am-2pm & 5-8pm Tue-Sat, 10am-2pm Sun Jul-Sep), housed in the 16th-century Casa de Miranda, contains some fine Gothic tombs and other archaeological artefacts covering a wide period.

PARQUE DE CASTILLO

This leafy hilltop park is crowned by the massive fortifications of the rebuilt **Castillo de Burgos** (☎ 947 28 88 74; adult/concession €3.50/2.50; 🕑 11am-2pm Sat & Sun Oct-Mar, 11am-2pm & 4-7pm Sat & Sun Apr-Sep). Dating from the 9th century, the castle has witnessed a turbulent history, suffering a fire in 1736 before finally being blown up by Napoleon's retreating troops in 1813. Just south of the car park is a **mirador** (lookout), which offers fine views over the town and helpful signposts to the major sights and further afield. Who knew that Burgos lies 3150km from Timbuktu…

Festivals & Events

Burgos' big fiestas occur in late June and early July to celebrate the **Festividad de San Pedro y San Pablo** (Feast of Saints Peter and Paul), with bullfights, processions and much merry-making, particularly on the first Sunday of July, the **Día de las Peñas**. Slightly more low-key is the **Festividad de San Lesmes** (for the city's patron saint) on 30 January.

Sleeping

Pensión Peña (☎ /fax 947 20 63 23; Calle de la Puebla 18; s/d without bathroom from €20/26) This impeccable little place with a motherly owner has rooms with delightful individual touches, such as hand-painted washbasins. The central location is also a plus.

Hostal Acacia (☎ 947 20 51 34; www.hostalacacia.com; Calle de Bernabé Perez Ortiz 1; d with shower & washbasin from €30, s/d with bathroom from €25/37) This place, which is especially popular with pilgrims, hasn't raised its prices in years, during which time the rooms have, if anything, improved. The simple rooms have dull bedspreads and mostly renovated bathrooms, and some have lovely ochre-painted walls. The loquacious Trotsky-lookalike proprietor is a star attraction.

our pick Hotel Norte y Londres (☎ 947 26 41 25; www.hotelnorteylondres.com; Plaza de Alonso Martínez 10; s €46-75, d €55-120; P 💻) Set in a former 16th-century palace and with understated period charm, this fine hotel promises spacious rooms with antique furnishings, polished wooden floors and pretty balconies; those on the 4th floor are more modern. The service is all about old-world civility to match. Parking costs €12.

Hotel Cabildo (☎ 947 25 78 40; www.hotelcabildo.com; Avenida del Cid Campeador 2; d €60-126; P ⊠ 💻) Relatively new to the Burgos hotel scene, Hotel Cabildo has quickly become one of the most comfortable places to stay in town. The rooms are large and stylish, combining natural light and suave, dark tones, and the service is obliging. It's a classy place. Parking costs €12.

Hotel Meson del Cid (☎ 947 20 87 15; www.mesondelcid.es; Plaza de Santa María 8; s €70-118, d €70-148; P ❄) The rooms here have a certain old-world architectural charm, and those facing the main cathedral facade (difficult to snaffle) promise the most comfortable front-row seats in Burgos. In years of visiting this place, we're yet to receive a smile. Parking costs €14.

Hotel La Puebla (☎ 947 20 00 11; www.hotellapuebla.com; Calle de la Puebla 20; s €58-70, d €73-106; P ❄ 💻) This boutique hotel adds a touch of style to the Burgos hotel scene, with professional service. The rooms aren't huge and most don't have views, but they're softly lit and supremely comfortable. They come in a range of styles, from colourful to minimalist black-and-white. Highly recommended. Parking costs €10.

NH Palacio de la Merced (☎ 947 47 99 00; www.nh-hotels.com; Calle de la Merced 13; d from €115; P ⊠ 💻) Brimful of the quality we've come to expect from the NH chain, the outstanding Palacio de la Merced is one of Burgos' most distinguished addresses. Housed in a 16th-century palace with high domed ceilings, the old-world elegance of the building is wedded to supermodern, supremely comfortable rooms with hardwood floors and muted shades.

Eating

Burgos is famous for its *queso* (cheese), *morcilla* (blood sausage made with rice and served with red peppers) and *cordero asado*.

TAPAS

our pick Cervecería Morito (☎ 947 26 75 55; Calle de la Sombrerería; 🕑 1-3.30pm & 7.30pm-midnight) Cervecería Morito is the undisputed king of Burgos tapas bars and it's always crowded, even on the quietest of nights; if it's full downstairs, there's more room on the 1st floor. A typical order is *alpargata* (lashings of cured ham with bread, tomato and olive oil; €2.70) and we challenge you to find better *calamares* (calamari) or *morcilla* elsewhere.

La Cabaña Arandino (Calle de la Sombrerería; 🕑 1-3.30pm & 7-11pm) Opposite Cervecería Morito, this place doesn't quite match the atmosphere, but it's popular and the tapas are good. Locals love the *tigres* (mussels with spicy sauce).

La Mejillonera (Calle de la Paloma 33; 🕑 11am-3pm & 6.30-11pm) Another popular stand-up place, La Mejillonera serves great mussels (€2.30 per plate), while the *patatas bravas* (potatoes with spicy tomato sauce) and *calamares* are other popular orders.

La Favorita (☎ 947 20 59 49; www.lafavorita-taberna.com in Spanish; Calle de Avellanos 8; 🕑 10am-midnight) Away from the main Burgos tapas hub close to the cathedral, La Favorita has an interior of exposed brick and wooden beams. There are plenty of *pinchos* (snacks) – the sirloin with foie gras (€2.80) is our favourite – plus *raciones* (€5.10 to €17.80) and *media raciones* (smaller tapas serving). The emphasis is on local cured meats and cheeses, and wine by the glass starts at €1.50.

RESTAURANTS

Chocolatería Candilejas (Calle de Fernán González 36; desserts from €2.80; 🕑 6.30-11pm Thu-Mon) Come here for killer cakes, *churros* and *batidos* (milkshakes; €3), all homemade.

Royal (Calle del Huerto del Rey 23; meals €10-15) If you can withstand the glaringly lit dining area, Royal serves a wide range of *raciones* (€3.20 to €7.70) and 18 choices of *bocadillo* (filled roll; €3.10 to €5.20) that contain everything from old Spanish classics to gourmet flourishes.

Casa Babylon (☎ 947 25 54 40; www.casababylon.es; Plaza de Santo Domingo 3; menús €15-18) Casa Babylon is a relative newcomer on the local restaurant scene, with fresh international tastes wedded to occasional local specialities. We especially like the lunch *and* dinner set menus during the week *and* on weekends, which is a great way to keep costs reasonable. You can also order à la carte.

La Fabula (☎ 947 26 30 92; Calle de la Puebla 18; meals €25-30) A good place for nouveau Castilian cuisine, La Fabula offers slimmed-down dishes in a light, modern dining room filled with classical music. Rice, fish and seafood dominate the menu.

our pick **Casa Ojeda** (☎ 947 20 90 52; www.grupojeda.com in Spanish; Calle de Vitoria 5; meals €30-40; ⏰ lunch & dinner Mon-Sat, lunch only Sun) This Burgos institution, all sheathed in dark wood, is one of the best places in town to try *cordero asado* (€21). The upstairs dining room has outstanding food and faultless service, although we're not sure what we think of a menu that lists the calories and cholesterol for each dish. A more limited range of *platos combinados* is available in the downstairs bar.

Drinking

CAFES

With its old-world elegance, **Café España** (Calle de Lain Calvo 12; ⏰ 10am-11pm) has been a bastion of the Burgos cafe scene for more than 80 years. Other good options include **Café Latino** (Calle de Lain Calvo 16; ⏰ 10am-11pm) and **Café de las Artes** (Calle de Lain Calvo 31; ⏰ 10am-midnight); the latter has a magazine rack, occasional live music and an artsy vibe.

BARS

To catch what's happening around town, pick up a copy of the Burgos edition of *Go!* (www.laguiago.com in Spanish), available from the tourist office and many hotels.

There are two main hubs of Burgos nightlife. The first is along Calle de San Juan and Calle de la Puebla, with plenty of bars to get your night started. Good options include **El Bosque Encantado** (Calle de San Juan 31; ⏰ 4.30pm-1am), which revels in its kitsch; **Urban Café** (Calle de San Juan 47; ⏰ 4pm-1am), which could be in Barcelona or Madrid with its refined sense of style; **Bardeblas** (Calle de la Puebla 29; ⏰ 4pm-1am), which plays alternative music; and **Café Marmedi** (Calle de le Puebla 20; ⏰ 4pm-1am), where the mojitos are a feature.

For later nights on weekends, Calle del Huerto del Rey, just northeast of the cathedral and known locally as Las Llanas, is the sort of street you'd hate to live above, with literally dozens of bars. We like **Buddha** (Calle del Huerto del Rey 8; ⏰ 11pm-4am Thu-Sat), but it only just shades around 10 others.

Shopping

Jorge Revilla (☎ 947 27 40 40; Calle de la Paloma 29; ⏰ 10am-2pm & 5-8pm Mon-Fri, 10am-2pm Sat) Local Burgos jewellery designer Jorge Revilla is making a name for himself beyond Spain's borders and it's not hard to see why – colourful silver pieces that are at once fun and sophisticated.

Casa Quintanilla (Calle de la Paloma 22; ⏰ 10am-8.30pm Mon-Sat, 10am-2pm Sun) This is the pick of many stores around the centre offering local produce that's ideal for a picnic or a gift for back home. If you're fortunate enough to be here when María Jesús, the owner, is in residence, expect a stream-of-consciousness sales pitch promising 'the best cheese in the world' and all manner of 'marvellous' local delicacies.

La Vieja Castilla (Calle de la Paloma 21; ⏰ 10am-2pm & 5-8pm Mon-Fri, 10am-2pm Sat) Next door to Casa Quintanilla, this place is similar but less entertaining.

Getting There & Away

BUS

From Burgos' **bus station** (Calle de Miranda 4), **ALSA** (☎ 947 26 63 70; www.alsa.es) runs regular buses to Madrid (€15.66, 2¾ hours), Vitoria (€7.37, 1½ hours), Bilbao (€11.16, two hours), San Sebastián (€14.88, 3½ hours), León (€13.31, 3¼ hours) and Valladolid (€8.16, two hours).

CAR & MOTORCYCLE

For Madrid, take the A1 directly south. The N234 branches off southeast to Soria and on to Zaragoza and ultimately Barcelona. The N623 leads north to Santander, while the AP1 *autopista* goes most of the way to Vitoria and hooks up with the AP68 *autopista* to Bilbao.

There's a convenient parking station beneath Plaza Mayor.

TRAIN

Burgos is connected with Madrid (from €23.10, four hours, up to seven daily), Bilbao (from €16.60, three hours, five daily), León (from €17.90, two hours, four daily), Valladolid (from €8.20, 1¼ hours, up to 13 daily) and Salamanca (from €20.10, 2½ hours, three daily).

Renfe (☎ 947 20 91 31; Calle de la Moneda 21; ⏰ 9.30am-1.30pm & 4.30-7.30pm Mon-Fri, 9.30am-1.30pm Sat) has a convenient sales office in the centre of town.

AROUND BURGOS

Quintanilla de las Viñas

If you take the N234 out of Burgos, a worthwhile stop some 35km out is the 7th-century **Ermita de Santa María de Lara** close to Quintanilla de las Viñas. This modest Visigothic hermitage has some fine bas-reliefs around its external walls, which are among the best surviving regional examples of religious art from the 7th century.

Covarrubias

pop 640 / elev 975m

The picturesque hamlet of Covarrubias is one of Castilla y León's hidden gems. Spread out along the shady banks of Río Arlanza, it's sprinkled with arcaded half-timbered houses overlooking intimate cobblestone squares. There's a small **tourist office** (☎ 947 40 64 61; www.ecovarrubias.com in Spanish; Calle de Monseñor Vargas; 🕐 10.30am-2pm & 4-7pm Tue-Sat, 11am-2.30pm Sun Mar-Jun & Sep-Dec, 10.30am-2.30pm & 4-7pm daily Jul & Aug) under the arches of the village's imposing northern gate, where you can pick up the free *Covarrubias: Castile Birthplace*, a handy pocket-sized guide to the sights around town. It also organises guided tours (€3 per person) of the village.

A good time to be here is the second weekend of July, when the village hosts its **Medieval Market & Cherry Festival**.

SIGHTS

Although the main attraction of Covarrubias is simply wandering its charming cobblestone streets, there are a few sights to provide focus for your visit. The squat 10th-century **Torreón de Doña Urraca** towers over the remains of the town's medieval walls, while the late-Gothic **Colegiata de San Cosme y Damián** (☎ 947 40 63 11; admission €2; 🕐 10.30am-2pm & 4-7pm Wed-Mon) hosts Castilla's oldest still-functioning church organ and has attractive cloisters. It also contains the stone tomb of Fernán González, the 10th-century founder of Castilla. **Casa Doña Sancha** is the best-preserved of Covarrubias' 15th-century half-timbered houses.

SLEEPING & EATING

Casa Galín (☎ 947 40 65 52; www.casagalin.com in Spanish; Plaza de Doña Urraca 4; s/d €25/42) A cut above your average provincial Castilian *hostal*, Casa Galín has comfortable, brightly painted rooms with renovated bathrooms in an old-fashioned timbered building overlooking the main plaza. It's home to a popular restaurant for tapas, fish and roasted meats, with a well-priced *menú* (€9).

Hotel Rey Chindasvinto (☎ 947 40 65 60; hotelchindas@wanadoo.es; Plaza del Rey Chindasvinto 5; s/d incl breakfast €35/55) The classiest hotel in town, the Rey Chindasvinto has lovely, spacious rooms with wooden beams and exposed brickwork, friendly owners and a good restaurant. This is ideal for those who want to enjoy Covarrubias after sunset, when the weekend crowds have returned home.

Los Castros (☎ 947 40 63 68; www.casaruralloscastros.com; Calle de los Castros 10; s/d incl breakfast €50/60) A historic *casa rural*, Los Castros has just five gorgeous doubles filled with all sorts of eclectic furnishings, which somehow reflect this enchanting town.

Restaurante de Galo (☎ 947 40 63 93; Plaza Mayor s/n; menú €10.50, meals €20-25) This fine restaurant in the heart of the village is recommended for its robust traditional dishes cooked in a wood-fired oven. This is a good place to sample the regional speciality of *cordero asado* (€14).

SHOPPING

La Alacena (☎ 947 40 65 63; Calle de Monseñor Vargas 8; 🕐 10am-2pm & 5-7.30pm Tue-Sun) For homemade chocolate and other tempting local foods, step inside this friendly shop in the centre of the village.

GETTING THERE & AWAY

Two buses travel between Burgos and Covarrubias on weekdays, and one runs on Saturday (€2.65, one hour).

Santo Domingo de Silos

pop 320

Nestled in the rolling hills south of Burgos, this tranquil, pretty village has an unusual claim to fame: monks from its monastery made the British pop charts in the mid-1990s

THE OLDEST EUROPEAN

The archaeological site of Atapuerca, around 15km west of Burgos, has long excited students of early human history. But archaeologists made their greatest discovery here in July 2007 when they uncovered a jawbone and teeth of what is believed to be the oldest-known European: 1.2 million years old, some 500,000 years older than any other remains discovered in Western Europe. A Unesco World Heritage–listed site, Atapuerca is still under excavation, although visits can be arranged through the municipal tourist office in Burgos (p255).

ONLY IN SPAIN...

Spain's weird and wonderful fiestas have always left the rest of the world shaking their heads, from the Running of the Bulls in Pamplona (p502) to the tomato-throwing extravaganza of La Tomatina (p619) in Buñol. But surely there's no festival quite as strange as the baby-jumping festival of Castrillo de Murcia, a small village just south of the A231, 25km west of Burgos.

Every year since 1620, this tiny village of around 250 inhabitants has marked the feast of Corpus Cristi by lining up the babies of the village on a mattress, while grown men dressed as 'El Colacho', a figure representing the devil, leap over up to six prostrate and, it must be said, somewhat bewildered babies at a time. Like all Spanish rites, it does have a purpose: the ritual is thought to ward off the devil. But why jumping over babies? We have no idea and the villagers aren't telling. They do, however, assure us that no baby has been injured in the recorded history of the fiesta.

with recordings of Gregorian chants. The monastery is one of the most famous in central Spain, known for its stunning cloister.

The local **tourist office** (☎ 947 39 00 70; Calle de Cuatro Cantones 10; 🕑 10am-1.30pm & 4-6pm Tue-Sun Apr-Oct) is helpful.

SIGHTS

The **church** (🕑 6am-2pm & 4.30-10pm), which is notable for its pleasingly unadorned Romanesque sanctuary dominated by a multidomed ceiling, is where you can hear the monks **chant** (admission free; 🕑 9am Mon-Fri, 1pm Sat, noon Sun).

The jewel in the attached monastery's crown is the two-storey **cloister** (☎ 947 39 00 68; admission €3; 🕑 guided tours 10am-1pm & 4.30-6pm Tue-Sat, 4.30-6pm Sun), a treasure chest of some of the most imaginative Romanesque art anywhere in the country. Although the overall effect is spectacular, the sculpted capitals are especially exquisite, with lions intermingled with floral and geometrical motifs betraying the never-distant influence of Islamic art in Spain. Look for the unusually twisted column on the western side. The pieces executed on the corner pillars represent episodes from the life of Christ, while the galleries are covered by Mudéjar ceilings from the 14th century. In the northeastern corner sits a 13th-century image of the Virgin Mary carved in stone, and nearby is the original burial spot of Santo Domingo.

Although much of the monastery is off-limits to visitors, the compulsory guided tour will show you inside the 17th-century **botica** (pharmacy) and a small **museum** containing religious artworks, Flemish tapestries and the odd medieval sarcophagus. Tours are available within the hours listed above and begin when there are enough people.

For sweeping views over the town, pass under the **Arco de San Juan** and climb the grassy hill to the south to the **Ermita del Camino y Via Crucis**.

SLEEPING & EATING

Hostal Cruces (☎ 947 39 00 64; Plaza Mayor 2; s/d €23/42) Decent if simple rooms – the cheapest in town – and friendly owners make this a good choice right in the heart of the village.

Hotel Santo Domingo de Silos (☎ 947 39 00 53; www.hotelsantodomingodesilos.com in Spanish; Calle de Santo Domingo s/n; hostal s/d from €26/36, hotel s/d from €39/52) This place combines a simple *hostal* with a three-star hotel with large, character-filled rooms, right opposite the monastery. It's a popular place so book ahead.

Hotel Tres Coronas (☎ 947 39 00 47; www.hoteltrescoronasdesilos.com in Spanish; Plaza Mayor 6; s/d from €53/68) This place is brimming with character (the suit of armour at the top of the grand staircase sets the scene), with rooms of thick stone walls and old-world charm. The rooms at the front have lovely views over the plaza. Service with a smile is not its strong point.

Men can rent a heated room (with meals, €28) in the monastery, but you'll need to book well ahead. Call the **Padre Hospedero** (☎ 947 39 00 68) between 11am and 1pm. You can stay for a period of three to 10 days.

The village's best, most atmospheric and most expensive restaurant is at the **Hotel Tres Coronas** (meals €20-30), although the cheaper **Hotel Santo Domingo de Silos** (meals €15-20) is not bad.

GETTING THERE & AWAY

Autobuses Arceredillo (☎ 947 48 52 66) runs one daily bus from Burgos to Santo Domingo de Silos (€5.10, 1½ hours) from Monday to Saturday.

Desfiladero de Yecla

A mere 1.3km down the back road (BU911) to Caleruega from Santo Domingo, the spectacular Desfiladero de Yecla, a splendid gorge of limestone cliffs, opens up. It's easily visited thanks to a walkway – the stairs lead down from just past the tunnel exit.

NORTH OF BURGOS

The N623 highway carves a pretty trail from Burgos, particularly between the mountain passes of **Portillo de Fresno** and **Puerto de Carrales**. About 15km north of the former, a side road takes you through a series of intriguing villages in the **Valle de Sedano**. The town of the same name has a fine 17th-century church, but more interesting is the little Romanesque one above **Moradillo de Sedano**: the sculpted main doorway is outstanding.

Villages flank the highway on the way north, but **Orbaneja del Castillo** is the area's best-kept secret. Take the turn-off for Escalada and follow the bumpy road until you reach the waterfall. Park where you can, then climb up beside the waterfall to the village, which is completely hidden from the road. A dramatic backdrop of strange rock walls lends this spot an enchanting air.

SOUTH TO RÍO DUERO

Lerma

pop 2720 / elev 827m

If you're travelling between Burgos and Madrid and finding the passing scenery none too eye-catching, Lerma rises up from the roadside like a welcome apparition.

An ancient settlement, Lerma hit the big time in the early 17th century when Grand Duke Don Francisco de Rojas y Sandoval, a minister under Felipe II, launched an ambitious project to create another El Escorial (see p199). He failed, but the cobbled streets and delightful plazas of the old town are his most enduring legacy.

The **tourist office** (☎ 947 17 70 02; www.citlerma.com in Spanish; Plaza de Santa Clara; ⏲ 10am-2pm & 4-7pm Tue-Sun Sep-Jun, 10am-2pm & 4-8pm daily Jul & Aug) is in the Convento de Santa Teresa. Guided tours (€3) of the town and most of its monuments depart from here.

SIGHTS

Pass through the **Arco de la Cárcel** (Prison Gate), off the main road to Burgos, climbing up the long Calle del General Mola to the massive **Plaza Mayor**, which is fronted by the oversized **Palacio Ducal**, now a *parador* notable for its courtyards and 210 balconies. To the right of the square is the Dominican nuns' **Convento de San Blas**, which can be visited as part of the tourist office tour.

A short distance northwest of Plaza Mayor, a pretty passageway and viewpoint, **Mirador de los Arcos**, opens up over Río Arlanza. Its arches connect with the 17th-century **Convento de Santa Teresa**.

The **Pasadizo de Duque de Lerma** (admission €2) is a restored 17th-century subterranean passage that connects the palace with the **Iglesia Colegial de San Pedro Apóstol** – buy tickets at the tourist office.

SLEEPING & EATING

Posada La Hacienda de Mi Señor (☎ 947 17 70 52; www.lahaciendademisenor.com in Spanish; Calle de El Barco 6; s/d with breakfast €50/75;) Apart from a few *casas rurales* dotted around the old town, this is your best midrange bet, with enormous rooms with free wi-fi in a renovated, historic building. The colour scheme will start to grate if you stay too long.

Parador de Lerma (⏲ 947 17 71 10; www.parador.es; Plaza Mayor 1; s/d from €128/160) Undoubtedly the most elegant place to stay is this *parador*, which occupies the renovated splendour of the old Palacio Ducal. As in any *parador*, the rooms have luxury and character and the service is impeccable.

You're in the heart of Castilian wood-fired-oven territory and Plaza Mayor is encircled by high-quality restaurants with *cordero asado* on the menu (€35 for two is a good price to pay). Our favourite is the cosy and friendly **Asador Casa Brigante** (☎ 947 17 05 94; Plaza Mayor 5; meals for 2 €60; ⏲ lunch only Sun-Fri, lunch & dinner Sat Sep-May, lunch & dinner Thu-Tue Jun-Aug) – you won't taste better roast lamb anywhere.

GETTING THERE & AWAY

There are eight daily **Continental Auto** (☎ 947 26 20 17) buses from Burgos (€3.10, 30 minutes), with only four on Saturday or Sunday. Some buses coming from Aranda de Duero or Madrid also pass through.

Aranda de Duero

pop 32,000 / elev 802m

The big attraction in this otherwise unattractive crossroads town is the main portal of the late-Gothic **Iglesia de Santa María** (☎ 947 50 05

05; 10am-2pm & 5-8pm Tue-Sun Jun-Sep, before & after Mass rest of year). Its remarkably rich sculptural flourish was executed in the 15th and 16th centuries. For more information on the city, visit the **tourist office** (947 51 04 76; Plaza Mayor; 9am-2pm & 3.30-7pm).

Other than that, Aranda de Duero is renowned as a bastion of classic Castilian cooking. Most of the better places serving *cordero* are on and around Plaza del Arco Isilla; look for the 'Asador' signs. Probably Aranda's premier *asador* is **Mesón de la Villa** (947 50 10 25; Calle de Rodríguez Valcarcel 3; meals €40; Tue-Sun), which does succulent lamb and complements it with excellent local wines. Reservations are essential on weekends.

Numerous buses and trains connect Aranda with Madrid (€10.16, two hours) and most major cities in Castilla y León.

Peñaranda de Duero

pop 560 / elev 877m

About 20km east of Aranda on the C111, the village of Peñaranda de Duero exudes considerable charm. Originally a Celtic fortress village, most of its surviving riches are grouped around the stately Plaza Mayor. The **Palacio Condes de Miranda** (947 55 20 13; admission free; 10am-2pm & 4-7.30pm Tue-Sun Apr-Sep, 10am-2pm & 3-6pm Tue-Sun Oct-Mar) is a grand Renaissance palace with a fine plateresque entrance, double-arched patio and beautiful ceilings in various styles. Obligatory guided tours run on the hour. The 16th-century **Iglesia de Santa Ana** integrates columns and busts found at the Roman settlement of Clunia into an otherwise baroque design. For superb views of the village and surrounding country, take a walk up to the 15th-century **castle** ruins. For more information, contact the **tourist office** (947 55 20 63; Calle de Trinquete 7; 10am-2pm & 4-8pm Tue & Thu-Sun Jan-Apr, 10am-2pm & 4-8pm Tue-Sun May-Dec).

There are at least six *casas rurales* in the area for you to choose from should you wish to stay. Most buses between Valladolid (€6.35, 1½ hours) and Soria (€6.25, 1½ hours) pass through town.

Sepúlveda

pop 1320 / elev 1313m

With its houses staggered along a ridge carved out by the gorge of Río Duratón, and famous for its *cordero asado* and *cochinillo*, Sepúlveda is a favourite weekend escape for *madrileños* (Madrid residents). Indeed, the warm ochre tones of Sepúlveda's public buildings, fronting the central Plaza de España, are an enviable setting for a hot Sunday roast.

The *ayuntamiento* backs onto what remains of the old castle, while high above it all rises the 11th-century **Iglesia del Salvador**. It's considered the prototype of Castilian Romanesque, marked by the single arched portico.

Most visitors don't stay overnight, but if you'd like to enjoy the town's sleepy post-crowd aspect, **Mirador del Castilla** (921 54 03 53; Calle del Conde Sepúlveda 26; s/d €43/55), just off Plaza de España, has comfortable rooms.

For the *cordero* feast, you can pretty much take your pick around Plaza de España (places serving mediocre *cordero* don't last long here), but **Restaurante Cristóbal** (921 54 01 00; Calle del Conde de Sepúlveda 9; meals €35) and **Restaurante Figón Zute el Mayor** (921 54 01 65; Calle de Lope Tablada 6; meals €35) are both long-standing favourites with good wine lists. Reservations are essential on weekends.

At least two buses link Sepúlveda daily with Madrid.

Parque Natural del Hoz del Duratón

A sizeable chunk of land northwest of Sepúlveda has been constituted as a natural park, the centrepiece of which is the **Hoz del Duratón** (Duratón Gorge). A dirt track leads 5km west from the hamlet of Villaseca to the **Ermita de San Frutos**. In ruins now, the hermitage was founded in the 7th century by San Frutos and his siblings, San Valentín and Santa Engracia. They lie buried in a tiny chapel nearby. This is a magical place, overlooking one of the many serpentine bends in the gorge, with squadrons of buzzards and eagles soaring above. It's a popular weekend excursion and some people take kayaks up to Burgomillodo to launch themselves down the waters of the canyon. There's a small but informative **Centro de Interpretación** (921 54 05 86; Calle del Conde de Sepúlveda 30; 10am-2pm & 4-7pm daily Jul-Sep, 10am-5pm Mon-Fri, 10am-2pm & 4-7pm Sat Oct-Jun) in Sepúlveda.

Castilnovo

Some 12km south of Sepúlveda, this rather cute little **castle** (921 53 11 33; admission €3; 9am-1pm & 4-6pm Mon-Fri) has the air of a private conceit by some moneyed eccentric. Originally built in the 14th century and largely Mudéjar, it has undergone a lot of alterations.

WEST ALONG RÍO DUERO

Peñafiel

pop 5520 / elev 758m

At the heart of the Ribera del Duero wine region, Peñafiel is home to the state-of-the-art **Museo Provincial del Vino** (☎ 983 88 11 99; www.museodelvinodevalladolid.es), cleverly ensconced within the walls of the mighty **Castillo de Peñafiel** (admission castle €3, incl museum €6; 🕒 11.30am-2pm & 4-7pm Tue-Sun Oct-Mar, 11am-2.30pm & 4.30-8.30pm Tue-Sun Apr-Sep). Telling a comprehensive story of the region's wines, this wonderful museum grabs the attention with interactive displays, dioramas, backlit panels and computer terminals. The pleasures of the end product are not neglected: wine tasting costs €9.

The castle itself, one of the longest and narrowest in Spain, is also worth exploring. Its crenellated walls and towers stretch over 200m, but are little more than 20m across, and were raised and modified over 400 years from the 11th century onwards. The sight of it in the distance alone is worth the effort of getting here.

Like the wine museum, the cool, classy **Hotel Ribera del Duero** (☎ 983 88 16 16; www.hotelriberadelduero.com; Avenida de Escalona 17; s/d €60/70) is an unexpected find in little Peñafiel, with understated but semiluxurious rooms, some with terrific views. It organises tours and tastings at local wineries, and its restaurant is the best place to eat in town.

Just north of Peñafiel, in the village of Curiel de Duero, **Hotel Castillo de Curiel** (☎ 983 88 04 01; www.castillodecuriel.com; d from €140) should be the hotel of choice for castle romantics. Occupying the oldest castle (9th century) in the region, the hotel has lovely rooms, all with sweeping views.

Four or five buses a day run to Valladolid (€4, 45 minutes), 60km west of here.

EAST ALONG RÍO DUERO

San Esteban de Gormaz

pop 3290 / elev 911m

The dusty little town of San Esteban de Gormaz contains a couple of Romanesque gems hidden away in its centre: the 11th-century **Iglesia de San Miguel** (🕒 11am-2pm & 5-7pm Jul-Nov) and **Iglesia de Nuestra Señora del Rivero** (🕒 11am-2pm & 5-7pm Jul-Nov). Both churches sport the porticoed side galleries that characterise the Romanesque style of the Segovia and Burgos areas.

El Burgo de Osma

pop 5060 / elev 943m

Some 12km east of San Esteban de Gormaz, El Burgo de Osma is a real surprise. Once important enough to host its own university, it's now a somewhat run-down little old town, dominated by a quite remarkable cathedral and infused with an air of decaying elegance.

The **tourist office** (☎ 975 36 01 16; Plaza Mayor 9; 🕒 10am-2pm & 4-8pm Wed-Sun) should be your first port of call.

SIGHTS

Your initiation into the old town is likely to be along **Calle Mayor**, its portico borne by an uneven phalanx of stone and wooden pillars. Not far along, it leads into **Plaza Mayor**, fronted by the 18th-century **ayuntamiento** and the more sumptuous **Hospital de San Agustín**.

On Plaza de San Pedro de Osma, the **catedral** (☎ 975 34 09 62; 🕒 10am-1pm & 4-6pm Tue-Sun Oct-Mar, 10am-1pm & 4-7pm Tue-Sun Apr-Sep) was begun in the 12th century as a Romanesque building, continued in a Gothic vein and finally topped with a weighty baroque tower that rivals many of the great cathedrals of Spain. The sanctuary is filled with art treasures, including the 16th-century main **altarpiece** and the so-called **Beato de Osma**, a precious 11th-century codex (manuscript) that can be seen in the Capilla Mayor. Also of note is the light-flooded, circular **Capilla de Palafox**, a rare example of the neoclassical style in this region.

If you exit El Burgo from near Plaza de San Pedro de Osma, take a left for the village of Osma, high above which stand the ruins of the 10th-century **Castillo de Osma**.

SLEEPING & EATING

Hostal Mayor 71 (☎ 975 36 80 24; www.mayor71.es in Spanish; Calle Mayor 71; s/d from €30/36) This is a cheap option and recommended as much for its central locale as for its tidy, well-kept rooms with bright bathrooms.

Posada del Canónigo (☎ 975 36 03 62; www.posadadelcanonigo.es; Plaza San Pedro de Osma 19; s €60-70, d €70-80) This is certainly the most imaginative choice, with some rooms overlooking the cathedral from an enchanting 17th-century building. The rooms have been lovingly restored and are overflowing with charm.

Hotel Il Virrey (☎ 975 34 13 11; www.virreypalafox.com; Calle Mayor 2; s €55-65, d €82-95, ste €115-135) This place possesses old Spanish charm, with its sweeping staircase and heavily gilded furniture. Hardwood floors and wrought-iron furnishings dominate and the bathrooms are newly renovated. Room rates soar on weekends in February and March, when people flock here for the ritual slaughter *(matanza)* of pigs, after which diners indulge in all-you-can-eat feasts. At €45 per head it's not bad for one of the more unusual dining experiences. There's even a pig museum…

Asador El Burgo (☎ 975 34 04 89; Calle Mayor 71; menú especial €25, meals €20-30; ⌚ lunch & dinner Fri-Sun) This place is popular with locals and does the usual meaty Castilian fare with aplomb, even if only on weekends.

GETTING THERE & AWAY

Therpasa (☎ 975 23 30 05) buses link El Burgo with Soria (€3.30, 50 minutes, two daily, one on Sunday) and **Linecar** (☎ 983 23 00 33) serves Valladolid (€9.30, two hours, three daily).

Parque Natural del Cañón del Río Lobos

Some 15km north of El Burgo de Osma, this park promises forbidding rockscapes and a magnificent, deep river canyon, not to mention abundant vultures and various other birds of prey. About 4km in from the road stands the Romanesque **Ermita de San Bartolomé**. You can walk deeper into the park but free camping is forbidden.

Camping Cañón del Río Lobos (☎ 975 36 35 65; sites per person/tent/car €5/5/6.25; ⌚ Easter–mid-Sep; 🏊) is near Ucero. If you're heading north along the switchback road that climbs up the canyon, you'll have some fine views back towards Ucero.

Gormaz

pop 20

Some 14km south of El Burgo, on Río Duero, is the virtual ghost town of Gormaz. The sprawling **castle** has 21 towers and was built by the Muslims in the 10th century and altered in the 13th. Its ruins still convey enormous dignity and the views alone justify the effort of getting here – this must have been a great perch for defending the surrounding country. The castle is reached via a winding road about 2km beyond the modern village.

Berlanga de Duero

pop 1060 / elev 978m

About 15km east of Gormaz, Berlanga de Duero is lorded over by an imposing but ruined **castle**. Down below, the squat **Colegiata de Santa María del Mercado** is a fine late-Gothic church, with star-shaped vaulting inside. The area around the pretty Plaza Mayor, with the occasional Renaissance house, is equally charming. To find out more, visit the **tourist office** (☎ 975 34 34 33; ⌚ 10am-2pm & 4-8pm Fri & Sat Easter-Jun & Oct-early Dec, 10am-2pm & 4-8pm daily Jul-Sep).

Hotel Fray Tomás (☎ 975 34 30 33; fax 975 34 31 69; Calle Real 16; s/d €33/52) has comfortable rooms in a modified 14th-century building.

Around Berlanga de Duero

About 8km southeast of Berlanga de Duero stands the **Ermita de San Baudelio** (admission €1; ⌚ 10am-2pm & 4-6pm Wed-Sat, 10am-2pm Sun Oct-Mar, 10am-2pm & 4-8pm Wed-Sat, 10am-2pm Sun Apr-Sep), where the simple exterior conceals a remarkable 11th-century Mozarabic interior. A great pillar in the centre of the only nave opens up at the top like a palm tree to create delicate horseshoe arches.

Another 17km south, the hilltop stone village of **Rello** retains much of its medieval defensive wall and feels like the place time forgot. The views from the village's southern ledge are superb. There's at least one *casa rural* if you love the peace and quiet.

The Road to Madrid

The N110 winds southwest from San Esteban de Gormaz to join up with the A1 highway between Madrid and Burgos.

The first village of note you'll come to is **Ayllón**, some 50km southwest of El Burgo de Osma; it bathes in the same orange glow that characterises El Burgo's townscape. You enter by a medieval **archway** and are immediately confronted on the right by the ornate facade of a late-15th-century noble family's **mansion**, built in Isabelline style. The uneven, porticoed Plaza Mayor is capped at one end by the Romanesque **Iglesia de San Miguel**, and nearby stands the Renaissance-era **Iglesia de Santa María la Mayor**. Turn right behind this and follow the narrow street for about 500m and you'll come to the extensive remains of another Romanesque **church**. The simple **Hostal Vellosillo** (☎ 921 55 30 62; Avenida Conde Vallellano s/n; s/d with washbasin €12/20, d with bathroom €32) is the better of the two *hostales* in town.

About 20km south of Ayllón, **Riaza** has a charmingly ramshackle and circular Plaza Mayor; the sandy arena in the centre is still used for bullfights.

SORIA

pop 38,200 / elev 1055m

Small-town Soria is one of Spain's smaller and least-visited provincial capitals. Set on Río Duero in the heart of backwoods Castilian countryside, it's a great place to escape tourist Spain, with an appealing and compact old centre, and a sprinkling of stunning monuments. Calm and laid-back by day, Soria has a surprisingly lively nightlife.

Information

Several banks are near the tourist office.

Cruz Roja (☎ 975 22 22 22; Calle Santo Domingo de Silos 3) For ambulances.

Emergency (☎ 112)

Hospital de Santa Barbara (☎ 975 23 43 00; Paseo de Santa Barbara s/n) Soria's most central hospital.

Main post office (☎ 975 23 36 40; Paseo del Espolón 6)

Tourist office (☎ 975 21 20 52; Calle de Medinaceli 2; 🕒 9am-2pm & 5-8pm daily mid-Sep–Jun, 9am-8pm Sun-Thu, 9am-9pm Fri & Sat Jul–mid-Sep)

Sights

CASCO VIEJO & AROUND

The narrow streets of Soria's **casco viejo** (old town) centre on Plaza Mayor. The plaza's appeal lies in its lack of uniformity, and in the attractive Renaissance-era **ayuntamiento** and the **Iglesia de Santa María la Mayor**, with its unadorned Romanesque facade and gloomy, though gilt-edge interior. A block north is the majestic, sandstone, 16th-century **Palacio de los Condes Gomara** (Calle de Aguirre).

Further north again is the city's most beautiful church, the Romanesque **Iglesia de Santo Domingo** (Calle de Santo Tomé Hospicio; 🕒 7am-9pm). Its small but exquisitely sculpted portal is something special, especially at sunset when its reddish stone seems to be aglow.

At the **Iglesia de San Juan de Rabanera** (Calle de San Juan de Rabanera), which was first built in the 12th century, hints of Gothic and even Byzantine art gleam through the mainly Romanesque hue.

Heading east towards Río Duero you pass the **Concatedral de San Pedro** (Calle de San Agustín), with its plateresque facade. The 12th-century **cloister** (admission €1; 🕒 11am-1pm Mon, 10.30am-1.30pm & 4.30-7.30pm Tue-Sun mid-Feb–Sep, shorter hours rest of year) is the most charming feature here. Its delicate arches are divided by slender double pillars topped with beautiful capitals adorned with floral, human and animal motifs.

MUSEO NUMANTINO

Archaeology buffs with a passable knowledge of Spanish should enjoy this well-organised **museum** (☎ 975 22 14 28; Paseo del Espolón 8; adult/concession €1.20/free; 🕒 10am-2pm & 4-7pm Tue-Sat, 10am-2pm Sun Oct-Jun, 10am-2pm & 5-8pm Tue-Sat, 10am-2pm Sun Jul-Sep), dedicated to finds from ancient sites across the province of Soria (especially Numancia; see p269). It has everything from mammoth bones to ceramics and jewellery, accompanied by detailed explanations of the historical developments in various major Celtiberian and Roman settlements.

BESIDE RÍO DUERO

The most striking of Soria's sights has to be the 12th-century **Monasterio de San Juan de Duero** (Camino Monte de las Ánimas; admission €0.60, free Sat & Sun; 🕒 10am-2pm & 4-7pm Tue-Sat, 10am-2pm Sun Oct-Jun, 10am-2pm & 5-8pm Tue-Sat, 10am-2pm Sun Jul-Sep). What most catches the eye are the exposed and gracefully interlaced arches of the monastery's partially ruined cloister, which artfully blends Mudéjar and Romanesque influences. Inside the church, the capitals are worth a closer look for their rather intense iconography.

A lovely riverside walk south for 2.3km will take you past the 13th-century church of the former Knights Templar, the **Monasterio de San Polo** (not open to the public), and on to the fascinating, baroque **Ermita de San Saturio** (Paseo de San Saturio; admission free; 🕒 10am-2pm & 4.30-8.30pm Tue-Sat, 10.30am-2pm Sun Jul & Aug, 10am-2pm & 4.30-7.30pm Tue-Sat, 10.30am-2pm Sun Apr-Jun, Sep & Oct, 10am-2pm & 4.30-6.30pm Tue-Sat, 10.30am-2pm Sun Nov-Mar). This octagonal structure perches right over the cave where Soria's patron saint spent much of his life.

Festivals & Events

Since the 13th century, the 12 *barrios* (districts) of Soria have celebrated, with considerable fervour, the **Fiestas de San Juan y de la Madre de Dios** during the second half of June. The main festivities take place on Jueves (Thursday) La Saca, when each of the districts presents a bull to be fought the next day. The day following the bullfight some of the animals' meat is auctioned off, after which general carousing continues until the small hours of Sunday. Hangovers and all, the *cuadrillas* (teams) parade in all their glorious finery and perform folk dances the next morning.

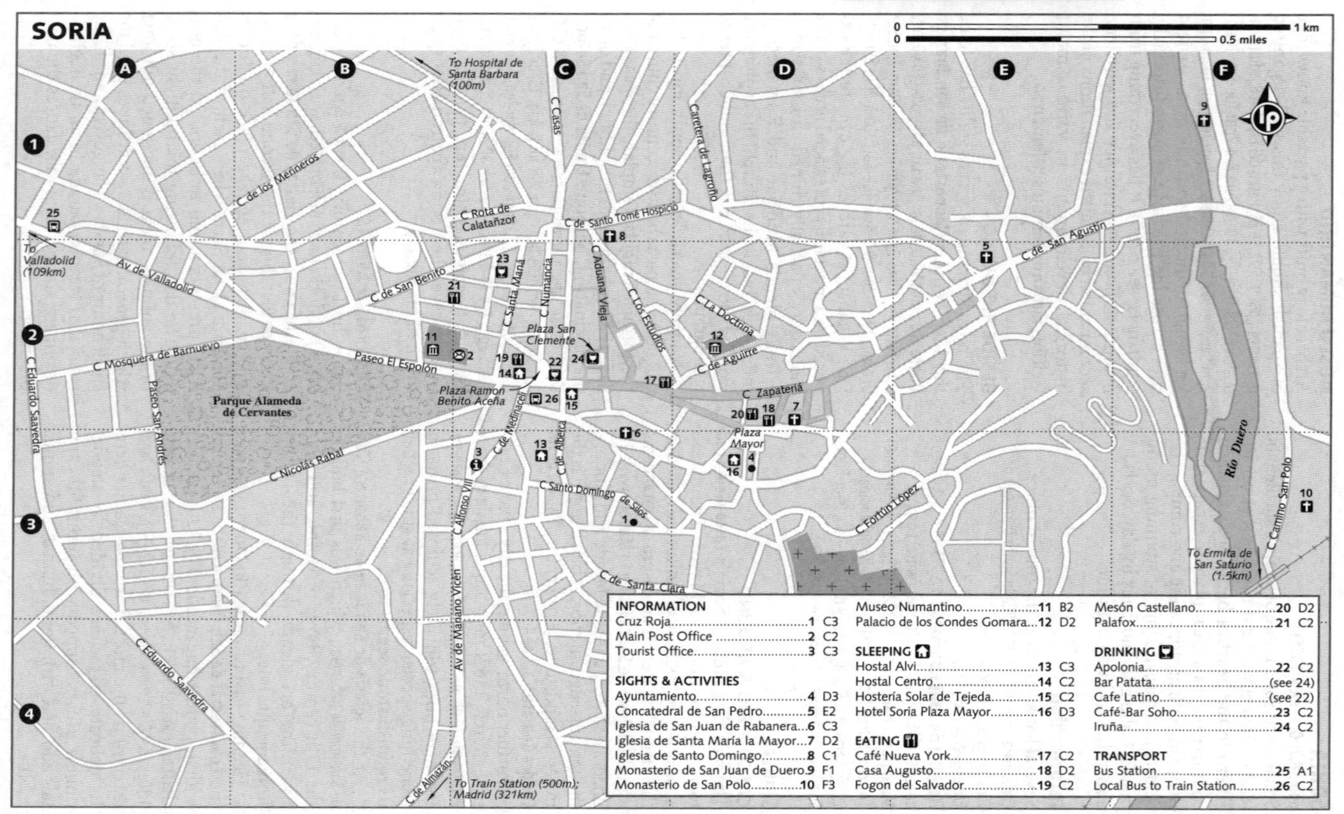
SORIA
0 1 km
0 0.5 miles
Río Duero
Parque Alameda de Cervantes
Plaza Mayor
Plaza San Clemente
Plaza Ramon Benito Aceña
Caretera de Lagroño
C de San Agustín
C Camino San Polo
C Fortún López
C Zapatería
C de Aguirre
C La Doctrina
C Los Estudios
C Aduana Vieja
C de Santo Tomé Hospicio
C Casas
C Numancia
C Santa María
C Rota de Calatañazor
C de San Benito
Paseo El Espolón
Av de Valladolid
C Mosquera de Barnuevo
Paseo San Andrés
C Nicolás Rabal
C Eduardo Saavedra
C de Medinaceli
C de Alberca
C Santo Domingo de Silos
C de Santa Clara
C Alfonso VIII
Av de Mariano Vicén
C de Almazán
To Valladolid (109km)
To Hospital de Santa Barbara (100m)
To Train Station (500m); Madrid (321km)
To Ermita de San Saturio (1.5km)
INFORMATION
Cruz Roja 1 C3
Main Post Office 2 C2
Tourist Office 3 C3
SIGHTS & ACTIVITIES
Ayuntamiento 4 D3
Concatedral de San Pedro 5 E2
Iglesia de San Juan de Rabanera 6 C3
Iglesia de Santa María la Mayor 7 D2
Iglesia de Santo Domingo 8 C1
Monasterio de San Juan de Duero 9 F1
Monasterio de San Polo 10 F3
Museo Numantino 11 B2
Palacio de los Condes Gomara 12 D2
SLEEPING
Hostal Alvi 13 C3
Hostal Centro 14 C2
Hostería Solar de Tejeda 15 C2
Hotel Soria Plaza Mayor 16 D3
EATING
Café Nueva York 17 C2
Casa Augusto 18 D2
Fogon del Salvador 19 C2
Mesón Castellano 20 D2
Palafox 21 C2
DRINKING
Apolonia 22 C2
Bar Patata (see 24)
Cafe Latino (see 22)
Café-Bar Soho 23 C2
Iruña 24 C2
TRANSPORT
Bus Station 25 A1
Local Bus to Train Station 26 C2

Sleeping

Hostal Alvi (☎ 975 22 81 12; hostalalvi@telefonica.net; Calle de Alberca 2; s/d €31/49) Spotless and central, this is one of the best-value places, with good rooms complete with TV and phone. The street itself is not Soria's prettiest, but you're a stone's throw from the centre.

Hostal Centro (☎ 975 22 61 22; www.soriadormir.com; Plaza Mariano Granados 2; s/d €50/55;) If you're looking for hotel quality at *hostal* prices, Hostal Centro, part of a chain of *hostales* across Soria, promises stylish rooms with outstanding bathrooms, a downtown location and double-glazed windows to keep out the noise.

our pick **Hostería Solar de Tejada** (☎ 975 23 00 54; www.hosteriasolardetejada.com; Calle de Claustrilla 1; s/d €52/56;) This charming boutique hotel right in the middle of the pedestrianised zone is one of the best choices in Soria. Individually designed rooms have whimsical decor, lots of Bohemian touches and beautifully tiled bathrooms.

Hotel Soria Plaza Mayor (☎ 975 24 08 64; www.hotelsoriaplazamayor.com; Plaza Mayor 10; s €73-95, d €84-105, ste €95-115;) This hotel has terrific rooms, each with its own style of decor and all overlooking either Plaza Mayor or a quiet side street. There are so many balconies in fact that even some bathrooms have them. The suites are *very* comfortable.

Eating

Café Nueva York (Plaza San Blas y el Rosel; 7am-6pm) This cafe serves up great breakfasts until noon and is also a good spot to fill up on divine pastries.

Palafox (☎ 975 22 00 76; Calle Vicente Tutor 2; menú from €9) This establishment makes substantial *bocadillos*, but also serves sit-down meals and tapas.

our pick **Casa Augusto** (☎ 975 21 30 41; Plaza Mayor 5; meals €15-25) This is a classy alternative, with an intimate dining area, an extensive wine list and professional service. If you can't decide what to eat, check out the list by the door of the year's most popular orders. For some reason, *la manita inocente* (pigs trotters) is always up there.

Fogon del Salvador (☎ 975 23 01 94; Plaza El Salvador 1; meals €25-30) Another Soria culinary stalwart, Fogon del Salvador has a wine list as long as your arm (literally) and a fabulous wood-fired oven churning out succulent meat-based dishes.

Mesón Castellano (☎ 975 21 30 45; Plaza Mayor 2; meals €25-35) With beamed ceilings and dangling flanks of ham, this local institution serves some of the best tapas in town and delicious full meals in its *comedor*. The *cabrito asado* (roast goat kid; €22) is a good order.

Drinking

Plaza San Clemente is perfect for kicking off the *marcha*. Of the handful of bars around here, **Iruña** (Plaza San Clemente 2) and **Bar Patata** (Plaza San Clemente 1) have the best range of tapas to go with your drinks.

Another good spot to start the evening is Plaza Ramon Benito Aceña, where you'll find the hugely popular Apolonia and the very cool Cafe Latino.

A supercool alternative is **Café-Bar Soho** (☎ 975 22 19 11; Calle de Campo 16; 8am-late Mon-Sat), which is good at any time of the day.

Getting There & Away

From the **bus station** (☎ 975 22 51 60; Avenida de Valladolid), a 15-minute walk west of the centre, there are regular services to Burgos (€11.20, 2¼ hours), Logroño (€7.05, 1¾ hours), Madrid (€14.80, 2½ hours) and Valladolid (€14.90, three hours). Provincial towns such as Medinaceli (€4.65, 45 minutes, two daily) and Almazán (€2.15, 30 minutes, two daily) are served as well.

If you're driving, take the N111 north for Logroño; for Madrid, the same road connects with the N11 south of Soria. The N122 goes west to El Burgo de Osma. Going east, it merges with the A68 to Zaragoza.

Trains connect Soria with Madrid (€13.85, three hours, three daily), but there are few other direct services. The **train station** (Carretera a Madrid) is 2.5km southwest of the city centre.

AROUND SORIA

Numancia

The mainly Roman ruins of **Numancia** (☎ 975 18 07 12; adult/concession €0.60/free, free Sat & Sun; 10am-2pm & 4-6pm Tue-Sat, 10am-2pm Sun Oct-Mar, 10am-2pm & 4-8pm Tue-Sat, 10am-2pm Sun Apr-Sep), 8km north of Soria, have a lonely, windswept aspect with little to suggest the long history of a settlement inhabited as early as the Bronze Age. Numancia proved one of the most resistant cities to Roman rule. Finally Scipio, who had crushed Carthage, starved the city into submission in 134 BC. Under Roman rule, Numancia was an important stop on the road from Caesaraugustus (Zaragoza) to Astúrica Augusta (Astorga). Now the city exists in outline only and will appeal more to budding archaeologists than to casual visitors.

To get here, take the N111 for around 5km north of Soria, then follow the signs to Garray.

Sierra de Urbión & Laguna Negra

The Sierra de Urbión, northwest of Soria, is home to the beautiful **Laguna Negra** (Black Lake), a small glacial lake that resembles a black mirror at the base of brooding rock walls amid partially wooded hills. Located 18km north of the village of **Vinuesa**, the lake is reached by a winding and scenic road (there's no public transport) that's bumpy in patches. The road ends at a car park, where there's a small information office. It's a further 2km uphill to the lake, either on foot or via the bus (return €1, departing every half-hour from 10am to 2pm and 4pm to 6.30pm), which leaves you 300m short of the lake. From the lake, a steep trail leads up to the Laguna de Urbión in La Rioja or to the summit of the Pico de Urbión, above the village of Duruelo de la Sierra, and on to a series of other tiny glacial lakes.

Vinuesa makes a good base for the area. **Hostal Virginia** (☎ 975 37 85 55; www.hotelvirginia.net; Avenida de la Generalitat 139; s/d €48/65) offers bright and pleasant rooms with wrought-iron beds; some rooms also have nice views. **Hostal Revinuesa** (☎ 975 37 81 47; s/d from €30/44), next door, has similarly pleasant rooms, some with nice wooden beams. Both have restaurants.

Camping El Cobijo (☎ 975 37 83 31; www.campingcobijo.com; sites per person/tent/car from €3.75/3.60/3.75, bungalows with kitchen from €80; Easter-Oct) is the nearest camping ground to the Laguna Negra (free camping is not permitted). It's a pleasant place set among ample greenery, 2km northwest of Vinuesa.

Calatañazor

pop 60 / elev 1071m

One of Castilla y León's most romantic tiny hilltop villages, Calatañazor, about 30km west of Soria, is a charming detour off the main road. It's hardly visible from the highway, just a kilometre away, and has a crumbling medieval air. Pass through the town gate and climb the crooked, cobbled lanes, wandering through a maze lined by ochre stone and adobe houses topped with red-tiled roofs and conical chimneys. Believe it or not, scenes from the movie *Doctor Zhivago* were shot here.

Towering above the village is the one-time Muslim fortress that gave Calatañazor its name (which comes from the Arabic Qala'at an-Nassur, literally 'the vulture's citadel'). Now in ruins, it has exceptional views from the walls and watchtowers, both down over the rooftops and north over a vast field called **Valle de la Sangre** (Valley of Blood). This was the setting of an epic 1002 battle that saw the Muslim ruler Almanzor defeated.

There's also a **church**, artisan shops selling local products and three *casas rurales* if Calatañazor has captured your imagination and you fancy staying the night.

There's no regular public transport to Calatañazor. If you're driving, the village lies around 1km north of the N122 – the well-signposted turn-off is about 29km west of Soria and about 27km northeast of El Burgo de Osma.

SOUTH OF SORIA

Almazán

pop 5830 / elev 940m

Three of this small town's massive gates remain to testify to a past more illustrious than the present in this quiet backwater. It frequently changed hands between the Muslims and Christians, and, improbably, for three short months was chosen by Fernando and Isabel as their residence.

The Romanesque **Iglesia de San Miguel** (☎ 975 31 07 02; Plaza Mayor; 10.30am-2pm & 5-7pm Tue-Sun Jul-Oct) sports an unusual octagonal cupola-cum-bell tower that reveals Mudéjar influences and a lovely circular apse. Inside is a bas-relief depicting the killing of Thomas à Becket at the hands of the British king Henry II. The work was commissioned by Henry's daughter, Eleanor of Aquitaine, the wife of Alfonso VIII, as a gesture of penance on behalf of her father.

The attractive facade of the Gothic–Renaissance **Palacio de los Hurtado de Mendoza** looks out over Plaza Mayor.

Hotel Villa de Almazán (☎ 975 30 06 11; www.hotelvilladealmazan.com; Avenida de Soria 29; s/d from €58/77) promises large, well-appointed modern rooms and the best restaurant in town.

There are four daily buses to/from Soria (€2.15, 30 minutes).

Medinaceli

pop 750 / elev 1270m

Modern Medinaceli, along a slip road just north of the A2 motorway, is the contemporary equivalent of a one-horse town, but don't be fooled: old Medinaceli is one of Castilla y León's most rustic and beautiful *pueblos* (villages), draped along a high, windswept ridge 3km to the north. Its most incongruous landmark is a 1st-century-AD **Arco Romano** (Roman triumphal arch), while there's also the moderately interesting Gothic **Colegiata de Santa María**. But Medinaceli's charm consists of rambling through tranquil cobblestone lanes and being surrounded by delightful stone houses redolent of the noble families that lived here after the town fell to the Reconquista in 1124. The area between Plaza de Santiueste and the lovely, partly colonnaded **Plaza Mayor** is Medinaceli at its best.

You can't miss the **tourist office** (☎ 689 734176; Calle Campo de San Nicolás; 🕑 10am-2pm & 4-8pm Wed-Sun) at the entrance to town, just around the corner from the arch.

Lovely **La Ceramica** (☎ 975 32 63 81; www.laceramicacasarural.es in Spanish; Calle de Santa Isabel 2; s/d €50/55, d incl breakfast & dinner €91) wins our vote for the friendliest staff, best location in the old town and all-round best deal. The rooms are intimate and comfortable, with a strong dose of rustic charm. There's usually a two-night minimum stay.

The style of the rooms at **Hostal Rural Bavieca** (☎ 975 32 61 06; www.hostalruralbabieca.com in Spanish; Calle Campo de San Nicolás 6; s/d incl breakfast €45/65, incl dinner €65/120) may not be to everyone's taste, but this is unmistakably a boutique hotel that offers high-quality rooms and ambience.

Both of the above sleeping options have good restaurants – again, La Ceramica is more cosy – but consider also **Asador de la Villa El Granero** (☎ 975 32 61 89; Calle de Yedra 10; meals €25-30; 🕑 lunch Wed-Mon Sep-Jun, lunch & dinner daily Jul & Aug), which is thought by many to be Medinaceli's best restaurant. The *setas de campo* (wild mushrooms) are something of a local speciality.

Two daily buses to Soria (€4.65, 45 minutes) leave from outside the *ayuntamiento* in the new town. There's no transport between the old and new towns; it's quite a hike.

Santa María de la Huerta

pop 390 / elev 818m

This largely insignificant village, just short of the Aragonese frontier, contains a wonderful **Cistercian monastery** (☎ 975 32 70 02; admission €3; 🕑 10am-1pm & 4-6.30pm Mon-Sat, 10-11.30am & 4-6.30pm Sun), founded in 1162, where monks lived until the monastery was expropriated in 1835. The order was allowed to return in 1930 and 25 Cistercians are now in residence. Before entering the monastery, note the church's impressive 12th-century facade with its magnificent rose window.

Inside the monastery, you pass through two cloisters, the second of which is the more beautiful. Known as the **Claustro de los Caballeros**, it's Spanish Gothic in style, although the medallions on the 2nd floor, bearing coats of arms and assorted illustrious busts, such as that of Christopher Columbus, are a successful plateresque touch. Off this cloister is the *refectorio* (dining hall). Built in the 13th century, it's notable for the absence of columns to support the vault.

A couple of buses per day connect the village with Almazán and Soria.

Castilla-La Mancha

Castilla-La Mancha acts as a natural buffer between the rich industrialism of northern Spain and Moorish, tourist-driven Andalucía. The landscape has a real Tolkienesque quality: undulating plains of rich henna-coloured earth, neatly striped and spotted with olive groves, golden wheat fields and grapevines, stretching to a horizon you never seem to reach. The story-book quality is intensified by the presence of solitary windmills and abundant (mostly ruined) castles. There are quiet mountainous stretches here as well, including the Montes de Toledo and the thickly carpeted valleys around Alcalá del Júcar.

The area's best-known city is glorious Toledo, Spain's spiritual capital and an open-air museum of medieval buildings and cultural sights. Cuenca is another wondrous place, seemingly about to topple off its eagle's-eyrie perch high above a gorge. In lovely Sigüenza, buildings and church spires are piled high on a hill, topped by a castle like a cherry on the cake. Further south is Almagro, home to one of Spain's more unusual and striking main squares.

Castilla-La Mancha is most famous as the home of the potty, errant and idealistic La Manchan knight Don Quijote. You can follow in his footsteps on the Quijote pilgrim trail. Quijote's windmills are everywhere to be seen, most evocatively in Consuegra and Campo de Criptana.

On a more sensory level, this is the region where saffron is grown, and it's also the capital of Spain's unrivalled Manchego cheese. The latter makes the perfect accompaniment to the local wines – Spain's largest vineyard is located here.

HIGHLIGHTS

- Stroll the tangle of medieval streets, exploring the museums and monuments, in **Toledo** (opposite)
- Revel in the unspoilt beauty of the **Parque Natural de las Lagunas de Ruidera** (p288), with its crystal-clear turquoise lakes
- Take *the* Don Quijote shot of the windmills overlooking **Consuegra** (p289)
- Kick back with a beer at a riverside bar beneath the cascade of houses in pretty **Alcalá del Júcar** (p291)
- Visit the exceptional **Museo de Arte Abstracto Español** (p293), housed in one of Cuenca's extraordinary hanging houses

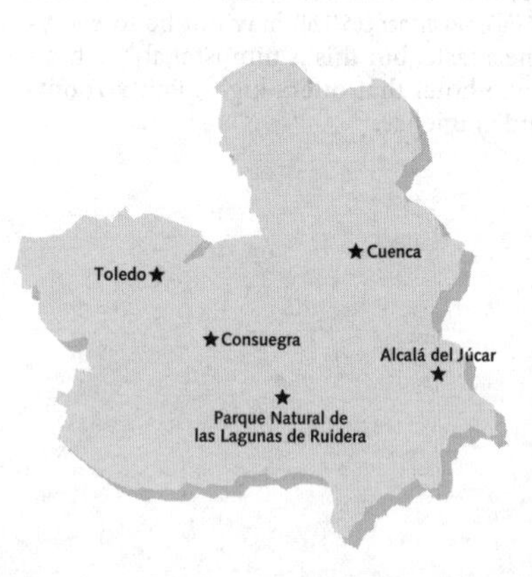

- AREA: 79,462 SQ KM
- AVE SUMMER TEMP: HIGH 34°C, LOW 16°C
- POP: 1.75 MILLION

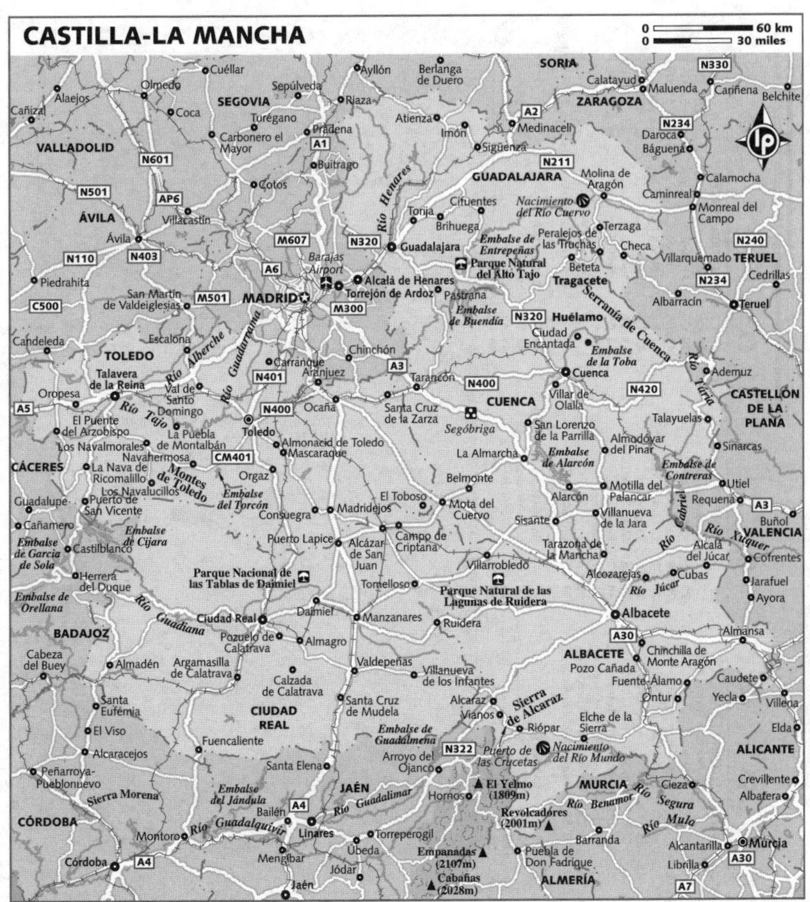

TOLEDO

pop 55,100 / elev 655m

Toledo is Spain's equivalent of a downsized Rome. You don't need a metro to cover the city's sights, only a pair of sturdy shoes. Toledo's labyrinth of narrow streets, plazas and inner patios is also reminiscent of the *medinas* (towns) of Damascus, Cairo or Morocco's Fez, although the historic diversity of Romans, Jews and Muslims equals an intriguing combination of synagogues and churches, as well as mosques. The artistic legacy bequeathed by the city's former inhabitants is reflected in its cultural values, as well as this mosaic of architecture. Add to this a lofty setting, high above Río Tajo, and it's no surprise that Toledo is one of Spain's most-visited cities.

Toledo's charms can be dampened if the streets are choked with tour groups. Try to stay till dusk, when the city returns to the locals and the streets take on a moody, other-worldly air.

HISTORY

Although the Romans were the first to single out this site as a strategic crossroads in Iberia, by the 6th century Visigothic King Atanagild had moved the site of his capital here from Seville. Over time, endless feuds between Visigothic nobles sent the kingdom into decline, resulting in the Muslims conquering Toledo, with little difficulty, after crossing the Strait of Gibraltar in 711.

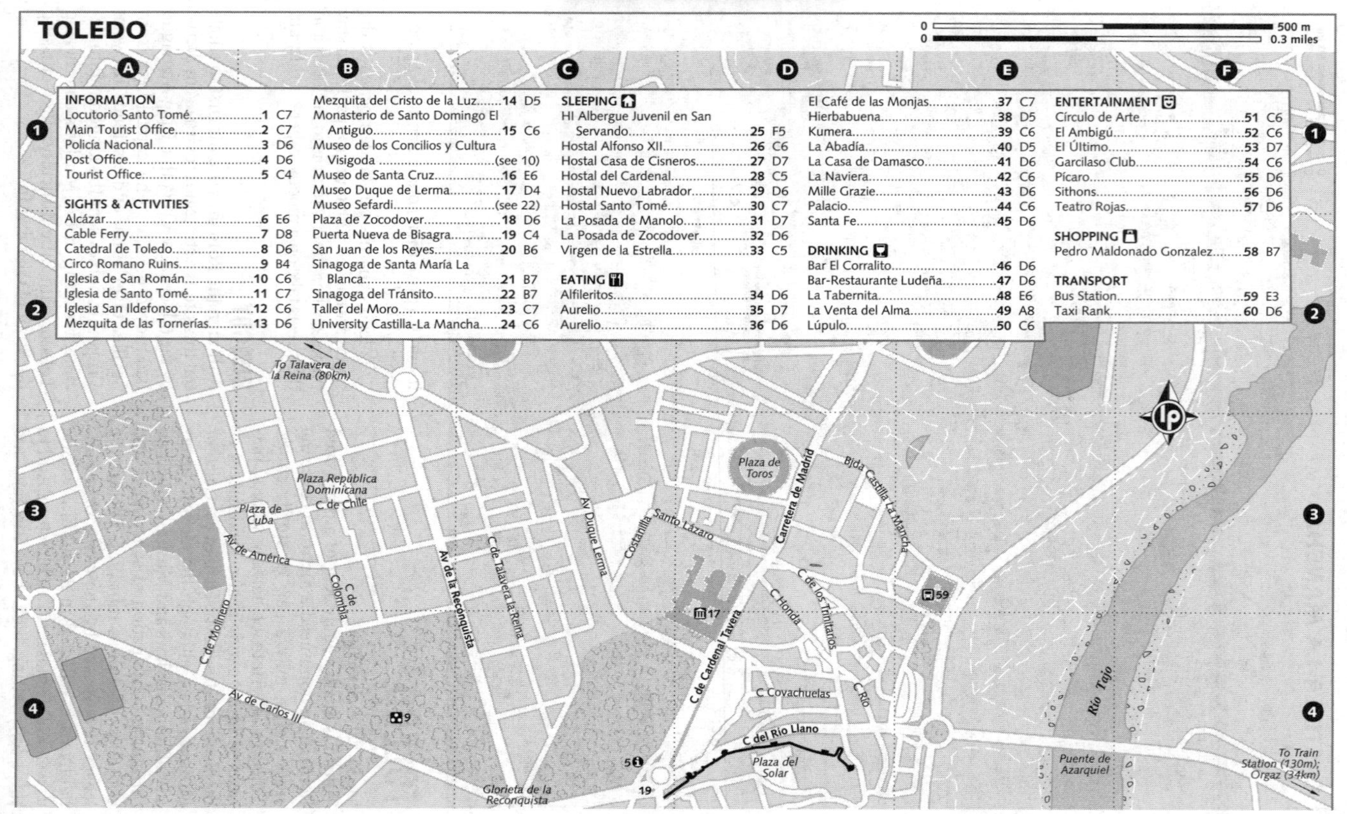
TOLEDO
0 500 m
0 0.3 miles
INFORMATION
Locutorio Santo Tomé 1 C7
Main Tourist Office 2 C7
Policía Nacional 3 D6
Post Office 4 D6
Tourist Office 5 C4
SIGHTS & ACTIVITIES
Alcázar 6 E6
Cable Ferry 7 D8
Catedral de Toledo 8 D6
Circo Romano Ruins 9 B4
Iglesia de San Román 10 C6
Iglesia de Santo Tomé 11 C7
Iglesia San Ildefonso 12 C6
Mezquita de las Tornerías 13 D6
Mezquita del Cristo de la Luz 14 D5
Monasterio de Santo Domingo El Antiguo 15 C6
Museo de los Concilios y Cultura Visigoda (see 10)
Museo de Santa Cruz 16 E6
Museo Duque de Lerma 17 D4
Museo Sefardí (see 22)
Plaza de Zocodover 18 D6
Puerta Nueva de Bisagra 19 C4
San Juan de los Reyes 20 B6
Sinagoga de Santa María La Blanca 21 B7
Sinagoga del Tránsito 22 B7
Taller del Moro 23 C7
University Castilla-La Mancha 24 C6
SLEEPING
HI Albergue Juvenil en San Servando 25 F5
Hostal Alfonso XII 26 C6
Hostal Casa de Cisneros 27 D7
Hostal del Cardenal 28 C5
Hostal Nuevo Labrador 29 D6
Hostal Santo Tomé 30 C7
La Posada de Manolo 31 D7
La Posada de Zocodover 32 D6
Virgen de la Estrella 33 C5
EATING
Alfileritos 34 D6
Aurelio 35 D7
Aurelio 36 D6
El Café de las Monjas 37 C7
Hierbabuena 38 D5
Kumera 39 C6
La Abadía 40 D5
La Casa de Damasco 41 D6
La Naviera 42 C6
Mille Grazie 43 D6
Palacio 44 C6
Santa Fe 45 D6
DRINKING
Bar El Corralito 46 D6
Bar-Restaurante Ludeña 47 D6
La Tabernita 48 E6
La Venta del Alma 49 A8
Lúpulo 50 C6
ENTERTAINMENT
Círculo de Arte 51 C6
El Ambigú 52 C6
El Último 53 D7
Garcilaso Club 54 C6
Pícaro 55 D6
Sithons 56 D6
Teatro Rojas 57 D6
SHOPPING
Pedro Maldonado Gonzalez 58 B7
TRANSPORT
Bus Station 59 E3
Taxi Rank 60 D6
To Talavera de la Reina (80km)
Plaza República Dominicana
Plaza de Cuba
C de Chile
Av de América
C de Colombia
C de Molinero
Av de Carlos III
Av de la Reconquista
C de Talavera la Reina
Glorieta de la Reconquista
Av Duque Lerma
Costanilla Santo Lázaro
Plaza de Toros
Carretera de Madrid
Bjda Castilla La Mancha
C de Cardenal Tavera
C Honda
C de los Trinitarios
C Covachuelas
C Río
C del Río Llano
Plaza del Solar
Río Tajo
Puente de Azarquiel
To Train Station (130m); Orgaz (34km)

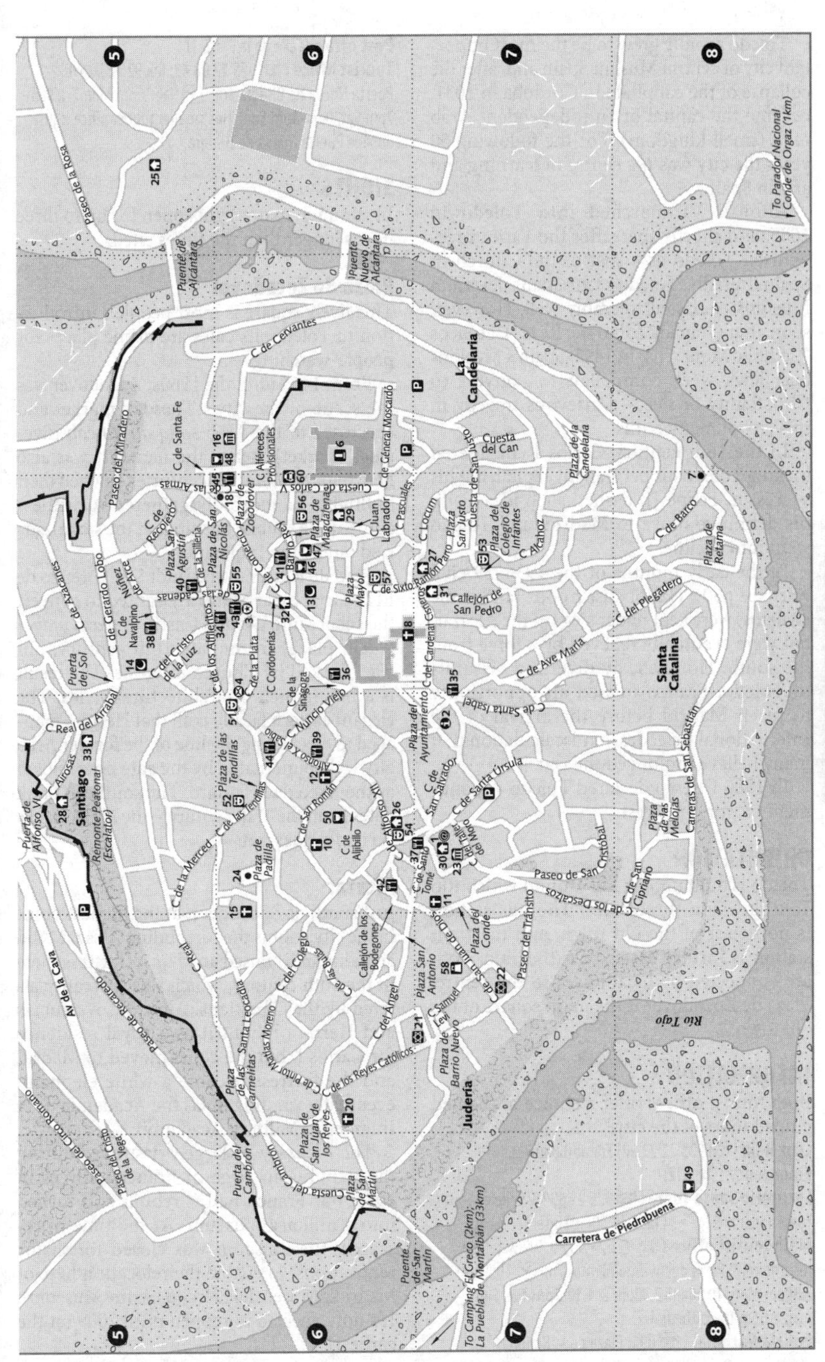

CASTILLA-LA MANCHA

Toledo rapidly grew to be the most important city of central Muslim Spain and, after the collapse of the caliphate in Córdoba in 1031, became the capital of an independent Arab *taifa* (small kingdom). For the following 50 years the city was *the* centre of learning and arts in Spain.

Alfonso VI marched into Toledo in 1085, and shortly thereafter the Vatican recognised Toledo as a seat of the Church in Spain. Initially, Toledo's Christians, Jews and Muslims coexisted tolerably well. However, soon after Granada fell to the Reyes Católicos (Catholic Monarchs) in 1492, Spain's Muslims and Jews were compelled to convert to Christianity or flee – a grievous tragedy in this city of many faiths.

In the 16th century Carlos I considered making Toledo his permanent capital, but his successor, Felipe II, dashed such ideas with his definitive move to Madrid, and Toledo went into decline.

In the early months of the 1936–39 civil war (see p50), Nationalist troops (and some civilians) were kept under siege in the Alcázar, but were eventually relieved by a force from the south. However, by diverting his units to Toledo, Franco missed an opportunity to reach Madrid before the arrival of the International Brigades, a miscalculation that many believe prolonged the war.

In 1986 Unesco declared Toledo a monument of world interest.

ORIENTATION

Toledo is built upon a hill around which Río Tajo flows on three sides. The bus station is northeast of the old town, and the train station is further east across the Tajo. Both are connected by local buses to the centre. Plaza de Zocodover is the main square of the old town.

INFORMATION

Both tourist offices offer a choice of themed guided tours of the city.

Cruz Roja (☎ 925 22 22 22) For ambulances.
Emergency (☎ 112)
Locutorio Santo Tomé (☎ 925 21 65 38; Calle de Santo Tomé 1; per hr €2; ⏰ 11am-10.30pm) Internet access.
Main tourist office (☎ 925 25 40 30; www.toledoturismo.com; Plaza del Ayuntamiento s/n; ⏰ 10.30am-2.30pm Mon, 10.30am-2.30pm & 4.30-7pm Tue-Sun) Across from the cathedral.
Policía Nacional (☎ 091; Plaza de la Ropería)
Post office (Calle de la Plata 1)
Tourist office (☎ 925 22 08 43; fax 925 25 26 48; Puerta Nueva de Bisagra s/n; ⏰ 9am-6pm Mon-Fri, 9am-7pm Sat, 9am-3pm Sun) This smaller tourist office is just outside Puerta Nueva de Bisagra.

SIGHTS

In summer, many sights open for up to three hours longer than the times cited.

Plaza de Zocodover

This lively square is most people's introduction to Toledo; its cafes are prime places for people-watching.

From 1465 until the 1960s, Zocodover was the scene of the city's Tuesday market and successor to the Arab *souq ad-dawab* (livestock market), hence the name. It was also here that *toledanos* for centuries enjoyed their bullfights or morbidly gathered to witness autos-da-fé (public burnings at the stake) carried out by the Inquisition.

Juan de Herrera, who built San Lorenzo de El Escorial (near Madrid), wanted to convert the square into a grand Castilian *plaza mayor* (main plaza) in the late 16th century, but was blocked by Church interests. The result is a hotchpotch of architectural styles. The elegant eastern facade is all that Herrera managed to erect along the line of the former Arab city wall, punctuated by the gate now known as the Arco de la Sangre. The southern flank dates from the 17th century – the McDonald's certainly does not.

Alcázar

Just south of Zocodover, at the highest point in the city, looms the foreboding Alcázar. Abd ar-Rahman III raised an *al-qasr* (fortress) here in the 10th century, which was thereafter altered by the Christians. Alonso Covarrubias and Herrera rebuilt it as a royal residence for Carlos I, but the court moved to Madrid and the fortress became a white elephant, eventually winding up as the Academia de la Infantería (Military Academy).

The Alcázar was largely destroyed during the Republican siege of Franco's forces in 1936, but Franco had it rebuilt and turned into a military museum. At the time of research, the museum was closed for major renovations, to enable the relocation here of Madrid's Museo del Ejército (Army Museum). It's not expected to reopen until 2009 (at the earliest).

Museo de Santa Cruz

Just off the Plaza de Zocodover, the **Museo de Santa Cruz** (☎ 925 22 10 36; Calle de Cervantes 3; admission free; 🕒 10am-6pm Mon-Sat, 10am-2pm Sun) was built in the early 16th century and is a beguiling combination of Gothic and Spanish Renaissance styles. The cloisters and carved wooden ceilings are superb, as are the upstairs displays of Spanish ceramics. The ground-level gallery contains a number of El Grecos (look for the *Asunción de la Virgen* and the superbly rendered *La Veronica*), a painting attributed to Goya *(Cristo Crucificado)*, the wonderful 15th-century *Tapestry of the Astrolabes*, and a mixed bag of religious objects.

Catedral de Toledo

Toledo's **catedral** (Plaza del Ayuntamiento; adult/under 12yr €7/free; 🕒 10.30am-6.30pm Mon-Sat, 2-6.30pm Sun) dominates the skyline, reflecting the city's historical significance as the heart of Catholic Spain.

From the earliest days of the Visigothic occupation, the modern site of the cathedral has been the city's centre of worship. During the three centuries of Muslim rule it contained Toledo's central mosque, which was subsequently destroyed in 1085. The construction of the cathedral dates from the 13th century.

Essentially a Gothic structure, the cathedral is nevertheless a melting pot of styles. Mudéjar elements are visible in the interior decoration, and the Spanish Renaissance is evident in the many chapels that line the church naves.

The cathedral's main nave is dominated by the **coro** (choir stalls), a feast of sculpture and carved wooden stalls. The 15th-century lower tier depicts the conquest of Granada, while the Renaissance upper level features images of saints and apostles.

Opposite is the **Capilla Mayor**, a chapel too small to accommodate the choir stalls as originally planned, but an extravagant work of art dating back to 1498. The masterpiece is the *retablo* (altarpiece) in Flemish Gothic style, depicting scenes from the lives of Christ and the Virgin Mary. The oldest of the cathedral's magnificent stained glass is the rose window above the **Puerta del Reloj**.

Behind the main altar lies a mesmerising piece of 18th-century *churrigueresco* (ornate style of baroque architecture), the **Transparente**, which also provides welcome light.

Other highlights include the gilded **Capilla de Reyes Nuevos**, the **Capilla de la Torre** and the **sacristía** (sacristy). The last contains a small gallery with paintings by such masters as El Greco, Zurbarán, Crespi, Titian, Rubens and Velázquez, while the Capilla de Reyes Nuevos houses the extraordinary **Custodia de Arfe**, by the celebrated goldsmith Enrique de Arfe. With 18kg of pure gold and 183kg of silver, this 16th-century conceit bristles with some 260 statuettes. Its big day out is the Feast of Corpus Christi (p280), when it is paraded around Toledo's streets.

The **sala capitular** (chapter house) features a remarkable 500-year-old *artesonado* (wooden Mudéjar ceiling) and Renaissance religious murals.

The cathedral's cool and pretty **claustro** (cloister) is entered through the **Puerta del Mollete** facing the square under the Arco del Palacio, which links the cathedral to the **Palacio Arzobispal** (Archbishop's Palace).

Iglesia San Ildefonso

The main attraction of this pretty 18th-century **church** (Plaza Juan de Mariana 1; admission €1.90; 🕒 10am-6.45pm), also known as the Iglesia de los Jesuítas, is the view from the top of the twin towers. This is the tallest point in the city (135 steps up); don't forget your camera.

Jewish Quarter

Toledo's former *judería* (Jewish quarter) was once home to 11 synagogues. The bulk of Toledo's Jews were tragically expelled in 1492.

Of the two synagogues remaining, don't miss **Sinagoga del Tránsito**, which was built in 1355 by special permission of Pedro I (construction of synagogues was by then prohibited in Christian Spain). From 1492 until 1877 it was variously used as a priory, hermitage and military barracks. The synagogue now houses the **Museo Sefardi** (☎ 925 22 36 65; www.museosefardi.net in Spanish; Calle Samuel Leví s/n; adult/under 12yr/12-25yr €2.40/free/1.20, audioguide €3; 🕒 10am-6pm Tue-Sat, 10am-2pm Sun). The vast main prayer hall has been expertly restored and the Mudéjar decoration and intricately carved (and colourful) wooden ceiling are striking. Exhibits provide an insight into the history of Jewish culture in Spain, and include archaeological finds, a memorial garden with tombstones inscribed in Hebrew, typical costumes of the Sephardic Jews and ceremonial artefacts.

Nearby, **Sinagoga de Santa María La Blanca** (☎ 925 22 72 57; Calle de los Reyes Católicos 4; admission

EL GRECO IN TOLEDO

Fortunately El Greco chose to change his name from the singularly unpronounceable Domenikos Theotokopoulos. Born in Crete in 1541, he moved to Venice in 1567 to be schooled as a Renaissance artist. He learned to extract the maximum effect from few colours, concentrating the observer's interest in the faces of his portraits and leaving the rest in relative obscurity – a characteristic that remained one of his hallmarks.

He came to Spain in 1577, hoping for a job decorating the palace-monastery complex of El Escorial outside Madrid, but was rejected as a court artist by Felipe II and settled in Toledo, where there were several patrons to support him. El Greco liked to hang around with the movers and shakers of the time and, by all reports, did not suffer from a lack of modesty: 'As surely as the rate of payment is inferior to the value of my sublime work, so will my name go down to posterity as one of the greatest geniuses of Spanish painting,' he pompously pronounced.

Arrogant and extravagant, El Greco liked the high life, and took rooms in a mansion on the Paseo del Tránsito. As Toledo's fortunes declined, however, so did the artist's personal finances (that's karma for you). Although his final paintings are among his best, he often found himself unable to pay the rent. He died in 1614, leaving his works scattered about the city, where many have remained to this day.

Iglesia de Santo Tomé (☎ 925 25 60 98; www.santotome.org; Plaza del Conde; admission €1.90; 🕒 10am-6pm) contains El Greco's masterpiece, *El Entierro del Conde de Orgaz* (The Burial of the Count of Orgaz). When the count was buried in 1322, Sts Augustine and Stephen supposedly descended from heaven to attend the funeral. El Greco's work depicts the event, complete with miracle guests including himself, his son and Cervantes.

One of the oldest convents in Toledo, the 11th-century **Monasterio de Santo Domingo El Antiguo** (☎ 925 22 29 30; Plaza de Santo Domingo el Antiguo; admission €2; 🕒 11am-1.30pm & 4-7pm Mon-Sat, 4-7pm Sun) includes some of El Greco's early commissions (most are copies). Visible through an iron grating is the crypt and wooden coffin of the painter himself.

Other spots in Toledo where you can contemplate El Greco's works include the Museo de Santa Cruz (p277), the *sacristía* of the Catedral de Toledo (p277) and the Museo Duque de Lerma (opposite).

CASTILLA-LA MANCHA

€2.30; 🕒 10am-6pm) is characterised by the horseshoe arches that delineate the five naves – classic Almohad architecture. Originally the upper arches opened onto rooms where women worshipped; the men worshipped down below.

SAN JUAN DE LOS REYES

North of the synagogues lies the Franciscan monastery and church of **San Juan de los Reyes** (☎ 925 22 38 02; Calle San Juan de los Reyes 2; admission €1.90; 🕒 10am-6pm), notable for its delightful cloisters.

Provocatively built in the heart of the Jewish quarter, San Juan de los Reyes was founded by Isabel and Fernando to demonstrate the supremacy of the Catholic faith in Spain. The rulers had planned to be buried here, but when they took the greater prize of Granada in 1492 they opted for the purpose-built Capilla Real.

Begun by the Breton architect Juan Güas in 1477, San Juan de los Reyes was only finished in 1606. Throughout the church and two-storey cloister the coat of arms of Isabel and Fernando dominates, and the chains of Christian prisoners liberated in Granada dangle from the walls. The prevalent late–Flemish Gothic style is enhanced with lavish Isabelline ornament and counterbalanced by unmistakable Mudéjar decoration, especially in the cloister, where typical geometric and vegetal designs stand out.

Islamic Toledo

Architectural traces of Toledo's medieval Muslim conquerors are still in evidence here. On the northern slopes of town you'll find the **Mezquita del Cristo de la Luz** (Cuesta de Carmelitas Descalzos 10; adult/under 12yr/12-25yr €1.90/free/1.40; 🕒 10am-6pm), a modest mosque that is nonetheless quite beautiful. Built in the 10th century, it suffered the usual fate of being converted to a church (hence the religious frescoes), but the original vaulting and arches have survived. The narrow, steep Calle del Cristo de la Luz continues past the mosque and its charming gardens, and via the Islamic-named **Bab al-Mardum** gate.

Outside the City Walls

Large portions of the city walls remain intact, including the imposing turrets of the **Puerta Nueva de Bisagra** (1550), emblazoned with Carlos I's coat of arms.

Just outside the gate is a shady park, the site of the Tuesday market. Down the hill to the west is another park, where you can see the ruins of the former **Circo Romano** (Roman Circus).

Nearby, on the road to Madrid, is the **Museo Duque de Lerma** (☎ 925 22 04 51; Calle de Cardenal Tavera 2; admission €4; ⏲ 10.30am-1.30pm & 3.30-6pm). Built in 1541, this former hospital contains an interesting array of art, including some of El Greco's last paintings.

For some of the best city views, head over the Puente de Alcántara to the other side of Río Tajo. Alternatively, in summer hop on the tiny, free **cable ferry** from near Hotel El Diamantista, and walk up the opposite bank. Scattered about this hinterland are many wealthy country estates.

WALKING TOUR

Stock up on Band-Aids and explore Toledo on foot, in a fascinating journey through history that could be completed in three hours or last all day.

Start off in central **Plaza de Zocodover** (**1**; p276), then pass through the **Arco de la Sangre (2)** on the eastern side of the square to the rewarding **Museo de Santa Cruz** (**3**; p277) on the left. Up the hill to the south is Toledo's signature **Alcázar** (**4**; p276), beyond which there are some fine views over the Río Tajo. Follow the spires down the hill to the west, passing the remnants of a mosque, **Mezquita de las Tornerías (5)**, before reaching the **Catedral de Toledo** (**6**; p277), the spiritual home of Catholic Spain. Twist your way west to the 14th-century **Taller del Moro** (**7**; ☎ 925 22 45 00; Calle del Taller del Moro s/n). Although the museum is closed for renovation (check at the tourist office for an update), the building is still interesting for its classic Islamic architecture, built in the Mudéjar style.

From here, you can detour northeast to the **Iglesia de San Román (8)**, an impressive hybrid of Mudéjar and Renaissance styles and home to the **Museo de los Concilios y Cultura Visigoda** (☎ 925 22 78 72; Calle de San Román; adult/child & senior €0.60/free; ⏲ 10am-2pm & 4-6.30pm Tue-Sat, 10am-2pm Sun), with Visigothic artefacts. Nearby is the **Monasterio de Santo Domingo El Antiguo** (**9**; opposite).

Down the hill is a must-see for El Greco enthusiasts – the wonderful **Iglesia de Santo Tomé** (**10**; opposite). From here you enter the heart of Toledo's old Jewish Quarter. The **Sinagoga del Tránsito** (**11**; p277) should not be missed, while

WALK FACTS

Start Plaza de Zocodover
Finish San Juan de los Reyes
Distance 2km
Duration From three hours

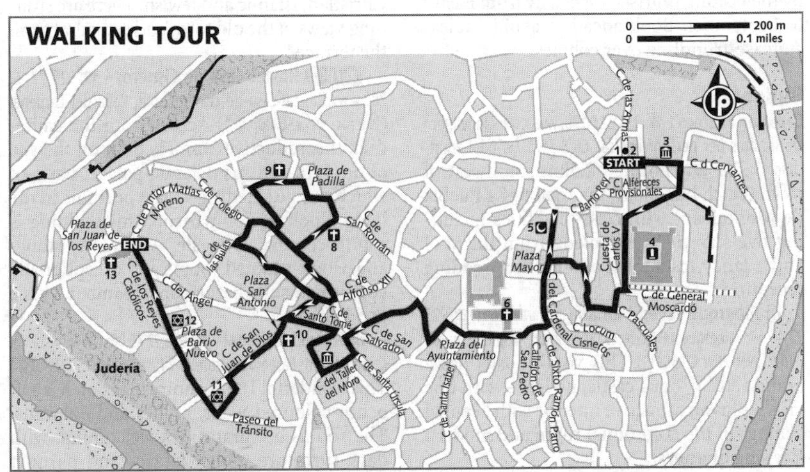

the **Sinagoga de Santa María La Blanca** (**12**; p277) is also worth a look. These synagogues take on special poignancy if you continue along Calle de los Reyes Católicos to the splendid **San Juan de los Reyes** (**13**; p278). Spain's Catholic rulers hoped this church would represent the ultimate endpoint of the city's history, so it seems a fitting spot to end your walk.

COURSES

The University Castilla-La Mancha runs an ESTO (Spanish in Toledo) program with various language courses. Visit www.uclm.es/fundacion/esto for more details.

FESTIVALS & EVENTS

The **Feast of Corpus Christi** falls on the Thursday of the ninth week after Easter and is one of the finest Corpus Christi celebrations in Spain. Several days of festivities reach a crescendo with a solemn procession featuring the massive Custodia de Arfe (see p277).

Semana Santa (Holy Week) in Toledo is also marked by several days of solemn processions by masked members of *cofradías* (brotherhoods). In the key days some of these processions occur around midnight.

The **Feast of the Assumption** is on 15 August, when you can drink of the cathedral's well water, believed to have miraculous qualities – the queues for a swig from an earthenware *botijo* (jug) can be equally astonishing.

SLEEPING

Toledo's plentiful accommodation is offset by the visiting tourists, especially from Easter to September. Book ahead to avoid endless suitcase-trundling over cobbles.

Budget

Camping El Greco (☎ 925 22 00 90; www.campingelgreco.ya.st; sites per person/tent/car €6/5.75/5.75, pool adult/child €3.50/2;) Located 2.5km southwest of town (catch bus 7), on the road to La Puebla de Montalbán, with classy facilities including five-star views of Toledo from the pool and a fancy restaurant popular for wedding receptions.

HI Albergue Juvenil en San Servando (☎ 925 22 45 54; ralberguesto@jccm.es; Subida del Hospital s/n; dm under/over 26yr €9.50/12) This youth hostel has a grand setting – in a castle, no less – with fine views, plus an attractive interior with beamed ceilings in the communal room and modern sleeping quarters.

Virgen de la Estrella (☎ 925 25 31 34; Calle Airosas 1; s & d without bathroom €30) The owner also runs the nearby restaurant of the same name, as well as a second, equally inexpensive, *pensión* (small private hotel). The plus here is a quieter, prettier location opposite the Santiago church.

La Posada de Zocodover (☎ 925 25 58 14; Calle Cordonerias 6; r €40) There are just seven clean and acceptable rooms at this superbly located place near the city's main square – which can require earplugs at weekends.

Midrange & Top End

Hostal Nuevo Labrador (☎ 925 22 26 20; fax 925 22 93 99; Calle Juan Labrador 10; s/d/tr €30/50/65;) A friendly hotel offering good value for money in a central location, with pleasant rooms decorated with pine furniture.

Hostal Santo Tomé (☎ 925 22 17 12; www.hostalsantotome.com; Calle de Santo Tomé 13; s/d €42/55; P) This good-value *hostal* (budget hotel) has larger-than-most rooms with light wood floors and furniture, plus bathrooms with five-star attitude offering extras like shoe polish and hairdryers.

Hostal Alfonso XII (☎ 925 25 25 09; www.hostal-alfonso12.com; Calle de Alfonso XII; r €65;) A gingerbread cottage of a place with original beams, terracotta tiles and stylish, albeit small, rooms decorated with impeccable taste.

La Posada de Manolo (☎ 925 28 22 50; www.laposadademanolo.com; Calle de Sixto Ramón Parro 8; s/d incl breakfast from €42/66) This boutique-style hotel has themed each floor with furnishings and decor reflecting one of the three cultures of Toledo: Christian, Islamic and Jewish. There are stunning views of the old town and cathedral from the terrace.

our pick **Hostal Casa de Cisneros** (☎ 925 22 88 28; www.hostal-casa-de-cisneros.com; Calle del Cardenal Cisneros; s/d €50/80;) Across from the cathedral, this seductive *hostal* is built on the site of an 11th-century Islamic palace, parts of which can be spied via a glass porthole in the lobby floor. In comparison, this building is a 16th-century youngster with pretty stone-and-wood-beamed rooms and exceptionally voguish en suite bathrooms. Number 23 is a good choice.

Hostal del Cardenal (☎ 925 22 49 00; www.hostaldelcardenal.com; Paseo de Recaredo 24; s/d €77/113; P) This wonderful 18th-century mansion has soft ochre-coloured walls, arches and columns. The rooms are grand, yet welcoming, with dark furniture, plush fabrics and parquet floors. Several overlook the garden, with its ponds, fountains and colourful flowers.

Parador Nacional Conde de Orgaz (☎ 925 22 18 50; www.parador.es; Cerro del Emperador s/n; s/d €114/159; P ✕) High above the southern bank of Río Tajo, Toledo's *parador* (luxurious state-owned hotel) boasts a classy interior and breathtaking city views. However, current renovation works could be a distraction; call first to ensure you are not sleeping within earshot of a pneumatic drill.

EATING

Avoid the plentiful restaurants that advertise various types of paella with a brightly coloured placard outside, as they will generally reflect an indifferent kitchen (these paellas are mass produced). Venues are open standard hours unless otherwise indicated.

Budget

El Café de las Monjas (☎ 925 21 34 24; Calle de Santo Tomé 2; 9am-9pm) An old-fashioned patisserie where you can taste such delights as marzipan cake and *chocolate con churros* (hot chocolate with spiral-shaped doughnuts for dunking).

Santa Fe (☎ 670 654216; Calle de Santa Fe 6; tapas €2, menú €8) You can eat better here and for half the price than in the restaurants on nearby Zocodover. Roll up your sleeves and join the workmen in the attractive half-tiled dining room enjoying tapas and dishes like tortilla with green pepper, homemade paella and *pollo al ajillo* (chicken in tomato and garlic sauce).

Mille Grazie (☎ 925 25 42 70; Calle de las Cadenas 2; pizzas from €6.50, pastas from €8) Despite the worrying inclusion of a Hawaiian pizza (with pineapple), the chef here *is* Italian and the dishes are tasty and good. Try the *panzotti Mille Grazie* (ravioli-style pasta stuffed with spinach and walnuts).

La Casa de Damasco (☎ 925 22 78 33; Sierpe 5; meals €12; V) Middle Eastern dishes here include the happily predictable felafel, hummus, *metabal* (aubergine-based dip), salads and doner kebab. Finish off with a puff on the hubble-bubble (€8).

our pick Palacio (☎ 925 21 59 72; Calle Alfonso X el Sabio 3; menú €13.90, meals €14-18) An unpretentious place where stained glass, beams and efficient old-fashioned service combine with traditional no-nonsense cuisine. Hungry? Try a gut-busting bowl of *judías con perdiz* (white beans with partridge) for starters.

Midrange & Top End

Kumera (☎ 925 25 75 53; Calle Alfonso X el Sabio 2; meals €18-25) The interior is all golden brick and stone, complemented by colourful artwork. The menu is similarly diverse, with choices such as tuna in soy sauce, crêpes with salmon, spinach and cheese, and venison with roast peppers.

Alfileritos (☎ 925 23 96 25; Calle de los Alfileritos 24; meals €18-25) Columns, beams and barrel-vault ceilings are happily combined with modern artwork here. The dining rooms are spread over four bright floors below a skylight, and the menu includes such delights as *langostinos con mojo* (large prawns in a spicy tomato and chilli sauce) and *sopa de fresas con helado de pimiento de Sichuan* (strawberry 'soup' with Szechuan pepper ice cream), which sure makes a change from the ubiquitous flan.

Hierbabuena (☎ 925 22 39 24; Calle de Navalpino 45; meals €18-25, menú €34.30; closed Sun night) A dress-for-dinner restaurant with tables set around a flower-filled patio. It dishes up classy cuisine such as artichokes stuffed with Catalan sausage and creamed leeks.

La Naviera (☎ 925 25 25 32; Calle de la Campana 8; meals €20-25; closed Mon) Diners swoop like seagulls on La Naviera's free tables, ready for the best seafood in Toledo, served in a suitably nautical atmosphere with nets and blue paintwork.

La Abadía (☎ 925 25 11 40; Plaza de San Nicolás 3; meals €25-30, menú €28; V) In a former 16th-century palace, this atmospheric bar and restaurant is ideal for romancing couples. Arches, niches and subtle lighting are spread over a warren of brick-and-stone-clad rooms. The menu includes meat and fish plates, as well as lightweight dishes like goat's cheese salad with pumpkin and sunflower seeds – perfect for small (distracted) appetites.

Aurelio (☎ 925 22 13 92; Plaza del Ayuntamiento 4; meals from €35; closed dinner Sun) The three restaurants under this name are among the best of Toledo's top-end eateries (the other locations are Calle de la Sinagoga 1 and 6). Game, fresh produce and traditional Toledan dishes are prepared with panache.

DRINKING & ENTERTAINMENT

Bars & Clubs

Toledo has enough bars and discos to ensure you miss bedtime.

Pícaro (☎ 925 22 13 01; Calle de las Cadenas 6) A popular cafe-theatre serving an eclectic range of *copas* (drinks). From Monday to Thursday it's perfect for a quiet beverage; the pace steps up on Friday and Saturday nights, when the disco ball starts spinning at 2.30am.

Lúpulo (☎ 925 25 71 36; Calle de Aljibillo 5) Serves a choice of more than 50 Spanish and foreign beers, and has a popular spill-over outside terrace.

La Venta del Alma (☎ 925 25 42 45; Carretera de Piedrabuena 35; closed Mon) For an older crowd, La Venta is mild-mannered during the day, but gets rowdy on Friday and Saturday when the full-on atmosphere hits a prolonged high. It's just outside the city: cross Puente de San Martín and turn left up the hill; the bar is about 200m up on your left.

Sithons (☎ 925 22 44 97; www.sithons.com; Callejón del Lucio 4; late-early Thu-Sat) Most revellers finish the night at Sithons, a *discoteca* (club) with a throbbing dance floor, animated DJ and pulsating lights.

El Ambigú (Calle de las Tendillas 8) Plays jazz and blues in an intimate half-tiled interior with artwork and arches.

La Tabernita (☎ 925 21 30 06; Calle de Santa Fe 10) A hole-in-the-wall bar that specialises in *sidra* (cider).

Also tempting in summer are the outdoor tables of the bars in the leafy courtyard just off Plaza de Magdalena, including Bar-Restaurante Ludeña and Bar El Corralito.

For the student-oriented bars, shimmy down to the streets around La Abadía, particularly Calle de los Alfileritos and Calle de la Sillería.

Theatre & Cinema

Teatro Rojas (☎ 925 22 39 70; Plaza Mayor;) Often has a rewarding program of theatre and dance. Tuesday nights are reserved for a 'film club', Toledo's only venue for original-soundtrack films. Check for weekend children's matinées.

Live Music

Círculo de Arte (☎ 925 21 43 29; www.circuloartetoledo.org; Plaza de San Vicente 2) There are several venues for enjoying foot-tapping live sounds, including this classy place with its regular classical, jazz and blues concerts.

Garcilaso Club (☎ 925 22 91 60; www.garcilasocafe.com; Calle Rojas 5) An easygoing, urbane crowd frequents this funky club with live rock bands, comedy nights and a dance space plus upstairs chill-out zone.

El Último (☎ 925 21 00 02; Plaza del Colegio de Infantes 4) Situated in a 16th-century building, El Último is a hotbed for live jazz, blues and soul.

SHOPPING

For centuries Toledo was renowned for the excellence of its swords, and you'll see them for sale everywhere. Another big seller is anything decorated with *damasquinado* (damascene), a fine encrustation of gold or silver in Arab artistic tradition. A reliable outlet is **Pedro Maldonado Gonzalez** (☎ 925 21 38 16; Calle de San Juan de Dios 10).

Toledo is also famed for its ceramics and marzipan, which every shop seems to sell regardless of the quality. The Santo Tomé marzipan brand is reputable and there are several outlets in town, including one on Zocodover. Even the local nuns get in on the marzipan act and most of the convents sell the sweets.

GETTING THERE & AWAY

For most major destinations, you'll need to backtrack to Madrid.

Bus

From Toledo's **bus station** (☎ 925 21 58 50; Avenida de Castilla la Mancha) buses depart for Madrid every half-hour from about 6am to 10pm daily (8.30am to 11.30pm Sunday and holidays). Direct buses (€4.53, one hour) run hourly; other services (1½ hours) go via villages along the way. Regular buses go to Consuegra (€4.34, one hour) and Talavera de la Reina (€5.95, 1¼ hours), while occasional buses go to Guadalajara (€8.10, 2¼ hours). There are also services on weekdays and Sunday to Albacete (€13.65, 2¾ hours), Ciudad Real (€7.50, 1½ hours) and Cuenca (€10.90, 2¼ hours).

Car & Motorcycle

The N401 connects Toledo with Madrid. If you want the A4 Autovía de Andalucía, the main motorway running south from Madrid to Córdoba and Seville, take the N400 for Aranjuez. The N403 heads northwest for Ávila and continues as the N501 for Salamanca.

Train

Built in 1920, the **train station** (☎ 902 24 02 02; Paseo de la Rosa) is a pretty introduction to the city. The high-speed AVE service runs every hour or so to Madrid's Atocha station (€9, 30 minutes).

GOLD ON A PLATE

Saffron is one of the most sensuous spices in the world: its intense colour, aroma and delicacy are accentuated by a wealth of nuances. It's also among the most expensive spices – hardly surprising when you consider that it takes some 160,000 flowers to produce just 1kg of commercial saffron.

Spain leads the European saffron market, while La Mancha is the region where the flowers are grown and cultivated, primarily around Cuenca and Albacete. Visit here in October and the surrounding fields are a sumptuous blanket of purple blooms. We talked with Fernando Sarasa, the quality and product manager of Safinter, one of Spain's largest saffron exporters.

How long has saffron been grown in La Mancha? I personally believe that Romans introduced the plant, but we can only be certain that the Moors cultivated the spice from the 9th century. It was subsequently exported to the Indian subcontinent – ironically travelling in the opposite direction to the traditional spice route.

Why La Mancha? The climate, soil and mainly the know-how of the generations of La Mancha farmers who have been growing saffron for several centuries.

How can you tell the difference between genuine high-quality saffron and the inferior cheaper brands? The proof is in the pudding. Good-quality saffron adds a delicate aroma and flavour to dishes, while cheaper brands are often adulterated by dyes, water and even sugar syrup. Study your saffron and you will also learn that the genuine product has a special texture, plus a crispness and subtly floral aroma with an initially bitter, but never astringent, taste. The yellow colour it produces is also all-important. You only need 50mg of pure saffron for a typical dish, so considering this, it is not so expensive!

And typical dishes that use saffron are...? In Italy, risotto Milanese; in France, bouillabaisse; in the UK, saffron cake; in Sweden, *lusserkatter* cake; and in Spain, numerous dishes, although the most famous just has to be the all-time traditional paella.

GETTING AROUND

Handy buses run between Plaza de Zocodover and the bus station (bus 5) and train station (buses 5 and 6).

A **remonte peatonal** (escalator; 7am-10pm Mon-Fri, 8am-10pm Sat & Sun), which starts near the Puerta de Alfonso VI and ends near the Monasterio de Santo Domingo El Antiguo, is another way you can minimise the steep uphill climb.

There are **taxi** (☎ 925 25 50 50) ranks south of Plaza de Zocodover and at the bus station.

AROUND TOLEDO

Carranque

Since 1983, archaeologists at **Carranque** (☎ 925 59 20 14; adult/child €4/free; 10am-9pm Tue-Sun 15 Apr-15 Sep, 10am-6pm Tue-Sat 16 Sep-14 Apr) have been excavating what they believe to be the foundations of a late-4th-century Roman basilica, which would make it the oldest in Spain. The skeletal remains of Roman villas and temple-fountains are among the site's other highlights, while the remains of a 12th-century monastery with some valuable mosaics are also undergoing excavation. The admission fee includes entrance to a small interpretation centre and museum. Carranque is just off the N401 highway 35km north of Toledo.

Castles

The area around Toledo is rich with castles in varying states of upkeep. Most are only accessible by car.

Situated some 20km southeast of Toledo along the CM400 is the dramatic ruined Arab castle of **Almonacid de Toledo**. There are legends that suggest El Cid lived here, but the lonely ruins have long been abandoned. A few kilometres further down the road is a smaller castle in the village of **Mascaraque**. Continue on to Mora, then take the CM410 for 10km to the village of **Orgaz**, which has a modest 15th-century **castle** (every 2nd Wed Apr-Nov) in good nick.

Around 30km southwest of Toledo, the hulking ruin of **Castillo de Montalbán**, believed to have been erected by the 12th-century Knights Templar, stands majestically over the Río Torcón valley. It's open only sporadically, but there's little to stop you wandering around at any time. To get there from Toledo, head for La Puebla de Montalbán, due west of the city, and follow the signs.

The town of **Escalona**, 52km northwest of Toledo on the N403, boasts a castle ruin of Arab origin, in a pretty location on the banks of Río Alberche.

THE WEST

Heavily wooded in parts and with a compelling combination of sweeping plains and dramatic mountains, the west of this region has plenty of surprises up its sleeve.

TALAVERA DE LA REINA

pop 90,000

Talavera de la Reina, with original city walls and Portuguese-style ceramic facades, has a laid-back appeal. Overrun by the Muslim Almoravid dynasty in the 12th century, Talavera was later the birthplace of Fernando de Rojas, whose *Celestina* (published in 1499) is judged by some as Europe's first great novel. In 1809 the town was the scene of a key battle between the Duke of Wellington's forces and the French.

These days, Talavera has settled into comfortable provinciality and has long been famous for its ceramic work, which adorns many buildings. The finest example is the gold-and-blue facade of the **Teatro Victoria**, just off Plaza del Padre Juan de Mariana.

Within the old city walls is **Museo Ruiz de Luna** (☎ 925 80 01 49; Calle de San Agustín el Viejo s/n; admission €0.60; 🕑 10am-2pm & 4-6.30pm Tue-Sat, 10am-2pm Sun), housing local ceramics dating from the 16th and 17th centuries. To buy contemporary ceramics check out the factories and shops along the road leading north to the A5 motorway. The **tourist office** (☎ 925 82 63 22; www.turismotalavera.org; Ronda del Cañello s/n; 🕑 10.30am-1.30pm & 4-6pm Mon-Sat, 10.30am-12.30pm Sun) doubles as a gallery displaying (you guessed it) ceramics.

Talavera's accommodation ranges from bland midrange options geared for business travellers to cheap no-frills places like **Hostal Edan** (☎ 925 80 69 89; Paseo de Extremadura 24; s/d €17/32), with simple, clean rooms. Reservations are recommended on weekends.

The bus station is in the town centre. Regular buses between Madrid and Badajoz stop in Talavera de la Reina, and up to nine leave daily for Toledo (€5.95, 1¼ hours). Buses also head to Cáceres, Mérida, Oropesa, Plasencia and Trujillo.

AROUND TALAVERA DE LA REINA

The delightful village of **Oropesa**, 34km west of Talavera, makes a more appealing overnight stop. Head first for a *cerveza* (beer) at one of the bars flanking lovely Plaza del Navarro, before tramping up to the hilltop 14th-century **castle** (☎ 925 45 00 06; www.e-oropesa.com; adult/under 12yr/12-25yr €2.50/free/1.25; 🕑 10am-2pm & 4-7pm Tue-Sun). It looks north across the plains to the mighty Sierra de Gredos and is a year-round venue for art exhibitions, plus concerts and theatre (including *zarzuela*, a mix of theatre, music and dance) during July and August.

Across from here is a 14th-century palace that houses Spain's second-oldest **parador** (☎ 925 43 00 00; www.parador.es; s/d €105/135; P ❄), which has managed to retain a heady historical feel without the 'over-heritaging' that typifies many Spanish *paradores*. The rooms are large and luxurious, with heavy brocade curtains and antiques. Read Somerset Maugham's rave review of the place in the lobby and ask to see San Pedro de Alcántara's sleeping quarters, hidden in the bowels of this former palace.

There's also **La Hostería** (☎/fax 925 43 08 75; www.lahosteriadeoropesa.com; Plaza del Palacio 5; s/d incl breakfast €50/65; P ❄), just below the castle, which has pretty, individually decorated rooms with beamed ceilings and a popular restaurant (meals €20) with tables spilling out into a flower-festooned courtyard.

From Talavera de la Reina, buses travel here three or four times daily. Drivers should follow the signs to the A5 motorway to Extremadura or Badajoz.

By Río Tajo just 14km south of Oropesa sits **El Puente del Arzobispo**, another well-known centre for ceramics with showrooms galore. The multi-arched bridge after which the town is named – and over which you're most likely to drive on your way out of town – was built in the 14th century.

MONTES DE TOLEDO

elev 1400m

The dramatic Montes de Toledo begin at the low foothills south of Toledo, rising westwards towards Extremadura. Exploring these hills takes you into the heart of some of the most sparsely populated country of Spain's interior. Long stretches of the region's roads are lined with terracotta-coloured earth dotted with olive trees, or green fields blanketed in spring with yellow and purple wildflowers. Most towns are served by the occasional bus from Toledo.

If you're travelling by car, the most straightforward route from Toledo is the CM401, which skirts the northern slopes of the Montes. Eleven kilometres short of Navahermosa, a trail leads south to **Embalse del Torcón**, a popular lakeshore picnic spot.

Beyond Navahermosa you have several options for branching south. Some of the more heavily wooded areas offer gorgeous vistas, and apart from in the odd tiny *pueblo* (village), you'll see more goats than folk. One longish route that gives a taste of the area starts south of the CM401 at Los Navalmorales. Take the CM4155 towards Los Navalucillos, and keep heading south past seemingly deserted villages until you hit a T-junction after 48km. Turning right (west), you wind 35km to the northern reaches of the huge **Embalse de Cijara**, part of a chain of reservoirs fed by Río Guadiana and actually part of Extremadura. Swing north towards **Puerto de San Vicente**, branching off west to the EX102 and the last curvy stretch towards Guadalupe.

THE SOUTH

This is the terrain that typifies La Mancha for many people: flat plains stretching to the horizon, punctuated by the occasional farmhouse or emblematic windmill. The southeast, however, is surprisingly verdant and lush with rivers, natural parks and some of the prettiest villages in the province.

CIUDAD REAL

pop 70,000

Despite being the one-time royal counterpart of Toledo, Ciudad Real is a fairly ordinary Spanish working town today, although this may well change when it is propelled into the spotlight with the completion of a Las Vegas–style gambling and leisure complex (see the boxed text, below). The centre is unlikely to alter, however, with its pedestrianised shopping streets and the quirky charm of Plaza Mayor, complete with carillon clock (topped by Cupid), flamboyant neo-Gothic town-hall facade and modern tiered fountain.

Information

Municipal tourist office (☎ 926 21 64 86; www.ayto-ciudadreal.es; Plaza Mayor 1; ⏲ 10am-2pm & 5-7pm Tue-Sat, 10am-2pm Sun) Can advise on city sights, hotels and restaurants.

Tourist office (☎ 926 20 00 37; Calle de Alarcos 21; ⏲ 10am-2pm & 4-7pm Mon-Sat, 10am-2pm Sun) Has plenty of information on the province.

Sights

Coming from the north, you'll enter Ciudad Real by the **Puerta de Toledo** (1328), the last remaining gate of the original eight, built in Mudéjar style by Alfonso X.

Museo Provincial (Calle del Prado 4) has archaeological exhibits but is closed until 2010. For Quijote fans, the **Museo del Quijote** (☎ 926 20 04 57; Ronda de Alarcos 1; admission free; ⏲ 10am-2pm & 6-9pm Mon-Sat, 10am-2pm Sun) has audiovisual displays, plus a Cervantes library stocked with hundreds of Don Quijote books, including some in Esperanto and Braille, and others dating back to 1724. It helps if you speak Spanish.

Of the swag of churches, the most striking is the 14th-century Gothic **Iglesia de San Pedro**

A GOOD BET (OR NOT…)

Tony Bennett may soon be adding Ciudad Real to his touring schedule when entertainment giant Harrah's applies its glittering touch to the Las Vegas–style Caesars Resort – reputed to be the most ambitious gambling and leisure centre to be built in Europe. Located just outside the city and due for completion in late 2008, its numbers are similarly big-time: a 4645-sq-metre casino, a 3000-seat theatre, a 2787-sq-metre spa, plus the inevitable shopping complex, multiple restaurants and bars. Several swimming pools and three golf courses are also in the pipeline; the latter is not such good news for this, one of the most arid regions in Spain.

Harrah's is obviously banking on the fact that millions of Spanish people have an interest in gambling, as evidenced by the popularity of the national lottery. The resort is a joint venture with local company El Reino, which has invested a hefty €567 million. It will be interesting to see if this is a gamble that pays off.

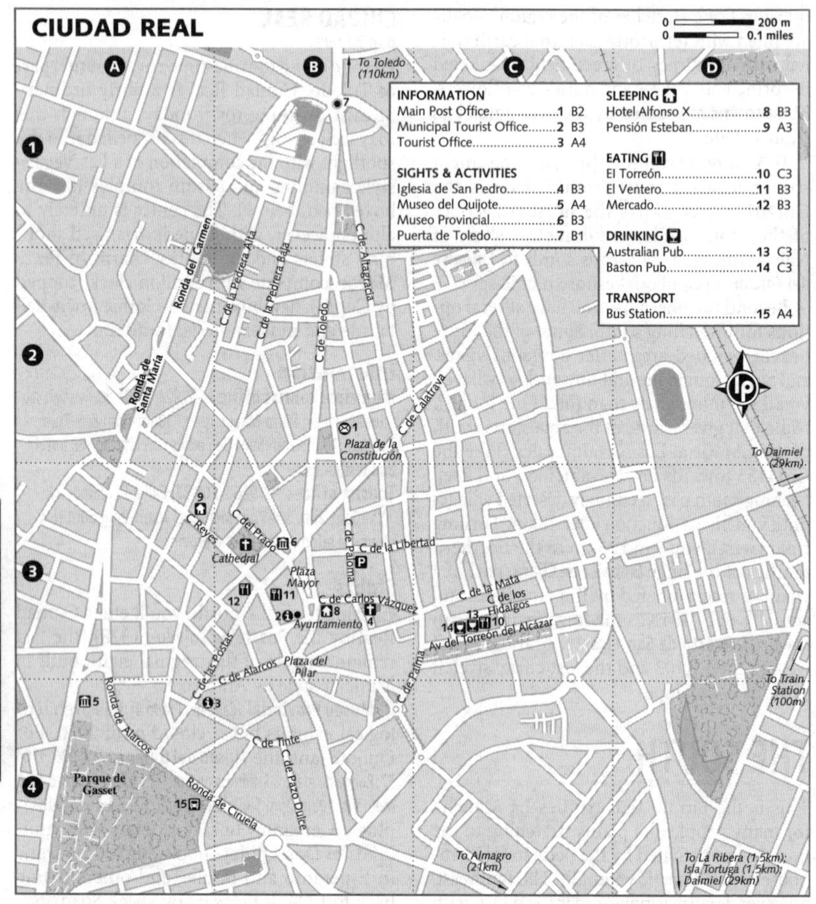

(Calle Ramón y Cajal General Rey; 11am-12pm & 8-8.30pm Mon-Fri, 11am-12pm & 7-7.30pm Sat, 9am-1pm Sun), with its three-part facade and three naves within, plus star-shaped vaults and gleaming 15th-century alabaster altarpiece.

Sleeping & Eating

Pensión Esteban (☎ 926 22 45 78; Calle Reyes 15; s/d €23/40) Within confessional distance of the cathedral, this no-nonsense *pensión* has a friendly owner, a flower-filled entrance and adequate rooms with pine furniture and sparkling bathrooms.

Hotel Alfonso X (☎ 926 22 42 81; Calle de Carlos Vázquez 8; s/d €60/120; P) This is an upmarket place where old facade meets renovated interior with success. The modern carpeted rooms come with all the swish trimmings, plus glossy marble bathrooms. The restaurant has a reasonable €17 daily *menú* (set meal). There's good access for travellers with disabilities.

El Ventero (☎ 926 21 65 88; Plaza Mayor 9; raciones €7) Time your chair on the square here to enjoy the carillon clock display (generally noon, 1pm, 2pm, 6pm and 8pm), when Don Quijote, Sancho and Cervantes emerge for a congenial spin around a small stage. The vast menu of *raciones* (large tapas servings) includes *salmorejo* (thick garlicky gazpacho), *almoronía* (similar to ratatouille topped with cheese) and *perdiz roja* (partridge in a sherry sauce).

The handful of cafe-bars along Calle de Palma serve some of the best-sized tapas in town. But for most of your dining and drinking pleasures, head for Avenida del Torreón del Alcázar and the parallel Calle de los Hidalgos. **El Torreón** (☎ 926 22 83 13; Avenida del Torreón del Alcázar 7; meals €25-30) is a good bet, specialising in game.

Self-caterers should head for the vast covered **mercado** (market; Calle de las Postas).

Drinking

You'll find clubs, discos and welcoming bars like **Australian Pub** (Avenida del Torreón del Alcázar 4) and the adjacent Baston Pub (with terrace) on lively Avenida del Torreón del Alcázar, flanking a park. Calle de los Hidalgos is another energetic street for bar-hopping. Move on to the city's best-known moving-and-shaking discos: La Ribera and Isla Tortuga in Playa Park, east of town beyond the train tracks.

Getting There & Away

BUS

The **bus station** (☎ 926 21 13 42) is southwest of the centre. Up to three daily buses head to Albacete (€13.50, 2¾ hours) and Toledo (€7.50, 1½ hours), and five per day head off to Madrid (€10.50, 2½ hours). Most surrounding towns, including Almagro (€2.10, 30 minutes, up to five daily), can be reached by bus.

TRAIN

The **train station** (☎ 926 22 02 02) lies east of the town centre. The bulk of trains linking Madrid with Andalucía stop at Ciudad Real. There are regular departures to Madrid (from €18.50, one hour) and Córdoba (from €23, one hour), and daily departures for Valencia (from €27, five hours, two daily) and southeast to Almagro (€2.30, 15 minutes).

Getting Around

Local bus 5 swings past both the train and bus stations bound for the town centre; catch it from Plaza del Pilar when you're leaving town.

CIUDAD REAL PROVINCE

Almagro

pop 9100

The jewel in Almagro's crown is the extraordinary Plaza Mayor with its wavy tiled roofs, stumpy columns and faded bottle-green porticoes. Although it looks quasi-oriental, the 16th-century plaza has Germanic roots, dating back to the reign of Carlos I, when several well-heeled bankers and traders moved here. The town is a delight to wander around, the relatively traffic-free cobbled streets flanked by Renaissance palaces, churches and shops selling local cheeses, embroidery and basketware.

INFORMATION

Tourist office (☎ 926 86 07 17; www.ciudad-almagro.com in Spanish; Plaza Mayor 1; 🕑 10am-2pm & 5-8pm Tue-Fri, 10am-2pm & 5-7pm Sat, 11am-2pm Sun) In the *ayuntamiento* (town hall), it can provide a map and information about the town sights, restaurants and hotels.

SIGHTS

Opening onto the plaza is the oldest theatre in Spain: the 17th-century **Corral de Comedias** (☎ 926 88 24 58; Plaza Mayor 18; adult/under 12yr/12-25yr incl audioguide in English €2.50/free/2; 🕑 10am-2pm & 5-7pm Tue-Sat, 11am-2pm & 5-7pm Sun Sep-Jun, 10am-2pm & 6-9pm Tue-Fri, 10am-2pm & 6-8pm Sat, 11am-2pm & 6-8pm Sun Jul & Aug), an evocative tribute to the Golden Age of Spanish theatre with rows of wooden balconies facing the original stage, complete with dressing rooms. It's still used for performances, especially during July's **Festival Internacional de Teatro Clásico** (www.festivaldealmagro.com in Spanish). The theatre is appropriately complemented by the **Museo de Teatro** (☎ 926 26 10 14; Calle de Gran Maestre 2; adult/under 12yr/12-25yr €2.50/free/1.20; 🕑 10am-2pm & 4-7pm Tue-Fri, 11am-2pm & 4-6pm Sat, 11am-2pm Sun), just across the square, with exhibits on Spanish theatre from the 18th century displayed in rooms surrounding a magnificent 13th-century courtyard.

Another imposing building is the 15th-century **Convento de la Asunción Almagro** (Calle de Ejido de Calatrava s/n; adult/under 12yr/12-25yr €1.50/free/1; 🕑 10am-2pm & 5-8pm Tue-Sat, 11am-2pm Sun), with its marble columned cloisters, simple church and upstairs salon crowned by an elaborate Mudéjar carved ceiling.

Almagro is also famed for its embroidery. Check it out at the **Museo de Encale** (☎ 926 88 25 33; Callejon del Villar s/n; adult/under 12yr/12-25yr €1.50/free/1; 🕑 10am-2pm & 5-8pm Tue-Fri, 10am-2pm & 5-7pm Sat, 11am-2pm Sun), which has some stunning examples of lacework and embroidery exhibited over three floors in well-lit exhibition spaces.

SLEEPING

Almagro's hotel prices increase by a whopping 50% during the July theatre festival and Semana Santa.

CASTILLA-LA MANCHA

La Posada de Almagro (☎/fax 926 26 12 01; www.laposadadealmagro.es; Calle de Gran Maestre 5; s/d from €35/55;) This 16th-century former coaching inn has retained its original character with open galleries, rustic beamed rooms and courtyards. The downstairs bar-restaurant is popular (and noisy).

Retiro del Maestre (☎ 926 26 11 85; www.retirodelmaestre.com in Spanish; Calle San Bartolomé 5; s/d incl breakfast €70/87; P) Enjoy five-star treatment and style here without the hurly-burly of a big hotel. The rooms are spacious and washed in warm yellow and blue; go for those on the upper floor with private balconies.

Parador (☎ 926 86 01 00; www.parador.es; Ronda de San Francisco 31; s/d €125/154; P) In a sumptuous ivy-clad convent in a quiet corner of Almagro, this *parador* has a luxurious, old-world charm despite the mildly incongruous, brightly coloured beams in the rooms.

Hospedería Almagro (☎ 926 88 20 87; Calle de Ejido de Calatrava s/n) Located in a 15th-century convent, this place has gone under the hammer, with new management set to revamp the place. Check at the tourist office for an update.

Also recommended is the **Hostal Rural San Bartolomé** (☎ 926 26 10 73; www.hostalsanbartoleme.com; Calle San Bartolomé 12; s/d €53/64;).

EATING

There are several cafes and bars spilling out onto Plaza Mayor. Most serve the usual suspects (*raciones, platos* etc) at the standard Plaza Mayor prices.

Bar Las Nieves (☎ 926 86 12 90; Plaza Mayor 52; snacks from €5, paella €5) One of the better Plaza Mayor bars, featuring chairs on the square and less-expensive light eats, plus paella on Sundays.

Meson Cepa Vieja (☎ 926 26 12 61; Ronda de Santo Domingo 77; meals €14-18; closed Tue) Better for a hot dinner than a hot date, this brightly lit place, complete with blaring TV, has a no-fuss, inexpensive menu. Try the excellent *pisto con huevo* (fried peppers, tomatoes, and garlic topped with a fried egg). Avoid the house wine unless you have onions to pickle.

El Corregidor (☎ 926 86 06 48; Calle de Jerónimo Ceballos 2; menú €30, meals €35-40; closed Mon except Jul) The town's best eating and drinking place, with several lively bars flanking a leafy central courtyard and a hotchpotch decor that somehow works. The upstairs restaurant features high-quality Manchegan cooking; check out the wall of culinary awards.

The restaurants at La Posada de Almagro and the *parador* are reliably good.

GETTING THERE & AWAY

Two trains go daily to Madrid (€13.65, 2¾ hours), with up to six to Ciudad Real (€2.30, 15 minutes) and two to Valencia (€25.20, 4¼ hours); for destinations to the south, change in Ciudad Real. Buses also run to Ciudad Real (€2.10, 30 minutes, up to five daily), but there are none on Sunday.

Castillo de Calatrava

About 30km south of Almagro, the fortress-like castle-monastery complex of **Castillo de Calatrava** (Calatrava La Nueva; admission free; 10am-2pm & 4-7pm Tue-Sun) commands magnificent views across the sierra (mountain range) of the same name. The complex was once a base of the medieval order of knights who controlled this frontier area during the Reconquista. Even if closed, it merits a visit for the site and view alone. From Calzada de Calatrava, travel 7km southwest along the CR504.

Parque Natural de las Lagunas de Ruidera

Consider a detour here; the scenery is stunning. A ribbon of 14 small lakes is surrounded by lush parkland, camping grounds, picnic areas and discreetly situated restaurants and hotels. Foreign tourists are rare; it's most popular as a chill-out zone for hot-and-bothered *madrileños* (Madrid residents).

The **tourist office** (☎ 926 52 81 16; Avenida Castilla La Mancha s/n, Ruidera; 10am-2pm & 4-6pm Wed-Sat, 10am-2pm Sun) has lots of glossy information on accommodation and activities, such as hiring rowing boats, kayaks or mountain bikes.

Camping Los Batanes (☎ 926 69 90 76; www.losbatanes.com; sites per person/tent/car €5.60/5/5.60, d bungalow €58; P) is a leafy campsite on Laguna Redondilla. During the summer months, an entertainment program for children is organised.

our pick **Hotel Albamanjon** (☎ 926 69 90 48; www.albamanjon.net; Laguna de San Pedro 16; d from €95, ste €159;) has a windmill suite with a view of the turquoise lake that's worth pushing the boat out for. All the rooms have private terraces and there's an excellent restaurant where you can sample owner Raúl's superb cooking. The hotel also has a bathing area with a jetty, offering pedal-boat and canoe rentals. Landlubbers can opt for the mountain bikes on loan.

THE WINES OF VALDEPEÑAS

Situated midway between Madrid and Córdoba, the large and otherwise uninviting town of Valdepeñas offers weary travellers one (and only one) good reason to break the journey. Surrounding the town is what some experts believe to be the largest expanse of vineyards in the world, although true aficionados of the humble grape argue that quantity does not easily translate into quality. There's an element of truth to this view – Valdepeñas has historically been to the mass market what La Rioja is to the quality end of the market (see the boxed text, p516).

That said, things are changing. You're still more likely to come across Valdepeñas wines in the cheap, cask variety than served in Spain's finest restaurants, but some of the Valdepeñas bodegas (cellars) have begun to make inroads into the quality end of the market. Most of the bodegas offer tours and tastings only by appointment and charge to boot. Check the websites for details to avoid going thirsty. **Bodegas Arúspide** (☎ 926 34 70 75; www.aruspide.com; Calle Franci Morales 102; tours per person €4.50) offers a tour of the bodega and a tasting of two or more wines.

La Vega (☎ 967 37 80 39; Calle San Pedro 7, Lagunas de Ruidera; meals from €12) is wonderfully situated on one of the larger lakes, with a large terrace and small beach. Expect a good grilling: barbecued meats are the speciality.

Villanueva de los Infantes

pop 6400

Villanueva de los Infantes is an attractive and busy provincial town. A highlight is **Plaza Mayor**, with its ochre-coloured buildings, wooden-and-stone balconies, and lively bars and restaurants.

Like Almagro, Villanueva is studded with the houses of old nobles. The **tourist office** (☎ 926 36 13 21; www.infantes.org in Spanish; Plaza Mayor s/n; 🕑 10am-2pm & 5-8pm Mon-Sat, 10am-2pm Sun) organises guided walks of the town. On the square stands the 15th-century **Iglesia de San Andrés**, where the 16th-century poet Francisco de Quevedo is buried.

Hospedería El Buscón Queveda (☎ 926 36 17 88; www.hosteriasreales.com; Calle Frailes 1; s/d from €50/65; ❄), a former convent four streets south of Plaza Mayor, has handsome regency-style rooms and magnificent public areas with original tapestries and oil paintings. On the downside, it can seem a little austere. Note that prices are higher at weekends.

Buses run to Ciudad Real three times daily from Monday to Friday (€5.50, 1½ hours).

SOUTHEAST TO ALBACETE

The sweeping, windswept plains of southeastern Castilla-La Mancha have an unfair reputation for being flat and boring. In fact, this landscape can have a very special drama with its rich abstract patterns and vibrant colours. Once you get off the highway, this is a land of ancient windmills, quiet villages and our favourite nutty knight – Don Quijote (see the boxed text, p290).

Consuegra

This is *the* place for the novice windmill-spotter, where you can get that classic shot of a dozen *molinos de vientos* (windmills) flanking the 13th-century **castle** (admission €2; 🕑 9.30am-1.30pm & 3.30-5.30pm; 🚸). Consuegra once belonged to the Knights of Malta; a few rooms in the castle have been done up to give a good indication of how the knights would have lived.

The **tourist office** (☎ 925 47 57 31; 🕑 9am-2pm & 4.30-7pm Mon-Fri, from 10.30am Sat & Sun) is in the Bolero mill (they all have names), which is the first you come to as the road winds up from the town. It can advise on *casas rurales* (village or farmstead accommodation) if you want to stay overnight. In windmill Rucio garrulous Pedro sells souvenirs and will show you round for €1.

Bar Castillo (☎ 926 48 14 79; Calle Sertorio 16; meals from €25) is located in town (turn left at the Guardia Civil), with a rustic-style dining room and robust local dishes. The *sopa de almendra* (almond soup) is excellent.

There are regular weekday buses (three on weekends) running between Consuegra and Toledo (€4.34, one hour), and up to seven buses daily to Madrid (€7, 2 hours).

Campo de Criptana & Around

Ten windmills straddle the town's summit, and their proximity to the surrounding houses makes an interesting contrast with Consuegra. The town is pleasant, if unexceptional. The **tourist office** (☎ 926 56 22 31; 🕑 10am-2pm & 5-8pm Tue-Sat, 10am-2pm Sun) is in the Poyatos mill.

If you want to stay overnight, lovely **Hospedería Casa de la Torrecilla** (☎ 926 58 91 30; www.casadelatorrecilla.com; Calle Cardenal Monescillo 17; s/d €35/53) has a vividly patterned and tiled interior patio. Housed in an early-20th-century nobleman's house, the rooms have parquet floors and are spacious and atmospheric; several have original stone fireplaces and balconies. Prices increase at weekends.

Campo de Criptana is served by the odd train and regional bus, but options are greater 8km away in Alcázar de San Juan. About four buses run daily between the two towns, but there are none on Sunday.

There are seven more pretty windmills gracing the horizon overlooking **Mota del Cuervo**, 29km northeast of Campo de Criptana, at the junction of the N301.

El Toboso

This is a town that has really cashed in on its Don Quijote heritage. Everywhere you look there seems to be a Quijote bar, a Quijote restaurant and several Quijote-themed small museums. Pilgrim or not, you'll find the most entertaining is the 16th-century **Casa-Museo de Dulcinea** (☎ 925 19 72 88; Calle Don Quijote 1; adult €0.60; 10am-2pm & 4.30-7.30pm Tue-Sat, 10am-2pm Sun). This was apparently the home of Doña Ana, the *señorita* who inspired Cervantes' Dulcinea, the platonic love of Quijote.

There are three direct buses every day to Madrid (€7.20, two hours). There's a small **tourist office** (☎ 925 56 82 26; Calle Daoíz y Velarde 3; 10am-2pm & 4-7pm Tue-Sat, 10am-2pm Sun).

Belmonte

About 25km northeast of Mota del Cuervo, Belmonte has one of the better-preserved 15th-century Castilian **castles** (adult/under 12yr/12-25yr €2/free/1; 10am-1.30pm & 5-8pm Tue-Sun Apr-Sep, 10am-1.30pm & 3.30-5.30pm Tue-Sun Oct-Mar). This is how castles *should* look, with turrets, largely intact walls and a commanding position over the village. Current restoration work within promises to reveal some fine Mudéjar architecture. The castle was once home to France's Empress Eugénie after her husband Napoleon III lost the French throne in 1871. Also well worth a visit is **Iglesia Colegial de San Bartolomé** (Colegiata; 11am-2pm & 4-8pm Tue-Sat, 4-8pm Sun), a magnificent golden-sandstone church with an impressive altarpiece.

La Muralla (☎ 967 17 10 45; Calle Osa de la Vega 1; s/d €20/40;) has plain comfortable rooms, with a cavernous downstairs bar where old men in flat caps play dominoes. The restaurant terrace gets packed with local families on Sundays and has a traditional menu (meals €20) with a predominance of game dishes.

Palacio Buenavista Hospedería (☎ 967 18 75 80; fax 967 18 75 88; Calle José Antonio González 2; s/d/ste incl breakfast from €50/77/104; P) is a classy boutique hotel set in a 17th-century palace next to the Colegiata. Rooms are stylish and set around a central patio with skylight. Go for a castle view.

By bus from Belmonte, you can get to Alcázar de San Juan (€2.20; 30 minutes) and Cuenca (€4.75; 1¼ hours).

ALBACETE

pop 165,000

This mildly down-at-heel provincial city is no star, but is useful as a transport hub and a place to pause between Spain's central plains and the Mediterranean coast. The **tourist office** (☎ 967 58 05 22; Calle del Tinte 2; 10am-2pm & 4.30-6.30pm Mon-Fri, to 6pm Sat, to 3pm Sun) should be able to muster more enthusiasm for the town than we can.

IN SEARCH OF DON QUIJOTE

Part of the charm of a visit to Castilla-La Mancha is the chance to track down the real-life locations into which Miguel de Cervantes placed his picaresque hero. These days it requires less puzzling over maps than previously: to celebrate the fourth centenary of this epic tale in 2007, the 250km Route of Don Quijote was created, with signposts that direct you along paths, cattle routes and historic routes throughout the region.

Out of all the places and sights you can ponder along the way, the *molinos de vientos* (windmills) are the most obvious, for it was these 'monstrous giants' that so haunted El Quijote and with which he tried to battle. Although Consuegra's are the most attractive, those that are specifically mentioned in Cervantes' novel are the windmills of **Campo de Criptana** (p289) and **Mota del Cuervo** (above). Other highlights on the trail include the castle of **Belmonte** (above) and **El Toboso** (above), where the knight discovered the lovely Dulcinea.

A BATTY CAVE

Forget stalagmites, cave drawings and coach tours – Alcalá's **Cuevas y Mirador del Diablo** (☎ 637 418297; San Lorenzo 7; admission €3;) is not your conventional cave. The first inkling comes when owner Juan José Martinez Garcia appears to collect your entrance fee sporting a sweeping Dalí-clone moustache. It transpires he grew up in the maestro's home town of Cadiques. OK, so that makes sense – sort of.

The real adventure starts with a 70m-long tunnel, which apparently dates back to Moorish times, when it was used for stabling animals. With the next exhibit the large no-smoking sign at the entrance suddenly makes sense. Don't take *any* drugs on this excursion. Spy through the porthole on your left and you are met with the astonishing sight of strobe lights in a quasi-disco setting, complete with throbbing music. Next you move into a bar (Juan has 10 children so there's no shortage of staff). After your free drink you can enjoy an extraordinary museum: a collectables heaven with old cameras, lottery tickets, farming implements, stuffed hens, cash registers, radios, sewing machines, news clippings and Juan's poems.

Next, climb several flights of stairs to emerge at a fabulous mirador (lookout) set into the side of the cave, complete with chairs for contemplating the vista. Then there's another passage (170m) and another bar (different children) where taxidermy seems to be the main theme, with stuffed goats, boars, foxes, badgers and wild cats on exhibit, among ancient farming implements and walls papered with photos of Juan with family, friends and uncertain-looking tourists. Juan has a stuffed gorilla as well, currently on show (as King Kong) at his second, rapidly expanding Museo del Cine (Museum of Cinema), just across the road.

There's something particularly apt about finding such an eccentric in the depths of La Mancha country – Cervantes would have definitely approved.

If you're passing through, the **cathedral**, with its four Ionic columns, is appealing enough. On a hot summer's afternoon, leafy **Parque de Abelardo Sánchez** (Calle de Tesifonte Gallego) offers some respite. It's home to the **Museo Provincial** (admission €1.20; 10am-2pm & 4.30-7pm Mon-Sat, 10am-2pm Sun), with well-documented archaeology, fine arts and ethnology exhibits.

If you want to stay, **Hotel Altozano** (☎ 967 21 04 62; Plaza del Altozano 7; r €48; P) has an ace location on a pretty main square. The rooms are modern with satellite TV.

The bus and train stations are next to each other at the northeastern end of town. Buses serve many major cities around the country. There are five daily buses to Cuenca (€10.90, two hours), three daily to Ciudad Real (€13.50, 2¾ hours), up to three to Toledo (€13.65, 2¾ hours, none on Saturday) and at least daily Monday-to-Friday services to Ruidera. Trains head to Ciudad Real (€18.65, 2¾ hours, five daily), Madrid (€30.70, three hours, hourly) and Valencia (€25.30, 1½ hours, up to 15 daily).

AROUND ALBACETE

Just off the N430 motorway to Valencia, a restored fortress overlooks **Chinchilla de Monte Aragón**, a whitewashed village with a beautiful Plaza Mayor. About 60km further on, a square-turreted castle built by the Muslims stands high above the town of **Almansa**. Both towns are served by bus from Albacete.

Alcalá del Júcar & Around

Northeast of Albacete, the deep, tree-filled gorge of Río Júcar makes a stunning detour. About halfway along the CM3218, the breathtaking town of **Alcalá del Júcar** comes into view as you descend via hairpin turns. Its restored 15th-century **castle** (admission €1; 11am-2pm & 5-8pm Mon-Fri, 11am-2pm & 4-8pm Sat & Sun), an unmistakable landmark, towers over the houses that spill down the steep bank of the Júcar gorge. At the foot of the town there's a leafy meeting-and-greeting plaza, home of a small **tourist office** (☎ 967 47 30 90; La Rambla s/n; 10.30am-2.30pm & 4-7pm Fri & Sat, 10.30am-2.30pm Sun) that has a wealth of information about *casas rurales* and activities in the region, including maps showing local walking trails.

There are several well-priced hotels, including **Hostal El Júcar** (☎ 967 47 30 55; Calle Batán 1; s/d incl breakfast €25/40), with pine-clad rooms, and **Hostal Rambla** (☎ 967 47 40 64; Paseo Los Robles 2; s/d incl breakfast €40/60;). Both have restaurants; the one at Hostal Rambla (meals €15 to €25) is particularly good, especially the char-grilled meats served with green peppers and potatoes. Larger parties can opt for a cave at **Maribel** (☎ 678 478104; www.casasruralesmaribel.net; Calle Batán 100; per week €475;), which sleeps 12 people in a series of three adjacent cave houses.

For an alternative route back to Albacete, a small back road takes you through the gorge, with houses cut into the cliff face. The more picturesque hamlets are at the western end, where the gorge narrows. Tiny **Cubas** has an intriguing ceramic-tiled and domed church hollowed out of the cliff, while **Alcozarejos** is famed for its trout fishing.

Sierra de Alcaraz

Stretching across the southern strip of Albacete province, the cool, green peaks of the Sierra de Alcaraz, laced with small, intensively farmed plots and dotted with villages, offer a great escape from the dusty plains around Albacete.

The most scenic countryside is to be found along the CM412, particularly between **Puerto de las Crucetas** (1300m) and **Elche de la Sierra**, although a detour to pretty **Vianos** is also worthwhile. Apart from in the wooded hills, donkey-mounted shepherds still watch their small flocks of sheep in the more remote corners of the sierra.

The largest choice of accommodation is in leafy **Riópar**, including the excellent **Camping Río Mundo** (☎ 967 43 32 30; www.campingriomundo.com; sites per person/tent/car €5.60/5/5.60;), where you can pick up a comprehensive booklet of routes for walking and cycling in the region. The campsite is located 6km east of town. The prettiest place to stay in these parts, however, is in sleepy hilltop **Alcaraz**, with its medieval Plaza Mayor and lattice of narrow cobbled streets. At the top of the village, sporting magnificent views, is modern **Los Rosales** (☎ 967 38 01 28; www.losrosalesalcaraz.com; Calle Granada s/n; s/d €43/48), with spruce and comfortably furnished rooms. Just down the hill, a handsome, mainly 16th-century building houses the **Mirador Sierra de Alcaraz** (☎ 967 38 00 17; Calle Padre Pareja; d/ste €65/72;), its central Moorish courtyard dating, incredibly, from the 9th century. The rooms have beamed ceilings, carved wooden bedheads and heavy period-style curtains and furnishings. The sumptuous suite is excellent value.

THE NORTHEAST

This region has a rich hinterland of craggy mountains and lush green valleys studded by unspoiled, pretty villages. It is also home to some of the country's most enchanting towns and *pueblos*.

CUENCA

pop 53,000

A World Heritage site, Cuenca is one of Spain's most enchanting cities, its old centre a stage set of evocative medieval buildings. Most emblematic are the *casas colgadas*, the hanging houses, which perch above the deep gorges that surround the town. As in so many Spanish cities, the surrounding new town is modern and forgettable, so keep the blinkers on during the approach – up the hill lies another world.

History

Probably inhabited in Roman times, Cuenca remained obscure until Muslim occupation early in the 11th century, when the city became a flourishing textile centre. The

THE BIRTH OF THE WORLD

Take a photo of you standing in front of the **Nacimiento del Río Mundo** (Birth of the River World; 10am-dusk;), send it to the folks back home and they will think that you have sidestepped to Niagara Falls for the day. To get to these amazing waterfalls, follow the signs just before Riópar for around 8km – past the amusing pictorial 'beware of the *amfibos* (frogs)' signs – until you reach the entrance and car park. It's a short walk through the forest of mainly coniferous trees to the bottom of the falls, where the water splashes and courses via several rock pools. There are two miradors; the first is at the base of the falls with neck-craning views of the dramatic waterfall above. It's a puff-you-out climb to the second mirador, but well worth it. At some 800m above sea level, the water emerges from the rocks just above the platform, almost close enough to touch, in a dramatic drop of some 24m (spraying you liberally en route). The falls are surrounded by dense forest stretching to a rocky horizon – all those sceptics who say La Mancha is flat and boring should definitely pay a visit here.

Christians took their time conquering the place, and it fell only in 1177 to Alfonso VIII. Like much of Spain's interior, 16th-century Cuenca slipped once again into decline and hardship, something from which it only began to recover during the 20th century.

Orientation

Cuenca is compact and easily negotiable. The old town is home to all the sights and occupies the narrow hill at the northeastern end of town, between the gorges of Ríos Júcar and Huécar. At the foot of the hill down which the old town tumbles, the new town spreads out to the south. Near Cuenca's southern outskirts (a 10-minute walk from the foot of the hill), the train and bus stations are almost opposite each other, southwest of Calle de Fermin Caballero.

Information

Cruz Roja (☎ 969 22 22 00) For ambulances.
Hospital de la Luz Virgen (☎ 969 17 99 00) Off Avenida de la Cruz Roja.
La Repro 11 (☎ 969 23 14 40; Calle Fray Luis de León 16; per hr €1.20; 10am-2pm & 5-8pm Mon-Sat) Internet access.
Main tourist office (☎ 969 32 31 19; www.aytocuenca.org in Spanish; Plaza Mayor s/n; 9am-9pm Mon-Sat, 9am-2.30pm Sun May-Sep, 9am-2pm & 5-8pm Mon-Sat, 9am-2pm Sun Oct-Apr) In the historic centre.
Policía Nacional (☎ 091)
Post office (cnr Calles del Parque de San Julián & del Dr Fleming)
Telephone office (Paseo de San Antonio 42)
Tourist office (☎ 969 23 58 15; Plaza Hispanidad; 10am-2pm & 5-8pm Mon-Thu, 10am-8pm Fri-Sun) In the new town.

Sights & Activities

CATEDRAL

The main facade of Cuenca's **catedral** (adult/under 12yr €2.50/free, audioguide €0.50; 9am-2pm & 4-7pm May-Oct, 9am-2pm & 4-6pm Nov-Apr) is hardly Spain's finest – a pastiche of unfortunate 16th-century Gothic experimentation and 20th-century restoration. Built on the site of a mosque, highlights within include several stunning stained-glass windows, the result of a competition among local artists in 1990. The abstract designs fuse well with the Gothic architecture and lofty fan vaulting. Don't miss the chapter house and Deep Chapel, both of which have ornate Mudéjar-style carved ceilings. The relatively unadorned nave dates back to the early 13th century, although other elements, such as the apse, were constructed in the mid-15th century.

CASAS COLGADAS

The most striking element of medieval Cuenca, the *casas colgadas* jut out precariously over the steep defile of Río Huécar. Dating from the 16th century, the houses with their layers of wooden balconies seem to emerge from the rock as if an extension of the cliffs. The finest restored examples now house an upmarket restaurant (p296) and an art museum (below), which make excellent use of what was once an economical adaptation of limited living space. For the best views of the *casas colgadas*, cross the **Puente de San Pablo** footbridge, or walk to the northernmost tip of the old town, where a **mirador** offers unparalleled views.

MUSEUMS

Although strolling around old Cuenca can feel like you've been dropped in the middle of a medieval museum, this is not just a place of ancient history.

The **Museo de Arte Abstracto Español** (Museum of Abstract Art; ☎ 969 21 29 83; www.march.es; adult/under 12yr/12-25yr €3/free/1.50; 11am-2pm & 4-6pm Tue-Fri, 11am-2pm & 4-8pm Sat, 11am-2.30pm Sun) has several superb gallery spaces occupying one of the *casas colgadas*. Begun as an attempt by Fernando Zóbel to unite the works of his fellow artists from the so-called Abstract Generation of the 1950s and '60s, the museum's constantly evolving displays include works by Chillida, Tápies and Millares. Don't miss the extraordinary landscapes by Eusebio Sempere (1924–85), which really capture the colourful patterned plains of La Mancha.

Beret-and-smock types can happily overdose in this town. The **Museo de Arte Contemporáneo** (Contemporary Art Museum; ☎ 969 23 06 19; www.dipucuenca.es; Ronda de Julián Romero 20; admission free; 11am-9pm Mon-Sun) has galleries spread over four floors within the former San Clemente convent. Spanish and international artists are represented in a mixed bag of mainly abstract paintings and sculptures.

Another innovative museum is the **Museo de Las Ciencias** (Science Museum; ☎ 969 24 03 20; Plaza de la Merced; adult/child €1.20/free, weekends free; 10am-2pm & 4-8pm Tue-Sat, 10am-2pm Sun;), where displays range from a time machine to plenty of interactive gadgets to keep the kiddies happy, as well as a **planetarium** (admission €1.20).

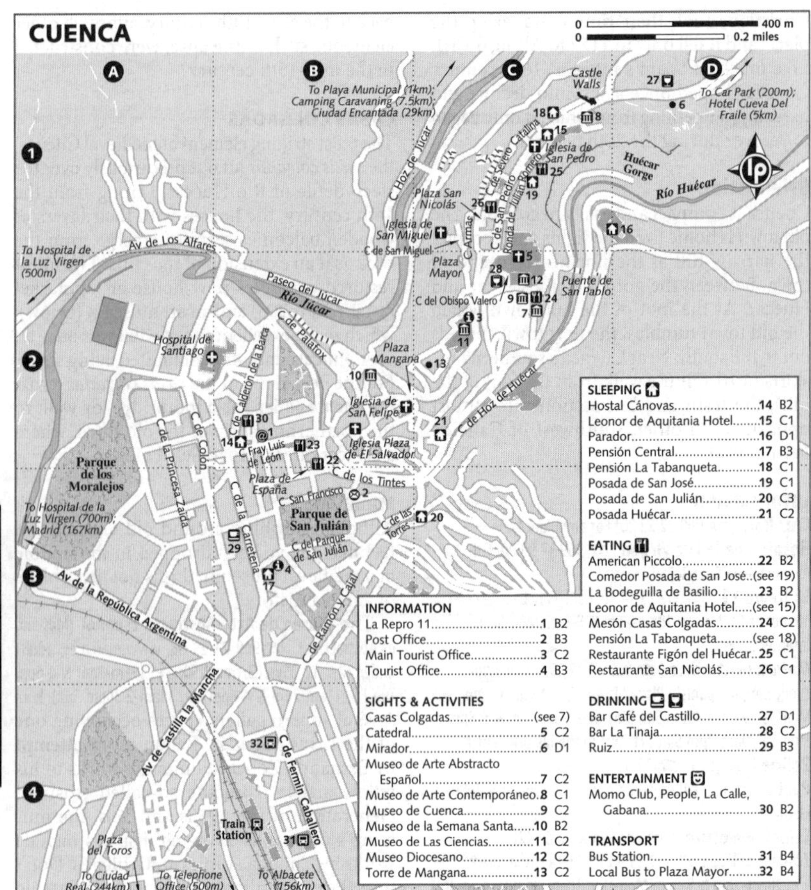

The **Museo de Cuenca** (☎ 969 21 30 69; Calle del Obispo Valero 6; adult/under 12yr/12-25yr €1.20/free/0.60; ⏰ 10am-2pm & 4-7pm Tue-Sat, 11am-2pm Sun) has exceptionally well-laid-out and well-documented (in Spanish) exhibits, ranging from the Bronze Age to the 18th century. Sala 7 is particularly awe-inspiring, with its original Roman statues, including Emperor Augustus, plus columns and pediments discovered at nearby Segóbriga (p297).

Appropriately close to the cathedral, the **Museo Diocesano** (☎ 969 22 42 10; Calle del Obispo Valero 3; adult/under 12yr/12-25yr €1.80/free/1.50; ⏰ 11am-2pm & 4-7pm Tue-Sat, 11am-2pm Sun) has exhibits of richly embroidered tapestries, plus sculptures, rugs and paintings, including two canvases by El Greco. A 14th-century Byzantine diptych is the jewel in the crown, however. How such a piece ended up in Cuenca is a mystery.

Cuenca's latest museum is the **Museo de la Semana Santa** (☎ 969 22 19 56; Calle Andrés de Cabrera; adult/under 12yr/12-25yr €3/free/1.50; ⏰ 11am-2pm & 4.30-7.30pm Wed-Sat), the next best thing to experiencing Semana Santa firsthand. Spread over two floors there are audiovisual displays showing the processions by local brotherhoods, against a background of sombre music. Displays include costumes and a 20-minute film (in Spanish) in which the locals explain their passion for this annual religious ritual.

TORRE DE MANGANA

The Torre de Mangana, near Plaza Mangana, is the last remnant of a fortress that was built by Cuenca's Muslim rulers. It is all that remains of Cuenca's days as a Muslim town.

PLAYA MUNICIPAL

Yep, you read that right. You can even get sand between your toes here. The **Playa Municipal** (admission €2.50; 8am-7pm;) is an artificial beach, complete with two swimming pools, located in a valley by the river 1km from town. Lie back and revel in the view of Cuenca and looming rocks above you. There is a handy restaurant and bar if you forgot to pack a picnic. To get here, follow the signs to Ciudad Encantada; the beach is signposted off to your right.

Festivals & Events

Cuenca's **Semana Santa** celebrations are renowned throughout Spain, particularly for the eerie, silent processions through the streets of the old town. Also gaining international acclaim is the **Semana de Música Religiosa de Cuenca**, the city's celebration of sacred music. Usually held in March or April, it attracts international performers and spectators and, if it's your thing, is a great time to be in town. Contact the tourist office for more information.

Sleeping

Aside from the possible disadvantage of lugging bags up the hill, the atmospheric old town is *the* place to stay. That said, there are some reasonable options down the hill. Most places increase their rates during Semana Santa and the summer.

If you decide to camp, **Camping Caravaning** (969 23 16 56; Carretera Cuenca-Tragacete, Km8; sites per person/tent/car €4.80/4.80/4.40;) has superb facilities, including a pool and tennis court. It's 8km out of town on the road towards Ciudad Encantada and is open year-round.

OLD TOWN

Many of the hotel rooms in the old town have stunning views, so always ask for a room with *una vista*.

Pensión La Tabanqueta (969 21 12 90; Calle de Trabuco 13; s/d without bathroom €15/30) The prices are the best you'll find in the historic centre and some rooms have five-star views of Río Júcar. In a listed building, this place is plain but charming, and there's a popular bar-restaurant attached.

Posada de San José (969 21 13 00; www.posadasanjose.com; Ronda de Julián Romero 4; s/d without bathroom from €25/38, with views from €55/86) Owned by Antonio and his Canadian wife, Jennifer, this 17th-century former choir school retains an extraordinary monastic charm with its crumbling portal, uneven floors and original tiles. Enjoy spectacular views and fresh flowers in the room in lieu of satellite TV. The restaurant is recommended (see p296).

Posada Huécar (969 21 42 01; www.posadahuecar.com; Paseo del Huécar 3; s/d €29/49; P) Feel luxurious on a tight budget. Located squarely between the old and new towns, this upbeat place has large rooms with terracotta tiles, rustic furnishings and river views. There's free internet use for guests, plus bicycles for rent (€4 for two hours).

Leonor de Aquitania Hotel (969 23 10 00; www.hotelleonordeaquitania.com; Calle de San Pedro 60; s/d incl breakfast €77/99;) In an 18th-century house, this is a well-aged classic, although the floral theme in the rooms may be a touch fussy for some of the chaps. Ask for room 105 or 106, with unequalled views of the gorge. The restaurant is excellent.

Parador (969 23 23 20; www.parador.es; Calle de Hoz de Huécar; d €143; P) This majestic former convent commands stunning view of the *casas colgadas*. The aesthetically revamped rooms have a luxury corporate feel, while the public areas are headily historic with giant tapestries and antiques.

NEW TOWN

Pensión Central (969 21 15 11; Calle de Alonso Chirino 7; s/d/tr without bathroom €14/24/31;) This is a cheap sleep in a clean and tidy *pensíon* in the new town. Rooms are adequate and clean, with TV and washbasin. Breakfast costs a whopping €2.

Posada de San Julián (969 21 17 04; Calle de las Torres 1; s/d €16/36) Just down the hill from the historic centre, revel in 16th-century surroundings with lofty ceilings, original columns, creaking staircases and atmospheric heavy-beamed rooms, some with balconies. It's family-run, and grandpa peels potatoes all day for the bustling restaurant downstairs (*menú* €10).

Hostal Cánovas (969 21 39 73; www.hostalcanovas.com; Calle Fray Luis de León 38; s/d €35/55;) This upbeat and welcoming *hostal* has spacious rooms with polished floorboards, a warm colour scheme and bright modern bathrooms.

Hotel Cueva Del Fraile (969 21 15 71; www.hotelcuevadelfraile.com; Hoz del Huécar s/n; s/d €87/115;

(P ✕ ✕) This 16th-century former convent is 5km from Cuenca. It's been resurrected as a chic, welcoming hotel with rooms washed in earth colours and excellent facilities, including tennis courts, minigolf and mountain bikes for hire.

Eating

There's plenty of choice in Cuenca, although the places in the historic quarter tend to hike up the price.

our pick **La Bodeguilla de Basilio** (☎ 969 23 52 74; Calle Fray Luis de León 3; raciones €10-13) Arrive here with an appetite, as you're presented with a complimentary plate of tapas when you order a drink, and not just a slice of dried-up cheese – typical freebies are a combo of quail eggs, ham, fried potatoes, lettuce hearts and courgettes. Understandably, it gets packed out, so head to the restaurant out back for more of the same (except you have to pay), including *patatas pobres* (fried potatoes with peppers, tomatoes and garlic). If you are bored with conversation, the walls are covered with fascinating clutter, ranging from old pics of Cuenca to farming tools.

Comedor Posada de San José (☎ 969 21 13 00; Ronda de Julián Romero 4; meals €12; 7-10pm) The Canadian owner has sensibly ensured that tourists can eat here according to their timetable back home. The food is uncomplicated and good, ranging from the reliable classic of fried eggs and (homemade) chips to *solomillo de cerdo a la sidra* (pork loin in cider). Wonderful views.

American Piccolo (☎ 969 21 28 55; Plaza de los Carros 4; meals €14) Weary of the ubiquitous meaty fare? This independent restaurant packs in young couples on an affordable date with its welcoming, diverse menu of Tex-Mex, Italian and Argentinean cuisine. Expect reliably acceptable rather than exceptional cuisine, with more than 125 dishes plus an adventurous wine list with plenty of imports.

Restaurante San Nicolás (☎ 969 24 05 19; Calle de San Pedro 15; menú €16, meals €25-35) Another fine establishment for solid Castilian-Manchegan food, although the service can be sniffy. The braised wild boar in a fennel and thyme sauce is particularly good.

Restaurante Figón del Huécar (☎ 969 24 00 62; Ronda de Julián Romero 6; menú €27, meals €30-35) Run by the same owners as Mesón Casas Colgadas, this dress-for-dinner place specialises in Castilian specialities like suckling pig with sweet potatoes, as well as more-international plates, including stir-fried vegetables. The chestnut cream with coffee and white chocolate should leave a smile on your face.

Mesón Casas Colgadas (☎ 969 22 35 52; Calle de los Canónigos 3; meals €25-35, menú €28) Housed in one of the *casas colgadas*, Cuenca's gourmet pride and joy fuses an amazing location with delicious traditional food, such as venison stew.

Also recommended are the restaurants at **Pensión La Tabanqueta** (menú €13) and **Leonor de Aquitania Hotel** (menú €22).

Drinking

You can join the under-26s who gather together along Calle de San Miguel (old town) or Plaza de España (new town) for loads of noisy evening *copas*. There's a gaggle of bars in both areas. The bars and cafes on Plaza Mayor are well placed for kicking back with a *cerveza*.

Bar La Tinaja (Calle del Obispo Valero 4) Enjoying an ace position beside the cathedral, this place is typically heaving with crusty locals here for the delicious (and free) tapas provided with every drink.

Bar Café del Castillo (☎ 969 24 34 47; Calle de Larga 13; closed Sun) Well sited for views from the large terrace, this spirited place is perfect for that late-night coffee, with a dozen of the spiked variety on offer.

Ruiz (Calle de Carretería 12; closed Sun) Popular with powdered ladies here for the delicious cakes, pastries and light snacks to accompany their *café con leche* (coffee with milk).

Entertainment

If you're looking to improve your dance moves, head for the disco-pubs on Calle del Doctor Galíndez, near Plaza de España. There is little to choose between Momo Club, People, La Calle and Gabana (to name but a few), but don't even consider shimmying down here until midnight. Early birds can head for nearby Calle San Francisco, where an energetic row of terrace bars has a preclubbing party feel from around 9pm onwards at weekends.

Getting There & Away

BUS

Up to nine buses daily serve Madrid (€10.50, two hours). Other services include Valencia (€11.95, 2½ hours, up to three a day) and Albacete (€10.90, two hours, up to three daily).

CASTILLA-LA MANCHA

There are also two buses to Toledo (€10.90, 2¼ hours) on weekdays and one on Sunday.

CAR & MOTORCYCLE

From Cuenca, the quickest route to Madrid is west along the N400, turning northwest onto the A3 at Tarancón.

TRAIN

Cuenca lies on the train line connecting Madrid and Valencia. Trains to Madrid's Atocha station (€10.65, 2½ hours) depart six times a day on weekdays and four times a day on weekends. Trains to Valencia leave four times daily (€11.75, 3¼ hours).

Getting Around

Local buses 1 and 2 do the circuit from the new town to Plaza Mayor (€0.70, every 30 minutes) with numerous stops, including outside the train station. There's free street parking at the top of the old town (follow the signs to *estacionamiento*).

AROUND CUENCA

Serranía de Cuenca

Spreading north and east of Cuenca, the Serranía de Cuenca is a heavily wooded and fertile zone of craggy mountains and green fields. Ríos Júcar and Huécar flow through Cuenca from the high hinterland, through landscapes that are well worth exploring if you have your own transport.

From Cuenca, take the CM2105 about 30km to the extraordinary **Ciudad Encantada** (Enchanted City; adult/child €3/free; 10am-sunset). Surrounded by pine woods, limestone rocks have been eroded into fantastical shapes by nature. If you let your imagination carry you away, it's possible to see a boat on its keel, a dog and a Roman bridge. The shaded 40-minute circuit around the open-air rock museum is great for breaking up a car journey. It's crowded with *madrileños* at weekends, and there are several overpriced places to eat and drink.

You could then head back to the CM2105 and turn right in the direction of Tragacete. This part of the province is very pretty, dotted with sleepy villages and the clear blue lake of the **Embalse de la Toba**. About 5km on from the eye-catching village **Huélamo**, a turn-off to the right (the sign says Teruel) leads 60km across the Montes Universales to the mesmerising medieval town of **Albarracín** (p465) – a perfect place to stroll at the end of a day's drive.

An alternative route to the road east to Teruel, the CM2105 continues north to the **Nacimiento del Río Cuervo** (17km), a couple of small waterfalls where Río Cuervo rises. From here you could loop around towards **Beteta** (29km) and the gorge of the same name, or cross the provincial frontier into Guadalajara to make for the pleasant, if unspectacular, **Parque Natural del Alto Tajo**.

Alarcón

One hundred kilometres or so south of Cuenca is the seductive village of Alarcón. Stop at the **tourist office** (☎ 969 33 03 01; Calle Posadas 6; 10am-2pm & 5-7pm Wed-Sat, 10am-2pm Sun May-Sep, 10am-2pm Wed-Sun Oct-Apr) for a map of walks around the village and beyond. Most famous here, however, is the triangle-based Islamic **castle**, which has been converted into a sumptuous **parador** (☎ 969 33 03 15; www.parador.es; d €219; P) offering old-world charm and supremely comfortable rooms with exposed brick-and-stone walls and plush fabrics and furnishings.

Segóbriga

These **ruins** (☎ 629 752257; adult/under 12yr/12-25yr €4/free/2; 9am-9pm Tue-Sun 15 Apr-15 Sep, 10am-6pm Tue-Sat 16 Sep-14 Apr) may date as far back as the 5th century BC. The best-preserved structures are a **Roman theatre** and **amphitheatre** on the fringes of the ancient city, looking out towards a wooded hillside. Other remains include the outlines of a Visigothic basilica and a section of the aqueduct, which helped keep the city green in what is otherwise a desert.

The site is near Saelices, 2km south of the A3 motorway between Madrid and Albacete. From Cuenca, drive west 55km on the N400, then turn south on the CM202.

GUADALAJARA

pop 69,600

Despite its romantic name, Guadalajara is, disappointingly, a modern, somewhat scruffy city, and of more historical than aesthetic interest.

Guadalajara (from the Arabic *wad al-hijaara*, or 'stony river') was, in its medieval Muslim heyday, the principal city of a large swath of northern Spain under the green banner of Islam at a time when Madrid was no more than a military observation point. In 1085 Alfonso VI finally took Guadalajara as the Reconquista moved ponderously south. The city was repeatedly sacked during the War of the Spanish Succession (1702–13), the Napoleonic occupation and the Spanish Civil War.

While little remains of Guadalajara's glory days, the much-restored **Palacio de los Duques del Infantado** (☎ 949 21 33 01; adult/under 12yr €2/free; 10am-2pm & 4-7pm Tue-Sat, 10am-2pm Sun), where the Mendoza family held court, is worth a visit if you're passing by. Its striking facade is a fine example of Gothic Mudéjar work, and the heavily ornamental patio is equally entrancing. The town's **tourist office** (☎ 949 21 16 26; Plaza de los Caídos 6; 10am-2pm & 4-7.30pm Mon-Sat, 10am-2pm Sun) is opposite the palace.

Guadalajara is a simple day trip from Madrid, but if you're stuck, check into **Hotel Pax** (☎ 949 24 80 60; www.hotelpaxchi.com in Spanish; Avenida de Venezuela 15; s/d €55/60;), with its air of all-round poshness and genteel pastel-coloured rooms.

The **bus station** (☎ 949 88 70 94; Calle del Dos de Mayo) is a short walk from the *palacio*. Regular buses depart for Madrid (€4.20, 50 minutes) throughout the day between 6.15am and 10pm. There are also buses to Sigüenza (€5.95, 1½ hours).

From the **train station** (☎ 949 21 28 50), 2km north of town, there are regular AVE fast trains to Madrid (€16.10, 30 minutes) from about 5am to 11.30pm, and far fewer slower trains (€10.80, 50 minutes).

CASTILLA-LA MANCHA

PASTRANA

pop 1080

Pastrana should not be missed. It's an unspoilt place that has a Tuscany feel, with twisting cobbled streets flanked by honey-coloured stone buildings. Forty-two kilometres south of Guadalajara along the CM200, the heart and soul of the place is the **Plaza de la Hora**, a large square dotted with acacias and fronted by the sturdy **Palacio Ducal**. It is here that the one-eyed princess of Éboli, Ana Mendoza de la Cerda, was confined in 1581 for a love affair with the Spanish King Felipe II's secretary. You can see the caged window of her 'cell', where she died 10 years later, and arrange a tour (Spanish only; €2) via the **tourist office** (☎ 949 37 06 72; www.pastrana.org in Spanish; Plaza de la Hora 5; 10am-2pm & 4-6pm Tue-Fri, 10am-2pm & 4-8pm Sat, 10am-2pm Sun).

Walk from the square along Calle Mayor and you'll soon reach the massive **Iglesia de Nuestra Señora de la Asunción** (Colegiata). Inside, the interesting little **museum** (adult/under 12yr €2.50/free; 11am-2pm & 5.30-8pm) contains the jewels of the princess, some exquisite 15th-century tapestries and even an El Greco.

Hostal Moratín (☎ 949 37 01 16; www.moratin.com; Calle de Moratín 7; s/d from €25/40;) is a family-owned *hostal* located on the main road into town, with comfortable, well-furnished rooms, a large terrace and a pool. There's a restaurant and adjacent bar.

Hostelería Real de Pastrana (☎/fax 949 37 10 60; Carretera C200 Pastrana-Zorita, s/d from €53/106; P) should be a *parador:* it's gorgeous, with original oil paintings and antiques throughout, and classic rooms with period touches and marshmallow-soft pillows. There's an adjacent museum of religious artefacts. If this fails to excite you'll need wheels – Pastrana is 2km away.

Pastrana has plenty of restaurants and bars. Don't miss the locals' local, **Casa Seco** (Calle Mayor 36; tapas from €2), papered with faded bullfighting posters and run by a wonderfully matriarchal lady who keeps the flat-cap clientele under control. You can also buy honey here. Round the corner, **Meson Castilla** (☎ 949 37 02 02; Calle Casino 2; meals from €20) is the pick of the restaurant bunch, its half-tiled dining room heaving with local families at weekends. Grilled meat is the speciality.

Two buses travel to Madrid (€4.50, 1½ hours) via Guadalajara every weekday morning.

AROUND PASTRANA

Some 20km northeast of Pastrana is the area's main reservoir, the white-rimmed **Embalse de Entrepeñas**, where swimming is more an attraction than the views. From here you can push north on the CM204 to **Cifuentes**, with its 14th-century castle.

An alternative, albeit longer, route to the lake goes via Guadalajara, from where you could follow the A2 northeast and turn off at **Torija**, which has a rather impressive castle out of proportion to the size of the town. The **museum** (admission free; 10am-2pm & 4-6pm Tue-Sat, 10am-2pm Sun) within the castle is dedicated to Cela's *Viaje a La Alcarria*. From here, take the CM201 for **Brihuega**, a leafy village with stretches of its medieval walls intact. The drive east along Río Tajuña is one of the more pleasant in this part of Castilla-La Mancha. The road forms a T-junction with the CM204, from where you can head north for Sigüenza or south to the Embalse de Entrepeñas.

SIGÜENZA

pop 5020

Sleepy, historic and filled with the ghosts of a turbulent past, Sigüenza is well worth a detour. The town is built on a low hill cradled by Río Henares, and boasts a castle, a cathedral and several excellent restaurants set among twisting lanes of honey-coloured medieval buildings. Start your ambling at the beautiful 16th-century Plaza Mayor.

History

Originally a Celtiberian settlement, Segontia (as the town was previously named) became an important Roman and, later, Visigothic military outpost. The 8th-century arrival of the Muslims put the town in the frontline provinces facing the Christians. Sigüenza stayed in Muslim hands for considerably longer than towns further southwest, such as Guadalajara and Toledo, resisting until the 1120s. After a period of Aragonese occupation, the town was later ceded to the Castilians, who turned Sigüenza and its hinterland into a vast Church property. The bishops remained complete masters – material and spiritual – of the town and land until the end of the 18th century. Sigüenza's decline was long and painful as the town found itself repeatedly in the way of advancing armies: again a frontline during the War of the Spanish Succession and the civil war, when fighting here was heavy.

Information

Both tourist offices can organise guided two-hour **town tours** (per person €7) for a minimum of six people.

Locotorio Sigüenza (☎ 949 39 15 83; Calle del Humilladero 21; per hr €1.80; ⌚ 10am-10pm Mon-Sat, 10am-8pm Sun) Check your emails cheaply here.

Main tourist office (☎ 949 34 70 07; www.siguenza.es in Spanish; Paseo de la Alameda; ⌚ 10am-2pm & 5-7pm Mon-Thu, 10am-2pm & 5-8pm Fri, 10am-2pm & 5-7pm Sat, 10am-2pm Sun) In the delightful Ermita del Humilladero.

Post office (Calle de la Villa Viciosa) Very central.

Tourist office (☎ 949 34 70 09; Calle de Medina 9; ⌚ 10am-2pm & 5-7pm Mon-Thu, 10am-2pm & 5-8pm Fri, 10am-2pm & 5-7pm Sat, 10am-2pm Sun Oct-Apr, closed Sun May-Sep) A smaller office just down the hill from the cathedral.

Sights

CATEDRAL

Rising up from the heart of the old town is the city's centrepiece, the **catedral** (⌚ 9.30am-2pm & 4-8pm Tue-Sat, noon-5.30pm Sun). Begun as a Romanesque structure in 1130, work continued for four centuries as the church was expanded and adorned. The largely Gothic result is laced with elements of other styles, from plateresque through Renaissance to Mudéjar. The church was heavily damaged during the civil war.

The dark (and very cold) **nave** has some fine stained-glass windows and an impressive 15th-century altarpiece along the south wall. To enter the chapels, sacristy and Gothic cloister, you'll need to join a Spanish-language-only **guided tour** (€4; ⌚ 11am, noon, 4.30pm & 5.30pm Tue-Sat). The highlights of the tour include the **Capilla Mayor**, home of the reclining marble statue of Don Martín Vázquez de Arce (the statue is named *El Doncel*), who died fighting the Muslims in the final stages of the Reconquista. Particularly beautiful is the **Sacristía de las Cabezas**, with a ceiling adorned with hundreds of heads sculpted by Covarrubias. The **Capilla del Espíritu Santo** boasts a doorway combining plateresque, Mudéjar and Gothic styles; inside is a remarkable dome and an *Anunciación* by El Greco.

MUSEO DIOCESANO DE ARTE

Across the square from the cathedral, this **museum** (☎ 949 39 10 23; admission €3; ⌚ 11am-2pm & 4-7pm Tue-Sun) has an impressive selection of religious art from Sigüenza and the surrounding area, including a series of mainly 15th-century altarpieces.

CASTILLO

Calle Mayor heads south up the hill from the cathedral to a magnificent-looking castle, which was originally built by the Roman and was, in turn, a Moorish Alcazar, royal palace, asylum and army barracks. Virtually destroyed during the Spanish Civil War, it was subsequently rebuilt under Franco as a *parador* (see p300).

Sleeping

As Sigüenza is a popular weekend jaunt for *madrileños*, accommodation gets quickly booked up.

Hostal El Doncel (☎ 949 39 00 01; www.eldoncel.com in Spanish; Paseo de la Alameda 3; s/d €40/55) Earth colours, spot lighting and shiny tiles – this family-owned place, opposite the tourist office, has class. Rooms on the 3rd floor have heady rooftop views.

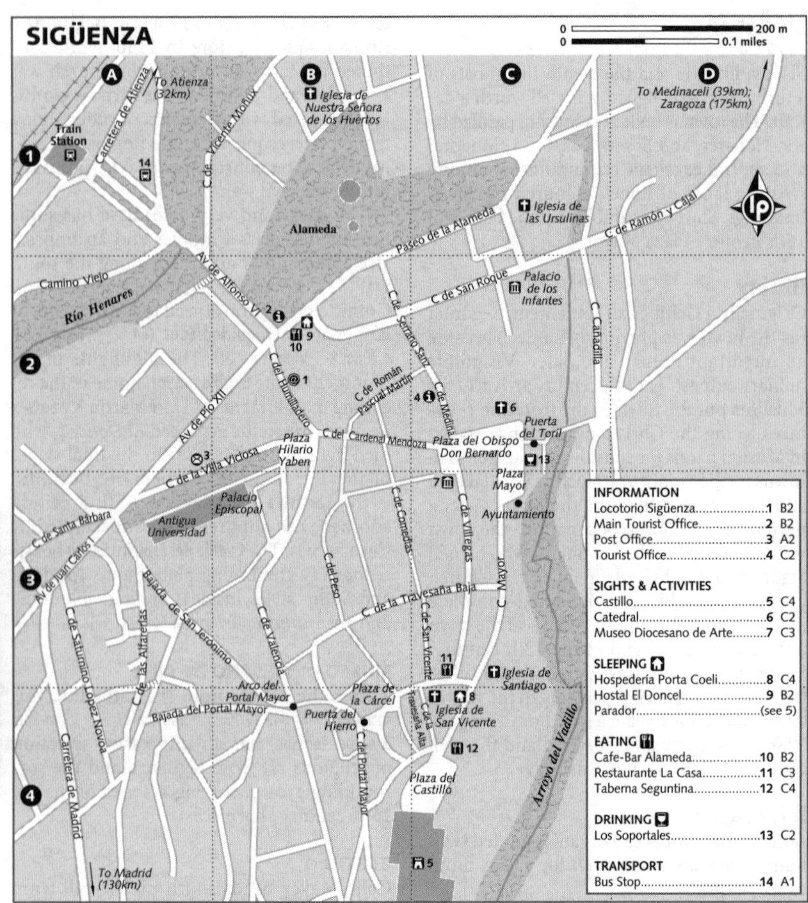

Hospedería Porta Coeli (☎ 949 39 18 75; Calle Mayor 50; s/d €54/69) Housed in a sumptuous historic building, the Hospedería Porta Coeli has light tiles and pale paintwork that provide a bright, fresh look to the good-sized bedrooms. The restaurant (meals cost €20; open weekends only) serves innovative dishes such as spinach-and-carrot flan with a truffle and oyster mushroom sauce.

Parador (☎ 949 39 01 00; www.parador.es; Plaza del Castillo s/n; s/d from €108/120) Sigüenza's *parador* ably provides its guests with the usual combination of luxury, attentive service and period furnishings. Set in the castle overlooking the town, its courtyard is a wonderful place to pass the time. The restaurant *menú* costs a reasonable €30.

Eating & Drinking

Finding somewhere to eat to fit your timetable can be problematic here. Several restaurants don't open until 10pm (locals eat dinner late), while those in the historic centre are geared more towards the weekend influx from Madrid and close several days during the week.

Los Soportales (☎ 949 39 17 42; Plaza Mayor 3; tapas €2-4) Great location under the arches, with tables on the square and free tapas with every drink.

Cafe-Bar Alameda (☎ 949 39 05 53; Paseo de la Alameda 2; snacks €5-10; 🕑 10am-midnight) Join the local card players at this down-home bar. Its counter heaves with tempting tapas and *pinchos* (snacks), including *caracoles* (snails) and *orejas* (pig's ears) for the intrepid, as well as more-digestible choices like stuffed green peppers and tortilla.

Taberna Seguntina (☎ 949 39 31 64; Calle Mayor 43; mains €8-15; lunch only Tue, closed Wed; V) A swallow's swoop from the castle, this restaurant has an innovative menu that includes vegetarian choices such as thistles with Asturian goat's cheese, and vegetable and almond soup, as well as the standard suckling pig.

Restaurante La Casa (☎ 949 39 03 10; Plazuela de San Vicente s/n; mains €15-20; closed Mon-Wed) Housed in a magnificent 12th-century house, it offers classic dishes such as *cabrito asado* (roasted kid) in a stone-clad dining room.

Getting There & Away

Buses are infrequent and mainly serve towns around Sigüenza, including Guadalajara. They stop on Avenida de Alfonso VI. Up to 10 regional trains go to Madrid's Chamartín station (€9.80, 1½ hours); some go on to Soria.

Sigüenza lies north of the A2 motorway. The main exits are the C204 (coming from the west) and the C114 (from the east). The C114 then heads north towards Almazán or Soria in Castilla y León.

AROUND SIGÜENZA

Imón

pop 40

This tiny gem of a hamlet, located 7km northwest of Sigüenza, has a surprising amount on offer, including several sophisticated restaurants (for weekending *madrileños*), a superb hotel and spa, and excellent walking and birdwatching potential.

our pick **Salinas de Imón** (☎ 949 39 73 11; www.salinasdeimon.com; Real 49; r from €85;) is housed in a mid-17th-century stone building. It has 13 rooms restored with sensitive integrity that retains the sense of history. There is nothing historic about the luxurious bathrooms or spa, however. A wide range of treatments is available, including massages (ayurvedic, sports, psycho-sensitive and aromatherapy) and reflexology. The garden is secluded and lovely, with lawns, a bower and a pool. A comment in the guest book says it all: 'Because I liked it so much I will tell my friend Dorothy,' writes Vicente, charmingly. Dinner is available.

For an easy walk, follow Don Quijote's path at the end of the main street (Calle Cervantes), heading north. The 4.5km pleasant stroll through fields leads to a magnificent 15th-century castle, La Riba de Santiuste, perched high on a rock above the partly abandoned village of the same name. The castle is partly in ruins and is fascinating to explore.

Atienza

pop 420

Some 10km northwest of Imón lies Atienza, a charming walled medieval village crowned by yet another castle ruin. The main square and former 16th-century market place, Plaza D Bruno Pascual Ruilopez, is overlooked by the Romanesque **Iglesia San Juan Bautista**, which has a lavish gilt *retablo*. For local bars and a couple of cavernous antique and gift shops, head to the adjacent Plaza de España. There are several more mostly Romanesque churches, plus three small **museums** (admission per museum €1.50, for all €3; 10.30am-1.30pm & 4.30-6.30pm) in the Iglesia de San Gil, Iglesia de San Bartolomé and Santísima Trinidad.

The best place to stay is the **Antiguo Palacio de Atienza** (☎ 949 39 91 80; Callejuelas de San Gil 47; r €80-120;), a former palace with handsome rooms featuring grey stone walls and beams. The variation in price relates to the size of the room and option of a Jacuzzi bath. Balconies overlook the lawns and pool.

El Mirador (☎ 949 39 90 38; Calle Barruelo s/n; d with/without bathroom €43/30) is the cheaper option, with small simple rooms. The excellent restaurant (meals €25) has creative dishes like *calabacines rellenos con mousse de pisto, hongas y queso ahumado* (stuffed courgettes with tomatoes, peppers, field mushrooms and smoked cheese), as well as the standard *cordero* (lamb) and *cabrito* (kid), accompanied by panoramic views.

A couple of buses leave early in the morning, bound for Guadalajara, Madrid and Sigüenza.

Barcelona

Set on a plain rising gently from the sea to a range of wooded hills, Barcelona is Spain's most cosmopolitan city and one of the Mediterranean's busiest ports. Restaurants, bars and clubs are always packed, as is the seaside in summer. You might get the impression it's dedicated exclusively to hedonism, but it's a hard-working, dynamic place hoping to place itself in the vanguard of 21st-century Europe with a heavy concentration of hi-tech and biomedical business.

It regards its long past with pride. From Roman town it passed to medieval trade juggernaut, and its old centre constitutes one of the greatest concentrations of Gothic architecture in Europe. Beyond this core are some of the world's more bizarre buildings: surreal spectacles capped by Antoni Gaudí's La Sagrada Família church.

Barcelona has been breaking ground in art, architecture and style since the late 19th century. From the marvels of Modernisme to the modern wonders of today, from Picasso to the likes of Susana Solano, the racing heart of Barcelona has barely skipped a beat. The city's avant-garde chefs whip up a storm that has even the French reaching for superlatives.

Barcelona is the capital of Catalonia, a region with its own language, character and history – many Catalans think of their home as a separate country. The city itself could keep you occupied for weeks but just outside it are sandy beaches, Sitges and the Montserrat mountain range.

HIGHLIGHTS

- Marvel at **La Sagrada Família** (p330), Antoni Gaudí's still-unfolding Modernista masterpiece
- Drink in the views from Gaudí's **Park Güell** (p334)
- Head out with the locals for a night of tippling and snacking in **L'Eixample** (p354)
- Study the earliest of Pablo's portraits in the **Museu Picasso** (p326)
- Grab your towel and tastebuds and head for **La Barceloneta** (p329)
- Get a spiritual lift in the strange soaring mountains of **Montserrat** (p367)
- Swan around inside the curvy **Casa Batlló** (p331), Gaudí's kookiest building
- Explore **Montjuïc** (p337), home to Romanesque art, a brooding fort, Miró and beautiful gardens
- Head down the coast for **Sitges** (p364), an outrageous beachside party resort

AREA: 477 SQ KM	AVE SUMMER TEMP: HIGH 28°C, LOW 20°C	POP: 1.59 MILLION

HISTORY

It is thought that Barcelona may have been founded by the Carthaginians in about 230 BC, taking the surname of Hamilcar Barca, Hannibal's father. Roman Barcelona (known as Barcino) covered an area within today's Barri Gòtic and was overshadowed by Tarraco (Tarragona), 90km to the southwest.

In the wake of Muslim occupation and then Frankish domination, Guifré el Pilós (Wilfrid the Hairy) founded the house of the Comtes de Barcelona (Counts of Barcelona) in AD 878. Barcelona grew rich on pickings from the collapse of the Muslim caliphate of Córdoba in the 11th century. Under Ramon Berenguer III (1082–1131), Catalonia launched its own fleet and sea trade developed.

In 1137 Ramon Berenguer IV married Petronilla, heiress of Aragón, creating a joint state and setting the scene for Catalonia's golden age. Jaume I (1213–76) wrenched the Balearic Islands and Valencia from the Muslims in the 1230s to '40s. Jaume I's son Pere II followed with Sicily in 1282. Then came a spectacular expansion of Catalonia's Mediterranean trade-based empire, albeit hampered at home by divisions in the ruling family, the odd clash with Castilla and trouble with the aristocracy in Aragón. Malta (1283), Athens (1310), Corsica (1323), Sardinia (1324) and Naples (1423) fell, for varying periods, under Catalan dominance.

The accession of the Aragonese noble Fernando to the throne in 1479 augured ill for Barcelona, and his marriage to Queen Isabel of Castilla more still. Catalonia effectively became a subordinate part of the Castilian state. In the War of the Spanish Succession (1702–13), Barcelona backed the wrong horse, was abandoned by its European allies and fell to Felipe V in September 1714. Felipe abolished the Generalitat (Parliament), built a huge fort, the Ciutadella, to watch over Barcelona, and banned the writing and teaching of Catalan.

Modernisme, Anarchy & Civil War

The 19th century brought economic resurgence. Wine, cotton, cork and iron industries developed, as did urban working-class poverty and unrest. To ease the crush, Barcelona's medieval walls were demolished in 1854, and in 1869 work began on L'Eixample, an extension of the city beyond Plaça de Catalunya. The flourishing bourgeoisie paid for lavish buildings, many of them in the unique Modernisme style, whose leading exponent was Antoni Gaudí (seven of his buildings in Barcelona together form a World Heritage site).

Modernisme was the most visible aspect of the Catalan Renaixença, a movement for the revival of Catalan language and culture in the late 19th century. By the turn of the 20th century, Barcelona was also Spain's hotbed of avant-garde art, with close ties to Paris.

In the decades around the turn of the century Barcelona became a vortex of anarchists, Republicans, bourgeois regionalists, gangsters, police terrorists, political *pistoleros* (gunmen), and meddling by Madrid.

Within days of the formation of Spain's Second Republic in 1931, Catalan nationalists, led by Francesc Macià and Lluís Companys, proclaimed Catalonia a republic within an imaginary 'Iberian Federation'. Madrid pressured them into accepting a unitary Spanish state, but Catalonia got a new regional government, with the old title of Generalitat.

For nearly a year after Franco's rise in 1936, Barcelona was run by revolutionary anarchists and the Partido Obrero de Unificación Marxista (POUM; Workers' Marxist Unification Party) Trotskyist militia, with Companys as president only in name. In 1937 the Catalan communist party (PSUC; Partit Socialista Unificat de Catalunya) took control and disarmed the anarchists and POUM. One of those to watch on in distress at this fratricidal conflict was George Orwell, who recorded his war efforts in his classic *Homage to Catalonia*. The city fell to Franco in 1939 and there followed a long period of repression.

From Franco to the Present

The big social change under Franco was the flood of immigrants, chiefly from Andalucía, attracted by economic growth in Catalonia. Some 750,000 people came to Barcelona in the '50s and '60s, and almost as many to the rest of Catalonia. Many lived in appalling conditions.

Three years after Franco's death in 1975, a new Spanish constitution created the autonomous community of Catalonia (Catalunya in Catalan, Cataluña in Castilian), with Barcelona as its capital, in the context of a new quasi-federation. The Generalitat has wide powers over agriculture, education, health, industry, tourism, local police and trade.

The autonomy statutes were renegotiated in 2006, moderately increasing Catalonia's fiscal independence.

Jordi Pujol's moderately right-wing nationalist Convergència i Unió (CiU) coalition won regional elections in 1980 and remained in control until late 2003, when a left-wing coalition under Pasqual Maragall's Partit Socialista de Catalunya (PSC, aligned with the national PSOE) took power. It collapsed in 2006 and fresh elections were called, the results of which were largely the same, but with José Montilla in Maragall's place. Barcelona itself has, since the return of democracy, always been run by a PSC-dominated council.

The 1992 Olympics spurred a burst of public works, bringing new life to areas such as Montjuïc, where the major events were held, and the once-shabby waterfront. The impetus has barely let up. The Fòrum area on the northeast waterfront has been transformed from wasteland into a high-rise residential and congress district with a new marina. Other spectacular buildings, such as Jean Nouvel's Torre Agbar, are just part of a continuing program of urban transformation: Toyo Ito is designing two landmark twisting towers for the new Fira 2 trade fair; Lord Richard Rogers has added the landmark business hotel, Hesperia Tower, in L'Hospitalet; and local boy Ricard Bofill is creating an 88m spinnaker-shaped hotel on the Mediterranean shoreline at the southern end of the Barceloneta beaches.

ORIENTATION

Barcelona's coastline runs roughly northeast to southwest, and many streets are parallel or perpendicular to it.

The focal axis is La Rambla, a 1.25km boulevard running northwest, and slightly uphill, from Port Vell (Old Harbour) to Plaça de Catalunya. The latter marks the boundary between Ciutat Vella (Old City) and L'Eixample, the grid extension into which Barcelona grew from the late 19th century.

Ciutat Vella, a warren of streets, centuries-old buildings, hotels, restaurants and bars, spreads either side of La Rambla. Its heart is the lower half of the section east of La Rambla, called the Barri Gòtic (Gothic Quarter). West of La Rambla is somewhat edgier El Raval. Ciutat Vella continues northeast of Barri Gòtic across Via Laietana to La Ribera, east of which lies the pretty Parc de la Ciutadella.

Port Vell (Old Port) has a great aquarium and two marinas. At its northeast end is La Barceloneta, the old sailors' and former industrial workers' quarter, from where beaches and a pedestrian promenade stretch 1km northeast to Port Olímpic, built for the Olympics and now surrounded by lively bars and restaurants.

You will find most of Barcelona's singular Modernista architecture, including La Sagrada Família, in L'Eixample.

Gràcia, beyond the wide Avinguda Diagonal on the northern edge of central L'Eixample, is a net of narrow streets and squares with a varied population, and can be a lively place to spend a Friday or Saturday night. Just north of Gràcia is Gaudí's Park Güell.

Two good landmarks are the hills of Montjuïc and Tibidabo. Montjuïc, the lower of the two, begins about 700m southwest of the bottom (southeast end) of La Rambla. Tibidabo, with its TV tower and church topped by a giant statue of Christ, is 6km northwest of Plaça de Catalunya. It's the high point of the Collserola range of wooded hills that forms the backdrop to the city.

El Prat airport is 12km to the southwest of central Barcelona.

Maps

Tourist offices hand out free city and transport maps but Lonely Planet's *Barcelona City Map* (1:24,000 with a complete index of streets and sights) is better. Also handy is Michelin's ring-bound *Barcelona*, scaled at 1:12,000.

INFORMATION

Bookshops

Altaïr (Map pp312-13; ☎ 93 342 71 71; www.altair.es; Gran Via de les Corts Catalanes 616) Excellent travel bookshop with maps, guides and travel literature.

Antinous (Map pp316-17; ☎ 93 301 90 70; www.antinouslibros.com; Carrer de Josep Anselm Clavé 6) Good gay bookshop and cafe.

Casa del Llibre (Map pp310-11; ☎ 902 02 64 07; www.casadellibro.com; Passeig de Gràcia 62) Enormous general bookshop.

Elephant (Map pp312-13; ☎ 93 443 05 94; www.lfant.biz; Carrer de la Creu dels Molers 12) A bright English-language bookshop.

Laie (Map pp310-11; ☎ 93 318 17 39; www.laie.es; Carrer de Pau Claris 85) Novels and books on architecture, art and film, in English and French, and a fine cafe.

Llibreria & Informaciò Cultural de la Generalitat de Catalunya (Map pp316-17; ☎ 93 302 64 62; La

Rambla dels Estudis 118) First stop for books on all things Catalan.
Quera (Map pp316-17; ☎ 93 318 07 43; Carrer de Petritxol 2) Map and guidebook specialist.

Cultural Centres

British Council (Map pp306-7; ☎ 93 241 99 72; www.britishcouncil.org/es/spain.htm; Carrer d'Amigó 83) Language school, library and occasional cultural events.
Institut Français de Barcelona (Map pp310-11; ☎ 93 567 77 77; www.institutfrances.org; Carrer de Moià 8) French-language school that puts on films, concerts and exhibitions.
Institute for North American Studies (Map pp310-11; ☎ 93 240 51 10; www.ien.es; Via Augusta 123) The main centre for learning North American English; also has library services.

Emergency

Tourists who want to report thefts need to go to the Catalan police, known as the **Mossos d'Esquadra** (Map pp312-13; ☎ 088; Carrer Nou de la Rambla 80), or the **Guàrdia Urbana** (Local Police; Map pp316-17; ☎ 092; La Rambla 43). See also p871 for a handy national police number and website.
Ambulance (☎ 061)
EU standard emergency number (☎ 112)
Fire Brigade (Bombers; ☎ 080, 085)
Institut Català de la Dona (Map pp316-17; ☎ 93 317 82 81; www.gencat.net/icdona; Plaça de Pere Coromines 1) For rape counselling.
Policía Nacional (☎ 091)

Internet Access

Bornet (Map pp316-17; ☎ 93 268 15 07; www.bornet-bcn.com; Carrer de Barra de Ferro 3; 1/10hr €2.80/20; 🕑 10am-11pm Mon-Fri, noon-11pm Sat, Sun & holidays) A cool little internet centre-cum-art gallery.
easyInternetcafé (www.easyeverything.com; per €2.50) Plaça de Catalunya (Map pp312-13; Ronda de l'Universitat 35; 🕑 8am-2am); El Raval (Map pp316-17; La Rambla 31; 🕑 8am-2.30am)

Internet Resources

www.bcn.cat The City of Barcelona's municipal website, with many links.
www.barcelonareporter.com A portal that gathers news articles from and about Barcelona and Catalonia.
www.lecool.com Subscribe for free to this site for weekly events listings.
www.rutadelmodernisme.com Web page of routes, monuments and events related to Modernisme.
www.bcn-nightlife.com Info on bars, clubs and parties across town.

Laundry

Lavaxpress (Map pp312-13; www.lavaxpres.com; Carrer de Ferlandina 34; 🕑 8am-11pm) An 8kg wash costs €3.50, drying is €3.50 for 30 minutes. It has five other branches around town.
Lavomatic Barri Gòtic (Map pp316-17; ☎ 93 342 51 19; Plaça de Joaquim Xirau 1; 🕑 9am-9pm); La Ribera (Map pp316-17; ☎ 93 268 47 68; Carrer del Consolat de Mar 43-45) A 7kg wash costs €5.50, drying is €0.85 for five minutes.
Wash'N Dry (Map pp310-11; ☎ 902 10 07 03; Carrer de Torrent de l'Olla 105; 🕑 7am-10pm) There are six other branches around town. An 8kg wash costs €4.50, drying is €1 per 10 minutes; there's a wash, dry and fold service for an extra fee.

Left Luggage

At the airport, **lockers** (in three sizes) can be found at the car park entrance opposite Terminal B. You pay €3.70/4.20/4.80 for 24 hours. There are plans to install special lockers for skis, snowboards and other bulky items.

Estació Sants, the train station, has **lockers** (🕑 5.30am-11pm) charging €3/4.50 per small/big item for 24 hours, as does the main bus station, Estació del Nord.

Lost Property

Oficina de Trovalles (Lost Property; Map pp316-17; ☎ 010; Carrer de la Ciutat 9; 🕑 9am-2pm Mon-Fri)
Taxis Lost Property (☎ 902 10 15 64)
TMB Bus & Metro Lost Property – Centre d'Atenció al Client (☎ 93 318 70 74)

Media

El País includes a daily supplement devoted to Catalonia, but the region has a lively home-grown press too. *La Vanguardia* and *El Periódico* are the main local Castilian-language dailies. The latter also publishes a Catalan version. *Avui* is the more conservative and Catalan-nationalist daily. *El Punt* concentrates on news in and around Barcelona.

Medical Services

Call ☎ 010 to find the nearest late-opening duty pharmacy. There are also several 24-hour pharmacies scattered across town.
Farmàcia Álvarez (Map pp310-11; ☎ 93 302 11 24; Passeig de Gràcia 26)
Farmàcia Clapés (Map pp316-17; ☎ 93 301 28 43; La Rambla de Sant Josep 98)
Farmàcia Torres (Map pp312-13; ☎ 93 453 92 20; www.farmaciaabierta24h.com; Carrer d'Aribau 62)

(Continued on page 318)

BARCELONA

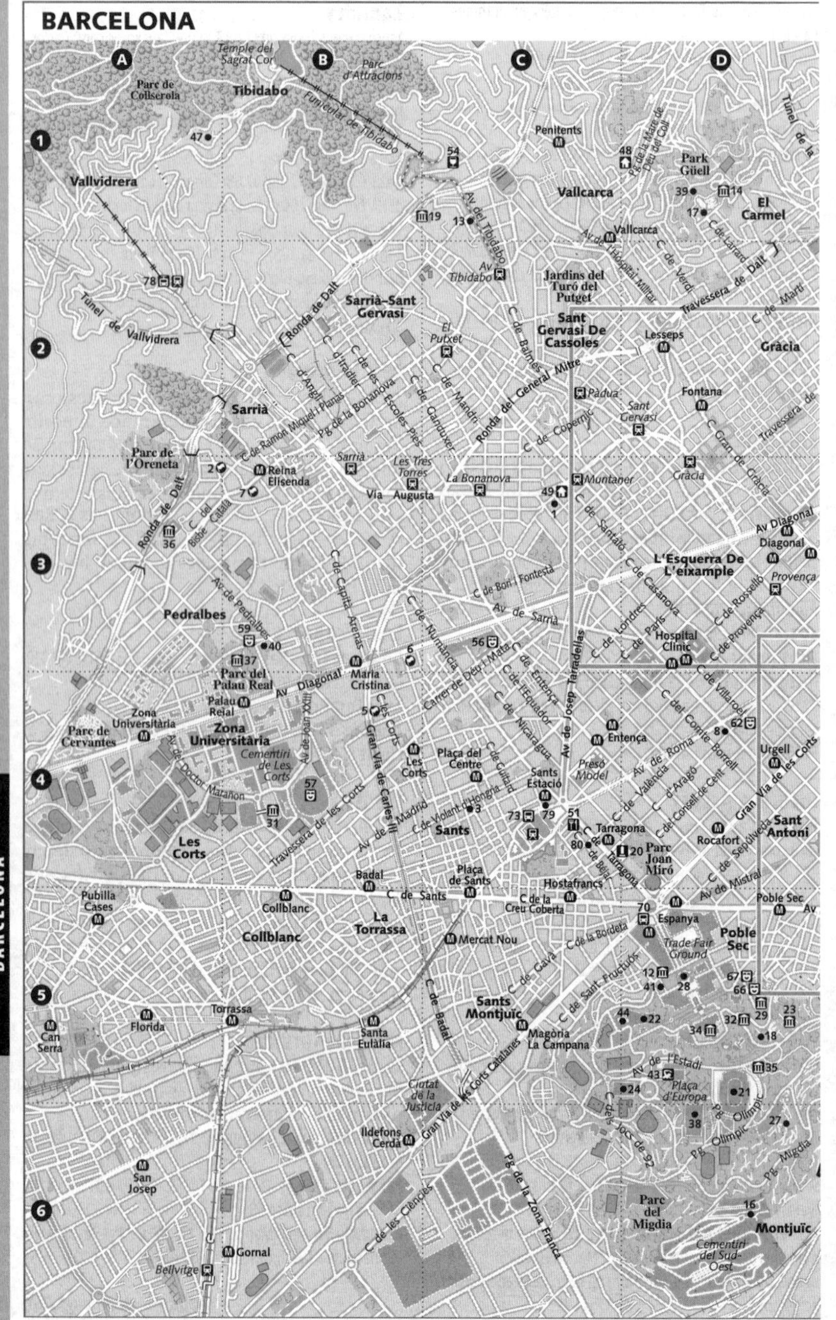

BARCELONA

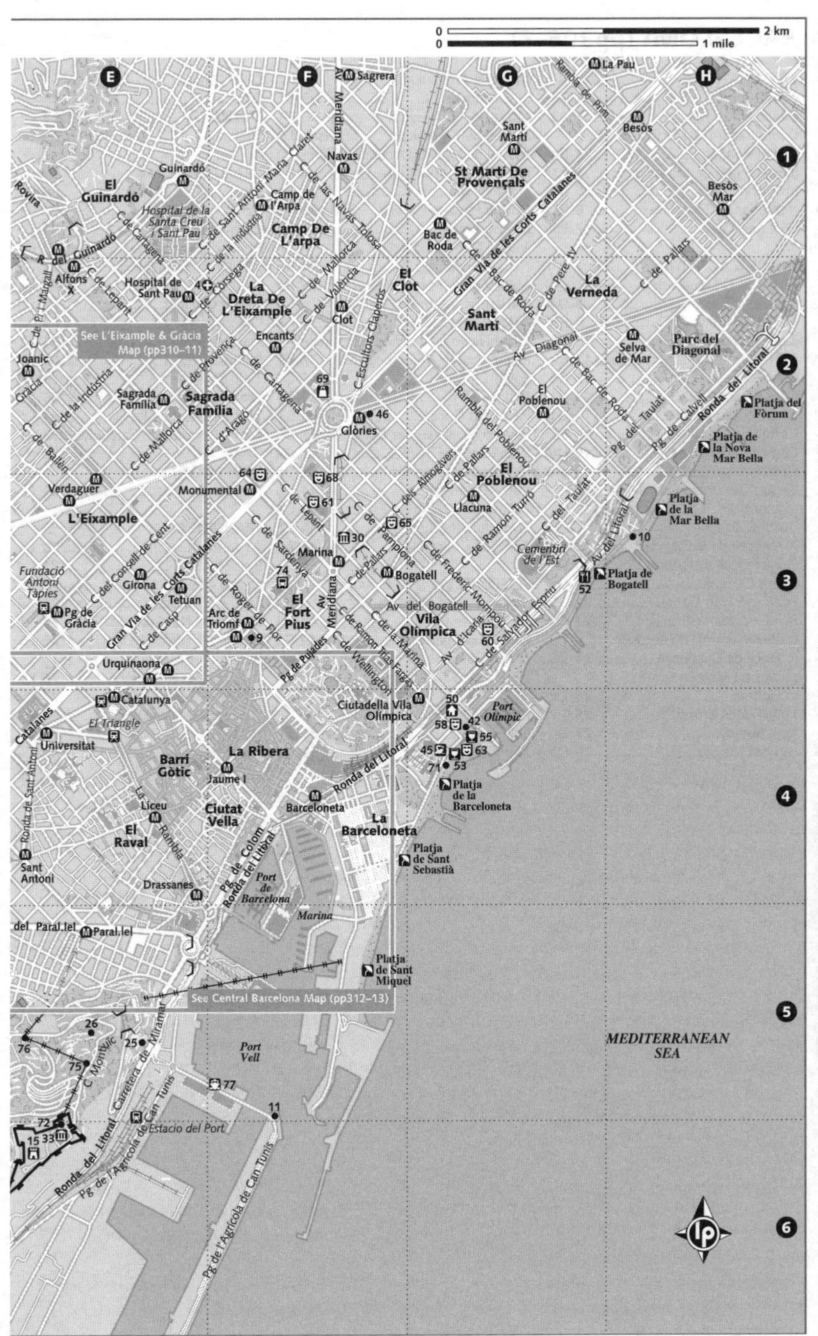

0 2 km
0 1 mile
E
F
G
H
1
2
3
4
5
6
El Guinardó
Guinardó
Hospital de la Santa Creu i Sant Pau
Hospital de Sant Pau
Alfons X
Camp de l'Arpa
Camp De L'arpa
La Dreta De L'Eixample
Navas
Sagrera
Av Meridiana
Sant Martí
St Martí De Provençals
La Pau
Besòs
Besòs Mar
Bac de Roda
El Clot
Clot
Encants
La Verneda
Sant Martí
Selva de Mar
Parc del Diagonal
Gran Via de les Corts Catalanes
Av Diagonal
See L'Eixample & Gràcia Map (pp310–11)
Joanic
Sagrada Família
El Poblenou
Glòries
Platja del Fòrum
Platja de la Nova Mar Bella
Verdaguer
Monumental
El Poblenou
Llacuna
Platja de la Mar Bella
L'Eixample
Cementiri de l'Est
Platja de Bogatell
Fundació Antoni Tàpies
Girona
Tetuan
Marina
Bogatell
Pg de Gràcia
Arc de Triomf
El Fort Pius
Vila Olímpica
Urquinaona
Catalunya
Ciutadella Vila Olímpica
Port Olímpic
El Triangle
Universitat
Barri Gòtic
La Ribera
Jaume I
Platja de la Barceloneta
Liceu
Ciutat Vella
Barceloneta
El Raval
La Barceloneta
Platja de Sant Sebastià
Sant Antoni
Drassanes
Port de Barcelona
Marina
Paral.lel
Platja de Sant Miquel
See Central Barcelona Map (pp312–13)
MEDITERRANEAN SEA
Port Vell
Estacio del Port
Ronda del Litoral
Pg de l'Agricola de Can Tunis
Carretera de Miramar
C Montjuïc
BARCELONA

BARCELONA (pp306–7)

INFORMATION

British Council....1 C3
Canadian Consulate....2 A3
Coordinadora Gai-Lesbiana Barcelona....3 C4
Hospital Dos de Maig....4 E2
Irish Consulate....5 B4
Netherlands Consulate....6 B3
US Consulate....7 B3

SIGHTS & ACTIVITIES

Antilla BCN Escuela de Baile....8 D4
Arc de Triomf....9 F3
Base Nautica Municipal....10 H3
BCN Skytour....11 F5
CaixaForum....12 D5
Casa Roviralta....13 C1
Casa-Museu Gaudí....14 D1
Castell de Montjuïc....15 E6
Cementiri del Sud-Oest....16 D6
Centre d'Acollida....17 D1
Centre Gestor del Parc de Montjuïc....18 D5
CosmoCaixa (Museu de la Ciència)....19 C1
Dona i Ocell Sculpture....20 D4
Estadi Olímpic....21 D5
Fundació Fran Daurel....22 D5
Fundació Joan Miró....23 D5
Institut Nacional d'Educació Física de Catalunya....24 D5
Jardins de Mossèn Costa i Llobera....25 E5
Jardins Joan Brossa....26 E5
Jardí Botànic....27 D6
La Font Mágica....28 D5
Museu d'Arqueologia de Catalunya....29 D5
Museu de Carrosses Fúnebres...30 F3
Museu de Ceràmica....(see 37)
Museu de les Arts Decoratives..(see 37)
Museu del Futbol Club Barcelona....31 B4
Museu Etnològic....32 D5
Museu Militar....33 E6
Museu Nacional d'Art de Catalunya....34 D5
Museu Olímpic i de lÉsport....35 D5
Museu-Monestir de Pedralbes....36 A3
Palau Nacional de Montjuic....(see 34)
Palau Reial de Pedralbes....37 B3
Palau Sant Jordi....38 D6
Park Güell....39 D1
Pavellons Güell....40 B3
Pavelló Mies van der Rohe....41 D5
Peix Sculpture....42 G4
Piscines Bernat Picornell....43 D5
Poble Espanyol....44 D5
Poliesportiu Marítim....45 G4
Torre Agbar....46 F2
Torre de Collserola....47 A1

SLEEPING

Alberg Mare de Déu de Montserrat....48 D1
Barcelona Apartments....49 C3
British Council....(see 1)
Hotel Arts Barcelona....50 G4

EATING

El Peixerot....51 C4
Xiringuito d'Escribà....52 G3

DRINKING

CDLC....53 G4
Mirablau....54 C1
Shôko....55 G4

ENTERTAINMENT

Bikini....56 C3
Camp Nou....57 B4
Catwalk....58 G4
Elephant....59 B3
Icària Yelmo Cineplex....60 G3
L'Auditori....61 F3
Méliès Cinemes....62 D4
Opium Mar....63 G4
Plaça de Braus Monumental....64 F3
Razzmatazz....65 F3
Tablao de Carmen....(see 44)
Teatre Lliure....66 D5
Teatre Mercat de les Flors....67 D5
Teatre Nacional de Catalunya....68 F3

SHOPPING

Els Encants Vells....69 F2

TRANSPORT

A1 Aerobús....70 D5
Biciclot....71 G4
Castell (Telefèric)....72 E6
Estació d'Autobusos de Sants....73 C4
Estació del Nord (Bus Station)...74 F3
Estació Mirador (Telefèric)....75 E5
Estació Parc Montjuïc (Funicular & Telefèric)....76 E5
Ferries to Genoa & Rome....77 F5
Funicular de Vallvidrera....78 A2
Hertz....79 C4
Pepecar....80 C4

L'EIXAMPLE & GRÀCIA (pp310–11)

INFORMATION
Australian Consulate........1 C3
Casa del Libre........2 F5
Farmàcia Álvarez........3 F6
German Consulate........4 D4
Halcón Viatges........5 G6
Hospital Clínic i Provincial........6 C6
Institut Français de Barcelona........7 C4
Institute for North American Studies........8 A3
Laie........9 G6
New Zealand Consulate........10 B4
Orixà........11 E6
Post Office........12 F5
Regional Tourist Office (Palau Robert)........13 D4
UK Consulate........14 A5
Wash'N Dry........15 D2

SIGHTS & ACTIVITIES
Casa Amatller........16 F6
Casa Batlló........17 F6
Casa de les Punxes (Casa Terrades)........18 E4
Casa Lleó Morera........19 F6
Casa Vicenç........20 B2
Església de Sant Joan........21 D1
Fundació Antoni Tàpies........22 E5
Fundació Suñol........23 E4
Fundación Francisco Godia........24 F6
La Pedrera (Casa Milà)........25 E4
Mercat de l'Abaceria........26 D2
Museu del Perfum........27 F6
Museu Egipci........28 F5
Museu Gaudí........29 H2
Palau del Baró Quadras (Casa Asia)........30 E4
Temple Expiatori de la Sagrada Família........31 H2

SLEEPING
Apartment Barcelona........32 F5
Barcelona On Line........33 G6
Centric Point........34 F6
Hostal Central........35 H4
Hostal Girona........36 H5
Hostal Goya........37 G6
Hostal Palacios........38 F6
Hotel Casa Fuster........39 D4
Hotel Claris........40 F5
Hotel Costanza........41 H6
Hotel d'Uxelles........42 H5
Hotel Hispanos Siete Suiza........43 G2
Hotel Omm........44 E4
Lodging Barcelona........45 E6

EATING
Bilbao........46 E3
Cata 1.81........47 D6
Cerveseria Catalana........48 E5
El Rincón Maya........49 D6
Envalira........50 D2
Goliard........51 E3
Koyuki........52 C5
L'Atzavara........53 C6
La Rita........54 F5
O! Gràcia........55 D2
Relais de Venise........56 F5
Saüc........57 B5
Taverna La Llesca........58 D2

DRINKING
Berlin........59 B5
Dry Martini........60 C5
La Cigale........61 E2
Les Gens Que J'Aime........62 F5
Michael Collins Pub........63 G2
Musical Maria........64 D3
New Chaps........65 E4
Premier........66 D6
Sabor a Cuba........67 D3

ENTERTAINMENT
DBoy........68 H6
Distrito Diagonal........69 E4
Filmoteca........70 A6
Luz de Gas........71 B5
Otto Zutz........72 B3
Sutton The Club........73 C4
Verdi........74 D2
Verdi Park........75 D2

SHOPPING
Antonio Miró........76 F6
Bulevard Rosa........77 E5
Camper........78 E5
Farrutx........79 D5
Joan Murrià........80 F5
Red Market........81 D2
Vinçon........82 E4
Xampany........83 D6

TRANSPORT
Avis........84 D5
Europcar........85 H5
TEISA Buses........86 F5
Vanguard........87 A6

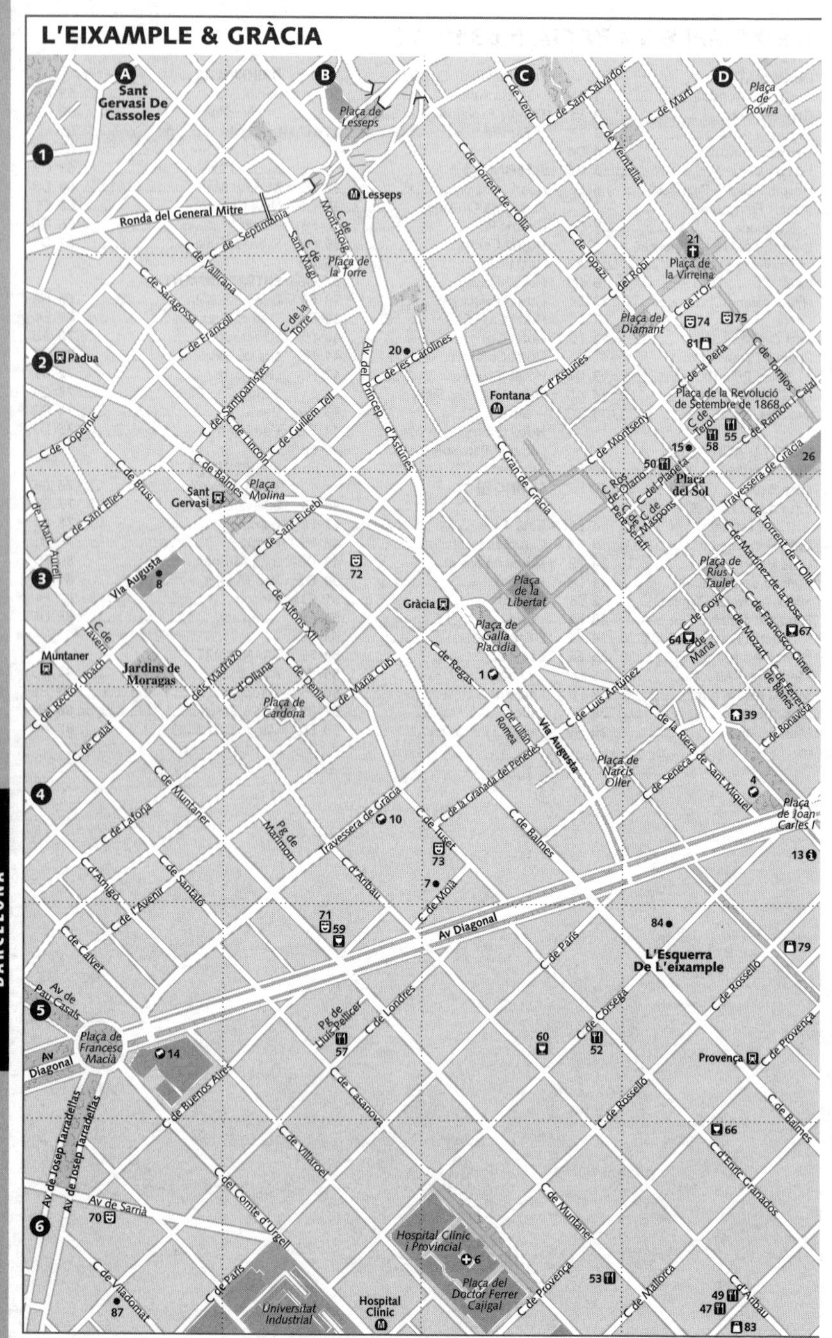
L'EIXAMPLE & GRÀCIA
Sant Gervasi De Cassoles
Plaça de Lesseps
Lesseps
Ronda del General Mitre
C de Septimània
C de Vallirana
C de Saragossa
C de Francolí
Sant Magí
C de Mont-Roig
Plaça de la Torre
C de la Torre
Pàdua
Av del Príncep d'Astúries
C de les Carolines
C de Verdi
C de Sant Salvador
C de Torrent de l'Olla
C de Verntallat
C de Martí
Plaça de Rovira
C de Topazi
C del Robí
Plaça de la Virreina
C de l'Or
Plaça del Diamant
C de la Perla
C de Torrijos
Plaça de la Revolució de Setembre de 1868
C de Ramon i Cajal
C de Terol
Fontana
C d'Astúries
C de Montseny
C del Planeta
Plaça del Sol
C Ros de Olano
C de Maspons
C de Pere Serafí
Travessera de Gràcia
C de Copèrnic
C del Santjoanistes
C de Lincoln
C de Guillem Tell
C de Brusi
C de Balmes
Sant Gervasi
Plaça Molina
C de Sant Eusebi
C de Sant Elies
C de Marc Aureli
Via Augusta
C de Alfons XII
Gran de Gràcia
Gràcia
Plaça de la Llibertat
Plaça de Galla Placídia
C de Martínez de la Rosa
C de Francisco Giner
Plaça de Rius i Taulet
C de Goya
C de Mozart
C de Maria
C de Ferrer de Blanes
C de Bonavista
C de Tavern
Muntaner
Jardins de Moragas
C del Rector Ubach
C dels Madrazo
C d'Oliana
C de Dènia
C de Maria Cubí
Plaça de Cardona
C de Regàs
C de Julián Romea
C de Luis Antúnez
C de la Riera de Sant Miquel
C de Sèneca
Plaça de Narcís Oller
C de la Granada del Penedès
C de Calaf
C de Muntaner
C de Laforja
Pg de Marimon
Travessera de Gràcia
C de Tuset
C de Balmes
Plaça de Joan Carles I
C d'Amigó
C de l'Avenir
C de Santaló
C d'Aribau
C de Molà
Av Diagonal
C de Calvet
C de París
L'Esquerra De L'eixample
C de Rosselló
Av de Pau Casals
Plaça de Francesc Macià
Av Diagonal
Pg de Lluís Pellicer
C de Londres
C de Còrsega
Provença
C de Provença
C de Buenos Aires
C de Casanova
C de Rosselló
C de Balmes
C de Villarroel
C d'Enric Granados
Av de Josep Tarradellas
Av de Sarrià
C del Comte d'Urgell
C de Muntaner
Hospital Clínic i Provincial
Plaça del Doctor Ferrer Cajigal
C de Viladomat
C de París
Universitat Industrial
Hospital Clínic
C de Provença
C de Mallorca
C d'Aribau

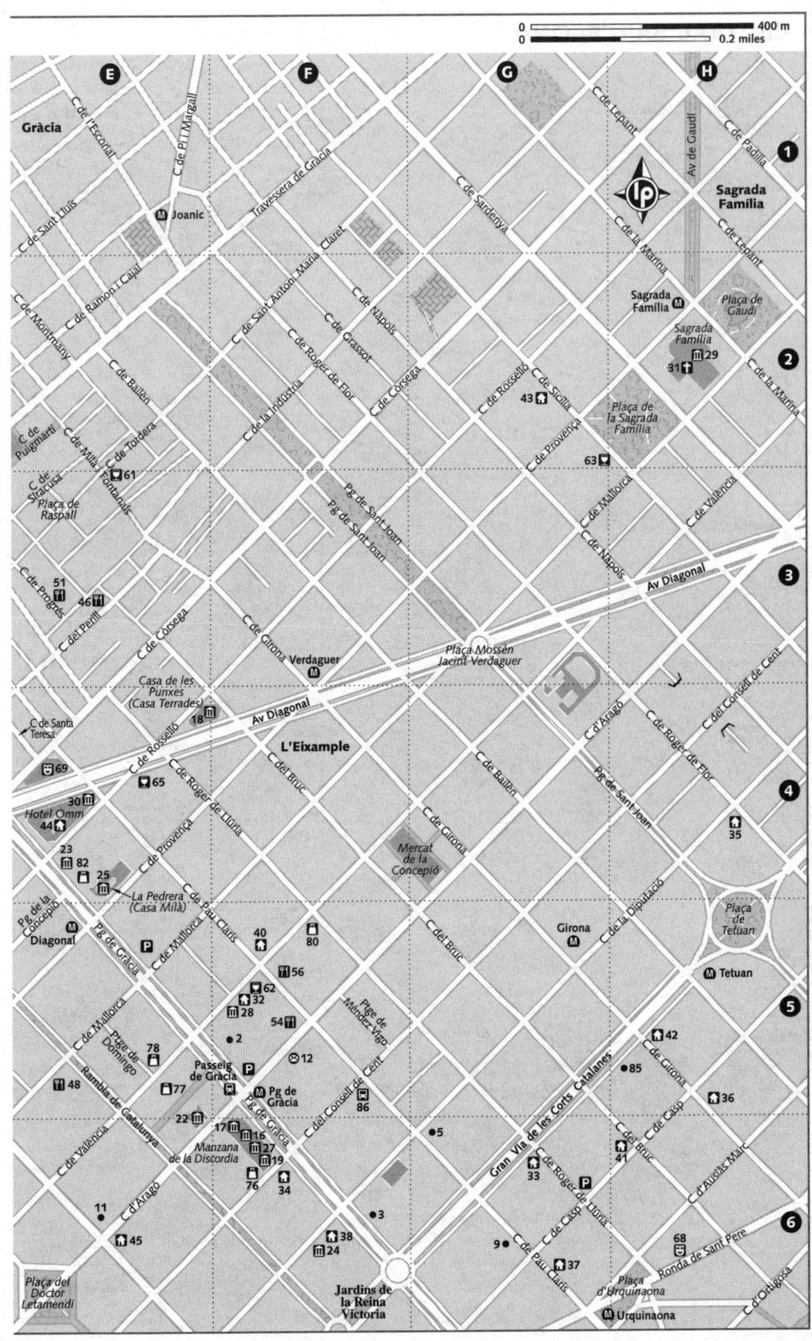

Gràcia
Joanic
Sagrada Família
Plaça de Gaudí
Plaça de la Sagrada Família
Plaça de Raspall
Verdaguer
Plaça Mossèn Jacint Verdaguer
Casa de les Punxes (Casa Terrades)
L'Eixample
Hotel Omm
La Pedrera (Casa Milà)
Mercat de la Concepció
Diagonal
Girona
Plaça de Tetuan
Tetuan
Passeig de Gràcia
Pg de Gràcia
Manzana de la Discordia
Gran Via de les Corts Catalanes
Plaça del Doctor Letamendi
Jardins de la Reina Victoria
Plaça d'Urquinaona
Urquinaona
Av Diagonal
Travessera de Gràcia
Pg de Sant Joan
BARCELONA

CENTRAL BARCELONA

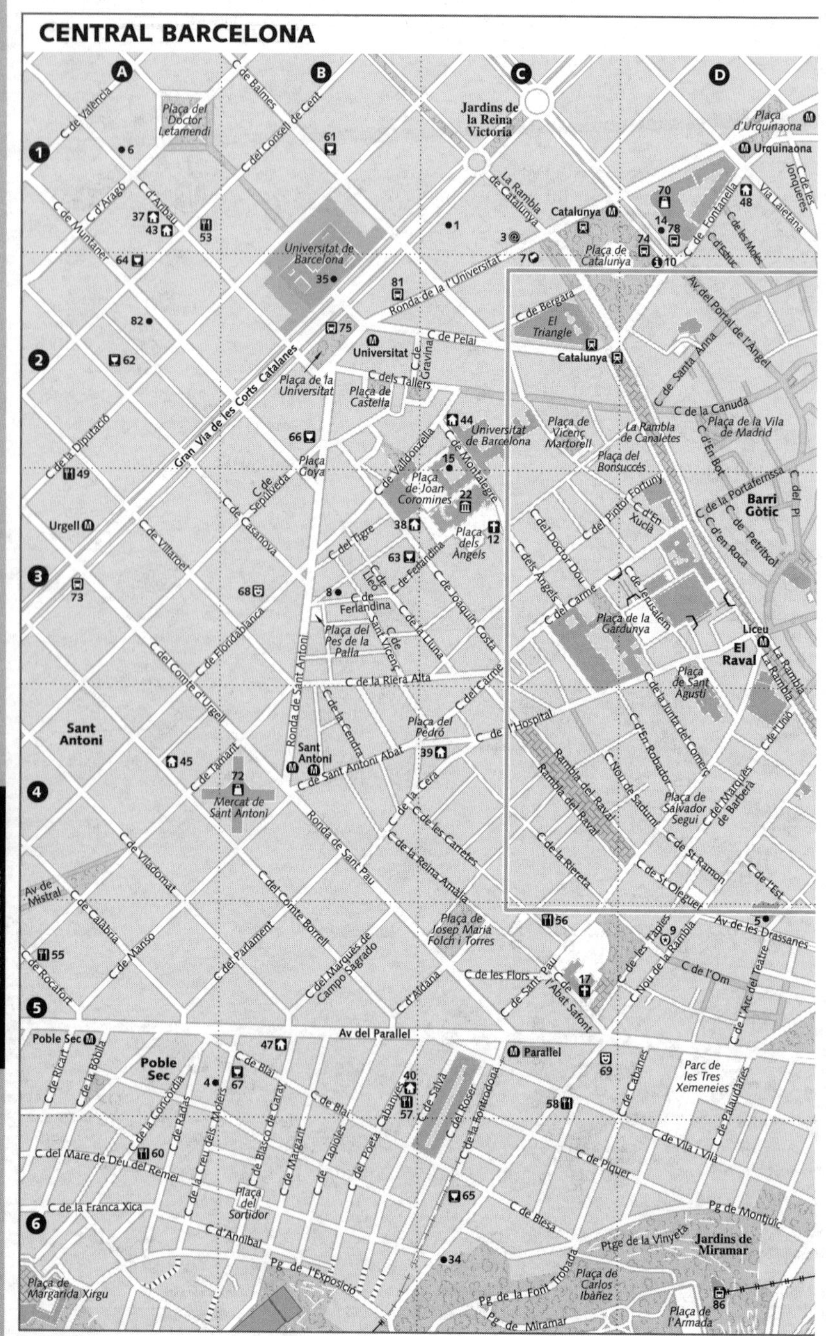

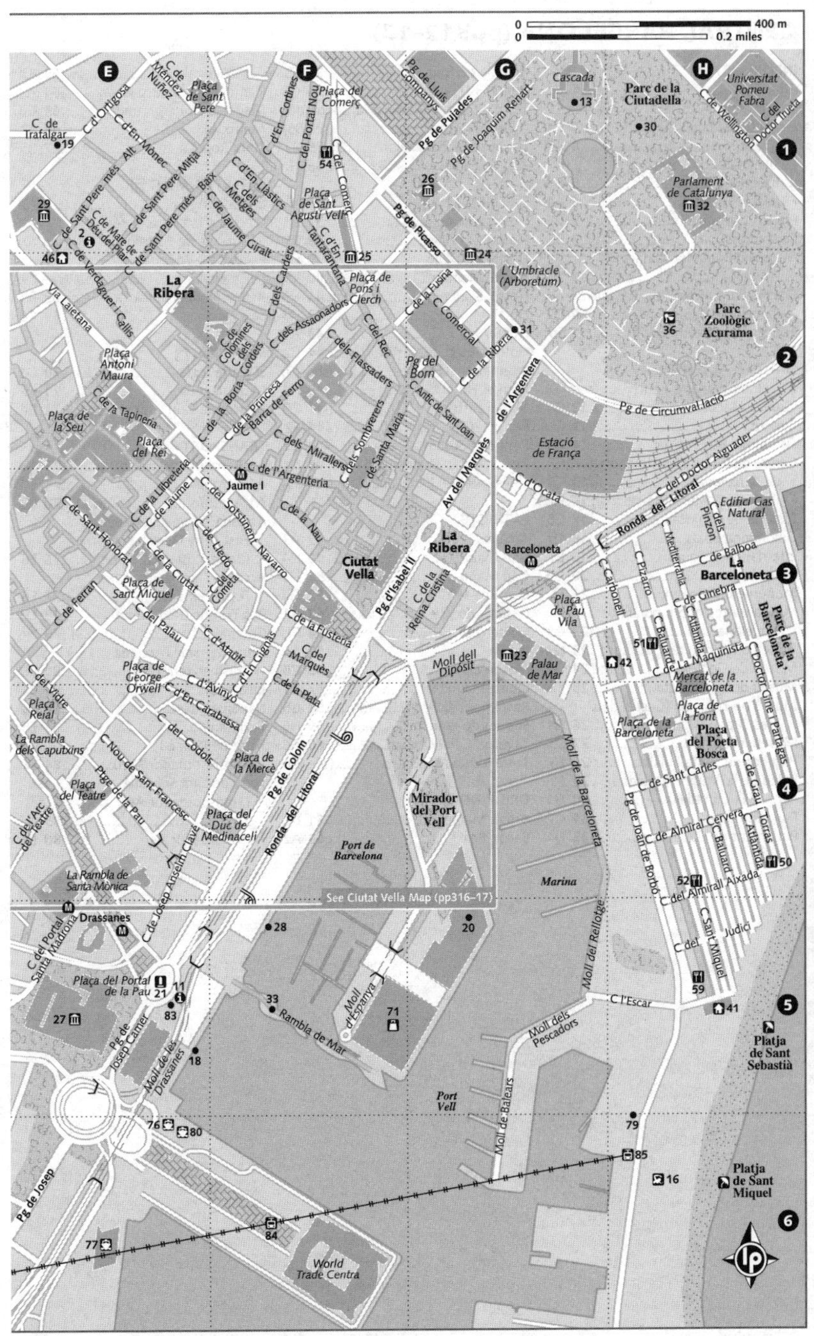

0 400 m
0 0.2 miles
Parc de la Ciutadella
Cascada
Universitat Pompeu Fabra
Parlament de Catalunya
L'Umbracle (Arboretum)
Parc Zoològic Acurama
Estació de França
La Ribera
Ciutat Vella
La Barceloneta
Parc de la Barceloneta
Edifici Gas Natural
Mercat de la Barceloneta
Plaça del Poeta Bosca
Palau de Mar
Mirador del Port Vell
Port de Barcelona
Marina
Port Vell
World Trade Centre
Platja de Sant Sebastià
Platja de Sant Miquel
Rambla de Mar
Moll d'Espanya
Moll de la Barceloneta
Moll dels Pescadors
Moll del Rellotge
Moll de Baleares
Moll de les Drassanes
Moll del Dipòsit
Pg de Colom
Ronda del Litoral
Pg d'Isabel II
Av del Marquès de l'Argentera
Pg de Picasso
Pg de Pujades
Pg de Circumval.lació
Pg de Joan de Borbó
Via Laietana
Plaça de la Seu
Plaça del Rei
Plaça de Sant Miquel
Plaça Reial
Plaça de George Orwell
Plaça de la Mercè
Plaça del Duc de Medinaceli
Plaça del Portal de la Pau
Plaça del Teatre
La Rambla dels Caputxins
La Rambla de Santa Mònica
Plaça de Pau Vila
Plaça de la Barceloneta
Plaça de la Font
Plaça Antoni Maura
Plaça de Sant Pere
Plaça del Comerç
Plaça de Sant Agustí Vell
Plaça de Pons i Clerch
Jaume I
Barceloneta
Drassanes
See Ciutat Vella Map (pp316–17)
BARCELONA

CENTRAL BARCELONA (pp312–13)

INFORMATION
Altäir....1 C1
Casal Lambda....2 E1
easyInternetcafé....3 C1
Elephant....4 A5
Escola Oficial d'Idiomes de Barcelona....5 D5
Farmàcia Torres....6 A1
French Consulate....7 C2
Lavaxpress....8 B3
Mossos d'Esquadra (Catalan Police)....9 D5
Oficina d'Informació de Turisme de Barcelona....10 D2
Tourist Information Booth....11 E5

SIGHTS & ACTIVITIES
Barcelona Walking Tours....(see 10)
Capella Macba....12 C3
Cascada....13 G1
Catalunya Bus Turístic....14 D1
Centre de Cultura Contemporània de Barcelona....15 C2
Club Natació Atlètic-Barcelona...16 H6
Església de Sant Pau....17 C5
Golondrina Boats....18 E5
International House....19 E1
L'Aquàrium....20 G5
Monument a Colom....21 E5
Museu d'Art Contemporàni de Barcelona....22 C3
Museu d'Història de Catalunya..23 G3
Museu de Geologia....24 G2
Museu de la Xocolata....25 F2
Museu de Zoologia (Castell dels Tres Dragons)....26 G1
Museu Marítim....27 E5
Pailebot de Santa Eulàlia....28 F5
Palau de la Música Catalana....29 E1
Parc de la Ciutadella....30 H1
Park Entrance....31 G2
Parlament de Catalunya....32 H1
Rambla de Mar....33 F5
Refugi 307....34 C6
Torre de Sant Sebastiá (Transbordador Aeri Tickets)....(see 85)
Universitat de Barcelona....35 B2
Zoo de Barcelona....36 H2

SLEEPING
Hostal Aribau....37 A1
Hostal Gat Raval....38 B3
Hostal Gat Xino....39 C4
Hostel Mambo Tango....40 B5
Hostel Sea Point....41 H5
Hotel 54....42 H3
Hotel Axel....43 A1
Hotel Mesón de Castilla....44 C2
International House....(see 19)
Market Hotel....45 A4
Melon District....(see 47)
Pensió 2000....46 E2
Rent a Bedroom....47 B5
Rent a Flat in Barcelona....48 D1
Universitat de Barcelona....(see 35)

EATING
Amaltea....49 A3
Can Majó....50 H4
Can Maño....51 H3
Can Ros 1911....52 H4
Casa Darío....53 A1
Comerç 24....54 F1
Inopia....55 A5
Mesón David....56 C5
Quimet i Quimet....57 B5
Restaurant Elche....58 C5
Suquet de l'Almirall....59 H5
Taverna Can Margarit....60 A6
Torre d'Alta Mar....(see 85)

DRINKING
Arena Madre....61 B1
Bacon Bear....62 A2
Casa Almirall....63 B3
Dietrich Gay Teatro Café....64 A2
Maumau Underground....65 C6
Metro....66 B2
Tinta Roja....67 B5

ENTERTAINMENT
El Corte Inglés....(see 70)
Oficina d'Informació de Turisme de Barcelona....(see 10)
Palau de la Música Catalana....(see 29)
Renoir Floridablanca....68 B3
Sala Apolo....69 C5

SHOPPING
El Corte Inglés....70 D1
Maremàgnum....71 F5
Mercat de Sant Antonì....72 B4

TRANSPORT
A1 Aerobús....73 A3
A1 Aerobús....74 D1
A1 Aerobús....75 B2
Acciona Trasmediterránea Fast Ferry Dock (Balearic Islands)....76 E6
Acciona Trasmediterránea Ferry Terminal....77 E6
Bus Turístic (Red Route)....78 D1
Cooltra....79 H6
Ferry Terminal (Acciona Trasmediterránea)....80 E6
Julià Tours....81 B2
National/Atesa....82 A2
Taxi Rank....83 E5
Torre de Jaume I (Transbordador Aeri)....84 F6
Torre de Sant Sebastiá (Transbordador Aeri Tickets)....85 H6
Transbordador Aeri....86 D6

BARCELONA

CIUTAT VELLA (pp316–17)

INFORMATION

5 Serveis 1 A1
Antinous 2 F6
Bornet 3 F2
easyInternetcafé 4 D5
Farmàcia Clapés 5 C4
Guàrdia Urbana (Local Police) 6 D5
Institut Català de la Dona 7 B6
Interchange 8 C4
Lavomatic 9 E6
Lavomatic 10 G3
Llibreria & Informació Cultural de la Generalitat de Catalunya 11 B3
Main Post Office 12 G4
Oficina de Trovalles 13 E3
Oficina d'Informació de Turisme de Barcelona 14 E3
Palau de la Virreina Arts Information Office (see 41)
Quera 15 C3

SIGHTS & ACTIVITIES

Ajuntament 16 E3
Antic Hospital de la Santa Creu 17 A4
Barcelona Vibes 18 F4
Capella Reial de Santa Àgata 19 E2
Casa de la Pia Almoina 20 E2
Casa de l'Ardiaca 21 D2
Casa Padellàs (see 36)
Catedral 22 E2
Centre d'Art Santa Mònica 23 D6
Centre d'Interpretació del Call 24 D3
Cook and Taste 25 D5
Església de Santa Maria del Mar 26 G2
Església de Santa Maria del Pi 27 C3
Galeria Maeght (see 44)
Institut d'Estudis Catalans 28 B4
La Capella 29 B4
Mercat de la Boqueria (see 81)
Mirador del Rei Martí 30 E2
Mosaïc de Miró 31 C4
Museu Barbier-Mueller d'Art Precolombi 32 G2
Museu de Cera 33 E6
Museu de l'Eròtica 34 C4
Museu del Rei de la Màgia 35 E2
Museu d'Història de la Ciutat 36 E2
Museu Diocesà (see 20)
Museu Frederic Marès 37 E2
Museu Picasso 38 G2
Palau de Dalmases 39 G2
Palau de la Generalitat 40 E3
Palau de la Virreina 41 B3
Palau del Bisbat 42 D2
Palau del Lloctinent 43 E2
Palau dels Cervelló 44 G2
Palau Güell 45 C5
Roman Tombs 46 C2
Roman Wall 47 F3
Roman Wall 48 E2
Saló del Tinell 49 E2
Sinagoga Major 50 D3
Temple Romà d'Augustí 51 E3

SLEEPING

Alberg Hostal Itaca 52 D2
Barcelona Mar Hostel 53 B6
Casa Camper 54 A3
Chic & Basic 55 G1
Hostal Campi 56 B2
Hotel Aneto 57 A3
Hotel Banys Orientals 58 F2
Hotel California 59 D4
Hotel Continental 60 B2
Hotel del Mar 61 H4
Hotel Jardí 62 C3
Hotel Neri 63 D3
Hotel Peninsular 64 C5
Hotel San Agustín 65 B4

EATING

Agut 66 F4
Bagel Shop 67 C2
Bar Celta 68 F5
Bar Pinotxo 69 B4
Biblioteca 70 B5
Cafè de l'Òpera 71 C4
Café Zurich 72 A1
Cal Pep 73 H2
Can Conesa 74 E3
Carrefour Express 75 B2
Casa Delfin 76 H2
Casa Leopoldo 77 A5
Centre Cultural Euskal Etxea 78 G2
El Xampanyet 79 G2
Maoz 80 D4
Mercat de la Boqueria 81 B4
Organic 82 B5
Orígen 83 H2
Pla 84 E3
Pla de la Garsa 85 F1
Restaurant El Cafetí 86 A5
Superservis 87 E4

DRINKING

Bar Marsella 88 B6
Barcelona Pipa Club 89 D5
Boadas 90 B2
Club Soul 91 E5
Gimlet 92 G1
Kentucky 93 D6
La Clandestina 94 F4
La Fianna 95 G2
La Vinya del Senyor 96 G3
London Bar 97 C6
Manchester 98 F4
Sinatra 99 D4
Vaixell Luz de Gas 100 H4

ENTERTAINMENT

Gran Teatre del Liceu 101 C5
Harlem Jazz Club 102 E4
Imax Cinema 103 H6
Jamboree 104 D5
Karma 105 D5
Monasterio 106 G4
Moog 107 D6
Palau de la Virreina (see 41)
Sala Tarantos 108 D5
Sidecar Factory Club 109 D4
Tablao Cordobés 110 D5
Teatre Romea 111 B4

SHOPPING

Casa Gispert 112 G2
Custo Barcelona 113 H2
FNAC 114 A1
Tanus 13 115 E3

TRANSPORT

BarcelonaBiking.com 116 E4
Barnabike 117 G4
Bike Tours Barcelona 118 H2
Bus Turístic (Blue Route) 119 A1
Fat Tire Bike Tours 120 E4
Gocar 121 E1
Pepecar 122 B1
Taxi Rank 123 B1

CIUTAT VELLA

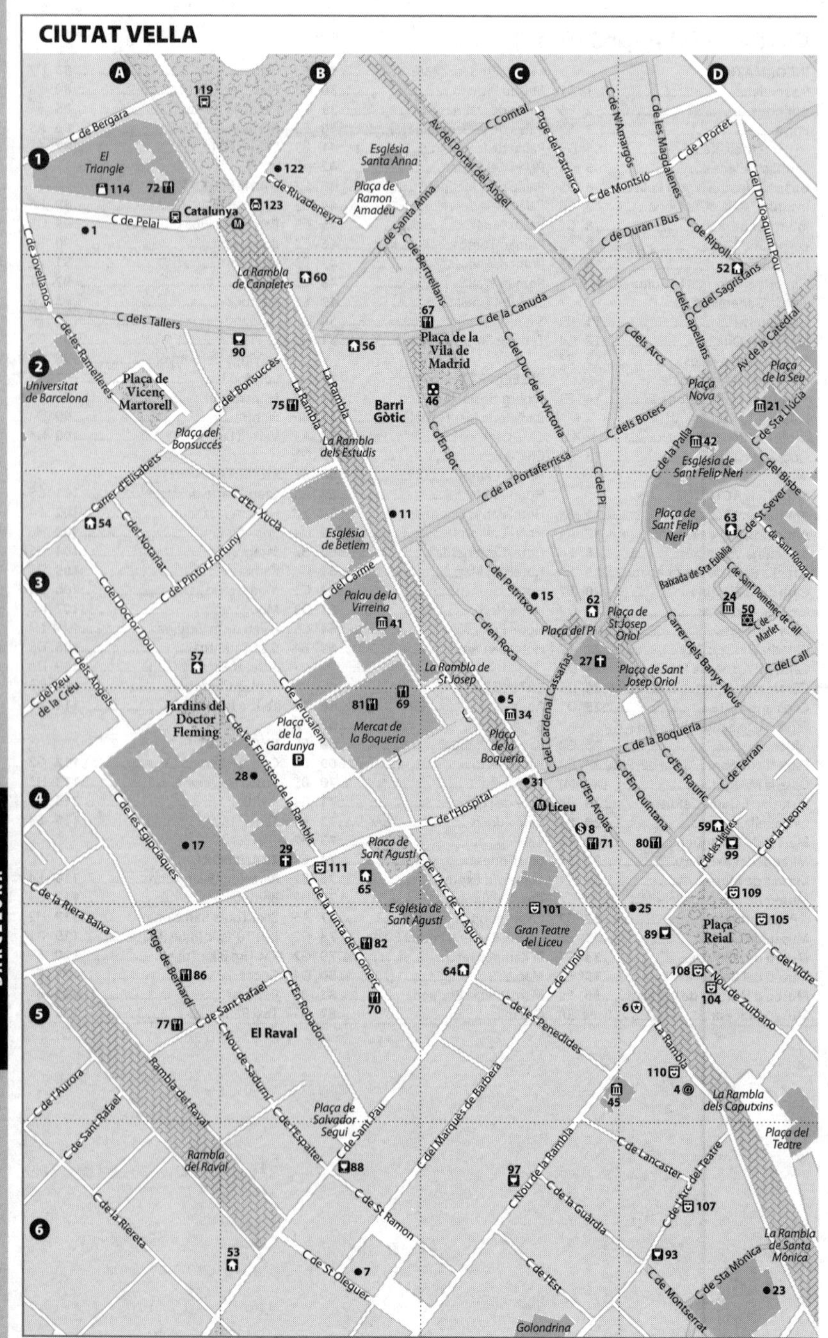

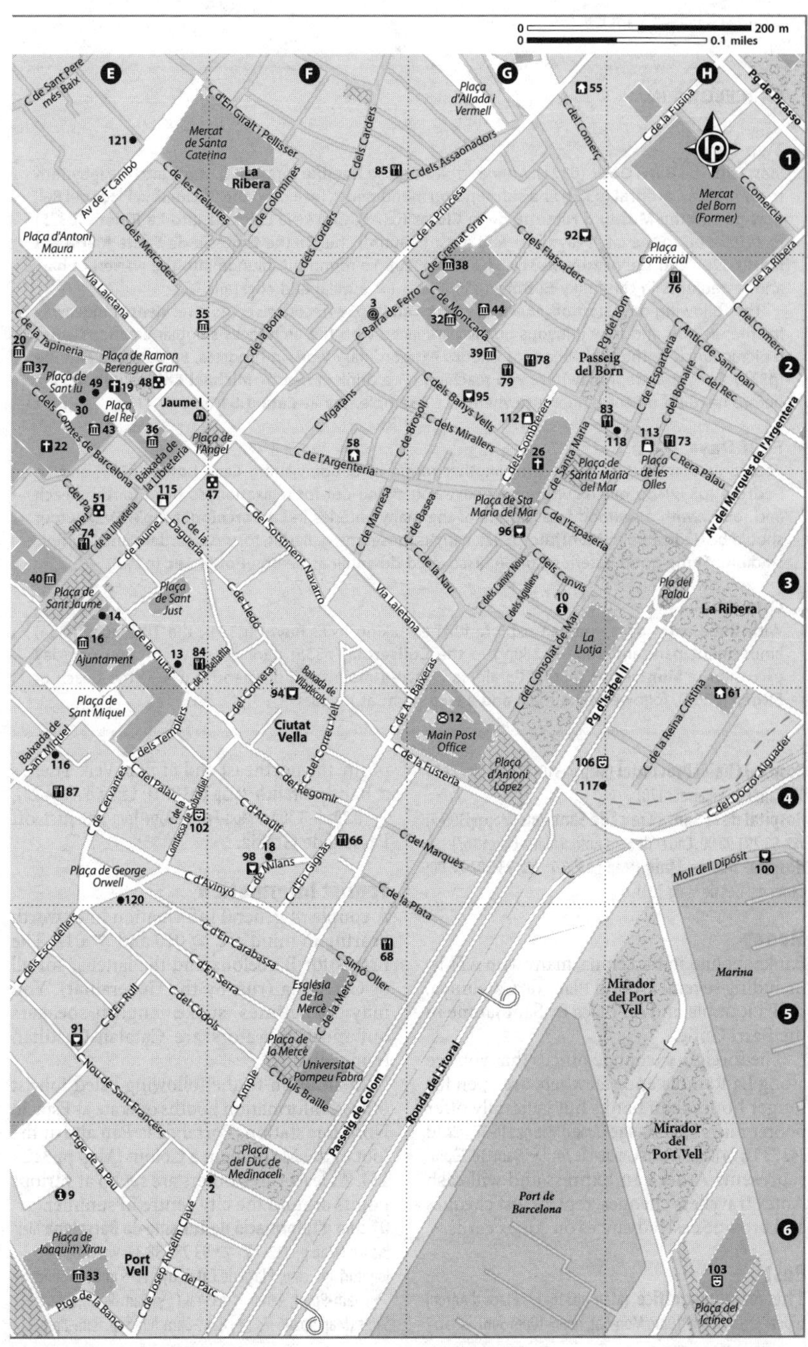

200 m
0.1 miles
Mercat de Santa Caterina
La Ribera
Plaça d'Allada i Vermell
Mercat del Born (Former)
Plaça d'Antoni Maura
Plaça Comercial
Plaça de Ramon Berenguer Gran
Plaça de Sant Iu
Plaça del Rei
Jaume I
Plaça de l'Àngel
Passeig del Born
Plaça de Santa Maria del Mar
Plaça de Sta Maria del Mar
Plaça de les Olles
Plaça de Sant Just
Plaça de Sant Jaume
Ajuntament
Plaça de Sant Miquel
Ciutat Vella
Main Post Office
Plaça d'Antoni López
La Llotja
Pla del Palau
Plaça de George Orwell
Església de la Mercè
Plaça de la Mercè
Universitat Pompeu Fabra
Plaça del Duc de Medinaceli
Plaça de Joaquim Xirau
Port Vell
Port de Barcelona
Mirador del Port Vell
Marina
Plaça del Ictíneo
Passeig de Colom
Ronda del Litoral
Pg d'Isabel II
Av del Marquès de l'Argentera
Via Laietana
Av de F Cambó
Moll dell Dipòsit
BARCELONA

(Continued from page 305)

BARCELONA IN...

Two Days

Start with the **Barri Gòtic** (p321). After a stroll along **La Rambla** (opposite), wade into the labyrinth to admire **La Catedral** (p322) and surrounding monuments, including the fascinating Plaça del Rei, now part of the **Museu d'Història de la Ciutat** (p323). Cross Via Laietana into **La Ribera** (p325) to square up to the city's favourite and most beautiful church, the **Església de Santa Maria del Mar** (p326), and the nearby **Museu Picasso** (p326). To round off, plunge into the warren of bars and restaurants in the funky **El Born** (p350) area for a meal and cocktails.

The following day, start off at Gaudí's **Park Güell** (p334), conceived as a residential hideaway for the well-off and now a joyous public park laced with the architect's singular creations. After a picnic lunch in the park, head for Gaudí's extraordinary work in progress, **La Sagrada Família** (p330). Such grandeur may have you reaching for a drink in nearby **Michael Collins Pub** (p354), before heading off for dinner elsewhere in L'Eixample, say at **Cata 1.81** (p351).

Four Days

You could start the third day with another round of Gaudí, visiting **Casa Batlló** (p331) and **La Pedrera** (p332). So much culture may have you crying out for relaxation, so head for the beach and follow with a seafood feast at one of the many eateries in **La Barceloneta** (p329). Day four should be dedicated to **Montjuïc** (p337), with its museums, galleries, fortress, gardens and Olympic stadium. Some good eateries can be discovered downhill at nearby **Poble Sec** (p352).

One Week

With three extra days you can explore further, taking in **El Raval** (p324), the **Tibidabo** (p334) amusement park and some walking in the **Collserola** (p335) parklands. A tempting one-day excursion is **Montserrat** (p367), Catalonia's 'sacred mountain', or spend a day at the beach at **Sitges** (p364), followed by a meal and a wild night at its bars.

Hospital Clínic i Provincial (Map pp310-11; ☎ 93 227 54 00; Carrer de Villarroel 170)
Hospital de la Santa Creu i de Sant Pau (Map pp306-7; ☎ 93 291 90 00; Carrer de Sant Antoni Maria Claret 167)
Hospital Dos de Maig (Map pp306-7; ☎ 93 507 27 00; Carrer del Dos de Maig 301)

Money

Banks abound in Barcelona, many with ATMs, including several around Plaça de Catalunya, on La Rambla and on Plaça de Sant Jaume in the Barri Gòtic.

The foreign-exchange offices that you see along La Rambla and elsewhere are open for longer hours than banks but generally offer poorer rates. **Interchange** (Amex; Map pp316-17; ☎ 93 342 73 11; La Rambla dels Caputxins 74; 🕓 9am-10.30pm) represents American Express and will cash Amex travellers cheques, replace lost cheques and provide cash advances on Amex cards.

Post

The **main post office** (Map pp316-17; Plaça d'Antoni López; 🕓 8.30am-10pm Mon-Sat, noon-10pm Sun) is opposite the northeast end of Port Vell. There's a handy **branch** (Map pp310-11; Carrer d'Aragó 282; 🕓 8.30am-8.30pm Mon-Fri, 9.30am-1pm Sat) just off Passeig de Gràcia.

Tourist Information

A couple of general information lines worth bearing in mind are ☎ 010 and ☎ 012. The first is for Barcelona and the latter is for all of Catalonia (run by the Generalitat). You may sometimes strike English-speakers but most operators are Catalan-Castilian bilingual only.

In addition to the following listed tourist offices, information booths operate at Estació Nord bus station, Portal de la Pau and at the foot of the Monument a Colom (Map pp312–13). At least three others are set up at various points around the city centre in summer.

Oficina d'Informació de Turisme de Barcelona Main Branch (Map pp312-13; ☎ 93 285 38 32; www.barcelonaturisme.com; Plaça de Catalunya 17-S underground; 🕓 9am-9pm); Aeroport del Prat (🕓 9am-9pm); Estació Sants (Map pp306-7; 🕓 8am-8pm Jun-Sep, 8am-8pm

Mon-Fri, 8am-2pm Sat, Sun & holidays Oct-May); Town Hall (Map pp316-17; Carrer de la Ciutat 2; 9am-8pm Mon-Fri, 10am-8pm Sat, 10am-2pm Sun & holidays) The main Barcelona tourist information office concentrates on city information and can help book accommodation. The branch in the airport's EU arrivals hall has information on all of Catalonia. A smaller office at the international arrivals hall opens the same hours. The train-station branch has limited city information. There's also a branch in the *ajuntament* (town hall).

Palau de la Virreina Arts Information Office (Map pp316-17; 93 301 77 75; La Rambla de Sant Josep 99; 10am-8pm) A useful office for events information and tickets.

Regional tourist office (Map pp310-11; 93 238 80 91; www.gencat.net/probert; Passeig de Gràcia 107; 10am-7pm Mon-Sat, 10am-2.30pm Sun) Housed in the Palau Robert, it has a host of material on Catalonia.

Travel Agencies

Halcón Viatges (Map pp310-11; 807 22 72 22; www.halconviajes.com in Spanish; Carrer de Pau Claris 108) Reliable chain of travel agents that sometimes has good deals. This is one of many branches around town.

Orixà (Map pp310-11; 93 487 00 22; www.orixa.com; Carrer d'Aragó 227) A good local independent travellers' agent.

SIGHTS

Barcelona could be divided up into thematic chunks. In Ciutat Vella (especially the Barri Gòtic and La Ribera) are clustered the bulk of the city's ancient and medieval splendours. Along with El Raval, on the other side of La Rambla, and Port Vell, where old Barcelona meets the sea, this is the core of the city's life, by day and by night.

L'Eixample is where the Modernistas went to town. Here the attractions are more spread out. Passeig de Gràcia is a concentrated showcase for some of the most outlandish of their work, but La Sagrada Família, Gaudí's masterpiece, and other outstanding buildings are scattered about.

The beaches and working-class district of La Barceloneta (which is riddled with seafood restaurants) form a separate summery side of the city, just as Montjuïc, with its gardens, museums, art galleries and Olympic Games sites, forms a microcosm on its own.

Gaudí's Park Güell is just beyond the area of Gràcia, whose narrow lanes and interlocking squares set the scene for much lively nightlife.

Further sights, ranging from FC Barcelona's Camp Nou football stadium to the peaceful haven of the Museu-Monestir de Pedralbes, glitter like distant stars away from the centre.

La Rambla

Head to Spain's most famous street for that first taste of Barcelona's vibrant atmosphere. Flanked by narrow traffic lanes, La Rambla (Map pp316–17) is a broad pedestrian boulevard, lined with cafes and restaurants, and crowded deep into the night with a cross-section of Barcelona's permanent and transient populace. It has to be said that the average *barcelonin* tends to stay away from La Rambla – under assault by tourists and the late-night party crowd, it has long ceased to be locals' favourite boulevard for a Sunday stroll. That doesn't take anything away from its liveliness, however. A visit to Barcelona wouldn't be right without at least one wander along La Rambla.

La Rambla gets its name from a seasonal stream (*raml* in Arabic) that once ran here. It was outside the city walls until the 14th century, and was built up with monastic buildings and palaces in the 16th to 18th centuries. Unofficially it's divided into five sections with their own names.

WARNING! AN EYE ON YOUR VALUABLES

Every year aggrieved readers write in with tales of woe from Barcelona. Petty crime and theft, with tourists as the prey of choice, is a problem, so you need to take a few common-sense precautions to avoid joining this regrettable list. Nine times out of 10 it is easy enough to avoid.

Thieves and pickpockets operate on airport trains and the metro, especially around stops popular with tourists (such as La Sagrada Família). The Old City (Ciutat Vella) is the pickpockets' and bag-snatchers' prime hunting ground. Take special care on and around La Rambla. Prostitutes working the lower (waterfront) end often do a double trade in wallet snatching. Also, stay well clear of the ball-and-three-cups *(trileros)* brigades on La Rambla. This is always a set-up and you will lose your money (and maybe have your pockets emptied as you watch the game).

From Plaça de Catalunya, La Rambla de Canaletes is named after an inconspicuous fount, whose drinking water (despite claims that anyone who drinks it will return to Barcelona) nowadays leaves much to be desired. Delirious football fans gather here to celebrate whenever the main home side, FC Barcelona, wins a cup or the league premiership. A block east along Carrer de la Canuda is Plaça de la Vila de Madrid, with a sunken garden where **Roman tombs** (Map pp316–17) lie exposed.

The second stretch, La Rambla dels Estudis, from below Carrer de la Canuda to Carrer de la Portaferrissa, is popularly known as La Rambla dels Ocells (Birds) because of its twittering bird market. From Carrer de la Portaferrissa to Plaça de la Boqueria, what is officially called La Rambla de Sant Josep (named after a now nonexistent monastery) is lined with flower stalls, which give it the alternative name Rambla de les Flors.

The **Palau de la Virreina** (La Rambla de Sant Josep 99; Ⓜ Liceu) is a grand 18th-century rococo mansion housing a municipal arts-entertainment information and ticket office. Next is the **Mercat de la Boqueria**, one of the best-stocked and most colourful produce markets in Europe. Plaça de la Boqueria, where four side streets meet just north of Liceu metro station, is your chance to walk all over a Miró – the colourful **Mosaïc de Miró** in the pavement, with one tile signed by the artist.

Barcelona takes pride in being a pleasure centre and in the **Museu de l'Eròtica** (Map pp316-17; ☎ 93 318 98 65; www.erotica-museum.com; La Rambla de Sant Josep 96; adult/senior & student €7.50/6.50; ⏲ 10am-midnight Jun-Sep, 11am-9pm Oct-May; Ⓜ Liceu) you can observe just how people have been enjoying themselves since ancient times – lots of Kama Sutra and 1920s porn flicks.

La Rambla dels Caputxins (named after yet another defunct monastery and also known as Rambla del Centre) runs from Plaça de la Boqueria to Carrer dels Escudellers. The west side is flanked by the Gran Teatre del Liceu (opposite).

Further south, on the east side of Rambla dels Caputxins, is the entrance to the palm-shaded Plaça Reial. Below this point La Rambla gets seedier, with a few strip clubs and peep shows. The final stretch, La Rambla

DISCOUNTS & OPENING TIMES

Students generally pay a little over half adult admission prices, as do children aged under 12 years and senior citizens (aged 65 and over) with appropriate ID. Several sights have free-entry days, often just once a month. For example, the Museu Picasso (p326) is free on the first Sunday of the month and the Museu Marítim (opposite) on the first Saturday.

Possession of a Bus Turístic ticket (see p343) entitles you to discounts to some museums.

Articket (www.articketbcn.org) gives you admission to seven important art galleries for €20 and is valid for six months. The galleries are the Museu Picasso, Museu Nacional d'Art de Catalunya (MNAC), the Museu d'Art Contemporani de Barcelona (Macba), the Fundació Antoni Tàpies, the Centre de Cultura Contemporània de Barcelona (CCCB), the Fundació Joan Miró and La Pedrera. You can pick up the ticket through **Tel-Entrada** (☎ 902 10 12 12; www.telentrada.com) and at the tourist offices on Plaça de Catalunya, Plaça de Sant Jaume and Sants train station.

ArqueoTicket is for those with a special interest in archaeology and ancient history. The ticket (€17) gets you entry to the Museu Marítim, Museu d'Història de la Ciutat, Museu d'Arqueologia de Catalunya, Museu Egipci and Museu Barbier-Mueller d'Art Precolombí. You can get it at participating museums and tourist offices.

If you want to get around Barcelona fast and visit multiple museums in the blink of an eye, the **Barcelona Card** (www.barcelonacard.com) might come in handy. It costs €24/29/33/36 for two/three/four/five days (a little less for children aged four to 12). You get free transport (and 20% off the A1 Aerobús) and discounted admission prices (up to 30% off) or free entry to many museums and other sights, as well as minor discounts on purchases at a small number of shops, restaurants and bars.

The Ruta del Modernisme pack (see the boxed text, p329) is well worth looking into.

Museum and art-gallery opening hours vary considerably, but as a rule of thumb you should be OK between 10am and 6pm, Tuesday to Saturday, in most places (some shut for lunch from around 2pm to 4pm). Many museums and galleries close all day Monday and from 2pm Sunday.

de Santa Mònica, widens out to approach the **Monument a Colom** overlooking Port Vell. La Rambla here is named after the Convent de Santa Mònica that once stood on the western flank of the street and has since been converted into an art gallery and cultural centre, the **Centre d'Art Santa Mònica** (Map pp316-17; ☎ 93 316 28 10; La Rambla de Santa Mònica 7; admission free; ⌚ 11am-8pm Tue-Sat, 11am-3pm Sun & holidays).

On the east side lurks the **Museu de Cera** (Map pp316-17; ☎ 93 317 26 49; www.museocerabcn.com; Passatge de la Banca 7; adult/under 5yr/senior & 5-11yr €7.50/free/4.50; ⌚ 10am-10pm daily Jun-Sep, 10am-1.30pm & 4-7.30pm Mon-Fri, 11am-2pm & 4.30-8.30pm Sat, Sun & holidays; Ⓜ Drassanes), a wax museum with a hall of horror and everyone from Lady Di to General Franco.

GRAN TEATRE DEL LICEU

Barcelona's grand **opera house** (Map pp316-17; ☎ 93 485 99 00; www.liceubarcelona.com; La Rambla dels Caputxins 51-59; admission with/without guide €8.50/4; ⌚ guided tours 10am, unguided visits 11.30am, noon, 12.30pm & 1pm; Ⓜ Liceu) was built in 1847, largely destroyed by fire in 1994 and reopened better than ever in 1999.

The Liceu launched such Catalan stars as Josep (aka José) Carreras and Montserrat Caballé, and can seat up to 2300. On the guided visit you are taken to the grand foyer, and then up the marble staircase to the glittering, neobaroque **Saló dels Miralls** (Hall of Mirrors). You are then led up to the 4th floor to admire the theatre in all its splendour from the high stalls. You finish off with a modest collection of Modernista art, El Cercle del Liceu.

MUSEU MARÍTIM

The once mighty Reials Drassanes (Royal Shipyards) are now home to the **Museu Marítim** (Map pp312-13; ☎ 93 342 99 20; www.museumaritimbarcelona.org; Avinguda de les Drassanes; adult/under 7yr/senior & student €6.50/free/3.25, admission free 3-8pm 1st Sat of month; ⌚ 10am-8pm; Ⓜ Drassanes; ♿), a rare work of civil Gothic architecture that was once the launch pad for medieval fleets. The museum, together with its setting, forms a fascinating tribute to the seafaring that shaped much of Barcelona's history. And you can take a load off afterwards in the pleasant restaurant-cafe.

The shipyards, first built in the 13th century, gained their present form (a series of long bays divided by stone arches) a century later. Extensions in the 17th century made them big enough to accommodate the building of 30 galleons. In their shipbuilding days (up to the 18th century) the sea came right up to them.

Inside is an impressive array of boats, models, maps, paintings and more, with areas devoted to ships' figureheads, Columbus and Magellan, and 16th-century galleons (the full-scale replica of Don Juan of Austria's royal galleon from the Battle of Lepanto is the highlight).

WHAT'S FREE?

- **Park Güell** (p334) – Gaudí's weird and wonderful landscaped park.
- **CaixaForum** (p339) – a grand gallery of modern art with constantly changing exhibitions.
- **Església de Santa Maria del Mar** (p326) – Barcelona's best example of Catalan Gothic.
- **Estadi Olímpic** (p339) – site of the 1992 Olympics.
- **Temple Romà d'Augustí** (p323) – the soaring columns left over from a great Roman temple.

MONUMENT A COLOM

The bottom end of La Rambla, and the harbour beyond, lie under the supervision of this late-19th-century **monument** (Map pp312-13; ☎ 93 302 52 24; Plaça del Portal de la Pau; lift adult/under 4yr/senior & 4-12yr €2.50/free/1.50; ⌚ 9am-8.30pm Jun-Sep, 10am-6.30pm Oct-May; Ⓜ Drassanes; ♿) to the glory of Christopher Columbus (who some Catalan historians insist came from Barcelona rather than Genoa in Italy). Take the lift to the top for spectacular views over the city.

Barri Gòtic

Barcelona's 'Gothic Quarter', east of La Rambla, is a medieval warren of narrow, winding streets, quaint *plaças* (plazas), and grand mansions and monuments from the city's golden age. Many of its great buildings date from the 15th century or earlier. The district is liberally seasoned with restaurants, cafes and bars, so sightseeing relief is always close to hand!

The Barri Gòtic stretches from La Rambla in the southwest to Via Laietana in the northeast; and from Plaça de Catalunya in the northwest to Passeig de Colom in the southeast. Carrer de Ferran and Carrer de Jaume I, cutting across the middle, form a halfway line: these streets and those to their northwest tend to be peppered with chic little shops, while those to their southeast become marginally seedier (but no less lively).

PLAÇA DE SANT JAUME

It's hard to imagine that on this very spot, a couple of thousand years ago, folk in togas would discuss the day's events and Roman politics. For hereabout lay the Roman-era Forum and the square as you see it today has again been Barcelona's political hub since at least the 15th century. Facing each other across it are the Palau de la Generalitat (the seat of Catalonia's government) on the north side, and the *ajuntament* on the south side. Both have fine Gothic interiors.

The **Palau de la Generalitat** (Map pp316-17; free guided visit 10am-1pm 2nd & 4th Sun of month plus 23 Apr, 11 Sep & 24 Sep; M Liceu or Jaume I), founded in the early 15th century, is open only on limited occasions. The most impressive of the ceremonial halls is the Saló de Sant Jordi, named after the region's patron saint, St George. At any time, however, you can admire the original Gothic main entrance on Carrer del Bisbe.

Outside, the only feature of the **ajuntament** (Map pp316-17; ☎ 010; admission free; 10am-1pm Sun; M Liceu or Jaume I) that's now worthy of note is the disused Gothic entrance on Carrer de la Ciutat. Inside you can visit, above all, the **Saló de Cent**, a fine arched hall created in the 14th century (but since remodelled) for the medieval city council, the Consell de Cent. Guided visits start every 30 minutes, and English and French speakers are catered for.

CATEDRAL & AROUND

You can reach Barcelona's **catedral** (Map pp316-17; ☎ 93 342 82 60; Plaça de la Seu; admission free, special visit €5; 8am-12.45pm & 5.15-8pm, special visit 1-5pm Mon-Sat, 2-5pm Sun & holidays; M Jaume I), one of its most magnificent Gothic structures, by following Carrer del Bisbe northwest from Plaça de Sant Jaume. The narrow old streets around the cathedral are traffic-free and dotted with occasionally very talented buskers.

The best view of the cathedral is from Plaça de la Seu beneath its main **northwest facade**. Unlike most of the building, which dates from between 1298 and 1460, this facade was not created until the 1870s! They say it is based on a 1408 design and it is odd in that it reflects northern-European Gothic styles rather than the sparer, Catalan version.

The interior of the cathedral is a broad, soaring space. It is divided into a central nave and two aisles by lines of elegant, thin pillars.

In the first chapel, on the right from the northwest entrance, the main Crucifixion figure above the altar is **Sant Crist de Lepant**, which was carried on the prow of the Spanish flagship at the Battle of Lepanto. It is said the figure acquired its odd stance by dodging an incoming cannonball. Further along this same wall, past the southwest transept, are the wooden **coffins** of Count Ramon Berenguer I and his wife Almodis, cofounders of the 11th-century Romanesque predecessor to the present cathedral.

Smack bang in the middle of the central nave is the late-14th-century, exquisitely sculpted timber **coro** (choir stall; admission €2.20). The coats of arms belong to members of the Barcelona chapter of the Order of the Golden Fleece.

The **crypt** beneath the main altar contains the remarkable alabaster tomb of Santa Eulàlia, one of Barcelona's patron saints and a good Christian lass of the 4th century, who suffered terrible tortures and death at the hands of the pagan Romans (or so the story goes). Some of these are depicted on the tomb.

For a bird's-eye (mind the poop) view of medieval Barcelona, visit the cathedral's **roof and tower** (admission €2.20) by a lift from the Capella de les Animes del Purgatori, near the northeast transept.

From the southwest transept, exit to the lovely **claustre** (cloister), with its trees, fountains and geese (there have been geese here for centuries). One of the cloister chapels commemorates 930 priests, monks and nuns martyred in the civil war.

Along the northern flank of the cloister you can enter the **Sala Capitular** (chapter house; admission €2; 10am-12.15pm & 5.15-7pm Mon-Sat, 10am-12.45pm & 5.15-7pm Sun). Although bathed in the rich reds of the carpet, and cosseted by fine-timber seating, the few artworks gathered here are of minor interest. Among them is a *Pietat* by Bartolomeo Bermejo.

You can visit the cathedral in one of two ways. In the morning or the afternoon, entrance is free and you can visit any combination of the choir stalls, chapter house and roof you choose. If you want to visit all three, it costs less (and is less crowded) to enter for the so-called 'special visit'.

At the northern end of Carrer del Bisbe, poke your head into the courtyards of the 16th-century **Casa de l'Ardiaca** (Archdeacon's House; Map pp316–17) and the 13th-century **Palau del Bispat** (Bishop's Palace; Map pp316–17). On the outside of both buildings, at the very end of Carrer del Bisbe, the foundations of the rounded towers that flanked a Roman gate are visible. The lower part of the Casa de l'Ardiaca's northwest wall was part of the **Roman walls** (9am-9pm Mon-Fri, 9am-2pm Sat). Inside the building itself you can see parts of the wall.

The walls ran along present-day Plaça de la Seu into what subsequently became the **Casa de la Pia Almoina** (Map pp316–17), a medieval almshouse that now contains the **Museu Diocesà** (Diocesan Museum; Map pp316-17; 93 315 22 13; www.arqbcn.org; Avinguda de la Catedral 4; adult/under 7yr/senior & student €6/free/3; 10am-2pm & 5-8pm Tue-Sat, 11am-2pm Sun; M Jaume I), where you can see a sparse collection of medieval religious art, usually supplemented by a temporary exposition or two.

Just beyond the southeast end of the cathedral stand four mighty columns of the **Temple Romà d'Augustí** (Roman Temple of Augustus; Map pp316-17; Carrer de Paradis 10; admission free; 10am-2pm Mon-Sat; M Jaume I), built in the first century AD.

PLAÇA DEL REI

A stone's throw east of the cathedral, Plaça del Rei is the courtyard of the former Palau Reial Major, the palace of the Counts of Barcelona and monarchs of Aragón.

Most of the tall, centuries-old buildings surrounding Plaça del Rei are now open to visitors as the **Museu d'Història de la Ciutat** (City History Museum; Map pp316-17; 93 256 21 00; www.museuhistoria.bcn.cat; Carrer del Veguer; adult/under 7yr/senior & student incl Museu-Monestir de Pedralbes & Park Güell Centre de Acollida €6/free/4, admission free from 4pm 1st Sat of month; 10am-2pm & 4-7pm Tue-Sat, 10am-3pm Sun Oct-Mar, 10am-8pm Tue-Sat, 10am-3pm Sun Apr-Sep; M Jaume I). This is one of Barcelona's most fascinating sights, combining large sections of the former palace with a subterranean walk through Roman and Visigothic Barcelona. Set aside at least an hour for the visit.

The entrance to the museum is through 16th-century **Casa Padellàs** (Map pp316–17), just south of Plaça del Rei. Casa Padellàs, with its courtyard typical of Barcelona's late-Gothic and baroque mansions, was moved here in the 1930s because of roadworks. The external courtyard staircase now leads to a restored Roman tower. Below ground awaits a remarkable walk through excavated Roman and Visigothic **ruins** – complete with sections of a Roman street, baths, shops, along with remains of a Visigothic basilica. You emerge inside the former palace on the north side of the Plaça del Rei. To your right is the Saló del Tinell and to the left ahead of you is the Capella Reial de Santa Àgata.

The **Saló del Tinell** (Map pp316–17) was the royal palace's throne hall, a masterpiece of strong, unfussy Catalan Gothic, built in the mid-14th century with wide, rounded arches holding up a wooden roof. The **Capella Reial de Santa Àgata**, whose spindly bell tower rises from the northeast side of Plaça del Rei, was the palace's chapel and dates from the same period. Rising above the Saló del Tinell is the multi-tiered **Mirador del Rei Martí** (Lookout Tower of King Martin), built in 1555. It is closed to the public.

The southwest side of Plaça del Rei is taken up by the **Palau del Lloctinent** (Viceroy's Palace; Map pp316-17; Carrer dels Comtes de Barcelona; admission free; 10am-7pm; M Jaume I), built in the 1550s as the residence of the Spanish viceroy of Catalonia and now home to part of the Arxiu de la Corona d'Aragón. This unique archive houses documents detailing the history of the Crown of Aragón and Catalonia, starting in the 12th century. Some of them often appear in temporary exhibitions held in the palace.

MUSEU FREDERIC MARÈS

A short distance north is the **Museu Frederic Marès** (Map pp316-17; 93 256 35 00; www.museumares.bcn.es; Plaça de Sant Lu 5-6; adult/under 16yr/senior & student €4.20/free/2.40, admission free Wed afternoon & 1st Sun of month; 10am-7pm Tue-Sat, 10am-3pm Sun & holidays; M Jaume I), in another part of the Palau Reial Major. Marès was a rich 20th-century Catalan sculptor and collector. He specialised in medieval Spanish sculpture, huge quantities of which are displayed on the ground and 1st floors. The top two floors, known as the Museu Sentimental, hold a mind-boggling array of other Marès knick-knacks, from toy soldiers and cribs to scissors and tarot cards, along with some of his own sculptures. Take a load off in the pleasant courtyard **cafe** (Apr-Oct).

ROMAN WALLS

From Plaça del Rei it's worth a detour to see the two best surviving stretches of Barcelona's Roman walls. One section (Map pp316–17) is on the southwest side of Plaça de Ramon Berenguer el Gran, with the Capella Reial de Santa Àgata on top. The other (Map pp316–17) is further south, by the north end of Carrer del Sotstinent Navarro. They date from the 3rd and 4th centuries, when the Romans rebuilt their walls after the first attacks by Germanic tribes from the north.

PLAÇA DE SANT JOSEP ORIOL & AROUND

This small plaza is the prettiest in the Barri Gòtic. Its bars and cafes attract buskers and artists, and make it a lively place to hang out for a while. It's surrounded by quaint streets, many of them dotted with appealing cafes, timeless restaurants and cavernous old shops. The plaza is dominated by the Gothic **Església de Santa Maria del Pi** (Map pp316-17; 8.30am-1pm & 4.30-9pm Mon-Sat, 9am-2pm & 5-9pm Sun & holidays; M Liceu), completed in the 16th century. The beautiful rose window above its entrance on Plaça del Pi is claimed to be the world's biggest. The inside of the church was gutted by anarchists' fire in 1936 and most of the stained glass is modern.

SINAGOGA MAJOR

The area between Carrer dels Banys Nous, to the east of the church, and Plaça de Sant Jaume is known as the Call, and was Barcelona's **Jewish quarter** – and centre of learning – from at least the 11th century until anti-Semitism saw the Jews expelled from it in 1424. Here the sparse remains of what is purported to be the medieval **Sinagoga Major** (Main Synagogue; Map pp316-17; ☎ 93 317 07 90; www.calldebarcelona.org; Carrer de Marlet 5; admission €2 donation; 11am-6pm Mon-Sat, 11am-3pm Sun; M Liceu) have been revealed and returned to occasional use as a functioning temple. Remnants of medieval and Roman-era walls remain, suggesting (given their orientation towards Jerusalem) that there may have been a Jewish place of worship here in Roman times. Historians are not agreed that this was in fact the site of the synagogue, so the claim is to be taken with a pinch of salt. Nearby at the **Centre d'Interpretació del Call** (Map pp316-17; ☎ 93 256 21 22; www.museuhistoria.bcn.cat; Placeta de Manuel Ribé s/n; admission free; 10am-2pm Wed-Fri, 11am-6pm Sat, 11am-3pm Sun & holidays; M Jaume I), you can learn something of the history of the one-time Jewish community in Barcelona through some explanatory panels. A small cabinet of Jewish artefacts and ceramic shards are all that is on show.

TOP FIVE MODERNISTA GEMS

- **La Sagrada Família** (p330)
- **Palau de la Música Catalana** (opposite)
- **La Pedrera** (p332)
- **Casa Batlló** (p331)
- **Park Güell** (p334)

PLAÇA REIAL & AROUND

Just south of Carrer de Ferran, **Plaça Reial** (Map pp316–17) is an elegant shady square surrounded by eateries, nightspots and budget accommodation. Its 19th-century neoclassical architecture (which replaced a centuries-old monastery) looks as if it would be at home in some Parisian quarter (but the palm trees wouldn't). The lampposts next to the central fountain are Gaudí's first known works.

Until 1990 the square and surrounding streets had long been a den of poverty, drug abuse and prostitution. A whiff of its dodgy past remains, in the form of a few down-and-outs and the occasional pickpocket. Today locals and tourists mostly fill the square's bars and restaurants with chatter and laughter, while coppers look on.

El Raval

West of La Rambla, Ciutat Vella spreads to Ronda de Sant Antoni, Ronda de Sant Pau and Avinguda del Parallel, which together trace the line of Barcelona's 14th-century walls. Known as El Raval, the area contains what remains of one of the city's slums, the dwindling but still seedy red-light zone and drug-abusers' haunt of the Barri Xinès, at its south end. It's not nearly as tricky as it once was, but watch your pockets nonetheless.

MUSEU D'ART CONTEMPORANI & AROUND

The vast, white **Museu d'Art Contemporani de Barcelona** (Macba; Map pp312-13; ☎ 93 412 08 10; www.macba.es; Plaça dels Àngels 1; adult/concession €7.50/6, Wed €3.50; 11am-8pm Mon & Wed, 11am-midnight Thu-Fri, 10am-8pm Sat, 10am-3pm Sun & holidays late Jun-late Sep, 11am-7.30pm Mon & Wed-Fri, 10am-8pm Sat, 10am-3pm Sun & holidays; M Universitat) is a temple to contemporary art. Artists frequently on show include

Antoni Tàpies, Miquel Barceló and a host of very now installation artists.

Behind the museum is the **Centre de Cultura Contemporània de Barcelona** (CCCB; Map pp312-13; ☎ 93 412 08 10; www.macba.es; Plaça dels Àngels 1; adult/concession €7.50/6, Wed €3.50; 🕑 11am-8pm Mon & Wed, 11am-midnight Thu-Fri, 10am-8pm Sat, 10am-3pm Sun & holidays late Jun-late Sep, 11am-7.30pm Mon & Wed-Fri, 10am-8pm Sat, 10am-3pm Sun & holidays; Ⓜ Universitat), a complex of auditoriums and exhibition and conference halls created in the early 1990s from an 18th-century hospice. The big courtyard, with a vast glass wall on one side, is spectacular. Exhibitions are held here regularly.

On the south side of the square is the Gothic shell of the 16th-century Convent dels Àngels, now known as the **Capella Macba** (Map pp312-13; Plaça dels Àngels), where part of the Macba's permanent exhibition is shown.

Two blocks southeast of Plaça dels Àngels is an architectural masterpiece from another age. Founded in the early 15th century as the city's main hospital, the **Antic Hospital de la Santa Creu** (Map pp316-17; ☎ 93 270 23 00; Carrer de l'Hospital 56; admission free; 🕑 library 9am-8pm Mon-Fri, 9am-2pm Sat) today houses the Biblioteca de Catalunya (Catalonia's national library). Take a look inside to admire some fine Catalan Gothic construction. The adjacent **Institut d'Estudis Catalans** was, in the 17th century, a house of convalescence. Take a look inside the tile-decorated main cloister if it's open.

La Capella (Map pp316-17; ☎ 93 442 71 71; www.bcn.es/virreinaexposicions; Carrer de l'Hospital 56; 🕑 noon-2pm & 4-8pm Tue-Sat, 11am-2pm Sun & holidays), the former hospital's now rather bare one-time chapel, is used for temporary exhibitions.

PALAU GÜELL

Gaudí's **Palau Güell** (Map pp316-17; ☎ 93 317 39 74; www.palauguell.cat; Carrer Nou de la Rambla 3-5; admission free; 🕑 10am-2.30pm Tue-Sat; Ⓜ Drassanes) is the only major Modernista building in Ciutat Vella. Gaudí built it in the late 1880s for his most constant patron, the industrialist Eusebi Güell. It lacks some of Gaudí's later playfulness but is still a characteristic riot of styles – art nouveau, Gothic, Islamic – and materials. After the civil war it was in police hands and political prisoners were tortured in its basement.

Features to look out for include the carved wooden ceilings and fireplace, the stonework, the use of mirrors, stained glass and wrought iron, and the main hall with its dome reaching right up to the roof. The roof is a weird world of fantastically shaped and polychrome-tiled chimneypots. At the time of writing, only the ground floor and basement could be visited due to ongoing restoration.

ESGLÉSIA DE SANT PAU

The best example of Romanesque architecture in the city is the dainty little cloister of this **church** (Map pp312-13; ☎ 93 441 00 01; Carrer de Sant Pau 101; admission free; 🕑 cloister 10am-2pm & 5-7pm Tue-Fri, 10am-2pm Sat; Ⓜ Parallel). Set in a somewhat dusty garden, the 12th-century church also boasts some Visigothic sculptural detail on the main entrance.

La Ribera

La Ribera is cut off from the Barri Gòtic by noisy Via Laietana, which was driven through the city in 1908. La Ribera, whose name refers to the waterfront that once lay much further inland, was the pumping commercial heart of medieval Barcelona. Its intriguing, narrow streets house major sights and a warren of good bars and restaurants, mainly in the too-cool-for-school El Born area.

PALAU DE LA MÚSICA CATALANA

The **Palau de la Música Catalana** (Palace of Catalan Music; Map pp312-13; ☎ 902 47 54 85; www.palaumusica.org; Carrer de Sant Francesc de Paula 2; adult/child/student incl guided tour €10/free/9; 🕑 50min tours every ½hr 10am-6pm Easter & Aug, 10am-3.30pm Sep-Jul; Ⓜ Urquinaona) is a Modernista high point and World Heritage site. It's not exactly a symphony, more a series of crescendos in tile, brick, sculptured stone and stained glass. Built between 1905 and 1908 by Lluís Domènech i Montaner for the Orfeo Català musical society, it was conceived as a temple for the Catalan Renaixença.

You can see some of its splendours – such as the main facade with its mosaics, floral capitals and sculpture cluster representing Catalan popular music – from the outside and wander into the foyer to admire the lovely tiled pillars and decor of the cafe and ticket office area.

Best of all, however, is the richly colourful auditorium upstairs, with its ceiling of blue-and-gold stained glass and, above a bust of Beethoven, a towering sculpture of Wagner's Valkyrie (Wagner was No 1 on the Renaixença charts). To see this, you need to attend a concert or join a guided tour.

MUSEU PICASSO

Barcelona's most visited **museum** (Map pp316-17; ☎ 93 256 30 00; www.museupicasso.bcn.es; Carrer de Montcada 15-23; adult/senior & under 16yr/student €9/free/3, temporary exhibitions adult €5.80, admission free 1st Sun of month; 10am-8pm Tue-Sun & holidays; M Jaume I) occupies five of the many fine medieval stone mansions (worth wandering into for their courtyards and galleries) on narrow Carrer de Montcada. The collection concentrates on Picasso's formative years and several specific moments in his later life. A word of warning on this – some visitors are disappointed at not seeing more of Picasso's better-known works, such as those from his cubist period. This collection is unique in giving such insight into the early period of his life but those interested primarily in cubism may not be satisfied. There are additional charges for special exhibitions. Allow two hours.

The museum's permanent collection is housed in the first three houses, the **Palau Aguilar**, **Palau del Baró de Castellet** and the **Palau Meca**, all dating back to the 14th century. The 18th-century **Casa Mauri**, built over some medieval remains (even some Roman leftovers have been identified), and the adjacent 14th-century **Palau Finestres** accommodate temporary exhibitions.

A visit starts, naturally enough, at the beginning, with sketches, oils and doodling from Picasso's earliest years in Málaga and La Coruña – most of it done between 1893 and 1895. Some of his self-portraits, and the portraits of his father, which date from 1896, are evidence enough of his precocious talent. The enormous *Ciència i Caritat* (Science and Charity) is proof to anyone that, had he wanted, Picasso would have made a fine mainstream artist. His first consciously thematic adventure, the Blue Period, is well covered. His nocturnal blue-tinted views of *Terrats de Barcelona* (The Rooftops of Barcelona) and *El Foll* (The Madman) are cold and cheerless, and yet somehow spectrally alive.

Among the later works, done in Cannes in 1957, there's a complex technical series *(Las Meninas)*, which are studies on Diego Velázquez's masterpiece of the same name (which hangs in the Prado in Madrid).

MUSEU BARBIER-MUELLER D'ART PRECOLOMBÍ

Occupying Palau Nadal, this **museum** (Map pp316-17; ☎ 93 310 45 16; www.barbier-mueller.ch; Carrer de Montcada 12-14; adult/under 16yr/senior & student €3/free/1.50, admission free 1st Sun of month; 11am-7pm Tue-Fri, 10am-7pm Sat, 10am-3pm Sun & holidays; M Jaume I) holds part of one of the world's most prestigious collections of pre-Colombian art, including gold jewellery, ceramics, statues and textiles. The artefacts from South American 'primitive' cultures come from the collections of the Swiss businessman Josef Mueller (1887–1977) and his son-in-law Jean-Paul Barbier, who directs the Musée Barbier-Mueller in Geneva. The museum is small but the pieces outstanding.

CARRER DE MONTCADA

Several other mansions on this once-wealthy street of Barcelona merchant barons are now commercial art galleries where you're welcome to browse. The 16th-century **Palau dels Cervelló**, for instance, houses the **Galeria Maeght** (Map pp316-17; Carrer de Montcada 25), a branch of the renowned Paris gallery. The baroque courtyard of the originally medieval **Palau de Dalmases** (Map pp316-17; Carrer de Montcada 20) is one of the finest on the strip and home to a rather baroque bar.

ESGLÉSIA DE SANTA MARIA DEL MAR

Carrer de Montcada opens at its southeast end into **Passeig del Born**, a plaza that once rang to the cheers and jeers of medieval jousting tournaments, today replaced at night by animated carousing. At its southwest tip rises Barcelona's finest Gothic church, the **Església de Santa Maria del Mar** (Map pp316-17; ☎ 93 319 05 16; Plaça de Santa Maria del Mar; admission free; 9am-1.30pm & 4.30-8pm; M Jaume I). Built in the 14th century, Santa Maria was lacking in superfluous decoration even before anarchists gutted it in 1909 and 1936. This only serves to highlight its fine proportions, purity of line and sense of space. You may occasionally catch an evening recital of baroque music here.

MERCAT DE SANTA CATERINA

A 19th-century market, built on the site of a 15th-century monastery, was replaced in 2005 with this original, colourful **market** (Map pp316-17; www.mercatsantacaterina.net; Avinguda de Francesc Cambó 16; 8am-2pm Mon, 8am-3.30pm Tue, Wed & Sat, 8am-8.30pm Thu & Fri; M Jaume I) designed by the adventurous Catalan architect Enric Miralles. The outstanding element is the bright, ceramic-covered, wavy roof – a splash of pastel loopiness. Out the back,

THE KING & QUEEN OF MAGIC

When he was 13, Josep Maria Martínez (now 62) was taken to an optician's on Carrer de la Princesa but his attention was captured by a little shop at No 11. With some trepidation, he dared to wander into El Rey de la Màgia (The King of Magic). 'It was a dark and mysterious place. The world of magic then was more secretive then than now and it was hard to get inside,' he remembers. 'I wanted to work in the shop, to help out and learn but he turned me down.'

He was Carles Bucheli (1903–81), better known by his stage name of Carlston, one of Spain's great magicians. Bucheli had taken over the store in 1932 from its founder, Joaquim Partagás (1848–1931), a showman who had taken his magic act all over Latin America before returning to Barcelona (where he was born) in 1878 and opening his magic shop in 1881. Until the 1950s El Rey de la Magia was *the* magic shop in all Spain. In Spain there wasn't a magician of note who did not have a connection with El Rey de la Màgia and its magician owners.

Martínez persisted. 'A great magician doesn't want to reveal his secrets to a little magician and a little magician doesn't want to reveal his secrets to a beginner! But if you really want to learn, you will, and you will find a magician to help!' His dreams eventually came true. He and his partner, Rosa Llop (54), forged a path in theatre but in 1977 began as a professional magic duo. Three years after Bucheli's death, they took over the shop.

It is pouring rain on a cold Saturday evening in May in La Ribera. In a tiny medieval dead-end lane, Carrer de l'Oli, some 40 people of all ages crowd into the minuscule theatre, to be enthralled by Martínez and Llop's show, the Capsa Màgica (Magic Box). The pair opened the theatre in a disused warehouse in 2002 and upstairs created a museum (p328). In the course of their one-hour show, they produce doves out of nowhere, pull rabbits out of hats, make torn-up newspapers whole, chop Ms Llop up in a magic box, levitate. The mystery of the magic continues. One of the audience, Pere, a design student, has come all the way from Solsona (in the central west of Catalonia) to see the show and talk to the artists.

Is there a future for magic? 'The golden age was from 1910 to the 1940s,' says Llop. The arrival of cinema put an end to big magic shows in major theatres but, according to Martínez, 'magic is enjoying a good period. It's coming back and a lot of people are interested in magic. It's still hard to reach a wide audience though.'

'Many young people who come to us have already started learning – in internet!' exclaims Llop. 'It's a good thing,' interjects Martínez. 'They are seeing videos and learning. That curiosity is breathing new life into the world of magic!'

Even after all these years, nothing is quite as easy as it seems. 'There are days when you don't feel like putting on the show,' says Martínez. 'It's work after all. And then, when you're in the dressing room, you start getting nervous…' Nervous?! 'Not beginner's nervousness,' Llop chimes in, 'but because of the responsibility of the show. It doesn't take much for something to go wrong.' Martínez: 'There are always problems. Everything hangs by a fine thread.'

Running the shop, theatre and museum, giving magic classes and promoting their cultural association is a lot of work. 'Given the amount we do, it's hardly profitable,' says Martínez. 'But we didn't want to let this all go,' says Llop. 'We have kept the shop as it was, and have this museum collection.'

Even magic can't escape real-world issues such as the Catalan language question. Says Llop: 'From the beginning we had the pledge to present our shows in Catalan.' Martínez adds: 'When we started professionally, magicians all did their shows in Castilian, which was considered more elegant.' Llop: 'And better still with a faked French accent!'

remnants of the monastery uncovered during excavations are on public show with explanatory panels.

MUSEU DE LA XOCOLATA

In the **Museu de la Xocolata** (Chocolate Museum; Map pp312-13; ☎ 93 268 78 78; http://pastisseria.com; Plaça de Pons i Clerch s/n; adult/under 7yr €3.90/free, admission free 1st Mon of month; 10am-7pm Mon & Wed-Sat, 10am-3pm Sun & holidays; M Jaume I;) you can trace the origins of this fundamental foodstuff and admire (but not chomp into!) somewhat cheesy chocolate models of things like La Sagrada Família.

MUSEU DEL REI DE LA MÀGIA

This **museum** (Map pp316-17; ☎ 93 319 73 93; www.elreydelamagia.com; Carrer de l'Oli 6; admission €3, incl show €8; 6-8pm Thu, incl show 6pm Sat & noon Sun;) is a timeless curio. Run by a magician couple who run a 19th-century magic shop at Carrer de la Princesa 11 (see the boxed text, p327), it is the scene of magic shows and home to a fascinating collection of magicians' paraphernalia dating back more than a century.

Parc de la Ciutadella

East of La Ribera and north of La Barceloneta, the gentle **Parc de la Ciutadella** (Map pp312-13; 8am-6pm Nov-Feb, 8am-8pm Oct & Mar, 8am-9pm Apr-Sep;) makes a fine antidote to the noise and bustle of the city.

After the War of the Spanish Succession, Felipe V built a huge fort (La Ciutadella) to keep watch over Barcelona. Only in 1869 did the government allow its demolition, after which the site was turned into a park and used to host the Universal Exhibition of 1888.

The monumental **Cascada** near the Passeig de les Pujades entrance was created between 1875 and 1881 by Josep Fontsère, with the help of a young Antoni Gaudí. It's a dramatic combination of classical statuary, rugged rocks, greenery and thundering water.

Southeast, in the fort's former arsenal, is the regional **Parlament de Catalunya** (Map pp312-13; ☎ 93 304 66 45; www.parlament.cat; free guided visit in Catalan 4-6pm 1st Fri of month). Head up the sweeping Escala d'Honor (Stairway of Honour) and through several solemn halls to the Saló de Sessions, the semicircular auditorium where parliament sits. It also opens on the first Friday of the month and on 11 and 12 September.

The south end of the park is occupied by the **Zoo de Barcelona** (Map pp312-13; ☎ 93 225 67 80; www.zoobarcelona.com; Passeig de Picasso & Carrer de Wellington; adult/under 4yr/senior/4-12yr €15.40/free/8.15/9.30; 10am-7pm Jun-Sep, 10am-6pm mid-Mar–May & Oct, 10am-5pm Nov–mid-Mar; Ⓜ Barceloneta;), which holds about 7500 living thingies, from gorillas to insects.

Along the Passeig de Picasso side of the park are several buildings created for the Universal Exhibition. These include two arboretums, the **Museu de Geologia** (Map pp312–13), for rock- and fossil-lovers; and the **Museu de Zoologia** (Map pp312–13), filled with stuffed animals and the like. The two constitute the **Museu de Ciències Naturals** (☎ 93 319 69 12; www.bcn.es/museuciencies; Passeig de Picasso; admission €3; 10am-2.30pm Tue, Wed & Fri-Sun, 10am-6.30pm Thu). The contents of the Zoology Museum are much less interesting than the building that contains them, the **Castell dels Tres Dragons** (Three Dragons Castle). It is a whimsical effort by Lluís Domènech i Montaner, who added medieval-castle trimmings on a pioneering steel frame for the Universal Exhibition. Designed as a temporary cafe to be knocked down after the exhibition, it has stood the test of time.

Northwest of the park is the imposing Modernista **Arc de Triomf** (Map pp306-7; Passeig de Lluís Companys), with unusual, Islamic-style brickwork.

Port Vell

Barcelona's old port at the bottom of La Rambla, once such an eyesore that it caused public protests, has been transformed since the 1980s into a people-friendly leisure zone.

For a view of the harbour from the water, you can take a **golondrina** (excursion boat; Map pp312-13; ☎ 93 442 31 06; www.lasgolondrinas.com; Moll de les Drassanes; adult/under 4yr/4-10yr/student & senior €10.50/free/4.80/7.70; Ⓜ Drassanes;) from in front of the Monument a Colom. The one-hour round trip takes you to Port Olímpic, the Fòrum and back again. The number of departures depends largely on season and demand. As a rule the trips are only done between March and November. Otherwise you can opt for a 35-minute excursion (adult/child under four years/child aged four to 10 years €5/free/2.50) to the breakwater and back. Neither trip is particularly exciting, but pleasant enough.

Northeast from the quay stretches the promenade **Moll de la Fusta**. Usually the **Pailebot de Santa Eulàlia** (Map pp312-13; Moll de la Fusta; adult/child €2.40/1.20, admission free with Museu Marítim ticket; noon-7.30pm Tue-Fri, 10am-7pm Sat & Sun & holidays May-Oct, noon-5.30pm Tue-Fri, 10am-5.30pm Sat & Sun &

TOP FIVE FOR ART-LOVERS

- **Museu Nacional d'Art de Catalunya** (MNAC; p337)
- **Museu Picasso** (p326)
- **Fundació Joan Miró** (p338)
- **Museu d'Art Contemporani de Barcelona** (Macba; p324)
- **Fundació Antoni Tàpies** (p332)

MODERNISME UNPACKED

Aficionados of Barcelona's Modernista heritage should consider the Ruta del Modernisme pack (www.rutadelmodernisme.com). For €12 you receive a guide to 115 Modernista buildings great and small, a map and discounts of up to 50% on the main Modernista sights in Barcelona, as well as some in other municipalities around Catalonia. The discounts are valid for a year. For €18 you get another guide and map, *Sortim,* which leads you to bars and restaurants located in Modernista buildings around the city. The proceeds of these packs go to the maintenance and refurbishment of Modernista buildings. The Ruta del Modernisme guide (in various languages) is available in bookstores. You can then take it to one of three Centres del Modernisme to obtain the discount cards, or you can buy the lot at those centres. They are located at the main tourist office at Plaça de Catalunya 17 (Map pp312–13), the Hospital de la Santa Creu i Sant Pau (Map pp306–7) and the Pavellons Güell in Pedralbes (Map pp306–7).

holidays Nov-Apr; Ⓜ Drassanes), a fully functioning 1918 schooner restored by the Museu Marítim, is moored here for visits, although sometimes it's off on the high seas. Admission is free with a Museu Marítim ticket.

At the centre of the redeveloped harbour is the **Moll d'Espanya**, a former wharf linked to Moll de la Fusta by a wave-shaped footbridge, **Rambla de Mar** (Map pp312–13), which rotates to let boats enter the marina behind it. At the end of Moll d'Espanya is the glossy Maremàgnum shopping and eating complex, but the major attraction is **L'Aquàrium** (Map pp312-13; ☎ 93 221 74 74; www.aquariumbcn.com; Moll d'Espanya; adult/under 4yr/4-12yr/over 60yr €16/free/11/12.50; ⌚ 9.30am-11pm Jul & Aug, 9.30am-9.30pm Jun & Sep, 9.30am-9pm Mon-Fri & 9.30am-9.30pm Sat & Sun Oct-May; Ⓜ Drassanes; 🚸), with its 80m-long shark tunnel. Short of diving among them (which can actually be arranged here too), this is as close as you can get to a set of shark teeth without being bitten. Beyond L'Aquàrium is the big-screen **Imax cinema**.

La Barceloneta & the Coast

It used to be said that Barcelona had 'turned its back on the sea', but the ambitious 1992 Olympics-inspired redevelopment program returned a long stretch of coast northeast of Port Vell to life. A similar process has largely turned around the city's once abandoned extreme northeast coastline, creating a high-rise residential district with parks, swimming areas and conference centre.

La Barceloneta, laid out in the 18th century and subsequently heavily overdeveloped, was long a factory-workers' and fishermen's quarter. It still retains a gritty flavour although the factories are a distant memory and there are unmistakable signs of gentrification. Some of the fishing families remain and the area is laced with seafood restaurants.

In the Palau de Mar building (former warehouses) facing the harbour is the **Museu d'Història de Catalunya** (Map pp312-13; ☎ 93 225 47 00; www.mhcat.net; Plaça de Pau Vila 3; adult/senior & under 7yr/student €4/free/3, admission free 1st Sun of month; ⌚ 10am-7pm Tue & Thu-Sat, 10am-8pm Wed, 10am-2.30pm Sun & holidays; Ⓜ Barceloneta). The place incorporates lots of audiovisuals and interactive information points in a series of colourful displays, recounting Catalonia's tumultuous past from prehistory to the 1980s. All sorts of scenes are recreated, from a prehistoric Pyrenean cave dwelling, through to a Roman house and a Spanish Civil War air-raid shelter. It's a little cheesy, and short on real artefacts, but engaging enough.

Barcelona's small fishing fleet ties up along the Moll del Rellotge, south of the museum. On La Barceloneta's seaward side are the first of Barcelona's **beaches**, which are popular on summer weekends. The pleasant **Passeig Marítim** (Map pp306–7), a 1.25km promenade from La Barceloneta to Port Olímpic, is a haunt for strollers and rollers, so bring your Rollerblades.

The **Transbordador Aeri** (Cable Car; Map pp312-13; Passeig Escullera; one way/return €9/12.50; ⌚ 11am-8pm mid-Jun–mid-Sep, 10.45am-7pm daily Mar–mid-Jun & mid-Sep–late Oct, 10.30am-5.45pm late Oct-Feb; Ⓜ Barceloneta or 🚌 17, 39, 64; 🚸), strung across the harbour to Montjuïc, provides a seagull's view of the city. Get tickets at Miramar (Map pp312–13) in Montjuïc and the **Torre de Sant Sebastiá** (Map pp312–13) in La Barceloneta.

Port Olímpic (Map pp306-7; Ⓜ Ciutadella-Vila Olímpica), a busy marina built for the Olympic sailing events, is surrounded by bars and restaurants. An eye-catcher on the approach from La Barceloneta is Frank Gehry's giant copper *Peix* (Fish; Map pp306–7) sculpture.

The area behind Port Olímpic, dominated by twin-tower blocks (the luxury Hotel Arts Barcelona and Torre Mapfre office block), is the former Vila Olímpica living quarters for the Olympic competitors, which has since been sold off as apartments.

More and better beaches stretch northeast along the coast from Port Olímpic. They reach the largely completed development project known variously as Diagonal Mar and **Fòrum** (M El Maresme-Fòrum). Aside from high-rise hotels and apartment blocks looking out to sea, highlights include the protected swimming area, a new marina, kids' playgrounds, good spots for rollerblading and skating, and the weird, triangular **Edifici Fòrum** building. The building is home to a permanent display on urban plans for Barcelona, **Barcelona Propera** (admission free; 11am-8pm Tue-Sun), including a huge scale model of the city and occasional temporary exhibitions. Eventually the city zoo will be relocated to a waterfront position here too.

L'Eixample

Stretching north, east and west of Plaça de Catalunya, L'Eixample (the Extension) was Barcelona's 19th-century answer to overcrowding in the medieval city.

Work on it began in 1869, following a design by architect Ildefons Cerdà, who specified a grid of wide streets with plazas that were formed by their cut-off corners. Cerdà also planned numerous public green spaces but few survived the ensuing scramble for real estate. Only now are some being recreated in the interior of some blocks.

L'Eixample has been inhabited from the start by the city's middle classes, many of whom still think it's the best thing about Barcelona. Along its grid of straight streets are the majority of the city's most expensive shops and hotels, plus a range of eateries and several concentrations of bars and clubs. The development of L'Eixample coincided with the city's Modernisme period and so it's home to many Modernista creations. These constitute the area's main sightseeing attractions and, apart from La Sagrada Família, the principal ones are clustered on or near L'Eixample's main avenue, Passeig de Gràcia.

LA SAGRADA FAMÍLIA

If you only have time for one sightseeing outing, this should be it. The **Temple Expiatori de la Sagrada Família** (Expiatory Temple of the Holy Family; Map pp310-11; 93 207 30 31; www.sagradafamilia.org; Carrer de Mallorca 401; adult/senior & student €8/5, incl Casa-Museu Gaudí in Park Güell €9/6; 9am-8pm Apr-Sep, 9am-6pm Oct-Mar; M Sagrada Família) inspires awe with its sheer verticality and, in the true manner of the great medieval cathedrals it emulates, it's still not finished after more than 100 years. Work is proceeding apace, however, and it might be done by anything between the 2020s and 2040s. It is Spain's most visited monu-

THE MODERNISTAS' MISSION

Antoni Gaudí (1852–1926), known above all for La Sagrada Família, was just one, albeit the most spectacular, of a generation of inventive architects who left an indelible mark on Barcelona between 1880 and the 1920s. They were called the Modernistas.

The local offshoot of the Europe-wide phenomenon of art nouveau, Modernisme was characterised by its taste for sinuous, flowing lines and (for the time) adventurous combinations of materials like tile, glass, brick, iron and steel. But Barcelona's Modernistas were also inspired by an astonishing variety of other styles too: Gothic and Islamic, Renaissance and Romanesque, Byzantine and baroque.

Gaudí and co were trying to create a specifically Catalan architecture, often looking back to Catalonia's medieval golden age for inspiration. It is no coincidence that Gaudí and the two other leading Modernista architects, Lluís Domènech i Montaner (1850–1923) and Josep Puig i Cadafalch (1867–1957), were prominent Catalan nationalists.

L'Eixample, where most of Barcelona's new building was happening at the time, is home to the bulk of the Modernistas' creations. Others in the city include Gaudí's Palau Güell (p325) and Park Güell (p334); Domènech i Montaner's Palau de la Música Catalana (p325); Castell dels Tres Dragons (p328) and the Hotel España restaurant (Carrer de Sant Pau 9-11, El Raval); and Puig i Cadafalch's Els Quatre Gats restaurant (Carrer de Montsió 3bis, Barri Gòtic).

ment and you could easily spend a couple of hours here.

The church was the project to which Antoni Gaudí dedicated the latter part of his life. He stuck to a basic Gothic cross-shaped ground plan, but devised a temple 95m long and 60m wide, which was able to seat 13,000 people. The completed sections and the museum can be explored at leisure. Guided tours (€3.50, 50 minutes, up to four daily) are offered. You can enter from Carrer de Sardenya and Carrer de la Marina. Audioguides (€3.50) are available and it costs a further €2 per ride on the lifts that take you up inside one of the towers on each side of the church.

The northeast, or **Nativity Facade**, is the Sagrada Família's artistic pinnacle, and was mostly done under Gaudí's personal supervision. You can climb high up inside some of the four towers by a combination of lifts and narrow spiral staircases – a vertiginous experience. The towers are destined to hold tubular bells capable of playing complicated music at great volume. Beneath the towers is a tall, three-part portal on the theme of Christ's birth and childhood. It seems to lean outwards as you stand beneath, looking up. Gaudí used real people and animals as models for many of the sculptures, along with the occasional corpse from the local morgue! The three sections of the portal represent, from left to right, Hope, Charity and Faith. Among the forest of sculpture on the Charity portal, you can make out, low down, the manger surrounded by an ox, an ass, the shepherds and kings, with angel musicians above.

The southwest **Passion Facade**, which has the theme of Christ's last days and death, has been constructed since the 1950s with, like the Nativity Facade, four needling towers and a large, sculpture-bedecked portal. The sculptor, Josep Subirachs, has not attempted to imitate Gaudí's work but has produced controversial (people like 'em or loathe 'em), angular images of his own. The sculptures, on three levels, are in an S-shaped sequence, starting with the Last Supper at bottom left and ending with Christ's burial at top right. Subirachs continues to add elements to the facade today.

The semicircular **apse** was the first part to be finished (in 1894). The interior of the church remains a building site but the nave has been roofed over, and a forest of extraordinary angled pillars is in place. The image of the tree is in no way fortuitous, for Gaudí's plan envisaged such an effect.

Work has begun on the **Glory Facade**. It will, like the others, be crowned by four towers – the total of 12 representing the 12 apostles. Further decoration will make the whole building a microcosmic symbol of the Christian church, with Christ represented by a massive 170m central tower above the transept, and the five remaining planned towers symbolising the Virgin Mary and the four Evangelists.

Open the same times as the church, the **Museu Gaudí** (Map pp310–11), below ground level, includes interesting material on Gaudí's life and other work, as well as models and photos of La Sagrada Família. You can see a good example of his plumb-line models, which showed him the stresses and strains he could get away with in construction. Gaudí is buried in the simple crypt at the far end.

CASA BATLLÓ & THE MANZANA DE LA DISCORDIA

If La Sagrada Família is his master symphony, the **Casa Batlló** (Map pp310-11; ☎ 93 216 03 66; www.casabatllo.es; Passeig de Gràcia 43; adult/student & senior €16.50/13.20; 🕑 9am-8pm; Ⓜ Passeig de Gràcia) is Gaudí's whimsical waltz. The facade, sprinkled with bits of blue, mauve and green tiles, and studded with wave-shaped window frames and balconies, rises to an uneven blue-tiled roof with a solitary tower. The roof represents Sant Jordi (St George) and the dragon, and if you stare long enough at the building, it almost seems a living being. Inside the main salon overlooking Passeig de Gràcia everything swirls. The ceiling is twisted into a vortex around a sun-like lamp. The doors, windows and skylights are dreamy waves of wood and coloured glass. The same themes continue in the other rooms and covered terrace. The roof, with its twisting chimneypots, is equally astonishing, and provides a chance for a close-up look at the St George-and-the-dragon motif that dominates the view from the street. Queues are frequent here, and on occasion opening hours can be shortened, so you may want to try turning up early in the morning.

Casa Batlló is the centrepiece of the so-called **Manzana de la Discordia** (Apple of Discord – in a play on words, *manzana* means both city block and apple), on the western side of Passeig de Gràcia between Carrer del Consell de Cent and Carrer d'Aragó. According to

Greek myth, the original Apple of Discord was tossed onto Mt Olympus by Eris (Discord) with orders that it be given to the most beautiful goddess, sparking jealousies that helped start the Trojan War.

On the same block are two utterly different houses (hence the discord) by the other two senior figures of Modernista architecture: Lluís Domènech i Montaner's **Casa Lleó Morera** (Map pp310-11; Passeig de Gràcia 35), which is closed to the public; and **Casa Amatller** (Map pp310-11; ☎ 93 487 72 17; www.amatller.org; Passeig de Gràcia 41; admission free; 10am-8pm Mon-Sat, 10am-3pm Sun; Ⓜ Passeig de Gràcia) by Josep Puig i Cadafalch. The former is swathed in art nouveau carving on the outside and has a bright, tiled lobby, in which floral motifs predominate. The latter is altogether different, with Gothic-style window frames, a stepped gable borrowed (deliberately) from the urban architecture of the Netherlands, and all sorts of unlikely sculptures and busts jutting out. The pillared foyer (which you can enter) and the staircase lit by stained glass are like the inside of some romantic castle. Exhibitions are held out the back and parts of the building might be opened to the public in the near future. You can join a guided tour (€8, times vary) of the foyer, original kitchen and Antoni Amatller's (the original owner) photo studio. All three buildings were completed between 1898 and 1906.

The **Museu del Perfum** (Map pp310-11; ☎ 93 216 01 21; www.museudelperfum.com; Passeig de Gràcia 39; adult/student & senior €5/3; 10.30am-2pm & 4.30-8pm Mon-Fri, 11am-2pm Sat; Ⓜ Passeig de Gràcia), in the Regia store, contains everything from ancient scent receptacles to classic eau-de-cologne bottles.

BARCELONA

LA PEDRERA

Back on Passeig de Gràcia is another Gaudí masterpiece, built between 1905 and 1910 as a combined apartment and office block. Formally called the Casa Milà, after the businessman who commissioned it, it's better known as **La Pedrera** (The Quarry; Map pp310-11; ☎ 902 40 09 73; www.fundaciocaixacatalunya.es; Carrer de Provença 261-265; adult/student & EU senior €8/4.50; 9am-8pm Mar-Oct, 9am-6.30pm Nov-Feb; Ⓜ Diagonal) because of its uneven grey-stone facade, which ripples around the corner of Carrer de Provença. The wave effect is emphasised by elaborate wrought-iron balconies. Queues are frequent here, so early morning is the best time to try to get in without too long a wait.

Visit the lavish top-floor flat, attic and roof, together known as the **Espai Gaudí** (Gaudí Space). The roof is the most extraordinary element, with its giant chimneypots looking like multicoloured medieval knights. One floor below, where you can appreciate Gaudí's gracious parabolic arches, is a modest museum dedicated to his work. You can see models and videos dealing with each of his buildings.

Downstairs on the next floor the apartment (El Pis de la Pedrera) spreads out. It is fascinating to wander around this elegantly furnished home, done up in the style a well-to-do family might have enjoyed in the early 20th century.

Some of the lower floors of the building, especially the grand 1st floor, often host temporary expositions. On hot August evenings, La Pedrera stages '30 Minuts de Música', miniconcerts held on the roof at 7, 8 and 9pm (€5).

FUNDACIÓ ANTONI TÀPIES

Around the corner from the Manzana de la Discordia, the **Fundació** (Map pp310-11; ☎ 93 487 03 15; www.fundaciotapies.org; Carrer d'Aragó 255; adult/under 16yr/senior & student €6/4; 10am-8pm Tue-Sun; Ⓜ Passeig de Gràcia) is a pioneering Modernista building of the early 1880s and a homage to, and by, a leading 20th-century Catalan artist. The collection spans the arc of Tàpies' creations (with more than 800 works) but only a small portion is ever on show, always in conjunction with several other temporary exhibitions. In the main exhibition area (Level 1, upstairs) you can see an ever-changing selection of about a dozen of Tàpies' later and grander works, often mystifying creations. For a historical perspective, head for the basement Level 3, where you'll find drawings and colourful canvases from the 1940s and 1950s.

PALAU DEL BARÓ QUADRAS & CASA DE LES PUNXES

A few blocks north and east of La Pedrera are two of Puig i Cadafalch's major buildings. **Palau del Baró Quadras** (Map pp310-11; ☎ 93 238 73 37; www.casaasia.es; Avinguda Diagonal 373; 10am-8pm Mon-Sat, 10am-2pm Sun; Ⓜ Diagonal) was built between 1902 and 1904 with fantastical neo-Gothic carvings on the facade and a fine stained-glass gallery. It houses Casa Asia, an Asia-Pacific cultural centre. Visiting the varied temporary exhibitions allows you to get a peek at the

TOP FIVE MUSEUMS

- **CosmoCaixa** (p334)
- **Museu Marítim** (p321)
- **Museu d'Història de la Ciutat** (p338)
- **Museu Barbier-Mueller d'Art Precolombí** (p326)
- **Palau Reial de Pedralbes** (p336)

inside of this intriguing building, which is full of surprising oriental themes.

Nearby Casa Terrades is better known as **Casa de les Punxes** (House of Spikes; Map pp310-11; Avinguda Diagonal 420) because of its pointed, witch's-hat turrets. This apartment block (1903–05) looks more like a fairy-tale castle.

HOSPITAL DE LA SANTA CREU I DE SANT PAU

Domènech i Montaner excelled himself as architect and philanthropist with the Modernista masterpiece **Hospital de la Santa Creu i de Sant Pau** (Map pp306-7; ☎ 902 07 66 21; www.santpau.es; Carrer de Cartagena; Ⓜ Hospital de Sant Pau), long one of the city's most important hospitals. The whole complex (a World Heritage site), including 16 pavilions, is lavishly decorated and each pavilion is unique. Among the many artists who contributed statuary, ceramics and artwork was the prolific Eusebi Arnau. You can wander around the grounds at any time, and it's well worth the stroll up Avinguda de Gaudí from La Sagrada Família.

The hospital facilities are gradually being transferred to new grounds nearby. Part of the historic site will become a museum dedicated to Montaner, medicine and the 600-year history of the hospital (which was first established in El Raval in the early 15th century; see p324), but not before 2009. You can join a guided tour for €5 (10.15am and 12.15pm in English, 11.15am in Catalan and 1.15pm in Spanish).

TORRE AGBAR

Jean Nouvel's glimmering cucumber-shaped **tower** (Map pp306-7; ☎ 93 342 21 29; www.torreagbar.com; Avinguda Diagonal 225; 🕑 10am-7pm Mon-Sat, 10am-2pm Sun; Ⓜ Glòries) has come to share the skyline limelight with La Sagrada Família, and it is now the most visible landmark in the city. You can generally get inside the foyer, where temporary exhibitions are often staged. It is best viewed at night, when its carapace is lit up in reds, purples and blues.

FUNDACIÓN FRANCISCO GODIA

Francisco Godia (1921–90) put together the intriguing mix of medieval art, ceramics and modern paintings at the **Fundación** (Map pp310-11; www.fundacionfgodia.org; Carrer de la Diputació 250; Ⓜ Passeig de Gràcia) in a lifetime of collecting. Godia's interests ranged from the Neapolitan baroque painter Luca Giordano through to Catalan Modernisme and Valencia's Joaquim Sorolla, not to mention fast cars. This new location for the collection should be open by 2009.

MUSEU EGIPCI

Hotel magnate Jordi Clos has spent much of his life collecting ancient Egyptian artefacts, brought together in this private **museum** (Map pp310-11; ☎ 93 488 01 88; www.fundclos.com; Carrer de València 284; adult/senior & student €7/5; 🕑 10am-8pm Mon-Sat, 10am-2pm Sun; Ⓜ Passeig de Gràcia), with some 700 objects spread over an airy seven-floor exhibition space. It's divided into different thematic areas (the pharaoh, religion, daily life etc).

FUNDACIÓ SUÑOL

Rotating exhibitions of portions of this private **collection** (Map pp310-11; ☎ 93 496 10 32; www.fundaciosunol.org; Passeig de Gràcia 98; adult/concession €5/2.50; 🕑 4-8pm Mon-Wed & Fri & Sat; Ⓜ Diagonal) of mostly 20th-century art (some 1200 works in total) offer the visitor anything from the photography of Man Ray to sculptures by Alberto Giacometti, and a hefty band of Spanish artists.

Gràcia

Gràcia lies north of L'Eixample. Once a separate village and in the 19th century an industrial district famous for its Republican and liberal ideas, it became fashionable among radical and bohemian types in the 1960s and '70s. Now more sedate and gentrified, it retains much of its style of 20 years ago, with a mixed-class population and very Catalan air. Gràcia's interest lies in the atmosphere of its narrow streets, small plazas and the multitude of bars and restaurants.

The liveliest plazas are Plaça del Sol, Plaça de Rius i Taulet with its **clock tower** (a favourite meeting place) and Plaça de la Virreina with the 17th-century **Església de Sant Joan** (Map pp310-11). Three blocks northeast of Plaça de Rius i Taulet there's a big covered market, the **Mercat del Abaceria** (Map pp310–11). West of Gràcia's main street, Carrer Gran de Gràcia, seek out an early Gaudí house, the turreted, vaguely Mudéjar **Casa Vicenç** (Map pp310-11; Carrer de les Carolines 22). It's not open to the public.

Park Güell

North of Gràcia, **Park Güell** (Map pp306-7; ☎ 93 413 24 00; Carrer d'Olot 7; admission free; ⏰ 10am-9pm Jun-Sep, 10am-8pm Apr, May & Oct, 10am-7pm Mar & Nov, 10am-6pm Dec-Feb; Ⓜ Lesseps or Vallcarca 🚌 24; ♿) is where Gaudí turned his hand to landscape gardening and the artificial almost seems more natural than the natural.

Park Güell originated in 1900 when Count Eusebi Güell bought a hillside property (then outside Barcelona) and hired Gaudí to create a miniature garden city of houses for the wealthy. The project was abandoned in 1914, but not before Gaudí had created 3km of roads and walks, steps and a plaza in his inimitable manner, plus the two Hansel-and-Gretel-style gatehouses on Carrer d'Olot.

Just inside the main entrance on Carrer d'Olot, visit the park's **Centre d'Interpretació** (☎ 93 285 68 99; adult/under 16yr/student €2/free/1.50; ⏰ 11am-3pm) in the **Pavelló de Consergeria**, the typically curvaceous, Gaudían former porter's home that hosts a display on Gaudí's building methods and the history of the park. There are nice views from the top floor. For €6 you get entry here and to the **Museu d'Història de la Ciutat** (p323) and the **Museu-Monestir de Pedralbes** (p336).

The steps up from the entrance, which is guarded by a mosaic dragon-lizard, lead to the **Sala Hipóstila**, a forest of 88 stone columns (some of them leaning at an angle), intended as a market. On top of the Sala Hipóstila is a broad open space; its highlight is the **Banc de Trencadís**, a tiled bench curving sinuously around its perimeter, which was designed by Gaudí's right-hand man, Josep Maria Jujol (1879–1949).

The spired house to the right is the **Casa-Museu Gaudí** (Map pp306-7; ☎ 93 219 38 11; admission €4; ⏰ 10am-8pm Apr-Sep, 10am-6pm Oct-Mar), where Gaudí lived for most of his last 20 years (1906–26). It contains furniture by him and other memorabilia. Bus 24 drops you at an entrance near the top of the park. Try coming here early on a weekday. On summer weekends it can be unpleasantly packed.

DEADLY SERIOUS

Probably the weirdest museum in town is the **Museu de Carrosses Fúnebres** (Map pp306-7; ☎ 902 07 69 02; Carrer de Sancho d'Àvila 2; admission free; ⏰ 10am-1pm & 4-6pm Mon-Fri, 10am-1pm Sat, Sun & holidays). This basement hearse museum is the place to come if you want to see how the great and good have been transported to their final resting places in Barcelona since the 18th century. Solemn, bewigged mannequins and life-size model horses accompany a serious of dark hearses.

Tibidabo

Tibidabo (512m) is the highest hill in the wooded range that forms the backdrop to Barcelona. It's a good place for some fresh air and fine views. Tibidabo gets its name from the devil, who, trying to tempt Christ, took him to a high place and said, in the Latin version: '*Haec omnia tibi dabo si cadens adoraberis me.*' ('All this I will give you, if you will fall down and worship me.')

COSMOCAIXA (MUSEU DE LA CIÈNCIA)

Located in a transformed Modernista building, this **science museum** (Map pp306-7; ☎ 93 212 60 50; www.fundacio.lacaixa.es; Carrer de Teodor Roviralta 47-51, Zona Alta; adult/student €3/2; ⏰ 10am-8pm Tue-Sun; 🚌 60 🚆 FGC Avinguda de Tibidabo; ♿) is a giant interactive paradise with knobs (and buttons and levers and lots more besides). Among the star attractions are the planetarium and the re-creation over 1 sq km of a chunk of flooded Amazon rainforest *(Bosc Inundat)*, with more than 100 species of Amazon flora and fauna (including anacondas and poisonous frogs). It has become one of the city's big draws and is perfect for kids of all ages.

PARC D'ATRACCIONS

Barcelonins (residents of Barcelona) come to Tibidabo for a bit of fresh air at this **funfair** (Map pp306-7; ☎ 93 211 79 42; www.tibidabo.es; Plaça de Tibidabo 3-4; adult/child shorter than 1.2m €24/9; ⏰ noon-10pm or 11pm Wed-Sun Jul-early Sep, other closing times vary (from 5pm to 9pm) Sat, Sun, holidays & some other days in warmer months; ♿). Give yourself a bit of a scare in the Hotel Krueger, a *hospedaje* (guesthouse) of horrors inhabited by actors playing out their Dracula, Hannibal Lecter and other fantasies. Stomach-churning and scream-inducing rides include the Pndol, and the planned new big dipper. A curious sideline is the Museu d'Autòmats, with around 50 automated puppets that go back as far as 1880 and are part of the original amusement park. You can still see some of these gizmos go.

TEMPLE DEL SAGRAT COR

The **Church of the Sacred Heart** (Map pp306-7; ☎ 93 417 56 86; Plaça de Tibidabo; 🕑 8am-7pm), looming above the top funicular station, is meant to be Barcelona's answer to Paris' Sacré Cœur. It's certainly equally as visible, and even more vilified by aesthetes (perhaps with good reason). It's actually two churches, one on top of the other. The top one is surmounted by a giant Christ and has a lift to the **roof** (tickets €2; 🕑 10am-2pm & 3-6pm Mon-Sat, 10am-2pm & 3-7pm Sun).

GETTING THERE & AWAY

Take one of the frequent Ferrocarrils de la Generalitat de Catalunya (FGC) trains to Avinguda de Tibidabo from Catalunya station on Plaça de Catalunya (€1.30, 10 minutes). Outside Avinguda de Tibidabo station, hop on the *tramvia blau*, Barcelona's last surviving old-style tram. It runs between fancy Modernista mansions – note particularly **Casa Roviralta** (Map pp306-7; Avinguda de Tibidabo 31), now home to a well-known grill restaurant – and Plaça del Doctor Andreu (one way/return €2.50/3.70; operating 10am to 8pm late June to early September, 10am to 6pm Saturday, Sunday and holidays mid-September to late June) and has been doing so since 1901. The tram runs every 15 or 30 minutes. On days and at times when the tram does not operate, a bus serves the route (€1.30).

From Plaça del Doctor Andreu, the Tibidabo funicular railway climbs through the woods to Plaça de Tibidabo at the top of the hill (one way/return €2/3, five minutes). Departures start at 10.45am and continue until shortly after the park's closing time.

An alternative is bus T2, the 'Tibibús', from Plaça de Catalunya to Plaça de Tibidabo (€2.30). It runs every 30 to 50 minutes on Saturday, Sunday and holidays year-round, and hourly from 10.30am Monday to Friday late June to early September; purchase tickets on the bus. The last bus down leaves Tibidabo 30 minutes after the Parc d'Atraccions closes. You can also buy a combined ticket that includes the bus and entry to the Parc d'Atraccions (€24).

Collserola

PARC DE COLLSEROLA

Stretching over 8000 hectares, this **park** (☎ 93 280 35 52; www.parccollserola.net; Carretera de l'Església 92; 🕑 Centre d'Interpretació 9.30am-3pm) makes an ideal escape hatch from the city, with ample walking and mountain-biking possibilities. Aside from the nature, the principal point of interest is the sprawling **Museu-Casa Verdaguer** (☎ 93 204 78 05; www.museuhistoria.bcn.es; Villa Joana, Carretera de l'Església 104; admission free; 🕑 10am-2pm Sat & Sun & holidays), 100m from the information centre and a short walk from the train station. In this late-18th-century country house, Catalonia's revered and reverend writer, Jacint Verdaguer, spent his last days before dying on 10 July 1902.

To get to the park, take the FGC train from Plaça de Catalunya to Peu de Funicular and then the Funicular to Baixador de Vallvidrera.

TORRE DE COLLSEROLA

The 288m **Torre de Collserola** (Map pp306-7; ☎ 93 211 79 42; www.torredecollserola.com; Carretera de Vallvidrera al Tibidabo; adult/child/senior €5/3/4; 🕑 11am-2.30pm & 3.30-6pm Wed-Sun Mar-Oct) telecommunications tower was completed by Norman Foster in 1992. An external glass lift whisks you up 115m to the visitors' observation area, from where you can see for 70km on a clear day. Take bus 111 from Funicular de Vallvidrera or from Plaça de Tibidabo.

Jardins del Laberint d'Horta

Laid out in the twilight years of the 18th century by Antoni Desvalls, Marquès d'Alfarras i de Llupià, this carefully manicured **park** (☎ 93 428 39 34; Carrer dels Germans Desvalls; adult/student €2/1.25, admission free Wed & Sun; 🕑 10am-sunset; Ⓜ Mundet; ♿) remained a private family idyll until the 1970s, when it was opened to the public. Many a fine party and theatrical performance was held here over the years, but now it serves as a kind of museum-park. The gardens take their name from a maze (which is very easy to get lost in!) in their centre, but other paths take you past a pleasant artificial lake or *estany*, waterfalls, a neoclassical pavilion and a false cemetery. The latter was inspired by 19th-century romanticism, often characterised by an obsession with a swooning, anaemic (some might say plain silly) vision of death.

Pedralbes

This is a wealthy residential area north of the Zona Universitària.

PALAU REIAL DE PEDRALBES

Across Avinguda Diagonal from the main campus of the Universitat de Barcelona, set in a lush, green park is the 20th-century **Palau Reial de Pedralbes** (Map pp306-7; ☎ 93 280 16 21; Avinguda Diagonal 686; ⌚ 10am-6pm Tue-Sat, 10am-3pm Sun & holidays, park 10am-6pm daily; Ⓜ Palau Reial), which belonged to the family of Eusebi Güell (Gaudí's patron) until they handed it over to the city in 1926. Then it served as a royal residence – King Alfonso XIII, the president of Catalonia and General Franco, among others, have been its guests.

Today the palace houses two museums. The **Museu de Ceràmica** (www.museuceramica.bcn.es; incl Museu de les Arts Decoratives adult/student €3.50/2, admission free 1st Sun of month) has a good collection of Spanish ceramics from the 13th to 19th centuries, including work by Picasso and Miró. Across the corridor, the **Museu de les Arts Decoratives** (www.museuartsdecoratives.bcn.es; incl Museu de Ceràmica; adult/student €3.50/2, admission free 1st Sun of month) brings together an eclectic assortment of furnishings, ornaments and knick-knacks dating as far back as the Romanesque period.

Over by Avinguda de Pedralbes are the Gaudí-designed stables and porter's lodge for the Finca Güell, as the Güell estate here was called. They were built in the mid-1880s, when Gaudí was strongly impressed by Islamic architecture, and are also known as the **Pavellons Güell** (Map pp306-7; ☎ 902 07 66 21; guided tours adult/senior & under 18yr €5/2.50; ⌚ 10.15am in English, 11.15am in Catalan, 12.15pm in English & 1.15pm in Spanish Fri-Mon). Outside visiting hours, there is nothing to stop you admiring Gaudí's wrought-iron dragon gate from the outside.

MUSEU-MONESTIR DE PEDRALBES

This peaceful old **convent** (Map pp306-7; ☎ 93 203 92 82; www.museuhistoria.bcn.es; Baixada del Monestir 9; admission incl Museu d'Història de la Ciutat & Park Güell Centre d'Interpretació €4; ⌚ 10am-5pm Tue-Sat, 10am-3pm Sun Jun-Sep, 10am-2pm Tue-Sat, 10am-3pm Sun Oct-May; 🚆 FGC Reina Elisenda, 🚌 22, 63, 64 or 75), founded in 1326 and now a museum of monastic life, stands at the top of Avinguda de Pedralbes in a divinely quiet corner of Barcelona. Displays are distributed in cells and dependencies around the elegant, three-storey cloister, a jewel of early-14th-century Catalan Gothic.

Upstairs is a grand hall that was once the **Dormidor**, or sleeping quarters. It was lined by tiny night cells but they were long ago removed. A modest collection of the monastery's art, especially Gothic devotional works, and furniture grace this space.

Camp Nou

One of Barcelona's most visited museums is the **Museu del Futbol Club Barcelona** (Map pp306-7; ☎ 93 496 36 00; www.fcbarcelona.es; Carrer d'Aristides Maillol; adult/child €8.50/6.80; ⌚ 10am-8pm Mon-Sat, 10am-2.30pm Sun & holidays mid-Apr–mid-Oct, 10am-6.30pm Mon-Sat, 10am-2.30pm Sun & holidays mid-Oct–mid-Apr; Ⓜ Collblanc), next to the club's giant Camp Nou stadium. Barça is one of Europe's top football clubs and its museum is a hit with fans the world over.

Camp Nou, built in 1957, is one of the world's biggest stadiums, holding 100,000 people, and the club has a world-record membership of 156,000. Soccer fans who can't get to a game (see p358) should find the museum worthwhile. The best bits are the photo section, goal videos and views over the stadium. Among the quirkier paraphernalia are old sports board games, the life-size diorama of old-time dressing rooms, magazines from way back and the *futbolín* (table-soccer) collection. You can join a guided **tour** (adult/child €13/10.40; ⌚ until 1hr before museum closing time) of the stadium, starting in the team's dressing rooms (pong!) then heading out through the tunnel, on to the pitch and winding up in the presidential box.

On match days there are no tours and the museum opens from 10am to 1pm.

Poble Sec

Draped on the eastern slopes of Montjuïc down to Avinguda del Parallel, working-class Poble Sec (Dry Village) is short on sights but hides several interesting bars and eateries. Until the 1960s the avenue was the centre of Barcelona nightlife, crammed with theatres and cabarets. A handful of theatres and cinemas survive and one, the Sala Apolo, managed to convert itself successfully into a club (p356).

REFUGI 307

This **air raid shelter** (Map pp312-13; Carrer Nou de la Rambla 169; admission €3; ⌚ 11am-2pm Sat & Sun; Ⓜ Parallel) was one of more than 1300 across the city during the civil war. The narrow and winding tunnels were slowly dug to a total of 200m over two years from March 1937. The half-hour tours (generally in Spanish or Catalan but you can book ahead for English or French) provide some fascinating insight into life in wartime Barcelona. Just being inside here and imagining bombs dropping outside is enough to give you the heebie-jeebies.

Montjuïc

Montjuïc, the hill overlooking the city centre from the southwest, is dotted with museums, soothing gardens and the main group of 1992 Olympic sites, along with a handful of theatres and clubs. It's worth at least a day of your time.

The name Montjuïc (Jewish Mountain) indicates there was once a Jewish cemetery, and possibly settlement, here. Montjuïc also has a darker history: its castle was used as a political prison and execution site by various governments, including the Republicans during the civil war and Franco thereafter.

The first main burst of building on Montjuïc came in the 1920s, when it was chosen as the stage for Barcelona's 1929 World Exhibition. The Estadi Olímpic, the Poble Espanyol and some museums all date from this time. Montjuïc got a facelift and more new buildings for the 1992 Olympics, and cosmetic surgery on the gardens since the late 1990s has made them beautiful and soothing places to walk, contemplate or just lie down and snooze.

Abundant roads and paths, with occasional escalators, plus buses and a chairlift, allow you to visit Montjuïc's sights in any order you choose. The main attractions – the Museu Nacional d'Art de Catalunya, CaixaForum, the Poble Espanyol, the Pavelló Mies van der Rohe, the Fundació Joan Miró, the Estadi Olímpic and the views from the castle – make for a full couple of days' sightseeing.

For information on the park, head for the **Centre Gestor del Parc de Montjuïc** (Map pp306-7; Passeig de Santa Madrona 28; ⌚ 10am-8pm Apr-Oct, 10am-6pm Nov-Mar) in the Font del Gat building, a short walk off Passeig de Santa Madrona, east of the Museu Etnològic. It also has a pleasant bar-restaurant. A handful of other information offices are scattered about the park, including at the castle (see p338).

AROUND PLAÇA D'ESPANYA

The approach to Montjuïc from Plaça d'Espanya gives you the full benefit of the landscaping on the hill's northern side and allows Montjuïc to unfold for you from the bottom up. On Plaça d'Espanya's northern side is the former **Plaça de Braus Les Arenes bullring**, built in 1900 and being converted into a shopping and leisure centre by Sir Richard Rogers.

Behind the bullring is **Parc Joan Miró**, created in the 1980s, and worth a quick detour for Miró's giant, highly phallic sculpture *Dona i Ocell* (Woman and Bird; Map pp306–7) in the northwest corner.

MUSEU NACIONAL D'ART DE CATALUNYA

The pompous-looking **Palau Nacional**, built in the 1920s for World Exhibition displays and designed to be a temporary structure, houses one of the city's most important **museums** (Map pp306-7; ☎ 93 622 03 76; www.mnac.es; Mirador del Palau Nacional; adult/senior & under 15yr/student €8.50/free/6, admission free 1st Sun of month; ⌚ 10am-7pm Tue-Sat, 10am-2.30pm Sun & holidays; Ⓜ Espanya). Its Romanesque art section consists mainly of 11th- and 12th-century murals, woodcarvings and altar frontals – painted, low-relief wooden panels that were forerunners of the elaborate *retablos* (altarpieces) that adorned later churches. Gathered from decaying rural churches in northern Catalonia early last century, they form one of Europe's greatest collections of Romanesque art. The two outstanding items are an image of Christ in majesty done around 1123 and taken from the apse of the Església de Sant Climent de Taüll in northwest Catalonia, and an apse image of the Virgin Mary and Christ child from the nearby Església de Santa Maria de Taüll.

The extensive Gothic-art section contains works by Catalan painters such as Bernat Martorell and Jaume Huguet. From here you pass through two eclectic private collections, the Cambò bequest and works from the Thyssen-Bornemisza collections. Works by the Venetian Renaissance masters Veronese (1528–88), Titian (1490–1557) and Canaletto (1697–1768), along with Rubens (1577–1640) and even England's Gainsborough (1727–88), feature.

Upstairs, after a series of minor works by a variety of classic 17th-century Spanish Old Masters, the collection turns to modern Catalan art. It is an uneven affair, but it is worth looking out for Modernista painters Ramon Casas and Santiago Rusiñol.

The photography section encompasses work from mostly Catalan snappers from the mid-19th century on. The Gabinet Numismàtic de Catalunya contains coins ranging from Roman Spain and medieval Catalonia to some engaging notes from civil war days.

FUNDACIÓ JOAN MIRÓ

Dedicated to one of the greatest artists to emerge in Barcelona in the 20th century, Joan Miró, the **Fundació Joan Miró** (Map pp306-7; ☎ 93 443 94 70; www.bcn.fjmiro.es; Plaça de Neptu; adult/senior & child €8/6, temporary exhibitions €4/3; ⏰ 10am-8pm Tue-Wed, Fri & Sat, 10am-9.30pm Thu, 10am-2.30pm Sun & holidays Jul-Sep, 10am-7pm Tue-Wed, Fri & Sat, 10am-9.30pm Thu, 10am-2.30pm Sun & holidays Oct-May; 🚌 50, 55, PM or Funicular) is a must-see gallery.

The collections include some 450 paintings, sculptures and textile works, and more than 7000 drawings, but only a selection is shown at any one time. The displays tend to concentrate on Miró's more settled last 20 years, but there are some important exceptions. The Sala Joan Prats and Sala Pilar Juncosa show work by the younger Miró that traces him moving away slowly from a *relative* realism towards his own later signature style. Transitional works from the 1930s and '40s are especially intriguing. Another interesting section is devoted to the 'Miró Papers', which include many preparatory drawings and sketches, some on bits of newspaper or cigarette packets. *A Joan Miró* is a collection of work by other contemporary artists, donated in tribute to Miró and displayed in a basement room.

Reckon on a couple of hours to take in the permanent and temporary exhibitions.

CASTELL DE MONTJUÏC & AROUND

The southeast of Montjuïc is dominated by the **castell** (Map pp306–7). For most of its existence the castle has been used to watch over the city and as a political prison and killing ground. The army opened it to the public as a museum in 1960.

The castle is surrounded by a network of ditches and walls, and houses the **Museu Militar** (Map pp306-7; ☎ 93 329 86 13; adult/senior & student €3/1.50; ⏰ 9.30am-8pm Tue-Sun late Mar-late Oct, Nov–mid-Mar, 9.30am-5pm Tue-Fri, 9.30am-7pm Sat & Sun & holidays late Oct-late Mar; 🚌 PM, Telefèric), which has a section on Catalan military history, old weapons collections, castle models and so on. A question mark hangs over the future of the Museu Militar, as the town hall plans to dismantle it now that the castle has been handed over from the Ministry of Defence. Best of all are the views from the castle ramparts of the port and city below. Make the charming walk along the base of the seaward walls along the Camí del Mar (a dirt trail), drinking in views of the city and the sea. On weekends a popular, chilled **bar** opens at the end of this trail.

Towards the foot of this part of Montjuïc, above the main road to Tarragona, the **Jardins de Mossèn Costa i Llobera** (Map pp306-7; admission free; ⏰ 10am-sunset) have a good collection of tropical and desert plants – including a veritable forest of cacti. Near the Estació Parc Montjuïc (funicular station) are the ornamental **Jardins de Mossèn Cinto Verdaguer** (Map pp306-7; admission free; ⏰ 10am-sunset), full of beautiful bulbs and aquatic plants. East across the road are the landscaped **Jardins Joan Brossa** (Map pp306-7; ⏰ 10am-sunset), set on the site of a former amusement park. These gardens contain many Mediterranean species, from cypresses to pines and a few palms. From the **Jardins del Mirador** (Map pp306–7), opposite the Estació Mirador, you have fine views over the port of Barcelona.

POBLE ESPANYOL

The so-called Spanish Village, **Poble Espanyol** (Map pp306-7; ☎ 93 508 63 30; www.poble-espanyol.com; Avinguda del Marquès de Comillas; adult/child/senior & student €8/5/6; ⏰ 9am-8pm Mon, 9am-2am Tue-Thu, 9am-4am Fri & Sat, 9am-midnight Sun; Ⓜ Espanya, 🚌 50, 61 or PM) is both a cheesy souvenir-hunters' haunt and an intriguing scrapbook of Spanish architecture. Built for the Spanish crafts section of the 1929 exhibition, it's composed of plazas and streets lined with surprisingly good copies of characteristic buildings from across the country's regions.

You enter from Avinguda del Marquès de Comillas, beneath a towered medieval gate from Ávila. Inside, to the right, is an information office with free maps. Straight ahead from the gate is a Plaza Mayor, or town square, surrounded by mainly Castilian and Aragonese buildings. Elsewhere you'll find an Andalucian *barrio* (district), a Basque street, Galician and Catalan quarters, and even – at the eastern end – a small Dominican monastery. The buildings house dozens of moderate-to-expensive restaurants, cafes, bars, craft shops and workshops, and a few souvenir stores.

The **Fundació Fran Daurel** (Map pp306-7; ☎ 93 423 41 72; www.fundaciofrandaurel.com; admission free; ⏰ 10am-7pm) is an eclectic collection of 200 works of art including sculptures, prints, ceramics and tapestries by artists ranging from Picasso to Miquel Barceló. The foundation also has a sculpture garden, boasting 27 pieces, nearby within the grounds of Poble Espanyol (look for the Montblanc gate).

LA FONT MÀGICA & AROUND

Avinguda de la Reina Maria Cristina, lined with exhibition and congress halls, leads from Plaça d'Espanya towards Montjuïc. On the hill ahead of you is the Palau Nacional de Montjuïc, and stretching up a series of terraces below it are Montjuïc's fountains, starting with the biggest, **La Font Màgica** (Map pp306-7; Avinguda de la Reina Maria Cristina; admission free; every 30min 7-8.30pm Fri & Sat Oct-late Jun, 9.30-11.30pm Thu-Sun late Jun-Sep), which comes alive with a 15-minute lights-water-and-music show repeated several times an evening.

Just to the west of La Font Màgica is the strange **Pavelló Mies van der Rohe** (Map pp306-7; 93 423 40 16; www.miesbcn.com; Avinguda del Marquès de Comillas; adult/under 18yr/student €4/free/2; 10am-8pm; M Espanya). Architect Ludwig Mies van der Rohe erected the Pavelló Alemany (German Pavilion) for the 1929 World Exhibition. It was a startling modern experiment. What you see now is a replica erected by an association of his fans in the 1980s.

CaixaForum (Map pp306-7; 93 476 86 00; www.fundacio.lacaixa.es in Spanish; Avinguda del Marquès de Comillas 6-8; admission free; 10am-8pm Tue-Fri & Sun, 10am-10pm Sat; M Espanya) hosts part of the Caixa bank's extensive collection of modern art from around the globe. It is housed in a remarkable former Modernista factory designed by Puig i Cadafalch. Constantly changing exhibitions are generally top quality and the elegant brick building itself warrants a wander even if the current exhibitions don't ring your bell.

MUSEU ETNOLÒGIC & MUSEU D'ARQUEOLOGIA

Down the hill east of the Museu Nacional d'Art, these museums are worth a visit if their subjects particularly interest you.

The **Museu Etnològic** (Ethnology Museum; Map pp306-7; 93 424 64 02; www.museuetnologic.bcn.es; Passeig de Santa Madrona 16-22; adult/under 12yr/senior & student €3.50/free/1.75, admission free 1st Sun of month; noon-8pm Tue-Sat, 11am-3pm Sun late Jun-late Sep, 10am-7pm Tue & Thu, 10am-2pm Wed, Fri-Sun late Sep-late Jun; 55) presents a wide-ranging, three-part exhibition with all sorts of traditional objects collected across Spain and around the world: anything from Australian boomerangs to ceramics from Andalucía.

The **Museu d'Arqueologia de Catalunya** (Archaeology Museum; Map pp306-7; 93 424 65 77; www.mac.es; Passeig de Santa Madrona 39-41; adult/child €3/2; 9.30am-7pm Tue-Sat, 10am-2.30pm Sun; 55 or PM) covers Catalonia and neighbouring areas in Spain. Items range from copies of pre-Neanderthal skulls to Carthaginian necklaces and Visigothic crosses. There's good material on the Balearic Islands and Empúries, and Roman finds dug up in Barcelona.

ANELLA OLÍMPICA

The 'Olympic Ring' is the group of sports installations where the main events of the 1992 Olympics were held. Westernmost is the **Institut Nacional d'Educació Física de Catalunya** (INEFC; Map pp306–7), a kind of sports university, designed by one of Catalonia's best-known contemporary architects, Ricardo Bofill. Past a circular arena, Plaça d'Europa, with the Torre Calatrava telecommunications tower behind it, is the **Piscines Bernat Picornell** (Map pp306–7), where the swimming and diving events were held. For details on swimming here, see p341.

Next comes a pleasant park, the Jardí d'Aclimatació, followed by the **Estadi Olímpic** (Map pp306-7; Avinguda de l'Estadi; admission free; 10am-6pm Oct-Mar, 10am-8pm Apr-Sep; 50, 61 or PM), the main stadium of the games (enter at the north end). If you saw the Olympics on TV, the 65,000-capacity stadium may seem surprisingly small. So may the Olympic flame-holder into which an archer spectacularly fired a flaming arrow during the opening ceremony. The stadium was opened in 1929 and restored for 1992.

Across the road from the stadium is the **Museu Olímpic i de l'Esport** (Map pp306-7; 93 292 53 79; www.fundaciobarcelonaolimpica.es; Avinguda de l'Estadi s/n; adult/senior & child/student €4/free/2.50; 10am-8pm Wed-Mon, Apr-Sep, 10am-6pm Wed-Mon Oct-Mar; 50, 61 or PM), an information-packed interactive museum dedicated to the history of sport and the Olympic Games. After picking up tickets you wander down a ramp that snakes below ground level and is lined with displays on the history of sport, starting with the ancients.

West of the stadium is the **Palau Sant Jordi** (Map pp306–7), a 17,000-capacity indoor sports, concert and exhibition hall designed by the Japanese architect Arata Isozaki.

JARDÍ BOTÀNIC

South across the road from the Estadi, this **botanic garden** (Map pp306-7; 93 426 49 35; www.jardibotanic.bcn.es; Carrer del Doctor Font i Quer 2; adult/under 16yr/student €3.50/free/1.70, admission free last Sun of month; 10am-8pm Jun-Aug, 10am-7pm Apr-May & Sep,

10am-6pm Feb-Mar & Oct, 10am-5pm Nov-Jan; 50, 61 or PM) was created atop an old municipal dump. The theme is 'Mediterranean' flora and the collection includes some 1500 species (40,000 plants) thriving in areas with a climate similar to that of the Mediterranean, including the Eastern Med, Spain (including the Balearic and Canary Islands), North Africa, Australia, California, Chile and South Africa.

CEMENTIRI DEL SUD-OEST

On the hill south of the Anella Olímpica you can see the top of a huge cemetery, the **Cementiri del Sud-Oest** (Map pp306-7; 93 484 17 00; 8am-5.30pm; PM), which extends right down the south side of the hill. It was opened in 1883, and is an odd combination of elaborate architect-designed tombs for rich families and small niches for the rest. It contains the graves of numerous Catalan artists and politicians, including Joan Miró, Carmen Amaya (the flamenco star from La Barceloneta) and Lluís Companys (a Nationalist president of Catalonia, who was executed by Franco's henchmen in the nearby Montjuïc castle in 1940).

GETTING THERE & AWAY

You *could* walk from Ciutat Vella (the foot of La Rambla is 700m from the eastern end of Montjuïc). Escalators run up to the Palau Nacional from Avinguda de Rius i Taulet and Passeig de les Cascades. They continue as far as Avinguda de l'Estadi.

Bus

Several buses make their way up here, including buses 50, 55 and 61. A local bus, the PM (Parc de Montjuïc) line, does a circle trip from Plaça d'Espanya to the castell.

Bus Montjuïc Turístic

Bus Montjuïc Turístic (adult/child €3/2) operates two hop-on, hop-off circuits (red and blue) in single-deck, open-top buses around the park. The blue line starts at Plaça d'Espanya and the red at Pla del Portal de la Pau, at the waterfront end of La Rambla. There are a total of 22 stops, five interconnecting the two routes. The service operates every 40 minutes, from 10am to 9pm, daily from May to September.

Metro & Funicular

Take the metro (lines 2 and 3) to Parallel station and get on the **funicular railway** (9am-10pm Apr-Oct, 9am-8pm Nov-Mar) from there to Estació Parc Montjuïc.

Transbordador Aeri

To get to the mountain from the beach, take the Transbordador Aeri (Telefèric; cable car). It runs between Torre de Sant Sebastiá in La Barceloneta (p329) and the Miramar stop on Montjuïc.

Telefèric de Montjuïc

From Estació Parc Montjuïc, this **cable car** (93 328 90 03; adult/child one way €5.70/4.50; 10am-9pm Jun-Sep, 10am-7pm Apr-May & Oct, 10am-6pm Nov-Mar) carries you to the Castell de Montjuïc via the mirador (lookout point).

ACTIVITIES

Cycling

For information on bicycle hire, see p362. Cycle lanes have been laid out along many main arteries across the city, although the network is far from complete – cyclists are often obliged to challenge the traffic or break the law by dodging (often rightly indignant) pedestrians. Montjuïc and the Parc de Collserola are both hilly but *much* less stressful than the rest of the city in terms of traffic. Indeed the latter is ideal for a little mountain-bike training.

Marathon

Runners converge on Barcelona annually to participate in the city's spring **marathon** (www.barcelonamarato.es); it usually starts and finishes at Plaça d'Espanya, passing Camp Nou, La Pedrera, La Sagrada Família, Torre Agbar, Fòrum, Parc de la Ciutadella, Plaça de Catalunya and La Rambla.

Rollerblading

The most popular parts of town for a gentle rollerblade are the esplanade along La Barceloneta beach and around Port Olímpic.

Sailing & Windsurfing

Head to **Base Nautica Municipal** (Map pp306-7; 93 221 04 32; www.basenautica.org; Avinguda Litoral s/n; M Poblenou), just back from Platja de la Mar Bella, for courses in pleasure-boat handling, kayaking or windsurfing (€179 for 10 hours' tuition).

Swimming

Down by La Barceloneta, **Club Natació Atlètic-Barcelona** (Map pp312-13; 93 221 00 10; www.cnab.org;

BICYCLE TOURS

Barcelona is awash with companies offering bicycle tours. Tours typically take two to four hours and generally stick to the old city, the Sagrada Família and the beaches. Operators include:

Barcelona By Bike (☎ 93 268 81 07; www.barcelonabybike.com)

BarcelonaBiking.com (Map pp316–17; ☎ 656 356300; www.barcelonabiking.com; Baixada de Sant Miquel 6)

Bike Tours Barcelona (Map pp316-17; ☎ 93 268 21 05; www.biketoursbarcelona.com; Carrer de l'Esparteria 3)

Fat Tire Bike Tours (Map pp316–17; ☎ 93 301 36 12; www.fattirebiketoursbarcelona.com; Carrer dels Escudellers 48)

Plaça de Mar s/n; adult/under 10yr €10.10/5.85; ⏲ 6.30am-11pm Mon-Fri, 7am-11pm Sat year-round, 8am-5pm Sun & holidays Oct–mid-May, 8am-8pm Sun & holidays mid-May–Sep; Ⓜ Barceloneta, 🚌 17, 39, 57, 64) has an indoor and two outdoor pools, a gym and private beach access.

Included in the standard price to Barcelona's Olympic pool, **Piscines Bernat Picornell** (Map pp306-7; ☎ 93 423 40 41; www.picornell.com in Catalan; Avinguda de l'Estadi 30-38; adult/senior & under 15yr/15-25yr €9.20/5.15/5.60, outdoor pool only Jun-Sep adult/6-14yr & senior €5.10/3.55; ⏲ 6.45am-midnight Mon-Fri, 7am-9pm Sat, 7.30am-4pm Sun; outdoor pool 10am-6pm Mon-Sat, 10am-4pm Sun Mar-Jun & Oct-Nov, 10am-4.30pm Mon-Sat, 10am-4pm Sun Dec-Mar, 9am-9pm Mon-Sat, 9am-8pm Sun Jun-Sep; 🚌 50, 61 or PM), is use of the gym, saunas and spa bath.

Water babies will adore the thalassotherapeutic sports centre, **Poliesportiu Marítim** (Map pp306-7; ☎ 93 224 04 40; www.claror.cat in Catalan; Passeig Marítim de la Barceloneta 33-35; admission Mon-Fri €14.40, Sat, Sun & holidays €17; ⏲ 7am-midnight Mon-Fri, 8am-9pm Sat, 8am-4pm Sun & holidays; Ⓜ Ciutadella-Vila Olímpica). Apart from the smallish training pool, the centre is a minor labyrinth of spa pools that are hot, warm and freezing cold, along with waterfalls for massage relief. When you're sufficiently relaxed, you can stumble outside and flop on to the beach.

WALKING TOUR

A great deal of what makes Barcelona fascinating is crowded into a relatively compact space, making an introductory strolling tour a great way to make the city's acquaintance (see Map p342). There's nothing wrong with following the crowds to start off with, so wander down La Rambla from **Plaça de Catalunya (1)**. Along the way, sniff around the **Mercat de la Boqueria** (**2**; p352), pop into the **Gran Teatre del Liceu** (**3**; p321) and visit one of Gaudí's earlier efforts, the **Palau Güell** (**4**; p325). From here, cross La Rambla and busy **Plaça Reial (5)** and make for **Plaça de Sant Jaume** (**6**; p322), at the core of the Barri Gòtic and the political heart of the city for 2000 years. You can examine the city's Roman origins in the nearby **Museu d'Història de la Ciutat** (**7**; p323). From the complex of buildings huddled around the museum and Plaça del Rei, you pass the **Museu Frederic Marès** (**8**; p323) en route for the main facade of the **Catedral** (**9**; p322). From there, make the loop down Via Laietana to admire what remains of the **Roman walls** (**10**; p324), and then branch off down Carrer de l'Argenteria to reach the splendid Gothic **Església de Santa Maria del Mar** (**11**; p326). Circle around it and up noble Carrer de Montcada, home to several museums including the **Museu Picasso** (**12**; p326). Proceed north past the **Mercat de Santa Caterina** (**13**; p326), a daring 21st-century reincarnation of a grand 19th-century produce market on the site of a medieval monastery; and then dogleg on to the stunning Modernista **Palau de la Música Catalana** (**14**; p325).

COURSES

Barcelona is bristling with schools offering Spanish- and Catalan-language courses:

Escola Oficial d'Idiomes de Barcelona (Map pp312-13; ☎ 93 324 93 30; www.eoibd.es in Spanish; Avinguda de les Drassanes s/n; Ⓜ Drassanes) Part-time courses (around 10 hours a week) in Spanish and Catalan (around €175 for a semester). Because of the demand for Spanish, there is no guarantee of a place.

International House (Map pp312-13; ☎ 93 268 45 11; www.ihes.com/bcn; Carrer de Trafalgar 14; Ⓜ Arc de Triomf) Intensive courses from around €390 for two weeks. Staff can also organise accommodation.

Universitat de Barcelona (Map pp312-13; Gran Via de les Corts Catalanes 585) Spanish (☎ 93 403 55 19; www.eh.ub.es); Catalan (☎ 93 403 54 78; www.ub.edu/slc) Intensive courses (40 hours' tuition over periods ranging from two weeks to a month; €413) in Spanish year-round. Longer Spanish and Catalan courses are also available.

And you can learn lots more in Barcelona, such as salsa and sauces:

Antilla BCN Escuela de Baile (Map pp306-7; ☎ 93 451 45 64, 610 900558; www.antillasalsa.com; Carrer d'Aragó 141) The place to learn salsa and other Caribbean dance. Ten weekly one-hour lessons cost €110.

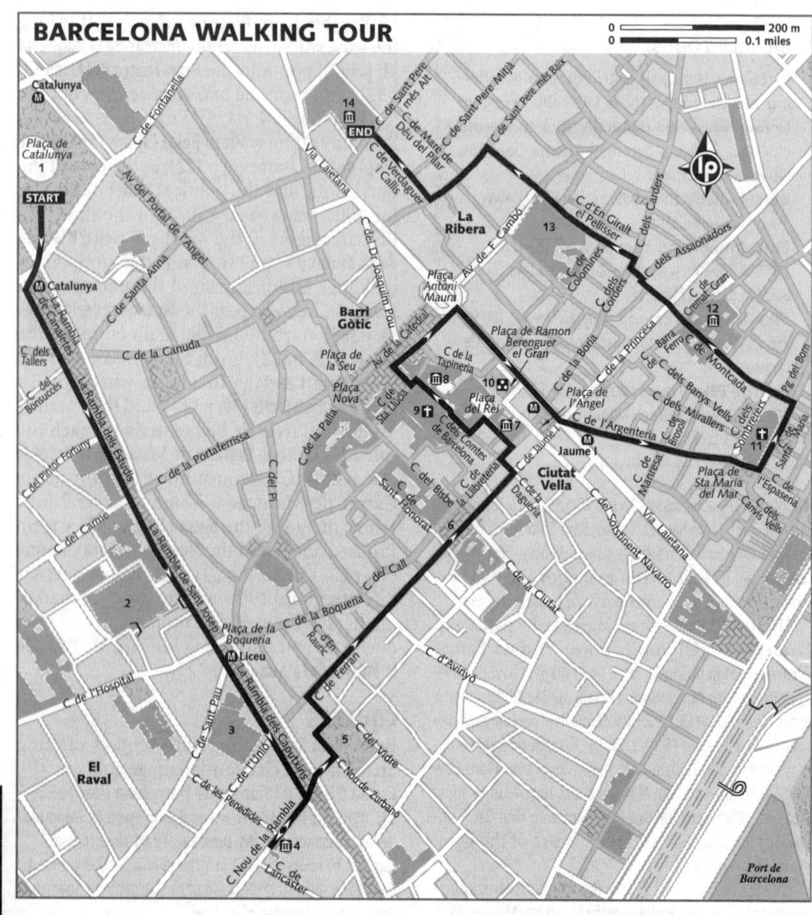

> **WALK FACTS**
>
> **Start** Plaça de Catalunya
> **Finish** Palau de la Música Catalana
> **Distance** 3.5km
> **Duration** 1½ hours

Cook and Taste (Map pp316-17; ☎ 93 302 13 20; www.cookandtaste.net; La Rambla 58; half-day workshop €60) Learn to whip up a paella or stir a gazpacho in this Spanish cookery school.

BARCELONA FOR CHILDREN

There's plenty to interest kids, from street theatre on La Rambla to the beaches. Transport is good, many attractions are huddled fairly close together and children are generally welcome in restaurants and cafes.

An initial stroll along La Rambla is full of potential distractions and wonders, from the bird stands to the living statues and buskers, and the **Museu de Cera** (Wax Museum; p321) is a classic diversion.

At the bottom end of La Rambla, more options present themselves: a ride up to the top of the **Monument a Colom** (p321) or seeing sharks at **L'Aquàrium** (p329).

The **Transbordador Aeri** (p329), strung across the harbour between La Barceloneta and Montjuïc, is an irresistible ride. Or scare the willies out of them with a ride in the Hotel Krueger horror house at Tibidabo's **Parc d'Atraccions** (p334) amusement park!

Of the city's museums, those most likely to capture children's imagination as much as that of their adult companions are the **Museu Marítim** (p321), the **Museu de la Xocolata** (p327) and the popular interactive **CosmoCaixa** (p334).

In the summer months you will doubtless be rewarded by squeals of delight if you take the bairns to one of the city's **swimming pools** (p340) and/or the **beach**. In cooler weather, parks can be a good choice. A walk in the gardens of Montjuïc, including some exploration of its **Castell** (p338), will appeal to everyone. Adults find the maze of the **Jardins del Laberint d'Horta** (p335) hard to work out too. Another old favourite with most children is a visit to see the animals at the **Zoo de Barcelona** (p328).

TOURS

Several tour options present themselves if you want a hand getting around the sights:

Barcelona Scooter (☎ 93 285 38 32; €45; ⏲ 10.30am Sat) Run by Cooltra (see p361); offers a four-hour tour around the city by scooter in conjunction with the city tourism office. Departure is from in front of the Sagrada Família on Carrer de Sardenya.

Barcelona Vibes (Map pp316-17; ☎ 93 310 37 47; www.barcelonavibes.com; Carrer de Milans 7) Offers everything from luxury private tours of the city in a chauffeur-driven Mercedes to trips around Catalonia. You can hire a Harley or sign for a city tour by Segway. If it can be booked or organised, it can probably do it.

Barcelona Walking Tours (Map pp312-13; ☎ 93 285 38 34; Plaça de Catalunya 17-S) The Oficina d'Informació de Turisme de Barcelona organises guided walking tours. One explores the Barri Gòtic (adult/child €11/4.50; ⏲ English 10am daily, Spanish and Catalan noon Saturday), another follows in Picasso's footsteps and winds up at the Museu Picasso, to which entry is included in the price (adult/child €15/6.50; ⏲ English 10.30am Tuesday to Sunday, Spanish and Catalan 11.30am Saturday) and a third takes in the main jewels of Modernisme (adult/child €11/4.50; ⏲ English 4pm Friday and Saturday, Spanish 4pm Saturday, all tours at 6pm June to September). It also offers a 'gourmet' tour of traditional purveyors of fine foodstuffs, from chocolate to sausages, across the old city (adult/child €15/6.50; ⏲ English 11am Friday and Saturday, Spanish and Catalan 11am Saturday). All tours last two hours and start at the tourist office.

BCN Skytour (Map pp306-7; ☎ 93 224 07 10; www.cathelicopters.com; Heliport, Passeig de l'Escullera; €80 per person; ⏲ 10am-7pm) A 10-minute thrill at 800m up in a helicopter will give a real bird's-eye view of the city. You can take the golondrina tour boats (p328) or a taxi to the heliport.

Bus Turístic (Map pp312-13; ☎ 010; www.tmb.net; one day adult/4-12yr €19/11, 2 consecutive days €23/15; ⏲ 9am-7.45pm) This hop-on, hop-off service covers three circuits (44 stops) linking virtually all the major tourist sights. Tourist offices, TMB transport authority offices and many hotels have leaflets explaining the system. Each of the two main circuits takes approximately two hours. The third circuit, from Port Olímpic to the Fòrum, runs from April to September and is less interesting.

Catalunya Bus Turístic (Map pp312-13; ☎ 93 285 38 32; www.tmb.net; tours €66) Two day-tour routes leaving from Plaça de Catalunya: Girona and Figueres; and Vilafranca del Penedès (Torres winery visit), Montserrat and Sitges. Both run daily (except Monday) from March to October, leaving at 8.30am and returning at 8pm.

Gocar (Map pp316-17; ☎ 902 30 13 33; www.gocartours.es; Carrer de Freixures 23bis; rental per hr/day €35/99) These GPS-guided 'cars' (really two-seat, three-wheel mopeds) allow you to tour around town and listen to commentaries on major sights as you go.

My Favourite Things (☎ 637 265405; www.myft.net; tours €26-32) These people offer tours (with no more than 10 participants) based on numerous themes: anything from design to food, rollerblading to sailing. Some of the more unusual activities cost more and times vary.

FESTIVALS & EVENTS

January

Reis/Reyes Epifanía (the Epiphany) on 6 January is also known as the Dia dels Reis Mags/Día de los Reyes Magos (Three Kings' Day). The night before, children delight in the Cavalcada dels Reis Mags (Parade of the Three Kings), a colourful parade of floats and music during which tons of sweets are thrown into the crowd of eager kids (and not a few adults!).

April

Dia de Sant Jordi This is the day of Catalonia's patron saint (George) and also the Day of the Book: men give women a rose, women give men a book, publishers launch new titles; La Rambla and Plaça de Sant Jaume are filled with book and flower stalls. Celebrated on 23 April.

BABYSITTING AGENCIES

Most of the midrange and top-end hotels in Barcelona can organise a babysitting service. A company that many hotels use, and which you can also contact directly, is **5 Serveis** (Map pp316-17; ☎ 93 412 56 76; Carrer de Pelai 50). Multilingual *canguros* (babysitters) are available. Reckon on paying about €10 an hour plus the cost of the babysitter's taxi ride home.

GAY & LESBIAN BARCELONA

The city's tourist board publishes *Barcelona – The Official Gay and Lesbian Tourist Guide* bi-annually. A couple of informative free magazines are in circulation in gay bookshops and bars. One is the biweekly *Shanguide*. It is jammed with listings and contact ads and aimed principally at readers in Barcelona and Madrid. For a listing of gay and lesbian websites, see p873.

Barcelona has a fairly busy gay scene, much of it concentrated in the 'Gaixample', between Carrer de Muntaner and Carrer de Balmes, around Carrer del Consell de Cent.

Arena Madre (Map pp312-13; ☎ 93 487 83 42; www.arenadisco.com; Carrer de Balmes 32; admission €6-12; ⏰ 12.30-6am) Popular with a young, cruisy gay crowd, Arena is one of the top gay clubs in town. Keep an eye on Wednesday's drag shows.

Bacon Bear (Map pp312-13; Carrer de Casanova 64; ⏰ 6pm-2.30am) Every bear needs a cave, and this is a friendly one. It's really just a big bar for burly gay folk.

Dietrich Gay Teatro Café (Map pp312-13; ☎ 93 451 77 07; Carrer del Consell de Cent 255; ⏰ 10.30pm-3am) It's show time at 1am, with at least one drag-queen gala a night at this cabaret-style locale dedicated to Marlene.

Metro (Map pp312-13; ☎ 93 323 52 27; www.metrodiscobcn.com; Carrer de Sepúlveda 185; ⏰ midnight-5am Sun-Thu, midnight-6am Fri & Sat) Metro attracts a casual crowd with its two dance floors, three bars and very dark room.

New Chaps (Map pp310-11; ☎ 93 215 53 65; Avinguda Diagonal 395; ⏰ 9pm-3am) Leather-lovers get in some close-quarters inspection on the dance floor and more especially in the dark room.

DBoy (Map pp310-11; www.dboyclub.com; Ronda de Sant Pere 19-21; ⏰ midnight-6am Fri-Sun & holidays) Beautiful boys and fluttering fag hags crowd into this completely renovated club. The La Madame Sunday session is especially big.

May

Primavera Sound (www.primaverasound.com) For three days late in May (or early June) the Auditori Fòrum and other locations around town become the combined stage for a host of international DJs and musicians.

June

Sónar (www.sonar.es) Sónar is Barcelona's celebration of electronic music and said to be Europe's biggest such event. Locations and dates change each year.

Dia de Sant Joan This is a colourful midsummer celebration on 24 June with bonfires, even in the squares of L'Eixample, and fireworks marking the evening preceding this holiday.

Dia per l'Alliberament Lesbià i Gai The city's big gay and lesbian festival and parade on the Saturday nearest 28 June.

June–August

Grec Arts Festival (www.barcelonafestival.com) Held from late June to August, the Grec Arts Festival involves music, dance and theatre at many locations across the city.

July

Summercase (www.summercase.com) Since 2006, this weekend music fest in mid-July has drawn big crowds for top contemporary acts (among those in 2008 were M.I.A, Mystery Jets and, in revival, The Stanglers) to the Parc del Fòrum.

August

Festa Major de Gràcia (www.festamajordegracia.org) This is a madcap local festival held in Gràcia around 15 August, with decorated streets, dancing and concerts.

September

La Diada Catalonia's national day on 11 September, marking the fall of Barcelona in 1714, is a fairly solemn holiday in Barcelona.

Festes de la Mercè (www.bcn.cat/merce) The city's biggest party involves around four days of concerts, dancing, *castellers* (human-castle builders), a fireworks display synchronised with the Montjuïc fountains, dances of giants on the Saturday, and *correfocs* – a parade of fireworks-spitting dragons and devils from all over Catalonia, on the Sunday. Held around 24 September.

SLEEPING

There is no shortage of hotels (with new ones opening seemingly every five minutes) in Barcelona, but its continuing status as one of Europe's city-break getaway flavours-of-the-month and its busy trade fair calendar mean that it is often a good idea to book in advance.

Those looking for cheaper accommodation close to the action should check out the Barri Gòtic and El Raval. Some good lower-end *pensiones* (small private hotels) are also scattered about L'Eixample. A growing range of boutique-style hotels with real charm in all categories has enriched the offerings in the past few years. A broad range of midrange and top-end places are spread across L'Eixample, most of them in easy striking distance of the old town. A growing range of options now makes it easier to stay in La Ribera and near the beaches at La Barceloneta.

La Rambla

Hotel Continental (Map pp316-17; ☎ 93 301 25 70; www.hotelcontinental.com; La Rambla 138; s/d €82/92;) Rooms in this classic old Barcelona hotel (where George Orwell stayed during the civil war) are spare but have romantic touches such as ceiling fans. Try for a double with balcony over La Rambla (for which you pay €20 extra). You can have breakfast in your room.

Barri Gòtic

Alberg Hostel Itaca (Map pp316-17; ☎ 93 301 97 51; www.jo-oh.com/itaca; Carrer de Ripoll 21; dm €18, d €50-55;) A bright option near La Catedral, Itaca has spacious dorms (sleeping six, eight or 12 people), with parquet floors, pleasant spring colours, and a couple of doubles with private bathroom. You can make use of the kitchen and exchange books.

Hostal Campi (Map pp316-17; ☎ 93 301 35 45; hcampi@terra.es; Carrer de la Canuda 4; d €62, s/d without bathroom €31/54) An excellent bottom-end deal. The best rooms are the doubles with their own loo and shower. Although basic, they are extremely roomy and bright.

Hotel California (Map pp316-17; ☎ 93 317 77 66; www.hotelcaliforniabcn.com; Carrer d'En Rauric 14; s/d €75/130;) A classic, central, gay-friendly establishment, the California offers simple but spotlessly kept rooms in light, neutral colours, with good-sized beds and a bustling breakfast room. Room service operates 24 hours.

Hotel Jardí (Map pp316-17; ☎ 93 301 59 00; www.hoteljardi-barcelona.com; Plaça de Sant Josep Oriol 1; d €79-106;) The best rooms in this attractively located spot are the doubles with a balcony over one of the prettiest squares in the city. The rest are dull.

Hotel Neri (Map pp316-17; ☎ 93 304 06 55; www.hotelneri.com; Carrer de Sant Sever 5; d from €248;) Occupying a beautifully adapted, centuries-old building, this stunningly renovated medieval mansion combines historic stone walls with sexy plasma TVs. Downstairs is a fine restaurant and you can take a drink and catch some rays on the roof deck.

El Raval

Barcelona Mar Hostel (Map pp316-17; ☎ 93 324 85 30; www.barcelonamar.com; Carrer de Sant Pau 80; dm €16-27, d €42-60;) Bunk down in no-nonsense double rooms and dorms for six to 16 people. You are within stumbling distance of plenty of bars on Rambla del Raval. It's open 24 hours and there's free access to internet, lockers, kitchen and luggage storage.

Hostal Gat Raval (Map pp312-13; ☎ 93 481 66 70; www.gataccommodation.com; Carrer de Joaquín Costa 44; d €80, s/d without bathroom €50/70;) There's a pea-green and lemon-lime colour scheme in this hip, young, 2nd-floor *hostal* deep in El Raval. Rooms are pleasant, secure and each is behind a green door, but only some have private bathroom. Across the road you have a choice of busy bars to while away the evenings.

Hotel Aneto (Map pp316-17; ☎ 93 301 99 89; www.hotelaneto.com; Carrer del Carme 38; s/d €55/75;) Nestled in a lively street in one of the nicer parts of El Raval, the Aneto is a good-value, simple base to range out from. The best rooms are the doubles with the shuttered street-side balconies.

Hotel Peninsular (Map pp316-17; ☎ 93 302 31 38; www.hpeninsular.com; Carrer de Sant Pau 34; s/d/tr/q €55/78/95/120;) The star attraction of this one-time convent is the plant-draped atrium extending the full height of the hotel, at the bottom of which you take breakfast in the morning. Rooms are simple, clean and (mostly) spacious.

Hostal Gat Xino (Map pp312-13; ☎ 93 324 88 33; www.gataccommodation.com; Carrer de l'Hospital 149-155; s/d €66/84, suite with terrace €130;) Better still than Gat Raval is this newer version. The lime-green theme continues but rooms are more spacious and all have bathroom. The suite has views to Montjuïc.

Hotel Mesón de Castilla (Map pp312-13; ☎ 93 318 21 82; www.husa.es; Carrer de Valldonzella 5; s/d €117/149; P) Some characterful Modernista touches remain on the 1st floor of this elegant hotel. Heavy wooden furniture across several timeless sitting rooms contrasts with playful stained glass and murals, and Gaudíesque window mouldings. Rooms have a classic charm and the best doubles are those with terraces out the back.

Hotel San Agustín (Map pp316-17; ☎ 93 318 16 58; www.hotelsa.com; Plaça de Sant Agustí 3; s/d €123/171;) Once an 18th-century monastery, this hotel opened in 1840, making it the city's oldest. The location is perfect: a quick stroll off La

Rambla on a curious square. Rooms sparkle, are mostly spacious and light and have parquet floors. Consider an attic double, with a sloping ceiling and bird's-eye views.

Casa Camper (Map pp316-17; ☎ 93 342 62 80; www.camper.es; Carrer d'Elisabets 11; s/d €240/284;) Run by the Mallorcan shoe people in the better end of El Raval, these designer digs offer rooms with a few surprises, like the Vinçon furniture. Across the corridor from each room is a separate, private sitting room, with balcony, TV and hammock.

La Ribera

Pensió 2000 (Map pp312-13; ☎ 93 310 74 66; www.pensio2000.com; Carrer de Sant Pere més Alt 6; s/d €66/86, without bathroom €54/67;) Sitting in front of the Modernista chocolate box that is the Palau de la Música Catalana (p325), this cheerful *pensión*, with its seven canary-yellow rooms, is a conveniently placed option. The best rooms have their own bathroom. You can also take time out on the little terrace.

Chic & Basic (Map pp316-17; ☎ 93 295 46 52; www.chicandbasic.com; Carrer de la Princesa 50; d €96-171;) In a completely renovated building with high vaults in the facade are 31 spotlessly white rooms. There are high ceilings, enormous beds (room types are classed as M, L and XL!) and lots of detailed touches (LED lighting, TFT TV screens and the retention of many beautiful old features of the original building, such as the marble staircase). Have a drink in its ground-floor White Bar, which is all white.

our pick **Hotel Banys Orientals** (Map pp316-17; ☎ 93 268 84 60; www.hotelbanysorientals.com; Carrer de l'Argenteria 37; s/d €89/107;) Cool blues and aquamarines combine with dark-hued parquet floors to lend this boutique beauty an understated charm. All rooms – admittedly on the small side but impeccably presented – look onto the street or back lanes. It has more spacious suites in two other nearby buildings.

Port Vell & the Coast

Hostel Sea Point (Map pp312-13; ☎ 93 231 20 45; www.seapointhostel.com; Plaça del Mar 1-4; dm €21.50;) What this youth hostel lacks in charm it makes up for in position. Set in an ugly high-rise and with rather tight dorms, it is right on the beach. The only other options in Barcelona that can make such a boast are five-star. It organises activities like bike rides.

Hotel del Mar (Map pp316-17; ☎ 93 319 33 02; www.gargallohotels.es; Plaça de Palau 19; s/d €102/118;) The 'Sea Hotel' is neatly placed between Port Vell and El Born. Some of the rooms in this classified building have balconies with waterfront views. It's no more than 10 minutes' walk from the beaches and seafood of La Barceloneta and the bars of El Born.

Hotel 54 (Map pp312-13; ☎ 93 225 00 54; www.hotel54barceloneta.com; Passeig de Joan de Borbó 54; s €135, d €145-190;) Location, location, location. Modern rooms, with dark tile floors, designer bathrooms and LCD TVs, are above all sought after for the marina and sunset views. Other rooms look out over the lanes of La Barceloneta and are cheaper. For those harbour views you can also sit on the roof terrace.

Hotel Arts Barcelona (Map pp306-7; ☎ 93 221 10 00; www.ritzcarlton.com; Carrer de la Marina 19-21; r €425; P) In one of the two sky-high towers that dominate Port Olímpic, these are Barcelona's most fashionable digs, frequented by VIPs from all over the planet. The rooms have unbeatable views. Prices vary greatly according to the size and position of the rooms. You can indulge in all sorts of extras, from massages to your own private bath butler.

L'Eixample

BUDGET

Centric Point (Map pp310-11; ☎ 93 215 65 38; www.centricpointhostel.com; Passeig de Gràcia 33; d €50, dm €21-27;) Stay on Barcelona's snootiest boulevard without paying the commensurate rent! One of four hostels run by the same people, this one offers 400 beds in a Modernista building close to Plaça de Catalunya. Linen is supplied and there is a lively bar on the premises.

Hostal Girona (Map pp310-11; ☎ 93 265 02 59; www.hostalgirona.com; Carrer de Girona 24; r up to €66) A 2nd-floor, family-run *hostal*, the Girona is a basic but clean and friendly spot. The atmosphere is Catalan and somewhat frozen in time but good value. Rooms range from poky singles with communal bathroom to airy doubles with balcony (beware of traffic noise in summer when you'll have to keep the windows open).

Hostal Aribau (Map pp312-13; ☎ 93 453 11 06; www.hostalaribau.com; Carrer de Aribau 37; s/d/tr €60/65/80, s/d without bathroom €45/55;) Handily located within brisk walking distance of Ciutat Vella and within a busy part of L'Eixample, this is a straightforward family-run *hostal* with smallish but clean rooms.

MIDRANGE

Hostal Central (Map pp310-11; ☎ 93 245 19 81; www.hostalcentralbarcelona.com; Carrer de la Diputació 346; s/d/tr €50/85/106; ⊠ ❄) In a pretty, early-20th-century apartment building you'll find 13 renovated rooms (all nonsmoking and mostly with own bathroom). They are not excessively big (and some rather teensy) but are pleasant and clean.

Market Hotel (Map pp312-13; ☎ 93 325 12 05; www.markethotel.com.es; Passatge de Sant Antoni Abad 10; s/d/ste €80/93/112; ❄ 💻) Attractively located in a renovated building along a narrow lane just north of the grand old Sant Antoni market (which unfortunately is going to be shut for years of much-needed works), this place has an air of simple chic. Room decor is a pleasing combination of white, dark nut-browns, light timber and reds.

Hostal Goya (Map pp310-11; ☎ 93 302 25 65; www.hostalgoya.com; Carrer de Pau Claris 74; s/d €70/96-113; ❄) The Goya is a gem of a spot on the chichi side of l'Eixample and a short stroll from Plaça de Catalunya. Rooms have parquet floors and a light colour scheme that varies from room to room. In the bathrooms, the original mosaic floors have largely been retained, combined with contemporary design features.

Hostal Palacios (Map pp310-11; ☎ 93 301 30 79; www.hostalpalacios.com; Rambla de Catalunya 27; s €69, d €99-129; ❄ 💻) This classy *hostal* offers fine, sunny rooms with high ceilings and old-style furnishings. The 'suites', which can be taken as triples, are roomy and worth the extra outlay.

Hotel d'Uxelles (Map pp310-11; ☎ 93 265 25 60; www.hotelduxelles.com; Gran Via de les Corts Catalanes 688; s/d €86/106; ❄ 💻) Wrought-iron bedsteads are overshadowed by flowing drapes in rooms that each have their own personal decor (from blues and whites to beige-and-cream combos). Some have little terraces. Get a back room as Gran Via is incredibly noisy.

Hotel Constanza (Map pp310-11; ☎ 93 270 19 10; www.hotelconstanza.com; Carrer del Bruc 33; s/d €90/120; ❄ 💻) Constanza is a boutique belle that has stolen the heart of many a visitor to Barcelona. Even smaller singles are made to feel special with broad mirrors and strong colours (reds and yellows, with black furniture).

Hotel Axel (Map pp312-13; ☎ 93 323 93 93; www.axelhotels.com; Carrer d'Aribau 33; s/d from €144/197; ❄ 💻 🏊) Fashion- and gay-friendly, the sleek-lined, corner-block Axel offers modern touches in its designer rooms. Plasma-screen TVs and (in the double rooms) king-size beds are just some of the pluses. Take a break in the rooftop pool, the Finnish sauna or the Jacuzzi. Or sip a cocktail at the summer skybar.

Hotel Hispanos Siete Suiza (Map pp310-11; ☎ 93 208 20 51; www.barcelona19apartments.com; Carrer de Sicilia 255; r for up to 4 people €214-278; P ❄ 💻 ♿) Near La Sagrada Família, this hotel's apartments have two double rooms and separate bathrooms, a lounge, a fully equipped kitchen and a terrace.

TOP END

Hotel Claris (Map pp310-11; ☎ 93 487 62 62; www.derbyhotels.es; Carrer de Pau Claris 150; d €251-401; P ❄ 🏊) Inside the fine 19th-century Palacio Verdura lurks one of the city's best-known designer digs (with a permanent art collection on show). Decor varies greatly: some rooms are strikingly modern, while others cede to more classic tastes in luxury.

Hotel Omm (Map pp310-11; ☎ 93 445 40 00; www.hotelomm.es; Carrer de Rosselló 265; d from €257; ❄ 🏊) The balconies look like strips of metallic skin peeled back from the shiny surface of the hotel – the sort of idea a latter-day Modernista might have had! Light, clear tones dominate in the ultramodern rooms, and the sprawling foyer bar is a popular evening meeting point for guests and outsiders alike.

Gràcia

Hotel Casa Fuster (Map pp310-11; ☎ 93 255 30 00; www.hotelcasafuster.com; Passeig de Gràcia 132; d from €407; P ❄ 💻 🏊) It is hard to believe the wrecking ball once threatened this Modernista mansion turned luxury hotel. Standard rooms are plush if smallish. Period features have been lovingly restored and complemented with hydromassage tubs and king-sized beds. Try for a room with a balcony looking down Passeig de Gràcia.

Tibidabo & Around

Alberg Mare de Déu de Montserrat (Map pp306-7; ☎ 93 210 51 51; www.xanascat.cat; Passeig de la Mare de Déu del Coll 41-51; dm under 26yr or ISIC card-holders/others up to €20.45/24.30; P 💻) Four kilometres north of the city centre, this hostel's main building is a magnificent former mansion with a Mudéjar-style lobby. Most rooms sleep six. Sitting outside on balmy summer nights makes a pleasant alternative to a trip into town. Take the metro to Vallcarca station and then bus 28 or 92.

Poble Sec

Hostel Mambo Tango (Map pp312-13; ☎ 93 442 51 64; www.hostelmambotango.com; Carrer del Poeta Cabanyes 23; dm €26;) A fun, international hostel to hang out in, the Mambo Tango has basic dorms (from six to 10 people) and a welcoming, somewhat chaotic atmosphere. The playful atmosphere is reflected in the kooky colour scheme in the bathrooms!

Melon District (Map pp312-13; ☎ 93 329 96 67; www.melondistrict.com; Avinguda Parallel 101; s/d €43/54;) Whiter than white seems to be the policy in this spanking-new student residence, where you can stay the night or book in for a year. Erasmus folks are attracted to this hostel-style spot, where the only objects in the rooms that aren't white are the green plastic chairs.

Camping

The nearest camping grounds to Barcelona lie some way out of town. A couple are on the main coast road heading for Sitges.

Camping Masnou (☎ 93 555 15 03; Camí Fabra 33, El Masnou; 2-person sites with car €30; year-round; P) Some 11km northeast of the city and only 200m from El Masnou train station (reached by *rodalies* trains from Catalunya station on Plaça de Catalunya), this camping ground offers some shade, is near the beach and is reasonable value.

Camping Tres Estrellas (☎ 93 633 06 37; www.camping3estrellas.com; Carretera C31, Km186.2, Viladecans; 2-person sites with car €33; mid-Mar–mid-Oct; P) This beachside camping ground is one of several located on a stretch starting about 12km southwest of Barcelona. It has shops, restaurants, bars, several pools and laundry facilities. There's a play area for kids and a basketball court. It's a comparatively green spot under shady pines. Bus L95 runs from the corner of Ronda de la Universitat and Rambla de Catalunya.

Apartments

An alternative accommodation option can be short-term apartment rental. Typical prices are around €80 to €100 for two people per night. If you're looking to do a short-term house swap, check out the ads on www.loquo.com. There are scores of rental services:

Apartment Barcelona (Map pp310-11; ☎ 93 215 79 34; www.apartmentbarcelona.com; Carrer de València 286)
Barcelona Apartments (Map pp306-7; ☎ 93 414 55 28; www.barcelonapartments.com; Via Augusta 173)
Barcelona On Line (Map pp310-11; ☎ 93 343 79 93/94; www.barcelona-on-line.es; Gran Via de les Corts Catalanes 662)
Lodging Barcelona (Map pp310-11; ☎ 93 467 78 00; www.lodgingbarcelona.com; Carrer de Balmes 62) Also offers accommodation options on boats in Port Vell (click on Apartamentos Flotantes)
Rent a Flat in Barcelona (Map pp312-13; ☎ 93 342 73 00; www.rentaflatinbarcelona.com; Carrer de Fontanella 18)

Long-Term Rentals

The **Universitat de Barcelona** (Map pp312-13; ☎ 93 402 11 00; Gran Via de les Corts Catalanes 585), the **British Council** (Map pp306-7; ☎ 93 241 99 77; Carrer d' Amigó 83) and **International House** (Map pp312-13; ☎ 93 268 45 11; Carrer de Trafalgar 14) have noticeboards with ads for flat shares.

Another option for students coming to Barcelona to study is **Rent a Bedroom** (Map pp312-13; ☎ 93 217 25 83; www.rentabedroom.com; Avinguda Parallel 101). Staff can organise rooms in share houses for between €300 and €700, inclusive of bills.

The free English-language monthly *Barcelona Metropolitan*, found in bars, some hotels, and occasionally at tourist offices, carries rental classifieds in English, as does another monthly freebie, *Catalunya Classified*. Check out the ads at www.loquo.com too. Otherwise, get hold of *Anuntis*, the weekly classifieds paper. The last few pages of the *Suplement Immobiliària* (Real-Estate Supplement) carry ads for shared accommodation under the heading *lloguer/hostes i vivendes a compartir*. Count on rent of €350 a month or more. To this, you need to add your share of bills (gas, electricity, water, phone and *comunidad* – building maintenance).

EATING

Barcelona was always a good place to eat but in recent years it has evolved into something of a foodies' paradise on earth, combining rich Catalan cooking traditions with a new wave of cutting-edge chefs at the vanguard of what has been dubbed *nueva cocina española*. The city has taken on quite a cosmopolitan hue too.

The main concentration of new and experimental cuisine is in El Born, the trendy, Boho lower side of La Ribera in the old city. More traditional restaurants, often not too demanding fiscally speaking, are scattered across the Barri Gòtic and there are some gems in El Raval too.

CAFES IN WHICH TO MEET

Located close to Plaça de Catalunya, **Café Zurich** (Map pp316-17; ☎ 93 317 91 53; Carrer de Pelai 39; coffee & pastries €3-4; 8pm-midnight) is a prime spot for coffee, newspaper and watching the passing street theatre at this crucial city crossroads. It's a visible place to meet and start a night out downtown.

Cafè de l'Òpera (Map pp316-17; ☎ 93 317 75 85; La Rambla 74), opposite the Gran Teatre del Liceu opera house, was founded in 1876. Although now somewhat neglected, it is pleasant for an early evening tipple or coffee and croissants. Head upstairs for a seat overlooking the boulevard.

Gràcia is also full of tempting eateries, among them a legion of Middle Eastern and Greek joints.

Across the broad expanse of L'Eixample and the Zona Alta, and further outlying districts, you'll find all sorts. The majority of the seriously top-level joints are to be found secreted away in such areas. You need to know where you are going, however, as wandering about aimlessly and picking whatever takes your fancy is not as feasible as in the old city.

Cartas (menus) may be in Catalan, Spanish or both; some establishments also have foreign-language menus.

Barri Gòtic

Can Conesa (Map pp316-17; ☎ 93 310 57 95; Carrer de la Llibreteria 1; entrepans & toasted sandwiches €3-5; Mon-Sat) This place has been doling out delicious *entrepans* (bread rolls with filling), frankfurters and toasted sandwiches here for more than 50 years – *barcelonins* swear by it and queue for them.

Maoz (Map pp316-17; Carrer de Ferran 13; falafels €3-4.50; noon-2am; V) There's a lot of goodness packed into a tiny space here. The extent to which you stuff yourself depends on just how much of the various fillings you can cram into your pitta.

Bagel Shop (Map pp316-17; ☎ 93 302 41 61; Carrer de la Canuda 25; meals €10; 9.30am-9.30pm Mon-Sat, 11am-4pm Sun; ☒) Searching for a smoked-salmon and cream-cheese bagel? You've found the spot for this and a whole array of savoury and sweet bagels using different types of bread.

Bar Celta (Map pp316-17; ☎ 93 315 00 06; Carrer de la Mercè 16; meals €20; noon-midnight) Specialists in *pulpo* (octopus) and other seaside delights from Galicia in the country's northwest; the waiters waste no time in serving up bottles of crisp white Ribeiro wine to wash down the *raciones* (large tapas serving).

Agut (Map pp316-17; ☎ 93 315 17 09; Carrer d'En Gignàs 16; meals €35; lunch & dinner Tue-Sat, lunch Sun; ☒) Contemporary paintings set a contrast with the fine traditional Catalan dishes offered in this timeless restaurant. You might start with something like the *bouillabaisse con cigalitas de playa* (little seawater crayfish) for €11 and follow with an oak-grilled meat dish.

Pla (Map pp316-17; ☎ 93 412 65 52; www.pla-repla.com; Carrer de Bellafila 5; meals €45-50; dinner daily; ☒) In this modern den of inventive cooking with music worthy of a club, the chefs present deliciously strange combinations such as *bacallà amb salsa de pomes verdes* (cod in a green apple sauce). Exotic meats like kangaroo turn up on the menu too.

El Raval

Organic (Map pp316-17; ☎ 93 301 09 02; www.antoniaorganickitchen.com; Carrer de la Junta de Comerç 11; meals €14-20; noon-midnight; ☒ V) A long sprawl of a vegetarian diner, Organic is always full. Choose from a limited range of options that change from day to day, and tuck into the all-you-can-eat salad bar in the middle of the restaurant. At night prices go up a tad and a full waiting service operates.

Mesón David (Map pp312-13; ☎ 93 441 59 34; Carrer de les Carretes 63; meals €15-20; Tue-Sun) With its timber ceiling and chaotic feel, this is a great slice of old Spain. Plonk yourself down on a bench for gregarious dining. It's no-nonsense cooking here, and house specialities include *lechazo asado*, a great lump of roast suckling lamb (€7).

Bar Pinotxo (Map pp316-17; ☎ 93 317 17 31; Mercat de la Boqueria; meals €15-20; 6am-5pm Mon-Sat Sep-Jul) Of the half-dozen or so tapas bars and informal eateries scattered about the market, this one near the Rambla entrance is the most popular. Dig into tapas and *raciones* of hearty market food.

Restaurant El Cafetí (Map pp316-17; ☎ 93 329 24 19; Passatge de Bernardí; meals €25-30, menú €12; lunch & dinner Tue-Sat, lunch Sun; ☒) This diminutive eatery is filled with antique furniture and offers traditional local cooking, with one or two unorthodox variations. Paella and other rice dishes dominate. It is down an arcade just off Carrer de Sant Rafael.

Biblioteca (Map pp316-17; ☎ 93 412 62 21; Carrer de la Junta de Comerç 28; meals €35-40; dinner Mon-Fri, lunch & dinner Sat) Exposed-brick and creamy-white decor dominate in the 'Library', where the food represents a broad sweep across Spain, with careful creative touches and a good wine list. A good sample is *bacallà confitat amb suc d'escamarlans i llegums de temporada* (pickled salted cod with crayfish juice and seasonal vegetables).

Casa Leopoldo (Map pp316-17; ☎ 93 441 30 14; www.casaleopoldo.com; Carrer de Sant Rafael 24; meals €50; lunch & dinner Tue-Sat, lunch Sun Sep-Jul; ⊠) Several rambling dining areas with magnificent tiled walls and exposed timber-beam ceilings make this a fine option. The seafood menu is extensive and the local wine list strong. This is an old-town classic beloved of writers and artists down the decades.

La Ribera

Casa Delfin (Map pp316-17; ☎ 93 319 50 88; Passeig del Born 36; meals €15-20, menú del día €11; 6am-7pm Mon-Sat) Under siege from triremes of ultra avant-garde cookeries, the 'Dolphin House' continues to do what it has always done best – a bountiful lunch from an extensive menu of Spanish favourites. No frills, just good tucker amid all the fancy folk.

El Xampanyet (Map pp316-17; ☎ 93 319 70 03; Carrer de Montcada 22; meals €15-20; lunch & dinner Tue-Sat, lunch Sun) Nothing much has changed in this, one of the city's best-known *cava* (sparkling wine) bars. Plant yourself at the bar or seek out a table jammed up against the old-style tiled walls for a glass or three of *cava* and an assortment of tapas, such as the tangy *boquerons en vinagre* (white anchovies in vinegar).

Orígen (Map pp316-17; ☎ 93 310 75 31; www.origen99.com; Carrer de la Vidrieria 6-8; meals €15-20; 12.30pm-1am; ⊠) With a treasure chest of Catalan regional products for sale, this place also has a long menu of bite-sized dishes (mostly around €5 to €8), such as *ànec amb naps* (duck and turnip) or *civet de senglar* (jugged boar), that you mix and match over wine by the glass. Orígen's opening branches all over town.

Pla de la Garsa (Map pp316-17; ☎ 93 315 24 13; Carrer dels Assaonadors 13; meals €25; dinner daily; ⊠) This 17th-century house is ideal for a romantic dinner. Timber beams, a peppering of tables around the dining area and soft ambient music combine to make an enchanting setting for traditional Catalan cooking. Try *bacallà amb cigronets del Pla de Llerona* (salted cod with chickpeas).

Centre Cultural Euskal Etxea (Map pp316-17; ☎ 93 310 21 85; Placeta de Montcada 1; tapas €20-25, meals €35-40; lunch & dinner Tue-Sat, lunch Sun) Barcelona has plenty of Basque and pseudo-Basque eateries, but this is the real deal. It captures the feel of San Sebastián better than many of its newer competitors. Choose your *pintxos* (snacks), sip *txacoli* wine, and keep the toothpicks so the staff can count them up and work out your bill.

Cal Pep (Map pp316-17; ☎ 93 310 79 61; www.calpep.com; Plaça de les Olles 8; meals €45; lunch & dinner Tue-Fri, dinner Mon, lunch Sat Sep-Jul; ⊠) This gourmet tapas bar is one of the most popular in town and difficult to snaffle a spot in. Pep recommends *cloïsses amb pernil* (clams and ham – seriously!) or the *trifàsic*, a combo of calamari, whitebait and prawns (€12).

Comerç 24 (Map pp312-13; ☎ 93 319 21 02; www.carlesabellan.com; Carrer del Comerç 24; meals €50-60; Tue-Sat; ⊠) The edgy black-red-yellow decor in the rear dining area lends this culinary cauldron a New York feel. Chef Carles Abellán whips up some eccentric dishes, inspired by everything from sushi to *crostini*. Plump for the tasting menu (€54) and leave it up to Abellán.

La Barceloneta & the Coast

Can Maño (Map pp312-13; ☎ 93 319 30 82; Carrer del Baluard 12; meals €15-20; Mon-Sat) You'll need to be prepared to wait before being squeezed in at a packed table for a raucous night of *raciones* (posted on a board at the back) over a bottle of *turbio* – a cloudy white plonk. You can breakfast on *gambes* (prawns), too, if you want!

Can Ros 1911 (Map pp312-13; ☎ 93 221 45 79; Carrer del Almirall Aixada 7; meals €30-35; Thu-Tue; ⊠) Little has changed over the decades in this seafood fave. In a restaurant where the decor is a reminder of simpler times, a simple rule guides – serve up succulent fresh fish cooked with a light touch. It does a chunky *fideuá amb cloïsses i gambes* (noodles with clams and prawns, €12.50).

Can Majó (Map pp312-13; ☎ 93 221 58 18; Carrer del Almirall Aixada 23; meals €30-40; lunch & dinner Tue-Sat, lunch Sun) Virtually on the beach (with tables outside in summer), Can Majó has a long and steady reputation for fine seafood, particularly its rice dishes (€14 to €20).

Xiringuito d'Escribà (Map pp306-7; ☎ 93 221 07 29; www.escriba.es; Platja de Bogatell, Ronda Litoral 42;

meals €40-50; ⏰ lunch daily) The Barcelona pastry family serves up top-quality seafood at this popular waterfront eatery. This is one of the few places where one person can order from their selection of paella and *fideuá* (normally a minimum of two people).

Suquet de l'Almirall (Map pp312-13; ☎ 93 221 62 33; Passeig de Joan de Borbó 65; meals €45-50; ⏰ lunch & dinner Tue-Sat, lunch Sun; ⊠) A family business run by one of the acolytes of Ferran Adrià's El Bulli restaurant (see p388), the order of the day is top-class seafood. A good option is the *pica pica marinera* (seafood mix, €36). The restaurant is closed for two weeks in August.

Torre d'Alta Mar (Map pp312-13; ☎ 93 221 00 07; www.torredealtamar.com; Torre de Sant Sebastià, Passeig de Joan de Borbó 88; meals €70-80; ⏰ lunch & dinner Tue-Sat, dinner Sun & Mon; ⊠) Head up to the top of the Torre de Sant Sebastiá and take a ringside seat for the best views of the city, and seafood. The setting alone makes this ideal for impressing a date.

L'Eixample

BUDGET

L'Atzavara (Map pp310-11; ☎ 93 454 59 25; Carrer de Muntaner 109; meals €10-15; ⏰ lunch Mon-Sat; ⊠ Ⓥ) A limited and varying *menú del día* (daily set menu; €9.90) is offered in this proper little place, and while servings are hardly gargantuan, the grub is tasty. The menu changes regularly but you might encounter a scrumptious *paella d'arròs integral amb verdures* (wholerice vegetable paella) or an oven-baked *pastís camperol* (vegetable pie).

Amaltea (Map pp312-13; ☎ 93 454 86 13; www.restaurantamaltea.com; Carrer de la Diputació 164; meals €10-15; ⏰ lunch Mon-Thu, lunch & dinner Fri & Sat; ⊠ Ⓥ) The weekday set lunch (€10) offers a series of dishes that change frequently with the seasons. Savour an *escalopa de seitan* (seitan escalope) and *empanadillas* (pastry pockets stuffed with spinach or hiziki algae and tofu).

MIDRANGE

La Rita (Map pp310-11; ☎ 93 487 23 76; Carrer d'Aragó 279; meals €20; ⊠) Locals line up to dine here, if only because the price–quality rapport is excellent. So join the queue to get inside this boisterous restaurant. You have a broad choice between classic local cooking and some more inventive dishes.

El Rincón Maya (Map pp310-11; ☎ 93 451 39 46; Carrer de València 183; meals €20; ⏰ lunch & dinner Tue-Sat, dinner Mon) The setting in this Mexican restaurant is warm and good-naturedly crowded. The nachos, guacamole and fajitas burst with flavour, and you may have to queue for a table.

Cerveseria Catalana (Map pp310-11; ☎ 93 216 03 68; Carrer de Mallorca 236; meals €25; ⊠) This 'Catalan brewery' is great for its cornucopia of tapas (€3 to €7) and *montaditos* (canapés, €1.80 to €3.50). You can sit at the bar, outside, or in the restaurant at the back. The variety of hot tapas, mouth-watering salads and other snacks draws a well-dressed crowd.

Koyuki (Map pp310-11; ☎ 93 237 84 90; Carrer de Còrsega 242; meals €25-30; ⏰ lunch & dinner Tue-Sat, dinner Sun) Take a seat at one of the long tables in this basement Japanese eatery that is as popular with Japanese visitors as it is with Catalans in the know. The *tempura udon* (€7.80) is a hearty thick noodle option.

Inopia (Map pp312-13; ☎ 93 424 52 31; www.barinopia.com; Carrer de Tamarit 104; meals €25-30; ⏰ dinner Tue-Fri, lunch & dinner Sat) Albert Adrià, brother of star chef Ferran, has his hands full with this constantly busy gourmet-tapas temple. Try the lightly fried, tempura-style vegetables, olive selections and *pincho moruno de pollo* (chicken on a skewer).

Relais de Venise (Map pp310-11; ☎ 93 467 21 62; Carrer de Pau Claris 142; meals €30; ⏰ Sep-Jul; ⊠) There's just one dish, a succulent beef entrecôte with a secret 'sauce Porte-Maillot' (named after the location of the original restaurant in Paris), chips and salad. It is served in slices and in two waves so that it doesn't go cold.

El Peixerot (Map pp306-7; ☎ 93 424 69 69; Carrer de Tarragona 177; meals €40-50; ⊠) With its sea-blue decor and long-standing fame for fresh seafood (sold by weight) and rice dishes (€17 to €29), this is a quality stop in the rather unlikely train-station area.

Cata 1.81 (Map pp310-11; ☎ 93 323 68 18; www.cata181.com; Carrer de València 181; meals €50; ⏰ dinner Mon-Sat Sep-Jul) Call ahead for the back room behind the kitchen. Surrounded by shelves of fine wines, you will be treated to a series of dainty gourmet dishes, such as *truita amb tòfona* (a thick potato tortilla with a delicate trace of truffle).

Casa Darío (Map pp312-13; ☎ 93 453 31 35; www.casadario.com; Carrer del Consell de Cent 256; meals €50-60; ⏰ Mon-Sat Sep-Jul; ⊠) Step into the timeless world of old-time silver service and ample helpings of the gifts of the sea. Opt for one of the set-menu feasts (around €50) and you will be served endless rounds of seafood wonders. Meat-eaters are catered for too.

TOP END

Saüc (Map pp310-11; ☎ 93 321 01 89; www.saucrestaurant.com; Passatge de Lluís Pellicer 12; meals €70-80; 🕑 Tue-Sat; ⊠) Pop down into this back-lane basement place and enter an upcoming gourmet landmark. The decor is sober but the dishes are sins for the senses. The €68 tasting menu comprises an appetiser and five courses, followed by a cheese selection and two desserts.

Gràcia

Taverna La Llesca (Map pp310-11; ☎ 93 285 02 46; Carrer de Terol 6; meals €15-20; 🕑 Mon-Sat) The name of the game is hearty servings of meat (which you can temper with a little salad if you want), washed down with some red (preferably not the house wine!). A good option is *entrecot de vedella* (beef entrecôte), best done with pepper.

Envalira (Map pp310-11; ☎ 93 218 58 13; Plaça del Sol 13; meals €25-30; 🕑 lunch & dinner Tue-Sat, lunch Sun) An inconspicuous, old-time eatery, Envalira specialises in fish and rice dishes, from *arròs a la milanesa* (a savoury rice dish with chicken, pork and a cheese gratiné) to *bullit de lluç*, a slice of white hake boiled with herb-laced rice and clams.

Goliard (Map pp310-11; ☎ 93 207 31 75; Carrer de Progrés 6; meals €30-35; 🕑 lunch & dinner Mon-Fri, dinner Sat & Sun; ⊠) This quiet diner is a haven of exquisite designer cooking at modest prices. Try the *filete de canguro con vinagreta de curry* (a kangaroo fillet in a curry vinaigrette). Book ahead.

O'Gràcia! (Map pp310-11; ☎ 93 213 30 44; Plaça de la Revolució de Setembre de 1868 15; meals €30-35; 🕑 Mon-Sat; ⊠) The *menú del día* is outstanding value for around €10. The *arròs negre de sepia* (black rice with cuttlefish) makes a good first course, followed by a limited set of meat and fish options with vegetable sides. *A la carta*, you have tasting-menu options at around €23 and €30.

Bilbao (Map pp310-11; ☎ 93 458 96 24; Carrer del Perill 33; meals €40; 🕑 Mon-Sat) Bilbao is a timeless classic: the back dining room, with bottle-lined walls, stout timber tables and a yellowing light evocative of distant country taverns, will appeal to carnivores especially. Opt for a *chuletón* (a massive T-bone steak) and wash it down with a good Spanish red.

Montjuïc & Poble Sec

Quimet i Quimet (Map pp312-13; ☎ 93 442 31 42; Carrer del Poeta Cabanyes 25; tapas €25-30; 🕑 lunch & dinner Mon-Fri, lunch Sat; ⊠) Quimet i Quimet is proof that good things come in small packages. Cram into this bottle-lined quad for gourmet tapas, fine wine and even a specially made dark Belgian beer.

Restaurant Elche (Map pp312-13; ☎ 93 441 30 89; Carrer de Vila i Vilà 71; meals €30) With tables spreading over two floors, and old-world style in service and settings, this spot has been doing some of Barcelona's best paella (of various types) and *fideuá* (vaguely similar to paella, but made with vermicelli noodles) since the 1960s.

Taverna Can Margarit (Map pp312-13; ☎ 93 441 67 23; Carrer de la Concòrdia 21; meals €30; 🕑 dinner Mon-Sat) Once a wine store, this tavern has for years attracted sometimes raucous dinner groups around its rough benches for dishes like *conejo a la jumillana* (fried rabbit served with garlic and various herbs).

Self-Catering

Shop in the **Mercat de la Boqueria** (Map pp316-17; La Rambla de Sant Josep; 🕑 8am-8pm Mon-Sat), one of the world's great produce markets, and complement with any other necessities from a local supermarket. Handy ones include **Carrefour Express** (Map pp316-17; La Rambla dels Estudis 113; 🕑 9am-10pm Mon-Sat), near the northern end of La Rambla; and **Superservis** (Map pp316-17; Carrer d'Avinyó 13; 🕑 8am-2pm & 4-8pm Mon-Sat) in the heart of Barri Gòtic.

For freshly baked bread, head for a *forn* or *panadería*. For a gourmet touch, the food sections of El Corte Inglés department stores (p359) have some tempting local and imported goodies.

DRINKING

Barcelona's bars run the gamut from wood-panelled wine cellars to bright waterfront places and trendy designer bars. Most are at their liveliest from about 10pm to 2am or 3am (later opening on Friday and Saturday), especially from Thursday to Saturday, as people get into their night-time stride.

The old town is jammed. The hippest area since the late 1990s has been El Born, in the lower end of La Ribera, but there is an impressive scattering of bars across the lower half of the Barri Gòtic and in El Raval too. The latter especially is home to some fine old drinking institutions as well as a new wave of funky, inner-city locales.

A word of warning on La Rambla: while it can be pleasant enough to tipple here, few locals would even think about it and bar prices

BEER FOR BARCELONA

Moritz, a crisp lager that was once Barcelona's most popular beer, has made an extraordinary comeback since 2004. Brewed since 1856 by a company founded by Louis Moritz, an Alsatian brewer, Moritz went belly-up in 1978 but Louis' descendants (who kept the brand) are back in action. The three late-19th-century buildings at Ronda Sant Antoni 39–43 (Map pp312–13) that once housed the subterranean brewery are being turned into a leisure and cultural centre (under the direction of French architect Jean Nouvel), with bar-restaurant (under Carles Abellán), demonstration brewery and museum, in addition to the company headquarters. The facades have been restored and the centre is due to open by 2009.

tend to be exorbitant – €25 for a carafe of sangria is not unheard of.

Elsewhere, the series of squares and some streets of Gràcia are loaded up with bars. In the broad expanse of L'Eixample you need to know where to go. The upper end of Carrer d'Aribau is the busiest area (late in the week), along with the area around its continuation northwest of Avinguda Diagonal. The main concentration of gay bars is on and around Carrer del Consell de Cent, between Carrer de Balmes and Carrer de Muntaner.

Some useful sources of information on bars, clubs and gigs include: **Lecool** (www.lecool.com), **Agentes de la Noche** (www.agentesdelanoche.com), **Barceloca** (www.barceloca.com), **BCN-Nightlife** (www.bcn-nightlife.com), **Barcelonarocks.com** (www.barcelonarocks.com), **Clubbingspain.com** (www.clubbingspain.com) and **LaNetro.com** (http://barcelon a.lanetro.com).

Barri Gòtic

Barcelona Pipa Club (Map pp316-17; ☎ 93 302 47 32; www.bpipaclub.com; Plaça Reial 3; ⏰ 11pm-4am Sun-Thu, 11pm-5am Fri & Sat) This pipe-smokers' club is like someone's flat, with all sorts of interconnecting rooms and knick-knacks – notably the pipes after which the place is named. You buzz at the door and head two floors up. It is for members only until 11pm.

Club Soul (Map pp316-17; ☎ 93 302 70 26; www.barceloca.com; Carrer Nou de Sant Francesc 7; ⏰ 10pm-2.30am Mon-Thu, 10pm-3am Fri & Sat, 8pm-2.30am Sun) One of the hippest club-style hang-outs in this part of town. Each night the DJs change the musical theme, ranging from deep funk to deeper house.

La Clandestina (Map pp316-17; ☎ 93 319 05 33; Baixada de Viladecols 2bis; ⏰ 10am-10pm Sun-Thu, 9am-midnight Fri & Sat) Opt for tea, a beer or a Middle Eastern *narghile* (the most elaborate way to smoke). You can even get a head massage or eat cake in this chilled teashop.

Manchester (Map pp316-17; ☎ 663 071748; www.manchesterbar.com; Carrer de Milans 5; ⏰ 7pm-2.30am Sun-Thu, 7pm-3am Fri & Sat) Settle in for a beer and the sounds of great Manchester bands, from Depeche Mode to Oasis. It has a pleasing rough-and-tumble feel, with tables jammed in every which way.

Sinatra (Map pp316-17; ☎ 93 412 52 79; Carrer de les Heures 4-10; ⏰ 9pm-2.30am) A block from Plaça Reial is this busy corner locale. The fauna is largely comprised of foreigners who flop into splotchy cowhide-pattern lounges, perch on long stools beneath the mirror ball and sip Desperados beer.

El Raval

Bar Marsella (Map pp316-17; Carrer de Sant Pau 65; ⏰ 10pm-2am Mon-Thu, 10pm-3am Fri & Sat) In business since 1820, the Marsella specialises in *absenta* (absinthe), a beverage known for its supposed narcotic qualities. Nothing much has changed here since the 19th century and the local tipple certainly has a kick.

Boadas (Map pp316-17; ☎ 93 318 88 26; Carrer dels Tallers 1; ⏰ noon-2am Mon-Thu, noon-3am Fri & Sat) Inside the unprepossessing entrance is one of the city's oldest cocktail bars (famed for its daiquiris). The bow-tied waiters have been serving up their poison since 1933, and both Joan Miró and Hemingway tippled here.

Casa Almirall (Map pp312-13; ☎ 93 318 99 17; Carrer de Joaquín Costa 33; ⏰ 7pm-2.30am) In business since the 1860s, this unchanged corner drinkery is dark and intriguing, with Modernista decor and a mixed clientele.

Kentucky (Map pp316-17; ☎ 93 318 28 78; Carrer de l'Arc del Teatre 11; ⏰ 10pm-3am Tue-Sat) All sorts of odd bods from the *barri* (district) and beyond squeeze into this long, narrow bar late at night. Opening times (which can mean until 5am) depend in part on the presence (or absence) of the law in the street.

London Bar (Map pp316-17; ☎ 93 318 52 61; Carrer Nou de la Rambla 34-36; ⏰ 7.30pm-3am Tue-Sun) If you still need a drink after 3am this is your best bet. Open since 1909, it started as a hang-out for circus hands and has some Modernista touches and the occasional music act way out back.

La Ribera

Gimlet (Map pp316-17; ☎ 93 310 10 27; Carrer del Rec 24; ⏰ 10pm-3am) Bar staff, with all the appropriate aplomb, will whip you up a gimlet, or any other classic cocktail your heart desires (around €8) as you crowd in around the curving, smoky bar.

La Fianna (Map pp316-17; ☎ 93 315 18 10; www.lafianna.com; Carrer dels Banys Vells 15; ⏰ 6pm-1.30am Sun-Wed, 6pm-2.30am Thu-Sat) There is something medieval-asian about this bar, with its bare stone walls, forged-iron candelabras and cushion-covered lounges. This place heaves and as the night wears on it's elbow room only.

La Vinya Del Senyor (Map pp316-17; ☎ 93 310 33 79; Plaça de Santa Maria del Mar 5; ⏰ noon-1am Tue-Sun) The wine list is as long as *War & Peace*, and the terrace lies in the shadow of Santa Maria del Mar. You can crowd inside the tiny wine bar itself or take a bottle upstairs to the one available table.

Port Vell & the Coast

The Barcelona beach scene, apart from the roasting of countless bodies, warms up to dance sounds in the summer months. In addition to waterfront restaurants and bars (especially on and near Port Olímpic), a string of *chiringuitos* (provisional bars) sets up along the beaches. Most serve food and some turn into miniclubs on the sand from the afternoon until about 1am. Most are strung along from Platja de Bogatell to Platja de Nova Mar Bella.

CDLC (Map pp306-7; ☎ 93 224 04 70; www.cdlcbarcelona.com; Passeig Marítim de la Barceloneta 32; ⏰ noon-3am) Seize the night by the scruff at the Carpe Diem Lounge Club, the perfect place for your first drink lounging back in semi-oriental surrounds. You could choose to eat too, but tables are shuffled away about midnight. Ideal for a warm-up before heading to the nearby clubs.

Shôko (Map pp306-7; ☎ 93 225 92 00; www.shoko.biz; Passeig Marítim de la Barceloneta 36; ⏰ 8pm-3am Tue-Sun) Wafting over your mixed Asian–Med food in this club-lounge-restaurant is an opiate mix of Shinto music and Japanese electro. As the food is cleared, the place turns into a funky beat kinda dance place.

Vaixell Luz De Gas (Map pp316-17; ☎ 93 209 77 11; moored on Moll del Dipósit; ⏰ noon-3am Mar-Nov) Sit on the top deck of this boat and let go of the day's cares. Sip wine or beer, nibble tapas and admire the yachts. On shore it plays some good dance music at night.

L'Eixample & Around

There are three main concentrations for carousers in L'Eixample, although bars are dotted about all over. The top end of Carrer d'Aribau and the area where it crosses Avinguda Diagonal attracts a heterogenous and mostly local crowd to its many bars and clubs. Carrer de Balmes is lined with clubs for a mostly teen 'n' twenties crowd. The city's gay-and-lesbian circuit is concentrated around Carrer del Consell de Cent (see p344).

Berlin (Map pp310-11; ☎ 93 200 65 42; Carrer de Muntaner 240; ⏰ 10am-1am Mon-Wed, 10am-3am Thu-Sat) This elegant corner bar attracts waves of night animals starting up for a long night. In warmer weather you can sit outside on the footpath, or head downstairs into the basement if the bar's too crowded.

Dry Martini (Map pp310-11; ☎ 93 217 50 72; Carrer d'Aribau 162-166; ⏰ 1pm-2am Sun-Thu, 1pm-3am Fri & Sat) Waiters serve up the best dry martini in town, or whatever else your heart desires, in this classic cocktail lounge. Sink into a leather lounge and nurse a huge G&T.

Les Gens Que J'aime (Map pp310-11; ☎ 93 215 68 79; Carrer de València 286; ⏰ 6pm-2.30am Sun-Thu, 6pm-3am Fri & Sat) This intimate relic of the 1960s offers jazz music in the background and a cosy scattering of velvet-backed lounges around tiny dark tables.

Michael Collins Pub (Map pp310-11; ☎ 93 459 19 64; Plaça de la Sagrada Família 4; ⏰ noon-2am Sun-Thu, noon-3am Fri & Sat) To be sure of a little Catalan-Irish craic, this barn-sized and storming pub is just the ticket.

Premier (Map pp310-11; ☎ 93 532 16 50; Carrer de Provença 236; ⏰ 6pm-2.30am Mon-Thu, 6pm-3am Fri & Sat) Relax at the bar or in a lounge in this funky little French-run wine bar.

Gràcia

La Cigale (Map pp310-11; ☎ 93 457 58 23; Carrer de Tordera 50; ⏰ 6pm-2.30am Sun-Thu, 6pm-3am Fri & Sat) A very civilised place for a cocktail (or two for €8 before 10pm). Prop up the zinc bar, sink into a secondhand lounge chair around a teeny table or head upstairs. Music is soothing and conversation lively.

Musical Maria (Map pp310-11; Carrer de Maria 5; ⏰ 9pm-3am) Even the music hasn't changed since this place got going in the late 1970s. Lovers of rock 'n' roll will enjoy sinking beers here, perhaps over a game of pool.

Sabor a Cuba (Map pp310-11; ☎ 600 262003; Carrer de Francisco Giner 32; 10pm-2.30am Mon-Thu, 10pm-3am Fri & Sat) A mixed crowd of Cubans and fans of the Caribbean island come to drink mojitos and shake their stuff in this home of *ron y son* (rum and sound).

Tibidabo & Around

Mirablau (Map pp306-7; ☎ 93 418 58 79; Plaça del Doctor Andreu; 11am-6am) Wander downstairs after 11pm to join the beautiful people in the squeeze-me small dance space. The views over sparkling Barcelona are magic.

Montjuïc & Poble Sec

Maumau Underground (Map pp312-13; ☎ 93 441 80 15; www.maumaunderground.com; Carrer de la Fontrodona 33; 11pm-2.30am Thu & Sun, 11pm-3am Fri & Sat) Funk, soul, hip hop and more are on the program in this Poble Sec music and dance haunt. Above the backlit bar a huge screen pours forth psychedelic images.

Tinta Roja (Map pp312-13; ☎ 93 443 32 43; www.tintaroja.net; Carrer de la Creu dels Molers 17; 8.30pm-2am Thu, 8.30pm-3am Fri & Sat) Sprinkled with an eclectic collection of furnishings, dimly lit in violets, reds and yellows, the 'Red Ink' is an intimate spot for a drink and the occasional show in the back.

ENTERTAINMENT

To keep up with what's on, pick up a copy of the weekly listings magazine, *Guía del Ocio* (€1) from newsstands. The daily papers also have listings sections and the **Palau de la Virreina** (Map pp316-17; ☎ 93 301 77 75; La Rambla de Sant Josep 99; 10am-8pm) information office can clue you in to present and forthcoming events.

The easiest way to get hold of *entradas* (tickets) for most venues throughout the city is through the **Caixa de Catalunya's Tel-Entrada** (☎ 902 10 12 12; www.telentrada.com) service or **Servi-Caixa** (☎ 902 33 22 11; www.servicaixa.com in Catalan & Spanish). Another one to try for concerts is **Tick Tack Ticket** (☎ 902 10 50 25; www.ticktackticket.com). There's a *venta de localidades* (ticket office) on the ground floor of the **El Corte Inglés** (Map pp312-13; ☎ 902 40 02 22; www.elcorteingles.es, click on entradas, in Spanish; Plaça de Catalunya) and at some of its other branches around town (you can also buy tickets through El Corte Inglés by phone and online); and at the **FNAC store** (Map pp316-17; ☎ 902 10 06 32; Plaça de Catalunya) in the El Triangle shopping centre on the same square.

You can purchase some half-price tickets at the Caixa de Catalunya desk in the **Oficina d'Informació de Turisme de Barcelona** (p318). To qualify, you must purchase the tickets in person no more than three hours before the start of the show you wish to see. The system is known as Tiquet-3.

Clubs

Barcelona clubs are spread a little more thinly than bars across the city. They tend to open from around midnight until 6am.

Catwalk (Map pp306-7; ☎ 93 224 07 40; www.clubcatwalk.net; Carrer de Ramon Trias Fargas 2-4; admission €15; midnight-6am Thu-Sun) A well-dressed crowd piles in here for good, danceable house, occasionally mellowed down with more body-hugging electro and funk. Alternatively, you can sink into a fat lounge for a quiet tipple and whisper. Popular local DJ Jekey leads the way most nights.

Distrito Diagonal (Map pp310-11; ☎ 607 113602; www.distritodiagonal.com; Avinguda Diagonal 442; admission after 4am €15; 11pm-8.30am Fri & Sat) It's hard to categorise this narrow, red-lit bar with the dance space up the back, but it's hard to resist a place that stays up so late on weekends, and for free if you're in before 4am! To move your booty to deep house and garage, slide past the long bar to the raised dance area out the back.

Elephant (Map pp306-7; ☎ 93 334 02 58; www.elephantbcn.com; Passeig dels Tillers 1; admission €15 Fri & Sat, free Wed, Thu & Sun; 11pm-3am Wed, 11pm-5am Thu-Sun) Getting in here is like being invited to some Beverly Hills private party. Models and wannabes mix freely, as do the drinks. A big tent-like dance space is the focus but mingle around the various garden bars too.

Karma (Map pp316-17; ☎ 93 302 56 80; www.karmadisco.com; Plaça Reial 10; admission €8; midnight-5.30am Tue-Sun) This basement place heaves to the sounds of indie, rock, punk and even '80s disco. Tunnel-shaped Karma is small and becomes quite packed.

Luz De Gas (Map pp310-11; ☎ 93 209 77 11; www.luzdegas.com; Carrer de Muntaner 244-246; admission up to €15; 11.30pm-6am) Set in a grand theatre that is frequently the scene of live acts, this club attracts a crowd of well-dressed beautiful people, whose tastes in music vary according to the night. Next door, Sala B is a separate dedicated clubbers' room open on Fridays and Saturdays only.

Moog (Map pp316-17; ☎ 93 301 72 82; www.masimas.com/moog; Carrer de l'Arc del Teatre 3; admission €12; ⌚ midnight-6am) This fun, minuscule club is a downtown hit. In the main downstairs dance area, DJs dish out house, techno and electro, while upstairs you can groove to indie and occasional classic pop.

Opium Mar (Map pp306-7; ☎ 902 26 74 86; www.opiummar.com; Passeig Marítim de la Barceloneta 34; ⌚ 8pm-6am; Ⓜ Ciutadella Villa Olímpica) All whites, shimmering silver and dark contrasts mark the decor in this barn of a seaside dance place. Clubbers from around town pile in here for the thumping beat of house and techno from 3am. It's best in summer.

Otto Zutz (Map pp310-11; ☎ 93 238 07 22; www.ottozutz.es; Carrer de Lincoln 15; admission €15; ⌚ midnight-5.30am Tue-Sat) Beautiful people only need apply for entry into this three-floor dance den. Head downstairs for house or upstairs for funk and soul. Wednesday and Thursday nights tend to be dominated by hip hop and R&B. Friday and Saturday the house shakes to house.

Razzmatazz (Map pp306-7; ☎ 93 272 09 10; www.salarazzmatazz.com; Carrer dels Almogàvers 122 or Carrer de Pamplona 88; admission €15; ⌚ 1-6am Fri & Sat) A half-dozen blocks back from Port Olímpic is this stalwart of Barcelona's club and concert scene, with five different clubs in one huge space.

Sala Apolo (Map pp312-13; ☎ 93 441 40 01; www.sala-apolo.com; Carrer Nou de la Rambla 113; admission €6-12; ⌚ 12.30am-6am Wed-Sat, 10.30pm-3.30am Sun) In this old theatre, the Nitsaclub team provides house, techno and break-beat sounds from Thursday to Sunday nights. Earlier in the evening concerts generally take place.

Sutton The Club (Map pp310-11; ☎ 93 414 42 17; www.thesuttonclub.com; Carrer de Tuset 13; admission €15; ⌚ 11.30pm-6am Tue-Sat) A classic club with mainstream sounds, this place inevitably attracts just about everyone pouring in and out of the nearby bars at some stage in the evening – if the bouncers let them, that is.

Cinemas

Foreign films, shown with subtitles and their original soundtrack, rather than dubbed, are marked VO *(versión original)* in movie listings. A ticket usually costs €6 to €7 but most cinemas have a weekly *día del espectador* (viewer's day), often Monday or Wednesday, when they charge €4.80 to €5.50. These cinemas show VO films:

TOP FIVE CLUBS

- **Elephant** (p355)
- **Otto Zutz** (left)
- **Razzmatazz** (left)
- **Sala Apolo** (left)
- **Sutton The Club** (left)

Filmoteca (Map pp310-11; ☎ 93 410 75 90; Avinguda de Sarrià 31-33; admission €4) Specialises in film seasons that concentrate on particular directors, styles and eras of film.

Icària Yelmo Cineplex (Map pp306-7; ☎ 93 221 75 85; www.yelmocineplex.es in Spanish; Carrer de Salvador Espriu 61) A massive complex where all the cinemas offer undubbed movies.

Imax (Map pp316-17; ☎ 93 225 11 11; Moll d'Espanya; www.imaxportvell.com) The city's 3-D big-screen experience.

Méliès Cinemes (Map pp306-7; ☎ 93 451 00 51; Carrer de Villarroel 102; admission €3-5) Old classics in the original.

Renoir Floridablanca (Map pp312-13; ☎ 93 426 33 37; www.cinesrenoir.com in Spanish; Carrer de Floridablanca 135) Art-house cinema on the edge of El Raval.

Verdi (Map pp310-11; ☎ 93 238 79 90; www.cines-verdi.com in Spanish; Carrer de Verdi 32) One of the most popular art-house cinemas in town, in the heart of Gràcia, and surrounded by bars and eateries.

Verdi Park (Map pp310-11; Carrer de Torrijos 49) Also operated by Verdi.

Theatre

Theatre is almost always performed in Catalan or Spanish. For more information on all that's happening in theatre, head for the information office at Palau de la Virreina (p318), where you'll find leaflets and *Teatre BCN*, the monthly listings guide.

Teatre Lliure (Map pp306-7; ☎ 93 289 27 70; www.teatrelliure.com; Plaça de Margarida Xirgu 1, Montjuïc; ⌚ box office 5-8pm) Consisting of two separate theatre spaces, the 'Free Theatre' puts on a variety of serious, quality drama, pretty much exclusively in Catalan.

Teatre Mercat de les Flors (Map pp306-7; ☎ 93 426 18 75; www.mercatflors.org; Carrer de Lleida 59) At the foot of Montjuïc, this is an important venue for contemporary dance. The box office opens one hour before the show.

Teatre Nacional de Catalunya (Map pp306-7; ☎ 93 306 57 00; www.tnc.es in Catalan & Spanish; Plaça de les Arts 1) Ricard Bofill's ultra-neoclassical theatre hosts a wide range of performances, principally drama but occasionally also dance and other performances.

Teatre Romea (Map pp316-17; ☎ 93 301 55 04; www.focus.es in Catalan & Spanish; Carrer de l'Hospital 51; box office 4.30-8pm Tue-Sun) This theatre is a reference point for quality drama in Barcelona. It puts on a range of interesting plays – usually classics with a contemporary flavour.

Live Music

There's a good choice most nights of the week. Many venues double as bars and/or clubs. Starting time is rarely before 10pm. Admission charges range from nothing to €20 – the higher prices often include a drink. Note that some of the clubs previously mentioned, including Razzmatazz (opposite), Sala Apolo (opposite) and Luz De Gas (p355) often stage concerts. Keep an eye on listings.

Big-name acts, either Spanish or from abroad, often perform at venues such as the 17,000-capacity Palau Sant Jordi (p339) on Montjuïc or the Teatre Mercat de les Flors (opposite).

Bikini (Map pp306-7; ☎ 93 322 08 00; www.bikinibcn.com; Carrer de Déu i Mata 105; admission €10-20; midnight-5am Wed-Sun) This multihall dance space frequently stages quality acts ranging from funk guitar to rock. Performances generally start around 10pm and the club then swings into gear around midnight.

Harlem Jazz Club (Map pp316-17; ☎ 93 310 07 55; Carrer de la Comtessa de Sobradiel 8; admission up to €10; 8pm-4am Tue-Thu & Sun, 8pm-5am Fri & Sat) This narrow, smoky, old-town dive is one of the best spots in town for jazz. Every now and then it mixes it up with a little rock, Latin or blues. There are usually two sessions in an evening.

Jamboree (Map pp316-17; ☎ 93 319 17 89; www.masimas.com/jamboree; Plaça Reial 17; admission €9; 9.30pm-6am) Concerts start at 11pm and proceed until about 2am at the latest, at which point attentive jazz fans convert themselves into clubbers. Some of the great names of jazz and blues have filled the air with their sonorous contributions.

Monasterio (Map pp316-17; ☎ 93 319 19 88; www.salamonasterio.com; Passeig d'Isabel II 4; 9pm-3am) Depending on the night, there's a little of everything in this basement jamming bar, from a fine flamenco session followed by samba on Sunday night to an anything-goes talent night on Mondays. It has Murphys on tap.

Sidecar Factory Club (Map pp316-17; ☎ 93 302 15 86; www.sidecarfactoryclub.com; Plaça Reial 7; admission €7-15; 10pm-3am Tue-Thu, 10pm-6am Fri & Sat) Downstairs from the bar and eatery are the red-tinged bowels of the club that opens for live music most nights. Just about anything goes, but rock and pop lead the way. Most shows start at 10pm (Thursday to Saturday).

FLAMENCO

Although numerous key flamenco artists grew up in the *barris* of Barcelona, opportunities for seeing good performances of this essentially Andalucian dance and music are limited. A few *tablaos* (tourist-oriented locales that stage flamenco performances) are scattered about. For more on flamenco, see p73.

Sala Tarantos (Map pp316-17; ☎ 93 319 17 89; http://masimas.com/tarantos; Plaça Reial 17; admission from €6; performances 8.30pm, 9.30pm & 10.30pm daily) This basement locale is the stage for some of the best flamenco to pass through Barcelona. You have to keep an eye out for quality acts, otherwise you can pop by for the more pedestrian regular performances. The place converts into a club later.

Tablao Cordobés (Map pp316-17; ☎ 93 317 57 11; www.tablaocordobes.com; La Rambla 35; show only €35, with dinner €68; shows 8.15pm, 10pm & 11.30pm) This long-standing *tablao* is typical of the genre. Generally people book for the dinner and show.

Tablao de Carmen (Map pp306-7; ☎ 93 325 68 95; www.tablaodecarmen.com; Carrer dels Arcs 9, Poble Espanyol; show only €35, with dinner €69-94 depending on the dinner option; shows 7.45pm & 10pm Tue-Sun) Named after the great Barcelona *bailaora* (flamenco dancer) Carmen Amaya, the set-up at this establishment is similar to that at the Tablao Cordobés.

CLASSICAL MUSIC & OPERA

Guía del Ocio has ample listings, but the monthly *Informatiu Musical* leaflet has the best coverage of classical music (as well as other genres). You can pick it up at tourist offices and the Palau de la Virreina (p318).

Gran Teatre del Liceu (Map pp316-17; ☎ 93 485 99 00; www.liceubarcelona.com; La Rambla dels Caputxins 51-59; box office 2-8.30pm Mon-Fri & 1hr before show Sat & Sun) Barcelona's grand opera house, rebuilt after a fire in 1999, has world-class opera, dance and classical-music recitals. Tickets can cost from €7.50 for a cheap seat behind a pillar, to €150 for a well-positioned night at the opera.

L'Auditori (Map pp306-7; ☎ 93 247 93 00; www.auditori.org; Carrer de Lepant 150; admission €17-65; box

POKING ABOUT THE MARKETS

Large **Els Encants Vells** ('The Old Charms'; Map pp306-7; 7am-6.45pm Mon, Wed, Fri & Sat), also known as the Fira de Bellcaire, is the city's principal flea market. There is an awful lot of junk, but you can turn up interesting items if you hunt around.

The Barri Gòtic is livened up by an **arts and crafts market** (Map pp316-17; Plaça de Sant Josep Oriol; 9am-8pm) on Saturday and Sunday; the antiques **Mercat Gòtic** (Map pp316-17; Plaça Nova; 9am-10pm) on Thursday; and a **coin- and stamp-collectors' market** (Map pp316-17; Plaça Reial; 9am-2pm) on Sunday morning. Just beyond the western edge of El Raval, the punters at the **Mercat de Sant Antoni** (Map pp312-13; 7am-8.30pm) dedicate Sunday morning to old maps, stamps, books and cards.

Once every fortnight, from Friday to Sunday, gourmands can poke about the homemade honey, sweets, cheese and other edible delights at the **Fira Alimentació** (Map pp316-17; Plaça del Pi).

office noon-9pm Mon-Sat) Barcelona's modern home for serious music lovers, L'Auditori puts on plenty of orchestral, chamber, religious and other music throughout the year.

Palau de la Música Catalana (Map pp312-13; 902 47 54 85; www.palaumusica.org; Carrer de Sant Francesc de Paula 2; box office 10am-9pm Mon-Sat) This Modernista delight is a traditional centre for classical and choral music, although nowadays you might see anything from South African dance to Portuguese *fado*.

Dance

The best chance you have of seeing people dancing the *sardana* (the Catalan folk dance) is at 7pm on Wednesday, 6.30pm on Saturday or noon on Sunday in front of the Catedral (p322). You can also see the dancers during some of the city's festivals. They join hands to form ever-widening circles, placing their bags or coats in the centre. The dance is intricate but hardly flamboyant.

Sport

BULLFIGHTING

Arguments over whether bullfighting should be banned in the city continue to rage in Barcelona but, for the moment, the show goes on. Fights are staged on Sunday afternoon in spring and summer at the **Plaça de Braus Monumental** (Map pp306-7; 93 245 58 02; cnr Gran Via de les Corts Catalanes & Carrer de la Marina; admission €20-120; tickets 11am-2pm & 4-8pm Mon-Fri, 11am-2pm & 4-7pm Sat). The 'fun' starts at around 6pm. Tickets are available at the arena or through **ServiCaixa** (902 33 22 11; www.servicaixa.com in Catalan & Spanish).

FOOTBALL

FC Barcelona (Barça for aficionados) has one of the best stadiums in Europe – the 100,000-capacity **Camp Nou** (Map pp306-7; 902 18 99 00, from abroad +34 93 496 36 00; www.fcbarcelona.com; tickets 9am-1.30pm & 3.30-6pm Mon-Fri) in the west of the city. Tickets for national-league games are available at the stadium, by phone or online. For the latter two options, nonmembers must book 15 days before the match. You can also obtain them through the ServiCaixa. Tickets can cost €14 to €170.

FORMULA ONE

Formula One drivers come to Barcelona every April/May to rip around the track at Montmeló, about a 30-minute drive north of the city. A seat for the Grand Prix race at the **Circuit de Catalunya** (93 571 97 71; www.circuitcat.com) can cost anything from €123 to €483, depending largely on how far in advance you book. Purchase by phone, at the track, or online with **ServiCaixa**. You can get a regular *rodalies* train to Montmeló (€1.40, 30 minutes) but will need to walk about 3km or find a local taxi (€10) to reach the track. On race days the **Sagalés bus company** (902 13 00 14; www.sagales.com) often puts on buses from Passeig de Sant Joan, between Carrer de la Diputació and Carrer del Consell de Cent.

SHOPPING

All of Barcelona seems to be lined with unending ranks of fashion boutiques and design stores. Alongside the latest modes and big national and international names in fashion, an assortment of curious traditional shops offer everything from coffee and nuts to candles, from sweets made in convents to amusing condoms.

Most of the mainstream fashion and design stores can be found on a shopping 'axis' that looks like the hands of a clock set at about twenty to five. From Plaça de Catalunya it heads along Passeig de Gràcia, turning left into Avinguda Diagonal. From here as far as Plaça de la Reina Maria Cristina, the Diagonal is jammed with shopping options.

Fashion does not end in the chic streets of L'Eixample and Avinguda Diagonal. The El Born area in La Ribera, especially on and around Carrer del Rec, is awash with tiny boutiques, especially those purveying young, fun fashion. A bubbling fashion strip is the Barri Gòtic's Carrer d'Avinyó. For second-hand stuff, head for El Raval, especially Carrer de la Riera Baixa. Carrer de Verdi in Gràcia is good for alternative shops too.

A squadron of antiques stores is scattered about Carrer dels Banys Nous in the Barri Gòtic, in whose labyrinthine lanes you can find all sorts of curious stores. For food, from cheese to nuts, some gems glitter in El Born.

The single best-known department store is **El Corte Inglés** (Plaça de Catalunya Map pp312-13; ☎ 93 306 38 00; www.elcorteingles.es; Plaça de Catalunya 14; 🕑 10am-10pm Mon-Sat; Plaça de la Reina Maria Cristina Map pp306-7; Avinguda Diagonal 617), with branches around town. **FNAC** (Map pp316-17; ☎ 93 344 18 00; Plaça de Catalunya 4; 🕑 10am-10pm Mon-Sat), the French book, CD and electronics emporium, has a couple of branches around town. **Bulevard Rosa** (Map pp310-11; ☎ 93 215 44 99; Passeig de Gràcia 55-57; 🕑 10am-8pm Mon-Sat) is one of the most interesting arcades, while the **Maremágnum** (☎ 93 225 81 00; www.maremagnum.es; Moll d'Espanya; 🕑 10am-10pm) shopping centre can be a diversion when wandering around Port Vell.

Winter sales officially start on or around 10 January and their summer equivalents on or around 5 July.

Art Galleries

Want some contemporary art? You'll find small galleries and designer stores around the Macba art museum (p324) on Carrer del Doctor Dou, Carrer d'Elisabets and Carrer dels Àngels (Map pp316–17). The classiest concentration of galleries is on and around the short stretch of Carrer del Consell de Cent between Rambla de Catalunya and Carrer de Balmes (Map pp310–11).

Fashion

Antonio Miró (Map pp310-11; ☎ 93 487 06 70; www.antoniomiro.es; Carrer del Consell de Cent 349) Mr Miró is one of Barcelona's haute-couture kings. He concentrates on light, natural fibres to produce smart, unpretentious men's and women's fashion.

Custo Barcelona (Map pp316-17; ☎ 93 268 78 93; www.custo-barcelona.com; Plaça de les Olles 7) Custo bewitches people the world over with a youthful, psychedelic panoply of women's and men's fashion. It has several branches around town.

Red Market (Map pp310-11; ☎ 93 218 63 33; Carrer de Verdi 20) Several funky fashion boutiques dot themselves along this street. Here you'll run into bright, uninhibited urban wear and accessories. Red dominates the decor more than the threads.

Tanus 13 (Map pp316-17; ☎ 93 315 01 55; Carrer de Jaume I 13) Handmade printed dresses and boldly coloured, handmade leather bags, purses and pouches fill this corner store. Those with an eye for the original, whether stylish uptown ladies or inner-city grunge lovers, will surely find something.

Food & Drink

Casa Gispert (Map pp316-17; ☎ 93 319 75 35; www.casagispert.com; Carrer dels Sombrerers 23) Prize-winning Casa Gispert has been toasting almonds and selling all manner of dried fruit since 1851. Pots and jars piled high on the shelves contain an unending variety of crunchy titbits.

Joan Murrià (Map pp310-11; ☎ 93 215 57 89; Carrer de Roger de Llúria 85) Ramon Casas designed the Modernista shop-front ads for this delicious delicatessen, where the shelves groan under the weight of speciality food from around Catalonia and beyond.

Xampany (Map pp310-11; ☎ 610 845011; Carrer de Valènica 200; 🕑 4.30-10pm Mon-Fri, 10am-2pm Sat) Since 1981 this 'Cathedral of Cava' has been a veritable Aladdin's cave of *cava*, with bottles of the stuff crammed high and into every possible chaotic corner of this dimly lit locale.

Homewares

Vinçon (Map pp310-11; ☎ 93 215 60 50; www.vincon.com; Passeig de Gràcia 96) Vinçon has the slickest designs in furniture and household goods, local and imported. The building once belonged to the Modernista artist Ramon Casas.

Shoes

Camper (Map pp310-11; ☎ 93 215 63 90; www.camper.com; Carrer de València 249) This Mallorcan success story is the Clarks of Spain. Its shoes range from the eminently sensible to the stylishly fashionable. It has stores all over town.

Farrutx (Map pp310-11; ☎ 93 215 06 85; www.farrutx.es; Carrer del Rosselló 218) Farrutx specialises in exclusive footwear for uptown gals.

GETTING THERE & AWAY

Air

Aeroport del Prat (☎ 902 40 47 04; www.aena.es) is 12km southwest of the centre at El Prat de Llobregat. Barcelona is a big international and domestic destination, with direct flights from North America as well as many European cities.

Several budget airlines, including Ryanair, use **Girona-Costa Brava airport**, 11km south of Girona and about 80km north of Barcelona. Buses connect with Barcelona's Estació del Nord bus station (right).

For general information on flights, see the Transport chapter (p883). See also Travel Agencies on p319.

Boat

BALEARIC ISLANDS

Regular passenger and vehicular ferries to/from the Balearic Islands, operated by **Acciona Trasmediterránea** (☎ 902 45 46 45; www.trasmediterranea.es), dock along both sides of the Moll de Barcelona wharf in Port Vell (Map pp312–13).

For information on schedules and fares, see p650.

ITALY

The Grimaldi group's **Grandi Navi Veloci** (☎ 902 41 02 00, 93 443 98 98, in Italy 010 209 4591; www1.gnv.it; Moll de San Beltran) runs a daily high-speed, roll-on, roll-off luxury ferry service that connects Genoa with Barcelona (18 hours). An economy-class airline-style seat can cost you as little as €16 in winter. A single cabin suite in high season can cost €199. The same company runs a weekly service between Barcelona and Tangier (Morocco). It leaves Tangier at midnight and Barcelona at 2pm. **Grimaldi Ferries** (☎ 902 53 13 33, in Italy 081 496444; www.grimaldi-ferries.com) has a similar service between Barcelona and Civitavecchia (for Rome, 20 hours) and Livorno (Tuscany, 19½ hours) up to six days a week. An economy-class airline-style seat costs from €29 in low season to €72 in high season on both routes.

Bus

Long-distance buses for destinations throughout Spain leave from the **Estació del Nord** (Map pp306-7; ☎ 902 30 32 22; www.barcelonanord.com; Carrer d'Ali Bei 80). A plethora of companies operates services to different parts of the country, although many come under the umbrella of **Alsa** (☎ 902 42 22 42; www.alsa.es). There are frequent services to Madrid, Valencia and Zaragoza (up to 20 a day) and several daily departures to such distant destinations as Burgos, Santiago de Compostela and Seville.

Eurolines (www.eurolines.com), in conjunction with local carriers all over Europe, is the main international carrier. It runs services across Europe and to Morocco departing from Estació del Nord and **Estació d'Autobusos de Sants** (Map pp306-7; Carrer de Viriat), which is next to Estació Sants Barcelona. For information and tickets in Barcelona, contact Alsa. Another carrier is **Linebús** (www.linebus.com).

Within Catalonia, much of the Pyrenees and the entire Costa Brava are served only by buses, as train services are limited to important railheads such as Girona, Figueres, Lleida, Ripoll and Puigcerdà. If there is a train, take it – they're usually more convenient. For bus fares and journey times from Barcelona, see the appropriate destinations in the Catalonia chapter (p370). Various bus companies operate across the region, mostly from Estació del Nord:

Alsina Graells (☎ 902 42 22 42; www2.alsa.es) Part of the Continental-Auto group, it runs buses from Barcelona to destinations west and northwest, such as Vielha, La Seu d'Urgell and Lleida.

Barcelona Bus (☎ 902 13 00 14; www.sagales.com in Catalan/Spanish) Runs buses from the capital to Girona (and Girona airport), Figueres, parts of the Costa Brava and northwest Catalonia.

Hispano-Igualadina (☎ 902 44 77 26; www.igualadina.net; Estació Sants & Plaça de la Reina Maria Cristina) Serves central Catalonia.

SARFA (☎ 902 30 20 25; www.sarfa.com) The main operator on and around the Costa Brava.

TEISA (Map pp310-11; ☎ 972 20 48 68; www.teisa-bus.com; Carrer de Pau Claris 117) Covers a large part of the eastern Catalan Pyrenees from Girona and Figueres. From Barcelona, buses head for Camprodon via Ripoll and Olot via Besalú.

Departures from Estació del Nord include the following (where frequencies vary, the lowest figure is usually for Sunday; fares quoted are the lowest available):

Destination	Frequency (per day)	Duration	Cost (one-way)
Almería	4-5	11¼-14hr	€59.97
Burgos	5-6	7¾-8½hr	€33.31
Granada	5-8	12-14½ hr	€65.96
Madrid	up to 16	7½-8hr	€27.08
Seville	1-2	15½-16 hr	€74
Valencia	up to 14	4¼-6¼hr	€24.35
Zaragoza	up to 22	3½ hr	€13.18

Car & Motorcycle

Autopistas (tollways) head out of Barcelona in most directions, including the C31/C32 to the southern Costa Brava; the C32 to Sitges; the C16 to Manresa (with a turn-off for Montserrat); and the AP7 north to Girona, Figueres and France, and south to Tarragona and Valencia (turn off along the AP2 for Lleida, Zaragoza and Madrid). The toll-free alternatives, such as the A2 north to Girona, Figueres and France, and west to Lleida and beyond, or the A7 to Tarragona, tend to be busy and slow.

RENTAL

Avis, Europcar, Hertz and several other big companies have desks at the airport, Estació Sants train station and Estació del Nord bus terminus:

Avis (Map pp310-11; ☎ 902 24 88 24, 93 237 56 80; www.avis.es; Carrer de Còrsega 293-295)

Cooltra (Map pp312-13; ☎ 93 221 40 70; www.cooltra.com; Passeig de Joan de Borbó 80-84) You can rent scooters here for around €20 a day, or as little as €90 a month in winter (low season). Add insurance. It also organises scooter tours.

Europcar (Map pp310-11; ☎ 93 302 05 43; www.europcar.es; Gran Via de les Corts Catalanes 680)

Hertz (Map pp306-7; ☎ 93 419 61 56; www.hertz.es; Carrer del Viriat 45)

National/Atesa (Map pp312-13; ☎ 902 10 01 01, 93 323 07 01; www.atesa.es; Carrer de Muntaner 45)

Pepecar (www.pepecar.com) La Rambla (Map pp316-17; ☎ 807 41 42 43; Plaça de Catalunya); Estació Sants Barcelona (Map pp306-7; Carrer de Béjar 68) This company specialises in cheap rentals. There's also an outlet near Aeroport del Prat at the Hotel Tryp Barcelona Aeropuerto.

Vanguard (Map pp310-11; ☎ 93 439 38 80; www.vanguardrent.com; Carrer de Viladomat 297) For motorbikes.

Train

The main international and domestic station is **Estació Sants** (Map pp306-7; Plaça dels Països Catalans), 2.5km west of La Rambla. Other stops on long-distance lines include **Catalunya** (Map pp312-13; Plaça de Catalunya) and **Passeig de Gràcia** (Map pp310-11; cnr Passeig de Gràcia & Carrer d'Aragó). Information windows operate at Estació Sants and Passeig de Gràcia station. Sants station has a **consigna** (left-luggage lockers; small/big locker per 24hr €3/4.50; 🕑 5.30am-11pm), a tourist office, a telephone and fax office, currency-exchange booths and ATMs.

INTERNATIONAL

For information on getting to Barcelona by rail from European cities, see the Transport chapter (p888).

One or two daily services connect Montpellier in France with Estació Sants (€51 each way in *turista* class, 4½ hours). A couple of other slower services (with a change of train at Portbou) also make this run. All stop in Perpignan.

From Estació Sants, up to eight trains daily run to Cerbère (from €9.60, 2½ hours), on the French side of the border, and five to Latour-de-Carol (€8.55, 3¼ hours). From these stations you have several onward connections to Paris via Montpellier and Toulouse, respectively.

DOMESTIC

There are trains to most large Spanish cities, with the usual huge range of train types and fares. Since early 2008 the high-speed AVE train between Barcelona and Madrid has provided some serious competition for that air route. Seventeen trains run in each direction, seven of them nonstop (two hours, 40 minutes). One-way prices range from around €40 (purchased online at least 15 days before travel) to €163 (open ticket valid for a year). All services depart from or pass through Estació Sants. Some other popular runs include (fares represent range of lowest fares depending on type of train):

Destination	Frequency (per day)	Duration	Cost (one-way)
Alicante	up to 8	4¾ -5½hr	€44-48.70
Burgos	4	8½-9hr	€38.50
Valencia	up to 15	3-3½hr	€32.50-38
Zaragoza	up to 16	1½-4¼hr	€25.40-56.60

GETTING AROUND

The metro is the easiest way of getting around and reaches most places you're likely to visit (although not the airport). For some trips you need buses or FGC suburban trains. The tourist office gives out the comprehensive *Guia d'Autobusos Urbans de Barcelona*, which has a metro map and all bus routes.

For public-transport information, make a call to ☎ 010.

To/From the Airport

The **A1 Aerobús** (Map pp312-13, Map pp306-7; ☎ 93 415 60 20; one-way €4.05; 30-40min) runs from the airport to Plaça de Catalunya via Plaça d'Espanya, Gran Via de les Corts Catalanes (on the corner of Carrer del Comte d'Urgell) and Plaça de la Universitat (six to 15 minutes depending on the time of day) from 6am to 1am. Departures from Plaça de Catalunya are from 5.30am to 12.15am and go via Plaça d'Espanya. Buy tickets on the bus or machines at the airport (if they are working!). Considerably slower local buses (such as bus 46 to/from Plaça d'Espanya and a night bus, the N17, to/from Plaça de Catalunya) also operate.

Renfe's *rodalies* line 10 runs between the airport and Estació de França in Barcelona (about 35 minutes), stopping at Estació Sants and Passeig de Gràcia. Tickets cost €2.60, unless you have a T-10 multitrip public-transport ticket. The service from the airport starts at 6am and ends at 10.29pm daily.

A taxi to/from the centre, about a half-hour ride depending on traffic, costs between €18 and €22.

Sagalés (☎ 902 13 00 14; www.sagales.com) runs direct Barcelona Bus services between Girona–Costa Brava Airport and Estació del Nord bus station in Barcelona (one way/return €12/21, 70 minutes), connecting with flights.

Bicycle

Bike lanes have been laid out along quite a few main roads (such as Gran Via de les Corts Catalanes, Avinguda Diagonal, Carrer d'Aragó, Avinguda de la Meridiana and Carrer de la Marina) and a growing web of secondary streets, so it is quite possible to get around on two ecological wheels.

Barnabike (Map pp316-17; ☎ 93 269 02 04; www.barnabike.com; Carrer del Pas de Sota la Muralla 3; per hr/24hr €4/18; 🕑 10am-9.30pm) Rents out an assortment of bikes (including kick bikes) and karts, Trikkes (odd three-wheel contraptions), electric bikes and bikes for kids.

Biciclot (Map pp306-7; ☎ 93 221 97 78; www.biciclot.net; Passeig Marítim 33; per hr/day €5.50/€18; 🕑 10am-3pm & 4-8pm Apr-Sep, to 6pm Oct-Nov, 10am-3pm Sat & Sun & holidays Dec-Mar) A handy seaside location.

Bus

The city transport authority, **TMB** (☎ 010; www.tmb.net), runs buses along most city routes every few minutes from 5am or 6am to 10pm or 11pm. Many routes pass through Plaça de Catalunya and/or Plaça de la Universitat (both on Map pp312–13). After 11pm, a reduced network of yellow *nitbusos* (night buses) runs until 3am or 5am. All *nitbus* routes pass through Plaça de Catalunya and most run about every 30 to 45 minutes.

Car & Motorcycle

An effective one-way system makes traffic flow fairly smoothly, but you'll often find yourself flowing the way you don't want to go, unless you happen to have an adept navigator and a map that shows one-way streets.

PARKING

Limited parking in the Ciutat Vella is virtually all for residents only, with some metered parking. The narrow streets of Gràcia are not much better. The broad boulevards of L'Eixample are divided into blue and green zones. For nonresidents they mean the same thing: limited meter parking. Fees vary but tend to hover around €2.35 to €2.85 per hour. Parking stations are also scattered all over L'Eixample, with a few in the old centre too. Prices vary from around €3 to €4 per hour.

Metro & FGC

The **Transports Metropolitans de Barcelona (TMB) metro** (☎ 010; www.tmb.net) has six numbered and colour-coded lines (see the map at the back of this book). It runs from 5am to midnight Sunday to Thursday, from 5am to 2am on Friday, and 5am to 5am on Saturday and days immediately preceding main holidays. Line 2 has access for disabled people and a handful of stations on other lines also have lifts. Line 11, a short suburban run, is automated, and in the future the other lines will also run without the need of a driver.

Suburban trains run by the **Ferrocarrils de la Generalitat de Catalunya** (FGC; ☎ 93 205 15 15; www.fgc.net) include a couple of useful city lines. One heads north from Plaça de Catalunya. A branch of it will get you to Tibidabo and another within spitting distance of the Monestir de Pedralbes. Some trains along this line run beyond Barcelona to Sant Cugat, Sabadell and Terrassa.

The other FGC line heads to Manresa from Plaça d'Espanya, and is handy for the trip to Montserrat (p367).

These trains run from about 5am (with only one or two services before 6am) to 11pm or midnight (depending on the line) Sunday to Thursday, and from 5am to about 1am (or a little later, depending on the line and stop) on Friday and Saturday.

Three **tram** (☎ 902 19 32 75; www.trambcn.com) lines run into the suburbs of greater Barcelona from Plaça de Francesc Macià and are of limited interest to visitors. Another line (T4) runs from behind the zoo near the Ciutadella-Vila Olímpica metro stop to Sant Adrià via Fòrum. The T5 line runs from Glòries to Badalona. All standard transport passes are valid.

Taxi

Taxis charge €1.75 flagfall (€1.85 from 9pm to 7am weekdays and all day Saturday, Sunday and holidays) plus meter charges of €0.78 per kilometre (€1 at night and on weekends). A further €3 is added for all trips to/from the airport and €0.90 for luggage bigger than 55cm x 35cm x 35cm. The trip from Estació Sants to Plaça de Catalunya, about 3km, costs about €8 to €10. You can call a **taxi** (☎ 93 225 00 00, 93 300 11 00, 93 303 30 33, 93 322 22 22, 704 10 11 12) or flag them down in the streets. General information is available on ☎ 010. The call-out charge is €3.09 (€3.86 at night and on weekends). In many taxis it is possible to pay with credit card.

Fono Taxi (☎ 93 300 11 00) is one of several taxi companies with taxis adapted for the disabled. **Taxi Amic** (☎ 93 420 80 88; www.terra.es/personal/taxiamic) is a special taxi service for the disabled or difficult situations (eg transport of big objects). Book at least 24 hours in advance if possible.

Tickets & Targetas

The metro, FGC trains, *rodalies/cercanías* (Renfe-run local trains) and buses come under one zoned fare regime. Single-ride tickets on all standard transport within Zone 1 (which extends beyond the airport), except on Renfe trains, cost €1.30.

Targetes are multitrip transport tickets. They are sold at most city-centre metro stations. The prices given here are for travel in Zone 1. Children under four travel free.

Targeta T-10 (€7.20) 10 rides (each valid for 1¼ hours) on the metro, buses and FGC trains. You can change between metro, FGC, *rodalies* and buses.

Targeta T-DIA (€5.50) Unlimited travel on all transport for one day.

Targeta T-50/30 (€29.80) For 50 trips within 30 days.

Two-/three-/four-/five-day tickets for unlimited travel on all transport except the A1 Aerobús cost €10/14.30/18.30/21.70. Buy them at metro stations and tourist offices.

Monthly transport pass (€46.25) For unlimited use of all public transport.

Train

Renfe runs local trains *(rodalies* or *cercanías)* to towns around Barcelona, as well as the airport. You can get information on times and fares at www.renfe.es. Search under Cercanías Barcelona. For the airports, see left.

Trixis

These three-wheeled **cycle taxis** (Map pp312-13; ☎ 93 310 13 79; www.trixi.info; per 30min/hr €10/18; 11am-8pm daily Mar-Nov) operate on the waterfront. They can take two passengers, and tickets for children aged three to 12 years are half-price. You can find trixis near the Monument a Colom. Other similar companies have also sprung up.

AROUND BARCELONA

Need a break from the hubbub? Several options within easy reach present themselves. Sitges is a pretty seaside town southwest of Barcelona with thumping nightlife. Wine-lovers may want to explore the Penedès wine-making region, famous for its *cava*. From the hedonistic to the heavenly, head north for Catalonia's sacred mountain range, Montserrat. Closer to home, admire the genius of Gaudí at Colònia Güell.

COLÒNIA GÜELL

Apart from La Sagrada Família, the last grand project Gaudí turned his hand to was the creation of a Utopian textile-workers' complex, known as the **Colònia Güell** (☎ 93 630 58 07; www.coloniaguellbarcelona.com; adult/student & senior crypt €4/2.50, 1hr tour of crypt €5/3.50, 2hr tour of crypt & Colònia Güell €8/6; crypt 10am-2pm & 3-7pm Mon-Fri, 10am-3pm Sat & Sun & holidays May-Oct, 10am-3pm Nov-Apr; FGC lines S4, S7, S8 or S33 from Plaça d'Espanya), outside Barcelona at Santa Coloma de Cervelló.

His main role was to erect the colony's church – the workers' housing and the local

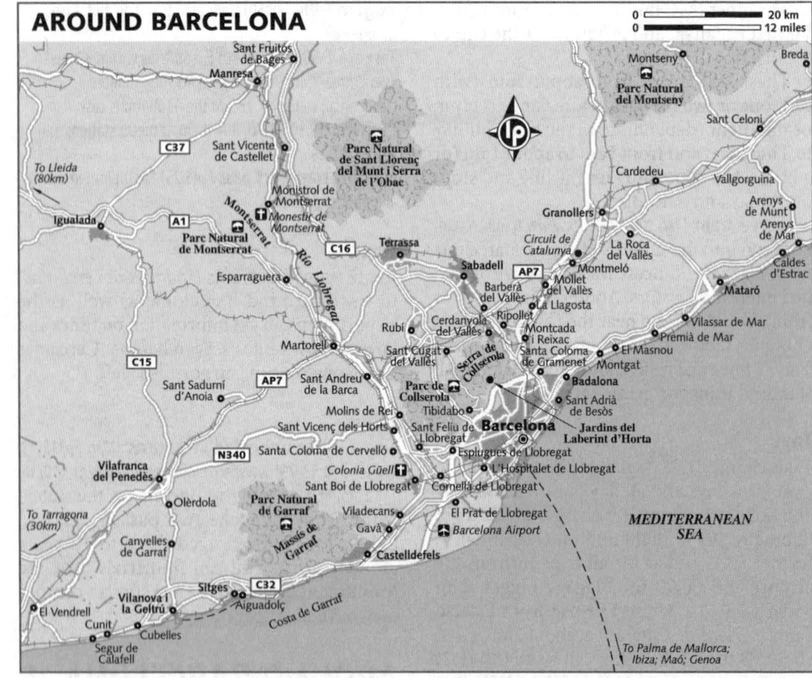

cooperative were in the hands of other architects. Work on the church's **crypt** started in 1908 and proceeded for eight years, at which point interest in the whole idea fizzled. The crypt serves as a working church.

This structure makes up an important part of Gaudí's oeuvre. The mostly brick-clad columns that support the ribbed vaults in the church's ceiling are inclined in much the way you might expect trees in a forest to lean at all angles (reminiscent also of Park Güell, which Gaudí was working on at much the same time).

Near the church are spread cute brick houses designed for the factory workers and still inhabited today. A short stroll away, the 23 factory buildings of a **Modernista industrial complex**, idle since the 1970s, have been brought back to life in a €60 million project under the direction of local building star Òscar Tusquets. Shops and businesses have moved into the renovated complex. You can pick up a map at the information centre and wander around or join guided visits of the crypt alone or the crypt and former factory complex at noon on weekends. Other tours take place at 10am and 2pm too if there are enough people. In theory, several languages are catered for but, for anything beyond Catalan and Spanish, you need to call ahead.

SITGES

pop 26,200

Sitges attracts everyone from jet-setters to young travellers, honeymooners to weekending families, and from Barcelona's night owls to an international gay crowd. The beach is long and sandy, the nightlife thumps until breakfast and there are lots of groovy boutiques if you need to spruce up your wardrobe. In winter Sitges can be dead, but it wakes up with a vengeance for Carnaval, when the gay crowd puts on an outrageous show.

Information

Policia Local (☎ 704 10 10 92; Plaça d'Ajuntament)

Main tourist office (☎ 93 810 93 40; www.sitgestur.com; Carrer de Sínia Morera 1; ⏰ 9am-8pm mid-Jun–mid-Sep, 9am-2pm & 4-6.30pm Mon-Fri Oct-Jun)

Tourist office (☎ 93 811 06 11; Passeig de la Ribera s/n; ⏰ 10am-2pm & 4-8pm daily mid-Jun–mid-Sep, 10am-2pm & 4-7pm Fri & Sat, 10am-2pm Sun-Thu mid-Sep–mid-Jun) A branch office.

Sights & Activities

MUSEUMS

Three **museums** (each adult/child/student €3.50/free/1.50; 10am-1.30pm & 3-6.30pm Tue-Fri, 10am-7pm Sat, 10am-3pm Sun Oct-Jun, 10am-2pm & 5-9pm Tue-Sun Jul-Sep), which offer a combined ticket (adult/child /student €6.40/free/3.50), make up the bulk of the cultural side of Sitges.

The **Museu Cau Ferrat** (93 894 03 64; Carrer de Fonollar) was built in the 1890s as a house-cum-studio by Santiago Rusiñol, Modernista artist and the man who attracted the art world to Sitges. In 1894 Rusiñol reawakened the public to the then unfashionable work of El Greco by parading two of the Cretan's canvases in from Sitges train station to Cau Ferrat. These are on show, along with the remainder of Rusiñol's rambling art-and-craft collection, which includes paintings by the likes of Picasso, Ramon Casas and Rusiñol himself.

Next door, the **Museu Maricel del Mar** (93 894 03 64; Carrer de Fonollar) houses art and handcrafts from the Middle Ages to the 20th century. The museum is part of the **Palau Maricel**, a stylistic fantasy built around 1910 by Miquel Utrillo, a companion of Casas and Rusiñol in Barcelona's art world at the turn of the 20th century.

The **Museu Romàntic** (93 894 29 69; Carrer de Sant Gaudenci 1) recreates the lifestyle of a 19th-century Catalan landowning family, and contains a collection of several hundred antique dolls.

BEACHES

The main beach is divided by a series of breakwaters into sections with different names. A pedestrian promenade runs its whole length. In the height of summer, especially on Saturday and Sunday, the end nearest the **Església de Sant Bartomeu i Santa Tecla** gets jam-packed. Crowds thin out slightly towards the southwest end.

Festivals & Events

Carnaval (19 to 25 February 2009; dates change from year to year) in Sitges is a week-long riot just made for the extrovert, ambiguous and exhibitionist, capped by an extravagant gay parade that's held on the last night. June sees the **Sitges International Theatre Festival**, with a strong experimental leaning. The town's **Festa Major** (Major Festival) in late August features a huge firework display on the 23rd. And early October is the time for Sitges' **International Film Festival** (www.cinemasitges.com).

Sleeping

Sitges has around 50 hotels and *hostales*, but many close from around October to April, then are full in July and August, when prices are at their highest and booking is advisable. Many, including the following, are gay-friendly without being exclusively so. Gay travellers looking for accommodation in Sitges can try **Throb** (www.throb.co.uk).

Pensió Maricel (93 894 36 27; www.milisa.com; Carrer d'En Tacó 13; d €60-70) This spot is one of the cheapest deals in town, just back from the beach in a tight lane. The 10 simple rooms are clean and spartan. Inside rooms are cheaper and have no view of anything, while from the exterior ones you can get sea glimpses if you lean out.

Romàntic Hotel (93 894 83 75; www.hotelromantic.com; Carrer de Sant Isidre 33; s/d €80/110, s/d without bathroom €68/95;) These three adjoining 19th-century villas are presented in sensuous period style, with a leafy dining courtyard. If it has no rooms, ask about its other charming boutique hotel, Hotel La Renaixença (Carrer d'Illa de Cuba 45), round the corner (the reception is at Romàntic Hotel). Indeed, it shares the street with several beautifully restored houses converted into enticing hotels.

Eating

Al Fresco (93 894 06 00; Carrer de Pau Barrabeig 4; meals €25-30; dinner Tue-Sat, lunch Sun mid-Jan–mid-Dec;) Hidden along a narrow stairway that masquerades as a street, it serves light curries and other surprises. It has a tasting menu (€29) on Wednesday nights.

Costa Dorada (93 894 35 43; Carrer del Port Alegre 27; meals €30; lunch & dinner Fri-Tue, lunch Wed Jan-Nov) Old-world service with 1970s atmosphere (lots of tiles and bottles of wine on display) and reliable standards make the 'Gold Coast' a safe bet, especially for seafood, paella and *fideuá*.

La Nansa (93 894 94 19 27; Carrer de la Carreta 24; meals €35; lunch & dinner Thu-Mon Feb-Dec) Cast just back from the waterfront up a little lane in a fine old house is this seafood specialist that does a good line in paella and other rice dishes.

Pic Nic (93 811 00 40; Passeig de la Ribera s/n; meals €35-40; lunch Sun-Thu, lunch & dinner Fri & Sat) With views straight out over the sea, this good-natured, rowdy seafood eatery is perfect for a group lunch. Fish and seafood rice dishes (paella and company) are the speciality here.

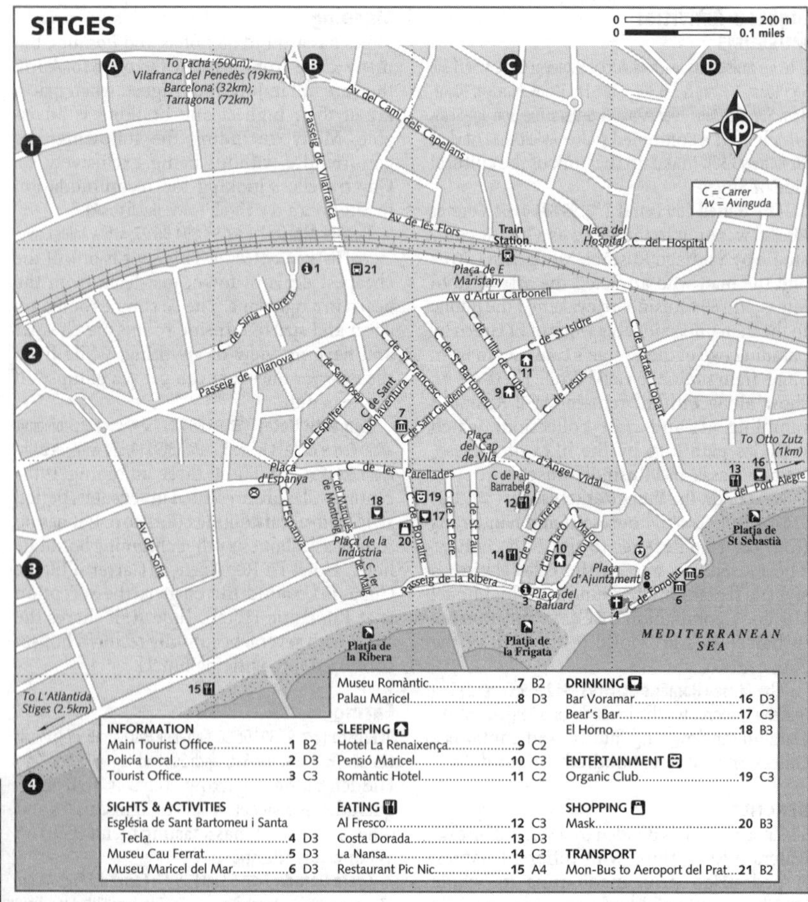

Drinking & Entertainment

Much of Sitges' nightlife happens on one short pedestrian strip packed with humanity right through the night in summer: Carrer del 1er de Maig, Plaça de la Industria and Carrer del Marqués de Montroig, all in a short line off the seafront. Carrer del 1er de Maig – also known as Calle del Pecado (Sin Street) – vibrates to the volume of 10 or so disco-bars, all trying to outdo each other in decibels. You'll find more of the same, if slightly less intense, around the corner on Carrer de les Parellades, Carrer de Bonaire and Carrer de Sant Pere. That said, virtually all bars shut by 3.30am.

On Platja de Sant Sebastià, **Bar Voramar** (www.pub-voramar.com; Carrer del Port Alegre 55) is a 1960s throwback with nautical decoration and good music. Check it out for live jazz sessions.

Afterwards, there's clubbing at the nearby **Otto Zutz** (Port d'Aiguadolç) on the waterfront and **Pachá** (☎ 93 894 22 98; www.pachasitges.com; Carrer de Sant Dídac, Vallpineda), north of the town centre. Equally popular is the beachside **L'Atlàntida Sitges** (☎ 93 894 26 77; www.clubatlantida.com; Platja Les Coves; Tue-Sun Jun-Sep), about 3.5km west of the centre. A shuttle bus runs here from Platja de Sant Sebastià on those nights it's open.

Gay and gay-friendly bars abound. **El Horno** (☎ 93 894 09 09; Carrer de Juan Tarrida Ferratges 6; 5.30pm-3am) has a dark room to fumble about in and you can make hirsute pursuits at **Bear's Bar** (www.bearsbarsitges.com; Carrer de Bonaire 17; 10pm-3.30am daily Jun-Sep, Fri & Sat Oct-May). For dancing late into the night, the **Organic Club** (Carrer de Bonaire 15; midnight-6am) is a popular gay club, one of two in town. If you need any toys, head for the **Mask** (93 811 34 32; Carrer de Bonaire 22) erotic shop.

Getting There & Away

From about 6am to 10pm, four *rodalies* per hour run from Passeig de Gràcia and Estació Sants in Barcelona to Sitges (€2.60, 38 to 46 minutes from Passeig de Gràcia depending on intermediate stops). The best road from Barcelona to Sitges is the C32 tollway. A direct bus run by Mon-Bus goes to Barcelona airport from near the tourist office.

MONTSERRAT

Montserrat (Serrated Mountain), 50km northwest of Barcelona, is a 1236m-high mountain of truly weird rock pillars, shaped by wind, rain and frost from a conglomeration of limestone, pebbles and sand that once lay under the sea. With the historic Benedictine Monestir de Montserrat, one of Catalonia's most important shrines, cradled at 725m on its side, it makes a great outing from Barcelona. From the mountain, on a clear day, you can see as far as the Pyrenees and even, if you're lucky, Mallorca.

Orientation & Information

The *cremallera* (rack-and-pinion train) arrives on the mountainside, just below the monastery. From there, the main road curves (past a snack bar, cafeteria, information office and the Espai Audiovisual) up to the right, passing the blocks of Celles Abat Marcel, to enter Plaça de Santa Maria, at the centre of the monastery complex.

The **information office** (93 877 77 01; www.abadiamontserrat.net; 9am-6pm) has information on the complex and walking trails.

Sights & Activities

MONESTIR DE MONTSERRAT

The monastery was founded in 1025 to commemorate a 'vision' of the Virgin on the mountain. Wrecked by Napoleon's troops in 1811, then abandoned as a result of anticlerical legislation in the 1830s, it was rebuilt from 1858. Today a community of about 80 monks lives here. Pilgrims come from far and wide to venerate *La Moreneta* (The Black Virgin), a 12th-century Romanesque wooden sculpture of Mary with the infant Jesus, which has been Catalonia's patron since 1881.

The two-part **Museu de Montserrat** (93 877 77 77; Plaça de Santa Maria; adult/student €6.50/5.50; 10am-6pm) has an excellent collection, ranging from an Egyptian mummy and Gothic altarpieces to art by El Greco, Monet, Degas and Picasso. The **Espai Audiovisual** (adult/senior & student €2/1.50, free with ticket to Museu de Montserrat; 9am-6pm) is a walk-through multimedia space (with images and sounds) that illustrates the daily life and activities of the monks and the history and spirituality of the monastery.

From Plaça de Santa Maria you enter the courtyard of the 16th-century **basilica** (admission incl La Moreneta €5; 9am-8.15pm Jul-Sep, earlier closing rest of yr), the monastery's church. The basilica's facade, with its carvings of Christ and the 12 Apostles, dates from 1901, despite its 16th-century plateresque style. Follow the signs to the **Cambril de la Mare de Déu** (8-10.30am & 12.15-6.30pm Mon-Sat, 8-10.30am, 12.15-6.30pm & 7.30-8.15pm Sun & holidays) to the right of the main basilica entrance to see the Black Virgin.

If you're around the basilica at the right time, you'll catch a brief performance by the **Montserrat Boys' Choir** (Escolania; www.escolania.net; admission free; performances 1pm & 6.45pm Mon-Fri, 11am & 6.45pm Sun, Sep-Jun), reckoned to be Europe's oldest music school.

On your way out, have a look in the room across the courtyard from the basilica entrance, filled with gifts and thank-you messages to the Montserrat Virgin, from people who give her the credit for all manner of happy events. The souvenirs range from plaster casts to wedding dresses.

To see where the holy image of the Virgin was discovered, take the **Santa Cova funicular** (one way/return €1.70/2.70; every 20min 10am-5.35pm Apr-Oct, 11am-4.25pm Nov-Mar) down from the main area.

THE MOUNTAIN

You can explore the mountain above the monastery on a web of paths leading to some of the peaks and to 13 empty and rather dilapidated hermitages. The **Funicular de Sant Joan** (one way/return €4.15/6.60; every 20min 10am-5.40pm Apr-Oct, to 7pm mid-Jul–Aug, 11am-4.30pm Nov-Mar) will carry you up the first 250m from the monastery. If you prefer to walk, the road past the funicular's bottom station leads to its top station in about one hour (3km).

From the Sant Joan top station, it's a 20-minute stroll (signposted) to the **Sant Joan chapel**, with fine westward views. More exciting is the one-hour walk northwest, along a path marked with occasional blobs of yellow paint, to Montserrat's highest peak, **Sant Jeroni**, from where there's an awesome sheer drop on the north face. The walk takes you across the upper part of the mountain, with a close-up experience of some of the weird rock pillars. Many have names: on your way to Sant Jeroni look over to the right for **La Prenyada** (The Pregnant Woman), **La Mòmia** (The Mummy), **L'Elefant** (The Elephant) and **El Cap de Mort** (The Death's Head).

Sleeping & Eating

Celles Abat Marcel (☎ 93 877 77 01; 2-/4-person apt €46.60/83.20; Ⓟ) Here you will find comfortable apartments equipped with full bathroom and kitchenette. Smaller studios go for €29.50/43.80 for one/two people.

Hotel Abat Cisneros (☎ 93 877 77 01; s/d €60.55/105.80; ✖ Ⓟ) The only hotel in the monastery complex has modern, comfortable rooms, some looking on to Plaça de Santa Maria. It has a restaurant (meals €30), a cafeteria (meals €15) for lunch and a couple of cafes for breakfast.

Getting There & Away

BUS

A daily bus from Barcelona with **Julià Tours** (Map pp312-13; ☎ 93 317 64 54; Ronda de l'Universitat 5) to the monastery (€43) leaves at 9.30am (returning at 3pm). The price includes travel, all entry prices, use of funiculars at Montserrat and a meal at the cafeteria.

CAR & MOTORCYCLE

The most straightforward route from Barcelona is by Avinguda Diagonal, Via Augusta, the Túnel de Vallvidrera and the C16. Shortly after Terrassa, follow the exit signs to Montserrat, which will put you on the C58 road. Follow it northwest to the C55. Then head 2km south on this road to Monistrol de Montserrat, from where a road snakes 7km up the mountain. You could leave the car at the parking station in Monistrol Vila and take the *cremallera* up to the top.

TRAIN & CREMALLERA

The R5 line trains operated by **FGC** (☎ 93 205 15 15) run from Plaça d'Espanya station in Barcelona to Monistrol de Montserrat up to 18 times daily starting at 5.24am. They connect with the rack-and-pinion train, or **cremallera** (☎ 902 31 20 20; www.cremallerademontserrat.com), which takes 17 minutes to make the upwards journey and costs €4.10/6.50 one way/return. One-way/return from Barcelona to Montserrat with the FGC train and *cremallera* costs €8.70/15.70. For various all-in ticket options, check out the above website or www.fg c.net.

PENEDÈS WINE COUNTRY

Some of Spain's finest wines come from Penedès plains southwest of Barcelona. Sant Sadurní d'Anoia, about a half-hour train ride west of Barcelona, is the capital of *cava*. Vilafranca del Penedès, 12km further down the track, is the heart of the Penedès *Denominación de Origen* (DO; Denomination of Origin) region, which produces noteworthy light whites. Some reasonable reds also come out of the area. Visitors are welcomed on tours of several wineries; there'll often be a free glass along the way and plenty more for sale. Several companies offer package trips to Barcelona that include winery tours of the Penedès, although it is cheaper to do it on your own. One such option for luxury-lovers is the four-day all-inclusive tour run by **Cellar Tours** (www.cellartours.com), which costs from €1500 per person up, depending on the number of people on the tour and style of accommodation. More accessible are 1½-day tours organised from Barcelona by **Spanish Fiestas** (www.spanish-fiestas.com), charging from €119 per person.

Sant Sadurní d'Anoia

pop 11,800

One hundred or so wineries around Sant Sadurní produce 140 million bottles of *cava* a year – something like 85% of the entire national output. *Cava* is made by the same method as French champagne. If you happen to be in town in October, you may catch the **Mostra de Caves i Gastronomia**, a *cava*- and food-tasting fest.

Freixenet (☎ 93 891 70 00; www.freixenet.es/web/eng/; Carrer de Joan Sala 2, Sant Sadurní d'Anoia; admission free; 🕑 1½hr tours 10am-1pm & 3-4.30pm Mon-Thu, 10am-1pm Fri-Sun), the best-known *cava* company, is right next to the train station.

Codorníu (☎ 93 891 33 42; www.codorniu.es; Avinguda de Jaume Codorníu s/n; admission free; 🕑 9am-5pm Mon-Fri, 9am-1pm Sat & Sun) is at Can Codorníu in a Modernista building at the entry to the town by road from Barcelona. Manuel Raventós, head of this firm back in 1872, was the first Spaniard to be successful in producing sparkling wine by the champagne method.

You can simply turn up for tours at either of these establishments.

Vilafranca del Penedès

pop 36,700

Vilafranca is larger than Sant Sadurní and more interesting. The **tourist office** (☎ 93 818 12 54; www.turismevilafranca.com; Carrer de la Fruita 13, Vilafranca; 9am-1pm & 4-7pm Tue-Sat, 4-7pm Sun) can provide tips on visiting some of the smaller wineries in the area.

SIGHTS

The mainly Gothic **Basilica de Santa Maria** (Plaça de Jaume I) stands at the heart of the old town. Begun in 1285, it has been much restored. It is possible to arrange visits of the bell tower in summer at around sunset. Ask at the tourist office.

The basilica faces the **Vinseum** (☎ 93 890 05 82; Plaça de Jaume I, Vilafranca; adult/under 12yr/12-17yr €5/free/3; 10am-2pm & 4-7pm Tue-Sat, 10am-2pm Sun & holidays) across Plaça de Jaume I. Housed in a fine Gothic building, a combination of museums here cover local archaeology, art, geology and birdlife, along with an excellent section on wine.

A statue on Plaça de Jaume I pays tribute to Vilafranca's famous *castellers*, who do their thing during Vilafranca's lively **Festa Major** (main annual festival) at the end of August. For more on castellers, see the boxed text, p425.

Vilafranca's premier winery is **Torres** (☎ 93 817 74 87; www.torres.es; tours per person €5; 9am-5pm Mon-Fri, 9am-6pm Sat, 9am-1pm Sun & holidays), 3km northwest of the town centre on the BP2121 near Pacs del Penedès. The Torres family revolutionised Spanish wine-making in the 1960s by introducing new temperature-controlled, stainless-steel technology and French grape varieties.

EATING

While there is no need to stay in Vilafranca and little attraction in doing so, eating is another story altogether. **Cal Ton** (☎ 93 890 37 41; Carrer Casal 8; meals €35-40; lunch & dinner Wed-Sat, lunch Sun & Tue) is one of several enticing options in town. Hidden away down a narrow side street, Cal Ton has a crisp, modern decor and offers inventive Mediterranean cuisine – all washed down with local wines!

Getting There & Away

Up to three *rodalies* trains an hour run from Estació Sants Barcelona to Sant Sadurní (€2.60, 45 minutes from Plaça de Catalunya in Barcelona) and Vilafranca (€3.20, 55 minutes). By car, take the AP7 and follow the exit signs.

Catalonia

From metropolitan Barcelona spreads a land of such diversity that you could spend weeks dissecting it and still feel you'd barely begun. The Costa Brava boasts much of the wild beauty that first drew visitors here, in spite of the occasional unsightly pocket of tourism-driven construction. Just inland are the medieval cities of Girona and Figueres, the latter home to the 'theatre-museum' of that city's zany son, Salvador Dalí.

Running across the north, the Pyrenees rise to mighty 3000m peaks from a series of green and often remote valleys, dotted with villages that retain a palpable rural and even medieval air. These mountains provide excellent opportunities for walking, skiing and climbing. Enchanting Romanesque churches are scattered across the valleys of the north (for tons of info, see www.romanicocatalan.com).

There's enough to keep you exploring in the far west and south for days, from the wetlands of the Ebro delta to the historic cities of Tarragona and Lleida. Strike out and you'll discover grand medieval monasteries, lush vineyards and remote hilltop villages rarely visited by outsiders.

Throughout Catalonia (Catalunya in Catalan, Cataluña in Castilian Spanish) the sense of difference from the rest of Spain is intense, not only in the use of Catalan (everyone speaks Castilian too) but in the festivals, cuisine and reminders of the region's unique history.

HIGHLIGHTS

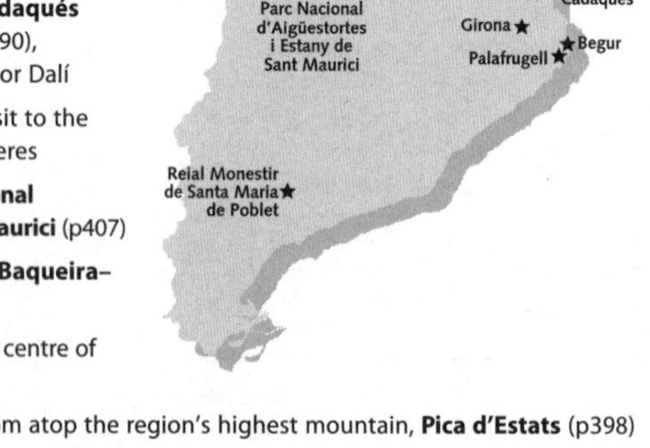

- Chill out on Costa Brava coves and beaches near **Palafrugell** (p377) or **Begur** (p379)
- Discover the magical village of **Cadaqués** (p388) and nearby **Port Lligat** (p390), haunted by the memory of Salvador Dalí
- Contemplate the absurd with a visit to the **Teatre-Museu Dalí** (p391) in Figueres
- Conquer the trails of the **Parc Nacional d'Aigüestortes i Estany de Sant Maurici** (p407)
- Ski the region's premier slopes at **Baqueira–Beret** (p413)
- Explore the compact medieval city centre of **Girona** (p380)
- Contemplate Spain and France from atop the region's highest mountain, **Pica d'Estats** (p398)
- Seek out the Romanesque churches around **Boí** and **Taüll** (p409)
- Wander the monastery complex of the **Reial Monestir de Santa Maria de Poblet** (p416)
- Take the *cremallera* (rack-and-pinion railway) up to **Vall de Núria** (p399)

AREA: 32,113 SQ KM	AVE SUMMER TEMP: HIGH 30°C, LOW 22°C	POP: 7.35 MILLION

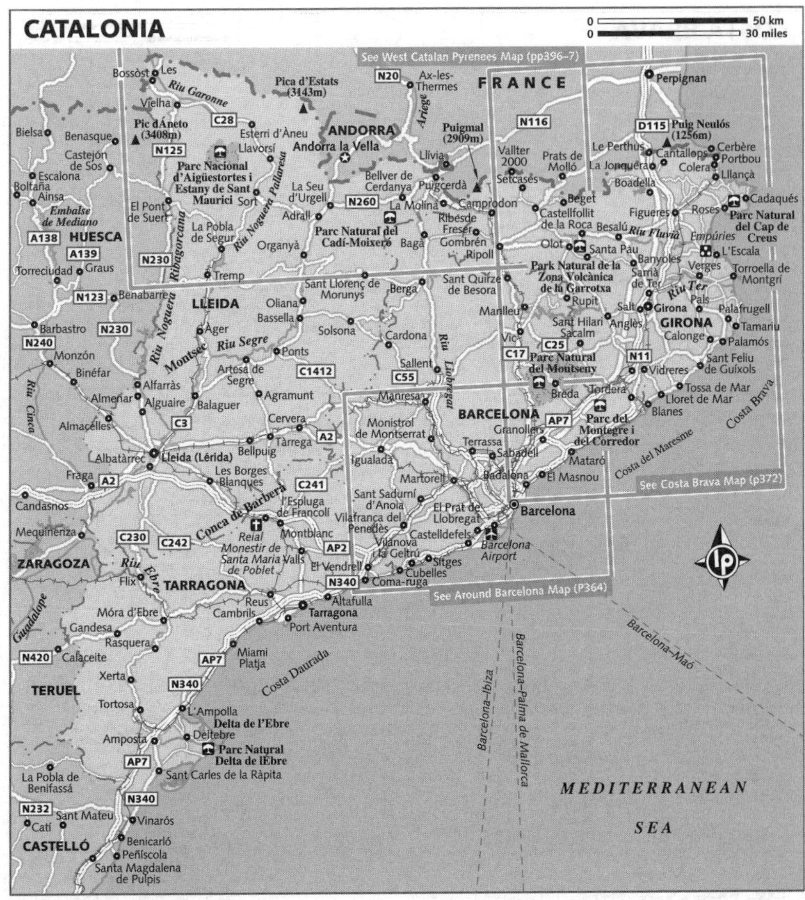

COSTA BRAVA

The Costa Brava (stretching from Blanes to the French border) ranks with the Costa Blanca and Costa del Sol as one of Spain's three great holiday coasts. But alongside some occasionally awful concrete development, English breakfasts and *Konditoreien* (pastry shops), the 'Rugged Coast' has some spectacular stretches.

Nestling in the hilly back country – green and covered in umbrella pine in the south, barer and browner in the north – are scattered charming stone villages, the towering monastery of St Pere de Rodes and Salvador Dalí's fantasy castle home at Púbol. A little further inland are the bigger towns of Girona (Castilian: Gerona), with a sizeable and strikingly well-preserved medieval centre, and Figueres (Castilian: Figueras), famous for its bizarre Teatre-Museu Dalí, the foremost of a series of sites associated with the eccentric surrealist artist Salvador Dalí.

The ruggedness of the Costa Brava continues under the sea and has some of the best diving in Spain. Diving centres with certified instructors operate at a dozen or more places. The Illes Medes, off L'Estartit, are protected islets with probably the most diverse sea life along the Spanish coast. Other top diving spots include the Illes Formigues (rocky islets off the coast between Palamós and Calella de Palafrugell with waters down to 45m) and Els Ullastres,

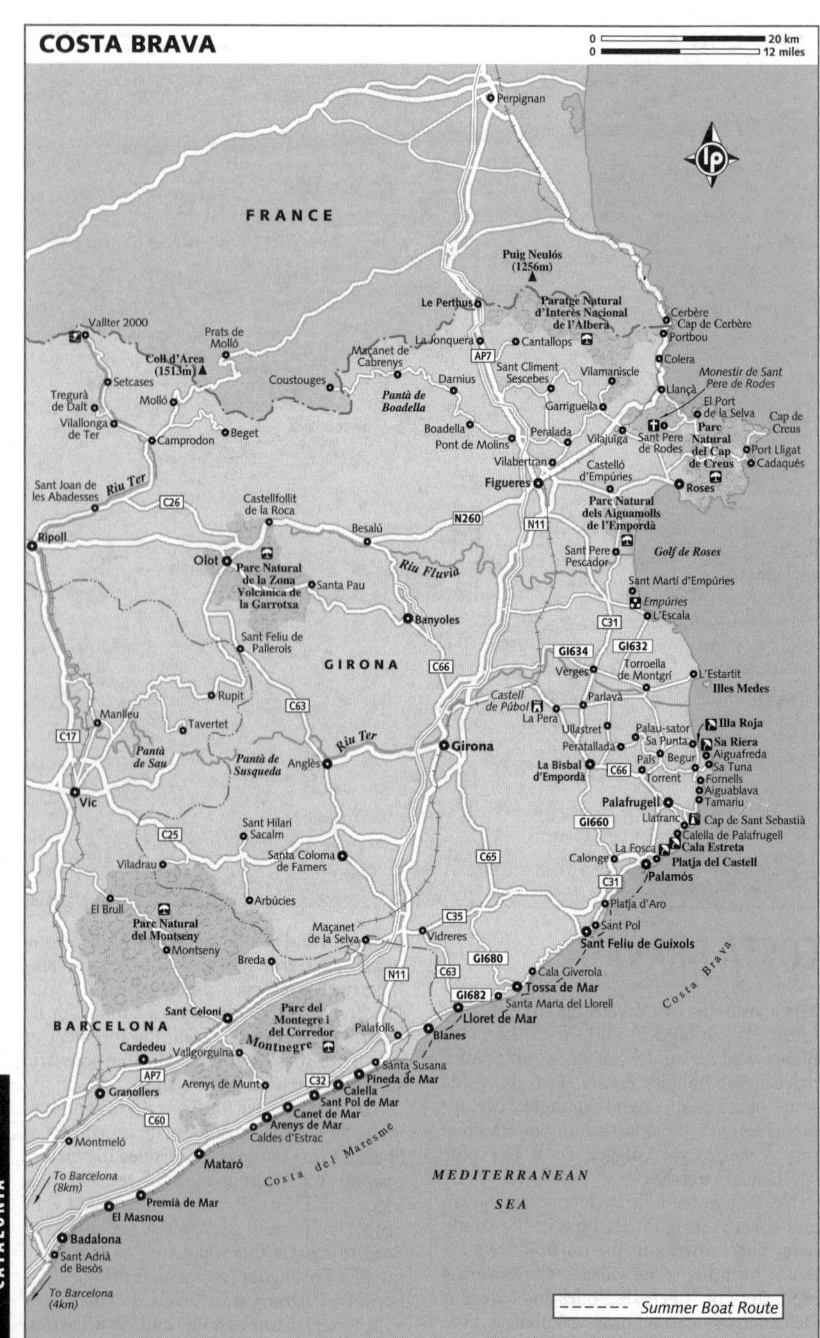
COSTA BRAVA
0 20 km
0 12 miles
FRANCE
Perpignan
Puig Neulós (1256m)
Le Perthus
Paratge Natural d'Interès Nacional de l'Albera
La Jonquera
Cantallops
AP7
Cerbère
Cap de Cerbère
Portbou
Colera
Llançà
Valter 2000
Prats de Molló
Coll d'Area (1513m)
Maçanet de Cabrenys
Coustouges
Darnius
Pantà de Boadella
Sant Climent Sescebes
Vilamaniscle
Garriguella
Monestir de Sant Pere de Rodes
El Port de la Selva
Cap de Creus
Setcases
Tregurà de Dalt
Molló
Vilallonga de Ter
Camprodon
Beget
Boadella
Pont de Molins
Peralada
Vilajuïga
Sant Pere de Rodes
Parc Natural del Cap de Creus
Port Lligat
Cadaqués
Vilabertran
Castelló d'Empúries
Figueres
Roses
Sant Joan de les Abadesses
Riu Ter
C26
Castellfollit de la Roca
N260
N11
Parc Natural dels Aiguamolls de l'Empordà
Ripoll
Besalú
Olot
Parc Natural de la Zona Volcànica de la Garrotxa
Santa Pau
Riu Fluvià
Sant Pere Pescador
Golf de Roses
Sant Martí d'Empúries
Empúries
L'Escala
C31
Banyoles
Sant Feliu de Pallerols
GI634
GI632
GIRONA
C66
Verges
Torroella de Montgrí
L'Estartit
Illes Medes
Rupit
C63
Castell de Púbol
La Pera
Parlavà
Manlleu
Tavertet
Ullastret
Palau-sator
Illa Roja
C17
Pantà de Sau
Pantà de Susqueda
Anglès
Riu Ter
Girona
Peratallada
Sa Punta
Sa Riera
Aiguafreda
La Bisbal d'Empordà
Pals
Begur
Sa Tuna
Torrent
Fornells
Aiguablava
Vic
Palafrugell
Tamariu
Llafranc
Cap de Sant Sebastià
Sant Hilari Sacalm
GI660
Calella de Palafrugell
C25
Cala Estreta
Viladrau
Santa Coloma de Farners
C65
La Fosca
Calonge
Platja del Castell
Palamós
C31
Arbúcies
El Brull
Parc Natural del Montseny
Platja d'Aro
C35
Sant Pol
Maçanet de la Selva
Vidreres
Sant Feliu de Guíxols
Montseny
Breda
GI680
Cala Giverola
N11
C63
Tossa de Mar
GI682
Santa Maria del Llorell
Costa Brava
Sant Celoni
Parc del Montegre i del Corredor
Lloret de Mar
BARCELONA
Montnegre
Palafolls
Blanes
Cardedeu
Vallgorguina
Santa Susana
AP7
Pineda de Mar
Arenys de Munt
C32
Calella
Granollers
Sant Pol de Mar
Canet de Mar
C60
Arenys de Mar
Caldes d'Estrac
Montmeló
Costa del Maresme
Mataró
MEDITERRANEAN SEA
To Barcelona (8km)
Premià de Mar
El Masnou
Badalona
Sant Adrià de Besòs
To Barcelona (4km)
Summer Boat Route

which has three underwater hills off Llafranc, with some sheer walls and depths to 54m.

Getting There & Away

Direct buses from Barcelona go to most towns on or near the Costa Brava. The train line between Barcelona and the coastal border town of Portbou runs inland, through Girona and Figueres, most of the way. From Girona and Figueres there are fairly good bus services to the coast.

In summer, you could take an alternative approach to the southern Costa Brava from Barcelona by a combination of *rodalies* (local trains) and boat.

The AP7 *autopista* (tollway) and the toll-free NII highway both run from Barcelona via Girona and Figueres to the French border, a few kilometres north of La Jonquera. The C32 *autopista* follows the NII up the coast as far as Blanes.

TOSSA DE MAR

pop 5660

Curving around a boat-speckled bay and guarded by a headland crowned with defensive medieval walls and towers (from which you can enjoy marvellous sunsets), Tossa de Mar is a picturesque village of crooked, narrow streets onto which tourism has tacked a larger, modern extension. In July and August it's hard to reach the water's edge without tripping over oily limbs, but it is heaven compared with Lloret de Mar 12km southeast – a

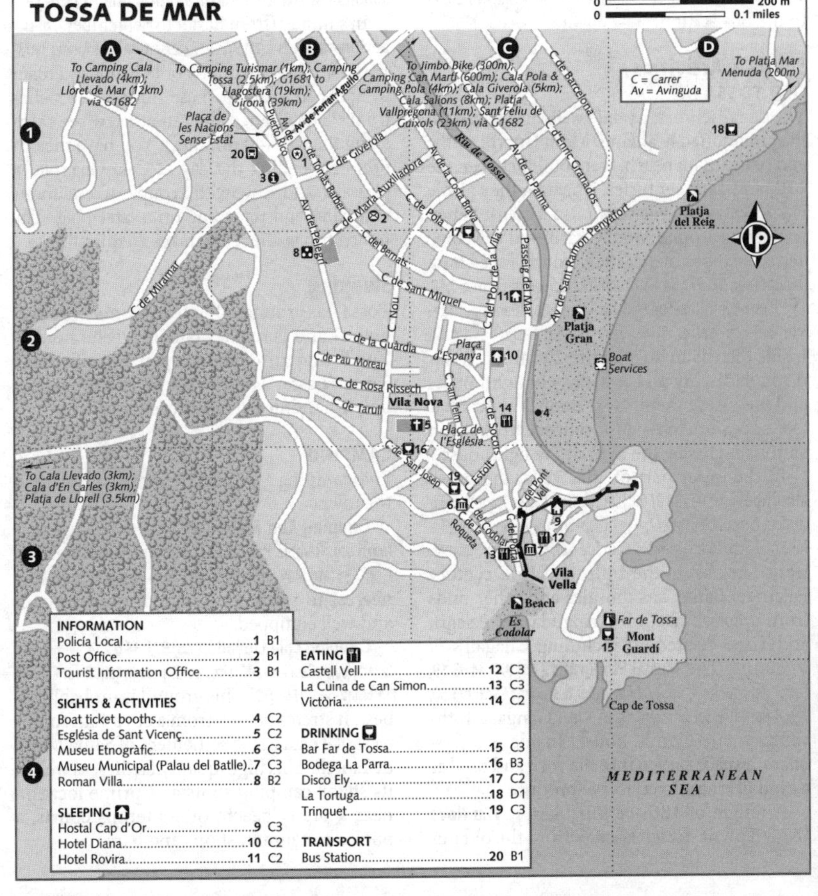

real concrete-and-neon jungle of Piccadilly pubs, *Bierkeller* and soccer chants.

Tossa was one of the first places on the Costa Brava to attract foreign visitors – a small colony of artists and writers gravitated towards what painter Marc Chagall dubbed 'Blue Paradise' in the 1930s. It retains much of that enchantment today, especially out of high season.

Orientation & Information

The bus station is beside the GI682, which leads to Lloret de Mar. The main beach, Platja Gran, and the older part of town are a 10-minute walk southeast.

The **tourist information office** (☎ 972 34 01 08; www.infotossa.com; Avinguda del Pelegrí 25; 9am-9pm Mon-Sat, 10am-2pm & 5-8pm Sun Jul-Aug, 9am-9pm Mon-Sat, 10am-2pm Sun Jun & Sep, 10am-2pm & 4-8pm Mon-Sat Apr-May & Oct, 10am-2pm & 4-7pm Mon-Sat Nov-Mar) is next to the bus station.

Sights & Activities

OLD TOSSA

The deep-ochre, fairy-tale **walls** and **towers** on the pine-dotted headland, Mont Guardí, at the end of the main beach, were built between the 12th and 14th centuries. The area they girdle is known as the **Vila Vella** (Old Town). When wandering around Mont Guardí you will come across vestiges of a castle, and the **Far de Tossa** (lighthouse; ☎ 972 34 12 97; adult/child/senior €3/free/1.50; 10am-10pm Tue-Sun mid-Jun–mid-Sep, 10am-6pm Tue-Sun mid-Sep–Easter, 10am-7pm Tue-Sat Easter–mid-Jun). Inside there is an imaginative 20-minute walk-through display on the history of lighthouses and life inside them. Next door is a great bar (see opposite). In August, concerts are held on various nights by the light of the lighthouse.

In the lower part of Vila Vella, the **Museu Municipal** (☎ 972 34 07 09; Plaça de Roig i Soler 1; adult/child/student & senior/€3/free/2; 10am-2pm & 4-8pm daily mid-Jun–mid-Sep, 10am-2pm & 4-6pm Tue-Sat, 10am-3pm Sun mid-Sep–mid-Jun), set in the 14th- and 15th-century Palau del Batlle, has mosaics and other finds from a **Roman villa**, off Avinguda del Pelegrí, and Tossa-related art including Chagall's *El Violinista*. The **Museu Etnogràfic** (☎ 972 34 33 59; Carrer del Codolar 4; adult/child/senior & student €3/free/1.50; 4-8pm Tue-Sat Jun-Sep) is in Can Ganga, a 16th-century, late-Gothic house. Inside is a *fresquera*, a space carved into the rock and used as a kind of fridge to conserve produce.

A tangle of 18th-century lanes, **Vila Nova** (New Town) stretches away from the old nucleus. Further north, northwest and northeast spreads the sprawl of the really new town.

BEACHES & COVES

The main town beach, golden **Platja Gran**, is pretty but tends to be busy. Further north along the same bay are the quieter and smaller **Platja del Reig** and **Platja Mar Menuda** at the end of Avinguda de Sant Ramon Penyafort. The coast to the northeast and southwest of Tossa is dotted by rocky coves, some with charming little beaches. You can walk cross-country from Tossa to **Cala Llevado** and **Cala d'En Carles** beaches, 3km southwest, or the longer **Platja de Llorell** (3.5km away), or drive down to Platja de Llorell from the GI682. To the northeast, you can walk down from the GI682 to sandy coves such as **Cala Pola** (4km), **Cala Giverola** (5km), **Cala Salions** (8km) and **Platja Vallpregona** (11km).

In summer (from Easter to September), **glass-bottomed boats** (☎ 972 34 22 29; return adult/under 3yr/3-12yr €12/free/8.50) run hourly or half-hourly (10am to 5pm) to some of these northeast beaches from Platja Gran, calling in at a few sea caves along the way (40 minutes). You have the option of spending the day at Cala Giverola (a pleasant sandy cove with a couple of restaurants and bars) and returning on a later boat. The return trip is direct and takes 20 minutes.

Sleeping

Tossa has around 60 hotels, *hostales* (budget hotels) and *pensiones* (small private hotels). You'll find all of them open from Semana Santa (Easter Holy Week) to October, but only a handful outside those months.

CAMPING

Five camping grounds are spread out around the town.

Camping Can Martí (☎ 972 34 08 51; www.canmarti.org; Rambla Pau Casals; sites per 2-person tent & car €32; late May–mid-Sep; P) This one is the nearest to town, 1km back from the beach and well equipped.

Camping Cala Llevadó (☎ 972 34 03 14; www.calallevado.com; Cala Llevadó; sites per 2-person tent & car €36.40; May-Sep; P) This ground is probably the best. It stretches back from a cove 4km southwest of Tossa in the settlement of Santa Maria de Llorell. This high-quality facility, as well as its shady camping spots and prime location near a pretty beach, offers tennis courts, a pool, a restaurant, shops and bars.

CATALONIA

The remaining ones, should you get stuck, are **Camping Tossa** (☎ 972 34 05 47; www.campingtossa.com; Carretera Llagostera, Km13; sites per 2-person tent & car €27; Apr-Sep), **Camping Turismar** (☎ 972 34 04 63; Carretera Llagostera, Km2; sites per 2-person tent & car €28; mid-Apr–mid-Sep) and **Camping Pola** (☎ 972 34 10 50; Carretera Sant Feliu, Km4; sites per 2-person tent & car €27; Jun-Sep). The latter is 4km out of town on a turquoise cove below the winding road northeast of Tossa.

HOSTALES & HOTELS

Hostal Cap d'Or (☎ 972 34 00 81; Passeig de la Vila Vella 1; s/d incl breakfast €49/93) Rub up against the town's history in this spot right in front of the walls. Rooms are comfortable and the best look straight onto the beach.

Hotel Rovira (☎ 972 34 02 61; www.hotelroviratossa.com; Carrer del Pou de la Vila 14; s/d €62/124; Apr-Nov; P) Like many of the midrange and upper-level hotels here, the centrally placed Rovira is sizeable and impersonal. Most rooms, however, enjoy lovely sea views from their balconies and are spacious if unexciting in decor. Families will appreciate the pool and kids' play area.

Hotel Diana (☎ 972 34 18 86; www.hotelesdante.com; Plaça d'Espanya 6; s/d €77/129, d with sea views incl breakfast €158; Apr-Nov) You'll relax simply on entering this small-scale, older hotel fronting Platja Gran. It has a Gaudí-built fireplace in the lounge and oozes Modernista decor and stained glass in the central covered courtyard. Half the rooms have beach views.

Eating

Look out for a local speciality, *cimitomba*, fish prepared in a garlic sauce.

Victòria (☎ 972 34 01 66; Passeig del Mar 23; meals €25-30) This eternal waterfront favourite is popular for its no-nonsense seafood cuisine. Try for a table with windows looking out to sea. Several other cheerful restaurants line this esplanade.

Castell Vell (☎ 972 34 10 30; Carrer del Abat Oliva 1; meals €30; lunch & dinner Tue-Sun, dinner Mon May-Oct) This rustic stone house lurks within the walls of the old town. Take your meal, which ranges from local cuisine to more international fare, out onto the terrace. Seafood predominates.

La Cuina de Can Simon (☎ 972 34 12 69; Carrer del Portal 24; meals €60-80; lunch & dinner Wed-Sat & Mon, lunch Sun) Tossa's culinary star (Michelin says so!) nestles by the old walls in a former fisherman's stone house. It serves an imaginative array of Mediterranean cuisine mixed in with traditional Catalan seaside cooking. The *besuc a la manera de Santurtzi* (sea bream with garlic chilli pepper tips and Modena vinegar) is a tangy fish number and the restaurant boasts good wines from around Spain.

Drinking & Entertainment

Many of the old town's lively bars, some with music, are along and near Carrer de Sant Josep.

Bodega La Parra (Carrer de Sant Josep 26; 9pm-3am Apr-Oct) This place manages to maintain an old-fashioned wine-cellar atmosphere.

La Tortuga (Avinguda de Sant Ramon de Penyafort 11; 8pm-3am Fri-Sun Apr-Jun, nightly Jul-Aug) For some sensual salsa and rumba sounds, head for the waterfront La Tortuga.

Trinquet (Carrer de Sant Josep; 9pm-3am Apr-Oct) For acid jazz, Trinquet is the place to go.

Bar Far de Tossa (☎ 972 34 12 97; 10am-10pm Tue-Sun May-Sep, 10am-6pm Oct-Apr) Next to the lighthouse is this groovy little bar with outdoor terrace and it's the best place for a morning coffee or sunrise wine. Light meals are also provided.

Disco Ely (☎ 972 34 00 09; Carrer de Pola; 10pm-5am Apr-Oct) This is one of a handful of clubs in town that puts on a wide range of mainstream dance music and plays some house in the mix.

Getting There & Away

BOAT

From April to October **Dolfi-Jet** (☎ 972 37 19 39) runs boats several times a day between Calella, Blanes, Lloret de Mar and Tossa de Mar (one to 1½ hours), with stops at a few points en route. You could catch one of the *rodalies* from Barcelona's Catalunya station to Calella or Blanes, then transfer to the boat. The return trip to Tossa from Calella costs €25. In many places the boats simply pull up at the beach (in Tossa, at Platja Gran) and tickets are sold at a booth there. From June to September a couple of other companies also kick in, some extending the route as far northeast of Tossa as Sant Feliu de Guíxols.

BUS

Sarfa (☎ 902 30 20 25; www.sarfa.com) runs to and from Barcelona's Estació del Nord up to

11 times daily via Lloret de Mar (€9.85, 1¼ hours). Otherwise there is only a handful of summer connections to Girona and Sant Feliu de Guíxols.

CAR & MOTORCYCLE

From Barcelona, the C32 *autopista*, which takes you almost to Blanes, saves a weary trudge on the toll-free A2. To the north, the 23km stretch of the GI682 to Sant Feliu de Guíxols is a great drive, winding its way up, down and around picturesque bays.

Getting Around

Jimbo Bike (☎ 972 34 30 44; Avinguda de Pau Casals 12; 9am-9pm mid-Jun–mid-Sep, 10am-1pm & 4-8pm Mon-Sat mid-Sep–Nov & Easter–mid-Jun) rents out mountain bikes for up to €21 for 24 hours.

SANT FELIU DE GUÍXOLS

pop 21,200

A snaking road hugs the spectacular ups and downs of the Costa Brava for the 23km from Tossa de Mar to Sant Feliu de Guíxols. On this road Rose Macaulay, author of *Fabled Shore*

WHAT'S COOKING IN CATALONIA?

Catalan cooking nudges Basque cuisine for the title of Spain's best. Its essence lies in its sauces for meat and fish. There are five main types: *sofregit,* of fried onion, tomato and garlic; *samfaina, sofregit* plus red pepper and aubergine or zucchini (courgette); *picada,* based on ground almonds, usually with garlic, parsley, pinenuts or hazelnuts, and sometimes breadcrumbs; *alioli,* garlic pounded with olive oil, often with egg yolk added to make a mayonnaise; and *romesco,* an almond, tomato, olive oil, garlic and vinegar sauce, also used as a salad dressing.

Romesco is used above all, however, with *calçots*. They are a type of long spring onion, delicious as a starter with *romesco* sauce and only in season in late winter/early spring. This is when Catalans get together for a *calçotada,* the local version of a barbecue. The *calçots* are the amusing part of the event, as the black ash in which they are grilled inevitably winds up on your hands and face! This is usually followed by an enormous meal with countless meat and sausage courses.

Catalans find it hard to understand why other people put mere butter on bread when *pa amb tomáquet,* bread slices rubbed with tomato, olive oil and garlic, is so easy. They eat it with almost everything.

Here are some typical dishes:

Starters

- *escalivada* – red peppers and aubergines (sometimes with onions and tomatoes), grilled, peeled, sliced and served lukewarm dressed with olive oil, salt and garlic
- *esqueixada* – salad of shredded salted cod *(bacallà)* with tomato, red pepper, onion, white beans, olives, olive oil and vinegar

Main Dishes

- *arròs a la cassola* or *arròs a la catalana* – Catalan paella, cooked in an earthenware pot, without saffron
- *arròs negre* – rice cooked in black cuttlefish ink; it sounds awful, but it's good
- *bacallà a la llauna* – salted cod baked in tomato, garlic, parsley, paprika and wine
- *botifarra amb mongetes* – pork sausage with fried white beans
- *cargols* – snails; a religion in parts of Catalonia
- *escudella* – a meat, sausage and vegetable stew
- *fideuá* – similar to paella, but using vermicelli noodles as the base
- *mandonguilles amb sipia* – meatballs with cuttlefish
- *sarsuela* (*zarzuela*) – mixed seafood cooked in *sofregit* with various seasonings
- *suquet* – a fish-and-potato hotpot, with generous clumps of both drenched in a tomato-based broth

(1950), 'met only one mule cart, laden with pine boughs, and two very polite *guardias civiles*'. Along the way are several enticing inlets and largely hidden beaches, where the water is emerald green. Easier ones to find include **Cala Pola** and **Cala Giverola**, on either side of Camping Pola (see p374). About 7km further north, at Km35.1, you'll find parking for the cliff-backed 800m-long naturists' beach, **Cala del Senyor Ramon**.

Sant Feliu itself has an attractive waterside promenade and a handful of curious leftovers from its long past, the most important being the so-called **Porta Ferrada** (Iron Gate): a wall and entrance, which is all that remains of a 10th-century monastery, the **Monestir de Sant Benet**. The gate lends its name to an annual music festival held every July since 1962. Lou Reed played here in 2008. With the help of a few local tips, you will discover some lovely beaches around here on either side of the town.

Sarfa buses call in here frequently (up to 12 from Easter to September) from Barcelona (€12.60, 1½ hours), on the way to Platja d'Aro or Palafrugell or both. They do *not* follow the coast road.

PLATJA D'ARO & PALAMÓS

These spots mark the two ends of one of the Costa Brava's party spots. The beaches are OK, the high-rises are standard issue and the nightlife is busy. The area tends to attract more Spanish tourism than foreign. Around the main broad beaches and their resorts are some magnificent stretches of coast with enticing coves. Both are stops on the frequent Barcelona–Palafrugell Sarfa bus route (€13 and €13.90 respectively, 1½ hours to Platja d'Aro and 15 minutes more to Palamós).

The 2km-long **Platja d'Aro** beach is big and sandy, but for something more secluded you could head north along the GRS92 coastal walking path, which winds along the high leafy coastline for about 4km to Sant Antoni de Calonge. The first beach you hit is **Platja Rovira**, and soon after, the smaller and more enchanting **Sa Cova**. A little further on again are two small nudist coves, **Platja d'en Ros** and **Platja d'es Canyers**.

If you should end up in Palamós and wonder how it happened, all is not lost. Pick up the GR92 trail and head north for **Platja del Castell**, a virtually untouched strand. If you don't fancy the walk, drive out of Palamós heading for Palafrugell and look for signs that lead right to the beach. Two kilometres of partly unsealed road get you there. The northern end of the beach is capped by a high wooded promontory that hides the 'castle' (the remains of a 6th- to 1st-century-BC Iberian settlement) after which the beach is named.

PALAFRUGELL & AROUND

North of Palamós begins one of the most beautiful stretches of the Costa Brava. The town of Palafrugell, 5km inland, is the main access point for a cluster of enticing beach spots. Calella de Palafrugell, Llafranc and Tamariu, one-time fishing villages squeezed into small bays, are three of the Costa Brava's most charming, low-key resorts.

Begur (p379), 7km northeast of Palafrugell, is a curious, tight-knit, castle-topped village with a cluster of less-developed beaches nearby (some of them splendid). Inland, seek out the charming villages of Pals and Peratallada.

Palafrugell

pop 19,300

Palafrugell is the main transport, shopping and service hub for the area but is of little interest in itself. The C66 Palamós–Girona road passes through the western side of Palafrugell, a 10-minute walk from the main square, Plaça Nova. The **tourist office** (☎ 972 30 02 28; www.turismepalafrugell.org; Carrer del Carrilet 2; ⏲ 9am-9pm Mon-Sat, 10am-1pm Sun Jul-Aug, 10am-1pm & 5-8pm Mon-Sat, 10am-1pm Sun May-Jun & Sep, 10am-1pm & 4-7pm Mon-Sat, 10am-1pm Sun Oct-Apr) is beside the C66 Hwy. The **bus station** (Carrer de Torres Jonama 67-9) is a short walk from the tourist office.

Sarfa runs to Palafrugell from Barcelona up to 16 times daily (€15.05, two hours). Many buses also run between Girona and Palafrugell (€5.70, one hour if you get the most direct service).

Calella de Palafrugell

pop 740

The low-slung buildings of Calella, the southernmost of Palafrugell's crown beach jewels, are strung Aegean-style around a bay of rocky points and small, pretty beaches, with a few fishing boats still hauled up on the sand. The **tourist office** (☎ 972 61 44 75; Carrer de les Voltes 4; ⏲ 10am-8pm daily Jul-Aug, 10am-1pm & 5-8pm Mon-Sat, 10am-1pm Sun Apr-Jun & Sep–mid-Oct) is housed in a curious 19th-century house, La Perola, near the seafront.

SIGHTS & ACTIVITIES

Apart from plonking on one of the beaches, you can stroll along pretty coastal footpaths northeast to Llafranc (20 or 30 minutes), or south to Platja del Golfet beach, close to Cap Roig (about 40 minutes). Atop Cap Roig, the **Jardí Botànic de Cap Roig** (☎ 972 61 45 82; adult/under 7yr/senior €6/free/3; 9am-7pm Jun-Sep, to 6pm Oct-May) is a beautiful garden of 500 Mediterranean species, set around the early-20th-century castle-palace of Nikolai Voevodsky. He was a tsarist colonel with expensive tastes, who fell out of grace in his homeland after the Russian Revolution.

FESTIVALS & EVENTS

Calella stages the Costa Brava's biggest summer **cantada de havaneres**. *Havaneres* are melancholy Caribbean sea shanties that became popular among Costa Brava sailors in the 19th century, when Catalonia maintained busy links with Cuba. These folksy concerts are traditionally accompanied by the drinking of *cremat* – a rum, coffee, sugar, lemon and cinnamon concoction that you set alight briefly before quaffing. Traditionally, Calella's *cantada* is held in August.

SLEEPING & EATING

Camping Moby Dick (☎ 972 61 43 07; www.campingmobydick.com; Carrer de la Costa Verde 16-28; sites per 2-person tent & car €23.70; Apr-Sep; P) Set in a pine-and-oak stand about 100m from the seaside, this camping ground is in an ideal location. It has tennis courts and offers the chance of diving and kayak excursions in the area.

Hotel Port Bo (☎ 972 61 49 62; www.hotelportbo.com; Carrer d'August Pi i Sunyer 6; s/d incl buffet breakfast €58/116; mid-Mar–Sep; P) Smack in the centre of the village, a few blocks back from the waterfront, this friendly hotel has 29 straightforward rooms with tile or parquet floors, balcony and simple furnishings.

Hotel La Torre (☎ 972 61 46 03; www.hotellatorre.com; Passeig de la Torre 28; s/d €68/136; Apr-Sep; P) Dominating a high point on the road leading north out of Calella, and in a leafy spot near an old watchtower, this hotel offers 28 rooms, most with extensive sea views and cheery balconies.

Restaurant Solimar (☎ 972 61 70 96; Carrer de Miramar 19; meals €25-30) Right on the beachfront, Solimar is a minuscule and no-frills spot where you can't help but get to know your fellow diners – it's that crammed. A lively, good-natured place with a handful of tables outside too, it's good for seafood and, especially, the catch of the day (ask what they have).

GETTING THERE & AWAY

Buses from Palafrugell run to Calella, then Llafranc, then back to Palafrugell (€1.30, 30 minutes). They leave every half-hour or so between 7.40am and 8.30pm in July and August; the service is steadily reduced to three or four buses a day from November to February.

Llafranc

pop 330

Barely 2km northeast of Calella de Palafrugell, and now merging with it along the roads back from the rocky coast between them, Llafranc has a smaller bay but a longer stretch of sand, cupped on either side by pine-dotted craggy coast. The **tourist office** (☎ 972 30 50 08; Carrer de Roger de Llúria; 10am-1pm & 5-9pm Mon-Sat, 10am-1pm Sun Jul-Aug, 10am-1pm & 5-8pm Mon-Sat, 10am-1pm Sun Apr-Jun & Sep–mid-Oct) is a kiosk just back from the western end of the beach.

From the **Far de Sant Sebastià** (a lighthouse) and **Ermita de Sant Sebastià** (a chapel now incorporated into a luxury hotel), up on Cap de Sant Sebastià (east of the town), there are tremendous **views** in both directions along the coast. It's a 40-minute walk up: follow the steps from the harbour and the road up to the right. You can walk on to Tamariu.

SLEEPING & EATING

Hostal Celimar (☎ 972 30 13 74; www.hostalcelimar.com; Carrer de Carudo 12-14; s/d €53.50/75) The sunset-yellow *hostal* is barely a stumble from the beach and offers bright rooms, with differing colour schemes from room to room, and spotless bathrooms. One of the cheapest deals in town, it also happens to be one of the best.

Hotel Far de Sant Sebastià (☎ 972 30 16 39; www.elfar.net; d €260-315; P) An 18th-century hostelry, with a chapel and defence tower, is now an elegant hotel (close to a lonely lighthouse) with magnificent clifftop views over the deep blue sea. The best rooms come with a spacious terrace, while some have a small balcony. Grand stone arches and sunny courtyards add a romantic touch.

Chez Tomás (☎ 972 30 62 15; Carrer de Lluís Marqués Carbó 2; meals €30; dinner daily Jun-Sep, lunch & dinner Fri-Sun Oct-May) As the name hints, the game here has a French flavour. Its strength is the use of fresh market produce to come up with 'such dishes as *filet de bou amb Torta de Casar trufada* (sirloin steak with a truffle-infused serving of a creamy cheese from Extremadura).

GETTING THERE & AWAY

See Calella de Palafrugell for information on bus services (opposite). The Llafranc bus stop is on Carrer de la Sirena, up the hill on the Calella side of town.

Tamariu

pop 270

About 3.5km north up the coast from Llafranc, as the crow flies, Tamariu is a small crescent cove surrounded by pine stands and other greenery. Its beach has some of the most translucent waters on Spain's Mediterranean coast. The **tourist office** (☎ 972 62 01 93; Carrer de la Riera; 10am-1pm & 5-8pm Mon-Sat, 10am-1pm Sun Jun-Sep) is in the middle of the village.

Hotel Es Furió (☎ 972 62 00 36; www.esfurio.com; Carrer del Foraió 5-7; s/d incl breakfast €80/140), a one-time fishing family's house converted into a hotel in 1934, is set just back from the beach and has spacious, cheerfully decorated rooms. Pale oranges, aqua tints and other seaside hues hold sway. It has its own restaurant and the beachfront is lined with seafood eateries.

Sarfa buses from Palafrugell run to Tamariu (€1.20, 15 minutes) three or four times daily, from mid-June to mid-September only. A rough road leads to the beach of Aiguablava (right).

Begur

pop 4090

The **castell** (castle), dating to the 10th century and towering above the roughly conical hill village, is in much the same state in which it was left by the Spanish troops who wrecked it to impede the advance of Napoleon's army in 1810. Dotted around the village are six or so towers built for defence against 16th- and 17th-century pirates. It is an engaging little town and well worth a stopover.

The **tourist office** (☎ 972 62 45 20; www.visitbegur.com; Avinguda del Onze de Setembre 5; 9am-2pm & 4-9pm Mon-Fri, 10am-2pm & 4-9pm Sat & Sun late Jun–mid-Sep, 10am-2pm daily mid-Sep–late Jun) has loads of information.

A few steps towards the castle from the central church is **Hotel Rosa** (☎ 972 62 30 15; www.hotel-rosa.com; Carrer de Pi i Ralló 19; s/d €75/92; Mar-Oct;), a little surprise package with well-kept, spacious rooms. You can get some sun upstairs on the terrace and relax in the Jacuzzi. Eat at its **Fonda Caner** (☎ 972 62 23 91; meals €35; dinner Mon-Fri, lunch & dinner Sat & Sun) at No 10.

Sarfa buses run up to four times a day from Barcelona (€15.85, two to 2¼ hours) via Palafrugell. On weekdays one Sarfa bus runs to Girona (€6.40, 1½ hours).

Around Begur

The enticing, heavily pine-wooded coast around Begur sparkles with an assortment of liquid gems. Take the turn-off east off the Palafrugell road 2km south of Begur. About 2km down is a turn-off to the black-sand **Platja Fonda** (1km). Half a kilometre further on is the turn-off to **Fornells** (1km), a hamlet on one of the most picturesque bays of the Costa Brava, with a marina, beach and transparent azure water.

One kilometre on from the Fornells turn-off is **Aiguablava**, with a slightly bigger and busier beach, and the **Parador Nacional de la Costa Brava** (☎ 972 62 21 62; www.parador.es; s/d €132/164), a modern luxury hotel enjoying superb views back across the Fornells bay (half-board obligatory in July and August).

Another road from Begur leads 2km east to **Aiguafreda**, a beach on a lovely cove backed by pine-covered hills. There's one modest, shady five-room hotel, **Hostal Sa Rascassa** (☎ 972 62 28 45; www.hostalsarascassa.com; d €100). A little further south comes the slightly more built-up **Sa Tuna**, on a quiet pebbly beach. You could stay in **Hostal Sa Tuna** (☎ 972 62 21 98; d €140) and gobble down a paella (around €19.50) in its convivial seaside eatery. A couple of kilometres north of Begur, there's another lovely sandy strand at **Sa Riera**. A walk along the coastal track brings you to the striking reddish sand of **Illa Roja** (Red Island), a nudist strip beyond which stretches the broad **Platja de Pals** to the north.

GETTING THERE & AWAY

A *bus platges* (beach bus) service runs from Plaça de Forgas in Begur between late June and mid-September.

Pals

pop 2540

About 6km inland from Begur (a five-minute ride on the Palafrugell bus, €1.30) is the pretty walled town of Pals. The main monument is the 15m **Torre de les Hores** (clock tower) but what makes the trip worthwhile is simply wandering around the uneven lanes and poking your nose into one medieval corner or another. From the **Mirador del Pedró** you can see northeast across the coastal plains to the sea, with the Illes Medes in the background. There are three basic *pensiones* in town.

Up to four Sarfa buses come here from Barcelona (€16.30, 2¼ hours) on weekdays.

Peratallada

pop 2540

The warm stone houses of Peratallada have made this village a favourite day trip for Catalans. Its beautifully preserved narrow streets, heavy stone arches, 12th-century Romanesque church and 11th-century castle-mansion (now a luxury hotel and restaurant) are supplemented by several places to stay, enticing restaurants and a sprinkling of low-key boutiques.

Ca l'Aliu (☎ 972 63 40 61; www.calaliu.com; Carrer de la Roca 6; d €64-86) is an 18th-century village home, where the old stone-and-timber frame has been teamed with modern comforts to create an atmospheric place with seven smallish but welcoming rooms. It is one of the more cheerful and most reasonably priced of the nine options here.

Peratallada is on the Begur–Girona bus route (see p379).

CASTELL DE PÚBOL

The **Castell de Púbol** (☎ 972 48 86 55; www.salvador-dali.org; La Pera; adult/student & senior €7/5; ⏰ 10.30am-7.15pm mid-Jun–mid-Sep, 10.30am-5.15pm Tue-Sun mid-Mar–mid-Jun & mid-Sep–Oct, 10.30am-4.15pm Tue-Sat Nov-Dec) is at La Pera, just south of the C66 and 22km northwest of Palafrugell. It forms the southernmost point of northeast Catalonia's 'Salvador Dalí triangle', whose other elements include the Teatre-Museu Dalí in Figueres and the Cadaqués area.

In 1968 Dalí bought this Gothic and Renaissance mansion, which includes a 14th-century church, and gave it to his wife, Gala, who lived here until her death. Local lore has it that the notoriously promiscuous Gala was still sending for young village men almost right up to the time she died in 1982, aged 88.

The castle was renovated by Dalí in his inimitable style, with lions' heads staring from the tops of cupboards, statues of elephants with giraffes' legs in the garden, and a stuffed giraffe staring at Gala's tomb in the crypt. In the garage is the blue Cadillac in which Dalí took Gala for a last drive here – after she died in Port Lligat. He had her buried in a crypt here and spent the next two years in maudlin mourning.

Sarfa buses between Palafrugell and Girona run along the C66.

GIRONA

pop 92,200

A tight huddle of ancient arcaded houses, grand churches, climbing cobbled streets and medieval baths, all enclosed by defensive walls and a lazy river, constitute a powerful reason for visiting north Catalonia's largest city, Girona (Castilian: Gerona).

The Roman town of Gerunda lay on Via Augusta, the highway from Rome to Cádiz (Carrer de la Força in Girona's old town follows part of Via Augusta). Taken from the Muslims by the Franks in AD 797, Girona became capital of one of Catalonia's most important counties, falling under the sway of Barcelona in the late 9th century. Its wealth in medieval times produced many fine Romanesque and Gothic buildings that have survived repeated attacks and sieges through the centuries.

Orientation

Girona sits in a verdant valley 36km inland from Palafrugell. The narrow streets of the old town climb above the east bank of Riu Onyar and are easy to explore on foot. Several road bridges and footbridges link it to the new town across the river. The train station is 1km southwest, on Plaça d'Espanya, off Carrer de Barcelona, with the bus station behind it on Carrer de Rafael Masó i Valentí.

Information

Parc Hospitalari Martí i Julià (Hospital; ☎ 972 18 25 00; Carrer del Doctor Castany s/n)

Policía Nacional (⏰ 091; Carrer de Sant Pau 2)

Tourist office (☎ 972 22 65 75; www.ajuntament.gi/turisme; Rambla de la Llibertat 1; ⏰ 8am-8pm Mon-Fri, 8am-2pm & 4-8pm Sat, 9am-2pm Sun)

> **FIVE IN ONE**
>
> The M5 ticket gives you half-price entry at four of Girona's five museums. You pay full price at the first museum you visit, where you pick up the ticket. It is valid for six months.

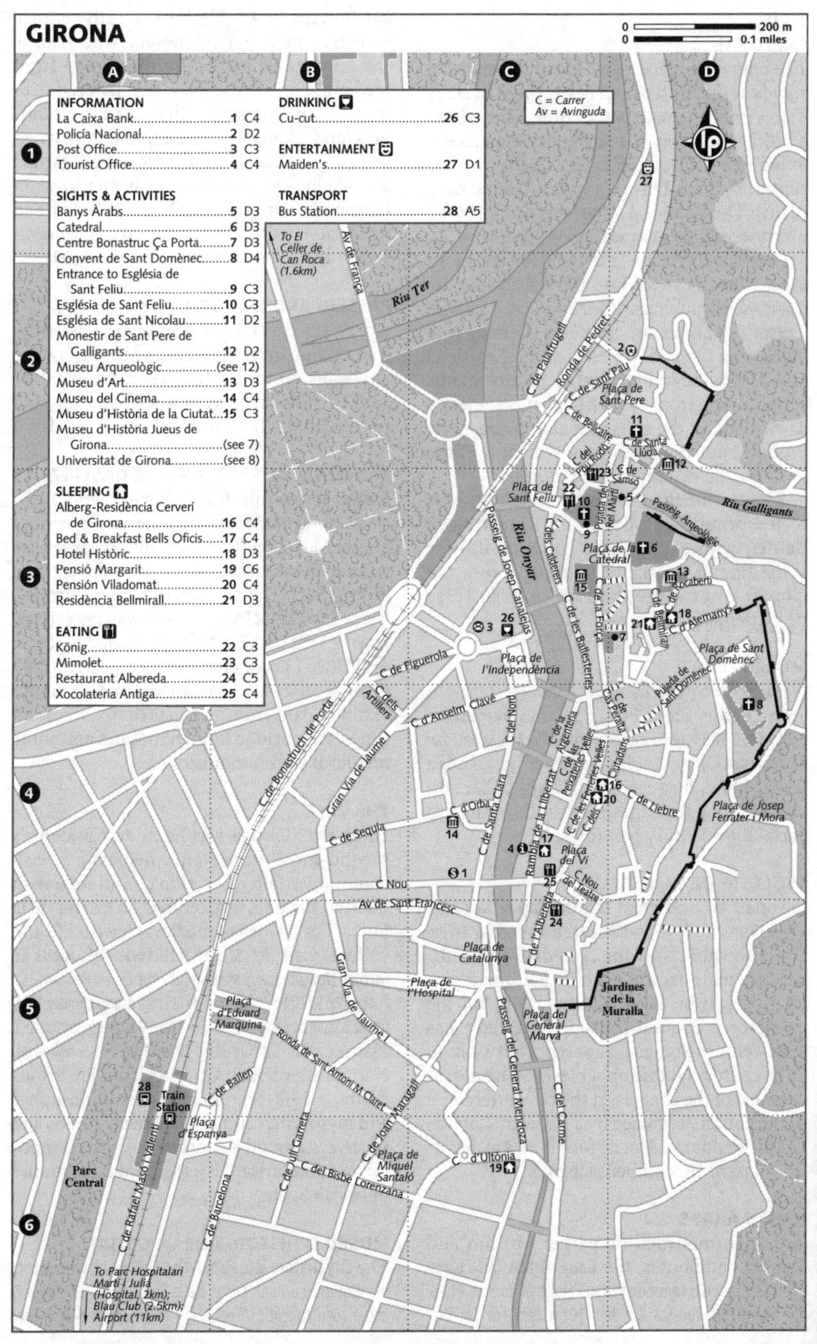
GIRONA
0 200 m
0 0.1 miles
INFORMATION
La Caixa Bank 1 C4
Policía Nacional 2 D2
Post Office 3 C3
Tourist Office 4 C4
SIGHTS & ACTIVITIES
Banys Àrabs 5 D3
Catedral 6 D3
Centre Bonastruc Ça Porta 7 D3
Convent de Sant Domènec 8 D4
Entrance to Església de Sant Feliu 9 C3
Església de Sant Feliu 10 C3
Església de Sant Nicolau 11 D2
Monestir de Sant Pere de Galligants 12 D2
Museu Arqueològic (see 12)
Museu d'Art 13 D3
Museu del Cinema 14 C4
Museu d'Història de la Ciutat 15 C3
Museu d'Història Jueus de Girona (see 7)
Universitat de Girona (see 8)
SLEEPING
Alberg-Residència Cerverí de Girona 16 C4
Bed & Breakfast Bells Oficis 17 C4
Hotel Històric 18 D3
Pensió Margarit 19 C6
Pensión Viladomat 20 C4
Residència Bellmirall 21 D3
EATING
König 22 C3
Mimolet 23 C3
Restaurant Albereda 24 C5
Xocolateria Antiga 25 C4
DRINKING
Cu-cut 26 C3
ENTERTAINMENT
Maiden's 27 D1
TRANSPORT
Bus Station 28 A5
C = Carrer
Av = Avinguda
To El Celler de Can Roca (1.6km)
Av de França
Riu Ter
C de Palafrugell
Ronda de Pedret
C de Sant Pau
Plaça de Sant Pere
C de Bellcaire
C de Santa Llúcia
C del Pou Rodó
C de Samsó
Plaça de Sant Feliu
Riu Galligants
Passeig Arqueològic
Pujada del Rei Martí
Passeig de Josep Canalejas
Riu Onyar
C dels Calderers
Plaça de la Catedral
C de Rocaberti
C de la Força
C de les Ballesteries
C de Bellmirall
C d'Alemanys
Plaça de Sant Domènec
Plaça de l'Independència
C de Figuerola
C dels Artillers
C d'Anselm Clavé
C del Nord
C de Cort Reial
Pujada de Sant Domènec
C de la Argenteria
C de les Peixateries Velles
C de les Ferreries Velles
C dels Ciutadans
C de Bonastruch de Porta
Gran Via de Jaume I
C de Llebre
Plaça de Josep Ferrater i Mora
C d'Orba
C de Santa Clara
C de Sequia
Rambla de la Llibertat
Plaça del Vi
C Nou del Teatre
C Nou
Av de Sant Francesc
C de l'Albereda
Plaça de Catalunya
Plaça de l'Hospital
Jardines de la Muralla
Plaça d'Eduard Marquina
Plaça del General Marva
Ronda de Sant Antoni M Claret
Passeig del General Mendoza
C del Carme
C de Ballen
Train Station
Plaça d'Espanya
C de Joan Maragall
C de Juli Garreta
Plaça de Miquel Santaló
C d'Ultònia
C del Bisbe Lorenzana
Parc Central
C de Rafael Masó i Valentí
C de Barcelona
To Parc Hospitalari Martí i Julià (Hospital, 2km); Blau Club (2.5km); Airport (11km)
CATALONIA

Sights

CATEDRAL

The billowing baroque facade of the **cathedral** stands at the head of a majestic flight of steps rising from Plaça de la Catedral. Most of the building, however, is much older than its exterior. Repeatedly rebuilt and altered down the centuries, it has Europe's widest Gothic nave (23m). The cathedral's **museum** (☎ 972 21 44 26; www.lacatedraldegirona.com; admission €4, admission free Sun; 🕑 10am-2pm & 4-7pm Tue-Sat Mar-Jun, 10am-8pm Tue-Sat Jul-Sep, 10am-2pm & 4-6pm Tue-Sat Oct-Feb, 10am-2pm Sun & holidays), through the door marked 'Claustre Tresor', contains the masterly Romanesque *Tapís de la Creació* (Tapestry of the Creation) and a Mozarabic illuminated *Beatus* manuscript, dating from 975. The Creation tapestry shows God at the epicentre and in the circle around Him the creation of Adam, Eve, the animals, the sky, light and darkness.

The fee for the museum also admits you to the beautiful 12th-century Romanesque **cloister**, whose 112 stone columns display some fine, if weathered, carving. From the cloister you can see the 13th-century Torre de Carlemany bell tower.

MUSEU D'ART

Next door to the cathedral, in the 12th- to 16th-century Palau Episcopal, the **art museum** (☎ 972 20 38 34; www.museuart.com; Plaça de la Catedral 12; admission €2; 🕑 10am-7pm Tue-Sat Mar-Sep, 10am-6pm Tue-Sat Oct-Feb, 10am-2pm Sun & holidays) collection ranges from Romanesque woodcarvings to early-20th-century paintings.

ESGLÉSIA DE SANT FELIU

Girona's second great **church** (Plaça de Sant Feliu; 🕑 9.30am-2pm & 4-7pm Mon-Sat, 10am-noon & 4-7pm Sun) is downhill from the cathedral. The 17th-century main facade, with its landmark single tower, is on Plaça de Sant Feliu, but the entrance is around the side. The nave has 13th-century Romanesque arches but 14th- to 16th-century Gothic upper levels. The northernmost of the chapels, at the far western end of the church, is graced by a masterly Catalan Gothic sculpture, Aloi de Montbrai's alabaster *Crist Jacent* (Recumbent Christ).

BANYS ÀRABS

Although modelled on earlier Muslim and Roman bathhouses, the **Banys Àrabs** (Arab baths; ☎ 972 21 32 62; Carrer de Ferran Catòlic; admission €1.80; 🕑 10am-7pm Tue-Sat Apr-Sep, 10am-2pm Tue-Sat Oct-Mar, 10am-2pm Sun & holidays) are a 12th-century Christian affair in Romanesque style. This is the only public bathhouse discovered from medieval Christian Spain, where, in reaction to the Muslim obsession with water and cleanliness (and a widely held view that water carried disease), washing almost came to be regarded as ungodly. The baths contain an *apodyterium* (changing room), followed by a *frigidarium* and *tepidarium* (with respectively cold and warm water) and a *caldarium* (a kind of sauna).

PASSEIG ARQUEOLÒGIC

Across the street from the Banys Àrabs, steps lead up into lovely gardens, which follow the city walls up to the 18th-century Portal de Sant Cristòfol gate, from where you can walk back down to the cathedral.

MONESTIR DE SANT PERE DE GALLIGANTS

Down across thin Riu Galligants, this 11th- and 12th-century Romanesque monastery has another lovely cloister with some marvellous animal and monster carvings on the capitals of its pillars. The monastery houses Girona's **Museu Arqueològic** (☎ 972 20 26 32; www.mac.es/girona; Carrer de Santa Llúcia s/n; adult/senior & child €2.30/free; 🕑 10.30am-1.30pm & 4-7pm Tue-Sat Jun-Sep, 10am-2pm & 4-6pm Tue-Sat Oct-May, 10am-2pm Sun & holidays), whose exhibits date from prehistoric to medieval times, and include Roman mosaics and some medieval Jewish tombstones.

THE CALL

Until 1492 Girona was home to Catalonia's second-most important medieval Jewish community (after Barcelona), and its Jewish quarter, the Call, was centred on Carrer de la Força. For an idea of medieval Jewish life and culture, visit the **Museu d'Història dels Jueus de Girona** (Jewish History Museum, aka the Centre Bonastruc Ça Porta; ☎ 972 21 67 61; Carrer de la Força 8; adult/under 16yr/senior & student €2/free/1.50; 🕑 10am-8pm Mon-Sat Jun-Oct, 10am-6pm Mon-Sat Nov-May, 10am-3pm Sun & holidays). Named after Jewish Girona's most illustrious figure, a 13th-century cabbalist philosopher and mystic, the centre – a warren of rooms and stairways around a courtyard – hosts temporary exhibitions and is a focal point for studies of Jewish Spain.

MUSEU D'HISTÒRIA DE LA CIUTAT

The **City History Museum** (☎ 972 22 22 29; www.ajuntament.gi/museuciutat; Carrer de la Força 27; adult/senior & under 16yr/student €3/free/2; 🕑 10am-2pm & 5-7pm Tue-

Sat, 10am-2pm Sun & holidays) has displays covering everything from the city's Roman origins, through the siege of the city by Napoleonic troops to the *sardana* (Catalonia's national folk-dance) tradition.

MUSEU DEL CINEMA

The Casa de les Aigües houses Spain's only **cinema museum** (☎ 972 41 27 77; www.museudelcinema.org; Carrer de Sèquia 1; adult/under 16yr/senior & student €4/free/4; 🕑 10am-8pm Tue-Sun May-Sep, 10am-6pm Tue-Fri, 10am-8pm Sat, 11am-3pm Sun Oct-Apr). The Col·lecció Tomàs Mallol includes not only displays tracing the history of cinema, but also a parade of hands-on items for indulging in shadow games, optical illusions and the like – it's great for kids.

Sleeping

Alberg-Residència Cerverí de Girona (☎ 972 21 80 03; www.xanascat.cat; Carrer dels Ciutadans 9; dm student & under 26yr/26yr & over €19/22; 💻) A modern youth hostel in the old town, it doubles for most of the year as a student residence.

Pensión Viladomat (☎ 972 20 31 76; Carrer dels Ciutadans 5; s/d without bathroom €22/40, d with bathroom €60) This is one of the nicest of the cheaper *pensiones* scattered about the southern end of the old town. It has eight simple but well-maintained rooms.

Pensió Margarit (☎ 972 20 10 66; Carrer d'Ultònia 1; s €33-37, d €50-70) A modern stopover placed near the river roughly halfway between the train station and south end of the old town, the Margarit offers a broad variety of rooms (28 in all) where there's rarely a need to book ahead.

Bed & Breakfast Bells Oficis (☎ 972 22 81 70; www.bellsoficis.com; Carrer dels Germans Busquets 2; r €35-85; ⊠ ❄ 💻) With just five rooms, this family-run option is perfectly placed just off Rambla de la Llibertat. The rooms are all very different. The two best ones have balconies overlooking the Rambla. The biggest (€85) has ample room for four people.

Residència Bellmirall (☎ 972 20 40 09; www.grn.es/bellmirall; Carrer de Bellmirall 3; s/d €40/75; 🕑 closed Jan-Feb; ❄) Carved out of a 14th-century building in the heart of the old city, this 'residence' of heavy stone blocks and timber beams oozes character. Rooms with shared bathroom are marginally cheaper.

Hotel Històric (☎ 972 22 35 83; www.hotelhistoric.com; Carrer de Bellmirall 4A; s/d €102/114; Ⓟ ❄ 💻) A bijou hotel in a historic building in old Girona, it has eight spacious rooms that are individually decorated. For a greater sense of home, you could opt for a small, self-contained apartment (starting at €90 for two people).

Eating

Xocolateria Antiga (☎ 972 21 66 81; Plaça del Vi 8; coffee & pastries €5-8; 🕑 7am-9pm Mon-Sat) Modernista decor, frilly lace in the windows and hot sticky cups of chocolate: time has stood still here. It's a great spot for breakfast.

König (☎ 972 22 57 82; Carrer dels Calderers 16; meals €8-15) For a quick sandwich, *entrepà* (filled roll) or simple hot dishes, 'King' boasts a broad outdoor terrace shaded by thick foliage. Or just stop by for a drink.

Mimolet (☎ 972 20 21 24; Carrer del Pou Rodó 12; meals €35-40; 🕑 Tue-Sat; ⊠ Ⓥ) For refined local cooking in a modern setting just within the old city walls, this is it. A stylish, designer spot, Mimolet offers an excellent wine menu to company the seasonally varied menu. It offers various carpaccios, some tempting salads, rice dishes and a set tasting menu (€62 with wines).

Restaurant Albereda (☎ 972 22 60 02; www.restaurantalbereda.com; Carrer de l'Albereda 9; meals €40; 🕑 lunch & dinner Tue-Sat, lunch Mon; ⊠) Elegant Albereda, one of the town's top restaurants, dishes up classic Catalan cuisine, such as the *fideuada de ceps i calamarcets* (a noodle dish with mushrooms and tiny squids). It also does tasting menus for €53.

El Celler de Can Roca (☎ 972 22 21 57; www.cellercanroca.com; Carrer Can Sunyer 46; meals €80-100; 🕑 Tue-Sat) About 2km west of the city centre (and not the easiest place to find), this two-star Michelin choice is one of Catalonia's top-ranking restaurants. Housed in a modernised *masia* (country house), it offers thoroughly inventive and ever-changing takes on Mediterranean cooking. How about *cigalas al humo de curry* (curry smoked crayfish)?

Drinking & Entertainment

Students make the nightlife here, so in summer things calm down. Thursday is the big night of the week, as most people head for the coast on weekends.

Cu-cut (☎ 972 22 85 25; Plaça de l'Independencia 10; 🕑 10pm-3am) This is a local classic with a mixed crowd of students and 30-somethings eager to get moving to anything from reggae through to pop and even, if you're not so fortunate, country.

Blau Club (☎ 972 24 92 11; www.blauclub.com; Camp de les Lloses 8; admission €12; 🕑 11pm-5am Thu-Sun) This

OF RUNNING FIRE, GIANTS & BIG-HEADS

Catalans get up to unusual tricks at *festa* time. Fire and fireworks play a big part in many Spanish festivals, but Catalonia adds a special twist with the *correfoc* (fire-running), in which devil and dragon figures run through the streets spitting fireworks at the crowds. (Wear protective clothes if you intend to get close!)

Correfocs are often part of the *festa major*, a town or village's main annual festival, which usually takes place in July or August. Part of the *festa major* fun are the *sardana* (Catalonia's national round-dance) and *gegants*, splendidly attired 5m-high giants that parade through the streets or dance in the squares. Giants tend to come in male-and-female pairs, such as a medieval king and queen. Almost every town and village has its own pair, or up to six pairs, of giants. They're accompanied by grotesque 'dwarfs' (known as *capsgrossos*, or 'big heads').

On La Nit de Sant Joan (23 June), big bonfires burn at crossroads and town squares in a combined midsummer and St John's Eve celebration, and fireworks explode all night. The supreme fire festival is the Patum in Berga. An evening of dancing and firework-spitting angels, devils, mulelike monsters, dwarfs, giants and men covered in grass culminates in a mass frenzy of fire and smoke. The 'real' Patum happens on Corpus Christi (the Thursday following the eighth Sunday after Easter Sunday) although there are simplified versions over the next two or three days. Unesco declared the Patum a World Heritage item in 2005.

club is in the southern 'burbs of town. There are three dark spaces that pump out a mix of drum and bass, techno and hip hop. The DJs tend to be local talent.

You can keep going until the wee hours near the river north of the old town, where you will find a string of bars (and restaurants) along Carrer de Palafrugell and Ronda de Pedret. **Maiden's** (for heavy-metal maniacs) at Carrer de Palafrugell 38 offers boisterous beer and thumping tunes from 10pm until about 3am.

Getting There & Away

AIR

Located 11km south of the centre is **Girona–Costa Brava airport**, and just off the AP7 and A2 is Ryanair's Spanish hub. **Sagalés** (☎ 902 13 00 14; www.sagales.com) operates hourly services from Girona–Costa Brava airport to Girona's main bus/train station (€2.05, 25 minutes) in connection with flights. See p362 for transport to/from Barcelona. Sarfa runs a couple of buses a day in summer, from the airport to coastal destinations, including Tossa de Mar (€8, 55 minutes) and Roses (€13, 1½ hours), as well as Figueres (€13, 55 minutes). A **taxi** (☎ 972 20 33 73, 972 22 23 33) to/from the airport to central Girona costs around €15.

BUS

Teisa (☎ 972 20 02 75; www.teisa-bus.com in Spanish) runs up to eight services daily (four on Sunday) to Besalú (€3.45, 50 minutes) and Olot (€5.90, 1¼ hours). Those planning to hang around the Girona area for an extended period may find multitrip passes useful (see www.atmgirona.cat).

TRAIN

Girona is on the train line between Barcelona, Figueres and Portbou on the French border. There are more than 20 trains per day to Figueres (€2.60 to €2.90, 30 to 40 minutes) and Barcelona (€5.90 to €6.70, 1½ hours), and about 15 to Portbou or Cerbère or both (€3.90 to €4.40, 50 minutes to one hour).

VERGES

pop 1180

About 15km east of Girona, the town of Verges has little to offer, but if you're in the area on Holy Thursday (Easter), do make an effort to see the macabre evening procession of the **Dansa de la Mort**. People dressed as skeletons perform the Dance of Death through the streets as part of a much bigger procession enacting Christ's way to Calvary. The fun starts around 10pm. Girona–Torroella buses pass through here.

TORROELLA DE MONTGRÍ

pop 10,900

On Riu Ter, about 30km northeast of Girona and 15km north of Palafrugell, the agreeable old town of Torroella de Montgrí is the funnel through which travellers to L'Estartit must pass.

Sights & Activities

Overlooking the town from the top of the 300m limestone Montgrí hills to the north, the impressive-but-empty **Castell de Montgrí** was built between 1294 and 1301 for King Jaume II, during his efforts to bring to heel the disobedient counts of Empúries, to the north. There's no road, and by foot it's a 40-minute climb from Torroella. Head north from Plaça del Lledoner along Carrer de Fàtima, at the end of which is a sign pointing the way.

In town, the **Museu de la Mediterrània** (☎ 972 75 51 80; www.museudelamediterrania.org; Carrer d'Ullà 31; admission free; ⌚ 10am-2pm & 6-9pm Mon-Sat, to 2pm Sun Jul-Aug, 10am-2pm & 5-8pm Wed-Sat & Mon, 11am-2pm Sun Sep-Jun) is a local museum and cultural centre housed in the Can Quintana mansion. The permanent exhibition on the 1st floor concentrates on local history, culture and music.

Getting There & Away

Ampsa (☎ 972 75 82 33; www.ampsa.org) runs buses about hourly (€1.30) to L'Estartit from June to September (half as often during the rest of the year). Sarfa has three or four daily buses to/from Barcelona (€17.65, 1¾ hours).

L'ESTARTIT & THE ILLES MEDES

pop 3050

L'Estartit, 6km east of Torroella de Montgrí, has a long, wide beach of fine sand but nothing over any other Costa Brava package resort – with the rather big exception of the Illes Medes (Islas Medes)! The group of rocky islets barely 1km offshore is home to some of the most abundant marine life on Spain's Mediterranean coast.

The main road in from Torroella de Montgrí is called Avinguda de Grècia as it approaches the beach; the beachfront road is Passeig Marítim, at the northern end of which is the **tourist office** (☎ 972 75 19 10; www.visitestartit.com; Passeig Marítim; ⌚ 9.30am-2pm & 4-8pm daily Jul-Sep, 9.30am-2pm & 4-7pm Mon-Sat, 10am-2pm Sun May-Jun & Oct, 9am-1pm & 3-6pm Mon-Fri, 10am-2pm Sat Oct-Apr).

Illes Medes

The shores and waters around these seven islets, an offshore continuation of the limestone Montgrí hills, have been protected since 1985 as a *reserva natural submarina* (underwater nature reserve), which has brought a proliferation in their marine life and made them Spain's most popular destination for snorkellers and divers. Some 1345 plant and animal species have been identified here. There's a big bird population too; one of the Mediterranean's largest colonies of yellow-legged gulls (8000 pairs) breeds here between March and May.

Kiosks by the harbour, at the northern end of L'Estartit beach, offer snorkelling and glass-bottomed boat trips to the islands. Other glass-bottomed boat trips go to a series of

DIVING OFF THE COSTA BRAVA

The range of depths (down to 50m) and underwater cavities and tunnels around the Illes Medes contribute much to their attraction. On and around rocks near the surface are colourful algae and sponges, as well as octopuses, crabs and various fish. Below 10m or 15m, cavities and caves harbour lobsters, scorpion fish and large conger eels and groupers. Some groupers and perch may feed from the hand. With luck, you'll spot some huge wrasse. If you get down to the sea floor, you may see angler fish, thornback rays or marbled electric rays. Be aware that this area gets pretty busy with divers, especially on summer weekends.

Several outfits in L'Estartit can take you out scuba diving, at the Medes or off the mainland coast; the tourist office has lists of them. It's worth shopping around before taking the plunge. Apart from price difference, try to assess the quality. Is the equipment in good shape or old? (There's nothing worse than a broken regulator.) Do they bother with safety checks? Do they provide guides? What is their attitude to touching coral and sea life? When doing courses, it is important to feel that safety aspects are properly taken into account. Sloppy dive shops often provide sloppy instruction.

If you're a qualified diver, a two-hour trip usually costs around €30 per person. Full gear rental can cost up to €45 a day. Night dives are possible (usually about €30 to €35). You generally pay extra to go with a guide and for insurance (if you don't have any). If you're a novice, do an introductory dive for around €55 to €60 or a full, five-day PADI Open Water Diver course for around €380.

caves along the coast to the north, or combine these with the Medes.

Sleeping & Eating

Les Medes (☎ 972 75 18 05; www.campinglesmedes.com; Paratge Camp de l'Arbre; sites per 2-person tent & car €32; Dec-Oct; P) Of the eight camping grounds in and around town, this is one of the best. It is set in a leafy location about 800m from the seaside and has a sauna as well as three pools. Bike rental and even massages are available.

Hostal Santa Clara (☎ 972 75 17 67; www.hostalsantaclara.com; Passeig Marítim 18; r half-board per person €37; P) On the waterfront and barely a 100yd dash to the beach, this friendly, bustling spot with its own bar-restaurant has three floors of standard rooms with balconies looking out to sea.

Hotel Les Illes (☎ 972 75 12 39; www.hotellesilles.com; Carrer de Les Illes 55; r per person incl breakfast €43) A decent, functional place with comfortable, if unspectacular, rooms, all with sparkling bathroom and balcony. It is basically a divers' hang-out that's in a good spot back from the port. It has its own dive shop.

The northern end of Passeig Marítim, by the roundabout, is swarming with eateries. These places are all pretty similar, presenting a mix of basic Spanish fare and chicken-and-chips-style meals.

Getting There & Around

Sarfa buses run to and from Barcelona once or twice daily (€17.65, two hours), rising to four times in peak season (July to August).

L'ESCALA

pop 8370

Travel back millennia in time to the ancient Greco-Roman site of Empúries (Castilian: Ampurias), set behind a near-virgin beach facing the Mediterranean. Its modern descendant, L'Escala, 11km north of Torroella de Montgrí, is a pleasant medium-sized resort (a good deal more attractive than better-known Roses to the north) on the often windswept southern shore of the Golf de Roses. Birdwatchers flock to the Parc Natural dels Aiguamolls de l'Empordà, coastal wetlands that lie about 10km north of Empùries.

Orientation & Information

If you arrive by Sarfa bus, you'll alight on L'Escala's Plaça de les Escoles, where you'll find the **tourist office** (☎ 972 77 06 03; Plaça de les Escoles 1; 9am-8.30pm daily mid-Jun–mid-Sep, 9am-1pm & 4-7pm Mon-Sat, 10am-1pm Sun mid-Sep–mid-Jun). Empúries is 1km around the coast to the northwest of the town centre.

Empúries

Empúries was probably the first, and certainly one of the most important, Greek colonies on the Iberian Peninsula. Early Greek traders, pushing on from a trading post at Masilia (Marseille in France), set up a new post around 600 BC at what is now the charming village of Sant Martí d'Empúries, then an island. Soon afterwards they founded a mainland colony, Emporion (Market), which remained an important trading centre, and conduit of Greek culture to the Iberians, for centuries.

In 218 BC, Roman legions clanked ashore here to cut off Hannibal's supply lines in the Second Punic War. About 195 BC, they set up a military camp and, by 100 BC, had added a town. A century later it had merged with the Greek one. Emporiae, as the place was then known, was abandoned in the late 3rd century AD, after raids by Germanic tribes. Later, an early Christian basilica and a cemetery stood on the site of the Greek town, before the whole place, after over a millennium of use, disappeared altogether.

Many of the ancient stones now laid bare don't rise more than knee-high. You need a little imagination – and perhaps the aid of a taped commentary (€1.50 from the ticket office) – to make the most of it.

THE SITE

During spring and summer there's a pedestrian entrance to the **site** (☎ 972 77 02 08; http://ftp.mac.es/empuries; adult/senior & child/student €3/free/2.50; 10am-8pm Jun-Sep, 10am-6pm Oct-May) from the seafront promenade in front of the ruins; just follow the coast from L'Escala to reach it. At other times the only way in is the vehicle approach from the Figueres road, about 1km from central L'Escala.

The **Greek town** lies in the lower part of the site, closer to the shore. Main points of interest include the thick southern defensive walls, the site of the Asklepion (a shrine to the god of medicine) with a copy of his statue found here, and the Agora (town square), with remnants of the early Christian basilica and the Greek *stoa* (market complex), beside it.

A **museum** (Barcelona's Museu d'Arqueologia de Catalunya, p339, has a bigger and better Empúries collection) separates the Greek town from the larger Roman town on the upper part of the site. Highlights of the **Roman town** include the mosaic floors of a 1st-century-BC house, the Forum and ancient walls. Outside the walls are the remains of an oval amphitheatre. A 2nd-century-AD bust in Carrara marble of the Roman god Bacchus was unearthed on the site in 2005.

A string of brown-sand beaches stretches along in front of the site. On one of the beaches, 1.2km from L'Escala, stands a Greek stone jetty. Nearby is where the 1992 Olympic flame was landed in a remake of an ancient Greek vessel amid great theatrical circumstance.

Another few hundred metres north along the beaches from Empúries brings you to a gem, the 15th-century seaside hamlet of **Sant Martí d'Empúries**, all bright stone houses and cobbled lanes. On Plaça Major, four restaurant-bars compete for your attention under the watchful gaze of the strange, squat facade of the local church.

Sleeping & Eating

L'Escala is famous for its *anchoas* (anchovies) and fresh fish, both of which are likely to crop up on menus. Plenty of eateries are scattered along the waterfront parade of Port d'en Perris, as well as some more sleeping options.

Pensió Vista Alegre (☎ 972 77 07 47; www.vistaalegre.biz; Carrer del Cargol 6; s/d €35/50) This is a cheap and cheerful spot barely a stumble from the beach. Rooms are simple but clean and the place is family-holiday oriented, so kids and pets are welcome.

Restaurant El Roser II (☎ 972 77 11 02; Passeig Lluís Albert 1; meals €35; lunch & dinner Tue-Sat, lunch Sun Mar-Jan) This is an excellent waterfront seafood eatery, with huge windows towards the sea and ideal for a hearty lunch of grilled catch of the day and *suquet* (fish-and-potato stew).

Els Pescadors (☎ 972 77 07 28; Port d'en Perris 5; meals €40-45; lunch & dinner Mon-Wed, Fri & Sat, lunch Sun Dec-Oct) If you're going to dig in to the town speciality of anchovies, this is the place to do it. It has a good *menú del día* (daily set menu) for €15.

Getting There & Away

Sarfa has one bus from Barcelona (via Palafrugell) on weekdays (€17.65, 1½ hours), and three on weekends (four daily July to August). Buses also run to and from Girona.

> **A RUN-DOWN OF CATALONIA'S PARKS & RESERVES**
>
> Catalonia boasts 17 parks, nature reserves, a marine reserve and areas of special interest. For a complete run-down on all of them, check out www.parcsdecatalunya.net, a very handy website full of useful background information.

PARC NATURAL DELS AIGUAMOLLS DE L'EMPORDÀ

This nature park preserves the remnants of mighty marshes that once covered the whole coastal plain of the Golf de Roses and is a key site for migrating birds. Birdwatchers have spotted over 100 species a day in the March to May and August to October migration periods, which bring big increases in the numbers of wading birds and even the occasional flamingo, glossy ibis, spoonbill or rare black stork. In all, in the migratory periods more than 300 species pass through (some 90 nest here). There are usually enough birds around to make a visit worthwhile at any time of year.

Head for the **El Cortalet information centre** (☎ 972 45 42 22; 9.30am-2pm & 4.30-7pm mid-Jun–mid-Sep, 9.30am-2pm & 3.30-6pm mid-Sep–mid-Jun), 1km east off the Sant Pere Pescador–Castelló d'Empúries road. Marked paths lead to a 2km stretch of beach and several *aguaits* (hides) with saltwater-marsh views. From the top of the **Observatori Senillosa**, a former silo, you can observe the whole park. The paths are always open, but morning and evening are the best times for birds (and mosquitoes!).

The nearest places to El Cortalet that can be reached by bus are Sant Pere Pescador, 6km south (served by four or five Sarfa buses daily from L'Escala and Figueres), and Castelló d'Empúries, 4km north.

CASTELLÓ D'EMPÚRIES

pop 3920

This well-preserved, tranquil ancient town was the capital of Empúries, a medieval Catalan county that maintained a large degree of independence up to the 14th century. The finest monument is the **Església de Santa Maria** on Plaça de Jacint Verdaguer. It's a voluminous 13th- and 14th-century Gothic church with a sturdy Romanesque bell tower.

Hotel Canet (☎ 972 25 03 40; www.hotelcanet.com; Plaça del Joc de la Pilota 2; s/d €48/75; P) is a

SEEING MICHELIN STARS

Once a simple bar and grill clutching on to a rocky perch high above the bare Mediterranean beach of Cala Montjoi and accessible only by dirt track from Roses, 6km to the west, **El Bulli** (☎ 972 15 04 57; www.elbulli.com; Cala Montjoi; meals €200; Apr-Sep;) is now one of the world's most sought-after dining experiences (usually fully booked a year in advance), thanks to star chef Ferran Adrià.

While easily Catalonia's internationally best-known dining experience, it has two stablemates as three-star Michelin eateries (in all Spain there are only six, the other three are in the Basque Country).

Can Fabes (☎ 93 867 28 51; www.canfabes.com; Carrer de Sant Joan 6, Sant Celoni; meals €120-150; Tue-Sat) has long attracted a steady stream of gastronauts from Barcelona (53km to the south). Chef Santi Santamaria (the first Catalan chef ever awarded three Michelin stars) is a local boy who started up here in 1981. Dishes based on local products (seafood landed at Blanes, for example) are at the core of his cooking.

Barely 25km east, on the coast at **Sant Pol de Mar**, is another foodies' fave. **Sant Pau** (☎ 93 760 06 62; Carrer Nou 10; meals €120-150; lunch & dinner Tue-Wed, Fri & Sat, dinner Thu, closed most of May & Nov) is a beautifully presented mansion whose garden overlooks the Mediterranean. Carme Ruscalleda is the driving force. Some 20 other restaurants scattered around Catalonia have a Michelin star (and just one has two), in addition to 14 in Barcelona!

modernised 17th-century mansion in the centre, with elegant rooms, low-slung stone arches and a sundeck. A soothing swimming pool glistens within the stone walls of the interior courtyard. It also has a decent restaurant offering mostly Catalan fare.

Sarfa runs from about 12 (fewer on Sunday and up to 28 in July and August) buses a day from Figueres (€1.30, 15 minutes), three or four (more in July and August) from Cadaqués (€3.40, 50 minutes) and up to four from Barcelona's Estació del Nord (€16.85, 1½ hours).

ROSES & AROUND

pop 18,100

Some believe Roses is the site of an ancient Greek settlement, Rodes, although nothing remains to confirm the hypothesis. The town does boast the impressive seaward wall of its 16th-century **citadel**, but is an otherwise listless place whose melancholy main entrance road is lined by tacky water parks. Although this middling holiday town's beaches are OK (the tourist office has endless lists of accommodation), Roses is, above all, a handy base for going elsewhere.

With a vehicle, you can get well beyond the crowds of Roses into the southern end of Parc Natural del Cap de Creus. About 6km east of Roses, a road runs up into the hills and along the rugged coast to **Cala Montjoi** and Spain's most renowned restaurant, **El Bulli** (see the boxed text, above).

Le Rachdingue (☎ 972 53 00 23; www.rachdingue.com; admission €10-15; Fri & Sat Jul-Aug, Sat Sep), about 8km northwest of Roses on the road to Vilajuïga, is a clubbing institution that celebrated 40 years in action in 2008. Name DJs from around Europe converge on this *masia* (country house) to spin sets of house, deep house and even deeper house (among other grooves and beats). Clubbers from all over the continent make an effort to get here. The pool comes in handy!

Sarfa buses from Barcelona run one to four times a day to Roses, depending on the day and season (€18.10, 1¾ hours). Plenty run between Roses and Figueres (€2.30, 30 minutes).

CADAQUÉS & AROUND

pop 2800

If you have time for only one stop on the Costa Brava, you can hardly do better than Cadaqués. A whitewashed village around a rocky bay, it and the surrounding area have a special magic – a fusion of wind, sea, light and rock – that isn't dissipated even by the throngs of mildly fashionable summer visitors.

A portion of that magic owes itself to Salvador Dalí, who spent family holidays in Cadaqués during his youth, and lived much of his later life at nearby Port Lligat. The empty moonscapes, odd-shaped rocks and barren shorelines that litter Dalí's paintings weren't just a product of his fertile imagination. They're strewn all round the Cadaqués area in what Dalí termed a 'grandiose geological delirium'.

The country here is drier than further south. The sparseness continues to dramatic Cap de Creus, 8km northeast of Cadaqués, lending itself to coastscapes of almost (ahem) surreal beauty.

Thanks to Dalí and other luminaries, Cadaqués pulled in a celebrity crowd for decades. One visit by the poet Paul Éluard and his Russian wife, Gala, in 1929 caused an earthquake in Dalí's life: he ran off to Paris with Gala (who was to become his lifelong obsession and, later, his wife) and joined the surrealist movement. In the 1950s the crowd he attracted was more jet-setting – Walt Disney, the Duke of Windsor and Greek shipowner Stavros Niarchos. In the 1970s Mick Jagger and Gabriel García Márquez popped by. Today the crowd is not quite as famous, and leans heavily to day-tripping French from across the border, but the enchantment of Cadaqués' atmosphere remains.

Information

Centre de Salut (☎ 972 25 88 07; Carrer Nou 6-10)
Policía Local (☎ 972 15 93 43; Carrer de Carles Rahola 9) Out of town, off the road to Port Lligat.
Tourist office (☎ 972 25 83 15; www.cadaques.org; Carrer del Cotxe 2; 9am-9pm Mon-Sat, 10am-1pm Sun Easter-Sep, 9.30am-1pm & 3-6pm Mon-Sat, 10am-1pm Sun Oct-Easter)

Sights

THE TOWN

Cadaqués is perfect for wandering, either around the town or along the coast (in either direction). The 16th- and 17th-century **Església de Santa Maria**, with a gilded baroque *retablo* (altarpiece), is the focus of the oldest part of town, with its narrow hilly streets. But wandering the little pedestrian-only lanes anywhere back from the waterfront is a delight.

The **Museu de Cadaqués** (☎ 972 25 88 77; Carrer de Narcís Monturiol 15; 10am-1.30pm & 4-7pm Mon-Sat) includes Dalí among other local artists. The admission fee depends on the temporary exhibition being held.

BEACHES

Cadaqués' main beach, and several others along the nearby coast, are small, with more pebbles than sand, but their picturesqueness and beautiful blue waters make up for that.

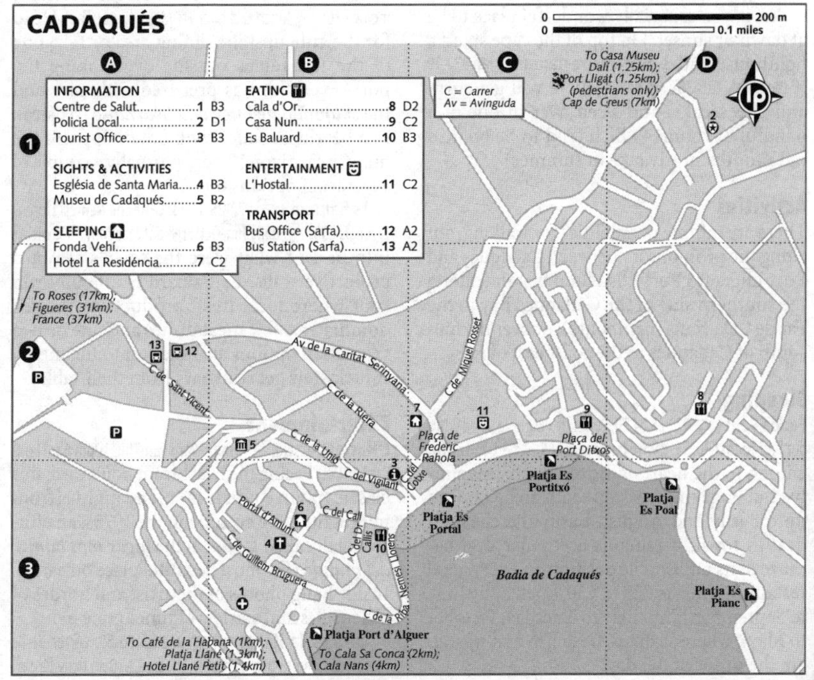

CATALONIA

Overlooking Platja Llané, to the south of the town centre, is Dalí's parents' holiday home. Out the front is a statue by Josep Subirachs dedicated to Federico García Lorca and in memory of his 1920s stay.

PORT LLIGAT

Port Lligat, a 1.25km walk from Cadaqués, is a tiny settlement around another lovely cove, with fishing boats pulled up on its beach. **Casa Museu Dalí** (☎ 972 25 10 15; www.salvador-dali.org; Port Lligat; adult/student & senior €10/8; ⏰ 10.30am-9pm mid-Jun–mid-Sep, 10.30am-6pm Tue-Sun mid-Sep–mid-Jan & mid-Mar–mid-Jun) began as a fisherman's hut and was steadily altered and enlarged by Dalí, who lived here from 1930 to 1982, apart from a dozen or so years abroad during and around the Spanish Civil War. It's the house with a lot of little white chimneypots and two egg-shaped towers, overlooking the western end of the beach. You must book ahead.

CAP DE CREUS

Cap de Creus is the most easterly point of the Spanish mainland and is a place of sublime, rugged beauty. With a steep, rocky coastline indented by dozens of turquoise-watered coves, it's an especially wonderful place to be at dawn or sunset. On top of the cape stand a lighthouse and a curious **restaurant** (☎ 972 19 90 05; meals €25-30; ⏰ daily) where you get curry and cheesecake, and sleep over in one of a handful of rooms (which tend to be booked out months in advance in summer).

Activities

There are infinite possibilities for walking: out along the promontory between Cadaqués and Port Lligat; to Port Lligat and beyond; along the southern side of the Cadaqués Bay to the Far de Cala Nans (lighthouse); or over the hills south of Cadaqués to the coast east of Roses.

Sleeping

Fonda Vehí (☎ 972 25 84 70; Carrer de l'Església 5; s/d without bathroom €30/55, d with bathroom €65; ❄) Near the church in the heart of the old town, this simple but engaging *pensión* tends to be booked up for July and August. Easily the cheapest deal in town, it remains a popular deal because of its unbeatable position and very good restaurant (meals €25 to €30; open daily June to September, Thursday to Tuesday, October to May), where seafood, fresh fish and *suquets* are the order of the day.

Hotel La Residència (☎ 972 25 83 12; www.laresidencia.net; Avinguda de la Caritat Serinyana 1; s/d €70/95; P ❄) In the heart of town, with just a dozen good-sized rooms, this hotel oozes history. It opened in 1904 and Picasso stayed here six years later. Nowadays the place has a studied, classy air. A beautiful stained-glass ceiling creates a light well in the main staircase, and decorative details range from Dalí to rococo. The best rooms look out to sea.

Hotel Llané Petit (☎ 972 25 10 20; www.llanepetit.com; Carrer del Doctor Bartomeus 37; d €120-132; P ❄ 💻) A four-storey place right on the bay, the hotel is perhaps not as 'petit' as all that (it has 35 rooms), but the location is splendid and all the rooms have a generous balcony to sit on. Otherwise, they are decidedly straightforward in a somewhat passé style.

Eating

Cala d'Or (☎ 972 25 81 49; Carrer de Sa Fitora 1; meals €20-25) Tucked away back from the waterfront, this knockabout place attracts swarms of local workers after a good solid lunch at tables dressed in classic gingham. Tuck into some *llobarro a la planxa* (grilled sea perch).

Casa Nun (☎ 972 25 88 56; Plaça del Port Ditxos 6; meals €30; ⏰ lunch & dinner Fri-Mon, dinner Thu) Head for the cute upstairs dining area or take one of the few tables outside overlooking the port. Everything is prepared with care and the *solomillo de buey a la béarnaise* (ox steak in a béarnaise sauce) will not disappoint the hungry carnivore. There is usually a couple of vegetarian options too.

Es Baluard (☎ 972 25 81 83; Carrer de Nemesi Llorens 2; meals €30; ⏰ daily Jun-Oct, Fri & Sat Mar-May) Tucked into part of what were the town's seaward protective walls, Es Baluard is a family-run spot where local fresh products of the sea dominate. A few meat dishes and one or two vegetarian options also sneak into the menu. A lucky few get sea views from their tables.

Entertainment

L'Hostal (Passeig; ⏰ 10pm-5am Sun-Thu, 10pm 6am Fri & Sat Apr-Oct) Facing the beachfront boulevard, this classic has live music on many nights (from midnight). One evening in the 1970s, an effusive Dalí called L'Hostal the *lugar más bonito del mundo* (the most beautiful place on earth). Inside hang photos of the artist and hordes of other stars and starlets of times gone by.

Café de la Habana (☎ 972 25 86 89; Carrer de Dr Bartomeus, Punta d'en Pampa; ⏰ 9pm-2.30am daily Easter-

Oct, 9pm-2.30am Fri-Sun Nov-Easter) One kilometre south of the town centre, this icon of Cadaqués' nightlife can get lively with Latin-music nights, art exhibitions and cool cocktails (not to mention the extensive range of Caribbean rums). Come along for Nanu's guitar session at 11pm on Saturday night (and most other nights in summer).

Getting There & Away

Sarfa buses to/from Barcelona (€19.90, 2¼ hours) leave twice daily (up to five daily in July and August). Buses also run to/from Figueres (€4.50, one hour) up to seven times daily (three in winter) via Castelló d'Empúries.

CADAQUÉS TO THE FRENCH BORDER

If you want to prolong the journey to France, **El Port de la Selva** and **Llançà** are pleasant, low-key beach resorts–cum–fishing towns. The former is backed by powerful mountains and filled with bobbing yachts, while the latter boasts a string of strands and coastal walking trail. Both have a range of accommodation. **Portbou**, on the French frontier, is rather less enticing. From El Port de la Selva you can undertake a wild and woolly walk high along the rugged coast. The trail, which is awkward at some points, leads east to Cap de Creus.

A spectacular stop is the **Monestir de Sant Pere de Rodes** (☎ 972 38 75 59; adult/senior/student €4.50/free/3, admission free Tue; ⏲ 10am-7.30pm Tue-Sun Jun-Sep, 10am-5pm Tue-Sun Oct-May), a classic piece of Romanesque architecture looming 500m up in the hills southwest of El Port de la Selva, with all-encompassing views. Founded in the 8th century, it later became the most powerful monastery between Figueres and Perpignan in France. The great triple-naved, barrel-vaulted basilica is flanked by the square Torre de Sant Miquel bell tower and a two-level cloister.

Getting There & Away

The monastery is on a back road over the hills between Vilajuïga, 8km to its west, and El Port de la Selva, 5km northeast. Each town is served by at least one Sarfa bus from Figueres daily, but there are no buses to the monastery. Vilajuïga is also on the train line between Figueres and Portbou.

FIGUERES

pop 41,120

Twelve kilometres inland from the Golf de Roses, Figueres (Castilian: Figueras) is a humdrum town (some might say a dive) with a single, unique and unmissable attraction: Salvador Dalí. In the 1960s and '70s Dalí created here, in the town of his birth, the extraordinary Teatre-Museu Dalí. Whatever your feelings about old Salvador, this is worth every cent and minute you can spare.

Information

Policía Nacional (Carrer de Pep Ventura 8)
Hospital (☎ 972 67 50 89; Ronda del Rector Aroles s/n)
Tourist office (☎ 972 50 31 55; www.figueresciutat.com; Plaça del Sol; ⏲ 9am-8pm Mon-Sat, 10am-2pm Sun Jul-Sep, 8am-3pm & 4.30-8pm Mon-Fri, 9.30am-1.30pm & 3.30-6.30pm Sat Easter-Jun & Oct, 8am-3pm Mon-Fri Nov-Easter) Hours can be unpredictable.

Sights

TEATRE-MUSEU DALÍ

A purple-pink building topped by giant boiled eggs and stylised Oscar statues? Smack in the middle of a dowdy provincial town? This can only mean one thing in these parts: Dalí!

Salvador Dalí was born in Figueres in 1904. Although his career took him to Madrid, Barcelona, Paris and the USA, he remained true to his roots and lived well over half his adult life at Port Lligat, east of Figueres on the coast. Between 1961 and 1974 Dalí converted Figueres' former municipal theatre, ruined by a fire at the end of the civil war in 1939, into the **Teatre-Museu Dalí** (☎ 972 67 75 00; www.salvador-dali.org; Plaça de Gala i Salvador Dalí 5; admission incl Dalí Joies & Museu de l'Empordà adult/student €11/8; ⏲ 9am-8pm Jul-Sep, 10.30am-6pm Tue-Sun Oct-Jun). 'Theatre-museum' is an apt label for this multidimensional trip through one of the most fertile (or disturbed) imaginations of the 20th century. It's full of surprises, tricks and illusions, and contains a substantial portion of his life's work. Readers have reported that queues are getting so long that opening hours have been extended on an ad hoc basis. Note that you can enter no later than 45 minutes before closing time.

Even outside, the building aims to surprise, from the collection of bizarre sculptures outside the entrance, on Plaça de Gala i Salvador Dalí, to the pink wall along Pujada del Castell, topped by a row of Dalí's trademark egg shapes and what appear to be sculptures of female gymnasts, and studded with what look like loaves of bread. The Torre Galatea, added in 1983, was where Dalí spent his final years.

Inside, the ground floor (1st level) includes a semicircular garden area on the site of the

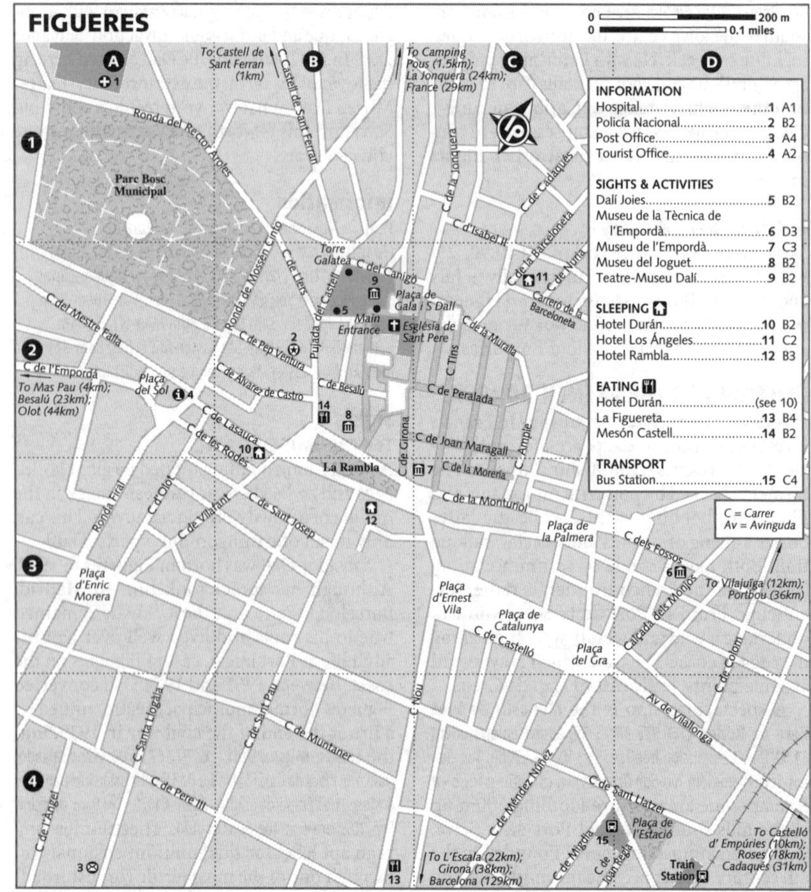

original theatre stalls. In its centre is a classic piece of weirdness called *Taxi Plujós* (Rainy Taxi), composed of an early Cadillac, which was said to have belonged to Al Capone, and a pile of tractor tyres; both are surmounted by statues, with a fishing boat balanced precariously above the tyres. Put a coin in the slot and water washes all over the inside of the car. The **Sala de Peixateries** (Fish Shop Room) off here holds a collection of Dalí oils, including the famous *Autoretrat Tou amb Tall de Bacon Fregit* (Soft Self-Portrait with Fried Bacon) and *Retrat de Picasso* (Portrait of Picasso). Beneath the former stage of the theatre is the crypt, with Dalí's plain tomb.

If proof were needed of Dalí's acute sense of the absurd, *Gala Mirando el Mar Mediterráneo* (Gala Looking at the Mediterranean Sea) on the 2nd level would be it. With the help of coin-operated viewfinders, the work appears, from the other end of the room, to be a portrait of Abraham Lincoln.

A separate entrance (same ticket and times) leads into the Owen Cheatham collection of 37 jewels, designed by Dalí, and called **Dalí Joies** (Dalí Jewels). Also on display are the designs themselves. Dalí did these on paper (his first commission was in 1941) and the jewellery was made by specialists in New York. Each piece, ranging from the disconcerting *Ull del Temps* (Eye of Time) through to the *Cor Reial* (Royal Heart), is unique.

In August the museum opens at night (admission €12, 10pm to 1am) for a maximum of

500 people (booking essential). You are treated to a glass of *cava* (sparkling wine).

MUSEU DE L'EMPORDÀ

This local **museum** (☎ 972 50 23 05; www.museuemporda.org; La Rambla 2; adult/senior & child/student €2/free/1; 11am-7pm Tue-Sat, 11am-2pm Sun & holidays) combines Greek, Roman and medieval archaeological finds with a sizeable collection of art, mainly by Catalan artists, but there are also some works on loan from the Prado in Madrid. Admission is free with a Teatre-Museu Dalí ticket.

MUSEU DEL JOGUET

Spain's only **toy museum** (☎ 972 50 45 85; www.mjc.cat; Carrer de Sant Pere 1; admission €5; 10am-6pm Mon-Fri, 10am-7pm Sat, 11am-6pm Sun Jun-Sep, 10am-6pm Tue-Fri, 10am-7pm Sat, 11am-2pm Sun & holidays Oct-May) has more than 3500 Catalonia- and Valencia-made toys from the pre-Barbie 19th and early 20th centuries. The Groucho Marx doll is an odd one!

MUSEU DE LA TÈCNICA DE L'EMPORDÀ

This technical **museum** (☎ 972 50 88 20; www.mte.cat; Carrer dels Fossos 12; adult/under 10yr/senior & student €3/free/2; 10am-7pm Tue-Fri, 10am-1pm & 4-7pm Sat, 11am-2pm Sun & holidays) is a treasure chest of old mechanical masterpieces, from typewriters and watches through to sewing machines, heaters and cash registers.

CASTELL DE SANT FERRAN

The sprawling 18th-century **fortress** (☎ 972 50 60 94; www.lesfortalesescatalanes.info; admission €3; 10.30am-8pm Easter & Jul–mid-Sep, 10.30am-3pm mid-Sep–Jun) stands on a low hill 1km northwest of the centre. Built in 1750, it saw no action in the following centuries. After abandoning Barcelona, Spain's Republican government held its final meeting of the civil war (1 February 1939) in the dungeons.

Sleeping

With some two dozen options, most of them uninspiring but inexpensive *pensiones*, finding a bed should not be too problematic.

Camping Pous (☎ 972 67 54 96; www.androl.internet-park.net; sites per 2-person tent & car €25; year-round) This small and leafy camping ground lies 1.5km north of the centre on the A2 towards La Jonquera. There is a little hotel (with doubles for up to €55) and restaurant on the same site.

Hotel Los Ángeles (☎ 972 51 06 61; www.hotelangeles.com; Carrer de la Barceloneta 10; s/d €44/60; P) Rooms are all much the same in these spick-and-span digs. White walls, brown floor tiles and sparkling attached bathroom are standard throughout. Throw in breakfast for €5.

Hotel Rambla (☎ 972 67 60 20; www.hotelrambla.net; La Rambla 33; s €56, d €70-85; P) Hiding behind an 1860 facade on the town's central boulevard, this hotel has pleasant rooms with crisp decor in blues and beiges. The superior rooms are spacious and light, but you can drop the price by taking a standard one.

Hotel Durán (☎ 972 50 12 50; www.hotelduran.com; Carrer de Lasauca 5; s/d €80/118; P) In business since the mid-19th century (on the site, it is said, of a wayside inn as far back as the 17th century), the hotel offers comfortable rooms with modern decorative touches (all soft beiges, browns and white), satellite TV and hairdryers in the bathroom.

Mas Pau (☎ 972 54 61 54; www.maspau.com; Avinyonet de Puigventós; s/d €88/105; P) Four kilometres west of Figueres along the road to Besalú, Mas Pau is an enchanting country hotel-restaurant, created inside the rough-hewn stone of a 16th-century *masia*, and set amid soothing gardens. The restaurant (meals €60 to €85; open Wednesday to Saturday, lunch only Sunday, dinner only Monday and Tuesday) has a great local reputation and offers elegant dishes based on local products and traditions.

Eating

La Figuereta (☎ 972 67 38 45; Carrer Nou 101; meals €25; lunch & dinner Tue-Sat, lunch Mon) Amid the hurly-burly of a busy, somewhat down-at-heel shopping street shines this elegant eatery, with bare brick walls and white table linen. On offer is a pleasing menu of mixed Mediterranean fare. The *salmó en mil fulles de gorgonzola i bacon* (salmon in a Gorgonzola cheese and bacon millefeuille) melts in the mouth.

Hotel Durán (☎ 972 50 12 50; Carrer de Lasauca 5; meals €30-40) More than a century of tradition has not tired the Durán clan of serving up fine traditional food. Frequently the stage of gastronomic events, this place offers much clever cooking. Try the succulent *confit de conill amb mostassa blanca i cireres de Terrades* (confit of rabbit with white mustard and local cherries). This is the place for *suquet* and rabbit with snails. See if you can arrange to visit the wine cellar (where it's also possible to dine), in which Salvador Dalí used to hang around quite a bit.

Mesón Castell (☎ 972 51 01 04; Pujada del Castell 4; meals €35-40; 🕑 Mon-Sat) A bustling, rustic eatery where you can sample tapas at the bar or head to the sit-down restaurant for robust local cooking (including lamb and suckling pig – grilled meats are the house speciality).

Getting There & Away

Sarfa buses serve Castelló d'Empúries (€1.30) 10 to 20 times daily and Cadaqués (€4.50, one hour) up to eight times daily.

Figueres is on the train line between Barcelona, Girona and Portbou on the French border, and there are regular connections to Girona (€2.60 to €2.90, 30 to 40 minutes) and Barcelona (€8.55 to €9.80, 2¼ hours) and to Portbou and the French border (€2 to €2.30, 25 minutes).

AROUND FIGUERES

It is hard to imagine that, just a few kilometres outside Figueres, such pleasant countryside should soothe the eyes. Take the C252 road northeast of town for a refreshing excursion.

In **Vilabertran**, 2.5km from central Figueres, there is what started life as an Augustinian **convent** (☎ 972 50 87 87; Carrer de l'Abadia 4; admission €2.40, free Tue; 🕑 10am-1.30pm & 3-6.30pm Tue-Sun Jun-Sep, 10am-1.30pm & 3-5.30pm Oct-May). The 11th-century Romanesque church, with its three naves and Lombard bell tower, is outstanding. Also of great charm is the cloister. This is the setting for an annual cycle of classical music by Schubert (www.schubertiada vilabertran.cat).

Five kilometres up the road, coquettish **Peralada** is known for the 16th-century **Castell-Palau dels Rocabertí**. The castle, with its round towers, has a rather French air and is given over to a casino and restaurant. The only way in, if you're not eating or gambling, is to turn up for a classical-music performance during the annual **Festival del Castell de Peralada** (☎ 93 503 86 46; www.festivalperalada.com; Carrer del Castell s/n; 🕑 Jul-Aug) in summer.

BESALÚ

pop 2270

The tall, crooked 11th-century **Pont Fortificat** (Fortified Bridge) over Río Fluvià in medieval Besalù, with its two tower gates, looks like something Tolkien might have invented. It is, however, quite real. As is the rest of this delightfully well-preserved town, which in the 10th and 11th centuries was the capital of an independent county that stretched as far west as Cerdanya before it came under Barcelona's control in 1111. The bridge is at the heart of a best-selling historical novel, *El Pont dels Jueus* (The Jews' Bridge), by local Martí Gironell – due to be translated into various languages and possibly filmed.

The **tourist office** (☎ 972 59 12 40; www.besalu.cat; Plaça de la Llibertat 1; 🕑 10am-2pm & 4-7pm) is on the arcaded central square. It has a decent map-brochure and offers guided visits to the **Miqvé**, a 12th-century Jewish ritual bath by the river around which remnants of the ancient **synagogue** were unearthed in excavations in 2005 (admission €1.50). Plans are afoot to create a small museum on the site. There are also guided tours of the bridge and the Romanesque **Església de Sant Vicenç**. The church and Miqvé are otherwise normally closed. Have a look at the 11th-century Romanesque church of the **Monestir de Sant Pere**, with an unusual ambulatory (walkway) behind the altar, and the 12th-century Romanesque **Casa Cornellà**.

A curious modern addition to the town's attractions is **Micromundi** (☎ 972 59 18 42; www.museuminiaturesbesalu.com; Plaça Prat de Sant Pere 15; adult/senior & child €3.50/2.50; 🕑 10am-7pm Mon-Sat Mar-Sep, 10.30am-6.30pm Mon-Sat Oct-Feb), a museum dedicated to miniatures. Peer through microscopes and magnifying glasses to look at such oddities as the incredibly detailed representation of Pinocchio and Gepetto's workshop (inside a pistachio nut) or a remake of Paris' Eiffel Tower hundreds of thousands time smaller than the real thing.

Sleeping & Eating

There are a couple of cheap *pensiones* in Besalú.

Els Jardins de la Martana (☎ 972 59 00 09; www.lamartana.com; Carrer del Pont 2; s/d €79/109; P ✖ 💻) You could try this charming mansion set on the out-of-town end of the grand old bridge. It has well-appointed rooms, with tiled floors, high ceilings and elegant curtains. Most offer views from balconies across the bridge to the town, and you'll find comfortable sitting rooms and peaceful garden terraces.

Pont Vell (☎ 972 59 10 27; Pont Vell 26; meals €25-30; 🕑 lunch & dinner Wed-Sun, lunch Mon, closed late Dec-late Jan) The views to the old bridge (after which the restaurant is named) are enough to tempt you to take a seat here, even without considering the wide-ranging, Michelin-approved menu. Starting from a base of standard local cuisine, the menu also offers more-intriguing options, like *conill agri-dolç* (sweet-and-sour rabbit).

Getting There & Away

The N260 road from Figueres to Olot meets the C66 from Girona at Besalú. See the Girona (p384) and Olot (p396) sections for information on Teisa bus services to Besalú.

THE PYRENEES

The Pyrenees in Catalonia encompass some awesomely beautiful mountains and valleys. Above all, the Parc Nacional d'Aigüestortes i Estany de Sant Maurici, in the northwest, is a jewel-like area of lakes and dramatic peaks. The area's highest mountain, the Pica d'Estats (3143m), is reached by a spectacular hike past glittering glacial lakes. On arrival at the top, you enjoy a privileged point with 360-degree views over France and Spain.

As well as the natural beauty of the mountains, and the obvious attractions of walking, skiing and other sports, the Catalan Pyrenees and their foothills have a rich cultural heritage, notably the countless lovely Romanesque churches and monasteries, often tucked away in remote valleys. They are mainly the product of a time of prosperity and optimism in this region in the 11th and 12th centuries, after Catalonia had broken ties with France in 988 and as the Muslim threat from the south receded.

When looking for a place to kip, keep an eye out for *cases rurals* or *cases de pagès* (country houses converted into accommodation), usually set in old village houses and peppered across the Pyrenees. The annual *Guia d'Establiments de Turisme Rural* guide, published by the Generalitat (regional Catalan government), covers most of them.

OLOT

pop 32,300 / elev 443m

The hills around Olot are little more than pimples, but pretty pimples indeed – the well-dormant volcanoes of the Parc Natural de la Zona Volcànica de la Garrotxa. The last time one burst was 11,500 years ago.

Information

Casal dels Volcans (☎ 972 26 62 02; Avinguda de Santa Coloma de Farners) For information about the Parc Natural de la Zona Volcànica de la Garrotxa. It's in the Jardí Botànic, 1km southwest of Plaça de Clarà. At the time of writing it was closed for refurbishment.

Patronat Municipal de Turisme (☎ 972 26 01 41; http://areadepromocio.olot.cat; Carrer del Hospici 8; 🕑 10am-8pm Mon-Sat, 10am-2pm Sun mid-Jul–mid-Sep, 10am-2pm & 4-7pm Mon-Sat, 11am-2pm Sun mid-Sep–mid-Jul). Near the bus station, it has some maps.

Sights

The **Museu Comarcal de la Garrotxa** (☎ 972 27 91 30; Carrer de l'Hospici 8; adult/student & child/senior €3/free/1.50; 🕑 11am-2pm & 5-7pm Mon-Sat, 11am-2pm Sun & holidays Jul-Sep, 10am-1pm & 3-6pm Tue-Fri, 11am-2pm & 4-7pm, 11am-2pm Sun & holidays Oct-Jun), in the same building as the tourist office, covers Olot's growth and development as an early textile centre and includes a collection of local 19th-century art.

The **Jardí Botànic**, a botanical garden of Olot-area flora, contains the interesting **Museu dels Volcans** (☎ 972 26 67 62; adult/student & child/senior €3/free/1.50; 🕑 10am-2pm & 4-7pm Tue-Sat, 10am-2pm Sun & holidays Jul-Sep, 10am-2pm & 3-6pm Tue-Fri, 10am-2pm & 4-7pm, 10am-2pm Sun & holidays Oct-Jun), which covers local flora and fauna as well as volcanoes and earthquakes. Combined tickets for these and other Olot museums are also available.

Four **volcanoes** stand sentry on the fringes of Olot. Head for Volcà Montsacopa, 500m north of the centre, or Volcà La Garrinada, 1km northeast of the centre. In both cases paths climb to their craters.

Sleeping & Eating

Several simple eateries are clustered around Plaça Major but the best restaurants are out of the town centre.

Torre Malagrida (☎ 972 26 42 00; Passeig de Barcelona 15; dm student & under 26yr/26yr & over €17.05/20.35) This youth hostel is set in an unusual early-20th-century Modernista building surrounded by gardens. The accommodation is unadorned dorm-style and you can purchase meals and rent bicycles.

Pensió La Vila (☎ 972 26 98 07; www.pensiolavila.com; Carrer de Sant Roc 1; s/d €39/56; ❄ 💻) Smack in the middle of town and overlooking Plaça Major, this straightforward *pensión* has perfectly comfortable rooms over three floors with satellite TV.

Les Cols (☎ 972 26 92 09; www.lescols.com; Carretera de la Canya s/n; meals €35-45; 🕑 lunch & dinner Wed-Sat, lunch only Mon-Tue; Ⓥ) Set in a converted *masia*, more than 100 years old, Les Cols is about

WEST CATALAN PYRENEES

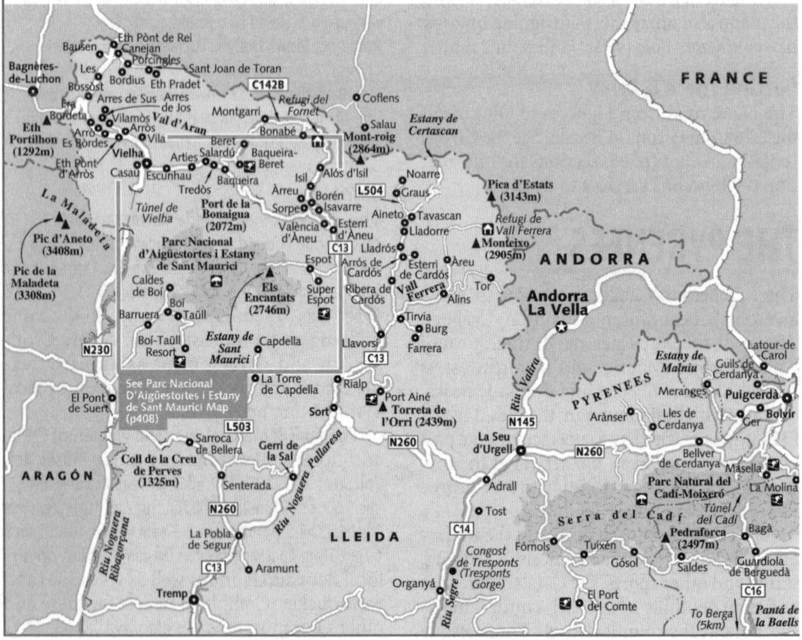

See Parc Nacional D'Aigüestortes i Estany de Sant Maurici Map (p408)

4km north of central Olot. Inside, the decor has a 21st-century edge, with iron and glass walls, a chilled-out ambience and gourmet ambitions. Dishes with local products are prepared with a silken touch, from chicken and duck to wild boar.

Getting There & Away

Teisa (☎ 972 26 01 96; www.teisa-bus.com) runs buses to/from Barcelona (via Banyoles) up to seven times a day (€12.85, two to 2¾ hours) and Girona via Banyoles and Besalú up to 15 times a day (€5.90, 1¼ hours). The easiest approach by car from Barcelona is by the AP7 and C63.

PARC NATURAL DE LA ZONA VOLCÀNICA DE LA GARROTXA

The park completely surrounds Olot but the most interesting area is between Olot and the village of Santa Pau, 10km southeast.

Volcanic eruptions began here about 350,000 years ago and the most recent one, at Volcà del Croscat, happened 11,500 years ago. In the park there are about 30 volcanic cones, up to 160m high and 1.5km wide. Together with the lush vegetation, a result of fertile soils and a damp climate, these create a landscape of unusual beauty. Between the woods are crop fields, a few hamlets and scattered old stone farmhouses.

The main park information office is the **Casal dels Volcans** in Olot. Another is the **Centre d'Informació Can Serra** (☎ 972 19 50 74), beside the GI524 Olot–Banyoles road 4.5km from the centre of Olot. Have a look also at www.turismeg arrotxa.com.

The old part of **Santa Pau** village, perched on a rocky outcrop, contains a porticoed plaza, the Romanesque Església de Santa Maria and a locked-up baronial castle.

Castellfollit de la Roca, on the N260 about 8km northeast of Olot, stands atop a crag composed of several layers of petrified lava – it's most easily viewed from the road north of the village.

Several good marked **walks**, which you can complete in less than a day, allow you to explore the park with ease. Inquire at the park information offices about routes.

Just off the GI524, and close to the most interesting parts of the park, are some pleasant,

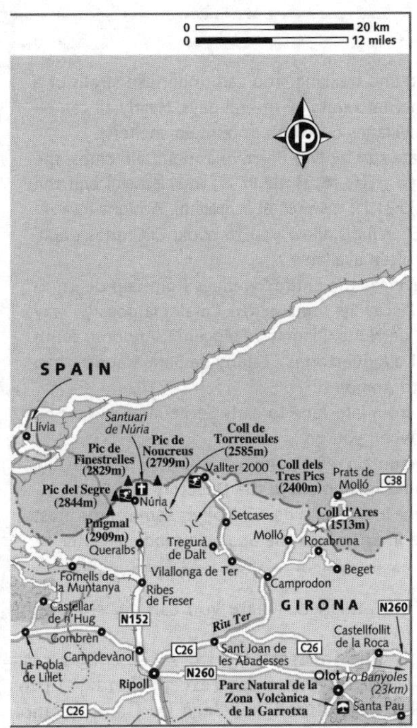

small country camping grounds. Wild camping is banned in the Garrotxa district, which stretches from east of Besalú to west of Olot, and from the French border to south of Sant Feliu de Pallerols. **Càmping La Fageda** (☎ 972 27 12 39; www.campinglafageda.com; Batet de la Serra; sites per 2-person tent & car €18.20; P), 4km east of the centre of Olot, has a pool, bar-restaurant, picnic areas and a children's playground.

RIPOLL

pop 10,900 / elev 691m

One of Spain's finest pieces of Romanesque art, in the Monestir de Santa Maria, is to be found at the medieval heart of this otherwise somewhat shabby industrial town.

Thirty kilometres west of Olot, Ripoll can claim, with some justice, to be the birthplace of Catalonia. In the 9th century, Ripoll was the power base from which the local strongman, Guifré el Pilós (Wilfred the Hairy), succeeded in uniting several counties of the Frankish March along the southern side of the Pyrenees. Guifré went on to become the first Count (Comte) of Barcelona. To encourage repopulation of the Pyrenees valleys, he founded the Monestir de Santa Maria, the most powerful monastery of medieval Catalonia.

Orientation & Information

The **tourist office** (☎ 972 70 23 51; www.elripolles.com, www.ajripoll.org; Plaça del Abat Oliba; 9.30am-1.30pm & 4-7pm Mon-Sat, 10am-2pm Sun) is by the Ribes de Freser–Sant Joan de les Abadesses road, which runs through the north of town. The Monestir de Santa Maria is virtually next door.

Sights

Following its founding in AD 879, the **Monestir de Santa Maria** grew rapidly rich, big and influential. From the mid-10th to mid-11th centuries it was Catalonia's spiritual and cultural heart. A five-naved basilica was built, and adorned in about 1100 with a stone portal that ranks among the high points of Romanesque art. Two fires had left the basilica in ruins by 1885, after which it was restored in a rather gloomy imitation of its former glory. The most interesting feature inside is the restored tomb of Guifré el Pilós.

You can visit the basilica and its great **portal** (admission free; 10am-1pm & 3-7pm Apr-Sep, to 6pm Oct-Mar), now protected by a wall of glass. A chart near the portal (in Catalan) helps to decipher the feast of sculpture: a medieval vision of the universe, from God the Creator, in the centre at the top, to the month-by-month scenes of daily rural life on the innermost pillars.

Down a few steps, to the right of the doorway, is the monastery's beautiful **claustre** (cloister; adult/child/senior & student €3/1/2). It's a two-storey affair, created in the 12th to 15th centuries, close to the tourist office.

Sleeping

Ca la Paula (☎ 972 70 00 11; www.elripolles.com/calapaula; Carrer dels Pirineus 6; s/d €28/45; P) This friendly family establishment is barely a stone's throw from the Monestir de Santa Maria. It has modern rooms with sparkling bathrooms and is the cheapest of the four options in town.

Getting There & Away

The bus and train stations are almost side by side on Carrer del Progrés, 600m southeast of the centre. Connections with Barcelona, Ribes de Freser and Puigcerdà are better by train. About 12 trains a day run to/from Barcelona (€5.90, about two hours), up to seven to Ribes de Freser (€2.10, 20 minutes) and six to Puigcerdà (€3.10, 1¼ hours).

OUT & ABOUT IN THE PYRENEES

The Catalan Pyrenees provide magnificent walking and trekking. You can undertake strolls of a few hours, or day walks that can be strung together into treks of several days. Nearly all can be done without camping gear, with nights spent in villages or *refugis* (mountain shelters).

Most of the *refugis* mentioned in this chapter are run by two Barcelona mountain clubs, the **Federació d'Entitats Excursionistes de Catalunya** (FEEC; ☎ 93 412 07 77; www.feec.org) and the **Centre Excursionista de Catalunya** (CEC; ☎ 93 315 23 11; www.cec.cat in Spanish). A night in a *refugi* costs around €12.50 to €17.50. Normally FEEC *refugis* allow you to cook; CEC ones don't. Moderately priced meals (around €15 to €17) are often available.

The coast-to-coast GR11 long-distance path traverses the entire Pyrenees from Cap de Creus on the Costa Brava to Hondarribia on the Bay of Biscay. Its route across Catalonia goes by way of La Jonquera, Albanyà, Beget, Setcases, the Vall de Núria, Planoles, Puigcerdà, Andorra, south of Pica d'Estats (3143m), over to the Parc Nacional d'Aigüestortes i Estany de Sant Maurici, then on to the southern flank of the Val d'Aran and into Aragón.

The season for walking in the high Pyrenees is from late June to early September. Always be prepared for fast-changing conditions, no matter when you go.

Local advice from tourist offices, park rangers, mountain *refugis* and other walkers is invaluable and you should look out for hiking maps of the kind mentioned in the Directory (p875).

There's boundless scope for **climbing** – Pedraforca in the Serra del Cadí offers some of the most exciting ascents. For more information on walking in Spain, see the Spain Outdoors chapter.

AROUND RIPOLL

A short way north of Ripoll, the GI401 branches west from Campdevànol, passes through Gombrèn and then proceeds in twisting and turning fashion on to **La Pobla de Lillet**, set a short way below the source of one of Catalonia's more important rivers, the Llobregat.

The grey stone village started life as a Roman outpost and grew to some importance as a local agricultural centre. People still cross its beautiful 12th-century Romanesque bridge and the town is also known for its delightful **Jardins Artigas**, a landscaped garden spread out along the river. Not any old landscaped garden, mind – but the handiwork of a certain Antoni Gaudí. You can sleep in one of three simple *pensiones*.

Follow the road up into the mountains from La Pobla de Lillet to the source of the Llobregat. Just 500m on and you reach the mountain hamlet of **Castellar de n'Hug**, over the shoulder from the La Molina ski resort (see p402). The hamlet was founded in the 13th century under the lords of Mataplana (based in Gombrèn). A tight web of alleys is bundled around the Romanesque **Església de Santa Maria** (much remodelled over the centuries), and from the square by the church you look north across a valley to the bare mountains beyond.

Six *pensiones* are gathered about the hamlet, three of them on Plaça Major. Most have a bar attached, where you can get something to eat.

One **Transports Mir** (☎ 972 70 30 12; www.autocarsmir.com) bus a day (except Sundays) runs between Ripoll and Bagà via Campdevànol, Gombrèn, Castellar de n'Hug and La Pobla de Lillet. The journey (€4.60) takes 1½ hours.

VALL ALTO DEL TER

This upper part of the Riu Ter valley reaches northeast from Ripoll to the pleasant towns of Sant Joan de les Abadesses and Camprodon, then northwest to the modest **Vallter 2000 ski centre** (☎ 972 13 60 75; www.vallter2000.com; day lift pass €29), just below the French border and at 2150m. It has 13 pistes of all grades, nine lifts and a ski school, but snow can be unreliable (most is usually artificial). The area makes a more pleasant overnight stop than Ripoll, and from the upper reaches there are some excellent walks to the Vall de Núria. Get the Editorial Alpina *Puigmal* map guide.

The C38 road leaves the Ter valley at Camprodon to head over the 1513m Collado d'Ares into France.

Sant Joan de les Abadesses

pop 3590

In Sant Joan de les Abadesses the restored 12th-century **bridge** over the Ter and the **Museu del Monestir** (☎ 972 72 00 13; Plaça de l'Abadessa; admission €2; 🕑 10am-2pm & 4-6pm Oct-Apr, 10am-2pm & 4-7pm May-

Jun & Sep, 10am-7pm Jul & Aug) are worth a look. This monastery, another founded by Guifré el Pilós, began life as a nunnery but the nuns were expelled in 1017 for alleged licentious conduct. Its elegant 12th-century church contains the marvellous *Santíssim Misteri*, a 13th-century polychrome woodcarving of the descent from the cross, composed of seven life-size figures. Also remarkable is the Gothic *retablo* of Santa Maria La Blanca, carved in alabaster. The elegant 15th-century late-Gothic cloister is charming.

Hostal Janpere (☎ 972 72 00 77; Carrer del Mestre Andreu 3; s/d per person €25), a basic but pleasant enough spot, is the only place to sleep here. It has good if somewhat clinical rooms.

Teisa (☎ 972 70 20 95) operates up to seven buses daily from Ripoll to Sant Joan de les Abadesses (€1.30, 15 minutes). One daily bus runs from Barcelona (Carrer de Pau Claris 117) at 7.15pm to Camprodon via Ripoll (€8.45, two hours).

Beget

Capping the end of a winding mountain lane that trails off here into a heavily wooded valley, this hamlet is a joy. The 12th-century Romanesque church is accompanied by an implausible array of roughly hewn houses, all scattered about stone-paved lanes. Through it gushes a mountain stream. Beget is on the GR11 walking route.

El Forn (☎ 972 74 12 31; Carrer de Josep Duñach 9; r per person €39), a well-kept cosy stone-and-timber house in the heart of the hamlet, is the best of the couple of accommodation and eating options. You can opt for half- or full board too.

There is no public transport to Beget.

VALL DE NÚRIA & RIBES DE FRESER

Around AD 700, the story goes, Sant Gil (St Giles) came from Nîmes in France to live in a cave in an isolated mountain valley 26km north of Ripoll, preaching the Gospel to shepherds. Before he left, four years later, apparently fleeing Visigothic persecution, Sant Gil hurriedly hid away a wooden Virgin-and-child image he had carved, a cross, his cooking pot and the bell he had used to summon the shepherds. They stayed hidden until 1079, when an ox led some shepherds to the spot. The statuette, the *Mare de Déu de Núria*, became the patron of Pyrenean shepherds and Núria's future was assured. The first historical mention of a shrine was made in 1162.

Sant Gil would recoil in shock if he came back today. The large, grey sanctuary complex squatting at the heart of the valley is an eyesore and the crowds would make anyone with hermitic leanings run a mile. But otherwise Núria remains almost pristine, a wide, green, mountain-ringed bowl that is the starting point for numerous walks. Getting there is fun too, either on foot up the Gorges de Núria – the green, rocky valley of the thundering Riu Núria – or from Ribes de Freser town, by the little *cremallera* (rack-and-pinion railway), which rises over 1000m on its 12km journey up the same valley.

Orientation

Unless you're walking across the mountains to Núria, you must approach from the small town of Ribes de Freser, on the N152 14km north of Ripoll. The *cremallera* to Núria starts at Ribes–Enllaç station, just off the N152 at the southern end of Ribes. There's a road from Ribes to Queralbs, but from there on it's the *cremallera* or your feet.

Information

Núria's **tourist office** (☎ 972 73 20 20; www.valldenuria.com; 🕑 8.30am-5.45pm mid-Sep–mid-Jul, 8.30am-6.30pm mid-Jul–mid-Sep) is in the sanctuary.

Sights

The large 19th- and 20th-century building that dominates the valley contains a hotel, restaurants and exhibition halls as well as the Santuari de Núria and its sacred *símbols de Núria*. The *santuari* (sanctuary) has the same opening hours as the information office. The Mare de Déu de Núria sits behind a glass screen above the altar and is in the Romanesque style of the 12th century, so either Sant Gil was centuries ahead of his time or this isn't his work! Steps lead up to the bell, cross and cooking pot (which all date from at least the 15th century). To have your prayer answered, put your head in the pot and ring the bell while you say it.

Activities

In winter, Núria is a small-scale ski resort with 10 short runs. A day lift pass costs €27.50.

Walkers should get Editorial Alpina's *Puigmal* map guide before coming to Núria. You can walk up the gorge to Núria but skip the first unexciting 6km from Ribes de Freser by taking the *cremallera* (or road) to Queralbs, thus saving your energies for the steepest and the most spectacular part of the approach, which is about three hours' walk up. Or take the *cremallera* up and walk down!

From the Vall de Núria, you can cap several 2700m-to-2900m peaks on the main Pyrenees ridge in about 2½ to four hours' walking for each (one way). The most popular is **Puigmal** (2909m).

Sleeping & Eating

Wild camping is banned in the whole Ribes de Freser–Núria area.

NÚRIA

Zona d'Acampada (☎ bookings 972 73 20 20; sites per adult/tent €3/3) Located behind the sanctuary, this is a basic camping area with limited facilities.

Alberg Pic de l'Àliga (☎ 972 73 20 48; dm student & under 26yr/26yr & over incl breakfast €20.45/24.30) The youth hostel is at the top of the *telecabina* (cable car) on the eastern side of the valley. Dorm rooms sleep from four to 14. The cable car runs from 9am to 6pm daily (to 7pm mid-July to mid-September). On Friday evenings it also runs to meet the *cremallera* train at around 7pm and 9pm.

Hotel Vall de Núria (☎ 972 73 20 20; half-board per person for 2 nights up to €171) Housed in the sanctuary building, the hotel has comfortable rooms with bathroom and satellite TV. Apartments are also available most of the year.

You'll find a couple of restaurants in the sanctuary building.

RIBES DE FRESER

Hotel Els Caçadors (☎ 972 72 70 77; www.hotelsderibes.com; Carrer de Balandrau 24; s/d €24/46, half-board per person from €41) A family-run business, this small hotel offers simple rooms with bathroom and TV. The buffet breakfast is grand – loads of cold meats, cheeses, juice, cereal and sweet pastries. Or try its three-star place across the road (half-board €59), where the best rooms are spacious, with parquet and timber, and, in some cases, have a hydromassage bathtub.

QUERALBS

This delightful hamlet of stone houses with slate roofs makes a prettier base. Try for a room at **Pensió L'Avet** (☎ 972 72 73 77; Carrer Major 7; half-board per person €40; 🕑 daily mid-Jun–mid-Sep, Sat, Sun & holidays rest of year). It's a pleasant old house that is the only option in the village itself (often open only at weekends and hard to get hold of). A couple of restaurants open up on weekends and during holiday periods.

Getting There & Away

Transports Mir runs services between Ripoll and Ribes de Freser, with two or three buses a day Monday to Friday, and one on Saturday.

Up to seven trains a day run to Ribes-Enllaç from Ripoll (€2.10, 20 minutes) and Barcelona (€6.55, 2¼ hours).

The **cremallera** (☎ 972 73 20 20) is a narrow-gauge electric-powered rack-and-pinion railway that has been operating since 1931. It runs from Ribes–Enllaç station to Núria and back six to 12 times a day; depending on the season (one way/return €12.20/19.50, 45 minutes one way). All trains stop at Ribes–Vila and Queralbs (1200m). It's a spectacular trip, particularly after Queralbs, as the train winds up the Gorges de Núria. Some services connect with Renfe trains at Ribes–Enllaç.

CERDANYA

Cerdanya, along with French Cerdagne across the border, occupies a low-lying basin between the higher reaches of the Pyrenees to the east and west. Although Cerdanya and Cerdagne, once a single Catalan county, were divided by the Treaty of the Pyrenees in 1659, they still have a lot in common. Walkers should get a hold of Editorial Alpina's *Cerdanya* map and guide booklet (scaled at 1:50,000).

Puigcerdà

pop 8950 / elev 1202m

Just 2km from the French border, Puigcerdà (puh-cher-*da*) is not much more than a way station, but it's a jolly one, particularly in summer and during the ski season. A dozen Spanish, Andorran and French ski resorts lie within 45km. At a height of just over 1200m, Puigcerdà is the capital of Cerdanya.

ORIENTATION & INFORMATION

Puigcerdà stands on a small hill, with the train station at the foot of its southwest side. A few minutes' climb up some flights of steps takes you to Plaça de l'Ajuntament, off which is the **tourist office** (☎ 972 88 05 42; Carrer de Querol 1; 🕑 10am-1pm & 4-7pm Mon-Fri, 10am-1pm & 4.30-7pm Sat, 10am-1pm Sun).

The **Hospital de Puigcerdà** (☎ 972 88 01 50; Plaça de Santa Maria 1) is up the road from the tourist office.

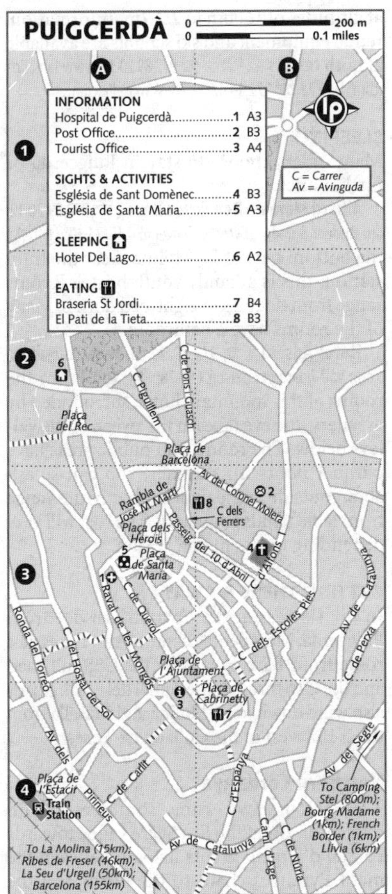

SIGHTS

The town was heavily damaged during the civil war and only the tower remains of the 17th-century **Església de Santa Maria** (Plaça de Santa Maria). The 13th-century Gothic **Església de Sant Domènec** (Passeig del 10 d'Abril) was also wrecked but later rebuilt. It contains 14th-century Gothic murals that somehow survived (opening times are erratic). The *estany* (lake) in the north of town, created back in 1380 for irrigation, is surrounded by turn-of-the-20th-century summer houses, built by wealthy Barcelona families.

SLEEPING

The town and the surrounding area is home to 17 varied hotels and *pensiones*.

Càmping Stel (☎ 972 88 23 61; www.stel.es; sites per 2-person tent & car €34.70; Jun-Sep; P) Out along the road to Llívia, this is the only nearby camping option, and a pleasant one, with a pool, basketball court and a football pitch. You can also rent bungalows by the month between October and May.

Hotel del Lago (☎ 972 88 10 00; www.hotellago.com; Avinguda del Dr Piguillem 7; s €91, d €107-128; P) Near the *estany*, this hotel has old-fashioned style and a nice leafy garden. The rooms vary greatly: some have heavy timber beams, while corner ones have windows opening in several directions out to the leafy exterior. The best doubles have Jacuzzis.

EATING

The adjoining squares of Plaça de Santa Maria and Plaça dels Herois are lined by cheerful bar-restaurants, some with unlikely names like Kennedy, Miami and Bier Garden!

El Pati de la Tieta (☎ 972 88 01 56; Carrer dels Ferrers 20; pizzas €9-11, meals €35-45; daily in high season, Thu-Sun Jul-May) One of the best choices, this understated restaurant offers a creative range of dishes, like the succulent *broquetes de cangur i verdures* (kangaroo on a skewer with vegetables).

Braseria St Jordi (☎ 972 14 03 66: Plaça de Cabrinetty 15; meals €25-30; Mon-Sat) A cheerful, cavernous spot for all sorts of meat goodies, this makes an inviting, modestly priced option. Try for a seat by the window for the valley views and tuck into a *filet de bou*. Or choose from a range of pasta, pizza and a series of cod dishes.

GETTING THERE & AWAY

Bus

Alsina Graells runs two daily buses (one at weekends) from Barcelona (€16.55, three hours) via the 5km Túnel del Cadí and two or three to La Seu d'Urgell (€5.60, one hour). They stop at the train station.

Car & Motorcycle

From Barcelona, the C16 approaches Puigcerdà through the Túnel del Cadí. Bicycles are not allowed in the tunnel, which is a tollway.

The N152 from Ribes de Freser climbs west along the northern flank of the Rigard valley, with the pine-covered Serra de Mogrony rising to the south, to the 1800m Collado de Toses (pass), then winds down to Puigcerdà.

The main crossing into France is at Bourg-Madame, immediately east of Puigcerdà, from where roads head to Perpignan and Toulouse.

Train

Six trains a day run from Barcelona to Puigcerdà (€8.55, 3¼ hours) via Ripoll and Ribes de Freser. Four in each direction make the seven-minute hop over the border to Latour-de-Carol in France, where they connect with trains from Toulouse or Paris, and with the narrow-gauge Train Jaune (yellow train) down the Têt Valley to Perpignan.

Llívia

pop 1390 / elev 1224m

Six kilometres northeast of Puigcerdà, across flat farmland, Llívia is a piece of Spain within France. Under the 1659 Treaty of the Pyrenees, Spain ceded 33 villages to France, but Llívia was a 'town' and so, together with the 13 sq km of its municipality, remained a Spanish possession.

The interest of Llívia's tiny medieval nucleus, near the top of the town, centres on the **Museu Municipal** (☎ 972 89 63 13; Carrer dels Forns 4; admission €1; 🕑 closed for restoration until mid-2009) and the 15th-century Gothic **Església de Nostra Senyora dels Àngels**, just above the museum. The museum is in what's claimed to be Europe's oldest pharmacy, the Farmacia Esteva, founded in 1415. From the church you can walk up to the ruined **Castell de Llívia** where, during the short-lived period of Islamic dominion in the Pyrenees, the Muslim governor Manussa enjoyed a secret dalliance with Lampègia, daughter of the Duke of Aquitaine (or so legend has it).

Dine on the balconies of **Restaurant Can Ventura** (☎ 972 89 61 78; Plaça Major 1; meals €35; 🕑 Wed-Sun), a ramshackle building dating from 1791. The food is delightful – traditional Catalan fare that comes from a discreetly hidden modern kitchen. Classics include local lamb slow-cooked in the oven for 12 hours.

Two or three buses a day run from Puigcerdà train station to Llívia. Otherwise, it's not a long walk, and the road is flat and quiet. You only cross about 2km of France before entering the Llívia enclave.

La Molina & Masella

These ski resorts lie either side of Tosa d'Alp (2537m), 15km south of Puigcerdà, and are linked by the Alp 2500 lift. The two resorts have a combined total of 101 runs (day lift pass for the whole area €36.50) of all grades at altitudes of 1600m to 2537m. Information, rental equipment and ski schools are available at both **resorts** (La Molina ☎ 972 89 20 31, www.lamolina.com; Masella ☎ 972 14 42 00, www.masella.com).

SLEEPING

Many skiers choose to stay in Puigcerdà or further afield.

Alberg Mare de Déu de les Neus (☎ 972 89 20 12; dm student & under 26yr/26yr & over €20.45/24.30; P) At the bottom part of La Molina, near the train station, this is a handy youth hostel. Rooms range from doubles to eight-bed dorms. Many of the rooms have a bathroom.

Hotel Adserà (☎ 972 89 20 01; www.hoteladsera.com; half-board per person €43-78; P) From the rooms of this mountain hotel, surrounded by greenery, the eye takes in the sweep of the valleys below. The rooms and public areas have parquet floors. In summer, you can splash about outside in the pool, and activities range from table tennis to archery. The cost will vary depending on room and season.

GETTING THERE & AWAY

In the ski season there's a bus service from Puigcerdà. Most people come by car; the easiest route from Barcelona is by the C58 toll road and the C16 through the Túnel del Cadí. Roads also wind down to La Molina and Masella from the N152 west of the Collado de Toses.

Northern Cerdanya

The N260 Hwy runs southwest from Puigcerdà along the Riu Segre valley towards La Seu d'Urgell. It cuts its path between the main Pyrenees chain to the north and the range made up mainly of the Serra del Cadí and Serra de Moixeró to the south. Up to three buses a day run along this valley between Puigcerdà and La Seu d'Urgell.

About 6km from Puigcerdà, **Bolvir** has a little Romanesque church and, more importantly, a luxurious and characterful place to stay, **Torre del Remei** (☎ 972 14 01 82; www.torredelremei.com; Camí Reial s/n, Bolvir; d from €294; P) This tastefully decorated Modernista mansion (which during the civil war was requisitioned as a school and later as a hospital by the Republican government) sits majestically amid tranquil gardens, and is a romantic luxury. The rooms, exquisitely furnished and each one different, are superb and the dining is equally tempting.

Another kilometre on from Bolvir, take the Ger turn-off for an excursion into the mountains. A minor asphalted road winds its way west and north through the broad, arid Valltova valley to **Meranges**, a dishevelled, stone farming village that makes few concessions to the passing tourist trade.

Those with cars can proceed along a sliver of road to the **Refugi de Malniu** (daily Jun-Sep, Sat & Sun rest of year), at 2130m. Right behind the *refugi* is the reed-covered **Estany Sec** (the misnamed Dry Lake). The *refugi* is on the path of the long-distance GR11 walk, which approaches from Guils de Cerdanya (also reachable by car) in the east, and continues west to Andorra.

SERRA DEL CADÍ

The N260 runs west along the wide Riu Segre valley from Puigcerdà to La Seu d'Urgell, with the Pyrenees climbing northwards towards Andorra, and the craggy pre-Pyrenees range of the Serra del Cadí rising steep and high along the southern flank. Although this face of the Cadí – rocky and fissured by ravines known as *canales* – looks daunting enough, the range's most spectacular peak is **Pedraforca** (2497m), a southern offshoot with the most challenging rock climbing in Catalonia. Pedraforca and the main Cadí range also offer some excellent mountain walking for those suitably equipped and experienced.

Orientation

The Pedraforca area is most easily reached from the C16, then along the B400, which heads west 1.5km south of Guardiola de Berguedà. Pedraforca looms mightily into view about halfway to the village of Saldes, which sits 1215m high at its foot, 15km from the C16. The main Cadí range runs east–west, about 5km north of Saldes. The Refugi Lluís Estasen (see right) nestles below the northern face of Pedraforca, 2.5km northwest of Saldes. You can reach it by footpath from Saldes or by a partly paved road that turns north off the B400 about 1km west of Saldes. Park at the Mirador de Gresolet (nice views), from where it's a 10-minute walk up to the refuge.

Information

The Parc Natural del Cadí-Moixeró's main **Centre d'Informació** (☎ 93 824 41 51; Carrer de la Vinya 1; 9am-1pm & 4-7pm Mon-Fri, 9am-1pm & 4-6.30pm Sat, 9am-1pm Sun & holidays Jun-Sep, 8am-3pm Mon, Wed & Thu, 8am-3pm & 4-6.30pm Tue & Fri, 9am-1pm & 4-6.30pm Sat, 9am-1pm Sun & holidays Oct-May) is in **Bagà**, a quiet village (walk down to the stone bridge that crosses the stream) 4km north of Guardiola de Berguedà on the C16.

In Saldes, the **Centre d'Informació Massís del Pedraforca** (☎ 93 825 80 46; 10am-2pm & 5.30-7.30pm Mon-Sat, 10am-2pm Sun Jul–mid-Sep, 10am-2pm & 5.30-7.30pm Sat, 10am-2pm Sun mid-Sep–Jun) has information on the Saldes and Pedraforca area only.

Sights

The B400 is paved from Saldes to the pretty stone village of **Gósol**, 6km further west. The original Gósol (Vila Vella), which dated back to at least the 9th century, is now abandoned on the hill south of the present village.

A road west from Gósol climbs the 1625m Coll de Josa pass, then descends past the picturesque hamlet of Josa del Cadí to **Tuixén** (1206m), another attractive village on a small hill and sometimes written Tuixent. From Tuixén, scenic paved roads lead northwest to La Seu d'Urgell (36km) and south to Sant Llorenç de Morunys (28km), which is on a beautiful cross-country road from Berga to Organyà.

Activities

The name Pedraforca means 'stone fork' and the approach from the east makes it clear why. Popular with rock climbers, the two separate rocky peaks – the northern Pollegó Superior (2497m) and the southern Pollegó Inferior (2400m) – are divided by a saddle called L'Enforcadura. The northern face, rising near vertically for 600m, has some classic rock climbs; the southern has a wall that sends alpinists into raptures.

Pedraforca is also an option for walkers. From Refugi Lluís Estasen you can reach the Pollegó Superior summit in about three strenuous hours – either southwards from the refuge, then up the middle of the fork from the southeast side (a path from Saldes joins this route); or westwards up to the Collada del Verdet, then south and east to the summit. The latter route has some hairy precipices and requires a good head for heights. It's not suitable for coming down: you must use the first route.

Sleeping & Eating

SALDES & AROUND

There are at least four **camping grounds** along the B400 between the C16 and Saldes, some open year-round. In Saldes you'll find a handful of *pensiones* and a larger hotel.

INTREPID TREMENTINAIRES

As late as the 1960s, Tuixén was known for its natural herbs and remedies and for the extraordinary women who would head off (often on foot) to sell them, the so-called Trementinaires (after *trementina,* or turpentine, one of their more popular items). From the late 19th century, these wandering saleswomen would leave for as long as four months and as far as Barcelona, leaving their menfolk behind to tend fields and animals, and only returned home when they had sold all their wares. Among the latter were *te de roca* ('rock tea' for upset tummies) and *orella d'ós* ('bear's ear' for coughs and colds). The women generally travelled in pairs, but even so, unaccompanied women travellers were otherwise virtually unheard of in Spain, much less from deep inland villages! The last Trementinaire, Sofia d'Ossera, undertook her final trip in 1982! Learn more in Tuixén's **Museu de les Trementinaires** (☎ 973 37 00 30; www.trementinaires.org; Plaça de la Serra del Cadí; admission free; 🕑 10am-2pm & 5-8pm Mon-Sat, 10am-2pm Sun Easter & Jul-Sep, 10am-2pm & 5-8pm Sat & Sun Oct-Jun).

Refugi Lluís Estasen (☎ 608 315312; 🕑 daily Jun-Sep, Sat, Sun & holidays rest of year) Run by the FEEC and near the Mirador de Gresolet, this *refugi* has 87 places, meals and a warden in summer. In winter it has about 30 places. When it's full you can sleep outside, but not in a tent.

GÓSOL & TUIXÉN

You'll find a handful of *cases rurals* in both villages, although some are rented out only on weekends or for a week at a time in summer.

Cal Farragetes (☎ 973 37 00 34; www.calfarragetes.com; Carrer del Coll 7, Tuixén; d per person €23; Ⓟ) A big, friendly stone place set over two floors around a sprawling courtyard, this country village house has smallish but immaculate rooms featuring iron bedsteads and wood panelling.

Forn Cal Moixó (☎ 973 37 02 74; Carrer del Canal 2, Gósol; meals €18-20; 🕑 daily) This bakery doubles as a homey restaurant. Tuck into filling and tasty local food, such as a tender *filet de vedella* (fillet of beef). The *menú del día* is good lunch value at €12.50.

Getting There & Around

You need your own vehicle to reach Saldes, Gósol or Tuixén.

LA SEU D'URGELL

pop 12,700 / elev 691m

The lively valley town of La Seu d'Urgell (la *se*-u dur-*zhey*) is Spain's gateway to Andorra, 10km to the north. It's a pleasant place to spend a night, with an admirable medieval cathedral.

When the Franks evicted the Muslims from this part of the Pyrenees, in the early 9th century, they made La Seu a bishopric and capital of the counts of Urgell. It has been an important market and cathedral town since the 11th century.

Information

Hospital (☎ 973 35 00 50; Passeig de Joan Brudieu 8)
Policía Municipal (☎ 973 35 04 26; Plaça dels Oms 1) In the Casa de la Ciutat (Town Hall).
Tourist office (☎ 973 35 15 11; www.laseu.org/coneix/turisme; Avinguda de les Valls d'Andorra 33; 🕑 9am-8pm Mon-Fri, 10am-2pm & 4-8pm Sat, 10am-2pm Sun Jul-Aug, 10am-2pm & 4-6pm Mon-Sat Sep-Jun) At the northern entrance to town.

Sights

On the southern side of Plaça dels Oms, the 12th-century **Catedral de Santa Maria & Museu Diocesà** (admission free; 🕑 10am-1pm & 4-7pm Mon-Sat, 10am-1pm Sun Jun-Sep, 10am-1pm & 4-6pm Mon-Sat, 10am-1pm Sun Oct-May) is one of Catalonia's outstanding Romanesque buildings despite various attempts at remodelling. It's one of more than a hundred Romanesque churches lining what has come to be known as the Ruta Románica, from Perpignan (France) to the Urgell district.

The fine western facade, through which you enter, is decorated in typical Lombard style. The inside is dark and plain but still impressive, with five apses, some murals in the southern transept, and a 13th-century Virgin-and-child sculpture in the central apse.

From inside the cathedral you can enter the **Museu Diocesà** (☎ 973 35 32 42; www.museudiocesaurgell.org; admission €3; 🕑 10am-1pm & 4-7pm Mon-Sat, 10am-1pm Sun Jun-Sep, 10am-1pm & 4-6pm Mon-Sat, 10am-1pm Sun Oct-May). This good museum encompasses the fine cloister and the 12th-century Romanesque **Església de Sant Miquel**, as well as some good medieval Pyrenean church murals, sculptures and altarpieces, and a rare

10th-century Mozarabic Beatus (illustrated manuscript of the Apocalypse).

Sleeping

Pensió Jové (☎ 973 35 02 60; Carrer dels Canonges 42; r per person €15) One of two basic digs on the same street in the old town, this place has clean, simple rooms with basin and shared bathroom.

Hotel Avenida (☎ 973 35 01 04; www.avenhotel.com; Avinguda de Pau Claris 24; s €40-65, d €55-100) This hotel has a range of mostly sunny rooms. Although not overly characterful, the rooms (some overhauled in 2007) are big enough and kept spick-and-span. Its Italian restaurant, Miscela, is not bad.

our pick **Casa Rural La Vall del Cadí** (☎ 973 35 0390; www.valldelcadi.com; Carretera de Tuixen s/n; d €55; P) Barely a 1km walk south of the hospital and across the Segre river, you are in another, protected, bucolic world in this stone country house. The cosy rooms, with terracotta floors, iron bedsteads and, in some cases, timber ceiling beams, have a nice winter detail – floor heating.

Hotel El Castell (☎ 973 35 00 00; www.hotelelcastell.com; Castellciutat; s/d from €180/225; P) Set in a castle in a hilltop jumble of lanes about 1.5km west of central La Seu, this spa hotel is a world of its own. Run by the Relais & Châteaux team, it is the classiest hotel for miles around, with soothing gardens, a gym, sauna and gourmet restaurant.

Eating

Ignasi (☎ 973 35 49 49; Carrer de Capdevila 17; meals €15; Mon-Sat) For a cheap and cheerful bite, you could try the savoury crêpes (€6.50) in this knockabout place – there are sweet ones for dessert too.

Cal Pacho (☎ 973 35 27 19; Carrer de la Font 11; meals €20-25; Mon-Sat) Hidden away in the old town, this is a marvellous den serving old-fashioned local grub. Try a dish of *cargols a la llauna* (baked snails €11) or *cabrit at forn* (roast kid €19). The *menú del día* offers a broad variety of options for €12.

Restaurant Les Tres Portes (☎ 973 35 56 58; Carrer de Garriga i Massou 7; meals €30-35; Thu-Sun) This is a homely spot, where you can chow down on mixed Spanish cuisine in the peaceful garden. Inside, the decor is bright but warm, with orange walls and yellow and red table linen.

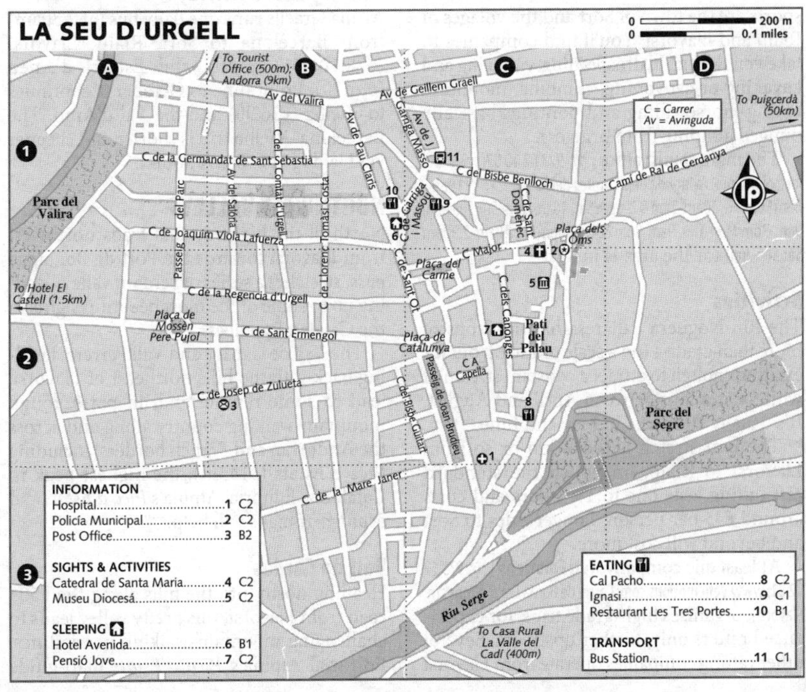

It presents an even array of options taking in fish, seafood and meat mains. The *mitjana de cavall amb alls* (horsemeat prepared in garlic) is hearty at €18.

Getting There & Away

BUS

The bus station is on the northern edge of the old town. Alsina Graells runs four or five buses daily to Barcelona (€22.90, 3½ hours): two each via Solsona and Ponts, and one, which does not run on Sunday, via the Túnel del Cadí. There are also three to Puigcerdà (€5.60, one hour) and two to Lleida (€15.60, 2½ hours).

CAR & MOTORCYCLE

The N260 Hwy heads 6km southwest to Adrall, then turns off west over the hills to Sort. The C14 carries on south to Lleida, threading the towering Tresponts gorge about 13km beyond Adrall.

VALL DE LA NOGUERA PALLARESA

The Riu Noguera Pallaresa, running south through a dramatic valley about 50km west of La Seu d'Urgell, is Spain's best-known white-water river. The main centres for white-water sports are the town of Sort and the villages of Rialp and Llavorsí. You'll find companies to take you rafting, hydrospeeding, canoeing and kayaking or canyoning, climbing, mountain biking, horse riding and ponting (basically bungee jumping from bridges).

The main **tourist office** (☎ 973 62 10 02; www.pallarssobira.info; Avinguda dels Comtes del Pallars 21; ⌚ 9am-8pm Mon-Fri, 10am-2pm & 3-6pm Sat, 10am-1pm Sun Jul-Aug, 9am-3pm Mon-Thu, 9am-3pm & 4-6.30pm Fri, 10am-2.30pm Sat Sep-Jun) for the area is in Sort.

Activities

The Riu Noguera Pallaresa has no drops of more than grade 4 (on a scale of 1 to 6), but it's exciting enough to attract a constant stream of white-water fans between April and August. It's usually at its best in May and June.

The best stretch is the 14km or so from Llavorsí to Rialp, on which the standard raft outing lasts one to 1½ hours and costs around €35 per person. Longer rides to Sort and beyond will cost more.

At least one company, **Yeti Emotions** (☎ 973 62 22 01; www.yetiemotions.com; Carrer de Borda Era d'Alfons s/n, Llavorsí), organises high-grade trips, for experienced rafters only, further upstream. Several other rafting companies operate from Llavorsí and other points like Sort. Canoeing trips on the same river start at €35.50 per hour.

You need to bring your own swimming costume, towel and a change of clothes. All other gear is usually provided.

Sleeping & Eating

Llavorsí is the most pleasant base, much more of a mountain village than Rialp or Sort, with a couple of camping grounds and four hotels. A couple of simple eateries can provide sustenance.

Camping Aigües Braves (☎ 973 62 21 53; sites per 2-person tent & car €19; ⌚ mid-Mar–Aug; P 🏊) About 1km north of Llavorsí proper, this pleasant riverside camping ground has a pool, restaurant and minimarket.

Hotel Riberies (☎ 973 62 20 51; www.riberies.com; Camí de Riberies s/n; s/d incl breakfast €93/152; P 💻 🏊) This is by far the most pleasant choice in the area. Timber ceilings and wooden floors give the spacious rooms a warm feel. Throw in comfort factors such as the verdant site, good restaurant and a heated swimming pool for an enjoyable stay.

Getting There & Away

Alsina Graells runs one daily bus (at 7.30am) from Barcelona to Sort, Rialp, Llavorsí (€28.10, 5½ hours) and Esterri d'Àneu (€31.20). From June to October it continues to Vielha (€36.90) and the Val d'Aran. The Barcelona–Vielha trip is shorter and cheaper via Lleida (€28.30, 5½ hours).

NORTHWEST VALLEYS

North of the highway that leads northwest from Llavorsí towards the Port de Bonaigua pass, stretches a series of verdant valleys leading up to some of the most beautiful sights in the Catalan Pyrenees.

The Vall de Cardòs and Vall Ferrera, heading back into the hills northeast of Llavorsí, lead to some remote and, in parts, tough mountain-walking country along and across the Andorran and French borders, including Pica d'Estats (3143m), the highest peak in Catalonia. Editorial Alpina's *Pica d'Estats* and *Montgarri* maps will help.

Vall de Cardòs

Heading north into the hills along the L504 road from Llavorsí, this pretty valley leads to challenging mountain-walking possibilities. Editorial Alpina's *Pica d'Estats* map-guide is useful here. There is no public transport up the valley.

Lladrós and **Lladorre**, the latter graced with a charming Romanesque church, are pretty stone hamlets oozing bucolic charm. **Tavascan** marks the end of the asphalt road. It's a huddle of well-kept houses and a launch pad for numerous excursions. The most stunning piece of scenery is a crystal-blue glacial lake (the largest in the Pyrenees), **Estany de Certascan**, about 13km away along a tough road best negotiated by 4WD. Just out of view of the lake is the **Refugi de Certascan** (☎ 973 62 13 89; www.certascan.com in Spanish; dm €13.50; ⏲ daily mid-Jun–mid-Sep, some weekends & holidays rest of year), which has room for 40 people, showers and offers meals. More trails and lakes await in this frontier mountain territory. The valley's towns are littered with charming *cases de pagès* (country guest houses), along with three hotels in Tavascan.

Vall Ferrera

Greener than the Vall de Cardòs and at the heart of the Parc Natural de l'Alt Pirineu (Catalonia's biggest nature reserve), this valley is another pleasant surprise, hiding several pretty villages and bringing even more good walking country within reach. The ascent of the **Pica d'Estats** (3143m), the region's highest peak, is generally undertaken from here. There is no public transport.

The prettiest hamlet, **Àreu**, is a popular base for walkers. It is divided into two separate settlements, each with a Romanesque church: Sant Climent is in the lower part and Sant Feliu de la Força up the road. The ascent of and return from the Pica d'Estats is an all-day affair and only for the fit. You need to be at the **Refugi de Vall Ferrera** (☎ 973 62 43 78; ⏲ Jul–mid-Oct), 10km to the north of Àreu, at dawn. On the way up you will pass glacial lakes, high pastures and ever-changing scenery, before ascending the bare rocky summit.

There are several *cases de pagès* and one hotel in Àreu, and more options in Alins. **Casa Besolí** (☎ 973 62 44 15; La Plaça s/n, Àreu; d €45), in the lower part of the village, is one of two that rents out rooms by the night. They are small but immaculately kept and cosy affairs.

Valls d'Àneu

To proceed to the next valleys west, you return to Llavorsí and the C13 Hwy, along which you proceed north. After 12km you pass the turn-off on the left for Espot – this is the most popular way into the Parc Nacional d'Aigüestortes i Estany de Sant Maurici.

Six kilometres further on from the turn-off, after passing an artificial lake on the right where you can hire rowing boats and canoes to potter about in, you'll arrive at **Esterri d'Àneu**, a popular, if distant, base for the ski fields of Baqueira–Beret (p413) in the Val d'Aran. Of the various valleys that make up the Valls d'Àneu, the **Vall d'Isil** is the most intriguing. Follow the C13 directly north through Esterri d'Àneu and it will lead you over a bridge across the Riu Noguera Pallaresa. You then follow this back road (the C147) up into a mountain valley, passing through the villages of **Borén**, **Isil** and the half-abandoned **Alós d'Isil**.

PARC NACIONAL D'AIGÜESTORTES I ESTANY DE SANT MAURICI & AROUND

Catalonia's only national park extends 20km east to west, and only 9km from north to south, but packs in more beauty than most areas 100 times its size. The product of glacial action over two million years, it's essentially two east–west valleys at 1600m to 2000m altitude lined by jagged 2600m to 2900m peaks of granite and slate. Against this backdrop, pine and fir forests, and open bush and grassland, bedecked with wildflowers in spring, combine with some 200 small *estanys* and countless streams and waterfalls to create a wilderness of rare splendour.

The national park, whose boundaries cover 141.2 sq km, lies at the core of a wider wilderness area, whose outer limit is known as the *zona perifèrica* and includes some magnificent high country to the north and south. The total area covered is 408.5 sq km and is monitored by park rangers.

You can find information (in Spanish) at http://reddeparquesnacionales.mma.es/parques.

Orientation

APPROACHES

The main approaches are via the village of Espot (1320m), 4km east of the park's eastern boundary, and Boí, 5.5km from the western side.

THE PARK

The two main valleys are those of the Riu Escrita in the east and the Riu de Sant Nicolau in the west. The Escrita flows out of the park's largest lake, the 1km-long **Estany de Sant Maurici**. The Sant Nicolau's main source is **Estany Llong**, 4km

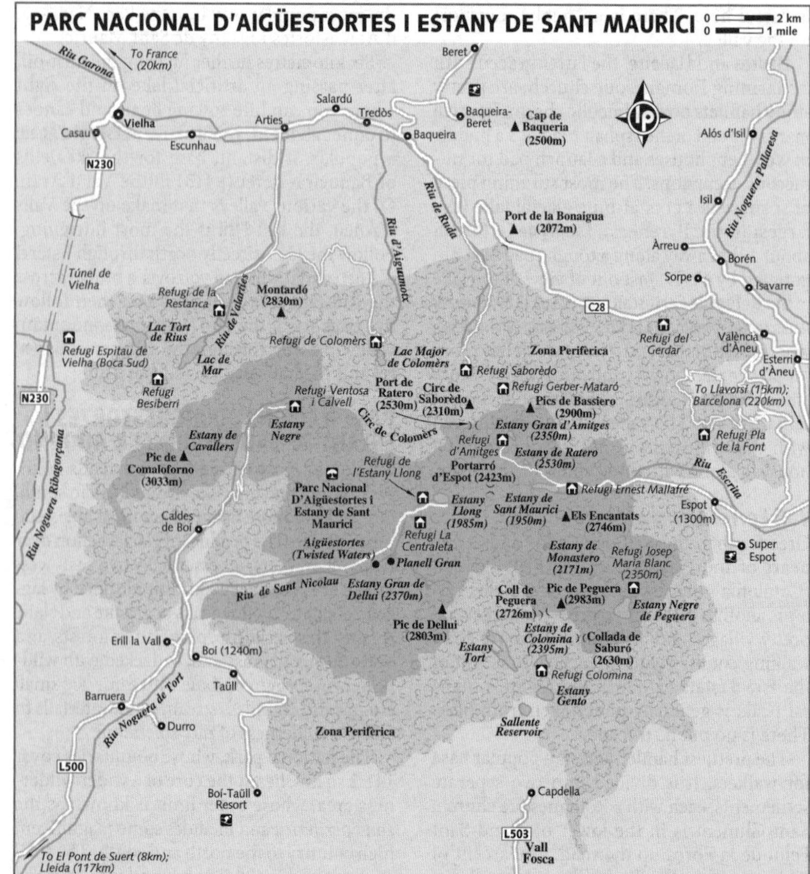

west of Estany de Sant Maurici across the 2423m Portarró d'Espot pass. Three kilometres downstream from Estany Llong, the Sant Nicolau runs through a particularly beautiful stretch known as **Aigüestortes** (Twisted Waters).

Apart from the valley openings at the eastern and western ends, virtually the whole perimeter of the park is mountain crests, with numerous spurs of almost equal height reaching in towards the centre. One of these, from the south, ends in the twin peaks **Els Encantats** (2746m and 2733m), towering over Estany de Sant Maurici.

MAPS & GUIDES

Editorial Alpina's map guides are adequate, although they don't show every single trail. *Sant Maurici – Els Encantats* covers the eastern half of the park and its approaches; *Vall de Boí* covers the western half and its approaches; *Montsent de Pallars* covers the northern Vall Fosca; and *Val d'Aran,* naturally, covers the Val d'Aran. A better map of the whole area is the Institut Cartogràfic de Catalunya's *Parc Nacional d'Aigüestortes i Estany de Sant Maurici,* scaled at 1:25,000 – but even it is not perfect. The help of guides can be enlisted at the Espot and Boí information offices.

Information

TOURIST INFORMATION

In Espot, there are **national park information offices** (☎ 973 62 40 36; 9am-1pm & 3.30-6.45pm daily Jun-Sep, 9am-2pm & 3.30-5.45pm Mon-Sat, 9am-2pm Sun

Oct-May) and **Boí** (☎ 973 69 61 89; 🕑 same as Espot office). The **tourist office** (☎ 973 69 40 00; 🕑 9am-2pm & 5-7pm Mon-Sat, 10am-2pm Sun) in Barruera, on the L500, 10km north from the N230, is a good source of information on the area around the west side of the park. A sub-branch is open at Taüll in Easter and June to September (same opening times). Offices south of the park are located in **El Pont de Suert** (☎ 973 69 06 40) and **La Pobla de Segur** (☎ 973 68 02 57).

PARK RULES

Private vehicles cannot enter the park. Wild camping is not allowed, nor are swimming or other 'aquatic activities' in the lakes and rivers. Hunting, fishing, mushroom-picking and just about every other kind of potentially harmful activity are banned.

Sights

The **Vall de Boí** (www.vallboi.com), southwest of the park, is dotted with some of Catalonia's loveliest little Romanesque churches, which together were declared a Unesco World Heritage site in 2000. Two of the finest are at Taüll, 3km east of Boí. **Sant Climent de Taüll**, at the entrance to the village, with its slender six-storey bell tower, is a gem, not only for its elegant, simple lines but also for the art that once graced its interior until the works were transferred to museums in the 20th century. The central apse contains a copy of a famous 1123 mural that now resides in Barcelona's Museu Nacional d'Art de Catalunya (see p337). At the church's centre is a *Pantocrator* (Christ figure), whose rich Mozarabic-influenced colours, and expressive but superhuman features, have become a virtual emblem of Catalan Romanesque art. Other art from this church has found its way to museums as far away as Boston in the USA!

Santa Maria de Taüll (admission free; 🕑 10am-8pm), up in the old village centre and possessing a five-storey tower, is also well represented in the Barcelona museum but lacks the in situ copies that add to the interest of Sant Climent.

Other worthwhile Romanesque churches in the area are at Boí (Sant Joan), Barruera (Sant Feliu), Durro (Nativitat) and Erill la Vall (Santa Eulàlia). The latter has a slender six-storey tower to rival Sant Climent's and slopes upwards to the altar. Next door is the **Centre d'Interpretació del Romànic** (☎ 973 69 67 15; www.centreromanic.com; Carrer del Batalló 5; 🕑 9am-2pm & 5-7pm Mon-Sat, 10am-2pm Sun), which has a small Romanesque art collection, and it's also where you can organise guided tours of the churches.

You can visit all the churches (with the exception of Santa Maria de Taüll) from 10am to 2pm and 4pm to 7pm daily (admission €1.20 each or €5 for all six churches).

Activities

WALKING

The park is criss-crossed by plenty of paths, ranging from well-marked to unmarked, enabling you to pick suitable routes.

East–West Traverse

You can walk right across the park in one day. The full Espot–Boí (or vice versa) walk is about 25km and takes nine hours, but you can shorten this by using Jeep-taxis to/from Estany de Sant Maurici or Aigüestortes (3km downstream from Estany Llong) or both. Espot (1300m) to Estany de Sant Maurici (1950m) is 8km (two hours). A path then climbs to the Portarró d'Espot pass (2423m), where there are fine views over both of the park's main valleys. From the pass you descend to Estany Llong and Aigüestortes (1820m; about 3½ hours from Estany de Sant Maurici). Then you have around 3.5km to the park entrance, 4km to the L500 and 2.5km south to Boí (1260m) – a total of about three hours.

Shorter Walks

Numerous good walks of three to five hours' return will take you up into spectacular side valleys from Estany de Sant Maurici or Aigüestortes.

From the eastern end of Estany de Sant Maurici, one path heads south 2.5km up the Monastero valley to **Estany de Monastero** (2171m), passing Els Encantats on the left. Another goes 3km northwest up by Estany de Ratero to **Estany Gran d'Amitges** (2350m). From **Planell Gran** (1850m), 1km up the Sant Nicolau valley from Aigüestortes, a path climbs 2.5km southeast to **Estany Gran de Dellui** (2370m). You can descend to **Estany Llong** (3km); it takes about four hours from Aigüestortes to Estany Llong.

SKIING

The **Boí-Taüll ski resort** (☎ 902 40 66 40; www.boitaullresort.com; day lift pass €32) is one of Catalonia's more promising areas, with 49 pistes (most fairly easy) covering 43km. You can also ski around **Espot** (☎ 973 62 40 58; www.espotesqui.net; day lift pass €31), which gives you a further 22 pistes over 23.5km.

Sleeping

CAMPING

There are four similarly priced camping grounds in and around Espot.

Camping Vorapark (☎ 973 62 41 08; www.voraparc.com; Prat del Vedat; sites per 2-person tent & car €23.65; Apr-Sep; P) This ground is about the best in Espot, around 1.5km out of town towards the park entrance. It has a pleasant swimming pool, as well as a pool hall, bar and minimarket.

MOUNTAIN REFUGIS

Six *refugis* in the park and nine more inside the *zona perifèrica* provide accommodation for walkers. They tend to be staffed from early or mid-June to September and for some weeks in the first half of the year for skiers. At other times several of them leave a section open where you can stay overnight; if you are unsure, call ahead or ask at the park information offices. Most charge €13.50 per person to stay overnight. The refuges in the park are listed here. Those outside are marked on the map, p408.

Refugi d'Amitges (☎ 973 25 01 09; www.amitges.com) At Estany Gran d'Amitges (2350m), in the north of the park, it's run by the Centre Excursionista de Catalunya (CEC). Meals and showers are available.

Refugi Ernest Mallafré (☎ 973 25 01 18) It's near the eastern end of Estany de Sant Maurici (1950m) and run by the FEEC. It has meals but no showers.

Refugi de l'Estany Llong (☎ reservations 629 374652, 973 29 95 45) It's near Estany Llong (1985m) and run by the national park; there's a kitchen and showers.

Refugi Josep Maria Blanc (☎ 973 25 01 08; www.jmblanc.com) It's near Estany Tort (2350m) and run by the CEC; meals available when staffed.

Refugi Ventosa i Calvell (☎ 973 29 70 90; www.refugiventosa.com) The CEC runs this *refugi* in the northwest of the park (2220m); it has a kitchen and showers.

Refugi La Centraleta is basic with bunks, mattresses and blankets, located 15 minutes south of Refugi de l'Estany Llong.

HOSTALES & HOTELS

The villages of Espot, Boí and Taüll have a range of accommodation options (including several midrange hotels in Espot). There are *hostales* and *cases de pagès* in Barruera, El Pont de Suert, Capdella and La Torre de Capdella.

Espot

Casa Felip (☎ 973 62 40 93; d incl breakfast Sep-Jun €30, d incl breakfast Jul-Aug €40) A friendly, family-run place in the heart of the village, this spot has clean rooms. It is one of three country homestays here. All of these accommodations charge about the same.

Taüll

Three kilometres uphill from Boí, Taüll is by far the most picturesque place to stay on the west side of the park. It has nine *cases de pagès* and over a dozen hotels and *pensiones,* either in the village itself or in the surrounding area.

Pensión Santa Maria (☎ 973 69 61 70; www.taull.com; Plaça Cap del Riu 3; d up to €123; P ☒) Through a shady entrance a grand stone archway leads into the quiet courtyard of this rambling country haven, with rose-draped balcony. The rooms are tastefully furnished and the building, all stonework with a timber-and-slate roof, oozes timeless character. For €9 the staff will pack you a picnic lunch.

Eating

Note that throughout the area many places close midweek and in the low season. Most of the towns have one or two fairly basic restaurants.

Restaurant Juquim (☎ 973 62 40 09; meals €20-25; daily Jun–mid-Oct, Wed-Mon mid-Oct–May) This classic on Espot's main square has a varied menu concentrating largely on hearty country fare, with generous winter servings of *olla pallaresa* (steaming hotpot) or *civet de senglar* (wild boar stew).

In Taüll, where there is a handful of eateries, try **El Mallador** (☎ 973 69 60 28; meals €20; daily Dec-Easter & Jul-Sep), in the shadow of the Sant Climent church and proffering a beautiful shady garden setting for its simple fare. Meat and salads dominate the menu, soft music wafts out from the ramshackle stone house (tables inside for chilly moments and, erm, winter).

Getting There & Away

BUS

Daily buses from Barcelona, Lleida and La Pobla de Segur to Esterri d'Àneu (and in summer to the Val d'Aran) will stop at the Espot turning on the C13. From there you have an 8km uphill walk (or hitch) to Espot.

Alsina Graells buses from Barcelona to La Pobla de Segur (€24.45, three to 4½ hours) run up to three times a day all year. From July to mid-September, a connecting bus runs daily from La Pobla de Segur to El Pont de Suert and from there to Barruera and the Boí turn-off (el Cruce de Boí) on the L500 (1km short of Boí).

Getting Around

Once you're close to the park, the easiest way of getting inside it is by Jeep-taxi from Espot or Boí. There's a more or less continuous shuttle service between Espot and Estany de Sant Maurici, and between Boí and Aigüestortes, saving you, respectively, 8km and 10km. The one-way fare for either trip is €4.85 per person and the services run from outside the park information offices in Espot and Boí (from July to September 8am to 7pm, other months 9am to 6pm).

VAL D'ARAN

pop 9820

This verdant valley, Catalonia's northernmost outpost, is surrounded by spectacular 2000m-plus mountains. In spite of massive tourism development since the 1964 opening of the Baqueira–Beret ski resort, especially in the valley and Vielha, it remains the lushest green corner of Catalonia. It's dotted with hill villages (many with exquisite little Romanesque churches – ask for a list in Vielha's tourist office) and is inspiringly beautiful when you get away from the tourist centres. From Aran's pretty side valleys, walkers can go over the mountains in any direction, notably southwards to the Parc Nacional d'Aigüestortes i Estany de Sant Maurici.

Its only natural opening is northwards to France, to which it gives its river, the Riu Garona (Garonne), flowing down to Bordeaux. Thanks in part to its geography, Aran's native language is not Catalan but Aranese *(aranés)*, which is a dialect of Occitan or the *langue d'oc*, the old Romance language of southern France. Mind you, not even all the locals still speak it, as interviewees chatting in Catalan on Aranese radio attest!

Despite this northward orientation, Aran has been tied politically to Catalonia since 1175, when Alfonso II took it under his protection to forestall the designs of rival counts on both sides of the Pyrenees. A major hiccup came with the Napoleonic occupation from 1810 to 1815.

The Val d'Aran is some 35km long and is considered to have three parts: Naut Aran (Upper Aran), the eastern part, aligned east-west; Mijaran (Middle Aran) around Vielha; and Baish Aran (Lower Aran), where the Garona flows northeast to France.

Vielha

pop 5390 / elev 974m

Vielha is Aran's junction capital, a barely controlled sprawl of holiday housing and apartments straggled along the valley and creeping up the sides. The tiny centre retains some charm but in general this is not the Vall d'Aran's highlight. The Aranese spelling of its name is more common than the Catalan and Castilian version, Viella.

INFORMATION

Hospital (☎ 973 64 00 04; Carrèr deth Espitau 5)

Mossos d'Esquadra (Catalan regional police; ☎ 973 35 72 85) Just north of the centre along the N230 to France.

Tourist office (☎ 973 64 01 10; www.torismearan.org; Carrèr de Sarriulèra 10; 🕑 9am-9pm)

SIGHTS

The small old quarter is around Plaça dèra Glèisa and across little Riu Nere, just west of the square. The **Glèisa de Sant Miquèu** (Plaça dèra Glèisa) is a church that displays a mix of 12th- to 18th-century styles, with a 13th-century main portal. It contains some notable medieval artwork, especially the 12th-century *Crist de Mijaran*, an almost life-sized wooden bust that is thought to have been part of a *Descent from the Cross* group. The **Musèu dèra Val d'Aran** (☎ 973 64 18 15; Carrèr Major 11; adult/senior & child €2/1; 🕑 10am-1pm & 5-8pm Tue-Sat, 11am-2pm Sun), housed in a turreted and somewhat decaying old mansion, tells the tale of Aran's history up to the present.

SLEEPING

About a third of the Val d'Aran's hotels are in the capital. For some of the cheaper places, head down Passeig dèra Llibertat, north off Avenguda de Castièro. High season for most is Christmas to New Year, Easter and a handful of other peak holiday periods: high summer (July to August) and much of the ski season (January to February). At other times, prices can as much as halve.

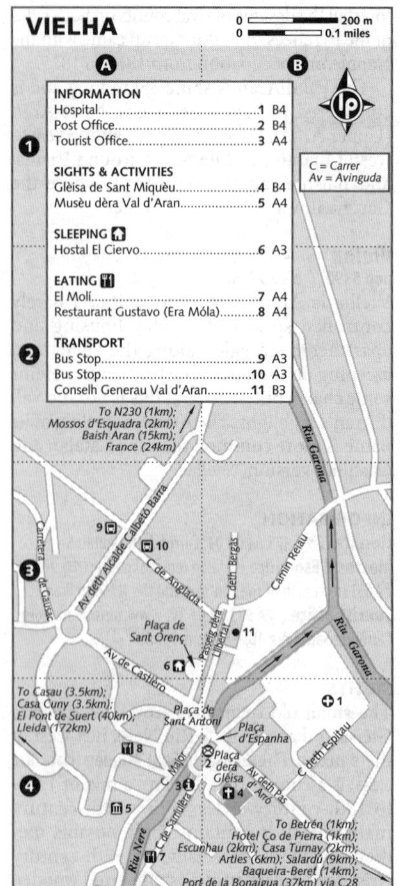

Hostal El Ciervo (☎ 973 64 01 65; Plaça de Sant Orenç 3; s/d €38/58) Some of the better rooms in this perfectly adequate, 18-room, old-style hotel overlooking a central square have the singular benefit of power showers.

You'll find some nice options just a few kilometres out of Vielha in the surrounding villages. In **Casau** (about 3.5km out of Vielha on the N230 road), high up above Vielha, you'll find three options, among them **Casa Cuny** (☎ 973 64 01 39; Carrèr Major 15; d €45), a three-storey whitewashed house with magnificent views over the city and valley below. In **Betrén**, a pretty village tacked on to the east end of Vielha's sprawl, seek out **Hotel Ço de Pierra** (☎ 973 64 13 34; www.hotelpierra.com; Carrèr Major 26; s/d €47/62), a new house that respects the stone-and-slate pattern of traditional housing. The 10 rooms combine stone, timber and terracotta for warmth. What's fabulous is that you are in a timeless village about a 15-minute walk from the centre of Vielha.

EATING

Quality dining is quite hard to come by in Vielha, but you will find no shortage of places serving average meals – many will dish up the local speciality, *olla aranesa* (a hearty hotpot).

El Molí (☎ 973 64 17 18; Carrèr de Sarriulera 26; meals €30) On the banks of Riu Nere, this eatery specialises in grilled meaty dishes and *llesques*, toasty bread with toppings like *ceps, jabugo i formatge fós* (mushrooms, top quality ham and melted cheese; €15).

Restaurant Gustavo (Era Mòla) (☎ 973 64 24 19; Carrèr de Marrèc 14; meals €30-35; 🕒 Thu-Tue mid-Jul–Sep & Dec-Apr) Easily the best restaurant in town, it is located in a low-slung stone house in the heart of the old town. Expect carefully prepared local cooking with a heavy French hand (you can't get more French than potted duck, ie *rillettes*). Savour the *solomillo de cerdo al Calvados* (pork fillet bathed in Calvados). The desserts rate a special mention.

Barely 2km out of town, in the attractive village of **Escunhau** (at whose summit stands a fine Romanesque church), you'll linger over your grub in the welcoming **Casa Turnay** (☎ 973 64 02 92; Carrèr de Sant Sebastià 2; meals €20-25; 🕒 daily mid-Jul–mid-Sep & Dec-Apr, weekends rest of the year). Inside is all stone walls, low timber beams, some marvels of antique furniture, a fireplace and good mountain cooking, with such classics as *civet de senglar* (pork stew) or a wild-goat version.

Arties

pop 490 / elev 1143m

Six kilometres east of Vielha, this village on the southern side of the highway sits astride the confluence of the Garona and Valarties Rivers. Among its cheerful stone houses is the Romanesque **Glèisa de Santa Maria**, with its three-storey belfry and triple apse.

Just nearby in a charming house atop the Valarties stream is **Hotel Besiberri** (☎ 973 64 08 29; www.hotelbesiberri.com; Carrèr deth Fòrt 4; s/d €75/96; 🕒 Dec-Apr & Jul-Sep; 💻 ⊠). This rustic place could almost be at home somewhere in Austria, with stone and timber trims. The staff can arrange for a babysitter when you're out wandering or skiing.

Another reason for coming to Arties is to eat at **Casa Irene** (☎ 973 64 43 64; Carrèr Major 20; meals €45-55; ⏰ Tue-Sun, closed Oct & May). The food at Casa Irene is sublime, featuring a tempting mix of sturdy local dishes and international flair.

Salardú

pop 460 / elev 1267m

Three kilometres east of Arties, Salardú's nucleus of old houses and narrow streets has largely resisted the temptation to sprawl. In May, June, October or November, however, you will find only a few hotels open. In the apse of the village's 12th- and 13th-century **Sant Andreu** church, you can admire the 13th-century *Crist de Salardú* crucifixion carving.

The town is a handy base for the Baqueira–Beret ski resort, 4km from here.

Alberg Era Garona (☎ 973 64 52 71; Carretera de Vielha s/n; dm student & under 26yr/26yr & over €22.45/26.30) is a large youth hostel built in local stone and slate. It has rooms of up to four beds, each with a bathroom.

Hotel deth Pais (☎ 973 64 58 36; Carrer de Santa Paula s/n; s/d €74/90; P) is in the middle of the original village; it's a pleasant slate-roofed hotel with straightforward rooms.

Baqueira–Beret

Baqueira (Vaquèira in Aranese), 3km east of Salardú, and Beret, 8km north of Baqueira, form Catalonia's premier **ski resort** (☎ 973 63 90 10; www.baquiera.es; day lift pass €42), favoured by the Spanish royal family, no less! Its good lift system gives access to 72 varied pistes totalling 104km (larger than any other Spanish resort), amid fine scenery at between 1500m and 2510m.

There's nowhere cheap to stay in Baqueira, and nowhere at all at Beret. Many skiers stay down the valley in Salardú, Arties or Vielha. If you want to rent an apartment, call the central booking number ☎ 973 63 90 00.

North of Vielha

The hills on either side of the highway up to the French frontier hide some exquisite countryside with fine walking trails and an assortment of curious villages.

ARRÒS, VILA & OTHER VILLAGES

Turn off the highway at Eth Pònt d'Arròs and climb a few kilometres into **Arròs** via Vila. This and other sleepy villages around here are full of charm with their stout old houses and rambling lanes. Rumbling tummies should call in at **El Raconet** (☎ 973 64 17 30; Carrèr de Crestalhera 3, Arròs; meals €25; ⏰ daily mid-Jul–mid-Sep & Dec–mid-Apr). Regulars keep coming back to this cosy stonewalled house converted into a charming country restaurant. The setting alone makes it worthwhile. Solid country cooking is on offer and the cooks have a special penchant for *bacalao* (dried and salted cod).

PLAN DERA ARTIGA DE LIN

Branch west, off the main highway at **Es Bòrdes**, a typical Aranese village, and keep following the road as it twists its way up into heavily wooded countryside. The drive alone is a real delight: follow the course of the Joèu stream, as you gain altitude, to reach the high mountain pastures of the Plan dera Artiga de Lin plain. Walking trails lead off into the tall forbidding mountains of the Aragonese Pyrenees, capped by the Pic d'Aneto (see p448).

Getting There & Around

BUS

Two Alsina Graells buses run daily between Barcelona and Vielha (€28.30, 5½ hours) via Lleida and El Pont de Suert. Lleida to Vielha (€11.59) takes three hours. From June to October, a daily Alsina Graells bus connects Barcelona and Vielha (€36.90, 7½ hours) via La Pobla de Segur, Llavorsí, the Espot turning on the C13, Port de la Bonaigua and Salardú.

A local bus service runs from four (at weekends) to nine times daily along the valley from Baqueira to Les or Pontaut (for Eth Pont de Rei) via Vielha and the intervening villages. Several others run from Vielha either to Baqueira or to Les/Pontaut. The trip from one end of the valley to the other takes up to an hour. A single ticket for any destination is €0.90 (or €8 for a book of 10 tickets – buy at the Conselh Generau Val d'Aran offices off Camin Reiau in Vielha).

CAR & MOTORCYCLE

The N230 Hwy from Lleida and El Pont de Suert reaches Aran through the 5.25km Túnel de Vielha, then heads north from Vielha to the French border at Eth Pont de Rei.

From the Vall de la Noguera Pallaresa, the C28 crosses the Port de la Bonaigua pass (2072m) – which is sometimes closed in winter – into Naut Aran, meeting the N230 Hwy at Vielha.

CENTRAL CATALONIA

Away from the beaches and mountains is a host of little-visited gems splashed across the Catalan hinterland. About halfway between Barcelona and the Pyrenees lies the graceful town of Vic, with its grand Plaça Major. Northwest of the capital, you can strike out for Manresa (just beyond Montserrat), Cardona (with its windy castle complex) and Solsona, en route to Lleida. An alternative route to Lleida takes you further south through the Conca de Barberà, littered with majestic medieval monasteries.

VIC

pop 38,320

Vic, with its attractive historic centre and some fine restaurants, dominates the flatlands of La Plana de Vic to the south of the Pyrenees. With some Roman remnants, medieval leftovers, a grand Gothic cloister, excellent art museum and reputation for fine food, it makes a rewarding day trip from Barcelona or first stop en route to the Pyrenees. The power of the bishops of Vic once stretched far and wide and explains the surprising number of churches crammed into the old town.

Information

Tourist office (☎ 93 886 20 91; www.victurisme.cat; Carrer de la Ciutat 4; 🕑 10am-2pm & 4-8pm Mon-Fri, 10am-2pm & 4-7pm Sat, 10am-1.30pm Sun)

Sights

Plaça Major, the largest of Catalonia's central squares, is lined with medieval, baroque and Modernista mansions. It's still the site of regular markets, hence its other name, Plaça del Mercadal. Around it swirl the serpentine streets of medieval Vic, lined by mansions, churches and chapels.

The **Catedral de Sant Pere** (☎ 93 886 44 49; Plaça de la Catedral s/n; admission €2; 🕑 10am-1pm & 4-7pm) is a neoclassical Goliath of gloomy taste, and flanked by a Romanesque bell tower. Inside, the dark, square-based pillars are lightened by murals by Josep Maria Sert (he had to do them twice because the first set was destroyed by fire in 1936). It is worth the admission fee to enter the Romanesque crypt, see the treasury rooms and wander into the stone lacework splendour of the Gothic cloister.

Across Carrer de Cloquer, the **Museu Episcopal** (☎ 93 886 93 60; www.museuepiscopalvic.com; Plaça del Bisbe Oliba 3; adult/child, student & senior €4/2; 🕑 10am-7pm Tue-Sat, 10am-2pm Sun Apr-Sep, 10am-1pm & 3-6pm Tue-Fri, 10am-7pm Sat, 10am-2pm Sun Oct-Mar) holds a marvellous collection of Romanesque and Gothic art, second only to the Museu Nacional d'Art de Catalunya collection (p337) in Barcelona. The Romanesque collection includes the vivid *Davallament*, a scene depicting the taking down of Christ from the cross. The Gothic collection contains works by such key figures as Lluís Borrassà and Jaume Huguet.

Festivals & Events

In the week running up to Palm Sunday, Plaça Major hosts the **Mercat del Ram** (Palm Market, a tradition that goes back to AD 875), selling palms and laurels. The square holds regular markets on Tuesdays and Saturdays. The Mercat del Ram is also the excuse for a major farm market, held out of the centre at the **El Sucre trade fair** (Carrer de la Llotja). The trade fair grounds host the annual **Fira d'Antiguitats de Vic** (www.fav.cat), one of Spain's biggest antiques markets, for a week over mid-August.

In September, the city hosts the **Mercat de Música Viva** (www.mmvv.net), a big if somewhat chaotic event over several days in which Catalan, national and foreign acts of various schools of Latin rock and pop get together to jam.

Sleeping & Eating

Vic is an easy day trip from Barcelona. The city is known for its disproportionate density of high-quality restaurants, and it's close enough to Barcelona for people from the big city to have an agreeable gourmet getaway.

Hostal Osona (☎ 93 883 28 45; Carrer de Remei 3; d €30) If you do need digs, this basic *hostal* has rooms with basin and shared showers in the hall. Otherwise there are three mid-level hotels.

La Taula (☎ 93 886 32 29, Plaça de Don Miguel de Clariana 4; meals €30; 🕑 daily Jul-Aug, Tue-Sat & lunch only Sun Oct-Jun, closed Feb) In a town that bristles with eateries, this is a bright star of traditional cooking, with fair prices and no pretensions (and considered by locals as one of the best in town). The *entrecot a la tòfona* (with truffles) is delicious. It has a *menú del día* for €11.

Melba (☎ 93 886 40 33; www.restaurantmelba.com; Carrer de Sant Miquel dels Sants 1; meals €35-40; 🕑 lunch & dinner Thu-Sat, lunch only Sun-Mon & Wed) Just off Plaça Major, Melba offers a mix of traditional Catalan and also more-creative dishes. It only uses freshly caught fish and local biofarm produce.

Getting There & Away

Regular *rodalies* (line C3) run from Barcelona (€4.10, up to 1½ hours).

AROUND VIC

Rupit

pop 330

An enchanting excursion northeast of Vic takes you 31km along the C153 to Rupit, a splendid old village set amid rugged grazing country. You cross a suspension footbridge to reach the village, which is full of quaint 17th-century houses, a baroque church and tucked-away squares. Especially enticing is Carrer del Fossar, which climbs the spine of the hill, along which part of the village is spread-eagled. Rupit is a good base for rambles in the area.

Getting here without your own vehicle is problematic. **Sagalés** (☎ 93 889 25 77) buses leave Carrer de Casp 30 in Barcelona at 3pm and 6pm Monday to Friday and at 11.20am on Saturday. Change buses in Vic. The trip (€9.50) takes about two hours from Barcelona.

MANRESA

pop 73,140

A big commercial centre in the Catalan heartland, Manresa was the scene of the first assembly of the nationalist Unió Catalanista (1897), which published the *Bases de Manresa,* a political manifesto for an autonomous Catalan state.

Not a great deal of the old town remains but you can't miss the great hulk that is the **Basílica de Santa Maria**, atop the Puig Cardener hill in the town centre. Its Gothic nave is second in size only to that of the cathedral in Girona. The unique Romanesque **Pont Vell**, whose eight arcs span the rather less-impressive Riu Cardener, was rebuilt after destruction in the civil war.

Rodalies from Barcelona (€4.10, 1¼ hours) via Terrassa run here regularly.

CARDONA

pop 5160

Long before arrival, you espy in the distance the outline of the impregnable 18th-century fortress high above Cardona, which itself lies next to the Muntanya de Sal (Salt Mountain). Until 1990 the salt mines were an important source of income.

The castle (follow the signs uphill to the **Parador Ducs de Cardona**, a lovely place to overnight) was built over an older predecessor. The single most remarkable element of the buildings is the lofty and spare Romanesque **Església de Sant Vicenç** (☎ 93 868 41 69; adult/child €3/2; ⏲ 10am-1pm & 3-6pm Tue-Sun Jun-Sep, 10am-1pm & 3-5pm Tue-Sun Oct-May). The bare stone walls were once covered in bright frescoes, some of which can be contemplated in the Museu Nacional d'Art de Catalunya (p337) in Barcelona.

Cardona is served by the Alsina Graells Barcelona–Manresa–Solsona bus route. Up to four run daily from Barcelona (€12, 1¾ hours) and 13 from Manresa (€4.10, 40 minutes). Up to four buses proceed to Solsona (€2.05, 25 minutes).

SOLSONA

pop 9000

They call the people of Solsona *matarucs* (donkey killers), which seems an odd tag until you hear what the townsfolk's favourite festive activity used to be.

Every February the high point of Solsona's Carnaval fun was the hoisting of a donkey, by the neck, up the town bell tower (Torre de les Hores). The donkey, literally scared to death, not unreasonably, would crap and piss on its way up, much to the delight of the drink-addled crowd below. To be hit by a glob of either substance was, they say, a sign of good fortune for the coming year. Nowadays the donkey is a water-spraying fake.

The **Catedral de Santa Maria** on Plaça de la Catedral (admission free; ⏲ 10am-1pm & 4-8pm) boasts Romanesque apses, a Gothic nave and a pretty cloister. Behind the cathedral is the neoclassical **Palau Episcopal** (☎ 973 48 21 01; Plaça del Palau; adult/senior & child €3/2; ⏲ 10am-1pm & 4-6pm Tue-Sat, 10am-2pm Sun Oct-Apr, 10am-1pm & 4.30-7pm Tue-Sat, 10am-2pm Sun May-Sep). Built in the 18th century, it houses a considerable collection of medieval art gathered from churches in the surrounding district.

Hotel Solsona Centre (☎ 973 48 43 40; www.hotelsolsonacentre.com; Carrer de Àngel Guimerà 3; s/d €39/48; P ❄ 💻) is a plain Jane of a place, but it's clean, secure and central.

Two to four Alsina Graells buses run daily from Barcelona (€14.10, two to 2½ hours) via Manresa (€6.20, 65 minutes) and Cardona to Solsona.

CATALAN TIPPLES

Avid tipplers will have come across a playful, relatively inexpensive bubbly called Freixenet. One of Spain's flagship exporters of *cava,* Freixenet is based at the heart of Catalonia's Penedès wine region, which alone produces the bulk of all Spain's sparkling white wines (see the Barcelona chapter, p368).

But Freixenet and bubbly are only the tip of the Catalan wineberg. Catalonia hosts 11 DO (Denominación de Origen) wine-producing zones and a remarkable variety of tipples. Less well-known outside Spain than Rioja drops, Catalan wines are full of pleasant surprises. The heavy, tannin-loaded, deep-coloured reds of El Priorat (www.doqpriorat.org) gained the much-desired DOC (Denominación de Origen Calificada) status long held only by Rioja wines in 2000. To further investigate El Priorat's wines, and wines from the adjacent Montsant DO region (which many in the know will tell you are just as good and much cheaper), head for the tourist office in **Falset** (☎ 977 83 10 23; www.priorat.org; Carrer de Sant Marcel 2) for information on local wine cellars. Falset, the capital of the Priorat area, offers some fine restaurant options too.

Catalonia's other DO wines come from points all over the region, spread as far apart as the Empordà area around Figueres in the north, and the Terra Alta zone around Gandesa in the southwest. The Penedès region pumps out almost two million hectolitres a year and thus doubles the combined output of the remaining DO regions.

Most of the grapes grown in Catalonia are native to Spain and include the white macabeo, garnacha and xarel lo (for white wines), and the black garnacha, monastrell and ull de llebre (hare's eye) red varieties. Foreign varieties (such as chardonnay, riesling, chenin blanc, cabernet sauvignon, merlot and pinot noir) are also widespread.

Beyond the Penedès region, look out for Raïmat, in the Costers del Segre DO area in Lleida province, for fine reds and a couple of notable whites. Good fortified wines come from around Tarragona; some pleasing fresh wines are also produced in the Empordà area in the north.

CONCA DE BARBERÀ

This hilly, green, wine-making district comes as a refreshing surprise in the otherwise drab flatlands of southwest Catalonia and makes an alternative route from Barcelona (or Tarragona) to Lleida and beyond. Vineyards and woods succeed one another across rolling green hills, studded by occasional medieval villages and monasteries.

Reial Monestir de Santa Maria de Poblet

The jewel in the crown is doubtless this imposing fortified **monastery** (☎ 977 87 00 89; adult/student €4.20/2.40; 🕒 10am-12.45pm & 3-6pm Mon-Sat, 10am-12.30pm & 3-5.30pm Sun & holidays mid-Mar–mid-Oct, 10am-12.45pm & 3-5.30pm Mon-Sat, 10am-12.30pm & 3-5.30pm Sun & holidays mid-Oct–mid-Mar), founded by Cistercian monks from southern France in 1151.

The walls of this abbey devoted to Santa Maria (a Unesco World Heritage site), were a defensive measure and also symbolised the monks' isolation from the vanities of the outside world. A grand portal gives access to a long uneven square, the Plaça Major, flanked by several dependencies including the small Romanesque **Capella de Santa Caterina**. The nearby **Porta Daurada** is so called because its bronze panels were overlaid with gold to suitably impress the visiting emperor Felipe II in 1564.

Once inside the **Porta Reial** (Royal Gate), flanked by hefty octagonal towers, you will be led through a worn Romanesque entrance to the grand cloister, of Romanesque origins but largely Gothic in style. With its peaceful fountain and pavilion, the two-level cloister is a marvellous haven. You will be led from the cloister to the head of the church, itself a typically tall and austere Cistercian Gothic creation, to witness the sculptural glory in alabaster that is the *retablo* and Panteón de los Reyes (Kings' Pantheon). The raised alabaster coffins, restored by Frederic Marès (see p323), contain such greats as Jaume I (the conqueror of Mallorca and Valencia) and Pere III.

Hostal Fonoll (☎ 977 87 03 33; www.hostalfonoll.com; Plaça de Ramon Berenguer IV 2; s/d €40/70; P ❄ 💻), opposite the monastery entrance, has simple but comfortable rooms. The dominating orange decor, especially in the bathrooms, is a little lurid! Or you can drop by for a coffee or food at the bar-restaurant downstairs. There's a Jacuzzi in the garden, access to a microwave and even a pool table.

Of six **Vibasa buses** (☎ 902 10 13 63; www.vibasa.es) from Tarragona to Montblanc, L'Espluga de Francolí (50 minutes) and on to Lleida on weekdays, three stop at the monastery (55 minutes, two make all stops on weekends). Regular trains from Barcelona (Ca4 regional line) stop at Montblanc and L'Espluga de Francolí (€8.20) – the monastery is a 40-minute walk from the latter.

Around Reial Monestir de Santa Maria de Poblet

It is worth spending time exploring the vicinity. **L'Espluga de Francolí**, 2.5km away from the monastery along a pleasant tree-lined country road that makes walking tempting, is a bright town with several small hotels. Above all else, it is home to the **Hostal del Senglar** (☎ 977 87 04 11; www.hostaldelsenglar.com; Plaça de Montserrat Canals 1; meals €30-35), an excellent Catalan restaurant for meat-lovers. The *filet de vedella al gust* (with a choice of tarragon, Armagnac or pepper sauce) is a thick, juicy slab of tender beef. The dining areas can be a little impersonal but the food and service are excellent. Kids can play in the gardens after lunch and the *hostal* also has 34 decent rooms if you need to stay overnight (single/double without breakfast €60/80).

More interesting still is **Montblanc**, 8km away. Surrounded by medieval battlements, this one-time royal residence is jammed with highlights, including a Gothic royal mansion and churches, as well as some vestiges of its Romanesque origins. The winding cross-country drive to **Prades** leads through lovely country.

More Monasteries

Two other fine Cistercian monasteries can be visited in the area. Following the AP7 motorway southwest from Vilafranca, take the AP2 fork about 18km west, then take exit 11 north for the medieval **Reial Monestir de Santes Creus** (Royal Monastery of the Holy Crosses; ☎ 977 63 83 29; Plaça de Jaume el Just s/n; adult/child €3.60/2.40, admission free Tue; 🕑 10am-1.30pm & 3-7pm Tue-Sun mid-Mar–mid-Sep, 10am-1.30pm & 3-5.30pm Tue-Sun mid-Sep–mid-Jan, 10am-1.30pm & 3-6pm Tue-Sun mid-Jan–mid-Mar). Cistercian monks moved in here in 1168 and from then on the monastery developed as a major centre of learning and a launch pad for the repopulation of the surrounding territory. Behind the Romanesque and Gothic facade lies a glorious 14th-century sandstone cloister, chapter house and royal apartments where the *comtes-reis* (count-kings; rulers of the joint state of Catalonia and Aragón) often stayed when they popped by during Holy Week. The church, begun in the 12th century, is a lofty Gothic structure in the French tradition. It's about 28km east of Montblanc.

North from Montblanc (take the C14 and then branch west along the LP2335), country roads guide you up through tough countryside into the low hills of the Serra del Tallat and towards yet another Cistercian complex, the **Reial Monestir de Santa Maria de Vallbona de les Monges** (Royal Monastery of St Mary of Vallbona of the Nuns; ☎ 973 33 02 66; adult/child €2.50/2; 🕑 10.30am-1.30pm & 4.30-6.45pm Tue-Sat, noon-1.30pm & 4.30-6.45pm Sun & holidays Mar-Oct, 10.30am-1.30pm & 4.30-6pm Tue-Sat, noon-1.30pm & 4.30-6pm Sun & holidays Nov-Feb), founded in the 12th century and where around 20 nuns still live and pray. You will be taken on a guided tour, probably in Catalan, in which it will become clear that it has even today not yet fully recovered from civil war damage.

A combined ticket to all these and the Poblet monastery is available for €7. For more information on the area around the monasteries, check out the Ruta del Cister (Cistercian Route) website (www.larutadel cister.info).

LLEIDA

pop 127,300

The hot, dry inland provincial capital Lleida (Castilian: Lérida) is a likeable place with a long and varied history. It's also the starting point of several beautiful scenic routes towards the Pyrenees. The old town is built around two hills, one topped by a mighty fortress-church and the other, a bit of a pimple by comparison, by another former fortress complex. The streets below offer a mix of curiosities. It's a funny place, with a slightly decrepit, rough feel of a Spain of yesteryear and a noticeable African migrant presence that is very much part of Spain's present.

Information

Centre d'Informació i Reserves (☎ 902 25 00 50; http://turisme.paeria.es; Carrer Major 31bis; 🕑 10am-2pm & 4-7pm Mon-Sat, 10am-1.30pm Sun & holidays) Turisme de Lleida provides information about the city.
Mossos d'Esquadra (regional police; ☎ 973 70 00 50; Carrer de Sant Hilari s/n)
Oficina Turisme de la Generalitat (☎ 973 24 88 40; Plaça de Ramon Berenguer IV; 🕑 10am-2pm & 3.30-7.30pm Mon-Fri, 10am-2pm Sat) For tips on the rest of Lleida province.

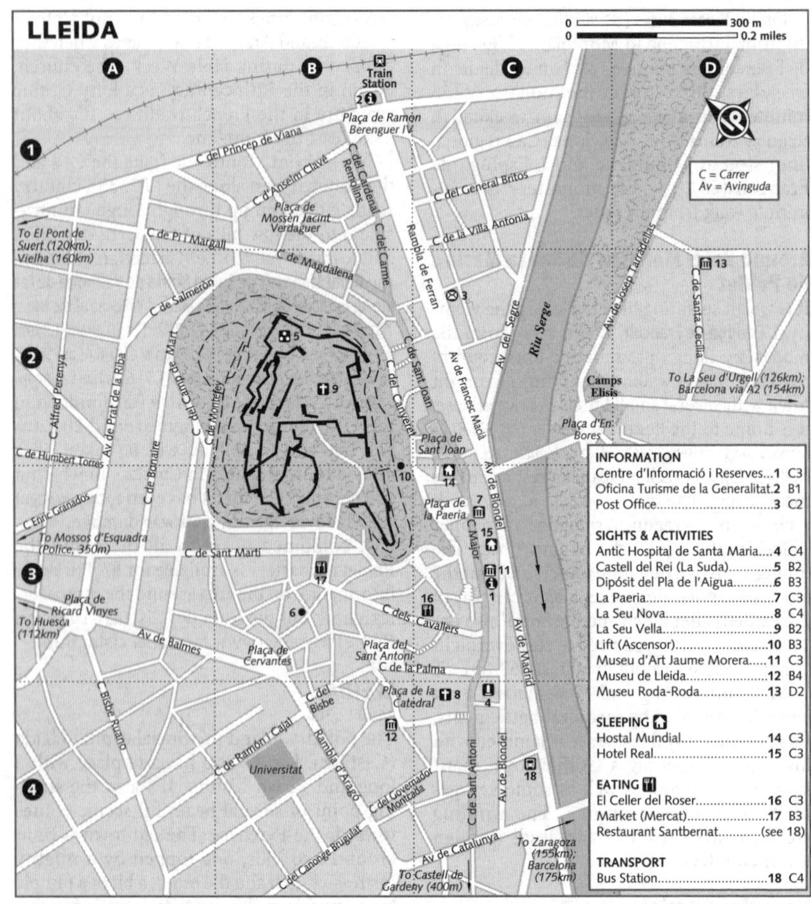

Post office (Rambla de Ferran 16; 8.30am-8.30pm Mon-Fri, 9.30am-2pm Sat)

Sights

LA SEU VELLA

Lleida's 'old cathedral', **La Seu Vella** (973 23 06 53; adult/under 7yr/senior & student €3/free/2; 10am-1.30pm & 3-5.30pm Tue-Sun Oct-May, 10am-1.30pm & 4-7.30pm Tue-Sun Jun-Sep) towers above everything else in position and grandeur. It stands within a *recinte* (compound) of defensive walls erected between the 12th and 19th centuries.

The main entrance to the **recinte** (admission free; 8am-9pm) is from Carrer de Monterey on its western side, but during the cathedral's opening hours you can use the extraordinarily ugly **ascensor** (lift; admission €0.20; 7am-9pm Sun-Wed, 7am-2am Thu-Sat) from above Plaça de Sant Joan.

The cathedral was built in sandy-coloured stone in the 13th to 15th centuries on the site of a former mosque (Lleida was under Islamic control from AD 719 to 1149). It's a masterpiece of the Transitional style, although it only recently recovered from 241 years' use as a barracks, which began as Felipe V's punishment for the city's opposition in the War of the Spanish Succession.

A 70m octagonal bell tower rises at the southwest end of the cloister, whose windows are laced with exceptional Gothic tracery. The spacious if austere interior, used as stables and dormitories during the military occupation, has a veritable forest of slender columns with carved capitals.

Above the cathedral are remains of the Islamic fortress and residence of the Muslim governors, known as the Castell del Rei or La Suda.

CASTELL DE GARDENY

The Knights Templar built a **monastery complex** (☎ 973 27 19 42; Turó de Gardeny; ⏰ 10am-1.30pm & 4-7.30pm Tue-Sat, to 6.30pm Mar-Apr & Oct, to 5.30pm Nov-Feb, 10am-2pm Sun May-Sep) here shortly after Lleida was taken from the Muslims in 1149. It was later expanded as a fortress in the 17th century. Today, you can still see the original Romanesque Església de Santa Maria de Gardeny and a hefty tower. An imaginative display lends insight into the monastic life of the Knights Templar.

MUSEU DE LLEIDA

This new **museum** (☎ 973 28 30 75; www.museudellleida.cat; Carrer de Sant Crist 1; adult/under 12yr /senior & student €3/free/1.50; ⏰ 10am-8pm Tue-Sat, 10am-2pm Sun Jun-Sep, 10am-7pm Tue-Sat, 10am-2pm Sun Oct-May) brings under one roof collections of artefacts that reach back to the Stone Age, and passing through a handful of Roman leftovers, medieval art and on to the 19th century.

CARRER MAJOR & AROUND

A 13th-century Gothic mansion, **La Paeria** has housed the city government almost since its inception. The 18th-century neoclassical **La Seu Nova** on Plaça de la Catedral was built when La Seu Vella was turned into a barracks. Opposite is the **Antic Hospital de Santa Maria** (Plaça de la Catedral), with some Gothic elements and beautiful courtyard. You can wander into the courtyard any time the premises are open and sometimes visit temporary exhibitions.

The **Museu d'Art Jaume Morera** (☎ 973 70 04 19; Carrer Major 31; admission free; ⏰ 11am-2pm & 5-8pm Tue-Sat, 11am-2pm Sun) is a varied collection of work by Lleida-associated artists.

OTHER SIGHTS

Lleida's 18th-century engineering wonder is the **Dipòsit del Pla de l'Aigua** (☎ 973 21 19 92; Carrer de Múrcia 10; adult/under 8yr/senior & student €1.60/free/1.05; ⏰ 11am-2pm Sat & Sun & hols), which long stored and supplied the city's drinking water via five public fountains. With 25 imposing stone pillars, it could hold nine million litres of water. No wonder they called it the Water Cathedral!

Chitty Chitty Bang Bang nostalgics might want to pop by the city's modest collection of classic cars and motorcycles, the **Museu Roda-Roda** (☎ 973 21 19 92; Carrer de Santa Cecília 22; admission free; ⏰ 11am-2pm & 5-8pm Tue-Sat, 11am-2pm Sun).

Sleeping

Hostal Mundial (☎ 973 24 27 00; Plaça de Sant Joan 4; s/d €24/42; **P**) Singles are smallish but have full bathrooms, which is not bad for a central little *hostal* like this one. Doubles are roomier and all are clean and neat.

Hotel Principal (☎ 973 23 08 00; www.hotelprincipal.com; Plaça de la Paeria 7; s/d €42/59) Right in the centre and once something of a grand old dame of the Lleida hotel business, this is a perfectly decent, sanitised version of what it once was.

Hotel Real (☎ 973 23 94 05; www.hotelreallleida.com; Avinguda de Blondel 22; s/d €68/107; **P** ❄ 💻) A modern mid-rise place with a pleasant garden, Hotel Real is aimed at business visitors and offers various classes of room. All are bright and clean, and the better ones have generous balconies. A couple of rooms have wheelchair access. Prices vary considerably depending on room and time of year.

Eating

Lleida is Catalonia's snail-eating capital. So many *cargols* are swallowed during the annual **Aplec del Cargol** (Snail Festival), held on a Sunday in early May, that some have to be imported.

Restaurant Santbernat (☎ 973 27 10 31; Carrer de Saracíbar; meals €20-30; ⏰ lunch & dinner Thu-Sun, lunch Mon; 👶) You would hardly expect to find a hearty eatery like this up on the 1st floor of the rather dour bus station. The star attractions are chargrilled meat dishes, which are sizzled up on a big open grill before your eyes. Choose anything from chicken (€7.50) to a juicy sirloin steak (€19.40). There's a set meal for kids (€16) too.

El Celler del Roser (☎ 973 23 90 70; Carrer dels Cavallers 24; meals €30; ⏰ lunch & dinner Mon-Sat, lunch Sun) While on the subject of snails, this classic specialises in the slithery delicacy, along with six possible permutations of its award-winning *bacallà* (cod).

Getting There & Away

BUS

For general bus-timetable information, call ☎ 973 26 85 00. Daily services by **Alsina Graells** include up to 14 buses (three on Sunday) to

Barcelona (€17.50, 2¼ to three hours); two to El Pont de Suert and Vielha (€11.59, 2¾ hours); one (except Sunday) to La Pobla de Segur, Sort, Llavorsí and Esterri d'Àneu (€18.35, three hours); and two to La Seu d'Urgell (€15.60, 2½ hours).

CAR & MOTORCYCLE

The quickest routes to Barcelona, Tarragona and Zaragoza are by the AP2, but you can avoid tolls by taking the A2 to Zaragoza or Barcelona or the N240 Hwy to Tarragona. The main northward roads are the C14 to La Seu d'Urgell, the N230 to Vielha and the N240 to Barbastro and Huesca (in Aragón).

TRAIN

Lleida is on the Barcelona–Madrid line. Up to 34 trains, ranging from slow regionals (3½ hours) to the high-speed AVE run daily to/from Barcelona, taking as little as one hour in the new Avant class trains (which costs half the price as the AVE and is almost as fast. Second-class one-way fares range from €9.60 to €20.40 (€42.10 in the AVE). These same trains proceed to Madrid via Zaragoza.

MONTSEC

This hilly range 65km north of Lleida is the main stage for hang-gliders and ultralights in Catalonia. It is also a popular area for walking, caving and climbing.

The focal point is **Àger**, a village in the valley of the same name. If coming via Balaguer, you'll see it to the northeast as you reach the top of **Coll d'Àger** (912m). The village is draped like a mantle over a hill, protruding from the top of which is the intriguing ruin of the **Església de Sant Pere**.

Montsec has a half-dozen take-off points, including one at the Sant Alís peak (1678m), the highest in the range. **Volàger** (☎ 973 32 02 30; www.volager.com; Camí de Castellnou s/n), based in Bellpuig, offers hang-gliding courses here and provides all the equipment. You can go hang-gliding with the school for a day (€80), while a full six-day course comes to €650.

A choice location for walkers and climbers is the stunning **Congost de Mont-Rebei**, a narrow gorge of 80m-high rock walls at the western end of the Montsec range. The Riu Noguera Ribagorçana flows into the gorge from the north, along the border with Aragón. Caves along the foot of the gorge, and around the dam to the south, attract speleologists.

You can stay at one of a handful of *cases de pagès* or a *hostal*. About the only way to get into and around the area is with your own wheels.

COSTA DAURADA

South of Sitges (p364) stretches the Costa Daurada (Golden Coast), a series of mostly quiet resorts with unending broad beaches along a mainly flat coast, capped by the delta of the mighty Riu Ebre (Ebro), which protrudes 20km out into the Mediterranean. Along the way is the old Roman capital of Tarragona, and the modern extravaganza of Port Aventura – Catalonia's answer to EuroDisney.

VILANOVA I LA GELTRÚ

pop 63,200

Six minutes west of Sitges by train, Vilanova is home to the culinary delicacy of *xató* (an almond-and-hazelnut sauce used on various dishes, particularly seafood), the much sought-after actor Sergi López and an esplanade lined by a trio of beautiful broad beaches.

There's a **tourist office** (☎ 93 815 45 17; www.vilanovaturisme.net; Passeig del Carme s/n; 🕒 10am-8pm Mon-Sat, 10am-2pm Sun) for information.

A few blocks inland from the beaches is Vilanova's main attraction, the **Museu del Ferrocarril** (Railway Museum; ☎ 93 815 84 91; Plaça d'Eduard Maristany; adult/student & child €5/4; 🕒 10.30am-2.30pm Tue-Fri & Sun, 10.30am-2.30pm & 4-6.30pm Sat Sep-Jul, 11am-2pm & 5-8pm daily Aug), in the 19th-century installations for the maintenance of steam trains, next to the train station. The collection of steam locomotives attracts kids of all ages.

Vilanova i la Geltrú stages a riotous Carnaval in February that lasts for 13 days. One of the high points is the **Batalla de Caramels** (Battle of the Sweets), when townsfolk in costume launch more than 100,000kg of sweeties at one another!

It's easy enough to pop down to Vilanova for the day from Barcelona or Sitges but there is one serious reason for hanging out a little longer…

Hotel Cèsar (☎ 93 815 11 25; www.hotelcesar.net; Carrer d'Isaac Peral 4-8; r €113-150; ☒ ☐ ☒) is the town's top hotel. It's set in a leafy, tranquil part of town just back from the waterfront. It offers a series of double rooms and suites in a variety of categories. The best rooms have their own computers with broadband internet access. Saunter to the sauna, or opt for a massage. The hotel is also home to **La Fitorra** (meals €35-40; Wed-Sun, dinner only Tue), one of the senior denizens of local cooking.

The town is just down the *rodalies* (line C2) from Sitges. From Barcelona the fare will set you back €2.60.

ALTAFULLA

pop 4140

Roman citizens of Tarragona who used to holiday here would no doubt still be tempted. A cheekily pretty medieval core, all cream and whitewashed walls with rose-coloured stone portals and windows, is capped by a 13th-century **castle**. Just 10km east of Tarragona, Altafulla was converted into a fortified settlement in the wake of the Muslim invasion.

Altafulla's broad **beach** (about 2km away on the other side of the freeway) is backed by a row of cheerful single-storey houses known as the **Botigues de Mar** (Sea Shops). Until well into the 19th century they served as warehouses but have since been converted into houses – many available for holiday let.

In the old part of town, **Alberg Casa Gran** (977 65 07 79; Plaçeta 12; dm student & under 26yr/26yr & over €19/22) is one of the region's more enchantingly placed youth hostels. Occupying a fine old mansion with a terrace, it even incorporates a tower belonging to the old town walls.

Housed in an 18th-century mansion built by *indianos* (locals who had made their fortune in the Americas) in the old town, **Faristol** (977 65 00 77; Carrer de Sant Martí 5, Altafulla; meals €30; lunch & dinner Jun-Sep, dinner Fri, lunch & dinner Sat & Sun Oct-May) offers traditional Catalan cooking with an emphasis on seafood. There are also some surprises thrown in, such as tandoori. Upstairs are five pretty rooms (single/double €50/60).

A host of local trains run to Altafulla from Tarragona (€1.60, 10 minutes).

TARRAGONA

pop 134,160

A seemingly eternally sunny port city, Tarragona is easily Catalonia's most important Roman site, starting with its amphitheatre. The medieval city, dominated by a beautiful cathedral that is surrounded by a compact warren of winding lanes, is another trip on its own. You could spend a day getting lost within its defensive walls. Or you might just want to flop on one of the town beaches. There are plenty of tempting food options, especially by the port, where night owls will also find an array of bars heaving into the wee hours.

History

Tarragona was first occupied by the Romans, who called it Tarraco, in 218 BC. In 27 BC Augustus made it the capital of his new Tarraconensis province (roughly all modern Spain) and stayed until 25 BC, directing campaigns in Cantabria and Asturias. Tarragona was abandoned when the Muslims arrived in AD 714, but reborn as the seat of a Christian archbishopric in 1089. Today its rich Roman remains and fine medieval cathedral make it an absorbing place.

Orientation

The main street is Rambla Nova, which runs roughly northwest from a clifftop overlooking the Mediterranean. A couple of blocks to the east, and parallel, is Rambla Vella, which marks the beginning of the old town and, incidentally, follows the line of the Via Augusta, the Roman road from Rome to Cádiz.

The train station is about 500m southwest of Rambla Nova, near the seafront, and the bus station is about 2km inland, just to the northwest, off Plaça Imperial de Tàrraco.

Information

Ciberespai (977 24 57 64; Carrer d'Estanislau Figueres 58; per hr €1; 9am-11pm Mon-Fri, 10am-11pm Sat & Sun) Internet access.

Guàrdia Urbana (977 24 03 45; Carrer de Prat de Riba 37) Police.

Hospital Joan XXIII (977 25 22 85; Carrer del Dr Mallafre Guasch 4)

Information kiosks (10am-2pm Sat & Sun Apr-Sep) These are scattered about town.

Post office (Plaça de Corsini; 8.30am-8.30pm Mon-Fri, 9.30am-2pm Sat)

Regional tourist office (977 23 34 15; Carrer de Fortuny 4; 9am-2pm & 4-6.30pm Mon-Fri, 9am-2pm Sat)

Tourist office (977 25 07 95; www.tarragonaturisme.cat; Carrer Major 39; 9am-9pm Mon-Sat, 10am-3pm Sun Jul-Sep, 10am-2pm & 4-7pm Mon-Sat, 10am-2pm Sun & holidays year-round)

Sights & Activities

Pick up the handy *Ruta Arqueològica Urbana* brochure from the tourist office. It details more than 30 locations throughout the old town where Roman remains can be viewed,

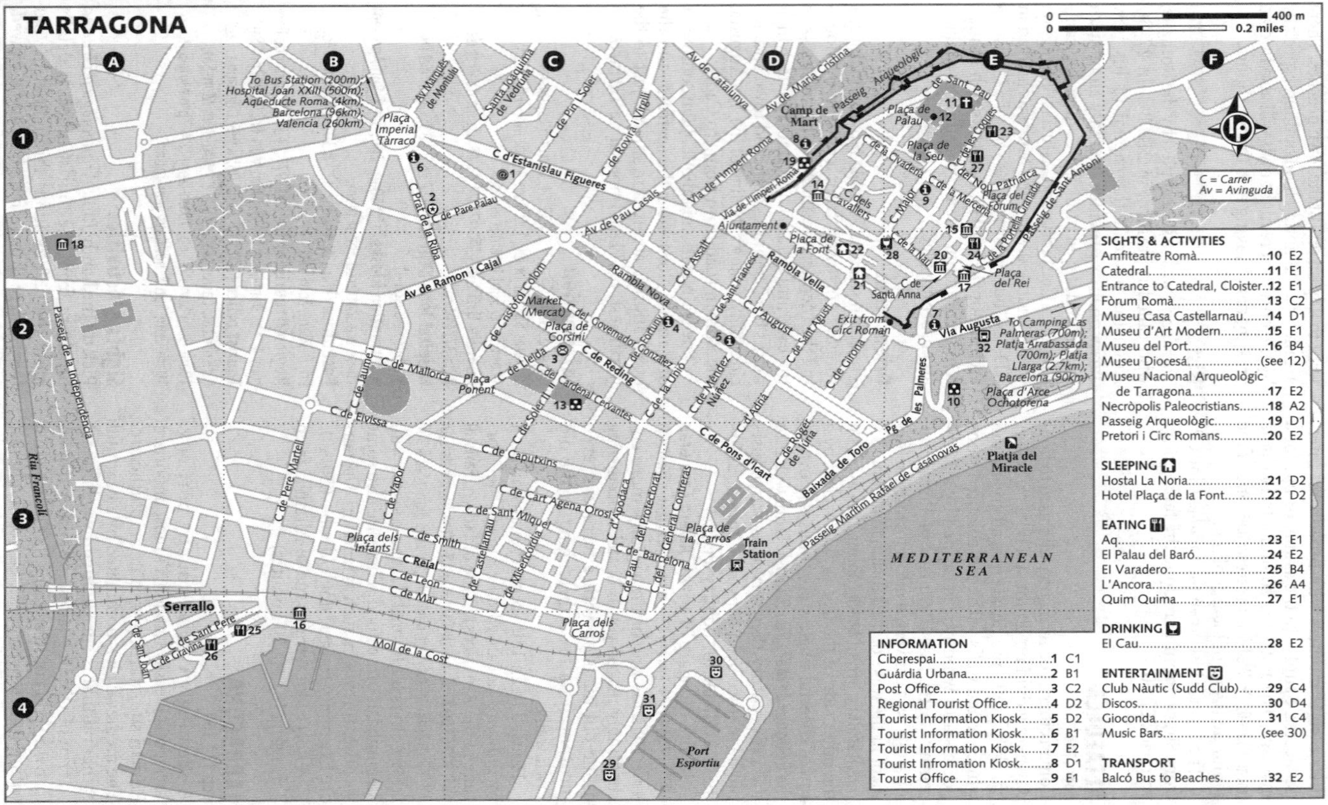

TARRAGONA

C = Carrer
Av = Avinguda

INFORMATION
Ciberespai....1 C1
Guàrdia Urbana....2 B1
Post Office....3 C2
Regional Tourist Office....4 D2
Tourist Information Kiosk....5 D2
Tourist Information Kiosk....6 B1
Tourist Information Kiosk....7 E2
Tourist Infromation Kiosk....8 D1
Tourist Office....9 E1

SIGHTS & ACTIVITIES
Amfiteatre Romà....10 E2
Catedral....11 E1
Entrance to Catedral, Cloister..12 E1
Fòrum Romà....13 C2
Museu Casa Castellarnau....14 D1
Museu d'Art Modern....15 E1
Museu del Port....16 B4
Museu Diocesá....(see 12)
Museu Nacional Arqueològic de Tarragona....17 E2
Necròpolis Paleocristians....18 A2
Passeig Arqueològic....19 D1
Pretori i Circ Romans....20 E2

SLEEPING
Hostal La Noria....21 D2
Hotel Plaça de la Font....22 D2

EATING
Aq....23 E1
El Palau del Baró....24 E2
El Varadero....25 B4
L'Ancora....26 A4
Quim Quima....27 E1

DRINKING
El Cau....28 E2

ENTERTAINMENT
Club Nàutic (Sudd Club)....29 C4
Discos....30 D4
Gioconda....31 C4
Music Bars....(see 30)

TRANSPORT
Balcó Bus to Beaches....32 E2

some of them in shops and restaurants. If they are not too busy with customers, shop owners are generally happy for individuals to drop by and take a look.

CATEDRAL

Sitting grandly at the top of the old town, Tarragona's **cathedral** (☎ 977 23 86 85; Pla de la Seu; admission €3.50; 🕑 10am-1pm & 4-7pm Mon-Sat mid-Mar–May, 10am-7pm Mon-Sat Jun–mid-Oct, 10am-5pm Mon-Sat mid-Oct–mid-Nov, 10am-2pm Mon-Sat mid-Nov–mid-Mar) is a treasure house deserving 1½ hours or more of your time, if you're to do it justice. Built between 1171 and 1331 on the site of a Roman temple, it combines Romanesque and Gothic features, as typified by the main facade on Pla de la Seu. The entrance is by the cloister on the northwest flank of the building.

The cloister has Gothic vaulting and Romanesque carved capitals, one of which shows rats conducting what they imagine to be a cat's funeral…until the cat comes back to life! The rooms off the cloister house the **Museu Diocesà**, with an extensive collection extending from Roman hairpins to some lovely 12th- to 14th-century polychrome woodcarvings of a breastfeeding Virgin.

The interior of the cathedral, over 100m long, is Romanesque at the northeast end and Gothic at the southwest. The aisles are lined with 14th- to 19th-century chapels and hung with 16th- and 17th-century tapestries from Brussels. The arm of St Thecla, Tarragona's patron saint, is normally kept in the **Capella de Santa Tecla** on the southeastern side. The choir in the centre of the nave has 15th-century carved walnut stalls. The marble main **altar** was carved in the 13th century with scenes from the life of St Thecla.

MUSEU D'HISTÒRIA DE TARRAGONA

This **museum** (www.museutgn.com; adult/concession per site €2.45/1.25, incl all MHT elements €9.25/4.60; 🕑 9am-9pm Mon-Sat, 9am-3pm Sun Easter-Sep, 9am-7pm Mon-Sat, 10am-3pm Sun & holidays Oct-Easter) comprises four separate Roman sites (which since 2000 together have constituted a Unesco World Heritage site) and a 14th-century noble mansion, which now serves as the **Museu Casa Castellarnau** (☎ 977 24 22 20; Carrer dels Cavallers 14).

Start with the **Pretori i Circ Romans** (☎ 977 23 01 71; Plaça del Rei), which includes part of the vaults of the Roman circus, where chariot races were held. The circus, 300m long, stretched from here to beyond Plaça de la Font to the west. Nearby Plaça del Fòrum was the location of the provincial forum and political heart of Tarraconensis province. Near the beach is the well-preserved **Amfiteatre Romà** (☎ 977 24 25 79; Plaça d'Arce Ochotorena), where gladiators battled each other, or wild animals, to the death. In its arena are the remains of 6th- and 12th-century churches built to commemorate the martyrdom of the Christian bishop Fructuosus and two deacons, who, they say, were burnt alive here in AD 259.

Southeast of Carrer de Lleida are remains of the **Fòrum Romà** (☎ 977 24 25 01; Carrer del Cardenal Cervantes), dominated by several imposing columns. The northwest half of this site was occupied by a judicial basilica (where legal disputes were settled), from which the rest of the forum stretched downhill to the southwest. Linked to the site by a footbridge is another excavated area with a stretch of Roman street. This forum was the hub of public and religious life for the Roman town. The discovery in 2006 of remains of the foundations of a temple to Jupiter, Juno and Minerva (the major triumvirate of gods at the time of the Roman republic) suggests the forum was much bigger and more important than previously assumed.

The **Passeig Arqueològic** is a peaceful walk around part of the perimeter of the old town between two lines of city walls; the inner ones are mainly Roman, while the outer ones were put up by the British during the War of the Spanish Succession.

MUSEU NACIONAL ARQUEOLÒGIC DE TARRAGONA

This carefully presented **museum** (☎ 977 23 62 09; www.mnat.es; Plaça del Rei 5; adult/senior & under 18yr/student €2.40/free/1.20; 🕑 9.30am-8.30pm Tue-Sat, 10am-2pm Sun & holidays Jun-Sep, 9.30am-1.30pm & 3.30-7pm Tue-Sat, 10am-2pm Sun & holidays Oct-May) gives further insight into Roman Tarraco. Exhibits include part of the Roman city walls, frescoes, sculpture and pottery. A highlight is the large, almost complete *Mosaic de Peixos de la Pineda,* showing fish and sea creatures. In the section on everyday arts you can admire ancient fertility aids including an outsized stone penis, symbol of the god Priapus.

Admission entitles you to enter the museum at the **Necròpolis Paleocristians** (☎ 977 21 11 75; Avinguda de Ramón i Cajal 80; adult/senior & under 18yr €2.40/free with Museu Nacional Arqueológic de Tarragona; 🕑 10am-8pm Tue-Sat, 10am-2pm Sun Jul-Sep, 10am-5.30pm Tue-Sat, 10am-2pm Sun Oct-Jun). This large Christian

TARRAGONA ALL IN ONE

The Tarragona Card (€14/19/24 for 24/48/72 hours) gives you free entry to all museums and other sights in the city, free local buses and a host of discounts on anything from participating restaurants to taxis. You also receive a guidebook on the city. For the pass to be worth your while, you have to be pretty sure you want to visit virtually everything in town.

cemetery of late-Roman and Visigothic times is on Passeig de la Independència on the western edge of town and boasts some surprisingly elaborate tombs. Unfortunately only its small museum is open.

MUSEU D'ART MODERN

This modest **art gallery** (☎ 977 23 50 32; Carrer de Santa Anna 8; admission free; ⏰ 10am-8pm Tue-Sat, 11am-2pm Sun & holidays) is at its most interesting when temporary exhibitions take place.

MUSEU DEL PORT

Down by the waterfront, this curious **museum** (☎ 977 25 94 42; Refugi 2 Moll de la Costa; adult/student €1.80/1.20; ⏰ 10am-2pm & 5-8pm Tue-Sat, 11am-2pm Sun & holidays Jun-Sep, 10am-2pm & 4-7pm Tue-Sat, 11am-2pm Sun & holidays Oct-May) is housed in a dockside shed. There's not a lot to it; there are some displays tracing the history of the port from Roman times (in Catalan and Castilian only), a few model boats and one or two other seafaring items.

PONT DEL DIABLE

The so-called Devil's Bridge is actually the **Aqüeducte Romà** (admission free; ⏰ 9am-dusk), yet another marvel left by the Romans. It sits, somewhat incongruously, in the leafy rough just off the AP7 freeway, which leads into Tarragona (near where it intersects with the N240). It is a fine stretch of two-tiered aqueduct (217m long and 27m high), along which you can totter to the other side. Bus 5 to Sant Salvador from Plaça Imperial de Tàrraco, running every 10 to 20 minutes, will take you to the vicinity, or park in one of the lay-bys marked on either side of the AP7, just outside the freeway toll gates.

BEACHES

The town beach, **Platja del Miracle**, is reasonably clean but can get terribly crowded. **Platja Arrabassada**, 1km northeast across the headland, is longer, and **Platja Llarga**, beginning 2km further out, stretches for about 3km. Buses 1 and 9 from the Balcó stop on Via Augusta go to both (€1.10). You can get the same buses from along Rambla Vella and Rambla Nova.

Sleeping

Tarragona has about 25 hotels, most of them scattered about newer parts of town and uninspiring. There's a handful of good choices in or near the old town.

Hostal La Noria (☎ 977 23 87 17; Plaça de la Font 53; s/d €30/48) For a bargain-basement position right on the old town's main square, you can't do much better than these corner digs. Rooms are simple enough but have their own attached clean bathroom, and those with a balcony assure you a window on old Tarragona's street life.

Camping Las Palmeras (☎ 977 20 80 81; www.laspalmeras.com; sites per 2-person tent & car €44; P ⓧ ⓧ) This cheerful camping ground lies at the far end of Platja Llarga (3km northeast of Tarragona) and is one of the better of eight camping grounds scattered behind the beaches northeast of the city. A big pool stretches out amid leafy parkland just back from the beach. The camping ground enjoys a 1.5km stretch of seaside frontage and untouched coastal woodland nearby. Windsurfing and kitesurfing classes are also on offer.

Hotel Plaça de la Font (☎ 977 24 61 34; www.hotelpdelafont.com; Plaça de la Font 26; s/d €55/70; ⓧ) A notch up and also on the town square is this crisp *pensión*. Rooms, although a trifle cramped, have a pleasing modern look, with soft colours, sturdy beds and, in the case of half of the rooms, little balconies overlooking the square.

Eating

Aq (☎ 977 21 59 54; Carrer de les Coques 7; meals €35-40; ⏰ Tue-Sat) is a bubbly designer haunt with stark colour contrasts (black, lemon and cream linen), slick lines and intriguing international plays on traditional cooking, such as *garrí al forn amb timbal d'albergínia i tomaquet* (oven-cooked suckling pig with aubergine and tomato timbal).

Quim Quima (☎ 977 25 21 21; Carrer de les Coques 1bis; meals €35, menú del día €14.90; ⏰ lunch Tue-Thu, lunch & dinner Fri & Sat) This renovated medieval mansion makes a marvellous setting for a meal. Huddle up to bare stone wall or opt for the shady little courtyard. The playful menu is wide-ranging, including sausage-and-cheese crêpes and lasagne.

El Palau del Baró (☎ 977 24 14 64; www.palaudelbaro.com; Carrer de Santa Anna 3; meals €35-45; ⏰ lunch & dinner Tue-Sat, lunch Sun) The Baron's palace, a centuries-old mansion, provides a romantic, sumptuous 19th-century setting. Dishes are served with aplomb, and range from paella to various fish options. The *confit d'ànec a la salsa d'oporto i fruits del bosc* (duck slices in a sauce of port and wild fruit) is an intense flavour hit.

A PASSION FOR HUMAN CONSTRUCTION

Miquel Ferret (37) has always had a passion for building castles. Human ones. Raised in Vilafranca del Penedès, he has been president of that town's champion *colla* (team or club, also known as the greens because of the shirts they wear) of *castellers* (human-castle builders) since early 2008.

'I entered the *colla* when I was 14, although I had followed the *castellers* from when I was a little boy,' he says, eyes twinkling. 'My great grandfather was a *casteller* with the Xiquets de Valls (from the town of Valls, the epicentre of *castell* culture). In August especially, they would tour, hired to perform at village festivals around central-southern Catalonia.'

With roots in the 18th century, this unique sport requires hundreds of participants to create complex human structures of up to 10 storeys! There are various ways of constructing a *castell:* those built without a *pinya, folre* or *manilles* (extra rings of support respectively for the first, second and third storeys) are tricky and termed *net* (clean). A completed *castell* is signalled by the child at the top (the *canalla* or *anxaneta*) raising their arm, a cue for tumultuous applause and cheering. A *castell* that manages to dismantle itself without collapsing in a heap is *descarregat*. Especially difficult is a *pilar,* a tower of one person per storey, which has a record of eight storeys. The big castles, like a *tres de deu* (three by 10), require around 600 people at the base *(pinya)*, 100 on the second floor *(folre)*, and 40 on the third level *(manilles)*.

The golden age of *castells* was in the 1860s. In the 1900s, interest declined as crisis hit and people left the country for the city to work. But there weren't just economic reasons. The rise of other sports contributed. It's easier to form teams of 11 to play football than get together 300 or more people to create a *colla*!

So what does it take to be a *casteller*? Ferret suggests 'strength, balance, courage and *seny* (good sense). It's like architecture. You have buttresses, a vault at the top. Each level has to be balanced and move as little as possible. I climb to the *manilles* – it's a nice position'. He adds, 'People do fall. But falls are cushioned by the *pinya.* What must never happen is that someone hits the ground.'

What about less-experienced *colles*?

'They are more dangerous!'

The death of a young girl *anxaneta* in a fall in 2006 unleashed heated debate on whether or not *anxanetes* (at least eight years old) should wear head protection. Says Ferret: 'A specially designed helmet is being examined, although many *colles* were initially against the idea. But others were already using some sort of helmet. The kids that climb to the top have to be very sharp, psychologically strong and alert.'

The line between a *colla* and spectators can be thin.

'Onlookers can join in the *pinya,*' Ferret notes. 'And if you come along for practice sessions for a few months, you'll soon be able to climb up to be part of the *castell* itself. It's easy to become part of a *colla*. No one is excluded for religious, political, economic or linguistic reasons. Or age. There are five-year-olds and 90-year-olds in the *colles*. The short and the tall, thin people and fat – there's a place for everyone.'

The top four *colles* (there are some 55) are the two from Valls (Joves Xiquets and Colla Vella), the Castellers de Vilafranca and the Minyons de Terrassa.

'The best place to feel the passion that team rivalry can unleash is in Valls,' says Ferret. 'There are no hooligans, but you can feel moments of great tension between supporters of the two Valls teams.'

Every two years a championship competition is held in Tarragona's bullring. The most successful club, the Castellers de Vilafranca, took their fourth successive title in 2008. The next one will be in October 2010. Otherwise, these and many other teams turn up at *festes* all over Catalonia.

L'Ancora (Carrer de Trafalgar 25; meals €25-30; 1pm-1am) and its sister establishment **El Varadero** (Carrer de Trafalgar 13) brim with mouth-watering seafood and open late. Go for a selection of dishes, which might include *tigres* (stuffed, breaded and fried mussels), *ostrón* (fat oyster) and *cigalas a la plancha* (grilled crayfish). You can sit inside (head upstairs) or take a seat at one of the outdoor tables. Hour-long queues at midnight on summer weekends are not unheard-of.

The quintessential Tarragona seafood experience can be had in Serrallo, the town's fishing port. About a dozen bars and restaurants here sell the day's catch, and on summer weekends in particular the place is packed. Most places close their kitchens by about 10.30pm.

Drinking & Entertainment

The main concentration of nightlife is the **bars** and **clubs** along the waterfront at the Port Esportiu (marina), and in some of the streets in front of the train station, such as along Carrer de la Pau del Protectorat.

El Cau (977 23 12 12; www.elcau.net; Carrer de Trinquet Vell 2; daily) Set in one of the vaults of the Roman circus, this is the best place for dancing in central Tarragona. Various DJs and acts perform on most nights (usually from midnight), ensuring that no two evenings are the same. Check the website for which maestro is on that particular night.

At the marina, head for the terrace at the **Club Nàutic**, where **Sudd Club** (admission free; 10pm-4am Thu-Sat) spins an electronic music dance session with views out to sea!

Gioconda (admission €8; 10pm-5am Wed-Sun) is one of the more popular clubs at the marina, bursting with fevered dancers on weekends especially.

Getting There & Away

Lying on main routes south from Barcelona, Tarragona is well connected. The train is generally the much easier option.

BUS

Bus services run to Barcelona, Valencia, Zaragoza, Madrid, Alicante, Pamplona, the main Andalucian cities, Andorra and the north coast. As a rule though, you are better off with the train.

TRAIN

At least 38 regional and long-distance trains per day run to/from Barcelona's Passeig de Gràcia via Sants. The cheapest fares (for regional and Catalunya Express trains) cost €5.15 to €5.80 and the journey takes one to 1½ hours. Long-distance trains (such as Talgo, Arco and Euromed trains) are faster but more expensive – as much as €17.70 in tourist (standard) class. Many of these trains continue on to Valencia, Alicante and a couple into Andalucía. Half a dozen trains connect with Lleida. High-speed Avant-class trains to Lleida and AVE trains on the Barcelona–Madrid line call at the new Camp de Tarragona station (about 20 minutes out of town by shuttle bus from the bus station).

PORT AVENTURA

One of Spain's most popular funfair adventure parks, **Port Aventura** (902 20 20 41, 902 20 22 20; www.portaventura.es; adult/senior & 5-12yr mid-Sep–mid-Jun €42/33.50, 2-day tickets €63/50.50; 10am-midnight Jul-Aug, 10am-8pm Easter-Jun & Sep, 10am-7pm Oct) lies 7km west of Tarragona. It makes an amusing day out, especially if you have children in tow. The park has plenty of spine-tingling rides and other attractions, such as the Furius Baco (in which they claim you experience the fastest acceleration of any ride in the world) and Hurakan Condor (at 100m one of the highest amusement park rides in Europe, and quite a drop!), spread across themed areas ranging from the Wild West to Polynesia.

Opening days and hours from November to March vary greatly but usually on weekends and public holidays only.

In addition to the main area, Port Aventura Park, the complex includes two hotels and **Caribe Aquatic Park** (adult/child & senior €21.50/17.50; 10am-7pm Jul-Aug, 10am-6pm mid-May–Jun & 1st half of Sep, 10am-5pm late Mar–mid-May), a waterworld with all sorts of wet rides, including some fear-inducing waterslides with more twists and turns than a Ken Follett mystery.

Trains run to Port Aventura's own station, about a 1km walk from the site, several times a day from Tarragona (€1.30 to €1.60, 10 to 15 minutes) and Barcelona (from €5.80 to €6.40, around 1½ hours). By road, take exit 35 from the AP7, or the N340 from Tarragona.

REUS & AROUND

pop 104,800

Reus was, for much of the second half of the 19th century, the second-most important city in Catalonia and a major export centre of textiles and brandy. Birthplace of Gaudí, it boasts a series of Modernista mansions. The **tourist**

office (☎ 902 36 02 00; turisme.reus.net; Plaça Mercadal 3; ⏲ 9.30am-8pm Mon-Sat, 10am-2pm Sun) can provide a map guiding you to 30-odd Modernista mansions around the town centre. The tourist office organises guided visits (sometimes in English and French) to some of the most interesting of these houses, for which you need to book in advance. Regular trains connect Reus with Tarragona (€1.40 to €1.60, 15 to 20 minutes).

About 35km northwest of Reus, above the pretty mountain village of **Siurana**, stand the remains of one of the last Islamic castles to fall to the reconquering Christians. To its west rise the rocky walls of the Serra de Montsant range, and the area attracts rock climbers and walkers. In Siurana you could stay in **Can Roig** (☎ 977 82 14 50; Carrer Major 6; d €38), a charming, refurbished stone house (one of two lodging options) in the middle of the village.

From Cornudella de Montsant, 9km from Siurana, a narrow and picturesque road (the TV7021) hugs the rugged southern face of the Montsant westwards to **Escaladei**, located in a valley below the mountain range, which produces some fine El Priorat reds. The evocative ruins of the **Cartoixa d'Escaladei** (☎ 977 82 70 06; adult/senior & under 6yr/student €3/free/2; ⏲ 10am-1.30pm & 4-7.30pm Tue-Sun Jun-Sep, 10am-1.30pm & 3-5.30pm Tue-Sun Oct-May), a 12th-century monastery complex, are a 1km walk out of the village.

To the southeast, 4km west of the village of **Riudecanyes**, stands the **Castell-Monestir de Sant Miquel d'Escornalbou** (☎ 977 83 40 07; adult/student & senior €3/2, weekends & holidays €5.10/4.10; ⏲ 10am-1.30pm & 4-7.30pm Tue-Sun Jun-Sep, 10am-1.30pm & 3-5.30pm Tue-Sun Oct-May). Dating from 1153, much of the castle-monastery complex is in ruins; parts have been rebuilt but hardly to exacting historical criteria. The most interesting elements are the church (from the 12th and 13th centuries), cloister and chapter house. You will be taken on a compulsory guided tour, probably in Catalan, of about half an hour.

There is no public transport to Siurana, Escaladei or Castell-Monestir de Sant Miquel d'Escornalbou.

CAMBRILS

pop 29,100

A sprawling tourist town (more or less an extension of the high-density tourist ghetto of Salou), inspired by the place's long beaches, has developed around the still-pretty original old village and fishing port, 18km southwest of Tarragona.

Although sun and sand are uppermost in many people's minds, the place rewards a bit of exploration, with several medieval towers, some Roman remains, the busy fishing port and, above all, something of a reputation as a culinary magnet.

For good seafood, try bustling **La Roca d'en Manel** (☎ 977 36 30 24; Passeig de Miramar 38; meals €25-30; ⏲ Tue-Sun), a few steps away from where the fishing boats tie up. Service can be abrupt, but the portions are tasty and generous. A step up in class is the nearby **Casa Gatell** (☎ 977 36 00 57; Passeig de Miramar 26; meals €45-55; ⏲ lunch & dinner Tue-Sat, lunch Sun), where you might succumb to the succulent *caldereta de bogavante*.

Cambrils is about 25 minutes from Tarragona by local train (€1.60 to €2.30).

TORTOSA

pop 34,800

Towering over this somewhat dusty inland town is a castle complex built by the Muslims when Tortosa, which was first settled by Iberian tribes more than 2000 years ago, was on the front line between the medieval Christian and Muslim Spain.

As well as the **tourist office** (☎ 977 44 96 48; www.turismetortosa.com; Plaça del Carrilet 1; ⏲ 10am-1.30pm & 4.30-7.30pm Tue-Sat, 10am-1.30pm Sun Easter-Oct, 10am-1.30pm & 3.30-6.30pm Tue-Sat, 10am-1.30pm Sun), there is an information office with similar hours in the Jardins del Príncep.

The old town, concentrated at the western end of the city, north of the Ebro, is watched over by the imposing **Castell de la Suda**, where a small medieval Arab cemetery has been unearthed and in whose grounds there now stands a fine **parador** (☎ 977 44 44 50; d €137-206; P ✗ ♿). The **Gothic cathedral** (Seu; ⏲ 9am-1pm & 4-8pm) dates back to 1347 and contains a pleasant cloister and some baroque additions. Other attractions include the **Palau Episcopal** and the lovely **Jardins del Príncep**, perfect for a stroll.

Hostal Virginia (☎ 977 44 41 86; www.hotelvirginia.net; Avinguda de la Generalitat 139; s/d €28/45; ✗ 💻) is a cheerful, central stop whose modern if somewhat antiseptic rooms boast good-sized beds and cool tile floors. There's a bar downstairs. If there's no room at this inn, you'll find three other, fairly antiseptic lower-midrange hotels elsewhere in town.

The train and bus stations are opposite each other on Ronda dels Docs. Trains to/from Barcelona, Lleida and Tarragona (€5.80, one

TAKING THE BULLS BY THE HORNS

Many Catalans advertise their loathing of bullfighting but some may not be aware that in the southern corner of their region, locals have indulged in their own summer bovine torment. In Amposta and neighbouring towns, people celebrate *bous capllaçats* and *bous embolats*, the former a kind of tug-of-war between a bull with ropes tied to its horns and townsfolk, the latter involving bulls running around with flaming torches attached to their horns. Denounced by animal rights groups, they are allowed by the Catalan government, which recognises the right to hold these *festas* because of their long history and the fact that the bulls are not killed. For more on bullfighting, see p61.

hour, five minutes) are more frequent than the buses. Two to four buses run into the Delta de l'Ebre area.

EBRO DELTA

The delta of the Río Ebro (Catalan: Delta de l'Ebre), formed by silt brought down by the river, sticks out 20km into the Mediterranean near Catalonia's southern border. Dotted with reedy lagoons and fringed by dune-backed beaches, this flat and exposed wetland is northern Spain's most important water-bird habitat. The migration season (October and November) sees the bird population peak, with an average of 53,000 ducks and 15,000 coots, but they are also numerous in winter and spring: 10% of all water birds wintering on the Iberian Peninsula choose to park themselves here.

Nearly half of the delta's 320 sq km is given over to rice-growing. Some 77 sq km, mostly along the coasts and around the lagoons, form the **Parc Natural Delta de l'Ebre**.

Orientation

The delta is a seaward-pointing arrowhead of land with the Ebro flowing eastwards across its middle. The town of Deltebre straggles about 5km along the northern bank of the river at the centre of the delta. Deltebre's western half is called Jesús i Maria and the eastern half La Cava. Facing Deltebre on the southern bank is Sant Jaume d'Enveja. Roads criss-cross the delta to Deltebre and beyond from the towns of L'Ampolla, Amposta and Sant Carles de la Ràpita, all on the N340. Three *transbordadors* (ferries), running from early morning until nightfall, link Deltebre to Sant Jaume d'Enveja (two people and a car €2.50).

Information

The **Centre d'Informació** (☎ 977 48 96 79; Carrer de Martí Buera 22, Deltebre; 🕑 10am-2pm & 3-7pm Mon-Sat, 10am-2pm Sun May-Sep, 10am-2pm & 3-6pm Mon-Sat, 10am-2pm Sun Oct-Apr) is combined with an **Ecomuseu** (admission €1.20; 🕑 same as Centre d'Informació), with displays describing the delta environment and an aquarium-terrarium of delta species.

There's another **information office** (☎ 977 48 21 81; 🕑 10am-2pm & 3-7pm Mon-Sat, 10am-2pm Sun May-Sep, 10am-2pm & 3-6pm Mon-Sat, 10am-2pm Sun Oct-Apr) with a permanent exposition (admission €1.50) on the delta's lagoons at La Casa de Fusta, beside L'Encanyissada lagoon, 10km southwest of Deltebre. Other offices are in Sant Carles de la Ràpita, Amposta and L'Ampolla.

Sights & Activities

Early morning and evening are the best times for **birdwatching**, and good areas include L'Encanyissada and La Tancada lagoons and Punta de la Banya, all in the south of the delta. L'Encanyissada has two observation towers and La Tancada one (others are marked on a map you can pick up at the Centre d'Informació). La Tancada and Punta de la Banya are generally the best places to see the **greater flamingos**, the delta's most spectacular birds. Almost 2000 of the birds nest here, and since 1992 the delta has been one of only five places in Europe where they reproduce. Punta de la Banya is joined to the delta by a 5km sand spit with the long, wide and sandy Platja de l'Eucaliptus at its northern end.

Olmos (☎ 977 48 05 48) is just one of a couple of companies that run daily tourist **boat trips** (€10 per person, 1½ hours) from Deltebre to the mouths of the Ebro and Illa de Buda at the delta's tip. Boats go daily, but the frequency depends on the season (and whether or not there are enough takers).

In El Poblenou del Delta, visit **Mas de la Cuixota** (☎ 977 26 10 26; Partida de l'Encanyissada). It rents out binoculars for birdwatching and runs organised trips along the delta canals in traditional, shallow-bottom boats, or *barques de perxar*. Several other places in Deltebre rent out bicycles too – prices hover around €10 per day.

Sleeping & Eating

Several camping grounds are scattered about Amposta, Deltebre and the surrounding countryside, along with a sprinkling of low-key hotels and rural accommodation. There are a few places to stay in Sant Carles de la Ràpita, a pleasant fishing town with a marina.

Lo Segador (☎ 636 517755; www.losegador.com; Carrer Major 14, El Poblenou del Delta; d/tr €45/63; P) A charming, six-room rural house with broad terraces, gardens and communal kitchen area, this spot offers simple accommodation in a friendly atmosphere.

Mas del Tancat (☎ 656 901014; www.toprural.com/masdeltancat; Camí dels Panissos s/n; d/tr €50/70; P) A converted historic farmhouse, Mas del Tancat has just five rooms with iron bedsteads, terracotta floors and a warm welcome. Sitting by the waters of the delta, it is a tranquil escape.

You'll find several eateries by Riumar and the mouth of the river. **Restaurant L'Alfacada** (☎ 977 26 10 62; Illa de Buda; meals €20-30; Tue-Sun Apr-Sep, Sun & holidays Oct-Mar) lies by a branch of the Ebre River whose opening on to the sea is now blocked by sand (the bank of sand allows us to walk across to what was a delta island, Illa de Buda). This rustic restaurant is perfect for local cooking, especially rice and eel (both abundant here!) concoctions.

Getting There & Away

The delta is easiest to get to and around with your own wheels, but it is possible to reach Tortosa by bus or a train/bus combination.

Autocars Hife (☎ 902 11 98 14; www.hife.es) runs buses to Jesús i Maria and La Cava from Tortosa (€2.70, 50 minutes) up to eight times daily (twice on Saturday, Sunday and holidays) and from Amposta (€1.30, 30 minutes) once daily.

Aragón

If you come to Spain and spend your entire time in Aragón, you'll experience an extraordinary breadth of quintessentially Spanish attractions and you certainly won't leave disappointed.

Aragón's heartbeat is Zaragoza, a city bursting with sound and fury yet still paying homage to high culture with a fine array of historical monuments. It's here in Aragón's largest city that the region's grand themes converge: a commitment to much-loved local cuisine that borders on the passionate; long nights of revelry; and a proliferation of extant glories from the great empires that give depth to Spanish history. The visual and culinary feast continues in Teruel, whose Mudéjar monuments are Spain's finest and where the streets course with life.

Away from the bustle of city life lies an altogether different world, one that's filled with quiet charm and splendid architecture. Stunning stone-walled villages line up across the countryside, from Sos del Rey Católico, Aínsa and Alquézar in the north to Daroca and Albarracín in the south and the small hamlets of Aragon's southeast. This is where Aragón is at its best, a timeless world where Old Spain lives and breathes.

Then there's the terrain that encompasses many of Spain's signature landscapes, beginning in the Pyrenees with some of Spain's most extraordinary mountain scenery and rolling down through the foothills to the arid mesas surrounding Teruel. The great mountains of the north cater for skiers and mountaineers while their valleys are a walkers' paradise of canyons, pretty villages, lonely castles and venerable monasteries with outstanding Romanesque architecture.

HIGHLIGHTS

- Hit buzzing streets and bars of **Zaragoza** (opposite) by night and visit its glorious monuments by day
- Veer off the beaten highway to fabulous old towns such as **Aínsa** (p450), **Sos del Rey Católico** (p460), **Daroca** (p461) and **Albarracín** (p465)
- Savour the Mudéjar architecture and wafer-thin perfection of the best *jamón* (ham) from **Teruel** (p461)
- Go quietly through the beautiful Pyrenean valleys of **Echo** and **Ansó** (p458)
- Walk the wilderness in the **Parque Nacional de Ordesa y Monte Perdido** (p451) in the Pyrenees

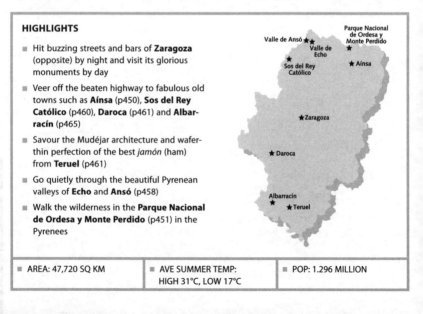

AREA: 47,720 SQ KM	AVE SUMMER TEMP: HIGH 31°C, LOW 17°C	POP: 1.296 MILLION

ZARAGOZA

pop 624,600 / elev 200m

Zaragoza (Saragossa) rocks and rolls. The feisty citizens of this great city on the banks of the mighty Río Ebro make up over half of Aragón's population and they live a fairly hectic lifestyle with great tapas bars and raucous nightlife. But Zaragoza is so much more than a city that loves to live the good life and there's a host of historical sights spanning the great civilisations (Roman, Islamic and Christian) that have left their indelible mark on the Spanish soul.

HISTORY

The Romans founded Caesaraugusta (from which 'Zaragoza' is derived – listen to it phonetically and you'll see what we mean) in 14 BC. As many as 25,000 people migrated to the prosperous Roman city whose river traffic brought the known world to the banks of Río Ebro. In Islamic times Zaragoza was capital of the Upper March, one of Al-Andalus' frontier territories. In 1118 it fell to Alfonso I 'El Batallador' (Battler), ruler of the expanding Christian kingdom of Aragón, and immediately became its capital. In the centuries that followed, Zaragoza grew to become one of inland Spain's most important economic and cultural hubs and a city popular with Catholic pilgrims. Now Spain's fifth-largest city, Zaragoza's growing confidence was reflected in its successful staging of Expo 2008, which thrust the city well and truly into the international spotlight.

ORIENTATION

The core of old Zaragoza, including the bulk of the city's historic monuments and most hotels and restaurants, lies south of Río Ebro, its former walls marked by Avenida de César Augusto to the west and El Coso to the south. Plaza del Pilar, dominated by Zaragoza's great churches, gives way southwards to a labyrinth of lanes and alleys whose heart is known as El Tubo. The major 'T-junction' of the modern city is south of the old town at Plaza de España. The Estación Intermodal Delicias train and bus stations are about 2km west of the old centre.

INFORMATION

Self-promotion is a Zaragoza speciality if the number of tourist offices is anything to go by. Only the most useful are listed in this section.

Conecta-T (☎ 976 20 59 79; Murallas Romanas 4; per hr €1.60; 🕑 10am-11pm Mon-Fri, 11am-11pm Sat & Sun) A well-organised facility with cheap international calls, mobile charge point and faxing. There's another branch (Paseo Calanda 27) close to the train and bus stations.

Estación Intermodal Delicias (☎ 976 32 44 68; 🕑 9am-9pm Easter-Oct, 9am-8pm Nov-Easter) Tourist office, in the train station.

Hellespontika (☎ 976 49 55 54; Plaza Ariño 1; wash & dry per 3kg load €12; 🕑 9.30am-1.30pm & 4.45-8pm Mon-Fri, 10am-2pm Sat) Laundry.

Hospital Clínico Universitario (☎ 976 35 75 01; Calle de San Juan Bosco 15)

Librería General (☎ 976 22 44 83; Paseo de la Independencia 22; 🕑 10am-1.30pm & 5-8.30pm Mon-Fri, 10am-1.30pm Sat) Bookshop with walking maps, guidebooks, and some English- and French-language novels.

Main post office (Paseo de la Independencia 33; 🕑 8.30am-8.30pm Mon-Fri, 9.30am-2pm Sat)

Oficina de Turismo de Aragón (☎ 976 28 21 81; www.turismodeAragon.com; Avenida de César Augusto 25; 🕑 9am-2pm & 5-8pm Mon-Fri, from 10am Sat & Sun) Tourist office.

Plaza del Pilar (☎ 976 39 35 37; www.zaragozaturismo.com; 🕑 9am-9pm Easter-Oct, 10am-8pm Nov-Easter) The city information office, opposite the basilica.

ZARAGOZA – CHEAP AND EASY

If time's tight, there are three options for making the most of Zaragoza without emptying your wallet. Information on all of the following options is available from any of the tourist offices listed above.

- **Zaragoza Card** (☎ 902 14 20 08; www.zaragozacard.com; 24-/48-/72hr €14/19/23) Free entry to all sights, travel on the Tourist Bus and discounts on hotels, restaurants and car rental.
- **Tourist Bus** (Bus Turístico; ☎ 976 20 12 00; adult/under 5yr €6/free) Hop-on, hop-off sightseeing bus that does two 75-minute city circuits daily in summer, less frequently the rest of the year.
- **BiziZaragoza** (☎ 902 31 99 31; www.bizizaragoza.com; subscription €6) Public bicycle rental from numerous pick-up and drop-off points around town.

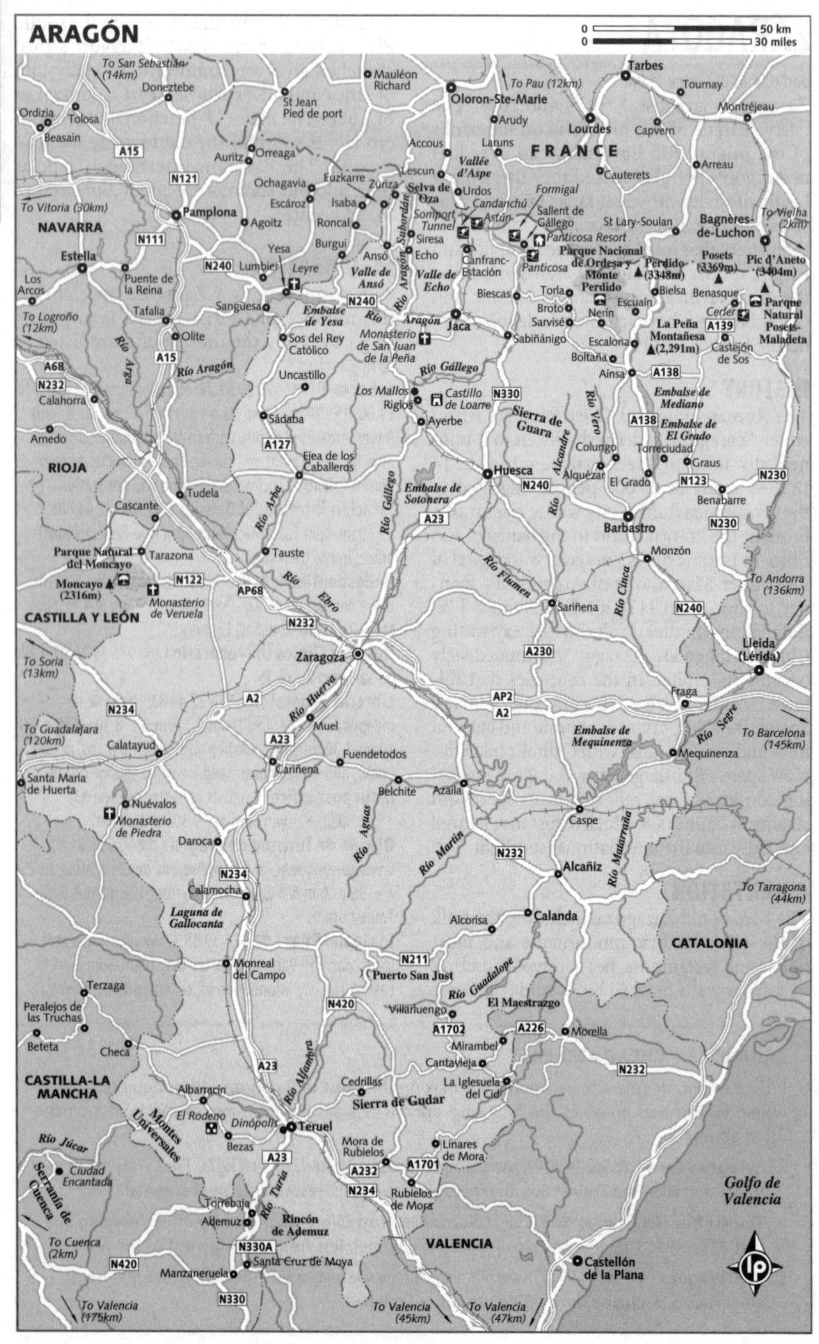
ARAGÓN
0 50 km
0 30 miles
FRANCE
NAVARRA
RIOJA
CASTILLA Y LEÓN
CASTILLA-LA MANCHA
VALENCIA
CATALONIA
Golfo de Valencia
Pamplona
Zaragoza
Huesca
Teruel
Jaca
Barbastro
Lleida (Lérida)
Tarbes
Lourdes
Oloron-Ste-Marie
Estella
Tudela
Tarazona
Calatayud
Daroca
Alcañiz
Calanda
Caspe
Fraga
Monzón
Ainsa
Castellón de la Plana
Albarracín
Sierra de Guara
Sierra de Gudar
El Maestrazgo
Parque Nacional de Ordesa y Monte Perdido
Parque Natural Posets-Maladeta
Parque Natural del Moncayo
Río Ebro
Río Aragón
Río Gállego
To Barcelona (145km)
To Valencia (175km)
To Tarragona (44km)
To Andorra (136km)

Torreón de la Zuda (☎ 976 20 12 00; Glorieta de Pío XII; 🕑 10am-2pm & 4.30-8pm Nov-Easter, 9am-9pm Easter-Oct) Subsidiary city information office in a 15th-century Mudéjar tower by the Roman walls. Climb the tower for panoramic views (free).

SIGHTS

The great eras of the city's colourful history – Roman, Islamic and Christian – all left enduring monuments in Zaragoza.

Christian Zaragoza

BASÍLICA DE NUESTRA SEÑORA DEL PILAR

Brace yourself for the saintly and the solemn in this great baroque cavern of Catholicism. It was here on 2 January AD 40, that Santiago (St James the Apostle) is believed by the faithful to have seen the Virgin Mary descend atop a marble *pilar* (pillar). A chapel was built around the remaining pillar, followed by a series of ever-more-grandiose churches, culminating in the enormous **basilica** (☎ 976 39 74 97; admission free; 🕑 6.45am-9.30pm) that you see today. Originally designed in 1681 by Felipe Sánchez y Herrera, it was greatly modified in the 18th century by the heavier hand of Ventura Rodríguez; the towers were not finished until the early 20th century. The exterior is another story altogether, its splendid main dome lording it over a flurry of 10 mini-domes, each encased in chunky blue, green, yellow and white tiles, creating a kind of rugged Byzantine effect.

The legendary **pilar** is hidden in the Capilla Santa, inside the east end of the basilica. A tiny oval-shaped portion of the *pilar* is exposed on the chapel's outer west side. A steady stream of people (with busloads of the faithful arriving at times) line up to brush lips with its polished and seamed cheek, which even popes have air-kissed. Parents also line up until 2pm most days to have their babies blessed next to the Virgin. More than the architecture, these symbols of the sacred and the devotion they inspire in the faithful are what makes this cathedral special.

Hung from the northeast column of the Capilla Santa are two wickedly slim shells that were lobbed at El Pilar during the civil war. They failed to explode. A miracle said the faithful: typical Czech munitions said the more cynical.

The basilica's finest artwork is a 16th-century alabaster altarpiece by Damián Forment. It stands at the outer west wall of the choir. Goya painted *La Reina de los Mártires* (Mary, Queen of Martyrs) in a cupola above the north aisle, outside the Sacristía de la Virgen.

A **lift** (admission €2; 🕑 9.30am-1.30pm & 4-6.30pm Sat-Thu) whisks you most of the way up the north tower (Torre Pilar) from where you climb to a superb viewpoint over the domes and out across this ever-expanding city.

LA SEO

Dominating the eastern end of Plaza del Pilar is the Catedral de San Salvador, more popularly known as **La Seo** (☎ 976 29 12 38; Plaza de la Seo; admission €2.50; 🕑 10am-6pm Tue-Fri, 10am-2pm & 3-6pm Sat, 10-11.30am & 2.30-6pm Sun Jun-Sep, shorter hr rest of year). Entry is at the eastern end.

La Seo may lack the fame of the Basílica de Nuestra Señora del Pilar, but it's easily its architectural superior. Built between the 12th and 17th centuries, it displays a fabulous spread of architectural styles from Romanesque to baroque. It stands on the site of Islamic Zaragoza's main mosque (which in turn stood upon the temple of the Roman forum). The northwest facade is a Mudéjar masterpiece, deploying classic dark brickwork and colourful ceramic decoration in eye-pleasing geometric patterns. All the chapels are framed by beautiful stonework and ring the changes from the eerie solemnity of the Capilla de San Marcos to the glorious Renaissance facade of the central Christ Chapel and the exquisite 15th-century high altarpiece in polychrome alabaster.

La Seo's **Museo de Tapices** (admission €2; 🕑 10am-8.30pm Tue-Sun Jun-Sep, shorter hr rest of year) has an impressive collection of 14th- to 17th- century Flemish and French tapestries.

OTHER CHURCHES

Several other Zaragoza churches are well worth a look. The **Iglesia de San Pablo** (cnr Calles de San Pablo & Miguel de Ara; 🕑 9am-1pm) has a delicate 14th-century Mudéjar tower and an early-16th-century *retablo* (altarpiece) by Damián Forment. The **Iglesia de La Magdalena**, **Iglesia de San Miguel** and **Iglesia de San Gil** also boast fine 14th- and 15th-century Mudéjar towers – at their best when floodlit at night.

Roman Zaragoza

The four museums dedicated to Zaragoza's Roman past form part of what's known as the Ruta de Cesaraugusta; a combined ticket costs €6.

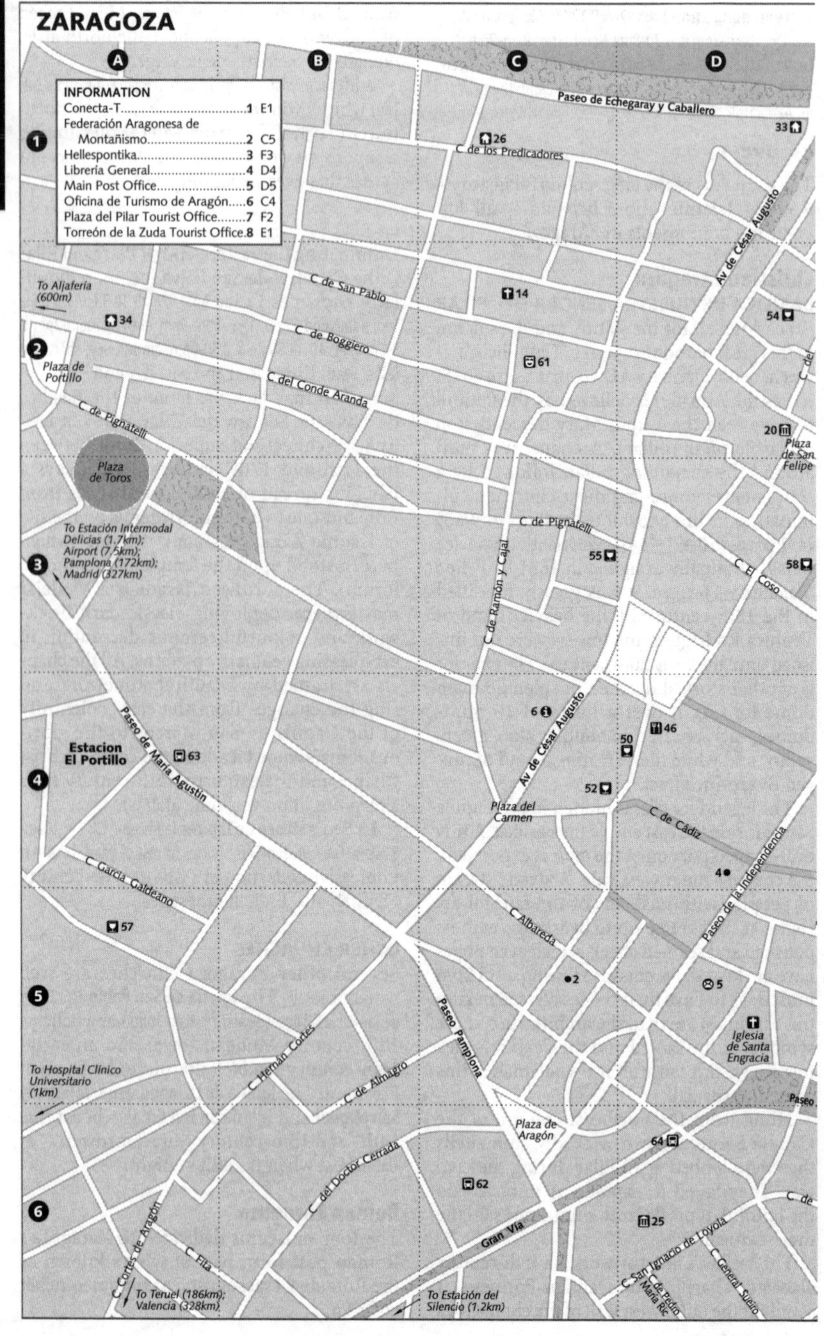
ZARAGOZA
INFORMATION
Conecta-T.....1 E1
Federación Aragonesa de Montañismo.....2 C5
Hellespontika.....3 F3
Librería General.....4 D4
Main Post Office.....5 D5
Oficina de Turismo de Aragón.....6 C4
Plaza del Pilar Tourist Office.....7 F2
Torreón de la Zuda Tourist Office.....8 E1
Paseo de Echegaray y Caballero
C de los Predicadores
Av de César Augusto
C de San Pablo
C de Boggiero
C del Conde Aranda
C de Pignatelli
To Aljafería (600m)
Plaza de Portillo
Plaza de Toros
To Estación Intermodal Delicias (1.7km); Airport (7.5km); Pamplona (172km); Madrid (327km)
C de Ramón y Cajal
Plaza de San Felipe
C El Coso
Paseo de María Agustín
Estacion El Portillo
Plaza del Carmen
C de Cádiz
C García Galdeano
C Albareda
Paseo de la Independencia
Iglesia de Santa Engracia
Paseo Pamplona
C Hernán Cortés
C de Almagro
To Hospital Clínico Universitario (1km)
Plaza de Aragón
C del Doctor Cerrada
Gran Vía
C Cortés de Aragón
C Fita
To Teruel (186km); Valencia (328km)
To Estación del Silencio (1.2km)
C San Ignacio de Loyola
C de Pedro María Ric
C General Sueiro

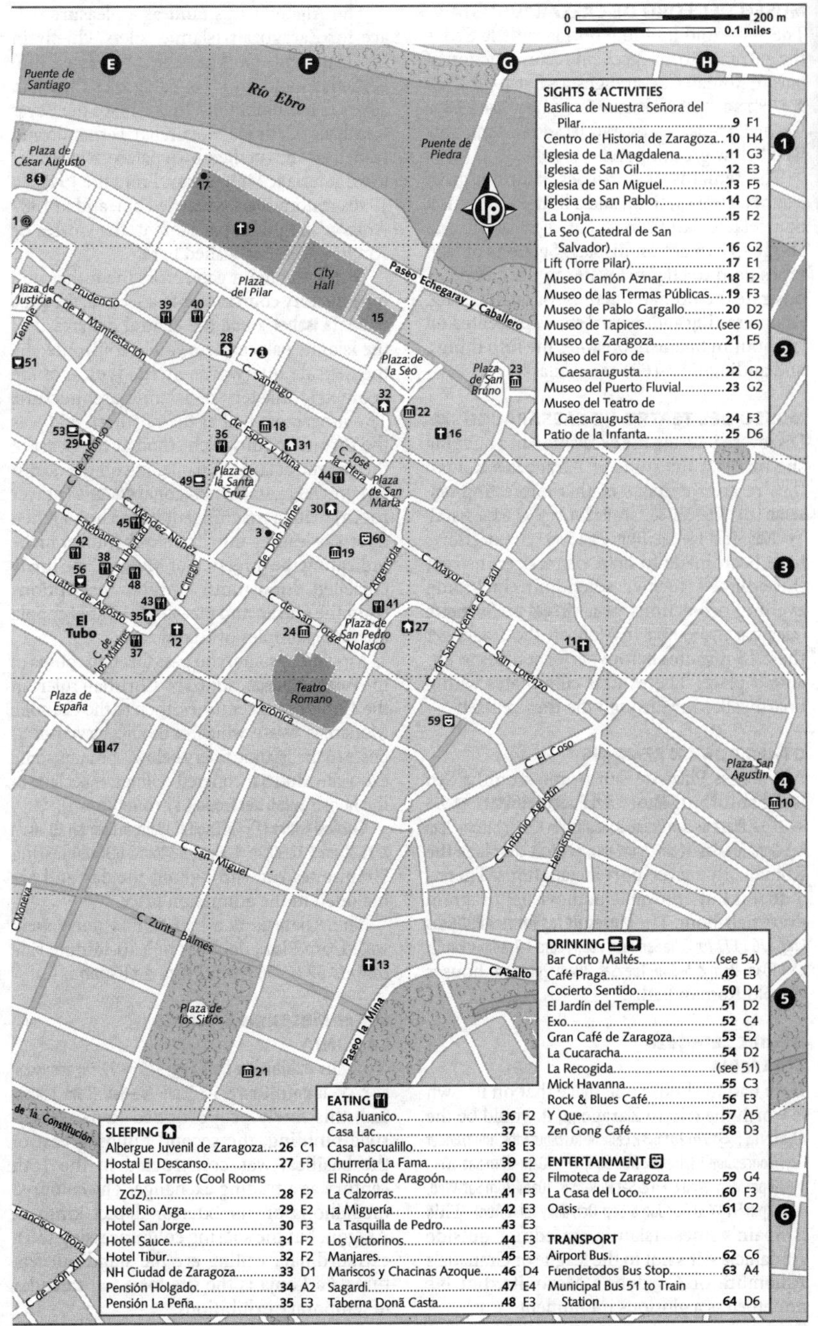
0 200 m
0 0.1 miles
E
F
G
H
1
2
3
4
5
6
Puente de Santiago
Río Ebro
Puente de Piedra
Plaza de César Augusto
Plaza del Pilar
City Hall
Paseo Echegaray y Caballero
Plaza de Justicia
C Prudencio
C de la Manifestación
Temple
Plaza de la Seo
Plaza de San Bruno
C Santiago
C de Espoz y Mina
C José la Hera
Plaza de San Marta
Plaza de la Santa Cruz
C de Alfonso I
C Estébanes
C Méndez Núñez
C de Don Jaime I
C de la Libertad
Cuatro de Agosto
C Cinegio
El Tubo
C de los Mártires
C Argensola
C Mayor
C de San Jorge
Plaza de San Pedro Nolasco
C de San Vicente de Paúl
C San Lorenzo
Teatro Romano
C Verónica
Plaza de España
C El Coso
C Antonio Agustín
C Heroísmo
Plaza San Agustín
C San Miguel
C Moneva
C Zurita Balmes
C Asalto
Paseo la Mina
Plaza de los Sitios
de la Constitución
Francisco Vitoria
C de León XIII
SIGHTS & ACTIVITIES
Basílica de Nuestra Señora del Pilar....9 F1
Centro de Historia de Zaragoza..10 H4
Iglesia de La Magdalena....11 G3
Iglesia de San Gil....12 E3
Iglesia de San Miguel....13 F5
Iglesia de San Pablo....14 C2
La Lonja....15 F2
La Seo (Catedral de San Salvador)....16 G2
Lift (Torre Pilar)....17 E1
Museo Camón Aznar....18 F2
Museo de las Termas Públicas....19 F3
Museo de Pablo Gargallo....20 D2
Museo de Tapices....(see 16)
Museo de Zaragoza....21 F5
Museo del Foro de Caesaraugusta....22 G2
Museo del Puerto Fluvial....23 G2
Museo del Teatro de Caesaraugusta....24 F3
Patio de la Infanta....25 D6
DRINKING
Bar Corto Maltés....(see 54)
Café Praga....49 E3
Cocierto Sentido....50 D4
El Jardín del Temple....51 D2
Exo....52 C4
Gran Café de Zaragoza....53 E2
La Cucaracha....54 D2
La Recogida....(see 51)
Mick Havanna....55 C3
Rock & Blues Café....56 E3
Y Que....57 A5
Zen Gong Café....58 D3
ENTERTAINMENT
Filmoteca de Zaragoza....59 G4
La Casa del Loco....60 F3
Oasis....61 C2
TRANSPORT
Airport Bus....62 C6
Fuendetodos Bus Stop....63 A4
Municipal Bus 51 to Train Station....64 D6
EATING
Casa Juanico....36 F2
Casa Lac....37 E3
Casa Pascualillo....38 E3
Churrería La Fama....39 E2
El Rincón de Aragoón....40 E2
La Calzorras....41 F3
La Miguería....42 E3
La Tasquilla de Pedro....43 E3
Los Victorinos....44 F3
Manjares....45 E3
Mariscos y Chacinas Azoque....46 D4
Sagardi....47 E4
Taberna Donã Casta....48 E3
SLEEPING
Albergue Juvenil de Zaragoza....26 C1
Hostal El Descanso....27 F3
Hotel Las Torres (Cool Rooms ZGZ)....28 F2
Hotel Rio Arga....29 E2
Hotel San Jorge....30 F3
Hotel Sauce....31 F2
Hotel Tibur....32 F2
NH Ciudad de Zaragoza....33 D1
Pensión Holgado....34 A2
Pensión La Peña....35 E3

MUSEO DEL FORO DE CAESARAUGUSTA

The trapezoid building on Plaza de la Seo is the entrance to an excellent reconstruction of part of Roman Caesaraugusta's **forum** (☎ 976 39 97 52; Plaza de la Seo 2; admission €2; 10am-2pm & 5-8pm Tue-Sat, 10am-2pm Sun, last entry 1hr before closing), now well below ground level.

The remains of porticoes, shops, a great *cloaca* (sewer) system, and a limited collection of artefacts dating from between 14 BC and about AD 15 are on display. Sections of lead pipes used to channel water to the city demonstrate the Romans' genius for engineering. An interesting audiovisual show, presented on the hour in Spanish, breathes life into things, and audioguides (€2) are available.

MUSEO DEL TEATRO DE CAESARAUGUSTA

Discovered during the excavation of a building site in 1972, the ruins of Zaragoza's Roman theatre are the focus of this interesting **museum** (☎ 976 20 50 88; Calle de San Jorge 12; admission €3; 10am-9pm Tue-Sat, 10am-2pm Sun). Great efforts have been made to help visitors reconstruct the edifice's former splendour, including evening projections of a **virtual performance** (admission €1; 10pm Fri & Sat) on the stage; get there 15 minutes before performances to ensure a place. The exhibit culminates with a boardwalk tour through the theatre itself.

OTHER ROMAN REMAINS

Just across Plaza de San Bruno from La Seo is the absorbing **Museo del Puerto Fluvial** (☎ 976 39 31 57; Plaza de San Bruno 8; admission €2; 10am-2pm & 5-8pm Tue-Sat, 10am-2pm Sun), which displays the Roman city's river-port installations. There's a quaint but enjoyable audiovisual program every half-hour. The **Museo de las Termas Públicas** (☎ 976 29 72 79; Calle San Juan y San Pedro 3-7; admission €2; 10am-2pm & 5-8pm Tue-Sat, 10am-2pm Sun) houses the old Roman baths.

Islamic Zaragoza

ALJAFERÍA

If we had to choose one place that on its own is worth the trip to Zaragoza, it would be the **Aljafería** (☎ 976 28 96 84; Calle de los Diputados; adult/under 12yr/concession €3/free/1, free Sun; 10am-2pm Sat-Wed, 4-6.30pm Mon-Wed & Fri & Sat Nov-Mar, 10am-2pm Sat-Wed, 4.30-8pm Fri-Wed Apr-Jun & Sep-Oct, daily Jul & Aug). This is Spain's finest Islamic-era edifice outside Andalucía – it's not in the league of Granada's Alhambra or Córdoba's Mezquita, but it's nonetheless a glorious monument.

The Aljafería was built as a pleasure palace for Zaragoza's Islamic rulers, chiefly in the 11th century. After the city passed into Christian hands in 1118, Zaragoza's Christian rulers made alterations. In the 1490s the Reyes Católicos (Catholic Monarchs), Fernando and Isabel, tacked on their own palace, whereafter the Aljafería fell into decay. From the 1940s to 1990s restoration was carried out, and in 1987 Aragón's regional parliament, the Cortes de Aragón, was established here.

Inside the main gate, cross the rather dull introductory courtyard into a second, the **Patio de Santa Isabel**, once the central courtyard of the Islamic palace. Here you're confronted by the delicate interwoven arches typical of the geometric mastery of Islamic architecture. The innermost hall at the northern end was the throne room which stood at the heart of the Islamic palace. Also opening off the northern porch is a small, octagonal **oratorio** (prayer room), with a magnificent horseshoe-arched doorway leading into its *mihrab* (prayer niche indicating the direction of Mecca). The finely chiselled floral motifs, Arabic inscriptions from the Quran and pleasingly simple cupola are fine examples of Islamic art.

Moving upstairs, you pass through rooms of the **Palacio Mudéjar**, added by Christian rulers in the 12th to 14th centuries, then to the Catholic Monarchs' **palace**, which, as though by way of riposte to the Islamic finery below, contains some exquisite Mudéjar coffered ceilings, especially in the lavish **Salón del Trono** (Throne Room).

Guided tours (in English 10am, in Spanish 10.30am & 11.30am & 12.30pm, 4.30pm, 5.30pm & 6.30pm) lasting 50 minutes run throughout the day and are included in the admission price.

The Aljafería is a half-hour's noisy walk west from Plaza del Pilar or a 10-minute ride on bus 32 or 36 from Plaza de España.

Other Museums & Sights

LA LONJA

Now an **exhibition hall** (☎ 976 39 72 39; admission free; 10am-1.30pm & 5-8.30pm Tue-Sat, 10am-1.30pm Sun), this finely proportioned Renaissance-style building, the second building east of the basilica, was constructed in the 16th century as a trading exchange. The coloured medallions on its exterior depict kings of Aragón, but the soaring columns rising to an extraordinary ceiling are the stand-out features. La Lonja is the site for a full calendar of temporary exhibitions.

THE SPANISH LAS VEGAS?

Overdevelopment in pursuit of the tourist dollar has blighted many coastal regions of eastern Spain, but plans for Europe's largest casino complex in the dusty badlands southeast of Zaragoza may just be the country's most controversial megaproject yet. 'Gran Scala' is the brainchild of International Leisure Development, a British-based consortium with dreams of a 2000-hectare town of 100,000 inhabitants, 32 casinos, 70 hotels, 232 restaurants and 500 shops by 2015. Mock Egyptian pyramids, Roman temples and even a replica of the Pentagon also form part of the €17-billion project. When finished, its advocates promise, it will draw 25 million visitors a year. Although approved by Aragón's regional government, Gran Scala has drawn fierce opposition from environmental groups, who have pointed out that this is one of Spain's driest regions, with already chronic water shortages.

MUSEO DE ZARAGOZA

Devoted to archaeology and fine arts, the **city museum** (☎ 976 22 21 81; Plaza de los Sitios 6; admission free; 🕑 10am-2pm & 5-8pm Tue-Sat, 10am-2pm Sun) displays artefacts from prehistoric to Islamic times, an important collection of Gothic art and a dozen Goya paintings.

MUSEO CAMÓN AZNAR

This eclectic **collection** (☎ 976 39 73 28; Calle de Espoz y Mina 23; admission free; 🕑 9am-2.15pm & 5-9.15pm Tue-Sat, 10am-2.15pm Sun) of Spanish art through the ages features a room of Goya etchings (on the top floor) and half a dozen paintings attributed to El Greco. It spreads over the three storeys of the Palacio de los Pardo, a Renaissance mansion.

PATIO DE LA INFANTA

This **exhibition** (☎ 976 76 76 76; Calle San Ignacio de Loyola 16; admission free; 🕑 8.30am-2pm & 6-8.30pm Mon-Fri, 11am-1.30pm & 6-8.30pm Sat, 11am-1.30pm Sun) is the Ibercaja bank's collection of Goya paintings, displayed in a lovely plateresque courtyard.

MUSEO DE PABLO GARGALLO

Within the 17th-century Palacio Argillo is a representative **display** (☎ 976 72 49 23; Plaza de San Felipe 3) of sculptures by Pablo Gargallo (1881–1934), probably Aragón's most gifted artistic son after Goya. It was closed for major renovations when we visited.

CENTRO DE HISTORIA DE ZARAGOZA

The old convent of San Agustín (only the neoclassical facade remains) is the site of this **museum** (Zaragoza History Centre; ☎ 976 20 56 40; Plaza San Agustín 2; admission free; 🕑 10am-2pm & 5-8.30pm Tue-Sat, 10am-2pm Sun). Each of the eight exhibit rooms focuses on a different aspect of the city's heritage, from trade and transport to popular celebrations. Of particular interest is a series of models depicting Zaragoza's physical transformation through four key phases of its development.

FESTIVALS & EVENTS

Zaragoza's biggest event is the **Fiestas del Pilar**, a week of full-on celebrations (religious and otherwise) peaking on 12 October, the **Día de Nuestra Señora del Pilar**. On 5 March Zaragozans celebrate **Cincomarzada**, commemorating the 1838 ousting of Carlist troops by a feisty populace. Thousands head for Parque Tio Jorge, north of the Ebro, for concerts, games, grilled sausage and wine.

SLEEPING

Zaragoza has good accommodation across a range of budgets, but there's little to really set the heart racing. With Expo 2008 out of the way, finding a room in Zaragoza has become a little easier, but reservations are always recommended.

Budget

Pensión La Peña (☎ 976 29 90 89; 1st fl, Calle de Cinegio 3; s/d without bathroom €15/30) Some of the cheapest beds in central Zaragoza are to be found here. You're in the heart of El Tubo with all the attendant noise and eating options, and rooms are basic but clean.

Albergue Juvenil de Zaragoza (Zaragoza Hostel; ☎ 976 28 20 43; www.alberguezaragoza.com; Calle de los Predicadores 70; d incl breakfast from €16.60; 💻) This dazzling new hostel opened in May 2008 and has super-new everything, save for some lovely original architectural features in the basement bar. Free breakfast, internet access and lockers are among the highlights.

Hostal El Descanso (☎ 976 29 17 41; Calle de San Lorenzo 2; s/d without bathroom €20/30) Simple, bright rooms, a family-run atmosphere and a central location overlooking a pretty plaza near the Roman theatre add up to a good budget deal.

Pensión Holgado (☎ 976 43 20 74; Calle del Conde de Aranda 126; s with/without bathroom €32/20, d with/without bathroom €44/33) Although slightly removed from the centre, this excellent *hostal* (budget hotel) is handy for the Aljafería and the rooms are simple and well tended. Depending on who you get at reception, service is not Zaragoza's warmest. To get here, take bus 22 (€1, eight minutes) from Plaza de España to Plaza del Portillo.

Hotel San Jorge (☎ 976 39 74 62; fax 976 39 85 77; Calle Mayor 4; s/d €34/42; P ✳) Not much to look at from the outside, this hotel has simple but well-sized rooms that were renovated in the not-too-distant past. Service is friendly but don't expect things like breakfast. Parking costs €9.

Midrange & Top End

Most of the following places either have on-site parking or can arrange discounts at nearby public parking stations; expect to pay €10 to €14.

Hotel Rio Arga (☎ 976 39 90 65; www.hotelrioarga.es; Contamina 20; s/d €43/60; P ✳ 💻) In a quiet location, yet ideal for all central needs, there are comfy rooms here. Most of the rooms have been renovated with flat-screen TVs and a modern look; those with recently overhauled bathrooms are the best.

Hotel Sauce (☎ 976 20 50 50; www.hotelsauce.com; Calle de Espoz y Mina 33; s/d €58.85/74.90; P ✳ 💻) This small hotel has good rooms with a mix of styles from traditional and cosy to pastel tones and a modern, classy look. Bookings are advisable. Breakfast costs €7.49.

Hotel Tibur (☎ 976 20 20 00; www.hoteltibur.com in Spanish; Plaza de la Seo 2; s/d from €70/80; P ✳ 💻) Business-standard rooms at this pleasant hotel, right on Plaza de la Seo, have minibars and plenty of space. Some rooms are starting to show their age, although more in the sense of style rather than maintenance.

our pick **Hotel Las Torres** (Cool Rooms ZGZ; ☎ 976 39 42 50; www.coolroomshotels.com; Plaza del Pilar 11; s €69-110, d €79-120; ✳ 💻) This place was a work-in-progress when we visited but it promises to be Zaragoza's best place to stay. Many of the rooms overlook Plaza del Pilar and all are being renovated with a designer, contemporary flourish. Laptops and hydromassage showers in every room are among the promised stand-out features and there are plans for a spa and gymnasium on site.

NH Ciudad de Zaragoza (☎ 976 44 21 00; www.nh-hoteles.com; Avenida de César Augusto 125; d from €117; ✳ 💻) If you've stayed in one of the NH Hotels before you know the deal: stylish rooms with clean lines and excellent service to go with all the necessary mod cons. Some rooms have views overlooking the Río Ebro, others look to the Basílica de Nuestra Señora de Pilar.

EATING

Tapas

Zaragoza has some terrific tapas bars, with dozens of places on or close to Plaza de Santa Marta and towards the southern end of Calle Heroísmo. Otherwise the narrow streets of El Tubo, north of Plaza de España, is tapas central.

our pick **Casa Pascualillo** (☎ 976 39 72 03; Calle de la Libertad 5; 🕑 lunch & dinner Tue-Sat, lunch Sun) When *Metropoli*, the respected weekend magazine of *El Mundo* newspaper, set out to find the best 50 tapas bars in Spain, it's no surprise that Casa Pascualillo made the final cut. The bar groans under the weight of every tapas variety imaginable, with seafood and meat in abundance, but the house speciality is El Pascualillo, a 'small' *bocadillo* of *jamón*, mushrooms and onion.

Los Victorinos (☎ 976 39 42 13; Calle José La Hera 6; 🕑 Mon-Sat) This place, tucked away in a pedestrian lane just west of Calle de Don Jaime I, also made *Metropoli*'s Top-50 list. Although there aren't as many options on the bar, there are plenty more on the menu, and choices for vegetarians.

Manjares (☎ 976 39 26 37; Calle Estébanes 7; 🕑 Tue-Sun) Promising 'pleasures in miniature', this slick place does a range of *tostadas*, *croquetas* and a range of creative tapas (€1.50 to €3). If you memorise its menu, you eat free, but it's no small task. It also has a good selection of wine by the glass.

Taberna Doña Casta (☎ 976 20 58 52; Calle Estébanes 6; 🕑 Tue-Sun) If you like your tapas without too many frills, this popular *taberna* (tavern) could become your culinary home in Zaragoza. The bottle of wine and six tapas for €25 is a terrific way to meet all your gastronomic needs at a reasonable price.

Other good places to try include:

Casa Juanico (☎ 976 29 50 88; Calle de Santiago 30-32; tapas from €2, menú del día €11) Everything from the best *jamón* to rice-based tapas.

La Calzorras (Plaza de San Pedro Nolasco) Plaza tables and tempting larger-than-tapas specialities for around €4.50.

WHAT'S COOKING IN ARAGÓN?

The kitchens and tables of Aragón are, like so many in inland Spain, dominated by meat. That's not to say you won't find fish and seafood and other Spanish staples. It's just that the *aragoneses* (people from Aragón) really get excited when offered *jamón de Teruel* (*jamón* from Teruel province, especially around Calamocha), *jarretes* (hock of ham or shanks) and above all *ternasco* (suckling lamb, usually served as a steak or ribs with potatoes). The latter is so beloved that there's even a website (www.iloveternascodearagon.com in Spanish) devoted to the dish with recipes and general adulation. Other popular dishes include *conejo a la montañesa* (rabbit mountain-style), *migas* (breadcrumbs, usually cooked with cured meats), *cardo* (cardoons) and *caracoles* (snails). Aragón also has five recognised wine-growing regions, the best-known of which is Somontano (see the boxed text, p448).

La Tasquilla de Pedro (☎ 976 39 06 58; Calle Cinegio s/n; tapas from €2) Cosy bar with specialities like asparagus stuffed with seafood or eggplant with foie gras.

Sagardi (☎ 976 23 16 77; Plaza de España 6) *Pintxos* (Basque tapas; €1.80) line up along the bar San-Sebastián-style with pleasant outdoor tables.

Restaurants

Churrería La Fama (☎ 976 39 37 54; Calle Prudencio 25; 3 churros €2; 🕑 8am-1pm & 5.30-9.30pm) La Fama, tucked away off Calle de Alfonso 1, is a good spot for fresh *churros* (long, deep-fried doughnuts) and chocolate to go with morning coffee; if you've been out all night, being here when it opens is a great way to begin (or end) your day.

La Miguería (☎ 976 20 07 36; Calle Estébanes 4; migas €5-10, raciones €6-19; 🕑 Mon-Sat) Who would have thought you could do so much with *migas* (breadcrumbs)… La Miguería serves this filling Aragonese quick-fix food in more than a dozen varieties, including drenched in olive oil, and topped with sardines and foie gras. It opens at 7.30pm, which may help those of you struggling to cope with late Spanish dinner times.

our pick **El Rincón de Aragón** (☎ 976 20 11 63; Calle de Santiago 3-5; menú del día €12.95)The sort of place that Spaniards love, El Rincón de Aragón does hearty Aragonese specialities. There's no time for unnecessary elaborations here – the decor is basic and the food stripped down to its essence – but the eating is top-notch and ideal for finding out why people get excited about Aragonese cooking. One house speciality among many is the *ternasco asado con patatas a la pobre* (roasted suckling lamb ribs with 'poor man's potatoes'). If you're feeling hungry, this and other local dishes usually appear on the three-course *menú Aragonés* (€19.90), which is a great order. El Rincón de Aragón is in the covered lane between Calle de Santiago and Plaza del Pilar.

Mariscos y Chacinas Azoque (☎ 976 48 38 38; Calle de Azoque 37; dishes €7-19) There's a pleasant Andalucían flavour to this fine restaurant where a cluster of dangling *jamónes* and a bar-top spread of seafood greet you. Relish the fishy wonders at the heart of landlocked Zaragoza.

Casa Lac (☎ 976 29 90 25; www.casalac.com in Spanish; Calle de los Mártires 12; meals €30-35; 🕑 dinner Mon-Fri, lunch & dinner Sat, lunch Sun) The grand old lady of the Zaragoza dining scene, Casa Lac pays homage to the 19th century with its seigneurial decor and impeccable service. The food revolves around Aragonese staples and the clientele is a Who's Who of Zaragoza society.

DRINKING

Cafes

Gran Café de Zaragoza (☎ 976 39 41 25; Calle de Alfonso I 25; breakfasts from €2.50; 🕑 8.30am-10pm Sun-Thu, 9am-2.30am Fri & Sat) This Zaragoza institution evokes the grand old cafes of Spain's past with a gold-plated facade and an old-style civility in the service. That said, it's a place to be seen by young and old alike and the elegant salon is a good place for morning coffee or breakfast.

Café Praga (☎ 976 20 02 51; Plaza de la Santa Cruz 13; 🕑 9am-1am Mon-Thu, 10am-3am Sat & Sun) One of Zaragoza's favourite cafes, Praga has a front-row seat on one of the city's most agreeable plazas and there's occasional live music in the main bar.

Bars

Calle del Temple, southwest of Plaza del Pilar, is the spiritual home of Zaragoza's roaring nightlife. This is where the city's considerable student population heads out to drink and there are more bars lined up along this street than anywhere else in Aragón. It's the sort of street you'll love after midnight, provided you don't live in one of the apartments up above.

Exo (Plaza del Carmen 11; 7am-1am Mon-Thu, 7am-3.30am Fri, 5pm-3.30am Sat, 5-11pm Sun) You don't need to be as sleek and cool as the bar staff or as shiny as the modernist decor at this smart but easygoing bar. There's a great friendly mood to go with the background Spanish rock.

Concierto Sentido (976 21 53 76; www.conciertosentido.com; Calle Azoque 6; 11am-late) A smooth, easy-listening bar with lots of subtle lighting and comfy seating by day, this happening place has themed party nights (eg Brazilian) and pop music on the first floor.

Rock & Blues Café (Cuatro de Agosto 5-9; 3pm-2.30am, later on weekends) Rock 'n' roll paraphernalia and homage to the likes of Jimi Hendrix set the tone for the music and style of this long-standing favourite. There's live pop, rock or blues on Thursdays at 10.30pm.

Zen Gong Café (976 39 25 90; Calle de Alfonso I 13; 7am-2am Sun-Thu, 8am-4.30am Fri & Sat) This place wouldn't look out of place in Madrid or Barcelona, with stylish decor, weird-and-wonderful lighting and a breadth of atmospheres from breakfast cafe to lunchtime wine bar and then on into pop, house and even drag acts by night.

Estación del Silencio (www.estaciondelsilencio.com; Calle de Catania 1; from 10pm) Paying homage to local music heroes Los Héroes de Silencio, this bar blends rock memorabilia with a mixed, dressed-down crowd of local celebrities. It's a real Zaragoza love-in, which makes up for it being a fair hike south of the centre.

On Calle del Temple, **Bar Corto Maltés** (Calle del Temple 23), **El Jardín del Temple** (Calle del Temple 18) and **La Recogida** (Calle del Temple 16) are always full and probably our favourites, while **La Cucaracha** (Calle del Temple 25) is great for well-priced cocktails. Zaragoza's gay bars include the lesbian-friendly **Y Que** (García Galdeano 13) and, closer to the old city, **Mick Havanna** (Calle de Ramón Pignatelli 7; from 5pm), a quiet, chatty place frequented by a mature crowd.

ENTERTAINMENT

The tourist office puts out the bimonthly *Agenda Cultural*, covering theatre, art, music and film events.

Filmoteca de Zaragoza (976 72 18 53; Plaza San Carlos 4; screenings from €2; Wed-Sat night) One of the few cinemas showing films in their original language (ie subtitled in Spanish, rather than dubbed).

La Casa del Loco (Calle Mayor 10-12; www.lacasadelloco.com; live music €8-13; midnight-5.30am Thu, midnight-6.30am Fri & Sat) Hugely popular, especially on Thursday nights when there's a regular live concert with mainly Spanish pop and rock bands. Friday and Saturday night it's still a lively late-night venue.

Oasis (976 43 95 34; Calle de Boggiero 28; cover €10; from midnight Fri & Sat) A few streets west of the old centre, Oasis began life long ago as a variety theatre. It's currently going strong as a disco with good techno house, but with a bit of 'anything goes'.

GETTING THERE & AWAY

Air

The **Zaragoza-Sanjurjo airport** (976 71 23 00) has direct **Ryanair** (www.ryanair.com) flights to/from London-Stansted, Brussels (Charleroi), Rome, Milan and Alicante. There are also **Iberia** (www.iberia.es) flights to/from Madrid, Barcelona, Paris and Frankfurt. **Air Europa** (www.aireuropa.com) flies to/from Palma de Mallorca.

Bus

Dozens of bus lines fan out across Spain from the bus station attached to the Estación Intermodal Delicias train station. The more-useful companies include:

Alosa (976 22 93 43; www.alosa.es in Spanish) At least eight buses to/from Huesca (€6.05, one hour), half of which continue to Jaca (€12.60, 2¼ hours).

ALSA (902 42 22 42; www.alsa.es) Frequent daily buses to/from Madrid (€14, 3¾ hours) and Barcelona (€13.50, 3¾ hours).

Train

Zaragoza's futuristic if rather impersonal **Estación Intermodal Delicias** (Calle Rioja 33) hosts a helpful tourist office.

Zaragoza is connected by almost hourly high-speed AVE services to Madrid (€50.90, 1½ hours, approximately 10 daily) and Barcelona (€58.90, one hour). There are also services to Valencia (€23.20, 4½ hours, two daily), Huesca (from €5.15, one hour, approximately four daily), Jaca (€11.20, 3½ hours, three daily) and Teruel (€12.25, 2¼ hours, three daily).

GETTING AROUND

Agreda Automóvil (976 55 45 88) runs airport buses (€2.15) to/from Paseo Pamplona via

DANCING IN THE DESERT

The rural town of Fraga in the relentless flatlands between Zaragoza and Valencia is the unlikely locale for **Florida 135** (☎ 974 47 02 50; www.f135.com in Spanish; Calle Sotet 2; admission €15; ⏰ from 11.30am Sat), the temple of Spanish techno. The windowless 3000-sq-metre graffiti-strewn space is the most recent incarnation of a dance hall that's been going since 1942. Bus loads of clubbers arrive for the club's main Saturday-night sessions. Check the website for the monthly program. In mid-July the **Monegros Desert Festival** (www.monegrosfestival.com), formerly called the Groove Parade, attracts dozens of Spanish and internationally renowned DJs and bands, who draw massive crowds at the event to Finca Les Peñetes, about 18km west of Fraga.

Plaza San Francisco and Gran Via 4 (the stop for municipal bus 30) that link with flights.

Bus 51 to/from Estación Intermodal Delicias begins/ends at Paseo de la Constitución, one block from Plaza de Aragón.

SOUTH OF ZARAGOZA

The A23 south towards Teruel passes through Campo de Cariñena, one of Aragón's premier wine-producing regions. Just off the motorway, the **Ermita de la Fuente** in **Muel** has some fine paintings of saints by the young Goya. If you take the slower but more tranquil N234 to **Cariñena**, **bodegas** (wine cellars) line the main road, and in Cariñena there's a good **Museo del Vino** (Wine Museum; ☎ 976 62 06 94; Camino de la Platera 7; admission €2; ⏰ 10am-1pm & 4-7pm Tue-Fri, 11am-2pm Sat & Sun).

Some 23km east of Cariñena along the A220 lies **Fuendetodos** (population 179), where Francisco José de Goya y Lucientes (Goya) began his days in 1746. The **Casa Natal de Goya** (☎ 976 14 38 30; Zuloaga 3; admission incl Museo del Grabado de Goya €2; ⏰ both 11am-2pm & 4-7pm Tue-Sun) stayed in his family until the early 20th century, when renowned artist Ignacio Zuloaga bought it. Down the road, the **Museo del Grabado de Goya** contains an important collection of the artist's engravings. Buses depart to Fuendetodos (€5.50, one hour, two daily) from Zaragoza's Paseo de María Agustín 20, outside the Museo Pablo Serrano.

A further 18km east, the twin towns of Belchite are an eloquent reminder of the destruction wrought in the Spanish Civil War. The ruins of the old town, which have been replaced by an adjacent new village, stand as a silent memorial to a brutal tug-o-war for possession of Aragón between Republican and Nationalist forces during the war. Abasa buses (€4.25, 45 minutes) arrive from Zaragoza three times daily.

WEST OF ZARAGOZA

Tarazona

pop 10,600 / elev 480m

The quiet, serpentine streets of Tarazona's old town are an evocative reminder of the layout of a medieval Spanish town. It has more than enough monuments to repay a stop.

The helpful **tourist office** (☎ 976 64 00 74; www.tarazona.org; Plaza San Francisco 1; ⏰ 9am-1.30pm & 4.30-7pm Mon-Fri, 10am-1.30pm & 4-6pm Sat & Sun) has lots of material on the town and area.

SIGHTS

Tarazona's **cathedral** is a fetching concoction of Romanesque, Gothic, Mudéjar and Renaissance styles. It has been closed for restoration for more than a decade while engineers undertake major stabilisation works. Nearby, the octagonal **Plaza de Toros Vieja** (Old Bullring) is made up of 32 houses built in the 1790s complete with ringside window seats.

A signposted walking route takes you around the twisting cobbled ways of the medieval 'high part' of the town, north of Río Queiles. From all around you can see the slender Mudéjar tower of the **Iglesia de Santa María Magdalena**. The **Palacio Episcopal** (Bishop's Palace), next door, was a fortified Islamic palace. Tarazona's medieval *judería* (Jewish quarter) is also exceptionally well preserved. The high balconied projections of the 'hanging houses' are remarkable.

SLEEPING & EATING

Hostal Palacete de los Arcedianos (☎ 976 64 23 03; www.palacetearcedianos.com in Spanish; Plaza de los Arcedianos 1; s/d €28/38) Up in the *judería*, this good budget choice offers unfussy, comfy rooms in a pleasant family-run place.

Hostal Santa Agueda (☎ 976 64 00 54; www.santaagueda.com; Calle Visconti 26; s/d from €65/75; ❄ 💻) Just off Plaza San Francisco, this 200-year-old

EIGHT PLACES TO ESCAPE THE MODERN WORLD

Aragón's essential charm is its beguiling sense of timelessness, whether getting close to nature or losing yourself in the labyrinth of one of its stone villages.

- **Parque Nacional de Ordesa y Monte Perdido** (p451) With just 1800 people allowed in this large park at once, it's all about you, the mountains and (if you're fit) a sense of well-being.
- **Sos del Rey Catolico** (p460) Cobblestone streets, the whiff of Spanish legend and a perch high above the madding crowd (except on summer weekends).
- **Aínsa** (p450) There's no more beautiful village in Aragón after the sun sets, the crowds go home and silence reigns.
- **Siresa** (p459) Soaring Pyrenean peaks you can contemplate free from the company of sweaty skiers and hikers.
- **Mirambel** p466) Spain's forgotten corner, where tourists are a rarity and every stone exudes a medieval tranquillity.
- **Daroca** (p461) Just when you thought Aragón's southern badlands have little to offer, Daroca embraces you within its walls.
- **Teruel's Fiesta Medieval** (p463) Dressed as princes and paupers, knights and damsels in distress, Teruel's inhabitants ward off the February cold.
- **Ésera Valley** (p450) Out of sight and earshot of the nearest road and surrounded by a cathedral of mountains, this Pyrenean valley hasn't changed in centuries.

home has lovely rooms with wooden beams and a charming proprietor. The little breakfast room is a glorious shrine to Raquel Meller, Aragón's queen of popular song during the early 20th century.

Hotel Condes de Visconti (☎ 976 64 49 08; www.condesdevisconti.com in Spanish; Calle Visconti 15; s/d €69/79; Ⓟ) Beautiful rooms, mostly with colourful individual decor, plus a preserved Renaissance patio, make this one-time 16th-century palace a fine stopover. It also has a good restaurant.

GETTING THERE & AWAY

Up to six **Therpasa** (☎ 976 64 11 00; www.therpasa.com) buses run daily to/from Zaragoza's Estación Intermodal Delicias (1¼ hours) and Soria (one hour).

Around Tarazona

Backed by the often snowcapped Sierra del Moncayo, the fortified **Monasterio de Veruela** (☎ 976 64 90 25; admission €2.50; 🕒 10.30am-6.30pm Wed-Mon), founded in the 12th century, looks more like a Castilian castle than a monastery. The rather stern Gothic church is flanked by a charming cloister, which has a lower Gothic level surmounted by a Renaissance upper gallery. There's a small wine museum within the complex. The monastery is 13km southeast of Tarazona and 1km from Vera de Moncayo. Two of Therpasa's daily Zaragoza–Tarazona buses stop in Vera itself; the others stop at the Vera turn-off on the N122, 4km from the monastery.

Those with a vehicle can visit **Parque Natural del Moncayo**; it has several walking trails on the flank of the 2300m-plus Sierra del Moncayo.

Calatayud

pop 20,700 / elev 530m

There's little to detain you in quiet Calatayud, just off the Zaragoza–Madrid A2 motorway, although its old town has three fine hotels in converted town houses. The **tourist office** (Plaza del Fuerte; 🕒 9.30am-1.30pm & 4-8pm) hands out the *Map-Guide Book of the town of Calatayud*, in English, to guide your visit. The prettily ramshackle Plaza de España marks the centre of the old town, while nearby the Mudéjar towers of the **Colegiata de Santa María** (Plaza de Santa María), **Iglesia de San Andrés** and the 14th-century **Iglesia de San Pedro** (Rua de Eduardo Dato) are worth a look. The baroque **Parroquia de San Juan El Real** (Calle Valentín Gómez 3; 🕒 10.30am-1pm & 4.30-7.30pm) features four Goya paintings of the fathers of the church, housed in the angles below its dome.

Budget travellers should look no further than **La Casa del Chaplin** (☎ 976 88 58 65; www.lacasadelchaplin.com; Calle de San Antón 9; d €38, menú del día €10.50), with simple, brightly painted rooms. For more character and comfort, **Hospedería**

El Pilar (☎ 976 89 70 20; www.hospederiaelpilar.com in Spanish; Calle Baltasar Gracián 15; s/d €36/68), **Hospedería Mesón de Dolores** (☎ 976 88 90 55; www.mesonladolores.com; Plaza de los Mesones; s/d €53/82) and **Posada Arco de San Miguel** (☎ 976 88 72 72; www.arcodesanmiguel.com; Calle de San Miguel 18; s/d €57/72; menú del dia €16) are wonderfully atmospheric places to sleep.

Calatayud's bus station is just off the central Plaza del Fuerte. Automóviles Zaragoza runs four or more buses daily to/from Zaragoza (€6.80, one hour).

Monasterio de Piedra

This one-time Cistercian **monastery** (☎ 902 19 60 52; park & monastery adult/child €12/8.50, monastery only adult €6.50; ⏰ park 9am-dusk, monastery 10.15am-1.15pm & 3.15-7.15pm), 28km southwest of Calatayud, dates from the 13th century but was abandoned in the 1830s and then sold into private hands in 1840. Subsequent owners laid out the ground as a formal wooded park full of caves and waterfalls, the latter fed by Río Piedra. It's a wonderful place to spend a day with kids, although it has something of a theme park's crassness on summer weekends. Incorporated into the complex is the **Hotel Monasterio de Piedra** (☎ 976 84 90 11; www.monasteriopiedra.com; s/d from €73/130).

On Tuesday, Thursday, Saturday and Sunday (or daily in summer), Automóviles Zaragoza runs a 9am bus from Zaragoza to the monastery (€12.15, 2½ hours) via Calatayud, returning at 5pm.

THE NORTH (THE PYRENEES)

Leaving behind Zaragoza's parched flatlands, a hint of green tinges the landscape and there's a growing anticipation of very big mountains somewhere ahead. And they are big. The Aragonese Pyrenees boast several peaks well over the 3000m mark and they're the most dramatic and rewarding on the Spanish side of the range. Viewed from the south their crenellated ridges fill the northern horizon wherever you turn and their valleys offer magnificent scenery, several decent ski resorts and great walking.

Activities

SKIING

Aragón has plenty of ski slopes in the Pyrenees, with resorts at Cerler (p449), Formigal (p458), Panticosa (p457), Astún (p457) and Candanchú (p457). Most hotels around the resorts offer packages that include ski passes and some meals.

WALKING

Aragón's mountains are more popular in summer than in winter. Some 6000km of long-distance trails (Grandes Recorridos; GR) and short-distance trails (Pequeños Recorridos; PR) are marked all across Aragón. The coast-to-coast GR11 traverses the most spectacular Aragón Pyrenees.

The optimum time for walking is mid-June to early September, though the more popular parks and paths can become crowded in midsummer. The weather can be unpredictable at any time of the year, so walkers should be prepared for extreme conditions at all times and always check the latest weather reports and local trail conditions.

Dotted throughout the mountains are several mountain *refugios* (refuges). Some are staffed and serve meals, while others are empty shacks providing shelter only. At holiday times staffed *refugios* are often full, so unless you've booked ahead, be prepared to camp. The **Federación Aragonesa de Montañismo** (FAM; ☎ 976 22 79 71; www.fam.es in Spanish; 4th fl, Calle Albareda 7, Zaragoza) in Zaragoza can provide information and a FAM card will get you substantial discounts on *refugio* stays.

The Aragonese publisher Prames produces some of the best maps for walkers.

HUESCA

pop 48,900 / elev 488m

Huesca is a provincial capital in more than name, a village writ large that shutters down during the afternoon hours and only stirs to life in the evenings. That said, its old centre retains some appeal and its location in north-central Aragón can serve as a launch pad for the Aragonese high country.

Orientation & Information

Old Huesca sits on a slight rise, with the bus and train stations sharing the modern Estación Intermodal, 500m south. There are several banks with ATMs along Calle de Zaragoza.

Ask the tourist office for a copy of *Radar*, which has a run-down of the month's music, theatre and arts events, or see its website at www.huescacultura.com (in Spanish).

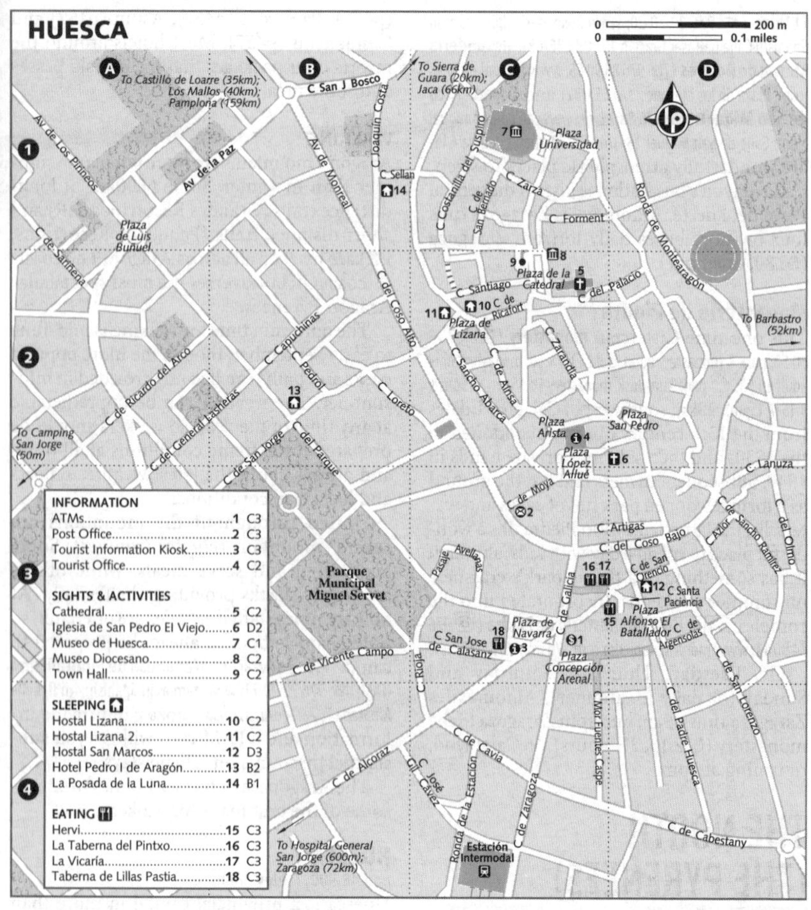

Hospital General San Jorge (☎ 974 24 70 00; Avenida Martínez de Velasco)

Post office (cnr Calles del Coso Alto & de Moya)

Tourist office (☎ 974 29 21 70; www.huescaturismo.com; Plaza López Allué 1; 🕑 9am-2pm & 4-8pm, sometimes open longer hours Jun-Sep) Also operates an information kiosk from June to September on Plaza de Navarra.

Sights

PLAZA DE LA CATEDRAL & AROUND

Somnambulant Plaza de la Catedral, at the heart of the old town, is presided over by the venerable Gothic **cathedral** (☎ 974 22 06 78; 🕑 10.30am-2pm & 3.30-5.30pm). The richly carved main portal dates from 1300. The stately interior features an astonishing, 16th-century alabaster *retablo* by Damián Forment that betrays a mix of Gothic and Renaissance styles. The adjoining **Museo Diocesano** (☎ 974 23 10 99; adult/concession €3/2; 🕑 10.30am-2pm & 4-7.30pm Mon-Fri, 10.30am-2pm Sat Jun-Sep, shorter hr rest of year) exhibits religious art from the Huesca diocese. The 16th-century **ayuntamiento** (town hall) across the square is an Aragonese gem of Renaissance detail. A little way north, the octagonal **Museo de Huesca** (☎ 974 22 05 86; Plaza Universidad 1; admission free; 🕑 10am-2pm & 5-8pm Tue-Sat, 10am-2pm Sun) is excellent, arrayed around a courtyard and containing a well-displayed collection (labels in Spanish only) covering the archaeology and art of Huesca province, including eight works by Goya (Room 7).

IGLESIA DE SAN PEDRO EL VIEJO

Another of the city's historical and architectural landmarks, the church of **San Pedro** (☎ 974 22 23 87; adult/concession €2/1; 🕑 10am-1.30pm & 4-7.30pm Jun-Sep, 10am-1.30pm Oct-May) is 12th-century Romanesque. Its cloister is adorned with beautiful Romanesque capitals attributed to the same maestro who carved those at the Monasterio de San Juan de la Peña (p458).

Tours

The tourist office (opposite) gives **guided tours** of the historic centre (adult/concession €2/1) in Spanish, English and French at 11am from mid-June until mid-September.

Tours by vintage bus (adult/concession €5/2.50, under 12 years free) run daily mid-June to September to the Castillo de Loarre (p446), Los Mallos (p446) and the Sierra de la Guara. Tickets can be bought at the tourist office.

Sleeping

Camping San Jorge (☎ 974 22 74 16; www.campingsanjorge.com in Spanish; Calle de Ricardo del Arco s/n; sites per person/tent/car €3.90/3.90/3.90; 🕑 Apr–mid-Oct) This well-run woodland site 1km west of the old town centre has good facilities. There's a restaurant offering everything from *bocadillos* (filled rolls) to sit-down meals.

Hostal San Marcos (☎ 974 22 29 31; www.hostalsanmarcos.es in Spanish; Calle de San Orencio 10; s/d/tr from €29/47/62; P ❄) In the heart of town, the San Marcos has 29 simple rooms with tiled floors and some have balconies overlooking the street. Parking costs €8; breakfast will set you back €4.

Hostal Lizana/Hostal Lizana 2 (☎ 974 22 07 76; www.hostal-lizana.com; Plaza de Lizana 6; s with/without bathroom €25/35, d with bathroom €50-60, tr €65; P ❄ 💻) Facing each other across a pleasant little plaza are these two worthwhile places, both with decent rooms – the rooms in Lizana 2 are newer, the bathrooms generally larger and you've a better chance of a balcony room here. Parking costs €10.

Hotel Pedro I de Aragón (☎ 974 22 03 00; www.gargallo-hotels.com in Spanish; Calle del Parque 34; s €68-100, d €90-150) Overlooking leafy Parque Municipal Miguel Servet, this is the place for modern, top-end comfort and one of the best locations in town. There are good restaurants and cafes on site.

our pick **La Posada de la Luna** (☎ 974 24 08 57; www.posadadelaluna.com; Calle Joaquin Costa 10; s/d from €95/130; P ❄ 💻) Our favourite hotel in Huesca, this lovely boutique place incorporates some original features of old Huesca architecture with a whimsical but contemporary feel. It's a comfortable, charming place, but there are just eight rooms, so book ahead. The breakfast buffet costs an excessive €15.

Eating

For the capital of a province that prides itself on its cuisine, Huesca has surprisingly few outstanding eateries. That doesn't, however, mean you'll leave hungry.

La Vicaría (☎ 974 22 51 95; Calle de San Orencio 9; tapas from €1.50; 🕑 Mon-Sat) Opposite Hervi and with a pleasing tile-and-wood-panelling interior, La Vicaría serves up great tapas and *raciones* (large tapas serving) (from €5.80).

La Taberna del Pintxo (☎ 974 22 60 63; Calle de San Orencio 7; tapas €2.80; 🕑 9am-4pm & 7pm-1am) Next door to La Vicaría, this engaging little bar has an eclectic menu that ranges from creative *bocadillos* (€4.10), such as steak with Roquefort and walnuts, *pintxos* (tapas; €2.80), *platos combinados* (€9), *cazuelas* (meals cooked in ceramic pots, €6 to €8) and a more traditional *menú del día* (€10.80).

Hervi (☎ 974 24 03 33; Calle Santa Paciencia 2; mains €13-21, menú €12; 🕑 Fri-Wed; V) A hugely popular lunchtime scene, Hervi offers a *menú del día* (daily set menu) where the servings are enormous and, unusually for Aragón, there is a range of vegetarian options.

Taberna de Lillas Pastia (☎ 974 21 16 91; Plaza de Navarra 4; mains €16-26, menú €33-63) Dress up just a little for this classy eatery in the town's old casino. The food is excellent, with a gastronome's touch in both presentation and taste. Meat, fish and attentive service are recurring themes, with special desserts that change daily.

Getting There & Away

BUS

Alosa (☎ 974 21 07 00; www.alosa.es in Spanish) runs numerous daily buses to/from Zaragoza (€6.05, 1¼ hours), Jaca (€6.55, 1¼ hours), Barbastro (from €3.89, 50 minutes), Lleida (Lérida; €9.15, 2¼ hours) and Barcelona (€15.60, 4¼ hours). There's also a daily service to Benasque (€11.13, three hours).

TRAIN

Nine trains a day run to/from Zaragoza (from €5.15, 1¼ hours), including two high-speed

AVE services (€13.40, 40 minutes). There are also AVE services to/from Madrid (€53.30, 2¼ hours, two daily), as well as regular services to Teruel (€17.10, 3¼ hours, one daily) and Valencia (€28.10, 5¾ hours, one daily). Three trains daily head north to Jaca (€7.75, 2½ hours).

AROUND HUESCA

Castillo de Loarre

The evocative **Castillo de Loarre** (☎ 974 34 21 61; www.castillodeloarre.com in Spanish; admission with/without guided tour €3.50/2; ⌚ 10am-2pm & 4-8pm mid-Jun–mid-Sep, 10am-2pm & 4-7pm mid-Sep–Oct & Mar–mid-Jun, 11am-2pm & 3.30-5.30pm Nov-Feb) broods above the southern plains across which Islamic raiders once rode. Raised in the 11th century by Sancho III of Navarra and Sancho Ramírez of Aragón, its resemblance to a crusader castle has considerable resonance with those times. Don't be surprised if it looks familiar – it starred in the 2005 Ridley Scott film *Kingdom of Heaven*, when the medieval fortress served as a backdrop for much of the action (though the film is set in 12th-century France). The banquet scenes were shot in the Iglesia de San Pedro.

A labyrinth of dungeons, tunnels and towers has been left in a state of partial restoration, giving it a suitably realistic atmosphere. Some parts are so dark that a torch (flashlight) would be useful. You can climb two towers for magnificent views.

The castle is a 5km drive, or a 2km, one-hour, uphill walk by the PR-HU105 footpath, from the village of Loarre, 35km from Huesca.

Camping Castillo de Loarre (☎ 974 38 27 23; www.campingloarre.com in Spanish; sites per person/tent/car €3.70/3.70/3.70) is a good site located halfway between the village and the castle. **Hospedería de Loarre** (☎ 974 38 27 06; www.hospederiadeloarre.com; Plaza Miguel Moya; s/d incl breakfast €58.50/73) is a charming, small hotel occupying a converted 16th-century mansion on Loarre village square. Its restaurant offers medium-priced to expensive meals and the hotel is wheelchair accessible.

Two buses run to Loarre village from Huesca (€2.70, 40 minutes) Monday to Friday; there's just one bus on Saturday.

Los Mallos

After a rather unexciting patch along the Huesca–Pamplona road, you come to a dramatic area along Río Gállego north of Ayerbe. On the eastern bank, huge rock towers known as Los Mallos (Mallets) rise up – they wouldn't look out of place in the Grand Canyon and are popular with serious rock climbers. For a closer look, head for Riglos.

ALQUÉZAR

pop 300 / elev 670m

Picturesque Alquézar, 20km northwest of Barbastro, means **canyoning** (*descenso de barrancos* in Spanish), which involves following canyons downstream by whatever means available – walking, abseiling, jumping, swimming, even diving. The Sierra de Guara, north of the Huesca–Barbastro road, is sliced through by more than 200 dramatic canyons of the Río Vero and other river systems; it is Europe's prime location for the sport, with the otherwise quiet village of Alquézar as its hub.

Information

The **tourist office** (☎ 974 31 89 40; Calle Arrabal; ⌚ 10am-1.30pm & 4.30-7.30pm Mon-Fri, 10am-2pm & 4.30-8pm Sat & Sun Jun-Oct, Sat, Sun & festivals only Nov-May) has useful information about the town in various languages. It also runs **guided tours** three times daily in summer (prices vary from €1.20 to €8 depending on the number of people) and can arrange **audioguides** (€4).

Sights

Even if you're not the canyoning type, Alquézar is a beautiful stone village, draped along a ridgeline and crowned by the **Colegiata de Santa María** (☎ 974 23 10 99; admission €2, incl Casa Fabián €3; ⌚ 11am-1.30pm & 4.30-7.30pm Wed-Mon Apr-Sep, 11am-1.30pm & 4-6pm Wed-Mon Oct-Mar), a large castle-monastery. Originally built as an *alcázar* (fortress) by the Arabs in the 9th century, it was conquered around 1060 by Sancho Ramírez. Remnants of the Augustinian monastery he established here in 1099 are still visible. The columns within its delicate cloister are crowned by perfectly preserved carved capitals depicting biblical scenes, and the walls are covered with spellbinding murals. On the upper level is a museum of sacred art. Visits are by guided tour only. The door is locked while tours are in progress, so simply wait for the next tour.

The charming **Casa Fabián** (☎ 974 31 89 13; Calle Baja 16; admission €1.50, incl Colegiata de Santa María €3; ⌚ 11am-2pm & 4-8pm Tue-Sun Apr-Oct, 11am-2pm Tue-Sun Nov-May), a folk museum in a 17th-century house, is full of intriguing artefacts of farming and domestic life and includes an old olive-oil works, dug out of the rocky foundations.

Activities

Several agencies offer guided canyoning and prices vary depending on the number of people and the graded difficulty of the trip. The main season is mid-June to mid-September and prices generally include gear, guide and insurance. Recommended places include:

Avalancha (☎ 974 31 82 99; www.avalancha.org; Calle Arrabal s/n; per person €42-65) Also organises rafting, trekking and mountain climbing.

Guías Boira (☎ 645 16 11 48; www.guiasboira.com in Spanish; per person €40-65) Also organises trekking, and rock and mountain climbing.

Vertientes (☎ 974 31 83 54; www.vertientesaventura.com; Calle San Gregorio 5; per person €42-70).

Sleeping & Eating

Camping Alquézar (☎ 974 31 83 00; www.alquezar.com; sites per person/tent/car €3.80/3.80/3.50) Just outside the village, this camping ground also has two- to six-person bungalows from €67.25 to €117.70. It organises canyon guiding and equipment rental.

Albergue Rural de Guara (☎ 974 31 83 96; www.albergueruraldeguara.com in Spanish; Calle Pilaseras s/n; bunks €12, breakfast €5) This cheerfully run *albergue* (refuge) is perched up above the village with fine views from the surrounds.

Hotel Villa de Alquézar (☎ /fax 974 31 84 16; www.villadealquezar.com in Spanish; Calle Pedro Arenal Cavero 12; s/d incl breakfast from €56/63; P) One of the best places in town, with a lot of style in its large airy rooms; several rooms have great balcony views and there are period touches throughout.

Hotel Santa María (☎ 974 31 84 36; www.hotel-santamaria.com; Calle Arrabal s/n; s/d €75/80) Hotel Santa María may lack the period charm of other places in this price category, but its rooms are light and airy and all but two boast terrific views.

Hotel Maribel (☎ 974 31 89 79; www.hotelmaribel.es; Calle Arrabal s/n; d from €120) This boutique hotel has plenty of charm and while the decor won't be to everyone's taste (following a wine theme and ranging from gorgeous to vaguely kitsch), every room is supremely comfortable.

Restaurants line up along the mirador (lookout) section of Calle Arrabal and you could pretty much take your pick with *menús* for €10 to €15. Up in the old town, **Restaurante Casa Gervasio** (☎ 974 31 82 82; Calle Pedro Arnal Cavero; menú €25-30) is possibly Alquézar's best.

Getting There & Away

Autocares Cortés (☎ 974 31 15 52) runs a bus to Alquézar from Barbastro (€1.66) daily except Sunday; check with the tourist office for times – it doubles as the local school bus and times change during holidays.

North of Alquézar, the road through Colungo to Aínsa is a delightful drive through pre-Pyrenean canyon country.

BARBASTRO & AROUND

pop 15,600 / elev 341m

Barbastro had a 350-year spell as one of Islamic Spain's most northerly outposts, but there are few traces today and it's a bit run-down, although its role as the capital of the Somontano wine region has breathed new life into the town. The area around Plaza del Mercado has some character and the 16th-century **cathedral** boasts a main altarpiece – an incomplete, yet still stunning, work by the Renaissance master Damián Forment.

The **tourist office** (☎ 974 30 83 50; turismo@barbastro.org; Avenida de la Merced 64; 10am-2pm & 4.30-7.30pm Tue-Sat Sep-Jun, daily Jul & Aug), next to the bullring, is combined with the **Espacio de Vino** (☎ 974 31 30 31; www.dosomontano.com in Spanish; 9am-8pm Mon-Fri, 11am-8pm Sat) wine museum, a **wine interpretation centre** and **wine shop** (10am-2pm & 4.30-7.30pm Tue-Sat Sep-Jun, daily Jul & Aug) all devoted to the local Somontano vintages; for more information see the boxed text, p448.

The central, wheelchair-accessible **Hostal Pirineos** (☎ 974 31 00 00; www.hostalpirineos.com; Calle General Ricardos 13; s/d €40/50; P) has bright decor and also runs the town's best cafe. For more comfort, the four-star **Gran Hotel Ciudad de Barbastro** (☎ 974 30 89 00; www.ghbarbastro.com; Plaza del Mercado 4; s/d/ste €61/82/133; P) is right on Plaza del Mercado; parking costs €6.

Monzón (population 14,650), 19km southeast of Barbastro, is home to a formidable **castle** (☎ 974 34 90 07; admission €2.50; 10am-1pm & 5-8pm Tue-Sat, 10am-1pm Sun Jul-Sep, 11.30am-1pm & 3-5pm Tue-Fri, 11.30am-1pm & 4-6pm Sat, 10am-2pm Sun Oct-Jun). Built by the Muslims, then taken for Aragón by Sancho Ramírez, it fell into the hands of the Knights Templar in 1143.

Getting There & Away

From Barbastro's **bus station** (☎ 974 31 12 93), **Alosa** (www.alosa.es in Spanish) operates buses to/from Huesca (from €3.89, 50 minutes), where you'll need to change for buses to Zaragoza and Jaca. There are also services to Monzón

SOMONTANO WINES

Somontano won the coveted Denominación de Origen (DO) status in 1984 and it has since become one of Aragón's most prestigious wine-growing regions. Centred around Barbastro, Somontano's 33 vineyards produce reds, whites and rosés from 13 different types of foreign and local grape varieties (including) chardonnay, cabernet sauvignon, syrah and pinot noir, often blending local grapes such as parreleta, a red grape indigenous to the Somontano region, with foreign varieties. It's a combination that marks out Somantano wines as different. Some of the better-known Somontano labels include Enate and Viñas del Vero.

The tourist office in Barbastro (p447) has brochures in Spanish, English and French outlining the various bodegas (wineries) that can be visited for sales and tasting. The Museo del Vino and interpretation centre attached to the tourist office also have audiovisual displays on Somontano wines, interactive grape-aroma displays and **wine tastings** (☎ 974 31 30 31; tastings €10; 🕑 6-8pm Sat); reservations are essential for the latter. You should also check out www.rutadelvinosomontano.com (in Spanish), which maps out possible wine itineraries through the region.

(€1.30, 25 mins, up to 18 daily), Lleida (Lérida, €5.26, 1½ hours, up to 10 daily), Benasque (€7.24, two hours, two daily); and one or two to Aínsa (€4.88, one hour).

BENASQUE

pop 1550 / elev 1140m

Aragón's northeastern corner is crammed with the highest and shapeliest peaks in the Pyrenees and Benasque (Benás in the local dialect) is perfectly sited to serve as gateway to the highest valleys. Even in midsummer these great mountains can be capped with snow and ice. The area, much of which is protected as the Parque Natural Posets-Maladeta, offers walkers almost limitless options and climbers a wide choice of peaks. Northeast of Benasque, the Pyrenees' highest peak, the Pic d'Aneto (3404m), towers above the massif. The village of Benasque itself occupies a broad green valley with rocky mountains rising on three sides. The location is more beautiful than the village itself, which has been over-touristed, although it does offer a range of services for walkers, climbers and skiers and can get pretty lively at night.

Information

Telecomunicaciones S&Z (☎ 974 55 14 59; Los Huertos 5; per hr €2; 🕑 3-10pm) Benasque's internet connection also offers cheap international calls.

Tourist office (☎ 974 55 12 89; www.turismobenasque.com in Spanish; Calle San Sebastián 5; 🕑 9.30am-1.30pm & 4.30-8pm) Information on walking routes.

Plenty of outfitters offer guides and instruction for climbing, skiing and other activities; most sell or rent clothing and equipment for the hills.

Barrabés (☎ 974 55 16 81; www.barrabes.com in Spanish; Avenida de Francia; 🕑 10.30am-1.30pm & 4.30-9pm) Gear, maps and guidebooks.

Casa de la Montaña (☎ 974 55 20 94; Avenida de los Tilos)

Compañía de Guías Valle de Benasque (☎ 974 55 13 36; www.guiasbenasque.com in Spanish; Avenida Luchón 19)

Gradodiez (☎ 629 182482; www.gradodiez.es; Avenida Luchón) Local branch of Cerler ski shop.

Sleeping

During the ski season most offer packages with *media pensión* (half-board).

Camping Aneto (☎ 974 55 11 41; www.campinganeto.com; sites per person/tent/car €5.60/5.60/5.60) The closest camping ground to town (3.5km away), Aneto is well equipped and has a shop and laundry.

Hotel Avenida (☎ 974 55 11 26; www.h-avenida.com in Spanish; Avenida de Los Tilos 14; s/d €35/45) Rooms here are handsomely furnished and the service is friendly. There's a restaurant attached and cheaper room rates for longer stays.

Hotel San Marsial (☎ 974 55 16 16; www.hotelsanmarsial.com in Spanish; Avenida de Francia 75; s/d incl buffet breakfast €55/110) The usual lodgelike touches are pleasantly done here in this comfortable, well-run hotel at the north end of town.

Eating & Drinking

The best places are along Avenida de los Tilos and its continuation, Calle Mayor.

Taberna del Ixarso (☎ 974 55 28 32; Calle Mayor 12) Meaty tapas such as *chorizo* and *salchichón* (sausage) help the drink go down at this lively little bar, where local aficionados happily mix with tourists.

La Buhardilla (☎ 974 55 13 20; Calle Mayor s/n; dishes €5-16) A plush crêperie at the heart of the old town, the 'attic's' sleek modern decor is softened by a big, open fire for chilly Pyrenean evenings. Sweet and savoury crêpes and fondues are what it's all about.

Restaurante El Fogaril (☎ 974 55 16 12; Calle Mayor 5; mains €18-29) Treat yourself at this elegant country dining room, which serves outstanding Aragonese fare. Its specialities include young venison and stuffed partridge, *cozal* (small deer) and freshwater fish, all superbly prepared and presented.

Bar La Compañía (☎ 974 55 29 00; Avenida Luchón 19; 2-11pm, closed Wed) Nicely worn decor and an upbeat atmosphere make this a popular drinking spot where rock and ice fanciers can thumb through copies of climbing mags while listening to background rock of the other sort.

Getting There & Away

Two buses operate Monday to Saturday, and one runs on Sunday, from Barbastro to Benasque (€7.24, two hours) and back. Buses to/from other destinations require a change in Bastro.

If you're driving, the approach from the south suddenly jumps out at you as the A139/N260 plunges through the Congosto de Ventamillo, a narrow defile carved by the crystalline Río Ésera. There's not much quarter given by traffic in either direction.

AROUND BENASQUE

Paragliding

South of Benasque, the village of Castejón de Sos is a paragliding centre with accommodation. For information on where to stay visit www.castejondesos.es, and for paragliding outfits try www.parapentepirineos.com (in Spanish) and www.volarenc astejon.com.

Skiing

Aragón's easternmost **ski resort** (☎ 974 55 10 12; www.cerler.com) has two centres: one at **Cerler** itself, at 1500m altitude, 6km southeast of Benasque; and another at **Ampriu**, 8km beyond Cerler, at 1900m. On offer are 45 varied runs, totalling 52km at altitudes up to 2630m, plus ski and snowboard schools and equipment rentals. With limited accommodation available, many people prefer to stay in Benasque. A bus service connects Benasque and the ski stations during ski season.

Walking & Climbing

From mid-June to mid-September, buses link Benasque with La Besurta (one-way/return €7.25/10.40), 16km north in the upper Ésera valley; and with the Refugio Pescadores (one-way/return €12.50/15.75) in the Valle de Vallibierna, 11km northeast of Benasque. The buses stop at camping grounds on the A139 north of Benasque – you can use them to reach many of the walks mentioned in this section. Check current timetables at Benasque's tourist office, opposite).

Good maps for northeast Aragón are *Aneto-Maladetas* and *Llardana-Posets* in Prames' 1:40,000 Mapa Excursionista series.

VALLE DE VALLIBIERNA

This valley runs southeast up from the A139 about 5.5km north of Benasque. Take the track towards Camping Ixeia, which leaves the A139 just before the Puente de San Jaime (or Chaime) bridge, 3km from Benasque. You're now on the GR11 coast-to-coast trail, which after a couple more kilometres diverges into Valle de Vallibierna. It's then about a 6km (2½-hour) walk, ascending nearly 600m, to the Refugio Pescadores or the Refugio Coronas, anglers' shelters that are small with no facilities. Three groups of mountain lakes, the Lagos (or Ibons) de Coronas, Llosás and Vallibierna, can each be reached in under two hours from the refuge.

GR11 TO BIELSA

Westbound, the GR11 leaves the A139 just after the Puente de San Jaime. It's an easy three-hour walk (600m ascent) up the Valle de Estós to **Refugio de Estós** (☎ 974 55 14 83; bunks adult/under 14yr €13.50/6), a good 115-bunk refuge (dinner €13.50) attended year-round. A further five hours bring you, via the 2592m Puerto de Gistaín (or Chistau) and some superb views of the Posets massif, to the excellent **Refugio de Viadós** (☎ 974 50 61 63; bunks €8, half-board €23.50; staffed Jun-Sep, Sat & Sun Easter-May). Viadós is a base for climbs on **Posets** (3369m), a serious undertaking that requires mountaineering skills, often requires crampons and long-shaft ice axes and is a hard six hours-plus to the summit, with potential altitude effect. Route finding is not that easy. The GR11 continues some six hours west to the hamlet of Parzán in the Bielsa valley, before heading into the Parque Nacional de Ordesa y Monte Perdido (p451).

Autocares Bergua (☎ 974 50 00 18) runs a bus from Bielsa to Aínsa at 6am Monday, Wednesday and Friday (daily, except Sunday, in July and August).

UPPER ÉSERA VALLEY & MALADETA MASSIF

North of Benasque, the A139 continues paved for about 12km. About 10km from Benasque, a side road leads 6km east along the pretty upper Ésera valley, ending at La Besurta, with a hut selling drinks and some food.

Hospital de Benasque (☎ 974 55 20 12; www.llanosdelhospital.com; bunks €20-30, s/d incl breakfast €115/140; P), a little under halfway from the A139 to La Besurta, is a large mountain lodge in a beautiful location, surrounded by handsome peaks. There's a bar, restaurant, and a variety of accommodation ranging from bunks to semi-luxurious rooms.

An exacting trail from Llanos del Hospital heads northeast and upwards to Peña Blanca, and from there winds steeply up to the 2445m Portillón de Benasque pass on the French frontier. This should take fit walkers about 2½ hours. You could return via the Puerto de la Picada, another pass to the east – or another 3½ hours north down past the Boums del Port lakes to the French town of Bagnères-de-Luchon.

South of La Besurta is the great Maladeta massif, a superb challenge for experienced climbers. This forbidding line of icy peaks, with glaciers suspended from the higher crests, culminates in **Aneto** (3404m), the highest peak in the Pyrenees.

Refugio de la Renclusa (☎ 974 55 21 06; bunks €14, half-board €32), staffed and serving meals from about June to mid-October and weekends from March to June, is a 40-minute walk from La Besurta. Experienced and properly equipped climbers can reach the top of Aneto from here in a minimum of five hours.

The massif offers other peaks, including Maladeta (3308m). From La Besurta or La Renclusa, walkers can follow paths southeast beneath the Maladeta massif, leading into Catalonia.

EAST OF THE PARK

Escalona, a roadside village at the park's southeastern corner, boasts several attractive lodgings. From Escalona you can head up the steep-sided Valle de Pineta, which is crowned by an impressive cirque. Along the way you'll find the shady **Camping Pineta** (☎ 974 50 10 89; www.campingpineta.com; sites per person/tent/car €4.80/4.80/4.80; Apr–mid-Oct), with some bungalows and double rooms; the always-attended **Refugio de Pineta** (☎ 974 50 12 03), with meals; and the luxurious **Parador de Bielsa** (☎ 974 50 10 11; d from €127).

Continuing north on the A138 takes you to the Túnel de Bielsa and into France.

AÍNSA

pop 1400 / elev 589m

The beautiful hilltop village of medieval Aínsa (L'Aínsa in the local dialect), which stands above the modern town of the same name, is one of Aragón's gems, a stunning village of uneven stone. From its perch, you'll have commanding panoramic views of the mountains, particularly of the great rock bastion of La Peña Montañesa. On weekends and throughout the main summer season the place is crammed with visitors.

Orientation & Information

You can drive up by road to a large car park behind the castle, which is the best option if you're staying overnight. Otherwise, the best way up is by foot, traversing cobbled streets between beautiful stone facades and eventually to the huge, arcaded Plaza Mayor and the castle.

There's an excellent **regional tourist office** (☎ 974 50 05 12; www.turismosobrarbe.com in Spanish; Plaza del Castillo 1, Torre Nordeste; 10am-2pm & 4-7pm) within the castle walls. Down in the new town, you'll find the helpful **tourist office** (☎ 974 50 07 67; ainsa@pirineo.com; Avenida Pirenáica 1; 9am-9pm Jul & Aug, 10am-2pm & 4-8pm Sep-Apr, closed Sun & Mon Nov-Mar).

Sights

The restored Romanesque **Iglesia de Santa María**, rising above the northeastern corner of Plaza Mayor, lights up when you pop a €1 coin into a box, with five minutes of Gregorian chants thrown in. The crypt and Gothic cloister are charming, while you can also climb the **belfry** (admission €1; approx 11am-1.30pm & 4-7pm) for stunning views of the mountains to the north and down over the terracotta rooftops of the old town; climb as close to sunset as the opening hours allow. Otherwise, simply wander down through the village along either Calle de Santa Cruz or Calle Mayor, pausing in the handful of artsy shops en route.

The **castle** and fortifications off the western end of the plaza mostly date from the 1600s, though the main tower is 11th century; there are some reasonable views from the wall. It contains an interesting **ecomuseum** (☎ 974 50 05 97; admission €2.50; 10.30am-2pm & 5-8.30pm Wed-Sun Easter-Oct) on Pyrenean fauna.

Sleeping

There's plenty of accommodation in the old town, but booking ahead is always advisable, partly because demand is high but also because hotel receptions here are rarely staffed around the clock. There was an **albergue** (youth hostel) close to completion down the eastern end of Calle Mayor when we visited, which will provide much-needed budget accommodation in the old town when it opens.

Casa El Hospital (☎/fax 974 50 07 50; Calle del Arco del Hospital; s €25-29, d €39-55) The cheapest place to stay in the old town, this place sits just off Plaza Mayor in a lovely stone building. There are six comfortable rooms with brass beds.

our pick **Hotel Los Siete Reyes** (☎ 974 50 06 81; www.lossietereyes.com in Spanish; Plaza Mayor s/n; d €90-120;) Set in one of the most charming stone buildings overlooking Plaza Mayor, this temple of style has stunning bathrooms, polished floorboards, flat-screen TVs and some lovely period detail wedded to a contemporary look (eg contemporary art adorning exposed stone walls). The attic rooms are enormous, but all are spacious and some have lovely views. Reasonable prices make this one of Aragón's best all-round choices.

Hotel Los Arcos (☎ 974 50 00 16; www.hotellosarcosainsa.com in Spanish; Plaza Mayor 23; s €85-96, d €107-160;) In a fine position on Plaza Mayor, this stylish hotel has luxurious rooms with canopied beds and good-sized bathrooms. In our view it doesn't quite scale the heights of its neighbour, Hotel Los Siete Reyes, and prices can be a little steep in high season, but it's still an outstanding place.

Other atmospheric places:

Hotel Villa Romanica (☎ 974 50 07 50; www.hotelvillaromanica.com in Spanish; Calle de Santa Cruz 21; s/d from €40/59;)

Posada Real (☎ 974 50 09 77; www.posadareal.com; Plaza Mayor s/n; d from €80;)

Eating & Drinking

In summer, there are plenty of outdoor tables around Plaza Mayor, a delightful place to eat in the cool of a summer evening, although prices can be steep.

our pick **L'Alfil** (☎ 974 50 02 99; Calle Traversa; raciones €6.50-11; Thu-Tue) A pretty little place with floral accompaniment to its outside tables, in a side street along from the church, this cafe-bar does a whole heap of *raciones* that are more creative than you'll find elsewhere, from ostrich chorizo, snails and deer sausage to wild boar paté and cured duck. It also serves good local wines.

Bodegas del Sobrarbe (☎ 974 50 09 37; www.bodegasdelsobrarbe.com; Plaza Mayor 2; mains from €13, menú €21.50) This fine restaurant off the southeastern corner of Plaza Mayor offers meaty Aragonese fare with a few fish dishes. The stuffed pork with foie and mushrooms is superb.

Bodegón de Mallacán (☎ 974 50 09 77; Plaza Mayor 6; menú €22, meals from €20) One of the most popular places on Plaza Mayor, this place has an extensive wine cellar, high-quality traditional local cooking and a number of pretty dining rooms.

L'Alverdadero (Calle Mayor; 6pm-late Mon-Fri, 3pm-late Sat & Sun) The outdoor terrace of this popular little bar, just down the hill from the Plaza Mayor, is our favourite Aínsa drinking hole. It also has free wi-fi for patrons.

Getting There & Away

ALOSA (☎ 902 21 07 00; www.alosa.es in Spanish) sends a daily bus to Aínsa from Barbastro (€4.88, one hour), while the same company also has one bus a day to Torla (€3.10, one hour). **Autocares Bergua** (☎ 974 50 06 01) has buses from Aínsa to Bielsa (€2.95, 45 minutes) on Monday, Wednesday and Friday; in July and August this service runs daily except Sunday.

PARQUE NACIONAL DE ORDESA Y MONTE PERDIDO

This is where the Spanish Pyrenees really take your breath away. At the heart of it all is a dragon's back of limestone peaks skirting the French border, with a southeastward spur that includes Monte Perdido (3348m), the third-highest peak in the Pyrenees. Deep valleys slice down from the high ground. Most were carved by glaciers and at their heads lie bowl-like glacial *circos* (cirques) backed by spectacular curtain walls of rock. Chief among the valleys are Pineta (east), Escuaín (southeast), Bellos (south), Ordesa (southwest), Bujaruelo (west) and Gavarnie (north, in France).

Orientation

The park's main jumping-off point is Torla (p454), 3km south of the southwest corner of the national park. For information about getting into the park, see p454.

From Escalona, 11km north of Aínsa on the A138, a minor paved road heads northwest across to Sarvisé, a few kilometres south of Torla. This road crosses the park's southern tip, with a narrow, sinuous section winding up the dramatic Bellos valley and giving access to walks in the spectacular Cañón de Añisclo (the upper reaches of the Bellos valley).

From Bielsa a 12km paved road runs up the Valle de Pineta in the park's northeastern corner.

MAPS

Ordesa y Monte Perdido Parque Nacional (1:25,000), published by the Ministerio de Fomento in 2000, costs around €7 and comes with a booklet detailing 20 walks. It's available in Torla shops.

If you're keen to traverse the park along the GR11, look for the strip maps *Senda Pyrenaica*, produced by Prames. Another good reference is the guidebook *Through the Spanish Pyrenees: GR11 – A Trekking Guidebook* by Paul Lucia and available from **Cicerone Press** (www.cicero ne.co.uk).

Information

Camping is allowed only above certain altitudes (1800m to 2500m), in small tents pitched at sunset and taken down at sunrise. Swimming in rivers or lakes, mountain biking, fishing and fires are banned.

In addition to the following park information centres, a large interpretation centre was due to open in the main car park in Torla soon after we visited, and the Centro de Visitantes El Parador (at Pradera de Ordesa) was to close.

Bielsa (☎ 974 50 10 43; 9am-1.30pm & 3-6pm Easter-Oct, 8am-3pm Mon-Fri Nov-Easter)

Centro de Visitantes El Molino (9am-1.30pm & 3-6pm Easter-Oct) In Tella in the Escuaín sector.

Escalona (☎ 974 50 51 31; 9am-1.30pm & 3-6pm Easter-Oct, 8am-3pm Mon-Fri Nov-Easter)

Torla (☎ 974 48 64 72; year-round 8am-3pm & 4-6pm Mon-Thu, 8am-3pm Fri, 9am-2pm & 4-7pm Sat & Sun) At the north end of Torla.

Walking & Climbing

CIRCO DE SOASO

A classic day walk follows the Valle de Ordesa to Circo de Soaso, a rocky balcony whose centrepiece is the **Cola del Caballo** (Horsetail) waterfall. From the eastern end of the Pradera de Ordesa, cross Río Arazas and climb steeply up through woods on the valley's south side. This hardest part, called the Senda de los Cazadores (Hunters' Path), in which you ascend 600m, takes an hour. Then it's level or downhill all the way along the high Faja de Pelay path to the *circo*. Return by the path along the bottom of the valley, passing several waterfalls. The circuit takes about seven hours.

REFUGIO DE GÓRIZ & MONTE PERDIDO

Fit walkers can climb a series of steep switchbacks (part of the GR11) to Circo de Soaso

PYRENEAN WILDLIFE

The vegetation range in the park's valleys is fascinating. Lush mixed forest gives way higher up to scattered stands of pines that cling to sheer cliffs in places. Above the treeline is the high mountain zone where edelweiss, gentians and other wildflowers sparkle with colour across the otherwise arid ground.

The park is home to at least 45 species of mammal and 130 bird species. Among the signature mammals is the chamois (*rebeco* in Spanish, *sarrio* in Aragonese), which wanders the park's upper reaches in herds of up to 50. It's not known whether the brown bear (*oso pardo* in Spanish), once prolific throughout the Pyrenees, has survived within the park's boundaries. Although some estimates place the number of brown bears at around 40, wildlife biologists suggest that the number may be as low as three and no more than 15 in the entire Pyrenean region straddling the Spanish–French border, including a handful of Slovenian brown bears introduced in the past decade. Bird species include the rare and formidable lammergeier or *quebrantahuesos* (bearded vulture) and the always-spectacular golden eagle.

Consider buying the excellent *Ecoguía del Parque Nacional de Ordesa y Monte Perdido* (in Spanish; €19), which is available in towns surrounding the park. It also details 100 walks.

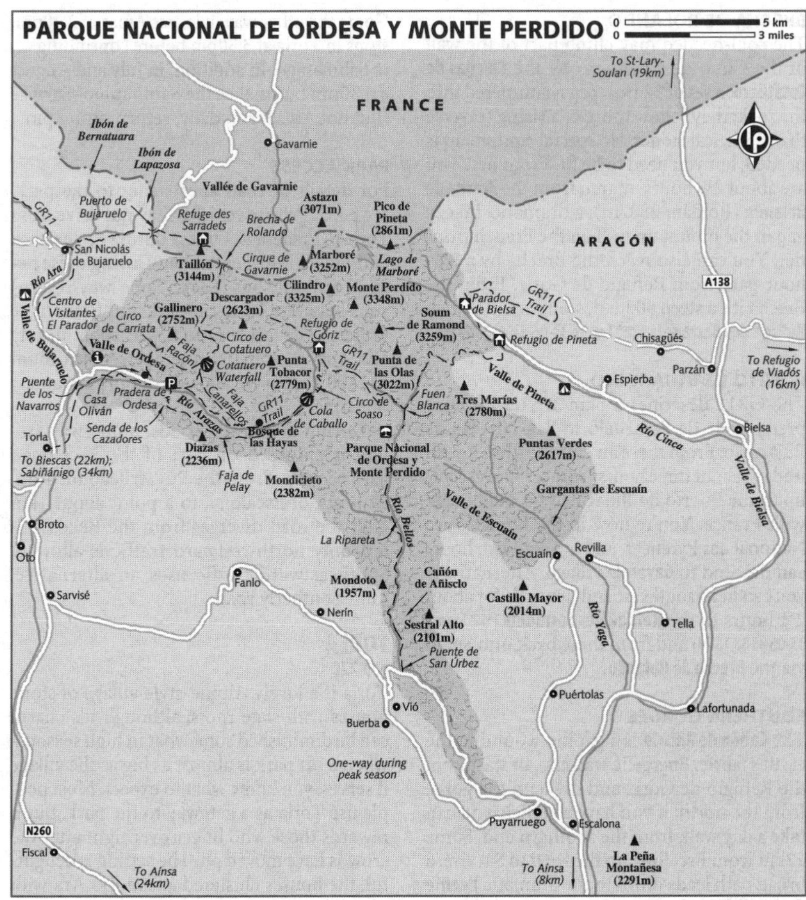

and up to the **Refugio de Góriz** (☎ 974 34 12 01; bunks €14), at 2200m. This 72-place refuge, attended and serving meals year-round, makes an obvious base for ascents of Monte Perdido. For July and August, book a month ahead. As with Posets (p449), Monte Perdido is a serious undertaking that requires mountaineering skills, crampons and ice axes.

FAJA RACÓN, CIRCO DE COTATUERO & FAJA CANARELLOS

This walk takes you along spectacular high-level paths on the north flank of the Valle de Ordesa. It takes about five or six hours, an hour less if you omit Faja Canalleros. It shouldn't be attempted in winter and spring, when there's a high risk of ice, falling rocks and avalanches.

From Pradera de Ordesa head 600m west back along the paved road to Casa Oliván, and take the path signed 'Tozal del Mallo, Circo de Carriata'. About 1½ hours up this fairly steep, zigzag path, diverge eastward along the path signed 'Faja Racón': this high-level route of about 3km brings you out below the Circo de Cotatuero's impressive 200m **waterfall**. From here head downhill to a wooden shelter. Here you can either continue down the Cotatuero *circo* to a path junction 600m east of Pradera de Ordesa or, if you're still energetic, cross a bridge opposite the shelter to follow another high-level path of 3km to 4km, Faja Canarellos. This brings you down to the Valle de Ordesa at Bosque de las Hayas, from where it's 4km westward, gently downhill, to Pradera de Ordesa.

BRECHA DE ROLANDO

The cool-headed may climb part of the wall of the Circo de Cotatuero by the **Clavijas de Cotatuero**, a set of 32 iron pegs hammered into the rock; they follow more of a rising traverse than a vertical ladder. No special equipment is needed, but you need to be fit. From here you are about 2½ hours' march from the **Brecha de Rolando** (Roldán; 2807m), a dramatic, breezy gap in the mountain wall on the French frontier. You can also reach the Brecha by a 3½-hour path from Refugio de Góriz. From the Brecha it's a steep 500m descent to the French **Refuge des Sarradets** (☎ France 33-06 83 38 13 24).

PUERTO DE BUJARUELO

The GR11 describes a 6km arc up the very pretty Valle de Bujaruelo to San Nicolás de Bujaruelo. From there an east–northeast path leads in about three hours (with a 950m ascent) up to the Puerto de Bujaruelo on the border with France. You're now in the French Parc National des Pyrénées, and in about two hours can descend to **Gavarnie** village. Alternatively you can head southeast and upwards for about 2½ hours to the **Refuge des Sarradets** (☎ France 33-06 83 38 13 24) and from there back into Spain via the **Brecha de Rolando**.

SOUTHERN GORGES

The **Cañón de Añisclo** is a gaping wound in the earth's fabric. Energetic walkers can start from the Refugio de Góriz and descend the gorge from the north; if you have a vehicle you can take a day walk from the southern end. Some 12km from Escalona on the road to Sarvisé, a broad path leads down to the dramatic **Puente de San Úrbez**, then up the canyon. You can walk as far north as La Ripareta and back in about five hours, or to Fuen Blanca and back in about eight hours.

The **Gargantas de Escuaín** is a smaller-scale but still-dramatic gorge on Río Yaga, further east. You can descend into the gorge in about an hour from the semi-abandoned hamlet of Escuaín, reached by a minor road off the Escalona–Sarvisé road.

Getting There & Away

BUS

One daily bus operated by **ALOSA** (☎ 902 21 07 00; www.alosa.es in Spanish) connects Torla to Aínsa (€3.10, one hour) and Sabiñanigo (€3.03, one hour). It departs Sabiñanigo at 11am, then continues on from Torla to Aínsa at noon. Going the other way, it leaves Aínsa at 2.30pm, stops in Torla at 3.30pm before continuing on to Sabiñanigo. In addition, in July and August a 6.30pm bus makes the Sabiñánigo–Sarvisé (but not Aínsa) run daily, returning at 8pm.

PARK ACCESS

For details of road approaches to the park, see p452. Private vehicles may not drive from Torla to Pradera de Ordesa during Easter week and July to mid-September. During these periods a shuttle bus (€3/4.50 one-way/return) runs between Torla car park and Pradera de Ordesa. The last run back is at 10pm in July and August, 9pm in September. A maximum of 1800 people are allowed in the park at any one time.

During the same periods, a one-way system is enforced on part of the Escalona–Sarvisé road. From the Puyarruego turn-off, 2km out of Escalona, to a point about 1km after the road diverges from the Bellos valley, only northwestward traffic is allowed. Southeastward traffic uses an alternative, more southerly road.

TORLA

pop 220

Torla is a lovely Alpine-style village of stone houses with slate roofs, although it's charm can be diminished somewhat in high season – when a car park is almost as big as the village it serves, you know what to expect. Most people use Torla as a gateway to the park, but it rewards those who linger overnight after the crowds have moved on. The setting is delightful, the houses clustered above Río Ara with a backdrop of the national park's mountains. In your ramblings around town, make for the 13th-century **Iglesia de San Salvador**; there are fine views from the small park on the church's northern side.

Sleeping & Eating

Reservations are essential during July and August. There are three camping grounds within 2km north of Torla (all closed from mid- or late October till Easter).

Hostal Alto Aragón (☎/fax 974 48 61 72; Calle de Capuvita; s/d from €30/38) Run in harness with Hotel Ballarín, with well-kept rooms.

Hotel Ballarín (☎/fax 974 48 61 55; Calle de Capuvita 11; s €32-42, d €40-50) Every bit as smart as Alto and has superb views from the top rooms. The welcome could be warmer.

Hotel Villa de Torla (☎ 974 48 61 56; www.hotelvilladetorla.com; Plaza de Aragón 1; s/d from €35/55;) The rooms here are tidy with a few nods to local character, but the undoubted highlight is the swimming pool and the bar terrace.

Hotel Villa Russell (☎ 974 48 67 70; www.hotelvillarussell.com; Calle de Capuvita; s/d from €57/80; P) Villa Russell has rooms that won't win a style contest, but they're enormous, come with sofas, microwave and hydromassage showers. Onsite parking costs €6.

The cheapest place to stay is **Refugio Lucien Briet** (☎ 974 48 62 21; www.refugiolucienbriet.com in Spanish; Calle de Francia; bunks €10, d €40), a French-managed refuge-style place in the village. It also has a couple of attractive *casas rurales* nearby.

All of the above places have restaurants with *menús* from €12 to €17. The charming **Restaurante El Duende** (☎ 974 48 60 32; www.elduenderestaurante.com in Spanish; Calle de la Iglesia; menú del día €18, meals €25-30) is the best restaurant in town, with fine local cuisine in a lovely 19th-century building.

Getting There & Away

For information on bus services from Torla, turn to opposite.

Around Torla

VALLE DE BUJARUELO

North of Torla and shadowing the eastern boundary of the park, Valle de Bujaruelo is another good base.

Camping Valle de Bujaruelo (☎ 974 48 63 48; www.campingvalledebujaruelo.com in Spanish; sites per person/tent/car €4.20/4.20/4.20, r €37-57; Easter–mid-Oct) Located 3.5km up the Valle de Bujaruelo, this camping ground features a refuge with bunks, a restaurant and a supermarket. The setting's lovely and the facilities are well maintained.

Mesón de Bujaruelo (☎ 974 48 64 12; www.mesondebujaruelo.com in Spanish; dm/s/d €12/18/36, half-board per person €28-37) At San Nicolás, 3km further up the valley, this old hostelry provides bunks and meals in a pretty location by the Puerto de Bujaruelo. Accommodation is too-cool-for-style mountain basics, but it's all about location here.

JACA

pop 11,800 / elev 820m

At once a gateway to the western valleys of the Aragonese Pyrenees and an agreeable town in its own right, Jaca has a pretty old town dotted with remnants of its past as the capital of the nascent 11th-century Aragón kingdom. These include an unusual fortress and some great places to eat. In February 2007 Jaca hosted the European Youth Olympic Winter Sports Festival and, on winter weekends, après-ski funsters provide a lively soundtrack.

Information

Ciberciva (Avenida del Regimiento de Galicia 2; per hr €2; 11am-1.30pm & 5pm-10pm Mon-Sat, 5.30-10pm Sun) Internet access.

Librería La Trastienda (☎ 974 36 34 38; Plaza de San Pedro 1; 10am-1.30pm & 5-8.30pm) Maps and guidebooks for the region.

Post office (Calle Universidad)

Tourist office (☎ 974 36 00 98; Plaza de San Pedro 11-13; 9am-1.30pm & 4.30-7.30pm Mon-Sat) Around the corner from the cathedral.

Sights & Activities

Jaca's 11th-century **cathedral** is a powerful building, its imposing facade typical of the sturdy stone architecture of northern Aragón. It was once more gracefully French Romanesque in style, but a Gothic overhaul in the 16th century bequeathed a hybrid look. The interior retains some fine features, in particular the side chapel dedicated to Santa Orosia, the city's patron saint, whose martyrdom is depicted in a series of mysterious murals. In the cloister, the **Museo Diocesano** has a remarkable collection of frescoes and sculpture from churches throughout the region; it was closed for restoration at the time of research.

The star-shaped, 16th-century **Ciudadela** (Citadel; www.museominiaturasjaca.es; adult/concession €10/5; 11am-2pm & 5-8pm Tue-Sun, closed second half Nov, last tickets sold at 1pm & 7pm) is Spain's only extant pentagonal fortress (the one in Pamplona is not complete) and one of only two in Europe. It now houses an army academy, but visits are permitted, with 40-minute guided tours (in English, Spanish or French). In the *ciudadela* the **Museo de Miniaturas Militares** (Museum of Military Miniatures) is an extraordinary collection of models and dioramas of battles ancient and otherwise, with over 32,000 toy soldiers on show. Deer graze in the moat surrounding the *ciudadela*.

There are some lovely old buildings in the streets of the **casco historico** (old city) that fans out south of the cathedral, including the 15th-century **Torre del Reloj** (clock tower; Plaza del Marqués

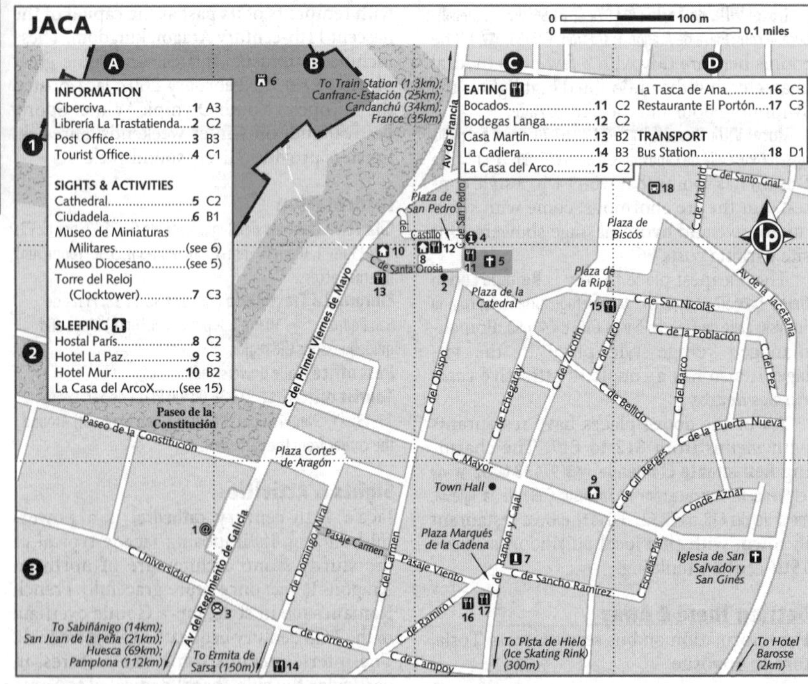

de la Cadena) and the charming little **Ermita de Sarsa** (Avenida Oroel).

The town's state-of-the-art **Pista de Hielo** (ice-skating rink), was closed for renovations when we visited but should be open by the time you read this.

Festivals & Events

Jaca puts on its party gear for the week-long **Fiesta de Santa Orosia**, which revolves round the saint's day of 25 June. To see displays of medieval archery visit on the first Friday of May, when Jaca celebrates a **Christian victory** over the Islamics in 760. The **Festival Folklórico de los Pirineos**, held in late July and early August, provides 1½ weeks of international music, dance, crafts and theatre. It's held on odd-numbered years.

Sleeping

It's worth booking ahead at weekends throughout the year, during the skiing season, and in July and August.

Hostal París (☎ 974 36 10 20; www.jaca.com/hostalparis in Spanish; Plaza San Pedro 5; s/d/tr without bathroom from €28/38/54) Close to the cathedral, this friendly, central option has spotless, ample-sized rooms and smart shared bathrooms (seven bathrooms for 20 rooms) that you'd swear were recently renovated. Breakfast costs €3.

La Casa del Arco (☎ 974 36 44 48; www.lacasadelarco.net in Spanish; Calle de San Nicolás 4; s without bathroom €20, d with/without bathroom €55/40; ☒) Rooms here at this fine all-round venue are cheerfully otherworldly, with a few bohemian touches.

Hotel Mur (☎ 974 36 01 00; www.hotelmur.com; Calle de Santa Orosia 1; s/d/tr incl breakfast €40/60/74) A pleasantly rambling place, this long-established hotel provides comfort and style, with light-filled rooms, some of which have views towards the *ciudadela;* those without exterior windows can be claustrophobic.

our pick **Hotel Barosse** (☎ 974 36 05 82; www.barosse.com in Spanish; s incl breakfast €77-117, d incl breakfast €95-141; ☒ ❄ 💻) In the quiet hamlet of Barós 2km south of Jaca, Hotel Barosse has six individually-styled rooms with lovely attention to detail, from exposed stone walls and splashes of colour to fine bathroom packages of goodies. There's a reading room, garden, an on-site Jacuzzi and sauna, and fine views of the Pyrenees. Best of all, José and Gustavo are wonderful hosts.

Eating

Bocados (☎ 974 36 52 17; Plaza de San Pedro 11-13; ⏲ 9am-midnight Thu-Tue) This cool little bar-cafe next to the cathedral serves up *bocadillos* (€4.30) and sweet and savoury crêpes (€3 to €8), as well as salads, pastries and fresh juices.

our pick La Tasca de Ana (☎ 974 36 36 21; Calle de Ramiro I 3; meals €10-15; ⏲ 7-11.30pm Mon-Fri, 12.30-3.30pm & 7-11.30pm Sat & Sun; ☒) One of Aragón's best tapas bars, La Tasca de Ana has tempting options lined up along the bar, more choices cooked to order and a carefully chosen list of local wines. Check out its '*tapas mas solicitados*' (most popular orders) listed on the blackboard. When we were there, the 'Rodolfito' (prawn in sauce) was top of the list and deservedly so, but there's so much here to get excited about.

La Cadiera (☎ 974 35 55 59; Calle de Domingo Miral 19; menú €10.10, meals €10-15; ⏲ lunch & dinner Tue & Thu-Sun, dinner Wed) The emphasis at this popular eatery is on meaty northern fare. Surefire bets include the garlic soup, *ternasco* (lamb), *migas* and *trucha de la Val* (trout).

La Casa del Arco (☎ 974 36 44 48; www.lacasadelarco.net in Spanish; Calle de San Nicolás 4; 2-/3-course menú from €15; ☒ Ⓥ) A haven of imaginative vegetarian food and with a delightfully alternative ambience, La Casa del Arco is terrific. Downstairs is a nice little bar, the Tetaría el Arco, which stages occasional music sessions and other events.

Restaurante El Portón (☎ 974 35 58 54; Plaza del Marqués de la Cadena 1; menú €13-36) Located in a little tree-shaded plaza, this classy venue serves haute-cuisine versions of Aragonese fare. Reservations are a must. Highly recommended.

Other good choices:

Bodegas Langa (☎ 974 36 04 94; Plaza de San Pedro 5) Gourmet-food-store-cum-summer-tapas-bar.

Casa Martín (☎ 974 35 69 04; Calle de Santa Orosia 2; menú del día €10.50, meals €20-30) Try the *guisado de jabalí* (wild boar stew; €9.90).

Getting There & Away

Five buses go to Huesca (€7.15, 1¼ hours) and Zaragoza (€13.20, 2¼ hours) most days, and two go to Pamplona (€7.75, 1¾ hours) from the central **bus station** (☎ 974 35 50 60; Plaza de Biscós).

AROUND JACA

The N330 leads north from Jaca, via the pretty Río Aragón valley, to the Somport road tunnel into France, passing **Canfranc-Estación** after 25km. Opened in 1928, this enormous station's distinctive architecture reflected the Modernista style. At the time it was Europe's second-largest station. The French unilaterally halted the service after an accident in 1970. There's talk of reopening the line, although more out of nostalgia than necessity. Two trains a day from Zaragoza via Huesca and Jaca stop here.

Ski Resorts

CANDANCHÚ & ASTÚN

A major winter sports stadium opened at **Candanchú** (☎ 974 37 31 94; www.candanchu.com) for the 2007 European Youth Olympic Winter Sports Festival, boosting the reputation of the resort, which lies 28km north of Jaca. Some 42km of widely varied pistes make it appealing to most grades of skiers.

One advantage of visiting Candanchú is that another good resort, **Astún** (☎ 974 37 30 88; www.astun.com in Spanish), is just 3km east. Astún's 42km of pistes are largely for capable skiers.

Five daily buses head from Jaca to Candanchú and Astún (€2.75, 45 minutes), via Canfranc-Estación.

GÁLLEGO VALLEY

From the regional centre of Biescas, north of Sabiñanigo, the A136 climbs gently towards the French border.

The small ski resort of **Panticosa** (☎ 974 48 72 48; www.panticosa-loslagos.com) occupies a pleasant perch at the confluence of two picturesque valleys. The runs here aren't too difficult, although the nearly 2km Mazaranuala ski run is a must for adept skiers.

A further 8km beyond the village is **Panticosa Resort** (☎ 902 25 25 22; www.panticosa.com), a stunning complex that includes the four-star **Hotel Continental** (d from €120),;five-star **Gran Hotel** (d from €350); three restaurants including **Restaurante del Lago** (meals start at around €65), watched over by star chef Pedro Subijana; bars; a casino; and the **Balneario** (Termas de Tiberio), a luxurious spa complex recently remodelled by star architect Rafael Moneo. Given its prestige, the Balneario's prices are surprisingly reasonable, with a €30 entry fee allowing access to the baths and gym, while a range of additional treatments is available. As well as such services, the setting is stunning, alongside a lake in an enclosed valley high in the Pyrenees.

Returning to the main A136, **Sallent de Gállego**, 3.5km north of the Panticosa turn-off, is a lovely stone village with a bubbling brook running through it. A little further on, a livelier ski resort with more infrastructure than Panticosa, **Formigal** (☎ 974 49 00 00; www.formigal.com) is a regular host for ski competitions, although like most ski towns it's a little quiet out of season. Here you have the full range of facilities, including restaurants, bars, discos and saunas, as well as 57km of ski runs and 22 lifts.

From Jaca, one or two daily buses wind over to Panticosa and Formigal (€5.30, two hours).

Monasterio de San Juan de la Peña

High in a mountain eyrie 21km southwest of Jaca, Monasterio de San Juan de la Peña is Aragón's most fascinating monastery. Gateway to the monastery is **Santa Cruz de la Serós**, a pretty village 4km south of the N240.

From Santa Cruz, a winding road climbs the Sierra de la Peña 7km to the **Monasterio Viejo** (Old Monastery; ☎ 974 35 51 19; www.monasteriosanjuan.com; adult/concession/child incl Iglesia de Santa María Nov-Easter €4.50/4/2.25, Easter-Oct €6/5/3; 10am-2pm & 4-7pm 6 Mar-May, Sep & Oct, 10am-2pm & 3-8pm Jun–mid-Jul, 10am-8pm mid-Jul–Aug, 10.30am-2pm & 3.30-5.30pm Nov-6 Mar), tucked under an overhanging lip of rock at a bend in the road.

The rock shelter where the Monasterio Viejo is built, perhaps used by Christian hermits as early as the 8th century, became a monastery in the 10th century, when the Mozarabic lower church was constructed. The monastery emerged as the early spiritual and organisational centre of the medieval kingdom of Aragón. A Romanesque church was built above it in the late 11th century. The highlight is the Romanesque **cloister**, with marvellous carved 12th- and 13th-century capitals depicting Genesis and the life of Christ. The first three kings of Aragón – Ramiro I (1036–64), Sancho Ramírez (1064–94) and Pedro I (1094–1104) – are among those buried here.

A fire in 1675 led the monks to abandon the old monastery and build a new one in brick further up the hill. **Monasterio Nuevo**, which keeps the same hours as Monasterio Viejo. It has a large visitors centre as well as the **Monastery Interpretation Centre** (adult/concession/child incl Iglesia de Santa María Nov-Easter €4.50/3/2, Easter-Oct €5/4/2.50), which documents the archaeological history of the site, and the **Kingdom of Aragón Interpretation Centre** (adult/concession/child incl Iglesia de Santa María Nov-Easter €4.50/3/2, Easter-Oct €5/4/2.50), devoted to the kings of Aragón.

A combined ticket for Monasterio Viejo, interpretation centres and Iglesia de Santa María costs €8/7/4 per adult/concession/child from November to Easter, €10/8/5 from Easter to October.

In Santa Cruz de la Serós, the 11th-century Romanesque **Iglesia de Santa María** (10am-2pm & 4-7pm) dominates the village. It has a stark beauty and you can climb the tower.

SLEEPING & EATING

Hostelería Santa Cruz (☎ 974 36 19 75; www.santacruzdelaseros.com; Calle Ordana; s/d €40/50), near the church in Santa Cruz de las Serós, is a beautiful place with friendly service and lovely rooms. Its restaurant serves a good *menú del día* (€12).

Hospedería Monasterio San Juan de la Peña (☎ 974 37 44 22; www.hospedriasdearagon.es; s/d €118/148;) Part of the Monasterio Nuevo, this recently opened four-star hotel has supremely comfortable rooms, a spa complex and good restaurant. It's wheelchair accessible.

GETTING THERE & AWAY

There's no public transport to the monastery, but if you buy your entry ticket for the monastery in the village it covers bus transport from the village, at least in high season.

At quiet times of year, drivers may be able to park on the roadside near the Monasterio Viejo; during high season you'll have to continue uphill for another 1.3km to the car park near the Monasterio Nuevo. At busy times a shuttle bus (€2) takes people down to Monasterio Viejo.

For walkers, a stiff 4km marked path (the GR65.3.2) leads up from Santa Cruz to the Monasterio Viejo in about 1½ hours, with an ascent of 350m.

VALLES DE ECHO & ANSÓ

The verdant Echo and Ansó valleys are mountain magic at its best, beginning with gentle climbs through the valleys and the accumulating charms of old stone villages punctuating slopes of dense mixed woods of beech, pine, rowan, elm and hazel. As the valleys narrow to the north, 2000m-plus peaks rise triumphantly at their heads. Go quietly through these beautiful valleys; they encourage a gentle touch and deserve less-conspicuous tourism than the more spectacular territory further east.

Most places to stay have good information on walking and exploring the area. Good map-guides include Prames' *Ansó-Echo Aragués-Jasa* or Alpina's *Ansó-Echo*.

A bus to Jaca leaves Ansó at 6.30am, Siresa at 6.53am and Echo at 7am, Monday to Saturday, returning from Jaca at 6.50pm. A road links Anso and Echo, a distance of about 12km.

Echo (Hecho)

pop 600 / elev 833m

Lovely Echo, the biggest village in the valley, is a place in which to linger, although you'll have company in the high season. It's, an attractive warren of solid stone houses with steep roofs and flower-decked balconies. There's a charming artistic riff in the form of street sculptures and a hillside sculpture park.

The helpful **tourist office** (☎ 974 37 55 05, 974 37 50 02; www.valledehecho.net in Spanish; Carretera Oza s/n; ⏰ 10am-1.30pm & 5.30-7pm Fri & Sat, 10am-1pm Sun) also contains the small **Museo de Arte Contemporáneo**, a basement art gallery of changing exhibitions. Alongside is the **Museo de Escultura al Aire Libre**, a hillside sculpture park. At the heart of the village is the endearing **Museo Etnológico Casa Mazo** (Calle Aire; admission €1.50; ⏰ 10.30am-1.30pm & 5-8pm), with displays on rural life including a terrific display of photographs of villagers from the 1920s and 1930s.

South of town, **Camping Valle de Hecho** (☎ 974 37 53 61; sites per adult/tent/car €4.50/4.50/4.50; 🅔) is a pleasant, well-kept camping ground.

The best place to stay in town is the charming **Casa Blasquico** (☎ 974 37 50 07; www.casablasquico.com; Plaza de la Fuente 1; d €49-53, tr €65; ⏰ closed 1st half Sep), with six charming rooms. Breakfast costs €5.50. Downstairs in the same building, the much-lauded **Restaurante Gaby** is a delightful place to eat (meals cost €20 to €30) with an intimate wood-beamed dining room and an extensive wine list that includes 17 local wines; specialities include *ensalada de perdiz* (pheasant salad; €13) and *conejo a la casera* (home-style rabbit; €12).

Next door, **Bar Subordán** does a range of *bocadillos* (€5), including local *longaniza* (sausage).

Siresa & Around

pop 120 / elev 850m

A couple of kilometres north of Echo, Siresa is another charming village, although on a smaller scale. The beautiful 11th-century **Iglesia de San Pedro** (admission €1.50; ⏰ 11am-1pm & 5-7pm Thu-Tue, 11am-1pm Wed) is the town's centrepiece; it originally comprised part of one of Aragón's earliest monasteries.

Albergue Siresa (☎/fax 974 37 53 85; www.alberguesiresa.com in Spanish & French; Calle Reclusa s/n; bunks incl breakfast €16, sheets €2; ⊠) is a cheerful hostel providing bunk-and-breakfast accommodation in clean conditions, with other meals available. It also rents mountain bikes (€12 per day).

Hotel Castillo d'Acher (☎ 974 37 53 13; www.castillodacher.com; Plaza Mayor; s with/without bathroom €45/30, d with/without bathroom €65/40) has a pleasant mix of rooms, some rather old-fashioned, others pine-clad and modern. It also has *casas rurales* (doubles €28) in the village. The big in-house restaurant does a good *menú del día* (€14).

There's perfect peace in fabulous surroundings at the outstanding **Hotel Usón** (☎ 974 37 53 58; www.hoteluson.com in Spanish; s/d incl breakfast €45/60, apt €75-125; ⏰ Easter-Oct; Ⓟ ⊠), high in the Echo valley, 5km north of Siresa on the road to the Selva de Oza. Peace extends to the total absence of TVs. The restaurant offers excellent home-cooked meals.

Selva de Oza

This top end of the Valle de Echo is particularly beautiful, the road running parallel to Río Aragón Subordán as it bubbles its way through thick woodlands. About 6km from Siresa is the **Centro de Interpretación del Megalitismo** (☎ 974 37 51 23; centromegalitismo@telefonica.net; ⏰ 11am-2pm & 4.30-8.30pm mid-Jun–mid-Sep, 11am-2pm & 4-6.30pm mid-Sep–mid-Jun), with displays, in Spanish, about the prehistoric stone burial chambers located throughout the area. About 14km from Siresa the paved road ends, shortly after it connects with the GR11 path en route between Candanchú and Zuriza. At least half a dozen mountain peaks sit in an arc to the north for strenuous day ascents.

Ansó

pop 500 / elev 860m

Ansó takes you even further into a world of high places and harmony. The rough-hewn stone houses here are in grey stone, their roofs are of red tiles. Some walls are whitewashed, making a pleasing checkerboard pattern. Forested slopes climb ever upwards from where Ansó straggles along a low escarpment above a partly covered streambed.

A grid of narrow streets surrounds the main square, Plaza Mayor, where there's a bank and ATM. The **tourist office** (☎ 974 37 02 25; Plaza Mayor; 9am-1.30pm & 5-8pm Easter & Jul-Sep) has information in Spanish.

Adjoining the rough-walled church, the delightful **Posada Magoria** (☎ 974 37 00 49; www.lospirineos.info/magoria in Spanish; Calle Milagros 32; s €35, d 48-53) is crammed with character and lovingly kept by a family with lots of local knowledge. In the kitchen *comedor* (dining room) you can enjoy an excellent €12 *menú* of organically sourced vegetarian dishes; vegans are catered for too. At **Casa Baretón** (☎ 974 37 01 38; www.casabareton.com; Calle Pascual Altemir 16; s/d €35/49), the craftsman owner of this lovingly restored stone house has retained a number of old features to add to the general comfort and charm of the rooms.

Bar Zuriza (☎ 639 284590; Calle Mayor 71), near the top end of the village, serves decent tapas.

SOS DEL REY CATÓLICO

pop 580 / elev 625m

If Sos del Rey Católico were in Tuscany, it would be a world-famous hill town. Sos, as the village is universally known, lies 80km west of Jaca, its old medieval town a glorious maze of twisting, cobbled lanes that wriggle between dark stone houses with deeply overhung eaves. But Sos has historical significance to go with its beauty: born here in 1452 was the other half of one of the most formidable double acts in history, Fernando II of Aragón. He and his wife, Isabel I of Castilla, became known as the Reyes Católicos (Catholic Monarchs). Together they conquered the last Islamic kingdom of Granada and united Spain.

The best way to experience Sos is to simply wander to get lost. The keep of the **Castillo de la Peña Feliciano** crowns the hilltop with fine views over the rooftops, and the Gothic **Iglesia de San Esteban** (admission €2; 10am-1pm & 3.30-5.30pm) below it, with a weathered Romanesque portal, has a deliciously gloomy crypt with terrific frescoes and huge wooden birds as light-holders.

Fernando is said to have been born in the **Casa Palacio de Sada**, now containing the **tourist office** (☎ 948 88 85 24; Plaza Hispanidad; 10am-2pm & 4-8pm Jun-Aug, 10am-1pm & 4-7pm Wed-Fri, 10am-2pm & 4-7pm Sat & Sun Sep-May) and an **interpretive centre** (adult/child/concession €2.40/1.20/1.80, incl guided tour of village €3.60/2.40/1.80), with fine exhibits on the history of Sos and the life of the king.

Sleeping & Eating

Albergue Juvenil (☎ 948 88 84 80; www.alberguedesos.com in Spanish; Calle de las Encinas; per person under/over 26yr €15/20) Enjoy life in a restored medieval tower in superb modern conditions at this excellent hostel that has bright, stylish decor. Free bicycle rental is available and meals are served.

As Bruixas (☎ 948 88 84 15; www.asbruixas.com in Spanish; Calle Mayor 25; d/ste €50/60;) Named 'The Witches' by its charming management, this terrific place has three rooms offering a refreshing blend of vivid style and comfort, with plump mattresses, gleaming bathtubs and bohemian objects fished out of thrift shops. Its similarly postmodern dining room offers cuisine that gives traditional ingredients a fresh twist.

Hostal Las Coronas (☎ 948 88 84 08; www.hostallascoronas.com in Spanish; Calle Pons Sorolla 2; s without/with plaza view €44/56, d €55/70) Run by the friendly Fernando, this *hostal* has attractive rooms with the barest hints of character and those with balconies overlooking the plaza are lovely. The downstairs bar serves *bocadillos* (€5 to €7), tapas (€3) and *raciones* (from €7).

Ruta del Tiempo (☎ 948 88 82 95; www.rutadeltiempo.es in Spanish; Calle Larraldía 1; s incl breakfast €47, d €60-100;) This charming family-run place next to the central Plaza de la Villa opened in late 2007. Rooms on the first floor are themed around three Aragonese kings, while the four second-floor rooms have decoration dedicated to four different continents; 'Asia' and 'Africa' are the largest and best rooms, but they're all good.

Parador de Sos del Rey Católico (☎ 948 88 80 11; www.parador.es; Calle Arquitecto Sainz de Vicuña 1; d from €130) A place that might just have pleased Los Reyes themselves, this grand building is modern but its style fits with the rest of Sos, the service is faultless and there's a terrific restaurant (set menus €25 to €45). Some rooms have fine villages and mountain views.

Outside of the hotel restaurants, **La Cocina del Principal** (Calle Mayor 17; mains from €14; lunch & dinner Tue-Sat, lunch Sun) is the best restaurant in town.

Getting There & Away

A **Gomez** (☎ 976 67 55 29) bus from Zaragoza to Sos del Rey Católico (€10.10) departs from below the old El Portillo train station at 7pm Monday to Friday. It returns from Sos at 7am.

THE SOUTH

Southern Aragón can seem, at first glance, to be flat by nature and flat by appeal, the vast sweeps of countryside immediately south of Zaragoza either dreary plains or bald, uninviting ridges. Head further south or southeast, however, and the landscape takes on a certain drama, along with some intriguing towns and villages.

DAROCA

pop 2260

Daroca is one of southern Aragón's best-kept secrets, a sleepy medieval town, one-time Islamic stronghold and, later, Christian Aragón's fortress town in the early medieval wars against Castilla. Its well-preserved old quarter is laden with historic references and the crumbling old city walls encircle the hill-tops; the walls once boasted 114 military towers. Coming from north or south, you slip quietly down off the N234 and enter Calle Mayor, the cobbled main street, through monumental gates and into another world. Here you'll find the **tourist office** (☎ 976 80 01 29; Plaza de España 4; 🕒 11am-2pm & 4.30-7.30pm), which offers maps for self-guided walks through town.

Sights & Activites

Of the walks, the best is the 45-minute **Ruta Monumental**, which gives a wonderful feel for the town and is well signposted. The other is the two-hour **Ruta del Castillo y Las Murallas**, a far more strenuous undertaking that climbs up to and follows the walls; the reward is magnificent views over Daroca. The tourist office also organises free **guided tours**, lasting 50 minutes, of the town at 11.15am on Saturdays and Sundays if 10 people show up.

The pretty Plaza de España is dominated by the large Romanesque Mudéjar Renaissance-style **Iglesia Colegiata de Santa María** (🕒 11am-1pm & 5.30-7pm Easter-Sep, noon-1pm & 5-7pm Oct-Easter), which boasts a lavish interior and organ. Further up the hill to the west, the 12th-century **Iglesia de San Miguel** is an austerely beautiful masterpiece of Romanesque architecture, but its greatest treasures are the Gothic frescoes within. Sadly, the church is kept closed, except if you join one of the tourist office's guided tours or for concerts during the town's festivals (see below).

Festivals & Events

The best time to be in Daroca is during the last week of July, when Calle Mayor is closed to traffic, locals don their medieval finery and concerts mark the **Feria Medieval** (Medieval Festival). In the first two weeks of August, Daroca hosts the **Festival Internacional de Música Antigua** (International Festival of Medieval Music) with courses and concerts in the two main churches.

Sleeping & Eating

La Posada del Almudí (☎ 976 80 06 06; www.posadadelalmudi.com; Grajera 5; s/d/duplex incl breakfast €45/65/120; ❄ 💻) A one-time 16th-century palace, this lovely old place has a personal touch. The rooms in the main building are lovingly restored and comfortable, although the larger duplexes with balcony are best. Across the lane it has a range of super-modern, smallish but comfortable rooms. The attached restaurant (menú €12) offers good traditional cuisine.

Hotel Cien Balcones (☎ 976 54 50 71; www.cienbalcones.com in Spanish; Calle Mayor 88; s/d incl breakfast €62/88; P ❄ 💻) Opened in August 2007, this stylish three-star hotel has large rooms with a minimalist designer flourish. There's a good restaurant (menú €16, mains from €15) and a cafe that serves up cheap *bocadillos* and pizza.

Getting There & Away

Buses stop outside the Mesón Félix bar, at Calle Mayor 104. Four daily buses run to Zaragoza and Teruel, Monday to Saturday.

LAGUNA DE GALLOCANTA

Some 20km south of Daroca and a similar distance west of Calamocha on the N234, this is Spain's largest natural lake, with an area of about 15 sq km (though it can almost dry up in summer). It's a winter home for some 70,000 cranes and many other waterfowl. A **Centro de Interpretación** (☎ 978 72 50 04; 🕒 10am-2pm & 4-8pm daily Nov & Feb, 10am-2pm & 4-8pm Sat & Sun rest of year), with information and exhibitions, is on the Tornos–Bello road near the southeast corner of the lake where the cranes gather. Take binoculars.

TERUEL

pop 32,400 / elev 917m

Teruel is one of Aragón's most engaging cities, an open-air museum of ornate Mudéjar monuments almost without peer in Spain. But this is a living museum where the streets are filled with life, a reflection of a city growing in confidence, reasserting itself with cultural attitude. For decades, Teruel had something of an image problem and an air of neglect, a place seemingly left behind by modern Spain's mainstream renaissance – '*Teruel existe!*' ('Teruel exists!') is still an oft-heard, only

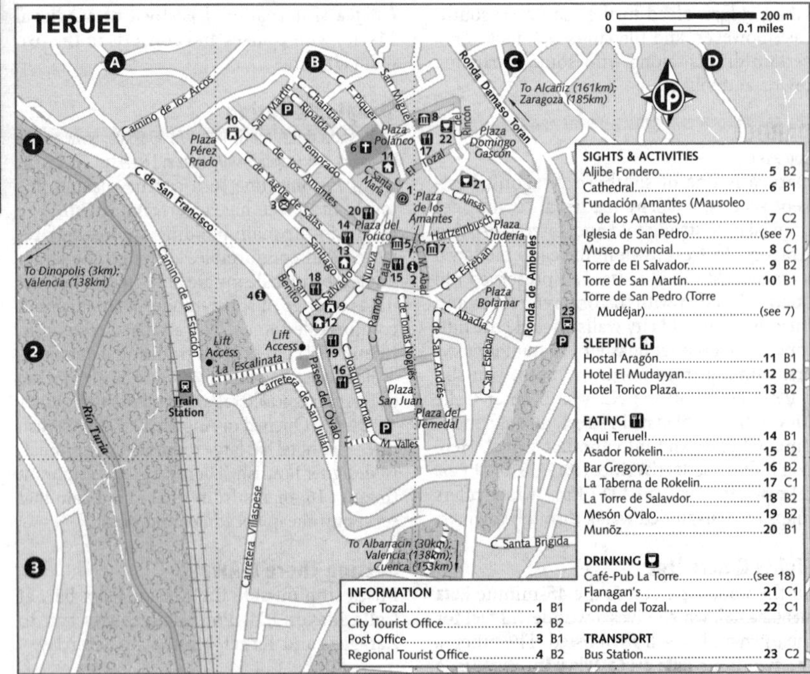

partly tongue-in-cheek refrain. But the city has pulled itself up by its boot-straps and it's well worth seeing what all of the fuss is about. In winter Teruel can be one of the coldest places in Spain, so come prepared.

Orientation

The train station is downhill on the western edge of the old town; a lift climbs up to the Paseo del Óvalo and the *casco historico* (old town). The bus station is on the eastern edge of town. Teruel's main square is Plaza del Torico (the name derives from a statue of what could be Spain's smallest bull), a lively focus of city life. From here the main street, Calle de Ramon y Cajal, leads to the big Plaza San Juan.

Information

Ciber Tozal (☎ 978 60 25 24; Calle El Tozal s/n; per hr €2; ⏲ 10.30am-2pm & 5-10pm Mon-Sat, 5-10pm Sun)

City tourist office (☎ 978 62 41 05; Plaza de los Amantes 6; ⏲ 10am-2pm & 4-8pm Sep-Jul, 10am-8pm Aug) Ask here for audioguides (€5) to the old city.

Post office (Calle de Yagüe de Salas 19)

Regional tourist office (☎ 978 64 14 61; Calle de San Francisco 1; ⏲ 9am-2pm & 4.30-7pm Mon-Sat, 10am-2pm & 4.30-7pm Sun mid-Sep–Jun, 10am-2pm & 4.45-7.45pm Mon-Sat, 10am-2pm & 4.45-7.45pm Sun Jul–mid-Sep) One hundred metres north of the top of La Escalinata staircase.

Sights

CATHEDRAL

Teruel's **cathedral** (☎ 978 61 80 16; Plaza de la Catedral; adult/child €3/2; ⏲ 11am-2pm & 4-8pm Easter-Oct, 11am-2pm & 4-7pm Nov-Easter) is a rich example of the Mudéjar imagination at work with its kaleidoscopic brickwork and colourful ceramic tiles. The superb 13th-century bell tower has hints of the Romanesque in its detail. Inside, the coffered roof of the nave is covered with paintings that add up to a medieval cosmography – from musical instruments and hunting scenes to coats of arms and Christ's crucifixion.

FUNDACIÓN AMANTES

Teruel's flagship attraction is the redesigned and somewhat curious **Mausoleo de los Amantes**, which under the umbrella of the **Fundación Amantes** (☎ 978 61 83 98; Calle Matías Abad 3; Mausoleo/Iglesia de San Pedro & Torre Mudéjar €4/5, combined ticket €8; ⏲ 10am-2pm & 4-8pm Sep-Jul, 10am-8pm Aug) pulls

THE LOVERS OF TERUEL

In the early 13th century Juan Diego de Marcilla and Isabel de Segura fell in love, but, in the manner of other star-crossed historical lovers, there was a catch: Isabel was the only daughter of a wealthy family, while poor old Juan Diego was, well, poor. Juan Diego convinced Isabel's reluctant father to postpone plans for Isabel's marriage to someone more appropriate for five years, during which time Juan Diego would seek his fortune. Not waiting a second longer than the five years, Isabel's father married off his daughter in 1217, only for Juan Diego to return, triumphant, immediately after the wedding. He begged Isabel for a kiss, which she refused, condemning Juan Diego to die of a broken heart. A final twist saw Isabel attend the funeral in mourning, whereupon she gave Juan Diego the kiss he had craved in life. Isabel promptly died and the two lovers were buried together.

out the stops on the city's famous legend of Isabel and Juan Diego (see the boxed text above). The 'Mausoleum of the Lovers' contains the mummified remains of the pair. They lie in modern alabaster tombs, sculpted by Juan de Ávalos, with their heads tilted endearingly towards each other. Round this centrepiece has been shaped a remarkable audiovisual exhibition, featuring music and theatre. It skates very close to glorious kitsch, but is entirely persuasive. The Mausoleo is wheelchair accessible.

Attached to the complex is the 14th-century **Iglesia de San Pedro**, with a stunning ceiling, baroque high altar and simple cloisters, as well as the **Torre de San Pedro** (Torre Mudéjar), from where there are fine views over central Teruel.

TORRE DE EL SALVADOR

The most impressive of Teruel's other Mudéjar monuments is the **Torre de El Salvador** (☎ 978 60 20 61; www.teruelmudejar.com in Spanish; Calle El Salvador; adult/child €2.50/1.80; 🕐 10am-2pm & 4-8pm mid-Jul–mid-Sep, 11am-2pm & 4.30-7.30pm Tue-Sat, 11am-2pm Sun rest of year), an early-14th-century extravaganza of brick and ceramics built around an older Islamic minaret. You climb the narrow stairways and passageways. Along the way, you'll find exhibits on Mudéjar art and architecture. The views from the summit are Teruel's best.

TORRE DE SAN MARTÍN

Although you can't climb it, **Torre de San Martín**, the northwestern gate of the old city, is almost as beautiful as the Torre de El Salvador. It was finished in 1316 and was incorporated into the city's walls in the 16th century.

MUSEO PROVINCIAL

Teruel's **Museo Provincial** (Provincial Museum; ☎ 978 60 01 50; Plaza Polanco; admission free; 🕐 10am-2pm & 4-7pm Tue-Fri, 10am-2pm Sat & Sun) is housed in the 16th-century Casa de la Comunidad, a fine work of Renaissance architecture. The archaeological sections are a highlight, and there are changing exhibitions of contemporary art.

ALJIBE FONDERO

Off the southeastern corner of Plaza del Torico is the metrolike entrance to the **Aljibe** (☎ 978 61 99 03; Calle Ramón y Cajal), a fascinating 14th-century underground water-storage facility. It was closed for works when we visited, with opening date unavailable.

LA ESCALINATA

The grand staircase that connects the Paseo del Óvalo on the old city's fringe to the train station, **La Escalinata** is a masterpiece of neo-Mudéjar monumental architecture. First built in 1920, it was painstakingly restored in the first years of the 21st century. Along with the redesigned Paseo del Óvalo, La Escalinata has won numerous awards, including the European Prize for Remodelled Urban Spaces in 2004, beating 169 candidates from 20 countries. Climb down the stairs, but take the lift back up to the Paseo.

DINÓPOLIS

It's fun for all at this large, modern **dinosaur theme park** (☎ 902 44 80 00; www.dinopolis.com; adult/child €22/17; 🕐 10am-8pm). It's 3km from the town centre, well signposted just off the Valencia road. A highlight is 'El Ride', a motorised trip through time spiced up with animated dinosaur robots.

Festivals & Events

On the weekend closest to 14 February, thousands of Teruel's inhabitants (and even more visitors from elsewhere) don medieval dress for the **Fiesta Medieval**. There are medieval markets and food stalls, but the centrepiece is the re-enactment of the Diego and Isabel legend (see the boxed text, p463).

The **Día de San Cristóbal** (St Christopher's Day; 10 July) is the hub of the week-long **Feria del Ángel**, which commemorates Teruel's founding.

Sleeping

Hostal Aragón (☎ 978 61 18 77; Calle Santa María 4; s with/without bathroom €25/22, d with/without bathroom €44/37) An unassuming place with well-kept wood-panelled rooms and on a narrow side street, this place drops its prices by a few euros midweek. We recommend booking at weekends and on holidays.

our pick **Hotel El Mudayyan** (☎ 978 62 30 42; www.elmudayyan.com in Spanish; Calle Nueva 18; s/d €60/90;) Easily the most character-filled of Teruel's hotels, El Mudayyan has lovely rooms with polished wood floors, wooden beams and charming interior design that's different in every room. It also has a *tetería* (teahouse) in the basement and a curious subterranean passage that dates back to earliest Teruel.

Hotel Torico Plaza (☎ 978 60 86 55; www.bacohoteles.com; Calle de Yagüe de Salas 5; s/d/ste €80/100/140;) It's hard to beat the location here, with some rooms looking out onto Plaza del Torico, but you don't expect missing light bulbs, pricey wi-fi and a near-empty minibar for this price.

Eating

Landlocked Teruel is utterly devoted to meat eating and promotes its local *jamón* and other *embutidos* (cured meats) with enthusiasm. One local speciality you'll find everywhere is *Las Delicias de Teruel* (local *jamón* with toasted bread and fresh tomato).

our pick **Muñoz** (☎ 978 60 11 30; www.dulcesdeteruel.com; Plaza del Torico 23; 9.30am-2pm & 5.30-9pm Mon-Sat, 9.30am-2pm Sun) Teruel's best place for breakfast or a deli snack in the early evening, Muñoz has a more classy feel to it (and better service) than other places around Plaza del Torico.

Bar Gregory (☎ 978 60 05 80; Paseo del Óvalo 6; raciones from €7; closed Tue) The pick of the tapas bars lined up along Paseo del Óvalo, this place has all the local staples, outdoor tables at which to enjoy them and good service.

Asador Rokelin (☎ 978 60 93 63; Calle Ramón y Cajal 7; dishes €8-15) This casual sit-down restaurant offers the whole range of meat dishes, but you'll no doubt be grateful for its enormous salad plates with, you guessed it, plentiful curls of *jamón*.

La Torre de Salvador (☎ 978 61 73 76; Calle El Salvador; dishes €10-19; Tue-Sun) Right opposite the Torre de El Salvador, this smart restaurant raises the stakes on style with its *nouveau cuisine Aragonese*, with subtle dishes such as quail in a fruity sauce and cod with mushrooms.

Mesón Óvalo (☎ 978 61 82 35; Paseo del Óvalo 8; menú €12, mains €12-18; lunch & dinner Tue-Sat, lunch Sun) There's a strong emphasis on regional Aragonese cuisine at this pleasant place, with meat and game dishes to the fore. One fine local speciality is *jarretes* (Mozarabic hock of lamb stewed with wild mushrooms).

Other temples to *jamón*:

La Taberna de Rokelin (☎ 978 78 60 60; Calle El Tozal 33; tapa/ración of ham €3.50/15)

Aqui Teruel! (Calle de Yagüe de Salas 4; tapa/ración €3.50/11)

Drinking

If you're fairly undiscerning about your night-time drinking holes, **Plaza Bolamar** has a bar on every doorstep with weekend crowds spilling over into the square.

Café-Pub La Torre (☎ 978 61 73 76; Calle El Salvador 20; 9am-1am Mon-Thu, noon-4am Fri & Sat, noon-1am Sun) This stylish place is our favourite bar in Teruel, as good for an afternoon drink as for a lively late-night vibe. Its eastern wall is the Torre de El Salvador, while the upstairs bar often has contemporary art installations.

Fonda del Tozal (Calle del Rincón 5; noon-late) The cavernous ground-floor bar is a rough-and-ready old place in which to unwind. It was formerly the stables of a very old inn and it's at its best when packed on weekend nights; on weekday afternoons, it can feel like the Wild West in a one-horse town.

Flanagan's (Calle Ainsas 2; 4pm-3.30am Sun-Thu, 5pm-4.30am Fri & Sat) We don't normally list Irish pubs, but this place rocks into the wee hours with the sort of music you're loathe to admit you like but dance to anyway.

Getting There & Away

From Teruel's **bus station** (☎ 978 61 07 89; www.estacionbus-teruel.com in Spanish), Autobuses Jiménez (www.grupo-jimenez.com in Spanish) runs up to five buses daily to/from Zaragoza (€11.50, 2½ hours); some go via Daroca. There also five buses to/from Valencia (€10.10, 2¼ hours) most days and four to/from Madrid (€19.90, 4½ hours).

Teruel is on the railway between Zaragoza (€12.25, two hours) and Valencia (€11, 2½ hours), with three trains each way daily.

RINCÓN DE ADEMUZ

Heading south from Teruel, the N330 crosses Sierra de la Matanza and enters the 'Ademuz Corner', a mountainous detached piece of Valencia province between the provinces of Teruel and Cuenca (Castilla-La Mancha). It makes a picturesque alternative route between Teruel town and Valencia or Cuenca provinces. The most spectacular stretch is the rough and winding 17km of the old N330A, south of the town of Ademuz to Santa Cruz de Moya.

The N420 west from the Rincón de Ademuz skirts the southern hills of the Serranía de Cuenca en route to Cuenca.

ALBARRACÍN

pop 970 / elev 1180m

Don't miss lovely hill town Albarracín. It takes time to get here, 38km west of Teruel, but it's worth it for the marvellous sense of timelessness that not even the modern onslaught of summer coach tours can erase. Ragged fortress walls rise up the surrounding slopes and the town's streets retain their mazelike charm, with centuries-old buildings leaning over them.

Built on a steep, rocky height carved out by a meander of Río Guadalaviar, Albarracín was, from 1012 to 1104, the seat of a tiny Islamic state ruled by the Berber Banu Razin dynasty. From 1170 to 1285 it was an independent Christian kingdom sandwiched between Castilla and Aragón.

Information

Post office (Calle de la Catedral)
Tourist office (☎ 978 71 02 62; Calle San Antonio s/n; ⌚ 10am-2pm & 4-7pm Tue-Sun except Sun afternoon)

Sights

The **cathedral** (⌚ 10.30am-2pm & 4-6pm except Sun afternoon, to 8pm Jul-Sep), with its cupola typical of the Spanish Levant, has an elaborate gilded altarpiece. The Palacio Episcopal (Bishop's Palace), to which it's connected, houses the **Museo Diocesano** (admission €2.50; ⌚ 10.30am-2pm & 4-6pm except Sun afternoon, to 8pm Jul-Sep). The **Museo de Albarracín** (Calle San Juan; admission €2.50; ⌚ 10.30am-1pm & 4-5.30pm except Sun afternoon), in the old city hospital, is devoted to the town's Islamic heritage.

The **castle**, near the southern end of town, and the **Torre del Andador** (Walkway Tower), at the top of the walls at the north, both date from the 9th century, when Albarracín was an important Islamic military post. Walk up to the Torre del Andador for wonderful panoramas. In the town itself, nearly every brick, stone, slab of concrete and slap of mortar in the place is in some earthy shade of red or pink, making for wonderful plays of colour, particularly in the evening.

Tours

El Andador (☎ 667 26 06 01; Calle de la Catedral 4) conducts worthwhile 1½-hour walks through Albarracín's medieval core for €3.50, departing from outside the tourist office at 11am, 12.45pm and 5pm.

Sleeping & Eating

For weekends in summer and all holiday times it's worth booking ahead.

Camping Ciudad de Albarracín (☎ 978 71 01 97; www.campingalbarracin.com; sites per person/tent/car €3.64/3.64/3.64; ⌚ Apr-Oct) Pleasant, small and shaded, the camping ground is 2km from the heart of Albarracín, off the Bezas road. It also has timbered four-person chalets for €65.

Habitaciones Los Palacios (☎ 978 70 03 27; www.montepalacios.com in Spanish; Calle Los Palacios 21; s/d/tr €28/45/52) This charming place has spotless rooms, some with balconies and gorgeous views. It's about 250m from Plaza Mayor, starting along Calle de Santiago and exiting through Portal de Molina.

Casa de Santiago (☎ 978 70 03 16; www.casadesantiago.net in Spanish; Subida a las Torres 11; s/d from €48/64; 💻) A beautiful place, with lots of exposed wood, tiled floors and with charming service to go with it, the Casa lies at the heart of the old town a few steps up from Plaza Mayor. You step off the street into an immediate comfort zone. The restaurant has a *menú* for €18.

our pick **La Casa del Tío Americano** (☎ 978 71 01 25; www.lacasadeltioamericano.com; Calle Los Palacios 9; d €95; 💻) An engaging place, 'The House of the American Uncle' boasts brightly painted rooms, some with exposed stone walls and special views, while all have hydromassage showers. The views of the village from the breakfast terrace are magnificent.

Other stylish options:

Posada del Adarve (☎ 978 70 03 04; www.posada-adarve.com; Calle Portal de Molina 23; s €35, d €50-75; 💻) An Albarracín town house lovingly restored by the Portal de Molina (Molina Gateway).

Hotel Arabia (☎ 978 71 02 12; www.montesunivers ales.com; Calle Bernardo Zapater 2; s/d/apt from €45/66/95; 🖳) Occupies a 17th-century convent with good rooms and enormous apartments with terrific views.

For something a little more special than the bars serving tapas and *raciones* around Plaza Mayor, which include **La Taberna** (☎ 978 70 03 17; Plaza Mayor 6; platos combinados €6.50-10), there's **Tiempo de Ensueño** (☎ 978 70 40 70; www.tiempodeensuenyo .com; menú €38, meals €30; 🕑 Thu-Tue), Albarracín's classiest restaurant, which serves a mix of traditional and nouvelle-cuisine dishes in its sleek, light-filled dining room.

Getting There & Away

Navarro buses leave daily, except Sunday, from Teruel for Albarracín (€3.65, 45 minutes) at 3.30pm, and from Albarracín for Teruel at 8.30am.

THE SOUTHEAST

The sparsely populated hills stretching east of Teruel into the Valencia region present a bleached maze of rocky peaks and dramatic gorges inhabited by quiet, ancient stone *pueblos* (villages) well away from well-trodden tourist trails. Unless you have a lot of time, you need a vehicle; although buses serve most places, they rarely do so more than once daily and often not at all on weekends.

A worthwhile route from Teruel for those with their own transport leads 43km southeast to **Mora de Rubielos** in the foothills of the Sierra de Gudar. A massive 14th-century **castle** (admission €1.50; 🕑 10am-2pm & 5-8pm Tue-Sun) towers over the village amid a sea of red and pink stone.

Another 14km southeast along the A232 is pretty **Rubielos de Mora**, a quiet web of narrow streets whose houses have typically small Aragonese balconies. The friendly **Hotel Los Leones** (☎ 978 80 44 77; www.losleones.info in Spanish; Plaza Igual y Gil 3; s/d €75/110) has attractive period decor and comfortable rooms, and has a fine restaurant with a €30 *menú*.

In the north of the region is **La Iglesuela del Cid**. Here you've entered El Maestrazgo, a medieval knightly domain centred on Sant Mateu (p626) in Castellón province. La Iglesuela's church and old town hall share a tight medieval plaza with the classy **Hospedería de la Iglesuela del Cid** (☎ 964 44 34 76; Ondevilla 4; s/d €85/125; 🅿) in an 18th-century mansion. It's accessible by wheelchair.

Cantavieja, 13km northwest of La Iglesuela, was reputedly founded by Hannibal and later became a seat of the Knights Templar. The best-preserved (and partly restored) part of town is the porticoed Plaza Cristo Rey.

If you're heading for Morella in the Valencian Maestrazgo, the A226 northeast of Cantavieja will take you, snaking down past ragged cliffs and then via **Mirambel**, a fine example of a gently decaying, walled medieval town.

Getting There & Away

A 3pm Monday-to-Friday bus runs from Teruel to La Iglesuela del Cid (€8.95, two hours) via Cantavieja (€8, 1½ hours). In the

LUIS BUÑUEL & THE DRUMS OF CALANDA

Luis Buñuel's earliest memories were of the drums of Calanda. In the centuries-old ritual of the lower Aragón town, the film director's birthplace, Good Friday noon marks the *rompida de la hora* (breaking of the hour). At that moment thousands commence banging on *tambores* (snare drums) and *bombos* (bass drums), together producing a thunderous din. The ceremony goes on for 24 hours, only ceasing for the passage of the standard Easter processions. The drumming rages all over the region, with drum parades at Alcañiz also.

'The drums, that amazing, resounding, cosmic phenomenon that brushes the collective subconscious, causes the earth to tremble beneath our feet,' Buñuel recalls in his memoir, *Mi Ultimo Suspiro* (My Last Sigh). 'One has only to place his hand on the wall of a house to feel the vibrations… Anyone who manages to fall asleep, lulled by the banging, awakes with a start when the sound trails off. At dawn, the drum skins are stained with blood: hands bleed after so much banging. And these are the rough hands of peasants.'

This clamour worked its way into Buñuel's dreams and nightmares, and eventually into his surreal films; the drums left their imprint, along with a taste for ritual, costumes and disguises.

opposite direction, the bus leaves La Iglesuela at 6.15am.

CALANDA

From Teruel the N420 heads north through mountainous terrain, reaching the foggy heights of Puerto San Just (1400m) pass before descending to meet the east–west N211, which leads to Calanda. The chief reason to visit Calanda is the **Centro Buñuel Calanda** (☎ 978 84 65 24; www.cbvirtual.com in Spanish; Calle Mayor 48; adult/concession €3.50/2.50; ⌚ 10.30am-1.30pm & 4-8pm Tue-Sun), a museum devoted to the life and films of Luis Buñuel. The museum tries to remain faithful to the surrealist spirit of the Calanda native (see the boxed text, opposite), cleverly weaving images from his oeuvre into the tour. For true aficionados, a filmography room has computers with details of all 32 of Buñuel's films, accompanied by screenings of key scenes and commentary by the director.

Calanda is served by buses (€9.15, two hours) from Teruel and Alcañiz.

ALCAÑIZ

pop 14,900

Alcañiz, the administrative centre for lower Aragón, is fairly overwhelmed by commerce, although it's a useful overnight stop. The huge castle is now a *parador*. A series of vivid, intricately detailed murals dating from the 14th century cover the walls of the **keep** (admission €5; ⌚ 10am-1.30pm & 4-6pm, longer hr in summer), which can be climbed for views.

The monumental **Iglesia de Santa María La Mayor**, with a huge baroque portal, dwarfs the central Plaza de España. A **tourist office** (⌚ 10am-2pm & 4-6pm Mon-Sat, 10am-2pm Sun) gives access to 'hidden Alcañiz', a series of **underground passages** (admission €2.50) once used as storerooms and ice store.

Of a dozen lodgings, **Hostal Aragón** (☎ 978 87 07 17; Calle Espejo 3; s/d €32/53) is an excellent, central choice – a tall, old house with sturdy balconies.

Up to four buses travel daily to/from Zaragoza, and two stop here (€10.75, 2½ hours) en route between Teruel and Barcelona.

Basque Country, Navarra & La Rioja

The jade green hills and drizzle-filled grey skies of this northeast pocket of Spain are quite a contrast to the flamenco- and castanet-filled clichés of the south. The Basques, the people who inhabit this corner, also consider themselves different. They claim to be the oldest Europeans, speaking the original European language and living in this mountainous fold on the borders of France and Spain since the days of prehistory. Whether or not this is actually the case remains unproven, but what is beyond doubt is that they live in a land of exceptional beauty and diversity. There are mountains watched over by almost-forgotten gods; cultured museums and art galleries; the finest surf breaks in Europe; street parties a million people strong; and the best food in Spain (some say in Europe). But despite all of these attractions, it's probably the people who'll leave the deepest impressions: kind, flamboyant and welcoming, the Basques are nothing if not proud. There is no denying that they are right when they say they are a special people in a special land.

Leave the rugged and wild north behind and feel the temperature rise as you hit the open, classically Spanish plains south of Pamplona. Here you enter the world of Navarra and La Rioja. It's a region awash with glorious wine, linked by geography to the more temperate north, yet persuasively Mediterranean in its sunburst colours; its dreamy landscape of vineyards, grassy hills and bone-white limestone escarpments; its medieval monasteries and enticing wine towns.

Wherever you choose to go in this remarkable region, one thing is assured: the experience will not be easily forgotten.

HIGHLIGHTS

- Play on a perfect beach, gorge on fabulous *pintxos* (Basque tapas), dance all night and wish you could stay forever in stylish **San Sebastián** (p484)
- Wish that you too could paint like a genius in the galleries of **Bilbao** (opposite)
- Get barrelled at **Mundaka** (p482) and re-create the Guggenheim in sand-castle form on a beautiful Basque **beach** (p483)
- Learn the secrets of a good drop in the museums and vineyards of **La Rioja** (p511)
- Roll back the years in the medieval fortress towns of **Olite** (p509) and **Ujué** (p509)
- Climb mist-shrouded slopes haunted by witches and vultures in the Navarran **Pyrenees** (p505)
- Pretend you're Hemingway during Pamplona's week of **Sanfermines** (p502) debauchery

AREA: 22,670 SQ KM	AVE SUMMER TEMP: HIGH 28°C, LOW 12°C	POP: 3.04 MILLION

BASQUE COUNTRY

No matter where you've just come from, be it the hot, southern plains of Spain or gentle and pristine France, the Basque Country is different. Known to Basques as Euskadi or Euskal Herria (the 'land of Basque Speakers'), and called El Pais Vasco in Spanish, this is where mountain peaks reach for the skies and sublime rocky coves are battered by mighty Atlantic swells. It's a place that demands exploration beyond the delightful and cosmopolitan main cities of Bilbao, Vitoria and San Sebastián. You travel through the Basque Country always curious, and always rewarded.

History

No one quite knows where the Basque people came from (they have no migration myth in their oral history), but their presence here is believed to predate even the earliest known migrations. The Romans left the hilly Basque Country more or less to itself, but the expansionist Castilian crown gained sovereignty over Basque territories during the Middle Ages (1000–1450), although with considerable difficulty; Navarra constituted a separate kingdom until 1512. Even when they came within the Castilian orbit, Navarra and the three Basque provinces (Guipúzcoa, Vizcaya and Álava) extracted broad autonomy arrangements, known as the *fueros* (the ancient laws of the Basques).

After the Second Carlist War in 1876 all provinces except Navarra were stripped of their coveted *fueros,* thereby fuelling nascent Basque nationalism. Yet, although the Partido Nacionalista Vasco (PNV; Basque Nationalist Party) was established in 1894, support was never uniform, as all Basque provinces included a considerable Castilian contingent.

When the Republican government in Madrid proposed the possibility of home rule (self-government) to the Basques in 1936, both Guipúzcoa and Vizcaya took up the offer. When the Spanish Civil War erupted, conservative rural Navarra and Álava supported Franco, while Vizcaya and Guipúzcoa sided with the Republicans, a decision they paid a high price for in the four decades that followed.

It was during the Franco days that Euskadi Ta Askatasuna (ETA; Basque Homeland and Freedom) was first born. It was originally set up to fight against the Franco regime, which suppressed the Basques through the banning of the language and almost all forms of Basque culture. After the overthrow of the dictator, ETA called for nothing less than total independence and continued its bloody fight against the Spanish government. A fight that, according to estimates by the Spanish government, has left some 800 people dead.

Today, despite several false ceasefires by ETA the violence continues – though there is almost no chance of a foreign visitor being caught up in it.

BILBAO

pop 354,200

Bilbao (Basque: Bilbo) had a tough upbringing. Growing up in an environment of heavy industry and industrial wastelands, it was abused for years by those in power and had to work hard to get anywhere. But, like the kid from the estates who made it big, Bilbao's graft paid off when a few wise investments left it with a shimmering titanium fish called the Museo Guggenheim and a horde of arty groupies around the world.

The Botxo (Hole), as it's fondly known to its inhabitants, has now matured into its role of major European art centre. However, in doing so, it hasn't gone all toffee-nosed and forgotten its past: at heart it remains a hard-working and, physically, rather ugly town, but it's one that has real character. And it's this down-to-earth soul, rather than its plethora of art galleries, that is the real attraction of the vital, exciting and cultured city of Bilbao.

History

Bilbao was granted the title of *villa* (a city-state) in 1300, and medieval *bilbaínos* went about their business in the bustle of Las Siete Calles, the original seven streets of the old town, and down on the wharves. The conquest of the Americas stimulated trade, and Basque fishers, merchants and settlers soon built strong links to such cities as Boston. By the late 19th century the smokestacks of steelworks, shipbuilding yards and chemical plants dominated the area's skyline.

From the Carlist Wars through to the Spanish Civil War, Bilbao was always considered the greatest prize in the north, largely for its industrial value. Franco took

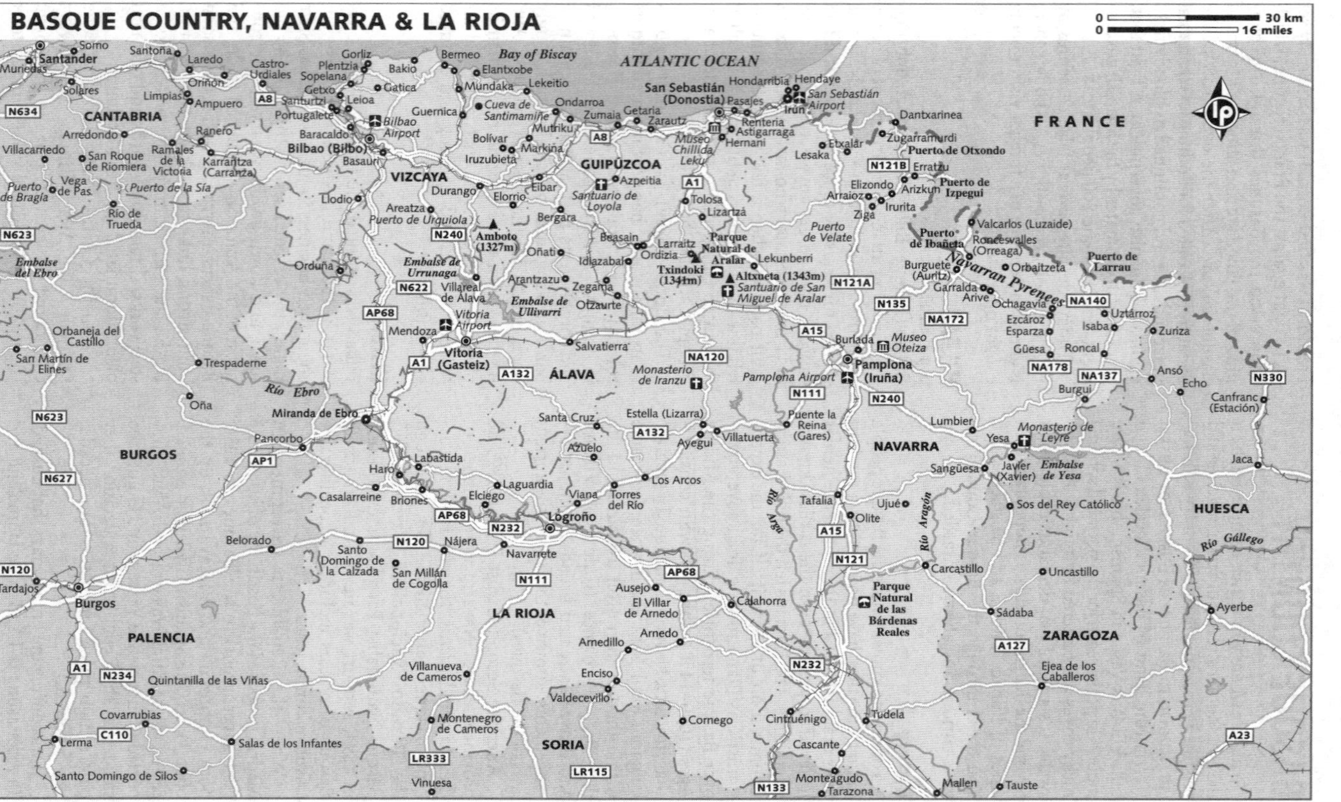
BASQUE COUNTRY, NAVARRA & LA RIOJA
0 30 km
0 16 miles
FRANCE
ATLANTIC OCEAN
Bay of Biscay
CANTABRIA
VIZCAYA
GUIPÚZCOA
ÁLAVA
NAVARRA
LA RIOJA
HUESCA
ZARAGOZA
SORIA
BURGOS
PALENCIA
Navarran Pyrenees
Santander
Muriedas
Somo
Santoña
Laredo
Oriñón
Castro-Urdiales
Limpias
Ampuero
Solares
Arredondo
Ramales de la Victoria
Karrantza (Carranza)
Ranero
San Roque de Riomiera
Vega de Pas
Villacarriedo
Puerto de Bragía
Puerto de la Sía
Río de Trueda
Embalse del Ebro
Orbaneja del Castillo
San Martín de Elines
Trespaderne
Oña
Portugalete
Santurtzi
Getxo
Sopelana
Plentzia
Gorliz
Leioa
Baracaldo
Bilbao (Bilbo)
Basauri
Bilbao Airport
Bakio
Gatica
Bermeo
Elantxobe
Mundaka
Guernica
Cueva de Santimamiñe
Lekeitio
Ondarroa
Mutriku
Markina
Bolívar
Iruzubieta
Durango
Elorrio
Areatza
Puerto de Urquiola
Llodio
Orduña
Amboto (1327m)
Eibar
Bergara
Zumaia
Getaria
Zarautz
Azpeitia
Santuario de Loyola
San Sebastián (Donostia)
Pasajes
Hondarribia
Hendaye
Irún
San Sebastián Airport
Rentería
Astigarraga
Hernani
Museo Chillida Leku
Tolosa
Lizartza
Oñati
Arantzazu
Zegama
Idiazabal
Beasain
Ordizia
Larraitz
Txindoki (1341m)
Parque Natural de Aralar
Altxueta (1343m)
Santuario de San Miguel de Aralar
Lekunberri
Otzaurte
Salvatierra
Embalse de Ullivarri
Embalse de Urrunaga
Villarreal de Álava
Vitoria Airport
Vitoria (Gasteiz)
Mendoza
Monasterio de Iranzu
Estella (Lizarra)
Ayegui
Villatuerta
Puente la Reina (Gares)
Pamplona Airport
Pamplona (Iruña)
Burlada
Museo Oteiza
Puerto de Velate
Lesaka
Etxalar
Arraioz
Ziga
Irurita
Elizondo
Arizkun
Erratzu
Zugarramurdi
Dantxarinea
Puerto de Otxondo
Puerto de Izpegui
Puerto de Ibañeta
Burguete (Auritz)
Roncesvalles (Orreaga)
Valcarlos (Luzaide)
Orbaitzeta
Garralda
Arive
Ochagavía
Ezcároz
Esparza
Güesa
Puerto de Larrau
Uztárroz
Isaba
Roncal
Burgui
Zuriza
Ansó
Echo
Canfranc (Estación)
Jaca
Río Gállego
Ayerbe
Monasterio de Leyre
Embalse de Yesa
Yesa
Javier (Xavier)
Sangüesa
Lumbier
Sos del Rey Católico
Uncastillo
Ejea de los Caballeros
Sádaba
Carcastillo
Río Aragón
Ujué
Olite
Tafalla
Río Arga
Parque Natural de las Bárdenas Reales
Tudela
Mallen
Tauste
Cintruénigo
Cascante
Monteagudo
Tarazona
Calahorra
Ausejo
El Villar de Arnedo
Arnedo
Cornego
Arnedillo
Enciso
Valdecevillo
Los Arcos
Torres del Río
Santa Cruz
Azuelo
Viana
Logroño
Laguardia
Elciego
Labastida
Navarrete
Nájera
Haro
Briones
Casalarreine
San Millán de Cogolla
Santo Domingo de la Calzada
Miranda de Ebro
Río Ebro
Pancorbo
Belorado
Villanueva de Cameros
Montenegro de Cameros
Vinuesa
Salas de los Infantes
Quintanilla de las Viñas
Covarrubias
Santo Domingo de Silos
Lerma
Burgos
Tardajos
N634
A8
N623
N240
N622
AP68
A1
A132
NA120
N111
A15
N121A
N121B
N135
NA172
NA178
NA140
NA137
N240
N330
A23
A127
N121
N232
N133
LR115
LR333
AP1
N120
N627
N234
C110

BASQUE NATIONALISM

Basque nationalism is many-faceted, yet at its heart its motivation lies in the Basque people's compelling sense of identity and of cultural uniqueness, a passion that becomes evident to even the most casual traveller through the northern Basque provinces.

In 1959 a small group of Basques set up an organisation that became known as Euskadi Ta Askatasuna (ETA; Basque Homeland and Freedom). Its goal was to carve out an independent Basque state from the Basque territories of northern Spain and southern France. In 1968 the group carried out its first successful terrorist attack. Thus began a cycle of violence that became increasingly self-defeating as wide-ranging autonomy was granted in the early 1980s and 1990s. The antithesis of ETA was the emergence of a powerful, though peaceful, nationalism, especially among the young, that saw the Basque language as the most potent symbol of nationhood and independence. The central government has granted much autonomy to the Basque region, including its own police force and government; the region is currently run by the PNV, a moderate nationalist party.

In the last 40 years, however, ETA's grisly war has (according to Spanish government estimates) killed more than 800 people. Sporadic 'ceasefires' and peace initiatives have foundered on the unwillingness of both ETA and the central government to make major concessions. Relations reached a nadir in March 2004 when the government of José María Aznar made a desperate, and ultimately failed, election play by trying to blame ETA for the terrorist bombings in Madrid (see p55).

In March 2006 ETA declared a 'final' ceasefire. The response of Prime Minister José Luis Rodríguez Zapatero was to state that the Madrid government had 'the best opportunity for a peace process for more than 30 years'. Unfortunately, his optimism was misplaced and by December that year the process collapsed with a car bombing at Madrid's Barajas airport that led to the deaths of two people. Since then there have been a number of shootings and a series of recent car-bomb attacks in Vitoria and other Basque towns. In January 2008 ETA stated again its call for independence and compared the Basque Country to Kosovo. In May 2008 a number of senior ETA members were arrested in the French city of Bordeaux.

No one would claim that all Basques are passionate nationalists, but with expanded autonomy on the cards for Catalonia, the realisation of the peaceful aspirations of a large majority of Basques seems more promising than ever. Complex and conflicting issues remain, however, not least the vexed question of the Madrid government's policy of imprisoning outside the Basque Country those whom many Basques see as political prisoners. The 2003 banning of Basque political party Batasuna for its alleged relationship to ETA and widely condemned support for terrorism has further aggravated the situation. Resolving this would be a major step forward.

the city in the spring of 1937 and reprisals against Basque nationalists were massive and long-lasting. Yet during the Franco era the city prospered as it fed Spanish industrial needs. This was followed by the seemingly terminal economic decline that has been so dynamically reversed in recent years.

Orientation

Bilbao's old quarter, the Casco Viejo, lies bundled up on the east bank of Ría de Bilbao, Río Nervión's channel to the sea. *Pensiones* (small private hotels), cafes, restaurants and bars cluster in the pedestrianised streets, Las Siete Calles. Between the Casco and the river is Plaza de Arenal, a broad open area in front of the handsome facade of the Teatro Arriaga. From here the Puente de Arenal spans the river and leads into the Abando area and Plaza Circular (Plaza de España). The plaza is the eastern hub of El Ensanche, the 19th-century 'extension' of Bilbao, with its swath of tall, handsome buildings. The main train stations are between Plaza Circular and the river. The main bus station, Termibus, is just over 1.5km west of Plaza Circular.

Information

BOOKSHOPS

Newsstands around Plaza Moyúa usually have a fair selection of foreign newspapers. There are well-stocked art bookshops at the Guggenheim and at the Museo de Bellas Artes.

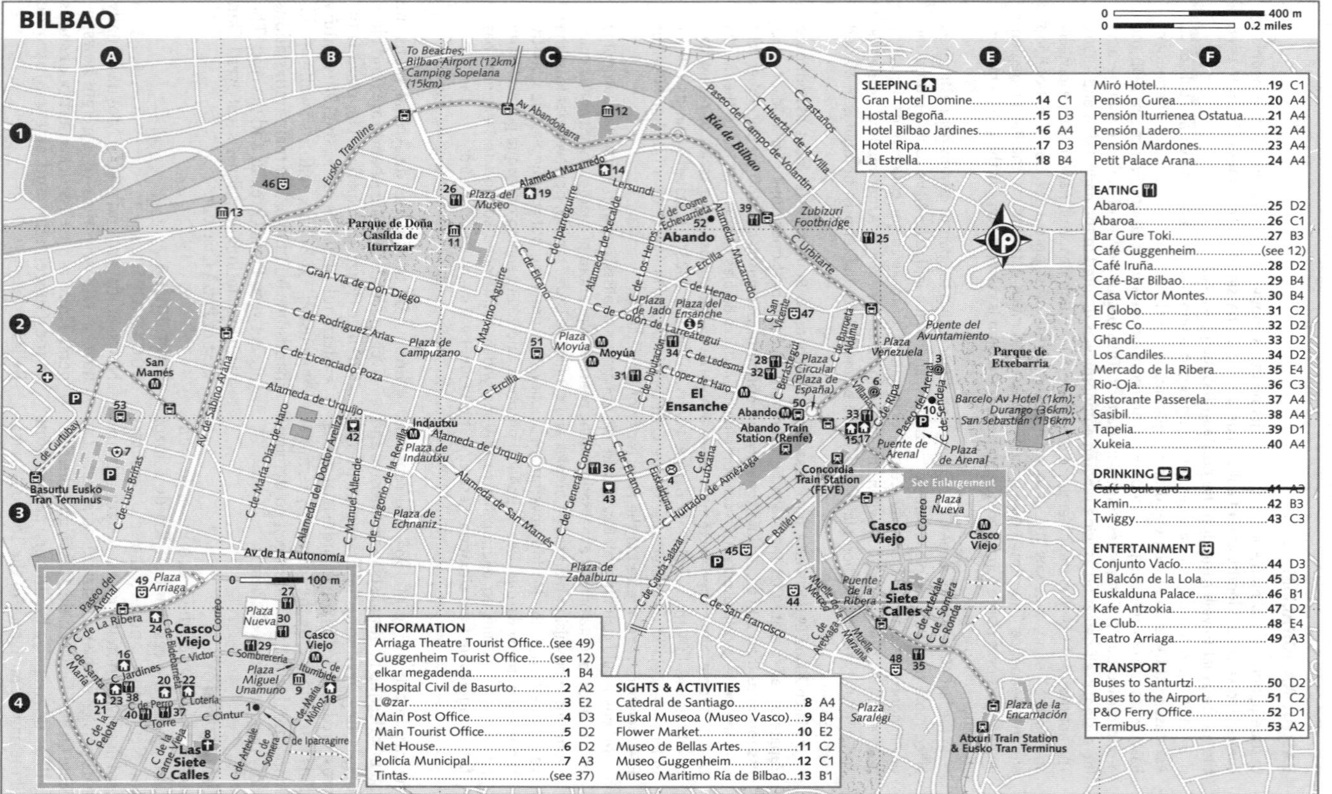
BILBAO
0 400 m
0 0.2 miles
SLEEPING
Gran Hotel Domine....14 C1
Hostal Begoña....15 D3
Hotel Bilbao Jardines....16 A4
Hotel Ripa....17 D3
La Estrella....18 B4
Miró Hotel....19 C1
Pensión Gurea....20 A4
Pensión Iturrienea Ostatua....21 A4
Pensión Ladero....22 A4
Pensión Mardones....23 A4
Petit Palace Arana....24 A4
EATING
Abaroa....25 D2
Abaroa....26 C1
Bar Gure Toki....27 B3
Café Guggenheim....(see 12)
Café Iruña....28 D2
Café-Bar Bilbao....29 B4
Casa Victor Montes....30 B4
El Globo....31 C2
Fresc Co....32 D2
Ghandi....33 D2
Los Candiles....34 D2
Mercado de la Ribera....35 E4
Rio-Oja....36 C3
Ristorante Passerela....37 A4
Sasibil....38 A4
Tapelia....39 D1
Xukeia....40 A4
DRINKING
Café Boulevard....41 A3
Kamin....42 B3
Twiggy....43 C3
ENTERTAINMENT
Conjunto Vacío....44 D3
El Balcón de la Lola....45 D3
Euskalduna Palace....46 B1
Kafe Antzokia....47 D2
Le Club....48 E4
Teatro Arriaga....49 A3
TRANSPORT
Buses to Santurtzi....50 D2
Buses to the Airport....51 C2
P&O Ferry Office....52 D1
Termibus....53 A2
INFORMATION
Arriaga Theatre Tourist Office..(see 49)
Guggenheim Tourist Office....(see 12)
elkar megadenda....1 B4
Hospital Civil de Basurto....2 A2
L@zar....3 E2
Main Post Office....4 D3
Main Tourist Office....5 D2
Net House....6 D2
Policía Municipal....7 A3
Tintas....(see 37)
SIGHTS & ACTIVITIES
Catedral de Santiago....8 A4
Euskal Museoa (Museo Vasco)....9 B4
Flower Market....10 E2
Museo de Bellas Artes....11 C2
Museo Guggenheim....12 C1
Museo Maritimo Ría de Bilbao....13 B1
To Beaches; Bilbao Airport (12km); Camping Sopelana (15km)
To Barcelo Av Hotel (1km); Durango (36km); San Sebastián (136km)
Ría de Bilbao
Parque de Doña Casilda de Iturrizar
Parque de Etxebarria
Abando
El Ensanche
Casco Viejo
Las Siete Calles
Abando Train Station (Renfe)
Concordia Train Station (FEVE)
Atxuri Train Station & Eusko Tran Terminus
Basurtu Eusko Tran Terminus
See Enlargement
0 100 m

BASQUE SIGNS

In many towns throughout the Basque region street names and signposts are changing from Castilian to Basque. Often this might be nothing more than Calle (street) becoming Kalle, with the actual name remaining unchanged, but not always. The problem is that not everyone uses these new names and many maps remain in Castilian. To make matters worse, it's often not the local council making these changes but people with aerosol cans. All this can make navigating a little confusing for tourists – San Sebastián and Bilbao are particularly hard. In this book we have attempted to stick with the most commonly used version or have included both Castilian and Basque. Below are some words that commonly appear on signs:

Basque	English	Spanish
aireportua	airport	*aeropuerto*
erdia	centre	*centro*
erdialdea	city centre	*centro de la ciudad*
jatetxea	restaurant	*restaurante*
kalle	street	*calle*
kalle nagusia	main street	*calle mayor*
komuna/k	toilet/s	*servicios*
kontuz!	caution/beware!	*!atención!*
nekazal turismoas	village or farmstead accommodation	*casas rurales*
ongi etorri	welcome	*bienvenido*
turismoa/turismo	tourism	*turismo*
turismo bulego	tourist office	*oficina de turismo*

elkar megadenda (☎ 944 24 02 28; Calle de Iparragirre 26) Basque publications are strongly represented here. It also stocks books in Spanish and a few in English, and there's an excellent map and travel section.

Tintas (☎ 944 44 95 41; Calle del Generál Concha 10) Travel bookshop with a broad selection of travel books, road maps and topographical maps for trekkers.

EMERGENCY

Cruz Roja (☎ 944 43 47 92) The Red Cross hospital.

Emergency (☎ 112)

Policía Municipal (☎ 092; Calle de Luís Briñas 14)

INTERNET ACCESS & TELEPHONE

L@zar (☎ 944 45 35 09; Calle de Sendeja 5; per min €0.06; 🕑 10.30am-1.30am Mon-Fri, 11am-1.30am Sat & Sun) Minimum 15 minutes' usage. Also has cheap international phone rates.

Net House (☎ 944 23 71 53; Calle Villarías 6; per hr €3; 🕑 10am-2pm & 4.30-10pm Mon-Fri, 10.30am-2pm Sat) Note that these hours seem a little flexible!

MEDICAL SERVICES

Hospital Civil de Basurto (☎ 944 00 60 00; Calle de Gurtubay)

MONEY

There are numerous banks, most with ATMs, in Bilbao, particularly around Plaza Circular.

POST

Main post office (☎ 944 22 05 48; Alameda de Urquijo 19)

TOURIST INFORMATION

Tourist office (☎ 944 79 57 60; www.bilbao.net/bilbaoturismo) Main Office (Plaza del Ensanche 11; 🕑 9am-2pm & 4-7.30pm Mon-Fri); Airport (☎ 944 71 03 01; 🕑 7.30am-11pm Mon-Fri, 8.30am-11pm Sat & Sun); Guggenheim (Avenida Abandoibarra 2; 🕑 10am-7pm Mon-Sat, 10am-6pm Sun Jul-Sep, 11am-6pm Tue-Fri, 11am-7pm Sat, 11am-3pm Sun Oct-May); Teatro Arriaga (Plaza Arriaga; 🕑 9.30am-2pm & 4-7.30pm daily Jun-Sep, 11am-2pm & 5-7.30pm Mon-Fri, 9.30am-2pm & 5-7.30pm Sat, 9.30am-2pm Sun Oct-May) Bilbao's friendly tourist-office staffers are extremely helpful, well informed and above all enthusiastic about their city. At all offices ask for the free bimonthly *Bilbao Guía*, with its entertainment listings plus tips on restaurants, bars and nightlife. There is also a call centre (☎ 944 71 03 01; 🕑 8.30am-11pm), which is on duty everyday and is equally helpful.

Sights

MUSEO GUGGENHEIM

Opened in September 1997, Bilbao's **Museo Guggenheim** (☎ 944 35 90 80; www.guggenheim-bilbao.es; Avenida Abandoibarra 2; adult/under 12yr/student €12.50/free/7.50; 🕑 10am-8pm daily Jul & Aug, 10am-8pm Tue-Sun Sep-Jun) lifted modern architecture and Bilbao into the 21st century – with sensation.

TRAVEL PASSES

The **Bilbacard** (1-/2-/3-day pass €6/10/12) entitles the user to reduced rates on all city transport as well as reductions at many of the sights. It can be purchased from any of the tourist offices. **Creditrans** give significant discounts on the metro, tram and city bus network. They are available in €5, €10 and €15 denominations from all metro and tram stations.

It boosted the city's already inspired regeneration and stimulated further development.

Some might say, probably quite rightly, that structure overwhelms function here and that the Guggenheim is probably more famous for its architecture than its content. But Canadian architect Frank Gehry's inspired use of flowing canopies, cliffs, promontories, ship shapes, towers and flying fins is irresistible.

Like all great architects, Gehry designed the Guggenheim with historical and geographical contexts in mind. The site was an industrial wasteland, part of Bilbao's wretched and decaying warehouse district on the banks of Ría de Bilbao. The city's historical industries of shipbuilding and fishing reflected Gehry's own interests, not least his engagement with industrial materials in previous works. The gleaming titanium tiles that sheathe most of the building like giant herring scales are said to have been inspired by the architect's childhood fascination with fish.

The interior of the Guggenheim is purposefully vast. The cathedral-like atrium is more than 45m high. Light pours in through the glass cliffs. Leading off from the atrium is Gallery 104, the Arcelor Gallery (formerly the Fish Gallery), a vast arena (128m by 30m) that houses Richard Serra's *Snake* and *The Matter of Time*. These installations comprise massive iron sheets arranged mazelike and mysteriously, between which you wander in a rust-red world of muffled, sibilant or clanging sound.

Galleries 103 and 105 house selections from the Guggenheim permanent collection, and can include works by Picasso, Braque, Mondrian, Miró, Rothko, Klee and Kandinsky. But for most people it is the temporary exhibitions that are the main attraction (check the Guggenheim's website for a full program of upcoming exhibitions).

Admission prices may vary depending on special exhibitions, and the last ticket sales are half an hour before closing. Free guided tours in English and French take place at 11am, 12.30pm, 4.30pm and 6.30pm; sign up half an hour before at the information desk. Groups are limited to 20, so get there early. Sign-language tours take place at 12.30pm on the last Sunday of each month. Excellent self-guided audio tours in various languages are free with admission. Entry queues can be horrendous, with wet summer days and Easter almost guaranteeing you a wait of over an hour. The museum is wheelchair accessible.

MUSEO DE BELLAS ARTES

A mere five minutes from Museo Guggenheim is Bilbao's **Museo de Bellas Artes** (Fine Arts Museum; ☎ 944 39 60 60; www.museobilbao.com; Plaza del Museo 2; adult/student €5.50/4, admission free Wed; 10am-8pm Tue-Sun). More than just a complement to the Guggenheim, it often seems to actually exceed its more famous cousin for content.

The museum houses a compelling collection that includes everything from Gothic sculptures to 20th-century pop art. There are three main subcollections: Classical Art, with works by Murillo, Zurbarán, El Greco, Goya and van Dyck; Contemporary Art, featuring works by Gauguin, Francis Bacon and Anthony Caro; and Basque Art, with the works of the great sculptors Jorge de Oteiza and Eduardo Chillida, and also strong paintings by the likes of Ignacio Zuloago and Juan de Echevarria. A useful audioguide costs €2. The museum is wheelchair accessible.

CASCO VIEJO

The compact Casco Viejo, Bilbao's atmospheric old quarter, is full of charming streets, boisterous bars, and plenty of quirky and independent shops. At the heart of the Casco are Bilbao's original 'seven streets', Las Siete Calles, which date from the 1400s.

The 14th-century Gothic **Catedral de Santiago** (10am-1pm & 4-7pm Tue-Sat, 10.30am-1.30pm Sun) has a splendid Renaissance portico and pretty little cloister. Further north, the 19th-century arcaded **Plaza Nueva** is a rewarding *pintxo* (Basque tapas) haunt. There's a lively Sunday-morning **flea market** here, which is full of secondhand book and record stalls, and pet 'shops' selling chirpy birds (some kept in old-fashioned wooden cages), fluffy mice and tiny baby terrapins. Elsewhere in the market children and adults alike swap and barter football cards and old stamps from countries you've never heard of; in between weave street performers and waiters with trays piled high. A sweeter-smelling **flower market** takes place on Sunday mornings in the nearby **Plaza del Arenal**.

EUSKAL MUSEOA (MUSEO VASCO)

This **museum** (Museum of Basque Archaeology, Ethnography & History; ☎ 944 15 54 23; www.euskal-museoa.org; Plaza Miguel Unamuno 4; adult/under 10yr/student €3/free/1.50, admission free Thu; 11am-5pm Tue-Sat, 11am-2pm Sun) is a complete and well-executed lesson in Basque history. The Basque story kicks off back in the days of prehistory and from this murky period the displays bound rapidly through to the modern age. The main problem with the museum is that unless you speak Spanish (or perhaps you studied Euskara at school?) it's all a little meaningless as, amazingly, there are no English or French translations!

The museum is housed in a fine old building, at whose centre is a peaceful cloister that was part of an original 17th-century Jesuit College. In the cloister is the **Mikeldi Idol**, a powerful pre-Christian, possibly Iron Age, symbolic figure.

The museum is wheelchair accessible.

MUSEO MARITIMO RIA DE BILBAO

The latest addition to Bilbao's ongoing restoration is the space-age **Museo Maritimo Ría de Bilbao** (Maritime Museum; ☎ 902 13 10 00; www.museomaritimobilbao.org; Muelle Ramón de la Sota 1; adult/child/senior & student €5/free/3.50; 10am-8pm Tue-Sun mid-Jun–mid-Sep, 10am-6.30pm Tue-Fri & Sun, 10am-8pm Sat mid-Sep–mid-Jun), appropriately sited down on the waterfront. Using bright and well-thought-out displays, the museum plunges into the watery depths of Bilbao and Basque maritime history and has enough interactive displays and activities to keep children smiling. There is also an outdoor section where children (and nautically inclined grown-ups) can clamber about a range of boats pretending to be pirates and sailors.

PARQUE DE DOÑA CASILDA DE ITURRIZAR

Floating on waves of peace and quiet just beyond the Museo de Bellas Artes is another work of fine art – the Parque de Doña Casilda de Iturrizar. The centrepiece of this whimsical park is the large pond filled with ornamental ducks and other waterfowl.

Festivals & Events

Held in February, **carnaval** is celebrated with vigour, but Bilbao's grandest fiesta begins on the first Saturday after 15 August and is known as the **Semana Grande** (Big Week). Traditional parades and music mix with a full program of cultural events over 10 days. Bilbao's biggest musical event is **Bilbao BKK Live** (www.bilbaobbklive.com), which takes place over three days in early July.

About 25km north of Bilbao, Getxo hosts a week-long **international jazz festival** in July, as well as a smaller **blues music festival** (June) and a **folk music festival** (September).

Sleeping

Bilbao, like the Basque Country in general, is increasingly popular, and it can be very hard to find decent accommodation (especially at

OPEN-AIR GALLERY

Part of the Guggenheim experience is a quiet wander around the outside of the building, appreciating the extraordinary imagination behind its design and catching the different colours reflected by the titanium tiles, limestone and glass.

Lying between the glass buttresses of the central atrium and Ría de Bilbao is a simple pool of water that emits at intervals a mist 'sculpture' by Fuyiko Nakaya. Nearby on the riverbank is a sculpture by Louise Bourgeois, a skeletal canopy representing a spider entitled *Maman,* said to symbolise a protective embrace. In the open area to the west of the museum a fountain sculpture fires off jets of water into the air randomly and youngsters leap to and fro across it. Beyond is a kids' playground.

On the Alameda Mazarredo, on the city side of the museum, is Jeff Koons' kitsch whimsy *Puppy,* a 12m tall highland terrier made up of thousands of begonias. Bilbao has hung on to 'El Poop', who was supposed to be a passing attraction as part of a world tour. With the fond, deprecating humour of citizens of all tough cities, *bilbainos* will tell you that El Poop came first – and then they had to build a kennel behind it…

weekends). You would be wise to book as far ahead as possible. The Bilbao tourism authority has a very useful **reservations department** (☎ 902 87 72 98; www.bilbaore servas.com).

BUDGET

Camping Sopelana (☎ 946 76 21 20; sites for 2 people, small tent & car €25.20;) This exposed site has a swimming pool and is within easy walking distance of Sopelana beach. Facilities are very good. It's on the metro line, 15km from Bilbao.

Pensión Ladero (☎ 944 15 09 32; Calle Lotería 1; s/d €24/36) The no-fuss rooms here are as cheap as Bilbao gets and represent good bang for your buck. After that mammoth climb up four storeys you can treat yourself to a dessert. Rooms cannot be reserved in advance.

Pensión Mardones (☎ 944 15 31 05; www.pension mardones.com; Calle Jardines 4; s/d €34/48;) This well-kept number has nice carved wooden wardrobes in the rooms and lots of exposed wooden roof beams. The cheerful owner is very helpful and all up it offers great value.

MIDRANGE

Hostal Begoña (☎ 944 23 01 34; www.hostalbegona.com; Calle de la Amistad 2; s/d from €53/64;) The owners of this outstanding place don't need voguish labels for their very stylish and individual creation. Begoña speaks for itself with colourful rooms decorated with modern artworks, all with funky tiled bathrooms and wrought-iron beds.

Pensión Gurea (☎ 944 16 32 99; hostalgurea@yahoo .es; Calle de Bidebarrieta 14; s/d €45/65;) It's a family affair at this bright and breezy *pensión*, where husband and wife run around trying to please you, and the kids just run around (don't worry: they're not noisy – normally!). It's well organised, with large rooms.

Hotel Ripa (☎ 944 23 96 77; www.hotel-ripa.com; Calle de Ripa 3; s/d €55/65; P) If you can snag a room with a river view then this is a good catch, but otherwise it lacks creative energy. The price is right though.

La Estrella (☎ 944 16 40 66; Calle de María Muñoz 6; s/d €40/68) Estrella has been around for a while and offers decent, colourful rooms that have no great character but are clean.

our pick Pensión Iturrienea Ostatua (☎ 944 16 15 00; www.iturrieneaostatua.com; Calle de Santa María 14; d/tr €70/96) Easily the most eccentric hotel in Bilbao, it's part farmyard, part old-fashioned toyshop, and a work of art in its own right. Try to get a room on the 1st floor; they are so full of character there'll be barely enough room for your own! The multilingual staff are amazingly helpful and friendly. If you do stay here, remember: whatever else you do, for goodness' sake don't let the sheep escape!

Barcelo Avenida Hotel (☎ 944 12 43 00; www .barceloavenida.com; Avenida Zumalacárregui 40; r from €75; P) OK, it's a chain hotel and, yes, they do find all sorts of extras to add onto the bill (you have to pay to park your car). But let's be fair: hotels of this quality don't come much cheaper than this. The rooms are slick, minimal and a perfect fit with Bilbao style. Though it's 1.5km from the centre, it's very close to a metro station.

Hotel Bilbao Jardines (☎ 944 79 42 10; www.hotel bilbaojardines.com; Calle Jardines 9; s/d €80/90; P) A welcome change from Casco Viejo's dusty facades, the Jardine's fresh, green decor and comfy furnishings offer a well-priced alternative to the sometimes worn charm of the quarter's long-serving *pensiones*.

Petit Palace Arana (☎ 944 15 64 11; www.ht hoteles.com; Calle de Bidebarrieta 2; s/d from €80/90;) A funky new business-level hotel, which brings the style of today to a building of yesterday. Rooms have large, soft beds and great zebra-striped bathrooms, and some come with river views.

TOP END

Miró Hotel (☎ 946 61 18 80; www.mirohotelbilbao.com; Alameda Mazarredo 77; s/d from €87/112; P) Dreamt up by fashion designer Antonio Miró, everything about this hotel is subtle, classy and absolutely in tune with the new Bilbao. It's the sort of place that makes you go home and try to redesign your own house! Book through the hotel website for the best rates.

Gran Hotel Domine (☎ 944 25 33 00; www.gran hoteldominebilbao.com; Alameda Mazarredo 61; d from €140; P) Designer chic all the way, from the Javier Mariscal main interiors to the Phillipe Starck and Arne Jacobsen fittings – and that's just in the loos. This stellar showpiece of the Silken chain has views of the Guggenheim from some of its pricier rooms and from the roof terrace.

Eating

In the world of trade and commerce the Basques are an outward-looking lot, but when it comes to food they refuse to believe that any other people could possibly match their culinary skills (and they may well have a point). This means that eating out in Bilbao is generally a choice of Basque, Basque or Basque food. Still, life could be worse, and there are some terrific places to get stuffed.

Though it lacks San Sebastián's stellar reputation for *pintxos*, prices are generally slightly lower here and the quality is about equal.

PINTXOS

Bar Gure Toki (☎ 944 15 80 37; Plaza Nueva 12) Tucked away in the northwest corner of Plaza Nueva is this cosy little *pintxo* bar that's grounded in Basque culture and tastes. There's a subtle but simple line in creative *pintxos* (€2).

Xukeia (☎ 944 15 97 72; Calle de Perro) One of the more character-infused places in the old town, it has something of the look of a small-town French bistro overlaid with raucous Spanish soul. The drool-inducing *pintxos* have won awards and at only €1 to €1.50 a go are cheaper than elsewhere.

Café-Bar Bilbao (☎ 944 15 16 71; Plaza Nueva 6) This place, with its cool blue southern tile work and warm northern atmosphere, prides itself on very creative *pintxos*, so plunge straight in, if you dare, for a taste of *mousse de pata sobre crema de melocotón y almendras* (duck, cream, peach and almond mousse). Don't ask; just eat…

Sasibil (☎ 944 15 56 05; Calle Jardines 8) Sasibil gets a more middle-aged clientele than some of its louder neighbours and, possibly because of this, instead of rock videos blaring on the TV you'll find informative films on the crafting of its superb *pintxos*.

Don't restrict your search for the perfect *pintxo* to the Casco Viejo: the El Ensanche area also has some good options. One of the best is **El Globo** (☎ 944 15 42 21; Calle de Diputación 8), a popular bar with a terrific range of *pintxos modernos*, including favourites such as *txangurro gratinado* (spider crab) and *morcilla rebozada* (blood sausage in light batter). **Los Candiles** (☎ 944 24 14 79; Calle de Diputación 1) is a narrow, low-key little bar, with some subtle *pintxos* filled with the taste of the sea.

RESTAURANTS

Fresc Co (☎ 944 23 30 01; Calle de Ledesma 12; mains €7-10; Ⓥ) You can cram your plate with salad and then scoop up soup, pasta and pizza as well as tasty desserts at this seductive budget venue. It's usually packed; pitch in around 4pm for some space.

our pick **Abaroa** (☎ 944 13 20 51; Paseo del Campo de Volantin 13; mains €7-12) This intimate and brightly furnished restaurant is a big name with locals. It specialises in hearty countryside fare, but with a twist of today. The result is that black pudding and a bowl of beans have never been so well presented or tasted so good. A full three-course meal with wine shouldn't cost more than €25 per person. There is a second, equally good branch on the Plaza del Museo.

Rio-Oja (☎ 944 15 08 71; Calle de Perro 4; mains €8-10) An institution that shouldn't be missed. It specialises in light Basque seafood and heavy Riojan fare, but to most foreigners the squid floating in pools of its own ink and sheep brains lying in its former owner's skull are the makings of a culinary adventure story they'll be recounting for years. Don't worry, though: it really does taste much better than it sounds.

Ghandi (☎ 944 23 39 34; Calle de la Amistad 6; mains €9) In an ocean of Basqueness it's nice to find an island of spice. One of the few curry houses in the Basque region, Ghandi has all your favourites, like rogan josh and chicken tikka.

Ristorante Passerela (☎ 944 44 03 46; Alameda de Urquijo 30; mains €10-13) Forget about sloppy pizzas, because this immensely popular hideaway is a real-deal Italian restaurant. As in Rome, you order a plate of pasta first and then one of meat or fish served on its own. Most of the pasta and all of the bread is freshly made. It's ideal for a filling lunch, but turn up early or book ahead.

Tapelia (☎ 944 23 08 20; www.tapelia.com; Calle Uribitarte 24; mains €10-15) This new restaurant, set on the banks of the Nervión, has a polished business exterior, but a stone-cottage country interior. It specialises in both excellent paella and the tastes of Alicante. It's essential to reserve a table in advance. The attached cafe serves up *pintxos* and simple snacks to those not lucky enough to get a seat for a meal.

Casa Victor Montes (☎ 944 15 56 03; www.victormontesbilbao.com; Plaza Nueva 8; mains €15) Part bar, part shop, part restaurant, total work of art. The Victor Montes is quite touristy but locals also appreciate its over-the-top decoration, its good food and the thousand or so bottles of wine lined up behind the bar. If you're stopping by for a full meal, book in advance and savour that Galician favourite, barnacles.

our pick **Café Guggenheim** (☎ 944 23 93 33; www.restauranteguggenheim.com; lunch menú €19, restaurant mains €30-35) El Goog's modernist, chic restaurant and cafe are under the direction of multi-Michelin-starred chef Martin Berasategui.

WILLY URIBE, PHOTOGRAPHER & WRITER

Willy Uribe is a well-known photographer and writer from the Basque Country. Much of his work concentrates on surfing and the surf lifestyle, and it has appeared in publications around the world. He is also a novelist and his latest book is called *Revancha*. You can find out more about him on his blog: www.unaimagenymilpalabras.blogspot.com.

Where are you from? I was born in Bilbao and grew up in the big urban area of Bilbao. The area close to the seaside. I'm still there.

What do you like most about Bilbao? The *ría* and the human activities along the *ría*. Bilbao has a very human scale. The size of the city is really nice and the *ría* is its heart. The *ría* is moving all day long and though you are 15km inland you can feel the sea. Bilbao even has tides.

How has Bilbao changed over the years? The big thing, the most important change, is that the harbour and the big factories have left the main area of the city and moved to the suburbs, disappeared or been converted. It was a radical change, but more for the landscape than the mentality of the people.

What do you like least about Bilbao? For me, it is a little bit sad to see all the foreigners coming to Bilbao only for the Guggenheim. Bilbao is not a tourist destination, at least not a classic one. Bilbao is a personal destination.

What is your favourite restaurant in Bilbao? Don't like restaurants too much. I prefer to eat a *bocadillo* (filled roll) overlooking the *ría*. But if I do go to one, I go to the Rio-Oja (p477) in the Casco Viejo.

Your work as a photographer means that you get to travel widely over the Basque Country. What is your favourite place and favourite thing to do in the Basque Country? The best part of the Basque Country, for me, is the seaside and the fishing villages. Walking along the coast is one of my favourite activities. There are beautiful coastal areas with good walks. Not too many guidebooks tell you about that, but if you know the places then you'll have a good experience.

What is your favourite thing to take photos of in the Basque? Surfing is forever my favourite, but I very much like taking photos of Basque rural sports, especially rowing competitions. They are really photogenic, diverse and full of strength, and with a lot of different angles from which to take photos.

Describe the Basque people. Gentlemen, but too proud of ourselves.

Do you speak Basque and do many of your friends speak it? I speak basic Euskara (Basque) and have some friends that speak a high level of Euskara.

Do you speak it on a daily basis with friends? In urban areas it is hard to hear Euskara. I usually speak Spanish with my friends. If I travel to rural areas, where Euskara is more present in conversation, I speak it. Franco's regime was terrible for those learning and speaking Euskara. Now, fortunately, all the kids learn to speak Euskara.

If you could change one thing about the Basque Country what would it be? The ETA violence. Without ETA, things will be better in the Basque Country.

What does the future hold for the Basque Country? It all depends on us. If we find peace, the future will be fine. If not…OK…let's find peace!

Needless to say, the *nueva cocina vasca* (Basque nouvelle cuisine) is breathtaking, including such mouth-waterers as roast vine tomato stuffed with baby squid with black risotto and fresh cream. Salivating yet? OK, so the food is good, but what about the costs? Well, that's the real beauty – it was decided that food of such exceptional quality shouldn't be available to just the elite, so prices, especially at lunchtime, are reasonable enough for everyone to afford. Reservations are essential in the evening, but at lunch it's on a first-come, first-served basis from 1.30pm.

CAFES

The porticoed Plaza Nueva is a good spot for coffee and people-watching, especially in summer.

Café Iruña (☎ 944 24 90 59; cnr Calles de Colón de Larreátegui & Berástegui) Moorish style and a century of gossip are the defining characteristics of this grande old dame of a cafe. It's the perfect place to sit down with a coffee and a work of highbrow literature and enjoy the people-watching. The *pinchos morunos* (spicy kebabs with bread; €2.20) magnetically draw people in every night.

SELF-CATERING

Mercado de la Ribera (Calle Ribera) For self-catering, try this market. Drifting round the fish section is a marvellous experience in itself.

Drinking

In the Casco Viejo, around Calles Barrenkale, Ronda and de Somera, there are plenty of terrific hole-in-the-wall, no-nonsense bars, often political, definitely alternative, and with a generally youngish crowd. Across the river in the Ensanche area, there's a more sophisticated slant on things in the numerous bars and cafes.

Twiggy (☎ 944 10 38 14; Alameda de Urquijo 35) Retro psychedelio! Happy post-hippy place with a cheerful mix of '60s kitsch for lovely people.

Kamin (☎ 944 44 41 21; Manuel Allende 8) Laid-back listening in rosy light among the Bilbao cognoscenti. The music trails sweetly through everything from rock and pop to alternative and fresh new sounds on the Basque scene.

Entertainment

CLUBS & LIVE MUSIC

There are plenty of clubs and live venues in Bilbao, and the vibe is friendly and generally easygoing. Websites usually have details of upcoming gigs.

Kafe Antzokia (☎ 944 24 46 25; www.kafeantzokia.com; Calle San Vicente 2) The vibrant heart of contemporary Basque Bilbao, featuring international rock bands, blues and reggae, but also the cream of Basque rock-pop. Weekend concerts run from 10pm to 1am, followed by DJs until 5am. Cover charge for concerts can range from about €4 upwards. During the day it's a cafe, restaurant and cultural centre all rolled into one and has frequent exciting events on.

Conjunto Vacío (Muelle de la Merced 4; around €10 at weekends) House is the spin here and there's a very style-conscious, confident, young, mixed gay-and-straight crowd.

Le Club (☎ 944 16 71 11; www.leclub.es; Muelle Marzana 4) Three floors to twist, gyrate and then relax on. The 1st floor has rock and '80s pop, the 2nd has dance music and the 3rd is the chill-out lounge. Entrance ranges from €8 to €12 with one drink included.

El Balcón de la Lola (☎ 946 08 67 20; Calle Bailén 10; around €10 at weekends) One of Bilbao's most popular mixed gay/straight clubs, this is the place to come if you're looking for hip industrial decor and a packed Saturday-night disco.

THEATRE

Bilbao offers regular performances of dance, opera and drama at the city's two principal theatres. Check the theatre websites for current information.

Teatro Arriaga (☎ 944 31 03 10; www.teatroarriaga.com; Plaza Arriaga) The baroque facade of this venue commands the open spaces of El Arenal between the Casco Viejo and the river.

Euskalduna Palace (☎ 902 54 05 39; www.euskalduna.net; Avenida Abandoibarra) About 600m downriver from the Guggenheim is another modernist gem, built on the riverbank in a style that echoes the great shipbuilding works of the 19th century. The Euskalduna houses the Bilbao Symphony Orchestra and the Basque Symphony Orchestra.

Getting There & Away

AIR

Bilbao's **airport** (☎ 944 86 96 64; www.aena.es) is near Sondika, 12km northeast of the city. Services are excellent. There's a first-class **tourist information office** (☎ 944 71 03 01; 7.30am-11pm Mon-Fri, 8.30am-11pm Sat & Sun), a medical centre, ATMs, shops, cafes, a restaurant and car-hire offices. **EasyJet** (www.easyjet.com) has cheap flights between London and Bilbao, although booking well ahead is advised.

BOAT

P&O ferries (☎ 902 02 04 61, 944 23 44 77; www.poportsmouth.com; Calle de Cosme Echevarrieta 1) leave three times a week for Portsmouth from Santurtzi. Ticket prices vary due to special offers, but a guide is €190 per passenger with cabin and €400 per car (with two passengers). Crossings from Portsmouth/Bilbao take 33/30 hours.

BUS

Bilbao's main bus station, **Termibus** (San Mamés), is west of the centre.

From Termibus there are regular services to Madrid (€26.11, 4¾ hours), Barcelona (€40.59, seven hours), Vitoria (€5.45, 50 minutes), Pamplona (€12.85, 1¾ hours), Logroño (€12.05, two hours), Irún and the French border (€7.91, two hours) and Santander (€9.27, 1½ hours). **Pesa** (☎ 902 10 12 10) operates services every 30 minutes to one hour to San Sebastián (€9.20, one hour) and also serves Durango (€3.50, 25 minutes), Elorrio (€3.50, 40 minutes) and Oñati (€5.50, 1¼ hours).

Bizkaibus (☎ 902 22 22 65) travels to destinations throughout the rural Basque Country, including coastal communities such as Lekeitio (€3.10) and Bermeo (€2.40).

TRAIN

The **Renfe** (☎ 902 24 02 02; www.renfe.es) Abando train station is just across the river from Plaza Arriaga and the Casco Viejo. There are two trains daily to Madrid (from €39.80, six hours) and Barcelona (€39.80, nine hours). Other cities served include Valladolid (€23.70, four hours) and Burgos (from €17.30, three hours).

Next door is the Concordia train station with its handsome art-nouveau facade of wrought iron and tiles. It is used by the **FEVE** (☎ 944 23 22 66; www.feve.es) private rail company for running trains west into Cantabria and Asturias.

The Atxuri train station is about 1km upriver from Casco Viejo. From here, **Eusko Tren/Ferrocarril Vasco** (ET/FV; ☎ 902 54 32 10; www.euskotren.es in Spanish & Basque) operates services every half-hour to Bermeo (€2.40, 1½ hours) via Guernica (€2.40, one hour) and Mundaka (€2.40, 1½ hours), and hourly to San Sebastián (€6.50, 2¾ hours) via Durango, Zumaia and Zarautz.

Getting Around

TO/FROM THE AIRPORT & PORT

The airport bus (Bizkaibus A3247; €1.25, 30 minutes) departs from a stand on the extreme right as you leave Arrivals. It runs through the northwestern section of the city, passing the Museo Guggenheim, stopping at Plaza Moyúa and terminating at the Termibus (bus station). It runs every 20 minutes from 5.20am to 10.20pm.

Taxis from the airport to the Casco Viejo cost about €25.

Buses for the port of Santurtzi leave from near the junction of Calle Hurtado de Amézaga and Plaza Circular.

METRO

There are metro stations at all the main focal points of the Ensanche and at Casco Viejo. Tickets start at €1.30. The metro was designed by architect Sir Norman Foster and opened in 1995. Locals instantly dubbed the concertina-style glass-and-chrome entrances 'Fosteritos'. The metro runs to the north coast from a number of stations on both sides of the river and makes it easy to get to the beaches closest to Bilbao.

TRAM

Bilbao's Eusko Tran tramline is a boon to locals and visitors alike. It runs to and fro between Basurtu, in the southwest of the city, and the Atxuri train station. Stops include the Termibus station, the Guggenheim and Teatro Arriaga by the Casco Viejo. Tickets cost €1 and need to be verified in the machine next to the ticket dispenser before boarding.

AROUND BILBAO

Beaches

Two reasonable beaches for swimming are **Azkorri** and **Sopelana**. The latter is the most consistent surf beach in the area. Better beaches can be found east of **Plentzia**. Also good is the sheltered beach at **Gorliz**, which has a pretty lighthouse and some fine views from the Astondo end of the beach. There are well-signposted tracks for walkers.

A worthwhile stop en route to the beaches is the newly restored **Puente Colgante**, the world's first transporter bridge, which opened in 1893 – it links Getxo and Portugalete. A platform, suspended from the actual bridge high above, is loaded with up to six cars plus foot passengers; it then glides silently over Río Nervión to the other bank. Rides cost €0.30 one way per person. You can also take a lift up to the superstructure at 46m (€4), and walk across the river and back (not for those prone to vertigo) for some great views. Another choice is to cross the river by small ferryboat (€0.30). The nearest metro stop from Bilbao is Areeta (€1.30) and the nearest Renfe stop is in Portugalete (€1.30).

Guernica

pop 15,600

Guernica (Basque: Gernika) is a state of mind as well as a place. At a glance it seems no more than a very ugly country town. Apparently, prior to the morning of 26 April

THE OLDEST LANGUAGE

'The Basque language is a country,' said Victor Hugo, and language certainly encapsulates all things Basque. Known as Euskara, the Basque language is acknowledged as being one of Europe's oldest and most quixotic languages, with no known relationship to the Indo-European family of languages. Its earliest written elements were thought to be 13th-century manuscripts found at the Monasterio de Suso (p515) at San Millán de Cogolla in La Rioja province, but discoveries in 2006 at the archaeological site of Iruña-Veleia near Vitoria included inscriptions in Basque dating from the 3rd century AD.

Suppressed by Franco, Basque was subsequently recognised as one of Spain's official languages. Although Franco's repression meant that many older Basques are unable to speak their native tongue, it has now become the language of choice, and of identity, among a growing number of young Basques, fuelling a dynamic cultural renaissance and a nonviolent political awareness. There are now Basque-language radio and TV stations and newspapers.

For more information on the Basque language, see the Language chapter, p900.

1937, Guernica wasn't quite so ugly, but the horrifying events of that day meant that the town was later reconstructed as fast as possible with little regard for aesthetics. Franco, who'd been having some problems with the Basques, decided to teach them a lesson by calling in his buddy Hitler. On that fateful morning planes from Hitler's Condor Legion flew backwards and forwards over the town demonstrating their new-found concept of saturation bombing. In the space of a few hours the town was destroyed and 1645 civilians killed. What makes this even more shocking is that it wasn't the first time this had happened. Just days earlier, the nearby town of Durango suffered a similar fate, but as there were no foreign observers the world simply did not believe what it was being told.

Franco chose Guernica for his 'lesson' because of its symbolic value to the Basques. It's the ancient seat of Basque democracy and the site at which the Basque parliament met beneath the branches of a sacred oak tree from medieval times until 1876. Today the original oak is nothing but a stump, but the Tree of Guernica lives on in the form of a young oak tree.

The tragedy of Guernica gained international resonance with Picasso's iconic painting *Guernica,* which has come to symbolise the violence of the 20th century. A copy of the painting now hangs in the entrance hall of the UN headquarters in New York, while the original hangs in the Centro de Arte Reina Sofía in Madrid. Many Basques had hoped that with the opening of the Guggenheim the painting would be moved to Bilbao, where it surely belongs, but this has never happened.

INFORMATION

The helpful **tourist office** (☎ 946 25 58 92; www.gernika-lumo.net; Artekalea 8; ⏰ 10am-8pm daily Jul & Aug, 10am-2pm & 4-7pm Mon-Sat, 10am-2pm Sun Sep-Jun) has friendly multilingual staff. It sells the Global Ticket (€5.25), a combined entry ticket for the town's sights.

SIGHTS

Guernica's seminal experience is a visit to the **Museo de la Paz de Gernika** (Guernica Peace Museum; ☎ 946 27 02 13; www.peacemuseumguernica.org; Plaza Foru 1; adult/child €4/2; ⏰ 10am-8pm Tue-Sat, 10am-3pm Sun Jul & Aug, 10am-2pm & 4-7pm Tue-Sat, 10am-2pm Sun Sep-Jun), where audiovisual displays calmly reveal the horror of war and hatred, both in the Basque Country and around the world. Display panels are in Castilian and Basque, but the ticket office hands out good English and French translations of almost all the captions. There are guided tours, in four languages, each day at 12pm and 5pm. The museum is wheelchair accessible.

A couple of blocks north, on Calle Allende Salazar, is a ceramic-tile version of Picasso's *Guernica.*

Further west along Calle Allende Salazar is the **Euskal Herriko Museoa** (☎ 946 25 54 51; Calle Allende Salazar; adult/child €3/1.50; ⏰ 10am-2pm & 4-7pm Tue-Sat, 11am-3pm Sun), housed in the 18th-century Palacio de Montefuerte. The comprehensive exhibitions on Basque history and culture are well worth a look, with fine old maps, engravings, and a range of other documents and portraits. The museum is wheelchair accessible.

The pleasant **Parque de los Pueblos de Europa** (⏰ 10am-7pm, to 9pm in summer) behind the museum contains a couple of typically curvaceous

sculptures by Henry Moore and other works by Eduardo Chillida. The park leads to the attractive **Casa de Juntas**, where the provincial government has met since 1979. Inside the chamber is a superb modern stained-glass window on a huge scale (235 sq metres). Outside is the famous **Tree of Guernica**, now a mere stump, sheltered by a neoclassical gazebo. Another tree was recently planted in the rear courtyard.

SLEEPING & EATING

The accommodation situation is in a pretty sorry state and most people sensibly visit as a day trip from Bilbao.

Hotel Boliña (☎ 946 25 03 00; www.hotelbolina.net; Calle de Barrencalle 3; s/d €37/48) In the centre of town, Boliña has dreary rooms that, one can only hope, have seen better days.

Pensión Akelarre (☎ 656 762217; Calle de Barrencalle 5; r from €54) Next door to the Boliña, Akelarre has equally uninspiring rooms. The reception is attended only from 9am to 1pm and from 6pm to 9pm. If you arrive outside of these hours you have to 'buy' a room through a weird credit-card swipe system on the door!

There are several simple restaurants and bars scattered around the main square and surrounding streets.

GETTING THERE & AWAY

Guernica is an easy day trip from Bilbao by ET/FV train from Atxuri train station (€2.40, one hour). Trains run every half-hour.

Cueva de Santimamiñe

The grotto of **Santimamiñe** (☎ 944 65 16 57; santimamiñe@bizkaia.net; 10am-2pm & 4-7pm Tue-Sun) is a crowd pleaser for its impressive stalactites, stalagmites and well-preserved prehistoric cave paintings. Guided tours (per person/per person within a group €5/3) ideally should be arranged in advance, though in reality you can often just rock up.

You'll need your own wheels to get here – take the BI638 to Kortezubi (4km northeast of Guernica), then turn off to the BI4244 just before town.

El Bosque Pintado de Oma

Near the grotto is one of the region's most unusual attractions, the 'Painted Forest' of Basque artist Agustín Ibarrola, who has adorned dozens of trees in the Oma Valley with rainbows, outlines of people and colourful abstract shapes. While at first they seem rather disjointed, several trees together form a complete picture.

The Bosque is accessible only on foot and a walk around the forest takes about two hours. To get there follow the signposted route to the Cueva de Santimamiñe; from a turn-off near the cave a marked forest track leads in 3km to the Bosque. Cars should not use this track.

Mundaka

pop 1800

Universally regarded as the home of the best wave in Europe, Mundaka is a name of legend for surfers across the world. The wave breaks on a perfectly tapering sandbar formed by the outflow of the Río Urdaibai and, on a good day, offers heavy, barrelling lefts that can reel off for hundreds of metres. The **Billabong Pro**, a stop on the World Championship Tour, is held here over 10 days in early October. If you're not quite up to world-champion standards then note that Mundaka is not a good place to get your first taste of surfing.

Despite all the focus being on the waves, Mundaka has done a sterling job of not turning itself into just another 'hey dude' surf town, and remains a resolutely Basque port with a pretty main square and harbour area. There's a small **tourist office** (☎ 946 17 72 01; www.mundaka.org; Calle Kepa Deuna).

For accommodation through the summer months most people cram, and we mean cram, into **Camping Portuondo** (☎ 946 87 77 01; www.campingportuondo.com; sites per person/tent & car €5.70/11.50, bungalows from €84;), though it does have lovely terraced grounds, a pool and a restaurant.

For more brick-based accommodation, the best place is **Hotel Mundaka** (☎ 946 87 67 00; www.hotelmundaka.com; Calle Florentíno Larrínaga 9; s/d €54/78), which has clean and reliable rooms, though with little character. It's just up from the main square. Several bars and restaurants can be found around the square and harbourfront.

Buses and ET/FV trains between Bilbao and Bermeo stop here.

Bermeo

pop 17,000

Located just a few minutes to the north of Mundaka and on the open coast proper, this tough fishing port is refreshingly down-to-earth and hasn't lost its soul to tourism. Though there are no beaches here it's an enjoyable place to while away a few hours

TOP PICKS FOR KIDS

With all those tiring outdoor activities, the Basque Country, Navarra and La Rioja are great places for children. In no particular order, here are our top picks.

- Hunting for dinosaurs in Enciso (p514).
- Playing dungeons and dragons in the castles of Olite (p509) and Javier (p505).
- Gawping at Nemo and Jaws in San Sebastián's aquarium (p485).
- Sand-castle building for the tots and learning to surf for the big boys and girls almost anywhere along the Basque coast (below).
- For older children, playing Jack and Jill went up the (very big) hill in the Pyrenees (p505).
- Turning your little sister into a frog with the witches of Zugarramurdi (p506).
- Fiesta, fiesta! The daylight hours of almost every fiesta are tailor made for children.

watching the boats bustle in and out of the harbour.

The **tourist office** (☎ 946 17 91 54; Askatasun Bidea 2; 10am-8pm Mon-Sat, 10am-2pm & 4-8pm Sun) is on the waterfront and has several excellent leaflets in French and English about the town. The absorbing **Museo del Pescador** (☎ 946 88 11 71; Plaza Torrontero 1; admission free; 10am-2pm & 4-7pm Tue-Sat, 10am-2pm Sun), in the handsome 15th-century **Torre Ercilla**, is steeply uphill from the tourist office. The **Aita Guria whaler** (☎ 946 17 91 54; adult/child €5/3; 10.30am-2pm & 4.30pm-7pm Tue-Sat, 11am-2pm Sun) is a replica of an old whaling ship that contains informative displays on how to catch your own whale. Children will love exploring it; adults less so. It's near the tourist office.

A few kilometres beyond Bermeo, the **Ermita de San Juan de Gaztelugatxe** stands on an islet that is connected to the mainland by a bridge. It also has two natural arches on its seaward side. Built by the Knights Templar in the 10th century, it has also served as a handy shelter for shipwrecked sailors.

For accommodation, the **Torre Ercilla Ostatua** (☎ 946 18 75 98; Calle Talaranzko 14; s/d €36/45) and the **Hotel Txaraka** (☎ 946 88 55 58; Calle Almike Bidea; s/d €51/68) both have happy rooms in the town centre.

Half-hourly buses and ET/FV trains run from Bermeo to Bilbao (€2.40, 1¼ hours).

THE CENTRAL BASQUE COAST

The coast road from Bilbao to San Sebastián is a glorious journey past spectacular seascapes, with cove after cove stretching east and verdant fields suddenly ending where cliffs plunge into the sea. *Casas rurales* (village or farmstead accommodation) and camping grounds are plentiful and well signposted.

Elantxobe

pop 460

The tiny hamlet of Elantxobe, with its colourful houses clasping like geckos to an almost sheer cliff face, is undeniably one of the most attractive spots along the entire coast. The difficulty of building here, and the lack of a beach, has meant that it has been saved from the worst of tourist-related development. Public-transport fans will be so excited by Elantxobe that the earth really will move for them – the streets are so narrow that buses don't have space to turn around, so the road spins around for them! See the Lekeitio section for bus connections.

Lekeitio

pop 7300

Bustling Lekeitio has an attractive old core centred on the unnaturally large and slightly odd-looking late-Gothic **Iglesia de Santa María de la Asunción**.

For most visitors it's the two beaches that are the main draw. The one just east of the river, with a small rocky mound of an island just offshore, is the prettier of the two.

Lekeitio's annual **Fiesta de San Antolín** (5 September) will appeal to animal-lovers everywhere – the highlight of the piece involves a tug of war with a goose. The 'fun and games' end when the goose's head falls off.

Accommodation is scarce and pricey. **Camping Endai** (☎ 946 84 24 69; sites per person/tent €3.80/3.80; mid-Jun–mid-Sep) is a smallish camping ground with a bar and a shop on Playa Mendexa, a few kilometres before you reach the town. The **tourist office** (☎ 946 84 40 17; Plaza Independancia) can point you in the direction of private rooms.

Bizkaibus A3513 (€3.10) leaves from Calle Hurtado de Amézaga, by Bilbao's Abando train station, about eight times a day (except Sunday) and goes via Guernica and Elantxobe. Fairly regular buses from Lekeitio run to San Sebastián (€7).

Ondarroa

Slotted into the coastal hills of Vizcaya province just inside the border with Guipúzcoa, Ondarroa is the Basque Country's biggest fishing port, a fascinating and gutsy place in every sense. The harbour is the vibrant focus and Río Artibai winds inland beneath two bridges: one is an ancient, iconic symbol of Basque resistance; the other a signature example of the modernist work of Santiago Calatrava.

The town beach, though hardly picturesque, heaves with bodies beautiful in the summer.

The **tourist office** (☎ 946 83 19 51; www.learjai.com; Kalea Erribera 9; 🕑 10am-2pm & 4-7pm Mon-Sat, 10am-2pm Sun mid-Jun–mid-Sep, 10.30am-1.30pm & 4-7pm Fri & Sat, 10.30am-2.30pm Sun mid-Sep–mid-Jun) has plenty of information about the area. Staff should be able to point you in the direction of some agrotourism in the nearby hills and villages.

Zumaia

pop 8700

First impressions of Zumaia are not great, but struggle through the industrial zone that hems the town and you'll find an attractive centre. For beach-lovers, further rewards await in the form of the **Playa de Izturun**, wedged in among slate cliffs, and the **Playa de Santiago**, a more traditional strand of soft sand a couple of kilometres east of the town centre. Next to the latter stands the surprising and richly rewarding **Museo de Zuloaga** (☎ 943 86 23 41; admission €6; 🕑 4-8pm Wed-Sun Apr-Sep), housed in the onetime studio of Basque artist Ignacio Zuloaga (1870–1945). It contains some of his important works, as well as a handful by other headliners, including El Greco and Zurbarán. If you want to visit outside the April-to-September period you can do so by appointment only.

Getaria

pop 2510

Getaria is a highly attractive medieval fishing settlement. The old village tilts gently downhill to a baby-sized harbour, at the end of which is a forested island known as El Ratón (Mouse), on account of its similarity to a mouse (a very big one then!).

It might have been this giant mouse that first encouraged the town's most famous son, the sailor Juan Sebastián Elcano, to take to the ocean waves. His adventures eventually culminated in him becoming the first man to sail around the world, after the captain of his ship, Magellan, died halfway through the endeavour.

A couple of local homes offer cheap beds, and there's **Pensión Guetariano** (☎ 943 14 05 67; Calle Herrieta 3; s/d €40/55), a charming, mellow yellow building with flower-filled balconies and comfortable rooms. Several harbourfront restaurants grill up the fresh catch of the day, which washes down well with a glass of crisp, locally produced *txakoli* (white wine).

Just a couple of kilometres further east, along a coastal road that battles with cliffs, ocean waves and several cavelike tunnels, is **Zarautz**, the north coast's answer to the Costas of the Mediterranean. It's a built-up and ugly place but has a wonderful, long beach with some of the most consistent surfing conditions in the area. Campers will find **Gran Camping Zarautz** (☎ 943 83 12 38; www.grancampingzarautz.com; sites for 2 people, tent & car €19.30), built on grassy terraces at the far eastern end of the town, with memorable views.

SAN SEBASTIÁN

pop 183, 300

It's said that nothing is impossible. This is wrong. It's impossible to lay eyes on San Sebastián (Basque: Donostia) and not fall madly in love. This stunning city is everything that grimy Bilbao is not: cool, svelte and flirtatious by night, charming and well mannered by day. Best of all is the summer fun on the beach. For it's setting, form and attitude, Playa de la Concha is the equal of any city beach in Europe. Then there's Playa de Gros, with its surfers and sultry beach-goers. As the sun falls on another sweltering summer's day, you'll sit back with a drink and an artistic *pintxo* and realise that yes, you too are in love with sexy San Sebastián.

History

San Sebastián was for centuries little more than a fishing village, but by 1174 it was granted self-governing status by the kingdom of Navarra, for whom the bay was the principal outlet to the sea. Whale and cod fishing were the main occupations, along with the export of Castilian products to European ports and then to the Americas. After years of knockabout trans-European conflicts that included the razing of the city by Anglo-Portuguese forces during the Peninsular War, San Sebastián was hoisted into 19th-century stardom as a fashionable watering hole by Spanish royalty dodging the searing heat of the southern *meseta* (tableland). By the close of the century, the city had been given a superb belle époque makeover that has left a legacy of elegant art-nouveau buildings and beachfront swagger.

After WWII the city's popularity sagged, but it's now undergoing a major revival and its overall style and excitement are giving it a growing reputation as a major venue for international cultural and commercial events. The beachfront area now contains some of the most expensive properties in Spain.

Orientation

San Sebastián has three main centres of action. The lively Parte Vieja (old town) lies across the neck of Monte Urgull, the bay's eastern headland. It is neatly underlined to the south by the Alameda del Boulevard, whose broad promenade leads into the pedestrianised Parque de Alderdi Eder, which in turn merges with the famous Paseo de la Concha with its elegant balustrades and background of well-manicured buildings.

South of the Alameda del Boulevard is the sleeker commercial and shopping district, the Centro Romántica, whose handsome grid of late-19th-century buildings extends from behind La Concha beach to the banks of Río Urumea. On the east side of the river is the district of Gros, a pleasant enclave that, with its relaxed ambience and the surfing beach of Playa de Gros (Playa de la Zurriola), makes a cheerful alternative to the honeypots on the west side of the river.

Information

BOOKSHOPS

The newsstand outside the Mercado de la Bretxa stocks the previous day's issue of many foreign newspapers. Also recommended:

elkar megadenda (☎ 943 42 00 80; Calle de Fermín Calbetón 21-30) Great selection of books, maps and music, including an excellent Basque section.

EMERGENCY

Emergency (☎ 112)

INTERNET ACCESS

Cibernetworld (☎ 943 42 06 51; Calle de Aldamar 3; per hr €3; 9am-12am Jun-Sep, 10.30am-12am Oct-May) As well as internet it also has luggage storage, general travel information and a foreign-language book exchange.

Donosti-Net (☎ 943 42 94 97; Calle de Narrica 3; per 10min/1hr €0.90/3.30; 9am-11pm) The best place for internet access. Also doubles as a supersavvy travellers' information centre, offering everything from a left-luggage service to money transfers and car hire.

Therow (☎ 943 29 18 09; Calle de Zabaleta 10; morning €1.50, after 2pm €2.30; 10am-10pm)

Zarranet (Calle de San Lorenzo 6; per hr €2; 10.30am-2pm & 3.30-9pm)

LAUNDRY

Wash'n Dry (☎ 943 29 31 50; Calle de Iparragirre 6; 8am-10pm) Just across the river in the Gros district, this is an excellent self-service laundry that has the bonus of being run like a de facto tourist office. There is a left-luggage service, book exchange and useful noticeboard.

MEDICAL SERVICES

Casa de Socorro (Calle Peñaflorida Bengoechea 4) Medical care.

MONEY

There are plenty of banks with ATMs throughout the city centre.

POST

Main post office (Calle de Urdaneta)

TOURIST INFORMATION

Centro de Atracción y Turismo (CAT; ☎ 943 48 11 66; www.sansebastianturismo.com; Blvd Reina Regente 3; 8.30am-8pm Mon-Sat, 10am-7pm Sun Jun-Sep, 9am-2pm & 3.30-7pm Mon-Sat, 10am-2pm Sun Oct-May) This friendly office offers comprehensive information on the city and the Basque Country in general.

Tourist kiosk (Paseo de la Concha; 10.30am-8.30pm Jul & Aug) Operates at the city end of the Paseo de la Concha.

Sights & Activities

The Donostia–San Sebastián Card (€10) entitles you to reduced admission rates at many of the city's sights and free citywide transport. The card is valid for three days and available at the tourist office.

AQUARIUM

In the city's excellent **aquarium** (☎ 943 44 00 99; www.aquariumss.com; Paseo del Muelle 34; adult/under 3yr/child/student €10/free/6/8; 10am-9pm daily Jul & Aug, 10am-8pm daily Apr-Jun & Sep, 10am-7pm Mon-Fri, 10am-8pm Sat & Sun Oct-Mar) you'll fear for your life as huge sharks bear down on you, and be tripped out by fancy fluoro jellyfish. The

SAN SEBASTIÁN

INFORMATION
Casa de Socorro 1 F3
Centro de Atracción y Turismo 2 F3
Cibernetworld 3 F3
Donosti-Net 4 H2
elkar megadenda 5 H2
Main Post Office 6 G5
Therow 7 G3
Tourist Kiosk 8 F4
Wash'n Dry 9 H3
Zarranet 10 H1

SIGHTS & ACTIVITIES
Aquarium 11 D3
Boats to Isla de Santa Clara 12 E3
Museo de San Telmo 13 F3
Museo Naval 14 E3
Pukas 15 H2
Pukas 16 G2

SLEEPING
Albergue La Sirena Ondarreta 17 B5
Hospedaje Ibai 18 H1
Hostal Alemana 19 E5
Hotel de Londres e Inglaterra 20 F5
Hotel Maria Cristina 21 G3
Olga's Place 22 H3
Pensión Aida 23 H4
Pensión Amaiur Ostatua 24 G1
Pensión Aries 25 G1
Pensión Bellas Artes 26 G5
Pensión Donostiarra 27 G4
Pensión Edorta 28 G2
Pensión Kursaal 29 G3
Pensión La Perla 30 F4
Pensión Larrea 31 H1
Pensión Loinaz 32 H2
Pensión Santa Clara 33 H1
Pensión Urkia 34 F4
Urban House 35 H2

EATING
Astelena 36 H1
Bar Goiz-Argi 37 H1
Bar La Cepa 38 H1
Bar Nagusía 39 H2
Bidebide 40 H1
Caravanserai 41 F5
Casa Valles 42 G5
Juantxo Taberna 43 H2
Kaskazuri 44 F3
La Cuchara de San Telmo 45 H1
La Mejíllonera 46 G2
La Zurri 47 G3
Mercado de la Bretxa 48 F3
Plaza Café 49 F5
Restaurante Alberto 50 H1
Restaurante Kursaal 51 G3
Restaurante Mariñela 52 E3
San Martin Centre 53 F4
Txandorra Restaurante 54 H1

DRINKING
Bar Ondarra 55 G3
Dioni's 56 G2

ENTERTAINMENT
Altxerri Jazz Bar 57 F3
Be Bop 58 F3
Etxekalte 59 E3
M.A.D. 60 G5
Splash 61 F5

SHOPPING
Divain 62 H2
nómada 63 H1
Trip 64 G1

TRANSPORT
Avis 65 F5
Bici Rent 66 G3
Buses 16 & 28 67 H2
Buses to Hernani, Astigarraga 68 G3
Buses to Hondarribia, Irún, Airport 69 F4
Europcar 70 G5

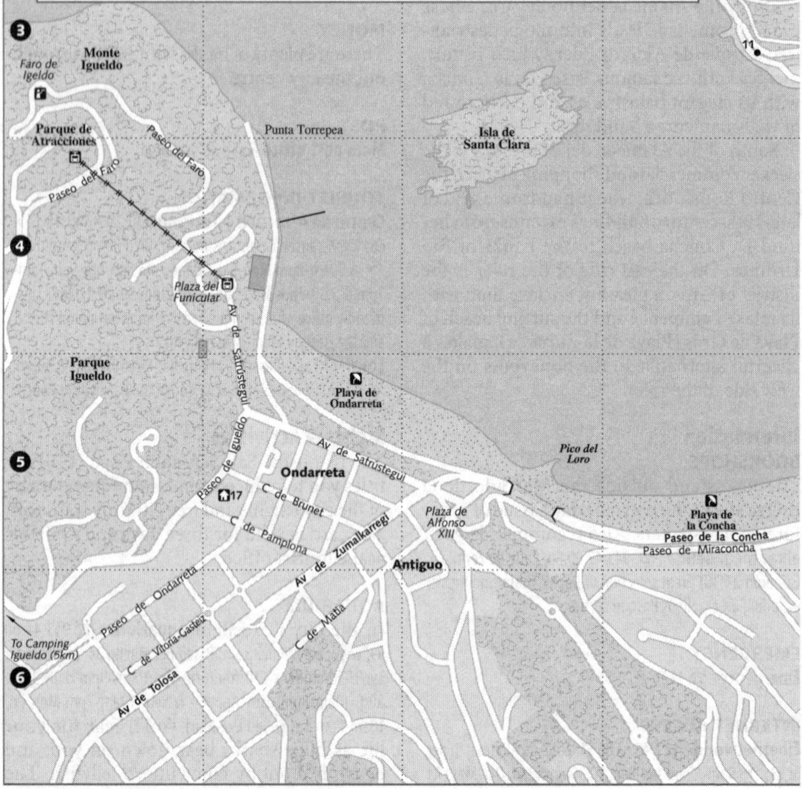

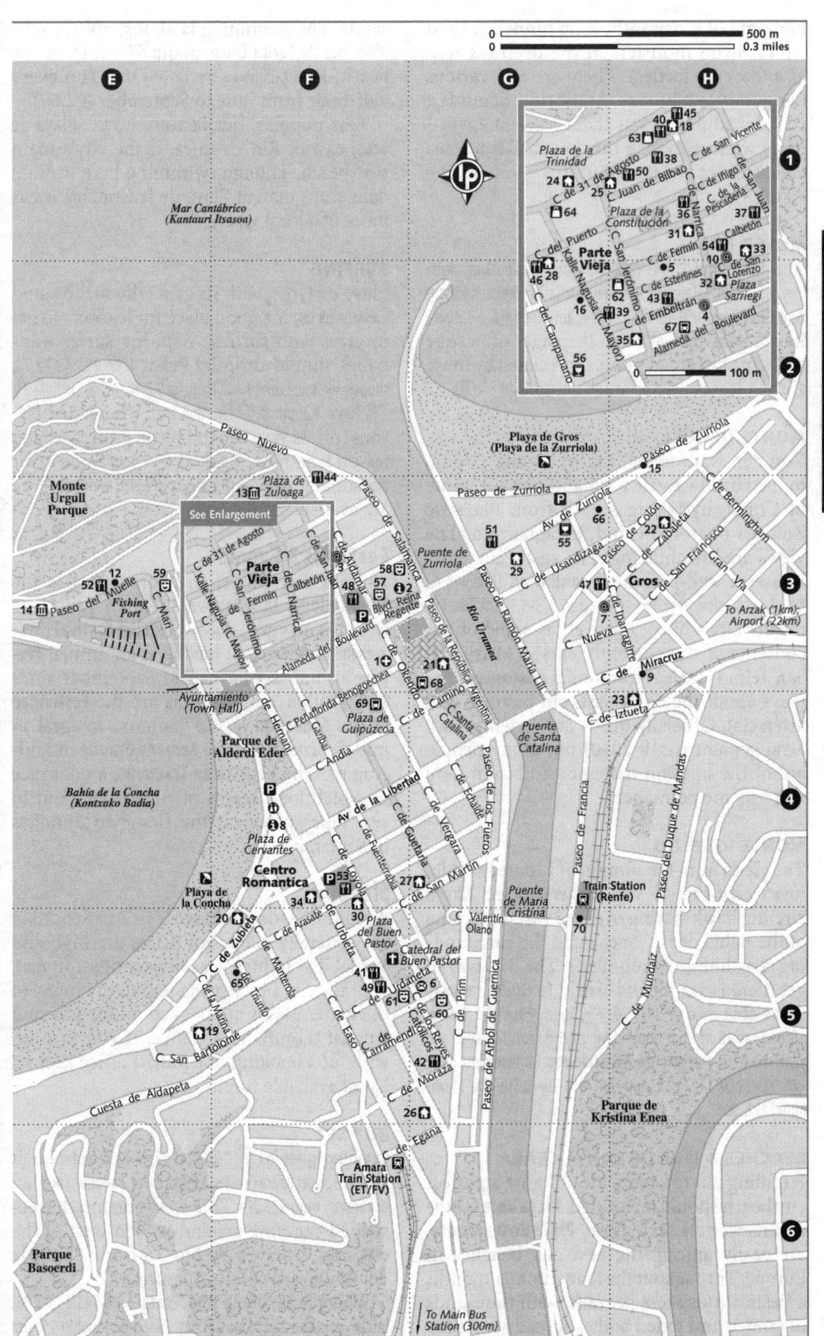

Mar Cantábrico (Kantauri Itsasoa)
Monte Urgull Parque
Paseo Nuevo
Plaza de Zuloaga
See Enlargement
Parte Vieja
Fishing Port
Paseo del Muelle
Ayuntamiento (Town Hall)
Parque de Alderdi Eder
Bahía de la Concha (Kontxako Badia)
Plaza de Cervantes
Centro Romantica
Playa de la Concha
Plaza de Guipúzcoa
Av de la Libertad
Plaza del Buen Pastor
Catedral del Buen Pastor
Puente de Zurriola
Río Urumea
Puente de Santa Catalina
Puente de María Cristina
Playa de Gros (Playa de la Zurriola)
Paseo de Zurriola
Gros
To Arzak (1km); Airport (22km)
Train Station (Renfe)
Paseo de Francia
Parque de Kristina Enea
Amara Train Station (ET/FV)
Parque Basoerdi
Cuesta de Aldapeta
To Main Bus Station (300m)
Plaza de la Trinidad
Plaza de la Constitución
Plaza Sarriegi
Alameda del Boulevard
500 m
0.3 miles
100 m

highlight of a visit is the long tunnel, around which swim monsters of the deep (as well as a few cute turtles). There are also various temporary exhibitions. At the time of our last visit the exhibition was about Ancient Egypt – quite what relevance this has to Basque sea creatures was unclear, but it was interesting all the same!

MUSEO NAVAL

This **museum** (☎ 943 43 00 51; http://um.gipuzkoakultura.net in Spanish & Basque; Paseo del Muelle 24; adult/child/student €1.20/free/0.60, free Thu; ⏲ 10am-1.30pm & 4-7.30pm Tue-Sat, 11am-2pm Sun) turns the pages of Basque seafaring history. It's best appreciated by those with at least basic Spanish-language skills.

MONTE URGULL

You can walk to the top of Monte Urgull, topped by low castle walls and a grand statue of Christ, by taking a path from Plaza de Zuloaga or from behind the aquarium. The views are breathtaking. The castle currently houses a well-presented **exhibition** (☎ 943 42 84 17; admission free; ⏲ 10am-2pm & 3-5.30pm Tue-Fri) on the city's history as well as some of the contents of the currently closed Museo de San Telmo (such as traditional costumes, displays about the city's past, old pictures and artefacts). Officially this is only a temporary arrangement (until 2010) but many people are of the opinion that the exhibition here will become permanent.

MONTE IGUELDO

The views from the summit of Monte Igueldo, just west of town, will make you feel like a circling hawk staring over the vast panorama of the Bahía de la Concha and the surrounding coastline and mountains. The best way to get there is via the old-world **funicular railway** (return adult/child €2.30/1.70; ⏲ 10am-10pm Jul & Aug, 10 or 11am-6 or 9pm depending on the month rest of the year) to the **Parque de Atracciones** (amusement park; ☎ 943 21 02 11; ⏲ 11am-6pm Mon-Tue & Thu-Fri, 11am-8pm Sat & Sun).

BEACHES & ISLA DE SANTA CLARA

Fulfilling almost every idea of how a perfect city beach should be formed, **Playa de la Concha** and its westerly extension, **Playa de Ondarreta**, are easily among the best city beaches in Europe. Throughout the long summer months a fiesta atmosphere prevails, with thousands of tanned and toned bodies spread across the sands. The swimming is almost always safe. The **Isla de Santa Clara**, about 700m from the beach, is accessible by boats that run every half-hour from June to September (€2.60).

Less popular, but just as showy, **Playa de Gros**, east of Río Urumea, is the city's main surf beach. Though swimming here is more dangerous than at Playa de la Concha, it has more of a local vibe.

SURFING

Playa de Gros, with its generally mellow and easy waves, is a good place for learners to get to grips with surfing. Aspiring surfer wannabes should drop by **Pukas** (☎ 943 42 72 28; shop@pukassurf.com; Kalle Nagusia 5 & Paseo de Zurriola 24; ⏲ 10am-1.30pm & 4-8pm Mon-Sat), where surf lessons (prices vary depending on group size and lesson length but peak at €49 for a one-hour personal lesson) and board and wetsuit hire are available.

Festivals & Events

Among San Sebastián's top draws is the **International Jazz Festival**, held in July. The world-renowned, two-week **Film Festival** (www.sansebastianfestival.com) has been an annual fixture in the second half of September since 1957. Other major fiestas are the **Festividad de San Sebastián** on 20 January, **carnaval** in mid-February and the **Semana Grande** in mid-August. The **Regatta de Traineras**, a boat race in which local teams of rowers race out to sea, takes place on the first two Sundays in September.

Sleeping

Accommodation standards in San Sebastián are generally good, but prices are high and availability in high season very tight. In fact, with the city's increasing popularity many of the better places are booked up for July and August months in advance. If you turn up without a booking, the tourist office keeps a list of available rooms.

BUDGET

Camping Igueldo (☎ 943 21 45 02; www.campingigueldo.com; Paseo del Padra Orkolaga 69; sites for 2 people, car & tent or caravan from €25.20) This well-organised, tree-shaded camping ground is 5km west of the city and is served by bus 16 from Alameda del Boulevard (€1.20, 30 minutes).

Albergue La Sirena Ondarreta (☎ 943 31 02 68; udala_youthhostel@donostia.org; Paseo de Igueldo 25; dm under/over 25yr from €17/18; P) San Sebastián's HI hostel is near Playa de Ondarreta and Monte Igueldo. It's immaculate and very secure. The midnight curfew extends to 4am on weekends, June to September.

our pick **Urban House** (☎ 943 42 81 54; www.enjoyeu.com; Alameda del Boulevard 24; dm/r €27/50;) Loud and colourful rooms set the tone for this superb party house where summer fun rules supreme. It's smack in the centre of the action and the young, multilingual staff will ensure you have a good time. They also organise a variety of city tours and surf lessons. During the high season it only offers beds in four-person dorms.

Olga's Place (☎ 943 32 67 25; Calle de Zabaleta 49; dm €30;) What you get here is the basics done exceedingly well; everything about this very popular hostel is immaculate. The common areas are probably the best news – there are a couple of terraces to kick back on and a stack of DVDs to watch (should you somehow find yourself lost for things to do in San Sebastián), and there's also a kitchen for guest use. Rooms come in a mixture of styles – some with vertigo-inspiring bunks and others with more down-to-earth soft beds.

Pensión La Perla (☎ 943 42 81 23; www.pensionlaperla.com; Calle de Loyola 10; s/d/tr €35/55/70) Brisk, old-fashioned service and clean, fairly plain rooms keep this well-located Centro Romantíca *pensión* busy. The no-nonsense woman who runs it is very helpful.

Pensión Urkia (☎ 943 42 44 36; www.pensionurkia.com; Calle de Urbieta 12; s/d €35/55;) This friendly family affair with cosy little rooms is a fashionista's delight – it's right opposite Zara! If it's full the owner will point you to somewhere with space.

Pensión Loinaz (☎ 943 42 67 14; pensionloinaz@telefonica.net; Calle de San Lorenzo 17; s/d €50/55;) Modern, small and immaculate, Pensión Loinaz is a very pleasant place, with friendly English-speaking proprietors, spotless bathrooms and bright rooms.

Pensión Aries (☎ 943 42 68 55; www.pensionaries.com; Calle San Jerónimo 22; s/d without bathroom €30/60) For single travellers especially this is a good find because it doesn't penalise you price-wise for going solo. The simple rooms are well soundproofed and one of the communal bathrooms has a massive bath to sink into the morning after the night before.

Hospedaje Ibai (☎ 943 42 62 53; www.reservasibai.e.telefonica.net; Calle de 31 de Agosto 16; s/d/tr without bathroom €40/60/80) This is one of the old town's larger establishments, so you can stop trudging around with that backpack. Rooms come in a plethora of simple styles, but all are well looked after. There are enough communal bathrooms to ensure no cross-legged queuing.

Pensión Larrea (☎ 943 42 26 94; Calle de Narrica 21; r €60;) An immaculate place, with the sort of kindly owner who'll fuss over you day and night and then break down into tears as you wave goodbye. The rooms facing the street might be a little noisy at night, so get out there and join the party!

MIDRANGE

our pick **Pensión Amaiur Ostatua** (☎ 943 42 96 54; www.pensionamaiur.com; Calle de 31 de Agosto 44; s/d without bathroom €55/60;) With only nine rooms, getting a space here is tough, but well worth the battle. The rooms are small but have had a great deal of thought put into them – there's chintzy wallpaper in the hallways, brazen primary colours in the bedrooms and everywhere a bizarre mix of African savannah and French street-scene paintings. Sounds weird? It is, but it works well. Try to get one of the street-facing rooms, where you can be completely enveloped in blushing red flowers. There's a kitchen for guest use and communal bathrooms only. In the high season you need to book months in advance.

Pensión Edorta (☎ 943 42 37 73; www.pensionedorta.com; Calle del Puerto 15; r with/without bathroom €60/80;) A fine *pensión* with rooms that are all tarted up in brash modern colours, but with a salute to the past in the stone walls and ceilings. It's very well cared for. Most rooms share common bathrooms.

Pensión Santa Clara (☎ 943 43 12 03; www.pensionsantaclara.com; Calle de San Lorenzo 6; s/d €50/65) This cheerful *pensión* has just a handful of rainbow-bright rooms and the owner is a mine of information. Santa Clara's so central that the smell of *pintxos* will virtually permeate your sleep.

Pensión Aida (☎ 943 32 78 00; www.pensionesconencanto.com; Calle de Iztueta 9; s/d €59/78;) The owners of this excellent *pensión* read the rule book on what makes a good hotel and have complied exactly. The rooms are bright and bold, full of exposed stone, and everything smells fresh and clean. The communal area, stuffed with soft sofas and mountains of information, is a big plus. For our money we'd say this one is hard to beat.

A PINTXO BY ANY OTHER NAME

Just rolling the word *pintxo* around your tongue defines the essence of this cheerful, cheeky little slice of Basque cuisine. The perfect *pintxo* should have exquisite taste, texture and appearance, and should be savoured in two elegant bites. The Basque version of a tapa, the *pintxo* transcends the commonplace by the sheer panache of its culinary campness. In San Sebastián especially, Basque chefs have refined the *pintxo* to an art form.

Many *pintxos* are bedded on small pieces of bread or on tiny half-baguettes upon which towering creations are constructed, often melded with flavoursome mayonnaise and then pinned in place by large toothpicks. Some bars specialise in seafood, with much use of marinated anchovies, prawns and strips of squid, all topped with anything from chopped crab to pâté. Others deal in mushroom delicacies, or simply offer a mix of everything.

Unfortunately such culinary brilliance no longer comes cheap, especially in San Sebastián. Expect to pay €2.50 to €3.50 for one *pintxo* and a glass of delicious *txakoli,* the young white wine of the Basque Country. Not so bad if you just take one, but is one ever enough!

Pensión Bellas Artes (☎ 943 47 49 05; www.pension-bellasartes.com; Calle de Urbieta 64; s/d from €59/79; 🖳) This has to be the friendliest hotel in town – particularly if you're English. Leire, the receptionist, lived in the UK and loves to chat about her time there. The rooms are also as welcoming as Leire! Highly recommended.

Pensión Kursaal (☎ 943 29 26 66; www.pensionesconencanto.com; Calle de Peña y Goñi 2; r €82; 🖳) This excellent place, full of light and colour, has magisterial rooms with a suitably refined edge. It's a short drunken stumble from the old town.

Pensión Donostiarra (☎ 943 42 61 67; www.pensiondonostiarra.com; Calle de San Martín 6; s/d €64/87) This *pensión,* with its imposing old-fashioned stairway and clanking lift, is a charmer. The rooms are plush sky-blue affairs and some have wonderful stained-glass doors leading onto little balconies.

Hostal Alemana (☎ 943 46 25 44; www.hostalalemana.com; Calle de San Martín 53; s/d €59/98; 🖳) A smart hotel that's opted for the white, minimalist look, which works very well and makes the rooms light and airy. Just a sandy footstep from the beach.

TOP END

Hotel de Londres e Inglaterra (☎ 943 44 07 70; www.hlondres.com; Calle de Zubieta 2; s/d from €175/225; P ❄ 🖳) Queen Isabel II set the tone for this hotel well over a century ago and things have stayed pretty regal ever since. It oozes class and some rooms have stunning views over Playa de la Concha.

Hotel Maria Cristina (☎ 943 43 76 00; www.starwoodhotels.com; Paseo de la República Argentina 4; s/d from €225/335; P ❄ 🖳) In case you're wondering what sort of hotels Lonely Planet authors normally stay in, the absolutely impeccable Maria Cristina, with its huge and luxurious rooms, is not one of them. However, don't be downhearted, because instead of hanging out with us, you'll get to mix with royalty and Hollywood stars. Yes, we know, it's still disappointing!

Eating

There are *pintxos* and then there are San Sebastián *pintxos* (see the boxed text, above). Though every city in Spain likes to boast about the quality of its own *pintxos* or tapas, all will grudgingly agree that those of San Sebastián stand on a pedestal above all others. To prove it's not just a one-trick pony, San Sebastián has some superb restaurants and is home to more Michelin stars than even Paris.

PINTXOS

The price varies for *pintxos,* depending on their size and quality. Heated *pintxos* usually cost more than the cold, ready-to-eat variety.

Bar La Cepa (Calle de 31 de Agosto 7) The best *jamón jabugo* (cured ham from southern Spain) does not disappoint here, and you eat beneath the blank eyes of a very large bull's head. The kitchens also produce decent no-frills *menús* for €13.50.

Casa Valles (Calle de los Reyes Católicos 10) Another meaty *pintxo* place beneath a forest of hung hams, this fine bar also does *raciones* (large tapas servings) and full meals (€13 to €30).

La Mejíllonera (Calle del Puerto 15) If you thought mussels came only with garlic sauce, come here and discover mussels (from €3) by the thousand in all their glorious forms.

Bar Goiz-Argi (Calle de Fermín Calbetón 4) *Gambas a la plancha* (prawns cooked on a hotplate) are the house speciality. Sounds simple, we know, but never have we tasted prawns cooked quite as perfectly as this.

our pick Astelena (Calle de Iñigo 1) The *pintxos* draped across the counter in this bar, tucked into the corner of Plaza de la Constitución, stand out as some of the best in the city. Many of them are a fusion of Basque and Asian inspirations, but the best of all are perhaps the foie-gras-based treats.

Bar Nagusía (Kalle Nagusia 4) This old-San-Sebastián-style bar has a counter that moans under the weight of its *pintxos*. You'll be moaning after a few as well – in sheer pleasure.

Txandorra Restaurante (Calle de Fermín Calbetón 7) *Pintxos* served in a gritty though memorable bar filled with one-armed bandits and other local characters.

our pick La Cuchara de San Telmo (☎ 943 42 08 40; Calle de 31 de Agosto 28) This unfussy, hidden-away bar offers miniature *nueva cocina vasca* from a supremely creative kitchen, where chefs Alex Montiel and Iñaki Gulin conjure up such delights as *carrílera de ternera al vino tinto* (calf cheeks in red wine), with meat so tender it starts to dissolve almost before it's past your lips. A percentage of profits goes to the worthy Fundación Vicente Ferrer charity.

RESTAURANTS

Bidebide (☎ 943 42 99 36; Calle de 31 de Agosto 22; mains €7.50-12) A change from all the traditional hanging-ham restaurants, this new place is light and cool, with slow sounds and a late-night-in-the-city vibe. There is a small but perfect range of *pintxos* and simple meals.

Restaurante Mariñela (☎ 943 42 73 83; Paseo del Muelle; mains €9-15) You pay for the fabulous harbourfront setting, but the location guarantees that the fish is so fresh it may well flop back off your plate and swim away.

La Zurri (☎ 943 29 38 86; Calle de Zabaleta 10; menú €9.50) Over the water in Gros, this ever-popular locals' restaurant has a menu as long as a conger eel and all of it is consistently good.

Restaurante Alberto (☎ 943 42 88 84; Calle de 31 de Agosto 19; mains from €15; 🕑 closed Tue) A charming old seafood restaurant with a fishmonger-style window display of the day's catch. It's small, dark and friendly, but much of the fish is sold by the kg so bring a friend.

Kaskazuri (☎ 943 42 08 94; Paseo de Salamanca 14; menús €20) Upmarket Basque seafood is all the rage in this flash restaurant, which is built on a raised platform allowing views of the former home of your dinner. Booking well in advance is essential.

Restaurante ni neu (☎ 943 00 31 62; Avenida de Zurriola 1; tasting menus from €48; 🕑 closed mid-Dec–mid-Jan) The Michelin-starred ni neu is another of top chef Martin Berasategui's outstations. Downstairs is what is being touted as a 'gastro pub' (open Sunday to Wednesday; *menú* from €24). A gastro pub with a Michelin-starred chef – we like that! The chic surroundings of the Kursaal Centre come for free with the meal.

Arzak (☎ 943 27 84 65; Avenida Alcalde Jose Elosegui 273; meals €100-160) With more Michelin stars than we've had hot dinners (well OK, three), acclaimed Chef Juan Mari Arzak takes some beating when it comes to *nueva cocina vasca*. Arzak is now assisted by his daughter Elena and they never cease to innovate. Reservations, well in advance, are obligatory. The restaurant is about 1.5km east of San Sebastián; it's closed for the last two weeks in June and for most of November. Prices are high, but then this man has cooked for the Queen of England.

TXOKO

Peek through the keyholes of enough Basque doors and eventually you'll come across an unusual sight: a large room full of men, and only men, seated around a table bending under the weight of food and drink. This is *Txoko* (Basque Gastronomic Society), and they are almost exclusively male preserves. The men who come here (who often wouldn't be seen dead in the kitchen at home) are normally highly accomplished amateur chefs who take turns cooking their own speciality for the critical consumption of the other members. It's often said that the best Basque food is to be found at the *Txoko*. Recently a very few women have started to enter the *Txoko*, but only as guests, and even then they are never allowed into the kitchen when the cooking is in process in case they distract the men. Women are, however, let into the kitchen afterwards – to do the washing-up!

QUICK EATS

Juantxo Taberna (Calle de Embeltrán 6; bocadillos from €2.50) You won't find starry cuisine here, but if you want rocket fuel then this much-loved bar offers rocket-sized *bocadillos* stuffed with tortillas and other great fillings.

Caravanserai (☎ 943 47 54 18; cnr Calle San Bartolomé & Plaza del Buen Pastor; bocadillos from €4, meals from €8.50) Does tasty burgers, sandwiches and pasta. It rubs shoulders in the cathedral plaza with the pleasant **Plaza Café** (☎ 943 44 57 12; Plaza del Buen Pastor 14; breakfasts €3.50-7), a popular breakfast spot with locals.

SELF-CATERING

At the heart of the Centro Romantíca, the smart **San Martin Centre** (Calle de Urbieta 9) has a very big supermarket. Mercado de la Bretxa, on the east side of the Parte Vieja, has an underground Lidl supermarket.

Drinking & Entertainment

It's said that San Sebastián's Parte Vieja contains more bars per square metre than anywhere else on Earth. Need we say more? It's hard to differentiate between most of these, as they all mutate through the day from calm morning-coffee hang-outs to *pintxo*-laden delights before finally finishing up as noisy bars full of writhing, sweaty bodies. Nights in San Sebastián start late and go on until well into the wee hours.

Dioni's (Calle Ijentea 2) More a spot for a black coffee in the early hours, this relaxed and very gay-friendly place has an '80s cocktail-bar ambience and is the perfect spot in which to watch the Eurovision Song Contest!

Bar Ondarra (Avenida de Zurriola 16) Head over to Gros for this terrific bar that's just across the road from the beach. There's a great chilled-out mixed crowd and in the rockin' downstairs bar every kind of sound gets aired.

Etxekalte (Calle Mari) A very late-night haunt near the harbour, which has hard dance and techno downstairs and funky jazz upstairs.

Altxerri Jazz Bar (Blvd Reina Regente 2; www.altxerri.com) This jazz and blues temple has regular live gigs by local and international stars. Jamming sessions take over on nonguest nights and there's an in-house art gallery.

Be Bop (Paseo de Salamanca 3) Grind your hips in this sultry bar/club tricked out in bright-red, green and cream and burnished by the evening sun. Cheesy pop anthems kick off the night and salsa turns things sexy later on.

Splash (Sánchez Toca 1) A brash, modern bar with outdoor seating and strong beats inside.

M.A.D (Calle de Larramendi 4) Musica, Arte and, well we're not sure what the D stands for, but otherwise it does what it says on the label. Alternative music blasts day and night, and photos and psychedelic art adorn the blood-red walls.

Shopping

Trip (☎ 943 42 94 43; Calle de 31 de Agosto 33) For souvenirs that balance happily between kitsch and authentic, try this place.

nómada (☎ 943 42 61 52; www.nomada.biz; Calle de 31 de Agosto 24) For something really special, check out the exquisite carpets, bags and other artefacts here, all ethically sourced by the proprietors. There are also superb artworks on fabric by Basque painters.

Divain (☎ 943 63 46 03; Calle San Jerónimo) Crammed full of outstanding ethnic-style furniture and jewellery from Argentina.

Getting There & Away

AIR

The city's **airport** (☎ 902 40 47 04) is 22km out of town, near Hondarribia. There are regular flights to Madrid and occasional charters to major European cities. Biarritz, just over the border in France, is served by Ryanair and EasyJet among various other budget airlines, and is generally much cheaper to fly into.

BUS

The main bus station, a 20-minute walk south of the Parte Vieja, is between Plaza de Pío XII and the river. Local bus 28 connects the bus station with Alameda del Boulevard (€1.10, 10 minutes).

Continental Auto (☎ 943 46 90 74) operates daily services to Madrid (from €30.54, six hours) and Vitoria (€7.51, 1½ hours).

La Roncalesa (☎ 943 46 10 64) has up to 10 buses daily to Pamplona (€6.50, one hour).

PESA (☎ 902 10 12 10) runs half-hourly services to Bilbao (€9.20, one hour) along the A8 *autopista* (tollway) from 6.30am to 10pm. It also has twice-daily buses to Hendaye (€2.75, 35 minutes), St Jean de Luz (€4.15, 50 minutes), Biarritz (€6.10, 75 minutes) and Bayonne (€7.10, 1½ hours) in France.

CAR

Several major car-hire companies are represented by agencies in San Sebastián, including

Avis (☎ 943 46 15 27; Calle del Triunfo 2) and **Europcar** (☎ 943 32 23 04; Renfe train station).

TRAIN

The main **Renfe train station** (Paseo de Francia) is just across Río Urumea, on a line linking Paris to Madrid. There are several services daily to Madrid (from €37.20, six hours) and two to Barcelona (from €38.20, eight hours).

There's only one direct train to Paris, but there are plenty more from the French border town of Hendaye (€1.55, 35 minutes), which is served by the private company **Eusko Tren/Ferrocarril Vasco** (ET/FV; ☎ 902 54 32 10; www.euskotren.es in Spanish & Basque) on a railway line nicknamed 'El Topo' (Mole). Trains depart every half-hour from Amara train station, about 1km south of the city centre, and also stop in Pasajes (€1.20, 12 minutes) and Irún (€1.35, 25 minutes). Another ET/FV railway line heads west to Bilbao (€6.50, 2½ hours, hourly) via Zarautz, Zumaia and Durango.

Getting Around

Interbus services to Hondarribia (€1.55, 45 minutes) and the airport (€1.55, 45 minutes) depart from Plaza de Guipúzcoa.

You can rent bicycles and mountain bikes at **Bici Rent** (☎ 655 724458; Avenida de Zurriola 22; per hr/day €4/17).

EAST OF SAN SEBASTIÁN

Pasajes

pop 16,100

Pasajes (Basque: Pasaia), where Río Oiartzun empties into the Atlantic, is the largest port in the province of Guipúzcoa. The main street and the area immediately around the central square are lined with pretty houses and colourful balconies, and are well worth a half-day's exploration. Nowadays it's virtually a suburb of San Sebastián and there are numerous buses.

Hondarribia

pop 16,100

Lethargic Hondarribia (Castilian: Fuenterrabía), staring across the estuary to France, has a heavy Gaelic fragrance and a charming Casco Antiguo (Old City), which makes it an excellent first or last port of call.

The **tourist office** (☎ 943 64 54 58; Calle de Javier Ugarte 6; 10am-8pm Mon-Fri, 10am-2pm & 4-8pm Sat & Sun Jul-Sep, 9.30am-1.30pm & 4-6.30pm Mon-Fri, 10am-2pm Sat & Sun Oct-Jun) is between the Casco and La Marina, the central harbour area. It has excellent information in several languages. You enter the Casco through an archway at the top of Calle San Compostela, just uphill from the tourist office, to reach the pretty Plaza de Gipuzkoa. Head straight on to Calle San Nicolás and go left to reach the bigger Plaza de Armas and the Gothic **Iglesia de Santa María de la Asunción**. The plaza is dominated by the sumptuous Parador El Emperador (below).

For La Marina, head the other way from the tourist office. This is Hondarribia's most picturesque quarter. Its main street, Calle San Pedro, is flanked by typical fishermen's houses, with facades painted bright green or blue and wooden balconies gaily decorated with flower boxes.

SLEEPING & EATING

Camping Faro de Higuer (☎ 943 64 10 08; Paseo del Faro 58; sites per person/small tent €4.10/5.50; P) You want a campsite with sea views? This camping ground, a few kilometres west of the town, is so close to the sea you'll be able to hear the fish breathing.

Pensión Zaragoza (☎ 943 64 13 41; Javier Ugarte 1; s/d €49/65) Located in a solid white building with breathtaking views to France, this is a simple guest house with a wiggly staircase and homely rooms.

Hotel San Nikolás (☎ 943 64 42 78; www.hotelsannikolas.com; Plaza de Armas 6; s/d €80/90; P) This enchanting, pretty, pink-and-blue hotel on the main square has rooms full of old furniture and bathrooms tiled in cool blue-and-white Andalucian-style tiles. The owner is a wealth of information in several languages.

Hotel Palacete (☎ 943 64 08 13; www.hotelpalacete.net; Plaza de Gipuzkoa; s/d €92/100) Set on a picturesque plaza, this is a hybrid hotel with a centuries-old winding stone staircase leading to modern, brightly painted rooms, some of which have curving French windows. There is a pleasant outside terrace.

Parador El Emperador (☎ 943 64 55 00; www.parador.es; Plaza de Armas 14; s/d €166/219) If the thought of being the king of the castle is appealing, then this is the place to do it. Behind the imposing 12th-century facade of this one-time palace is a flower-bedecked inner courtyard and a swath of luxurious rooms.

Sebastián (☎ 943 64 01 67; Calle Mayor 11; mains €20; lunch Tue-Sun) This one-time grocery store has retained much of its original interior as a nice backdrop to classy food. Great fish dishes, especially *merluza* (hake), are complemented by equally fine meat and game dishes.

There is a swath of popular and cheaper restaurants serving up decent snacks and meals along Calle de San Pedro and the quieter Calle de Santiago, one block west.

GETTING THERE & AWAY

Buses leave every 20 minutes from near the post office for Irún (€1, 10 minutes) and San Sebastián (€1.55, 45 minutes), and occasionally for Hendaye, across the border in France. In summer you can catch a boat to Hendaye (€1.50, 10 minutes).

SOUTH OF SAN SEBASTIÁN

Museo Chillida Leku

This open-air **museum** (☎ 943 33 60 06; www.museochillidaleku.com; adult/child/student €8.50/free/6.50; 10.30am-8pm Mon-Sat, 10.30am-3pm Sun Jul & Aug, 10.30am-3pm Wed-Mon Sep-Jun) is the most engaging museum in rural Basque Country. Amid the beech, oak and magnolia trees, you'll find 40 sculptures of granite and iron created by the renowned Basque sculptor Eduardo Chillida. Many more of Chillida's works appear inside the renovated 16th-century farmhouse.

To get here, take the G2 bus (€1.25) for Hernani from Calle de Okendo in San Sebastián and get off at Zabalaga. If you're driving, take the A1 south from San Sebastián. After 7km, take the turn-off southwest for Hernani (GI3132). The museum is 600m along on your left.

Walking in the Hills

Thirty kilometres south of San Sebastián and served by frequent buses, **Ordizia** is the best base from which to visit the hills to the east. A popular 1½-hour walk leads up to the top of Monte Txindoki (1341m), one of the highest peaks in the Sierra de Aralar. The walk begins from the village of **Larraitz**, about 8km to the east (follow the signs for Zaldibia). A few buses make the run from Ordizia to Larraitz (weekends only).

The Interior

The hills rising to the south between San Sebastián and Bilbao offer a number of appealing towns. There are plenty of *nekazal turismoas* (*casas rurales*; family homes in rural areas with rooms to rent).

SANTUARIO DE LOYOLA

Just outside Azpeitia (12km south of the A8 motorway along the GI631) lies the portentous **Santuario de Loyola** (10am-noon & 4-7pm), dedicated to St Ignatius, the founder of the Jesuit order. The dark, sooty basilica laden with grey marble and plenty of carved ornamentation is monstrous rather than attractive. The house where the saint was born in 1490 is preserved in one of the two wings of the sanctuary. Weekends are the most interesting times to come, as the sanctuary fills up with pilgrims.

OÑATI

pop10,500

If your Basque experiences have so far been limited to a crawl around some San Sebastián bars and Bilbao galleries then you might be wondering what this ETA fuss is all about. If so, the small town of Oñati is a good place to experience the darker side of Euskadi.

On first impressions the town, set in a bowl in the surrounding mountains, is a charmer, but walk down its streets during a grey and drizzly lunchtime when all is shut up tight and you'll quickly see another side to the place. Almost every square centimetre of wall space is covered in Nationalist graffiti calling for independence. With every passing step you'll be confronted with a poster graphically revealing Spanish state torture or calling for Basque prisoners to be returned to the Basque Country. Against such a backdrop it's hard to imagine how real, lasting peace can be achieved.

Away from politics there are further reasons for visiting Oñati, the main one being the Renaissance treasure of the **Universidad de Sancti Spiritus**. Built in the 16th century, it was the first university in the Basque Country and, until its closure in 1902, alumni here were schooled in philosophy, law and medicine. Today it's been taken over as local council offices, but you can still enter the **Mudéjar courtyard** (9am-2pm & 3-4.30pm Mon-Thu, 9am-2pm Fri) and admire its plateresque facade and courtyard. The **tourist office** (☎ 943 78 34 53; Calle San Juan 14; 10am-2pm & 3.30-7.30pm Mon-Fri, 10am-2pm & 4.30-6.30pm Sat, 10am-2pm Sun Apr-Sep, 10am-1pm & 4-7pm Mon-Fri, 11am-2pm Sat & Sun Oct-Mar), opposite the *universidad*, can organise guided tours (€6) with a few hours' notice.

Nearby is the **Iglesia de San Miguel**, a late-Gothic confection whose cloister was built over the river. The church faces onto the main square, Foruen Enparantza, dominated by the eye-catching baroque **ayuntamiento** (town hall).

Ongi Ostatua (☎ 943 71 82 85; Calle Zaharra 19; s/d €30/42) is an excellent stopover, with big, bright rooms that smell of polish. Downstairs is a bar popular with the town's young people, which has a big-screen TV for sporting events. For rural luxury you won't beat **Arregi** (☎ 943 78 36 57; www.nekatur.net/arregi; Garagaltza 21; s/d €32/42), a splendid agrotourism home 2km south of town. The nicely restored farmhouse sits in a green valley full of brown cows with big eyelashes, and has sheer views of bold mountainsides. The rooms themselves are spacious and nicely decorated, and there's a kitchen for guest use and a sitting room with a big log fire. You'll need your own transport.

There are daily buses to/from San Sebastián, Vitoria and Bilbao.

SANTUARIO DE ARANTZAZU & ARRIKRUTZ CAVES

About 10km south of Oñati is the love-it-or-loathe-it pilgrimage site of **Santuario de Arantzazu**, a fabulous conflation of piety with avant-garde art. The sanctuary was built in the 1950s on the site where, in 1468, a shepherd found a statue of the Virgin under a hawthorn bush – on which the sanctuary's design is supposed to be based (maybe 15th-century hawthorn bushes looked different from today's?). The overwhelming impression of the building is of spiky towers and hollow halls guarded by 14 strange-looking, chiselled apostles and, inside, a dramatic-looking Jesus – sculptures that caused a bit of headache for the Vatican.

The road up and the setting are worth the trip themselves, and the whole area lends itself to excellent walking – the Oñati tourist office has information on routes. If you do go for a walk around here be a little careful, because there's more to these spectacular hills than meets the eye – one of the numerous caves that litter the slopes is supposedly the home of Mari, the pre-Christian goddess of the Basques, who is said to control the weather. If you get lost while out walking just shout out her name three times and she'll appear in the skies above you to guide you in the right direction. If, however, you stumble upon her cave home, don't enter as she'll get very angry. Trust us, you really don't want to see what an angry Basque goddess looks like!

While we're on the subject of caves, a slightly safer cavern system can be found a couple of kilometres back down the road towards Oñati. The **Arrikrutz caves** (☎ 943 08 20 00; adult/under 3yr/child & senior €8/free/6; 🕑 10am-2pm & 3-7pm Tue-Sun Jun-Sep, 10am-2pm & 3-6pm Tue-Sun March-May & Oct, 10am-2pm & 3-5pm Tue-Sun Nov-Feb) don't contain any goddesses, but they do have numerous slow-growing stalagmites and stalactites.

VITORIA

pop 229,500 / elev 512m

Vitoria (Basque: Gasteiz) has a habit of falling off the radar, yet it's actually the capital of not just the southern Basque province of Álava (Basque: Araba) but also the entire Basque Country. Maybe it was given this honour precisely because it is so forgotten, but if that's the case then prepare for some big changes. With an art gallery whose contents frequently supersede those of the more famous Bilbao galleries, a delightful old quarter, dozens of great *pintxo* bars and restaurants, a large student contingent and a friendly local population, you have the makings of a perfect city – it surely won't be long until the world catches on!

History

Vitoria's name may well derive from the Basque word *beturia*, meaning height, a reference to the hill on which the old town stands. It was so named by the Visigoths. Sancho VI of Navarra settled things by founding a 'New Vitoria' in the 12th century. Thereafter, Vitoria bounced to and fro between the Castilian and Navarran crowns. The economic advances of the late 19th century triggered Vitoria's expansion, which carried over into the 20th century. The city's historic and well-preserved nature made it a good choice for capital of the Basque autonomous government in 1981. The University of the Basque Country also has its base here.

Orientation

From the central adjoining squares of Plaza de la Virgen Blanca and the late-18th-century Plaza de España (Plaza Nueva to the Basques), the Casco Viejo (the medieval town) rises in a series of concentric ellipses, a spider's web of narrow streets leading to the 14th-century Catedral de Santa María. South of the plazas is Vitoria's 19th-century extension, which counts some wonderful parks and leafy promenades as complements to its grid of pleasant streets. The central Calle de Eduardo Dato, main artery of the evening *paseo* (stroll), leads arrow-straight to the Renfe train station. The bus station is right on the eastern edge of the Casco.

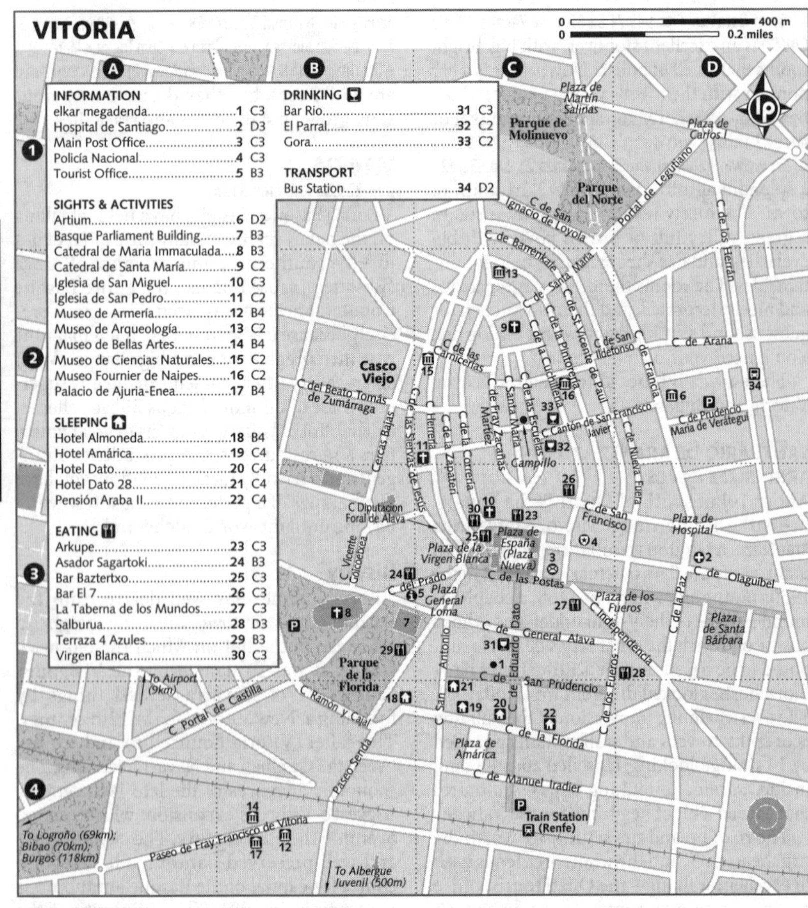

Information

When it's time to top up your wallet, there are plenty of banks with ATMs located in the newer part of town.

elkar megadenda (☎ 945 14 45 01; Calle de San Prudencio 7) For books, maps and music.

Emergency (☎ 112)

Hospital de Santiago (☎ 945 25 36 00; cnr Calles de la Paz & de Olaguíbel)

Main post office (Calle de las Postas)

Policía Nacional (☎ 091) Near the Hospital de Santiago.

Tourist office (☎ 945 16 15 98; www.vitoria-gasteiz.org/turismo; Plaza General Loma 1; 🕒 10am-7pm daily Jul-Sep, 10am-7pm Mon-Sat, 11am-2pm Sun Oct-Jun) Opposite the Basque Parliament Building.

Sights

GOVERNMENT BUILDINGS

As befits the Basque capital, Vitoria boasts some important buildings: essential administrative centres, but of great symbolic significance. They include the **Basque Parliament Building** (Calle de General Alava), built in 1853 in the Parque de la Florida, and the 1920 **Palacio de Ajuria-Enea** (Paseo de Fray Francisco de Vitoria), residence of the *lehendakari* (president of the regional government).

ART GALLERIES

Unlike some famous Basque art galleries, Vitoria's palace of modern art, the **Artium** (☎ 945 20 90 20; www.artium.org; Calle de Francia 24; adult/student €4.50/2.20, admission free Wed; 🕒 11am-8pm

Tue-Sun), doesn't need to dress to impress and knows that it's what's on the inside that really counts. As such its ever-changing collections have a robust, frontline ethos that frequently leaves the Guggenheim for dead. The large subterranean galleries are filled with engrossing works by Basque, Spanish and international artists, displaying some fairly intense modernist work that the more mainstream Guggenheim could never get away with. For example, at the time of research the collection included a photographic exhibition of 'erotic art', which it was indeed! Guided tours, in Spanish, run several times a day. The gallery is wheelchair accessible.

Housed in a fine old building, the absorbing **Museo de Bellas Artes** (☎ 945 18 19 18; Paseo de Fray Francisco de Vitoria; admission free; 🕑 10am-2pm & 4-6.30pm Tue-Fri, 10am-2pm & 5-8pm Sat, 11am-2pm Sun & holidays) has Basque paintings and sculpture from the 18th and 19th centuries. The works of local son Fernando de Amaríca are given good space and reflect an engaging romanticism that manages to mix drama with great warmth of colour and composition.

CHURCHES

At the base of Vitoria's medieval Casco Viejo is the delightful **Plaza de la Virgen Blanca**. It's lorded over by the 14th-century **Iglesia de San Miguel**, whose statue of the Virgen Blanca lends its name to the plaza below and is the city's patron saint.

The 14th-century **Iglesia de San Pedro** (Calle Herrería) is the city's oldest church and has a fabulous Gothic frontispiece on its eastern facade.

At the summit of the old town and dominating its skyline is the medieval **Catedral de Santa María** (☎ 945 25 51 35; www.catedralvitoria.com; 🕑 11am-2pm & 5-8pm). The cathedral is undergoing a lengthy, but much-praised, restoration project that's unlikely to be completed for some years yet. There are excellent guided tours (€3) that give an insight into the excitement of restoration and discovery as well as providing some contact with the cathedral's interior. You must book in advance either by telephone or via the website.

The **Catedral de María Immaculada** (☎ 945 15 06 31; Cadena y Eleta s/n; 🕑 10am-2pm & 4-6.30pm Tue-Fri, 10am-2pm Sat, 11am-2pm Sun) might look old but in fact only dates from the early 1970s. There are some impressive, fairly adventurous stained-glass windows and a neck-stretching high nave. More interesting, though, is the attached museum of sacred art, which contains some early Christian stone carvings and Basque crosses, detailed paintings of Biblical scenes and a glittering ensemble of crucifixes and ceremonial crosses – all of which come from the Basque Country.

MUSEUMS

Vitoria has a sprinkling of interesting **museums** (admission free; 🕑 10am-2pm & 4-6.30pm Tue-Fri, 10am-2pm Sat, 11am-2pm Sun), notably the brick-and-timber **Museo de Arqueología** (☎ 945 18 19 22; Calle de la Correría 116), which is housed in a former armoury. The **Museo de Ciencias Naturales** (Natural Sciences Museum; ☎ 945 18 19 24; Calle de las Siervas de Jesús 24), in the Torre de Doña Oxtanda, gives you an overview of Navarra's nonhuman neighbours, while the **Museo de Armería** (☎ 945 18 19 25; Paseo de Fray Francisco de Vitoria) is one for jousting fans. The eccentric **Museo Fournier de Naipes** (Card Museum; ☎ 945 18 19 20; Calle de la Cuchillería 54) is in the 16th-century Palacio de Bendaña, with an impressive collection of historic presses and playing cards, including some of the oldest European decks. At the time of writing the last two museums were closed for renovations, but both should have reopened by the time you read this.

Festivals & Events

The calm sophistication of Vitoria takes a back seat during the boisterous **Fiestas de la Virgen Blanca**, held from 4 to 9 August, with a range of fireworks, bullfights, concerts and street dancing. All of this is preceded by the symbolic descent of Celedón, a Basque effigy that flies down on strings from the Iglesia de San Miguel into the plaza below.

A **jazz festival** is held in July. A fairly new gig is the **Azkena Rock Festival** (www.azkenarockfestival.com) held at the end of August to early September. It features a rather lively mix of Basque and Spanish bands, plus headliners who have included Iggy Pop and Deep Purple in the past.

Sleeping

Albergue Juvenil (☎ 945 14 81 00; ifj@alava.net; cnr Calles de Escultor Isaac Diéz & Salvatierrabide; dm under/over 18 €13.50/18) About 600m southwest of the train station, this well-kept, well-secured, red-brick building is the cheapest deal in town, and with 100 beds on offer it should never be full.

Pensión Araba II (☎ 945 23 25 88; Calle de la Florida 25; s/d €30/42) A charming *pensión* that's run as a real family affair and is full of frilly decorations. If it's full then you'll be directed to decent, nearby alternatives.

Hotel Dato/Hotel Dato 28 (☎ 945 14 72 30; www.hoteldato.com; Calle de Eduardo Dato 28; s/d €37/52; 💻) Two gorgeous twin-sister hotels on parallel streets. It's hard to know if the extravagant art-deco style, full of seminaked nymphs, Roman pots and frilly fittings is tacky or classy. Either way it works well here, and the whole ensemble produces an exceptionally good-value and memorable hotel. Reception for both hotels is at Hotel Dato.

Hotel Amárica (☎ 945 13 05 06; fax 945 13 05 48; Calle de la Florida 11; s/d €37/55) Functional, user-friendly rooms and the strategically positioned Buddhas help to keep your karma in check. The receptionist is often hanging out over the road so you might have to wait a minute or two for him to turn up.

Hotel Almoneda (☎ 945 15 40 84; www.hotelalmoneda.com; Calle de la Florida 7; s incl breakfast €52-63, d incl breakfast €75-100; 💻) This confident business-level hotel is a smidgen overpriced but otherwise decent enough. The rooms have creaky, polished wooden floors and beds as soft as a cloud, but the bathrooms are cramped in the extreme. A percentage of profits goes to Amnesty International.

Eating

Head for the west sides of Plaza de España and the adjacent Plaza de la Virgen Blanca for breakfast and morning coffee in the bright light of day. Switch to the east sides for afternoon sun and stronger drinks.

Terraza 4 Azules (☎ 945 14 88 48; Parque de la Florida; coffee & coissant €3; 🕑 8.30am-11pm; 💻) What nicer place can there be to sit and drink and dine al fresco than under the calming trees of the pretty Parque de la Florida? It's a great breakfast spot: if it's a typically cold Vitoria morning move indoors for coffee, croissants and chilled beats.

Bar Baztertxo (☎ 628 120237; Plaza de España 14; dishes €10-15) A very welcoming restaurant backing right onto the main square, with outdoor tables for fine-weather drinking and dining, and long wooden tables and benches for dark-day indoor dining. The duck in honey sauce is very tasty.

La Taberna de los Mundos (☎ 945 13 93 42; www.delosmundos.com; Calle Independencía 14; menú €11) A warm and inviting place in which to indulge in some gut-busting lunch *menus*, including vegetarian options. As the name implies, the decor is inspired by the wider world and includes frequent photo exhibitions of faraway, exotic locales. Despite such worldly-wise backdrops the food stays much closer to home.

Virgen Blanca (☎ 945 28 61 99; Plaza de la Virgen Blanca; menú €14) An eternally popular restaurant on the main square, with a perfectly formed Basque lunch *menú* that is particularly recommended. For once there is plenty of space and advance reservations are rarely needed.

Arkupe (☎ 945 23 00 80; Calle Mateo Benigno de Moraza 13; mains from €17) For superb Basque cooking check out this moderately upmarket establishment. The rough wood exterior belies a formal and slightly chic atmosphere. There is an extensive wine list, with all the offerings racked up against the back wall.

Asador Sagartoki (☎ 945 28 86 76; Calle del Prado 18; mains €18) A marvellous *sidrería* (cider house) that has one of the most creative menus around and an atmosphere to go with it. The dining room stretches way beyond the busy front bar and the *pintxos* are sublime award-winners. Marvel as the bar staff, arms akimbo, orchestrate jets of cider from the big barrels to the glasses in their outstretched hands; then try it yourself in the restaurant. Like most *sidrerías*, this is a place to come with friends.

You can get *pintxos* and *menús del día* at many of the bars in the Casco Viejo. A good place is **Bar El 7** (☎ 945 27 22 98; Calle de la Cuchillería 3; menú €11), which is well liked by the young and not just on account of its supervalue lunch *menús*. At night it morphs into a drink-heavy bar. The top spot is **Salburua** (☎ 945 28 64 60; Calle de los Fueros 19), which has picked up several awards for its *pintxos* and has an old-Basque-bar feel with *jamones* (hams) swinging gently from hooks behind the bar.

Drinking

There's a strong politico-arty vibe in the Casco Viejo, where a lively student cadre keeps things swerving with creative street posters and action.

El Parral (☎ 945 27 68 33; Cantón de San Francisco Javier) This is the 'grape arbor', though all the grapes are in the flowing wine that fuels lively discussion and late-night rock, reggae and Spanish pop. It sometimes has live music.

Gora (☎ 945 12 14 52; Cantón de San Francisco Javier) Mutates from busy and noisy rock-filled nights to a more refined daytime restaurant/

bar with alternative leanings and €10 *menú del día*. The alien green planets floating about lend a trippy air to proceedings.

Bar Río (Calle de Eduardo Dato 20) A more sophisticated and sedate nightspot and a good place to kick things off or slow them down again. The bar is a bejewelled, tiled affair. Attracts all age ranges.

Getting There & Away

Vitoria's **airport** (☎ 945 16 35 00) is at Foronda, about 9km northwest of the city, with connections to Madrid and Barcelona. There are car-hire offices and an ATM at the airport. Buses (€3) to town meet flights; taxis cost day/night €15/20.

There are car parks by the train station, by the Artium and just east of the cathedral.

Vitoria's **bus station** (☎ 945 25 84 00; Calle de los Herrán) has regular services to Madrid (€23.79, four hours, up to 13 daily), Barcelona (€37.65, seven hours), Pamplona (€6.85, 1¾ hours) and Bilbao (€5.45, 55 minutes).

Trains go to Madrid (from €30.55, 4¾ hours, eight daily), San Sebastián (€8.85, 1¾ hours, up to 10 daily) and Pamplona (€4.40, one hour, four daily).

NAVARRA

Several Spains intersect in Navarra (Basque: Nafarroa). The soft greens and bracing climate of the Navarran Pyrenees lie like a cool compress across the sunstruck brow of the south, which is all stark plains, cereal crops and vineyards, sliced by high sierras with cockscombs of raw limestone. Navarra is also pilgrim territory: for centuries the faithful have used the pass at Roncesvalles to cross from France on their way to Santiago de Compostela (see Camino de Santiago, p118).

Navarra was historically the heartland of the Basques, but dynastic struggles and trimming due to reactionary politics, including Francoism, has left it as a semi-autonomous province, with the north being Basque by nature while the south leans towards Castilian Spain. The centre hangs between and Navarra seems intrinsically uncommitted to the vision of a Basque future.

The Navarran capital, Pamplona, tends to grab the headlines with its world-famous running of the bulls, but the region's real charm is in its peppering of small towns and villages, each one with a unique history and an iconography that covers every kind of architecture.

PAMPLONA

pop 195,800 / elev 456m

Senses are heightened in Pamplona (Basque: Iruña), capital of the fiercely independent Kingdom of Navarra, alert constantly to the fearful sound of thundering bulls clattering like tanks down cobbled streets and causing mayhem and bloodshed all the way. Of course, visit outside the eight days that fall between 6 and 14 July, when the legendary festival of Sanfermines (see the boxed text, p502) takes over the minds and souls of a million people, and the closest you'll come to a bloodthirsty bull is a photograph. For those who do dare venture here outside fiesta time, despite the overriding feeling that you're the one who missed the party, you'll find Pamplona a fascinating place. And for those of you who come during fiesta week? Welcome to one of the biggest and most famous festivals in the world – if you hadn't drunk so much it would be a week you'd remember forever!

History

The Romans called the city Pompaelo, after its founder Pompey the Great. They were succeeded by the Visigoths and then, briefly, by the Muslims. Navarra has been a melting pot of dynastic, political and cultural aspirations and tensions ever since Charlemagne rampaged across the Pyrenees from France in 778. The city achieved great things under Sancho III in the 11th century and its position on the Camino de Santiago ensured its prosperity. Twentieth-century affluence saw an expansion of the city.

Orientation

The compact old-city centre is marked off to the north and east by Río Arga and what remains of the old defensive wall. To the west it's bordered by parks and the Ciudadela, the former citadel. The main square is the enormous Plaza del Castillo, with its central bandstand. Its south side extends southwest to the wide Paseo de Sarasate, roughly marking the division between the old town and the 19th-century Ensanche, the 'extension'. The train station is a kilometre northwest of the city centre. The main bus station is a few minutes' walk south of Paseo de Sarasate.

Information

There are several banks with exchange services and ATMs along Paseo de Sarasate and numerous ATMs throughout the newer part of town.

elkar megadenda (☎ 948 22 41 67; Calle Comedias 14) Excellent branch of this chain bookshop, with music and maps too.

Emergency (☎ 112)

Hospital de Navarra (☎ 848 42 21 00; Calle de Irunlarrea 3)

Kuria.Net (☎ 948 22 30 77; Calle Curia 15; per hr €2.50; ⏰ 10am-10pm Mon-Fri, 10am-2pm & 3pm-10pm Sat) A more stylish internet cafe would be hard to find.

Main post office (☎ 948 20 68 40; cnr Paseo de Sarasate & Calle de Vínculo)

Policía Nacional (☎ 091; Calle del General Chinchilla 3)

Telephone Locutorio (Plaza de Castillo; ⏰ 9am-11pm)

Tourist office (☎ 848 42 04 20; www.navarra.es; Calle de Esclava 1; ⏰ 10am-2pm & 4-7pm Mon-Sat, 10am-2pm Sun) This extremely well-organised office has English-speaking staff and plenty of information about the city and Navarra.

Sights

CATHEDRAL

Pamplona's main **cathedral** (☎ 948 22 29 90; Calle Dormitalería; guided tours €4.40; ⏰ 10am-7pm Mon-Fri, 10am-2.30pm Sat mid-Jul–mid-Sep, 10am-2pm & 4-7pm Mon-Fri, 10am-2pm Sat mid-Sep–mid-Jul) stands on a rise just inside the city ramparts amid a dark thicket of narrow streets. The cathedral is a late-medieval Gothic gem spoiled only by its rather dull neoclassical facade, an 18th-century appendage. The vast interior reveals some fine artefacts, including a silver-plated Virgin and the splendid 15th-century tomb of Carlos III of Navarra and his wife Doña Leonor. The real joy is the Gothic cloister, where there is marvellous delicacy in the stonework. The **Museo Diocesano** occupies the former refectory and kitchen, and houses an assortment of religious art, including some fine Gothic woodcarvings.

MUSEO DE NAVARRA

Housed in a former medieval hospital, this **museum** (☎ 848 42 64 92; www.cfnavarra.es; Calle Santo Domingo 47; adult/student €2/1, admission free Sat afternoon & Sun; ⏰ 9.30am-2pm & 5-7pm Tue-Sat, 11am-2pm Sun) has an eclectic collection of archaeological finds (including a Roman mosaic), as well as a selection of art including Goya's *Marqués de San Adrián*.

CIUDADELA & PARKS

The walls and bulwarks of the grand fortified citadel, the star-shaped **Ciudadela** (Avenida del Ejército; admission free; ⏰ 7.30am-9.30pm Mon-Sat, 9am-9.30pm Sun), lurk amid the verdant grass and trees in what is now a charming park, the portal to three more parks that unfold to the north and lend the city a beautiful green escape.

MUSEO OTEIZA

Around 9km northeast of Pamplona in the town of Alzuza, this impressive **museum** (☎ 948 33 20 74; www.museooteiza.org; Calle de la Cuesta 7; adult/child/student €4/free/2, admission free Fri; ⏰ 11am-7pm Tue-Sun Jun-Sep, 10am-3pm Tue-Fri, 11am-7pm Sat & Sun Oct-May) contains almost 3000 pieces by the renowned Navarran sculptor Jorge Oteiza. As well as his workshop, this beautifully designed gallery incorporates the artist's former home in a lovely rural setting.

Rio Irati (☎ 948 22 14 70) has at least one bus a day to Alzuza from Pamplona's bus station. If you're driving, Alzuza is signposted north off the NA150, just east of Huarte.

Sleeping

During Los Sanfermines hotels raise their rates mercilessly – all quadruple their normal rack rates and many increase them five-fold – and it can be near impossible to get a room without reserving between six months and a year in advance. A patch of rubbish-strewn pavement may suddenly look like a very inviting bed! If that doesn't appeal, then the tourist office maintains a list of private houses with rooms to rent during this period, and touts hang around the bus and train stations offering rooms. With numerous 'San Fermín' buses travelling up from all nearby Spanish and French cities, it's actually not a bad idea to stay in a different town altogether and catch a ride on these party buses. Ask local tourist offices for details of departure times and costs.

At any other time of year Pamplona is packed with good-value accommodation and it's rarely worth booking ahead.

BUDGET

Ezcaba (☎ 948 33 03 15; www.campingezcaba.com; sites per person/tent/car €4.90/5.35/4.90) On the banks of Río Ulzama, about 7km north on the N121, this is the nearest camping ground. Bus 4 runs four times daily (more during Sanfermines) from Plaza de las Merindades by the BBVA bank. Prices double during Sanfermines.

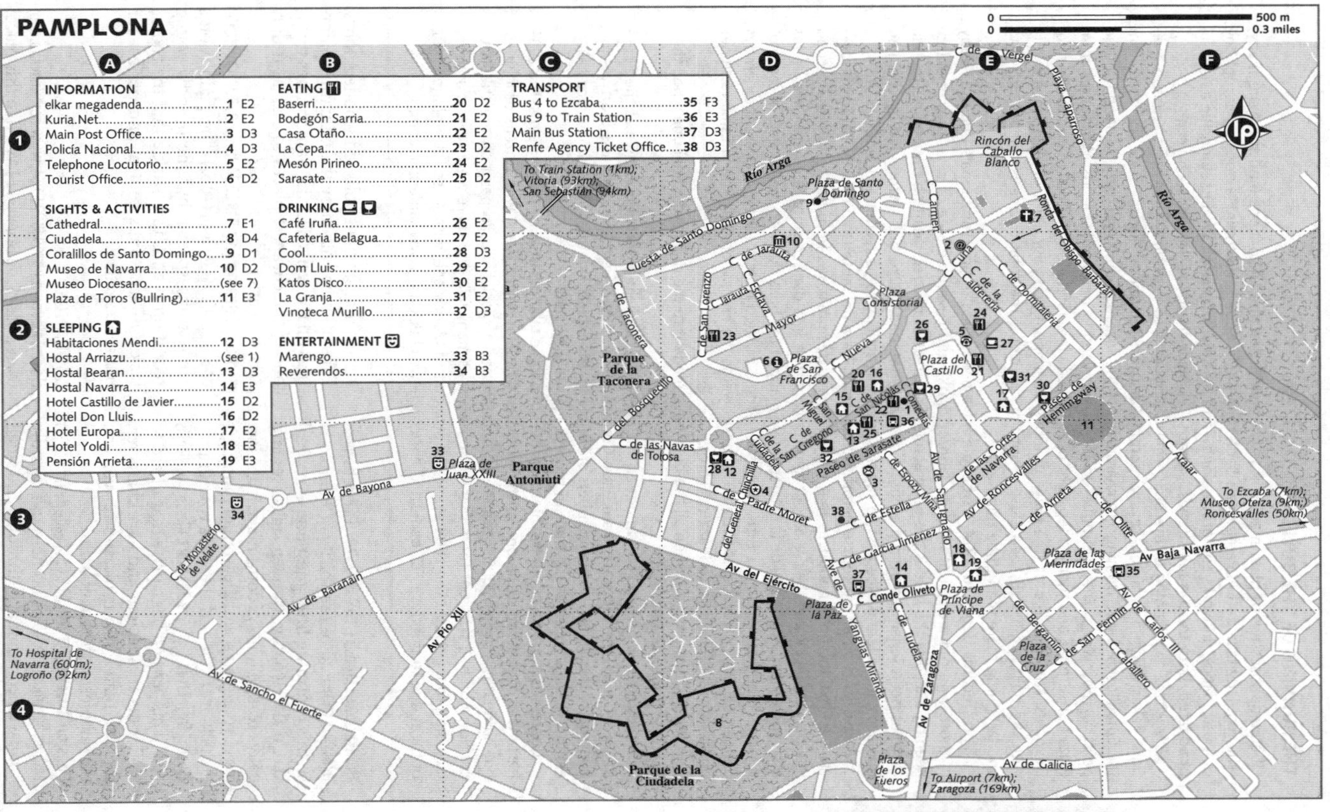
PAMPLONA
INFORMATION
elkar megadenda 1 E2
Kuria.Net 2 E2
Main Post Office 3 D3
Policía Nacional 4 D3
Telephone Locutorio 5 E2
Tourist Office 6 D2
SIGHTS & ACTIVITIES
Cathedral 7 E1
Ciudadela 8 D4
Coralillos de Santo Domingo 9 D1
Museo de Navarra 10 D2
Museo Diocesano (see 7)
Plaza de Toros (Bullring) 11 E3
SLEEPING
Habitaciones Mendi 12 D3
Hostal Arriazu (see 1)
Hostal Bearan 13 D3
Hostal Navarra 14 E3
Hotel Castillo de Javier 15 D2
Hotel Don Lluis 16 D2
Hotel Europa 17 E2
Hotel Yoldi 18 E3
Pensión Arrieta 19 E3
EATING
Baserri 20 D2
Bodegón Sarria 21 E2
Casa Otaño 22 E2
La Cepa 23 D2
Mesón Pirineo 24 E2
Sarasate 25 D2
DRINKING
Café Iruña 26 E2
Cafeteria Belagua 27 E2
Cool 28 D3
Dom Lluis 29 E2
Katos Disco 30 E2
La Granja 31 E2
Vinoteca Murillo 32 D3
ENTERTAINMENT
Marengo 33 B3
Reverendos 34 B3
TRANSPORT
Bus 4 to Ezcaba 35 F3
Bus 9 to Train Station 36 E3
Main Bus Station 37 D3
Renfe Agency Ticket Office 38 D3
500 m
0.3 miles
Río Arga
Parque de la Taconera
Parque Antoniuti
Parque de la Ciudadela
Plaza del Castillo
Plaza de Santo Domingo
Plaza Consistorial
Plaza de San Francisco
Plaza de Juan XXIII
Plaza de los Fueros
Plaza de la Paz
Plaza de Príncipe de Viana
Plaza de las Merindades
Plaza de la Cruz
Rincón del Caballo Blanco
Playa Caparroso
Cuesta de Santo Domingo
Ronda del Obispo Barbazán
Paseo de Hemingway
Paseo de Sarasate
Av del Ejército
Av Pío XII
Av de Bayona
Av de Zaragoza
Av de San Ignacio
Av Baja Navarra
Av de Carlos III
Av de Galicia
Av de Sancho el Fuerte
Av de Barañain
Av de Roncesvalles
To Train Station (1km); Vitoria (93km); San Sebastián (94km)
To Ezcaba (7km); Museo Oteiza (9km); Roncesvalles (50km)
To Airport (7km); Zaragoza (169km)
To Hospital de Navarra (600m); Logroño (92km)

THE RUNNING OF THE BULLS

Liberated, obsessive or plain mad is how you might describe aficionados (and there are many) who regularly take part in Pamplona's Sanfermines (Fiesta de San Fermín), a nonstop cacophony of music, dance, fireworks and processions – and the small matter of running alongside a handful of agitated, horn-tossing *toros* (bulls) – that takes place from 6 to 14 July each year.

El encierro, the running of the bulls from their corrals to the bullring for the afternoon bullfight, takes place in Pamplona every morning during Sanfermines. Six bulls are let loose from the Coralillos de Santo Domingo to charge across the square of the same name (a good vantage point for observers). They continue up the street, veering onto Calle de los Mercaderes from Plaza Consistorial, and then sweep right onto Calle de la Estafeta for the final charge to the ring. Devotees, known as *mozos* (the brave or foolish, depending on your point of view), race madly with the bulls, aiming to keep close – but not too close. The total course is some 825m long and lasts little more than three minutes.

Since records began in 1924, 13 people have been killed during Pamplona's bull run. Many of those who run are full of bravado (and/or drink), and have little idea of what they're doing. Keeping ahead of the herd is the general rule. The greatest danger is getting trapped near a bull that has been separated from the herd – a lone, frightened, 500kg bull surrounded by charging humans can be lethal. Needless to say this is not an activity to be recommended.

Participants enter the course before 7.30am from Plaza de Santo Domingo. At 8am two rockets are fired: the first announces that the bulls have been released from the corrals; the second lets participants know they're all out and running. The first danger point is where Calle de los Mercaderes leads into Calle de la Estafeta. Here many of the bulls skid into the barriers because of their headlong speed on the turn. They can become isolated from the herd and are then always dangerous. A very treacherous stretch comes towards the end, where Calle de la Estafeta slopes down into the final turn to Plaza de Toros.

A third rocket goes off when all the bulls have made it to the ring, and a final one when they have been rounded up in the stalls.

Sanfermines winds up at midnight on 14 July with a candlelit procession, known as the Pobre de Mí (Poor Me), which starts from Plaza Consistorial. Another event, often no less pretty, is the Running of the Nudes, where members of People for the Ethical Treatment of Animals race naked along the same route as the bulls in protest against the event.

Concern has grown about the high numbers of people taking part in recent *encierros.* The 2004 fiesta was considered to be one of the most dangerous in recent years, with dozens of injuries, but no deaths. For the 2005 fiesta the authorities used a special antislip paint on the streets to cut down on bull skid, but there seemed to be just as many falls and there were several injuries, including four gorings. The 2008 event was also quite a bloody one, with 45 serious injuries (four of them due to gorings). For dedicated *encierro* news check out www.sanfermin.com.

Habitaciones Mendi (☎ 948 22 52 97; Calle de las Navas de Tolosa 9; r €40) Full of the spirits of Pamplona past, this charming little guest house is a real find. Creaky, wobbly, wooden staircases and equally creaky, chintzy rooms make it just like being at your gran's, and the woman running it will cluck over you as if she were your gran.

Hostal Don Lluis (☎ 679 385157; Calle de San Nicolás 24; r €40) This *pensión* has a price that's hard to beat. Rooms are spacious and have character, and rather than a boring old shower you can make bubbles in the small baths.

Pensión Arrieta (☎ 948 22 84 59; Calle de Arrieta 27; s/d without bathroom €35/45) A homely and friendly *pensión* with communal bathrooms and small rooms that smell of polished wooden floors. Fans of India will enjoy the miniature paintings on the walls. During Sanfermines this is one of the cheapest places to stay as it only raises its prices three times.

Hostal Bearan (☎ 948 22 34 28; fax 948 22 43 02; Calle de San Nicolás 25; s/d from €40/52) The plain rooms are nothing special, but the friendly young receptionist adds the sparkle that the rooms lack. Otherwise it's central and perfect for budget travellers.

MIDRANGE

Hostal Navarra (☎ 948 22 51 64; www.hostalnavarra.com; Calle de Tudela 9; s/d €45/60; 💻) We like this place!

Why? Firstly because it's immaculately clean; secondly because the manager makes sure that everyone is kept happy no matter what their requirements; and thirdly because not only are the rooms colourful and comfortable, but the communal areas have open fireplaces and mountains of literature to dive into.

Hotel Castillo de Javier (☎ 948 20 30 40; www.hotelcastillodejavier.com; Calle de San Nicolás 50; s/d €45/62;) On a street of cheap digs this slick hotel shows a touch of class. The reception area is modern through and through, and the rooms typical of a business-class hotel but, and it's a big but, they've stuffed too many rooms into too small a space and the result is a tin of sardines.

Hostal Arriazu (☎ 948 21 02 02; www.hostalarriazu.com; Calle Comedias 14; s/d incl breakfast €55/65;) Falling somewhere between a budget *pensión* and a midrange hotel, there is superb value to be found in this former theatre. The rooms are plain but the bathrooms as good as you'll find. The communal lounge area has a big-screen TV and, if running with bulls just isn't for you, then you can spend a quiet evening reading through the numerous scholarly looking books.

Hotel Yoldi (☎ 948 22 48 00; www.hotelyoldi.com in Spanish; Avenida de San Ignacio 11; s/d €60/88 + 7% tax;) A bustling business hotel with CD players, flat-screen TVs and other such complicated stuff in each room, and showers that look like Niagara Falls when in full flow. The downstairs cafe is one of those classic city meeting points.

Hotel Europa (☎ 948 22 18 00; www.hreuropa.com; Calle de Espoz y Mina 11; s/d €87/95;) Wow – that's all we can say! What a bizarre concoction of fake marble, equally fake gold-framed portraits of historical figures and photographs of the famous and not-so famous visitors to the hotel. Despite all this, the comfortable rooms are good value.

Eating

Bodegón Sarria (☎ 948 22 77 13; Calle de la Estafeta 50; mains from €9) It could be the cured hams hanging from the ceiling and the used napkins thrown haphazardly on the floor, or it could be the pictures of Hemingway and bull bravado. Whatever it is, it certainly makes for a macho air about this place – as well as a bar bursting with *pintxos* and some simple lunch *menús*.

La Cepa (☎ 948 21 31 45; Calle de San Lorenzo 2; menú €10) A grungy bar full of hardcore Basque hairdos (after a while in the Basque Country you'll know what we mean!) and simple meals appealing to young pockets. Alternative music scene at night.

Sarasate (☎ 948 22 57 27; Calle de San Nicolás 21; menú €11-17; V) This bright, uncluttered vegetarian restaurant on the 1st floor offers excellent veggie dishes and gluten-free options. It's run by the same people as the Baserri so the quality is undoubted.

our pick **Baserri** (☎ 948 22 20 21; Calle de San Nicolás 32; menú del día €14) This place has won enough food awards that we could fill this entire book listing them. In fact, it's staggering to know that so many food awards actually exist! As you'd expect from such a certificate-studded bar, the meals and the *pintxos* are superb and for once won't break the bank. A *menú degustación* (a sampler of *pintxos*) costs €24; or just pick away at such treats as venison with wild mushrooms or ostrich with Idiázabal cheese. There are also gluten-free options.

Mesón Pirineo (☎ 948 22 20 45; Calle de la Estafeta 41; menú €16) There's nothing fancy and modern about this place; it's just old Navarran style and superb *pintxos* all the way.

Casa Otaño (☎ 948 22 50 95; Calle de San Nicolás 5; mains €16-20) A little pricier than many on this street but worth the extra. Its formal atmosphere is eased by the dazzling array of pink and red flowers spilling off the balcony. Great dishes include that salty favourite, *bacalao* (dried and salted cod), with a Viscaína sauce (€17.50), and there's a variety of heavy meat dishes. The attached *pensión* (singles/doubles €30/48) is definitely run as something of an afterthought to the restaurant.

Drinking

Pamplona's resident student population ensures a lively after-dark scene year-round. There's a strong Basque vibe in the bars around Calle Carmen and Calle de la Calderería and up towards the cathedral.

Cool (☎ 948 22 46 22; www.coolounge.com; Calle de las Navas de Tolosa 11) As the name suggests, this clean steel bar on the edge of the old city is a place to lounge around, seeing and being seen.

Café Iruña (☎ 948 22 20 64; Plaza del Castillo 44) Opened on the eve of Sanfermines in 1888, Café Iruña's dominant position, powerful sense of history and frilly belle époque decor make this by far the most famous and popular watering hole in the city.

Cafeteria Belegua (☎ 948 22 32 82; Calle de la Estafeta 49) This is where young mothers and other tired sorts come for a caffeine pick-me-up and a cake in the late afternoon.

Vinoteca Murillo (☎ 948 22 10 15; cnr Calle de San Gregorio & Plaza de San Nicolás; 🕑 9am-1.45pm & 4-8pm Mon-Sat) For penny-pinching partygoers, this wine shop supplies 5L containers of fiesta-quality wine for only €6.50. But if you're the sort who thinks wine shouldn't taste like vinegar, then they can sort you out too.

Other good bars include the intimate **Dom Lluis** (cnr Calles de San Nicolás & de Pozo Blanco), which rolls on through the night when many others are safely tucked up at home, and **La Granja** (Calle de la Estafeta 71), which despite its modern outlook is full of old-timers propping up the bar. For something louder and drunker, the **Katos Disco** (Paseo de Hemingway) should fit the bill late into the night.

Entertainment

Most of Pamplona's clubs are a walk or short taxi ride south and west of the old city centre, in the direction of the university. Doors at these places are usually open after 11pm Thursday to Saturday, and the cover charge tends to be around €8 to €12, depending on the night.

Reverendos (Calle de Monasterio de Velate 5; 🕑 11.30pm-6.30am) This is the big number for the 20- to 30-year-old dance and techno fiends.

Marengo (Avenida de Bayona 2) This venue gets the crowds going with Latin rhythms and cheesy pop.

Getting There & Away

AIR

Pamplona's **airport** (☎ 948 16 87 00), about 7km south of the city, has regular flights to Madrid and Barcelona. There's an ATM as well as car-rental desks. Bus 21 (€1) travels between the city (from the bus station) and the airport. A taxi costs about €13.

BUS

From the **main bus station** (☎ 948 22 38 54; Calle Conde Oliveto 8), buses leave for most towns throughout Navarra, although service is restricted on Sunday.

Regular bus services travel to Bilbao (€12.85, 1¾ hours), Vitoria (€6.85, 1¾ hours), Logroño (€7.69, 1½ hours), San Sebastián (€6.50, one hour). Regional destinations include Olite (€3.40, 40 minutes, 16 daily) and Estella (€3.69, one hour, 10 daily).

TRAIN

Pamplona's train station is linked to the city centre by bus 9 from Paseo de Sarasate every 15 minutes. Tickets are also sold at the **Renfe agency** (☎ 902 24 02 02; Calle de Estella 8; 🕑 9am-1.30pm & 4.30-7.30pm Mon-Fri, 9am-1pm Sat).

Trains run to/from Madrid (€51.80, three hours, three daily), San Sebastián (from €14.70, two hours, three daily), Vitoria (€4.40, one hour, four daily) and Tudela (from €6.40, 1¼ hours, five daily).

NORTH OF PAMPLONA

Sierra de Aralar

One of Navarra's many natural parks, the scenic Sierra de Aralar offers pleasant walking. There's not much to **Lekunberri**, the area's main town, except a gaggle of solid Basque farmhouses in the old quarter and an ever-growing estate of soulless modern housing beyond. The **tourist office** (☎ 948 50 72 04; oit.lekunberri@cfnavarra.es; Calle de Plazaola 21) here is very helpful and can advise on the numerous fantastic walks the area offers.

For most people the main reason for visiting is to travel the bendy back road NA1510, which leads southwest through a tapestry of mixed deciduous and evergreen forests to culminate (after 21km) in the austere and very bleak 9th-century **Santuario de San Miguel de Aralar** (☎ 948 39 60 28; 🕑 10am-2pm & 4-8pm Jun-Sep, 10am-2pm & 4-7pm Apr, May & Oct, 10am-2pm & 4-6pm Nov-Mar), which lies in the shadow of Monte Altxueta (1343m). Despite its attractive naves and 800-year-old altarpiece, it isn't the sort of place you'd want to visit on a moonless night. There are some spectacular views down onto the plains to the south.

Lekunberri has a number of hotels and restaurants. Hang with the ghosts of Sanfermines past at the beautiful **Hotel Ayestarán** (☎ 948 50 41 27; www.hotelayestaran.com; Calle de Aralar 27; s/d from €46/74), where Hemingway stayed en route to the party. A signed photograph of him standing outside the hotel hangs on the wall. The attached restaurant is equally superb.

Most buses between Pamplona and San Sebastián stop in Lekunberri, but you'll need your own vehicle to explore the sierra.

Sierra de Andia

Looking south from the Santuario de San Miguel de Aralar it's impossible to miss the tempting massif rising up off the plains. This is the Sierra de Andia, and it too offers wonderful walking opportunities. To get there take the very narrow, vertigo-inducing dirt road leading south from the *sanctuario* (do not attempt to drive this route in icy, foggy or very wet conditions) and then join the NA120, which runs, eventually, on to Estella via a laborious clamber up onto the sierra. The sheer mountainsides keep vultures and eagles hanging like mobiles on the thermals, and the limestone heights are a chaos of karst caves that once provided a home to witches. Once up on the plateau things calm down considerably and you'll find a number of wild walks clearly signposted from the first car park you pass.

EAST OF PAMPLONA

Javier

pop 80 / elev 448m

Tiny Javier (Xavier), 11km northeast of Sangüesa, is a quiet rural village set in gentle green countryside. It's utterly dominated by a childhood-fantasy castle that is so perfectly preserved you half expect the drawbridge to come crashing down and a knight in armour to gallop out on a white steed. As well as being an inspiration for fairy-tale dreams, this is also the birthplace of the patron saint of Navarra, San Francisco Xavier, who was born in the village in 1506. Xavier spent much of his life travelling, preaching, teaching and healing in Asia, and today his body lies in a miraculous state of preservation in a cathedral in Goa, India. The **Castillo de Javier** (☎ 948 88 40 24; admission €2; ⌚ 10am-1.30pm & 3.30-6.30pm Apr-Sep, 10am-12.30pm & 4-5.30pm Oct-Mar) houses a small museum dedicated to the life of the saint.

If you want to stay, the red-brick, ivy-clad **Hotel Xabier** (☎ 948 88 40 06; www.hotelxabier.com; s/d €50/81; P 🖳) has small and dated rooms that are a little overpriced, though we can forgive them this because staying here does allow you to peer out of your window on a moonlit night and look for ghosts flitting around the castle keep.

Monasterio de Leyre

Totally swamped with visitors on public holidays, the **Monasterio de Leyre** (☎ 948 88 41 50; adult/child €2.10/0.50; ⌚ 10.15am-2pm & 3.30-7pm Mon-Fri, 10.15am-2pm & 4-7pm Sat & Sun Mar-Nov, 10.15am-2pm & 3.30-6pm Mon-Fri, 10.15am-2pm & 4-6.30pm Sat & Sun Nov-Mar) is in an attractive setting in the shadow of the Sierra de Leyre, about 4km from Yesa on the N240. The early-Romanesque crypt has a three-nave structure with a low roof, and the 12th-century main portal of the church is a fine example of Romanesque artistry.

Accommodation is available at the refined **Hospederia de Leyre** (☎ 948 88 41 00; www.monasteriodeleyre.com; s/d €40/79), which is housed in part of the monastery complex and also has a reasonable restaurant.

Look down from the monastery, towards the main road, and you won't fail to notice the **Embalse de Yesa**, an enormous expanse of water that is perfect for swimming.

There's an early-morning bus from Yesa to Pamplona, as well as one to Huesca. Virtually no buses run on Sunday, and there are none at all from Yesa to the monastery.

NAVARRA'S CASAS RURALES

Navarra has an excellent selection of *casas rurales* (village houses or farmsteads with rooms to let), which are often well-kept, beautiful houses in mountain villages. You can recognise *casas rurales* by one of two small plaques: one has 'CR' in white on a dark-green background; the more modern one, in brown, olive-green and white, displays the letter 'C' and the outline of a house.

A copy of the *Guía de Alojamientos* is available free from most tourist offices in Navarra, and it lists all the private homes and farmsteads that rent out rooms. Reservations are recommended at peak periods.

THE PYRENEES

Awash in greens and often concealed in mists, the rolling hills, ribboned cliffs, clammy forests and snow-plastered mountains that make up the Navarran Pyrenees are a playground for outdoor enthusiasts and pilgrims on the Camino de Santiago. Despite being firmly Basque in history, culture and outlook, there is something of a different feeling to the tiny towns and villages that hug these slopes. Perhaps it's their proximity to France, but in general they seem somehow more prim and proper than many of the lowland towns. This only adds to the charm of exploring what are without doubt some of the most delightful and least exploited mountains in Europe.

Trekkers and skiers should be thoroughly equipped at any time of the year and note emergency numbers in case of difficulties: ☎ 112 in Navarra or ☎ 17 in Aquitaine (France).

WALKING

There are numerous walking trails of mixed lengths and difficulties in the Pyrenees, and it's even possible to follow high-altitude trails across the entire breadth of the range in around 45 days. If you are intending to do some proper walking then keep in mind that the weather up here changes alarmingly fast. Even in August a beautiful morning can quickly slide into an afternoon of violent storms. For even fairly moderate exploration, a two-season sleeping bag and all-weather gear are essential – even in summer.

Finding a suitable place to begin hiking can be a little confusing, and without a dedicated guidebook, a decent map and a compass, the most rewarding walks will elude you. Fortunately almost every newsagent, bookshop and tourist office in the region has a full stock of such guides, but they are all in Spanish or French only, and to understand the routes they describe you must speak one of these languages to a very high level. Some of the shorter and more popular walks are more clearly signposted and accessible to the non-linguist; otherwise tourist offices can sometimes supply basic maps of short walks.

We have not attempted to describe any walking routes here and have focused instead on mountain areas and villages accessible to visitors with their own car.

Further information on these wonderful mountains can be obtained from the **Federación Navarra de Deportes de Montaña y Escalada** (☎ in Pamplona 948 22 46 83, in San Sebastián 943 47 42 79; www.fed me.es).

The Northern Foothills

VALLE DEL BAZTÁN

This is rural Basque Country at its most typical, a landscape of splotchy reds and greens. Minor roads take you in and out of charming little villages, such as **Arraioz** (known for the fortified Casa Jaureguizar) and **Ziga**, with its 16th-century church.

Just beyond Irurita on the N121B is the valley's biggest town, **Elizondo**, given a distinctly urban air by its tall half-timbered buildings. It's a good base for exploring the area. There's accommodation at the **Antxitónea Hostal** (☎ 948 58 18 07; www.antxitonea.com; Calle Braulío Iríarte 16; d from €68), which has plain rooms with flower-coated balconies. The attached restaurant has an excellent-value €10 *menú del día*. Buses from Elizondo go to Pamplona up to three times daily (€4.15, 1½ hours), stopping in many of the smaller villages up and down the valley.

Beyond Elizondo, the NA2600 road meanders dreamily about picturesque farms, villages and hills before climbing sharply to the French border-pass of **Puerto de Izpegui**, where the world becomes a spectacular collision of crags, peaks and valleys. At the pass you can stop for a short hike up to the top of **Mt Izpegui**. You'll find a good number of *casas rurales* throughout the area, as well as **Camping Baztan** (☎ 948 45 31 33; sites for 2 people, car & tent €18.20; 🕒 closed end Oct–mid-Mar) in Erratzu.

The N121B continues northwards to the Puerto de Otxondo and the border crossing into France at Dantxarinea. Just before the border a minor road veers west to the almost overly pretty village of **Zugarramurdi**, home to the decidedly less pretty **Cuevas de Las Brujas** (Witches' Caves; ☎ 948 59 93 05; adult/child €3.50/2; 🕒 11am-dusk). The caves were once, according to the Inquisition, the scene of evil debauchery. Having established this, the perverse masters of the Inquisition promptly tortured and burned scores of alleged witches. Playing on the flying-broomstick theme is the **Museo de las Brujas** (☎ 948 59 90 04; adult/child €4/2; 🕒 11am-6pm Wed-Sun), a fascinating delve into the mysterious cauldron of witchcraft in the Pyrenees.

Zugarramurdi has plenty of *casas rurales* but no public transport.

To France via Roncesvalles

As you bear northeast out of Pamplona on the N135 and ascend into the Pyrenees, the yellows, browns and olive greens of lower Navarra begin to give way to more-luxuriant vegetation, before the mountains thunder up to great Pyrenean heights. It would be fair to say that this route, which follows the Camino de Santiago, is more for culture vultures than mountain walkers and dawdlers.

BURGUETE

The main road runs tightly between neat, whitewashed houses with bare cornerstones at Burguete (Basque: Auritz), lending a more sober French air to things. Despite lacking the history, it actually makes a better night's halt than nearby Roncesvalles. There's a supermarket, a bank, an ATM and some decent accommodation.

Camping Urrobi (☎ 948 76 02 00; www.campingurrobi.com; sites per person/tent/car €4.50/4.50/4.50; 🕒 Apr-Oct; 💻) is a few kilometres south. In the town itself, as well as a sprinkling of *casas rurales*, **Hostal Juandeaburre** (☎ 948 76 00 78; Calle de San Nicolás 38; s/d with washbasin €16/27), run by a lovely old woman, is as cheap as Spain gets and has simple flowery rooms that smell of mothballs. Easily the best place to stay is the new **Don Jauregui** (☎ 948 76 00 31; www.donjaureguideburguete.com; Calle de San Nicolás 32; s/d €35/45), which has bright, youthful rooms and plenty of friendly chit-chat from the owners. The more sophisticated, but less interesting, **Hotel Loizu** (☎ 948 76 00 08; www.hotelloizu.com; Calle de San Nicolás 13; s/d from €59/82) is a proper hotel whose upper rooms have attractive beams and exposed stone walls. The formal hotel restaurant offers a *menú del día* for €15.

Restaurante Txikipolit (☎ 948 76 00 19; Calle de San Nicolás 52; menú €18), on the main road, has tasty mains and specialises in foie gras.

RONCESVALLES

There is an air of accomplishment to Roncesvalles (Basque: Orreaga), but it isn't one of artistic achievement, because the famous monastery is actually a squat and ugly affair. Rather it's the accomplishment of the millions of pilgrims who, over the years, have successfully conquered the Pyrenees, one of the hardest parts of the Camino de Santiago.

Despite its ugliness the main event is the **monastery complex** (admission to cloister, chapter house & museum €2.30, guided tours adult/child €4.50/2.30; 🕑 10am-1.30pm & 3.30-7pm). It's open shorter hours from October to March. The 13th-century Gothic **Real Colegiata de Santa María** (🕑 10am-8.30pm) contains a much-revered, silver-covered statue of the Virgin beneath a modernist-looking canopy worthy of Frank Gehry. Also of interest is the cloister, which contains the tomb of King Sancho VII (El Fuerte) of Navarra, the apparently 2.25m-tall victor in the Battle of Las Navas de Tolosa, fought against the Muslims in 1212. Nearby is the 12th-century **Capilla de Sancti Spiritus**. A few steps away in an old mill house is the **tourist office** (☎ 948 76 03 01; 🕑 10am-2pm & 4-7pm Mon-Sat, 10am-2pm Sun).

As might be expected in such a tourist hotspot, the rooms at the **Hostal Casa Sabina** (☎ 948 76 00 12; tw €50) aren't great value and it's twin beds only – possibly to stop any hanky-panky so close to a monastery? The bar and restaurant get more lively than the bedrooms. **La Posada** (☎ 948 76 02 25; www.laposadaderoncesvalles.com; s/d €43/54; 💻) is a much more appealing option. The simple rooms have some gentle country charm and the staff are equally gentle.

A bus departs Roncesvalles at 9.20am every morning except Sundays for Pamplona (€5.40, 1 hour 40 minutes) via Burguete, and returns in the late afternoon.

PUERTO DE IBAÑETA & VALCARLOS

From Roncesvalles the road climbs to the Puerto de Ibañeta, from where you have magnificent views across the border. The last town before the frontier is Valcarlos (Basque: Luzaide). Built on the side of the slippery slope leading to France, this is a sleepy but pretty spot. Of the numerous *casas rurales* in town, the tree-framed **Casa Etxezuria** (☎ 948 79 00 11; www.etxezuria.com in Spanish; r €35), with mountain-flavoured rooms, is the most reliable – many of the others never seem to have anyone around to help you.

THE ROADS TO OCHAGAVÍA

Happy wanderers on wheels can drift around a network of quiet country roads, with pretty villages along the way, in the area east of the main Roncesvalles road. A couple of kilometres south of Burguete, the NA140 branches off east to Garralda. Push on to **Arive**, a charming hamlet, from where you could continue east to the Valle del Salazar, or go south along Río Irati past the fine Romanesque church near **Nagore**. Another option is to take a loop northeast through the beautiful **Bosque de Irati** forest, with its thousands of beech trees that turn the slopes a flaming orange every autumn and invite exploration on foot. Eventually this route will link you up with the Valle del Salazar at Ochagavía. If you stick to the NA140 between Arive and Ochagavía, **Abaurregaina** and **Jaurrieta** are particularly picturesque. Most villages along the route have *casas rurales*.

Ochagavía

This charming Pyrenean town lying astride narrow Río Zatoya sets itself quite apart from the villages further south. Grey stone, slate and cobblestones dominate the old centre, which straddles a bubbling stream crossed by a pleasant medieval bridge. The town's sober dignity is reinforced by the looming presence of the **Iglesia de San Juan Evangelista**.

This is a popular base for walkers and even skiers, so there are plenty of *casas rurales*. For a list of options and hiking opportunities in the region, visit the **Centro de Interpretación**

de la Naturaleza (☎ 948 89 06 80; oit.ochagavia@cfnavarra.es; 🕑 10am-2pm & 4.30-8.30pm Mon-Sat,10am-2pm Sun). **Camping Osate** (☎ 948 89 01 84; sites per person/tent €4.30/4.20) also has two-person cabins from €43.

To reach France, take the NA140 northeast from Ochagavía into the Sierra de Abodi and cross at the Puerto de Larrau (1585m), a majestically bleak pass. Four kilometres short of the border there's a seasonal restaurant and bar for skiers.

Valle del Salazar

If you've made your way to Ochagavía, a good choice for heading south is the Valle del Salazar, many of whose hamlets contain gems of medieval handiwork with quiet cobbled streets and little plazas. **Esparza**, with its mansions, medieval bridge and restored Iglesia de San Andrés, is particularly rewarding, while **Ezcároz**, **Sarriés**, **Güesa** and nearby **Igal** (off the main road) are also worth an amble. A daily bus runs the length of the Valle del Salazar between Pamplona and Ochagavía.

Valle del Roncal

Navarra's most spectacular mountain area is around Roncal, and this easternmost valley is an alternative route for leaving or entering the Navarran Pyrenees. One bus leaves Pamplona at 5pm Monday to Saturday, passing through all the Valle del Roncal towns on its way to Uztárroz. It returns early in the morning. For details of *casas rurales* in the valley, visit the **Roncal-Salazar** (www.roncal-salazar.com) website.

BURGUI

The gateway to this part of the Pyrenees is Burgui – an enchanting huddle of stone houses built beside a clear, gushing stream (the Río Esca) bursting with frogs and fish and crossed via a humpbacked Roman bridge. You can swim from a small beach on the banks of the stream. The village is renowned for its almonds and on **almond day** (3 May) it even throws a little fiesta for them. **Hostal El Almadiero** (☎ 948 47 70 86; www.almadiero.com; Plaza Mayor; d half-board €120), in the heart of the village, has slightly overpriced but bright and colourful rooms with 19th-century bathrooms (though with mod cons like hot water!).

RONCAL

The largest centre along this road, though still firmly a village, Roncal is a place of cobblestone alleyways that twist and turn between dark stone houses and meander down to a river full of trout. Roncal is renowned for its Queso de Roncal, a sheep's-milk cheese that's sold in the village.

The **tourist office** (☎ 948 47 52 56; www.vallederoncal.es; 🕑 10am-2pm & 4.30-8.30pm Mon-Sat, 10am-2pm Sun mid-Jun–mid-Sep, 10am-2pm Mon-Thu & Sun, 10am-2pm & 4.30-7.30pm Fri & Sat mid-Sep–mid-Jun), on the main road towards the Isaba exit from town, has an excellent interpretation centre (€1.20). There's a bank with an ATM in the village.

Across the river on the southern exit from Roncal is **Hostal Zaltua** (☎ 948 47 50 08; www.zaltua.com; Calle de Castillo 23; s/d €35/50), which has cute rooms, some with river views. Outside of the high season it's closed on Sundays.

ISABA

Lording it over the other villages in the valley, lofty Isaba, lying above the confluence of Ríos Belagua and Uztárroz, is another popular base for walkers and skiers. The closest reliable cross-country skiing is about 12km away in Belagua. There are a few banks with ATMs and a **tourist office** (☎ 948 89 32 51; 🕑 10am-2pm & 4.30-8.30pm Mon-Sat, 10am-2pm Sun mid-Jun–mid-Sep, 10am-2pm Mon-Thu & Sun, 10am-2pm & 4.30-7.30pm Fri & Sat mid-Sep–mid-Jun).

There are plenty of sleeping places, but many are block-booked during the skiing season. An excellent, character-infused option is the **Hostal Onki Xin** (☎ 948 89 33 20; www.onkixin.com; d €55), housed inside a converted traditional house with fancily painted rooms and lots of wrinkly old wood and open stone walls. **Camping Asolaze** (☎ 948 89 30 34; www.campingasolaze.com; sites per person/tent/car €4.20/4.20/4.20) is at Km6 on the road to France.

SOUTH OF PAMPLONA

Take the A15 south of Pamplona and you only have to drive for 15 minutes to enter an entirely new world. Within the space of just a few kilometres, the deep greens that you will have grown to love in the Basque regions and northern Navarra vanish and are replaced with a lighter and more Mediterranean ochre. As the sunlight becomes more dazzling (and more commonly seen!) the shark's-teeth hills of the north flatten into tranquil lowland plains, the wet forests become scorched vineyards and olive groves, and even the people change – they're more gregarious and, as the graffiti ascertains, often fiercely anti-Basque.

For the traveller it feels as if you are finally arriving in the Spain of the clichés.

Olite

pop 3440 / elev 365m

Bursting off the pages of a fairy tale, the turrets and spires of Olite are filled with stories of kings and queens, brave knights and beautiful princesses. Though it might seem a little hard to believe today, this insignificant, honey-coloured village was once the home of the royal families of Navarra and the walled old quarter is crowded with their memories.

Founded by the Romans (parts of the town wall date back to Roman times), Olite first attracted the attention of royalty in 1276 but didn't really take off until it caught the fancy of King Carlos III (Carlos the Noble) in the 15th century. Carlos wasn't just noble; he was also very ambitious and it's him that we must thank for the exceptional **Palacio Real** (Castillo de Olite; ☎ 948 74 00 35; adult/child €3.50/2; 10am-8pm daily Jul & Aug, 10am-7pm Mon-Fri, 10am-8pm Sat & Sun Apr-Jun & Sep, 10am-6pm Mon-Fri, 10am-6.30pm Sat & Sun Oct-Mar), which towers over the village. Back in Carlos' day the inhabitants of the castle included not just princes and jesters but also lions, giraffes and other exotic pets, as well as Babylon-inspired hanging gardens. Today, though the princesses and lionesses are sadly missing, some of the hanging gardens remain. Integrated into the castle is the **Iglesia de Santa María la Real**, which has a superbly detailed Gothic portal. There are guided tours of the church; check with the tourist office for times.

At the other end of the medieval luxury scale are the **Galerías Subterráneas** (Plaza Carlos III; adult/child €1.50/1; 11am-1pm Tue-Fri, 11am-2pm & 5-7pm Sat, Sun & public holidays), a series of underground galleries whose origin and use remain something of a mystery. Today they contain a small museum explaining the town's medieval life, which basically illustrates that if you had blue blood or were rich then life was one jolly round of wine, food and things that your mother wouldn't approve of, and if you weren't – well, life sucked.

If all this talk of medieval drinking binges has piqued your interest in wine, don't miss the superb **Museo del Vino** (☎ 948 74 12 73; Plaza de los Teobaldos 10; adult/child €3.50/2; 10am-2pm & 4-7pm Mon-Sat, 10am-2pm Sun Easter-Oct, 10am-5pm Mon-Fri, 10am-2pm Sat Nov-Easter), which is a fascinating journey through wine and wine culture. Everything is well labelled and laid out and there are lots of flashy, beeping interactive displays. The entrance ticket to the Palacio Real entitles you to a €1 discount and a free bottle of wine.

Olite has a friendly and helpful **tourist office** (☎ 948 74 17 03; Plaza de los Teobaldos 10; 10am-2pm & 4-7pm Mon-Sat, 10am-2pm Sun Easter-Oct, 10am-5pm Mon-Fri, 10am-2pm Sat Nov-Easter), in the same building as the wine museum.

Excellent stopovers include **Hotel Casa Zanito** (☎ 948 74 00 02; www.casazanito.com; Rúa Mayor 10; s/d €67/80), where good-value rooms make copious use of dark, carved wood to create the almost obligatory olde-worlde feel. It has a restaurant serving traditional cuisine.

Hotel Merindad de Olite (☎ 948 74 07 35; www.hotel-merindaddeolite.com; Rúa de la Judería 11; s/d from €68/78;) is a charming place with very comfortable rooms and masses of period style. It's popularity has led the owners to open a new establishment, **Hotel El Juglar** (☎ 948 74 18 55; Rua Romana 39; r €125; P), a few minutes' walk into the new suburbs, which might well offer the best deal in town. The handful of rooms on offer here are all slightly different from one another – some have big round whirlpool baths, others old-fashioned stone baths, and some have elaborate walk-in showers. All have four-poster beds and lots of fancy decorations. It's so new that we were actually the very first guests.

As with all *paradores* (luxurious state-owned hotels), the **Principe de Viana** (☎ 948 74 00 00; olite@parador.es; Plaza de los Teobaldos 2; s/d incl breakfast from €138/184;), situated in a wing of the castle (though some of the cheaper rooms are in a newer extension), is in a sumptuous, atmospheric class of its own. Though there might be equally good rooms available elsewhere in town for considerably fewer euros, they don't come with a castle attached.

El Preboste (Asador Pizzeria; ☎ 948 71 22 50; www.elpreboste.com; Rúa de Mirapies 8; mains €10), with its typical Spanish dishes mixed with sheets of thin-based pizza, is easily the locals' favourite eating haunt.

Up to nine buses a day run between Olite and Pamplona (€3.40, 40 minutes to one hour).

Ujué

Balancing atop a hill criss-crossed with terraced fields, the tiny village of Ujué, some 18km east of Olite and overlooking the plains of southern Navarra, is a perfect example of a fortified medieval village. Today the almost immaculately preserved village is sleepy and pretty, with steep, narrow streets tumbling down the hillside, but what gives it something special is the hybrid **Iglesia de Santa María**, a fortified church of mixed Romanesque-Gothic style. The church contains a rare statue of the black Virgin, which is said to have been discovered by a shepherd who was led to the statue by a dove. In addition to the Virgin, the church also contains the heart of Carlos II.

The village plays host to a fascinating *romería* (pilgrimage) on the first Sunday after St Mark's Day (25 April), when hundreds of people walk through the night from Tudela to celebrate Mass in the village church.

Unfortunately there is no accommodation in the village, but it makes a great lunch stop. **Mesón las Migas** (☎ 948 73 90 44; Calle Jesús Echauri; mains €12-15), which serves traditional south Navarran food, is the best place to eat. Try the *migas de pastor* (fried breadcrumbs with herbs and spices) and the *conejo en salsa de almendras* (rabbit in almond sauce). A full meal with wine for two will cost around €50.

Monasterio de la Oliva

The 12th-century **Monasterio de la Oliva** (☎ 948 72 50 06; guided tours €2; 🕒 9am-12.30pm & 3.30-6.15pm Mon-Sat, 9-11.45am & 4-6.15pm Sun), 2km from Carcastillo, was founded by Cistercian monks and is still functioning as a community. Its austere church gives onto a peaceful and pleasing Gothic cloister. The monks are dressed in exotic white hooded robes. There are two or three buses daily between Pamplona and Carcastillo.

Parque Natural de las Bárdenas Reales

In a region largely dominated by wet mountain slopes, the last thing you'd expect to find is a sunburnt desert, but in the Parque Natural de las Bárdenas Reales a desert is exactly what you'll find. Established as a natural park in 1999 and as a UN Biosphere Reserve in 2000, the Bárdenas Reales is a desiccated landscape of blank table-top hills, open gravel plains and snakelike gorges that covers over 41,000 hectares of southeastern Navarra. As well as spectacular scenery, the park plays host to numerous birds and animals, including the great bustard, golden eagles, Egyptian and griffon vultures, numerous reptiles, mountain cats and wild boar. There are a couple of dirt motor tracks and numerous hiking and cycling trails, all of which are only vaguely signposted. The tourist offices in Olite (p509) and Tudela (below) are the best places to pick up reliable information and maps.

Tudela

pop 32,800 / elev 243m

The outskirts of Tudela are depressing indeed and almost enough to make you turn around. But persevere: thanks to Islam, things do improve! Tudela was in Muslim hands for some 400 years and the Islamic genius for serpentine street creation makes the old quarter a pleasure to wander through. There's an excellent **tourist office** (☎ 948 84 80 58; oit.tudela@navarra.es; Calle de Juicio 4; 🕒 9.30am-2pm & 4-8pm Mon-Fri, 10am-2pm & 4-8pm Sat, 10am-2pm Sun Easter–mid-Oct, 9.30am-2pm & 4-7pm Mon-Fri, 10am-2pm & 4-7pm Sat, 10am-1pm Sun mid-Oct–Easter) opposite the cathedral.

The brightly decorated, 17th-century **Plaza de los Fueros** has coloured panels high on its walls, depicting coats-of-arms and bullfight scenes from the days when the square was used as a bullring. Today plenty of cheerful cafes encircle the plaza. In former incarnations the 16th-century **Iglesia de Santa María** was both a mosque and a synagogue. A short distance away is the **cathedral**, a sombre 12th-century Gothic pile. The western Puerta del Juicio is particularly striking, with its many sculpted figures looking decidedly uneasy about their participation in the Last Judgment, and positively agonised on the right-hand side, where little devils are boiling them in oil.

Take time to wander the streets, as there are some fine old mansions, many with Aragónese-style *aleros* (awnings) jutting out from the roof – the **Palacio del Marqués de San Adrián** (☎ 948 82 15 35; Calle de Magallón 10) is an impressive example.

Hostal Remigio (☎ 948 82 08 50; www.hostalremigio.com; Calle de Gaztambide 4; s/d €32/52), just off Plaza de los Fueros, has plenty of sturdy, good-value rooms. Its old dining room does a filling *menú del día* for €15.

Around six or seven trains run daily to/from Pamplona (from €6.40, 1½ hours). Buses to Pamplona (€8, 1¼ hours, eight daily) operate from next to the train station, southeast of the town centre.

WEST OF PAMPLONA

Puente la Reina

pop 2670 / elev 421m

The spectacular six-arched medieval bridge at Puente la Reina (Basque: Gares), 22km southwest of Pamplona on the A12, throngs with the ghosts of a multitude of pilgrims. Over the centuries they approached from Roncesvalles to the north and Aragón to the east, and then united to take the one main route west to Santiago de Compostela. Their first stop here was at the late-Romanesque **Iglesia del Crucifijo**, erected by the Knights Templar and still containing one of the finest Gothic crucifixes in existence.

Estella

pop 14,000 / elev 483m

Estella (Basque: Lizarra) was known as 'La Bella' in medieval times because of the splendour of its monuments and buildings, and though the old dear has lost some of its *bella* to modern suburbs, it's not without its charms. During the 11th century, Estella became a main reception point for the growing flood of pilgrims along the Camino de Santiago. Today most visitors are continuing that same plodding tradition.

The **tourist office** (☎ 948 55 63 01; www.navarra.es; Calle de San Nicolás 1; ⏰ 10am-8pm Mon-Sat, 10am-2pm Sun Jul & Aug, 10am-2pm & 4-7pm Mon-Sat, 10am-2pm Sun Sep & Easter-Jun, 10am-5pm Mon-Sat, 10am-2pm Sun Oct-Easter) is on the western bank of the river below the 12th-century **Iglesia de San Pedro de la Rúa**, the most important monument in Estella. Adjacent to the tourist office is the **Palacio de los Reyes** (☎ 948 54 60 37; www.museogustavodemaeztu.com; Calle de San Nicolás 2; admission free; ⏰ 11am-1pm & 5-7pm Tue-Sat, 11am-1.30pm Sun), a rare example of Romanesque civil construction. It houses an intriguing collection of paintings by Gustavo de Maeztu y Whitney (1887–1947), who was of Cuban-English parentage but emphatically Basque in upbringing and identity. Landscapes, portraits and full-bodied nudes reflect Maeztu's engaging sensual romanticism. Across the river and overlooking the town is the **Iglesia de San Miguel**, with a fine Romanesque north door.

Every year from 31 July to 8 August, Estella hosts a **feria** (fair) with its own **encierro**, the running of the bulls.

Decent hotels include **Pensión San Andrés** (☎ 948 55 41 58; Plaza Santiago 58; s with/without bathroom €32/20, d with/without bathroom €40/32), with very simple, clean rooms that you'll be lucky to get into without a reservation, and the **Hotel Yerri** (⏰ 948 54 60 34; fax 948 55 50 81; Avenida de Yerri 35; s/d €35/60), a large place a few minutes' walk from the old centre. The Yerri's rooms are very comfortable though not terribly interesting.

Astarriaga Asador (☎ 948 55 08 02; Plaza de Los Fueros 12; menú €13.30), on the main square, is a very popular restaurant with Galicia-bound pilgrims on account of its energy-enhancing *menús* (served at lunch and dinner). Meat eaters will love the steak selections – some are almost the size of a cow.

About 10 buses leave from the **bus station** (Plaza Coronación) for Pamplona (€3.69, one hour) Monday to Friday, and four on Saturday and Sunday.

Around Estella

The countryside around Estella is littered with monasteries. One of the best is the **Monasterio de Irache** (☎ 948 55 44 64; admission free; ⏰ 9am-1.30pm Tue, 9am-1.30pm & 5-7pm Wed-Sun, closed 15 Dec-31 Jan), 3km southwest of Estella, near Ayegui. This ancient Benedictine monastery has a lovely 16th-century plateresque cloister, and its Puerta Especiosa is decorated with delicate sculptures.

About 10km north of Estella, near Abárzuza, is the **Monasterio de Iranzu** (☎ 948 52 00 47; www.monasterio-iranzu.com; adult/child €2.50/1.50; ⏰ 10am-2pm & 4-8pm May-Sep, 10am-2pm & 4-6pm Oct-Apr). Originally founded way back in the 11th century, but recently restored, this sandy-coloured monastery with beautiful cloisters is so calm and tranquil that it could inspire religious meditation in Lucifer himself.

LA RIOJA

Get out the *copas* (glasses) for La Rioja and for some of the best red wines produced in the country. Wine goes well with the region's ochre earth and vast blue skies, which seem far more Mediterranean than the Basque greens further north. In fact, it's hard not to feel as if you're in a different country altogether. The bulk of the vineyards line Río Ebro around the town of Haro, but extend also into neighbouring Navarra and the Basque province of Álava. This diverse region offers more than just the pleasures of the grape, though, and a few days here can see you mixing it up in lively towns and quiet pilgrim churches, and even hunting for the remains of giant reptiles.

LOGROÑO

pop 147,100

Logroño doesn't feel the need to be loud and brash. Instead it's a stately town with a heart of tree-studded squares, narrow streets and hidden corners. There are few monuments, but there are some fine restaurants and tapas/*pintxos* bars in plenty, while the citizens are unfailingly friendly. It's the sort of place that you cannot help but feel contented in – and it's not just the wine.

Orientation

If you arrive at the train or bus station, first head up Avenida de España and then Calle del General Vara de Rey until you reach the Espolón, a large, parklike square lavish with plane trees. The Casco Viejo starts just to the north; the main area here is the pedestrianised Calle de Portales with the cathedral as its focus.

Information

There are two tourist offices in Logroño: a regional office and a relatively new office run by the town council.

Main post office (Plaza de San Agustín 1) In the old town.

Oficina de Información Logroño (☎ 941 27 33 53; www.logroturismo.org; Calle de Portales 50; 9am-2pm & 5-8pm Jul–mid-Sep, 10am-2pm & 4.30-7.30pm mid-Sep–Jun) The town office.

Tourist Office of La Rioja (☎ 941 24 43 84; www.lariojaturismo.com; Paseo del Espolón; 10am-2pm & 4-7pm Mon-Fri, 10am-2pm & 5-8pm Sat, 10am-2pm & 5-7pm Sun) The regional office.

Sights

The **Catedral de Santa María de La Redonda** (Calle de Portales; 8am-1pm & 6.30-7.30pm Mon-Sat) started life as a Gothic church before maturing into a full-blown cathedral. Inside you'll find it a little dark and overpowering. Outside it seems lighter and friendlier, thanks, no doubt, to the huge square it sits proudly in.

The impressive main entrance to the 13th-century **Iglesia de San Bartolomé** (Calle de Rodríguez Paterna) has a splendid portico of deeply receding orders and an expressive collection of statuary.

A stroll around the old town and down to the river is a pleasant diversion. The **Museo de la Rioja** (Plaza de San Agustín) was closed for renovations at the time of research.

Festivals & Events

Logroño's week-long **Fiesta de San Mateo** starts on 21 September and doubles as a harvest festival, during which all of La Rioja comes to town to watch the grape-crushing ceremonies in the Espolón and to drink ample quantities of wine. The **Feast of San Bernabé** is held on 11 June and commemorates the French siege of Logroño in 1521. **Actual**, a program of cultural, musical and artistic events, is a much more sober festival that takes place through the first week of January.

Sleeping

Pensión La Bilbaina (☎ 941 25 42 26; Calle de Capitán Gallarza 10; s €25-30, d €36-40) A cute little place with clean and pleasing rooms. The grand entrance is an impressive mess of tile work.

our pick Hostal La Numantina (☎ 941 25 14 11; Calle de Sagasta 4; s/d €35/55) This professional operation caters perfectly to the traveller's needs. The rooms are comfortable and homely, with crazy patterned wardrobes and pool-sized baths. The best aspects, though, are the communal TV room and the ample tourist info.

Hotel Marqués de Vallejo (☎ 941 24 83 33; www.hotelmarquesdevallejo.com; Calle del Marqués de Vallejo 8; s/d €59/64; 💻) From the driftwood art in the communal spaces to the lollipops and raunchy red pouffes in the rooms, a huge amount of thought and effort has gone into the design of this stylish modern hotel.

Hostal Niza (☎ 941 20 60 44; www.hostalniza.com; Calle de Capitán Gallarza 13; s €43-54, d €64-75) Simple and smart rooms, which come with tea- and coffee-making facilities. Right in the heart of the action.

Eating

Logroño is a *pintxo*-lover's delight. The chief streets of delicacies are Calle Laurel and Calle de San Juan.

Bar Soriano (Travesía de Laurel 2) The smell of frying food will suck you into this bar, which has been serving up the same delicious mushroom tapa, topped with a shrimp, for more than 30 years.

Lorenzo (Travesía de Laurel 4-6) This old-fashioned place serves the delicious *tío agus* (roasted pork in a secret sauce). There is another, much more modern branch around the corner on Calle de San Agustín.

La Taberna de Baco (☎ 941 21 35 44; Calle de San Agustín 10) This place has a cracking list of tapas, including *bombitas* (potatoes stuffed with mushrooms) and *rabas de pollo* (fried chicken slices marinated in spices and lemon juice). You'll also find some delicious casseroles and salads.

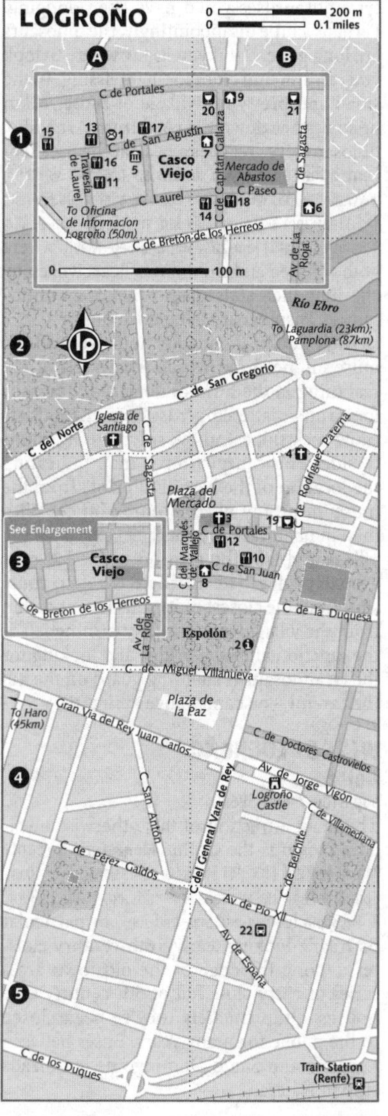

INFORMATION
Main Post Office ... 1 A1
Tourist Office of La Rioja ... 2 B3

SIGHTS & ACTIVITIES
Catedral de Santa María Redonda ... 3 B3
Iglesia de San Bartolomé ... 4 B2
Museo de la Rioja ... 5 A1

SLEEPING
Hostal La Numantina ... 6 B1
Hostal Niza ... 7 B1
Hotel Marqués de Vallejo ... 8 B3
Pensión La Bilbaina ... 9 B1

EATING
Bar A Tu Gusto ... 10 B3
Bar Charly ... (see 11)
Bar Soriano ... 11 A1
La Sacristía ... 12 B3
La Taberna de Baco ... 13 A1
La Taberna del Laurel ... 14 B1
Lorenzo ... 15 A1
Lorenzo ... 16 A1
Vinos de Rioja ... 17 A1
Vinos El Peso ... 18 B1

DRINKING
Café Picasso ... 19 B3
Noche y Día ... 20 B1
Steel ... 21 B1

TRANSPORT
Bus Station ... 22 B5

La Sacristía (☎ 941 24 87 16; Calle de Portales 25; menú €12) The bullfighting and flamenco memorabilia provide a pleasant setting in which your taste buds can salivate over gorgeous seafood dishes. The lunch *menú* is particularly good.

Other excellent *pintxo* bars include the yellow wonderland that is the **Bar Charly** (Travesía de Laurel 2), renowned for its *pimientos rellenos* (spicy red peppers stuffed full of meat). It's open in the evenings only. The speciality at **La Taberna del Laurel** (Calle Laurel 7) is *patatas bravas* (potatoes in a spicy tomato sauce). They're not just good; they're damn near divine. **Bar A Tu Gusto** (Calle de San Juan 21) serves delicious shellfish in an Andalucian-flavoured bar.

For self-catering there's the **Mercado de Abastos** (Calle Peso), with a fish-and-meat section and superb fruit-and-veg shops. There are countless wine outlets in town, but two excellent shops are **Vinos de Rioja** (Plaza San Agustín 4; 10am-2pm & 5-8pm Tue-Sat) and **Vinos El Peso** (☎ 941 22 82 54; cnr Calles Laurel & de Capitán Gallarza; 9am-9pm Mon-Fri, 9am-4pm Sat, 9am-2pm Sun).

Drinking

The bars along Calle Laurel are great places to start your evening, as most offer good local wines for bargain prices.

Steel (Calle de Portales 49) This bar is a glass fashion emporium with city style and a young vibe.

Noche y Día (Calle de Portales 63) This popular coffee and drinks place lives up to its name, at least until 2am (fairly late for La Rioja). The clientele is older and tamer than at the others.

Café Picasso (☎ 941 24 79 92; Calle de Portales 4) This place plays on for a bit later and morphs from trendy cafe during the day to a still-trendier bar at night.

Getting There & Away

Up to five buses leave daily for Burgos (€5.95, two hours), Bilbao (€12.05, two hours) and Pamplona (€7.69, 1½ hours). There are also connections to/from Haro (€2.60, one hour) and Santo Domingo de la Calzada (€2.50, 45 minutes).

By train, Logroño is regularly connected to Zaragoza (€17.30, two hours), Madrid (€51.80, 3½ hours), Bilbao (€17.10, three hours) and Burgos (€17.30, 2½ hours).

SOUTH OF LOGROÑO

For those with their own transport, heading south for Soria leads through some stunning countryside. One route, which takes in shades of the Arab world and reminders of the prehistoric, heads southeast of Logroño and past the large and ugly town of Calahorra, on the N232. From here head southwest, via Arnedo, to perfect **Arnedillo**, a small spa village surrounded by slowly eroding hills, terraced in olive groves and watched over by circling hawks and vultures. It's an ideal place to spend a peaceful day or two walking and dinosaur hunting. There is a small **museum** and, in the same building, a **tourist office** (☎ 941 39 42 26; 9.30am-2.30pm Tue-Thu, 9.30am-2.30pm & 4-6pm Fri & Sat, 10am-2pm Sun).

For accommodation, the tourist office can supply details of nearby *casas rurales;* otherwise try the funky **Casa Rural La Fuente** (☎ 941 39 41 38; casarurallafuentearnedillo@hotmail.com; r €40-45), where you get an art-stuffed room, kitchen use and a primitive sitting room.

our pick **Hospederia Las Pedrolas** (☎ 941 39 44 01; fax 941 39 44 01; Plaza Felix Merino 16; s/d incl breakfast €54/86;), a couple of doors down from La Fuente, is an immaculately restored house full of tasteful furnishings and crooked roof beams. Comfortable rooms splashed in glaring whitewash leave you feeling as if you're sleeping inside a Mr Whippy ice cream.

Just beyond Arnedillo is the hamlet of **Peroblasco**, confidently perched in a defensive posture on the crown of a hill and well worth a wander.

Never mind dodging crazy truck drivers; if you'd been driving around these parts 120 million years ago it would have been crazy tyrannosauruses you'd have been dodging. Perhaps a little disappointingly, the dinosaurs are long gone, but if you know where to look you can still find clues to their passing. In the small and pretty hill village of **Enciso**, 10km or so further down the road from Arnedillo, dinosaur fever reaches a peak at the excellent **Centro Paleontológico de Enciso** (☎ 941 39 60 93; www.dinosaurios-larioja.org in Spanish; adult/child €3/1.50; 11am-2pm & 5-8pm daily Jun–mid-Sep, 11am-2pm & 3-6pm Mon-Sat, 11am-2pm Sun mid-Sep–May), where both children and children-at-heart will enjoy checking their stats against that of a brontosaurus. Displays are in Spanish only.

After you've done your homework in the museum, head out to see what's left of the real thing in the form of dozens of dinosaur footprints scattered across former mudflats (now rock slopes) in the surrounding countryside. You can pick up a map indicating the location of the best dino prints from the museum or any nearby tourist office. With map in hand take the southern exit from the village and take the turn-off to the left over a small bridge. This is where the dino route starts, but the closest footprints (around 3km from the village) are found by turning left at the junction after the bridge and looking for the tyrannosaurus standing guard on the hill (be careful – he comes alive at night!).

WEST OF LOGROÑO

Nájera

pop 8100 / elev 506m

The main attraction of this otherwise unexciting town is the Gothic **Monasterio de Santa María la Real** (☎ 941 36 36 50; admission €3; 10am-1pm & 4-7pm Tue-Sun mid-Jun–mid-Sep, 10am-12.30pm & 4-6.30pm Tue-Sun mid-Sep–mid-Jun), in particular its fragile-looking, early-16th-century cloisters. Along the edge of the old town are a series of rusty cliffs full of 6th-century cave houses. Unfortunately they've been closed to the public for many years. Buses between Logroño and Santo Domingo de la Calzada stop in Nájera.

San Millán de Cogolla

pop 270 / elev 733m

About 16km southwest of Nájera are two remarkable monasteries in the hamlet of San Millán de Cogolla, framed by a beautiful valley.

The **Monasterio de Yuso** (☎ 941 37 30 49; adult/child €4/1.50; 10.30am-1.30pm & 4-6.30pm Jun-Sep, 10.30am-

1pm & 4-6pm Oct-May), sometimes presumptuously called El Escorial de La Rioja, contains numerous treasures in its museum. You can only visit as part of a guided tour (in Spanish only; non-Spanish speakers will be given an information sheet). Tours last 50 minutes and run every half-hour or so.

A short distance away is the **Monasterio de Suso** (☎ 941 37 30 82; admission €3; 9.30am-1.30pm & 3.30-6.30pm Tue-Sun Jun-Sep, 9.30am-1.30pm & 3.30-6pm Tue-Sun Oct-May). Built above the caves where San Millán once lived, it was consecrated in the 10th century. It's believed that in the 13th century a monk named Gonzalo de Berceo wrote the first Castilian words here, although recent discoveries suggest otherwise (see the boxed text, p481). Again, it can only be visited on a guided tour. Tickets, which include the short bus ride up to the monastery, are sold by the very helpful **tourist office** (☎ 941 37 32 59) at the Monasterio de Yuso. Maps detailing short walks in the region can also be obtained at the tourist office.

Santo Domingo de la Calzada

pop 6260 / elev 630m

Santo Domingo is small-town Spain at its very best. A large number of the inhabitants continue to live in the partially walled old quarter, a labyrinth of medieval streets where the past is alive and vibrant and the sense of community is strong. It's the kind of place where you can be certain that the baker knows all his customers by name and that everyone will turn up for María's christening. Santiago-bound pilgrims have long been a part of the fabric of this town and that tradition continues to this day, with most visitors being foot-weary pilgrims. All this helps to make Santo Domingo one of the most enjoyable places in La Rioja.

The morose, monumental **cathedral** and its attached **museum** (adult/student €3.50/2.50, admission free Sun; 9.30am-1.30pm & 4-6.30pm Mon-Sat) glitter with gold that attests to the great wealth the Camino has bestowed on otherwise backwater towns. The cathedral's most eccentric feature is the Disneyesque white rooster and hen that forage in a glass-fronted cage opposite the entrance to the crypt. These two celebrate a longstanding legend, the Miracle of the Rooster, which tells of a young man who was unfairly executed only to recover miraculously, while the broiled cock and hen on the plate of his judge suddenly leapt up and chickened off, fully fledged.

If your idea of a religious-run hotel includes lumpy beds, 5am prayers and severe sisters then forget it, because the **Hospedería Sta Teresita** (☎ 941 34 07 00; Calle Pinar 2; s/d €32/54) is much more about elevators, swipe cards and business-standard rooms. **Hostal R Pedro** (☎ 941 34 11 60; www.hostalpedroprimero.es; Calle San Roque 9; s/d €50/61;) is a newly renovated town house with superb-value, terracotta-coloured rooms, wooden roof beams and entirely modern bathrooms.

our pick **Parador Santo Domingo Bernado de Fresneda** (☎ 941 34 11 50; www.parador.es; Plaza de San Francisco 1; s/d incl breakfast & dinner €95/139; P) is the antithesis of the town's general air of piety. Occupying a former monastery, the palatial hotel offers far and away the best *parador* value in the region. Why? Because it's used as a training centre for chefs, waiters and others to gain experience in the *parador* chain, which means that prices are kept artificially low and meals are included. You might imagine that this inexperience leads to poor service, but in fact it's quite the opposite, and we found this to be the most welcoming and least snooty of all the *paradores*.

There are a few lacklustre cafes and bars in the modern centre of town by the bus stop, but **Restaurante Río** (☎ 941 34 02 77; Calle Alberto Etchegoyen 2; menú €10) is a suitably small-town-Spain eating experience, with old men drinking wine before 10am, and fussing family owners.

Buses run to Burgos (€3.80, one hour, five daily), Logroño (€2.50, 45 minutes via Nájera, up to 13 daily on weekdays, fewer on weekends) and Haro (€1.20, 25 minutes, four daily).

WINE REGION

La Rioja wine rolls on and off the tongue with ease, by name as well by taste. All wine fanciers know the famous wines of La Rioja, where the vine has been cultivated since Roman times. The region is classic vine country and vineyards cover the hinterland of Río Ebro. On the river's north bank, the region is part of the Basque Country and known as La Rioja Alavesa.

Haro

pop 11,500 / elev 426m

Despite its fame in the wine world, there's not much of a heady bouquet to Haro, the capital of La Rioja's wine-producing region. But the town has a cheerful pace, and the compact old

IN SEARCH OF THE FINEST DROP

La Rioja is as much about serious wine drinking as it is holidaymaking. Well, there's a downside to everything!

Such research should be conducted only after proper training, so we recommend you begin at one or all of the region's wine museums. In Navarra there is the exceptional **Museo del Vino** (p509), in Olite, and **Quaderna Via** (☎ 948 55 40 83; fax 948 55 65 40; admission free; 🕑 8am-2pm & 4-7pm Mon-Fri, 10am-2pm Sat & Sun), around 4km west of Estella, near Igúzquiza. In La Rioja proper is Haro's excellent **Museo del Vino** (below) and, finally, the big daddy of them all, **Dinastía Vivanco** (opposite).

After all that history you'll be needing a drink. What will it be? Wine categories in La Rioja are termed Young, Crianza, Reserva and Gran Reserva. Young wines are in their first or second year and are inevitably a touch 'fresh'. Crianzas must have matured into their third year and have spent at least one year in the cask, followed by a few months resting in the bottle. Reservas pay homage to the best vintages and must mature for at least three full years in cask and bottle, with at least one year in the cask. Gran Reservas depend on the very best vintages, and are matured for at least two years in the cask followed by three years in the bottle. These are the 'velvet' wines.

Experts have developed a classification system for the years in which the wine was particularly good. Five stars (the maximum) were awarded in 1982, 1994, 1995, 2001 and 2004. Four-star years include 1981, 1987, 1991, 1996 and 1998.

The tourist offices in Haro, Laguardia and Logroño have lists of bodegas that can be visited throughout the region, although it usually requires ringing in advance to arrange a time. One exception is **Bodegas Muga** (below), which has set times for guided tours and tastings.

quarter, leading off Plaza de la Paz, has some intriguing alleyways with bars and wine shops in plenty. Keep an eye peeled for the huge stork's nest perched on the roof of the tourist office – if you have arrived here from the north then this is about the first place where you'll start to see these wonderful birds.

The **tourist office** (☎ 941 30 33 66; Plaza de Florentino Rodríguez; 🕑 10am-2pm & 4.30-7.30pm Tue-Sat, 10am-2pm Sun Jul-Sep, 10am-2pm Tue-Fri, 10am-2pm & 4-7pm Sat, 10am-2pm Sun Oct-Jun) is a couple of hundred metres along the road from Plaza de la Paz and has plenty of excellent information, including a list of wineries open to the public.

SIGHTS

The **Museo del Vino** (☎ 941 31 05 47; Bretón; admission €3, free Wed; 🕑 10am-2pm & 4-8pm Mon-Sat, 10am-2pm Sun), near the bus station, houses a detailed display on how wine is made and has helpful information in Spanish, French and English.

The winery **Bodegas Muga** (☎ 941 31 04 98; www.bodegasmuga.com), just after the railway bridge on the way out of town, gives guided tours and tastings in Spanish at 11.30am and 4.30pm Monday to Thursday and at 11.30am on Fridays. Technically you should book in advance, especially in low season, but in high season you can often just turn up and tack onto the back of a tour. For an English-language tour it's essential to book several days ahead.

FESTIVALS & EVENTS

On 29 June the otherwise mild-mannered citizens of Haro go temporarily berserk during the **Batalla del Vino** (Wine Battle), squirting and chucking wine all over each other in the name of San Juan, San Felices and San Pedro. Plenty of it goes down the right way too.

SLEEPING & EATING

Hostal La Peña (☎ 941 31 00 22; Calle La Vega 1; s/d €30/40) Just off Plaza de la Paz is this family-run, slightly old-fashioned place tiled in bold blue and white. Singles have shared bathrooms only.

Los Agustinos (☎ 941 31 13 08; hotelagustinos.com; Calle San Augustín 2; s/d/tr €96/120/155; P 💻) History hangs in the air of this luxurious hotel. The rooms are simply perfect but it's the stunning covered courtyard of this former monastery that steals the show. The only let-down is the reception, which is as snooty as you would expect from a posh address in a wine town.

Restaurante Beethoven I & II (☎ 941 31 11 81; Calle de Santo Tomás 5 & 10; menú from €16) The best places to fill hungry tummies in Haro are these two restaurants facing each other across the narrow street. Number II is more formal, but both offer excellent La Riojan cuisine, all of it complemented by the very best local wines.

There are plenty of cafes and bars around Plaza de la Paz and the surrounding streets.

GETTING THERE & AWAY

Regular trains connect Haro with Logroño (€3.65, 45 minutes), and buses additionally serve Vitoria, Bilbao, Santo Domingo de la Calzada and Laguardia.

Briones

pop 900 / elev 501m

One man's dream is putting the small, obscenely quaint village of Briones firmly on the Spanish wine and tourism map. The sunset-gold village crawls gently up a hillside and offers commanding views over the surrounding vine-carpeted plains, where you will find the fantastic **Dinastía Vivanco** (Museo de la Cultura del Vino; ☎ 902 32 00 01; adult/child/student €7.50/free/6.50; 10am-8pm Tue-Sun Jun-Sep, 10am-6pm Tue-Thu & Sun, 10am-8pm Fri & Sat Oct-May). This space-age museum is the creation of Pedro Vivanco Paracuello. As he relates in the cheesy introductory film, he wanted to leave a legacy to the land that has provided for his family for generations. This museum is that legacy and it truly is an incredible one. There can be few more advanced private museums in the country. Over several floors and numerous rooms you will learn all about the history and culture of wine and the various processes that go into its production. All of this is done through interesting displays brought to life with the latest in computer technology. The treasures on display include Picasso-designed wine jugs; Roman and Byzantine mosaics; gold-draped, wine-inspired religious artefacts; and the world's largest collection of corkscrews, including several in the shape of amusingly large penises (yes, we're easily entertained). At the end of the tour you can enjoy some wine tasting and, by booking in advance, you can join a tour of the winery (€6.50; in Spanish only).

The village itself is also worth exploring with the 16th-century **Iglesia de Santa María de la Asunción**, which contains a magnificent organ, an equally impressive altar, and a side chapel painted from head to toe with the great and good of the local Christian world. At the far end of the village are the very battered remains of an 11th-century **castle**, which now hide a small garden.

Currently the only place to rest wine-heavy heads is **Los Calaos de Briones** (☎ 941 32 21 31; www.loscalaosdebriones.com; Calle San Juan 13; r €58), which has pleasant rooms in shades of peach and sky-blue. Some have suitably romantic four-posters. The attached restaurant is stuffed with excellent locally inspired cuisine (mains €12 to €13).

The village is several kilometres southeast of Haro and a couple of buses a day trundle out here.

Laguardia

pop 1490 / elev 557m

It's easy to spin back the wheels of time in the medieval fortress town of Laguardia, or the 'Guard of Navarra' as it was once appropriately known, sitting proudly on its rocky hilltop.

THE NEW GUGGENHEIM

Its setting seems a little incongruous, but the tiny farming village of Elciego is the home of northern Spain's second Guggenheim. When the owner of the Bodegas Marqués de Riscal decided he wanted to create something special, he certainly didn't hold back. The result is the spectacular Frank Gehry–designed **Hotel Marqués de Riscal** (☎ 945 18 08 80; www.starwoodhotels.com/luxury; r €595). Costing around €85 million to construct and now managed by the Starwood chain, the building is a flamboyant wave of multicoloured titanium sheets that stands in utter contrast to the creaky old village behind it. Like the Guggenheim, this building is having a radical effect on the surrounding countryside, and has led to more tourists, more jobs, more wine sales and more money appearing in the hands of locals. Casual visitors are not, however, welcome at the hotel. If you want a closer look you have three options. The easiest is to join one of the bodega's **wine tours** (☎ 945 18 08 88; www.marquesderiscal.com; tours per person €10) – it's necessary to book in advance. You won't get inside the building, but you will get to see its exterior from some distance. A much closer look can be obtained by reserving a table at the expensive but excellent restaurant (*menú* €85) or the bistro (*menú* €50). For the most intimate look at the building, you'll need to reserve a room for the night, but be prepared to part with some serious cash!

The walled old quarter, which makes up most of the town, is virtually traffic-free and a sheer joy to wander around, but as well as memories of long-lost yesterdays, the town further entices with its wine-producing present.

The **tourist office** (☎ 945 60 08 45; Plaza de San Juan; 10am-2pm & 4-7pm Mon-Fri, 10am-2pm & 5-7pm Sat, 10.45am-5pm Sun) has a list of bodegas that can be visited in the local area. There are several ATMs around the town.

SIGHTS

Maybe the most impressive feature of the town is the castlelike **Puerta de San Juan**, one of the most stunning city gates in Spain. Equally impressive is the **Iglesia de Santa María de los Reyes** (☎ 945 50 08 45; guided tours €2), which has a breathtaking late-14th-century Gothic doorway, thronged with beautiful sculptures of the disciples and other motifs. The statue of Santa María de los Reyes has the looks of a heartbreaker. Just alongside the entrance to the church is a little plaza with a metal **sculpture** by the Vitoria artist Koko Rico, a delightful collection of casually displayed bags and boots.

SLEEPING & EATING

Laguardia has only a few places to stay, so if you are determined to stay here it may be wise to book ahead, especially at weekends and during holidays.

Restaurante Hostal Biazteri (☎ 945 60 00 26; www.biazteri.com; cnr Calles Mayor & Berberana; s/d €32/54) The calm rooms found here are the cheapest and simplest in town. The attached restaurant is about the most popular place to eat.

our pick **Casa Rural Legado de Ugarte** (☎ 945 60 01 14; legadodeugarte@hotmail.com; Calle Mayor 17; r incl breakfast €75) This is one that you're going to either love or hate – we love it. Recently renovated, the entrance and reception have more of the same olde-worlde flavour you'll be starting to get bored of, but the bright and very comfortable rooms are an arresting mix of purple, silver and gold pomp. If that sounds a little too much, it also has a more classic blue-and-white room. The gregarious host is charming.

Posada Mayor de Migueloa (☎ 945 62 11 75; www.mayordemigueloa.com; Mayor de Migueloa 20; s/d €90/115; P) For the ultimate in gracious La Rioja living, this old mansion-hotel is simply irresistible. Couples will be delighted to know that guests are supplied with a full range of massage oils and instructions on how to use them! The in-house restaurant offers fine local cuisine with meals starting at about €20.

GETTING THERE & AWAY

Six slow daily buses connecting Vitoria and Logroño pass through Laguardia.

Around Laguardia

Your own transport is essential for exploring here. There are several wine cellars that can be visited, often with advance notice – contact the tourist office in Laguardia for details. **Bodegas Palacio** (☎ 945 60 00 57; Carretera de Elciego), only 1km from Laguardia on the Elciego road, is one of the most receptive to visitors. The real stellar attraction of the area, though, is the **Bodegas Marqués de Riscal** (☎ 945 60 60 00; www.marquesderiscal.com), on the edge of the village of Elciego, 6km southwest of Laguardia (see the boxed text, p517).

Cantabria & Asturias

Rolling meadows and cattle pasture, craggy hills, cider-drinking and bagpipes. It might be an advertisement for a composite of Ireland and Wales, but no, it is the flip side of the typical image of Spain. The verdant emerald strip (between Galicia to the west and the Basque Country to the east) formed by Cantabria and Asturias is as beautiful as it is surprising.

The two regions share a spectacular coastline along the Bay of Biscay, alternating between sheer cliffs, tiny coves, small fishing and resort towns, and scores of sandy beaches. Stone villages dot the roads leading inland towards the chain-mail wall of mountains that forms the regions' southern boundary, the Cordillera Cantábrica – beyond which the landscape changes with amazing abruptness to the parched plains of the *meseta* (tableland). The mountains reach their greatest heights and grandeur in the Picos de Europa, a northern spur of the cordillera straddling southeast Asturias, southwest Cantabria and the north of Castilla y León.

It's not just bucolic beauty that attracts people here. From the prehistoric art of Altamira to the medieval splendours of Santillana del Mar, the area is dotted with man-made gems. The big three cities of Santander, Oviedo and Gijón all offer plenty of sightseeing and nocturnal diversions in their restaurants and bars.

The only drawback to 'green Spain' is what makes it green: the rain. Even in August you might endure a week of grey skies and showers, especially inland.

HIGHLIGHTS

- Sidle up for cider poured in the convivial **sidrerías** (cider houses; p538) of Asturias
- Ignore the pong and savour the tangy **Cabrales cheese** (p535
- Travel by train along the **Santander–Oviedo coastal corridor** (p895)
- Walk the **Garganta del Cares** (p558) in the Picos de Europa
- Let the medieval town of **Santillana del Mar** (p529) bewitch you with its charms
- Bathe at secluded **Playa del Silencio** (p548)
- Admire the ancient rock paintings at **Cueva de Altamira** (p532) and **Puente Viesgo** (p527)
- Take the plunge and canoe down the rapids of **Río Sella** (p555) near Ribadesella
- Marvel at the pre-Romanesque churches of **Oviedo** (p535)
- Admire a little Modernista madness in the buildings of Gaudí and Co at **Comillas** (p532)

■ AREA: 15,925 SQ KM	■ AVE SUMMER TEMP: HIGH 22°C, LOW 14°C	■ POP: 1.66 MILLION

CANTABRIA

It is no wonder the Romans had a hard time subduing the Cantabrian tribes. The lushness of the vegetation belies the difficulty of much of Cantabria's terrain. Sliced up by deep mountain valleys dotted with the occasional settlement, the region remained until recently virtually untouched by the modern legions of visitors that flock to Spain each year.

It offers a little of everything for the traveller looking for an escape. Some pretty beaches make summer seaside days quite possible (unreliable weather permitting), while the inland valleys, sprinkled with quiet towns and villages, offer a feast of natural beauty for the eyes, whether you choose to drive the country roads or walk the trails. The rugged ranges culminate in the west in the abrupt mountainous walls of the Picos de Europa.

The capital, Santander, offers a slice of urban life with its bustling bodegas (wine cellars) and handful of sights. The towns of Santillana del Mar and Comillas entice with their medieval and Modernista trappings. The remarkable cave paintings of the Cueva de Altamira, off limits to the public, can be admired in impressive replica form near the site.

Dotted around the region are more than 400 often beautifully restored country homes (which go by various names, such as *casas rurales* and *posadas*) to stay in. Check out www.turismocantabria.net, www.turismoruralcantabria.com or www.cantabriarural.com for listings. For camping grounds across the region, see www.campingsdecantabria.com (in Spanish). A good source of general information on the region is www.culturadecantabria.com (in Spanish).

The Romans, as reported, finally carried the day against the proud Cantabrians and pacified the area by around 19 BC. In more recent centuries, Cantabria was long regarded simply as a coastal extension of Castilla and as its direct gateway to what was confidently known as the Mar de Castilla (Castilian Sea). Cantabria became a separate region under Spain's 1978 constitution.

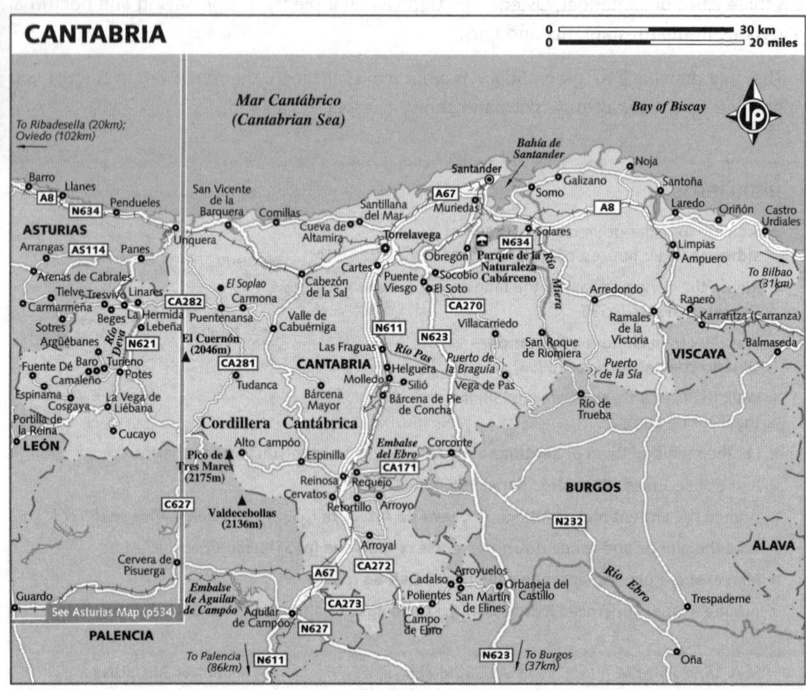

WHAT'S COOKING IN CANTABRIA?

Cantabria's eating habits vary considerably from the coast to the interior. *Sorropotún,* a northern tuna *(bonito)* and potato-based stew that fishermen used to take with them on long fishing expeditions in the Atlantic, is nowadays a speciality of San Vicente de la Barquera. Santander is perhaps the best place for fresh seafood, while the rivers inland are the source of trout and salmon. Perhaps the most popular mountain dish is *cocido montañés,* a hearty stew of white beans, cabbage, potato, chorizo, black pudding and sometimes port. Smelly-cheese lovers seek *queso picón* (a mix of cow's, sheep's and goat's milk), made in eastern Cantabria, especially in the villages of Tresviso and Beges (or Bejes).

SANTANDER

pop 181,800

Most of modern Santander, with its bustling centre, clanking port and shapeless suburbs, stands in drab contrast to its pretty beaches and, in particular, to the old-world elegance of El Sardinero. A huge fire raged through the city back in 1941, but what remains of the 'old' centre is now a lively source of entertainment for both the palate and the liver, and there's an atmosphere well worth stopping to savour. All up, however, Santander is a good deal more staid than its resort cousin, San Sebastián (p484).

History

When the Romans landed here in 21 BC, they named the place Portus Victoriae (Victory Harbour) and, indeed, within two years they had vanquished the Cantabrian tribes that had given them such strife.

From that time, Santander, as the city became known, led a modestly successful existence. Its heyday came rather late, when King Alfonso XIII made a habit of spending summer here in the 1900s. The locals were so pleased they gave him the Península de la Magdalena and built him a little palace there. Everyone who wanted to see and be seen converged on Santander, giving rise to a belle époque building boom – most evident around El Sardinero.

Orientation

The city stretches along the northern side of the handsome Bahía de Santander out to the Península de la Magdalena. North of the peninsula, Playa del Sardinero, the main beach, faces the open sea.

The ferry, train and bus stations are all within 500m of each other in the southwest part of the central district. A 10-minute walk northeast brings you to the heart of older Santander, then it's a half-hour stroll to the beaches. Most of the cheaper places to stay and many good restaurants and bars are in a compact area taking in the bus and train stations and the old quarter.

Information

Banks cluster in the newer part of central Santander around Avenida de Calvo Sotelo.

Ciberlope (www.ciberlope.com; Calle de Lope de Vega 14; from €1.20 per 30min; 10.30am-midnight Mon-Fri, 11.30am-midnight Sat, 5pm-midnight Sun) Internet access.

Hospital Marqués de Valdecilla (942 20 25 20; Avenida de Valdecilla 25)

Municipal tourist office (942 20 30 00; www.ayto-santander.es in Spanish; Jardines de Pereda; 9am-9pm daily mid-Jun–mid-Sep, 8.30am-1.30pm & 4-7pm Mon-Fri, 10am-2pm Sat mid-Sep–Easter, 8.30am-1.30pm & 4-7pm Mon-Fri, 10am-7pm Sat Easter–mid-Jun) A branch office in El Sardinero, opposite Plaza de Italia, operates in summer.

Post office (Plaza Alfonso XIII; 8.30am-8.30pm Mon-Fri, 9.30am-2pm Sat)

Regional tourist office (901 11 11 12, 942 31 07 08; www.turismodecantabria.com in Spanish; Calle de Hernán Cortés 4; 9am-9pm Jul-Sep, 9.30am-1.30pm & 4-7pm Oct-Jun) Located inside the rebuilt, originally 19th-century Mercado del Este. The telephone service is open from 9am to 9pm year-round.

Sights

The **cathedral** (942 22 60 24; Plaza del Obispo José Eguino y Trecu s/n; 10am-1pm & 4-8pm Mon-Fri, 10am-1pm & 4.30-8pm Sat, 10am-1.30pm & 5-9pm Sun & holidays) is composed of two 13th-century Gothic churches, one above the other. The upper church, off which is a 14th-century cloister, was extensively rebuilt after the 1941 fire. In the lower **Iglesia del Santísimo Cristo** (942 21 15 63; Calle de Somorrostro s/n; 8am-1pm & 4-8pm Jun-Sep, 8am-1pm & 5-8pm Oct-May) glass panels reveal excavated bits of Roman Santander under the floor. Displayed nearby are silver vessels containing the skulls of the early Christian martyrs San Emeterio and San Celedonio, Santander's patron saints.

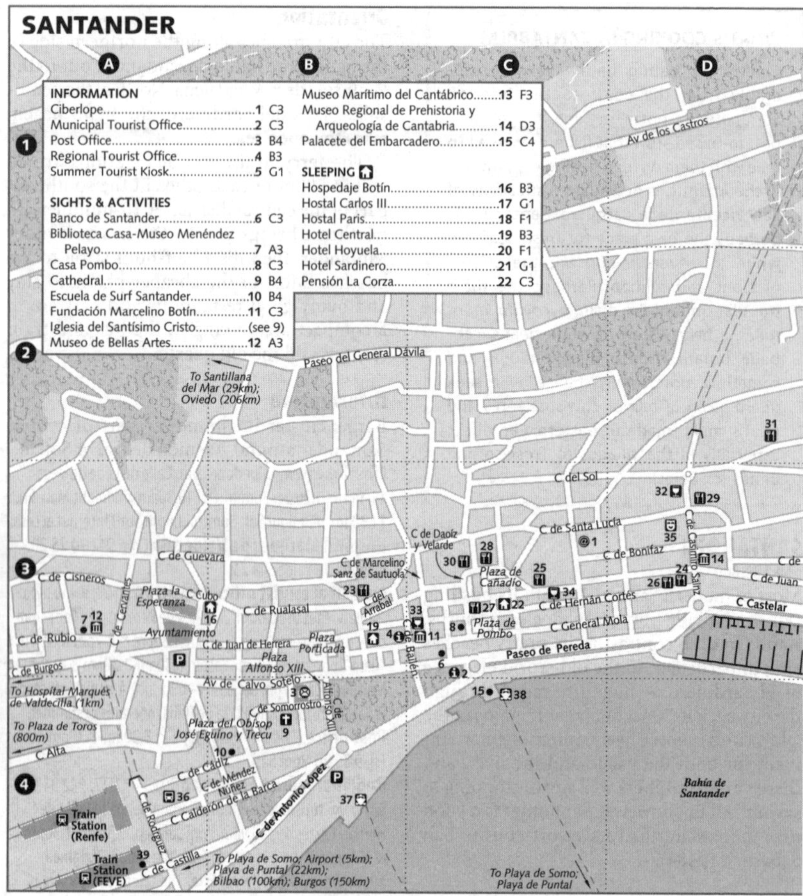

The care of these holy relics, found on this site, prompted the construction of the monastery that previously stood here.

To the east spreads the lovely **Jardines de Pereda**, named after the Cantabrian writer José María de Pereda, whose seminal work, *Escenas Montañesas,* is illustrated in bronze and stone here. You can't miss the grand **Banco de Santander** building (built in 1875), with the grand arch in the middle, across the road from the park. The facade is crowned by four statues representing the arts, culture, commerce and navigation. The Santander is one of Spain's biggest banks and a significant world player, so the architectural grandiloquence is not entirely misplaced.

One block north of the gardens is the stately **Plaza Porticada**, surrounded by 64 porticoes. It was created after the disastrous fire of 1941. A short walk east of here is one of the most pleasant corners of the old heart of Santander. Delightful **Plaza de Pombo** is dominated by the 19th-century **Casa Pombo** and its cafe terraces are perfect for a morning coffee. Nearby, lively **Plaza de Cañadío** is brimming with bars and gets quite boisterous at night.

Under one roof, the **Museo Regional de Prehistoria y Arqueología de Cantabria** (☎ 942 20 71 09; Calle de Casimiro Sainz 4) brings together collections of prehistoric finds from across the region, including some elements from the Cueva de Altamira (p532). Among the highlights are

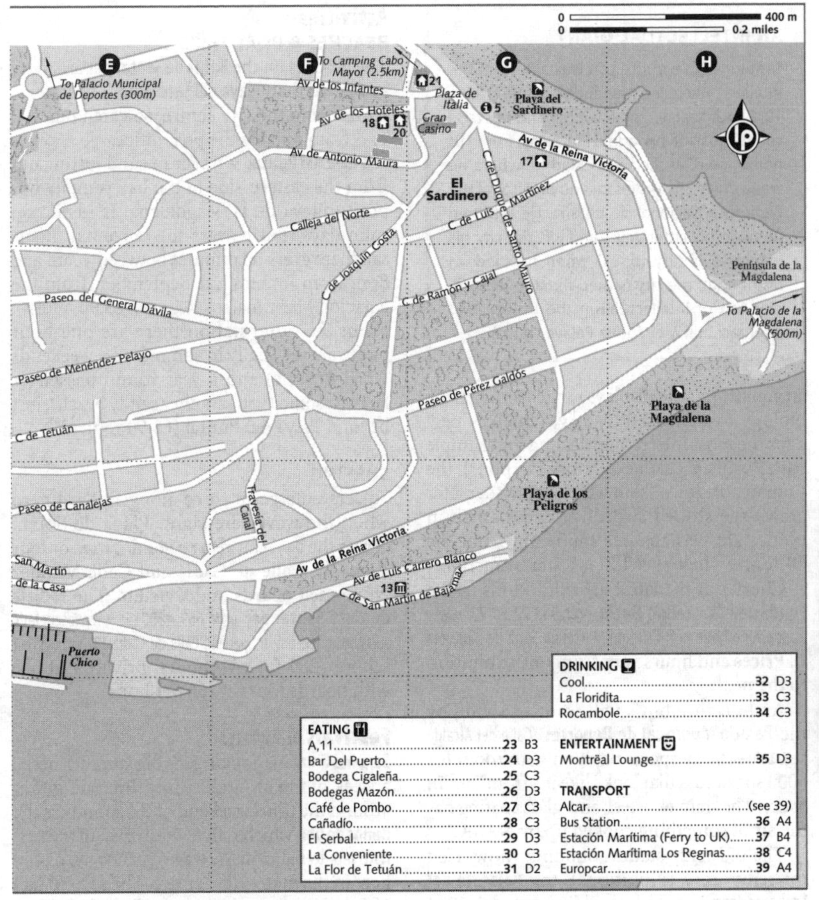

copies of cave paintings and some Roman stellae, accompanied by interpretations of their texts. There are (stalled) plans to transfer the collection to another location, and the museum was closed at the time of writing.

Make a giant leap closer to our times with a visit to the **Museo de Bellas Artes** (☎ 942 20 31 20; Calle de Rubio 6; admission free; 🕑 10.15am-1pm & 5.30-9pm Mon-Fri, 10am-1pm Sat), a sometimes fusty but eclectic art collection spanning the 16th to 20th centuries. Much of what's on show is secondary Spanish art: from about 1920 on the 1st floor; 1860–1920 on the 2nd floor; and earlier stuff, mixed in with a few Flemish, Italian and French works, on the 3rd floor. You'll find the odd curio, such as Goya's portrait of King Fernando VII. In an equally portentous building at the same address is the **Biblioteca Casa-Museo de Menéndez Pelayo** (☎ 942 23 45 34; Calle de Rubio 6; admission free; 🕑 9am-11.30pm), a vast old library that belonged to this learned local, whose one-time house and office stands next door. Upon his death in 1912, Pelayo left the city this precious library of 40,000 volumes. See the boxed text, p524.

If seafaring is your thing, visit the **Museo Marítimo del Cantábrico** (☎ 942 27 49 62; www.museosdecantabria.com in Spanish; Calle San Martín de Bajamar s/n; adult/senior, student & 4-12yr €6/4; 🕑 10am-7.30pm Tue-Sun May-Sep, 10am-6pm Tue-Sun Oct-Apr), near the bay beaches. The four-floor museum covers all facets of navigation in Cantabria, and includes

AN INTELLECTUAL GIANT

Santander's favourite son was a hero of the intellect. Marcelino Menéndez Pelayo (1856–1912) was teacher, philosopher and poet. He spent most of his adult life away from his home town, especially in Madrid, where he was a university professor and director of the Biblioteca Nacional de España. He returned home in his latter years and left the city his extensive library (p523) when he died. In his honour, the city named the annual summer fest of intellectualism the Universidad Internacional Menéndez Pelayo (right).

an aquarium. The displays range from marine biology to maritime history, which is perhaps the most interesting, dealing for example with Portus Victoriae (Victory Harbour), the Roman port town from which Santander later grew. The stuffed swordfish and starfish in bottles are perhaps less captivating, but the 60-tonne whale skeleton is a star attraction.

Check out the latest art exhibitions in the **Fundación Marcelino Botín** (☎ 942 22 60 72; www.fundacionmbotin.org; Calle de Marcelino Sanz de Sautuola 3). Prices and hours vary from one exhibition to the next.

Architecture buffs will want to swing by the **Palacio Municipal de Deportes** (Calle del Alcalde Vega Lamera s/n), a sports pavilion with room for 6000 spectators that looks like it's from *Lost in Space*. The stainless-steel-and-glass coating has the air of something cooked up by NASA.

The old ferry station building (now used for temporary exhibitions), the **Palacete del Embarcadero**, is a quirky building raised in 1932 that recalls another era and even another place – there's a touch of Brighton about it. The bayfront promenade that stretched east to the Puerto Chico (Little Port) is lined with opulent buildings, characterised by their glassed-in balconies, the fruit of early-20th-century boom times.

The **Península de la Magdalena** (🕑 8am-10pm Jun-Sep, 8am-8.30pm Oct-May) parklands are perfect for a stroll and popular with picnickers. Kids will enjoy the sea lions and the little train that choo-choos around the headland. The peninsula is crowned by the **Palacio de la Magdalena**, the former royal palace. It's an exuberant and eclectic pile, built from 1908 to 1912 and used by the royal family every summer until 1930.

Activities

BEACHES & BOAT TRIPS

The beaches on the **Bahía de Santander** are more protected than **Playa del Sardinero**. The latter is a hike from the city centre, so catch bus 1, 2 or 3 from outside the post office.

Playa del Puntal, a finger of sand jutting out from the eastern side of the bay roughly opposite Playa de la Magdalena, is idyllic on calm days (but beware the currents). Boats sail there every 30 minutes between 10am and 8pm from June to late September, from the Estación Marítima Los Reginas (€3.90 return). From the same station there are one-hour bay tours (€8) daily in summer (on weekends April to June) and a year-round passenger ferry to Somo (with another sandy beach), just beyond Playa del Puntal (€3.90 return).

SURFING

Surfers emerge in force along El Sardinero when the waves are right. Playa de Somo, across the bay, can also be good. Three or four shops on Calle de Cádiz and Calle Méndez Núñez sell boards and wetsuits. The **Escuela de Surf Santander** (☎ 669 488015; www.escueladesurfsantander.com in Spanish; Calle de Cádiz 19) is a surf school (€50 for two hours' private tuition) with boards for rent (€6 per hour).

Festivals & Events

Semana Grande is Santander's big summer fiesta, a week of fun around 25 July. Preceding this, around the third weekend of the month, is the **Baños de Ola**, which relives the arrival of the first tourists to bathe in the waves (hence the name) here in the mid-19th century. The second half of July is also marked by the **Feria de Santiago** bullfighting competitions held in the **Plaza de Toros** (☎ 942 33 22 89; Calle de Montevideo). Right through summer, the Palacio de la Magdalena hosts the **Universidad Internacional Menéndez Pelayo** (www.uimp.es in Spanish), a global get-together for specialists in all sorts of disciplines. The **Festival Internacional de Santander** (www.festivalsantander.com) is a sweeping musical review in August, covering everything from jazz to chamber music.

Sleeping

Loads of budget spots can be found around the train and bus stations. Down by fashionable Playa del Sardinero, the cheaper places tend to close from about October to mid-May. The pick of the middle- and top-range digs are also down that way.

Camping Cabo Mayor (☎ 942 39 15 42; www.cabomayor.com; Avenida del Faro s/n; sites per 2 adults, car & tent €21; P) This place is out towards the Cabo Mayor lighthouse, beyond Playa del Sardinero. Take bus 9 from Jardines de Pereda. It provides free hot showers, a supermarket and laundry facilities. It also has bungalows that sleep two and four. It's about a 300m walk to the beach.

Hospedaje Botín (☎ 942 21 00 94; www.hospedajebotin.com; Calle de Isabel II 1; s/d €38/55) The homey Botín has some spacious rooms with showers and *galerías* (glassed-in balconies).

Pensión La Corza (☎ 942 21 29 50; Calle de Hernán Cortés 25; r with/without bathroom €55/42) The best deal around, La Corza is on pleasant Plaza de Pombo. It has high-ceilinged, handsomely furnished rooms up on the 3rd floor, some with balconies overlooking the square.

Hostal Carlos III (☎/fax 942 27 16 16; Avenida de la Reina Victoria 135; s/d €57/76; Easter-Oct) Frosted-glass fixtures and painted mouldings adorn this vintage (and somewhat worn), turreted structure. Some rooms are in the ugly front building but you will be rewarded with sea views.

Hostal Paris (☎ 942 27 23 50; www.hparis.net; Avenida de los Hoteles 6; s/d €85/112; P) This charmer in off-white boasts rooms dominated by the same colour theme. Otherwise they are quite different from one another, but the overall effect is a lingering sensation of the late 19th century. Parquet floors, spare but elegant furnishings and, in some cases, nice architectural touches (such as the setting of the sleeping area in an alcove) make this an attractive choice.

Hotel Sardinero (☎ 942 27 11 00; www.gruposardinero.com; Plaza de Italia 1; d €130-155) This grand old seaside hotel evokes the area's golden age. Rooms are a trifle small but pleasingly furnished, with high ceilings. Try for those with sea views. Single rates (from €66) are available outside of the July–August peak season.

Hotel Central (☎ 942 22 24 00; www.elcentral.com; Calle General Mola 5; s/d €95/147) A century-old hotel of a startling blue hue, the Central is what its name suggests, smack in the heart of the city. Rooms are spacious and originally decorated (with steel blues in the colour scheme in some). Singles are smallish. Top-floor terrace rooms (€157) with unbeatable bay views are worth the extra.

Hotel Hoyuela (☎ 942 28 26 28; www.gruposardinero.com; Avenida de los Hoteles 7; d €239; P) The Hoyuela emanates the classic sense of Santander's golden seaside age and elegance. The cream decor and soft carpet make for soothing rooms. Downstairs is an equally elegant restaurant, and you're not far from the beach. Prices drop to as little €75 in the low season.

Eating

You can sit down for a few snacks in a tapas bar, dig into hearty local food in a no-nonsense bodega or head further upmarket in any number of restaurants. Santander's waterfront promenades brim with cafes and ice-cream stands.

BUDGET

Café de Pombo (☎ 942 22 32 24; Calle de Hernán Cortés 21; 8am-midnight) On the square of the same name, this is one of the city's most pleasant and elegant lingering breakfast stops. A hot chocolate on the square comes in at €1.75.

A,11 (☎ 942 07 43 62; Calle del Arrabal 11; tapas & raciones €1.30-12; Mon-Sat) Gourmet sophistication and big-city-style bright lights have landed here, a respectful distance from the classic bodegas but packed to screaming point with locals after something a little different.

Bodega Cigaleña (☎ 942 21 30 62; Calle de Daoíz y Velarde 19; pinchos from €2; Mon-Sat) A lovely and classic bar for tapas, wine and laughter, this is one of the best and most popular of its ilk in the old town.

Bodegas Mazón (☎ 942 21 57 52; Calle de Hernán Cortés 57; raciones €5-12) This cavernous wine cellar serves up varied *raciones* (large tapas servings) at a long timber bar. The selections are chalked on great lumbering vats and behind you are piled huge barrels of wine and sherry. Proceed out the back for a sit-down meal.

our pick **La Conveniente** (☎ 942 21 28 87; Calle de Gómez Oreña 9; meals €15-20; dinner Mon-Sat) This cavernous bodega has high stone walls, wooden pillars and beams, and more wine bottles than you may ever have seen in one place. Squeeze into the tramlike enclosure at the front or line up for a seat out back (or just snack at the bar). You might go for a cheese *tabla* (platter) or other classic *raciones*. Servings are generous.

MIDRANGE & TOP END

La Flor de Tetuán (☎ 942 21 83 53; Calle de Tetuán 25; meals €30-40; Mon-Sat) This is a simple seafood delight, offering anything from a salad filled with crayfish to a slab of catch-of-the-day lightly grilled. Most items are sold by weight. This is the best of a series of four seafood eateries on this strip.

Bar Del Puerto (☎ 942 21 30 01; Calle de Hernán Cortés 63; meals €35-45; ⏰ lunch & dinner daily Jun-Sep, lunch & dinner Tue-Sat, lunch Sun Oct-Apr) With its grand windows looking out over the waterfront of the Puerto Chico, this is the perfect spot for damn near perfect seafood. Your choice of critter will have a huge influence on the fiscal outlay.

Cañadío (☎ 942 31 41 49; www.restaurantecanadio.com; Calle de Gómez Oreña 15; meals €45; ⏰ Mon-Sat) A tastefully modernised place with art on the red walls, high-backed chairs, fine linen and timber floors, Cañadío offers creative cooking with local inspiration. They prepare hake every which way.

El Serbal (☎ 942 22 25 15; www.elserbal.com; Calle de Andrés del Río 7; meals €50; ⏰ lunch & dinner Tue-Sat, lunch Sun, closed Feb) Probably the best restaurant in town, this is an elegantly understated place beneath a brick high-rise apartment block. It offers modern, imaginative twists on essentially typical northern Spanish food – like tossing *calçots,* a quintessentially Catalan item, into a wok with seafood, pine nuts and *romesco* sauce (see the boxed text, p376). You could let rip with a tasting menu (€60).

Drinking & Entertainment

Plaza de Cañadío is home to several *bares de copas,* where you can enjoy an outdoor beer in the evening. Calle de Santa Lucía, along with Calle del Río de la Pila and its immediate neighbourhood, also teems with bars of all descriptions. Most stay open until between 3am and 4am.

La Floridita (☎ 942 22 33 09; www.floriditasantander.com; Calle de Bailén 4) A tropically themed nightspot attracting a broad age group, Floridita has a luminous green bar, big cocktails and wi-fi.

Cool (Calle de San Emeterio 3) Despite the beyond-capacity crowds, this small hash-infused club stays pretty relaxed, with everyone getting their dose of funky music and sweet fumes.

Rocambole (☎ 942 36 49 61; Calle de Hernán Cortés 37; ⏰ 10pm-5am) The action often goes on till dawn at this dimly lit, basement rock-music bar. Make for the jazz 'n' jam sessions from 10pm on Thursdays.

Montrëal Lounge (Calle de Santa Lucía; ⏰ 1am-6.30am Thu-Sat) For clubbing, you could head to this inner-city hang-out, which attracts a boisterous and fairly young crowd.

Getting There & Away

AIR

The airport is about 5km south of town at Parayas. A handful of daily flights serve Madrid and Barcelona. Ryanair has flights from Dublin, London Stansted, Frankfurt (Hahn), Bergamo (for Milan) and Rome (Ciampino).

BOAT

From Plymouth in the UK, **Brittany Ferries** (☎ UK 0870 907 6103, Spain 942 36 06 11; www.brittany-ferries.co.uk) runs a twice-weekly car ferry to Santander (20½ hours) from mid-March to mid-November. Fares can vary enormously. Two people travelling with a car in August might pay UK£454 one way for a standard interior cabin when booking in May.

BUS

From the **bus station** (☎ 942 21 19 95; www.santandereabus.com), ALSA runs at least six buses daily to/from Madrid (€26.50 to €39, 5¼ to 6½ hours). Frequent runs connect with Bilbao (€6.50, 1½ to two hours) and at least six daily with San Sebastián (€12.50, 2½ to four hours), Irún and the French border. ALSA also runs at least seven times daily to Oviedo (€12.60 to €21.70, 2¼ to 3¼ hours), with most buses stopping in Llanes, but only two or three daily calling in at Arriondas and Ribadesella.

CAR & MOTORCYCLE

Heading west, take the A67 for Torrelavega for a quick getaway. The N623 to Burgos – a pretty route – is the main road south. All traffic heads out of the city along the south side of the train station.

Europcar (☎ 942 21 78 17) is inside the FEVE train station. Next door, local company **Alcar** (☎ 942 21 47 06) rents small cars (like Peugeot 107s) for €45 a day.

TRAIN

There are two train stations. **Renfe** (☎ 902 24 02 02; www.renfe.es) has three trains daily to/from Madrid (€43.90, 4½ to 5¼ hours) via Palencia and Reinosa. Three trains run daily to/from Valladolid (€26.20, 3¼ hours).

FEVE (☎ 942 20 95 22; www.feve.es), next door, operates two trains daily to/from San Vicente de la Barquera, Llanes and Oviedo (€13.20, 4¾ hours), and three to/from Bilbao (€7.25, 2½ to three hours).

Getting Around

Santander **buses** (www.tusantander.es in Spanish) cost €1 per ride. Purchase a 10-ride ticket for €5.80 at tobacco stands throughout the city.

AROUND SANTANDER

Puente Viesgo & Around

pop 2650

The valley town of Puente Viesgo, 25km south of Santander on the N623 towards Burgos, lies at the foot of the conical Monte Castillo. About 1.5km up this mountain stretch the impressive **Cuevas del Castillo** (☎ 942 59 84 25; each cave adult/under 4yr/4-12yr €3/free/1.50; 9.30am-8pm daily May-Sep, 9.30am-5pm Wed-Sun Oct-Apr). The two caves on view, El Castillo and La Moneda, contain prehistoric wall paintings of various animals that are just as breathtaking as those at Cueva de Altamira (p532), but these are the genuine article rather than copies. In between the art, there's a labyrinth of stalactites and stalagmites in an astounding array of shapes. El Castillo has more paintings. In summer it's mandatory to book a day ahead.

The town also has some local fame for the medicinal qualities of its baths, and its salmon and trout farms. To pamper yourself, visit or stay at the **Gran Hotel Balneario** (☎ 942 59 80 61; www.balneariodepuenteviesgo.com; Calle de Manuel Pérez Mazo s/n; s/d €140/170; baths 8.30am-9pm; P), where you can indulge in all sorts of treatments, from a simple paddle in hot baths (€15 for about 20 minutes) to mixed sessions of anything from shiatsu to specific treatments for backache.

Seven buses run to Puente Viesgo from Santander Monday to Friday (€1.95, 35 to 45 minutes), with fewer on weekends.

Those with a vehicle should head northeast of Puente Viesgo about 3km to admire the 12th-century **Colegiata de Santa Cruz de Castañeda** in the village of Socobio. It is one of the finest Romanesque churches in Cantabria, and displays elements of later periods too. About a 1km walk away is the **Palacio de Alvear**, a 16th-century tower with surrounding buildings in a pleasant park.

Langre

About 20km east of Santander by car (follow the signs for Somo and then proceed to Galizano) are the wild beaches of Langre, backed by cliffs topped with green fields. Most people head for Langre Grande (car park €3), although nearby Langre Pequeña is more protected.

Parque de la Naturaleza Cabárceno

This open-air **zoo** (☎ 902 21 01 12; www.parquedecabarceno.com; adult/under 6yr/6-12yr Mar-Oct €18/free/12, Nov-Feb €12/free/8; 9.30am-7pm Apr-Sep, 9.30am-6pm Oct-Mar) is a curious experiment, a free-range home on the site of former open-cut mines for everything from buffaloes to watussis (big-horned African quadrupeds). In 2005 an elephant was born in captivity here. Buses run the 20km from Santander to Obregón (€1.40, 30 to 50 minutes), from where you can enter the park.

EASTERN CANTABRIA

The 95km stretch of coast between Santander and Bilbao offers jaded citizens of both cities several seaside bolt holes. Some, such as Noja, are little more than beaches fronted by rows of holiday flats.

Santoña

The fishing port of Santoña is dominated by two forts, **Fuerte de San Martín** and, further north, the abandoned **Fuerte de San Carlos**. You can take a pleasant walk around both, or plonk yourself on sandy Playa de San Martín. You could also head off for a hike in the hilly parkland east of the town centre. Otherwise, head north along the C141 to **Playa Berria**, a magnificent sweep of sand on the open Mar Cantábrico. Down here, one of the best sleeping options is **Hotel Juan de la Cosa** (☎ 942 66 12 38; www.hoteljuandelacosa.com; Playa de Berria 14; s/d €88/116). It's a brutish-looking building, but inside the blue-hued rooms are generally spacious (shame about the carpet!). From the 2nd floor up you have nice views of the beach.

Nine buses run Monday to Saturday (four on Sundays) to/from Santander (€3.60, 50 to 65 minutes), and a regular passenger ferry (9am to 8pm May to September) crosses the estuary to the western end of Laredo beach (€1.50). Hourly buses link Santoña with Playa Berria.

Laredo

Tacked on to one end of a long sandy beach, the compact, cobblestoned *puebla vieja* (old town) of Laredo makes for a pleasant stroll. Locals gather in several bars on Rua Mayor for early-evening tipples and banter. For an abundant *arroz con bogavante* (lobster and seafood rice) for two (€45), call in at the stone-walled **Restaurante La Abadía** (☎ 942 61 14 89; Rua Mayor 18; meals €35-40; ⏰ Thu-Tue). If they could just turn the telly down!

Several buses from Santander (€3.80, 40 minutes) call in here.

Playa de Oriñón

One of the nicer beaches along this coast is at Oriñón, 14km east of Laredo. Popular on summer weekends, the broad sandy strip is set deep behind protective headlands, making the water calm and *comparatively* warm. In contrast, you'll find a chilly sea and some surfable waves on the windward side of the western headland. The settlement itself is made up of drab holiday flats. Up to 10 buses a day head from Castro Urdiales to Oriñón (30 minutes).

Castro Urdiales

pop 29,700

The haughty Gothic jumble that is the **Iglesia de Santa María de la Asunción** (⏰ 10am-1.30pm & 4-7pm Jul & Aug, 4-6pm Sep-Jun) stands out above the harbour and the tangle of narrow lanes that make up the medieval centre of Castro Urdiales. It could be a seaside set for *The Name of the Rose*. The church shares its little headland with the ruins of what was for centuries the town's defensive bastion, now supporting a lighthouse.

Of the two beaches, the westerly **Playa de Ostende** is the more attractive. High above and all around the old town rise the serried ranks of high-density housing (mostly aimed at commuters to Bilbao) that have gone up since the late 1990s, blighting various parts of the Cantabrian coast. Even the bursting of the property bubble in 2008 can't seem to put a stop to the continuing (and frequently illegal) scenic massacre.

Find out about other beaches in the area at the **tourist office** (☎ 942 87 15 12; Avenida de la Constitución 1; ⏰ 9am-9pm Jul–mid-Sep, 9am-2pm & 5-7pm mid-Sep–Jun), by the fishing port in the heart of the town.

Several places to stay are scattered about the old centre. **Hostal La Mar** (☎ 942 87 05 24; Calle de la Mar 27; s/d €36/56) is one of the best. It's one block from the waterfront and has crisp and functional, if unexciting, rooms, some of which look onto the narrow pedestrian street.

Traditional fare, such as *sopa de pescado* (fish soup) and *pudín de cabracho* (seafood pâté), abounds in *mesones* (old-style eateries) and *tabernas* (taverns) along Calle de la Mar and Calle de Ardigales, and in front of the fishing boats at Plaza del Ayuntamiento.

ALSA (Calle de Leonardo Rucabado 2) runs up to 10 buses daily to/from Santander (€5.35, one hour). Bizkaibus has buses to/from Bilbao (€3.10, one hour) every half-hour, making various stops in town, including at Bar La Ronda, on the corner of Calle La Ronda and Calle de Benito Pérez Galdós.

Eastern Valleys

Short on specific sights but rich in unspoiled rural splendour, the little-visited valleys of eastern Cantabria are ripe for exploration. Plenty of routes suggest themselves: what follows is but a sample.

From El Soto, on the N623 just south of Puente Viesgo, take the CA270 southeast towards Vega de Pas. The town is of minimal interest, but the drive is something. The views from the **Puerto de la Braguía pass** in particular are stunning. From Vega de Pas continue southeast, briefly crossing into Castilla y León, before turning north again at Río de Trueba,

TOOLING ABOUT IN CAVES

Cantabria is laced with caves (9000 according to one estimate) and the area around the Río Asón accounts for about half of them. Around 10 have been selected for incorporation into the **Red de Cuevas de Alto Asón** (☎ 942 64 65 04; www.altoason.com in Spanish). The caves range from easy to difficult and guided visits with speleologists can be organised – in advance. One that is easy to visit (but should still be booked) is the **Cueva Cullavera** (☎ 902 99 92 22; adult/child €6/4; ⏰ 9.40am-1.40pm & 4-7pm May-Sep, 10am-1pm & 3-4pm Oct-Apr). The 400m walk from the centre of the town of **Ramales de la Victória** is considered part of one-hour visit. The cave is a huge cavity with some signs of prehistoric art. For more information on this and other Cantabrian caves, check out www.cuevasdecantabria.es. Ramales is an hour's bus ride from Santander (€4.95) but there are only one or two departures a day. It's a wonderful scenic route with some great lookout points.

CANTABRIA & ASTURIAS

then following Río Miera down through San Roque de Riomiera towards Santander.

Another option from Río de Trueba is to take the BU571 road up over the Puerto de la Sía pass towards Arredondo. This road is full of switchbacks, a couple of mountain passes and isolated farmhouses.

SOUTHERN CANTABRIA

Fine panoramas of high peaks and deep river valleys flanked by patchwork quilts of green await the traveller penetrating the Cantabrian interior. Every imaginable shade of green seems to have been employed to set this stage, strewn with warm stone villages and held together by a network of narrow country roads.

From the industrial centre of Torrelavega, the N611 road winds south along the Río Besaya. This has long been the traditional route between the coast and Castilla – during their wars with Cantabrian tribes, the Romans built a road from Palencia province in Castilla y León to Suances. Parts of it are still visible today.

On the way south to Reinosa, curiosities include the Palacio de Hornillos in **Las Fraguas**, built by an English gent in the 19th century and indeed looking very much like an English country seat. A few kilometres further south, in **Helguera**, is a rare 10th-century Mozarabic church. After another few kilometres, a turn to the east takes you to **Silió**, site of a much renovated Romanesque church. If you manage to be here on the first Sunday of January you may catch the Vijanera, an ancient Carnival-like celebration in which locals dress up in spooky masks and outfits as part of a ritual to chase off the old year and welcome the new.

Reinosa (population 10,200), the main town in southern Cantabria, is dreary, with little to stop for, except perhaps to look at the mansions around the central Plaza de España. But the **Colegiata de San Pedro** in Cervatos, 5km south, is one of Cantabria's finest Romanesque churches.

Inquire at Reinosa's **tourist office** (☎ 942 75 52 15; http://turismoreinosa.es; Avenida del Puente de Carlos III 23; 9.30am-2.30pm Mon-Fri) for information on *senderos* (walking routes) if a little rambling in the area appeals to you.

If you get stuck in Reinosa, you'll find a half-dozen sleeping options. Set in a charmingly restored, turn-of-the-20th-century Modernista building, the **Villa Rosa** (☎ 942 75 47 47; www.villarosa.com; Calle de los Héroes de la Guardia Civil 4; d €80) is what it says it is – pink. It looks more like something you'd expect in central Europe and the 12 rooms have an inviting period feel. It's also handy for the train and bus stations.

Three regional trains (€5.15, 1½ hours) and two or three more expensive long-distance trains head to/from Santander daily. Up to 11 buses (€5.35, up to 1½ hours) head to/from Santander.

Along the Río Ebro

The Río Ebro (from whence 'Iberia' stems) rises about 6km west of Reinosa, fills the Embalse del Ebro reservoir and then meanders south and east into Castilla y León. You can follow its course along minor roads out of Reinosa.

Head first along the CA171 towards Corconte, then turn right at Requejo to cross over to the reservoir. Follow the southern shore towards Arroyo and you quickly reach the ruins of Roman **Julióbriga** (adult/child €3/1.50; 10.30am-12.30pm & 4-7pm Wed-Sun), just outside Retortillo. A *domus* (Roman house) has been recreated here and it contains a small museum.

Just before Arroyo, turn right (south). Along this exceedingly narrow route, you encounter the **Monasterio de Montes Claros**, dating from the 9th century. Next, descend to Arroyal and finally hit a T-junction where the CA272 meets the CA273. About 13km east is **Polientes**, where you'll find banks, a petrol station and four places to stay. Along or just off the road, several medieval chapels hewn from the rock can be visited. The best example, the **Iglesia de Santa María de Valverde**, is actually about 10km west of the T-junction. Eastwards, there are chapels at **Campo de Ebro** and, beyond Polientes, **Cadalso** and **Arroyuelos**.

Across the Ebro from Arroyuelos, **San Martín de Elines** has a fine Romanesque church and marks the end of the line for a daily bus from Reinosa via Polientes. With your own transport you can push on for Orbaneja del Castillo (p263) in Castilla y León.

WESTERN CANTABRIA

Santillana del Mar

pop 4000

They say this is the city of the three lies, since it is not holy *(santi)*, flat *(llana)* or on the sea *(del mar)*! Some good-looking liar! This medieval jewel is in such a perfect state of preservation, with its bright cobbled streets and tanned stone and brick buildings huddling in a muddle of centuries of history, that it seems too good to be true. Surely it's a film set! Well, no. People still live here, passing their precious houses down from generation to generation.

You could easily pass by on the motorway and never be the wiser. Strict town planning rules were first introduced back in 1575, and today they include the stipulation that only residents or guests in hotels with garages may bring in their vehicles. Other hotel guests may drive to unload luggage and must then return to the car park at the town entrance.

Santillana is a bijou in its own right, but makes an obvious overnight base for visiting the nearby Cueva de Altamira too.

Banks, a post office, telephones and a bookshop all cluster on or near the handsome Plaza de Ramón Pelayo (aka Plaza Mayor). You'll find an informative **tourist office** (☎ 942 81 88 12; Calle del Escultor Jesús Otero 20; 🕑 9am-9pm Jul-Sep, 9.30am-1.30pm & 4-7pm Oct-Jun) at the main car park. You can also get information on the town at www.santilla nadelmar.com.

SIGHTS

A stroll along the cobbled main street, past solemn nobles' houses from the 15th to 18th centuries, leads you to the lovely 12th-century Romanesque **Colegiata de Santa Juliana** (admission €3; 🕑 10am-1.30pm & 4-7.30pm daily Jun-Sep, 10am-1.30pm & 4-6.30pm Tue-Sun Oct-May). The drawcard in this former monastery is the cloister, a formidable storehouse of Romanesque handiwork, with the capitals of its columns carved into a huge variety of figures. The sepulchre of Santa Juliana, a 3rd-century Christian martyr from Turkey (and the real source of the name Santillana), stands in the centre of the church. The monastery and town grew up around the saint's relics, which arrived here after her death.

Admission to the Colegiata includes entry to the **Museo Diocesano** (☎ 942 84 03 17; www.santil lanamuseodiocesano.com; Calle del Cruce; 🕑 10am-1.30pm & 4-7.30pm daily Jun-Sep, 10am-1.30pm & 4-6.30pm Tue-Sun Oct-May) at the other end of town. The former Dominican monastery contains a fascinating collection of 'popular' polychrome wooden statuary, some of it quite bizarre.

Santillana also hosts an eclectic bunch of museums, cultural foundations and exhibitions. The **Museo El Solar** (☎ 942 84 02 73; Calle del Escultor Jesús Otero 1; adult/under 13yr/senior & student €3.60/free/2.40; 🕑 10am-9pm Apr-Sep, 10.30am-8pm Oct-Mar) houses an exhibition on the Inquisition, displaying more than 70 charming instruments of torture used in its unremitting battle against heresy. The **Fundación Santillana** (☎ 942 81 82 03; Plaza de Ramón Pelayo; admission free; 🕑 9am-2pm & 3.30-7.15pm Mon-Thu, 9am-3pm Fri) and the **Palacio Caja Cantabria** (☎ 942 81 81 71; Calle de Santo Domingo 8; adult/child €2.50/free; 🕑 11am-2pm & 4-8pm Tue-Sun) stage temporary exhibitions from around the world. The 14th-century **Torre del Merino** (☎ 942 81 82 89; Plaza de Ramón Pelayo) is a medieval tower also sometimes used for temporary exhibitions; it was closed at time of writing.

SLEEPING

There are dozens of places to stay, an inordinate number of them in atmospheric historic buildings converted for your comfort and pleasure. They are scattered about the old part of town and along the roads towards the Cueva de Altamira and Santander. Some close from about November to February.

Camping Santillana (☎ 942 81 82 50; www.can tabria.com/complejosantillana; sites per 2 people, car & tent €23; P 🏊) Just west of Santillana del Mar on the Comillas road, this camping ground has good facilities, including bungalows, supermarket, kids' playground, tennis court and restaurant.

Posada Santa Juliana (☎ 942 84 01 06; Calle Carrera 19; d €57) A short walk in from the main road, this charming *casona* (medieval house) has six smallish but tastefully restored doubles with creaking timber floors and wooden furniture. Inquire at Los Nobles restaurant opposite.

Posada La Solana (☎ 942 81 81 06; www.posadala solana.com; Camino de los Hornos 12; d €73; P) Smack in the heart of old Santillana, this two-storey grey stone house has 10 fairly simple but welcoming rooms, with tile floors and, in some cases, ceilings with timber beams. Room prices almost halve in the low-season.

Hotel Siglo XVIII (☎ 942 84 02 10; www.hotelsigloxviii .com; Calle de Revolgo 38; s/d €48/78; 🕑 closed mid-Dec–Feb; P 🏊) This has to be one of the better deals in Santillana. Surrounded by a garden, this stone mansion, although quite new, is faithful to the town's style. Rooms are inviting, with antique furniture, and access to a pool at these prices is a bonus.

our pick **La Casa del Organista** (☎ 942 84 03 52; www.casadelorganista.com; Camino de Los Hornos 4; s/d

€79/96; P) Rooms at this elegant 18th-century house, once home to the *colegiata*'s organist, are particularly attractive, with wood-rail balconies, plush rugs, antique furniture and plenty of exposed heavy beams and stonework. Some rooms look across fields towards the *colegiata*.

Casa del Marqués (☎ 942 81 88 88; www.turismosantillanadelmar.com; Calle del Cantón 26; s/d €188/208; closed mid-Dec–Feb; P) Feel like the lord or lady of the manor in this 15th-century Gothic mansion, once home to the Marquis of Santillana. Exposed timber beams, thick stone walls and cool terracotta floors contribute to the atmosphere of the rooms, all of which are quite different from one another.

EATING

Santillana has many humdrum eateries catering to the passing tourist trade, and you should be able to get a full meal at most for around €20 to €25. There are some better options, however.

La Villa (☎ 942 81 83 64; Plaza de la Gándara s/n; meals €25-30; Thu-Tue) Wander through the great timber doors into the courtyard. To your left is a bar with benches; to the right and upstairs is the dining area. They're brought together as though under a big top of heavy, dark timber beams. The meat dishes, such as the *solomillo con salsa de queso* (sirloin in cheese sauce; €15), are its strong suit.

Casa Uzquiza (☎ 942 84 03 56; Calle del Escultor Jesús Otero 11; meals €30-35; daily Jun-Aug, Wed-Mon Sep-Jan & Mar-May, closed Feb) This upstairs restaurant with red-and-blue walls and somewhat harsh lighting offers many of the usual local suspects, such as *cocido montañés* (a hearty stew of white beans, cabbage, potato, chorizo, black pudding and sometimes port), and surprises with an elegant touch, such as *lomo de bacalao en pil-pil de erizo* (soft steamed cod drenched in a thick yellow sea urchin sauce). There's a *menú del día* (daily set menu) for €14.50 and the lemon tart is to die for.

Restaurante Gran Duque (☎ 942 84 03 86; www.granduque.com; Calle del Escultor Jesús Otero 5; meals €35; lunch & dinner daily Jul-Aug, lunch & dinner Tue-Sat, lunch Sun, dinner Mon Sep-Jun) The food is high-quality local fare and what sets it apart is the setting, a grand stone house with noble trappings and nice decorative touches such as the exposed brick and beams. There is a reasonable balance of surf or turf options, but the latter are better.

GETTING THERE & AWAY

Autobuses La Cantábrica (☎ 942 72 08 22) has buses four times a day Monday to Friday, with three on Saturday and Sunday, from Santander to Santillana (€2.15, 35 minutes), and on to Comillas and San Vicente de la Barquera. They stop on Avenida de Antonio Sandí, opposite the medical centre.

ART PREHISTORY

When archaeologists stumbled across them in 1879, they dismissed the vivid rock paintings in the Cueva de Altamira (p532) as a hoax. They were just too good to be the handiwork of primitive people tens of thousands of years ago. Wrong. These works are the real McCoy and so precious that the Unesco World Heritage site has been closed to the public (a replica has been created nearby).

Around 50 similar sites have been found around Cantabria, and others in Asturias, but few can be visited. The region's mild climate and limestone caves provided a convenient habitat for Palaeolithic settlers, when ice still covered much of the earth's surface. Ensconced in this environment, some of these early inhabitants felt the need to express themselves using the materials at hand.

The most spectacular images, covering the ceiling of the Cueva de Altamira, are thought to be the work of a single artist, done 14,500 years ago. Most of the thousands of paintings found at Altamira and elsewhere (some dating as far back as 20,000 years ago) are stylised depictions of animals, usually deer, bison, boars and bulls, rendered in red, black and ochre tones. Other motifs also appear. At the Cuevas del Castillo (p527) there are 53 negative handprints (produced by what was surely the world's first air-brush), and a series of crimson discs that one theory (among many) suggests could have been used as a lunar calendar. The **Museo de Altamira website** (http://museodealtamira.mcu.es) details other caves that can be visited in Cantabria (click on 'Information' then 'Other places to visit').

Museo & Cueva de Altamira

The country's finest prehistoric art, in the Cueva de Altamira (Altamira Cave), 2km southwest of Santillana del Mar, is now off limits to all but the scientific community.

Since 2001, however, the **Museo Altamira** (☎ 942 81 80 05; http://museodealtamira.mcu.es; adult/senior & under 18yr/student €2.40/free/1.20, Sun & from 2.30pm Sat free; 9.30am-8pm Tue-Sat, 9.30am-3pm Sun & holidays May-Oct, 9.30am-6pm Tue-Sat, 9.30am-3pm Sun & holidays Nov-Apr; P) has allowed all comers to view the inspired, 14,500-year-old depictions of bison, horses and other beasts (or rather, their replicas) in this full-size, dazzling re-creation of the cave's most interesting chamber, the Sala de Polícromos (Polychrome Hall). The viewing is enhanced by the museum's excellent interactive exhibits on prehistoric humanity and cave art around the world, from Altamira to Australia.

Visits to the replica cave, called the Neocueva, are guided; you will be assigned a tour time with your ticket. Tours are in Spanish but you can request tours in other languages, including English. During Easter and from July to September it's worth purchasing tickets in advance at branches of **Banco de Santander** (☎ 902 24 24 24; www.bancosantander.es in Spanish), or by phoning or visiting the website (click on 'Get your tickets'). Those without vehicles must walk or take a taxi from Santillana del Mar.

Comillas

pop 2470

Take the CA131 16km from Santillana through verdant countryside to reach Comillas. You first sight the town's fine, golden beach, but there is much more: a pleasant, cobbled old village centre and, separated from it by verdant valleys, hilltops crowned by some of the most original buildings in Cantabria. Comillas was dubbed the 'town of archbishops' in the 18th century because at least five of the town's sons had been made archbishops by then.

The **tourist office** (☎ 942 72 07 68; www.comillas.es; Calle de Aldea 6; 10.30am-1.30pm & 5-8pm daily Jul-Aug, 10.30am-1.30pm & 5-8pm Wed-Mon Sep-Jun) has local information, and there's a **branch** (Plaza de Joaquín del Piélagos; 9am-2pm & 4-6pm Mon-Sat, 10am-2pm Sun Jul-Aug) behind the town hall. Take the official opening times with a pinch of salt, as at the time of writing they opened in summer only (June to September).

SIGHTS

Antoni Gaudí left few reminders of his genius beyond Catalonia, but of those that he did, the 1885 **Capricho de Gaudí** (Gaudí's Caprice) in Comillas is easily the most flamboyant, if modest in stature. The brick building, originally a summerhouse for the Marqués de Comillas and now a top-end restaurant (opposite), is liberally striped with ceramic bands of alternating sunflowers and green leaves. The building is on a rise southwest of the town centre.

The Capricho was one of several buildings commissioned from leading Catalan Modernista architects by the first Marqués de Comillas, who was born here as plain Antonio López, made a fortune in Cuba and returned to beautify his home town. In the same hillside parklands stand the wonderful neo-Gothic **Palacio de Sobrellano** (☎ 942 72 03 39; admission €3; 10am-9pm Jun-Sep, 10.30am-2pm & 4-7.30pm Oct-May) and **Capilla Panteón de los Marqueses de Comillas** (admission €3; 10am-9pm Jun-Sep, 10.30am-2pm & 4-7.30pm Oct-May), both designed by Joan Martorell. With the *palacio* (palace), Martorell truly managed to out-Gothic real Gothic. Visits to both buildings are by guided tour.

Martorell also had a hand in what was long the **Universidad Pontificia**, on the hill opposite, but Lluís Domènech i Montaner, another Catalan Modernista, contributed the medieval flavour to this elaborate building. The former seminary, in whose grounds you can stroll, is now being converted from pontifical university to international Spanish-language study centre, the Fundación Campus Comillas.

Comillas' compact medieval centre is full of its own little pleasures. **Plaza de la Constitución** is its focal point, a sloping, cobbled square flanked by the town hall, the Iglesia de San Cristóbal and old sandstone houses with flower-bedecked balconies.

Comillas boasts a teeny fishing port and fine beach, a 10-minute walk from the Plaza.

SLEEPING

Camping Comillas (☎ 942 72 00 74; www.campingcomillas.com; sites per 2 people, car & tent €22; Easter & Jun-Sep) A simple grassy spot run by a friendly fellow on the eastern edge of town, the camping ground spreads to a clifftop area overlooking part of the beach in July and August (minimum stay in that part five days).

Pensión La Aldea (☎ 942 72 10 46; La Aldea 5; d without/with bathroom €35/40) This homey guesthouse offers simple rooms with hardwood floors, and there's a little *comedor* (dining room) downstairs. It runs a second, slightly fancier place over on Calle de Díaz de la Campa.

Hostal Esmeralda (☎ 942 72 00 97; www.hostalesmeralda.com; Calle de Antonio López 7; s/d €60/80) A short distance east of the town centre, this handsomely restored *hostal* (budget hotel) contains large, old-fashioned rooms. It's in a fine, stone building partly covered in ivy.

EATING

The obvious place for morning coffee is the Plaza de la Rabia, behind the cathedral. A couple of simple seafood restaurants line the waterfront.

Restaurante Gurea (☎ 942 72 24 46; Calle Ignacio Fernández de Castro 11; meals €40; lunch & dinner daily Jun-Sep, lunch & dinner Tue-Sat, lunch Sun Oct-May) In a backstreet behind Hostal Esmeralda, this elegant restaurant dishes up a mix of Basque and *montañés* (Cantabrian-style mountain) fare. Try the delicate *carpaccio de buey al aroma de trufa* (beef carpaccio seasoned with truffle) or the tasting menu (€35). The lunchtime *menú del día* (€19) is also good.

El Capricho de Gaudí (☎ 942 72 03 65; meals €40-45; lunch & dinner daily Jul-Aug, lunch & dinner Mon-Sat, lunch Sun Sep-Jun) You can't visit Gaudí's Capricho, but you can eat there! Of course, the dining area is curved (no straight lines for Gaudí) and has a modestly elegant air. There's a *menú del día* for €23.

GETTING THERE & AWAY

Comillas is served by the same buses as Santillana del Mar (€3.40, 55 minutes from Santander). The main stop is on Calle del Marqués de Comillas, near the driveway to the Capricho de Gaudí.

Around Comillas

Out of several beaches around Comillas, the long, sandy **Playa de Oyambre**, 5km west, is decidedly superior. Two year-round camping grounds operate behind the beach.

A little further west, the wilder, less crowded and clothing-optional **Playa de Merón** and its continuation, **Playa del Rosal**, stretch 3km to the estuary at San Vicente de la Barquera. Heed the warning signs about currents.

San Vicente de la Barquera

pop 4560

Just 10km further west from Comillas, follow the CA131 through the green and humid estuary land of the Parque Natural de Oyambre. As you approach from a height, you see how a broad swath of sea water has cut a gash through the coast at San Vicente de la Barquera. The main estuary is spanned by the long, low-slung, 15th-century Puente de la Maza. On its east side, out of view of the main road, runs a long, golden strand. The town huddles between the bridge and another narrow inlet on the west side.

San Vicente was an important fishing port throughout the Middle Ages and later became one of the so-called Cuatro Villas de la Costa – converted by Carlos III into the province of Cantabria in 1779.

The **tourist office** (☎ 942 71 07 97; www.sanvicentedelabarquera.org; Avenida del Generalísimo 20; 10am-1.30pm & 4.30-7pm Mon-Sat, 11am-2pm Sun) doubles as an agent for *casas rurales* (country homes) in the area. The weekend opening times are, erm, flexible.

The old part of town is topped by a **castle** (adult/child €1.40/0.70; 11am-2pm & 5-8pm Tue-Sun) and some remnants of the old city walls, but its outstanding monument is the largely 13th-century **Iglesia de Santa María de los Ángeles**, further inland. Although Gothic, it sports a pair of impressive Romanesque doorways. In one of the chapels, the lifelike statue of 16th-century Inquisitor Antonio del Corro (reclining on one elbow, reading) is deemed to be the best piece of Renaissance funerary art in the country.

Just after the bridge and before you hit the central Plaza de José Antonio, **Hotel Luzón** (☎ 942 71 00 50; www.hotelluzon.net; Calle de Miramar 1; s/d €45/70) is a stately looking stone-fronted home possessing an air of older times with its high ceilings and quiet drawing rooms. Rooms are fusty but most have a sense of space and many have broad views over town and water.

El Pescador (☎ 942 71 00 05; Calle Antonio Garrelly s/n; meals €20; lunch & dinner daily Jun-Aug, lunch & dinner Wed-Sun, lunch Mon Sep-May) is the liveliest of seafood restaurants with tables overlooking the estuary. Stand around in the good-natured bar area knocking back tapas, or make your way out back to the dining area overlooking the water.

San Vicente bus station, by the Puente de la Maza, is served by five to seven daily ALSA services on the Gijón–San Sebastián route (€4.45, 1¼ hours from Santander; €8.85, 1¾ to two hours from Oviedo). Autobuses Palomera also stops here en route between Santander and Potes (€3.20, 1½ hours to/from Potes). Two FEVE trains stop in San Vicente daily en route between Santander (€4.20, 1½ hours) and Oviedo (€9.10, three hours, 20 minutes).

Western Valleys

Generally ignored by holidaymakers, who concentrate their attention on the Picos de Europa further west, the valleys of Río Saja and, next west, Río Nansa, make a soft contrast to the craggy majesty of the Picos.

A beautiful drive starting from the Picos de Europa is the CA282, which snakes up high and eastwards from La Hermida on Río Deva. The village of **Puentenansa** forms a crossroads. Fifteen kilometres north (turn east at Rábago and climb 7km) is **El Soplao** (☎ 902 82 02 82; www.soplao.com; adult/senior, student & child €9.50/7; 🕑 10am-2pm & 3-5pm), a 12km stretch of caves full of stalactites and stalagmites, and until 1979 a lead and zinc mine. The Cantabrian government and speleological club are slowly opening the caves up to the public – the first chamber was opened in 2005 and visits take about 45 minutes. A separate tour of about 3km (2½ hours) for groups of no more than 20 (€30) opens up an extraordinary subterranean world.

The CA281 south from Puentenansa follows Río Nansa upstream. Along the way, a short detour east leads to the attractive hamlet of **Tudanca**, dominated by the white, 18th-century rural mansion or **Casona** (☎ 942 72 90 25; adult/to 14yr €3/1.50; 🕑 11am-2pm & 4-6.15pm daily May-Sep, 11am-2pm & 4-5.30pm Tue-Sun Oct-Apr). Visits are guided and last 45 minutes. Inside you'll see all sorts of centuries-old furniture and diverse objects. The house was built by an *indiano*, that is, someone who had made a fortune in Spain's Latin American colonies (in this case Peru) and returned. The chapel contains a baroque *retablo* (altarpiece).

The CA281 eventually meets the C627, on which you can head south to Cervera de Pisuerga (p246) or turn northwest back to the Picos.

Proceeding east from Puentenansa takes you through **Carmona**, with many fine stone mansions. When you reach the village of Valle de Cabuérniga and Río Saja, head south towards Reinosa. The views are magnificent. The hamlet of **Bárcena Mayor**, about 9km east of the main road, is a popular spot with a couple of *casas rurales* to stay in and great *mesones*, where you should try the *cocido montañés*.

ASTURIAS

'Ser español es un orgullo', the saying goes, *'ser asturiano es un título'*. 'If being Spanish is a matter of pride, to be Asturian is a title', or so some of the locals would have you think.

Asturias' beauty lies in its stunning countryside. Much of the Picos de Europa are on Asturian territory, and fishing villages such as Llanes and Cudillero make great bases for exploring the lovely coast, dotted with picture-postcard coves (it is said there are more than

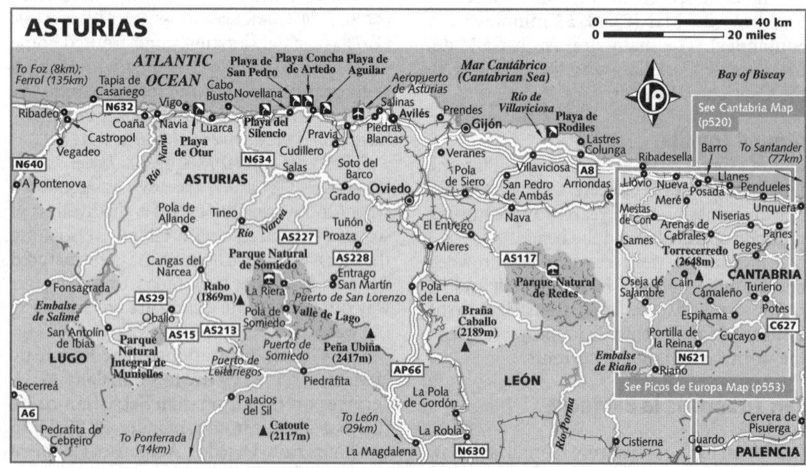

WHAT'S COOKING IN ASTURIAS?

Traditional Asturian food is simple peasant fare. Best known is the *fabada asturiana,* a hearty bean dish jazzed up with meat and sausage. A broth version that goes lighter on the beans is *pote asturiano. Cachopo* (breaded veal stuffed with ham, cheese and vegetables) is a carnivore's dream, with vegetables to boot! As in Cantabria, the rivers of Asturias provide trout, salmon and eels.

The region is also famed for the many varieties of untreated cow's milk cheese, *queso de Cabrales*. There are some 30 varieties, some mixed with goat's and/or sheep's milk and most fairly strong. You can learn more about Cabrales cheesemaking at the **Cueva El Cares** (☎ 985 84 67 02; adult/child €2.50/1.50; 10am-2pm & 4-8pm Apr-Sep, Sat & Sun only Oct-Mar), an exhibition cave south of Arenas de Cabrales (p557) along the Poncebos road.

Cider is the Asturian tipple of preference, but some young red and white wine is made around Cangas del Narcea in the west.

600 beaches on the Asturian coast) and inlets. For the architecture buff, Asturias is the land of the pre-Romanesque – modest but unique survivors of early medieval building and decoration. The region's pretty capital, Oviedo, is an interesting enough town, with its old centre and elegant squares.

Bucolically green though much of it is, Asturias also has its gritty industrial side. The Oviedo–Gijón–Avilés triangle is the heart of industrial Asturias and mines still operate in various spots, especially in the southwest.

Like neighbouring Galicia, Asturias was Celtic territory before the arrival of the Romans. It's also the sole patch of Spain never conquered by the Muslims. Ever since King Pelayo warded them off in the Battle of Covadonga in AD 722 and laid the foundations of Christian Spain's 800-year comeback, Asturians have thought of themselves – or have been perceived to think of themselves – as a cut above the rest of the peninsula's inhabitants. Asturias, they say, is the real Spain; the rest is simply *tierra de la reconquista* (reconquered land).

The Reconquista's southwards progress left Asturias increasingly a backwater. As a concession, Juan I of Castilla y León made Asturias a *principado* (principality) in 1388, and to this day the heir to the Spanish throne holds the title Príncipe de Asturias (just as Prince Charlie is the Prince of Wales). Annual awards handed out by the prince to personalities of distinction are Spain's equivalent of the Nobel prizes.

Asturias of the 20th century was at once rural backwater and industrial hotbed. Mining and steel production scarred the area between Avilés and Gijón. A miners' revolt in 1934 was crushed by a certain General Franco, who two years later launched the civil war. In 1962, with all Spain well under Franco's thumb, the miners again revolted in strikes that lasted months and were, again, mercilessly crushed.

Asturias' regional tourism office maintains an excellent website, www.infoasturias.com. The regional government's site (www.asturias.es) also has plenty of material. Another useful site is www.vivirasturias.com (in Spanish).

For hotel accommodation, you could try **Nuestros Hoteles en Asturias** (www.ehotelesasturias.com). The countryside and small towns are peppered with *casas rurales,* known quaintly as *casas de aldea* (hamlet houses), which you can search at www.casasdealdea.com. More than 50 camping grounds are scattered across Asturias.

OVIEDO

pop 216,700 / elev 232m

The elegant parks and modern shopping streets of Asturias' capital are agreeably offset by what remains of the *casco antiguo* (old town). Out on the periphery, the hum and heave of factories is a strong reminder that Oviedo is a key producer of textiles, metal goods, sugar and chocolate.

History

When Asturian king Alfonso II El Casto (the Chaste; AD 791–842) defeated a Muslim detachment that practically razed Oviedo, he was sufficiently impressed by the site to rebuild and expand it, and move his court there from Pravia. It stayed until 910, when it moved to León. The university opened around 1600, and industry took off in the 19th century. The 1934 miners' revolt and a nasty siege in the first months of the Spanish Civil War led to the destruction of much of the old town.

Orientation

From the train station, Oviedo's main drag, Calle de Uría, leads southeast to the Campo de San Francisco (a park) and the old town. The ALSA bus station is east of the train station on Calle de Pepe Cosmen.

Information

Ciberexpress (1st fl, train station; per hr €2.40; 10.30am-3pm & 5-9.30pm Mon-Fri, 11am-3pm & 5-9pm Sat) Internet access.
Farmacia Nestares (985 22 39 25; Calle de Uría 36; 9am-midnight)
Hospital Central de Asturias (985 10 61 00; Avenida de Julián Clavería)
Main post office (Calle de Alonso Quintanilla 1; 8.30am-8.30pm Mon-Fri, 9.30am-2pm Sat) While under renovation, the nearest office is at Calle de Santa Susana 18.
Oficina Municipal de Turismo (985 22 75 86; http://turismo.ayto-oviedo.es; Calle de Marqués de Santa Cruz 1; 9.30am-2pm & 4.30-8pm mid-Jun–mid-Sep, 10am-2pm & 4.30-7pm mid-Sep–mid-Jun) In a kiosk off Campo de San Francisco. You can download some MP3 files from the website on to your MP3 player to use as a tour guide round the city.
Policía Nacional (Calle del General Yagüe 5-7)
Regional tourist office (985 21 33 85; www.infoasturias.com; Calle de Cimadevilla 4; 10am-8pm mid-Jun–mid-Sep, 10am-7pm mid-Sep–mid-Jun)

Sights

CATEDRAL DE SAN SALVADOR

In a sense, the mainly Gothic edifice you see today forms the outer casing of a many-layered history in stone of Spanish Christianity. Its origins lie in the Cámara Santa, a chapel built by Alfonso II to house holy relics. The chapel is now the inner sanctuary of the **cathedral** (10am-7pm Mon-Sat mid-May–Sep, 10am-1pm & 4-7pm Mon-Fri, 10am-1pm & 4-6pm Sat Sep–mid-May), which was chiefly built between the 14th and 16th centuries. The **cloister** is pure 14th-century Gothic, rare enough in Asturias, and just off it the *sala capitular* (chapter house) contains some well-restored Flemish Gothic choir stalls.

The **Cámara Santa** (985 22 10 33; admission incl Museo Diocesano adult/under 10yr/10-15yr €2.50/free/1, free Thu afternoon; 10am-1pm & 4-6pm or 7pm Mon-Sat) contains some key symbols of medieval Spanish Christianity. Alfonso II presented the Cruz de los Ángeles (Cross of the Angels) to Oviedo in 808, and it's still the city's emblem. A century later Alfonso III donated the Cruz de la Victoria (Cross of Victory), which in turn became the sign of Asturias.

These and other items can be viewed from the Sala Apostolar, whose remarkable sculptures of the apostles are the work of Maestro Mateo, creator of the Pórtico de la Gloria in the cathedral of Santiago de Compostela. Turning to leave, you'll see three heads sculpted out of a single block of stone above the doorway. This strikingly simple work depicts, from left to right, the Virgin Mary, Christ and St John on Calvary. You can pay just to enter the Cámara Santa (adult/child €1.25/free).

The **Museo Diocesano** (985 20 31 17; admission incl Cámara Santa adult/under 10yr/10-15yr €2.50/free/1, free Thu afternoon 10am-8pm Mon-Fri, 10am-6pm Sat Jul-Sep, 10am-1pm & 4-8pm Mon-Fri, 10am-1pm & 4-6pm Sat May-Jun, 10am-1pm & 4-6pm or 7pm Mon-Sat Oct-Apr), on the top floor of the cloister, houses some interesting ecclesiastical artefacts.

One vestige of the original 9th-century structure is a Romanesque tower on the south side, best approached via the Tránsito de Santa Barbara.

AROUND THE CATHEDRAL

Plaza de Alfonso II El Casto and neighbouring Plaza de Porlier are fronted by elegant palaces dating from the 17th and 18th centuries. The nearby **Museo de Bellas Artes de Asturias** (985 21 30 61; www.museobbaa.com in Spanish; Calle de Santa Ana 1; admission free; 11am-2.30pm & 5-9pm Tue-Sat, 11am-2.30pm Sun Jul & Aug, 10.30am-2pm & 4.30-8.30pm Tue-Fri, 11.30am-2pm & 5-8pm Sat, 11.30am-2.30pm Sun Sep-Jun), itself housed in two buildings dating to the 17th and 18th centuries, respectively, rewards a visit. Its collection includes paintings by Goya, Murillo and other Spanish greats, and plenty by Asturians, such as Evaristo Valle, plus a roomful of El Grecos.

Behind the cathedral, the 16th-century Benedictine Monasterio de San Vicente houses the **Museo Arqueológico** (closed indefinitely for restoration).

PLAZAS

Explore the old town's nooks and crannies. **Plaza de la Constitución** occupies a barely perceptible rise close to the heart of old Oviedo, capped at one end by the **Iglesia de San Isidoro**, and fronted by an eclectic collection of old shops, cafes and the 17th-century

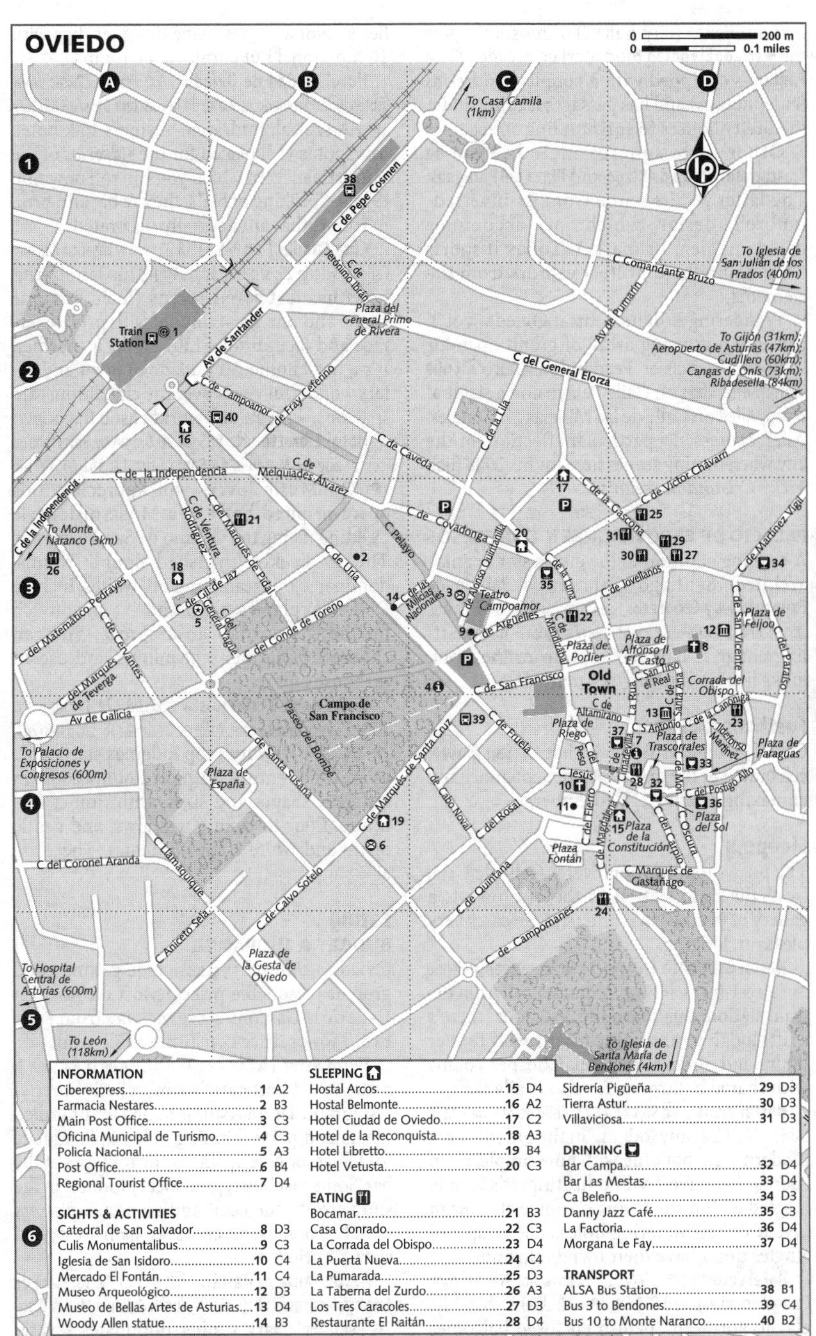
OVIEDO
0 200 m
0 0.1 miles
A
B
C
D
1
2
3
4
5
6
To Casa Camila (1km)
C de Pepe Cosmen
C de Jerónimo Ibrán
Plaza del General Primo de Rivera
Train Station
Av de Santander
C Comandante Bruzo
To Iglesia de San Julián de los Prados (400m)
Av de Pumarín
To Gijón (31km); Aeropuerto de Asturias (47km); Cudillero (60km); Cangas de Onís (73km); Ribadesella (84km)
C del General Elorza
C de Campoamor
C de Fray Ceferino
C de la Lila
C de Caveda
C de la Independencia
C de Melquiades Álvarez
C de Ventura Rodríguez
C del Marqués de Pidal
C Pelayo
C de Covadonga
C de Alonso Quintanilla
C de la Gascona
C de Victor Chávarri
C de Martínez Vigil
To Monte Naranco (3km)
C de Uría
C de las Milicias Nacionales
Teatro Campoamor
C de la Luna
C de Jovellanos
C del Matemático Pedrayes
C de Gil de Jaz
C del General Yagüe
C de Argüelles
C de Mendizábal
Plaza de Porlier
Plaza de Alfonso II El Casto
C de San Vicente
Plaza de Feijoo
C del Paraíso
C de Cervantes
C del Conde de Toreno
C del Marqués de Teverga
Av de Galicia
Campo de San Francisco
C de San Francisco
Old Town
C San Tirso el Real
C de Santa Ana
Corrada del Obispo
C de Altamirano
La Rúa
C de la Canóniga
To Palacio de Exposiciones y Congresos (600m)
Paseo del Bombé
C de Fruela
Plaza de Riego
C S Antonio
C Ildefonso Martínez
Plaza de Paraguas
Plaza de Trascorrales
C de Santa Susana
Plaza de España
C de Marqués de Santa Cruz
C de Cabo Noval
C del Peso
C de Cimadevilla
C Jesús
C del Rosal
C de Mon
C del Postigo Alto
C del Fierro
C de Magdalena
Plaza de la Constitución
C del Campillo
C Oscura
Plaza del Sol
C Llamaquique
C del Coronel Aranda
Plaza Fontán
C de Quintana
C Marqués de Gastañago
C de Calvo Sotelo
C Aniceto Sela
C de Campomanes
Plaza de la Gesta de Oviedo
To Hospital Central de Asturias (600m)
To León (118km)
To Iglesia de Santa María de Bendones (4km)
INFORMATION
Ciberexpress 1 A2
Farmacia Nestares 2 B3
Main Post Office 3 C3
Oficina Municipal de Turismo 4 C3
Policía Nacional 5 A3
Post Office 6 B4
Regional Tourist Office 7 D4
SIGHTS & ACTIVITIES
Catedral de San Salvador 8 D3
Culis Monumentalibus 9 C3
Iglesia de San Isidoro 10 C4
Mercado El Fontán 11 C4
Museo Arqueológico 12 D3
Museo de Bellas Artes de Asturias 13 D4
Woody Allen statue 14 B3
SLEEPING
Hostal Arcos 15 D4
Hostal Belmonte 16 A2
Hotel Ciudad de Oviedo 17 C2
Hotel de la Reconquista 18 A3
Hotel Libretto 19 B4
Hotel Vetusta 20 C3
EATING
Bocamar 21 B3
Casa Conrado 22 C3
La Corrada del Obispo 23 D4
La Puerta Nueva 24 C4
La Pumarada 25 D3
La Taberna del Zurdo 26 A3
Los Tres Caracoles 27 D3
Restaurante El Raitán 28 D4
Sidrería Pigüeña 29 D3
Tierra Astur 30 D3
Villaviciosa 31 D3
DRINKING
Bar Campa 32 D4
Bar Las Mestas 33 D4
Ca Beleño 34 D3
Danny Jazz Café 35 C3
La Factoria 36 D4
Morgana Le Fay 37 D4
TRANSPORT
ALSA Bus Station 38 B1
Bus 3 to Bendones 39 C4
Bus 10 to Monte Naranco 40 B2

ayuntamiento (city hall). To the south, past the **Mercado El Fontán** food market, arcaded **Plaza Fontán** is equipped with a couple of *sidrerías* (cider houses) and has passages leading under the pretty houses to surrounding streets.

Other little squares include **Plaza de Trascorrales**, **Plaza de Riego** and **Plaza del Paraguas**. The latter got its name from its inverted-umbrella design, which once accommodated an open-air market. Today it sports a big umbrella to protect visitors from the elements.

Wandering around central Oviedo, you'll run into a growing array of grand open-air sculptures, such as Fernando Botero's **Culis Monumentalibus** on Calle Pelayo and a **statue of Woody Allen** on Calle de las Milicias Nacionales. Allen expressed a particular affection for the city when filming scenes here for his 2008 flick *Vicky Cristina Barcelona.*

PALACIO DE EXPOSICIONES Y CONGRESOS

A dashing addition to the city is star Spanish architect Santiago Calatrava's **Palacio de Exposiciones y Congresos** (Exhibition and Congress Palace; ☎ 985 24 15 43; Calle de José Ramón Zaragoza 8-10), a startling congress complex that, from the front, looks like a white praying mantis.

Festivals & Events

Oviedo's biggest fiesta is that of **San Mateo**, celebrated in the third week of September and climaxing around 21 September.

Sleeping

The busy shopping boulevard, Calle de Uría, from the train station to the old town is a gallery of inexpensive, and in some cases very pleasant, lodgings.

Hostal Belmonte (☎ 985 24 10 20; calogon@teleline.es; Calle de Uría 31; s/d €39/49) A quick stroll from the train station, this charming 3rd-floor (there's a lift) lodging offers cosy rooms with timber floors and an at-home feel. Cheaper rooms with shared bathroom are also available.

Hostal Arcos (☎ 985 21 47 73; Calle de Magdalena 3; s/d €35/50) The only lodging in the old town is a modern brick building with nine simple, clean rooms that have TV and heating. It's ideally located within stumbling distance of some of Oviedo's best watering holes. The couple of singles don't have their own bathroom.

Hotel Vetusta (☎ 985 22 22 29; www.hotelvetusta.com; Calle de Covadonga 2; d €64-80; P ⌘ 🖳) Behind its classic northern Spanish enclosed balconies lies a somewhat wannabe designer digs with 16 functional but comfortable rooms.

Hotel Ciudad de Oviedo (☎ 985 22 22 24; www.hotelciudaddeoviedo.es; Calle de la Gascona 21; s/d €83/100; P) A typical, midrange business-folk hotel, this spot is well placed for the *sidrerías* of the same street, from which you can roll downhill to bed. Speaking of beds, they're big and firm, in rooms that are neutrally decorated.

Casa Camila (☎ 985 11 48 22; www.casacamila.com; Calle de Fitoria 29; s/d €78/104; P) This family-run hotel has just seven rooms (including one single and one great double with private terrace and Jacuzzi for €130) and is a charmer. It's a few kilometres outside of town and offers wonderful views over the city. Rooms are spacious, with an old-world rustic flavour.

Hotel Libretto (☎ 985 20 20 04; www.librettohotel.com; Calle de Marqués de Santa Cruz 12; s/d €150/160; P 🖳) Music lovers will appreciate this opera-inspired hotel in a Modernista-style building facing the Campo de San Francisco. The 15 sleekly furnished double rooms, dominated by creams and off-whites, include DVD/CD players, wi-fi and – a nice touch for the wet north – an umbrella. You can choose from a menu of pillows and use an in-house laptop.

Hotel de la Reconquista (☎ 985 24 11 00; www.hoteldelareconquista.com; Calle de Gil de Jaz 16; s/d €193/241; P ⌘ 🖳) The city's top lodgings started life as an 18th-century hospice. Rooms come in different shapes and sizes, with timber furniture, floor-to-ceiling windows, and gentle ochre and white colour schemes. There are also suites.

Eating

BUDGET & MIDRANGE

Oviedo's *sidrería* rules include getting good grub at reasonable prices. Most of those on Calle de la Gascona serve *raciones* from €8 to €18. Two or three constitute a full meal.

Tierra Astur (☎ 985 20 25 02; Calle de la Gascona 1; meals €20-25) A particularly atmospheric *sidrería*/restaurant, Tierra Astur is famed for its grilled meats and prize-winning cider. Folks queue for tables, or give up and settle for tapas at the bar. Some just buy typical local products in the shop area to the right and go home. Platters of Asturian sausage, cheese or ham are a good starter option.

Restaurante El Raitán (☎ 985 21 42 18; Plaza de Trascorrales 6; meals €30-35; 🕑 lunch & dinner Mon & Wed-Sat, lunch Sun) Dark timber dominates several labyrinthine dining areas. The menu is extensive, with tonnes of starters and a good range of fish and meat options. The *solomillo* (sirloin medallions) are melt-in-the-mouth tender and the salads enormous.

Casa Conrado (☎ 985 22 39 19; Calle de Argüelles 1; meals €35-40; ⌚ Mon-Sat, closed Aug) A classic, where black-jacketed waiters will deliver carefully assembled Asturian dishes to your table. It offers variations on hake and plenty of other seafood. Meat-eaters could try the *solomillo de carne roja con foie fresco de pato y salsa de oporto* (sirloin with fresh duck foie gras and port sauce; €24.50).

A boisterous cider bar and restaurant, **Sidrería Pigüeña** (☎ 985 21 03 41; Calle de la Gascona 2; meals €30-35; ⌚ Thu-Tue) is jammed most nights, especially weekends, with a broad mix of locals, from labourers to lovers, hoeing into seafood and *rollitos de verdura con marisco* (seafood-stuffed vegetable tubes), and slurping bottles of cider. Let the waiters serve the cider though! In a similar vein are **La Pumarada** (Calle de la Gascona 8; ⌚ Tue-Sun) and **Villaviciosa** (Calle de la Gascona 7).

TOP END

La Corrada del Obispo (☎ 985 22 00 48; Calle de la Canóniga 18; meals €40; ⌚ lunch & dinner Mon-Sat, lunch Sun) Modern decor combines with the exposed stone walls of this 18th-century house to provide a welcoming setting for fine local cooking. They do a succulent *pixín* (monkfish) and you might be able to snare a table in the upstairs gallery. It's an Oviedo classic; Woody Allen shot some scenes for his 2008 film *Vicky Cristina Barcelona* here.

our pick **Bocamar** (☎ 985 27 16 11; www.bocamar.es; Calle del Marqués de Pidal 20; meals €40-45; ⌚ Mon-Sat) Allen also dined at Bocamar, a sober-enough-looking place from the outside and with a decidedly maritime air. Indeed, this is probably the best seafood restaurant in town, where all items (fresh from the sea to the north) are prepared with a lightness of touch that makes all the difference.

La Taberna del Zurdo (☎ 985 96 30 96; www.latabernadelzurdo.com; Calle de Cervantes 27; meals €40-45; ⌚ Mon-Sat) A mix of tradition and innovation, where you might munch *calamares en*

IN A PRE-ROMANESQUE WORLD OF THEIR OWN

Largely cut off from the rest of Christian Europe by the Muslim invasion, the tough and tiny kingdom that emerged in 8th-century Asturias gave rise to a unique style of art and architecture.

The 14 buildings, mostly churches (and collectively a World Heritage site), that survive from the two centuries of the Asturian kingdom take some inspiration from other sources, but have no real siblings. Typical are the straight lines of their profiles and floor plans – no apses or cylinders here – although their semicircular arches and complete vaulting of the nave are obvious forerunners of Romanesque.

Roman and Visigothic elements *are* visible. In many cases the bases and capitals of columns, with their Corinthian or floral motifs, were simply cannibalised from earlier structures. Another adaptation, which owes something to developments in Muslim Spain, was the use of lattice windows as a design effect. Their Eastern progenitors were inspired by the desire to maintain privacy from the outside world – hardly an issue in a church.

Some of the best representatives of the pre-Romanesque style are found in or near Oviedo. The **Iglesia de San Julián de los Prados** (adult/child €1.20/0.60, Mon free; ⌚ 10am-1pm Mon-Fri, 9.30am-12.30pm & 3.30-5.30pm Sat, 4-7pm holidays May-Sep, 10am-12.30pm Mon, 9.30-11.30am & 4-5.30pm daily Oct-Apr) in Oviedo, just above the road to Gijón, is the largest remaining pre-Romanesque church, and one of the oldest, built under Alfonso II. It is flanked by two porches – another Asturian touch – and the inside is covered with frescoes. It's about a 1.2km walk from Campo de San Francisco. The **Iglesia de Santa María de Bendones**, southeast of Oviedo (take bus 3 from Calle de Marqués de Santa Cruz), is unique for its extrawide nave, a result of Roman influence. It can only be seen from outside. On the slopes of Monte Naranco, 3km northwest of central Oviedo, the tall, narrow **Palacio de Santa María del Naranco** and the **Iglesia de San Miguel de Lillo** (admission to both adult/child €3/2, Mon free; ⌚ 9.30am-1pm Sun & Mon, 9.30am-1pm & 3.30-7pm Tue-Sat Apr-Sep, 10am-12.30pm Sun & Mon, 10am-12.30pm & 3.30-7pm Tue-Sat Oct-Mar) were built by Ramiro I (842–50), Alfonso II's successor, and mark an advance in Asturian art. An outstanding feature of the decoration in the former is the *sogueado,* the sculptural motif imitating rope used in its columns. To get here, take bus 10 from Calle de Uría near the train station.

su tinta (calamari in squid ink), fished out of the Bay of Biscay, or duck with pear. Try the homemade cheesecake to finish. Or you can drop by for gourmet tapas (which won a national snacks prize – yes, there is such a thing – in 2008).

La Puerta Nueva (☎ 985 22 52 27; Calle de Leopoldo Alas 2; meals €40-50; ⌚ lunch & dinner Mon-Sat, lunch Sun) A gourmet experience, mixing northern with Mediterranean cooking in a homey, welcoming atmosphere. The best option is to tackle the tasting menu. Market supplies largely determine what appears on the menu.

Los Tres Caracoles (☎ 985 20 77 89; Calle de Jovellanos 25; meals €45-50; ⌚ Mon-Sat, closed Jan) The Three Snails offers pleasingly presented permutations of Asturian cuisine, such as *bogavante sobre crosta de arroz y Parmesano* (lobster on a rice crust with Parmesan cheese), under 1950s lighting. Sit at the bar, perch on a high stool at high tables for two or three, or head out back. Half portions are available.

Drinking & Entertainment

The narrow pedestrian streets of the old town are thronged with people having a great time inside and outside dozens of bars on weekends. The main axis is Calle de Mon, with wall-to-wall bars, and its extension, the slightly less manic Calle Oscura (aptly named 'Dark Street'). During the week, bars are generally open 11pm to 3.30am and can be quiet. On Fridays and Saturdays they mostly stay open until 5.30am and are jammed.

Bar Campa (Plaza del Sol 3) A good place to start the night, this is a straightforward beer bar that fills with boisterous locals.

La Factoria (Calle del Postigo Alto) A square, bare stone basement bar that gets jammed so tight that the DJ's efforts seem pointless (if he's hoping to encourage dancing).

Morgana Le Fay (Calle de Cimadevilla 15) A long bar with multicoloured lighting and mainstream dance tunes (it even has a doorman, although this ain't a club), this places fills with a mixed, eclectic crowd.

Ca Beleño (Calle de Martínez Vigil 4) This is a well-established venue for Celtic music, whether of Asturian, Galician or Irish extraction. It hosts occasional jam sessions.

Bar Las Mestas (Calle del Mon 10) An enormous, big-windowed, old-time bar, it is quite untypical of the generally small joints on this street but has the same blasting music.

Danny Jazz Café (Calle de la Luna 13) With its low lights sprinkled about, small tables, background music and mixed-age crowd, Danny's doesn't always have jazz but it does boast a pleasing, conspiratorial feel.

Getting There & Away

AIR

The Aeropuerto de Asturias is at Santiago del Monte, 47km northwest of Oviedo and 40km west of Gijón. There are flights to Madrid, Barcelona, Palma de Mallorca and several other Spanish destinations, along with services to London and Geneva (easyJet), destinations in Germany (Air Berlin), and Paris and Brussels (Iberia).

BUS

From the **ALSA bus station** (☎ 902 42 22 42; Calle de Pepe Cosmen), direct services head up the motorway to Gijón (€1.99, 25 to 30 minutes) every 10 or 15 minutes from 6.30am to 10.45pm.

Other daily buses head to/from Galicia, Cantabria and elsewhere. Up to nine go to León (€8.04, 1½ to two hours), 10 to Madrid (€29.89 to €47.50, 5¼ to 5½ hours), up to 10 to Santander (€12.60 to €21.70, 2¼ to 3¼ hours) and four to Santiago de Compostela (€25.12 to €36.40, 4¾ to 7¼ hours). Buses to Cangas de Onís (€5.70, one hour 10 minutes to 1½ hours) and Covadonga (€6.55, 1¾ hours) also run from Oviedo.

TRAIN

One train station serves both rail companies, Renfe and FEVE, the latter located on the upper level. For Gijón, it's best to use the Renfe *cercanías* (local trains that serve large cities; €2.45, 35 minutes), which run until after 10pm.

FEVE (☎ 985 98 23 81; www.feve.es) runs four daily trains to/from Arriondas (€4.20, 1½ hours), Ribadesella (€5.40, two hours) and Llanes (€6.95, 2½ hours), with two continuing to Santander (€13.20, 4¼ hours) and one to Bilbao. Westbound, FEVE trains link up with trains from Gijón at Pravia, with three daily runs to Cudillero (€2.60, 1¼ hours) and Luarca (€6.05, 2¼ hours).

Getting Around

Buses run regularly between the ALSA bus station and the Aeropuerto de Asturias (€5.95, 45 minutes).

SAMPLING CIDER

Ancient documents show Asturians were sipping cider as far back as the 8th century! The region, which produces 80% of Spanish cider (the rest is made in Galicia, the Basque Country and Navarra), churns out anything up to 30 million litres a year, depending on the apple harvest. Apples are reaped in autumn and crushed to a pulp (about three-quarters of the apple winds up as apple juice). A mix of bitter, sour and sweet apples is used. The cider is fermented in *pipes* (barrels) kept in *llagares* (the place where the cider is made) over winter. It takes about 800kg of apples to fill a 450-litre *pipa,* which makes 600 bottles.

Traditionally, the *pipes* were transported to *chigres* (cider taverns) all over Asturias, and punters would be served direct from the *pipa*. The *chigre* is dying out, though, and most cider is now served in bottles in *sidrerías* (cider houses), usually with tapas or full meals. The cider is *estanciado,* that is, served by pouring it from the bottle, which the barman holds overhead, into a glass held low. This gives it some fizz. Such a glass of cider is known as a *culete* or *culín* and should be knocked back in one hit.

AROUND OVIEDO

El Entrego

Asturias has a proud mining history, an industry that promoted the arrival of the railways and opened the region up to the rest of the country. You can plunge into that history at the **Museo de la Minería y de la Industria** (☎ 985 66 31 33; www.mumi.es in Spanish; Calle El Trabanquín s/n; adult/child €4/2; 10am-8pm Tue-Sat, 10am-2pm Sun Jul-Sep, 10am-2pm & 4-7pm Tue-Sat, 10am-2pm Sun Oct-Jun). The displays, life-sized models of machinery and a replica of a mineshaft, bring to life the tough story of mining in Asturias.

Renfe and FEVE trains to/from Oviedo call in at El Entrego.

Nava

This nondescript railway town 33km east of Oviedo also happens to be Asturias' biggest centre of cider production. The only reason for popping by is to look into the **Museo de la Sidra** (Cider Museum; ☎ 985 71 74 22; www.museodelasidra.com; Plaza del Príncipe de Asturias s/n; adult/6-16yr €3/2, Tue free; 11am-2pm & 4-8pm Tue-Sun mid-Jun–mid-Sep, 11am-2pm & 4-7pm Tue-Fri, 11am-3pm & 4.30-8pm Sat, 11am-2pm Sun mid-Sep–mid-Jun). With beautiful old timber presses, explanatory films and the chance to crush your own apple, it is an entertaining display on the history of cider. Kids will like the virtual game of Asturian bowling and the *juego de la rana,* an ancestral Asturian pastime in which you try to throw metal disks into the mouth of a metal frog. You finish the tour with a fresh glass of cider.

Regular buses run to Nava from Oviedo (€2.40, 25 to 35 minutes). FEVE trains also call by.

Drivers looking for a treat should head south out of Nava along the narrow, winding AS251 road 22km south to Barredos, and then the AS117 southeast. The second half of this 46km route to the regional frontier with Castilla y León is a paradise of green, partly constituted as the **Parque Natural de Redes** (www.parquenatu ralderedes.es).

GIJÓN

pop 274,100

Bigger, busier and gutsier than Oviedo, Gijón (khi-*hon*) produces iron, steel and chemicals, and is the main loading terminal for Asturian coal. But Gijón is emerging like a phoenix from its industrial setting, having given itself a face-lift with pedestrianised streets, parks and seafront walks. The place is something of a minor party town too, and in summer puts on a vast entertainment program.

Information

In addition to the tourist office mentioned here, information booths open at Playa de San Lorenzo and elsewhere in town in summer. There is no shortage of banks with ATMs around central Gijón, including at the train station.

Ciber Capua (Calle de Capua 4; per hr €2; 11am-midnight Mon-Sat) Check email here. Quite a few bars have wi-fi too.

Hospital de Cabueñes (☎ 985 18 50 00; Calle de Cabueñes s/n) Four kilometres east of the city centre.

Municipal tourist office (☎ 985 34 17 71, 902 01 35 00; www.gijon.info; Espigón Central de Fomento; 9am-10pm Jul–mid-Sep, 9am-8pm mid-Sep–Jun) On a pier of the Puerto Deportivo (marina).

Policía Local (☎ 985 18 11 00; Calle San José 2) South of the centre of town.
Post office (Plaza del Seis de Agosto; 🕓 8.30am-8.30pm Mon-Fri, 9.30am-2pm Sat)
www.gijonasturias.com This website (in Spanish) is worth a look.

Sights & Activities

The ancient core of Gijón is concentrated on the headland known as **Cimadevilla**. At the top of this, you'll find what was once a fortified military zone has been converted into an attractive park. At the edge of the promontory stands the **Elogio del Horizonte**, a monumental concrete sculpture by Basque artist Eduardo Chillida that has become a symbol of the city. Wrapped around the landward side is an enticing web of narrow lanes and small squares.

Plaza de Jovellanos is dominated by the home of 18th-century Enlightenment politician Gaspar Melchor de Jovellanos, now housing the **Museo Casa Natal de Jovellanos** (☎ 985 34 63 13; www.jovellanos.net in Spanish; Plaza de Jovellanos 2; admission free), devoted mainly to Asturian art and Jovellanos himself.

To the east, underneath Campo Valdés, are the town's **Termas Romanas** (Roman Baths; ☎ 985 18 51 51; adult/senior & student €2.40/1.40, Sun free), built in the 1st to 4th centuries AD.

West of the baths spreads the harmonious **Plaza Mayor**, with porticoes on three sides and the **casa consistorial** (town hall) on the fourth. Further west, the impressive 18th-century

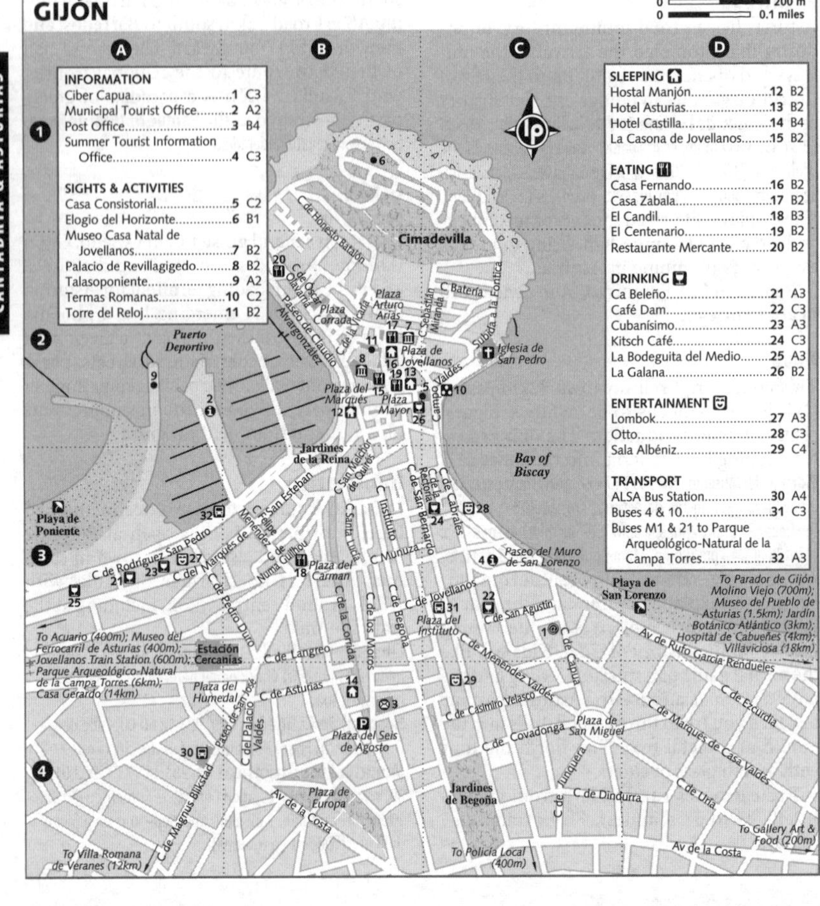

GIJÓN MUSEUMS & ALL-IN-ONE CARD

All Gijón museums are closed on Monday. Opening hours on other days vary but the typical timetable is 10am to 1pm (or 11am to 2pm) and 5pm to 7pm, 8pm or 9pm (depending on the season) Tuesday to Saturday, and 11am to 2pm (and sometimes 5pm to 7pm) on Sunday. A single ticket to three/four/five museums or archaeological sites costs €4.20/5.70/7.10 for adults and €2.05/2.80/3.50 for seniors, students and under 16s and is available at the sites.

The Gijón Card (€10/12/15, valid for one/two/three days) gives you entry to all museums and attractions in the city (except the aquarium, for which you get 30% off) and discounts on others throughout Asturias, free use of town buses, and discounts on a whole range of restaurants and *sidrerías* (cider houses). If you make use of the last, it could work as a money-saver. Available at tourist offices and online at www.gijon.info.

Palacio de Revillagigedo (☎ 985 34 69 21; Plaza del Marqués 2) is now a lively cultural centre, hosting modern art exhibitions and the occasional play or concert. The **Torre del Reloj** (Clock Tower; ☎ 985 18 13 29; Calle de Recoletas 5; admission free), just behind it, houses a six-floor exhibition on Gijón's history, with a viewing platform at the top.

The **Museo del Ferrocarril de Asturias** (☎ 985 30 85 75; Calle de Dionisio Fernández Nespral Aza s/n; adult/senior & student €2.40/1.40, Sun free) explores the role of railways in Asturian history, with 50 locomotives and carriages, and plenty of choo-choo paraphernalia. It's housed in Gijón's old Renfe train station, just a few minutes' walk west of the city centre.

On Playa de Poniente, a little further on from the Museo del Ferrocarril, is the city's **Acuario** (☎ 958 18 52 20; www.acuariodegijon.com; adult/child €12/6; ⏰ 10am-10pm daily Jul-Aug, 10am-7pm Mon-Fri, 10am-8pm Sat, Sun & holidays Sep-Jun). This singular aquarium has 4000 specimens (from Cantabrian otters to grey sharks and penguins) in 50 tanks ranging over 12 separate underwater environments, from the Bay of Biscay to the tropics. It also incorporates an Asturian freshwater river environment with trout and salmon. Large plastic bubbles have been inserted into the seabed so that you can get a sea-snail's-eye view of proceedings.

The **Museo del Pueblo de Asturias** (☎ 985 18 29 60; Paseo del Dr Fleming 877, La Huelga; adult/senior & student €2.40/1.40, free Sun), on a large woodland site 2km east of the city centre, is a regional ethnographic museum with several traditional buildings. One contains the **Museo de la Gaita**, with bagpipes from Asturias and elsewhere. Take bus 10 from Plaza del Instituto to the Grupo Cultura Covadonga stop, about 400m from the museum.

Parque Arqueológico-Natural de la Campa Torres (☎ 985 30 16 82; adult/senior & student €2.40/1.40, Sun free), on the Cabo Torres headland 6km northwest of the city centre, is Gijón's birthplace – a Roman and pre-Roman site where you can examine remains of dwellings and cisterns. Take bus M1 or 21 from in front of the marina. Another archaeological site is the **Villa Romana de Veranes** (☎ 985 18 51 29; adult/senior & student €2.40/1.40, Sun free; ⏰ 10am-8pm Tue-Fri, 11am-8pm Sat & Sun), 12km southwest of Gijón, about 500m north off the AS18 road to Oviedo. The main remaining building, which was transformed into a church in the Middle Ages, is thought by some to have been an early Christian church or perhaps even baths. Some original Roman mosaics have survived. Hourly ALSA buses run to Veranes (€1.20, 15 minutes).

The **Jardín Botánico Atlántico** (Atlantic Botanical Garden; ☎ 985 13 07 13; www.botanicoatlantico.com; adult/senior & student €5.70/2.80; ⏰ 10am-9pm Tue-Sun Jun-Sep, 10am-6pm Tue-Sun Oct-May), 3km east of the city centre, provides an excellent introduction to Cantabrian flora. The grand finale is the Jardín de la Isla, a landscaped park laced with pools and streams, based on the plans of 19th-century industrialist Florencio Valdés. Take bus 4 from Plaza del Instituto.

For swimming, **Playa de San Lorenzo** is a surprisingly good, clean city beach, but rather thin when the tide comes in. **Playa de Poniente**, west of the Puerto Deportivo, has imported sand and is much broader. **Talasoponiente** (www.talasoponiente.com), at the eastern extreme of the beach, is a modern thalassotherapy centre, with all sorts of baths, saunas and related treatment options. The basic entrance price is €7, which gives access to a pool and gym. For €19.50 you have 1½ hours in the rest of the complex.

Festivals & Events

Throughout the summer, Gijón finds some excuse for a fiesta almost every week, from the **Semana Negra** (Black Week) arts festival in early July, focusing on detective novels, to the **Fiesta de la Sidra Natural** (Natural Cider Festival) in late August. Varied musical programs and plenty of partying accompany all these events. The biggest week of all is **Semana Grande** (early to mid-August).

Sleeping

Getting a room in August can be a challenge, so book ahead. Prices tumble outside summer.

Hostal Manjón (☎ 985 35 23 78; Plaza del Marqués 1; s/d €37/49) Though basic and in a rather ugly high-rise (1st floor), it is in a handy location, with some rooms overlooking the marina and others facing Palacio de Revillagigedo.

Hotel Asturias (☎ 985 35 06 00; www.hotelasturiasgijon.es; Plaza Mayor 11; s/d €64/86) Touched with elegance, the Asturias' spacious rooms, with parquet floors, overlook Cimadevilla's main square. One room is adapted for guests with disabilities.

our pick La Casona de Jovellanos (☎ 985 34 20 24; www.lacasonadejovellanos.com; Plaza de Jovellanos 1; s/d €65/87; P) This antique-furnished 16th-century house is one of only two hotels in the old heart of town. It's on one of Cimadevilla's nicest squares, and there's a lively *chigre* (cider tavern) downstairs.

Hotel Castilla (☎ 985 34 62 00; www.hotelcastillagijon.com; Calle de la Corrida 50; s/d €62/90; 💻) Standing beside the lively Plaza Seis del Agosto, the Castilla is dated but cosy, with friendly service and good-sized rooms on seven floors.

Parador de Gijón Molino Viejo (☎ 985 37 05 11; www.parador.es; Parque de Isabel la Católica s/n; s/d €123/154; P ❄) In a building that spreads out discreetly at one end of the city's most pleasing park, these are the nicest top-end digs. Rooms are modern and comfortable; those with park views cost another €23.

Eating

The newer part of the city centre offers many options, but the most atmospheric area is Cimadevilla.

Restaurante Mercante (☎ 985 35 02 44; Cuesta del Cholo 2; meals €30-35) For views of the port while you munch on your fish and seafood, this is a great spot. On warm days, grab a table on the cobbled terrace, otherwise head upstairs. It's a bit of a knockabout place, full of atmosphere and always packed. It does a huge *parrillada de pescado* (mixed fish grill; €40 for two).

El Candil (☎ 985 35 30 38; www.elcandilgijon.es; Calle Numa Guilhou 1; meals €35-40; 🕑 Mon-Sat) A mix of local and Basque cooking is served up in this warm little eatery. Paintings of fish and copper pans decorate the yellow walls. Start with *almejas con alcachofas* (clams and artichokes) and follow with the catch of the day.

our pick Casa Zabala (☎ 985 34 17 31; Calle del Vizconde de Campo Grande 2; meals €35-45; 🕑 lunch & dinner Tue-Sat, lunch Sun) A fine eatery, nestled in among the many estimable *sidrerías* around Cimadevilla, Casa Zabala is good for seafood and fish of a more sophisticated ilk than you generally encounter hereabouts. The old-time looks have been maintained, and it's not everywhere you'll be served mullet in a *txacoli* (Basque white wine) sauce.

Casa Gerardo (☎ 985 88 77 97; Carretera AS19, Prendes; meals €45-70; 🕑 lunch Tue-Thu & Sun, lunch & dinner Fri & Sat) About 14km northwest of Gijón, this stone-fronted house has been serving up good local cooking since 1882. Five generations of the Morán family have refined their art to the point of snagging a Michelin star. Regular ALSA buses make the 20-minute run (€1.20) until 8.30pm.

Gallery Art & Food (☎ 985 19 66 66; www.galleryartandfood.com; Avenida de la Costa 118; meals €60-100; 🕑 lunch & dinner Thu-Sat, lunch Mon-Wed Sep-Jun, lunch & dinner Mon-Sat Jul-Aug) Tucked deep inside the basement of a nondescript building, this designer restaurant run by Alejandro García is the talk of the town. Even the menu will grab your attention, with dishes like *pig pop art* (roast suckling pig).

Casa Fernando (☎ 985 34 59 13; Plaza del Marqués 5) and **El Centenario** (☎ 985 34 35 61; Plaza Mayor 7; 🕑 lunch & dinner Wed-Sun, dinner Tue) are two typical seafood joints in Cimadevilla. Among more exotic local specialities are *oricios* (sea urchins) and *centollos* (spider crabs). *Raciones* go for around €5 to €15; cider for €2.50 per bottle. More *sidrerías* are found a bit further up in Cimadevilla and indeed all over town.

Drinking & Entertainment

Normal bars shut by 1.30am Sunday to Thursday and 3.30am on weekends. Those licensed to have bands and DJs (many fall into this category) can remain open until 3.30am during the week and 5.30am on weekends. Clubs disgorge their punters at 7.30am. The folks here really are deprived!

The *sidrerías* in Cimadevilla and around town are a fun way to start the night (and inject some food), and further up in Cimadevilla, a youthful music-bar scene flourishes in spots around Plaza Corrada and down Calle de la Vicaría.

An excellent traditional *sidrería* is **La Galana** (☎ 985 17 24 29; Plaza Mayor 10). The atmosphere is always boisterous in here and you can nibble on bar snacks to accompany the torrents of cider that bar staff pour into your glass.

Kitsch Café (Calle de la Rectoría 8; ⏰ 11am-1.30am Sun-Thu, 5pm-3.30am Fri & Sat) provides a suitably low-lit ambience before clubbing, while **Café Dam** (www.cafedam.net in Spanish; Calle de San Agustín 14; ⏰ 5.30pm-1am Sun-Thu, 5.30pm-5.30am Fri & Sat) is a great den for live music and DJs.

A more mature crowd descends upon the string of back-to-back bars and clubs along Calle de Rodríguez San Pedro – ranging from salsa dens **Cubanísimo** (☎ 985 17 25 17; Calle de Rodríguez San Pedro 35) and **La Bodeguita del Medio** (☎ 985 35 21 46; Calle de Rodríguez San Pedro 43; ⏰ 11pm-3.30am Mon-Wed, 11pm-4.30am Thu, 11pm-5.30am Fri & Sat) to **Ca Beleño** (☎ 984 29 22 53; Calle de Rodríguez San Pedro 39; ⏰ 5pm-1.30am Mon-Wed, 5pm-2.30am Thu-Sat), with jazz and Celtic sounds.

Sala Albéniz (☎ 985 35 65 13; www.sala-albeniz.com in Spanish; Calle de San Bernardo 62; cover €6-15; ⏰ 1am-7.30am Fri & Sat, 6.30pm-2am Sun), a large nightclub built into what was a classic old theatre, is a venue for touring bands. Otherwise, DJs keep the place hopping on Fridays and Saturdays with a broad range of music (although house is the dominant theme). Alternatives include salsa-oriented **Otto** (⏰ noon-7.30am Fri & Sat) on the waterfront and chilled **Lombok** (Calle de Rodríguez San Pedro 31; ⏰ 11pm-7.30am Fri & Sat).

Getting There & Away

BUS

Buses fan out across Asturias and beyond from the **ALSA bus station** (Calle de Magnus Blikstad). Hourly buses run to Villaviciosa (€2.45, 45 minutes) and there are six to 10 daily to Ribadesella (€5.60 to €6.56, 1½ to 1¾ hours). Six buses a day run to Llanes (€7.91, 1¾ to two hours) en route to Santander and San Sebastián. Plenty more express buses also run to Santander (€13.71 to €23.94, 3 to 4½ hours), stopping only in Oviedo (€1.99, 25 to 30 minutes). Westwards, up to 9 (three only on Sundays) daily services go to Cudillero (€4.55, one hour and 10 minutes) and Luarca (€8.75, 1½ hours).

TRAIN

The main train station is **Estación Cercanías** (Plaza del Humedal), though it isn't only used by suburban trains. The other station, Jovellanos, is 600m west. See p540 for trains between Oviedo and Gijón.

FEVE (www.feve.es), using Estación Cercanías only, runs *cercanías* to/from Cudillero (€2.60, 1½ hours) hourly on weekdays, half as often on weekends. Others run as far as Ferrol (€19.95, 6½ hours).

EAST COAST

Mostly Spanish holidaymakers seek out a summer spot on the beaches and coves along the coast east of Gijón, backed by the Picos de Europa, which rise as little as 15km inland.

Villaviciosa & Around

pop 14,600

Apart from the Iglesia de Santa María, a late-Romanesque structure, Villaviciosa's pretty centre is mostly a child of the 18th century. Calle García Caveda, the main street in the old town, is lined with noble houses.

The surrounding area is sprinkled with often diminutive and ancient churches. One that should not be missed is the pre-Romanesque **Iglesia de San Salvador de Valdediós** (☎ 985 89 23 24; admission €2; ⏰ 11am-1.30pm & 4-6.30pm Tue-Sun Apr-Sep, 11.15am-1pm Tue-Fri, 4-5.30pm Sat & Sun Oct-Mar), about 9km southwest, off the road to Pola de Siero. It was built in AD 893 as part of a palace complex for Alfonso III El Magno in what Asturians dubbed 'God's Valley', but archaeologists have failed to find any remnant beyond this simple church. Next door is the Romanesque **Iglesia y Monasterio de Santa María**, of the Cistercian persuasion, open for occasional guided tours. Oviedo-bound buses from Villaviciosa can drop you at San Pedro de Ambás, from where it's a 2km walk to the site.

Another fine Romanesque church is the **Iglesia de San Juan de Amandi**, 1.5km south of Villaviciosa in Amandi.

In Villaviciosa itself, which you could easily leave off your itinerary, there are 14 hotels and *pensiones* (small private hotels). One of the most attractive is the **Hotel Casa España** (☎ 985 89 20 30; www.hcasaespana.com; Plaza de Carlos I 3; s/d €57/71), with old-style rooms in the prettiest part of town.

La Casona de Amandi (☎ 985 89 01 30; Calle de San Juan 6; s/d €90/130; ⊠), a 19th-century farmhouse in Amandi, is a treat. Rooms, all of which ooze their own character and vary in size, contain Isabelline furnishings.

Facing the sea on the western side of the Ría de Villaviciosa is the minute port village of **Tazones**, 11km north of Villaviciosa along the AS256 and then the VV5. Carlos I supposedly first landed in Spain here in 1517. It's a popular spot with a cluster of seafood restaurants and three places to stay, including the twin portside hotel-restaurants **Hotel Imperial** (☎ 985 89 71 16) and **Hotel El Pescador** (☎ 985 89 70 77). In either a simple double will cost up to €55 in August. The best restaurant is the portside **Restaurante Rompeolas** (☎ 985 89 70 13; Calle de San Miguel 21; meals €30-40; Wed-Mon). Opening times in all spots outside the high summer period can be dodgy.

The eastern side of the estuary is covered by the broad golden sands of the **Playa de Rodiles**. Surfers might catch a wave here in late summer. **Camping La Ensenada** (☎ 985 99 61 56; sites per 2 people, car & tent €16; Feb–mid-Dec) is a beachfront camping ground that has laundry facilities and a restaurant.

GETTING THERE & AWAY

ALSA provides up to 11 buses daily to/from Oviedo (€3.50, 35 minutes to one hour) and Ribadesella (€3.20, 30 to 55 minutes), as well as an hourly service to/from Gijón (€2.45, 30 to 45 minutes). From early July to early September a 12.45pm bus runs to Playa de Rodiles, returning six hours later.

Lastres

In addition to various sandy beaches, the main stop along the 40km stretch between Villaviciosa and Ribadesella is the precarious cliffside fishing village of Lastres, a scruffier version of Cudillero (p548), with a couple of 16th-century churches thrown in.

Ribadesella

pop 6290

Unless you've booked in advance, it's best to stay away from Ribadesella on the first weekend after 2 August, when the place goes mad for the **Descenso Internacional del Sella** (p555), a canoeing festival. Otherwise, Ribadesella is a low-key resort. Its two halves, split by the Río Sella's estuary, are joined by a long, low bridge. The western half has a good, expansive beach, Playa de Santa Marina, while the older part of town and fishing harbour are on the eastern side.

The **tourist office** (☎ 985 86 00 38; www.ayto-ribadesella.es; Paseo Princesa Letizia s/n; 10am-10pm daily Jul-Sep, 10am-2pm & 5-8pm Mon-Sat, 11am-2pm Sun Oct-Jun) is at the eastern end of the Sella bridge.

SIGHTS & ACTIVITIES

To see some real cave paintings (as opposed to the copies at Altamira in Cantabria), plan on visiting the **Cueva de Tito Bustillo** (☎ 985 86 11 20; http://titobustillo.com; adult/senior, student & child €4/2; 10am-5.15pm Wed-Sun Apr–mid-Sep). The cave drawings here, mostly of horses, are roughly 14,000 years old.

The site is a short distance south of the western end of the Sella bridge. Groups enter the cave every 25 minutes. The hour-long, 1.5km tour includes some slippery stretches, and is not recommended for children under 11. There's a limit of 360 visitors daily, so turn up early in August, or book by phone or through www.asturias.es (click on What to See under Visit Asturias, then Archaeological Sites on the second page of listings).

Several companies can set you up with canoe trips along the Río Sella, rent you a bike, take you canyoning and so on. Try **Turaventura** (☎ 985 86 02 67; www.turaventura.com in Spanish; Calle de Manuel Caso de la Villa 50).

SLEEPING

Albergue Roberto Frassinelli (☎ 985 86 11 05; www.albergueribadesella.com; Calle de Ricardo Canga; per person under/over 30yr with hostelling card €13.50/16;) Housed in a grand *palacio de indianos* (mansion built by a returnee from the Americas), this REAJ hostel backs onto Playa de Santa Marina. It has two-, four- and six-bed rooms. Meals cost €6 to €7.

Hotel Covadonga (☎ 985 86 01 10; Calle de Manuel Caso de la Villa 9; d €55) About 100m back from the port in the older part of town, the Covadonga is a step back in time, a little dusty but full of character and generally booked in August. Downstairs is a boisterous *sidrería*.

EATING

The busy waterfront *sidrerías* on the eastern side of the river are a good bet for seafood.

Casa Gaspar (☎ 985 86 06 76; Calle de López Muñiz 6; meals €20; Fri-Wed) If waves of fish leave you nauseous, you could opt for tapas and cider in copious quantities at Casa Gaspar, in the heart of the old town. On summer nights especially it gets rollickingly busy.

Casa Tista (☎ 985 86 09 54; meals €35; Wed-Mon) Want a local tip? For the best in straightforward, fresh fish (grilled or lightly baked) or seafood (sold by weight) head for Casa Tista, 5km east of Ribadesella along the AS263, just after the hamlet of Toriello. Sit inside or under the leafy pergola.

GETTING THERE & AWAY

The **bus station** (☎ 985 86 13 03; Avenida del Palacio Valdés) is about 300m south of the bridge. There are three to six services daily to/from Arriondas (€1.50, 25 minutes), up to nine for Oviedo (€6.55, 65 minutes to 2¼ hours) and Gijón (€5.60 to €6.56, 1½ to 1¾ hours), and plenty east to/from Llanes (€2.25, 30 to 40 minutes). Only a couple run to San Vicente de la Barquera (€3.98) and Santander (€7.75, 1½ to 2½ hours). In July and August a couple of daily buses run to/from Cangas de Onís.

FEVE trains run at least thrice daily to/from Llanes and Oviedo, and twice to/from Santander.

Ribadesella to Llanes

Several little beaches and coves await discovery between Ribadesella and Llanes by those with transport and time. About 10km short of Llanes, **Playa de San Antolín** is a vast, unprotected beach where you might pick up the odd wave. A couple of kilometres further on you hit the hamlet of Niembro. Nearby is **Playa de Torimbia**, a beautiful, golden crescent backed by green hills. Some bathers shed all. One kilometre further on is the village-cum-understated-holiday-resort of **Barro**. The beach is beaut but the ranks of apartments that have sprung up about 500m inland are less so.

Llanes

pop 13,700

Inhabited since ancient times, Llanes was for a long period an independent-minded town and whaling port with its own charter awarded by Alfonso IX of León in 1206. Today, with a small medieval core and bustling harbour, it's one of northern Spain's more popular holiday destinations – a handy base for some very pretty beaches and with the Picos de Europa close at hand.

The **tourist office** (☎ 985 40 01 64; www.llanes.com; Calle Alfonso IX s/n; 🕓 10am-2pm & 5-9pm daily mid-Jun–mid-Sep, 10am-2pm & 4-6.30pm Mon-Sat, 10am-2pm Sun mid-Sep–mid-Jun) is in La Torre, a tower left over from Llanes' 13th-century defences.

Of the three town beaches, **Playa de Toró** to the east, its limpid waters dotted with jutting pillars of rock, is easily the best.

La Basílica (Plaza de Cristo Rey), the town's main and mostly Gothic church, was begun in 1240 and is worth a quick inspection if you find it open.

Strewn alongside the far end of the pier like a set of children's blocks are the **Cubes of Memory**, painter Agustín Ibarrola's playful public artwork using the port's breakwater as his canvas.

SLEEPING & EATING

In the June to mid-September period, booking is virtually essential, especially at weekends, as Llanes fills to the brim.

Pensión La Guía (☎ 985 40 25 77; www.pensionlaguia.com; Plaza de Parres Sobrino 1; d €65) Just west of the river, this 300-year-old house has plenty of charm, with glassed-in balconies overlooking the plaza. The structure is a web of dark timber beams and terracotta floors, although the rooms themselves are plainer. Everything is kept religiously spick and span.

El Bodegón (☎ 985 40 01 85; Calle Mayor 14; tapas €4-8; 🕓 Fri-Wed) A rollicking good-fun place for cider and chips (and more). El Bodegón is very social, especially if you crowd onto the terrace situated out the back in a pretty cobbled square.

Plenty of lively *marisquerías* (seafood eateries) and *sidrerías* line Calles Mayor and de Manuel Cué, so stoking up on sea critters and washing them down with cascades of cider is an easy task.

GETTING THERE & AWAY

The **bus station** (Calle La Bolera) is east of the river. Five daily ALSA buses stop in Llanes between Gijón (€7.91, 1¾ hours) and Santander (€5.92, 1½ to two hours). Regular services also run to/from Oviedo (€8.80, 1¼ to 2¼ hours).

Three or four FEVE trains come here daily from Oviedo and Ribadesella, two of them continuing to Santander.

East of Llanes

The 350m-long **Playa La Ballota** is a particularly attractive beach a few kilometres east of Llanes, hemmed in by green cliffs and accessible by dirt track. Part of it is for nudists. On the coast by **Vidiago**, search out **Arenillas**, where a geiser-style jet of seawater is pumped up rhythmically by the sea through a tunnel in the limestone. **Playa de la Franca**, further towards Cantabria, is also nice and has a summer camping ground.

WEST COAST

Avilés

pop 85,000

In the 1950s, with the steel industry in full swing, Avilés was reckoned to be one of the most polluted cities in Europe. Today its compact old town, nestling next to the Ría de Avilés estuary that was once a heaving port, has been cleaned up and makes for an attractive few hours' strolling, especially along colonnaded streets like Calle de Bances Candamo and Calle de la Ferrería. Plaza de España is fronted by two elegant 17th-century buildings, one of which is home to the town hall. Locals gather on Plaza de Carbayedo to wine, dine and chat.

The big news, however, is the future. By 2011 the **Centro Niemeyer** (www.niemeyercenter.org), across the estuary on once-industrial land, will open its doors and become a cultural rival for Bilbao's Museo Guggenheim. Exhibitions are already being organised for this extraordinary 21st-century gift from Brazil's Oscar Niemeyer.

You'll find 16 hotels and *pensiones* here. A great place to sample the local atmosphere and food is **Casa Tataguyo** (☎ 985 56 48 15; www.tataguyo.com; Plaza de Carbayedo 6; meals €40-45), in business since 1845. Seafood lovers should make for neighbouring Salinas, a coastal suburb, and the century-old **Real Balneario de Salinas** (☎ 985 51 86 13; www.restaurantebalneario.com; Avenida de San Juan Sitges 3; meals €35-40; 🕑 lunch & dinner Tue-Sat, lunch Sun). Opened as a bathing and social centre right on the beach by King Alfonso XIII in 1916, it's a top seafood restaurant today. Ask for the day's catch and salivate!

ALSA buses run every half hour to/from Gijón (€1.95, 30 minutes). There are plenty for Oviedo (€2.06, 45 to 60 minutes) too. FEVE trains also connect with Gijón and Oviedo.

Cudillero

pop 1710

Cudillero is the most picturesque fishing village on the Asturian coast, and it knows it. The houses, painted in varying pastel shades, cascade down to a tiny port on a narrow inlet. Despite its touristy feel, Cudillero is cute and remains reasonably relaxed, even in mid-August when almost every room in town is occupied. For a good map of area beaches, stop by the **tourist office** (☎ 985 59 13 77; www.ayuntamientodecudillero.org; 🕑 10am-9pm daily Jul-Sep, 10am-2pm & 5-8pm Mon-Sat, 11am-2pm Sun Oct-Jun) by the port, which is also the only place to park.

The main activity is watching the fishing boats come in (between 5pm and 8pm) and unload their catch, then sampling fish, molluscs and urchins at the *sidrerías*. The former *lonja* (fish market) is now a minor but not uninteresting fishing museum, **Los Pixuetos y la Mar** (admission €1; 🕑 9am-2pm & 4-7pm Tue-Sun), all in Spanish only.

BEACHES

The coast around here is a particularly appealing sequence of cliffs and beaches. The nearest beach is the fine, sandy **Playa de Aguilar**, a 3km drive or walk east. Those to the west include **Playa Concha de Artedo** (4km) and the pretty **Playa de San Pedro** (10km).

Playa del Silencio (also called El Gavieiru), 15km west of Cudillero, could certainly qualify as one of Spain's most beautiful beaches: a long sandy cove backed by a natural rock amphitheatre. Take the exit for Novellana and follow signs to Castañeras.

SLEEPING

Accommodation in the village of Cudillero is limited, especially during the low season, when some places shut down.

Camping L'Amuravela (☎ 985 59 09 95; www.lamuravela.com; sites per 2 people, car & tent €22.50; 🕑 Mar-Nov; P) At the village of El Pito, about 1.5km southeast (uphill) from the town centre, this is the closest camping ground to town. Facilities include a big playground and bungalows for up to five people.

Hotel Casa Prendes (☎ 985 59 15 00; Calle San José 4; d €82) This blue-fronted stop is a nicely maintained port hotel. Single rates (€48 to €58) are available outside August. The owners also rent apartments.

La Casona de Pío (☎ 985 59 15 12; www.arrakis.es/~casonadepio in Spanish; Calle del Ríofrío; s/d €66/84) Just back from the port area is this charming stone house, featuring 11 very comfortable rooms with a rustic touch, and a good restaurant.

Plenty of hotels, *casas de aldea* (village houses), *pensiones* and apartments are scattered around the countryside within a few kilometres.

EATING

There's no shortage of eateries down towards the port. A meal with drinks is likely to cost you around €25 to €35 in most places.

Sidrería El Patrón (Calle de Suárez Inclán 2; meals €20) Back up the road a bit from the port, this is where many locals hang out for *raciones* of seafood or cheese, and sausage or ham platters (€6 to €16).

El Faro (☎ 985 59 15 32; Calle del Ríofrío; meals €30; ⏰ Thu-Tue) This is an attractive eatery hidden one street back from the port. A combination of stone, timber and blue decor creates a welcoming atmosphere in which to dig into an *arroz caldoso* (a seafood and rice stew).

GETTING THERE & AWAY

The bus station is at the top of the hill, 800m from the port, and the FEVE train station is 1km further inland. See p545.

Luarca

pop 4510

More dishevelled than Cudillero, Luarca has a similar setting in a deep valley running down to a larger harbour full of small fishing boats. It's a base for some good nearby beaches.

The **tourist office** (☎ 985 64 00 83; www.turismoluarcavaldes.com in Spanish; Calle Caleros 11; ⏰ 10am-2pm & 4.30-6.30pm Tue-Fri, 10.30am-2pm & 5-7pm Sat, noon-2pm Sun) is behind the town hall.

The **Aula del Mar** (☎ 985 64 04 47; www.cepesma.com), 1.5km uphill in the Villar district, features a collection of giant squid, along with some 700 other marine species. It was closed at time of writing.

BEACHES

Sandy, 600m-long **Playa de Cueva**, 7km east of Luarca, is one of the best beaches in the district, with cliffs, caves and occasional decent surf. Five kilometres further on, **Cabo Busto** will give you some sense of the Asturian coast's wildness as waves crash onto the jagged, rocky cliffs. **Playa de Otur**, 8km west of Luarca, and **Playa de Barayo**, 1km further, are good sandy beaches in pretty bays. Barayo is a protected natural reserve at the mouth of a river winding through wetlands and dunes. To reach it, turn off the N634 at Puerto de Vega and head for the village of Vigo, then follow signs (which are painted on the road) for the beach. From the car park, the beach is accessible by a well-marked 30-minute nature hike.

SLEEPING & EATING

At least seven hotels and *hostales* are on or just off the central Plaza de Alfonso X, including three cheapies in Calle Crucero. Several seafood eateries dot the waterfront.

Hotel La Colmena (☎ 985 64 02 78; Calle de Uría 2; s/d €45/60; 💻) On the corner of the street and Plaza de Alfonso X, this comfortable hotel has some nice touches, such as the dark parquet floors, high ceilings and tall windows.

Hotel Cabo Busto (☎ 985 47 55 22; www.cabobusto.com; Valdés s/n; d €65; Ⓟ) About 10km east of Luarca in Busto, on the windswept cape of the same, this is a lovely, tranquil retreat. Tastefully decorated and spacious rooms with dark hardwood floors are kept in perfect nick by Joaquina, who also serves up a smashing breakfast in the welcoming lounge-dining area.

our pick **Hotel Villa La Argentina** (☎ 985 64 01 02; www.villalaargentina.com; s/d/ste €88/95/127; Ⓟ) This 1899 *casa de indianos* is now a comfy 12-room hotel amid lovely gardens that drips with belle époque elegance. Antique furniture brings warmth to the rooms, with their high ceilings, chandeliers and understated decoration. It's in the Villar district about 1.5km southeast (uphill) from Luarca.

El Barómetro (☎ 985 47 06 62; Paseo del Muelle 5; meals €30-35; ⏰ lunch & dinner Thu-Tue, lunch Sun) A great spot for *calamares en potera* (calamari in squid ink), this one-storey, portside house is a simple, cheerful affair. Enter the marine-blue house and sit down for Asturian cooking with a seaside leaning. A classic is *fabes con almejas* (beans and clams). It might not sound great but try it!

our pick **Restaurante Sport** (☎ 985 64 10 78; Calle de Rivero 8; meals €40-50; ⏰ lunch & dinner Thu-Tue, lunch Sun) This family seafood restaurant, hidden a few steps away from the waterfront, has been pleasing customers since the early 1950s. Slurp a half-dozen oysters (€9) as a starter. Catch of the day is sold at €6 per 100g, as are such north-coast delicacies as *percebes* (goose barnacles; €12). The *bonito en rollo con salsa de tomate* (delicious patties of northern tuna mixed with vegetables and drowned in fresh tomato sauce) is a traditional local dish.

GETTING THERE & AWAY

Up to seven daily ALSA buses run to/from Oviedo (€8.10, 1½ hours) and along the coast as far as Ribadeo (Galicia). Up to nine come from Gijón, too. The FEVE train station is 800m south of the town centre. Three trains run daily to/from Cudillero and Oviedo, and two along the coast to/from Ferrol (Galicia).

Coaña & Río Navia

The small town of Coaña lies about 4km inland of the port of Navia, west of Luarca.

A couple of kilometres beyond is the **Castro de Coaña** (☎ 985 97 84 01; adult/child €3/1.50, Wed free; 11am-2pm & 4-7pm Tue-Sun Apr-Sep, 11am-3pm Tue-Sun Oct-Mar), one of the best-preserved Celtic settlements in northern Spain and well worth visiting.

From the *castro* (Celtic-fortified village), a road snakes its way high above the cobalt-blue Río Navia, through classic Asturian countryside – meadows alternating with rocky precipices – to Lugo in Galicia, crossing some of Galicia's least-visited and wildest territory, around the town of **Fonsagrada**.

Tapia de Casariego

pop 4250

This welcoming fishing haven makes a pleasant lunch stop if you're driving, but little more. If you get stuck here, you'll find a half-dozen options for stopping overnight. Beaches along the next few kilometres west, such as **Playa Anguileiro**, **Playa La Paloma**, **Playa de Serantes** and **Playa de Santa Gadea**, all boast surfable waves, and there are several surf shops in Tapia.

Castropol & Around

pop 3920

Ría de Ribadeo marks the frontier between Asturias and Galicia. Spanning the broad mouth of this, the first of the many grand estuaries that slice into Galicia's coast, is the Puente de los Santos.

Whitewashed Castropol village, on a rise a few kilometres up the eastern side of the *ría* (estuary), is a tranquil alternative to Ribadeo, Galicia, the town on the other side. From Castropol, the N640 southwest to Lugo forms a little-travelled back route into Galicia.

Camping Playa Penarronda (☎ 985 62 30 22; www.campingplayapenarronda.com; sites per 2 people, car & tent €20; Easter-Sep) is set on the fringe of the broad, open Playa de Penarronda beach, 7km northeast of Castropol, and offers a cafe and shop as well as bicycle hire.

One of two hotels at the northern entrance into Castropol, **Hotel Casa Vicente** (☎ 985 63 50 51; Carretera General; s/d €37/55) has 14 rooms, half of which give matchless views of the *ría*.

Like a haughty countess, the early-20th-century mansion complex **Palacete Peñalba** (☎ 985 63 61 25; www.hotelpalacetepenalba.com; Calle Granda s/n; d €120-130) stands amid almost 2 sq km of sculpted gardens studded with palms, magnolias and statues in Figueras del Mar, 4km north of Castropol and 200m from the beach. A total of 19 rooms are spread out over two buildings, one of them a Modernista gem.

INLAND WESTERN ASTURIAS

Although it's mostly difficult to reach unless you're driving, there's some gorgeous country in southwest Asturias. Even just passing through on alternative routes into Castilla y León, such as the AS226 via the 1587m Puerto Ventana, the AS227 via the beautiful 1486m Puerto de Somiedo, or the AS213 via the 1525m Puerto de Leitariegos, can be rewarding.

Salas

pop 6080

Between Oviedo and Luarca drivers could take, instead of the standard highways, the pretty N634, which snakes up and down lush valleys northwest of Oviedo. At Salas, 48km from Oviedo, it soon becomes clear that the town's most famous son was Grand Inquisitor Fernando de Valdés Salas, who also founded Oviedo's university in the 16th century. His **castle** has been converted into the Hotel Castillo de Valdés Salas, and his elaborate alabaster tomb is inside the nearby **Colegiata de Santa María**.

Charming **Hotel Castillo de Valdés Salas** (☎ 985 83 01 73; www.castillovaldesalas.com; Plaza Campa; s/d €68/85), gathered around a quiet courtyard lined by a polished timber gallery, is in a beautiful 16th-century building. Rooms are simple enough but attractive, with parquet and iron bed heads. The enchantment is in the rest of the building.

Regular ALSA buses run to/from Oviedo (€3.90, 1¼ hours).

Senda del Oso

Between the villages of Tuñón and Entrago, southwest of Oviedo, the Senda del Oso is a 20km walking and cycling path that follows the course of a former mine railway through fields, riverbank woodlands and canyons. About 5km south of Tuñón, the path passes the **Monte del Oso** (Bear Mountain), where Paca and Tola, two Cantabrian brown bears orphaned by a hunter in 1996, are the only bears in the area to live in a 40,000-sq-metre compound (other bears here are wild and hard to see). Each day around noon, except during their hibernation from about December to February, the bears are fed at a spot where their compound borders the path (look for the 'Cercado del Oso' sign) and you stand an excellent chance of seeing them. At the time of writing you could see them in a small enclosed area with a male

THERE'S A BEAR IN THERE

The wild mountain area of southwest Asturias and northern Castilla y León is the main remaining bastion of the Cantabrian version of the brown bear *(oso pardo)*, of which an estimated 105 to 130 remain. Loved by ecologists and loathed by farmers, this lumbering beast can reach 200kg and live an average of 25 to 30 years. The bear population (which in the 1990s had dropped to 70) is not out of the woods, despite rarely being hunted nowadays. Increasingly used to people, bears have become more daring in recent years, occasionally popping up in villages and on farms, attacking honeycombs, livestock and rubbish containers. Part of the reason seems to be the reduction of blueberries in the forest, due, it is thought, to global warming, which is pushing bears to look for other sources of food. Conservationists fear for the bears if they come to depend on humans for food. Unregulated tours through the Parque Natural de Somiedo in search of bears are also beginning and many fear the arrival of tour groups will make things worse, especially if organisers leave food out to attract the bears.

The **Fundación Oso Pardo** (☎ 942 23 49 00; www.fundacionosopardo.org) organises hikes through the Somiedo park but doesn't guarantee sightings. Indeed, the hikes are not specifically aimed at spotting bears (though you could get lucky).

bear transferred out of captivity to attempt mating. When we passed through, the three bears (!) didn't seem too interested in a roll in the hay. One kilometre southwest of this spot, in Proaza, is the **Casa del Oso** (☎ 985 76 10 53; admission free; ⌚ 10am-2pm & 4-7pm), with exhibits (in Spanish only) on Spanish brown bears.

GETTING THERE & AROUND

The bear-feeding spot is a 15-minute walk from the AS228 Trubia–Tuñón–Entrago road, 2km north of Proaza: watch for the 'Cercado del Osero' sign and car park. Three daily buses run from Oviedo bus station to Entrago via Tuñón and Proaza.

Parque Natural de Somiedo

If you fancy exploring dramatic mountain country that few foreigners know, consider this 300-sq-km protected area on the northern flank of the Cordillera Cantábrica. Composed of five valleys descending from the cordillera's 2000m-plus main ridge, the park is characterised by lush woodlands and high pastures dotted with (now largely abandoned) thatched shepherds' shelters *(tietos)*. It's also the main habitat of Spain's remaining brown bear population (see the boxed text, above).

Each of the valleys has a number of marked walking trails, which you can find out about at the park's **Centro de Recepción** (☎ 985 76 34 06; www.somiedo.es; ⌚ 10am-2.30pm & 4-9pm daily mid-Jun–mid-Sep, 10am-2pm & 4-7pm Mon-Fri & Sun, 10am-2.30pm & 4-9pm Sat mid-Sep–mid-Jun) in the centre of the surprisingly unimpressive village of **Pola de Somiedo**. Pola also has a bank, a supermarket and half-a-dozen budget and midrange places to stay.

One of the best (and most popular) walking areas is the **Valle del Lago**, whose upper reaches contain a number of glacial lakes and high summer pastures. There is a camping ground and several other places to stay and eat in Valle del Lago hamlet, a wonderful 8km drive southeast of Pola de Somiedo that winds and climbs to about 1300m. The hamlet is a good (and in summer very popular) starting point for walks.

One or two daily buses (weekdays) run between Oviedo and Pola de Somiedo (€6.85, 1¼ to two hours). From Proaza, with your own wheels, the most spectacular route takes you along the AS228 road, through the Desfiladero del Teverga gorge and, from San Martín, along the high mountain road that crosses the Puerto de San Lorenzo pass (1894m, often snowed under in winter) and runs past tiny rural hamlets. The pass marks the northeast boundary of the park. The mountain road reaches the AS227 road at La Riera, 8km north of Pola de Somiedo.

Cangas del Narcea & Around

Busy town Cangas del Narcea, 85km southwest of Oviedo and capital of Asturias' modest wine production, is not a pretty place. However, the roads leading south out of town are another matter. In particular, follow the AS15 and Río Narcea south for 6km and then cut west along the AS29. A loop of about 75km takes you over seven mountain passes, past huddles of slate-roofed houses and lush vegetation. San Antolín

THE LAST OF THE CATTLE FARMERS?

Ramiro sits nonchalantly astride his donkey as he surveys the rooftops of his mountain village, Orderias.

'Only seven of the houses are inhabited now, two here [in the upper part] and five down in the lower *barrio* (district). The other one [high up on the other side of the road] is abandoned,' he recounts. 'We're oldies, mostly retired. Some others come on weekends…'

'We still live off cattle farming. That's all there is here. In summer we let them graze in the fields around here and up around the [San Lorenzo] pass, and go up every two or three days to check on them. In winter, we have to bring them down to the village and keep them in the *cuadras* (stables). That's much more work.'

It's late May and still bitingly cold. This afternoon a heavy hailstorm has left the pass white.

'The good thing about this is that you have no boss or timetable. Cattle don't care if they're fed at nine or ten [o'clock]. In August we have to keep a watch for wolves, as they come down then to teach their young to hunt.'

'The young people left to find work in Oviedo and Gijón. I guess we'll keep working with the cattle. That's all there is here. Until we move on to that other place.' Ramiro looks skyward. 'Can't be too bad there,' he smiles, 'because no one ever comes back!' With that, he shuffles off on his donkey between the stone houses and timber *hórreos* (grain storage huts on stilts).

Further down the road, in La Morteras, Susana, one of the area's few women farmers (she and her husband raise horses, and a filly was just born yesterday), says she wouldn't be in the cattle game. 'Without subsidies, you just can't make a living.' But she loves this country. To the south, she points to where most of the Somiedo bear population lives. 'You sometimes see them here.' To the north is wolf territory and wild boar abound. Susana and her husband generally sell their horses to the abattoirs. 'But not this filly – I am hanging on to her!'

de Ibias, on the AS384, has a couple of places to eat. Here you turn east along the AS384 through densely forested country, part of which falls within the **Parque Natural de las Fuentes del Narcea** (www.fuentesdelnarcea.org). The heartland of this area is the unique **Parque Natural Integral de Muniellos** (about 6km west of the of AS15 along the AS384 road, near the town of Moal). It is considered the biggest and best-preserved oak forest in Europe and was declared a Unesco Biosphere in 2000. Visits are guided and limited to 20 people per day. Call ☎ 012 (or ☎ +34 985 27 91 00 from outside Asturias) to book a place. You can get information on the park at the **Centro de Interpretación** (11am-7pm), about 7km west of the AS15 road, just after you turn-off for the hamlet of Oballo.

PICOS DE EUROPA

These jagged, deeply fissured mountains straddling Asturias, Cantabria and the northeast of Castilla y León province amount to some of the finest walking country in Spain, offering plentiful short and long outings for striders of all levels, plus lots of scope for climbers and cavers, too.

Beginning only 15km from the coast, and stretching little more than 40km from east to west and 25km north to south, the Picos still encompass enough spectacular mountain and gorge scenery to ensure a continual flow of Spanish and international visitors. They comprise three limestone massifs, whose geological structure is unique in Spain and similar to that of the Alps: the eastern Macizo Andara, with a summit of 2444m; the western Macizo El Cornión, rising to 2596m; and the particularly rocky Macizo Central or Macizo Los Urrieles, reaching 2648m. The 647-sq-km Parque Nacional de los Picos de Europa covers all three massifs and is Spain's second-biggest national park. Some websites worth checking out include www.turismopicosdeeuropa.com (in Spanish), www.liebanaypicosdeeuropa.com and www.picosdeeuropa.com (in Spanish).

Virtually deserted in winter, the area is full to bursting in August and you should always try to book ahead, whether you are heading for a hotel or a mountain *refugio* (refuge).

Orientation

The main access towns for the Picos are Cangas de Onís in the northwest, Arenas de Cabrales in the central north and Potes in the southeast. Paved roads lead from Cangas southeast up to Covadonga, Lago de Enol and Lago de la Ercina; from Arenas south up to Poncebos then east up to Sotres and Tresviso; and from Potes west to Fuente Dé. The mountains are roughly bounded on the western side by Río Sella and the N625 Cangas de Onís–Riaño road; on the north by the AS114 Cangas de Onís–Arenas de Cabrales–Panes road; and on the east by Río Deva and the N621 Panes–Potes road.

MAPS

The best maps of the Picos, sold in shops in Cangas de Onís, Potes and elsewhere for €4 to €5 each, are Adrados Ediciones' *Picos de Europa* (1:80,000), *Picos de Europa Macizos Central y Oriental* (1:25,000) and *Picos de Europa Macizo Occidental* (1:25,000).

Information

The national park's main information office, in Cangas de Onís, is **Casa Dago** (☎ 985 84 86 14; Avenida de Covadonga 43; 🕑 9am-2.30pm). Sometimes it opens in the afternoon too. Other park information offices are in **Posada de Valdeón** (☎ 987 74 05 49; Travesía de los Llanos; 🕑 9am-5pm daily Jul & Aug, 9am-2pm Sat & Sun Sep-Jun) in the southwest, where hours can vary considerably, and in **Tama** (☎ 942 73 81 09; Avenida Luis Cuevas 2A; 🕑 9am-8pm Jun-Sep, 9am-6pm Oct-May) in east Cantabria. Basic information on walks and accommodation is available at these offices. Local tourist offices can usually provide information too.

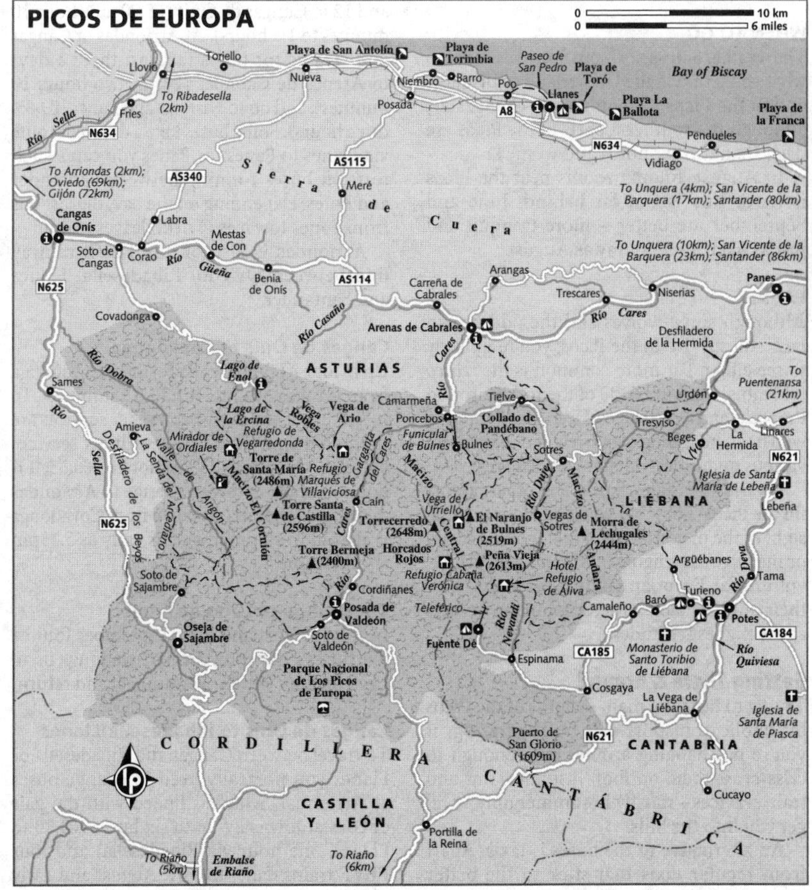

WARNING

Picos weather is notoriously changeable, and mist, rain, cold and snow are common problems. Higher up, few trails are marked and water sources are rare. Paying insufficient attention to these details has cost several lives over the years.

Cangas de Onís, Arenas de Cabrales and Potes all have banks, ATMs and supermarkets. Cangas and Potes are the best places to buy outdoor equipment.

Camping within the national park is permitted only above 1600m and only overnight: tents can only be erected in the evening and must be taken down in the morning.

WHEN TO GO

The weather across northern Spain is similar to what you'd find in the UK, Ireland or Brittany, and in the Picos it's notoriously changeable, although the southeast parts of the Picos are drier than further north and west.

In August, finding rooms near the Picos is hard. July is not far behind. June and September are better – more tranquil and just as likely to be sunny as August.

FAUNA

Although some wolves and the odd brown bear still survive in the Picos, you're unlikely to see either. Far more common is the *rebeco* (chamois). Around 6500 of them skip around the rocks and steep slopes. Deer, foxes, badgers, wild boar, hedgehogs, squirrels and martens, in various quantities, inhabit wooded areas.

A variety of eagles, hawks and other raptors fill the Picos' skies, but you'd be lucky to catch sight of the majestic *águila real* (golden eagle) or the huge scavenging *buitre leonado* (griffon vulture) or Egyptian vulture. Choughs, with their unmistakable caws, accompany walkers at the highest altitudes.

Getting There & Around

Trying to taste the main delights of the Picos by public transport can be frustrating, if you're not hanging around long enough to criss-cross them on foot. Just a few bus and train services – mostly in summer only – will get you into the hills.

An alternative to the buses is taxis. Apart from regular taxis that stick to the better roads, such as **Taxitur** (☎ 985 84 87 97, 689 143881) in Cangas, there are also 4WD taxi services that can manage some of the mountain tracks. One of the latter is operated by Casa Cipriano (p559) in Sotres. A regular taxi costs €28 from Cangas de Onís to the Lagos de Covadonga, and about €20 from Arenas de Cabrales to Sotres, or Potes to Fuente Dé.

BUS & TRAIN

Details of the following bus and train services change from time to time, but the broad outlines described below are likely to be maintained.

Oviedo to Panes

From Oviedo, ALSA has up to 13 buses daily to Arriondas (€5.10, one hour to 1¼ hours) and 12 to Cangas de Onís (€5.70, one hour 10 minutes to 1½ hours). At Arriondas or Cangas you change for buses (at least three a day) to Arenas de Cabrales (€8.10, two hours 10 minutes), and on to Niserias and Panes (€9.85, three hours). Some buses take a different route via Llanes to Panes. At Panes you can switch to/from buses running between Santander and Potes. Depending on the day, the last bus from Panes towards Oviedo leaves at 4pm.

Arriondas is also on the FEVE railway line between Oviedo, Ribadesella, Llanes and Santander.

Cangas de Onís to Covadonga

Up to four ALSA buses daily run to Covadonga from Cangas de Onís (€1.20, 15 minutes). In July, August and early September services are more frequent. There are few direct services between Oviedo and Covadonga (€6.55, 1¾ hours) – most involve a change in Arriondas or Cangas. The last bus down from Covadonga is at 8pm in summer, and as early as 5.15pm at other times.

Covadonga to Lago de Enol

In July, August and early September four or five buses a day travel from Covadonga up to Lago de Enol (€1.85, 30 minutes) and return.

Cangas de Onís to Ribadesella/Llanes

To travel between Cangas and Ribadesella or Llanes you normally need to change buses at Arriondas, which is linked with the pair of coastal towns by up to six buses (€3.70 to Llanes, one hour via Ribadesella) and four FEVE trains daily. In July, August and early

September, however, up to three daily buses run from Cangas to Ribadesella and return.

Cangas de Onís to Oseja de Sajambre

On weekdays, one bus a day (two a day from late June to early September) links these two spots (€2.45, one hour).

Poncebos & Garganta del Cares

From July to early September up to three buses go between Arenas de Cabrales and Poncebos Monday to Friday (but only one on weekends). In the same period a daily ALSA bus runs in the morning from Oviedo to Cangas de Onís and Posada de Valdeón, then in the afternoon/evening from Poncebos back to Cangas and Oviedo. The idea is that you walk the 8km road along the Cares valley from Posada to Caín, then along the Garganta del Cares gorge to Poncebos, and be picked up at the end. Buses to/from Llanes, Ribadesella and Gijón connect with this service at Cangas de Onís.

Arenas de Cabrales to Llanes

ALSA buses link Arenas de Cabrales with Llanes once or twice daily (€2.80 to €5.25, one to two hours depending on the route).

Santander to Picos

From Santander, **Autobuses Palomera** (☎ 942 88 06 11; www.autobusespalomera.com) travels via San Vicente de la Barquera to Panes, Urdón, La Hermida, Lebeña and Potes (€7.05, 2½ hours), and returns, two or three times daily. In July and August, the line is sometimes extended to Fuente Dé and one or two return services between Potes and Fuente Dé (about 50 minutes) are added.

WESTERN PICOS

Arriondas

pop 2580

Arriondas is the starting point for easy and popular **canoe trips** down pretty Río Sella to various end points between Fries and Llovio (13km to 16km). That is about the limit of the interest in this otherwise dreary provincial town.

At least a dozen agencies in town will rent you a canoe, paddle, life jacket and waterproof container, show you how to paddle and bring you back to Arriondas at the end. Try **Astur Aventura** (☎ 985 84 10 02; www.asturaventura.net in Spanish; Calle Río Piloña) or **Jaire** (☎ 985 84 14 64; www.canoasdelsella.com in Spanish; Calle Juan Carlos I 7). The standard charge, including a picnic lunch, is around €25 per person. Excursions set off around 11am. Bring a change of clothes. Agencies in Cangas de Onís and nearby coastal towns offer much the same deal, including transport to Arriondas and return.

This stretch of the Sella has a few entertaining minor rapids, but it's not a serious white-water affair, and anyone from about eight years old can enjoy this outing.

The river is at its busiest on the first Saturday after 2 August, when 1500 canoes head downriver from Arriondas to Ribadesella, in the **Descenso Internacional del Sella** (www.descensodelsella.com), an international canoeing event.

Arriondas has a range of accommodation, including the basic **Camping Sella** (☎ 985 84 09 68; www.campingsella.info; sites per 2 people, car & tent €17; 🕑 mid-Jun–mid-Sep), about 100m from Río Sella, and **Hotel La Estrada** (☎ 985 84 07 67; www.laestradahotel.com; Calle Inocencio del Valle 1; s/d incl breakfast €45/80; 🅿). The best place in town for a feed is the eclectic **El Corral del Indiano** (☎ 985 84 10 72; www.elcorraldelindianu.com; Avenida de Europa 14; meals €35; 🕑 Fri-Wed). The garden is beautiful for summertime meals. Inside, the decor is startling, with contemporary art on deep aquamarine walls, bear stone and dark-hued parquet. You might start with a *sopa de navajas, regaliz y pistachos* (razor clam soup with liquorice and pistachios) and follow with fish of the day.

Cangas de Onís

pop 6600

Good King Pelayo, after his victory at Covadonga, moved about 12km down the hill to settle the base of his nascent Asturian kingdom at Cangas in AD 722. Cangas' big moment in history lasted 70 years or so, until the capital was moved elsewhere. Its second boom time arrived in the late 20th century with the invasion of Picos de Europa tourists. In August, especially, the largely modern and rather drab town is full to bursting with trekkers, campers and holidaymakers, many desperately searching for a room – a common story throughout eastern Asturias in high summer.

INFORMATION

The **tourist office** (☎ 985 84 80 05; www.cangasdeonis.com; Jardines del Ayuntamiento 2; 🕑 10am-9pm daily Jul & Aug, 10am-2pm & 4-7pm Mon-Sat, 10am-2pm Sun Sep-Jun) is just off the main street, Avenida de

Covadonga. **Casa Dago** (☎ 985 84 86 14; Avenida de Covadonga 43; 9am-2.30pm, sometimes open in afternoon) provides national park information. Cangas has a fair smattering of banks with ATMs.

SIGHTS

The so-called **Puente Romano** spanning Río Sella, which arches like a cat in fright, is almost certainly medieval rather than Roman, but no less impressive for the mistaken identity. From it hangs a copy of the Cruz de la Victoria, the symbol of Asturias, which resides in Oviedo's cathedral.

The tiny **Capilla de Santa Cruz** (Avenida Contranquil; 10am-1pm & 3-6.30pm Tue-Sun Jul–mid-Sep, 10am-1pm & 3-6.30pm Sat & Sun mid-Sep–Jun) marks the site of a millennia-old shrine, though the chapel itself was placed there in the 1940s. Within the crypt is a megalithic tomb.

Parque de la Naturaleza La Grandera (☎ 985 94 00 17; 11am-8pm daily Easter-Sep, 11am-8pm Tue-Sun Oct-Easter) at Soto de Cangas, 3km east on the Covadonga road, offers the chance to observe captive bears, wolves, birds of prey and other Spanish wildlife that you would be pretty lucky to see on the trail. Injured animals are brought here for care.

ACTIVITIES

Many agencies offer a range of activities, including canoeing on Río Sella (around €28 per person), horse riding (€15 per hour), canyoning (€36 for two to three hours) and caving (€22 to €25 for two to three hours). **Cangas Aventura** (☎ 985 84 92 61; http://cangasaventura.galeon.com in Spanish; Avenida de Covadonga 17) is a fairly typical agency.

SLEEPING

Cangas has loads of hotels and a few *pensiones*, and there are plenty more of both, plus numerous *casas rurales*, in nearby villages. Along the road towards Arenas de Cabrales, Soto de Cangas, Mestas de Con and Benia de Onís all have several options. Most places in town can also inform you of rental apartments.

Hostal de Casa Fermín (☎ 985 84 84 91, 676 015377; Paseo de Contranquil 3; d €50) Located 500m past the Capilla de Santa Cruz, in a vaguely bucolic setting, this brick structure has bright, simple rooms and a popular summer *sidrería*.

Hotel Santa Cruz (☎ 985 84 94 17; www.hotelsantacruz.net; Avenida Constantino González 11; s/d €67/90) Between the Capilla de Santa Cruz and a big riverside playground, this modern hotel goes for the rustic look. You can increase the comfort factor by opting for a double with its own Jacuzzi (€120).

Hotel Los Lagos (☎ 985 84 92 77; www.loslagos.as; Jardines del Ayuntamiento 3; s/d €88/103;) A standard, mid-ranking hotel offering a range of rooms. The better doubles are quite spacious and spotless; others are a little cramped. Lodgings are above the best restaurant in town, Los Arcos.

EATING

Mesón Puente Romano (☎ 985 84 81 10; menú del día €12) The terrace is just below the bridge, or you could opt for the lugubrious cellarlike dining room. The set lunch is *fabada* (a hefty Asturian bean stew) followed by *arroz con leche* (rice pudding). The management warns that both dishes are 'abundant'.

Los Arcos (☎ 985 84 92 77; Jardines del Ayuntamiento 3; meals €35) This prize-winning eatery will win you over with such cunning contemporary interpretations of traditional cooking as *ventresca de atún con crema de espárragos, polvo de jamón y cubitos de melón* (a tasty cut of tuna stomach with cream of asparagus, ham powder and cubes of melon).

GETTING THERE & AWAY

You will find the bus stop and local ALSA bus company office opposite the Jardines del Ayuntamiento on Avenida de Covadonga.

Covadonga

The importance of Covadonga, 12km southeast of Cangas de Onís, lies in what it represents rather than what it is. Somewhere hereabouts, in approximately AD 722, the Muslims received their first defeat in Spain at the hands of King Pelayo, who set up the Asturian kingdom, which is considered to be the beginning of the Reconquista – a mere 800-year project.

The place is an object of pilgrimage, for in a cave here, the **Santa Cueva**, the Virgin supposedly appeared to Pelayo's warriors before the battle. On weekends and in summer the queues at the cave, now with a chapel installed, are matched only by the line of cars crawling past towards the Lagos de Covadonga. The **Fuente de Siete Caños** spring, by the pool below the cave, is supposed to ensure marriage within one year to women who drink from it.

Landslides destroyed much of Covadonga in the 19th century and the main church here now, the **Basílica de Covadonga**, is a neo-Romanesque affair built between 1877 and 1901. About 100m from the basilica is the

Museo de Covadonga (☎ 985 84 60 96; adult/child €3/2; ⏲ 10.30am-2pm & 4-7pm Tue-Sun), filled with all sorts of items, mostly donations by the illustrious faithful.

Lagos de Covadonga

Don't let summer traffic queues deter you from continuing the 10km uphill from Covadonga to these two beautiful little lakes. Most of the day trippers don't get past patting a few cows' noses near the lakes, so walking here is as nice as anywhere else in the Picos. In August the road can close for an hour or two when the car parks near the lakes can't accept any more vehicles.

Lago de Enol is the first lake you reach. It's linked to **Lago de la Ercina**, 1km away, not only by the paved road but also by a footpath via the **Centro de Visitantes Pedro Pidal** (⏲ 10am-6pm Easter-early Dec), which has information and displays on the Picos and a bookshop. There are rustic restaurants near both lakes, closed in winter. Bathing in the lakes is banned.

When mist descends, the lakes, surrounded by the green pasture and bald rock that characterise this part of the Picos, take on an eerie appearance.

WALKS FROM THE LAKES

Two relatively easy trails begin and end at the lakes. The first leads about 5km southeast, with an ascent of 600m, from Lago de la Ercina to the **Vega de Ario**, where the **Refugio Marqués de Villaviciosa** (Refugio Vega de Ario; ☎ 650 900760; bunks €10), attended and with meal service daily from Easter to early December, has sleeping space for 40 people. The reward for about 2½ hours' effort is magnificent views across the Garganta del Cares (Cares Gorge) to the Macizo Central of the Picos.

The alternative walk takes you roughly south from Lago de Enol to the **Refugio de Vegarredonda** (☎ 985 92 29 52; www.vegarredonda.com; bunks €10, meals €14) and on to the **Mirador de Ordiales**, a lookout point over a 1km sheer drop into the Valle de Angón. It's about a 3½-hour walk (one way) – relatively easy along a mule track as far as the *refugio*, then a little more challenging on up to the mirador. The 58-place *refugio* is attended year-round.

Desfiladero de los Beyos

The N625 south from Cangas de Onís follows Río Sella upstream through one of the most extraordinary defiles in Europe. The road through the Desfiladero de los Beyos gorge is a remarkable feat of engineering. Towards the southern end of the defile, you cross from Asturias into Castilla y León.

Hotel Puente Vidosa (☎ 985 94 47 35; www.puentevidosa.com; s/d €64/77; P ♿), gloriously perched on a bend in the Sella by a waterfall, is 20km south of Cangas. The converted stone house contains 19 lovely rustic rooms with gorge(ous) views and wood panelling. A pool, sauna and Jacuzzi add to the value.

Oseja de Sajambre

pop 290 / elev 650m

Once inside the region of Castilla y León you'll soon strike Oseja de Sajambre, an average place with magnificent views across the gorge. There's a *hostal*, a couple of restaurants and grocery shops.

Soto de Sajambre

pop 100 / elev 930m

Pressing on 4km north from Oseja de Sajambre, you reach this much prettier village by a freshwater stream, a great base for hikers. Walks from Soto de Sajambre include La Senda del Arcediano, a very scenic trip of five or six hours north to Amieva, manageable by most walkers, and a more difficult trail east to Posada de Valdeón. There is a handful of sleeping options here.

CENTRAL PICOS

A star attraction of the Picos' central massif is the gorge that divides it from the western Macizo El Cornión. The popular Garganta del Cares (Cares Gorge) trail can be busy in summer, but the walk is worthwhile. This part of the Picos also has plenty of less heavily tramped paths and climbing challenges once you've 'done' the Cares. Arenas de Cabrales (or just plain Arenas) and Poncebos are obvious bases.

Arenas de Cabrales

pop 810

Arenas de Cabrales lies at the confluence of Ríos Cares and Casaño, 30km east of Cangas de Onís. The busy main road is lined with hotels, restaurants and bars, and just off it lies a little tangle of quiet squares and back lanes. Buses stop next to the **tourist office** (☎ 985 84 64 84; ⏲ 10am-2pm & 4-8pm Tue-Sun Easter & Jul-Sep), which is a kiosk in the middle of town at the junction of the Poncebos road.

On the second-last or last Sunday in August, the **Certamen del Queso** (Cheese Festival) is held in this home of fine smelly cheese. Thousands come to enjoy the exhibitions, processions, cheesemaking demonstrations and tastings.

SLEEPING & EATING

Arenas has a camping ground and about 10 other accommodation options, as well as holiday apartments.

Camping Naranjo de Bulnes (☎ 985 84 65 78; sites per 2 people, car & tent €24.50) This large and efficiently run camping ground sits within a chestnut grove, 1.5km east of the town centre on the Panes road.

Hostal Naturaleza (☎ 985 84 64 87; d €36) About 800m from the centre of Arenas along the road to Poncebos is this quiet little house with a series of smallish but well-scrubbed rooms. The owner, Fina, also has a couple of houses for rent in Arenas.

Hotel Rural El Torrejón (☎ 985 84 64 11; www.eltorrejon.com in Spanish; r incl breakfast €55) A bright-red country house welcomes the weary traveller with tastefully decorated rooms in a rural style with lots of fragrant wood. The setting is idyllic, beside Río Casaño, a couple of minutes' walk from the village centre.

Restaurante Cares (☎ 985 84 66 28; meals €25-30; daily Jun-Sep, Tue-Sun Oct-May) On the western approach into town, this is one of the best restaurants for miles around. Dig into a hearty *cachopo* (breaded veal stuffed with ham, cheese and vegetables) and finish with *delicias de limón* (between lemon mousse and yogurt).

Garganta del Cares

Nine kilometres of well-maintained path high above Río Cares between Poncebos and Caín constitute, perhaps unfortunately, the most popular mountain walk in Spain; in August the experience is akin to London's Oxford St on a Saturday morning. If you do arrive with the holiday rush, try not to be put off – the walk is a spectacular excursion between two of the Picos' three massifs. If you're feeling fit (or need to get back to your car), it's quite possible to walk the whole 9km and return as a (somewhat tiring) day's outing; it takes about seven hours plus stops.

PONCEBOS & FUNICULAR DE BULNES

Poncebos, a straggle of buildings at the northern end of the gorge, set amid already spectacular scenery, is exclusively dedicated to Picos tourism. A road turning uphill just above the Pensión Garganta del Cares leads 1.5km up to the hamlet of **Camarmeña**, where there's a lookout with views to El Naranjo de Bulnes in the Macizo Central.

A few metres up the Sotres road, just below Poncebos, is the lower end of the **Funicular de Bulnes** (☎ 985 84 68 00; adult/child return €18/5.40; 10am-8pm Easter & Jul-Sep, 10am-12.30pm & 2-6pm rest of year), a tunnel railway that climbs 2km inside the mountain to the hamlet of Bulnes (opposite), which is inaccessible by road. The funicular functions year-round, making the seven-minute trip every half-hour in either direction.

Hotel Garganta del Cares (☎ /fax 985 84 64 63; Calle de Poncebos; s/d €38/62; closed 10 Dec-15 Jan; P) offers beds and meals (*menú del día* €9.50) that are the closest to the Garganta del Cares trail. A classier hotel lies next door.

GARGANTA DEL CARES WALK

By doing the walk from north to south, you save the best till last. Follow the 'Ruta de Cares' sign pointing uphill about 700m along the road from the top end of Poncebos. The beginning involves a steady climb upwards in the wide and mostly bare early stages of the gorge. After about 3km you'll reach some abandoned houses. A little further and you're over the highest point of the walk. You should encounter a couple of drink stands along the way (the stuff is transported by horse).

As you approach the regional boundary with Castilla y León, the gorge becomes narrower and its walls thick with vegetation, creating greater contrast with the alpine heights above. The last stages of the walk are possibly the prettiest, and as you descend nearer the valley floor, you pass through a series of low, wet tunnels to emerge at the end of the gorge among the meadows of Caín.

CAÍN

If you're coming from the south, the trailhead of the walk is at Caín, where the rickety (and picturesque) road from Posada de Valdeón comes to an end.

Casa Cuevas (☎ 987 74 27 20; d €40) has basic rooms. There are at least two fancier places to stay, plus a couple of bars and restaurants. You'll find further lodgings in the string of villages south of Caín, including Cordiñanes and the rather drab Posada de Valdeón.

Sotres

A side road heads up 11km from Poncebos to Sotres, the highest village in the Picos at

1045m and the starting point for a number of good walks. There are five places to stay, most with their own restaurant.

Casa Cipriano (☎ 985 94 50 24; www.casacipriano.com; s/d €30/50) is a favourite haunt of mountain aficionados. Aside from the simple but cheerful rooms, the staff offers a professional mountain-and-caving guide service and simple restaurant.

Hotel Peña Castil (☎ 985 94 50 80; www.hotel.penacastil.com; s/d €40/60) offers 10 impeccable if smallish rooms in a renovated stone house. The rooms have graciously tiled floors, some wood panelling and fine showers, and some have perky balconies.

WALKS AROUND SOTRES

A popular route goes east to the village of **Tresviso** and on to **Urdón**, on the Potes–Panes road. As far as Tresviso (10km) it's a paved road, but the final 6km is a dramatic walking trail, the **Ruta de Tresviso**, snaking 850m down to the Desfiladero de la Hermida (right). Doing this in the upward direction, starting from Urdón, is at least as popular. An alternative track winds off the Sotres–Tresviso road and down via the hamlet of Beges to La Hermida, also in the Desfiladero de la Hermida.

Many walkers head west from Sotres to the **Collado de Pandébano**, about 90 minutes' walk away up on the far side of the Duje valley. From Pandébano it's possible to see the 2519m rock finger called **El Naranjo de Bulnes** (Pico Urriello), an emblem of the Picos de Europa and a classic challenge for climbers.

Few walkers can resist the temptation to get even closer to El Naranjo. It's possible to walk in around three hours from Pandébano to the **Vega de Urriellu**, at the foot of the northwestern face of the mountain, where the **Refugio de la Vega de Urriellu** (☎ 985 92 52 00; www.picuurriellu.com; bunks €10, breakfast €6, dinner €14) is attended, with meal service, year-round.

Otherwise, you can descend for about an hour west to **Bulnes**. Bulnes is divided into two parts, the upper Barrio del Castillo and the lower La Villa. All amenities are in La Villa, including the six-room **La Casa del Chiflón** (☎ 985 84 59 43; www.casadelchiflon.com; d/tr/q €59/70/80; 🕐 Mar-Nov, Sat & Sun by reservation Dec-Feb) *casa rural* and **Bar Bulnes** (☎ 985 84 59 34; 🕐 daily Jun-Aug, Tue-Sun Sep-May), with good home cooking. You can also get to Bulnes by walking southeast up from Poncebos (about 1¼ hours), or by taking the Funicular de Bulnes (opposite).

Niserias

East of Arenas de Cabrales, the AS114 winds along the verdant Río Cares valley downstream towards Panes. The stretch between Arenas and Trescares is especially beautiful. Keep an eye out for the **Puente La Vidre**, about 9.5km east of Arenas and shortly before Trescares. It is a high, arching, early medieval bridge built in place of a probably imperial Roman predecessor. A fine walking trail leads up into the Picos de Europa here.

About 5.5km further on from the bridge is the peaceful hamlet of Niserias, at a particularly pretty bend in the Cares. You can't miss the cheerful, deep-yellow country house **Casa Julián** (www.casajulian.com). In business since 1949, it's long been part shop, part digs for fishermen coming to try their luck in Río Cares. Today it's a welcoming stop for modern travellers, divided into **hotel** (☎ 985 41 57 97; s/d €50/70) and **hostal** (☎ 985 41 57 79; d €50), the latter across the road. In August single-occupancy rates are not available. The restaurant does great fish dishes.

La Tahona de Besnes (☎ 985 41 57 49; www.latahonadebesnes.com; d €69-116) comprises a beautifully renovated set of old stone bakery buildings in a leafy river valley 1.75km north of Niserias (take the Alles road and follow the signs). It has attractive double rooms, a few apartments and a good restaurant. You can go horse riding here, too.

EASTERN PICOS

Panes

Panes is where the AS114 from Cangas and Arenas meets the N621 running from the coast south to Potes. It has a range of accommodation. Hotel Trespalacios on the main street is the main bus stop.

Desfiladero de la Hermida

The N621 south from Panes follows Río Deva and enters the impressive Desfiladero de la Hermida gorge. You cross into Cantabria here at Urdón, the bottom end of the Ruta de Tresviso path (left), 2km before the hamlet of **La Hermida**. There's not much at La Hermida but the bubbling Deva, the Picos looming to the west and a couple of *pensiones*. Just outside, on the road to Potes, there is also the rather large **Hotel La Hermida** (☎ 942 73 36 25; www.balneariolahermida.com), which has thermal baths. A circuit of various baths, saunas, steam baths etc costs €30.

Lebeña

About 8.5km south of La Hermida is a spot that warrants visiting. A kilometre east of the N621 stands the fascinating little **Iglesia de Santa María de Lebeña** (admission €1; 10am-1.30pm & 4.30-7.30pm Tue-Sun), built in the 9th century. The horseshoe arches in the church are a telltale sign of its Mozarabic style – rarely seen this far north in Spain. The floral motifs on the columns are Visigothic, while below the main *retablo* stands a Celtic stone engraving. They say the big yew tree outside was planted 1000 years ago.

Potes

pop 1500 / elev 291m

Overrun in peak periods, but with some charm in the old centre (restored in attractive traditional stone and slate after considerable damage during the civil war), Potes is a popular staging post on the southeast edge of the Picos. Spanned by the medieval San Cayetano bridge, Río Quiviesa joins Río Deva at the heart of the village, with the Macizo Andara (also called Macizo Oriental) rising close at hand.

The **tourist office** (942 73 07 87; Plaza de la Serna; 10am-2pm & 4-7pm Mon & Thu-Sat, 10am-2pm Sun) shares a building with the bus station on the west side of town. Inquire there about the various adventure outfits operating from Potes and offering everything from horse riding and quad biking to canoeing and canyoning.

Right in the centre of town, the squat **Torre del Infantado** was built as a defensive tower in the 15th century and is now the town hall, having long served as a prison. A bit further down the river, the 14th-century **Iglesia de San Vicente**, deconsecrated in the 19th century, is a nice example of rustic Gothic architecture.

SLEEPING & EATING

With 13 hotels and *pensiones*, there is no shortage of accommodation here. They are by and large simple, straightforward places, all clustered fairly close to one another.

our pick **Casa Cayo** (942 73 01 50; www.casacayo.com; Calle Cántabra 6; s/d €30/50) This is the pick of the bunch in Potes, with helpful service and attractive, comfy, wood-beamed rooms. Open the timber window shutters early in the morning to listen to the nearby burbling river. You can eat well in the excellent restaurant for about €20. Try the *cocido lebaniego completo* (€14), a feast that starts with unlimited noodle soup followed by a plate loaded with meat, sausage, chickpeas, potato, cabbage and spinach.

Tasca Cántabra (942 73 07 14; Calle Cántabra; meals €20; Thu-Tue) For a cheerful meal try this old town eatery; try local faves *cocido lebaniego* or *lengua con tomate* (tongue with tomato).

Around Potes

The Valle de Liébana, of which Potes is in a sense the 'capital', lies between the southeast side of the Picos de Europa and the main spine of the Cordillera Cantábrica. Christian refugees from Muslim-occupied Spain to the south fled to this frontline valley in the 8th century. The Muslim army defeated at Covadonga is said to have been wiped out while retreating through this valley by a massive landslide near Cosgaya (an event immediately attributed to the Almighty by the Christians).

The settlers brought with them the Lígnum Crucis, purportedly the single biggest chunk of Christ's cross, which had supposedly been transported from Jerusalem by Bishop Toribio of Astorga in the 4th century. The holy relic has been housed ever since in the **Monasterio de Santo Toribio de Liébana** (10am-2pm & 4-7pm), 3km west of Potes (signposted off the Fuente Dé road). About 500m further on is the tiny **Ermita de San Miguel**, a chapel with great valley views.

The relic, which according to tradition features the hole made by the nail that passed through Christ's left hand, is an extraordinary magnet for the faithful. It's kept inside a crucifix of gold-plated silver, which is housed in a lavish 18th-century baroque chapel off the monastery's austere Gothic church (dating from 1256).

Head of the monastery in the latter half of the 8th century was Beato de Liébana, who won fame in medieval Europe for his lavishly illustrated *Commentary on the Apocalypse*. Copies of this illustrated tome were distributed throughout Europe and came to be known as Beatos. Around 30 survive today, scattered across Europe, but the original was lost.

The Romanesque **Iglesia de Santa María de Piasca**, 2.5km off the CA184 road about 8km southeast of Potes, was at the heart of the other main medieval monastery established here, but now gone. Its sculpture is among the most exquisite in the region.

Potes to Fuente Dé

The 23km CA185 from Potes to Fuente Dé is a beautiful trip, with several places to stay (including three camping grounds) along the way. At **Camaleño** is the **Hostal El Caserío** (☎ 942 73 30 48; s/d €30/45), housed in a cluster of beautifully restored old structures, including what used to be the town's cantina. **Cosgaya**, 13km southwest of Potes, is home to the majestic twin stone townhouses of the **Hotel del Oso** (☎ 942 73 30 18; www.hoteldeloso.com; s/d €64/81; P), which face each other across Río Deva and the road. Spacious rooms with timber floors and finishings are very inviting.

ESPINAMA

This is the last stop of any significance before Fuente Dé, and probably makes a more appealing base if you have your own transport. A 4WD track from here leads about 7km north and uphill to the Hotel Refugio de Áliva and on to Sotres.

There's a surprising choice of decent places to stay in Espinama, all with restaurants. The family-run **Hostal Remoña** (☎ 942 73 66 05; s/d €25/45) has large rooms, some with balconies over rushing Río Nevandi.

Fuente Dé & the Teleférico

At 1078m, Fuente Dé lies at the foot of the stark southern wall of the Macizo Central. In four minutes the **Teleférico de Fuente Dé** (cable car; ☎ 942 73 66 10; return adult/under 6yr/6-12yr €14/free/5; 9am-8pm Easter & Jul-Sep, 10am-6pm rest of year, closed 7 Jan-Feb) here whisks people 762m to the top of that wall, from where walkers and climbers can make their way deeper into the central massif.

Be warned that during the high season (especially August) you can wait for hours at the bottom to get a seat. Coming down, you simply join the queue and wait – OK on a sunny day, but a little unpleasant if the queue is long.

WALKING & CLIMBING

It's a walk of 3.5km from the top of the *teleférico* to the Hotel Refugio de Áliva, or you might catch one of the private 4WD shuttles that do the trip for €4 per person. From the hotel, two trails descend into the valley that separates the central massif from its eastern cousin. The first winds its way some 7km south down to Espinama, while the other will take you north to Sotres via Vegas de Sotres. If there is a demand, 4WDs cover the Sotres and Espinama routes.

Other possibilities for the suitably prepared include climbing Peña Vieja (2613m) and making your way across the massif to El Naranjo de Bulnes. This requires proper equipment and experience – Peña Vieja has claimed more climbers' lives than any other mountain in the Picos. Less exacting is the route of about two hours leading northwest from the *teleférico*, passing below Peña Vieja by marked trails to the tiny (three-place) Refugio Cabaña Verónica at 2325m near Horcados Rojos.

SLEEPING & EATING

Fuente Dé has one camping ground and two hotels (including an ugly *parador* – a luxury, state-owned hotel), both of which offer 4WD trips into the mountains.

Hotel Rebeco (☎ 942 73 66 01; s/d €54/70; P) This handsome stone lodge is the better-value option (over the *parador*). Eleven of the 30 rooms include loft levels that are suitable for kids.

Hotel Refugio de Áliva (☎ 942 73 09 99; s/d €47/75; Jun–mid-Oct) Set 1700m high, this 27-room hotel features a restaurant and cafe as well as a sun deck. It's reached from the top of the *teleférico* (see left).

Potes to Posada de Valdeón

Drivers will be rewarded by a drive from Potes around to the southern approaches to the Picos. Take the N621 (direction Riaño) south of Potes and you are soon on a narrow road winding through the verdant Valle de Liébana. After about 8km, you reach the cute crossroads hamlet of **La Vega de Liébana** (ALSA buses call in here), with a handful of places to stay. Branch east to drive the 12km to **Cucayo** via **Dobres** (11km), a lovely trip that rises to about 900m. Cucayo is the end of the road. Around you are scarred mountain peaks and green fields below. Stay at the marvellous **Posada de Cucayo** (☎ 942 73 62 46; www.laposadadecucayo.com; d up to €64), where nine of the 10 spacious and tasteful doubles enjoy sweeping views. The owners will also have you making bread, jams, cheese and heaven knows what else if you truly want a taste of rural bliss!

Back in La Vega, the road southwest quickly penetrates a gorge before rising to the often fog-bound **Puerto de San Glorio** pass (1609m). It then drops down quickly on the Castilian side of the frontier. At **Portilla de la Reina**, take the narrow and still pretty country lane northwest to **Posada de Valdeón**, where you are at the southern gateway to the Picos.

Galicia

Imagine a place that blends the vibrant green landscapes of Ireland, the dramatic coastline of Brittany and the friendly, late-night-loving attitude of Andalucía. You've just concocted a pretty clear picture of Galicia. The epitome of 'Green Spain', Galicia is blessed with wide rivers, lush valleys, abrupt seascapes and densely forested land just begging to be explored.

Galicia's spiritual, cultural and official capital is Santiago de Compostela, the destination of thousands of pilgrims who set out on the famous Camino de Santiago. This magical city is crowned with Spain's most impressive cathedral and its beauty is unparalleled. But don't make the mistake of bypassing the rest of Galicia. Enchanting cities like A Coruña, Vigo, Pontevedra, Lugo and Ourense are easy to reach. Along the coast, dramatic shorelines and enticing fishing villages make excellent sea-and-sand destinations. And for those with a healthy dose of wanderlust, Galicia's unspoilt interior is a trip back in time through country lanes and alongside medieval monasteries. Perhaps more than any other Spanish region, Galicia appeals to those travellers who long to mark their own paths.

Galicia's wild coastline is frayed up and down its length by a series of majestic *rías* (inlets or estuaries). In the south, Río Miño divides Galicia from Portugal, and in the east Galicia is separated from Spain's *meseta* (central tableland) by the western end of the Cordillera Cantábrica.

Galicia is culturally separate as well. With its own language, ties to Celtic culture, and a focus on fishing and shipbuilding, Galicia at times seems to have little in common with the rest of the Iberian Peninsula. A rich and spirited land, it rewards travellers with a unique mix of ancient history, excellent gastronomy and verdant natural beauty.

HIGHLIGHTS

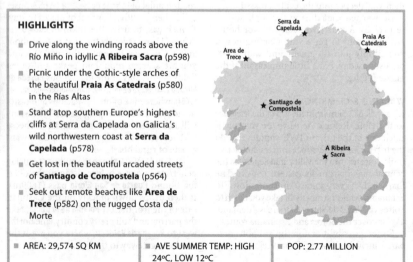

- Drive along the winding roads above the Río Miño in idyllic **A Ribeira Sacra** (p598)
- Picnic under the Gothic-style arches of the beautiful **Praia As Catedrais** (p580) in the Rías Altas
- Stand atop southern Europe's highest cliffs at Serra da Capelada on Galicia's wild northwestern coast at **Serra da Capelada** (p578)
- Get lost in the beautiful arcaded streets of **Santiago de Compostela** (p564)
- Seek out remote beaches like **Area de Trece** (p582) on the rugged Costa da Morte

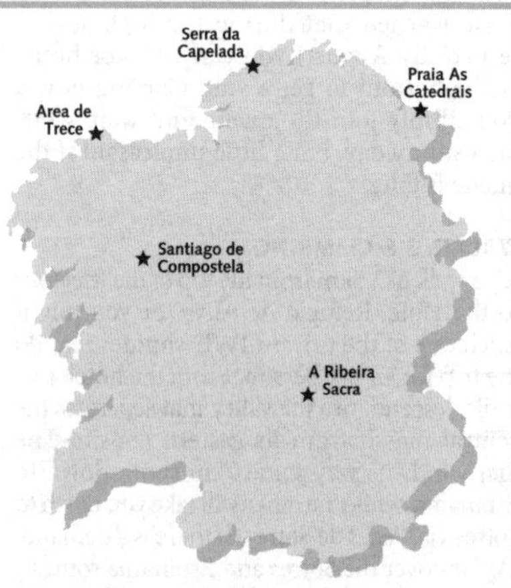

AREA: 29,574 SQ KM	AVE SUMMER TEMP: HIGH 24°C, LOW 12°C	POP: 2.77 MILLION

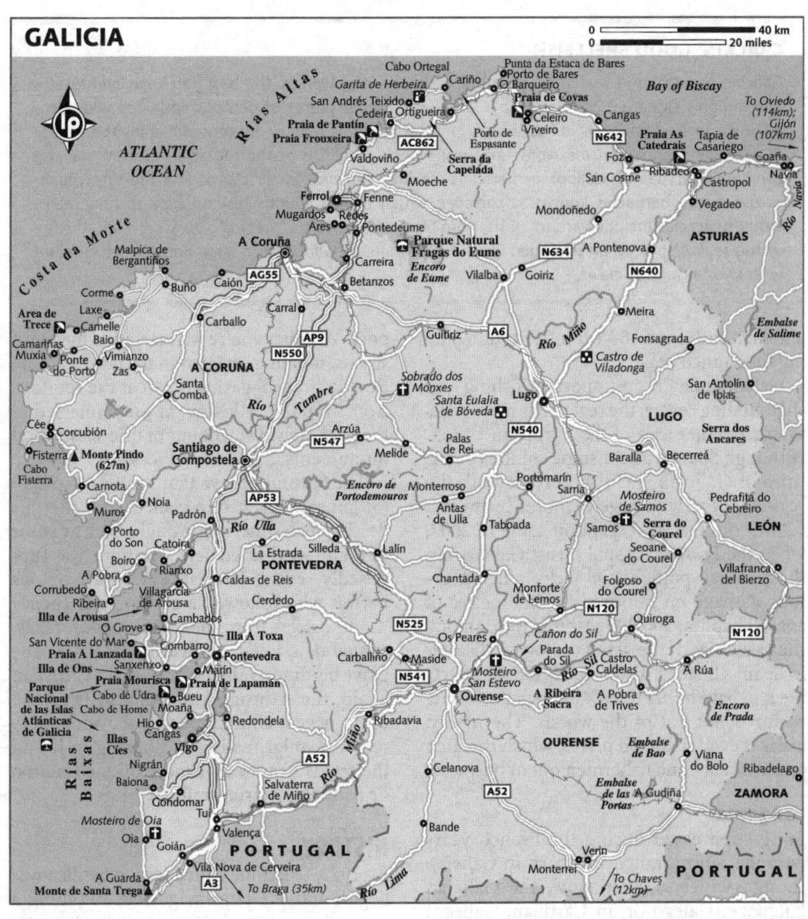

History

Galicia's history stretches back to the Iron Age, when many *castros* (protected settlements of circular stone huts) were built. Most Galicians say these ancestors were Celts, though sceptics claim Galicia's Celtic origins are exaggerations of romantic nationalists.

The Romans united 'Gallaecia' in the first century BC, founding cities like Lucas Augusti (Lugo). The region was ruled by the Germanic Suevi for most of the 5th and 6th centuries AD, before the Visigoths asserted themselves. Little touched by the 8th-century Muslim invasion, Galicia was under the control of the Christian kingdom of Asturias by 866.

The big event in the area's medieval history was the 'rediscovery' of the grave of Santiago Apóstol (St James the Apostle) in 813, at what would become Santiago de Compostela. The site grew into a rallying symbol for the Christian Reconquista of Spain, and pilgrims from all over Europe began trekking to Santiago, which rivalled Rome and even Jerusalem as a pilgrimage site. For more, see the Camino de Santiago chapter (p118).

By the time the Reconquista was completed in 1492, Galicia had become an impoverished backwater in which Spain's centralist-minded Catholic Monarchs (Reyes Católicos), Isabel and Fernando, had already begun to supplant the local tongue and traditions with Castilian methods and language. The Rexurdimento, an awakening of Galician national consciousness, did not surface until late in the 19th century,

CRACKIN' GOOD SHELLFISH

Galician shellfish and seafood is plentiful, fresh and may well be the best you have ever tasted. The region's signature dish is *pulpo a la gallega,* tender pieces of octopus sprinkled with olive oil and paprika (*pulpo á feira has* chunks of potato added). Mollusc mavens will enjoy the variety of *ameixas* (clams) and *mexillons* (mussels). Special shellfish of the region include *vieiras* and *zamburiñas* (types of scallop), *berberechos* (cockles), *navajas* (razor clams) and the tiny, much-prized goose barnacles known as *percebes,* which bear a curious resemblance to fingernails. Other delicacies include various crabs, from little *necoras* to the great big *buey del mar* – the 'ox of the sea'. Also keep an eye open for the *bogavante* or *lubrigante,* a large, lobster-like creature with two enormous claws.

and then suffered a 40-year interruption during the Franco era.

Galicia today is an important fishing and shipbuilding centre; the region has more ports than any other area of the European Union. Although Spaniards consume copious quantities of Galician shellfish and seafood, the region is otherwise largely ignored by the rest of the country. An exception came in 2002, when the *Prestige* oil spill thrust Galicia into the national spotlight. Oil slicks inflicted serious damage on hundreds of kilometres of coastal habitat; 300,000 seabirds were among the casualties of the worst ecological disaster in Spain's history. Today the *Prestige*'s effects seem to have been erased, although the fishing sector is not out of the woods. The newest crisis is ever-rising oil prices, which threaten to put small-time fishermen out of business.

Language

Long suppressed during the Franco years (strange, since Franco was born in Galicia), though widely spoken now, the Galician language (Galego or, in Castilian, Gallego) is a Romance language that seems to cross Portuguese and Castilian. In this chapter we use the names you're likely to encounter during your travels. By and large, this means Galician spellings for towns, villages and geographical features.

SANTIAGO DE COMPOSTELA

pop 88,000 / elev 260m

Locals say the arcaded, stone streets of Santiago de Compostela are at their most beautiful in the rain, when the old city glistens. Most would agree, however, that it's hard to catch the Galician capital in a bad pose. Whether you're wandering its medieval streets, nibbling on tapas in the taverns along Rúa do Franco, gazing down at the rooftops from atop the cathedral, or are immersed in the gold-tinged splendour of its ecclesiastical monuments, Santiago seduces.

The faithful believe that Santiago Apóstol (St James) preached in Galicia and, after his death in Palestine, was brought back by stone boat and was buried here. The tomb was supposedly rediscovered in 813 by a religious hermit who followed a guiding star (hence 'Compostela', from the Latin *campus stellae, campo de estrella,* or field of the star). The grave became a rallying symbol for Christian Spain, the Asturian king Alfonso II turned up to have a church erected above the holy remains, pilgrims began flocking to it and the rest is history. For more on the Camino de Santiago pilgrim trail, see p118.

HISTORY

By 1075, when the Romanesque basilica was begun and the pilgrimage was becoming a major European phenomenon, Santiago de Compostela had been raided on various occasions by Normans and Muslims. Bishop Gelmírez obtained archbishopric status for Santiago in 1100 and added numerous churches in the 12th century, when homage paid to its saint brought in a flood of funds. Enthusiasm for the pilgrimage peaked around then, and the following centuries were marked by squabbling between rival nobles, dampened down by Isabel and Fernando after the Reconquista. After misguidedly siding with the Carlists in the 1830s, Santiago de Compostela slipped into the background. Only since the 1980s, as capital of the autonomous region of Galicia and a rediscovered tourist and pilgrimage site, has the city been revitalised. Each year some 100,000 pilgrims make the journey here.

ORIENTATION

Santiago's compact old town, focused on the cathedral and its surrounding squares and almost completely pedestrianised, contains most of the monuments and places to stay and eat. Praza de Galicia marks the boundary between the old town and the modern shopping area to its south.

The train station is about a 15-minute walk downhill (south) from the city centre, and the bus station is marginally further to the northeast of the centre.

INFORMATION

Ciber Mundonet (☎ 981 58 32 8; Rúa Xelmírez 19; per hr €1.50; ⏲ 9am-midnight) Leave luggage here for €2 per day per piece.

City tourist office (☎ 981 55 51 29; www.santiagoturismo.com; Rúa do Vilar 63; ⏲ 9am-9pm Jun-Sep, 9am-2pm & 4-7pm Oct-May)

Cyber Nova 50 (☎ 981 56 41 33; Rúa Nova 50; per hr €1.20; ⏲ 9am-midnight Mon-Fri, 10am-11pm Sat & Sun) Internet access.

Farmácia Bescansa (☎ 981 58 5940; Cantón do Toural 11; ⏲ 24 hr)

Hospital Clínico Universitario (☎ 981 95 00 00; http://chusantiago.sergas.es; Travesa da Choupana s/n)

Pilgrims' Reception Office (Oficina de Acogida de Peregrinos; ☎ 981 56 88 46; www.archicompostela.org/peregrinos; Rúa do Vilar 1; ⏲ 9am-9pm) People who have covered at least the last 100km of the Camino de Santiago on foot, or the last 200km by bicycle, with spiritual or religious motives can obtain their 'Compostela' certificate to prove it here.

Policía Nacional (☎ 981 55 11 00; Avenida de Rodrigo de Padrón 3)

Post office (Rúa das Orfas 17; ⏲ 8.30am-8.30pm Mon-Fri, 9.30am-2pm Sat)

Regional tourist office (☎ 981 58 40 81 or 902 33 20 10 toll-free from within Spain; www.turgalicia.es; Rúa do Vilar 30-32; ⏲ 10am-8pm Mon-Fri, 11am-2pm & 5-7pm Sat, 11am-2pm Sun) This is the place for the scoop on all things Galicia as well as on the Camino de Santiago.

SIGHTS

Catedral de Santiago de Compostela

The grand heart of Santiago, the **cathedral** (Praza do Obradoiro; www.catedraldesantiago.es; ⏲ 7am-9pm) soars above the city centre in a splendid jumble of moss-covered spires and statues. Though Galicia's grandest monument was built piecemeal through the centuries, its beauty is only enhanced by the enticing mix of Romanesque, baroque and Gothic flourishes. What you see before you is actually the fourth church to stand on this spot. The bulk of it was built between 1075 and 1211, in Romanesque style with a traditional Latin-cross layout and three naves. Much of the 'bunting' (the domes, statues and endless trimmings) came later. Its artistic and architectural riches fill guidebooks of their own; you'd need days to see it all.

Most people enter via the lavish staircase and facade on the Praza do Obradoiro. Just behind the grand doorway is the artistically unparalleled **Pórtico de la Gloria** (Galician: Porta da Gloria), the original entryway. Its impact is undoubtedly muted by the exterior baroque facade, which protects the 200 sculptures of Maestro Mateo, the architect and sculptor placed in charge of the cathedral-building program in the late 12th century by Fernando II of León. At the time of writing, restoration of the portal was imminent; visitors may find it shrouded.

The main figure in the portico's central archway is a throned Christ, as depicted in Revelations. He's surrounded by the four Evangelists, angels and symbols of Jesus' passion. In an arc above are the 24 musicians said in the Apocalypse to sit around the heavenly throne. Below Christ's feet is

THE BOTAFUMEIRO

Santiago's iconic censer, the *botafumeiro* (loosely 'smoke spitter'), dates from the 13th century, at which time covering up the odours of road-weary pilgrims who slept and cooked inside the cathedral was more than a mere ceremonial act. Weighing in at 62kg the silver-coated vessel reaches a speed of 68km/h, misses hitting the north and south transept vaults by only 51cm while reaching an angle of 82 degrees, and swings a minimum of 25 days per year. It's fallen only twice – in 1499 and 1622 – and is a perfect, gigantic pendulum conceived three centuries before pendulum physics was worked out. To see it best, be sure to stand in the north or south transept. When not in action, the Botafumeiro is kept in the cathedral library, part of the Museo da Catedral (p567).

In holy years (next in 2010), it's swung daily after the pilgrim's mass at noon. It may also be swung on holidays and if a pilgrimage group donates €240.

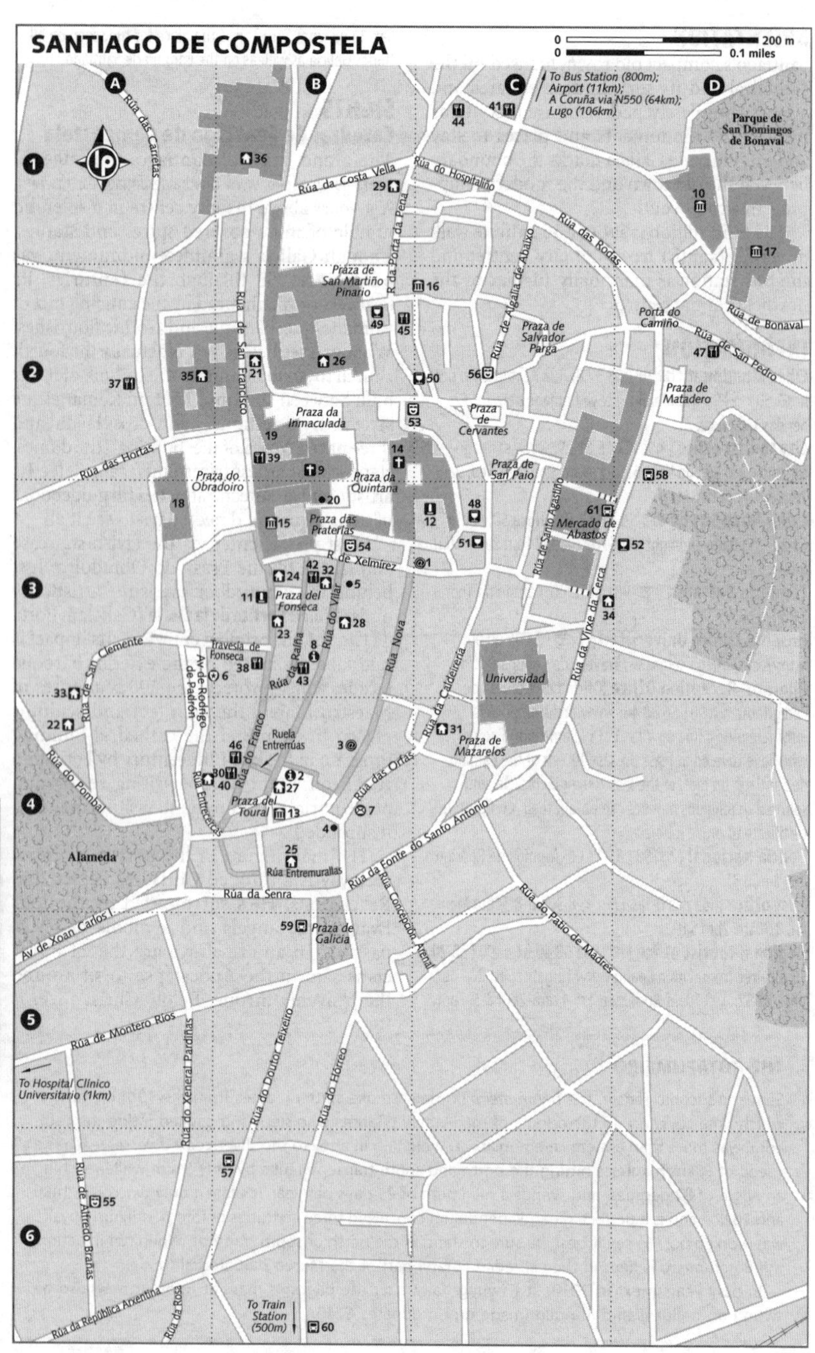
SANTIAGO DE COMPOSTELA
0 200 m
0 0.1 miles
To Bus Station (800m); Airport (11km); A Coruña via N550 (64km); Lugo (106km)
Parque de San Domingos de Bonaval
Rúa das Carretas
Rúa da Costa Vella
Rúa do Hospitaliño
Rúa das Rodas
R. da Porta da Pena
Praza de San Martiño Pinario
Rúa de Algalia de Abaixo
Rúa de San Francisco
Porta do Camiño
Rúa de Bonaval
Rúa de San Pedro
Praza de Salvador Parga
Praza de Matadero
Praza da Inmaculada
Praza de Cervantes
Rúa das Hortas
Praza do Obradoiro
Praza da Quintana
Praza de San Paio
Rúa de Santo Agostiño
Mercado de Abastos
Praza das Praterías
R. de Xelmírez
Praza del Fonseca
Rúa do Vilar
Rúa da Raíña
Rúa Nova
Rúa da Virxe da Cerca
Travesía de Fonseca
Av de Rodrigo de Padrón
Rúa de San Clemente
Rúa da Caldeirería
Universidad
Praza de Mazarelos
Rúa do Franco
Ruela Entrerrúas
Rúa Entrerrúas
Rúa das Orfas
Rúa do Pombal
Praza del Toural
Rúa da Fonte do Santo Antonio
Alameda
Rúa Entremurallas
Rúa da Senra
Av de Xoan Carlos I
Praza de Galicia
Rúa Concepción Arenal
Rúa do Patio de Madres
Rúa de Montero Ríos
To Hospital Clínico Universitario (1km)
Rúa do Xeneral Pardiñas
Rúa do Doutor Teixeiro
Rúa do Hórreo
Rúa de Alfredo Brañas
Rúa da República Arxentina
Rúa da Rosa
To Train Station (500m)
GALICIA

INFORMATION
Ciber Mundonet....1 C3
City Tourist Office....2 B4
Cyber Nova 50....3 B4
Farmácia Bescansa....4 B4
Pilgrims' Reception Office....5 B3
Policía Nacional....6 A3
Post Office....7 B4
Regional Tourist Office....8 B3

SIGHTS & ACTIVITIES
Catedral de Santiago de Compostela....9 B2
Centro Galego de Arte Contemporánea....10 D1
Colexio de Fonesca....11 B3
Fuente de los Caballos....12 C3
Fundación Eugenio Granell....13 B4
Galicia Dixital....(see 26)
Hostal dos Reis Católicos....(see 35)
Mosteiro de San Martiño Pinario....(see 26)
Mosteiro de San Paio de Antealtares....14 B2
Museo da Catedral....15 B3
Museo das Peregrinacións....16 C2
Museo do Pobo Galego....17 D1
Pazo de Raxoi....18 A3
Pazo de Xelmírez....19 B2
Puerta Santa....20 B3

SLEEPING
Casa-Hotel As Artes....21 B2
Hostal Alameda....22 A4
Hostal Barbantes....23 B3
Hostal Libredón....24 B3
Hostal Mapoula....25 B4
Hostal Seminario Mayor....26 B2
Hostal Suso....27 B4
Hotel Airas Nunes....28 B3
Hotel Costa Vella....29 B1
Hotel Entrecercas....30 A4
Hotel Real....31 C4
Hotel Rúa Villar....32 B3
Hotel San Clemente....33 A3
Hotel Virxe da Cerca....34 C3
Parador Hostal dos Reis Católicos....35 A2
San Francisco Hotel Monumento....36 B1

EATING
Carretas....37 A2
Casa Rosalía....38 B3
Cre-Cottê Creperie....39 B2
El Pasaje....40 B4
La Bodeguilla de San Roque....41 C1
O Beiro....42 B3
O Gato Negro....43 B3
O Triángulo Das Verduras....44 C1
Restaurant Sobrinos del Padre....45 B2
Restaurante Ó 42....46 B4
Restaurante Ó Dezaseis....47 D2

DRINKING
Borriquita de Belém....48 C3
Café Atlántico....49 B2
hs....50 C2
Modus Vivendi....51 C3
Momo....52 D3

ENTERTAINMENT
A Casa das Crechas....53 B2
Conga 8....54 B3
Dado Dadá....55 A6
Garigolo....56 C2

TRANSPORT
Airport Bus Stop....57 B6
Bus 5 to Bus Station....58 D2
Bus 5 to Bus Station....59 B5
Bus 6 to Centre....60 B6
Bus 6 to Train Station....61 C3

Santiago and below him, Hercules (holding open the mouths of two lions). On the other side of the central pillar is Maestro Mateo. For centuries, tradition called for visitors to bump heads with the maestro to acquire some of his smarts. But countless noggin knocks led to Mateo's notably flat nose; he is now blocked off behind a metal barrier. Another tradition called for a brief prayer as you place your fingers in the five holes created above Hercules' head by the repetition of this very act by millions of faithful over the centuries. It too is now blocked off.

The remarkably lifelike figures on the right side of the portico are apostles, while those to the left represent Old Testament prophets. The only female statue depicts Queen Esther, who local lore assures was the inspiration for Galicia's iconic *tetilla* cheese ('titty cheese'). Supposedly, her stone breasts were originally much larger. When local leaders deemed them inappropriate and filed them down, townspeople responded by creating the cone-shaped cheese in Esther's honour.

Approaching the Churrigueresque **Altar Mayor** (Main Altar), a small staircase on the right side leads to a 13th-century **statue of Santiago**. You emerge on the left side then proceed down some steps to contemplate what you are assured is his **tomb**. Nearby is the **Puerta Santa** (Holy Door), which opens onto the Praza da Quintana and is cracked only in holy years (next in 2010). In 2004 a bronze door with scenes of Santiago's life replaced a simpler stone version.

A special pilgrims' Mass is celebrated at noon daily. Other High-Altar masses take place Monday through Saturday at 9.30am and 7.30pm and on Sundays at 10am. Chapel masses are celebrated daily at 7.30am, 8am, 8.30am, 9am and 11am. You may catch one of the special Masses where the world's greatest dispenser of incense, the **botafumeiro**, is swung across the church (p565).

MUSEO DA CATEDRAL

The sprawling **Museo da Catedral** (Cathedral Museum; ☎ 981 56 05 27; Praza do Obradoiro; adult/child €5/1; 10am-2pm & 4-8pm Jun-Sep, 10am-1.30pm & 4-6.30pm Oct-May, closed Sun afternoon) encompasses several different spaces. Head to the right side of the Obradoira facade to enter the **cloister**, home to displays on the cathedral's development, an impressive collection of religious art (including the *botafumeiro*) and the lavishly decorated 18th-century *sala capitular* (chapter house). Maestro Mateo's original stone *coro* (choir) is on view beside the main entrance. From the cloister, you have access to the **treasury**, **Chapel of Relics** and **Royal Pantheon**. The **crypt**, entered from the foot of the cathedral's Praza do Obradoiro steps, is notable for its 12th-century architecture and rich decoration.

Around the Cathedral

A stroll around the cathedral leads to some of Santiago's most inviting squares. The grand **Praza do Obradoiro** (Worker's Plaza) earned its name because it was under construction for a full century while the grand palaces on it were constructed. On the northern end, the Renaissance **Hostal dos Reis Católicos** was built in the early 16th century by Isabel and Ferdinand. A symbol of the crown's power in this ecclesiastical city, it was built as a hospital for the poor and infirm. Now, it shelters well-off travellers instead, as a luxurious *parador* (p570). Along the western side of the square is the elegant 18th-century **Pazo de Raxoi**, now the city hall.

South of the cathedral, stop in the cafe-lined Praza de Fonseca to peek into the **Colexio de Fonseca** (☎ 981 56 31 00; admission free; 🕑 11am-2pm & 5-8.30pm Tue-Sat, 11am-2pm Sun), the original seat of Santiago's university (founded in 1495), with a beautiful courtyard and exhibition gallery.

Around the corner, the **Praza das Praterías** (Silversmiths' Square) is marked with the **Fuente de los Caballos** (1829) fountain. The cathedral's south facade, up the steps, is an original, if weathered, Romanesque masterpiece. Curiously, the building facing it on the lower side of the square is a fake. Since there was no space to build a proper palace here, this is simple a 2m-wide facade.

Following the cathedral walls you enter **Praza da Quintana**. Across the plaza is the long, stark wall of the **Mosteiro de San Paio de Antealtares**, founded by Alfonso II for Benedictine monks to look after St James' relics, and converted to a nunnery in 1499. Climbing the steps at the top of the plaza you'll find the entrance to the convent. Inside, the **sacred art museum** (Vía Sacra 5; admission €1.50; 🕑 10.30am-1.30pm & 4-7pm Mon-Sat Apr-Dec) contains the original altar raised over the Santiago relics. The church itself is of relatively simple design, with the exception of its main altar – a frenzy of gilded baroque. Stop by in the evening to hear the nuns singing **vespers** (🕑 8pm Mon-Fri, 7.30pm Sat & Sun).

Keep following the cathedral walls northwards to reach **Praza da Inmaculada**, known for its *azabeche* (jet) shops. Pilgrims arriving via the Camino Francés (French Route) are met first with this view of the cathedral. Opposite its facade looms the huge Benedictine **Mosteiro de San Martiño Pinario**, a seminary that's closed to the public except in summer, when it opens as a *hostal* (opposite). The monastery's elaborate baroque **church** (☎ 981 58 30 08; admission €2; 🕑 10am-2pm & 4-6pm) now operates as a museum featuring the beautifully carved Renaissance choir stalls originally used in the cathedral. Another museum, the kid-friendly **Galicia Dixital** (☎ 981 55 40 48; admission free; 🕑 10.30am-2pm & 4-8.30pm Mon-Sat), occupies the left flank of the monastery and is an interactive space with attractions like a 3-D 'experience' of Galicia's marine life.

Other Attractions

Santiago's greatest pleasures are simply wandering its arcaded streets and drifting in and out of the tapas bars along the Rúas Franco and Raíña. If you have a couple of days to explore, there are also worthwhile museums, monuments and parks.

The **Museo das Peregrinacións** (☎ 981 58 15 58; Rúa de San Miguel 4; admission €2.40; 🕑 10am-8pm Tue-Fri, 10.30am-1.30pm & 5-8pm Sat, 10.30am-1.30pm Sun) explores the Camino de Santiago phenomenon over the centuries. The **Fundación Eugenio Granell** (☎ 981 57 21 24; Praza del Toural; adult/child €2/free, Sun free; 🕑 11am-9pm Wed-Sat & Mon, 11am-2pm Sun Oct-May, 11am-9pm Wed-Mon Jun-Sep) includes the artist's broad body of work as well as his collections of surrealist and ethnic art.

A short walk northeast of the old town, the former Convento de San Domingo de Bonaval houses the **Museo do Pobo Galego** (Galician Folk Museum; ☎ 981 58 36 20; Rúa San Domingos de Bonaval; admission free; 🕑 10am-2pm & 4-8pm Tue-Sat, 11am-2pm Sun), with exhibits on Galician life and arts ranging from the fishing industry to music and traditional costumes. Facing the museum, the **Centro Galego de Arte Contemporánea** (☎ 981 54 66 19; Rúa de Ramón del Valle-Inclán; admission free; 🕑 11am-8pm Tue-Sun) hosts temporary exhibitions of modern art.

Of Santiago's many verdant parks, the largest is the **Alameda**, which sprawls west of the old town in a tidy grid of tree-lined promenades like the Paseo da Ferradura, offering peerless views of the cathedral spires.

TOURS

Several public and private entities organise walking tours in the old town. Two-hour walks led by **Compostur** (☎ 981 56 98 90; adult/child €10/free; 🕑 in English noon & 6pm Tue & Sun Easter-Oct, 4pm Sun Nov-Easter, in Spanish noon & 6pm Apr–mid-Oct, noon mid-Oct-Mar) from Praza das Praterias offer a fascinating glimpse into the legends and stories behind Santiago's old stone walls.

For an unforgettable bird's-eye view of the city, take the **cathedral rooftop tour** (☎ 981 55 29 85; www.archicompostela.com; per person €10; ⌚ 10am-2pm & 4-8pm) organised by the Museo da Catedral. This tour is the only way to visit the Gothic **Pazo de Xelmírez** (1120), where the main banquet hall is adorned with exquisite little wall busts depicting feasters, musicians, kings and jugglers.

Pick up the monthly *Culturall* brochure, available at the municipal tourist office and many bars around town, for details on themed summer-only tours of the centre.

FESTIVALS & EVENTS

July is Santiago's busiest month. The **Feast of Saint James** (Día de Santiago) is on 25 July and is simultaneously Galicia's 'national' day. Two weeks of festivities surround the festival, which culminates in a spectacular fireworks display on July 24.

SLEEPING

From cheap *hostales* to chic hotels, Santiago boasts an excellent range of accommodation options. It's always wise to book ahead, especially in July when the number of pilgrims swells.

Budget

Hostal Suso (☎ 981 58 66 11; Rúa do Vilar 65; s/d €20/40) Stacked above a bar, this family-run *hostal* represents the best deal in town. Immaculate rooms with spic-and-span bathrooms have firm beds and modern wood furniture. Light sleepers should request an interior room.

Hostal Seminario Mayor (☎ 981 58 30 09; www.viajesatlantico.com/pinario; Praza da Inmaculada 5; s/d/tr incl breakfast €30/47/60; ⌚ Jul-Sep) Rooms are basic, but this *hostal* offers the rare experience of staying inside a Benedictine monastery. With 126 rooms it's a good bet when everywhere else is full.

Hostal Alameda (☎ 981 58 81 00; www.alameda32.com in Spanish; Rúa de San Clemente 32; d/tr €53/71, s without bathroom €24) Great value, with exceptionally large rooms, the family-run Alameda backs up to a park. Try to book one of the modern, queen-bed rooms rather than a twin, which have kept 1980s-style ruffled bedspreads and gold curtains.

Hostal Mapoula (☎ 981 58 01 24; www.mapoula.com; Rúa Entremurallas 10; s/d/tr/q €32/42/55/65; 💻) Rooms at this stylish third-floor *hostal* are small but decorated with flair in a sunny orange-and-rust-red colour scheme. The bathrooms are a tight squeeze but clean.

Midrange

Hostal Libredón (☎ 981 57 65 20; www.libredonbarbantes.com; Praza de Fonseca 5; s/d €45/65) The bright, fresh-feeling rooms (many with balconies) are basic yet inviting, but the real reason to book here is its location on a lively little square. Downsides include squishy mattresses and cramped bathrooms.

Hostal Barbantes (Rúa do Franco 3; s €43-54, d €65) Sharing the Libredón's reception office, the Barbantes offers the same deal, though rooms are newer and boast a pinch of contemporary pizzazz. Request a cathedral view.

Hotel Real (☎ 981 56 92 90; www.hotelreal.com; Rúa da Caldeirería 49; s/d €50/70) The sunny rooms are on the small side, but they feature old-fashioned charm in the form of wrought-iron beds, oriental-style carpets and balconies overlooking the cobblestone street below.

Hotel Airas Nunes (☎ 902 40 58 58, 981 55 47 06; www.pousadasdecompostela.com; Rúa do Vilar 17; s/d €70/80; 💻) For laid-back elegance, this is a great choice. The spiralling granite staircase leads to 10 appealing rooms with garnet-and-green colour schemes, buttery yellow walls, warm wooden furniture and wood-beam ceilings. For other stylish hotels run by the same company, see p570.

Hotel Costa Vella (☎ 981 56 95 30; www.costavella.com; Rúa da Porta da Pena 17; s €51 d €69-85; ✿) The tranquil, thoughtfully designed rooms (some with galleries) and a lovely garden cafe (open 8am to 11pm) make this a wonderful option. Even if you don't stay, it's an ideal spot for breakfast (€5) or coffee.

Hotel Entrecercas (☎ 981 57 11 51; Rúa Entrecercas 11; s/d incl breakfast €66/86; P 💻) A homey, family-run place, the Entrecercas inhabits a restored 600-year-old house near the Praza da Galicia. Exposed stone walls and flowered curtains lend the comfy rooms a rustic touch. It's wheelchair accessible.

our pick **Casa-Hotel As Artes** (☎ 981 55 52 54; www.asartes.com; Travesía de Dos Puertas 2; r €88-98; 💻) Located on a quiet street close to the cathedral, the Casa Hotel As Artes' lovely stone-walled rooms exude a romantic rustic air. Breakfast

(€9) is served in a homey dining room overlooking the street.

Other Pousadas de Compostela–run hotels are also recommended:

Hotel Virxe da Cerca (☎ 902 40 58 58; www.pousadasdecompostela.com; Rúa da Virxe da Cerca 27; s €80-105, d €105-130; P ✠ ☐) Backed by tranquil gardens where breakfast is served, this elegant hotel at the edge of the old quarter was an 18th-century Jesuit residence.

Hotel San Clemente (☎ 981 56 92 60; www.pousadasdecompostela.com; Rúa de San Clemente 28; s/d €70/80) With the Pousada group's standard elegance, it's on a tranquil street at the edge of the old quarter.

Top End

Hotel Rúa Villar (☎ 981 51 98 58; www.hotelruavillar.com in Spanish; Rúa do Vilar 8-10; s/d incl breakfast €96/161; ✠ ☐) Rúa Villar is in an artfully restored 18th-century building whose focal point is a central patio capped with a splendid stained-glass skylight. The 14 rooms, with soft beds and original elements like stone walls, are cosy and inviting, if not spacious.

San Francisco Hotel Monumento (☎ 981 58 16 34; www.sanfranciscohm.com; Campillo San Francisco 3; s/d €130/170; P ✠ ☐ ☐) The stone hallways, with their low lights and stone door frames, recall the hotel's former life as a 16th-century monastery. But rooms, minimalist and modern, are all about contemporary comfort, and it's wheelchair friendly.

Parador Hostal dos Reis Católicos (☎ 981 58 22 00; www.parador.es; Praza do Obradoiro 1; r €225; P ✠ ☐) Built in 1499 and rubbing shoulders with the cathedral, the palatial *parador* is Santiago's top hotel. Even if you don't book one of its regal rooms, stop in for tea at the elegant cafe.

EATING

Central Santiago is packed with eateries, especially along Rúa do Franco (named for the French, not the dictator) and parallel Rúa da Raíña. Don't leave without trying a *tarta de Santiago*, an iconic almond cake.

TAPAS

O Gato Negro (☎ 981 58 31 05; Rúa da Raíña; raciones €3-9) Marked only with a green door and a black cat, this old-town haunt serves plates of seafood, ham, cheese or peppers on five sought-after tables.

Casa Rosalía (☎ 981 568 441; Rúa do Franco 10; raciones €3-15) With a sleeker, more contemporary style than other nearby bars, Rosalía draws crowds for tapas and *raciones* like *pulpo*, salads and fried cuttlefish.

O Beiro (☎ 981 58 13 70; Rúa da Raíña 3; mains €11-24) The house speciality is *tablas* (trays) of delectable cheeses and sausages, but you can also get tapas and *raciones* at this friendly two-storey tavern and *viñoteca* (wine bar).

RESTAURANTS

Restaurante Ó 42 (☎ 981 57 06 65; Rúa do Franco 42; mains €5-18) With tapas, *raciones* and a solid menu of local favourites like empanadas, shellfish, octopus and tortillas, this stylish place stands out from the crowd.

Restaurant Sobrinos del Padre (☎ 981 58 35 66; Rúa da Fonte de San Miguel 7; mains €6-10, menú €10.50) Octopus rules at this no-frills bar-cum-eatery, though you can also get meatier dishes like roasted lamb or Galician-style tripe.

O Triángulo Das Verduras (☎ 981 57 62 12; Praciña das Peñas 2; menú €11.50, mains €7; ⏲ closed Mon evening & Sun; V) Lacklustre service and decor aside, this below-street-level restaurant is a herbivore's best shot at a varied meal – hummus, stuffed eggplant and veggie soups are a few of the dishes available.

Cre-Cotté Creperie (☎ 981 57 76 43; Praza da Quintana 1; mains €8-14; V) A dozen different salads and a wide range of sweet and savoury crepes make this second-storey eatery a hit with vegetarians, though meat dishes are served as well.

La Bodeguilla de San Roque (☎ 981 56 43 79; Rúa de San Roque 13; mains €8-15) Northeast of the old town, this busy two-storey restaurant serves an eclectic range of excellent dishes ranging from salads and scrambled eggs to Galician veal fillet or *zorza* (chopped pork).

Carretas (☎ 981 56 31 11; Rúa das Carretas 21; mains €10-18, menú €18) Located at the edge of the old town, this classic *marisquería* (seafood eatery) is known for its shellfish platters (€48 per person) and excellent *ría*-fresh fish.

our pick Restaurante Ó Dezaseis (☎ 981 56 48 80; Rúa de San Pedro 16; mains €11-13, menú €11.50) Wood-beam ceilings and exposed stone walls give an invitingly rustic air to this popular tavern just beyond the touristy buzz. The mixed crowd tucks into specialities like *caldo gallego* (Galician soup) and *lacón con grelos* (ham with greens).

El Pasaje (☎ 981 55 70 81; Rúa do Franco 54; mains €14-25) For a special meal, this classic spot offers melt-in-your-mouth Galician seafood, shellfish and steaks. A series of intimate din-

GALICIA'S STRANGEST DINING EXPERIENCE

Getting there is half the fun at **Fogar do Santiso** (☎ 981 80 59 48; www.fogardosantiso.es; Trasellas, Luóu-Teo; raciones €2-8; dinner only), a rambling shack-like eatery located 20 minutes south of the city in what feels like the middle of nowhere (check online for directions and a map). Oddities like old farm equipment, cobweb-draped pigs' heads and rusty antiques fill every inch of the place, creating what's got to be Galicia's most striking dining environment. While the mixed crowd downs simple dishes like *criollo* sausage, french fries and *pulpo*, the quirky owner and his entourage walk around playing the *gaita* (Galician bagpipes). Come around midnight on Saturdays for the *queimada*, when this traditional flambé liquor is made following a comically spooky ritual.

ing rooms scattered over several floors ensures a tranquil setting.

DRINKING

The centre is packed with bars and cafes. If you're after tapas and wine, graze along the Rúas do Franco and da Raíña. For people-watching, hit the cafes along Praza da Quinatana and Rúa do Vilar. The liveliest area lies east of Praza da Quintana, especially along Rúa de San Paio de Antealtares, a hot spot for live music. Things get lively after dinner, especially Thursday to Sunday nights, when Santiago's large student population comes out in full force.

Borriquita de Belém (Rúa de San Paio de Antealtares 22) Just south of Praza de San Paio, this is an inviting little jazz club serving mojitos.

Modus Vivendi (Praza de Feixóo 1) A Santiago classic, this atmospheric pub in the stables of an 18th-century mansion attracts all types with wide-ranging music.

Café Atlántico (☎ 981 57 73 96; Rúa da Fonte de San Miguel 9) This multi-level bar pulls in a hip, attractive 20s set, with music ranging from Cajun blues to Spanish indie rock.

hs (Rúa da Troia) This high-spirited club is a bastion of Santiago's gay scene.

Momo (Rúa da Virxe da Cerca 23) It has a wonderful big garden area open in warmer weather with views over parks and monasteries, plus two bars, a pool and football tables and rock music.

ENTERTAINMENT

Cultural events and festivals go on year-round. For details, pick up *Culturall* or check the agenda on www.santiagoturismo.com. In summer, look out for frequent alfresco concerts; popular venues include the Prazas Toral, Quintana and Obradoiro. In the new town, people gravitate towards the clubs along Rúas da República Arxentina and Nova de Abaixo.

Conga 8 (Rúa da Conga 8) Head to the downstairs dance floor for Latin and salsa beats.

A Casa das Crechas (www.casadascrechas.com in Galician; Vía Sacra 3) There's no better place for Celtic music. Jam sessions and concerts are scheduled regularly.

Dado Dadá (Rúa de Alfredo Brañas 19) Jazz fans should head for this Santiago mainstay, featuring jam sessions starting at 11pm Tuesday.

Garigolo (Praciña da Algalia de Arriba 1) This chill cafe morphs into a concert venue at night, when mainly local acts take the stage.

GETTING THERE & AWAY

Air

The **Lavacolla airport** (☎ 981 54 75 00; www.aena.es) is 11km east of the city and connects Santiago with Spanish and European destinations. Ryanair flies in from London, Liverpool, Frankfurt, Rome and Valencia; Aer Lingus connects with Dublin; and Air Europa has routes to the Canary Islands. Barcelona and Madrid are served by Iberia and Spanair; Vueling also flies to Barcelona. Other destinations include Bilbao, Malaga, Menorca, Mallorca, Paris, Seville and Zurich.

Bus

Several companies operate out of Santiago's **bus station** (☎ 981 54 24 16; www.tussa.org; Rúa San Caetano). **Castromil-Monbus** (☎ 902 29 29 00, 981 58 90 90; www.monbus.es) links the capital to the rest of Galicia, with services to destinations including A Coruña (€6.15, 50 to 90 minutes, up to 30 daily), Pontevedra (€5, 50 to 90 minutes, up to 28 daily) and Ourense (€9.95, two hours, up to six daily).

Alsa (☎ 902 42 22 42; www.alsa.es) operates further afield, with daily buses to Spanish cities like Madrid (€57, 8½ hours, two daily), Oviedo (€25 to €41, 5½ to 7½ hours, up to six daily) and Salamanca (€23 to €28, six to eight hours, two daily). Alsa also heads to European destinations including Porto, Lisbon, Paris, London, Brussels, Amsterdam and Zürich.

Further daily services head for places along the Costa da Morte and Rías Baixas, and destinations to the east such as Lugo, Santander, San Sebastián and Burgos.

Car & Motorcycle

The main motorway into the city is the AP9 toll road. Slower and free of cost is the N550. Street parking anywhere near the centre of the city is difficult, but you can pay to park in underground lots, such as the one in the Praza da Galicia.

Train

Renfe (www.renfe.es) travels to/from Madrid (Chamartín station; €45) on a daytime Talgo (seven hours) or an overnight Trenhotel (nine hours).

Regional trains run roughly every hour up and down the coast, linking Santiago with Vigo (€5.90 to €8, 90 minutes), Pontevedra (€3.90 to €5.25, 50 minutes) and A Coruña (€3.90 to €5.25, 45 to 70 minutes).

GETTING AROUND

Santiago de Compostela is walkable, although it's a bit of a hike from the train and bus stations to the centre.

Up to 21 **Empresa Freire** (☎ 981 58 81 11) buses run daily between Lavacolla airport and the bus station (€1.70). About half of them continue to/depart from Rúa do Doutor Teixeiro, southwest of Praza de Galicia. Taxis charge around €20.

The city's **Tralusa** (☎ 901 12 00 54; www.tussa.org in Spanish) bus 6 runs every 20 to 30 minutes from Rúa do Hórreo near the train station to Rúa da Virxe da Cerca on the eastern edge of the old town. Bus 5 runs every 15 to 30 minutes between Praza de Galicia and the bus station, via Rúa da Virxe da Cerca. Tickets cost €0.90.

A CORUÑA & THE RÍAS ALTAS

In few places do land and sea meet in such abrupt beauty. The striking scenery of the Rías Altas, with their untamed beaches, towering sea cliffs and powerful waves, are certainly more dramatic than the landscapes of the Rías Bajas. Combine that with the allure of maritime A Coruña and the lively resort hubs along the eastern and northern shores, and you'll be puzzling over why more visitors don't journey north.

A CORUÑA

pop 252,000

A Coruña (Castilian: La Coruña) is hard to pin down. It's a port city and a beachy hot spot; a buzzing commercial centre and an interesting cultural enclave, a historical city and a buzzing modern metropolis. And its superb maritime location (along with a thriving cultural and nightlife scene) is responsible for bringing in thousands of cruise tourists each summer.

Britain looms large on A Coruña's horizon. In 1588 the ill-fated Spanish Armada weighed anchor here, and the following year Sir Francis Drake tried to occupy the town, but was seen off by María Pita, a heroine whose name lives on in the town's main square. In the 19th and 20th centuries, A Coruña's port was the gateway through which hundreds of thousands of Galician emigrants left for new lives in the Americas. Home to the world's second-biggest textile company, Inditex, and Galicia's biggest banks and building companies, today this is the region's wealthiest city.

Orientation

Although this is a sprawling city, most of what you'll want to see is concentrated along a narrow isthmus and mushroom-shaped headland. The *ciudad vieja* (old city) huddles in the southeast of the headland, while hotels, restaurants and bars predominate at the centre of the isthmus, which is bordered by the port to the southeast and beaches to the northwest. The train and bus stations are 2km southwest of the city centre.

Information

Cyber Zalate@Net (Calle de Zalaeta 7; per hr €1.50; 🕒 10.30am-1.30am)

Farmacia Velasco (☎ 981 22 21 34; Calle Real 92; 🕒 8am-3am) Late-opening pharmacy.

Main post office (☎ 981 22 51 75; Calle Alcalde Manuel Casas; 🕒 8.30am-8.30pm Mon-Fri, 9.30am-2pm Sat)

Municipal tourist office (☎ 618 79 06 65; www.turismocoruna.com; Plaza de María Pita; 🕒 9am-8.30pm Mon-Fri Feb-Oct, 9am-2.30pm & 4-8.30pm Mon-Fri Nov-Jan, 10am-2pm & 4-8pm Sat, 10am-3pm Sun year-round) The tourist office organises several free guided tours in

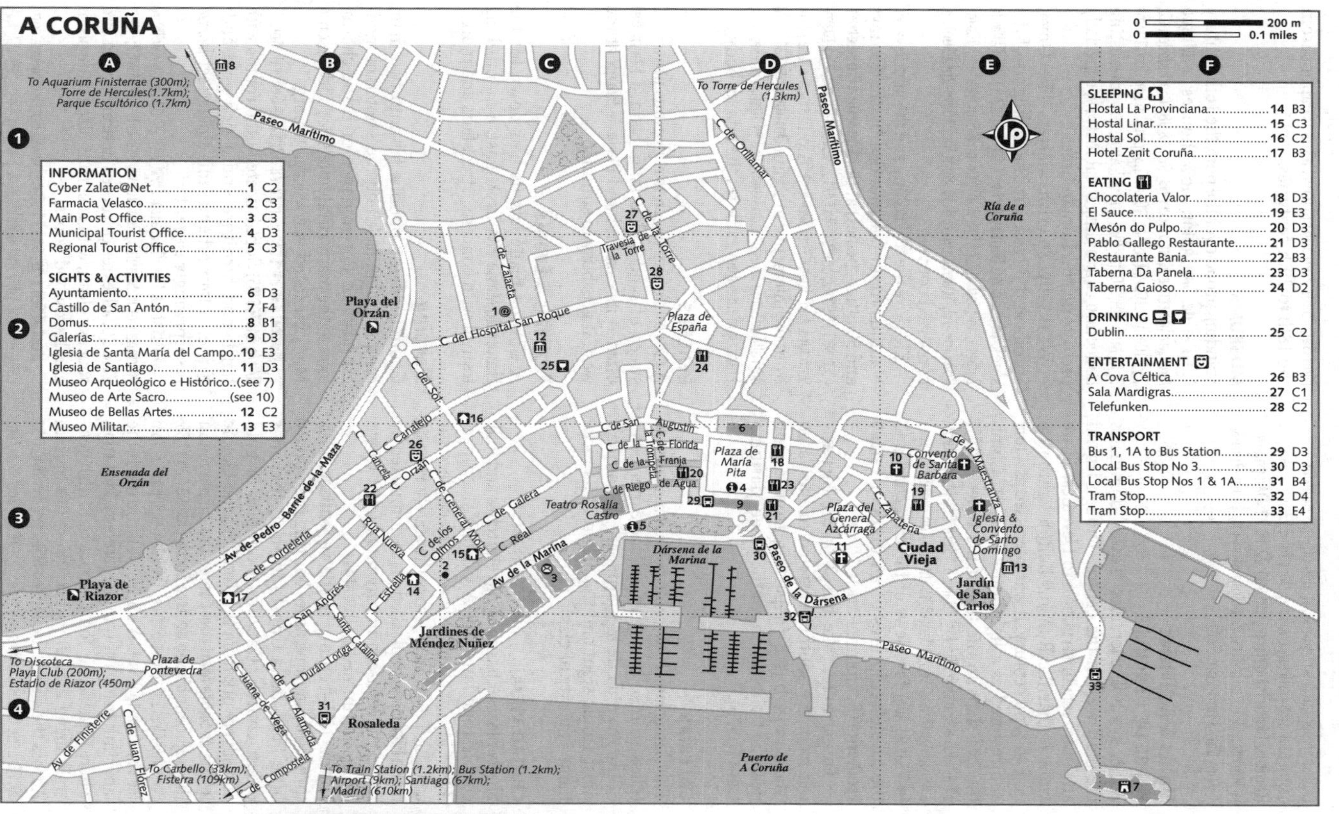
A CORUÑA
0 200 m
0 0.1 miles
INFORMATION
Cyber Zalate@Net....1 C2
Farmacia Velasco....2 C3
Main Post Office....3 C3
Municipal Tourist Office....4 D3
Regional Tourist Office....5 C3
SIGHTS & ACTIVITIES
Ayuntamiento....6 D3
Castillo de San Antón....7 F4
Domus....8 B1
Galerías....9 D3
Iglesia de Santa María del Campo..10 E3
Iglesia de Santiago....11 D3
Museo Arqueológico e Histórico..(see 7)
Museo de Arte Sacro....(see 10)
Museo de Bellas Artes....12 C2
Museo Militar....13 E3
SLEEPING
Hostal La Provinciana....14 B3
Hostal Linar....15 C3
Hostal Sol....16 C2
Hotel Zenit Coruña....17 B3
EATING
Chocolatería Valor....18 D3
El Sauce....19 E3
Mesón do Pulpo....20 D3
Pablo Gallego Restaurante....21 D3
Restaurante Bania....22 B3
Taberna Da Panela....23 D3
Taberna Gaioso....24 D2
DRINKING
Dublin....25 C2
ENTERTAINMENT
A Cova Céltica....26 B3
Sala Mardigras....27 C1
Telefunken....28 C2
TRANSPORT
Bus 1, 1A to Bus Station....29 D3
Local Bus Stop No 3....30 D3
Local Bus Stop Nos 1 & 1A....31 B4
Tram Stop....32 D4
Tram Stop....33 E4
To Aquarium Finisterrae (300m); Torre de Hercules(1.7km); Parque Escultórico (1.7km)
To Torre de Hercules (1.3km)
To Discoteca Playa Club (200m); Estadio de Riazor (450m)
To Carbello (33km); Fisterra (109km)
To Train Station (1.2km); Bus Station (1.2km); Airport (9km); Santiago (67km); Madrid (610km)
Paseo Marítimo
Ría de a Coruña
Ensenada del Orzán
Playa del Orzán
Playa de Riazor
Plaza de España
Plaza de María Pita
Plaza del General Azcárraga
Plaza de Pontevedra
Ciudad Vieja
Convento de Santa Barbara
Iglesia & Convento de Santo Domingo
Jardín de San Carlos
Jardines de Méndez Nuñez
Rosaleda
Teatro Rosalía Castro
Dársena de la Marina
Puerto de A Coruña
Paseo de la Dársena
Av de la Marina
Av de Pedro Barrie de la Maza
Av de Finisterre
C de Orillamar
C de la Torre
Travesía de la Torre
C de Zalaeta
C del Hospital San Roque
C del Sol
C Canalejo
C Cancela
C Orzán
C de General Mola
C de Galera
C Real
C de los Olmos
Rúa Nueva
C Estrella
C San Andrés
C Santa Catalina
C Durán Loriga
C de la Alameda
C Juana de Vega
C de Cordelería
C de Juan Flórez
C de Compostela
C de San Augustín
C de la Florida
C de la Trompeta
C de la Franja
C de Riego de Agua
C Zapatería
C de la Maestranza

GALICIA

English; reservations required. It also offers a popular gastro tour and Galician cooking class for €12.

Regional tourist office (☎ 981 22 18 22; Dársena de la Marina; ⏰ 10am-2pm & 4-7pm Mon-Fri, 11am-2pm & 4-7pm Sat, 11am-2pm Sun)

Sights & Activities

TORRE DE HÉRCULES

A city symbol, 'Hercules' Tower' dominates the bluff west of the centre. Though legend attributes its construction to Hercules, all we *know* is that the Romans built a lighthouse here the 2nd century. It was later used as a fort and restored as a lighthouse in 1791. Climb the 234 steps to the top of the **tower** (☎ 981 22 37 30; admission €2; ⏰ 10am-5.45pm Oct-Mar, 10am-6.45pm Apr-Jun & Sep, 10am-8.45pm Jul-Aug, until 11.45pm Fri & Sat Jul-Aug) for views of the city, coast and the lovely sculptures of an outdoor **Parque Escultórico** (Sculpture Park).

To get here, take bus 3 or 3A (departing from the southern stretch of the Paseo Marítimo), bus 5 (departing from a stop near the train station) or the Paseo Marítimo tram (p576).

GALERÍAS

The classic late-19th-century Galician *galerías* (glass-fronted balconies) on the eastern end of the Avenida de la Marina are A Coruña's most-iconic sight and the origin of its nickname, 'the city of glass'.

CIUDAD VIEJA

Shady plazas, charming old churches and hilly cobblestone lanes fill A Coruña's compact 'Old City', making this the perfect place for a stroll. To get here, cross the stately **Plaza de María Pita**, a sun-splashed plaza dominated by the early-20th-century *ayuntamiento* (town hall) and rimmed with cafes.

The 12th-century **Iglesia de Santiago**, with three Romanesque apses backing onto pretty little Plaza de la Constitución, is the city's oldest church. Dazzling examples of gold and silverwork from the Romanesque-Gothic **Iglesia de Santa María del Campo** are displayed in the adjacent **Museo de Arte Sacro** (☎ 981 20 31 86; Puerta de Aires 23; admission free; ⏰ 10am-1.30pm & 5-7pm Tue-Fri, 10am-1pm Sat). A short walk through the labyrinth brings you to the **Jardín de San Carlos**, where General Sir John Moore (a British general during the Peninsular War) lies buried. Across the street, the **Museo Militar** (☎ 981 20 53 00; Plaza de Carlos I; admission free; ⏰ 10am-2pm & 4-7pm Mon-Sat, 10am-2pm Sun) showcases weapons from the 18th to 20th centuries.

MUSEUMS

Standing proud over the port, the 16th-century **Castillo de San Antón** now houses a **Museo Arqueológico e Histórico** (☎ 981 18 98 50; admission €2; ⏰ 10am-7.30pm Tue-Sat, 10am-2.30pm Sun Sep-Jun, 10am-9pm Mon-Sat, 10am-3pm Sun Jul-Aug), an interesting collection canvassing local history, especially prehistoric and Roman times.

Works by Spanish masters like Goya, Sorolla and Picasso are the highlights of the sleek **Museo de Bellas Artes** (☎ 981 22 37 23; Calle de Zalaeta; admission €2.40, Sat afternoon & Sun free; ⏰ 10am-8pm Tue-Fri, 10am-2pm & 4.30-8pm Sat, 10am-2pm Sun), a converted convent.

Kids love the seal colony and the underwater Nautilus room (surrounded by sharks, rays and 50 other species) at the **Aquarium Finisterrae** (☎ 981 18 98 42; adult/child €4/10; Paseo Marítimo; ⏰ 10am-9pm Jul & Aug, 10am-7pm Sep-Jun). Along the same seafront the interactive museum **Domus** (☎ 981 18 98 40; Calle de Santa Teresa 1; admission €2; ⏰ 10am-7pm Sep-Jun, 11am-9pm Jul & Aug) explores the human body.

BEACHES

A Coruña's city beach is a glorious protected sweep of sand 1.4km long. Named **Playa del Orzán** at its east end and **Playa de Riazor** at the west, it gets busy in summer.

Festivals & Events

A Coruña really lets its hair down for the **Fiestas de María Pita** in August, a month-long festival with concerts, street fairs and more.

Sleeping

Central lodging options fall into two main camps: straightjacket business hotels or modest *hostales*. For romance or rustic charm, look to the many rural hotels beyond the city. Many are listed at www.aga tur.org.

Hostal Linar (☎ 981 22 78 37; Calle General Mola 7; d/tr/q €45/65/85) Sophisticated little rooms with hardwood furniture and a rich gold-and-garnet colour scheme; this side-street *hostal* is surprisingly elegant.

Hostal La Provinciana (☎ 981 22 04 00; www.laprovinciana.net in Spanish; Rúa Nueva 9; s/d/tr €37/49/67; P) The 20, all-exterior rooms here are bright and squeaky clean, with generous-sized bathrooms and hardwood floors.

Hostal Sol (☎ 981 21 03 62; www.hotelsolcoruna.com; Calle del Sol 10; r incl breakfast & parking €87; P 💻) A friendly, family-run place with unpretentious yet comfortable rooms (some with terraces), the Sol is a good deal, especially in low season.

Hotel Zenit Coruña (☎ 981 21 84 84; www.zenithoteles.com; Calle Comandante Fontanes 19; r €85-105; P) The sunny, stylishly minimalist rooms have glass wash basins and elegant wallpaper, and it's all just a block from Orzán beach.

Eating

Popular seafood eateries line the Plaza de María Pita. For tapas, *raciones* and cheap lunch *menús*, hit the narrow lanes west of the plaza, especially Calle de la Franja.

Chocolateria Valor (☎ 981 20 86 23; Plaza de María Pita 5; hot chocolate €2.50-5; 9am-1pm & 4.30-9.30pm) With lusciously thick chocolate with *churros*, indulgent ice creams, milkshakes and great coffee, Valor is ideal for breakfast or an afternoon pick-me-up.

Mesón do Pulpo (☎ 981 20 24 44; Calle de la Franja 9; raciones €4-12; closed Sun) Here it's all about octopus, as the name suggests. Eat it classically prepared with paprika, rock salt and olive oil.

Restaurante Bania (☎ 981 22 13 01; Calle de Cordelería 7; mains €4-15, menú €9.25; closed dinner Mon & lunch & dinner Sun; V) Interesting salads, tofu dishes and vegetable ensembles are the heart of this classy all-vegetarian eatery a short walk from the main drag.

our pick **El Sauce** (☎ 981 22 09 20; Rúa Sinagoga 8; mains €6-8, menú €9; V) Red-and-white chequered tablecloths and a wall full of antiques lend an inviting country air to the five-table Sauce, tucked away in a small plaza in the old quarter. The menu centres on simple yet inventive fare like salads and scrambled eggs with cheese or vegetables.

Taberna Da Penela (☎ 981 20 92 00; Plaza de María Pita 12; mains €7-18; closed Mon) Get tasty, typical dishes like *pulpo*, *caldo gallego* and hake at this popular plaza-side spot. The wine list is surprisingly varied, with lots of Spanish and Galician brands to choose from.

Taberna Gaioso (☎ 981 21 33 55; Plaza de España 15; tapas & raciones €11-20; closed dinner Sun & lunch & dinner Mon) A cut above your typical tavern, this stylish spot serves innovative tapas like 'cod confit with spinach'.

Pablo Gallego Restaurante (☎ 981 20 88 88; Plaza de María Pita 11; mains €10-29; closed Sun) The classiest choice on the plaza, this serene, stone-walled dining room prepares 21st-century updates on traditional Galician ingredients. Try lobster croquettes, braised sea bass or grilled eel.

Drinking & Entertainment

At night, A Coruña is buzzing with taverns, bars and clubs. Head to Plaza de María Pita for low-key drinks and unbeatable people-watching, or navigate the Zona de los Vinos (Wine District), as the area centred around Calles de la Franja, Barrera and Galera is known. Dozens of pubs on Calle del Sol, Calle Canalejo, Calle del Orzán and other streets behind Playa del Orzán party on from around midnight till 3am or 4am at the weekend.

Sala Mardigras (☎ 981 20 38 77; www.salamardigras.com in Spanish; Travesía de la Torre 8; admission varies; from 10pm Thu-Sat) Crowds pack this dark little bar to hear blues, rock and country bands play.

A Cova Céltica (Rúa Orzán 82; mains €10-29; closed Sun) Galician folk music sets the tone at this popular neighbourhood tavern.

Dublin (☎ 981 20 32 74; Calle Panaderas 50) This Irish pub stages Galician folk nights some Tuesdays. Music starts around 10pm.

Telefunken (www.housecafemusic.com; Calle Alcalde Folla Yordi 8; midnight-4am Thu-Sat) House lovers flock to this cool club.

Discoteca Playa Club (☎ 981 27 75 14; www.playaclub.net in Spanish; Playa de Riazor; admission €6.50; 3am-6am Thu-Sat) As the pubs close, the discos start to fill. This ever-popular spot boasts views over the bay and a dance-inducing musical mix of alternative pop, soul-jazz, funk and electronica.

Deportivo La Coruña (☎ 981 22 94 10; www.canaldeportivo.com in Spanish; Estadio de Riazor, Calle de Manuel Murguía) A Coruña is justly proud of its football team, which mixes it with Europe's best.

Getting There & Away

AIR

From A Coruña's **Alvedro airport** (☎ 981 18 72 00), Iberia has at least three flights daily to/from Madrid, plus daily direct services to/from London with its low-cost arm, Clickair. There are further Madrid and Barcelona flights on Spanair, and daily flights to Lisbon by Tap-Air Portugal.

BUS

From the **bus station** (☎ 981 18 43 35; Calle Caballeros 21), **Monbus-Castromil** (☎ 902 29 29 00; www.monbus.es) operates services to southern cities including Santiago de Compostela (€5.75 to €6.70, one to 1½ hours, approximately hourly) and Vigo (€14.30, 2½ hours, up to nine daily). **Arriva** (☎ 902 27 74 82; www.arriva.es) serves the Rías Altas and Costa da Morte, while **ALSA** (☎ 902 42 22 42; www.alsa.es) heads further afield to destinations including Madrid (€39 to €57, 6½ to 8½ hours, up to six daily).

CAR & MOTORCYCLE

The AP9 tollway heading for Santiago de Compostela is the quickest way out of town to the south. Before Betanzos another tollway heads north to Ferrol. The N550 to Santiago is prettier and there's no charge.

TRAIN

Renfe (☎ 902 24 02 02; www.renfe.es) heads down south about hourly, stopping in Santiago de Compostela (from €3.90, one hour), Pontevedra (from €8.55, two to 2½ hours) and Vigo (from €9.60, 2½ to three hours). Up to a half-dozen trains also head to destinations like Lugo (from €6.50, two hours) and Ourense (from €13.85, two to three hours). Long-distance routes include Madrid (from €48, nine to 10 hours, three daily), and Barcelona (from €51, 16 to 17 hours, two daily).

Getting Around

Buses (€1.15) run every half-hour from 7.15am until 9.45pm (10.30pm on weekends) between the airport and the centre. A taxi costs about €15.

Local buses 5, 5A and 11 link the train station with central A Coruña; they stop diagonally opposite the station. Buses 1, 1A, 12 and 14 stop outside the bus station en route to the city centre. Rides cost €1.

Daily from mid-June to sometime in October, and on weekends the rest of the year, trams (€1) run along Paseo Marítimo from the port area right round the large headland north of the city centre to the beach Playa de Riazor.

GALICIA

RÍAS ALTAS

If you're seeking dramatic scenery, look no further. Here, towering forests open to views of sheer sea cliffs, sweeping beaches and vivid green fields studded with farmhouses. Add in medieval villages like Betanzos and Pontedeume and the constant roar of the Atlantic, and it's easy to see why the Rías Altas may be Galicia's most beautiful area. The water may be colder up here, but beaches are far less crowded, making this an ideal destination for travellers yearning to get off the beaten path.

TOP FIVE BEACHES

Of Galicia's 1200km of coastline and 275km of beaches, these five stand out from the crowd.

- **Illas Cíes** (p593), for strolling.
- **Praia A Lanzada** (p589), for swimming.
- **Praia de Pantín** (p578), for surfing.
- **Praia As Catedrais** (p580), for stellar picnics.
- **Area de Trece** (p582), for seclusion.

Betanzos

pop 13,300

The medieval city of Betanzos straddles the Ríos Mendo and Mandeo, which meet here to flow north into the Ría de Betanzos. Once a thriving port rivalling A Coruña (until that city eclipsed it), Betanzos today offers a well-preserved old town, although its best face is seen by strolling along the riverbank, sipping local wines in its taverns, or enjoying the sunlight on your face in one of the cafes in the centre.

Get a map at the **tourist office** (☎ 981 77 66 66; Praza da Galicia 1; 10am-2pm & 4-7pm Oct-May, 10-2pm & 5-8pm Jun-Sep).

SIGHTS

Start your visit in the sprawling main square, Praza dos Irmáns García Naveira (named for the town's early-20th-century benefactors), with its multi-storey houses glassed in by classic *galerías*. Around 50,000 people cram into the square at midnight on 16 August to witness the releasing of an enormous, decorated paper hot-air balloon from the tower of Santo Domingo church in the **Fiesta de San Roque**.

Just around the corner, the **Museo das Mariñas** (adult/child €1.20/free; 10am-2pm & 4-8pm Mon-Fri, 10.30am-1pm Sat), occupies the 16th-century Santo Domingo convent. With exhibits ranging from the mundane (old coffee mugs) to the culturally significant (typical costumes), the museum peeks into traditional Galician life.

Take Rúa Castro into the old town. Sunny Praza da Constitución is flanked by several appealing cafes along with the neoclassical

Casa do Concello and Romanesque/Gothic **Igrexa de Santiago**. A short stroll northeast, the photogenic Praza de Fernán Pérez de Andrade sits between the Gothic churches **Santa María do Azougue** and **San Francisco**. The latter, a cross-shaped church that's beautiful in its simplicity, is famous for holding the carved stone tomb of Fernán Pérez de Andrade 'O Boo' (The Good), the powerful 14th-century potentate who had all three of these Gothic churches built along with a slew of other works.

Beyond the centre, the **Parque O Pasatempo** (9am-8pm) is a park filled with sculpture and fountains. For more natural beauty, take the riverside walkway that begins at the end of Rúa Ánxeles and leads 3km (about 45 minutes) to **Os Caneiros**, the destination of a popular summertime *romería* (pilgrimage).

SLEEPING & EATING

A 10-minute walk from the old town, the **San Roque** (981 77 55 55; www.complejosanroque.com; s/d €81/91; P), a modernist-mansion-turned-hotel, has sleek, sunny rooms with a vaguely maritime air. The peachy facade is unmissable from the main road. It's wheelchair friendly.

In town, **Hotel Garelos** (981 77 59 30; www.hotelgarelos.com; Calle Alfonso IX 8; s/d incl breakfast €79/90; P) has spic-and-span rooms endowed with parquet floors, marble bathrooms and countryside views. It's wheelchair accessible.

A string of terrace cafes flanks the expansive Praza Irmáns Garcia Naviera. Amid the sidewalk tables dart two narrow alleyways, Venela Campo and Travesia do Progreso. The taverns here are popular for drinks, tapas (€2 to €3) or larger *raciones* (€4 to €15). Be sure to try the local *tortilla de patata*, a runny potato omelette that's Betanzo's culinary claim to fame. The very best place to try it is **La Casilla** (981 77 01 61; Carretera de Castilla 90; mains €8-18) a homey restaurant on the highway outside of town.

GETTING THERE & AWAY

Arriva (902 27 74 82; www.arriva.es in Spanish) buses to/from A Coruña (€2.30, 35 minutes, every half-hour) stop in the Praza dos Irmáns García Naveira. Several buses head daily to Viveiro, Lugo and Ferrol.

Betanzos Cidade train station is northwest of the old town, across Río Mendo. Five trains go daily to Ferrol and A Coruña (both €2.60, 45 minutes).

Pontedeume

pop 8600

Another pleasant stop, this medieval hillside town overlooks the Eume estuary, where fishing boats bob. The old town is a maze of narrow streets, the main one being the porticoed Rúa Real, which climbs past a cheerful little square to the 18th-century **Iglesia de Santiago**. Down near the waterfront rises the **Torreón dos Andrade**, the keep of what was once the palace-castle of the local feudal lords, the Andrades. It houses a **tourist office** (981 43 02 70; 10am-2pm & 4-6pm Mon-Fri, 10am-2.30pm Sat, 11am-2pm Sun Sep-May, 10am-2pm & 5-7pm Mon-Fri, 10am-2.30pm Sat, 11am-2pm Sun Jun-Aug).

On Saturdays, Pontedeume comes alive with a **street market** that takes over the town centre with stalls of flea-market-style junk alongside local cheeses, honeys, breads and sausages. Pick up the town speciality, *proia mantecada*, a sweet bread sprinkled with grainy sugar.

Rúa Real is lined with taverns and eateries. At the top of the street, the bohemian-aired **Taberna Tostaky** (981 43 44 45; Rúa Real 34; mains €5-9; closed Sun night & Mon) serves chicken and veggie curry alongside traditional tapas and seafood.

To sleep nearby, your best bet is a rural hotel like the enchanting **Casa do Castelo de Andrade** (981 43 38 39; www.casteloandrade.com; Lugar Castelo de Andrade; r €95-110), 7km from town. This pretty stone farmhouse has 10 immaculate rooms near the Fragas do Eume natural park.

Parque Natural Fragas do Eume

Just beyond Pontedeume, the 91-sq-km of the **Fragas do Eume** park flank the broad Río Eume. This natural wonderland is famous for its Atlantic coastal forest. For details on the many **walking trails** traversing the park, stop at the **Centro de Interpretación** (981 43 25 28; 8.30am-3pm & 4-8pm Mon-Fri, 10am-2pm & 4-8pm Sat & Sun) on the Ombre–Caaveiro highway. Next door, the **Andarubel cafeteria** (981 43 39 69; mains €7-20) rents **bikes** for €5 per hour. From here, you can bike, walk or take the free, half-hourly buses up the mostly flat, paved road to the ruins of the 10th-century **Mosteiro de Caaveiro** (which was being restored at the time of writing). This is the only part of the park most visitors ever see, but to really experience the forest's splendour you're better off planning a hike that dives further in.

The Eume is famous for its reo (large maritime trout) and trout **fishing**. For fishing permits, contact the **Consellería de Pesca** (☎ 981 54 54 00).

There's family-friendly **kayaking** in the calm waters of the Eume Reservoir. Rent equipment at the **Club Deportivo Fragas do Eume** (☎ 671 49 71 47; www.cdfragasdoeume.com in Spanish; Carretera de Eiras; kayak rental €30 per day; 9am-8pm daily Jun-Sep, weekends only Oct-May), located 9km from the 10th-century **Mosteiro de Monfero**.

Cedeira & Around

pop 7500

Heading north, the coast is studded with small maritime towns and pretty beaches worth exploring. Along the Ría de Ares, you could stop in the tiny fishing hamlet of **Redes**. Nearby, on the Ría de Ferrol, **Mugardos** is famous for its local octopus recipe.

The Rías Altas' largest hub is the naval port of **Ferrol**, just 17km north of Pontedeume. It's the western terminus of the FEVE railway from the Basque Country and was the birthplace of General Franco, but it has little to detain you.

Continuing north, you'll come to **Valdoviño**, with the beautiful Praia Frouxeira. Just beyond Valdoviño, **Praia de Pantín** hosts an international surfing competition in early September.

Some 38km from Ferrol is the Rías Alta's biggest resort, **Cedeira**. The old town fronts the west bank of Río Condomiñas with traditional *galerías,* while across two parallel bridges on the modern side of town is the popular **Praia da Magdalena**. Around the headland to the south is the more appealing **Praia de Vilarrube**, a protected dunes and wetlands area.

Cedeira's **tourist office** (☎ 981 48 21 87; Calle Ezequiel López 17; 10.30am-1.30pm & 5-8pm Mon-Fri, 10.30am-2pm Sat, 12-2pm Sun) is in the old town.

For a nice hour or two's stroll, walk oceanward along the waterfront to the fishing port, climb up beside the old fort above it and then walk out onto the headland overlooking the mouth of Ría de Cedeira. The rocky coast around here produces rich harvests of *percebes* (goose barnacles), a much-coveted delicacy.

SLEEPING & EATING

Cedeira is full of bars and cafes, especially around the river mouth and on the Praza Roja, behind the Praia da Magdalena.

Cordobelas (☎ 981 48 06 07; Rúa Cordobelas 29; d €45-70, apt €80-130; P) Just 1km out of Cedeira, this endearingly rustic B&B has converted four century-old houses into an enticing spot with a fabulous garden. Homey rooms have wooden ceilings and it's wheelchair friendly.

our pick **Herbeira** (☎ 981 49 21 67; Rúa Cordobelas; s/d €60/80; P) As sleek as Galicia gets, this contemporary, wheelchair-accessible family-run hotel outside Cedeira boasts 16 minimalist rooms with wenge-coloured furniture, glassed-in galleries and stunning views over the *ría*.

Mesón Muiño Kilowatio (☎ 981 48 26 90; Rúa do Mariñeiro 9; tapas €4-8) This tiny bar packs 'em in for generous servings of *marraxo* (a type of shark), *raxo* and *zorza* (types of grilled pork) and other Galician delights.

El Naútico (☎ 981 48 00 11; Rúa do Mariñeiro 7; mains €9-20) Of the several justifiably popular seafood eateries flanking the river, this is the best-known. Succulent shellfish – most notably *percebes* – and tuna top the menu.

GETTING THERE & AWAY

By bus from the south, you'll need to change in Ferrol, from where **Rialsa** (www.rialsa.com) runs up to nine buses daily (€2.65, 45 minutes) to Cedeira. **Arriva** (☎ 902 27 74 82; www.arriva.es) serves the Cedeira/Cariño route (€3, 50 minutes, up to six daily).

Serra da Capelada

The wild, rugged coastline that the Rías Altas are famous for begin above Cedeira. If you have your own car (or even better, time for long-distance hikes), Galicia's northwestern corner is truly a captivating place to explore, with lush forests, vertigo-inducing cliffs and stunning oceanscapes.

SAN ANDRÉS DE TEIXIDO & GARITA HERBEIRA

In summer, busloads of tourists descend on the hamlet of Texeido (12km past Cediera), a jumble of stone houses renowned as a sanctuary of relics of St Andrew. The faithful draw spring water from the **Fonte do Santo** and buy locally made amulets called *sanandreses*. Though the town has an important place in Galician's hearts, it doesn't take long to see, and the church is a simple affair.

More exciting is its natural setting. Hit the winding CP-2205 highway, a lovely road that runs northwest towards Cariño and the Cabo Ortegal, for incredible views. Six kilometres beyond San Andrés is the must-see **Garita Herbeira Mirador**, 600m above sea level. This is the best place to wow over southern Europe's

GALICIA

highest sea cliffs. Further on, make a 9km detour to the **Mirador da Miranda**, a sublime vantage point over the Estaca de Bares that's only slightly marred by the presence of two communications towers.

CABO ORTEGAL

The magnificent cape where the Atlantic Ocean meets the Bay of Biscay, **Cabo Ortegal** overlooks the craggy coastline from its perch above tall cliffs. Just offshore, **Os Tres Aguillóns**, three islets, provide a home to hundreds of **marine birds** like yellow-leg seagulls and storm petrels. If you come with binoculars, you may also spot dolphins or whales near the cape.

Sitting 4km beyond the workaday town of **Cariño**, the cape is worth visiting just for the views, but there are also some lovely walks out here. On the road out stop at the first *mirador* (viewpoint) to take the 3.2km/30-minute clifftop trail to the **San Xiáo de Trebo** chapel. This well-marked path traverses a forest, crosses the Soutullo River and affords grand views. The vastly more ambitious **GR-50** long-distance ramblers' trail also begins nearby; its endpoint in Betanzos is some 23 hours' walk away.

Rural hotels are the way to go in the area. **Río da Cruz** (☎ 981 42 80 57; www.riodacruz.com; Landoi; r €60-80; Ⓟ) offers six rooms in a rustic country house 15 minutes outside Cariño. The old-fashioned kitchen and sitting room are cosy. Like the bedrooms, they feature solid, if slightly careworn, wooden furnishings.

Cariño to Viveiro

From Cariño the road roughly follows Ría de Ortigueira southwards to Río Mera. The major town is **Ortigueira**, a fishing port and host of the **Festival de Ortigueira** the second weekend in July (see the boxed text, right).

Further on, several detours off the AC-862 highway lead to small but breathtaking beaches like the **Praia de Santo António** in Porto de Espesante. For a very chill base near the coast, book a room at the aged but well-kept **Orillamar** (☎ 981 40 80 14; Praia de Santo António; s/d incl breakfast €55/75), whose restaurant (mains €7 to €22) serves excellent seafood and shellfish.

Continue northeast to **O Barqueiro**, a storybook Galician fishing village where white houses with slate-tile roofs cascade down to the port. There's little to do but stroll along the coast and watch the day's catch come in. FEVE's Ferrol–Viveiro trains and Arriva buses service the town.

> **PIPERS & FIDDLERS**
>
> Much of Galician folk music has Celtic roots, and the sounds of the *gaita* (bagpipe), *bombo* (big drum) and *zanfona* (accordion-like instrument) provide the soundtrack to many festivals and cultural events. Several summer folk music festivals liven up the summer months. The biggest and best is held in July in Ortigueira – see www.festivaldeortigueira.com for details. Other festivals worth seeking out include Intercéltico (www.interceltico.com) in Moaña (Ría de Vigo) and the Festa da Carbelleira (www.festadacarbelleira.com) in Zas (Costa da Morte). Both are held on the first weekend of August.

For an even quieter base, push north to **Porto de Bares**. Little more than a beach with a few boats belly-up in the sand, this is the lowest of low-key bases; the nosiest things around are the seagulls. For a treat, book a room in the contemporary naval-base-turned-hotel **Semaforo de Bares** (☎ 981 41 71 47; www.semaforobares.com; Estaca de Bares; r €65-150; 🕑 closed Christmas & February; Ⓟ), where six indulgent rooms sit 3km above town on a bluff commandeering impressive views of the *rías*. In town and overlooking the water, **Restaurante Centro** (☎ 981 41 40 23; Porto de Bares; mains €5-22) is humble spot whose menu ranges from *callos* (tripe) to fresh shellfish.

The **Estaca de Bares** peninsula has several good walking trails and is a birding hot spot; some 100,000 birds pass through from late summer to early autumn.

Viveiro

pop 15,700

This sprawling town at the mouth of the Río Landro is really three destinations in one. The heart of Viveiro is its historic quarter, but the municipality also incorporates the beach resort of **Praia de Covas**, west of the river, and the fishing and leisure port of **Celeiro**, past Viveiro proper off the C-642 highway.

Strolling old Viveiro is a pleasure. Behind the grand **Puerta de Carlos V** (the most impressive of Viveiro's three remaining old gates) there's a cluster of cobbled lanes and plazas. Not too much has changed since the town was rebuilt after a fire in 1540. Directly up the street past Praza Maior is the 12th-century

Iglesia de Santa María do Campo, displaying Romanesque and Gothic features. Nearby is 1925 reproduction of the shrine of Lourdes, perpetually decorated with wax figures representing the faithfuls' prayer requests.

A well-stocked **tourist office** (☎ 982 56 08 79; www.viveiro.es in Spanish; Avenida Ramón Canosa; 🕑 11am-2pm & 4.30-7.30pm Mon-Fri, 11am-2pm & 5-7pm Sat Sep-Jun, 10am-2pm & 4.30-8pm Mon-Fri, 11am-2pm & 5-7pm Sat, 11.30am-1.30pm Sun Jul-Aug) is opposite the small bus station (north along the waterfront from the Puerta de Carlos V). Viveiro is famous for its elaborate Easter week celebrations, which fill the town with processions and decorations.

Hotel Vila (☎ 982 56 13 31; www.hotel-vila.net; Avenida Nicolás Cora Montenegro 57; s/d €40/53; P), just down from the FEVE station, is an unfussy one-star with bright, yellow-walled rooms and up-to-date furnishings. Prices are slashed in the low season. Several camping grounds sprawl near the beaches outside town, particularly at Praia de Covas.

Even better, head to one of the many rural hotels nearby. **Pazo da Trave** (☎ 982 59 81 63; www.pazodatrave.com; Galdo; r €145; P), 3km inland (off the LU-540 highway, roughly south of Viveiro), is a converted 15th-century manor house where original artwork adds flair to the rustic-chic rooms.

In town, you can get either tapas or a real sit-down meal at the popular tavern-like **Casa Serra** (☎ 982 56 03 74; Rúa de Antonio Bas; mains €6-20). Unfussy pan-grilled meat and fish dishes are served alongside splashier shellfish treats.

If you have a car or a desire to tackle a 3.5km uphill climb, follow signs to the **Monte San Roque**, a gorgeous kid-friendly park with enviable ría views. If it's lunchtime, you can picnic on the stone tables or feast on grilled meats at the rustic **Mirador San Roque** (☎ 608 25 43 96; mains €8-18).

FEVE heads to/from Ferrol (€5.40, two hours, four daily) and Oviedo (€13.80, 4½ hours, two daily), stopping at the coastal resorts along the way. Four or five daily buses fan out to other destinations along the Rías Baixas.

The North Coast

Heading east along the N-642 highway, there are no big resorts or important towns to detain you, though you will get to savour occasional glimpses of the brilliant blue Cantabrian Sea (Bay of Biscay). If it's mealtime, pull over at the **Mesón O'Paseo** (☎ 982 13 57 40; Km 40.5 N-642 Hwy; menú €10, mains €25) a delightful highway-side restaurant near Cangas. As you eat grilled seafood, shellfish or meat you can soak in the view of a pristine little beach bordered by low cliffs.

Ribadeo

pop 9700

This lively port town, a sun-seeker magnet in summer, marks the Galician–Cantabrian border. Though Ribadeo itself is beachless (a small leisure port and larger fishing port dominate the waterfront), it's surrounded by incredible shoreline. Get the scoop at the **tourist office** (☎ 982 12 86 89; www.ribadeo.org; Praza de España 7; 🕑 10.30am-2pm & 4-7pm).

The old city is an attractive mix of maritime charm and eclectic 20th-century architecture. Ribadeo's tranquil, palm-studded central square, **Praza de España**, is highlighted by the modernist **Torre de los Moreno** with a glazed ceramic dome. For sea and sand, you'll have to head out of town, but you won't be disappointed with the spectacular beaches, especially **Praia As Catedrais** (Cathedral Beach), a 1.5km sandy stretch with whose rock arches are awesome Gothic-looking creations best seen at low tide. A 5km-long **boardwalk** backs the beach, connecting it to others nearby.

This area has plenty of camping grounds, beachy *hostales* and appealing hotels. One of the best is **A Cortiña** (☎ 982 13 01 87; www.cantalarrana.com; Pazo Lanzo s/n, Grañol; r €68; P), an adorable country house with loads of charm (think quilts, gingham curtains and antique furniture). It's a 15-minute walk from town and a short stroll from the FEVE train station. Overlooking the Ría de Ribadeo is the elegant state-run **Parador** (☎ 982 12 88 25; www.parador.es; Rúa de Amador Fernández 7; r €160; P), where rooms, some with galleries and views, are decorated in a classy if aged style. It's wheelchair accessible.

Just up from the leisure port, you can get fine seafood, grilled meats and pasta dishes in the cosy upstairs dining room at **Solana** (☎ 982 12 88 35; Rúa de Antonio Otero 41; mains €9-22). The smoky tavern downstairs serves drinks and tapas.

FEVE trains operate to/from Oviedo (€10, 3½ hours. two daily) and Ferrol (€9.10, three hours, four daily), stopping at all the main coastal towns along the way. Half a dozen daily buses head to/from Oviedo, Luarca and (except Sunday) Viveiro, and a few go to/from Lugo.

Mondoñedo

pop 4700 / elev 139m

Northern Galicia's inland charms have a hard time rivalling those along the coast, although there are exceptions, like **Mondoñedo**, a compact historical village surrounded by green hills.

The prettiest sight is the **Praza da Catedral**, a quaintly lopsided plaza rimmed with porticoed, galleried houses and flanked by the majestic **Catedral Basílica de la Asunción** (9am-1pm & 4-8pm), a stylistic mongrel ranging from 13th-century Romanesque to 18th-century baroque. A handful of bars and the **tourist office** (982 50 71 77; www.emondonedo.com in Spanish; Praza da Catedral 34; 10.30am-2pm & 4.30-7pm) are here too.

Get an airy, tranquil room at the **Hospedaxe Seminario** (982 52 10 00; Praza do Seminario; s/d €22/38), a *hostal* inside 18th-century Santa Catalina seminary, a huge building that also operates as a retired priests' residence and a functioning seminary. Rooms are surprisingly modern and some have cloister views.

Right by the Praza do Concello, **Mesón Os Arcos** (982 50 70 12; Rúa de Alfonso VII 6; menú €10, mains €7-14) specialises in tasty *carnes a la brasa* (barbecued meats).

A few daily buses operate to Lugo, Ribadeo, Viveiro and A Coruña.

COSTA DA MORTE

Long, remote beaches broken up by ragged, rocky points and peaks make up the eerily beautiful 'Coast of Death', the relatively isolated and unspoilt shore that runs from Caión down to Muros. This is a land of legends, like the one telling the story of villagers who put out lamps to lure passing ships to their doom on deadly rocks; though the locals are hardly to blame, this treacherous coast has certainly seen more than its share of shipwrecks. The idyllic landscape can undergo a rapid transformation when ocean mists blow in.

If you're looking for a quiet base from which to explore the region, consider staying in a rural hotel. Many are listed online at www.turismocostadamorte.com.

Although **Arriva** (902 27 74 82; www.arriva.es) runs buses from Santiago de Compostela and A Coruña to many places on the Costa da Morte, you really need your own wheels (or strong legs) to reach the area's most beautiful sights.

MALPICA DE BERGANTIÑOS & AROUND

Malpica itself is a ramshackle town whose port and centre are more functional than scenic. Still, there's a good beach and several excellent seafood restaurants. Get lunch at the unassuming but eternally popular **O'Burato** (981 72 00 57; Praza Villar Amigo; mains €10-15), overlooking the port. It knows its niche: fish and shellfish. Nothing else (not even a vegetable) appears on the menu.

Far more rewarding than the town itself is **Cabo de Santo Hadrian**, a windy bluff past Malpica. Follow the signs to the **Faro de Sisgarde**; the road leads to glorious views of the coast and the **Illas Sisargas**, known as a nesting spot for gulls.

PONTECESO TO LAXE

The sinuous highways weaving across the Costa da Morte aren't the easiest to navigate, but if you've got a good sense of direction, this is a marvellous area to explore. Heading southeast, stop for a memorable meal at **Mar de Ardora** (981 75 43 11; As Revoltas-Canduas; mains €13-20; Tue-Sun for lunch, Thu-Sat lunch & dinner), where innovative Galician cuisine is served in an impeccably restored farmhouse perched above the Atlantic on the AC-430 highway between Ponteceso and Canduas.

Steer towards the inland crossroads town of **Baio** to pass the turn-off points for interesting cultural sights, like the 6000-year-old **Dolmen de Dombate** (11am-2pm & 4-8pm), considered a 'cathedral' of the Galician megalithic and one of the best-preserved ancient constructions in all of Spain (it's currently being restored – and is expected to be for a while with no set finishing date – but can still be visited). Nearby, you can poke around the **Castro A Cidá**, a 5th-century settlement. Both are signposted off the AC-430 highway. If you have time, you can see both sites along with a handful of others on the four-hour, circular **Archaeological Route**. Get a walking map from the Bar Paredes, 500m from the Castro.

A sweeping beach is the focal point of the laid-back resort in **Laxe**, where the 15th-century Gothic church of **Santa María da Atalaia** stands guard over the harbour. The lively waterfront makes this a good base from which to explore the coast. Stay in the sleek, three-star

Playa de Laxe Hotel (☎ 981 73 90 00; www.playadelaxe.com; Avenida Cesáreo Pondal 27; s €70, d €80-90; P ❄ 💻), just off the beach. The 40 rooms have parquet floors and clean-lined décor, and are wheelchair accessible. It's worth paying a bit extra for 'superior' rooms, which have ocean views and more space. For fresh fish and seafood, head to the **Casa do Arco** (☎ 981 70 69 04; Rúa Real 1; mains €12-18; 🕑 closed Tue) overlooking the bay.

This area's true appeal, however, lies beyond its towns and is best explored on foot. From Laxe, you could take the PR-G70 loop trail (5.2km, two hours) around the Monte da Insua. The longer (but poorly maintained in parts) PR-G38 trail runs along the coast.

CAMELLE TO CAMARIÑAS

The sleepy fishing village of **Camelle** has no great charm; it's just a blip of construction along an amazingly beautiful coastal stretch. Its one claim to fame is the quirky though neglected **Museo do Alemán**, a sculpture garden made by 'Man', an eccentric long-time German resident. Locals say the sculptor was so devastated by the *Prestige* spill, which splotched his fanciful figures black, that he died shortly afterwards. The museum (now oil-free) has been left to fend for itself, although it has inspired a cultural centre and annual art exhibit. On the main road, get a tasty seafood meal at **Chalana** (☎ 981 71 05 12; Rúa Principal 2; menú €9).

Much more enticing is the rugged coast west of town. You can walk, bike or drive the **coastal road** (part of which is marked as the PR-G38 Costa da Morte trail) that parallels some of Galicia's most beautiful coastline and culminates in the **Cabo Vilán** lighthouse. From Arou, a little-visited fishing village, head west. This spectacular road winds its way above secluded beaches (like **Area de Trece**), windswept hillsides and weathered rock formations; it's guaranteed to keep your camera clicking. There are many places to stop along the way, such as the **Cementerio dos Ingleses** (English Cemetery), the burial ground from a 1890 British shipwreck.

Five kilometres past the lighthouse, you reach the fishing village of **Camariñas**, known for its traditional *encaixe* (lacework). Several shops specialise in lace and there's a **Museo do Encaixe** (Lace Museum; ☎ 981 73 63 40; Praza Insuela; admission €1.20; 🕑 11am-2pm & 4-7pm Tue-Sat, 11am-2pm & 4-6pm Sun) by the town hall.

The best spot to lay your head is the **Puerto Arnela** (☎ 981 70 54 77; www.puertoarnela.com; Plaza del Carmen 20; r incl breakfast €35-40), right on the waterfront. A stone manor house with delightfully rustic rooms, this family-run spot also has a simple restaurant (mains €5 to €12) serving basics like grilled chicken and seafood. The hotel is wheelchair friendly.

Vázquez (☎ 981 14 84 70) runs up to four daily buses to/from A Coruña, while **Aucasa** (☎ 981 58 88 11) sends one bus to Santiago via Baio, and **Monbus** (☎ 902 29 29 00) heads once or twice a day to Muxía and Cee.

MUXÍA & AROUND

From Camariñas, it's a short drive to the quaint village of **Muxía**. On the way, you'll pass through the pretty hamlet of **Cereixo**. From here, you could detour down to **Leis**, an idyllic country hamlet studded with *hórreos* (traditional stone grain stores) and farmhouses. These country lanes twist and turn almost all the way to Muxía. Along this enchanting route you'll pass turn-offs towards inviting beaches like **Praia do Lago** and **Praia de Barreiros**.

Muxía itself is a photogenic little fishing port with a handful of cosy bars. Continue along the waterfront, following the signs to Santuario da Barca, to reach one of Galicia's most beloved pilgrimage points: **Punta da Barca**, where the baroque **Santuario da Virxe da Barca** marks the spot where legend attests that the Virgin Mary arrived in a stone boat and appeared to St James. The boat's hull and sail are supposedly here among the rocks strewn about the coast, and some believe they have healing powers.

West of Muxía, the magical **Praia de Lourido** is a long, unspoilt stretch of sand perfect for a romantic stroll.

Just outside town, you can get both a fabulous seafood meal and a good bed at **Tira da Barca** (☎ 981 74 23 23; www.tiradabarca.com; Cereixo–Muxía highway; r €65; P), a seven-room hotel whose high-end restaurant (mains €17 to €25, menú €26) draws local executive types for top-quality shellfish.

For even more charm, try the inviting **Casa de Trillo** (☎ 981 72 77 78; www.casadetrillo.com; r €60-75; P 💻), in nearby Santa Mariña. This 16th-century manor house has lovely gardens and cosy, well-appointed rooms; it's wheelchair accessible.

FISTERRA & AROUND

Spain's Land's End, **Cabo Fisterra** (Castilian: Cabo Finisterre), is the western edge of Spain,

GALICIA

at least in popular imagination. The real westernmost point is Cabo de la Nave, 5km north, but that doesn't keep throngs of day-trippers from making the trek out to this beautiful, windswept cape, which is also kilometre 0 of the 86km Fisterra variant of the Camino de Santiago.

Most people drive out (it's 3.5km past the town of Fisterra), but a challenging **walking trail** provides a more tranquil route, especially on summer weekends when the highway is clogged with buses. On the way out is the 12th-century **Igrexa de Santa María das Areas**, a mix of Romanesque, Gothic and baroque. The best views of the coast are to be had by climbing up the track, beginning 600m past the church, to **Monte Facho** and **Monte de San Guillerme**. The area is laced with myth and superstition, and they say childless couples used to come up here to improve their chances of conception.

The town of **Fisterra** itself is a small maritime centre whose waterfront is studded with seafood eateries. With a prime spot overlooking the waterfront, the classic **Casa Velay** (☎ 981 74 01 27; Paseo del Puerto; mains €10-15) is known for various fish dishes served *en cazuela* – swimming in a tasty tomato sauce. There are terrace tables in fine weather. Stylish **O Centolo** (☎ 981 74 04 52; Paseo del Puerto s/n; mains €14-25), with its breezy street-side terrace by the port, is popular with families. It offers a huge range of dishes, from the ubiquitous Galician seafood specialities to rices and grilled meats.

Fisterra town has a dozen places to stay. The best is **Hotel Rústico Ínsula Finisterrae** (☎ 981 71 22 11; www.insulafinisterrae.com in Spanish; Lugar da Ínsua 76; r incl breakfast €84-99; P 💻 ♿), a century-old converted farmhouse at the top of the village. The spacious, sunny rooms have brass beds, fresh white linen, stone walls and a charming country air. The rooms with galleries have fantastic views over town and the Atlantic, and there's wheelchair access.

Enticing area beaches include the **Praia de Estorde**, near the village of Cee.

MUROS & CARNOTA

Continue south towards **Carnota**, renowned as home to Galicia's longest *hórreo*. Exactly 34.5m long, it was built late in the 18th century. There are several good beaches nearby, like the all-natural **Praia de Porto Ancho**.

The Costa da Morte ends in the municipality of **Muros**, long an important port for Santiago de Compostela. These days, the town is best known as a quiet spot for a seaside meal after a morning spent sunbathing on one of the area beaches. At **Pachanga** (☎ 981 82 60 48; Avenida Castelao 29), on the waterfront, crowds wash down plates of octopus with glasses of light Albariño wine.

RÍAS BAIXAS

Wide beaches and relatively calm, warm waters have made the Rías Baixas (Castilian: Rías Bajas) Galicia's best-known tourist area. It boasts way more hotels, rental apartments and restaurants than other stretches of the Galician coast, so it's no surprise that so many visitors end up here. The downside to such convenience is that the area's natural beauty is all too often hidden by the tourist sprawl. Still, the mix of pretty villages, sandy beaches and good eating keep most people happy. Throw in the Illas Cíes, lovely old Pontevedra and bustling Vigo, and you have a tempting travel cocktail.

The following sections start at the inland end of each *ría* and work outwards, but if you have a vehicle and plenty of time you could simply follow the coast around from one *ría* to the next: the coastal road runs some 360km from Cée on the Costa da Morte to Tui on the Portuguese border – a straight-line distance of just 110km!

Get lots of information about the area, including links to rural hotels, online at www.riasbaixas.depo.es.

TOP FIVE VILLAGES

There's steep competition here for the title of prettiest village, but if you're yearning for old-world charm, there's no beating the following:

- **Muxía** (opposite), a lovely and laid-back fishing port.
- **Cambados** (p585), where you'll get a taste of Galician wine country.
- **Combarro** (p588), great seafood in a picture-perfect setting.
- **Ribadavia** (p600), home to Galicia's best-preserved medieval Jewish quarter.
- **Castro Caldelas** (p599), story-book charm nestled in the hills.

RÍA DE MUROS Y NOIA

Noia

pop 14,800

On the banks of the Noia River, this beach-less town was Santiago de Compostela's de facto port for centuries. Now, the crooked streets of its historic centre make a pleasing place for a stroll.

Two must-see monuments are the Gothic **Igrexa de San Martiño** (closed for renovation at time of writing), which dominates the old town's Praza do Tapal, and the **Igrexa de Santa María A Nova** (Carreiriña do Escultor Ferreiro; 10.30am-1.30pm & 4-6pm Mon-Fri, 10.30am-1.30pm Sat, 11am-1.30pm Sun), which rests peacefully in the town centre along with its romantic cemetery.

Noia has a lively tapas scene, and several popular bars cluster around the 14th-century Pazo de Costa, down the street from the Igrexa de San Martiño. The best is **Tasca Típica** (☎ 981 82 18 42; Rúa Cantón 15). A dark, stone-walled tavern, it's great for a drink, snacks or even a sit-down meal; there are a handful of tables in the candle-lit dining room.

South Shore

The coast here isn't completely unspoilt, but it's pleasantly low-key, with several small beaches (like the **Praia de Aguieira**, 2km past Portosín) and villages worth the stop. In **Porto do Son**, whose busy port, small beach and diminutive old town jumble together by the *ría*, you'll find several good tapas bars and informal restaurants. **Hotel Villa del Son** (☎ 981 85 30 49; www.hotelvilladelson.com; Rúa de Trincherpe 11, Porto do Son; s/d €35/55) has tidy rooms with cool tile floors, bright bathrooms and a cheery blue-and-yellow decor. For fair-priced grilled fish and meat dishes, pizzas and fresh shellfish, try popular **Hórreo** (☎ 981 76 72 15; Rúa de Felipe II; mains €6-12).

Two kilometres southwest of Porto do Son, you'll reach the turn-off for the spectacular **Castro de Baroña** prehistoric settlement. Park by the cafeteria and take the rocky path down to the seaside ruins. Celts or not (the debate rages on), Galicia's ancients sure knew how to choose real estate. The settlement is poised majestically on a wind-blasted headland overlooking the crashing waves of the Atlantic. The **Centro de Interpretación do Castro de Baroña** (Calle de Fernando Fariña; admission €0.60; 11am-2pm & 7-9pm Jul-Sep), in Porto do Son, provides background.

Stretching south from the *castro*, **Praia Area Longa** is the first of a small string of surfing beaches down this side of the *ría*.

Drivers could detour to the **Dolmen de Axeitos**, a well-preserved megalithic monument, signposted between Xuño and Ribeira; and on to **Corrubedo** at the tip of the peninsula, with beaches either side of town, a lighthouse at the end of the road and a few relaxed bars around its small harbour.

RÍA DE AROUSA

Padrón

pop 9000

As the story goes, this is where Santiago's corpse sailed in to Galicia on a stone boat. These days, it's best known for its tiny green peppers, *pimientos de padrón*, which were imported from Mexico by 16th-century Franciscan friars and are now grown all around town. When fried up and sprinkled with coarse salt, they're one of Spain's favourite tapas. Just beware of the odd spicy one.

Padrón itself won't keep you long, but there are a couple of tempting restaurants. **Chef Rivera** (☎ 981 81 04 13; Elace Parque 7; mains €14-21) is one of Galicia's most elite eateries. Signposted from the main highway, it's famous for wonderfully presented renditions of local specialities. The decor is as classic as they come except for the interesting collection of Galician artwork adorning the walls.

At Km3 of the AC-301 highway linking Padrón and Noia, the rustic, century-old **Casa Ramallo** (☎ 981 80 41 80; Carretera Padrón-Noia; mains €8-20) tempts you inside. The menu makes the rounds of predictable Galician specialities, such as *lacón con grelos* (ham with greens), *cocido gallego* (hearty meat, potato and chickpea stew) and *cazuela de pescado* (fish stew).

Five kilometres out of town is the 19th-century country house **A Casa da Meixida** (☎ 609 12 34 41; www.casadameixida.com; Muiños-Esclavitud; s €48, d €59-75), whose five inviting rooms are decorated with simple beige furnishings and a warm rustic style.

Buses run up to eight times daily to/from Santiago de Compostela and Pontevedra, and a few travel daily to/from Noia, Cambados and O Grove.

Illa de Arousa

Southwest of **Catoira**, a town known for its medieval castle, the Illa de Arousa is an island connected to the mainland by a 2km-long bridge. You can skip the town and head straight to the lovely **Parque Natural Carreirón**, where walking trails meander among dunes, beaches and marshlands known for their bird life. There are a couple of good camping grounds nearby.

Monbus (☎ 902 29 29 00) has a few daily buses linking the island with Vilanova de Arousa and Vilagarcía de Arousa, both of which have connections for Santiago de Compostela, Cambados and O Grove. **Autocares Núñez Barros** (☎ 986 54 31 00) operates to/from Pontevedra.

Cambados & Around

pop 13,600

The capital of the **Albariño wine country**, a region famed for its fruity whites, **Cambados** is a pretty seaside village founded by the Visigoths. You can visit a handful of wineries in and around town, and a popular **wine festival** takes place at the end of July.

Though better-known wineries lie beyond the city centre, the most accessible are both on the sprawling Praza de Fefiñáns at the northern end of town. **Bodegas del Palacio de Fefinañes** (☎ 986 54 22 04; www.fefinanes.com; 10am-2pm & 4-8pm Mon-Sat mid-Mar-Dec) and **Gil Armada** (☎ 986 52 48 77; 10.30am-2pm & 5.30-8pm Mon-Sat, 11am-2pm Sun) offer tours (call ahead) and small gift shops.

A short drive away, you could visit Galicia's best-known winery, **Martín Códax** (☎ 986 52 60 40; www.martincodax.com; Rúa Burgáns 91, Vilariño; 11am-7pm Mon-Fri, 11am-1pm Sat Jun-Sep, closed Sat Oct-May). For more details on wine routes through the Rías Baixas, see www.rutadelvinoriasbaixas.com.

Cambados has five **museums** (joint admission €3; 11am-2.30pm & 4.30-7.30pm Tue-Sun), mainly devoted to wine and fishing but there's also one preserving an old tide-operated cereal mill. Yet the best Cambados has to offer may be the pedestrian-friendly streets like Rúa Príncipe and Rúa Real, which are lined with touristy seafood eateries.

If you want to be based in the area, consider a rural hotel like **Pazo A Capitana** (☎ 986 52 05 13; www.pazoacapitana.com in Spanish; Rúa Sabugueiro 46; s/d incl breakfast €70/90; P). This 15th-century country house at the edge of town has stately rooms and an on-site winery. The elegant **Parador de Cambados** (☎ 986 54 22 50; www.parador.es; Paseo Calzada; s/d incl breakfast €142/190; P V), in a 17th-century mansion in the heart of Cambados, is also a great option, with modern rooms and an excellent restaurant. Both are wheelchair accessible.

The town of Cambados is linked by bus to Santiago de Compostela, Pontevedra and O Grove (some via Sanxenxo).

O Grove

pop 11,000

The more than two dozen sandy beaches, including the spectacular **Praia a Lanzada** (p589) around O Grove, have made this seaside village and the mostly unspoilt peninsula surrounding it a buzzing summer destination.

Before coming into the resort proper, you could cross the bridge leading to the **Illa A Toxa**, a manicured island known for its spas, golf course and swanky hotels. Take a stroll in the gardens surrounding the **Capilla de las Conchas**, a church completely plastered with *vieira* (clam) shells.

The **tourist office** (☎ 986 73 14 15; www.turismogrove.com; Praza do Corgo 1; 10am-7pm Tue-Sat, 10am-2pm Mon-Sun) is near the fishing harbour in the heart of O Grove. Lively fish auctions are staged in the nearby **Lonxa** (Fish Market) when the day's catch comes in, around 5pm.

In fine weather from April to November, numerous companies depart from the harbour on *ría* cruises, chiefly to look at the **bateas** – platforms where mussels, oysters and scallops are cultivated. Tours, including mussel tastings, cost €13/6 per adult/child and last 75 minutes. Sailing, scuba, surf and kayak enthusiasts can head to the **Pedras Negras leisure port** (☎ 98673 84 30), across the O Grove peninsula in San Vicente do Mar, for rentals and classes. Stay to stroll along the scenic **boardwalk** that curves around the tip of the peninsula.

To learn more about the area's marine life, visit **Acquariumgalicia** (☎ 986 73 15 15; admission €9; 10am-2pm & 4-7pm Mon-Fri, 10am-2pm & 4-8pm Sat) at Punta Moreiras on the northwest side of the O Grove peninsula, where some 95 species of mostly Galician marine life are showcased. The visit lasts about an hour.

From Punta Moreiras, several **walking trails** descend to the shore. For more wonderful views, hit the trails that begin near the **Mirador A Siradella**, sitting 159m above O Grove and signposted from town. This is also a popular birdwatching site.

A dozen camping grounds sprawl along the west side of the O Grove peninsula. In town, accommodation is mostly spread along Rúa Castelao, running between the centre and the bridge to Illa A Toxa. Even better are the many rural lodgings in the area.

O Grove is famous for its shellfish, and you can sample delicacies like *berberechos* (cockles) and *centollo* (spider crab) in restaurants. In mid-October the town hosts the

Festa do Marisco shellfish festival. Of the slew of large seafood houses facing the water, one good option is **Restaurante Xantar da Ría** (☎ 986 73 11 69; Rúa Beiramar; 34; mains €7-16). In a homey dining room near the bus station it serves up very reasonably priced grilled or Galician-style seafood along with chicken, beef and rice dishes.

Monbus-Castromil (☎ 902 29 29 00; www.monbus.es) runs up to 19 buses daily to Pontevedra (€3.70, one hour) and up to six to Santiago de Compostela (€7, two hours 20 min). The bus station (☎ 986 68 04 11) is on Rúa Beiramar, by the port.

PONTEVEDRA

pop 80,200

Galicia's smallest provincial capital may have a story-book old quarter, but it's no sleepy museum city. The interlocking lanes and plazas of the compact city centre are abuzz with shops and markets, cafes and tapas bars. An inviting riverside city, Pontevedra effortlessly combines history, culture and cosmopolitan style into an ideal base for exploring the Rías Baixas.

History

In the 16th century Pontevedra was the biggest city in Galicia and an important port. Columbus' flagship, the *Santa María,* was built here. In the 17th century the city began to decline in the face of growing competition in the *ría* and the silting up of its port. Nevertheless, Pontevedra was made provincial capital in 1835 and today tourism is a healthy boon.

Information

Ciber Dobleclick (Rúa da Virgen del Camino 21; per hr €1.95; 🕒 10am-midnight Mon-Sat, 4pm-midnight Sun)

Municipal tourist information kiosks (Praza de España & Praza de Ourense; 🕒 10am-2pm & 4-8.30pm daily mid-Jun–mid-Sep only)

Post office (Rúa Oliva)

Turismo Rías Baixas (☎ 986 84 26 90; www.riasbaixas.org; Praza de Santa María; 🕒 9am-8pm Mon-Fri, 10am-2pm Sat & Sun mid-Jun–mid-Sep, 9am-9pm Mon-Fri, 10am-2.30pm & 4.30-8pm Sat & Sun mid-Sep–mid-Jun) Heaps of information on all Pontevedra province.

Sights

Pontevedra's pedestrianised historic centre was once enclosed behind medieval walls, though scarce remnants stand today. More than a dozen plazas dot the old quarter – the liveliest are the Prazas da Verdura, da Pedreira, da Leña and da Ferraría.

Starting at the southeastern edge of the old town, you can't miss the distinctive curved facade of the **Santuario da Virxe Peregrina**, an 18th-century caprice with a distinctly Portuguese flavour. The broad, part-colonnaded **Praza da Ferrería**, nearby, displays an eclectic collection of buildings dating as far back as the 15th century. Set back from Praza da Ferrería in its own gardens is the 14th-century **Igrexa de San Francisco** (🕒 7.30am-12.45pm & 5.30-9pm), said to have been founded personally by St Francis of Assisi when on pilgrimage to Santiago de Compostela. What was the adjacent convent is now the local tax office.

Head down Rúa da Pasantería and you emerge in **Praza da Leña**, one of Pontevedra's most enchanting niches, partly colonnaded and with a *cruceiro* (wayside crucifix) in the middle. Just off it is the main entrance to the **Museo de Pontevedra** (☎ 986 85 14 55; Rúa da Pasantería 2-12; admission free; 🕒 10am-2pm & 4.30-8.30pm (until 7pm Oct-May) Tue-Sat, 11am-2pm Sun), an eclectic collection scattered through five centre-city buildings. From Bronze Age archaeological finds to Galician crafts and Renaissance painting, this museum has it all.

Up Rúa de Isabel II stands the **Basílica de Santa María la Maior** (🕒 10am-1pm & 6-8.30pm Mon-Sat, 10am-2pm & 7-9pm Sun). Although temporarily draped in scaffolding, it's a mainly Gothic church with a whiff of plateresque and Portuguese Manueline influences.

Festivals & Events

The **Festas da Peregrina**, held here for a week in the middle of August, feature a big funfair on the Alameda and concerts in Praza da Ferrería. In late July, the **Festival Internacional de Jazz e Blues de Pontevedra** (www.jazzpontevedra.com) attracts top-notch musicians from around the world.

Sleeping

Hospedaje Casa Maruja (☎ 986 85 49 01; Avenida de Santa María 12; s €15-25, d €30-38) Though the beds are lumpy and the linen might be older that you are, this clean and friendly budget option has sublime views onto a shady plaza.

Hotel Rúas (☎ 986 84 64 16; hotelruas@terra.es; Rúa de Padre Sarmiento 37; s/d €40/65; 🅿 ✖ 💻) Surprisingly classy one-star rooms, most with idyllic plaza views, have shiny wooden floors, unfussy fur-

GALICIA

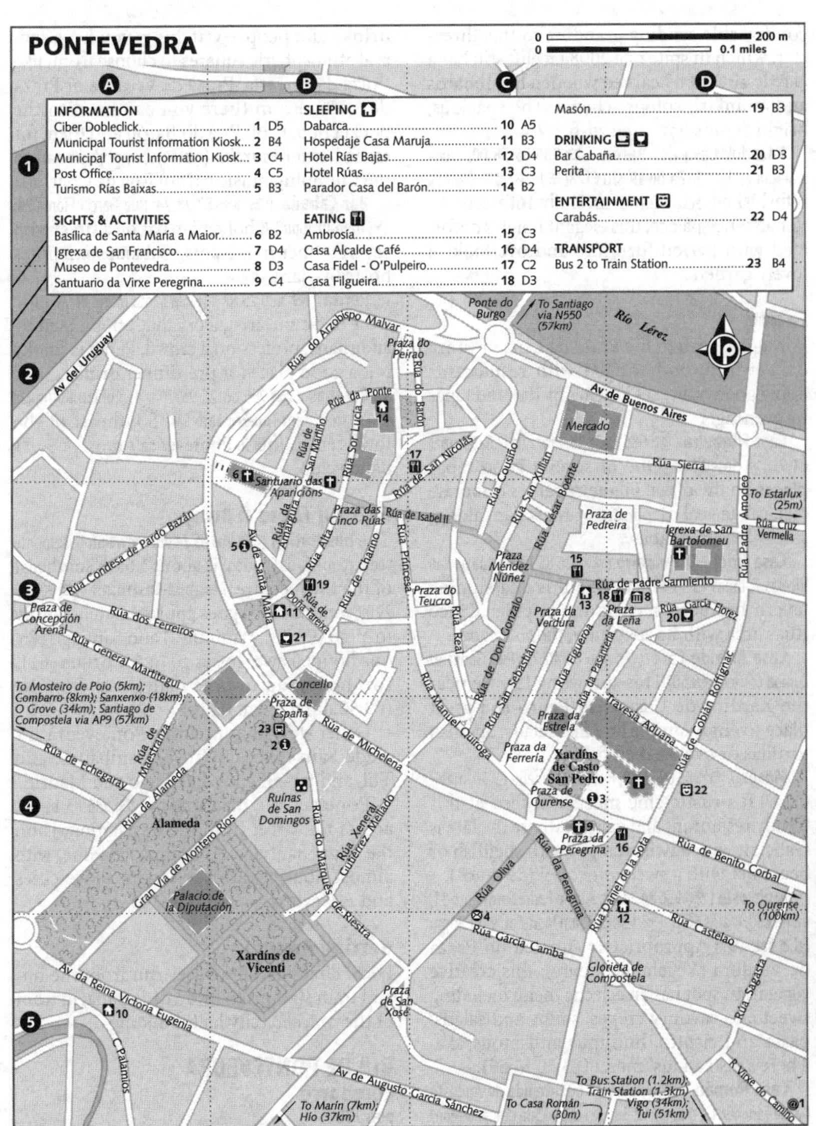

nishings, large bathrooms and wi-fi. The hotel is wheelchair accessible and its restaurant does a very good set lunch for €12.

our pick Dabarca (☎ 986 86 97 23; www.hoteldabarca.com; Calle Palamios 2; s/d/tr €90/95/120;) Run like a hotel but offering apartments instead of standard rooms, this sleek spot is ideal for families (there's a small surcharge per child). Apartments are fitted with a small kitchenette, washing machine, free wi-fi and beige Ikea-inspired furniture. There's a stylish cafeteria for the nights you don't want to cook.

Hotel Rías Bajas (☎ 986 85 51 00; hotelriasbajas.com; Rúa Daniel de la Sota 7; s/d €70/100; P) You'd feel comfortable sending grandma to this three-star, which in spite of a 2008 facelift still has a classic air lent by carved wooden headboards and a pinkish colour scheme. The spacious, bright rooms have free wi-fi.

Parador Casa del Barón (☎ 986 85 58 00; www.parador.es; Rúa do Barón 19; s/d €128/160; P ✕ 💻) A refurbished, wheelchair-friendly 16th-century Renaissance palace, this elegant hotel is decorated with period furniture and overlooks a lovely garden.

Eating

For tapas, head to the Praza da Leña or Praza da Verdura, both ringed with restaurants doing good-value set lunches by day and tapas by evening.

Casa Filgueira (☎ 986 85 88 15; Praza da Leña 2; tapas €3-9; 🕒 closed Sun) One of several good tapas places on the plaza, Filgueira serves elaborate dishes like veal carpaccio or roast ham alongside salads and tapas.

Casa Fidel – O' Pulpeiro (☎ 986 85 12 34; Rúa de San Nicolás 7; tapas €3-9) Since 1956 this unassuming tavern has been serving the popular Cinco Rúas area with its speciality, *pulpo a feiro*.

Casa Alcalde Café (☎ 986 86 46 72; Rúa González Zúñiga 6; menú €8.50) This sprawling terrace near the Xardíns de Casto San Pedro is a great place to enjoy simple fare like salads, Spanish tortillas or oven-baked fish.

Masón (☎ 986 89 66 10; Rúa Alta 4; menú €9.50, mains €10-17) It's rustic-chic meets art deco at this trendy restaurant and gallery, where the fare is Galician with a twist (crepes with shellfish or beef fillet with a sweet *mencía* wine sauce).

Ambrosía (☎ 986 84 24 80; Rúa de Padre Sarmiento 31; menú €10, mains €6-8; 🕒 1.30-3.45pm Mon-Sat, 9-11.30pm Fri & Sat; V) Appropriately situated on Praza da Verdura (Vegetable Square), this creative vegetarian spot has an eclectic menu including sweet and savoury crepes, soups and salads, pasta and risotto, hummus and moussaka. There's also a kids' menu (€3.50 to €5).

Casa Román (☎ 986 84 35 60; Avenida de Augusto García Sánchez 12; mains €12-36; 🕒 closed Sun dinner & Mon) Widely considered Pontevedra's best table, the discretely elegant Román is a culinary tour through the best of Galician cuisine. Many seafood and meat dishes are priced by the kilo.

Drinking & Entertainment

The crossroads plaza **As Cinco Rúas** is a hub of Pontevedra nightlife. For coffee, laid-back drinks and people-watching, you have several atmospheric squares to choose from, like Praza da Ferrería, Praza da Verdura or Praza da Leña. From there you can head to the pocket of bars on Rúa do Barón and then, for some heftier *marcha* (action), up the road to the thumping music bars of Rúa de Charino.

Bar Cabaña (☎ 986 85 28 24; Rúa García Flórez 22; 🕒 from 10.30pm) A bohemian bar on a street with several other nightspots, Cabaña sometimes hosts live jazz.

Perita (☎ 660 25 87 11; Rúa Santa Maria 4) A chic wine bar-cum-art-gallery that's populated by an urbane, professional crowd, Perita is smoky but a good place for pre-dinner drinks.

Carabás (☎ 986 86 26 95; Rúa de Cobián Roffignac 4; 🕒 from 1am Thu-Fri, 3am Sat) Southeast of the town centre, this is Pontevedra's most popular dance club.

Getting There & Away

The **bus station** (☎ 986 85 24 08; www.autobusespontevedra.com; Rúa da Estación) is about 1.5km southeast of the town centre. **Monbus-Castromil** (☎ 902 29 29 00; www.monbus.es) goes approximately hourly to Vigo (€2.85; 30 minutes) and Santiago (€5, one hour). Fewer buses go to A Coruña (€11, two hours, up to nine daily) and Ourense (€9.50, up to eight daily).

Other destinations from Pontevedra include Sanxenxo, O Grove, Cambados, and Tui, and far-off cities like Lugo and Madrid.

Pontevedra's **train station** (☎ 986 85 13 13), across the street from the bus station, is on the Vigo–Santiago de Compostela line, with almost hourly train services to those cities and A Coruña.

Getting Around

Local circular-route buses run from the bus and train stations to Praza de España, in front of the *concello* (city hall) building.

RÍA DE PONTEVEDRA

Combarro

pop 1200

Near Pontevedra, the postcard-perfect village of Combarro unfurls around a tidy bay. With a jumble of seaside *hórreos*, a historic quarter that looks like it was plucked straight out of the Middle Ages, and crooked lanes (some of them hewn directly out of the rock bed) dotted with *cruceiros* and wonderful little restaurants, this is many people's favourite stop in the Rias Baixas.

The main activity here is eating, and you have several excellent choices. Savour excellent fish, rice and meat dishes at spots like **O Peirao** (☎ 986 77 07 32; Peirao da Chouza 43; mains €15-25), among the waterfront *hórreos*.

Just beyond Combarro, veer down towards the **Praia de Covelo** to reach a locally revered but humble-looking **El Caracol** (☎ 986 74 15 59; Rúa do Peirao Samiera; mains €18-28), a tavern with a porch-like terrace overlooking the water. The house speciality is baked fish, but it's also known for rice dishes, such as *codillo* and *jarreta a la antigua*.

Campsites and *hostales* are dotted along the road west towards Sanxenxo. Monbus buses between Pontevedra and Sanxenxo stop at Combarro.

Sanxenxo

pop 17,000

Whoever nicknamed Sanxenxo (Castilian: Sangenjo) the 'Marbella of Galicia' has probably never seen the real thing. With a busy leisure port, several inviting beaches, and a long buzzing waterfront, the town indeed takes a page from the book of Mediterranean-style resorts. But the metaphor doesn't extend much further.

Sanxenxo boasts a fine, sandy beach – the busy **Praia de Silgar**. West, towards Portonovo, the dune-backed **Praia de Baltar** is a bit quieter. There's a **tourist office** (☎ 986 72 02 85; www.sanxenxo.org; Porto Juan Carlos I; 9am-2pm & 4-7pm Tue-Sun Oct-May, 10am-9pm daily Jun-Sep), plus a large car park in the shiny new marina development immediately east of the beach.

For a seafront location, the stylish and comfortable **Hotel Rotilio** (☎ 986 72 02 00; www.hotelrotilio.com; Avenida do Porto 7; s €65, d €110-165; P) overlooks both Praia de Silgar and the marina. All 40 rooms are exterior and the majority have balconies. Its restaurant, **La Taberna de Rotilio** (mains €15-25; closed Sun & Mon) serves up terrific Galician seafood and meat with a creative touch. **Portonovo**, 2km west, has many tapas bars and seafood eateries.

Buses between Pontevedra and O Grove (over 20 a day in summer) stop in Sanxenxo.

Praia A Lanzada & Around

The highway linking Sanxenxo and O Grove parallels the wave-battered shore at the tip of the *ría*, although sand-and-sea views are limited because of the non-stop parade of hotels, *hostales* and general tourist sprawl. Occasional stretches of development-free coastline hint at how beautiful this area can be, revealing patchwork fields rimmed in low stone walls, green hillsides slipping into the ocean and the rumbling Atlantic pounding the sand. The hamlet of **Montalvo** is one such unspoilt place.

A better-known reprieve to the overdevelopment is the dune-backed **Praia A Lanzada**, the longest beach in the Ría de Pontevedra. Stretching 2.3km along the west side of the isthmus leading to the O Grove promontory, the beach is enticingly natural, but it's not exactly deserted, as the mammoth car park attests. O Grove-bound buses will drop you here.

Illa de Ons

In summer, you can hop a boat out to vehicle-free Ons island, with its sandy beaches, cliffs, ruins, walking trails and rich bird life. Campers who are wanting to pitch at the **camping ground** (☎ 986 68 76 96; Jul-Sep) must obtain a *tarjeta de acampada* (camping card) with their boat ticket.

Weather permitting, **Cruceros Rías Baixas** (☎ 986 73 13 43; www.crucerosriasbaixas.com in Spanish; adult/child €14/7; 10.15am-1pm & 4.14-7.45pm Jul-Sep) sails to/from Illa de Ons several times daily from Sanxenxo and Portonovo.

South Shore

BEACHES

Zip past the sprawl surrounding Marín to discover the quiet appeal of the *ría*'s southern shore, where you can stop at beaches like the wide **Praia de Lapamán** or in maritime towns like **Bueu**, with its pretty beach and busy waterfront. Venture past the fishing hamlet of Beluso towards the **Cabo de Udra**, where the jagged shoreline is adorned with a backdrop of the Illa de Ons and there are several secluded (though not secret) beaches like the clear-watered **Praia Mourisca**.

HÍO & AROUND

At the far tip of the *ría*, the peaceful village of Hío draws visitors who want a glimpse of Galicia's most-famous **cruceiro**, a small but elaborate cross that stands outside the **San Andrés de Hío** church. Sculpted during the 19th century from a single block of stone, it narrates key passages of Christian teaching, from Adam and Eve to the taking down of Christ from the cross.

Numerous sandy beaches are signposted in the area. About 2.5km north of Hío by paved road is a tranquil sandy beach, **Praia Areabrava**.

Continue west through the hamlet of Donón and towards the windswept **Cabo de Home**, a rocky cape with an archaeological site, views of the Illas Cíes and several walking trails, including a portion of the GR-59 long-distance ramblers' trail.

Near the beach and the famous *cruceiro*, **Hotel Doade** (☎ 986 32 83 02; www.hoteldoade.com; Bajada Praia de Arneles 1, Hío; r incl breakfast €55-70; P) has spacious, spic-and-span rooms with peach-coloured walls and fresh, white linen. The restaurant specialises in *ria*-fresh seafood.

RÍA DE VIGO

The AP-9 motorway's Puente de Rande suspension bridge brings the *ría*'s northern shore into easy reach of the city, and taking a drive along the seaside PO-551 highway is a pleasant day out. Humble seaside towns like **Moaña** and **Cangas** are convenient places to stop for provisions, but the real draw here is the area's natural beauty.

From Moaña you could head a few kilometres inland to the **Mirador de Cotorredondo**, a lookout commanding magical views over the Rías de Vigo and Pontevedra. Continue west to ramble around the **Cabo de Home** or visit the famous **Cruceiro de Hío** (see p589).

VIGO

pop 294,800

Depending on where you aim your viewfinder, Vigo is a gritty port city, a cosmopolitan art centre, or a noble and historic capital. Galicia's most-populous metropolis and the home of Europe's largest fishing fleet, this is an axis of trade and commerce in northern Spain. Yet it is also walkable and compact, and it boasts some of the best shellfish and seafood in all the world.

People started to notice Vigo in the Middle Ages when it began to overtake Baiona as a major port. Although the first industries started up here in the 18th century, Vigo's major development was in the 20th century, during which its population grew fifteen-fold.

Orientation

The train station is 800m southeast of the old centre. The bus station is on Avenida de Madrid, about 1.4km beyond. From near the train station, Rúa do Urzáiz and its pedestrianised continuation, Rúa do Príncipe (an outdoor mall of sorts), lead down to Praza da Porta do Sol, the gateway to the old centre and port area. The heart of the modern town is immediately east of the old centre, between Rúa do Príncipe and the waterfront.

Information

CiberStation (☎ 986 22 36 35; Praza da Princesa 3; per hr €1.80; 9am-midnight Mon-Fri, 11am-12.30am Sat & Sun)
Hospital Xeral-Cíes (☎ 986 81 60 00; Rúa do Pizarro 22)
Municipal tourist office (☎ 986 22 47 57; www.turismodevigo.org; Rúa de Teófilo Llorente 5; 10am-2pm & 3.30-7.30pm Mon-Sat)
Policía Local (☎ 986 43 22 11 or 092; Praza do Rei)
Post office (Rúa de García Barbón 53)
Regional tourist office (☎ 986 43 05 77; oficina.turismo.vigo@xunta.es; Rúa Cánovas del Castillo 22; 9.30am-2.30pm & 4.30-6.30pm Mon-Fri, 10am-1.30pm Sat, also 4.30-6.30pm Sat, 10am-1.30pm Sun Jul-Aug)

Sights & Activities

Vigo's greatest charms are its simplest: navigating the steep streets of the **Casco Vello** (Old Town); watching the boats come and go in the **harbour**; poking around the **Lonja de Pescado** (Fish Market) in the early morning; slurping oysters on lively **Rúa Pescadería**; and window shopping along the busy **Rúa do Príncipe**.

The heart of the old town is the elegant **Praza da Constitución**, a perfect spot for a coffee. Head north down **Rúa dos Cesteiros**, famous for its wicker shops, and you'll come upon the **Igrexa de Santa María**, built in 1816 – long after its Romanesque predecessor had been burnt down by Sir Francis Drake. Nearby **Praza da Almeida** is home to a few art galleries.

Vigo has a well-earned reputation as Galicia's art centre, and there are several top-line museums and galleries to prove it. Pick up the month's *Guía del Ocio* (in Spanish) at the tourist office for full exhibit listings. If you have time for just one artistic stop, make it at the **Museo de Arte Contemporánea de Vigo** (Marco; ☎ 986 11 39 00; www.marcovigo.com; Rúa de Príncipe 54; admission free; 11am-9pm Tue-Sat, 11am-3pm Sun), a prime venue for exhibitions ranging from painting and sculpture to cinema, fashion and design. It's wheelchair accessible.

Directly south (and uphill) of the old town you can wander in the verdant **Parque do Castro**, where you can inspect a **castro** dating to the 3rd century BC and poke around the medieval

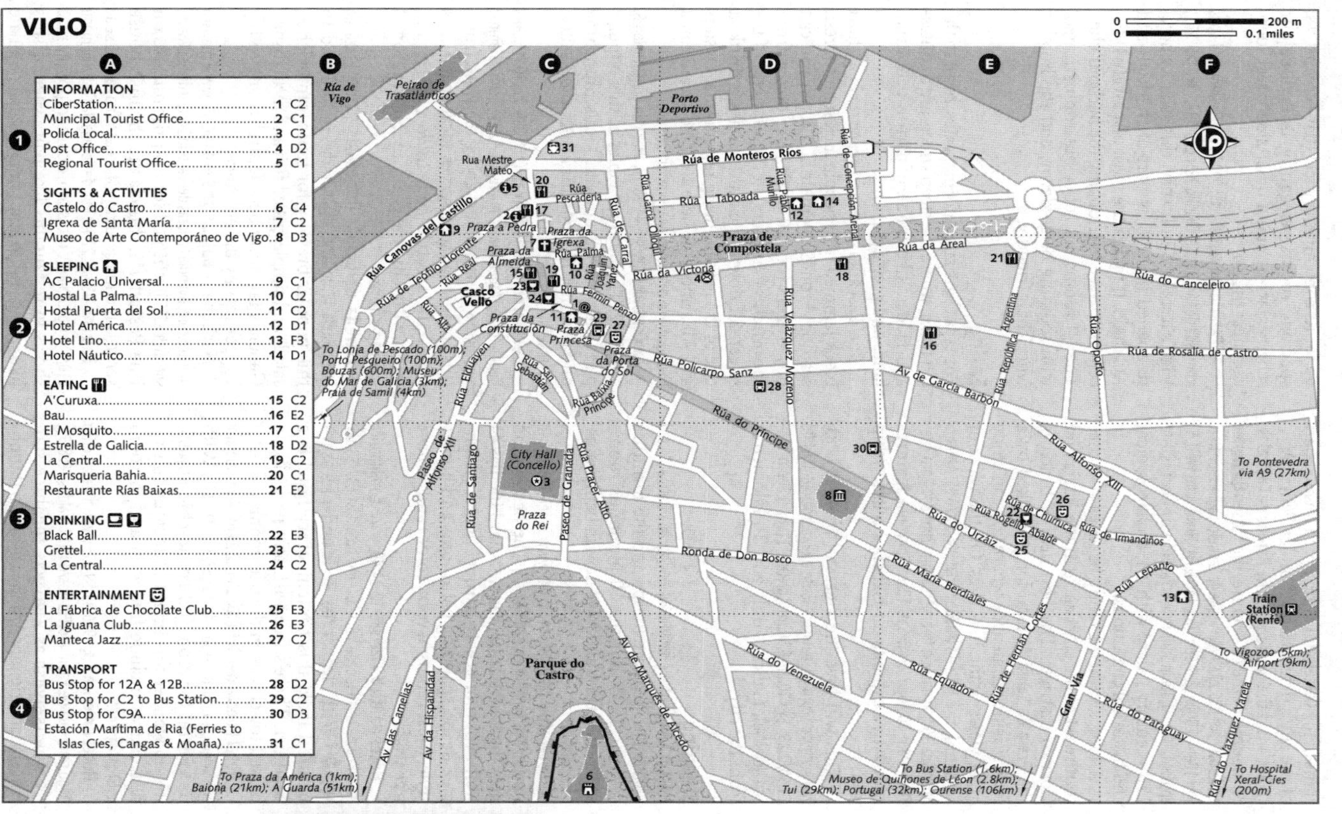
VIGO
0 200 m
0 0.1 miles
INFORMATION
CiberStation....1 C2
Municipal Tourist Office....2 C1
Policía Local....3 C3
Post Office....4 D2
Regional Tourist Office....5 C1
SIGHTS & ACTIVITIES
Castelo do Castro....6 C4
Igrexa de Santa María....7 C2
Museo de Arte Contemporáneo de Vigo..8 D3
SLEEPING
AC Palacio Universal....9 C1
Hostal La Palma....10 C2
Hostal Puerta del Sol....11 C2
Hotel América....12 D1
Hotel Lino....13 F3
Hotel Náutico....14 D1
EATING
A'Curuxa....15 C2
Bau....16 E2
El Mosquito....17 C1
Estrella de Galicia....18 D2
La Central....19 C2
Marisqueria Bahia....20 C1
Restaurante Rías Baixas....21 E2
DRINKING
Black Ball....22 E3
Grettel....23 C2
La Central....24 C2
ENTERTAINMENT
La Fábrica de Chocolate Club....25 E3
La Iguana Club....26 E3
Manteca Jazz....27 C2
TRANSPORT
Bus Stop for 12A & 12B....28 D2
Bus Stop for C2 to Bus Station....29 C2
Bus Stop for C9A....30 D3
Estación Marítima de Ria (Ferries to Islas Cíes, Cangas & Moaña)....31 C1
Ría de Vigo
Peirao de Trasatlánticos
Porto Deportivo
Rúa de Monteros Ríos
Rúa Taboada
Rúa Pablo Murillo
Rúa de Concepción Arenal
Praza de Compostela
Rúa da Areal
Rúa do Canceleiro
Rúa da Victoria
Rúa García Olloqui
Rúa de Carral
Rua Mestre Mateo
Rúa Pescadería
Rúa Canovas del Castillo
Rúa de Teófilo Llorente
Rúa Real
Rúa Alta
Casco Vello
Praza a Pedra
Praza da Igrexa
Rúa Palma
Praza da Almeida
Rúa Joaquín Yanez
Rúa Fermín Penzol
Praza da Constitución
Praza Princesa
Praza da Porta do Sol
Rúa Policarpo Sanz
Rúa Velázquez Moreno
Rúa República Argentina
Rúa Oporto
Rúa de Rosalía de Castro
Av de García Barbón
Rúa do Príncipe
Rúa Baixa Príncipe
Rúa San Sebastián
Rúa Elduayen
Paseo de Alfonso XII
Rúa de Santiago
City Hall (Concello)
Praza do Rei
Paseo de Granada
Rúa Pracer Alto
Rúa Alfonso XIII
Rúa de Churruca
Rúa Rogelio Abalde
Rúa de Irmandiños
Rúa do Urzáiz
Ronda de Don Bosco
Rúa María Berdiales
Rúa Lepanto
Rúa de Hernán Cortes
Gran Vía
Rúa do Paraguay
Rúa do Vazquez Varela
Rúa Equador
Rúa do Venezuela
Parque do Castro
Av de Marqués de Alcedo
Av das Camelias
Av da Hispanidad
Train Station (Renfe)
To Pontevedra via A9 (27km)
To Vigozoo (5km); Airport (9km)
To Hospital Xeral-Cíes (200m)
To Bus Station (1.6km); Museo de Quiñones de León (2.8km); Tui (29km); Portugal (32km); Ourense (106km)
To Praza da América (1km); Baiona (21km); A Guarda (51km)
To Lonja de Pescado (100m); Porto Pesqueiro (100m); Bouzas (600m); Museu do Mar de Galicia (3km); Praia de Samil (4km)

GALICIA

ruins of the **Castelo do Castro**, which formed part of the city's defences built under Felipe IV.

Set amid the gardens of the **Parque de Castrelos**, 3km south of the city centre, the **Museo Quiñones de León** (☎ 986 29 50 70; Parque de Castrelos; admission free; ⏲ 10am-1.30pm & 5-8pm Tue, Thu & Fri, 10am-8pm Wed, 5-8pm Sat, 10am-1.30pm Sun) is a wheelchair accessible 17th-century palace with art, archaeological and historical collections.

A long swathe of sandy beaches stretches southwest of the city centre in the Vavia and Coruxo districts. The best nearby beach is the **Praia de Samil** (1.2km long), backed by a long seaside promenade where you can enjoy great views of the Illas Cíes. On the way out to Samil, the **Museo do Mar** (☎ 986 24 76 95; Avenida Atlántida 160; admission free; ⏲ 10am-2pm & 4-8pm Tue-Thu, 10am-10.30pm Fri & Sat, 10am-9pm Sun) features innovative exhibits on Galicia's relationship with the sea.

Kids will love the **Vigozoo** (☎ 986 26 77 83; www.vigozoo.com in Spanish; Monte da Madroa; adult/child €4.50/2.25; ⏲ 10am-8.30pm Apr-Oct, 11am-6.30pm Tue-Sun Nov-Mar), Galicia's only zoo, 10 kilometres from the city.

Sleeping

Hostal La Palma (☎ 986 43 06 78; Rúa Palma 7; s/d €20/28) The beds are lumpy and the furniture seems c 1975, but the 10 luminous rooms are fresh feeling and have newish bathrooms. No elevator.

Hotel Lino (☎ 986 44 70 04; www.hotel-lino.com in Spanish; Rúa Lepanto 26; s/d €42/48) The best option near the train station, the two-star Lino has 44 well-kept rooms with parquet floors, denim-blue decor, sparkling bathrooms and homey style. Most rooms have balconies and all have free wi-fi.

Hotel Náutico (☎ 986 12 24 49; www.hotelnautico.net; Rúa de Luis Taboada 28; s/d/tr incl breakfast €37/53/66; P 💻) With clean, crisp style and a pleasant nautical look, this contemporary hotel is a solid bet. There's free wi-fi and perks like a heated towel rack in the bathroom.

Hotel Puerta del Sol (☎ 986 22 23 64; www.alojamientosvigo.com; Porta do Sol 14; s/d €53/71; P 💻) With its central location and rustic-chic appeal, it's no wonder this bright little hotel fills up fast. Extras include free wi-fi and in-room CD players.

Hotel América (☎ 986 43 89 22; www.hotelamerica-vigo.com; Rúa de Pablo Morillo 6; s/d incl breakfast €68/93; ♿ 💻) As stylish as Vigo gets, the three-star, wheelchair-friendly América gets two thumbs up for its contemporary feel (flat-screen TVs, spacious rooms, elegantly muted colour schemes, wi-fi) and a quiet side-street location near the port.

AC Palacio Universal (☎ 902 29 22 93; www.ac-hotels.com; Rúa de Cánovas del Castillo 28; r €78-132; P ♿ 💻) Vigo's last word in luxury, this swanky hotel re-opened in 2006 as part of the high-end AC chain. It makes the most of a lovely 19th-century palace overlooking the harbour club. The 69 rooms are sober but sophisticated, with soothing beige decor, and the hotel is wheelchair friendly.

Eating

For tapas bars and informal cafes, head to the old town, where the steep streets are a chutes-and-ladders-like jumble of narrow pedestrian lanes and pretty plazas.

Rúa Pescadería, near the port, is a short block jammed with people tucking into fresh seafood. From 9.30am until 3.30pm you can buy oysters for €10 to €12 per dozen from the *ostreras* (shuckers) at the west end of the street. Sit down to eat them with a drink at one of the neighbouring restaurants. Oysters and Albariño wine here are Vigo's traditional Sunday-morning hangover cure.

La Central (☎ 986 44 28 17; Praza da Constitucion 8; tapas €4-12) The outdoor tables at this popular plaza-side bar fill up with locals munching on favourites like potatoes with *alioli* sauce, mussels and octopus.

Restaurante Rías Baixas (☎ 986 22 30 41; Rúa República de Argentina 2; mains €5-12; ⏲ closed dinner Sun, lunch & dinner Wed) Just above the waterfront, this traditional spot serves local specialities like Galician-style cod, *caldo gallego*, and tripe with chickpeas in an old-fashioned dining room.

Estrella de Galicia (☎ 986 11 72 67; Praza da Compostela 17; raciones & sandwiches €6-14) Head to this popular brewery for tapas, sandwiches, salads and simple grilled fish and meat dishes. Galicia's favourite beer (Estrella) sits in big copper vats by the entrance.

Marisqueria Bahia (☎ 986 44 96 55; www.mariscomarisco.com; Avendia Cánoras del Castillo 24; fish dishes €8-16, shellfish €5-50) With tables near the *ostreras* on Rúa Pescaderia, this classic shellfish house serves an endless array of treats from the sea.

Bau (☎ 986 22 22 14; Rúa de Rosalía de Castro 6; menú €10; ⏲ closed Sun) Vigo's more contemporary face shows in restaurants like Bau, where dishes like spring risotto and Waldorf salad populate the internationally flavoured menu. A dozen sidewalks tables add to the ambience.

A'Curuxa (☎ 986 43 88 57; Rúa dos Cesteiros 7; menú €12, mains €8-16; closed Tue) This delightful stone tavern mixes the traditional and contemporary in both its decor and menu. Try either Galician favourites like *caldos* (soups) and *cocidos* (stews), or opt for chicken kabobs and guacamole. Great atmosphere but slow service.

El Mosquito (☎ 986 43 35 70; Praza da Pedra 4; mains €12-26) Popular with the business lunch crowd, this local establishment focuses on fish and shellfish but also offers a smattering of other dishes, like oven-roasted kid goat and hearty steaks.

Drinking & Entertainment

Vigo's nightlife is hopping. Start off slow at one of several enticing cafe-bars on the Praza da Constitución. Bohemian-aired **Grettel** (☎ 986 226 508; Praza da Constitución 10) serves fresh juices and teas by day and cocktails such as mojitos, daiquiris and caipirinhas by night. The taverns along nearby Rúas Real and Teófilo Llorente are also good low-key options, or head over to Rúa Carral for jazz gigs and concerts Wednesdays through Sundays at **Manteca Jazz** (Rúa Carral 3; admission usually free). In summer, hit the terraces along Rúa de Montero Ríos (opposite the waterfront).

The real *zona de marcha* is southeast around the Churraca district: the Praza do Portugal and Rúas de Churraca, Rogelio Abide and Imagines. You might start at the retro lounge-style **Black Ball** (Rúa de Churruca 8), then stop into **La Fábrica de Chocolate Club** (Rúa de Rogelio Abalde 22) which hosts a live band or two each week (usually Thursday to Sunday nights). Most nights you can catch a live show at the ever-varied **La Iguana Club** (Rúa da Churraca 14; admission €3-20).

Other popular nightspots cluster around Rúas Arial and Rosalía de Castro district, the Samil beach/Avenida de Europa district, and along Gran Vía.

Getting There & Away

AIR

Vigo's **Picador airport** (☎ 986 26 82 00) is about 9km east of the centre. Iberia flies to/from Bilbao, Valencia Barcelona and Madrid. Spanair also serves Barcelona, Madrid and Tenerife. Air France and Air Europa have flights to/from Paris.

BOAT

Naviera Mar de Ons (☎ 986 22 52 72; www.mardeons.com) ferries to Cangas (€4.20 return, 20 minutes) run every half-hour weekdays (hourly on weekends) from 6.30am to 10.30pm; ferries to Moaña (€4 return, 15 minutes) sail hourly from 6.30am until 10.30pm (from 8.30am weekends). For details on ferries to the Illas Cíes, see p594.

BUS

Several companies service Vigo's **bus station** (☎ 986 37 34 11; www.vigobus.com; Avenida de Madrid 57). **Avanza** (www.avanzabus.com) heads to Madrid (€42, seven hours, at least one daily) and **Mobus-Castromil** (www.monbus.es) make several trips daily to all major Galician cities, including Pontevedra (€2.50, 30 minutes), Santiago de Compostela (€7.95, 1½ hours), A Coruña (€14.30, 2½ hours) and the coastal resorts.

Autna (www.autna.com) runs four times daily Monday to Friday (once daily on weekends) to/from Porto, Portugal (€10, 2½ hours), with connections there for Lisbon.

Other buses, many run by **Alsa** (www.alsa.es), head for Oviedo, Santander, Bilbao, Pamplona, Barcelona, Salamanca, Seville and elsewhere.

TRAIN

Renfe (www.renfe.es) runs approximately hourly to Pontevedra (€2 to €3, 30 minutes), Santiago de Compostela (€6 to €8, approximately 90 minutes) and A Coruña (€10 to €13, two to three hours), and eight times daily to Ourense (€8 to €18, approximately two hours). There are twice-daily trains to Madrid (€45, nine hours) and Barcelona (€60 to €67, 15½ hours).

Getting Around

Vitrasa (☎ 986 29 16 00; www.vitrasa.es in Spanish; per ride €1.08) covers the city centre. Bus C9A runs between the Praza da América and the airport; bus C2 links the centre and the bus station; and line 11 joins the centre with Rúa do Urzáiz close to the train station. See the Vigo Map p591 for locations of stops or visit the **information kiosk** (9am-2pm & 4-7pm) in the Porta do Sol, itself a major hub.

ILLAS CÍES

A beautiful bird sanctuary and the home to some of Galicia's most privileged beaches, the Illas Cíes are a 45-minute ferry ride from Vigo. Sitting just 14km offshore, this small archipelago constitutes the main attraction of the **Parque Nacional de las Islas Atlánticas de Galicia** (☎ 986 24 65 17), a national park that also includes the Ons, Sálvora and Cortegada archipelagos further north.

The three Cíes islands (Illa do San Martiño, Illa do Faro and Illa de Monteagudo) form a 6km breakwater that protects Vigo and its *ría* from the Atlantic's fury. The lack of development here makes it an ideal spot for dune strolling, birdwatching and lolling on the pristine beaches.

You can only visit the Illas Cíes during Semana Santa, on weekends from May to early June and daily from early June to early September. To stay overnight you must book at **Camping Illas Cíes** (☎ 986 43 83 58, www.campingislascies.com in Spanish; sites per person/tent €7.15/7.45) through the camping ground's office at the Illas Cíes boat terminal in Vigo. The camping ground is wheelchair friendly, and has a restaurant and supermarket, and a capacity of 800 people – often filled in August.

Naviera Mar de Ons (☎ 986 22 52 72; www.mardeons.com in Spanish) runs boats to the island. In summer and Semana Santa, weather permitting, up to eight daily trips are made from Vigo (45 minutes one way, adult/child €17.50/free), and beginning in July, up to four each from Baiona and Cangas. Wherever you start, return tickets cost €16.50.

THE SOUTHWEST

From Vigo, the PO-552 highway dives south, skimming a rocky coast that, while beautiful, has largely resisted tourist development because of a lack of sandy beaches. Nevertheless, it's home to several tempting stops.

BAIONA

pop 11,800

Crowned with a spectacular seaside fortress, Baiona (Castilian: Bayona) is a popular resort that balances coast and culture. Its shining moment came on 1 March 1493, when Christopher Columbus' *Pinta* arrived bearing the remarkable news that the explorer had made it to the Indies (in fact, he had bumped into the Americas). Then an important trading port, Baiona was later eclipsed by Vigo. These days, you can visit a replica of the **Pinta** (admission €.80; ⏲ 10am-8pm mid-Jun–mid-Sep), which sits moored in Baiona's harbour.

A tangle of inviting lanes makes up Baiona's **casco histórico** (historic district). There are a handful of 16th- and 17th-century houses and chapels, with cafes, restaurants and artisans' shops scattered about.

You can't miss the pine-covered promontory **Monte Boi**, dominated by **Fortaleza de Monterreal** (pedestrian/car €1/5; ⏲ 10.30am-8.30pm Oct-Jun, 10.30am-9.30pm Jul-Sep). The fortress, erected between the 11th and 17th centuries, is protected by an impenetrable 3km circle of walls. Also within the precinct today is a luxurious Parador Hotel (see below). An enticing 40-minute walking trail loops the area, skimming a rocky shoreline broken up by a few small beaches.

For better beaches, take the seaside promenade towards the **Praia Ladeira**, 1.5km from the centre. Some 2.5km further on is the magnificent sweep of **Praia América** at Nigrán. Most buses between Baiona and Vigo stop at these beaches.

Get maps and more at the **tourist office** (☎ 986 68 70 67; www.baiona.org in Spanish; Paseo da Ribeira; ⏲ 10am-2pm & 3-7pm Mon-Sat, 11am-2pm & 4-7pm Sun Jan-Mar & Oct-Dec, 10am-2pm & 4-8pm Mon-Sat, 11am-2pm & 4-8pm Sun Apr-Jun & Sep, 10am-3pm & 4-9pm Jul-Aug), on the approach to Mont Boi.

Sleeping & Eating

Many of Baiona's hotels are clustered near the harbour-front drive. A couple of blocks inland is **Casa Soto** (☎ 696 79 51 31; www.casasoto.com; Rúa Laxe 7; apt for 2/3/4/6 people €85/95/115/150), whose inviting apartments are decorated in a beachy style and are ideal for families.

The privileged **Parador de Baiona** (☎ 986 35 50 00; www.parador.es; Monte Boi; s €165, d €219-312) stands high above the bay in the centre of the Monte Boi. The grandiose rooms boast canopied beds and wonderful views, while the sophisticated restaurant (mains €10 to €26) offers a sampling of local specialities like *vieiras asadas al horno* (oven-roasted clams).

The cobbled lanes in the centre of town, including Rúa do Conde and Rúa de Ventura Misa, are full of restaurants, tapas bars and watering holes. Try the rustic and cosy **El Túnel** (☎ 986 35 51 09; Rúa de Ventura Misa; mains €9-60), where you'll spot all the usual suspects of Galician shellfish and seafood.

Getting There & Away

ATSA (☎ 986 35 53 30) buses run north to Vigo (€2) every 30 minutes till 9pm most days, and a couple go south daily to A Guarda from in front of the *lonja* (fish market) by the harbour. In summer boats sail to the Illas Cíes (see p593).

A GUARDA

pop 10,000

A fishing port just north of where the Río Miño spills into the Atlantic, A Guarda (Castilian: La Guardia) is a ho-hum town with several good seafood restaurants. Its draw is the nearby **Monte de Santa Trega** (admission in vehicle per person Tue-Sun Easter-early Dec €0.80, other times free), a beautiful hilltop 3.5km from the town.

Drive or take the 45-minute trail walk from the base of the Monte. On the way up, poke around the **Castro de Santa Tegra** where a couple of the primitive circular dwellings have been restored. Past the ancient site, the road continues to the mount's peak, where a **castle** and **chapel** (11am-2pm & 4-7pm Semana Santa-Dec) stand watch. There's also a small **museum** (9am-9pm Jun-Sep, 10am-7.30pm Oct-Dec & Feb-May, closed Jan). The beauty of this place is slightly marred by chintzy souvenir shops and busloads of retirees, but it's still worth visiting (especially at sunset). Two cafeterias make convenient places for a pick-me-up. But best of all are the magnificent views up the Miño, across to Portugal and out over the Atlantic.

A real treat, **Hotel Convento de San Benito** (986 61 11 66; www.hotelsanbenito.es; Praza de San Bieito; s €53, d €77-108; P) is housed in a 16th-century convent down by the harbour. Its 24 elegant rooms are romantic and individually decorated, with period furniture and original architectural elements like exposed stone walls.

More than a dozen eateries line up in front of the less-than-picturesque harbour. This is a great place to try local *bogavante* (lobster). At one end of the harbour sits the humble **Porto Guardés** (986 61 34 88; Rúa do Porto 1; fish dishes €5-11), where grilled swordfish, tuna, cod and other seafood are served in a tavern-like atmosphere. Head to the opposite end of the harbour for upscale shellfish at the **Marisquería Anduriña** (986 61 11 08; Rúa do Porto 58; fish dishes €13-21), where tanks of live *bogavante* tempt.

Most **ATSA** (986 61 02 55) buses to/from Vigo (€5.20, 80 minutes, approximately half hourly) run via Tui, but a few go via Baiona. Service is reduced at weekends.

TUI

pop 17,000

Sitting above the banks of the majestic Miño River, the border village of Tui (Castilian: Tuy) draws Portuguese and Spanish day trippers with its lively cafe scene, tightly packed medieval centre and magnificent cathedral. Just across the bridge is Portugal's equally appealing Valença.

There's a **regional tourist office** (986 60 17 89; Rúa Colón 2; 9.30am-1.30pm & 4.30-6.30pm Mon-Fri, 10.30am-12.30pm Sat) almost opposite the Hotel Colón.

Sights

Heading towards the old town, you'll come first to the plaza-like Paseo Calvo Sotelo, better known as the **Corredoira**, where several terrace bars make tempting spots for a cold drink. From here, enter the historic district via the **Porta da Pía**, a gate in the 12th-century defensive wall.

The highlight of the old town is the fortress-like **Catedral de Santa Maria** (admission €2, Jul–mid-Sep €3; 11am-1.30pm & 4-7pm Oct-Apr, 11am-2pm & 4-8pm May, 11am-2pm & 4-9pm Jun-Sep), which reigns over the Praza San Fernando. Begun in the 12th century, it reflects a stoic Romanesque style in most of its construction, although the portal is ornate Gothic. It was much altered in the 15th century and extra stone bracing was added after the Lisbon earthquake in 1755. It's worth the ticket price to visit the Gothic cloister, Romanesque chapter house, tower and gardens with views over the river, and the **Museo Diocesano** (Easter–mid-Oct), across the street, with its archaeology and art collection.

From the cathedral, Tui slides downhill towards the Miño. A smattering of bars and artisans' shops inject its sloping stone streets with life. There are also several *cruceiros* and various chapels including the **Iglesia de San Telmo**, containing relics of the patron saint of sailors.

Sleeping & Eating

There are several inviting places to eat near the cathedral. On Friday to Sunday nights, Entrefornos and other quaint cobblestone streets behind the cathedral are the scene of some major partying.

O Novo Cabalo Furado (627 07 23 32; www.cabalofurado.com; Rúa Seijas 3; s €30-40, d €50-80) In the heart of the old town, the rooms and apartments at this intimate guesthouse are simple but inviting, with all-wood furnishings and sparkly new bathrooms.

Hotel Colón (986 60 02 23; www.hotelcolontuy.com; Rúa Colón 11; s €50-68, d €85, apt for 2 €95; P)

The stylish lobby is a bit deceiving, as the 45 rooms themselves have changed little since the hotel opened in 1983. Apartments, however, are fresh in a Nordic-minimalist way. Rooms and apartments are sunny with tranquil views overlooking the tennis court and countryside. It's a half-kilometre from the centre.

Quinta do Ramo (☎ 902 02 70 75; www.quintadoramo.com in Spanish; Lugar de Ramo 5, Forcadela (Tomiño); s/d incl breakfast €65/110; P) An exquisite garden alive with fruit trees and flowery bushes surrounds this elegant rural hotel 10km from Tui. The 14th-cenutury stone house has six cosy, country-style rooms and an upscale restaurant (mains €13 to €27) serving excellent meat and fish dishes like grilled sole and Galician-style hake.

O Vello Cabalo Furado (☎ 986 60 38 00; Rúa Seijas 2; mains €5-16, menú €12; closed Tue & Sun pm Sep-Jun, closed Sun Jul-Aug) Not to be confused with the inferior O Cabalo Furado around the corner, this large inviting dining hall serves hearty specialities such as *cocido gallego*, roasted ham and a long list of local fish dishes.

Getting There & Away

Frequent **ATSA** (☎ 986 61 02 55) buses to Vigo (€2.80, 40 minutes approximately every half hour) and A Guarda (€2.80, 40 minutes, approximately every half hour) stop on Paseo de Calvo Sotelo, opposite Librería Byblos. Service is reduced at weekends.

THE EAST

Although often overshadowed by the glorious coastline or by the better-known attractions in Santiago de Compostela or A Coruña, eastern Galicia is a treasure-trove of enticing provincial cities, spectacular natural landscapes and old-fashioned rural enclaves. It's the ideal destination for travellers who like digging out their own hidden gems.

OURENSE

pop 107,000

The impeccable historic quarter, lively tapas scene and tempting thermal baths of Galicia's third-largest city will have you wondering why it ranks so low on most visitors' agendas. Although founded by the Romans, who were the first to take advantage of the healing waters that surge from the ground here, Ourense (Castilian: Orense) only came into its own as a Castilian trading centre in the 11th century. Rising above the banks of the Río Miño, old Ourense is compact and packed with cultural sites, thanks in large part to the city's long ecclesiastical tradition. The recent years' efforts to polish up historic monuments of the old quarter mean that Ourense is more enticing now than ever.

Orientation

The train station is 500m north of Río Miño and the bus station a further 1km northwest. On foot you can approach the city centre across Ponte Romano, which is actually a medieval bridge constructed in place of an older Roman one. Climb towards the Catedral do San Martiño, around which the old town unfolds.

Information

Ciber Eclipse (Rúa Monte Cabeza de Manzaneda 2; per hr €2; 9am-midnight) Coin-operated internet access.
Municipal tourist office (☎ 988 36 60 64; www.ourense.es; Rúa As Burgas 12; 9am-2pm & 3-8pm Mon-Fri 11am-2pm Sat & Sun)
Policía Local (☎ 988 38 81 38; Rúa de Victoria Kent 1)
Post office (Rúa do Progreso 53; 8.30am-8.30pm Mon-Fri, 9.30am-2pm Sat)
Regional tourist office (☎ 988 37 20 20; 9am-2pm Mon-Fri) On the Ponte Romano.

Sights & Activities

Head to the 12th-century **Catedral do San Martiño** (8.30am-1.30pm & 4.30-8.30pm; admission free). Begun in 1160 and consecrated in 1188, the crucifix-shaped cathedral is the epicentre of the old quarter. Its highlight is the gilded Santo Cristo chapel, near the northern entrance. At the west end is the Pórtico do Paraíso, a Gothic copy of Santiago de Compostela's Pórtico de la Glória. Seek out a sacristan to see the cathedral's **museum** (noon-1pm & 4.30-7pm).

Radiating away from the cathedral is a maze of narrow streets begging to be explored. Intriguing churches like the concave-facaded **Igrexa de Santa Eufemia**, the baroque **Santa María la Madre**, the 10th-century **Santísima Trinidad**, or the renaissance **Santo Domingo** dot the centre and are accompanied by well-kept gardens and beguiling squares. The largest is Praza Maior, a sloping plaza rimmed by cafes and crowned by the **Casa do Concello** (town hall).

The main commercial streets are the wide pedestrianised Rúa do Paseo and the Rúa Santo Domingo, where you'll find traditional

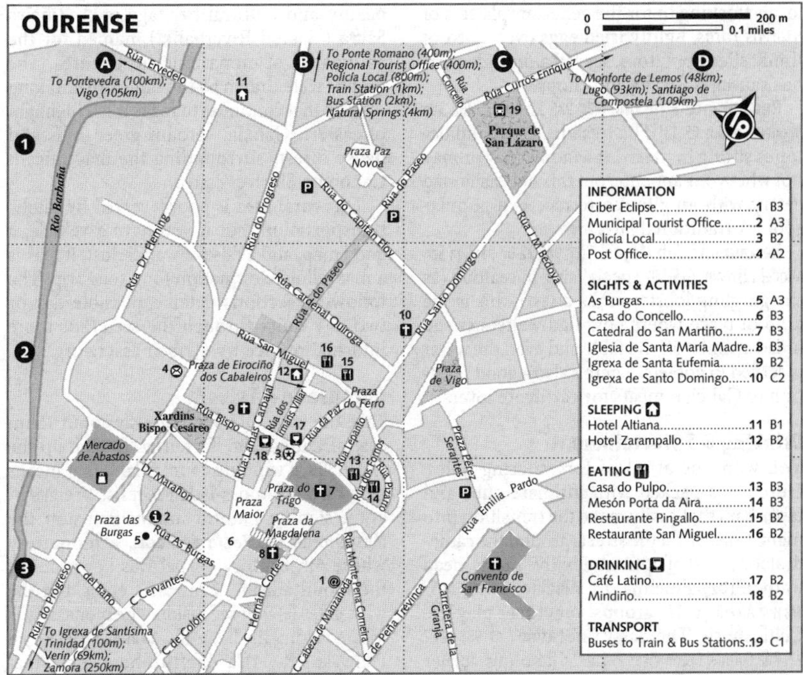

and contemporary shops, cafes and restaurants. In the evening, the Rúa do Paseo is a long promenade packed with families.

Ourense's original raison d'être is the fountain **As Burgas**, which gushes out 67°C waters that locals use to heal a myriad of ailments. Just out of town, along the Río Miño, are a string of other **natural springs** that have been beautifully landscaped and provide the perfect spot to unwind. With the exception of one private spring, these hot (60°C) and cold pools are free and open 24 hours a day. A 3km-long riverside path leads the way there. Cars aren't allowed, but you can walk, bike or take the **tourist train** (admission €0.73; at least 11am-1pm & 5-9pm) that departs from the Praza Maior.

Sleeping

Ourense's hotels are a bit of a letdown given the city's cultural flavour. For better options, look to the rural areas beyond the city sprawl (p598).

Hotel Altiana (☎ 988 37 09 52, 988 37 01 28; Rúa Erveldo 14; s/d/tr €32/45/60) This modest two-star on the fringe of the old town offers free (and fast) wi-fi. Decor, however, is uninspired, with worn parquet floors, narrow balconies overlooking a busy street and clean but careworn bathrooms.

Hotel Zarampallo (☎ 988 23 00 08; www.zarampallo.com in Spanish; Rúa dos Irmáns Villar 19; s/d €30/50) With a great city-centre location, this contemporary family-run hotel has modern rooms with peach-coloured walls, narrow balconies overlooking a pedestrian street, clean white bathrooms, and local art hanging on the walls.

Eating

Ir de tapeo ('going for tapas') is a way of life in Ourense, and central streets like Fornos, La Paz, Lepanto, Viriato and San Miguel are brimming with smoky taverns where having to push and shove your way to the bar is seen as a sign of quality. Tapas run from €2 to €10, depending on what you order, and are nearly always washed down with a glass of local wine.

Casa do Pulpo (☎ 988 25 52 42; Rúa Juan de Austria 15) Specialises in octopus *(pulpo)*.

Mesón Porta da Aira (☎ 988 25 07 49; Rúa dos Fornos 2; tapas €2-14, dishes €8-22) This tiny eatery has locals flocking in for the generous platters of *huevos rotos,* lightly fried eggs over a bed of thinly sliced potatoes, served alongside various sausages, steaks and chops.

Restaurante Pingallo (☎ 988 22 00 57; Rúa San Miguel 6; mains €5-13) The fresh hake, eel and octopus sitting in the front window may or may not whet your appetite, but this old-fashioned eatery with an alfresco terrace is a popular spot for traditional fare.

Restaurante San Miguel (☎ 988 22 07 95; Rúa San Miguel 12; mains €15-38) Specialising in seafood (as the gurgling lobster tanks attest), this is the kind of place where bow-tied waiters sweep bread crumbs off the table and even the water is served in goblets. There's also a good selection of Galician meats for carnivore lovers.

Drinking & Entertainment

You won't be at a loss for watering holes; Ourense is packed with intimate pubs and tapas bars that easily make the transition into night-time. Stroll the streets around the cathedral for a host of options. For live music, head to the Praza Eufemia. At **Mindiño** (☎ 988 24 55 36; Rúa Arcediagos 13), groups sometimes play live Celtic music. The classy **Café Latino** (☎ 988 22 67 21; Rúa Coronel Ceano Vivas 7) has a fabulous corner stage that hosts groups playing jazz and other styles. It does double duty as a daytime cafe.

Getting There & Away

Ourense's **bus station** (☎ 988 21 60 27; Carretera de Vigo 1) has service throughout the province and to Galicia's main cities. **Monbus** (www.monbus.es) runs to Santiago (€10, two hours, six daily), Vigo (€9.50, 75 minutes, 10 daily) and Pontevedra (€9.50, 90 minutes, eight daily). **Avanza** (www.avanzabus.com) journeys to Madrid (€30 to €37, fivehours, four daily) and other Spanish cities.

Renfe (www.renfe.es) runs trains to Santiago (€7 to €18, up to two hours, six daily), A Coruña (€14 to €22, up to three hours, four daily) and Vigo (€8 to €18, up to two hours, eight daily) as well as Spanish cities further afield.

Getting Around

Local buses 1, 3, 6, 8 and 12 run between the train station and Parque de San Lázaro in the city centre. Buses 6 and 12 also serve the bus station.

A RIBEIRA SACRA & CAÑÓN DO SIL

Northeast of Ourense, along the Miño and Sil Rivers, unfolds the unrivalled natural beauty and cultural heritage of A Ribeira Sacra ('Sacred Riverbank'), named for the abundance of monasteries in the area. The monks were drawn by the same breathtaking scenery that continues to make this a highlight of eastern Galicia: verdant green hills and dense forests surrounding the magnificent Cañón do Sil river canyon.

This rural area is poorly served by public transportation, but if you have a vehicle, a good map, and a dose of wanderlust, it makes a marvellous destination for a road trip. The following sections detail a possible day or two-day route through the area. For more information, see www.ribeir asacra.org.

Ourense to A Teixera

Take the wide OU-536 highway about 15km east of Ourense to Tarreirigo to pick up the OU-0509, a winding country land that meanders through moss-laden forests. Veer right at the sign for Luintra and the first stop, the **Mosteiro de San Pedro de Rocas**, a monastery whose 6th-century chapel was hewn out of the mountainside. You can't enter, but the wide gates let you see inside. The monastery is located along the beautiful **Camino Real** (Royal Path; aka PR-G4), a 9km/two-hour circuit that loops around the area.

Back on the highway, continue towards Luintra and veer right on the OU-0508 towards the Benedictine **Mosteiro San Estevo** (opposite) now a Parador Hotel. Though a monastery may have stood here as early as the 6th century, the mammoth construction you see today dates to the 12th century and was greatly modified through the years, with three magnificent cloisters (one Romanesque, one Gothic, one Renaissance) and an 18th-century baroque facade.

Continue along the OU-0508, following the signs towards Loureiro to reach the **Cañón do Sil** (Sil River Canyon), where small boats make cruises. To reach the canyon's bottom, follow the sign down to the *embarcaderos* (jetties). At the end of a scenic if sinuous highway, **Hemisferios cruise boats** (☎ 982 25 45 45; www.hemisferios.es; adult €11-14, child €8-11; 🕒 12.30pm & 4.30pm or 11am & 6pm Tue-Sun Mar-Nov) make 90-minute tours of the river canyon. In the same complex is a **tourist office** (🕒 10am-2pm & 4-6.30pm Sat & Sun) and a small cafeteria.

The river canyon is perhaps even more beautiful from above. Continue along the main highway as it winds its way through moss-drenched forests and along a ridge high above the gorge. Several *miradores*, including the spectacular **Balcón de Madrid**, provide vantage points along the way. When the highway ends, turn left on the OU-0605. Just 200m further on, before you reach **Parado do Sil**, turn left towards the **Mosteiro Santa Cristina**. In 4.5km you reach the ruins of this medieval monastery and Romanesque church hidden among the trees above the canyon and looking romantically forlorn. You can freely explore it inside and out.

Castro Caldelas & Around

The OU-0605 continues along another dreamy stretch of highway, passing waterfalls, farm plots divided by crumbling stone walls, story-book villages and occasional jaw-dropping vistas of the gorge below.

At the intersection with OU-0606, veer left towards A Teixeira, and follow the signs towards **Castro Caldelas**, a delightful village with the requisite cobblestone streets, glassed-in Gallegan balconies and well-tended flower boxes. Explore the historic centre, crowned by the **Igrexa Santa Isabel** and a 15th-century **castle**, which oddly enough has several free public computers. The town's small **tourist office** (☎ 988 20 46 30; Praza da Torre s/n; ⏰ 10am-2pm & 5-8pm Mon-Fri, 11am-2pm & 5-8pm Sat & Sun) has information about the whole Ribeira Sacra area.

Towards Monforte de Lemos

From Castro Caldelas, pick up the OU-903 highway towards **Monforte de Lemos**, a historic crossroads town. The road winds down to the river canyon, where **catamarans** (☎ 982 26 01 96; www.rutasdelosembalses.com; per person €9; ⏰ 11.30am, 12pm, 12.15pm, 4.30pm, 5pm, 5.15pm daily Jun-Oct, 11.30am weekends Nov-May) take 2½-hour tours of the gorge. As you cross the river, the highway becomes the LU-903 and climbs out of the gorge, leaving the river's deep green waters far behind as it cuts across the impossibly steep **vineyards** that characterise the area. A half-hour further on, the monuments of Monforte come into view.

The Río Cabe cuts through the heart of town and the 16th-century **Ponte Vella** (old bridge) spanning it is one of the loveliest sights of the centre. Once an important rail junction, the city is neither as compact nor as pristine as other stops on the route, but its cultural monuments make it well worth a visit. Most important is the monumental area of **San Vicente**, which stands watch over the city from a low mountain beside the river. The **Pazo Condal**, formerly the residence of the counts of Lemos, is now a Parador Hotel (see Parador de Monforte de Lemos, p600). Flanking it is the Renaissance facade of the **Mosteiro Beneditino de San Vicente** and the 8th-century **Torre da Homenaxe**, a defensive tower left as the last vestige of the castle that once stood here. Monforte's **tourist office** (☎ 982 40 47 15; www.concellodemonforte.com; Rúa Campo da Compañía; ⏰ 10am-2pm & 4-7pm Mon-Sat) organises guided tours of the **tower** (⏰ 11am & 4pm Mon-Sat, 11am Sun).

North of the N-120, the natural paradise hugging the Río Miño constitutes the rest of the Ribeira Sacra. The towns of Taboada, Chantada, Nogueira do Miño and Os Peares are the main centres along a route that, like the one described above, cuts through soul-stirring rural scenery and a handful of interesting monasteries.

Sleeping & Eating

Hotel Puente Romano (☎ 982 41 11 67; www.hpuenteromano.com in Spanish; Paseo do Malecón, Monforte de Lemos; s/d €27/42; Ⓟ) In the heart of Monforte, overlooking the river, this humble hotel has 33 comfortable rooms.

Pousada Vicente Risco (☎ 988 20 33 60; www.pousadavicenterisco.com; Rúa Grande 4, Castro Caldelas; s/d incl breakfast €35/45) One of three charming guesthouses in the centre of Castro Caldelas, this quaint spot has eight well-kept rooms with classic-style furniture and some rustic touches, like exposed stone walls.

Hotel Rústico a Forxa (☎ 988 20 10 25; www.hotelaforxa.com; Praza Maior 12, Luíntra; r incl breakfast €36-78; Ⓟ) Antique wooden furniture decorates the nine simple rooms at this family-run hotel in the heart of the tiny hamlet of Luíntra. The hotel's restaurant (mains €6 to €14) serves tried-and-true dishes like lamb chops or roast chicken.

Casa Grande Cristosende (☎ 988 20 75 29; Cristosende, Teixeira; r €48-77; Ⓟ) A charming, wheelchair-friendly stone manor house near A Teixeira, this rural hotel has seven inviting rooms that are monastic in their simplicity. The restaurant (*menú* €16) serves hearty Galician fare.

Parador San Estevo (☎ 988 01 01 10; www.parador.es; Nogueria de Ramuín; s/d €136/170; Ⓟ) Ribeira Sacra's best-known monastery is also an indulgent hotel with all the comforts and a wonderful setting above the river canyon. Its excellent restaurant (mains €17 to €20) serves local specialities like *caldo gallego* as well as special options for vegetarians and coeliacs. The *parador* is wheelchair accessible.

Parador de Monforte de Lemos (☎ 982 41 84 84; www.parador.es; Plaza Luis de Góngora y Argote s/n, Monforte de Lemos; s/d €127/159; P ♿) Perched high above town, this 16th-century palace has spacious, welcoming rooms, and the restaurant (mains €17 to €20) is a wonderful place to sample regional fare like *vieiras a la gallega* or *cachelos y chorizo*. The hotel is wheelchair accessible.

Polar (☎ 982 40 00 01; Rúa Cardenal Rodrigo de Castro 13, Monforte de Lemos; mains €6-12) Pleases everyone with a huge range including pizzas, tapas, pasta, salads and local dishes like octopus and cod.

Restaurante O Grelo (☎ 982 40 47 01; Campo de la Virgen s/n, Monforte de Lemos; mains €14-20) In a rustic stone building just below the Monasterio de San Vicente do Pino, this character-filled place specialises in game like partridge and wild boar. This being Galicia, there are also wonderful seafood dishes and traditional dishes like *lacon con greldos* (ham with greens).

Getting There & Away

From Monforte, the wide N-120 highway zips back to Ourense. Buses head north to Lugo and southwest to Ourense about once an hour on weekdays, and a few others travel east to Ponferrada and León. Although this was once an important train stop, now mainly trains bound for Ourense (€3.15, 40 minutes, up to nine) call in. Both stations are north of the castle.

RIBADAVIA & DO RIBEIRO

The headquarters of the Ribeiro wine region, where some of Galicia's best whites are made, Ribadavia sits tucked between the Avia and Miño Rivers in a verdant valley. Its historic centre is an enticing maze of narrow stone streets lined with heavy stone arcades and broken up by diminutive plazas; it's all that's left of Galicia's largest Jewish quarter.

The enthusiastic **tourist office** (☎ 988 47 12 75; www.ribadavia.com; Praza Maior 7; 🕑 9.30am-2.30pm & 4-6.30pm Mon-Fri, 10.30am-2.30pm & 4-6.30pm Sat, 10.30am-2.30pm Sun) is in a 17th-century palace on the main square. Upstairs is the **Centro de Información Xudía** (admission €1), with an exhibition on the Jews of Galicia.

The **Barrio Xudío** (Jewish Quarter) occupies the zone between the south wall and Praza Magdalena, where a house once served as the community synagogue. The **Casa da Inquisición** fronts nearby Praza de García Boente. Of several churches, the Romanesque **Igrexa de Santiago** and **Igrexa de San Xoán** stand out. The **Museo Etnolóxico** (☎ 988 47 18 43; Rúa Santiago 10; admission €2.40; 🕑 10am-2.30pm & 4-9pm Tue-Fri, 11am-2.30pm Sat & Sun), just down the street from the Igrexa de Santiago, with its Galician folk history collection, is worth a look, too. The remains of the **Castelo dos Condes de Ribadavia**, closed for repairs at the time of writing, date from the 15th century.

Relax with a stroll along the 5km-long **riverside path** that runs by the gurgling Río Avia.

In early July, Ribadavia stages Galicia's biggest wine festival, the **Feria del Vino del Ribeiro**.

For a meal or tapas, head to the Praza Maior, a glorious open square ringed by cafes and restaurants like **Restaurante Plaza** (☎ 988 47 05 76; Praza Maior; s/d €20/30; mains €5-10), where you can get Galician specialities.

There are several wonderful rural hotels in the area. Just 10 minutes outside town, you can kill several birds with one stone at the **Casal de Armán** (☎ 988 49 18 09; www.casaldearman.net; O Cotiño, San Andrés; mains €9-16; r incl breakfast €75), a dignified stone house that serves as a rural hotel, restaurant and wine cellar rolled into one. Traditional Galician fare is served with style in its rustic-chic dining room, while the five rooms overlook the countryside. The winery is open for visits outside meal times and with prior arrangement.

Up to 10 buses and five trains run daily to Ourense and Vigo from stations in the east of town, just over Río Avia.

LUGO

pop 93,900 / elev 475m

The grand Roman walls encircling old Lugo are considered the world's best-preserved and are the number one reason visitors land here. Yet within the fortress is a beautifully preserved labyrinth of streets and squares, most of them traffic-free and ideal for strolling. First established over an ancient *castro* in the 1st century BC, Lugo today is a quiet but engaging city.

Information

Hospital Xeral Calde (☎ 982 29 60 00; Rúa Doutor Ochoa)

Policía Municipal (☎ 982 29 71 10; Praza da Constitución)

Regional tourist office (☎ 982 23 13 61; www.lugoturismo.com; Rúa de Conde Pallarés 2; 🕑 10am-2pm & 4-7pm Mon-Sat Sep-Jun, 10am-2pm & 4-8pm daily Jul & Aug)

GALICIA

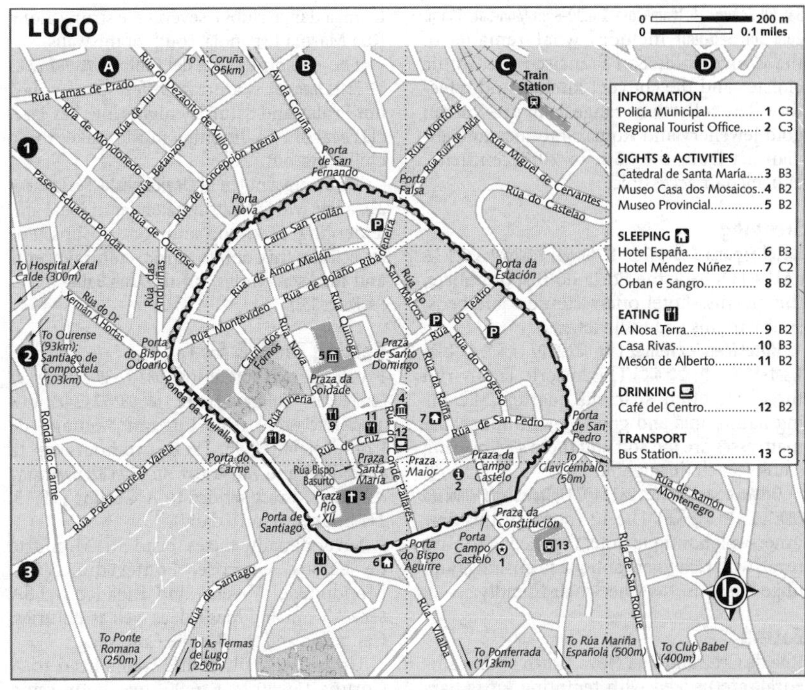

Sights

ROMAN REMAINS

The path running along the top of the **Roman walls** is to Lugo what a maritime promenade is to a seaside resort: a place to jog, take an evening stroll, see and be seen. Several staircases and a ramp access the walkway; one is the **Porta de Santiago** (Santiago Gate) near the cathedral.

The walls, which make a 2.25km loop around the old city, rise 15m high, are studded with 82 stout towers and represent 18 centuries of history. First erected in the 3rd century, the walls were used and improved through the years, although they were never very successful at their task of protecting the city. Lugo was invaded by the Suevi in 460 and the Muslims 300 years later. Until well into the 19th century the city gates were closed at night and tolls were charged to bring in goods from outside.

Newly excavated underground ruins are the heart of the **Museo Casa dos Mosaicos** (☎ 982 29 73 47; Rúa de Doctor Castro 20; 🕑 11am-2pm & 5-7pm Tue-Sun), which offers a peek into the daily life of Roman Lugo.

Southwest of the centre cluster more Roman remains. Cross the 1st-century **Ponte Romana** (Roman bridge), spanning the Río Miño, to access **As Termas de Lugo** (☎ 982 22 12 28; Barrio da Ponte s/n; admission free; 🕑 9am-1pm & 6.30-8.30pm), where ancient baths taking advantage of the 44°C sulphurous waters are hidden inside the modern spa of the Balneario de Lugo hotel.

CATHEDRAL

The **Catedral de Santa María** (🕑 8.30am-8pm), inspired by Santiago's grand cathedral, was begun in 1129, though work continued for centuries, resulting in the aesthetic architectural mix that includes dashes of styles ranging from Romanesque (see the northern doorway) to neoclassical (as in the main facade). Inside, the walnut choir stalls are a baroque masterpiece. For access to the cloister and treasury, get a ticket to the cathedral's **museum** (☎ 982 22 04 66; adult/child €1.50/free; 🕑 11am-1pm Mon-Sat).

MUSEO PROVINCIAL

Lugo's **museum** (☎ 982 24 21 12; Praza da Soidade; admission free; 🕑 11am-2pm & 5-8pm Mon-Fri, 10am-2pm

Sat Jul & Aug, 10.30am-2pm & 4.30-8pm Mon-Sat, 11am-2pm Sun Sep-Jun) includes what remains of the Convento de San Francisco – a Gothic cloister and the convent kitchen and refectory. The collections range from pre-Roman gold jewellery and Roman mosaics to Galician art from the 15th to 20th centuries. Wheelchair accessible.

Sleeping

Hotel España (☎ 982 23 15 40; Rúa Vilalba 2; s €22-32, d €32-40) Outside the Porta do Bispo Aguirre, this no-fuss hotel offers comfortable beds, sunny rooms and wall views.

Hotel Méndez Núñez (☎ 982 23 07 11; Rúa da Raíña 1; s/d €50/60; P ✖ 🖳) This historic, family-run three-star offers spacious quarters, gleaming bathrooms and good views, though the mattresses are too soft and there's a lingering smoky smell throughout.

Orban e Sangro (☎ 982 24 02 17; Travesía do Miño; s/d €80/100; P ✖ 🖳) The 12 rooms of this new inner-wall boutique hotel (opened 2008) are regal, with rich linen, antique furnishings and huge 2m beds. It's wheelchair friendly.

Eating

Rúa de Cruz and Rúa Nova, north of the cathedral, are packed with tempting tapas bars and restaurants.

Casa Rivas (☎ 982 22 10 58; Ronda Muralla 177; menú €8) Stepping through the doorway of this family-run spot is like crossing into 1970s Spain. A neighbourhood crowd files in to the mustard-coloured dining room for noodle soup, grilled veal, fried hake, squid or chickpea stew.

A Nosa Terra (☎ 982 22 92 35; Rúa Nova 8; mains €7-18) A dark but inviting bar with a long by-the-glass wine list, this popular spot doles out good tapas (free with a drink). The downstairs bodega is a good place to try *pulpo á feira* or *lacón con grelos*.

Mesón de Alberto (☎ 982 22 83 10; Rúa da Cruz 4; menú €13, mains €14-25; ⏲ closed dinner Tue, lunch & dinner Sun) One of several restaurants on this street, Alberto serves great traditional fare alongside informal tapas.

Drinking & Entertainment

Weekend nights, things get lively near the cathedral, especially along the Rúa Nova, Praza do Campo, Praza do Campo Castelo, Rúa da Cruz and Rúa Bispo Basulto. Start with tapas and drinks, then hit the bars or *chundas* (electronica dance clubs); several are strung along Rúa Mariña Española, south of the walls.

The old-timey **Café del Centro** (☎ 982 22 83 39; Praza Maior 9) is a great coffee spot by day, but Friday and Saturday nights low-key jazz, classical or easy-listening music makes this a chill hang-out.

Take it up a notch at **Clavicémbalo** (Rúa Paxariños 23), a bar with a healthy calendar of local and 'emerging' jazz, pop and rock groups. For an eclectic mix of live music, cultural events and film screenings, hit the **Club Babel** (Rúa de San Roque 153).

Getting There & Away

From the **bus station** (☎ 982 22 39 85; Praza da Constitución), **Empresa Freire** (☎ 982 22 03 00; www.empresafreire.com) runs to/from Santiago de Compostela (€7.95, 1½ to two hours, up to 10 daily), and **Arriva** (☎ 902 27 74 82; www.arriva.es) offers direct service to A Coruña (€9.15, 1¼ hours, up to 10 daily).

Several daily buses head to Monforte de Lemos, Ourense, Pontevedra, Vigo, Mondoñedo, Viveiro and Ribadeo. ALSA serves León and Madrid, as well as Asturias, Cantabria and the Basque Country.

Up to five daily Renfe trains head to A Coruña (€6.50 to €16.90, two hours) and Monforte de Lemos (€3.60 to €13.50, one hour). An Atlantico overnight train goes all the way to Madrid (€52, nine hours).

AROUND LUGO

The **Terres do Miño** Unesco Biosphere Reserve wraps around Lugo like a doughnut, hiding within its green folds beautiful natural areas and several worthy cultural sites, like the **Castro de Viladonga**, a prehistoric settlement 24km northeast of Lugo; the **Santa Eulalia de Bóveda** Roman ruins, 14km southwest of Lugo; and, to the southeast, the **Mosteiro de Samos**, a grand Benedictine monastery built in Romanesque, Gothic, Renaissance and baroque styles over many centuries.

Nearby, sitting on the Galician border, are two of northern Spain's most famous natural areas, the **Serra dos Ancares** and the **Serra do Courel**. These beautiful mountainous regions are crossed by long- and short-distance hiking trails and are truly rewarding destinations for those who want to dive into 'green Spain'. For more information, go to www.turgalicia.com or www.lugo tur.com.

Valencia

So many of the more than 5.5 million overseas visitors to the Comunidad Valenciana (Valencia region) each year confine themselves to the resorts of the thin coastal strip, where they stay put – except, perhaps, for a day trip to Valencia city. The more enterprising rent a bike or car, leave behind the coastal hedonism and explore the region's rich interior.

Valencia is both of Spain and distinct from Spain. In Muslim hands for five centuries, its Christian European history has been shaped as much by Catalonia, its neighbour to the north, as by Castilla. The region's flag bears the red and yellow stripes of Catalonia and the mother tongue of many is Valenciano, a dialect of Catalan.

Valencia city, the region's capital, is famed for its nightlife, the wild Las Fallas spring festival and the stunning architecture of its Ciudad de las Artes y las Ciencias.

To the north, along the Costa del Azahar (Orange Blossom Coast), is a string of low-key resorts, plus the historic site of Sagunto. Southwards along the Costa Blanca (White Coast) stretch some of Spain's finest beaches. You can bar-hop and party in international resorts such as Benidorm, Torrevieja and the lively provincial capital of Alicante. Others, such as Denia and Gandia, still retain a much more Spanish flavour.

Inland lies a world where mountains buckle and castles crown hilltops: there's Morella, girt by intact medieval walls; Xàtiva, with its splendid castle; Montanejos, a tiny spa town that draws rock climbers from around Europe; and Elche, with Europe's most extensive palm groves.

HIGHLIGHTS

- Fling fireworks and suffer serious sleep deprivation at **Las Fallas** (p611), Europe's wildest spring festival
- Sway on the smart new tram that runs along the spectacular coastline between **Alicante** and **Benidorm** (p640)
- Bring your tent and shake your booty at **Festival Internacional de Benicàssim** (p623), Benicàssim's outdoor international music festival
- Gasp at the daring architecture of **Valencia city** (p607) in the Ciudad de las Artes y las Ciencias, and immerse yourself in the Oceanogràfic, Europe's largest aquarium
- Savour your first glimpse of the medieval fortress town of **Morella** (p627) from afar

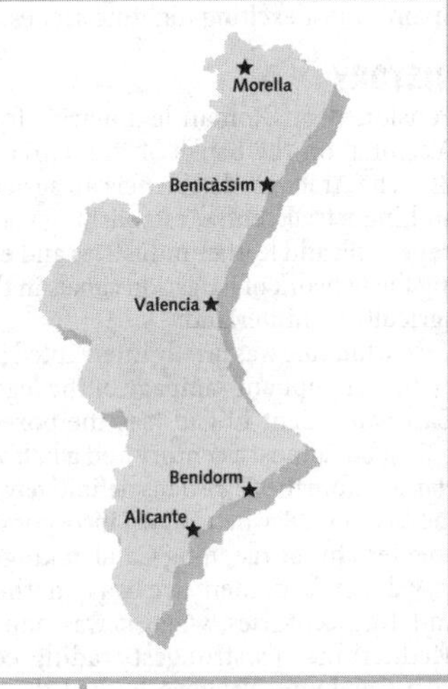

AREA: 23,255 SQ KM	AVE SUMMER TEMP: HIGH 32°C, LOW 19°C	POP: 4.4 MILLION

VALENCIA CITY

pop 805,300

Valencia, Spain's third-largest city, for ages languished in the long shadows cast by Madrid, Spain's political capital, and Barcelona, the country's cultural and economic powerhouse. No longer. Stunning public buildings have changed the city's skyline – Sir Norman Foster's Palacio de Congresos, David Chipperfield's award-winning Veles i Vents structure beside the inner port, and, on the grandest scale of all, the Ciudad de las Artes y las Ciencas, designed in the main by Santiago Calatrava, local boy made good.

Events too have raised Valencia's profile. In 2007 the eyes of the world were upon the town as it hosted the America's Cup sailing races, while in 2008 the city hosted both the World Indoor Athletics Championships and the first European Grand Prix, where Formula One cars hurtled around an urban circuit that threads in and around the radically transformed inner port.

An increasingly popular short-break venue (the number of overseas visitors has almost doubled in the last four years), Valencia is where paella first simmered over a wood fire. It's a vibrant, friendly, mildly chaotic place with two outstanding fine-arts museums, an accessible old quarter, Europe's newest cultural and scientific complex – and one of Spain's most exciting nightlife scenes.

HISTORY

Pensioned-off Roman legionaries founded 'Valentia' on the banks of Río Turia in 138 BC. The Arabs made Valencia an agricultural and industrial centre, establishing ceramics, paper, silk and leather industries and extending the network of irrigation canals in the rich agricultural hinterland.

Muslim rule was briefly interrupted in 1094 by the triumphant rampage of the legendary Castilian knight El Cid (see the boxed text, p258), but almost a century and a half were to elapse before the Christians definitively retook the city in 1238, when Jaime I incorporated the area into his burgeoning Catalan kingdom.

Valencia's golden age was in the 15th and 16th centuries, when it was one of the Mediterranean's strongest trading centres. Like Catalonia, Valencia backed the wrong horse in the War of the Spanish Succession (1702–13) and in retribution the victorious Bourbon king Felipe V abolished the *fueros*, the autonomous privileges the city had enjoyed. The Spanish Civil War proved similarly unlucky; Valencia, having sided with the Republicans (and acting as seat of the Republican government from November 1936 until October 1937) was slighted for years by successive nationalist governments.

The *fueros* may not have been restored but, benefiting from the decentralisation that followed Franco's death, Valencia today enjoys a high degree of autonomy.

ORIENTATION

The 'action' part of the city is an oval area bounded by the old course of Río Turia, and the sickle-shaped inner ring road of Calles de Colón, Xàtiva and de Guillem de Castro. Within this oval are three major squares: Plazas del Ayuntamiento, de la Reina (also known as Plaza de Zaragoza) and de la Virgen.

INFORMATION

Call ☎ 902 12 32 12 throughout the region for tourist information (at premium rates).

Casa del Llibre (Map p608; ☎ 96 353 00 80; Passeig Russafa 11) Offspring of the giant Madrid mother store, with a reasonable stock of books in English.

Laundry Stop (Map p608; Calle Baja 17; 🕑 9.30am-10pm) Surf the net (per hr €1.50) or wi-fi as your clothes spin.

Librería Patagonia (Map p608; ☎ 96 393 60 52; Calle Hospital 1) An excellent travel bookshop with some guides in English, including Lonely Planet titles.

Main post office (Map p608; Plaza del Ayuntamiento)

Ono (Map p608; Calle San Vicente Mártir 22; per hr €3.50; 🕑 10am-10pm) Internet access.

Region of Valencia (www.comunitatvalenciana.com) The Valencia region's excellent official tourism site.

Regional tourist office (Map p608; ☎ 96 398 64 22; Calle Paz 48; 🕑 9am-2.30pm & 4.30-8pm Mon-Fri)

CREEPING CATALAN

More and more town halls are replacing street signs in Spanish with the Valenciano/Catalan equivalent. While the difference between the two versions is often minimal, this can sometimes be confusing for visitors. Occasionally we use the Valenciano form where it's clearly the dominant one. But since Spanish is the version every local understands and the majority uses, we've elected to stick with it in most cases.

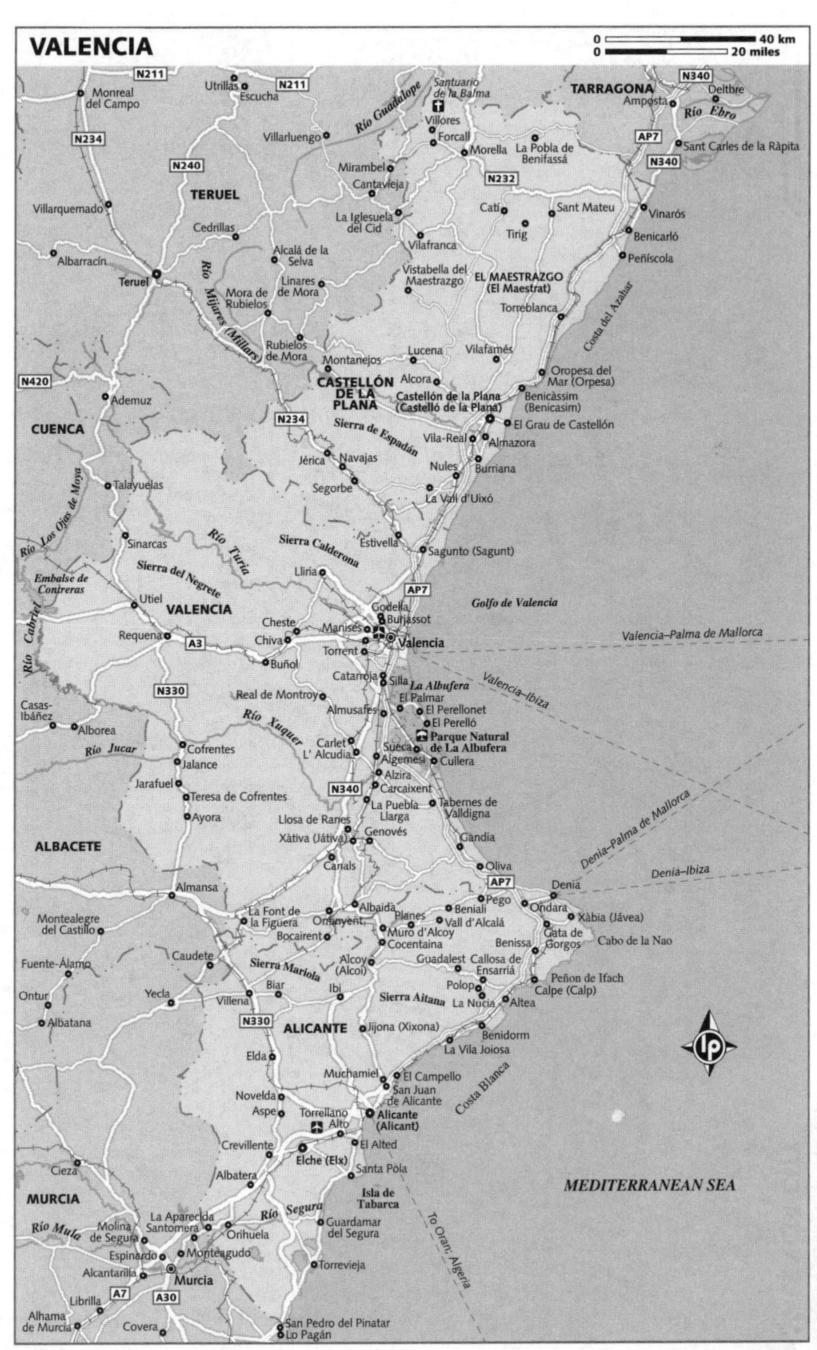
VALENCIA
0 40 km
0 20 miles
N211
Utrillas
Escucha
Monreal del Campo
Río Guadalope
Santuario de la Balma
Villores
Forcall
Morella
La Pobla de Benifassá
TARRAGONA
N340
Amposta
Deltbre
Río Ebro
AP7
Sant Carles de la Ràpita
N234
Villarluengo
Mirambel
Cantavieja
N240
N232
TERUEL
Villarquemado
Cedrillas
La Iglesuela del Cid
Catí
Tirig
Sant Mateu
Vinarós
Benicarló
Peñíscola
Vilafranca
Albarracín
Teruel
Alcalá de la Selva
Linares de Mora
Mora de Rubielos
Río Mijares (Millars)
Vistabella del Maestrazgo
EL MAESTRAZGO (El Maestrat)
Torreblanca
Costa del Azahar
Rubielos de Mora
Montanejos
Lucena
Vilafamés
Alcora
Oropesa del Mar (Orpesa)
N420
Ademuz
CASTELLÓN DE LA PLANA
Castellón de la Plana (Castelló de la Plana)
Benicàssim (Benicasim)
El Grau de Castellón
CUENCA
N234
Sierra de Espadán
Vila-Real
Almazora
Jérica
Navajas
Nules
Burriana
Talayuelas
Segorbe
La Vall d'Uixó
Río Los Ojos de Moya
Sinarcas
Río Turia
Sierra Calderona
Estivella
Sagunto (Sagunt)
Sierra del Negrete
Llíria
Embalse de Contreras
AP7
Utiel
VALENCIA
Golfo de Valencia
Godella
Burjassot
Río Cabriel
Cheste
Manises
Requena
Chiva
Valencia
A3
Torrent
Valencia–Palma de Mallorca
Buñol
Catarroja
Silla
La Albufera
Valencia–Ibiza
N330
Real de Montroy
El Palmar
Casas-Ibáñez
Alborea
Almusafes
El Perellonet
El Perelló
Río Xuquer
Parque Natural de La Albufera
Cofrentes
Carlet
Sueca
L' Alcudia
Algemesí
Cullera
Río Jucar
Jalance
Alzira
Jarafuel
Carcaixent
N340
Teresa de Cofrentes
La Puebla Llarga
Tabernes de Valldigna
Ayora
Llosa de Ranes
Genovés
Xàtiva (Játiva)
Gandia
ALBACETE
Denia–Palma de Mallorca
Canals
Oliva
AP7
Denia–Ibiza
Almansa
Denia
Pego
Ondara
La Font de la Figuera
Albaida
Beniali
Xàbia (Jávea)
Montealegre del Castillo
Onteniente
Planes
Vall d'Alcalá
Muro d'Alcoy
Gata de Gorgos
Bocairent
Cocentaina
Benissa
Cabo de la Nao
Caudete
Fuente-Álamo
Alcoy (Alcoi)
Guadalest
Callosa de Ensarriá
Sierra Mariola
Peñon de Ifach
Calpe (Calp)
Ontur
Yecla
Biar
Polop
Villena
Ibi
Sierra Aitana
La Nucia
Altea
Albatana
N330
ALICANTE
Jijona (Xixona)
Benidorm
La Vila Joiosa
Elda
Muchamiel
El Campello
San Juan de Alicante
Costa Blanca
Novelda
Aspe
Torrellano
Alicante (Alicant)
Alto
Crevillente
El Alted
Elche (Elx)
Cieza
Santa Pola
Albatera
MURCIA
Isla de Tabarca
MEDITERRANEAN SEA
La Aparecida
Río Segura
Río Mula
Molina de Segura
Santomera
Orihuela
Guardamar del Segura
Espinardo
Monteagudo
To Oran, Algeria
Alcantarilla
Murcia
Torrevieja
Librilla
A7
A30
Alhama de Murcia
Covera
San Pedro del Pinatar
Lo Pagán

VALENCIA

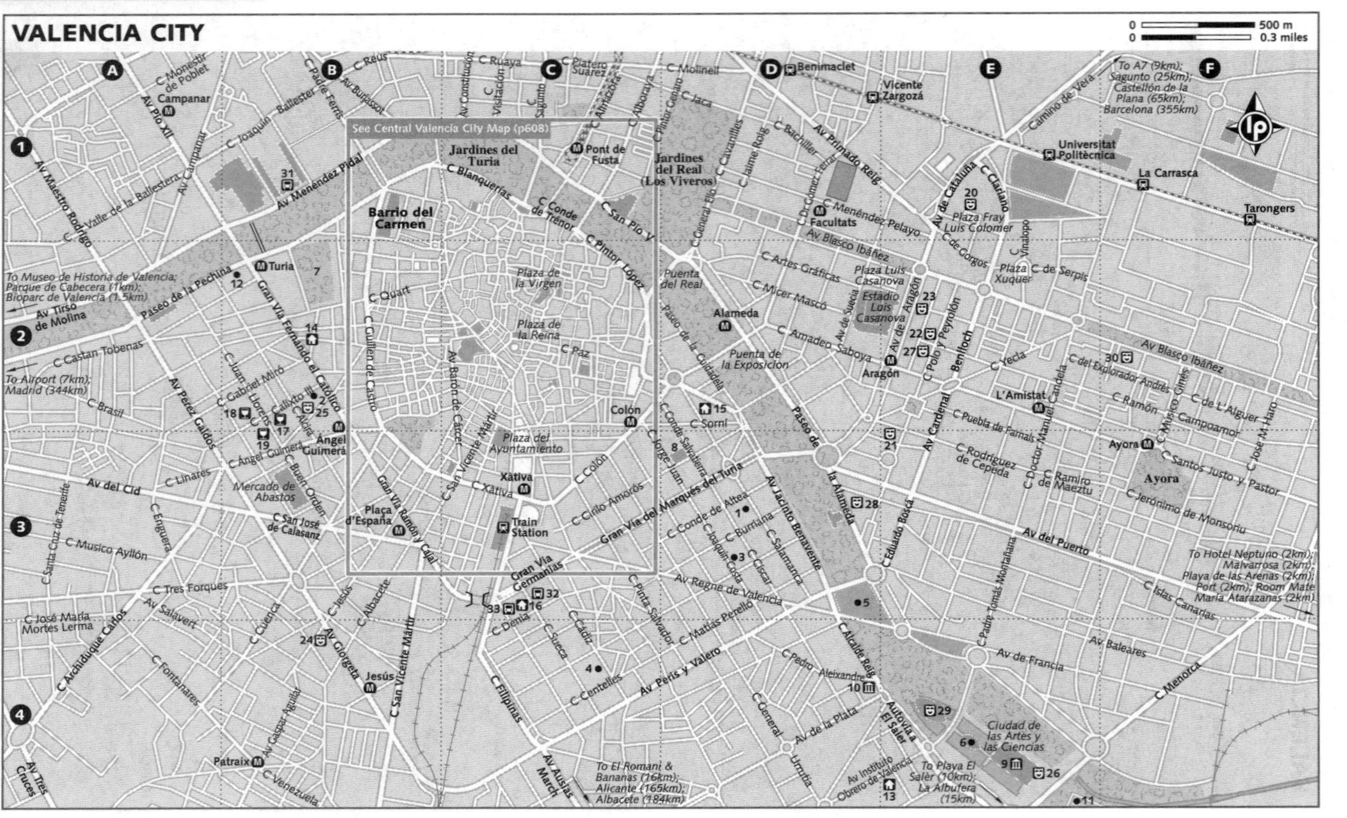
VALENCIA CITY
0 500 m
0 0.3 miles
See Central Valencia City Map (p608)
To A7 (9km); Sagunto (25km); Castellón de la Plana (65km); Barcelona (355km)
To Museo de Historia de Valencia; Parque de Cabecera (1km); Bioparc de Valencia (1.5km)
To Airport (7km); Madrid (344km)
To El Romaní & Bananas (16km); Alicante (165km); Albacete (184km)
To Playa El Saler (10km); La Albufera (15km)
To Hotel Neptuno (2km); Malvarrosa (2km); Playa de las Arenas (2km); Port (2km); Room Mate Marina Atarazanas (2km)
Barrio del Carmen
Jardines del Turia
Jardines del Real (Los Viveros)
Plaza de la Virgen
Plaza de la Reina
Plaza del Ayuntamiento
Plaça d'España
Mercado de Abastos
Ciudad de las Artes y las Ciencias
Estadio Luis Casanova
Plaza Luis Casanova
Plaza Fray Luis Colomer
Plaza Xuquer
Universitat Politècnica
Ayora
Train Station
Campanar
Turia
Pont de Fusta
Colón
Xàtiva
Alameda
Facultats
Benimaclet
Vicente Zargozá
La Carrasca
Tarongers
Aragón
L'Amistat
Àngel Guimerá
Jesús
Patraix
Av Pío XII
Av Maestro Rodrigo
Av Campanar
Av Menéndez Pidal
Paseo de la Pechina
Av Tirso de Molina
Av Pérez Galdós
Gran Vía Fernando el Católico
Gran Vía Ramón y Cajal
Gran Vía del Marqués del Turia
Gran Vía Germanías
Av del Cid
Av Giorgeta
Av Blasco Ibáñez
Av Primado Reig
Av de Cataluña
Paseo de la Alameda
Av Jacinto Benavente
Av del Puerto
Av de Francia
Av Baleares
Av Peris y Valero
Av Regne de Valencia
Av de Aragón
Av Cardenal Benlloch
C Filipinas
Av Ausiàs March
Av Tres Cruces
Av Barón de Cárcer
Autovía a El Saler
Av de la Plata
Puente del Real
Puente de la Exposición
Paseo de la Ciudadela
C Guillem de Castro
C Quart
C Blanquerías
C San Vicente Mártir
C Colón
C Xàtiva
C Pinta Salvador
C Sueca
C Cádiz
C Archiduque Carlos
C Menorca
C Islas Canarias
C Jerónimo de Monsoriu
C Eduardo Boscá
C Clariano
C Alcalde Reig
C Pedro Aleixandre
C Salamanca
C Císcar
C Conde de Altea
C Joaquín Costa
C Sorní
C Conde Salvatierra
C Jorge Juan
C Pintor López
C San Pío V
C Conde de Trénor
Camino de Vera

SIGHTS & ACTIVITIES
Academia de Baile Maria Cruz Alcalá....1 D3
Centre Professional de Dansa Valenciá....2 B2
Escuela de Cocina Eneldo....3 D3
Estudio de Danza Maria Carbonell....4 C4
Gulliver....5 D3
Hemisfèric....6 E4
Jardín Botánico....7 B2
Mercado de Colón....8 D3
Museo de las Ciencias Príncipe Felipe....9 E4
Museo Fallero....10 D4
Oceanogràfic....11 E4
Palau de les Arts Reina Sofía....(see 29)
Valencia Guías....12 B2

SLEEPING
40flats.com....13 E4
Chill Art Jardín Botánico....14 B2
Palau del Mar....15 D2
Petit Palace Germanías....16 C3
Rôôms de Luxe....(see 13)

DRINKING
Akuarela....17 B2
Anubis....18 B2
Café Carioca....19 B3

ENTERTAINMENT
Albatros....20 E1
Babel....21 E2
Black Note....22 E2
Caribbean's....23 E2
Dub Club....24 B4
El Loco....25 B2
L'Umbracle Terraza....26 E4
Mosquito....27 E2
Palau de la Música....28 D3
Palau de les Arts Reina Sofía....29 E4
Rumbo 144....30 F2

TRANSPORT
Bus Station....31 B1
Bus to Playa El Salér....32 C3
Buses to the Airport....33 C3

Turismo Valencia (VLC) tourist office (☎ 96 315 39 31; www.turisvalencia.es) Plaza de la Reina (Map p608; Plaza de la Reina 19; 9am-7pm Mon-Sat, 10am-2pm Sun); Train Station (Map p608; Calle Xàtiva) Also has a branch at the airport arrivals area.
Valencia city (www.turisvalencia.com) Best of several competing tourism sites about the city.
Work Center (Map p608; Calle Xàtiva 19; per hr €3; 24 hr Mon-Thu, 7am-11pm Fri, noon-2pm & 5-9pm Sat & Sun) Internet access.

SIGHTS & ACTIVITIES

Ciudad de las Artes y las Ciencias

The aesthetically stunning **Ciudad de las Artes y las Ciencias** (City of Arts & Sciences; Map p606; ☎ reservations 902 10 00 31; www.cac.es; Autovía a El Saler; combined ticket for all 3 attractions adult/child €30.60/23.30) occupies a massive 350,000-sq-metre swath of the old Turia riverbed. It's mostly the work of local architect Santiago Calatrava, designer of, among many other exciting creations around the world, the transport terminal for the new World Trade Center site in New York.

The **Hemisfèric** (Map p606; adult/child €7.50/5.80) is planetarium, IMAX cinema and laser show, all in one. Optional English commentary.

The **Museo de las Ciencias Príncipe Felipe** (Map p606; adult/child €7.50/5.80; 10am-7pm or 9pm) is an interactive science museum where each section has a pamphlet in English summarising its contents.

Highlight of the complex, especially if you have young children, will probably be the **Oceanogràfic** (Map p606; adult/child €23.30/17.60; 10am-6pm or 8pm Sep–mid-Jul, 10am-midnight mid-Jul–Aug). The aquariums of this watery world have sufficient water sloshing around to fill 15 Olympic-size swimming pools. There are also polar zones, a dolphinarium, a Red Sea aquarium, a Mediterranean seascape – and a couple of underwater tunnels, one 70m long, where the fish have the chance to gawp at visitors.

The **Palau de les Arts Reina Sofía** (Map p606; ☎ 902 20 23 83; www.lesarts.com; Autovía a El Saler) broods over the riverbed like a giant beetle, its shell shimmering with translucent mosaic tiles. With four auditoriums and seating for 4400, it's exceeded in capacity only by the Sydney Opera House.

Take bus 35 from Plaza del Ayuntamiento or bus 95 from Torres de Serranos or Plaza de América.

Museo de Historia de Valencia

Above the riverbed Parque de Cabecera, the **Museo de Historia de Valencia** (☎ 96 370 11 05; Calle Valencia 42; adult/child €2/1; admission free Sat & Sun; 10am-2pm & 4.30-8.30pm Tue-Sat, 10am-3pm Sun) plots more than 2000 years of the city's history. Hands-on and with lots of film and video, it's great fun. Ask to borrow the museum's informative folder in English. Take bus 3, 81 or 95 or get off at the Nou d'Octubre metro stop.

Museo de Bellas Artes

Bright and spacious (and with a great little cafe for a drink or snack lunch), the **Museo de Bellas Artes** (Fine Arts Museum; Map p608; ☎ 96 378 03 00; Calle San Pío V 9; admission free; 10am-8pm Tue-Sun) ranks among Spain's best. Its highlights include the grandiose Roman *Mosaic of the Nine Muses*, a collection of magnificent late medieval altarpieces and works by El Greco, Goya, Velázquez, Murillo, Ribalta, plus artists such as Sorolla and Pinazo of the Valencian Impressionist school.

Instituto Valenciano de Arte Moderno (IVAM)

IVAM (Map p608; ☎ 96 386 30 00; www.ivam.es; Calle Guillem de Castro 118; adult/student €2/1, free Sun;

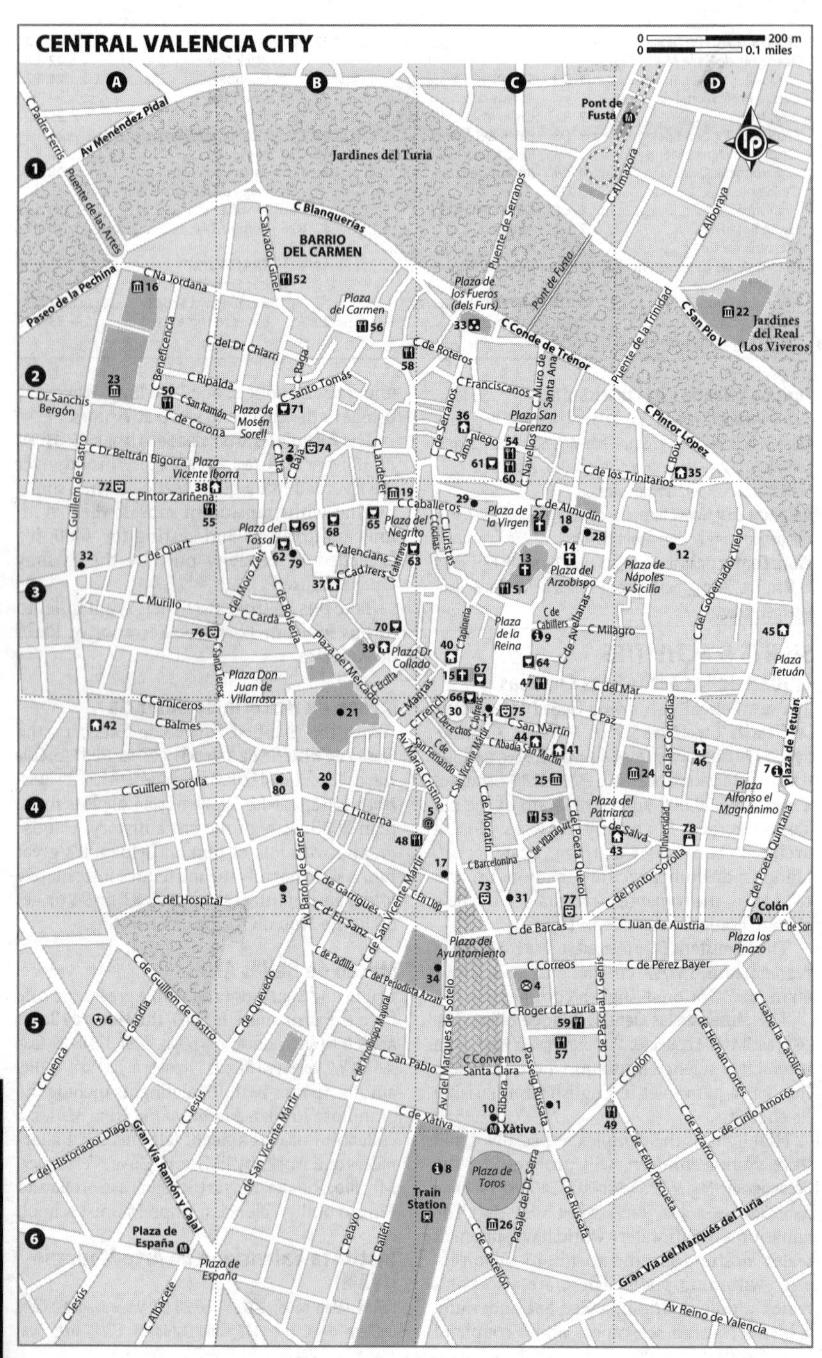
CENTRAL VALENCIA CITY
0 200 m
0 0.1 miles
Jardines del Turia
BARRIO DEL CARMEN
Av Menéndez Pidal
C Padre Ferris
Puente de las Artes
Paseo de la Pechina
C Blanquerías
C Salvador Giner
Pont de Fusta
C Almazora
Puente de Serranos
Plaza de los Fueros (dels Furs)
C Conde de Trénor
C San Pío V
Jardines del Real (Los Viveros)
C Alboraya
Puente de la Trinidad
C Pintor López
Plaza del Carmen
C Na Jordana
C Beneficencia
C del Dr Chiarri
C Ripalda
C Dr Sanchis Bergón
C de Corona
C Santo Tomás
Plaza de Mosén Sorell
C de Roteros
C Franciscanos
C Muro de Santa Ana
Plaza San Lorenzo
C Dr Beltrán Bigorra
Plaza Vicente Iborra
C Pintor Zariñena
C Guillem de Castro
C de Quart
Plaza del Tossal
C Valencians
C Cadirers
Plaza del Negrito
C Caballeros
Plaza de la Virgen
C de Almudín
Plaza del Arzobispo
Plaza de Nápoles y Sicilia
C del Gobernador Viejo
C de los Trinitarios
C Murillo
C Cardà
C de Bolsería
Plaza del Mercado
Plaza Dr Collado
Plaza de la Reina
C Milagro
C de Avellanas
Plaza Tetuán
Plaza Don Juan de Villarrasa
C Carniceros
C Balmes
C del Mar
C Paz
C San Martín
C de las Comedias
Plaza de Tetuán
Plaza Alfonso el Magnánimo
C Guillem Sorolla
C Linterna
Av María Cristina
C de Moratín
Plaza del Patriarca
C de Salvá
C del Poeta Querol
C del Pintor Sorolla
C del Poeta Quintana
C del Hospital
C de Garrigues
C d'En Sanz
Av Barón de Cárcer
C de San Vicente Mártir
Plaza del Ayuntamiento
C de Barcas
C Juan de Austria
Colón
Plaza los Pinazo
C Correos
C de Perez Bayer
C Roger de Lauria
C de Guillem de Castro
C de Quevedo
C San Pablo
C Convento Santa Clara
Av del Marques de Sotelo
C de Pascual y Genís
C de Hernán Cortés
C Isabel la Católica
C Colón
C de Cirilo Amorós
C de Xàtiva
Xàtiva
C Ribera
Passeig Russafa
C Cuenca
C Jesús
C del Historiador Diago
Gran Vía Ramón y Cajal
Train Station
Plaza de Toros
Pasaje del Dr Serra
C de Russafa
C de Félix Pizcueta
C de Pizarro
Gran Vía del Marqués del Turia
Plaza de España
C Pelayo
C Bailén
C de Castellón
Av Reino de Valencia
C Albacete
VALENCIA

INFORMATION
Casa del Llibre ... 1 C5
Laundry Stop ... 2 B2
Librería Patagonia ... 3 B4
Main Post Office ... 4 C5
Ono ... 5 C4
Police Station ... 6 A5
Regional Tourist Office ... 7 D4
Turismo Valencia (VLC) Tourist Office ... 8 C6
Turismo Valencia (VLC) Tourist Office ... 9 C3
Work Center ... 10 C5

SIGHTS & ACTIVITIES
Babylon Idiomas ... 11 C4
Baños del Almirante ... 12 D3
Cathedral ... 13 C3
Cripta de la Cárcel de San Vicente Mártir ... 14 C3
Iglesia de Santa Catalina ... 15 C3
Instituto Valenciano de Arte Moderno (IVAM) ... 16 A2
Intereuropa ... 17 C4
La Almoina ... 18 C3
L'Iber (Toy Soldiers Museum) ... 19 B3
Lonja ... 20 B4
Mercado Central ... 21 B4
Museo de Bellas Artes ... 22 D2
Museo de Prehistoria (La Beneficencia) ... 23 A2
Museo del Patriarca ... 24 D4
Museo Nacional de Cerámica ... 25 C4
Museo Taurino ... 26 C6
Nuestra Señora de los Desamparados ... 27 C3
Orange Bikes ... (see 80)
Palacio del Marqués de Campo ... 28 C3
Palacio del Marqués de Dos Aguas ... (see 25)
Palau de la Generalitat ... 29 C3
Plaza Redonda ... 30 C4
Route 66 Idiomas ... 31 C4
Torres de Quart ... 32 A3
Torres de Serranos ... 33 C2
Town Hall ... 34 C5

SLEEPING
Ad Hoc ... 35 D2
Center Valencia ... 36 C2
Hilux Hotel ... 37 B3
Hôme Backpackers ... 38 A3
Hôme Youth Hostel ... 39 B3
Hostal Antigua Morellana ... 40 C3
Hotel Melia Inglés ... 41 C4
Indigo Youth Hostel ... 42 A4
Pensión París ... 43 C4
Petit Palace Bristol ... 44 C4
Purple Nest Hostel ... 45 D3
Red Nest Hostel ... 46 D4

EATING
Burdeos in Love ... 47 C3
En Bandeja ... 48 B4
Fresc Co ... 49 C5
La Lluna ... 50 A2
La Lola ... 51 C3
La Tastaolletes ... 52 B2
La Utielana ... 53 C4
Las Cuevas ... 54 C2
L'Hamadríada ... 55 A3
Luna Carmen ... 56 B2
Marisquería Civera ... 57 C5
Mattilda ... 58 B2
Mercado Central ... (see 21)
Palacio de la Bellota ... 59 C5
Seu-Xerea ... 60 C2

DRINKING
Café de las Horas ... 61 C2
Café Infanta ... 62 B3
Café-Bar Negrito ... 63 B3
Finnegan's ... 64 C3
Fox Congo ... 65 B3
Horchatería de Santa Catalina ... 66 C3
Horchatería el Siglo ... 67 C3
Johnny Maracas ... 68 B3
San Jaume ... 69 B3
The Lounge ... 70 B3
Xino Xano ... 71 B2

ENTERTAINMENT
Disco City ... 72 A3
Filmoteca ... 73 C4
Jimmy Glass ... 74 B2
La Claca ... 75 C4
Radio City ... 76 A3
Teatro Principal ... 77 C4
Teatro Rialto ... (see 73)

SHOPPING
Valencia Club de Fútbol Shop ... 78 D4

TRANSPORT
Do You Bike ... 79 B3
Orange Bikes ... 80 B4

(10am-8pm or 10pm Tue-Sun), pronounced 'ee-bam', houses an impressive permanent collection of 20th-century Spanish art and hosts excellent temporary exhibitions.

Cathedral

Valencia's **cathedral** (Map p608; adult/under 3yr/3-12yr incl audioguide €4/free/2.70; 10am-5.30pm or 6.30pm Mon-Sat, 2-5.30pm Sun) is a microcosm of the city's architectural history: the Puerta del Palau on the east side is pure Romanesque; the dome, tower and Puerta de los Apóstoles on Plaza de la Virgen are Gothic; the presbytery and main entrance on Plaza de la Reina are baroque; and there are a couple of Renaissance chapels inside.

Don't miss the recently revealed Italianate frescoes above the main altarpiece. In the flamboyant Gothic Capilla del Santo Cáliz, right of the main entrance, is what's claimed to be the **Holy Grail**, the chalice from which Christ sipped during the Last Supper. The next chapel north, La Capilla de San Francisco de Borja, has a pair of particularly sensitive Goyas.

Left of the main portal is the entrance to the **Miguelete bell tower** (adult/under 14yr €2/1; 10am-7.30pm). Climb the 207 steps of its spiral staircase for great city-and-skyline views.

As for over a thousand years, the **Tribunal de las Aguas** (Water Court) meets every Thursday exactly at noon outside the cathedral's Puerta de los Apóstoles. Here, local farmers' irrigation disputes are settled in Valenciano.

Plaza de la Virgen & Around

This busy plaza was once the forum of Roman Valencia, the axis where the main north–south and east–west highways met. Beside the cathedral is the church of **Nuestra Señora de los Desamparados** (Map p608; 7am-2pm & 4.30-9pm). Above the altar is a highly venerated statue of the Virgin, patron of the city. Opposite is the handsome 15th-century Gothic – and much amended – **Palau de la Generalitat** (Map p608), seat of government for the Valencia region. The reclining figure in the central fountain represents Río Turia, while the eight maidens with their gushing pots symbolise the main irrigation canals flowing from it.

Beneath the adjacent, interconnecting square of **La Almoina** (Map p608), the archaeological remains of the kernel of Roman, Visigoth and Islamic Valencia shimmer through a shallow veil of water. **Guided tours** (☎ 96 208 41 73; adult/under 7yr/7-16yr €2/free/1; 🕑 10am-2pm & 5-8pm Tue-Sat, 10am-3pm Sun) explore this underground area. Ring to book a visit in English.

Beside it, the **Cripta de la Cárcel de San Vicente Mártir** (Map p608; ☎ 96 394 14 17; Plaza del Arzobispo 1; adult/child €2/1, free Sat & Sun; 🕑 9.30am-2pm & 5.30-8pm Tue-Sat, 9.30am-2pm Sun) was reputedly used as a prison for the 4th-century martyr San Vicente. Although the crypt of this Visigoth chapel isn't particularly memorable in itself, it's worth taking in the multimedia show that presents Valencia's history and the saint's life and death. Reserve by phone or at the **Palacio del Marqués de Campo** (Map p608), just opposite, and ask for a showing in English.

Palacio del Marqués de Dos Aguas

A pair of wonderfully extravagant rococo caryatids prop up the main entrance surround of the **Palacio del Marqués de Dos Aguas** (Map p608). Inside, the **Museo Nacional de Cerámica** (Map p608; ☎ 96 351 35 12; Calle Poeta Querol 2; adult/child €2.40/1.20, free Sat afternoon & Sun; 🕑 10am-2pm & 4-8pm Tue-Sat, 10am-2pm Sun) displays ceramics from around the world – and especially of the renowned local production centres of Manises, Alcora and Paterna.

Plaza del Mercado

Facing each other across Plaza del Mercado are two emblematic buildings, each a masterpiece of its era. Pop into the 15th-century Gothic **Lonja** (Map p608; adult/child €2/1, free Sat & Sun; 🕑 10am-2pm & 4.30-8.30pm Mon-Sat, 10am-3pm Sun), an early Valencian commodity exchange, now a World Heritage site, with its striking colonnaded hall. And set aside time to prowl the **Mercado Central** (Map p608; Plaza del Mercado; 🕑 7.30am-2.30pm Mon-Sat), Valencia's Modernista covered market. Constructed in 1928, it's a swirl of smells, movement and colour. The **Mercado de Colón** (Map p606; Calle de Cirilo Amorós), also a market in its time and now colonised by boutiques and cafes, is an even finer Modernista building.

Torres de Serranos & Torres de Quart

Two imposing, twin-towered stone gates are all that remain of Valencia's old city walls. Once the main exit to Barcelona and the north, the 14th-century **Torres de Serranos** (Map p608; adult/child €2/1, free Sat & Sun; 🕑 9.30am-2pm & 5.30-9pm Tue-Sat, 9.30am-2pm Sun Apr-Sep, 10am-2pm & 4.30-8.30pm Tue-Sat, 10am-3pm Sun Oct-Mar) overlook the former bed of Río Turia. Further west, you can also clamber to the top of the 15th-century **Torres de Quart** (Map p608; admission free; same hr), which face towards Madrid and the setting sun. Up high, you can still see the pockmarks caused by French cannonballs during the 19th-century Napoleonic invasion.

Bioparc

Valencia's latest megaproject is its new **zoo** (☎ 902 25 03 40; www.bioparcvalencia.es in Spanish; Avenida Pio Baroja 3; adult/child €20/15; 🕑 10am-dusk), if that's not too old-fashioned a term for such a state of the art, ecofriendly space. Six years in gestation and costing 60 million euros, it let the public loose on its animals for the first time in 2008. Take bus 3, 81 or 95 or get off at the Nou d'Octubre metro stop.

Parks & Gardens

The **Jardines del Turia** (Maps p606 and p608) in the former riverbed are a 9km-long lung of green, a mix of playing fields, cycling, jogging and walking paths, fountains, lawns and playgrounds. See Lilliputian kids scrambling over a magnificent, ever-patient **Gulliver** (Map p606) east of the Palau de la Música.

Reaching down to the riverbed are the **Jardines del Real** (Royal Gardens; Map p606), usually called Los Viveros and another lovely spot for a stroll.

The **Jardín Botánico** (Map p606; Calle Quart 80; adult/under 7yr €1/free; 🕑 10am-dusk Tue-Sun), established in 1802, was Spain's first botanic garden. With mature trees and plants, an extensive cactus garden and a wary colony of feral cats, it's a shady, tranquil place to relax.

Beaches

Spread your towel on broad **Playa de la Malvarrosa** running into **Playa de las Arenas**, each bordered by the **Paseo Marítimo** promenade and a string of restaurants. One block back, lively bars and discos thump out the beat in summer. Take buses 1, 2 or 19, or the high-speed tram from Pont de Fusta or the Benimaclet Metro junction. Buses 20, 21 and 22 are additional summer-only services.

Playa El Salér, 10km south, is backed by shady pine woods. **Autocares Herca** (☎ 96 349 12 50; www.autocaresherca.com in Spanish) buses run between Valencia and Perelló hourly (half-

LAS FALLAS

The exuberant, anarchic swirl of **Las Fallas de San José** – fireworks, music, festive bonfires and all-night partying – is a must if you (together with some two million other visitors) are in Spain between 12 and 19 March.

The *fallas* themselves are huge sculptures of papier mâché on wood (with, increasingly, environmentally damaging polystyrene), built by teams of local artists. In 2007, the combined cost of their construction was an estimated 9.75 million euros. Each neighbourhood sponsors its own *falla*, and when the town wakes after the *plantà* (overnight construction of the *fallas*) on the morning of 16 March, more than 350 have been erected. Reaching up to 15m in height, with the most expensive costing more than €120,000 (oh yes, we've got those eurozeros right!), these grotesque, colourful effigies satirise celebrities, current affairs and local customs.

Around-the-clock festivities include street parties, paella-cooking competitions, parades, open-air concerts, bullfights and nightly free firework displays. Valencia considers itself the pyrotechnic capital of the world and each day at 2pm from 1 to 19 March a *mascletà* (over five minutes of deafening thumps and explosions) shakes the window panes of Plaza del Ayuntamiento.

After midnight on the final day each *falla* goes up in flames – backed by yet more fireworks.

hourly in summer), calling by El Salér village (€1.10, 30 minutes). They stop (look for the Herca sign) at the junction of Gran Vía de las Germanias and Calle Sueca, beside Plaza de Cánovas and in front of the Ciudad de las Artes y Las Ciencias.

Other Attractions

The **Estación del Norte** (Map p608) is another impressive Modernista building. Opened in 1917, the train station's main foyer is decorated with ceramic mosaics and murals – and mosaic 'bon voyage' wishes in all major European languages.

The bijou **Museo del Patriarca** (Map p608; Calle la Nave 1; admission €1.20; 11am-1.30pm) is particularly strong on Spanish and Flemish Renaissance painting, including canvases by El Greco, Juan de Juanes and Ribalta.

Each Fallas, only one of the thousands of *ninots*, near-life-size figurines that strut and pose at the base of each *falla* (the huge statues of papier-mâché on wood), is saved from the flames by popular vote. Those reprieved over the years are displayed in the **Museo Fallero** (Map p606; Plaza Monteolivete 4; adult/child €2/1, free Sat & Sun; 10am-2pm & 4.30-8.30pm Tue-Sat, 10am-3pm Sun).

The small **Museo Taurino** (Map p608; Pasaje Doctor Serra 10; admission free; 10am-8pm Tue-Sun), behind Plaza de Toros, holds a collection of bullfighting memorabilia.

At the **Museo de Prehistoria** and **Museo de Etnología** (Map p608; ☎ 96 388 35 65; Calle Corona 36; admission free; 10am-8pm or 9pm Tue-Sun), which share premises usually called La Beneficencia, there's a wealth of finds from the Palaeolithic period, plus Roman and Iberian artefacts.

Baños del Almirante (Map p608; ☎ 605 275784; Calle Baños del Almirante 3-5; admission free; 10am-2pm & 6-8pm Tue-Sat, 10am-2pm Sun) are Arab-style baths, constructed in 1313, that functioned continuously as public bathing facilities until 1959. There's an excellent audiovisual presentation with optional English commentary every half-hour.

L'Iber, also called the **Museo de Soldaditos de Plomo** (Map p608; ☎ 96 391 86 75; Calle Caballeros 20-22; admission €4; 11am-2pm & 4-7pm Tue-Sat, 11am-2pm Sun) plausibly claims to be the world's largest collection of toy soldiers. The vast 4.7m x 2.8m set piece of the Battle of Almansa (1707) has more than 9000 combatants and cases teem with rank upon rank, battalion following battalion, of toy soldiers, each set resembling so many computer-generated clones.

Off Plaza de la Reina is **Iglesia de Santa Catalina** (Map p608), its striking 18th-century baroque belfry one of the city's best-known landmarks. Nearby, stalls in the small circular **Plaza Redonda** (Map p608) sell bits and bobs, buttons and bows, clothes and locally made crafts and ceramics. At the time of writing, it was undergoing an elaborate facelift.

WALKING TOUR

From **Plaza de la Virgen** (**1**; p609), head west along Calle Caballeros (Street of the Knights), the main thoroughfare of medieval Valencia. Turn right into Calle Serranos and continue to **Plaza de los Fueros (2)**, overshadowed by the **Torres de Serranos** (**3**; p610). Go left into Calle

WALK FACTS

Start/Finish Plaza de la Virgen
Distance 3km
Duration 1½ hours comfortably

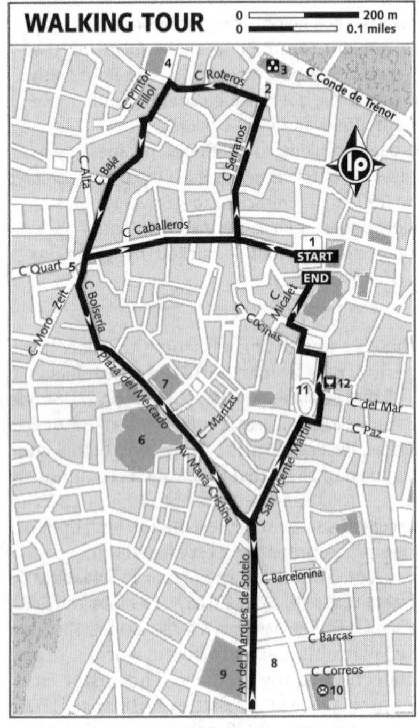

Roteros, sleepy by day but a buzz of restaurants and bars after dark, and continue to **Plaza del Carmen (4)**, where the baroque facade of the old convent and the Palacio de Pineda stare each other out. Turn left (south) into Calle Pintor Fillol, which becomes Calle Baja (Valenciano: Baix, Low St). This and its twin, Calle Alta (Valenciano: Dalt – you've guessed it, High St), were also important medieval thoroughfares. At **Plaza del Tossal** (**5**; Square of the Hill, though the gradient's all but imperceptible) you can take a drink in one of the swanky bars, then either short-cut eastwards back along Calle Caballeros (admiring the fine mansions as you go) or continue down Calle Bolsería. Turn left into Plaza del Mercado and allow yourself time to browse around the **Mercado Central** (**6**; p615) and **Lonja** (**7**; p610).

Bear right at the junction with Calle San Vicente Mártir to detour briefly and take in **Plaza del Ayuntamiento (8)**, where the neoclassical **town hall (9)** looks across to the neobaroque splendour of Valencia's **main post office (10)**. Dip inside to savour its interior – more like a theatre foyer than a place to post a letter – and raise your eyes to the magnificent leaded-glass dome. Returning, head north up Calle San Vicente Mártir to **Plaza de la Reina (11)**, wide and a bit soulless – something that can't be said for **Finnegan's** (**12**; p617). With the walk's end almost in sight, you might want to reward yourself with a Guinness at this Irish bar. Otherwise, slip up the lane that runs to the left (west) of the cathedral to rejoin your starting point.

COURSES

Cooking

Escuela de Cocina Eneldo (Map p606; ☎ 96 395 54 57; www.cocinaeneldo.com in Spanish; Calle Joaquín Costa 45) Cooking's a very demonstrable discipline, so even if your Spanish isn't up to scratch, pitch in and get your hands floury.

Dance

Academia de Baile Maria Cruz Alcalá (Map p606; ☎ 96 334 42 31; www.maricruzalcala.com in Spanish; Calle Salamanca 20) Runs three dance schools around Valencia city.

Centre Professional de Dansa Valencià (Map p606; ☎ 96 385 80 54; www.centreprofessionaldansavalencia.com in Spanish; Calle Calixto III 11-13) Offers everything from traditional Spanish to belly dancing.

Estudio de Danza Maria Carbonell (Map p606; ☎ 96 380 58 43; www.mariacarbonell.com in Spanish; Calle Cádiz 54) Forming dancers for over 20 years.

Language

Babylon Idiomas (Map p608; ☎ 96 315 33 32; www.babylon-idiomas.com; Calle San Vicente Mártir 2)

Intereuropa (Map p608; ☎ 96 394 49 95; www.intereuropa.es; 1st fl, Plaza del Ayuntamiento 5)

Route 66 Idiomas (Map p608; ☎ 96 342 73 68; www.route66idiomas.com; Calle Moratín 15) Hey, it even throws in free bike hire for the duration of your course.

VALENCIA FOR CHILDREN

Beaches (p610), of course: nearest is the combined beach of Malvarrosa and Las Arenas (the latter meaning 'sand'), a shortish bus or tram ride from the centre. The high-speed tram is fun: feel the G-force as it surges along. The other great playground, year-round, is the diverted Río Turia's former 9km riverbed. Of its formal playgrounds, **Gulliver** (p610) just asks to be clambered all over.

Within the **Jardines del Real** (Los Viveros gardens, p610), there's a miniature road system, complete with traffic signs and bridges. You have to take your own bike, trike or pedal car, but it's great fun – and a learning experience too. The **Jardín Botánico** (p610) is altogether more peaceful; mind the cactuses and feral cats, play hide-and-seek among the trees and keep an eye out for frogs in the fountain.

Of the **Ciudad de las Artes y las Ciencias'** diversions (p607), the Oceanogràfic, with more than 45,000 aquatic beasts and plants, has something for all ages. The science museum, reasonably documented in English, is more for over-12s (we've seen primary-school kids innocently and casually wrecking the hands-on exhibits), while the IMAX cinema offers thrills for all. The fun is far from free, however, so do research the range of family and combined tickets.

TOURS

Bicycle Tours

Valencia Guías (Map p606; ☎ 96 385 17 40; www.valenciaguias.com; Paseo de la Pechina 32) conducts 3½-hour guided bicycle tours (€25 including rental) of Valencia in English, leaving from its premises at 10am. It will turn out daily and requires a minimum of only two cyclists.

Orange Bikes (Map p608; ☎ 96 391 75 51; www.orangebikes.net; Calle Editor Manuel Aguilar 1) runs similar guided visits and also rents out audioguides to the city (€10).

Bus Tours

Valencia Bus Turístico (☎ 96 341 44 00; www.valenciabusturistic.com; adult/under 7yr/7-11yr €14/free/6) runs 90-minute city bus tours with a recorded commentary in eight languages. Buses leave from Plaza de la Reina, tickets are valid for 24 hours and you can hop off and on at five sites en route.

It also does a similar multilingual two-hour **tour** (adult//under 7yr/7-11yr €14/free/10) of **La Albufera** (p619), including a half-hour boat trip on the lagoon.

Walking Tours

Valencia Guías (Map p606; ☎ 96 385 17 40; www.valenciaguias.com; Paseo de la Pechina 32) does two-hour walking tours in Spanish and English (adult/child €15/7.50), leaving Plaza de la Reina tourist office at 10am each Saturday.

FESTIVALS & EVENTS

March/April

Las Fallas See the boxed text, p611.

Semana Santa Elaborate Easter Holy Week processions in the seaside district of La Malvarrosa.

Fiesta de San Vicente Ferrer Colourful parades and miracle plays performed around town on the Sunday after Easter.

May

Fiesta de la Virgen The effigy of the Virgen de los Desamparados, hemmed in by fervent believers struggling to touch her, makes the short journey across Plaza de la Virgen to the cathedral on the second Sunday of May.

June

Corpus Christi Celebrated with an elaborate procession and mystery plays on the ninth Sunday after Easter.

Día de San Juan From 23 to 24 June, Midsummer's Day is celebrated; thousands mark the longest day with bonfires on the beach.

July

Feria de Julio Performing arts, brass-band competitions, bullfights, fireworks and a 'battle of the flowers' in the second half of July.

October

Día de la Comunidad Commemorates the city's 1238 liberation from the Arabs on 9 October.

Festival of Mediterranean Cinema A week of films from around the Mediterranean.

Valencia Bienial Held in October to November in odd-numbered years, this is a festival of modern visual arts with exhibitions all over town.

SLEEPING

Budget

Valencia is particularly well endowed with well-priced and well-run private hostels.

Red Nest Hostel (Map p608; ☎ 96 342 71 68; www.nesthostelsvalencia.com; Calle Paz 36; dm €14-21, d €41-65, q €68-100) This hugely welcoming hostel has brightly decorated rooms ranging from doubles to dorms accommodating 12.

Purple Nest Hostel (Map p608; ☎ 96 353 25 61; Plaza Tetuan 5; dm €14-21, d €41-65, q €68-100; ❄) Red Nest's big brother, slightly more sophisticated and just round the corner, observes the same rates. All rooms have air-con and some (specify when you reserve) come with en suite bathroom. Its bar has three kinds of draught beer including Guinness.

Hôme Backpackers (Map p608; ☎ 96 391 37 97; www.likeathome.net; Calle Santa Cristina s/n; dm €17.80; 💻)

This, the simplest of the Hôme team's three excellent budget hostels, each with self-catering facilities, has 170 beds and a large roof terrace for chilling out or soaking in the sun.

Pensión París (Map p608; ☎ 96 352 67 66; www.pensionparis.com; 1st & 3rd fl, Calle Salvá 12; basic s/d/tr €22/32/48, d/tr with shower €38/51, d with bathroom €40) Welcoming, with spotless rooms – most with corridor bathrooms, some with en suite facilities – this family-run option on a quiet street is the antithesis of the crowded, pack-'em-in hostel.

Hostal Antigua Morellana (Map p608; ☎ 96 391 57 73; www.hostalam.com; Calle En Bou 2; s €45-55, d €55-65; ✱) The friendly, family-run 18-room Hostal Antigua Morellana is tucked away near the central market. Occupying a renovated 18th-century *posada* (a place where wealthier merchants bringing their produce to the nearby food market could spend the night), it has cosy, good-sized rooms, most with balconies.

Other recommended budget choices:

Indigo Youth Hostel (Map p608; ☎ 96 315 39 88; www.indigohostel.com; Calle Guillem de Castro 64; dm €14-21) Independent and friendly.

Hôme Youth Hostel (Map p608; ☎ 96 391 62 29; www.likeathome.net; Calle Lonja 4; dm €15-24)

Center Valencia (Map p608; ☎ 96 391 49 15: www.center-valencia.com; Calle Samaniego 18; r €17-22) Valencia's newest budget choice.

Hilux (Map p608; ☎ 96 391 46 91; www.feetuphostels.com; Calle Cadirers 11; d incl breakfast €48-60)

Midrange

Since Valencia is a business centre, big hotels struggle to fill rooms at weekends and most offer fat weekend and high-summer discounts.

Hotel Melia Inglés (Map p608; ☎ 96 351 64 26; www.meliaingles.solmelia.com; Calle Marqués de Dos Aguas 6; r €60-130; ⊠ ✱ 💻) In a stylishly renovated, much modified 18th-century palace, the Hotel Inglés has 63 rooms, each with parquet floor, dark, stained-wood bedhead and a large glass-topped working table. The congenial cafe and some bedrooms overlook the glorious rococo main entrance to the Palacio del Marqués de Dos Aguas.

Petit Palace Germánias (Map p606; ☎ 96 351 36 38; www.hthotels.com; Calle Sueca 14; r €65-120; P ⊠ ✱ 💻) Younger sister to Petit Palace Bristol, this equally nice boutique hotel, just that little bit further from the centre, has equally seductive charms. Guests can borrow bikes for free. Parking is €14.

Rôôms de Luxe (Map p606; ☎ 96 381 53 39; www.roomsdeluxe.com; Avenida del Instituto Obrero 20; d/tr incl breakfast from €70/100; P ⊠ ✱ 💻) Free wi-fi and parking. Scarcely a stone's throw from the City of Arts and Sciences, this place indeed justifies the label de luxe. Each of its 28 rooms has been designed with huge flair and originality by a different artist. Scan the website and pick the one that appeals to you most.

Ad Hoc (Map p608; ☎ 963 91 91 40; www.adhochoteles.com; Calle Boix 4; s €76-101, d €89-125; ✱) Friendly, welcoming Ad Hoc offers comfort and charm deep within the old quarter and also runs a splendid small restaurant. The late-19th-century building has been restored to its former splendour with great sensitivity, revealing original ceilings, mellow brickwork and solid wooden beams.

Petit Palace Bristol (Map p608; ☎ 96 394 51 00; www.hthoteles.com; Calle Abadía San Martín 3; s €80-120, d €90-140; ⊠ ✱ 💻) Hip, minimalist and friendly, this lovely boutique hotel, a comprehensively made-over 19th-century mansion, retains the best of its past and does a particularly scrumptious buffet breakfast. It's well worthwhile paying €10 extra for one of the superior doubles on the top floor with its broad wooden terrace giving panoramic views over the city.

Chill Art Jardín Botánico (Map p606; ☎ 96 315 40 12; www.hoteljardinbotanico.com; Calle Doctor Peset Cervera 6; s €94-133, d €94-149; ⊠ ✱) Welcoming and mega-cool, this intimate – only 16 rooms – hotel is furnished with great flair. Candles flicker in the lounge and each bedroom has original art work. Understandably, the Instituto Valenciano de Arte Moderno (IVAM), an easy walk away, regularly selects it as a venue for its guests.

Room Mate María Atarazanas (☎ 96 320 30 10; www.room-matehotels.com; Plaza Tribunal de las Aguas 5; r €70-130) The cream walls and fabrics of each bedroom contrast with the dark, stained woodwork. Sybaritic bathrooms have deep tubs with hydromassage and the broad shower-head is as big as a discus. From the breezy rooftop terrace there's a magnificent wrap-around view of sea and city.

If you prefer to be independent, **40flats.com** (Map p606; ☎ 96 335 67 93; www.40flats.com; Avenida Instituto Obrero de Valencia 20; 2-/4-/6-person apt €85/125/145; P ✱), scarcely a stone's throw from the City of Arts and Sciences, has brand-new, fully equipped apartments with no minimum rental period.

Top End

Neptuno (☎ 96 356 77 77; www.hotelneptunovalencia.com; Paseo de Neptuno 2; s €110-180, d €110-225; P) Neptuno, ultramodern and ultracool, overlooks the beach and America's Cup port. Ideal for mixing cultural tourism with a little beach frolicking.

Palau del Mar (Map p606; ☎ 96 316 28 84; www.hospes.es; Calle Navarro Reverter 14; r €160-350;) Created by the merging of two elegant 19th-century mansions (with 18 very similar rooms, newly constructed, surrounding a tranquil internal garden), this boutique hotel, all black, white, soft fuscous and beige, is cool, confident and ultramodern. There's a sauna, Jacuzzi – and a pool scarcely bigger than your bathtub.

EATING

Valencia is the capital of La Huerta, a fertile coastal agricultural plain that supplies the city with delightfully fresh fruit and vegetables.

Around Plaza del Ayuntamiento

En Bandeja (Map p608; ☎ 96 394 06 95; Calle San Vicente Mártir 24; breakfasts €3, lunches €10.20; 8.30am-9pm Mon-Sat Sep-May, 8.30am-9pm Mon-Fri Jun-Aug) This relaxed self-service place does excellent-value continental breakfasts and lunches (lunch price includes a drink and coffee).

Fresc Co (Map p608; ☎ 96 310 63 88; Calle Felix Pizcueta 6; buffet lunches €8.50, mains €10) Fresc Co's all-you-can eat buffet offers a veritable kitchen garden of salad items and a choice of pasta or pizza. With its bare, mellow brickwork, it's an agreeable, excellent-value place, though you're not encouraged to linger once dessert's over.

La Utielana (Map p608; ☎ 96 352 94 14; Plaza Picadero dos Aguas 3; menú €10, meals €15; lunch & dinner Mon-Fri, lunch Sat) Tucked away off Calle Prócida and not easy to track down, La Utielana well merits a minute or two's sleuthing. Very Valencian, it packs in the crowds, drawn by the wholesome fare and exceptional value for money. Arrive early as it doesn't take reservations.

There's a cluster of superb upmarket seafood restaurants along pedestrianised Calle Mosén Femades, including **Palacio de la Bellota** (Map p608; ☎ 96 351 53 61; Calle Mosén Femades 7; Mon-Sat) and **Marisquería Civera** (Map p608; ☎ 96 352 97 64; Calle Mosén Femades 10). For both, count on at least €50 per head, including wine.

A visit to the magnificent covered market, the **Mercado Central** (Map p608; Plaza del Mercado; 7.30am-2.30pm Mon-Sat), is a must, even if you only browse.

Around Plaza de la Virgen

Las Cuevas (Map p608; ☎ 96 391 71 96; Calle Samaniego 9; tapas €3-7) 'The Caves', low-ceilinged, semi-basement and aptly named, carries a huge range of fresh tapas.

La Lola (Map p608; ☎ 96 391 80 45; Subida del Toledano 8; mains €17-22; Tue-Sat) Up an alley beside the cathedral, here's a very suave number where cool jazz warbles. The all-white walls and furnishings offset stark reds, blacks and giant polka dots, and the food (save a space for one of the gooey desserts) is equally innovative. There's live flamenco on Thursday and Friday nights and, on Saturday, a DJ spins lounge, electronic and pop.

Seu-Xerea (Map p608; ☎ 96 392 40 00; Calle Conde Almodóvar 4; menú €22-49, mains €20-24; lunch & dinner Mon-Fri, dinner Sat) This welcoming restaurant is favourably quoted in almost every English-language press article about Valencia city. Its creative, regularly changing à la carte menu features dishes both international and rooted in Spain.

Burdeos in Love (Map p608; ☎ 96 391 43 50; Calle del Mar 4; menú €35-45, mains €17-21; lunch & dinner Mon-Fri, lunch Sat) At this smart restaurant with its modern, clean-lined decor, the *menú degustación* (tasting menu; €45) is particularly good value and there's an impressive wine list, especially of Spanish reds.

WHAT'S COOKING IN VALENCIA?

Arroz (rice) underwrites much Valencian cuisine – such as paella, first simmered here and exported to the world. For a more original experience, try alternatives such as *arroz a banda* (simmered in a fish stock); *arroz negro* (with squid, including its ink); *arroz al horno* (baked in the oven). For *fideuá,* Valencian cooks simply substitute noodles for rice.

Other regional specialities include *horchata,* an opaque sugary drink made from pressed *chufas* (tiger nuts), into which you dip large finger-shaped buns called *fartons.* Finally, despite its name, *Agua de Valencia* couldn't be further from water. The local take on Buck's Fizz, it mixes *cava* (sparkling Champagne-method wine), orange juice, gin and vodka.

Elsewhere in El Barrio del Carmen

La Tastaolletes (Map p608; ☎ 96 392 18 62; Calle Salvador Giner 6; tapas €5-9, mains €8-10; lunch & dinner Tue-Sat, dinner Mon; V) This tiny place does a creative range of vegetarian tapas. Pleasantly informal, it's worth visiting for the friendly atmosphere and good, wholesome food created from quality prime ingredients. Salads are frondy and the cheesecake with stewed fruits, a dream.

Luna Carmen (Map p608; ☎ 96 336 62 13; Plaza del Carmen; menú €9, mains €10-18; Mon-Sat) Pick at a tapa or two, select a salad or go for a full meal either within the stylish, minuscule interior or outside, overlooking Plaza del Carmen. Dishes are creative and the wine list is short but particularly well chosen. At lunchtime, it offers a magnificent-value €9 *menú* (set menu).

L'Hamadríada (Map p608 ☎ 96 326 08 91; www.hamadriada.com in Spanish; Plaza Vicente Iborra 3; lunch menú €10, menú degustación €26-40; lunch daily, dinner Wed-Sat) Staff are well-informed and attentive at L'Hamadríada (the wood nymph), a local favourite where everybody seems to know everyone else. Down a short, blind alley, this slim white rectangle of a place does an innovative midday *menú*, perfectly simmered rice dishes that change daily, and grills where the meat, like the vegetables, is of prime quality.

Mattilda (Map p608; ☎ 96 382 31 68; Calle Roteros 21; menú €11, mains €15-19; lunch & dinner Mon-Fri, dinner Sat) The decor is stylish and modern at Mattilda, run by a cheery young team. There's an imaginative à la carte selection and a particularly good-value lunch *menú*.

La Lluna (Map p608; ☎ 96 392 21 46; Calle San Ramón 23; meals around €15; Mon-Sat; V) It's smoking on the top floor, smoke-free downstairs and the compromise works well at La Lluna. Friendly and full of regulars, with walls of clashing tilework, it's been serving quality, reasonably priced vegetarian fare (including a superb-value four-course lunch menu at €7) for over 25 years.

Las Arenas

At weekends, locals in their hundreds head for Las Arenas, just north of the port, where a long line of restaurants overlooking the beach all serve up authentic paella in a three-course meal costing around €15.

Lonja del Pescado (☎ 96 355 35 35; Calle Eugenia Viñes 243; meals around €20; dinner Tue-Fri, lunch & dinner Sat & Sun Mar-Oct, lunch & dinner Sat & Sun Nov-Feb) One block back from the beach at Malvarrosa, this busy, informal place in what's little more than an adorned tin shack offers unbeatable value for fresh fish. Grab an order form as you enter and fill it in at your table.

La Pepica (☎ 96 371 03 66; Paseo Neptuno 6; meals around €25; lunch & dinner Mon-Sat, lunch Sun) More expensive than its competitors and run for over a century by three generations of the same family, La Pepica, renowned for its rice dishes and seafood, is where Ernest Hemingway, among many other luminaries, once strutted. Between courses, browse through the photos and tributes that plaster the walls.

our pick **Tridente** (☎ 96 371 03 66; Paseo Neptuno; menú €45-65, mains €22-30) Begin with an aperitif on the broad beachfront terrace of Tridente, restaurant of Neptuno hotel (p615), then move inside, where filtered sunlight bathes its soothing cream decor. There's an ample à la carte selection but you won't find details of the day's *menús* in front of you – they're delivered orally by the maître, who speaks good English. Dishes with their combinations of colours and blending of sweet and savoury are creative and delightfully presented and portions are generous.

DRINKING

Fuelled by a large student population, Valencia's nightlife has a justified reputation way beyond its borders.

The Barrio del Carmen has both the grungiest and grooviest collection of bars. The other major area is around the university; Avenidas de Aragón and Blasco Ibáñez and surrounding streets have enough bars and *discotecas* (clubs) to keep you busy beyond sunrise.

Another zone well worth checking out is around the Mercado de Abastos, while in summer the new port area and Malvarrosa leap to life.

Barrio del Carmen

'El Carmé' has everything from designer pubs to grungy thrash-metal haunts. On weekends, Calle Caballeros, the main street, seethes with punters seeking *la marcha* (the action).

Cafe-Bar Negrito (Map p608; Plaza del Negrito) At this bar, which traditionally attracts a more left-wing, intellectual clientele, the crowd spills out onto the square.

Xino Xano (Map p608; Calle Alta 28) The genial owner, a well-known DJ in his own right, picks from his collection of dub, reggae and funk.

Plaza del Tossal is rimmed by sophisticated bars. The interior of **Café Infanta** (Map p608) is a clutter of cinema memorabilia. The first floor of **San Jaume** (Map p608), a converted pharmacy, is all quiet crannies and poky passageways. Both have great people-watching terraces.

On Calle Caballeros are a couple of bars for beautiful people: **Johnny Maracas** (Map p608; Calle Caballeros 39) is a suave salsa place with fish tanks on the bar. **Fox Congo** (Map p608; Calle Caballeros 35), also great for dancing, has a cool back-lit alabaster bar and walls clad in leather and sheet-metal. Wednesday is student night.

Other Areas

Café de las Horas (Map p608; Calle Conde de Almodóvar 1) This place offers high baroque, tapestries, music of all genres, candelabras and a long list of exotic cocktails.

Finnegan's (Map p608; Plaza de la Reina) Longest established of Valencia's several Irish bars, it's a popular meeting place for English speakers.

The Lounge (Map p608; ☎ 96 391 80 94; Calle Estameñaría Vieja 2; ⏲ 5pm-1.30am) A true Irish bar without a false fiddle or unread copy of James Joyce in sight, this friendly place with an internet terminal is where locals and visitors interact with weekly conversational interchanges – and, if you hit the right night, speed dating!

Two traditional places to sample *horchata* (p615) in the heart of town are **Horchatería de Santa Catalina** (Map p608) and **Horchatería el Siglo** (Map p608), facing each other in eternal rivalry on Plaza Santa Catalina.

Near the Mercado de Abastos (Map p606), just west of the town centre, Calle Juan Lloréns (Map p606) and surrounding streets are another hip area where bars abound. Drop into **Akuarela** (Calle Juan Lloréns 49), strong on Spanish and international pop, **Café Carioca** (Calle Juan Lloréns 52), a dance-bar that plays eclectic pop, or, for a little Pharaonic frenzy, **Anubis** (Calle Juan Lloréns 34) with its ancient Egyptian theme.

ENTERTAINMENT

Best of the online 'what's on' guides is www.thisisvalencia.com. *La Turia* and *Que y Donde* are weekly guides in Spanish on sale at kiosks and newsagents. *Hello Valencia* (Spanish and English) and *24-7 Valencia* (in English) are free monthlies. Both are available in tourist offices and selected bars and clubs.

Dance Clubs & Discotecas

Radio City (Map p608; www.radiocityvalencia.com; Calle Santa Teresa 19; ⏲ 10pm-3.30am) Radio City is a great place to drop in for a drink and has a free disco that's good for post-bar dancing to salsa and house. There's live flamenco every Tuesday.

Disco City (Map p606; Calle Pintor Zariñena 16; ⏲ 1-7.30am) At weekends, Radio City's recently opened sibling beats until dawn to funk, break beats, electronic and house. Free entry until 3am, Thursday to Saturday.

Caribbean's (Map p606; Calle Bélgica 5; ⏲ Tue-Sat) Drinks (try the mojitos) are decently priced at this small, below-ground and usually jam-packed dance-bar that blends house, hip hop and R&B. Wednesday night is student night.

Mosquito (Map p606; Calle Polo y Peyrolón 11) DJs at this tiny box of a place dispense classic soul, R&B and a leavening of hip hop. However many shots you knock back, you'll know you're in the right place by the giant papier mâché mosquito hovering above its circular bar.

Rumbo 144 (Map p606; Avenida Blasco Ibáñez 146; ⏲ Thu-Sat Sep-Jul) This is a funky, large-floored place with a light show. Thursday is student night.

Bananas (☎ 96 178 17 06; Carretera Valencia-Alicante, El Romani; ⏲ from midnight Fri & Sat) Just about the maxiest maxidisco you'll ever party at, Bananas packs in dancers by the thousand, playing techno with a dash of house. Forget taxi lines: take the special train that leaves Estación del Norte at 1.15am, go Bananas and return on the early bird at 6.15am.

Dub Club (Map p606; www.dubclubvalencia.com in Spanish; Calle Jesús 91; ⏲ Thu-Sun) With the slogan 'We play music not noise', this is a bar that has great music: reggae (Thursday), dub, drum 'n' bass, funk and more. Tuesday is live jazz jamming night.

La Claca (Map p608; ☎ 669 325079; www.laclaca.com in Spanish; Calle San Vicente Mártir 3; ⏲ 7pm-3.30am) La Claca, central and popular with overseas visitors, has nightly DJs playing funk, hip hop and indie. Earmark Sunday evening for some of the best live flamenco in town.

L'Umbracle Terraza (Map p606; ⏲ from 8pm Jun-Sep) Within the City of Arts and Sciences, this a cool, sophisticated spot to spend a hot summer night. Catch the evening breeze under the stars on the terrace, then drop below to **Mya**, a top-of-the-line club with an awesome sound system. Admission (€18) covers both venues.

For more life after 3am, head to the university area along and around Avenidas Blasco Ibáñez and de Aragón. Most clubs have cover charges (€10 to €20), so keep an eye out for discounted passes, carried by many local bars.

Cinemas

Filmoteca (Map p608; ☎ 96 399 55 77; Plaza del Ayuntamiento; admission €1.50) This cinema, on the 4th floor of the Teatro Rialto building, screens undubbed classic, art-house and experimental films – and hasn't raised its admission price in 20 years! At the time of writing, it was temporarily housed in IVAM (p607) while its auditorium was being refurbished.

Valencia has two multiscreen cinemas that show exclusively undubbed films and share a website (www.cinesalbatrosbabel.com in Spanish): **Albatros** (Map p606; ☎ 96 393 26 77; Plaza Fray Luis Colomer) and **Babel** (Map p606; ☎ 96 362 67 95; Calle Vicente Sancho Tello 10). Admission prices are lower on Monday.

Theatre & Opera

Teatro Principal (Map p608; ☎ 96 353 92 00; Calle Barcas 15) is Valencia's main venue for theatre. **Palau de la Música** (Map p606; ☎ 96 337 50 20; www.palaudevalencia.com in Spanish; Paseo de la Alameda 30) hosts mainly classical music recitals. **Palau de les Arts Reina Sofía** (Map p606; ☎ 902 10 00 31; Autovía a El Saler) with its four auditoriums is a spectacular arts venue offering mostly opera.

Live Music

Black Note (Map p606; ☎ 96 393 36 63; Calle Polo y Peyrolón 15) Valencia city's most active jazz venue, Black Note has live music Monday to Thursday and good canned jazz, blues and soul on Friday and Saturday.

Jimmy Glass (Map p608; Calle Baja 28) Playing cool jazz from the owner's vast CD collection, Jimmy Glass also has regular live performances.

El Loco (Map p606; ☎ 96 326 05 26; www.lococlub.org in Spanish; Calle Erudito Orellena 12) This place puts on live concerts from Wednesday to Saturday.

Football

Valencia Club de Fútbol is the city's major football team. You can pick up a scarf, woolly hat, shirt or other memento from the club's **shop** (Calle Pintor Sorolla 24).

Valencia's other professional club, Levante, a minnow by comparison, has lately bounced in and out of the Spanish first division. Do take in a game – again down in the second, they need all the support they can get.

GETTING THERE & AWAY

Air

Valencia's **Aeropuerto de Manises** (☎ 96 159 85 00) is 10km west of the city centre along the A3, direction Madrid.

EasyJet flies to/from Bristol and London (Gatwick and Stansted), Ryanair serves Dublin, Liverpool and London (Stansted), Jet2.com flies to Leeds and Clickair to London (Heathrow). Other budget flights serve major European destinations such as Milan, Rome, Amsterdam and Geneva.

Boat

Acciona Trasmediterránea (☎ 902 45 46 45; www.acciona-trasmediterranea.es) operates car and passenger ferries to Mallorca and Ibiza. Buy your ticket online, at its Muelle de Poniente passenger terminal (☎ 96 316 48 59) or at any travel agency.

Bus

Valencia's **bus station** (Map p606; ☎ 96 346 62 66) is beside the riverbed on Avenida Menéndez Pidal. Bus 8 connects it to Plaza del Ayuntamiento.

Avanza (☎ 902 02 00 52; www.avanzabus.com) operates hourly bus services to/from Madrid (€23 to €29, four hours). **ALSA** (☎ 902 42 22 42; www.alsa.es) has up to 20 daily buses to/from Barcelona (€25.15 to €38.50, four to 5½ hours) and over 10 to Alicante (€17.60 to €20, 2½ hours), most passing by Benidorm (€14 to €15.75, 1¾ hours).

Train

From Valencia's Estación del Norte (Map p608), up to 10 Alaris express trains travel daily to/from Madrid (€43.50, 3½ hours), at least 12 to Barcelona (€35.30 to €39.60, three to 3¾ hours) and 10 to Alicante (€26.30, 1¾ hours).

Trains run every half-hour to Castellón (€3.95, up to one hour) via Sagunto (€2.60, 30 minutes).

GETTING AROUND

Valencia has an integrated bus, tram and metro network. EMT buses ply town routes, while MetroBus serves outlying towns and villages. Tourist offices stock maps for both services.

Tourist offices of **Turismo Valencia (VLC)** (p607) sell the Valencia Card (€8/14/18 per one/two/three days), entitling you to free urban travel and discounts at participating sights, shops and restaurants.

To/From the Airport

Metro line 5 connects the airport, downtown and the port. A taxi into the centre costs around €17 (there's a supplement of €2.50 above the metered fee for journeys originating at the airport).

Bicycle

Orange Bikes (Map p608; ☎ 96 391 75 51; www.orangebikes.net; Calle Editor Manuel Aguilar 1) rents out mountain bikes and town bikes (€9 to €12 per day, €45 to €55 per week) and electric bikes (€15 per day). The initiative of an engaging Anglo-Valenciano couple, this is also a good place to buy a secondhand cycle.

Valencia Guías (Map p606; ☎ 96 385 17 40; www.valenciaguias.com; Paseo de la Pechina 32) also rents out reliable town bikes (€15/36/56 per day/three days/week) from its office and from several other outlets around town (see the website for details).

Do You Bike (Map p608; ☎ 96 315 55 51; www.doyoubike.com; Plaza Horno San Nicolás; per day/week €15/40) also has a couple more outlets in the city.

Car & Motorcycle

Street parking is a real pain. There are large underground car parks beneath Plazas de la Reina and Alfonso el Magnánimo and, biggest of all, near the train station, covering the area between Calle Xàtiva and the Gran Vía.

Reliable local companies operating from Valencia airport include **Javea Cars** (☎ 96 579 3312; www.javeacars.com), **Solmar** (☎ 96 153 90 42; www.solmar.es) and **Victoria Cars** (☎ 96 583 02 54; www.victoriacars.com). They are usually substantially less expensive than the multinationals.

Public Transport

Most **EMT** (☎ 96 352 83 99; www.emtvalencia.es) buses run until about 10pm, with night services continuing on seven routes until around 1am. A single journey costs €1.20. *Estancos* (tobacconists) and some kiosks sell T1s (one-day pass; €3.30) or a 10-trip Bonobus (€5.65).

The high-speed tram is a pleasant way to get to the beach, paella restaurants of Las Arenas and the port. Pick it up at Pont de Fusta or where it intersects with the metro at Benimaclet.

Metro lines serve the outer suburbs. The closest stations to the centre are Ángel Guimerá, Xàtiva (for the train station), Colón and Pont de Fusta.

Taxi

Call **Radio-Taxi** (☎ 96 370 33 33) or **Valencia Taxi** (☎ 96 357 13 13).

AROUND VALENCIA CITY

La Albufera

About 15km south of Valencia, La Albufera is a huge freshwater lagoon separated from the sea by La Devesa, a narrow strip of sand dunes and pine forests. The lake and its shores are a breeding ground and sanctuary for migrating and indigenous birds. Keen birdwatchers flock to the **Parque Natural de la Albufera**, where around 90 species regularly nest while more than 250 others use it as a staging post on their migrations.

LA TOMATINA

Buñol? It'll make you see red.

The last Wednesday in August marks Spain's messiest and most bizarre festival. Held in Buñol, an otherwise drab industrial town 40km west of Valencia city, La Tomatina is a tomato-throwing orgy that attracts more than 40,000 visitors to a town of just 9000 inhabitants.

At precisely 11am a rocket swooshes skywards and over 100 tonnes of ripe, squishy tomatoes are tipped from trucks to the waiting crowd. For precisely one hour, until a second rocket is fired, everyone joins in a frenzied, cheerful, anarchic tomato battle. After being pounded with pulp, expect to be sluiced down with hoses by the local fire brigade.

The mayhem takes place on the town's main square and Calle del Cid. Most people come for the day, arriving on the morning train from Valencia and heading back in the afternoon. Don't forget a set of fresh clothes and perhaps a pair of goggles to protect the eyes.

Alternatively, you can watch the spectacle in dry comfort on Canal 9, Valencia's local TV channel.

Sunsets can be spectacular. You can take a boat trip out on the lagoon, joining the local fisherfolk, who use flat-bottomed boats and nets to harvest fish and eels from the shallow waters.

Surrounded by rice fields, La Albufera was the birthplace of paella. Every second house in the villages of **El Palmar** and **El Perellonet** is a restaurant, often run by ex- or part-time fisherfolk, serving paella and other rice and seafood dishes.

Autocares Herca buses for Playa El Salér (p610) are also good for La Albufera, and go on to either El Palmar (six daily) or Perello (hourly or half-hourly), further down the coast.

Sagunto

pop 63,400

You come to Sagunto (Valenciano: Sagunt), 25km north of Valencia, primarily to enjoy the spectacular panorama of the town, coast and green sea of orange groves from its hilltop castle complex. It's usually visited as a day or half-day excursion from Valencia.

Now a sleepy spot, Sagunto was once a thriving Iberian community (called – infelicitously, with hindsight – Arse) that traded with Greeks and Phoenicians. In 219 BC Hannibal besieged the town for eight months. The inhabitants were eventually wiped out and their town destroyed, sparking the Second Punic War between Carthage and Rome. Rome won, named the town Saguntum and set about rebuilding it.

From the train station it's a 15-minute walk to the **tourist office** (☎ 96 266 22 13; www.sagunt.es in Spanish; Plaza Cronista Chabret; 🕒 9am-2.30pm & 4.30-6.30pm Mon-Fri, 9am-2pm Sat & Sun). A further 10-minute uphill walk – detour into the small *judería,* the former Jewish quarter – brings you to the **Roman theatre**. Its modern 'restoration' is controversial but the acoustics remain outstanding and it's the main venue for Sagunto's three-week, open-air August **arts festival**.

Higher up, the stone walls of the **castle complex** (admission free; 🕒 10am-dusk Tue-Sat, 10am-2pm Sun) girdle the hilltop for almost a kilometre. Mostly in ruins, the rambling complex's seven sections each speak of a different period in Sagunto's long history.

GETTING THERE & AWAY

There are frequent trains between Valencia and Sagunto (one-way/return €2.60/4.15) and **AVSA** (☎ 96 267 14 16) runs a service (€2.15, half-hourly) from Valencia's bus station.

Segorbe

pop 8900 / elev 395m

Segorbe, 33km northwest of Sagunto and 56km from Valencia, has a substantial baroque **cathedral**. Within its more delicate Gothic cloister is a fine **ecclesiastical museum** (adult/child €3/2; 🕒 11am-1.30pm & 5-7pm Tue-Sun) with a sculpture of the Virgin and Child by Donatello and several colourful altarpieces.

At the western corner of the old town is a pair of cylindrical **towers** (guided visit adult/under 12yr €2/free; 🕒 noon Tue-Sun). The **Torre de la Carcel** for a time served as the town's lock-up while the town executioner, for those whose fate was even worse, lived nearby in the **Torre del Verdugo**.

The **Museo del Aceite** (☎ 96 471 20 45; Plaza Belluga 3; adult/under 12yr €2/free; 🕒 11am-2pm & 5-8pm Tue-Sun), in a former olive mill, is a multimedia tribute to the area's staple crop. Its shop is the place to pick up local hams, sausages, wines and, of course, virgin olive oil.

Segorbe's **medieval aqueduct**, of which a healthy hunk remains, brought water from the fountain of **La Esperanza** (Hope), from where it still springs eternal.

The town's major fiesta is its **Entrada de Toros y Caballos** (Entry of Bulls and Horses). Prompt at 2pm for seven days in the first half of September, skilled horsemen guide and prod the bulls down Calle Colón between two human walls of spectators. The **Centro de Interpretación de la Entrada de Toros y Caballos** (adult/under 12yr €2/free), sharing premises with the tourist office and observing the same hours, is a thrilling multilingual evocation of this rumbustious spectacle.

The **tourist office** (☎ 964 71 32 54; Calle Marcelino Blasco 3; 🕒 9am-2pm & 4-6pm Mon-Fri, 10am-2pm Sat, 10.30am-1.30pm Sun) is beside the town hall.

Requena

pop 20,400 / elev 690m

Until 1851, when its citizens decided to identify themselves with Valencia, Requena, 65km west of Valencia, was part of Castilla La Mancha. From its heart rears La Villa, its medieval nucleus, jumbled and irregular with twisting streets and blind alleys. Requena's former wealth came from silk; at one time it had 800 active looms, making this tiny town Spain's fourth-biggest producer. Nowadays it's primarily wine and livestock country, producing robust reds, sparkling *cavas* and rich hunks of sausage and spicy meats.

The second weekend in February marks the **Muestra del Embutido**, the Sausage Show; when an estimated 10,000kg of sausage and 25,000 servings of roast pork are gobbled up. In late August/early September, Requena's **Fiesta de la Vendimia** is 12 days of hearty bacchanal, celebrating the end of the grape harvest.

The **tourist office** (☎ 96 230 38 51; www.requena.es; Calle García Montés s/n; 9.30am-2pm Tue-Thu, 9.30am-2pm & 4-7pm or 5-8pm Fri & Sat) is below the main entrance to the old town. Ask for the English version of its *Sensaciones para Descubrir*, a helpful guide to La Villa.

SIGHTS

Enter the old quarter from its northern side, passing by the 10th-century Islamic **Torre del Homenaje**. Within the town walls are the Gothic **Santa María and San Salvador churches**, each with a magnificent if much weathered main portal, and sturdy noblemen's mansions such as the **Casa del Arte Mayor de la Seda** (Silk Guild House) and **Palacio del Cid**, destined to one day house the town's new wine museum.

Plaza de la Villa, also called Plaza Albornoz, hides in its intestines a network of interlinked cellars, once used as storerooms and, during strife, hideouts. **Guided visits** (adult/child €3/2; 3-6 times daily Tue-Sun) descend from the entrance on the eastern side of the old quarter's main square. Ask at the tourist office for times.

Ferevin (☎ 96 230 57 06; Calle Castillo; admission free; 11am-2pm Tue-Sun plus 5-7pm Sat), showroom for Utiel-Requena's association of wine producers, carries a good selection of the region's best vintages and has free sampling, each week highlighting a different bodega.

Requena's **Museo de Arte Contemporáneo** (☎ 96 230 30 32; Cuesta del Ángel 2; adult/child €3/2; 11am-2pm & 5.30-9.30pm Tue-Sat, 11am-2pm Sun) has canvases mainly by Spanish artists, including Picasso, Miró, Sempere, Tàpies and Dalí.

The **Museo Municipal** (Calle Carmen s/n; adult/child €3/2; 11am-2pm Tue-Sun) has a rich collection of traditional costumes, re-creations of a bourgeois town house and country dwellings and exhibits illustrating Requena's silk weaving past.

SLEEPING & EATING

On the old town's main square are two attractive sleeping options, each with a good restaurant.

Hôtel La Villa (☎ 96 230 03 74; www.hotellavillarestaurante.com in Spanish; Plaza Albornoz 8; s/d €36/55;) Until recently this hotel was a family home; now it offers 18 attractive rooms and a couple of suites, all furnished in rustic style.

Hôtel Doña Anita (☎ 96 230 53 47; www.tubal.net; Plaza Albornoz 15; s/d €45/72) Across the square, in a new building despite its antique air, Doña Anita offers greater luxury.

Mesón La Villa (☎ 96 230 21 32; Plaza Albornoz 13; mains €7.50-14) If you can't visit Requena's cellars, dine here and ask your hosts to let you see theirs (admission €1), briefly used by the local branch of the Inquisition (see the Papal coat of arms on the facade) to turn the screws on heretics.

Mesón del Vino (☎ 96 230 00 01; Avenida Arrabal 11; lunch & dinner Wed-Sun, lunch Mon; P) Down on the main street, drop in here for a drink or a full-scale meal at this splendidly democratic spot, tiled floor to ceiling. A huge stuffed bull's head greets everyone from local intellectuals to blue collar workers as they enter.

GETTING THERE & AWAY

Up to 14 buses (€4.20, one hour) and seven trains (€3.95, 1½ hours) run daily to/from Valencia.

COSTA DEL AZAHAR

Inland from the Costa del Azahar, 'the orange blossom coast', spread citrus groves, from whose headily scented flowers the region takes its name. The busy, developed – not always harmoniously – seaside resorts are enticing if you're after sun and sand. By contrast, the high hinterland, especially the wild, sparsely populated lands of the Maestrazgo, offer great walking, solitude and hearty mountain cooking.

Getting There & Away

The Valencia to Barcelona train line follows the coast and regional trains stop at all main towns. From Valencia, trains run every half-hour to Castellón de la Plana. At least six trains daily call at Benicàssim, Oropesa, Benicarló/Peñíscola and Vinaròs train stations.

CASTELLÓN DE LA PLANA

pop 147,700

The outskirts of Castellón de la Plana are grim, industrial and rambling, so the centre comes as a pleasant surprise if you penetrate to the heart of this commercial town.

Orientation & Information

Plaza Mayor and, just to its south, Plaza Santa Clara, form the nucleus of what matters to the visitor. Bus and train stations, one above the other, are about 1km northwest, beyond leafy Parque Ribalta.

Main tourist office (☎ 964 35 86 88; Plaza María Agustina 5; 9am-7pm Mon-Fri, 10am-2pm Sat Jul-Aug, 9am-2pm & 4-7pm Mon-Fri, 10am-2pm Sat Sep-Jun)

Sights

The **Museo de Bellas Artes** (☎ 964 72 75 00; Avenida Hermanos Bou 28; admission free; 10am-8pm Mon-Sat, 10am-2pm Sun) is in a striking award-winning contemporary building. Highlights are its large ceramics section, reflecting the region's major industry, two magnificently wrought silver crosses and a set of 10 magnificent canvases by Zurbarán.

Two other galleries that show temporary exhibitions also impress by their architecture. The **Espai d'Art Contemporani** (☎ 96 472 35 40; Calle Prim s/n; admission free) is a dazzling piece of contemporary design. By contrast, the freshly and sensitively restored **Llotja del Cánem** (Calle Caballeros 1), in the shadow of the cathedral, brings new life to what was originally Castellón's hemp exchange.

From Plaza Mayor, bordered by the early 18th-century town hall and the busy covered market, thrusts the long finger of **El Fadrí** (1604), an octagonal bell tower and symbol of the city. Beside the tower is the reconstructed **Concatedral de Santa María**, shattered in the civil war and now restored to its original state.

El Grau de Castellón, Castellón's port and 4km east of the centre, handles this industrial region's exports as well as the local fishing fleet. The beaches start north of here.

Sleeping & Eating

Hostal La Esperanza (☎ 964 22 20 31; Calle Trinidad 37; basic s/d/tr €19/32/48) This welcoming *hostal* (budget hotel) has spotless rooms with corridor facilities above a cosy, family-run bar-restaurant (*menú* €8; open Monday to Saturday) with a great range of tapas. Phone first, as the owners have serious thoughts of retirement.

Hotel Intur Castellón (☎ 964 22 50 00; www.intur.com in Spanish; Calle Herrero 20; r €60-€75; P ⊠ ❄ 💻) Although stark from the outside, there's a bright, spacious central atrium within, onto which give, receding upwards, each of the 120 rooms. Weekend rates and summer tariffs are particular bargains. Parking is €10.

Julivert (☎ 964 23 52 72; Calle Caballeros 41; menú €9.80; 8.30am-4.30pm Mon-Thu, 8.30am-4.30pm & 8.30pm-12.30am Fri & Sat; V) This tiny place does a good three-course *menú* with vegetarian option.

La Casita de Gredos (☎ 964 22 09 33; Calle Gracia 26; menú €21, mains €14-23; lunch Mon-Sat, dinner Fri & Sat) With an enticing lunch *menú* that changes daily and creative fish and meat dishes based upon fresh local produce, this long, low, welcoming place is renowned for its *bacalao* (dried and salted cod) dishes and select wine list. Reservations essential.

La Cambra dels Vins (Calle Caballeros 24; Mon-Fri & morning Sat) carries a carefully chosen selection of Spanish wines – malt whiskies too – plus exotic cans and jars of picnic enhancers. **Carnicería Charcutería Miguel** (73 Calle Navarra) is another treasure chest of wines, honeys, pâtés and (rare in Spain) vintage cheeses.

With three busy restaurants around town, **Mesón Navarro** (Calle Amadeo ☎ 964 25 09 66; Calle Amadeo I 8; Calle Sanchis Abella ☎ 964 26 11 33; Calle Sanchis Abella 4; Plaza Tetuán ☎ 964 21 31 15; Plaza Tetuán 26) is excellent value (mains €9 to €13), especially for meat dishes.

Getting There & Around

Long-distance services use the **bus station** (☎ 964 24 07 78). Frequent buses for Benicàssim set out from Plaza Fadrell. For both Valencia and resorts to the north, except for Benicàssim, trains are swifter and more frequent.

AROUND CASTELLÓN DE LA PLANA

Vilafamés

pop 1500

What draws visitors to Vilafamés, a hillside village 26km north of Castellón, is its excellent **Museo de Arte Contemporáneo** (☎ 964 32 91 52; Calle Diputació 20; adult/child €2/free; 10am-1.30pm & 4-7pm Tue-Sun). Within the 15th-century Palacio de la Bailía, worth a visit in its own right, is a wonderful, highly eclectic collection of contemporary paintings and sculpture.

The **tourist office** (☎ 964 32 99 70; www.villafames.com in Spanish; Plaza del Ayuntamiento 2) is beside the town hall.

The village is an agreeable clutter of whitewashed houses and civic buildings in rust-red stone. From Plaza de la Sangre, steep steps take you up to the ruined **castle** and a sensational panorama.

Each of the 11 rooms of recently opened **L'Antic Portal** (☎ 964 32 93 84; www.anticportal.com in Spanish; Calle de la Fuente 6; r €70; ⊠ ❄) is pleasingly contemporary in design. Within the shell of an antique building (a huge hunk of original rock contributes to one of the walls), each has a small balcony. It belongs to neighbouring **Hotel El Rullo** (☎ 964 32 93 84; Calle de la Fuente 2; s/d €22/42), a modest family hotel that offers cheaper, simpler rooms and does an economical *menú*.

Montanejos

pop 400 / elev 460m

It's a spectacular drive along the CV20 from Castellón up Río Mijares gorges to this resort, spa village and rock-climbing base at the heart of the Sierra de Espadán. Surrounded by craggy, pine-clad mountains, its cool, fresh mountain air attracts summer visitors in plenty and there's bathing for free in the 25°C waters of **Fuente de los Baños**, 1km north.

The **tourist office** (☎ 964 13 11 53; Carretera Tales s/n; www.montanejos.com in Spanish) is within the **balneario** (spa; ☎ 902 74 74 03), which draws its waters from the natural springs of Fuente de los Baños and offers a huge range of watery health-inducing treatments.

Geoextrem.com (☎ 696 421361; www.geoextrem.com in Spanish) offers outdoor thrills including, kayaking, canyon descents, rock climbing and caving. Operating year-round, it has a base at Fuente de los Baños in summer.

Albergue el Refugio (☎ 964 13 13 17; www.refugio-montanejos.com in Spanish; sites per tent/person €4/3, B&B/half-board per person dm €12/20, cabin €20/28; year-round) This popular pad for climbers and walkers, run by Alexandra and Pascal, refugees from urban life in Geneva, is the place to meet friendly outdoor folk. There's limited camping space. It serves sandwiches and snacks to all comers and does meals (€8 to €14) to order and regularly for Saturday dinner and Sunday lunch.

Most hotels open only in summer and at weekends. **Hotel Rosaleda del Mijares** (☎ 964 13 10 79; www.hotelesrosaleda.com in Spanish; Carretera Tales 28; s incl breakfast €60-66, d €80-92; mid-Feb–mid-Dec), barely 100m from the *balneario*, lays on a filling *menú* (€15; mains €10 to €15) in its vast dining room. Its 81 rooms are attractive and comfortable with large beds. The hotel has its own pool and gym and also offers a fistful of spa packages.

Gruta de San José

The **Gruta de San José** (Valenciano: Coves de Sant Josep; ☎ 964 69 67 61; adult/under 4yr/4-13yr €9/free/4; 11am-1.15pm & 3.30-6.30pm or 7.15pm Jun-Sep, to 5.45pm Oct-May) is a winding tunnel, scoured naturally through the karst. On the outskirts of La Vall d'Uixó, 35km southwest of Castellón, it bores into the hillside for 2.75km. Boats glide through the first subtly lit 800m, followed by a walk.

BENICÀSSIM

pop 12,400

Benicàssim has been a popular resort since the 19th century, when wealthy Valencian families built summer residences here. To this day, around 80% of summer visitors are Spanish and many people from Madrid, Valencia and nearby Castellón own summer apartments here.

Orientation & Information

Benicàssim's beaches and accompanying development, scarcely a couple of blocks wide, stretch for 6km along the coast.

Main tourist office (☎ 964 30 09 62; www.benicassim.org; Calle Santo Tomás 74; 9am-2pm & 5.30-8.30pm mid-Jun–mid-Sep, 9am-2pm & 4.30-7.30pm Mon-Sat, 10.30am-1.30pm Sun rest of year) One km inland in the old town.

Sights & Activities

Those 6km of broad beach are the main attraction. Bordering the promenade at the northeastern end are **Las Villas**, exuberant, sometimes frivolous holiday homes built by wealthy Valencians at the end of the 19th century and into the 20th. Ask for the tourist office leaflet, *The Las Villas Path*.

Aquarama water park (☎ 964 30 33 21; www.aquarama.net in Spanish; day below/above 1.4m €12.50/18, half-day €8.80/12; 11am-7pm mid-Jun–Aug) is just south of town, off the N340.

The **Desierto de las Palmas**, about 6km inland, is a mountain range – cooler than the coast, on occasion misty – with a Carmelite monastery (1697) at its heart. Nowadays a nature reserve and far from desert (for the monks it meant a place for mystic withdrawal), it's a green, outdoor activities area. From **Monte Bartolo** (728m), its highest point, there are staggering views. Ask at the tourist office for its handout *The Desert de les Palmes Nature Reserve*, which illustrates three worthwhile, signed walking trails.

Festivals & Events

In late July or early August, fans by the tens of thousands gather for the annual four-day **Festival Internacional de Benicàssim** (FIB; www.fiberfib.com), one of Europe's top outdoor music festivals. Top acts in 2008 included Morrissey, Babyshambles, My Bloody Valentine, Siouxsie and Hot Chip.

Sleeping & Eating

Benicàssim's six camping grounds are all within walking distance of the beaches.

Camping Azahar (☎ 964 30 31 96; sites per person/tent/car €3.75/11.90/3.70; year-round;) Extensive sites are shaded by mature mulberry trees. There's a restaurant, a large pool and toilet blocks (including one that's equipped for disabled travellers) that are kept scrupulously clean.

Hotel Tramontana (☎ 964 30 03 00; www.hoteltramontana.com; Paseo Marítimo Ferrandis Salvador 6; s/d/tr incl breakfast from €32/52/72; mid-Feb–Oct; P) Only half a block from the shore, the Tramontana is also family-owned. Although something of a time warp with dowdy decor, it has three aces: its nearness to the beach, its very reasonable rates and its friendliness.

Hotel Avenida (☎ 964 30 00 47; www.hotelecoavenida.com; Avenida Castellón 2; d €36-74; mid-Feb–Oct; P) This appealing family-owned hotel, just off the old town's main street, has a pool, Jacuzzi and shady courtyard. Rooms are large, parking's free and it's excellent value. The entrance is on Calle Quatro Caminos.

Hotel Voramar (☎ 964 30 01 50; www.voramar.net in Spanish; Paseo Marítimo Pilar Coloma 1; s/d €51/94; P) Venerable (run by the same family for four generations) and blooded in battle (it functioned as a hospital in the Spanish Civil War), the Voramar has more character than most of Benicàssim's modern upstarts and is the only hotel that faces directly onto the sands. The dining room, where the cuisine is first class, has large windows overlooking the sea. Parking is €8 to €12.

Torreón (☎ 964 30 03 42; Avenida Ferrandis Salvador 2; mains around €16) Overlooking the 16th-century Torre San Vicente watchtower that gives this café-restaurant its name, it's a great spot to catch the sea breezes while nibbling on a snack, sipping a drink or tucking into a full meal. If you're dining, book in advance to enjoy a place on its smaller, less crowded terrace.

Plenty of economical restaurants line Calle de Santo Tomás and Calle Castellón, the old town's main street.

Drinking

In summer and at weekends, Benicàssim rocks. The eastern end of Calle de los Dolores in the old town is cheek-by-jowl bars including El Único, Vogue, Scratch Sessions, Cactus and Resaca (the perhaps appropriately named 'Hangover'). The town's biggest *discoteca*, **The End**, is beside Aquarama (p623).

Getting There & Away

Buses run every half-hour (every 15 minutes in summer) to Castellón, from where train connections are more plentiful.

OROPESA DEL MAR

It's a fine scenic drive from Benicàssim to Oropesa (Valenciano: Orpesa) along a narrow road winding around the rocky coastline. The resort is expanding rapidly and none too prettily northwards, embracing the massive spa and resort of **Marina d'Oro**.

The main **tourist office** (☎ 964 31 23 20; Plaza París; 9.30am-2pm & 4.30-6.30pm or 5-8pm) is beside Playa de la Concha.

Naturhiscope (☎ 964 31 30 26; Plaza de la Iglesia; adult/under 8yr/8-12yr €3/free/1.50; 10.30am-2pm & 6-9pm Jul & Aug, 10am-2pm & 4-7pm Sep-Jun) is a collection of photos and everyday objects, interpreting the town and its relationship with the sea in a high-tech context. Inspirational for some, pretentious flummery for others.

Two tiny museums, also in the old town, are each run by passionate, eccentric amateurs. The **Museo del Naipe** (Playing Card Museum; ☎ 626 564749; Calle Hospital 1; adult/child €3/1.50; 11am-1.30pm & 6-8pm Jun-Sep) has over 5000 different packs and other memorabilia from around the world, explained with beguiling enthusiasm. Outside opening times, just knock; the owner lives above.

Luis Elvira, another collecting squirrel, has assembled a unique collection of cogs and grills, shields and other items in metal at the **Museo del Hierro** (Metalwork Museum; ☎ 964 31 07 51; Calle Ramón y Cajal 12; adult/under 6yr €3/2; 10am-2pm Mon-Fri).

PEÑÍSCOLA

pop 4800

Peñíscola's old town, all cobbled streets and whitewashed houses, huddles within stone walls that protect the rocky promontory jutting into the sea. It's pretty as a postcard – and just as commercial, with ranks of souvenir and ceramics shops (one favourite: a pot with a – oh dear – stiff penis for a spout, a pun that doesn't even work in Spanish). In stark contrast, the high-rises sprouting northwards along the coast are mostly leaden and charmless. But the **Paseo Marítimo** promenade makes pleasant walking, and the beach, which extends as far as neighbouring Benicarló, is sandy and over 5km long.

Information

Que La Fuerza Te Acompañe (Avenida Papa Luna 4; per hr €2; noon-10.30pm) Internet access. Opens at 3pm at various times of the year.

Main tourist office (964 48 02 08; www.peniscola.es; 9am-8pm daily mid-Jun–mid-Sep, 9.30am-1.30pm & 4-7pm Mon-Sat, 10am-1pm Sun rest of year) At south end of Paseo Marítimo. Pick up its descriptive booklet, *The Old City*.

Sights & Activities

The rambling 14th-century **castle** (adult/under 10yr €3.50/free; 9.30am-9.30pm Easter–mid-Oct, 10.30am-5.30pm rest of year) was built by the Knights Templar on Arab foundations and later became home to Pedro de Luna ('Papa Luna', the deposed Pope Benedict XIII).

The **Museu de la Mar** (Maritime Museum; Calle Principe s/n; admission free; 10am-2pm & 4pm-dusk daily Apr-Sep, Tue-Sun Oct-Mar) illustrates the town's fishing and seafaring heritage from Phoenician times to the present. The high point for children will be the three small aquariums, where diaphanous shrimps dart and octopuses ooze and flow.

From the port, **Golondrinas Super Bonanza & Damiana Sanz** (964 48 06 64, 651 961050) do daily 30-minute boat trips (€7) from the port and, in summer, sail to Las Islas Columbretes (adult/child €50/45), a protected offshore archipelago and nature reserve.

The **Sierra de Irta**, running south from Peñíscola, is both nature park and protected marine reserve. It's one of the last unspoilt stretches of coastline in the Comunidad Valenciana, best explored on foot or by mountain bike. You can attack the full 26km of the circular PR V-194 trail or slip in one or more shorter loops. Ask at the tourist office for its *Paths Through Irta* brochure.

Sleeping & Eating

There are two great alternatives to the beachside concrete towers. Since they're small, do reserve.

Chiki Bar Restaurante (964 48 02 84, 605 280295; Calle Mayor 3-5; r €40-50) High in the old town, Chiki Bar has, in addition to its engaging name, seven spotless, modern rooms with views. You might want your earplugs since the nearby parish church chimes tinnily, on the hour, every hour. From March to October, it runs an attractive restaurant (mains from €8.50, closed Tuesday except July to September) with a great-value three-course *menú* (€11).

Hotel-Restaurante Simó (964 48 06 20; www.restaurantesimo.es in Spanish; Calle Porteta 5; s €44-62, d €55-76; Mar-Dec) At the base of the castle pile and right beside the sea, the Simó has a restaurant (mains €11.50 to €18) with magnificent views across the bay. All its nine simple, unfussy and relatively spacious rooms have balconies and seven enjoy equally impressive vistas.

Hostería del Mar (964 48 06 00; www.hosteriadelmar.net; Avenida Papa Luna 18; s €49-100, d €68-133; P) Once, this friendly, four-star, family-owned place was the only hotel along the promenade. And it still preserves more character than most of its undistinguished multistorey neighbours on the north beach. Nearly all rooms have balconies overlooking the beach.

Hogar del Pescador (964 48 95 88; Plaza Lonja Vieja; fish from €10, menú €20) This popular fisherfolk's cafe by day is great value for everything fishy. For the maximum taste sensation for two, share firstly a *mariscada* (seafood special; €35), then a *combinado degustación* (€21), a magnificent platter of mixed fish and shellfish.

Casa Jaime (964 48 00 30; Avenida Papa Luna 5; mains €18.50-23.50; daily mid-Jun–mid-Sep, closed Wed & dinner Sun mid-Sep–mid-Jun) Dine on the ample outside terrace or in the cosy dining room, where you can see mum and dad (once a fisherman who learnt his trade cooking for the crew) at work in the kitchen. They're renowned for their *suquet de peix* (fish stew; €22.50; minimum two people), and other rice and simmered fish dishes.

Getting There & Around

Year-round, local buses run at least every half-hour between Peñíscola, Benicarló and Vinaròs. From July to mid-September, there's an hourly run to Peñíscola/Benicarló train station.

To patrol the long beach front, hire a bike or scooter from **Diver Sport** (609 622225; Avenida Estación 17).

VINARÒS

pop 22,100

Unlike its luxury-loving neighbours, Vinaròs is a working town, and a fairly grim one. Redeeming features are its active fishing port, famous for *langostinos* (king prawns), and a pair of small, sandy beaches.

KING OF ALL THE PRAWNS

The *langostinos* (king prawns) that make it as far as Vinaròs' wholesale fish market (around 15 tonnes of them annually) have had a hard time of it. They hatch in the sandy beds of Río Ebro delta, to the north, where the estuary's low salinity enhances their flavour and plumpness of flesh. Once mature, they leave its relative comfort to scrabble their way over rocky promontories and struggle against strong currents and waves, only to be scooped up and netted and find their way, sizzling and grilled or simply boiled, to your plate.

So prized is this delicacy with its reputedly aphrodisiac qualities that it's been designated as the town's official tourist emblem and is well on the way to being awarded DO (Denominación de Origen) status, just like a fine wine or cheese.

The **Iglesia Arciprestal** (Plaza del Ayuntamiento) is a stocky baroque fortified church with a tall bell tower and elaborate main doorway decorated with candy-twist columns. Opposite is the Modernista **Casa Giner** (1914), garnished with floral motifs and fine *miradores* (enclosed balconies). These days a Benetton shop, its original stained glass proclaims its earlier quaint function as *paquetería* and *mercería* (haberdasher and draper).

From here, pedestrianised Calle Mayor leads past the Modernista **covered market**, active and ideal for self-caterers and picnickers, to the **Playa del Fortí**, sandy and bordered by a splendid, wide, recently pedestrianised promenade that many a better endowed tourist resort should envy.

The **tourist office** (☎ 964 45 33 34; www.turisme.vinaros.es; Plaza Jovellar 2; 🕑 10am-1.30pm & 5.30-8pm daily Jun-Sep, 10am-2pm & 5-7pm Tue-Sat, 10am-2pm Sun Oct-May) is round the corner from Iglesia Arciprestal.

Vinaròs has two big annual bashes. Forty days before the privations of Lent, the town erupts with one of Spain's biggest and most exuberant carnivals, culminating in three days of intensive strutting and parading. From 10 to 13 August, the Fiestas del Langostino celebrate Vinaròs' prime catch with seaside samplings and plenty of other outdoor fun.

You've plenty of eating choices on the waterfront, most specialising in seafood.

A well-lobbed *langostino* from the quayside fish market, **Bar Puerto** (☎ 964 45 56 72; Calle Costa Borrás 60; mains €7-10), small, friendly and informal, and its equally tempting neighbour, **Bar Folet**, do a great range of tapas and fishy mains.

Just across the road, **El Faro** (☎ 964 45 63 62; Zona Portuaria s/n; menú €25-30, mains €15-18; 🕑 Tue-Sat & lunch Sun), in the base of a former lighthouse, serves up both traditional Mediterranean dishes and more innovative fare with a strong emphasis on what's pulled from the sea.

La Cuina (☎ 964 45 47 36; Paseo Blasco Ibañez 12; menú €20-37, mains €15.30-24.60; 🕑 lunch & dinner Mon-Sat & lunch Sun) beside the promenade and bedecked with crisp white tablecloths and napkins, is in more classic mode. To enjoy the riches hauled from the Mediterranean, invest in the six-course fish and seafood *menú degustación* (€37, minimum two people).

EL MAESTRAZGO

Straddling northwestern Valencia and southeast Aragón, El Maestrazgo (Valenciano: El Maestrat) is a mountainous land, a world away from the coastal fleshpots, that's fertile territory for cyclists and walkers. Here ancient *pueblos* (villages) huddle on rocky outcrops and ridges. One such place, Sant Mateu, was chosen in the 14th century by the maestro (hence the name El Maestrazgo) of the Montesa order of knights as his seat of power.

SANT MATEU

pop 1850 / elev 325m

A drive 5km south from the N232 along the CV132 brings you to Sant Mateu, once capital of the Maestrazgo. Its solid mansions and elaborate facades recall the town's more illustrious past and former wealth, based upon the wool trade. From colonnaded Plaza Mayor, ringed with cafe terraces, signs point to four small **municipal museums** (adult/under 14yr €1.50/free; 🕑 10am-noon & 4-6pm Tue-Sun): the **Museo Paleontológico**, **Museo Arciprestal** of religious art (in Casa Abadía, beside the parish church tower), **Museo les Presons** in the former jail and **Museo Histórico Municipal**, entered via the tourist office.

Radiating from the village are three signed circular walking trails of between 2½ and five hours that lead through the surrounding hills. Ask for the free tourist office pamphlet *Senderos de Sant Mateu*.

The **tourist office** (☎ 964 41 66 58; www.santmateu.com in Spanish; Calle Historiador Betí 10; 🕑 10am-2pm & 4-6pm Tue-Sat, 10am-2pm Sun) is just off Plaza Mayor, in **Palacio Borrull**, a stalwart 15th-century building.

Family-run (see the blown-up photos of its three generations around the tiled dining room), **Hotel-Restaurante La Perdi** (☎ 964 41 60 82; laperdicb@hotmail.com; Calle Historiador Betí 9; s/d €24/36) is a bargain with five modern, comfortable rooms and a restaurant (mains €6 to €14.40) that does a decent *menú* for only €9. Room reservations are essential.

Follow signs from Plaza Mayor to the **Ermita de la Mare de Déu dels Àngels**, perched on a rocky hillside, a 2.5km drive or considerably shorter walk. A monastery until the Spanish Civil War (take a peep at its over-the-top baroque chapel), it's nowadays a quality **restaurant** (☎ 626 525219; menú €21-35; 🕑 10.30am-7pm Wed-Sun & 8pm-midnight Fri & Sat) offering incomparable views of the surrounding plain.

Getting There & Away

Weekdays, **Autos Mediterráneo** (☎ 964 22 00 54) buses link San Mateu with Vinaròs (€2.40, 35 minutes, four daily), Castellón (€4.60, 1½ hours, three daily) and Morella (€3, 45 minutes, two daily). On Saturday, one bus runs from Castellón to Morella via Sant Mateu. The bus stop is 100m east of Hotel Restaurante Montesa.

MORELLA

pop 2700 / elev 1000m

Bitingly cold in winter and refreshingly cool in summer, Morella is the Maestrazgo's principal town. This outstanding example of a medieval fortress town, perched on a hilltop and crowned by a castle, is girdled by an intact rampart wall over 2km long.

Orientation & Information

Morella's walls are broken only by their seven entrance gates. The town is a pleasantly confusing, compact jumble of narrow streets, alleys and steep steps. Its main street runs east–west between Puerta San Miguel and Puerta de los Estudios. Bordered by shops selling mountain honey, perfumes, cheeses, pickles and pâtés, skeins of sausages and fat hams, it compounds the confusion by assuming five different names in less than 1km.

The **tourist office** (☎ 964 17 30 32; www.morella.net; Plaza San Miguel 3; 🕑 10am-2pm & 4-6pm or 7pm Mon-Sat, 10am-2pm Sun daily Apr-Oct, closed Mon Nov-Mar) is just behind Torres de San Miguel, twin 14th-century towers flanking the main entrance gate.

Ciberlocutori Nou (Calle San Julián 2; per hr €2; 🕑 10am-2pm & 5.30-9.30pm) has internet access.

Sights & Activities

Morella's **castle** (adult/under 16yr €2/1.50; 🕑 11am-7pm Apr-Oct, 11am-5pm Nov-Mar), though badly knocked about, well merits the strenuous ascent to savour the breathtaking views of the town and surrounding countryside. At its base is the bare church and cloister of the **Convento de San Francisco**, destined to become a *parador* hotel.

Museo del Sexenni (adult/under 16yr €2/1.50; 🕑 irregular; consult the tourist office), in the former Church of Sant Nicolau, displays models, photos and items associated with this major fiesta (see below).

In **Museo Tiempo de Dinosaurios** (adult/under 16yr €2/1.50; 🕑 11am-2pm & 4-6pm or 7pm daily Apr-Oct, closed Mon Nov-Mar), opposite the tourist office, are dinosaur bones and fossils – the Maestrazgo's remote hills have been a treasure trove for palaeontologists – together with an informative video (in Spanish).

The imposing Gothic **Basílica de Santa María la Mayor** (Plaza Arciprestal; 🕑 11am-2pm & 4-6pm or 7pm) has two elaborately sculpted doorways on its south facade. A richly carved polychrome stone staircase leads to the elaborately sculpted overhead choir, while cherubs clamber and peek all over the gilded altarpiece. Its ecclesiastical treasure is kept within the **Museo Arciprestal** (admission €1.50).

Among several imposing civil buildings are the 14th-century **Casa del Consell** (town hall; Calle Segura Barreda 28) and manorial houses such as the **Casa de la Cofradía de Labradores** (House of the Farmers' Guild; Calle de la Confraría).

On the outskirts of town stretch the arches of a handsome 13th-century **aqueduct**.

Festivals & Events

Morella's major festival is the **Sexenni**, held during August every six years without interruption since 1673 (the next is in 2012) in honour of the Virgen de Vallivana. Visit the Museo del Sexenni to get the flavour of this major celebration with its tonnes of confetti and elaborate compositions in crêpe paper.

Annually in August, there's a **baroque music festival**, starring the Basílica de Santa María la Mayor's huge organ.

JASON WEBSTER, AUTHOR

In the early 1990s, British author Jason Webster, straight down from Oxford, immersed himself in Spanish and *gitano* (Roma) culture. Three tempestuous years in Spain inspired his best-selling first book, *Duende,* translated into 12 languages.

As he settled back into Britain and a steady BBC job, the Iberian years might possibly have been no more than a youthful fling. 'So what brought you back? And why Valencia?', I ask as we lick ice cream on a cafe terrace ('best place for ices in all Valencia', he assures me). 'Love, in a word', he replies. In England, he had met Salud, actress and flamenco dancer (it was a postponed interview date; Salud, with the fine timing of her profession, had given birth to their first child on the day of our original rendezvous). 'We had the choice between Reading or Valencia, my wife's home town. It was a no brainer.'

Valencia has been home to them both for nearly a decade now. But Jason finds the Valencia of today a different city from the one he first identified with. 'Then, it was all a bit grubby, decayed and unkempt. That very scruffiness appealed to something inside me. My *barrio* of Russafa was more like a village. I was constantly bumping into people I knew, there was a haberdasher, a knife grinder, a man who sold nothing but potatoes. They've all gone.' Today, he argues with but a dash of nostalgia, Valencia has lost its Cinderella complex yet manages to maintain the spark and energy that first appealed to him.

Like tens of thousands of Spaniards, Jason and Salud have bought themselves a second, country home – but one that couldn't be more different from your typical holiday villa. 'I needed an escape route, somewhere greener, cooler and quieter, somewhere where nobody obeyed the rules.' So in 2004 they bought themselves half a mountainside, at the end of a dirt track in the deepest hinterland of Castellón province. The land was long neglected and the dilapidated farmhouse threatened to tumble into the valley bottom.

Jason's fourth and latest book, *Sacred Sierra: A Year on a Spanish Mountain* tells of the transformation. 'But isn't the genre – the experiences, droll or challenging, of an expatriate somewhere in Europe – exhausted?', I ask. 'Such books tend to be rather egocentric, the locals seen as characters, viewed from the outside. I come from a different perspective', he retorts. 'And I feel the need to put something back into Spain, the land that has given me so much.' On a practical level, he and Salud have planted and nurtured more than 250 trees in an effort to create an arboretum of native species. 'In the book I try to illustrate and document the last remains of a mountain culture that's destined to disappear. I started from scratch; no one, not even most Spaniards, knows this remote, primarily oral culture with its own folklore, stories, beliefs and customs.'

To this, I'd add another difference. Webster writes about Spain without a whiff of patronising his subjects. And from the inside, as someone deeply immersed in his adopted country. As he observed just a trifle ruefully, 'Weeks pass when I don't speak a word of English. I sometimes fear for the quality of my prose.'

Sleeping & Eating

Hostal La Muralla (☎ 964 16 02 43; www.hostalmuralla.com; Calle la Muralla 12; s/d €30/46) Hostal La Muralla's rooms, on two floors and mostly overlooking the town walls, are spruce and comfortable.

Hotel El Cid (☎ 964 16 01 25; www.hotelelcidmorella.com; Puerta San Mateu 3; s/d €33/56.60) Beside the ramparts and above its popular bar and restaurant, Hotel El Cid has smart, attractively furnished modern rooms and strictly contemporary bathrooms. Most rooms have balconies and top-floor ones have magnificent views of the surrounding countryside.

Hotel Cardenal Ram (☎ 964 17 30 85; www.cardenalram.com; Cuesta Suñer 1; s/d €45/70; ❄) This venerable hotel with its ancient stone floors, high ceilings and antique furniture is a wonderfully transformed 16th-century cardinal's palace. Attractively decorated rooms have sensual power showers. Its restaurant (mains €7 to €14; open lunch and dinner Tuesday to Saturday and lunch Sunday, September to July, daily in August) does a first-class *menú degustación* (€30, minimum two people) and a tempting *menú del día* (€15). Parking is €9.

Mesón del Pastor (☎ 964 16 02 49; Cuesta Jovaní 5-7; mains €8.35-15.50; ⏰ lunch Thu-Tue, dinner Sat) The stuffed boar and wild goat heads balefully eyeing your plate hint at the glories within the kitchen. It's all about strong mountain cuisine, thick gruels in winter, rabbit, juicy sausages, partridge and, yes, wild boar and goat. In February, you can eat truffle-flavoured dishes from starter to dessert. Ditto for wild mushrooms during peak autumn collecting time.

Restaurante Casa Roque (☎ 964 16 03 36; Cuesta San Juan 1; mains €9.65-19.25; 🕑 lunch & dinner Tue-Sat & lunch Sun) Within a vast 17th-century mansion, Casa Roque does a good-value weekday *menú* (€11.70) and rich mountain *menús* (€21 and €26) offering typical Els Ports dishes such as *cordero relleno con ciruela pasa y guarnación de setas* (stuffed lamb with prunes, garnished with seta mushrooms) and *conejo al Maestrazgo con caracoles* (rabbit with snails stewed in a rich, herbed sauce).

Getting There & Around

On weekdays, **Autos Mediterráneo** (☎ 964 22 00 54) runs two daily buses to/from Castellón (€7.60, 2¼ hours) with a change in Sant Mateu for Vinaròs (€4.55). There's also one Saturday service to/from Castellón.

ELS PORTS

Morella is the ancient capital of Els Ports, the 'mountain passes', a rugged region offering some outstanding scenic drives and strenuous cycling excursions, plus excellent possibilities for walkers.

Fábrica de Giner

On the Forcall road, 4.5km west of Morella, is the Fábrica de Giner complex, a former textile factory.

The HI-affiliated **Youth Hostel** (☎ 902 22 55 52; creserves_ivaj@gva.es; dm under/over 25yr €7.45/10.60; 🕑 daily Jun–mid-Sep, alternate Fri-Sun mid-Sep–May) has been converted from what used to be factory workers' housing. Rooms sleep from four to 14 and there's a pool and large, grassy children's playground in the complex.

Saltapins (☎ 964 17 32 56; adult/child €17/15; 🕑 10am-8pm daily mid-Jun–mid-Sep, 10am-6pm Sat & Sun Apr–mid-Jun & mid-Sep–Oct) is an adventure centre up in the woods across a small river. There are two gentle circuits for children (€10 to €14) and an altogether more challenging one (€18) with creepers to swing from, suspended gangplanks to teeter over and barrels to wriggle through.

Tirig

The **Museo de Valltorta** (☎ 964 76 10 25; admission free; 🕑 10am-2pm & 4pm-7pm or 5pm-8pm Tue-Sun), 10km southwest of Sant Mateu, illustrates the Maestrazgo's rich heritage of rock paintings, recognised as a Unesco World Heritage treasure. There are also guided walks to the clifftop overhangs twice daily.

COSTA BLANCA

The long stripe of the Costa Blanca (White Coast) is one of Europe's most heavily visited areas. If you're after a secluded midsummer beach, stay away – or head inland to enjoy traditional villages and towns that have scarcely heard the word tourism. Then again, if you're looking for a lively social scene, good beaches and a suntan…

It isn't all concrete and package deals. Although the original fishing villages have long been engulfed by the sprawl of resorts, a few old town kernels, such as those of Xàbia (Jávea) and Altea, still survive.

In July and August it can be tough finding accommodation if you haven't booked. Out of season, those places remaining open usually charge far less than in high summer.

Most buses linking Valencia and Alicante head down the motorway, making a stop in Benidorm. A few, however, call by other intervening coastal towns. A smart new tram plies the scenic route between Alicante and Benidorm, from where a narrow-gauge train runs northwards to Denia. Both stop at all *pueblos* en route. Renfe trains connect Valencia with Gandia.

Inland Trips from the Costa Blanca, by Derek Workman, describes 20 one-day car excursions into the interior in detail and with flair. His *Small Hotels and Inns of Eastern Spain* is also worth packing if you'd like to linger and spend the night away from the crowds.

GANDIA

pop 77,400

Gandia, 67km south of Valencia, is a tale of two cities. The main town, once home to a branch of the Borja dynasty (more familiar as the infamous Borgias), is a prosperous commercial centre.

Four kilometres away on the coast, Playa de Gandia has a long, broad beach of fine sand, groomed daily by a fleet of tractors. It's a popular and predominantly Spanish resort with a good summer and weekend nightlife.

Information

Playa de Gandia tourist office (☎ 96 284 24 07; www.gandiaturismo.com; Paseo de Neptuna 45; ⌚ 9.30am-8.30pm Mon-Sat, 9.30am-1.30pm Sun Jul-Sep, 9.30am-2pm & 4-7.30pm Mon-Fri, 9.30am-1.30pm Sat & Sun Mar-Jun, 9.30am-1.30pm Tue & Thu-Sun Oct-Feb)

Town tourist office (☎ 96 287 77 88; ⌚ 9.30am-1.30pm & 3.30-7.30pm or 4-8pm Mon-Fri, 9.30am-1.30pm Sat) Opposite the bus/train station.

Sights

Gandia's magnificent **Palacio Ducal de los Borja** (☎ 96 287 14 65; Calle Duc Alfons el Vell 1; guided tour adult/under 9yr/9-12yr/13-18yr €6/free/4/5; ⌚ 10am-2pm & 4-8pm or 6.30-7.30pm Mon-Sat, 10am-2pm Sun) was the 15th-century home of Duque Francisco de Borja. Highlights include its finely carved *artesonado* ceilings and rich ceramic work – look out for the vivid *mapa universal* floor composition. One-hour guided tours in Spanish, with an accompanying leaflet in English, take place about every half-hour.

Festivals & Events

In a miniature version of Valencia city's Las Fallas festival (see the boxed text, p611), more than 20 *fallas* decorate – nay, block – the streets of Gandia between 11 and 19 March.

Sleeping

Albergue Mar i Vent (☎ 96 283 17 48; albergpiles_ivaj@gva.es; dm under/over 26 €7.45/10.60; ⌚ year-round) This sterling 90-bed beachfront youth hostel is around 10km south of Gandia, overlooking Playa de Piles. Rooms sleep from three to six and there's a water sports centre right next door. Take La Amistad bus from Gandia's bus station.

Camping L'Alquería (☎ 96 284 04 70; www.lalqueria.com; Carretera del Grau de Gandia s/n; sites €13.50-22.65; ⌚ year-round; 🏊) About 1km inland, this camping ground has reasonable shade and – a rarity hereabouts – a heated indoor pool.

Hostal El Nido (☎ 96 284 46 40; Calle Alcoy 22; s €35-50, d €45/65) The 10 rooms, equipped with standing fans in summer, are as cheerful as the owners at this modest place, a block back from the beach. Between June and September it also runs a small bar for guests.

Hotel Riviera (☎ 96 284 50 42; www.hotelesrh.com in Spanish; Paseo de Neptuno 28; half-board per person €39-90; P ❄ 💻 🏊) It's well worth paying the few coppers extra for half-board at this 72-room beachside hotel, one of Denia's earliest but comprehensively renovated over the years. Invest an extra €5.25 per person for one of the eight full-frontal sea-view rooms. Parking is €8 to €10.

Hotel Bayren 1 (☎ 96 284 03 00; www.hotelesrh.com in Spanish; Paseo de Neptuno 62; half-board per person €40-95.60; P ❄ 💻 🏊) Rooms, most with balconies, are comfortable and there's a gym, spa and pool at this good, if a little monolithic, four-star hotel that also faces the beach. Parking is €9 to €15.

Eating

Eating choices abound in Paseo Marítimo Neptuno. You'll also find a few longer-established places at the western end of the port and along Calle Verge.

Restaurante Emilio (☎ 96 284 07 61; Bloque F-5, Avenida Vicente Calderón; mains €15-21; ⌚ lunch & dinner Thu-Tue, daily Jul–mid-Sep) Despite a cupboardful of gastronomic accolades, Emilio, his wife and three children manage to preserve a family atmosphere in this traditionally furnished restaurant where you'll eat very well indeed.

Arrop (☎ 96 295 07 68; Calle Sant Joan de Ribera 20; meals around €55; ⌚ lunch & dinner Wed-Sat, Mon & lunch Tue), inland in the main town, justifiably earns one Michelin star. Choose its *menú gastronómico* (€49.80), let chef Ricard Camarens make the decisions and savour its exciting, innovatory take on traditional Valenciano cuisine.

Drinking

There's great summer and weekend nightlife at Playa de Gandia, with bars, including Paco Paco Paco, Mama Ya Lo Sabe and Ke Caramba, clustered around Plaza del Castell, barely 300m inland from the beach. After they close, head for one of the through-the-night discos such as **Bacarrá** (Calle Legazpi 7), two blocks from the beach, or **La Diva** (Cami Vell de Valencia), further inland.

Getting There & Around

Trains run between Gandia and Valencia (€3.95) every half-hour (hourly at weekends). The combined bus and train station is opposite the town tourist office. Stopping beside the office, La Marina Gandiense buses for Playa de Gandia run every 20 minutes.

DENIA

pop 42,700

Denia, the Comunidad Valenciana's major passenger port, has the shortest sea crossings to the Balearic Islands. The beaches of La Marina, to its north, are good and sandy, while southwards the fretted coastline of Las Rotas and beyond offers less-frequented rocky coves.

Orientation & Information

The **tourist office** (☎ 96 642 23 67; www.denia.net; Plaza Oculista Buigues 9; ⌚ 9.30am-2pm & 5-8pm Jul–mid-Sep, 9.30am-1.30pm & 4-7pm Mon-Sat, 9.30am-1.30pm Sun mid-Sep–Jun) is near the waterfront. Both train station and ferry terminal are close by.

Mon Blau (1st fl, Calle Marqués de Campo 23; per hr €1.50; ⌚ 9am-1am) has internet access.

Sights & Activities

From Plaza de la Constitución, steps lead up to the ruins of Denia's **castle** (admission free; ⌚ 10am-1.30pm & 5-8.30pm Jul & Aug, 10am-1pm & 4-6pm Sep-Jun), from where there's a great overview of the town and coast.

To catch the sea breezes, sign on with **Mundo Marino** (☎ 96 642 30 66), which does return catamaran trips to/from Xàbia (adult/child €15/7.50; 40 minutes), some of which continue to Calpe (€25/12.50) and Altea (€30/15).

For more active fun, cycle the circumference of the Parc Natural del Montgó, following a 26km signed route along traffic-free paths that links Denia and Xàbia, then return to Denia on the Mundo Marino catamaran.

Sleeping

Costa Blanca (☎ 96 578 03 36; www.hotelcostablanca.com in Spanish; Calle Pintor Llorens 3; r from €58; P ⊠ ❄) Beside the train station, this is an excellent-value option except in high summer, when prices soar to €92. Rooms are comfortable and cosily furnished, there's a small, well-stocked bar and the port is but a few steps away. Parking is €12.

our pick **Hotel Chamarel** (☎ 96 643 50 07; www.hotelchamarel.com; Calle Cavallers 13; r incl breakfast from €85; P ⊠ ❄) This delightful hotel, tastefully furnished in period style by a pair of seasoned travellers, occupies an attractive 19th-century bourgeois mansion. Its 14 rooms surround a tranquil, plant-shaded internal patio. The vast internal salon with its correspondingly large marble-topped bar is equally relaxing. The whole is a capacious gallery for the paintings of artist and owner Mila Vidallach, whose canvases decorate bedrooms and public areas. Ask for room 201, under the eaves, Japanese in mood and positively breathing feng shui. Parking is €15.

Posada del Mar (☎ 96 643 29 66; www.laposadadelmar.com; Plaza Drassanes 2; s/d incl breakfast from €110/120; P ⊠ ❄ 💻) This sensitively renovated hotel occupies a 13th-century building that last functioned as Denia's customs house. Each of its 25 rooms is individually decorated with a nautical theme and light streams through large windows that overlook the harbour. Parking is €15.

Eating

There's a clutch of tempting restaurants, catering for all pockets, along harbour-facing Explanada Cervantes and Calle Bellavista, extending to Plaza del Raset. Many began life as simple bars for the fisherfolk from the old fish market, just across the road.

El Raset (☎ 96 578 50 40; Calle Bellavista 7; menú €23.50-30, mains €22.50-27.50) Eat on the wide terrace or within the cool, air-conditioned interior of El Raset, reputed for its rice dishes. Its excellent four-course lunch *menú* includes, as starters, a variety of tapas such as marinated sardines, octopus on a bed of peppers and baby cannelloni stuffed with seafood. Dishes are attractively presented and service is genial and helpful.

Asador del Puerto (☎ 96 642 34 82; Plaza del Raset 10-11; menú €26.75-38.50, mains €19-24) This is an excellent choice for either meat, roasted in a wood-fired oven, or fish dishes. Try the *cochinillo* (suckling pig; €23.50), crispy on the outside, juicy within and roasted to a turn.

Another splendid option is **Sal de Mar** (☎ 96 642 77 66; menú €15-42), gourmet restaurant of Hotel Posada del Mar (above).

Getting There & Away

From the station, seven trains daily follow the scenic route southwards to Benidorm (€3.15, 1¼ hours), connecting with the tram for Alicante (€6.30, 2½ hours).

For the Balearic Islands, **Balearia Lines** (☎ 902 16 01 80; www.balearia.net) has regular and high-speed ferries to/from Mallorca and Ibiza, while **Iscomar** (☎ 902 119128; www.iscomar.com) runs to/from Ibiza.

XÀBIA

pop 29,900

With a third of its resident population and over two-thirds of its annual visitors non-Spanish (every second shop seems to be an estate agent/realtor), Xàbia (Spanish: Jávea) isn't the best place to meet the locals. That said, it's gentle, family-oriented and well worth a visit early in the season, when the sun shines but the masses have yet to arrive.

Xàbia comes in three parts: the small old town 2km inland; El Puerto (the port), directly east of the old quarter; and the beach zone of El Arenal, a couple of km south of the harbour. Further south, there are spectacular seascapes from the promontory of Cabo de La Nao.

Information

Bookworld (☎ 96 646 22 53; Avenida Amanecer de España 13) English bookshop in the old town.

Connections (Calle Santísimo Cristo del Mar 29, El Puerto; per hr €2.50; 9.30am-2pm & 3-7pm Mon-Fri, 10am-2pm Sat) Internet access.

Lavandería Los Delfines (Avenida del Pla s/n, El Arenal; 9am-1pm & 4-6pm Mon-Fri, 9am-1pm Sat) Laundrette.

Tourist offices (www.xabia.org; 9am-1.30pm & 4-7.30pm or 4.30-8pm Mon-Fri, 10am-1.30pm Sat) El Arenal (☎ 96 646 06 05; Carretera Cabo de la Nao); Old Town (☎ 96 579 43 56; Plaza de la Iglesia); Port (☎ 96 579 07 36; Plaza Almirante Bastareche 11; also 10am-1.30pm Sun)

Activities

In addition to sun fun on El Arenal's broad beach, the old town merits a brief wander. The tourist office carries a pack titled *Xàbia: Nature Areas Network* (in English), containing five brochures, each describing a waymarked route in the area, including an ascent of Montgó, the craggy mountain that looms over the town. Year-round, the tourist office leads free guided walks at least twice weekly.

Sleeping

Camping Naranjal (☎ 96 579 29 89; www.campingelnaranjal.com; Carretera Cabo de la Nao s/n; sites €11.60-13.60; year-round;) A 10-minute walk from El Arenal's beach and surrounded by orange groves, this camping ground has a restaurant, shop, pool and children's playground.

Pensión la Marina (☎ 96 579 31 39; www.pensionlamarina.com; Av Marina Española 8; s €29, d €39-69;) This small, English-owned place has eight rooms plus a couple of family options, all with ceiling fans. Its huge plus is its position, right beside the pedestrianised promenade (rooms with sea views are €10 extra). For dinner, go no further than the restaurant below, which serves tasty food with an Italian slant.

Hotel Miramar (☎/fax 96 579 01 02; Plaza Almirante Bastarreche 12; s €30-40 55, d €55-67;) This imposing family-run building, right beside the port, almost tumbles into the sea. Its 26 rooms, eight with balcony, are cosy (those overlooking the bay carry a €10 to €15 supplement) and there's a bar and restaurant.

Parador de Jávea (☎ 96 579 02 00; www.paradores.es; Avenida del Mediterráneo 233; s/d from €109/136) Architecturally, Xàbia's boxy, once-modern *parador* is unexciting but it enjoys a magnificent site, on a headland overlooking the bay of El Arenal, and has all the usual *parador* comforts.

Eating & Drinking

The old town has several enticing tapas bars, while bars and restaurants flank Avenida de la Marina Española, the pedestrianised promenade south of the port. In El Arenal, cafes and restaurants hug the rim of beachside Paseo Marítimo.

La Bombonería (☎ 96 579 16 47; Avenida Lepanto 20; mains €14.50-18.50; Mon-Sat) Near the port and set back from the road, this restaurant offers good traditional cuisine with a creative twist. You can dine inside or on its ivy-clad terrace.

Amarre 152 (☎ 96 579 06 29; Port de la Fontana s/n; meals €30) At the end of a backwater in El Arenal, this is a delightful retreat (just count your way along the moorings to number 152), with a designer interior and tiny quayside terrace. Great for rice dishes, its fish is the freshest: nothing from the freezer and not even a minnow from a fish farm.

In the old town, **Temptacions** (☎ 96 579 29 20; Plaza de la Iglesia 10), indeed a tempting place for a tapa or a drink, is adapted from two old houses (only their doorway arches, curving over the interior, still survive). Nearby (go down the steps beside the tourist office), neighbours **Bar Imperial** (☎ 96 646 11 81; Plaza de Baix 2) and **Tertulia** (☎ 96 646 07 61; Plaza de Baix 3) have pleasant terraces and serve both tapas and full meals.

Getting There & Around

At least five buses run daily to both Valencia (€9.85) and Alicante (€8.35). They stop on Avenida Óndara, at Rotonda del Olivo, with a large olive tree at its heart.

You can rent a cycle at **Xàbia's Bike Centre** (☎ 96 646 11 50; www.xabiabike.com; Avenida Lepanto 21; per day/week from €7/42) in the port area.

CALPE

pop 27,800

The Gibraltaresque Peñon de Ifach, a giant molar protruding from the sea, rears up from the seaside resort of Calpe (Valenciano: Calp).

Two large bays sprawl either side of the Peñon: Playa Arenal on the southern side is backed by the old town, while Playa Levante, to the north, has most of the more recent development.

Information

DIP Digital Center (Calle Benidorm 15; per hr €3; 10am-9pm Mon-Sat) Internet access.

Librería Europa (☎ 96 583 58 24; www.libreria-europa-calpe.com; Calle Oscar Esplá 2) Good stock of titles in English and other European languages.

Main tourist office (☎ 96 583 85 32; www.calpe.es in Spanish; Plaza del Mosquit; 9am-2pm & 5-8.30pm Mon-Sat Jul-Sep, 9am-3pm & 4-7.30pm Mon-Sat Oct-Jun) In the old town.

Sights

A fairly strenuous trail – allow 2½ hours for the round trip – climbs from the Peñon's **Aula de Naturaleza** (Nature Centre) towards the 332m summit, offering great seascapes from its end point at the end of a dark tunnel. In July and August walkers depart in batches of 20 every 20 minutes, so you may have a short wait.

Sleeping

Pensión Centrica (☎ 96 583 55 28; mjpiffet@telefonica.net; Plaza de Ifach 5; basic s/d €13/26;) This welcoming, French-run place just off Avenida Gabriel Miró has 13 well-maintained rooms with ceiling fans and corridor bathrooms. There's a fridge and microwave for guests' use. Look out for the giant pet tortoise and iguana…

Hostal Terra de Mar (☎ 96 587 59 28; www.hostalterrademar.com in Spanish; Calle Paternina 31; s/d incl breakfast €55/80;) You're greeted by a giant mural of bangled hands, from which rose petals flutter, and fresh orchids flourish in reception at this stylish recent addition to Calpe's sleeping options. Each floor has its own style (climb the stairs and you can travel from Japan to Morocco to Africa and Paris). The low-season tariff for its 12 rooms (single/double with breakfast €35/55 October to May) is anexcellent deal.

Hotel Esmeralda (☎ 96 583 61 01; www.rocaesmeralda.com; Calle Ponent 1; s incl breakfast €67-100, d €87.20-131.50; P) At the northern limit of Playa Levante, the huge Esmeralda, as much leisure complex as hotel, is particularly suited to families with children. If the sea fails to call, there are three outside pools and a heated indoor one too, plus a gym, a couple of restaurants and a cafe.

Eating

There are plenty of restaurants and bars around Plaza de la Constitución and along main Avenida de Gabriel Miró, plus a cluster of good fish places down by the port.

Los Zapatos (☎ 96 583 15 07; www.loszapatos.com; Calle Santa María 7; mains €12.75-18.75; dinner Thu-Tue, lunch Sun mid-Jun–mid-Sep, lunch & dinner Thu-Mon mid-Sep–mid-Jun) Highly recommended, this German-run restaurant has a short, specialised à la carte menu and a carefully selected wine list of mainly Spanish vintages. In season it does a tempting *menú caza y pescado* (hunting and fish menu) with wild boar and fish of the day. Alternatively, home in on the 'Menu for Fish Freaks'.

La Cambra (☎ 96 583 06 05; Calle Delfín 2; mains €15-21; Mon-Sat Jul-Sep, lunch Mon-Thu, lunch & dinner Fri & Sat Oct-Jun) All antique wood and tiles, traditional La Cambra specialises in rice dishes (€10 to €12) and also has a rich à la carte selection of Basque and Valencian dishes.

Getting There & Away

Seven narrow-gauge trains travel daily northwards to Denia (€2, 50 minutes) and south to Benidorm (€2, one hour), connecting with the tram for Alicante (€5.35, two hours).

Buses connect Calpe with both Alicante (€5.95, 1½ hours, seven daily) and Valencia (€11.10, 3½ hours, five daily). The **bus station** (Avenida de la Generalitat Valenciana) is just off the ring road.

ALTEA

pop 26,600

Altea, separated from Benidorm only by the thick wedge of the Sierra Helada, could be a couple of moons away. Altogether quieter, its beaches are mostly of pebbles. The modern part, extending along the coast, is a bog-standard coastal resort. By contrast, the whitewashed old town, perched on a hilltop overlooking the sea, is just about the prettiest *pueblo* in all the Comunidad Valenciana.

The **tourist office** (☎ 96 584 41 14; Calle San Pedro 9; ⏰ 10am-2pm & 5-7.30pm or 8pm Mon-Fri, 10am-1pm Sat) is on the beachfront.

Spain's first organic hotel, **Aparthotel & Restaurante Venus Albir** (☎ 96 686 48 20; www.venusalbir.com; Plaza Venus, Albir-Alfaz del Pi; d €47-90, tr €63-121; P ⊠ ✤ ⛶) was awarded a national prize for its ecofriendliness. Located in Albir, a continuation of Altea southwards, its 24 comfortable apartments have self-catering facilities and a balcony and you can indulge in a variety of healthy, de-stressing activities. At its restaurant (mains €13.50 to €23), open to all, ingredients are strictly organic. It does an excellent-value four-course lunch *menú* (€14.50 including a couple of glasses of wine) and the small shop sells organic products that feature in its cuisine.

Off Plaza de la Iglesia in Altea's old town, and especially down Calle Major, there's a profusion of cute little restaurants, many open for dinner only except in high summer.

BENIDORM

pop 69,100

It's easy to be snobbish about Benidorm, which long ago sold its birthright to mass package tourism. An estimated 1.2 million Britons alone visit the town each year and in Europe only London and Paris have more hotel beds. But the old girl, though violated most summer nights by louts from northern Europe, still manages to retain a certain dignity. The foreshore is magnificent as the twin sweeps of Playa del Levante and the longer Playa del Poniente – 5km of white sandy beaches – meet beneath Plaza del Castillo, where the land juts into the bay like a ship's prow.

In winter half of all visitors are over 60, mostly from northern Europe. During summer Benidorm is for all ages.

Information

El Otro Mondo de Jaime (Calle Ruzafa 2; per hr €3; ⏰ 8am-1am) Internet access.

Laundrette (Calle Ibiza 14; ⏰ 9am-8pm Mon-Fri, 9am-2pm Sat)

Main tourist office (☎ 96 585 13 11; www.benidorm.org; Avenida Martínez Alejos 16; ⏰ 9am-9pm Mon-Fri, 10am-1.30pm Sat) Also tourist office kiosks on Avenida de Europa and in Rincòn de Loix.

Vic Center (Calle Lepanto 9; per hr €2; ⏰ 9.30am-11pm) Internet access.

Sights & Activities

Terra Mítica (Mythical Land; ☎ 902 02 02 20; www.terramiticapark.com; adult/under 5yr/5-10yr €34/free/25.50; ⏰ 10am-1am Jul–mid-Sep, 10am-8pm mid-Mar–Jun, Sep & Oct), Spain's biggest theme park, is the Costa Blanca's answer to Disneyland. A fun day out, especially if you're with children, it's Mediterranean in theme, with plenty of scary rides, street entertainment and areas devoted to ancient Egypt, Greece, Rome, Iberia and the islands. Take bus 1 or 41.

Terra Natura (☎ 902 50 04 14; www.terranatura.com; adult/under 4yr/4-12yr €23/free/18; ⏰ 10am-dusk) is a rival theme park, also on the grand scale. Over 1500 animals live in habitats approximating their natural environment, there's a water park (€6 supplement) and, for the brave, the chance to swim with sharks (fairly small and benign, no visitors yet lost).

Aqualandia (☎ 96 586 01 00; www.aqualandia.net; adult/under 3yr/3-12yr €25/free/18; ⏰ 10am-dusk mid-May–mid-Oct) is Europe's largest water park. Beside it is **Mundomar** (☎ 96 586 01 00; www.mundomar.es in Spanish; adult/child €22/16; ⏰ 10am-dusk mid-Feb–mid-Dec), a marine and animal park with parrots, dolphins, sea lions, even bats – and no, they're not mermaids but a bevy of girls doing synchronised swimming with dolphins. Each park is worth a full day. Take bus 1 or 4.

Excursiones Marítimas Benidorm (☎ 96 585 00 52; Paseo de Colón) has hourly boats (adult/child return €12.50/10) to the Isla de Benidorm, a cruise up the coast to Calpe (€20/13) and a full-day outing to the island of Tabarca (p641) for €25/16.

Should Benidorm's frenetic pace get you down, pick up a free copy of *Routes Across Sierra Helada* from the tourist office and stride out into the hills north of town for superb bay views.

Sleeping

Almost everyone's on a package deal so accommodation can be expensive for the independent traveller. Book online through **Benidorm Spotlight** (www.benidorm-spotlight.com) for significant discounts.

Hotel Iris (☎ 96 586 52 51; www.iris-hotel.net; Calle Palma 47; s €25-45, d €25-60; ✤ ⛶) Here's a friendly budget choice on a fairly quiet

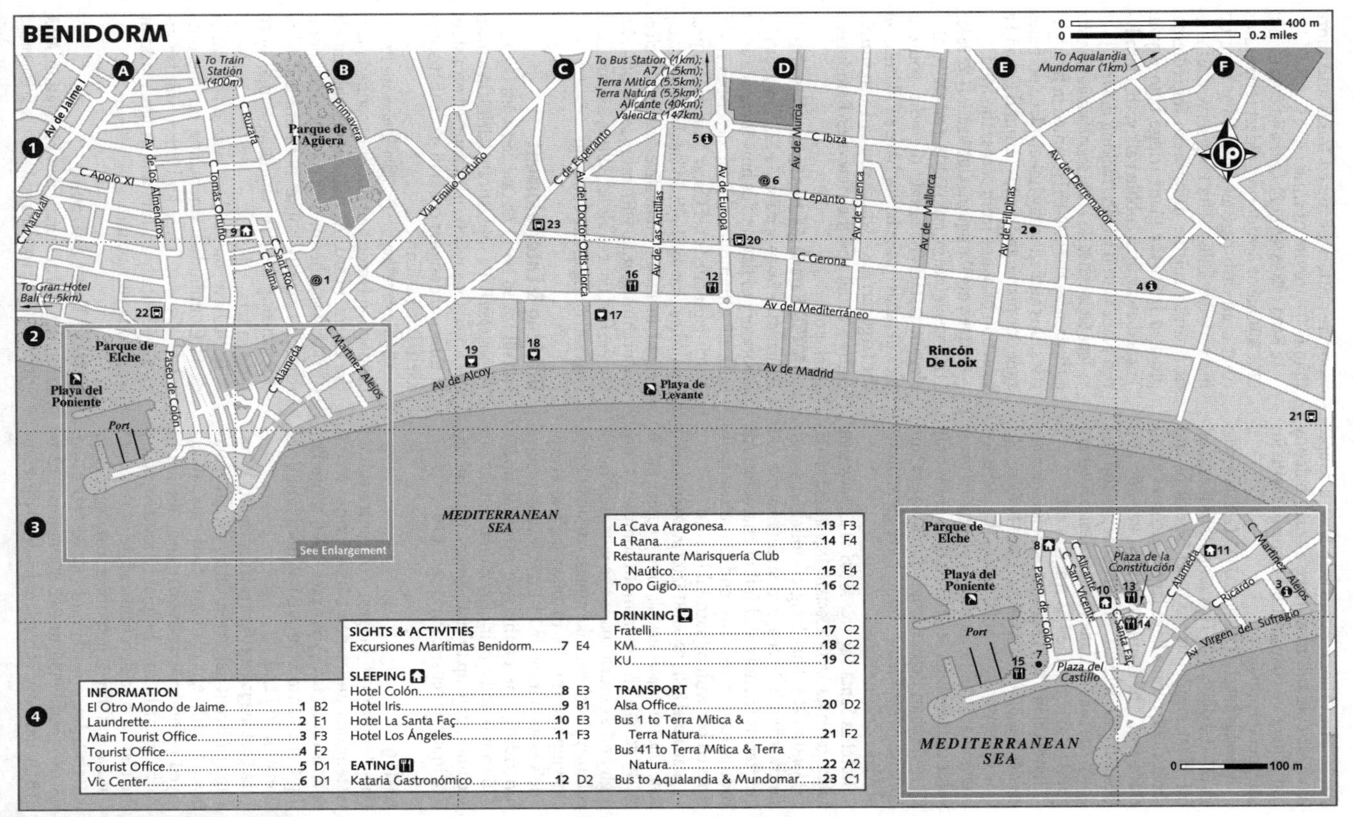

BENIDORM
0 400 m
0 0.2 miles
To Train Station (400m)
To Bus Station (1km); A7 (1.5km); Terra Mítica (5.5km); Terra Natura (5.5km); Alicante (40km); Valencia (147km)
To Aqualandia Mundomar (1km)
To Gran Hotel Bali (1.5km)
Av de Jaime I
C Apolo XI
C Maravall
Av de los Almendros
C Tomás Ortuño
C Ruzafa
C Sant Roc
C Palma
C de Primavera
Parque de l'Agüera
Vía Emilio Ortuño
C de Esperanto
Av del Doctor Ortis Llorca
Av de Las Antillas
Av de Europa
Av de Murcia
Av de Cuenca
Av de Mallorca
Av de Filipinas
Av del Derremador
C Ibiza
C Lepanto
C Gerona
Av del Mediterráneo
Av de Madrid
Av de Alcoy
Rincón De Loix
Playa de Levante
Parque de Elche
Playa del Poniente
Paseo de Colón
C Alameda
C Martínez Alejos
Port
MEDITERRANEAN SEA
See Enlargement
INFORMATION
El Otro Mondo de Jaime 1 B2
Laundrette 2 E1
Main Tourist Office 3 F3
Tourist Office 4 F2
Tourist Office 5 D1
Vic Center 6 D1
SIGHTS & ACTIVITIES
Excursiones Marítimas Benidorm 7 E4
SLEEPING
Hotel Colón 8 E3
Hotel Iris 9 B1
Hotel La Santa Faç 10 E3
Hotel Los Ángeles 11 F3
EATING
Kataria Gastronómico 12 D2
La Cava Aragonesa 13 F3
La Rana 14 F4
Restaurante Marisquería Club Naútico 15 E4
Topo Gigio 16 C2
DRINKING
Fratelli 17 C2
KM 18 C2
KU 19 C2
TRANSPORT
Alsa Office 20 D2
Bus 1 to Terra Mítica & Terra Natura 21 F2
Bus 41 to Terra Mítica & Terra Natura 22 A2
Bus to Aqualandia & Mundomar 23 C1
Plaza de la Constitución
C Alicante
C San Vicente
C Santa Faç
C Ricardo
Av Virgen del Sufragio
Plaza del Castillo
0 100 m

street. Most rooms come with fans, a couple have air-con and most have a small balcony too. There's a cosy ground-floor bar with an internet terminal.

Hotel Los Ángeles (☎ 96 680 74 33; Calle Los Ángeles 3; s €27-43, d €50-76; ❄) This is another pleasant, informal, family-owned hotel. The fifth- and sixth-floor rooms have large balconies at no extra cost. The family also runs Pensión and Restaurante del Mar, slightly cheaper and just down the road at Calle Pintor Lozano 5, where guests staying at the Los Ángeles eat.

Hotel Colón (☎ 96 585 04 12; www.hotelcolon.net; Paseo de Colón 3; s €38-62, d €48-96; 🕒 mid-Mar–Oct; ❄) Conveniently positioned where the old town meets Playa del Poniente, the Colón is great value outside high season. Half-board is only €4 more than B&B, though don't expect fine cuisine. West-facing rooms have great views of Playa del Poniente.

Hotel La Santa Faç (☎ 96 585 40 63; www.santafazhotel.com in Spanish; Calle Santa Faç 18; s/d/tr €50/85/125; 🕒 Apr-Oct; ❄) This long-established hotel, sandwiched between two streets in the old quarter, is friendly and full of character. All rooms have a balcony and there's a well-stocked bar with billiard table.

Gran Hotel Bali (☎ 96 681 52 00; www.granhotelbali.com; Calle Luis Prendes s/n; half-board per person €46.50-95; P ❄ 🏊) This mammoth complex, 186m high and as much space-age village as hotel, is Europe's tallest. Like a massive silver knife cleaving the sky, its vastness isn't to everyone's taste but, with 23 lifts/elevators (have fun riding one of the two external ones), 776 rooms and a pair of restaurants that can accommodate up to 1000 diners, it's superlative in many senses. Parking is €10.

Eating

For Benidorm's biggest concentration of restaurants and tapas bars serving decent Spanish fare, take your pick from those lining Calle Santo Domingo at the Plaza de la Constitución end.

La Cava Aragonesa (Plaza de la Constitución) What a magnificent selection of tapas, fat canapés, 20 different plates of cold cuts, all arrayed before you at the bar and labelled in both Spanish and English! Good wine by the glass too (a decent measure of standard Catalan bubbly is just one euro). Next door is its sit-down restaurant (☎ 96 680 12 06; lunch *menú* €9.80 to €12.80, mains €12 to €18), where you can select from 20 different wooden platters of mixed foods and more than 600 varieties of wine.

La Rana (☎ 96 586 81 20; Costero del Barco 6; mains €8-16.60) One of Benidorm's oldest restaurants (that aged cash register must have rung up the very first bills), The Frog serves authentic Spanish cuisine using fresh ingredients, plucked from the giant fridge before you. Tucked away up a cobbled alley, this family-run place is well worth tracking down.

Topo Gigio (☎ 96 585 71 68; Edificio Marianne 9, Avenida del Mediterráneo; mains €10-19) Hemmed in by high-rises, this authentically Italian place prepares superior pizzas and pastas (around €8) and a selection of mains from across the Med.

Restaurante Marisquería Club Naútico (☎ 96 585 54 25; Paseo de Colón s/n; mains €12-18, menú €20) At this elegant restaurant beside the port, you can pick at tapas by the bar or have a full meal on the large terrace – where you can also simply enjoy a drink and the view over Benidorm's small port.

our pick **Kataria Gastronómica** (☎ 96 683 13 72; Avenida de Europa 5; mains €16-22; 🕒 Mon-Sat) 'A laboratory of flavours' is how this restaurant with its ultramodern decor describes itself. Much-garlanded chef Oscar Marcos conjures up dishes that are both a visual and culinary delight, including innovative creations such as sea urchins gratiné with mousseline of leeks. On the first floor of Hotel Belroy, its ambience is as satisfying as the cooking.

Drinking & Entertainment

Fratelli (☎ 96 585 39 79; Calle Doctor Orts Llorca s/n; 🕒 from 6pm) For a sophisticated drink in a town not noted for subtlety, park yourself on a stool at this cool designer cocktail place that styles itself 'Bar Fashion'.

KU (Avenida de Alcoy s/n; 🕒 10am-5am), with its reproduction Hindu and Buddhist statues, plays the oriental card. At its near neighbour **KM** (🕒 10am-5am), the music's eclectic until 6pm, when it's strictly house. Both are laid-back cafes during the day, changing tempo once the sun sets.

Both have mega *discotecas* on Avenida de la Comunidad Valenciana on the outskirts of town. They and other similar giants open daily in July and August, and at weekends year-round.

Getting There & Around

From Benidorm's smart new bus station, **ALSA** (☎ 96 680 39 55; www.alsa.es; Avenida de la Comunidad

Europea 2) direct buses (€8, 13 daily) go to Alicante airport and Valencia airport (€16.30, two daily). They also run north and south along the Costa Blanca to/from Valencia (€14 to €15.75, 1¾ hours) and Alicante (€3.80, one hour, frequent).

Alternatively, you can take the tram to Alicante (€4, 1¼ hours every 30 minutes) or the little train to Denia (€3.15, 1¼ hours, seven daily).

For the bus station, take local bus 41 or 47.

For a taxi phone ☎ 96 586 18 18.

ALICANTE

pop 322,700

Alicante (Valenciano: Alacant) lives for much more than tourism alone. Dynamic, it's transformed itself from a somewhat seedy port to an attractive provincial town, the Valencia region's second-largest. In 2008, in a fillip to local pride, it was the starting point of the Volvo Ocean Race, the world's toughest round-the-world yacht competition. Try to fit in at least one overnight stay to experience its frenetic – and unmistakably Spanish – nightlife.

Orientation

Palm trees shade pedestrianised Paseo Explanada de España, running parallel to the harbour. Around Catedral de San Nicolás are the narrow streets of El Barrio (the old quarter), bordered by the Rambla de Méndez Núñez, the principal north–south artery.

Information

Main post office (Calle de Alemania)

Municipal tourist office (www.alicanteturismo.com) Branches at bus station and train station.

Regional tourist office (☎ 96 520 00 00; Rambla de Méndez Núñez 23; 9am-8pm Mon-Sat, 10am-2pm Sun)

Xplorer Cyber Café (Calle de San Vicente 46; per hr €1.20; 9am-midnight)

Sights & Activities

Museu de Fogueres (Museo de las Hogueras; ☎ 96 514 68 28; Rambla de Méndez Núñez 29; admission free; 10am-2pm & 5-7.45pm or 6-9pm Tue-Sat, 10am-1.45pm Sun) has a great audiovisual presentation of what the Fiesta de Sant Joan (right), all fire and partying, means to *alicantinos*.

From the 16th-century **Castillo de Santa Bárbara** (admission free; 10am-9.30pm May-Sep, 9am-6.30pm Nov-Mar) there are sweeping views over the city. Inside is a permanent display of contemporary Spanish sculpture. A lift/elevator (€2.40 return; closed for renovation at the time of writing), reached by a footbridge opposite Playa del Postiguet, rises through the bowels of the mountain. Otherwise, it's a pleasant walk through Parque de la Ereta via Calle San Rafael to Plaza del Carmen.

MARQ (Museo Arqueológico Provincial; ☎ 96 514 90 00; Plaza Doctor Gómez Ulla s/n; adult/child €3/1.50; 11am-2pm & 6pm-midnight Tue-Sun Jul & Aug, 10am-7pm Tue-Sat, 10am-2pm Sun Sep-Jun), very visual and hi-tech, well merits a visit even though there's little information in English. Buses 2, 6, 9, 20 and 23 pass by.

MUBAG (Museo de Bellas Artes Gravina; ☎ 96 514 67 80; Calle Gravina 13-15; admission free; 10am-2pm & 4-8pm or 5-9pm Mon-Sat, 10am-2pm Sun), Alicante's stimulating fine-arts museum, is within an 18th-century mansion.

Nearby, the **Iglesia de Santa María** (admission €1; 10am-12.30pm & 6-8.30pm) has a flamboyant, 18th-century facade and an ornate, gilded altarpiece, both contrasting with the nave's Gothic simplicity.

From the harbour, **Kon Tiki** (☎ 96 521 63 96) makes the 45-minute boat trip (€16 return) to the popular island of Tabarca (p641).

A pleasant harbourside promenade and tiled walkway (separated only by a hideously busy road) follow the curve of the port. On the western mole is **Panoramis**, a vast shopping and leisure complex.

Immediately north of the port is the sandy beach of **Playa del Postiguet**. Larger and less-crowded beaches are at **Playa de San Juan**, easily reached by the tram.

The splendid waterside bronze figure of a pin-headed **Icarus bearing a surfboard**, emerging from the water is by contemporary sculptor Esperanza d'Ors.

The **Pozos de Garrigós** (☎ 96 514 37 87; Plaza del Puente; admission free; 11.30am-2pm & 5-8.30pm Jul & Aug, 10am-2pm & 5-7.30pm Sep-Jun) are three vast water cisterns, built to collect run-off from Monte Benacantil and nowadays used as a venue for temporary exhibitions.

Festivals & Events

Alicante's major festival is the **Fiesta de Sant Joan**, spread either side of 24 June, the longest day, when the city stages its own version of Las Fallas (see the boxed text, p611), with fireworks and satirical effigies (Valenciano: *fogueres*, Spanish: *hogueras*) going up in smoke all over town.

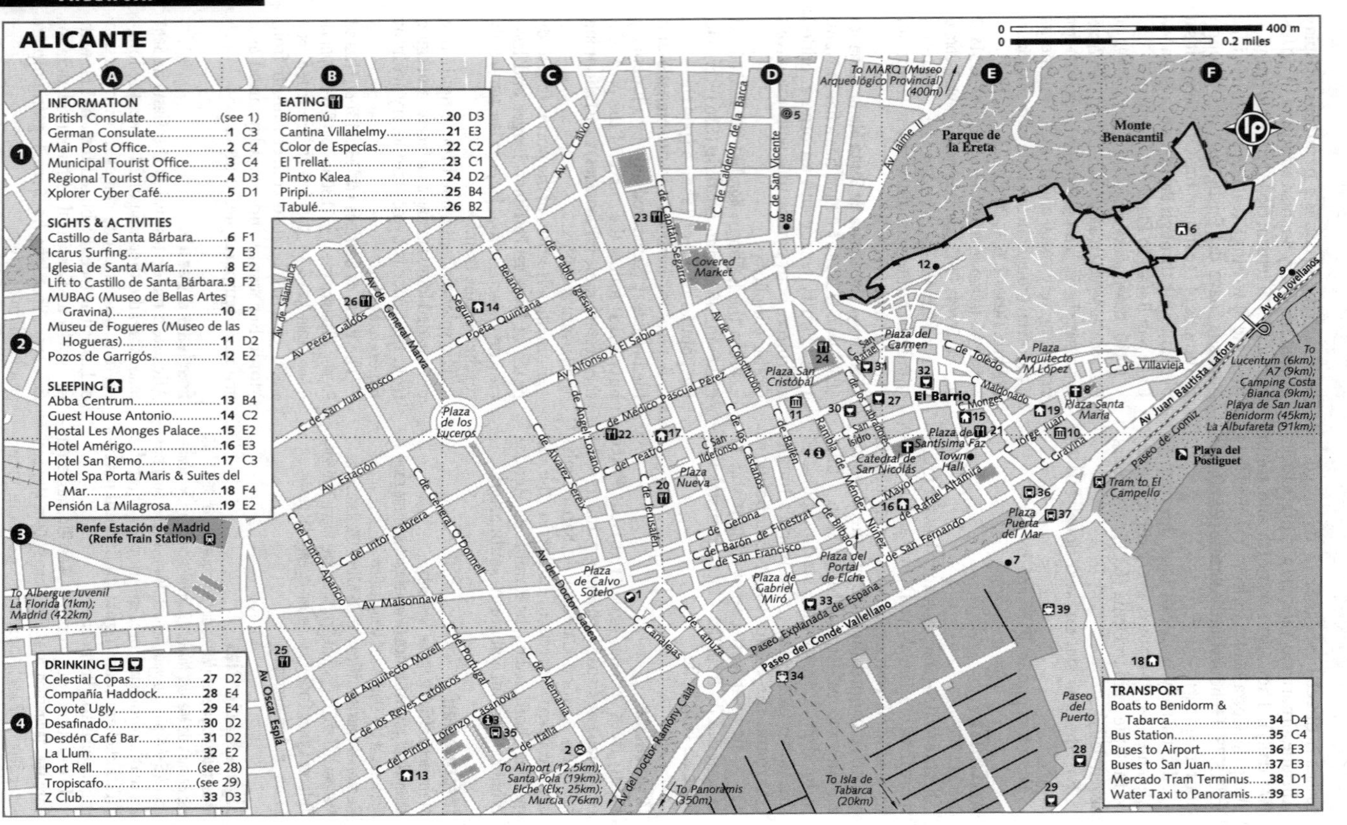
ALICANTE
0 400 m
0 0.2 miles
INFORMATION
British Consulate (see 1)
German Consulate 1 C3
Main Post Office 2 C4
Municipal Tourist Office 3 C4
Regional Tourist Office 4 D3
Xplorer Cyber Café 5 D1
SIGHTS & ACTIVITIES
Castillo de Santa Bárbara 6 F1
Icarus Surfing 7 E3
Iglesia de Santa María 8 E2
Lift to Castillo de Santa Bárbara 9 F2
MUBAG (Museo de Bellas Artes Gravina) 10 E2
Museu de Fogueres (Museo de las Hogueras) 11 D2
Pozos de Garrigós 12 E2
SLEEPING
Abba Centrum 13 B4
Guest House Antonio 14 C2
Hostal Les Monges Palace 15 E2
Hotel Amérigo 16 E3
Hotel San Remo 17 C3
Hotel Spa Porta Maris & Suites del Mar 18 F4
Pensión La Milagrosa 19 E2
EATING
Bíomenú 20 D3
Cantina Villahelmy 21 E3
Color de Especías 22 C2
El Trellat 23 C1
Pintxo Kalea 24 D2
Piripi 25 B4
Tabulé 26 B2
DRINKING
Celestial Copas 27 D2
Compañía Haddock 28 E4
Coyote Ugly 29 E4
Desafinado 30 D2
Desdén Café Bar 31 D2
La Llum 32 E2
Port Rell (see 28)
Tropiscafo (see 29)
Z Club 33 D3
TRANSPORT
Boats to Benidorm & Tabarca 34 D4
Bus Station 35 C4
Buses to Airport 36 E3
Buses to San Juan 37 E3
Mercado Tram Terminus 38 D1
Water Taxi to Panoramis 39 E3
To MARQ (Museo Arqueológico Provincial) (400m)
Parque de la Ereta
Monte Benacantil
Renfe Estación de Madrid (Renfe Train Station)
To Albergue Juvenil La Florida (1km); Madrid (422km)
To Lucentum (6km); A7 (9km); Camping Costa Blanca (9km); Playa de San Juan Benidorm (45km); La Albufareta (91km)
To Airport (12.5km); Santa Pola (19km); Elche (Elx; 25km); Murcia (76km)
To Panoramis (350m)
To Isla de Tabarca (20km)
Tram to El Campello
Playa del Postiguet
Paseo del Puerto
Covered Market
El Barrio
Plaza de los Luceros
Plaza Nueva
Plaza de Calvo Sotelo
Plaza de Gabriel Miró
Plaza del Portal de Elche
Plaza San Cristóbal
Plaza del Carmen
Plaza Arquitecto M López
Plaza Santa María
Plaza de Santísima Faz
Plaza Puerta del Mar
Catedral de San Nicolás
Town Hall
Av Jaime II
Av de Jovellanos
Av Juan Bautista Lafora
Paseo de Gomiz
Paseo Explanada de España
Paseo del Conde Vallellano
Av del Doctor Ramony Calal
Av del Doctor Gadea
Av Maisonnave
Av Oscar Esplá
Av Estación
Av de General Marva
Av Alfonso X El Sabio
Av de la Constitución
Av Perez Galdós
Av de Salamanca
Av C Calvo
C de Calderón de la Barca
C de San Vicente
C de Capitán Segarra
C de Pablo Iglesias
C Belando
C Segura
C Poeta Quintana
C de San Juan Bosco
C de Médico Pascual Pérez
C de Ángel Lozano
C de Álvarez Sereix
C de General O'Donnell
C del Intor Cabrera
C del Pintor Aparicio
C del Arquitecto Morell
C de los Reyes Católicos
C del Pintor Lorenzo Casanova
C del Portugal
C de Alemania
C de Italia
C Canalejas
C de Lanuza
C de Jerusalén
C del Teatro
C San Ildefonso
C de los Castaños
C de Bailén
Rambla de Méndez Núñez
C de los Labradores
C San Isidro
C San Rafael
C de Toledo
C Maldonado
C Monges
C Jorge Juan
C Gravina
C Mayor
C de Rafael Altamira
C de San Fernando
C de Bilbao
C de Gerona
C del Barón de Finestrat
C de San Francisco
C de Villavieja

Sleeping

BUDGET

Camping Costa Blanca (☎ 965 63 06 70; www.campingcostablanca.com; Calle Convento, Campello; sites per person/tent/car €5.65/8.25/5.65;) This large camping ground, about 10km north of Alicante, has a poolside bar, restaurant, mini-market and mini-library, where you can exchange your holiday reading. The tram passes right by.

Albergue Juvenil La Florida (☎ 902 22 55 52, 96 511 30 44; Avenida Orihuela 59; under/over 26yr €7.45/10.60) Around 2km west of the centre and normally a student residence, La Florida functions as a youth hostel between July and mid-September. Facilities are excellent, with most beds in single rooms. Take bus 2 or 3, both of which pass by bus and train stations.

Guest House Antonio (☎ 650 718353; www.guesthousealicante.com; Calle Segura 20; s €33-40, d €43-48;) Here's a magnificent budget choice. Each of the eight large, tastefully decorated rooms has a safe, full-size fridge and free beverage-making facilities. The five apartments (€70 to €80), two with their own patio, have a mini-kitchen and washing machine and are exceptional value. Antonio also has two other apartments, one nearby, the other handy to the bus station.

Pensión La Milagrosa (☎ 96 521 69 18; www.hostallamilagrosa.com; Calle de Villavieja 8; s/d €20/40, with bathroom €30/50;) The Miracle is a great central budget choice with simple rooms, a small guest kitchen, washing machine and roof terrace. It also has three apartments (€60) that can sleep up to six (per extra person €20).

our pick **Hostal Les Monges Palace** (☎ 96 521 50 46; www.lesmonges.net; Calle San Agustín 4; s €30-44, d €45-56; P) This agreeably quirky place is a treasure with its winding corridors, tiles, mosaics and antique furniture. Each room is individually and tastefully decorated and reception couldn't be more welcoming. To really pamper yourself, choose one of the two rooms with sauna and Jacuzzi (€97). Look out for the small Dalí original beside the reception desk.

MIDRANGE & TOP END

Hotel San Remo (☎ 96 520 95 00; www.hotelsanremo.net; Calle Navas 30; s €35-43, d €45-58, tr €60-75;) This friendly, family-run hotel has 27 spruce, well-maintained, if smallish, rooms. Although it doesn't offer breakfast, there's a coffee machine near reception that dispenses the real brew.

Abba Centrum (☎ 96 513 04 40; www.abbahoteles.com; Calle del Pintor Lorenzo Casanova 31; r €83-125; P) Abba Centrum is a hugely attractive option, right by the bus station and with the train station a short walk away. Popular with business visitors, its weekend rates (August too) drop to a bargain €65 per room. Parking is €11.50.

Hotel Spa Porta Maris & Suites del Mar (☎ 96 514 70 21; www.hotelspaportamaris.com; Plaza Puerta del Mar 3; s €90-139, d €90-155;) Each of the 138 rooms has a balcony overlooking either beach or marina. Among the many facilities at this hyperhealthy four-star option are pools, gym and a Wellness Center. Then again, no one will care if you simply slob around.

Hotel Amérigo (☎ 96 514 65 70; www.hospes.es; Calle de Rafael Altamira 7; r from €140; P) Within an old Dominican convent, this glorious five-star choice, voted best-designed European hotel by Conde Nast Johansens in 2007, harmoniously blends the traditional and ultramodern. Enjoy the views from the rooftop pool, itself a work of art, or build up a sweat in the fitness area – if you can tear yourself away from the comfort of your stunningly designed room. Parking is €28.

Eating

Bíomenú (☎ 96 521 31 44; Calle Navas 17; mains €4.60-6.80, salads €15; 9.30am-4.30pm Mon-Sat; V) This ultracheap option is both vegetarian restaurant (load your plate from its varied pay-by-weight salad bar) and shop specialising in organic produce.

Cantina Villahelmy (☎ 965 21 25 29; Calle Mayor 37; mains €8-16; lunch & dinner Tue-Sat & lunch Sun) One wall's rough stone, another bright orange and navy blue, painted with skeletons, creepy-crawlies and a frieze of classical figures. Intimate, funky and popular, the Villahelmy has lots of snacks, excellent salads and a menu that features dishes from couscous to octopus.

El Trellat (☎ 965 20 62 75; Calle de Capitán Segarra 19; lunch menú €11.50, dinner menú €17.50; lunch Mon-Sat, dinner Fri & Sat) Beside the covered market, this small, friendly place does creative three-course *menús:* first course a serve-yourself buffet, then an ample choice of inventive mains. For dessert, trust Manuel, the chef/owner; he previously worked in Alicante's premier cake shop.

Pintxo Kalea (☎ 96 514 58 41; Plaza San Cristóbal 11; menú €12) Basque music wails and jigs in the background at this modern, stylish bar and restaurant, which does a wonderful selection of juicy *pinchos* (canapés), salads, steaks and, being Basque, cod prepared in four different ways.

Piripi (☎ 96 522 79 40; Avenida Oscar Esplá 30; mains €13-23) This highly regarded restaurant is strong on stylish tapas and dishes of rice, seafood and fish, which arrives fresh and daily from the wholesale markets of Denia and Santa Pola. There's a local speciality, changing daily (eat here on Tuesday and its *guisado de la abuela*, grandmother's stew).

Color de Especías (☎ 96 520 72 01; Calle de Médico Pascual Pérez 25; menú €15, mains €16-21; lunch & dinner Mon-Fri & lunch Sat) Eat in the sensual surroundings of this restaurant with its deep red decor and intimate lighting. Dishes, such as confit of duck in a mango and pear coulis, are truly creative, blending in harmony sweet and sour, salt and vinegar.

Tabulé (☎ 96 513 34 45; Avenida Pérez Galdós 52; menú €18; lunch Mon & Tue, lunch & dinner Wed-Sat; V) Service is swift and friendly at this vegetarian restaurant, run by an all-girl team, where you take what's on offer on the day's *menú*, which includes a drink and coffee. You won't repeat yourself; it's original, inventive and changes weekly.

Self-caterers can browse around Alicante's huge, art nouveau twin-storey **covered market** (Avenida Alfonso X El Sabio).

Drinking

The old quarter around Catedral de San Nicolás is wall-to-wall bars. Down by the harbour, the Paseo del Puerto, tranquil by day, is a double-decker line of bars, cafes and night-time discos.

Early opener **Desdén Café Bar** (Calle de los Labradores 22) is a friendly place to kick off the evening, while **La Llum** (cnr Calles Montengon & Padre Maltés) is a tiny sweatbox dance-bar that goes wild late into the night.

Celestial Copas (Calle San Pascual 1) is heavenly and decidedly weird, with a kitsch collection of religious art/junk and great music. Nearby, **Desafinado** (Santo Tomas 6) is another heaving dance bar with DJs that also offer good jazz.

An easy walk away, **Z Club** (Calle Coloma; Tue-Sun) is a slick *discoteca* with a dress code. Don't turn up before 3am unless you want to dance alone.

In the port area, if you don't recognise **Compañía Haddock** by the din, you will from the image of Tintin's pipe-smoking companion. Sitting above it – and risking bringing the roof down on a good night – is **Port Rell**.

A couple of doors along, **Tropiscafo** beams out good recorded jazz, while beside it **Coyote Ugly** sometimes has live music.

If you're still on your feet, take the night ferry over to the Panoramis complex, where the opportunities for nocturnal action are almost as rich.

Getting There & Away

AIR

Alicante's **El Altet airport** (☎ 902 40 47 04), gateway to the Costa Blanca, is served by budget airlines, charters and scheduled flights from all over Europe.

BOAT

Romeu (☎ 96 520 04 01) runs regular ferries to/from Oran in Algeria.

BUS

From the **bus station** (☎ 96 513 07 00) more than 10 motorway buses go daily to Valencia (€17.60 to €20, 2½ hours). Others, much slower, pass through Costa Blanca coastal towns such as Benidorm (€3.80, one hour, frequent). At least seven fast services run to/from Murcia (€5.20, one hour) and at least 10 serve Madrid (€26.30, 5¼ hours).

TRAIN & TRAM

Destinations from the main **Renfe Estación de Madrid** (Avenida de Salamanca) include Murcia (€4.30, 1¼ hours, hourly) via Orihuela and Elche, Valencia (€26.30, 1¾ hours, 10 daily) via Villena and Xàtiva, Madrid (€41, 3¾ hours, seven daily) and Barcelona (€50.70, 4¾ hours, eight daily).

TRAM (☎ 900 72 04 72) runs a smart new tram to Benidorm (€4, every half-hour) along a coastal route that's scenically stunning at times. Take it from the new Mercado terminus beside the covered market or from Puerto Plaza del Mar, changing at La Isleta or Lucentum.

Getting Around

El Altet airport is around 12km southwest of the centre. Bus C-6 runs every 40 minutes between Plaza Puerta del Mar and the airport, passing by the north side of the bus station.

Reliable and very economical local car-hire companies operating from the airport include **Javea Cars** (☎ 96 579 33 12; www.javeacars.com), **Solmar** (☎ 96 646 10 00; www.solmar.es) and **Victoria Cars** (☎ 96 583 02 54; www.victoriacars.com).

Buquebus (one-way/return €2/2.50, 7pm-2am Mon-Fri, noon-2am Sat & Sun), a water taxi, makes the 10-minute crossing from Paseo del Puerto to Panoramis.

For a taxi call ☎ 96 525 25 11.

AROUND ALICANTE

Isla de Tabarca

A trip to Tabarca, around 20km south of Alicante as the seagull flies, makes for a pleasant day trip – as much for the boat ride itself as for the island, which heaves with tourists in summer. Pack your towel and face-mask. Much of the waters that lap this small island, 1800m long and 400m wide at its widest point, are protected and no-go areas. But fish don't understand such boundaries and you'll enjoy some great underwater viewing in permitted areas.

In summer, daily boats visit the island from Alicante, Benidorm and Torrevieja, and there are less-regular sailings year-round.

Lucentum

On and around the Tossal de Manises spread the remains of the Roman town of **Lucentum** (☎ 96 526 24 34; adult/under 7yr/7-15yr €2/free/1.20; 9am-noon & 7-10pm Tue-Sat, 9am-noon Sun Jun–mid-Sep, 10am-2pm & 4-6pm Mon-Sat, 10am-2pm Sun rest of year), forerunner of Alicante, where excavations have revealed a rich wealth of pottery. You can make out its clearly defined streets and town plan. Take the tram, or bus 9 or 21.

TORREVIEJA

pop 94,000

Torrevieja, set on a wide coastal plain between two lagoons, one pink, one emerald, has good beaches. Sea salt production remains an important element of its economy.

The main **tourist office** (☎ 96 570 34 33; Plaza de Capdepont; 8am-8pm Mon-Fri, 10am-2pm Sat) is near the waterfront.

Sights & Activities

To appreciate why salt still means so much to *torrevejenses*, visit the **Museo del Mar y de la Sal** (Sea & Salt Museum; ☎ 96 670 68 38; Calle Patricio Pérez 12; admission free; 10am-2pm & 5-9pm Mon-Sat, 10am-1.30pm Sun), an appealing clutter of mementoes and bric-a-brac. The **Centro de Interpretación de la Industria Salinera** (☎ 96 570 58 88; Avenida de la Estación; admission free; 8.30am-2pm Mon-Fri) is more didactic, yet with a lightness of touch. It's in Torrevieja's former train station.

Aquópolis (☎ 902 34 50 08; Av Delfina Viudes; adult/under 4yr/4-10yr €21/free/16; 11am-7pm Jun-Aug, 11am-6pm Sep) – say it aloud and the pun will make you wince – is a fun water park on the outskirts of town. It offers free transport from the bus station.

El Delfín (admission free; 5-10pm Wed-Sun Jun-Sep, 9am-2pm Oct-May) is a decommissioned navy submarine that you can prowl around.

The **Via Verde** is a 6km-long walking and cycling track that follows an old train line, down which the last train steamed over 50 years ago. Running beside the lagoon and through the salt pans, it makes for a great half-day outing. Rent a bike from **Family Bike Hire.com** (☎ 96 677 45 98; www.familybikehire.com; per day/3 days/week €15/30/49), who will deliver to your hotel.

Just to the south of the tourist office is a large parking area and the jetty from which boats of **Marítimas Torrevieja** (☎ 96 670 21 22; adult/child €21/15 return; mid-Mar–mid-Nov) leave for day trips to the island of **Tabarca** (left).

Sleeping

Hotel Cano (☎ 96 670 09 58; www.hotelcano.com; Calle Zoa 53; s €30-40, d €40-60; P) Five blocks west of the bus station, the Cano has 57 trim, modern rooms, many with balcony. Those in the newer wing have fresh furniture and plenty of pleasing woodwork. Parking is €8.

Hotel Madrid (☎ 96 571 00 38; www.ansahotel.com in Spanish; Calle Villa Madrid 15; s incl breakfast €46-60, d €67.40-92; P) The Madrid is a friendly, family-run option with 40 comfortable, fairly spacious rooms, one equipped for travellers with disabilities. There's also a top-floor Jacuzzi and, just across the road, the hotel's brand-new swimming pool. Guests can hire a bike for a bargain €6 per day. Parking is €7.

Hotel Masa Internacional (☎ 96 692 15 37; www.hotelmasa.com; Avenida Alfredo Nobel 150; s €58-83, d €81-108; P) This smart clifftop hotel, 3.5km northeast of Torrevieja, is a lovely luxury choice, remote from all the downtown frenzy. Rooms overlooking the sea come at no extra cost. Parking is €6.

Eating

Plenty of restaurants around the waterfront offer cheap meals and international menus. On Plaza Isabel II, park yourself on a patio and enjoy great grilled fresh fish.

Restaurante Vegetariano (☎ 96 670 66 83; Calle Pedro Lorca 13; mains €10, salads €5.50-9.50; Tue-Sun; V) One block back from the beachfront, this little vegetarian haven serving salads, sandwiches, pizzas, pastas, pâtés and tasty mains is run by a Spanish–Australian couple.

Mesón de la Costa (☎ 96 670 35 98; Calle Ramón y Cajal 23; meals around €20; ⏰ Thu-Tue) Hams dangle from the roof of this low-beamed house of plenty. Greeting you as you enter are salvers and tureens of chicken, snails, grilled vegetables, fresh seafood on ice, and a cornucopia of fruit lies behind the glass doors of the refrigerator. Set one block back from the promenade, it's an authentically, enticingly Spanish restaurant that prides itself on the prime quality of its raw materials.

Mercado de Abastos (Plaza Isabel II),Torrevieja's covered market, is a great basket-filler for self-caterers.

Getting There & Away

From the **bus station** (☎ 96 571 01 46; Calle Antonio Machado), Autocares Costa Azul runs eight buses daily to Cartagena (€4, 1¼ hours) and Alicante (€3.50, one hour).

INLAND FROM THE COSTA BLANCA

The borderline between the holiday *costa* and the interior is, perhaps appropriately, a motorway. Venture away from the Med, west of the A7, to find yourself in a different, truly Spanish world. By far the easiest way to explore this hinterland is with your own transport.

XÀTIVA

pop 28,600

Xàtiva (Spanish Játiva) makes an easy and rewarding 50km day trip from Valencia. It has a small historic quarter and a mighty castle strung along the crest of the Serra Vernissa, at whose base the town snuggles.

The Muslims established Europe's first paper manufacturing plant in Xàtiva, which is also famous as the birthplace of the Borgia Popes Calixtus III and Alexander VI. The town's glory days ended in 1707 when Felipe V's troops torched most of the town.

Information

Tourist office (☎ 96 227 33 46; www.xativa.es in Spanish; Alameda Jaime I 50; ⏰ 10am-2.30pm Tue-Sun mid-Jun–mid-Sep, 10am-1.30pm & 4-6pm Tue-Fri, 10am-1.30pm Sat & Sun rest of year) On the Alameda, Xàtiva's shady main avenue.

Sights & Activities

What's interesting lies south and uphill from the Alameda. Ask at the tourist office for its English brochure *Xàtiva: Monumental Town.*

In the **Museo del Almudín** (☎ 96 227 65 97; Calle Corretgería 46; adult/child €2.10/1.10; ⏰ 9.30am-2.30pm Tue-Fri, 10am-2.30pm Sat & Sun mid-Jun–mid-Sep, 10am-2pm & 4-6pm Tue-Fri, 10am-2pm Sat & Sun mid-Sep–mid-Jun) items of most interest, including a couple of fine portraits by Ribera, are up on the penultimate floor. You can't miss the portrait of Felipe V, hung upside down in retribution for his torching the town.

The 16th-century **Colegiata Basílica** (Collegiate Church; ⏰ 10.30am-1pm) impresses by its sheer size but little else. Outside are a couple of fine statues of Xàtiva's two Borgia Popes, while in a couple of side chapels are 20th-century portraits of clerics assassinated by the Republican side during the Spanish civil war.

It's a long climb to the **castle** (adult/child €2.10/1.10; ⏰ 10am-6pm or 7pm Tue-Sun), from where the views are sensational. On the way up, on your left is the 18th-century **Ermita de San José** and, to the right, the lovely Romanesque **Iglesia de Sant Feliu** (1269), Xàtiva's oldest church. Alternatively, hop aboard the little tourist train (€4 return) that heads up from the tourist office at 12.30pm and 4.30pm (5.30pm June to September) or call a taxi (☎ 96 227 16 81) and stride back down.

Sleeping & Eating

Hotel Huerto Virgen de las Nieves (☎ 96 228 70 58; www.huertodelavirgendelasnieves.com in Spanish; Avenida Ribera 6; s/d €85/90; ❄ 💻 🏊) This intimate hotel (it has only nine rooms), all warm brick, woodwork and cobbled floors, gives onto a secluded garden shaded by palm trees and cypresses. Bedrooms are large (though the well-equipped bathrooms are tiny), blending traditional furniture with bright, contemporary artwork.

Hostería Mont Sant (☎ 96 227 50 81; www.mont-sant.com; r €103-149.50; P ❄ 🏊) On the road to the castle, this place sits charmingly amid extensive groves of palm and orange. Stay in the main building, once a farm, or in one of the spacious modern wooden cabins. There's a splendid restaurant, divided into intimate crannies. Sip your sundowner beside the mirador (viewing platform) with its plunging view of the plains.

Casa la Abuela (☎ 96 228 10 85; Calle de la Reina 17; mains €13-19, menú €15; ⏲ mid-Aug–mid-Jul) Renowned for its rice dishes, 'Grandmother's House' is equally strong on meat options, such as its ultra-tender *media paletilla de cordero confitada a bajo temperatura,* half a shoulder of lamb simmered/roasted at low temperature.

Two restaurants, both with broad terraces and open daily, stand out among those bordering Xàtiva's broad, tree-lined main avenue. **Canela y Clavo** (☎ 96 228 24 26; Albereda Jaume I 64; mains €11-18), staffed by black-clad waiters, does particularly creative mains and an excellent-value four-course lunch *menú* (€16). Its near neighbour, recently opened **Pebre Negre** (☎ 96 228 07 23; menú €16, mains €11-18), equally stylish, offers more than 20 rice dishes.

Getting There & Away

The train is by far your best bet. Frequent regional trains connect Xàtiva with Valencia (€3.65, 40 minutes, half-hourly) and most Valencia–Madrid trains stop here too. You can also reach Alicante (€8.85 to €19.60, 1½ hours, six daily).

VILLENA

pop 32,650

Villena, on the N330 between Alicante and Albacete, is the most attractive of the towns along the corridor of the Val de Vinalopó.

Plaza de Santiago is at the heart of the old quarter. The **tourist office** (☎ 96 615 02 36; ⏲ 8am-3pm Mon-Fri, 10.30am-1.30pm Sat & Sun) is at No 5. Within the imposing 16th-century **Palacio Municipal** (Plaza de Santiago 2) is Villena's **Museo Arqueológico** (admission free; ⏲ 10am-2pm Tue-Fri, 11am-2pm Sat & Sun). Pride of its collection are 60 gold artefacts weighing over 10kg, dating from around 1000 BC and found by chance in an old riverbed. Perched high above the town, the 12th-century **Castillo de la Atalaya** (admission free by guided visit) is splendidly lit at night. Guided visits, in Spanish with English summary, take place three times each morning, Tuesday to Sunday.

Villena celebrates its **Moros y Cristianos** fiesta from 5 to 9 September (see the boxed text, p644).

Hotel Restaurante Salvadora (☎ 96 580 09 50; www.hotelsalvadora.com in Spanish; cnr Calles Luis García & Jacinto Benavente; r €55) is the town's sole hotel, featuring simple, clean, well-priced rooms, popular bar with a great range of tapas, and gourmet restaurant (mains €13 to €20, four-course *menú degustación* €26) that does a mean *triguico picao* (€6.50), the local speciality – a thick gruel of wheat, beans, pork and turnip.

ELDA

pop 51,600

Elda vies with Elche for the title of shoemaking capital of Spain. Foot fetishists shouldn't miss the **Museo del Calzado** (Shoe Museum; ☎ 96 538 30 21; Avenida Chapí 32; adult/child €2.50/1.25; ⏲ 10am-2pm & 4-8pm Tue-Sat, 11am-2pm Sun Sep-Jul, 10am-2pm Tue-Fri Aug). Above the mezzanine floor with its rows of Heath Robinson drills, stamps and sewing machines, it's wall-to-wall footwear: boots through the ages; shoes from around the world; fanciful designs that must have been agony to wear; and donated cast-offs from matadors, flamenco dancers, King Juan Carlos, Queen Sofia and other well-shod greats.

NOVELDA

pop 24,800

Novelda was once an affluent town that derived its wealth from the saffron trade. Just 25km from Alicante, it's rich in art nouveau (more often known as *Modernismo* in Spanish) sights. At **Casa-Museo Modernista** (☎ 96 560 02 37; Calle Mayor 24; admission free; ⏲ guided visits hourly 10am-1pm Tue-Sat), a bourgeois mansion completed in 1903, the stained glass, soft shapes in wood, period furniture and magnificent spiralling wrought-iron staircase take the breath away.

Novelda's **tourist office** (☎ 96 560 92 28; www.novelda.es; Calle Mayor 6; ⏲ 9am-2pm & 4.30-6pm Mon-Fri, 10am-2pm Sat) is within the town's Centro Cultural, itself a lovely Modernista building. Admire too the exterior of the headquarters of the local **Cruz Roja** (Spanish Red Cross; Plaza Vieja 9) and make the smallest of detours to take in the glorious **Santuario de Santa María Magdalena** (⏲ 10am-1.45pm & 4-6.45pm), the carefully crafted equivalent, on a doll's-house scale, of Gaudí's famous Sagrada Família in Barcelona (p330).

JIJONA

pop 7200

If you love all things sweet, you really ought to make a pilgrimage to Jijona (Valenciano: Xixona), on the N340 more or less midway between Alicante and Alcoy. This small town has two claims to fame. Nowadays, it's Spain's principal producer of *turrón*, a kind of nougat with both soft and crunchy variants. In the past, the place was also a stopover for porters bearing ice from the high hinterland to assuage the heat of a coastal summer. And so it lent its name to Jijona, a popular brand of ice cream that sells by the hectolitre throughout the land.

To learn about *turrón* production and crunch on a sample or two, visit the **Museo del Turrón** (☎ 965 61 02 25; www.museodelturron.com; adult/under 12yr €1/free; 10am-7.30pm Jul-Nov, 10am-2pm & 4-8pm Dec-Jun), mounted by the company that makes *1880* and *El Lobo*, two of the tastiest brands.

ALCOY

pop 58,350 / elev 565m

For 51¾ weeks a year, there's not a lot to entice you to the industrial town of Alcoy (Valenciano: Alcoi), 54km north of Alicante. But there's everything to draw you here between 22 and 24 April, when the town holds its resplendent **Moros y Cristianos** festival (see the boxed text, below).

To get a feel for this exuberant fiesta, visit the comprehensively renovated **Museu Alcoià de la Festa** (☎ 96 554 08 12; Calle Sant Miquel 60; adult/child €3/1.50; 10am-2pm & 4-7pm Tue-Sat, 11am-2pm Sun) with its posters, musical instruments, resplendent costumes and a stirring, noisily evocative 20-minute film of the action.

Alcoy's **tourist office** (☎ 96 553 71 55; alcoi@touristinfo.net; Calle San Lorenzo 2; 10am-2pm & 4-6pm Mon-Fri, 11am-2pm Sat & Sun) is just off the main Plaza de España.

The ultramodern **Hotel AC Ciutat d'Alcoi** (☎ 96 533 36 06; www.ac-hotels.com; Calle Colón 1; r €80-105; P ⊠ ✻ 💻) was once an electricity substation, though you'd never believe it. The black and chestnut brown of bedroom furnishings contrast pleasingly with crisp white sheets. It also runs a superlative restaurant, **La Llum** (☎ 96 533 45 40; menú €22.25, mains €10.50-16.10; lunch & dinner Mon-Sat & lunch Sun). Parking is €10.50.

Hostal Savoy (☎ 96 554 72 72; www.hostalsavoy.com in Spanish; Calle Casablanca 9; s/d/tr with bathroom €35/50/65; P ✻) is a friendly place, one block south of Plaza de España. Its 24 rooms, eight of which have air-con, are trim, well kept and have a bathtub. Its cafe does a bargain lunch *menú* (€8) and there's locked parking (€6) a short walk away.

Immediately west of Plaza de España, **Plaxa de Dins**, arcaded and more intimate, is packed with drinkers and diners on warm summer evenings.

There are four trains daily to/from Valencia (€7.15, two hours) via Xàtiva. From the nearby bus station, six daily services run to Valencia (€9, 1¾ hours), at least eight to Alicante (€6.30; 1¾ hours) and a couple to Gandia (€4; 1¾ hours).

GUADALEST

pop 200

You'll be far from the first to discover the village of Guadalest; nowadays coaches, heading up from the Costa Blanca resorts, disgorge more than two million visitors every year. But get there early, or stay around after the last bus has pulled out and the place will be almost your own.

MOROS Y CRISTIANOS

More than 80 towns and villages in the south of Valencia hold their own Fiesta de Moros y Cristianos (Moors and Christians festival) to celebrate the Reconquista, the region's liberation from Muslim rule.

Biggest and best known is Alcoy's (22 to 24 April), when hundreds of locals dress up in elaborate traditional costumes representing different 'factions' – Muslim and Christian soldiers, slaves, guild groups, town criers, heralds, bands – and march through the streets in colourful processions with mock battles.

Processions converge upon Alcoy's main plaza and its huge, temporary wooden fortress. It's an exhilarating spectacle of sights and sounds: soldiers in shining armour, white-cloaked Muslim warriors bearing scimitars and shields, turban-topped Arabs, scantily clad wenches, brass bands, exploding blunderbusses, firework displays and confetti showering down on the crowds.

Each town has its own variation on the format, steeped in traditions that allude to the events of the Reconquista. So, for example, Villena's festival (5 to 9 September) features midnight parades, while La Vila Joiosa (24 to 31 July), near Benidorm, re-enacts the landing of Muslim ships on the beaches.

Crowds come because Guadalest, reached by a natural tunnel and overlooked by the **Castillo de San José** (adult/under 7yr/7-12yr €4/free/2; 10am-6pm or 8pm), is indeed very pretty, and it's a joy to stroll through a traffic-free village.

One little jewel amid so much day-tripper-oriented tackiness is the diminutive **Museo Etnológico** (☎ 96 588 52 38; admission free, donations welcome; 10am-6.30pm daily Jun-Oct, Sun-Fri Nov-May), a sensitive presentation of what life in Guadalest was like before the coach parties came along.

ELCHE

pop 194,700

Precisely 23km southwest of Alicante, Elche (Valenciano: Elx) is a Unesco World Heritage site twice over: for the Misteri d'Elx, its annual mystery play (see the boxed text, p646) and for its extensive palm groves, Europe's largest, originally planted by the Phoenecians and extended by the Arabs. Islamic irrigation systems converted the region into a rich agricultural district that still produces citrus fruit, figs, almonds, dates – and 85% of Spain's pomegranates.

Though its suburbs are drear and soulless, Elche's heart is green and open, with parks, date groves and public gardens. Its sights are comprehensively signed in English.

Orientation & Information

The town is split north–south by the channelled trickle of Río Vinalopó. The older quarter and most of the parks and monuments lie on its eastern side.

Train and bus stations are beside each other on Avenida de la Libertad (also called Avenida del Ferrocarril), north of the centre. From either, go south along Avenida de la Libertad, then down Paseo de la Estación to reach the tourist office and town centre.

The **tourist office** (☎ 96 665 81 96; www.turismedelx.com; 9am-7pm Mon-Fri, 10am-7pm Sat, 10am-2pm Sun) is located at the southeast corner of Parque Municipal (Town Park).

Sights & Activities

Well over 200,000 palm trees, some shaggy and in need of a haircut, most trim and clipped, each with a lifespan of some 250 years, make the heart of this busy industrial town a veritable oasis. A signed 3km walking trail (ask at the tourist office for its leaflet *Historic Palm Groves Route*) leads you through the groves.

Opposite the hotel of the same name, the **Huerto del Cura** (Porta de la Morera 49; adult/under 5yr/5-14yr incl audioguide €5/free/2.50; 9am-sunset Mar-Oct, 9.30am-5pm Nov-Feb) is a lovely private garden with tended lawns and colourful flowerbeds. More instructive is the **Museo del Palmeral** (☎ 96 542 22 40; Porta de la Morera 12; adult/child €1/0.50; 10am-1.30pm & 4.30-8pm Tue-Sat, 10.30am-1.30pm Sun). In a former farmhouse, it's all about the date palm and the intricate blanched, woven fronds used throughout Spain in Palm Sunday rites. Wander through the delightful adjacent palm grove and orchard with its gurgling irrigation channels and typical fruit trees of the *huerta*.

The **Museo Arqueológico y de Historia de Elche** (MAHE; ☎ 96 665 82 03; Diagonal del Palau 7; adult/child €3/1; same as Museo del Palmeral), well signed in Spanish and English, recounts Elche's history through selected artefacts, touch screens and giant computer animations.

For an alternative overview of the town, call by the **Centro de Visitantes** (admission free; 10am-7pm Mon-Sat, 10am-2pm Sun). This Arab-style building, in the park behind the tourist office, runs a 10-minute audiovisual presentation with multilingual commentary.

The 12th-century **Baños Árabes** (Arab Baths; ☎ 96 545 28 87; Passeig de les Eres de Santa Lucía 13; adult/child €1/0.50; same as Museo del Palmeral) runs an enjoyable audiovisual presentation with optional English soundtrack.

The vast baroque **Basílica de Santa María** (7am-1.30pm & 5.30-9pm) is used for performances of the Misteri d'Elx. Climb up its **tower** (adult/under 5yr/5-10yr €2/free/1; 11am-6pm or 7pm) for a pigeon's-eye view over the palms.

The well-documented **Alcúdia archaeological site** is 3.5km south of the town centre. Here was unearthed the Dama de Elche, a masterpiece of Iberian art that's now in Madrid's Museo Arqueológico Nacional collection (see p158). Visit the site's excellent **Museo Arqueológico** (☎ 96 661 15 06; adult/child €3/1; 10am-8pm). The museum displays the rich findings from a settlement that was occupied continuously from Neolithic to late-Visigoth times.

Sleeping & Eating

Pensión Faro (☎ 96 546 62 63; Camí dels Magros 24; basic s/d €15/30) This friendly nine-room family-run place is a little gem with simple, spotless rooms and corridor bathrooms.

Hotel Huerto del Cura (☎ 96 661 00 11; www.huertodelcura.com; Porta de la Morera 14; r Mon-Thu €112, Fri-Sun

MISTERI D'ELX

The *Misteri d'Elx,* a two-act lyric drama dating from the Middle Ages, is performed annually in Elche's Basílica de Santa María.

One distant day, according to legend, a casket was washed up on Elche's Mediterranean shore. Inside were a statue of the Virgin and the *Consueta,* the music and libretto of a mystery play describing Our Lady's death, assumption into heaven and coronation.

The story tells how the Virgin, realising that death is near, asks God to allow her to see the apostles one last time. They arrive one by one from distant lands and, in their company, she dies at peace. Once received into paradise, she is crowned Queen of Heaven and Earth to swelling music, the ringing of bells, cheers all round and – hey, we're in the Valencia region – spectacular fireworks.

The mystery's two acts, *La Vespra* (the eve of her death) and *La Festa* (the celebration of her assumption and coronation), are performed in Valenciano by the people of Elche themselves on 14 and 15 August respectively (with public rehearsals on the three previous days).

You can see a multimedia presentation – complete with virtual apostle – in the **Museu de la Festa** (☎ 96 545 34 64; Carrer Major de la Vila 25; adult/child €3/1; ⏰ 10am-1.30pm & 4.30-8pm Tue-Sat, 10.30am-1.30pm Sun), about a block west of the basilica. The show lasts 35 minutes and is repeated several times daily, with optional English commentary.

€102-132; P ⊠ ✇ ▣ ◙) Accommodation is in trim bungalows within lush, palm-shaded gardens. It's a family-friendly place with playground, large pool and babysitting service. Complete the cosseting at Elche's longest-standing luxury hotel by dining in **Els Capellans**, its renowned restaurant. Parking is €12.

Restaurante Dátil de Oro (☎ 96 545 34 15; mains €12-20, menú €16-30) Within the municipal park, this vast emporium to eating can accommodate almost 800 diners. Even so, the cuisine is far from institutional and it's one of the best places in town to sample local dishes, such as *arroz con costra* (rice with a crusty egg topping).

El Granaíno (☎ 96 666 40 80; Calle Josep María Buck 40; ⏰ lunch & dinner Tue-Sat & lunch Mon Sep–mid-Aug) The tiled exterior of this long-established favourite hints at the classic, quintessentially Spanish cuisine of this family-run restaurant with its impressively long bar and bodega of more than 7000 bottles.

Carrer Mare de Déu del Carmé (Calle Nuestra Señora del Carmen) has a cluster of cheap and cheerful eateries. On summer evenings almost the whole length of this short street is set with tables.

Getting There & Around

SuBús operates buses at least every hour to/from Alicante (€1.85). **ALSA** (www.alsa.es) runs seven buses daily to Valencia (€10.95) via Elda and Villena and seven to/from Murcia (€3.80).

Elche is on the Alicante–Murcia train line. Around 20 trains daily rattle through, bound for Alicante (€1.85) or Murcia (€2.65) via Orihuela (€1.85).

ORIHUELA

pop 54,400

Beside Río Segura and flush with the base of a barren mountain of rock, the historical heart of Orihuela with its Gothic, Renaissance and, especially, baroque buildings well merits a short detour.

The **tourist office** (☎ 96 530 27 47; Calle Francisco Die 25; ⏰ 8am-2.30pm or 3pm & 4-7pm or 5-8pm Mon-Fri, 10am-2pm Sat) is opposite Iglesia de Santiago Apostól.

Sights

The 16th-century **Convento de Santo Domingo** (Calle Adolfo Claravana s/n; ⏰ 9.30am-1.30pm & 4-7pm or 5-8pm Tue-Fri, 10am-2pm Sat) has two fine Renaissance cloisters and a refectory rich in 18th-century tilework.

Other splendid ecclesiastical buildings include the 14th-century Catalan Gothic **Catedral de San Salvador** (Calle Doctor Sarget; ⏰ 10.30am-2pm & 4-6.30pm or 5-8pm Tue-Fri, 10am-2pm Sat) with three finely carved portals, a lovely little cloister and the **Museo de Arte Sacro** (admission €2), whose collection includes Velázquez' *Temptation of St Thomas*.

The **Iglesia de las Santas Justa y Rufina** (Plaza Salesas 1; ⏰ 10am-2pm & 4-7pm or 5-8pm Tue-Fri, 10am-2pm Sat) has a Renaissance facade and a Gothic tower graced with gargoyles. Also noteworthy are the sober baroque facade of the **Palacio Episcopal** (Calle Ramón y Cajal), the 14th-century **Iglesia de Santiago Apóstol** (Plaza de Santiago 2) and, crowning the mountain, the ruins of a **castle** originally constructed by the Muslims.

Access to Orihuela's **Museo de la Muralla** (☎ 96 530 46 98; Calle del Río s/n; admission free; ⏰ 10am-2pm & 4-7pm or 5-8pm Tue-Sat, 10am-2pm Sun) is through the main door to the Universidad Miguel Hernandez. A 20-minute guided tour in Spanish (ask for the English leaflet) leads you through the vast underground remains of the city walls, Arab baths, domestic buildings and a Gothic palace.

Sleeping & Eating

Hostal Rey Teodomiro (☎/fax 96 674 33 48; 1st fl, Avenida Rey Teodomiro 10; s/d €32.10/53.50; ❄) In the modern part of town and handy for bus and train stations, this is an excellent-value budget option, with air-con in all 23 rooms. Those facing the grassy square have balconies.

Hotel Melia Palacio de Tudemir (☎ 96 673 80 10; www.solmelia.com; Calle Alfonso XIII 1; r €85; ⊠ ❄) Palace is indeed the word for this tastefully renovated 18th-century building. There's a pleasant cafe (open 8am to midnight) offering tasty snacks and a restaurant (menú €17 to €20, mains €18 to €21; open lunch only) that's the best of Orihuela's limited dining options.

Barra Restaurante Joaquín (☎ 96 674 34 15; Avenida Rey Teodomiro 18; mains €15-21; ⏰ closed dinner Wed, lunch & dinner Sun) For food that is grilled, roasted, or at most garnished with a simple sauce meunière. The Joaquin's reputation rests upon the superb quality of its fresh meat, fish and seafood, served unadorned and without fancy sauces. Dine in the convivial bar or in the more restrained surroundings of the rear restaurant.

Getting There & Away

Bus and train stations are combined at the Intermodal, an airy structure at the end of Avenida de Teodomiro. Orihuela is on the Alicante–Murcia train line and has frequent services to both places. Tickets cost €3.15 to Alicante and €1.20 to Murcia.

Balearic Islands

Each of these four islands (Islas Baleares in Spanish; Illes Balears in Catalan), floating serenely in the glittering Mediterranean, could be said to have a theme. Mallorca is the senior island, combining a little of everything, from spectacular mountain scenery and hiking through to the standard sea 'n' sun tourism. Ibiza is synonymous with clubbing, the island that gave Europe the rave. Menorca is a haven of tranquillity – splendid isolated beaches and coves, and prehistoric monuments standing as taciturn reminders of how small we are in the grand scheme of things. And tiny Formentera, a chill-out island, where some people lose themselves for the entire summer, needing little more to keep them happy than white beaches and sunset parties.

Each year a massive multinational force invades the islands in search of a piece of this multifaceted paradise. The total population of the isles barely stands over the million mark, but many times that number are involved in a round-the-clock airlift and disembarkation of sun- and fun-seekers from Easter to October.

Surprisingly, the islands have managed to maintain much of their intrinsic beauty. Beyond the high-rise resort hotels, bars and more popular beaches are Gothic cathedrals, Stone Age ruins, fishing villages, spectacular walks, secluded coves, endless olive and almond groves and citrus orchards. And a growing spread of elegant, rural retreats and A-list eateries are attracting a range of visitors beyond the party package crowd.

HIGHLIGHTS

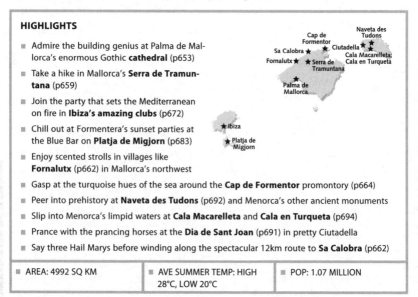

- Admire the building genius at Palma de Mallorca's enormous Gothic **cathedral** (p653)
- Take a hike in Mallorca's **Serra de Tramuntana** (p659)
- Join the party that sets the Mediterranean on fire in **Ibiza's amazing clubs** (p672)
- Chill out at Formentera's sunset parties at the Blue Bar on **Platja de Migjorn** (p683)
- Enjoy scented strolls in villages like **Fornalutx** (p662) in Mallorca's northwest
- Gasp at the turquoise hues of the sea around the **Cap de Formentor** promontory (p664)
- Peer into prehistory at **Naveta des Tudons** (p692) and Menorca's other ancient monuments
- Slip into Menorca's limpid waters at **Cala Macarelleta** and **Cala en Turqueta** (p694)
- Prance with the prancing horses at the **Dia de Sant Joan** (p691) in pretty Ciutadella
- Say three Hail Marys before winding along the spectacular 12km route to **Sa Calobra** (p662)

AREA: 4992 SQ KM	AVE SUMMER TEMP: HIGH 28°C, LOW 20°C	POP: 1.07 MILLION

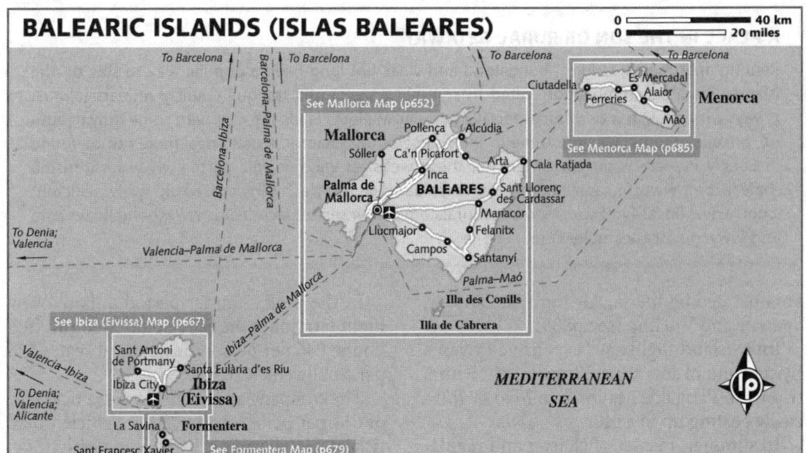

History

Archaeologists believe the first human settlements in the Balearic Islands date from around 5000 BC and the islands were later regular ports of call for Phoenician traders. The Carthaginians followed and founded Ibiza City in 654 BC, making it one of the Mediterranean's major trading ports. Next came the Romans, who, in turn, were overwhelmed by the Visigoths.

Three centuries of Muslim domination ended with the Christian Reconquista, led by Jaume I of Catalonia and Aragón, who took Palma de Mallorca in 1229 and sponsored the invasion of Ibiza in 1235. Menorca was the last to fall: Alfons III took it in 1287 in a nasty Vietnam-style campaign, completing the islands' incorporation into the Catalan world.

After their initial boom as trading centres and Catalan colonies, the islands had fallen on hard times by the 15th century. Isolation from the mainland, famines and frequent raids by pirates contributed to their decline. During the 16th century Menorca's two major towns were virtually destroyed by Turkish forces and Ibiza City's fortified walls were built. After a succession of bloody raids, Formentera was abandoned.

After backing the Habsburgs in the War of Spanish Succession (1702–13), Mallorca and Ibiza were occupied by the victorious Bourbon monarchy in 1715. Menorca was granted to the British along with Gibraltar in 1713 under the Treaty of Utrecht. British rule lasted until 1802, with the exception of the Seven Years War (1756–63), during which the French moved in, and a brief Spanish reconquest after that. In the Spanish Civil War, Menorca was the last of the islands to succumb to Franco's forces.

Tourism since the 1950s has brought considerable wealth. The islanders now enjoy – by some estimates – the highest standard of living in Spain, but 80% of their economy is based on tourism (14 million arrivals each year). This has led to thoughtless (and continuing) construction on the islands (the term *balearización* has been coined to illustrate this short-termism and wanton destruction of the archipelago's prime resource – its beautiful coastlines).

The islands' foreign admirers have their preferences. If the Germans have set their sights on Mallorca, Formentera becomes Little Italy in July and August. The Brits are numerous in Mallorca, but have a special affection for Menorca. Ibiza's clubs, on the other hand, attract an international brigade of hedonists.

Place names and addresses in this chapter are in Catalan, the main language spoken (with regional variations). The major exceptions are Ibiza and Ibiza City – both are called Eivissa in Catalan but we use the better-known Spanish rendition.

Getting There & Around

AIR

If your main goal in Spain is to visit the Balearic Islands, it makes *no* sense to fly via the mainland. If already in Spain, scheduled flights from major cities on the mainland

A PLACE IN THE SUN OR RURAL GETAWAY

Renting apartments, studios, bungalows and villas has long been a popular way to stay on the islands. Rural accommodation, often in stylishly transformed tranquil country retreats (almost always with pool), has become especially popular. Mallorca leads the way, with some truly beautiful, bucolic options. We note some in the course of this chapter. A great deal more can be found in Lonely Planet's *Mallorca*. Otherwise, these websites will get you started: www.agroturismo-balear.com, www.fincamallorca.de, www.baleares.com/fincas, www.mfh.co.uk, www.rusticrent.com, www.fincas4you.com, www.toprural.com, www.secretplaces.com, www.homelidays.com and www.guiascasasrurales.com.

are operated by Iberia, Air Europa, Clickair, Spanair and Vueling (see p883).

Inter-island flights are expensive (given a flying time of less than 30 minutes), with a trip from Palma de Mallorca to Maó or Ibiza easily costing up to €140.

In summer, masses of charter and regular flights converge on Palma de Mallorca and Ibiza from all over Europe.

BOAT

The main ferry company, **Acciona Trasmediterránea** (☎ 902 45 46 45; www.trasmediterranea.es), runs services between Barcelona and Valencia on the mainland, and Ibiza City, Maó and Palma de Mallorca. Tickets can be purchased from any travel agency or online. Timetables and fares vary constantly.

From Barcelona, two daily services run to Palma de Mallorca from about Easter to late October. A high-speed catamaran leaves at 4pm (€90 for standard seat, €180 for small car; four hours), while an overnight ferry leaves at 11pm (€47 for standard seat, €154 for small car; 7¼ hours). The return trips from Palma are at 10am or 11.30am (catamaran) and 1pm (ferry). Between late October and Easter, only the overnight ferry continues to run most days. All these ferries continue to Ibiza. You pay the same price as for Mallorca but add three hours to the journey time.

From Valencia, a high-speed catamaran leaves for Palma (six hours) via Ibiza (3½ hours) at 4pm and a direct overnight ferry at 11pm (7½ hours). The fast ferry operates Thursday to Tuesday and the overnight Monday to Saturday. The return catamaran trip from Palma leaves at 7.30am, while the ferry departs at 11.45am (seven hours) or midnight (eight hours). Prices are similar to those from Barcelona. In August, a direct València–Mallorca catamaran service is usually added.

In the peak summer period a daily overnight ferry does the Barcelona–Maó run (9½ hours; €46 per person in standard seat; €176 per small vehicle).

The company adds a cheeky extra ticket fee of €11 per person and €13 per vehicle on all tickets. Get discounts by booking early.

Acciona Trasmediterránea runs two fast ferries or catamarans a day between Palma and Ibiza City (generally leaving Ibiza at 7am and 7.45pm, and Palma at 7.30am and 8.45pm) from Easter to the end of October (€61 for standard seat, €116 for small car; 2¼ hours). Curiously, the service drops to one a day in August.

The inter-island booking fee is €6 per person and €9 per vehicle.

Baleària (☎ 902 16 01 80; www.balearia.com) operates ferries to Palma de Mallorca from Barcelona, Valencia and Denia (via Ibiza). You can check all fares and departure times online. Prices can be considerably lower than those with Acciona Mediterránea if you book far enough ahead.

One fast ferry (two hours) and one conventional boat (five hours) link Palma to Ibiza from mid-March to October. Up to two other fast ferries are added to this run in July and August. There is a daily ferry between Alcúdia, in northeast Mallorca, and Ciutadella in the same period.

Iscomar (☎ 902 11 91 28; www.iscomar.com) has a ferry service from Barcelona to Palma (€48, €140 per small car, 7½ hours, daily in summer). There are sometimes services to Ibiza and Maó too. From Valencia (nine hours, six days a week in summer) the prices are similar. One or two daily ferries shuttle between Ciutadella on Menorca and Port d'Alcúdia on Mallorca (up to €55 per person and up to €90 per small car one-way, 2½ hours) between mid-March and mid-December.

Cala Ratjada Tours (☎ 902 10 04 44; www.calaratjadatours.es) operates two fast ferries daily between Cala Ratjada, in eastern Mallorca, and Ciutadella, in Menorca, from May to September. The crossing (one-way/return up to €80/120) takes 55 minutes. Same-day returns cost €60 and other tickets cost less if bought at least one day in advance.

You can compare prices and look for deals at **Direct Ferries** (www.directf erries.es).

For details of ferries between Ibiza and Formentera, see p678.

MALLORCA

In 1950 the first charter flight landed on a small airstrip on Mallorca, the largest of the Balearic Islands (3620 sq km). The number of annual visitors today hovers around 10 million – most in search of the three S's: sun, sand and sea, and swamping the local island populace of some 814,280 people (nearly half of whom live in the capital, Palma de Mallorca).

However, there's much more to Mallorca than the beach. Palma de Mallorca (or simply Palma) is the main centre and a charming stop. The northwest coast, dominated by the Serra de Tramuntana mountain range, is a beautiful region of olive groves, pine forests and ochre villages, with a spectacularly rugged coastline.

Most of Mallorca's best beaches are on the north and east coasts and, although many have been swallowed up by tourist developments, you can still find the occasional exception. There is also a scattering of fine beaches along parts of the south coast.

Check out websites like www.illesbalears .es, www.baleares.com, www.abc-mallorca .com and www.newsmallorca.com. For hotels, check www.mallorcahotelguide.com and www.reisdem allorca.com.

Orientation

The capital, Palma de Mallorca, is on the south side of the island, on a bay known for its brilliant sunsets.

Locals, who call their island *sa Roqueta* (Little Rock), refer to what lies beyond the capital as the *part forana,* the 'part outside'. A series of rocky coves and harbours punctuate the short southwest coastline. Offshore from the island's westernmost point is the large, uninhabited Illa de Sa Dragonera.

The spectacular Serra de Tramuntana mountain range runs parallel with the northwest coast and Puig Major (1445m) is its highest point. The northeast coast is largely made up of two bays, the Badia de Pollença and the larger Badia d'Alcúdia.

The east coast is an almost continuous string of sandy bays and open beaches, which explains the densely packed tourist developments. Most of the south coast is lined with rocky cliffs interrupted by beaches and coves, and the interior is largely made up of the fertile plain known as Es Pla.

Getting Around

BOAT

Palma and the major resorts and beaches around the island are connected by boat tours and water-taxi services. Some of these are detailed in the *Excursions En Barca* brochure, available at tourist offices. **Cruceros Iberia** (☎ 971 71 71 90; ⏰ Tue, Thu & Fri mid-May–mid-Oct) organises day trips to Sant Elm, leaving at 9.30am and returning at 5pm, for €52.50 per person including lunch and hotel transfers.

BUS

Most of the island is accessible by bus from Palma. All buses depart from (or near) the **bus station** (Carrer d'Eusebi Estada). For information contact **Transport de les Illes Balears** (TIB; ☎ 971 17 77 77; http://tib .caib.es).

BUSIER THAN BEN HUR

The Balearics in high summer (from late June to about halfway into September) can be incredibly busy. Palma de Mallorca alone turns around some 40 inbound and outbound flights a day. It is no coincidence that local bus and taxi drivers occasionally choose to strike around this time. Most of the millions of visitors have prebooked package accommodation and the strain on local infrastructure can make it tricky for the independent traveller. It is wise to book at least the first couple of nights around this time to avoid an uncomfortable start. In July and August, some hotels push the boat out on prices. This chapter reflects such high-season maxima, which means that in some places you can expect to pay considerably less in quieter times.

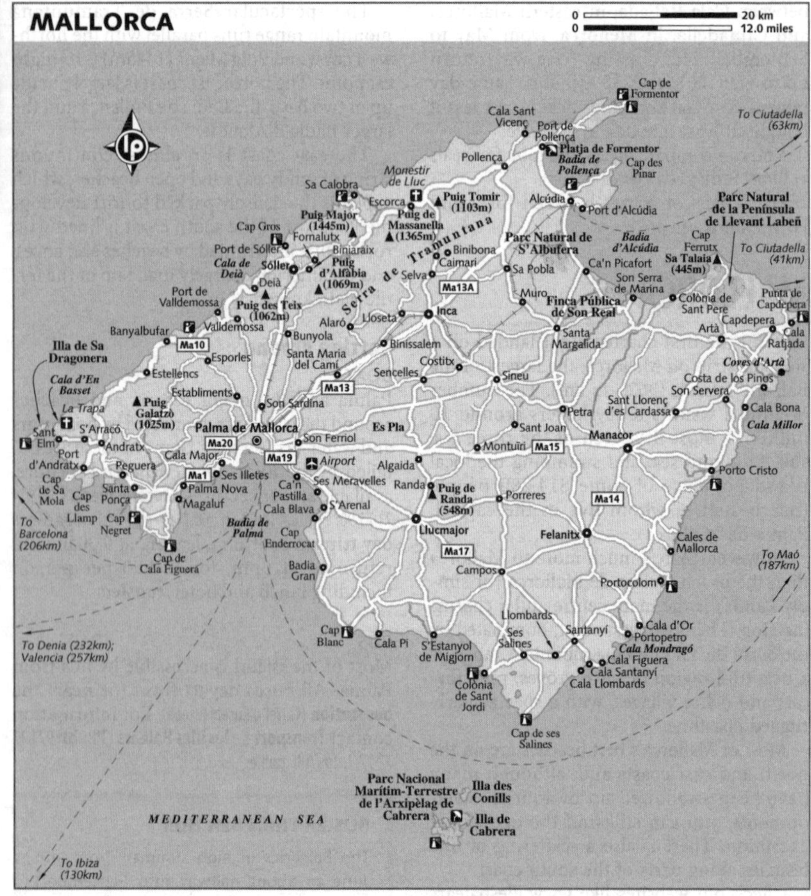

One-way fares from Palma include Cala Ratjada (€9.50), Ca'n Picafort (€4.65), Port de Pollença (€4.90) and Port d'Andratx (€3.80).

CAR & MOTORCYCLE

About 30 vehicle-hire agencies operate in Palma. The big league has representatives at the airport and along Passeig Marítim, along with several cheaper companies.

One of the best deals is **Hasso** (☎ 902 20 30 12; www.hasso-rentacar.com). **Pepecar** (☎ 807 41 42 43; www.pepecar.com) has several rental outlets, including the airport (look for the Centauro counter).

You can rent scooters from **Europa Moto Rent** (☎ 971 28 71 29; Avinguda d'Argentina 9).

TAXI

You can get around the island by taxi, but it's costly. Prices are posted at central points in many towns. You're looking at €86 (or €97 for the night rate) from the airport to Cala Ratjada.

TRAIN

Two train lines run from Plaça d'Espanya in Palma de Mallorca. The popular, old train runs to Sóller (see the boxed text, opposite) and is a pretty ride. A more prosaic **train line** (☎ 971 17 77 77) runs inland to Inca (€1.80), where the line splits with a branch to Sa Pobla (€2.65, 58 minutes) and another to Manacor (€3.70, one hour six minutes).

THE SLOW CHUG NORTH TO SÓLLER

A delightful journey into the past is also a pleasing way to head north from Palma de Mallorca for Sóller (p661). Since 1912, a **narrow-gauge train** (☎ 971 75 20 51, 902 36 47 11; http//:trendesoller.com; one-way/return €9/14, 3-6yr half-price, under 3yr free) has trundled along this winding 27.3km route. The teetering timber-panelled train departs from Plaça de l'Estació seven times daily and takes 1¼ hours. You pass through ever-changing countryside that becomes dramatic in the north as it crosses the Serra de Alfàbia, offering fabulous views over Sóller and the sea on the final descent into town.

PALMA DE MALLORCA

pop 383,100

Palma de Mallorca is the islands' only true city. Central Palma's old quarter is an enchanting blend of tree-lined boulevards and cobbled laneways, Gothic churches and baroque palaces, designer bars and slick boutiques.

The only bad news is that you'll have to take a bus to get to most beaches.

Orientation

Central Palma stretches from the harbour to Plaça d'Espanya, home to the train stations and 200m from the bus station. The airport bus stops here, too. It has a tourist office, and frequent buses run to the central Plaça de la Reina (a 20-minute walk).

Information

Airport tourist office (☎ 971 78 95 56; 🕑 8.30am-8pm Mon-Sat, 9am-1.30pm Sun)

Azul Cybercafé (☎ 971 71 29 27; www.azulgroup.com; Carrer de la Soledat 4; per hr €2.90; 🕑 8.30am-8pm Mon-Fri, noon-6pm Sat).

Consell de Mallorca tourist office (☎ 971 71 22 16; www.infomallorca.net; Plaça de la Reina 2; 🕑 9am-8pm Mon-Fri, 9am-2pm Sat) Covers the whole island.

Hospital Son Dureta (☎ 971 17 50 00; Carrer de Andrea Doria 55)

Municipal tourist office (☎ 902 10 23 65; www.palmademallorca.es) Main office (Casal Solleric, Passeig d'es Born 27; 🕑 9am-8pm); Branch office (Parc de les Estacions; 🕑 9am-8pm)

Post office (Carrer de la Constitució 6; 🕑 8.30am-8.30pm Mon-Fri, 9.30am-2pm Sat).

www.palmademallorca.es The official site of the city of Palma *(ajuntament)*, with plenty of links and an interactive city map.

www.visit-palma.com Asociación Hotelera de Palma de Mallorca website, with hotel and general information for Palma de Mallorca.

Numerous countries maintain consular agencies here; see Directory p872 and Map p654.

Sights

Central Palma is especially known for the elegant courtyards, or *patis*, of its many noble houses and mansions. Most are in private hands, but a peek into a *pati* is often possible. Ask for a booklet pinpointing the most interesting ones at the tourist office.

CATEDRAL & AROUND

Palma's enormous **catedral** (La Seu; ☎ 971 72 31 30; www.catedraldemallorca.org; Carrer del Palau Reial 9; adult/under 10yr/student €4/free/3; 🕑 10am-6.30pm Mon-Fri, 10am-2.30pm Sat Jun-Sep, 10am-5.30pm Mon-Fri, 10am-2.30pm Sat Apr-May & Oct, 10am-2.30pm Mon-Fri, 10am-2.30pm Sat Nov-Mar) is often likened to a huge ship moored at the city's edge. Construction on what had been the site of the main mosque started in 1300 but wasn't completed until 1601. This awesome structure is predominantly Gothic, apart from the main facade (replaced after an earthquake in 1851) and parts of the interior (renovated in Modernista style by Antoni Gaudí at the beginning of the 20th century).

Entry is via a small, three-room **museum**, which holds a rich collection of religious artwork and precious gold and silver effects. Interesting items include a portable altar, thought to have belonged to Jaume I. Its little compartments contain saints' relics. Other reliquaries can be seen too, including one purporting to hold three thorns from Christ's crown of thorns.

The cathedral's interior is stunning, with a series of narrow columns supporting the soaring ceiling and framing three levels of elaborate stained-glass windows. The front altar's centrepiece, a rather odd twisting wrought-iron sculpture suspended from the ceiling and periodically lit with fairy lights, has been widely acclaimed, mainly because it was Gaudí's handiwork. It doesn't happen often, but Gaudí is completely upstaged by the island's top contemporary artist, Miquel

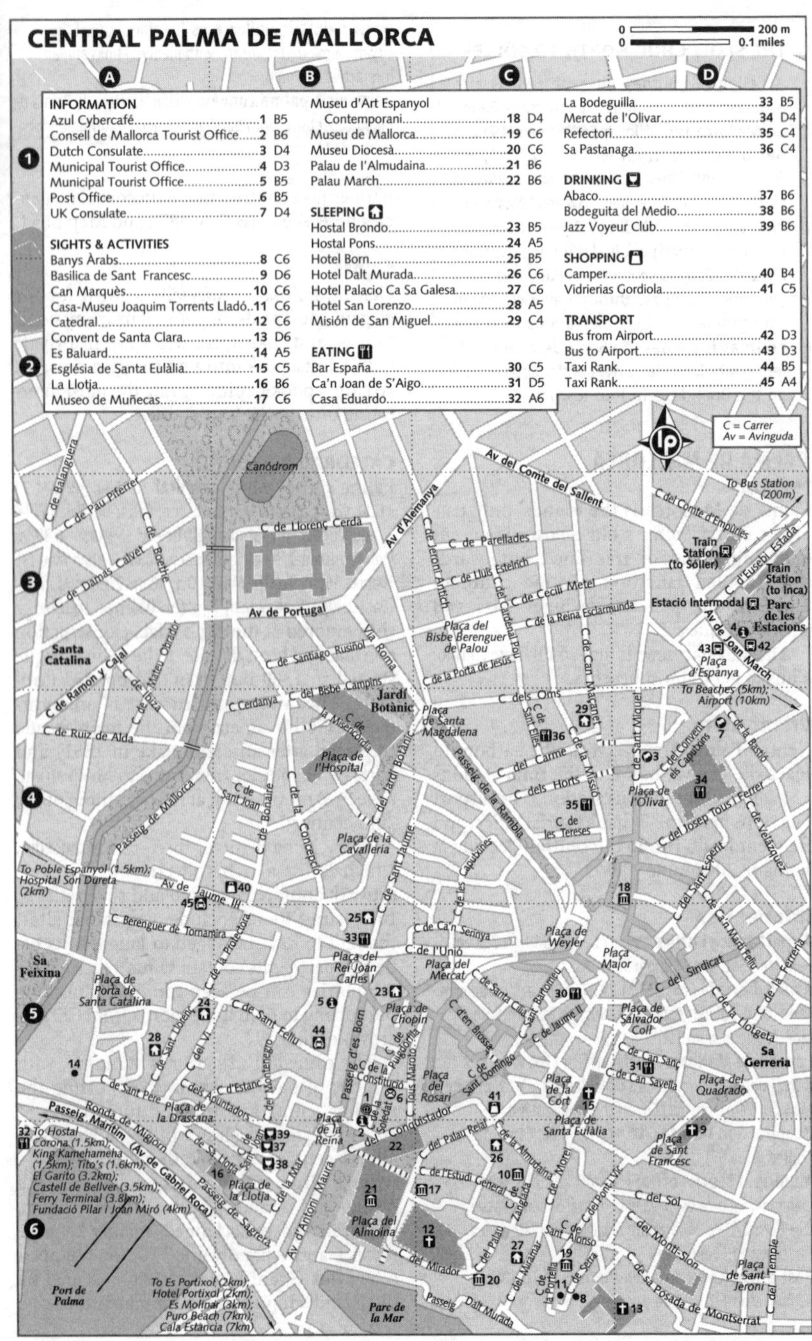

CENTRAL PALMA DE MALLORCA
0 200 m
0 0.1 miles
A
B
C
D
1
2
3
4
5
6
INFORMATION
Azul Cybercafé....1 B5
Consell de Mallorca Tourist Office....2 B6
Dutch Consulate....3 D4
Municipal Tourist Office....4 D3
Municipal Tourist Office....5 B5
Post Office....6 B5
UK Consulate....7 D4
SIGHTS & ACTIVITIES
Banys Àrabs....8 C6
Basilica de Sant Francesc....9 D6
Can Marquès....10 C6
Casa-Museu Joaquim Torrents Lladó..11 C6
Catedral....12 C6
Convent de Santa Clara....13 D6
Es Baluard....14 A5
Església de Santa Eulàlia....15 C5
La Llotja....16 B6
Museo de Muñecas....17 C6
Museu d'Art Espanyol Contemporani....18 D4
Museu de Mallorca....19 C6
Museu Diocesà....20 C6
Palau de l'Almudaina....21 B6
Palau March....22 B6
SLEEPING
Hostal Brondo....23 B5
Hostal Pons....24 A5
Hotel Born....25 B5
Hotel Dalt Murada....26 C6
Hotel Palacio Ca Sa Galesa....27 C6
Hotel San Lorenzo....28 A5
Misión de San Miguel....29 C4
EATING
Bar España....30 C5
Ca'n Joan de S'Aigo....31 D5
Casa Eduardo....32 A6
La Bodeguilla....33 B5
Mercat de l'Olivar....34 D4
Refectori....35 C4
Sa Pastanaga....36 C4
DRINKING
Abaco....37 B6
Bodeguita del Medio....38 B6
Jazz Voyeur Club....39 B6
SHOPPING
Camper....40 B4
Vidrierias Gordiola....41 C5
TRANSPORT
Bus from Airport....42 D3
Bus to Airport....43 D3
Taxi Rank....44 B5
Taxi Rank....45 A4
C = Carrer
Av = Avinguda
Canódrom
Av del Comte del Sallent
To Bus Station (200m)
C del Comte d'Empúries
Train Station (to Sóller)
Train Station (to Inca)
Estació Intermodal
Parc de les Estacions
Av de Joan March
Plaça d'Espanya
To Beaches (5km); Airport (10km)
Av d'Alemanya
C de Llorenç Cerdà
C de Parellades
C de Lluís Estelrich
C de Cecili Metel
C de la Reina Esclarmunda
Av de Portugal
Plaça del Bisbe Berenguer de Palou
C de la Porta de Jesús
C de Jeroni Antich
C del Cardenal Pou
C de Can Maçanet
C de Balanguera
C de Pau Piferrer
C de Damas Calvet
C de Boethe
Santa Catalina
C de Ramon y Cajal
C de Mateu Obrador
C de Ibiza
C de Ruiz de Alda
C de Santiago Rusiñol
Via Roma
C del Bisbe Campins
C Cerdanya
Jardí Botànic
Plaça de Santa Magdalena
C dels Oms
C de Sant Elies
C de la Misericòrdia
Plaça de l'Hospital
C del Jardí Botànic
Passeig de la Rambla
C del Carme
C dels Horts
C de la Missió
C de Sant Miquel
C del Convent els Caputxins
C de la Bastió
Plaça de l'Olivar
C del Josep Tous i Ferrer
C de Velázquez
C de les Tereses
Passeig de Mallorca
C de Sant Joan
C de Bonaire
C de la Concepció
Plaça de la Cavalleria
C de Sant Jaume
C de les Caputxines
To Poble Espanyol (1.5km); Hospital Son Dureta (2km)
Av de Jaume III
C Berenguer de Tornamira
C de la Protectora
C de Ca'n Serinya
C de l'Unió
Plaça de Weyler
Plaça Major
C del Sant Esperit
C de Ca'n Martí Feliu
C de la Ferreria
C del Sindicat
Sa Feixina
Plaça de Porta de Santa Catalina
Plaça del Rei Joan Carles I
Plaça del Mercat
C de Santa Clara
C de Sant Bartomeu
C de Jaume II
Plaça de Salvador Coll
C de la Llotgeta
Sa Gerreria
C de Sant Feliu
C de Sant Llorenç
C del Vi
C del Montenegro
Plaça de Chopin
Passeig d'es Born
C de la Puigdorfila
C de Tous Maroto
C d'en Brossa
C de Sant Domingo
C de Can Sanç
C de Can Savella
Plaça del Quadrado
C de Sant Pere
C d'Estanc
C dels Apuntadors
Plaça de la Drassana
C de la Constitució
C de la Soledat
Plaça del Rosari
Plaça de la Cort
Plaça de Santa Eulàlia
Plaça de Sant Francesc
Ronda de Migjorn
Passeig Marítim (Av de Gabriel Roca)
To Hostal Corona (1.5km); King Kamehameha (1.5km); Tito's (1.6km); El Garito (3.2km); Castell de Bellver (3.5km); Ferry Terminal (3.8km); Fundació Pilar i Joan Miró (4km)
C de Sa Llotja
C de Sant Joan
C de la Mar
Plaça de la Llotja
Passeig de Sagrera
Plaça de la Reina
C del Conquistador
C del Palau Reial
C de l'Estudi General
C de la Almudaina
C de Zanglada
C de Morei
C del Pont i Vic
C del Sol
C del Monti-Sion
Av d'Antoni Maura
Plaça del Almoina
C del Mirador
C del Palau
C del Miramar
C de Sant Alonso
C de la Portella
C de Serra
Plaça de Sant Jeroni
C del Temple
C de sa Posada de Montserrat
Port de Palma
To Es Portixol (2km); Hotel Portixol (2km); Es Molinar (3km); Puro Beach (7km); Cala Estància (7km)
Parc de la Mar
Passeig Dalt Murada

Barceló, who completely reworked the Capella del Santíssim i Sant Pere, at the rear of the south aisle, in a dream-fantasy ceramic rendition of the miracle of the loaves and fishes.

In front of the cathedral stands the **Palau de l'Almudaina** (☎ 971 21 41 34; www.patrimonionacional.es; Carrer del Palau Reial s/n; adult/student €3.20/2.30, audioguide €2; ⏲ 10am-6pm Mon-Fri, 10am-2pm Sat Apr-Sep, 10am-2pm & 4-6pm Mon-Fri, 10am-2pm Sat Oct-Mar), an Islamic fort converted into a residence for the Mallorcan monarchs at the end of the 13th century. It is still occasionally used for official functions when King Juan Carlos is in town, but otherwise you can wander through a series of cavernous and austere stone-walled rooms, a chapel with a rare Romanesque entrance, and upstairs royal apartments kitted out with Flemish tapestries and period furniture.

The **Banys Àrabs** (☎ 971 72 15 49; Carrer de Serra 7; adult/child €1.50/free; ⏲ 9am-7.30pm Apr-Nov, 9am-6pm Dec-Mar), modest remains of Arab baths, are one of the few reminders of Muslim domination of the island. All that remains are two small underground chambers, one with a domed ceiling supported by a dozen columns, some of whose capitals were recycled from demolished Roman buildings.

MUSEUMS

Opened in 2007 in its magnificent new home of the Palau Episcopal (bishop's residence), the **Museu Diocesà** (☎ 971 21 31 00; Carrer del Mirador 5; admission €3; ⏲ 10am-2pm Tue-Fri) is a fascinating excursion for those interested in Mallorca's Christian art history. The first thing you see is a mind-boggling *retaule* (altarpiece) depicting the Passion of Christ (c 1290–1305) and taken from the Convent de Santa Clara. Christ flailed looks utterly unperturbed, while the image of his being nailed to the cross is unsettling as He looks right at…you. Pere Niçard's *Sant Jordi* (St George), done around 1468–70, is remarkable for its busy detail. The city of Mallorca (ie Palma) is shown in the background.

Es Baluard (Museu d'Art Modern i Contemporani; ☎ 971 90 82 00; www.esbaluard.org; Porta de Santa Catalina 10; adult/student & senior €6/4.50, temporary exhibitions €4/3; ⏲ 10am-10pm Tue-Sun mid-Jun–Sep, 10am-8pm Tue-Sun Oct–mid-Jun) takes the grand Renaissance-era seaward fortifications as its setting. A 21st-century concrete complex has been built into the walls, and is a playful game of light, surfaces and perspective – the perfect framework for this big and mixed exhibition. It starts with Catalan and other landscape artists at work in Mallorca in the 19th and 20th centuries and continues with a revolving band of 20th-century greats – you might see works by anyone from Oskar Kokoschka to Amedeo Modigliani. The views from the ramparts and cafe are splendid.

Housed in a converted 15th-century palace, the **Museu de Mallorca** (☎ 971 71 75 40; www.museudemallorca.es in Spanish; Carrer de la Portella 5; ⏲ 10am-7pm Tue-Sat, 10am-2pm Sun) holds an extensive collection of archaeological artefacts, religious art, antiques and ceramics. Upstairs is a portrait gallery of local identities and painters. Much of the museum is temporarily off-limits due to ongoing renovation but all the archaeology section is open, including an outstanding collection of 4th-century-BC bronze statuettes; admission is free during the work.

Once one of several residences of the phenomenally wealthy March family, **Palau March** (☎ 971 71 11 22; www.fundbmarch.es; Carrer de Palau Reial 18; admission €3.60; ⏲ 10am-6.30pm Mon-Fri, 10am-2pm Sat Apr-Oct, 10am-5pm Mon-Fri, 10am-2pm Sat Nov-Mar) boasts an outdoor terrace display of modern sculpture and, inside, an odd mix. The only permanent item inside is the extraordinary 18th-century Neapolitan baroque *belén* (nativity scene).

Housed in an 18th-century mansion, the **Museu d'Art Espanyol Contemporani** (☎ 971 71 35 15; www.march.es/arte/palma; Carrer de Sant Miquel 11; admission free; ⏲ 10am-6.30pm Mon-Fri, 10.30am-2pm Sat) offers a good introduction to Spanish modern art. On permanent display are some 70 pieces held by the Fundación Juan March, a veritable who's who of mostly 20th-century artists, including Picasso, Miró, Juan Gris (of cubism fame), the sculptor Julio González and Salvador Dalí.

Near the cathedral, the **Museo de Muñecas** (☎ 971 72 98 50; Carrer del Palau Reial 27; adult/under 6yr/child €3.50/free/2.50; ⏲ 10am-6pm Tue-Sun; 🚸) is a shop-cum-museum dedicated to old dolls.

The gorgeous Gothic **La Llotja** (☎ 971 71 17 05; Plaça de la Llotja s/n; ⏲ 11am-1.45pm & 5-8.45pm Tue-Sat, 11am-1.45pm Sun for exhibitions only), opposite the waterfront, was built as a merchants' stock exchange and is used for temporary exhibitions.

OLD PALMA HOUSES

Can Marquès (☎ 971 71 62 47; www.casasconhistoria.net; Carrer de Zanglada 2A; adult/student & senior €6/5; ⏲ 10am-3pm Mon-Fri, 11am-2pm Sat) is one of few such places in Palma open to visitors. Dating to the 14th century, it gives a fascinating insight into how the well-to-do lived around the turn of the 20th century. The building shows elements of Gothic, baroque and even Modernista influences.

Another fine mansion houses the **Casa-Museu Joaquim Torrents Lladó** (☎ 971 72 98 35; www.jtorrentsllado.com; Carrer de la Portella 9; adult/student & senior €3/1.80; 🕑 11am-7pm Tue-Fri, 10am-2pm Sat mid-Jun–mid-Sep, 10am-6pm Tue-Fri, 10am-2pm Sat mid-Sep–mid-Jun), with a timber gallery overlooking a courtyard. It once belonged to the Catalan artist of the same name (1946–93) and has been largely preserved as he left it.

CHURCHES

Two of Palma's oldest churches are the soaring Gothic **Església de Santa Eulàlia** (☎ 971 71 46 25; Plaça de Santa Eulàlia 2; 🕑 9am-10.30pm & 5-8pm) and the nearby **Basílica de Sant Francesc** (☎ 971 71 26 95; Plaça de Sant Francesc 7; admission €1; 🕑 9.30am-12.30pm & 3.30-6pm Mon-Sat, 9.30am-12.30pm Sun & holidays). The latter was begun in 1281 in Gothic style and its baroque facade was added in 1700. You enter by the beautiful, two-tiered, trapezoid cloister. Inside is the tomb of, and monument to, the 13th-century scholar Ramon Llull.

OTHER ATTRACTIONS

In the west of the city, **Poble Espanyol** (☎ 971 73 70 75; Carrer del Poble Espanyol 39; adult/student & senior €5/3; 🕑 9am-7pm Apr-Sep, 9am-6pm Oct-Mar) is a copy of the village of the same name in Barcelona. It contains replicas of famous monuments and other buildings representative of a variety of Spanish architectural styles, not to mention souvenir shops galore.

Further south, the circular **Castell de Bellver** (☎ 971 73 06 57; adult/senior & student €2/1; 🕑 8am-8.30pm Mon-Sat, 10am-7pm Sun & holidays Apr-Sep, 8am-7.15pm Mon-Sat, 10am-5pm Sun & holidays Oct-Mar) is an unusual, circular 14th-century castle (with a unique round tower) set atop a pleasant park. Parts of the castle are shut on Sunday. It is the stage for a summer **classical music festival** in July.

The **Fundació Pilar i Joan Miró** (☎ 971 70 14 20; http://miro.palmademallorca.es; Carrer de Joan de Saridakis 29; adult/under 17yr/student & senior €6/free/3; 🕑 10am-7pm Tue-Sat, 10am-3pm Sun & holidays mid-May–mid-Sep, 10am-6pm Tue-Sat, 10am-3pm Sun & holidays mid-Sep–mid-May) in Cala Major (about 4km southwest of the city centre) is housed in a modern complex on the site of Joan Miró's former studios. On show is a permanent collection of the works stored here at the time of his death. Take bus 3 or 46 from Plaça d'Espanya.

Sleeping

Central Palma is by far the best area to stay. Avoid the string of glossy (and not-so-glossy) tourist hotels around the waterfront east and west of the city centre – they're a long way from anything (except each other).

BUDGET

Hostal Pons (☎ 971 72 26 58; Carrer del Vi 8; s/d without bathroom €25/45) This *hostal* (budget hotel) seems unchanged since the 1880s. The downstairs chambers are cluttered with antiques and artworks, and the quaint bedrooms all have timber bedsteads and rickety tiled floors.

Hostal Corona (☎ 971 73 19 35; www.hostal-corona.com; Carrer de Josep Villalonga 22; s €30, d €45-55) With its palm trees and cornucopia of plants, the generous courtyard garden of this little hotel (the house was once a private villa) has a faraway feel. The rooms are simple, with timber furnishings and old tiled floors. Grab the suite (€69) and hang around in the evening, when the courtyard turns into a popular, chilled-out bar (open 6pm to 1am Tuesday to Sunday). The nearest bus stop is at Avinguda de Joan Miró 24 (take buses 3 or 46 from Plaça d'Espanya).

Hostal Brondo (☎ 971 71 90 43; www.hostalbrondo.net; Carrer de Ca'n Brondo 1; s/d without bathroom €40/55, d with bathroom €70) Climb the courtyard stairs to arrive in a homey sitting room overlooking the narrow lane. High-ceilinged rooms (No 3 with a glassed-in gallery) furnished in varying styles (from Mallorcan to vaguely Moroccan) are atmospheric.

MIDRANGE & TOP END

Hotel Born (☎ 971 71 29 42; www.hotelborn.com; Carrer de Sant Jaume 3; s €55, d €80-100) A superb place in the heart of the city, this hotel is in an 18th-century palace. The rooms combine elegance and history, with all the mod cons. The best rooms have an engaging view on to the courtyard.

Hotel San Lorenzo (☎ 971 72 82 00; www.hotelsanlorenzo.com; Carrer de Sant Llorenç 14; s/d from €118/140; ❄ 🏊) Tucked away inside the old quarter, this hotel is in a beautifully restored 17th-century building, and has a marvellous Mallorcan courtyard, its own bar, dining room and rooftop terrace with swimming pool.

our pick **Misión de San Miguel** (☎ 971 21 48 48; www.hotelmisiondesanmiguel.com; Carrer de Can Maçanet

1; r €125-130; P) The hotel is on a side alley off Carrer Oms and its spacious rooms are quiet, with free wi-fi, firm mattresses and rain showers. The restaurant serves a fabulous made-to-order breakfast and the patio area is romantic and relaxing.

Hotel Portixol (971 27 18 00; www.portixol.com; Carrer de la Sirena 27; s/d from €135/225;) Boasting one of the trendiest seafood restaurants around, Portixol is also one of the hippest hotels in town. It's a fine exercise in cool, streamlined minimalism. The best rooms have sea views, and a drink on the terrace bar is a pleasant way to begin the evening.

Hotel Dalt Murada (971 42 53 00; www.daltmurada.com; Carrer de la Almudaina 6; d from €159) Gathered around a medieval courtyard, this carefully restored old town house is a gorgeous if tiny option, with just a handful of doubles and suites. The penthouse suite has a Jacuzzi and views of the cathedral.

Hotel Palacio Ca Sa Galesa (971 71 54 00; www.palaciocasagalesa.com; Carrer del Miramar 8; s/d €261/332; P) Welcome to the classiest act in town. This enchanting 16th-century mansion has five doubles and two singles arranged around a cool patio garden. A genteel air wafts through the elegant rooms, with antiques, artwork and silk bed throws.

Eating

A mess of eateries and bars cater to Palma's visitors in the maze of streets between Plaça de la Reina and the port. Take a look around the *barrio* (district) of Santa Catalina, west of Passeig de Mallorca, especially around the east end of Carrer de la Fàbrica. Also pleasant is the seaside Es Molinar area around Es Portixol, where you'll find cheerful seafood eateries and laid-back bars.

At lunchtime Monday to Saturday, head to the Mercat de l'Olivar, which houses several lively tapas bars serving fresh food to market workers and shoppers.

Ca'n Joan de S'Aigo (971 71 07 59; Carrer de Can Sanç 10; hot chocolates €1.40; 8am-9pm Wed-Mon) This is *the* place for a hot chocolate in what can only be described as an antique-filled milk bar dating from 1700. The house speciality is *quarts*, a feather-soft sponge cake item that children love with almond-flavoured ice cream (served in a glass with a spoon).

Sa Pastanaga (971 72 41 94; Carrer de Sant Elies 6B; meals €12.20; lunch Mon-Fri; V) Locals queue for vegetarian set lunches. Yellow walls and exposed beams lend a huggy feel to the place. Starters (juice or salad) could be followed by *crema de carbassò i pèsols* (pumpkin and peas cream) and a main course of *burritos de verdura amb salsa de formatge* (vegetable burritos in a cheese sauce).

Bar España (971 72 42 34; Carrer de Ca'n Escurrac 12; meals €15-20; 6pm-midnight Mon, 10am-midnight Tue-Sat) Pick your *pintxos* (Basque tapas) at the bar (where you can't smoke) and sample with house wine. Or take them to a table (smoker-friendly). Bullfight posters adorn the walls and it fills to bursting at lunch and on weekend evenings.

La Bodeguilla (971 71 82 74; Carrer de Sant Jaume 1-3; meals €35-45; 1-11.30pm Mon-Sat;) This gourmet eatery does lightly creative interpretations of dishes from across Spain (such as *cochinillo,* suckling pig, from Segovia, and *lechazo,* young lamb, baked Córdoba-style in rosemary).

Casa Eduardo (971 72 11 82; Travessia Pesquera (Mollet); meals €35-45; lunch & dinner Tue-Sat, lunch Sun) What better place to get stuck into fish than behind the fresh fish market? Casa Eduardo has been serving meals since the 1940s and

WHAT'S COOKING IN THE BALEARIC ISLANDS?

Fish and seafood are the lead items in many a Balearic kitchen. In the marshlands of S'Albufera, in eastern Mallorca, rice and eels are traditional mainstays. The former is used in many dishes, while the latter most usually pops up in the *espinagada*, an eel-and-spinach pie. Valldemossa is famous for its versions of *coca*, a pizza-like snack that you will find around the island. One of the local specialities is the potato version, *coca de patata*. Menorca is especially known for its cheeses and *caldereta de llagosta*, a juicy lobster stew. A favourite in Ibiza is *frito de pulpo* (a baked dish of octopus, potatoes, paprika and herbs). Another is *bullit de peix*, a fresh fish and potato stew.

The interior of Mallorca is serious wine country, with two Denominación de Orígen (DO) areas, Binissalem and Pla i Llevant (roughly the southeast sector of the island). Limited quantities of wine (some very good) are also made in Menorca, Ibiza and Formentera (try the whites here).

comes up with such things as lobster paella (€25 a head)! Waiters in black vests move about swiftly on the roof terrace below ceiling fans and neon lights.

our pick **Refectori** (971 22 73 47; Carrer de la Missió 7A; meals €70-80; lunch & dinner Mon-Fri, dinner Sat;) Lovingly prepared Mediterranean grub with a special touch is the order of the day in the convent refectory. Alleluia! The restaurant has a modern air, with angular high-back chairs and rigorously white, black and timber decor.

Drinking & Entertainment

The old quarter is the city's most vibrant nightlife zone. Particularly along the narrow streets that lie between Plaça de la Reina and Plaça de la Drassana, you'll find an enormous selection of bars, pubs and bodegas (wine cellars). Look around the Santa Catalina (especially Carrer de Sant Magí) and Es Molinar districts too. There is one caveat. Most bars shut by 1am Sunday to Thursday (3am Friday and Saturday).

S'Arenal and Magaluf (Map p652), the amorphous seaside tourist haunts to the east and west of Palma respectively, are full of bars and discos filled to bursting with the lobster-hued package-tourist crowd.

Abaco (971 71 59 47; Carrer de Sant Joan 1; cocktails €15; 8pm-1am Tue-Thu, 8pm-3am Fri & Sat) Behind a set of ancient timber doors is the bar of your wildest dreams. Inside, a Mallorcan *pati* and candlelit courtyard are crammed with elaborate floral arrangements, cascading towers of fresh fruit and bizarre artworks.

Jazz Voyeur Club (971 90 52 92; www.jazzvoyeur.com; Carrer dels Apuntadors 5) A tiny club no bigger than most people's living rooms, Voyeur hosts live jazz bands nightly, starting at 10pm. Red candles burn on the tables and a few plush chairs are scattered about; though you should get here early if you want one.

Bodeguita del Medio (971 71 78 32; Carrer de Vallseca 18; 9pm-3am) For a taste of Cuba, head in here for a mojito (rum, lemon, mint and ice, one of Hemingway's faves) or three.

our pick **Puro Beach** (971 74 47 44; www.purobeach.com; 11am-2am) One marvellous exception is this uber-laid-back, sunset chill lounge – an all-white bar with a tapering outdoor promontory area that is perfect for sunset cocktails, DJ sessions and fusion food escapes. Blend in with the monochrome decor and wear white, emphasising your designer tan. It is just a two-minute walk east of Cala Estancia (itself just east of Ca'n Pastilla).

About 2km west of the old quarter along and behind Passeig Marítim (aka Avinguda de Gabriel Roca) is a concentration of taverns, girlie bars and clubs. A classic among the latter is **El Garito** (971 73 69 12; www.garitocafe.com; Dàrsena de Can Barberà; 7pm-4.30am). DJs and live performers doing anything from jazz rock to disco classics and electro beats heat up the scene from around 10pm; admission is generally free. **King Kamehameha** (971 93 92 00; www.king-kamehameha.com; Passeig Marítim 29; midnight-5am), pulsating with up-to-the-minute electronic tracks and a young, international crowd, is a big hit. Another classic club is **Tito's** (971 73 00 17; Passeig Marítim 33; 11.30pm-6am Jun-Sep, 11.30pm-6am Thu-Sun Oct-May).

Shopping

Camper (971 71 46 35, Avinguda de Jaume III 16) The best known of Mallorca's famed shoe brands, funky, eco-chic Campers are now trendy worldwide.

Vidrierias Gordiola (971 71 15 41; Carrer de la Victoria 8; closed Sat pm) Mallorca's best-known glassmakers offer everything from traditional goblets and vases to surprisingly modern works of art.

Getting There & Away

Sant Joan airport is about 10km east of Palma. For trains and buses to other parts of the island, see Getting Around (p651).

Getting Around

TO/FROM THE AIRPORT

Bus 1 runs every 15 minutes between Sant Joan airport and Plaça d'Espanya in central Palma (€1.85, 15 minutes) and on to the ferry terminal. Alternatively, a taxi will charge you around €15 to €18 for the trip.

BUS

There are 25 local bus services around Palma and its bay suburbs with **EMT** (971 21 44 44; www.emtpalma.es). Single-trip tickets cost €1.10, or you can buy a 10-trip card for €8. For the beaches at S'Arenal, take bus 15 from Plaça d'Espanya.

TAXI

There are a few numbers to call for a **taxi** (971 72 80 81, 971 75 54 40, 971 40 14 14).

MALLORCA'S TOP FIVE BEACHES

- **Platja de Formentor** (p664)
- **Cala Llombards** (p666)
- **Cala de Sant Vicenç** (p663)
- **Cala de Deià** (p661)
- **Es Trenc** (p666)

SOUTHWEST COAST

A freeway skirts around the Badia de Palma towards Mallorca's southwest coast. Along the way you'll pass the resorts of Cala Major, Ses Illetes (lovely little beaches), Palma Nova and Magaluf (nice long beaches and mass British tourism), basically a continuation of Palma's urban sprawl. From the inland town of Andratx (worth a stop for a taste of an inland Mallorca town, especially busy in the early evening when people sit around for drinks at terraces on Plaça d'Espanya and Plaça des Pou), two turn-offs lead down to the coast: one goes to Port d'Andratx and the other to Sant Elm.

Port d'Andratx

pop 2680

Port d'Andratx is set on low hills surrounding a narrow bay. Yachties hang out here and the bay makes a nice setting for a meal and/or drinks. A couple of dive schools are based here.

A couple of hundred metres back from the harbour, **Hostal-Residencia Catalina Vera** (☎ 971 67 19 18; Carrer de Isaac Peral 63; s/d €42/68) is a lovely guesthouse retreat with rooms set around a tranquil garden courtyard. The best doubles have balconies and prices haven't budged in years.

A couple of blocks inland from the waterfront, **Restaurante La Gallega** (☎ 971 67 13 38; Carrer de Isaac Peral 52; meals €30; Tue-Sun, closed Nov) is a popular local seafood restaurant overlooked by most foreigners, who prefer the pricier waterfront alternatives. Try northern Spanish seafood faves, such as a quarter-kilo of *percebes* (a strange-looking mollusc) for €37.

Sant Elm

pop 80

The seaside hamlet of Sant Elm is popular for day trips from Palma. The last part of the drive (7km) across from Andratx via the sleepy village of S'Arracó (with a couple of attractive restaurants) is a spectacular, winding route through leafy hills. If you'd rather walk this section, take a regular bus to Andratx (€3.90, 20 daily, 30 minutes).

Sant Elm's sandy beach is pleasant, but can get crowded. Just offshore is a small rocky islet – within swimming distance for the fit. Further north is a small dock from where you can join a **glass-bottomed boat tour** or take a **boat** (☎ 639 617545; admission €10; 15 min, 3-4 times daily Feb-Nov) to the imposing and uninhabited **Illa Sa Dragonera**, which is criss-crossed with good walking trails. You can also take the boat between Sant Elm and Port d'Andratx (€7, 20 minutes, once daily February to November).

Some nice hikes lead northwest out of the town to **La Trapa**, a former monastery, and pebbly **Cala d'En Basset** cove. Reckon on an hour each way for both walks.

There are two hotels and plenty of restaurants to choose from.

NORTHWEST COAST & SERRA DE TRAMUNTANA

Dominated by the rugged Serra de Tramuntana range, Mallorca's northwest coast and its hinterland make up 'the other Mallorca'. No sandy beach resorts here. The coastline is rocky and largely inaccessible, the villages are mostly built of local stone, and the mountainous interior is much loved by walkers for its beautiful landscapes of pine forests, olive groves and spring wildflowers. Beautiful in summer, it is a peaceful, virtually year-round destination for walkers.

The main road through the mountains (the Ma10) starts at Andratx and runs roughly parallel to the coast to Pollença. It's a stunning scenic drive and a popular cycling route, especially during spring, when the muted mountain backdrop of browns, greys and greens is splashed with the bright colours of yellow wattles and blood-red poppies. Plenty of miradors (lookout points) recommend themselves as stops to punctuate the trip.

Estellencs

pop 350

Estellencs is a pretty village of stone buildings scattered around rolling hills below the **Puig Galatzó** (1025m) peak. It's a popular base for walkers and cyclists. A rugged walk of about 1km leads down to the local 'beach', a cove with crystal-clear water.

RUTA DE PEDRA EN SEC

A walkers' week would see you traverse the entire mountainous northwest, from Cap de Formentor to Sant Elm (p660). Old mule trails constitute the bulk of the (still incomplete) 150km GR221 walking route, aka the Ruta de Pedra en Sec (Dry Stone Route). The 'dry stone' refers to an age-old building method throughout the island. In the mountains you'll see paved ways, farming terraces, houses, walls and more built of stone without mortar. Good maps and a compass are necessary, and in the cooler months you need to be prepared for cold weather, rain and, sometimes, even a little ice and snow. Check out www.conselldemallorca.net/mediambient/pedra.

The higgledy-piggledy, stone **Petit Hotel Sa Plana** (☎ 971 61 86 66; www.saplana.com; Carrer de Eusebi Pascual; d up to €98; P ❄ ♿) dominates a rise that catches the evening sun. Rooms (there are five) are quite different and tastefully decorated with period furnishings. Other options and a few eateries present themselves in the village.

Banyalbufar

pop 460

Eight kilometres northeast of Estellencs, Banyalbufar is similarly positioned high above the coast. Surrounded by steep, stone-walled farming terraces carved into the hillside, the town is home to a cluster of bars and cafes, and three hotels.

Located part of the way down the road to the village cove, **Hotel Sa Coma** (☎ 971 61 80 34; www.hotelsacoma.com; Camí des Molí 3; s/d €76/118; 🕑 Mar-Oct; P ❄ 💻 ♿) boasts unbeatable sea views from its rooms' balconies. The accommodation is basic but reasonably sized and spotless (running water is a trickle).

The four guest rooms in the charming stone **Ca Madò Paula** (☎ 971 14 87 17; www.camadopaula.com; Carrer de la Constitució 11; d up to €138; ❄ 💻) are decorated simply with a few antique touches and have sea views. The small dining room is like what you might expect at your Mallorcan granny's place.

The Palma–Estellencs bus (€3.35, one hour 20 minutes) passes through Banyalbufar. It runs from four to 11 times a day.

Valldemossa

pop 1710

Valldemossa is an attractive blend of tree-lined streets, old stone houses and impressive new villas. It owes most of its fame to the fact that the ailing composer Frédéric Chopin and his lover, writer George Sand, spent their 'winter of discontent' here in 1838–39.

They stayed in the **Cartoixa de Valldemossa** (aka Cartuja; ☎ 971 61 21 06; www.valldemossa.com; adult/student & child €7.50/3; 🕑 9.30am-6.30pm Mon-Sat, 10am-1pm Sun Jun-Sep, 9.30am-4.30pm Mon-Sat, 10am-1pm Sun Oct-May), a grand monastery that had been turned into rental accommodation after its monks were expelled in 1835. Their stay wasn't entirely happy and Sand later wrote *Un Hiver à Mallorque* (Winter in Mallorca), which, if nothing else, made her perennially unpopular with Mallorcans.

Tour buses arrive in droves to visit the monastery, a beautiful building with lovely gardens and fine views. In the couple's former quarters are Chopin's piano (which, due to shipping delays, arrived only three weeks before their departure), his death mask and several original manuscripts. Entry includes piano recitals (eight times daily in summer) and entry to the adjacent 14th-century **Palau del Rei Sanxo** (King Sancho's Palace) and local **museum**.

From Valldemossa, a tortuous 7km drive leads down to the rocky cove of **Port de Valldemossa**, with a dozen or so buildings, including the popular **Restaurant Es Port** (☎ 971 61 61 94; meals €30-35; 🕑 Feb-Nov).

Es Petit Hotel (☎ 971 61 24 79; www.espetithotel-valldemossa.com; Carrer d'Uetam 1; s/d from €113/125; ❄ 💻) is an enticing stone town house; the 'little hotel' is a great midrange option. The buffet breakfast bursts with variety and you get the feeling that everything is done with an eye to detail and comfort.

A sprinkling of cheerful restaurants decorates the streets. About 2.5km out of Valldemossa on the road to Deià, **Ca'n Costa** (☎ 971 61 23 63; meals €30; 🕑 Wed-Mon) makes a great roadside rustic stop for *porcelleta al forn* (suckling pig). The Valldemossa–Deià buses stop outside.

Bus 210 from Palma to Valldemossa (€1.55, 30 minutes) runs four to nine times daily.

Miramar & Can Marroig

Five kilometres north of Valldemossa on the road to Deià is **Miramar** (☎ 971 61 60 73, 649 913832;

www.sonmarroig.com in Spanish; admission €3; 9.30am-7pm Tue-Sun May-Oct, 10.30am-6pm Tue-Sun Nov-Mar), one of Habsburg Archduke Luis Salvador's former residences. The archduke built this home on the site of a 13th-century monastery, of which only a small part of the cloister remains.

Two kilometres further on is one of the archduke's other residences, **Can Marroig** (971 63 91 58; www.sonmarroig.com; admission €3; 9.30am-7.30pm Mon-Sat & holidays Apr-Sep, 9.30am-2pm & 3-5.30pm Mon-Sat & holidays Oct-Mar). It is a delightful, rambling mansion, jammed with furniture and period items. The views are the stuff of dreams. Wander 3km down to the **Foradada**, the strange hole-in-the-rock formation by the water.

Deià

pop 650

Deià is perhaps Mallorca's most famous village. Its setting is idyllic, with a cluster of stone buildings cowering beneath steep hillsides terraced with vegetable gardens, vineyards and fruit orchards.

Such beauty has always been a drawcard, and Deià was once a second home to an international colony of writers, actors, musicians and the like. The most famous member was the English poet Robert Graves, who died here in 1985 and is buried in the town's hillside cemetery. Check out **Deià Mallorca** (www.deia.info) and **Enjoy Deià** (www.deia-ma llorca.com).

SIGHTS & ACTIVITIES

The Ma10 passes though the town centre, where it becomes the main street and is lined with bars and shops, expensive restaurants and ritzy boutiques. Several pricey **artists' workshops** and **galleries** flog locally produced work. The steep cobbled lanes lead to the parish church and attached **museum**.

Graves moved to Deià in 1929 and three years later had a house built here. The **Casa Robert Graves** (971 63 61 85; www.fundaciorobertgraves.com; Ca N'Alluny; admission €5; 10am-5pm), a five-minute walk out along the road to Sóller, is now a museum.

On the coast, **Cala de Deià** is a popular swimming spot and hosts a couple of busy summertime bar-restaurants. The steep walking track from town takes about half an hour. You can also drive down (3km from central Deià) but competition for a parking spot (€5 for the day) can be intense. Some fine walks criss-cross the area, such as the gentle **Deià Coastal Path** to the pleasant hamlet of **Lluc Alcari** (three hours return).

SLEEPING

our pick **Hostal Miramar** (971 63 90 84; www.pensionmiramar.com; Carrer de Can Oliver s/n; d €84) Hidden up in what could almost be described as the jungle above the main road and with views across to Deià's hillside church and beyond to the sun-kissed sea, this 19th-century stone house with gardens is a shady retreat. Various artists have chosen to stay in one of the nine rooms down the years.

S'Hotel des Puig (971 63 94 09; www.hoteldespuig.com; Carrer des Puig 4; s/d €88/140; Feb-Nov) Rooms in this gem in the middle of the old town ooze a muted modern taste within ancient stone walls. Out the back are secrets impossible to divine from the street, such as the cool pool and terrace.

Hotel Costa d'Or (971 63 90 25; www.hoposa.es; s/d from €100/154; Mar-Oct; P) This secluded spot is on the coast 3km north of Deià, in the hamlet of Lluc Alcari. Designer rooms are encased in a stone building that backs on to woods high above the Med. Rooms with sea views cost considerably more but you get the same views from the restaurant and pool. A 15-minute walk through a pine forest takes you down to a little pebbly beach with crystal-clear water.

EATING

El Barrigón de Xelini (971 63 91 39; Avinguda del Arxiduc Lluís Salvador 19; meals €20; 12.30pm-12.30am Tue-Sun) You never quite know what to expect here, but tapas is at the core. It has a penchant for mains of lamb too. In the evenings, you may encounter a bit of live jazz.

Sebastian (971 63 94 17; Carrer de Felip Bauzà 2; meals €45-50; dinner Thu-Tue, closed late Nov-Feb) In restrained fashion, Sebastian meets the designer gourmet's requirements, with subtle dishes like *suprema de rodaballo con risotto de espárragos blancos y salsa de trufa* (turbot supreme with white asparagus risotto and truffle sauce).

Sóller

pop 8170

The shady ochre town of Sóller is set amid citrus orchards in a broad valley basin behind which rise the stone walls of the Serra de Tramuntana. It has a bustling feel and makes a fine base for exploration of the northwest, whether on foot or by vehicle.

The main square, Plaça de la Constitució, is 100m downhill from the train station, which itself hosts a couple of intriguing **art exhibits** (10am-6.30pm), the **Sala Picasso** (ceramics) and **Sala Miró** (prints) The square is surrounded by bars and restaurants, and is home to the *ajuntament* (town hall). Also here is the large 16th-century **Església Parroquial de San Bartolomé**, with a beautiful Gothic interior and a Modernista facade.

A pleasant 1km stroll west of the square leads to the **Jardí Botànic** (971 63 40 14; www.jardibotanicdesoller.org; adult/under 11yr €5/free; 10am-6pm Tue-Sat, 10am-2pm Sun), a peaceful botanical garden, with collections of flowers and other plants native to the islands.

Most visitors take a ride on one of Sóller's open-sided old trams, which shuttle 2km down to **Port de Sóller** on the coast (€3). They depart from the train station every 30 minutes between 7am and 9pm.

FESTIVALS & EVENTS

Around the second weekend of May, Sóller is invaded by a motley crew of Muslim pirates. This conflict (involving about 1200 townsfolk) between *pagesos* (town and country folk) and *moros* (Moors), known as **Es Firó**, is full of good-humoured drama and not a little drinking. It re-enacts an assault on the town that was repulsed on 11 May 1561.

SLEEPING & EATING

Sóller and the surrounding countryside is jammed with boutique hotels in historic buildings or set in country houses. Many are listed on www.sollernet.com.

Hotel El Guía (971 63 02 27; www.sollernet.com/elguia; Carrer del Castañer 2; s/d €51/80) Handily located beside the train station, this is a good place to meet fellow walkers. Its bright rooms feature timber trims and modern bathrooms.

Ca's Carreter (971 63 51 33; Carrer del Cetre 9; meals €25-30; lunch & dinner Tue-Sat, lunch Sun) Set in a leafy, corner cart workshop (founded in 1914), this is a cool and welcoming spot for modest local cooking, with fresh local fish, a couple of meat options and such specials as *calabacines rellenos de espinacas y pescado* (spinach and fish stuffed courgettes).

The Port de Sóller waterfront is lined with eateries and hotels.

Biniaraix & Fornalutx

From Sóller it's a pleasant 2km drive, pedal or stroll through narrow laneways up to the hamlet of Biniaraix. From there, another narrow and scenic route continues north to Fornalutx, through terraced groves crowded with orange and lemon trees. Various other walking options also exist.

Fornalutx is a pretty village of distinctive stone houses with green shutters, colourful flower boxes and well-kept gardens, many now owned by expats. Who can blame them?

A delightfully converted former convent just off the main street, **Fornalutx Petit Hotel** (971 63 19 97; www.fornalutxpetithotel.com; Carrer de l'Alba 22; s/d €79/144; P) is a friendly, tranquil place to stay. Rooms glow with the warmth of terracotta floors and stonework. Room decor is mostly sober white but soothing. Have a snooze in the garden hammock.

Ca N'Antuna (971 63 30 68; Carrer de Arbona Colom 8; meals €35-40; lunch & dinner Tue-Sat, lunch Sun), half a kilometre out of the centre on the Ma2121 road leading northeast out of town, does a bubbling cauldron of *caldereta de llagosta* (lobster stew) or a vegetable version of the same thing, but is locally famous for oven-cooked lamb and other meats.

Sa Calobra

The 12km road from route Ma10 across and down to the small port of Sa Calobra is a spectacular scenic drive. The serpentine road has been carved through the weird mountainous rock formations, skirting narrow ridges before twisting down to the coast in an eternal series of hairpin bends.

You won't be alone. NATO would be proud to organise such an operation. Divisions of buses and fleets of pleasure boats disgorge battalion after battalion of tireless tourists. It makes D-Day look like play lunch, and all that's missing are the choppers playing *Ride of the Valkyrie*. Sa Calobra must be wonderful on a quiet, bright, midwinter morning.

From the northern end of the road a short trail leads around the coast to a river gorge, the **Torrent de Pareis**, and a small cove with some fabulous (but usually crowded) swimming spots.

If you have wheels, skip the crowd scenes and, 2km before arriving, follow a turn-off west for **Cala Tuent**, a tranquil emerald-green inlet in the shadow of Puig Major.

Boats make excursions to Sa Calobra and Cala Tuent from Port de Sóller.

Monestir de Lluc & Around

In the 13th century, a local shepherd claimed to have seen an image of the Virgin Mary in the sky. Later, a similar image appeared on a rock. 'It's a miracle!' everyone cried, and a chapel was built to commemorate it. A monastery was established shortly thereafter. Since then thousands of pilgrims have come every year to pay homage to the 14th-century **statue of the Virgin of Lluc**, known as *La Moreneta* because of her dark complexion.

The present **monastery** (☎ 971 87 15 25; www.lluc.net; admission free; ⏰ 8.30am-8pm), a huge austere complex, dates from the 18th century. Off the central courtyard is the entrance to the **Basílica de la Mare de Déu**, which contains the statue. There is also a **museum** (admission €3.30; ⏰ 10am-1.30pm & 2.30-5pm) with archaeological bits and bobs and a modest art collection.

Santuari de Lluc (☎ 971 87 15 25; s/d from €13.50/23.50) is the monastery's accommodation section, with 97 rooms (of all sizes and some with kitchen access), and is popular with school groups, walkers and pilgrims. The downstairs rooms are dark and best avoided. Several restaurants and cafeterias cater to your tummy's demands.

About 15km south of the monastery, the scenic Ma2130 road leads (follow the signs) to the once near-abandoned Binibona village. The area is dotted with some fine rural retreats (www.som7.com). One of them, **Es Castell** (☎ 971 87 51 54; www.fincaescastell.com; Carrer de Binibona s/n; s/d €110/145; P ⛶ 💻 🏊) is on a 14th-century farm estate, encompassing a muddle of sturdy stone houses and 300ha dominated by olive trees.

Up to two buses a day (May to October) run from Ca'n Picafort to the Monestir de Lluc (€5.25, 1¾ hours) on their way to Sóller and Port Sóller. From Palma, two all-stops buses (bus 330) to Inca continue to Lluc via Caimari on weekends only (or take the train to Inca and change to bus 332).

Pollença

pop 9250

Next stop on the Mallorcan pilgrimage is this attractive inland town. The devout climb up **Calvari** (Calvary), 365 stone steps leading from the town up to a hilltop chapel. The views from the top are worth it. Otherwise, the central Plaça Major is a good place to relax, with several cafes and restaurants. A handful of museums are scattered about the town. A 1.5km road, which is almost undriveable, climbs south of the town up to the former monastery of **Santuari de la Mare de Déu des Puig** (☎ 971 18 41 32; d €20), where you can stay in basic former cells. Booking is mandatory.

> **MOORS & CHRISTIANS IN IMMORTAL COMBAT**
>
> The beginning of August sees the staging of one of the most colourful of Mallorca's festivals. This version of **Moros i Cristians** (Moors and Christians) celebrates a famous victory by townsfolk of Pollença over a Moorish raiding party led by the infamous Turkish pirate Dragut (1500–1565) in 1550. The 'battle' is the highpoint of the **Festes de la Patrona** (the Feast of the Patron Saint, ie the Virgin Mary). Locals dress up as scimitar-waving Moorish pirates and pole-toting villagers engage in several mock engagements, to the thunder of drums and blunderbusses, on the afternoon of 2 August. The night before, the town centre is the scene of one almighty piss-up!

Several hotel options (none especially cheap) are available in town. Otherwise, **Finca Son Brull** (☎ 971 53 53 53; www.sonbrull.com; Carretera Palma-Pollença Km49.8; s/d €308/362; P ⛶ 💻 🏊) is an exquisite retreat set in a grand 18th-century *possessió* (typical Mallorcan farmhouse) about 1.5km south of Pollença. It also boasts a spa, one of the island's top restaurants and a bar set by the old olive press. Lop €100 or more off in low season.

Restaurant Eu Centro (☎ 971 53 50 82; Carrer del Temple 3; meals €25, menú del día €8; ⏰ Thu-Tue) offers Mallorcan cooking and tapas. All the old faves are here, from *tumbet* (layered mixed vegetable bake) to *frit mallorquí* (lamb offal and vegetable fry-up). Meat-lovers might want to have a go at the *porcella* (suckling pig).

Pollença is on the Ca'n Picafort–Sóller bus route.

Cala de Sant Vicenç

pop 260

A series of four jewel-like *cales* (coves), this is a tranquil resort in a magnificent setting. Yes, the inevitable English breakfast and German bratwurst problem is in evidence, but it's minimal compared with the big beaches further southeast. And the water is so limpid you feel you could see to the centre of the world.

Hostal los Pinos (☎ 971 53 12 10; www.hostal-lospinos.com; s/d up to €44/72; P) is set on a leafy hillside back off the road between Cala Molins and Cala Carbo. The best of the simple rooms have partial sea views and are technically suites, with separate sleeping and lounge areas and balconies to hang up your beach towel.

Up to six buses (the 340 Palma–Port de Pollença service) run to Cala Sant Vicenç (€1.15, 15 minutes) from Pollença and likewise from Port de Pollença.

Port de Pollença

pop 6520

On the north shore of the Badia de Pollença, this resort is popular with British families soothed by fish and chips and pints of ale. Sailboards and yachts can be hired on the beaches. South of town, the bay's shoreline becomes quite rocky and the beaches are less attractive.

Cap de Formentor

A splendid drive leads from Port de Pollença out high along this rocky promontory. Stop at the **Mirador de Sa Creueta** (232m), 3km out of Port de Pollença, for the views. Midway along the promontory is the historic **Hotel Formentor**, a jewel of pre-WWII days, and the nearby shady strand of **Platja de Formentor** (aka Platja del Pi, parking €4). Another spectacular 11km bring you to the lighthouse on the cape that marks Mallorca's northernmost tip.

BADIA D'ALCÚDIA

The long beaches of this huge bay dominate Mallorca's northeast coast, its broad sweeps of sand stretching from Port d'Alcúdia to Ca'n Picafort.

Alcúdia

pop 11,100

Wedged between the Badia de Pollença and Badia d'Alcúdia, busy Alcúdia was once a Roman settlement. Remnants of the Roman theatre can be seen and the old town is still partly protected by (largely rebuilt) medieval walls. Wander through the Roman ruins of **Pollentia** (☎ 971 89 71 02; www.pollentia.net; adult/student & senior incl museum €2/1.25; 9.30am-8.20pm Tue-Sun May-Sep, 10am-4pm Tue-Fri, 10am-2pm Sat & Sun Oct-Apr), just outside the walls. The pleasant town centre is worth a look too.

Cheap, comfortable beds can be had at **Fonda Llabres** (☎ 971 54 50 00; www.fondallabres.com; Plaça de sa Constitució; s/d €30/36;). Cheaper rooms without bathrooms are also available.

The 351 bus from Palma to Platja de Muro calls at Alcúdia (€4.60, one hour) from five to 16 times a day.

Port d'Alcúdia

pop 4260

A large harbour dominates the town centre and imparts a slightly chic maritime flavour, with boat trips leaving daily to various points, especially Platja de Formentor (anything up to €26 depending on time spent out, the route, and whether or not you take the lunch option). Hunt around the waterfront.

Explore **Cap des Pinar**, a pretty peninsula (with a youth hostel) that lends itself to cycling and hiking. The **Parc Natural de S'Albufera** (9am-7pm Apr-Sep, 9am-5pm Oct-Mar), just south of Port d'Alcúdia, is home to a bustling selection of birdlife.

Friendly managers run the tidy **Hostal Vista Alegre** (☎ 971 54 73 47; www.hvista-alegre.com; Passeig Marítim 22; s/d €20/35;). The singles are pokey and have no air-con, while the doubles have either sea views (and breeze) or air-con. The doubles have their own bathroom. There are zillions of other places to stay in and around Port d'Alcúdia.

Ca'n Picafort & Around

A smaller version of Port d'Alcúdia, Ca'n Picafort is a package-tour frontier town, and somewhat raw and soulless, but the beaches are pretty good. About 5km further south along the coast is Son Serra de Marina, whose southeast edge is capped by a fine 2km beach favoured by windsurfers.

EAST COAST

Most (but not all!) of the fine beaches along Mallorca's east coast have succumbed to the ravages of mass tourism. Much of the northern half of this stretch of coastline is home to a series of concrete jungles that rivals the worst excesses of the Costa del Sol on the mainland. Further south the coastline is corrugated with a series of smaller coves and ports, saving it from the same fate.

Artà

pop 6730

The quiet inland town of Artà is dominated by a 14th-century hilltop fortress and **Església de San Salvador**, from where you have wonderful views across the town, countryside and out to sea.

On the coast 10km southeast are the **Coves d'Artà** (☎ 971 84 12 93; www.cuevasdearta.com; adult/under 6yr/6-13yr €10/free/5; 10am-6pm May-Oct, 10am-5pm Nov-Apr), rivalling Porto Cristo's Coves del Drac (below). Tours of the caves leave every 30 minutes.

our pick **Hotel Casal d'Artà** (☎ 971 82 91 63; www.casaldarta.de; Carrer de Rafael Blanes 19; s/d €46/86;) is a wonderful old mansion in the centre of town away from the seaside fish-and-chips scene.

Bus 411 runs up to five times daily from Palma to Artà (€8.30, one hour 20 minutes).

Cala Ratjada

pop 5960

The main streets in this busy but not unattractive resort are wall-to-wall souvenir shops, and the pretty beaches are carpeted with sizzling flesh. Head for beaches out of town, like **Cala Mesquida**. A few kilometres inland, **Capdepera** is marked by the walls of the 13th-century **castle** (☎ 971 81 87 46; adult/child €2/1.50; 9am-7.30pm Apr-Oct, 9am-4.45pm Nov-Mar) above the town.

You can make last-minute online accommodation booking in Cala Ratjada at the local hotel association's site, www.firstsunmallorca.com.

Line 411 links Palma de Mallorca and Cala Ratjada, via Artà, with up to five runs daily in each direction (€9.80 return, two hours). In summer, boats run to Ciutadella in Menorca. See p650.

Porto Cristo

pop 6620

During the day, this place teems with day trippers but by late afternoon when the hordes have disappeared it can be quite nice. The town cradles a small sandy beach and boat harbour.

The **Coves del Drac** (Dragon's Caves; ☎ 971 82 07 53; www.cuevasdeldrach.com; Carretera de les Coves s/n; adult/under 7yr €10.50/free; 10am-5pm mid-Mar–Oct, 10.45am-4.30pm Nov–mid-Mar) are on the southern outskirts of town. One-hour tours are held hourly.

In between the town's modest aquarium and the caves is the cheerful, roadside **Hotel Sol i Vida** (☎ 971 82 10 74; Avinguda de Joan Servera Camps 11; s/d up to €38/45;), with a pool, bar-restaurant and tennis court.

Portocolom

pop 3810

A tranquil village set on a generous harbour, Portocolom has managed to resist the tourist onslaught with dignity. Various restaurants dot the long bay, and within a couple of kilometres are some fine beaches, such as the immaculate cove of **Cala Marçal**.

Right on the waterfront, **Hostal Porto Colom** (☎ 971 82 53 23; www.hostalportocolom.com; Carrer d'en Cristòfol Colom 5; s/d €55/90;) offers breezy rooms with parquet floors, big beds and sunny decor. Downstairs opens out to a too-cool-for-school restaurant (sandwiches €5, mains €15 to €20) and lounge bar.

Up to seven buses run here daily from Palma via Felanitx (€5.15, 1¾ hours).

Cala d'Or to Cala Mondragó

Once a quaint fishing village, **Cala d'Or** is now an overblown big-dollar resort. Its sleek marina is lined with glistening megayachts and the surrounding hills are crowded with blindingly whitewashed villas. Plenty of lifestyle, little substance.

Immediately south of Cala d'Or (and virtually joined to it by urban sprawl) is the smaller and more tranquil **Portopetro**. Centred on a boat-lined inlet and surrounded by residential estates, it has a cluster of harbourside bars and restaurants, and a couple of small beaches nearby.

Two kilometres south of Portopetro, **Cala Mondragó** is one of the most attractive coves on the east coast. Sheltered by large rocky outcrops and fringed by pine trees, a string of three protected sandy beaches (two with a bar each and one with a restaurant) connected by coast footpaths await you.

The five-storey **Hostal Playa Mondragó** (☎ 971 65 77 52; www.playamondrago.com; Cala Mondragó; s/d €59/88; P) is barely 50m back from one of the beaches. It's a tranquil option, and the better rooms have balconies and fine sea views.

Regular local buses travel Monday to Saturday between Cala d'Or and Cala Mondragó via Portopetro.

Cala Figuera

The fisherfolk here really still fish, threading their way down the winding inlet before dawn while the predominantly German tourists sleep off the previous night's food and drink. What has probably kept the place in one piece is the fact that the nearest beach, pretty **Cala Santanyí**, is a few kilometres drive southwest.

Nicer still is **Cala Llombards**, which you can walk to (scaling endless stairs) from Cala Santanyí or drive to via Santanyí (follow the signs to Llombards and then Cala Llombards).

Simple but spacious rooms with bathrooms and balconies at **Hostal Ca'n Jordi** (☎ 971 64 50 35; www.osteria-hostal-canjordi.com; Carrer de la Virgen del Carmen 58; s/d €28/42) offer splendid views over the inlet. The owners also rent out a few apartments and villas.

Bus 502 makes the trip from Palma (€6.15, 1½ hours), via Colònia de Sant Jordi and Santanyí no more than three times a day, Monday to Saturday.

Colònia de Sant Jordi

pop 2380

On the southeast coast, the resort town of Colònia de Sant Jordi is unexciting. Some good beaches lurk nearby, however, particularly **Ses Arenes** and **Es Trenc** (with a nudist strip), both a few kilometres up the coast towards Palma.

From Colònia de Sant Jordi you can take full-day **boat trips** (☎ 971 64 90 34; www.excursionsacabrera.com; Carrer de l'Explanada del Port; adult/child €31/15; 9.30am-4.30pm May-Oct) to the former prison island of **Cabrera**, where more than 5000 French soldiers died after being abandoned in 1809 towards the end of the Peninsular War. Illa Cabrera and its surrounding islets now form the **Parc Nacional Marítim-Terrestre de l'Arxipèlag de Cabrera**. The boats leave the port at 9am and return at 3.30pm – the trip takes an hour each way.

THE INTERIOR

East of the Serra de Tramuntana, Mallorca's interior is a largely flat and fertile plain. Dominated by (partly abandoned) farmland and often fairly unremarkable agricultural townships, it marks its own time and holds various low-key gems for those not obsessed with bucket-and-spade holidays.

Several of the island's major inland towns are well-known for their specialised products. **Binissalem** is a major centre of the island's wine industry (which produces small quantities of at times great whites and reds). Ugly **Inca** holds a popular market each Thursday and is, more importantly, the seat of much of Spain's leather and shoe production. You can browse plenty of outlets and shops. Check out Gran Via de Colom and Avinguda del General Luque. **Felanitx** has a name for ceramics and is at the heart of another wine-making area.

Industrial and melancholy **Manacor** is known for its manufactured pearl industry (including the Majorica factory) and is home to many of the island's furniture manufacturers. Majorica has a huge shop just inside town on the road in from Palma.

Binissalem and several other towns offer fine boutique accommodation. Better still is the growing network of beautiful hotels housed in centuries-old stone houses on farm estates (some of which still work as farms). See the boxed text, p650, at the beginning of this chapter for some websites to get you started on your search.

IBIZA (EIVISSA)

For many, Ibiza means endless partying in Mediterranean macro-clubs. There is, however, another side to the island.

The Greeks called Ibiza and Formentera the Islas Pitiusas (Islands of Pine Trees). The landscape is harsh and rocky. Alongside hardy pines, the most common crops are olives, figs and almonds. Perhaps surprisingly, about half the island (especially the comparatively unspoilt northeast) remains covered by thick woods.

In 1956, the island boasted 12 cars and in the 1960s the first hippies from mainland Europe began to discover its idyllic beaches. A mixed World Heritage site because of Ibiza City's architecture and the island's rich sea life, the island soon latched on to the money-spinner of bulk tourism. Today the island populace of 117,700 watches on as millions (more than four million passengers are regist-

IBIZA'S TOP FIVE BEACHES

- **Cala Benirràs** (p675)
- **Cala Mastella** (p674)
- **Cala de Boix** (p674)
- **Cala Xarraca** (p675)
- **Cala Codolars** (p677)

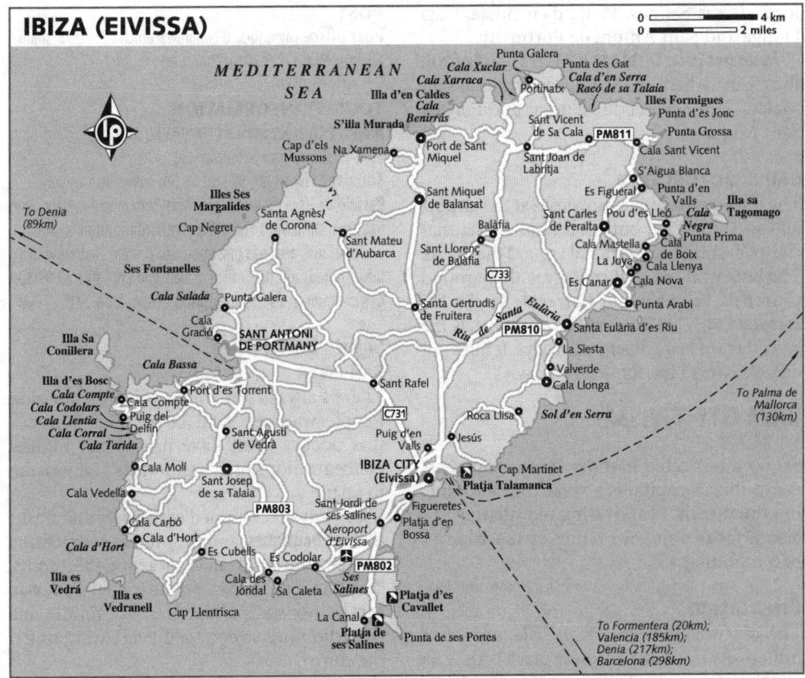

ered annually through the airport alone) pour through S'Illa Blanca (White Island) each year.

Birthplace of the rave, Ibiza is home to some of Spain's most (in)famous clubs and plenty of bars. But coastal walking trails, woods and quiet (if not deserted) beaches allow you to elude Ministry of Sound–style madness too.

Interesting websites include www.ibiza holidays.com, www.ibiza-spotlight.com and www.ecoi biza.com.

Although not as numerous as in Mallorca, rural hotels (about 30 in all) are gaining favour in Ibiza. Most are concentrated in the tranquil northeast. Search at www.ibizaruralvillas .com and www.casasruralesibiza.com (Spanish only). For more-standard accommodation, start at www.ibizahot elsguide.com.

Orientation

Ibiza City and its airport are on the southwest coast. The city, Sant Antoni de Portmany to its north and the highway between the two via Sant Rafel account for the bulk of the clubs and nightlife. Various attractive beaches dot the west coast, while the south coast from Ibiza City via Santa Eulària d'es Riu to Es Canar is built up. Ibiza City is at the heart of partying, with a 20- to 30-something crowd, and the area around Es Canar is more family-oriented. The northeast half of the island is the quietest, laced with winding back roads, heavily wooded forests and dotted with sleepy hamlets. It is a rural idyll – not what one associates with Ibiza at all!

Getting Around

BUS

Four bus companies operate and fares don't exceed €3 for the longest journey. Grab a copy of *Horario y Líneas de Autobuses* (the bus timetable) from tourist offices or check out www.ibiz abus.com.

Autobuses Empresas HF Vilas (☎ 971 30 19 16) operates from Ibiza City to Santa Eulària d'es Riu, Es Canar, Cala Sant Vicent, Portinatx, and other eastern and northern beaches. It also does the Santa Eulària d'es Riu–Sant Antoni de Portmany run.

Autobuses San Antonio (☎ 971 34 05 10) runs from Ibiza City to Sant Antoni de Portmany.

Autobuses Voramar El Gaucho (☎ 971 34 03 82) operates from Ibiza City to the airport, Sant

Jordi de ses Salines, Platja d'en Bossa, Cala Llonga and Sant Antoni de Portmany.

Autocares Lucas Costa (☎ 971 31 27 55) runs from Ibiza City to Santa Gertrudis de Fruitera, Sant Mateu, Sant Miquel de Balansat and Port de Sant Miquel.

CAR & MOTORCYCLE

The big boys have car-hire desks at the airport and in Ibiza City, but local (and sometimes cheaper) outfits are scattered around the island. The bulk of those in Ibiza City gather around Carrer de Felipe II and Carrer de Carles III. **Europcar** (☎ 971 19 22 55; Carrer de Carles III 13) has the advantage of being open seven days. It hires out an Opel Corsa for about €48 a day.

IBIZA CITY (EIVISSA)

pop 44,100

Set on a protected harbour on the southeast coast, Ibiza's capital is a vivacious, enchanting town with a captivating old quarter. It's also a focal point for some of the island's best nightlife.

Orientation

The old walled town, D'Alt Vila, crowns a hilltop overlooking all. Between D'Alt Vila and the harbour lies Sa Penya, a jumble of narrow streets and lanes lined with whitewashed shops, bars and restaurants.

The broad Passeig de Vara de Rei runs westward from Sa Penya to Avinguda d'Espanya, which in turn takes you out of the city towards the airport, 7km southwest. The new town spreads west of the old centre.

Information

EMERGENCY

Policía Nacional (Avinguda de la Pau s/n)

INTERNET ACCESS

Surf@Net (☎ 971 19 49 20; Carrer de Riambau 8; per hr €2.40; 🕑 11am-11pm Mon-Fri, 3-11pm Sat)

INTERNET RESOURCES

www.eivissa.org Ibiza city's town hall website.
www.eivissaweb.com Multilingual Ibiza search engine.
www.ibiza-online.com Another general search engine.

MEDICAL SERVICES

Farmacia Juan Tur Viñas (☎ 971 31 03 26; Carrer d'Antoni Palau 1; 🕑 7am-3am)
Hospital Can Misses (☎ 971 39 70 00; Carrer de la Corona, Barri Can Misses)

POST

Post office (Avinguda d'Isidor Macabich 67; 🕑 8.30am-8.30pm Mon-Fri, 9.30am-2pm Sat)

TOURIST INFORMATION

Airport tourist office (☎ 971 80 91 18; 🕑 9am-8pm Mon-Fri, 9am-7pm Sat May-Sep)
Tourist office (☎ 971 30 19 00; www.ibiza.travel; Passeig de Vara de Rei 1; 🕑 9am-8pm Mon-Fri, 9am-7pm Sat, 9am-3pm Sun) The office, with information on the entire island, also has plasma touch screens loaded with info. There is another office in Dalt Vila (☎ 971 39 92 32; Carrer Major 2; 🕑 10am-2pm & 6-8pm Mon-Sat).

Sights & Activities

SA PENYA

There's always something going on portside. People-watchers will be right at home – this pocket must have one of the highest concentrations of exhibitionists and weirdos in Spain.

Sa Penya is crammed with funky and trashy **clothing boutiques**, and the intense competition between the locally made gear and the imports keeps a lid on prices. The so-called **hippy markets**, street stalls along Carrer d'Enmig and the adjoining streets, sell everything under the sun.

D'ALT VILA & AROUND

From Sa Penya wander up into D'Alt Vila, the old walled town (and Unesco World Heritage site). The Romans were the first to fortify this hilltop, but the existing walls were raised by Felipe II in the 16th century to protect against invasion by French and Turkish forces.

A ramp leads from Plaça de sa Font in Sa Penya up to the **Portal de ses Taules** gateway, the main entrance. Above it hangs a commemorative plaque bearing Felipe II's coat of arms and an inscription recording the 1585 completion date of the fortification – seven artillery bastions joined by thick protective walls up to 22m in height. You can **walk** the entire perimeter of these impressive Renaissance-era walls (with great views along the way), designed to withstand heavy artillery. In the **Baluard de Sant Jaume** (🕑 10am-2pm & 5-8pm Mon-Sat, 10am-2pm Sun), an interesting military display includes soldiers' cuirasses that you can try for size (and weight!), cannonballs to lift and a video on the German bombing of Guernica (Gernika) during the civil war.

Along the perimeter walk, above the Portal de ses Taules, the **Museu d'Art Contemporani**

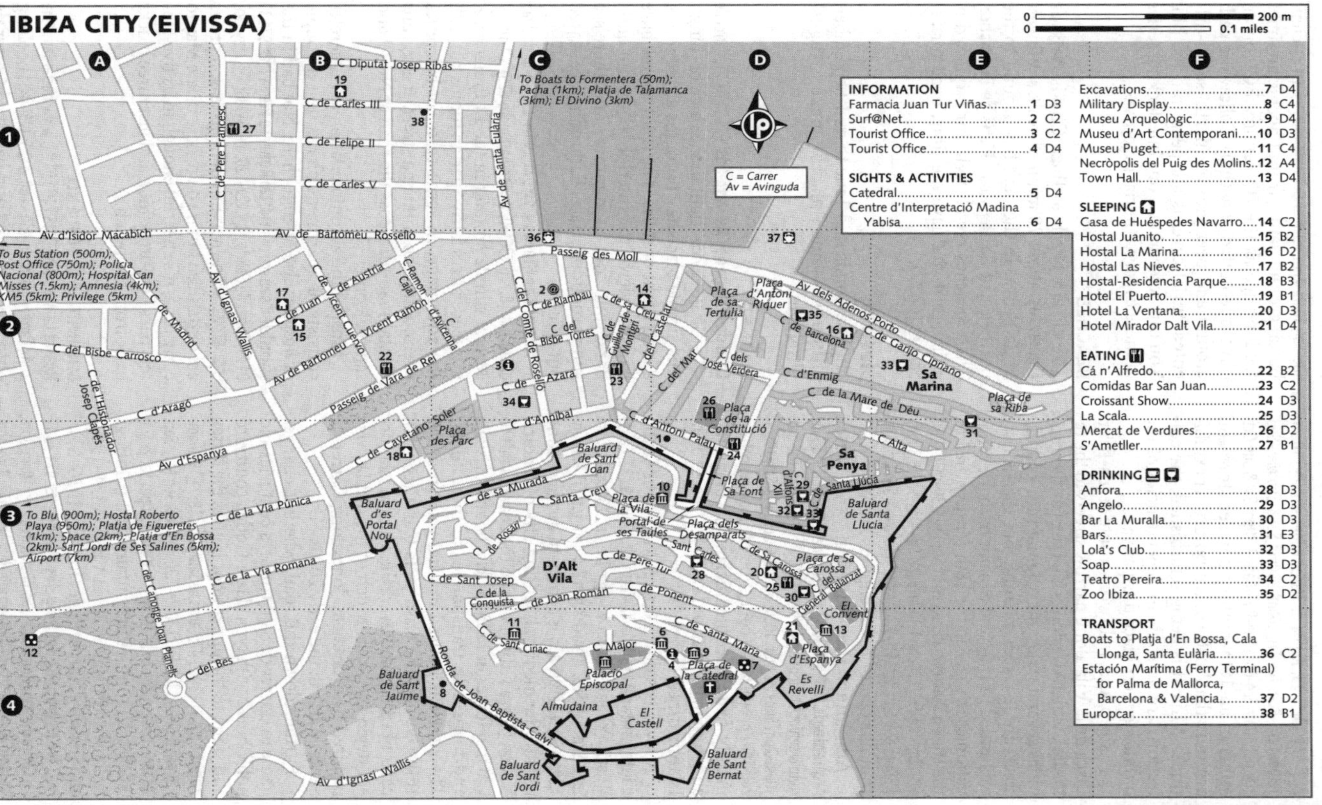
IBIZA CITY (EIVISSA)
0 200 m
0 0.1 miles
C = Carrer
Av = Avinguda
INFORMATION
Farmacia Juan Tur Viñas....1 D3
Surf@Net....2 C2
Tourist Office....3 C2
Tourist Office....4 D4
SIGHTS & ACTIVITIES
Catedral....5 D4
Centre d'Interpretació Madina Yabisa....6 D4
Excavations....7 D4
Military Display....8 C4
Museu Arqueològic....9 D4
Museu d'Art Contemporani....10 D3
Museu Puget....11 C4
Necròpolis del Puig des Molins..12 A4
Town Hall....13 D4
SLEEPING
Casa de Huéspedes Navarro....14 C2
Hostal Juanito....15 B2
Hostal La Marina....16 D2
Hostal Las Nieves....17 B2
Hostal-Residencia Parque....18 B3
Hotel El Puerto....19 B1
Hotel La Ventana....20 D3
Hotel Mirador Dalt Vila....21 D4
EATING
Cá n'Alfredo....22 B2
Comidas Bar San Juan....23 C2
Croissant Show....24 D3
La Scala....25 D3
Mercat de Verdures....26 D2
S'Ametller....27 B1
DRINKING
Anfora....28 D3
Angelo....29 D3
Bar La Muralla....30 D3
Bars....31 E3
Lola's Club....32 D3
Soap....33 D3
Teatro Pereira....34 C2
Zoo Ibiza....35 D2
TRANSPORT
Boats to Platja d'En Bossa, Cala Llonga, Santa Eulària....36 C2
Estación Marítima (Ferry Terminal) for Palma de Mallorca, Barcelona & Valencia....37 D2
Europcar....38 B1
To Boats to Formentera (50m); Pacha (1km); Platja de Talamanca (3km); El Divino (3km)
To Bus Station (500m); Post Office (750m); Policía Nacional (800m); Hospital Can Misses (1.5km); Amnesia (4km); KM5 (5km); Privilege (5km)
To Blu (900m); Hostal Roberto Playa (950m); Platja de Figueretes (1km); Space (2km); Platja d'En Bossa (2km); Sant Jordi de Ses Salines (5km); Airport (7km)
Sa Marina
Sa Penya
D'Alt Vila
El Castell
Almudaina
Palacio Episcopal
El Convent
Es Revell
Passeig des Moll
Av dels Adenos Porto
Av d'Espanya
Av d'Ignasi Wallis
Av d'Isidor Macabich
Av de Bartomeu Rosselló
Ronda de Joan Baptista Calvi
Baluard de Sant Joan
Baluard d'es Portal Nou
Baluard de Sant Jaume
Baluard de Sant Jordi
Baluard de Sant Bernat
Baluard de Santa Llúcia
Plaça de la Catedral
Plaça d'Espanya
Plaça de la Constitució
Plaça des Parc
Plaça de sa Riba

(☎ 971 30 27 23; Ronda de Narcís Puget s/n; 🕑 10am-1.30pm & 5-8pm Tue-Fri, 10am-1.30pm Sat & Sun May-Sep, 10am-1.30pm & 4-6pm Tue-Fri, 10am-1.30pm Sat & Sun Oct-Apr) is in an 18th-century powder store and armoury that hosts contemporary art exhibitions. While it is being refurbished, the collections are on show in dependencies of the *ajuntament* on Plaça d'Espanya.

A steep and well-worn route leads from Plaça de la Vila along narrow streets to the **cathedral**, which overlooks all. It elegantly combines several styles: the original 14th-century structure is Catalan Gothic but the sacristy was added in 1592 and a major baroque renovation took place in the 18th century. Inside, the **Museu Diocesà** (admission €1.50; 🕑 9.30am-1.30pm & 5-8pm Tue-Fri, 9.30am-1.30pm Sat & Sun May-Sep, 9.30am-1.30pm & 4-6pm Tue-Fri, 9.30am-1.30pm Sat & Sun Oct-Apr) contains centuries of religious art.

Adjoining the cathedral, the **Museu Arqueològic** (☎ 971 30 17 71; Plaça de la Catedral 3; adult/child & senior/student €2.40/free/1.20; 🕑 9am-3pm Tue-Sat, 10am-2pm Sun Oct-Mar, 10am-2pm & 6-8pm Tue-Sat, 10am-2pm Sun Apr-Sep) has a collection of ancient relics, mainly from the Phoenician, Carthaginian and Roman periods, but also a few pieces from Islamic times.

A few steps down Carrer Major, the **Centre d'Interpretació Madina Yasiba** (☎ 971 39 92 32; Carrer Major 2; 🕑 10am-1.30pm & 5-8pm Tue-Fri, 9.30am-1.30pm Sat & Sun May-Sep, 10am-1.30pm & 4-6pm Tue-Fri, 9.30am-1.30pm Sat & Sun Oct-Apr) is a modern display taking us into the medieval Muslim city of Madina Yasiba (Ibiza City), prior to the island's fall to Catalan forces in 1235. Artefacts, audiovisuals and maps help transport us to those times. The centre is housed in what was, from the 16th century, the Casa de la Cúria (courts), parts of whose walls were the original Islamic-era defensive walls. Much of the display was inspired by **excavations** done along Carrer de Santa Maria in the early 2000s.

Further down the road, where it changes name to Carrer de Sant Ciriac, a centuries-old noble house with typical late-Gothic courtyard and stairs to the upper floor houses the **Museu Puget** (☎ 971 39 21 47; Carrer de Sant Ciriac 18; 🕑 9.30am-1.30pm & 5-8pm Tue-Fri, 9.30am-1.30pm Sat & Sun May-Sep, 9.30am-1.30pm & 4-6pm Tue-Fri, 9.30am-1.30pm Sat & Sun Oct-Apr). The museum contains 130 paintings by local artist Narcís Puget Viñas (1874–1960) and his son, Narcís Puget Riquer (1916–83).

The **Necròpolis del Puig des Molins** (☎ 971 30 17 71; Carrer de la Via Romana 31; admission free; 🕑 10am-2pm & 6-8pm Tue-Sat, 10am-2pm Sun mid-Mar–mid-Oct; 9am-3pm Tue-Sat, 10am-2pm Sun mid-Oct–mid-Mar) is an ancient burial ground dating from Phoenician times (as long ago as the 7th century BC), on an olive-tree-dotted *puig* (hill). Follow the path around and peer into the north–south-oriented burial caverns cut deep into the hill. You can descend into one interlocking series of these *hypogea* (burial caverns).

BEACHES

The closest beach to Ibiza City is **Platja de Figueretes**, about 20 minutes' walk southwest of Sa Penya. In the next bay around to the northeast of Sa Penya is **Platja de Talamanca**. These beaches are all right for a quick dip, although if you have the time, head for **Ses Salines** (p677).

Sleeping

High season is mid-June to mid-September, although some places make August ultrahigh.

BUDGET

Casa de Huéspedes Navarro (☎ 971 31 07 71; Carrer de sa Creu 20; s/d €30/55) Right in the thick of things, this simple place has 10 rooms at the top of a long flight of stairs. The front rooms have harbour views, the interior rooms are quite dark (but cool in summer) and there's a sunny rooftop terrace. Bathrooms are shared but spotless.

Hostal Las Nieves (☎ 971 19 03 19; Carrer de Juan de Austria 18; s/d €30/60, d with bathroom €75) One of several simple *hostales* in the El Pratet area, this place offers fairly Spartan rooms but with the advantage, in some cases, of balconies overlooking the animated street. It also runs Hostal Juanito, across the road at No 19 and sans balconies.

Most of the accommodation at Figueretes consists of apartment blocks, but a couple of *hostales* also operate there. Not bad in the shoulder season is **Hostal Roberto Playa** (☎ 971 39 04 21; Carrer de Galicia 22; s €27-120, d €35-186; 🕑 May-Oct; ❄ 💻 🅿). The maximum high-season prices are outlandish but if you're here in late May to early June, it's cheerful enough in its five-storey, pack-'em-in fashion and just three blocks back from the beach.

MIDRANGE & TOP END

Hostal La Marina (☎ 971 31 01 72; www.hostal-lamarina.com; Carrer de Barcelona 7; s €68, d €85-175; ❄) Looking onto the waterfront and bar-lined Carrer de

Barcelona, this mid-19th-century building has all sorts of brightly coloured rooms. A handful of singles look onto the street, as do some doubles (with the predictable noise problem) but you can opt for pricier doubles and attics with terraces and panoramic port and/or town views. The same people run other simpler lodging options in the same street.

Hostal-Residencia Parque (☎ 971 30 13 58; www.hostalparque.com; Carrer de Vicent Cuervo 3; s €60, d with bathroom €110-170) The best doubles here overlook pleasant Plaça des Parc from above the eponymous cafe. Doubles are comfortable but singles are predictably pokey. The best are the attic rooms with their own terrace and views of the old town.

Hotel El Puerto (☎ 971 31 38 12; www.ibizaelpuerto.com; Carrer de Carles III 24; s/d €91/145;) This place offers more than 90 rooms and a series of apartments (from €152 for two people) just outside the old town and handy for the Formentera ferry. Rooms are fairly standard but some are generous in size and the pool is a plus.

Hotel La Ventana (☎ 971 39 08 57; www.laventanaibiza.com; Carrer de Sa Carossa 13; d from €177; P) Just wander into this charming 15th-century mansion in the old town, set on a little tree-shaded square. Some rooms come with stylish four-poster beds and mosquito nets, and the rooftop terrace, gardens and restaurant are added reasons to choose this spot.

Hotel Mirador Dalt Vila (☎ 971 30 30 45; www.hotelmiradoribiza.com; Plaça d'Espanya 4; d €270-450; Apr-Dec;) The Fajarnés family has lived in this rose-hued mansion since the 19th century. Situated on a shady square, the present building dates to 1905 and offers 13 prettily decked-out rooms. Parquet floors with throw rugs and oodles of art on the walls are common features. The Jacuzzi-pool has a counter-current swimjet for the active.

Eating

Croissant Show (☎ 971 31 76 65; Plaça de la Constitució s/n; 6am-11pm) Opposite the food market, this is where *everyone* goes for an impressive range of pastries and other breakfast, post-partying goodies. It is quite a scene all on its own.

our pick **Comidas Bar San Juan** (☎ 971 31 16 03; Carrer de Guillem de Montgri 8; meals €15-20; lunch & dinner Mon-Sat) A family-run operation with two small dining rooms, this simple eatery offers outstanding value, with fish dishes for around €10 and many small mains for €6 or less.

S'Ametller (☎ 971 31 17 80; Carrer de Pere Francesc 12; meals €30-35; lunch Mon-Thu, lunch & dinner Fri & Sat) 'The Almond Tree', resting uneasily next door to a cheap Chinese eatery, offers local cooking with fresh market produce. On offer are a couple of tasting menus, at €35 and €42.

La Scala (☎ 971 30 03 83; Plaça de sa Carrossa 6; meals €40; dinner Wed-Mon) This candlelit place serves international cuisine with a central-European bent, and a highlight is the meat dishes. There's a pretty open-air terrace and the clientele is predominantly, but not exclusively, gay.

Ca' n'Alfredo (☎ 971 31 12 74; Passeig de Vara de Rei 16; meals €40-45; lunch & dinner Tue-Sat, lunch Sun) Locals have been flocking to Alfredo's place since 1934. This is no new-wave Thai-fusion experience, but a great place for the freshest of seafood and other island cuisine that's so good it's essential to book. Try the *filetes de gallo de San Pedro en salsa de almendras* (fillets of fine local white fish in almond sauce).

Mercat de Verdures (Plaça de la Constitució; 7am-7pm Mon-Sat) Buy fresh fruit and vegies from this open-air market, opposite the entrance to D'Alt Vila.

Drinking & Entertainment

Sa Penya is the nightlife centre. Dozens of bars keep the port area jumping from sunset until the early hours. Alternatively, various bars at Platja d'En Bossa combine sounds, sand, sea and sangria (among other tipples). After they wind down, you can continue at one of the island's world-famous discos.

BARS

Carrer de Barcelona, parallel with the harbour, is lined with high-energy bars. Most have tall tables on the street and pump out loud music. Touts do their damndest to 'invite' passers-by to join them for a drink, sometimes with the lure of discounted passes to the clubs. A popular one is Zoo Ibiza (Plaça d'Antoni Riquer). They all open nightly from early evening until 3am to 4am, May to September. Those along Carrer de Garijo Cipriano are a little less in your face.

Lola's Club (Via de Alfonso XII 10) Anyone who remembers Ibiza in the '80s will have fond memories of Lola's Club, one of the first on the island. It's a hip miniclub (with a gay leaning).

Teatro Pereira (☎ 971 19 14 68; www.teatropereyra.com; Carrer del Comte de Rosselló 3) Away from the waterfront hubbub, this is a lively bar, packed most nights with a more eclectic crowd than the standard preclubbing bunch. It often has live music sessions. Out back is the much abandoned 1893 theatre. For years there has been talk of restoring it.

Blu (www.blu-ibiza.com; Carrer de Navarra 27, Figueretes; 10pm-4am nightly Jun-Sep, Fri & Sat Oct-May) A one-time strip joint, Blu is a recent addition to the preclubbing scene. It works with some of the island's top promoters to bring good DJ sets to the dance floor. It is also at the lower price end – you can frequently get in for €15 (including first drink)! It's one block south of Avinguda d'Espanya down Carrer del País Basc.

Bora Bora Beach Club At Platja d'en Bossa, about 2km from the old town, this is *the* place – a long beachside bar where sun- and fun-worshippers work off hangovers and prepare new ones. The ambience is chilled, with low-key club sounds wafting over the sand. From midnight, everyone crowds inside. It's off Carrer del Fumarell.

our pick KM5 (☎ 971 39 63 49; www.km5-lounge.com; Carretera de Sant Josep Km5.6; 8pm-4am May-Sep) The bar named after its highway location is where you go to glam it up. Head out of town towards Sant Josep and dance in the gardens as you gear up for the clubs. Lounging is the second major activity, and there are plenty of pillows and candles strewn about the tents for this sort of thing.

CLUBS

In summer (late May to the end of September) the west of the island is a continuous party from sunset to sunrise and back again. Entrepreneurs have built an amazing collection of clubs – huge, throbbing temples to which thousands of disciples flock to pay homage to the gods of hedonism. In 2007, the International Dance Music Awards named three Ibiza clubs (Amnesia, Pacha and Space) among the top five in the world.

The major clubs operate nightly from around 1am to 6am. Each has something different to offer. Theme nights, fancy-dress parties and foam parties (where you are half-drowned in the stuff) are regular features. Some places go a step or two further, with go-go girls (and boys), striptease acts and even live sex as a climax (ahem).

Entertainment Ibiza-style doesn't come cheaply. Admission can cost anything from €25 to €60 (and mixed drinks/cocktails then go for around €10 to €15). If you hang out around the right bars in Sa Penya, you might score a flier that entitles you to discounted admission handed out by sometimes scantily clad club promoters and touts – if they think you've got the look.

Amnesia (☎ 971 19 80 41; www.amnesia.es; nightly early Jun-Sep) Four kilometres out on the road to Sant Rafel, with a sound system that seems to give your body a sound massage. A huge glass-house-like internal terrace, filled with palms and bars, surrounds the central dance area, a seething mass of mostly tireless 20-something dancers. It gets heated in here, so every now and then icy air is pumped through.

Es Paradis (☎ 971 34 66 00; www.esparadis.com; Carrer de Salvador Espriu 2, Sant Antoni; nightly mid-May-Sep) This club boasts an equally amazing sound system, fountains and outdoor feel (there's no roof, but then in summer it doesn't rain anyway). It's one of the prettiest of the macro-clubs, with loads of marble, a glass pyramid and plenty of greenery. Queues to get in can be enormous, so get in early. Es Paradis is known for its water parties, when the dance floor is flooded.

Pacha (www.pacha.com; nightly Jun-Sep, Fri & Sat Oct-May) In business on the northern side of Ibiza City's port since 1973, Pacha contains 15 bars (!) and various dance spaces that can hold 3000 people. The main dance floor, a sea of colour, mirror balls and veils draped from the ceiling, heaves to deep techno. Those needing a break can step out onto the terrace, with more-gentle, relaxing sounds.

Privilege (☎ 971 19 81 60; www.privilegeibiza.com) One kilometre further north of Ibiza City from Amnesia, this club claims to be the world's largest (with a mere 20 bars and a pool inside, and capacity for up to 10,000 gyrating clubbers). It's quite a spectacle! Head down-stairs into the main domed dance temple, an enormous, pulsating area where the DJ's cabin is suspended above the pool.

Space (☎ 971 39 67 93; www.space-ibiza.es; 4.30pm-6am Jun–mid-Oct) One of the biggest of them all, south of Ibiza City in Platja d'en Bossa, with as many as 40 DJs and up to 12,000 clubbers – the action here starts in the mid-afternoon! Regular daytime boats make the trip between Platja d'en Bossa and Ibiza City (€7 return).

Different DJ teams make the rounds of the big clubs. One of the best known in Ibiza, **Manumission** (www.manumission.com), is known for its sexy acts and has a popular morning slot at least one day a week at Space.

A good website is **Ibiza Spotlight** (www.ibiza-spotlight.com). Another is www.discotecasdeibiza.com.

Ibiza's **Discobus** (☎ 971 31 34 47) operates nightly from midnight until 6am (June to September), doing circuits between the major discos, bars and hotels in Ibiza City, Platja d'en Bossa, Sant Rafel, Santa Eulària d'es Riu (and an extension to Es Canar) and Sant Antoni.

GAY BARS & CLUBS

The gay scene is based towards the east end of Sa Penya, particularly along the far end of Carrer de la Mare de Déu and around Carrer de Santa Llúcia. Many of the big clubs have special gay nights. Check out www.gayibiza.net.

Bar La Muralla (☎ 971 30 18 82; Carrer de Sa Carossa 3; 🕑 11pm-4am Mon-Sat) A gay sex club with dark room, labyrinth and sling cage.

Anfora (Carrer de Sant Carles 7; 🕑 10pm-4am) Seemingly dug out of walls of rock, this is a favourite gay dance haunt high up D'Alt Vila. Heteros are welcome to hang about too. From 1.30am you pay €12 admission (includes first drink).

In the shadow of the old city walls, **Angelo** (Carrer de Santa Llúcia 12) is a busy gay bar with several levels. The atmosphere is relaxed and heteros wind up here too. It is surrounded by a handful of other gay-leaning bars, such as the slicker **Soap** (Carrer de Santa Llúcia 12).

Getting There & Away

Ibiza's airport (Aeroport d'Eivissa) is 7km southwest of the capital and receives direct flights from various mainland Spanish cities as well as London and a host of European centres.

Boats for Formentera leave from a separate terminal 300m north of the centre. For information on other inter-island ferries, see Getting There & Around (p650).

Cruceros Santa Eulalia (☎ 971 33 22 51; www.ferrysantaeulalia.com) runs boats to Cala Llonga, Santa Eulària d'es Riu and Es Canar up to four times daily (all €13 return) from May to mid-October.

Buses to other parts of the island depart from a series of stops along Avinguda d'Isidoro Macabich (the western continuation of Avinguda de Bartomeu Rosselló).

For information on car hire, see p668.

Getting Around

Buses between the airport and the central port area via Platja d'en Bossa operate hourly between 6.30am and 11.30pm (€1.50, 20 to 25 minutes). Other buses run direct from the airport to Sant Antoni de Portmany and Es Canar. A taxi from the airport costs around €12 to €14. You can call a **taxi** (☎ 971 39 83 40, 971 30 66 02).

EAST COAST

A busy highway (C733) speeds you north out of Ibiza City towards Santa Eulària d'es Riu on the east coast. Alternatively, you could take the slower but more scenic coastal road via Cala Llonga – take the turn-off to Jesús a couple of kilometres northwest of Ibiza City. This route winds through low hills and olive groves, with detours along the way to several beaches, including the pleasant **Sol d'en Serra**.

Cala Llonga is set on an attractive bay with high rocky cliffs sheltering a lovely sandy beach, but the town itself has many high-rise hotels.

Santa Eulària d'es Riu

pop 13,900

Ibiza's third-largest town, Santa Eulària d'es Riu is a bustling place with reasonable

THE GREEN CARD

In 2005 the nonprofit Fundació pel Desenvolupament Sostenible de les Illes Balears (Sustainable Development Foundation for the Balearic Islands) introduced the **Targeta Verda** (Green Card; ☎ 902 92 99 28; www.targetaverda.com). Anyone can buy the card (€10) from hotels, airline desks, newspaper stands and post offices. It entitles holders to discounts at many sights, restaurants and shops throughout the Balearic Islands. Proceeds go to environmental protection and sustainable projects. The most important of these so far has been the improvement of infrastructure and protection at Mallorca's Parc Natural de S'Albufera (p664), at a cost of around €1 million. In Ibiza, the *Greenheart Guide* (www.greenheart.info) promotes projects and attractions in Ibiza and Formentera with ecofriendly credentials.

beaches, a large harbour and plenty of 20th-century tourist-resort architecture.

ORIENTATION & INFORMATION

The main highway, known as Carrer de Sant Jaume as it passes through town, is a hectic traffic artery lined with souvenir shops.

The **tourist office** (☎ 971 33 07 28; www.santaeulalia.net; Carrer de Marià Riquer Wallis 4; 9.30am-1.30pm & 5-7.30pm Mon-Fri, 9.30am-1pm Sat) is just off the highway.

SIGHTS

A world away from the beaches is the core of the original town, the hilltop **Puig de Missa**, 1km from the bus station (signposted). As well as the cute 16th-century church, the **Església de Santa Eulària**, you'll find the **Museu Barrau** (9.30am-1.30pm Tue-Sat), a white house with blue shutters dedicated to local artist Laureà Barrau, and the **Museu Etnogràfic** (☎ 971 33 28 45; 10am-2pm & 5.30-8pm Mon-Sat, 11am-1.30pm Sun Apr-Sep, 10am-2pm Mon-Sat, 11am-1.30pm Sun Oct-Mar), with farming and household instruments.

SLEEPING & EATING

Modern hotels and apartments crowd the Santa Eulària beachfront, but you will find a cluster of affordable *hostales* a couple of blocks inland.

Most of the restaurants and cafes along the beachfront are tacky and overpriced. Four blocks back, there are plenty of decent eateries along Carrer de Sant Vicent.

Hostal-Residencia Sa Rota (☎ 971 33 00 22; Carrer de Sant Vincent 59; s/d €45/74) A good-value *hostal*, this place features bright generous rooms (the doubles in particular) with modern bath or shower. The downstairs cafe has a nice outdoor extension with a pergola.

Ca's Català (☎ 971 33 10 06; www.cascatala.com; Carrer del Sol s/n; s €53.50, d €80-118;) A British-run place with 12 rooms (with ceiling fans and all nonsmoking), this place is a find. It has the feel of a private villa, with colourful flowerpots, rooms overlooking a garden courtyard and a pool (with bar).

El Naranjo (☎ 971 33 03 24; Carrer de Sant Josep 31; meals €40-45; dinner Tue-Sun mid-Jun–Sep, lunch & dinner Tue-Sun Oct–mid-Jun) Enjoy well-prepared seafood meals in a shady garden at 'The Orange', a tranquil gourmet escape. Carpaccios of various kinds of meat are a house speciality. The *lechona al horno con puré de manzana* (suckling pig with apple purée) melts in the mouth.

ENTERTAINMENT

Guaraná (www.guaranaibiza.com; Passeig Marítim; 8pm-6am) Right by the marina, this a cool club away from the Ibiza-Sant Rafel-Sant Antoni circuit, with occasionally mellow tones.

GETTING THERE & AWAY

Regular buses (every 30 to 60 minutes) connect Santa Eulària's **bus stop** (Carrer de sa Església) with Ibiza City, Sant Antoni and the northern beaches.

Santa Eulària d'es Riu to S'Aigua Blanca

Northwest of Santa Eulària d'es Riu is the resort town of **Es Canar**, which is heavily developed and probably best avoided, although a couple of camping grounds are located nearby.

Further north on the main road is the sleepy village of **Sant Carles de Peralta**. Just outside the village, at Km12 on the road to Santa Eulària, is the **Las Dalias** (www.lasdalias.es; 10am-8pm Sat & 8pm-1.30am Mon Jun-Sep) market, held on Saturday, and Monday night.

Side roads lead off to the pleasant **Cala Llenya** and the serene **Cala Mastella** beaches. Boats run to the former from Santa Eulària five times daily (€8 return) from June to September. At the latter you could walk around the rocks from the left (northern) end of the pretty beach to reach **Es Bigote** (meals €30; 2pm lunch May-Sep). Offering *bullit de peix* (three or four types of fish caught that morning cooked up with herbs and potatoes in a huge vat), followed by *arròs caldós* (saffron rice cooked in the broth of the *bullit de peix*), this eatery is known far and wide. Finish off with *cafè de caleta* (coffee prepared with lemon zest, cinnamon and burned brandy). You need to turn up here in person at least the day before to book a spot.

The road to Cala Mastella continues on a couple of kilometres up to **Cala de Boix**, the only true black-sand beach in the Balearic Islands. Alternatively, there is another turn-off to Cala de Boix about 1km after Sant Carles.

Back on the main road, the next turn-off leads to the low-key resort area of **Platja Es Figueral**, with a golden sand beach and turquoise water. A little further on a handwritten sign marks the turn-off to the still lovelier beaches of **S'Aigua Blanca**, where clothing is optional. A couple of shacks act as seaside daytime bars.

Sitting out to sea east of Platja Es Figueral, **Illa sa Tagomago** is an uninhabited island. If you can hitch a boat ride, the transparent water on the protected west side of the island is paradise for swimming.

By day, especially on weekends and from July to August, all these beaches can be surprisingly busy.

SLEEPING & EATING

Camping Cala Nova (☎ 971 33 17 74; www.campingcalanova.com; sites per 2 people, tent & car €26.15) Just back from the Cala Nova beach and about 1km north of Es Canar, this is the best of the camping grounds here. There is a play area for the kids and tennis courts for the grown-ups.

Hostal Es Alocs (☎ 971 33 50 79; www.hostalalocs.com; s/d €35/55; May-Oct) This place is right on the beach at Platja Es Figueral. Rooms are simple, with bathrooms, over a couple of floors. Downstairs there is a bar-restaurant with a shady terrace.

our pick **Hostal Cala Boix** (☎ 971 33 52 24; www.hostalcalaboix.com; d incl breakfast €68; P) Set uphill and back from the beach, this solitary place could not be further from Ibiza madness. All rooms have bathrooms and some have sea views. It has a hearty restaurant (one of three here) – watch for the Thursday barbecues. On the beach you'll find a daytime bar.

Can Curreu (☎ 971 33 52 80; www.cancurreu.com; Carretera de Sant Carles Km12; d from €278; P) This Ibizan farmstead lies 1.5km south of Sant Carles, just off the main road from Santa Eulària. Rooms are tastefully decorated and furnished, and the suites are a luxury home in the country, with such extras as CD player, Jacuzzi and fireplace (for the winter).

Bar Anita (☎ 971 33 50 90; Sant Carles de Peralta; meals €20-25) A timeless tavern opposite the village church, this restaurant and bar has been attracting all sorts from around the island for decades. They come for pizza, pasta or slabs of *entrecote con salsa de pimiento* (entrecote in a pepper sauce; €15), or simply to drink and chat.

Osteria Es Figueral (☎ 971 33 59 55; Carrer de Platja Es Figueral 6; Platja Es Figueral; meals €30; daily May-Sep, dinner Fri-Sun Oct-Dec) Pull up a little blue wood-and-wicker chair on the shady roadside terrace, listen to Paolo Conte sing and tuck into excellent pizzas or such Italian faves as *saltimbocca a la romana* (slices of pork oven-cooked with prosciutto and parmesan cheese).

Cala Sant Vicent

The package-tour resort of Cala Sant Vicent is built around the shores of a protected bay on the northeast coast, a long stretch of sandy beach backed by a string of modern midrise hotels. The beach is a pleasant place for a swim. A 2.5km drive north winds through a leafy residential area high up to **Punta Grossa**, with spectacular views over the coast and east out to sea.

NORTH COAST & INTERIOR

The north of Ibiza contains some of the island's most attractive landscapes. The area's coastal hills and inland mountains are popular with bushwalkers and cyclists.

Cala Sant Vicent to Portinatx

The PM811 road heads west from Cala Sant Vicent, passing by the unremarkable village of **Sant Vicent de Sa Cala** before hitting the main north–south highway. From here you can head south to Ibiza City or north to **Portinatx**. The latter is the north coast's major tourist resort, with phalanxes of hotels around its three adjoining beaches – S'Arenal Petit, S'Arenal Gran and Platja Es Port. The beaches themselves are beautiful but can get crowded.

Cala Xarraca, just west of Portinatx, is set in a picturesque, partly protected bay with a rocky shoreline and a dark-sand beach. Development is limited to a solitary bar-restaurant and a couple of private houses.

Sant Miquel de Balansat & Port de Sant Miquel

One of the largest inland towns, Sant Miquel is overlooked by a shimmering white, boxlike 14th-century **church** that is worth the climb. Inside, the restored early 17th-century frescoes in the Capella de Benirràs are worth a look if you get lucky and the church is open. On the pretty patio, demonstrations of traditional island dances are held at 6pm on Thursday. Several kilometres north, the fine beaches of Port de Sant Miquel are dominated by the huge **Hotel Club San Miguel**.

A turn-off to the right just before you enter town, coming from the south, takes you around a headland to the entrance to the **Cova de Can Marçà** (☎ 971 33 47 76; adult/child €7.50/4; 10.30am-7.30pm Jun-Sep, 11am-6pm Oct-May), a collection of underground caverns spectacularly lit by coloured lights. Tours in various languages take around 30 to 40 minutes.

Beyond the caves, an unsealed road continues 4km around the coast to the unspoiled bay of **Cala Benirrás**. A sealed road to Cala Benirrás leads off the Sant Joan–Sant Miquel road, midway between the towns. High, forested cliffs and a couple of bar-restaurants back the beach. On Sunday at sunset you may well encounter groups of hippies with bongos banging out a greeting to the sunset, something they have been doing for decades.

The country mansion of **Can Planells** (☎ 971 33 49 24; www.canplanells.com; Carrer de Venda Rubió 2; d €178-290; P), just 1.5km outside Sant Miquel on the road to Sant Mateu d'Aubarca, oozes a relaxed rural luxury in its handful of tastefully arranged doubles and suites. The best suites have private terraces, and the place is set amid delightful gardens and fruit-tree groves.

Sant Llorenç de Balàfia

This quiet hamlet is dominated by a white Ibizan fortress church dating to the 18th century, when attacks by Moorish pirates were the scourge of the island. If it's open, climb to the roof. One kilometre northeast on a dirt track is the tiny, onetime fortified, hamlet of **Balàfia**, with two towers, a feast of flowers and lots of *privado* signs around the half-dozen houses.

Head 500m on to the C733 road and you reach the shady open-air restaurant of **Cana Pepeta** (☎ 971 32 50 23; Km15.4; meals €25; Wed-Mon), where the *frito de pulpo* (a baked dish of octopus, potatoes, paprika and herbs) is delicious.

If it's a slap-up grill you want, we recommend **Balafía** (☎ 971 32 50 19; meals €30-35; 8-11pm Mon-Sat), a simple restaurant about 50m along the dirt road. Enjoy sizzling grills on the terrace. Booking is essential.

In Sant Llorenç is the delightful **Paloma Café** (☎ 971 32 55 43; meals €15-20; 9am-4pm, Tue-Sun; V), about 100m downhill from the brilliant-white village church. The laid-back Ibiza spirit pervades this place, where you can snack on anything from quiche to carrot cake in the shade of the overgrown terrace. You can take away too.

East of Sant Llorenç and 2.2km off the C733 (signposted at Km15) is one of the island's more luxurious chill-out havens. **Atzaró** (☎ 971 33 88 38; www.atzaro.com; d €353; P) offers various grades of accommodation over its generous grounds, which with their ponds and Eastern statuary give the impression of being more temple than rural hotel! The spa is delightful (nonguests can use it all day for €30), the restaurant enticing and the very laid-back bar soothing.

Santa Gertrudis de Fruitera

If you blinked at the wrong time you could easily miss tiny Santa Gertrudis, south of Sant Miquel. Clustered around the central, pedestrianised Plaça de l'Església you'll find an unusual collection of **art-and-craft galleries** and antique and bric-a-brac shops, plus several good bars, among which the perennial favourite is **Bar Costa** (Plaça de l'Església 11), with art on the walls and somewhat erratic opening times. **Casi Todo** (☎ 971 19 70 23; www.casitodo.com; Plaça de l'Església 20; meals €25-30; 6-11pm Sun-Fri), run by the same British gent who operates the auction house next door, offers simple dishes with an international range and using local products.

Sant Rafel

pop 1780

Midway between Ibiza City and Sant Antoni de Portmany, Sant Rafel is internationally known as the nearest geographical point to two of Ibiza's biggest and best discos, Privilege (p672) and Amnesia (p672). By day, the town is known as a craft centre.

When clubbers are ready to take a breather, some like to chill and feed at **El Ayoun** (☎ 971 19 83 35; www.elayoun.com; Carre d'Isidor Macabich 6, Sant Rafel; meals €30-40; 8pm-4am mid-Mar–Oct), a relaxed Moroccan restaurant (with sushi bar). The Middle Eastern food is just the beginning (kitchen closes around midnight). The huge garden terrace is another attraction.

WEST COAST

Sant Antoni de Portmany

pop 19,900

Sant Antoni (San Antonio in Spanish), widely known as 'San An', is big and about as Spanish as bangers and mash. The locals joke that even football hooligans need holidays, and somehow they seem to end up in San An. It's the perfect destination if you've come in search of booze-ups, brawls and hangovers. The bulk of punters are young and from the UK (as the many flags hanging off hotel and apartment balconies attest).

About the only sight in town is the pretty, white 14th-century **Església de Sant Antoni** (Plaça de S'Església), a couple of blocks in from the marina.

Not far north of Sant Antoni are several undeveloped beaches, such as **Cala Salada**, a wide bay with sandy shores backed by pine forest. From here, a rough track continues further north to the beach at **Ses Fontanelles**. Closer to Sant Antoni are the pretty inlet beaches of **Cala Gració** and **Cala Gracioneta**, separated by a small rocky promontory.

SLEEPING & EATING

There is no shortage of mid-rise hotels, holiday apartment blocks and cheap-as-chips eateries all over Sant Antoni. All the sunset bars mentioned below serve food.

Hotel Pikes (☎ 971 34 22 22; www.pikeshotel.com; Camí de sa Vorera Km12; d from €246; P) An extraordinary hotel about 2km south of Sant Antoni off the road to Santa Gertrudis, Pikes offers a range of doubles and suites (all with varying themes, names like Honeysuckle and Sunset, and some with prices reaching for the stars). The stone country mansion has a gym, garden with bar and a translucent pool. The hotel's bar sessions (finishing as late as 2am) are renowned.

Villa Mercedes (☎ 971 34 85 43; www.villamercedesibiza.com; Molls dels Pescadors s/n; meals €35-40; 7pm-3am; V) This place stands out because it really looks like a villa in among the sometimes horrendous muddle of Sant Antoni. It looks over the marina and offers eclectic cooking, from wok-fried vegetables through rice and noodle dishes to local catch of the day.

DRINKING

Head for the small rock-and-sand strip on the north shore to join hundreds of others for sunset drinks at a string of chilled bars. A new pedestrian walkway makes it easy to head around from the port.

our pick **Café del Mar** (☎ 971 34 25 16; www.cafedelmar.es; 5pm-4am) remains the best-knownplace.

Others include **Café Mambo** (☎ 971 34 66 38; www.cafemamboibiza.com; 2pm-4am) and **Savannah Café** (☎ 971 34 80 31; www.savannahibiza.com; 2pm-4am). They are getting stiff competition from another set of stylish lounge bars about 300m further north along the pedestrian walkway. Places such as **Coastline Café**, **Sun Beach Bar** and **Kanya** all have pools and attract plenty of punters. After the sun goes down all turn up the rhythmic heat and pound on until 4am, from about June to October.

Around the other side of the bay at Cala de Bou is **Kumharas** (☎ 971 80 57 40; www.kumharas.org; Carrer de Lugo 2), where you can eat, drink and soak in the final rays of the day. Sunday night is best, with live performances (especially fire-dancers). Look for the Rodeo Vaca Loca sign on the main road and turn down Carrer de Lugo towards the sea.

GETTING THERE & AWAY

Local buses run every 15 to 30 minutes to Ibiza City and take about 30 to 40 minutes. There are seven or eight buses a day to Cala Bassa and Cala Compte from June to October. They take about 20 minutes, depending on stops and traffic.

Cruceros Portmany boats (☎ 971 34 34 71; www.crucerosportmany.com) run to local beaches, such as Cala Bassa and Cala Compte (€9 return to either).

Cala Bassa to Cala d'Hort

Heading west and south from Sant Antoni, you'll come to the rocky and popular bay of **Cala Bassa**. The next few coves around the coast hide some extremely pretty beaches – **Cala Compte**, with its translucent water, and the popular **Cala Codolars** are among the best. All are accessible by local bus and/or boat from Sant Antoni.

Further south, **Cala Vedella** is a modest resort with a fine beach in the centre of town, backed by a couple of restaurants. It gets pretty jammed. A little further south, **Cala d'Hort** has a spectacular setting overlooking two rugged rocky islets, **Es Vedrá** and **Es Vedranell**. The water here is an inviting shade of blue, and the beach a long arc of sand sprinkled with pebbles and rocks. The developers still haven't ruined this place, and there's little here apart from two relaxed bar-restaurants. But like Cala Vedella, it gets crowded.

SOUTH COAST

Ses Salines

pop 4300

Platja de ses Salines and the adjacent Platja d'es Cavallet, at the southernmost tip of the island, are the best beaches within easy striking distance of Ibiza City. The area takes its name from the salt pans exploited here since Carthaginian times – big business until tourism came along.

The local bus from Ibiza City drops you at the western end of Ses Salines beside a small bar. Across the road, on the other side of the sand dunes, a long crescent-shaped bay stretches into the distance, with a broad sandy beach broken by patches of rocks. These beaches are popular with Ibiza's party-hard crowd and four or five open-air beach bars are spread around the bay. Swimsuits become less common the further east you go. Stroll on if the au naturel look appeals to you: **Platja d'es Cavallet**, the next bay around to the east, is Ibiza's official nudist beach.

Hostal Mar y Sal (☎ 971 39 65 84; d incl breakfast €65; ⏰ May-Sep) is handy for the beach, and has its own bar and restaurant. It's frequently booked months in advance for July and August.

Sa Trinxa, at the eastern end of the beach, remains the coolest of the four bars on this stretch of sand. It serves burgers, *bocadillos* (filled rolls), salads and fruit smoothies. It also does somewhat stronger drinks, and when the DJ gets into gear (from 2pm) things can get kind of wild.

Autobuses Voramar El Gaucho runs eight to 10 buses daily (line 11) to Ses Salines from Ibiza City (€1.50).

Platja des Codolar & Around

Northwest of Ses Salines stretches a 3km grey stone beach, **Platja des Codolar**, at the north end of which you'll espy the circus-style tents of **Macao Café** (www.macaocafemusic.com), which keeps a chilled-out crowd (seemingly oblivious to the low-flying jets landing and taking off overhead) happy with music, drinks and snacks. Bus 26 runs by from Ibiza City, but it's easier to drive. Follow the PM803 road towards Sant Josep de sa Talaia. Take the turn-off left marking the airport only (if you pass the Km5 bar on your left, you've missed the turn – no problem, take the next for Sa Caleta). Two kilometres down this road, take a right and in another 2km you're at Macao Café. Less than 1km west, you hit **Sa Caleta**, a tiny, pretty beach with restaurant. A 200m walk east of the beach is a fishing inlet with boats pulled up in front of protective huts. You'll also find the remains of Phoenician settlement, founded in the late 8th century BC. Another 500m west is the stony beach of **Cala des Jondal**, backed by three very Ibiza-style chilled lounge-bar eateries.

FORMENTERA

A short boat ride south of Ibiza, Formentera is the smallest and least-developed of the four main Balearic Islands, with a population of 8440. This idyll is laced with sandy beaches and some relaxing short walking and cycling trails. It's a popular day trip from Ibiza and gets crowded in midsummer (especially with the Italian contingent, for whom Formentera is what Bali is to Australians), but most of the time it is still possible to find yourself a strip of sand out of sight and earshot of other tourists.

Formentera's predominantly flat landscape is rugged and at times bleak. The coast is alternately fringed with jagged cliffs and beaches backed by low dunes. A handful of farmers scrape a living from the land in the centre and east, but elsewhere the island is a patchwork of pine plantations, sun-bleached salt beds, low stone walls and mostly vacant fields.

Orientation & Information

Formentera is less than 20km across from east to west. Most ferries arrive at La Savina, a harbour town wedged between two large salt lakes, the Estany d'es Peix and Estany Pudent (the aptly named Smelly Lake). Three kilometres south of La Savina is the island's administrative capital, Sant Francesc Xavier, and another 5km southwest is Cap de Barbaria, the southernmost point. Es Pujols, the main tourist resort, is 3km east of La Savina.

The main road (PM820) runs down the middle of the island, passing by the fine beaches of Platja de Migjorn along the south coast and through the fishing village of Es Caló (13km southeast of La Savina) before climbing to Sa Talaia (192m), the island's highest point. The eastern end of the island is marked by the Far de sa Mola lighthouse.

Formentera's **tourist office** (☎ 971 32 20 57; www.turismoformentera.com; ⏰ 9am-7pm Mon-Fri, 9am-3pm Sat & Sun May-Sep) is in La Savina, hidden behind the row of vehicle-hire agencies that line the port. Opening hours vary seasonally. A branch with the same hours opens in **Es Pujols** and another opposite the church in **Sant Francesc Xavier**, where you'll also find most of the banks. There is a clinic, **Centro Médico** (☎ 902 07 90 79; ⏰ 8am-8pm Mon-Fri), 3km south of La Savina.

Getting There & Around

Baleària-Trasmapi (☎ 902 160191; www.balearia.com, www.trasmapi.com) runs around 15 daily fast ferries (one-way/return €21.60/41, 25 minutes) between Ibiza City and Formentera (La Savina). It also runs a few from Ibiza City direct to Cala Saona (same prices). Slightly slower vessels that take vehicles also make the run. Fares for vehicles cost €73 for a small car one-way and €32 for motorcycles under 250cc.

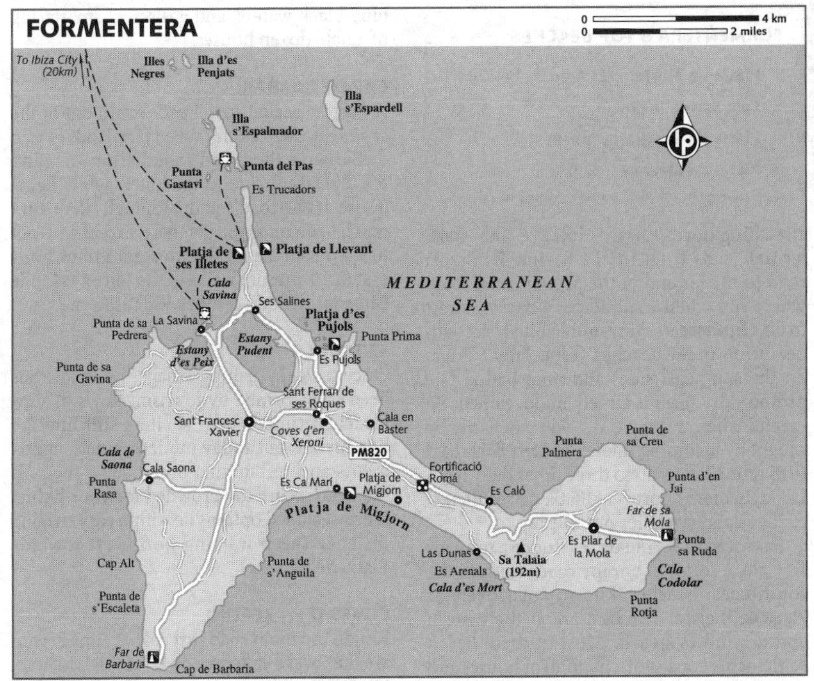

Bicycles go free of charge. On the fast ferries in particular, there are sometimes special offers. The first ferry leaves Ibiza City at 7am and the last one returns from Formentera at 10pm (Sunday 7.30pm).

Mediterranea-Pitiusa SL (☎ 971 32 24 43; www.medpitiusa.net) runs up to nine fast ferries daily between Ibiza and Formentera (€19.60 to €21.50 each way, 25 to 35 minutes).

Autocares Paya (☎ 971 32 31 81; www.autocarespaya.com) runs a regular bus service connecting the main towns, but scooter and bicycle are the preferred options.

Vehicle-hire agencies are all over the island, including a string of places opposite the harbour in La Savina. Local agencies include **Moto Rent Mitjorn** (☎ 971 32 23 06), **Moto Rent La Savina** (☎ 971 32 22 75) and **Formotor** (☎ 971 32 29 29). Daily rates are around €6 to €8 for a bike, €10 for a mountain bike, €20 to €25 for a motor scooter and up to €55 for a motorcycle. A car is superfluous on this tiny island, but they are available for rent, as are quads (at around €60 to €80 a day).

You can also call a **taxi** (☎ 971 32 20 16, 971 32 80 16, 971 32 23 42).

Sights & Activities

Apart from walking, cycling and lying on beaches, activities are limited. Points of interest include a series of crumbling stone **watchtowers** along the coastline, a ruined **Roman fortress** (Fortificació Romà), on the south coast, and 40 minor **archaeological sites** (most signposted off the main roads). Divers could approach **Diving Center Formentera** (☎ 971 32 11 68; www.blue-adventure.com; Carrer d'Almadraba 67-71, La Savina; dive with rental gear €45), one of a handful of island dive centres. **Wet4Fun** (☎ 971 32 18 09; 🕑 10am-6pm Mon-Sat, Jun-Sep) offers the chance to learn windsurfing and kitesurfing, as well as sailing on small catamarans. You can hire windsurf or kitesurf gear if you are already experienced (€24 per hour). There are also outlets at Es Pujols, Ca' Mari (west end of Migjorn beaches) and Es Arenals (east end of Migjorn).

BEACHES

Among the island's best beaches are **Platja de Llevant** and **Platja de ses Illetes** – beautiful strips of white sand that line the eastern and western sides, respectively, of the narrow promontory

FORMENTERA'S TOP BEACHES

- **Platja de Migjorn** (Es Arenals; below)
- **Cala Saona** (below)
- **Platja de Ses Illetes** (p679)
- **Platja de Llevant** (p679)

stretching north towards Ibiza. A 4km **walking trail** leads from the La Savina–Es Pujols road to the far end of the promontory, from where you could wade across a narrow strait to **Illa s'Espalmador**, a tiny uninhabited islet with beautiful, quiet beaches (especially S'Alga, on the southeast side) and mud baths. The promontory itself is largely undeveloped. Be careful when wading out – you can easily be caught by incoming tides. The **Barca Bahia boat** (€15 return) runs up to three times daily from La Savina ferry port (via Platja de ses Illetes) to the island (weather permitting).

East of Sant Ferran de ses Roques, towards Es Caló, a series of bumpy roads leads to the south-coast beaches, known collectively as **Platja de Migjorn**. The best are at the eastern end around **Es Arenals**. Most of these beach settlements consist of a handful of houses and apartments, a couple of bar-restaurants and the odd *hostal*.

Nudism is fairly common on many of the island's beaches. It's not mandatory but no one bats an eyelid if you shed all.

SANT FRANCESC XAVIER

pop 2350

Formentera's capital and biggest population centre, Sant Francesc Xavier is an attractive whitewashed village with some good cafes overlooking small, sunny plazas. The town's older buildings include a 14th-century **chapel**, an 18th-century **fortress**, and the **Museu Etnològic** (☎ 971 32 26 70; Carrer de Jaume I 17; admission free; 🕑 10am-2pm & 7-9pm Mon-Fri, Jun-Sep, 9am-3pm Mon-Fri Oct-Apr), a modest ethnological museum devoted to the traditional aspects of predominantly rural island life.

CALA SAONA

On the road south of Sant Francesc Xavier, one-third of the way to Cap de Barbaria, turn west to the delectable cove of Cala Saona. The beach is one of the island's best, with just one big hotel (see opposite), a couple of bar-restaurants overlooking the aqua-and-blue-black waters, and a discreet smattering of a half-dozen houses.

CAP DE BARBARIA

A narrow sealed road heads south out of the capital through stone-walled farmlands to Cap de Barbaria, the island's southernmost point. It's a pleasant ride to the lonely white lighthouse at the road's end, although there ain't much to do once you get there, except gaze out to sea. From the *far* (lighthouse) a track leads east (a 10-minute walk) to the **Torre d'es Cap de Barbaria**, an 18th-century watchtower.

ES PUJOLS

Once a sleepy fishing village, Es Pujols has been transformed by tourism. Rows of sun-bleached timber boat shelters still line the beachfront, but today modern hotels, apartments and restaurants overshadow them. If the beaches are too crowded for your liking, more-secluded options lie within easy striking distance (keep walking northwest towards Platja de Llevant).

COVES D'EN XERONI

Beside the main road just east of Sant Ferran are the **Coves d'en Xeroni** (☎ 971 32 82 14; adult/under 12yr €4/2.50; 🕑 10am-1.30pm & 2.30-7pm Mon-Sat May-Oct), an unexceptional series of underground caves with stalactites and all. Treat opening times with a large grain of salt. How many organised visits a day (the most likely time is 1pm) depends on demand and whether or not the guide is around.

EASTERN END

The fishing settlement of Es Caló is set on a tiny rocky cove ringed by faded timber boat shelters. The coastline is jagged, but immediately west of Es Caló you'll find some good swimming holes and rock pools with small patches of sand.

From Es Caló, the road twists up to the island's highest point. Close to the top, Restaurante El Mirador offers spectacular views along the length of the island, whose eastern extremity is an elevated limestone plateau. Most of the coastline is only accessible by boat, and pine stands and farms mainly take up the interior. A road runs arrow-straight to the island's eastern tip, passing through **Es Pilar de la Mola**, which comes alive for hippy markets on Wednesday and Sunday (open 4pm to 9pm). At the end of the road stand the **Far de sa Mola** lighthouse, a **monument** to Jules Verne (who used this setting in one of his novels), a bar and spectacular cliffside views.

Sleeping

Camping is prohibited. Most accommodation caters to package-tour agencies, so is overpriced and/or booked out in midsummer. Single rooms are as rare as hens' teeth in summer, and rental apartments (a better deal for stays of a week or more) are more common than *hostales* and hotels (of which there are just over 50). Check out www.formenterahotels guide.com and www.guiafor mentera.com.

Astbury Formentera (☎ UK 01642-210163; www.formentera.co.uk; 31 Baker St, Middlesbrough TS1 2LF) is a UK-based specialist in house and apartment rentals in Formentera.

SANT FRANCESC XAVIER

Several *hostales* are scattered about this pleasant town and prices are more realistic than at some of the beach locations.

Casa Rafal (☎ 971 32 22 05; Carrer d'Isidoro Macabich; d €65; ❄) Just off sleepy Plaça de sa Constitució, this modest two-storey spot is friendly and offers good, clean rooms with bathroom and breakfast. There is a restaurant downstairs.

ES PUJOLS

Hostal Voramar (☎ 971 32 81 19; voramar@interbook.net; Carrer de Miramar; s/d incl breakfast €115/150; 🕑 May-Oct; ❄ 💻 🏊) About 100m inland from the beach, this ochre-fronted hotel has comfortable rooms, most with balcony. Have a workout in the small gym.

The same people own the simpler **Fonda Pinatar** (s/d €88/113), almost next door.

SANT FERRAN DE SES ROQUES

Hostal Pepe (☎ 971 32 80 33; Carrer Major 68; s/d incl breakfast €46/60) Located on the pleasant (and on summer nights lively) main street near the village's old sandstone church, this whitewashed place with flashes of blue has 45 simple and breezy rooms with bathrooms. Most have a balcony too. It's been a classic for decades.

CALA SAONA

Hotel Cala Saona (☎ 971 32 20 30; www.hotelcalasaona.com; s/d €120/170; 🕑 May-Oct; P ❄ 🏊) A white behemoth, this hotel is set back from the beach and offers 116 rooms, pool, tennis courts and restaurant. From the best rooms the view is straight across the beach and out to sea. Prices halve in low season. The beach bar-restaurants are perfect for a sunset sangria.

PLATJA DE MIGJORN

A spattering of *hostales* and apartments is spread along Formentera's south beach but most only deal with tour operators.

Hostal Ca Marí (☎ 971 32 81 80; Es Ca Marí; s/d €80.50/125; ❄ 🏊) This is actually three comfortable *hostales* in one: its rooms and apartments all share a central bar, restaurant, pool and grocery shop in the little settlement of the same name.

ES CALÓ

our pick **Fonda Rafalet** (☎ 971 32 70 16; s/d €64/107) Overlooking a small rocky harbour, this guest house has spacious rooms (many with sea views), and also incorporates a bar and popular seafood restaurant with portside terrace. The owners also run a couple of other *hostales* and apartments in this diminutive fishing hamlet.

Eating

Mostly waterfront eateries offer a standard range of seafood and paella-style options. Reckon on an average of €30 to €40 a head or more for a full meal in the bulk of restaurants, most of which open from May to October only.

SANT FRANCESC XAVIER

Plenty of Italian-run pasta and pizza joints and a couple of lazy cafes with terraces make it easy to fuel up here.

ES PUJOLS

The waterfront is lined with restaurants of greater or lesser interest. Most serve seafood.

El Caminito (☎ 971 32 81 06; Carretera La Savina-Es Pujols; meals €40-50; 🕑 dinner Apr-Nov) A touch of the Pampa in the Med, this Argentine meat grill is one of the best restaurants on the island, serving succulent slabs of meat in all its known forms. It is barely 1km outside Es Pujols on the road to La Savina.

SANT FERRAN DE SES ROQUES

On pedestrianised Carrer Major you'll find a string of summertime eateries.

Can Forn (☎ 971 32 81 55; Carrer Major 39; meals €30-35; 🕑 lunch & dinner Mon-Sat & dinner only Sun May-Oct)

A WANING WAY OF LIFE

Pep Campanitx (54), president of the Formentera fishing cooperative, is a deeply tanned, softly spoken and sprightly man. His *llaüt* (a small, single-sail fishing boat) is hauled up at the tiny rocky cove of Es Caló, one of about 25 fishing vessels still in service around Formentera. They fish along the coast, no more than six or seven nautical miles out to sea. Three larger trawlers based in La Savina fish on a grander scale and further away.

'The flavour of fish depends on what they eat. Here (and in Ibiza), the fields of *posidonia* (poseidon grass) are in good condition and the fish feed in it. It gives the fish a nice flavour,' he smiles. 'When we eat fish elsewhere, it's not the same thing!'

In July and August, when the island's temporary population can reach 40,000 ('too many!' says Campanitx), the local fishermen barely provide 10% of the fish eaten. In winter, when half the local population is on holiday elsewhere, fishermen have to flog their catch to Ibiza!

It could be a dying art. On the one hand, moves are under way to create marine reserves and restrict fishing at certain times to allow repopulation. On the other, few young people take up this tough trade. 'If you don't inherit a boat and mooring, together worth around €90,000, it's virtually impossible for a young lad to get started,' muses Campanitx. 'In the 1980s, when we set up the cooperative, we had 100 members and 60 vessels. Now we are half that number.'

'We are losing our identity. This is an island of fishermen. Before tourism, most islanders were self-sufficient. Fishermen had a bit of land and farmers did a little fishing. But how can you expect young people to get into something from which it is hard to make a living? For months on end you can be without work. Without government subsidies, the future of fishing here doesn't look good.

'You have to be out to sea by 4am, which means you're up preparing the boat at 3am. Nowadays, young folks are just coming home from a night out at that hour,' he laughs.

On the land, if anything, things are grimmer still. 'Fields are abandoned; only six or seven retired people continue to work the land a little. There's still a few sheep around, but basically all our meat, fruit and vegetables are imported,' says Campanitx.

And those tasty island wines? 'People from elsewhere started growing vines and making wine, mostly up on La Mola, about 10 years ago. I can't imagine it is profitable.'

Not all the news is bad. Young people are moving away, as you might have expected on a tough, small island. 'About 90% of those who go away to study elsewhere come back. Islanders have strong roots here. Now that we have a hospital and a new government needing specialised staff, even more will return. But they might not be tempted to hit the high seas!'

The best dishes here are the *calamar a la bruta* ('dirty calamari', with potato, Mallorcan sausage and squid ink) and *calamar a la payesa* (similar, but with an onion sauce and tomato instead of the ink).

PLATJA DE SES ILLETES

A 3km, partly dirt road winds north of the La Savina–Es Pujols road, just behind the string of beaches leading to Platja de ses Illetes and providing access to four beachside restaurants and a trio of bars along the way.

Es Molí de Sal (☎ 971 18 74 91; meals €40-50; ⏲ May-Oct) In this tastefully renovated mill boasting a lovely terrace and magnificent sea views you will discover some of the finest seafood on the island. Try one of the rice dishes or the house speciality, *caldereta de llagosta*.

SOUTH COAST

Vogamari (☎ 971 32 90 53; Km9.5; meals €30-35; ⏲ lunch & dinner Wed-Mon, lunch only Tue May-Oct) A simple island eatery with a broad verandah set amid a greenery-filled dune, this is great for fresh fish, paella or solid meat dishes.

our pick **Sa Platgeta** (☎ 971 18 76 14; Platja de Migjorn, Es Ca Marí; meals €35; ⏲ Mon-Sat May-Oct) According to some locals, this is one of the best spots on the island for fresh fish. It is a simple spot set amid pines just back from a narrow and rock-studded beach and also has a pleasant shady terrace. Sa Platgeta is 500m west of Es Ca Marí (follow the signs through the backstreets or walk along the waterfront).

Restaurante Es Cupiná (☎ 971 32 72 21; Plajta de Migjorn; meals €35-40; ⏲ May-Oct) At the eastern extremity of the beach, this is a big name on the island, noted especially for the lobster (unfortunately not always available) and freshly cooked fish of the day.

10.7 Vista y Sol (☎ 971 32 84 85; www.vistaysol.com; meals €40-50; ⌚ Apr-Oct) Milan meets the sea in this Italian eatery (with an international wine list). DJ sounds, black-and-white decor and a relaxed vibe make it perfect for lingering.

ES CALÓ

our pick **S'Eufabi** (☎ 971 32 70 56; Carretera La Mola Km12.5; meals €25-30; ⌚ lunch & dinner Wed-Mon, dinner only Tue) For some of the best paella and *fideuá* (a fine noodle version) on Formentera at a reasonable price, head for this shady eatery about 1km east of Es Caló. It's on the left as you begin the gentle ascent towards Es Pilar de la Mola.

ES PILAR DE LA MOLA

Formentera's easternmost town has a handful of bars and restaurants.

Pequeña Isla (☎ 971 32 70 68; Avinguda del Pilar 111; meals €30-35; Ⓥ ♿) Easily the best restaurant in town, with a shady roadside terrace, the 'Little Island' dishes up hearty meat dishes, fresh grilled fish, paella (and other rice dishes), and various island specialities, including lamb dishes and fried octopus.

Entertainment

ES PUJOLS

In summer Es Pujols gets lively, offering an intense tangle of intertwined bars along or just off Carrer d'Espardell (just back from the waterfront) that stay open until 3am or 4am. Customers are 90% Italian – indeed you'd hardly know you were in Spain! A favourite since 1994 is the red and rocking **Indiana Café**, with its high tables and stools. Next door, newcomer **Neroopaco** is all black and white, low lounges and deep house. The end effect is like being in one huge semi-open-air drinking saloon with themed spaces. Nearby Carrer de Roca Plana also has a few bars, of which boisterous **Pachanka** is a good one to keep in mind for later in the evening. **Vivi Club** (☎ 691 046904; Avinguda Miramar) is a pleasant bar-lounge-restaurant with pine trees in the garden. The purple lighting tinges everything, even your cocktails.

SANT FERRAN DE SES ROQUES

Fonda Pepe (☎ 971 32 80 33; Carrer Major 55; ⌚ May-Oct) Welcome to the island classic, a knock-about bar connected with the *hostal* (across the street) of the same name. It has been serving *pomades* (gin and lemon) for decades and attracts a lively crowd of locals and foreigners of all ages and persuasions.

PLATJA DE SES ILLETES

One of the island beachside rituals is sipping on sangria while observing the sunset.

Bigsurlife (⌚ 10.30am-sunset May-Oct) This bar attracts a good-natured beautiful Italian crowd, and serves nachos all day and Italian dishes at lunchtime. It's such a hit with the *dolce vita* mob that they have brought out their own chill-out CDs. The daily event is drinks (huge glass steins of mojito) on the beach for sunset. About 20m before the turn-off for Platja de ses Illetes from the La Savina–Es Pujols road, a parking area is signposted to the left. Another 30m brings you to the beach and bar.

Tiburón (⌚ 10am-sunset May-Oct) About 200m further up the beach, this is an equally fun beach tavern that tends to attract more locals for fish, salads, sangria and, of course, sunsets.

PLATJA DE MIGJORN

This long strand is littered with bars, ranging from rather sophisticated (often Italian-run) chill-out scenes for sipping cocktails to relaxed club sounds and the sunset, to more rough-and-ready affairs.

our pick **Blue Bar** (☎ 971 18 70 11; www.bluebarformentera.com; Km8; ⌚ noon-4am Apr-Oct) This is a Formentera classic, offering good seafood, paella and spadefuls of *buen rollito* (good vibes). It is the south's chill-out bar par excellence, and everything is blue – the seats, the sunshades, the tables, lounges, loos, walls.

Xiringuito Bartolo (⌚ May-Oct) At the eastern extremity of the beach, this must be the world's tiniest beach bar and is much loved by islanders. Sitting cheerfully on stilts, it hosts two longish tables. But Bartolo serves up drinks and snacks to wander away with if there's nowhere to sit.

MENORCA

Menorca (population 90,240) is the least overrun and most tranquil of the Balearics. In 1993 Unesco declared it a Biosphere Reserve, aiming to preserve environmental areas, such as the Parc Natural S'Albufera d'es Grau wetlands and the island's unique archaeological sites.

The untouched beaches, coves and ravines around its 216km coastline allow the more adventurous the occasional sense of discovery! This must be one of the few places in the Mediterranean where it is possible to have a beautiful beach largely to yourself in summer. Some say the island owes much to Franco for not being overrun with tourist development. While neighbouring Mallorca went over to the Nationalists almost at the outset of the civil war, Menorca resisted. Franco later 'rewarded' Mallorca with a construction free-for-all and penalised Menorca by blocking development!

The second-largest and northernmost of the Balearics, Menorca also has a wetter climate and is usually a few degrees cooler than the other islands. Particularly in the low season, the 'windy island' is relentlessly buffeted by *tramuntana* winds from the north.

Check out the tourist information website www.e-menorca.org and the island's official accommodation website, www.visitmenorca.com. Within Spain, you can also try the **call centre** (☎ 902 92 90 15; 🕑 10am-6pm). For activities, have a look at Menorca Activa (www.menorca activa.com).

Orientation

The capital, Maó (Castilian: Mahón), is at the eastern end of the island. Ferries from the mainland and Palma de Mallorca arrive at Maó's busy port, and Menorca's airport is 7km southwest of the city. The main road (ME1) runs along the middle of the island to Ciutadella, Menorca's second town, with secondary roads leading north and south to the resorts and beaches.

The northern half of Menorca is an undulating area of green rolling hills, with a rugged and rocky coastline. The southern half of the island is flatter and drier, with a smoother coastline and sandy beaches between high cliffs.

Getting Around

TO/FROM THE AIRPORT

Menorca's airport is served by buses to the bus station in Maó (€1.55, 15 minutes) every half-hour from 5.55am to 10.25pm and then (June to September only) hourly to 12.25am.

BUS

Do not expect to move around the island fast on the buses. You can get to quite a few destinations from Maó, but, with a few exceptions, services are infrequent and sluggish.

> **MENORCA'S TOP FIVE BEACHES**
>
> - **Cala Macarelleta** (p694)
> - **Cala en Turqueta** (p694)
> - **Cala Pregonda** (p693)
> - **Cala Presili** (p693)
> - **Cala Morell** (p692)

CAR & MOTORCYCLE

In Maó, try **Autos Valls** (☎ 971 35 42 44; www.autosvalls.com; Plaça d'Espanya 13) or **Autosmenorsur** (☎ 971 36 56 66; Moll de Llevant 35). All the biggies have representatives at the airport. Daily hire can cost €35 to €45 for something like a Hyundai Atos.

MAÓ

pop 28,300

The British have invaded Menorca four times (if you count the modest campaign that began with the first charter flight from London in 1953). As a result Maó, the capital, is an unusual blend of Anglo and Spanish characteristics.

The British made it the capital in 1713, and the influence of their almost 100-year presence (the island reverted to Spanish rule in 1802) is still evident in the town's architecture, traditions and culture. Even today the majority of Maó's visitors come from Britain.

Maó's harbour is its most impressive feature and was the drawcard for the Brits. The deep, well-protected waters handle everything from small fishing boats to tankers. The town is built atop the cliffs that line the harbour's southern shore. Although some older buildings still remain, the majority of the architecture is in the restrained 18th-century Georgian style (note the sash windows!).

Information

Centre de Salut Verge del Toro (☎ 971 15 77 00; Carrer de Barcelona 3) A central general clinic.
Hospital Mateu Orfila (☎ 971 48 70 00; Ronda de Malbúguer 1) On the ring road.
Policía Nacional (Carrer de la Concepciò 1)
Post office (Carrer del Bon Aire 15; 🕑 8.30am-8.30pm Mon-Fri, 9.30am-2pm Sat)
Tourist office airport (☎ 971 15 71 15; 🕑 8am-10pm daily Jul-Aug, 8am-10pm Mon-Fri, 8am-2pm Sat May-Jun

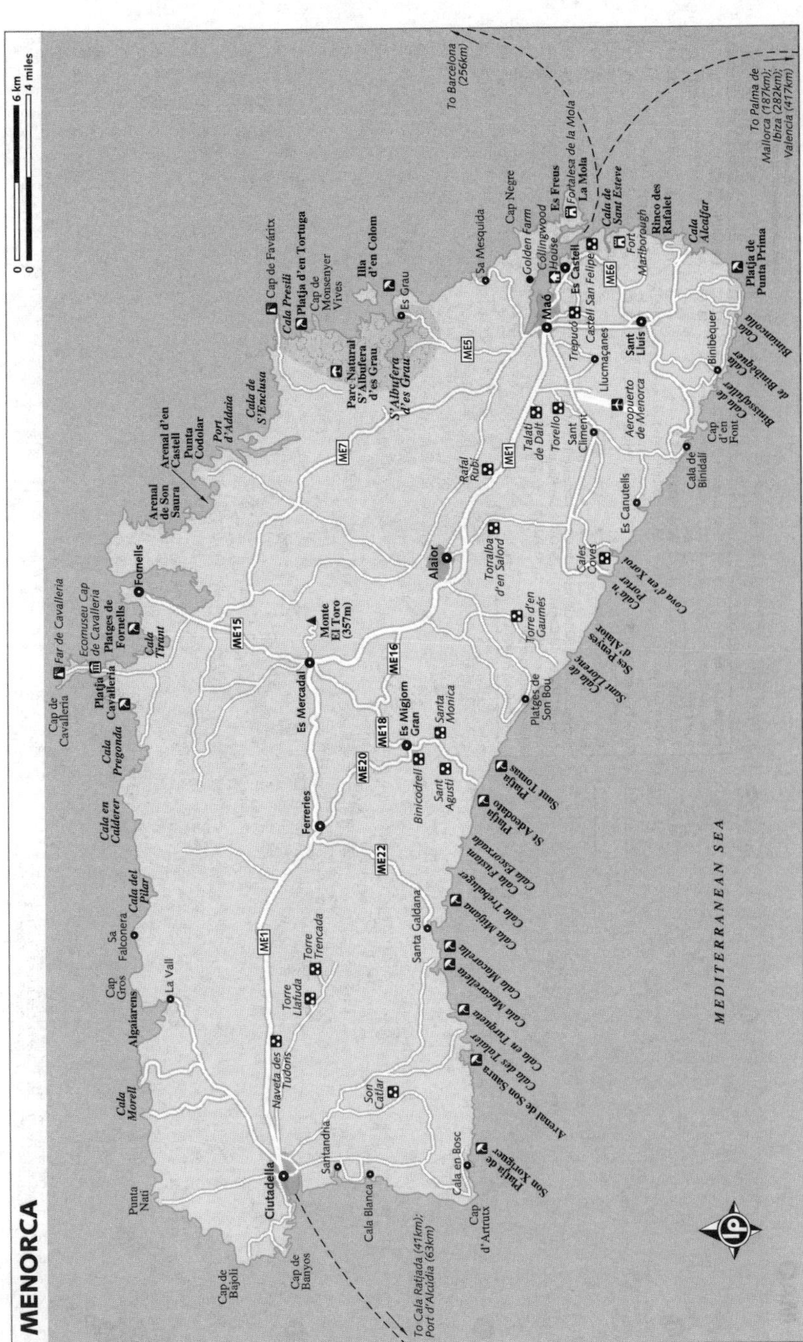
MENORCA
0 6 km
0 4 miles
To Barcelona (256km)
To Palma de Mallorca (187km); Ibiza (282km); Valencia (417km)
To Cala Ratjada (41km); Port d'Alcúdia (63km)
MEDITERRANEAN SEA
Ciutadella
Punta Nati
Cap de Bajolí
Cap de Banyos
Cala Blanca
Santandria
Cala en Bosc
Cap d'Artrutx
Platja de Son Xoriguer
Arenal de Son Saura
Cala des Talaier
Cala en Turqueta
Cala Macarelleta
Cala Macarella
Santa Galdana
Cala Mitjana
Cala Trebalúger
Cala Fustam
Cala Escorxada
Platja St Adeodato
Platja Sant Tomàs
Son Catlar
Naveta des Tudons
Torre Llafuda
Torre Trencada
Cala Morell
Algaiarens
Cap Gros
La Vall
Sa Falconera
Cala del Pilar
Cala en Calderer
Cala Pregonda
Cap de Cavalleria
Platja Cavalleria
Far de Cavalleria
Ecomuseu Cap de Cavalleria
Platges de Fornells
Cala Tirant
Fornells
Ferreries
Binicodrell
Sant Agustí
Es Migjorn Gran
Santa Monica
Es Mercadal
Monte El Toro (357m)
Platges de Son Bou
Sant Llorenç
Cala de Sant Llorenç
Ses Penyes d'Alaior
Torre d'en Gaumés
Torralba d'en Salord
Alaior
Cala'n Porter
Cova d'en Xoroi
Cales Coves
Es Canutells
Cala de Binidalí
Cap d'en Font
Cala de Binissafúller
Cala de Binibèquer
Cala Binancolla
Binibèquer
Sant Lluís
Aeropuerto de Menorca
Sant Climent
Torelló
Talatí de Dalt
Rafal Rubí
Llucmaçanes
Trepucó
Castell San Felipe
Maó
Es Castell
Fort Marlborough
Platja de Punta Prima
Cala Alcalfar
Rinco des Rafalet
Cala de Sant Esteve
Fortalesa de la Mola
La Mola
Es Freus
Collingwood House
Golden Farm
Cap Negre
Sa Mesquida
Es Grau
Illa d'en Colom
Parc Natural S'Albufera d'es Grau
S'Albufera d'es Grau
Cap de Monsenyer Vives
Platja d'en Tortuga
Cala Presili
Cap de Favàritx
Cala de S'Enclusa
Port d'Addaia
Punta Codolar
Arenal d'en Castell
Arenal de Son Saura
ME1
ME5
ME6
ME7
ME15
ME16
ME18
ME20
ME22

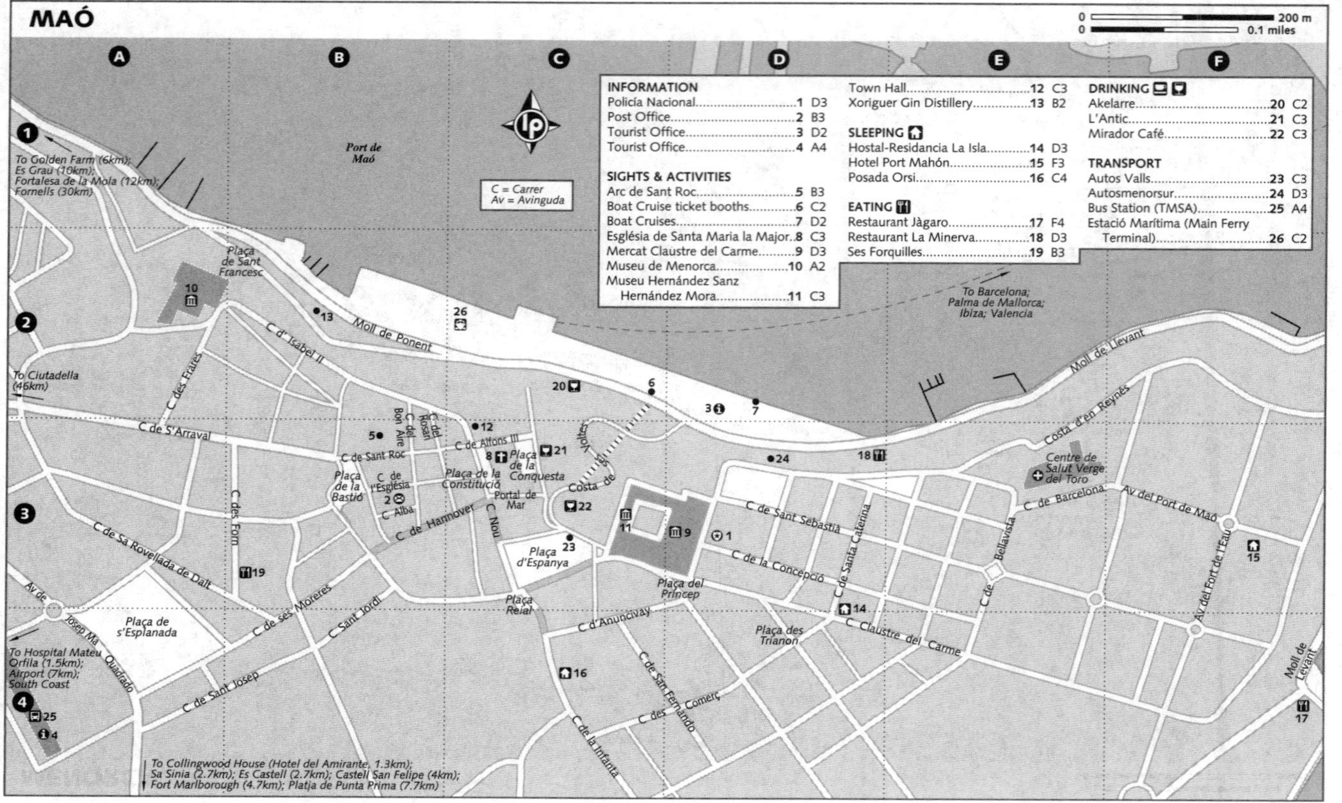
MAÓ
0 200 m
0 0.1 miles
INFORMATION
Policía Nacional 1 D3
Post Office 2 B3
Tourist Office 3 D2
Tourist Office 4 A4
SIGHTS & ACTIVITIES
Arc de Sant Roc 5 B3
Boat Cruise ticket booths 6 C2
Boat Cruises 7 D2
Església de Santa Maria la Major 8 C3
Mercat Claustre del Carme 9 D3
Museu de Menorca 10 A2
Museu Hernández Sanz Hernández Mora 11 C3
Town Hall 12 C3
Xoriguer Gin Distillery 13 B2
SLEEPING
Hostal-Residancia La Isla 14 D3
Hotel Port Mahón 15 F3
Posada Orsi 16 C4
EATING
Restaurant Jàgaro 17 F4
Restaurant La Minerva 18 D3
Ses Forquilles 19 B3
DRINKING
Akelarre 20 C2
L'Antic 21 C3
Mirador Café 22 C3
TRANSPORT
Autos Valls 23 C3
Autosmenorsur 24 D3
Bus Station (TMSA) 25 A4
Estació Marítima (Main Ferry Terminal) 26 C2
C = Carrer
Av = Avinguda
Port de Maó
To Golden Farm (6km); Es Grau (10km); Fortalesa de la Mola (12km); Fornells (30km)
To Ciutadella (46km)
To Hospital Mateu Orfila (1.5km); Airport (7km); South Coast
To Barcelona; Palma de Mallorca; Ibiza; Valencia
To Collingwood House (Hotel del Amirante, 1.3km); Sa Sinia (2.7km); Es Castell (2.7km); Castell San Felipe (4km); Fort Marlborough (4.7km); Platja de Punta Prima (7.7km)
Plaça de Sant Francesc
Moll de Ponent
C d' Isabel II
Moll de Llevant
Costa d'en Reynés
Centre de Salut Verge del Toro
C de Barcelona
Av del Port de Maó
Av del Fort de l'Eau
Moll de Levant
C des Frares
C de S'Arraval
C de Sant Roc
C del Bon Aire
C del Rosari
C de Alfons III
Plaça de la Conquesta
Plaça de la Constitució
Plaça de la Bastió
C de l'Església
C Alba
Portal de Mar
Costa de ses Voltes
C de Hannover
C Nou
Plaça d'Espanya
C de Sant Sebastià
C de Santa Caterina
C de la Concepció
C de Bellavista
Plaça del Príncep
C Claustre del Carme
Plaça des Trianon
C d'Anunciavay
C de San Fernando
C des Comerç
C de la Infanta
Plaça Reial
C des Forn
C de Sa Rovellada de Dalt
C de ses Moreres
C Sant Jordi
C de Sant Josep
Av de Josep Ma Quadrado
Plaça de s'Esplanada

& Sep-Oct); bus station (☎ 971 36 37 90; 9am-1pm & 4-6.30pm Mon-Fri, 10am-1.30pm Sat May-Oct); Moll de Llevant (Moll de Llevant 2; 8am-8.30pm Tue-Sat, 8am-1pm Sun-Mon) The office at the airport is the main office. Opening hours from November to April are hit and miss.

Sights & Activities

OLD QUARTER

Maó's main plaza is the large Plaça de s'Esplanada. A **craft and clothing market** is held here every Saturday.

The narrow streets to the east comprise the oldest part of Maó. The **Arc de Sant Roc**, a 16th-century archway at the top end of Carrer de Sant Roc, is the only remaining relic of the medieval walls that once surrounded the old city.

The **Església de Santa Maria la Major** (Plaça de la Constitució), further east, was completed in 1287, but rebuilt during the 18th century. It houses a massive organ built in Barcelona and shipped across in 1810. At the northern end of this plaza is the **ajuntament** (town hall).

PLAÇA D'ESPANYA

Just off Plaça d'Espanya is the **Mercat Claustre del Carme**, where former church cloisters have been imaginatively converted into a market and shopping centre. Upstairs enjoy temporary art exhibitions and the modest **Museu Hernández Sanz Hernández Mora** (☎ 971 35 05 97; admission free; 10am-1pm Mon-Sat), devoted to Menorcan themes and dominated by artworks, maps and decorative items going as far back as the 18th century. You may find it open on Sunday too.

MUSEU DE MENORCA

This former 15th-century Franciscan **monastery** (☎ 971 35 09 55; Plaça de Sant Francesc; adult/child & senior €2.40/free, admission free Sat afternoon & Sun; 10am-2pm & 6-8.30pm Tue-Sat, 10am-2pm Sun & holidays) has a chequered history. From the time the Franciscans were obliged to abandon the premises in 1835 after Mendizábal's expropriations, the buildings embarked on a colourful career path – ranging from nautical school and public library to high school and children's home.

The permanent museum collection covers the earliest history of the island, the Roman and Byzantine eras and Islamic Menorca, and includes paintings and other material from more-recent times, too.

XORIGUER GIN DISTILLERY

On the waterfront, head to the **distillery** (☎ 971 36 21 97; Moll de Ponent 93; 8am-7pm Mon-Fri, 9am-1pm Sat May-Oct, 9am-1pm & 4-6pm Mon-Fri Nov-Apr), where you can try the local gin, another British legacy. At the front is a liquor outlet and souvenir shop where visitors can help themselves to free samples. Menorcan gin is distinctively aromatic and very tasty. You can also try various strange liqueurs and tonics.

BEACHES

The closest decent beaches to the capital are **Es Grau** to the north and **Platja de Punta Prima** to the south. Both are connected to Maó by local bus. There are around eight buses a day to Punta Prima.

HARBOUR CRUISES

Numerous operators offer glass-bottomed boat cruises around the harbour next to the ferry terminal. These can be a pleasant way to kill an hour or two and generally cost around €10/5 per adult/child for an hour.

Sleeping

Posada Orsi (☎ 971 36 47 51; Carrer de la Infanta 19; s/d with washbasin €30/49, d with bathroom €60;) Pastel colours are all the go here, and you may pick up the scent of incense. Rooms are equally bright (with lots of pink, hot orange and sky blue), mosquito nets (handy) and a no-smoking policy (and no hot water after midnight).

Hostal-Residencia La Isla (☎ 971 36 64 92; Carrer de Santa Caterina 4; s/d €30/52;) This large, family-run *hostal* is excellent value, with spacious rooms (all with their own bathroom). Decor is uninspiring but the folks are friendly and run a bustling cafe-bar downstairs.

Hotel Port Mahón (☎ 971 36 26 00; www.sethotels.com; Avinguda del Port de Maó; s/d from €143/195, d with port views €196;) This fine hotel has 82 nicely turned-out rooms, a pool and pleasant gardens. It also has luxurious suites. Try to get a room fronted by a balcony with a grand view over the port. Decor varies between the rooms.

Eating

Maó's harbour is lined with restaurants and bars; most offer alfresco dining. Also worth investigating are the many waterfront eateries in Cales Fonts, just 3km away in Es Castell.

Ses Forquilles (☎ 971 35 27 11; Carrer de Sa Rovellada de Dalt 20; meals €30-35; lunch & dinner Thu-Sat, lunch Mon-Wed) This self-proclaimed 'gastronomic space' offers tasty snacks, a handful of dishes ranging from steak tartar to *fideuá de sépia* *negra* (a noodle and cuttlefish dish). There's also a good gourmet set lunch for €16.

Restaurant La Minerva (☎ 971 35 19 95; Moll de Llevant 87; meals €40-45;) Dine out on seafood on this boat moored to the waterfront. It may all look a bit cheesy (it is), but this doesn't stop the kitchen from pouring out good fish and seafood – cooked lightly, just as it should be.

Restaurant Jàgaro (☎ 971 36 23 90; Moll de Llevant 334; meals €40-45) The last in the long line of eateries on the harbour is a timeless place but the goodies still leave mouths watering. Seafood in any combination is the order of the day.

Drinking & Entertainment

Nightlife in Maó is low-key in comparison to Mallorca or Ibiza. Most of the action is on the waterfront.

Mirador Café (☎ 971 35 21 07; Plaça d'Espanya 9; 10am-2am Mon-Sat) In a laneway between the top of Costa de ses Voltes and the Mercat Claustre del Carme, this is a popular music bar with a cave-like interior carved out of the old walls above the harbour. Best of all, take a ringside seat outside and drink in the port views with your beer.

L'Antic (Plaça de la Conquesta 5; 10am-11.30pm Mon-Sat) A relaxed crowd of Rasta-types and hippies hangs out here over beers, herbal teas

FORTS & MANSIONS

From the time Great Britain took control of Menorca, Maó's value as a port was clear. And so they built **Fort Marlborough** (☎ 971 36 04 62; adult/under 7yr/senior & student €3/free/1.80; 9.30am-8.30pm Tue-Sat, 9.30am-3pm Sun-Mon Jun-Sep, 10am-2.30pm Tue-Sun Oct-Apr) above the charming emerald-green inlet, Cala de Sant Esteve (2.5km beyond Es Castell, which to the Brits was Georgetown), southeast of Maó. Most of the fortress was excavated into the rock below surface level. It is well worth wandering around the fort, and the cheesy video provides a modicum of information.

Not far off (1.3km) is the **Castell San Felipe** (☎ 971 36 21 00; www.museomilitarmenorca.com; adult/under 12yr/senior €5/free/2.50), which under British control became one of the largest fortresses in Europe. When Spain recovered the island, King Carlos III had the fort largely destroyed. However, the labyrinth of underground tunnels has remained more or less intact and occasional guided visits are possible – call or check the website for latest times (usually not more than a couple of times a week). Night-time **torchlit tours** (adult/child/senior €20/10/15; 9.30pm-midnight, Sat in Spanish, Sun in English mid-Jun–mid-Sep), complete with actors playing soldiers and the acrid whiff of gunpowder, take you into the bowels of this once mighty fortress.

To more fully immerse yourself in the area's British colonial past, stop at **Collingwood House** (Hotel del Almirante; ☎ 971 36 27 00; www.hoteldelalmirante.com; Fonduco, Es Castell; s/d €80/105; P), once the residence of Nelson's fellow commander-at-sea and now a charming hotel, replete with maritime reminiscences, pool, terrace, bar, restaurant and wonderful views over the port of Maó. With its heavy carpets, dark-timber doors and furniture, and countless paintings and sketches of great vessels and their commanders, you could almost be in a minor museum. It's on the road about halfway between Maó and Es Castell, and the two are connected by regular local buses (€1.30, 15 minutes).

In the 19th century Queen Isabel II ordered the construction of a new fortress (completed 1848–75), the **Fortalesa de la Mola** (☎ 971 36 40 40, 686 659400; www.fortalesalamola.com; adult/under 12yr/senior & student €7/free/4.75; 10am-8pm Jun-Sep, 10am-6pm May & Oct, 10am-2pm Tue-Sun Nov-Apr), out on the promontory of the same name on the northern shore of the bay. It's about a 12km drive from Maó, so you'll want to set aside a couple of hours for the visit and use one of the audioguides (€1.75). Wear comfortable shoes and bring a torch (flashlight) for the tunnels. You will go rambling through galleries, gun emplacements and barracks. In July and August staff sometimes organise torchlit night tours. The only way here is by car, unless you want to call a **water taxi** (☎ 616 428891, return €15). They will come to various points in Maó and Es Castell.

On the way back towards Maó you'll notice a rose-coloured stately home surrounded by gardens on a high point near Sant Antoni. **Golden Farm** (Granja Dorada) is private property and can't be visited, but they say Nelson and his lover Lady Hamilton enjoyed a tryst here in 1799.

and the odd snack. A scattering of marble tables and odds and ends of furniture inside are one option, but a table in the pretty square is better still.

our pick **Akelarre** (☎ 971 36 85 20; www.akelarrejazz.es; Moll de Ponent 41-43; 🕑 3pm-4am daily Jun-Sep, 7pm-4am Thu-Sat, 7pm-3am Sun-Wed Oct-May) Ambient and jazz dance music dominate the wee hours in this place, made welcoming by the warm stone interior. Live music frequently enlivens proceedings earlier in the evening (starting around 11pm, and costing €10). Thursday night is blues jam night. Five other bars line up next door.

Sa Sínia (Carrer de Sant Jordi s/n, Es Castell; 🕑 8pm-3am Tue-Sun) At the entrance to Es Castell in an old white house with a pleasant terrace, this is not a bad spot for a drink and a little music. A range of (mostly local) DJs spin anything from '80s hits to hip hop.

Getting There & Away

You can catch **TMSA** (☎ 971 36 04 75; www.tmsa.es) buses from the bus station just off the southwest end of Plaça de s'Esplanada. In summer (May to October), at least eight go to Ciutadella (€4.40, one hour) via Alaior (€1.35), Es Mercadal (€2.25) and Ferreries (€2.90). The company also operates regular services to the south-coast beaches, including Platja de Punta Prima (€1.45). A handful of bus services run to Santa Galdana (€3.65, one hour). Two to five **Autos Fornells** (www.autosfornells.com) services run each day to/from Fornells (€2.80, one hour). All services drop from November to April.

THE INTERIOR – MAÓ TO CIUTADELLA

Menorca's main road, from Maó to Ciutadella, divides the island into north and south. It passes through Alaior, Es Mercadal and Ferreries, and along the way smaller roads branch off towards the beaches and resorts of the north and south coasts.

Many of the most significant archaeological relics are signposted off the main road.

Alaior is home to the local cheese and shoe industries. The main cheese manufacturer is **Coinga** (☎ 971 37 12 27; www.coinga.com; Carretera Nova s/n; 🕑 9am-2pm Mon-Fri). Factory visits are organised at 11.30am on Tuesday and Thursday.

Es Mercadal is one of the oldest villages on the island (a market has been held here since at least 1300) and is at the turn-off north for Fornells. You also turn here to get to **Monte El Toro** (all of a towering 357m), Menorca's highest point. A twisting road leads to the summit, which is shared by a 16th-century **church** and formerly **Augustine monastery** (now run by a handful of Franciscan nuns), a cluster of satellite dishes and radio towers, and a statue of Christ (built to honour the dead of the civil war). On a clear day you can see Mallorca. In town are several good places to eat.

our pick **Restaurant N'Aguedet** (☎ 971 37 53 91; Carrer de Lepanto 30; meals €35-40) is an elegant den of island cooking that has the stamp of approval of Catalan megachef Ferran Adrià (see p388). Head up the graceful marble stairway to the first-floor dining room, where you can sample seafood but should probably try some typical island meat dishes, such as the melt-in-your-mouth *lechón* (suckling pig, €16) or *conejo con cebolla y alcaparras* (rabbit in onion and capers).

Ferreries is Menorca's highest town. Each Saturday morning the **Mercat de Ferreries** takes place, with stallholders selling fresh produce, along with traditional Menorcan crafts and artworks. This is also a centre of cheese, shoes and leather goods production. The turn-off to the resort of Santa Galdana is just west of here.

our pick **Restaurante El Gallo** (☎ 971 37 30 39; meals €30-35; 🕑 lunch & dinner Tue-Sun Oct-May, dinner only Tue-Fri, lunch & dinner Sat & Sun Jun-Sep) is a beautiful 200-year-old rambling white-washed house with pretty garden. Even if you're not headed for Santa Galdana, head down the turn-off 1.5km and stop here. Your main objective should be the *filet amb formatge de Maó* (steak cooked in local cheese).

CIUTADELLA

pop 28,000

Founded by Carthaginians and known to the Muslims as Medina Minurqa, Ciutadella was almost destroyed following the 1558 Turkish invasion and much of the city was subsequently rebuilt in the 17th century. It was Menorca's capital until the British arrived.

Known as Vella i Bella (The Old and the Beautiful), Ciutadella is an attractive and distinctly Spanish city with a picturesque port and an engaging old quarter. Its character is quite distinct from that of Maó, and its historic centre is far more appealing.

Information

Policía Local (Ajuntament, Plaça d'es Born)
Post office (Plaça d'es Born 9; 8.30am-8.30pm Mon-Fri, 9.30am-1pm Sat)
Tourist office (971 38 26 93; Plaça de la Catedral 5; 9am-2pm & 4-9pm Mon-Fri, 9am-2pm Sat May-Sep, 9am-1pm & 5-7pm Mon-Fri Oct-Apr); Port (10.30am-2pm & 6.30-9pm Tue-Sat, 10am-3pm Sun May-Sep) The port office is located where boats from Mallorca land.

Sights & Activities

The main square, Plaça d'es Born, is surrounded by palm trees and gracious 19th-century buildings, including the post office, the **ajuntament** (town hall) and the **Palau Torresaura**. In the centre of the square is an **obelisk**, raised to commemorate those townsfolk who died trying to ward off the Turks on 9 July 1558.

Costa d'es Moll takes you down to the port from Plaça d'es Born. Heading in the other direction, the narrow cobbled laneways and streets between Plaça d'es Born and Plaça d'Alfons III hold plenty of interest, with simple whitewashed buildings alongside ornate churches and elegant palaces. The pedestrian walkway of **Ses Voltes** (The Arches) has a vaguely North African flavour, and is lined with glamorous shops and boutiques, restaurants and smoky bars.

Architectural landmarks worth looking out for include the 14th-century **cathedral** (971 38 07 39; Plaça de la Catedral; 8am-1pm & 6-9pm), built in Catalan Gothic style (although with a baroque facade) on the site of Medina Minurqa's central mosque. There are also the baroque 17th-century churches **Església dels Socors** (971 48 12 97; Carrer del Seminari 9), behind the town produce market and home to the **Museu Diocesà** (971 48 12 97; adult/student/senior €2.40/1.80/1.20; 10.30am-1.30pm Tue-Sat); and **Església del Roser** (Carrer del Roser), now used as an occasional exhibition gallery. Impressive noble families' mansions, such as **Palau Martorell** (Carrer del Santíssim 7) and **Palau Saura** (Carrer del Santíssim 2) are sometimes used for temporary exhibitions.

The **Museu Municipal** (971 38 02 97; Bastió de sa Font; adult/under 12yr/senior €2.25/free/1.30; 10am-2pm & 6-9pm Tue-Sat May-Sep, 10am-2pm Tue-Sat Oct-Apr) contains displays recounting the island's story from prehistory to medieval times.

West of the town centre, the southern head of the port entrance is dominated by the stout

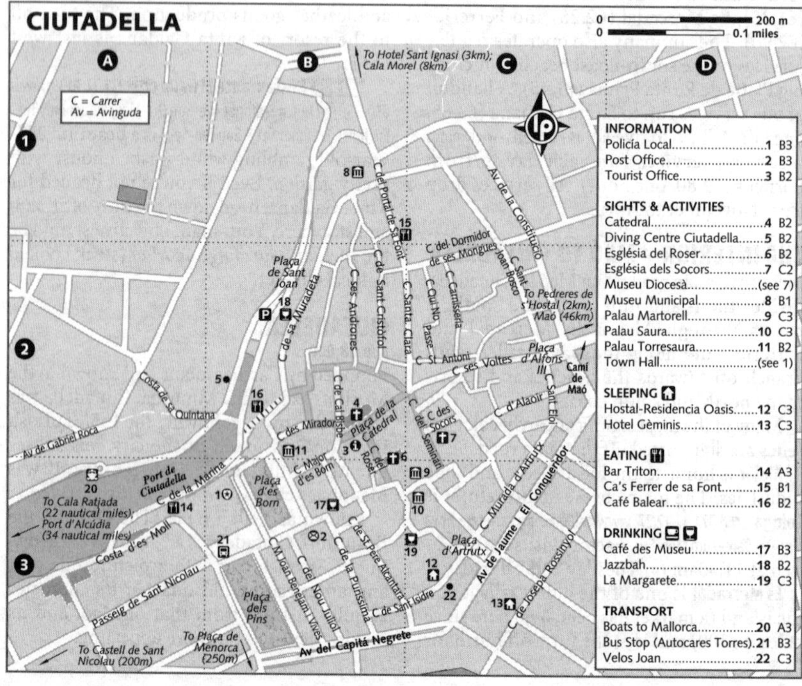

little **Castell de Sant Nicolau** (☎ 676 807649; Plaça del Almirante Ferragut; admission free; ⏰ 10am-1pm & 5-9pm Tue-Sat May-Sep). The views west to Mallorca and south down the coast are lovely.

About 2km east of the town centre is an original 'monument'. The **Pedreres de s'Hostal** (☎ 971 48 15 78; www.lithica.es; Camí Vell; adult/under 10yr/senior €4/free/2; ⏰ 9.30am-sunset Mon-Sat, 9.30am-2.30pm Sun & holidays) is an extensive series of stone quarries. The bleached *marés* stone, extracted here and in other quarries around the island, has historically been Menorca's main building material. This quarry was in action until 1994. The bizarre shapes cut into the rock were first hewn by strong men with picks (as long as 200 years ago) and later with machinery. In the latter, which are a series of giant, deep pits, concerts are organised (the acoustics are great). In the older quarry a **botanical garden**, with endemic Menorcan species, grows amid the weird 'sculpture'.

Three dive centres operate in and around Ciutadella. **Diving Centre Ciutadella** (☎ 971 38 60 30; www.menorcatech.com; Plaça de Sant Joan 10; per dive €47) is handily located in the town port.

Festivals & Events

The **Dia de Sant Joan** is held in Ciutadella in the third to last week of June. The high point is 23 June, the eve of the saint's feast day, although the atmosphere in the streets builds over preceding evenings. It is one of Spain's best-known and most traditional festivals, featuring busy processions, prancing horses (Menorcans pride themselves on their riding skills), performances of traditional music and dancing, and lots of partying.

Sleeping

Hostal-Residencia Oasis (☎ 971 38 21 97; Carrer de Sant Isidre 33; s/d €40/55) Set around a spacious garden courtyard, this quiet place close to the heart of the old quarter has pleasant rooms, some of them done up in the past two years and most with bathrooms.

Hotel Gèminis (☎ 971 38 46 44; www.hotelgeminismenorca.com; Carrer de Josepa Rossinyol 4; s/d €65/96;) A friendly, stylish two-star place on a backstreet, this graceful, three-storey, rose-white lodging offers comfortable if somewhat neutral rooms just a short walk away from the city centre. The best rooms have a nice balcony to boot.

Hotel Sant Ignasi (☎ 971 38 55 75; www.santignasi.com; Carretera de Cala Morell s/n; s/d per person €158/252; P) This tranquil rural hotel is a fine retreat 3km outside Ciutadella. It boasts a good restaurant, a pleasant garden, bar and pool. Prices more than halve over winter months.

Eating

Ciutadella's small port is teeming with restaurants and cafes, many of which are set in the old city walls or carved out of the cliffs that line the waterfront.

Bar Triton (☎ 971 38 00 02; Carrer de la Marina 55; meals €20-25) Join local fishermen and other folks as they hang out here and down generous serves of seafood and such house specialities as *pilotes* (micro meatballs in tomato sauce).

our pick **Café Balear** (☎ 971 38 00 05; Placa de Sant Joan 15; meals €25-30; ⏰ Mon-Sat) Sometimes the old timers are the best. Set apart from the town's more frenetic restaurant activity, this remains one of Ciutadella's classic seafood stops. You can eat outside and admire the old quarter towering before you while tucking into local prawns or *navalles* (razor clams). Ask what is fresh that day.

Ca's Ferrer de sa Font (☎ 971 48 07 84; Carrer del Portal de Sa Font 16; meals €35; ⏰ lunch & dinner Tue-Sat, dinner Sun) Located in an 18th-century two-storey building with timber shutters, this is a romantic place offering a mix of quality inventive Mediterranean cooking.

Drinking & Entertainment

The bulk of the town's nightlife is concentrated along the waterfront and in particular around Plaça de San Joan, on either side of which you will encounter phalanxes of bars and clubs.

Jazzbah (Plaça de San Joan 3; admission €10; ⏰ 11pm-5am) This venue is worth watching for its live concerts, happening house nights and chill-out sessions. The latter take place on the terrace.

Café des Museu (Carreró d'es Palau 4; ⏰ 10pm-3.30am) In the old town, this is a charming cocktail bar tucked away down a tight lane and occasionally host to live gigs – anything from acid jazz to bossanova.

our pick **La Margarete** (Carrer de Sant Joan 6; ⏰ 10pm-3.30am) This is a stylish option, with modern, arty decor and a pleasant internal lawn.

Getting There & Away

Boats for Mallorca (Port d'Alcúdia and Cala Ratjada) leave from the northern side of the Port de Ciutadella. For details, see p650.

TMSA runs regular buses between Ciutadella and Maó. **Autocares Torres** (☎ 971 38 64 61; €1.70;

MENORCA'S PREHISTORIC MYSTERIES

As long ago as 2000 BC, people were enjoying Menorca's pristine beaches in between stints of hunting and gathering. The island's interior remains sprinkled with reminders of those times. Many of the most significant sites are open to the public (and free). In winter, the bulk of the paying sites are unattended and can be visited freely (and free of charge).

The monuments are linked to three main periods: the Pre-Talayotic Period (or cave era) from 2000 BC to 1300 BC; the Talayotic Period (Bronze Age) from 1300 BC to 800 BC; and the Post-Talayotic Period (Iron Age) from 800 BC to around 100 BC. Similarly, there are three general types of structures: *navetas, talayots* and *taulas.*

Navetas, built from large rocks in the shape of upturned boat hulls, are thought to have been used as tombs or meeting places – perhaps both. *Talayots,* large stone mounds found all over the island (and elsewhere in the Balearics), were perhaps used as watchtowers. Unique to Menorca, *taulas* are huge stone tablets precisely balanced in the shape of a 'T'. They could have been used as sacrificial altars but nobody is sure how these enormous stone slabs were moved or what they signify.

Off the ME1 road 3km west of Maó, the Talayotic settlement of **Talatí de Dalt** (adult/under 8yr/student & senior €4/free/3; 9am-sunset; P) is one of the most interesting and its main feature is a well-preserved *taula.*

About 4km further along on the north side of the road is **Rafal Rubí**, a pair of well-preserved burial *navetas.*

The nearby **Torralba d'en Salord** (971 37 83 85; adult/under 16yr/student & senior €3.50/free/2; 10am-8pm Apr-Sep) is a Talayotic settlement whose outstanding feature is an impressive *taula.*

South of Alaior, the **Torre d'en Gaumès** (adult/under 16yr/student & senior €2.40/free/1.20, admission free Sun; 9am-9pm Tue-Sat, 9am-3pm Sun-Mon May-Sep, 9am-3pm Tue-Sun Apr & Oct) settlement includes three *talayots* on a hilltop and a collection of circular dwellings. It's free to visit every day from October to April, and on Sunday from May to September.

Further south on the coast at **Cales Coves**, some 90 caves dug into the coastal cliffs were apparently used for ritual burials. More recently some of the caves have been homes to hippy colonies, and nearby the large **Cova d'en Xoroi** (971 37 72 36; www.covadenxoroi.com; Cala'n Porter; admission with drink adult/child €5.80/3.50; 11.30am-9pm Jun-Sep) can be visited as a sight by day or as a club by night. The sunset chill-out scene starts around 8pm and the disco gets into action around midnight to 5am. Foreign DJs make regular summer appearances.

South of Ciutadella (from the *ronda*, or ring road, follow the road for Macarella and after 2.8km veer right), **Son Catlar** (admission free; 10am-sunset) is the largest Talayotic settlement in the Balearic Islands. Its five *talayots* and the remains of its dwellings cover around six hectares. East of Ciutadella (near the Km40 road marker), the **Naveta des Tudons** (adult/under 8yr/senior & 8-16yr €2/free/1, admission free Sun; 9am-9pm Tue-Sat, 9am-3pm Sun-Mon May-Sep, 9am-3pm Tue-Sun Apr & Oct) is a stone burial chamber.

20-30 min) buses serve the coast south of Ciutadella as far as Son Xoriguer. All buses terminate in and leave from Plaça dels Pins.

Getting Around

You can hire mountain bikes from **Velos Joan** (971 38 15 76; Carrer de Sant Isidre 28) for €10 per day, as well as Vespas and scooters (€58 to €74 for two days, depending on the model).

AROUND CIUTADELLA

North of Ciutadella, **Cala Morell** is a low-key development of whitewashed villas. Steep steps lead to the small port and beach, backed by a couple of bar-restaurants. More intriguing is the **Cala Morell Necropolis**, prehistoric burial caves hacked into the coastal cliffs along a track leading away from the beach.

Before reaching Cala Morell, a right turn to **Algaiarens** leads you about 6km to a privately owned car park, about a 500m walk short of a pair of crescent-shaped, white-sand beaches.

NORTH COAST

Menorca's north coast is rugged and rocky, dotted with small and scenic coves. It's less developed than the south and, with your own transport and a bit of footwork, you'll discover some of the Balearics' best off-the-beaten-track beaches.

Maó to Fornells

North of Maó, head first for **Es Grau**, a plain hamlet on an open bay. The beach is OK and you can kick back at a couple of bar-restaurants. Head for **Bar Es Moll** (Carrer d'es Pescadors 5; meals €20-25), a basic place with plastic tables and chairs facing the water. Come for fresh fish and seafood, whatever has been brought in that day, nothing fancy.

Inland from Es Grau and separated from the coast by a barrier of high sand dunes is the **Parc Natural S'Albufera d'es Grau**, the largest freshwater lagoon in the Balearic Islands. Home to many species of wetland birds and an important stopover for migrating species, S'Albufera and the surrounding countryside form the 'nucleus zone' of Menorca's Biosphere Reserve, a natural park protected from the threat of development. **Illa d'en Colom**, a couple of hundred metres offshore, is considered part of the park.

The drive up to **Cap de Favàritx**, a narrow rocky cape at the top of the Parc Natural S'Albufera d'es Grau zone, is a treat. The last leg is across a lunarlike landscape of black rock. At the end of the road a **lighthouse** stands watch as the sea pounds relentlessly against the impassive cliffs.

South of the cape stretch some fine sandy bays and beaches, including **Cala Presili** and **Platja d'en Tortuga**, reachable on foot.

Cap de Cavalleria & Around

Three kilometres shy of Fornells, turn west and follow the signs for 7km to reach a parking area for the stunning little double-crescent, golden beach of **Platja Cavalleria** (a five-minute walk from the car park). One kilometre further north is the **Ecomuseu Cap de Cavalleria** (☎ 971 35 99 99; www.ecomuseudecavalleria.com; adult/child/senior €3/free/2; ⏰ 10am-8pm Jul-Sep, 10am-7pm Apr-Jun & Oct), with displays and videos on the north coast, its fauna, the lighthouse, ancient inhabitants and Romans. The remains of the latter's settlement, **Sanisena** (today Sanitja), have been excavated nearby. At the museum you'll receive a detailed area map showing you how to wander to the ruins and round about. In 2008 the museum ran various excavation campaigns open to amateurs who wish to learn about archaeology in practice (in English and Spanish). Check the website to see if similar programs are planned in coming years.

Another 2km drive north brings you to the abrupt cliffs, *far* (lighthouse) and a series of crumbling civil war Republican gun emplacements. A side road from the Cap de Cavalleria road leads about 3km to **Cala Binimella**, an OK beach with a nearby bar-restaurant. You can walk from there to the much prettier **Cala Pregonda**.

Fornells

pop 940

This picturesque whitewashed village is on a large, shallow bay popular with windsurfers. Fornells has come to be known for its waterfront seafood restaurants, most of which serve up the local (and rather pricey) speciality, *caldereta de llagosta*.

SIGHTS & ACTIVITIES

If the sight of those fishing boats bobbing in the bay stirs the seawolf in your soul, embark on a three- to four-hour catamaran trip with **Catamaran Charter** (☎ 626 486426; www.catamarancharter.net; Passeig Marítim 69; adult/child €60/35). You can also hire kayaks and bicycles here. For underwater fun, check out **Diving Center Fornells** (☎ 971 37 64 31; www.divingfornells.com; Passeig Marítim 68).

At the edge of town stands the squat, round defensive tower, the **Torre de Fornells** (admission €2.40; ⏰ 11am-2pm & 5-8pm Tue-Sun Jun-Sep).

A couple of kilometres west at **Platges de Fornells**, the development frenzy has been unleashed on the coastal hills surrounding a small beach. The exclusive villas of the Menorca Country Club resort dominate this ritzy *urbanització* (urban development).

SLEEPING & EATING

The restaurants along the foreshore are all pretty expensive, and if you're here to try *caldereta de llagosta*, you are looking at €60 to €69.

Hostal La Palma (☎ 971 37 66 34; Plaça S'Algaret 3; s/d €48/84; ❄ 🏊) Out the back of this bar-restaurant are cheerful rooms with bathrooms, balconies and views of the surrounding countryside. Singles aren't available in summer.

Hostal S'Algaret (☎ 971 37 65 52; www.hostal-salgaret.com; Plaça de S'Algaret; s/d €65/100; ⏰ May-Oct; ❄ 💻 🏊) In business since the 1950s, this pleasant, simple *hostal* has crisp, clean rooms with balconies. The pool out the back is a big

FANCY FOOTWORK

Mallorca is better known for its shoemaking tradition (especially with the international success of the Camper company) but Menorca too has long had its share of cobblers. The best-loved local product is *avarques*, loose, comfortable slip-on sandals that cover the front of the foot and strap around the heel. They make great summer shoes and shops sell them all over the island (and indeed all over the Balearics).

plus and the restaurant is a bustling spot for your seafood hit. It's open year-round (prices halve outside summer).

Es Port (☎ 971 37 64 03; Passeig Marítim 10; meals €30-35; ⏰ Sat-Thu) Some fine fresh fish and seafood are done here. Try the tender white meat of the *gall de Sant Pere*, a popular Balearic catch (€20.50). Of course, it does *caldereta de llagosta* (€61). Less fiscal outlay goes into a sizzling *paella de llomanto* (lobster paella; €35).

S'Ancora (☎ 971 37 66 70; Passeig Marítim 7-8; meals €35-45) A more upmarket setting next door to Es Port, with dark-brown wicker chairs and elegant table settings, it does much the same basic items (seafood), with a slicker presentation of dishes.

SOUTH COAST

Menorca's southern flank tends to have the better beaches – and thus the greater concentration of development. The recurring image is of a jagged coastline, occasionally interrupted by a small inlet with a sandy beach and backed by a cluster of gleaming-white villas. Menorca has largely opted for small-scale developments in the 'Moorish-Mediterranean' style, modelled on the resort of Binibèquer (or Binibeca), near the southeast corner, designed by the architect Antonio Sintes in 1972.

Ciutadella to Platges de Son Bou

The rugged coastline south of Ciutadella gives way to a couple of smallish beaches at the resorts of **Santandria** and **Cala Blanca**. On the island's southwest corner looms the large resort of **Cala en Bosc**, a busy boating and diving centre. Not far east are the popular beaches of **Platja de Son Xoriguer**, connected to Ciutadella by frequent buses.

Between Son Xoriguer and Santa Galdana lies some of the least accessible southern coast. A narrow country road leads south of Ciutadella (follow the 'Platjes' sign from the *ronda*, or ringroad) and then forks twice to (almost) reach the unspoiled beaches (from west to east) of **Arenal de Son Saura**, **Cala en Turqueta**, **Cala des Es Talaier**, **Cala Macarelleta** and **Cala Macarella**.

For Cala Macarella, for instance, you arrive at a car park and must walk 15 minutes to the beach (which has a restaurant). You can walk or swim around to the still prettier Cala Macarelleta. The walk between Cala Macarella and Cala en Turqueta takes an hour.

Day cruises (☎ 971 38 52 59) to these beaches run from Ciutadella in summer for €40 per person. The full-day trip takes in various beaches with a lunch of paella thrown in.

Southwest of Ferreries is **Santa Galdana**, just the place if karaoke, English pubs and mini-golf are your idea of fun. In fairness, the beach is beautiful and the tack mild. A walking track leads west along the coast to Cala Macarella (30 minutes). To the east of Santa Galdana, **Cala Mitjana** is another enticing strand.

Pleasant **Camping S'Atalaia** (☎ 971 37 42 32; www.campingsatalaia.com; sites per 2 people, tent & car €23.20; P 🏊), shaded by pine trees, is two-thirds of the way down the Ferreries–Santa Galdana road.

The resort of **Platges de Son Bou**, south of Alaior, boasts the island's longest beach and most depressing development. Just back from the beach are the remains of a 5th-century **Christian basilica**.

South of Maó

Most of the coast south of Maó is more intensively developed. Regular buses sidle down to **Platja de Punta Prima**, which has a nice beach (you can even catch the occasional wave!). If you pass through **Sant Lluís** (a bright, white town built by the French during their brief occupation of the island between 1756 and 1763), you may want to stop to savour one of several fine eateries. West around the coast is **Binibèquer**, touted as a charming old fishing town. It has been given several coats of whitewash and turned into a tourist beehive, but the curious houses and narrow lanes, not to mention the little boat harbour with its transparent water, are attractive. A few kilometres further west lies **Cala de Binidalí**. The village is no big deal and the beach small, but the water is so enticingly azure it makes you want to dive in and swim out to the open sea.

Murcia

Situated with the modesty of a maiden aunt between the boisterous resorts of Valencia's Costa Blanca to the north and the high-profile beaches of Almería to the south, Murcia is one of the least visited and, La Manga apart, least touristy corners of Spain.

This blip of absenteeism is even more surprising given that the Costa Cálida (Hot Coast) guarantees approximately 3000 hours of sunshine annually. Plus, for those seeking more stimulus than a sun-basting on the beach, the province has plenty of historical and cultural highlights. Away from the resorts, foodies will also be pleasantly surprised by the sophistication of the *murciana* cuisine.

The name Murcia derives from the Latin *murtae* (mulberry). For centuries, the region's mulberry leaves were feed for silkworms, enabling a flourishing silk industry that lasted until well after WWII. Today, the main crops are citrus fruits and grapes grown in the El Guadalentín valley, watered by an irrigation system comprising waterwheels, aqueducts and canals dating back to the 11th century,. Far less aesthetic are the vast plastic greenhouses, south of Cartagena, which grow tomatoes and other cheap crops by the tonne today.

Blinker out this synthetic eyesore and explore the busy capital with its splendid cathedral. Cartagena also has plenty of appeal and is busy excavating, digging deep to reveal its rich classical heritage; inland, pretty Lorca is famous for its Easter processions. Nature-lovers should head for the dramatic unspoilt beauty of the natural parks.

HIGHLIGHTS

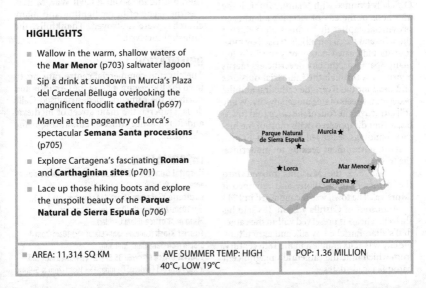

- Wallow in the warm, shallow waters of the **Mar Menor** (p703) saltwater lagoon
- Sip a drink at sundown in Murcia's Plaza del Cardenal Belluga overlooking the magnificent floodlit **cathedral** (p697)
- Marvel at the pageantry of Lorca's spectacular **Semana Santa processions** (p705)
- Explore Cartagena's fascinating **Roman** and **Carthaginian sites** (p701)
- Lace up those hiking boots and explore the unspoilt beauty of the **Parque Natural de Sierra Espuña** (p706)

AREA: 11,314 SQ KM	AVE SUMMER TEMP: HIGH 40°C, LOW 19°C	POP: 1.36 MILLION

MURCIA CITY

pop 417,000

Officially twinned with Miami, Murcia is the antithesis of the city of vice; it's a laid-back provincial capital that comes alive during the weekend *paseo* (stroll). Bypassed by most tourists and treated as a country cousin by too many Spaniards, the city nevertheless merits a visit. Pass through the industrial outskirts and head for the river, the cathedral and the pedestrian streets of this university city. While still attractive, the soul of the *casco* (old town) has all but disappeared, with most of the historic buildings destroyed by the post-Franco socialist government seeking to 'modernise' the town.

In AD 825 the Muslims moved into the former Roman colony and renamed it 'Mursiya'. The town was reconquered in 1243 by Alfonso X of Castilla y León. It's said his shrivelled heart is preserved within the cathedral's altar. Enriched by silk and agriculture, the city was at its grandest in the 18th century, from which time the cathedral's magnificent baroque facade dates.

Looted by Napoleonic troops in 1810, then overcome by plague and cholera, the city subsequently fell into decline. A century later, during the Spanish Civil War, Murcia was the scene of bitter fighting and many churches were destroyed. Thankfully, the cathedral survived.

ORIENTATION

The city and commercial centre runs north from the Río Segura. East of the Gran Via and north of the cathedral, pedestrianised Calle de la Trapería, the main street of medieval and Renaissance Murcia, cuts through the old town.

INFORMATION

Hospital General (☎ 968 35 90 00; Avenida Intendente Jorge Palacios 1)

Locutorio Viajacom (Plaza de Camachos; per hr €1; 🕑 10am-2pm & 4.30-10pm) Internet access.

Main post office (Plaza Circular)

Tourist kiosk (Calle de Santa Clara; 🕑 10am-2pm & 5-8pm Mon-Sat, 10am-2pm Sun)

Tourist office (☎ 968 35 87 49; www.murciaciudad.com; Plaza del Cardenal Belluga; 🕑 10am-2pm & 5-9pm

Mon-Sat, 10am-2pm Sun Jun-Sep, 10am-2pm & 4.30-8.30pm Mon-Sat, 10am-2pm Sun Oct-May)
www.murciaturistica.es The regional tourist authority website.

SIGHTS

Catedral de Santa María

Murcia's sumptuous **cathedral** (Plaza del Cardinal Belluga; 7am-1pm & 5-8pm) was built in 1394 on the site of a mosque. The initial Gothic architecture was given a playful facelift in 1748, receiving an exuberant baroque facade complete with tumbling cherubs. The 15th-century Capilla de los Vélez is a highlight; the chapel's flutes and curls resemble piped icing. The **Museo de la Catedral** (10am-2pm & 5-8pm Tue-Sat, 10am-2pm Sun) displays religious artefacts but is most striking for the excavations on display: the remains of an 11th-century Moorish dwelling and of a small *mezquita* (mosque), evocatively visible below a, thankfully, sturdy glass walkway.

Museums

Inaugurated in late 2007, the **Museo Arqueológico** (968 23 46 02; www.museoarqueologicomurcia.com; Avenida Alfonso X El Sabio 7; admission free; 10am-8pm Tue-Sat, 10am-2pm Sun) has exhibits that are exceptionally well laid out and well documented. Starting with Palaeolithic times, and including audiovisual displays, they spread over two floors.

Museo de Bellas Artes (968 23 93 46; Calle del Obispo Frutos 12; admission free; 10am-8.30pm Tue-Sat, 10am-2pm Sun) is an inviting, well-lit gallery devoted to Spanish artists. The 2nd floor Siglo de Oro gallery includes canvases by Murillo, Zurbarán and 'Lo Spagnoletto', José (Jusepe) de Ribera. For a break from all that religious piety, don't miss the superbly kitsch dazzle of glamorous señoritas on the 3rd floor by, among others, Julio Romero de Torres.

Located in the baroque chapel of Ermita de Jesús, **Museo Salzillo** (968 29 18 93; www.museosalzillo.es in Spanish; Plaza de San Agustín 1-3; admission free; 10am-2pm & 5-8pm Tue-Fri, 10am-2pm Sat) is devoted to the Murcian sculptor Francisco Salzillo (1707–83). The highlights are his exquisite *pasos* (figures carried in Semana Santa processions) and his nativity figurines – all 550 carved in wood.

Beside the river, **Museo de la Ciencia y del Agua** (968 21 19 98; Plaza de la Ciencia 1; adult/ under 12yr/12-25yr €1.20/free/0.60; 10am-2pm & 5-8pm Tue-Sat, 11am-2pm Sun;) is one for the children. Although everything's in Spanish, this small hands-on science museum has plenty of buttons to press and knobs to twirl, plus fish tanks and a small planetarium.

FESTIVALS & EVENTS

Murcia's **Semana Santa** processions rival Cartagena's in their fervour. Two days after Easter Sunday, the mood changes as the city celebrates the **Bando de la Huerta**, recalling its agricultural heritage with parades, food stalls, folklore and carafe-fulls of fiesta spirit.

SLEEPING

Pensión Segura (968 21 12 81; Plaza de Camachos 14; s/d €36/44;) A centrally located *pension* (small private hotel) where the owners have made the best of the small boxy rooms with yellow-and-white paintwork, sparkling floor tiles and slimline wardrobes and bathrooms.

Pensión Murcia (968 21 99 63; Calle Vinadel 6; s with/without bathroom €43/25, d with/without bathroom €50/40;) Tucked into a quiet elbow near bars and shops, this 16-room *pensíon* has tidy rooms with floral bedspreads, modern bathrooms and more space than most cheap sleeps in the city.

our pick **Hotel Casa Emilio** (968 22 06 31; www.hotelcasaemilio.com; Alameda de Colón 9; s/d €45/55; P) Across from the leafy Floridablanca gardens, near the river, this is a nicely designed and well-maintained hotel with spacious, brightly lit rooms, large bathrooms and good firm mattresses.

Hotel Hispano II (968 21 61 52; www.hotelhispano.net in Spanish; Calle Radio Murcia 3; s €48-54, d €52-70; P) Hotel Hispano II and Pensión Hispano I, around the corner (closed for refurbishment until early 2009) share a garage (parking €12). The trim, modern Hispano II is famous for its excellent restaurant (p699), and popular with business travellers. The traditional-style rooms have shiny dark-wood furnishings and plush fabrics.

El Churra (968 23 84 00; www.elchurra.net; Avenida Marqués de los Vélez 12; s €54, d €54-€75; P) Take a look at the photos in the lobby of when Churra was a rough-and-ready snack bar surrounded by fields and orchards. Fifty years on, this slickly run hotel has small stylish rooms.

Arco de San Juan (968 21 04 55; www.arcosanjuan.com; Plaza de Ceballos 10; s/d €75/130; P) This four-star hotel in a former palace hints of its palatial past with a massive 5m-high original

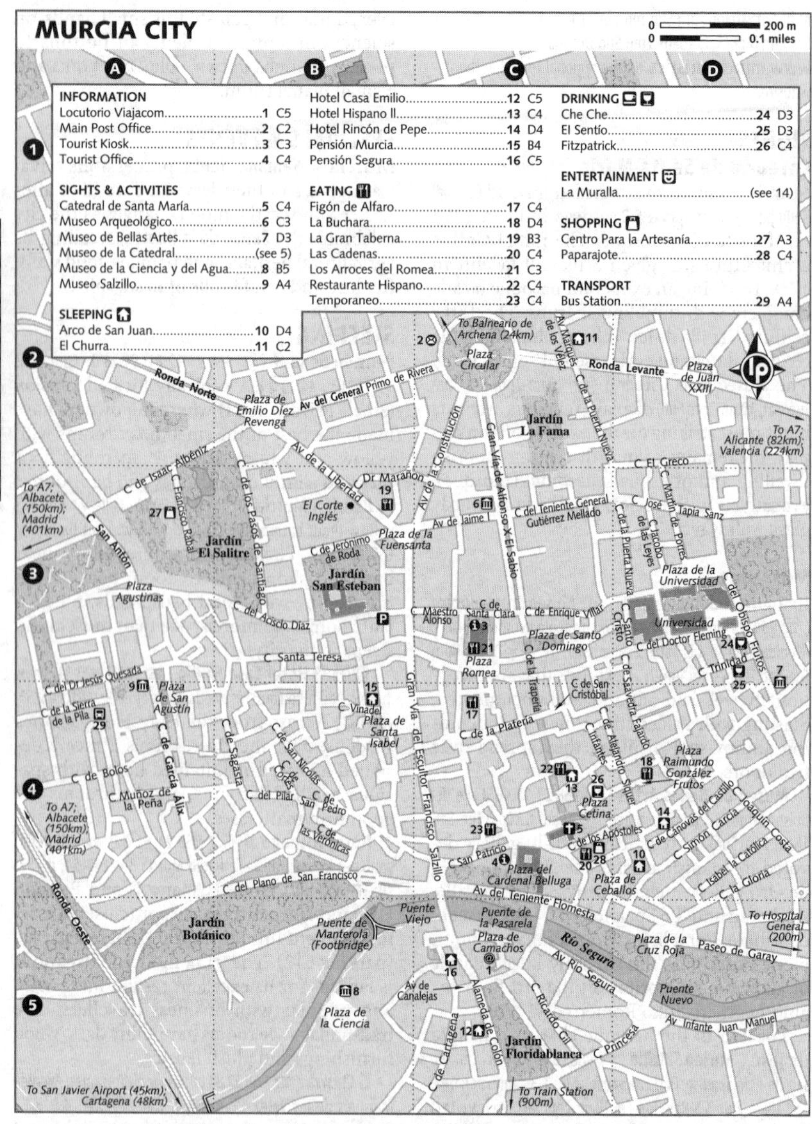

door and some hefty repro columns. The rooms are classic and comfortable with hardwood details and classy fabrics.

Hotel Rincón de Pepe (☎ 968 21 22 39; www.nh-hotels.com; Calle de los Apóstoles 34; r €95-126; P ✈ 💻) Acres of marble lobby greet guests at this corporate-style hotel. Rooms have shiny parquet floors and large luxurious bathrooms. The hotel restaurant promises a gourmet dining experience.

EATING

Murcia has some outstanding restaurants and bars that serve innovative, sophisticated dishes far cheaper than you find in better-known gourmet hot spots.

Figón de Alfaro (☎ 968 21 68 62; Calle Alfaro 7; meals €12-15; closed dinner Sun) Popular with all ages and budgets, Figón de Alfaro offers a chaotic bar area or a more sedate interconnecting dining room. Choose from full meals, a range of juicy *montaditos* (minirolls) or innovative one-offs such as *pastel de berejena con salsa de calabacín* (aubergine pie with a courgette sauce).

Temporaneo (☎ 968 90 99 09; Plaza Apostoles 5; meals €15) Lying within confessional distance of the cathedral, Temporaneo attracts hip young things with its slick black furnishings, challenging artwork and moody background music. The menu similarly exudes plenty of attitude, including dishes such as sashimi.

Restaurante Hispano (☎ 968 21 61 52; Calle Arquitecto Cerdán; meals €16-25; closed dinner Sun) The warm and inviting bar area here has some wonderfully inventive *raciones* (large tapas serving), such as baby broad beans sautéed with artichokes and onion. The smarter restaurant beyond has an appealing combination of similarly creative and more traditional dishes.

La Buchara (☎ 968 21 23 77; Plaza Raimundo González Frutos 5; meals €18-25; closed dinner Sun) Despite its location on a drab modern square, this restaurant has a fashionable feel with its brick-clad dining room and open-plan kitchen. Go for a seafood dish, such as sea bass with garlic. The hot chocolate cake with violet sorbet is worth the extra notch on your belt.

Los Arroces del Romea (☎ 968 21 84 99; Plaza Romea s/n; meals €20-25; V) Watch the speciality paella-style rice dishes being prepared in cartwheel-sized pans over the flames while you munch on circular *murciano* bread drizzled with olive oil. There are five rice dishes to choose from, including vegetarian.

Las Cadenas (☎ 968 22 09 24; Calle de los Apóstoles 10; meals €20-28; Mon-Sat) Las Cadenas has leaded windows, tasteful artwork and an elegant dress-for-dinner feel. The menu should suit the fussiest of families, with dishes including pasta, *pulpo a la gallega* (Galician-style octopus) and that ultimate comfort food – *tortilla de patatas* (potato and onion omelette).

La Gran Taberna (☎ 968 24 45 22; Avenida de la Libertad 6; meals €30-35; closed Sun & dinner Tue) Located in a modern square, opposite El Corte Inglés department store. The walls here host an attractive clutter of old menus, posters, programs and framed lacework. Work your way through the magnificent *menú tradicional* (traditional set menu; €34), chalked up on the blackboard and constant for more than a decade.

DRINKING & ENTERTAINMENT

Most through-the-night-life buzzes around the university. There are some vibrant bars, including **Che Che** (Calle del Doctor Fleming 16) and **El Sentío** (Calle Trinidad 14). For sophisticated jazz nights **La Muralla** (☎ 968 21 22 39; Thu 10.30pm to late), located in the bowels of Hotel Rincón de Pepe (opposite), has its cocktail bar snuggled up against the original city walls. Nearby, **Fitzpatrick** (☎ 968 21 47 70; Plaza Cetina) has a suitably blarney atmosphere and all the predictable ales on tap.

SHOPPING

For local handicrafts try **Centro Para la Artesanía** (☎ 968 35 75 19; Calle Francisco Rabal 8), which is both an exhibition space and sales outlet, and **Paparajote** (☎ 968 21 58 25; Calle de los Apóstoles 14), which also sells gourmet goodies.

GETTING THERE & AWAY

Air

Murcia's **San Javier airport** (☎ 968 17 20 00) is situated beside the Mar Menor, closer to Cartagena than Murcia city. Connections to the UK include:

easyjet (www.easyjet.com) London (Gatwick, Luton and Stansted), Birmingham, Bournemouth, Bristol, East Midlands, Edinburgh, Liverpool, Manchester, Newcastle and Bristol.

Jet2.com (www.jet2.com) Blackpool, Edinburgh, Leeds, Manchester and Newcastle.

Ryanair (www.ryanair.com) London (Luton and Stansted), Dublin, Leeds, Glasgow and Liverpool.

Bus

For bus information call ☎ 968 29 22 11. At least 10 buses run daily to both Cartagena (€3.40, one hour) and Lorca (€4.95, 1½ hours).

ALSA has daily buses to Granada (€18.75, 3½ hours, seven daily), Valencia (€14.50, 3¾ hours, four to six daily) and Madrid (€24, five hours, 10 daily).

Train

Up to five trains travel daily to/from Madrid (€41.30, 4¼ hours). Hourly trains operate to/from Lorca (€14.50, one hour).

GETTING AROUND

A taxi between the airport and Murcia city costs around €40.

From the bus station, take bus 3 into town; from the train station hop aboard bus 9 or 39.

SUMPTUOUS SPA

Surrounded by lofty eucalyptus and palm trees 24km north of Murcia, the **Balneario de Archena** (☎ 902 33 32 22; www.balneariodearchena.com) is a green oasis hidden in the depths of a desertlike landscape of barefaced mountains framing arid plains. The spa's history bubbles back to the 5th century BC and today it retains an appropriate Roman-toga feel, thanks to the fashion of white towelling dressing gowns and flip-flops (thongs) – even in the outside bar areas. There are three hotels interconnected by underground tunnels where most of the treatments take place.

If you don't want to fork out for a hotel-cum-treatment package (starting at €203 per day), you can enjoy the modern Balneatermalium (thermal bath complex). Opened in late 2007, it comprises a circuit that includes Russian, Finnish and Aztec saunas, hot and cold pools and Jacuzzi. Massages may also be reserved. Book at least a day in advance for the Balneatermalium (€36 for three hours; massages from €38).

MURCIA REGION

The Murcia region offers a tantalising choice of landscapes, ranging from the chill-out beaches of the Costa Cálida to the medieval magic of its towns. To best appreciate the unspoiled hinterland, you will need your own wheels.

CARTAGENA

pop 208,600

This is a city where you should walk with your eyes raised to the skyline (when you're not looking down at the map). The Modernista buildings, with their domes, swirly decorations and pastel colours add a sumptuous quality to the architecture. The city is equally laden with archaeological sites, as well as excellent restaurants and sights. This appealing potpourri continues to attract cruise passengers and day trippers, distinctive for their holiday-golf clothes, from nearby La Manga Club. Cartagena also has a sizeable North African population, largely employed in the surrounding agricultural industry.

The city has a chequered economic history. The mining boom of the late 19th century all but ceased by the late 1920s, while the naval presence of dollar-rich sailors on R&R also wained. Growing increasingly dingy and neglected, Cartagena's closed shops and dilapidated buildings all spoke of recession.

But the town is picking itself up while digging deep into the past: excavations are stripping back more and more of its old quarter to reveal a long-buried – and fascinating – Roman and Carthaginian heritage.

History

In 223 BC Hasdrubal marched his invading army into the Iberian settlement of Mastia and renamed it Carthago Nova. The town prospered during Roman occupation and, under Muslim rule, became the independent emirate of Cartajana. The Arabs improved agriculture and established the town's reputation for building warships before being expelled by the Catholics in 1242. The defensive walls were raised in the 18th century. Although the city was badly bombed in the civil war, industry and the population flourished during the 1950s and '60s.

Information

Exit (Plaza del Rey 5; per hr €2; 🕑 noon-midnight Mon-Sat, 4pm-midnight Sun) Internet access.
Post office (Plaza del Rey)
Tourist office (☎ 968 50 64 83; www.cartagena.es; Plaza del Almirante Bastarreche; 🕑 10am-2pm & 4-6pm or 5-7pm Mon-Fri, 10am-1pm Sat)
Tourist office kiosk (Paseo de Alfonso XII; 🕑 10am-2pm & 4-6pm or 5-7pm Mon-Fri, 10am-1pm Sat, 10am-2pm Sun)

Sights & Activities

Cartagena is rich in Modernista buildings, including **Casa Cervantes** (Calle Mayor 11); the **Casino** (Calle Mayor 13), which has a cafeteria; **Casa Llagostera** (Calle Mayor 25); the zinc-domed **Gran Hotel** (Calle del Aire s/n); the strawberries-and-cream confection of **Casa Clares** (Calle del Aire 4); and the resplendent **Palacio Aguirre** (Plaza de la Merced), now an exhibition space for modern art.

Puerto de Culturas (🕑 968 50 00 93; www.puertoculturas.com) offers four different combined tick-

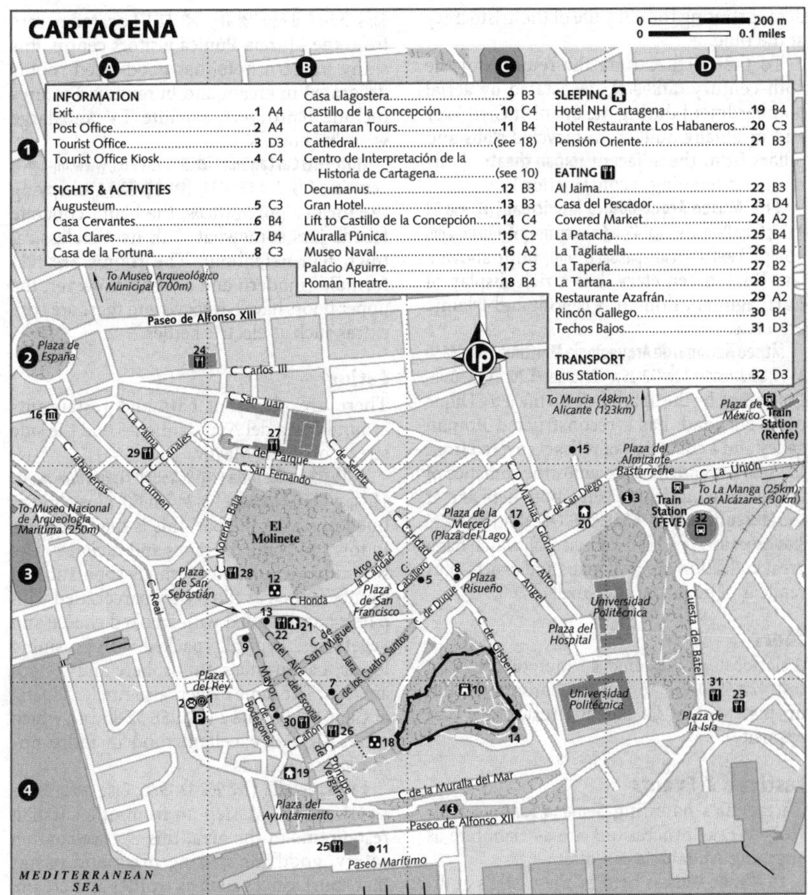

ets (€11 to €18) covering Murcia's sights and tours. Tickets are available at each venue or at the tourist office.

For a sweeping panoramic view, stride up to **Castillo de la Concepción**, or hop on the lift (€1). Within the castle's gardens, decorated by strutting peacocks, the **Centro de Interpretación de la Historia de Cartagena** (☎ 968 52 53 26; adult/under 12yr/12-25yr €3.50/free/2.50; 10am-2.30pm & 4-8.30pm daily Jul-Sep, 10am-2.30pm & 4-6.30pm Tue-Sun Oct-Jun) offers a mid-tech potted history of Cartegena through the centuries via audio screens and a 10-minute film (in English and Spanish).

A similar visitors centre, the **Muralla Púnica** (☎ 968 52 54 77; Calle de San Diego; adult/under 12yr/12-25yr €3.50/free/2.50; 10am-2.30pm & 4-8.30pm daily Jul-Sep, 10am-2.30pm & 4-6.30pm Tue-Sun Oct-Jun), built around a section of the old Punic wall, concentrates on the town's Carthaginian and Roman legacy.

Other Roman sites include the **Augusteum** (Calle Caballero; adult/under 12yr/12-25yr €2.50/free/2; 10am-2.30pm Tue-Sun Jul-Sep, 4-6.30pm Tue-Sun Oct-Jun), which has an exhibition on the Roman Forum; the **Decumanus** (adult/12-25yr/under 12yr €2/1/free; 10am-2.30pm & 4-6pm Tue-Sun Jul-Sep, 10am-2.30pm Tue-Sun Oct-Jun), shop-lined remains of one of the town's main Roman streets, located just off Calle Honda; and the **Casa de la Fortuna** (Plaza Risueño; adult/under 12yr/12-25yr €2.50/free/2; 10am-2.30pm & 4-8.30pm Tue-Sun Jul-Sep, 10am-2.30pm Tue-Sun Oct-Jun), a Roman villa dating back to the 2nd and 3rd centuries AD, demonstrating the daily life of the aristocracy at the time.

To the northeast are the remains of the 13th-century **cathedral**, devastated by aerial bombardment during the Spanish Civil War and originally built from recycled slabs and pillars from the adjacent **roman theatre** (currently undergoing reconstruction).

The **Museo Arqueológico Municipal** (☎ 968 53 90 27; Calle Ramón y Cajal 45; admission free; 🕑 10am-2pm & 5-8pm Tue-Fri, 11am-2pm Sat & Sun), built above a late-Roman cemetery, has a rich display of Carthaginian, Roman, Visigoth and Islamic artefacts.

Museo Nacional de Arqueología Marítima (☎ 968 50 84 15; adult/under 12yr/12-25yr €2.40/free/1.20; 🕑 9.30am-3pm Tue-Sun), by the lighthouse on the jetty Dique de la Navidad, has a reconstructed Roman galley and a collection of relics recovered from the sea. Kids are likely to enjoy the romance of discovering hidden treasure, both here and at the **Museo Naval** (☎ 968 58 20 00; Calle Menéndez Pelayo 8; admission free; 🕑 10am-1.30pm Tue-Sun), which has a great collection of naval maps and charts, plus replicas of boats big and small.

Tours

A sleek catamaran offers 45-minute **tours** (adult/under 12yr €5.50/4.50; 🚸) of the harbour. Pick it up just west of La Patacha restaurant (see opposite).

Festivals & Events

Cartagena's haunting **Semana Santa** (Easter Holy Week) processions are as elaborate as anything Andalucía can offer.

La Mar de Músicas held in the castle's auditorium brings the best of world music to Cartagena throughout July.

For 10 days in the second half of September, the townsfolk play war games, reenacting the battles between rival Carthaginian and Roman occupiers in the spectacular **Carthagineses y Romanos** fiesta.

Sleeping

Pensión Oriente (☎/fax 968 50 24 69; 2nd fl, Calle Jara 27; s/d without bathroom €25/34) The Oriente has 12 simple rooms with high ceilings, pine furniture and fans. The one spacious double en suite (€38) is worth the extra, although all the rooms could do with a lick of paint.

Hotel Restaurante Los Habaneros (☎ 968 50 52 50; www.hotelhabaneros.com in Spanish; Calle de San Diego 60; s €52-57, d €69-73; P ❄ 💻) Located across from the Murcia Púnica visitors centre, this shiny modern hotel has good-sized rooms decorated in cream and burgundy. Features include hairdryers, satellite TV and large walk-in showers.

Hotel NH Cartagena (☎ 968 12 09 08; www.nh-hotels.com; Calle Real 2; d €81-131; P ❄ 💻) Occupying the former port offices, the bland concrete facade jars somewhat with its neoclassical town hall neighbour. The rooms are NH formula (modern and stylish); however, the upper floors have bay views and there are cosy extras such as electric kettles.

Eating

There are plenty of bars and restaurants around Plaza del Ayuntamiento and the side streets off Calle Mayor.

our pick **La Tartana** (☎ 968 50 00 11; Puerta de Murcia 14; tapas €1.50, raciones €4-8) With 60-plus choices lined up along the bar, this is the best place in town to come for tapas and *raciones*. The selection includes surprisingly sophisticated numbers such as filo pastry parcels tied with parsley and stuffed with smoked cheese and vegetables. Typically packed with gossiping locals, La Tartana's atmosphere and service are tops. The same owners also run La Tapería at Calle del Parque 2 (☎ 968 52 86 14), which offers similar excellent food in more upmarket surrounds.

La Tagliatella (☎ 968 12 19 95; Calle Cañon 4; pizzas €11, pasta €13) A step up from other Italian restaurants in the area, this is a welcoming eatery, good for sharing pizza and pastas that sport sauces such as truffles and cream, and pesto with walnuts and gorgonzola. The pizzas are crispy based with robust, tasty toppings.

Rincón Gallego (☎ 667 725596; Calle Cañon 13; meals €12-15; 🕑 Mon-Sat) The arm-long menu of fish dishes includes several ways of preparing the speciality – octopus – including the deliciously simple grilled octopus with fresh lemons. Avoid the house wine, which is better for pickling grandma (sorry, onions).

Al Jaima (☎ 968 08 40 20; Calle Jara 27; meals €15-20; 🕑 Mon-Sat; V) Boho-arty decor with sink-into sofas and colourful cushions. The Moroccan menu of vegetable tagines, couscous and side dishes such as hummus and *foul belkamu* (broad beans with garlic) is gastro-heaven for vegetarians.

La Patacha (☎ 968 10 39 71; Muelle Alfonso XII; meals €25-38) This permanently moored boat has a shiny wooden interior. Pillars are masked with coiled ropes and the ceiling lights are suspended from an upside-down canoe. The choice is (obviously) seafood and fish, and the dishes are with well prepared – the simpler the better.

Restaurante Azafrán (☎ 968 52 31 72; Calle La Palma 3; meals €35; closed Sun year-round, dinner Mon May-Sep) Despite the residential location, the Saffron has a far from pedestrian feel with its dramatic black-and-white display of photos, background jazz and shady terrace. The cuisine offers an innovative twist to traditional dishes, such as pork cutlets in a creamy truffle sauce.

Plaza de la Isla has two large popular fish restaurants where you can indulge in the catch of the day: **Casa del Pescador** (☎ 968 50 63 75; meals €20-35; closed dinner Sun & Mon year-round, lunch & dinner Tue Aug) and its cheaper neighbour **Techos Bajos** (☎ 968 50 50 20; meals €15-20; lunch Tue-Sun, dinner Fri & Sat).

Cartagena has a handy **covered market** (Calle Carlos III; 7am-2pm Mon-Sat) that is good for self-caterers.

Getting There & Away

BUS

Buses run eight times daily to/from Alicante (€7.75, two hours) via Los Alcázares (€1.50, 30 minutes) and Torrevieja (€4.20, 1¼ hours). At least 10 motorway buses go to/from Murcia (€3.40, one hour) daily and **ALSA** (☎ 902 42 22 42; www.alsa.es) runs services to/from La Manga (€2.95 to €3.45, one hour, at least 10 daily). Contact the **bus station** (☎ 968 50 56 56; Plaza Bastarrecho) for more info.

TAXI

A taxi to or from San Javier airport will cost you approximately €35.

TRAIN

For Renfe train destinations, change in Murcia (€4.20, 50 minutes, four to seven daily). Beware: take the local train as the Talgo express alternative costs €14.20!

Local FEVE trains make the short run to Los Nietos (€1.75, 30 minutes, every 40 minutes) on the Mar Menor.

COSTA CÁLIDA

With more than 300 days of annual sunshine and an average temperature of 18°C, the Hot Coast is aptly named.

Mar Menor

The Mar Menor is a 170-sq-km saltwater lagoon. Its waters are a good 5°C warmer than the open sea and excellent for water sports, including jet-skiing, kayaking and waterskiing. Check the Sports category on the comprehensive www.marmenor.net website for more information. The lagoon is separated by **La Manga** (Sleeve), a 22km sliver of land punctuated by small beaches but overdeveloped with high-rise accommodation; the world would lose little if the whole isthmus one day cut loose and drifted away. The reality is that it just may sink – see the boxed text, p704.

Cabo de Palos, at the peninsula's southern limit, has a small harbour filled with pleasure boats and surrounded by low-rise restaurants and holiday apartments. The waters around the tiny offshore (and protected) **Islas Hormigas** (Ant Islands) are great for scuba diving. **Atura-Sub** (☎ 968 56 48 23; www.aturasub.com in Spanish; La Bocana 28) and nearby **BuceaYa** (☎ 968 34 70 33; www.buceaya.com in Spanish), located beside the marina, offer dives from €40. Both offices are staffed sporadically; book through the websites.

At the northern end of the lagoon, **Lo Pagán** is a mellow low-rise resort with a long promenade, pleasant beach and plenty of bars and restaurants. Avoid July and August when it gets packed out with *madrileños* (people from Madrid). There is also the added attraction (for some) of natural, and free, mud treatments. Head north of the promenade where a 2km walkway sticks out into the lagoon. Have a dip on the west side of the path and coat yourself in mud. Let it dry, wash it off, then to really tone yourself up take a dip in the lagoon opposite. The mud's high salt and iodine content is supposedly very therapeutic.

Just east of here lie the **Salinas de San Pedro** (salt pans) where you can follow a well-signposted *senda verde* (footpath). This relatively easy walk of just over 4km passes by several lagoons favoured by flocks of pink flamingos.

Time your visit to check out the summer season of cultural events at **San Javier**, around 5km southwest of the salt pans. During June, July and August the town plays host to the San Javier Jazz Festival, the Pecata Minuta Pop Festival and the Festival of Theatre, Music

ALEJANDRO AGUERA PARRÓN, KAYAKER

Born and raised in Cartagena, Alejandro Aguera Parrón believes the Mar Menor is the best place in Spain for canoeing and kayaking. 'This salty lake has a perimeter of some 65km, an average air temperature of 18 degrees, consistently warm water, a perfect depth and is surrounded by beautiful natural parks.'

A previous holder of the Spanish Cup for *kayak de mar* (sea-kayaking), Alejandro explains the appeal of the sport.

'What I love most is the sensation of tranquillity out on the water. Each year I go on trips of up to 10 days throughout Spain. I carry everything I need, including water, dehydrated food and a fishing rod. Last year I kayaked from Ibiza to Formentera, camping on wild beaches inaccessible by land.'

Not everything is so swimmingly idyllic, however: Alejandro fears the environmental changes impacting the Mar Menor.

'Erosion is continuing to take place,' he says. 'In Roman times, the water depth was some 60m, today it is only 7m. Also, with increased tourism, there are more jet skis and yachts which contaminate the water. Until recently, the level of salt in the Mar Menor was 7% more than the Mediterranean, which created fauna endemic to the lake. Recently, affluent yacht owners have insisted that the channel from the sea to the lake be deepened, which would cause the salinity level to drop.'

Ironically, there is one otherwise negative environmental factor that may actually help the Mar Menor. 'If the level of the sea rises, people will no longer want to buy houses near the beach for fear of a tsunami. For some people it may already be too late; studies have shown that the overbuilt La Manga is a catastrophe waiting to happen, and that what should have been created here is a natural park, like Doñana in Andalucía.'

and Dance. Check out www.marmenor.net for more information.

Golfo de Mazarrón

The rugged coast west of Cartagena is fretted with small coves and unspoilt beaches, best reached by car. Inland, where agricultural business prevails, the shimmering silver lakes prove to be entire valleys sheathed in plastic where vegetables are force-grown in greenhouses for local and export markets.

If speed matters, take the AP7 toll motorway. Otherwise, opt for the more picturesque N332, which swoops and snakes through the coastal mountains. Both bring you to **Puerto de Mazarrón**, a bustling, likeable resort with shops and restaurants. Head west of the centre for the best beaches. At **Playa La Ermita,** the beachfront **Centro de Buceo del Sureste** (☎ 968 15 40 78; www.buceosureste.com) offers dives from €40. Five kilometres west, tiny **Bolnuevo** has surreal sandstone-sculptured rocks eroded over millions of years, known as the **Gredas de Bolnuevo** (Enchanted City of Bolnuevo). It's easy to find; there are signs everywhere. The beach opposite is long and sandy. Just 1km further west, a cove for naturists is appropriately well secluded. Around 30km on **Águilas**, with its coves and beaches flanking the town, is similarly good for getting sand between the toes.

LORCA

pop 89,900 / elev 330m

This appealing market town is the site of some of Spain's most flamboyant Semana Santa (Holy Week) celebrations, which may be appreciated via various museums, if you can't make the dates. Well worth a stopover, the old quarter is partly pedestrianised with some fine baroque buildings crowned by a 13th-century castle.

Lorca's economy is primarily based on the export of pork products and textiles, although tourists dip in regularly from the holiday resorts and the town fills its coffers at Easter time.

Orientation & Information

The historic district clings to the slopes between Calle Lope Gisbert and the castle in the northwest.

The train and bus stations lie 200m southwest of the **tourist office** (☎ 968 46 61 57; www.lorca.es; Calle Lope Gisbert 10; ⏰ 9.30am-2pm & 5.30-7.30pm Mon-Sat, 10am-3pm Sun). The **Centro de Visitantes** (☎ 902

40 00 47; www.lorcatallerdeltiempo.com; 9.30am-2pm & 4-7pm Tue-Sun), located in a former convent, is an informative visitors centre and has a **multimedia exhibition** (adult/under 12yr/12-25yr €3/free/2.30;) illustrating Lorca's long history.

Sights

The Centro de Visitantes sells various combined tickets (€12 to €24) to the sights. A **tourist train** (adult/under 12yr €3/2.30) provides a painless chug up to the castle. You can pick it up at various sights throughout town, including by the Puente de la Alberca (outside the Centro de Visitantes).

Peculiar to Lorca are four small museums exhibiting the magnificent Semana Santa costumes. Some cloaks are up to 5m in length and all are elaborately hand-embroidered in silk, depicting colourful religious and historical scenes. The two largest of these museums are the **Museo de Bordados del Paso Azul** (968 47 20 77; Calle Nogalte 7; adult/under 12yr/12-25yr €3/free/2.50; 10am-2pm & 5-7.30pm Tue-Sat, 10am-2pm Sun), which competes in splendour with the **Museo de Bordados del Paso Blanco** (650 272004; Calle Santo Domingo 8; adult/under 12yr/12-25yr €3/free/2.50; 10am-2pm & 5-7.30pm Tue-Sat, 10am-2pm Sun), annexed to the church of Santo Doming. For more on Semana Santa, see the boxed text, below.

Behind the baroque facade of the 17th-century **Casa de Guevara** (968 44 19 14; Calle Lope Gisbert s/n; adult/under 12yr €3/2.50) is a fascinating palace that includes a harmonious patio, a (transplanted) late-19th-century pharmacy (complete with bottles of medicinal potions, including cocaine), and plush rooms with fine paintings, furniture and artefacts.

You'll find more splendid baroque buildings around **Plaza de España**, including the **Pósito**, a 16th-century former granary; the 18th-century **Casa del Corregidor**; and the town hall. Lording over the square is the golden limestone **Colegiata de San Patricio** (11am-1pm & 4.30-6pm), a church with a handsome baroque facade and predominantly Renaissance interior.

The town's **castle** has been transformed into a veritable theme park – **La Fortaleza del Sol** (968 47 74 37; adult/under 12yr €10/free; 10.30am-6.30pm Tue-Sun; closed Jan-Mar;) offers dioramas, actors in costume and various gadgetry. While children will probably enjoy all the jollity, adults may ponder the days when visiting the castle was a less contrived, more contemplative experience.

Lorca's **Museo Arqueológico** (968 40 62 67; Plaza de Juan Moreno s/n; adult/under 12yr/12-25yr €2/free/1.50; 10am-2pm & 5-7.30pm Tue-Sat, 10am-2pm Sun), set in the grand 16th-century Casa de los Salazar, provides an insight into the city's ancient history, which dates back to the mid-Palaeolithic period and through to the final years of Muslim Lorca.

Sleeping & Eating

Pensión del Carmen (968 46 64 59; Rincón de los Valientes 3; s/d €18/35;) A great budget choice. Cheerful and family-run, Carmen has seven doubles and seven singles, all spotless. You'll find it in a tiny square just off Calle Nogalte.

Hotel Alameda (968 40 66 00; www.hotel-alameda.com; 1st fl, Calle Musso Valiente 8; s/d/tr €30/50/65; P) Look beyond the insipid chip-marble flooring and dated floral fabrics, as the rooms here are large, good value and excellently located.

Jardines de Lorca (968 47 05 99; www.sercotelhoteles.com; Alameda de Rafael Méndez; s/d €140/165; P) This angular, modern red-brick hotel is in an affluent residential area around 200m south of the bullring. Popular with business travellers, the rooms

ADDING COLOUR TO SEMANA SANTA

In Lorca you'll find issues are clearly blue and white – the colours of the two major brotherhoods that have competed every year since 1855 to see who can stage the most lavish Semana Santa display.

Lorca's Easter parades beat to a different rhythm, distinct from the slow, sombre processions of Andalucía and elsewhere in Murcia. While still deeply reverential, they're full of colour and vitality, mixing Old and New Testament legend with the Passion story.

If you hail from Lorca, you're passionately Blanco (White) or Azul (Blue). Each of the brotherhoods has a statue of the Virgin (one draped in a blue mantle, the other in white, naturally), a banner and a spectacular museum. The result of this intense and mostly genial year-round rivalry is just about the most dramatic Semana Santa you'll see anywhere in Spain.

are slick and corporate; there's a spa for post-boardroom relaxation.

Restaurante Juan de Toledo (☎ 968 47 02 15; Calle Juan de Toledo 14; meals €25; ⏰ Tue-Sat, lunch Sun) Situated within an atmospheric old building, generally decorated by upstairs' daily wash, the *menú* (set menu) here is meatily uncomplicated. Choose from dishes such as *rabo de toro estofado* (oxtail stew) and *solomillo a la brasa* (grilled fillet steak). Lightweights can opt for a bowl of gazpacho with all the trimmings.

Shopping

The cavernous **Centro de Artesanía** (☎ 968 46 39 12; Calle Lope Gisbert s/n; ⏰ 10am-2pm & 5-7pm Mon-Sat, 10am-2pm Sun), beside the tourist office, sells local traditional crafts.

Getting There & Around

Hourly buses (€4.95, 1½ hours) and trains (€4.25, 1¼ hours) run between Lorca and Murcia.

There's a large **underground car park** (Plaza Colón) 200m west of the tourist office.

PARQUE NATURAL DE SIERRA ESPUÑA

The park is a 40-minute drive southwest of Murcia towards Lorca. Just north of the N340, it has more than 250 sq km of unspoilt highlands covered with trails that are popular with walkers and climbers.

Limestone formations tower above its sprawling forests. In the northwest of the park are 26 Pozos de la Nieve (ice houses) where, until the arrival of industrial refrigeration, snow was compressed into ice then taken to nearby towns in summer.

Access to the park is best via Alhama de Murcia. Visit the fab **Ricardo Codorniu Visitors Centre** (☎ 968 42 54 55; www.sierraespuna.com; ⏰ 10am-2pm & 5-7pm Mon-Sat, 10am-2pm Sun) located in a traditional country house in the heart of the park.

The nearby village of **El Berro** has a couple of restaurants and the friendly **Camping Sierra Espuña** (☎ 968 66 80 38; www.campingsierraespuna.com; sites per person/tent/car €3.50/3.50/3.50, 2-person bungalow €46; 🏊), which has superb facilities for families including barbecue pits, swimming pool, minigolf, playground and cafeteria.

Andalucía

What aspect of Spain does Andalucía represent? To millions of visitors, this southern powerhouse *is* Spain. Since the country began to reinvent itself as a major destination in the 1950s Andalucía has been the generator of national stereotypes. Now, as the 21st century gets under way, it's providing fresh images and startling contrasts.

There's Cádiz, Europe's oldest living city, contrasting the shiny new metropolises of the Costa del Sol still waiting to be inhabited. The narrow streets of Andalucía's provincial capitals, rich in historic treasures left by Phoenician, Roman, Moorish, Jewish and Catholic conquerors, offset a vast outdoor adventure playground with Spain's widest swathes of protected land, the mainland's highest mountain, and Europe's stiffest breezes powering kitesurfing in Tarifa.

Andalucía is a clash of sensory impressions as fierce as its searing light and impenetrable shade. It's scrambled brains and testicles in a classic *tortilla de Sacromonte* omelette; sleek silver trams swishing past 15th-century cathedrals; the flat tinkle of an Alpujarran goat bell in a main shopping street; wind farms, wax tapers, and world-famous names headlining at music festivals; and wild eagles in Doñana National Park. Andalucía's both superstitious and irreligious. Yet it's not sentimental and its young people are impatient for change. Andalucía is taking its place in 21st-century Spain – the past can come along if it likes.

HIGHLIGHTS

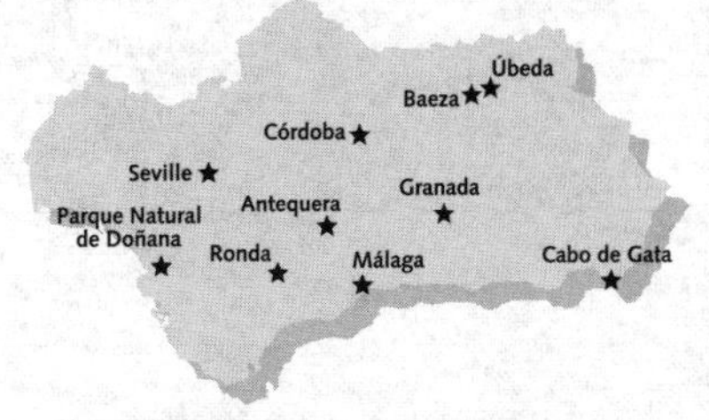

- Watch exotic birds soar over the moody marismas marshlands of Huelva's **Parque Nacional de Doñana** (p733)
- Savour Seville's medieval supremacy in the exquisite architecture and gardens of the city's **Alcázar** (p718)
- Visit the **Picasso Museum** (p768) then follow the contemporary art trail through culture-mad Málaga
- Walk the beautiful volcanic coastline of **Cabo de Gata** (p828) and contemplate stone, sea and sky
- Immerse yourself in the scented sensuality of Córdoba's exquisite hammam baths, the **Baños Arabes** (p791)
- Enter some of Europe's largest megalithic tombs near **Antequera** (p785) in Málaga and step into prehistory
- Reconstruct the splendour of Renaissance Spain in the magnificent Jaén towns of **Úbeda** (p819) and **Baeza** (p818)
- Live life on the edge in **Ronda** (p780) as you drink cocktails at the parador overlooking plunging El Tajo gorge

AREA: 87,000 SQ KM	AVE SUMMER TEMP: HIGH 36°C, LOW 20°C (SEVILLE	POP: 7.9 MILLION

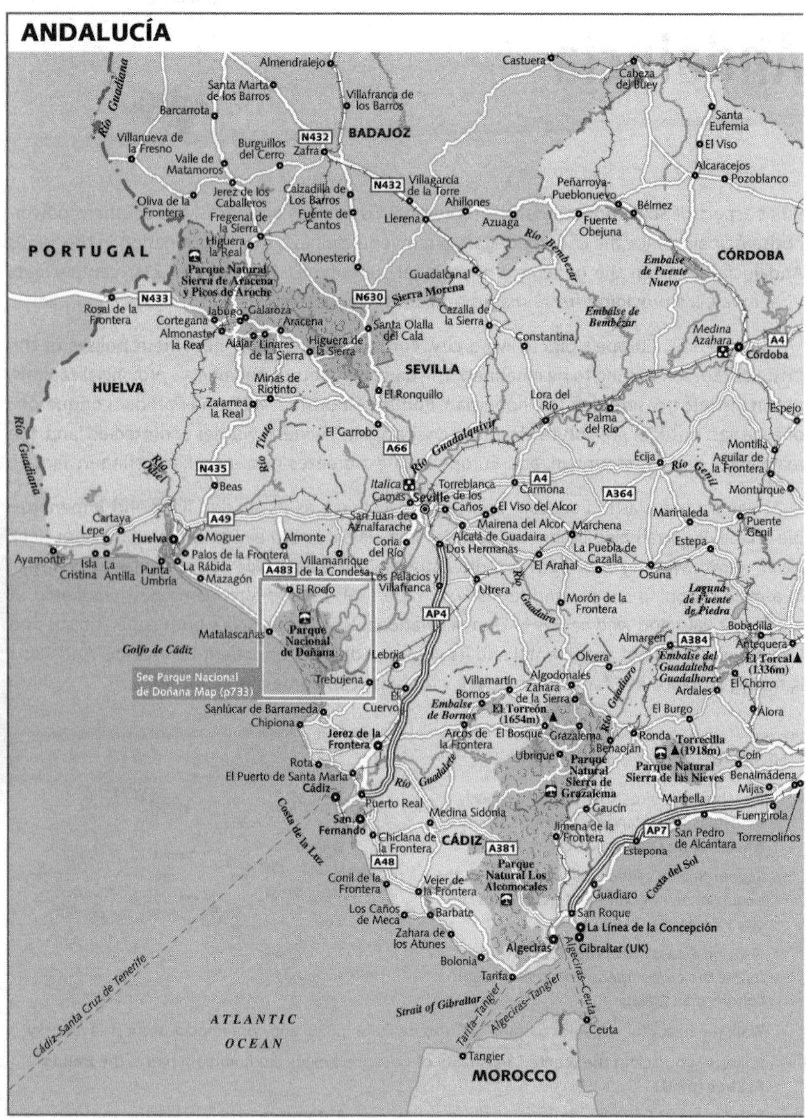

History

Around 1000 or 900 BC, Andalucía's agricultural and mining wealth attracted Phoenician trading colonies to coastal sites such as Cádiz, Huelva and Málaga. In the 8th and 7th centuries BC Phoenician influence gave rise to the mysterious, legendarily wealthy Tartessos civilisation somewhere in western Andalucía. From the 3rd century BC to the 5th century AD Andalucía, governed from Córdoba, was one of the most civilised and wealthiest areas of the Roman Empire.

Andalucía was the obvious base for the Muslim invaders who surged onto the Iberian Peninsula from Africa in 711 under Arab general Tariq ibn Ziyad, who landed at Gibraltar

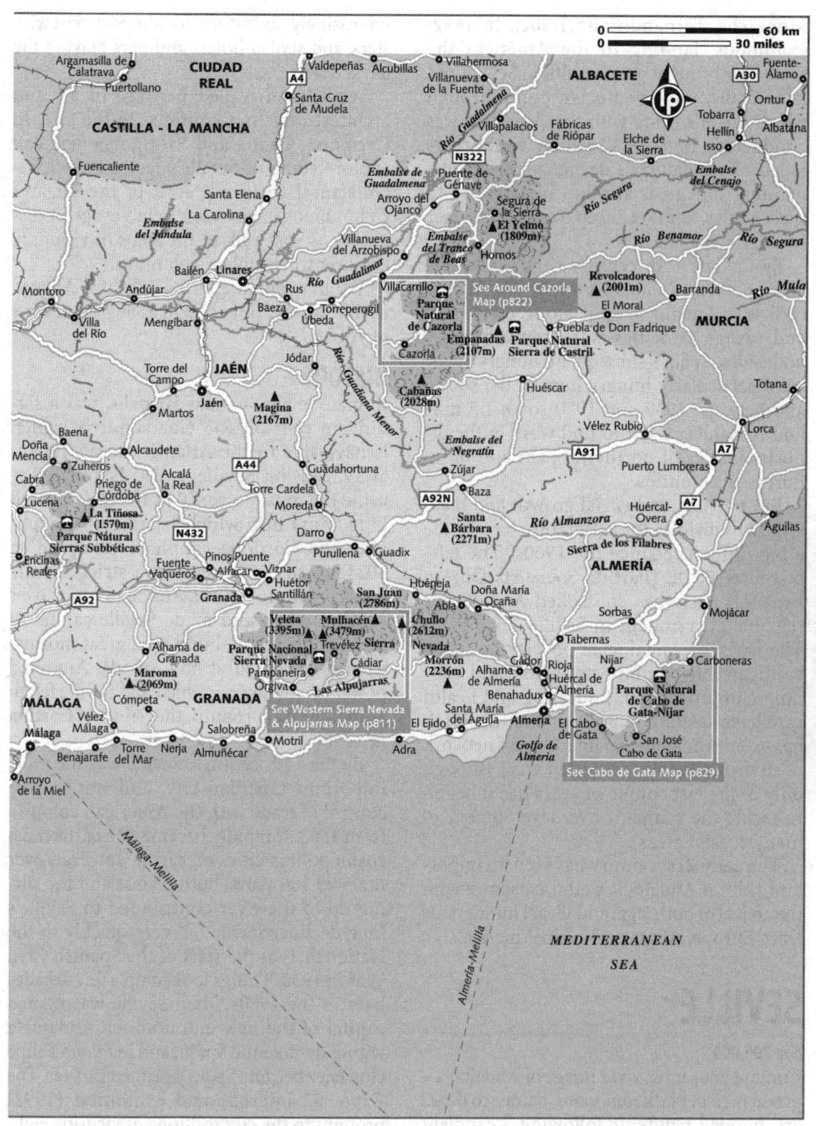

with around 10,000 men, mostly Berbers (indigenous North Africans). Until the 11th century Córdoba was the leading city of Islamic Spain, followed by Seville until the 13th and finally Granada until the 15th centuries. At its peak in the 10th century, Córdoba was the most dazzling city in Western Europe, famed for its 'three cultures' coexistence of Muslims, Jews and Christians. Islamic civilisation lasted longer in Andalucía than anywhere else on the Iberian Peninsula, and it's from the medieval name for the Muslim areas of the peninsula, Al-Andalus, that the name Andalucía comes.

The Emirate of Granada, the last bastion of Al-Andalus, finally fell to the Catholic

Monarchs, Fernando and Isabel, in 1492. Columbus' landing in the Americas the same year brought great wealth to Seville and later Cádiz, the Andalucian ports through which Spain's trade with the Americas was conducted. But the Castilian conquerors killed off Andalucía's deeper prosperity by handing out great swathes of territory to their nobles, who set sheep to run on former food-growing lands.

By the late 19th century rural Andalucía was a hotbed of anarchist unrest. During the civil war Andalucía split along class lines and savage atrocities were committed by both sides. Spain's subsequent 'hungry years' were particularly hungry here in the south, and between 1950 and 1970 some 1.5 million Andalucians left to find work in the industrial cities of northern Spain and other European countries.

But tourism, industrial growth and massive EU subsidies for agriculture have made a big difference since the 1960s. The left-of-centre PSOE (Partido Socialista Obrero Español) party has controlled Andalucía's regional government in Seville since 1982. The worst of Andalucian poverty has been eradicated by welfare provision and economic improvement. Education and health care have steadily improved, and the PSOE has given Andalucía Spain's biggest network of environmentally protected areas (though only in the last couple of years has it begun to tackle the rampant overdevelopment of many coastal areas).

The early 21st century has seen an important shift in Andalucía's ethnic balance with the arrival of both legal and illegal immigrants from Europe, Africa and Latin America.

SEVILLE

pop 700,000

Conjure your most vivid image of Andalucía – proud men in black *sombreros,* flamenco dancers, hooded penitents following a candlelit statue of the Virgin, a matador unfurling his scarlet cape – and it comes alive in Seville. All this and more is played out with intense passion in Andalucía's capital city, especially during the city's Semana Santa (Holy Week) and its annual *feria* (fair) in spring. Yet Seville doesn't rest on its historic laurels; increasingly, its historic buildings coexist with stark and stylish hotels and bars playing the latest beats.

Seville's unrivalled heritage of art and architecture is not confined to the city. In Carmona, Osuna and Santiponce you can explore some of Seville's lesser-known architectural treasures. And in the Lugares Colombinos, make your own voyage of discovery as you walk in the steps of visionary explorer Christopher Columbus.

Try to avoid sweltering July and August. Seville is quite hot enough at any other time of year!

HISTORY

Roman Seville, named Hispalis, was a significant port on Río Guadalquivir, which is navigable to the Atlantic Ocean 100km away. Muslim Seville, called Ishbiliya, became the most powerful of the *taifas* (small kingdoms) into which Islamic Spain split after the Córdoba caliphate collapsed in 1031. In the 12th century a strict Islamic sect from Morocco, the Almohads, took over Muslim Spain and made Seville capital of their whole realm, building a great mosque where the cathedral now stands. Almohad power eventually crumbled and Seville fell to Fernando III (El Santo, the Saint) of Castilla in 1248.

By the 14th century, Seville was the most important Castilian city, and was in sole control of trade with the American colonies from 1503. It rapidly became one of the most cosmopolitan cities on earth. However, over the next 300 years, both plague and the silting up of the river contributed to Seville's long decline. Seville fell very quickly to the Nationalists at the start of the Spanish Civil War in 1936. Things looked up a few decades later in the 1980s when Seville was named capital of the new autonomous Andalucía within democratic Spain, and *sevillano* Felipe González became Spain's prime minister. The Expo '92 international exhibition (1992) brought to the city millions of visitors, eight new bridges across the Guadalquivir and the speedy AVE rail link to Madrid. And in the new century, where less is more, Seville is already experimenting with green initiatives, including trams (p730) that glide quietly alongside the city's antique monuments to past glory.

ORIENTATION

Seville straddles Río Guadalquivir, with most places of interest found on the river's east bank. The central area is a tangle of narrow, twisting old streets and small squares, with the exception of Plaza Nueva and the broad, straight Avenida de la Constitución. Just east of Constitución are the city's major monuments: the cathedral, La Giralda and the Alcázar fortress-palace. The quaint Barrio de Santa Cruz, east of the cathedral and the Alcázar, is a popular place to stay and eat. The true centre of Seville, El Centro, is a little further north, around Plaza de San Francisco and Plaza Salvador. The area between Avenida de la Constitución and the river is called El Arenal.

The train station and the two bus stations are on the periphery of the central area, all served by city buses that circle the centre (p729): Prado de San Sebastián bus station is 650m southeast of the cathedral and within walking distance of the Barrio de Santa Cruz; Plaza de Armas bus station is 900m northwest of the cathedral, within walking distance of El Arenal; and Santa Justa train station is 1.5km northeast of the cathedral.

INFORMATION

Bookshops

Casa del Libro (Map pp714-15; ☎ 954 50 29 50; Calle Velázquez 8; 9.30am-9.30pm Mon-Sat) Maps and guidebooks

LTC (Map pp714-15; ☎ 954 42 59 64; Avenida Menéndez Pelayo 46; closed Sat) Andalucía's top map shop.

Emergency (☎ 112)

Ambulance (☎ 061)

Policía Local (☎ 092)

Policía Nacional (☎ 091)

Internet Access

Internetia (Map pp712-13; Avenida Menéndez Pelayo 45; per hr €2; 11am-11pm every day)

Sevilla Internet Center (Map pp714-15; ☎ 954 50 02 75; 1st fl, Calle Almirantazgo 2 (cnr Avenida Constitución & Calle Almirantazgo); per min €0.05; 9am-10pm Mon-Fri, 10am-10pm Sat & Sun)

Internet Resources

Discover Sevilla (www.discoversevilla.com) This is an excellent, comprehensive site.

Explore Seville (www.exploreseville.com)

Seville Tourism (www.turismo.sevilla.org) The city's informative official tourism site.

Laundry

Laundries here do the job for you (usually in half a day), with washing, drying and folding included in their prices.

Lavandería Roma (Map pp714-15; ☎ 954 21 05 35; Calle Castelar 2C; per load €6; 9.30am-1.30pm & 5-8.30pm Mon-Fri, 9am-2pm Sat)

La Segunda Vera (Map pp714-15; ☎ 954 53 63 76; Avenida Menendez Pelayo; per load €10; 9am-2pm & 5.30-8.30pm Mon-Fri, closed Sat)

SEVILLE IN...

Two Days

On your first morning, visit the **cathedral** (p717) and **Giralda** (p717) then wander through the **Barrio de Santa Cruz** (p719) and enjoy lunch at the **Corral del Agua** (p725) or **Restaurante La Albahaca** (p725). In the afternoon head over to Río Guadalquivir and visit the **Plaza de Toros** (p720) or the **Museo de Bellas Artes** (p720). Devote the evening to a relaxed tour of a few tapas bars!

Give your second morning to the **Alcázar** (p718) before heading up to El Centro to visit the **Palacio de la Condesa de Lebrija** (p720) and some of the city-centre shops. In the evening take in a flamenco performance and check out some of the bars in **El Centro** (p727) or around the **Alameda de Hércules** (p727).

Four Days

On day three relax with a visit to the leafy **Parque de María Luisa** (p720) and its museums, followed by whichever of the sights you missed on day one. Treat yourself to dinner at a classy restaurant such as the **Egaña Oriza** (p725) or **Enrique Becerra** (p726). On day four venture out to Santiponce to explore the Roman **Itálica** (p730) and **Monasterio de San Isidoro del Campo** (p730). Wind up with a night out enjoying some live music and, if it's the weekend, a **nightclub** (p727).

ANDALUCÍA

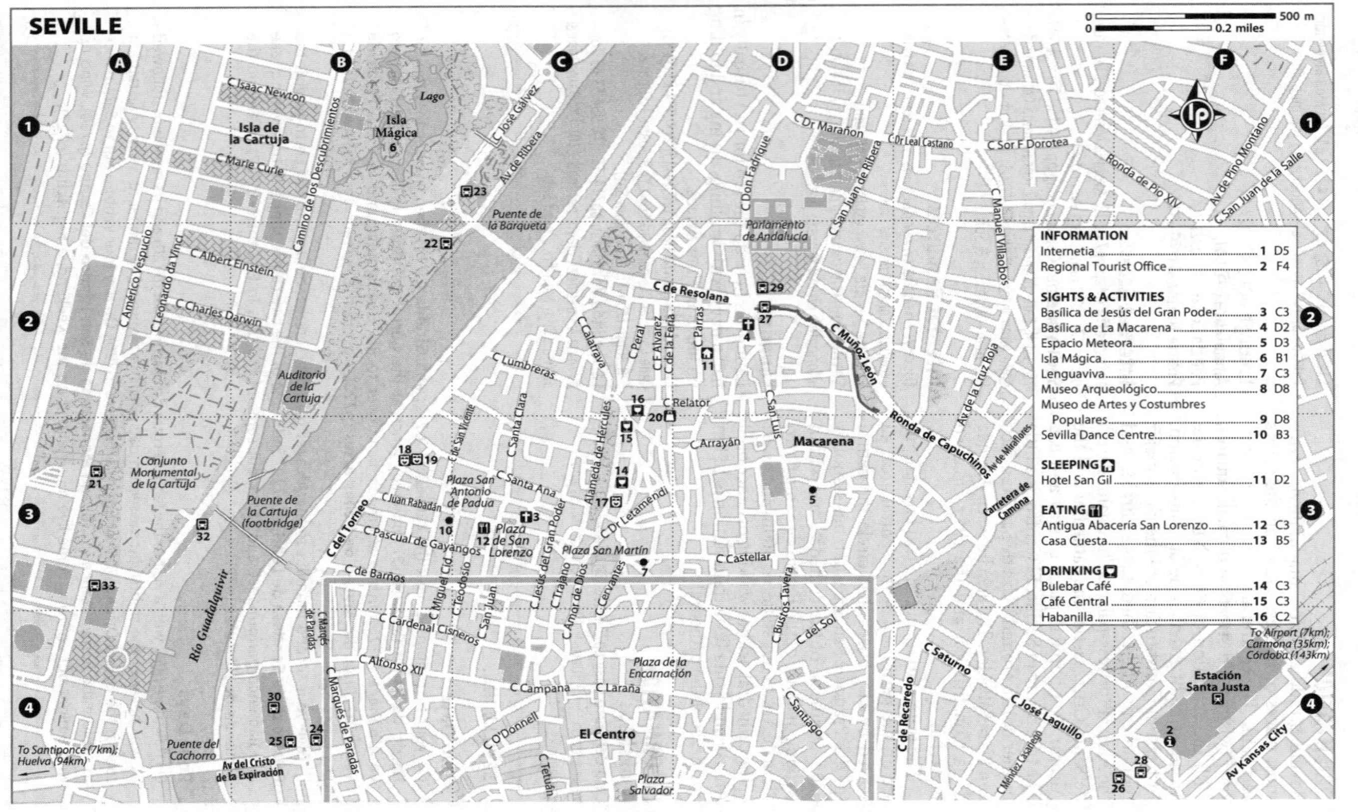
SEVILLE
0 500 m
0 0.2 miles
INFORMATION
Internetia 1 D5
Regional Tourist Office 2 F4
SIGHTS & ACTIVITIES
Basílica de Jesús del Gran Poder 3 C3
Basílica de La Macarena 4 D2
Espacio Meteora 5 D3
Isla Mágica 6 B1
Lenguaviva 7 C3
Museo Arqueológico 8 D8
Museo de Artes y Costumbres Populares 9 D8
Sevilla Dance Centre 10 B3
SLEEPING
Hotel San Gil 11 D2
EATING
Antigua Abacería San Lorenzo 12 C3
Casa Cuesta 13 B5
DRINKING
Bulebar Café 14 C3
Café Central 15 C3
Habanilla 16 C2
To Airport (7km); Carmona (35km); Córdoba (143km)
To Santiponce (7km); Huelva (94km)
Isla de la Cartuja
Isla Mágica
Lago
Auditorio de la Cartuja
Conjunto Monumental de la Cartuja
Puente de la Cartuja (footbridge)
Puente de la Barqueta
Puente del Cachorro
Río Guadalquivir
Parlamento de Andalucía
Macarena
El Centro
Estación Santa Justa
Plaza de la Encarnación
Plaza Salvador
Plaza San Martín
Plaza de San Lorenzo
Plaza San Antonio de Padua
Alameda de Hércules
Camino de los Descubrimientos
C Américo Vespucio
C Leonardo da Vinci
C Charles Darwin
C Albert Einstein
C Marie Curie
C Isaac Newton
C José Gálvez
Av de Ribera
C del Torneo
C de Resolana
C Muñoz León
Ronda de Capuchinos
Av de Miraflores
Ronda de Pío XII
Av de Pino Montano
C San Juan de la Salle
C San Juan de Ribera
C Dr Marañon
C Dr Leal Castano
C Don Fadrique
C Manuel Villaobos
C Sor F Dorotea
Av de la Cruz Roja
Carretera de Carmona
C San Luis
C de Recaredo
C Saturno
C José Laguillo
C Méndez Casariego
Av Kansas City
C Bustos Tavera
C del Sol
C Santiago
C Castellar
C Arrayán
C Relator
C Parras
C de la Feria
C F Alvarez
C Peral
C Calatrava
C Lumbreras
C Santa Clara
C Santa Ana
C de San Vicente
C Jesús del Gran Poder
C Trajano
C Amor de Dios
C Cervantes
C Dr Letamendi
C Teodosio
C San Juan
C Miguel Cid
C Cardenal Cisneros
C Alfonso XII
C Marqués de Paradas
C Pascual de Gayangos
C Juan Rabadán
C de Baños
C Campana
C Laraña
C O'Donnell
C Tetuán
Av del Cristo de la Expiración

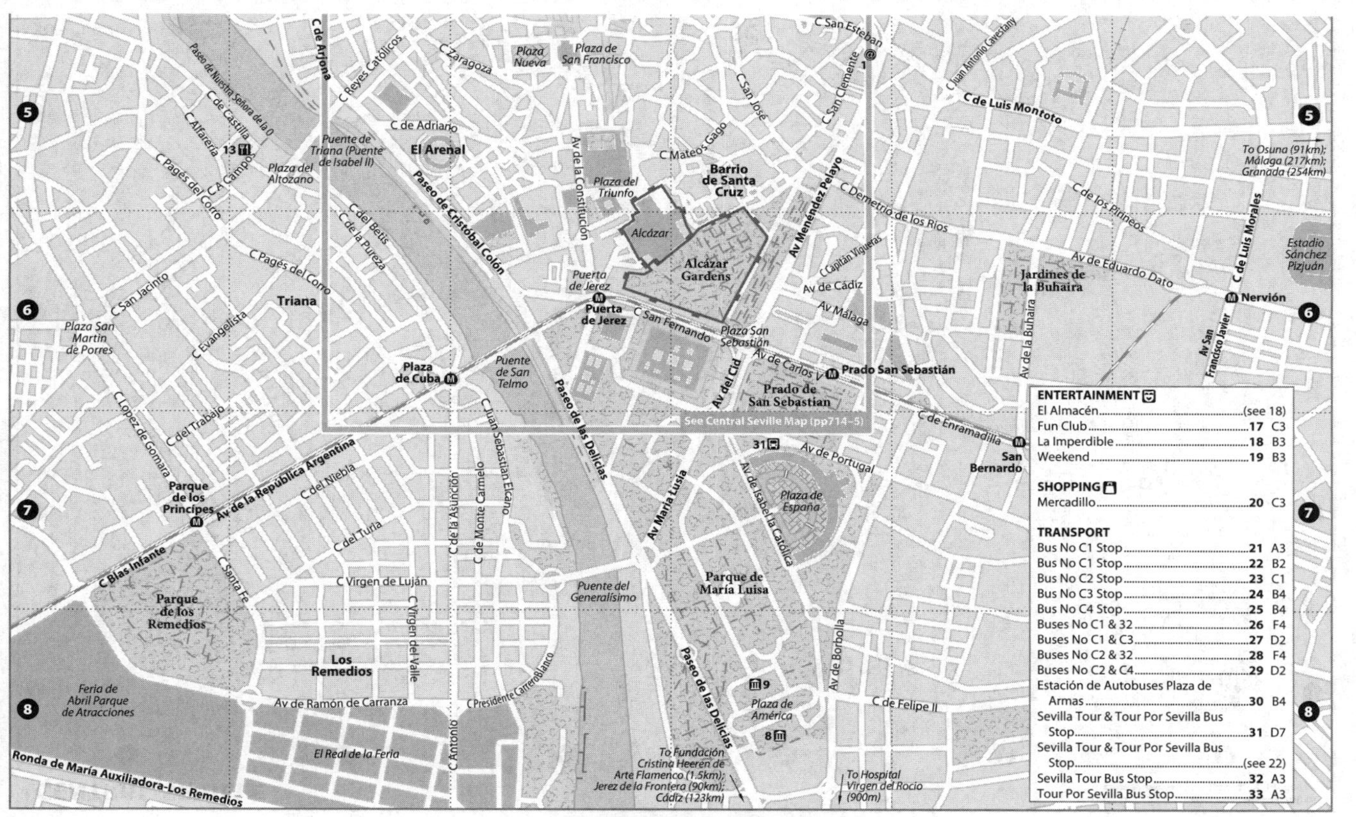
ENTERTAINMENT
El Almacén (see 18)
Fun Club 17 C3
La Imperdible 18 B3
Weekend 19 B3
SHOPPING
Mercadillo 20 C3
TRANSPORT
Bus No C1 Stop 21 A3
Bus No C1 Stop 22 B2
Bus No C2 Stop 23 C1
Bus No C3 Stop 24 B4
Bus No C4 Stop 25 B4
Buses No C1 & 32 26 F4
Buses No C1 & C3 27 D2
Buses No C2 & 32 28 F4
Buses No C2 & C4 29 D2
Estación de Autobuses Plaza de Armas 30 B4
Sevilla Tour & Tour Por Sevilla Bus Stop 31 D7
Sevilla Tour & Tour Por Sevilla Bus Stop (see 22)
Sevilla Tour Bus Stop 32 A3
Tour Por Sevilla Bus Stop 33 A3
See Central Seville Map (pp714–5)
To Osuna (91km); Málaga (217km); Granada (254km)
To Hospital Virgen del Rocio (900m)
To Fundación Cristina Heeren de Arte Flamenco (1.5km); Jerez de la Frontera (90km); Cádiz (123km)
Estadio Sánchez Pizjuán
Nervión
San Bernardo
Prado San Sebastián
Puerta de Jerez
Plaza de Cuba
Parque de los Príncipes
Jardines de la Buhaira
Barrio de Santa Cruz
Alcázar Gardens
Alcázar
Prado de San Sebastian
Plaza de España
Parque de María Luisa
Plaza de América
El Arenal
Triana
Los Remedios
Parque de los Remedios
El Real de la Feria
Feria de Abril Parque de Atracciones
Paseo de las Delicias
Paseo de Cristóbal Colón
Av de la Constitución
Av Menéndez Pelayo
Av de Eduardo Dato
C de Luis Montoto
C de Luis Morales
Av de Isabel la Católica
Av María Lusia
Av de la República Argentina
Ronda de María Auxiliadora-Los Remedios
Puente de Triana (Puente de Isabel II)
Puente de San Telmo
Puente del Generalísimo

ANDALUCÍA

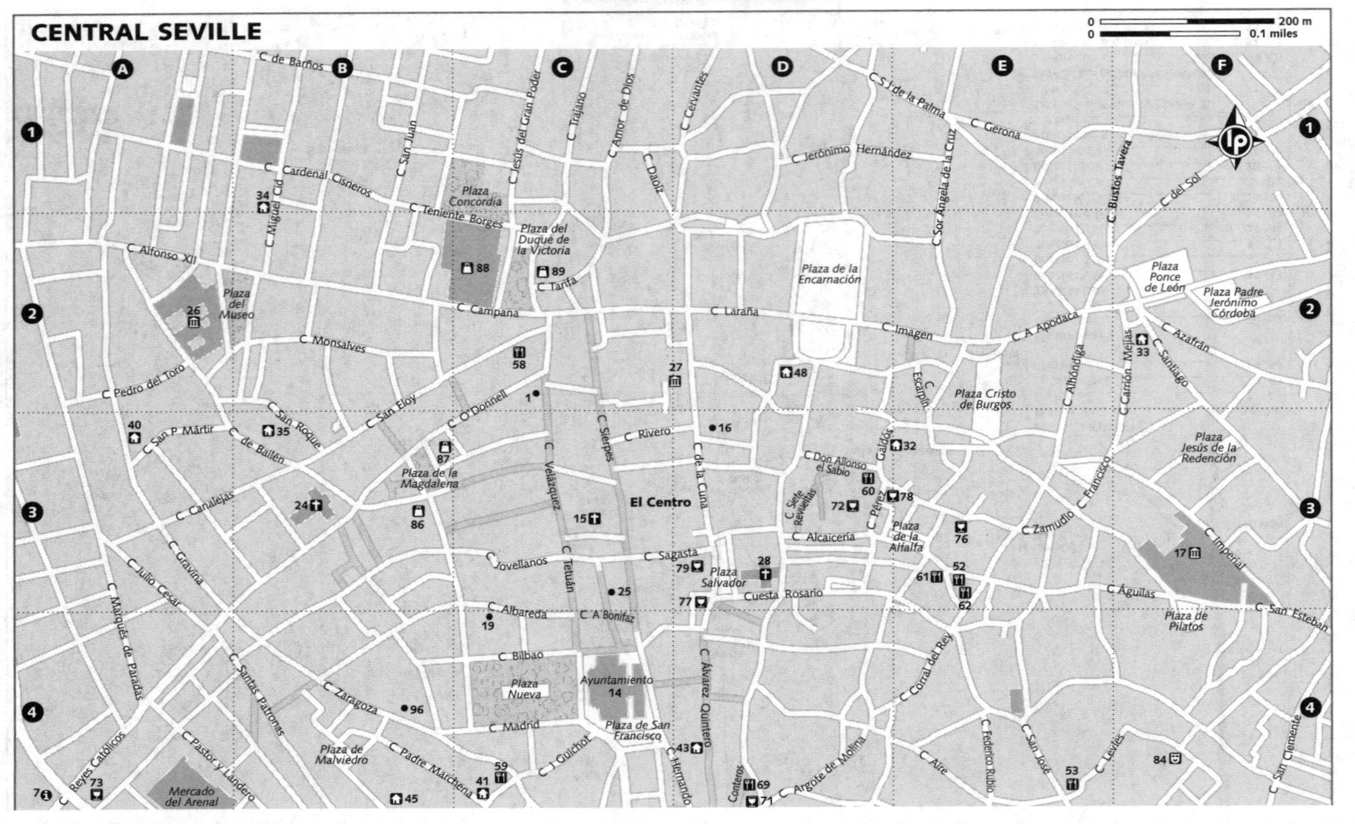
CENTRAL SEVILLE
0 200 m
0 0.1 miles
C de Baños
C Cardenal Cisneros
C Miguel Cid
C San Juan
C Teniente Borges
Plaza Concordia
C Jesús del Gran Poder
C Trajano
C Amor de Dios
C Daoíz
C Cervantes
C Jerónimo Hernández
C S J de la Palma
C Gerona
C Sor Ángela de la Cruz
C Bustos Tavera
C del Sol
Plaza del Duque de la Victoria
C Tarifa
C Alfonso XII
Plaza del Museo
C Campana
C Laraña
Plaza de la Encarnación
C Imagen
C A Apodaca
Plaza Ponce de León
Plaza Padre Jerónimo Córdoba
C Azafrán
C Santiago
C Carlón Mejías
C Alhóndiga
C Monsalves
C Pedro del Toro
C San Eloy
C O'Donnell
C Escarpín
Plaza Cristo de Burgos
C San P Mártir
C San Roque
C de Bailén
C Sierpes
C Rivero
C de la Cuna
C Don Alfonso el Sabio
C Galdós
Plaza Jesús de la Redención
C Francisco
Plaza de la Magdalena
C Velázquez
El Centro
C Siete Revueltas
C Pérez
C Zamudio
C Canalejas
C Alcaicería
Plaza de la Alfalfa
C Imperial
C Gravina
C Jovellanos
C Sagasta
C Tetuán
Plaza Salvador
C Julio César
Cuesta Rosario
C Águilas
C Marqués de Paradas
C Albareda
C A Bonifaz
Plaza de Pilatos
C San Esteban
C Bilbao
C Santas Patronas
Plaza Nueva
Ayuntamiento
C Álvarez Quintero
C Corral del Rey
C Zaragoza
C Madrid
Plaza de San Francisco
C Reyes Católicos
C Pastor y Landero
Plaza de Malviedro
C Padre Marchena
C J Guichot
C Hernando
C Contreros
C Argote de Molina
C Aire
C Federico Rubio
C San José
C Levíes
C San Clemente
Mercado del Arenal

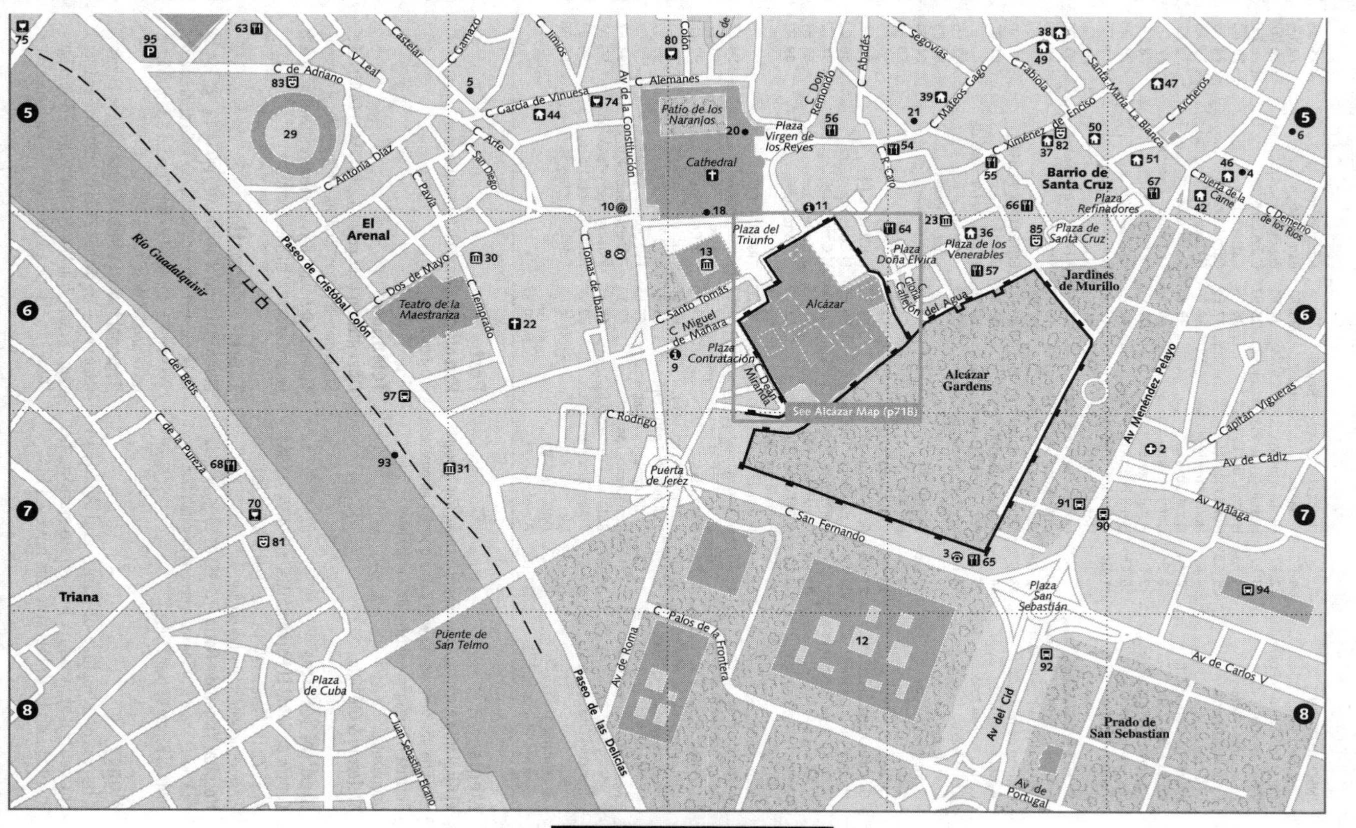
Barrio de Santa Cruz
Plaza Refinadores
Plaza de Santa Cruz
Plaza de los Venerables
Jardines de Murillo
Alcázar Gardens
Alcázar
See Alcázar Map (p718)
Plaza Doña Elvira
Callejón del Agua
C Gloria
Plaza del Triunfo
C Deán Miranda
Plaza Contratación
Cathedral
Patio de los Naranjos
Plaza Virgen de los Reyes
Av de la Constitución
Colón
C Alemanes
C Santo Tomás
C Miguel de Mañara
C Tomas de Ibarra
C Rodrigo
Puerta de Jerez
C San Fernando
C Palos de la Frontera
Av de Roma
Paseo de las Delicias
Puente de San Telmo
C Juan Sebastián Elcano
Plaza de Cuba
Plaza San Sebastián
Av del Cid
Av de Portugal
Prado de San Sebastian
Av de Carlos V
Av Málaga
Av de Cádiz
C Capitán Vigueras
Av Menéndez Pelayo
C Demetrio de los Ríos
C Puerta de la Carne
C Archeros
C Santa María La Blanca
C Fabiola
C Ximénez de Enciso
C Mateos Gago
C Segovias
C Abades
C R Caro
C Don Remondo
C Jimios
C García de Vinuesa
C Arfe
C San Diego
C Gamazo
C Castelar
C Pavía
C Temprado
Teatro de la Maestranza
C Dos de Mayo
El Arenal
C Antonia Díaz
C V Leal
C de Adriano
Paseo de Cristóbal Colón
Río Guadalquivir
C del Betis
C de la Pureza
Triana
ANDALUCÍA

INFORMATION
Casa del Libro 1 C2
Centro de Salud El Porvenir 2 F7
Ciber Alcázar 3 E7
La Segunda Vera 4 F5
Lavandería Roma 5 C5
LTC 6 F5
Municipal Tourist Office 7 A4
Post Office 8 C6
Regional Tourist Office 9 D6
Seville Internet Center 10 C5
Turismo Sevilla 11 D5

SIGHTS & ACTIVITIES
Antigua Fábrica de Tabacos (Universidad de Sevilla) 12 D8
Archivo de Indias 13 D6
Ayuntamiento 14 C4
Capilla de San José 15 C3
Carpe Diem 16 D3
Casa de Pilatos 17 F3
Cathedral Entrance 18 D5
CLIC 19 C4
Giralda 20 D5
Giralda Center 21 E5
Hospital de la Caridad 22 C6
Hospital de los Venerables Sacerdotes 23 E6
Iglesia de la Magdalena 24 B3
LINC 25 C3
Maritime Museum (see 31)
Museo de Bellas Artes 26 A2
Palacio de la Condesa de Lebrija 27 D2
Parroquia del Salvador 28 D3
Plaza de Toros de la Real Maestranza 29 B5
Reales Atarazanas (Royal Shipyards) 30 C6
Torre del Oro 31 C7

SLEEPING
Casa Sol y Luna 32 D3
Hospas las Casas del Rey de Baeza 33 F2
Hostal Museo 34 B1
Hostal Residencia Naranjo 35 B3
Hostería del Laurel 36 E6
Hotel Alcántara 37 E5
Hotel Amadeus 38 E5
Hotel Goya 39 E5
Hotel Madrid 40 A3
Hotel Maestranza 41 C4
Hotel Puerta de Sevilla 42 F5
Hotel San Francisco 43 D4
Hotel Simón 44 C5
Hotel Vincci La Rábida 45 B4
Huéspedes Dulces Sueños 46 F5
Las Casas de la Judería 47 F5
Oasis Backpackers Hostel 48 D2
Pensión Córdoba 49 E5
Pensión San Pancracio 50 E5
Un Patio en Santa Cruz 51 F5

EATING
Bar Alfalfa 52 E3
Bar Levíes 53 E4
Bodega Santa Cruz 54 E5
Café Bar Las Teresas 55 E5
Cervecería Giralda 56 D5
Corral del Agua 57 E6
El Patio San Eloy 58 C2
Enrique Becerra 59 C4
Habanita 60 D3
La Bodega 61 E3
La Trastienda 62 E3
Porta Rossa 63 B5
Restaurant La Cueva 64 E6
Restaurante Egaña Oriza 65 E7
Restaurante La Albahaca 66 E5
Restaurante Modesto 67 F5
Ristorante Cosa Nostra 68 B7
Robles Placentines 69 D4

DRINKING
Alambique 70 B7
Antigüedades 71 D5
Bare Nostrum 72 D3
Big Ben (see 70)
Cabo Loco (see 72)
Café Isbiliyya 73 A4
Casa Morales 74 C5
El Capote 75 A5
El Garlochi 76 E3
La Antigua Bodeguita 77 D3
La Rebótica 78 D3
La Sapotales 79 D3
Muí d'Aquí (see 70)
Nao (see 72)
P Flaherty Irish Pub 80 D5
Sirocca (see 70)

ENTERTAINMENT
Boss 81 B7
Casa de la Memoria de Al-Andalus 82 E5
Empresa Pagés 83 B5
La Carbonería 84 F4
Los Gallos 85 E6

SHOPPING
El Corte Inglés 86 C2
El Corte Inglés 87 C2
El Corte Inglés 88 B3
El Corte Inglés 89 B3

TRANSPORT
Bus 1 Stop 90 E7
Bus 36/37 Stop 91 E7
Bus C4 Stop 92 E8
Cruceros Turísticos Torre del Oro 93 B7
Estación de Autobuses Prado de San Sebastián 94 F7
Parking Paseo de Colón 95 A5
Renfe Ticket Office 96 B4
Sevilla Tour Bus Stop 97 B6

Media

El Giraldillo Andalucía-wide what's-on mag, free at tourist offices and some hotels, with a strong Seville emphasis.
Tourist Free mag for tourists with worthwhile information.
Welcome & Olé Ditto.

Medical Services

Centro de Salud El Porvenir (Map pp714-15; ☎ 954 71 23 23; cnr Avenidas Menéndez y Pelayo & de Cádiz) Public clinic with emergency service.
Hospital Virgen del Rocío (☎ 955 01 20 00; Avenida de Manuel Siurot s/n) The main general hospital, 1km south of Parque de María Luisa.

Money

There's no shortage of banks and ATMs in the central area. Santa Justa train station, the airport and both bus stations have ATMs.

Post

Post office (Map pp714-15; Avenida de la Constitución 32)

Telephone

Ciber Alcázar (Map pp714-15; ☎ 954 21 04 01; Calle San Fernando 35; 10.00am-11.00pm Mon-Fri, noon-11.00pm Sat & Sun) offers inexpensive international calls (as well as several internet booths).

Tourist Information

Municipal tourist office (Map pp714-15; ☎ 954 22 17 14; barranco.turismo@sevilla.org; Calle de Arjona 28; 9am-7.30pm Mon-Fri, 9am-2pm Sat & Sun, reduced hrs during Semana Santa & Feria de Abril)
Regional tourist offices Avenida de la Constitución 21 (Map pp714-15; ☎ 954 22 14 04; otsevilla@andalucia.org; 9am-7pm Mon-Fri, 10am-2pm & 3-7pm Sat, 10am-2pm Sun, closed holidays); Estación Santa Justa

(Map pp712-13; ☎ 954 53 76 26; ⏲ 9am-8pm Mon-Fri, 10am-2pm Sat & Sun, closed holidays).

Turismo Sevilla (Map pp714-15; ☎ 954 21 00 05; www.turismosevilla.org; Plaza del Triunfo 1; ⏲ 10.30am-7pm Mon-Fri)

SIGHTS

Seville's major monuments, the cathedral, the Giralda and the Alcázar complex, are all just east of Avenida de la Constitución and south of the city's true centre (El Centro). But there's plenty more to see and do in El Centro and around.

Cathedral & Giralda

After Seville fell to the Christians in 1248 its main mosque was used as a church until 1401 when, in view of its decaying state, the church authorities decided to knock it down and start again. Seville's **cathedral** (Map pp714-15; ☎ 954 21 49 71; adult/concession/under 12yr €7.50/1.50/free, admission free Sun; ⏲ 11am-6pm Mon-Sat, 2.30-7pm Sun Sep-Jun, 9.30am-4.30pm Mon-Sat, 2.30-7pm Sun Jul & Aug) is one of the largest in the world: the main building is 126m long and 83m wide. It was completed by 1507 and was originally Gothic, though work done after its central dome collapsed in 1511 was mostly in the Renaissance style. The original mosque's beautiful minaret, La Giralda, still stands on its eastern side (see right). There is wheelchair access.

SALA DEL PABELLÓN

Selected treasures from the cathedral's art collection are exhibited in this first room after the ticket office.

CATHEDRAL CHAPELS & STAINED GLASS

The sheer size of the broad, five-naved cathedral is obscured by a welter of interior decoration typical of Spanish cathedrals. Near the western end of the northern side is the **Capilla de San Antonio**, with Murillo's large 1666 canvas depicting the vision of St Anthony of Padua; thieves excised the kneeling saint in 1874 but he was found in New York and put back.

COLUMBUS' TOMB

Inside the cathedral's southern door stands the elaborate tomb of Christopher Columbus, dating from 1902. However, the remains within the tomb are the subject of heated debate, with some arguing that the explorer is (mainly) buried in the Dominican Republic.

CAPILLA MAYOR

Towards the east end of the main nave is the Capilla Mayor, whose Gothic altarpiece is the jewel of the cathedral and reckoned to be the biggest altarpiece in the world. Begun by Flemish sculptor Pieter Dancart in 1482 and completed by others by 1564, this sea of gilded and polychromed wood holds more than 1000 carved biblical figures.

SACRISTIES & CHAPTER HOUSE

South of the Capilla Mayor you'll find rooms containing many of the cathedral's art treasures. The westernmost of these is the **Sacristía de los Cálices** (Sacristy of the Chalices), where Goya's 1817 painting of the Seville martyrs *Santas Justa y Rufina* (potter sisters who died at the hands of the Romans in AD 287) hangs above the altar. A lion licks Rufina's feet, as reputedly happened when she was thrown to the said beasts during her travails. The room's centrepiece is the **Custodia de Juan de Arfe**, a huge 475kg silver monstrance made in the 1580s by Renaissance metal smith Juan de Arfe. Displayed in a glass case are the city keys handed to the conquering Fernando III in 1248.

The beautifully domed **cabildo** (chapter house), in the southeastern corner of the cathedral, was built between 1558 and 1592 to the designs of Hernán Ruiz, architect of the Giralda belfry. High above the archbishop's throne at the southern end is a Murillo masterpiece, *La Inmaculada*. Eight Murillo saints adorn the dome.

GIRALDA

In the northeastern corner of the cathedral interior you'll find the passage for the climb up the Giralda. The ascent is quite easy, as a series of ramps – built so that the guards could ride up on horseback – goes all the way up. The climb affords great views.

Over 90m high, La Giralda was the minaret of the mosque that stood on the site before the cathedral, constructed in brick by Almohad caliph Yusuf Yacub al-Mansur between 1184 and 1198. Its proportions, decoration and colour make it perhaps Spain's most perfect Islamic building. The topmost parts (from the bell level up) were added in the 16th century. At the very top is **El Giraldillo**, a 16th-century bronze weathervane, which represents Faith and is a symbol of Seville.

PATIO DE LOS NARANJOS

Planted with over 60 orange trees, this was originally the courtyard where Muslims performed ablutions before entering the mosque. On its north side is the beautiful Islamic Puerta del Perdón.

Alcázar

Residence of many generations of kings and caliphs, the **Alcázar** (Map pp714-15; ☎ 954 50 23 23; adult/under 16yr, senior, student, disabled €7/free; 🕒 9.30am-8pm Tue-Sat, to 6pm Sun & holidays Apr-Sep, to 6pm Tue-Sat, to 2.30pm Sun & holidays Oct-Mar) is Seville's answer to Granada's Alhambra. It stands south of the cathedral across Plaza del Triunfo and is wheelchair accessible. This intriguing complex is intimately associated with the life and loves of the extraordinary Pedro I of Castilla (1350–69).

Originally founded as a fort for the Cordoban governors of Seville in 913, the Alcázar has been expanded and rebuilt many times in its 11 centuries of existence. The Catholic Monarchs, Fernando and Isabel, set up court here in the 1480s as they prepared for the conquest of Granada. Later rulers created the Alcázar's lovely gardens.

PATIO DEL LEÓN

The Lion Patio was the garrison yard of the Al-Muwarak palace. Off here, the **Sala de la Justicia** (Hall of Justice), with beautiful Mudéjar plasterwork, was built in the 1340s by Alfonso XI, who disported here with his mistress Leonor de Guzmán. Alfonso's dalliances left his heir Pedro I (El Cruel/Justiciero) with five half-brothers and a severe case of sibling rivalry. One of the half-brothers, Don Fadrique, died in the Sala de la Justicia. The room gives on to the pretty **Patio del Yeso**, a 19th-century reconstruction of part of the 12th-century Almohad palace.

PATIO DE LA MONTERÍA

The rooms on the western side of this patio were part of the Casa de la Contratación, founded by the Catholic Monarchs in 1503 to control American trade. The **Sala de Audiencias** contains the earliest known painting on the discovery of the Americas (by Alejo Fernández, 1530s), in which Columbus, Fernando El Católico, Carlos I, Amerigo Vespucci and Native Americans can be seen sheltered beneath the Virgin in her role as protector of sailors.

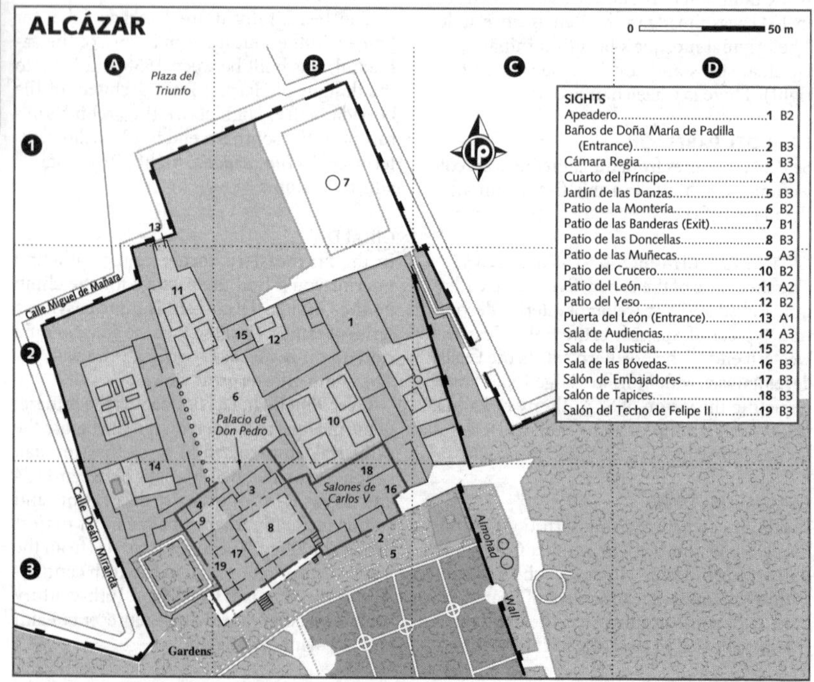

PALACIO DE DON PEDRO (MUDEJAR PALACE)

He might have been 'the Cruel', but between 1360 and 1364 Pedro I humbly built his exquisite palace in 'perishable' ceramics, plaster and wood, obedient to the Quran's prohibition against 'eternal' structures, reserved for the Creator.

At the heart of the palace is the wonderful **Patio de las Doncellas** (Patio of the Maidens), surrounded by beautiful arches and exquisite plasterwork and tiling. In 2004 archaeologists uncovered its original sunken garden from beneath a 16th-century marble covering.

The **Cámara Regia** (King's Quarters) on the northern side of the patio has two rooms with stunning ceilings. Just west is the small **Patio de las Muñecas** (Patio of the Dolls), the heart of the palace's private quarters, with delicate Granada-style decoration; indeed, plasterwork was actually brought here from the Alhambra in the 19th century. The **Cuarto del Príncipe** (Prince's Quarters), to its north, has a excellent wooden cupola ceiling recreating a starlit night sky and was probably the queen's bedroom.

The spectacular **Salón de Embajadores** (Hall of Ambassadors), off the western end of the Patio de las Doncellas, was Pedro I's throne room and incorporates caliphal-style door arches from the earlier Al-Muwarak palace. Its fabulous wooden dome of multiple star patterns, symbolising the universe, was added in 1427. On its western side, the beautiful **Arco de Pavones**, with peacock motifs, leads into the **Salón del Techo de Felipe II**.

SALONES DE CARLOS V

Reached by a staircase from the Patio de las Doncellas, these are the rooms of Alfonso X's 13th-century Gothic palace, much remodelled since his time. It was here that Alfonso's intellectual court gathered and, a century later, Pedro I installed the mistress he loved, María de Padilla. The **Sala de las Bóvedas** (Hall of the Vault) is adorned with beautiful 1570s tiling, while the **Salón de Tapices** (Tapestry Room) has huge 18th-century tapestries showing Carlos I's 1535 conquest of Tunis.

GARDENS & EXIT

From the Salones de Carlos V, enter the Alcázar's large gardens. Those in front of the Salones de Carlos V and Palacio de Don Pedro were mostly brought to their present form in the 16th and 17th centuries, while those to the east are 20th-century creations. From the little **Jardín de las Danzas** (Garden of the Dances) a passage runs beneath the Salones de Carlos V to the grotto known as the **Baños de Doña María de Padilla**.

From the new gardens you can leave the Alcázar via the **Apeadero**, a 17th-century entrance hall, and the **Patio de las Banderas** (Patio of the Banners).

Archivo de Indias

On the western side of Plaza del Triunfo, the **Archivo de Indias** (Map pp714-15; ☎ 954 21 12 34; Calle Santo Tomás, admission free; ⌚ 10am-4pm Mon-Sat, 10am-2pm Sun & holidays, closed 25 Dec, 1 & 6 Jan & Good Friday) is the main archive on Spain's American empire, with 80 million pages of documents dating from 1492 through to the end of the empire in the 19th century: a most effective statement of Spain's power and influence during its Golden Age.

Barrio de Santa Cruz

Seville's medieval *judería* (Map pp714–15; Jewish quarter), east of the cathedral and Alcázar, is today a tangle of quaint, winding streets and lovely plant-decked plazas perfumed with orange blossom. Its most characteristic plaza today is **Plaza de Santa Cruz**, which gives the *barrio* its name.

The 17th-century **Hospital de los Venerables Sacerdotes** (Map pp714-15; ☎ 954 56 26 96; Plaza de los Venerables 8; adult/student & senior/under 12yr €4.75/2.40/free, admission free Sun afternoon; ⌚ 10am-2pm & 4-8pm) was a residence for aged priests, and has a lovely central courtyard.

El Centro

The real centre of Seville is the densely packed zone of narrow streets north of the cathedral (Map pp714–15).

PLAZA DE SAN FRANCISCO & CALLE SIERPES

Plaza de San Francisco has been Seville's main public square since the 16th century. The southern end of the **ayuntamiento** (town hall; Map pp714-15) here is encrusted with lovely Renaissance carving from the 1520s and '30s.

Pedestrianised Calle Sierpes, heading north from the plaza, and the parallel Calle Tetuán/Velázquez are the hub of Seville's fanciest shopping zone. Between the two streets is the 18th-century **Capilla de San**

José (Map pp714-15; Calle Jovellanos; 8am-12.30pm & 6.30-8.30pm), with breathtakingly intense baroque ornamentation.

The **Palacio de la Condesa de Lebrija** (Map pp714-15; ☎ 954 22 78 02; Calle de la Cuna 8; whole bldg/ground fl only admission €8/4; 10.30am-1.30pm & 5-8pm Mon-Fri, 10am-1.30pm Sat), a block east of Calle Sierpes, is a 16th-century noble mansion remodelled in 1914 by traveller and art connoisseur Doña Regla Manjón, Countess of Lebrija.

PLAZA SALVADOR

This plaza, which has a few popular bars, was once the forum of Roman Hispalis. It's dominated by the **Parroquia del Salvador** (Map pp714–15), a big baroque church built between 1674 and 1712 on the site of Muslim Ishbiliya's main mosque. The interior reveals a fantastic richness of carving and gilding. At sunset, colour from stained glass windows plays on the carvings to enhance their surreal beauty.

CASA DE PILATOS

Another of the city's finest noble **mansions** (Map pp714-15; ☎ 954 22 52 98; Calle Águilas; whole house/lower fl only admission €8/5, EU citizen 1-5pm Tue free; 9am-7pm Apr-Oct, 9am-6pm Nov-Mar), 500m northeast of the cathedral, is still occupied by the ducal Medinaceli family. This extensive and splendid 16th-century building is a mixture of diverse architectural styles.

ANDALUCÍA

El Arenal

A short walk west from Avenida de la Constitución brings you to the bank of Río Guadalquivir, lined by a pleasant footpath. The nearby district of El Arenal (Map pp714–15) is home to some of Seville's most interesting sights.

TORRE DEL ORO

This 13th-century riverbank Islamic watchtower supposedly had a dome covered in golden tiles, hence 'Tower of Gold'. Inside is a small **maritime museum** (Map pp714-15; ☎ 954 22 24 19; admission adult/students & seniors, €2/1; 10am-2pm Tue-Fri, 11am-2pm Sat & Sun, closed Mon, holidays & all Aug).

ROYAL SHIPYARDS

King Alfonso X 'the Wise' commissioned the **Royal Shipyards** (Map pp714-15; ☎ 954 21 66 72; Calle Temprado 1; admission free; 10am-6pm Mon-Sat, to 2pm Sun & holidays) in 1252. In all, 17 *naves* or bays were built on what were then the sandy banks of the Guadalquivir. After some years as a customs shed, it became an army arsenal and warehouse in the 18th century, then languished until 1993. It's now being restored and is destined to be the splendid new home of the city's maritime museum.

HOSPITAL DE LA CARIDAD

A marvellous sample of Sevillean golden-age art adorns the church in this **charity hospice** (Map pp714-15; ☎ 954 22 32 32; Calle Temprado 3; admission €5 with audioguide, free Sun & holidays for EU citizens; 9am-1.30pm & 3.30-7.30pm Mon-Sat, to 1pm Sun & holidays) a block from the river. The hospital was founded in the 17th century by Miguel de Mañara, a legendary libertine who changed his ways after experiencing a vision of his own funeral procession. Seventeenth-century masterpieces include Valdés Leal's frightening *In Ictu Oculi* (In the Blink of an Eye) and *Finis Gloriae Mundi* (The End of Earthly Glory).

PLAZA DE TOROS DE LA REAL MAESTRANZA

Seville's **bullring** (Map pp714-15; ☎ 954 22 45 77; www.realmaestranza.es; Paseo de Cristóbal Colón 12; tours adult/over-65 €5/4; half-hourly 9.30am-7pm Nov-Apr, 9.30am-8pm, May-Oct, 9.30am-3pm bullfighting days, closed Good Friday & Christmas Day) is one of the most handsome in Spain and probably the oldest (building began in 1758). It was here, and in the ring at Ronda, that bullfighting on foot (instead of horseback) began in the 18th century.

MUSEO DE BELLAS ARTES

Set in a beautiful former convent, Seville's **fine-arts museum** (Map pp714-15; ☎ 954 78 65 00; Plaza del Museo 9; adult/EU citizen, retired, students, €1.50/free; 2.30-8.30pm Tue, 9am-8.30pm Wed-Sat, to 2.30pm Sun, closed Mon) does full justice to Seville's leading role in Spain's artistic golden age. The museum is wheelchair accessible.

South of the Centre

ANTIGUA FÁBRICA DE TABACOS

Seville's massive former **tobacco factory** (Map pp714-15; Calle San Fernando; admission free; 8am-9.30pm Mon-Fri, to 2pm Sat) – workplace of Bizet's passionate operatic heroine, Carmen – was built in the 18th century. It's wheelchair accessible.

PARQUE DE MARÍA LUISA & PLAZA DE ESPAÑA

A large area south of the tobacco factory was transformed for Seville's 1929 international fair, the Exposición Iberoamericana, when architects adorned it with fantastical buildings, many of them harking back to Seville's past glory or imitating the native styles of Spain's former colonies. In its midst is the large **Parque de María Luisa** (Map pp712-13; 8am-10pm, to midnight Jul & Aug), a living expression of Seville's Moorish and Christian past.

Plaza de España, one of the city's favourite relaxation spots, faces the park across Avenida de Isabel la Católica. Around it is the most grandiose of the 1929 buildings, a semicircular brick-and-tile confection featuring Seville tilework at its gaudiest.

On Plaza de América, at the southern end of the park, is Seville's **Museo Arqueológico** (Map pp712-13; ☎ 954 78 64 74; adult/EU citizen, under 16yr & senior €1.50/free; 2.30-8.30pm Tue, 9am-8.30pm Wed-Sat, to 2.30pm Sun & holidays), with plenty to interest. Facing it is the **Museo de Artes y Costumbres Populares** (Map pp712-13; ☎ 954 23 25 76; adult/EU citizen €1.50/free; 3-8pm Tue, 9am-8pm Wed-Sat, to 2.30pm Sun & holidays). Both are wheelchair accessible.

Isla Mágica

This Disney-goes-Spanish-colonial **amusement park** (Map pp712-13; ☎ 902 16 17 16; www.islamagica.es; adult/under 16yr & senior late Jun–mid-Sep all day €23.50/17-19, evening €17-19/12-14, late Sep-late Oct all day €23.50/17, evening €17/12; 11am-7pm Tue-Fri, to 10pm Sat & Sun Apr-late Jun, to 11pm Mon-Fri & Sun, to midnight Sat late Jun-early Sep, to 9pm Fri & Sat early Sep-Oct, closed Nov-Mar) provides a great day out for kids and all lovers of white-knuckle rides. Confirm times before going.

Both buses C1 and C2 (p729) run to Isla Mágica.

WALKING TOUR

This route will acquaint you with the main central neighbourhoods of Seville as a preliminary to more in-depth investigations. In addition, **Turismo Sevilla** (☎ 954 21 00 05; www.turismosevilla.org; Plaza del Triunfo 1; 10.30am-7pm Mon-Fri) publishes an excellent pocket booklet with self-guided walks around the city

WALK FACTS

Start Plaza del Triunfo
Finish Cathedral
Distance 4km
Duration Two hours plus stops

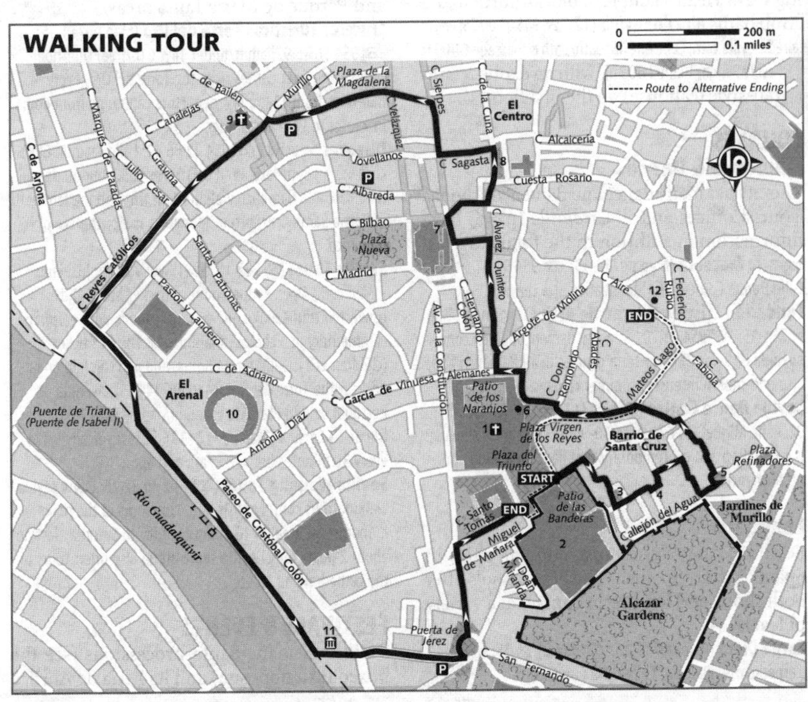

defined by special interests, including the Jewish Quarter, Triana and the River, and the Parque de Maria Luisa.

Start on Plaza del Triunfo, flanked by Seville's two great monuments, the **cathedral** (**1**; p717) and the **Alcázar** (**2**; p718). From here, wander through the narrow lanes and pretty plazas of the Barrio de Santa Cruz – **Plaza Doña Elvira** (**3**; **p719**), **Plaza de los Venerables** (**4**) and **Plaza de Santa Cruz** (**5**; p719), Calle Santa Teresa and Calle Mateos Gago. You'll very likely want to return to some of the bars, restaurants and shops here later. Calle Mateos Gago brings you out front of **La Giralda** (**6**; p717). Now head up pedestrian Calle Álvarez Quintero to El Centro, the age-old true centre of Seville, for **Plaza de San Francisco** (**7**; p719) and **Plaza Salvador** (**8**; p719). Stroll north along Calle Sierpes, a key downtown shopping street. Turn west along Calle Rioja to **Iglesia de la Magdalena** (**9**; opposite), then head southwest to Río Guadalquivir. Follow the river southeast along the walking path, passing **Plaza de Toros de la Real Maestranza** (**10**; p720), as far as the **Torre del Oro** (**11**; p720), from where it's a short walk east back to the cathedral. Time to give those weary sightseeing muscles a soothing soak? Head a couple of blocks north to the Arab baths **Aire de Sevilla** (**12**; ☎ 955 01 00 25; www.airedesevilla.com; Calle Aire 15; bath/bath & massage €18/31; ⏰ every 90min, 10am-1.30am), with an exotic *teteria* (Arab-style teahouse) on the first floor.

ANDALUCÍA

COURSES

Flamenco & Dance

The city has many dance and flamenco schools. Tourist offices and *El Giraldillo* (p716) have information in addition to the following:

Espacio Meteora (Map pp712-13; ☎ 954 90 41 83; Calle Duque Cornejo 16A) Innovative arts centre.

Fundación Cristina Heeren de Arte Flamenco (Map pp714-15; ☎ 954 21 70 58; www.flamencoheeren.com; Avenida de Jerez 2) Long-term courses in all flamenco arts, also one-month intensive summer courses.

Sevilla Dance Centre (Map pp712-13; ☎ 954 38 39 02; Calle Miguel Cid 67; ⏰ 5.30-9pm) The Centre's focus is on hip hop and contemporary/jazz dance teaching and performance.

Language

Seville is one of the most popular cities in Spain to study Spanish. The best schools offer both short- and long-term courses at a variety of levels:

Carpe Diem (Map pp714-15; ☎ 954 21 85 15; www.carpediemsevilla.com; Calle de la Cuna 13)

CLIC (Map pp714-15; ☎ 954 50 21 31; www.clic.es; Calle Albareda 19)

Giralda Center (Map pp714-15; ☎ 954 22 13 46/954 21 31 65; www.giraldacenter.com; Calle Mateos Gago 17)

Lenguaviva (Map pp712-13; ☎ 954 90 51 31; www.lenguaviva.net; Calle Viriato 24)

LINC (Map pp714-15; ☎ 954 50 04 59; www.linc.es; Calle General Polavieja 13)

SEVILLE FOR CHILDREN

Open spaces such as the banks of the Guadalquivir, Parque María Luisa (p720) and the Alcázar gardens (p719) are great places for young children to let off some steam. They'll enjoy feeding the doves at Plaza de América in Parque María Luisa. Isla Mágica (p721) is a huge day of fun: those aged over 10 will get the most out of the rides. Another sure hit is a city tour (below) in an open-top double-decker or horse-drawn carriage.

TOURS

Horse-drawn carriages wait near the cathedral, Plaza de España and Puerta de Jerez, charging €40 for up to four people for a one-hour trot around the Barrio de Santa Cruz and Parque de María Luisa areas.

Cruceros Turísticos Torre del Oro (Map pp714-15; ☎ 954 56 16 92; adult/under 14yr €16/free) One-hour sightseeing river cruises from the Torre del Oro, every half-hour from 11am; last departure can range from 6pm in winter to 9pm in summer.

Discover Sevilla (☎ 954 22 66 42; Calle Joaquín Guichot 6; ⏰ 8pm-late, Wed & Fri). For €59, your guide will take you on a flamenco walking tour through the labyrinth of Barrio Santa Cruz, often claimed as the birthplace of flamenco.

Sevilla Tour (☎ 902 10 10 81; www.citysightseeing-spain.com) Open-topped double-decker buses and converted trams make one-hour city tours, with earphone commentary in a choice of languages. The €15 ticket (children €6) is valid for 24 hours, and you can hop on or off near the Torre del Oro (Map pp714–15), Avenida de Portugal behind Plaza de España (Map pp712–13) or the Isla de La Cartuja (Map pp712–13). Buses typically leave every 30 minutes between 7am and 8pm.

Sevilla Walking Tours (☎ 902 15 82 26; www.sevillawalkingtours.com) English-language tours of the main monumental area, at 10.30am Monday to Saturday lasting about 2 hours for €12. The same group also offers tours of the cathedral and Alcázar.

FESTIVALS & EVENTS

Seville's Semana Santa processions (see the boxed text, opposite) and its Feria de Abril, a week or two later, are worth travelling a long way for, as is the Bienal de Flamenco.

Feria de Abril

In the second half of the month, the **Feria de Abril** (April Fair) is the joyful celebration after the solemnity of Semana Santa. The biggest and most colourful of all Andalucía's *ferias*, it takes place on a special site, El Real de la Feria, in the Los Remedios area southwest of the city centre. The ceremonial lighting of the *feria* grounds on the Monday night is the starting gun for six nights of partying. Much of the site is occupied by private *casetas* (enclosures), but there are also public ones. There's also a huge fairground.

During the afternoon, from aroud 1pm, those with horses and carriages parade about the *feria* grounds in their finery (horses are dressed up, too). It is also during the *feria*

SEMANA SANTA IN SEVILLE

Nowhere in Spain is Holy Week marked with quite such intense spectacle, solemnity and joy as in Seville.

Every day from Palm Sunday to Easter Sunday, large, richly bedecked images and life-size tableaux from the Easter story are carried from Seville's churches through the streets to the cathedral, accompanied by processions that may take more than an hour to pass. These rites have been going on in their present form since the 17th century, when many of the images were created.

The processions are organised by over 50 different *hermandades* or *cofradías* (brotherhoods, some of which include women), each normally with two *pasos* (sculptural representations of events from Christ's Passion).

The first *paso* focuses on Christ; the second is an image of the Virgin. They are carried by teams of about 40 bearers called *costaleros,* who work in relays as each supports a weight of about 50kg. The *pasos* move with a hypnotic swaying motion to the rhythm of their accompanying bands and the commands of their bell-striking *capataz* (leader).

Each pair of *pasos* has up to 2500 costumed followers, called *nazarenos*. Many of these wear tall capes, notoriously copied later by the Ku Klux Klan, which cover their heads (except for eye slits), implying that the identity of the penitent is known only to God. The most contrite go barefoot and carry crosses.

From Palm Sunday to Good Friday, about eight brotherhoods leave their churches in the afternoon or early evening, arriving between 5pm and 11pm at Calle Campana, at the northern end of Calle Sierpes. This is the start of the *carrera oficial* (official route), which all then follow along Calle Sierpes, Plaza San Francisco and Avenida de la Constitución to the cathedral. They enter the cathedral at its western end and leave at the east, emerging on Plaza Virgen de los Reyes. They get back to their churches some time between 10pm and 3am.

The climax of the week is the *madrugada* (early hours) of Good Friday, when some of the most respected brotherhoods file through the city. The first to reach the *carrera oficial,* at about 1.30am, is the oldest brotherhood, El Silencio, which goes in complete silence. At about 2am comes Jesús del Gran Poder, whose 17th-century Christ is a masterpiece of Sevillan sculpture. Around 3am comes La Macarena, whose much adored Virgin is Seville's supreme representation of the grieving-yet-hoping mother of Christ. Then come El Calvario, from the Iglesia de la Magdalena, then Esperanza de Triana and finally, at about 6am, Los Gitanos, the *gitano* (Roma) brotherhood.

On the Saturday evening, just four brotherhoods make their way to the cathedral, and finally, on Easter Sunday morning, only one, the Hermandad de la Resurrección.

Procession schedules are widely available during Semana Santa, and the website www.semana-santa.org (in Spanish) is devoted to Holy Week in Seville. Arrive near the cathedral early evening for a better view.

If you're not in Seville for Semana Santa, you can see what it's about from some of the churches housing the famous images. The **Basílica de La Macarena** (Map pp712-13; ☎ 954 90 18 00; Calle Bécquer 1; museum €3; 🕑 9am-2pm & 5-9pm) and the **Basílica de Jesús del Gran Poder** (Map pp712-13; ☎ 954 91 56 72; Plaza de San Lorenzo 13; 🕑 8am-1.30pm & 6-9pm Sat-Thu, 7.30am-10pm Fri) are both north of the centre. The **Iglesia de la Magdalena** (Map pp714-15; Calle San Pablo 12; 🕑 usually 8am-11.30am & 6.30-9pm) is a few streets south of the Museo de Bellas Artes.

that Seville's major bullfighting season takes place.

Bienal de Flamenco

Spain's biggest flamenco festival, the **Bienal de Flamenco** (www.bienal-flamenco.org), is staged for a month in September of even-numbered years, and brings together the best of classical and experimental music and dance.

SLEEPING

There's a good range of places to stay in all three of the most attractive areas – Barrio de Santa Cruz (close to the Alcázar and within walking distance of Prado de San Sebastián bus station), El Arenal (convenient for Plaza de Armas bus station) and El Centro.

Room rates in this section are for each establishment's high season – typically from March to June and again from September to October. Just about every room in Seville costs even more during Semana Santa and the Feria de Abril, and sometimes between the two as well, so try to book ahead for this time.

Renting a tourist apartment here can be good value: typically costing under €100 a night for four people, or between €30 and €70 for two. Try **Apartamentos Embrujo de Sevilla** (☎ 627 569919; www.embrujodesevilla.com), which specialises in historic town mansion apartments, or **Sevilla5.com** (☎ 637 011091, 954 22 62 87; www.sevilla5.com).

Barrio de Santa Cruz

BUDGET

Huéspedes Dulces Sueños (Map pp714-15; ☎ 954 41 93 93; Calle Santa María La Blanca 21; s/d with bathroom €40/50, without bathroom €20/45;) 'Sweet Dreams' is a friendly little *hostal* (budget hotel) with spotless rooms. Only the doubles have air-conditioning.

Pensión San Pancracio (Map pp714-15; ☎ /fax 954 41 31 04; Plaza de las Cruces 9; d with bathroom €50, s/d without bathroom €25/35) The furnishings are almost as old as the rambling family house, but it's all cheerful and clean.

Pensión Córdoba (Map pp714-15; ☎ 954 22 74 98; Calle Farnesio 12; s/d with bathroom €55/75, s/d without bathroom €40/60;) Run for the past 30 years by a friendly older couple. It's located on a quiet pedestrian street. Rooms are basic but spotless.

MIDRANGE & TOP END

Hotel Puerta de Sevilla (Map pp714-15; ☎ 954 98 72 70; www.hotelpuertadesevilla.com; Calle Puerta de la Carne 2; s/d €66/86; P) A small shiny hotel in a great location, the Puerta de Sevilla is all flower-pattern textiles and wrought-iron beds.

Hotel Goya (Map pp714-15; ☎ 954 21 11 70 www.hotelgoyasevilla.com; Calle Mateos Gago 31; s/d €55/90;) The gleaming Goya is more popular than ever. Pets are welcome. Book ahead.

Hotel Alcántara (Map pp714-15; ☎ 954 50 05 95; www.hotelalcantara.net; Calle Ximénez de Enciso 28; s/d €68/89;) This small, friendly hotel on a pedestrian street punches above its weight with sparkling modern bathrooms, windows on to the hotel's patio and pretty floral curtains. It's also wheelchair accessible.

Un Patio en Santa Cruz (Map pp714-15; ☎ 954 53 94 13; www.patiosantacruz.com; Calle Doncellas 15; s/d €78/128;) An understated hotel defying the elaborate traditions of Andalucian decor.

Hotel Amadeus (Map pp714-15; ☎ 954 50 14 43; www.hotelamadeussevilla.com; Calle Farnesio 6; s/d €80/90; P) This musician family converted their 18th-century mansion into a stylish hotel with 14 elegant rooms. Five new rooms have been added, one or two soundproofed for piano or violin practice.

Hostería del Laurel (Map pp714-15; ☎ 954 22 02 95; www.hosteriadellaurel.com; Plaza de los Venerables 5; s/d incl breakfast €73/104;) Above a characterful old bar of the same name on a small Santa Cruz plaza, the Laurel has spacious if uninspired rooms and good-sized bathrooms on one of the city's prettiest plazas.

Las Casas de la Judería (Map pp714-15; ☎ 954 41 51 50; www.casasypalacios.com; Callejón Dos Hermanas 7; s/d from €140/175; P) This charming five-star hotel is in fact a series of luxuriously restored houses and mansions based around several patios and fountains.

El Arenal

Hotel Madrid (Map pp714-15; ☎ 954 21 43 06; www.hotelmadridsevilla.com; Calle San Pedro Mártir 22; s/d €40/55; P) This friendly hotel remains pretty good value. All the good-sized rooms have firm beds, fresh decor and spacious bathrooms.

Hostal Museo (Map pp714-15; ☎ 954 91 55 26; www.hostalmuseo.com; Calle Abad Gordillo 17; s/d €48/60;) The immaculate rooms are endowed with solid wooden furniture and comfortable beds.

Hostal Residencia Naranjo (Map pp714-15; ☎ 954 22 58 40; Calle San Roque 11; s/d €49/65;) Homely pine furniture and restful colours add a touch of warmth.

Hotel Maestranza (Map pp714-15; ☎ 954 56 10 70; www.hotel-maestranza.es; Calle Gamazo 12; s/d €53/87;

) A small, friendly hotel on a quietish street, the Maestranza has spotless, plain rooms.

Hotel Simón (Map pp714-15; 954 22 66 60; www.hotelsimonsevilla.com; Calle García de Vinuesa 19; s €60-70, d €95-110;) A charming small hotel in a grand old 18th-century house, with spotless and comfortable rooms. Even the light filtering into the antique patio seems dipped in tea.

Hotel Vincci La Rábida (Map pp714-15; 954 50 12 80; www.vinccihoteles.com; Calle Castelar 24; s/d €159/195;) A beautiful four-storey columned atrium-lounge greets you in this converted 18th-century palace.

El Centro

Oasis Backpackers' Hostel (Map pp714-15; 954 29 37 77; www.oasissevilla.com; Plaza de la Encarnación 29, dm/d incl breakfast €20/46;) Seville's offbeat, buzzing backpacker central offers 24-hour free internet access. The new location is in Plaza Encarnación, a narrow street behind the Church of the Anunciación. Each dorm bed has a personal safe, and there is a small rooftop pool. Oasis also has several apartments at Calle Don Alonso el Sabio 1A (Map pp714–15).

Casa Sol y Luna (Map pp714-15; 954 21 06 82; www.casasolyluna1.com; Calle Pérez Galdós 1A; d with bathroom €45, s/d/tr without bathroom €22/38/60) This is a first-rate *hostal* in a beautifully decorated house dating from 1911, with embroidered white linen that makes you feel as if you're staying at your grandma's. Pay special attention to the 24-hour booking confirmation policy.

Hotel San Francisco (Map pp714-15; /fax 954 50 15 41; www.sanfranciscoh.com; Calle Álvarez Quintero 38; s/d €55/68; closed Aug;) This good-value hotel on a pedestrianised street occupies an 18th-century home and is wheelchair accessible.

Hospas Casas del Rey de Baeza (Map pp714-15; 954 56 14 96; www.hospes.es; Plaza Jesús de la Redención 2; s/d €168/210;) This expertly run and marvellously designed hotel off Calle Santiago occupies former communal housing patios dating from the 18th century. The large rooms boast attractive modern art, CD player, DVD and wi-fi. Public areas include a lounge and a gorgeous pool.

North of the Centre

Hotel San Gil (Map pp712-13; 954 90 68 11; www.hotelsangil.com; Calle Parras 28; s/d €141/176;) Around the corner from the Basílica de la Macarena, this renovated early-20th-century building focuses on a pretty courtyard. Rooms are hushed, spacious and decorated in relaxing neutrals.

EATING

Seville is one of Spain's tapas capitals, so plunge straight in and follow the winding tapas trail. Most tapas bars open at lunchtime as well as in the evening.

For a sit-down meal, modern restaurants preparing Spanish food with enlivening international touches abound. Don't bother looking for dinner until at least 9pm, nearer 10pm in summer.

Barrio de Santa Cruz & Around

Bodega Santa Cruz (Map pp714-15; 954 21 32 46; Calle Mateos Gago; tapas €1.50-2) Established neighbourhood tapas haunt with smoke-tempered paintwork, obligatory TV and religious pin-ups. The long bar props up local workers and tourists.

Café Bar Las Teresas (Map pp714-15; 954 21 30 69; Calle Santa Teresa 2; tapas €2.20-4) Head barman Pepe has served thousands of punters here since 1962, including Edward Kennedy in 1964. He will be happy to share the experience with you in this convivial corner of old Seville.

Cervecería Giralda (Map pp714-15; 954 22 82 50; Calle Mateos Gago 1; tapas €3.50-5) Exotic tapas variations are merged with traditional dishes in this one-time Muslim bathhouse.

Restaurant La Cueva (Map pp714-15; 954 21 31 43; Calle Rodrigo Caro 18 & Plaza de Doña Elvira, 1; mains €11-24, menú €16) This popular bull's head-festooned eatery cooks up a storming fish *zarzuela* (casserole; €30 for two people) and a hearty *caldereta* (lamb stew; €14.90).

Restaurante Modesto (Map pp714-15; 954 41 68 11; Calle Cano y Cueto 5 (Puerta de la Carne); mains €11-34) This bustling, unpretentious place is famed for its lobster and monkfish stew.

Corral del Agua (Map pp714-15; 954 22 48 41; Callejón del Agua 6; mains €16.50-22; lunch & dinner Mon-Sat) Inventive Al-Andalus and traditional dishes are served in a semitropical courtyard under a twining canopy of vines and jacaranda.

Restaurante La Albahaca (Map pp714-15; 954 22 07 14; Plaza de Santa Cruz 12; mains €20-30) Gastronomic invention is the mainstay of this elegant, gilded restaurant with its azure blue interior. Try the leg of duck confit in a sauce of bitter orange and rosemary honey.

Restaurante Egaña Oriza (Map pp714-15; 954 22 72 11; Calle San Fernando 41; mains €22-32; closed Sat lunch & Sun) Regarded as one of the city's best restaurants, Egaña Oriza cooks up superb Andalucian–Basque cuisine, including lasagne with seafood, lobster and truffles.

El Arenal

Mesón Cinco Jotas (Map pp714-15; ☎ 954 21 05 21; Calle Castelar 1; tapas/media raciones €3.80/9.45) Try some of the best *jamón* in town here and move on to the *solomillo ibérico* (Iberian pork sirloin) in sweet Pedro Ximénez wine for the peak of porcine flavour.

Porta Rossa (Map pp714-15; ☎ 954 21 61 39; Calle Pastor y Landero 20; mains €8.50-19) Excellent ingredients make a fine basis for authentic Italian classics starring a tender steak salad with arugula in a tart balsamic and lemon dressing. The owners and staff are friendly and attentive. It's best to reserve early.

Enrique Becerra (Map pp714-15; ☎ 954 21 30 49; Calle Gamazo 2; mains €16.50-24; closed Sat & Sun) Adding a smart touch to El Arenal, Enrique Becerra cooks up hearty Andalucian dishes. The lamb drenched in honey sauce and stuffed with spinach and pine nuts is delectable.

El Centro

Plaza de la Alfalfa is the hub of the tapas scene, with a flush of first-rate bars serving tapas from around €1.80 to €3. On Calle Alfalfa just off the plaza, hop from sea-themed La Trastienda to the intimate Bar Alfalfa and on to La Bodega where you can mix head-spinning quantities of ham and sherry.

El Patio San Eloy (Map pp714-15; Calle San Eloy 9; tapas €1.50-3) Patches of old tiling remain at the always-busy Patio San Eloy, where you can sit on the tiled steps at the back and feast on a fine array of *burguillos* (small filled rolls).

Bar Levíes (Map pp714-15; ☎ 954 21 53 08; Calle San José 15; tapas €2-5) The ultimate student tapas bar, crowded Levíes serves a tapa of *solomillo al whisky* as big as a ración – and beer in big glasses.

Robles Placentines (Map pp714-15; ☎ 954 21 31 62; Calle Placentines 2; tapas €2.90) Modelled on a Jerez wine cellar, this popular haunt serves up tempting dishes such as white asparagus from the Sierra de Córdoba.

Alameda de Hércules

Antigua Abacería de San Lorenzo (Map pp712-13; ☎ 954 38 00 67; www.antiguaabaceriadesanlorenzo.com; Calle Teodosio 53; tapas €1-5; 9.30am-midnight every day, closed 5pm-8pm Sat & Sun Jun-Sep) A traditional combination of provisions store/deli/tapas bar and prepared food takeaway in a cleverly restored 17th-century house.

Habanita (Map pp714-15; ☎ 606 716456; Calle Golfo 3; raciones €8-15; closed Sun evening; V) This top restaurant serves a winning variety of Cuban, Andalucian and vegetarian food.

Triana

There are several big riverside restaurants along Calle del Betis, all serving much the same fried seafood and other traditional dishes. Beware of overpriced venues with indifferent food.

Ristorante Cosa Nostra (Map pp714-15; ☎ 954 27 07 52; Calle del Betis 52; pizzas €8.50-12; closed Mon) Popular and reasonably priced, Cosa Nostra has an intimate feel that neighbouring pizza-and-pasta joints lack.

Casa Cuesta (Map pp712-13; ☎ 954 33 33 37; Calle de Castilla 3-5; mains €9-10) Something about the carefully buffed wooden bar and gleaming beer pumps suggests the owners are proud of Casa Cuesta. They should be; it's a real find for food and wine lovers alike.

DRINKING

Bars usually open 6pm to 2am weekdays, 8pm till 3am at the weekend. Drinking and partying really get going around midnight on Friday and Saturday (daily when it's hot). In summer, dozens of open-air late-night bars *(terrazas de verano)* spring up along both banks of the river.

Barrio de Santa Cruz

P Flaherty Irish Pub (Map pp714-15; ☎ 954 21 04 17; Calle Alemanes 7) The location right next to the cathedral makes this one of the busiest – and biggest – bars around. If there's a football game on, the atmosphere is fun.

Antigüedades (Map pp714-15; Calle Argote de Molina 40) Blending mellow beats with offbeat decor, the tiled window seats with a view of the busy street are the best place to nurse your drink.

El Arenal

our pick **Casa Morales** (Map pp714-15; ☎ 954 22 12 42; García de Vinuesa 11) Founded in 1850, not much has changed in this defiantly old-world bar, with charming anachronisms wherever you look. Towering clay *tinajas* (wine storage jars) carry the chalked-up tapas choices of the day. Locals sweat it out on summer nights like true *sevillanos*.

El Capote (Map pp714-15; Calle de Arjona) A beach-side ambience complete with palm trees makes for relaxed *al fresco* drinking right next to Puente de Triana.

Café Isbiliyya (Map pp714-15; ☎ 954 21 04 60; Paseo de Cristóbal Colón 2) Cupid welcomes you to this gay music bar, which puts on extravagant drag-queen shows on Thursday and Sunday nights.

El Centro

Plaza del Salvador is brimful of drinkers from mid-evening to 1am. Grab a drink from **La Antigua Bodeguita** (Map pp714-15; ☎ 954 56 18 33) or **La Sapotales** next door and sit on the steps of the Parroquia del Salvador.

Calle Pérez Galdós, off Plaza de la Alfalfa, has a handful of pulsating bars: **Bare Nostrum** (Map pp714-15; Calle Pérez Galdós 26), **Cabo Loco** (Map pp714-15; Calle Pérez Galdós 26), **Nao** (Map pp714-15; Calle Pérez Galdós 28) and **La Rebótica** (Map pp714-15; Calle Pérez Galdós 11).

El Garlochi (Map pp714-15; Calle Boteros 4) Named after the *gitano* word for 'heart', this deeply camp bar hits you with clouds of incense, Jesus and Virgin images displayed on scarlet walls, and potent cocktails with names like Sangre de Cristo (Blood of Christ).

Alameda de Hércules

In terms of hipness and trendy places to go out, the slightly shabby Alameda is where it's at, and it's also the heartbeat of gay Seville.

Bulebar Café (Map pp712-13; Alameda de Hércules 83; 🕑 4pm-late) This place fills up with young sweaty bodies at night, but is pleasantly chilled in the early evening, with friendly staff.

Café Central (Map pp712-13; ☎ 954 37 09 99; Alameda de Hércules 64) One of the oldest and most popular along the street, Central has yellow bar lights, wooden flea-market chairs and a massive crowd that gathers at weekends.

Habanilla (Map pp712-13; ☎ 954 90 27 18; Alameda de Hércules 63; 🕑 8am-2am) Habanilla's subversive charm is encapsulated in the cheeky beer-bottle chandelier that dominates the room.

Triana

If you want a change from the slicker watering holes of the city proper, try the raffish, ripe-for-development Triana riverfront. The wall overlooking the river along Calle del Betis forms a makeshift bar. Carry your drink out from one of the following places: Alambique, Big Ben, Sirocca and Muí d'Aquí. They're all clustered at Calle del Betis 54 (Map pp714–15) and open from 9pm.

ENTERTAINMENT

Seville comes to life at night with live music, experimental theatre and steamy flamenco. See www.discoversevilla.com or www.exploreseville.com for the latest action.

Clubs

Clubs in Seville come and go fast but a few stand the test of time. The partying starts between 2am and 3am at the weekend. Dress smarter (so no sportswear) at the weekend as clubs become pickier about their punters.

Boss (Map pp714-15; Calle del Betis 67; admission free with flyer; 🕑 8pm-7am Tue-Sun) Make it past the two gruff bouncers and you'll find Boss a top dance spot. The music is a total mix.

Weekend (Map pp712-13; ☎ 954 37 88 73; Calle del Torneo 43; admission €7; 🕑 11pm-8am Thu-Sat) This is one of Seville's top live-music and DJ spots.

Aduana (Map pp712-13; ☎ 954 23 85 82; www.aduana.net; Avenida de la Raza s/n; admission varies; 🕑 midnight-late Thu-Sat) Aduana is where Seville's best-dressed party-goers show off their moves. This huge dance venue, 1km south of Parque de María Luisa, hosts all-night revels from Thursday to Sunday.

Live Music

Fun Club (Map pp712-13; ☎ 958 25 02 49; Alameda de Hércules 86; admission live-band nights €3-6, other nights free; 🕑 11.30pm-late Thu-Sun, from 9.30pm live-band nights) With funk, Latino, hip hop and jazz bands taking the stage it's not surprising that this little dance warehouse is a music-lovers' favourite.

La Imperdible (Map pp712-13; ☎ 954 38 82 19; Curtidurías 12; admission €8-10) This epicentre of experimental arts stages lots of contemporary dance, usually around 9pm.

El Almacén (Map pp712-13; ☎ 954 90 04 34; admission free) The bar of La Imperdible hosts varied music events from around 11pm Thursday to Saturday.

Flamenco

La Carbonería (Map pp714-15; ☎ 954 21 44 60; Calle Levíes 18; admission free; 🕑 about 8pm-4am) A converted coal yard in the Barrio de Santa Cruz with two large bars, thronged nearly every night, which offer live flamenco from about 8pm to 4am.

Casa de la Memoria de Al-Andalus (Map pp714-15; ☎ 954 56 06 70; Calle Ximénez de Enciso 28; adult/child €14/8;

(🕘 9pm & 10.30pm) Authentic nightly shows with a focus on medieval and Sephardic Al-Andalus styles, in a room of shifting shadows. Space is limited, so reserve tickets in advance.

Hotels and tourist offices tend to steer you towards *tablaos* (expensive, tourist-oriented flamenco venues), which can lack atmosphere, though **Los Gallos** (Map pp714-15; ☎ 954 21 69 81; www.tablaolosgallos.com; Plaza de Santa Cruz 11; admission incl 1 drink €30; 🕘 2hr shows 8-10pm & 10.30pm-12.30am) is a cut above the average. Seville also stages the biggest of all Spain's flamenco festivals, the month-long Bienal de Flamenco (p724).

Bullfights

Fights at Seville's ancient, elegant, 14,000-seat **Plaza de Toros de la Real Maestranza** (Map pp714-15; Paseo de Cristóbal Colón 12; www.realmaestranza.com) are among the biggest in Spain. Seville's crowds are some of the most knowledgeable in the bullfighting world. The season runs from Easter Sunday to early October, with fights every Sunday, usually at 7pm, and every day during the Feria de Abril and the week before it.

From the start of the season until late June/early July, nearly all the fights are by fully fledged matadors. Seats cost €32.50 to €110 but only cheap *sol* seats (those in the sun at the start of proceedings) may be available to those who don't hold season tickets. Most of the rest of the season, *novilleras* (novice bullfights) are held, with tickets costing €4 to €26. Tickets are sold in advance at **Empresa Pagés** (Map pp714-15; ☎ 954 50 13 82; Calle de Adriano 37) and from 4.30pm on fight days at the bullring itself.

Whether you appreciate this as sport for the brave or view it is a form of animal cruelty is a matter for debate. Either way, it is certainly an important aspect of Spanish tradition. For more information on bullfighting, see p61.

SHOPPING

The craft shops in the Barrio de Santa Cruz are inevitably tourist-oriented, but many sell attractive ceramics and tiles.

El Centro has a pretty cluster of pedestrianised shopping streets. Calles Sierpes, Cuna, Velázquez and Tetuán have a host of small shops selling everything from polka-dot flamenco dresses to diamond rings. **El Corte Inglés** department store (Map pp714–15) occupies four separate buildings a little west, on Plaza de la Magdalena and Plaza del Duque de la Victoria. Further north, Calle Amor de Dios and Calle Doctor Letamendi (Map pp712–13) have more alternative shops.

The large Thursday **mercadillo** (flea market; Map pp712-13) in Calle de la Feria near the Alameda de Hércules is worth a visit.

In the traditional **tile-making area** of Triana, a dozen shops and workshops still offer charming, artful ceramics around the junction of Calle Alfarería and Calle Antillano Campos.

GETTING THERE & AWAY

Air

Seville's **Aeropuerto San Pablo** (☎ 902 40 47 04; 🕘 24-hr) has a fair range of international and domestic flights. **Iberia** (☎ 902 40 05 00; www.iberia.com) flies direct to Barcelona, Madrid and half a dozen other Spanish cities as well as to London and Paris. **Spanair** (☎ 954 44 91 38; www.spanair.com) also flies to Madrid and, along with **Air Europa** (☎ 902 40 15 01; www.air-europa.com) and **Vueling** (☎ 902 33 39 33; www.vueling.com), to Barcelona. Vueling also covers Paris, Rome, Amsterdam and Brussels to Seville.

From the British Isles there are flights with **British Airways** (☎ 902 11 13 33; www.ba.com) from London Gatwick, **Ryanair** (☎ 807 22 00 32; www.ryanair.com) from Liverpool and London Stansted, and **Aer Lingus** (☎ 902 50 27 37; www.aerlingus.com) from Dublin. **Air-Berlin** (☎ 954 26 07 03; www.airberlin.com) flies to several major German, Swiss and Austrian cities. **Transavia** (☎ 902 11 44 78; www.transavia.com) comes from Amsterdam and **SN Brussels Airlines** (☎ 902 90 14 92; www.flysn.com) from Brussels. Carrier and schedule information changes frequently, so it's best to check with specific airlines or major online bookers.

Bus

From the **Estación de Autobuses Prado de San Sebastián** (Map pp714-15; ☎ 954 41 71 11; Plaza San Sebastián), there are 12 or more buses daily to/from Cádiz (€10.95, 1¾ hours), Córdoba (€9.43, 2 hours), Granada (€18.57, 3½ hours), Jerez de la Frontera (€7.20, 1¼ hours), Ronda (€10.50, 2½ hours, five or more daily) and Málaga (€14.75, 2¾ hours). This is also the station for other towns in Cádiz province, the east of Sevilla province, and destinations along the Mediterranean coast from the Costa del Sol to Barcelona.

From the **Estación de Autobuses Plaza de Armas** (Map pp712-13; ☎ 954 90 80 40; Avenida del Cristo de la Expiración), destinations include Madrid (€18.65, six hours, 14 daily), El Rocío (€5.10, 1½ hours, three to five daily), Aracena (€5.67, 1¼ hours, two daily) and other places in Huelva province, Mérida (€11, three hours, 12 daily), Cáceres (€15, four hours, six daily) and northwestern Spain. This is also the station for buses to Portugal. **ALSA** (www.alsa.es) runs two daily buses to Lisbon (€41, seven hours daily), one via Badajoz and Évora, the other (overnight) via Faro. **Casal** (www.autocarescasal.com) has a daily service between Seville and the border at Rosal de la Frontera (west of Aracena), where you can connect with Portuguese buses to/from Lisbon for a total journey time of 10 hours, costing €23. **Damas** (www.damas-sa.es) runs twice daily (except Saturday, Sunday and holidays from October to May) to/from Lagos (€18, 5½ hours) via Faro and Albufeira. Finally, **Eurolines** (www.eurolines.es) will take you to Germany, Belgium, France, Holland and Sofia, capital of Bulgaria.

Train

The **Estación de Santa Justa** (Map pp712-13; ☎ 902 24 02 02; Avenida Kansas City) is 1.5km northeast of the city centre. There's also a city-centre **Renfe ticket office** (Map pp714-15; Calle Zaragoza 29).

Twenty or more superfast AVE trains, reaching speeds of 280km/h, whiz daily to/from Madrid (€75.10, 2½ hours). There are cheaper 'Altaria' services (€58.90, 3½ hours). Other destinations include Barcelona (€57.50 to €88, 10½ to 13 hours, three daily) and the AVE (€128.30, 6½ hours, one daily), Cádiz (€9.80, 1¾ hours, 13 daily), Córdoba (€8.20 to €28.30, 40 minutes to 1½ hours, 21 or more daily), Granada (€21.65, three hours, four daily), Huelva (€7.50, 1½ hours, three daily), Jerez de la Frontera (€6.70, 1¼ hours, nine daily), Málaga (€17.30 to €33, 2½ hours/2 hours, five daily) as well as Mérida (€13, five hours, one daily).

GETTING AROUND

To/From the Airport

The airport is 7km east of the city centre on the A4 Córdoba road. **Amarillos Tour** (☎ 902 21 03 17) runs buses between the airport and the Puerta de Jerez (€2.20 to €2.50, 30 to 40 minutes, at least 15 daily). A taxi costs about €18.

Bus

Buses run by Seville's urban transport authority (**Tussam**; ☎ 902 45 99 54; www.tussam.es), C1, C2, C3 and C4, do useful circular routes linking the main transport terminals and the city centre. The C1, from in front of Estación de Santa Justa, follows a clockwise route via Avenida de Carlos V (close to Prado de San Sebastián bus station and the Barrio de Santa Cruz), Avenida de María Luisa, Triana, Isla Mágica and Calle de Resolana. The C2, heading west from in front of Estación de Santa Justa, follows the same route in reverse. Bus 32, also from outside Santa Justa, runs to/from Plaza de la Encarnación in El Centro.

The clockwise number C3 will take you from Puerta Carmona (near Prado de San Sebastián bus station and the Barrio de Santa Cruz) to Puerta La Carne and Puerto Jerez. The C4 does the same circuit anticlockwise except that from Estación de Autobuses Plaza de Armas it heads south along Calle de Arjona and Paseo de Cristóbal Colón, instead of crossing the river to Triana.

Bus rides cost €1.10.

Car & Motorcycle

Hotels with parking usually charge you €12-18 a day for the privilege – no cheaper than some public car parks but at least your vehicle will be close at hand. **Parking Paseo de Colón** (Map pp714-15; cnr Paseo de Cristóbal Colón & Calle Adriano; per hr up to 10 hr €1.20, 10-24 hr €13.50) is a relatively inexpensive underground car park.

Cycle

SeVici (☎ 902 01 10 32; www.sevici.es; 7am-9pm) is a bright green idea from Seville's urban authority: a cycle hire network comprising almost 200 fully automated pick-up/drop-off points dotted all over the city (clearly shown on a nifty folding pocket map). A one-week subscription costs €5. Your first 30 minutes cycling is free, the next hour costs €1, second and subsequent hours are €2 per hour. Alternatively, you can pay €10 and sign up for a year (forms available at Tourist Information Offices or online). In that case, your first hour will cost €0.50 and subsequent hours €1. A clear, compact cycle route map of the city is available from tourist information centres.

Quieter, cleaner and infinitely more stylish than fuming amid traffic fumes, the SeVici cycle network is an idea all Spanish cities would do well to follow. The only possible drawback is the €150 deposit for both long- and short-term hires. Use a credit card, which 'freezes' the deduction, instead of a debit card.

Metro

Seville's long-awaited light **metro** (www.sevilla21.com/metro in Spanish) is gradually becoming a reality. Line 1 will run west to south, from Ciudad Expo to Olivar de Quinto (the suburb of Dos Hermanas). It is expected to be running from the end of 2008. Three further lines should then begin construction; Line 2 running west to east, Line 3, north to south, and Line 4, a semicircular route running above ground.

Tram

Tussam's **Tranvia** (www.tussam.es in Spanish), the city's sleek, environmentally sustainable tram service, was launched in 2007. As yet just two lines are operating, with plans to construct several more routes over the next five years. T1 and T4 swish back and forth between the Plaza Nueva (near the *ayuntamiento*) and along Avenida de la Constitución to the Archivo de Indias and Puerta de Jerez, then down San Fernando to the bus station at Prado de San Sebastian. Individual rides cost €1.10, or you can buy a *Bono* (travel pass offering five rides for €5) from many newspaper stands and tobacconists.

AROUND SEVILLE

You'll find Andalucía's best Roman ruins at Itálica and, on the rolling agricultural plains east of Seville, fascinating old towns such as Carmona and Osuna that bespeak many epochs of history.

Santiponce

pop 7000

The small town of Santiponce, 8km northwest of Seville, is the location of Itálica and of the historic Monasterio de San Isidoro del Campo.

Itálica (☎ 955 99 73 76; adult/EU citizen €1.50/free; 🕓 8.30am-8.30pm Tue-Sat, 9am-3pm Sun Apr-Sep, 9am-5.30pm Tue-Sat, 10am-4pm Sun Oct-Mar), on the northern edge of Santiponce, was the first Roman town in Spain. Founded in 206 BC, Itálica was also the home town of the 2nd-century-AD Roman emperors Trajan and Hadrian. The partly reconstructed ruins include one of the biggest of all the Roman amphitheatres, broad paved streets, ruins of several houses with beautiful mosaics and a theatre.

The **Monasterio de San Isidro del Campo** (☎ 955 99 69 20; adult/students & seniors €2/1; 🕓 10am-2pm Wed & Thu, to 2pm & 5.30-8.30pm Fri & Sat, to 3pm Sun & holidays, also 4-7pm Fri & Sat Oct-Mar) is at the southern end of Santiponce (the end nearest Seville), 1.5km from the Itálica entrance. Founded in 1301, it contains a rare set of 15th-century murals showing saints and Mudéjar geometric and floral designs. The dark wood stalls in the choir are particularly imposing.

Casa Venancio (☎ 955 99 67 06; Avenida Extremadura 9; mains €6.50-18), opposite the Itálica entrance, does good rabbit or partridge with rice (€18 for two).

Buses run to Santiponce (€1.20, 40 minutes) from Seville's Plaza de Armas bus station, at least twice an hour from 6.35am to 11pm Monday to Friday, and a little less often at weekends. They stop near the monastery and outside the Itálica entrance.

CARMONA

pop 26,000 / elev 250m

Long-civilised Carmona, continuously inhabited since the Neolithic era and fortified since the 8th century BC, perches on a low hill dotted with venerable palaces and impressive monuments 38km east of Seville off the A4 to Córdoba.

The helpful **tourist office** (☎ 954 19 09 55; www.turismo.carmona.org; 🕓 10am-3pm & 4.30-6pm Mon-Sat, 10am-3pm Sun & holidays) is in the Puerta de Sevilla at the main entrance to the old part of town. Buses from Seville's Prado de San Sebastián bus station (€2.55, 45 minutes, 20 a day Monday to Friday, 10 on Saturday, seven on Sunday) stop 300m west of here, on Paseo del Estatuto.

Sights

Just over 1km southwest of the Puerta de Sevilla is Carmona's impressive **Roman necropolis** (☎ 954 14 08 11; Avenida de Jorge Bonsor; admission free; 🕓 9am-2pm Tue-Sat 15 Jun-14 Sep, to 5pm Tue-Fri, 10am-2pm Sat & Sun rest of year, closed 1 Jul-31 Aug holidays). You can climb down into a dozen family tombs, hewn from the rock.

The tourist office in the **Puerta de Sevilla**, the impressive fortified main gate of the old town, sells tickets (adults/students & seniors, €2/1) for the gate's interesting upper levels.

Up into the old town from here, the 17th-century **ayuntamiento** (Town Hall; Calle El Salvador; admission free; 🕓 8am-3pm Mon-Fri), contains a large, very fine Roman mosaic of the Gorgon Medusa. The splendid **Iglesia Prioral de Santa María** (Calle Martín López de Córdoba; admission €3; 🕓 10am-2pm & 5.30-7.30pm Mon-Fri, to 2pm Sat, closed 20 Aug-19 Sep) was built mainly in the 15th and 16th centuries. But its Patio de los Naranjos was originally a mosque's courtyard and has a Visigothic calendar carved into one of its pillars. Particularly beautiful are the embossed and inlaid pair of bible covers from around 1400. Behind Santa María, the **Museo de la Ciudad** (City History Museum; ☎ 954 14 01 28; Calle San Ildefonso 1; admission €2, free Tue; 10am-2pm Mon, 10am-2pm & 6.30-8.30 Tue-Thu, 9.30am-2pm Sat & holidays) provides extensive background for explorations of the town.

The **Puerta de Córdoba** in Calle Dolores Quintanilla at the end of the street passing the Iglesia de Santa María, is an original Roman gate in marvellous repair, framing the fertile Seville countryside that unfolds like a precious, faded rug. South of here is the stark, ruined **Alcázar**, an Almohad fort that Pedro I turned into a country palace. Brought down by earthquakes in 1504 and 1755, it's now the site of the luxurious *parador* (government-owned luxury hotel).

Sleeping & Eating

Hostal Comercio (☎ 954 14 00 18; Calle Torre del Oro 56; s/d €32/45;) This lovely old tiled building near the Puerta de Sevilla provides 14 cosy, clean rooms hosted by the fourth generation of this courteous family.

Hospedería Palacio Marques de las Torres (☎ 954 19 62 48; www.hospederiamarquesdelastorres.com; Calle Fermin Molpeceres 2; dm/d incl breakfast €27.90/57.25;) Modern comforts amid 18th-century graciousness make for a handsome mix. Surprising dorm cabins rub shoulders with comfortable hotel rooms containing plush beds in a converted *palacio*, plus a fabulous turquoise pool in the sunny garden.

Parador Alcázar del Rey Don Pedro (☎ 954 14 10 10; www.parador.es; s/d €127.54/159.43-170.13; P) Carmona's luxuriously equipped *parador* feels even more luxurious for the ruined Alcázar in its grounds. The refectory-style dining room (*menú del día* €31) is one of the best in town.

Casa de Carmona (☎ 954 19 10 00; www.casadecarmona.com; Plaza de Lasso 1; r incl breakfast €175-180; P) A superluxurious hotel in a beautiful 16th-century palace, the Casa de Carmona feels like the aristocratic home that it used to be. Its elegant restaurant (mains €18 to €25) serves *haute cuisine* with an *andaluz* (Andalucian) touch.

Carmona offers its very own tapas tour – the map is available from the Tourist Office. Start at cool, dark **Bodega L'Antigua** (Plaza del Palanque; tapas/raciones €1.50-3.00) opposite the Tourist Office and see if you can work your way around the 20 featured bars by closing time!

OSUNA

pop 18,000 / elev 330m

Just off the A92 towards Granada, 91km from Seville, Osuna is the loveliest of Sevilla province's country towns, with beautifully preserved baroque mansions and an amazing Spanish Renaissance monastery. Several of the most impressive buildings were created by its ducal family, one of Spain's richest since the 16th century. About 100m north of Plaza Mayor in the characterful setting of the 18th-century granary, or El Posito, the **Oficina Municipal de Turismo** (☎ 954 81 57 32; 9am-2pm Mon-Sat) and the **Asociación Turístico Cultural Osuna** (☎ 954 81 28 52; 10am-2pm & 5-8pm Mon-Fri, to 2pm Sat, closed Sun) both provide tourist information and hand out useful guides.

Sights

The massive buildings on the hill overlooking the centre graphically symbolise the weight of various kinds of authority in old Spain. On the way up from Plaza Mayor, the **Museo Arqueológico** (☎ 954 81 12 07; Plaza de la Duquesa; admission €1.50; 11.30am-1.30pm & 5-6.30pm Tue-Sun, closed Sun afternoon Jul & Aug) in the 12th-century Torre del Agua has a good collection of mainly Iberian and Roman reliefs, glassware and coins, as well as the original of the town's symbol, the Bull of Osuna. Further up the same hill, the 16th-century **Colegiata de Santa María de la Asunción** (☎ 954 81 04 44; Plaza de la Encarnación; admission by guided tour only €2; 10am-1.30pm & 4-6.30pm Tue-Sun, closed Sun afternoon Jul & Aug), contains a wealth of sacred art, including several paintings by José de Ribera. The visit includes the lugubrious Sepulcro Ducal, the Osuna family vault. Opposite the Colegiata is the **Monasterio de la Encarnación** (☎ 954 81 11 21; admission €2; same as Colegiata), now Osuna's museum of religious art, with beautiful tile work and a rich collection of baroque art. Just down the road, the pointy blue-and-white-tiled towers of the Antigua Universidad fascinate like illustrations in a sinister fairy tale.

Sleeping

Hostal Caballo Blanco (☎ 954 81 01 84; Calle Granada 1; s/d €40/58; P) The friendly 'White Horse Inn' is an historic coaching inn with courtyard parking, comfy rooms and surprisingly spacious bathrooms.

Hotel Palacio Marqués de la Gomera (☎ 954 81 22 23; www.hotelpalaciodelmarques.com; Calle San Pedro 20; s/d €85/130; P) This luxury hotel occupies one of Osuna's finest baroque mansions. It is exceptionally handsome, with rooms of princely proportions and quiet luxury. It even boasts its own ornate private chapel, well-upholstered library and billiard room.

Getting There & Away

The **bus station** (☎ 954 81 01 46; Avenida de la Constitución) is 500m southeast of Plaza Mayor. Up to 11 daily buses run to Seville (Prado de San Sebastián, €6.61, 1½ hours). The **train station** (Avenida de la Estación) is 1km southwest of the centre, with six trains a day to Seville (€8, one hour).

HUELVA PROVINCE

Andalucía's little-known westernmost province – an afterthought to most travellers who are not on the way to or from Portugal – is in fact a land of many and surprising rewards. Around half the excellent, sandy Atlantic beaches of the Costa de la Luz lie along Huelva's coast, and the longest run of dunes in Europe is at one of those beaches, Castilla. Also here is most of that beautiful and hugely important wildlife sanctuary, the Parque Nacional de Doñana. Anyone with a historical leaning will be fascinated by the Columbus sites outside Huelva city. And northern Huelva, focused on the town of Aracena, is a beautiful rolling hill-country district just waiting to be discovered on foot.

HUELVA

pop 146,700

The province's unspectacular but amiable capital is very much a working port and industrial city. It was probably founded by the Phoenicians as a trading settlement about 3000 years ago. What's here today, however, has almost all been built since the devastating Lisbon earthquake of 1755.

Orientation & Information

Huelva stands between the Odiel and Tinto estuaries. The central area is about 1km square, with the bus station at its western edge, on Calle Doctor Rubio, and the train station at its southern edge on Avenida de Italia. The main street is Avenida Martín Alonso Pinzón (also called Gran Vía). The nearby **regional tourist office** (☎ 959 65 02 00; Plaza Alcalde Coto Mora 2; 9am-7.30pm Mon-Fri, 10am-2pm Sat & Sun) is outstandingly well informed and helpful.

Sights

The **Museo Provincial** (☎ 959 25 93 00; Alameda Sundheim 13; admission free; 2.30-8.00pm Tue, 9.00am-8.00pm Wed-Sat & Sun) focuses on Huelva province's archaeological pedigree, especially its millennia of mining history (see p736).

Sleeping & Eating

Instalación Juvenil de Huelva (☎ 959 65 00 10; www.inturjoven.com; Avenida Marchena Colombo 14; per person incl breakfast under 26yr €16, over 26yr €20;) This is a good, modern, wheelchair-accessible youth hostel where all rooms have a bathroom and absolutely no frills. It's 2km north of the bus station: city bus 6 (€0.80) from there stops just around the corner from the hostel, on Calle JS Elcano.

Hotel Los Condes (☎ 959 28 24 00; Alameda Sundheim 14; s/d incl breakfast €47.50/63; P) Large, bright, modern rooms, with big gleaming bathrooms, plus friendly reception, free internet and a reasonable restaurant, add up to a good-value hotel.

NH Luz Huelva (☎ 959 25 00 11; www.nh-hotels.com; Alameda Sundheim 26; s/d €100/135; P) This is the best hotel Huelva has to offer, with cool, spacious rooms in a boxy building. Ring ahead to bag a parking spot.

Taberna El Condado (☎ 959 26 11 23; Calle Sor Ángela de la Cruz 3; tapas €2.00, raciones €10-16; closed Sun) An atmospheric tapas dispensary of just two small rooms dominated by a ham-heavy bar, specialising in tasty local meats.

Trattoria Fuentevieja (Avenida Martín Alonso Pinzón; mains €6-11; closed Sun dinner) This ultra-popular Italian spot serves a good range of salads as well as pizza, pasta and meat dishes. Good value *menú del día* at €8, 12 or 16.

Getting There & Away

From the **bus station** (☎ 959 25 69 00) at least 18 daily buses head to Seville (€7.14, 1¼ hours) and four to Madrid (€21.80, seven hours). Two (except Saturday, Sunday and holidays from October to May) head for Lagos (€13 to €14, four hours) in Portugal via Faro and Albufeira. From the **train station** (☎ 902 24 02 02) three daily trains head to Seville (€7.50, 1½ hours).

LUGARES COLOMBINOS

The Lugares Colombinos (Columbus Sites) are the three townships of La Rábida, Palos de la Frontera and Moguer, along the eastern bank of the Tinto estuary east of Huelva. All three played key roles in the discovery of the

Americas and can be combined in a single day trip from Huelva, the Doñana area or the nearby coast.

La Rabida

pop 600

In this pretty and peaceful town, don't miss the 14th-century **Monasterio de La Rábida** (☎ 959 35 04 11; admission €3; 🕑 10am-1pm & 4-7pm Tue-Sat Apr-Jul & Sep, 10am-1pm to 6.15pm Tue-Sat Oct-Mar, 10am-1pm & 4.45-8pm Tue-Sat Aug, 10.45am-1pm Sun year-round), visited several times by Columbus before his great voyage of discovery. On the waterfront below the monastery is the **Muelle de las Carabelas** (Wharf of the Caravels; ☎ 959 53 05 97; admission €3.30; 🕑 10am-2pm & 5-9pm Tue-Fri, 11am-8pm Sat, Sun & holidays Jun-Sep, 10am-7pm Tue-Sun Oct-May), where you can board replicas of Columbus' tiny three-ship fleet, crewed by ludicrous mannequins.

Palos de la Frontera

pop 8500

La Rabida's neighbouring town boasts the **Casa Museo Martín Alonso Pinzón** (☎ 959 10 00 41; Calle Colón 24; admission €2; 🕑 10am-2pm Tue-Sat), once the home of the *Pinta*'s captain. Further along Calle Colón is the 15th-century **Iglesia de San Jorge** where Columbus and his men took communion before embarking for their great voyage.

Stop to take on supplies yourself at **El Bodegón** (☎ 959 53 11 05; Calle Rábida 46; mains €10-23; 🕑 closed Tue), a noisy, atmospheric cavern of a restaurant that cooks up fish and meat on wood-fired grills.

Moguer

pop 16,300

Sleepy **Moguer** provided many of Columbus' crew. There's a helpful **tourist office** (☎ 959 37 18 98; Calle Castillo s/n; 🕑 10am-2pm & 5-7pm Mon-Sat, 10am-3pm Sun, Mon & holidays) a couple of blocks south of the central Plaza del Cabildo, in Moguer's **Castillo**, a dramatic, bare walled enclosure of Almohad origin, expanded in the 14th century.

The 14th-century **Monasterio de Santa Clara** (☎ 959 37 01 07; Plaza de las Monjas; guided tour €3; 🕑 11am-2pm & 5-7pm Mon-Fri) is where Columbus kept a prayerful vigil the night after returning from his first voyage in March 1493.

Mesón El Lobito (☎ 959 37 06 60; Calle Rábida 31; raciones €4-12; 🕑 closed Wed), 'the Wolf', is a characterful place to sample good country cooking under the gaze of its snarling, stuffed namesake.

Getting There & Away

At least 10 buses a day leave Huelva for La Rábida (€1, 30 minutes), with half of them continuing to Palos de la Frontera (€1, 35 minutes) and Moguer (€1.20, 30 minutes). The others go on to Mazagón.

PARQUE NACIONAL DE DOÑANA

Spain's most celebrated and in many ways most important wildlife refuge, the Doñana National Park, created in 1969, is one of Europe's last remaining great wetlands. Covering 542 sq km in the southeast of Huelva province and neighbouring Sevilla province, this World Heritage site is a vital refuge for such endangered species as the Spanish imperial eagle. It offers a unique combination of ecosystems and a place of haunting beauty that is well worth the effort of getting to. To visit the national park you must take a tour from the Centro de Visitantes El Acebuche (p735) on the western side of the park, or from El Rocío (p734) at the park's northwest corner, or from Sanlúcar de Barrameda (p745) at its southeast corner.

Half the park consists of *marismas* (wetlands) of the Guadalquivir delta, the largest area of wetlands in Europe. Almost dry from July to October, in autumn the *marismas* fill with water, attracting hundreds of thousands of wintering water birds from the north. As the waters sink in spring, other birds – greater flamingos, spoonbills, storks – arrive, many to nest. The park also has a 28km Atlantic beach, separated from the *marismas* by a band

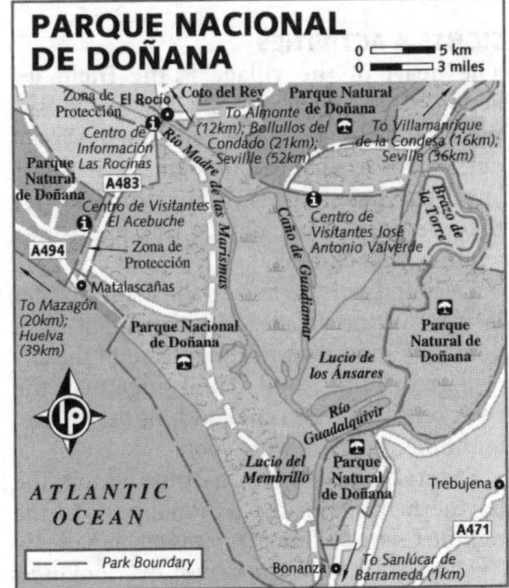

of sand dunes up to 5km wide; and 144 sq km of *coto* (woodland and scrub), which harbours many mammals, including deer, wild boar and semiwild horses.

Interesting areas surrounding the national park are included in the 540-sq-km Parque Natural de Doñana, a separate protected area comprising four distinct zones.

El Rocío

pop 1200

The village of El Rocío overlooks a section of the Doñana *marismas* at the park's northwestern corner. The village's sandy streets bear as many hoof prints as tyre marks, and they are lined with rows of verandahed buildings that are empty most of the time. But this is no ghost town: most of the houses belong to the 90-odd *hermandades* of pilgrim-revellers and their families, who converge on El Rocío every year in the extraordinary Romería del Rocío (see right). In fact, a party atmosphere pervades the village at most weekends as *hermandades* arrive to carry out lesser ceremonial acts.

INFORMATION

The **tourist office** (☎ 959 44 38 08; www.turismodedonana.com; Avenida de la Canaliega s/n; ⌚ 9.30am-1.30pm & 3-5pm Mon-Fri) is by the main road at the western end of the village. It can make reservations for park tours. The **Centro de Información Las Rocinas** (☎ 959 43 95 70; ⌚ 9am-3pm & 4-7pm, to 8pm or 9pm Apr-Aug, to 3pm Sun 15 Jun-14 Sep), 1km south on the A483, has national park information and paths to nearby birdwatching hides.

SIGHTS & ACTIVITIES

The heart of the village is the **Ermita del Rocío** (⌚ 8am-10.30pm Apr-Sep, 8.30am-8pm Oct-Mar), the church housing the celebrated Virgen del Rocío, a tiny wooden image in long, jewel-encrusted robes. Many come to pay their respects every day in this handsome white-walled church.

Deer and horses graze in the shallow water in front of the village, and you might see a flock of flamingos wheeling through the sky in a great pink cloud. The bridge over the river on the A483, 1km south of the village, is another good viewing spot.

Several operators run tours along the northern fringe of the national park to the remote **Centro de Visitantes José Antonio Valverde** (⌚ 10am-7pm, to 8pm or 9pm Apr-Aug), overlooking a year-round lake. On these trips you have high chances of seeing deer and boar and will definitely see a great diversity of birds. January, April and May are the best months.

Recommended operators:

Discovering Doñana (☎ 959 44 24 66; www.discoveringdonana.com; Calle Águila Imperial 150, El Rocío; 6hr trip 1-3 people €120) Expert English-speaking guides; most trips are of broad interest, and their website carries glowing testimonials to guides' enthusiasm and dedication.

Doñana Nature (☎ 959 44 21 60; www.donana-nature.com; Calle Las Carretas 10, El Rocío; 3½hr trip per person adult/under 16 €25/12.50) Half-day trips, at 8am and 6pm daily (3.30pm in winter), are of general interest; English- and French-speaking guides available.

Doñana Ecuestre (☎ 959 44 24 74; Avenida de la Canaliega s/n; per 1hr/2hr/half-day €20/30/40) Offers enjoyable guided horse rides through the woodlands west of El Rocío, some led by qualified biologists.

FESTIVALS & EVENTS

Every Pentecost (Whitsuntide), the seventh weekend after Easter, El Rocío is inundated with up to a million pilgrim-revellers from all corners of Spain in the **Romería del Rocío** (Pilgrimage to El Rocío). This vast cult festivity revolves around the tiny image of Nuestra Señora del Rocío, which was found here in a tree by a hunter from Almonte back in the 13th century. Carrying it home, the hunter stopped for a rest and the statue miraculously made its own way back to the tree. Before long a chapel was built where the tree had stood (now El Rocío) and pilgrims were making for it.

Today almost 100 *hermandades* from around and beyond Andalucía, some comprising several thousand men and women, travel to El Rocío each year on foot, on horseback and in gaily decorated covered wagons pulled by cattle or horses, using cross-country tracks.

Solemn is the last word you'd apply to this quintessentially Andalucian event. The 'pilgrims' dress in bright Andalucian costume and sing, dance, drink and romance their way to El Rocío.

Things reach an ecstatic climax in the early hours of the Monday. Members of the *hermandad* of Almonte, which claims the Virgin for its own, barge into the church and bear her out on a float. Chaotic struggles ensue as others battle with the Almonte lads for the honour of carrying La Blanca Paloma, but somehow good humour survives and the

Virgin is carried round to each of the brotherhood buildings, finally returning to the Ermita in the afternoon.

SLEEPING & EATING

Don't bother even trying for a room at Romería time.

Camping La Aldea (☎ 959 44 26 77; www.campinglaaldea.com; Carretera El Rocío Km25; sites per adult/tent/car €6.50/6.50/6.50, cabin or bungalow for 4 or 5 adults €115-30; P ✻ 💻 🏊) At the north end of the village, well-equipped La Aldea has a range of cosy cabins and bungalows as well as over 250 camping spaces.

Pensión Cristina (☎ 959 44 24 13; Calle El Real 58; s/d €30/36) Just east of the Ermita, the Cristina provides reasonably comfortable budget rooms and a popular restaurant (mains €5 to €15) serving paella, venison, seafood and more.

Hotel & Restaurante Toruño (☎ 959 44 23 23; Plaza Acebuchal 22; s/d incl breakfast €65/105; P ✻ 💻) An attractive villa overlooking the *marismas*, Toruño has 30 well-appointed rooms. Some have marsh views, so you can see the spoonbills having their breakfast when you wake. Across the road, the restaurant (mains €12 to €22) dishes up generous portions of well-prepared country and coastal fare. Served proudly on a plate, the *salmorejo* soup is surely the richest and thickest in all Andalucía, as red and fragrant as a kiss.

Aires de Doñana (☎ 959 44 27 19; Avenida de la Canaliega 1; mains €15-19; 🕑 closed Mon) Aires de Doñana stands out among El Rocío eateries with its picture windows right over the *marismas*, polished service and successfully imaginative menu.

Centro de Visitantes El Acebuche

Twelve kilometres south of El Rocío on the A483, then 1.6km west, **El Acebuche** (☎ 959 44 87 11; 🕑 8am-9pm May-Sep, to 7pm Oct-Apr) is the national park's main visitor centre. It has an interactive exhibit on the park and paths to birdwatching hides, plus a film show of Iberian lynxes at El Acebuche – the closest visitors can get to them.

NATIONAL PARK TOURS

Trips in 20-person all-terrain vehicles from El Acebuche are the only way for ordinary folk to get into the interior of the national park from the western side. Book ahead through **Cooperativa Marismas del Rocío** (☎ 959 43 04 32/51; 4hr tour per person €25; 🕑 8.30am Tue-Sun year-round, 3pm Oct-Apr, 5pm May-Sep). During spring, summer and holidays, book at least a month ahead, but otherwise a week is usually plenty of notice. Bring binoculars if you can, drinking water in summer and mosquito protection except in winter. Most guides speak Spanish only. The tour normally starts with a long beach drive, before moving inland. You can be pretty certain of seeing deer and boar, but ornithologists may be disappointed by the limited bird-observation opportunities.

Matalascañas & Mazagón

These two small resorts on the long, sandy beach running northwest from the national park provide alternative bases to El Rocío. Matalascañas town itself is a sad contrast to the adjacent wildernesses, but Mazagón, 28km up the coast, is lower-key. At **Cuesta de Maneli**, between the two, a 1.2km boardwalk leads across 100m-high dunes from a car park to the beach through glorious pines and junipers.

Both towns have large camping grounds and a range of hotels.

Hotel Albaida (☎ 959 37 60 29; www.hotelalbaida.com; Carretera Huelva-Matalascañas, Mazagón; s €44-65, d €55-90, all incl breakfast; P ✻) has airy rooms and welcoming staff; among pines just off the highway and close to the beach. Book ahead for **Hotel Doñana Blues** (☎ 959 44 98 17; www.donanablues.com; Sector I, Parcela 129, Matalascañas; r €105; ✻ 💻 🏊), a small hotel in comfortable yet appealingly rustic style, set in pretty gardens.

The interior and exterior of the **Parador de Mazagón** (☎ 959 53 63 00; www.parador.es; Playa de Mazagón; s/d €129/159; P ✻ 💻 🏊), 6km east of central Mazagón, blend pleasingly with its splendid natural surroundings and the luxurious rooms all have sea views.

Getting There & Away

Three daily buses run between Seville (Plaza de Armas) and Matalascañas (€6.50, 1¾ hours) via El Rocío (€6, 1½ hours). One or two further services along the A483 between Almonte and Matalascañas also stop at El Rocío. All these buses will stop on request outside El Acebuche visitors centre.

From Huelva, buses go to Mazagón (€2.10, 35 minutes, up to 13 daily), with just two of these (Monday to Friday only) continuing to Matalascañas (€4.30, 50 minutes). Extra services may run in summer. You can travel between Huelva and El Rocío by changing buses at Almonte.

THE BODEGAS OF BOLLULLOS

For the hungry traveller heading west on the E1/A49 from Seville towards Huelva and the Portuguese border, **Bollullos Par del Condada** is the place to stop for a hearty and well-priced lunch. Along Calle 28 Febrero in the centre of town, a series of bodegas (old wine warehouses) have been converted into huge, bustling eating halls hosting holiday-happy diners from Seville, Huelva and even Madrid. Great value grilled meats and seafood from nearby Huelva feature on the simple menus (from around €8). Don't be lured into the 'posh' restaurant side; stick to the long tables in the main hall for a feast of good food and Spanish family-watching. Try **Bodegón Abeulo Curro** at number 97. To reach the bodegas, take exit 48 on the A483 turnoff south towards Almonte.

WEST OF HUELVA

The coast between Huelva and the Portuguese border, 53km to the west, is lined nearly all the way by a superb, broad, sandy beach backed for long stretches by dunes and trees. The coastal settlements emphasise tourism but also retain port character.

Punta Umbría, Huelva's summer playground, has a friendly atmosphere and an attractive location between the Atlantic beach and the peninsular wetlands of the Marismas del Odiel, creating an agreeable mix of seaside and countryside activities in one location. Further west, **Isla Cristina** has a bustling fishing port and plenty more of the same great beach. **Ayamonte**, the most westerly resort on the Andalucian coast, stands beside the broad Río Guadiana, which divides Spain from Portugal. A free road bridge crosses the river 2km north of Ayamonte, but there's also a ferry from the town (€4.50 for a car and driver, €1.35 for pedestrians).

Recommended is **Hotel El Paraíso Playa** (☎ 959 33 02 35; www.hotelparaisoplaya.com; Avenida de la Playa, Isla Cristina; s/d €50-65/80-129 incl breakfast; P) a friendly and attractive two-storey hotel, with restaurant, a stone's throw from Playa Central. (Rates dip by 25% to 50% outside July and August.)

MINAS DE RIOTINTO

pop 6200 / elev 420m

Tucked away on the fringe of Huelva's northern hills is one of the world's oldest mining districts – an unearthly, sculpted and scarred landscape that makes a fascinating stop. Copper was being dug up here at least 4000 years ago, iron has been mined since at least Roman times, and in the 19th century the British-dominated Rio Tinto Company turned the area into one of the world's great copper-mining centres.

The area's hub is the town of Minas de Riotinto, 68km northeast of Huelva.

Sights & Activities

The attractions are run by the **Parque Minero de Riotinto** (☎ 959 59 00 25; www.parquemineroderiotinto.sigadel.com in Spanish), headquartered at the well-signposted **Museo Minero** (Plaza Ernest Lluch; adult/under 13yr €4/3; 10.30am-3pm & 4-7pm). The fascinating museum, which was the Riotinto company hospital between 1873 and 1954, takes you right through the Riotinto area's unique history from megalithic tombs to the Roman and British colonial eras and finally the closure of the mines in 2001. Its best features include a 200m-long re-creation of a Roman mine, and the Vagón del Maharajah, a luxurious carriage used by Alfonso XIII to visit the mines.

An easy and fun way to see the mining area is to ride the **Ferrocarril Turístico-Minero** (adult/child €10/9; 1.30pm 1 Jun-15 Jul; 1.30pm & 5.30pm 16 Jul-30 Sep; 1pm Mon-Fri, 4pm Sat, Sun & holidays 1 Oct-30 Nov), taking visitors on the 22km round-trip through the surreal landscape in restored early-20th-century railway carriages. Trips start at Talleres Minas, 2.5km east of Minas de Riotinto. Another trip is to the old copper and sulphur mines of **Peña de Hierro** (adult/child €8/7; 12-1.30pm & 5.30-7pm daily), 9km from Minas de Riotinto. Here you see the source of Río Tinto, an 85m-deep open-cast mine, and are taken into a 200m-long underground mine gallery. For both these trips it's essential to book ahead, and schedules may change.

The Parque Minero is not running trips to the **Corta Atalaya**, 1km west of the town. But you can still get a peep at this awesome opencast mine, 1.2km long and 335m deep, if you follow the sign to it as you enter Minas de Riotinto from the southwest.

ANDALUCÍA

Sleeping & Eating

Hostal Galán (☎ 959 59 08 40; www.hostalrestaurantegalan.com; Avenida La Esquila 10; s/d €30/42; ❄) Just around the corner from the Museo Minero, Minas de Riotinto's only accommodation has plain but acceptable rooms and a handy restaurant (menú €10.50).

Hotel Vázquez Díaz (☎/fax 959 58 09 27; personal.telefonica.terra.es/web/hotelvazquezdiaz; Calle Cañadilla 51, Nerva; s/d €38/48; ❄ 💻) A welcoming, well-run hotel with decent rooms and its own good restaurant (*menú* €14), in Nerva, 5km east of Minas.

Getting There & Away

Up to six daily buses run from Huelva to Minas de Riotinto (€5.50, 1½ hours) and Nerva (€6, 1¾ hours) and vice versa. **Casal** (☎ 954 99 92 62) has three daily buses from Seville (Plaza de Armas) to Nerva (€4, 1½ hours) and Minas de Riotinto (€4.50, 1¾ hours).

ARACENA

pop 6300 / elev 730m

This appealing, whitewashed old market town, spreading around the skirts of Cerro del Castillo, makes a good base for exploring the lovely, rolling hill country of northern Huelva. Most of the hill country lies within the 1840-sq-km **Parque Natural Sierra de Aracena y Picos de Aroche**, Andalucía's second-largest protected area.

Aracena's **Municipal tourist office** (☎ 959 12 82 06; Calle Pozo de la Nieve; 🕑 10am-2pm & 4-6.30pm) faces the entrance to the Gruta de las Maravillas (see below) and sells some maps of the area.

> **THE MARTE PROJECT**
>
> On trips to Peña de Hierro you'll see the area where since 2003 scientists from the USA's NASA and Spain's Centro de Astrobiología in Madrid have been conducting a research program called MARTE (Mars Analog Research & Technology Experiment) in preparation for seeking life on Mars. It's thought that the high acid levels that give Río Tinto its rust-red colour (the action of acid on iron) are a product of underground microorganisms comparable with those that may exist below the surface of Mars. Experiments in locating these microbes up to 150m below ground level are helping to develop techniques for seeking similar subterranean life on the red planet.

Sights & Activities

Aracena's biggest tourist attraction, the **Gruta de las Maravillas** (Cave of Marvels; ☎ 959 12 83 55; Calle Pozo de la Nieve; tour adult/under 19yr €8/5.50 🕑 tours every hr or ½hr 10am-1.30pm & 3-6pm), ranks among Spain's most picturesque cave systems, and is beautifully lit for maximum theatricality. The **Cerro del Castillo** is an extremely romantic-looking white village crowned by a beautiful Gothic Mudéjar church and a ruined castle, both built around 1300.

Sleeping & Eating

Molino del Bombo (☎ 959 12 84 78; www.molinodelbombo.com in Spanish; Calle Ancha 4; s/d €21/42; ❄ 💻) Rustic as a farmhouse fireside, the Molino stands near the top of the town and offers charming country-style rooms at extremely reasonable prices.

Hospedería Reina de los Ángeles (☎ 959 12 83 67; www.hospederiareinadelosangeles; Avenida Reina de los Ángeles s/n; s/d €25/41.50; 💻) This former residence for school students, opened as a hotel in 2005, provides 90 utilitarian but spotless rooms with phone and TV and a convivial cafe-bar – a good budget deal.

Finca Valbono (☎ 959 12 77 11; www.fincavalbono.com; Carretera Carboneras Km1; s/d €75/90.16, 4-person apt €157; P ❄ 💻 🏊) A converted farmhouse 1km northeast of town, this is Aracena's most charming accommodation. Facilities include a pool, riding stables and a good, medium-priced restaurant (mains €8 to €18). It's also wheelchair accessible.

Café-Bar Manzano (☎ 959 12 63 37; Plaza del Marqués de Aracena; tapas €1.80-3.50, raciones €9-18; 🕑 8am-8pm or later Wed-Sat & Mon, 10am-8pm Sun) This terrace cafe on the main plaza is a fine spot to watch Aracena go by and enjoy varied tapas and *raciones* that celebrate wild mushrooms and other regional fare.

Restaurante José Vicente (☎ 959 12 84 55; Avenida de Andalucía 53; 3-course menú €20; 🕑 closed Sun evening, last week Jun & 1st week Jul) The proprietor is an expert on *sierra* cuisine, and the fixed-price *menú* (which includes a drink) is excellent. It's advisable to book.

Getting There & Away

The **bus station** (Avenida de Sevilla) is towards the southeast edge of town. Two daily buses come from Seville (Plaza de Armas; €5.67, 1¼ hours), one or two from Huelva (€6.75, 2¼ hours), and up to three from Minas de Riotinto (€2.30, one hour). A Casal bus leaves at 10.30am to the Portuguese border just beyond Rosal de la Frontera, where you can change to onward buses for Lisbon (€18.50, nine hours from Aracena).

WEST OF ARACENA

The hills, valleys and villages of Huelva's portion of the Sierra Morena form one of Andalucía's most surprisingly beautiful landscapes. Most of the villages grew up around fortress-like churches, or hilltop castles constructed in medieval times to deter the Portuguese. The area is threaded by well-maintained walking trails with ever-changing vistas. Good walking routes are particularly thick in the area between Aracena and Cortegana, making attractive villages such as Alájar, Castaño del Robledo and Almonaster la Real good bases. Discovery Walking Guides' *Sierra de Aracena* and accompanying *Sierra de Aracena Tour & Trail Map* are terrific aids to the walker here.

One kilometre above Alájar (towards Fuenteheridos), the **Peña de Arias Montano** has magical views, as does **Cerro de San Cristóbal** (915m), a 4km uphill drive from Almonaster. Almonaster's 10th-century **mezquita** (mosque; 8.30am-7pm approx) is a gem of Islamic architecture and features the oldest *mihrab*, or prayer niche, in Spain. *Jamón serrano* from nearby **Jabugo** is acclaimed as the best in Spain, and the village's Carretera San Juan del Puerto is lined with bars and restaurants waiting for *your* verdict!

There are a few recommended lodgings: **Posada del Castaño** (☎ 959 46 55 02; www.posadadelcastano.com; Calle José Sánchez Calvo 33, Castaño del Robledo; s/d incl breakfast €40/50;) is a characterfully converted village house whose helpful young British owners have walkers foremost in mind. **Hotel Casa García** (☎ 959 14 31 09; Avenida San Martín 2, Almonaster la Real; s/d €37/53; mains €10-12; P) is a small, stylish hotel with a highly regarded restaurant. **La Posada** (☎ 959 12 57 12; www.laposadadealajar.com; Calle Médico Emilio González 2, Alájar; s/d incl breakfast €45/60) is a very cosy inn whose owners are keen walkers themselves and speak very good English. Local live music acts play at weekends; its shop sells maps and regional recipe books.

Daily **Casal** (☎ Seville 954 99 92 62) buses connect nearly all these villages with Aracena and Seville (Plaza de Armas).

CÁDIZ PROVINCE

It's hard to fathom how an area little more than 100km from north to south or east to west can encompass such variety. Cosmopolitan, cultured, fun-loving Cádiz city can seem a world away from nearby Jerez de la Frontera, where aristocratic, sherry-quaffing, equestrian elegance rubs shoulders with poor quarters that have nurtured some of the great flamenco artists; and neither city has much in common with the unromantic industrial port of Algeciras. The colourful, bustling towns of the 'sherry triangle' give way to the long, sandy beaches of the Atlantic coast and the hip international surf scene of Tarifa. Inland, the majestic cork forests of Los Alcornocales yield to the rugged peaks and pristine white villages of the Sierra de Grazalema. Active travellers in Cádiz can enjoy Europe's best windsurfing, hike dramatic mountains, trek the countryside on horseback or train their binoculars on some of Spain's most spectacular birds. Meanwhile, the province's fascinating and diverse history is ever-present in the shape of thrillingly sited hilltop castles, beautiful churches and medieval mosques.

CÁDIZ

pop 128,600

Once past the coastal marshes and industrial sprawl around Cádiz, you emerge into an elegant, historic port city of largely 18th- and 19th-century construction. The old part of Cádiz is crammed onto the head of a promontory like some huge, crowded, ocean-going ship, and the tang of salty air and ocean vistas are never far away. Cádiz has a long and fascinating history, absorbing monuments and museums and plenty of enjoyable places to eat and drink. It is enjoying a top-notch urban renovation program in preparation for the 200th anniversary of the Cádiz parliament in 2012.

History

Cádiz may be the oldest city in Europe. Historians date its founding to the arrival of Phoenician traders in 800 BC.

In less-distant times, Cádiz began to boom after Columbus' trips to the Americas. He sailed from here on his second and fourth voyages. Cádiz attracted Spain's enemies too: in 1587 England's Sir Francis Drake 'singed the king of Spain's beard' with a raid on the

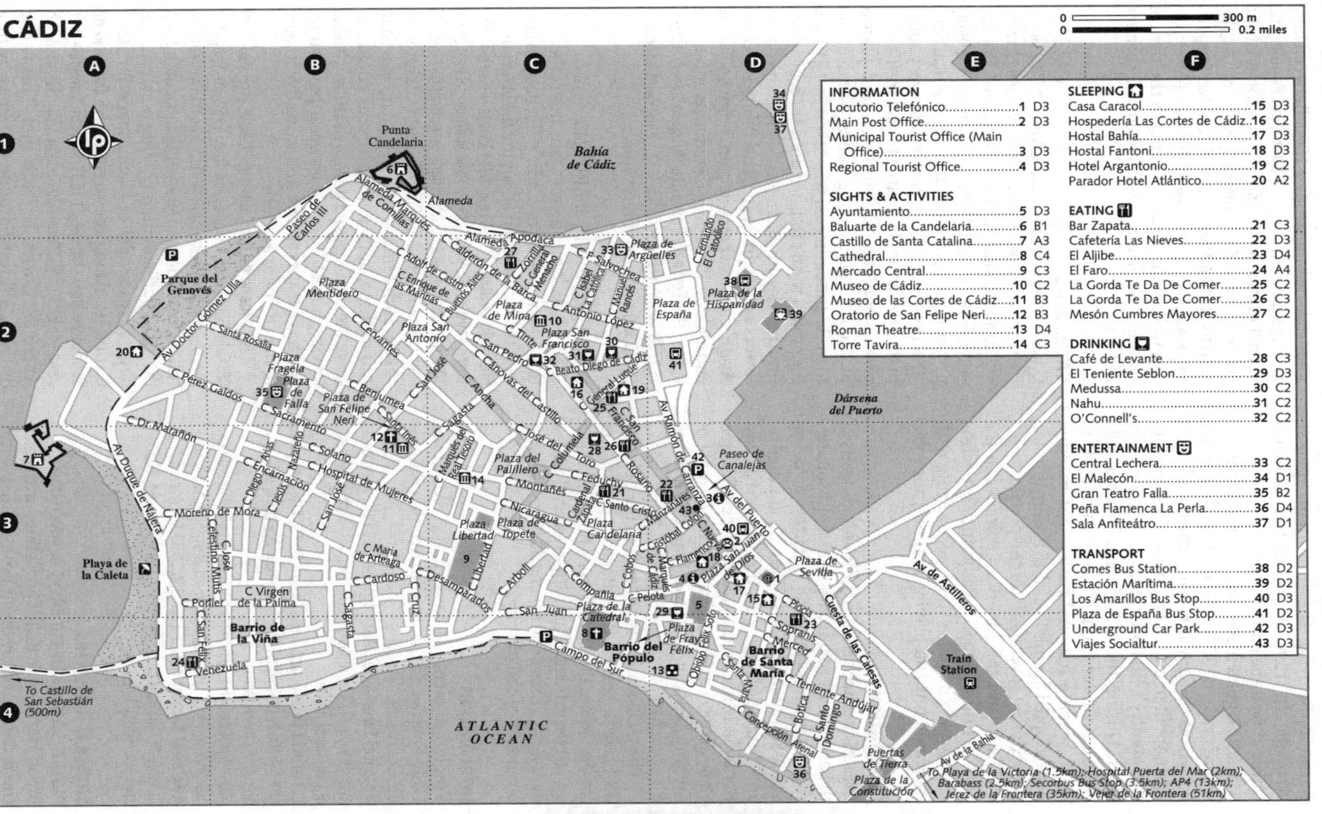
CÁDIZ
0 300 m
0 0.2 miles
INFORMATION
Locutorio Telefónico 1 D3
Main Post Office 2 D3
Municipal Tourist Office (Main Office) 3 D3
Regional Tourist Office 4 D3
SIGHTS & ACTIVITIES
Ayuntamiento 5 D3
Baluarte de la Candelaria 6 B1
Castillo de Santa Catalina 7 A3
Cathedral 8 C4
Mercado Central 9 C3
Museo de Cádiz 10 C2
Museo de las Cortes de Cádiz 11 B3
Oratorio de San Felipe Neri 12 B3
Roman Theatre 13 D4
Torre Tavira 14 C3
SLEEPING
Casa Caracol 15 D3
Hospedería Las Cortes de Cádiz 16 C2
Hostal Bahía 17 D3
Hostal Fantoni 18 D3
Hotel Argantonio 19 C2
Parador Hotel Atlántico 20 A2
EATING
Bar Zapata 21 C3
Cafetería Las Nieves 22 D3
El Aljibe 23 D4
El Faro 24 A4
La Gorda Te Da De Comer 25 C2
La Gorda Te Da De Comer 26 C3
Mesón Cumbres Mayores 27 C2
DRINKING
Café de Levante 28 C3
El Teniente Seblon 29 D3
Medussa 30 C2
Nahu 31 C2
O'Connell's 32 C2
ENTERTAINMENT
Central Lechera 33 C2
El Malecón 34 D1
Gran Teatro Falla 35 B2
Peña Flamenca La Perla 36 D4
Sala Anfiteátro 37 D1
TRANSPORT
Comes Bus Station 38 D2
Estación Marítima 39 D2
Los Amarillos Bus Stop 40 D3
Plaza de España Bus Stop 41 D2
Underground Car Park 42 D3
Viajes Socialtur 43 D3
Bahía de Cádiz
ATLANTIC OCEAN
Dársena del Puerto
Punta Candelaria
Alameda
Playa de la Caleta
Parque del Genovés
Barrio de la Viña
Barrio del Pópulo
Barrio de Santa María
Train Station
Puertas de Tierra
Plaza de la Constitución
Av de Astilleros
Cuesta de las Calesas
Av Ramón de Carranza
Av del Puerto
Av Duque de Nájera
Av Doctor Gómez Ulla
Campo del Sur
Paseo de Canalejas
Plaza de España
Plaza de la Hispanidad
Plaza de Argüelles
Plaza de Sevilla
Plaza San Juan de Dios
Plaza de Mina
Plaza de Falla
Plaza Mentidero
Plaza San Antonio
Plaza San Francisco
Plaza de Topete
Plaza Libertad
To Castillo de San Sebastián (500m)
To Playa de la Victoria (1.5km); Hospital Puerta del Mar (2km); Barabass (2.5km); Secorbus Bus Stop (3.5km); AP4 (13km); Jerez de la Frontera (35km); Vejer de la Frontera (51km)

ANDALUCÍA

harbour, delaying the imminent Spanish Armada. In 1596 Anglo-Dutch attackers burnt almost the entire city.

Cádiz's golden age was the 18th century, when it enjoyed 75% of Spanish trade with the Americas. It grew into the richest and most cosmopolitan city in Spain and gave birth to the country's first progressive, liberal middle class. During the Napoleonic Wars, Cádiz held out under French siege from 1810 to 1812, when a national parliament meeting here adopted Spain's liberal 1812 constitution, proclaiming sovereignty of the people.

The loss of the American colonies in the 19th century plunged Cádiz into a decline from which it is only today recovering, with increased tourism playing a significant role.

Orientation

Breathing space between the huddled streets of the old city is provided by numerous squares; the most important for orientation being Plaza San Juan de Dios, Plaza de la Catedral and Plaza de Topete in the southeast, and Plaza de Mina in the north. Pedestrianised Calles Nueva and San Francisco run most of the way between Plaza San Juan de Dios and Plaza de Mina.

The train station is just east of the old city, off Plaza de Sevilla, with the main bus station (of the Comes line) 900m to its north on Plaza de la Hispanidad. The 18th-century Puertas de Tierra (Land Gates) mark the southern boundary of the old city.

Information

You'll find plenty of banks and ATMs along Calle Nueva and the parallel Avenida Ramón de Carranza.

Hospital Puerta del Mar (☎ 956 00 21 00; Avenida Ana de Viya 21) The main general hospital, 2km southeast of Puertas de Tierra.

Locutorio Telefónico (Calle Lázaro Dou 1; internet per hr €2; h10am-midnight) Also has phone booths & sells discount phone cards.

Municipal tourist office (☎ 956 24 10 01; Paseo de Canalejas s/n; ⏰ 8.30am-6pm Mon-Fri, 9am-5pm Sat & Sun)

Regional tourist office (☎ 956 20 31 91; Avenida Ramón de Carranza s/n; ⏰ 9am-7.30pm Mon-Fri, 10am-2pm Sat, Sun & holidays)

Sights & Activities

PLAZA SAN JUAN DE DIOS & AROUND

Broad Plaza San Juan de Dios is lined with cafes and is dominated by the imposing neoclassical **ayuntamiento** built around 1800. Between here and the cathedral is the **Barrio del Pópulo**, the kernel of medieval Cádiz and a focus of the city's recent sprucing-up program. At the nearby **Roman Theatre** (☎ 956 25 17 88; Campo del Sur; admission free; ⏰ 10am-2.30pm Wed-Mon) you can walk along a gallery beneath the tiers of seating. The theatre was discovered by chance in 1980.

CATHEDRAL

Cádiz's yellow-domed **cathedral** (☎ 956 28 61 54; Plaza de la Catedral; adult/student €5/3, free during services; ⏰ 10am-6.30pm Mon-Fri, 10am-4.30pm Sat, 1-6.30pm Sun, services 7-8pm Tue-Fri, 11am-1pm Sun) is an impressively proportioned baroque-cum-neoclassical construction but by Spanish standards very sober in its decoration. It fronts a broad, traffic-free plaza where the cathedral's ground-plan is picked out in the paving stones. The decision to build the cathedral was taken in 1716 but the project wasn't finished until 1838, by which time neoclassical elements, such as the dome, towers and main facade, had diluted Vicente Acero's original baroque plan. From a separate entrance on Plaza de la Catedral, climb to the top of the **Torre de Poniente** (Western Tower; ☎ 956 25 17 88; adult/child/senior €4/3/3; ⏰ 10am-6pm, to 8pm 15 Jun-15 Sep) for marvellous vistas.

PLAZA DE TOPETE & AROUND

A short walk northwest from the cathedral, this square is one of Cádiz's liveliest, bright with flower stalls and adjoining the large, lively **Mercado Central** (Central Market). Nearby, the **Torre Tavira** (☎ 956 21 29 10; Calle Marqués del Real Tesoro 10; adult/student €4/3.30; ⏰ 10am-6pm, to 8pm 15 Jun-15 Sep) is the highest of Cádiz's old watchtowers (in the 18th century the city had no less than 160 of these, built so that citizens could observe the comings and goings of ships without leaving home). It provides great panoramas and has a **camera obscura** projecting live images of the city onto a screen.

The **Museo de las Cortes de Cádiz** (☎ 956 22 17 88; Calle Santa Inés 9; admission free; ⏰ 9am-1pm Tue-Sun, 5-7pm Tue-Fri Jun-Sep, 4-7pm Tue-Fri Oct-May) is full of historical memorabilia focusing on the 1812 parliament, including a marvellous large 1770s model of Cádiz, made for King Carlos III. Along the street is the **Oratorio de San Felipe Neri** (☎ 956 21 16 12; Plaza de San Felipe Neri; admission €2.50; ⏰ 10am-1.30pm Mon-Sat), the church where the Cortes de Cádiz met. This is one of Cádiz's finest baroque churches, with a beautiful dome, an unusual oval interior and a Murillo *Inmaculada* on the altarpiece.

MUSEO DE CÁDIZ

Cádiz's excellent major **museum** (☎ 956 20 33 68; Plaza de Mina; EU citizen/other free/€1.50; 🕒 2.30-8.30pm Tue, 9am-8.30pm Wed-Sat, 9.30am-2.30pm Sun) faces one of the city's largest and leafiest squares. The stars of the ground-floor archaeology section are two Phoenician marble sarcophagi, carved in human likeness, and a monumental statue of the Roman emperor Trajan, from Baelo Claudia (p756). The fine arts collection upstairs has 21 superb canvases by Francisco de Zurbarán and the painting that cost Murillo his life – the altarpiece from Cádiz's Convento de Capuchinas. The baroque maestro died from injuries received in a fall from scaffolding while working on this in 1682.

COASTAL WALK

This airy 4.5km walk takes at least 1¼ hours. Go north from Plaza de Mina to the city's northern seafront, with views across the Bahía de Cádiz. Head west along the **Alameda** gardens to the **Baluarte de la Candelaria**, then turn southwest to the **Parque del Genovés**, a semitropical garden with waterfalls and quirkily clipped trees. Continue to the **Castillo de Santa Catalina** (☎ 956 22 63 33; admission free; 🕒 10.30am-8.30pm, to 7.45pm Nov-Feb), built after the 1596 sacking; inside are an interesting historical exhibit on Cádiz and the sea, and a gallery for exhibitions. Sandy **Playa de la Caleta** (very crowded in summer) separates Santa Catalina from the 18th-century **Castillo de San Sebastián**. You can't enter San Sebastián but do walk along the breezy 750m causeway to its gate. Finally, follow the broad promenade along **Campo del Sur** to the cathedral.

PLAYA DE LA VICTORIA

This lovely, wide ocean beach of fine Atlantic sand stretches about 4km along the peninsula from its beginning 1.5km beyond the Puertas de Tierra. At weekends in summer almost the whole city seems to be out here. Bus 1 (Plaza España–Cortadura) from Plaza de España will get you there.

Festivals & Events

No other Spanish city celebrates **Carnaval** with the enthusiasm and originality of Cádiz, where it turns into a 10-day party spanning two weekends. The fun, abetted by huge quantities of alcohol, is infectious. Groups called *murgas*, in fantastic costumes, tour the city on foot or on floats, singing witty satirical ditties, dancing or performing sketches. In addition to the 300 or so officially recognised *murgas*, judged by a panel in the Gran Teatro Falla, there are also the *ilegales* – any group that fancies taking to the streets and trying to play or sing.

Some of the liveliest scenes are in the working-class Barrio de la Viña and on Calle Ancha and Calle Columela, where *ilegales* tend to congregate.

Rooms in Cádiz get booked months in advance for Carnaval, even though prices can be double their summer rates. If you don't manage to snatch one, you could just visit for the night from anywhere else within striking distance. Plenty of other people do this.

Sleeping

Casa Caracol (☎ 956 26 11 66; www.caracolcasa.com; Calle Suárez de Salazar 4; dm/hammock incl breakfast €16/10; 💻) Casa Caracol is the only backpacker hostel in the old town. Friendly and crowded, it has bunk dorms for four and eight, a communal kitchen, free internet and a roof terrace with hammocks. It's advisable to book through www.hostelworld.com or www.hostelbookers.com as the hostel often fills up.

Hostal Fantoni (☎ 956 28 27 04; www.hostalfantoni.net; Calle Flamenco 5; s/d €45/70; ❄) The Fantoni offers a dozen attractive and spotless rooms, all with air-con, in an attractively modernised 18th-century house. The panoramic roof terrace catches a breeze in summer.

Hostal Bahía (☎ 956 25 90 61; Calle Plocia 5; s/d €60/76; 🚭 ❄ 💻) All rooms are exterior and impeccably looked-after, and have phone, TV and built-in wardrobes. It's plain and straightforward but good value.

Hotel Argantonio (☎ 956 21 16 40; www.hotelargantonio.com in Spanish; Calle Argantonio 3; s/d incl breakfast €74/101; ❄ 💻) A very attractive small new hotel in the old city with an appealing Mudéjar accent to its decor. Staff are welcoming, and the rooms are comfortable with wi-fi access and flat-screen TVs.

Parador Hotel Atlántico (☎ 956 22 69 05; www.parador.es; Avenida Duque de Nájera 9; s/d €110/137; 🅿 ❄ 💻 🏊) Cádiz's modern *parador* is comfortable and spacious, if architecturally bland. All rooms have a terrace with a sea view of some sort, and the pool sits in a lawn overlooking the ocean.

Hospedería Las Cortes de Cádiz (☎ 956 21 26 68; www.hotellascortes.com; Calle San Francisco 9; s/d incl breakfast €109/148; P ✱ ▣) This excellent hotel occupies a remodelled 1850s mansion. The 36 rooms, each themed around a figure, place or event associated with the Cortes de Cádiz, sport classical furnishings and modern comforts. The hotel also has a roof terrace, Jacuzzi and small gym.

Eating

Bar Zapata (Plaza Candelaria; montaditos €1.60-2, raciones €10-12; ⏰ closed Sun) The crowd often spills out the door at this highly popular tapas joint. The scrumptious *montaditos* (open sandwiches) and *revueltos* (scrambled-egg dishes) are a speciality, and the jazz-rock-blues soundtrack adds to the atmosphere.

Cafetería Las Nieves (☎ 956 26 12 55; Plaza Mendizábal 4; coffee & tostada €2; ⏰ 7.45am-10pm Mon-Fri, 9am-1.30pm Sat) Near Plaza San Juan de Dios, this cosy cafe with decor of brick, tile and prints is one of the city's most inviting breakfast spots. Enjoy *tostadas* or *molletes* (soft toasted rolls) with a big range of spreads.

Mesón Cumbres Mayores (☎ 956 21 32 70; Calle Zorrilla 4; tapas €1.50-2, mains €9-18) The wood-beamed Cumbres Mayores has an excellent tapas bar in the front and a small restaurant in the back. It's hard to beat the ham and cheese *montaditos*. In the restaurant, there are great salads, seafood, barbecued meats and *guisos* (stews).

El Aljibe (☎ 956 26 66 56; www.pablogrosso.com; Calle Plocia 25; tapas €2-3.50, mains €10-15) *Gaditano* chef Pablo Grosso concocts delicious combinations of the traditional and the adventurous. He stuffs his pheasant breast with dates and his *solomillo ibérico* (Iberian pork sirloin) with Emmental cheese, ham and piquant peppers. You can enjoy his creations as tapas in the stone-walled downstairs bar.

El Faro (☎ 956 22 99 16; Calle San Félix 15; mains €15-25) Over in Barrio de la Viña, El Faro has a famous and excellent seafood restaurant, decorated with pretty ceramics, and an adjoining, less-pricey, tapas bar.

Also recommended, **La Gorda Te Da De Comer** (tapas €2-2.40, media raciones €6) Luque (Calle General Luque 1; ⏰ 9-11.30pm Mon, 1.30-4pm & 9-11.30pm Tue-Sat); Rosario (cnr Calles Rosario & Marqués de Valdeiñigo; ⏰ 1-4pm & 9-11.30pm Tue-Sat) has incredibly tasty food at low prices amid trendy pop design at both its locations. Try the *solomillo* in creamy mushroom sauce or the curried chicken strips with Marie-Rose dip.

Drinking

In the old city the Plaza de Mina–Plaza San Francisco–Plaza de España area is the main hub of the nocturnal bar scene; things start to get going around midnight at most places, but can be quiet in the first half of the week.

Medussa (cnr Calles Manuel Rancés & Beato Diego; www.medussa.com; ⏰ closed Mon) Medussa is the late-night magnet for an alternative and student crowd; red walls and banks of lime-green fluorescent lighting set the tone. DJs vary, and there is occasional live music – from garage and funk to punk and indie-rock.

Nahu (☎ 856 07 90 22; Calle Beato Diego 8; ⏰ from 5pm) An African-themed music cafe that's consistently popular. DJs spin different rhythms each night, from reggae or world to hip hop or chillout.

Café de Levante (☎ 956 22 02 27; www.cafelevante.com; Calle Rosario 35; ⏰ from 8pm) A cosy little bar with an artsy and student clientele and walls adorned with all sorts of curious photos and posters.

O'Connell's (☎ 956 22 49 61; Plaza San Francisco; ⏰ from 1pm) A convivial, wood-panelled Irish pub, O'Connell's always has a good crowd. There's rock music and sport on the TVs.

El Teniente Seblon (☎ 956 26 58 39; Calle Posadilla 4) This arty, gay-friendly bar is one of the liveliest evening spots in the Barrio del Pópulo.

The second hot spot is down Playa de la Victoria, along Paseo Marítimo and nearby in the Hotel Playa Victoria area, about 2.5km from the Puertas de Tierra. The hippest bars include glamorous **Barabass** (☎ 856 07 90 26; www.barabass.es; Calle General Muñoz Arenillas 4-6; admission incl 1 drink €8; ⏰ 6pm-6am).

Entertainment

Head out late, Thursday to Saturday, to Punta de San Felipe (known as La Punta) on the northern side of the harbour. Here, a line of disco bars and the big disco **Sala Anfiteátro** (Paseo Pascual Pery; admission €6-8) pack with an 18-to-25 crowd from around 3am to 6am, while **El Malecón** (☎ 956 22 45 51; Paseo Pascual Pery; admission €8-10) is the place for salsa and gets going a bit earlier, with free salsa classes at midnight Saturday.

Peña Flamenca La Perla (☎ 956 25 91 01; www.perladecadiz.com in Spanish; Calle Carlos Ollero s/n) The cavernlike Peña La Perla hosts flamenco nights at 10pm on many Fridays in spring and summer. Check with the tourist offices for other flamenco events.

The **Gran Teatro Falla** (☎ 956 22 08 34; Plaza de Falla) and the **Central Lechera** (☎ 956 22 06 28; Plaza de Argüelles s/n) host busy and varied programs of theatre, dance and music.

Getting There & Around

BOAT

See p744 for details of the passenger ferries heading across the bay to El Puerto de Santa María.

BUS

Most buses are run by **Comes** (☎ 956 80 70 59; Plaza de la Hispanidad). Destinations include Seville (€10.65, 1¾ hours, 10 daily), El Puerto de Santa María (€1.85, 30 to 40 minutes, 19 or more daily), Jerez de la Frontera (€2.85, 40 minutes, nine or more daily), Tarifa (€7.91, two hours, five daily) and other places down the Cádiz coast, Arcos de la Frontera (€5.28, 1¼ hours, five daily Monday to Friday, two daily Saturday and Sunday), Ronda (€12.61, three hours, two daily), Málaga (€19.58, four hours, six daily) and Granada (€27.90, five hours, four daily).

Los Amarillos, from its stop by the southern end of Avenida Ramón de Carranza, operates up to four further daily buses to Arcos de la Frontera (€4.37, 1¼ hours) and El Bosque (€6.83, two hours), plus up to 13 daily to Sanlúcar de Barrameda (€3, 1¼ hours). Some services go less often on Saturday and Sunday. Information is available at **Viajes Socialtur** (☎ 956 29 08 00; Avenida Ramón de Carranza 31).

Secorbus (☎ 956 25 74 15; Avenida José León de Carranza 20) runs three buses daily to Madrid (€22.30, eight hours). The stop is 3.6km southeast of the Puertas de Tierra – to reach it take city bus 1 (€0.93) from Plaza de España to its last stop.

CAR & MOTORCYCLE

The AP4 motorway from Seville to Puerto Real on the eastern side of the Bahía de Cádiz carries a €5.50 toll. The toll-free A4 is slower.

There's a handily placed **underground car park** (Paseo de Canalejas; per 24hr €9) near the port area.

TRAIN

From the **train station** (☎ 902 24 02 02) up to 36 trains run daily to El Puerto de Santa María (€2.35 to €2.90, 40 minutes) and Jerez de la Frontera (€2.90 to €3.65, 50 minutes), up to 15 to Seville (€9.80, two hours), three to Córdoba (€34 to €43, three hours) and two to Madrid (€63, five hours).

EL PUERTO DE SANTA MARÍA

pop 85,100

El Puerto, across the bay and 10km northeast of Cádiz (22km by road), is one of Cádiz province's triangle of sherry-making towns and its excellent beaches, sherry bodegas and tapas bars make it a fine outing from Cádiz or Jerez. In summer it jumps with a series of festivals, and *sevillanos* and people from all round Cádiz province come to the coast for a good time. El Puerto is easily and enjoyably reached by ferry from Cádiz.

Orientation & Information

The heart of the town is on the northwestern bank of Río Guadalete. The ferry *El Vapor* arrives at the Muelle del Vapor jetty, on Plaza de las Galeras Reales. The train station is beside the Jerez road on the northeast side of town, about 700m from Plaza de las Galeras Reales. The good **tourist office** (☎ 956 54 24 13; www.turismoelpuerto.com; Calle Luna 22; 🕐 10am-2pm & 6-8pm May-Sep, 10am-2pm & 5.30-7.30pm Oct-Apr) is 2½ blocks straight ahead from the Muelle del Vapor.

Sights & Activities

The four-spouted **Fuente de las Galeras Reales** (Fountain of the Royal Galleys), by the Muelle del Vapor, once supplied water to America-bound ships.

The **Castillo de San Marcos** (☎ 956 85 17 51; Plaza Alfonso El Sabio 3; admission €5; 🕐 10.30am-1.30pm Thu & Sat) is open for half-hour guided tours two days a week, with a sampling of Caballero sherry included (the company owns the castle). The castle's highlight is the pre-13th-century mosque (now a church) preserved inside. The **Fundación Rafael Alberti** (☎ 956 85 07 11; Calle Santo Domingo 25; admission €3; 🕐 11am-2.30pm Tue-Sun), a few blocks further inland, has interesting exhibits on Rafael Alberti (1902–99), one of the great poets of Spain's 'Generation of 27', who grew up here. The exhibits are well displayed and audioguides in English, German or Spanish (€2) are available. El Puerto's most splendid church, the 15th- to 18th-century **Iglesia Mayor Prioral** (🕐 8.30am-12.45pm Mon-Fri, 8.30am-noon Sat, 8.30am-1.45pm Sun, 6-8.30pm daily), dominates nearby Plaza de España. Four blocks southwest from there, the grand 19th-century **Plaza de Toros** (Bullring; ☎ 956 54 15 78; Plaza Elías Ahuja; admission free; 🕐 11am-1.30pm & 5.30-7pm Tue-Sun) is one of the most celebrated in Spain. Top matadors fight here every Sunday in July and August:

the ring is closed for visits the day before and after fights.

The best known of El Puerto's seven sherry wineries, **Osborne** (☎ 956 86 91 00; www.osborne.es in Spanish; Calle Los Moros 7; tours in English/Spanish/German €6; 10.30am, noon & 12.30pm Mon-Fri) and **Terry** (☎ 956 15 15 00; Calle Toneleros 1; tours in English & Spanish €8; 10.30am & 12.30pm Mon-Thu), offer weekday tours and sometimes add extra tours, including on Saturday, in summer. For Osborne you need to phone ahead; for Terry you don't.

The nearest beach is pine-flanked **Playa de la Puntilla**, a half-hour walk from the centre – or take bus 26 (€0.80) along Avenida Aramburu de Mora. In high summer the beaches furthest out, such as **Playa Fuenterrabía**, reached by bus 35 from the centre, are least hectic.

Sleeping

The tourist office's accommodation list and website helpfully highlight places with wheelchair access.

Hostal Costa Luz (☎ 956 05 47 01; www.hostalcostaluz.com in Spanish; Calle Niño del Matadero 2; s/d €42.50/65; P) Friendly, modern *hostal* in the bullring vicinity with 11 nicely done, medium-sized rooms and a cafe for breakfast.

Casa No 6 (☎ 956 87 70 84; www.casano6.com; Calle San Bartolomé 14; s/d/q incl breakfast €70/80/140; P) This beautifully renovated 19th-century house provides a friendly welcome and charming, spacious and spotless rooms. There's usually a three-night minimum stay in high summer.

Casa del Regidor Hotel (☎ 956 87 73 33; www.hotelcasadelregidor.com; Ribera del Río 30; s/d €65/95; P) A converted 18th-century mansion with its original patio. The excellent rooms have all mod cons and solar-heated hot water.

Hotel Monasterio San Miguel (☎ 956 54 04 40; www.hotelesjale.com; Calle Virgen de los Milagros 27; s/d €148/196; P) A gourmet restaurant, a pool in a semi-tropical garden, and classically elegant rooms await your pleasure at this luxurious converted 18th-century monastery.

Eating

Romerijo (☎ 956 54 12 54; Plaza de la Herrería; seafood per 250g from €4.50) A huge, always busy El Puerto institution, Romerijo has two buildings, one boiling the seafood, the other frying it. Choose from the displays and buy by the quarter-kilogram in paper cones.

Casa Flores (☎ 956 54 35 12; Ribera del Río 9; mains €20-30) For more formal dining, go for tile-bedecked Casa Flores. Fish and seafood are the specialities, but there are good choices for meat eaters too.

El Puerto has one of the best collections of tapas bars of any town of its size in Andalucía. The main streets to look in are the central Calle Luna; Calle Misericordia and Ribera del Marisco to its north; and Avenidas Bajamar and Aramburu de Mora to its south. Don't miss **Mesón Leonés** (☎ 956 85 96 36; Calle Luna 4; tapas €1.50-2; closed Wed) for its cured meats and cheeses; **Cervecería El Puerto** (☎ 956 85 89 39; Calle Luna 13; tapas €2; closed Thu) for seafood; **Mesón del Asador** (☎ 956 54 03 27; tapas €2.20; Calle Misericordia 2) for grilled meats; or the tightly packed **Casa Luis** (☎ 956 87 20 09; Ribera del Marisco s/n; tapas €3; closed Mon) with innovative concoctions like *paté de cabracho* (scorpion fish paté). Mesón del Asador also has a sit-down restaurant with grilled meats for €11 to €18.

Getting There & Away

BOAT

The small ferry *Adriano III*, known as **El Vapor** (☎ 629 468014; www.vapordeelpuerto.com), a decades-old symbol of El Puerto, sails to El Puerto (one-way/return €3/4, 40 minutes) from Cádiz's Estación Marítima (Passenger Port) five or six times daily from early February to early December (except Mondays from late September to late May). The faster Catamarán (€1.85, 25 min), operated by the public **Consorcio de Transportes Bahía de Cádiz** (☎ 902 45 05 50; www.cmtbc.com), sails between Cádiz (Terminal Marítima, near the train station) and El Puerto 18 times a day Monday to Friday, six times on Saturday and five on Sunday and holidays. In El Puerto, the Catamarán docks on the river 400m southwest (downstream) from the Muelle del Vapor.

BUS

Buses run to Cádiz (€1.85, 30 to 40 minutes) from the Plaza de Toros (Bullring) about half-hourly, 6.45am to 10.30pm (7.15am to 8.30pm Saturday, 8.45am to 8.45pm Sunday). For Jerez de la Frontera (€1.10, 20 minutes) there are nine to 17 daily buses from the train station, plus six (Monday to Friday only) from the bullring. Buses for Sanlúcar de Barrameda (€1.64, 30 minutes, five to 13 daily) depart from the bullring. Buses to Seville (€8.50, 1½ hours, three daily) go from the train station.

TRAIN

Up to 36 trains travel daily to Jerez (€1.40, 15 minutes) and Cádiz (€2.35 to €2.90, 40 minutes), and up to 15 daily to Seville (€8.20, 1½ hours).

SANLÚCAR DE BARRAMEDA

pop 67,000

Sanlúcar, 23km northwest of El Puerto de Santa María, is the northern tip of the sherry triangle. It looks across the Guadalquivir estuary to the Parque Nacional de Doñana and is one of the two starting points for 4WD tours in the national park – the other is El Acebuche (p735).

Sanlúcar's nautical history is proud. Columbus sailed from Sanlúcar in 1498 on his third voyage to the Caribbean. So, in 1519, did the Portuguese Ferdinand Magellan, seeking – as Columbus had – a westerly route to the Asian spice islands. Magellan succeeded, but was killed in the Philippines. His pilot, Juan Sebastián Del Cano, completed the first circumnavigation of the globe by returning to Sanlúcar in 1522 with just one of the five ships, the *Vittoria*.

Orientation & Information

Sanlúcar stretches 2.5km along the southeastern side of the Guadalquivir estuary, fronted by a long, sandy beach. Calzada del Ejército (La Calzada), running inland from the seafront Paseo Marítimo, is the main avenue. A block beyond its inland end is Plaza del Cabildo, the central square. The bus station is on Avenida de la Estación, 100m southwest of the middle of La Calzada. The multilingual and very helpful **tourist office** (☎ 956 36 61 10; www.turismosanlucar.com in Spanish; 10am-2pm & 6-8pm Mon-Fri Jun-Oct, 10am-2pm & 4-6pm Mon-Fri Nov-Feb, 10am-2pm & 5-7pm Mon-Fri Mar-May, 10am-12.45pm Sat & 10am-2pm Sun all year) is on Calzada del Ejército.

The old fishing quarter, Bajo de Guía, site of Sanlúcar's best restaurants and boat departures for the Parque Nacional de Doñana, is 750m northeast from La Calzada. Here, the **Centro de Visitantes Fábrica de Hielo** (☎ 956 38 65 77; www.parquenacionaldonana.es; 9am-8pm) provides displays and information on the Parque Nacional de Doñana.

Sights

From Plaza del Cabildo, cross Calle Ancha to Plaza San Roque and head up Calle Bretones, which becomes Calle Cuesta de Belén and doglegs up to the **Palacio de Orleans y Borbón** (admission free; 10am-2.30pm Mon-Fri), a beautiful neo-Mudéjar palace that was built as a summer home for the aristocratic Montpensier family in the 19th century and is now Sanlúcar's town hall. A block to the left along Calle Caballeros is the medieval **Iglesia de Nuestra Señora de la O** (mass 8pm Mon-Sat, 9am, noon & 8pm Sun), which stands out among Sanlúcar's churches for its beautiful Gothic Mudéjar main portal, created in the 1360s, and the richness of its interior decoration, including the Mudéjar *artesonado* ceilings. Next door is the **Palacio de los Duques de Medina Sidonia** (☎ 956 36 01 61; www.fcmedinasidonia.com in Spanish; Plaza Condes de Niebla 1; tour €3; 11am & noon Sun), the rambling home of the aristocratic family that once owned more of Spain than anyone else. The house, mostly dating to the 17th century, bursts with antiques and paintings by Goya, Zurbarán and other famous Spanish artists.

Some 200m further along the street, amid buildings of the Barbadillo sherry company, is the 15th-century **Castillo de Santiago** (☎ 956 08 83 29; Plaza del Castillo; tour €7; h10am-1pm Tue-Sat), recently opened after many years of intermittent restoration work. There are great views from the hexagonal Torre del Homenaje (Keep).

Tours

SHERRY BODEGAS

Sanlúcar produces a distinctive sherrylike wine, manzanilla. Several bodegas give tours for which you don't need to book ahead, including these:

Barbadillo (☎ 956 38 55 00; Calle Luis de Eguilaz 11; tours €3; in English 11am Tue-Sat, in Spanish noon & 1pm Tue-Sat) Near the castle, Barbadillo is the oldest & biggest manzanilla firm. There's also a good manzanilla museum (10am-3pm Tue-Sat) here, which you can visit independently of the tour.

Hidalgo-La Gitana (☎ 956 38 53 04; Calzada del Ejército; tours in English & Spanish €5; 11am & noon Mon-Fri, noon Sat)

Pedro Romero (☎ 956 36 07 36; Calle Trasbolsa 84; tours €6; in English & Spanish noon Mon-Sat, 6pm Tue-Fri, in German 11am Wed & Fri, noon Mon) This bodega also holds 2½-hour tasting sessions (€20 per person) at noon on Tuesday, Thursday and Saturday.

PARQUE NACIONAL DE DOÑANA

From Bajo de Guía, **Viajes Doñana** (☎ 956 36 25 40; Calle San Juan 20; tours per person €36; office 9am-2pm & 5-8.30pm Mon-Fri, 10am-1pm Sat) and **Viajes Correcaminos** (☎ 956 38 20 40; Calle Ramón y Cajal 4) operate 3½-hour tours into the national park, at 8.30am and 2.30pm on Tuesday and Friday (the afternoon trips go at 4.30pm from May to mid-September). After the river crossing, the trip is by 20-person 4WD vehicle, visiting much the same spots as the tours from El Acebuche. On the trip, either take mosquito repellent or cover up.

Festivals & Events

The Sanlúcar summer gets going with the **Feria de la Manzanilla**, in late May or early June, and blossoms in July and August with jazz, flamenco and classical-music festivals, one-off concerts by top Spanish bands, and Sanlúcar's unique horse races, the **Carreras de Caballo** (www.carrerassanlucar.es), in which thoroughbred racehorses thunder along the beach during two three-day evening meetings during August.

Sleeping

Book well ahead at holiday times.

Hostal La Bohemia (☎ 956 36 95 99; Calle Don Claudio 5; s/d €30/44;) Pretty, folksy-painted chairs dot the corridors of this little upstairs *hostal*, on a side street 300m northeast of Plaza del Cabildo; rooms are neat, clean and air-conditioned.

Hotel Barrameda (☎ 956 38 58 78; www.hotelbarrameda.com; Calle Ancha 10; s/d incl breakfast €54/81;) This new 30-room hotel is a welcome addition. The ground-floor reception gives onto a patio; rooms have stylish modern furnishings, marble floors, framed art prints and wi-fi access, and there's a roof terrace too.

Hotel Posada de Palacio (☎ 956 36 48 40; www.posadadepalacio.com; Calle Caballeros 11; s/d from €88/109; P) Sanlúcar's most atmospheric lodging is this rambling 18th-century mansion, with pretty patios and terraces, plenty of antiques, and rooms kitted out with period furnishings. Staff can be a little offhand.

Tartaneros Hotel (☎ 956 38 53 93; www.hoteltartaneros.com; Calle Tartaneros 8; s/d from €97/129; P) A century-old industrialist's mansion with assorted quirky artefacts and comfortable rooms, at the inland end of Calzada del Ejército.

Eating

Spain holds few dreamier dining experiences than tucking into succulent seafood while watching the sun go down over the Guadalquivir at Bajo de Guía.

Restaurante Virgen del Carmen (☎ 956 38 22 72; Bajo de Guía s/n; fish mains €9-15) This is one of the best of several restaurants at Bajo de Guía. Dine on the downstairs *terraza* or in the upstairs dining room. Decide whether you want your fish *plancha* (grilled) or *frito* (fried), and don't skip the starters: *langostinos* (king prawns, €10) and *coquines al ajillo* (clams in garlic, €9) are specialities.

Casa Bigote (☎ 956 36 26 96; Bajo de Guía 10; fish mains €7-14; closed Sun) The food here gets excellent reviews from everyone. Do try the house speciality – *hamburguesas de bacalao con salsa* (codburgers with sauce; €8.50).

Cafetería Guzmán El Bueno (☎ 956 36 01 61; Plaza Condes de Niebla 1; dishes €3-8; 8.30am-9pm, to early am Sat & Jul-Aug) Sink into plump cushions surrounded by antique furnishings at the cafe in the Palacio de los Duques de Medina Sidonia (p745). Fare is simple – omelettes, cheese, ham – but the setting is uniquely atmospheric.

Cafes and bars, many serving manzanilla from the barrel, surround Plaza del Cabildo and Plaza San Roque behind it: **Casa Balbino** (Plaza del Cabildo 11; tapas €2-3) is a must for tapas.

Entertainment

There are some lively music bars on and around Calzada del Ejército and Plaza del Cabildo, and lots of concerts in summer.

Getting There & Away

Buses from Sanlúcar include services to El Puerto de Santa María (€1.64, 30 minutes, five to 12 daily), Cádiz (€3, 1¼ hours, five to 12 daily), Jerez de la Frontera (€1.68, 30 minutes, seven to 15 daily) and Seville (€7.06, 1½ hours, five to 10 daily).

JEREZ DE LA FRONTERA

pop 202,700

Jerez (heh-*reth*), 36km northeast of Cádiz, is a beguiling town with a uniquely eclectic and intense character. Visitors come to see its famous sherry bodegas, but Jerez is also Andalucía's horse capital and has a creative artistic and nightlife scene and a large *gitano* community that is one of the hotbeds of flamenco. It stages fantastic, showy, hedonistic fiestas with sleek horses, beautiful people, fine food and drink and passionate music. Wealth and contemporary style rub shoulders here with poverty, tradition and history, and it all adds up to an enthralling compound that can be a hard to get a handle on at first but bountifully repays time taken getting to know it.

Orientation & Information

The central axis of Jerez is Calle Larga and Calle Lancería, pedestrianised streets lined

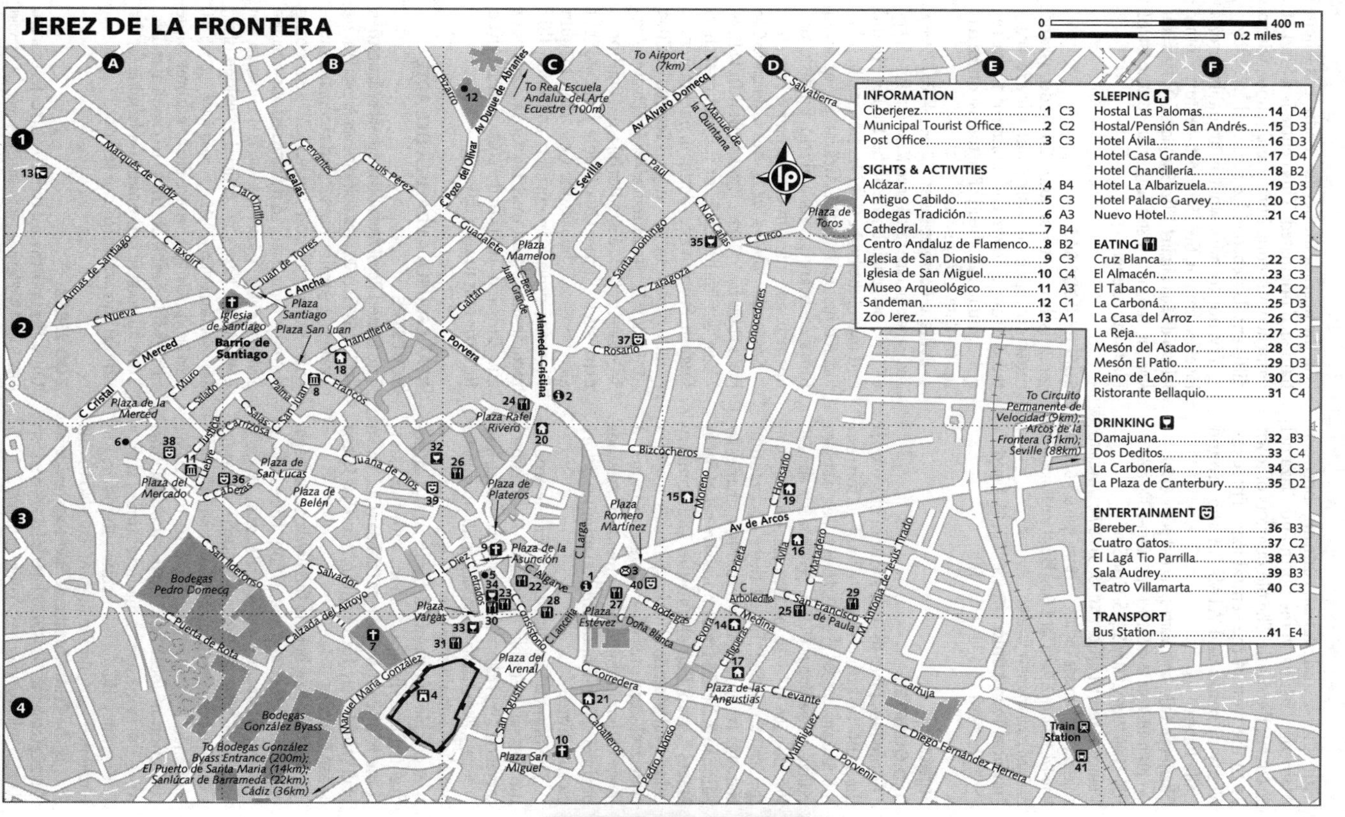
JEREZ DE LA FRONTERA
0 400 m
0 0.2 miles
INFORMATION
Ciberjerez....1 C3
Municipal Tourist Office....2 C2
Post Office....3 C3
SIGHTS & ACTIVITIES
Alcázar....4 B4
Antiguo Cabildo....5 C3
Bodegas Tradición....6 A3
Cathedral....7 B4
Centro Andaluz de Flamenco....8 B2
Iglesia de San Dionisio....9 C3
Iglesia de San Miguel....10 C4
Museo Arqueológico....11 A3
Sandeman....12 C1
Zoo Jerez....13 A1
SLEEPING
Hostal Las Palomas....14 D4
Hostal/Pensión San Andrés....15 D3
Hotel Ávila....16 D3
Hotel Casa Grande....17 D4
Hotel Chancillería....18 B2
Hotel La Albarizuela....19 D3
Hotel Palacio Garvey....20 C3
Nuevo Hotel....21 C4
EATING
Cruz Blanca....22 C3
El Almacén....23 C3
El Tabanco....24 C2
La Carboná....25 D3
La Casa del Arroz....26 C3
La Reja....27 C3
Mesón del Asador....28 C3
Mesón El Patio....29 D3
Reino de León....30 C3
Ristorante Bellaquio....31 C4
DRINKING
Damajuana....32 B3
Dos Deditos....33 C4
La Carbonería....34 C3
La Plaza de Canterbury....35 D2
ENTERTAINMENT
Bereber....36 B3
Cuatro Gatos....37 C2
El Lagá Tio Parrilla....38 A3
Sala Audrey....39 B3
Teatro Villamarta....40 C3
TRANSPORT
Bus Station....41 E4
To Airport (7km)
To Real Escuela Andaluz del Arte Ecuestre (100m)
To Circuito Permanente de Velocidad (9km); Arcos de la Frontera (31km); Seville (88km)
To Bodegas González Byass Entrance (200m); El Puerto de Santa María (14km); Sanlúcar de Barrameda (22km); Cádiz (36km)
Av Álvaro Domecq
Alameda Cristina
Av de Arcos
Barrio de Santiago
Plaza de Toros
Plaza Mamelon
Plaza Santiago
Plaza San Juan
Plaza Rafael Rivero
Plaza de Plateros
Plaza Romero Martínez
Plaza de la Asunción
Plaza Vargas
Plaza Estévez
Plaza del Arenal
Plaza San Miguel
Plaza de las Angustias
Plaza de la Merced
Plaza del Mercado
Plaza de San Lucas
Plaza de Belén
Iglesia de Santiago
Bodegas Pedro Domecq
Bodegas González Byass
Train Station
C Marqués de Cádiz
C Armas de Santiago
C Taxdirt
C Nueva
C Merced
C Cristal
C Lealas
C Cervantes
C Luis Pérez
C Jardinillo
C Juan de Torres
C Ancha
C Chancillería
C Porvera
C Pozo del Olivar
Av Duque de Abrantes
C Pizarro
C Guadalete
C Beato Juan Grande
C Gaitán
C Sevilla
C Paul
C Manuel de la Quintana
C Salvatierra
C Santo Domingo
C N de Cañas
C Circo
C Zaragoza
C Rosario
C Conocedores
C Bizcocheros
C Moreno
C Honsario
C Prieta
C Ávila
C Matadero
C M Antonia de Jesús Tirado
C Arboledilla
C San Francisco de Paula
C Medina
C Evora
C Higueras
C Bodegas
C Doña Blanca
C Larga
C Lancería
C Consistorio
C Algarve
C Letrados
C L Díez
C Salvador
C Calzada del Arroyo
C San Ildefonso
C Puerta de Rota
C Manuel María González
C San Agustín
C Corredera
C Caballeros
C Pedro Alonso
C Mariñíguez
C Levante
C Porvenir
C Cartuja
C Diego Fernández Herrera
C Juana de Dios
C Francos
C Palma
C San Juan
C Salas
C Carrizosa
C Justicia
C Liebre
C Cabezas
C Muro
C Salado

ANDALUCÍA

with shops and cafes, running between Alameda Cristina in the north and Plaza del Arenal in the south. The old quarters of town lie to the west of the central axis. There are plenty of banks and ATMs on and around Calle Larga.

Ciberjerez (Calle Santa María 3, internet per hr €1.80; 10am-10.30pm Mon-Sat Oct-Apr, 10am-2.30pm & 5.30-11pm Mon-Sat May-Sep, 5-10pm Sun)

Municipal tourist office (956 33 88 74; www.turismojerez.com; Alameda Cristina; 9am-3pm & 5-6.30pm Mon-Fri, 9.30am-2.30pm Sat & Sun) Expert multilingual staff and comprehensive website.

Provincial Tourist Office (956 18 68 08; Airport; 8.15am-2pm & 5-6.30pm Mon-Fri)

Sights

OLD QUARTER

The obvious place to start a tour of old Jerez is the 11th- or 12th-century Almohad fortress, the **Alcázar** (956 35 01 33; Alameda Vieja; admission incl/excl camera obscura €5.40/3; 10am-6pm Mon-Sat, 10am-3pm Sun 16 Sep-30 Apr; 10am-8pm Mon-Sat, 10am-3pm Sun 1 May-15 Sep). Inside there's a beautiful **mezquita** (mosque), converted to a chapel by Alfonso X in 1264, an impressive set of **Baños Árabes** (Arab Baths) and the 18th-century **Palacio Villavicencio**. In the palace's tower a **camera obscura** provides a live panorama of Jerez, with multilingual commentary. Sessions begin every half-hour until 30 minutes before closing time.

The orange tree–lined promenade around the Alcázar overlooks the mainly 18th-century **cathedral** (11.30am-1pm & 6.30-8pm Mon-Sat, Mass 11.30am, 1.30pm, 7.30pm & 9pm Sun), built on the site of Scheris' main mosque.

A couple of blocks northeast of the cathedral is Plaza de la Asunción, with the handsome 16th-century **Antiguo Cabildo** (Old Town Hall) and lovely 15th-century Mudéjar **Iglesia de San Dionisio**.

Northwest of here is the **Barrio de Santiago**, with a sizeable *gitano* population. The excellent **Museo Arqueológico** (Archaeological Museum; 956 35 01 33; Plaza del Mercado) here was closed for extension works at research time but should have reopened by the end of 2008. Its impressive collection of local finds spans the millennia from the stone age to medieval times, with a 7th-century-BC Greek helmet, found in Río Guadalete, among the highlights. Also in this area is the **Centro Andaluz de Flamenco** (Andalucian Flamenco Centre; 956 34 92 65; http://caf.cica.es in Spanish; Plaza San Juan 1; admission free; 9am-2pm Mon-Fri). Jerez is at the heart of the Seville–Cádiz axis where flamenco originated. This centre is a kind of flamenco museum, library and school, with a different flamenco video screened each day.

Try not to miss what is arguably Jerez's loveliest church, the 15th/16th-century Gothic **Iglesia de San Miguel** (Plaza San Miguel; Mass 8pm Mon-Sat, 9am, noon & 8pm Sun), just southeast of Plaza del Arenal.

SHERRY BODEGAS

Jerez is home to around 20 bodegas and most are open to visits, but they're scattered around town and many of them require you to call ahead. The tourist office has up-to-date information.

Bodegas González Byass (902 44 00 77; www.bodegastiopepe.com; Calle Manuel María González 12; tour €10; 11am-6pm) is home of the Tio Pepe brand and one of the biggest sherry houses, handily located just west of the Alcázar. Six or seven tours each are given daily in English and Spanish, and a few in German and French.

Sandeman (956 31 29 95; www.sandeman.eu; Calle Pizarro 10; tour €6; 11am-2.15pm Mon, Wed & Fri, 10.15am-2.15pm Tue & Thu) has three or four tours each in English, Spanish and German, one in French. Another interesting bodega is **Bodegas Tradición** (956 16 86 28; www.bodegastradicion.com; Plaza Cordobeses 3; 9am-2pm & 4.30-6.30pm Mon-Fri) – not only for its extra-aged sherries (20 or more years old) but also because it houses the Colección Joaquín Rivera, a private Spanish art collection that includes important works by Goya, Velázquez and Zurbarán. Tours of the collection are given three or four times a day.

REAL ESCUELA ANDALUZA DEL ARTE ECUESTRE

The famed **Royal Andalucian School of Equestrian Art** (956 31 80 08; www.realescuela.org; Avenida Duque de Abrantes;) trains horses and riders in equestrian skills, and you can watch them going through their paces in **training sessions** (admission adult/child €10/6; 11am-1pm Mon, Wed & Fri Sep-Jul, Mon & Wed Aug). There's an official **exhibición** (show; admission adult/child €24/15, noon Tue & Thu Sep-Jul, noon Tue, Thu & Fri Aug), where the handsome white horses show off their tricks to classical music. You can book tickets online – advisable for the official shows, which can sell out.

ZOO JEREZ

Only 1km northwest of the centre, Jerez's **zoo** (956 14 97 85; www.zoobotanicojerez.com; Calle Taxdirt s/n; adult/child €9/6; 10am-6pm Tue-Sun May-Sep, 10am-8pm Tue-sun Jun-Aug;) houses 1300 beasts and has well-established gardens and a recuperation centre for wild animals.

Festivals & Events

Jerez has a big calendar of festive events. These are the biggest highlights:

Festival de Jerez (www.festivaldejerez.es in Spanish) Late February/early March – Jerez's biggest celebration of flamenco.

Motorcycle Grand Prix Usually March, April or May – Jerez's **Circuito Permanente de Velocidad** (Racing Circuit; 956 15 11 00; www.circuitodejerez.com), on the A382 10km east of town, hosts several motorcycle and car-racing events each year, including one of the Grand Prix races of the World Motorcycle Championship.

Feria del Caballo Late April or first half of May – Jerez's week-long Horse Fair is one of Andalucía's biggest festivals, with music, dance and bullfights as well as all kinds of equestrian competitions and parades.

Fiestas de la Vendimia September – The two-week Grape-Harvest Festivals involve the traditional treading of the first grapes on Plaza de la Asunción.

Sleeping

Many places almost double their rates for the Motorcycle Grand Prix and Feria del Caballo, and you need to book ahead.

Hostal/Pensión San Andrés (956 34 09 83; www.hotelsanandres.es in Spanish; Calle Moreno 12; s €22-26, d €30-40;) The friendly San Andrés has three pretty, plant-filled patios and a range of rooms including economical shared-bath options. The hotel section is cosier than the pensión.

Hostal Las Palomas (956 34 37 73; www.hostal-las-palomas.com; Calle Higueras 17; s with/without bathroom €25/20 d with/without bathroom €35/30) A faint Moroccan theme, touches of art, earthy colours and a good roof terrace are among the pluses of this recently revamped hostal.

Hotel Ávila (956 33 48 08; www.hotelavila.com; Calle Ávila 3; s/d €43/64;) A friendly welcome and comfy, well-kept if unexciting rooms make this hotel on a quiet side street an excellent deal.

Hotel La Albarizuela (956 34 68 62; www.hotelalbarizuela.com; Calle Honsario 6; s/d €106/149;) A contemporary place popular with an under-30s crowd. Deep discounts (often around 60% from mid-October to mid-April) are frequently offered, so email or phone for the best deals.

Nuevo Hotel (956 33 16 00; www.nuevohotel.com; Calle Caballeros 23; s/d €35/50;) This popular, family-run hotel provides comfortable rooms with TV and winter heating. Most rooms are plain, with the glorious exception of the spectacular Muslim-style stucco work in No 208. It's best to book ahead.

Hotel Casa Grande (956 34 50 70; www.casagrande.com.es; Plaza de las Angustias 3; s €75, d €97-105;) This hotel occupies a carefully restored and strikingly decorated 1920s mansion centred on a bright patio. Rooms vary in style, and there's a great roof terrace. The breakfasts (€9) are special too.

Hotel Chancillería (956 30 10 38; www.hotelchancilleria.com; Calle Chancillería 21; s/d incl breakfast €65/90;) This 14-room hotel in the atmospheric Barrio de Santiago is a great addition to Jerez's accommodation. Full of lovely original crafts, it has many eco-friendly touches including solar water heating and grey-water recycling. It's also extremely well set up for wheelchair users. The hotel's restaurant, Sabores (956 32 98 35), has a prize-winning young chef; mains cost €14 to €18 and include a good vege selection.

Hotel Palacio Garvey (956 32 67 00; www.sferahoteles.net; Calle Tornería 24; s/d €224/293;) The Garvey is a sensational conversion of the 19th-century neoclassical palace of one of Jerez's sherry families. The 16 rooms are superluxurious.

Eating

The sherry trade has introduced English and French accents into the local cuisine. Jerez also prizes its cured and grilled meats and fish.

La Casa del Arroz (956 34 85 12; Calle Francos 10; mains €9-14;) This polished restaurant specialises in very well-prepared paella and other rice dishes, with some creative touches.

Mesón El Patio (956 34 07 36; Calle San Francisco de Paula 7; mains €8-17; closed Sun evening & Mon) Convivial yet a touch refined, El Patio serves terrific fish and meat dishes.

La Carboná (956 34 74 75; Calle San Francísco de Paula 2; mains €10-16; closed Tue) This popular, cavernous restaurant, with an eccentric menu and young waitstaff, occupies a wood-beamed former tavern. Specialities include charcoal-grilled Cantabrian meats and fresh fish.

Ristorante Bellaquio (956 34 40 03; Plaza Monti 12; mains €10-18; closed Sun evening & Mon) For a change from Jerez's staple meat and fish, head to this stylish Italian joint near the Alcázar, with original compositions like cannelloni with prawns and wild mushrooms.

Central Jerez is littered with great tapas bars. The pedestrian streets just north of Plaza del Arenal are a fine place to start. Head for the cavelike **El Almacén** (☎ 956 18 71 43; Calle Latorre 8; tapas €3; 🕑 1-4pm Thu & Fri, 8.30pm-1.30am daily; Ⓥ) or **Reino de León** (☎ 956 32 29 15; Calle Latorre 8; tapas €3) next door. Close by, **Cruz Blanca** (☎ 956 32 45 35; Plaza de la Yerva; tapas €1.80/3) whips up good fish, egg, meat and salad offerings and has tables on a quiet little plaza. Busy **Mesón del Asador** (☎ 956 32 26 58; Calle Remedios 2; tapas €2.15) is tops for grilled meats and also has a sit-down restaurant section. Atmospheric **La Reja** (Calle Mesones 6; tapas €1.80; 🕑 8pm-11pm or later) offers 32 varieties of tasty filled rolls called *enrejados*.

About 500m north, further brilliant tapas bars surround little Plaza Rafael Rivero. Head here at lunchtime or after 9.30pm. Don't miss the *montaditos* (mini toasted rolls) at **El Tabanco** (☎ 956 33 44 20; tapas €2-2.50).

Drinking

A few bars in the narrow streets north of Plaza del Arenal can get lively with an under-30 crowd: try beer bar **Dos Deditos** (Plaza Vargas 1) and wine bar **La Carbonería** (Calle Letrados 7). **Damajuana** (☎ 956 32 04 64; www.damajuanacafebar.com; Calle Francos 18; 🕑 4.30pm-3am Tue-Sun) has a studenty, artsy vibe, with exhibitions and occasional live music.

Northeast of the centre, La Plaza de Canterbury has bars around a central courtyard that attract a 20s clientele, while music bars northeast on Avenida de Méjico are the late-night headquarters for the 18–25 crowd.

Entertainment

The tourist office is very helpful with what's-on information; also visit www.turismojerez.com and look out for posters. Several *peñas flamencas* (flamenco clubs) welcome genuinely interested visitors: ask at the tourist office about events.

El Lagá Tio Parrilla (☎ 956 33 83 34; Plaza del Mercado; show & 2 drinks €18; 🕑 10.30pm Mon-Sat) The best of the places staging regular flamenco shows. The emphasis is on the more upbeat styles such as *bulería*, but this is still the genuine article with gutsy performers.

Bereber (☎ 956 34 00 16; www.tablaodelbereber.com; Calle Cabezas 10; 🕑 4.30pm-late) An amazing reformed palace in the Barrio de San Mateo, mixing noble and Islamic style with several patios, rooms and bars, some open to the sky. The flamenco show at 9pm (€70) includes dinner and drinks.

Teatro Villamarta (☎ 956 35 02 72; www.villamarta.com; Plaza Romero Martínez) Stages a busy program of music, dance and drama.

Cuatro Gatos (Calle Santa Rosa 10; 🕑 9pm-late Mon-Sat) For more informal musical nights, try this club where the almost-nightly live music ranges from world music to Beatles covers and jam sessions.

Sala Audrey (☎ 956 34 04 11; www.salaaudrey.com; Calle Carmen 22; 🕑 10pm-late Wed-Sat) This hip little venue is dedicated to Audrey Hepburn, and has DJs spinning house, funk or reggae.

Getting There & Around

AIR

Jerez airport (☎ 956 15 00 00), 7km northeast of town on the NIV, is increasingly busy with flights from European cities and has at least six car rental offices. **Ryanair** (☎ 956 15 01 52) flies here daily from London Stansted, and a variety of airlines come from Amsterdam, Brussels, Paris and several German airports. **Iberia** (☎ 902 40 05 00), **Vueling** (☎ 902 33 39 33) and **Spanair** (☎ 956 15 01 30) fly direct from Madrid and Barcelona.

BUS

A useful airport bus service runs 16 times daily (six times on Saturday and Sunday) from the airport to Jerez bus station (€0.95, 30 minutes), with three services daily continuing to El Puerto de Santa María train station (from the airport €1.10, 50 minutes) and six or more to Cádiz's Comes bus station (€2.85, 1¼ hours).

Jerez's **bus station** (☎ 956 33 91 61; Plaza de la Estación) is 1.3km southeast of the centre. Destinations include Seville (€7.20, 1¼ hours, 11 or more daily), Sanlúcar de Barrameda (€1.68, 30 minutes, seven or more daily), El Puerto de Santa María (€1.10, 20 minutes, 15 or more daily), Cádiz (€2.85, 40 minutes, nine or more daily), Arcos de la Frontera (€2.40, 45 minutes, 13 or more daily), El Bosque (€5.20, two hours, three or more daily) and Ronda (€19.50, 2½ hours, three daily).

TRAIN

Jerez **train station** (☎ 956 34 23 19; Plaza de la Estación) is beside the bus station, with up to 36 daily trains to El Puerto de Santa María (€1.40,

15 minutes) and Cádiz (€2.90 to €3.65, 50 minutes), and 10 or more to Seville (€6.50 to €16.80, 1¼ hours).

ARCOS DE LA FRONTERA

pop 29,900 / elev 185m

Bathed in burning white light the walled, hill-top town of Arcos, 30km east of Jerez, could not be more thrillingly sited: it perches on a high, unassailable ridge with sheer precipices plummeting away on both sides. Always prized for its strategic position, Arcos was briefly, during the 11th century, an independent Berber-ruled kingdom before being absorbed by Seville, then Christian Alfonso X took the town in 1255. When the last Duque de Arcos died in 1780, his cousin, the Duquesa de Benavente, took over his lands. With her help, agriculture around Arcos diversified and more profitable crops and horse breeding replaced sheep farming.

Arcos' charm today lies in exploring the mazelike upper town with its whitewashed houses and spectacular setting.

Orientation & Information

From the bus station it's a 1.5km uphill walk to the old town. Paseo de los Boliches and Calle Debajo del Corral (becoming Calle Corredera) both lead east up to the old town's main square, Plaza del Cabildo.

The **tourist office** (☎ 956 70 22 64; Plaza del Cabildo; 🕑 10am-2.30pm & 5.30-8pm Mon-Fri, 10.30am-1.30pm & 5-7pm Sat, 10.30am-1.30pm Sun) is on the old town's main square. There's also a **tourist information kiosk** (Paseo de Andalucía).

Banks and ATMs are along Calle Debajo del Corral and Calle Corredera.

Sights

The old town is a delight to get lost in with every turn revealing something new. The centre of this quarter is the Plaza del Cabildo. The square itself has been somewhat spoilt by being turned into a car park, but the surrounding fine old buildings and a vertiginous **mirador** (lookout) with views over Río Guadalete make up for a lot. The 11th-century **Castillo de los Duques** is firmly closed to the public. On the plaza's northern side is the Gothic-cum-baroque **Basíllica-Parroquia de Santa María**, which was closed for renovations at the time of research. On the eastern side, the **Parador Casa del Corregidor** hotel (see p752) is a reconstruction of a 16th-century magistrate's house. From the gate leading onto the mirador you can get all high-tech and put yourself live on the internet for your friends to see! See the sign on the gate for instructions.

Along the streets east of here, take time to seek out lovely buildings such as the **Iglesia de San Pedro** (Calle Núñez de Prado; admission €1; 🕑 10am-1pm & 4-7pm Mon-Sat, to 1.30pm Sun), another Gothic baroque confection, and the 17th-century **Palacio Mayorazgo**, now a community building, with a Renaissance facade and pretty patios.

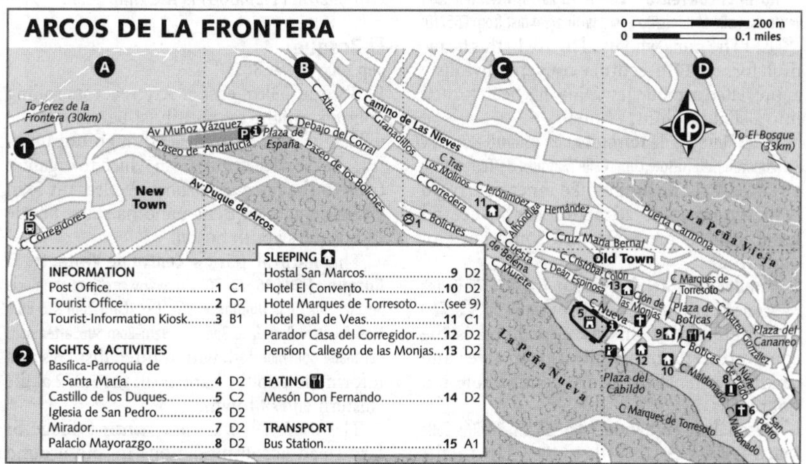

Tours

One-hour guided tours (€7) of the old town's monuments and pretty patios start from the tourist office at 11am Monday to Friday.

Festivals & Events

Semana Santa Holy Week processions through the narrow old streets are dramatic; on Easter Sunday there's a hair-raising running of the bulls.
Fiesta de la Virgen de las Nieves Three-day festival in early August includes a top-class flamenco night in Plaza del Cabildo.
Feria de San Miguel Arcos celebrates its patron saint, San Miguel, with a four-day fair at the end of September.

Sleeping & Eating

Pensíon Callegón de las Monjas (☎ 956 70 23 02; Calle Deán Espinosa 4; s/d from €25/35;) A great value budget base. Some of the rooms have little balconies with massive views to the plains below. Room rates are negotiable if times are slow.

Hostal San Marcos (☎ 956 70 07 21; Calle Marqués de Torresoto 6; s/d €35/45;) A simple old-town *hostal*, there are four pretty rooms and a roof terrace. The attached restaurant is a delight of wrinkled old characters.

our pick **Hotel Real de Veas** (☎ 956 71 73 70; www.hotelrealdeveas.com; Calle Corredera 12; s/d €48/55;) A superb option inside a lovingly restored building. The dozen or so rooms are arranged around a glass-covered patio and are cool and comfortable. It's one of the few places that has easy car access. The price includes a decent breakfast.

Hotel El Convento (☎ 956 70 23 33; www.hotelconvento.es; Calle Maldonado 2; s/d with breakfast from €55/70;) The nuns who used to live in this beautiful, former 17th-century convent obviously appreciated a good view. Now it's been turned into a slightly chintzy hotel.

Hotel Marques de Torresoto (☎ 956 70 07 17; www.hotelmarquesdtorresoto.com; Calle Marqués de Torresoto 4; s/d €55/75;) The jungle-like inner courtyard is the *numero uno* attraction of this central hotel. Rooms are plain and some have an odd layout.

Parador Casa del Corregidor (☎ 956 70 05 00; www.parador.es; Plaza del Cabildo; r from €128;) The highlight of this *parador* hotel is the courtyard restaurant full of palm trees and tinkling water. Rooms are comfortable but not plush.

Mesón Don Fernando (☎ 956 71 73 26; Calle Boticas 5; mains €9-11, closed Mon) Up in the old-town maze, Mesón Don Fernando has a lively Spanish atmosphere. You can enjoy treats like rabbit stew and deer steaks while sitting on an outside table relishing the evening breeze.

Getting There & Away

Services from the **bus station** (☎ 956 70 49 77; Calle Corregidores) run to Jerez (€2.55, 45 minutes, 12–15 daily), Cádiz (€5.59, 1¼ hours, 5 daily), El Bosque (€2.55, one hour, 7 daily), Ronda (€8.14, two hours, 3 daily) and Seville (€7.45, two hours, 2 daily). Frequencies to some destinations are reduced on Saturday and Sunday.

PARQUE NATURAL SIERRA DE GRAZALEMA

The mountains of the Parque Natural Sierra de Grazalema rise abruptly off the plains northeast of Cádiz in a rugged mess of peaks and rocky pillars. It's one of Andalucía's greenest areas with a landscape of pastoral river valleys and precipitous gorges. This is fine walking country (the best months are May, June, September and October), and there are opportunities for climbing, caving, canyoning, kayaking and paragliding.

The park extends into northwestern Málaga province, where it includes the Cueva de la Pileta (p784). Useful walking guides include *Walking in Andalucía* by Guy Hunter-Watts and *Eight Walks from Grazalema* by RE Bradshaw. Editorial Alpina's *Sierra de Grazalema* (1:25,000) is the map pick.

El Bosque

pop 2000 / elev 385m

El Bosque, 33km east of Arcos across rolling country, might be prettily situated, but the village itself is a modern (though not unattractive) service centre from which to organise trips to the *parque natural*. A pleasant 5km riverside path to Benamahoma starts beside El Bosque's youth hostel.

The natural park's **Centro de Visitantes El Bosque** (☎ 956 72 70 29; www.cma.jnta.andalucia.es; Avenida de la Diputación s/n; 10am-2pm & 6-8pm Mon-Fri, 9am-2pm & to 8pm Sat, 9am-2pm Sun, afternoons Oct-Mar 4-6pm Mon-Sat), with limited displays and information on the park, is off the A372 at the western end of town.

There are several *casa rurals* (village or farmstead accommodation) in and around

GRAZALEMA RESERVE AREA WALKS

Three of the Sierra de Grazalema's best day walks are the ascent of El Torreón (1654m), the highest peak in Cádiz province; the route from Grazalema to Benamahoma via Spain's best-preserved *pinsapar* (woodland of the rare Spanish fir); and the trip into the Garganta Verde, a deep ravine south of Zahara de la Sierra, with a large colony of griffon vultures. All these walks are within a 38-sq-km reserve area with restricted access, meaning that to do any of them you must obtain a (free) permit from the El Bosque visitors centre (opposite). You can call or visit El Bosque up to 15 days in advance for this and, if you wish, it will fax permits to be collected at the Zahara information office (p754) or Grazalema tourist office (below). Staff might speak only Spanish. It's normally necessary to book ahead only for walking on a weekend or public holiday. Authorised local guide companies such as Horizon (below) and Al-qutun (p754) will guide you on these walks, but you can also do them on your own with a decent map and map-reading skills. Do-it-yourselfers should obtain a decent map such as Editorial Alpina's *Sierra de Grazalema* (1:25,000), which is available locally and includes a walking guide booklet in English and Spanish. The entire park is closed to independent travellers between 1 July and the middle of October due to the high fire risk. To visit at this time of year (when it's probably too hot to be enjoyable anyway) a guide from an authorised company is obligatory – though even then the Torreón route is out of bounds.

the village that the tourist office can point you towards. Otherwise the following all get our vote of approval.

Near the park information office, **Hotel Enrique Calvillo** (☎ 956 71 61 05; Avenida Diputación 5; s/d €35/50; ❄ 💻) has tasteful rooms featuring large walk-in showers and exposed wooden roof beams. The popular restaurant is full of gently swaying, hanging hams. **Hotel Las Truchas** (☎ 956 71 60 61; www.tugasa.com/index2.htm; Avenida Diputación s/n; s/d €35/59; ❄ P) offers rooms that are a bit staid but some have nice views, and the clincher, on hot summer afternoons, is its inviting pool.

Casa Calvillo (☎ 956 71 60 10; Avenida Diputación s/n; mains €9-12) is a very popular lunch spot, especially at weekends when local families pile in for some pleasing countryside tastes.

Grazalema

pop 2240 / elev 825m

For good reason Grazalema is the most popular travellers' base in the *sierra*: the red-roofed village, hunched up under an enormous shaft of rock, is so pretty it looks like it's from a fairy tale. Local products include pure wool blankets and rugs.

The village centre is the pretty Plaza de España, overlooked by the 18th-century Iglesia de la Aurora. Here you'll find the **tourist office** (☎ 956 13 20 73; 🕐 10am-2pm & 4-9pm), with a shop selling local products. Two banks on Plaza de España have ATMs.

Horizon (☎/fax 956 13 23 63; www.horizonaventura.com; Calle Corrales Terceros 29) is a highly experienced adventure firm that will take you climbing, bungee jumping, canyoning, caving, paragliding or walking, with English-speaking guides.

If you're hanging around for a while, and you'll want too, then look out for the very useful *What to See and Do in Grazalema* (€2), which is available at many hotels.

SLEEPING & EATING

Casa de las Piedras (☎/fax 956 13 20 14; www.casadelaspiedras.net; Calle Las Piedras 32; s with/without bathroom €35/13, d with/without bathroom €48/25; ❄ 💻) It's hard to find fault with this well-run hotel. Rooms are pretty perfect and the geranium-clad patio even more so. The common areas often play host to small art exhibitions.

Hotel Peñón Grande (☎ 956 13 24 34; www.hotelgrazalema.com; Plaza Pequeña 7; s/d €36/53; ❄) A small, friendly hotel with functional rooms just off Plaza de España.

our pick La Mejorana (☎ 956 13 23 27; www.lamejorana.net; Calle Santa Clara 6; r incl breakfast €52; 💻) This is the sort of dreamy hotel you'd choose for a romantic weekend break. There are only five rooms, all of which are full of Spanish charm, and a very tempting pool hidden under a cover of shady green plants. It's tucked away at the top of the village.

Mesón El Simancón (☎ 956 13 24 21; Plaza Asomaderos; mains €6-15, menú €12.90; 🕐 closed Tue) There are plenty of places to eat and drink around Plaza de España and on Calle Agua. The Simancón, right by the car park, serves well-prepared ham, beef, quail, venison, wild boar and *revueltos*.

Zahara de la Sierra

pop 1600 / elev 550m

Topped by a crag with a ruined castle, Zahara is the most dramatically sited of the area's villages. The 18km drive from Grazalema via the vertiginous 1331m Puerto de los Palomas (Doves' Pass) is otherworldly and full of spectacular switchbacks. The village centres on Calle San Juan, where you'll find the natural park's helpful **Punto de Información Zahara de la Sierra** (☎/fax 956 12 31 14; Plaza del Rey 3; 9am-2pm & 4-7pm).

Zahara's streets invite investigation, with vistas framed by tall palms and hot-pink bougainvillea. To climb to the 12th-century **castle keep**, take the path almost opposite the Hotel Arco de la Villa – it's a steady 10- to 15-minute climb. The castle's recapture from the Christians by Abu al-Hasan of Granada, in a night raid in 1481, provoked the Catholic Monarchs to launch the last phase of the Reconquista, which ended with the fall of Granada.

Adventure-tourism firm **Al-qutun** (☎ 956 13 78 82; www.al-qutun.com), in Algodonales, 7km north of Zahara, organises canyoning, guided walks, kayaking, paragliding, caving and climbing. Get in touch for the schedule. Another memorable way of seeing the Sierra is from the saddle of a horse. Riders can arrange tours through **Rutas a Caballo Santiago** (☎ 608 840376; www.zaharadelasierra.info/caballos).

Accommodation options include **Hostal Marqués de Zahara** (☎/fax 956 12 30 61; www.marquesdezahara.com; Calle San Juan 3; r incl breakfast €50;), a rambling old place in the village centre whose rooms have seen better days. The 17 rooms at modern **Hotel Arco de la Villa** (☎ 956 12 32 30; www.tugasa.com; Paseo Nazarí s/n; s/d €35/59; P), which is partially built into the rock face, have jaw-dropping views but little rural character.

Restaurante Los Naranjos (☎ 956 12 33 14; Calle San Juan 12; mains €8-12; 9am-11pm) serves hearty hill-country platefuls both indoors and outside under the orange trees. It's often the only place with any sign of life in the entire village!

Getting There & Around

Los Amarillos (☎ 902 21 03 17) runs buses to El Bosque from Jerez (€5.60, two hours, six daily) and Arcos (€2.55, one hour, 11 daily). From El Bosque, buses leave for Grazalema (€2.10, 30 minutes) at 3.30pm Monday to Saturday. Grazalema to El Bosque buses depart at 5.30am Monday to Friday and 7pm Friday.

There's no bus service between Zahara and Grazalema.

SOUTHERN COSTA DE LA LUZ

The 90km coast between Cádiz and Tarifa is Andalucía's finest, and miraculously mass tourism development has no more than a toehold here. Apart from the relatively large towns of Conil de la Frontera and Barbate, most of the scattered settlements are still beach villages. The coast can be windy, and its Atlantic waters are cooler than the Mediterranean, but these are small prices to pay for a wild stretch of coastline where you can enjoy a host of water- and land-based activities. Andalucian holidaymakers swarm in with a fiesta atmosphere in July and August and on other holidays from spring to autumn (phone ahead for rooms at these times), and a growing number of foreigners are choosing to settle here.

Vejer de la Frontera

pop 12,800 / elev 190m

This ancient white town looms mysteriously atop a rocky hill above the busy N340, 50km from Cádiz. A quaint labyrinth of twisting old streets, it has experienced a minor influx of foreign residents, some of whom have set up boutique hotels. There's an eclectic bunch of restaurants too. Buses stop beside the **tourist office** (☎ 956 45 17 36; www.turismovejer.com; Avenida Los Remedios 2; 10am-2pm daily, 6-8pm Mon-Sat approx May-Oct), about 500m below the town centre. Also here is a convenient large, free car park.

Vejer's much-reworked **castle** (admission free; approx 10am-9pm Jun-Sep) has great views from its battlements. Its erratically open small museum preserves one of the black cloaks that Vejer women wore until just a couple of decades ago (covering everything but the eyes). When the castle is not open, you can still visit it on daily one-hour **guided walks** (in English/Spanish €4/3; noon & 7pm) from the tourist office.

SLEEPING & EATING

Hostal La Janda (☎ 956 45 01 42; Calle Machado s/n; s/d €40/50; P) A friendly, economical and impeccably clean place. Some of the 36 rooms afford town vistas, and there's a restaurant.

ANDALUCÍA

La Botica de Vejer (☎ 956 45 02 25; www.laboticadevejer.com; Calle Canalejas 13; s/d incl breakfast €80/90; ❄) La Botica offers appealingly bright and colourful rooms set around a patio where breakfast is served. There's a roof terrace with rural views.

Hotel La Casa del Califa (☎ 956 44 77 30; www.lacasadelcalifa.com; Plaza de España 16; s €60-98, d €79-115, incl breakfast; ❄ 💻) Rambling over several floors, this gorgeous hotel oozes character. Rooms are peaceful and very comfortable, with Islamic decorative touches. It also has a superb Middle Eastern restaurant, **El Jardín del Califa** (mains €8-16; V).

Restaurante Trafalgar (☎ 956 44 76 38; Plaza de España 31; mains €11-18) The Trafalgar has some tables outside on Vejer's happening plaza, and prepares typical Cádiz fish, seafood and meat with a contemporary flourish.

GETTING THERE & AWAY

From Avenida Los Remedios, buses run to Cádiz (€4.53, 50 minutes) five or six times a day. Buses for Tarifa (€3.71, 45 minutes, 10 daily), Algeciras (€5.84, 1¼ hours, 10 daily), Jerez de la Frontera (€5.88, 1½ hours, two daily), Málaga (€16, 2¾ hours, two daily) and Seville (€12.59, 2¼ hours, four daily) stop at La Barca de Vejer, on the N340 at the bottom of the hill. It's a steep 20-minute walk up to town from there.

Los Caños de Meca

pop 200

The superchilled beach village of Los Caños straggles along a series of spectacular open beaches southwest of Vejer. Once a hippie hideaway, Los Caños still has a highly alternative, hedonistic scene especially in summer. Out of season, it's often very sleepy. Windsurfing, kitesurfing, surfing, horse riding and hikes in the nearby Parque Natural de la Breña y Marismas de Barbate are all among the activities you can pursue here.

At the western end of Los Caños a side road leads out to a lighthouse on an unremarkable spit of land with a famous name – **Cabo de Trafalgar**, which marks the site of the eponymous battle in 1805. Wonderful beaches stretch either side of Cabo de Trafalgar.

Some 5km along the coast northwest of Los Caños, the long beach at **El Palmar** has Andalucía's best board-surfing waves from about October to May. Several places rent boards and give surfing classes: try **Escuela de Surf 9 Pies** (☎ 620 104241; www.9piesescueladesurf.com in Spanish; board & wetsuit rental per 2/4hr €12/18, classes 2/4hr €27/52), open all year towards the north end of the beach. **Trafalgar Surf** (☎ 666 942849; www.trafalgarsurftrip.com; beginners' classes 1½/4½hr €40/105) offers classes in English at the area's best surfing beach on the day, with free pick-up anywhere along the coast from Los Caños to La Barrosa.

SLEEPING

Hostal Mini-Golf (☎ 956 43 70 83; Avenida Trafalgar 251; www.hostalminigolf.com; s/d €50/70; P ❄) This budget place opposite the Cabo de Trafalgar turn-off has fresh, clean rooms, with TV and winter heating, around a simple Spanish patio. There's a cafe and, yes, minigolf in the front garden.

Casas Karen (☎ 956 43 70 67; www.casaskaren.com; Camino del Monte 6; d per 2 nights €190-290, per week €520-825, q per 2 nights €330-470, per week €935-1470; P) This eccentric gem has nine different studios, bungalows and *chozas* (traditional thatched dwellings) each with a kitchen, lounge, outdoor sitting area and casual *andaluz*–Moroccan decor. It's about 500m off the main road, well signposted 500m east of Cabo de Trafalgar.

Hotel Madreselva (☎ 956 43 72 55; www.madreselvahotel.com; Avenida Trafalgar 102; s/d incl breakfast €79/96; closed Nov-Feb; P ❄) The 18 rooms at this artistically designed place have their own garden-patios. There's a good pool, and mountain biking, horse riding, massages and surfing can be arranged.

Sajorami Beach (☎ 956 43 74 24; www.sajoramibeach.com; Playa de Zahora; r €98-168; P) Rooms, apartments and studios around beachfront gardens at Zahora, 2km northwest of the main part of Los Caños (turn off the main road by Camping Caños de Meca). There's a popular restaurant here too (closed mid-October to mid-February).

For further accommodation options check www.playasdetrafalgar.com or www.placerdetrafalgar.com.

EATING

La Pequeña Lulu (☎ 956 43 73 55; Avenida Trafalgar 2; dishes €6-15) This funky French-run cafe-bar at the far eastern end of the village serves excellent light meals from crêpes to couscous on a lovely terrace.

Bar Saboy (☎ 956 43 71 38; Carril de Mangueta, Zahora; dishes €10-15) The Saboy, 300m from the main road about 3km northwest of Los Caños, with a spacious thatched roof and fireplace, serves up good snacks and meals of the fish, seafood and meat variety.

Restaurante El Caña (☎ 956 43 73 98; Avenida Trafalgar s/n; mains €9-13; ⌚ Easter-Sep, closed Wed Easter-Jun & Sep) This has a super position atop the small cliff above the eastern part of Los Caños beach. Lots of fish and seafood.

Restaurante Trafalgar (☎ 956 43 71 21; Avenida Trafalgar 86; mains €10-23; ⌚ Apr-Sep, closed lunch Mon-Fri Apr-20 Jun) A high-standard restaurant that has a summer patio and serves creative Mediterranean cuisine. Internet facilities out the back.

DRINKING & ENTERTAINMENT

Good bars include **Los Castillejos** (⌚ Easter-Oct) towards the eastern end of Avenida Trafalgar and **Ketama** (⌚ Mar-Dec). Open year-round are superrelaxed **Las Dunas** on the road out to Cabo de Trafalgar, and **Bar Saboy** and **La Pequeña Lulu** (see p755), both often hosting live music of various kinds from about midnight. All these places stay open till 2 or 3am.

GETTING THERE & AWAY

Monday to Friday, there are two Comes buses to/from Cádiz (€5, 1¼ hours) to El Palmar (€4.53, 1¼ hours) and Los Caños (€4.99, 1½ hours). There's also one morning bus, Monday to Friday, running between Vejer and both places. There may be extra services from Cádiz and even Seville from mid-June to early September.

Zahara de los Atunes

pop 1200

Sitting in the middle of a broad, 12km, sandy beach, Zahara is an elemental place. At its heart stands the crumbling old Castillo de las Almadrabas, once a refuge against pirate attacks and a depot for the local tuna fishers. Today the nearest tuna fleet is at Barbate, and Zahara has become a fashionable Spanish summer resort, with more of a family ambience than Los Caños de Meca. There's an old-fashioned core of narrow streets around the ruined castle. The southern end of town, known as Atlanterra, is being developed somewhat unsympathetically, but the pristine beaches and walking trails beyond Atlanterra are well worth exploring.

SLEEPING & EATING

Camping Bahía de la Plata (☎ 956 43 90 40; www.campingbahiadelaplata.com; Carretera de Atlanterra; sites per adult/tent/car €7/5.50/4.50, bungalow €120) Good treed camping ground fronting the beach at the southern end of Zahara.

Hotels Almadraba & Almadrabeta (☎ 956 43 92 74; www.hotelesalmadraba.es; Calle María Luisa 13 & 15; s/d Almadraba €65/80, Almadrabeta €45/70; P ❄) These two neighbouring hotels, under one management, provide 25 simple but pleasing rooms with TV and winter heating. The restaurant here, specialising in fish and meat, is one of the best in town.

Hotel Doña Lola (☎ 956 43 90 09; www.donalolazahara.com; Plaza Thompson 1; r €100-160; P ❄ 🏊) At the entrance to town but only two minutes from the beach, this modern hotel has rooms in an old-fashioned style and lovely grounds.

Hotel Gran Sol (☎ 956 43 93 09; www.gransolhotel.com; Avenida de la Playa s/n; r incl breakfast €107-145; P ❄ 🏊) The Gran Sol occupies the prime beach spot. Its large, bright, comfortable rooms all come with balconies.

Most restaurants in the old part are on or near Plaza de Tamarón, near Hotel Doña Lola, and most offer similar *andaluz* fare.

Restaurante La Jabega (☎ 956 43 94 42; Calle Tomillo 7; raciones €10-13, mains €9-30) Just back from the beach north of the Hotel Gran Sol, the Jabega is acclaimed for its seafood especially its scrumptious *albóndigas de choco* (cuttlefish fishballs).

ENTERTAINMENT

In July and August the beachfront bars get pretty lively from about midnight. Some have live flamenco or other music.

GETTING THERE & AWAY

Comes runs up to three daily buses to and from Cádiz (€6.55, two hours) via Vejer de la Frontera and Barbate, and one to/from Tarifa (€3.24, 40 minutes). There are usually extra services mid-June to September.

Bolonia

pop 125

This village, hidden on a beautiful bay about 20km up the coast from Tarifa, has a long white-sand beach and the ruins of the most complete Roman town yet uncovered in Spain: **Baelo Claudia** (☎ 956 10 67 97; adult/EU citizen €1.50/free; ⌚ 10am-8pm Tue-Sat Jun-Sep, 10am-7pm Tue-Sat Mar-May & Oct, 10am-6pm Tue-Sat Nov-Feb, 10am-2pm Sun & holidays). The ruins include a theatre where plays are still sometimes staged, a market, forum, temples, and workshops that turned out the products that made Baelo Claudia famous in the Roman world: salted fish and *garum*, a prized condiment made from fish entrails. There's a good recently opened museum too.

You can walk up the big sand dune at the far end of the beach, or out to Punta Camarinal, the headland protecting the west end of the bay. You can also walk 8km along the coast to or from Ensenada de Valdevaqueros (p758) via Punta Paloma.

SLEEPING & EATING

Many places at Bolonia open only seasonally but the following are open all year.

La Posada de Lola (☎ 956 68 85 36; www.hostallola.com; El Lentiscal 26; r with shared/private bathroom €45/55; Ⓟ) Friendly Lola's pretty garden is flower-filled and the rooms are simple but attractive. There's a Moroccan-inspired sitting area too. Follow the signs on giant surfboards to find it. A seven-night minimum is required for reservations in July and August.

Apartamentos Isabel (☎ 956 68 85 69; El Lentiscal 6; apt €80-110; Ⓟ) Isabel, right on the beach, provides six bright, well-fitted, one- and two-bedroom apartments, all with kitchen.

La Hormiga Voladora (☎ 956 68 85 62; El Lentiscal 15; r €70-83, apt for 3 €105; Ⓟ) Extending back from the seafront, the 'Flying Ant' is a lovable warren of simple but carefully decorated rooms and apartments, set around various courtyards.

Las Rejas (☎ 956 68 85 46; El Lentiscal 8; salad €7, paella per person €12) The fish and seafood here are terrific, and the waiters willingly suggest the day's best options.

GETTING THERE & AWAY

A hilly 7km side road to Bolonia heads west off the N340, 15km from Tarifa. A couple of local buses run daily from Tarifa to Bolonia in July and August only. Times and stops are changeable: check with Tarifa tourist office.

TARIFA

pop17,200

Set at mainland Spain's southernmost tip, Tarifa has grown in two decades from a down-at-heel coastal town into Europe's hip kitesurfing and windsurfing capital. The near-constant *levante* (easterly) or *poniente* (westerly) winds blowing through the Strait of Gibraltar create ideal conditions for these sports. A creative international scene has grown up around the surf activities, resulting in some original lodgings, eclectic eateries, chilled bars and clubs, and quite a party scene, especially in summer.

Add the setting of a quaint, whitewashed old town, stunning white-sand beaches, views of Morocco, and rolling green countryside, and you'll understand why for a growing number of people Tarifa has a magic unique in Spain. To boot, it's one of the best places in Europe for watching not just birds but also dolphins and whales. The only negative can be the wind, which can be ruinous for a relaxed sit on the beach and tiring if you're simply wandering around. August, however, can be blessedly still.

Tarifa takes its name from Tariq ibn Malik, who led a Muslim raid in 710, the year before the main Islamic invasion of the peninsula.

Orientation

Two roads head into the town of Tarifa from the N340. The one from the northwest becomes Calle Batalla del Salado, which is lined with surf shops and kite schools and ends at Avenida de Andalucía, where the Puerta de Jerez leads through the walls into the old town. The one from the northeast becomes Calle Amador de los Ríos, meeting Calle Batalla del Salado in front of the Puerta de Jerez. The main street of the old town is Calle Sancho IV El Bravo. To the southwest of town protrudes the Isla de las Palomas, a military-occupied promontory that is the southernmost point of continental Europe. Northwest of Tarifa stretches 10km of spectacular beach comprising Playa de los Lances and its continuations as far as the bay Ensenada de Valdevaqueros.

Information

Centro de Salud (Health Centre; ☎ 956 02 70 00; Calle Amador de los Ríos) Has emergency service.
Pandora (Calle Sancho IV El Bravo 13A; internet per hr €2; 🕑 10am-2.30pm & 5-9.30pm)
Policía Local (☎ 956 61 21 74; Ayuntamiento, Plaza de Santa María)
Tourist office (☎ 956 68 09 93; www.aytotarifa.com in Spanish; Paseo de la Alameda; 🕑 10am-2pm daily, 4-6pm Mon-Fri Oct-May, 6-8pm Mon-Fri Jun-Sep)

Sights

A wander round the old town's narrow streets, of mainly Islamic origin, is a must. The Mudéjar **Puerta de Jerez** was built after the Reconquista. Look in at the bustling **market** (Calle Colón) before wending your way to the mainly 15th-century **Iglesia de San Mateo** (Calle

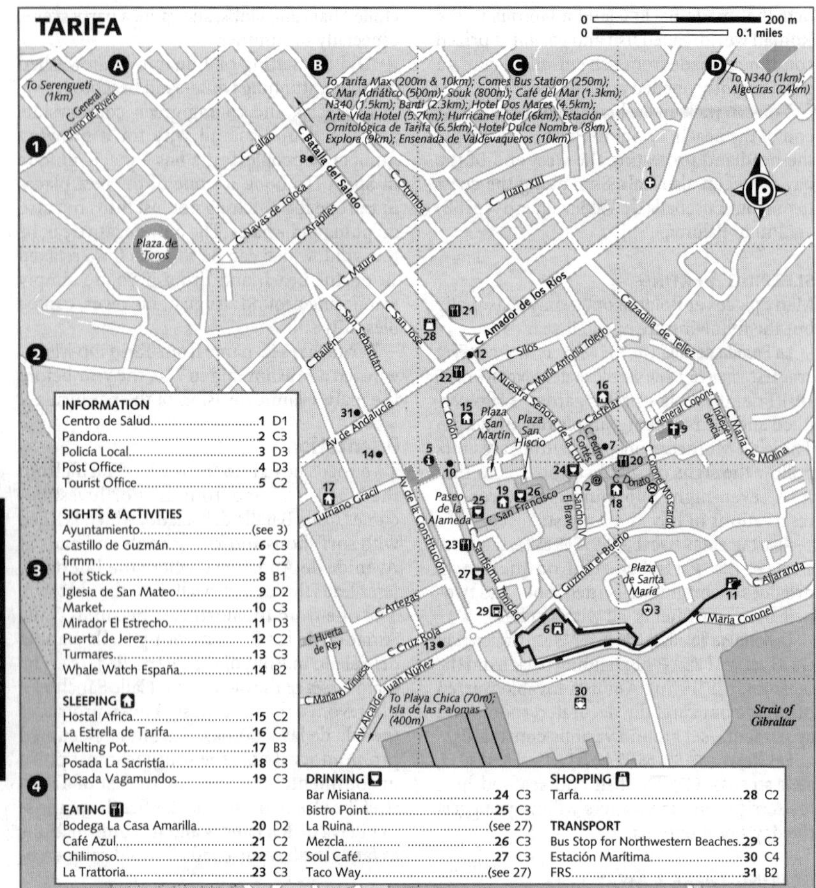

Sancho IV El Bravo; 9am-1pm & 5.30-8.30pm). South of the church, the **Mirador El Estrecho**, atop part of the castle walls, has spectacular views across to Africa, only 14km away.

The **Castillo de Guzmán** (Calle Guzmán El Bueno) is named after the Reconquista hero Guzmán El Bueno. In 1294, when threatened with the death of his captured son unless he surrendered the castle to attacking Islamic forces, El Bueno threw down his own dagger for the deed to be done. Guzmán's descendants became the Duques de Medina Sidonia, one of Spain's most powerful families. The imposing fortress was closed for refurbishment at research time. It may be open by 2009: ask the tourist office. It was originally built in 960 on the orders of Cordoban caliph Abd ar-Rahman III.

Activities

BEACHES

On the isthmus leading out to Isla de las Palomas, **Playa Chica** is sheltered but very small indeed. From here the spectacular **Playa de los Lances** stretches northwest to the huge sand dune at **Ensenada de Valdevaqueros**.

KITESURFING & WINDSURFING

Most of the action occurs along the coast between Tarifa and Punta Paloma, 11km northwest. The best spots depend on the day's winds and tides: El Porro on Ensenada de Valdevaqueros is one of the most popular, with easy parking. Both wind- and kitesurfing are practised year round, but the biggest season is from about April to October.

Tarifa now has around 30 kitesurf and windsurf schools, many of them with offices or shops along Calle Batalla del Salado or on Calle Mar Adriático. Others are based along the coast. Many rent and sell equipment. It's essential for kitesurfing beginners to take classes. An eight-hour beginners' course in groups of up to four, usually over two days, costs around €200 including equipment. Full equipment rental is around €80 for one day. Two-hour windsurfing classes in groups of up to four are around €50; board-and-sail rental for two/four hours is around €45/60, or €60/75 if you need a wetsuit and harness too. Some experienced, recommended schools:

Spin Out/Adrenalina Valdevaqueros (☎ 956 23 63 52; www.tarifaspinout.com; El Porro Beach, Ensenada de Valdevaqueros, N340 Km75) Windsurf and kitesurf.

Club Mistral (www.club-mistral.com) Hurricane (☎ 956 68 90 98; Hurricane Hotel, N340 Km78) Valdevaqueros (☎ 619 340913; Cortijo Valdevaqueros, Ensenada de Valdevaqueros, N340 Km75) Windsurf and kitesurf.

Tarifa Max (☎ 696 558227; www.tarifamax.net) Town (O'Neill shop, Calle Tinto 1); N340 (Hotel Copacabana, N340 Km75) Kitesurf.

Hot Stick Town (☎ 956 68 04 19; www.hotsticktarifa.com; Calle Batalla del Salado 41) Offers six-hr kitesurf courses with lower rates; windsurf classes too.

HORSE RIDING

On Playa de los Lances, **Aventura Ecuestre** (☎ 956 23 66 32; www.aventuraecuestre.com; Hotel Dos Mares, N340 Km79.5) and **Hurricane Hípica** (☎ 646 964279; Hurricane Hotel, N340 Km78) both rent well-kept horses with excellent guides. An hour's beach ride costs €30. Three- or four-hour inland rides are €70.

WHALE-WATCHING

The Strait of Gibraltar is a top site for viewing whales and dolphins. Killer whales visit in July and August, huge sperm and fin whales lurk here from spring to autumn, and pilot whales and three types of dolphin stay all year. Several organisations in Tarifa run daily two- to 2½-hour boat trips to observe these marine mammals, and most offer a free second trip if you don't at least see dolphins. Most trips cost €27/18 for over/under 14 years; special 3½-hour killer-whale trips in July and August are around €40/30. At holiday times you may need to book two or three days ahead. If the strait is too rough, the boats may head for the Bahía de Algeciras with its groups of dolphins.

firmm (☎ 956 62 70 08; www.firmm.org; Calle Pedro Cortés 4; ⏰ Mar-Oct) Uses every trip to record data.

Turmares (☎ 956 68 07 41; www.turmares.com; Avenida Alcalde Juan Núñez 3; ⏰ Jan-Nov) Has the largest boats (one with a glass bottom), holding 40 & 60 people.

Whale Watch España (☎ 956 62 70 13; www.whalewatchtarifa.net; Avenida de la Constitución 6; ⏰ Apr-Oct)

BIRDWATCHING

From March to May and August to October, if the *levante* is blowing or there's little wind, the Tarifa area, including the spectacular Mirador del Estrecho lookout point, is great for watching bird migrations across the Strait of Gibraltar. The volunteer-staffed **Estación Ornitológica de Tarifa** (☎ 639 859350; cocn.tarifainfo.com; N340 Km78.5; ⏰ 5-9pm Tue-Sat, 10am-2pm Sun), 5km northwest of town, provides lots of information on the area's birds. **Andalucian Guides** (☎ 956 43 29 49; www.andalucianguides.com) leads recommended birdwatching outings in the area.

Sleeping

High season is typically from the beginning of July to mid-September, and it's essential to phone ahead in August.

IN TOWN

Melting Pot (☎ 956 68 29 06; www.meltingpothostels.com; Calle Turriano Gracil 5; dm €22-25, d €54, incl breakfast; 💻) The Melting Pot is a friendly, well-equipped hostel just off the Alameda. The five dorms, for five to eight people, have bunks and there's one for women only. A good kitchen adjoins the cosy bar-lounge, and all guests get their own keys.

Hostal Africa (☎ 956 68 02 20; hostal_africa@hotmail.com; Calle María Antonia Toledo 12; s with/without bathroom €50/35, d with/without bathroom €65/50; ⏰ closed 24 Dec-31 Jan) The well-travelled owners of this revamped house know just what travellers need. Rooms are attractive and there's an expansive terrace with wonderful views. Short-term storage for boards, bicycles and baggage available.

La Estrella de Tarifa (☎ 956 68 19 85; www.laestrelladetarifa.com in Spanish; Calle San Rosendo 2; r €75-110, ste €120-145, incl breakfast) Full of intriguing nooks and crannies, this comfortable small hotel in an old townhouse rambles up and down over four floors with Moroccan decor in soothing blue and white.

Posada Vagamundos (☎ 956 68 15 13; Calle San Francisco 18; www.posadavagamundos.com; s/d/ste incl breakfast €91/102/123) Right in the centre in a carefully restored 18th-century convent building, Vagamundos has 11 exotic rooms with African-Asian-Islamic decor and a wi-fi-equipped cafe.

Posada La Sacristía (☎ 956 68 17 59; www.lasacristia.net; Calle San Donato 8; r incl breakfast €115-135) Tarifa's most elegant accommodation is in a beautifully renovated 17th-century townhouse. The 10 white rooms have some lovely details. There's a new in-house massage and therapy centre too. It also offers 10 other rooms, suites and apartments scattered around the old town.

ALONG THE COAST

Six year-round **camping grounds** (www.campingsdetarifa.com in Spanish), with room for more than 4000 campers, and several, mostly expensive, hotels are dotted along the beach and on and near the N340 within 10km northwest of Tarifa.

Hotel Dulce Nombre (☎ 956 68 53 44; www.hoteldulcenombre.com; N340 Km76.1; r or apt incl breakfast €122-159; P) Set 300m inland from the N340, 8km northwest of town, the Dulce Nombre still enjoys sea views and provides good-sized, fairly plain rooms. There's an excellent pool, and prices drop considerably outside August.

Arte Vida Hotel (☎ 956 68 52 46; www.hotelartevidatarifa.com; N340 Km79.3; s/d incl breakfast €120/140; P) The stylish Arte Vida, just over 5km from the town centre, combines attractive, medium-sized rooms with an excellent restaurant that has stunning views. Its grassy garden opens right on to the beach.

Hurricane Hotel (☎ 956 68 49 19; www.hotelhurricane.com; N340 Km78; r incl breakfast land/ocean side €162/178; P) This classy Moroccan-style hotel, 6km from town, is the place to go if you're feeling flush. Set in semitropical gardens, it has large rooms, two pools, two restaurants and on-site riding stables and a kitesurf and windsurf school. The buffet breakfast is probably the best you'll ever have.

Hotel Dos Mares (☎ 956 68 40 35; www.dosmareshotel.com; N340 Km79.5; r or bungalow incl breakfast €175-195; P) On the beach about 4.5km from Tarifa, Islamic-themed Dos Mares offers rooms and bungalows outside. The bar, with views to Africa, is a popular hang-out, and there's a good beachside *chiringuito* (small, open-air bar) too. The hotel also boasts tennis and paddle courts, a gym and its own stables.

Eating

Tarifa tempts your tastebuds with a great array of international cuisines.

Café Azul (Calle Batalla del Salado 8; breakfast €3.50-5; 9am-3pm) This little Italian-owned place packs 'em in every day for Tarifa's best breakfasts. The muesli, fruit salad and yogurt is large and tasty, or choose one of the excellent crepes. There's good coffee, juices and shakes, plus *bocadillos* (filled rolls) and cakes.

Chilimoso (☎ 956 68 50 92; Calle Peso 6; dishes €4-6; V) This tiny place serves tasty vegan and vegetarian food with oriental leanings. Try the falafel with hummus, tzatziki and salad.

Souk (☎ 956 62 70 65; Calle Mar Tirreno 46; dishes €8-15; from 8pm Wed-Mon V) In the unlikely residential setting north of town, Souk serves terrific Moroccan- and Asian-inspired food. There's a bright upstairs bar for drinks too.

La Trattoria (☎ 956 68 22 25; Paseo de la Alameda; pasta & pizza €7-11, mains €14-18.50) The Alameda is lined with restaurants and cafes. First-class food and efficient service make La Trattoria one of the best and busiest Italian eateries in town.

Miramar (☎ 956 68 52 46; Arte Vida Hotel, N340 Km79.3; mains €8-18) The Miramar's chefs whip up a

SHOPPING TARIFA

Tarifa's a great place to shop. The streets of the old town are dotted with jewellery, contemporary fashion and curio shops. Stroll along **Calle Batalla del Salado** to find countless surf shops and boutiques offering casual fashion and beachwear. Surf brands such as Rick Shapes, No Work Team and El Niño are well-known names in Spain, and most were founded in Tarifa. Rip Curl, Billabong and Quiksilver are also represented.

A few stores sell groovy homewares and even furniture. **Tarfa** (☎ 956 62 70 63; Calle Batalla del Salado 13) is excellent for gifts. Some warehouse-like stores on the N340 northwest of town stock anything from thatch-roofed Balinese platform shelters (around €6000) to chair-shaped hammocks – check **Explora** (☎ 956 68 91 32; N340 Km76.2), which also offers beach volleyball and a chillout zone.

ANDALUCÍA

range of pasta, meat and fish dishes – and the expansive beach and ocean views double your enjoyment.

Bodega La Casa Amarilla (☎ 956 68 19 93; Calle Sancho IV El Bravo 9; mains €14-18) With an attractive, flowery patio, this is a top place in town for local grilled meats and fish, good *revueltos* (scrambled egg dishes) and tapas.

Drinking & Entertainment

The lively downtown bar scene focuses on narrow Calle Santísima Trinidad and Calle San Francisco, just east of the Alameda. Most places here get busy after 11pm and stay open till 2 or 3am. Many are closed on Sunday. Don't miss the hip, Italian-owned bar-club **Soul Café** (Calle Santísima Trinidad 9) with good cocktails and international music: you may hear guest DJs from Milan play their stuff. Right next door are the relaxed little **Taco Way**, known for its mojitos, and **La Ruina**, with good electro dance music. **Bistro Point** (cnr Calles Santísima Trinidad & San Francisco) has a friendly international crowd and serves good crepes (€2 to €4) too. Also check out Irish and Italian-owned **Mezcla** (Calle San Francisco 12), with sport screens, tapas and wi-fi.

A handful of more clublike bars stay open longer. Fashionable **Bar Misiana** (☎ 956 62 70 83; Hotel Misiana, Calle Sancho IV El Bravo 18) is one of *the* places to be seen. DJs spin till 3 or 4am. Top of the late and cool list, though oddly located, is Ibiza-inspired **Café del Mar** (☎ 956 62 72 16; Polígono La Vega; from 6pm Mon-Sat), which includes a couple of bars and a nikkei (Japanese-Peruvian) restaurant as well as a night club with resident house DJs.

There are further bar and club possibilities on Playa de los Lances and outside town. The line-up is ever-changing, but two apparent spring and summer fixtures are the open-air **Serengueti**, on the beach, and spacious **Banti** (☎ 956 68 15 09; www.bantitarifa.com; N340 Km82.7), which is also an Asian restaurant and small hotel.

Getting There & Around

BOAT

FRS (☎ 956 68 18 30; www.frs.es; Avenida Andalucía) runs a fast ferry between Tarifa and Tangier, Morocco (passenger/car/motorcycle one-way €31/85/31, 35 minutes), eight times daily, often with more sailings in July and August. FRS also offers daily one-day tours to Tangier including the ferry round trip, a guide and lunch, for €55. You can get information and tickets at the Estación Marítima (Passenger Port), where the ships sail from. All ferry passengers need a passport except EU citizens on FRS excursions, for whom national ID cards are sufficient.

TOP 10 ANDALUCIAN BEACHES

- **Ensenada de Valdevaqueros** (p758)
- **Bolonia** (p756)
- **Zahara de los Atunes** (p756)
- **Playa del Playazo** (p830)
- **Cuesta de Maneli** (p735)
- **Cabo de Trafalgar** (p755)
- **Calas del Barronal** (p830)
- **Playa de la Victoria** (p741)
- **Agua Amarga** (p830)
- **Isla Cristina** (p736)

BUS

Comes (☎ 902 19 92 08, 956 68 40 38; Calle Batalla del Salado 13) runs six or more daily buses to Cádiz (€7.91, 1¾ hours), Algeciras (€1.90, 30 minutes) and La Línea de la Concepción (€3.59, 45 minutes), four to Seville (€15.30, three hours), two each to Jerez de la Frontera (€8.34, 2½ hours) and Málaga (€12.45, two hours), and one to Zahara de los Atunes (€3.24, 40 minutes).

In July and August local buses run about every 1½ hours northwest along the coast as far as Camping Jardín de las Dunas on Ensenada de Valdevaqueros. There's a bus stop at the bottom of the Paseo de Alameda; another stop is at the Comes bus station, where a timetable and prices should be posted.

ALGECIRAS

pop 111,300

Let's be honest about this – nobody comes to Algeciras for its beauty. This major port linking Spain with Africa is an ugly industrial town and fishing port. If you come here you do so only to leave again by catching a ferry to Morocco. If for some reason you do have some time to kill here then make for the palm-fringed main square, Plaza Alta. It should be said that in the tradition of seedy ports the world over Algeciras isn't entirely safe, and you should keep your wits about

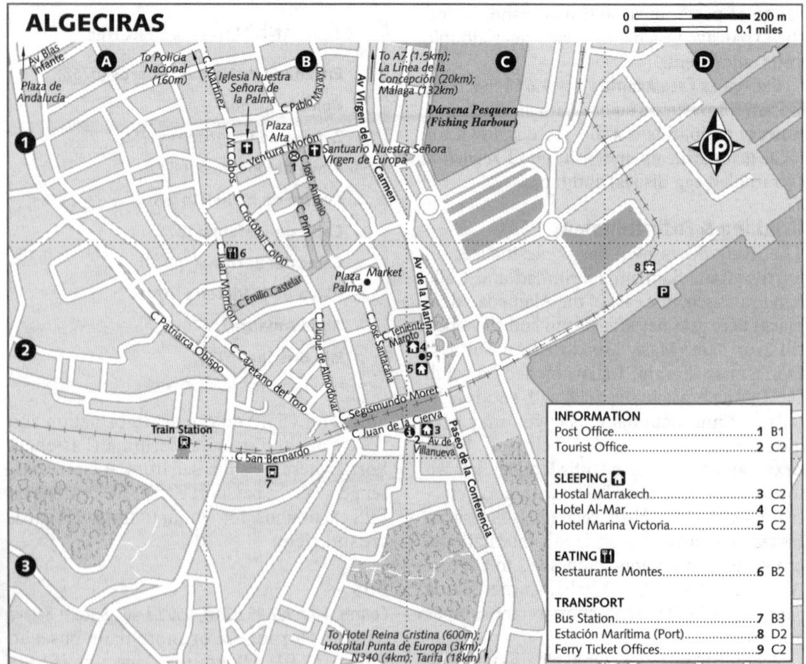

you in the port, bus station and market. It's also even more important than normal not to leave any valuables in your car and, if you are driving, never, ever pick up any hitch-hikers around here.

Algeciras was taken by Alfonso XI from the Merenids of Morocco in 1344, but later razed by Mohammed V of Granada. In 1704 it was repopulated by many of those who left Gibraltar after it was taken by the British.

During summer the port is hectic, as hundreds of thousands of Moroccans working in Europe return home for summer holidays.

Information

If you're going to arrive in Morocco at night, take some dirham with you. Exchange rates for buying dirham in Algeciras are best at banks. There are banks and ATMs on Avenida Virgen del Carmen and around Plaza Alta, plus a couple of ATMs inside the port.

Hospital Punta de Europa (☎ 956 02 50 00; Carretera de Getares s/n) 3km west of the centre.

Left Luggage (Estación Maritima; per item €2-3; 🕒 7am-9-30pm) Bags must be secured. There are lockers (€3) nearby and also luggage storage at the bus station.

Policía Nacional (☎ 956 66 04 00; Avenida de las Fuerzas Armadas 6)

Tourist office (☎ 956 57 32 41; Calle Juan de la Cierva s/n; 🕒 9am-7.30pm Mon-Fri, 9.30am-3pm Sat & Sun) English-speaking; has a message board.

Sleeping & Eating

The accommodation scene in Algeciras is pretty dire.

Hostal Marrakech (☎ 956 57 34 74; Calle Juan de la Cierva 5; s/d €25/40) If you have to stay the night then do yourself favour and stay here. The Moroccan family who run this place have a handful of bold and tarty rooms with communal bathrooms only.

Hotel Marina Victoria (☎ 956 63 28 65; www.hotelmarinavictoria.com; Avenida de la Marina 7; s/d €32/50; ❄) Shades of the '70s prevail at this rundown hotel. Still, it's handy for the port…

Hotel Al-Mar (☎ 956 65 46 61; Avenida de la Marina 2-3; s/d €53/94; P ❄) Following in the lead of its neighbour, the Marina Victoria, the rooms in this lacklustre hotel also opt for the '70s disaster-film look.

Hotel Reina Cristina (☎ 956 60 26 22; www.hotelesglobales.com; Paseo de la Conferencia s/n; s/d €89/149;

P) For olde-worlde ambience head south to this colonial-style hotel with two swimming pools. Big discounts are often available by booking through their website.

Restaurante Montes (☎ 956 65 42 07; Calle Juan Morrison 27; menú €9.50, mains €15) The Montes has a hugely fishy lunch *menú* consisting of three courses, bread and wine. There is also a long list of tempting à la carte seafood.

Getting There & Away

BOAT

Companies such as **Trasmediterránea** (☎ 902 45 46 45; www.trasmediterranea.es) and **EuroFerrys** (☎ 956 65 23 24; www.euroferrys.com) operate frequent daily passenger and vehicle ferries to/from Tangier, Morocco (2½-hour ferry passenger/car and passenger €42/160; 1¼-hour fast ferry passenger/car and passenger €42/160) and Ceuta, the Spanish enclave on the Moroccan coast (35-minute fast ferry passenger/car and passenger €39.50/146.10). **Buquebus** (☎ 956 65 24 73) operates a similar Ceuta service at least six times daily. From mid-June to September there are ferries almost round the clock to cater for the Moroccan holiday migration – you may have to queue for up to three hours. Buy your ticket in the port or at the agencies on Avenida de la Marina: prices are the same everywhere.

BUS

The bus station is on Calle San Bernardo. **Comes** (☎ 956 65 34 56) has buses for La Línea (€1.86, 30 minutes) every half-hour (every 45 minutes at weekends). Other daily buses include up to 13 each to Tarifa (€1.86, 30 minutes) and Cádiz (€10.59, 2½ hours), six to Seville (€16.52, 2½ hours), and one Monday to Friday to Ronda (€9.39, two to three hours). **Daibus** (☎ 956 58 78 97) runs four daily buses to Madrid (€27.55, eight to nine hours), starting from the port then calling at the bus station. **Portillo** (☎ 902 14 31 44) operates numerous buses up and down the Andalucian Mediterranean coast.

TRAIN

From the **station** (☎ 956 63 10 05), adjacent to Calle San Bernardo, trains run to/from Madrid (€38.10 to €63.50, six or 11 hours, two daily) and Granada (€18.35, four hours, three daily). All go through Ronda (€6.70 to €17.40, 1¾ hours) and Bobadilla (€11, 2¾ hours), where you can change for Málaga, Córdoba or Seville.

LA LÍNEA DE LA CONCEPCIÓN

pop 63,000

La Línea, 20km east of Algeciras, is the stepping stone to Gibraltar. A left turn as you exit the bus station brings you onto Avenida 20 de Abril, which runs the 300m or so from the main square, Plaza de la Constitución, to the Gibraltar border. The **municipal tourist office** (☎ 956 17 19 98; Avenida Príncipe Felipe s/n; 8am-8pm Mon-Fri, 9am-2pm Sat) faces the border.

Buses run about every 30 minutes to/from Algeciras (€1.86, 30 minutes).

To save queuing at the border, many visitors to Gibraltar park in La Línea, then walk across. The underground **Parking Fo Cona**, just off Avenida 20 de Abril, is the safest place to leave your wheels.

GIBRALTAR

When English poet Laurie Lee visited Gibraltar on his first journey through Spain in the mid-1930s, he described it as looking like 'it had been towed out from Portsmouth and anchored off-shore still wearing its own grey roof of weather'.

Despite bobbies on the beat and red post boxes, Gibraltar is actually a cultural cocktail with Genoese, Spanish, North African and other elements creating a rich blend. Naturally, the main sight is the awesome Rock, a vast limestone ridge that rises to 426m, with sheer cliffs on its northern and eastern sides. For the ancient Greeks and Romans this was one of the two Pillars of Hercules, split from the other, Jebel Musa in Morocco, in the course of Hercules' arduous Twelve Labours. The two great rocks marked the edge of the ancient world. Gibraltar's location and highly defensible nature have attracted the covetous gaze of military strategists ever since.

Gibraltarians (77% of the population) speak both English and Spanish and, often, a curious mix of the two. Signs are in English.

History

In 711 Tariq ibn Ziyad, the Muslim governor of Tangier, landed at Gibraltar to launch the Islamic invasion of the Iberian Peninsula. The name Gibraltar is derived from Jebel Tariq (Tariq's Mountain).

Castilla wrested the Rock from the Muslims in 1462. Then in 1704 an Anglo-Dutch fleet captured Gibraltar during the War of the

Spanish Succession. Spain ceded the Rock to Britain in 1713, but didn't abandon military attempts to regain it until the failure of the Great Siege of 1779–83. Britain developed it into an important naval base (bringing in a community of Genoese ship repairers). During the Franco period, Gibraltar was an extremely sore point between Britain and Spain: the border was closed from 1967 to 1985. In 1969 Gibraltarians voted, by 12,138 to 44, in favour of British rather than Spanish sovereignty, and a new constitution gave Gibraltar domestic self-government. In 2002 the UK and Spain held talks about a possible future sharing of sovereignty over Gibraltar, but Gibraltarians expressed *their* feelings in a referendum (not recognised by Britain or Spain), which voted resoundingly against any such idea.

In December 2005 the governments of the UK, Spain and Gibraltar set up a new, trilateral process of dialogue. The three parties have reached agreement on some issues but tricky topics remain, not the least Britain's military installations and 'ownership' of Gibraltar airport. Gibraltarians want self-determination and to retain British citizenship, making joint sovereignty improbable. Few foresee a change in the status quo but at least relations are less strained. On 18 September 2006 a three-way deal was signed by Spain, Gibraltar and Britain relating to telecommunications on the Rock, Gibraltar airport and other issues, but not sovereignty. Gibraltar airport will be expanded across the border into Spain, and flights from Spanish cities and other European destinations direct to Gibraltar airport will be introduced. The mainstays of Gibraltar's economy are tourism, the port and financial services (including, Spanish police complain, the laundering of proceeds from organised crime, though Gibraltar counters that money laundering is tightly controlled). Investment on the Rock continues apace with a huge luxury waterfront development on its western side.

Orientation

To reach Gibraltar by land you must pass through the Spanish border town of La Línea de la Concepción (p763). Just south of the border, the road crosses Gibraltar airport runway. Gibraltar's town and harbours lie along the Rock's less steep western side, facing Bahía de Algeciras (Bay of Gibraltar). From Casemates Sq, just inside Grand Casemates Gate, Main St, with all the shops, runs south for about 1km.

Information

BOOKSHOPS

Bell Books (☎ 76707; 11 Bell Lane)
Gibraltar Bookshop (☎ 71894; 300 Main St)

ELECTRICITY

Electric current is the same as in Britain: 220V or 240V, with plugs of three flat pins.

EMERGENCY

Emergency (☎ 199) For police or ambulance.
Police station (120 Irish Town)

INTERNET ACCESS

PC Clinic & Computer Centre (☎ 49991; 17 Convent Place; 🕑 9.30am-6.30pm Mon-Fri; per hr £3)

MEDICAL SERVICES

St Bernard's Hospital (☎ 79700; Europort) 24-hour emergency facilities.

MONEY

The currencies are the Gibraltar pound (£) and pound sterling, which are interchangeable. You can spend euros (except in pay phones and post offices) but conversion rates are poor. Change unspent Gibraltar currency before leaving. Banks are generally open from 9am to 3.30pm weekdays. There are several on Main St.

POST

Post office (104 Main St; 🕑 9am-4.30pm Mon-Fri & 10am-1pm Sat, closes at 2.15pm Mon-Fri mid-Jun–mid-Sep)

TELEPHONE

To dial Gibraltar from Spain, you now precede the five-digit local number with the code ☎ 00350; from other countries, dial the international access code, then the Gibraltar country code (☎ 350) and local number. To phone Spain from Gibraltar, just dial the nine-digit Spanish number.

TOURIST INFORMATION

Gibraltar has several helpful tourist offices.
Gibraltar Tourist Board (☎ 45000, 74950; www.gibraltar.gov.uk; Duke of Kent House, Cathedral Sq; 🕑 9am-5.30pm Mon-Thu, to 5.15pm Fri)
Information booth (☎ 73026; airport; 🕑 Mon-Fri, mornings only)

ANDALUCÍA

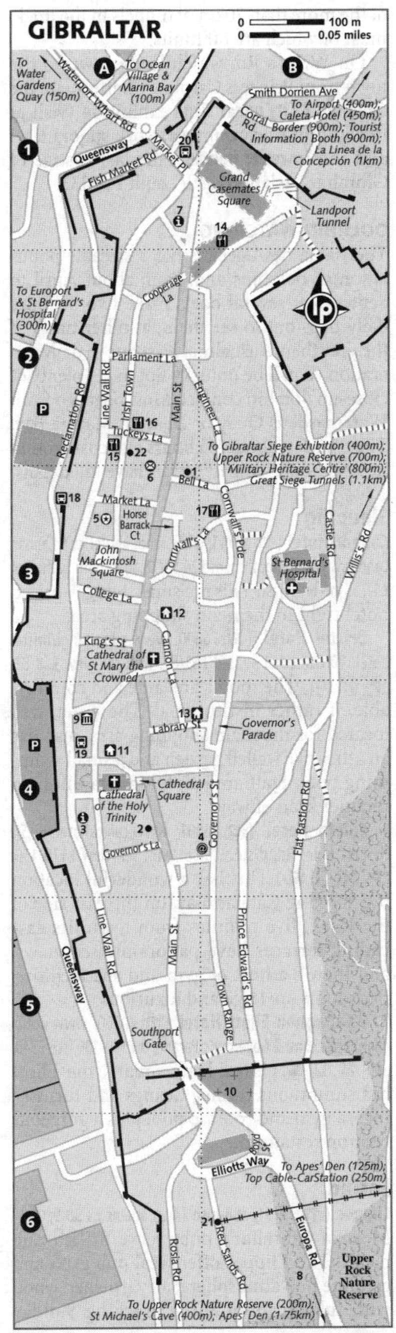

INFORMATION
Bell Books....1 A3
Gibraltar Bookshop....2 A4
Gibraltar Tourist Board....3 A4
PC Clinic & Computer Centre....4 B4
Police Station....5 A3
Post Office....6 A3
Tourist Office....7 A1

SIGHTS & ACTIVITIES
Alameda Botanical Gardens....8 B6
Gibraltar Museum....9 A4
Trafalgar Cemetery....10 B5

SLEEPING
Bristol Hotel....11 A4
Cannon Hotel....12 A3
O'Callaghan Eliott Hotel....13 A4

EATING
Café Solo....14 B1
Clipper....15 A2
House of Sacarello....16 A2
Thyme....17 B3

TRANSPORT
Bus 10....18 A3
Bus 3....19 A4
Bus 9....20 A1
Lower Cable-Car Station....21 B6
Turner & Co....22 A2

Information booth (☎ 50762; Customs House, Frontier; 9am-4.30pm Mon-Fri, 10am-1pm Sat)
Tourist office (☎ 74982; Grand Casemates Sq; 9am-5.30pm Mon-Fri, 10am-3pm Sat, to 1pm Sun & holidays) Several information desks provide all the information you need about Gibraltar, with plenty of pleasant cafes in the same square where you can read through it all at leisure.

VISAS & DOCUMENTS

To enter Gibraltar, you need a passport or EU national identity card. EU, USA, Canadian, Australian, New Zealand and South African passport-holders are among those who do not need visas for Gibraltar. For further information contact Gibraltar's **Immigration Department** (☎ 51725).

Sights & Activities

THE TOWN

Pedestrianised Main St has an emphatically British appearance, but the Spanish lilt in the air is a reminder that this is still Mediterranean Europe. Most Spanish and Islamic buildings on Gibraltar were destroyed in 18th-century sieges, but the Rock bristles with British fortifications, gates and gun emplacements.

In the **Gibraltar Museum** (Bomb House Lane; adult/under 12yr £2/1; 10am-6pm Mon-Fri, to 2pm Sat), a labyrinth of rooms large and small, the story of Gibraltar unfolds from Neanderthal to medieval artefacts, with plenty more of its later military and naval history. Don't miss the well-preserved Muslim bathhouse and an intricately painted 7th-century BC-Egyptian mummy washed up here in the late 1800s. The **Trafalgar Cemetery** (Prince Edward's Rd; 9am-7pm) gives a more poignant history lesson, with its graves of British sailors who died at Gibraltar after the Battle of Trafalgar in 1805. The lush **Alameda Botanic Gardens** (Europa Rd; admission free; 8am-sunset) are a short distance south.

UPPER ROCK NATURE RESERVE

The most exciting thing about Gibraltar is the Rock itself. Most of the upper Rock, starting just above the town, is a **nature reserve** (adult/child incl attractions £8/4, vehicle £1.50, pedestrian excl attractions £1; 9.30am-7pm), with spectacular views and several interesting spots to visit. A great way to get up here is by the cable car (opposite). During a westerly wind the Rock is often a fine spot for observing migrations of birds, especially raptors and storks, between Africa and Europe. January to early June is the time for northbound migrations, and late July to early November for southbound migrations. White storks sometimes congregate in flocks of 3000 to cross the strait.

The Rock's most famous inhabitants are its colony of Barbary macaques, the only wild primates in Europe (probably introduced from North Africa in the 18th century). Some of these hang around the **Apes' Den**, near the middle cable-car station; others lurk at the top cable-car station or the Great Siege Tunnels. Touchingly human in their ways, they groom their young with frowns of absorption, snack on blackened banana skins, or pose for your camera, looking wistfully out to sea.

About 20 minutes' walk south down St Michael's Rd from the top cable-car station (or 20 minutes up from the Apes' Den), **St Michael's Cave** is a big natural grotto that was once home to Neolithic inhabitants of the Rock. Giant fingers of stone plunge deep and soar high, with atmospheric lighting to add drama as you pace the walkway on a 15-minute tour. Princess Caroline's Battery, a half-hour walk north (downhill) from the top cable-car station, houses a **Military Heritage Centre**. From here a road leads up to the impressive **Great Siege Tunnels**, hand-hewn by the British for gun emplacements during the siege of 1779–83. They constitute a tiny proportion of the more than 70km of tunnels in the Rock, most of which are off limits.

On Willis's Rd, which leads down to the town from Princess Caroline's Battery, are the **Gibraltar, A City under Siege** exhibition (visit at twilight for maximum waxwork spookiness) and the **Tower of Homage**, the last vestige of Gibraltar's Islamic castle, built in 1333.

DOLPHIN-WATCHING

The Bahía de Algeciras has a sizeable population of dolphins and, from about April to September, several boats make two or more daily trips out to see them; at other times of the year there's usually at least one in daily operation. You'll be unlucky not to get plenty of close-up dolphin contact. Most boats go from Watergardens Quay or adjacent Marina Bay. The trips last about 1½ hours and cost around £20 per adult. Tourist offices have full details.

Sleeping

Cannon Hotel (51711; www.cannonhotel.gi; 9 Cannon Lane; s/d without bathroom £26.50/38.50, d with bathroom £47, all incl breakfast) This is a small, budget-priced hotel right in the main shopping area.

Bristol Hotel (76800; www.gibraltar.gi/bristolhotel; 10 Cathedral Sq; s/d £63/81, with sea view £68/87; P) The rooms are large and comfortable, if rather institutional. The hotel, well located for the main shopping area, also has an attractive walled garden and a small swimming pool. Staff are helpful in a faithful old retainer kind of way.

Caleta Hotel (76501; www.caletahotel.gi; Sir Herbert Miles Rd; d/ste without/with sea view £110/150; P) This has a wonderful location overlooking Catalan Bay, on the east side of the Rock, five minutes from town. Its cascading terraces have panoramic sea views, and there's a host of gym and spa facilities. Bedrooms are large and luxurious.

O'Callaghan Eliott Hotel (70500; www.ocallaghanhotels.com; 2 Governor's Parade; d £140-180, ste £340; P) On a leafy square, the Eliott has sumptuous rooms, fittings and furnishings, a gym and rooftop pool plus a gorgeous rooftop restaurant.

Eating

Clipper (79791; 78B Irish Town; mains £3.50-9; V) Most of Gibraltar's pubs serve British pub meals. The Clipper offers real pub grub and genuine pub atmosphere, all varnished wood with full-on footy and a cracking Sunday roast. Vegetarians should go for the Greek salad wrap. Full English breakfast is served from 9.30 to 11am.

House of Sacarello (☎ 70625; 57 Irish Town; daily specials £7-11.50; 9am-7.30pm Mon-Fri, 9am-3pm Sat, closed Sun) A chic place in a converted coffee warehouse with light lunches including pastas and salads. You can linger over afternoon tea (£4) between 3pm and 7.30pm.

Café Solo (☎ 44449; Grand Casemates Sq 3; pastas £8-12) With tables inside the exposed brick and wood cafe and out on the bustling square, this is a good place to stop for coffees, continental beers and a variety of interesting pastas and salads, including vegetarian goodies. It's also a great place for breakfast, with mellow jazz piped in.

Nuno's (☎ 76501; Caleta Hotel, Sir Herbert Miles Rd; mains £11-15) A top-class, formal Italian restaurant in the Caleta Hotel, with fabulous terrace views. Delicious homemade pastas and risottos are accompanied by an extensive wine list. Try the breast of duck with fig ravioli.

our pick **Thyme** (☎ 49199; www.dineatthyme.com; 5 Cornwall's Lane; mains £12-22); closed Sun) Middle Eastern, Italian, Spanish or Thai – Thyme's menu reflects Gibraltar's joyful muddle of ethnicities, and does it brilliantly. Share the Seafood Slammer – seven large shot glasses filled with miniature masterpieces, including a musically crisp prawn tempura with a red onion marmalade, and sea bass with homemade tartare sauce. Move on (slowly) to chilli and lime-roasted chicken on a bed of Thai risotto with a tomato and coriander salsa. Add chilled jazz, a warm welcome, the smart decor, and you have an extraordinary experience.

Several pleasant waterside eateries also line Marina Bay.

Shopping

Gibraltar has lots of British high-street stores, such as Next, Marks & Spencer, Monsoon and Mothercare (all on or just off Main St) and a huge Morrisons store (in Europort at the northern end of the main harbour). Shops are normally open 9am to 7.30pm weekdays, and until 1pm Saturday.

Getting There & Away

AIR

Easyjet (www.easyjet.com), **Iberia** (www.iberia.com) and **Monarch** fly daily to/from London Gatwick. **Monarch Airlines** (☎ 47477; www.flymonarch.com) flies daily to/from London Luton and Manchester.

BOAT

FRS (☎ 956 68 18 30 in Tarifa, Spain; www.frs.es) operates one ferry a week between Gibraltar and Tangier, departing Gibraltar at 9pm Friday for the 70-minute crossing, and returning at the same time on Sunday. One-way/return fares are adult £32/57, child £21/38, car £83/150. The ferry departs from the terminal in front of the coach park. Purchase tickets from **Turner & Co** (☎ 78305; 67 Irish Town, 8am-3-pm Mon-Fri Jun-Oct, 9am-1pm & 2-5pm Nov-May).

BUS

There are no regular buses to Gibraltar, but La Línea de la Concepción bus station (p763) is only a five-minute walk from the border.

CAR & MOTORCYCLE

Snaking vehicle queues at the 24-hour border and congested traffic in Gibraltar often make it easier to park in La Línea and walk across the border. To take a car into Gibraltar (free) you need an insurance certificate, registration document, nationality plate and driving licence.

Getting Around

The 1.5km walk from the border to the town centre crosses the airport runway. A left turn off Corral Rd takes you through the pedestrian Landport Tunnel into Grand Casemates Sq. Alternatively, several local bus lines (adult/child/senior 70p/50p/40p) run from the border into town about every 15 minutes (every 30 minutes on Saturday and Sunday), until 9pm. Bus 9 goes to Market Pl; number 3 goes to Cathedral Sq and the lower cable-car station; and number 10, a red double-decker, runs to Europort (stopping at Morrisons), then Reclamation Rd near the city centre.

All of Gibraltar can be covered on foot, and much of it (including the upper Rock) by car or motorcycle. You can also ascend, weather permitting, by the **cable car** (Red Sands Rd; adult return £8, child £4.50; every few min 9.30am-8pm Mon-Sat; last cable up, 7.15pm, last cable down 7.45pm, to 5pm Oct-Apr). For the Apes' Den, disembark at the middle station.

MÁLAGA PROVINCE

To many travellers, until quite recently, Málaga was just a Spanish airport, their last stop on the way to the sun, sea and sand package holiday on the Costa del Sol. But that perception is changing as fast as the area's increasingly sophisticated city life, arts venues and construction of cutting-edge hotels. Inland, by contrast, time often seems to stand still, captured in the historic treasures of Ronda and Antequera, and in the sprinkling of white villages in the surrounding hills. Nevertheless, Málaga's coastal resorts, from Torremolinos to Nerja, are undeniably obsessed with holidays – yours. So you get a huge choice of good accommodation and loads to see and do by day and night, especially if you are holidaying as a family. Olé!

MÁLAGA

pop 720,000

This exuberant and very Spanish port city, set against a sparkling blue Mediterranean, is both historic and pulsing with modern life; more than any other major Andalucian city, Málaga seems to be focusing on the future, though with plenty to boast about from the past. The centre presents the visitor with narrow old streets and wide, leafy boulevards, beautiful gardens and impressive monuments, fashionable shops and a burgeoning cultural life. The austere and beautiful Picasso Museum, devoted to Málaga's most illustrious son, is leading a mini-galaxy of contemporary arts venues and events in its energetic wake, including a fascinating museum of contemporary art and a new fine arts museum pending. The historic centre is being restored and much of it pedestrianised, and the port is being developed as a leisure zone. The city's terrific bars and nightlife, the last word in Málaga *joie de vivre,* stay open very late.

ANDALUCÍA

History

Probably founded by Phoenicians, Málaga has long had a commercial vocation. It flourished in the Islamic era, especially as the chief port of the Emirate of Granada, later reasserting itself as an entrepreneurial centre in the 19th century when a dynamic middle class founded textile factories, sugar and steel mills and shipyards. Málaga dessert wine ('mountain sack') was popular in Victorian England. During the civil war Málaga was initially a Republican stronghold. Hundreds of Nationalist sympathisers were killed before the city fell in February 1937 after being bombed by Italian planes. Vicious reprisals followed.

Málaga has enjoyed a steadily increasing economic spin-off from the mass tourism launched on the nearby Costa del Sol in the 1950s. In recent years, the city has become an important destination in itself.

Orientation

The tree-lined Paseo del Parque and Alameda Principal run along the southern edge of the old town. The main streets leading north into the old town are Calle Marqués de Larios and Calle Molina Lario. The Gibralfaro hill rising above the eastern half of Paseo del Parque dominates the central area. Avenida de Andalucía continues the Paseo del Parque–Alameda Principal axis west of Río Guadalmedina. The main train and bus stations are around 600m south of Avenida de Andalucía, and the airport is 9km southwest.

Information

There are plenty of banks with ATMs on Calle Puerta del Mar and Calle Marqués de Larios, and ATMs in the airport arrivals hall.

Hospital Carlos Haya (☎ 951 03 01 00; Avenida de Carlos Haya) The main hospital, 2km west of the centre.

Librería Luces (Map p770; Alameda Principal 16) Bookshop with some English titles and a good travel section, both on the ground floor.

Meeting Point (Map p770; Plaza de la Merced 20; internet per min/hr €0.20/1-2; 10am-11pm Mon-Sat, 1.30-11pm Sun) Twenty-five internet stations in a big bright centre with video game stations in front of the store.

Municipal tourist office (www.malagaturismo.com in Spanish) Plaza de la Marina (Map p770; ☎ 952 12 20 20; 9am-7pm Mon-Fri, 10am-7pm Sat & Sun Apr-Oct, to 6pm Mon-Fri, 10am-6pm Sat & Sun, Nov-Mar) Casita del Jardinero (Map p770; ☎ 952 13 47 31; Avenida de Cervantes 1; same hr) Also information booths at the bus station and around town.

Policía Local (Map p769; ☎ 952 12 65 00; Avenida de la Rosaleda 19)

Post office (Map p769; Avenida de Andalucía 1; 8.30am-8.30pm Mon-Fri, 9.30am-2pm Sat)

Regional tourist office (Map p770; ☎ 951 30 89 11; Pasaje de Chinitas 4; www.andalucia.org; 9am-7.30pm Mon-Fri, 10am-7pm Sat, to 2pm Sun) There is another branch at the airport; these cover the whole of Málaga and all of Andalucía.

Sights

MUSEO PICASSO MÁLAGA

The hottest attraction on Málaga's tourist scene is tucked away on a pedestrian street in what was medieval Málaga's *judería.* The **Museo Picasso Málaga** (Map p770; ☎ 902 44 33 77; www.museopicassomalaga.org; Palacio de Buenavista, Calle

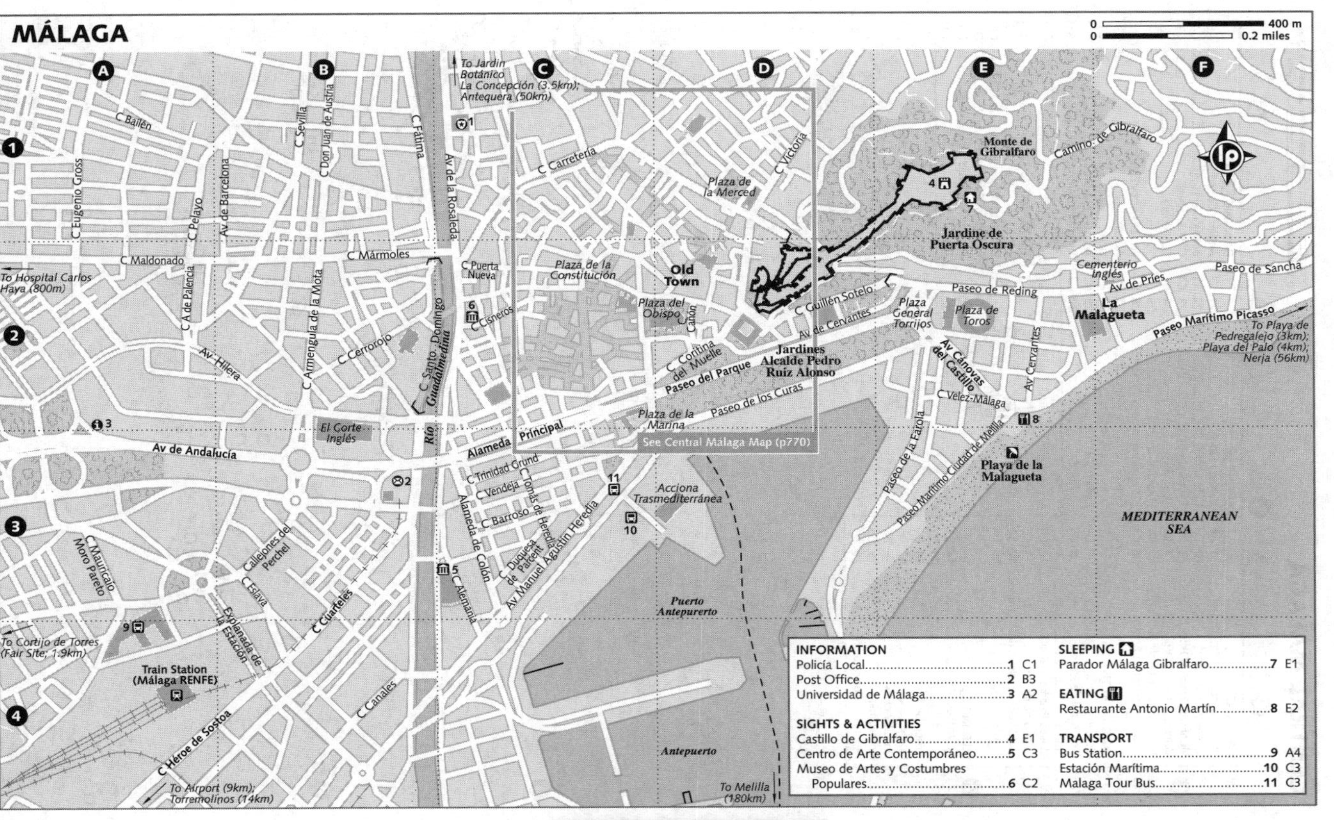
MÁLAGA
0 400 m
0 0.2 miles
INFORMATION
Policía Local..........1 C1
Post Office..........2 B3
Universidad de Málaga..........3 A2
SIGHTS & ACTIVITIES
Castillo de Gibralfaro..........4 E1
Centro de Arte Contemporáneo..........5 C3
Museo de Artes y Costumbres Populares..........6 C2
SLEEPING
Parador Málaga Gibralfaro..........7 E1
EATING
Restaurante Antonio Martín..........8 E2
TRANSPORT
Bus Station..........9 A4
Estación Marítima..........10 C3
Malaga Tour Bus..........11 C3
MEDITERRANEAN SEA
Old Town
See Central Málaga Map (p770)
Monte de Gibralfaro
Jardine de Puerta Oscura
La Malagueta
Playa de la Malagueta
Plaza de Toros
Plaza General Torrijos
Jardines Alcalde Pedro Ruiz Alonso
Paseo del Parque
Paseo de los Curas
Plaza de la Marina
Plaza del Obispo
Plaza de la Constitución
Plaza de la Merced
Cementerio Inglés
Puerto Antepurerto
Antepuerto
Acciona Trasmediterránea
El Corte Inglés
Train Station (Málaga RENFE)
Río Guadalmedina
Alameda Principal
Av de Andalucía
Av de la Rosaleda
Alameda de Colón
Paseo Marítimo Picasso
Paseo de Sancha
Paseo de Reding
Av Cánovas del Castillo
Paseo Marítimo Ciudad de Melilla
Paseo de la Farola
Av Cervantes
Av de Cervantes
Camino de Gibralfaro
Av de Pries
C Guillén Sotelo
C Velez-Málaga
C Victoria
C Carretería
C Cisneros
C Puerta Nueva
C Mármoles
C Fátima
C Santo Domingo
C Cerrojo
C Armengual de la Mota
C Don Juan de Austria
C Sevilla
Av de Barcelona
C Pelayo
C A de Palencia
Av Hilera
C Maldonado
C Bailén
C Eugenio Gross
C Mauricio Moro Pareto
Explanada de la Estación
C Eslava
Callejones del Perchel
C Cuarteles
C Canales
C Héroe de Sostoa
C Alemania
Av Manuel Agustín Heredia
C Duquesa de Parcent
C Barroso
C Vendeja
C Trinidad Grund
C Tomás de Heredia
C Cortina del Muelle
C Cañón
To Jardín Botánico La Concepción (3.5km); Antequera (50km)
To Hospital Carlos Haya (800m)
To Cortijo de Torres (Fair Site; 1.9km)
To Airport (9km); Torremolinos (14km)
To Melilla (180km)
To Playa de Pedregalejo (3km); Playa del Palo (4km); Nerja (56km)

ANDALUCÍA

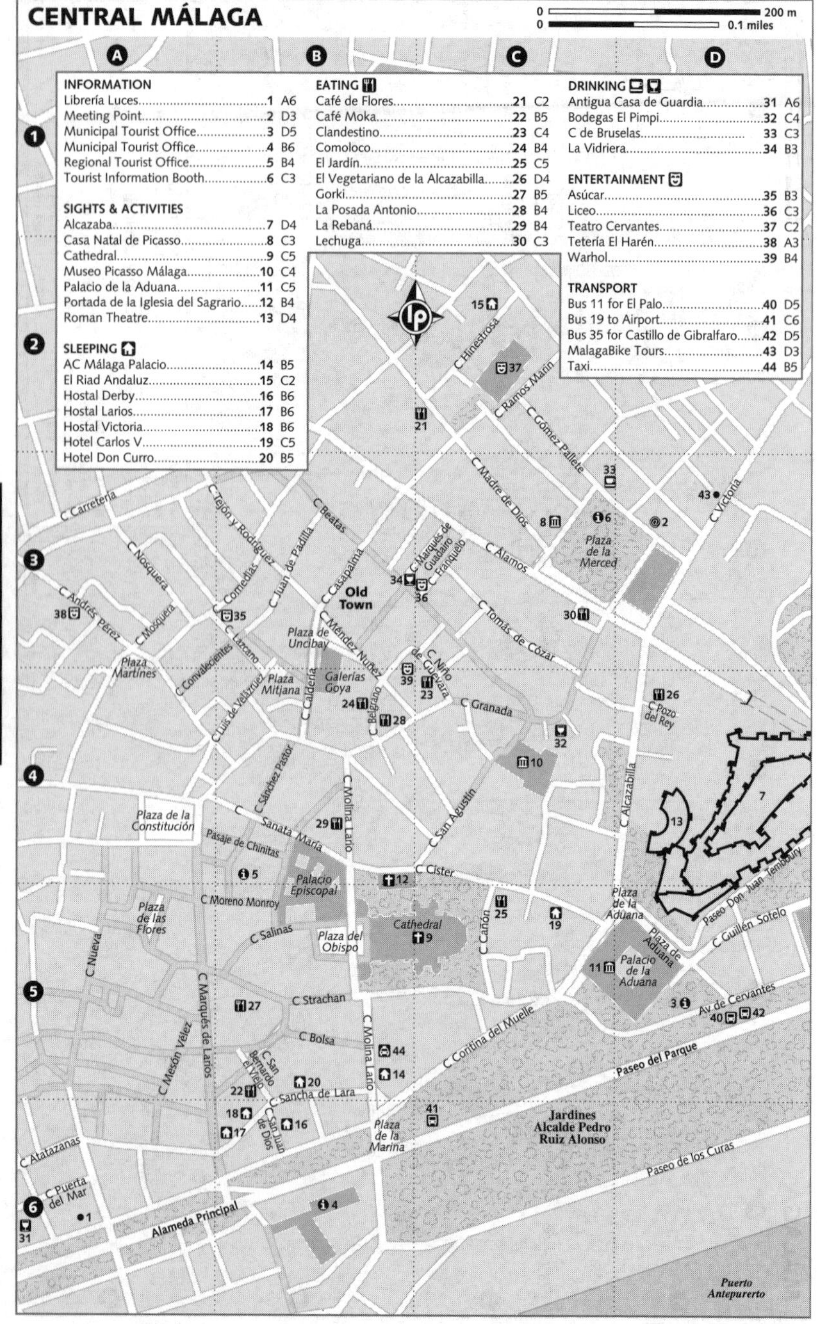
CENTRAL MÁLAGA
0 200 m
0 0.1 miles
A
B
C
D
1
2
3
4
5
6
INFORMATION
Librería Luces....1 A6
Meeting Point....2 D3
Municipal Tourist Office....3 D5
Municipal Tourist Office....4 B6
Regional Tourist Office....5 B4
Tourist Information Booth....6 C3
SIGHTS & ACTIVITIES
Alcazaba....7 D4
Casa Natal de Picasso....8 C3
Cathedral....9 C5
Museo Picasso Málaga....10 C4
Palacio de la Aduana....11 C5
Portada de la Iglesia del Sagrario....12 B4
Roman Theatre....13 D4
SLEEPING
AC Málaga Palacio....14 B5
El Riad Andaluz....15 C2
Hostal Derby....16 B6
Hostal Larios....17 B6
Hostal Victoria....18 B6
Hotel Carlos V....19 C5
Hotel Don Curro....20 B5
EATING
Café de Flores....21 C2
Café Moka....22 B5
Clandestino....23 C4
Comoloco....24 B4
El Jardín....25 C5
El Vegetariano de la Alcazabilla....26 D4
Gorki....27 B5
La Posada Antonio....28 B4
La Rebaná....29 B4
Lechuga....30 C3
DRINKING
Antigua Casa de Guardia....31 A6
Bodegas El Pimpi....32 C4
C de Bruselas....33 C3
La Vidriera....34 B3
ENTERTAINMENT
Asúcar....35 B3
Liceo....36 C3
Teatro Cervantes....37 C2
Tetería El Harén....38 A3
Warhol....39 B4
TRANSPORT
Bus 11 for El Palo....40 D5
Bus 19 to Airport....41 C6
Bus 35 for Castillo de Gibralfaro....42 D5
MalagaBike Tours....43 D3
Taxi....44 B5
C Hinestrosa
C Ramos Marín
C Gómez Pallete
C Madre de Dios
C Victoria
C Carretería
C Tejón y Rodríguez
C Beatas
C Marqués de Guadiaro
C Franquelo
C Álamos
Plaza de la Merced
C Nosquera
C Comedias
C Juan de Padilla
C Casapalma
Old Town
C Tomás de Cózar
C Andrés Pérez
C Mosquera
C Lazcano
Plaza de Uncibay
C Méndez Núñez
C Niño de Guevara
Plaza Martínez
C Convalecientes
C Luis de Velázquez
Plaza Mitjana
C Calderería
Galerías Goya
C Belgrano
C Granada
C Pozo del Rey
C Sánchez Pastor
C Molina Lario
C San Agustín
C Alcazabilla
Plaza de la Constitución
C Sanata María
Pasaje de Chinitas
C Císter
Palacio Episcopal
C Moreno Monroy
Plaza de las Flores
C Salinas
Plaza del Obispo
Cathedral
C Cañón
Plaza de la Aduana
Paseo Don Juan Temboury
C Guillén Sotelo
Plaza de Aduana
Palacio de la Aduana
C Nueva
C Marqués de Larios
C Strachan
C Bolsa
C Mesón Vélez
C San Bernardo el Viejo
C Sancha de Lara
C San Juan de Dios
C Cortina del Muelle
Av de Cervantes
Paseo del Parque
Plaza de la Marina
Jardines Alcalde Pedro Ruiz Alonso
C Atatazanas
C Puerta del Mar
Alameda Principal
Paseo de los Curas
Puerto Antepurerto

San Agustín 8; permanent collection €6, temporary exhibition €4.50, combined ticket €8, seniors & under-26 students half price; 10am-8pm Tue-Thu & Sun, to 9pm Fri & Sat) has 204 Picasso works, donated and lent by his daughter-in-law Christine Ruiz-Picasso and grandson Bernard Ruiz-Picasso, and also stages high-quality temporary exhibitions on Picasso themes. The Picasso paintings, drawings, engravings, sculptures and ceramics on show (many never previously on public display) span almost every phase and influence of the artist's colourful career – blue period, cubism, surrealism and more, with a fascinating emphasis on early, formative works. Gaze at *'Niña con su muñeca'* and marvel. The museum is housed in the 16th-century Palacio de Buenavista, sensationally restored at a cost of €66 million. Picasso was born in Málaga in 1881 but moved to northern Spain with his family when he was nine.

CATHEDRAL

Málaga's **cathedral** (Map p770; 952 21 59 17; www.3planalfa.es/catedralmalaga; Calle Molina Lario, entrance Calle Císter; admission €3.50; 10am-5.30pm Mon-Fri, to 5pm Fri, closed Sun & holidays) was begun in the 16th century on the former site of the main mosque. Building continued for two centuries, so while the northern door, **Portada de la Iglesia del Sagrario**, is Gothic, and the interior, with a soaring 40m dome, is Gothic and Renaissance, the facade is 18th-century baroque. The cathedral is known as La Manquita (the One-Armed), since its southern tower was never completed. Inside, note the 17th-century wooden choir stalls, as dark and smooth as chocolate, finely carved by the popular Andalucian sculptor Pedro de Mena. The chapels vie with each other in splendour. Pause at the Chapel of the Virgin of the Kings (numbered 18 in the Cathedral guide) to look at a large painting depicting the beheading of St Paul – violent, graphic and strangely beautiful.

ALCAZABA

At the lower, western end of the Gibralfaro hill, the wheelchair-accessible **Alcazaba** (Map p770; 952 22 51 06; Calle Alcazabilla; admission €2, incl Castillo de Gibralfaro €3.20; 9.30am-8pm Tue-Sun Apr-Oct, 8.30am-7pm Tue-Sun Nov-Mar, closed Mon & major holidays) was the palace-fortress of Málaga's Muslim governors, dating from 1057. The brick path winds uphill, interspersed with arches and stone walls and refreshingly cool in summer. Roman artefacts and fleeting views of the harbour and city enliven the walk, while honeysuckle, roses and jasmine perfume the air. Go before noon during the hot months, to avoid the crowds as well as the worst of the heat, and watch out for low, unprotected parapets, especially if you are taking kids. A lift (elevator) from Calle Guillén Sotelo brings you out in the heart of the Alcazaba.

Below the Alcazaba is a **Roman theatre**.

CASTILLO DE GIBRALFARO

Above the Alcazaba rises the older **Castillo de Gibralfaro** (Map p769; 952 22 72 30; admission €2; 9am-9pm Apr-Sep, to 6pm Oct-Mar), built by Abd ar-Rahman I, the 8th-century Cordoban emir, and rebuilt in the 14th and 15th centuries. Nothing much remains of the interior of the castle, but the walkway around the ramparts affords exhilarating views and there's a tiny museum with a military focus.

To walk up to the Castillo, take the road immediately right of the Alcazaba entrance, and where it bends left into a tunnel, take the steps on the right; or take bus 35 from Avenida de Cervantes (roughly every 45 minutes). The walk is long and steeply uphill. There is a small cafe with outdoor seating and toilets at the Castillo.

OTHER MUSEUMS

Casa Natal de Picasso (Map p770; 952 06 02 15; Plaza de la Merced 15; admission free; 9.30am-7.45pm, closed major holidays), Picasso's birthplace, is a centre for exhibitions and academic research on contemporary art, with a few compelling items of personal memorabilia and a well-stocked shop.

Centro de Arte Contemporáneo (Map p769; 952 12 00 55; Calle Alemania; admission free; 10am-8pm, 10am-2pm & 5-9pm 20 Jun-24 Sep, Tue-Sun) is a coolly minimal museum of international 20th- and 21st-century art housed in a skilfully converted 1930s market. The large and diverse museum shop and suitably stark cafe are good stops to complete your visit.

Located in a 17th-century inn, the speciality of **Museo de Artes y Costumbres Populares** (Museum of Popular Arts & Customs; Map p769; 952 21 71 37; www.museoartespopulares.com; Pasillo de Santa Isabel 10; adult/under 14yr/senior €2/free/1; 10am-1.30pm & 4-7pm Mon-Fri Jun-Sep, to 8pm Oct-May, 10am-1.30pm Sat) is everyday rural and urban life of the past; note the painted clay figures *(barros)* of characters from Málaga folklore.

The **Palacio de la Aduana** (Map p770; Paseo del Parque; admission free; 3-8pm Tue, 9am-8pm Wed-Fri,

9am-3pm Sat & Sun) is set to become the permanent home of the city's museum, but not until 2012. Art exhibitions have been suspended, but meanwhile, you can marvel at one of Andalucía's largest and most magnificent patios, and take shelter from the sun under glossy, broad-leafed plants.

BEACHES

Sandy city beaches stretch several kilometres in each direction from the port. **Playa de la Malagueta**, handy to the city centre, has some excellent bars and restaurants close by. **Playa de Pedregalejo** and **Playa del Palo**, about 4km east of the centre, are popular and reachable by bus 11 from Paseo del Parque.

JARDÍN BOTÁNICO LA CONCEPCIÓN

The largely tropical **Jardín Botánico** (☎ 952 25 21 48; adult/under 16 yrs/senior €4/2/2; 🕑 9.30am-5.30pm Oct-Mar, 9.30am-8.30pm (last entry 7pm) Apr-Sep, closed Mon), 4km north of the city centre, feature towering trees (including hundreds of palms), 5000 tropical plants, waterfalls, lakes and spectacular seasonal blooms – especially the purple wisteria in spring. You can visit solo or by 1½-hour guided tour in English, costing an extra €2.50.

By car, take the N331 Antequera road north from the Málaga ring road (A7) to Km166 and follow the signs. Alternatively, the MálagaTour bus (below) runs from the bus station to the gardens.

Courses

There are many private language schools in Málaga; the main tourist offices have contact lists. The **Universidad de Málaga** (Map p769; ☎ 952 27 82 11; www.uma.es/estudios/extranj/extranjeros.htm; Avenida de Andalucía 24) also runs very popular courses.

Tours

To pick up the child-friendly, open-topped **MalagaTour bus** (Map p769; ☎ 902 10 10 81; www.malaga-tour.com; adult/child €15/7; 🕑 every 30 min 9.30am-8pm), head for Avenida Manuel Agustín Heredia or the eastern end of the Paseo del Parque. This hop-on-hop-off tour does a circuit of the city, stopping at all the sights. Tickets are valid for 24 hours. If you're happier on two wheels, you can try **MalagaBike Tours** (☎ 606 978513; www.malagabiketours.eu; Calle Victoria 15; €23). In four hours you can tour the Jewish quarter and the Arab city, breathe sea air along the prom and quaff a free drink in a typical *malagueño* bar. Book 24 hours ahead. Or you can travel in old-fashioned style, with a **horse-and-carriage tour** of the city that lasts 45 minutes and costs €30. Carriages line up at the Plaza de la Marina end of the Jardines Alcalde Pedro Ruiz Alonzo, along the Paseo del Parque.

Festivals & Events

Semana Santa (Holy Week) Solemn and spectacular: the platforms bearing the holy images *(tronos)* are large and heavy, each needing up to 150 bearers. Every night from Palm Sunday to Good Friday, six or seven *tronos* are carried through the city, watched by big crowds. Witness this event on the Alameda Principal, between 7pm and midnight.

Feria de Málaga (mid- to late August) Lasting nine days, this is the biggest and most ebullient of Andalucía's summer fairs. During daytime, especially on the two Saturdays, celebrations take over the city centre, with music, dancing and horses. At night the fun switches to large *feria* grounds at Cortijo de Torres, 4km southwest of the city centre, with fairground rides, music and dancing.

Sleeping

Hostal Derby (Map p770; ☎ 952 22 13 01; Calle San Juan de Dios 1, 4th fl; s/d €36/49; 🖳) A good-value *hostal* with spacious rooms and big windows, some overlooking the harbour.

Hotel Carlos V (Map p770; ☎ 952 21 51 20; carlosv@spa.es; Calle Císter 10; s €36, d €59; P ❄ 🖳) Close to the cathedral and Picasso museum, the Carlos V is enduringly popular. Renovated in 2008, bathrooms sparkle in their new uniform of cream-and-white tiles. Excellent standard for the price and helpful staff make this hotel a winner.

Hostal Larios (Map p770; ☎ 952 22 54 90; www.hostallarios.com; Calle Marqués de Larios 9; s/d/tr with bathroom €48/58/78; s/d without bathroom €39/49; P ❄ 🖳). This central *hostal* outclasses all others in the budget range. The 12 rooms are painted apricot and blue.

Hostal Victoria (Map p770; ☎ 952 22 42 24; hostalvictoria@hostalvictoria.net; Calle Sancha de Lara 3; s/d €55/69; ❄) Centrally located, the Victoria provides basic, comfortable rooms with bathtubs.

El Riad Andaluz (Map p770; ☎ 952 21 36 40; www.elriadandaluz.com; Calle Hinestrosa 24; s/d 70/90; ❄ 🖳) Colourful and exotic, this gorgeous restored monastery offers eight rooms with Moroccan decor set around an atmospheric patio, with tea and coffee on tap all day. Situated in the rapidly gentrifying Centro Historico, it's an easy stroll to all the funkiest bars and restaurants in surrounding plazas. The French owner and his family infuse the Riad with a special magic.

Hotel Don Curro (Map p770; ☎ 952 22 72 00; www.hoteldoncurro.com; Calle Sancha de Lara 7; s/d €80/110; P ✻ 💻) Big, busy Don Curro is efficient, comfortable and central, with well-appointed, spacious rooms, and substantial breakfasts just a few steps away at its own Café Moka.

AC Málaga Palacio (Map p770; ☎ 952 21 51 85; www.achotels.com; Calle Cortina del Muelle 1; d €137; P ✻ 🏊) This sleek, 15-storey hotel has sensational views over the busy seafront. Design in the public areas tends towards bling, but the rooms are quietly elegant, there is a top-floor terrace for drinks and dining, and body pampering facilities complete its luxury offerings.

Parador Málaga Gibralfaro (Map p769; ☎ 952 22 19 02; www.parador.es; Castillo de Gibralfaro, s/n; s/d €134/170; P ✻ 🏊) With an unbeatable location up on the pine-forested Gibralfaro hill, Málaga's modern but rustic *parador* provides spectacular views of city and harbour from its upper floors, an excellent terrace restaurant and a rooftop pool.

Eating

TAPAS

La Rebaná (Map p770; Calle Molina Lario 5; tapas €4.20-8.50, raciones €7-11.50) A great, noisy tapas bar near the Picasso Museum and the cathedral. Dark wood, tall windows and exposed brick walls create a modern, minimal but laid-back space. Try the foie gras with salted nougat for a unique tapa.

Gorki (Map p770; ☎ 952 22 14 66; Calle Strachan 6; platos combinados €7.50-16) A popular upmarket tapas bar with pavement tables and a modern interior full of wine-barrel tables and stools.

Lechuga (Map p770; Plaza de la Merced 1; tapas €2.50-3.60, raciones €8-9.50; V) In this calm retreat, vegetables reign supreme and the chef does wonderful things with them, as with hummus, Indian-style *bhajis* and various inventive salads.

RESTAURANTS

Málaga's restaurants are well priced and of a good standard due to the largely local clientele. A speciality here is fish fried quickly in olive oil. *Fritura malagueña* consists of fried fish, anchovies and squid.

Comoloco (Map p770; Calle Denis Belgrano 17; salads €8-10 & pittas €5-6; 🕑 1pm-1am, V) This place with huge windows onto the little street is packed out at lunchtime. The menu also features a vegetarian's delight of salads and generously filled pitta wraps at a good price amid industrial decor.

El Vegetariano de la Alcazabilla (Map p770; ☎ 952 21 48 58; Calle Pozo del Rey 5; mains €9.50-12.50; 🕑 closed Sun; V) Laid-back veggie/vegan restaurant combining friendly service with good food in a shabby-chic setting just a cannonball throw from the Alcazaba walls. Do try the 'meatballs of Seitan'.

El Jardín (Map p770; ☎ 952 22 04 19; Calle Cañón 1; mains €12.50; 🕑 9am-midnight Mon-Thu, to 2pm & 5pm-midnight Fri & Sat, 5pm-midnight Sun) Beautiful Viennese-style cafe next to the palm-filled gardens behind the cathedral. Lace tablecloths and walls lined with old photographs add up to an evocative ambience, but not great food. Sip a coffee or a glass of wine earlier in the day and soak up the atmosphere.

Clandestino (Map p770; ☎ 952 21 93 90; Calle Niño de Guevara 3; mains €9-17; 🕑 1pm-1am; V) A trendy warehouse-style restaurant with an exciting menu that fuses northern European and Latin cuisines. A good selection of vegetarian dishes is headed by silky felafel patties on a salad dressed with alfalfa sprouts and a dill yogurt vinaigrette.

Cafe de Flores (Map p770; ☎ 952 60 85 24; Calle Madre de Dios 29; menú €9.50, mains €14-23; 🕑 1.30pm-late, closed Mon) Formerly La Casa del Ángel, the once eccentric interior has been replaced with sleek plexiglass furniture, abstract art and a highly rated DJ to become a haunt of smart young *malagueños* in up-and-coming Plaza Madre de Dios, right opposite the blue-and-gold Teatro Cervantes. By day it's a coffee bar and lunch place, by night good food is complemented by great sounds.

Restaurante Antonio Martín (Map p769; ☎ 952 22 73 98; Playa de la Malagueta; mains €22-29; 🕑 closed Sun Nov-Apr) On the beach and with a large terrace, Antonio Martín is a somewhat stuffy dress-up-and-be-seen restaurant serving a range of fried fish and meat in a starched tablecloth zone.

Drinking

On weekend nights, the web of narrow old streets north of Plaza de la Constitución comes alive. Look for bars around Plaza de la Merced, Plaza Mitjana and Plaza de Uncibay.

Antigua Casa de Guardia (Map p770; ☎ 952 21 46 80; Alameda Central 18) This venerable old tavern has been serving Málaga's sweet dessert wines since 1840. Try the dark brown, sherry-like *seco* complemented by a simple plate of prawns.

Bodegas El Pimpi (Map p770; ☎ 952 22 89 90; Calle Granada 62; 7pm-2am) A Málaga institution with a warren of charming rooms and mini-patios, El Pimpi attracts a fun-loving crowd of all nationalities and generations with its sweet wine and traditional music.

Calle de Brusellas (Map p770; ☎ 952 60 39 48; Plaza de la Merced 16; 9am-2am) This is a retro Belgian bar that woos a bohemian crowd. During the day it caters to the coffee scene with pavement tables, then at night the dark little bar comes to life. Good tapas include a generous helping of fresh Greek feta salad.

Café Moka (Map p770; ☎ 952 21 40 02; Calle San Bernardo El Viejo 2) Just off the Calle Larios, this busy little retro cafe caters to a mainly Spanish crowd. In the mornings, it does brisk breakfast business with savoury-filled soft rolls (*molletes*), croissants and strong, creamy coffee, starting at around €3.50.

La Vidriera (Map770; ☎ 952 228 943; Marqués de Guadiaro 2; midnight-late) Next to the popular Liceo music bar in this lively part of the city, each table in the long upper room of this bar is fitted with its own tap for pulling long cold glasses of Alhambra beer. A range of *raciones* is available for soaking up the amber liquid, from around €4 to €12.

ANDALUCÍA

Entertainment

Teatro Cervantes (Map p770; ☎ 952 36 02 95; www.teatrocervantes.com; Calle Ramos Marín s/n; closed mid-Jul–Aug) The palatial Cervantes has a fine program of music, theatre and dance.

Liceo (Map p770; Calle Beatas 21; 9pm-1am Thu-Sat) A grand old mansion turned young music bar, which buzzes with a student crowd after midnight. Go up the winding staircase and discover more rooms.

Warhol (Map p770; Calle Niño de Guevara; 11pm-late Thu-Sat) A stylish haunt for gay clubbers who want an upmarket atmosphere in which to enjoy the funky house beats mixed by dreadlocked DJs.

Asúcar (Map p770; cnr Calles Convalescientes & Luzcano; 9pm-late) Salsa fans need go no further. Casual salsa classes from 9pm to 10.30pm Tuesday to Saturday.

Tetería El Harén (Map p769; Calle Andrés Pérez 3) A large teahouse that rambles over several floors with lots of private nooks. Live music Thursday to Saturday evenings.

Getting There & Away

AIR

Málaga's busy **airport** (☎ 952 04 88 38), the main international gateway to Andalucía, receives flights by dozens of airlines (budget and otherwise) from around Europe (see p883).

BOAT

Trasmediterránea (☎ 952 22 74 77, 902 45 46 45; www.trasmediterranea.com; Estación Marítima, Local E1) operates a fast ferry (four hours) and a slower ferry (7½ hours) daily year-round to/from Melilla (passenger, fast ferry/ferry €55/33.50; car, fast ferry/ferry €174/156).

BUS

Málaga's **bus station** (Map p769; ☎ 952 35 00 61; Paseo de los Tilos) is just 1km southwest of the city centre. Frequent buses travel along the coasts, and others go to Seville (€16, 2½ hours, nine or more daily), Granada (€10, 1½ to two hours, 17 daily), Córdoba (€12.50, 2½ hours, five daily), Antequera (€5, 1 hour, 13 daily) and Ronda (€9.50, 2½ hours, nine or more daily). Nine buses also run daily to Madrid (€21.50, six hours), and a few go up Spain's Mediterranean coast. There are services to France, Germany, Holland, Portugal and Morocco too.

CAR

Numerous international and local agencies have desks at the airport, many with small cars for around €170 per week.

TRAIN

The main station, **Málaga-Renfe** (Map p769; ☎ 952 36 02 02; Explanada de la Estación), renamed the María Zambrano in 2007, is round the corner from the bus station. The superfast AVE service runs to Madrid (€71.20 to €79.20, 2½ hours, six daily).

Trains also go to Córdoba (€19, 1 hour, 10 daily), Seville (€17.30/33, 2½ hours/2 hours, five daily) and Barcelona (€58.40 to €129.40, 13/6½ hours, two daily). For Granada (€13.45, 2½ hours) and Ronda (€8.85, 1½ hours minimum) you need to change at Bobadilla.

Getting Around

TO/FROM THE AIRPORT

The Aeropuerto train station on the Málaga–Fuengirola line is a five-minute walk from the airport (follow signs from the departures hall). Trains run about every half-hour, 6.49am to 11.49pm, to Málaga-Renfe station (€2, 11 minutes) and Málaga-Centro station. Trains depart for the airport between 5.45am and 10.30pm.

Bus 19 to the city centre (€1.10, 20 minutes) leaves from the 'City Bus' stop outside the arrivals hall, every 20 or 30 minutes, 6.35am to 11.45pm, stopping at Málaga-Renfe train station and the bus station en route. Going out to the airport, you can catch the bus at the western end of Paseo del Parque and from outside the stations, about every half-hour from 6.30am to 11.30pm.

A taxi from the airport to the city centre costs €20 to €24 depending on traffic and pickup location.

Metro Málaga (☎ 902 93 49 44; www.metrodemalaga.info) Málaga is responding to green issues and citizen pressure by building its own Metro system, with the first section of track, from the port towards the city centre and including the train station, set to launch in 2010.

Even greener initiatives include guided cycle tours of the city (see p772), which offer access to fascinating hidden corners of the city that other forms of transport just can't reach.

Another fun way to get around Málaga is to hire a Trixi through **Tricosol** (☎ 657 440605; www.bike2malaga.com; Calle Victoria 15; 🕑 11am-8pm daily) These curvaceous electric-powered cars can be hired for anything from a 15-minute trixi ride (€6) to a one-hour guided tour of the city (€18), with pedal-power provided. They offer a green and pleasant way of touring Málaga, and can normally be hailed from in front of the cathedral.

COSTA DEL SOL

Strewn along the seaboard from Málaga almost to Gibraltar, the Costa del Sol stretches like a wall of wedding cakes several kilometres thick. Its recipe for success is sunshine, convenient beaches (of grey-brown sand), cheap package deals and bountiful nightlife and entertainment. The *costa* (coast) is also a haven for sport lovers, with around 40 golf clubs, several busy marinas, tennis courts, riding schools, swimming pools, gyms and beaches offering every imaginable water sport.

The resorts were once fishing villages, but there's little evidence of that now. The Costa del Sol was launched as a 1950s development drive for impoverished Andalucía, and it has succeeded very well indeed, at the cost of turning a spectacular coastline into an eye-stinging, unbroken series of untidy, crowded townscapes. In July and August it's best to ring ahead for a room. Outside these peak months, many room rates drop sharply.

A convenient train service links Málaga's Renfe and Aeropuerto stations with Torremolinos (€1.20), Arroyo de la Miel (€1.35) and Fuengirola (€2.50). Buses from Málaga link all the resorts, and services to places such as Ronda, Cádiz, Seville and Granada go from the main resorts.

The AP7 Autopista del Sol motorway bypasses all the *costa* towns, with tolls amounting to €9.00 (€14 from June to September and during Semana Santa) for the full 80km. The old coast road, the N340, continues to carry plenty of traffic and you need to take care on it: don't let other drivers force you into going too fast, and watch out for animals and inebriated pedestrians.

Torremolinos

pop 48,000

'Torrie', which led the Costa del Sol's mass tourism boom of the 1950s and '60s, is a concrete high-rise jungle designed to squeeze as many paying customers as possible into the smallest possible space. It spruced itself up somewhat in the 1990s, and a pleasant seafront walk, the Paseo Marítimo, now extends for nearly 7km and gives some cohesion and character to the resort. Torremolinos has a big gay scene.

ORIENTATION & INFORMATION

Torremolinos' main pedestrian artery is Calle San Miguel, running most of the 500m from Plaza Costa del Sol (on the main road through town) down to Playa del Bajondillo. Southwest of Playa del Bajondillo is Playa de la Carihuela, once the fishing quarter.

The **bus station** (☎ 952 38 24 19; Calle Hoyo) is northeast of Plaza Costa del Sol. Buses to Marbella stop on Avenida Palma de Mallorca, 200m southwest of Plaza Costa del Sol. The **train station** (Avenida Jesús Santos Rein) is off Calle San Miguel.

Tourist office (☎ 952 37 95 12; www.ayto-torremolinos.org; Plaza Pablo Picasso; 🕑 9.30am-12.30pm Mon-Fri, Oct-May, 10am-2pm & 6-8pm every day Jun-Sep) In the town hall. There are also offices on **Playa Bajondillo** (☎ 952 37 19 09; 🕑 10am-2pm) and **Playa Carihuela** (☎ 952 37 29 56; 🕑 10am-2pm).

SIGHTS & ACTIVITIES

Torrie's **beaches** are wider, longer and a slightly paler shade of grey-brown than most on the *costa*, and they get very crowded. The local attractions are mostly child-oriented. In the more upmarket Puerto Deportivo (marina) at Benalmádena Costa, just southwest of Torremolinos, **Sea Life** (☎ 952 56 01 50; www.sealifeeurope.com; adult/child €11.95/8.85; 10am-10pm Jun, to midnight Jul-Sep, to 6pm Oct-May) is a good modern aquarium of mainly Mediterranean marine creatures, with organised games and shark feeding. **Tivoli World** (☎ 952 57 70 16; www.tivolico.es; Avenida de Tivoli; admission €6; noon-7pm Sun Oct-Apr, 12-8pm May; 5pm-1am Jun, 6pm-2am Jul-Sep), just five minutes' walk from Benalmádena-Arroyo de la Miel train station, is the biggest amusement park on the *costa*. The Supertivolino ticket (€12) gives unlimited access to more than 35 rides.

SLEEPING & EATING

A couple of dozen *hostales* and hotels are within a few minutes' walk of Torremolinos' train and bus stations. The tourist offices have lists.

Red Parrot (☎ 952 37 54 45; www.theredparrot.net; Avenida Los Manantiales 4; s/d €35-50/46-60;) Newly refurbished and central, this place offers comfortable balconied rooms around a patio, and it has a pool.

Hotel Miami (☎ 952 38 52 55; www.residencia-miami.com; Calle Aladino 14, Torremolinos; s/d €41/62;) A white castle-style villa amid tropical gardens, 100m from La Carihuela beach.

La Fonda Benalmádena (☎ /fax 952 56 82 73; www.fondahotel.com; Calle Santo Domingo 7, Benalmádena Pueblo; s/d incl breakfast €73/103; P) Charming hotel with large rooms built around Islamic-style patios with fountains, and an excellent, moderately priced restaurant.

Besides British breakfasts and beer, Torremolinos has no shortage of good seafood places, many of them lining the Paseo Marítimo in La Carihuela.

ENTERTAINMENT

The weekend nightlife at Benalmádena Costa's Puerto Deportivo pulls a youthful, zesty crowd from all along the coast. The bars start to throb after midnight on Friday and Saturday. International visitors come to Torremolinos to party hard. **Passion** (Avenida Palma de Mallorca 18) and **Palladium** (Avenida Palma de Mallorca 36), two of Torremolinos' hottest clubs, boast two floors, three different atmospheres, international DJs, live performances, swimming pools, go-go dancers and singers in both venues. The gay 'in crowd' hangs out in the new bars and clubs in **La Nogalera**, the area close to Torremolinos train station. Check out the trendy **El Gato Lounge** (La Nogalera, from 4pm till late) or girls' bar **Ánfora**.

Fuengirola

pop 65,000

Fuengirola, 18km down the coast from Torremolinos, has more of a family scene but is just as densely packed. The streets between the beach and Avenida Matías Sáenz de Tejada (where the bus station is) delineate what's left of the old town, with Plaza de la Constitución at its centre. The **train station** (Avenida Jesús Santos Rein) is a block further inland. The **tourist office** (☎ 952 46 74 57; Avenida Jesús Santos Rein 6; 9.30am-2pm & 5-7pm Mon-Fri, 10am-1pm Sat) is near the train station.

The **Hipódromo Costa del Sol** (☎ 952 59 27 00; www.carreraentertainment.com; Urbanización El Chaparral; admission €5; 10pm-2am Sat Jul-Sep, 11.30am-4pm Sun Oct-Jun), Andalucía's leading horse-racing track with regular racing, is off the N340 at the southwestern end of Fuengirola.

SLEEPING & EATING

Hostal Italia (☎ 952 47 41 93; Calle de la Cruz 1; s/d €37/57;) Welcoming and notably friendly, this clean and comfortable budget option in old-fashioned Spanish style is a couple of blocks from the beach. There's a big, tiled sun terrace on the roof.

Hostal Marbella (☎ 952 66 45 03; www.hostalmarbella.info; Calle Marbella 34; s €44-53, d €64-73;) Run by a dedicated Swedish couple, this place is also excellent value for money, with big, spotless rooms and gleaming bathrooms. It's in the centre of town, just minutes from the beach.

Hotel El Puerto (☎ 952 47 01 00; www.hotel-elpuerto.com; Paseo Maritimo 32; s incl breakfast €75-82, d incl breakfast €104-134;) A big, modern, three-star hotel on the beach with sea views and a rooftop pool.

Restaurante Portofino (☎ 952 47 06 43; Paseo Marítimo 29; mains €15-20; closed Mon) An international menu features an ocean of classic fish dishes, and white tablecloths and aproned waiters denote a slightly smarter dress code than beachwear.

Mijas

This village of winding Muslim-origin streets and white buildings situated in the hills 8km

ANDALUCÍA

north of Fuengirola is now surrounded by villas and *urbanizaciones* (housing estates) and full of busloads up from the *costa*. But it remains a strikingly pretty place, and the **Casa Museo de Mijas** (☎ 952 59 03 80; Calle Málaga; admission free; 10am-2pm & 4-7pm Sep-Mar, afternoons 5-8pm Apr-Jun, 6-9pm Jul-Aug) gives a poignant glimpse into life in the area before the 1960s tourist deluge. There are good hotels and lots of restaurants, cafes and craft shops. Frequent buses run from Fuengirola (€1, 25 minutes).

Parque Acuático Mijas (☎ 952 46 04 04; www.aquamijas.com; N340, km209, Mijas Costa, Málaga; admission adult/under 12/under 4 €16/11/free; 10.30am-5.30pm 28 Apr-31 May, 10am-5pm Jun, 10am-7pm Jul-Aug, 10am-6pm Sep) A big leisure park dedicated to water and happily screaming kids. Attractions include the Labyrinth toboggan slide, gentler kiddie slides and river thrills. There are two big self-service restaurants and picnic facilities. The park is just minutes from Fuengirola's bus and train terminals, with ample free parking, or you can catch the Acuático bus from Fuengirola bus station. This runs every half hour from 10.15am to 4.30pm, and costs €1.25.

Marbella

pop 132,000

Overlooked by the dramatic Sierra Blanca 28km west of Fuengirola, Marbella has been the Costa del Sol's glossiest resort since the 1950s. Yet Marbella proper and its Casco Antiguo or old town has little to do with the conspicuous consumption of the notorious Golden Mile, heading west towards Puerto Banús. Instead, you can enjoy a resort where Spanish holidaymakers balance the international visitors and a variety of shops, bars and restaurants offer real-world food and goods at real world prices.

ORIENTATION

The N340 through town takes the names Avenida Ramón y Cajal and Avenida Ricardo Soriano. The old town is centred on Plaza de los Naranjos.

INFORMATION

Hospital Costa del Sol (☎ 952 82 82 50; Carretera N340 Km187) Big public hospital 6km east of the centre.

Municipal tourist office (www.marbella.es in Spanish; 9am-9pm Mon-Fri, 9.30am-2.30pm Sat, closed Sun); Fontanilla (☎ 952 77 14 42; Glorieta de la Fontanilla); Naranjos (☎ 952 82 35 50; Plaza de los Naranjos 1)

SIGHTS & ACTIVITIES

Pretty **Plaza de los Naranjos**, with its 16th-century town hall, is at the heart of the largely pedestrianised, postcard-perfect old town. Nearby are the **Iglesia de la Encarnación** (Plaza de la Iglesia), begun in the 16th century, and the **Museo del Grabado Español Contemporáneo** (Museum of Contemporary Spanish Prints; ☎ 952 76 57 41; Calle Hospital Bazán s/n; admission €3, free Sat; 9am-2pm & 6-9pm Tue-Fri, 9am-2pm Mon & Sat). In beautifully uncluttered vaulted rooms, you can see work by Picasso, Joan Miró and Salvador Dalí, among others.

The charming **Museo Bonsai** (☎ 952 86 29 26; adult/child €4/2; 10.30am-1.30pm & 4-6.30pm, evenings Jul-Aug 5-8pm), devoted to the Japanese miniature-tree art, is in Parque Arroyo de la Represa just northeast of the old town. Stroll through this fascinating, open-air art gallery – and take as many photos as you like. It's wheelchair accessible.

Avenida del Mar, leading down to the central **Playa de Venus**, a standard Costa del Sol beach, is peppered with crazed **sculptures** by Salvador Dalí. For a longer, broader stretch of sand walk to the 800m **Playa de la Fontanilla**, or **Playa de Casablanca** beyond Playa de la Fontanilla. All walks along the seafront are full of life, noise and colour, especially when it cools down after 8pm in high summer.

Puerto Banús, the Costa del Sol's flashiest marina, is 6km west of Marbella. Some truly enormous floating palaces are tied up here. Marbella's 'spend, be seen, have fun' ethos is at its purest in Puerto Banús, with a constant parade of the glamorous, the would-be glamorous and the normal in front of the boutiques and busy restaurants strung along the waterfront.

There are good **walks** in the Sierra Blanca, starting from the Refugio de Juanar, a 17km drive north of Marbella.

SLEEPING

Hostal Paco (☎ 952 77 12 00; www.hostalpacomarbella.com; Calle Isaac Peral 16; s/d 40/65;) Located in a pleasant, pedestrianised part of the old town, Hostal Paco has good-sized rooms and very good bathrooms. Staff are helpful. Marvel at the great black-and-white photos in reception.

Hostal Berlin (☎ 952 82 13 10; www.hostalberlin.com; Calle San Ramón 21; s/d/tr €45/65/80; P) A very friendly *hostal* simply but brightly furnished and with spotless shower rooms, on a quiet street parallel to Calle La Luna. Breakfast is €3.

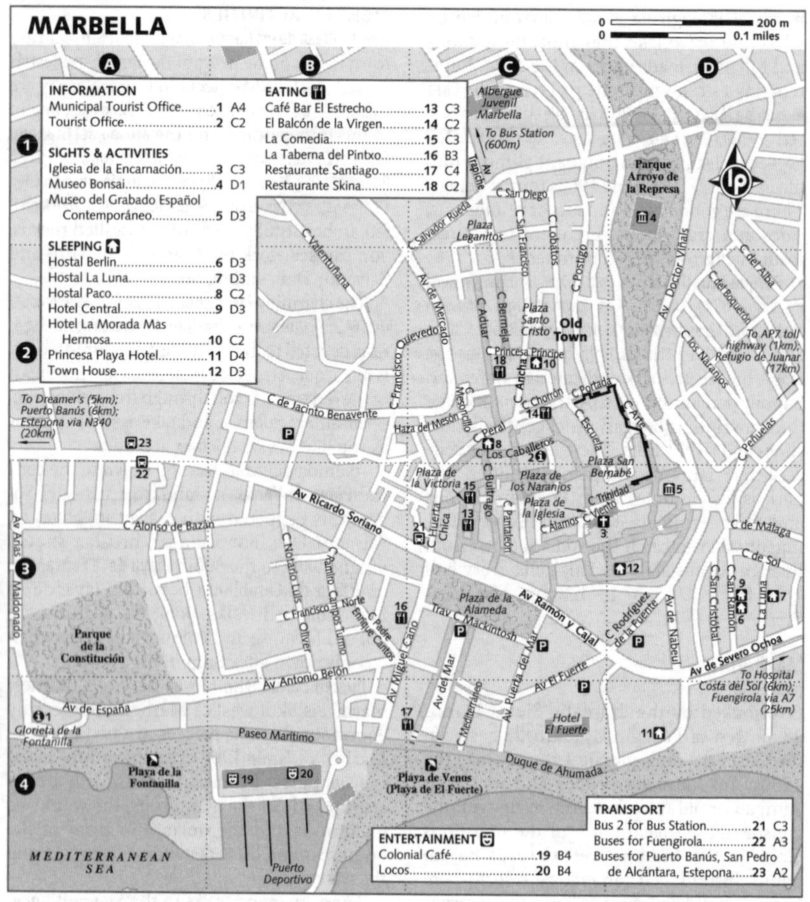

Hostal La Luna (☎ 952 82 57 78; Calle La Luna 7; s/d/q €56/75/100;) Calle La Luna is one of four pedestrian lanes dotted with decent *hostales* just east of the centre and close to the beach. Big, balconied rooms with fridges and spotless bathrooms overlook an internal patio, everything is well looked after and it's a peaceful spot.

Hotel Central (☎ 952 90 24 42; www.hotelcentralmarbella.com; Calle San Ramón 15; s/d €63/78;) A cut above the neighbouring *hostales*, Hotel Central enjoys the same quiet location but has 15 large, tasteful rooms, all with airy black-and-white tiled bathrooms.

Hotel La Morada Mas Hermosa (☎ 952 92 44 67; www.lamoradamashermosa.com; Calle Montenebros 16A; s/d €80/99;) A small, personable hotel on a tranquil, flowery, old-town street. Just six rooms, some with spiral stairs up to the bathrooms, with decor as warm and friendly as the staff.

our pick **Town House** (☎ 952 90 17 91; www.townhouse.nu; Calle Alderete 7; s/d incl breakfast €115/130;) Occupying a traditional town house, with nine chic rooms, the Swedish-owned Town House reminds you what a luxury hotel is for: to pamper you with feather bedding and leather sofas, cashmere throws and great coffee; to serve you a healthy fruit and Greek yogurt breakfast, and to send you out again at peace with yourself and the whole world. This is a high-class hotel with heart and is worth every centimo.

Princesa Playa Hotel (☎ 952 82 09 44; www.princesaplaya.com; Avenida Puerta del Mar s/n; s €117-59, apt €133-99; P ✱ 💻 ♿) With great sea views, this modern apartment hotel represents relatively good value for money on the seafront. Rooms are very well equipped and bathrooms are newly refurbished.

EATING

Dining in Marbella doesn't necessarily mean chichi interiors and bikini-size portions at whale-sized prices. There are some authentic tapas bars and a few trendy restaurants doing delicious, good-value cuisine.

Café Bar El Estrecho (☎ 952 77 00 04; Calle San Lázaro 12; tapas €2.10-2.60) This is a good, busy old-town tapas bar.

La Taberna del Pintxo (Avenida Miguel Cano 7; tapas €1-2) Grab a table and a plate and choose from a huge range of hot and cold tapas, such as the goats' cheese tart with cranberry jelly. At the end of the evening, the little swords or toothpicks from each tapa are counted and you are charged accordingly. This big, busy bar is just a block or two from the beach and all the evening *paseo* action.

El Balcón de la Virgen (☎ 952 77 60 52; Calle Virgen de los Dolores; mains €9-18; 🕑 closed Sun) One of the best restaurants near Plaza de los Naranjos, this has a lovely summer *terraza* overlooked by a 300-year-old grieving Virgin and a large bougainvillea, vibrant pink against the bright blue paintwork. The fare is typical Andalucian.

La Comedia (☎ 952 77 64 78; www.lacomedia.net; Plaza de la Victoria; mains €10.50-20) Along with popular first-floor tables looking down on the little plaza, a charming candlelit room, and a mix of interesting art and photography on the walls, you get a very warm welcome from the Irish hosts and good selection of classic, Spanish and international dishes for carnivores and vegetarians alike.

Restaurante Santiago (☎ 952 77 00 78; Paseo Marítimo 5; mains €18-28; 🕑 closed Nov) Santiago is right on the seafront, offering top-class seafood. The waiters wear black and the tables wear white, so you need to dress accordingly.

Restaurante Skina (☎ 952 76 52 77; Calle Aduar 12; mains €25-29; 🕑 7-11.30pm Mon-Sat) A good bet for an imaginative meal, tiny Skina is great for outdoor dining on summer evenings. Try sole with lime and ginger or suckling pig with 'a trio of textured apples'.

DRINKING & ENTERTAINMENT

Marbella's revamped Puerto Deportivo (marina) now provides an entertaining after-dark scene without the sleaze. Head for **Colonial Café** (☎ 952 86 85 77; 🕑 6pm-3am or later), a hip disco-pub playing funky-house and reggae-dub, or **Locos** (🕑 1.30pm-4am or later), at the back of the marina, with an alternative feel. In the old town, Calle Pantaleón has a string of popular *cervecerías* (beer bars).

The busiest nightlife zone in the Marbella area is at Puerto Banús, where dozens of pubs and varied dance clubs cluster along a couple of narrow lanes behind the marina. The serious big-name clubs cluster around the 'Golden Mile' (the 5km road between Marbella and Puerto Banús). **Dreamer's** (☎ 952 81 20 80; www.dreamers-disco.com in Spanish; Carretera de Cádiz 175, Río Verde) mix of tribal, vocal and light shows, bongo beats and an ever-changing menu of DJs gives house-lovers a chance to truly let their hair down.

GETTING THERE & AROUND

Half-hourly buses to Fuengirola (€2.65, 1¼ hours), Puerto Banús (€1.10, 20 minutes) and Estepona (€2.51, 1¼ hours) have stops on Avenida Ricardo Soriano. Other services use the **bus station** (☎ 952 76 44 00; Avenida Trapiche), 1.2km north of Plaza de los Naranjos. Bus 7 (€1.10) runs between the bus station and the central **Fuengirola/Estepona bus stop** (Avenida Ricardo Soriano); returning to the bus station, take bus 2 from Avenida Ramón y Cajal.

Marbella's streets are notoriously traffic-clogged. Fortunately there are a number of pay car parks (Map p778) where you can take refuge on arrival.

Estepona

pop 50,000

Estepona, southwest of Marbella, has controlled its development relatively carefully and remains a fairly agreeable seaside town. The big attraction here is the popular safari park, **Selwo Aventura** (☎ 902 19 04 82; www.selwo.es; Carretera A7 (Autovia Costa del Sol) Km162.5, Las Lomas del Monte; admission €33, 3-7yr €23; 🕑 10am-6pm mid Feb-Jun & Oct, to 8pm Jul-Sep, closed early Dec-early Feb), 6km east of town, with over 200 exotic animal species. Buses 110 and 120 (Autobuses Portillo) run to Selwo from Málaga via Torremolinos, Fuengirola and Marbella (phone Selwo for information).

EL CHORRO & BOBASTRO

pop (El Chorro) 100

Fifty kilometres northwest of Málaga, Río Guadalhorce and the main railway in and out of Málaga both pass through the awesome **Garganta del Chorro** (El Chorro Gorge), which is 4km long, up to 400m deep and as little as 10m wide. The gorge is a magnet for rock climbers, with hundreds of varied routes of almost every grade of difficulty. Anyone can view the gorge by walking along the railway from the tiny El Chorro village (ask locally for directions). The view provides an adrenaline rush all by itself.

Swiss-owned **Finca La Campana** (right), which is popular with adventure-lovers, offers climbing courses, climbing, caving, kayaking and mountain-bike trips, and bike rentals (€8 to €18 per day). One thrilling outing is its five-hour climbing trip along the Camino del Rey (King's Path), a crumbling concrete catwalk clinging to the gorge wall 100m above the river – worth every céntimo of the €90 (one to three people).

Near El Chorro is **Bobastro**, the hilltop redoubt of the 9th-century rebel, Omar ibn Hafsun, a sort of Islamic Robin Hood, who led a prolonged revolt against Cordoban rule. Ibn Hafsun at one stage controlled territory from Cartagena to the Strait of Gibraltar. From El Chorro village, follow the road up the far (western) side of the valley and after 3km take the signed Bobastro turning. Nearly 3km up here, an 'Iglesia Mozárabe' sign indicates a 500m path to the remains of a remarkable little Mozarabic church cut from the rock, the shape so blurred by time that it appears to have been shaped by the wind alone. It's thought that Ibn Hafsun converted from Islam to Christianity (thus becoming a Mozarab) before his death in 917 and was buried here. When Córdoba finally conquered Bobastro in 927, the poor chap's remains were taken for grisly posthumous crucifixion outside Córdoba's Mezquita. At the top of the hill, 2.5km further up the road and with unbelievable views, are faint traces of Ibn Hafsun's rectangular Alcázar (fortress).

Sleeping & Eating

Pensión Estación (☎ 952 49 50 04; r without bathroom €25) At tiny El Chorro station, this *pensión* has clean, basic rooms run by a helpful family, and its **Bar Isabel**, a renowned climbers' gathering place, serves *platos combinados* (€5 to €7).

Apartamentos La Garganta (☎ 952 49 50 00; www.lagarganta.com; 2-/4-person apt €75/115; mains €12; P ✿ ✿) The best option in El Chorro, this converted flour mill has beautifully decorated apartments and excellent food.

Finca La Campana (☎ 952 11 20 19; www.el-chorro.com; dm €12, d €29, 2-8-person apt €42-96; ✿ ✿) More than just a great place to stay, with cottage-style accommodation in one of Andalucía's most stunning landscapes, this is also a club of like-minded adrenaline junkies, with a cult following to show. During the climbing season (October to March) the Finca is very busy, so book ahead. To get there follow signs from behind Apartamentos La Garganta.

Getting There & Away

Trains run to El Chorro from Málaga (€3.65, 45 minutes, two daily except Sunday and holidays), from Ronda (€5.80, 70 minutes, one daily except Sunday and holidays) and Seville (€14.45, two hours, one daily). No buses run to El Chorro. Drivers can get there via Álora (south of El Chorro) or Ardales (west of El Chorro).

RONDA

pop 37,000 / elev 744m

Perched on an inland plateau riven by the 100m fissure of El Tajo gorge and surrounded by the beautiful Serranía de Ronda, Ronda is the most dramatically sited of all the *pueblos blancos*. Just an hour north of the Costa del Sol, it is nevertheless a world away from the coastal scene. Ronda attracts its quota of visitors, many of them weekenders from Seville, Málaga or Córdoba, especially during the hotter months.

With its setting, quaint old Islamic town and a romantic place in Spanish folklore, Ronda has fascinated travellers from Dumas to Hemingway and beyond. For most of the Islamic period, it was the capital of an independent statelet, and its near-impregnable position kept it out of Christian hands until 1485. Modern-day alternative-lifestylers have set up home in and around the town, adding an artsy touch.

Orientation

The old Muslim town, called La Ciudad, stands on the southern side of El Tajo. The newer town to the north has most of the accommodation and restaurants, and the bus and train stations. Three bridges span the gorge, the main one being the Puente Nuevo. Both parts of town end abruptly on their western side in cliffs plunging away to the valley of Río Guadalevín.

ANDALUCÍA

Information

Banks and ATMs are mainly on Calle Virgen de la Paz and Plaza Carmen Abela.

Municipal tourist office (☎ 952 18 71 19; www.turismoderonda.es; Paseo de Blas Infante; 🕓 10am-7.30pm Mon-Fri May-Sep, to 6pm Oct-Apr, 10.15am-2pm & 3.30-6.30pm Sat, Sun & holidays) Helpful and friendly staff with a wealth of information on the town and region.

Regional tourist office (☎ 952 87 12 72; www.andalucia.org; Plaza de España 1; 🕓 9am-7.30pm Mon-Fri May-Sep, to 6pm Oct-Apr, 10am-2pm Sat)

Sights

PLAZA DE ESPAÑA & PUENTE NUEVO

The majestic Puente Nuevo (New Bridge), spanning El Tajo from Plaza de España, the

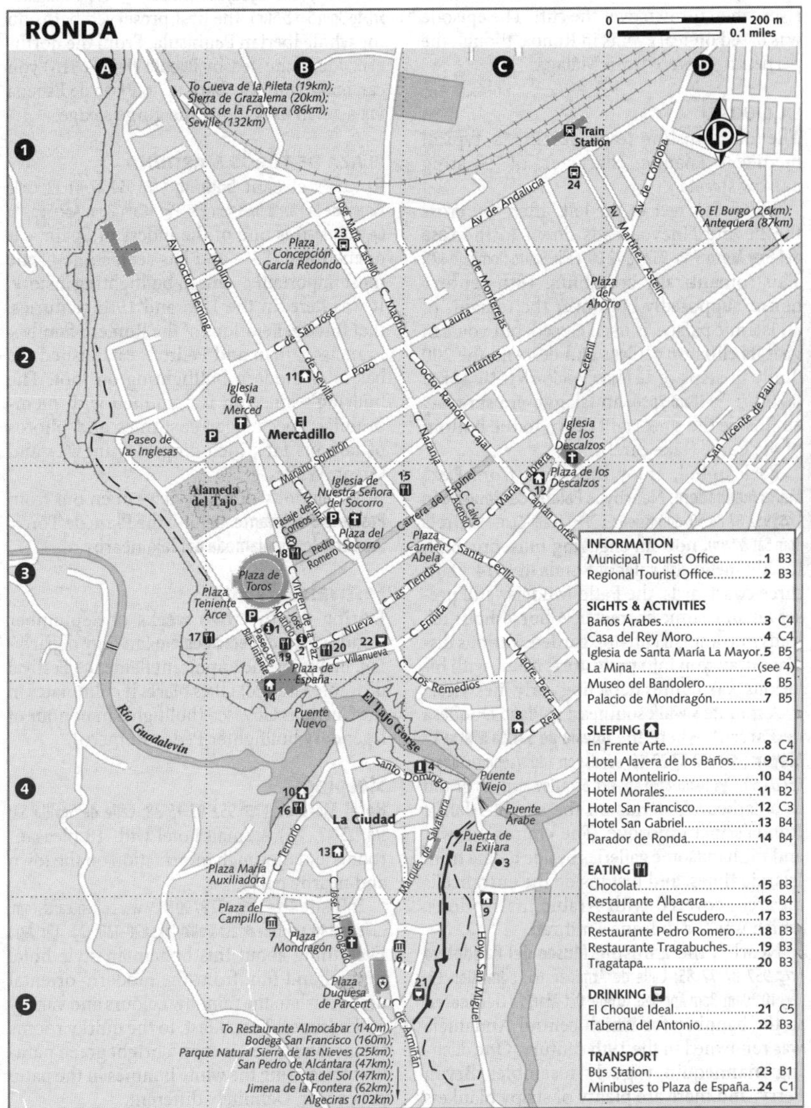

main square on the north side of the gorge, was completed in 1793. Folklore claims that its architect, Martín de Aldehuela, fell to his death while trying to engrave the date on the bridge's side. Chapter 10 of Hemingway's *For Whom the Bell Tolls* tells how, early in the Spanish Civil War, the 'fascists' of a small town were clubbed and flailed by townspeople 'in the plaza on the top of the cliff above the river', then thrown over the cliff. The episode was based on real events in Ronda, though the perpetrators were from Málaga.

LA CIUDAD

The old Muslim town retains a typical medieval Islamic character of twisting narrow streets.

The first street to the left, after you cross the Puente Nuevo, leads down to the **Casa del Rey Moro** (☎ 952 18 72 00; Calle Santo Domingo 17). This romantically crumbling 18th-century house, supposedly built over the remains of an Islamic palace, is itself closed, but you can visit its cliff-top **gardens** and descend the 200 dimly lit steps of **La Mina** (gardens & La Mina adult/child €4/2; 10am-7pm), an Islamic-era stairway cut inside the rock right down to the bottom of the gorge (take care!).

Back uphill, enjoy the views from **Plaza María Auxiliadora**. Nearby is **Palacio de Mondragón** (☎ 952 87 84 50; admission €2; 10am-6pm Mon-Fri, to 3pm Sat & Sun), now an engaging museum, built for Abomelic, the ruler of Ronda in 1314. Of its three courtyards, the Patio Mudéjar still preserves an Islamic character. A horseshoe arch leads into a small cliff-top garden. Various displays draw you into prehistoric caves, with hilarious wax figures depicting early lifestyles.

A minute's walk southeast is Plaza Duquesa de Parcent, where the **Iglesia de Santa María La Mayor** (☎ 952 87 22 46; admission adult/senior/student €3/2/1.50; 10am-8pm Apr-Oct, 6pm Nov-Mar), as grand as a cathedral, stands on the site of Islamic Ronda's main mosque. The church's tower and the handsome galleries beside it date from Islamic times, and just inside the entrance is an arch, covered with Arabic inscriptions, which was the mosque's mihrab.

Nearby, the amusing **Museo del Bandolero** (☎ 952 87 77 85; Calle de Armiñán 65; admission €3; 10.30am-8pm Apr-Sep, to 6pm Oct-Mar) is dedicated to the banditry for which central Andalucía was renowned in the 19th century. One dashing mannequin vaguely resembles Bryan Ferry, and there are plenty of stripy blankets flung over shoulders, together with the tools of the bandit trade, and some of their spoils. The museum is wheelchair accessible.

Beside the museum, a long flight of cobbled steps leads down to an impressive stretch of La Ciudad's old **walls**. Follow the path down to the beautiful horseshoe arches of the 13th- and 14th-century **Baños Árabes** (Arab Baths; ☎ 656 950937; Hoyo San Miguel; admission €3; 10am-7pm Mon-Fri, to 3pm Sat & Sun), the best preserved baths on the whole Iberian Peninsula. From the northern side of the nearby **Puente Viejo** (1616) you can make your way back up to Plaza de España via a small park along the gorge's edge.

PLAZA DE TOROS & AROUND

Ronda's elegant **bullring** (☎ 952 87 41 32; Calle Virgen de la Paz; admission €6; 10am-8pm Apr-Sep, to 6pm Oct-Mar) is one of the oldest in Spain – it opened in 1785 – and has seen some of the most important events in bullfighting history. It was here, in the 18th and 19th centuries, that three generations of the Romero family – Francisco, Juan and Pedro – established the basics of modern bullfighting on foot. The bullring's museum is crammed with memorabilia, spectacular costumes and photos of famous fans including Hemingway and Orson Welles.

Vertiginous cliff-top views open out from **Paseo de Blas Infante**, behind the Plaza de Toros, and the leafy **Alameda del Tajo** nearby.

Festivals & Events

During the first two weeks of September Ronda's **Feria de Pedro Romero** (an orgy of partying, including the important flamenco Festival de Cante Grande) takes place. It culminates in the Corridas Goyesca (bullfights in honour of legendary bullfighter Pedro Romero).

Sleeping

Hotel Morales (☎ 952 87 15 38; Calle de Sevilla 51; s/d €25/42;) A small hotel with 18 pleasant rooms and thorough information on the town and nearby parks.

EnFrente Arte (☎ 952 87 90 88; www.enfrentearte.com; Calle Real 40; r incl breakfast & all drinks €70-130;) Everything about this bohemian-style hotel is vivid and fun, from the modern-oriental decor clash to the rainbow colours and variety of the (superb) breakfast, to the quirky rooms themselves. There's even a bright green parakeet terrorising the white bunnies in the patio pet corner. Definitely different.

ANDALUCÍA

Hotel San Francisco (☎ 952 87 32 99; www.hotelsanfranciscoronda.com; Calle María Cabrera 18; s/d incl breakfast €38/60;) This is possibly the best budget option in Ronda, offering a warm welcome. It was recently refurbished and upgraded from *hostal* to hotel, with facilities to match including wheelchair access.

Hotel Alavera de los Baños (☎ 952 87 91 43; www.andalucia.com/alavera; Hoyo San Miguel s/n; s/d incl breakfast €65/85;) A magical hotel with style echoes of the Arab baths next door, this one-time tannery is sumptuously decorated, with a flower-filled patio and pool. The sultan-sized baths are carved from a type of stucco, and their pink tinge is due to natural pigments. A place to pamper yourself.

Hotel San Gabriel (☎ 952 19 03 92; www.hotelsangabriel.com; Calle José M Holgado 19; s/d €68/96;) This charming, historic hotel with a country house ambience is filled with antiques and photographs chronicling Ronda's history. There is a poetry collection and deep armchairs to read in, you can watch old movies in the miniature cinema and your breakfast croissant comes from an artisan baker. This attention to detail extends to the elegant rooms to create a very special place to stay.

Hotel Montelirio (☎ 952 87 38 55; www.hotelmontelirio.com; Calle Tenorio 8; s/d €100/150-165; P) Sensitively converted mansion with sumptuous fittings and magical views of Ronda's gorge from rooms that cost a little more. Charming rooms incorporate antique accessories, there is an inviting bar and restaurant, and staff seem to enjoy looking after you.

Parador de Ronda (☎ 952 87 75 00; www.parador.es; Plaza de España s/n; s/d €127/159; P) Acres of shining marble and deep-cushioned furniture give this modern *parador* a certain appeal. The terrace is a wonderful place to drink in views of the gorge with your coffee or wine, especially at night.

Eating

Traditional Ronda food is hearty mountain fare that's big on stews, trout, game such as rabbit, partridge and quail, and, of course, oxtail.

Chocolat (Calle de Seville 18; breakfast from €2.20) An elegant cafe where you can choose from a long list of teas, coffees, breakfasts and a boggling array of cakes and pastries.

our pick **Bar Restaurant Almocábar** (☎ 952 87 59 77; Calle Ruedo Alameda 5; tapas €2, mains €12-20; 1.30-5pm & 8pm-1am Wed-Mon, closed Aug; V) In the Barrio San Francisco, a little off the tourist path, tiny Almocábar features inspired and exceptional cooking, with a surprising range of vegetarian salads, as well as meaty classics and fish. The salad with goats' cheese, walnuts, apples and mango purée is outstanding. Finish your meal with a tangerine sorbet that tastes like all the tangerines in the world concentrated into one shimmering scoop. Booking advisable.

Restaurante Pedro Romero (☎ 952 87 11 10; Calle Virgen de la Paz 18; mains €17.50-22; closed Sun & Mon dinner Jul/Aug) This celebrated eatery, dedicated to bullfighting, turns out classic Ronda dishes – a good place to try the famously man-food oxtail dish, *rabo de toro*.

Restaurante Albacara (☎ 952 16 11 84; Calle Tenorio 8; meals €18-22) Situated in the old stables of gorge-side Hotel Montelirio, the Albacara serves up creative meals in an elegant environment, with plate-glass windows designed to make the most of the stupendous views.

Restaurante del Escudero (☎ 952 87 13 67; Paseo de Blas Infante 1; mains €18-25, menú €13.50; closed Sun evening & Mon) Sister restaurant of Restaurante Tragabuches with more reasonable prices, set in an attractive garden.

Restaurante Tragabuches (☎ 952 19 02 91; Calle José Aparicio 1; mains €27-32; closed Mon) Sleek, modern Tragabuches is famous for its creativity. Try venison and sweet potatoes or pork trotters with squid and sunflower seeds.

Drinking

El Choque Ideal (☎ 952 16 19 18; www.elchoqueideal.com; Calle Espíritu Santo 9; 9.30am-3am Feb-Oct, 1pm-1am Nov-Jan) This funky cafe has fantastic views. It puts on a host of events from films out on the terrace to live bands.

In Calle Los Remedios you can stop for a cold *cerveza* at ever-popular **Taberna del Antonio** (Calle Los Remedios 22). Down in the Barrio San Francisco try the heaving **Bodega San Francisco** (Calle Ruedo Alameda). Several jolly cafes and restaurants spill out on pedestrianised Calle Nueva in the newer north side of town. Try **Tragatapa** at No 4, with inventive tapas such as salmon marinaded in vanilla with lime zest.

Getting There & Away

BUS

From the **bus station** (Plaza Concepción García Redondo 2), **Los Amarillos** (☎ 952 18 70 61) goes to Málaga (€9.11, two hours, at least four daily), Grazalema (€2.46, 35 minutes, two daily) and Seville (€10.85, 2½ hours, three to six daily);

Comes (☎ 952 87 19 92) has three or four buses daily to Arcos de la Frontera (€8.14, two hours), Jerez (€10.67, 2½ hours) and Cádiz (€13.74, 2½ hours); and **Portillo** (☎ 952 87 22 62) runs to Málaga (€10.21, 1½ hours, at least three daily) via Marbella.

TRAIN

The **train station** (☎ 952 87 16 73; Avenida de Andalucía) is on the highly scenic Granada–Algeciras line. Trains run to/from Algeciras (€6.70 to €17.50, 1¾ hours, six daily), Granada (€12.25, 2½ hours, three daily) via Antequera, Córdoba (€18 to €29.50, 2½ hours, two daily) and Málaga (€8.85, two hours, one daily except Sunday). For Seville, change at Bobadilla or Antequera.

Getting Around

Minibuses operate every 30 minutes to Plaza de España from Avenida Martínez Astein, across the road from the train station.

ANDALUCÍA

AROUND RONDA

The beautiful green hills of the Serranía de Ronda, scattered with sugar-cube white villages, stretch in all directions from Ronda. This area has many traditional houses converted into gorgeous rural accommodation. For information try Ronda's municipal tourist office, www.serraniaronda.org and www.rusticblue.com.

Cueva de la Pileta

Palaeolithic paintings of horses, goats, fish and even a seal, dating from 20,000 to 25,000 years ago, are preserved in this large **cave** (☎ 952 16 73 43; adult/student/child €8/5/5; hourly tours 10am-1pm & 4-6pm), 20km southwest of Ronda. You'll be guided by kerosene lamp and one of the knowledgeable Bullón family from the farm in the valley below. A family member found the paintings in 1905. The Cueva de la Pileta is 250m (signposted) off the Benaoján–Cortes de la Frontera road, 4km from Benaoján. Guides speak a little English. If it's busy, you may have to wait, but you can phone ahead to book a particular time.

Parque Natural Sierra de las Nieves

This precious area of rare natural diversity, a Unesco Biosphere Reserve, also has an unusual history of human endeavour. For hundreds of years before refrigeration, the snow sellers of the region would gather at the end of the winter to shovel tonnes of snow into containers and transport it to huge pits, where it was pressed and compacted to form ice. Tightly covered until summer, mule teams would then transport huge blocks of ice into neighbouring towns, to sell at astronomical prices. Today, this 180-sq-km protected area, southeast of Ronda, offers some excellent walks. Torrecilla (1910m), the highest peak in the western half of Andalucía, is a five- to six-hour (return) walk from Área Recreativa Los Quejigales, which is 10km east by unpaved road from the A376 Ronda–San Pedro de Alcántara road.

Cerro de Hijar (☎ 952 11 21 11; www.cerrodehijar.com/eng; Carretera del Balneario, Sierra de las Nieves; d €86; P) Just above the dazzling white village of Tolox and just within the park, at 650m above sea level, this tastefully decorated hotel is generous with its room sizes, decoration, sweeping views and the range of activities it cheerfully organises for guests, including mountain biking, guided walks and 4WD excursions.

ANTEQUERA

pop 43,000 / elev 575m

Set on the edge of a plain 50km north of Málaga, with rugged mountains to the south and east, the handsome provincial town of Antequera is a mass of red-tiled roofs punctuated by 30 church towers. Here hides one of the richest historical legacies in Andalucía. Antequera's 'golden age' was during the 15th and 16th centuries.

Orientation & Information

The old heart of Antequera is below the northwestern side of the hill, crowned by the Islamic Alcazaba, which dominates the townscape, as big and simple as a child's drawing. The main street, Calle Infante Don Fernando, runs northwest from Plaza de San Sebastián.

Tourist office (☎ 952 70 25 05; www.antequera.es; Plaza de San Sebastián 7; 11am-2pm & 5-8pm Mon-Sat, to 2pm Sun)

Sights

The main approach to the **Alcazaba** (Fortress) passes through the **Arco de los Gigantes**, built in 1585 and incorporating stones with Roman inscriptions. What remains of the Alcazaba affords great views. Just below it is the **Colegiata de Santa María la Mayor** (Plaza Santa María; 10am-2pm & 4.30-6.30pm Tue-Fri, 10.30am-2pm Sat, 11.30am-2pm Sun), a 16th-century church with a beautiful Renaissance facade.

The pride of the **Museo Municipal** (Plaza del Coso Viejo; tour €3; 10am-1.30pm & 9-11pm Wed & Fri, 10-1.30pm Sat, 11am-1.30pm Sun) is *Efebo,* a beautiful 1.4m bronze Roman statue of a patrician's 'toy boy', unearthed near Antequera in the 1950s – one of the finest pieces of Roman sculpture found in Spain.

Only the most jaded would fail to be impressed by the **Iglesia del Carmen** (Plaza del Carmen; admission €1.50; 10am-2pm) and its marvellous 18th-century Churrigueresque retable. Carved in red pine and in beautiful detail by Antequera's Antonio Primo, it is encrusted with angels, saints, popes and bishops who seem to fly through the air, so finely rendered are their garments.

Some of Europe's largest megalithic tombs stand on the fringes of Antequera. The **Dolmen de Menga** and **Dolmen de Viera** (admission free; 9am-5.45pm Tue-Sat, 9.30am-2.15pm Sun) are 1km from the city centre, on the road leading northeast to the A45. In about 2500 or 2000 BC the local folk managed to transport dozens of huge rocks from nearby hills to construct these earth-covered tombs for their chieftains. Menga is 25m long, 4m high and composed of 32 slabs, the largest weighing 180 tonnes. You can walk across the utterly modern marble courtyard to enter this simple yet powerful relic of an unimaginably distant past. It could have been built yesterday to house one of Andalucía's proliferating dance venues.

Sleeping & Eating

You can't get much more central than the smartly refurbished **Hotel San Sebastián** (/fax 952 84 42 39; Plaza de San Sebastián 5; s/d €27/43;) Its terrace is the best perch on the plaza to watch the evening *paseo*. At **Hotel Coso Viejo** (952 Calle Encarnación 9; www.hotelcosoviejo.es; s/d incl breakfast €50/65; P), a converted 17th-century neoclassical palace in the heart of Antequera, rooms are set around a handsome patio with a fountain; there's a pleasant cafeteria and restaurant. In a quiet area north of the bullring, the ultra-modern **Parador de Antequera** (952 84 02 61; www.parador.es; Paseo García del Olmo s/n; s/d €95/118; P) is set amid pleasant gardens with wonderful views. It's due to reopen after its refurbishment by November 2008.

Restaurante La Espuela (952 70 30 31; Calle San Agustín 1; mains €12-21; closed Mon) In a charming cul-de-sac off Calle Infante Don Fernando, La Espuela plays background jazz and offers a fine selection of Antequeran specialities and international fare. A pleasant, traffic-free spot for lunch or dinner.

Getting There & Away

The **bus station** (Paseo Garcí de Olmo s/n) is 1km north of the city centre. At least 12 daily buses run to/from Málaga (€6.75, one hour), and three to five each to/from Osuna (€6.50, one hour), Seville (Prado de San Sebastián; €10.75, two hours), Granada (€8.25, 1¼ hours) and Córdoba (€8.25, 1½ hours). The ticket offices shut down completely between 2pm and 5pm.

The **train station** (Avenida de la Estación) is 1.5km north of the city centre. Two to four trains a day travel to/from Granada (€8, 1½ hours), Seville (€13, 1¾ hours) and Ronda (€5.80, 1¼ hours). For Málaga or Córdoba, change at Bobadilla.

AROUND ANTEQUERA

El Torcal

Sixteen kilometres south of Antequera, Nature has sculpted this 1336m **mountain** into some of the weirdest, most wonderful rock formations you'll see anywhere. Its 12 sq km of gnarled, pillared and deeply fissured limestone began life as seabed about 150 million years ago.

Two marked walking trails, the 1.5km 'Ruta Verde' (Green Route) and the 3km 'Ruta Amarilla' (Yellow Route), start and end near the information centre.

Laguna de Fuente de Piedra

This shallow lake, close to the A92 20km northwest of Antequera, is one of Europe's two main breeding grounds for the spectacular **greater flamingo** (the other is France's Camargue). After a wet winter as many as 20,000 pairs of flamingos breed at the lake. They arrive in January or February, with the chicks hatching in April and May, and stay till about August.

The **Centro de Información Fuente de Piedra** (952 11 17 15; 10am-2pm & 6-8pm), at the lake, on the edge of Fuente de Piedra village, hires out binoculars. Three to six daily buses (€1.10, 30 minutes) run between Antequera bus station and Fuente de Piedra village.

EAST OF MÁLAGA

The coast east of Málaga, sometimes called the Costa del Sol Oriental, is less developed than the coast to the west, but is striving hard to fill the gaps.

Behind the coast, **La Axarquía**, a region dotted with white villages (of Islamic origin) linked by snaking mountain roads, climbs to the *sierras* along the border of Granada province. There's good walking here (best in April and May, and from mid-September to late October). Once impoverished and forgotten, La Axarquía has experienced a surge of tourism and an influx of expat residents in recent years.

Nerja

pop 16,500

Nerja, 56km east of Málaga, is older, whiter and a little more charming than the towns to its west, though still inundated by (mainly British) tourism. The **tourist office** (☎ 952 52 15 31; www.nerja.org; Puerta del Mar; ⌚ 10am-2pm & 6-10pm Mon-Sat, 10am-2pm Sun May-Oct, 10am-2pm & 5-8pm Nov-Apr) is just off the Balcón de Europa promenade and lookout point, which has gorgeous coastal vistas. The best beach is **Playa Burriana**, on the eastern side of town.

SLEEPING

Rooms in the better hotels get booked up well in advance for the summer period.

Hostal Mena (☎ 952 52 05 41; hostalmena@hotmail.com; Calle El Barrio 15; s/d €25/40;) A short distance west of the tourist office, this friendly *hostal* has immaculate rooms (some with sea views) and a pleasant garden. One of the oldest hotels in town, it offers a tranquil retreat from the bustling beach life outside.

Hostal Miguel (☎ 952 52 15 23; www.hostalmiguel.com; Calle Almirante Ferrandiz 31; s/d €38/52) Straddled between two streets in the old town, this friendly English-run place has good rooms with a Moroccan theme and a pleasant roof terrace. The proprietor is friendly and helpful, with loads of information on things to see and do around Nerja.

Hostal Marissal (☎ 952 52 01 99; www.marissal.com; Balcón de Europa; s/d €45/60;) Right by the Balcón de Europa, the Marissal delights with its soothingly clean, quiet and comfortable rooms decked with tasteful art, and a good restaurant. This is hotel accommodation at hostal prices.

Hotel Carabeo (☎ 952 52 54 44; www.hotelcarabeo.com; Calle Carabeo 34; d/ste incl breakfast €91/198; P) This small, chic hotel is full of stylish antiques and set above well-tended gardens right on the cliff-edge. Its **Restaurante 34** (mains €17.50-25.50, ⌚ closed end Oct-Apr) offers delicious and exotic food combinations but nouvelle-size portions in a gorgeous setting overlooking the sea.

Hotel Paraíso del Mar (☎ 952 52 16 21; www.hotelparaisodelmar.com; Calle Prolongación de Carabeo; s/d €105-123/120-135 incl breakfast; P) To the east of the centre above Playa Carabeo, the Paraíso del Mar has great sea views and a range of spa facilities, as well as beautifully decorated Jacuzzi bathrooms. There is a private access gate to Burriana beach and a pool overlooking the sea.

EATING

Merendero Ayo (☎ 952 52 12 53; Playa Burriana; mains €9-13) One of the best feeds in town is at this always-busy open-air restaurant on Nerja's best beach. You can down a plate of paella, cooked on the spot in great sizzling pans, then go back for a refill.

Casa Luque (Plaza Cavana 2; mains €15-21; ⌚ closed Sun lunch & Wed) Casa Luque has a wonderfully panoramic terrace and, with an elegant haute-Med menu, more character than most Nerja eateries. The interior, with its high ceilings, is a cool and classy refuge from the ever-bustling streets.

A Taste of India (☎ 952 52 00 43; Calle Carabeo 51; mains €8-13, ⌚ closed Tue) This fantastic Goan-style Indian place serves delicious coconut curry and a range of curry favourites cooked on the spot. It has deservedly kept its popularity for some years.

ENTERTAINMENT

Nightlife focuses on the aptly named Tutti-Frutti Plaza, with an international clutch of bars and clubs. Check out what's on at the admirable **Centro Cultural Villa de Nerja** (☎ 952 52 38 63; Calle Granada 45).

GETTING THERE & AWAY

From the N340 near the top of Calle Pintada, **Alsina Graells** (☎ 952 52 15 04) runs to Málaga (€3.69, one hour, 14 daily), Almuñécar (€2.40, 25 minutes, up to 13 daily), Almería (€11.68, 2½ hours, nine daily) and Granada (€8.85, 1½ hours, two to three daily).

Around Nerja

The big tourist attraction is the **Cueva de Nerja** (☎ 952 52 95 20; www.cuevadenerja.es; adult/child €7/3.50; ⌚ 10am-2pm & 4-6.30pm, later in Jul & Aug), just off the N340, 3km east of town on the slopes of the Sierra Almijara mountains. This enormous cavern remains impressive, like some vast underground cathedral, 225 million years in the making. Large-scale performances including ballet and flamenco are staged there throughout the summer. About 14 buses run daily from Málaga and Nerja, except Sunday. The whole site is very well organised for large-scale tourism and has a huge restaurant and car park. A full tour of the caves takes about 45 minutes.

Further east the coast becomes more rugged, and with your own wheels you can head out to **Playa El Cañuelo** and other scenic, if stony, beaches down tracks from the N340, about 8km to 10km from Nerja.

Cómpeta & Around

pop 3500 / elev 640m

The hill village of Cómpeta, 17km inland, is a popular base for exploring La Axarquía and the mountains, although it's in danger of being overwhelmed by heavy construction traffic and estate agents as the *costa* building boom spreads uncontrollably up the inland valleys. It is very popular with summer home owners from northern Europe, with a sizeable Danish community. There's a **tourist office** (☎ 952 55 36 85; Avenida de la Constitución; ⏰ 10am-2pm & 3-6pm Wed-Sun, Tue-Sat Jul-Sep) by the bus stop at the foot of the village. Three or four buses run daily from Málaga (€3.50, two hours) via Torre del Mar.

SIGHTS & ACTIVITIES

A few kilometres down the valley from Cómpeta, **Árchez** has a beautiful Almohad minaret next to its church. From Árchez a road winds 8km southwest to **Arenas**, where a steep but driveable track climbs to the ruined Islamic **Castillo de Bentomiz**, which crowns a hilltop. **Los Caballos del Mosquín** (☎ 608 658108; www.horseriding-andalucia.com), just outside Canillas de Albaida, 2km northwest of Cómpeta, offers horse rides in the mountains lasting from one hour to several days. An exhilarating long walk is up the dramatically peaked **El Lucero** (1779m), from whose summit, on a clear day, you can see both Granada and Morocco. This is a demanding full-day return walk from Cómpeta, but it's possible to drive as far up as Puerto Blanquillo pass (1200m) via a slightly hairy mountain track from Canillas de Albaida. From Puerto Blanquillo a path climbs 200m to another pass, the Puerto de Cómpeta. One kilometre down from there, past a quarry, the summit path (1½ hours), marked by a signboard, diverges to the right across a stream bed.

SLEEPING & EATING

Hotel Balcón de Cómpeta (☎ 952 55 35 35; www.hotel-competa.com; Calle San Antonio 75; s/d €50/68; P ❄ ♿ ●) Cómpeta's only hotel has comfortable rooms with balconies, a good restaurant, a bar, a big pool and a tennis court. Staff are friendly and helpful and speak good English. It's also wheelchair accessible.

You can book houses, apartments and rooms through **Cómpeta Direct** (www.competadirect.com).

The two best restaurants, both serving excellent and varied Spanish/international food, are **El Pilón** (☎ 952 55 35 12; Calle Laberinto; mains €11-18.50; ⏰ 8-12pm) and **Cortijo Paco** (☎ 952 55 36 47; Avenida Canillas 6; mains €10-15; ⏰ 8-12pm, closed Mon). In summer ask for an upstairs terrace table at either place.

CÓRDOBA PROVINCE

Córdoba city was capital of Al-Andalus and at its zenith was home to the glittering court of Abd ar-Rahman III. While history remains the tourist magnet, Córdoba also celebrates new talent in its prestigious annual Guitar Festival, its daring fusion cuisine, and startling glimpses of steel, glass and rusty metal architecture. Beyond the city stretches an essentially rural province that produces some of Andalucía's best olive oil and wine.

CÓRDOBA

pop 302,000 / elev 110m

Standing on a sweep of Río Guadalquivir Córdoba is a handsome, conservative city. Apart from its great historical attractions, it also features some of the region's best restaurants and taverns, though there is a small but growing nightlife scene. The best time to visit is between temperate mid-April and mid-June, when the city's patios and lanes, like the Calleja de las Flores, are at their fragrant best.

History

The Roman colony of Corduba, founded in 152 BC, became capital of Baetica province, covering most of today's Andalucía. In 711 Córdoba fell to the Muslim invaders and soon became the Islamic capital on the Iberian Peninsula. It was here in 756 that Abd ar-Rahman I set himself up as emir of Al-Andalus.

Córdoba's heyday came under Abd ar-Rahman III (912–61). The biggest city in Western Europe had dazzling mosques, libraries, observatories and aqueducts, a university and highly skilled artisans in leather, metal, textiles and glazed tiles. And the multicultural court was frequented by Jewish, Arab and Christian scholars.

Towards the end of the 10th century, Al-Mansour (Almanzor), a fearsome general, took the reins of power and struck terror into Christian Spain with over 50 *razzias* (forays) in 20 years. But after his death bands of Berber troops terrorised Córdoba and the caliphate descended into anarchy.

Córdoba's intellectual traditions, however, lived on. Twelfth-century Córdoba produced two of the most celebrated of all Al-Andalus scholars: the Muslim Averroës (Ibn Rushd) and the Jewish Maimonides. These polymaths are best remembered for their philosophical efforts to harmonise religious faith with reason.

In 1236, Córdoba was captured by Fernando III of Castilla and became a provincial town of shrinking importance. The decline began to be reversed only with the arrival of industry in the late 19th century. In common with other Andalucian cities in recent years, the culture, artefacts and traditions of Al-Andalus have enjoyed a growing revival of scholarly and popular interest. In fact, in 2016, when Córdoba aspires to be the European Capital of Culture, its status may well have come full circle.

Orientation

The fascinating part of Córdoba is the World Heritage–listed medieval city, a labyrinth of narrow streets focused on the Mezquita, which is immediately north of Río Guadalquivir. The main square of modern Córdoba is Plaza de las Tendillas, 500m north of the Mezquita.

Information

Most banks and ATMs are around Plaza de las Tendillas and Avenida del Gran Capitán. The bus and train stations have ATMs.

Ch@t (Calle Claudio Marcelo 15; per hr €1.80; 9am-1.30pm & 4.30-8.30pm Mon-Fri Nov-Mar, 9.30am-1.30pm & 5.30-8.30pm Apr-Oct, 10am-1.30pm Sat) Many terminals and efficient internet access, although no internet access available if you are on Mac.

Hospital Reina Sofía (957 21 70 00; Avenida de Menéndez Pidal s/n) Located 1.5km southwest of the Mezquita.

Luque Libros (Calle José Cruz Conde 19; 9.45am-1.30pm & 5pm-8.30pm, to 1.30pm Sat) Sells city and Michelin maps cheaper than the tourist shops near the Mezquita.

Municipal tourist office (957 20 05 22; Plaza de Judá Levi; 8.30am-2.30pm Mon-Fri)

Policía Nacional (95 747 75 00; Avenida Doctor Fleming 2)

Post office (Calle José Cruz Conde 15)

Regional tourist office (957 35 51 79; Calle de Torrijos 10; 9am-7.30pm Mon-Fri, 9.30am-3pm Sat, Sun & holidays) Facing the western side of the Mezquita, this helpful office offers information on the city and surrounding countryside.

Sights & Activities

Opening hours for Córdoba's sights change frequently, so check with the tourist offices for updated times. Most places (except the Mezquita) close on Monday. Closing times are generally an hour or two earlier in winter than summer.

MEZQUITA

It's hard to exaggerate the beauty of the Córdoba **mosque** (957 47 05 12; adult/child €8/4; 10am-7pm Mon-Sat Apr-Oct, to 6pm Mon-Sat Nov-Mar, 9-10.45am & 1.30-6.30pm Sun year-round), one of the great creations of Islamic architecture, with its shimmering golden mosaics and rows of red-and-white-striped arches disappearing into infinity.

Emir Abd ar-Rahman I founded the Mezquita in 785 on the site of a Visigothic church that had been partitioned between Muslims and Christians. In the 9th and 10th centuries, the Mezquita was enlarged and embellished until it extended over nearly 23,000 sq metres in total, making it one of the biggest mosques in the world. Its 14,000-sq-metre prayer hall incorporated 1293 columns, some of which had stood in the Visigothic church, in Roman buildings in Córdoba and even in ancient Carthage. Today 856 of the columns remain.

What we see today is the Mezquita's original architectural form with two big changes: a 16th-century cathedral plonked right in the middle (which explains the often-used description 'Mezquita-Catedral'); and the closing

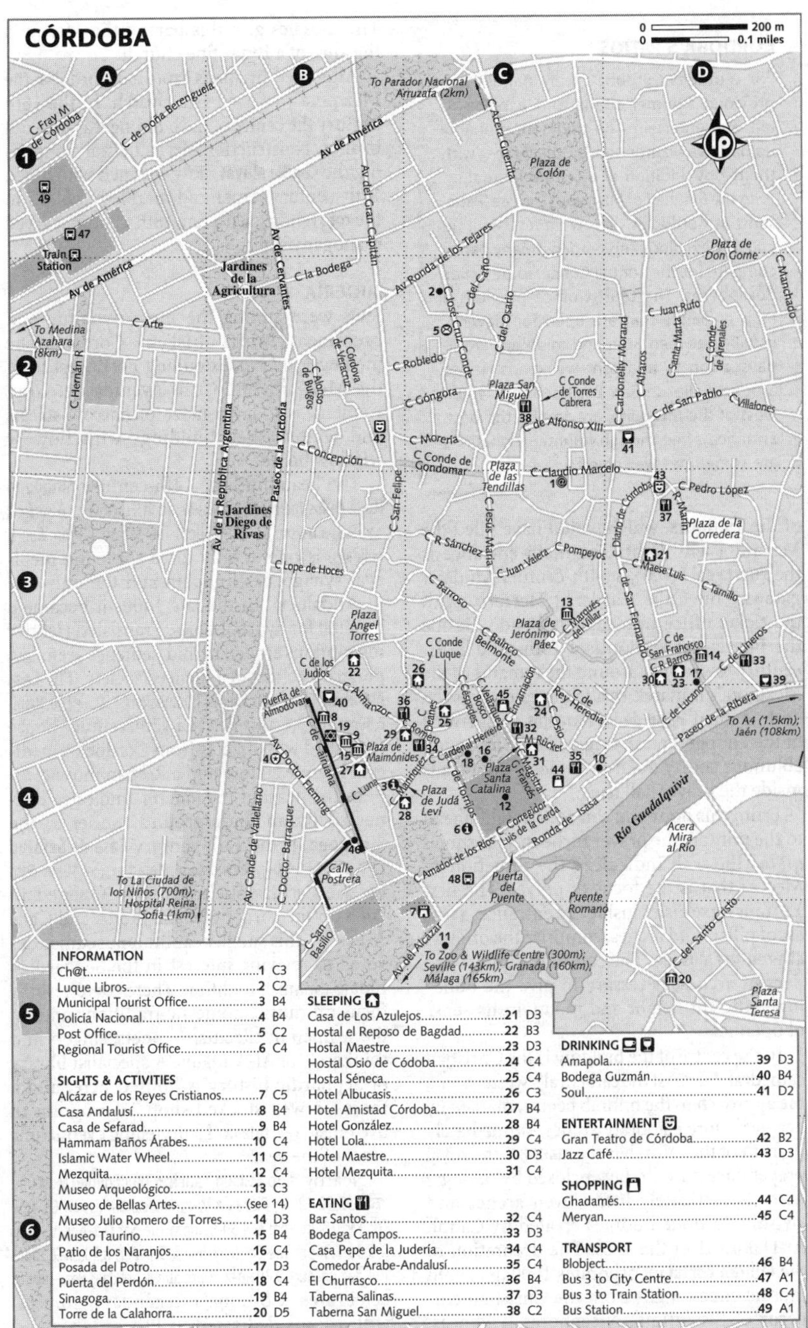

INFORMATION

Ch@t....................1 C3
Luque Libros....................2 C2
Municipal Tourist Office....................3 B4
Policía Nacional....................4 B4
Post Office....................5 C2
Regional Tourist Office....................6 C4

SIGHTS & ACTIVITIES

Alcázar de los Reyes Cristianos....................7 C5
Casa Andalusí....................8 B4
Casa de Sefarad....................9 B4
Hammam Baños Árabes....................10 C4
Islamic Water Wheel....................11 C5
Mezquita....................12 C4
Museo Arqueológico....................13 C3
Museo de Bellas Artes....................(see 14)
Museo Julio Romero de Torres....................14 D3
Museo Taurino....................15 B4
Patio de los Naranjos....................16 C4
Posada del Potro....................17 D3
Puerta del Perdón....................18 C4
Sinagoga....................19 B4
Torre de la Calahorra....................20 D5

SLEEPING

Casa de Los Azulejos....................21 D3
Hostal el Reposo de Bagdad....................22 B3
Hostal Maestre....................23 D3
Hostal Osio de Códoba....................24 C4
Hostal Séneca....................25 C4
Hotel Albucasis....................26 C3
Hotel Amistad Córdoba....................27 B4
Hotel González....................28 B4
Hotel Lola....................29 C4
Hotel Maestre....................30 D3
Hotel Mezquita....................31 C4

EATING

Bar Santos....................32 C4
Bodega Campos....................33 D3
Casa Pepe de la Judería....................34 C4
Comedor Árabe-Andalusí....................35 C4
El Churrasco....................36 B4
Taberna Salinas....................37 D3
Taberna San Miguel....................38 C2

DRINKING

Amapola....................39 D3
Bodega Guzmán....................40 B4
Soul....................41 D2

ENTERTAINMENT

Gran Teatro de Córdoba....................42 B2
Jazz Café....................43 D3

SHOPPING

Ghadamés....................44 C4
Meryan....................45 C4

TRANSPORT

Blobject....................46 B4
Bus 3 to City Centre....................47 A1
Bus 3 to Train Station....................48 C4
Bus Station....................49 A1

CÓRDOBA'S PATIOS

For centuries Córdoba's leafy patios have provided summer shade and a place to talk and entertain. The tradition, probably Roman, was continued by the Arabs, with the happy addition of a central fountain.

In the first half of May, you'll notice 'Patio' signs in Córdoba's narrow streets, inviting you to view blooming gardens. Many patios compete for the annual Concurso de Patios Cordobéses. The tourist office provides a map of patios that are open for viewing, usually between 5pm and midnight weekdays, noon to midnight weekends. Those around Calle de San Basilio, about 400m west of the Mezquita, are among the best. Entrance is free, though voluntary donations are sometimes welcomed.

of the 19 doors, which would have filled the Mezquita with light. The main entrance is the **Puerta del Perdón**, a 14th-century Mudéjar gateway on Calle Cardenal Herrero, with the ticket office immediately inside. Beside the Puerta del Perdón is a 16th- and 17th-century tower built around the remains of the Mezquita's minaret. Inside the gateway is the aptly named **Patio de los Naranjos** (Courtyard of the Orange Trees), originally the mosque's ablutions courtyard, from which a door leads inside the prayer hall itself.

From this door you can see straight ahead to the mihrab, the prayer niche in a mosque's *qibla* (the wall indicating the direction of Mecca) that is the focus of prayer. The first 12 transverse aisles inside the entrance, a forest of pillars and arches, comprise the original **8th-century mosque**. The columns support two tiers of arches, necessary to give the building sufficient height and maintain its sense of openness.

In the centre of the building is the Christian cathedral. Just past the cathedral's western end, the approach to the mihrab begins, marked by heavier, more elaborate arches. Immediately in front of the mihrab is the **maksura**, the royal prayer enclosure (today enclosed by railings) with its intricately interwoven arches and lavishly decorated domes created by Caliph Al-Hakim II in the 960s. The decoration of the **mihrab portal** incorporates 1600kg of gold mosaic cubes, a gift from the Christian emperor of Byzantium, Nicephoras II Phocas. The mosaics give this part of the Mezquita the aura of a Byzantine church.

After the Christians captured Córdoba, the Mezquita was used as a church. In the 16th century the centre of the building was torn out to allow construction of a cathedral comprising the **Capilla Mayor**, now adorned with a rich 17th-century jasper and marble *retablo*, and the **coro** (choir), with fine 18th-century carved mahogany stalls.

JUDERÍA

Jews were among the most dynamic and prominent citizens of Islamic Córdoba. The medieval *judería*, extending northwest from the Mezquita almost to Avenida del Gran Capitán, is today a maze of narrow streets and whitewashed buildings with flowery window boxes.

The beautiful little 14th-century **Sinagoga** (Calle de los Judíos 20; admission adult/EU citizen €0.30/free; 9.30am-2pm & 3.30-5.30pm Tue-Sat, to 1.30pm Sun & holidays) is one of only three surviving medieval synagogues in Spain and the only one in Andalucía. In the late 1400s it became a hospital for hydrophobics. Translated Hebrew inscriptions eroded in mid-sentence seem like poignant echoes of a silenced society. The **Casa Andalusí** (Calle de los Judíos 12; admission €2.50; 10.30am-8.30pm, to 6.30pm Nov-Mar) is a 12th-century house furnished with objects from Córdoba's medieval Islamic culture and a Roman mosaic.

In the heart of the *judería*, and once connected by an underground tunnel to the Sinagoga, is the 14th-century **Casa de Sefarad** (957 42 14 04; www.casadesefarad.es; 10am-6pm Mon-Sat, 11am-2pm Sun; admission €4) Opened in 2008 on the corner of Calle Judios and Calle Averroes, this small, beautiful museum is devoted to reviving interest in the Sephardic–Judaic–Spanish tradition. There is a refreshing focus on music, domestic traditions and on the women intellectuals – poets, singers and thinkers – of Al-Andalus. A specialist library of Sephardic history is housed here, and a there's a well-stocked shop. A program of live music recitals and storytelling events runs most of the year.

Nearby, the **Museo Taurino** (Bullfighting Museum; 957 20 10 56; Plaza de Maimónides; admission €3, free Fri; 10am-2pm & 4.30-6.30pm Tue-Sat Oct-Apr, to 2pm & 5.30-7.30pm Tue-Sat May-Jun & Sep-Oct, 8.30am-2.30pm Tue-Sat Jul-Aug, 9.30am-2.30pm Sun & holidays year-round) celebrates Córdoba's legendary *toreros*, with rooms dedicated to El Cordobés and

Manolete, and even the forlorn, pegged-out hide of Islero, the bull that fatally gored Manolete in 1947. Closed throughout 2008 and much of 2009 for extensive repairs.

ALCÁZAR DE LOS REYES CRISTIANOS

Just southwest of the Mezquita, the **Alcázar,** or **Castle of the Christian Monarchs** (☎ 957 42 01 51; Campo Santo de Los Mártires s/n; admission adults/students/senior €4/2, free Fri; ⏰ 10am-2pm & 4.30-6.30pm Tue-Sat mid-Oct–Apr, 10am-2pm & 5.30-7.30pm Tue-Sat May-Jun & Sep–mid-Oct, 8.30am-2.30pm Tue-Sat Jul-Aug, 9.30am-2.30pm Sun & holidays year-round), began as a palace and fort for Alfonso X in the 13th century. From 1490 to 1821 the Inquisition operated from here. Today its gardens are among the most beautiful in Andalucía. The building houses an old royal bathhouse, the Baños Califales. Take time to gaze at the third-century Roman sarcophagus, with its reflections on life and death.

PUENTE ROMANO & AROUND

Just south of the Mezquita is the much-restored **Puente Romano** (Roman Bridge) crosses the Guadalquivir. Just downstream, near the northern bank, is a restored **Islamic water wheel**.

At the southern end of the bridge is the **Torre de la Calahorra** (☎ 957 29 39 29; Puente Romano s/n; adult/child €4/2.50; ⏰ 10am-2pm & 4.30-8.30pm May-Sep, to 6pm Oct-Apr), a 14th-century tower with the curious Roger Garaudy Museum of the Three Cultures highlighting the intellectual achievements of Islamic Córdoba.

MUSEO ARQUEOLÓGICO

Córdoba's excellent **archaeological museum** (☎ 957 47 40 11; Plaza de Jerónimo Páez 7; adult/EU citizen €1.50/free; ⏰ 3-8pm Tue, 9am-8pm Wed-Sat, to 3pm Sun & holidays), provides a real insight into pre-Islamic Córdoba in the suitably historic setting of a Renaissance palace. The upstairs is devoted to medieval Córdoba.

PLAZA DEL POTRO

This pedestrianised plaza, 400m northeast of the Mezquita, was a celebrated hang-out for traders and adventurers in the 16th and 17th centuries. Miguel de Cervantes lived for a while in the **Posada del Potro** (☎ 957 48 50 18; Plaza del Potro 10; admission free; ⏰ 10am-2pm & 5-8pm Mon-Fri Aug-May), then an inn (which he described in *Don Quijote* as a 'den of thieves') and today a more respectable exhibition hall.

A former hospital houses what is, surprisingly enough, Córdoba's most visited museum, the **Museo Julio Romero de Torres** (☎ 957 49 19 09; Plaza del Potro 1; admission €3, free Fri; ⏰ 10am-2pm & 4.30-6.30pm Tue-Sat mid-Oct-Apr, to 2pm & 5.30-7.30pm Tue-Sat May-Jun & Sep–mid-Oct, 8.30am-2.30pm Jul-Aug, 9.30am-2.30pm Sun & holidays year-round), devoted to revered local painter Julio Romero de Torres (1873–1930). Romero de Torres specialised in sensual yet sympathetic portraits of Cordoban women. In the same building is the **Museo de Bellas Artes** (Fine Arts Museum; adult/EU citizen €1.50/free; ⏰ 2.30-8.30pm Tue, 9am-8.30pm Wed-Sat, to 2.30pm Sun & holidays), which exhibits Cordoban artists' work from the 14th to the 20th century.

HAMMAM BAÑOS ÁRABES

Follow the lead of the medieval Cordobans and indulge your senses at the beautifully renovated **Arab baths** (☎ 957 48 47 46; www.hammamspain.com/cordoba; Calle Corregidor Luis de la Cerda 51; bath/bath & massage €25/32; ⏰ 2hr sessions at 10am, noon, 2pm, 4pm, 6pm, 8pm & 10pm) where you can enjoy an aromatherapy massage, with tea, hookah and Arabic sweets in the cafe later.

Festivals & Events

Spring and early summer is the chief festival time for Córdoba.

Concurso & Festival de Patios Cordobeses (Early May) See the boxed text, opposite; at the same time there's a busy cultural program.

Feria de Mayo (Last week of May/first days of June) Ten days of party time for Córdoba, with a giant fair, concerts and bullfights.

Festival Internacional de Guitarra (Late June/early July) Two-week celebration of the guitar, with live classical, flamenco, rock, blues and more; top names play in the Alcázar gardens at night.

Semana Santa (Holy Week) Every evening during Holy Week, between around 8pm and midnight, up to 12 processions accompany their *pasos* (elaborate platforms bearing religious images) on an official route through the city. Processions peak between 4am and 6am on Good Friday.

Cordoba for Children

When you and the kids just don't want to look at old stones a moment longer, it's time to head a little way out of town and leave the past behind. Just southwest of the city centre and adjoining the city **Zoo and Wildlife Centre** (Avenida de Linneo; admission adult/child/senior €4/2; ⏰ 10am-7pm Tue-Sun Apr & May, to 8pm Jun, Jul, Aug, to 7pm Sep, to 5-6pm Oct-Mar), historic buildings morph into brightly coloured climbing equipment.

Welcome to **La Ciudad de los Niños** (☎ 663 035709; laciudaddelosninos@educasur.es; Avenida Menéndez Pidal; admission free; 10am-2pm & 7-11pm Jun-mid-Sep, 10am-6pm Nov-Mar), Córdoba's City for Kids. A calendar of special events aimed at 4 to 12 year olds runs throughout the summer – check its website for details, or ask at the regional tourist office. Buses 2 and 5 (heading to Hospital Reina Sofia) from the city centre stop here.

Sleeping

There is plenty of budget accommodation in Córdoba (though finding single rooms for a decent price is not easy). Many lodgings are built around some of the city's charming patios. Booking ahead is wise from March to October and essential during the main festivals. Prices are generally reduced from November to mid-March, and some places also cut their rates during hot July and August.

ANDALUCÍA

BUDGET

Hostal El Reposo de Bagdad (☎ 957 20 28 54; www.hostalbagdad.eresmas.com; Calle Fernández Ruano 11; s/d €30/45) Hidden in a tiny street in the *judería,* this 200-year-old house feels thrillingly Moorish. The rooms are simple but clean.

Hostal Séneca (☎/fax 957 47 32 34; Calle Conde y Luque 7; s/d incl breakfast €36/48; closed one week Aug & Christmas week) The charming, friendly Séneca occupies a rambling house with a marvellous pebbled patio that's filled with greenery. Some rooms have air-conditioning. A small cafe-bar supplies breakfast and drinks on the patio.

Hostal Osio de Córdoba (☎/fax 957 48 51 65; Calle Osio 6; d/tr €45/60) Great facilities are available here at a very reasonable price. This hotel is a refurbished mansion with two cool patios, and the proprietor speaks English.

Hotel Maestre (☎ 957 47 24 10; Calle Romero Barros 4; s/d €38/52, apt €58; P) This place has comfortably furnished rooms with all the mod cons, although bathrooms are grudging of both space and supplies. The reception staff speak some English.

MIDRANGE

Hotel González (☎ 957 47 98 19; hotelgonzalez@wanadoo.es; Calle Manríquez 3; s €35-37, d €49-66) Rich baroque decor lends a graciousness to this well-priced hotel. The restaurant is set in the pretty flower-filled patio and the friendly proprietors speak fluent English.

Hotel Mezquita (☎ 957 47 55 85; hotelmezquita@wanadoo.es; Plaza Santa Catalina 1; s €37-39, d €53-74) One of the best-value places in town, this hotel is right opposite the Mezquita itself. The 16th-century mansion has sparkling bathrooms and elegant rooms, some with views of the great mosque.

Hotel Albucasis (☎/fax 957 47 86 25; Calle Buen Pastor 11; s/d €50/70; P) Tucked away in a quiet location in the *judería,* the decor is austere and restful, with modest rooms decorated primarily in white and pale green. The ivy-festooned patio is a great spot for breakfast.

Hotel Lola (☎ 957 20 03 05; www.hotelconencantolola.com; Calle Romero 3; d incl breakfast €114; P) A quirky hotel with large antique beds and full of smaller items that you just wish you could take home. You can eat your breakfast on the roof terrace overlooking the Mezquita bell tower.

Casa de los Azulejos (☎ 957 47 00 00; www.casadelosazulejos.com/marco.htm; Calle Fernando Colón 5; s/d €100/120) Andalucía meets Mexico in this stylish hotel, where the patio is all banana trees, fluffy ferns and tall palms. The rooms are in a colonial style, and there's a good Mexican restaurant downstairs.

TOP END

Hotel Amistad Córdoba (☎ 957 42 03 35; www.nh-hoteles.com; Plaza de Maimónides 3; s/d €118; P) Occupying two 18th-century mansions with original Mudéjar patios, the Amistad is part of the modern NH chain with elegant rooms and all the requisite luxury hotel facilities including babysitting. Closed at the time of research; however, renovations will have been completed by the time you read this.

Parador Nacional Arruzafa (☎ 957 27 59 00; www.parador.es; Avenida de la Arruzafa s/n; s/d €116/145; P) Best if you're driving, the *parador* is 3km north of the city centre. It's fabulously situated on the site of Abd ar-Rahman I's summer palace but is a modern affair (rather disappointing in such an historic city) amid lush green gardens where Europe's first palm trees were planted. It's wheelchair accessible.

Eating

Dishes common to most Cordoban restaurants include *salmorejo,* a very thick tomato-based gazpacho (cold vegetable soup), and *rabo de toro.* Some restaurants feature recipes from Al-Andalus such as garlic soup with raisins, honeyed lamb, or meat stuffed with dates and nuts. The local tipple is wine from nearby Montilla and Moriles, similar to sherry but unfortified.

There are lots of places to eat right by the Mezquita, but beware inflated prices and uninspired food.

Bar Santos (Calle Magistral González Francés 3; tortillas €2.50) The legendary Santos serves the biggest *tortilla de patata* in town – eaten with plastic forks on paper plates, while gazing at the Mezquita. Don't miss it.

Taberna Salinas (☎ 957 48 01 35; Calle Tundidores 3; tapas/raciones €2.50/8; closed Sun & Aug) Dating back to 1879, this large patio restaurant fills up fast. Try the delicious aubergines with honey or potatoes with garlic. The tavern side is quieter in the early evening, and the friendly bar staff will fill your glass with local Montilla whenever you look thirsty.

Taberna San Miguel (☎ 957 47 01 66; Plaza San Miguel 1; tapas €2-5 media raciones €5.50-10; closed Sun & Aug) Córdoba prides itself on its tabernas. The San Miguel has been going strong since 1880, with a good base of local regulars for a friendly ambience.

Comedor Árabe-Andalusí (☎ 957 47 51 62; Calle Alfayatas 6; mains €8-11) Indulge your North African tastes at this low-seated eatery where you can choose from *kofte*, falafel, tagines or bowls of fluffy couscous with chicken, lamb, greens and herbs.

Casa Pepe de la Judería (☎ 957 20 07 44; Calle Romero 1; tapas/media raciones €2.50-9.50, mains €11-18, menú €27.82) A great roof-terrace with views of the Mezquita and a labyrinth of busy dining rooms. Down a complimentary glass of Montilla before launching into the house specials, including Cordoban oxtails or venison fillets.

El Churrasco (☎ 957 29 08 19; Calle Romero 16; mains €15-24; closed Aug) The food is rich, the portions generous and service in the shady patio room is old-school attentive. White gazpacho made from pine nuts and garnished with raisins and apple chunks is as soft and creamy as angels' wings. In contrast, meaty dishes include the eponymous *churrasco*, a barbecued pork fillet with a wickedly scarlet Arabian sauce.

Bodega Campos (☎ 957 49 75 00; Calle de Lineros 32; tapas/raciones €6.50-16, mains €17.50-29; closed Sun evening) This many-roomed, atmospheric winery-cum-restaurant offers the peak dining experience in Cordoba. Corridors and rooms are lined with oak barrels, signed by the Spanish royal family and Tony Blair, among other immortals, and the establishment offers its own house Montilla.

Drinking & Entertainment

Córdoba's liveliest bars are mostly scattered around the newer parts of town and come alive at about 11pm or midnight at weekends. Most bars in the medieval centre close around midnight.

Amapola (☎ 957 47 37 40; Paseo de la Ribera 9; 9am-3pm Mon-Fri, 5pm-4am Sat & Sun) This is where the young and beautiful lounge on green leather sofas and consume elaborate cocktails. The DJ whips up a storm. Party in style till late at night.

Soul (☎ 957 49 15 80; Calle de Alfonso XIII 3; 9am-3am Mon-Fri & 10am-4am Sat & Sun, closed Aug) Sparsely furnished, student-filled DJ bar that gets hot and busy at weekends, attracting a more alternative and younger crowd.

Bodega Guzmán (Calle de los Judíos 7) Don't miss this atmospheric old-city favourite, with Montilla from the barrel.

Jazz Café (☎ 957 47 19 28; Calle Espartería s/n; admission free; 8am-late) This fabulous, cavernous bar puts on regular live jazz and jam sessions.

Gran Teatro de Córdoba (☎ 957 48 02 37; www.teatrocordoba.com in Spanish; Avenida del Gran Capitán 3) This theatre hosts a busy program of concerts, theatre, dance and film, mostly geared to popular Spanish tastes.

Shopping

Córdoba is known for its *cuero repujado* (embossed leather) goods, silver jewellery (particularly filigree) and attractive pottery. Craft shops congregate around the Mezquita.

Meryan (☎ 95 747 59 02; Calleja de las Flores) A top place for quality embossed leather, although it is factory-produced (on a relatively small scale).

Ghadamés (☎ 957 48 16 07; www.cuerrosghadames.com; Corregidor Luis de la Cerda 52; 10am-1pm & 5.30pm-8pm, to 1pm Apr-Sep) Here in his tiny workshop, enthusiastic Rafael Varo is one of a handful of dedicated craftsmen reviving the lost art of *guadamecíes*. This is a technique invented in Córdoba during the 13th century for curing leather so that intricate designs can be painted, engraved or inlaid on it. Pieces start at around €200.

Getting There & Away

BUS

The **bus station** (☎ 957 40 40 40; Glorieta de las Tres Culturas) is 1km northwest of Plaza de las Tendillas, behind the train station. Destinations include Seville (€9.96, 1¾ hours, six daily),

Granada (€12.04 to €16.60, 2½ hours, seven daily), Madrid (€14.40, 4½ hours, six daily), Málaga (€12.21, 2¾ hours, five daily) and Jaén (€8.22, 1½ hours, seven daily).

TRAIN

Córdoba's **train station** (☎ 957 40 02 02; Avenida de América) is on the high-speed AVE line between Madrid and Seville. Rail destinations include Seville (€27.80, 90 minutes, 23 or more daily), Madrid (€48.40 to €61.80, 1¾ to 6¼ hours, 23 or more daily), Málaga (€19.05 to €22.30, 2½ hours, nine daily), Barcelona (€55.40 to €124.50, 10½ hours, four daily) and Jaén (€8.85, 1½ hours, one daily). For Granada (€32, four hours), change at Bobadilla.

Getting Around

Bus 3 (€1), from the street between the train and bus stations, runs to Plaza de las Tendillas and down Calle de San Fernando, east of the Mezquita. For the return trip, you can pick it up on Ronda de Isasa, just south of the Mezquita.

Taxis from the bus or train station to the Mezquita cost around €6.

For drivers, Córdoba's one-way system is nightmarish, but routes to many hotels and *hostales* are fairly well signposted with a 'P' if they have parking. Hotels charge about €12 to €18 per day for parking.

Blobjects (☎ 957 76 00 33; www.blobject.es; Avenida Dr Fleming; €25-50, one-day hire €100) The jaunty, rounded Blobject is an American-made Gem electric car (top speed around 20mph). Equipped with GPS technology and a USB port for plugging in flash drive information in your chosen European language, the Blobject is a safe, environmentally friendly and fun way to see, hear and smell this city of flowers. Blobjects for one, two or four passengers can be collected and returned to several major tourist sites around the city. Ask at a tourist information office for details of routes. The same company is experimenting with the strange-but-cute Segway, an electrical scooter controlled by leaning movements of the driver, with full training and safety helmets provided before setting off.

AROUND CÓRDOBA

Medina Azahara

Even in the cicada-shrill heat and stillness of a summer afternoon, the Madinat al-Zahra whispers of the power and vision of its founder, Abd ar-Rahman III. The self-proclaimed caliph began the construction of a magnificent new capital 8km west of Córdoba around 936, and took up full residence around 945. **Medina Azahara** (Madinat al-Zahra; ☎ 957 32 91 30; adult/EU citizen €1.50/free; 🕑 10am-6.30pm Tue-Sat, to 8.30pm May–mid-Sep, to 2pm Sun) was a resounding declaration of his status, a magnificent trapping of power.

The new capital was amazingly short-lived. Between 1010 and 1013, during the caliphate's collapse, Medina Azahara was wrecked by Berber soldiers. Today, though less than a tenth of it has been excavated, and only about a quarter of that is open to visitors, Medina Azahara is still a fascinating place to visit.

The visitor route leads down to the **Dar al-Wuzara** (House of the Viziers), a substantial building with several horseshoe arches, fronted by a square garden, and on to the most impressive building, the painstakingly restored **Salón de Abd ar-Rahman III**, the caliph's throne hall, with delicate horseshoe arching framing elaborate gardens, and exquisitely carved stuccowork, of a lavishness hitherto unprecedented in the Islamic world.

Since much of the site is in full sun, try to avoid visiting after 11am in July and August, thus avoiding both crowds and extreme heat. It's also advisable to wear comfortable walking shoes to negotiate some uneven paths and rough ground around the monuments.

Medina Azahara is signposted on Avenida de Medina Azahara, which leads west out of Córdoba onto the A431.

A taxi costs €37 for the return trip, with one hour to view the site, or you can book a three-hour coach tour for €6.50 to €10 through many Córdoba hotels. Guided visits can also be arranged for around €15.

GRANADA PROVINCE

Granada province houses two of Andalucía's crown jewels – the Alhambra and the mainland's highest mountain range and ski resort. But there is much more to delight: the sleeping beauty of the Alpujarra valleys and the province's own Mediterranean resort area, the Costa Tropical, are, like the skiing, both less than an hour's drive from the city. Even at the height of summer, night-times and early mornings bring reviving mountain breezes, the tapas are still free, and the people are friendly and open to new influences.

GRANADA

pop 300,000 / elev 685m

Spain's most visited monument, the Alhambra palace, presides over a city full of architectural and historic treasures. Today, Granada's Islamic past is being reinvented for the 21st century in the shops, restaurants, tearooms and mosque of a growing North African community in and around the Albayzín. Alongside them flourish smart new tapas bars, tiny flamenco dives and chrome-and-neon clubs that support a dynamic student and gay scene.

History

Granada's history reads like a thriller. Granada began life as an Iberian settlement in the Albayzín district. Muslim forces took over from the Visigoths in 711, with the aid of the Jewish community around the foot of the Alhambra hill in what was called Garnata al Jahud, from which the name Granada derives; *granada* also happens to be Spanish for pomegranate, the fruit on the city's coat of arms.

After the fall of Córdoba (1236) and Seville (1248), Muslims sought refuge in Granada, where Mohammed ibn Yusuf ibn Nasr had set up an independent emirate. Stretching from the Strait of Gibraltar to east of Almería, this 'Nasrid' emirate became the final remnant of Al-Andalus, ruled from the increasingly lavish Alhambra palace for 250 years. Granada became one of the richest cities in medieval Europe.

However, in the 15th century the economy stagnated and violent rivalry developed over the succession. One faction supported the emir, Abu al-Hasan, and his harem favourite Zoraya. The other faction backed Boabdil, Abu al-Hasan's son by his wife Aixa. In 1482 Boabdil rebelled, setting off a confused civil war. The Christian armies invading the emirate took advantage, besieging towns and devastating the countryside, and in 1491 they finally laid siege to Granada. After eight months, Boabdil agreed to surrender the city in return for the Alpujarras valleys and 30,000 gold coins, plus political and religious freedom for his subjects. On 2 January 1492 the conquering Catholic Monarchs, Isabel and Fernando, entered Granada ceremonially in Muslim dress. They set up court in the Alhambra for several years.

Jews and Muslims were steadily persecuted, and both groups had been expelled by the 17th century. Granada sank into a deep decline until the Romantics revived interest in its Islamic heritage during the 1830s, when tourism took hold.

When the Nationalists took over Granada at the start of the civil war, an estimated 4000 *granadinos* (Granada residents) with left or liberal connections were killed, among them Federico García Lorca, Granada's most famous writer. Granada has a reputation for political conservatism.

Orientation

The two major central streets, Gran Vía de Colón and Calle Reyes Católicos, meet at Plaza Isabel La Católica. From here Calle Reyes Católicos runs southwest to Puerta Real, an important intersection, and northeast to Plaza Nueva. Cuesta de Gomérez leads northeast up from Plaza Nueva towards the Alhambra on its hilltop. The old Muslim district, the Albayzín, rambles over another hill that rises north of Plaza Nueva.

The bus station (northwest) and train station (west) are both out of the city centre but linked by buses.

Information

BOOKSHOPS

Cartográfica del Sur (☎ 958 20 49 01; Calle Valle Inclán 2; 🕒 10am-2pm & 5-8.30pm, Mon-Fri, to 1.30 Sat) Granada's best map shop, in the south of the city, just off Camino de Ronda. Wide range of high-quality Sierra Nevada, walking and trekking maps.

Metro (Map p801; ☎ 958 26 15 65; Calle de Gracia 31) Stocks an excellent range of English-language novels, guidebooks and books on Spain, plus plenty of books in French.

EMERGENCY

Policía Nacional (Map p801; ☎ 958 80 80 00; Plaza de los Campos) The most central police station.

INTERNET ACCESS

Thanks to Granada's 60,000 students, internet cafes are cheap and stay open for long hours.

Cyberlocutorio (Map p801; Puerta Elvira, Plaza del Triunfo 5; per hr €1; 🕒 9am-midnight Mon-Thu, 9am-2pm & 4pm-midnight Fri, 11am-midnight Sat, Sun & holidays)

Cyberlocutorio Alhambra (Map p801; Calle Joaquin Costa 40; per hr €1.50; 🕒 10.30am-midnight every day)

INTERNET RESOURCES

Where2 (www.where2.es) Excellent, comprehensive English-language website with information on 'Where To' eat, sleep, find entertainment or even buy property in Granada.

GRANADA

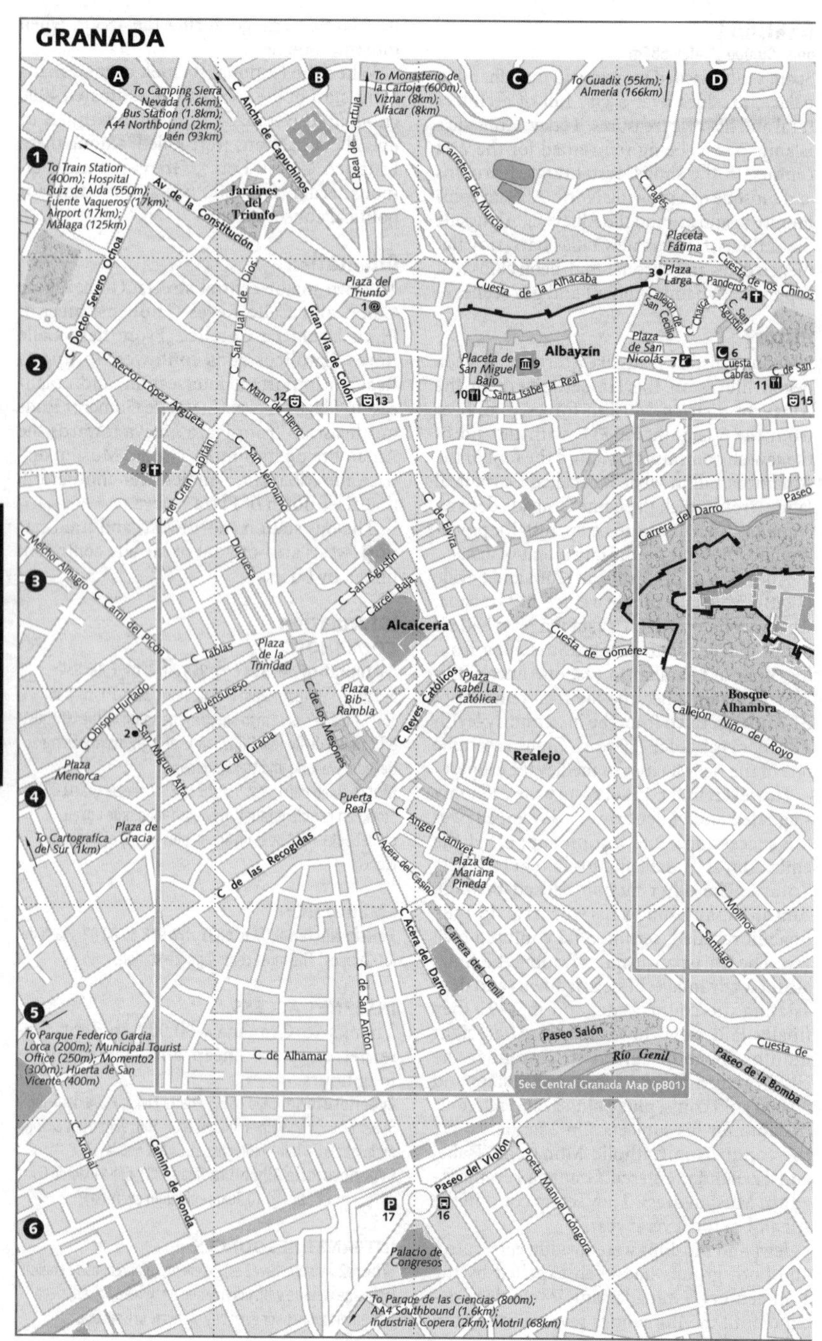

To Camping Sierra Nevada (1.6km); Bus Station (1.8km); A44 Northbound (2km); Jaén (93km)
To Monasterio de la Cartoja (600m); Víznar (8km); Alfacar (8km)
To Guadix (55km); Almería (166km)
To Train Station (400m); Hospital Ruiz de Alda (550m); Fuente Vaqueros (17km); Airport (17km); Málaga (125km)
C Ancha de Capuchinos
C Real de Cartuja
Carretera de Murcia
Jardines del Triunfo
Av de la Constitución
C Pagés
Placeta Fátima
Cuesta de los Chinos
Plaza Larga
C Panderos
Cuesta de la Alhacaba
Plaza del Triunfo
C San Juan de Dios
Gran Vía de Colón
C Doctor Severo Ochoa
Callejón de San Cecilio
C Chauca
C San Agustín
Plaza de San Nicolás
Placeta de San Miguel Bajo
Albayzín
Cuesta Cabras
C de San
C Santa Isabel la Real
C Rector López Argueta
C Mano de Hierro
C San Jerónimo
C del Gran Capitán
C de Elvira
Paseo
Carrera del Darro
C Duquesa
C Melchor Almagro
C Caril del Picón
C San Agustín
C Cárcel Baja
Alcaicería
Cuesta de Gomérez
C Tablas
Plaza de la Trinidad
Plaza Bib-Rambla
C de los Mesones
C Reyes Católicos
Plaza Isabel La Católica
Bosque Alhambra
Callejón Niño del Royo
C Buensuceso
C Obispo Hurtado
C San Miguel Alta
C de Gracia
Realejo
Plaza Menorca
Puerta Real
C Ángel Ganivet
Plaza de Gracia
To Cartografica del Sur (1km)
C Acera del Casino
Plaza de Mariana Pineda
C de las Recogidas
C Molinos
C Santiago
C Acera del Darro
Carrera del Genil
C de San Antón
To Parque Federico García Lorca (200m); Municipal Tourist Office (250m); Momento2 (300m); Huerta de San Vicente (400m)
Paseo Salón
Río Genil
C de Alhamar
See Central Granada Map (p801)
Cuesta de
Paseo de la Bomba
C Arabial
Camino de Ronda
Paseo del Violón
C Poeta Manuel Góngora
Palacio de Congresos
To Parque de las Ciencias (800m); AA4 Southbound (1.6km); Industrial Copera (2km); Motril (68km)

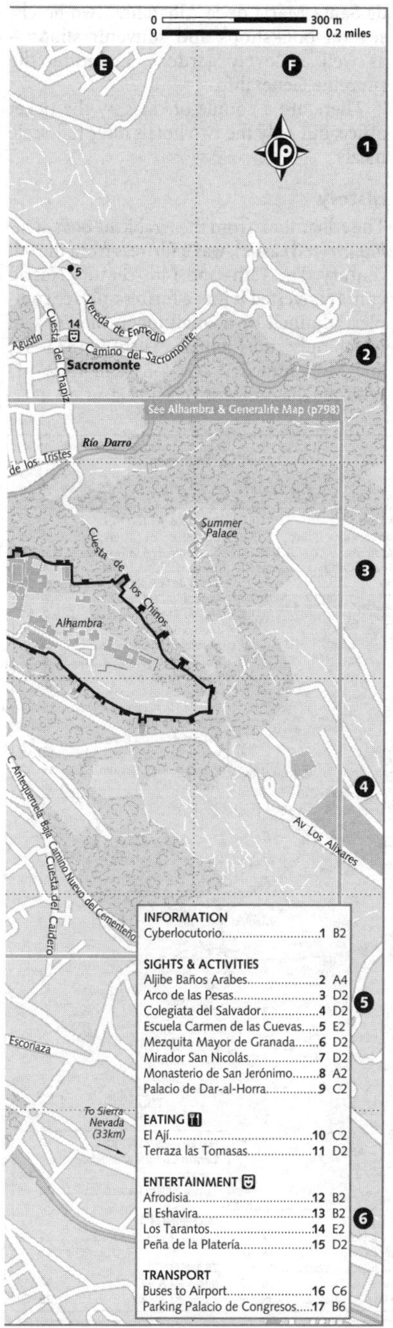

Turismo de Granada (www.turismodegranada.org) Good website of the provincial tourist office, although deeper layers of information are sketchy.

MEDIA

Where2 Magazine Excellent free English-language pocket guide to Granada, published bi-monthly. Where2 is stuffed with information on 'where to' indulge your eyes, ears and taste buds in Granada. It's available at tourist offices and at major sights.

MEDICAL SERVICES

Hospital Ruiz de Alda (☎ 958 02 00 09, 958 24 11 00; Avenida de la Constitución 100) Central, with good emergency facilities.

MONEY

There are plenty of banks and ATMs on Gran Vía de Colón, Plaza Isabel La Católica and Calle Reyes Católicos.

POST

Post office (Map p801; Puerta Real s/n; 🕑 8.30am-8.30pm Mon-Fri, 9.30am-2pm Sat) Often has long queues.

TOURIST INFORMATION

Provincial tourist office (Map p801; ☎ 958 24 71 28; www.turismodegranada.org; Plaza de Mariana Pineda 10; 🕑 9am-8pm Mon-Fri, 10am-2pm & 4-7pm Sat, 10am-3pm Sun May-Sep, 9am-8pm Mon-Fri, 10am-1pm Sat, to 3pm Sun Nov-Apr) Helpful staff with information on the whole Granada region; a short walk east of Puerta Real.

Regional tourist office Plaza Nueva (Map p801; ☎ 958 22 10 22; Calle Santa Ana 1; 🕑 9am-7.30pm Mon-Sat, 9.30am-3pm Sun & holidays); Alhambra (Map p798; ☎ 958 22 95 75; ticket-office bldg, Avenida del Generalife s/n; 🕑 8am-7.30pm Mon-Fri, to 2pm & 4-7.30pm Sat & Sun, closes at 6pm Nov-Feb, 9am-1pm holidays) Information on all of Andalucía.

Municipal tourist office (Map pp796-7; ☎ 958 22 52 17; www.granadatur.com; Calle Almona del Campillo, 2; 🕑 9am-7pm Mon-Fri, to 6pm Sat, 10am-2pm Sun, holidays) Sleek, efficient centre opposite the city's Parque Federico Garcia Lorca.

Sights & Activities

Most major sights are within walking distance of the city centre, though there are buses to save you walking uphill.

ALHAMBRA

Stretched along the top of the hill known as La Sabika, the **Alhambra** (Map p798; ☎ 902 441221;

Advance ticket purchase: www.alhambra-tickets.es & www.servicaixa.com, €13; adult/EU senior/EU student €12/9/9, disabled & under 8yr free, Generalife only €6; 8.30am-8pm Mar-Oct, to 6pm Nov-Feb, closed 25 Dec & 1 Jan) is the stuff of fairy tales. From outside, its red fortress towers and walls appear plain, if imposing, rising from woods of cypress and elm, with the Sierra Nevada forming a magnificent backdrop.

Try to visit first thing in the morning (8.30am) or late in the afternoon to avoid the crowds, or treat yourself to a magical night by visiting the Palacio Nazaríes (opposite for details).

The Alhambra contains two outstanding sets of buildings: the Palacio Nazaríes and the Alcazaba (Citadel). Also within its walls you'll find the Palacio de Carlos V, the Iglesia de Santa María de la Alhambra, two hotels, several bookshops and souvenir shops – as well as lovely gardens, including the supreme Generalife.

There are a couple of cafes by the ticket office, but only the two hotels offer full-scale meals.

History

The Alhambra, from the Arabic *al-qala'at al-hamra* (red castle), was a fortress from the 9th century. The 13th- and 14th-century Nasrid emirs converted it into a fortress-palace complex adjoined by a small town *(medina)*, of which only ruins remain. Yusuf I (1333–54) and Mohammed V (1354–59 and 1362–91) built the magnificent Palacio Nazaríes.

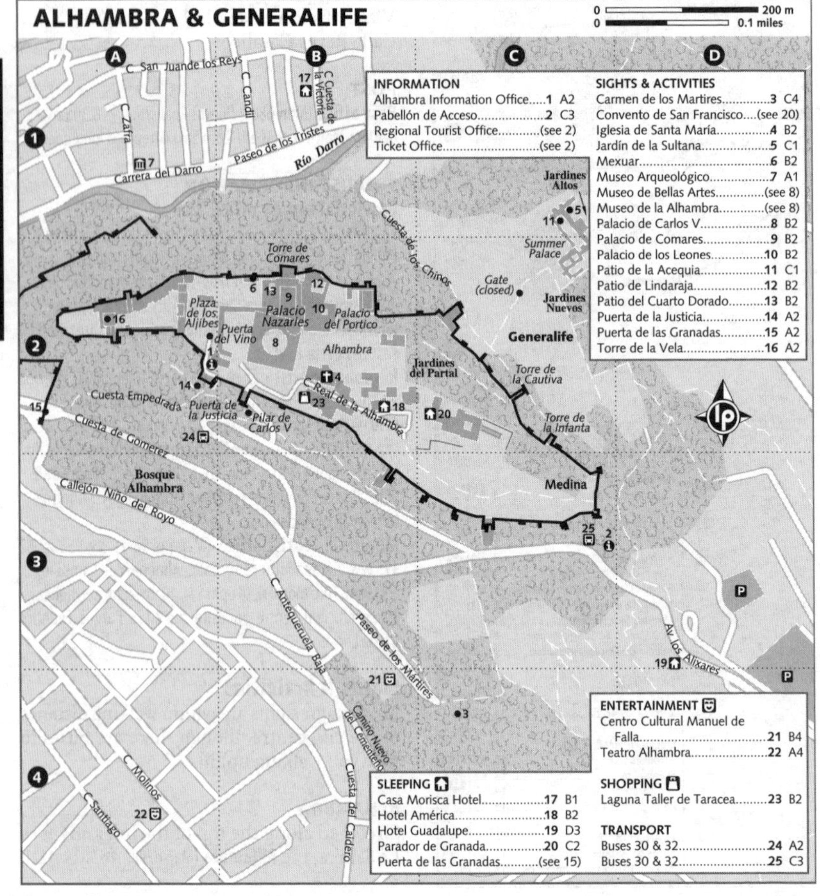

After the Christian conquest the Alhambra's mosque was replaced with a church and the Convento de San Francisco (now the Parador de Granada) was built. Carlos I, grandson of Isabel I and Fernando II, had a wing of the Palacio Nazaríes destroyed to make space for a huge Renaissance palace, the Palacio de Carlos V (using his title as Holy Roman Emperor).

In the 18th century the Alhambra was abandoned to thieves and beggars. During the Napoleonic occupation it was used as a barracks and narrowly escaped being blown up. In 1870 it was declared a national monument as a result of the huge interest stirred by Romantic writers such as Washington Irving, who wrote the entrancing *Tales of the Alhambra* in the Palacio Nazaríes during his brief stay in the 1820s. Since then the Alhambra has been salvaged and very heavily restored. Together with the Generalife gardens and the Albayzín, it now enjoys Unesco World Heritage status.

Admission

Some areas of the Alhambra can be visited at any time without a ticket, but the highlight areas can be entered only with a ticket. Up to 6600 tickets are available for each day. At least 2000 of these are sold at the ticket office on the day, but in Easter week, June, July, August and September these sell out early and you need to start queuing by 7am to be reasonably sure of getting one.

It's highly advisable to book in advance (€1 extra per ticket). You can book up to a year ahead in two ways:

Alhambra Advance Booking (☎ 902 88 80 01 for national calls, 0034 934 92 37 50 for international calls; 🕑 8am-9pm every day)

Servicaixa (www.servicaixa.com). Online booking in Spanish and English. You can also buy tickets in advance from Servicaixa cash machines, but only in the Alhambra grounds (🕑 8am-7pm Mar-Oct, 8am-5pm Nov-Feb)

For internet or phone bookings you need a Visa card, MasterCard or Eurocard. You receive a reference number, which you must show, along with your passport, national identity card or credit card, at the Alhambra ticket office when you pick up the ticket on the day of your visit.

Every ticket is stamped with a half-hour time slot for entry to the Palacio Nazaríes. Once inside the *palacio,* you can stay as long as you like. Each ticket is also either a *billete de mañana* (morning ticket), valid for entry to the Generalife or Alcazaba from 8.30am until 2pm, or a *billete de tarde,* for entry after 2pm.

The Palacio Nazaríes is also open for **night visits** (🕑 10pm-11.30pm Tue-Sat Mar-Oct, 8pm-9.30pm Fri & Sat Nov-Feb). Tickets cost the same as daytime tickets: the ticket office opens 30 minutes before the palace's opening time, closing 30 minutes after it. You can book ahead for night visits in the same ways as for day visits.

Alcazaba

The ramparts and several towers are all that remain of the citadel. The most important is the **Torre de la Vela** (Watchtower), with a winding staircase to its top terrace, which has splendid views. The cross and banners of the Reconquista were raised here in January 1492. In the past the tower's bell chimes controlled the irrigation system of Granada's fertile plain, the Vega.

Palacio Nazaríes

This is the Alhambra's true gem, the most brilliant Islamic building in Europe, with its perfectly proportioned rooms and courtyards, intricately moulded stucco walls, beautiful tiling, fine carved wooden ceilings and elaborate stalactite-like *muqarnas* vaulting, all worked in mesmerising, symbolic, geometrical patterns. Arabic inscriptions proliferate in the stuccowork.

The **Mexuar**, through which you normally enter the palace, dates from the 14th century and was used as a council chamber and antechamber for audiences with the emir. The public would have gone no further.

From the Mexuar you pass into the **Patio del Cuarto Dorado**, a courtyard where the emirs gave audiences, with the **Cuarto Dorado** (Golden Room) on the left. Opposite the Cuarto Dorado is the entrance to the Palacio de Comares through a beautiful facade of glazed tiles, stucco and carved wood.

Built for Emir Yusuf I, the **Palacio de Comares** served as a private residence for the ruler. It's built around the lovely **Patio de los Arrayanes** (Patio of the Myrtles) with its rectangular pool. The southern end of the patio is overshadowed by the walls of the Palacio de Carlos V. Inside the northern **Torre de Comares** (Comares Tower), the **Sala de la Barca** (Hall of the Blessing), with a beautiful wooden ceiling, leads into the **Salón de Comares** (Comares Hall), where the emirs would have conducted negotiations with Christian emissaries. This room's marvellous domed marquetry ceiling contains more than 8000 cedar pieces in a pattern of stars representing the seven heavens of Islam.

The Patio de los Arrayanes leads into the **Palacio de los Leones** (Palace of the Lions), built under Mohammed V – by some accounts as the royal harem. The palace rooms surround the famous **Patio de los Leones** (Lion Courtyard), with its marble fountain channelling water through the mouths of 12 marble lions. The palace symbolises the Islamic paradise, which is divided into four parts by rivers (represented by water channels meeting at the fountain). Of the four halls around the patio, the southern **Sala de los Abencerrajes** is the legendary site of the murders of the noble Abencerraj family, whose leader, the story goes, dared to dally with Zoraya, Abu al-Hasan's favourite. At the eastern end of the patio is the **Sala de los Reyes** (Hall of the Kings), with leather-lined ceilings painted by 14th-century Christian artists. The name comes from the painting on the central alcove, thought to depict 10 Nasrid emirs. On the northern side of the patio is the richly decorated **Sala de Dos Hermanas** (Hall of Two Sisters), probably named after the slabs of white marble at either side of its fountain. It features a fantastic *muqarnas* dome with a central star and 5000 tiny cells, reminiscent of the constellations. This may have been the room of the emir's favourite paramour. At its far end is the **Sala de los Ajimeces**, with low-slung windows through which the favoured lady could look over the Albayzín and countryside while reclining on ottomans and cushions.

From the Sala de Dos Hermanas a passage leads through the **Estancias del Emperador** (Emperor's Chambers), built for Carlos I in the 1520s, some of them later used by Washington Irving. From here, descend to the **Patio de la Reja** (Patio of the Grille) and **Patio de Lindaraja** and emerge into the **Jardines del Partal**, an area of terraced gardens. Leave the Partal gardens by a gate facing the Palacio de Carlos V, or continue along a path to the Generalife.

Palacio de Carlos V

This huge Renaissance palace was begun in 1527 by Pedro Machuca, a Toledo architect, and was never completed. The imposing building is square but contains a surprising circular, two-tiered courtyard with 32 columns. Were the palace in a different setting, its merits might be more readily appreciated.

On the ground floor, the **Museo de la Alhambra** (☎ 958 22 75 27; admission free; ⏰ 9am-2.30pm Tue-Sat) has an absorbing collection of Islamic artefacts from the Alhambra, Granada province and Córdoba, with explanatory texts in English and Spanish.

Upstairs, the **Museo de Bellas Artes** (☎ 958 22 48 43; admission, adults/EU €1.50/free; ⏰ 2.30-8pm Tue, 9am-8pm Wed-Sat, 9am-2.30pm Sun & holidays Mar-Oct, 2.30-6pm Tue, 9am-6pm Wed-Sat, 9am-2.30pm Sun & holidays Nov-Feb) is worth a visit for its impressive collection of Granada-related paintings and sculptures.

Other Christian Buildings

The **Iglesia de Santa María** was built between 1581 and 1617 on the site of the former palace mosque. The **Convento de San Francisco**, now the Parador de Granada hotel (p806), was erected over an Islamic palace. Isabel and Fernando were buried in the patio before being transferred to the Capilla Real (p802).

Generalife

The name Generalife means 'Architect's Garden'. It's the perfect place to end an Alhambra visit. The Muslim rulers' summer palace is in the corner furthest from the entrance. Within the palace, the **Patio de la Acequia** (Court of the Water Channel) has a long pool framed by flowerbeds and 19th-century fountains, whose shapes sensuously echo the arched porticos at each end. Off this patio is the **Jardín de la Sultana** (Sultana's Garden), with the trunk of a 700-year-old cypress tree, where Abu al-Hasan supposedly caught his lover, Zoraya, with the head of the Abencerraj clan, leading to the murders in the Sala de los Abencerrajes.

Getting There & Away

Buses 30 and 32 (€1.10) both run between Plaza Nueva and the Alhambra ticket office every five to nine minutes from 7.15am to 11pm.

If you opt to walk up Cuesta de Gomérez from Plaza Nueva you soon reach the **Puerta de las Granadas** (Gate of the Pomegranates), built by Carlos I. Above this are the Bosque Alhambra woods. If you already have your Alhambra ticket, you can climb the Cuesta Empedrada path up to the left and pass through the austere **Puerta de la Justicia** (Gate of Justice), constructed in 1348 as the Alhambra's main entrance.

If you need to go to the ticket office, in the **Pabellón de Acceso** (Access Pavilion), continue on for about 900m from the Puerta de las

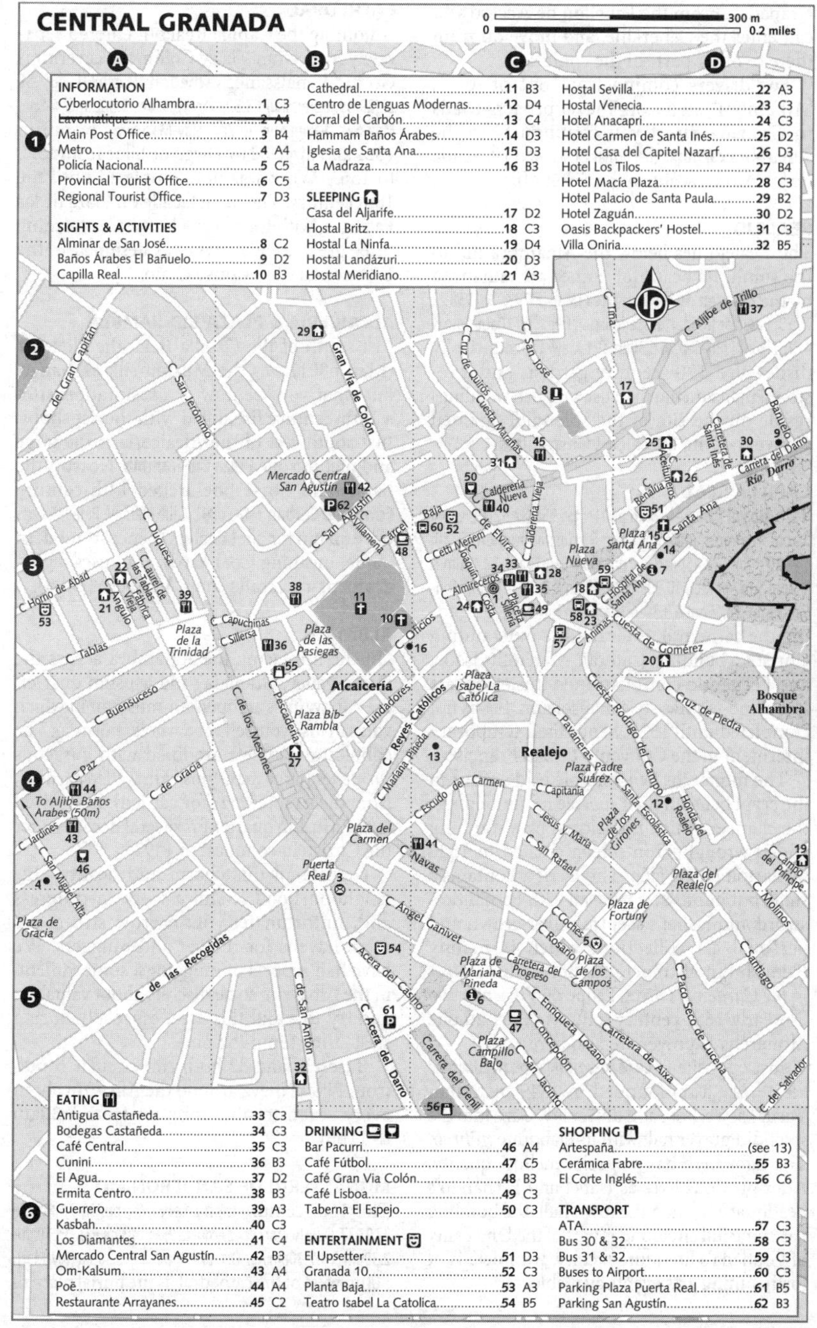
CENTRAL GRANADA
0 300 m
0 0.2 miles
A
B
C
D
1
2
3
4
5
6
INFORMATION
Cyberlocutorio Alhambra 1 C3
~~Lavomatique 2 A4~~
Main Post Office 3 B4
Metro 4 A4
Policía Nacional 5 C5
Provincial Tourist Office 6 C5
Regional Tourist Office 7 D3
SIGHTS & ACTIVITIES
Alminar de San José 8 C2
Baños Árabes El Bañuelo 9 D2
Capilla Real 10 B3
Cathedral 11 B3
Centro de Lenguas Modernas 12 D4
Corral del Carbón 13 C4
Hammam Baños Árabes 14 D3
Iglesia de Santa Ana 15 D3
La Madraza 16 B3
SLEEPING
Casa del Aljarife 17 D2
Hostal Britz 18 C3
Hostal La Ninfa 19 D4
Hostal Landázuri 20 D3
Hostal Meridiano 21 A3
Hostal Sevilla 22 A3
Hostal Venecia 23 C3
Hotel Anacapri 24 C3
Hotel Carmen de Santa Inés 25 D2
Hotel Casa del Capitel Nazarí 26 D3
Hotel Los Tilos 27 B4
Hotel Macía Plaza 28 C3
Hotel Palacio de Santa Paula 29 B2
Hotel Zaguán 30 D2
Oasis Backpackers' Hostel 31 C3
Villa Oniria 32 B5
EATING
Antigua Castañeda 33 C3
Bodegas Castañeda 34 C3
Café Central 35 C3
Cunini 36 B3
El Agua 37 D2
Ermita Centro 38 B3
Guerrero 39 A3
Kasbah 40 C3
Los Diamantes 41 C4
Mercado Central San Agustín 42 B3
Om-Kalsum 43 A4
Poë 44 A4
Restaurante Arrayanes 45 C2
DRINKING
Bar Pacurri 46 A4
Café Fútbol 47 C5
Café Gran Via Colón 48 B3
Café Lisboa 49 C3
Taberna El Espejo 50 C3
ENTERTAINMENT
El Upsetter 51 D3
Granada 10 52 C3
Planta Baja 53 A3
Teatro Isabel La Catolica 54 B5
SHOPPING
Artespaña (see 13)
Cerámica Fabre 55 B3
El Corte Inglés 56 C6
TRANSPORT
ATA 57 C3
Bus 30 & 32 58 C3
Bus 31 & 32 59 C3
Buses to Airport 60 C3
Parking Plaza Puerta Real 61 B5
Parking San Agustín 62 B3
Gran Vía de Colón
Mercado Central San Agustín
Plaza de la Trinidad
Plaza de las Pasiegas
Alcaicería
Plaza Bib-Rambla
Plaza Isabel La Católica
Plaza Nueva
Plaza Santa Ana
Río Darro
Bosque Alhambra
Realejo
Plaza Padre Suárez
Plaza de los Girones
Plaza del Realejo
Plaza de Fortuny
Plaza del Carmen
Puerta Real
Plaza de Gracia
To Aljibe Baños Arabes (50m)
Plaza de Mariana Pineda
Plaza de los Campos
Plaza Campillo Bajo
C de las Recogidas
C Reyes Católicos
C del Gran Capitán
C San Jerónimo
C Duquesa
C Tablas
C Buensuceso
C de Gracia
C San Antón
C Acera del Darro
C Acera del Casino
C Ángel Ganivet
Carrera del Genil
Carretera de Aixa
Cuesta de Gomérez
C Cruz de Piedra
Cuesta Rodrigo del Campo
C Santa Ana
Carrera del Darro
C Elvira
C San José
C Tina
C Aljibe de Trillo
C Paco Seco de Lucena
C Santiago
C Molinos
C Campo del Príncipe
ANDALUCÍA

Granadas. From the Pabellón de Acceso you can enter the Generalife, and move on from there to other parts of the complex.

For drivers coming from out of town, 'Alhambra' signs on the approach roads to Granada direct you circuitously to the Alhambra **car parks** (per hr/day €1.40/14) on Avenida de los Alixares, above the ticket office.

REALEJO

The Realejo lies below the Alhambra hill to the south. Its beautiful homes are enhanced by the **Carmen de los Martires** (Map pp798; ☎ 958 22 79 53; Paseo de los Martires; admission free; 🕑 10am-1pm & 4.30-7.30pm Jun-Sep, to 6.30pm Oct-May) Romantically dishevelled 19th-century gardens and a restored mansion much in use for posh weddings reside on the site of the splendidly named Convent of the Discalced Carmelites.

CAPILLA REAL

The **Royal Chapel** (Map p801; ☎ 958 22 92 39; www.capillareal.granada.com; Calle Oficios; admission €3.50; 🕑 10.30am-12.45pm & 4-7pm Mon-Sat, 11am-12.45pm & 4-7pm Sun Apr-Oct, 10.30am-12.45pm & 3.30-6.15pm Mon-Sat, 11am-12.45pm & 3.30-6.15pm Sun Nov-Mar), adjoining the cathedral, is Granada's outstanding Christian building. Catholic Monarchs Isabel and Fernando commissioned this elaborate Isabelline-Gothic-style mausoleum. It was not completed until 1521, hence their temporary interment in the Convento de San Francisco.

The monarchs lie in simple lead coffins in the crypt beneath their marble monuments in the chancel, which is enclosed by a stunning gilded wrought-iron screen created in 1520 by Bartolomé de Jaén. The sacristy contains a small but impressive **museum** with Fernando's sword and Isabel's sceptre, silver crown and personal art collection, which is mainly Flemish but also includes Botticelli's *Prayer in the Garden of Olives*. Felipe de Vigarni's two fine early-16th-century statues of the Catholic Monarchs at prayer are also here.

Just opposite is **La Madraza** (Map p801; admission free; 🕑 8am-10pm) founded in 1349 by Sultan Yusuf I as a school and university. Gaze into the splendid prayer hall with its elaborate *mihrab*. The light here has a special mellow quality. After previous lives as Isabel and Fernando's headquarters, then the town hall, the building has come full circle and is part of the University of Granada's literature faculty, with details of forthcoming arts events available.

CATHEDRAL

Adjoining the Capilla Real but entered separately from Gran Vía de Colón, the cavernous Gothic-Renaissance **cathedral** (Map p801; ☎ 958 22 29 59; admission €3.50; 🕑 10.45am-1.30pm & 4-8pm Mon-Sat, 4-8pm Sun, to 7pm Nov-Mar) was begun in 1521 and directed by Diego de Siloé from 1528 to 1563. Work was not completed until the 18th century. The main facade on Plaza de las Pasiegas, with four heavy buttresses forming three great arched bays, was designed in the 17th century by Alonso Cano.

ALCAICERÍA & PLAZA BIB-RAMBLA

Just south of the Capilla Real, the **Alcaicería** (Map p801) was the Muslim silk exchange, but what you see now is a restoration after a 19th-century fire, filled with tourist shops. Just southwest of the Alcaicería is the large and picturesque **Plaza Bib-Rambla**. Nearby, the handsome, horseshoe-arched 14th-century **Corral del Carbon** (Map p801; Calle Mariana Pineda) was once an inn for coal dealers (hence its modern name, meaning Coal Yard). It houses a government-run crafts shop, **Artespaña** (p808).

ALBAYZÍN

On the hill facing the Alhambra across the Darro valley, Granada's old Muslim quarter, the Albayzín, is an open-air museum in which you can lose yourself for a whole morning. The cobblestone streets are lined with gorgeous *cármenes* (large mansions with walled gardens, from the Arabic *karm* for garden). It survived as the Muslim quarter for several decades after the Christian conquest in 1492.

Despite all this charm and beauty, this neighbourhood is still a work-in-progress and, unfortunately, its narrow streets are often havens for thieves and muggers. We have had reports of muggings, some violent, in the Albayzín, so be discreet about valuables and try to avoid this area, especially during siesta time (3pm to 5pm).

Buses 31 and 32 both run circular routes from Plaza Nueva around the Albayzín about every seven to nine minutes from 7.30am to 11pm.

MONASTERIO DE SAN JERÓNIMO

This 16th-century **monastery** (Map pp796-7; ☎ 958 27 93 37; Calle Rector López Argueta 9; admission €3; 🕑 10am-2.30pm & 4-7.30pm Apr-Oct, to 2.30pm & 3-6.30pm Nov-Mar), 500m west of the cathedral, is the burial place of

THE BIG POMEGRANATE

Dark-haired and boyishly handsome, Lorenzo Vera Franco breaks off every few minutes to exchange greetings with friends passing our table. We are chatting over glasses of chilled *Rueda* (white wine) at trendy Ermita Centro (p807) in Plaza Romanilla. A network of gay and straight friends is just one of the changes Lorenzo appreciates in the 14 years he has lived here. 'I came to university here in 1994 from Miranda de Ebro in Burgos to do medieval Arab studies, but also to get away from being a gay guy in a small city,' he says. 'Granada had two gay clubs then – private, you had to ring the bell – but today I'd say it's the gay capital of Andalucía.' Back then, the city lived up to its reputation for dour conservatism. 'Then in the late 1990s the council started a major campaign to clean up the city, and plant trees and flowers everywhere.' Literally and figuratively, says Lorenzo, Granada has been blooming ever since.

During the week, Lorenzo works as personal assistant and event organiser for the head of Granada's local government body, the Diputación de Granada. The job has enabled him to buy and start restoring a 1930s house in San Miguel Bajo in the Albayzin, which together with the city's Realejo neighbourhood, on the southern flank of the Alhambra hill, is home to a significant number of Granada's gay community.

Weekends are for rest and relaxation, though there are plenty of arts events to attend, especially during university term time. 'This city's biorhythms are ruled by the university year, even more than by the tourist season,' says Lorenzo. But these days, summer is busy too. The increasingly popular Festival de Musica y Danza (www.granadafestival.org) takes place mid-June.

Saturdays begin in or around Plaza Larga in the heart of the Albayzin, with *churros* (freshly deep-fried doughnut) dunked in thick creamy cocoa. 'Then, if friends are staying, we might go to the Alhambra – again! But really, the light is always changing with the seasons; it's different every time.'

Saturday nights offer an ever wider range of hip gay bars, though these days Lorenzo prefers to meet friends at just a few favourite places. He might start the evening at Taberna El Espejo (p807) a small, artsy bar where he feels very much at home.

Lorenzo loves to spend Sundays out of doors whenever he can, especially in Granada's mild spring and autumn days. 'Mornings, I often take my book and a picnic to the Carmen de los Martires (opposite). I feel at home here.'

'On Sunday evening, everyone in this town seems to go to the movies. Because of the university we get really good independent movies here. And around mid-June we have the Cines del Sur film festival here (www.cinesdelsur.com).

'I love Granada as a gay city, but there are cliques. Here in the Albayzin, though, it's different. Everybody knows your name. Some weekends we don't even bother going to the centre, we just hang out here. In fact, the old people who have lived here all their lives say, "I'm going to Granada" as though it were another city altogether.'

El Gran Capitán (the Great Captain), Gonzalo Fernández de Córdoba, the military right-hand man of the Catholic Monarchs. It's a treat for fans of Gothic and Renaissance architecture and stone carving. The formal gardens are as beautiful in winter as in summer.

MONASTERIO DE LA CARTUJA

Another architectural gem stands 2km northwest of the city centre, reached by bus 8 from Gran Vía de Colón. **La Cartuja Monastery** (☎ 958 16 19 32; Paseo de la Cartuja; admission €3.50; 🕒 10am-1pm & 4-8pm every day Apr-Oct, to 1pm & 3-6pm Nov-Mar) was built between the 16th and 18th centuries and features a church bursting with gold, marble and sculptures and an exuberantly baroque sacristy.

HUERTA DE SAN VICENTE

This **house** (☎ 958 25 84 66; Calle Virgen Blanca s/n; admission €3, free Wed) where Federico García Lorca spent summers and wrote some of his best-known works, is a 15-minute walk south of the city centre, though it still retains the evocative aura of an early 20th-century country villa. Today the modern but handsome **Parque Federico García Lorca** separates it from whizzing traffic.

To get there, head 700m down Calle de las Recogidas from Puerta Real, turn right along Calle del Arabial, then take the first left into Calle Virgen Blanca.

Walking Tour

Plaza Nueva extends northeast into Plaza de Santa Ana, where the **Iglesia de Santa Ana (1)** incorporates a mosque's minaret in its belltower. Along narrow Carrera del Darro, stop by the 11th-century Muslim bathhouse, the **Baños Árabes El Bañuelo** (**2**; ☎ 958 22 97 38; Carrera del Darro 31; admission free; ⏰ 10am-2pm Tue-Sat). Further along is the **Museo Arqueológico** (**3**; Archaeological Museum; ☎ 958 22 56 03; Carrera del Darro 43; adult/EU citizen €1.50/free; ⏰ 2.30-8.30pm Tue, 9.30am-8.30pm Wed-Sat, to 2.30pm Sun), displaying finds from Granada province.

Shortly past the museum, Carrera del Darro becomes Paseo de los Tristes. Turn up Calle Candil and climb, via Placeta de Toqueros and Carril de San Agustín, to Plaza del Salvador, near the top of the Albayzín. Plaza del Salvador is dominated by the **Colegiata del Salvador** (**4**; ☎ 958 27 86 44; admission €0.75; ⏰ 10.30am-1pm & 4.30pm-7.30pm Mon-Sat, Apr-Oct, 10.30am-1pm & 4.30-7.30pm Mon-Sat Nov-Mar), a 16th-century church on the site of the Albayzín's main mosque; the mosque's horseshoe-arched patio, cool and peaceful, survives at its western end. From here head west to Plaza Larga and through the **Arco de las Pesas (5)**, an impressive gateway in the Albayzín's 11th-century defensive wall. Callejón de San Cecilio leads to the **Mirador San Nicolás (6)**, a lookout with unbeatable views of the Alhambra and Sierra Nevada. Come back here later for sunset (you can't miss the trail then!). At any time of day take care: skilful, well-organised wallet-lifters and bag-snatchers operate here.

Just east of Mirador San Nicolás, off Cuesta de las Cabras, the Albayzín's first new mosque in 500 years, the **Mezquita Mayor de Granada** (**7**; ☎ 958 20 23 31; ⏰ gardens 11am-2pm & 6-9.30pm) has been built to serve modern Granada's growing Muslim population.

Return to the lookout, take the steps down beside it and follow the street down to Camino Nuevo de San Nicolás. Turn right and head downhill to **Placeta de San Miguel Bajo (8)**, with its lively cafe-restaurants. Leave the square by Callejón del Gallo, turn right at the end of this short lane, and you'll come to the 15th-century **Palacio de Dar-al-Horra** (**9**; Callejón de las Monjas s/n; admission free; ⏰ 10am-2pm Mon-Fri), a romantically dishevelled mini-Alhambra that was home to the mother of Boabdil, Granada's last Muslim ruler.

Return to Placeta de San Miguel Bajo and head down Placeta Cauchiles de San Miguel, which becomes Calle San José, where the lovely **Alminar de San José** (**10**; San José Minaret) survives from an 11th-century mosque. Calle San José meets the top of **Calle Calderería Nueva (11)**, which is lined with *teterías* (Middle Eastern–style teahouses serving a rainbow of tea flavours and tiny, sugar-enamelled pastries) and shops brimming with slippers, hookahs, jewellery and North African pottery. Stop for a Moroccan mint tea, or head back to Plaza Nueva.

WALK FACTS

Start/Finish Plaza Nueva
Distance 5.5km
Duration four to five hours including stops

WALKING TOUR

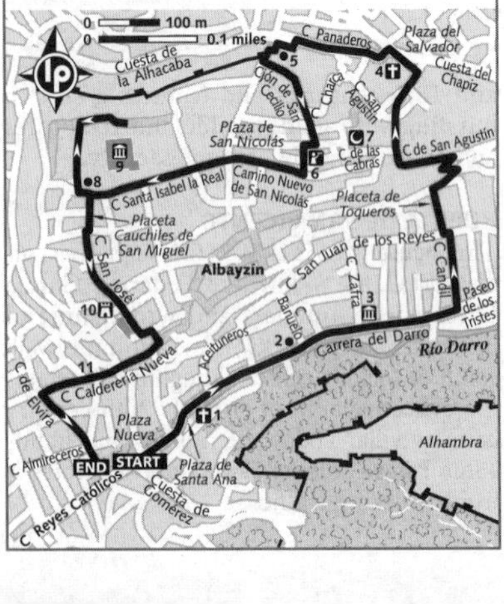

Courses

Granada is a great place to study Spanish. It also has several Spanish dance schools. The provincial tourist office has lists of schools, or check out www.granadaspanish.org and www.spanishc ourses.info.

Centro de Lenguas Modernas (Modern Languages Centre; Map p801; ☎ 958 21 56 60; www.clm-granada.com; Placeta del Hospicio Viejo s/n) Granada University's modern-language department offers a variety of popular Spanish-language courses, at all levels, starting from 10 days (40 hours of classes) for €346.

ANDALUCÍA

HAMMAMS

Granada has two *baños Árabes* (Arabic baths), and a visit to one of these is a must for the sheer lazy pleasure of it. Both baths offer a bath and aromatherapy massage that lasts for two hours (bath 1 hour 45 minutes, massage 15 minutes), and both need advance reservations. Swimwear is obligatory (you can rent it), towels are provided and all sessions are mixed. The better of the pair is **Aljibe Baños Árabes** (Map p801; ☎ 958 52 28 67; www.aljibesanmiguel.es; Calle San Miguel Alta 41; bath/bath & massage €15/22). **Hammam Baños Árabes** (Map p801; ☎ 958 22 99 78; www.hammamspain.com/granada in Spanish; Calle Santa Ana 16; bath/bath & massage €16/25) is older and smaller.

Escuela Carmen de las Cuevas (Map pp796-7; ☎ 958 22 10 62; www.carmencuevas.com; Cuesta de los Chinos 15, Albayzin) This private school attracts students from as far away as the United States, and no wonder. The passion and enthusiasm of staff and students is extraordinary. The school teaches Spanish language and culture, and flamenco dance and guitar from beginners to advanced. A two-week intensive language course (40 hours) costs €300.

Tours

Granavisión (☎ 902 33 00 02) Offers guided tours of the Alhambra and Generalife (€49) and Historic Granada tours (€48). Phone direct or book through a travel agent.

City Sightseeing Granada (☎ 902 10 10 81) Operates Granada's double-decker city tour bus. It has 20 stops outside the main sights. Hop on and off where you like; the ticket (€15) is valid for 24 hours.

Granada Tapas Tours (☎ 619 444984; www.granadapastours.com). Friendly and fluent in both Scots and Spanish, your guide will steer you to independently chosen favourite bars for drinks, tapas and information about the city, starting at around €65 for two including drinks and tapas.

Festivals & Events

Semana Santa (Holy Week) This and the Feria de Corpus Christi are the big two. Benches are set up in Plaza del Carmen to view the Semana Santa processions.

Día de la Cruz (Day of the Cross) Squares, patios and balconies are adorned with floral crosses (the Cruces de Mayo) and become the setting for typical *andaluz* revelry on 3 May.

Feria de Corpus Christi (Corpus Christi Fair) Fairgrounds, bullfights, more drinking and *sevillanas*. Next celebrated 11 June 2009, 3 June 2010.

Festival Internacional de Música y Danza (www.granadafestival.org) Running for 2½ weeks from late June to early July, this festival features mainly classical performances, some free, many in historic locations. Explore the website early as popular performances are sold out very quickly.

Granada for Children

With four buildings and eight interactive exhibition areas, Granada's popular **Parque de las Ciencias** (☎ 958 13 19 00; www.parqueciencias.com; Avenida del Mediterráneo s/n; admission adult/under 18 €4.50/3.50; 🕑 10am-7pm Tue-Sat, 10am-3pm Sun & holidays) should keep the kids happily absorbed for hours. Playing giant chess or threading the Plant Labyrinth are just two activities they can do here. It's about 900 metres south of the centre, near the Palacio de Congresos conference centre.

If even less intellectual exertion is called for, then **Parque Federico Garcia Lorca** (p803) offers refreshing, flat open space for both children and parents. The park abounds in broad paved paths and is also a great place to study *granadinos* at leisure.

Sleeping

Granada is almost oversupplied with hotels, however, it's definitely worthwhile booking ahead from March to October, and especially during Semana Santa and Christmas.

BUDGET

At busy times, prime-location rooms tend to fill up before noon, especially on Cuesta de Gomérez.

Camping Sierra Nevada (☎ 958 15 00 62; Avenida de Madrid 107; per adult/child/tent/car €5.70/4.85/5.70/5.75; ♿) Close to the bus station, 2.5km northwest of the centre, this camping ground is big, jolly and well run. Bathrooms are plain and clean, and there is a laundrette. Gates close at midnight and reopen at 7.00am. Bus 3 runs between here and the centre.

Hostal Venecia (Map p801; ☎ 958 22 39 87; Cuesta de Gomérez 2; r €32, s/d/tr/q without bathroom €19/30/53/60) A lovely *hostal* with friendly hosts and flower-and-picture-filled turquoise corridors, just off Plaza Nueva.

Hostal Britz (Map p801; ☎ /fax 958 22 36 52; Cuesta de Gomérez 1; s/d €25/35, s/d without bathroom €32/46) The friendly, efficient Britz has 22 clean, functional rooms with double glazing, gleaming wooden surfaces and central heating. There's also a lift.

Oasis Backpackers' Hostel (Map p801; ☎ 958 21 58 48; www.oasisgranada.com; Placeta Correo Viejo 3; dm €18, d €40;) Seconds away from the Caldererías and bars on Calle Elvira. There's free internet access, a rooftop terrace and personal safes. The location is tricky – best to walk up Caldereria Nueva, then left down narrow Calle Correo Viejo into the *placeta* itself.

Hostal Landázuri (Map p801; ☎ /fax 958 22 14 06; Cuesta de Gomérez 24; s/d €36/45, s/d without bathroom €24/34, t €60, q €70; P €10) This homely place boasts a terrace with Alhambra views, a cafe and a helpful mother-daughter team.

Hostal Sevilla (Map p801; ☎ 958 27 85 13; Calle Fábrica Vieja 18; hostalsevilla@telefonica.net; s/d €27/38, without bathroom €22/31; P) The friendly, clean Sevilla, run by a young couple, has pretty tiles and lampshades; there's a great, large attic double.

Hostal Meridiano (Map p801; ☎ /fax 958 25 05 44; www.hostalpensionmeridiano.com; Calle Angulo 9; r €38, s/d without bathroom €18/32, 4-/6-person apt €35/40; P) The energetic couple who run this hostal seem to genuinely like helping their guests.

ANDALUCÍA

MIDRANGE

Hostal La Ninfa (Map p801; ☎ 958 22 79 85; Calle Campo del Príncipe s/n; s/d €46/70;) A rustic place covered inside and out with brightly painted ceramic stars and plates. It has clean, cosy rooms, friendly owners and an attractive breakfast room.

Puerta de las Granadas (Map p801; ☎ 958 21 62 30; www.hotelpuertadelasgranadas.com; Calle Cuesta de Gomérez 14; s/d €77/99, superior r €107-80;) This 19th-century building, renovated in modern-minimalist style, has wooden shutters and elegant furnishings

Hotel América (Map p798; ☎ 958 22 74 71; www.hotelamericagranada.com; Calle Real de la Alhambra 53; s/d €70/115; Mar-Nov;) Within the Alhambra grounds, the early 19th-century building creates a restful ambience in contrast to the busy Alhambra foot traffic. Reserve well in advance, as rooms are limited.

Hotel Guadalupe (Map p798; ☎ 958 22 34 23; www.hotelguadalupe.es; Avenida Los Alixares s/n; s/d €72/111; P) Almost on the Alhambra's doorstep, Guadalupe has a bright atmosphere. Rooms are subdued and elegant in shades of pumpkin and cream, with Alhambra or olive-grove views.

There are several hotels in beautiful renovated Albayzín mansions, including **Hotel Casa del Capitel Nazarí** (Map p801; ☎ 958 21 52 60; www.hotelcasacapitel.com; Cuesta Aceituneros 6; s/d €73/91;), **Casa del Aljarife** (Map p801; ☎ /fax 958 22 24 25; www.granadainfo.com/most; Placeta de la Cruz Verde 2; r €96.30;) and **Hotel Zaguán** (Map p801; ☎ 958 21 57 30; www.hotelzaguan.com; Carrera del Darro; s €55, r €95;).

A little less characterful but more central, **Hotel Los Tilos** (Map p801; ☎ 958 26 67 12; Plaza Bib-Rambla 4; www.hotellostilos.com; s/d €55/80;), **Hotel Maciá Plaza** (Map p801; ☎ 958 22 75 36; www.maciahoteles.com; Plaza Nueva 4; s/d €66.50/96; P) and **Hotel Anacapri** (Map p801; ☎ 958 22 74 77; www.hotelanacapri.com; Calle Joaquín Costa 7; s/d €66.34/96.30;) are all centrally located and provide the usual modern hotel comforts.

TOP END

Casa Morisca Hotel (Map p798; ☎ 958 22 11 00; www.hotelcasamorisca.com; Cuesta de la Victoria 9; d interior/exterior €118/148;) The hotel occupies a late-15th-century Albayzín mansion, with 14 stylish rooms centred on an atmospheric patio with an ornamental pool and wooden galleries.

Villa Oniria (Map p801; ☎ 958 53 53 58; www.villaoniria.com; Calle San Anton 28; s/d €140/200; P) Cream and brown predominate in the spacious rooms and public areas. The dining terrace is designed around oblong ponds ripplilng with cool water. There is even a basement spa.

Hotel Carmen de Santa Inés (Map p801; ☎ 958 22 63 80; www.carmensantaines.com; Placeta de Porras 7; s/d €80/96, r with sitting room €140-222;) This Islamic-era house, extended in the 16th and 17th centuries, offers a lovely breakfast patio in a garden of myrtles, fruit trees and fountains.

Parador de Granada (Map p798; ☎ 958 22 14 40; www.parador.es; Calle Real de la Alhambra s/n; s/d €220/310; P) The most expensive *parador* in Spain can't be beaten for its location within the Alhambra and its historical connections. Book ahead.

Hotel Palacio de Santa Paula (Map p801; ☎ 902 29 22 93; www.ac-hotels.com; Gran Vía de Colón; r from €276; P) This five-star hotel, part of a chain, occupies a former 16th-century convent, some 14th-century houses with patios and wooden balconies, and a 19th-century aristocratic house, all with a contemporary overlay and modern luxuries.

Eating

Granada is one of the last bastions of that fantastic practice of free tapas with every drink, and some have an international flavour.

RESTAURANTS

Near Plaza Nueva

Café Central (Map p801; ☎ 958 22 97 06; Calle de Elvira; tapas €2.90-3.60, raciones €7.90-9.80) Perk up with a strong morning coffee (€1.60) at this laid-back cafe with a feeling of yesteryear to it.

Bodegas Castañeda (Map p801; Calle Almireceros; raciones from €6) An institution, and reputedly the oldest bar in Granada, this kitchen whips up traditional food in a typical bodega setting. Their free tapa of paella is almost enough for a light lunch. Get a table before 2pm as it gets very busy then.

Antigua Castañeda (Map p801; Calle de Elvira; raciones €8-16) Soak up potent 'Costa' wine from the Contraviesa with a few *montaditos* (small sandwiches; €5 to €6).

For fresh fruit and veg, head for the large covered **Mercado Central San Agustín** (Map p801; Calle San Agustín; 8am-2pm Mon-Sat), a block west of the cathedral.

Albayzín

The labyrinthine Albayzín holds a wealth of eateries all tucked away in the narrow streets. Calle Caldereria Nueva is a fascinating muddle of *teterías*, leather shops and Arabic-influenced takeaways.

Kasbah (Map p801; Calle Caldereria Nueva 4; tea €2.30-5) A great choice for light snacks. It's open 'from noon until the candles burn down'.

Restaurante Arrayanes (Map p801; ☎ 958 22 84 01; Cuesta Marañas 4; mains €8.50-19; from 8pm) Pop in to fill up on delicious Moroccan tagine casseroles. Note that Restaurante Arrayanes does not serve alcohol.

El Ají (Map pp796-7; ☎ 958 29 29 30; San Miguel Bajo 9; menú €10.50, mains €10-20; V) We like the cool, modern interior, soft jazz, and its menu of nontraditional meat and lively vegetarian choices.

El Agua (Map p801; ☎ 958 22 33 58; Plaza Aljibe de Trillo 7; fondues per person €14-19, minimum 2 people; lunch Wed-Mon, dinner daily) and **Terraza las Tomasas** (Map pp796-7; ☎ 958 22 41 08; Carril de San Agustín 4; mains €18-22; dinner Wed-Sat) offer fabulous views of the Alhambra.

Plaza Bib Rambla & Around

In the heart of modern Granada, the plaza and its surrounding network of streets cater to a range of tastes and pockets from student to executive.

Poë (Map p801; Calle Paz; media raciones €3) British–Angolan Poë offers Brazilian favourites such as *feijoada* or chicken stew with polenta and a trendy multicultural vibe.

Om-Kalsum (Map p801; Calle Jardines 17; media raciones €3) A few doors away from Poë, Om-Kalsum sticks to Arabic-influenced favourites such as lamb mini-tagines and chicken kebabs.

Guerrero (Map p801; ☎ 958 28 14 60; Plaza de la Trinidad 7; raciones €3.50-12, breakfast €5.50) This is where you come for coffee and tostadas, or an English or 'American' breakfast if you're homesick.

Cunini (Map p801; ☎ 958 25 07 77; Plaza de Pescadería 14; menú €19, mains €11-23) This place dishes up first-class fish and seafood as tapas if you stand at the bar, or full meals out back.

Los Diamantes (Map p801; ☎ 958 22 70 70; Calle Navas 26; media raciones €6) shines when it comes to fried fish; **Ermita Centro** (☎ 958 27 00 29; www.ermitacentro.com; Plaza Romanilla, Calle Carcel Baja 1; raciones €7.50-11) serves modern twists on traditional dishes.

Camino del Ronda/Neptuno

our pick **Momento2** (Map pp796-7; ☎ 958 52 30 09; www.momento2.com; Calle Neptuno; tapas €1.50-2.50; restaurant mains €11-35; 8am-11pm Mon-Fri, 10am-midnight Sat & Sun) Right next to Neptuno parking (just off the A44-E902 at Exit 129 and near a taxi stop, 5 minutes into the centre) you can avoid getting snarled in Granada traffic *and* have some of the best food in Granada. Try the morcilla blood sausage tapa with date pesto, cherry compote and a wafer of fried milk.

CAFES

Good cafes can be surprisingly elusive in Granada, but the following offer authentic atmosphere and good breakfast fare. Try **Cafe Futbol** (Map p801; Plaza Mariana Pineda 6, opposite tourist office) for art-nouveau decor and fresh *churros*, **Café Lisboa** (Map p801; cnr Reyes Catolicos & Plaza Nueva) for its luscious apple strudel and **Café Gran Via Colón** (Map p801; Gran Via 13) for substantial breakfasts.

Drinking

The best street for drinking is rather scruffy Calle Elvira (try above-average **Taberna El Espejo** at number 40) but other chilled bars line Río Darro at the base of the Albayzín and Campo del Príncipe attracts a sophisticated bunch.

Bodegas Castañeda (Calle Almireceros) – see left – and **Antigua Castañeda** (Calle de Elvira) – see left – are the most inviting and atmospheric, with out-of-the-barrel wine and generous tapas to keep things going. Perch at **Bar Pacurri** (Map p801; ☎ 958 25 27 75; Calle de Gracia 21; tapas €2.50-5; 1pm-1am), a small, arty bar, and munch on above-average tapas with well-chosen wines.

Entertainment

The excellent monthly *Guía de Granada* (€1), available from kiosks, lists entertainment venues and places to eat, including tapas bars.

CLUBS

Look out for posters and leaflets around town advertising live music and nontouristy flamenco.

Sala Industrial Copera (☎ 958 25 84 49; www.industrialcopera.net; Carretera Armilla, Calle la Paz, warehouse 7; admission varied; 🕑 12pm-late, Fri & Sat) This warehouse club is where serious clubbers go for all-nighters, with a constantly changing schedule of live acts. You can count on lots of techno and hip hop, and DJs from Ibiza, Madrid and Barcelona. Get a cab.

Granada 10 (Map p801; Calle Cárcel Baja; admission €6; 🕑 from midnight, closed mid-Jul & Aug) A glittery converted cinema is now Granada's top club for the glam crowd, who recline on the gold sofas and go crazy to cheesy Spanish pop tunes.

Planta Baja (Map p801; ☎ 630 950824; Calle Horno de Abad 11; www.plantabaja.net; admission €5; 🕑 12.30am-6am Tue-Sat) Planta Baja's popularity never seems to wane, and it's no wonder since it caters to a diverse crowd *and* has top DJs like Vadim. There's old school, hip hop, funk and electroglam downstairs, and lazy lounge sessions on the top floor.

Afrodisia (Map pp796-7; www.afrodisiaclub.com; Edificio Corona, Calle Almona del Boquerón; admission free; 🕑 11pm-late) If you dig Granada's ganja-driven scene, this is where you'll find a like-minded lot. DJs spin hip hop, ska, reggae, funk and even jazz on Sundays.

FLAMENCO

El Eshavira (Map pp796-7; ☎ 958 29 08 29; www.eshavira.com; Postigo de la Cuna 2; 🕑 from 10pm) Duck down a spooky alley to this shadowy haunt of flamenco and jazz. It is jam-packed on Thursday and Sunday, the performance nights.

El Upsetter (Map p801; ☎ 958 22 72 96; Carrera del Darro 7; admission for flamenco show €12; 🕑 11pm-late) The Upsetter has a decent nightly flamenco show from 10pm to midnight only, and doubles as a dreadlock-swinging reggae bar for the rest of the week.

Peña de la Platería (Map pp796-7; ☎ 958 21 06 50; Placeta de Toqueros 7) Buried deep in the Albayzín warren, this is a genuine aficionados' club with a large outdoor patio. Catch a 9.30pm performance on Thursday or Saturday.

Situated above and to the northwest of the city centre, and offering panoramic views over the Alhambra, the Sacromonte is Granada's centuries-old *gitano* quarter. The Sacromonte caves harbour touristy flamenco haunts for which you can pre-book through hotels and travel agencies, some of whom offer free transport. Try the Friday or Saturday midnight shows at **Los Tarantos** (Map pp796-7; ☎ 958 22 45 25 day, 958 22 24 92 night; Camino del Sacromonte 9; admission €24) for a lively experience.

OTHER ENTERTAINMENT

Centro Cultural Manuel de Falla (Map p798; ☎ 958 22 00 22; Paseo de los Mártires s/n) A haven for classical music lovers, this venue near the Alhambra presents weekly orchestral concerts in a leafy and tranquil setting.

Teatro Alhambra (Map pp798; ☎ 958 22 04 47; Calle de Molinos 56) and the more central **Teatro Isabel La Católica** (Map p801; ☎ 958 22 15 14; Acera del Casino) have ongoing programs of theatre and concerts (sometimes flamenco) and a reputation for more adventurous programming than similar venues in Granada.

Shopping

Classic pots with distinctive *granadino* green or blue-and-white glazing can be bought at **Cerámica Fabre** (Map p801; Calle Pescadería s/n). A distinctive local craft is *taracea* (marquetry), used on boxes, tables and more – the best have shell, silver or mother-of-pearl inlays. Marquetry experts can be seen at work in **Laguna Taller de Taracea** (Map p798). Other *granadino* crafts include embossed leather, guitars, wrought iron, brass and copper ware, basket weaving and textiles. Look out for these in the Alcaicería and Albayzín, on Cuesta de Gomérez and in the government-run **Artespaña** in Corral del Carbón (Map p801).

The Plaza Nueva area is awash with jewellery vendors, selling from rugs laid out on the pavement, and ethnic-clothing shops.

For general shopping try pedestrianised Calle de los Mesones or expensive department store El Corte Inglés (Map p801).

Getting There & Away

AIR

Iberia (☎ 902 40 05 00; www.iberia.com) flies daily to and from Madrid and Barcelona. From the UK, **Ryanair** (www.rynanair.com) flies daily to Granada.

BUS

Granada's **bus station** (Map pp796-7; Carretera de Jaén) is nearly 3km northwest of the city centre. All services operate from here, except those going to a few nearby destinations, such as Fuente Vaqueros (p810). **Alsina Graells** (☎ 958 18 54 80) runs to Córdoba (€12 to €16.60, 2¾ hours direct, nine daily), Seville (€18.57, three hours direct, 8 daily), Málaga (€9, 1½ hours direct, 16 daily) and Las Alpujarras (see p812 for details). Alsina also handles buses to destinations in Jaén province and on the Granada, Málaga and Almería coasts, and to Madrid (€15.66, five to six hours, 10 to 13 daily).

ALSA (☎ 902 42 22 42; www.alsa.es) operates buses up the Mediterranean coast to Barcelona (€65.96 to €76.99, seven to 10 hours, four daily) and to many international destinations.

CAR

Car rental is expensive. **ATA** (Map p801; ☎ 958 22 40 04; Plaza Cuchilleros 1) has small cars (e.g. Renault Clio) for €72.70/46.30/34.90 per day for one/two/seven days. You would be better advised to take a taxi to the airport (€18 to €22) where four or five good car-hire operators have offices.

TRAIN

The **train station** (Map pp796-7; ☎ 958 24 02 02; Avenida de Andaluces) is 1.5km west of the centre, off Avenida de la Constitución. Four trains run daily to/from Seville (€21.65, three hours) and Almería (€14.45, 2¼ hours) via Guadix, and six daily to/from Antequera (€6.70 to €8, 1½ hours). Three go to Ronda (€12.25, three hours) and Algeciras (€18.35, 4½ hours). For Málaga (€13.45, 2½ hours) or Córdoba (€16.40, four hours) take an Algeciras train and change at Bobadilla (€8.25, 1½ hours). One or two trains go to each of Madrid (€62.20, four to five hours), Valencia (€46.10 to €72.30, 7½ to eight hours) and Barcelona (€56.30 to €104.30, 12 to 14½ hours).

Getting Around

TO/FROM THE AIRPORT

The **airport** (☎ 958 24 52 23) is 17km west of the city on the A92. **Autocares J González** (☎ 958 49 01 64) runs buses between the airport and a stop near the Palacio de Congresos (€3, five daily), with a stop in the city centre on Gran Vía de Colón, where a schedule is posted opposite the cathedral, and at the entrance to the bus station. A taxi costs €18 to €22 depending on traffic conditions and pickup point.

BUS

City buses cost €1.10. Tourist offices have leaflets showing routes. Bus 3 runs between the bus station and the Palacio de Congresos conference centre, via Gran Vía de Colón in the city centre. To reach the city centre from the train station, walk to Avenida de la Constitución and pick up bus 4, 6, 7, 9 or 11 going to the right (east). From the centre (Gran Vía de Colón) to the train station, take number 3, 4, 6, 9 or 11. Routes 30, 31, 32 and 34 are special tourist minibuses plying in and around the Alhambra and the Albayzin. Route 33 takes you to and from the bus station, through the centre of the city, and northeast towards the Sierra Nevada.

CAR & MOTORCYCLE

Vehicle access to the Plaza Nueva area is restricted by red lights and little black posts known as *pilonas,* which block certain streets during certain times of the day. If you are going to stay at a hotel near Plaza Nueva, press the button next to your hotel's name beside the *pilonas* to contact reception, which will be able to lower the *pilonas* for you.

Many hotels, especially in the midrange and above, have their own parking facilities. Central underground public car parks include **Parking San Agustín** (Calle San Agustín; per hr/day €1/16), **Parking Neptuno** (Calle Neptuno, A44-E902, exit 129) and **Parking Plaza Puerta Real** (Acera del Darro; per hr/day €1/12). Free parking is available at the Alhambra car parks.

TAXI

If you're after a taxi, head for Plaza Nueva, where they line up. Most fares within the city cost between €4.50 and €8.50.

AROUND GRANADA

Granada is surrounded by a fertile plain called La Vega, planted with poplar groves and crops ranging from melons to tobacco. The Vega was an inspiration to Federico García Lorca, who was born and died here. The **Parque Federico García Lorca**, between the villages of Víznar and Alfacar (about 2.5km from each), marks the site where Lorca and hundreds, possibly thousands, of others are believed to have been shot and buried by the Nationalists, at the start of the civil war.

Fuente Vaqueros

The touchingly modest house where Lorca was born in 1898, in this otherwise unremarkable suburb 17km west of Granada, is now the **Casa Museo Federico García Lorca** (☎ 958 51 64 53; www.museogarcialorca.org in Spanish; Calle Poeta Federico García Lorca 4; admission €1.80; guided visits hourly 10am-1pm & 5-7pm Tue-Sat Apr-Jun, to 2pm & 6-8pm Tue-Sat Jul-Sep, 10am-1pm & 4-6pm Tue-Sat Oct-Mar). The place brings his spirit to life, with numerous charming photos, posters and costumes from his plays and paintings illustrating his poems. A short video captures him in action with the touring Teatro Barraca.

Buses to Fuente Vaqueros (€1.50, 20 minutes) by **Ureña** (☎ 958 45 41 54) leave from Avenida de Andaluces in front of Granada train station, roughly once an hour from 9am during the week, and at 9am, 11am, 1pm and 5pm at weekends and holidays.

SIERRA NEVADA

The Sierra Nevada, which includes mainland Spain's highest peak, Mulhacén (3479m), forms an almost year-round snowy southeastern backdrop to Granada. The range stretches about 75km from west to east, extending into Almería province. All its highest peaks (3000m or more) are towards the Granada end. The upper reaches of the range form the 862-sq-km **Parque Nacional Sierra Nevada**, Spain's biggest national park, with a rare high-altitude environment that is home to about 2100 of Spain's 7000 plant species. Andalucía's largest ibex population (about 5000) is here too. Surrounding the national park at lower altitudes is the 848-sq-km **Parque Natural Sierra Nevada**. The mountains and the Alpujarras valleys (p812) comprise one of the most spectacular areas in Spain, and the area offers wonderful opportunities for walking, horse riding, climbing, mountain biking and, in winter, good skiing and snowboarding.

The **Centro de Visitantes El Dornajo** (☎ 958 34 06 25; ⏲ 10am-2pm & 6-8pm Apr-Sep, 10am-2pm & 4-6pm Oct-Mar), about 23km from Granada, on the A395 towards the ski station, has plenty of information on the Sierra Nevada. Knowledgeable, English-speaking staff are happy to help.

Estación de Esquí Sierra Nevada

The **Sierra Nevada Ski Station** (☎ 958 24 91 36; www.sierranevadaski.com; ⏲ 10am-2pm & 4pm-6pm), at Pradollano, 33km southeast of Granada, is one of Spain's biggest and liveliest ski resorts. It can get overcrowded at weekends and holiday times. The ski season normally lasts from December to April.

The resort has 70 marked downhill runs (mainly red and blue with a few black and green) totalling over 80km, a dedicated snowboarding area and some cross-country routes. Some runs start almost at the top of Veleta, the Sierra Nevada's second-highest peak. A one-day ski pass plus rental of skis, boots and stocks or snowboard costs €50 to €60 depending when you go. The resort has several ski and snowboard schools: six hours' skiing instruction in group classes costs €63.

Nonskiers can ride cable cars up from Pradollano (2100m) to Borreguiles (2645m) for €10 return, and then ice-skate, dogsled or snowshoe. One cable car has wheelchair access. Outside the ski season **Sierra Nevada Activa** (www.sierranevadaactiva.com in Spanish) operates a host of warmer-weather activities, such as mountain biking, trekking, horse riding and canyoning.

The ski station has around 20 hotels, *hostales* and apartment-hotels. None are cheap (double rooms mostly start at €80) and reservations are always advisable. Ski packages, which can be booked through the station's website or phone number, start at around €150 per person for two days and two nights, with half board and lift passes. Book two weeks ahead, if you can.

Dorm rooms at youth hostel **Instalación Juvenil Sierra Nevada** (☎ 958 57 51 16; Calle Peñones 22; dm incl breakfast under/over 26yr €25/30; Ⓟ) sleep from two to four, including six doubles with wheelchair access. The stark modern exterior encloses a stark, modern interior, and many school groups use this hostal. **Albergue Universitario** (☎ 958 48 01 22; Peñones de San Francisco, Monachil; www.nevadensis.com/albergue_sierra_nevada.html; ⏲ all year; dm €25/38, d €25/45 half-board; Ⓟ), a big chalet-style *hostal*, offers plain, comfortable accommodation in a remote setting. Adventure days out can be booked here. At **Hotel Apartamentos Trevenque** (☎ 958 48 08 62; www.cetursa.es; Plaza de Andalucía 6; s/d €114/147; Ⓟ) studios for two come complete with kitchenette, TV and DVD, plus good food and views. Alpine-style **Hotel Ziryab** (☎ 958 48 05 12; www.cetursa.es; Plaza de Andalucía; s/d €128/179; ⏲ late Nov-early May; ♿) near the foot of the resort provides soaring views from the cosy bar/restaurant. Ice skating, dog sledding and sleigh rides can all be booked here, and it's wheelchair accessible.

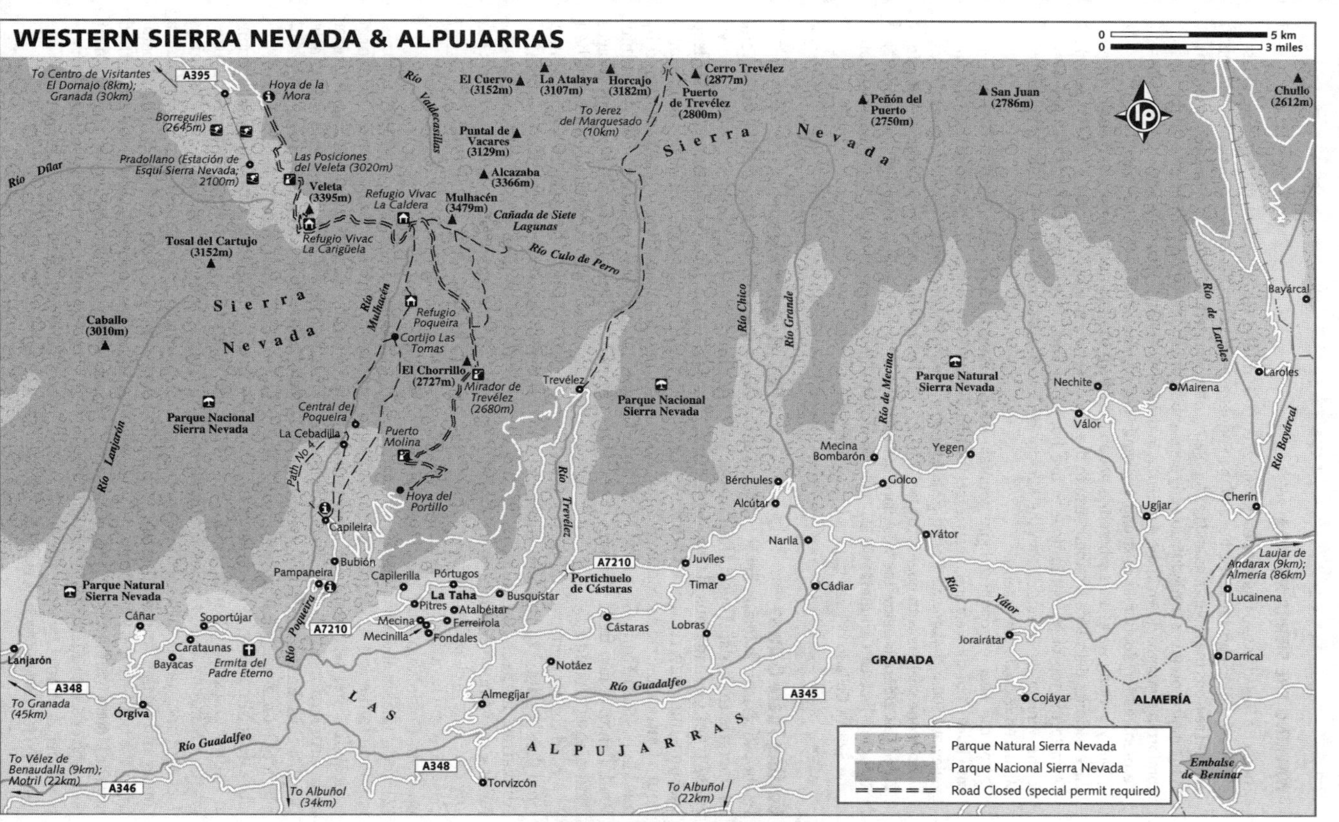
WESTERN SIERRA NEVADA & ALPUJARRAS
0 5 km
0 3 miles
To Centro de Visitantes El Dornajo (8km); Granada (30km)
A395
Hoya de la Mora
Borreguiles (2645m)
Pradollano (Estación de Esquí Sierra Nevada; 2100m)
Río Dílar
Las Posiciones del Veleta (3020m)
Veleta (3395m)
Refugio Vivac La Caldera
Refugio Vivac La Carigüela
Río Valdecasillas
El Cuervo (3152m)
La Atalaya (3107m)
Horcajo (3182m)
Cerro Trevélez (2877m)
Puerto de Trevélez (2800m)
To Jerez del Marquesado (10km)
Peñón del Puerto (2750m)
San Juan (2786m)
Chullo (2612m)
Puntal de Vacares (3129m)
Alcazaba (3366m)
Mulhacén (3479m)
Cañada de Siete Lagunas
Río Culo de Perro
Tosal del Cartujo (3152m)
Sierra Nevada
Caballo (3010m)
Río Mulhacén
Refugio Poqueira
Cortijo Las Tomas
El Chorrillo (2727m)
Mirador de Trevélez (2680m)
Trevélez
Parque Nacional Sierra Nevada
Parque Natural Sierra Nevada
Río Chico
Río Grande
Río de Mecina
Río de Laroles
Bayárcal
Laroles
Nechite
Mairena
Válor
Río Bayárcal
Central de Poqueira
La Cebadilla
Puerto Molina
Path No 4
Hoya del Portillo
Río Lanjarón
Río Trevélez
Mecina Bombarón
Yegen
Bérchules
Golco
Alcútar
Ugíjar
Cherín
Capileira
Yátor
Narila
Bubión
A7210
Juviles
Laujar de Andarax (9km); Almería (86km)
Pampaneira
Capilerilla
Pórtugos
Portichuelo de Cástaras
Tímar
Cádiar
Lucainena
La Taha
Busquístar
Pitres
Atalbéitar
Río Yátor
Cáñar
Soportújar
Río Poqueira
Mecina
Ferreirola
Cástaras
Lobras
Mecinilla
Fondales
Jorairátar
Lanjarón
Caratáunas
Bayacas
Ermita del Padre Eterno
Darrical
Notáez
GRANADA
A348
Río Guadalfeo
To Granada (45km)
Órgiva
Almegíjar
A345
Cojáyar
ALMERÍA
Las Alpujarras
To Vélez de Benaudalla (9km); Motril (22km)
A346
To Albuñol (34km)
Torvizcón
To Albuñol (22km)
Parque Natural Sierra Nevada
Parque Nacional Sierra Nevada
Road Closed (special permit required)
Embalse de Beninar

WALKING THE SIERRA NEVADA

The Sierra Nevada's two highest peaks, Mulhacén (3479m) and Veleta (3395m), rise to the southeast of the ski station and above the head of the Poqueira valley in Las Alpujarras to their south. In the warmer seasons the mountains and Las Alpujarras offer wonderful walking, but the best conditions in the high mountains (early July to early September) unfortunately don't coincide with the most comfortable months down in the Alpujarras. In the Sierra Nevada – which are serious mountains – be prepared for cloud, rain or strong, icy winds *any* day, and come well equipped.

Many exciting walks start where the national park shuttle bus routes drop you (below). From the Posiciones del Veleta it's about 4km to the top of Veleta, an ascent of some 370m (1½ hours), 14km to the top of Mulhacén (four to five hours), or about 15km (six hours) all the way over to the Mirador de Trevélez. From the Mirador de Trevélez it's around three hours to the top of Mulhacén (6km, 800m ascent).

You can sleep overnight in high-mountain refuges. **Refugio Poqueira** (☎ 958 34 33 49; dm €9), with bunks, hot showers and meals (breakfast/dinner €3.50/10), is towards the top of the Poqueira valley at 2500m, a 4km walk from the Mirador de Trevélez. Phone ahead if possible. Two *refugios vivac* (stone shelters with boards to sleep on) are free but reservations are not possible: **Refugio Vivac La Caldera** is below the west flank of Mulhacén, a 1½-hour walk up from Refugio Poqueira; **Refugio Vivac La Carigüela** is a 2½-hour walk west along the road from Refugio La Caldera, at the 3200m Collado del Veleta pass below the summit of Veleta.

Getting There & Away

In the ski season **Autocares Bonal** (☎ 958 46 50 22) operates three daily buses (four at weekends) from Granada bus station to the ski station (one way/return €4.20/7.50, one hour). Outside the ski season there's just one bus daily (9am from Granada, 5pm from Pradollano). A taxi from Granada to the ski station costs around €45.

A road climbs right over the Sierra Nevada from the ski station to Capileira village in Las Alpujarras, on the southern side of the range, but it's snowbound much of the year and in any case always closed to private motor vehicles between Hoya de la Mora (2550m), 3km up from Pradollano, and Hoya del Portillo (2150m), 12.5km above Capileira. From about late June to the end of October the national park shuttle-bus services, called the Servicio de Interpretación Ambiental Altas Cumbres (High Peaks Environmental Interpretation Service), run about 6km up the road from Hoya de la Mora (to the Posiciones del Veleta, at 3020m) and some 21km up from Capileira (to the Mirador de Trevélez, at 2680m). Tickets (one way/return €4.50/7 on either route) and further information are available from the national park information posts at **Hoya de la Mora** (☎ 630 959739; 🕑 during bus-service season approx 8.30am-2.30pm & 3.30-7.30pm) and at Hoya del Portillo, **Capileira** (☎ 958 76 34 86, 686 414576; 🕑 year-round approx 9am-2pm & 4.30-7.30pm).

LAS ALPUJARRAS

Below the southern flank of the Sierra Nevada lies the 70km-long jumble of valleys known as Las Alpujarras. Arid hillsides split by deep ravines alternate with oasis-like white villages set beside rapid streams and surrounded by gardens, orchards and woodlands. An infinity of good walking routes links valley villages and heads up into the Sierra Nevada: the best times to visit are between April and mid-June, and mid-September and early November.

A recent upsurge in tourism, New Age settlers and foreign (mainly British) settlers has given the area a new dimension.

History

In the 10th and 11th centuries the Alpujarras, settled by Berbers, was a great silkworm farm for the workshops of Almería. But after Granada fell to Ferdinand and Isabella in 1492, the industry languished and many villages were abandoned.

South from Granada by Gerald Brenan, an Englishman who lived in the Alpujarras village of Yegen in the 1920s and '30s, gives a fascinating picture of what was then a very isolated, superstitious corner of Spain. Another Englishman, Chris Stewart, settled here more recently, as a sheep farmer near Órgiva. His entertaining best-selling *Driving over Lemons* tells of life as a foreigner in Las Alpujarras in the '90s.

Lanjarón

Known as 'the gateway to the Alpujarras', Lanjarón's heyday was during the late 19th and early 20th centuries, when it was a fashionable *balneario* or spa. Today, although Lanjarón water is sold all over Spain, the spa is visited largely by elderly Spanish cure-seekers. Yet the town has authentic charms. Traditional family life is lived along its main streets, Avenida Alpujarra and Avenida Andalucía. The **tourist office** (☎ 958 77 04 62; Avenida de la Alpujarra) opposite the *balneario* provides comprehensive information on outdoor activities and accommodation for the entire Alpujarras region.

Eat at seafood restaurant **Los Mariscos** in Avenida de la Alpujarra, where 70-something Granny Callejón still presides over the homely kitchen and everything is cooked from fresh ingredients. A good vegetarian option is friendly **Bar Health** at the other end of town in Calle Señor de la Expiración, with generous salads and pastas.

Órgiva

pop 6500 / elev 725m

The western Alpujarras' main town, Órgiva, is a scruffy but bustling place with a big hippy–New Age element. Good places to eat include **El Limonero** where the chef's passion for local ingredients is put to good use in a handsome room; **La Almazara** (Avenida González Robles; menú €12), with inventive dishes and excellent pizza served in an orange grove all summer; and vegetarian brunch/lunch options at welcoming **Café Libertad** in Calle Libertad.

Stay at **Hotel Taray Botánico** (☎ 958 78 45 25; www.hoteltaray.com; A348 Km18.5; s/d €70/83; P ✻ 💻 ♿), where the owners love their hotel and it shows. Set in lush gardens just south of the centre, with rustic-style rooms and a good restaurant, plus two lovely big pools. Book well ahead in summer. A cheaper option is **Camping Puerta de las Alpujarras** (☎ 958 78 44 50; www.puertalpujarra.com; A348 Carretera Lanjarón-Orgiva; adult/under 11 years/tent & car €4.50/3/9), handily located for the High Alpujarras with a big pool, pleasant restaurant.

Pampaneira, Bubión & Capileira

pop 1270 / elev 1200-1440m

These small villages clinging to the side of the deep Barranco de Poqueira valley, 14km to 20km northeast of Órgiva, are three of the prettiest, most dramatically sited (and most touristy) in Las Alpujarras. Capileira is the best base for walks.

INFORMATION

You'll find ATMs outside the car-park entrance in Pampaneira, and in Capileira at **La General** (Calle Doctor Castilla).

Punto de Información Parque Nacional de Sierra Nevada (☎ 958 76 31 27; www.nevadensis.com; Plaza de la Libertad, Pampaneira; 🕑 10am-2pm & 4-6pm Tue-Sat, to 3pm Sun & Mon, Oct-March) Plenty of information about Las Alpujarras and Sierra Nevada; outdoor gear, maps and books for sale.

Servicio de Interpretación de Altos Cumbres (☎ 958 76 34 86, 686 41 45 76; 🕑 approx 9am-2pm & 4.30-7.30pm) By the main road in Capileira; information mainly about the national park, but also on Las Alpujarras.

SIGHTS & ACTIVITIES

All three villages have solid 16th-century **Mudéjar churches** (🕑 Mass times). They also have small **weaving workshops**, descendants of a textile tradition that goes back to Islamic times, and plentiful **craft shops**. In Bubión, get a marvellous glimpse of bygone Alpujarras life at the excellent little folk museum, **Casa Alpujarreña** (Calle Real; admission €2; 🕑 11am-2pm Sun-Thu, to 2pm & 5-7pm Fri, Sat & holidays), beside the church.

Eight **walking trails**, ranging from 4km to 23km (two to eight hours), are marked out in the beautiful Barranco de Poqueira with little colour-coded posts. Their starting points can be hard to find, but they are marked and described on Editorial Alpina's *Sierra Nevada, La Alpujarra* map (see the boxed text, p814). **Nevadensis** (☎ 958 76 31 27; www.nevadensis.com), at the information office in Pampaneira, offers hikes and treks, 4WD trips, horse riding, mountain biking, climbing and canyoning, with knowledgeable guides.

SLEEPING & EATING

Book ahead for rooms around Easter and from July to September. Many villages have apartments and houses for rent; ask in tourist offices or check websites such as **Turgranada** (www.turgranada.com) or **Rustic Blue** (www.rustic blue.com).

Pampaneira

A good value *hostal* at the entrance to the village is **Hostal Pampaneira** (☎ 958 76 30 02; Avenida Alpujarra 1; s/d €28/40 incl. breakfast) with a friendly local owner. **Restaurante Casa Diego** (☎ 958 76

30 15; Plaza de la Libertad 3; mains €6.50-13.50), along the street, has a pleasant upstairs terrace and serves local trout and ham.

Bubión

Hostal Las Terrazas (☎ 958 76 30 34; www.terrazasalpujarra.com; Plaza del Sol 7; s/d €22/33, 2-/4-/6-person apt €48/59/77) is located below the main road and near the car park. Traditional **Teide Restaurant** (☎ 958 76 30 37; Carretera de Sierra Nevada 2; menú €10) has a good *menú del dia* while **Estación 4** (☎ 958 76 31 16; Calle Estación 4; mains €7-12) inhabits an old village house.

Capileira

Hostal Atalaya (☎ 958 76 30 25; www.hostalatalaya.com; Calle Perchel 3; s/d incl breakfast; s/d with view €30/38, without view €18/30) is a good budget option, while **Finca Los Llanos** (☎ 958 76 30 71; www.hotelfincalosllanos.com; Carretera de Sierra Nevada; s/d €50/75; P) has tasteful rooms, a pool and a good restaurant. It's also an official Sierra Nevada information point. Renovated farmhouse **Cortijo Catifalarga** (☎ 958 34 33 57; www.catifalarga.com; d €80-95, apt from €95; mains €8-16; P V) is stunning. The driveway begins 750m up the Sierra Nevada road from the top of Capileira, and both the views and its eclectic food are way up there. At **Restaurante Ibero-Fusión** (☎ 958 76 32 56; Calle Parra 1; salads €7-10, mains €10-12.50 dinner, closed Tue; V) just below the church, enjoy a rare *andaluz*, Arabic and Indian fusion restaurant with plenty of vegetarian specialities and great views from the pleasant upstairs dining room.

Pitres & La Taha

pop 800

Pitres (elevation 1245m) is a break from the tourism and souvenirs in the Poqueira Gorge villages, although not quite as pretty.

> **SIERRA NEVADA & ALPUJARRAS MAPS**
>
> The best overall maps of the area are Editorial Alpina's *Sierra Nevada, La Alpujarra* (1:40,000) and Editorial Penibética's *Sierra Nevada* (1:50,000). Both come with booklets, in English or Spanish, describing walking, biking and skiing routes. An invaluable resource is *34 Alpujarras Walks* by Charles Davis, published by Discovery Walking Guides, which has an accompanying Tours & Trails map.

The beautiful valley below it, with five tranquil hamlets (Mecina, Mecinilla, Fondales, Ferreirola and Atalbéitar), all grouped with Pitres in the *municipio* called La Taha, is particularly fascinating to explore. Its ancient pathways are a walkers' delight.

In an ancient village house, welcoming French-run guesthouse **L'Atelier** (☎ 958 85 75 01; www.ivu.org/atelier; Calle Alberca 21, Mecina; s/d €35/50, incl breakfast; dinner Wed-Mon; V) also serves gourmet vegetarian meals and has an art gallery. In peaceful Ferreirola, **Sierra y Mar** (☎ 958 76 61 71; www.sierraymar.com; Calle Albaicín, Ferreirola; s/d/t incl breakfast €36/56/76) has just nine rooms set around patios and gardens. Back in Mecina, **Hotel Albergue de Mecina** (☎ 958 76 62 41; Calle La Fuente s/n, Mecina; s/d/tr €60/88/107; P) is modern and comfortable with a helpful English-speaking owner and wheelchair access.

Trevélez

pop 1150 / elev 1476m

Trevélez, in a valley almost as impressive as the Poqueira Gorge, claims to be the highest village in Spain (although Valdelinares, Aragón, reaches above 1700m) and produces famous *jamón serrano*.

On a leafy, terraced hillside 1km west of Trevélez, **Camping Trevélez** (☎/fax 958 85 87 35; www.campingtrevelez.net; Carretera Trevélez-Órgiva Km1; sites per adult/tent/car/cabin €4.50/5/3.80/19; closed Jan-mid Feb; P) has ecologically minded owners and a good-value restaurant. Walkers' favourite **Hotel La Fragua I & II** (☎ 958 85 86 26; Calle San Antonio 4; s/d €30/40, Fragua II, d/tr €50/65, mains €7.50-12.50) provides pine-furnished rooms, with a more upmarket annex at La Fragua II. Its restaurant, **Mesón La Fragua**, a few doors away, is one of the best in town and worth searching out. More central **Hotel Pepe Álvarez** (☎ 958 85 85 03; www.andalucia.co.uk; Plaza Francisco Abellán s/n; s/d €25/45, mains €6-11) has some terraces overlooking the busy plaza.

East of Trevélez

East of Trevélez the landscape becomes barer and more arid, yet there are still oases of greenery around the villages. The central and eastern Alpujarras have their own magic but see far fewer tourists than the western villages.

BÉRCHULES

Seventeen kilometres from Trevélez, Bérchules is in a green valley stretching far back into the hills, with attractive walks. **Hotel Los Bérchules**

(☎ 958 85 25 30; www.hotelberchules.com; Carretera s/n; s/d/apt €35/50/75; mains €7.50-12; P), by the main road, has bright rooms, helpful English-speaking hosts who can help with activities, and an excellent restaurant (try local rabbit in garlic sauce).

YEGEN

Gerald Brenan's home in the 1920s is 12km east of Bérchules, off the main plaza with the fountain. Several walking routes have been marked out locally, including a 2km 'Sendero de Gerald Brenan'. **El Rincón de Yegen** (☎ 958 85 12 70; www.aldearural.com/rincondeyegen; s/d/apt €30/42/90; mains €8-16, closed Feb, restaurant closed Tue; P), on the eastern edge of the village, has simply furnished rooms and an excellent, medium-priced restaurant.

Getting There & Away

Alsina Graells (☎ 958 18 54 80) runs three daily buses from Granada to Órgiva (€4, 1½ hours), Pampaneira (€5, two hours), Bubión (€5.50, 2¼ hours), Capileira (€5.50, 2½ hours) and Pitres (€5.50, 2¾ hours). Two of these continue to Trevélez (€6.50, 3¼ hours) and Bérchules (€7.50, 3¾ hours). The return buses start from Bérchules at 5am and 5pm, and from Pitres at 3.30pm. Alsina also runs twice-daily buses from Granada to Cádiar (€7, three hours) and Yegen (€8, 3½ hours).

THE COAST

Granada's rugged, cliff-lined, 80km coast has a few reasonably attractive beach towns, linked by several daily buses to Granada, Málaga and Almería.

Salobreña

pop 11,000

On a crag overlooking the Mediterranean, old Salobreña's white houses seem scattered from an overturned sugar bowl. The very helpful **tourist office** (☎ 958 61 03 14; Plaza de Goya; 9.30am-1.30pm & 4.30-6.30pm Tue-Sun, to 1.30pm Mon) is 200m off the N340. Up at the top of the town is the impressive 13th-century **Castillo Árabe** (admission €2.80; 10.30am-1.30pm & 6-9pm Jun-Oct, 4-7pm Nov-May). The ticket also includes the nearby **Museo Arqueológico**, open the same hours. Below all this are two **beaches**, separated by a rocky promontory, one pebbly, one sandy, and both extremely popular with *granadinos* in August.

A fine place to stay is the spick-and-span **Hostal San Juan** (☎ 958 61 17 29; www.hostalsanjuan.com in Spanish; Calle Jardines 1; s/d €34-42/42-58;), on a quiet street about 400m from the tourist office. Its French owners have entirely replaced conventional power with solar energy. Well-sited **Hotel Avenida** (☎ 958 61 15 44; www.hotelavenidatropical.com; Avenida Mediterráneo 35; s/d/tr €42-60/60-95/80-115; P) offers phone, satellite TV and bathtub, plus its own cafe-restaurant and wheelchair access. There are loads of restaurants and beachside *chiringuitos* on and near the beachfront. Two of the best are **La Bahia** and **El Peñon**, which face each other.

Almuñécar

pop 23,000

From the highway Almuñécar seems an uninviting group of apartment blocks with pebbly beaches, but it has a more attractive older heart around the 16th-century castle. The **bus station** (☎ 958 63 01 40; Avenida Juan Carlos I 1) is just south of the N340. The **main tourist office** (☎ 958 63 11 25; www.almunecar.info; Avenida Europa s/n; 10am-2pm all year & 6-9pm, Jul-mid Sep, 5-8pm mid-Sep–end Oct & Apr-end Jun, 4.30-7pm Nov-Mar) is 1km southwest, just back from Playa de San Cristóbal, in a rose-pink 19th-century *palacete* with lovely gardens that is a tourist sight in its own right.

Just behind Playa de San Cristóbal is a tropical-bird aviary, **Parque Ornitológico Loro-Sexi** (☎ 958 63 02 80; adult/child €4/2; 11am-2pm all year & 6-9pm approx Jul–mid-Sep, 5-7pm approx mid-Sep–Oct & Apr-Jun, 4-6pm Nov-Mar).

You can paraglide, windsurf, dive, sail, ride a horse or descend canyons in and around Almuñécar and nearby La Herradura. The tourist office and its website have plenty of information.

Just off the winding N340 coast road, **Hostal California** (☎ 958 88 10 38; www.hotelcaliforniaspain.com; Carretera N340 Km313; s/d €38/56; P V) is refreshingly different, with colourful touches of Moroccan style and tasty food, including vegetarian options. The hotel offers special packages for paragliders as the owner is an expert and enthusiast. In town, streamlined **Hotel Casablanca** (☎ 958 63 55 75; www.almunecar.info/casablanca; Plaza de San Cristóbal 4; s/d €48/70; P) is furnished in distinctive Al-Andalus style, with sea views from some rooms.

If you tire of seafood on the beach, **Los Geraneos** (☎ 958 63 40 20; Plaza de La Rosa 4; mains €9.50-15; 1-5pm & 7.30-late, closed Sun evening & Mon) is a pleasantly blue-trimmed townhouse restaurant. The best first-floor tables view the plaza through long French windows.

JAÉN PROVINCE

Though life here has traditionally been a struggle, both nature and history have lavished their gifts on Jaén. Set on Andalucía's border with Castilla-La Mancha, Jaén alternates between wild mountain ranges, ravishing Renaissance towns and rolling country covered with lines of olive trees (Jaén *alone* produces about 10% of the world's olive oil). Nature has blessed the eye as well as the palate, with the dramatic mountain ranges of the Parque Natural de Cazorla in the east of the province. Jaén's diet includes plenty of game (partridge, venison, wild boar) meats.

JAÉN

pop 116,500 / elev 575m

The provincial capital is a bustling university city with some excellent tapas tucked away in its narrowest streets.

Orientation

Old Jaén, dominated by the huge cathedral, huddles beneath the high, castle-crowned Cerro de Santa Catalina. The focal point of the newer part of town is Plaza de la Constitución, 200m northeast and downhill from the cathedral. From here the main artery of the new city, Calle Roldán y Marín, becoming Paseo de la Estación, heads northwest to the train station, 1km away.

Information

There's no shortage of banks or ATMs around Plaza de la Constitución.

Cyber Cu@k (Calle de Adarves Bajos 24; per 30min €1.20; 🕒 10.30am-3pm & 5.00pm-1am Mon-Fri, 11am-3pm & 4.30pm-12am Sat, Sun)

Librería Metrópolis (Calle del Cerón 17) Good for maps.

Tourist office (☎ 953 19 04 55; otjaen@andalucia.org; Calle Ramón y Cajal 1; 🕒 10am-8pm Mon-Fri, to 7pm Oct-Mar, to 1pm Sat, Sun & holidays) Helpful, multilingual staff with plenty of free information about the city and province.

Sights

Jaén's huge **cathedral** (☎ 953 23 42 33; 🕒 8.30am-1pm & 4-7pm Mon-Sat Oct-Mar, to 1pm & 5-8pm Mon-Sat Apr-Sep, 9am-1pm & 5-7pm Sun) was built mainly in the 16th and 17th centuries, and mainly to the Renaissance designs of Andrés de Vandelvira – though the southwestern facade on Plaza de Santa María sports a dramatic array of 17th-century baroque statuary.

The Renaissance **Palacio de Villardompardo** (☎ 953 23 62 92; Plaza de Santa Luisa de Marillac; admission free with passport; 🕒 9am-8pm Tue-Fri, 9.30am-2.30pm Sat & Sun, closed holidays) houses three excellent attractions and is worth tracking down: the beautiful 11th-century **Baños Árabes** (Arab Baths), with a transparent walkway for viewing the excavated baths; the **Museo de Artes y Costumbres Populares**, devoted to the artefacts of the harsh rural lifestyle of pre-industrial Jaén province; and the **Museo Internacional de Arte Naïf**, with a large international collection of colourful and witty naive art. You can spend hours lost in the everyday detail so playfully depicted in these works.

The **Museo Provincial** (☎ 953 31 33 39; Paseo de la Estación 27; adult/EU citizen €1.50/free; 🕒 2.30-8.30pm Tue, 9am-8.30pm Wed-Sat, to 2.30pm Sun) has the finest collection of 5th-century-BC Iberian sculptures in Spain. Found in Porcuna, they show a clear Greek influence in their fluid form and graceful design.

Jaén's most exhilarating spot is the top of the Cerro de Santa Catalina, where the **Castillo de Santa Catalina** (☎ 953 12 07 33; admission €3; 🕒 10am-2pm & 5-9pm Tue-Sun Apr-Sep, 3.30-7pm

MASS FERVOUR IN THE SIERRA MORENA

On the last Sunday of every April, around half a million people converge on a remote shrine in the Sierra Morena in the northwest of Jaén province for one of Spain's biggest religious gatherings, the festive pilgrimage known as the Romería de la Virgen de la Cabeza. The original 13th-century Santuario de la Virgen de la Cabeza, 31km north of Andújar, was destroyed in the civil war, when Francoist troops occupying it were besieged by the Republicans for eight months, but the shrine has since been rebuilt. The annual festivities see a tiny statue of the Virgin Mary, known as La Morenita (the Little Brown One), being carried around the Cerro del Cabezo for about four hours from about 11am. It's a festive and emotive occasion, with children and items of clothing being passed over the heads of the crowd to priests who touch them to the Virgin's mantle.

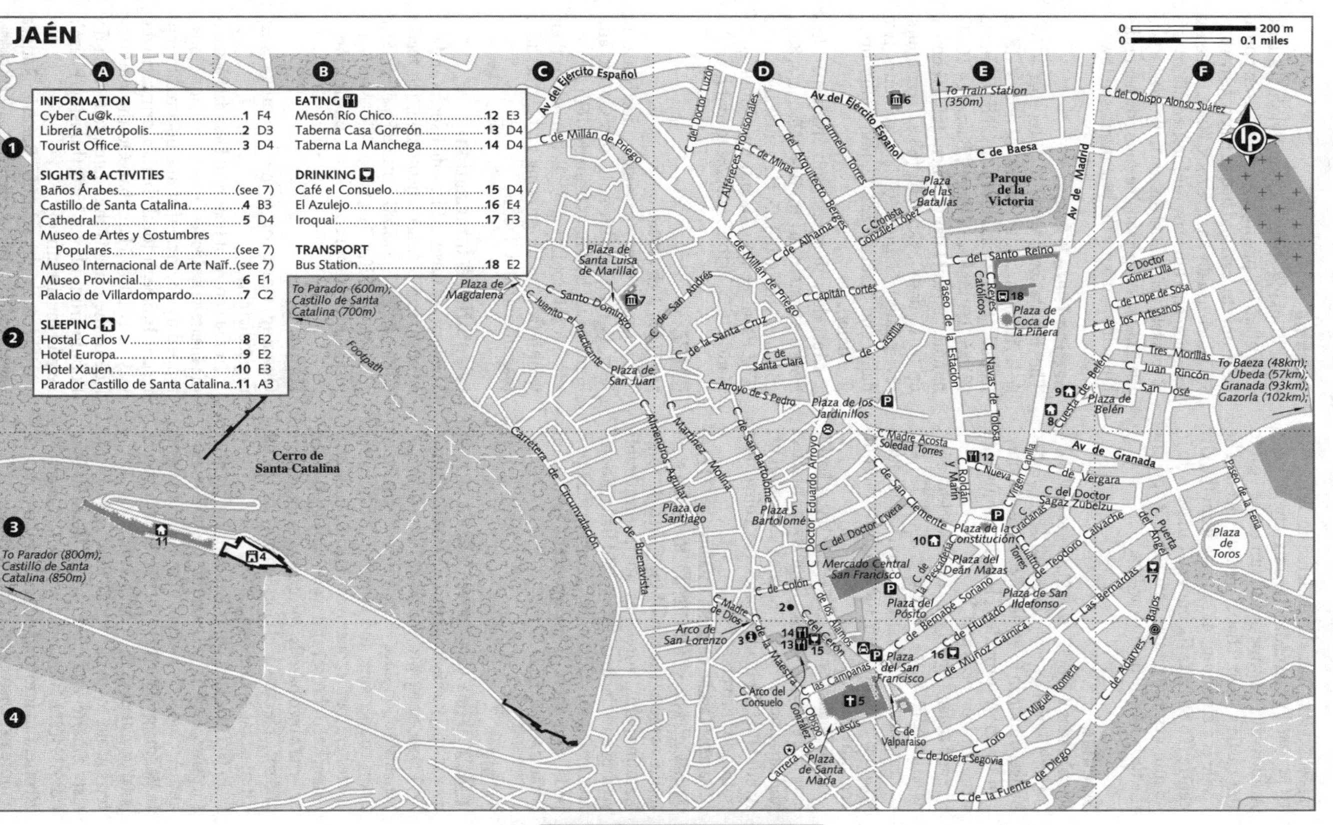
JAÉN
INFORMATION
Cyber Cu@k 1 F4
Librería Metrópolis 2 D3
Tourist Office 3 D4
SIGHTS & ACTIVITIES
Baños Árabes (see 7)
Castillo de Santa Catalina 4 B3
Cathedral 5 D4
Museo de Artes y Costumbres Populares (see 7)
Museo Internacional de Arte Naïf (see 7)
Museo Provincial 6 E1
Palacio de Villardompardo 7 C2
SLEEPING
Hostal Carlos V 8 E2
Hotel Europa 9 E2
Hotel Xauen 10 E3
Parador Castillo de Santa Catalina 11 A3
EATING
Mesón Río Chico 12 E3
Taberna Casa Gorreón 13 D4
Taberna La Manchega 14 D4
DRINKING
Café el Consuelo 15 D4
El Azulejo 16 E4
Iroquai 17 F3
TRANSPORT
Bus Station 18 E2
200 m
0.1 miles
To Train Station (350m)
To Baeza (48km); Úbeda (57km); Granada (93km); Gazorla (102km);
To Parador (600m); Castillo de Santa Catalina (700m)
To Parador (800m); Castillo de Santa Catalina (850m)
Cerro de Santa Catalina
Footpath
Parque de la Victoria
Plaza de las Batallas
Plaza de Toros
Paseo de la Feria
Av de Madrid
Av de Granada
Av del Ejército Español
C de Baesa
Paseo de la Estación
C Navas de Tolosa
C Reyes Católicos
Plaza de Coca de la Piñera
C del Santo Reino
C Roldán y Marín
C Madre Acosta Soledad Torres
Plaza de los Jardinillos
C de San Clemente
Plaza de la Constitución
Plaza del Deán Mazas
Mercado Central San Francisco
Plaza del Pósito
Plaza del San Francisco
Plaza de Santa María
C Doctor Eduardo Arroyo
C de los Álamos
C del Cerón
C de la Maestra
C de Colón
Plaza S Bartolomé
C de San Bartolomé
C Martínez Molina
C Almendros Aguilar
Plaza de Santiago
C de Buenavista
Carretera de Circunvalación
Plaza de San Juan
C Juanito el Practicante
C Santo Domingo
Plaza de Santa Luisa de Marillac
Plaza de Magdalena
C de Millán de Priego
C Alféreces Provisionales
C del Doctor Luzón
C Carmelo Torres
C del Arquitecto Berges
C de Alhama
C de Minas
C Cronista González López
C de Castilla
C Capitán Cortés
C Arroyo de S Pedro
C de Santa Clara
C de la Santa Cruz
C de San Andrés
Arco de San Lorenzo
C Madre de Dios
C Arco del Consuelo
C Obispo González
Carrera de Jesús
C las Campanas
C de Valparaíso
C de Josefa Segovia
C de la Fuente de Diego
C Toro
C Miguel Romera
C de Adarves Bajos
C Las Bernardas
C Puerta del Ángel
C de Vergara
C del Doctor Sagaz Zubelzu
C de Teodoro Calvache
C Cuatro Torres
C Gracianas
C Virgen Capilla
C Nueva
C de la Pescadería
C de Bernabé Soriano
C de Hurtado
C de Muñoz Garnica
Plaza de San Ildefonso
Cuesta de Belén
Plaza de Belén
C del Obispo Alonso Suárez
C Tres Morillas
C Juan Rincón
C San José
C de los Artesanos
C de Lope de Sosa
C Doctor Gómez Ulla
ANDALUCÍA

Tue-Sun Oct-Mar) was surrendered to Fernando III in 1246 by Granada after a six-month siege. Audiovisual gimmicks add fun to the visit to the castle's keep, chapel and dungeon. The castle is a circuitous 4km drive from the city centre (€6.50 by taxi), but you can walk up in 45 minutes using a steep path almost opposite the top of Calle de Buenavista.

Sleeping

Hostal Carlos V (☎ 953 22 20 91; Avenida de Madrid 4, 2nd fl; s/d without bathroom €24/38;) The best budget option in town, the well-located family-run Carlos V provides pleasant rooms with wrought-iron beds and TV.

Hotel Xauen (☎ 953 24 07 89; www.hotelxauenjaen.com; Plaza del Deán Mazas 3; s/d €56/84; P) The central, business-oriented Xauen has adequate facilities for a stopover, though the bathrooms are rather tired.

Hotel Europa (☎ 953 22 27 00; www.husa.es; Plaza de Belén 1; s/d €41/65; P) Rooms are attractive and spacious, and the Europa's location off Avenida de Granada makes it a convenient option for drivers.

Parador Castillo de Santa Catalina (☎ 953 23 00 00; www.parador.es; s/d €119/149; P) Next to the castle at the top of the Cerro de Santa Catalina, this hotel has an incomparable setting and theatrically vaulted halls. Rooms are luxuriously dignified, featuring four-post beds, and there is an excellent restaurant (mains €16 to €32).

Eating

our pick Taberna Casa Gorreón (☎ 953 23 20 00; www.tabernagorrion.es in Spanish; Calle Arco del Consuelo 7; 1.30pm-5pm Tue, Wed, Thu, 8am-12.30pm Sun & Mon) A Jaén institution since 1888, with its original tiled floor, copper sink and long bar. Aficionados come here for the topaz-yellow *queso manchego* (Manchego cheese) and sweet wine aged in the taverna's own barrels. Attracting an interesting and sociable crowd, El Gorreón may well be the ultimate tapas experience.

In fact, the Jaén tapas trail is full of pleasant surprises, especially along tiny Calle del Cerón and Arco del Consuelo. One such is **Taberna La Manchega** (☎ 953 23 21 92; Calle Bernardo López 12; platos combinados €7.50; lunch & dinner Wed-Mon), a terrific old-town bar where food is cheap and tasty. Smarter and more central, **Mesón Río Chico** (☎ 953 24 08 02; Calle Nueva 12; raciones €12-18, mains €14-24) offers an informal downstairs taberna and a more expensive restaurant upstairs.

Drinking

Cool drinking spots include stylish **El Azulejo** (Calle de Hurtado 8) playing everything from pop to electronic to jazz, and **Iroquai** (Calle de Adarves Bajos 53), which usually has live rock, blues, flamenco or fusion on Thursday. And at streamlined **Café el Consuelo** (Calle Arco del Consuelo 12; breakfast 9am-1pm, 8pm-3am) the personable young owner prides himself on making the best mojitos in town.

Getting There & Away

The **bus station** (☎ 953 25 01 06; Plaza de Coca de la Piñera) is 250m north of Plaza de la Constitución. Destinations include Granada (€7.85, 1½ hours, 14 daily), Baeza (€4.10, 45 minutes, up to 11 daily), Úbeda (€5, 1¼ hours, up to 12 daily), Córdoba (€8.22, 1½ hours, seven daily), Cazorla (€7.50, two hours, two daily) and Madrid (€23.02, four hours, up to five daily).

Most days there are only five departures from the **train station** (☎ 902 24 02 02); one, at 8am, goes to Córdoba (€8.85, 1½ hours) and Seville (€17.10, three hours), and up to four go to Madrid (€23.20 to €27.40, 2¾ to four hours).

BAEZA

pop 17,000 / elev 790m

This country town, 48km northeast of Jaén, is replete with gorgeous Gothic and Renaissance buildings from the 16th century, when local nobility ploughed much of their wealth from grain-growing and textiles into magnificent architecture.

Orientation & Information

The heart of town is Plaza de España and the adjacent Paseo de la Constitución. The **tourist office** (☎ 953 77 99 82/83; Plaza del Pópulo; 9am-7.30pm Mon-Fri, 9.30am-3pm, Sat, Sun & fiestas Apr-Sep) is just southwest of Paseo de la Constitución.

Sights

Opening times of some buildings vary unpredictably.

In the centre of beautiful **Plaza del Pópulo** is the **Fuente de los Leones** (Fountain of the Lions), topped by an ancient statue believed to represent Imilce, a local Iberian princess who was married to Hannibal. On the southern side of the plaza is the Plateresque Casa del Pópulo from about 1540 (housing Baeza's helpful tourist office).

Now a high school, Baeza's **Antigua Universidad** (Old University; Calle Beato Juan de Ávila; admis-

ANDALUCÍA

sion free; 10am-1pm & 4-6pm Thu-Tue) was founded in 1538. The main patio has two levels of elegant Renaissance arches. Round the corner is the early-16th-century **Palacio de Jabalquinto** (Plaza Santa Cruz; admission free; 9am-2pm Mon-Fri), a mansion with a flamboyant Isabelline-Gothic facade and lovely Renaissance patio with a fantastically carved baroque stairway. Across the square, the 13th-century **Iglesia de la Santa Cruz** (11am-1.00pm & 4.30-6pm Mon-Sat, 11am-1pm Sun), one of the first churches to be built in Andalucía after the Reconquista, may be the only Romanesque church in Andalucía.

Baeza's eclectic **cathedral** (Plaza de Santa María; donations welcome; 10.30am-1pm & 5-7pm Apr-Sep) is chiefly in 16th-century Renaissance style, with an interior designed by Andrés de Vandelvira and Jerónimo del Prado. One chapel displays a life-size Last Supper, with finely detailed wax figures and Mary in Victorian flounces of cream lace and pearls.

A block north of Paseo de la Constitución, the **ayuntamiento** (Town Hall; Paseo del Cardenal Benavides 9) has a marvellous plateresque facade.

Sleeping & Eating

With such a wealth of built heritage, there are several beautifully restored hotel conversions to choose from in Baeza.

Stylishly restored **Hotel Palacete Santa Ana** (953 74 16 57; www.palacetesantana.com; Calle Santa Ana Vieja 9; s/d €42/66;) has its own museum in what was a 16th-century nunnery. **Hospedería Fuentenueva** (953 74 31 00; www.fuentenueva.com; Calle del Carmen 15; s/d incl breakfast €52/78;), a former women's prison, now has big, beautiful rooms with matt-black slate shower rooms. **Hotel Baeza Monumental** (953 74 72 82; www.hotelbaezamonumental.com; Calle Cuesta de Prieto, 6; s/d Mon-Thu €46/50, Fri-Sun-€70-95; P) is a slick, modern revamp. **Hotel Puerta de la Luna** (953 74 70 19; www.hotelpuertadelaluna.com in Spanish; Calle Canónigo Melgares Raya s/n; s/d Mon-Thu €75/95, Fri-Sun €105/129; P) is quietly luxurious, with crisp damask sheets and antique accessories.

Hearty meals are found at **La Góndola** (953 74 29 84; Portales Carbonería 13, Paseo de la Constitución; mains €12-20) The terrific local atmosphere here is helped along by the glowing wood-burning grill, cheerful service and good food. At restored convent **Restaurante Vandelvira** (953 74 81 72; Calle de San Francisco 14; mains €8-22; closed Sun night & Mon) treat yourself to dishes such as partridge pâté salad or *solomillo al carbón* (char-grilled steak).

Getting There & Away

From the **bus station** (953 74 04 68; Paseo Arco del Agua), 700m east of Plaza de España, buses go to Jaén (€3.85, 45 minutes, 11 daily), Úbeda (€1.10, 30 minutes, 15 daily), Cazorla (€4.41, 2¼ hours, two daily) and Granada (€11.34, 2¼ hours, five daily)

Linares-Baeza train station (953 65 02 02) is 13km northwest. Buses connect with most trains Monday to Saturday; a taxi is €15.

ÚBEDA

pop 35,000 / elev 760m

Just 9km east of Baeza, Úbeda's architecture rivals its neighbour's. Sixteenth century grandee Francisco de los Cobos y Molina became first secretary to Carlos I; his nephew, Juan Vázquez de Molina, succeeded him in the job and kept it under Felipe II. They lavished their wealth on a profusion of Renaissance mansions and churches – many of them designed by Jaén's Renaissance master, Andrés de Vandelvira (b. 1509).

Orientation & Information

The fine architecture is mostly in the southeastern old part of town, a web of narrow streets and expansive plazas. Budget accommodation and the bus station are in the more down-to-earth new town in the west and north.

The **tourist office** (953 77 92 04; Calle Baja del Marqués 4; 9am-7.30pm Mon-Fri, 9.30am-3pm Sat, Sun & holidays) is in the 18th-century Palacio Marqués de Contadero in the old town.

Sights

PLAZA VÁZQUEZ DE MOLINA

This plaza, Úbeda's crown jewel, is surrounded by beautiful 15th- and 16th-century buildings.

The **Capilla de El Salvador** (admission €2.25; 10am-2pm & 4.30-7pm) faces the eastern end of the plaza. Founded in the 1540s by Francisco de los Cobos y Molina as his family funerary chapel, it was Vandelvira's first commission in Úbeda. The basic concept is by Diego de Siloé, architect of Granada cathedral, but Vandelvira added plenty of his own touches, including the elaborate main facade, an outstanding piece of plateresque design. Lit up at night, the whole facade seems to come to life. The sacristy, by Vandelvira, has a portrait of Francisco de los Cobos y Molina. The Cobos family crypt lies beneath the nave.

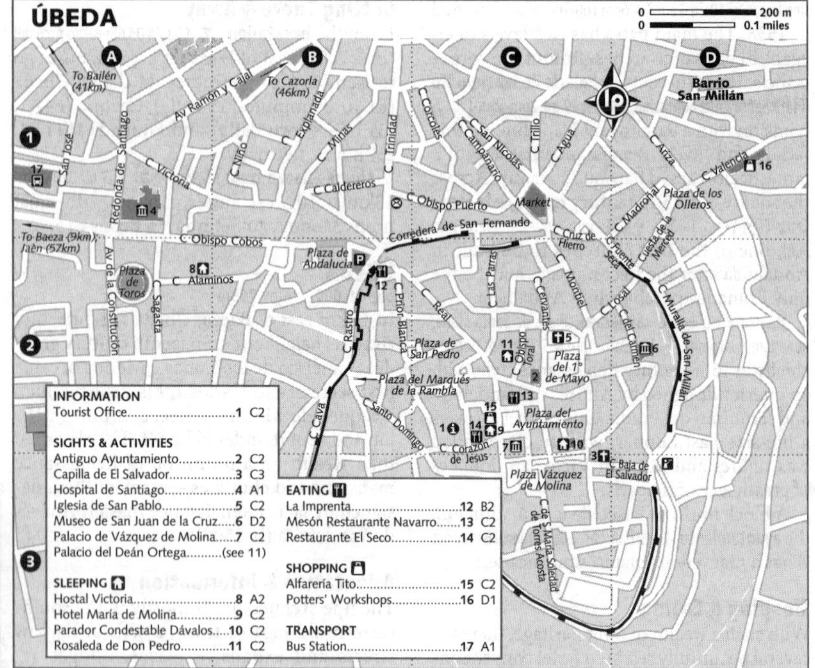

Next to the Capilla de El Salvador stands what was the abode of its chaplains – in fact one of Vandelvira's best palaces, the **Palacio del Deán Ortega**. It's now Úbeda's *parador*.

The harmonious proportions of the Italianate **Palacio de Vázquez de Molina** (10am-2pm & 5-8pm Mon-Sat, 10am-2pm Sun), at the western end of the plaza, make it one of the finest buildings in the town. Now Úbeda's town hall, it was built around 1562 by Vandelvira for Juan Vázquez de Molina, whose coat of arms surmounts the doorway.

PLAZA 1 DE MAYO & AROUND

Plaza 1 de Mayo used to be Úbeda's market square and bullring, and the Inquisition burnt heretics where its kiosk now stands. Worthies would watch from the gallery of the elegant 16th-century **Antiguo Ayuntamiento** (Old Town Hall) in the southwestern corner. Along the top (northern) side of the square is the **Iglesia de San Pablo** (11am-1.30pm & 7-8pm Mon-Sat), with a fine late-Gothic portal from 1511.

The **Museo de San Juan de la Cruz** (953 75 06 15; Calle del Carmen; admission €1.50; 11am-1pm & 5-7pm Tue-Sun) is devoted to the mystic and religious reformer St John of the Cross, who died here in 1591. Even if you can't understand the Spanish-speaking monks who guide all visits, you'll still get to marvel at some of the saint's mystical memorabilia.

HOSPITAL DE SANTIAGO

Completed in 1575, Andrés de Vandelvira's last **building** (Calle Obispo Cobos; admission free; 8am-2.30pm & 5-10pm Mon-Fri, 11am-3pm Sat & Sun) is on the western side of town. This impressive late-Renaissance masterpiece has been dubbed the 'Escorial of Andalucía'. Off the classic Vandelvira two-level patio are a chapel, now restored as an auditorium (the hospital is now a busy cultural centre), and a staircase with colourful frescoes.

Sleeping & Eating

Hostal Victoria (953 75 29 52; Calle Alaminos 5; s/d €26/40; P) Superfriendly Señora Victoria has run this backpackers' choice for over 20 years. It's near the bullring just behind the main shopping street, a cafe-studded stroll from the historic old quarter, and offers wheelchair access.

Rosaleda de Don Pedro (☎ 953 79 61 11; www.rosaledadedonpedro.com; Calle Obispo Toral 2; s €65-80, d €80-115; P ❄ 🖳 ♿) Back in the old town, this option offers three-star facilities, wheelchair access, a good restaurant and the only pool in the historic centre. All standard rooms are adapted for wheelchair users.

Hotel María de Molina (☎ 953 79 53 56; www.hotel-maria-de-molina.com in Spanish; Plaza del Ayuntamiento; s €53-61, d €84-94; ❄ 🖳) This handsome hotel occupies a 16th-century *palacio* on picturesque Plaza Ayuntamiento. Well-appointed rooms are arranged around a typical patio, and the hotel has a good restaurant.

Parador Condestable Dávalos (☎ 953 75 03 45; www.parador.es; Plaza Vázquez de Molina; s/d €114/159; ❄ 🖳) Overlooks the magnificent Plaza Vázquez de Molina and its restaurant serves up elegant dishes (around €14 to €22). Try local specialities such as *carruécano* (green peppers stuffed with partridge) or *cabrito guisado con piñones* (stewed kid with pine nuts).

Mesón Restaurante Navarro (☎ 953 79 06 38; Plaza del Ayuntamiento 2; raciones €6-14) Less exalted perhaps but great fun, this is a no-frills local favourite. Best *ración* is *tortitas de camarones* (crisply fried prawn mini-omelettes).

Restaurante El Seco (☎ 953 79 14 52; Calle Corazón de Jesús 8; menú €14) Has good traditional dishes such as steaming *carne de monte* (usually venison) with a rich tomato sauce.

La Imprenta (☎ 953 75 55 00; Plaza del Doctor Quesada 1; mains €16-25; 🕙 closed Tue) A renovated number, formerly Ubeda's print works, La Imprenta serves an inspired fusion menu of local ingredients.

Shopping

The typical green glaze on Úbeda's attractive pottery dates back to Islamic times. Several workshops on Cuesta de la Merced and Calle Valencia in the Barrio San Millán, the potters' quarter northeast of the old town, sell their wares on the spot, and the potters are often willing to explain some of the ancient techniques they still use. **Alfarería Tito** (Plaza del Ayuntamiento 12) has a large selection too. Tito's intricately made blue-and-cream ware is particularly covetable.

Getting There & Away

The **bus station** (☎ 953 75 21 57; Calle San José 6) is in the new part of town. Destinations include Baeza (€0.90, 30 minutes, 15 daily), Jaén (€4.50, 1¼ hours, up to 12 daily), Cazorla (€3.46, 45 minutes, up to 10 daily) and Granada (€11.34, 2¾ hours, seven daily).

CAZORLA

pop. 8250 / elev 885m

Cazorla, 45km east of Úbeda, is the main gateway to the Parque Natural de Cazorla and a quaintly intriguing hillside town of narrow old streets in its own right. It can get pretty busy at Spanish holiday times. Hunting and shooting are the dominant pastimes here, with game proudly displayed on restaurant walls and plates all over town.

Orientation & Information

Three plazas delineate the town's central axis: Plaza de la Constitución is the main square of the northern, newer part of town; Plaza de la Corredera is 150m further south along Calle Doctor Muñoz; and Plaza de Santa María, downhill through narrow, winding streets another 300m southeast, is the heart of the oldest part of town.

The **Oficina de Turismo Municipal** (☎ 953 72 08 75; Calle Narra 8; 🕙 10am-1pm & 5.00-7.30pm) is 200m north of Plaza de la Constitución.

Sights

At one end of lovely **Plaza de Santa María** is the large shell of the **Iglesia de Santa María.** It was built by Andrés de Vandelvira in the 16th century but wrecked by Napoleonic troops. A short walk up from here, the ancient **Castillo de la Yedra** houses the **Museo del Alto Guadalquivir** (adult/EU citizen €1.50/free; 🕙 2.30-8pm Tue, 9am-8pm Wed-Sat, to 2pm Sun & holidays), with art and relics of past local life.

Sleeping & Eating

Hotel Guadalquivir (☎ 953 72 02 68; www.hguadalquivir.com in Spanish; Calle Nueva 6; s/d €36/48; ❄) The Guadalquivir has comfortable, pine-furnished rooms and big bathrooms. The singles can be a bit cramped, but it's good value in an excellent location seconds from the Plaza de la Corredera.

Hotel Tharsis (☎ 953 721 313; www.tharsiscazorla.com in Spanish; Calle Hilario Marco 51-53; s/d €50/65 + IVA, incl breakfast; 🕙 closed Jan; P ❄ 🖳) This midrange, midtown hotel is a boon for motorists with its ample parking, friendly management and pleasant modern rooms behind its rather dull facade.

Molino la Farraga (☎ 953 72 12 49; www.molinolafarraga.com; Calle Camino de la Hoz s/n; d €70 incl breakfast; 🕙 closed mid-Dec–25 Feb; 🖳 ♿) The tranquil old La Farraga mill, set in romantic gardens, is

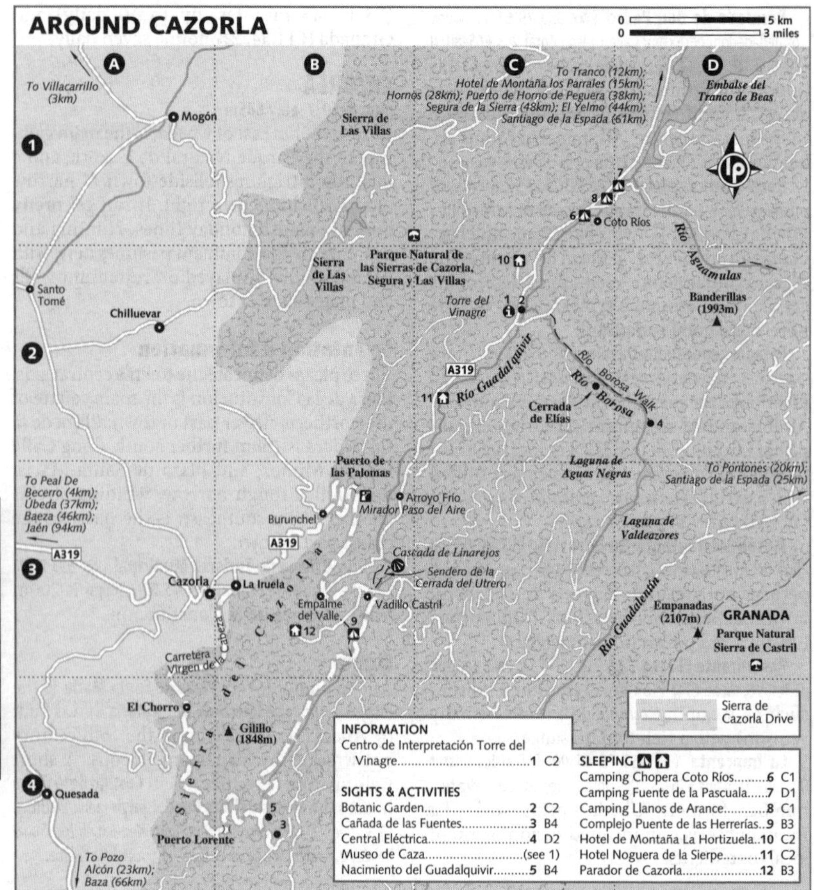

just up the valley from Plaza Santa María. You have to park in the public spaces and walk 100 metres up the steep path, but waiting for you is an exquisite house and the warmest of welcomes from Marisa.

Hotel Ciudad de Cazorla (☎ 953 72 17 00; Plaza de la Corredera 9; s/d incl breakfast €63/74; P) This modern structure on mansion-ruled Plaza de Corredera has had resistance from tradition-minded locals, but it's a good building with spacious rooms and all the requisite facilities.

Rincón Serrano (Plaza de la Corredera; raciones €8) Several bars on Cazorla's three main squares serve good tapas and *raciones*. Rincón Serrano has the best location: perched high in the southeast corner of the Plaza with commanding views over this bustling square.

Mesón Don Chema (☎ 953 72 00 68; Calle Escaleras del Mercado 2; mains €10-18) Down a lane off Calle Doctor Muñoz, this hunting-themed restaurant in a hunting-mad town serves up classic local fare; try the *ciervo* (venison) in an intense wine sauce with pine nuts.

Mesón Leandro (☎ 953 72 06 32; Plaza de Santa Maria; mains €7-18.50; closed Tue) Tucked away in the furthest corner of this pretty plaza near the ruins of Iglesia Santa Maria, Mesón Leandro serves reasonably good and well-priced traditional food in a handsome, tranquil room with classical music.

Getting There & Away

Alsina Graells runs buses to/from Úbeda (€3.35, 45 minutes, up to 10 daily), Jaén

(€7.37, two hours, two daily) and Granada (€14.12, 3½ hours, two daily). The main stop in Cazorla is Plaza de la Constitución; the tourist office has timetables.

PARQUE NATURAL DE CAZORLA

The **Parque Natural de las Sierras de Cazorla, Segura y Las Villas,** filling almost all the east side of Jaén province, is a stunning region of rugged mountain ranges divided by high plains and deep, forested valleys, and it's one of the best places in Spain for spotting wildlife. At 2143 sq km, it's also the biggest protected area in the country. Walkers stand a good chance of seeing wild boar, red and fallow deer, ibex and mouflon (a large wild sheep). The park also supports 2300 plant species.

The Guadalquivir, Andalucía's longest river, rises in the south of the park and flows north into the Embalse del Tranco de Beas reservoir, then west towards the Atlantic.

Admittedly, you do need wheels to reach some of the most spectacular areas and walks. The best times to visit are between late April and June, and September and October, when the vegetation flourishes and the weather is at its best. In spring, the flowers are magnificent. Peak visitor periods are Semana Santa, July and August.

Orientation & Information

Entering the park from Cazorla, the A319 winds over the 1200m Puerto de las Palomas pass and down to the Empalme del Valle junction, where it turns north and follows the Guadalquivir valley.

The main information centre is the **Centro de Interpretación Torre del Vinagre** (☎ 953 71 30 40; ⌚ 10am-2pm & 4-7pm Apr-Jun, 10am-2pm & 5-8pm Jul-Aug, 10am-2pm & 4-6pm Nov-Mar), 16km north of Empalme del Valle on the A319. Kids will enjoy the interactive AV exhibits about the park's flora and fauna. The **Museo de Caza** (Hunting Museum) with stuffed park wildlife, is in an adjoining building; a more-cheerful **botanic garden** is just along the road.

Editorial Alpina's 1:40,000 *Sierra de Cazorla,* which covers the south of the park and is available in English, and *Sierra de Segura,* which covers the north, are the best maps, showing selected walks that are described in accompanying booklets. You may be able to get the maps locally, but don't count on it.

Sights & Activities

SIERRA DE CAZORLA DRIVE

For those with wheels, this itinerary of about 60km is a good introduction to the parts of the park nearest Cazorla, with a couple of stops to stretch your legs. It's all passable for ordinary cars, if bumpy in places.

Head first up to La Iruela, 1km east of Cazorla, and turn right along Carretera Virgen de la Cabeza. About 12km along here, during which the road ceases to be paved, is **El Chorro**, a gorge that's good for watching vultures. Just beyond El Chorro, ignore another dirt road forking down to the right. Your track winds round over the **Puerto Lorente** pass and down to a junction after 12km. Fork right here, and after about 200m a 'Nacimiento del Guadalquivir' sign to your left points down to the official **source of the Guadalquivir**.

The road heads a short distance past the Nacimiento to the **Cañada de las Fuentes** picnic area, a convenient stop. From here head back northward down the beautiful valley of the infant Guadalquivir. At a T-junction after 14km, about 1km beyond the northern end of the **Complejo Puente de las Herrerías**, go left; after 400m the **Sendero de la Cerrada del Utrero** begins on the right. This marked 2km-loop walk takes you under imposing cliffs to the **Cascada de Linarejos**, then above a narrow reservoir on the Guadalquivir and back to the road. Another 3.5km west along the road and you're at Empalme del Valle, from which it's 17km back to Cazorla.

RÍO BOROSA WALK

Though it gets busy at weekends and holidays, this walk of about seven hours return (plus stops) is the park's most popular for good reason. It follows the course of Río Borosa upstream to two beautiful mountain lakes: an ascent of 500m in the course of 12km from Torre del Vinagre. Using the bus to Torre del Vinagre, you can do it as a day trip from Cazorla (but confirm bus schedules before setting off). You can top up your water bottle at good, drinkable springs along the walk; the last is at the Central Eléctrica hydroelectric station.

A road signed 'Central Eléctrica', opposite Torre del Vinagre, soon crosses the Guadalquivir and, within 1km, reaches the marked start of the walk, on your right beside Río Borosa. The first section is an unpaved road, crisscrossing the tumbling river on bridges. After 4km, where the road starts climbing to the left, take a path forking right. This takes you through a beautiful 1.5km section, where the valley narrows to a gorge, **Cerrada de Elías**, and the path takes to a wooden walkway to save you from swimming. Rejoining the main track, continue for 3km to the Central Eléctrica hydroelectric station. Just past this, a sign points you on up towards the Laguna de Valdeazores. This path will lead you, via some dramatic mountain scenery and two tunnels supplying water to the power station (there's room to stay dry as you go through), to reservoir **Laguna de Aguas Negras**, then the natural **Laguna de Valdeazores.**

HORNOS & EL YELMO

The small village of Hornos sits atop a high rocky outcrop with a romantic ruined castle and panoramic views over the northern end of the Embalse del Tranco. The southern approach is awe-inspiring. About 10km northeast of Hornos is the Puerto de Horno de Peguera pass and junction. One kilometre north from here, a dirt road turns left to the top of El Yelmo (1809m), one of the most distinctive mountains in the north of the park. It's 5km to the top, an ascent of 360m – driveable, but better as a walk, with superb views and griffon vultures wheeling around the skies (plus paragliders and hang-gliders at weekends). At a fork after 1.75km, go right.

ANDALUCÍA

SEGURA DE LA SIERRA

The most spectacular village inside the park, Segura sits 20km north of Hornos, perched on an 1100m hill crowned by a castle. When taken in 1214 by the Knights of Santiago, Segura was one of the very first Christian conquests in Andalucía.

As you reach the upper part of the village, there's a **tourist office** (☎ 953 12 60 53; 🕑 10.30am-2pm & 6.30-8.30pm) beside the Puerta Nueva arch. Segura's two main monuments are normally left open all day every day, but you should check this before proceeding.

The **Baño Moro** (Muslim Bathhouse; Calle Caballeros Santiaguistas), built about 1150, has three elegant rooms (for cold, tepid and hot baths) with horseshoe arches and barrel vaults studded with skylights. The **castle**, at the top of the village, has Islamic (or maybe even earlier) origins. From its three-storey keep there are great views across to El Yelmo and far to the west.

Tours

A number of operators offer trips to some of the park's less accessible areas, plus other activities. Hotels and camping grounds in the park can often arrange for them to pick you up.

Excursiones Bujarkay (☎ 953 72 11 11; www.guiasnativos.com; Calle Martinez Falero, 28, Cazorla) Walking, 4WD, biking and horse-riding trips with 'native' guides.

Tierraventura (☎ 953 72 20 11/953 71 00 73; www.tierraventuracazorla.com in Spanish; Calle Ximénez de Rada 17, Cazorla) Multiadventure activities including canoeing, hiking, canyon descents and rock climbing.

TurisNat (☎ 953 72 13 51; www.turisnat.org in Spanish; Paseo del Santo Cristo 17 Bajo, Edificio Parque, Cazorla) Offers wildlife spotting trips, photo-safaris and 4WD trips to *zonas restringidas* (areas where vehicles are not normally allowed) for €28/47 per person per half/full day.

Sleeping & Eating

There's plenty of accommodation in the park, much of it dotted along the A319 north of Empalme del Valle. At peak times it's worth booking ahead. Most restaurants in the park are part of hotels or *hostales*.

CAMPING

Camping is not allowed outside the organised camping grounds. From October to April you should check ahead that these are open.

Complejo Puente de las Herrerías (☎/fax 953 72 70 90; near Vadillo Castril; sites per adult/tent/car €4.80/4.40/4.40, caravan €5.20-6.20, 2-person cabin €48, rooms €50; P ⛞ ⛱) This is the largest camping ground in the park, with room for about 1000 people, plus a restaurant and a pool. You can arrange horse riding, canoeing, canyoning and climbing here.

Just off the A319, between 3km and 7km north of Torre del Vinagre, are three medium-sized camping grounds beside the Guadalquivir, all charging between €13 and €15 for two people with a tent and car:

Camping Chopera Coto Ríos (☎ 953 71 30 05)
Camping Fuente de la Pascuala (☎ 953 71 30 28)
Camping Llanos de Arance (☎ 953 71 31 39)

HOTELS & APARTMENTS

El Parral (☎ 953 72 72 65; Arroyo Frío; 4-person apt €70; P ⛞ ⛱) Attractive, spacious apartments that have well-equipped kitchens and scenic terraces.

Hotel de Montaña Los Parrales (☎ 953 12 61 70/699 83 40 49; www.turismoencazorla.com/parrales.html in Spanish; Carretera del Tranco Km78; s/d €35/44, half/full board €12.50/22.50 per day extra; P ⛞) North of Tranco along the road towards Hornos, cheerful Los

Parrales has idyllic views of the reservoir and a country-style dining room.

Hotel de Montaña La Hortizuela (☎ 953 71 30 13; www.lahortizuela.com in Spanish; Carretera del Tranco Km50.5; s/d €38/58; P ✤ ☒) This cosy hotel with a well-kept terrace has a tranquil setting, 1km along a signed track off the A319, 2km north of Torre del Vinagre. The restaurant serves a *menú* at €12.

Los Enebros (☎ 953 72 71 10; www.lfhoteles.com in Spanish; Arroyo Frío; s/d half-board €54/58, 4-person apt €111; P ✤ ☒) At the northern end of Arroyo Frío village on the A319, this complex has a hotel, apartments, chalets and a small camping ground. The accommodation is spartan but has two pools and a playground. A huge range of activities can be arranged here.

Los Huertos de Segura (☎ 953 48 04 02; www.loshuertosdesegura.com; Calle Castillo 11, Segura de la Sierra; 2-/4-person apt €58/78; P ✤) Excellent apartments whose genuinely friendly and helpful owners are full of information about tours and walking in the area. Excellent English spoken.

Hotel Noguera de la Sierpe (☎ 953 71 30 21; www.lfhoteles.com in Spanish; Carretera del Tranco Km 44; s/d €60/90; P ✤ ☒) This curious hotel, overlooking a picturesque little lake 5km north of Arroyo Frío, is a hunters' favourite and decked out with trophies. The rooms are comfortable, if not exactly cosy. You can arrange riding sessions at the hotel's stables, and there is a good rustic restaurant.

Parador de Cazorla (☎ 953 72 70 75; www.parador.es; s/d €109.57/128; P ☒) This hunting-lodge–style *parador* has a lovely pine forest setting, grassy garden and good pool, but only nine of the 33 rooms have views. It's at the end of the JF7094, near Vadillo Castril.

Getting There & Away

Carcesa (☎ 953 72 11 42) runs two daily buses (except Sunday) from Cazorla's Plaza de la Constitución to Empalme del Valle (€1.80, 30 minutes), Arroyo Frío (€2.13, 45 minutes), Torre del Vinagre (€3.49, one hour) and Coto Ríos (€3.49, 70 minutes). Pick up the latest timetable from the Cazorla tourist office.

ALMERÍA PROVINCE

Arid, inhospitable Almeria has achieved a spectacular economic comeback in recent years, embracing tourism and mass horticulture in its *invernaderos,* the shiny oceans of plastic greenhouses further inland. Though some of the coast has suffered from dreary Costa-del-Sol–style development, the dramatic Cabo de Gata promontory remains more or less pristine.

ALMERÍA

pop 175,000

The hefty, cliff-ringed Alcazaba fortress dominating Almería is a dramatic reminder of past glories. As the chief port of the Córdoba caliphate and, later, capital of an 11th-century *taifa,* Islamic Almariya grew wealthy weaving silk from the silkworms of the Alpujarras. Devastated by an earthquake in 1522, Almería is today an increasingly prosperous port city and magnet for migrant job-seekers. Agri-euros from the province's horticulture are helping to fund a revival, and chic bars and clubs stay open till dawn.

Orientation

The city centre lies between the Alcazaba and the Rambla de Belén, a broad promenade created from a dry riverbed. Paseo de Almería, cutting northwest from Rambla de Belén to the Puerta de Purchena intersection, is the main city-centre artery. The bus and train stations are together on Plaza de la Estación, east of Rambla de Belén.

Information

There are numerous banks on Paseo de Almería.

El Libro Picasso (☎ 950 23 56 00; Calle Reyes Católicos 9) Excellent book and map shop with a small English-language book selection.

Internet Saram Corazon (Junction Calle de las Tiendas & Calle Azara; per hr €1; ⏲ 10am-2.30pm & 6pm-midnight) Ten booths, efficient service despite low-tech sweet-shop frontage.

Main post office (Behind Plaza Ecuador)

Municipal tourist office (☎ 950 28 07 48; Rambla de Belén; ⏲ 8.30am-2pm & 5pm-7.30pm Mon-Fri, 8.30am-2pm Sat)

Regional tourist office (☎ 950 27 43 55; Parque de Nicolás Salmerón s/n; ⏲ 9am-7pm Mon-Fri, 10am-2pm Sat & Sun)

Policía Local (☎ 950 21 00 19; Calle Santos Zárate)

Sights & Activities

ALCAZABA

The founding of the **Alcazaba** (☎ 950 17 55 00; Calle Almanzor s/n; adult/EU citizen €1.50/free; ⏲ 9-8.30pm Apr-Oct & 9am-6.30pm Nov-Mar) by the Córdoba caliph

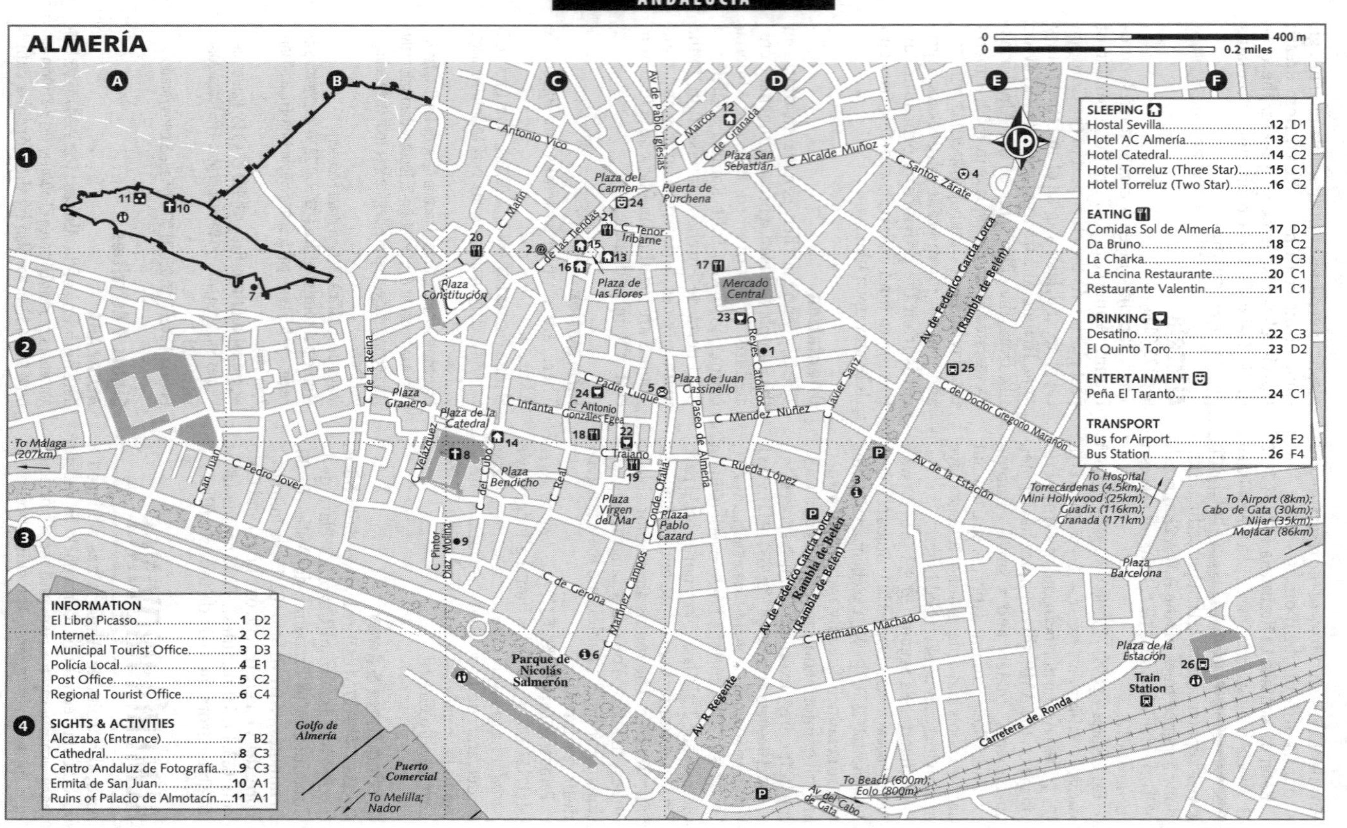
ALMERÍA
0 400 m
0 0.2 miles
SLEEPING
Hostal Sevilla....12 D1
Hotel AC Almería....13 C2
Hotel Catedral....14 C2
Hotel Torreluz (Three Star)....15 C1
Hotel Torreluz (Two Star)....16 C2
EATING
Comidas Sol de Almería....17 D2
Da Bruno....18 C2
La Charka....19 C3
La Encina Restaurante....20 C1
Restaurante Valentin....21 C1
DRINKING
Desatino....22 C3
El Quinto Toro....23 D2
ENTERTAINMENT
Peña El Taranto....24 C1
TRANSPORT
Bus for Airport....25 E2
Bus Station....26 F4
INFORMATION
El Libro Picasso....1 D2
Internet....2 C2
Municipal Tourist Office....3 D3
Policía Local....4 E1
Post Office....5 C2
Regional Tourist Office....6 C4
SIGHTS & ACTIVITIES
Alcazaba (Entrance)....7 B2
Cathedral....8 C3
Centro Andaluz de Fotografía....9 C3
Ermita de San Juan....10 A1
Ruins of Palacio de Almotacín....11 A1
C Antonio Vico
C Marín
Plaza del Carmen
Puerta de Purchena
Av de Pablo Iglesias
C Marcos
C de Granada
Plaza San Sebastián
C Alcalde Muñoz
C Santos Zárate
C de las Tiendas
C Tenor Iribarne
Plaza de las Flores
Plaza Constitución
Mercado Central
C Reyes Católicos
Av de Federico García Lorca
(Rambla de Belén)
C de la Reina
Plaza Granero
Plaza de la Catedral
C Infanta
C Padre Luque
C Antonio Gonzáles Egea
Plaza de Juan Cassinello
Paseo de Almería
C Mendez Nuñez
C Javier Sanz
C del Doctor Gregorio Marañón
To Málaga (207km)
C San Juan
C Pedro Jover
C Velázquez
C del Cubo
Plaza Bendicho
C Real
C Trajano
C Conde Ofalia
C Rueda López
Av de la Estación
To Hospital Torrecárdenas (4.5km); Mini Hollywood (25km); Guadix (116km); Granada (171km)
To Airport (8km); Cabo de Gata (30km); Níjar (35km); Mojácar (86km)
C Pintor Díaz Molina
Plaza Virgen del Mar
Plaza Pablo Cazard
C de Gerona
C Martínez Campos
Rambla de Belén
Plaza Barcelona
C Hermanos Machado
Plaza de la Estación
Train Station
Parque de Nicolás Salmerón
Av R Regente
Carretera de Ronda
Golfo de Almería
Puerto Comercial
To Melilla; Nador
To Beach (600m); Eolo (800m)
Av del Cabo de Gata

Abd ar-Rahman III in 955 was what turned Almería into the major port of Al-Andalus. It still rises triumphantly from impregnable cliffs and commands exhilarating views, though earthquakes and time have spared little of its internal splendour.

The lowest of the Alcazaba's three compounds, the Primer Recinto, originally served as a military camp in times of siege. The Segundo Recinto was the heart of the Alcazaba. At its eastern end is the **Ermita de San Juan** chapel, which was converted from a mosque by the Catholic Monarchs, who took Almería in 1489. On its northern side are the remains of the Muslim rulers' palace, the **Palacio de Almotacín**. The Tercer Recinto, at the top end of the Alcazaba, is a fortress added by the Catholic Monarchs.

CATHEDRAL

Almería's weighty **cathedral** (Plaza de la Catedral; admission €2; 10am-2pm & 4pm-5.30pm, Mon-Fri, to 1pm Sat) is at the heart of the old part of the city below the Alcazaba. Begun in 1524, its fortresslike appearance, with six towers, reflects the prevalence of pirate raids from North Africa during this era.

The interior has a Gothic ribbed ceiling and is trimmed with jasper and local marble. The chapel behind the main altar contains the tomb of Bishop Diego Villalán, the cathedral's founder, whose broken-nosed image is the work of Juan de Orea, who also created the Sacristía Mayor with its fine carved stonework.

Centro Andaluz de Fotografía (Andalucian Photographic Centre; 950 26 96 80; Calle Pintor Diaz Molina, 9; admission free; 11am-2pm & 5.30pm-9.30pm Mon-Sun) Whether you are a keen photographer or an overheated sightseer, you will enjoy the edgy and memorable images.

BEACHES

A long, grey-sand beach fronts the palm-lined Paseo Marítimo, east of the city's centre. **Eolo** (950 26 17 35; www.eolo-wind.com; Avenida del Cabo de Gata 187), nearby, organises out-of-town trips (€39 to €90) with English-speaking staff to explore some of the dramatic cliffs and beaches of the Parque Natural Cabo de Gata-Níjar by windsurfing, kayaking, catamaran and other water-related activities.

Sleeping

Hostal Sevilla (950 23 00 09; Calle de Granada 23; s/d €38/54;) This best budget bet is a cheerful and efficient place that offers clean rooms and a good central location. Bathrooms are minuscule but modern.

Hotel Torreluz (950 23 43 99; www.torreluz.com; Plaza de las Flores 2 & 3; s/d 2-star €39/64, 3-star €56/74; P) Burnt-plum-coloured walls, comfortable beds and good prices make this one of Almería's best-value places to stay.

Hotel AC Almeria (950 23 49 99; www.acalmeria.com; Plaza de las Flores 5; s/d €100; P) A grand four-star place with lots of brass and marble and a huge sweeping staircase, this is a favourite with business clientele, and prices are reduced by up to 40% at weekends.

Hotel Catedral (950 27 81 78: www.hotelcatedral.net; Plaza de la Catedral 8; s/d €110/140;) Superbly located, this elegantly restored former 19th-century house offers spacious rooms all with broadband and satellite TV. A smart bar and restaurant with funky touches serves light modern Mediterranean dishes.

Eating

La Charka (950 25 60 45; Calle Trajano 8; drink & tapa €1.50) This very popular tapas haunt in Almería's busiest bar area is a great spot to graze in the earlier part of the evening.

Da Bruno Ristorante/Pizzeria (950 27 72 09; Calle Martinez Almagro 8; mains €6-11.50; 12pm-4.30 & 8pm-12.30am) Big, cheerful, noisy pizzeria serving surprisingly good salads, pizza and pasta, including an untamed, spicy *arrabiatta*. Kids will love it.

Comidas Sol de Almería (Calle Circunvalación, Mercado Central; menú €10.50; 12.30pm-4pm, closed Sun) A jolly restaurant, opposite the busy covered market, with a large sunlit yet sheltered patio behind it. Hungry shoppers stream in for the extensive and hearty lunch *menú*.

Restaurante Valentín (950 26 44 75; Calle Tenor Iribarne 19; mains €10-15; closed Mon & Sep) A secluded, intimate fish restaurant with stylish service and good food.

La Encina Restaurante (950 27 34 29; Calle Marín 3; mains €16-27; closed Sun dinner & Mon) Good traditional dishes with a twist, including a seven-fungi sauté. If you have space, finish with coconut sorbet in a moat of red berry sauce.

Drinking & Entertainment

El Quinto Toro (950 23 91 35; Calle Juan Leal 6; 12-4pm, 8-12pm, closed Sat evening & Sun) Authentic, bull-fight-flavoured tapas bar that has been a local institution since 1947. Good selection of tapas and friendly third-generation owner.

Desatino (Calle Trajano 14; 8pm-late) A trendy bar with mirrored windows, playing Cuban rumbas. It doesn't open or fill up until late.

Peña El Taranto (950 23 50 57; Calle Tenor Iribarne 20) Hidden in the renovated Aljibes Árabes (Arab Water Cisterns), this is Almería's top flamenco club. Live performances (€20), open to the public, often happen at weekends.

Getting There & Away

AIR

Almería **airport** (950 21 37 00) 10km east of the city centre receives flights from several European countries. **Easyjet** (www.easyjet.com) flies from London Gatwick and Stansted, **Ryanair** (www.ryanair.com) from Stansted, **Jet2** (www.jet2.com) from Leeds/Bradford and **Monarch Airlines** (www.flymonarch.com) from Birmingham and Manchester, **Air-Berlin** (www.airberlin.com) flies from Berlin and **Transavia** (www.transavia.com) from Amsterdam. **Iberia** (www.iberia.com) flies direct to/from Barcelona, Madrid and Melilla.

BOAT

Trasmediterránea (950 23 61 55; www.trasmediterranea.es; Estación Marítima) sails daily to/from Melilla and twice daily most days from June to September. The trip takes up to eight hours on the slow ferry and three hours on the fast ferry. A *butaca* (seat) costs €33.20 one way; car fares start at €189.20 for a small vehicle and driver. Three Moroccan lines sail to/from Nador, the Moroccan town neighbouring Melilla, with similar frequency and prices. Trasmediterránea also has summer sailings to Ghazaouet, Algeria.

BUS

Destinations served from the clean, efficient **bus station** (950 26 20 98) include Granada (€10.95 to €13, 2¼ hours, 10 daily), Málaga (€15.85, 3¼ hours, 10 daily), Murcia (€5.50, 2½ hours, 10 daily), Madrid (€25, seven hours, five daily) and Valencia (€33 to €39.50, 8½ hours, five daily).

TRAIN

Four daily trains run to Granada (€14.45, 2¼ hours) and Seville (€34.80, 5½ hours); two run to Madrid (€40.80 to €54, 6¾ to 10 hours).

Getting Around

The airport is 8km east of the city; the number 20 'Alquián' bus (€0.90 runs from Calle Doctor Gregorio Marañón to the airport every 40 to 50 minutes from 6.35am to 10.40pm (but less frequently on Saturday and Sunday). The last bus from the airport to the city leaves at 10.33pm (10.22pm Saturday and Sunday).

AROUND ALMERÍA

Mini Hollywood

Beyond Benahadux, north of Almería, the landscape becomes a series of canyons and rocky wastes that look straight out of the Arizona badlands, and in the 1960s and '70s moviemakers shot around 150 Westerns here.

The movie industry has left behind three Wild West town sets that are open as tourist attractions. **Mini Hollywood** (950 36 52 36; poblado@playasenator.com; adult/child €19/9; 10am-9pm Apr-Oct, to 7pm Tue-Sun Nov-Mar), the best known and the best preserved of these, is 25km from Almería on the N340 Tabernas road. Parts of more than 100 movies, including *A Fistful of Dollars* and *The Good, the Bad and the Ugly*, were filmed here. At 5pm (and 8pm from mid-June to mid-September) a hammed-up bank hold-up and shootout is staged (dialogue in Spanish of course). Rather bizarrely, the ticket also includes entry to the adjoining **Reserva Zoológica**. You will need your own vehicle to visit from Almería.

Níjar

Attractive and unusual glazed pottery and colourful striped cotton rugs, known as *jarapas*, are made and sold in this small town 34km northeast of Almería. Worth a detour – Nijar was also the real-life setting for the story that became Federico Garcia Lorca's *Blood Wedding*.

CABO DE GATA

Some of Spain's most beautiful and least crowded beaches are strung between grand cliffs and capes east of Almería city, where dark volcanic hills tumble into a sparkling turquoise sea. Though Cabo de Gata is not undiscovered, it still has a wild, elemental feel and, with a couple of exceptions in July and August, its scattered villages remain low-key. You can walk along, or not far from, the coast right round from Retamar in the northwest to Agua Amarga in the northeast (61km), but in summer there's little shade.

It's worth calling ahead for accommodation over Easter and in July and August.

The **Parque Natural de Cabo de Gata-Níjar** covers Cabo de Gata's 60km coast plus a slice of hinterland. The park's main information centre is the **Centro de Interpretación Las Amoladeras** (☎ 950 16 04 35; ⏰ 10am-2pm & 5.30-9pm mid-Jul–mid-Sep, to 3pm Tue-Sun mid-Sep–mid-Jul), about 2.5km west of Ruescas.

El Cabo de Gata Village

Fronted by a long straight beach, this village (officially San Miguel de Cabo de Gata) is composed largely of holiday houses and apartments (deserted out of season), but has an old nucleus, with a small fishing fleet, at the southern end. The **Oficina de Información** (☎ 950 38 00 04; Avenida Miramar 88; ⏰ 10am-2.30pm & 5.30-9pm) rents out bicycles (€5/14 per two hours/day) – a nice way to explore the area.

South of the village stretch the **Salinas de Cabo de Gata**, which are salt-extraction lagoons. In spring many migrating greater flamingos and other birds call in here: by late August there can be 1000 flamingos here. There's a public viewing hide just off the road, 3km south of the village.

You should see a good variety of birds from here any time except winter, when the *salinas* (salt-extraction lagoons) are drained, but you really need binoculars to appreciate the scene.

There are a couple of decent options for accommodation: **Hostal Las Dunas** (☎ 950 37 00 72; www.lasdunas.net; Calle Barrio Nuevo 58; s/d €36/51; P), a friendly, family-run hotel with spotless modern rooms, huge bathrooms and crazy balustraded balconies carved in marble and wreathed with flowers. For camping, try the extremely well-run **Camping Cabo de Gata** (☎ 950 16 04 43; site for adult/tent or caravan/car & electricity €17.28, bungalow €71-112; P), 1km from the beach; it has all the necessary amenities including a restaurant. It's 2.5km north of the village by dirt roads.

Located right at the entrance to the village, **El Naranjero** (☎ 950 37 01 11; Calle Iglesia 1; mains €12-27; ⏰ closed Sun), specialises in fish and seafood dishes.

Faro de Cabo de Gata & Around

Beyond the Salinas de Cabo de Gata, a narrow road winds 4km round the cliffs to the **Faro de Cabo de Gata**, the lighthouse at the promontory's tip. A turning by Café Bar El Faro, just before the lighthouse, leads to the **Torre Vigía Vela Blanca**,

ANDALUCÍA

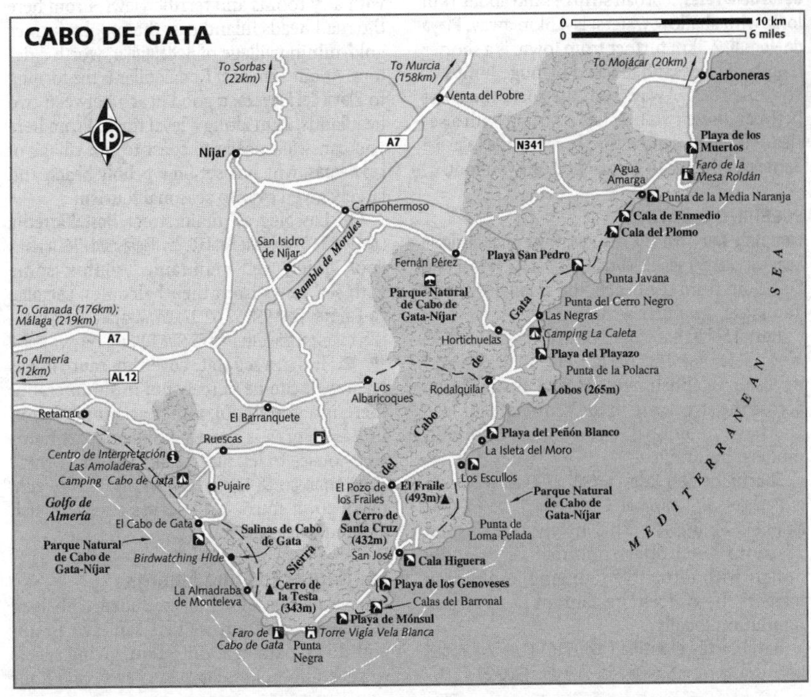

an 18th-century watchtower atop 200m cliffs, with awesome views. Here the road ends but a walking and cycling track continues down to Playa de Mónsul (one hour on foot).

San José

pop 550

San José, spreading round a bay on the eastern side of Cabo de Gata, is a mildly chic resort in summer, but it remains a small, pleasant, low-rise place and is a base for both watery and land-bound activities. Out of season you may have the place almost to yourself.

The road from the north becomes San José's main street, Avenida de San José, with the beach and harbour a couple of blocks down to the left. On Avenida de San José you'll find a **Natural Park information office** (☎ 950 38 02 99; Calle Correo; ⏰ 10am-2pm & 5-9.30pm Mon-Sat, to 2pm Sun), a bank and an ATM. The information office can tell you about bicycle rental, horse riding, boat trips and diving.

BEACHES

Some of the best beaches on Cabo de Gata lie along a dirt road southwest from San José. **Playa de los Genoveses**, a broad strip of sand about 1km long with shallow waters, is 4.5km away. **Playa de Mónsul**, 2.5km further from town, is a shorter length of grey sand, backed by huge lumps of volcanic rock. Away from the road, the coast between these two beaches is strung with a series of isolated, sandy, cove beaches, the **Calas del Barronal**, which can be reached only on foot.

SLEEPING & EATING

Camping Tau (☎ 950 38 01 66; www.parquenaturale.com/tau; sites per adult/tent/car €4.75/6/4.50; ⏰ Apr-Sep) Set 250m from the beach, the small but shady Tau is very popular with families.

Hostal Sol Bahía (☎ 950 38 03 07, fax 950 38 03 06; Avenida de San José; d €40-70; ❄) The Sol Bahía and its sister establishment, Hostal Bahía Plaza, across the street, are in the centre of San José and have functional, clean rooms in bright, modern buildings.

Sanctuario San Jośe (☎ 902 87 73 88; www.elsantuariosanjose.es; Camino de Calahiguera 9; s/d €55/100; mains €15-24; P ❄) This newly refurbished 28-room hotel offers minimal yet friendly design with attractive lounging and dining terraces. Its Anicette restaurant has a strong reputation locally.

Hotel Cortijo el Sotillo (☎ 950 61 11 00; www.hotelsotillo.com; Carretera Entrada a San José s/n; s €100-20, d €117-41; mains €15-25; P ❄ 🏊) This smart but fun ranch-style complex, popular with families, has a host of great facilities, on-site riding and an excellent restaurant.

Restaurante Mediterraneo (☎ 950 38 00 93; Puerto Deportivo de San José; mains €10-22) Last stop in a run of similarly good seafood restaurants near the marina, this one has particularly friendly staff and a less frantic atmosphere than some of its neighbours.

San José to Las Negras

The rugged coast northeast of San José allows only two small settlements, the odd fort and a few beaches before the village of Las Negras, 17km away as the crow flies. The road spends most of its time ducking inland.

The hamlet of **Los Escullos** has a short beach. You can walk here from San José, along a track starting at Cala Higuera bay. One kilometre beyond Los Escullos, **La Isleta del Moro** is a tiny village with a beach and a couple of fishing boats. **Casa Café de la Loma** (☎ 950 38 98 31; www.degata.com/laloma; s/d €35-57), on a small hill above the village and five minutes from the beach, is a 200-year-old house restored in Al-Andalus style with airy rooms and terrific views. From here the road heads inland past the spooky former gold-mining village of **Rodalquilar**, worth a detour. About 1km past Rodalquilar is the turning to **Playa del Playazo**, a good beach between two headlands, 2km along a level track. From here you can walk near the coast to the village of **Las Negras**, which is set on a pebbly beach and largely given over to seasonal tourism.

On Las Negras' main street, **Hostal Arrecife** (☎ 950 38 81 40; Calle Bahía 6, Las Negras; s/d €26/38) has cool, quiet, well-maintained rooms, some with sea views from their balconies. **Camping La Caleta** (☎ 950 52 52 37; www.vayacamping.net/lacaleta; sites per adult/tent/car €5.60/6.70/5.60; ⏰ year-round; P 🏊) lies in a separate cove 1km south of Las Negras. It can be fiercely hot in summer, but there is a good pool. Other accommodation in Las Negras is mostly holiday apartments and houses to let. **Restaurante La Palma** (☎ 950 38 80 42; mains €8-12), overlooking the beach, plays good music and serves excellent fish at good prices.

Las Negras to Agua Amarga

There's no road along this secluded, cliff-lined stretch of coast, but walkers can take an up-and-down path of about 11km, giving access to several beaches. **Playa San Pedro**, one hour from Las Negras, is the site of a ruined hamlet (with castle), inhabited erratically by hippies and naturists. It's 1½ hours on from there to **Cala del Plomo** beach, with another tiny village, then 1½ hours further to **Agua Amarga**.

Drivers must head inland from Las Negras through Hortichuelas. A mostly unsealed road heads northeast, cross-country from the bus shelter in Fernán Pérez. Keep to the main track at all turnings, and after 10km you'll reach a sealed road running down from the N341 to Agua Amarga, a chic and expensive but still low-key former fishing village on a straight sandy beach.

Breezy, beachfront **Hostal Restaurante La Palmera** (☎ 950 13 82 08; Calle Aguada s/n; d low/high season €60/90; mains €10-18; ❄) has 10 bright rooms, and its restaurant is Agua Amarga's most popular lunch spot. And although **Hotel Family** (☎ 950 13 80 14; www.sawdays.co.uk; Calle La Lomilla; d incl breakfast €85/120; 🕓 closed 5 Nov-10 Dec; mains €17-26, 🕓 closed Tue & Wed; P 🏊) appears to have been furnished by a frugal maiden aunt, it is a cheerful place, set in mature gardens and just a short stroll from the beach.

Chic, slick **miKasa** (☎ 950 13 80 73; www.mikasasuites.com; Carretera Carboneras s/n; d incl breakfast €120-240; P ❄ 🏊) is an elegant, really comfortable, romantic hideaway for the long-weekend crowd. Wi-fi in suites only.

Many miKasa guests will no doubt be eating at **Restaurante Playa** (☎ 950 13 81 67; mains €8-23; 🕓 closed Jan & Feb). With its long terrace right on the beach and minimal yet friendly restaurant, this is the coolest dinner date in town.

Getting There & Away

From Almería bus station buses run to El Cabo de Gata (€2, 30 minutes, 10 daily), San José (€3.16, 1¼ hours, four daily Monday to Saturday), Las Negras (€4.25, 1¼ hours, one daily Monday to Saturday) and Agua Amarga (€4.95, 1¼ hours, one daily Monday to Friday).

MOJÁCAR

Pop 6500

Mojácar, northeast of Cabo de Gata, is actually two towns: the old Mojácar Pueblo, a jumble of white, cube-shaped houses on a hilltop 2km inland, and Mojácar Playa, a modern beach resort strip 7km long but only a few blocks wide. Though dominated by tourism, the *pueblo* is exceptionally pretty with its mazelike streets and bougainvillea-swathed balconies.

From the 13th to 15th centuries, Mojácar found itself on the Granada emirate's eastern frontier, finally falling to the Catholic Monarchs in 1488. Tucked away in an isolated corner of one of Spain's most backward regions, it was decaying and half-abandoned by the mid-20th century, before its mayor started luring artists and others with giveaway property offers.

Orientation & Information

Pueblo and Playa are joined by a road that heads uphill from the Parque Comercial shopping centre, towards the northern end of Mojácar Playa.

The very helpful **tourist office** (☎ 950 61 50 25; www.mojacar.es; Calle Glorieta 1; 🕓 10am-2pm & 5-7.30pm Mon-Fri, 10.30am-1.30pm Sat) is just off Mojácar Pueblo's main square, Plaza Nueva. In the same building are the post office and **Policía Local** (☎ 950 47 20 00). **CiberKoko** (☎ 950 47 84 55; Multicentro, Plaza Nueva 9; per hour €1; 🕓 11.30am-2.30pm & 4.30pm-11.30pm) is a pleasant internet cafe with eight booths complete with functioning printer, and a friendly, helpful owner.

Sights & Activities

Exploring the *pueblo* is mainly a matter of wandering the winding streets, with their flower-decked balconies, and nosing into craft shops, galleries and boutiques. The **Mirador El Castillo**, at the topmost point, provides magnificent views. The fortress-style **Iglesia de Santa María** (Calle Iglesia) dates from 1560 and may have once been a mosque.

The most touching spot is the **Fuente Mora** (Moorish Fountain; Calle La Fuente) in the lower part of the *pueblo*. Though remodelled in modern times, it maintains the medieval Islamic tradition of making art out of flowing water.

For good windsurfing equipment (per hour €12), canoeing, sailing and water-skiing (per session €20) check out **Samoa Surf** (☎ 666 442263; Playa de las Ventánicas) in Mojácar Playa.

Sleeping & Eating

MOJÁCAR PUEBLO

Hostal Arco Plaza (☎ 950 47 27 77; fax 950 47 27 17; Calle Aire Bajo 1, Plaza Nueva; s/d €36/52; ❄) Bang in the centre of the village, the Arco Plaza has rooms in pretty pastel shades with spacious bathrooms and crisp, white linen. Management and staff seem incredibly friendly and efficient.

Pensión El Torreón (☎ 950 47 52 59; Calle Jazmín 4; d without bathroom €60; 💻) This beautiful *hostal*, with its five quaint rooms and stained-glass windows, is timeless. It was allegedly the birthplace of Walt Disney, whom locals maintain was the love child of a village girl and a wealthy landowner.

El Mirador del Castillo (☎ 950 47 30 22; www.elcastillomojacar.com; Mirador El Castillo; d €60-68;) A laid-back *hostal* with a no-fuss bohemian atmosphere and fantastic views.

Hostal Mamabel's (☎ 950 47 24 48; www.mamabels.com; Calle Embajadores 5; d/ste €70/90) This small hotel hugs the very edge of the *pueblo*, with rooms seemingly piled on top of each other. All are individually styled, with amazing views.

El Horno (mains €11-19) The restaurant at Hostal Mamabel's offers dinner and good breakfasts.

La Taberna (☎ 647 724367; Plaza del Cano 1; tapas & platos combinados from €4; V) This thriving little eatery, inside a warren of cavelike rooms, serves extremely well-prepared meals with plenty of tasty vegetarian options.

Restaurante El Viento del Desierto (Plaza Frontón; mains from €7.50; closed Sun & Jan) Good value long-established Moroccan-cum-Spanish eatery just by the church.

Restaurante El Palacio (☎ 950 47 28 46; Plaza de Caño; mains €9.75-19.75; dinner) Decorated in more white fabric than a wedding and situated next to the old Town Gate, this discreet restaurant breathes romance. Dishes include Caesar salad and fresh salmon in prune sauce.

MOJÁCAR PLAYA

Hotel Río Abajo (☎ 950 47 89 28; Calle Río Abajo; d €60-70; P) Budget option and looks like it. However, jolly chalets are dotted among lush gardens with direct access to the broad sandy beach at the far north end of Mojácar Playa. A good place for kids.

Hotel Puntazo (☎ 950 47 82 65; www.hotelpuntazo.com; Paseo del Mediterraneo, 257; s/d €116/144;) Sixty rooms, some with sea views, and a huge restaurant, cater especially well for families. An efficient if somewhat impersonal ambience.

Tito's (☎ 950 61 50 30; www.elbeachbar.com; Playa de las Ventanicas; Apr-Oct) Weathered, warm-hearted ex-Californian Tito creates the perfect laid-back atmosphere for this cane-canopied beach bar. Very popular for both lunch and dinner. Live music on Saturday and Sunday evenings.

Drinking & Entertainment

Classical music, live comedy acts and jazz concerts are staged at the lively **Café Bar Mirador del Castillo** (☎ 950 47 30 22; 11am-11pm or later) in Mojácar Pueblo. The *pueblo*'s better bars (open evenings only, from around 8pm) include **La Muralla**, which boasts the most romantic views from its terrace, and slick chrome-and-wood **Jazz Life Café** in Calle Embajadores. Tiny **Time & Place** (Plaza de las Flores) is as cute as a crooked smile, wreathed in bougainvillea. Try the 'Teeny Weeny Woo Woo' of vodka, peach schnapps and cranberry juice, then lurch on to alcoholic jellies and puddings.

On weekend nights at the beach, imbibe to the beat of live world music at **Aku Aku** (☎ 950 47 89 81; Playa del Cantal; to 3am summer).

Getting There & Around

Long-distance buses stop at the Parque Comercial (Mojácar Playa) and the Fuente stop at the foot of Mojácar Pueblo. The tourist office has timetables. Destinations include Murcia (€10.17, 2½ hours, five daily), Almería (€6.41, 1¾ hours, two daily), Granada (€15, four hours, two daily) and Madrid (€34.13, eight hours, two daily).

A local bus service (€1.10) runs a circuit from the southern to northern ends of Mojácar Playa, then back to the Parque Comercial, up to the *pueblo* (Calle Glorieta), then back down to the Parque Comercial and the southern end of the Playa. It runs every half-hour, 9am to 11.30pm, from April to September, and every hour from 9.30am to 7.30pm between October and March.

Extremadura

The fourth largest, yet least populated, autonomous region in Spain, Extremadura is also one of the least visited by tourists; partly because it's a considerable sidestep from Madrid's international airport. The result is that this part of Spain still feels like a place with hidden corners to discover: remote villages tucked away in the mountains where locals stare and there's no signal for your phone.

This is a region of big skies and vast swathes of sparsely populated land where isolated farmhouses resemble solitary dice against a gently undulating chequerboard of wheat fields, green valleys and grasslands. Wooded sierras rise along the region's northern, eastern and southern fringes, while two of Spain's major rivers, the Tajo and the Guadiana, cross Extremadura from east to west. On the urban front, cities and towns like Trujillo, Cáceres, Guadalupe and Zafra are rich in Roman, medieval and Moorish history, while the craggy Parque Nacional de Monfragüe, between Plasencia and Trujillo, has some of Spain's most spectacular bird life.

Reconquered from the Muslims in the 13th century, Extremadura was handed to knights who turned it into one great sheep pen. Those who did not work the land often had only one choice – migration. Small wonder that many 16th-century conquistadors, including Pizarro and Cortés, sprang from here. The riches they brought back from the Americas are reflected in the lavish mansions they constructed as a result of this booty.

If your bank balance is not quite at conquistador level, do not fret. Extremadura also happens to be, arguably, the cheapest place to eat and sleep in Spain.

HIGHLIGHTS

- Stroll the Ciudad Monumental's evocative cobbled streets in **Cáceres** (p844)
- Clamber over Spain's finest Roman ruins in **Mérida** (p855)
- Travel to **Trujillo** (p849), home town of some of Latin America's most (in)famous conquistadors
- Spot majestic birds of prey as they wheel over the **Parque Nacional de Monfragüe** (p843)
- Wander among the gleaming white buildings in the southern town of **Zafra** (p861)

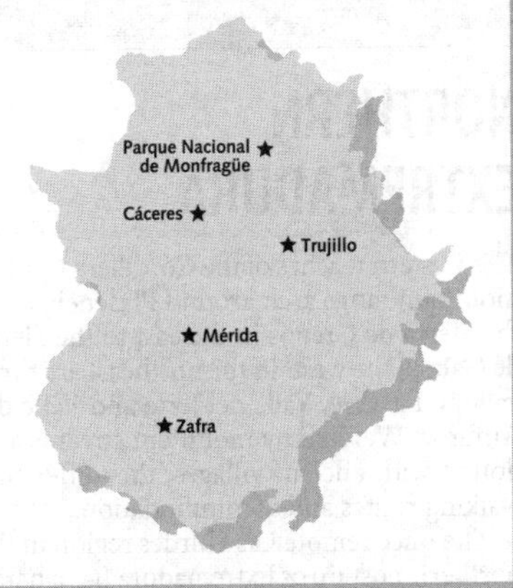

AREA: 41,634 SQ KM	AVE SUMMER TEMP: HIGH 38°C, LOW 26°C	POP: 1.084 MILLION

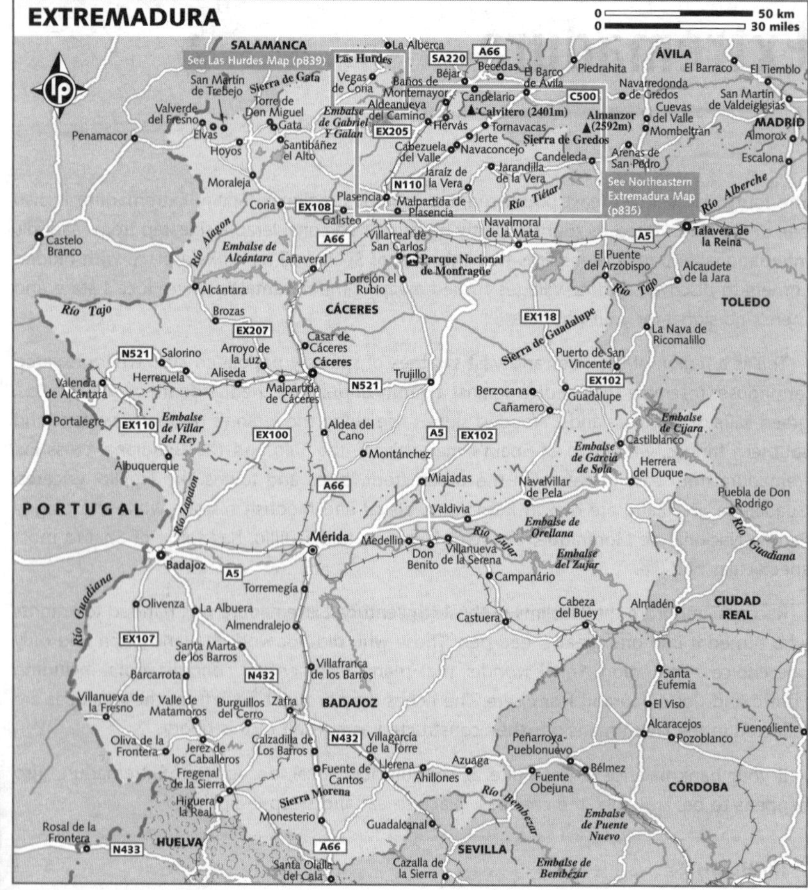

NORTHERN EXTREMADURA

The western reaches of the Cordillera Central mountain range arch around Plasencia from the Sierra de Gredos in the east to the Sierra de Gata in the west. In the northeast are three valleys: La Vera, Valle del Jerte and Valle del Ambroz. Watered by mountain streams and dotted with ancient villages, they offer fine walking routes and accommodation.

The once remote Las Hurdes region in the northernmost tip of Extremadura has a harsh beauty, while the Sierra de Gata in the northwest is pretty and more fertile.

LA VERA

Surrounded by mountains often still capped with snow as late as May, the fertile La Vera, on the northern side of Río Tiétar valley, produces raspberries, asparagus and, above all, paprika *(pimentón)* sold in charming old-fashioned tins. Here too grows 80% of Spain's tobacco (look out for the brick drying sheds with their honeycombs of air vents).

Typical too of La Vera are half-timbered houses leaning at odd angles, their overhanging upper storeys supported by timber or stone pillars.

Information

Asociación de Turismo de la Vera (www.aturive.com in Spanish) Useful website for activities.

Comarca de la Vera (www.comarcadelavera.com) Another recommended website.

Tourist office (☎ 927 17 05 87; Avenida de la Constitución 167, Jaraíz de la Vera; ⏰ 9.30am-2pm & 4.30-6.30pm Mon-Fri, 10am-2pm Sat & Sun) Lots of information, including local walking maps.

Tourist office (☎ 927 56 04 60; www.jarandilla.com in Spanish; Plaza de la Constitución 1, Jarandilla de la Vera; ⏰ 10am-2pm & 4-6pm Tue-Sun)

Sights & Activities

Pasarón de la Vera is a pretty, tranquil village nestled in a valley 32km northeast of Plasencia. It is home to the emotive 16th-century palace Condes de Osorno, featuring an open-arcaded gallery decorated with medallions. Head 20km north on the EX203 for **Cuacos de Yuste**, rich in typical La Vera half-timbered houses. Seek out lovely **Plaza Fuente Los Chorros**, its half-timbered houses surrounding a 16th-century fountain, and **Plaza Juan de Austria**, built on a rock, with its bust of Carlos I.

The **Monasterio de Yuste** (☎ 927 17 21 97; 30min guided tour in Spanish €2.50; ⏰ 10am-6pm Tue-Sun Apr-Sep, 10.30am-5.30pm Tue-Sun Oct-Mar) is 2km northwest of Cuacos. The gouty Carlos I of Spain (also known, confusingly, as Carlos V of Austria, Emperor of the Holy Roman Empire) withdrew here in 1557 to spend his dying years, having divided the world's biggest empire between his brother, Ferdinand, and his legitimate son, Felipe II. A closed order of Hieronymite monks occupies the monastery itself, but you can visit the outlying church with its Gothic and plateresque cloisters, and the modest royal chambers where the ailing monarch's bed was placed to give him a direct view of the altar. Ask for the accompanying pamphlet in English.

A narrow road with spectacular views continues 7km beyond the monastery to **Garganta la Olla**, a picturesque, steeply pitched village with ancient door lintels inscribed with the 16th-century date of construction and name of the original owner. Seek out the Casa de las Muñecas at No 3 on the main street. The House of the Dolls gets its name from the much-weathered female carving on the stone archway. Painted in blue, the come-on colour of the time, it was a brothel in Carlos I's time and now houses a far drearier souvenir shop. Another distinctive house is the Casa de Postas Posada de Viajeros (look for the plaque at the top of the street) a travelling inn reputedly used by Carlos I. From the village you can make the spectacular drive over the 1269m **Puerto de Piornal** pass to the Valle del Jerte.

Jarandilla de la Vera, 10km northeast of Cuacos de Yuste, has a 15th-century fortified church on Plaza de la Constitución and a magnificent *parador* (p836).

The **Ruta del Emperador**, a 10km walking trail, replicates the emperor's route from Jarandilla to the Monasterio de Yuste. Follow the sign south from the church below the town's *parador* and turn right at a T-junction to leave town via Calle Marina.

Other La Vera villages with fine traditional architecture are **Valverde de la Vera** and

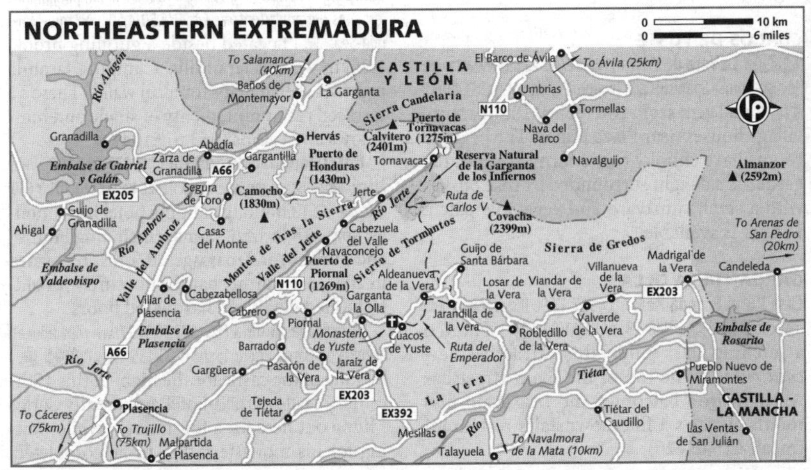

EASTER SUFFERING

On the day before Good Friday Villanueva de la Vera is the scene of one of the more bizarre of Spain's religious festivities, **Los Empalaos** (literally 'the Impaled'). Several penitent locals strap their arms to a beam (from a plough) while their near-naked bodies are wrapped tight with cords from waist to armpits, and all along the arms to the fingertips. Barefoot, veiled, with two swords strapped to their backs and – to top it all – wearing a crown of thorns, these 'walking crucifixes' follow a painful Way of the Cross. Hanging from the timber are chains of iron that clank in a sinister fashion as the penitents make their painful progress watched by the crowds. Guided by *cirineos* (guides who light the way and help them if they fall), the *empalaos* occasionally cross paths. When this happens they kneel and rise again to continue their laborious journey. Doctors stay on hand, as being so tightly strapped does nothing for blood circulation.

Villanueva de la Vera. The former is particularly engaging; lovely Plaza de España is lined with timber balconies, and water gushes down ruts etched into the cobbled lanes.

Sleeping & Eating

Most of the villages have well-signposted and excellent camping grounds, often with lovely riverside positions. There are also some fine *casas rurales* (country home, village or farmstead accommodation) with rooms to let.

PASARÓN DE LA VERA

La Casa de Pasarón (☎ 927 46 94 07; www.pasaron.com; La Magdalena 18; d/tr €70/85; P ❄ 🏊 V) Follow the signs through the village to this handsome family house run by granddaughter Susana. The ground floor dates from 1890. Rooms are bathed in light with terracotta tiles and lashings of white linen and paintwork. A nightly optional menu (€12) includes vegetarian choices.

CUACOS DE YUSTE

our pick **La Vera de Yuste** (☎ 927 17 22 89; www.laveradeyuste.com in Spanish; Calle Teodoro Perianez 17; s/d €40/60; ❄) A real gem set in two typical 18th-century village houses near Plaza Major. The beamed rooms have chunky rustic furniture, and the garden is a delight surrounded by rose bushes with a small courtyard and vegetable patch. Dinner is available.

GARGANTA LA OLLA

Casa Rural Parada Real (☎ 927 17 96 05; www.paradareal.com; Calle Chorrillo 28; s/d €40/50; ❄) Painted a fetching dark pink, this attractive new *casa rural* at the top of the main street has wrought-iron balconies and bright no-fuss rooms. There's a fine downstairs restaurant (meals €15 to €20).

Restaurante La Fragua (☎ 927 17 95 71; Calle de Toril 4; meals €20-25) Offering good local cooking in a busy dining room, Restaurante La Fragua is all timber beams and exposed stone walls. Whet your appetite with *berenjenas a la miel* (fried aubergines with honey) topped with the creamily delicious *Torta del Casar* cheese.

JARAÍZ DE LA VERA

Finca Valvellidos (☎ 927 19 41 43; www.valvellidos.com in Spanish; d €56-68; P ⊠ ❄) This impeccably restored farmhouse has five spacious double rooms, plus bungalows and self-contained apartments (€65 to €80), in a gentle country setting, 2km along a dirt track off the EX392, 2km south of Jaraíz. The restaurant prepares dishes using the *finca's* organic produce; weather permitting, guests eat outside at a long communal table.

JARANDILLA DE LA VERA

Camping Jaranda (☎ 927 56 04 54; www.campingjaranda.es; sites per adult/tent/car €4.50/4.50/4.50; 🕑 mid-Mar–mid-Sep; 🏊) Located beside a gurgling brook, 1.25km west of Jarandilla, Camping Jaranda provides sketch maps for local walks. There's a terraced restaurant, plenty of shade and bungalows and cabins (€63 to €104).

Hotel Don Juan de Austria (☎ 927 56 02 06; www.donjuandeaustria.com; Avenida Soledad Vega Ortiz 101; r €80; ❄ 💻 🏊) This longstanding hotel has a modest spa with Jacuzzi, saunas (including Finnish and Turkish) and massages. Rooms (renovated in 2007) are warmly bathed in ochre with old-fashioned detail and hardwood floors.

Parador Jarandilla (☎ 927 56 01 17; www.parador.es; Avenida de García Prieto 1; s/d €108/135; P ⊠ ❄ 🏊) Be king of the castle for the night at this 15th-century castle-turned-hotel. Apparently Carlos I hung out here for a few months while waiting for his monastery digs to be completed.

Within the stout walls and turrets are period-furnished rooms, plus a classic courtyard where you can dine on royal fantasies from the gourmet restaurant menu.

Getting There & Away

Up to three buses daily run between lower La Vera villages and Plasencia. There is one daily bus from Plasencia to Madrigal de la Vera (€7, 1¾ hours), the most distant village.

VALLE DEL JERTE

This valley, separated by the Sierra de Tormantos from La Vera, grows half of Spain's cherries and is a sea of white blossom in early spring. Visit in May and every second house is busy boxing the ripe fruit.

The Plasencia–Ávila N110 runs up the valley, crossing into Castilla y León by the Puerto de Tornavacas (1275m).

Information

Tourist office (☎ 927 47 25 58; www.turismovalledeljerte.com in Spanish; ⌚ 10am-3pm Mon, 10am- 3pm & 4-5.30pm Tue-Fri, 10am-2pm Sat) Located 600m north of Cabezuela del Valle on the N110; covers the whole valley.

Valle del Jerte tourism (www.elvalledeljerte.com) Another useful website.

Sights & Activities

Piornal (1200m), on the southeast flank of the valley and famous for its Serrano ham, is well placed for walks along the Sierra de Tormantos.

In **Cabezuela del Valle**, the Plaza de Extremadura area has some fine houses with overhanging wooden balconies. A spectacular, winding 35km road leads from just north of Cabezuela over the 1430m Puerto de Honduras to Hervás in the Valle del Ambroz.

Jerte has another excellent base for walks within the nature reserve: **Reserva Natural de la Garganta de los Infiernos** (Hell's Gorge). The **Centro de Interpretácion de la Naturaleza** (☎ 927 01 49 36; ⌚ 10am-2pm & 5.30-7.30pm Apr-Sep, 9am-1pm & 3-6pm Oct-Mar) beside Camping Valle del Jerte has an illustrated display and can provide a map highlighting eight walks. An easy 1½-hour 7km return walk from the office takes you to Los Pilones, with its strange, smooth rock formations and winding emerald-and-sapphire-coloured stream.

Tornavacas, yet another Extremaduran village with a huddled old quarter, is the starting point of the **Ruta de Carlos V**. Twenty-eight kilometres long, the trail (PR1) follows the route by which Carlos I was borne over the mountains to Cuacos de Yuste (p835) via Jarandilla de la Vera. You can walk it in one day – just as Carlos' bearers did in the 1550s. The route crosses the Sierra de Tormantos by the 1479m Collado (or Puerto) de las Yeguas.

Sleeping & Eating

Camping Río Jerte (☎ 927 17 30 06; www.campingriojerte.com; sites per adult/tent/car €4.50/4.50/4.50, 4-6 person bungalows €80-100;) Located 1.5km southwest of Navaconcejo, facilities include a volleyball court. To cool off, choose from the adjacent natural riverside pool or a standard artificial one.

Hotel Aljama (☎ 927 47 22 91; Calle Federico Bajo s/n, Cabezuela del Valle; s/d €35/50;) Almost touching the church across the street as it overhangs the very narrow lane, this hotel has traditional cork floors, wooden shutters and beams. Rooms are simple and rustic, and the restaurant offers generous inexpensive mains like *lomo de cerdo* (pork loin) for €6.

Hospedería La Serrana (☎ 927 47 60 34; www.hospederialaserrana.com in Spanish; Carretera Garganta la Olla s/n; s/d with breakfast €40/64; P) A former sanatorium for TB patients, this low-rise country house just east of Piornal has dated, rather stuffy, decor but is good value and well placed for local hikes.

El Cerezal de los Sotos (☎ 927 47 04 29; www.elcerezaldelossotos.net in Spanish; Calle de las Vegas, Jerte; d with breakfast €81; P) The valley is known for *casas rurales* like this one. It is a homey stone house dating from 1890 with beams, open fireplace and spacious attractive rooms set amid cherry orchards and sweeping lawns above the river. Follow the signs over the bridge from Jerte and the N110. Dinner is available (€20).

Valle del Jerte (☎ 927 47 04 48; Gargantilla 16, Jerte; meals €20-25) This family-run traditional restaurant is *the* place to taste local specialties like trout and *cabrito* (kid). The superb desserts include a classic cherry-and-goat's-cheese tart topped with cherry-flavoured honey.

Getting There & Away

From Plasencia there's one weekday bus to Piornal (€2.40, one hour) and up to five daily Monday to Friday along the valley as far as Tornavacas (€2.80, one hour 20 minutes).

VALLE DEL AMBROZ

This broader valley west of the Valle del Jerte, once split by the Roman Vía de la Plata (see

RUTA DE LA PLATA

The name of this ancient highway, also called the Vía de la Plata, derives from the Arabic *bilath,* meaning tiled or paved. But it was the Romans in the first century who originally laid this 1000km-long artery, linking Seville in the south with the coast of Cantabria and Bay of Biscay. Along its length moved goods, troops, travellers and traders. Later, it also served as an alternative pilgrim route for the faithful walking from Andalucía to Santiago de Compostela.

Nowadays it's closely paralleled by the A66 highway, although much of the original remains and alternative walking tracks have been introduced. Entering Extremadura south of Zafra, it passes through Mérida, Cáceres and Plasencia, then heads for Salamanca in Castilla y León.

Neglected and virtually abandoned when cars arrived on the scene, it's now justifiably promoted. Take a look at www.rutadelaplata.com or pick up the guide (€3) from tourist offices on the route. And should you be tempted to trek a stretch or two, pack *Walking the Vía de la Plata* by Ben Cole and Bethan Davies.

the boxed text, above), is nowadays home to the N630 and A66 motorway; the latter is still under construction. The area's **tourist office** (☎ 927 47 36 18; www.valleambroz.com in Spanish; Calle Braulio Navas 6; 10am-2pm & 4.30-7.30pm Tue-Fri, 10am-2pm Sat & Sun) is in Hervás.

Hervás

pop 4100

This colourful town has Extremadura's best surviving **barrio judío** (Jewish quarter), which thrived until the tragic 1492 expulsion of the Jews, when most families fled to Portugal. Seek out Calles Rabilero and Cuestecilla then, for a fine view, climb up to the **Iglesia de Santa María**, on the site of a ruined Knights Templar castle. Note that many of the streets in this *barrio* have the Star of David next to the street name.

Within an impressive 18th-century mansion, the **Museo Pérez Comendador-Leroux** (☎ 927 48 16 55; Calle Asensio Neila; admission €1.20; 4-8pm Tue, 11am-2pm & 4-8pm Wed-Fri, 10.30am-2pm Sat & Sun), houses works of Hervás-born 20th-century sculptor Enrique Pérez Comendador and his wife, the French painter Magdalena Leroux.

The **Museo de la Moto Clásica** (☎ 927 48 12 06; www.museomotoclasica.com; Carretera de la Garganta; adult/12-25yr/under 12yr €10/5/free; 10.30am-1.30pm & 4-8pm Mon-Fri, 10.30am-8pm Sat & Sun) is set in distinctive conical-roofed buildings 200m north of the river. Classic motorcycles, ranging from Harleys to Zundapps, are on show, plus collections of classic cars and horse-drawn carriages.

SLEEPING & EATING

Several agencies can arrange apartment rentals including **La Platea** (☎ 927 47 31 91; Avenida Francisco Sanz López 6; www.espaciorural.com; 2-bed apt from €50).

Camping El Pinajarro (☎ 927 48 16 73; www.campingelpinajarro.com in Spanish; sites per adult/tent/car €4/4/4, 2-/4-person bungalows €44/61; mid-Mar–Sep, Fri-Sun Oct–mid-Mar) On the EX205, 1.5km southwest of Hervás, this superb camping ground, shaded by lofty sycamore trees, is run by a welcoming couple. With a shop, restaurant (July and August), nature walks and plenty of children's activities, it's warmly recommended.

Albergue de la Via de la Plata (☎ 927 47 34 70; www.alberguesviaplata.com; Paseo de la Estación s/n; per person €20; P) Owner Carlos runs this delightful hostel with warmth and enthusiasm. The setting is an evocative converted train station overlooking the overgrown tracks, not in use since 1984. Rooms and the communal areas are brightly furnished, and there's a bar, as well as self-catering facilities.

El Jardín del Convento (☎ 927 47 49 92; www.eljardindelconvento.com; Plaza del Convento 22; s/d €60/95; P) Dating from 1860, this stunningly restored former convent has just six rooms, plus a small cottage. The former are large with wooden floors, exposed stone walls, period furniture and a well-concealed TV. Several overlook the exquisite gardens with beds of roses, a vegetable patch and plenty of tranquil seating space. Dinner is available in summer.

Granadilla

About 25km west of Hervás, **Granadilla** is a picturesque village complete with its own turreted **castle** (admission free; 10am-1pm & 5-7pm Mon-Fri, 5-7pm Sat, 10am-1pm Sun). Located in a lush green setting amid pinewoods but abandoned in the 1960s after the creation of the reservoir that laps around it, Granadilla is gradually being restored thanks to enthusiastic student projects.

Baños de Montemayor

This elegant spa town 7km north of Hervás has an Alpine air with handsome buildings straddling the base of steep pine-clad mountains. Its two springs, both dispensing sulphurous waters at 43°C, were first tapped by the Romans, whose baths soothed the muscles of weary travellers along the Vía de la Plata. At the **Balneario de Baños de Montemayor** (☎ 923 42 83 02; www.villatermal.com; Avenida de las Termas 57; Mar–mid-Dec) you can wallow in a 45-minute water-based relaxation program (€30) in a former Roman bathhouse.

Hostal Eloy (☎ 927 48 80 02; www.hostaleloy.com; Avenida de las Termas 59; s/d €37/53; P) Located next to the baths, you can walk there wearing your robe (others do). In a wisteria-cloaked ochre-and-stone building, the rooms here are spacious and light.

Be wary of the wicker shops along the main street. Much of what's on sale here is overpriced and imported.

Getting There & Away

Up to five buses daily run between Cáceres, Plasencia and Salamanca via the Valle del Ambroz, calling by Hervás (€2.65) and Baños de Montemayor (€2.80).

LAS HURDES

Las Hurdes has taken nearly a century to shake off its image of poverty, disease and chilling tales of witchcraft, even cannibalism. In 1922 the miserable existence of the *hurdanos* prompted Alfonso XIII to declare during a horseback tour, 'I can bear to see no more'.

The austere, rocky terrain yields only small terraces of cultivable land along the riverbanks. The few remaining original, squat stone houses resemble slate-roofed sheep pens as much as human dwellings, and are increasingly being replaced by anonymous modern houses. In the hilly terrain, donkeys and mules remain more practical than tractors while clusters of beehives produce high-quality honey. Overall living standards have substantially increased in this region, although outsiders are still a rare enough phenomenon to cause some serious curtain twitching.

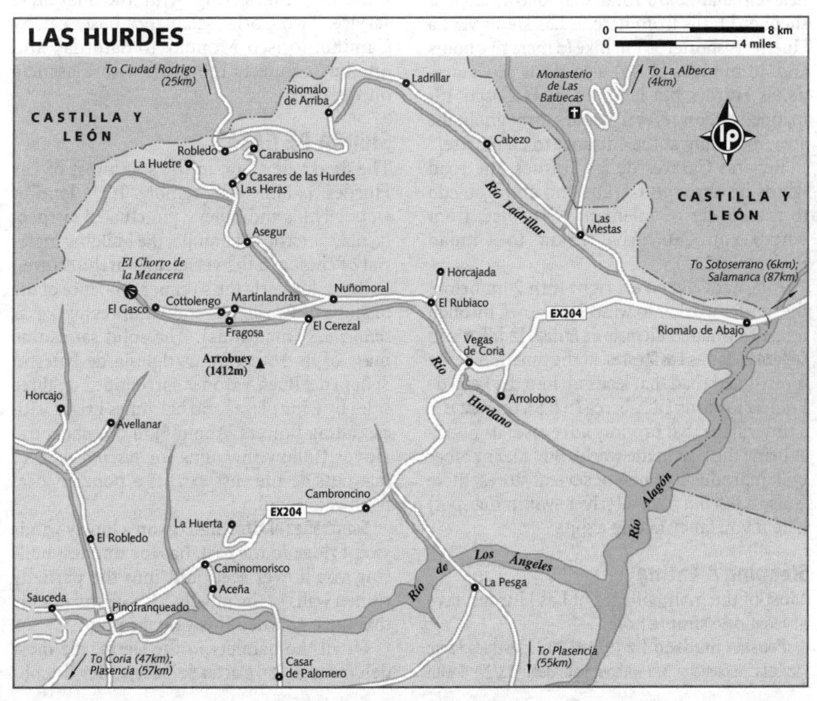

Information

The **tourist office** (☎ 927 43 53 29; www.todohurdes.com; Avenida de Las Hurdes s/n; 10am-2pm & 4.30-7pm Tue-Sat, 11am-1.30pm Sun), beside the EX204 in Caminomorisco, is the area's lone information office and has a useful map outlining local walks and drives.

Sights & Activities

The valley of Río Hurdano, slicing northwest from Vegas de Coria and cut by the EX204, is at the heart of Las Hurdes. From **Nuñomoral**, 7.5km up the valley, a road heads west up a side valley to **El Gasco**, from where there's a particularly good one-hour return walk to **El Chorro de la Meancera**, a 70m waterfall. This side valley, the most picturesque of the area, has farming terraces carved out of the ravine's steep banks and clusters of traditional stone and slate-roofed houses huddled together in hamlets such as **Cottolengo** and **La Huetre**.

Back in the main valley, **Casares de las Hurdes**, climbs 9km northwest of Nuñomoral. The main square has good views down the valley. To get a feel for Las Hurdes at the pace it demands, set aside a day to walk the PR40, a near-circular 28km route that follows ancient shepherd trails from here to Las Heras via La Huetre. A shorter 17km hike (a mere five hours and 40 minutes or so) also starts at Casares de las Hurdes but lands up at El Gasco. It's mapped out on several plaques throughout the area, including at the entrance to La Huetre.

Beyond Casares de las Hurdes, the road winds up through Carabusino and Robledo to the border of Salamanca province, from where you can drive 25km to Ciudad Rodrigo (p223).

Alternatively, take a right turn 20m before the border marker to wind 9km down through forest to isolated **Riomalo de Arriba**, **Ladrillar** and **Cabezo** as far as **Las Mestas**, at the junction of the forest-lined road that leads up into the Peña de Francia towards La Alberca (p225). **Las Mestas** is a tiny village that proudly advertises its honey as being the best in the world. Buy a jar or other pollen products at one of several stores; there is also a *piscina natural* (river swimming spot) here if you fancy taking a dip.

Sleeping & Eating

Most of the main villages of Las Hurdes have at least one simple hotel.

Pensión Hurdano (☎ 927 43 30 12; Avenida Padre Rizabala; Nuñomoral; s/d without bathroom €18/27, d with bathroom €30) This is a plain place in the centre of town run by a friendly couple. There is also a bar and restaurant (menu €10).

Hostal Montesol (☎ 927 67 61 93; Calle Lindón 7, Casares de las Hurdes; r without/with bathroom €30/32; P) Located on the edge of this austere valley, the rooms are nothing memorable but most have big sky views. The vast restaurant serves groaning platefuls of dishes like *patatas meneas a tipico* (roasted potatoes with peppers and garlic).

Las Cabañas de Mestas (☎ 927 43 40 25; www.lasmestas.com; Finca La Viña Grande; Las Mestas cabins €45-55; P) Surrounded by olive trees, the cabins accommodate up to four people and have a porch, kitchen and postage-stamp-sized garden. To book in person head for Las Cabanas de Mestas bar just out of town, direction La Alberca.

Getting There & Away

Transport is not prolific in these parts. On weekdays, one bus runs daily between Plasencia and Vegas de Coria (€5.10, 1½ hours) and Casares de las Hurdes (€6.30, 2¼ hours). Another runs between Riomalo de Arriba and Vegas de Coria (€2.65, 30 minutes), connecting with the Plasencia service. Two Coria–Salamanca buses call by Caminomorisco Monday to Saturday and one bus connects the town with Plasencia on weekdays.

SIERRA DE GATA

The Sierra de Gata, to the southwest of Las Hurdes, is almost as remote. It's a land of wooded hills and valleys, punctuated by spectacular outcrops of granite, the building material of choice in the vernacular architecture.

Hoyos, formerly the summer residence of the bishops of Coria, has some impressive *casas señoriales* (mansions). The solid sandstone mass of its 16th-century Iglesia de Nuestra Señora del Buen Varón is surrounded on three sides by wide plazas and balconies bright with cascading flowers. About 5km out of central Hoyos (follow the signs for *piscina natural* just outside the east exit) is a popular local freshwater pool.

Santibáñez el Alto, high up on a lonely windswept ridge to the east, has the dinkiest bullring you'll ever see, built into the partially ruined walls of the mostly 13th-century castle that once guarded this vantage point.

Of all the hamlets in the sierra, the most delightful is **San Martín de Trebejo**. Beside cobblestone lanes with water coursing down central grooves, traditional houses jut out upon timber-and-stone supports. Around five *casas rurales* offer rooms in the old village centre including lovely **Casa Antolina** (☎ 927 51 05 29; www.casa-antolina.com; Calle La Fuente 1; s/d/ste €60/65/95) with its tastefully restored rustic rooms. On the northern edge of the village you can stroll out along an original Roman road. Here and in the two next villages looking west, **Elvas** and **Valverde del Fresno**, the folk speak their own isolated dialect, a strange mix of Spanish and Portuguese.

Getting There & Away

From Coria, four buses run daily to Hoyos (€2.45, 35 minutes) and one or two to Valverde del Fresno (€4.65, 1¾ hours). There's one bus daily on weekdays from Plasencia to Valverde del Fresno (€6, 1¾ hours) via San Martín de Trevejo. Two run from Plasencia to Hoyos (€5, 1¼ hours) and another to Santibáñez (€3, 35 minutes).

CORIA & AROUND

pop 13,200

This pretty, small market town lies south of the Sierra de Gata. Massive and largely intact protective walls, marked by four gates, enclose the historic quarter of town. The Romans called the place Caurium; after a period of decay its splendour was revived under the Moors, when it was briefly the capital of a small Muslim state. Today it seems an altogether more modest place.

Information

Esitat-Coria (Calle Almanzor 12; per hr €3; 🕒 11am-2pm & 4-11pm) Internet access.

Tourist office (☎ 927 50 13 51; Avenida de Extremadura 39; 🕒 9am-2pm & 5-7pm Mon-Fri, 10am-2pm Sat & Sun) Pick up a map and guide to the town.

Sights & Activities

The **cathedral** (Plaza de la Catedral; 🕒 10am-1pm & 4-6.30pm), primarily Gothic, has intricate plateresque decoration around its north portal. Attached is a small **ecclesiastical museum** (admission €2). On the plain below is a fine stone bridge, abandoned in the 17th century by Río Alagón, which now takes a more southerly course.

The **Convento de la Madre de Dios** (Calle de las Monjas s/n; admission €1.50; 🕒 10am-12.45pm & 4.15-6.45pm Sun-Fri, 4.15-6.45pm Sat) is a thriving 16th-century convent with an elegant cloister. The sisters sell a variety of delicious home-made sweets and pastries.

The **Museo de la Carcel Real** (☎ 927 50 80 29; Calle de las Monjas 2; admission €1.20; 🕒 10.30am-2pm & 5.30-8.30pm Wed-Sun; ♿), once the town's lock-up, houses Coria's tiny two-storey archaeological museum. Step inside the dark, poky *celda del castigo* (punishment cell), then see how the cushy 1st- floor cells differed from the plebs' prison below.

Galisteo, 26km east of Coria on the EX109, has near-intact Muslim-era walls, the remains of a 14th-century fort with a curiously disproportionate cone-shaped tower (added later) and a Mudéjar brick apse in its old church.

Sleeping & Eating

Palacio Coria (☎ 927 50 64 49; www.hotelpalaciocoria.es; Plaza de la Catedral s/n; s/d €70/85; P ❄) Opened in early 2008 in a 17th-century former bishop's palace next to the cathedral, this sumptuous accommodation successfully couples modern comfort and convenience within heady palatial surrounds. There are excellent weekend deals.

Casa Campana (☎ 927 50 00 38; Plaza San Pedro 5; meals €20-25) Don the blinkers for the dazzling red decor in the bar. The restaurant has a less edgy ambience with its vaulted ceiling and stone walls. Winner of several gastronomic awards, the fine country cooking specialises in roasted meats.

El Bobo de Coria (☎ 927 50 07 95; Calle de las Monjas 6; meals €25-30; 🕒 Tue-Sun) Particularly strong on local mushroom dishes in season, the Idiot of Coria (named after a Velazquez painting) is also rich in traditional Extremadura dishes. The food's safe here; the walls are scarcely visible for the collection of locks, keys and bolts that adorn them.

Getting There & Away

The **bus station** (☎ 927 50 01 10; Calle de Chile s/n) is in the new part of town. Buses run to/from Plasencia (€4.25, 50 minutes, three daily) and Cáceres (€6, 3½ hours, five daily).

PLASENCIA

pop 40,100

This pleasant, bustling town is the natural hub of northern Extremadura. Rising above a bend of Río Jerte, it retains long sections of its defensive walls. Founded in 1186 by Alfonso VIII of Castilla, Plasencia lost out to Cáceres as Extremadura's premier town only in the

19th century. It has an earthy and attractive old quarter of narrow streets and stately stone buildings, many emblazoned with noble coats of arms. Less admirable is all the emblazoned graffiti in town. On a happier note, Plasencia seems to be competing with Madrid with its number of bars, particularly around the historic centre.

Information

Municipal tourist office (☎ 927 42 38 43; www.aytoplasencia.es/turismo in Spanish; Calle Santa Clara 2; 9am-9pm Mon-Fri, 10am-2pm & 4-8pm Sat & Sun)
Regional tourist office (☎ 927 01 78 40; www.turismoextremadura.com; off Avenida del Ejército; 9am-2pm & 5-7pm Mon-Fri, 9.45am-2pm Sat & Sun Jun-Sep, 9am-2pm & 4-6pm Mon-Fri Oct-Apr) Within Torre Lucia.

Sights

In Plasencia life flows finally to the lively, arcaded **Plaza Mayor**, meeting place of 10 streets and scene of a Tuesday farmers market since the 12th century. The jaunty fellow who strikes the hour on top of the much-restored Gothic transitional **town hall** is El Abuelo Mayorga (Grandpa Mayorga), an unofficial symbol of the town.

Plasencia's **cathedral** (Plaza de la Catedral; 9am-1pm & 5-7pm Mon-Sat, 9am-1pm Sun May-Sep, 9am-2pm & 4-6pm Mon-Sat, 9am-1pm Sun Oct-Apr) is actually two in one. The 16th-century **Catedral Nueva** (under restoration until 2010) is mainly Gothic with a handsome plateresque facade. Within the Romanesque **Catedral Vieja** (admission €1.50; 9am-1pm & 5-7pm) are the classic 13th-century cloisters surrounding a trickling fountain and lemon trees. Also on view is the soaring octagonal Capilla de San Pablo with the dramatic 1569 Caravaggio painting of John the Baptist.

Nearby is the **Museo Etnográfico-Textil** (☎ 927 42 18 43; Plazuela Marqués de la Puebla; admission free; 11am-2pm & 5-8pm Wed-Sat, 11am- 2pm Sun), with three floors of well-displayed local handicrafts and costumes, including exquisite embroidery on the 1st floor. Don't miss the footwear, also here – the elaborate patchwork leather boots look straight from 1960s Carnaby St.

The **Centro de Interpretación Torre Lucia** (☎ 927 41 68 40; Calle Torre Lucia s/n; admission free; 10am-2pm & 5-7pm Tue-Sat;), located just off Avenida del Ejército, tells the history of medieval Plasencia through a video, models and artefacts and provides access to a hunk of the city wall, which you can walk along.

Sleeping

Hotel Rincón Extremeño (☎ 927 41 11 50; www.hotelrincon.com in Spanish; Calle Vidrieras 6; s/d €35/45;) This unpretentious hotel just off Plaza Mayor has clean, if unmemorable, rooms, although its popular restaurant is more daring with frogs legs and white truffles with garlic on the menu (meals €25).

Hotel Alfonso VIII (☎ 927 41 02 50; www.hotelalfonsoviii.com in Spanish; Avenida Alfonso VIII 32; s €76-88, d €125-145; P) Located on a busy street just outside the old city walls, this early-20th-century hotel offers well-equipped spacious rooms, though the decor looks a little tired. It runs a highly regarded restaurant.

Parador (☎ 927 42 58 70; www.parador.es; Plaza San Vicente Ferrer s/n; s/d €112/140; P) This *parador* is a classic – still oozing the atmosphere and austerity of its 15th-century convent roots with massive stone columns, soaring ceilings and a traditional Renaissance cloister. The rooms are far from monastic, being luxuriously furnished with rugs and rich fabrics.

Eating

At lunchtime and sunset the bars and terraces surrounding Plaza Mayor fill up with eager punters, downing *cañas* (a small draught beer) or the local *pitarra* red while munching complimentary *pinchos* (tapas) and watching life pass by.

Corral (☎ 927 41 52 69; Calle Vidrieras 11; meals €10) A no-frills restaurant with paper tablecloths and bright lights, but the food is good and astonishingly cheap. Try the *sopa extremeño* with garlic, bread, ham, asparagus and egg (€4).

Casa Juan (☎ 927 42 40 42; Calle Arenillas 5; meals €25-30; Fri-Wed) Tucked down a quiet cobbled lane, French-owned Casa Juan does well-prepared *extremeño* meat dishes such as shoulder of lamb and suckling pig. Try the homemade melt-in-the-mouth *foie gras* or Parisian authentic *snails au gratin*. Eat in the vast dining room or on the smaller rear terrace surrounded by pot plants.

Shopping

Casa del Jamón (☎ 927 42 55 35; Calle Zapatería 15) This is a pleasantly pungent delicatessen with a great selection of goodies including cherry liquor from the valley.

Getting There & Away

The **bus station** (☎ 927 41 45 50; Calle de Tornavacas 2) is about 750km east of Plaza Mayor. The train station is off the Cáceres road, about 1km southwest of town.

Up to five buses daily run to/from Cáceres (€3.50, 50 minutes) and five to seven to/from Madrid (€22, 5½ hours).

Local services, weekdays only, include La Vera (up to three daily), Hervás (up to five daily), Coria (€4.25, 50 minutes, three daily), Hoyos (€5, 1¼ hours, one daily) and one each to Caminomorisco and Valverde del Fresno (€6, 1¾ hours). Up to five services run to Salamanca (€7.40, 2½ hours).

Trains depart from Plasencia to Madrid (€18.10, three to 3½ hours, two to six daily), Cáceres (€4.35, 1½ hours, up to five daily) and Mérida (€7.20, 2½ hours, two to three daily).

PARQUE NACIONAL DE MONFRAGÜE

Spain's 14th and newest national park, created in 2007, is a hilly paradise for birdwatchers. Straddling the Tajo valley, it's home to some of Spain's most spectacular colonies of raptors and more than 75% of Spain's protected species. Among some 175 feathered varieties are around 300 pairs of black vultures (the largest concentration of Europe's biggest bird of prey) and populations of two other rare large birds: the Spanish imperial eagle and the black stork. The best time to visit is between March and October since storks and several raptors winter in Africa.

The park **information centre** (☎ 927 19 91 34; www.monfrague.com; 🕑 9am-7.30pm Apr-Oct, 9am-6.30pm Nov-Mar) is in the hamlet of Villarreal de San Carlos on the EX208 Plasencia–Trujillo road. Request the English version of its excellent illustrated map, which describes three signed walking trails of between 2½ and 3½ hours and shorter loops too (also available on the website). You can drive to several of the hides and lookout points, such as the hilltop **Castillo de Monfragüe**, a ruined 9th-century Muslim fort. Alternatively, it's 20 minutes on foot from the castle car park or an attractive 1½-hour walk from Villarreal. On the Peña Falcón crag, over on the opposite (west) bank of Río Tajo, are griffon vultures, black storks, Egyptian vultures, peregrine falcons, golden eagles and eagle owls.

The park maintains a couple of **Centros de Interpretación**, one about water (its video has an optional English soundtrack) and the other presenting the park's natural environment.

The nearest towns with accommodation are Torrejón el Rubio, 16km south of Villarreal, and Malpartida de Plasencia, 18.5km north. Villarreal has a couple of *casas rurales;* reservations are normally essential.

Al Mofrag (☎ 927 19 90 86; www.casaruralalmofrag.com in Spanish; Cañada Real 19; s/d incl breakfast €35/50;) There are six cosy rooms in this fully renovated house with snug warmly painted

MARTIN KELSEY, ORNITHOLOGIST

Despite the rich and varied birdlife in Extremadura, Martin Kelsey OBE is one of only a handful of professional ornithologists living here.

'Extremadura is excellent for birdlife, although the Monfragüe National Park is the jewel in the crown. You don't have to travel far to discover superb habitats. For example we even have rice fields, which are popular feeding grounds for a wide variety of birds.'

As Martin explains, at certain times of the year birdwatching takes on a real drama of its own. 'Around November over 80,000 cranes fly in from Scandinavia and Western Russia to winter here feeding on rice stubble and acorns. Other migrating birds include thousands of geese here to escape the bitter cold of the Norwegian winters.'

Martin is constantly in demand from birdwatchers who come to Extremadura from all over the world, particularly Britain, Norway and Sweden. 'I like to work with just two or three people so I can customise their trip according to their preferred pace, which birds they are most interested in, and so on.'

Birdwatcher or not, visitors to Extremadura are inevitably intrigued by the storks. Their enormous nests are perched atop spires, steeples, towers and even telephone masts. The local government has thoughtfully placed small platforms on the latter for the storks to use. 'This is in part to discourage them from nesting on house chimneys as they can bring snakes and rubbish to the nest.'

As well as conducting tours, Martin helps the Sociedad Española de Ornitología (SEO) gathering information and statistics and promoting interest in birds among the local community.

rooms, a kitchen for guests' use and a pool for cooling off after a day's hike.

El Cabrerín (☎/fax 927 19 90 02; www.elcabrerin.com; Calle Villarreal 3; s/d €38/55) El Cabrerín is a simple stone cottage with just four low-key rustic rooms, plus an attractively tiled dining room where guests can enjoy breakfast.

Camping Monfragüe (☎ 927 45 92 33; www.camping monfrague.com in Spanish; sites per adult/tent/car €4/4/4, 4-person bungalows €80; year-round;) Precisely 14km north of Villarreal on the EX208 is this shady camping ground with restaurant, shop and pool, plus homey bungalows complete with front porches. It rents out bikes and does inexpensive four-hour 4WD guided tours of the park (€25), including a picnic.

CENTRAL EXTREMADURA

If you have time to visit just one region, make it this one; the heart of Extremadura is home to arguably its most stunning towns: Cáceres, Trujillo and Guadalupe, as well as some dramatic scenery punctuated by pretty unspoiled villages.

CÁCERES

pop 89,000

Extremadura's largest city after Badajoz, Cáceres is also a lively place with a sizeable student population, good restaurants and a spirited nightlife.

The Ciudad Monumental (old town) here is truly extraordinary. The narrow cobbled streets twist and climb among ancient stone walls lined with palaces and mansions while the skyline is decorated with turrets, spires, gargoyles and enormous storks' nests. Protected by defensive walls, it has survived almost intact from its 16th-century heyday. Established by the Romans, adapted by the Moors and enriched by the migrating nobles from León in the wake of the Reconquest, the old town retains tangible evidence of all three cultures. Stretching at its feet, arcaded Plaza Mayor is one of Spain's finest public squares.

Orientation

The Ciudad Monumental rises above the 150m-long Plaza Mayor. Around both, a tangle of streets, mostly pedestrianised, extends to Avenida de España. From Plaza de América, at its southern end, Avenida de Alemania runs 1km southwest to the train and bus stations.

Information

Junta de Extremadura tourist office (☎ 927 01 08 34; www.ayto-caceres.es; Plaza Mayor 3; 9am-2pm & 4-6pm or 5-7pm Mon-Fri, 9.45am-2pm Sat & Sun)

Main post office (Paseo Primo de Rivera 2)

Municipal tourist office (☎ 927 24 71 72; Calle Ancha 7; 10am-2pm & 4.30-7.30pm or 5.30-8.30pm Tue-Sun)

Yass (Calle del General Ezponda 12; per hr €1; 10am-10pm) Internet access.

Sights

Ciudad Monumental's name captures it all. The Monumental City's churches, palaces and towers are indeed huge and hugely impressive although, ironically, few people actually live here and there are just a handful of bars and restaurants. The place merits at least two visits: first by day, then by night to enjoy the buildings illuminated.

PLAZA DE SANTA MARÍA

Enter the Ciudad Monumental from Plaza Mayor through the 18th-century **Arco de la Estrella**, built this wide for the passage of carriages. The **Concatedral de Santa María** (Plaza de Santa María; 10am-1pm & 5-8pm Mon-Sat, 9.30am-2pm & 5-8pm Sun), 15th-century Gothic cathedral creates an impressive opening scene. On its southwest corner is a modern statue of San Pedro de Alcántara, a 16th-century *extremeño* ascetic (his toes worn shiny by the hands and lips of the faithful). Inside, drop €1 in the slot to the right of the Santa Rita chapel to light up the magnificent carved 16th-century cedar altarpiece. There are several fine noble tombs and a small **ecclesiastical museum** (admission €1).

Also on the plaza are the **Palacio Episcopal** (Bishop's Palace), the **Palacio de Mayoralgo** and the **Palacio de Ovando**, all in 16th-century Renaissance style. Just off the plaza's northeast corner is the **Palacio Carvajal** (☎ 927 25 55 97; Calle de l'Amargura 1; admission free; 9am-9pm Mon-Fr, 10am-2pm & 5-8pm Sat, 10am-2pm Sun). Within this late-15th-century mansion, rooms have been restored with period furnishings and artwork, and there is a permanent exhibition about sites of interest throughout northern Extremadura.

Just to the west of the plaza lies the domed **Palacio Toledo-Moctezuma** (Calle Canilleros), once the home of a daughter of the Aztec emperor Moctezuma, who was brought to Cáceres as a conquistador's bride. Heading back through Arco de la Estrella, you can climb the 12th-century **Torre de Bujaco** (Plaza Mayor; adult/under 12yr €2/free; 10am-2pm & 5.30-8.30pm

Mon-Sat, 10am-2pm Sun Apr-Sep, 10am-2pm & 4.30-7.30pm Mon-Sat, 10am-2pm Sun Oct-Mar,). From the top of this tower, there's a good bird's-eye view (literally: you're within feather-ruffling distance of a couple of stork nests) of the Plaza Mayor.

PLAZA DE SAN JORGE

Southeast of Plaza de Santa María, past the Renaissance-style **Palacio de la Diputación**, is Plaza de San Jorge, above which rises the **Iglesia de San Francisco Javier**, an 18th-century Jesuit church. Beside it, the 15th-century **Casa de los Becerra** (Plaza de San Jorge 2) is a restored mansion, now functioning as a cultural centre with occasional free exhibitions. Due east on Cuesta del Marqués is the **Arco del Cristo**, a Roman gate.

PLAZA DE SAN MATEO & PLAZA DE LAS VELETAS

From Plaza de San Jorge, Cuesta de la Compañía climbs to Plaza de San Mateo and the **Iglesia de San Mateo**, traditionally the church of the land-owning nobility and built on the site of the town's Islamic mosque.

Just to the east is the **Torre de las Cigüeñas** (Tower of the Storks). This was the only Cáceres tower to retain its battlements when the rest were lopped off in the late 15th century.

Below the square is the excellent **Museo de Cáceres** (927 01 08 77; Plaza de las Veletas 1; admission/EU citizens €1.20/free; 9am-2.30pm & 4-7.15pm Tue-Sat, 10.15am-2.30pm Sun) in a 16th-century mansion built over an evocative (if musty) 12th-century *aljibe* (cistern), the only surviving element of Cáceres' Muslim castle. It has an impressive archaeological section, rooms devoted to traditional crafts and costumes, and an excellent fine-arts display, with works by El Greco, Picasso and Miró.

OTHER BUILDINGS

Check out the **Palacio de los Golfines de Arriba** (Calle de los Olmos 2), where Franco was declared head of state in 1936; the ground floor is now a sophisticated restaurant. The nearby **Casa Mudéjar** (Cuesta de Aldana 14) still reflects its Islamic influence in its brickwork and 1st-floor window arches. On opposite sides of Plaza de los Caldereros are the **Palacio de la Generala** and **Casa de los Rivera**, now university administrative buildings.

Tours

The **Asociación de Guías Turísticas** (Tourist Guides Association; 927 21 72 37; Plaza Mayor 2) leads regular 1½- to two-hour tours (€5) in Spanish of the Ciudad Monumental, starting from its office on Plaza Mayor. Tours in English can be arranged with advance notice.

Festivals & Events

For three fiesta-fuelled days in early May, Cáceres stages the Spanish edition of **Womad** (World of Music, Arts and Dance; www.granteatrocc.com in Spanish), with international bands ranging from reggae and Celtic to African, Indian and Indigenous Australian, playing in the old city's squares.

From 21 to 23 April the town celebrates the **Fiesta de San Jorge** in honour of its patron saint.

Sleeping

Albergue Turístico Las Veletas (927 21 12 10; Calle del General Maragallo 36; dm €20; Tue-Sun;) This modern hostel with its homey rear garden with flowers offers agreeable accommodation in rooms of two, four or more. Reserve in advance, especially out of season, since it works primarily with groups.

Hotel Don Carlos (927 22 55 27; www.hoteldoncarloscaceres.net in Spanish; Calle Donoso Cortés 15; s €33-48, d €48-65;) Rooms are tastefully decorated with bare brick and stone at this welcoming small hotel, sensitively created from a long-abandoned early-19th-century house. There are two artists among the owner's family, hence plenty of original art work.

Hostal Alameda (927 21 12 62; Plaza Mayor 33; s/d €45/60;) Survive the puff-you-out climb to the 3rd floor, and this place is a good deal. There are six rooms recently refurbished with green paintwork, cool beige tiles and antiques. Go for spacious number 15 with its superb view of the square.

Hotel Iberia (927 24 76 34; www.iberiahotel.com in Spanish; Calle de los Pintores 2; s/d €46/65;) Located in an 18th-century former palace just off Plaza Mayor, this 36-room hotel has plush, if quirky, public areas, decorated with collections of teapots, brass knockers, framed embroidery, fans and moody family portraits. The rooms are more traditional with parquet floors, cream walls and pale-grey tiled bathrooms.

Alameda Palacete (927 21 16 74; www.alamedapalacete.com; Calle General Maragallo 45; s/d/tr/q €50/65/75/85;) Two reclining lion statues greet you at this tastefully restored early-20th-century townhouse with its original richly

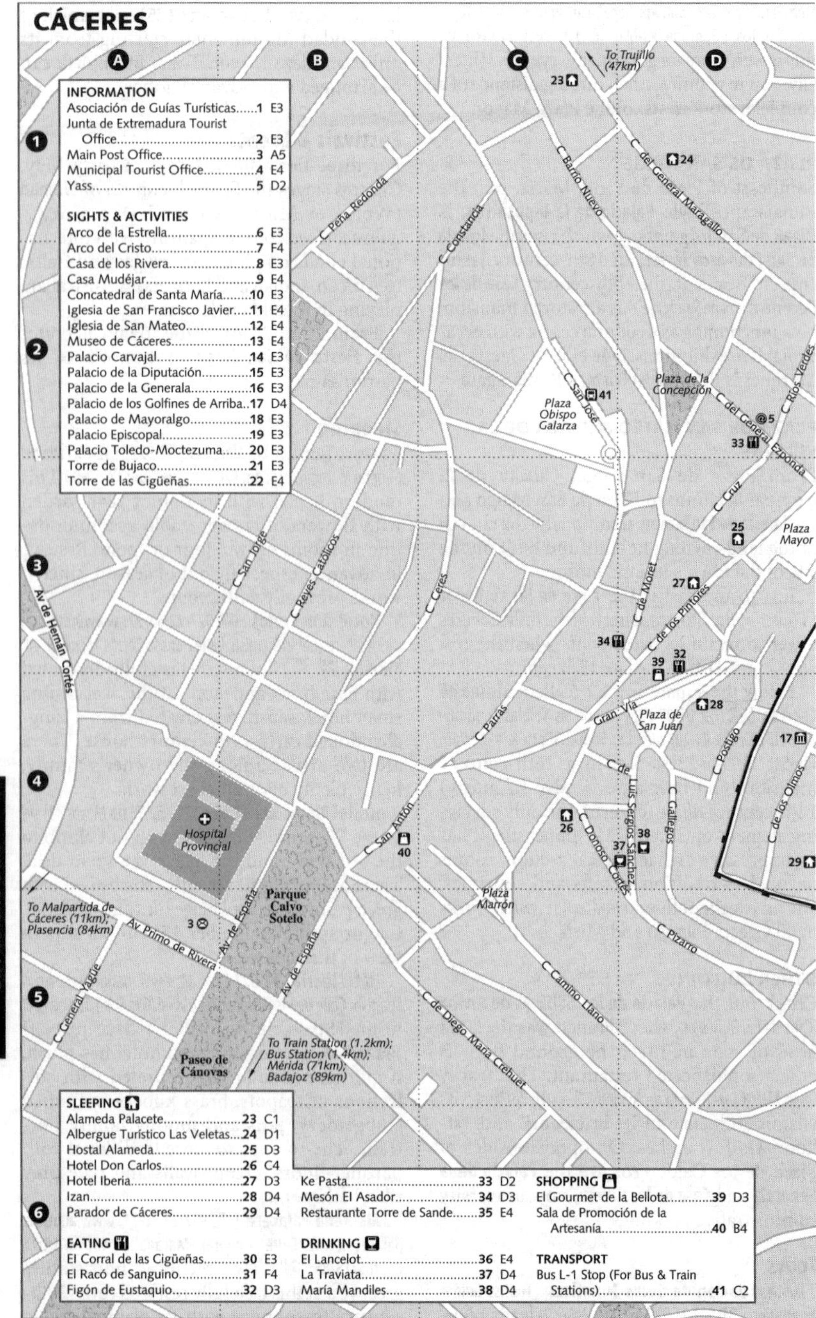
CÁCERES
INFORMATION
Asociación de Guías Turísticas.....1 E3
Junta de Extremadura Tourist Office.....2 E3
Main Post Office.....3 A5
Municipal Tourist Office.....4 E4
Yass.....5 D2
SIGHTS & ACTIVITIES
Arco de la Estrella.....6 E3
Arco del Cristo.....7 F4
Casa de los Rivera.....8 E3
Casa Mudéjar.....9 E4
Concatedral de Santa María.....10 E3
Iglesia de San Francisco Javier.....11 E4
Iglesia de San Mateo.....12 E4
Museo de Cáceres.....13 E4
Palacio Carvajal.....14 E3
Palacio de la Diputación.....15 E3
Palacio de la Generala.....16 E3
Palacio de los Golfines de Arriba..17 D4
Palacio de Mayoralgo.....18 E3
Palacio Episcopal.....19 E3
Palacio Toledo-Moctezuma.....20 E3
Torre de Bujaco.....21 E3
Torre de las Cigüeñas.....22 E4
SLEEPING
Alameda Palacete.....23 C1
Albergue Turístico Las Veletas.....24 D1
Hostal Alameda.....25 D3
Hotel Don Carlos.....26 C4
Hotel Iberia.....27 D3
Izan.....28 D4
Parador de Cáceres.....29 D4
EATING
El Corral de las Cigüeñas.....30 E3
El Racó de Sanguino.....31 F4
Figón de Eustaquio.....32 D3
Ke Pasta.....33 D2
Mesón El Asador.....34 D3
Restaurante Torre de Sande.....35 E4
DRINKING
El Lancelot.....36 E4
La Traviata.....37 D4
María Mandiles.....38 D4
SHOPPING
El Gourmet de la Bellota.....39 D3
Sala de Promoción de la Artesanía.....40 B4
TRANSPORT
Bus L-1 Stop (For Bus & Train Stations).....41 C2
To Trujillo (47km)
C Barrio Nuevo
C del General Margallo
C Peña Redonda
C Constancia
Plaza de la Concepción
C Ríos Verdes
C del General Ezponda
C San José
Plaza Obispo Galarza
C Cruz
Plaza Mayor
C San Jorge
C Reyes Católicos
C Ceres
C de Moret
C de los Pintores
Av de Hernán Cortés
Gran Vía
Plaza de San Juan
C Parras
C Postigo
C de Luis Sergios Sánchez
C Gallegos
C de los Olmos
Hospital Provincial
C San Antón
C Donoso Cortés
Parque Calvo Sotelo
Plaza Marrón
To Malpartida de Cáceres (11km); Plasencia (84km)
Av Primo de Rivera
Av de España
C Pizarro
C Camino Llano
C General Yagüe
C de Diego María Crehuet
Paseo de Cánovas
To Train Station (1.2km); Bus Station (1.4km); Mérida (71km); Badajoz (89km)

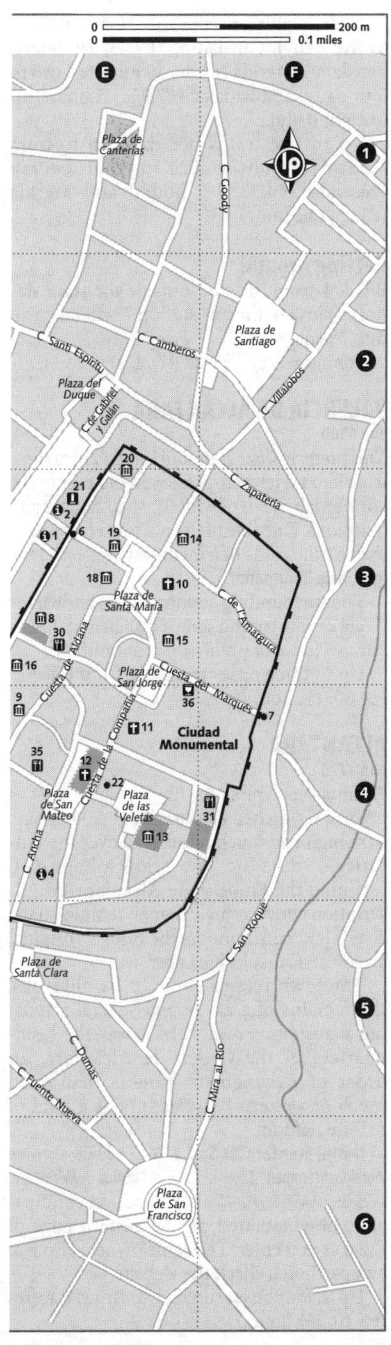

patterned floor tiles. The rooms are bathed in light with high ceilings.

Izán (☎ 927 21 58 00; www.izanhoteles.es; Plaza de San Juan 11; s/d €90/100; P) This boutique hotel (formerly part of the Melia chain) is in a 16th-century palace aesthetically revamped with vaulted brick ceilings, columns and arches. The rooms are luxurious and carpeted.

Parador de Cáceres (☎ 927 21 17 59; www.parador.es; Calle Ancha 6; s/d €128/154; P) A grand 14th-century Gothic stone building houses this elegant accommodation located deep in the walled town across from the tourist office. Stone and wooden floors, dark-wood antiques and a grand fireplace in the Great Hall add to the palatial atmosphere.

Eating

From the restaurants and cafes flanking Plaza Mayor you can watch the swallows and storks swoop and glide among the turrets of the old city. Stick to a drink and simple tapa, however, as the food here tends to be overpriced and indifferent.

El Corral de las Cigüeñas (Cuesta de Aldana 6; 8am-1pm Mon-Fri, 7pm-3am Tue-Sat, 5-11pm Sun) The secluded courtyard with its lofty palm trees and ivy-covered walls is the perfect spot for one of the best-value breakfasts around: there are seven versions to choose from, including the basic *madrileño:* fresh orange juice, coffee and *porros* (doughnut type pastries), for just €2.20!

Mesón El Asador (☎ 927 22 38 37; Calle de Moret 34; raciones €6-8, meals €18-25; closed Sun) Enter the dining room and you get the picture right away: one wall is covered with hung hams. You won't taste better roast pork (or lamb) in town. Its bar also serves *bocadillos* (bread rolls with filling) and a wide range of *raciones.*

Figón de Eustaquio (☎ 927 24 43 62; Plaza de San Juan 14; menú €17-19, meals €30) The walls are papered with photos of famous diners, including Spanish royalty, at this venerable, multi-roomed option. You'll be treated to such dishes as *vacuno a la crema de anchoa,* strange bedfellows of steak in a cream of anchovy sauce. Round off with *técula mécula,* a divine dessert made of egg yolk, almonds and acorns.

Ke Pasta (☎ 927 22 03 44; Calle del General Ezponda 7; meals €18-25; closed Sun) If you have grown a tad weary of piggy fare, then this Italian restaurant dishes up good pasta dishes, if not quite in the Neapolitan league. More unusual options include tortellini with *rúcula* and *fiocchi* (pasta) with cheese and pear.

El Racó de Sanguino (☎ 927 22 76 82; www.racodesanguino.es; Plaza de las Veletas 4; meals €30-40; ⏲ lunch & dinner Tue-Sat & lunch Sun) Tables and wicker chairs spread beneath the sloping, timber ceiling within, while romantics can head for the candlelit tables outside. Carlos Sanguino has created a traditional *extremeño* menu with an innovative twist like codfish scented with fresh rosemary with a potato mousse (a nice change from fries).

Restaurante Torre de Sande (☎ 927 21 11 47; www.torredesande.com; Calle Condes 3; meals €35-45; ⏲ lunch & dinner Tue-Sat & lunch Sun) Dine in the pretty courtyard on dishes like *salmorejo de cerezas del jerte con queso de cabra* (cherry-based cold soup with goat's cheese) and *raviolis de perdiz* (partridge) at this elegant gourmet restaurant. More modestly, stop for a drink and a tapa (€4.50) at their interconnecting Tapería.

Drinking

The streets at the northern end of Plaza Mayor are lined with lively late-night bars.

Just beyond the walls on the south side of the Ciudad Monumental popular hang-outs include **La Traviata** (Calle Luis Sergios Sánchez s/n) with its floral wallpaper, original tiles, arches and terrace, and nearby **María Mandiles** (☎ 649 241680; Calle Luis Sergios Sánchez s/n), located on the corner of Calle Gallegos, which packs them in with its dark red interior and funky art work.

For a touch of the Irish head to **El Lancelot** (☎ 927 24 49 80; Rincón de la Monja 2; ⏲ 8pm-1am Wed-Mon). Surrounded by stained wood and rustic panelling, this is a great spot for a tipple and live Celtic music on Sunday (9.30pm). If you are after atmosphere, check out **El Corral de las Cigüeñas** (Cuesta de Aldana 6), which occasionally stages live music.

The new part of the city also offers plenty of action, including several clubs, in an area known as La Madrila on and around Calle Doctor Fleming.

Shopping

El Gourmet de la Bellota (⏲ 927 24 07 24; Plaza de San Juan 6) One of several places to stock up on gourmet goodies, like creamy *Torta de Casar* (cheese).

Sala de Promoción de la Artesanía (⏲ 927 24 35 28; Calle San Antón 17) Run by the provincial government; stocks typical *extremeño* handicrafts.

Getting There & Away

The **bus station** (⏲ 927 23 25 50; Carretera de Sevilla) has services to Trujillo (€3.55, 45 minutes, eight daily), Plasencia (€3.50, 50 minutes, up to five daily), Guadalupe (€9.35, 2½ hours, one daily), Mérida (€4.80, 50 minutes, two to four daily) and Badajoz (€7.95, 1¼ hours, up to eight daily).

Up to five trains per day run to/from Madrid (€17.80 to €24.50, four hours), Plasencia (€4.35, 1½ hours) and Mérida (€5.25, one hour).

Getting Around

Bus L-1 from the stop outside the train station – close to the bus station – will take you into town.

For a taxi, call ⏲ 927 21 21 21.

VALENCIA DE ALCÁNTARA

pop 6100

This pretty town is 7km short of the Portuguese frontier and its well-preserved old centre is a curious labyrinth of whitewashed houses and mansions. One side of the old town is watched over by the ruins of a medieval castle and the **Iglesia de Rocamador**.

The surrounding countryside is known for its cork industry and some 50 ancient dolmens (stone circles of prehistoric monoliths).

Up to three buses run daily from Cáceres (€4.80, 1½ hours).

ALCÁNTARA

pop 1770

Alcántara is Arabic for 'the Bridge'. West of town, a six-arched **Roman bridge** – 204m long, 61m high and much reinforced over the centuries – spans Río Tajo below a huge dam retaining the Embalse de Alcántara. An inscription above a small Roman temple on the river's left bank honours the bridge's original architect, Caius Julius Lacer.

The town retains some of its old walls, the remains of a castle and several imposing mansions. From 1218 it was the headquarters of the Orden de Alcántara, an order of Reconquista knights that ruled much of western Extremadura as a kind of private fiefdom.

Hostal Kantara Al Saif (☎ 927 39 08 33; www.hotelpuenteromanosl.com in Spanish; Avenida de Mérida s/n; s €25-35, d €45-50; P ❄) is a bland, yet comfortable, hotel situated on the eastern edge of town as you enter. The same owners also run an aparthotel; check the website.

Up to four buses run daily to/from Cáceres (€5.10, 1½ hours).

TRUJILLO

pop 9700

Wander into Plaza Major here and you could be forgiven for thinking that you had stumbled onto the filmset of a medieval blockbuster. The square is surrounded by baroque and Renaissance stone buildings topped with a skyline of towers, turrets, cupolas, crenulations and nesting storks. Stretching beyond the square the illusion continues with a labyrinth of mansions, leafy courtyards, fruit gardens, churches and convents; Trujillo truly is one of the most captivating small towns in Spain.

The town came into its own only with the conquest of the Americas. Then, Francisco Pizarro and his co-conquistadors enriched the city with a grand new square and imposing Renaissance mansions that look down confidently upon the town today.

Information

Ciberalia (☎ 927 65 90 87; Calle de Tiendas 18; per hr €2; 🕒 11am-midnight) Internet access.

Post office (Calle de la Encarnación 28)

Tourist office (☎ 927 32 26 77; www.ayto-trujillo.com in Spanish; Plaza Mayor s/n; 🕒 10am-2pm & 4-7pm Oct-May, 10am-2pm & 5-8pm Jun-Sep)

Sights

PLAZA MAYOR

There are a handful of feeble museums in Trujillo. If you are tempted they are well signposted but, aside from the one mentioned

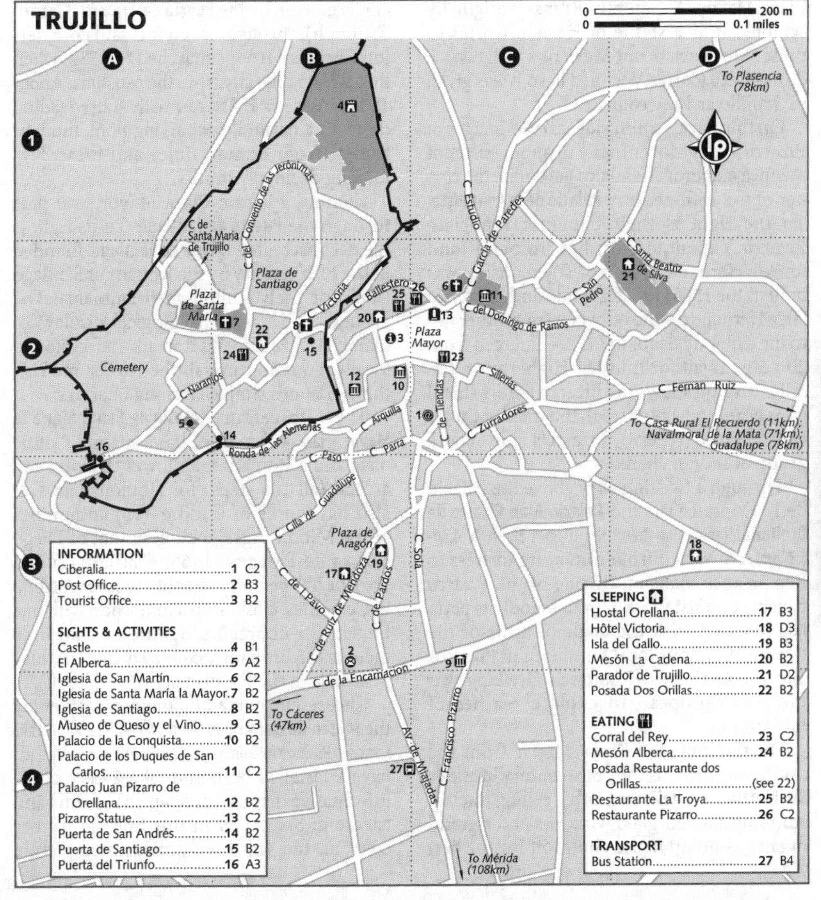

TIMES & TICKETS

A combined ticket (€4.70 to €5.30), which includes a comprehensive guidebook available in English, covers entry to most of the sights, including the castle. It's €6.75 if you want to join a guided tour (in Spanish). Tickets are on sale at the tourist office.

Unless we indicate otherwise, tariffs and times are constant for all **sights** (adult/under 12yr €1.40/free; 10am-2pm & 4.30-7.30pm or 5-8pm).

below, arguably not as rewarding as the sights noted below.

A large equestrian **Pizarro statue** by American Charles Rumsey looks down over Plaza Mayor. Apparently Rumsey originally sculpted it as a statue of Hernán Cortés to present to Mexico, but Mexico, which takes a dim view of Cortés, declined it, so it was given to Trujillo as Pizarro instead.

On the plaza's south side, carved images of Pizarro and his lover Inés Yupanqui (sister of the Inca emperor Atahualpa) decorate the corner of the 16th-century **Palacio de la Conquista**. To the right is their daughter Francisca Pizarro Yupanqui with her husband (and uncle), Hernando Pizarro. The mansion was built in the 1560s for Hernando and Francisca after Hernando – the only Pizarro brother not to die a bloody death in Peru – emerged from 20 years in jail for murder. Higher up, a bas relief carving shows the Pizarro family shield (two bears and a pine tree), the walls of Cuzco (in present-day Peru), Pizarro's ships and a group of Indian chiefs.

Through a twisting alley above the Palacio de la Conquista is the **Palacio Juan Pizarro de Orellana** (admission free; 10am-1.30pm & 4.30-6.30pm), converted from miniature fortress to Renaissance mansion by one of the Pizarro cousin conquistadors. Now a school, its patio is decorated with the coats of arms of the two most famous local families: the Pizarros and the Orellanas (Francisco Orellana was the first European to explore reaches of the Amazon).

Overlooking the Plaza Mayor from the northeast corner is the 16th-century **Iglesia de San Martín** with delicate Gothic ceiling tracing, stunning stained-glass windows and a grand organ (climb up to the choir loft for the best view). It's one of the few churches in Trujillo still functioning as a place of worship.

Across the street rears the solid presence of the 16th-century **Palacio de los Duques de San Carlos** (admission €1; 10am-1pm & 4.30-6.30pm), nowadays a convent for the Jerónimo order but open for visits and for selling their homemade biscuits. Its treasures are the sober classical patio and a grand granite staircase crowned with a painting of the family crest: a two-headed eagle. The distinctive brick chimneys were built in late Mudéjar and Gothic style.

UPPER TOWN

The 900m of walls circling the upper town date from Muslim times. Here, the newly settled noble families built their mansions and churches after the Reconquista. The western end is marked by the **Puerta del Triunfo** (Gate of Triumph), through which it is said conquering Christian troops marched in 1232, when they wrested the city from the Muslims. About 100m inside is **El Alberca**, with stairs leading down to a naturally occurring pool, thought to date from Roman times and these days looking decidedly murky.

Coming up from Plaza Mayor, you pass through the **Puerta de Santiago**. To its right is the deconsecrated **Iglesia de Santiago**, founded in the 13th century by the Knights of Santiago (look for their scallop-shell emblem). The ground level has archaeological displays of mainly Bronze Age and Roman artefacts found locally. You can climb the bell tower and visit the sacristan's simple sleeping quarters.

The 13th-century **Iglesia de Santa María la Mayor** (Plaza de Santa María) has a mainly Gothic nave and a Romanesque tower that you can ascend (all 106 steps) for fabulous views. It also has tombs of leading Trujillo families of the Middle Ages, including that of Diego García de Paredes (1466–1530), a Trujillo warrior of legendary strength who, according to Cervantes, could stop a mill wheel with one finger. The church's magnificent altarpiece includes 25 brilliantly coloured 15th-century paintings in the Flemish style.

Cheese-and-wine aficionados may enjoy the **Museo de Queso y el Vino** (☎ 927 32 30 31; Calle Francisco Pizarro s/n; admission €2.30) where you can have a taster of both and take a look at the informative display (in Spanish) of wine and cheese in Spain. Set in this fine old former convent, the 4m three-dimensional picture of a jolly Don Quijote is the stunning work of local artist Francisco Blanco.

At the top of the hill Trujillo's **castle** (☎ 927 32 26 77; Calle del Convento de las Jerónimas 12;) of 10th-century Muslim origin (evident by the horseshoe-arch gateway just inside the main entrance) and later strengthened by the Christians, is impressive, although bare but for a lone fig tree. Patrol the battlements for magnificent 360-degree sweeping views. One of the towers contains the hermitage of Our Lady of the Victory, the patron saint of Trujillo.

Festivals & Events

The last weekend in April is a pungent period as cheesemakers from all over Spain and elsewhere display their best at Trujillo's **Feria del Queso** (Cheese Fair). The town's annual **Fiestas de Trujillo**, with music, theatre and plenty of partying, are spread over a few days around the first Saturday in September.

Sleeping

Hostal Orellana (☎ 927 32 07 53; Calle de Ruiz de Mendoza 2; s/d €30/45;) The comfortable rooms in this 16th-century house have exposed stone, dark timber and warm decor with terracotta tiles and butter-coloured paintwork. It's located a short walk from the centre above a same-name bar and restaurant.

Mesón La Cadena (☎ 927 32 14 63; fax 927 32 31 16; Plaza Mayor 8; s/d €36/46;) Occupying part of a 16th-century mansion on the plaza, the rooms have cool grey-and-white floor tiles and beams. Go for rooms 206 or 207 with their sweeping views of the square. The downstairs restaurant offers inexpensive, if predictable, local cuisine (meals €15 to €20).

Hôtel Victoria (☎/fax 927 32 18 19; Plaza del Campillo 22; s/d €58/72; P) The marble-clad rooms at this hotel open onto a central light-filled atrium with neoclassical columns and delicate wrought-ironwork. The rooms on the ground floor are more spacious. The reliably good restaurant has some amusing English translations like *sopa de picadillo* (hash soup, no less).

Casa Rural El Recuerdo (☎ 927 31 93 49; www.casaruralelrecuerdo.com; Pago de San Clemente; r €69; P) The decor is a fusion combination of South American, Indian and Spanish – the ornithologist owner, Martin Kelsey (see the boxed text, p843) and his wife, Claudia, are well travelled. Rooms have original tiles and the dining room, originally a bodega, still has the trough where the wine was collected. To get here take the EX208 for Guadalupe. After 10km take the road signposted to San Clemente and the *casa rural*.

Isla del Gallo (☎ 927 32 02 43; www.isladelgallo.com; Plaza de Aragón 3; s/d €70/80; P) Yet another former 17th-century convent tastefully restored as a boutique-style hotel. Rooms are large with parquet floors, wrought-iron beds and dark wood furniture. The colour scheme throughout is warm earth colours, and the tranquil patio is shaded by lemon and olive trees.

our pick **Posada Dos Orillas** (☎ 927 65 90 79; www.dosorillas.com; Calle de Cambrones 6; d €70-107;) This tastefully renovated 16th-century mansion in the walled town once served as a silk-weaving centre. The rooms replicate Spanish colonial taste; those in the older wing bear the names of the 'seven Trujillos' of Extremadura and the Americas. Unsurprisingly, 'Extremadura' is the largest and most luxurious. Relax on the sunny patio or dine in its courtyard restaurant (below).

Parador de Trujillo (☎ 927 32 13 50; trujillo@parador.es; Calle Santa Beatriz de Silva 1; s/d €96/120; P) No surprise that this *parador* is a former 16th-century convent; there's an agreeable overdose in this town. It's located in the winding back streets of the old town allows you to enjoy a peaceful cloistered courtyard and gently bubbling fountains.

Eating

Restaurante La Troya (☎ 927 32 13 64; Plaza Mayor 10; menú €15) The restaurant and its founder, the late Concha Álvarez, are *extremeño* institutions. You will be directed to one of several dining areas and there, without warning, be presented with a plate of tortilla, chorizo and salad, followed by a three-course menu (with truly gargantuan portions) and including wine and water. If it all sounds a bit too girth-expanding, opt for one of the tapas at the bar (€2) instead.

Posada Restaurante Dos Orillas (☎ 927 65 90 79; www.dosorillas.com; Calle de Cambrones 6; meals €25-30; lunch & dinner Tue-Sat, lunch Sun; V) Just as the hotel is a gem, so the restaurant is a place of quiet, refined eating, whether al fresco on the patio or in dining room with its soft-hued fabrics. Vegetarian dishes include pasta with

EXTREMADURA & AMERICA

Extremeños jumped at the opportunities opened up by Columbus' discovery of the Americas in 1492.

In 1501 Fray Nicolás de Ovando from Cáceres was named governor of all the Indies. He set up his capital, Santo Domingo, on the Caribbean island of Hispaniola. With him went 2500 followers, many of them from Extremadura, including Francisco Pizarro, the illegitimate son of a minor noble family from Trujillo. In 1504 Hernán Cortés, from a similar family in Medellín, arrived in Santo Domingo.

Both young men prospered. Cortés took part in the conquest of Cuba in 1511 and settled there. Pizarro, in 1513, accompanied Vasco Núñez de Balboa (from Jerez de los Caballeros) to Darién (Panama), where they discovered the Pacific Ocean. In 1519 Cortés led a small expedition to what's now Mexico, rumoured to be full of gold and silver. By 1524, with combined fortitude, cunning, luck and ruthlessness, Cortés and his band had subdued the Aztec empire. Though initially named governor of all he had conquered, Cortés soon found royal officials arriving to usurp him.

He returned to Spain and, before returning to Panama, visited Trujillo, where he received a hero's welcome and collected his four half-brothers, as well as other relatives and friends. Their expedition set off from Panama in 1531, with just 180 men and 37 horses, and managed to capture the Inca emperor Atahualpa, despite the emperor having a 30,000-strong army. The Inca empire, with its capital in Cuzco and extending from Colombia to Chile, resisted until 1545, by which time Francisco had died (he is buried in the cathedral of Lima, Peru).

About 600 people of Trujillo made their way to the Americas in the 16th century, so it's no surprise that there are about seven Trujillos in North, Central and South America. There are even more Guadalupes, for conquistadors and colonists from all over Spain took with them the cult of the Virgen de Guadalupe in eastern Extremadura, one that remains widespread throughout Latin America.

broccoli and cheese and courgettes stuffed with oyster mushrooms; carnivores won't go hungry.

Restaurante Pizarro (☎ 927 32 02 55; Plaza Mayor 13; meals €25-35; ⏰ Wed-Mon) Next door to La Troya and with arguably better food (hence winning gastronomic awards since 1985); the dining room is pleasantly unpretentious, while the menu includes dishes like chicken stuffed with truffles, tomato soup with figs, and *frito de cordero* (lamb stew).

Mesón Alberca (☎ 927 32 22 09; Calle de Cambrones 8; meals €30-40, menú €17.50; ⏰ Thu-Sun) A pretty ivy-clad terrace or dark-timber tables laid with gingham cloths create a choice of warm atmospheres for sampling classic *extremeño* cooking. The specialities are oven roasts and *solomillo ibérico con Torta del Casar* (pork sirloin with creamy sheep's milk cheese).

Corral del Rey (☎ 927 32 17 80; Corral del Rey 2; meals €35-40; ⏰ lunch & dinner Mon-Sat, lunch Sun & Wed) Located just off the main square, this classic restaurant has four intimate dining rooms. Settle for the *menú del día* (€24) or choose from a tempting range of grills, roasts and fish dishes; the latter speciality being *bacalao Corral del Rey* (grilled cod with a courgette and roasted garlic sauce).

Getting There & Away

The **bus station** (☎ 927 32 12 02; Avenida de Miajadas) is 500m south of Plaza Mayor. There are services to/from Madrid (€15.20 to €19, three to 4¼ hours, up to 10 daily), Guadalupe (€5.75, 1½ hours, two daily), Cáceres (€3.55, 45 minutes, eight daily) and Mérida (€7.35, 1½ hours, three daily).

GUADALUPE

pop 2250

This sparkling white village is like a bright jewel set in the green crown of the surrounding ranges and ridges of the Sierra de Villuercas. There are thick woods of chestnut, oak and cork meshed with olive groves and vineyards. Guadalupe (from the Arabic meaning 'hidden river') appears as though from nowhere, huddled around the massive stone hulk of the Real Monasterio de Santa María de Guadalupe. It's a small place, and you can easily visit the sights and stroll its cobbled streets in a day. Start at its heart: the

Plaza Santa María de Guadalupe, known more simply as Plaza Mayor, located at the base of the monastery steps. The central 15th-century fountain is where Columbus baptised his two American Indian servants in 1496.

Information

Fotobías (☎ 927 15 42 90; Calle Gregorio López 24; per hr €1.80; ⌚ 10am-2pm & 5-8.30pm Mon-Sat) Internet access.

Tourist office (☎ 927 15 41 28; www.puebladeguadalupe.net; Plaza Mayor s/n; ⌚ 10am-2pm & 4-6pm Mon-Fri, Sep-Jun, 10am-2pm & 5-7pm Mon-Fri, Jul-Aug 10am-2pm Sat & Sun)

Sights

The **Real Monasterio de Santa María de Guadalupe** (☎ 927 36 70 00; Plaza Santa María de Guadalupe; ⌚ 9am-8pm), a Unesco World Heritage site, was founded in 1340 by Alfonso XI on the spot where, according to legend, a shepherd found an effigy of the Virgin, hidden years earlier by Christians fleeing the Muslims. It remains one of Spain's most important pilgrimage sites.

In the 16th century, the Virgin of Guadalupe was so revered that she was made patron of all Spain's New World territories. On 29 July 1496, Columbus's Indian servants were baptised in the fountain in front of the monastery, an event registered in the monastery's first book of baptisms. The Virgin of Guadalupe, patron of Extremadura, remains a key figure for many South American Catholics.

Inside the **church** (admission free) the Virgin's image occupies the place of honour lit up within the soaring *retablo* (altarpiece). There is a five-minute audio explanation available in several languages for €1 (to the right of the entrance) plus a 45-minute **guided tour** (adult/under 12yr/12-25yr €3/free/1.50; ⌚ tours 9.30am-1pm & 3.30-6.30pm in Spanish). To get the most out of the latter, buy the English version of the visitors guide (€2) in advance, which, in stilted English, describes the route followed.

At the centre of the monastery is a 15th-century Mudéjar cloister with three museums. The **Museo de Bordados** displays wonderfully embroidered altar cloths and vestments from the 14th to 18th centuries, mostly made in convents. The **Museo de Libros Miniados** has a fine collection of illuminated choral songbooks from the 15th century onwards, and the **Museo de Pintura y Escultura** includes three paintings by El Greco, a Goya and a beautiful little ivory crucifixion attributed to Michelangelo.

In the elaborately decorated baroque **sacristía** (sacristy) hang eight portraits (1638–47) by Francisco de Zurbarán of leading monks of the Hieronymite order. Also here is a lantern captured from the Turkish flagship at the 1571 Battle of Lepanto (notice the twin holes made by the bullet that passed right through it). The **Relicario-Tesoro** houses a variety of other treasures, including a snaking 18th-century Italian chandelier and a 200,000-pearl cape for the Virgin. Finally the tour reaches the **camarín**, a chamber behind the altarpiece where the image of the Virgin is revolved for the faithful to contemplate her at close quarters and kiss a fragment of her mantle.

Activities

One splendid walking option is to take the Madrid–Miajadas bus to the village of **Cañamero**, southwest of Guadalupe, and hike back along a well-signed 17km trail. The **Ruta de Isabel la Católica** retraces the steps of pilgrims coming to Guadalupe from the south (including Isabel and Fernando after the fall of Moorish Granada). The tourist office has maps describing other shorter and easier circular routes of three to five hours.

Festivals & Events

Colourful processions wind through the heart of the town during Easter Week, between 6 and 8 September in honour of the Virgin of Guadalupe, and on 12 October, the Día de la Hispanidad, celebrated throughout the Spanish-speaking world. Wednesday is the local market day.

Sleeping

Should you want to stay, Guadalupe has some excellent-value choices.

Camping Las Villuercas (☎ 927 36 71 39; sites per adult/tent/car €3/3/2.50; ⌚ Apr-Dec;) This is the nearest camping option to Guadalupe, with a tennis court, swimming pool, bar-restaurant and sites shaded by lofty mature trees. It's 3km south of the village off the EX102.

Cerezo (☎ 927 36 73 79; www.hostalcerezo.com in Spanish; Calle Gregorio López 20; s/d/tr €29/43/52;) This 16-room *hostal* (budget hotel), a mere 50m from the Plaza Mayor, has small rooms with pine furniture, all with bathtub. Ask for one at the rear, overlooking the gently rolling countryside (104 is a good choice). Its more-than-decent restaurant (menú €10 to €19, mains €8.40 to €15.20) has a picture window offering the same view beyond a tangle of citrus and fig trees.

Cerezo II (☎ 927 15 41 77; www.hostalcerezo2meson.com; Plaza Mayor 23; s/d €35/48;) Owned by another Cerezo brother and on the main square, Cerezo II has more attractive modern rooms, decorated in earth colours with classy thick quilts.

Hospedería del Real Monasterio (☎ 927 36 70 00; www.monasterioguadalupe.com; Plaza Juan Carlos I; s/d/tr €43/62/83; P) Centred on the monastery's beautiful 16th-century Gothic cloister with high-ceilinged luxurious rooms (all different), this is *the* sleeping option in Guadalupe. The prices are astonishingly reasonable and the public areas are stunning; don't miss the flower-filled patio just off the lobby.

Posada del Rincón (☎ 927 36 71 14; www.posadadelrincon.com in Spanish; Plaza Mayor 11; s €45-49, d €68-75;) Behind its tiny facade, Posada del Rincón, first mentioned in writing in the late 15th century, has 20 warm-coloured rooms with exposed brick and stonework, dark-timber furniture and oak ceilings. Rooms 3, 4 and 5 overlook the bijou internal patio.

Parador de Guadalupe (☎ 927 36 70 75; www.parador.es; Calle Marqués de la Romana 12; s/d €109/136; P) Also known as Parador Zurbarán, this place occupies a converted 15th-century hospital and 16th-century religious school opposite the monastery. Spacious rooms are tastefully decorated, and the cobbled courtyard is delightful with its lemon and orange trees surrounded by a cloister-like colonnade with arches.

Eating

In addition to the following, the restaurants in the Parador de Guadalupe and Posada del Rincón are quality eateries. There are several tempting-looking bakeries around Plaza Major town selling freshly made *tortas de anis* (aniseed biscuits) and similar.

Panaderia Ntra Sra de Guadalupe (Calle Alfonso el Onceno 11) Join the queue at this tiny place dating from 1933 and serving delicious traditional cakes and pastries (as well as fresh bread).

La Marina (☎ 927 36 71 30; Gregorio López 21; menú €9, mains €4.80-9) An earthy dress-down restaurant where toothy wild boars and antlers decorate the dining room. Hearty starters like the tasty *lentejas estofadas* (lentil stew) and *garbanzos guisados con chorizo* (chick peas with chorizo) will set you up for the day for the price of a couple of *vinos*.

Hospedería del Real Monasterio (☎ 927 36 70 00; www.monasterioguadalupe.com; Plaza Juan Carlos I; meals €25) Dine grandly under the arches of the magnificent Gothic cloister or in the dining halls, rich with 17th-century timber furnishings and antique ceramics. There's a competent range of both meat and fish dishes, and most of the desserts are rustled up in the kitchens.

Shopping

Amid the imported Taiwanese baskets and *recuerdo de Guadalupe* ashtrays are some fine food products, including local *pitarra* wine, goats' cheese and various honeys and liqueurs produced in the monastery. Take your pick of the goodies at **Atrium** (☎ 927 36 70 40; Calle Alfonso El Onceno 6), also an elegant cafe.

Getting There & Away

Buses stop on Avenida Conde de Barcelona near the town hall, a two-minute walk from Plaza Mayor. **Mirat** (☎ 927 23 48 63) runs two daily services to/from Cáceres (€9.35, 2½ hours) via Trujillo (€5.75). **La Sepulvedana** (☎ 902 22 22 82) has two daily buses to/from Madrid (€14.85, 3¾ hours). Timetables are displayed in the tourist office window.

SOUTHERN EXTREMADURA

The landscape in this region is a beguiling combination of flat plains, which, further south, subtly change to a gentle, more pastoral, landscape.

MÉRIDA

pop 74,900

Mérida, seat of the Junta de Extremadura, is remarkable for its archaeological remains. Founded as Augusta Emerita in 25 BC for veterans of Rome's campaigns in Cantabria, it has Spain's most complete Roman ruins and a magnificent classical museum.

One can only wonder what still lies buried under the modern anonymous city that is Mérida today. Although there are some attractive cobbled streets around Plaza de España, overall it is an ordinary Spanish working town with little to hint of the illustrious days when Mérida was the capital of the Roman province of Lusitania; the largest

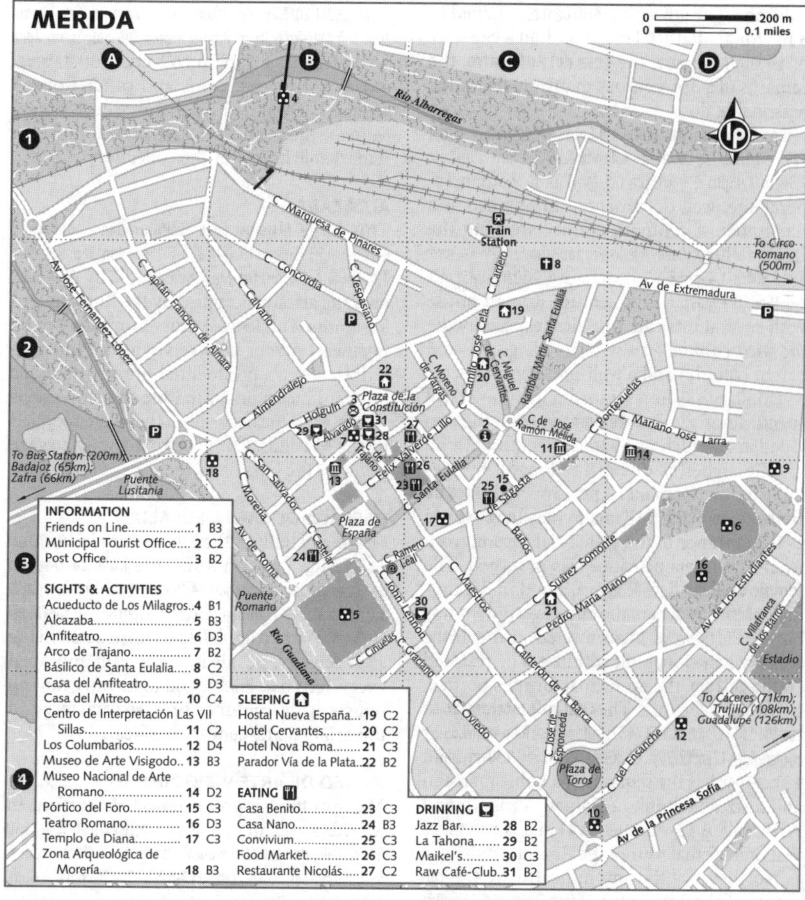

city on the Iberian Peninsula, with more than 40,000 inhabitants.

Orientation

The train station is a 10-minute walk from central Plaza de España. From the **bus station** (☎ 924 37 14 04; Avenida de la Libertad), 150m west of Río Guadiana, a 15-minute walk takes in a spectacular view of the Puente Romano from the Puente Lusitania, a sleekly modern suspension bridge designed by the famed Spanish architect Santiago Calatrava.

The most important Roman ruins are within easy walking distance of each other on the east side of town. Pedestrianised Calle Santa Eulalia, heading northeast from Plaza de España, is the main shopping street.

Information

Friends on Line (Calle Romero Leal 5; per hr €2; 🕑 11am-2pm & 4pm-midnight) Internet access.
Municipal tourist office (☎ 924 33 07 22; Calle Santa Eulalia 64; 🕑 9.30am-2pm & 4-7pm or 5-8pm)
Post office (Plaza de la Constitución)

Sights

ROMAN REMAINS

The **Teatro Romano** (Calle Alvarez S. de Buruaga; adult/under 12yr €7/free, incl Los Columbarios, Casa de Mitreo, Alcazaba, Zona Arqueológica de Morería, Basilica de Santa Eulalia & Circo Romano adult/under 12yr €10/free; 🕑 9.30am-1.45pm & 5-7.15pm Jun-Sep, 9.30am-1.45pm & 4-6.15pm Oct-May; 🚸), built around 15 BC to seat 6000 spectators, has a dramatic and well-preserved two-tier backdrop of stone columns. The adjoining **Anfiteatro**, opened in 8 BC for gladiatorial contests, had a capacity of 14,000. Nearby, the **Casa del Anfiteatro**, the remains of a 3rd-century mansion, has some reasonable floor mosaics.

Los Columbarios (Calle del Ensanche s/n; adult/under 12yr €4/free; 9.30am-1.45pm & 5-7.15pm Jun-Sep, 9.30am-1.45pm & 4-6.15pm Oct-May) is a Roman funeral site, well documented in Spanish and illustrated. A footpath connects it with the **Casa del Mitreo** (Calle Oviedo s/n; adult/under 12yr €4/free; 9.30am-1.45pm & 5-7.15pm Jun-Sep, 9.30am-1.45pm & 4-6.15pm Oct-May), a 2nd-century Roman house with several intricate mosaics (especially the *mosaico cosmológico* with its allegories and bright colours) and a well-preserved fresco.

Don't miss the extraordinarily powerful spectacle of the **Puente Romano** over the Río Guadiana, which at 792m in length with 60 granite arches, is one of the longest bridges built by the Romans. The 15m-high **Arco de Trajano** over Calle de Trajano may have served as the entrance to the provincial forum, from where Lusitania province was governed. The **Templo de Diana** (Calle de Sagasta) stood in the municipal forum, where the city government was based. Parts were incorporated into a 16th-century mansion, built within it. The restored **Pórtico del Foro**, the municipal forum's portico, is just along the road. The **Centro de Interpretación Las VII Sillas** (608 73 74 32; Calle de José Ramón Mélida 20; adult/under 12yr/12-25yr €2.40/free/1.20; 9.30am-2pm & 4.30pm-7pm) has the remains of a noble mansion and a sizeable hunk of Roman, Visigoth and Arab wall. A 13-minute DVD in Spanish takes you on a virtual tour of the Roman city.

Northeast of the amphitheatre are the remains of the 1st-century **Circo Romano** (Avenida Juan Carlos; adult/child €4/free; 9.30am-1.45pm & 5-7.15pm Jun-Sep, 9.30am-1.45pm & 4-6.15pm Oct-May), the only surviving hippodrome of its kind in Spain, which could accommodate 30,000 spectators. Inside you can see brief footage in Spanish about Diocles, a champion *auriga* (chariot racer) who served his apprenticeship in Mérida before going on to the big league in Rome. Further west, the **Acueducto de Los Milagros** (Calle Marquesa de Pinares), highly favoured by nesting storks, once supplied the Roman city with water from the dam at Lago Proserpina, about 5km out of town.

MUSEO NACIONAL DE ARTE ROMANO

This excellent **museum** (924 31 16 90; www.mnar.es; Calle de José Ramón Mélida; adult/senior & 18-25yr/under 18yr €2.40/1.20/1.20; 10am-2pm, 5-7pm Tue-Sat, 10am-2pm Sun Mar-Nov, 10am-2pm & 4-6pm Tue-Sat, 10am-2pm Sun Dec-Feb) has a superb collection of statues, mosaics, frescoes, coins and other Roman artefacts. Designed by the architect Rafael Moneo, the grand brick structure makes a remarkable home for the collection.

ALCAZABA

This large **Muslim fort** (Calle Graciano; adult/child €4/free; 9.30am-1.45pm & 5-7.15pm Jun-Sep, 9.30am-1.45pm & 4-6.15pm Oct-May) was built in AD 835 on a site already occupied by the Romans and Visigoths. The 15th-century monastery in its northeast corner now serves as the Junta de Extremadura's presidential offices. Its *aljibe* (cistern) incorporates marble and stone slabs with Visigothic decoration that were recycled by the Muslims. Climb up to the walls to gaze out over the Guadiana.

BÁSILICA DE SANTA EULALIA

Originally built in the 5th century in honour of Mérida's patron saint, the **básilica** (Avenida de Extremadura; adult/child €4/free; 9.30am-1.45pm & 5-7.15pm Mon-Sat Jun-Sep, 9.30am-1.45pm & 4-6.15pm Mon-Sat Oct-May) was completely reconstructed in the 13th century. Beside it, a museum and open excavated areas enable you to identify Roman houses, a 4th-century Christian cemetery and the original 5th-century basilica.

MUSEO DE ARTE VISIGODO

Many of the Visigothic objects unearthed in Mérida are exhibited in this **museum** (924 30 01 06; Calle de Santa Julia; admission free; 10am-2pm & 5-7pm Mon-Sat, 10am-2pm Sun Jun-Sep, 10am-2pm & 4-6pm, 10am-2pm Sun Oct-May), just off Plaza de España.

ZONA ARQUEOLÓGICA DE MORERÍA

This excavated **Moorish quarter** (Avenida de Roma; adult/child €4/free; 9.30am-1.45pm & 5-7.15pm Jun-Sep, 9.30am-1.45pm & 4-6.15pm Oct-May) contains the remains of a cemetery, walls and houses dating from Roman to post-Islamic times.

Festivals & Events

The prestigious summer **Festival de Teatro Clásico** (www.festivaldemerida.es in Spanish; admission €12-39; around 11pm most nights Jul & Aug), at the Roman theatre and amphitheatre, features Greek and more recent drama classics, plus music and dance. Mérida lets its hair down a little later than most of Extremadura at its **Feria de Septiembre** (September Fair; 1 to 15 September).

Sleeping

Hostal Nueva España (☎ 924 31 33 56; Avenida de Extremadura 6; s/d €25/38; ❄) Well positioned and with friendly family owners, the rooms are spick and span, although the bedspreads are threadbare and the bare bulb lighting pretty bleak. Ask for an interior room away from the busy road.

Hotel Cervantes (☎ 924 31 49 61; www.hotelcervantes.com; Calle Camilo José Cela 8; s €40-50, d €60-70; P ❄) Best deal in this price bracket with attractive half-panelled rooms with marble floors, full baths and dark-wood furniture. The bar-restaurant serves a bacon-and-egg breakfast.

Hotel Velada (☎ 924 31 51 10; www.veladahoteles.com; Avenida Reina Sofia s/n; r €60-85; P ⊠ 💻 ❄) The city's newest hotel is just 600m from the Teatro Romano and has a faux-temple exterior complete with columns. The rooms are modern, carpeted and comfortable with perks like a trouser press (no jeans please) and gleaming marble bathrooms. The buffet breakfast is more generous than most.

Hotel Nova Roma (☎ 924 31 12 61; www.novaroma.com in Spanish; Calle Suárez Somonte 42; s/d €72/89; ❄) Love it or loathe it, the pseudo–Roman Empire interior is all heavy layers of marble and headless statues. The rooms are less kitsch: bright and spacious with light pastel-coloured decor. The restaurant *menú del día* is also excellent value at €11.50 with a six-starter and main choice, plus dessert.

Parador Vía de la Plata (☎ 924 31 38 00; www.parador.es; Plaza de la Constitución 3; s/d €118/142; P ⊠ ❄ ♿) You're sleeping on the site of a Roman temple in a building that started life as a convent; the lounge was a former chapel, then served as both hospital and prison. In the gardens, the assembled hunks of Roman, Visigoth and Mudéjar give a brief canter through Mérida's architectural history. Rear-room balconies look onto a quiet garden with fountains.

Eating

Convivium (☎ 648 23 13 90; Calle de Sagasta 21; tortillinas €1.50, raciones €5-12) Head straight for the pretty patio with tables set under a large lemon tree. Try the speciality *tortillinas* (mini-omelettes with fillings including cod, salami, spinach, aubergines and prawns). The *raciones* are more traditional.

Casa Benito (☎ 924 33 07 69; Calle San Francisco 3; tapas €2.60) Squeeze onto a tiny stool in the wood-panelled dining room, prop up the bar or relax on the sunny terrace for tapas at this bullfight enthusiasts' hang-out, its walls plastered with photos, posters and memorabilia from the ring. The adjacent *asador* specialises in roasts including *rabo de toro* (bull's tail) – no surprises there (€12.75).

Casa Nano (☎ 924 31 82 57; Calle San Salvador Castelar 3; meals €15-20; 🕑 Mon-Sat) Tucked behind Plaza de España, the *simpatico* staff here serve dishes like *cordero a la ciruela* (lamb with plums), various *bacalao* (cod) dishes and *patatas al rebujón* (wedges of thick potato omelette). Don your shades and brave the bright lights of the dining room or head outside for a table on this quiet pedestrian street.

Restaurante Nicolás (☎ 924 31 96 10; Calle Felix Valverde Lillo 15; meals €20-25; 🕑 lunch & dinner Mon-Sat, lunch Sun) Long admired as a local favourite, this is one of the classier city dining options. Its relaxing ground-floor bar serves *raciones* while upstairs the food is decidedly more exciting than the restaurant's rather drab decor.

Self-caterers can ferret out plenty of delights in Mérida's busy **food market** (Calle Felix Valverde Lillo).

Drinking

The best place to enjoy an early evening drink is at one of the four kiosk-bars on Plaza de España. You'll find a more diverse selection of bars in and around Plaza de la Constitución.

La Tahona (Calle Alvarado 5; 🕑 9pm-late) There's a classy courtyard draped with bougainvillea at La Tahona, plus a cavernous bar area with a stage for regular live gigs ranging from flamenco to blues and jazz.

Raw Café-Club (☎ 924 33 01 35; Plaza de la Constitución 2; 🕑 6pm-late Tue-Sun) A spirited and edgily grungy bar in an incongruous lavishly tiled and historic town house. It attracts the teens/early 20s gang with live gigs nightly.

Head to the **Jazz Bar** (☎ 666 706392; Calle Alvarado 10; 🕑 4pm-2am Tue-Sat) for a more sophisticated scene with regular exhibitions, and jazz every Thursday at 10pm. **Maikel's** (Calle John Lennon 19; 🕑 10pm-5am Thu-Sat) is the place to move your booty in downtown Mérida. Look for the twinkling orange globe outside.

Getting There & Around

Bus destinations include Badajoz (€4.25, one hour, five to nine daily), Seville (€11.95, 2½ hours, five daily), Cáceres (€4.80, 50 minutes, two to four daily), Trujillo (€7.35, 1¼ hours, three daily) and Madrid (€20.65 to €27, four to five hours, eight daily). The bus station is located across the river, along Avenida de Libertad.

There are four trains to Madrid (€28.75 to €31.80, 4½ to 5½ hours) and two to Seville (€12.15, five hours) via Zafra (€3.80). Up to six trains run to/from Cáceres (€5.25, one hour).

For a taxi, call ☎ 924 37 11 11.

BADAJOZ

pop 145,300

Badajoz, provincial capital of the southern half of Extremadura, straddles Río Guadiana just 4km from Portugal. While the shell is sprawling and industrial, the historic centre around the cathedral has a beguiling charm, with narrow pedestrian streets lined with shops, bars and restaurants. Even the former dilapidated neighbourhood below the Alcazaba is gradually being spruced up, thanks to generous local and European Union investment.

The town has had more than its share of strife. After centuries of Muslim occupation, it was first occupied by Portugal in 1385, then again in 1396, 1542 and 1660. It was besieged during the War of the Spanish Succession, then three times by the French in the Peninsular War. In 1812 the British expelled the French in a bloody battle that cost 6000 lives. In the Spanish Civil War, the Nationalists carried out atrocious massacres when they took Badajoz in 1936. The

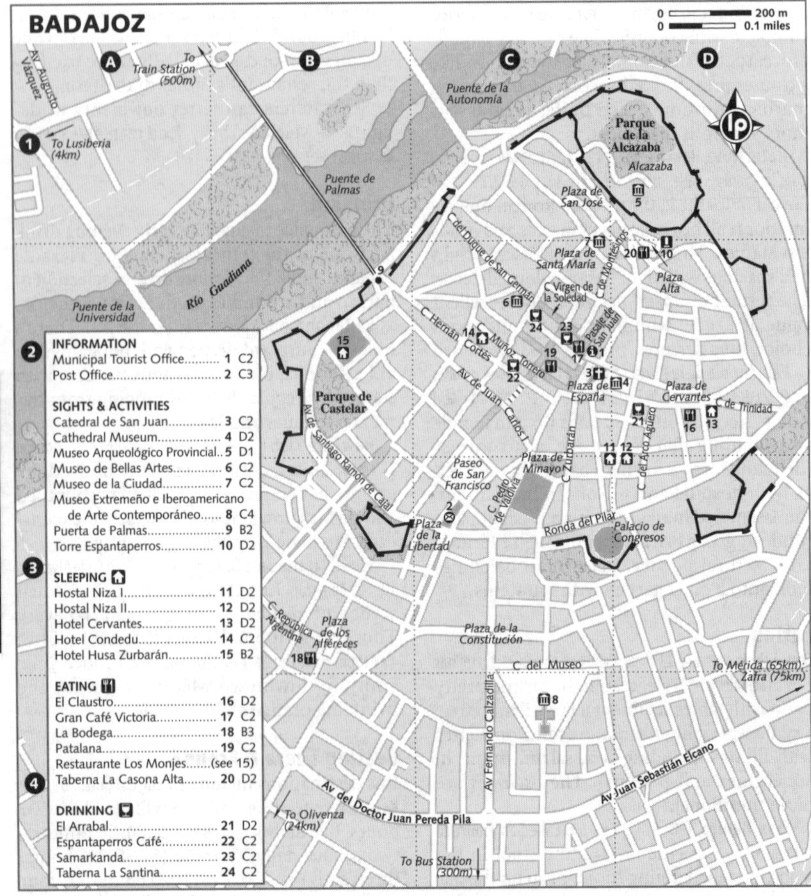

latest of its many trials was in 1997 when Río Guadiana burst its banks and flash floods coursed through the city causing 24 deaths.

Orientation

Plaza de España is the centre of the old town. The pedestrianised streets to its west are full of restaurants and bars. The main commercial centre is to the south, around Avenida de Juan Carlos I and Paseo de San Francisco.

The **bus station** (☎ 924 25 86 61; Calle José Rebollo López) is 1km south of the city centre. The **train station** (Avenida de Carolina Coronado) is 1.5km northwest of the city centre, across the river.

Information

Municipal tourist office (☎ 924 22 49 81; www.turismobadajoz.com; Pasaje de San Juan s/n; 10am-2pm & 4-6pm or 6-8pm Mon-Fri, 10am-2pm Sat)
Post office (Plaza de la Libertad)

Sights

What a treat: admission to all Badajoz's sights, except for the cathedral museum, is free.

The **Catedral de San Juan** (Plaza de España) was built in the 13th century on the site of a mosque and subsequently much altered, including a worryingly perfect-looking faux limestone exterior. It is currently closed for reformation; check with the tourist office for an update. Its **museum** (entry from Calle de San Blas; adult/student €3/1; 11am-1pm & 5-7pm Tue-Sat) contains a treasure chest of religious objects and artworks.

The magnificent walled **Alcazaba** lords it on the hilltop, north of the centre. Walk around the ramparts enclosing the 8-hectare site with its well-labelled ruins and banks of wild rosemary and flowers and ponder on what must still lie beneath this partially excavated site – once a thriving community with *medinas*, baths, mosques and houses. Guarding all is the **Torre Espantaperros** (Scare-Dogs Tower), symbol of Badajoz, constructed by the Arabs and topped by a 16th-century Mudéjar bell tower. At its feet is the **Plaza Alta**, dating back to 1681 with its like-it-or-loathe-it highly decorative burgundy, grey and white dizzily painted facades. Within the fort area, a restored Renaissance palace houses the **Museo Arqueológico Provincial** (☎ 924 00 19 08; admission free; 10am-3pm Tue-Sun), with artefacts from prehistoric times through to Roman, Islamic and medieval Christian periods.

The **Museo de Bellas Artes** (☎ 924 21 24 69; Calle del Duque de San Germán 3; admission free; 10am-2pm & 4-6pm or 6-8pm Tue-Fri, to 2pm Sat & Sun) is an excellent gallery with works by Zurbarán, Morales, Picasso, Dalí, plus striking works by the 19th-century Badajoz-born artist Felipe Checa.

The **Puente de Palmas**, an impressive 582m-long granite bridge built in 1596, leads over Río Guadiana from the 16th-century **Puerta de Palmas** city gate, so insensitively over-restored that it could be an import from Disneyland.

Badajoz's pride and joy is the **Museo Extremeño e Iberoamericano de Arte Contemporáneo** (MEIAC; ☎ 924 01 30 60; Calle Virgen de Guadalupe 7; admission free; 10am-1.30pm & 5-8pm Tue-Sat, 10.30am-1.30pm Sun). This commanding modern building, dedicated to Spanish, Portuguese and Latin American contemporary art, houses a wide-ranging collection of avant-garde painting and sculpture.

The **Museo de la Ciudad** (City Museum; ☎ 924 20 06 87; Plaza de Santa María; admission free; 10am-2pm & 4.30-7.30pm or 5-8pm Tue-Sat, to 2pm Sun; ♿) is housed in a modern block that jars with the historic, if shabby surrounds. Painstakingly created, the exhibits recount the story of the city through illustrative panels and interactive displays (all in Spanish), taking you through the glory days of Islamic Badajoz and the Reconquista to today. Don't miss the blow-up newspaper replicas on the first floor with top stories like Franco's death.

Lusiberia (☎ 924 28 60 98; Avenida de Elvas, Antigua Frontera de Caya; adult/child €14/10; 11.30am-8.30pm mid-Jun–mid-Sep, 2-8pm Sat & Sun mid-Sep–mid-Jun) is a gigantic family theme and water park, bang up against the Portuguese frontier.

Festivals & Events

Badajoz's big bash is the **Feria de San Juan**, celebrated for a full week around 24 June.

Running a close second are the town's **Carnaval** celebrations, among the most elaborate in Spain, in the build-up to Lent.

Sleeping

Hostal Niza II (☎ 924 22 31 73; Calle del Arco Agüero 45; s/d €27/43) Look beyond the bland chip marble floors and anaemic colour scheme as the rooms here are clean and comfortable. Hostal Niza I across the road at No 34 is basically a spill-over in a more recent building, with virtually identical decor.

Hotel Cervantes (☎ 924 22 37 10; Calle de Trinidad 2; s/d €29/42; P) You can't miss the candy floss Modernista exterior of this atmospheric rambling hotel on the corner of a leafy square. Original tilework and green timber are evocative reminders of its former days as a grand private house. Rooms are charmingly dated in the old half and quieter and better equipped in the newer wing.

Hotel Condedu (☎ 924 20 72 47; www.hotelcondedu.com; Calle Muñoz Torrero 27; s/d €40/55; P) Look beyond the bland concrete exterior of this 1970s hotel, as the rooms are a pleasant surprise with strong colours, parquet floors, interesting art work and expensively tiled bathrooms.

Hotel Husa Zurbarán (☎ 924 00 14 00; www.husa.es; Paseo Castelar s/n; r from €70-85; P) Something of a concrete monster from street level, the Zurbarán is considerably warmer and more attractive within; the majority of the rooms have been tastefully reformed with lots of dazzling white and soft earth colours. The hotel's Restaurante Los Monjes is, by common consent, Badajoz's finest restaurant.

Eating

Gran Café Victoria (☎ 924 26 32 23; Calle Obispo San Juan de Ribera 3; breakfasts €2-3) With its huge central lamp arrangement, tall dark pillars and wine-red couches, this cafe has a dignified ambience for your morning coffee and croissant.

Patalana (☎ 617 17 62 67; Melendez Valdes 9; tortilla €6, meals €10-14) Head to a table outside this small, mildly shabby-looking place and order one of the 14-plus choice of traditional potato and egg tortillas, with fillings including spinach, bacon, peppers and onion, prawns, oregano and cheese. Mains are less innovative but passable and cheap.

La Bodega (☎ 924 22 48 07; Plaza de los Alfereces 8; menú €11, meals €18-25) The appropriately named La Bodega is one of several restaurants with sprawling terraces that ring this pretty square with its maple trees and fountain. Within, you can dine economically among wine barrels and wood, on the set lunchtime menu that varies daily.

El Claustro (☎ 924 20 17 21; Plaza de Cervantes 13A; tapas €2.50, meals €22-25; 12am-12pm Mon-Sat) The fashionable stone-clad interior is hung with edgy art work and fronted by a buzzy tapas bar serving generous, innovative snacks like *salmon con mouse de queso y vinagreta de tomato* (salmon mousse with cream cheese and tomato vinaigrette). The chandelier-lit dining room dishes up larger portions of similar tastebud treats.

Taberna La Casona Alta (☎ 670 71 30 96; Plaza Alta; raciones from €6, meals €25-30; lunch & dinner Mon-Sat, lunch Sun) With chairs on the square and a bustling bar area with barrel tables, here you can choose from a healthy menu of *raciones* or more substantial dishes in the downstairs Moorish-style restaurant, like Portuguese-style *bacalao* (cod), prepared a variety of ways.

Drinking

Taberna La Santina (☎ 924 25 76 57; Calle Virgen de la Soledad 25; Mon-Sat) Bullfighting memorabilia bedecks this inviting Andalucian-style bar, its hams hanging behind the bar gently curing in cigarette smoke.

Late-night bars are scattered around the streets near the cathedral. Among the liveliest are **Espantaperros Café** (☎ 924 27 30 31; Calle Hernán Cortés 14; 8pm-3am Mon-Thu & 4pm-4am Fri-Sun), which has live jazz nightly; sophisticated **El Arrabal** (Calle de San Blas 14; 10pm-2.30am Mon-Sat), with its garden bar; and **Samarkanda** (☎ 607 28 15 93; Calle Virgen de la Soledad 9; 4.30pm-2.30am), its moody dark-red paintwork overlooked by a serene Buddha statue.

Getting There & Around

You can get buses to most main points in the region from Badajoz. Further afield, buses run to/from Mérida (€4.25, one hour, five to nine daily), Madrid (€24.20, 4½ to 5½ hours; nine daily), Lisbon (€24.75, three hours, three daily) and Seville (€13.60, three hours; six daily) via Zafra (€5.75; 1¼ hours).

Trains are much less frequent and the station awkwardly placed.

For a taxi, call ☎ 924 24 31 01.

AROUND BADAJOZ

Albuquerque

pop 5700

Looming large above the small town, 38km north of Badajoz, is the intact **Castillo de la Luna** (admission free; guided visits in Spanish 11am-1pm & 4-6pm Tue-Sun). The centrepiece of a complex frontier defence system of forts, the castle was built on the site of its Muslim predecessor in the 13th century and subsequently expanded. From the top, views dominate the Portuguese frontier (the Portuguese actually took the town for a few years in the early 18th century). Among many curiosities is a hole set in the wall of one of the towers. It was used by the castle's masters as a toilet – sending an unpleasant message to hostile forces below when under siege.

Up to four buses a day (€3.75, 45 minutes) between Badajoz and San Vicente de Alcántara stop by.

Olivenza

pop 11,400

Pretty Olivenza, 24km south of Badajoz, clings to its strong Portuguese heritage – it has only been Spanish since 1801. The cobbled centre is distinctive for its whitewashed houses, typical turreted defensive walls and penchant for blue-and-white ceramic tilework.

The town was fortified due to its strategic position as a Portuguese outpost on the fertile Guadiana plain. Smack bang in its centre is the 14th-century **castle**, dominated by the **Torre del Homenaje**, 37m high, from which there are fine views. The castle houses an **ethnographic museum** (☎ 924 49 02 22; admission €1; 🕒 11am-2pm & 4-7pm or 5-8pm Tue-Fri, 10am-2pm Sun). Eternal Peter Pans will savour the collection of toy cars on the 1st floor. The most impressive section of the original **defensive walls** is around the 18th-century **Puerta del Calvario**, on the west side of town.

Restaurante Hostal Dosca (☎ 924 49 10 65; www.hoteldosca.com; Plaza de la Constitución 15; s/d €40/50; ❄), on the corner of one of the town's most evocative squares, complete with fountain, makes an excellent lunch stop (*menú del día* €13 to €25) or overnight stay. The rooms here are prettily furnished and have lovely views.

Buses to Badajoz (€1.85, 30 minutes) run almost hourly during the week from the bus station on Calle Avelino, five minutes' walk east of Plaza de España.

ZAFRA

pop 16,400

Gleaming white Zafra resembles an Andalucían *pueblo blanco,* except that the sea is 160km away. The narrow streets are lined with baroque churches, old-fashioned shops and traditional houses decorated by the brilliant red splashes of geraniums. Originally a Muslim settlement, the town makes a serene, attractive stop between Seville and Mérida.

The **tourist office** (☎ 924 55 10 36; www.ayto-zafra.com in Spanish; 🕒 9.30am-2pm & 4-7pm or 5-8pm Mon-Fri, 10am-1.30pm & 5-7pm or 6-8pm Sat & Sun) is on Plaza de España, the main square.

Zafra's 15th-century **castle**, now the town's *parador,* was built over the former Muslim Alcázar and dominates the town. **Plaza Grande** and the adjoining **Plaza Chica**, arcaded and bordered by bars, are the place to see Zafra life, from old men in flat caps playing dominoes to children playing football and decorating the ground with pipas (sunflower) shells. Peek into the courtyard of the **ayuntamiento** (town hall; Plaza Pilar Redondo), its brick arches supported by slender pillars, and the 16th-century **Iglesia de la Candelaria** (Calle Tetuán; 🕒 10.30am-1pm & 5.30-7.30pm or 6.30-8.30pm Thu-Tue) with its fine altarpieces.

Sleeping & Eating

Albergue Convento San Francisco (☎ 924 02 98 17; Calle Ancha 1; dm €18-32; 💻) Open to all, this former monastery is the choice of walkers along the Ruta Vía de la Plata (see the boxed text, p838). It has a choice of dorms or en suite doubles in pleasant, brightly furnished surroundings.

Hotel Plaza Grande (☎ 924 56 31 63; Calle Pasteleros 2; s/d €30/60; ❄) The new owner has created a gem of a hotel here. Go for room 108 with its corner windows overlooking the plaza. Decor is terracotta accentuated by cream paintwork and muted earth colours. The downstairs restaurant and bar are reliably good.

Hotel Huerta Honda (☎ 924 55 41 00; www.hotelhuertahonda.com; Calle López Asme 1; s €59, d €74-105; P ⊠ ❄ 🏊) There are two grades of rooms here: standards are fashionably modern with lots of browns and beiges while superiors are sumptuous with four-poster beds, timber ceilings and antiques. The bougainvillea-draped courtyard has views of the castle.

Parador Hernán Cortés (☎ 924 55 45 40; www.parador.es; Plaza Corazón de María 7; s/d €115/144; ⊠ ❄ 🏊) They say a man's home is his castle: here it's the reverse. The large rooms are richly decorated with burgundy-coloured fabrics and antiques. The marble-pillared courtyard is truly magnificent while the secluded pool is surrounded by ivy and turrets. Both the *parador* and Hotel Huerta Honda have excellent restaurants.

La Rebotica (☎ 924 55 42 89; Calle Boticas 12; meals €35; 🕒 lunch & dinner Tue-Sat, lunch Sun) This restaurant offers a traditional meaty menu including *rabo de toro* (ox tail) and five different pork fillet dishes subtly prepared by Dutch chef Rudy Koster. It's just off delightful Plaza Chica, where you can whet your appetite with a drink at one of four earthy local bars.

Getting There & Away

Zafra is on the main bus and train routes linking Seville to the south with Mérida (€4.55, 65 minutes) and Badajoz (€5.75, 1¼ hours).

AROUND ZAFRA

Roads through the rolling Sierra Morena into Andalucía head southwest through Fregenal de la Sierra into northern Huelva province, and southeast into the Parque Natural Sierra Norte in Sevilla province.

In **Fregenal de la Sierra** highlights include the 13th-century castle with seven turrets and adjacent Santa María church. On Tuesday and Friday mornings there is a lively market in the main square. Walled and hilly **Jerez de los Caballeros**, 42km west of Zafra, was a cradle of conquistadors. It has a Knights Templar castle and several handsome churches, three with towers emulating the Giralda in Seville. Quiet **Burguillos del Cerro**, southwest of Zafra, is overlooked by a 15th-century castle atop a grassy hill. Just outside **Casas de Reina** on the Guadalcanal road are impressive remains of a Roman theatre and a hilltop Muslim castle.

One weekday bus runs between Zafra and Fregenal de la Sierra (€2.80, one hour), Jerez de los Caballeros (€2.85, one hour) and Burguillos del Cerro (€1.45, 30 minutes).

Directory

CONTENTS

ACCOMMODATION

There's generally no need to book ahead for a room in the low or shoulder seasons, but when things get busier it's advisable (and in high periods it can be essential) to make a reservation if you want to avoid a wearisome search for a room. At most places a phone call earlier the same day is all that's needed: they'll probably ask your approximate time of arrival and will tell you that they'll hold the room for you until a specific hour. Some may ask for a credit card number. Many hotels take reservations by email.

Prices throughout this guidebook are high-season maximums. You may be pleasantly surprised if you travel at other times. What constitutes low or high season depends on where and when. Most of the year is high season in Barcelona, especially during trade fairs. August can be dead in the cities. Winter is high season in the Pyrenees and low season in the Balearic Islands (indeed, the islands seem to shut down between November and Easter). July and August in the Balearics offer sun and fun, but finding a place to stay without booking ahead can be a pain. Weekends are high season for boutique hotels and *casas rurales* (country home, village or farmstead accommodation; see p864), but bad for business hotels (which often offer generous specials then) in Madrid and Barcelona.

We divide accommodation categories into budget, midrange and top end. As prices vary greatly from one part of the country to another, the dividing line is somewhat arbitrary. In places such as Barcelona and Madrid, and other popular tourist locations, a budget place can mean anything up to €40/60 for an *individual/doble* (single/double). At the higher end of this range you can generally expect to find good, comfortable rooms with private bathrooms. Shave a few euros off and you may find the place only has shared bathrooms in the corridor. In less-travelled regions, such as Extremadura, Murcia and Castilla-La Mancha, it can be relatively easy to find perfectly acceptable single/double rooms (usually with shared bathroom) for around €30/45. If you want to go for rock bottom then youth hostels, where a bed can cost anything up to €27 but more often around €12 to €21, are probably the best bet.

Midrange places in the big cities can cost up to about €200 for a fine double, and there are plenty of good and on occasion outright charming options for less. Anything above that price takes you into luxury level. Again, though, much depends on the location and period. Cities like Madrid and Barcelona, with busy trade fair calendars, can become more expensive still during such fairs. In many other parts of Spain you'd be hard-pressed to pay more than €150 for the best double in town. Within each area we have divided up the offerings on the basis of local conditions. A double in a *parador* (see p866) in Castilla-La Mancha at around €100 might be rated top end; the same price will get you a nice but smallish midrange room in Madrid.

A *habitación doble* (double room) is frequently just that: a room with two beds (which you can often shove together). If you want to be sure of a double bed *(cama matrimonial)*, ask for it!

Two websites with online hotel booking facilities are **Hotelkey** (☎ in Spain 902 303555; www.hotelkey.com) and **Madeinspain** (www.madeinspain.net). The national tourist office website (www.spain.info) is another option.

BOOK YOUR STAY ONLINE

For more accommodation reviews and recommendations by Lonely Planet authors, check out the online booking service at www.lonelyplanet.com/hotels. You'll find the true, insider lowdown on the best places to stay. Reviews are thorough and independent. Best of all, you can book online.

Apartments, Villas & Casas Rurales

Throughout Spain you can rent self-catering apartments and houses from one night upwards. Villas and houses are widely available on the main holiday coasts and in popular country areas.

A simple one-bedroom apartment in a coastal resort for two or three people might cost as little as €30 per night, although more often you'll be looking at nearly twice that much, and prices can jump even further in high season. More luxurious options with a swimming pool might come in at anything between €200 and €400 for four people. These options are most worth considering if you plan to stay several days or more.

Rural tourism has become immensely popular, with accommodation available in many new and often charming *casas rurales*. These are usually comfortably renovated village houses or farmhouses with a handful of rooms. They often go by other names, such as *cases de pagès* in Catalonia, *casas de aldea* in Asturias, *posadas* and *casonas* in Cantabria and so on. Some just provide rooms, while others offer meals or self-catering accommodation. Lower-end prices typically hover around €30/50 (single/double) per night, but classy boutique establishments can easily charge €100 or more for a double. Many are rented out by the week.

Tourist offices can supply lists of places for rent, and in Britain the travel sections of the broadsheet press carry private ads for such places. Agencies include:

Apartments-Spain (www.apartments-spain.com)
Associació Agroturisme Balear (☎ 971 721508; www.agroturismo-balear.com)
Atlas Rural (www.atlasrural.com)
Casas Cantabricas (☎ in UK 01223 328 721; www.casas.co.uk)
Cases Rurals de Catalunya (www.casesrurals.com)
Fincas 4 You (www.fincas4you.com)
Guías Casas Rurales (www.guiascasasrurales.com in Spanish)
Holiday Serviced Apartments (☎ in UK 0845 470 4477; www.holidayapartments.co.uk)
Individual Travellers Company (☎ 08700 780 194; www.individualtravellers.com)
Owners Direct (www.ownersdirect.co.uk)
Rustic Rent (☎ 971 768040; www.rusticrent.com)
Secret Destinations (☎ in UK 0845 612 9000; www.secretdestinations.com)
Secret Places (www.secretplaces.com)
Simply Travel (☎ 0871 231 4050; www.simplytravel.co.uk)
Top Rural (www.toprural.com)
Traum Ferienwohnungen (www.traum-ferienwohnungen.de)
Vintage (☎ in UK 0845 344 0460; www.vintagetravel.co.uk)

Camping & Caravan Parks

Spain has around 1000 officially graded *campings* (camping grounds). Some are well located in woodland or near beaches or rivers, but others are on the outskirts of towns or along highways. Few are near city centres, and camping isn't particularly convenient if you're relying on public transport.

Camping grounds are officially rated as first class (1ªC), second class (2ªC) or third class (3ªC). There are also a few that are not officially graded, usually equivalent to third class. Facilities generally range from reasonable to very good, although any camping ground can be crowded and noisy at busy times (especially July and August). Even a third-class camping ground is likely to have hot showers, electrical hook-ups and a cafe. The best ones have heated swimming pools, supermarkets, restaurants, laundry service, children's playgrounds and tennis courts. Sizes range from a capacity of under 100 people to over 5000.

Camping grounds usually charge per person, per tent and per vehicle – typically €4 to

€8.50 for each. Children usually pay a bit less than adults. Many camping grounds close from around October to Easter.

The annual *Guía Oficial de Campings*, available in bookshops around the country, lists most of Spain's camping grounds and their facilities and prices. Tourist offices can always direct you to the nearest camping ground.

You sometimes come across a *zona de acampada* or *área de acampada*, a country camping ground with minimal facilities (maybe just tap water or a couple of barbecues), little or no supervision and little or no charge. If it's in an environmentally protected area, you may need to obtain permission from the local environmental authority to camp there.

With certain exceptions – such as many beaches and environmentally protected areas and a few municipalities that ban it – it is legal to camp outside camping grounds (but not within 1km of official ones!). Signs usually indicate where wild camping is not allowed. If in doubt you can always check with tourist offices. You'll need permission to camp on private land.

Various websites list camping grounds around the country, including www.campinguia.com and www.campingsonline.com/espana. The former contains comments (mostly in Spanish) and links, while you can book on the latter.

Hostels

Spain's 250 or so youth hostels – *albergues juveniles*, not be confused with *hostales* (budget hotels) – are often the cheapest places for lone travellers, but two people can usually get a double room elsewhere for a similar price. Some hostels are only moderate value, lacking in privacy, often heavily booked by school groups, and with night-time curfews and no cooking facilities (although if there is nowhere to cook there is usually a cafeteria). Others, however, are conveniently located, open 24 hours and composed mainly of double rooms or small dorms, often with a private bathroom. An increasing number have rooms adapted for people with disabilities. Some even occupy fine historic buildings.

Most Spanish youth hostels are members of the **Red Española de Albergues Juveniles** (REAJ, Spanish Youth Hostel Network; www.reaj.com), the Spanish representative of **Hostelling International** (HI; www.hihostels.com).

Most of the REAJ member hostels are also members of the youth hostel association of their region (Andalucía, Catalonia, Valencia etc). Each region usually sets its own price structure and has a central booking service where you can make reservations for most of its hostels. You can also book directly with hostels themselves. Central booking services include:

Andalucía (☎ 902 510000; www.inturjoven.com)
Catalonia (☎ 93 483 83 41; www.xanascat.cat)
Valencia (☎ 902 225552; www.ivaj.es in Spanish)

Just a few youth hostels are independent of regional associations – although they may still be REAJ and HI members! A growing number of hostel-style places not connected with HI or REAJ often have individual rooms as well the more typical dormitory options. Prices can vary greatly as, not being affiliated to any organisation, they are not subject to any pricing system. A good website for seeking out hostels, affiliated or otherwise, is www.hostel world.com.

Prices at youth hostels often depend on the season, and vary between about €12 and €21 for under-26s (the lower rate is usually applied to people with ISIC cards too – see p872) and between €16 and €27 for those 26 and over. In some hostels the price includes breakfast. A few hostels require you to rent sheets (around €2 to €4 for your stay) if you don't have your own or a sleeping bag.

Most hostels require you to have an HI card or a membership card from your home country's youth hostel association; others don't require a card (even though they may be HI hostels), but may charge more if you don't have one. You can obtain an HI card in Spain at most hostels.

You will sometimes find independent *albergues* offering basic dormitory accommodation for around €10 to €18, usually in villages in areas that attract plenty of Spanish walkers and climbers. These are not specifically youth hostels – although the clientele tends to be under 35. They're a kind of halfway house between a youth hostel and a *refugio* (mountain shelter; see p867). Some will rent you sheets for a couple of euros if you need them.

Hotels, Hostales, Pensiones & Hospedajes

Officially, places to stay are classified into *hoteles* (hotels; one to five stars), *hostales*

PRACTICALITIES

- Use the metric system for weights and measures.
- Bring an international adaptor because plugs have two round pins; the electric current is 220V, 50Hz.
- If your Spanish is up to it, try the following newspapers: *El País* (or the free, constantly updated, downloadable version, *24 Horas,* on www.elpais.es), the country's leading daily and left-of-centre oriented; *ABC,* for a right-wing view of life; Barcelona-based *La Vanguardia,* which on Friday has a great listings magazine for that city; and *Marca,* an all-sports (especially football) paper.
- Tune into: Radio Nacional de España (RNE)'s Radio 1, with general interest and current affairs programs; Radio 5, with sport and entertainment; and Radio 3 ('Radio d'Espop'), with admirably varied pop and rock music. The most popular commercial pop and rock stations are 40 Principales, Cadena 100 and Onda Cero.
- Switch on the box to watch Spain's state-run Televisión Española (TVE1 and La 2) or the independent commercial stations (Antena 3, Tele 5, Cuatro, La Sexta and Canal Plus). Regional governments run local stations, such as Madrid's Telemadrid, Catalonia's TV-3 and Canal 33 (both in Catalan), Galicia's TVG, the Basque Country's ETB-1 and ETB-2, Valencia's Canal 9 and Andalucía's Canal Sur. Cable and satellite TV is becoming more widespread.

(one to three stars) and *pensiones* (basically small private hotels, often family businesses in rambling apartments; one or two stars). These are the categories used by the annual *Guía Oficial de Hoteles,* sold in bookshops, which lists almost every such establishment in Spain, except for one-star *pensiones,* with approximate prices.

In practice, places listing accommodation use all sorts of overlapping names to describe themselves, especially at the budget end of the market. In broad terms, the cheapest are usually places just advertising *camas* (beds), *fondas* (traditionally a basic eatery and inn combined, though one of these functions is now often missing) and *casas de huéspedes* or *hospedajes* (guesthouses). Most such places will be bare and basic. Bathrooms are likely to be shared. Your room may be small, possibly lacking a window, and it may have alarming electrical fittings and erratic hot water – but in most cases it will be kept pretty clean. The beds may make you feel as though you're lying diagonally across a bumpy hillside – or they may be firm, flat and comfortable. In winter don't hesitate to ask for extra blankets. Singles/doubles in these places generally cost from around €15/25 to €25/40.

A *pensión* is usually a small step up from the above types in standard and price. Some cheap establishments forget to provide soap, toilet paper or towels. Don't hesitate to ask for these necessities. *Hostales* are in much the same category. In both cases the better ones can be bright and spotless, with rooms boasting full en suite bathroom. Prices can range up to €40/60 for singles/doubles in more popular/expensive locations.

The remainder of establishments call themselves *hoteles* and run the gamut of quality, from straightforward roadside places, bland but clean, through charming boutique jobbies and on to superluxury hotels. Even in the cheapest hotels, rooms are likely to have an attached bathroom and there'll probably be a restaurant. Among the more tempting hotels for those with a little fiscal room to manoeuvre are the 90 or so **Paradores** (☎ in Spain 902 547979; www.parador.es), a state-funded chain of hotels in often stunning locations, among them towering castles and former medieval convents. Similarly, you can find beautiful hotels in restored country homes and old city mansions, and these are not always particularly expensive. A raft of cutting-edge, hip design hotels with androgynous staff and a feel à la New York can be found in the big cities and major resort areas.

Many places to stay of all types have a range of rooms at different prices. At the budget end, prices will vary according to whether the room has only a *lavabo* (washbasin), *ducha* (shower) or *baño completo* (full bathroom – that is, bath/shower, basin and loo. At the top end you may pay more for a room with a view (especially sea views or with a *balcón* (balcony)) and will often have the option of a suite. Many places have rooms for three, four or more people where the per-person cost is lower than in a single or double, which is good news for families.

Checkout time is generally between 11am and noon.

Monasteries

An offbeat possibility is staying in a monastery. In spite of the expropriations of the 19th century and a sometimes rough run in the 20th, plenty of monastic orders have survived (albeit in diminishing numbers) across the country. Some offer rooms to outsiders – often fairly austere monks' or nuns' cells.

Monastery accommodation is generally a single-sex arrangement, and the idea in quite a few is to seek refuge from the outside world and indulge in quiet contemplation and meditation. On occasion, where the religious order continues ancient tradition by working on farmland, orchards and/or vineyards, you may have the opportunity to work too! A good place to start your search is www.guiasmonasterios.com (in Spanish). Or look for the guidebook, *Alojamientos Monásticos de España,* by Javier de Sagastizabal and José Antonio Egaña.

Refugios

Mountain shelters *(refugios)* for walkers and climbers are liberally scattered around most of the popular mountain areas (mainly the Pyrenees), except in Andalucía, which has only a handful. They're mostly run by mountaineering and walking organisations. Accommodation – usually bunks squeezed into a dorm – is often on a first-come, first-served basis, although for some *refugios* you can book ahead. In busy seasons (July and August in most areas) they can fill up quickly, and you should try to book in advance or arrive by mid-afternoon to be sure of a place. Prices per person range from nothing to €12.50 a night. Many *refugios* have a bar and offer meals (dinner typically costs around €8 to €10), as well as a cooking area (but not cooking equipment). Blankets are usually provided, but you'll have to bring any other bedding yourself. Bring a torch too.

BUSINESS HOURS

Generally, Spaniards work Monday to Friday from about 9am to 2pm and then again from 4pm or 5pm for another three hours. Shops and travel agencies are usually open similar hours on Saturday as well, although many skip the evening session. The further south you go, the longer the afternoon break tends to be, with shops and the like staying closed until 6pm or so.

Big supermarkets and department stores, such as the nationwide El Corte Inglés chain, are open from about 10am to 10pm Monday to Saturday. Shops in tourist resorts sometimes open on Sunday too.

Many government offices don't bother opening in the afternoon, any day of the year. In summer offices tend to go on to *horario intensivo,* which means they can start as early as 7am and finish up for the day by 2pm.

Museums all have their own opening hours: major ones tend to open for something like normal Spanish business hours (with or without the afternoon break), but often have their weekly closing day on Monday.

Pharmacies have a wide variety of opening hours. The standard hours follow those of other shops. In the bigger centres you will find several that are open 24 hours a day. Some have extended hours, say 8am to 10pm, usually on a rota basis. To find out where late-opening pharmacies are in the cities and bigger towns, pick up the local paper. Otherwise, pharmacies with normal opening hours post details of the nearest late-opening pharmacies.

For bank and post office opening hours, respectively, see p876 and p877.

As a general rule, restaurants open their kitchens for lunch from 1pm to 4pm and for dinner from 8pm to midnight. The further south you go, the later locals tend to go out to eat. While restaurants in Barcelona may already be busy by 9.30pm, their Madrid counterparts are still half empty at this time. At lunch and dinner you can generally linger quite a while after the kitchen closes. Some, but by no means all, places close one or two days a week. Some also shut for a few weeks' annual holiday – the most common period for this is during August.

Bars have a wider range of hours. Those that serve as cafes and snack bars can open from about 8am to the early evening. Those that are more nightlife bars may open in the early evening and generally close around 2am to 3am. Some places combine the two roles. As the bars close the clubs open (generally from around midnight or 1am to around 5am or 6am).

Reviews in this guidebook won't list business hours unless they differ from these standards.

CHILDREN

Practicalities

As a rule Spaniards are very friendly to children. Any child whose hair is less than jet black will be dubbed *rubio/rubia* (blond/e). Accompanied children are welcome at all kinds of accommodation, as well as in many cafes, bars and restaurants, where outside tables often allow kids a bit of space and freedom while the grown-ups sit and eat or drink. Spanish children stay up late, and at fiestas it's common to see even tiny ones toddling the streets at 2am or 3am. Visiting kids like this idea too – but can't always cope with it quite so readily.

Always make a point of asking staff at tourist offices if they know of family activities and for suggestions on hotels that cater for kids. Discounts are available for children (usually under 12) on public transport and for admission to sights. Those under four generally go free.

You can hire car seats for infants and children from most car-rental firms, but you should always book them in advance. You cannot rely on restaurants having high chairs, and few have nappy-changing facilities. That said, few Spanish restaurants will turn up their noses to families and children.

In better hotels you can generally arrange for childcare and in some places child-minding agencies cater to temporary visitors.

You can buy baby formula in powder or liquid form, as well as sterilising solutions such as Milton, at *farmacias* (pharmacies). Disposable nappies (diapers) are widely available at supermarkets and *farmacias*. Fresh cow's milk is sold in cartons and plastic bottles in supermarkets in big cities, but can be hard to find in small towns, where UHT is often the only option.

Throughout the book, we have added a child-friendly icon ( ) to sights and sleeping options that seem to be particularly appropriate for children or go out of their way to welcome kids. This does not imply that other places in the book are not child-friendly. As most restaurants are child-friendly but few make any special effort to, say, cater for infants, we have not used such icons there.

Sights & Activities

As well as the obvious attractions of beaches (and all the seaside activities), swimming pools and playgrounds, there are plenty of other good options for kids. Aquaparks, zoos and aquariums are generally winners. Barcelona's L'Aquàrium (p329), with its extraordinary walk-through shark-infested tunnel, is one of the best in all Europe. Valencia also has a marvellous aquarium, Oceanogràfic (p607).

Most kids and not a few adults succumb to the siren call of extravagant theme parks like Catalonia's Port Aventura (p426) or Terra Mítica in Benidorm (p634). On a slightly different note are Mini Hollywood (p828) and other Western movie sets in the Almería desert.

Keep an eye out for sights that might be of special interest to children. Castles, of which Spain is full (they are especially numerous across the two Castillas), are often the easiest sights to sell to young ones.

Certain museums will also interest kids. The Museu Marítim (p321) and CosmoCaixa (p334) interactive science museum in Barcelona have imaginative and engaging displays. Equally, Valencia's Ciudad de las Artes y las Ciencias (p607) is a magnificent attraction.

A walk in the park can be fun. Madrid's Parque de Buen Retiro (p156) is full of diversion. You can potter about in boats in the little lake and at weekends in summer you may encounter puppet shows.

Football-addicted youngsters (and many of their parents) will probably want to visit either FC Barcelona's Camp Nou (p336) or Real Madrid's Santiago Bernabéu (p193) football stadiums or, better still, go to a match.

Most younger children are fascinated by the ubiquitous street-corner *kioscos* selling sweets or *gusanitos* (corn puffs) for a few *céntimos* (cents). The magnetism of these places often overcomes a child's inhibitions enough for them to carry out their own first Spanish transactions. Town fairs and festivals are also great fun for kids.

For further information, see Lonely Planet's *Travel with Children* or visit the websites www.travelwithyourkids.com and www.familytravelnetwork.com.

CLIMATE CHARTS

The *meseta* (high tableland of central Spain) and Ebro basin have a continental climate: scorching in summer, cold in winter, and dry. Madrid regularly freezes in December, January and February, and temperatures climb above 30°C in July and August. Valladolid on the northern *meseta* and Zaragoza in the

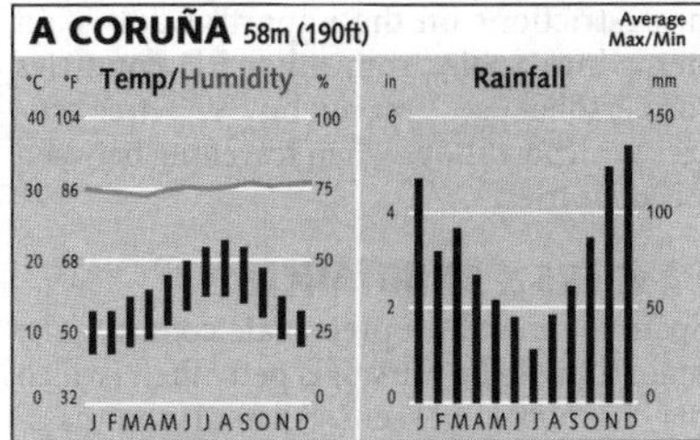

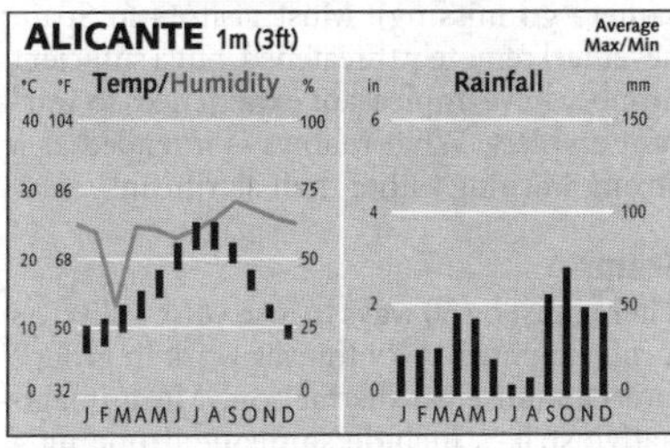

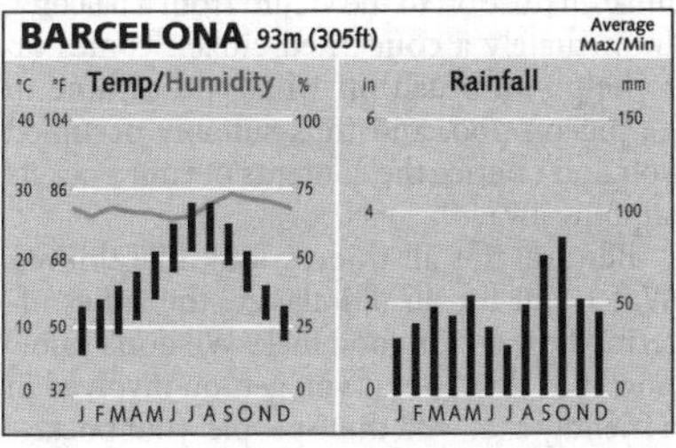

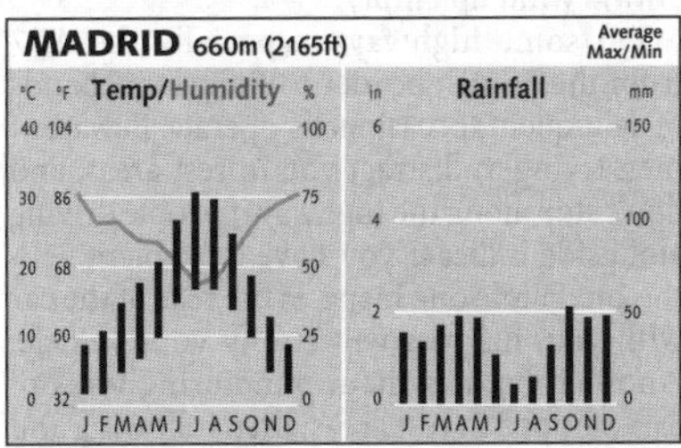

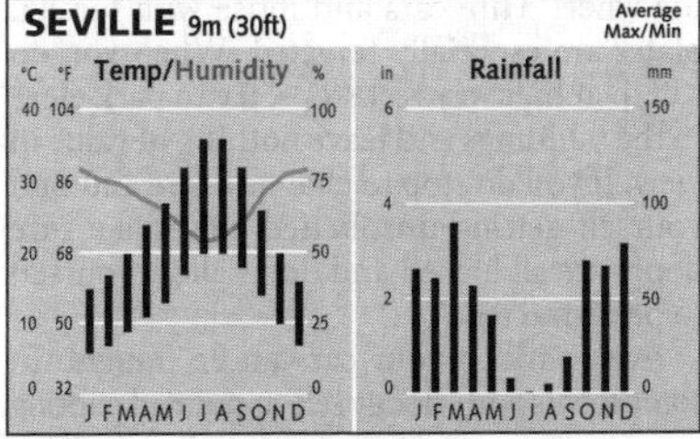

Ebro basin are even drier, with only around 300mm of rain a year (little more than Alice Springs in Australia). The Guadalquivir basin in Andalucía is only a little wetter and positively broils in high summer, with temperatures of 35°C-plus in Seville that kill people every year.

The Pyrenees and the Cordillera Cantábrica, backing the Bay of Biscay, bear the brunt of cold northern and northwestern airstreams, which bring moderate temperatures and heavy rainfall (three or four times as much as Madrid's) to the north coast. Even in high summer you never know when you might get a shower.

The Mediterranean coast and Balearic Islands get a little more rain than Madrid, and the south can be even hotter in summer. The Mediterranean, particularly around Alicante, also provides Spain's warmest waters (reaching 27°C or so in August). Barcelona's weather is typical of the coast – milder than in inland cities but more humid.

In general you can usually rely on pleasant or hot temperatures just about everywhere from April to early November. In Andalucía there are plenty of warm, sunny days right through winter. In July and August temperatures can get unpleasantly hot inland.

Snowfalls in the mountains can start as early as October and some snow cover lasts all year on the highest peaks.

For more tips on the best times to travel, see p20.

COURSES

A spot of study in Spain is an excellent way to meet people – Spaniards as well as other travellers – and learn something more about the country and culture. More than anything else, people are drawn to Spain from all over Europe and North America for language courses – after all, Spanish is the world's third most spoken tongue after Chinese and English!

The **Instituto Cervantes** (www.cervantes.es in Spanish), with branches in over 30 cities around the world, promotes the Spanish language and culture. It's mainly involved in Spanish teaching and in library and information services. The institute's London branch has a **library** (☎ 020-7235 0353; http://londres.Cervantes.es; 102 Eaton Sq, London SW1 W9AN) with a wide range of reference books, periodicals, videos and DVDs (including feature films), language-teaching material, electronic databases and music CDs. You can find more addresses on the institute's website.

A number of Spanish universities offer good-value language courses. Barcelona (p341), Granada (p804), Madrid (p163), Salamanca (p219) and Seville (p722) are popular locations. The **Escuela Oficial de Idiomas** (EOI; www.eeooiinet.com in Spanish) is a nationwide language institution where you can learn Spanish and locals other languages. Classes can be large and busy but are generally fairly cheap. There are branches in many major cities. On the website's opening page, hit Centros under Comunidad and then Centros en la Red to get to a list of schools.

Private language schools as well as universities cater for a wide range of levels, course lengths, times of year, intensity and special requirements. Many courses have a cultural component as well as language. University courses often last a semester, although some are as short as two weeks or as long as a year. Private colleges can be more flexible. One with a good reputation is **¿?don Quijote** (www.donquijote.com), with branches in Barcelona, Granada, Madrid, Salamanca and Valencia.

Costs vary widely. A typical 40-hour course over two to four weeks will cost around €350 to €450 at a university. At private schools you could be looking at up to €1000 for a month of tuition at 30 hours a week. Accommodation can be arranged with families, or in student flats or residences. You might pay €450 per month in a shared student flat or €800 to €1000 for full board with a family.

It's also worth finding out whether your course will lead to any formal certificate of competence. The Diploma de Español como Lengua Extranjera (DELE) is recognised by Spain's Ministry of Education and Science.

Of course, language is not the only learning route you can follow. You might join salsa classes in Barcelona, a flamenco school in Madrid or cooking courses in Valencia city. Many language schools offer combinations of language tuition with anything from cooking to diving.

CUSTOMS

Duty-free allowances for travellers entering Spain from outside the EU include 2L of wine (or 1L of wine and 1L of spirits), and 200 cigarettes or 50 cigars or 250g of tobacco.

There are no duty-free allowances for travel between EU countries but equally no restrictions on the import of duty-paid items into Spain from other EU countries for personal use. You *can* buy VAT-free articles at airport shops when travelling between EU countries.

DANGERS & ANNOYANCES

Spain is generally a pretty safe country. The main thing to be wary of is petty theft (which may of course not seem so petty if your passport, cash, travellers cheques, credit card and camera go missing). Most visitors to Spain never feel remotely threatened, but a sufficient number have unpleasant experiences to warrant an alert. What follows is intended as a strong warning rather than alarmism.

Scams

There must be 50 ways to lose your wallet. As a rule, talented petty thieves work in groups and capitalise on distraction. More imaginative strikes include someone dropping a milk mixture on to the victim from a balcony. Immediately a concerned citizen comes up to help you brush off what you assume to be pigeon poo, and thus suitably occupied you don't notice the contents of your pockets slipping away.

Beware: not all thieves look like thieves. Watch out for an old classic: the ladies offering flowers for good luck. We don't know how they do it, but if you get too involved in a friendly chat with these people, your pockets always wind up empty.

On some highways, especially the AP7 from the French border to Barcelona, bands of delinquents occasionally operate. Beware of men trying to distract you in rest areas, and don't stop along the highway if people driving alongside indicate you have a problem with the car. While one inspects the rear of the car with you, his pals will empty your vehicle. Another gag has them puncturing tyres of cars stopped in rest areas, then following and 'helping' the victim when they stop to change the wheel. Hire cars and those with foreign plates are especially targeted. When you do call in at highway rest stops, try to park close to the buildings and leave nothing of value in view. If you do stop to change a tyre and find yourself getting unsolicited aid, make sure doors are all locked and don't allow yourself to be distracted.

Even parking your car can be fraught. In some towns fairly dodgy self-appointed parking attendants operate in central areas where you may want to park. They will direct you frantically to a spot. If possible, ignore them and find your own. If unavoidable, you may well want to pay them some token not to scratch or otherwise damage your vehicle after you've walked away. You definitely don't want to leave anything visible in the car (or open the boot (trunk) if you intend to leave luggage or anything else in it) under these circumstances.

Terrorism

International terrorism struck with a vengeance in Madrid in March 2004 when a series of bombs placed by suspected Al-Qaeda members ruptured three early-morning commuter trains and left 190 people dead.

But Spain has long had its own homegrown terrorism problem. The Basque terrorist organisation ETA frequently issues chilling warnings to tourists to stay away from Spain.

Repeated arrests of ETA members and a tough stance by the central government and French authorities have dented the group's capacity to strike. However, ETA ended a temporary ceasefire in 2007 and have since shown they still have the capacity to make fatal strikes. Several bomb attacks have taken place and, at the time of writing, their principal targets appeared to be members of the ruling Socialist party and police.

Overall, the chances of being in the wrong place at the wrong time are not much greater nowadays than in any other Western country.

Theft & Loss

Theft is mostly a risk in tourist resorts, big cities and when you first arrive in the country or at a new city and may be off your guard. You are at your most vulnerable when dragging around luggage to or from your hotel. Barcelona, Madrid and Seville have the worst reputations for theft and, on isolated occasions, muggings.

The main things to guard against are pickpockets, bag snatchers and theft from cars (see Scams, opposite). Theft can occur around the sights and areas frequented by tourists and on the metro (trains and stations). Some thieves operate in groups and have no scruples about attacking in broad daylight. Unfortunately, police are thin on the ground and generally seem fairly blasé about such incidents (they've seen it all before).

Carry valuables under your clothes if possible – not in a back pocket, a daypack or anything that can easily be snatched away. Don't leave baggage unattended and avoid crushes (eg on public transport). Be cautious with people who start talking to you for no obviously good reason. This could be an attempt to distract you and make you an easier victim. Ignore demands to see your passport unless they come from a uniformed police officer (thieves posing as police have been a problem recently); some gangs recycle stolen passports.

Always remove the radio and cassette player from your car and never leave any belongings visible when you leave the car.

Anything left lying on the beach can disappear in a flash when your back is turned. Avoid dingy, empty city alleys and backstreets, or anywhere that just doesn't feel 100% safe, at night.

You can also help yourself by not leaving anything valuable lying around your room, above all in any hostel-type place. Use a safe if one is available.

Report thefts to the national police. You are unlikely to recover your goods but you need to make this formal *denuncia* for insurance purposes. To avoid endless queues at the *comisaría* (police station), you can make the report by phone (☎ 902 102112) in various languages or on the Web at www.policia.es (click on Denuncias). The following day you go to the station of your choice to pick up and sign the report, without queuing.

If your passport has gone, contact your embassy or consulate for help in issuing a replacement. Embassies and consulates can also give help of various kinds in other emergencies, but as a rule cannot advance you money to get home. Many countries have consulates in cities around Spain (such as Alicante, Barcelona, Málaga, Palma de Mallorca, Seville and Valencia), and your embassy can tell you where the nearest one is (see p872).

DISCOUNT CARDS

At museums, never hesitate to ask if there are discounts for students, young people, children, families or seniors.

Senior Cards

There are reduced prices for people over 60, 63 or 65 (depending on the place) at various museums and attractions (sometimes restricted to EU citizens only) and occasionally on transport. You should also seek information in your own country on travel packages and discounts for senior travellers, through senior citizens' organisations and travel agents.

Student & Youth Cards

At some sights discounts (usually half the normal fee) are available to students and people under 18. You will need some kind of identification to prove age or student status. An ISIC (International Student Identity Card; www.isic.org) may come in handy for travel discounts but is not accepted at many sights. There is also a teachers' version, ITIC.

You'll have more luck with a Euro<26 (www.euro26.org) card (known as Carnet Joven in Spain), which is useful for those under 26. For instance, Euro<26 card holders enjoy 20% or 25% off most 2nd-class train fares; 10% or 20% off many ferries and some bus fares; good discounts at some museums; and discounts of up to 20% at some youth hostels.

For nonstudent travellers under 25 there is also the International Youth Travel Card (IYTC; www.istc.org), which offers similar benefits.

Student cards are issued by hostelling organisations, student unions and some youth travel agencies worldwide.

EMBASSIES & CONSULATES

Spanish Embassies & Consulates

To find the details of any Spanish embassy or consulate, check out the Ministry of Foreign Affairs Web page (www.maec.es), click on Servicios Consulares and then choose the country you want. Among those with representation are:

Andorra (☎ 800 030; Carrer Prat de la Creu 34, Andorra la Vella)

Australia Canberra (☎ 02-6273 3555; www.embaspain.au; 15 Arkana St, Yarralumla ACT 2600); Melbourne (☎ 03-9347 1966; 146 Elgin St, Vic 3053); Sydney (☎ 02-9261 2433; Level 24, St Martin's Tower, 31 Market St, NSW 2000)

Canada Ottawa (☎ 613-747 2252; http://spain.embassyincanada.com; 74 Stanley Ave, Ontario K1M 1P4); Montreal (☎ 514-935 5235; Ste 1456, 1 Westmount Sq, Québec H3Z 2P9); Toronto (☎ 416-977 1661; 2 Bloor St East, Ste 1201, Ontario M4W 1A8)

France (☎ 01 44 43 18 00; www.amb-espagne.fr; 22 Ave Marceau, 75008 Paris)

Germany Berlin (☎ 030-254 00 70; www.info-spanischebotschaft.de; Lichtensteinallee 1, 10787); Düsseldorf (☎ 0211-43 90 80; Hombergerstr 16, 40474); Frankfurt am Main (☎ 069-959 16 60; Niebelungenplatz 3, 60318); Munich (☎ 089-998 47 90; Oberföhringerstr 45, 81925)

Ireland (☎ 01-269 1640; emb.dublin.info@mace.es; 17A Merlyn Park, Ballsbridge, Dublin 4)

Japan (☎ 03-3583 8531; emb.tokio@maec.es; 1-3-29 Roppongi Minato-ku, Tokyo 106-0032)

Morocco Rabat (☎ 07-63 39 00; emb.rabat@mae.es; rue Ain Khalouiya, Route des Zaërs, Km5.3, Souissi); Casablanca (☎ 02-22 07 52; 31 rue d'Alger); Tangier (☎ 09-93 70 00; 85 Ave Président Habib Bourghiba)

Netherlands (☎ 070-302 49 99; www.claboral.nl; Lange Voorhout 50, The Hague 2514 EG)

New Zealand (☎ 913 11 67; emb.wellington@maec.es; 56 Victoria St, Wellington 6142)

Portugal (☎ 01-347 2381; emb.lisboa@mae.es; Rua do Salitre 1, Lisbon 1269-052)

UK London (☎ 020-7235 5555; http://spain.embassyhomepage.com; 39 Chesham Pl, SW1X 8SB); Edinburgh (☎ 0131-220 1843; 63 North Castle St, EH2 3LJ); London consulate (☎ 020-7589 8989; 20 Draycott Pl, SW3 2RZ); Manchester (☎ 0161-236 1262; 1a Brook House, 70 Spring Gardens, M2 2BQ)

USA Washington DC (☎ 202-728 2340; embespus@mail.mae.es; 2375 Pennsylvania Ave NW, 20037); Boston (☎ 617-536 2506); Chicago (☎ 312-782 4588); Houston (☎ 713-783 6200); Los Angeles (☎ 213-938 0158); Miami (☎ 305-446 5511); New York (☎ 212-355 4080); San Francisco (☎ 415-922 2995)

Embassies & Consulates in Spain

The embassies are in Madrid. Some countries also maintain consulates in major cities, particularly in Barcelona. Embassies and consulates include:

Australia Madrid (Map p133; ☎ 91 353 66 00; www.spain.embassy.gov.au; Plaza del Descubridor Diego de Ordás 3); Barcelona (Map pp310-11; ☎ 93 490 90 13; Plaça de Galla Placidia 1)

Canada Madrid (Map p140); ☎ 91 423 32 50; www.canada-es.org; Calle de Núñez de Balboa 35); Barcelona (Map pp306-7; ☎ 93 204 27 00; Carrer d'Elisenda de Pinós 10; FGC Reina Elisenda)

France Madrid (Map p140); ☎ 91 423 89 00; www.ambafrance-es.org; Calle de Salustiano Olózaga 9); Barcelona (Map pp312-13; ☎ 93 270 30 00; Ronda de l'Universitat 22B)

Germany Madrid (Map p140); ☎ 91 557 90 00; www.madrid.diplo.de; Calle de Fortuny 8); Barcelona (Map pp310-11; ☎ 93 292 10 00; Passeig de Gràcia 111)

Ireland Madrid (Map pp134-5; ☎ 91 436 40 93; Paseo de la Castellana 46); Barcelona (Map pp306-7; ☎ 93 491 50 21; Gran Via de Carles III 94)

Japan (Map p133; ☎ 91 590 76 00; www.es.emb-japan.go.jp; Calle de Serrano 109, Madrid)

Morocco (Map p133; ☎ 91 563 10 90; www.embajada-marruecos.es; Calle de Serrano 179, Madrid)
Netherlands Madrid (Map p132; ☎ 91 353 75 00; www.embajadapaisesbajos.es; Avenida del Comandante Franco 32); Barcelona (Map pp306-7; ☎ 93 363 54 20; Avinguda Diagonal 601); Palma de Mallorca (Map p654; ☎ 971 71 64 93; Calle de San Miquel 36)
New Zealand Madrid (Map p133; ☎ 91 523 02 26; www.nzembassy.com; Calle del Pinar 7); Barcelona (Map pp310-11; ☎ 93 209 03 99; Travessera de Gràcia 64)
Portugal (Map pp134-5; ☎ 91 782 49 60; www.embajadaportugal-madrid.org; Calle del Pinar 1, Madrid)
UK Madrid (Map p140); ☎ 91 700 82 00; www.ukinspain.com; Calle de Fernando el Santo 16); Consulate (Map p140); ☎ 91 524 97 00; Paseo de Recoletos 7/9); Barcelona (Map pp310-11; ☎ 93 366 62 00; Avinguda Diagonal 477); Palma de Mallorca (Map p654; ☎ 971 71 24 45; Carrer del Convent dels Caputxins 4, Edifici B)
USA Madrid (Map pp134-5; ☎ 91 587 22 00; www.embusa.es; Calle de Serrano 75); Barcelona (Map pp306-7; ☎ 93 280 22 27; Passeig de la Reina Elisenda de Montcada 23-25; FGC Reina Elisenda) Consular Agencies in A Coruña, Fuengirola, Palma de Mallorca, Sevilla and Valencia.

FOOD

Glorious food. There's plenty of it in Spain and the regional variety is remarkable. From myriad seafood curiosities in Galicia to the venison of Castilla and the avant-garde *nueva cocina* that's cooking in Barcelona, Madrid and the Basque Country, Spain offers no shortage of surprises. For an overview of what's in store in Spain's kitchens, see Food & Drink (p92) and the special colour cuisine section, Local Flavours (p77; also look out for the What's Cooking…? boxed texts in destination chapters.

Throughout this guidebook we present a broad selection of eateries. In order to provide a guide to what you might pay for your grub, we divide listings into budget (roughly up to €15 for a full meal), midrange (around €16 to €50) and top end (around €51 and up). There is a good amount of regional variation, however, so a degree of flexibility is built in to these divisions. Some places are costlier than others. You may well find yourself eating like royalty in out-of-the-way towns and spending less than this split would indicate. A budget place in Madrid might well cost the same as a lower midrange joint in Murcia. On some occasions, dining listings have been ordered by type (cafe, restaurant etc) and this division is based on the situation in the bigger cities. We define a meal as three courses (including dessert) and house wine.

GAY & LESBIAN TRAVELLERS

Homosexuality is legal in Spain and the age of consent is 13, as for heterosexuals. In 2005 the Socialist president, José Luis Rodríguez Zapatero, gave the country's conservative Catholic foundations a shake with the legalisation of same-sex marriages in Spain.

Lesbians and gay men generally keep a fairly low profile, but are more open in the cities. Madrid, Barcelona, Sitges, Torremolinos and Ibiza have particularly lively scenes. Sitges is a major destination on the international gay party circuit; gays take a leading role in the wild Carnaval there in February/March (p365). As well, there are gay parades, marches and events in several cities on and around the last Saturday in June, when Madrid's gay and lesbian pride march takes place (p173).

Worth looking for is *Guía Gay de España*, a countrywide guide published by Shangay, a gay publishing group; and *El País* for gay and gay-friendly bars, restaurants, hotels and shops around the country.

A couple of informative free magazines are in circulation in gay bookshops and gay and gay-friendly bars. One is the biweekly *Shanguide*. It is jammed with listings and contact ads and aimed principally at readers in Madrid and, to a lesser extent, in Barcelona. Barcelona's tourist board also publishes *Barcelona – The Official Gay and Lesbian Tourist Guide* bi-annually. The annual, worldwide *Spartacus* guide is often on sale at newsstands along La Rambla.

For more information, check out the following sites on the internet:
Chueca (www.chueca.com in Spanish) You have to become a member of the site if you want to access the site's Guía Nocturna for bars and clubs.
Coordinadora Gai-Lesbiana (www.cogailes.org) A good site presented by Barcelona's main gay and lesbian organisation, with nationwide links. Here you can zero in on information ranging from bar, sauna and hotel listings through to contacts pages.
GayBarcelona (www.gaybarcelona.com) News and views and an extensive listings section covering bars, saunas, shops and more in Barcelona and Sitges.
Gays Abroad (www.gays-abroad.com) For gay men moving to Barcelona.
LesboNet (www.lesbonet.org in Spanish) A lesbian site with contacts, forums and listings.
Mensual (www.mensual.com) Click on Guía de España to search for bars, restaurants and more.
Nación Gay (www.naciongay.com in Spanish) News on the gay community across Spain.

Shangay (http://shangay.com in Spanish) For news, art reviews, contacts and *Shanguide* listings. You have to register to get full access.
Universo Gay (http://guia.universogay.com in Spanish) Listings around the country, along with videos, personals, opinions and more.
Voz Gay (www.vozgay.com in Spanish) A Spanish community website with listings for the whole country.

Organisations

Casal Lambda (Map pp312-13; ☎ 93 319 55 50; www.lambdaweb.org; Carrer de Verdaguer i Callis 10). A gay and lesbian social, cultural and information centre in Barcelona.
Colectivo de Gais y Lesbianas de Madrid (Map pp142-3; ☎ 91 523 00 70; www.cogam.org; Calle de la Puebla 9) Has an information office and social centre.
Coordinadora Gai-Lesbiana (Map pp306-7; ☎ 93 298 00 29; www.cogailes.org; Carrer de Violant d'Hongria 156). Barcelona's main coordinating body for gay and lesbian groups. It also runs an information line, the Línia Rosa (☎ 900 60 16 01).
Fundación Triángulo (Map pp134-5; ☎ 91 593 05 40; www.fundaciontriangulo.es; Calle de Eloy Gonzalo 25) Another source of information on gay issues in Madrid.

HOLIDAYS

The two main periods when Spaniards go on holiday are Semana Santa (the week leading up to Easter Sunday) and August. At these times accommodation in resorts can be scarce and transport heavily booked, but other places are often half-empty.

There are at least 14 official holidays a year – some observed nationwide, some locally. When a holiday falls close to a weekend, Spaniards like to make a *puente* (bridge), meaning they take the intervening day off too. Occasionally when some holidays fall close, they make an *acueducto* (aqueduct)! National holidays are:

Año Nuevo (New Year's Day) 1 January
Viernes Santo (Good Friday) March/April
Fiesta del Trabajo (Labour Day) 1 May
La Asunción (Feast of the Assumption) 15 August
Fiesta Nacional de España (National Day) 12 October
La Inmaculada Concepción (Feast of the Immaculate Conception) 8 December
Navidad (Christmas) 25 December

Regional governments set five holidays and local councils two more. Common dates for widely observed holidays include:

Epifanía (Epiphany) or **Día de los Reyes Magos** (Three Kings' Day) 6 January
Día de San José (St Joseph's Day) 19 March
Jueves Santo (Good Thursday) March/April. Not observed in Catalonia and Valencia.
Corpus Christi June. This is the Thursday after the eighth Sunday after Easter Sunday.
Día de San Juan Bautista (Feast of St John the Baptist) 24 June
Día de Santiago Apóstol (Feast of St James the Apostle) 25 July
Día de Todos los Santos (All Saints Day) 1 November
Día de la Constitución (Constitution Day) 6 December

INSURANCE

A travel-insurance policy to cover theft, loss and medical problems is a good idea. It may also cover you for cancellation or delays to your travel arrangements. Paying for your ticket with a credit card can often provide limited travel-accident insurance and you may be able to reclaim the payment if the operator doesn't deliver. Ask your credit card company what it will cover. Worldwide travel insurance is available at lonelyplanet.com/travel_services. You can buy, extend and claim online anytime – even if you're on the road.

For details of car and health insurance, respectively, see p893 and p897.

INTERNET ACCESS

Travelling with a laptop is a great way to stay in touch with life back home. Make sure you have a universal AC adaptor, a two-pin plug adaptor for Europe and a reputable 'global' modem if you plan to use dial-up. Spanish telephone sockets are the US RJ-11 type. Most laptops now come equipped with wi-fi, meaning you can log on to hotspots where they're available. These are still relatively thin on the ground in Spain, and in some cases (such as in airports and some hotels) you must pay a fee to access the internet this way. Still, a growing number of cafes, bars and restaurants in the bigger cities and tourist resorts offer free wi-fi to customers.

The number of hotels equipped with internet availability (in rooms or in the foyer) is growing rapidly. Hotels in this guide with such services are indicated with an icon (💻).

If you intend to rely on cybercafes (commonly referred to as *cibers*), you'll need three pieces of information: your incoming (POP or IMAP) mail-server name, your account name and your password. Most travellers make constant use of internet cafes and free Web-based email such as Yahoo (www

.yahoo.com), Hotmail (www.hotmail.com) or Google's Gmail (www.gmail.com). You typically have to pay about €1.50 to €3 per hour to go online in most cybercafes.

Check out the websites on p23 before arriving in Spain.

LEGAL MATTERS

If you're arrested you will be allotted the free services of an *abogado de oficio* (duty solicitor), who may speak only Spanish. You're also entitled to make a phone call. If you use this to contact your embassy or consulate, the staff will probably be able to do no more than refer you to a lawyer who speaks your language. If you end up in court, the authorities are obliged to provide a translator.

In theory, you are supposed to have your national ID card or passport with you at all times. If asked for it by the police, you are supposed to be able to produce it on the spot. In practice it is rarely an issue and many people choose to leave passports in hotel safes.

The legal age for voting and for driving is 18 years. The age of consent is 13 years, for both heterosexual and homosexual relations. Note that there are some limitations on the age of consent laws, particularly regarding sexual relations between adults and minors. In this sense the age of consent for young teenagers is understood as consent between two minors – it's a tricky area of the law. Travellers should note that they can be prosecuted under the laws of their home country regarding age of consent, even when abroad.

Drugs

The only legal drug is cannabis and only for personal use, which means very small amounts. Public consumption of any drug is illegal, although in a few bars you may find people smoking joints openly. Travellers entering Spain from Morocco should be prepared for drug searches, especially if they have a vehicle.

Police

Spain is well endowed with police forces. The Policía Local or Policía Municipal operates at a local level and deals with such issues as traffic infringements and minor crime. If your car has been towed, it's because these guys called for a tow truck.

The Policía Nacional (☎ 091) is the state police force, dealing with major crime and operating primarily in the cities. The military-linked Guardia Civil (created in the 19th century to deal with banditry) is largely responsible for highway patrols, borders and security, and often has a presence in more remote areas where there is no *comisaría* (Policía Nacional station). They also deal with major crime and terrorism, and there is frequently an overlap (and occasional bickering) with the Policía Nacional.

Just to complicate matters, several regions have their own police forces, such as the Mossos d'Esquadra in Catalonia, the Ertaintxa in the Basque Country and, at some point in the future, a new force in Galicia (a law approving the creation of such a force was approved in 2007).

MAPS

Make sure you get hold of the latest versions of country maps, as a series of highway code changes in 2004 caused considerable confusion for a while.

City Maps

For finding your way around cities, the free maps handed out by tourist offices are often adequate, although more detailed maps are sold widely in bookshops. The best Spanish series of maps are produced by Telstar, Alpina and Everest, while Lonely Planet produces a sturdy and helpful *Barcelona City Map*.

Small-Scale Maps

Some of the best maps for travellers are by Michelin, which produces the 1:1,000,000 *Spain Portugal* map and six 1:400,000 regional maps covering the whole country. These are all pretty accurate, even down to the state of minor country roads, and are frequently updated and detailed yet easy to read. They're widely available in Spain. Also good are the GeoCenter maps published by Germany's RV Verlag.

Probably the best physical map of Spain is *Península Ibérica, Baleares y Canarias* published by the Centro Nacional de Información Geográfica (CNIG, www.cnig.es), the publishing arm of the Instituto Geográfico Nacional (IGN, www.ign.es). Ask for it in good bookshops.

Walking Maps

Useful for hiking and exploring some areas (particularly in the Pyrenees) are Editorial

Alpina's *Guía Cartográfica* and *Guía Excursionista y Turística* series. The series combines information booklets in Spanish (and sometimes Catalan) with detailed maps at scales ranging from 1:25,000 (1cm to 250m) to 1:50,000 (1cm to 500m). They are an indispensable hikers' tool but have their inaccuracies. The Institut Cartogràfic de Catalunya puts out some decent maps for hiking in the Catalan Pyrenees that are often better than their Editorial Alpina counterparts. Remember that for hiking only maps scaled at 1:25,000 are seriously useful. The CNIG also covers most of the country in 1:25,000 sheets.

You can often pick up Editorial Alpina publications and CNIG maps at bookshops near trekking areas, and at specialist bookshops such as **Librería Desnivel** (☎ 902 248848; www.libreriadesnivel.com; Plaza de Matute 6) or **Altaïr** (☎ 93 342 71 71; www.altair.es; Gran Via de les Corts Catalanes 616) or **Quera** (☎ 93 318 07 43; www.llibreriaquera.com; Carrer de Petritxol 2) in Barcelona. Some map specialists in other countries, such as **Stanfords** (☎ 020-7836 1321; www.stanfords.co.uk; 12-14 Long Acre, London WC2E 9LP) in the UK, also have a good range of Spain maps.

MONEY

As in 14 other EU nations the euro is Spain's currency. The euro is divided into 100 cents. Coin denominations are one, two, five, 10, 20 and 50 cents, €1 and €2. The notes are €5, €10, €20, €50, €100, €200 and €500. You'll find exchange rates on the inside front cover of this book and a guide to costs on p20.

Spain's international airports have bank branches, ATMs and exchange offices. They're less frequent at road crossings now as Spain's neighbours – Andorra, Portugal and France – all use the euro. If you're coming from Morocco, get rid of any dirham before you leave (it can't be converted outside the country).

Banks and building societies tend to offer the best exchange rates, and are plentiful: even small villages often have at least one. They mostly open from about 8.30am to 2pm Monday to Friday. Some also open Thursday evening (about 4pm to 7pm) or Saturday morning (9am to 2pm). Ask about commissions before changing (especially in exchange bureaux).

Prices in this guidebook are quoted in euros (€), unless otherwise stated.

ATMs

Many credit and debit cards (Visa and MasterCard are the most widely accepted) can be used for withdrawing money from *cajeros automáticos* (automatic telling machines). This is handy because many banks do not offer an over-the-counter cash advance service on foreign cards (and where they do, the process can be wearisome). The exchange rate used for credit and debit card transactions is usually more in your favour than that for cash exchanges. Bear in mind, however, the costs involved. There is usually a charge (hovering around 1.5% to 2%) on ATM cash withdrawals abroad. This charge may appear on your statements.

Cash

There is little advantage in bringing foreign cash into Spain. True, exchange commissions are often lower than for travellers cheques, but the danger of losing the lot far outweighs such gains.

Credit & Debit Cards

You can use plastic to pay for many purchases (including meals and rooms, especially from the middle price-range up). You'll often be asked to show your passport or some other form of identification when using cards. Among the most widely accepted are Visa, MasterCard, American Express (Amex), Cirrus, Maestro, Plus, Diners Club and JCB. Many institutions add 2.5% or more to all transactions (cash advance or purchases) on cards used abroad – this charge does not generally appear on your bank statements.

If your card is lost, stolen or swallowed by an ATM, you can telephone toll free to have an immediate stop put on its use. For MasterCard the number in Spain is ☎ 900 971231, for Visa ☎ 900 991124, for Amex ☎ 900 994426 and for Diners Club ☎ 901 101011.

Moneychangers

As well as at banks, you can exchange both cash and travellers cheques at exchange offices – usually indicated by the word *cambio* (exchange). They abound in tourist resorts and other places that attract high numbers of foreigners. Generally they offer longer opening hours and quicker service than banks, but worse exchange rates. Their commissions are, on occasion, outrageous.

Taxes & Refunds

In Spain, value-added tax (VAT) is known as IVA (*ee*-ba; *impuesto sobre el valor añadido*).

On accommodation and restaurant prices, it's 7% and is often included in quoted prices. On retail goods and car hire, IVA is 16%. To ask 'Is IVA included?', say *'¿Está incluido el IVA?'*.

Visitors are entitled to a refund of the 16% IVA on purchases costing more than €90.16 from any shop if they are taking them out of the EU within three months. Ask the shop for a cash back (or similar) refund form showing the price and IVA paid for each item, and identifying the vendor and purchaser. Then present the refund form to the customs booth for IVA refunds at the airport, port or border from which you leave the EU. This works best at airports, where you will need your passport and a boarding card that shows you are leaving the EU. The officer will stamp the invoice and you hand it in at a specified bank at the departure point for immediate reimbursement. Otherwise you will have to send the forms off from your home country and have the amount credited to your credit card.

Tipping

The law requires menu prices to include a service charge; tipping is a matter of choice. Most people leave some small change if they're satisfied: 5% is normally fine and 10% generous. Porters will generally be happy with €1. Taxi drivers don't have to be tipped but a little rounding up won't go amiss.

Travellers Cheques

Travellers cheques usually bring only a slightly better exchange rate than cash, usually offset by the charges for buying them in the first place and the commission you may have to pay to cash them in. Plastic has by now largely supplanted travellers cheques for travel in Spain but the ultra-cautious may see them as a useful back-up measure in case of something going wrong with one's debit and/or credit cards.

The advantage of travellers cheques, of course, is that they protect your money because they can be replaced if lost or stolen. Visa, Amex and Travelex are widely accepted brands with (usually) efficient replacement policies. Remember to take along your passport when you cash travellers cheques.

Get most of your cheques in fairly large denominations (the equivalent of €100 or more) to save on any per-cheque commission charges.

If you lose your Amex cheques, call a 24-hour freephone number (☎ 900 994426). For Visa cheques call ☎ 900 948973 and for MasterCard cheques call ☎ 900 948971. It's vital to keep your initial receipt, and a record of your cheque numbers and the ones you have used, separate from the cheques themselves.

POST

The Spanish postal system, **Correos** (☎ 902 197197; www.correos.es), is generally reliable, if a little slow at times. Central post offices in most cities open around 8.30am to 10pm, Monday to Saturday. Many branch post offices open 8am to 2pm, Monday to Friday, although there are variations depending on the branch.

Postal Rates & Services

A postcard or letter weighing up to 20g costs €0.60 from Spain to other European countries and €0.78 to the rest of the world. The same would cost €2.84 and €3.02, respectively, for registered *(certificado)* mail. Sending such letters *urgente*, which means your mail may arrive two or three days sooner than usual, costs €3.10 and €3, respectively. You can send mail both *certificado* and *urgente* if you wish. Stamps for regular letters, including those being sent abroad, can also be bought at most tobacconists *(estancos)* – look for the 'Tabacos' sign.

Receiving Mail

Delivery times are similar to those for outbound mail. All Spanish addresses have five-digit postcodes; using postcodes will help your mail arrive more quickly.

Lista de correos (poste restante) mail can be addressed to you anywhere in Spain that has a post office. It will be delivered to the place's main post office, unless another is specified in the address. Take your passport when you pick up mail. A typical *lista de correos* address looks like this:

Jenny JONES
Lista de Correos
28080 Madrid
Spain

Sending Mail

Delivery times are erratic but ordinary mail to other Western European countries can take up to a week (although often as little as three days); to North America up to 10 days; and to Australia or New Zealand (NZ) up to two weeks.

SHOPPING

There are some excellent *mercadillos* and *rastros* (flea markets) around the country, and craft shops can be found in many villages and towns. You may also pick up crafts at weekly or daily markets. The single most likely place you'll find any particular item in most cities is the nationwide department store El Corte Inglés (but not necessarily at bargain basement prices!).

Bargaining

Bargaining is not an option in department stores and high street shops. At markets and more souvenir-oriented stores you can try your luck (you've got nothing to lose, after all).

Clothes & Textiles

Label lovers and fashion victims can keep themselves well occupied in the big cities, such as Madrid and Barcelona, where local and international names present a broad range of options. Ibiza in summer is also a bit of a magnet for clubbing and summer-wear seekers.

Inexpensive rugs, blankets and hangings are made all over the country, notably in Andalucía and Galicia. In Andalucía head for Las Alpujarras and Níjar for colourful items. *Jarapas* (rugs) feature weft threads made of different types of cloth. Other textiles include lace tablecloths and pillowcases (especially from Galicia) and embroidery. Places particularly known for their embroidery include Segovia, La Alberca (Salamanca province), Carbajales (Zamora province), and Lagartera, Oropesa and Talavera (Toledo province).

In Andalucía, every major city centre has a cluster of flamenco shops, selling embroidered shawls, hand-painted fans, flat-top Cordoban hats and of course lots of flouncy dresses *(batas de cola)*.

Leather

Prices of leather goods aren't as low as they used to be, but you can get good deals on jackets, bags, wallets, belts, shoes and boots in many places. Mallorcan shoe brands like Camper and Farrutx have become international beacons – their products are stylish, moderately priced and, especially in the case of Camper, easily found all over Spain. The island of Mallorca is especially known for its leather production – head to the inland town of Inca and you'll find plenty of stores and outlets selling everything from purses to pants.

Pottery

Crockery, jugs, plant pots, window boxes and tiles are cheap. Islamic influence on design and colour is evident in much of the country. Original techniques include the use of metallic glazes and *cuerda seca* (dry cord), in which lines of manganese or fat are used to separate areas of different colour. Toledo, Talavera de la Reina, Seville, Granada and Úbeda are major centres of production but many other small ceramics centres are sprinkled across the country.

Other Crafts

Damascene weapons (made of steel encrusted with gold, silver or copper) are still being produced in Toledo. Very pleasing woodwork is available, such as Granada's marquetry boxes, tables and chess sets, some of which are inlaid with bone or mother-of-pearl. Baskets and furniture made from plant fibres are produced throughout Spain but are most common near the coasts.

SOLO TRAVELLERS

About the only real practical disadvantage of travelling solo in Spain is the cost of accommodation. As a rule, single rooms (or doubles let as single rooms) cost around two-thirds of the price of a double. Some hotels make little or no discount on double-room rates.

Females travelling alone shouldn't encounter problems either, at least in more travelled parts of Spain. In more out-of-the-way places, the sight of a lone female traveller may raise local eyebrows. You should be choosy about your accommodation too. Bottom-end fleapits with all-male staff can be insalubrious locations to bed down for the night. Lone women should also take care in city streets at night – stick with the crowds. Hitching for solo women travellers, while feasible, is risky.

TELEPHONE

The ubiquitous blue payphones are easy to use for international and domestic calls. They accept coins, phonecards *(tarjetas telefónicas)* issued by the national phone company Telefónica and, in some cases, various credit cards. Phonecards come in €6 and €12 denominations and, like postage stamps, are sold at post offices and tobacconists.

Mobile Phones

Spaniards adore *teléfonos móviles* (mobile or cell phones), and shops on every high street sell phones with prepaid cards. The most basic models of mobile phones start from around €80 (if you're buying a prepaid SIM card – they are often free for residents taking out a contract).

Spain uses GSM 900/1800, which is compatible with the rest of Europe and Australia but not with the North American GSM 1900 or the system used in Japan. From those countries, you will need to travel with a tri-band or quadric-band phone.

You can rent a mobile phone by calling the Madrid-based **Cellphone Rental** (www.onspanishtime.com/web). It will deliver the phone to a hotel or apartment anywhere in Spain.

Phone Codes

Dial the international access code (☎ 00 in most countries), followed by the code for Spain (☎ 34) and the full number (including the code, 91, which is an integral part of the number). For example to call the number ☎ 91 455 67 83 in Madrid, you need to dial the international access code followed by ☎ 34 91 455 67 83.

The access code for international calls from Spain is ☎ 00. To make an international call, dial the access code, wait for a new dialling tone, then dial the country code, area code and number you want.

International collect calls are simple. Dial 99 00 followed by the code for the country you're calling:

Australia ☎ 99 00 61
Canada ☎ 99 00 15
France ☎ 99 00 33
Germany ☎ 99 00 49
Ireland ☎ 99 03 53
Israel ☎ 99 09 72
New Zealand ☎ 99 00 64
UK for BT ☎ 99 00 44
USA for AT&T ☎ 99 00 11, for Sprint and various others ☎ 99 00 13

You'll get straight through to an operator in the country you're calling. The same numbers can be used with direct-dial calling cards.

If for some reason the above information doesn't work for you, in most places you can get an English-speaking Spanish international operator by dialling ☎ 1008 (for calls within Europe) or ☎ 1005 (rest of the world).

For international directory inquiries dial ☎ 11825. Be warned: a call to this number costs €2!

Dial ☎ 1009 to speak to a domestic operator, including for a domestic reverse-charge (collect) call *(llamada por cobro revertido)*. For national directory inquiries dial ☎ 11818.

Mobile phone numbers start with 6. Numbers starting with 900 are national toll-free numbers, while those starting 901 to 905 come with varying conditions. A common one is 902, which is a national standard rate number. In a similar category are numbers starting with 803, 806 and 807.

Phonecards

Cut-rate prepaid phonecards can be good value for international calls. They can be bought from *estancos* (tobacconists) and newsstands in the main cities and tourist resorts. If possible, try to compare rates because some are better than others. *Locutorios* (private call centres) that specialise in cut-rate overseas calls have popped up all over the place in the centre of bigger cities. Again, compare rates – as a rule the phonecards are better value and generally more convenient.

TAKING YOUR MOBILE PHONE

If you plan to take your own mobile phone to Spain, check in advance with your mobile network provider that your phone is enabled for international roaming, which allows you to make and receive calls and messages abroad. Ask what you have to dial in order to use international roaming.

- Consider buying an alternative SIM card for use on a local network in Spain. If your phone is not blocked (make sure you check this out before leaving home), you can buy any local pay-as-you-go SIM card.
- Take an international adaptor for the charger plug.
- Note your phone's number and serial number (IMEI number) and your operator's customer services number. This will help if your phone is stolen.
- For more advice on using mobile phones abroad go to www.ofcom.org.uk.

TIME

Mainland Spain and the Balearic Islands have the same time as most of the rest of Western Europe: GMT/UTC plus one hour during winter and GMT/UTC plus two hours during the daylight-saving period, which runs from the last Sunday in March to the last Sunday in October.

The UK, Ireland, Portugal and the Canary Islands are one hour behind mainland Spain. Morocco is on GMT/UTC year-round. From the last Sunday in March to the last Sunday in October, subtract two hours from Spanish time to get Moroccan time; the rest of the year, subtract one hour.

Spanish time is USA Eastern Time plus six hours and USA Pacific Time plus nine hours.

During the Australian winter (Spanish summer), subtract eight hours from Australian Eastern Standard Time to get Spanish time; during the Australian summer, subtract 10 hours.

Although the 24-hour clock is used in most official situations, you'll find people generally use the 12-hour clock in everyday conversation.

TOURIST INFORMATION

Local Tourist Offices

All cities and many smaller towns have an *oficina de turismo* or *oficina de información turística*. In the country's provincial capitals you'll sometimes find more than one tourist office – one specialising in information on the city alone, the other carrying mostly provincial or regional information. National and natural parks also often have visitor centres offering useful information. Their opening hours and quality of information vary widely.

Turespaña (www.spain.info, www.tourspain.es), the country's national tourism body, presents a variety of general information and links on the entire country in its Web pages.

Tourist Offices Abroad

Information on Spain is available from the following branches of Turespaña abroad:

Canada (☎ 416-961 3131; www.tourspain.toronto.on.ca; 2 Bloor St W, Ste 3042, Toronto M4W 3E2)

France (☎ 01 45 03 82 50; www.spain.info/TourSpain/?Language=fr; 43 rue Decamps, 75784 Paris)

Germany (☎ 030-882 6543; berlin@tourspain.es; Kurfürstendamm 63, 10707 Berlin) Branches in Düsseldorf, Frankfurt am Main and Munich.

Netherlands (☎ 070-346 59 00; www.spaansverkeersbureau.nl; Laan van Meerdervoor 8a, 2517 The Hague)

Portugal (☎ 21-354 1992; lisboa@tourspain.es; Avenida Sidónio Pais 28 3° Dto, 1050-215 Lisbon)

UK (☎ 020-7486 8077; www.spain.info/uk/tourspain; you may visit the office by appointment only)

USA (☎ 212-265 8822; www.okspain.org; 666 Fifth Ave, 35th fl, New York, NY 10103) Branches in Chicago, Los Angeles and Miami.

TRAVELLERS WITH DISABILITIES

Spain is not overly accommodating for travellers with disabilities but some things are slowly changing. For example, disabled access to some museums, official buildings and hotels represents something of a sea change in local thinking. In major cities more is slowly being done to facilitate disabled access to public transport and taxis. A growing number of sights and hotels have made at least some effort to meet the needs of the wheelchair-bound. It is sometimes possible to obtain lists of hotels with wheelchair access from local or regional tourist offices. Many hotels also mention this on their websites too. You need to be a little circumspect about hotels who advertise themselves as being disabled-friendly, as this can mean as little as wide doors to rooms and bathrooms, or other token efforts.

Organisations

Accessible Barcelona (☎ 93 428 52 27; www.accessiblebarcelona.com) Craig Grimes, a T6 paraplegic and inveterate traveller, created this Barcelona-specific accessible travel site, easily the most useful doorway into the city for the disabled. It can also help with the surrounding region of Catalonia.

Accessible Travel & Leisure (☎ 01452-729739; www.accessibletravel.co.uk; Avionics House, Naas Lane, Gloucester GL2 2SN) Claims to be the biggest UK travel agent dealing with travel for the disabled and encourages the disabled to travel independently.

ONCE (☎ 91 436 53 00; www.once.es; Calle de José Ortega y Gasset 18, Madrid) The Spanish association for the blind. You may be able to get hold of guides in Braille to a handful of cities, including Madrid and Barcelona, although they are not published every year.

Society for Accessible Travel & Hospitality (☎ 212 447 7284; www.sath.org; 347 Fifth Ave, Ste 605, New York, NY 10016) Although largely concentrated on the USA, this organisation can provide general information.

VISAS

Spain is one of 24 member countries of the Schengen Convention, under which 22 EU countries (all but Bulgaria, Cyprus, Ireland, Romania and the UK) plus Iceland and Norway have abolished checks at common borders. Switzerland is in the process of becoming a member and Cyprus was set to join by the end of 2008. For detailed information on the EU, including which countries are member states, visit http://eur opa.eu.int.

EU, Norwegian, Swiss and Icelandic nationals need no visa, regardless of the length or purpose of their visit to Spain. If they stay beyond 90 days, they are required to register with the police (although many do not). Legal residents of one Schengen country (regardless of their nationality) do not require a visa for another Schengen country.

Nationals of many other countries, including Australia, Canada, Israel, Japan, NZ and the USA, do not need a visa for tourist visits of up to 90 days in Spain, although some of these nationalities may be subject to restrictions in other Schengen countries and should check with consulates of all Schengen countries they plan to visit. If you wish to work or study in Spain, you may need a specific visa, so contact a Spanish consulate before travel. If you are a citizen of a country not mentioned in this section, check with a Spanish consulate whether you need a visa.

The standard tourist visa issued by Spanish consulates is the Schengen visa, valid for up to 90 days. A Schengen visa issued by one Schengen country is generally valid for travel in all other Schengen countries.

Those needing a visa must apply *in person* at the consulate in the country where they are resident. You may be required to provide proof of sufficient funds, an itinerary or hotel bookings, return tickets and a letter of recommendation from a host in Spain. Issue of the visa does *not*, however, guarantee entry.

Coming from Morocco, you are unlikely to get into Spain's North African enclaves of Ceuta or Melilla without a Spanish visa (if you are supposed to have one), and passports are generally checked again when you head on to the peninsula. You may well be able to board a boat from Tangier (Morocco) to Algeciras and certainly to Gibraltar but, again, passports are generally closely checked by the Spaniards at Algeciras and you could be sent back to Morocco.

Extensions & Residence

Schengen visas cannot be extended. You can apply for no more than two visas in any 12-month period and they are not renewable once in Spain. Various transit visas also exist. Nationals of EU countries, Iceland, Norway and Switzerland can enter and leave Spain at will and don't need to apply for a *tarjeta de residencia* (residence card), although they are supposed to apply for residence papers. They are not issued with a Spanish residence card and use national ID in their everyday transactions. In some cases (such as when purchasing property) they may need the residence papers that, otherwise, remain safely in the drawer.

People of other nationalities who want to stay in Spain longer than 90 days are supposed to get a residence card, and for them it can be a drawn-out process, starting with an appropriate visa issued by a Spanish consulate in their country of residence. Start the process well in advance.

Photocopies

All important documents (passport data page and visa page, credit cards, travel insurance policy, driving licence etc) should be photocopied before you leave home. Leave one copy with someone at home and keep another with you, separate from the originals.

VOLUNTEERING

Several possibilities for volunteering to participate in projects present themselves in Spain. A good website to start your research, with options ranging from excavations in Mallorca to work on restoring the wetlands of Manga del Mar Menor, is **Transitions Abroad** (www.transitions abroad.com). At **Pueblo Inglés** (www.puebloingles.com) volunteers spend their days conversing with Spaniards in English at various locations in Spain. Monitor the presence of the bearded vulture in Andalucía and learn about other endangered species in Spain with **Global Vision International** (www.gvi.co.uk). You could spend a couple of weeks on archaeological digs in Mallorca through the **Earthwatch Institute** (www .earthwatch.org). **Sunseed Desert Technology** (www .sunseed.org.uk) is a UK-run project, developing sustainable ways to live in semi-arid environments, and is based in the hamlet of Los Molinos del Río Agua in Almería.

WOMEN TRAVELLERS

Travelling in Spain is as easy as travelling anywhere in the Western world. Spanish women now travel widely around their own country without men, and Spaniards are quite accustomed to foreign women travelling in Spain without men. Spanish men under about 40, who've grown up in the liberated post-Franco era, conform less to old-fashioned sexual stereotypes, although you might notice that sexual stereotyping becomes more pronounced as you move from north to south in Spain, and from city to country. And in terms of equality of the sexes, Spain still has some way to go. The Socialist Zapatero government has introduced measures to promote equality in employment for women and took a lead in 2008 when it appointed a cabinet in which women ministers outnumbered their male counterparts eight to seven. Zapatero also named the country's first ever woman defence minister. Still, few women reach top positions in private enterprise and women's wages remain lower than those of men for the same kind of work.

Women travellers should be ready to ignore stares, catcalls and unnecessary comments. Learn the word for help *(socorro)* in case you need to draw other people's attention.

By and large, Spanish women have a highly developed sense of style and put considerable effort into looking their best. While topless bathing and skimpy clothes are in fashion in many coastal resorts, people tend to dress more modestly elsewhere.

There are women's bookshops in Madrid, Barcelona and a few other cities that are also useful sources of information on women's organisations and activities. The websites of many women's organisations can be reached through the feminist website www.nodo50.org/mujeresred.

WORK

Nationals of EU countries, Switzerland, Norway and Iceland may freely work in Spain. If you are offered a contract, your employer will normally steer you through any bureaucracy.

Virtually everyone else is supposed to obtain, from a Spanish consulate in their country of residence, a work permit and, if they plan to stay more than 90 days, a residence visa. These procedures are well-nigh impossible unless you have a job contract lined up before you begin them.

You could look for casual work in fruit picking, harvests or construction, but this is generally done with imported labour from Morocco and Eastern Europe, with pay and conditions that can often best be described as dire.

Translating and interpreting could be an option if you are fluent in Spanish and a language in demand.

You can start a job search on the Web, for instance at **Think Spain** (www.thinkspain.com).

Language Teaching

This type of work is an obvious option for which language-teaching qualifications are a big help. Language schools abound and are listed under 'Academias de Idiomas' in the Yellow Pages. Getting a job is harder if you're not an EU citizen. Giving private lessons is another avenue, but is unlikely to bring you a living wage straight away.

Sources of information on possible teaching work – in a school or as a private tutor – include foreign cultural centres, such as the British Council, Alliance Française etc, foreign-language bookshops, universities and language schools. Many have noticeboards where you may find work opportunities or can advertise your own services.

Tourist Resorts

Summer work on the Mediterranean coasts is a possibility, especially if you arrive early in the season and are prepared to stay a while. Many bars (especially of the British and Irish persuasion), restaurants and other businesses are run by foreigners. Check any local press in foreign languages, such as the Costa del Sol's *Sur In English,* which lists ads for waiters, nannies, chefs, babysitters, cleaners and the like.

Yacht Crewing

It is possible to stumble upon work as crew on yachts and cruisers. The best ports to look include (in descending order) Palma de Mallorca, Gibraltar and Puerto Banús.

In summer the voyages tend to be restricted to the Mediterranean but, from about November to January, many boats head for the Caribbean. Such work is usually unpaid and about the only way to find it is to ask around on the docks. Paid work is more in the line of repairs, cleaning and maintenance of such boats in port. It is not well paid and most people doing it anticipate having the chance to sail at some point.

Transport

CONTENTS

GETTING THERE & AWAY

Spain is one of Europe's top holiday destinations and is well linked to other European countries by air, rail and road. Regular car ferries and hydrofoils run to and from Morocco, and there are ferry links to the UK, Italy, the Canary Islands and Algeria.

The existence of budget airlines has revolutionised travel in Europe. Flying is generally the fastest and cheapest way of reaching Spain from elsewhere in Europe. On the other hand, the per-person carbon emissions are greater than travelling, say, by train.

Some good direct flights are available from North America. Those coming from Australasia will usually have to make at least one change of flight.

Flights, tours and rail tickets can be booked online at www.lonelyplanet.com/travel_services.

ENTERING THE COUNTRY

Passport

Citizens of the 27 European Union (EU) member states and Switzerland can travel to Spain with their national identity card alone. If such countries do not issue ID cards – as in the UK – travellers must carry a full valid passport. All other nationalities must have a full valid passport.

If applying for a visa (see p880), check that your passport's expiry date is at least six months away. If not an EU citizen, you may be required to fill out a landing card (at airports).

By law you are supposed to have your passport or ID card with you at all times. It doesn't happen often, but it could be embarrassing if you are asked by the police to produce a document and you don't have it with you. You will need one of these documents for police registration when you take a hotel room.

AIR

High season in Spain generally means Christmas, New Year, Easter and roughly June to September. This varies, depending on the specific destination. You may find reasonably priced flights to Madrid available in August because it is stinking hot and everyone else has fled to the mountains or the sea. As a general rule, November to March is when airfares to Spain are likely to be at their lowest, and the intervening months can be considered shoulder periods.

Airports & Airlines

The main gateway to Spain is Madrid's **Barajas airport** (Aeropuerto de Barajas; ☎ nationwide flight information 902 40 47 04; www.aena.es), although many European direct flights serve other centres, particularly Barcelona's Aeroport del Prat, Málaga, Palma de Mallorca and Valencia. Charter flights and low-cost airlines (mostly from the UK) fly direct to a growing

> **THINGS CHANGE...**
>
> The information in this chapter is particularly vulnerable to change. Check directly with the airline or a travel agent to make sure you understand how a fare (and ticket you may buy) works and be aware of the security requirements for international travel. Shop carefully. The details given in this chapter should be regarded as pointers and are not a substitute for your own careful, up-to-date research.

CLIMATE CHANGE & TRAVEL

Climate change is a serious threat to the ecosystems that humans rely upon, and air travel is the fastest-growing contributor to the problem. Lonely Planet regards travel, overall, as a global benefit, but believes we all have a responsibility to limit our personal impact on global warming.

Flying & Climate Change

Pretty much every form of motor travel generates CO_2 (the main cause of human-induced climate change) but planes are far and away the worst offenders, not just because of the sheer distances they allow us to travel, but because they release greenhouse gases high into the atmosphere. The statistics are frightening: two people taking a return flight between Europe and the US will contribute as much to climate change as an average household's gas and electricity consumption over a whole year.

Carbon Offset Schemes

Climatecare.org and other websites use 'carbon calculators' that allow jetsetters to offset the greenhouse gases they are responsible for with contributions to energy-saving projects and other climate-friendly initiatives in the developing world – including projects in India, Honduras, Kazakhstan and Uganda.

Lonely Planet, together with Rough Guides and other concerned partners in the travel industry, supports the carbon offset scheme run by climatecare.org. Lonely Planet offsets all of its staff and author travel.

For more information check out our website: lonelyplanet.com.

number of regional airports, including A Coruña, Alicante, Almería, Asturias, Bilbao, Girona (for the Costa Brava and Barcelona), Ibiza, Jerez de la Frontera, Murcia, Reus and Seville.

Iberia, Spain's national carrier, flies to most Spanish cities (many via Madrid) from around the world but is generally the expensive way to go.

Among the airlines that fly to and from Spain are the following:

Aer Lingus (EI; ☎ in Ireland 0818 365000; www.aerlingus.com)
Air Berlin (AB; ☎ 902 32 07 37, in Germany 01805 737800; www.airberlin.com)
Air Europa (UX; ☎ 902 40 15 01; www.aireuropa.com)
Air Nostrum (IB; ☎ 902 40 05 00; www.airnostrum.es)
Alpi Eagles (E8; ☎ in Italy 899 500058; www.alpieagles.com)
American Airlines (AA; ☎ in the USA 800 433 7300; www.aa.com)
BMI (BD; ☎ 91 275 46 29, in the UK 0870 607 0555; www.flybmi.com)
British Airways (BA; ☎ 902 11 13 33, in the UK 0870 850 9850; www.britishairways.com)
Brussels Airlines (SN; ☎ 807 22 00 03, in Belgium 0902 516000; www.flysn.com)
Clickair (XG; ☎ 902 25 42 52; www.clickair.com)
Continental (CO; ☎ 900 96 12 66, in the USA 800 231 0856; www.continental.com)
Delta (DL; ☎ 901 11 69 46, in the USA 800 221 1212; www.delta.com)
EasyJet (U2; ☎ 807 26 00 26, in the UK 0905 821 0905; www.easyjet.com)
FlyGlobeSpan (Y2; ☎ in the UK 0871 271 0415; www.flyglobespan.com)
Germanwings (4U; ☎ 91 625 97 04, in Germany 0900 1919100; www.germanwings.com)
Iberia (IB; ☎ 902 40 05 00; www.iberia.es)
Jet2 (LS; ☎ 902 88 12 69, in the UK 0871 226 1737; www.jet2.com)
Lufthansa (LX; ☎ 902 22 01 01, in Germany 01805 838426; www.lufthansa.com)
Meridiana (IG; ☎ in Italy 892928; www.meridiana.it)
Monarch (ZB; ☎ 800 09 92 60, in the UK 0870 040 5040; www.flymonarch.com)
MyAir (8I; ☎ in Italy 899 500060; www.myair.com)
Norwegian Air Shuttle (DY; ☎ in Norway 815 21815; www.norwegian.no)
Royal Air Maroc (AT; www.royalairmaroc.com)
Ryanair (FR; ☎ 807 22 00 32, in the UK 0871 246 0000, in Ireland 0818 303030; www.ryanair.com)
Singapore Airlines (SQ; ☎ 902 01 25 14; www.singaporeair.com)
Sky Europe (NE; ☎ 807 00 12 04, in Slovakia 02 3301 7301, in Hungary 06 1777 7000; www.skyeurope.com)

Spanair (JK; ☎ 902 13 14 15; www.spanair.com)
Sterling Airlines (NB; ☎ 91 749 66 43, in Denmark 70 10 84 84; www.sterlingticket.com)
Swiss (LX; ☎ 901 11 67 12, in Switzerland 0848 700700; www.swiss.com)
Thomson Fly (BY; ☎ in the UK 0871 231 4691; www.thomsonfly.com)
Transavia (HV; ☎ 807 07 50 22, in the Netherlands 0900 0737; www.transavia.com)
US Airways (US; ☎ 901 11 70 73, in the USA 800 428 4322; www.usairways.com)
Vueling (VY; ☎ 902 33 39 33; www.vueling.com)
Windjet (IV; ☎ 900 99 69 33; w2.volawindjet.it)
Wizz (W6; ☎ 807 45 00 10, in Hungary 06 9018 1181; http://wizzair.com)

Tickets

The internet is increasingly the easiest way of locating and booking reasonably priced seats. This is especially so for flights from around Europe, regardless of whether you are flying with major carriers like Iberia or low-cost airlines.

Full-time students and those under 26 sometimes have access to discounted fares, especially on longer-haul flights from beyond Europe. You have to show a document proving your date of birth or a valid International Student Identity Card (ISIC) when buying your ticket. Other cheap deals include the discounted tickets released to travel agents and specialist discount agencies.

There is no shortage of online agents:

www.cheaptickets.com
www.ebookers.com
www.expedia.com
www.flightline.co.uk
www.flynow.com
www.lastminute.com
www.openjet.com
www.opodo.com
www.planesimple.co.uk
www.skyscanner.net
www.travelocity.co.uk
www.tripadvisor.com

Africa

From South Africa a host of major airlines service Spain, usually via European hubs like Frankfurt, London and Paris. British Airways and Lufthansa are among the airlines offering the best deals out of Cape Town, Durban and Johannesburg. **Flight Centre** (www.flightcentre.co.za), **STA Travel** (www.statravel.co.za) and **Rennies Travel** (www.renniestravel.com) have offices throughout southern Africa.

Morocco's national airline, Royal Air Maroc (RAM), dominates the flying trade to major Spanish cities, with flights to Barcelona, Madrid, Málaga and Valencia. Most of the direct flights are from Casablanca.

Iberia flies to Málaga, Almería, Granada, Madrid, Seville and Valencia from Melilla, the Spanish enclave on the Moroccan coast. The Moroccan crossing point into Melilla is the neighbouring town of Nador.

Asia

STA Travel proliferates in Asia, with branches in **Bangkok** (☎ 02-236 0262; www.statravel.co.th), **Singapore** (☎ 6737 7188; www.statravel.com.sg), **Hong Kong** (☎ 2736 1618; www.statravel.com.hk) and **Japan** (☎ 03 5391 2922; www.statravel.co.jp). Another resource in Japan is **No 1 Travel** (☎ 03 3205 6073; www.no1-travel.com); in Hong Kong try **Four Seas Tours** (☎ 2200 7760; www.fourseas travel.com).

Australia

Cheap flights from Australia to Europe generally go via Southeast Asian capitals. There are hardly any direct flights. Singapore Airlines, however, does fly direct to Barcelona via Singapore.

STA Travel (☎ 1300 733 035; www.statravel.com.au) and **Flight Centre** (☎ 133 133; www.flightcentre.com.au) are major dealers in cheap airfares, although discounted fares can also be found at your local travel agent. For online bookings, try www.travel.com.au.

Canada

Scan the travel agencies' advertisements in the *Globe & Mail*, *Toronto Star* and *Vancouver Sun*. **Travel Cuts** (☎ 1-866 246 9762; www.travelcuts.com), called Voyages Campus in Quebec, has offices in all major cities in Canada. For online bookings try www.expedia.ca and www.travelocity.ca.

Iberia has daily flights from Toronto via London to Madrid. Other major European airlines offer competitive fares to most Spanish destinations via other European capitals.

Canary Islands

Few visitors to the Canary Islands combine their trip with another to mainland Spain (or vice versa). There is no financial incentive to do so, as flights from other parts of Europe to the Canaries are often cheaper than those between the islands and the mainland.

Iberia, Spanair, Air Europa and charters fly from Santa Cruz de Tenerife, Las Palmas de Gran Canaria and, less frequently, Lanzarote and Fuerteventura to Madrid, Barcelona and other mainland destinations.

Continental Europe

Air travel between Spain and other places in continental Europe is worth considering if you are short of time. Short hops can be expensive, but for longer journeys you can often find airfares that beat overland alternatives.

In France, have a look at **Anyway** (☎ 0892 302 301; http://voyages.anyway.com), **Lastminute** (☎ 0892 707 505; www.lastminute.fr), **Nouvelles Frontières** (☎ 0825 000 747; www.nouvelles-frontieres.fr) and **Voyageurs du Monde** (☎ 0892 235 656; www.vdm.com).

In Germany, **STA Travel** (☎ 069 7430 3292; www.statravel.de) is one of the best student and discount travel agencies. **Just Travel** (☎ 089 747 3330; www.justtravel.de) is also worth a look.

Amsterdam is a popular departure point and a good budget-flight centre. Try the bucket shops along Rokin, or try **Air Fair** (☎ 0900 7717717; www.airfair.nl). **Kilroy Travels** (☎ 0900 0400636; www.kilroytravels.nl) is also worth checking out.

The best place to look for cheap fares in Italy is **CTS** (Centro Turistico Studentesco e Giovanile; ☎ 199 501150; www.cts.it), which has branches in cities throughout the country.

In Portugal, **Tagus** (☎ 707 220000; www.viagenstagus.pt) is a reputable travel agency with branches around the country.

New Zealand

There are no direct flights between New Zealand and Spain. The *New Zealand Herald* has a travel section with ads. **STA Travel** (☎ 0800 474 400; www.statravel.co.nz) and **Flight Centre** (☎ 0800 243 544; www.flightcentre.co.nz) have branches in Auckland and throughout the country.

South America

Iberia and a series of South American national airlines connect Spain with Latin America. Most flights converge on Madrid, although some continue to Barcelona.

Asatej (www.asatej.com) is a Hispanic youth travel organisation, with offices in Argentina and Mexico.

UK & Ireland

Discount air travel is big business in London. Advertisements for many travel agencies appear in the travel pages of the weekend newspapers, such as the *Independent*, the *Guardian* on Saturday and the *Sunday Times*.

STA Travel (☎ 0871 230 0040; www.statravel.co.uk) and **Trailfinders** (☎ 0845 058 5858; www.trailfinders.com), both of which have offices throughout the UK, sell discounted and student tickets. Other recommended travel agencies include **ebookers.com** (☎ 0800 074 4444; www.ebookers.com) and **Flight Centre** (☎ 0870 499 0040; www.flightcentre.co.uk).

Most British travel agents are registered with the Association of British Travel Agents (ABTA). If you've paid for your flight with an ABTA-registered agent who goes bust, ABTA will guarantee a refund or an alternative.

No-frills airlines are big business for travel between the UK and Spain. EasyJet and Ryanair are the main operators, getting some competition from smaller outfits like Jet2. Prices vary wildly according to season and also depend on how far in advance you book.

The two national airlines linking the UK and Spain are British Airways and Iberia. They both operate regular direct flights to Madrid and Barcelona, as well as a range of other centres.

Good agencies for charter flights from the UK to Spain include **Avro** (☎ 0871 423 8550; www.avro.com), **Thomas Cook** (www.thomascook.com) and **Thomson** (☎ 0871 231 4691; www.thomson.co.uk).

From Ireland, check out offers from Aer Lingus and Ryanair.

USA

Several airlines fly 'direct' (many flights involve a stop elsewhere in Europe en route) to Spain, landing in Madrid and Barcelona. These include KLM, British Airways and Iberia.

Discount travel agencies in the USA are known as consolidators. San Francisco is the ticket-consolidator capital of America, although some good deals can be found in other big cities. The *New York Times, Los Angeles Times, Chicago Tribune* and *San Francisco Examiner* all produce weekly travel sections. **STA Travel** (☎ 800 781 4040; www.statravel.com) has offices around the country. **Travel Cuts** (☎ 800 592 2887; www.travelcuts.com) is a similar operation.

Discount and rock-bottom options from the USA include charter, stand-by and courier flights. Stand-by fares are often sold at 60% of the normal price for one-way tickets. **Courier Travel** (www.couriertravel.org) is a search engine for courier and stand-by flights. You can also check out the **International Association of Air Travel Couriers** (www.courier.org).

LAND

You can enter Spain by train, bus and private vehicle along various points of its northern border with France (and Andorra) and the western frontier with Portugal. Bus is generally the cheapest option but the train is more comfortable, especially for long-haul trips.

Border Crossings

The main road crossing into Spain from France is the highway that links up with Spain's AP7 tollway, which runs down to Barcelona and follows the Spanish coast south (with a branch, the AP2, going to Madrid via Zaragoza). A series of links cut across the Pyrenees from France and Andorra into Spain, as does a coastal route that runs from Biarritz in France into the Spanish Basque Country.

The A5 freeway linking Madrid with Badajoz crosses the Portuguese frontier and continues on to Lisbon, and there are many other road connections up and down the length of the Hispano-Portuguese frontier.

As Spain, France and Portugal are members of the EU and the Schengen area (see p880) there are usually no border controls between them. The tiny principality of Andorra is not in the EU, so border controls (and customs checks for contraband) remain in place.

Bus

Eurolines (www.eurolines.com) and its partner bus companies run an extensive network of international buses across most of Western Europe and Morocco. In Spain they serve many destinations from the rest of Europe, although services often run only a few times a week.

See individual country sections for more information on bus transport.

Car & Motorcycle

When driving in Europe, always carry proof of ownership of a private vehicle. Third-party motor insurance is required throughout Europe (see p893).

Every vehicle should display a nationality plate of its country of registration. A warning triangle (to be used in case of breakdown) is compulsory. In Spain a reflective jacket is also compulsory. Other recommended accessories are a first-aid kit, spare-bulb kit and fire extinguisher.

Prebooking a rental car before leaving home will enable you to find the cheapest deals (for multinational agencies, see p893). No matter where you hire your car, make sure you understand what is included in the price and your liabilities.

Spain is great for motorcycle touring, and motorcyclists swarm into the country in summer. With a bike you rarely have to book ahead for ferries and can enter restricted traffic areas in cities.

An interesting website packed with advice for people planning to drive in Europe is **Ideamerge** (www.ideamerge.com), with information on the Renault company's car-leasing plan, motor-home rental and much more.

Your vehicle could be searched on arrival from Andorra. Spanish customs look out for contraband duty-free products destined for illegal resale in Spain. The same generally goes on arrival from Morocco or the Spanish North African enclaves of Ceuta and Melilla. In this case the search is for controlled substances.

BUS PASSES

Travellers planning broader European tours that include Spain could find one of the following passes useful.

Busabout (☎ in the UK 020 7950 1661; www.busabout.com; 258 Vauxhall Bridge Rd, London SW1V 1BS) is a UK-based hop-on, hop-off bus service aimed at younger travellers. It has passes of varying duration allowing you to use a network of 36 cities in 11 countries. The main passes are of interest only to those travelling a lot beyond Spain (where there are four stops). A Western Loop pass taking in Spain, France and Switzerland costs €459. A seven-day Spain & Portugal Adventure pass, which takes in Madrid and the south, costs €619. Other tours tailor-made for certain parts of the country are also available.

Eurolines (www.eurolines.com) offers a low-season pass valid for 15/30 days that costs UK£139/209 (UK£119/159 for under-26s and seniors over 60). This pass allows unlimited travel between 40 European cities. The only Spanish cities included are Barcelona and Madrid. Fares increase to UK£229/299 (UK£189/249) between June and mid-September.

See p892 for comprehensive information on road rules, petrol, insurance and other driving tips for Spain.

Train

The principal rail crossings into Spain pierce the Franco-Spanish frontier along the Mediterranean coast and via the Basque Country. Another minor rail route runs inland across the Pyrenees from Latour-de-Carol to Barcelona. From Portugal, the main line runs from Lisbon across Extremadura to Madrid.

Direct trains link Barcelona with Paris, Geneva, Zürich, Turin and Milan at least three times a week. Direct overnight trains also connect Paris with Madrid. Check details on the website of **Renfe** (☎ for international trips 902 24 34 02; www.renfe.es), the Spanish national railway company.

Andorra

Regular buses connect Andorra with Barcelona (including winter ski buses and direct services to the airport) and other destinations in Spain (including Madrid) and France. Regular buses run between Andorra and Estació d'Autobusos de Sants bus station (€21; 3¼ to four hours).

France

BUS

Eurolines (www.eurolines.fr) heads to Spain from Paris and more than 20 other French cities and towns. It connects with Madrid (17¾ hours), Barcelona (14¾ hours) and many other destinations. There is at least one departure per day for main destinations.

TRAIN

About the only truly direct trains to Madrid and Barcelona are the *trenhoteles*, which are expensive sleeper trains. The Barcelona service leaves from Paris Austerlitz at 8.32pm daily and arrives at 8.24am (stopping at Orléans, Limoges, Perpignan, Figueres, Girona and Barcelona Sants). The Madrid equivalent leaves from Paris at 7.43pm daily and arrives in Madrid Chamartín at 9.13am (stopping at Orléans, Blois, Poitiers, Vitoria, Burgos and Valladolid).

There are several other less luxurious possibilities. Two or three TGV (high-speed) trains leave from Paris Montparnasse for Irún, where you change to a normal train for the Basque Country and on towards Madrid. Up to three TGVs also put you on track to Barcelona (leaving from Paris Gare

RAIL PASSES

InterRail (www.interrail.net) passes are available to people who have lived in Europe for six months or more. They can be bought at most major stations and student travel outlets, as well as online.

Eurail (www.eurail.com) passes are for those who've lived in Europe for less than six months and are supposed to be bought outside Europe. They're available from leading travel agencies and online.

Seniors travelling from the UK should ask at the **Rail Europe Travel Centre** (☎ 0844 848 4064; www.raileurope.co.uk) about possible discounts on rail travel in continental Europe.

InterRail Passes

InterRail has a Global Pass encompassing 30 countries that comes in four versions, ranging from five days' travel in 10 days to a full month's travel. These in turn come with three prices: adult 1st class, adult 2nd class and youth 2nd class. The one-month pass costs, respectively, €809/599/399.

The InterRail one-country pass for Spain can be used for three, four, six or eight days in one month. For the eight-day pass you pay €309/229/149/154.50/114.50 for adult 1st class/adult 2nd class/youth 2nd class/child 1st class/child 2nd class. Children's passes are for children aged four to 11, youth passes for people aged 12 to 25 and adult passes for those 26 and over. Children aged three and under travel for free. Cardholders get discounts on travel in the country where they purchase the ticket.

Eurail Global Pass

Eurail Global Passes are good for travel in 20 European countries (not including the UK); forget it if you intend to travel mainly in Spain. People aged 26 and over pay for a 1st-class Global Pass and those aged under 26 for a 2nd-class version. Passes are valid for 15 or 21 days, or for one, de Lyon), with a change of train at Montpellier or Narbonne. One or two daily direct services connect Montpellier with Barcelona (and on to Murcia). A slow overnight train runs from Paris to Latour-de-Carol, where you change for a local regional train to Barcelona.

For more information on French rail services check out the **SNCF** (www.voyages-sncf.com) website.

Morocco

Buses from several Moroccan cities converge on Tangier to make the ferry crossing to Algeciras, and then fan out to the main Spanish centres. Several companies, including **ALSA** (www.alsa.es), run these routes.

Portugal

BUS

Avanza (☎ in Spain & Portugal 902 02 09 99; www.avanzabus.com) runs one or two buses a day from Lisbon to Madrid via Badajoz. The trip takes 7½ to nine hours.

Other services from the Portuguese capital run to Seville via Aracena; to Málaga via Badajoz, Seville, Cádiz, Algeciras and the Costa del Sol; and to Granada via Albufeira, Huelva, Seville, Málaga and Almuñécar.

Another service runs north via Porto to Tui, Santiago de Compostela and A Coruña in Galicia. Local buses cross the border from towns such as Huelva in Andalucía, Badajoz in Extremadura and Ourense in Galicia.

TRAIN

An overnight sleeper train runs daily from Lisbon to Madrid, and another train connects the Portuguese capital with Irún. See **Renfe** (www.renfe.es) for details.

UK

BUS

Eurolines (www.nationalexpress.com/eurolines) runs buses to Barcelona, Madrid and other Spanish destinations several times a week. The London terminal is at **Victoria Coach Station** (Buckingham Palace Rd). Journey times (including a wait in Paris of up to two hours) can range from 24 to 26 hours to Barcelona and from 25 to 30 hours to Madrid.

CAR & MOTORCYCLE

You can take your car across to France by ferry or via the Channel Tunnel on **Eurotunnel** (☎ 0870 535 3535; www.eurotunnel.com). The latter runs four crossings (35 minutes)

two or three months. These cost €503/653/810/1145/1413, respectively, for the 1st-class adult pass. The 2nd-class youth version comes in at €327/423/527/745/920. Children aged between four and 11 pay half-price for the 1st-class passes. The 1st-class saver is for groups of two or more and brings a 15% reduction in the standard Global Pass adult prices.

Another option is a Global Pass for 10/15 days' travel within two months, which costs €594/781. The 15-day pass costs €665/508 for the saver/2nd-class youth versions.

Eurail Select Pass

This provides between five and 15 days of unlimited travel within a two-month period in three to five bordering countries (from a total of 23 possible countries). As with Global Passes, those aged 26 and over pay for a 1st-class pass, while those aged under 26 can get a cheaper 2nd-class pass. The basic five-day pass for three countries costs €319/270/207 for the 1st-class adult/saver/2nd-class youth version.

Eurail Regional & National Passes

Eurail also offers a Spain national pass and several two-country regional passes (Spain-France, Spain-Italy and Spain-Portugal). You can choose from three to 10 days' train travel in a two-month period for any of these passes. The 10-day national pass costs €388/313 for 1st-class adult/2nd-class youth. Regional passes come in five versions: 1st- and 2nd-class adult, 1st- and 2nd-class adult saver and 2nd-class youth. The 10-day regional pass for Spain and France, for instance, costs €433/379/379/332/288. As with all Eurail passes, you want to be sure you will be covering a lot of ground to make these worthwhile. Check some sample prices in euros for the places you intend to travel on the **Renfe** (www.renfe.es) website to compare.

an hour between Folkestone and Calais in the high season.

For breakdown assistance both the **AA** (☎ 0800 085 7253; www.theaa.com) and the **RAC** (☎ 0870 572 2722; www.rac.co.uk) offer comprehensive cover in Europe.

TRAIN

The passenger-train service **Eurostar** (☎ 0870 518 6186; www.eurostar.com) travels between London and Paris, from where you can connect with trains to Spain. Alternatively, you can purchase a train ticket that includes crossing the English Channel by ferry, SeaCat or hovercraft.

For the latest fare information on journeys to Spain, including the Eurostar, contact the **Rail Europe Travel Centre** (☎ 0844 848 4064; www.raileurope.co.uk). Another source of rail information for all of Europe is **Rail Choice** (www.railchoice.com). Travel times depend in large measure on which connections you make in Paris.

SEA

Ferries run to mainland Spain regularly from the Canary Islands, Italy, North Africa (Algeria, Morocco and the Spanish enclaves of Ceuta and Melilla) and the UK. Most services are run by the Spanish national ferry company, **Acciona Trasmediterránea** (☎ 902 45 46 45; www.trasmediterranea.es).

Algeria

Acciona Trasmediterránea runs daily ferries from Alicante to Oran (nine hours, leaving at 11pm or noon) from late June to early September, and to Ghazaouet (eight hours, leaving at midnight) from late June to August. There are one or two weekly departures for Ghazaouet in May–June as well.

Canary Islands

An Acciona Trasmediterránea car ferry leaves from Santa Cruz de Tenerife (2pm) every Thursday and from Las Palmas de Gran Canaria (8am) every Monday for Cádiz. It's a long and bumpy ride, taking about 44 hours from Santa Cruz (with a stop in Santa Cruz de Palma) and 34 from Las Palmas (with a stop in Arrecife).

Italy

Ferries run daily from Genoa to Barcelona, and up to six times a week from Civitavecchia (near Rome) and Livorno (for Florence and Pisa). For more information see p360.

Morocco

You can sail from the Moroccan ports of Tangier Al Hoceima and Nador, and from Ceuta or Melilla (Spanish enclaves on the Moroccan coast), to Almería, Málaga, Algeciras, Gibraltar and Tarifa. The routes are Melilla–Almería, Al Hoceima–Almería, Nador–Almería, Melilla–Málaga, Tangier–Gibraltar, Tangier–Algeciras, Ceuta–Algeciras and Tangier–Tarifa. All routes usually take vehicles as well.

The most frequent sailings are from Algeciras to Tangier (taking 1¼ to 2½ hours) and Ceuta (35 to 45 minutes). Extra services are put on during the peak summer period (mid-June to mid-September) to cater for the stream of Moroccans resident in Europe heading home for the holidays, and the Tangier–Tarifa route may be restricted to people with EU passports or EU residence papers during this period.

Acciona Trasmediterránea and various other companies compete for business. For more details, see the appropriate sections in the Andalucía chapter.

Grandi Navi Veloci (Grimaldi) runs a weekly ferry service between Barcelona and Tangier (24 hours); see p360 for details.

UK

PLYMOUTH TO SANTANDER

From Milbay Docks in Plymouth, **Brittany Ferries** (☎ 0870 907 6103; www.brittany-ferries.co.uk) runs a car ferry twice a week to Santander from mid-March to mid-November. See also p526.

PORTSMOUTH TO BILBAO

P&O Ferries (☎ 0871 664 5645; www.poferries.com) operates a service from Portsmouth to Bilbao. As a rule there are sailings every three days, year-round. You leave Portsmouth at 9.15pm and arrive at 8am two mornings later. See also p479.

VIA FRANCE

You can transport your car by ferry to France from the UK. **Norfolkline** (☎ 0870 870 1020; www.norfolkline.com) fast boats take about 1¾ hours to cross from Dover to Dunkirk. **P&O Ferries** (☎ 0871 664 5645; www.poferries.com) has frequent car ferries from Dover to Calais (1¼ hours).

GETTING AROUND

You can reach almost any destination in Spain by train or bus, and services are efficient and, generally, cheap. Money is being poured into expanding the high-speed train network. Domestic air services are plentiful over longer distances and on routes that are more complicated by land. While rail prices have climbed considerably in the past few years (along with efficiency, speed and comfort, it should be added!), airfares have become more competitive. However, your own wheels give you the most freedom.

AIR

Airlines in Spain

Iberia and its subsidiary, Iberia Regional-Air Nostrum, have an extensive network covering all of Spain. Competing with Iberia are Spanair and Air Europa, as well as the low-cost companies Clickair (another Iberia subsidiary) and Vueling. Between them they cover a host of Spanish destinations. The busiest route by far, in spite of strong competition from the high-speed AVE train, is the Barcelona–Madrid *puente* (bridge).

The UK low-cost airline EasyJet has a hub in Madrid and offers domestic flights to Oviedo, Ibiza and A Coruña. Ireland's Ryanair also runs a handful of domestic Spanish flights, including Alicante–Zaragoza, Girona–Granada, Girona–Madrid, Madrid–Santander, Reus–Palma de Mallorca, Reus–Santander, Reus–Santiago de Compostela, Reus–Seville and Valencia–Santiago de Compostela.

Generally, domestic flights are most easily booked on the airlines' websites. It is worth shopping around, and for return flights there is nothing to stop you booking each leg with a different airline. For airline contact details see p883.

Typical cheaper return fares between Madrid and Barcelona hover around €80 to €120, but can range up to €250. Occasionally you find real *gangas* (bargains). Cheaper tickets are generally nonrefundable, must be booked up to two weeks in advance and allow no changes. All applicable airport taxes are factored into the price of your ticket.

BICYCLE

Years of highway improvement programs across the country have made cycling a much easier prospect than it once was. There are plenty of options, from mountain biking in the Pyrenees to distance riding along the coast.

If you get tired of pedalling it is often possible to take your bike on the train. All regional trains have space for bikes (usually marked by a bicycle logo on the carriage), where you can simply load the bike. Bikes are also permitted on most *cercanías* (local-area trains around big cities such as Madrid and Barcelona). On long-distance trains there are more restrictions. As a rule you have to be travelling overnight in a sleeper or couchette to have the (dismantled) bike accepted as normal luggage. Otherwise, it can only be sent separately as a parcel. It's often possible to take your bike on a bus – usually you'll just be asked to remove the front wheel.

In the UK, the **Cyclists' Touring Club** (CTC; ☎ 0870 873 0061; www.ctc.org.uk; Parklands, Railton Rd, Guildford, Surrey GU2 9JX) can help you plan your own bike tour or organise guided tours. Membership costs UK£35 per annum (UK£12 for those under 18 or students under 26).

Hire & Purchase

Bicycle rental is not as common as you might expect in Spain, although it is becoming more so, especially in the case of mountain bikes *(bici todo terreno)* and in the more popular regions, such as Andalucía and coastal spots like Barcelona. Costs vary considerably, but you can be looking at around €10 per hour, €15 to €20 per day, or €50 to €60 per week.

You can purchase any kind of bicycle you want in the bigger centres, and prices are average by European standards. A basic city bike with no gears won't come for much less than €100. For a decent mountain bike with 16 gears you're looking at €250 or more, and racing bikes can be more expensive still.

BOAT

Ferries and hydrofoils link the mainland (La Península) with the Balearic Islands and Spain's North African enclaves of Ceuta and Melilla. For details of the latter, see opposite and the relevant sections in the Andalucía chapter (p763, p774 and p828). For more on ferries between the mainland and the Balearics, see p650.

The main national ferry company is **Acciona Trasmediterránea** (☎ 902 45 46 45; www.trasmediterranea.es). It runs a combination of slower car ferries and modern, high-speed, passenger-only fast ferries and hydrofoils. On overnight services between the mainland and the Balearic Islands you can opt for seating or sleeping accommodation in a cabin.

BUS

A plethora of companies provide bus links, from local routes between villages to fast intercity connections. It is often cheaper to travel by bus than by train, particularly on long-haul runs, but also less comfortable.

Local services can get you just about anywhere, but most buses connecting villages and provincial towns are not geared to tourist needs. Frequent weekday services drop off to a trickle on Saturday and Sunday. Often just one bus runs daily between smaller places during the week, and none operate on Sundays. It's usually unnecessary to make reservations; just arrive early enough to get a seat.

On many regular runs (say, from Madrid to Toledo) the ticket you buy is for the next bus due to leave and *cannot* be used on a later bus. Advance purchase in such cases is generally not possible.

For longer trips (such as Madrid to Seville or to the coast), and certainly in peak holiday season, you can (and should) buy your ticket in advance. On some routes you have the choice between express and all-stops services.

In most larger towns and cities, buses leave from a single bus station *(estación de autobuses)*. In smaller places, buses tend to operate from a set street or plaza, often unmarked. Locals will know where to go. Usually a specific bar sells tickets, although in some cases you may have to purchase tickets on the bus.

Bus travel within Spain is not overly costly. The trip from Madrid to Barcelona costs around €27 one way. From Barcelona to Seville, one of the longest trips you could do (15 to 16 hours), you pay up to €74 one way.

People under 26 should inquire about discounts on long-distance trips. Occasionally a return ticket is cheaper than two singles.

Bus companies operating in Spain:

ALSA (☎ 902 42 22 42; www.alsa.es) By far the biggest player, this company has routes all over the country, which it operates in association with various other companies. From Madrid it runs buses to Alcalá de Henares, Alicante, Ávila, Barcelona, Burgos, the Basque Country, towns all over Galicia, Guadalajara, Granada (and most of Andalucía), León, Logroño, Murcia, Navarra, Santander, Segovia, Soria, Tarragona, Toledo, Valladolid and Zaragoza. From Seville buses run up through Extremadura and Salamanca into Galicia, as well as through Córdoba through the east of the country to Barcelona.

Alsina Graells (☎ 902 42 22 42; www.alsa.es) Part of the ALSA group. It runs buses from Barcelona across Catalonia to destinations west and northwest, such as Vielha, La Seu d'Urgell and Lleida.

Avanza (☎ in Spain & Portugal 902 02 09 99; www.avanzabus.com) Operates buses from Madrid to Extremadura, western Castilla y León (eg Tordesillas, Salamanca, Zamora) and Valencia via eastern Castilla-La Mancha (eg Cuenca).

La Sepulvedana (☎ 902 22 22 82; www.lasepulvedana.es) Buses to Segovia, parts of Castilla-La Mancha, Extremadura and some parts of Andalucía from Madrid.

Socibus & Secorbus (☎ 902 22 92 92; www.socibus.es) These two companies jointly operate services between Madrid and western Andalucía, including Cádiz, Córdoba, Huelva and Seville.

CAR & MOTORCYCLE

Automobile Associations

The **Real Automóvil Club de España** (RACE; Map pp134-5; ☎ 902 40 45 45; www.race.es; Calle de Eloy Gonzalo 32, Madrid) is the national automobile club. They may well come to assist you in case of breakdown, but in any event you should obtain an emergency telephone number for Spain from your own insurer.

Bring Your Own Vehicle

If bringing your own car, remember to have your insurance and other papers in order (see p887).

Driving Licence

All EU member states' driving licences are fully recognised throughout Europe. Those with a non-EU licence are supposed to obtain a 12-month International Driving Permit (IDP) to accompany their national licence, which your national automobile association can issue. People who have held residency in Spain for one year or more must apply for a Spanish driving licence. If you want to hire a car or motorcycle you will need to produce your driving licence.

Fuel & Spare Parts

Petrol *(gasolina)* in Spain is pricey, but generally cheaper than in its major EU neighbours (including France, Germany, Italy and the UK). About 30 companies, including several foreign operators, run petrol stations in Spain, but the two biggest are the home-grown Repsol and Cepsa.

Prices vary between service stations *(gasolineras)*. Lead-free (*sin plomo*; 95 octane) costs up to €1.21 per litre. A 98-octane variant costs as much as €1.32 per litre. Diesel *(gasóleo)* comes in at €1.25 per litre. As world oil prices climb, so do the tank prices.

Petrol is about 10% cheaper in Gibraltar than in Spain and 15% cheaper in Andorra. It's

ROAD DISTANCES (km)

	Alicante	Badajoz	Barcelona	Bilbao	Córdoba	Granada	A Coruña	León	Madrid	Málaga	Oviedo	Pamplona	San Sebastián	Seville	Toledo	Valencia	Valladolid
Badajoz	696																
Barcelona	515	1022															
Bilbao	817	649	620														
Córdoba	525	272	908	795													
Granada	353	438	868	829	166												
A Coruña	1031	772	1118	644	995	1043											
León	755	496	784	359	733	761	334										
Madrid	422	401	621	395	400	434	609	333									
Málaga	482	436	997	939	187	129	1153	877	544								
Oviedo	873	614	902	304	851	885	340	118	451	995							
Pamplona	673	755	437	159	807	841	738	404	407	951	463						
San Sebastián	766	768	529	119	869	903	763	433	469	13	423	92					
Seville	609	217	1046	933	138	256	947	671	538	219	789	945	1007				
Toledo	411	368	692	466	320	397	675	392	71	507	510	478	540	458			
Valencia	166	716	349	633	545	519	961	685	352	648	803	501	594	697	372		
Valladolid	615	414	663	280	578	627	455	134	193	737	252	325	354	589	258	545	
Zaragoza	498	726	296	324	725	759	833	488	325	869	604	175	268	863	396	326	367

about 35% cheaper in Spain's tax-free enclaves of Ceuta and Melilla in North Africa.

You can pay with major credit cards at most service stations.

Hire

A selection of multinational car rental agencies is listed below.

Autos Abroad (☎ in the UK 0870 066 7788; www.autosabroad.com)
Avis (☎ 902 24 88 24; www.avis.es)
Budget (☎ in the USA 800 472 3325; www.budget.com)
Europcar (☎ 902 10 50 55; www.europcar.es)
Hertz (☎ 91 372 93 00; www.hertz.es)
National/Atesa (☎ 902 10 01 01; www.atesa.es)
Pepecar (☎ 807 41 42 43; www.pepecar.com) A local low-cost company.

To rent a car in Spain you have to have a licence, be aged 21 or over and, for the major companies at least, have a credit or debit card. Smaller firms in areas where car hire is particularly common (such as the Balearic Islands) can sometimes live without this last requirement. Although those with a non-EU licence should also have an IDP, you will find that national licences from countries like Australia, Canada, New Zealand and the USA are often accepted.

Insurance

Third-party motor insurance is a minimum requirement in Spain and throughout Europe. Ask your insurer for a European Accident Statement form, which can simplify matters in the event of an accident. A European breakdown-assistance policy such as the AA Five Star Service or RAC Eurocover Motoring Assistance is a good investment.

Car-hire companies also provide this minimum insurance, but be careful to understand what your liabilities and excess are, and what waivers you are entitled to in case of accident or damage to the hire vehicle.

Road Rules

Drive on the right. In built-up areas the speed limit is 50km/h (and in some cases, such as inner-city Barcelona, 30km/h), which increases to 100km/h on major roads and up to

120km/h on *autovías* and *autopistas* (toll-free and tolled dual-lane highways, respectively). Cars towing caravans are restricted to a maximum speed of 80km/h. The minimum driving age is 18 years.

Motorcyclists must use headlights at all times and wear a helmet if riding a bike of 125cc or more. The minimum age for riding motorbikes and scooters of 80cc and over is 16; for those 50cc and under it's 14. A licence is required.

Spanish truck drivers often have the courtesy to turn on their right indicator to show that the way ahead of them is clear for overtaking (and the left one if it is not and you are attempting this manoeuvre).

At traffic circles (roundabouts), vehicles already in the circle have the right of way.

The blood-alcohol limit is 0.05%. Breath tests are common, and if found to be over the limit you can be judged, condemned, fined and deprived of your licence within 24 hours. Fines range up to around €600 for serious offences. Nonresident foreigners will be required to pay up on the spot (at 30% off the full fine). Pleading linguistic ignorance will not help – your traffic cop will produce a list of infringements and fines in as many languages as you like. If you don't pay, or don't have a Spanish resident to act as guarantor for you, your vehicle could be impounded.

HITCHING

Hitching is never entirely safe in any country in the world, and we don't recommend it. Travellers who decide to hitch should understand that they are taking a small but potentially dangerous risk. People who do choose to hitch will be safer if they travel in pairs and let someone know where they are planning to go.

Hitching is illegal on *autopistas* and *autovías*, and difficult on other major highways. Choose a spot where cars can safely stop before highway slipways, or use minor roads. The going can be slow on the latter, as the traffic is often light. Overall, Spain is not a hitchhiker's paradise.

LOCAL TRANSPORT

All the major cities have good local transport. Madrid and Barcelona have extensive bus and metro systems, and other major cities also benefit from generally efficient public transport.

Bicycle

Few of the big cities offer much in the way of encouragement to cycle. Barcelona is an exception, where cycling lanes (albeit insufficient) have been laid out along main roads and various hire outlets make it possible for visitors to enjoy them. Barcelona and Seville have introduced public bicycle systems (but in Barcelona it is for residents only). Driver attitudes are not always so enlightened, so beware.

Bus

Cities and provincial capitals all have reasonable bus networks. You can buy single tickets (up to €1.30, depending on the city) on the buses or at tobacconists, but in cities such as Madrid and Barcelona you are better off buying combined 10-trip tickets (see Metro, below) that allow the use of a combination of bus and metro, and which work out cheaper per ride. These can be purchased in any metro station.

Regular buses run from about 6am to shortly before midnight. In the big cities a night bus service generally kicks in on a limited number of lines in the wee hours. In Madrid they are known as *búhos* (owls) and in Barcelona more prosaically as *nitbusos* (night buses).

Metro

Madrid has the country's most extensive metro network. Barcelona follows in second place with a reasonable system. Valencia, Bilbao and Palma de Mallorca also have limited metros, and Seville is building one (due to open by the end of 2008). Tickets must be bought in metro stations (from counters or vending machines). Single tickets cost the same as for buses (up to €1.30). The best value for visitors wanting to move around the major cities over a few days are the 10-trip tickets, known in Madrid as Metrobús (€6.70) and in Barcelona as T-10 (€7.20). Monthly and season passes are also available.

Taxi

You can usually find taxi ranks at train and bus stations, or you can telephone for radio taxis. In larger cities taxi ranks are also scattered about the centre, and taxis will stop if you hail them in the street. Look for the green light and/or the *libre* sign on the passenger side of the windscreen. The bigger cities are well populated with taxis, although finding one when you need to get home late on a Friday or Saturday night in places such as Madrid and Barcelona can be tricky. No more than four people are allowed in a taxi.

Daytime flagfall (generally to 10pm) is around €1.30 to €1.95. After 10pm and on weekends and holidays (in some cities, including Madrid and Barcelona), the price can rise to €2.95. You then pay around €0.80 to €1 per kilometre depending on the time of day. There are airport and luggage surcharges. A cross-town ride in a major city will cost about €5 to €8, while a taxi between the city centre and airport in either Madrid or Barcelona will cost €20 to €25 with luggage.

Tram

Trams were stripped out of Spanish cities decades ago, but they are making a timid comeback in some. Barcelona has a couple of new suburban tram services in addition to its tourist Tramvia Blau run to Tibidabo. Valencia has some useful trams to the beach. Various limited lines, often of little use to visitors, run in places like Bilbao, suburban Madrid and Murcia.

TRAIN

Renfe (☎ 902 24 02 02; www.renfe.es) is the national train system that runs most of the services in Spain. A handful of small private railway lines are noted throughout this book.

Spain has several types of trains. For short hops, bigger cities such as Madrid, Barcelona, Bilbao, Málaga and Valencia have local networks known as *cercanías*. Long-distance (aka *largo recorrido* or Grandes Líneas) trains come in all sorts of different flavours. They range from all-stops *regionales* operating within one region to the high-speed Tren de Alta Velocidad Española (AVE) trains that link Madrid with Barcelona, Burgos, Huesca (via Zaragoza), Málaga, Seville and Valladolid (and in coming years Madrid–Valencia via Cuenca, and Madrid–Bilbao). Similar to the AVE trains used on conventional Spanish tracks (which differ from the standard European gauge) connect Barcelona with Valencia and Alicante in the Euromed service. A whole host of modern intermediate-speed services (Alaris, Altaria, Alvia, Arco and Avant) offer an increasingly speedy and comfortable service around the country, and have improved services vastly on such shorter-distance runs as Madrid–Toledo and Barcelona–Lleida. Slower long-distance trains include the Talgo and Intercity.

You'll find *consignas* (left-luggage facilities) at all main train stations. They are usually open from about 6am to midnight and charge from €3 to €4.50 per day per piece of luggage.

Classes & Costs

All long-distance trains have 2nd and 1st classes, known as *turista* and *preferente*, respectively. The latter is 20% to 40% more expensive. Some services have a third, superior category, called *club*. Fares vary enormously depending on the service (faster trains cost considerably more) and, in the case of some high-speed services such as the AVE, on the time and day of travel. If you get a return ticket, it is worth checking whether your return journey is by the same kind of train. If you return on a slower train than the outward-bound trip you may be entitled to a modest refund on the return leg. Alternatively, if you return by a

A MEMORABLE NORTHERN TRAIN JOURNEY

The romantically inclined could opt for an opulent and slow-moving, old-time rail adventure in the colourful north of Spain.

Catch the **Transcantábrico** (www.transcantabrico.feve.es) for a journey on a picturesque narrow-gauge rail route, from Santiago de Compostela (by bus as far as O Ferrol) via Oviedo, Santander and Bilbao along the coast, and then a long inland stretch to finish in León. The eight-day trip costs €3500/5000 per single/double, and can also be done in reverse. There are departures up to four times a month from April to October. The package includes various visits along the way, including the Museo Guggenheim in Bilbao, the Cuevas de Altamira, Santillana del Mar, and the Covadonga lakes in the Picos de Europa. The food is as pleasurable for the palate as the sights are for the eyes, with some meals being eaten on board but most in various locations.

The trains don't travel at night, making sleeping aboard easy and providing the opportunity to stay out at night.

TRAIN ROUTES

faster train you will need to pay more to make your return ticket valid for that train.

Tickets for AVE trains are by far the most expensive. A one-way trip in 2nd class from Madrid to Barcelona (on which route only AVE trains run) could cost as must as €160 (less if booked ahead on the web). Flying is often cheaper (although more of a hassle) and the bus certainly is. By contrast, the trip on the slower but much longer run from Barcelona to Oviedo costs a very reasonable €56.

Children aged between four and 12 years are entitled to a 40% discount; those aged under four travel for free (except on high-speed trains, for which they pay the same as those aged four to 12). Buying a return ticket often gives you a 10% to 20% discount on the return trip. Students and people up to 25 years of age with a Euro<26 Card (Carnet Joven in Spain) are entitled to 20% to 25% off most ticket prices.

Buying tickets in advance on the internet can also bring significant discounts (as much as 60% on some AVE services for tickets bought as least 15 days in advance).

On overnight trips within Spain on *trenhoteles* it's worth paying extra for a *litera* (couchette; a sleeping berth in a six- or four-bed compartment) or, if available, single or double cabins in *preferente* or *gran clase* class. The cost depends on the class of accommodation, type of train and length of journey. The lines covered are Madrid–La Coruña, Barcelona–Córdoba–Seville, Barcelona–Madrid (and on to Lisbon) and Barcelona–Málaga.

Reservations

Reservations are recommended for long-distance trips, and you can make them in train stations, Renfe offices and travel agencies, as well as online (which can be a little complicated). In a growing number of stations you can pick up prebooked tickets from machines scattered about the station concourse.

Health

CONTENTS

BEFORE YOU GO

Prevention is the key to staying healthy while abroad. Some predeparture planning will save trouble later. See your dentist before a long trip; carry a spare pair of contact lenses and glasses; and take your optical prescription with you. Bring medications in their original, clearly labelled containers. A signed and dated letter from your physi cian describing your medical conditions and medications, including generic names, is also a good idea. If carrying syringes or needles, be sure to have a physician's letter documenting their medical necessity.

INSURANCE

If you're an EU citizen, a European Health Insurance Card, available from health centres or, in the UK, post offices, covers you for most medical care in public hospitals. It will not cover you for non-emergencies or emergency repatriation. So even with the card, you will still have to pay for medicine bought from pharmacies, even if prescribed, and perhaps for a few tests and procedures. The card is no good for private medical consultations and treatment in Spain; this includes virtually all dentists and some of the better clinics and surgeries. Citizens from other countries should find out if there is a reciprocal arrangement for free medical care between their country and Spain. If you do need health insurance, strongly consider a policy that covers you for ambulances and the worst possible scenario, such as an accident requiring an emergency flight home.

Find out in advance if your insurance plan will make payments directly to providers or reimburse you later for overseas health expenditures; if you have to claim later make sure you keep all documentation. The former option is generally preferable, as it doesn't require you to pay out of your own pocket in a foreign country.

Worldwide travel insurance is available at www.lonelyplanet.com/travel_services. You can buy, extend and claim online anywhere – even if you're already on the road.

RECOMMENDED VACCINATIONS

No jabs are necessary for Spain. However, the World Health Organization (WHO) recommends that all travellers should be covered for diphtheria, tetanus, measles, mumps, rubella and polio, regardless of their destination. Since most vaccines don't produce immunity until at least two weeks after they're given, visit a physician at least six weeks before departure.

INTERNET RESOURCES

International Travel and Health, a WHO publication, is revised annually and is available online at www.who.int/ith. Other useful websites:

Age Concern (www.ageconcern.org.uk) Advice on travel for the elderly.

Fit for Travel (www.fitfortravel.scot.nhs.uk) General travel advice for the layperson.

Marie Stopes International (www.mariestopes.org.uk) Information on women's health and contraception.

MD Travel Health (www.mdtravelhealth.com) Travel health recommendations for every country; updated daily.

IN TRANSIT

DEEP VEIN THROMBOSIS (DVT)

Blood clots may form in the legs during flights, chiefly because of prolonged immobility. The chief symptom of DVT is swelling or pain of the foot, ankle or calf, usually but not always on just one side. When a blood clot travels to the lungs, it may cause chest pain and breathing difficulties. Travellers with any of these symptoms should immediately seek medical attention.

To prevent the development of DVT on long flights you should walk about the cabin, contract your leg muscles while sitting, drink plenty of fluids, and avoid alcohol and tobacco.

IN SPAIN

AVAILABILITY & COST OF HEALTH CARE

If you need an ambulance, call ☎ 061. For emergency treatment go straight to the *urgencias* (casualty) section of the nearest hospital.

Good health care is readily available, and *farmacias* (pharmacies) offer valuable advice and sell over-the-counter medication. In Spain, a system of *farmacias de guardia* (duty pharmacies) operates so that each district has one open all the time. When a pharmacy is closed, it posts the name of the nearest open one on the door.

Medical costs are lower in Spain than many other European countries, but can still mount quickly if you are uninsured.

TRAVELLER'S DIARRHOEA

If you develop diarrhoea, be sure to drink plenty of fluids, preferably an oral rehydration solution, such as Dioralyte. If diarrhoea is bloody, persists for more than 72 hours or is accompanied by a fever, shaking, chills or severe abdominal pain, you should seek medical attention.

ENVIRONMENTAL HAZARDS

Altitude Sickness

Lack of oxygen at high altitudes (over 2500m) affects most people to some extent. Symptoms of Acute Mountain Sickness (AMS) usually develop during the first 24 hours at altitude but may be delayed up to three weeks. Mild symptoms include headache, lethargy, dizziness, difficulty sleeping and loss of appetite. AMS may become more severe without warning and can be fatal. Severe symptoms include breathlessness, a dry, irritative cough (which may progress to the production of pink, frothy sputum), severe headache, lack of coordination and balance, confusion, irrational behaviour, vomiting, drowsiness and unconsciousness. There is no hard-and-fast rule as to what is too high: AMS has been fatal at 3000m, although 3500m to 4500m is the usual range.

Treat mild symptoms by resting at the same altitude until recovery, usually for a day or two. Paracetamol or aspirin can be taken for headaches. If symptoms persist or become worse *immediate descent is necessary*; even 500m can help. Drug treatments should never be used to avoid descent or to enable further ascent.

Diamox (acetazolamide) reduces the headache caused by AMS and helps the body acclimatise to the lack of oxygen. It is only available on prescription, and those who are allergic to the sulphonamide antibiotics may also be allergic to Diamox.

In the UK, fact sheets are available from the **British Mountaineering Council** (☎ 0870 010 4878; www.thebmc.co.uk; 177-179 Burton Rd, Manchester, M20 2BB).

Heat Exhaustion & Heatstroke

Heat exhaustion occurs following excessive fluid loss with inadequate replacement of fluids and salt. Symptoms include headache, dizziness and tiredness. Dehydration is happening by the time you feel thirsty – aim to drink sufficient water to produce pale, diluted urine. Replace lost fluids by drinking water and/or fruit juice, and cool the body with cold water and fans. Treat salt loss with salty fluids, such as soup, or add a little more table salt to foods than usual.

Heatstroke is much more serious, resulting in irrational and hyperactive behaviour, and eventually loss of consciousness and death. Rapid cooling by spraying the body with water and fanning is ideal. Emergency fluid and electrolyte replacement by intravenous drip is recommended.

Bites & Stings

Bees and wasps only cause real problems to those with a severe allergy (anaphylaxis). If you have a severe allergy to bee or wasp stings, carry an 'epipen' or similar adrenaline injection.

In forested areas watch out for the hairy reddish-brown caterpillars of the pine processionary moth. They live in silvery nests up in the pine trees and, come spring, leave the nest to march in long lines (hence the name). Touching the caterpillars' hairs sets off a severely irritating allergic skin reaction.

Some Spanish centipedes have a very nasty but nonfatal sting. The ones to watch out for are those with clearly defined segments, which may be patterned with, for instance, black and yellow stripes.

Jellyfish, which have stinging tentacles, generally occur in large numbers or hardly at all, so it's fairly easy to know when not to go in the sea.

Mosquitoes are found in most parts of Europe. They may not carry malaria, but can cause irritation and infected bites. Use a DEET-based insect repellent.

Sandflies are found around the Mediterranean beaches. They usually cause only a nasty itchy bite but can carry a rare skin disorder called cutaneous leishmaniasis.

Scorpions are found in Spain. Their sting can be distressingly painful, but is not considered fatal.

The only venomous snake that is even relatively common in Spain is Lataste's viper. It has a triangular-shaped head, grows up to 75cm long, and is grey with a zigzag pattern. It lives in dry, rocky areas, away from humans. Its bite can be fatal and needs to be treated with a serum, which state clinics in major towns keep in stock. Also to be avoided is the Montpellier snake, which is blue with a white underside and prominent ridges over the eyes. It lives mainly in scrub and sandy areas, but keeps a low profile and is unlikely to be a threat unless trodden on.

Check for ticks if you have been walking where sheep and goats graze: they can cause skin infections and other more serious diseases.

Hypothermia

The weather in Spain's mountains can be extremely changeable at any time of year. Proper preparation will reduce the risks of getting hypothermia. Even on a hot day the weather can change rapidly; carry waterproof garments and warm layers, and inform others of your route.

Hypothermia starts with shivering, loss of judgment and clumsiness. Unless rewarming occurs, the sufferer deteriorates into apathy, confusion and coma. Prevent further heat loss by seeking shelter, warm dry clothing, hot sweet drinks and shared body warmth.

Water

Tap water is generally safe to drink in Spain. If you are in any doubt, ask *¿Es potable el agua (de grifo)?* (Is the (tap) water drinkable?) Do not drink water from rivers or lakes as it may contain bacteria or viruses that can cause diarrhoea or vomiting.

TRAVELLING WITH CHILDREN

Make sure your children are up to date with routine vaccinations, and discuss possible travel vaccines well before departure as some are not suitable for children under one year of age.

WOMEN'S HEALTH

Travelling during pregnancy is usually possible but always seek a medical check-up before planning your trip. The most risky times for travel are during the first 12 weeks of pregnancy and after 30 weeks.

SEXUAL HEALTH

Condoms are widely available, but emergency contraception may not be, so take the necessary precautions. When buying condoms, look for a European CE mark, which means they have been rigorously tested. Remember to also keep them in a cool, dry place so that they don't crack and perish.

Language

CONTENTS

Spanish *(español)*, or Castilian *(castellano)* as it is more precisely called, is spoken throughout Spain, but there are also three important regional languages: Catalan *(català)*, another Romance language with close ties to French, spoken in Catalonia, the Balearic Islands and Valencia; Galician *(galego)*, similar enough to Portuguese to be regarded by some as a dialect, spoken in Galicia; and Basque *(euskara)*, of obscure, non-Latin origin, spoken in the Basque Country and Navarra.

English isn't as widely spoken as many travellers expect, though you're more likely to find people who speak some English in the main cities and tourist areas. Generally, however, you'll be better received if you try to communicate in Spanish.

For a more comprehensive guide to the Spanish language than we're able to offer here, get a copy of Lonely Planet's *Spanish Phrasebook*. For information on language courses available in Spain, see p869.

PRONUNCIATION

Spanish pronunciation isn't difficult – many Spanish sounds are similar to their English counterparts, and there's a clear and consistent relationship between pronunciation and spelling. If you stick to the following rules you should have very few problems making yourself understood.

Vowels

Unlike English, each of the vowels in Spanish has a uniform pronunciation that doesn't vary. For example, the Spanish **a** has only one pronunciation, similar to the 'u' in 'nut'. Many Spanish words are written with an acute accent (eg *días*) – this normally indicates a stressed syllable and doesn't change the sound of the vowel. Vowels are pronounced clearly even if they are unstressed.

Spanish Pronunciation Guide

a	a	as the 'u' in 'nut'
ai	ai	as in 'aisle'
au	ow	as in 'cow'
e	e	as in 'met'
ei	ey	as in 'they'
i	ee	as in 'keep'
ia	ya	as in 'yard'
ie	ye	as in 'yes'
o	o	as in 'hot'
oy	oy	as in 'boy'
u	oo	as in 'hoof'
	–	silent after **q** and in *gue/gui*
ue	we	as in 'wet'
uy	ooy	as the 'oy' in 'boy'
ü	w	as in 'wet'

Semiconsonant

Spanish also has the semiconsonant **y**. When occuring at the end of a word or standing alone (meaning 'and') it's pronounced like the Spanish **i**. As a consonant, it's somewhere between the 'y' in 'yonder' and the 'g' in 'beige', depending on the region you're in.

Consonants

Some Spanish consonants are pronounced the same as their English counterparts. The pronunciation of others varies according to which vowel follows and which part of Spain you happen to be in. The Spanish alphabet also contains three consonants that are not found within the English alphabet: **ch**, **ll** and **ñ**. In newer dictionaries the letters **ch** and **ll** are listed under **c** and **l** respectively, but **ñ** is still treated as a separate letter and comes after **n**.

Spanish Pronunciation Guide

b	b	as in 'book' when at the start of a word or preceded by **m** or **n**; elsewhere as the 'v' in 'van'
c	k	as in 'cat' when followed by **a**, **o**, **u** or a consonant
	th	as in 'thin' before **e** and **i**
ch	ch	as in 'church'
cu	kw	as the 'qu' in 'quite'
d	d	as in 'dog' when word-initial or when preceded by **l** or **n**
	th	as in 'then'
	–	not pronounced in some words ending in -ado, eg *complicado* (complicated) is often pronounced kom·plee·*ka*·o
f	f	as in 'frame'
g	g	as in 'get' when initial and before **a**, **o** and **u**
	kh	as the 'ch' in the Scottish *loch* before **e** or **i**
h	–	always silent
j	kh	as the 'ch' in the Scottish *loch*
l	l	as in 'let'
ll	ly	as the 'lli' in 'million'; some people pronounce it like the 'y' in 'yellow'
m	m	as in 'many'
n	n	as in 'nana'
ñ	ny	as the 'ni' in 'onion'
p	p	as in 'pop'
q	k	as in 'kick'
r	r	a rolled 'r' sound; longer when initial or doubled
s	s	as in 'see'
t	t	as in 'top'
v	b	as in 'bus'
vu	vw	as the 'voi' in the French *voir*
x	ks	as in 'taxi' when between two vowels
	s	as in 'see' when preceding a consonant
z	th	as in 'thin'

WORD STRESS

Stress is indicated by italics in the pronunciation guides included with all the words and phrases in this language guide. In general, words ending in vowels or the letters **n** or **s** have stress on the next-to-last syllable, while those with other endings have stress on the last syllable. Thus *vaca* (cow) and *caballos* (horses) both carry stress on the next-to-last syllable, while *ciudad* (city) and *infeliz* (unhappy) are both stressed on the last syllable.

Written accents indicate a stressed syllable, and will almost always appear in words that don't follow these rules, eg *sótano* (basement) and *porción* (portion).

GENDER & PLURALS

Spanish nouns are marked for gender (masculine or feminine) and adjectives will vary according to the gender of the noun they modify. There are a few rules to help determine gender – with exceptions, of course! Feminine nouns generally end with **-a** or with the groups **-ción**, **-sión** or **-dad**. Other endings typically signify a masculine noun. Endings for adjectives also change to agree with the gender of the noun they modify (masculine/feminine **-o/-a**).

Where necessary, both forms are given for the words and phrases below, separated by a slash and with the masculine form first, eg *perdido/a* (lost).

If a noun or adjective ends in a vowel, the plural is formed by adding **s** to the end. If it ends in a consonant, the plural is formed by adding **es** to the end.

ACCOMMODATION

I'm looking for ...	*Estoy buscando ...*	e·*stoy* boos·*kan*·do ...
Where is ...?	*¿Dónde hay ...?*	*don*·de ai ...
a hotel	*un hotel*	oon o·*tel*
a boarding house	*una pensión/ un hospedaje*	*oo*·na pen·*syon*/ oon os·pe·*da*·khe
a youth hostel	*un albergue juvenil*	oon al·*ber*·ge khoo·ve·*neel*

I'd like a ... room.	*Quisiera una habitación ...*	kee·*sye*·ra *oo*·na a·bee·ta·*thyon* ...
double	*doble*	*do*·ble
single	*individual*	een·dee·vee·*dwal*
twin	*con dos camas*	kon dos *ka*·mas

How much is it per ...?	*¿Cuánto cuesta por ...?*	*kwan*·to *kwes*·ta por ...
night	*noche*	*no*·che
person	*persona*	per·*so*·na
week	*semana*	se·*ma*·na

May I see the room?
¿Puedo ver la habitación? — *pwe*·do ver la a·bee·ta·*thyon*

LANGUAGE

MAKING A RESERVATION

(for phone or written requests)

To ...	*A ...*
From ...	*De ...*
Date	*Fecha*
I'd like to book ...	*Quisiera reservar ...* (see Accommodation, p901, for bed/room options)
in the name of ...	*en nombre de ...*
for the nights of ...	*para las noches del ...*
credit card ...	*tarjeta de crédito ...*
number	*número*
expiry date	*fecha de caducidad*
Please confirm ...	*Puede confirmar ...*
availability	*la disponibilidad*
price	*el precio*

Does it include breakfast?
¿Incluye el desayuno? een·*kloo*·ye el de·sa·*yoo*·no
I don't like it.
No me gusta. no me *goos*·ta
It's fine. I'll take it.
Vale. La cojo. *va*·le la *ko*·kho
I'm leaving now.
Me voy ahora. me *voy* a·o·ra

full board	*pensión completa*	pen·*syon* kom·*ple*·ta
private/shared bathroom	*baño privado/ compartido*	*ba*·nyo pree·*va*·do/ kom·par·*tee*·do
too expensive	*demasiado caro*	de·ma·*sya*·do *ka*·ro
cheaper	*más económico*	mas e·ko·*no*·mee·ko
discount	*descuento*	des·*kwen*·to

CONVERSATION & ESSENTIALS

When talking to people familiar to you or younger than you, use the informal form of 'you', *tú*, rather than the polite form *Usted*. Wait for your Spanish friends to suggest you use the *tú* form. The polite form is used in all cases in this guide; where options are given, the form is indicated by the abbreviations 'pol' and 'inf'.

Hello.	*Hola.*	*o*·la
Good morning.	*Buenos días.*	*bwe*·nos *dee*·as
Good afternoon.	*Buenas tardes.*	*bwe*·nas *tar*·des
Good evening/ night.	*Buenas noches.*	*bwe*·nas *no*·ches
Goodbye.	*Adiós.*	a·*dyos*
Bye/See you soon.	*Hasta luego.*	*as*·ta *lwe*·go
Yes.	*Sí.*	see
No.	*No.*	no
Please.	*Por favor.*	por fa·*vor*
Thank you.	*Gracias.*	*gra*·thyas
Many thanks.	*Muchas gracias.*	*moo*·chas *gra*·thyas
You're welcome.	*De nada.*	de *na*·da
Pardon me. (getting attention)	*Perdón/ Discúlpeme.*	per·*don*/ dees·*kool*·pe·me
Sorry. (when apologising)	*Lo siento.*	lo see·*en*·to
Excuse me. (when asking to get past someone)	*Permiso.*	per·*mee*·so

How are things?
¿Qué tal? ke tal
What's your name?
¿Cómo se llama Usted? *ko*·mo se *lya*·ma *oo*·ste (pol)
¿Cómo te llamas? *ko*·mo te *lya*·mas (inf)
My name is ...
Me llamo ... me *lya*·mo ...
It's a pleasure to meet you.
Encantado/a. en·kan·*ta*·do/a
Where are you from?
¿De dónde es/eres? de *don*·de *es*/*e*·res (pol/inf)
I'm from ...
Soy de ... soy de ...
Where are you staying?
¿Dónde está alojado/a? *don*·de es·*ta* a·lo·*kha*·do/da (pol)
¿Dónde estás alojado/a? *don*·de es·*tas* a·lo·*kha*·do/da (inf)
May I take a photo?
¿Puedo hacer una foto? *pwe*·do a·*ther* *oo*·na *fo*·to

DIRECTIONS

How do I get to ...?
¿Cómo puedo llegar a ...? *ko*·mo *pwe*·do lye·*gar* a ...
Is it far?
¿Está lejos? es·*ta* *le*·khos
Go straight ahead.
Siga/Vaya todo recto. *see*·ga/*va*·ya *to*·do *rek*·to
Turn left.
Gire a la izquierda. *khee*·re a la eeth·*kyer*·da
Turn right.
Gire a la derecha. *khee*·re a la de·*re*·cha
Can you show me (on the map)?
¿Me lo podría indicar (en el mapa)? me lo po·*dree*·a een·dee·*kar* (en el *ma*·pa)

here	*aquí*	a·*kee*
there	*allí*	a·*lyee*
avenue	*avenida*	a·ve·*nee*·da
street	*calle/paseo*	*ka*·lye/pa·*se*·o
traffic lights	*semáforos*	se·*ma*·fo·ros
north	*norte*	*nor*·te
south	*sur*	soor
east	*este*	*es*·te
west	*oeste*	o·*es*·te

EMERGENCIES

Help!	*¡Socorro!*	so·*ko*·ro
Fire!	*¡Incendio!*	een·*then*·dyo
Go away!	*¡Vete!/¡Fuera!*	*ve*·te/*fwe*·ra

Call ...!
¡Llame a ...! *lya*·me a
an ambulance
una ambulancia oo·na am·boo·*lan*·thya
a doctor
un médico oon *me*·dee·ko
the police
la policía la po·lee·*thee*·a

It's an emergency.
Es una emergencia.
es *oo*·na e·mer·*khen*·thya
Could you help me, please?
¿Me puede ayudar, por favor?
me *pwe*·de a·yoo·*dar* por fa·*vor*
I'm lost.
Me he perdido.
me e per·*dee*·do
Where are the toilets?
¿Dónde están los baños?
don·de es·*tan* los *ba*·nyos

HEALTH

I'm sick.
Estoy enfermo/a. es·*toy* en·*fer*·mo/ma
I need a doctor (who speaks English).
Necesito un médico (que hable inglés). ne·the·*see*·to oon *me*·dee·ko (ke *a*·ble een·*gles*)
Where's the hospital?
¿Dónde está el hospital? *don*·de es·*ta* el os·pee·*tal*
I'm pregnant.
Estoy embarazada. es·*toy* em·ba·ra·*tha*·da
I've been vaccinated.
Estoy vacunado/a. es·*toy* va·koo·*na*·do/da

I'm allergic to ...
Soy alérgico/a a ... soy a·*ler*·khee·ko/ka a ...
antibiotics
los antibióticos los an·tee·*byo*·tee·kos
penicillin
la penicilina la pe·nee·thee·*lee*·na
nuts
las nueces las *nwe*·thes
peanuts
los cacahuetes los ka·ka·*we*·tes

I'm ...	*Soy ...*	soy ...
asthmatic	*asmático/a*	as·*ma*·tee·ko/ka
diabetic	*diabético/a*	dya·*be*·tee·ko/ka
epileptic	*epiléptico/a*	e·pee·*lep*·tee·ko/ka

I have ...	*Tengo ...*	*ten*·go ...
a cough	*tos*	tos
diarrhoea	*diarrea*	dee·a·*re*·a
a headache	*dolor de cabeza*	do·*lor* de ka·*be*·tha
nausea	*náusea*	*now*·se·a

LANGUAGE DIFFICULTIES

Do you speak (English)?
¿Habla/Hablas (inglés)? *a*·bla/*a*·blas (een·*gles*) (pol/inf)
Does anyone here speak English?
¿Hay alguien que hable inglés? ai al·*gyen* ke *a*·ble een·*gles*
I (don't) understand.
Yo (no) entiendo. yo (no) en·*tyen*·do
How do you say ...?
¿Cómo se dice ...? *ko*·mo se *dee*·the ...
What does ... mean?
¿Qué quiere decir ...? ke *kye*·re de·*theer* ...

Could you please ...?
¿Puede ..., por favor? *pwe*·de ... por *fa*·vor
repeat that
repetirlo re·pe·*teer*·lo
speak more slowly
hablar más despacio a·*blar* mas des·*pa*·thyo
write it down
escribirlo es·kree·*beer*·lo

NUMBERS

0	*zero*	*the*·ro
1	*uno*	*oo*·no
2	*dos*	dos
3	*tres*	tres
4	*cuatro*	*kwa*·tro
5	*cinco*	*theen*·ko
6	*seis*	seys
7	*siete*	*sye*·te
8	*ocho*	*o*·cho
9	*nueve*	*nwe*·be
10	*diez*	dyeth
11	*once*	*on*·the
12	*doce*	*do*·the
13	*trece*	*tre*·the
14	*catorce*	ka·*tor*·the
15	*quince*	*keen*·the
16	*dieciséis*	dye·thee·*seys*
17	*diecisiete*	dye·thee·*sye*·te
18	*dieciocho*	dye·thee·*o*·cho
19	*diecinueve*	dye·thee·*nwe*·be

20	*veinte*	*veyn*·te
21	*veintiuno*	veyn·*tyoo*·no
30	*treinta*	*treyn*·ta
31	*treinta y uno*	*treyn*·tai *oo*·no
40	*cuarenta*	kwa·*ren*·ta
50	*cincuenta*	theen·*kwen*·ta
60	*sesenta*	se·*sen*·ta
70	*setenta*	se·*ten*·ta
80	*ochenta*	o·*chen*·ta
90	*noventa*	no·*ven*·ta
100	*cien*	thyen
101	*ciento uno*	thyen·to *oo*·no
200	*doscientos*	dos·*thyen*·tos
500	*quinientos*	keen·*yen*·tos
1000	*mil*	meel
5000	*cinco mil*	*theen*·ko meel

SHOPPING & SERVICES

I'd like to buy ...
Quisiera comprar ... kee·*sye*·ra kom·*prar* ...
I'm just looking.
Sólo estoy mirando. *so*·lo es·*toy* mee·*ran*·do
May I look at it?
¿Puedo mirar(lo/la)? *pwe*·do mee·*rar*·(lo/la)
How much is it?
¿Cuánto cuesta? *kwan*·to *kwes*·ta
That's too expensive for me.
Es demasiado caro para mí. es de·ma·*sya*·do *ka*·ro *pa*·ra mee
Could you lower the price?
¿Podría bajar un poco el precio? po·*dree*·a ba·*khar* oon *po*·ko el *pre*·thyo
I don't like it.
No me gusta. no me *goos*·ta
I'll take it.
Lo llevo. lo *lye*·vo

Do you accept ...?
¿Aceptan ...? a·thep·*tan* ...
credit cards
tarjetas de crédito tar·*khe*·tas de *kre*·dee·to
debit cards
tarjetas de débito tar·*khe*·tas de *de*·bee·to

less	*menos*	*me*·nos
more	*más*	mas
large	*grande*	*gran*·de
small	*pequeño/a*	pe·*ke*·nyo/nya

I'm looking for the ...
Estoy buscando ... es·*toy* boos·*kan*·do ...
ATM
el cajero automático el ka·*khe*·ro ow·to·*ma*·tee·ko
bank
el banco el *ban*·ko
bookstore
la librería la lee·bre·*ree*·a
chemist/pharmacy
la farmacia la far·*ma*·thya
embassy
la embajada la em·ba·*kha*·da
laundry
la lavandería la la·van·de·*ree*·a
market
el mercado el mer·*ka*·do
post office
correos ko·*re*·os
supermarket
el supermercado el soo·per·mer·*ka*·do
tourist office
la oficina de turismo la o·fee·*thee*·na de too·*rees*·mo

What time does it open/close?
¿A qué hora abre/cierra?
a ke *o*·ra *a*·bre/*thye*·ra
I want to change some money/travellers cheques.
Quiero cambiar dinero/cheques de viajero.
kye·ro kam·*byar* dee·*ne*·ro/*che*·kes de vya·*khe*·ro
What is the exchange rate?
¿Cuál es el tipo de cambio?
kwal es el *tee*·po de *kam*·byo
I want to call ...
Quiero llamar a ...
kye·ro lya·*mar* a ...

airmail	*correo aéreo*	ko·*re*·o a·*e*·re·o
letter	*carta*	*kar*·ta
registered mail	*correo certificado*	ko·*re*·o ther·tee·fee·*ka*·do
stamps	*sellos*	*se*·lyos

TIME & DATES

What time is it?
¿Qué hora es? ke *o*·ra es
It's one o'clock.
Es la una. es la *oo*·na
It's seven o'clock.
Son las siete. son las *sye*·te
midnight
medianoche me·dya·*no*·che
noon
mediodía me·dyo·*dee*·a
half past two
dos y media dos ee *me*·dya

today	*hoy*	oy
tonight	*esta noche*	*es*·ta *no*·che
tomorrow	*mañana*	ma·*nya*·na
yesterday	*ayer*	a·*yer*

LANGUAGE

SIGNS

Abierto	Open
Cerrado	Closed
Comisaría	Police Station
Entrada	Entrance
Prohibido	Prohibited
Prohibido Fumar	No Smoking
Salida	Exit
Servicios/Aseos	Toilets
Hombres	Men
Mujeres	Women

Monday	*lunes*	*loo*·nes
Tuesday	*martes*	*mar*·tes
Wednesday	*miércoles*	*myer*·ko·les
Thursday	*jueves*	*khwe*·bes
Friday	*viernes*	*vyer*·nes
Saturday	*sábado*	*sa*·ba·do
Sunday	*domingo*	do·*meen*·go

January	*enero*	e·*ne*·ro
February	*febrero*	fe·*bre*·ro
March	*marzo*	*mar*·tho
April	*abril*	a·*breel*
May	*mayo*	*ma*·yo
June	*junio*	*khoo*·nyo
July	*julio*	*khoo*·lyo
August	*agosto*	a·*gos*·to
September	*septiembre*	sep·*tyem*·bre
October	*octubre*	ok·*too*·bre
November	*noviembre*	no·*vyem*·bre
December	*diciembre*	dee·*thyem*·bre

TRANSPORT

Public Transport

What time does ... leave/arrive?	*¿A qué hora sale/llega ...?*	a ke *o*·ra *sa*·le/*lye*·ga ...?
the bus	*el autobús*	el ow·to·*boos*
the plane	*el avión*	el a·*vyon*
the ship	*el barco*	el *bar*·ko
the train	*el tren*	el tren

airport
el aeropuerto — el a·e·ro·*pwer*·to

bus station
la estación de autobuses — la es·ta·*thyon* de ow·to·*boo*·ses

bus stop
la parada de autobuses — la pa·*ra*·da de ow·to·*boo*·ses

luggage check room
la onsigna — la kon·*seeg*·na

taxi rank
la parada de taxi — la pa·*ra*·da de *tak*·see

ticket office
la taquilla — la ta·*kee*·lya

train station
la estación de trenes — la es·ta·*thyon* de *tre*·nes

The ... is delayed.
El/La ... está retrasado/a. — el/la ... es·*ta* re·tra·*sa*·do/da

I'd like a ticket to ...
Quiero un billete a ... — *kye*·ro oon bee·*lye*·te a ...

Is this taxi free?
¿Está libre este taxi? — e·*sta lee*·bre *es*·te *tak*·see

What's the fare to ...?
¿Cuánto cuesta hasta ...? — *kwan*·to *kwes*·ta *a*·sta ...

Please put the meter on.
Por favor, ponga el taxímetro. — por fa·*vor pon*·ga el tak·*see*·me·tro

a ... ticket	*un billete de ...*	oon bee·*lye*·te de ...
one-way	*ida*	*ee*·da
return	*ida y vuelta*	*ee*·da ee *vwel*·ta
1st-class	*primera clase*	pree·*me*·ra *kla*·se
2nd-class	*segunda clase*	se·*goon*·da *kla*·se
student	*estudiante*	es·too·*dyan*·te

Private Transport

I'd like to hire a/an ...
Quisiera alquilar ... — kee·*sye*·ra al·kee·*lar* ...

4WD
un todoterreno — oon *to*·do·te·*re*·no

car
un coche — oon *ko*·che

motorbike
una moto — *oo*·na *mo*·to

bicycle
una bicicleta — *oo*·na bee·thee *kle*·ta

diesel	*gasóleo*	ga·*so*·lyo
petrol	*gasolina*	ga·so·*lee*·na

Where's a petrol station?
¿Dónde hay una gasolinera?
don·de ai *oo*·na ga·so·lee·*ne*·ra

Please fill it up.
Lleno, por favor.
lye·no por fa·*vor*

I'd like (20) litres.
Quiero (veinte) litros.
kye·ro (*veyn*·te) *lee*·tros

Is this the road to ...?
¿Se va a ... por esta carretera?
se va a ... por *es*·ta ka·re·*te*·ra

(How long) Can I park here?
¿(Por cuánto tiempo) Puedo aparcar aquí?
(por *kwan*·to *tyem*·po) *pwe*·do a·par·*kar* a·*kee*

Where do I pay?
¿Dónde se paga?
don·de se *pa*·ga

ROAD SIGNS

Acceso	Entrance
Aparcamiento	Parking
Ceda el Paso	Give Way
Despacio	Slow
Desvío	Detour
Dirección Única	One Way
Modere Su Velocidad	Slow Down
No Adelantar	No Overtaking
Peaje	Toll
Peligro	Danger
Prohibido Aparcar	No Parking
Prohibido el Paso	No Entry
Salida	Exit (Freeway/Motorway)

I need a mechanic.
Necesito un mecánico.
ne·the·*see*·to oon me·*ka*·nee·ko

The car has broken down at ...
El coche se ha averiado en ...
el *ko*·che se a a·ve·*rya*·do en ...

The motorbike won't start.
No arranca la moto.
no a·*ran*·ka la *mo*·to

I have a flat tyre.
Tengo un pinchazo.
ten·go oon peen·*cha*·tho

I've run out of petrol.
Me he quedado sin gasolina.
me e ke·*da*·do seen ga·so·*lee*·na

I've had an accident.
He tenido un accidente.
e te·*nee*·do oon ak·thee·*den*·te

TRAVEL WITH CHILDREN

I need ...
Necesito ... ne·*the*·see·to ...

Do you have ...?
¿Hay ...? ai ...

a car baby seat
un asiento de seguridad para bebés
oon a·*thyen*·to de se·goo·ree·*da pa*·ra be·*bes*

a child-minding service
un servicio de cuidado de niños
oon ser·*vee*·thyo de kwee·*da*·do de *nee*·nyos

a children's menu
un menú infantil
oon me·*noo* een·fan·*teel*

a crèche
una guardería
oo·na gwar·de·*ree*·a

(disposable) nappies/diapers
pañales (de usar y tirar)
pa·*nya*·les (de oo·*sar* ee tee·*rar*)

an (English-speaking) babysitter
un canguro (de habla inglesa)
oon kan·*goo*·ro (de *a*·bla een·*gle*·sa)

formula (milk)
leche en polvo
le·che en *pol*·vo

a highchair
una trona
oo·na *tro*·na

a potty
un orinal de niños
oon o·*ree*·nal de *nee*·nyos

a stroller
un cochecito
oon ko·che·*thee*·to

Do you mind if I breastfeed here?
¿Le molesta que dé de pecho aquí?
le mo·*les*·ta ke de de *pe*·cho a·*kee*

Are children allowed?
¿Se admiten niños?
se ad·*mee*·ten *nee*·nyos

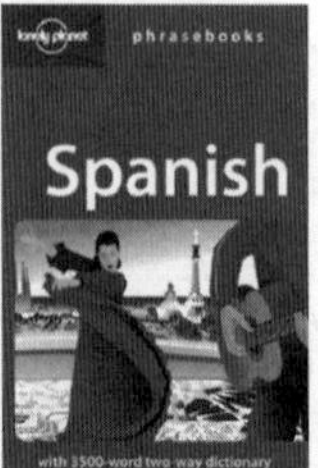

Also available from Lonely Planet:
Spanish Phrasebook

Glossary

Unless otherwise indicated, these terms are in Castilian Spanish.

abierto – open
agroturismo – rural tourism; see also *turismo rural*
ajuntament – Catalan for *ayuntamiento*
alameda – tree-lined street
albergue – refuge
albergue juvenil – youth hostel
alcalde – mayor
alcázar – Muslim-era fortress
aljibe – cistern
armadura – wooden Mudéjar ceiling
artesonado – wooden Mudéjar ceiling with interlaced beams leaving a pattern of spaces for decoration
autonomía – autonomous community or region: Spain's 50 *provincias* are grouped into 17 of these
autopista – tollway
autovía – toll-free highway
AVE – Tren de Alta Velocidad Española; high-speed train
ayuntamiento – city or town hall

bailaor – male flamenco dancer
bailaora – female flamenco dancer
baile – dance in a flamenco context
balneario – spa
barrio – district/quarter (of a town or city)
biblioteca – library
bici todo terreno (BTT) – mountain bike
bodega – cellar (especially wine cellar); also a winery or a traditional wine bar likely to serve wine from the barrel
bomberos – fire brigade
búhos – night-bus routes

cabrito – kid
cala – cove
calle – street
callejón – lane
cama – bed
cambio – change; also currency exchange
caña – small glass of beer
capilla – chapel
capilla mayor – chapel containing the high altar of a church
carmen – walled villa with gardens, in Granada
Carnaval – traditional festive period that precedes the start of Lent; carnival
carretera – highway
carta – menu
casa de huéspedes – guesthouse; see also *hospedaje*
casa de labranza – *casa rural* in Cantabria
casa de pagès – *casa rural* in Catalonia
casa rural – village, country house or farmstead with rooms to let
casco – literally 'helmet'; often used to refer to the old part of a city; more correctly, *casco antiguo/histórico/viejo*
castellano – Castilian; used in preference to *español* to describe the national language
castellers – Catalan human-castle builders
Castile – Castilla (the province)
castillo – castle
castro – Celtic fortified village
català – Catalan language; a native of Catalonia
catedral – cathedral
cercanías – local train network
cerrado – closed
cervecería – beer bar
churrigueresco – ornate style of baroque architecture named after the brothers Alberto and José Churriguera
ciudad – city
claustro – cloister
CNIG – Centro Nacional de Información Geográfica; producers of good-quality maps
cofradía – see *hermandad*
colegiata – collegiate church
coll – Catalan for *collado*
collado – mountain pass
comarca – district; grouping of *municipios*
comedor – dining room
completo – full
comunidad – fixed charge for maintenance of rental accommodation (sometimes included in rent); community
comunidad autónoma – see *autonomía*
conquistador – conqueror
copa – drink; literally 'glass'
cordillera – mountain range
coro – choir: part of a church, usually the middle
correos – post office
Cortes – national parliament
costa – coast
cruceiro – standing crucifix found at many crossroads in Galicia
cuenta – bill, cheque
cuesta – lane, usually on a hill
custodia – monstrance

día del espectador – cut-price ticket day at cinemas; literally 'viewer's day'
dolmen – prehistoric megalithic tomb

embalse – reservoir
encierro – running of the bulls Pamplona-style; also happens in many other places around Spain
entrada – entrance
ermita – hermitage or chapel
església – Catalan for *iglesia*
estació – Catalan for *estación*
estación – station
estación de autobuses – bus station
estación de esquí – ski station or resort
estación de ferrocarril – train station
estación marítima – ferry terminal
estany – lake
Euskadi Ta Askatasuna (ETA) – the name stands for Basque Homeland & Freedom
extremeño – Extremaduran; a native of Extremadura

fallas – huge sculptures of papier-mâché (or nowadays more often polystyrene) on wood used in Las Fallas festival of Valencia
farmacia – pharmacy
faro – lighthouse
feria – fair; can refer to trade fairs as well as to city, town or village fairs that are basically several days of merrymaking; can also mean a bullfight or festival stretching over days or weeks
ferrocarril – railway
festa – Catalan for *fiesta*
FEVE – Ferrocarriles de Vía Estrecha; a private train company in northern Spain
fiesta – festival, public holiday or party
fútbol – football (soccer)

gaditano – person from Cádiz
gaita – Galician version of the bagpipes
gallego – Galician; a native of Galicia
gato – literally 'cat'; also a colloquial name for *madrileño*
gitanos – the Roma people
glorieta – big roundabout/traffic circle
Gran Vía – main thoroughfare
GRs – (senderos de) Gran Recorrido; long-distance hiking paths
guardia civil – military police

habitaciones libres – literally 'rooms available'
hermandad – brotherhood (including men and women), in particular one that takes part in religious processions
hórreo – Galician or Asturian grain store
hospedaje – guesthouse
hostal – cheap hotel
hostal-residencia – *hostal* without any kind of restaurant
huerta – market garden; orchard

iglesia – church
infanta/infante – princess/prince
IVA – *impuesto sobre el valor añadido,* or value-added tax

jai-alai – Basque name for *pelota vasca*
jardín – garden
judería – Jewish *barrio* in medieval Spain

kiosco – kiosk; newspaper stand

lavandería – laundrette
levante – easterly
librería – bookshop
lidia – the art of bullfighting
locutorio – private telephone centre
luz – light; also a common name for household electricity

madrileño/a – a person from Madrid
manchego – La Manchan; a person from La Mancha
marcha – action, life, 'the scene'
marismas – wetlands
marisquería – seafood eatery
medina – Arabic word for town or city
mercado – market
mercat – Catalan for *mercado*
meseta – plateau; the high tableland of central Spain
mihrab – prayer niche in a mosque indicating the direction of Mecca
mirador – lookout point
Modernisme – literally 'modernism'; the architectural and artistic style, influenced by art nouveau and sometimes known as Catalan Modernism, whose leading practitioner was Antoni Gaudí
Modernista – an exponent of *modernisme*
monasterio – monastery
morería – former Islamic quarter in a town
movida – similar to *marcha;* a *zona de movida* is an area of a town where lively bars and discos are clustered
Mozarab – Christian living under Muslim rule in early medieval Spain
Mozarabic – style of architecture developed by Mozarabs, adopting elements of classic Islamic construction to Christian architecture
Mudéjar – Muslims who remained behind in territory reconquered by Christians; also refers to a decorative style of architecture using elements of Islamic building style applied to buildings constructed in Christian Spain
muelle – wharf or pier
municipio – municipality, Spain's basic local administrative unit
muralla – city wall
murgas – costumed groups
museo – museum
museu – Catalan for *museo*

nitbus – Catalan for night bus

oficina de turismo – tourist office; also *oficina de información turística*

Pantocrator – Christ the All-Ruler or Christ in Majesty, a central emblem of Romanesque art
parador – luxurious state-owned hotels, many of them in historic buildings
parque nacional – national park; strictly controlled protected area
parque natural – natural park; a protected environmental area
paseo – promenade or boulevard; to stroll
paso – mountain pass
pasos – figures carried in Semana Santa parades
pelota vasca – Basque form of handball, also known simply as *pelota,* or *jai-alai* in Basque
peña – a club, usually of flamenco aficionados or Real Madrid or Barcelona football fans; sometimes a dining club
pensión – small private hotel
pincho – snack
pintxos – Basque tapas
piscina – swimming pool
plaça – Catalan for *plaza*
plateresque – early phase of Renaissance architecture noted for its intricately decorated facades
platja – Catalan for *playa*
playa – beach
plaza – square
plaza de toros – bullring
poniente – westerly
port – Catalan for *puerto*
PP – Partido Popular (People's Party)
PRs – *(senderos de) Pequeño Recorrido;* short distance hiking paths
presa – dam
prohibido – prohibited
provincia – province; Spain is divided into 50 of them
PSOE – Partido Socialista Obrero Español (Spanish Socialist Workers Party)
pueblo – village
puente – bridge; also means the extra day or two off that many people take when a holiday falls close to a weekend
puerta – gate or door
puerto – port or mountain pass
punta – point or promontory

rambla – avenue or riverbed
rastro – flea market; car-boot sale
REAJ – Red Española de Albergues Juveniles, which is the Spanish HI youth hostel network
real – royal
Reconquista – the Christian reconquest of the Iberian Peninsula from the Muslims (8th to 15th centuries)
refugi – Catalan for *refugio*
refugio – mountain shelter, hut or refuge
refugios vivac – stone shelters with boards to sleep on
Renfe – Red Nacional de los Ferrocarriles Españoles; the national rail network
reservas nacional de caza – national hunting reserves, where hunting is permitted but controlled
retablo – altarpiece
Reyes Católicos – Catholic monarchs; Isabel and Fernando
ría – estuary
río – river
riu – Catalan for *río*
rodalies – Catalan for *cercanías*
romería – festive pilgrimage or procession
ronda – ring road

sacristía – sacristy; the part of a church in which vestments, sacred objects and other valuables are kept
sagrario – sanctuary
sala capitular – chapter house
salida – exit or departure
salinas – salt-extraction lagoons
santuario – shrine or sanctuary
según mercado – meaning 'according to market price'
Semana Santa – Holy Week, the week leading up to Easter Sunday
Sephardic Jews – Jews of Spanish origin
seu – cathedral (Catalan)
sidra – cider
sidrería – cider house
sierra – mountain range
s/m – on menus, an abbreviation for *según mercado*
s/n – sin número (without number), sometimes seen in addresses
supermercado – supermarket

tablao – tourist-oriented flamenco performances
taifa – small Muslim kingdom in medieval Spain
tajines – earthenware dishes with pointed lids
tapeo – tapas-bar crawl
tasca – tapas bar
techumbre – roof; specifically a common type of *armadura*
teleférico – cable car; also called *funicular aereo*
temporada alta/media/baja – high/mid/low season
terraza – terrace; pavement cafe
terrazas de verano – open-air late-night bars
tetería – teahouse, usually in Middle Eastern style, with low seats around low tables
toreros – bullfighters
torre – tower

transept – the two wings of a cruciform church at right angles to the nave
trascoro – screen behind the *coro*
trono – literally 'throne'; also the platform on which an image is carried during a religious procession
turismo – means both tourism and saloon car; *el turismo* can also mean 'tourist office'
turismo rural – rural tourism; usually refers to accommodation in a *casa rural* and associated activities, such as walking and horse riding

urbanización – suburban housing development
urgencia – emergency

vall – Catalan for *valle*
valle – valley
villa – small town
VO – abbreviation of *versión original;* a foreign-language film subtitled in Spanish

zarzuela – Spanish mix of theatre, music and dance

The Authors

DAMIEN SIMONIS

Coordinating Author

Barcelona, Catalonia, Cantabria & Asturias, Balearic Islands

The spark was lit on a short trip over the Pyrenees to Barcelona during a summer jaunt in southern France. It was Damien's first taste of Spain and he found something irresistible about the place – the way the people moved, talked and enjoyed themselves. Damien came back years later, living in medieval Toledo, frenetic Madrid and, finally, settling in Barcelona. He has ranged across the country, from the Picos de Europa to the Sierra Nevada, from Córdoba to Cáceres, and slurped cider in Asturias and gin in the Balearic Islands. For this edition of *Spain* he also wrote the Getting Started, Events Calendar, Itineraries, Culture, Architecture, Directory and Transport chapters. Damien has authored *Barcelona, Madrid, Mallorca, Canary Islands* and the now-defunct *Catalunya & the Costa Brava* for Lonely Planet.

SARAH ANDREWS

Galicia

Sarah Andrews has been living in and writing about Spain since 2000, when she moved to Barcelona from North Carolina. Since then, she's worked on many Spain-related titles for Lonely Planet and other publishers, but authoring the Galicia chapter was her first immersion in *gallego* culture. After weeks of soaking in stunning scenery, visiting incredible cities such as Santiago de Compostela, and getting her fill of specialities like *caldo gallego* (Galician soup), she's hooked. Read her recent work online at www.sarahandrews.com.

LONELY PLANET AUTHORS

Why is our travel information the best in the world? It's simple: our authors are passionate, dedicated travellers. They don't take freebies in exchange for positive coverage so you can be sure the advice you're given is impartial. They travel widely to all the popular spots, and off the beaten track. They don't research using just the internet or phone. They discover new places not included in any other guidebook. They personally visit thousands of hotels, restaurants, palaces, trails, galleries, temples and more. They speak with dozens of locals every day to make sure you get the kind of insider knowledge only a local could tell you. They take pride in getting all the details right, and in telling it how it is. Think you can do it? Find out how at **lonelyplanet.com**.

STUART BUTLER

Basque Country, Navarra & La Rioja, Andalucía, Environment, Spain Outdoors

Stuart's first visit to the Basque Country, as a nipper, led to his first taste of surfing. He quickly became addicted to both. When he was older he spent every summer on the beaches in and around both the French and Spanish Basque Country until one day he found himself so hooked on the waves, climate, landscapes and beach 'attractions' that he was unable to leave – he has been there ever since. When not writing for Lonely Planet he drags himself away from home to search for uncharted surf on remote coastlines. The results of these trips appear frequently in the world's surf media. His website is www.oceansurfpublications.co.uk.

ANTHONY HAM

Madrid, Castilla y León, Aragón, Food & Drink

In 2001 Anthony fell irretrievably in love with Madrid on his first visit to the city. Less than a year later, he arrived there on a one-way ticket, with not a word of Spanish and not knowing a single person in the city. Now Anthony speaks Spanish with a Madrid accent and is married to Marina, a *madrileña;* together with their daughter Carlota, they live overlooking their favourite plaza in the city. When he's not writing for Lonely Planet, Anthony is the Madrid stringer for Melbourne's *Age* newspaper and writes about and photographs Madrid, Africa and the Middle East for newspapers and magazines around the world. Anthony also wrote Destination Spain and the Local Flavours and Green Getaways colour chapters.

JOHN NOBLE

Andalucía, History

In the mid-1990s John, originally from England's Ribble Valley, and his wife Susan Forsyth decided to try life in an Andalucían mountain village. A writer specialising in Spain and Latin America, John has travelled throughout Spain and loves its fascinatingly historic cities, wild, empty back country, isolated villages and castles, rugged coasts, and its music, art, tapas, wine and football.

JOSEPHINE QUINTERO

Castilla-La Mancha, Murcia, Extremadura

Josephine started travelling with a backpack and guitar in the late '60s. Further travels took her to Kuwait, where she was held hostage during the Iraq invasion. Josephine moved to the relaxed shores of Andalucía shortly thereafter, from where she has explored most of the country. She loves Castilla-La Mancha for its dramatic landscape and because it is a beautiful, yet largely undiscovered, region where you still need to speak Spanish to order a beer.

MILES RODDIS

Valencia

Miles and his wife Ingrid have lived for more than 15 years in a shoebox-sized apartment in the Barrio del Carmen, Valencia's oldest and most vibrant quarter. Having cut his Lonely Planet teeth on tough African stuff such as Chad, the Central African Republic and Sudan, he nowadays writes about softer Mediterranean lands – Spain, France and Italy. He's the author or coauthor of more than 30 Lonely Planet guidebooks, including *Valencia & the Costa Blanca, Best of Valencia, Walking in Spain, Canary Islands* and five editions of the book you're holding. He loves Fallas about twice a decade and gets the hell out of town in intervening years.

ARPI ARMENAKIAN SHIVELY

Andalucía

Arpi, her partner Fred Shively and their bearded collie Macduff arrived in the Andalucían spa town of Lanjarón more or less by accident in 2003, via previous writing lives in London and Washington DC. They quickly fell in love with the dramatic Alpujarran landscape, the simplicity of life and the warmth of the community, plus free supplies of Lanjarón's coveted mineral water. As half of a freelance writer and photographer team, Arpi has written many articles about Andalucía's people, places and lifestyles for magazines in Spain and the UK, and plans to write many more as she continues to explore her adopted region in this beautiful country.

CONTRIBUTING AUTHOR

Nancy Frey wrote the Camino de Santiago chapter. She earned her PhD in cultural anthropology from UC Berkeley and wrote *Pilgrim Stories: On and Off the Road to Santiago*. For nine years Nancy and her partner Jose Placer have led hundreds down the Camino with their walking tours company On Foot in Spain. They have three kids and live on the Galician coast.

Behind the Scenes

THIS BOOK

The 7th edition of *Spain* was researched and written by a stellar team of authors. Damien Simonis coordinated the group, which comprised Anthony Ham, John Noble, Josephine Quintero, Miles Roddis, Sarah Andrews, Stuart Butler and Arpi Armenakian Shively. Nancy Frey wrote the Camino de Santiago chapter; Clifton Wilkinson helped update the History chapter; and Paula Hardy coordinated the Andalucía chapter. Damien, John, Miles, Sarah and Susan Forsyth all made major contributions to previous editions, as did Fiona Adams, Mark Armstrong, Fionn Davenport, Tim Nollen, Andrea Schulte-Peevers, Corinne Simcock, Daniel C Schecter, Des Hannigan, Richard Sterling and Elizabeth Swan. The Health chapter was written by Dr Caroline Evans. This guidebook was commissioned in Lonely Planet's London office and produced by the following:

Commissioning Editors Korina Miller, Lucy Monie, Clifton Wilkinson
Coordinating Editor Susan Paterson
Coordinating Cartographer Anthony Phelan
Coordinating Layout Designer Carlos Solarte
Managing Editor Imogen Bannister
Managing Cartographer Mark Griffiths, Alison Lyall
Managing Layout Designer Laura Jane
Assisting Editors David Andrew, Cathryn Game, Kim Hutchins, Stephanie Pearson, Helen Yeates
Assisting Cartographers Csanad Csutoros, Tony Fankhauser, Simon Goslin, Valentina Kremenchutskaya, Erin McManus, Brendan Streager
Assisting Layout Designer Carol Jackson
Cover Designer Pepi Bluck
Project Manager Fabrice Rocher
Language Content Coordinator Quentin Frayne

Thanks to Sally Darmony, James Hardy, Paula Hardy, Jim Hsu, Rachel Imeson, Lisa Knights, Robyn Loughnane, Charity Mackinnon, Wayne Murphy, Trent Paton, Sally Schafer, Lyahna Spencer, Geoff Stringer, Branislava Vladisavljevic, Celia Wood

THANKS

DAMIEN SIMONIS

In Barcelona, countless folks keep me on my toes and make rediscovering the city as fun as it is challenging. They include: Anna Arcarons, María Barbosa Pérez and Enric Muñoz, Sandra Canudas, Dominique Cerri, Paolo Cesco, Rebecca and Elsa Daraspe, Manon Deblois, Oscar Elias, Veronica Farré, Damien Harris, Ralf Himburg and Lilian Müller (and the Thursday gang), Edith López García (and

THE LONELY PLANET STORY

Fresh from an epic journey across Europe, Asia and Australia in 1972, Tony and Maureen Wheeler sat at their kitchen table stapling together notes. The first Lonely Planet guidebook, *Across Asia on the Cheap,* was born.

Travellers snapped up the guides. Inspired by their success, the Wheelers began publishing books to Southeast Asia, India and beyond. Demand was prodigious, and the Wheelers expanded the business rapidly to keep up. Over the years, Lonely Planet extended its coverage to every country and into the virtual world via lonelyplanet.com and the Thorn Tree message board.

As Lonely Planet became a globally loved brand, Tony and Maureen received several offers for the company. But it wasn't until 2007 that they found a partner whom they trusted to remain true to the company's principles of travelling widely, treading lightly and giving sustainably. In October of that year, BBC Worldwide acquired a 75% share in the company, pledging to uphold Lonely Planet's commitment to independent travel, trustworthy advice and editorial independence.

Today, Lonely Planet has offices in Melbourne, London and Oakland, with over 500 staff members and 300 authors. Tony and Maureen are still actively involved with Lonely Planet. They're travelling more often than ever, and they're devoting their spare time to charitable projects. And the company is still driven by the philosophy of *Across Asia on the Cheap*: 'All you've got to do is decide to go and the hardest part is over. So go!'

family – another memorable *calçotada!*), Antonio Marin and Ana Pina (and SCIJ Espanya), Soledad Moreiro, Teresa Moreno Quintana and Carlos Sanagustín, Niko von Mosch and Small World, Steven Muller and Veronika Brinkmann, Sonya Müller-Salget, Nicole Neuefeind, Brian O'Hare and Marta Cervera, Susana Pellicer (with Albert and friends), David Poveda, John Rochlin (and ASBA), Gemma Sesplugues, Peter (don't call me 'the Greek') Sotirakis, Armin Teichmann, José María Toro, Matthew Tree, Michael van Laake and Rocío Vázquez, Nuria Vilches and Simona Volonterio.

In Cantabria and Asturias, *gracias a* Ricardo, Begoña, Esperanza and Juan for a memorable last night of cider and *baile vaquiero,* and to the friendly people of Somiedo. In Mallorca, thanks go to Roberto Fortea, Verónica García, Carlos García, Felipe Amorós, Miquel Àngel Part, Antonio Bauzá, Alessandra Natale, Verónica Carretero, Bartomeu (Tolo) Alcover and Nati Barbosa, Javier Terrasa, Andreu Villalonga and James Hiscock. In Ibiza, *mille mercis* to the multicultural Daraspe family: Rebecca, André and Cherie. In Menorca, Alfredo López had some fine tips.

A big thanks to the *Spain* 7 team, who made coordinating a breeze, and to Korina Miller for her patience and flexibility in HQ.

This is for Janique, who shared car breakdowns, rain and even some lazy beach days.

SARAH ANDREWS

I had some fabulous on-the-road help in Galicia, and for that I'm truly grateful! I owe a big *'gracias'* to many strangers and tourist office staff along the way, but in particular I'd like to thank local experts Courtney Edwards and José Tojo for introducing me to so many great Santiago haunts and for all their Galician advice. To my road-trip-companion Amy Blaise, I owe you a pair of dry shoes after so much time spent trooping around in the rain. It was all in the name of research – thanks! And to my wonderful husband Miquel, here's to beautiful hikes and fish-filled rivers. We'll go back again soon, I promise.

STUART BUTLER

Firstly, a huge thank you to Heather for her continued support in everything as well as her devotion in making sure I got the shopping and *pintxos* information spot on! Thank you also to Willy Uribe for his time, the staff of numerous tourist offices and hotels for information, Laura for helping Heather with the shopping and *pintxos,* Maarten for his gay nightlife advice, Korina and everyone else at Lonely Planet London, the Spanish police for stopping me three times in one day and, finally, the people of the Basque regions for everything they've done for me over the years.

ANTHONY HAM

Thanks to Fernando at Café Comercial and Oriol Balaguer for taking the time to answer my questions, and to Javier Degen whose help was invaluable. Thanks also to my fellow authors, especially Damien, Josephine and Miles, and to my editor Korina. James Nicol's intimate knowledge of the culinary and nightlife scenes in Zaragoza was also a huge help. The good people of Madrid, Aragón and Castilla y León went beyond the call of duty to help wherever possible. And to Marina and Carlota who accompanied me on so many trails and are my wonderful daily companions in Madrid – *gracias, gracias, gracias.*

JOSEPHINE QUINTERO

A very special *gracias* to the especially helpful tourist offices in Trujillo and Cuenca, as well as the tour guide organisation in Cáceres. I would also like to thank Jaime García in Murcia for introducing me to some of the best tapas in Spain and Mary Gordon for her hospitality in Toledo. At Lonely Planet, Korina Miller and Damien Simonis were helpful and supportive and, finally *un beso* for Robin Chapman for sharing observations, ideas – and a regular bottle of wine at the end of a long day on the road.

MILES RODDIS

Huge appreciation and thanks to Ingrid, who drove me the length and breadth of the Comunidad Valenciana and proofread my prose with the eye of a benign eagle. Poppy and Lily Birch (a tribute too to Lolita and Anita) set me wise about the club scene. Tourist office staff were, as always, a pleasure to learn from. Big thank yous to David (Xàtiva), Miguel Ángel (Villena), Marcial (Alicante), Paco and Pablo (Benidorm), Lucía (Jávea), Maria-José (Denia), Maria-Jesús (Requena), Paquita and María (Segorbe), Carmina (Castellón), Iván (San Mateu), Vanessa (Morella), Anais (Peñiscola) and all the ladies in the Benicássim office.

ARPI ARMENAKIAN SHIVELY

Many thanks to Korina Miller, Mark Griffiths and all the team at Lonely Planet for their courteous and patient handling, especially as the deadline approached! Thanks too to John Noble, for his great work on Cádiz. To Tash, who kept dogs, plants and home flourishing in our absence. And most of all to my partner Fred, for his steadfast organisation, navigation and inspiration – without him I would still be going round in circles.

SEND US YOUR FEEDBACK

We love to hear from travellers – your comments keep us on our toes and help make our books better. Our well-travelled team reads every word on what you loved or loathed about this book. Although we cannot reply individually to postal submissions, we always guarantee that your feedback goes straight to the appropriate authors, in time for the next edition. Each person who sends us information is thanked in the next edition – and the most useful submissions are rewarded with a free book.

To send us your updates – and find out about Lonely Planet events, newsletters and travel news – visit our award-winning website: **lonelyplanet.com/contact**.

Note: we may edit, reproduce and incorporate your comments in Lonely Planet products such as guidebooks, websites and digital products, so let us know if you don't want your comments reproduced or your name acknowledged. For a copy of our privacy policy visit lonelyplanet.com/privacy.

OUR READERS

Many thanks to the travellers who used the last edition and wrote to us with helpful hints, useful advice and interesting anecdotes:

A James Ace, Janet Adams, Mira Airola, Alistair Aitken, Michael Asbury **B** Anthony Barnes, Bruce Bartrug, Maryam Benganga, Anthony Bishop, Rebecca Blakeway-Long, William Blyth, Gina Bolotinsky, Susan Booth, Laura Borowiec, Bettina Breuninger, Pamela Brice, Gillian Brown, Margo Buckles, Marjon Buis, Paul Butler **C** Tony Camblor, Elle Carrington, Simon Carstens, Andrew Chen, Berangere Chevallier, Justin Clark, Siobhan Conaghan, Tony Cotterill, Nathalie Coulembier, Murray Cox, Cherisse Crockett, Andrew Curran **D** Nathalie D'Adelhart Toorop, Gun Nidhi Dalmia, Donelda Day, Victoria De La Horra Veldman, Wouter De Sutter, Ewoud Dekker, Ann Ditondo, Julie Doherty **E** Clive Earl, Lars Edman, Amy-Jane Egan **F** Carlota Fernandez, Julia Flores, Carl Foreman, Dennie Fornwald, Martina Forstner, James Franklyn, Philipp Fröhling, Mechthild Fuchs **G** Ronan Gawronski, Jeff Geha, Anne Gibbins, Sepi Gilani, Chris Godlington, Richard Gould, Anna Lisa Grech **H** Marianne Hall, Bree Hancock, Malcolm Hayes, Kate Henderson, Per Høegh Henriksen, Sherri Horbachewsky, Michiel Humblet, Rachel Hunt **J** Danielle Jackson, Laura Jeffery, Brian Jones, Maria Jose Romeo **K** Dimitris Kaliakoudas, Zvi Kam, Mariusz Kamionka, Sharon Keld, Jessie Knapp **L** Marie Larvin, Xabier Legarreta, Erik Lehtinen, Sue Lewis, Maribel Lopez **M** Catharina Magnusson, Luke McCarthy, Meridyth McIntosh, John Mead, Duncan Melville, James Midgley, Laura Moreno, Jose Morente **N** Katharina Nagele, Belinda Naiken, Serhat Narsap **O** Christian Oberdanner, Lodewijk Olthof **P** Charlotte Padelsi, Marcos Palomo, Gordon Payne, Yaron Pedhazur, Matt Pepe, Steve Perkins, Libby Phillips **R** Katrine Hassenkam Rasmussen, Dawn Renfrew, Anton Rijsdijk, Thom Roep, Angelo Rossini, Dakota Rubin **S** Elizabeth Sandaver, Andrea Santini, Jutta Schall-Emden, Volker Schmidt-Wellenburg, Patrick Sclater, Piet Sibbles, Rodrigo Sisdel, Katie Jo Slaughter, Vince Smeaton, Shona Smith, Lester Soo, Melissa Stewart, Laura Street, Marta Sueiras, Darius Sunawala, Julia Swanson, Judy Szende **T** Pete Teele, John Templeman, Graham Tillotson, Stephen Tomlinson, Liz Turner **V** Mike Verbeeck **W** Cathie Wajsberg, Ray Walker, Jeanette Wall, Rosemary Wallace, Andrew Wraight **Y** Carole Yude **Z** Serena Zimmermann.

ACKNOWLEDGMENTS

Many thanks to the following for the use of their content:

Globe on title page © Mountain High Maps 1993 Digital Wisdom, Inc.

Madrid Metro Map © 2008 Metro de Madrid SA

Barcelona Metro Map © TMB 2008

Internal photographs p11 (#3) by Francesc Muntada/CORBIS. All other photographs by Lonely Planet Images, and by Chris Mellor p5; Dale Buckton p6 (#1); Eoin Clarke p7 (#2); Greg Elms p7 (#3); Krzysztof Dydynski p8 (#1); Neil Setchfield p8 (#3); Paul Bernhardt p9 (#6); Bruce Esbin p9 (#7); Matthew Schoenfelder p10 (#2); Eoin Clarke p11 (#1); LPI photographer p12 (#3).

All images are the copyright of the photographers unless otherwise indicated. Many of the images in this guide are available for licensing from Lonely Planet Images: www.lonelyplanetimages.com.

Index

000 Map pages
000 Photograph pages

INDEX

000 Map pages
000 Photograph pages

INDEX

M

INDEX

000 Map pages
000 Photograph pages

INDEX

INDEX

INDEX

INDEX

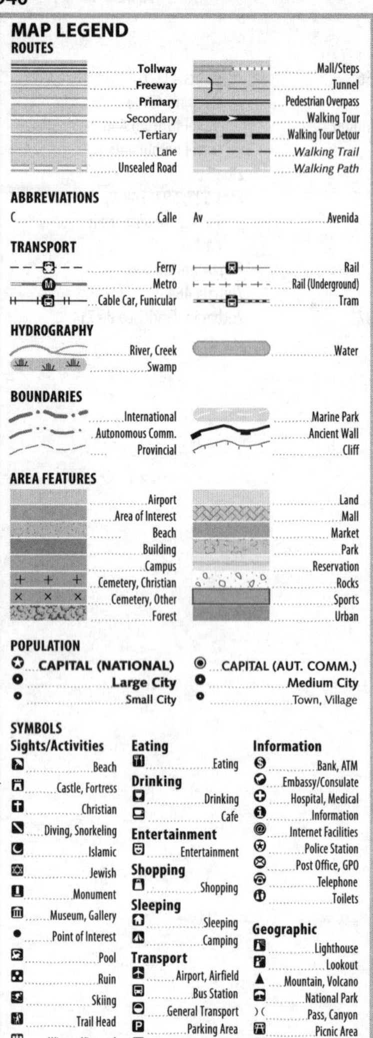

LONELY PLANET OFFICES

Australia
Head Office
Locked Bag 1, Footscray, Victoria 3011
☎ 03 8379 8000, fax 03 8379 8111
talk2us@lonelyplanet.com.au

USA
150 Linden St, Oakland, CA 94607
☎ 510 250 6400, toll free 800 275 8555
fax 510 893 8572
info@lonelyplanet.com

UK
2nd fl, 186 City Rd,
London EC1V 2NT
☎ 020 7106 2100, fax 020 7106 2101
go@lonelyplanet.co.uk

Published by Lonely Planet Publications Pty Ltd
ABN 36 005 607 983

Cover photograph: Feria de Abril, Seville, Spain, Alan Copson/Photolibrary. Many of the images in this guide are available for licensing from Lonely Planet Images: www.lonelyplanetimages.com.

Printed by Toppan Security Printing Pte. Ltd., Singapore.

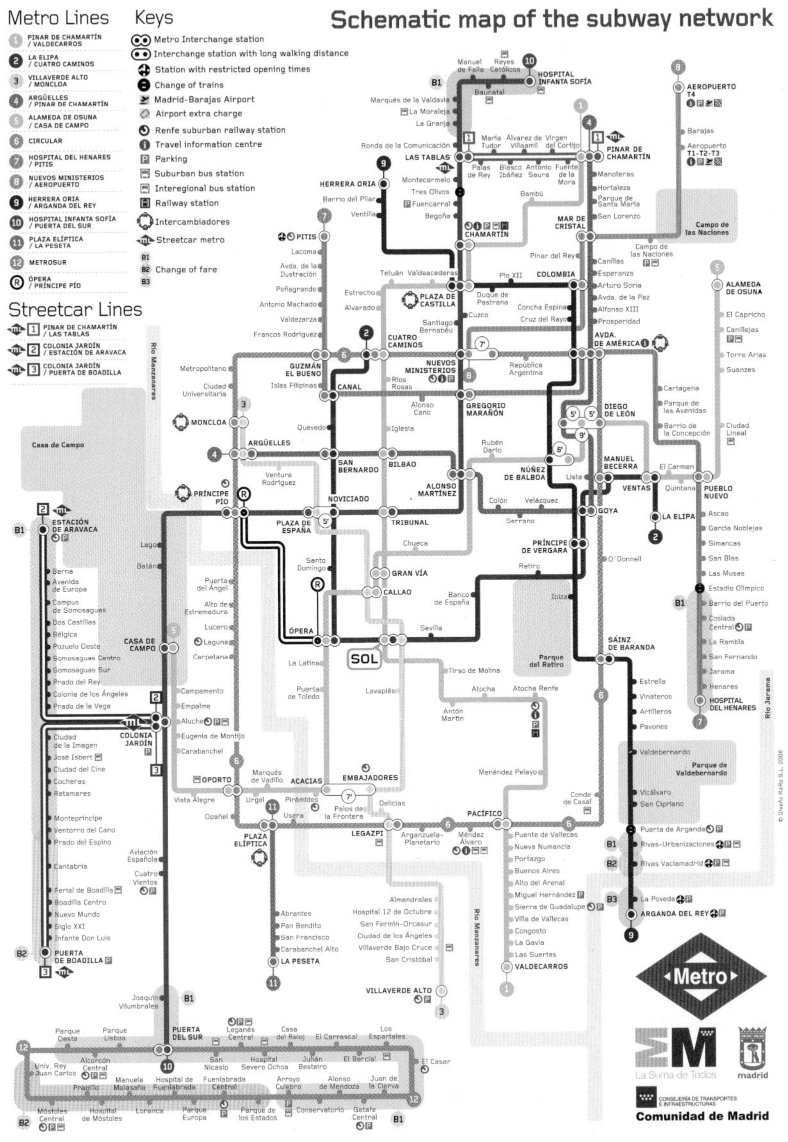

Metro Lines
1 PINAR DE CHAMARTÍN / VALDECARROS
2 LA ELIPA / CUATRO CAMINOS
3 VILLAVERDE ALTO / MONCLOA
4 ARGÜELLES / PINAR DE CHAMARTÍN
5 ALAMEDA DE OSUNA / CASA DE CAMPO
6 CIRCULAR
7 HOSPITAL DEL HENARES / PITIS
8 NUEVOS MINISTERIOS / AEROPUERTO
9 HERRERA ORIA / ARGANDA DEL REY
10 HOSPITAL INFANTA SOFÍA / PUERTA DEL SUR
11 PLAZA ELÍPTICA / LA PESETA
12 METROSUR
R ÓPERA / PRÍNCIPE PÍO
Keys
Metro Interchange station
Interchange station with long walking distance
Station with restricted opening times
Change of trains
Madrid-Barajas Airport
Airport extra charge
Renfe suburban railway station
Travel information centre
Parking
Suburban bus station
Interegional bus station
Railway station
Intercambiadores
Streetcar metro
B1 B2 B3 Change of fare
Streetcar Lines
1 PINAR DE CHAMARTÍN / LAS TABLAS
2 COLONIA JARDÍN / ESTACIÓN DE ARAVACA
3 COLONIA JARDÍN / PUERTA DE BOADILLA
Schematic map of the subway network
Río Manzanares
Casa de Campo
Campo de las Naciones
Parque del Retiro
Parque de Valdebernardo
Río Jarama
HOSPITAL INFANTA SOFÍA
Manuel de Falla
Reyes Católicos
Baunatal
Marqués de la Valdavia
La Moraleja
La Granja
Ronda de la Comunicación
LAS TABLAS
María Tudor
Álvarez de Villaamil
Virgen del Cortijo
PINAR DE CHAMARTÍN
Palas de Rey
Blasco Ibáñez
Antonio Saura
Fuente de la Mora
HERRERA ORIA
Barrio del Pilar
Ventilla
Montecarmelo
Tres Olivos
Fuencarral
Begoña
CHAMARTÍN
Bambú
Manoteras
Hortaleza
Parque de Santa María
San Lorenzo
MAR DE CRISTAL
AEROPUERTO T4
Barajas
Aeropuerto T1-T2-T3
Campo de las Naciones
Pinar del Rey
Canillas
Esperanza
Arturo Soria
Avda. de la Paz
Alfonso XIII
Prosperidad
AVDA. DE AMÉRICA
PITIS
Lacoma
Avda. de la Ilustración
Peñagrande
Antonio Machado
Valdezarza
Francos Rodríguez
Tetuán
Valdeacederas
Estrecho
Alvarado
PLAZA DE CASTILLA
Duque de Pastrana
Pío XII
COLOMBIA
Concha Espina
Cruz del Rayo
Cuzco
Santiago Bernabéu
CUATRO CAMINOS
ALAMEDA DE OSUNA
El Capricho
Canillejas
Torre Arias
Suanzes
Metropolitano
Ciudad Universitaria
GUZMÁN EL BUENO
Islas Filipinas
CANAL
Ríos Rosas
NUEVOS MINISTERIOS
República Argentina
Alonso Cano
GREGORIO MARAÑÓN
DIEGO DE LEÓN
Cartagena
Parque de las Avenidas
Barrio de la Concepción
Ciudad Lineal
MONCLOA
Quevedo
Iglesia
Rubén Darío
ARGÜELLES
SAN BERNARDO
BILBAO
ALONSO MARTÍNEZ
NÚÑEZ DE BALBOA
MANUEL BECERRA
El Carmen
Lista
VENTAS
Quintana
PUEBLO NUEVO
Ventura Rodríguez
PRÍNCIPE PÍO
NOVICIADO
Colón
Velázquez
GOYA
LA ELIPA
PLAZA DE ESPAÑA
TRIBUNAL
Serrano
Ascao
García Noblejas
Simancas
San Blas
Las Musas
Estadio Olímpico
Barrio del Puerto
Coslada Central
La Rambla
San Fernando
Jarama
Henares
HOSPITAL DEL HENARES
ESTACIÓN DE ARAVACA
Lago
Batán
Chueca
PRÍNCIPE DE VERGARA
O'Donnell
Santo Domingo
GRAN VÍA
Retiro
Puerta del Ángel
CALLAO
Banco de España
Ibiza
Alto de Extremadura
Lucero
Laguna
Carpetana
ÓPERA
Sevilla
SOL
SÁINZ DE BARANDA
CASA DE CAMPO
La Latina
Tirso de Molina
Estrella
Vinateros
Artilleros
Pavones
Berna
Avenida de Europa
Campus de Somosaguas
Dos Castillas
Bélgica
Pozuelo Oeste
Somosaguas Centro
Somosaguas Sur
Prado del Rey
Colonia de los Ángeles
Prado de la Vega
Campamento
Empalme
Aluche
Eugenia de Montijo
Carabanchel
Puerta de Toledo
Lavapiés
Antón Martín
Atocha
Atocha Renfe
Valdebernardo
Vicálvaro
San Cipriano
COLONIA JARDÍN
Ciudad de la Imagen
José Isbert
Ciudad del Cine
Cocheras
Retamares
Montepríncipe
Ventorro del Cano
Prado del Espino
Cantabria
Ferial de Boadilla
Boadilla Centro
Nuevo Mundo
Siglo XXI
Infante Don Luis
PUERTA DE BOADILLA
OPORTO
Marqués de Vadillo
ACACIAS
EMBAJADORES
Menéndez Pelayo
Vista Alegre
Urgel
Pirámides
Usera
Palos de la Frontera
Delicias
Conde de Casal
Opañel
PLAZA ELÍPTICA
LEGAZPI
Arganzuela-Planetario
Méndez Álvaro
PACÍFICO
Puente de Vallecas
Nueva Numancia
Portazgo
Buenos Aires
Alto del Arenal
Miguel Hernández
Sierra de Guadalupe
Villa de Vallecas
Congosto
La Gavia
Las Suertes
VALDECARROS
Puerta de Arganda
Rivas-Urbanizaciones
Rivas Vaciamadrid
La Poveda
ARGANDA DEL REY
Aviación Española
Cuatro Vientos
Abrantes
Pan Bendito
San Francisco
Carabanchel Alto
LA PESETA
Almendrales
Hospital 12 de Octubre
San Fermín-Orcasur
Ciudad de los Ángeles
Villaverde Bajo Cruce
San Cristóbal
VILLAVERDE ALTO
Joaquín Vilumbrales
Parque Oeste
Parque Lisboa
PUERTA DEL SUR
Leganés Central
Casa del Reloj
El Carrascal
Los Espartales
Univ. Rey Juan Carlos
Alcorcón Central
San Nicasio
Hospital Severo Ochoa
Julián Besteiro
El Bercial
El Casar
Manuela Malasaña
Hospital de Fuenlabrada
Fuenlabrada Central
Arroyo Culebro
Alonso de Mendoza
Juan de la Cierva
Pradillo
Móstoles Central
Hospital de Móstoles
Loranca
Parque Europa
Parque de los Estados
Conservatorio
Getafe Central
Metro
La Suma de Todos
madrid
CONSEJERÍA DE TRANSPORTES E INFRAESTRUCTURAS
Comunidad de Madrid
© Diseño RaRo S.L. 2008

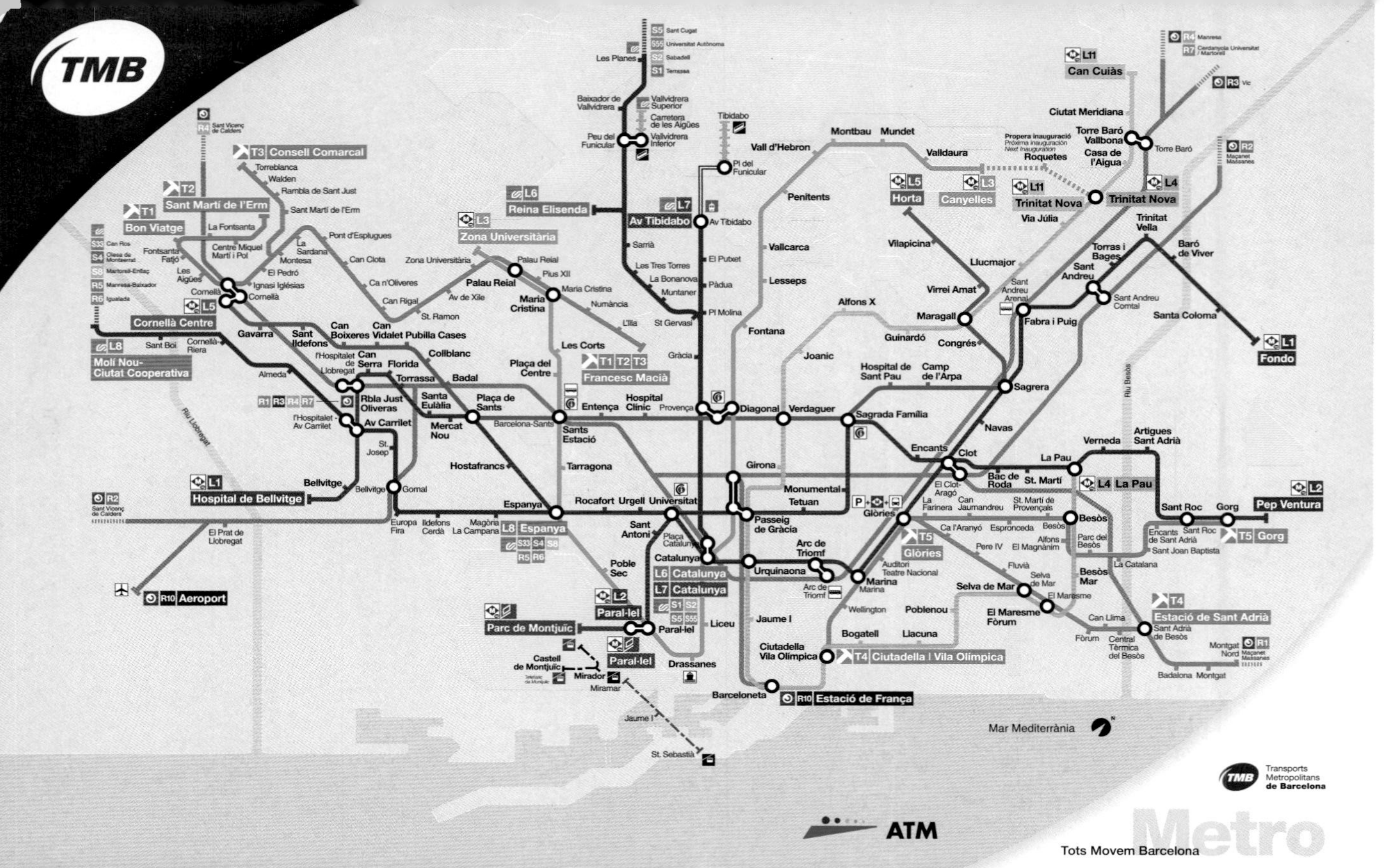

TMB
T3 Consell Comarcal
T2 Sant Martí de l'Erm
T1 Bon Viatge
L5 Cornellà Centre
L8 Molí Nou-Ciutat Cooperativa
L6 Reina Elisenda
L7 Av Tibidabo
L3 Zona Universitària
T1 T2 T3 Francesc Macià
L1 Hospital de Bellvitge
R10 Aeroport
L8 Espanya
L2 Paral·lel
Parc de Montjuïc
Paral·lel
L6 Catalunya
L7 Catalunya
R10 Estació de França
T4 Ciutadella | Vila Olímpica
T5 Glòries
L4 La Pau
L2 Pep Ventura
T5 Gorg
T4 Estació de Sant Adrià
L1 Fondo
L5 Horta
L3 Canyelles
L11 Trinitat Nova
L4 Trinitat Nova
L11 Can Cuiàs
Les Planes
Baixador de Vallvidrera
Peu del Funicular
Vallvidrera Superior
Carretera de les Aigües
Vallvidrera Inferior
Tibidabo
Pl del Funicular
Av Tibidabo
Sarrià
Les Tres Torres
La Bonanova
Muntaner
St Gervasi
El Putxet
Pàdua
Pl Molina
Gràcia
Provença
Torreblanca
Walden
Rambla de Sant Just
Sant Martí de l'Erm
La Fontsanta
Centre Miquel Martí i Pol
Fontsanta Fatjó
Les Aigües
Cornellà
Ignasi Iglésias
El Pedró
Montesa
La Sardana
Pont d'Esplugues
Can Clota
Ca n'Oliveres
Can Rigal
St. Ramon
Av de Xile
Zona Universitària
Palau Reial
Pius XII
Maria Cristina
Numància
L'Illa
Gavarra
Sant Ildefons
Sant Boi
Cornellà-Riera
Almeda
Can Boixeres
Can Vidalet
Pubilla Cases
Collblanc
Badal
l'Hospitalet de Llobregat
Can Serra
Florida
Torrassa
Santa Eulàlia
Plaça de Sants
Rbla Just Oliveras
l'Hospitalet Av Carrilet
Av Carrilet
Mercat Nou
St. Josep
Bellvitge
Gornal
Hostafrancs
Plaça del Centre
Les Corts
Entença
Hospital Clínic
Barcelona-Sants
Sants Estació
Tarragona
Espanya
Rocafort
Urgell
Universitat
Europa Fira
Ildefons Cerdà
Magòria La Campana
El Prat de Llobregat
Riu Llobregat
Sant Antoni
Plaça Catalunya
Catalunya
Poble Sec
Liceu
Drassanes
Castell de Montjuïc
Mirador
Miramar
Jaume I
St. Sebastià
Barceloneta
Vall d'Hebron
Montbau
Mundet
Valldaura
Penitents
Vallcarca
Lesseps
Fontana
Joanic
Alfons X
Guinardó
Congrés
Maragall
Vilapicina
Llucmajor
Virrei Amat
Hospital de Sant Pau
Camp de l'Arpa
Sagrada Família
Diagonal
Verdaguer
Girona
Monumental
Tetuan
Passeig de Gràcia
Arc de Triomf
Urquinaona
Jaume I
Ciutadella Vila Olímpica
Bogatell
Llacuna
Poblenou
Wellington
Marina
Auditori Teatre Nacional
Glòries
Ca l'Aranyó
Espronceda
Pere IV
El Magnànim
Alfons
Fluvià
Selva de Mar
El Maresme
El Maresme Fòrum
La Farinera
Can Jaumandreu
St. Martí de Provençals
Besòs
Parc del Besòs
Besòs Mar
La Catalana
Encants
Clot
El Clot-Aragó
Bac de Roda
St. Martí
Navas
Sagrera
Fabra i Puig
Sant Andreu Arenal
Sant Andreu
Sant Andreu Comtal
Torras i Bages
Trinitat Vella
Baró de Viver
Santa Coloma
Via Júlia
Roquetes
Propera inauguració
Casa de l'Aigua
Torre Baró Vallbona
Torre Baró
Ciutat Meridiana
La Pau
Verneda
Artigues Sant Adrià
Sant Roc
Gorg
Encants de Sant Adrià
Sant Joan Baptista
Can Llima
Fòrum
Central Tèrmica del Besòs
Sant Adrià de Besòs
Badalona
Montgat
Montgat Nord
Riu Besòs
Mar Mediterrània
ATM
Transports Metropolitans de Barcelona
Metro
Tots Movem Barcelona